For Reference

Not to be taken from this room

The Molding of American Banking

History of American Economy: Studies and Materials for Study
A series of reprints of the important studies
and source books relating to the growth of the
American economic system.

General Editor: William N. Parker

THE MOLDING OF AMERICAN BANKING

MEN AND IDEAS

By
FRITZ REDLICH

In Two Parts

With a New Introduction by the Author

JOHNSON REPRINT CORPORATION

New York and London

1968

CARNEGIE LIBRARY
LIVINGSTONE COLLEGE
SALISBURY, N. C. 28144

© 1947, 1951 by Fritz Redlich

© 1968 by Johnson Reprint Corporation
All Rights Reserved

Library of Congress Catalog Card Number: 68-28936

Printed in the U.S.A.

Ref.
332.1
R 317

PREFACE TO THE SECOND EDITION

Needless to say, the author is highly gratified by the opportunity of bringing out a new edition of this book which has been out of print for several years. Originally a revised and enlarged one had been planned. Such an edition would have made it possible to revise in some chapters the style of the presentation, to eliminate misprints, to make small changes and insertions, and to merge the old and the new on the basis of the author's present outlook and knowledge. But this project proved too expensive and it entailed a certain risk. The work would have taken at least two years and, because of his age, the author might not have been able to finish it. Since the very best was unattainable, the second best has been chosen, and I wish to express my appreciation to Professor William N. Parker for his assistance toward this end. This second best, then, is a reprint of the work, with an introduction to bring the original publication up to date by presenting and evaluating the banking literature published since the two volumes first came out.

Of the manuscripts whose use was acknowledged in the preface of volume II, one has since been published; Irene Neu's manuscript is now available under the title, Erastus Corning, Merchant and Financier, 1794-1872 (Ithaca, New York, 1960).

May 1, 1968   Fritz Redlich

103719

Introduction to the Reprint

THE HISTORY OF AMERICAN BANKING IN THE
LITERATURE OF THE LAST FIFTEEN YEARS: A SURVEY*

I

Not much work on the history of American banking has been done since the first publication of the volumes reprinted here. Although some recent works are interesting and significant contributions, the picture as a whole has changed hardly at all. Only two books have come into the market which deal with American banking history in its totality; of these only one is of real importance, and that one does not carry the story beyond 1865. It is Bray Hammond's Banks and Politics in America from the Revolution to the Civil War (Princeton, 1957).[1] As the title indicates, the volume looks at American banking history from a point of view different from that which guides the present investigation. The second publication, sponsored by the American Bankers' Association to celebrate the hundredth anniversary of the National Currency Act, was written by Paul B. Trescott and appeared under the title Financing American Enterprise: The Story of Commercial Banking (New York, 1963). It is designed for popular consumption and lacks scholarly depth, facts being provided mostly in an anecdotal form. Yet the book has a theme: the contribution of American commercial banking to capital formation and thereby to economic development. It deals also with the first half of the twentieth century.

As indicated by the subtitle of my book, I never intended to go into banking statistics, let alone do primary research in the field. But I would have presented telling figures, especially in the chapters on the general characteristics of the various periods, had quantitative information been accessible. This gap is in the process of being filled. Valuable time series are now available in the Historical Statistics of the United States, Colonial Times to 1957, edited by the U.S. Department of Commerce, Bureau of the Census (1960), Chapter X. Its introduction is worth reading, too, since it informs the student as to some of the sources and problems of banking statistics (pp. 615 ff.).

Moreover, J. Van Fenstermaker has recently done primary quantitative research on early United States banking. The results are contained in the mimeographed publication A Statistical Summary of the Commercial Banks Incorporated in the United States prior to 1819, Kent State University, Bureau of Economic and Business Research, Research Papers, No. 2 (Kent, Ohio, 1965)

---

*It should be appreciated that the author is not a bibliographer and that this survey is not meant to be a complete bibliography of recent publications on American banking history. The survey is merely an introduction to this type of literature. In particular, the periodicals on local and regional history have not been systematically covered.

It will also be understood that this book deals with American banking history to the establishment of the Federal Reserve System. Consequently this survey of the recent banking literature omits such items as deal with the decades after 1910.

and in his book The Development of American Commercial Banking: 1782-1837.
The latter was issued by the same university and the same research organization
in its Printed Series No. 5 (Kent, Ohio, 1965). It is surprising how much
quantitative information Fenstermaker could glean from state archives and
printed sources, mainly state documents. Yet I have doubts as to the reliability of some and as to the significance of other material, for example, of
the information on bank capital authorized in the charters. Quite useful is
the presentation of nonquantitative material in tabulated form such as "State
laws restricting non-incorporated banking," banks in which states owned considerable amounts of shares, Bank reports and their character by states, "Records"
of individual banks, and others. In his most recent publication, "The Statistics of American Commercial Banking, 1782-1818" in the Journal of Economic
History, XXV (1965), 400 ff., Fenstermaker presented the following time series:
number of commercial banks; size of their capital stock (i.e., total authorized
capital); size of their monetary reserves (i.e., capital account and liabilities
of reporting state-chartered banks, the ratio of bank notes in circulation and
deposits to paid-in capital stock--figures meaningful only in the context of
eighteenth-century banking thought--[2] and the ratio of such items to specie,
one which interests modern theorists). Finally he reports on the relative
importance of bank notes to demand deposits in Boston, Providence, and Philadelphia, figures which I consider entirely atypical, if United States banking
of the early period prior to 1818 is considered as a whole.

II

(Chapters I-V)

     Surprisingly little monographic work has been done recently on the
periods and topics treated in Chapters I through V of this book. There is a
paper by Theodore Thayer on "The Land-Bank System in the American Colonies" in
the Journal of Economic History, XIII (1953), 145 ff. I myself investigated
more carefully than before the early history of the American check, focusing
attention on its formal characteristics. Combined with this paper was one by
Webster M. Christman III who found among the Girard Bank papers an unexpectedly
large number of checks drawn on the bank, so that a statistical breakdown under
several heads was possible. Both papers appeared together in the Business
History Review, XLI (1967) 285 ff. under the title "The Early American Check
and an Example of Its Use." The reason for the greater amount of checks
surviving in the Girard Bank papers is explained in Christman's essay. It was
the result of Hamburg influence brought to bear on Girard by David Parish, a
friend of his. It is suggested that future researchers and archivists pay
attention to and preserve, respectively, for statistical purposes, any similar
accumulation of checks which they may find in bank records so far untouched.
Yet it is possible that the collection of early American checks in the Girard
Bank papers is unique for the United States. The item, just cited, was followed
up by James P. Baughman in a paper "Early American Checks: Forms and Functions"
published in the same periodical, XLI(1967), 421 ff.
     An obiter dictum is here in order. We know now for certain that checks
were used for several purposes in the American commercial centers by 1800. But

there was no creation of deposit money as yet. It did not make its appearance
in the East before the late 1830's. Thereafter checks and deposit currency
became common in the various parts of the country at very different periods; and
within each area and period checks and deposit currency were probably used in
cities earlier than in the surrounding countryside. We do know, for example,
that check and deposit currency were not adopted in Chicago before the 1850's,[3]
and that they came to the South only some time after the Civil War. An investigation of the adoption of the check and deposit currency in the various parts
of the country would prove an interesting research topic; and I contend as
before that in the Biddle era the check was mostly used as domestic exchange,
a position which remains to be disproved.

    A few more items are noteworthy in the context of this section. Stuart
Weems Bruchey in his Robert Oliver, Merchant of Baltimore 1783-1819 (Johns Hopkins Studies in Historical and Political Science, Series LXXIV, No. 1, Chapter
III), deals in a special part with banking and money. He draws attention to
certain bank and financial policies of merchants, customary by 1800, which have
not been generally observed. Beatrice G. Reubens's article, "Burr, Hamilton and
the Manhattan Company" in Political Science Quarterly, LXXII (1957), 578 ff.,
and LXXIII (1958), 100 ff., describes episodes of the same period, the chartering
and launching of that renowned New York bank. The two-volume work of Merrill
Denison, Canada's First Bank, A History of the Bank of Montreal (Toronto-
Montreal, 1966 and 1967) now permits the comparison of early United States banking with its beginnings in Canada.

                                   III

                              (Chapter VI)

    In contrast to the paucity of recent research on the earliest periods
of American banking and the topics of my Chapters I to V there is an abundance
of new research on what I have treated in Chapter VI under the head of "Early
American Central Banking."

    The First Bank of the United States is attracting attention again.
There is a paper by H. Wayne Morgan on "The Origins and Establishment of the
First Bank of the United States" in the Business History Review, XXX (1956),
472 ff. But of real importance is the fact that Stuart Bruchey has taken over
the task of working up the material collected on that bank over many years by
the late Professor James O. Wettereau. As Bruchey was good enough to inform me
by letter, his analysis of Wettereau's material will not lead to a radical
change in the traditional picture. Its interest, I am told, lies in rich novel
statistical information on government deposits, not only in the Bank of the
United States but also in all other depositories, and in such figures as will
illumine the working of the various branches. We can expect new knowledge as to
the relationship of the national bank and the then existing state banks as well
as an improved view of the First Bank of the United States as a central bank and
of the simultaneously performed central banking functions of the Treasury-- the
latter, to be sure, not a subject treated in these volumes.

    Interest in the Second Bank of the United States, the Bank War, and its
aftermath proceeds unabated. This interest is reflected in the comparatively
large number of recent publications in these fields, publications often inspired

by the fact that new sources have become available. What remains of the papers
of William Jones, first president of the Second Bank of the United States, was
deposited in the Historical Society of Pennsylvania at Philadelphia. I myself
used these documents and, to the extent that they contained pertinent material,
reported on it in a paper entitled "William Jones' Resignation from the Presidency of the Second Bank of the United States," Pennsylvania Magazine of History
and Biography LXXI (1947), 223 ff. The papers do not contain anything startling,
but it is clear that Jones did not flee his job "in affright." He was at the
critical moment, the time of the publication of the Spencer Report, laid up by an
eye disease and tendered his resignation in a formal letter to the President,
a letter which survives in the National Archives.

        A few years later the papers of the Cheves family were turned over to
the South Carolina Historical Society in Charleston, S.C. This collection contains only a few letters by Langdon Cheves, the second president of the Second
Bank of the United States, written during the time of his presidency. Of these,
photocopies were made available; they contain nothing which throws light on his
leadership of the Bank. I conjecture that his letterbooks remained in the Bank
and were destroyed together with the Bank's papers. My attempt to have the
letters which Cheves received between 1819 and 1822 microfilmed was unsuccessful;
other methods of getting at them would have entailed prohibitive costs, and the
task of working up these papers remains to be done.

        More than a decade ago there appeared a new monograph on the Second
Bank of the United States, written by Walter Buckingham Smith and entitled
Economic Aspects of the Second Bank of the United States (Cambridge, Mass.,
1953). The author's intent was to examine the relation of the Bank to American
economic development, its effect on business and industrial activity, its
efficiency as the fiscal agent of government, its relation to other banks, and
its role as the country's central bank (page 1). The book was conceived in the
1920's and had an unusually long gestation period which deprived it somewhat of
the influence it would have had, had it appeared earlier. The program itself
would have fared better by a topical treatment, which, however, would have
demanded theoretical underpinning and refined statistical methods. Since the
author did not make use of sophisticated tools but preferred simple nonanalytical
description, he had to organize his material by time periods, namely 1816-1818,
1819-1822, 1823-1829, 1830-1836, and 1836-1841. This organization alone would
have worked against an efficient execution of the program.

        While W.B. Smith deals with the history of the Second Bank of the
United States from its beginnings to its end and beyond, David McCord Wright
chose to focus his attention on a few years only of its existence, namely those
during which Langdon Cheves was at its head. Stung by the low opinion in which
posterity has held his ancestor, this economist decided to right a supposed
wrong. For this purpose, after studying the extant primary material, he published a paper, "Langdon Cheves and Nicholas Biddle: New Data for a New Interpretation" in Journal of Economic History, XIII (1953), 305 ff. It appears to
me that, while some of the data are new, they by no means warrant a new interpretation. To be sure, the ridiculous often quoted statement by William M.
Gouge that "the Bank was saved and the people were ruined" by the policy of
contraction, inaugurated even before Cheves took over, has already been expressly
rejected by Walter B. Smith. Yet he only described Cheves' activities as the
president of the Second Bank of the United States without analyzing the effects.[4]

On the other hand, while Bray Hammond simply cites Gouge's saying, his criticism of it can be read between the lines.[5]

Wright objects to considering Cheves untutored in, or at least inarticulate on, economic matters. He reports that Cheves' library contained American reprints of most of the outstanding contemporary books on economics, such as Adam Smith's Wealth of Nations and his Theory of Moral Sentiment, Ricardo's Principles and his High Price of Bullion, Malthus's Principles of Population, an item by Lauderdale, translations of Say's Traité d' économie politique and Ganilh's Des Systèmes d' économie politique. Moreover he owned the Bullion Report, some pamphlets on the bullion controversy, and an important American item, Blodget's Economica. Finally, Wright has dug up articles on economic matters written by Cheves under the pseudonym of "Say" for the Philadelphia National Gazette in September, October, and November 1820, i.e., at a time when he was already president of the Bank. To be sure, for the "unbeliever" it is disquieting that the series of articles came to a stop at the very moment when the discussion reached the topics of money and banking. One would have expected that the president of the national bank, if secure in his convictions, would have eagerly grasped the opportunity to promote his ideas on the subject.[6]

I agree with Wright that crucial for the interpretation of Cheves' activities is a memorial drawn up in the fall of 1820 (p. 312 of the article "Langdon Cheves and Nicholas Biddle..."). It is crucial also for the understanding of the developing conflict between Cheves, the president of the Bank, and Biddle, one of its most influential directors. The memorial contains a reform proposal which Wright considers "formidable." In contrast, I think three of the four proposals were paltry (the third abolishing the principle of rotation in office for the Bank's directors aroused opposition immediately). For the purpose of understanding and judging the plan, attention must be focused on the fourth proposal, "limiting the obligation of the Bank to receive its branch notes in payment of federal taxes and requiring that these need be accepted for taxes only in the district in which initially issued." This implies that Cheves wanted to make the Bank a regular contemporary "money bank" with interstate branches. From recent research, to be cited forthwith, it has been established beyond doubt that the Bank of England assumed central banking functions as early as the eighteenth century. A national bank, founded in the United States in the 1810's, had to turn in the same direction or it was meaningless. Cheves did not see that, but Biddle had this vision; and the disagreement between the two men really turned, when expressed in modern terms, on the question of whether the national bank should be ready to assume central banking functions (Biddle), or be run like a large commercial bank with branches (Cheves). Regardless of Wright's protest against such an interpretation (p. 318 of the same article), it appears to me that Cheves actually did not understand Biddle. Wright's presentation falls flat and is best countered with Cheves' own words to be found in Niles Register of 1837, passages which Bray Hammond quoted:[7] Said Cheves "I have ... almost as little ambition to be considered an eminently skillful banker as an eminently skillful physician;" and he went on: "I am free to declare that I am opposed to a national bank in any shape. I always believed it to be unconstitutional, and my experience and observation have satisfied me that it is inexpedient, unnecessary, and dangerous." Cheves' opinion was certainly not as articulate in 1820-1822 as it was in 1837, but "the constitutional lawyer and political theorist," that Cheves was in Wright's words,[8] had probably inhibitions while at the head of the bank and was therefore not the

right man for that position. He himself claimed in 1837 that he "determined in
a few weeks after [he] entered the Bank to leave it" as soon as the task was
finished. The fact that toward the end of his life Cheves became a champion of
slavery and secession is not in any way indicative of a sense of reality. At
all events, after a careful study of Wright's article and an equally careful
reading of the pertinent sections of Hammond's and Smith's books I have to maintain in all essentials my own presentation of Cheves and his activities contained
in this book.

Just as I am unable to accept a new interpretation of Cheves, I must
reject the new interpretation of Biddle contained in Thomas Payne Govan's
Nicholas Biddle: Nationalist and Public Banker 1786-1844 (Chicago, 1959).
Govan has presented us with the first full-fledged biography of Biddle; he has
exhaustively studied the pertinent primary sources; and he has provided a good
deal of fresh information. In the introduction of his book (p.viii) he sums up
his interpretation of the great banker. While the earlier authors who respected
Biddle's genius had found that his weaknesses, mistakes in judgment, and faults
in character explained the ultimate disaster, Govan, while not denying Biddle's
faults, weaknesses, and mistakes, concluded that none of them accounted for the
final result. I cannot see this and must again stand by my own analysis.

My own interpretation of Biddle pivots around his own intuitive recognition of his role as a central banker. Bray Hammond has credited me with
pioneering with this interpretation at which he himself arrived independently;[9]
and both Walter B. Smith[10] in his book on the Second Bank of the United States
and Milton S. Heath[11] in his history of Georgia banking followed suit.

The question of whether the First and Second Banks of the United States
were "true" central banks, has recently been posed again, this time by Harold
Barger who, incidentally, took no notice of the present book. In his work
entitled The Management of Money: A Survey of the American Experience (Chicago,
1964), after describing the pertinent actions of the banks, Barger cautiously
answered the question "in the negative" and added: "No more, of course, was the
Bank of England at that period." One can certainly not argue about the word
"true" which in this case might be called a "weasel word." But the statement
about the Bank of England is incorrect. In his methodologically exceedingly
interesting article, "The Role of the Bank of England as Lender of Last Resort
in the Crises of the Eighteenth Century," published in Explorations in Entrepreneurial History, X (1957/1958), 8 ff., Michael C. Lovell has shown convincingly
by statistical inference that as early as the eighteenth century the Bank of
England had at least advanced to that status. I would draw the conclusion that
it was already then acting as a central bank, just as the Bank of the United
States did somewhat later under the leadership of Biddle.

At the very moment when the Second Bank of the United States was
approaching its end, implying at the same time the end of nineteenth century
American central banking, a strange episode developed in the State of New York.
There, in the critical years of the 1830's, the Canal Fund moved temporarily
into the position of a kind of state central bank. The story has been told in
the attractive book by Nathan Miller, The Enterprise of a Free People: Aspects
of Economic Development in New York State During the Canal Period, 1792-1838
(Ithaca, N.Y., 1962), 115 ff. This volume is the source of what follows.[12]

The Canal Fund Commissioners, appointed to manage the fund, were unable
in the early 1830's to repurchase canal bonds because of the high price which

they commanded in the market.   On the other hand, under the law the commissioners had only a few possibilities of investing the accumulating sums, and so these were deposited in a great number of New York banks which paid interest thereon. By the end of 1833 deposits of the Canal Fund were made in seventeen banks located all over the state, banks which held anywhere between $56,000 and $184,000 apiece.   Originally these deposits were interest-bearing demand deposits, while from 1831 on they became to a certain extent "loans" to banks, i.e., time deposits which could be withdrawn only sixty days after notice.   By that time the accumulated funds amounted to about $2,000,000.   In 1836 the banks reached the peak of their indebtedness to the Canal Fund, amounting to a little more than $3,600,000 the largest proportion of which was on deposit or on "loan" in New York City, Albany, Troy, Utica, Syracuse, Lockport, Rochester, and Buffalo, where there was the greatest demand for loanable funds.   The Canal Fund added considerably to the resources available through the banks to these communities.   In adopting and executing this policy of lending surplus canal funds to the New York banks, the Commissioners were aware of their heavy responsibility and of dangers ahead; and they were anxious to accept any offer of canal stock, if made at a reasonable rate, to reduce the available surplus funds prior to the due dates of the securities.

Bankers and businessmen all over the state were aware by that time that the Canal Fund had moved into the position of a kind of development bank.   But it was during the crisis of 1834, when the Second Bank of the United States contracted its loans and discounts in the course of the Bank War, and again during the crisis of 1837, that the Canal Fund assumed central banking functions. In order to counteract the contraction of 1834 the New York Canal Fund Commissioners, backed in this policy by the Democratic state government, decided to leave "loans" and deposits with the banks concerned to the largest possible extent, meeting themselves only the most urgent payments and maintenance charges. Moreover in 1837 their lending policy became distinctly counter-cyclical, after the experience with relief action for New York City, struck by the great fire of 1835, had paved the way.

When the panic of 1837 was approaching, the Canal Fund Commissioners were prevailed upon and consented to lend the banks $3,395,000 in canal stock, originally issued to finance additions to the Erie Canal system, but not sold as yet.   That is to say, the Canal Fund Commissioners were willing to lend the credit of the Canal Fund to the banks, which, in turn, would take those bonds at par and pay the interest thereon until the bonds were restored to the Canal Fund.   The banks would provide such cash as was required for the construction of the works.   The bonds were to be distributed among eight New York City banks pro rata of their capital, and these banks would issue certificates of indebtedness to businessmen.   The latter, in turn, were expected to use them to pay their own debts to foreigners.   The plan came to naught when the suspension of specie payments was announced, for then the Fund could receive from the banks only debased currency when drawing on them, i.e., demanding payment of its deposits.   The Fund Commissioners suggested that the banks pay the difference between the value of notes and that of specie, but the banks refused to do so. Nevertheless the Canal Fund itself weathered the storm, proceeded to pay specie on its obligations, and thereby upheld the credit of the state.

When it came to the resumption of specie payments, the abortive plan of 1837 was resuscitated, and $2,230,526.55 worth of canal stock was lent to solvent banks in the City of New York.   The pertinent transactions, as

described, seem to justify the characterization of the Canal Fund as a temporary
rudimentary central bank for the State of New York.

Returning once more to the Second Bank of the United States, we find
the Bank War described again in the books of Govan, Hammond, and Smith. One
particular aspect of Hammond's interpretation has aroused the criticism of Frank
Otto Gatell. Asking the question cui bono?, Hammond suggested[13] that Van Buren
might have been the master mind behind the Bank War, as the result of which Wall
Street was freed from the tyranny of Chestnut Street. In his paper, "Sober
Second Thoughts on Van Buren, the Albany Regency, and the Wall Street Conspiracy"
in The Journal of American History, LIII (1966), 19 ff., Gatell rejects this
proposition which in much detail he tries to prove untenable. Assuming that
under these circumstances the responsibility shifts back to President Jackson
himself, we are bound to take an interest in an article by Charles G. Sellers,
Jr., "Banking and Politics in Jackson's Tennessee 1817-1827" in Mississippi
Historical Review, XLI (1954/55), 61 ff. The author of this paper concludes
that in the last analysis Jackson's attitude toward banks was rooted in earlier
experience gained in Tennessee in the years following the War of 1812.[13a]

In her book Biddle's Bank: the Crucial Years (New York and London,
1967) Jean Alexander Wilburn asks a question neglected by earlier investigators
of the Bank War, namely, who supported the Bank of the United States when in
1832 it applied for a new charter. She comes to the conclusion that "the Bank
was supported by most state legislatures, by a majority in both Houses of the
United States Congress, by an impressive number of state banks, and by more
direct expressions of pro-Bank than anti-Bank feeling among the people at large."
Particularly, she has proved that, in contrast to what has been assumed so far,
the majority of state banks in the South and West were in 1832 friends of the
Bank. Be it stressed, however, that the author's findings refer to one year
only and are arrived at by measurement which is not unimpeachable.[13b]

Another presentation of the Bank War (to my mind an overworked subject,
in any case) is contained in a biography of Taney, by Walker Lewis, Without Fear
or Favor: A Biography of Chief Justice Roger Brooke Taney (Boston, 1965). In
this book (Part II, pp. 129 ff.) interest is centered on the role played by
Taney who, as the adviser of President Jackson in his capacities of Attorney
General and later Secretary of the Treasury, prepared and executed the removal
of the government deposits from the Second Bank of the United States. Lewis's
uncritical admiration for Taney colors his description of the Bank War, just as
Govan's admiration for Biddle is reflected in his biography Nicholas Biddle ....

The role which Taney played in the Bank War has recently been reinvesti-
gated by other researchers. Taney was supposed to have written or at least
played a role in the drafting of the Veto Message which destroyed the Second
Bank of the United States once and for all. A document written by Taney himself
years after the event seemed to fortify this assumption.[14] But drafts of the
Veto Message recently found in the Andrew Jackson Donelson papers are supposed
to indicate that actually Kendall was the author.[15]

Biddle's use of the press in his defense of the Bank was widely attacked
by its enemies in the course of the Bank War. The customary accusation has now
been investigated by James L. Crouthamel, "Did the Second Bank of the United
States Bribe the Press?" in Journalism Quarterly, XXXVI (1959), 35 ff. The
question is answered in the negative. On the other hand, a widely presumed result of the Bank War, the American monetary disturbances in the 1830's and early
1840's, have recently been assigned rather to external influences by

George Macesich. His paper, "Sources of Monetary Disturbances in the United States, 1834-1845," appeared in The Journal of Economic History, XX (1960), 407 ff.

Once removed from the Second Bank of the United States the government deposits were transferred to state-chartered banks which, as is generally known, were designated by contemporaries as "pet banks." As a matter of fact, the pet bank system, the details of which had not been investigated until recently, has now attracted a good deal of attention. Harry N. Scheiber, in his article "The Pet Banks in Jacksonian Politics and Finance, 1833-1841" in The Journal of Economic History, XXIII (1963), 196 ff., has shown that of the first seven deposit banks selected by the Treasury Department, six were dominated by friends of the administration. Therefore the nickname was originally justified, although, later, politics played a smaller role in the selection. Scheiber himself has treated a bank which became a depository of government funds without any affiliation of its leading men with Democratic politics in his paper, "George Bancroft and the Bank of Michigan 1837-41" in Michigan History, XLIV (1960), pp. 82 ff. It is not our task here to report on further details presented in these essays.

Besides Scheiber, Frank Otto Gatell carefully investigated the pertinent material. In Volume LXXX (1964/1965), 35 ff., of the American Historical Review he published a paper, "Spoils of the Bank War: Political Bias in the Selection of Pet Banks," which he followed up by one on "Secretary Taney and the Baltimore Pets: A Study in Banking and Politics: in Business History Review, XXXIX (1965), 207 ff. In the first-named paper Gatell, who on certain points differs with Scheiber, confirmed Scheiber's general statement on the selection of the first deposit banks giving slightly different figures and going further in the explanation of the pertinent policy of the Treasury Department. The value of his earlier paper lies in his investigation of the selected deposit banks, city by city, and in distinguishing three periods of selection prior to the Deposit Act of 1836. He arrives at the conclusion that "geographically determined, they [the pet banks] showed a mixed picture of politics." In the second paper Gatell concentrates on Baltimore. This implies that Thomas Ellicott, president of the Union Bank of Baltimore (treated also in this work), and his relations to Taney moved into the center of interest, since Ellicott, a personal friend of Taney, played a considerable role in planning the removal of the deposits and in the establishment of the pet bank system. It is a rather unsavory story which cannot be retold here. For his second paper Gatell was able to use a document published by Stuart Bruchey: "Roger Brooke Taney's Account of his Relations with Thomas Ellicott in the Bank War" in Maryland Historical Magazine, LIII (1958), 58 ff. and 131 ff. Of course, Taney's relations with Ellicott are also described in Lewis' biography of Jackson's Secretary of the Treasury. His presentation is mainly based on material emanating from Taney himself.

At this point a paper on a minor, almost forgotten, and hardly respectable man must be mentioned. Written by John M. Mc Faul and Frank Otto Gatell it is entitled "The Outcast Insider Reuben M. Whitney and the Bank War" and appeared in the Pennsylvania Magazine of History and Biography, XCI (1967), 115-144. Whitney, a bankrupt merchant and politician, acted as the agent of the Pet Banks.

IV

(Chapters VIII and XII)

Certain problems of Southern, more specifically Louisiana, banking history are being re-investigated by Irene D. Neu. She has established beyond doubt that the term "plantation banks" which I used as the heading of Chapter VIII of Volume I is a misnomer. The appropriate term should have been the alternative "property banks." These were founded by New Orleans merchants to create additional lending facilities which they themselves would control and through which they could borrow on the basis of both city real property and plantations. Actually the emphasis was on the former.

On page 207 of Volume I of this book I quoted a contemporary statement according to which one J.B. Moussier devised the new and efficient type of bank. Irene Neu followed up this clue in her article, "J.B. Moussier and the Property Banks of Louisiana" in Business History Review, XXXV (1961) 550 ff. She found that Moussier was a merchant and sugar planter but that his primary interests were mercantile. Actually, it was he who in the 1820's drew up the charter of the Consolidated Association of Planters, the first property bank on which the later ones were modeled; and he prepared the necessary exhibits for the legislature, acting in the interest of the New Orleans mercantile community. Moussier did not manage his business as successfully as he devised a new and efficient type of bank. He died sometime before the end of 1831 leaving an entangled estate.[16]

Miss Neu is now working on a biography of Edmond John Forstall, and her research is based both on local primary sources and on material she found in the archives of the Barings and the Hopes in London and Amsterdam, respectively. Her work can be expected to revise my own presentation in Volume II, Chapter XII; and one erroneous statement can be put right here. The Forstall family was not of French origin, as I stated following the then available information. The Forstalls are an Irish family who went to Louisiana by way of Martinique. Edmond J. played a role in connection with the Louisiana Banking Act of 1842 which in the older literature is universally praised. Younger students of banking, influenced by the present-day interest in economic development, are less favorably inclined toward what was a remarkable achievement. These critics, supposedly historians, forget about history, namely that the Act was the creative reaction to the horrible experiences which the merchants and the state had suffered during the preceding decade. The critics feel, and probably rightly so, that the Act retarded economic development in the state. No doubt, inflationary banking is a boon to economic development, and I myself have stated so somewhere in this work. But America had to pay a very high price for inflationary banking and for a very fast economic development, and under the given circumstances it appears healthy to me, just as before, that the brakes were put on at least in one, and a relatively advanced, state. Typical of the approach of the young generation seems to be the report by George D. Green on his thesis, the report having been published under the title, "Banking and Finance in Antebellum Louisiana: Their Influence on the Course of Economic Development" in Journal of Economic History, XXVI (1966), 579-581. The basic error of the author is a lack of understanding of the fact that every kind of theory useful in historical research is itself historical in character. Mid-twentieth century banking theory is inapplicable, if one wants to understand banking practice of the mid-nineteenth century, just as mid-nineteenth century banking theory does not fit banking of the 1960's. Although of basic importance for the analytical economic historian, this rule is often forgotten. Green's criticism of the stand which I have taken is beside the point and is due to lack of epistemological insight.

V

(Chapters VII and IX)

I have not come across a single recent item on Free Banking, but since the Equal Rights Party, the so-called Locofocos, played a role in the establishment of Free Banking in the State of New York, the article by Carl N. Degler, "The Locofocos: Urban 'Agragians'" in Journal of Economic History, XVI (1956), 322 ff., is of tangential interest to the historian of American banking.

In a paper entitled "The Trustee Savings Banks 1817-1861" in the Journal of Economic History, XXI (1961), 26 ff., Albert Fishlow has shown that English savings banks, established to assist the poor, actually became a boon for the lower middle classes. This article should inspire younger American historians to make similar investigations into the early American savings banks, if the extant material permits. I would not dare make guesses in advance as to the result. Even more important would be a historical investigation of the American stock savings banks of the nineteenth century. I am not aware that any historical material on this type of savings bank has been analyzed or even compiled. In these savings banks the savers seem to have been neglected and the institutions seem to have enabled aggressive businessmen to collect funds for other enterprises of their own from the smallest rivulets into which savings of the impecunious lower strata could be directed. I wonder what one could learn about American business methods from a pertinent investigation.

While what appears to me as the most urgent research in this area of banking seems to have been neglected, some investigations have been conducted by Peter Lester Payne and Lance Edwin Davis: The Savings Bank of Baltimore 1818-1866, A Historical and Analytical Study, The Johns Hopkins University Studies in Historical and Political Science, Series LXXII, No. 2 (Baltimore, 1956) and "From Benevolence to Business: The Story of Two Savings Banks" in the Business History Review, XXXII (1958), 386 ff. The latter study compares the Savings Bank of Baltimore with the Provident Institution for Savings in the Town of Boston, focusing attention on objectives, administration, and policies considered typical of savings banking in ante-bellum America. (For further titles, see the bibliography Studies in Enterprise by Lorna Daniells cited on page XXVI(a) of this paper.)

VI

(Chapters X and XI)

There are a number of items which are hard to subsume because events or institutions treated therein had their start in the 1830's and carried over

into the 1840's and 1850's, that is, they began in what is characterized in
this book as the second period of American banking and continued into what is
here called the third period. I am thinking of such items as

Macesich, George, "Sources of Monetary Disturbances in the United States, 1834-
    1845, Journal of Economic History, XX (1960), 407 ff.
Scheiber, Harry, "The Commercial Bank of Lake Erie, 1831-1843, Business History
    Review, XL (1966), 47 ff.
Warburton, Clark, "Variations in Economic Growth and Banking Developments in
    the United States from 1835 to 1885" Journal of Economic History, XVIII
    (1958), 283 ff.

   Studying the period between 1840 and 1860 one is bound to feel a gap
in knowledge; one lacks a history of the trust company then becoming important.
Trust companies had no note privilege but were de facto regular banks which
could, at least in principle, create purchasing power by way of deposits. The
fact that very little is known about the beginnings is disturbing also to the
student of later banking prior to 1912.

   I am not aware of any recent significant research in the fields
covered by Chapters X and XI of my book.

VII

(Chapters XIII - XVII)

   What has been said about the lack of new research on the general
characteristics of banking between 1840 and 1860 and on the Middle Western
state banks with branches, holds true also for the subjects treated in this
book in Chapters XIII to XVII. With two exceptions there is little to report.

   First, in Chapter XIV on Private Banking I dealt with the Scottish
immigrant George Smith as one of the few note-issuing private bankers in the
United States. He himself, his associates, and his business activities as a
land speculator and banker, are now treated in a very satisfactory monograph
by Alice E. Smith, George Smith's Money: A Scottish Investor in America
(Madison, Wisconsin, 1966). The subtitle is somewhat misleading, for Smith was
not merely an investor, he was a financier of first rank in an area that was in
the process of being opened up. On the other hand, there is a kernel of truth
in the characterization: I do think that his ultimate extraordinary success
was to a large extent due to the fact that in the beginning he had more capital
at his disposal than the average moneyed immigrant of the 1830's brought to
Illinois or Wisconsin.

   The new book does not change completely the traditional picture, but
it alters it somewhat and is very revealing. Smith came to America first in
1833 on his own account bringing some funds with which he very successfully
speculated in Illinois, especially Chicago, and Wisconsin real estate. After
three years he returned to Aberdeen for a short stay and induced Scottish
promoters to establish a joint-stock company, the Illinois Investment Company,
through which Scottish capital was set aside for speculative enterprise in
American real estate. Smith returned to the United States as a shareholder and
as its master mind, but he does seem to have been officially an agent or
employee. Under his influence what was meant to be a real estate office was

soon made over into a banking and commission business without the knowledge of
the shareholders. Scottish money was now also used for establishing, under
Smith's presidency, the Wisconsin Marine and Fire Insurance Company, de facto
a bank in a bankless area.

The book is full of details of how the pseudo-banking enterprise was
run. By issuing "certificates of deposit" in small round denominations the
company created purchasing power (a circulating medium) as any other bank did.
It kept specie for redemption purposes at the rate of 20 per cent of the capital,
i.e., in the 1840's Smith still adhered to Mercantilist banking theory which
related note issue to capital; capital and not specific reserves was considered
the ultimate backing of note issues. Through the Smith monograph we gain insight into profit rates, into interest rates charged, running as high as 12 per
cent per annum, and into Smith's lending and dividend policies. The concern
operated out of Chicago and Milwaukee and used a number of agencies (actually
branches) whose main task was to circulate the "certificates of deposit" of the
Wisconsin Marine and Fire Insurance Company. Mainly for the purpose of dealing
in domestic exchange the head offices were interlocked with the New York brokerage house of Strachan and Scot, which was merely the American style of the
Illinois Investment Company, of which both Strachan and Scot were employees.
(They were meant to do a real estate business in Chicago but, without knowledge
of the managing committee of the Scottish shareholders, had changed both the
domicile and the purpose of their activities.)

It is implied that the author, reporting these and other damaging facts,
does not gloss over shady aspects of the business. In the late 1830's, during
the depression, Smith unloaded onto his Scottish partners as his share in the
company's capital personally owned real estate at his own price and without their
knowledge. That there was not a penny of deposits behind the circulating
"certificates of deposit" was, of course, already known. They were promises to
pay but, in contrast to what many contemporary American banks did, the promises
were kept and could be kept because of Smith's highly efficient entrepreneurship.
That was the secret of the success of the business leader prior to the deepening
of the depression. What happened at the depth of the depression of the 1840's
is not much to the credit of the de facto trustees of the Scottish capitalists.
When a confidant of the investors arrived in America he found the concern in
very bad shape. Not only had the New York office (Strachan and Scot) shown very
poor judgment in its lending, but the misdeeds of the senior manager also came
to light. It is doubtful whether Smith himself had acted in an unimpeachable
way. At all events he benefited when the disgusted Scottish investors decided
to dissolve their company and, after having received a pittance on their shares,
released the managers from further responsibility.

What remained after such bloodletting survived the depression and was
carried to tremendous success in the next boom. Smith now specialized in
creating a paper currency and deriving extraordinary profit therefrom. In the
1840's and 1850's he came more and more under fire and was fought tooth and claw
by state authorities, newspapers, and competing enterprises, although at the
same time, he also had friends and defenders. While he always sustained the convertibility of his issues, his activities came closer and closer to wildcat
banking.

Smith, who probably understood the fine points of banking better than
any contemporary in what was then the American West, is described by his
biographer as a wily and not too scrupulous man appearing "forbidding" to all

but his few collaborators. He had a remarkable sense of timing which permitted him to liquidate his business a few months before the crisis broke in 1857. He was, in fact, a money-making automaton cooperating with an in-group of Scots who, with one exception (Alexander Mitchell) never became Americanized, never married, and returned home with stuffed pocketbooks after a pretty long excursion to the New World. Other and younger Scots complemented his staff. Smith's later activities as an investor in Middle Western railroads do not concern us here.

In the same Chapter XIV on Private Banking in which I dealt with George Smith, I described on pp. 78/79 more recent developments in the field of installment credit. An article by Robert A. Lynn, "Installment Credit before 1870" in Business History Review, XXXII (1958), 414 ff., seems to indicate that installment credit originated by the middle of the nineteenth century in connection with the marketing of expensive farm implements and machines and the selling of consumers' capital such as sewing machines and pianos. It was not necessarily a line for private bankers.

The second important contribution to the topics treated in this section and in the pertinent chapters of this book is the article by Phillip Cagan "The First Fifty Years of the National Banking System: An Historical Appraisal" in Banking and Monetary Studies, ed. by Deane Carson (see footnote 1), 15 ff.

In the framework of a conference, called by the Eleutherian Mills-Hagley Foundation, the Proceedings of which were published under the title Economic Change in the Civil War Era, edited by David T. Gilchrist and W. David Lewis (Grenville, Delaware, 1965), commercial banking was discussed by Robert P. Sharkey and the author of the present volume. Their presentations hardly brought new information; but the recorded discussion raised some interesting points (see pages 29-40). The topic of the conference overlapped my Chapters X, XVI, and XVIII. [17]

VIII

(Chapters XVIII - XX)

Irwin Unger in a book which he himself characterizes as "primarily a political ... history" (p. 7) has provided a wealth of background information for banking history between the end of the Civil War and 1880. It is entitled The Greenback Era: A Social and Political History of American Finance, 1865-1879 (Princeton, 1964).

Of a very different character and presented with much more sophistication is the background information contained in A Monetary History of the United States 1867-1960 by Milton Friedman and Anna Jacobson Schwartz, being "a study of the National Bureau of Economic Research" (Princeton, 1963). It focuses attention on the "stock of money in the United States" and deals in its first 188 pages with the decades from the end of the Civil War to the establishment of the Federal Reserve System. Since deposits are generally held to belong to the stock of money and the authors deal with a period treated in this book also, the volume deserves attention here. To be sure, the authors include in the "stock of money" savings-banks deposits also. This does not appear to me as a good idea, although I would agree that a certain percentage of savings-banks deposits can and should be included. I think an investigation of extant saving-bank records of various periods as to the ratio of withdrawals to total deposits might reveal the pertinent percentage.

It is noteworthy that the authors consider the earlier notes of National Banks, backed as they were by government bonds, as indirect government liabilities rather than "liabilities of banks comparable to their deposits" (p. 50). On the whole, they are less interested in bank money than in other kinds and in the totals. But they studied the rise of deposit money (pp. 122, 164), the actual, as opposed to the legal, reserve ratios (see index under "deposit currency, ratio"). They deal with central-banking activities of the Treasury which can be traced back to the times of Hamilton and Gallatin.[18] Of course, the resumption of specie payments in 1879 is treated by Friedman and Schwartz in great detail.[19] On the whole the book is valuable for the bank historian by providing quantitative background information rather than essential new knowledge on banking.

A different statement is in order when we evaluate the paper by Lance E. Davis, "The Investment Market, 1870-1914: The Evolution of a National Market" in Journal of Economic History, XXV (1965), 355 ff. He shows that until about 1900 the interest rates on short-term loans paid by the banks of the major American cities were different, varying between an average of 4.854 per cent in New England and 8.991 per cent in the Western States. But thereafter the growth of a national market for short-term capital substantially reduced the rate differentials. In contrast, a national market for long-term capital developed less quickly before World War I, although there was a trend in this direction also; this was due to the activities of the large insurance companies and the rise of investment banking. That this development was not equally fast and complete may have been due to a falling behind of mortgage banking.

A history of banking such as the present one is, of course, specifically concerned with the role which bankers played at various opportunities. I myself described the actions of the New York banking community in the last stages of resumption during which they assisted the Secretary of the Treasury. (See "'Translating' Economic Policy into Business Policy: An Illustration from the Resumption of Specie Payments in 1879" in Bulletin of the Business Historical Society, XX [1946], 190 ff.) Another pertinent presentation goes further back. In Chapter VI (pp. 221 ff.) of his book Money, Class, and Party, an Economic Study of Civil War and Reconstruction, Johns Hopkins University Studies in Historical and Political Science, Series LXVII, No. 59, Robert P. Sharkey asks: What role did the American bankers play in the post-Civil War contraction of the currency preparing the ultimate resumption of specie payments? He found that there were differences of opinion, particularly between Eastern and Western bankers. On the whole, however, banking opinion was originally distinctly for contraction. In fact the bankers' backing and their providing "the constitutional rational for [their] opinion" was a valuable assistance to McCulloch and and his policy (p. 271).[20] In the later stages of the development toward resumption bankers opinion was, according to Unger, divided.

Let us stress then that bankers played a role in favoring contraction which for some while became United States policy after the Civil War, and that ultimately they helped in the resumption of specie payments. One and a half decades later, in 1895, Morgan and Belmont at the head of a syndicate of bankers, defended the gold standard, as described in this work, Volume II, page 370. Yet in 1896 the gold standard was again jeopardized during the election campaign, when William Jennings Bryan became a presidential candidate on a bimetallist platform. Mathew Simon, in an article entitled, "The Hot Money Movement and the Private Exchange Pool Proposal of 1896" in Journal of Economic History, XX (1960), 31 ff., deals with the reaction of influential bankers, an episode not known to me when I wrote this book. In fact, in July 1896 the "international bankers," i.e., the big exchange dealers, met under the leadership of Morgan who had invited them to his office. These men, most of whom were simultaneously investment bankers, formed a pool, to be managed by the houses of Morgan, Belmont, von Hoffmann & Co., Kuhn, Loeb and Company, and Lazard Frères, to prevent the shipment of gold. It handled the situation on the basis of the experience gained by the Morgan-Belmont syndicate of the previous year, sabotaged by gold exports of W. H. Crossmann and Bros. The rather tight pool borrowed short-term funds in Europe and sold sight drafts and cable transfers at rates lower than the gold export point. It rightly figured that the European advances could be made good by claims on Europe arising from the export of the new cotton crop within the next two months. The expectation came true and confidence was restored.

When, in Chapter XVIII of Volume II, pp. 186 ff. of the first edition of this book, I treated the bank consolidations taking place by 1900, I was not aware of what had happened in Philadelphia so that there is a gap on page 192. In the meantime this information has been provided by Nicholas B. Wainwright in his book on the History of the Philadelphia National Bank, A Century and a Half of Philadelphia Banking 1803-1953 (p.p., Philadelphia, 1953), 146, 150. According to Wainwright, the Fourth Street National Bank of Philadelphia, founded in 1886, absorbed several smaller banks in its quick rise. In 1898 it took over the National Bank of the Republic, the Seventh and the Commercial National Banks. The Merchants' National Bank acquired the National Bank of Commerce in 1899, thereby becoming a large financial institution.

The material presented in this book on Boston consolidations (Volume II, p. 190) has been supplemented by an article by Marion W. Sears, "The National Shawmut Bank Consolidation of 1898" in Business History Review, XXXIX (1965), 368 ff. This paper is valuable, since it describes the motivation behind the move. Massachusetts savings banks which had invested in Boston bank stock and were disappointed by dropping prices of the shares and low dividends, took the lead. The process by which the consolidation took place is well presented.

The balanced article by Joel A. Tarr, "John R. Walsh of Chicago: A Case Study in Banking and Politics, 1881-1905" in Business History Review, XL (1966), 451 ff., describes in detail the rise and fall of a Chicago chain of banks which is only touched upon in the second volume of this work. Its fate is seen as the result of the owner's overcommitment in unprofitable enterprises, for the benefit of which the banks were drawn upon, but also as the outcome of undue reliance of a businessman on the favors of the ruling party machine.

IX

(Chapter XXI)

Extensive research on American investment banking is being conducted by Vincent P. Carosso whose study emphasizes the twentieth century; but the early chapters of his coming book deal with the nineteenth century, too, and also with the first decade of the twentieth century. To that extent, as Carosso has informed me, his findings confirm the presentation in this work. On the other hand, recent research in the field has shown that my material could have been periodized. What I described in Section VIII (pages 333 ff.) of my chapter on investment banking could be seen as its first American period, characterized by the fact that government securities (those of the Federal and state governments alike) were the main stock in trade.[21] In the 1830's this first period overlapped with the second in which railroad securities became a more important article than state stock for the firms concerned. This second period, in turn, passed through three phases prior to the Civil War.

This fact has been pointed out by Alfred D. Chandler, Jr. in his paper, "Patterns of American Railroad Finance, 1830-1850" in Business History Review, XXVIII (1954), 248 ff. In the first phase Philadelphia was leading, due to the activities of Nicholas Biddle and of Thomas Biddle and Company. Chandler goes so far as to call Nicholas Biddle "America's pioneer investment banker" (p. 253). I do not think that one can rightly say that, since it would mean overlooking what I have called above the first period of American investment banking. I myself (Volume II, p. 337) speak of Biddle as this country's first "full-fledged" investment banker.

Turning to Thomas Biddle and Company, whose outstanding role in the field is pointed out in this work, we find it now treated in a company history by Harold A. West entitled Two Hundred Years 1764-1964. The Story of Yarnall, Biddle & Co., Investment Bankers (p.p., Philadelphia, 1965). The Biddle firm that has existed more than two hundred years used different styles during its career. As mentioned in this work also, it originated in 1764 as a typical colonial mercantile and shipping house. By 1820 it had developed into a banking and brokerage business dealing in the shares of banks, turnpike companies, government obligations, canal stock, and some others, for example, stock of the Philadelphia, Dover & Norfolk Steam Boat and Transportation Company. Thomas Biddle (1776-1857), since 1806 at the head of the firm, acted as the broker of his cousin Nicholas Biddle, whose adviser and confidant he was at the same time. Between 1830 and 1857 Thomas Biddle guided the firm, then styled Thomas Biddle & Co. It was in this period that he became one of the early American railroad financiers. A good deal of additional information on Thomas Biddle & Co. is contained in this work (see its index).

On pages 341 and 342 of its second volume I speak of two regular banks which, besides the Bank of the United States of Pennsylvania in the late 1830's, had reached the status of genuine investment banks: the Morris Canal and Banking Company and the North American Trust and Banking Company of New York. About this latter firm additional information has been collected, since this book first appeared.[22] The North American Trust and Banking Company was established in 1838 under the New York Free Banking Act with an authorized capital of $50,000,000 divided into $100 shares. Actually $3,285,900 was subscribed, a large amount for the time. Among the directors were Anson G. Phelps, founder of Phelps, Dodge and Company; John Lorimer Graham; and Melvil Wilson, one of the partners of the London firm of Thomas Wilson and Company which failed in the crisis of 1837. Palmer, McKillop, Dent and Company of London, headed by Sir Horsley Palmer who had made some arrangements with the Wilson partners, became the agents of the newly founded New York bank. One of its main functions may have been facilitating the realization of the frozen assets of Thomas Wilson and Company. The cash capital of the new bank was rather small, since subscriptions could be made in state bonds and in 7 per cent personal bonds secured by unencumbered real estate. The cash capital amounted to about $250,000, almost all of which came from British subscribers.

The new enterprise immediately entered the field of investment banking. Its first extensive transaction was the purchase of $1,000,000 of Arkansas bonds, followed by that of large numbers of Indiana, Ohio, Louisiana, and Florida bonds. These were mostly bought on credit and paid for by interest-bearing certificates of deposit and post notes; then they were consigned to Europe, especially to the Palmer firm. The latter also received for sale in Europe convertible bonds and other credit instruments of the New York bank which, however, could have been sold only at "ruinous" prices. Therefore advances were made by Palmer, McKillop, Dent and Company, and bills of exchange drawn on them by the New York bank.

Joseph D. Beers, whose pre-crisis investment activities are discussed in this book, was the first president of the North American Trust and Banking Company. From the outset his policy was highly speculative and possibly even shady. To be sure the former Wilson partners, who played a role in the enterprise, were trying to influence the management of the bank's affairs in the interest of the creditors of their old firm.

After this detour let us return to the main line of thought. After Nicholas Biddle's retirement the center of railroad finance shifted to Boston. The predominance of this city in the field characterizes the second phase of the second period of American investment banking. One aspect of the Boston phase of the development, and what evolved from it over a period of several decades, is the subject of a study by Arthur M. Johnson and Barry E. Supple, Boston Capitalists and Western Railroads: A Study in the Nineteenth Century Railroad Investment Process, Harvard Studies in Business History, No. 23 (Cambridge, Mass., 1967). The title of this book is in a way unfortunate, since it may cause students of financial history to overlook it. In fact, the study deals with the process by which New England capital amassed in trade and mobilized by individuals was applied to early Western railroads. Its contribution lies in the identification of investor-types and its analysis of their behavior over a considerable span of time. Furthermore, it covers the transition from direct investing by individuals allied by kinship and trade relationships to the development of institutional arrangements for amassing and applying capital, exemplified by the important role of investment banking houses in financing Western railroads by the end of the nineteenth century.

A new phase of railroad finance, which implies a new phase of the second period of American investment banking, started when New York, overtaking Boston, became the center of railroad finance. The move to New York started by 1850. The first decade of this phase, i.e., the ante-bellum decade of American investment banking, has attracted the attention of quite a few recent researchers. In this connection the firm of Winslow, Lanier and Company moved very much into the limelight, actually to a larger extent than implied in my own presentation. Vincent P. Carosso warned me in a letter that I was underestimating the post-Civil-War activities of this company which continued to be important in this period but lost its leadership. It disbanded only at some point between 1929 and 1931. I must confess that in writing this book I overlooked the autobiography of James Franklin Doughly Lanier, Sketch of the Life of J.F.D. Lanier (printed for the use of the family only).[23]

On the other hand, a doubt must be raised. Is it perhaps possible that the importance of Winslow, Lanier and Company has recently been overestimated by historians?[24] According to Lanier himself, his company was the first in the

field and "created" the negotiating of railroad securities in the New York
market. So it was bound to attract the lion's share of attention, even if
Lanier's autobiography had been written in a more modest tone. But very soon
there arose keen competition in the field, and the leaders among the competitors
of Winslow, Lanier and Company have not yet been carefully investigated. I mean
such firms as Morris Ketchum and Company, Duncan Sherman and Company, Dulaney &
Clark, and a good many others.

As a matter of fact between about 1850 and 1860 there were three groups
of investment bankers active in New York. One consisted of genuinely American
firms, of which some have just been mentioned. Another group consisted of Swiss
bankers who took American securities to the Continent. No details are known
about these men and their enterprises. The third was made up of Anglo-American
merchant bankers. On these we now have an attractive paper by Ralph W. and
Muriel E. Hidy, entitled "Anglo-American Merchant Bankers and Railroads in the
Old North West, 1848-1860" published in the Business History Review, XXXIV
(1960), 150 ff. Leading firms among these were Baring Brothers & Company and
George Peabody & Company, but they were joined in marketing American securities
in Europe by about half a dozen other companies. Their pertinent business consisted of a web of mercantile and financial transactions largely conducted in
partnership with American houses.

But the investment banking business did not seem to have been concentrated in New York to the exclusion of all other locations. One immediately
thinks of Boston, but there was also, for example, the firm of Robert Garret &
Sons in Baltimore, whose activities were described in the company history by
Harold A. Williams, Robert Garret & Sons: Origin and Development 1840-1965
(p.p., Baltimore, 1965). One is almost inclined to say, "of course" this
company too started as a mercantile house. It traded very actively with the
West but also with other areas of North and Central America. Since it was
located in Baltimore and did business with the West, the well-to-do owners were
bound to take an interest in the Baltimore and Ohio Railroad; and thence they
were drawn into railroad finance. Bonds of several railroads, especially those
connecting with the B. & O., were disposed of in American markets including
New York, and it is interesting to learn how these markets were opened up (p.27).
The pertinent European business was done with the Barings and the Peabodys.
In the middle of the 1850's the firm was winding up its grocery business with
the West and began emphasizing investment banking and such other financial
transactions as were then commonly undertaken by private bankers.[25] In the
1860's it cooperated with J. Pierpont Morgan & Company of New York. But specialization did not as yet go beyond a certain point. Only in New York, and to a
less extent in Philadelphia and Boston, was the volume of trade in securities
large enough to permit far-reaching specialization. The Garrets of Baltimore
had to round out their business by trade in coffee, sugar, flour, and cotton;
once in a while they acted as shipping brokers, and they had extensive real estate interests. But even the New York firms, taking a particular interest in
private banking and even more specifically in investment banking, embarked on a
good many transactions in rails. These they purchased in England for the American railroads, the securities of which they floated in the European markets.

Before we turn to what can be considered the third period of American
investment banking, attention must be drawn to a paper by Harry H. Pierce,
"Foreign Investments in American Enterprise," presented at the Eleutherian-Mills
Conference of 1964, mentioned above and printed in the conference record.[26]

The paper is full of very detailed information on the placing of railroad securities in England and on the Continent, carrying the story from 1827 through about 1880. Yet attention is not focused on the investment banker.

A third period of American investment banking started with the "Rise of a Market for Industrial Securities, 1887-1902," this being the title of a paper by Thomas R. Navin and Marion V. Sears in Business History Review, XXIX (1955), 105 ff. The essay contains mostly background information; but it touches also upon some of the leading promoters of the period and some of the important flotations. It was already known that the then big investment bankers were slow in entering the new field. The authors come to the conclusion that what we have called here the third period of American investment banking, in which industrials slowly gained a larger and larger share in the market without crowding out railroad securities as the most important stock in trade, experienced four developmental phases succeeding each other.[27] This conclusion is, of course, predicated on the kind of criterion used in the periodization.

Our third period of investment banking, thus established, is, when seen from another angle, the period of financial capitalism, the era ruled by the giants of investment banking. As James P. Baughman has suggested to me in private conversations, their rise in the post-bellum period may have been due first to the tremendous amount of government securities to be handled if not refunded. In a later stage it was, of course, the result of the widening market in securities, due largely to the rise of the big insurance companies and to some extent that of the investment trusts.

Douglass C. North in a paper, "Life Insurance and Investment Banking at the Time of the Armstrong Investigation of 1905-1906" in Journal of Economic History, XIV (1954), 209 ff., has stressed that connection. He points out that the big three insurance companies, the Mutual, the Equitable, and the New York Life, which commanded a considerable share in the country's new savings, played a role in the ascendency of the investment banking community. This they did not only by putting funds at the disposal of the investment bankers, but also by the flexibility with which they could be used: on the one hand, as members of syndicates; on the other, as providers of a market for securities once floated. But they were unable to rise to a controlling position and remained dependent, to be sure, on the investment banking community rather than on particular investment bankers.[28]

The individual giants of investment banking have not been neglected by recent researchers. The foremost among them and his enterprise have been treated in the new book by Edwin P. Hoyt, Jr., The House of Morgan (New York, 1966), a journalistic performance; it hardly goes beyond the older one on the same subject by Frederick Lewis Allen which is cited in the list of references of Volume II of this work, except that it carries the story to the present. Moreover Jonathan Hughes has dealt with Morgan and his actions in the eighth chapter, entitled "J. Pierpont Morgan, the Investment Banker as Statesman," in his book The Vital Few, American Progress and Its Protagonists (Boston, 1966).[29]

On the other hand, the Jewish giants and exponents of financial capitalism are treated in the brilliant paper by Barry E. Supple, "A Business Elite: German-Jewish Financiers in Nineteenth-Century New York" in Business History Review, XXXI (1957), 143 ff. The author investigated the "social and economic influences which fashioned the ultimate business activities of the German-Jewish investment bankers." The group, whose prominent member was Kuhn, Loeb & Co., was second only to its Yankee competitors led by Morgan and Baker, as described in this work. More recently Stephen Birmingham has treated the same subject in his book 'Our Crowd:' The Great Jewish Families of New York (New York, 1967). He has emphasized the families of the Jewish investment bankers, rather than their business, and the rise of these immigrant families in American society. An old paper on August Belmont came only recently to the attention of the author: Ludwig Frank, "Silhuetten deutsch-amerikanischer Banquiers: August Belmont." It is to be found in Feuilleton Beilage zur "New Yorker Handelszeitung," October 27, November 10, December 1, 1877.

        It is needless to stress here again, that the house of J. & W. Seligman & Co. belonged to the small number of outstanding Jewish investment bankers. The hundredth anniversary of the banking house of the family, founded in 1864, was celebrated by the company in an anniversary publication written by Ross L. Muir and Carl J. White, Over the Long Term... the Story of J. & W. Seligman & Co. (p.p., New York, 1964). It brings out a good deal of previously unknown information on the beginnings and the development of the family businesses between 1837, when Joseph Seligman as the first of eight brothers arrived in the United States, and 1864 when the international banking and investment firm was founded. Like the Guggenheims and Albert D. Lasker's father, the Seligmans started as pack peddlers.

        Information has been made available on an investment bank which in the pre-World War I days possessed importance without belonging to the small number of leading houses. We refer to Spencer Trask and Company, New York, which developed out of a stock brokerage firm. Active as an early backer of Edison, it led in the introduction of electric light, and from then on took a special interest in the handling of securities of public utilities. Influential in the company, besides Spencer Trask himself and after the latter's death, was George Foster Peabody (1854-1938).[30]

                                    X

        There have appeared in recent years a few histories of banking in particular states or regions. Outstanding among the presentations is the banking history of Georgia contained in Milton Sydney Heath's Constructive Liberalism: The Role of the State in Economic Development in Georgia to 1860 (Cambridge, Mass., 1954), pp. 159-230.[31] This piece goes in depth far beyond what can be found in the common run of histories of banking in the various states.

        Banking in Texas deserves special attention, since its evolution there was very different from the development elsewhere in the United States. As early as the fall of 1822 the governor of the province of Texas, then still part of Mexico, independent of Spain since 1821, issued a degree establishing the Banco Nacional de Texas. It actually issued close to $12,000 in notes, the first of which were used to pay overdue soldiers' wages. It was expected that the silver ultimately to be sent by the national government to settle the soldier's claims would be used to redeem the notes. But when the Mexican government decided to issue paper money which was declared legal tender, the bank came to an unceremonious end and payment of the notes was tendered in government paper money. After the note holders steadfastly refused to accept this paper, their claims were ultimately settled in 1829.[32]

        The next banking episode in Texas grew out of the mercantile activities of the House of McKinney & Williams, which played a large role when Texas was

fighting for independence and during the time it was an independent country.
This mercantile partnership received a charter for the Banco di Commercio y
Agricultura, the first legally incorporated, privately owned bank in Texas. It
had an authorized capital of $1,000,000 and operated in Galveston between 1847
and 1859, at which date its charter was declared invalid. Thereupon it liquidated and transferred its good will to a private bank.[33]

This fate of the bank was due to the fact that the Texas constitution
of 1845 prohibited the chartering of banks and authorized the legislation to
forbid the issue of notes by private bankers, an action which the legislature
took the following year. Only under the rule of a new and later constitution,
that of 1869, did the incorporation of banks become possible. More than forty
state banks were chartered from 1870 through 1875. Yet from 1876 to 1904 it
again was legally impossible to establish chartered banks in Texas. Under these
circumstances private banks gained greater importance in that state than in the
other American states. There were 86 private banks at the end of 1873, 145 in
1891, and 184 in 1904. Of course the constitutional prohibition did not extend
to National Banks, the first of which was established in 1865 (The First National
Bank of Galveston). Their number grew to 207 in 1891 and to 421 in 1904.[34]

The following is a list of recent publications on banking in various
states:

Andersen, Theodore A. A Century of Banking in Wisconsin. Madison, 1954.

Arrington, Leonard J. "Banking Enterprise in Utah, 1847-1860," Business History
    Review, XXIX (1955), 312 ff.

Basalou, F.W. "The Concentration of Banking Power in Nevada: A Historical
    Analysis," Business History Review, XXIX (1955), 350 ff.

Brantley, William H. Banking in Alabama 1816-1860. Birmingham, 1961.

Cole, David M. The Development of Banking in the District of Columbia. New York,
    1959.

Dovell, Junius E. History of Banking in Florida, 1828-1954. Orlando, 1955.

Federal Reserve Bank of Boston, Commercial Banking in New England, 1784-1958.
    Boston, Mass., 1959.

French, Bruce H. Banking and Insurance in New Jersey: A History. Princeton, 1965.

Hasse, William F. A History of Money and Banking in Connecticut. New Haven, 1957.

To these must be added a few more, inserted in non-national periodicals, the
titles of which can be found in the bibliography by Lorna Daniells to be cited
forthwith.

Larger is the number of histories of individual banks (company histories) the titles of which need not be presented here, since they are to be
found in Lorna Daniells, Studies in Enterprise. A Selected Bibliography of
American and Canadian Company Histories and Biographies of Businessmen (Boston,
Mass., 1957); see section VII, pp. 87-104, "Finance." Continuations have
appeared in the Business History Review, XXXIII (1959), 217 ff.; XXXIV (1960),
219; XXV (1961), 265; XXXVI (1962), 216; XXXVII (1963), 252; and XXXVIII (1964),
356. The titles in question can be found under the head of "Banking" on the
pages cited here, except in Vol. XXXIII (1959) which lacks topical entries.
The bibliography will be continued but no longer on a yearly basis.

Only after the appearance of the original edition of this book, was a
key to extant bank records provided for the first time by the National Union
Catalogue of Manuscripts, listed under the index heading "Banks and Banking."
A cumulative index for the first two volumes (1959 through 1962) appeared in
1964, while the individual volumes have their own indexes. Additional material

will be listed in later volumes, when reported by the owning institutions. In passing it may be mentioned that the early credit records of Dunn and Bradstreet have been deposited in the manuscript collections of Baker Library, Graduate School of Business Administration, Harvard University. The credit reports on contemporary banks may prove useful to some researchers in the field; they go back to the 1840's.

May 1, 1968.   Fritz Redlich

Introduction

Footnotes

1. Incidentally, there is a paper by Bray Hammond "Banking Before the Civil War" in Deane Carson, ed., Banking and Monetary Studies, a Project of the Department of Banking and Economic Research, Office of the Comptroller of the Currency (Homewood, Illinois, 1963), 1 ff.

2. See this work, Volume II, 42, footnote 49.

3. See page 134 of Alice E. Smith, George Smith's Money: A Scottish Investor in America (Madison, Wis., 1966).

4. W. B. Smith, Economic Aspects, 124.

5. Hammond, Banks and Politics, 254.

6. Wright, "Cheves and Biddle," 309, 310; also his (mimeographed) The Economic Library of the President of the Bank of the United States, 1819-1823. An Address before the Bibliographical Society of the University of Virginia November 7, 1950 (Charlottesville, Virginia, 1950), passim.

7. Hammond, Banks and Politics, 278; for the original, see Niles Register, LIII (1837), 8, 9.

8. Wright, "Cheves and Biddle," 318.

9. Hammond, Banks and Politics, 532.

10. See this introduction above, page viii(a)

11. Milton S. Heath, Constructive Liberalism: The Role of the State in Economic Development in Georgia to 1860 (Cambridge, Mass., 1954). Incidentally, J. Z. Rowe in his book The Public-Private Character of United States Central Banking (New Brunswick, N. J., 1965) designates the First and Second Banks of the United States as "central banks," i.e. puts these words in quotation marks.

12. The Canal Fund was one in which the revenue of the Erie and other New York canals accumulated and was held ready for the redemption of the bonds on the proceeds of which the canals had been built.

13. Hammond, Banks and Politics, 332, 354.

13a. Robert V. Rimini, in his book, Andrew Jackson and the Bank War: A Study in the Growth of Presidential Power (New York, 1967) focuses attention on the President's role in the struggle and stresses the political problem involved, namely, the use of the "veto power as an important presidential instrument in controlling legislation."

13b. Incidentally, Miss Wilburn has pointed in passing to the important role played in those years by the Albany banker, Thomas W. Olcott. Since some of the records of his enterprises are now available at Columbia University, he could and should be treated in a paper.

14. "Roger B. Taney's 'Bank War Manuscript'" ed. Carl Brent Swisher in Maryland Historical Magazine, LIII (1958), 103 ff., 215 ff.

15. Lynn L. Marshall, "The Authorship of Jackson's Bank Veto Message," Mississippi Valley Historical Review, L (1963/64), 466 ff.

16. There is new material available on the Real Estate Bank of Arkansas which I mentioned as one of the late plantation (better, property) banks; see Ted B. Worley, "The Control of the Real Estate Bank of Arkansas 1836-1855," in Mississippi Valley Historical Review, L (1963/64), 466 ff.

17. In my Chapter XVI on National Banking I mentioned Orlando B. Potter who played a minor role in its initiation. The few data which I could find on this man are to be found in Volume II, page 148, footnote 24. In the meantime

Andrew Barrie Jack informed me by letter that Potter was the financial and marketing partner of Grover and Baker, one of the early large sewing machine companies. He is, again according to Professor Jack, credited with what is probably the first patent pool, that of 1854 in which his company and the main other sewing machine producers participated.

18. Central banking activities of the Treasury are the subject of a book by Esther Taus which I have cited in the list of references, Volume I, page 326. H. Barger, The Management of Money: A Survey of the American Experience (Chicago, 1964), 16,17 mentions them again. I have not considered it my task to discuss the matter in this book.

19. A compilation of "Newspaper Accounts of the Resumption of Specie Payment in the United States on January 1, 1879" by Donald L. Kemmerer is in Monetary Notes, ed. Walter E. Spahr, XII, No. 5, May 1, 1962.

20. The paper by Richard H. Timberlake, Jr., "Ideological Factors in Specie Resumption and Treasury Policy" in Journal of Economic History, XXIV (1964), 29 ff., provides background information only.

On the other hand, that by James K. Kindahl, "Economic Factors in Specie Resumption [in] the United States, 1865-1879," Journal of Political Economy, LXIX (1961), 30 ff., provides a useful economic analysis of the necessary preconditions of successful resumption.

21. In contrast, what has been described in sections VI and VII, pages 323-333, would then appear as the prehistory.

A very interesting episode, so far entirely neglected, has been described by Milton Sydney Heath in his book Constructive Liberalism: The Role of the State in Economic Development in Georgia to 1860 (Cambridge, Mass., 1954). On pages 190-201 and 211-223 he describes the history of the Central Bank of Georgia which he interprets as representing an attempt at "investment banking on the basis of public credit" (p.229).

In Volume II, page 326 I touch upon the so-called improvement banks which up to this moment have not been adequately investigated. But Heath (on pages 201, 202, and 262-266) deals with the Georgia railroad banks belonging to the type. He arrives at the conclusion that, in the Georgia cases, note issues did not contribute to making construction possible.

22. The following presentation replaces Volume II, page 342, column 1, lines 11-17, and column 2, lines 1-3.

23. I have come across two editions, one of 1870 and another of 1871.

24. Alfred D. Chandler, Jr., reprints in his source book, The Railroads: The Nation's First Big Business, Sources and Readings (New York, 1965), passages from Lanier's autobiography (pp. 65 ff.) and comments on this piece on page 47.

25. Harold A. Williams, Robert Garret & Sons, 23 ff.

26. See Pierce, "Foreign Investment," 41 ff. in Eleutherian Mills, Proceedings (see this introduction page xviii(a)).

27. Navin-Sears, "Market for Industrial Securities" 137 ff.

28. Here tie in some aspects of the paper on The Investment Market... by Lance E. Davis treated here on page xix(a).

29. Egisto P. Fabbri is mentioned on page 385 of Volume II of this work as one of the important early Morgan partners. A biographical sketch is included in Henry Hall, America's Successful Men of Affairs (New York, 1895). Fabbri was born in Florence, Italy in 1834, the son of a silk merchant, and he came to the United States in the 1850's. He started as a bookkeeper, rose to

independence, and in 1875 became a partner in Drexel, Morgan & Co. He retired in 1885 because of ill health.

It is regrettable that the Drexels of Philadelphia who belonged to the giants have not been treated in recent years.

30. Eugene J. Koop, History of Spencer Trask and Company (p.p., New York, 1941), Louise Ware, George Foster Peabody: Banker, Philanthropist, Publiciest (Athens, Georgia, 1951), one of those anecdotal and laudatory entrepreneurial biographies which do not delight the historian.

31. On pages 188, 189 one finds interesting information on Georgia branch banking.

32. Carlo E. Castañeda, "The First Chartered Bank West of the Mississippi: Banco Nacional de Texas," Bulletin of the Business Historical Society, XXV (1951), 242 ff.

33. Joe B. Frantz, "The Mercantile House of McKinney & Williams, Underwriters of the Texas Revolution," Bulletin of the Business Historical Society, XXVI (1952), 1 ff.

34. This material was compiled by Frank A. Ross in a University of Texas Ph.D. thesis: "Texas Banking Legislation 1833-1953." I owe this reference to Prof. James P. Baughman who kindly permitted me to use his excerpt.

HISTORY OF AMERICAN BUSINESS LEADERS

A SERIES OF STUDIES

VOLUME 2

PART I

BANKING

1781 - 1840

THE MOLDING OF AMERICAN BANKING

BANKING

MEN AND IDEAS

By
FRITZ REDLICH

Part I

1781 - 1840

Second Imprint

HAFNER PUBLISHING COMPANY, INC.
NEW YORK
1951

Copyright 1947
Fritz Redlich

"But I have promises to keep."

                                Robert Frost.

PREFACE

There are a few to whom the author must express his gratitude for assistance during the time he was working on this book. He is especially indebted to Professor Arthur H. Cole who in innumerable ways provided help without which this volume would never have come to completion.

At the very beginning Mrs. Hope Brown-Constable Ferguson aided the author and at the end Miss Ruth Crandall helped to edit the manuscript. While simple justice demands that the aid of the former, entirely without monetary remuneration, must be acknowledged, the contribution of the latter far exceeded what she could be recompensed.

A grant-in-aid was received at an early date from the Social Science Research Council for which the author expresses his appreciation as well as for the confidence thus reposed in him. It is indeed remarkable that this Council could see merits in the project when barely conceived while hardly any one else saw them at a later date when tangible results were in evidence. This grant financed one quarter's work in the Harvard libraries, but more than half a dozen times as much had to be invested by the author himself, a financial burden which at times was all out of proportion to his income. This point is stressed not for personal reasons so much as to show in a specific case how the policy of our foundations either contributes to the fragmentization of knowledge in the social sciences or leads to outright waste of funds. Only small analytical projects can be undertaken by the average American student, while large synthetical ones, if started at all, are liable to break down for lack of funds before completion, thus entailing a concomitant loss of the capital previously invested. With all due gratitude to the Social Science Research Council, it must be stated that without the unreasonable financial sacrifices of the author the grant to him would have been lost.

Research as it is presented in this volume required very much help on the part of numerous libraries and their staffs. It is impossible to enumerate all the librarians who during the past years have assisted the author in one way or another. But the librarians or reference librarians of the following institutions should be mentioned: Columbia University (School of Business), Historical Society of Pennsylvania, New York Public Library, State Library of New York, and the Library of the University of Louisiana. While in all these cases assistance was given in the form of answering specific questions, the research itself was carried on in the libraries of Harvard University, and without the hospitality which Widener and Baker Libraries have extended to the author for many years the work would have been impossible. For this hospitality the author wishes to express thanks to Mr. Robert H. Haynes and, again, to Professor Arthur H. Cole.

The author furthermore owes gratitude to the Boston Clearing House and its members, especially Thomas P. Beal, its president, Herbert B. Stone, its secretary, and Henry Otte, its manager, for

having opened their records to him. The same debt of gratitude is
due to the Philadelphia Clearing House and especially to Mr. Charles
P. Blinn, Jr., Executive Vice President of the Philadelphia National
Bank, and Mr. Herbert E. Amidon, Manager of the Philadelphia Clearing
House Association.

This book takes up controversial matters. Controversial is
the underlying philosophy, the denial of determinism in history and
the conviction of the role of individuals and ideas in economic
development. Moot are the personality and the actions of Nicholas
Biddle and so is the question whether or not the First and Second
Banks of the United States were central banks. Different opinions
are held among American scholars on the degree of American dependence
on Europe during the nineteenth century. Contested is the author's
conviction that Mercantilist banking theory was back of early American banking practice. There is no doubt in the author's mind that
some, perhaps even many of his interpretations and explanations will
be disputed, but discussion is the lifeblood of science and if this
book does nothing except to provoke controversy the author will be
satisfied.

Massachusetts State College   Fritz Redlich
        at Fort Devens

TABLE OF CONTENTS

		Page
INTRODUCTION.		1

CHAPTER

I	FIRST PERIOD, GENERAL CHARACTERISTICS	5
	Some of the Social Implications of Early American Banking	7
	The Banking Business.	10
	Organization.	17
	The Emergence of the American Banking System.	20
II	BANK FOUNDERS AND BANK PERSONNEL IN THE FIRST PERIOD.	24
	Bank Founders	24
	Bank Personnel.	36
	Presidents	36
	Directors.	38
	Cashiers	39
III	SECOND PERIOD, GENERAL CHARACTERISTICS.	43
	Banking Transactions.	44
	Banking Organization.	55
	Banking Philosophy.	64
IV	THE PROBLEM OF COUNTRY NOTES AND THE SUFFOLK BANK SYSTEM	67
V	THE SAFETY FUND SYSTEM.	88
VI	EARLY AMERICAN CENTRAL BANKING.	96
	I. The Beginnings	96
	II. Intermediary Period.	101
	III. Nicholas Biddle and the Heyday of American Central Banking	110
	Biddle, the Chief Executive.	113
	Biddle, the Banker	124
	Biddle, the Central Bank President	127
	Biddle, the Politician	145
	Biddle's Personality and his End	156
	IV. Andrew Jackson and the Destruction of American Central Banking.	162
	V. The Debates of the 1830's and 1840's on the Need of a National Bank and their Significance.	178
	Appendices.	181
VII	FREE BANKING.	187
VIII	THE SOUTHERN PLANTATION BANKS	205
IX	SAVINGS BANKS	209
	Footnotes	231
	Bibliography.	305

INTRODUCTION

The book of which the first volume is presented herewith is a second study in the author's series: <u>History of American Business Leaders</u>. The second volume of this second <u>study</u> is in preparation, but further work on the <u>series</u> will not be forthcoming: the author's interest has shifted to a related field.

It may be advisable to stress once more the basic theoretical and philosophical presuppositions of this research. The problem in which this author has been interested for about fifteen years is: the personal element in economic development. This interest derives from a denial on his part of determinism and the working of blind forces in history. On the other hand, the author does not accept the Great Men theory in its radical form. In the appendix to his <u>Essays in American Economic History</u> he has explained the basis of his thinking. It may be accepted or rejected; but those who agree that human beings, not anonymous forces, determine the course of history will have to recognize ideas as the driving forces back of the actions of history-making men. This book on the personal and ideological elements in the development of American banking is predicated on the above presuppositions; for what is true of history in general is true also of economic history.

If it is granted that this aspect of economic history is correct, there can be no doubt that in the capitalistic era,[1] with which this book is concerned, business leaders (entrepreneurs) have determined its course to a large extent. In the first chapter of the first volume of this series the author has discussed at great length the theory of the entrepreneur as it has been developed in the last hundred and fifty years. For the purpose of his research he characterized the entrepreneur as the man who (alone or in conjunction with others) shapes and reshapes his enterprise, establishes its relations with other enterprises and fits it into the market and the national economy; as the man who directs it and determines its spirit and its strategy by making the major decisions.[2]

Of course, not every entrepreneur, nor every businessman, to use the sloppy vernacular, in so doing has influenced economic development. Tens of thousands, if not hundreds of thousands, have passed the stage of history, but only a few hundred have left a more or less permanent trace of their activities. The business leaders, the men who determined the course of economic history, have been called by Professor Schumpeter "entrepreneurs." This author prefers the term "creative entrepreneur" and, of late, the word "innovator" had been proposed to cover this type of men. In an article which this author hopes to publish soon, he has tried to analyze it further and has come to distinguish between creative entrepreneur, creative manager, and creative capitalist.[3] Terms, as such, are, of course, immaterial as long as the economic and historical phenomenon covered by such terms is clearly understood, as it is in this case: the business leader who contributes to economic development.

In the first volume of this series, the interest was focused on these men. Soon after work was begun on the second volume, however, it became apparent that the field of investigation had to be broadened. Banking has been so much under the influence of state governments and, in certain periods, under that of the national government, and, on the other hand, was so intensely intertwined with social life as a whole, that no history of the personal element in banking could be complete without including all the men who have influenced the development of banking, regardless of whether or not they were business leaders. Therefore, in addition to business leaders, two other groups of personalities had to be taken into account. First, men in public life had to be considered, such as statesmen, politicians, government administrators, who in one way or another through their actions have influenced economic development. (That destructive actions determine the course of history just as well as creative ones goes without saying.) Secondly, thinkers, the originators of ideas, had to be studied too, if their ideas through the medium of men of action (entrepreneurs, statesmen, etc.) had gained influence on the history of banking, However, ideas rarely ever emerge in a form ready for immediate adoption. As a rule, they require repeated reformulation before reaching that stage, or, to state it differently, they have histories of their own. Thus an element of Geistesgeschichte[4] necessarily entered into this research, a branch of history so masterfully practiced by Friedrich Meinicke. The distinguishing element between a history of banking ideas, as presented, for instance, by Miller, and that history of ideas on the subject which has become part of the research presented in this book, is a difference in interest and emphasis. Only those ideas which, regardless of their inherent worth, influenced economic development are of interest here. It is the propelling idea that counts in connection with this research, regardless of whether its logic was good or bad and regardless of its wholesome or unwholesome consequences.

In this connection there comes up the question of the relative importance of really new ideas for economic development. Of course they are important. But most ideas when they become propelling ideas are not actually new. Frank Albert Fetter, speaking in a recent publication[5] on economic doctrines, remarked keenly that they appear and reappear like the pieces of colored glass in a kaleidoscope. The same in detail they nevertheless show themselves in ever changing settings. This statement is true not only with respect to economic doctrines, but also with respect to the many ideas currently picked up by business leaders and statesmen to help them in dealing with the problems of the day. Walther Rathenau,[6] himself a business leader and statesman and a deep thinker besides, had a very clear understanding of the fact that remarkable achievements in business which gain influence on economic development are not as a rule the result of really new ideas. What actually makes the great business leader and statesman is the instinct for choosing the idea suited to the day or the ability to effect a new combination of ideas, a combination in which an older thought can suddenly become a propelling one.

These men who formulated ideas which became important for the development and those men in public life and business who tried to shape the world with their help, as a matter of fact do their work within society. Since the principle of interaction (in contrast to that of cause and effect) determines social life, studying the history of certain ideas and their realization by certain men leads to "circular" reasoning. Such reasoning is required by social reality for men shape the development of society and, in turn, are molded by that society. Society provides an institutional set-up for each generation. The contribution of the creative men of the respective generations is the alteration within a limited range of possibilities of the given set-up. Thus a new institutional set-up is provided for the next generation. The creative members of this generation, in turn, alter the new set-up, and so on ad infinitum.

Thus the question whether economic development is a social process or the work of individuals is not put correctly if the two possible answers are understood to be mutually exclusive. Both possible answers are equally correct if they are understood as supplementing each other and as presenting only the same phenomenon from two different angles. There is no doubt in the mind of this author that economic development is the work of individuals. In some cases these individuals can be easily identified and there can be no argument about their achievements. But even in the most extreme case of this kind the individuals in question are themselves, as has just been mentioned, the product of the society which has molded them and presented them with the problem which they as individuals came to solve. That is to say, seen from the other angle, society poses the problem and solves it through the agency of these individuals. In other cases, economic development was the result of an accumulation of changes, each of which by itself was almost imperceptible. Again in other cases, the necessity of change was so obvious and urgent that several people accomplished it at the same time. They may have cooperated to the desired end or, acting independently, may or may not have influenced each other. In these cases, to the superficial observer, development seems to have been a social process; but, nevertheless, individuals, concrete individuals, have wrought the change in question even if the historian cannot put his finger on any one of them. Thus even in the extreme cases of both characters, economic development is just as much an individual achievement as a social process; the only difference is the point of view of the historian.

Incidentally what is true of these two aspects of economic development is equally true of two others in that they also supplement each other. Economic history can be studied and described in two different ways. Interest can be focused on the change of conditions as such, or, in other words, on the result of a process, or it can be focused on the process itself. Most publications in the field of economic history fall into the former category, while this study belongs to the latter.

The theoretical and philosophical presuppositions of this research, discussed elsewhere as mentioned above, cannot be repeated here in detail, but some methodological discussions may be inserted at this point: This author does not primarily aim at unearthing unknown facts although he is certain that this book contributes to our factual knowledge of banking by adding information overlooked so far. What this author really aims at is _understanding_ of banking history. There were generations of economists which hunted for economic laws, immutable as long as mankind needed food, clothing, and shelter. Recently, economists have come to the fore who are searching for the laws of change. This author confesses to being a disbeliever in any economic laws be they static or dynamic. To him the social sciences have one foremost goal: _understanding_ of social reality. The term _understanding_ in the field of economic history has two implications: First, it implies seeing with the eyes and speaking in the language of the contemporaries of an event, or in other words, realizing their intentions, their open and hidden presuppositions, and their ideas and ideals. Or, expressed differently, if by some miracle the historian could be removed into an era gone by, he should be able to talk to the people by whom he would then be surrounded. Secondly, it implies seeing the significance of an event of the past in the development which led to the present. It implies putting an event in its right place, in its true perspective, and giving it its right weight. In consequence of historical change, the past takes on a new aspect from generation to

generation so that history needs to be rewritten by each succeeding one (but _understanding_ in the former sense is more or less final). To give an example: ever since the middle of the nineteenth century, even in America, economic life has been moving away from rugged individualism and has been absorbing more and more collectivistic features. Therefore the history of one hundred and fifty years of cooperation among banks (to be described in the second volume of this book) has entered the horizon of this historian. As long as America thought exclusively in terms of individualism these cooperative actions of bankers were not seen, or when seen, were considered so irrelevant that they were neglected by historians.

If the historian studies social or economic sources with the purpose of _understanding_ them (this term being used in the first sense described above) he will discover that thereby he gains an opportunity of dating the beginning of new social processes and institutions, a method which to the knowledge of this author has not been used heretofore. When something new comes into existence, contemporaries find great difficulty in describing it and even greater in giving it a precise name. Therefore, whenever one finds at any given time that a certain social or economic phenomenon is generally described in rather awkward terms, one may be sure that the phenomenon is still in its infancy, and one will find invariably in later sources better descriptions and, finally, the precise term. When the historian first meets this precise term he can draw the conclusion that the institution or process has reached a certain maturity and has entered a second stage.[7]

Closely connected with the purpose of this research, gaining _understanding_ of economic development in the field of banking, are the sources used. This author anticipates criticism as to his use of secondary ones. He is glad to concede that he did so, and in fact he _had_ to do so. Professor Nef in a paper recently read before the Economic History Association rightly spoke of the "fragmentization" of knowledge brought about by our scientific procedure. This fragmentization has reached a point where it becomes a real research job to go over previous research with the view of combining the fragments into one whole. The job is comparable to the work of the architect who makes use of bricks and other valuable structural material when erecting a building. In the present stage of our knowledge much more scholarship will have to be exerted in the direction of synthesis than ever before. It is sad to see, for instance, about a hundred men having worked on banking histories of various states with hardly one of them having thought of comparing his results with the findings of his neighbor. Consequently, most of these men do not even know if facts which they have found are typical or atypical, let alone see lines of influence.

In regard to the use of sources this author has been guided by the following principles: When a fact has been established by the previous research of reliable students he took the result at its face value. For instance, the claim that Samuel Hooper was responsible for the Massachusetts banking act of 1858 was taken as established and not rechecked on the basis of primary sources. But, on the other hand, when it came to the specific research job which this author meant to tackle, namely, the question: What ideas prompted Hooper when he took those actions, of course only primary sources were used. Never was an interpretation based on anything but primary sources. These were also consulted in cases of doubt or whenever an important source had never been used before, as in the case of the clearing house records, or, as in the case of the letterbooks of Nicholas Biddle, not used to answer these specific questions.

The goal was to strike a happy medium between becoming bogged down by using primary sources for the confirmation of facts already established or primary sources which are of limited value for the purpose of this research, on the one hand, and uncritical reliance on other people's monographs, on the other. A recently deceased reputable writer when surveying a broad field of social history was guilty of the former mistake. As one of his critics rightly stressed, by meticulous avoidance of secondary sources he missed the point again and again, taking as he did no cognizance of the result of important research in his field. It is left to the reviewers of this book to decide to what extent this author has succeeded in avoiding both of the dangers which threatened him.

There are scholars who like to dig in and unearth treasures, while others prefer to climb the mountains to enjoy the larger view. In each case the technique used differs: the former will require a spade, the latter a pick and rope. The former, as a matter of fact, will love to dig in virgin soil; while the latter must necessarily first climb hills and mountains which others have already scaled, before he can reach the hitherto unconquered peak. Those who dig within well-circumscribed boundaries need much less guidance than those who essay the mountains; this means that the latter need far more the directional guidance of well-elaborated theory and of previous research. Both may fail in their endeavors: those who dig may unearth worthless rock; while those who climb may miss the path and arrive on a summit from which they see only what others have seen before. The results achieved by both these groups are of course liable to criticism; but for one to tell the other that his method and goal are without value would be unjustifiable. Actually they complement each other. As to the goal of this present research, the author wishes to stress once more that understanding of economic development in the field of banking is its purpose. This statement implies in which direction he would wish criticism to be leveled.

Chapter I

FIRST PERIOD

GENERAL CHARACTERISTICS

It is customary among historians to begin the history of American banking with a description of the founding of both the so-called Pennsylvania Bank and of its successor, the Bank of North America in Philadelphia. This procedure, however, is correct only if applied cum grano salis. The creation of these enterprises cannot be understood except as they are seen belonging to a chain of events of which they were important links.

The history of American banking begins with the discussions on land banks which took place in this country in and after the 1680's. Different as was the Bank of North America from the early eighteenth-century land banks, planned or set up before the extension of the "Bubble Act" to the colonies in 1741 made them illegal,[1] they nevertheless have one element in common: the Bank of North America as well as the earlier colonial land banks were children of the same Mercantilist banking theory which dominated American banking down to the War of 1812 and the influence of which can be traced as late as about 1840. It is hard to understand how this connection could have been overlooked for so long. Mercantilist banking theory found expression in numerous pamphlets published during the second half of the seventeenth and the first half of the eighteenth centuries both in England and in America. The American material is well known to our scholars through the research of Andrew MacFarland Davis, but strangely enough it has not been used in the interpretation of early American banking history.

Mercantilist banking theory, as contained in the above-mentioned pamphlet literature, was summed up in Book III of Sir James Steuart's Inquiry into the Principles of Political Economy (London, 1765). This work was well known in America by 1800 and its influence on American thought could well be made the subject of research. Sir James Steuart's elaborate banking theory of 1765 embraced whatever was then known on the subject of banking, and was therefore a remarkable achievement (regardless of what we think of it today). In comparison, the corresponding chapter[2] in Adams Smith's Wealth of Nations of 1776 was short and not too impressive for practical bankers. This statement holds true except for the passages on Scotch banking which became so influential and the systematic elaboration of the theory that banks should restrict their advances to short-term commercial paper. The importance of Adam Smith's chapter on banking lies especially in the facts that he clearly recognized which tenets of the established theory had no future and that he dropped what was no longer tenable. But such was the character of this chapter of the Wealth of Nations that not even in England did it crowd out Mercantilist banking theory from contemporary thinking. Sir James Steuart's Book III on banking was reprinted in London as late as 1810 and 1812 because it was considered "justly celebrated for its elementary accuracy."[3]. Furthermore, when one keeps in mind that Ricardo did not appear as an economic writer prior to 1809, that the Bullion Report, that landmark of modern monetary and banking theory, did not come out before 1810, and that Ricardo's main work was not issued until 1817, one cannot see how American banking before 1812 could have been influenced by anything except Mercantilist theory.[3a]

The connection between Mercantilist thought and early American banking has been described elsewhere by this author.[4] There he has tried to prove the influence of Mercantilist theory on early American banking by juxtaposing theory and practice. The congruity of Mercantilist theory and early American banking practice was to make the connection self-evident. Additional research has made it possible to show undeniable cases of the dependence of American banking thought on Mercantilist theory: On January 5, 1784 Thomas Willing, one of the

founders and president of the Bank of North
America in Philadelphia, wrote to William
Phillips and other promoters of the Bank of
Massachusetts a letter which will be discussed in more detail later. This letter
proves beyond doubt that the founders of
the Bank of North America consulted books
before embarking on their venture.[5] Since
the only material on banks then available
in print, besides such remarks as could be
found in books on business, was the English
and American pamphlet literature published
after 1650 and Book III of Sir James
Steuart's great work, the founders can
hardly have avoided reading the Mercantilist theory expressed therein. The statement could even go further, for James
Wilson, the Philadelphia jurist and another
founder of the Bank of North America, is
said to have known Sir James Steuart's
book.[6] As a matter of fact Wilson's memorandum on banking[7] which was circulated
among members of the Pennsylvania legislature in December, 1780 clearly shows his
dependence on Steuart whose very words
he used. In the same period, in 1786,
Sir James Steuart was cited in John
Witherspoon's Essay on Money and although
Steuart was criticized the passage in question shows the high regard in which he was
held.[8] For the years around 1810 proof of
Steuart's influence on American thought
accumulates. In the Debate in the House
of Representatives of Pennsylvania on Mr.
Holgate's Resolutions relative to the Bank
of the United States on January 4, 1811 no
lesser person than Nicholas Biddle referred
to Sir James Steuart as "one of the most
intelligent political economists."[9] This
speech of Biddle's was a masterpiece and
the maturest discussion of banking which
can be found in America in that period.
Furthermore Sir James Steuart was quoted,
on one page with Adam Smith, in an article
in Walsh's Review of History and Politics
of 1812, which may well have been contributed by Eric Bollmann.[10] A few years later
(in 1815) Ferris Pell, writing under the
pseudonym of Publicola, quoted Sir James
Steuart repeatedly in his Letter to Albert
Gallatin and incidentally, once in one
breath with Adam Smith.[11] As late as 1831
in a booklet published in New York on The
Most Prominent Banks in Europe and...the
Bank of North America Sir James Steuart
was alluded to as the "celebrated Sir James
Stewart" (sic).[12]

　　Mercantilist banking theory, as

summed up by Steuart can be outlined as
follows:[13] Important among its tenets was the
distinction between money banks and land
banks, or, synonymously, the distinction
between "banking on mercantile credit," on
the one side, and "banking on land and merchandise" or "banking on private credit"
or "banking on real and personal estates,"
on the other. These terms will be applied
repeatedly and alternatively in this book
and are used throughout in the sense of
Sir James Steuart. Money banks, as represented by the eighteenth century Bank of
England, hardly interested Steuart, who
devoted the largest part of his Book III to
land banks. Money banks, according to
Mercantilist theory, issued notes on the
basis of obligations of merchants and manufacturers, in contrast to land banks which
issued their notes on the basis of land and
personal estates. The latter type of banking was considered preferable to "banking
on mercantile credit" because land banks
were supposed to stand on solid ground and
not to depend on the success of their borrowers as did the money banks. The principle of "banking on private credit" was
"to give credit to those who have property
and a desire to melt it down" for improvements of all sorts. This was the fundamental idea back of this type of Mercantilist banking, and such banks came into
existence when men of property joined together and, for the security of the noteholders, formed a stock which, in the words
of Steuart, "might consist indifferently
of any species of property." In addition
to this stock the founders also provided
in proportion to the notes issued a sum of
coin which they judged sufficient to answer
such notes as should return for payment.
There was some doubt in Steuart's mind
whether land banks should actually redeem
their notes in specie. "When paper issued
for domestic circulation returns to a bank,
were it not for the profits of their trade,
I see no reason why a bank should pay in
any other species of property than what
it received." "The regular method" by
which a bank should acquire the obligation
embodied in the notes was by restoring to
the debtor the security granted at their
issuance when he returned them in payment
for his debt.

　　As to the management of "banks on
real and personal estates," Steuart gave
the following advice: "It is plain that it
is both the office and the interest of banks

to give credit to all who can give good security for it.[14] After credit is given "the capitals due the banks must not be demanded by the bank as long as the interest is regularly paid." This was still in line with older thought: that the mortgagor of land may not be distressed to his undoing, is the formulation which we find for the same idea in a pamphlet which dates as far back as the 1680's.[15]

Capital, according to Sir James Steuart, plays only a minor part in banking upon private credit. The capital stock of a bank serves as collateral security for the notes issued and as a pledge for the faithful discharge of the trust reposed in the bank. The value of notes, however, rests primarily on value received. Consequently, "a man without a shilling of property may carry on a bank of domestic circulation to as good purpose as if he had a million; and his paper will be every bit as good as that of the Bank of England. Every note he issues is secured on good private security." If the notes return to him they will find the securities taken by him at the time he issued the notes. A large capital serves only to establish credit for the bank in question and to create confidence on the part of the public.[16]

The purpose of this type of bank is to enable every man of property to circulate his capital for the advancement of industry,[17] or, as stated in another context, it is the "unspeakable advantage" of banks of circulation that they supply money for the encouragement of industry or for improvements of all sorts, at all times, to those who have property and want to melt it down. This supply of money may be kept constantly at a "due proportion to alienation."[18] Translated into modern language, this means: it is the advantage of banking on land and merchandise that it finances the process of capital formation and that the supply of funds is elastic.

Such were the ideas of the men who stood at the cradle of American banking, and their choice lay between "banking on mercantile credit" or "banking on real and personal estates" or an attempt at compromise. It was in choosing the first possibility that they made history, regardless of the fact that their successors and followers did not stick to that choice. Or, to put it differently, if one looks at the pre-history, if you please, and early history of American banking as belonging to

the Mercantilist era, the historical importance of the foundation of the Bank of North America does not lie in the fact that thereby was established American banking. The great importance of this bank actually lay in its representing the first money bank in this country.[19] As a money bank, it was modeled on the Bank of England, the prototype of the Mercantilist money bank, and at the same time it improved on the organization of the latter by opening with a specie capital, which the Bank of England had not possessed.[20] The Bank of North America blazed the trail which led to modern commercial banking in America.

Some of the Social Implications of Early American Banking

The earliest American banks were chartered because they were considered as some sort of public utility, as public blessings, to use the terminology of the late eighteenth and early nineteenth centuries.[21] Applications for and preambles[22] to early charters evidence this fact.[23] When after the Revolutionary War the charter of the Bank of North America was to be repealed because of popular clamor, its defenders pointed to its war record, to its loans to the government, to its assistance to the state of Pennsylvania, to its aid in restoring a sound currency, and to its support of trade and commerce. Its charter was restored when the utility of the institution to the Commonwealth and to individuals had been shown convincingly and when it was willing to take a less liberal charter.[24] At about the same time the petitioners for the charter of the Massachusetts Bank stressed the proven usefulness of the Bank of North America as a reason why the institution planned for Boston should receive corporate rights and privileges. They set forth four advantages to be derived from banks: borrowers would be protected against usurers; banks would inculcate the habit of punctuality among debtors; banks would provide a safe place of deposit for capitalists; and they would furnish an increased medium of exchange. This latter statement is of particular interest showing as it does the spirit of Mercantilism behind early American banking.[25]

In 1789, to give one more example, the already-existing Bank of New York applied for a charter. It believed it would

strengthen its case by the statement that
the experience of other nations had
"evinced the utility" of banks, among whose
essential objects was that of affording financial aid to governments in exigencies.
The incorporation of the bank was urged as
an "indispensable step toward enabling it
to give aid to the government of the United
States," which had just come into existence.[26]

    The maturest expression of the idea
that banks were business enterprises with
semipublic functions, and by far the best
contemporary description of the economic
advantages expected from banks, can be
found in Alexander Hamilton's Report on a
National Bank; and Madison's enumeration
of the advantages and disadvantages of
banks contained in a speech of 1791 equally
illuminates the thought of that time.[27]
Hamilton's point of view dominated a large
portion of public opinion for decades to
come. As late as 1829, for instance,
Joshua Forman proposed dealing with banks
as public institutions.[28]

    As a matter of fact, not many peo-
ple were as farsighted as was Hamilton,
and in the course of the first period this
aspect was abandoned more and more. In
1812 Governor Tompkins of New York stated
that "to facilitate commercial operations
...was the only justification for granting
bank charters;"[29] and when the second period opened Dallas recommended a new national bank, contrasting his project with
a "commercial bank" and characterizing it
as "not an institution created for the
purposes of commerce and profit alone, but
much more for the purposes of national policy." The implications of these statements
with regard to the average bank then chartered need no comment. By 1834 the outlook
had been so completely changed that Levi
Woodbury in an official document could
claim that banks were incorporated chiefly
for the benefit of the "wealthier and more
commercial classes."[30]

    Throughout the first period, how-
ever, and during much of the second, the
concept of the double status of banks as
business enterprises with semi-public
functions had far-reaching consequences.
The common man came to regard "a bank rather in the light of a benevolent than of a
money making institution and as possessing
recognized special claims on public and
legislative favor and therefore bound to

accommodate the public."[31] For this and
other reasons[32] legislators in several
states were induced to enact the participation of their respective states in banking
enterprises[33] (the fact that New York banks
had to donate shares to educational institutions ties in here);[34] and, finally, bank
promoters had to pay at least lip service
to the idea of banks as semi-public institutions chartered because of their advantages for the common weal.[35] Actually, of
course, most of the bank founders were then,
as later, after profit only and the average
legislator of 1800 in all probability believed that the foremost advantage to be
derived from banks was the creation of an
additional medium of exchange[36] (in their
making money plentiful, in their "melting
down property" for improvements of all
sorts). It will be remembered that the advantage of banks creating an additional medium of exchange was frankly stated in the
above-cited application for a charter of
the Massachusetts Bank. A similar statement can be found in the preamble to the
charter of the Providence Bank. This idea
was to have a long life. As late as 1834
the then Secretary of the Treasury set
forth that it was "computed by many, whether justly or wisely need not here be discussed, that through the issues of paper
over the amount of specie in the vaults of
banks the public is enabled to obtain a
temporary use of so much more money, as if
to that extent...it were a real addition
to the specie capital."[37]

    The point of view that banks were
instruments to further the common weal
survived for decades in spite of much bitter experience. Even in the first period,
a few years after banks had come into existence and had begun multiplying all over the
country, it became obvious that they were
no undisguised blessings, and a large portion of public opinion came to look on
banks as curses rather than as public
blessings.[38] At an early moment it was
seen and stressed that banks influenced
the price level, that banks "regulated
money." "A regulation of money is always
a regulation of prices and an interposition
by law in the economy of individuals,"[39]
as John Taylor of Caroline County put it.
Or in the words of James Sullivan: banks
have it "in their power to swell and lessen
the medium of the country...and consequently
to raise or fall the price of articles of

commerce as they [see] fit."[40] The second main objection was a social one. A contemporary economist[41] explained that a man who acquired bank stock acquired the power of compelling somebody in the world to labor for him. "The objection to these institutions, however, is not so much that they facilitate this increase of power as that they afford this facility to the rich and not to the poor in equal proportions... that they operate as an exclusive privilege." Finally, there were specific reasons for complaint. The early banks in this country were, as will be remembered, "money banks" which banked "on mercantile credit." They made high profits and undoubtedly under these circumstances capitalists often preferred to invest their funds in banks instead of lending them on mortgage as they had done in the past. That is to say, the then-very-limited loanable funds were shifted from investment in agriculture to the financing of international commerce. This change was, as a matter of fact, detrimental to farmers who felt aggrieved and complained vociferously. Contemporary statements to the effect that banks had destroyed "private credit"[42] are telling, for by 1800 private credit meant, cum grano salis, what is called mortgage credit today. The fact that a keen, disinterested foreign observer, such as Talleyrand,[43] took up that complaint shows its validity. Finally, when it is remembered that at least in the case of the Bank of New York a money bank crowded out a land bank project,[44] and that the existence of banks precluded loan offices, a type of credit institutions which was considered by agrarians as the proper solution of their credit problems, the bitter feelings of these classes can well be understood.[45]

     In consequence thereof, lingering Mercantilist landbank traditions were soon revived in the average American country bank as it existed down to about 1860. It combined heterogeneous functions, at the same time extending short-term commercial credit and long-term investment credit, issuing bank notes indiscriminately on the basis of both types of obligations of its debtors.[46] That combination of heterogeneous functions was noted as early as the 1830's when Forstall described the banks as having two important functions to perform; namely, "as loan offices, on

mortgage and otherwise" and "as banks of discount for the mercantile and industrial interest."[47] It has been shown in detail in a previous volume by the present author[48] how this combination of functions was rooted in Mercantilist banking practice. (Even the Bank of England in the first years of its existence had been anxious to get hold of the mortgage business.[49]) But these concessions, that is to say, the building up of a specific type of hybrid bank to meet their needs, could not allay the hostility of certain strata of the population against all banks, a hostility which began in the first period and reached its greatest importance in the second. The early American money banks were exponents of the coming capitalistic order and by their mere existence forced a capitalistic spirit on a population inimical to the economic and psychological change which this spirit entailed. Similar geistige developments took place in Europe at the same time, but, of course, the anti-capitalistic spirit of historically older social classes found different expression in the countries with older civilizations.[50] In America, in the 1790's, banks were attacked because they destroyed the "confidence, forbearance and compassion" previously shown to debtors by creditors. This complaint referred mainly to the punctuality enforced by banks.[51] That is to say, while the merchants praised the banks for bringing into business that punctuality which was a prerequisite for capitalistic development, the pre-capitalistic strata complained about it because it destroyed the world to which they were accustomed. "Our laws and habits countenance long credit and afford slow methods of recovering debts," as a representative of agriculture put it in 1786.[52] Since the common man was inarticulate then, as he is now, he tried to put his grievances in simple formulae. Thus, when the Bank of New York had barely come into existence it was branded as working in the interests of British capitalists,[53] and for decades to come such and similar claims, i.e., flag-waving, became effective as propaganda weapons against the most important banks. Again, the fight against the First Bank of the United States in 1810 and 1811 was widely seen as "a war of the middle and poorer classes of society against the rich."[54]

     Thus originated during the first period the different attitudes of the public toward banks which were to determine the history of American banking for years to come and especially for the 1820's and 1830's.[55] They were rooted in Mercantilist or pre-capitalistic tradition, and they were shaped in reaction to the necessities of the expanding capitalistic order, on the one hand, and the disappointment of pre-capitalistic and early capitalistic social strata, on the other. The latter were enthusiastic about banks as long as they were built and run on the principles of Mercantilist "banking on private credit" and consequently would be used as a device for making money plentiful; but they abhorred modern commercial banks, the successors of Mercantilist "money banks" and exponents of the coming high-capitalistic era. The backers of the latter type of bank, on the other hand, fought and checked that sort of banking which the former strata desired. Each group tried to build banks to suit its needs; each was forced to compromise; and the American bank typical of the years between about 1820 and 1840 was the result.

The *geistige* genealogy as well as this compromise must be kept in mind by the student who tried to understand and explain banking business and bank organization down to 1814.

The Banking Business

The earliest American banks, as should be stressed once more, were "money banks." Their character implied that they were established with sufficient capital, in contrast to the country banks[56] which made their appearance first in the 1790's and soon became heirs to the tradition of Mercantilist "banking on private credit." The character of the earlier American "money banks," furthermore implied that they at least began their operations on a specie basis, regardless of the fact that, following the example of the Bank of England, the capitals of some of them consisted partly of government obligations. Through having a specie capital they were, as mentioned above, distinct from their model. Reference is made to the material published by Professor Gras with respect to the Massachusetts Bank[57] which shows that between 1785 and 1791 the specie reserves of that bank dropped from 144.9 per cent to 20.1 per cent of circulation

and deposits. These figures are not only interesting *per se*, but also for the trend they show. To the extent that the early "money banks" in the trade centers along the Altantic coast were supplemented by country banks representing a relapse into Mercantilist "banking on private credit," the specie reserves back of the American banking system as a whole, and those back of individual banks, became smaller and smaller until, for some years after the suspension of 1814, American banks went off specie completely.[58]

However, the fact that the first American banks were "money banks" had still another implication. Money banks represented not only banking on sufficient capital and on a specie basis, but at the same time "banking on mercantile credit," i.e., on short term obligations of merchants; or in other words the first American banks were the true forerunners of modern commercial banks. In turn this character of theirs was reflected in their lending policy, and these various features combined made for comparatively liquid banking.

Rules and regulations for the large mercantile banks of the 1780's and early 1790's have survived together with other documentary material so that the student is able to gain a clear picture of that policy.[59] At the beginning, stress was laid on the discounting of "real paper,"[60] i.e., non-renewable paper originating from short-term business transactions between merchants who during the eighteenth century, had made the bill of exchange their indispensable tool. Such paper was necessarily "double-name paper." However, in America [in contrast to Europe] "double-name paper," which the early banks preferred, also included promissory notes, endorsed by the maker and by the merchant who had received the note in payment for goods. The use of this sort of "double-name paper" did not lack danger since it opened the way for the so-called accommodation paper, to be described forthwith, which on its face could not be distinguished from the former. Paper offered for discount was supposed to run for no more than thirty or sixty days, a period which would be considered too short today. "Sometimes through tenderness the credit [was] prolonged."[61] The interest rate was fixed at 6 per cent, since in those decades and for many to come, American banks had to comply with legal interest requirements. (Even the Bank of England did not have a flexible interest rate at that time.) Bills and notes were not offered for discount daily, but on a certain day or certain days during each week. On the following, the so-called discount, day the boards of directors assembled and passed on the offers. The procedure which they followed was sometimes so odd that to the historian it seems that of a secret society rather than of a business enterprise.[62] The directors were supposed to base their decision on the intrinsic value of the paper offered. But numerous complaints were registered in that period that the directors showed favoritism[63] and accorded preferential treatment to members of their party or creed, or to good friends in general. Discounts were originally payable at the discounting bank in specie or in its notes, a logical procedure, in line with Mercantilist tradition and banking theory.[64]

As early as the 1790's accommodation paper, as mentioned before, started to creep into the portfolios of all banks, even those that were truly mercantile. The way had not only been paved by the custom of taking promissory notes, as opposed to bills of exchange, but also by the practice of renewing paper when due, a practice frowned upon by the earliest banks.[65]

In America the term "accommodation paper" had a meaning different from that which it possessed in England in the early nineteenth century.[66] In America the term referred to promissory notes representing loans unconnected with specific business transactions.[67] James Alexander Hamilton, in 1829, coined a nice definition of this sort of paper. According to him, accommodation paper produced business in contrast to genuine trade paper that sprang from business.[68] Accommodation loans were medium or long-term loans, disguised under the form of two or three-month notes, which it was understood would be renewed regularly at maturity.[69] Such loans were given for the development of capital resources and slowly repaid, if ever, in installments over a period of several years. So common were accommodation loans that in 1811[70] Mathew Carey took it for granted that funds borrowed from the First Bank of the United States had been sunk in machinery, houses, and ships.[71] Occasionally, in cases where

banks financed voyages, as in Rhode Island, even the notes of merchants approximated accommodation paper.[72]

When the discounting of accommodation paper began with the country banks of the 1790's, and the genuine money banks followed suit, American banking deviated from the original course set in the 1780's. In the Bank of New York and the Bank of Massachusetts[73] the wise rule that no bill or note would be renewed was quickly discarded; and the Bank of North America was all but crippled for some time in the 1790's because a few powerful customers met their maturing obligations by renewal upon renewal until they had monopolized the funds of the bank.[74] With the adoption of the practice of discounting accommodation paper, American banking started veering in the direction which became typical of its course down to Civil War times. Thus the lending of funds for the development of capital resources became the primary function of country banks; while the combination of lending on goods in transitu with lending for the former purpose, which combination has been rightly characterized by Bray Hammond as hybridization of bank functions, became the characteristic feature of city banking. This set-up was a step backward, even behind English eighteenth-century practice. Then and there loans for the development of capital resources had been considered the domain of "banking on real and personal estates" and not as that of money banks. In contrast to sound English commercial banking practice, permanent bank loans in this country became well-nigh universal in the late eighteenth century and so remained for decades to come.

The early American banks do not seem to have required special security when lending on "real paper." In this case they lent on "personal security" to use the contemporary term; but there was a tendency to make such loans on shorter terms.[75] In contrast, collateral for accommodation loans had to be given in the form of bullion, stocks, merchandise, and in the form of non-marketable securities, "securities not merchandized" (personal bonds and mortgages). Lending on merchandise, traditionally the domain of "banking on land and merchandize" as had been the lending on bond and mortgage, was thus adopted by the early American money banks. In the Bank of New York, lending on merchandise became so important that in 1804 a special department was organized to handle this business.[76] Lending on stocks,[77] which term according to the custom of the time included what today are called government bonds[78] opened up a road fraught with danger, but which, on the other hand, also led to modern lending on stock collateral. The danger alluded to lay in the lending on stock of the lending bank,[79] especially in order to facilitate the payment of the installments by the holders of this same stock. This widely adopted practice was the back door through which reentered into American commercial banking the Mercantilist concept that capital was superfluous for "banking on private credit."

These heterogeneous lending activities resulted in the combination, already mentioned, of short, medium, and long-term credit in the same banking enterprises. The practice of issuing notes to all borrowers regardless of the character of their loans, which will be discussed shortly, coming as it did on the top of that dangerous lending policy, saddled American banking in the first period with a serious defect which remained its Achilles' heel down to Civil War times. The pressure of those groups which were not benefited by mercantile banking, as first set up, was primarily responsible for that development. At the end, the only difference between the portfolio of a mercantile bank along the Eastern seaboard, the descendant of the Mercantilist "money bank," and that of a country bank, the descendant of the Mercantilist land bank, was the different distribution between the real and accommodation paper carried therein. The latter type of bank often enough had no real paper at all among its loans.

The foregoing description does not exhaust the lending activities of banks in the first period, since many of them lent to Federal, state, and local governments.[80] So did the Bank of North American when it was founded, and hardly had Hamilton taken over the office of the Secretary of the Treasury before he borrowed funds from the Bank of New York and again from the Bank of North America. It has been described above how the intention of making loans to the newly-created Federal government was one of the reasons why the stockholders of the Bank of New York considered themselves entitled to receive corporate privileges.

A few years later the First Bank of the United States was created for that very purpose, made fourteen successive loans to the Federal government for an aggregate amount of more than 13 1/2 million dollars, and would have been crippled had not Thomas Willing, warned by his experience in the Bank of North America, insisted on repayment.[81] Just as the Bank of North America and later the First Bank of the United States were launched for the purpose of making loans to the Federal government, state banks were created or at least bound by their charters, to extend credit to the commonwealth from which they received their charters. As examples[82] out of many cases the Philadelphia Bank of 1803 and the State Bank of Boston of 1811 may be mentioned. The lending of bank funds to state governments was common practice in the first period, and similar lending to local governments took place occasionally.

Since modern American banking came into existence against the background of colonial loan offices and land banks, both of which had issued circulating notes, and since it followed English practice, the lending of funds in the form of bank notes became the essential feature of American banking from the outset. For decades to come, in America banking was synonymous with note issue and one cannot understand the contemporary sources before the Civil War unless this specific American meaning of the term "banking" is kept in mind. As might be expected, some difficulties had to be overcome before the public became accustomed to bank notes. For example, the first issues of the Bank of North America or the Hartford Bank did not circulate readily.[83] Hamilton's actions as Secretary of the Treasury undoubtedly contributed to promoting their use.[84] Two ways of extending credit were excluded in America from the beginning. First, the lending by way of overdrafts, although there were occasional exceptions which, however, were always considered illegitimate. (In fact, some of the early banks, as the Bank of New York, expressly forbade them.)[85] Secondly, banking on the basis of book credits, as developed in the Low Countries from medieval times and practiced with perfection in the eighteenth century, was not adopted on a large scale in this country by incorporated banks, although it was repeatedly suggested.[86] Eric Bollmann, a

Hanoverian who was acquainted with the methods of the Bank of Hamburg, made such a proposal in 1812. He claimed that bank credits were a more convenient circulating medium than specie or even bank notes, and while the public preferred bank notes to specie it preferred bank credits to both.[87] A few years later, in 1816, Mathew Carey's recommendation that notes be replaced by book credits indicated keen interest in this type of banking at that time.[88] It is probable that some banks in larger cities in the 1790's and 1800's practiced banking based to a limited extent on book credits; and private bankers must have adopted this method of banking, when note issue by enterprises other than incorporated banks became forbidden in practically every state after 1800.

Thus for chartered banks the issue of notes became the typically American way of extending credit down to Civil War times. However, when American banking began in the 1780's bank notes were not standardized as yet even in England. Sir James Steuart treated deviations from what later became the standard form under the heading: optional clauses on bank notes; and Adam Smith also devoted some space to the irregular types. This situation was reflected in the early American bank-note issues: first of all, practically all banks during the first period issued (besides demand notes) so-called post notes, i.e., notes payable to order on a specified later date.[90] But still other irregular note issues were put into circulation in those decades. The directors of the Massachusetts Bank in Boston, for instance, resolved on June 21, 1785 to issue notes with the following tenor: "This note shall at all times be received in discharge of debts due to the Bank and entitles the possessor to (blank) dollars in specie from the bank stock when it shall be divided."[91] Notes of such tenor were nothing but expressions of Mercantilist banking thought as characterized above.[92] Similar notes, known under the name of "facility notes" circulated as late as the 1810's.[93]

Distinct from the lending activities were the investment activities of early American "money banks." From the outset some of them, such as the First and Second Banks of the United States, invested a considerable part of their capital in government obligations, by taking them from subscribers in lieu of specie for the payments of bank shares. Or to give another example, the State of Pennsylvania subscribed $300,000 to the Philadelphia Bank and paid for this subscription in United States 6 per cent stock.[84] Once more the Bank of England had served as a model, but the American followers invested in government obligations only a part of, and not the whole, capital. The State Bank of Boston, to be sure, by 1815 had invested five-eighths of its capital in loans to the Federal government and to the Commonwealth of Massachusetts.[95] The policy of using a part of the capital for more or less permanent investment, outside of the regular banking business, is typical of banks founded with the avowed purpose to serve government finance. It was adopted by other early banks also and was especially widespread in the 1810's.[96] The Massachusetts Bank, for example, invested funds in shares of the First Bank of the United States and later in those of the Manufacturers and Mechanics Bank,[97] and the Philadelphia Bank invested in stocks of turnpike and bridge companies. Those among the few banks which in the first period were setting aside reserves tended to invest them in the same way. An early transaction of the Massachusetts Bank amounts to this, and the 1816 balance sheet of the Philadelphia Bank contains under assets the item: Stock bought on Account of Contingent Fund.[98]

So much for the lending and investment business of the early American banks. It was supplemented by a second important line, the deposit business. The earliest American banks were brought into being with the avowed purpose of providing safe depositories for the funds of capitalists.[99] Thereby American banks following the example of the Bank of England[100] from the start combined two sets of activities which in large parts of Europe were then kept separate. The distinction between banks of deposit (the Bank of Amsterdam and Hamburg), banks of discount, and banks of circulation was soon to become common in this country.[101] Because of the combination of functions, the American banks followed a practice different from that of the Continental banks of deposit in that no charge was made to the depositor. The Massachusetts Bank, which had promised in its charter application of 1784 to follow this policy, deviated only temporarily from it and for a few years charged a small fee to depositors payable at the withdrawal of the deposits.[102]

One can distinguish for the first period three different types of deposits.[103] Banks took what the Roman law knew under the name of depositum regulare. That is to say, bullion (gold ignots and silver bars) or plate or valuable articles of small bulk were deposited for safekeeping with the banks with the understanding that the depositor would receive back the identical bullion, plate or valuables.[104] More important, as a matter of fact, were genuine deposits which corresponded to the depositum irregulare of the Roman law and which will be discussed in detail later: Gold and silver coin, notes of the bank with which the deposit was made, notes of other banks in the same place, items payable at such banks, and notes of the First Bank of the United States were, as a rule, credited to the depositor as cash.[105] This phrase is self-explanatory and synonymous with the above term.

In addition to these two types of deposits there existed in the first period, and also in the first years of the second, a third type: the "special deposit" which can perhaps be characterized as a hybrid between the depositum regulare and the depositum irregulare. Banks would refuse to credit notes of distant banks as cash, but would take them on special deposit.[106] This meant that the depositor, who in the case of the Massachusetts Bank of Boston had to present a list of such notes as deposited, could withdraw identical notes or notes of the same bank or of banks of similar description.[107] Alternatively such notes could be credited as cash after deduction of a certain discount[108] and when the latter practice expanded in the course of the second period the special deposit became obsolete.[109]

There was a good deal of disagreement as to the true character of these special deposits especially around 1817. At that time the institution was widely used because of conditions created by the previous suspension of specie payments. The question was whether a special deposit was a depositum regulare or a depositum irregulare, although these terms were unknown. In 1817 the cashier of the Pittsburgh branch of the Bank of Pennsylvania refused to touch a special deposit of the United States Treasury without the latter's permission. That is to say, he treated that deposit as a depositum regulare and this was the construction which Crawford, the Secretary of the Treasury, gave to such deposits.[110] In contrast the Bank of the State of Tennessee considered a special deposit as a depositum irregulare, as can be seen from the following illuminating letter by its president, H. L. White (dated March 17, 1817):

No list of these notes deposited was ever kept, nor were the notes thus deposited laid by as ones to which the Treasurer of the United States had a specific claim. The bank used such notes whenever opportunity offered, in the same manner they would have used money received on general deposit, holding itself at liberty when drawn upon by the Treasurer to pay in notes upon other banks a sum equal to that which had been thus deposited, and never did conceive that it was under obligation to retain and pay to such drafts the identical notes which it had received. Such a construction...would have created trouble and responsibility...without any possibility of benefit to the bank. The meaning therefore of the term special deposits in notes on other banks, as we always practiced upon it, both as it respects the United States and all others from whom such deposits have been made is, that so far as we have received notes on other banks to the same extent are we at liberty to pay in notes on other banks.[111]

In consideration of the prevailing practice[112] this author is inclined to hold the following interpretation: From the point of view of the individual depositor the special deposit was in most cases a depositum irregulare, since on the whole he would not receive back the identical notes which he had deposited. From the point of view of the depositors as a group, however, the special deposits represented a depositum regulare, for, so to speak, they contributed to a pool of a certain type of bank money lodged with a particular bank. As a group, they would receive the identical notes which they had deposited.

Special deposits were the result of the monetary confusion of that era; they date back as far as the 1780's, the time of financial instability under the Articles of Confederation.[113] The beginnings are reflected in the directors' records of the Massachusetts Bank. On June 26, 1784 the directors resolved:

> that any person who shall deposit money in the Bank shall have a right to take out the same kind of money as that which they deposited, to the amount of what may be due to him on account of that particular deposit at the time of his demanding the kind of money he deposited, and provided that such kind of money shall then be in the bank.[114]

The same situation which led in this case to the establishment of rudimentary special deposits induced the Bank of New York to make up two separate balance sheets in which it kept paper and specie transactions apart. It distinguished between "paper bank" and "specie bank," the term "bank" connoting in this context what is called "fund" today. The former balance sheet was kept in dollars and referred to the transactions in state paper money; the latter was kept in pounds sterling, the distinction implying that the bank must have kept two different sets of books. The bank building is to be found in the balance sheet of the "paper bank," probably because it was bought with paper money. Capital and discounts are to be found in the balance sheet of the "specie bank," while deposits and profit are shown on both.[115] The monetary confusion of the Revolutionary period had hardly cleared away when country notes became a disturbing factor and resulted in the establishment of the first full-fledged special deposits.[116] In the 1800's in the case of the Boston Exchange Office, described below[117] a complete enterprise was built on the basis of special deposits of country money.

During the War of 1812, under the rule of suspension specie was turned over to banks on special deposit, a type of transaction which had not been unknown in the 1800's but must have multiplied during the war, without becoming widespread.[118] But when, after resumption in 1817, a new monetary confusion similar to that encountered in and after the 1780's threatened businessmen and bankers, the special deposit of notes was revived and gained considerable importance for a short while. At the same time this institution, meant to be a protective device for the banks, became instead a serious problem for them.

On March 17, 1817 Secretary Crawford wrote to President Jones of the Second Bank of the United States: "I agree with you entirely in the opinion...on the nature of the risk and responsibility which the banks of the interior have incurred by receiving special deposits."[119] When the monetary conditions became stabilized in the 1820's the special deposit disappeared for good, more or less.[120]

Turning now to genuine deposits, one is surprised to find from the very beginning all the various types which exist today.[121] There were time deposits and demand deposits, although contemporary bankers did not yet make this distinction. Actually most deposits were time deposits in character, i.e., funds entrusted to banks for safekeeping; but demand deposits liable to draft by checks were common, at least in the eastern trade centers. (Besides regular checks,[122] cashiers' checks were known.) As a rule, demand deposits were[123] lodged deposits, but created deposits did exist.[124] They were rare, however, and in most cases, as expressed in the Rules and Regulations of 1811 of the Massachusetts Bank, discounts were "paid off" in notes.[125] Again the terms "lodged" and "created" deposits, as such, were, of course, unknown. Although the various types of deposits were in existence, the deposit business as a whole was still in its infancy. In the 1780's and 1790's the Massachusetts Bank, for example, charged depositors a fee, then abandoned it; it restricted deposits to $300 and checks to $100, restrictions which also were dropped again after a few years.[126] If we knew more about other banks similar cases would probably be on record. Anyway Noah Webster deemed it necessary to describe in detail the mechanism of money transfers by check.[127]

In addition to deposits of private capitalists, which formed the bulk of all deposits, the first American banks (the Bank of North America, the Bank of New York, the Massachusetts Bank, the Bank of Providence and the Bank of Maryland, as well as the First Bank of the United States) also held deposits of federal funds.[128] While during most of the period these funds were concentrated in the Bank of the United States, except in certain places where it had no branches, after its dissolution in 1811 the business in government deposits became important for a number of banks.

Furthermore some banks, such as the Bank of New York, the Massachusetts Bank, and the Philadelphia Bank, also kept deposits of state funds.[129] Occasionally state deposits originated from loan transactions.

It comes as rather a surprise to find that as early as the 1790's banks themselves were depositors in other banks. In 1792 the Massachusetts Bank deposited with the Boston branch of the First Bank of the United States notes of that bank under the condition that the deposit could at any time be withdrawn in silver.[130] In the years following, country banks deposited funds with city brokers for the purpose of buying up or redeeming and circulating their notes. One could suspect that the earliest bankers' balances, i.e., deposits of banks with other banks, developed from funds kept for such purposes by country banks with city brokers, for it is a fact that by 1800 banks had invaded the note brokerage business. Be that as it may, material published by Professor Gras[131] for Massachusetts in the years 1808-1813 shows clearly that before the outbreak of the War of 1812 deposits of banks with other banks were quite common. Massachusetts country banks kept deposits with Boston banks and Boston banks kept deposits with each other (probably on the basis of arrangements similar to that between the Massachusetts Bank and the Boston branch of the First Bank of the United States just described). In addition there existed inter-state bank relations. In 1813 the Massachusetts Bank kept deposits with the Bank of New York and with the Bank of North America in Philadelphia; the Union Bank of Boston kept deposits with the Mechanics Bank and the Manhattan Company, both of New York, and with the Farmers and Mechanics Bank of Philadelphia. This author does not know of any material for New York and Pennsylvania which would be equally conclusive with that for Massachusetts. But enough data have survived to prove that inter-bank deposits and incipient correspondent relationships existed in these states also as early as the 1800's. In 1803 the newly-founded Philadelphia Bank proposed to the young Merchants Bank of New York the "establishment of mutual credit and mutual reception of notes," and it opened an account with the latter.[132] In the same year the Manhattan Company and the

Merchants Bank, both of New York, competed for the deposits of the newly-founded State Bank of Albany.[133] When in 1811 Stephen Girard opened his Banking House, the Barings of London, the Bank of South Carolina in Charleston, and the City Bank and the Bank of America in New York became its correspondents in addition to banks in Baltimore, Lancaster, and Wilmington.[134] Thus the beginnings of modern networks of correspondents and banker's balances date back as far as the 1800's.[135] So much for the deposit business!

The question of whether or not banks themselves should and could become borrowers came up at a very early moment although it did not then agitate public opinion as it was to do in the second period. As early as 1784 the "laws" of the Massachusetts Bank contained a clause: "that the directors may borrow money for the use of the bank on the credit of its stock whenever it shall be thought necessary." Actually a transaction of that type was concluded as early as 1797.[136] Prior to that date the First Bank of the United States had already embarked on similar borrowings. It had loaned so large a percentage of its capital to the Federal government that it needed operating funds if it wanted to build up a regular commercial banking business also. Thus in the years 1793-1795, hypothecating United States 6 per cent stock, it borrowed $746,000 in Amsterdam, a loan which was repaid by 1803.[137] William Bingham, then a director of the Bank of the United States, is supposed to have been the driving force in this transaction.

But still other methods of borrowing became available in the first period. Beginning in 1795 the Bank of Maryland received "at different times" loans from the stockholders amounting to $85,000, reimbursable in 1805.[138] In Connecticut in 1807 the General Assembly permitted the use of post notes in order to counteract the depression created by the Embargo, and a pamphlet of 1810 permits the conclusions that post notes were used to a considerable extent as a means of borrowing funds prior to the War of 1812.[139] The taking of deposits was not yet considered as the borrowing of funds; but under certain circumstances it was identical with so doing. Whenever the issue of notes was limited to

100 per cent of capital and deposits and the banks issued notes on the basis of the latter or whenever they voluntarily adopted this policy as the first American banks did, they had actually borrowed such deposits. This holds true of the First Bank of the United States, of the Rhode Island banks under the law of 1809, and in general of the earliest banks in their early years.[140] The Hartford Bank, for instance, learned that it could loan with safety two-thirds of its deposits.[141] The statement, however, would not hold true for those banks which by their charters were permitted to lend 200 or 300 per cent of their capitals (or capitals and deposits, respectively) since experience showed that such large note issues could not be kept in circulation anyway.[142]

In conclusion, some minor lines of the American banking business of 1800 should be mentioned. Banks in the first period were building up a collection business,[143] and issued special-purpose post notes to their customers in order to facilitate the transmission of money.[144] Some of them also dabbled in stocks[145] on their own account or, like the Bank of New York, as an agent of the Secretary of the Treasury. Even the business in foreign exchange, which the New York merchants had intended to reserve for themselves, was entered into by the banks in the first period. In New York the branch of the First Bank of the United States sold to merchants foreign exchange, resulting from government drafts on Amsterdam.

Organization

The social status and the individual standing of the average stockholder in the early American city bank were determined by the following facts: Shares of such banks as the Bank of North America, the Bank of New York, the Massachusetts Bank, the First Bank of the United States, and the Hartford Bank had the high face value of four or five hundred dollars and a good deal of vision and courage was required for the investment in enterprises of an unheard-of type. Those qualities in conjunction with wealth could then be found in America only in the merchant class. This class therefore provided the early American banks with stockholders who

were partly men of inherited wealth, accumulated in the colonial era, and partly nouveaux riches.[146] The composition of stockholders in individual banks, on the other hand, was usually influenced by social and family ties among the old and prominent families of the cities in question. As has been shown by East, this social pattern was established with the foundation of the Bank of North America through the activities of Robert Morris; and the fact that the early American banks had been dominated by socially prominent cliques exerted in time a considerable influence on the history of American banking, especially in and immediately after the 1830's. These stockholders, well versed in business, considered themselves "proprietors" of their enterprises.[147] One surmises that the rather even distribution of stock among a considerable number of members of the wealthy mercantile class, as is typical of the early banks (with the exception of the Bank of North America), was intentional[148] and contributed to this attitude.[149] Consequently the interest of these men in the enterprises in which they held stock went further than that of modern stockholders,[150] so that occasionally a stockholders' meeting could influence the policy of the bank in question. In the First Bank of the United States, for instance, the decision to create branches was made in a stockholders' meeting. When in the 1790's and 1800's bank shares became smaller and smaller in value the prevailing type of bank shareholder and his attitude toward his enterprise underwent a change.

According to the conception of that time the stockholders delegated their powers to boards of directors.[151] But during the debates of 1786 in the Pennsylvania legislature on the fate of the Bank of North America it was still claimed that that bank was "managed...by the stockholders," while in the same discussion Robert Morris stated that as a stockholder he had no share in the management "unless when the stockholders are called together." It is very significant that the term "banker," which in the eighteenth century meant proprietor of a bank,[152] was used in these debates to connote the bank stockholder.[153] A few years later this outlook was abandoned, however, and boards of directors were generally conceived of as

administrative bodies acting for the stockholders. James Sullivan speaks of "acting
proprietors" when he refers to bank directors.[154] They actually ran the banks,[155]
a statement which will be qualified shortly. The fact that the directors were expected to take an active part in the administration of the banks was recognized, for
instance, by the stockholders of the
Massachusetts Bank, who at their meeting of
January 6, 1790 voted to pay the directors
$100 "for their services in the last
year."[156] The boards met once or twice a
week when they determined the policy of
their enterprises and made decisions with
regard to the current business. The discounting of bills of exchange and of promissory notes was typically the function of
the boards of directors, and all the extant
rules and regulations of early banks stress
this fact. It is characteristic of the importance of the boards that twelve out of
nineteen articles of the Ordinance and By-
Laws for the Regulation of the First Bank
of the United States and fifteen out of
sixteen articles of the "Laws" of 1784 of
the Massachusetts Bank deal with the functions of the board.[157]

The members of a typical bank board
of the first period were merchants, with a
sprinkling of lawyers.[158] They were all
wealthy men. The fact that of the fifteen
New Yorkers who were reputed to have kept
carriages in 1806 four were or had been
directors of the Bank of New York[159] illuminates both the social standing of these
men and the reasons for the violent antagonism to banks displayed by those less
fortunate.

Bank directors had businesses of
their own to conduct, and so while as a
body they set the policy and administered
their banks (going so far as to draft important letters to be signed by the president), they soon delegated the actual management thereof to the cashiers. Before long,
however, even the general administration of
banks by the boards became cumbersome, and
organizational development turned in two
directions. Following the precedent established by the Bank of England boards began
to delegate part of their functions to committees. As a matter of fact in the Massachusetts Bank the appointment of committees
of the board started as early as 1784.[161]
In the Bank of the United States it was a

committee which performed the supervisory
functions of the board and, as described by
Professor Wettereau, the board of this bank
referred all questions brought before it
to some committee for study and report.
The fact that committees of bank boards
were set up in the first period (actually
after the 1780's) is of considerable interest. As will be shown later, the administration of banks by committees was to become one of the typical features of bank
organization in the second period. In the
first period, however, committees of bank
boards were hardly what one could characterize as standing committees. They were
appointed for particular purposes whenever
necessary.[162] Such purposes were partly
of vital importance: to examine the state
of the bank; to determine the dividends to
be paid; to burn worn out notes; to plan
and supervise the erection of bank buildings; to represent the bank in negotiations
with the public authorities and committees
of other banks; to attend meetings of
stockholders of the bank in which the represented bank held shares; to buy government stock or bank stock; and so on.
Committees also acted on minor matters
(they assisted the cashier in the final
settlement of books or decided whether the
bank room should be enlarged) and they even
performed such completely unimportant tasks
as taking care of the repairing of a fence,
of writing a letter, or paying a creditor
(1787).[163] Although as a rule committees
of the bank boards were appointed for special purposes, the repeated appointment of
the same committees whenever a certain job
had to be done, and the appointment of the
same men to these same committees again
and again, paved the way to the standing
committees of the second period, committees
which stood ready to fulfill certain specific functions.[164] Committees on the
state of the bank and dividend committees
especially seem to have been rather common
in the first period, even attaining a semi-
permanent status.[165]

While administration of banks by
committees was one possible solution of the
organizational problems of those days,
there were still other possibilities. One
was the administration by cashiers, although
originally they had not been considered as
important cogs in the administrative wheels
of banks. In the Ordinance of the First

Bank of the United States the cashier is not even mentioned. Tench Francis, the cashier of the Bank of North American and America's first bank cashier, did not receive more than $1000 as his salary. ($1100 was the salary of the cashier of the Massachusetts Bank in 1792.)[166] Yet it was the cashiers who became the first professional bankers in this country and the progenitors of the modern banking profession. Some of them developed remarkable administrative abilities. A few years after the position of bank cashiers had been created they started to rise and to gain considerable importance. As the historian of the Bridgeport Bank put it: "The whole business of the bank was conducted by [the cashier] (the directors superintending the discounts)."[167] In some banks, as, for instance, the Philadelphia Bank and the State Bank in Boston, the cashiers received salaries higher than those of the presidents,[168] and by 1800 their salaries were, on the whole, considerably higher than they had been around 1790. In the 1800's $2000 was a fair salary for a cashier in a big city bank, while those in country banks, of course, received less. The cashier of the Hartford Bank earned $800 in 1794, $900 in 1800, and $1000 in 1801. The cashier of the Bridgeport Bank was given $700 in 1807 and was raised to $1000 in 1810. The cashier of the Phoenix Bank in Hartford received $800 in 1814, a low salary which is due perhaps to the fact that the president of that bank rose from a cashiership himself and was planning to do part of the job then usually done by cashiers. Sometimes the cashiers in addition to their salaries were given rent-free lodgings in the bank building.[169] There is a further indication of the rise of the cashiers in the early American banks. While originally they do not seem to have attended board meetings they were soon made secretaries of the boards: in the Massachusetts Bank (of 1784) in 1789 and in the Philadelphia Bank (of 1803) in 1807.[170]

There remained still another organizational possibility which was practised, for instance, by the Massachusetts Bank,[171] but which does not seem to have become common custom. In this bank every week one of the directors "in rotation in alphabetical order" acted as the sitting director (also called the director of the week), and as some sort of chief executive officer administered the bank for that week. He "decide[d] on such business as [was] not acted on by the board at their sitting,...examine[d] the securities offered, and...transact[ed] such other business as [was] requisite." This organizational setup resulted in a personnel policy different from that of all the other banks in the same period whose organization is known to this author. In the Massachusetts Bank, bank officers were annually appointed by the new board and could not "remain in their offices longer then the directors continue in theirs" (1784). Thus the cashiers in that bank became de facto exalted tellers and accountants, although the Rules and Regulations of 1811 defined the cashier's functions as "superintending the affairs of the bank."[172] They represented with the exception of the first two cashiers, a distinctly lower type of employee than their colleagues in other banks. Consequently while elsewhere cashiers stayed on for decades, the Massachusetts Bank had four cashiers in the first ten years of its existence and in 1814 a cashier had to be fired for defalcations.[173]

If one wishes to understand how the position of the sitting director came into being, one must go back to Robert Morris's original bank plan of the spring of 1781.[174] According to this plan the board of the "national bank" to be founded (the Bank of North America) was to be a policy-making body pure and simple.[175] It was to meet only quarterly for the purpose of "regulating the affairs of the bank." At these quarterly meetings the board was also to "choose two directors to inspect and control the business of the bank for the ensuing three months." That is to say, the policy-making board of directors was to select two of its members (designated by Robert Morris as "inspectors")[176] to serve as the bank's administrators, a logical procedure following the example of the Committee in Waiting of the Bank of England. (This committee was a "rota" of directors to superintend the current business, including discounting.)[177] However, when the Bank of North America, the Massachusetts Bank, and other American institutions took over this device and appointed sitting directors they changed the significance of

Morris's proposal, because the boards themselves had been set up as administrative bodies. Thus the sitting directors of the Massachusetts Bank and of other banks following this practice became the representatives of administrative bodies, instead of administrators elected by policy-making bodies.

The president of a bank in the first period had nothing to do with the administration of his enterprise. He was elected by the directors, was considered _primus inter pares_, and held typically a position of trust and confidence. The Ordinance of the First Bank of the United States quoted above devoted only one article to describing his functions: he had the power to convoke the board of directors on special occasions; with approbation of the board he assembled and affixed to documents the seal of the corporation which he kept in his custody. So unimportant was the president of the early American bank that the Rules of the Massachusetts Bank of 1784, 1786, and 1811 hardly mention him.[178] One will find an "entrepreneur" among the bank presidents of the first period only as an exception.[179] It is typical that in 1797 when the president of the Massachusetts Bank was to sign a certain letter he was expressly authorized to do so "in behalf of the board." He himself did not draft the letter for it had previously been "reported" to the board. Similarly when in the same year the same president was to take action on a specific matter the board appointed him a committee of one.[180] A few years later when Thomas Willing resigned in 1807 as president of the First Bank of the United States, his colleagues praised his "impartial conduct" observed "as well during their procedures as in coinciding with their decisions."[181] The earliest indications that the position of the bank president was about to change can be found in the exceptions alluded to before and to be discussed later, and in the practice of the president becoming a member of important committees of the board. A new stage in the development was reached in 1812 when the president and the cashier, instead of a committee of its directors, represented the Bank of New York in a meeting with other banks, and again in 1814 when, probably for the first time, a bank cashier resigned to become the president of a rival bank.[182]

While bank presidents of the first period were not the administrators of their institutions, the fact that they held this position indicated in a few cases that they controlled the enterprises in question. The mere existence of such control at that early moment is noteworthy, for most of the old charters tried to exclude it through the limitation of the voting power and, sometimes, as in the case of the Hartford Bank, even by the limitation of stockholdings.[183] Professor Gras had described how William Phillips, a founder and (in 1785) the largest stockholder of the Massachusetts Bank, became its second president (1785-1791), how he was succeeded by his son-in-law; and how later his son was the sixth and his grandson the eighth president.[184] One understands why Gras characterized this bank as a sort of Phillips bank from 1784 to 1840. This control over the Massachusetts Bank by the Phillips family seems to have begun when the Massachusetts Bank experienced a capital reduction in 1785.[185] A few years later, in 1791, the Providence Bank came into being. It was from the outset in the hands of the Brown family of Providence and remained so for ninety-two years[186] as evidenced in the succession of presidents from the Brown family, beginning with John Brown. Again the facts that John Nixon during the years 1791-1808 was the second president of the Bank of North America and that in 1822 his son Henry became the fourth seem to indicate control of that bank by the Nixon family of Philadelphia. Finally, in the early nineteenth century the Phoenix Bank of Hartford was obviously under the domination of the Bunce family: Russell Bunce, an original director, married the widow of the first president and his son later became a president of the bank.[187] These data indicate that not only did bank control exist in the first period, but that it was already becoming hereditary.

The Emergence of the American Banking System

The first period saw emerge not only a specific type of bank but also a banking system, although there was not, as yet, any action consciously directed toward that end. For years after the first banks had been created, it was even doubtful whether this country would possess a multiplicity of banks or, to use a modern term, its complement, a banking system.

When in 1781 the Bank of North America came into being as the first mercantile bank in this country it was endowed with a national monopoly for the duration of the Revolutionary War. But the underlying idea survived the war, namely, that it might be advantageous to have but one incorporated bank in this country, just as England had at the time only the Bank of England. When the Bank of New York was founded and its cashier went to Philadelphia to be trained in the Bank of North America for his job, Gouverneur Morris suggested to him that the Bank of New York become a branch of the Bank of North America.[188] In the following decade a national banking monopoly of the First Bank of the United States seemed possible and was widely desired by Federalist merchants.[189] As late as 1802 Jefferson, who in contrast considered the "monopoly of a single bank...an evil,"[190] expressed to Gallatin the fear that "the Bank of the United States might swallow up the others and monopolize the whole banking business of the United States."[191] Actually, by that time, it had already become evident that a banking monopoly on a national basis could not be established in America. But then at least local monopolies seemed desirable to many representatives of early American banking. Consequently, the men in charge of the Bank of North America successfully fought the first project to launch a second bank in Philadelphia in 1784. Similarly Hamilton was upset in 1791 when informed that a second bank was planned for New York.[192] In the same year some of the directors of both the Bank of New York and the Massachusetts Bank, first aiming at a national monopoly, favored a merger with the Bank of the United States. When this plan did not materialize the Bank of New York offered the Bank of the United States a number of shares at par (as did the Providence Bank also) for the obvious purpose of becoming sole agent in New York, of precluding the creation of a branch, and of upholding its own local monopoly.[193] The Massachusetts Bank, on the other hand, invested in stock of the national bank, so as to exclude the possibility of competition by interlocking interest. As a matter of fact, the second banks in Boston and Philadelphia came into

existence only in 1792 and 1793, respectively; while the first bank in each city had opened for business in 1782 and 1784. In the very year 1792 in which the Union Bank of Boston was established as the second bank of that city, James Sullivan still broached the plan for a monopolistic public bank in Masschusetts,[194] and the act establishing the Bank of Pennsylvania, the second in Philadelphia, authorized the Bank of North American to relinquish its own charter and to become absorbed into the new bank.[195] In New York even two attempts at founding a second bank failed until in 1799 (fifteen years after the first), the Bank of the Manhattan Company was brought into being in that city, by devious means.[196] The Browns of Providence tried to uphold the local monopoly of the Providence Bank as late as 1800[197] and the Hartford Bank, finally, enjoyed a local monopoly for a period of twenty-two years.[198]

In the late 1790's the idea of local banking monopolies was on the point of being abandoned.[199] In the meantime, almost simultaneously with the multiplication of banks, the first steps had been taken toward building a banking system, and at the beginning voluntary cooperation, which will be described in a later volume, was a more important integrating factor than legislative action. There were at first very few restrictions imposed on banks and the few that were imposed were embodied in the bank charters. (General banking laws did not come into existence prior to the second period.) But just the same the tendency to model charters of newer banks on those of certain older ones led to integration.[200] In fact some bank charters became models for whole groups of banks in the same state and even elsewhere. Another important early step toward the organization of a banking system was the enactment of what were called in New York state "restraining acts," acts which reserved to incorporated banks[201] the right to issue notes.

Division of labor among banks further contributed to integration: First of all there was both a geographical and a functional division of labor between city and country banks. Or in other words: instead of the country being financed in the cities, it became financed locally, with the result, unfortunately, that less sound credit methods were used than would probably have been worked out otherwise. The creation of country banks precluded the development of banking functions on the part of city merchants.[202] Once local credit institutions had spread all over the country, they came to specialize in certain transactions and left the city banks to specialize in others (banking on "private" as against banking on "mercantile" credit). On the other hand, the trend toward division of labor among banks was thwarted by charter conditions which forced city banks to loan a certain percentage of their capital to agricultural and manufacturing interests not residing in the city.[203]

In the 1790's and 1800's when banks began multiplying even in one and the same place, they tended to cater to different groups of customers. Occasionally they selected the latter along party lines (Republican as against Federalist banks), as will be discussed shortly. Besides such aberration from sound business practice, there was real specialization among the several banks in the same city. In Philadelphia, for instance, the big importers were customers of the Bank of the United States; while the Philadelphia Bank worked with the shopkeepers. Firm names, such as Merchants Bank, Mechanics Bank, Farmers Bank, Farmers and Mechanics Bank, Merchants and Mechanics Bank, were significant, indicating the type of people with whom the bank in question wished to deal.[204] While division of labor was at that time a more powerful integrating factor, the creation of the first bankers' balances also contributed to the emergence of a banking system.

The "political bank" mentioned above must be discussed in passing because of its great, though indirect, influence on the history of American banking. As described above, the first mercantile banks were launched by merchants who were Federalists almost by necessity. Consequently when in the 1790's the American party alignment took place and much bitter feeling was engendered, there was undoubtedly a tendency on the part of bank directors to discriminate against those applicants for discounts who were their political enemies. In New York it was claimed (whether correctly or incorrectly does not matter in this context) that "it was impossible for traders to express Republican sentiments without material injury to their business"[205] and conversely, as soon as the Republicans controlled a bank they retaliated in kind.[206] Such behavior by bank directors together with the fact that banks were considered semi-public institutions, could not but make them subject to the political struggle. Thus by 1800 the chartering of a bank could easily become a political affair, as is exemplified by the fight for and against the charter of the Merchants Bank of New York.[207] In 1803 President Jefferson schemed to make all banks Republican by having them share in the public deposits according to their political disposition.[208] The political maneuvers in 1812 of Republican Governor Daniel D. Tompkins of New York to counteract the chartering of the Bank of America, which he considered Federalist, are typical.[209]

This was the atmosphere in which the "political bank"[210] came into being. A few examples will be given to sketch the type. The Manhattan Company of New York of 1799 was created by Aaron Burr and Brockholst Livingston, two names which meant a political program. On the board of this bank was Samuel Osgood, who had started his career among the representatives of Federalism, but later was guided by fear of centralized power and aristocratic influence. Another political bank of great importance was the State Bank of Boston. It came into being in 1811 after the Democratic-Republicans complained that all the existing Boston banks had been founded by their political enemies. When subscriptions were opened a circular stated "that the establishment of the present institution should be so conducted that [in accordance with the expectation of the legislature] its benefits shall be diffused as extensively as possible among the friends of the government..."[211] The political character of this bank was unblushingly blazoned abroad in 1812 when it applied for national deposits. The application to the Secretary of the Treasury signed by William Gray contained the following passage: the bank "is the property of sixteen hundred freemen of the respectable State of Massachusetts, all of them advocates of the then existing federal administration, associated not solely for the purpose of advancing their pecuniary interests, but for the more noble purpose of cherishing republican men and republican measures against the wiles and machinations of a party which has obtained the direction of the moneyed institutions of the State and used them to check the growth of republicanism and thus indirectly to weaken the constituted authorities of the nation."[212] One more example, this time in the field of country banking: Elkanah Watson, the founder of the Bank of Albany, disagreed with his collaborators in that bank, the leading Federalist Dutch citizens of Albany. Leaving the bank, he conceived and launched in 1803 the Albany State Bank as a Republican institution to compete with the earlier Federalist enterprise. Such political banks were typical of the first period[213] and the conviction that banks were chartered as instruments of party politics survived with the public for years. This conviction played a considerable part in the fight against the Second Bank of the United States.

The development toward a banking system alluded to before took place in two stages: during the first period neither banks nor legislatures were aware of what was in the making; in the second they became conscious of the trend. Lack of awareness and awareness, respectively, distinguish the two stages. Actually by the end of the first period American banks already represented a banking system, as described by Mathew Carey in 1811: if one bank in a city reduced its discounts the others had to follow since otherwise they would have been deprived of their specie. That is to say, by 1810 banks were already dependent on each other to such an extent that they had lost that freedom of action which, for instance, the Bank of North America, the Massachusetts Bank or the Bank of New York had had for about a decade, during which they possessed regional monopolies. This statement is but another way of saying that by 1810 American banks had become part and parcel of a banking system.

Chapter II

BANK FOUNDERS AND BANK PERSONNEL IN
THE FIRST PERIOD

Able authors have repeatedly described how the first mercantile bank of
this country, the Bank of North American in
Philadelphia, grew out of a patriotic purchasing agency called the Pennsylvania
Bank and founded in 1780. The term "bank"
in this firm name, according to the custom
of the eighteenth century, connoted only
what is today called a "fund." But the
enterprise issued 6 per cent post notes in
exchange for money contributed, and possibly also for deposits (funds borrowed); and
a real bank, the Bank of North America, was
its natural successor. The Philadelphians
who backed both the Pennsylvania Bank and
the Bank of North America have also been
the subject of chapters in books and paragraphs of articles, and most of this material needs no repetition.[1]

I

Bank Founders[2]

Foremost in founding the Bank of
North American stood Robert Morris, the
first of the three great leaders among the
originators of American banking. His
achievement, however, was not a creation
ab ovo and consequently can be understood
only against the background of the earlier
stage of the development: As shown by
Andrew MacFarland Davis, land banks as well
as several money banks had at least been
planned in America during the colonial era.
It is in this setting that one must look at
Morris's first bank scheme of 1763.[3] In a
speech before the Pennsylvania Assembly in
1786 referring to it Morris himself stated:
"I...laid the foundation for one [bank] and
established a credit in Europe for the purpose. From the execution of this design, I
was prevented only by the Revolution."
This promotion must have had at least the
one advantage of making Morris familiar
with the principles of Mercantilist money
banks, the successful introduction of which
into America in 1781 was his great achievement.[4]

In a letter of July 13, 1781 to
John Jay,[5] Morris described in detail the
background of his actions as well as his
motives in promoting the Bank of North
America. First there was a serious lack
of a sound circulating medium because, due
to extensive issues of paper money (Continental Currency), specie had become a commodity to be exported or hoarded. Secondly,
the government had no credit and therefore
could not borrow the means of prosecuting
the war. "Under the pressure of these difficulties," as Morris expressed it later in
1786 before the Pennsylvania legislature,
"the idea of a public or national bank suggested itself as a measure that might be
extremely useful in my attempts to regain
for the united states [sic!] that credit
which had been lost."[6] He expected "that
the small sums advanced by the holders of
bank stock [might] be multiplied in the
usual manner by the means of their credit,
so as to increase the resource which the
government can draw from it, and at the
same time by placing the collective mass of
private credit between the lenders and borrowers supply at once the want of ability
in the one and of credit in the other." Or
to put it more concretely, as Morris himself did, he planned to borrow from the
bank and to anticipate the payment of taxes
and other income by discounting the notes
of individuals and receiving, in turn,
"paper that [could not] depreciate."
Thirdly, to use modern terms, he wished to
replace an unsound currency by a sound one;
and last, but not least, he wanted "to
unite the several states more closely together in one general money connexion and
indissolubly to attach many powerful individuals to the cause of our country by
the strong principle of self-love and the
immediate sense of private interest."[7]
Thus back of Morris's thinking were motives
of financial and economic, as well as of
general, policy, the unification of the
country. Moreover, the new enterprise was
not to be a war measure only, like the

Pennsylvania Bank; it was to serve in future peace times also. Morris expected the bank to become "an institution that most probably will continue as long as the United States and that will become as useful to commerce and agriculture in the days of peace as it must be to the government during the war."

In order to understand Morris's political intentions, one must keep in mind that not only the Superintendent of Finance but also all the other founders of the Bank of North America belonged to that group of conservative men who aimed at a centralistic, or to use their terminology, at a national (as opposed to a federal) government. As early as 1781, when Robert Morris became Superintendent of Finance, Gouverneur Morris became his assistant. In 1775 the latter had drafted the report of the New York Provincial Congress which contains the following passage: "Whenever a paper currency has been emitted and obtained general credit it will be a new bond to the Associated Colonies."[8] Thus it might well be inferred that by creating the bank these men meant ·to issue paper money of general credit which would contribute to the integration of the sovereign American states. Be that as it may, the bank "immediately began to act as a national reagent in politics," as East puts it.[9] With its help Robert Morris drew wealthy individuals from all over the country into an enterprise national in scope and character. Capitalists from the various northern states such as William Duer and Philip Schuyler of New York, Jeremiah Wadsworth of Connecticut, John Langdom of New Hampshire, and the clique of Philadelphia merchants of high social standing pivoting around Thomas Willing became stockholders of the bank and were thereby tied together by common interest.

However, Robert Morris did more than conceive and promote the first American bank. His actions included seeing the plan through Congress, an activity which was to become typical of those which succeeding founders of early American banks had to undertake. Furthermore, without Morris the Bank of North America, though established, would not have been able to open for business. He it was who made an arrangement with the directors and subscribers of the Pennsylvania Bank by which the latter transferred their subscriptions to the "national bank." In turn he guaranteed that they would receive from Congress what was due them, so that they could pay up the transferred subscriptions. In addition to making private investments possible, he invested considerable government specie funds in the venture when private capitalists were unable or unwilling to provide the money needed for the start. Finally, Morris contributed to early American banking some organizational features which were to become typical of the first and second periods. In his original plan of 1781, which was embodied in the charter of the Bank of North America, there can be found proxy voting and the sitting director. The former became a general feature of early American banking, while the latter was adopted by quite a few banks, as described above. Another rule which later became common and exerted a profound influence, namely, that directors (including the president) should not receive any remuneration except by resolution of the stockholders, was also conceived by Morris. He wanted to render these offices "honorable rather than lucrative." Honor as well as "their own interest as stockholders" was expected to "induce the first characters to accept the direction." Morris's plan stipulated that supervision of the bank by the Superintendent of Finance be established. This measure was taken over into the charters of the First and Second Banks of the United States as a function of the Secretary of the Treasury and undoubtedly influenced later state legislators to institute supervision by legislative committees, whenever the state in question invested funds in the bank concerned. In this connection Morris introduced into early American banking the element of secrecy which remained its characteristic feature for decades to come.[10] Supervision by the Superintendent of Finance was expected to avoid "public inspection" which would make business impossible "amidst the continued interruption" and yet to guard against the ill consequences of mismanagement.[11] Morris's partner, Thomas Willing, passed this idea on to the founders of the Massachusetts Bank when he wrote to them in 1784 that the world was apt to see in banking a greater mystery than there was and added: "perhaps it is right that they should do so and wonder on."[12]

In promoting the Bank of North America, Morris, of course, did not act alone. Gouverneur Morris, then his assistant, claimed to have drafted the plan of the bank, just discussed. To what extent[13] Alexander Hamilton's letter suggesting the creation of a bank influenced the Superintendent of Finance cannot be determined, although the wording of Morris's letter to Hamilton[14] permits the conclusion that such influence, if any, was not considerable. There can hardly be any doubt, however, about the importance of the cooperation of James Wilson (1742-1798), the great Philadelphia jurist. In 1780 when Morris set up the Pennsylvania Bank, the repeatedly-mentioned patriotic purchasing agency, Wilson who at that time promoted the establishment of a bank on his own, was Morris's legal adviser. The latter's communication to members of the Pennsylvania legislature has been mentioned previously as an important proof of the influence of Sir James Steuart on the originators of American banking.[15] In this letter Wilson pointed out to his friends the desirability of chartering in America a bank modeled on the Bank of England, that is to say, of a money bank.

While there is agreement among most students about the importance of James Wilson's contribution to the beginnings of American banking, this author is reluctant to adopt the universally held view as to that of Thomas Willing (1731-1821). He believes that John Nixon (1733-1808) and George Clymer (1739-1813), then directors of the Pennsylvania Bank and recipients of subscriptions for the "national bank" worked harder for it than did Thomas Willing.[16] Although he does not want to be dogmatic on this point, he feels certain that Thomas Willing's role in connection with the foundation of the Bank of North America has been overestimated and over-stressed. As far as this author can see, Willing was not a leader and did not possess those qualities of a creative entrepreneur needed to play a decisive part in this movement. His letters to Morris, written at a trying moment, show him rather weak and unable to master difficulties once the real head of his enterprise - Robert Morris - had left.[17] It is significant that in 1791 his election to the presidency of the First Bank of the United States was opposed because he was considered to be dominated by Morris who then was under suspicion as being a reckless speculator.[18] Neither does Willing's role in that bank present the picture of a leader among[19] leaders. The heir to a great fortune and an important business enterprise, Willing, in the opinion of this author, is an example of those businessmen who are able to retain and even to augment inherited wealth and business reputation which they would have been unable to build up themselves. Willing himself modestly wrote the following lines: "My success in life has not been derived from superior abilities or extensive knowledge...it can only be ascribed to a steady application to whatever I have undertaken and an honest and upright conduct in every transaction of life."[20] These words, which throw a most favorable light on the man, at the same time permit the historian to understand what Willing actually contributed to Morris's great achievement in creating American banking: viz., his solid mercantile reputation, some of his wealth, and his family and business connections. To be sure, his eleven shares, when compared with the 395 of the four largest individual subscribers, show him not only cautious, but rather reluctant.[21] But the fact that he not only invested in the new enterprise, but even became its president, publicly announced to the business community that the Bank of North America was not a wild and cockeyed scheme, but a sound enterprise. This expression of confidence drew other important men to its support.

Alexander Hamilton was the second of the three great bank founders and his letters to Morris, to be discussed presently, may even have exerted some influence on the Superintendent of Finance, as indicated above. In 1780 when Hamilton made his first proposal for the creation of a bank in America he was under the influence of Mercantilist banking theory, with which he had become acquainted through "some reading on the subjects of commerce and finance." While it is not known from which books and papers sprang Hamilton's original knowledge which inspired his thinking on banks and banking, the further development of his thought can be traced step by step.

Hamilton's first bank plan was embodied in a letter to Robert Morris, and resulted from his deep concern about the inflated Continental Currency.[22] Hamilton considered it urgent and, at the same time, possible to stop further depreciation, if one could only make it the immediate interest of the moneyed men of the country to cooperate with the government in its support. He believed that with regard to that money America was then in the same predicament as France had been previous to the launching of John Law's Mississippi scheme. Thus this scheme became the starting point for Hamilton's first suggestions on banking, a significant fact which will be explained later.[23] His favorable interpretation of Law and the latter's plan differed rather widely from that of today. According to young Hamilton, John Law had possessed more "penetration" than honesty: his plan had been essentially sound. Interpreting Law's actions in the light of his own intentions, Hamilton expressed the opinion that Law meant to unite the interest and credit of rich men to those of the state. In this respect he was, of course, just as mistaken as in his belief that Law's banking theory was essentially the same as that of the Bank of England.

Hamilton had not yet learned to distinguish between "money banks" and "land banks." What he actually proposed to Morris was not a land bank, like John Law's, but rather a money bank; for his institution was to bank partly on a foreign loan and partly on a subscription of Continental Currency.[24] Following the example of the Bank of England, Hamilton's enterprise was to lend funds to the government and to private individuals on "good securities." Different as was this project from that of Law, one element was actually taken from the latter's design, namely the combination of bank and trading company: Hamilton's bank was to use the whole or part of its stock in commerce. The proposal was essentially a funding scheme for the Continental Currency. The funding was to be entrusted to an enterprise which was at the same time a money bank and a non-monopolistic trading company; whereas Law combined a land bank with a monopolistic trading company. Loaning on land as security, however, was not excluded from the activities of Hamilton's money bank. The resultant combination of these heterogeneous functions was soon to become typical of early American banking.

Hamilton's plan of 1780 was soon discarded by its author, who submitted a new one to Morris in 1781. This second project had at least one trait in common with the first: it was "to unite interest and influence of the moneyed men" in the "establishment and preservation" of "government paper credit." The basic idea was soon to become one of the leitmotifs of Hamilton's public career.[25] At the time of his second proposal his theoretical knowledge of banking had improved, but was still hazy. For instance, he did not yet understand the difference between the deposit banks of Venice, Genoa, Amsterdam, and Hamburg on the one side and the Bank of England on the other. In a way his new scheme[26] (of April 30, 1781) was even a step backward, for it envisaged a mongrel institution, half land bank and half money-bank.

The capital of the newly-suggested bank was to be paid as follows: up to five shares, in specie; six to fifteen shares, one-half in specie and one-half in good landed security; sixteen or more shares, two-sixths in specie, one-sixth in good European bills of exchange, and three-sixths in good landed security. In either case specie and domestic and foreign bills of exchange could be substituted for landed security. The explanation of this project breathed the spirit of Mercantilist banking on land, and in a way this second plan of Hamilton's was closer to Law's banking theory than his first; but this time Law was not mentioned. Says Hamilton:

> By admitting landed security as a part of the bank stock, while we establish solid funds for the money emitted, we at the same time supply the defect of specie, and we give a strong inducement to moneyed men to advance their money; because, not only the money actually deposited [i.e., invested] is to be employed for their benefit, but on the credit of their landed security...may be raised an equal amount in cash, to be also employed for their benefit; by which artifice they have the use of their land..., and the use of the value of it in a representative cash...[27]

The preceding quotation is not the only proof that Mercantilist thought was behind Hamilton's second plan, as it had been back of his first. This fact is evident also in various details of the scheme of 1781, as, for instance, in the suggestion that notes above 20 shillings should bear interest (Article VII), interest-bearing banking notes being a typically eighteenth-century, and therefore Mercantilist, banking device. Again, the stock of the bank was to be protected against any attachment or seizure although the holders of notes could sue any stockholder who in turn (after having paid the obligation) might recover the debt out of his property mortgaged to the bank for the purpose of acquiring stock (Article IV). Back of this article is the Mercantilist theory that notes should be paid out and, if possible, in that form of property which having become part of the bank's capital served as security for the noteholder. Finally, the clause in Article VIII that the "aggregate of the notes" was "never to exceed the bank stock" also reflects Mercantilist banking philosophy. According to that school the exclusive function of a bank's capital was to serve as security for the noteholders, and this security would have been diminished by issuing notes to a larger amount than the capital. In conclusion: Hamilton's bank plan of 1780 envisaged a combination of Mercantilist money bank and trading company; while that of 1781 entailed a cross of money bank with land bank.

In the years following Hamilton grew wiser, and in 1784 for the first time he became active in behalf of a genuine money bank. In that year his draft for the charter of the Bank of New York[28] planned from the outset the conduct of "banking on mercantile credit" (Article II). There is only one clause of this charter of particular interest in view of the future development of American banking: Article VII forbade the bank to deal in foreign exchange. This business was considered the domain of those merchants who backed the project and who could not be expected to create a competitor to themselves.

It would be interesting to know to whom or to which experiences and studies was due the remarkable development of Hamilton's ideas on banking in the few years between 1781 and 1784. Possibly his English brother-in-law, John Barker Church, exerted some influence. A letter from Hamilton to Church (dated March 10, 1784)[29] indicates that Hamilton acted as the agent of his brother-in-law, who then planned to set up a bank in New York, as will be described later. At that time Hamilton had not only acquired a clear perception of the difference between land banks and money banks and their respective repercussions on

the various economic classes, but had also drawn the practical consequences therefrom. With a view to his brother-in-law's project and "for the sake of the commercial interests" of the state he initiated political opposition against a then pending land-bank scheme broached by Chancellor Livingston. To this end he enlisted the cooperation of the "most intelligent merchants" of the city of New York, and so convincing were his warnings on the "absurdity and inconvenience" for the commercial interests of the impending land-bank scheme that the merchants as a counterstroke started to organize a money bank on their own. This was rather embarrassing for Hamilton. Although he had probably provided the original incentive, only in an advanced stage was he called upon to subscribe to the bank. However, he felt it wise to fall in with the merchants even though thereby he was forced to abandon as an independent venture Church's project with which by that time he seems to have identified himself and of which no details are known. Instead he now became a director of the Bank of New York, the institution started by the merchants, and drew up its charter as already mentioned. Thus he became active in the second mercantile, or as we would say today, commercial bank in this country.[30]

Thereafter Hamilton became one of the leading exponents of money banks as opposed to land banks, or to use the synonymous Mercantilist terms, he promoted "banking on mercantile credit," as opposed to "banking on private credit." Thus the First Bank of the United States, the child of his brain, chartered in 1791, was modeled on the Bank of England, the prototype of the Mercantilist money bank. Hamilton's draft as presented in the "Report on a National Bank" and the actual charter show Mercantilist influence at every turn. For instance, in describing the advantages to be derived from banks Hamilton states as "a well-established fact that banks in good credit can circulate a far greater sum than the actual quantum of their capital in gold and silver."[37] That is to say, as late as 1790 Hamilton took his start from a discovery made by Englishmen as early as 1650. At that time Italian, Dutch, and Hamburg experience along this line became known in England and the discovery resulted in the first public discussion on banking.[32] Mercantilist influence can be discerned equally in the proposition that the projected bank would increase the quantity of the circulating medium and quicken the circulation, and that it would thereby be of "general benefit."

As a whole the bank plan of 1790 aimed at a Mercantilist money bank, as represented by the Bank of England.[33] However, while some of the arguments presented in its favor embodied Mercantilist thought, as described above, many of them breathe a different spirit. By that time Hamilton had become thoroughly acquainted with Adam Smith's great work. A recent statement that whereas Hamilton's ideas were mostly Smithian, "colored by Mercantilist reminiscences and inclinations," his policy was purely Mercantilist,[34] is undoubtedly correct with regard to his banking policy.

Adam Smith's influence can be seen, for example, in Hamilton's expectation that the bank would augment the active or productive capital of the country.[35] Therein he quoted Adam Smith, and when he stated that gold and silver, when employed merely as instruments of exchange and alienation, had not been improperly denominated "dead stock," he was again making a direct reference to the Wealth of Nations.[36] In the Report on Public Credit, Hamilton recommended the proposed national bank as an "indispensable engine in the administration of the finances." This again smacks of Adam Smith who spoke of the Bank of England as "a great engine of the state."[37] Finally, the suggestion that the proposed national bank "shall be under a private, not a public direction - under the guidance of individual interest, not of public policy," - the warning against the dangers of "public direction," and the praise of the "magnetic sense" of the interest of the proprietors, all, of course, breathe the spirit of the great Scot.[38]

Most of the other founders of the American pioneer banks belonged, like Morris, to that group of aggressive businessmen who had joined the Revolution and either in official capacity or as private contractors, or at one time in one and at another time in the other capacity, had taken care of the supply and financial side of the war. Thus they had learned to do business on an unheard-of scale and to cooperate with other merchants for business purposes. Fortified by their war experience, these men took the lead in the capitalistic development of the country after the war, as if to prove Werner Sombart's thesis of the connection between war and the development of capitalism. Among the new types of business activities which they evolved, banking ranked high.

None of them, as a matter of fact, can be compared in importance with Robert Morris or Alexander Hamilton; but Jeremiah Wadsworth stands out in the crowd as in a class by himself and by this author is considered as the third of the great originators of American banking. Jeremiah Wadsworth[39] (1743-1804), the son of a Hartford minister, had started his career by following the sea and at the age of thirty had settled in Hartford. Championing colonial rights at an early date and possessing an exceptional knowledge of business affairs, he was appointed by the Connecticut legislature in 1775 as commissary to the Revolutionary forces raised in that state. In 1777 the Continental Congress elected him deputy commissary general of purchases; in 1778 he advanced to commissary general. The commissions received in this connection aroused resentment and in 1779 he resigned "amid the usual complaints." From then on as a private agent he supplied the army with provisions. He gained outstanding mercantile importance when Rochambeau requested him to become commissary to the French troops at the same time. The latter connection almost hit a snag when a dashing young Englishman, John Barker Church, alias John Carter, started to interfere. Church (Carter) had come to America to join the Revolution and had just eloped with one of General Philip Schuyler's daughters, whose sister married Alexander Hamilton. Wadsworth was clever enough to avoid a fight by entering into a business association with the dangerous competitor in 1780. From this partnership was to grow later cooperation in banking enterprises. The two men paid for their purchases for the French army partly with metallic money and partly with bills of exchange drawn on the French government which they received from the French military authorities. These dealings in foreign exchange may have been responsible for Wadsworth's initial interest in banking since they resulted in his contact with a French banking firm. Furthermore, by using subcontractors the Wadsworth-Carter partnership made Wadsworth the center of a whole group of Connecticut businessmen. These relations must have led to all sorts of financial transactions

which, like his contact with a French
banker, may well have drawn Wadsworth's
attention to the usefulness of banks. In
1783, finally, Wadsworth went to France to
settle his accounts with the French government, whose debts were remitted by French
bankers in pounds sterling through English
houses. This business experience, too,
must have contributed to Wadsworth's knowledge of banking; but to what extent, if
any, his trip to England in 1784 made a
similar contribution is not known.

        In the meantime, acting as a crea-
tive capitalist, Wadsworth had become interested in America's first commercial bank,
the Bank of North America. When Morris
invited leading capitalists from all over
the country to make funds available for
that enterprise he found feeble response,
except among the Philadelphia businessmen
pivoting around his partner Thomas Willing
and among a few non-Philadelphians who together provided much of the original capital of the Bank of North America.[40]
(This limited distribution of subscriptions,
incidentally, was very different from that
typical of the first banks to follow.)
Among the creative capitalists who by their
subscriptions made the Bank of North
America possible, Wadsworth stood highest
with his 104 shares, followed by his partner, John Barker Church (Carter), who had
98 shares. Besides becoming the largest
single stockholder of the Bank of North
America he also collected subscriptions in
Connecticut for the bank.[41]

        This, however, was only the begin-
ning of Wadsworth's activities in the field
of banking. The next bank in which he became interested was the Bank of New York.
Probably his former partner, John Barker
Church, drew him into this scheme. While
Wadsworth was abroad, Church promoted a
commercial bank in New York and, as described above, enlisted the help of Alexander
Hamilton, his brother-in-law. Hamilton, in
turn, was instrumental in getting Church to
join a group of New York merchants working
toward the same end, so that in 1784 both
Church and Hamilton participated in setting
up the Bank of New York. It is not known
when and how Wadsworth himself was brought
into the enterprise. Although not among
the original subscribers of the Bank of
New York, he became its second president,
an office which he held for one year.
Later, in 1792, Wadsworth became the founder

of the Hartford Bank, which was first suggested to Hartford businessmen by his
clerk. When the presidency of the bank was
offered to him, however, he declined, although at about the same time (1791) he
accepted a directorship on the first board
of the First Bank of the United States, the
fourth bank with which he became connected.
According to Professor Wettereau's material,
however, he did not play an important part
in this bank and was a director for only
two years. Incidentally, his refusal of a
presidency and acceptance of a directorship
shed light on the evaluation of the former
position by a highly active and creative
business leader of the 1790's.

        The minor founders of early
American banks can be grouped according to
the motives which dominated their activities and these activities were promotional
and organizational, as well as political.[42]
The fact that practically all of the men
were interested in profits does not make
impossible such distinction. For some of
them political motives ranked high; but
this group can be further subdivided. It
contained some men who were guided by motives of national interest, while others
acted under the impulse of narrow party
politics. The former, following Morris
and Hamilton, planned banking for the purpose of establishing the young nation
firmly, of financing it, and of making it
independent by promoting its commerce and
industry. Undoubtedly there were among the
founders of the banks of the 1780's and
early 1790's quite a few men who played a
part in the public life of the young
Republic and who, when working for banks,
had the public welfare at heart. There is
furthermore no doubt that among the economic motives of these men overcoming the
alleged lack of a circulating medium ranked
rather high.

        Governor William C.C. Claiborne of
Louisiana presents a unique example of a
de facto bank founder for purely political
reasons. When in 1804 the leading citizens
of New Orleans petitioned for a bank because of lack of circulating medium which
had resulted from the stoppage of silver
imports from Vera Cruz, he acceded to their
request. On March 9 and March 16, 1804,
respectively, he thus reported on his
actions to Madison, then Secretary of State;
"I am inclined to indulge the people on
this occasion [the petition for a bank].

The bank would be so pleasing and so much engross the public attention that if Congress should permit the province to remain in its present situation for months it seems to me the citizens would not be desposed to complain." And a few days later: "I discovered that efforts were making to render the people discontented with the present state of things and to impress them with the opinion that their interests were not attended to by Congress...I thought that the best means of speedily allaying discontent was the passing...some popular ordinances. The project of a bank presented itself..." Thus the Bank of Louisiana was chartered as the first bank in New Orleans.[43]

The Browns of Providence on the other hand, furnish an example of bank founders who, while interested in the common weal, interpreted the latter on a narrow local basis. John Brown (1736-1803), the most enterprising of the five brothers, was one of the first merchants to engage in the East Asia and China trade. As early as 1784, in cooperation with other leading merchants, he had tried to get a bank for Providence. His plan miscarried, but was revived in 1791. While on a trip to Philadelphia, he was urged to obtain for his home town a branch of the First Bank of the United States. In this situation he wrote to his brother Moses that the best means of inducing the directors of the national bank to come to Providence would be the establishment of a local bank. Nevertheless he was somewhat reluctant to work for such a one, since he considered the town too small to carry such an institution; but he added: "by our exertions and favoring a good and substantial foundation for the commercial, manufacturing, and mechanical rising generation, it may in time become no inconsiderable capital, but without a spring to promote our young men in business here, they must and will continue to go to such places as will aid them with the means of business; and in short all our wealth, I mean the wealth as fast as acquired in this state, must be transferred to other states who by their banks promote all the valuable arts of mankind."[44] (The latter sentence is very interesting as an indication of contemporary public opinion.) In consequence both John and Moses Brown studied the charters and regulations of the existing American banks and of the Bank of England; and when they founded the Providence Bank they modeled it closely on the Bank of the United States.

As already indicated, those bank founders who were prompted by considerations of national or local economic and financial policy must be distinguished from those who came to the fore about a decade later and who were mainly stimulated by party politics. This is true of the Burrs, Osgoods, and Brockholst Livingstons, who originated the Manhattan Company of New York; and of William Gray and Elkanah Watson when they launched the State Bank of Boston and the State Bank of Albany, respectively.

On analyzing the business motives of early bank founders, the student will find a whole array of incentives. Some of them wanted to profit from banking as such (investment of funds in banking), others from increased borrowing facilities, and still others from speculation in bank stocks. Governor Daniel D. Tompkins of New York thus described the intentions of the latter type of men:[45]

Having disposed of [the] stock [acquired by participation in earlier banks] at a lucrative advance...they became more importunate in every fresh attempt to obtain an opportunity of renewing the speculations.

Those men, on the other hand, who became bank founders in order to profit from banking activities as such could set up banks in places where they had not existed before (as Jeremiah Wadsworth did when originating the Hartford Bank), or they could try to break up existing local bank monopolies. In 1814, for example, the applicants for the Phoenix Bank of Hartford stated: "and they [the petitioners] ask for a new bank...thinking it more congenial to true republican principles that a new bank be granted thereby diffusing...privileges ...[and] promoting competition which creates an increased endeavour to accommodate the public."[46] Breaking up existing monopolies, like opening banks in new locations, provided not only profit from banking as such (which in the former case had been monopolized by the stockholders of the earlier monopolistic bank), but often also bank accommodations where none had been obtainable before. The original banks in some places, because of their truly

mercantile character, may not have catered
to such groups as farmers and mechanics; or
they may not have considered smaller merchants, such as shopkeepers, worthy of
credit; or the party spirit dominating
their boards may have resulted in excluding
certain businessmen from accommodations.
In all such cases, men interested in profitable investment, businessmen seeking accommodations, and politicians could easily
join hands in establishing new banks for
the purpose of creating new lending facilities. The Philadelphia Bank of 1803 is an
example of one founded to cater to business
groups (shopkeepers) which so far had had
no access to banks; while the Lynn Mechanics Bank of 1814 was founded to make the
shoe manufacturers of that place independent
of the "factor" who had previously been the
sole source of credit.

Examples of bank founders prompted
mainly by business motives may be seen in
the men who originated the Massachusetts
Bank and who were led by William Phillips;
or those who established the Bank of Maryland or the Bank of Alexandria.[47] Regarding Massachusetts, Professor Gras[48] has
drawn attention to the close connection
between the origin and early development of
marine insurance and of banking. As a
matter of fact, two Boston insurance offices
were back of the foundation of the Massachusetts Bank, and some of the founders and
early directors of the bank were regular
insurance underwriters. William Gray, the
great Massachusetts merchant who had been
a member of one of these Boston insurance
offices, became the president of the newly-
founded Essex Bank in Salem in 1792 and in
1803 was one of the incorporators of the
Essex Fire and Marine Insurance Company of
the same city.[49]

Close connection between these two
lines of business existed in Connecticut
and Rhode Island, also. The same Jeremiah
Wadsworth who took an interest in four of
the earliest American banks and who was
the founder of the Hartford Bank, opened an
office in 1794 for the purpose of insuring
houses, furniture, merchandize, and so on
against fire. A partner in this enterprise
was Peleg Sanford, then a director of the
Hartford Bank. Somewhat earlier, while
still Wadsworth's clerk, Sanford had represented his employer in that meeting of
Hartford businessmen at which it was decided
to apply for the charter of the Hartford

Bank. A year later Wadsworth entered into
a copartnership for underwriting marine
insurance. In this concern his partners
were the same men who with him had been
instrumental in founding that bank and who
were now its directors (including the
president).[50] Finally, an organized local
marine insurance business, which started
in Hartford in 1799, was in the hands of
such men as Caldwell, president of the
Hartford Bank, and Normand Knox, who later
was to become the president of the Phoenix
Bank of Hartford. A comparison shows that
while in Boston, insurance came first and
banking second, in Connecticut it was just
opposite; and Rhode Island followed the
Connecticut pattern. The first bank in
Rhode Island, the Providence Bank, opened
for business in 1792; while the first
insurance company, the Providence Insurance
Company, was not organized before 1799. It
soon bought stock in the Providence Bank.
From then on interlocking interest between
banking and insurance became a standard
feature in Rhode Island business. The second bank in Providence, the Exchange Bank,
was started by the Washington Insurance
Company (chartered in 1801) whose backers
were not on friendly terms with the Browns.
In 1804 the Newport Bank was organized and
its president and directors were authorized to launch also the Rhode Island
Insurance Company, while the latter enterprise received the right to invest in the
stock of the bank.[51]

The close connection between banking and insurance for which the state of
Rhode Island provides still a few more
examples can easily be explained: premiums
were at that time often paid in notes instead of in specie, and the capital of the
early insurance companies to a certain extent consisted of stock notes. Consequently a bank controlled by the same men who
controlled an insurance concern became the
means of converting credit instruments into
money. Furthermore, as soon as the insurance companies accumulated reserves, they
were interested in having an outlet for
such funds by investing them in banks.
Besides the various Rhode Island companies,
the Hartford Fire Insurance Company and
several Massachusetts insurance companies
(in 1807) followed this practice.[52] The
banks, on the other hand, wished to have
permanent access to paper which was by its
character self-liquidating like that given

in the payment of premiums: and at least in Rhode Island banks profited from being fiscal agents of the early insurance companies. Occasionally there was a sort of division of labor between allied banks and insurance companies, the former making commercial, the latter permanent loans, thus running a kind of banking business, without issuing notes, and deriving most of their profit therefrom.[52a]

One of the minor early bank founders deserves special attention because he it was who introduced banking into a new type of location, the small inland market town, thus paving the way for country banking which was soon to follow. This man was Elkanah Watson. Watson (1758-1842) was a New Englander of Pilgrim stock from Plymouth. A former apprentice to John Brown of Providence, he was a highly successful (but finally bankrupt) shipping merchant in Nantes, France, and a widely traveled man, both in America and Europe. In 1789 he settled in Albany because he recognized its strategical location as an inland trade center. Watson was one of America's early promoters and, at least for his time, the foremost example of the "romantic" type of entrepreneur. As described by his biographer, he was a man of vision rather than an administrator, a seer of uncanny prevision rather than a patient architect of his enterprises; all of which were planned to contribute to the common weal.[53] Thus while incessantly disseminating ideas for the public benefit and for the advantage of others, he was unable to reap adequate profits for himself.

It is not known in detail what ideas prompted Watson's actions when he promoted the creation of the Bank of Albany, chartered in 1792; nor is it known by what means he was able to gain the support of leading Dutch families, such as the Rensselaers and Schuylers. He himself emphasized the cooperation of General Philip Schuyler, whose "powerful influence and talents...forced [the charter] through both houses of the legislature." Since, as mentioned above, all of Watson's projects were intended to serve the common weal, and since banks were then widely considered to be semi-public tools to that end, considerations of this character may well have played a certain part. They were undoubtedly decisive with Chancellor Livingston for, convinced by Watson of the propriety of the charter, he saw that it was not lost in the Council of Revision.[54]

The Bank of Albany was not the only bank which Watson founded. He soon lost the backing of his Dutch partners, partly for political reasons since he was the leader of the Yankees in Albany, partly because his incessant drives for improvements and innovations frightened the conservative Dutchmen and warned them of his instability. Consequently he conceived the idea of a second, political, bank in Albany dominated by Yankee interests, a Republican bank as against the existing Federalist Bank of Albany. Through his activities the Albany State Bank came into existence in 1803 as a Republican bank and represents an early example of the political bank typical of the second half of the first period. Incidentally, the methods applied by Watson in getting this charter were later to become common: he bribed the legislators by selling them stock at cheap prices. While in the Bank of Albany the Rensselaers and Schuylers had been Watson's associates, in his second banking enterprise he cooperated with such men as John Tayler, a former Indian trader and Indian agent, state senator, and later Lieutenant Governor and acting Governor of New York.[55]

In a recently published paper this author tried to show how as late as the first half of the nineteenth century economic development in Europe was predicated on personal contacts. This is equally true for America, and the first two decades of American banking afford proof of this contention. The Bank of North America, to be sure, which was modeled on the Bank of England, was not the result of any personal contacts between the founders of the American enterprises and the directors of the Bank of England. Printed material and information acquired in connection with the business activities of its promoters took the place of personal intercourse. Professor Gras has drawn attention to a passage in James Sullivan's Path to Riches of 1792: "The history of the Bank of England[56] I have taken from acts of the British Parliament respecting it." That source and the literature discussed in the preceding chapter was available in Philadelphia also. As mentioned by F. C. James, the Philadelphia jurist, James Wilson, who played an important role among the founders of the Bank of North America, had been acquainted with the activities of the Bank of England ever since his student days in Edinburgh.

From the Bank of North America, however, further development for years to come took place by the agency of personal contacts. From the point of view of the present research a letter[57] written by Thomas Willing, president of the Bank of North America, on January 6, 1784 to William Phillips and other promoters of the Massachusetts Bank is one of the most interesting business documents of the eighteenth century. In that letter Willing gave information on the organization and administration of the Bank of North America. He also sent the by-laws and the rules and regulations of that bank, thus facilitating the work of the Boston promoters and enabling them to model their enterprise on the Bank of North America.[58] Moreover, Samuel Osgood, one of the directors of the Bank of North America, was called to Boston to serve as the first cashier of the Massachusetts Bank; and the accountant of the latter enterprise was sent to Philadelphia to be trained there.

In addition there was still another line of influence leading from the Bank of North America to the Massachusetts Bank. One of the founders of the latter was Thomas Russell, (1740-1796) originally a Charlestown merchant who had risen to commercial importance in Boston during the war and who was to rise even higher after the war as a participant in the Baltic trade and as one of the first to trade with the Isle de France. In the war years Russell became the confidential agent of Robert Morris and a subcontractor or agent of Jeremiah Wadsworth in connection with the latter's business dealings with the army and with the French forces. Thus he came in contact with two of the three men who stood out among all the founders of American banking. Russell not only collected subscriptions in Boston for the Bank of North America but himself became a subscriber; while in turn when he helped to found the Massachusetts Bank, Robert Morris subscribed to the latter.[59]

Similar in character was the line which led from the Bank of North America to the Bank of New York. The way in which Jeremiah Wadsworth and John Barker Church, as creative capitalists, contributed to the foundation of the Bank of North America has already been described, as has the manner by which they became tied up with the Bank of New York. However, this was not the only line of connection between the two banks. Soon after William Seton had been selected as cashier of the new bank he was sent to Philadelphia with a letter of introduction from Hamilton to Thomas Fitzsimmons, one of the directors of the Bank of North America. Although Seton arrived at rather an awkward moment, it cannot be doubted that at the end he received some training from the hands of Tench Francis, the bank's cashier.

The First Bank of the United States of 1791, the next of the early American banks, was tied to the Bank of New York through its founder, Alexander Hamilton, who had been a director of the latter bank and who had drafted its charter. On the other hand, the First Bank of the United States was tied to the Bank of North America through both its president and its cashier. Thomas Willing, the first president of the Bank of North America, became the first president of the First Bank of the United States, resigning from the former enterprise; while George Simpson, an officer of the Bank of North America, became first an officer and after a few years the cashier of the Bank of the United States. Again, William Bingham, a founder and director of the Bank of North America, became one of the most influential directors of the First Bank of the United States. Finally, Jeremiah Wadsworth, who became a director of the Bank of the United States, represented influences leading down both from the Bank of North America and the Bank of New York.[60]

The Boston branch of the national bank was tied to the Massachusetts Bank both by its president, Thomas Russell,[61] and by Peter Roe Dalton, its cashier, who in his person also linked that branch with the Bank of North America. Dalton started his banking career in 1784 as an accountant in the Massachusetts Bank and was sent at once to receive training in the Bank of North America. He was the cashier of the Massachusetts Bank from 1785 to 1792, and secretary to the board from 1789 to 1792.[62]

The banks started between 1784 and 1791 (the Bank of New York, the Massachusetts Bank, the First Bank of the United States, and the Bank of Maryland in Baltimore) were set up more or less under the influence of the Bank of North America and can be considered as a second crop of banks. From these banks in turn there sprang in one way or another a third crop, appearing between 1792 and about 1800.[63] While the second crop of banks consisted

of the first banks in the main commercial
centers of the northern and middle states
and the national bank, the third crop included the second banks in these centers
(the Union Bank of Boston, the Manhattan
Company of New York, the Bank of Pennsylvania in Philadelphia, and the Bank of
Baltimore). It included, furthermore, the
first banks in the main commercial centers
of the South (such as Charleston and Alexandria). Finally it comprised the first
banks in smaller marts along the northern
seacoast, as, for instance, the banks in
New Haven, New London, Providence, Newport,
Salem, Newburyport, Portsmouth, and, on the
other hand, those in the inland trade centers of the northern and middle states, as
Albany, Hartford, and Middletown, Connecticut.[64] Only after this third crop of banks,
after about 1800, came the indiscriminate
multiplication of banks,[65] (the banks at
Hudson, New York and at Bristol and
Westerly, both in Rhode Island, were the
very first ones in economically insignificant places).[66]

With such expansion of banking all
over the country indirect and impersonal
influence, of course, was added to the
direct and personal. (After what has already been said on the status of stockholders in early American banks it will not
be surprising to find stockholders among
the influence carriers.)[67] Indirect and
impersonal lines of influence may have resulted from familiarity with banks through
contacts as depositor, borrower, or even
unsuccessful applicant for loans, or
through third persons; from knowledge acquired through newspaper articles, and
pamphlets; from imformation gathered as
legislators; or, in case of country banking,
through conversations around the pot-bellied
stove of the country store. John Brown of
Providence, perhaps, and certainly Elkanah
Watson of Albany[68] were among the earliest
bank founders who were without direct personal contact with the former founders or
administrators of banks.

In Massachusetts, as a matter of
fact, the third crop of banks depended more
or less on the Massachusetts Bank.[69]
Thomas Russell, who connected the Bank of
North America with the Massachusetts Bank,
as described above, later turned his support to the Union Bank, the second bank
chartered in Massachusetts. Russell had
been connected with the insurance office

of one John Hurd, where another participant
was William Gray,[70] the great Massachusetts
merchant and politician. Since John Hurd's
office was one of the largest original
subscribers to the Massachusetts Bank, Gray
must have been well informed regarding the
latter enterprise. In 1792 he was among the
founders of the Essex Bank in Salem; in
1810 he became president of the Penobscot
Bank when it had run into difficulties; a
year later he assumed the presidency of the
State Bank of Boston; and in 1816 we find
him as the president of the Boston branch
of the Second Bank of the United States.

In New York City the Bank of New
York became an important center of influence. Aaron Burr and Richard Harrison,
later New York City treasurer, who were
founders of the Manhattan Company of 1799,
the second bank in the city of New York,
had both been stockholders of the Bank of
New York. This is true also of Richard
Varick,[71] one of the first directors and
later a president of the Merchants Bank
of New York. Alexander Hamilton, once a
director of the Bank of New York, drew up
the articles of association of the Merchants
Bank in 1803. Another director of this
bank was James Roosevelt, son of Isaac
Roosevelt, who had been president of the
Bank of New York. However, the Merchants
Bank of New York was also connected with
the Manhattan Company through John Swartout,
a politician and the confidante of Burr.
He had been one of the directors of the
Manhattan Company and had lost his seat
there "after a hotly contested election,"[72]
whereupon he became a founder and director
of the Merchants Bank. From the Merchants
Bank of New York, in turn, the line leads
through Isaac Bronson to the Bridgeport
Bank. Bronson had been a founder of the
Merchants Bank before becoming the controlling president of the Bridgeport Bank in
1807, thus showing interest in both city
and country banking.

Another center of influence was
the First Bank of the United States. The
parent bank in Philadelphia became, after
its dissolution, the Banking House of
Stephen Girard and the exponent of the continuity was George Simpson, the efficient
cashier of the Bank of the United States
who became the cashier and actual head of
the latter enterprise. The New York branch
of the First Bank of the United States, on
the other hand, became the Bank of America.

Here the continuity was represented again by the cashier, Jonathan Burrall, who was taken over from the former enterprise, and also by Archibald Gracie and William Bayard who had been directors of the New York branch of the First Bank of the United States and became directors of the succeeding enterprise. Since Oliver Wolcott, formerly a president of the Merchants Bank, became the first president of the Bank of America, there was also a link connecting the Bank of America to the Merchants Bank. Later, in 1816, the New York branch of the Second Bank of the United States took from the Merchants Bank its cashier, Lynde Catlin, who after a few years returned to the Merchants Bank as its president.

It has already been shown that Jeremiah Wadsworth was connected with the Bank of North America, the Bank of New York, and the First Bank of the United States, and that he was the founder of the Hartford Bank. This latter bank copied the articles of association of the Bank of New York which, as will be remembered, were the work of Alexander Hamilton. The cashier of the Hartford Bank from 1799-1814 was one Normand Knox who resigned in 1814 to become the first president of the newly-founded Phoenix Bank of Hartford. This bank was the second in that city and represents, so to speak, an example of the fourth generation of American banks.[73]

One can look at the same phenomenon from still another angle: many of the men who were most instrumental in creating American mercantile banking were linked to more than one bank. Jeremiah Wadsworth and William Gray were each interested in four, as described above. Alexander Hamilton, Samuel Osgood, and Oliver Wolcott were connected with three banks each. Hamilton was a founder and a director of the Bank of New York, the founder of the First Bank of the United States, and he drew up the charter of the Merchants Bank of New York. Osgood was a director of the Bank of North America, the first cashier of the Massachusetts Bank, and a director of the Manhattan Company. Oliver Wolcott, Hamilton's close friend, was instrumental in making the First Bank of the United States a branch bank; he was the first president of the Merchants Bank of New York in 1803, and he played a prominent part in launching the Bank of America which succeeded the New York branch of the First Bank of the United States. The many men who were in one way or another participants

in two banks will not be enumerated again: their names are to be found in the preceding paragraphs. Incidentally the connection of certain men with more than one bank was well known to contemporaries, as can be seen from a speech of Governor Daniel D. Tompkins of New York: "Prominent men who seek the incorporation of new banks are the very same who have deeply participated in the original stock of most of the previously established banks..."[74]

The diagram inserted on page 42 at the end of this chapter presents the pertinent material in graphic form. Although this chart merely sums up what has previously been written, some additional comment seems necessary. The chart does not claim to be complete. Undoubtedly there were additional lines of personal influence which could be discovered through minute research. Moreover, indirect and impersonal influence which became very important after 1792 is not indicated except in two cases. The lines of influence down to about 1792 show, first of all the transfer of the idea of banking as such, or, in other words, the fact that the process of expansion was predicated on personal contact. In addition, down to 1792 bank organization and bank policy, as well as experiences in banking, were thus bequeathed from older to younger enterprises. After that date there may or may not have been a transfer of the idea of banking as such or of business organization and policy by the individual who linked together an older and a younger banking enterprise. This was the case, for example, when Hamilton drew up the charter of the Merchants Bank. At all events, however, when an individual with experience in one bank joined another he must have been influenced either positively or negatively by such experience. A negative influence (this or that ought not to happen here) is of course just as important as positive influence, and may account for cases where possible developments (possible transfer of ideas) did not take place.

II

Bank Personnel

Presidents

The functions of bank presidents described in the preceding chapter determined the men to be selected for this position. Such selections, furthermore, reflected the double status of banks as business enterprises with semi-public functions. Thus in the first period bank presidents were either men who had attained a high rank in public life and therefore enjoyed public confidence, or they were merchants. In the former case the semi-public status of banks was stressed; in the latter their character as business enterprises. Early examples of the former type of bank president were James Bowdoin (1727-1790) and Alexander McDougall (1732-1786). Bowdoin, the Massachusetts statesman who holds "a secure place among the founders of the republic," became the first president of the Massachusetts Bank in 1784. The next year he was elected governor of the Commonwealth, and withdrew as stockholder and president of the bank.[75] McDougall, the revolutionary agitator and soldier, was the first president of the Bank of New York and held this office from 1784 to 1785.

This type of bank president still existed in the 1800's, and even survived into the second period. In the 1800's[76] Oliver Wolcott (1760-1833), Secretary of the Treasury from 1792 to 1800, judge of the Supreme Court the next two years, and later (1817-1822) governor of Connecticut, was president of even two banks, the Merchants Bank (1802-1804) and the Bank of America (1812-1814), both of New York. In the same decade Richard Varick (1753-1831) became the president of the Merchants Bank of New York a position which he held from 1808 to 1822. He had been military secretary to General Philip Schuyler, muster master-general of the Northern Department, Washington's recording secretary, recorder of the City of New York in 1784, speaker of the New York Assembly in 1787, attorney general of the state in 1788 and 1789, and mayor of New York City in 1801. At the turn of the period, in the early months of 1815, to give a final example, Joseph Story (1779-1845) became the second president of the Merchants Bank of Salem. He was to become a famous jurist, judge of the United States Supreme Court, and Harvard law professor. He owed his position as bank president, which he held for many years (1815-1835), to the fact that he was a leading Republican politician in Massachusetts. Incidentally, he and Wolcott are representatives of the few cases in which jurists became bank presidents in this early period.[77]

Fortunately, a statement has survived which shows clearly what motives guided early bank directors in electing men of public confidence as presidents. One Samuel F. Smith, for half a century a director, president, and again director of the Philadelphia Bank, with which be became connected first in 1807, wrote in a valedictory upon his retirement in 1861: "And in order to give character to the institution they [the directors] selected and elected for their president a gentleman of an exalted character, a patriot of the Revolution...," namely George Clymer.[78]

Thus leading men in public life did not consider it beneath their dignity to become bank presidents; nevertheless most bank presidents were merchants. It was a merchant who became the very first bank president and this merchant, Thomas Willing, established a pattern for decades to come upon assuming the presidency of the Bank of North America. When a merchant became a bank president in the first period he owed his election not only to the fact that he had been successful in business, but also, and perhaps even more, to the wide family and business connections such as Willing had possessed.[79] Thereby he was expected to inspire confidence and to attract business to his bank.

As examples of merchants who became early bank presidents may be cited John Nixon, who in 1792 succeeded Thomas Willing as president of the Bank of North America when the latter became president of the First Bank of the United States; or his one-time colleague as director of the Pennsylvania Bank, George Clymer, who became president of the Philadelphia Bank in 1803. In both cases, however, it is questionable whether they owed their election to the fact that they were successful merchants or to their role in the revolutionary struggle.[80] In fact, the latter is more probable. There can be no doubt, however, that William Phillips, (1722-1804), the second president of the Massachusetts Bank, became its president mainly because he was a successful and wealthy merchant - retailer, wholesaler, underwriter of marine insurance - a heavy stockholder, and one of the founders of the bank.[81] But at the same time, this descendant of prominent New England divines, a member of the leading society family that founded Phillips Academy in Andover, had taken " a decided and active part in the proceedings which preceded and attended the revolution, was on many committees appointed by the town of Boston in those trying times, and often contributed liberally of his money to carry forward the measures which issued in the establishment of our independence."[82] Moreover in the decade when he became president of the Massachusetts Bank William Phillips was embarking on a political career which made him state representative, senator, and governor's councillor. He was also a member of the two conventions which framed the state constitution and adopted the Federal one. However, this career (except as representative) was still in the future when he became president of the Massachusetts Bank, undoubtedly because of his success as a merchant. The same is true of John Brown (1786-1803), the first president of the Providence Bank, a highly creative and successful entrepreneur who as a member of a clan of influential merchants was in a way the Providence counterpart of Thomas Willing; and of John Caldwell (1755-1838), who was a ship-owning merchant engaged in the West Indies trade and the first president of the Hartford Bank.

While the foregoing examples are taken from the beginnings of the first period the situation was not different when that period ended. As one example out of many, William Gray may be mentioned. He was, in the words of Timothy Pickering, "for mercantile talents and extent of business the first merchant in the United States." Nevertheless in this case again it is doubtful whether he attained the position because of his being a leading merchant or a party leader (lieutenant governor of Massachusetts).[83] The same is true of Benjamin William Crowinshield (1772-1851), from 1811-1814 the first president of the Merchants Bank of Salem. He belonged to a family which had replaced the Derbys as the leading merchant family of Salem, and, on the other hand, was a politician and (like other members of his family) a staunch Republican, who became Secretary of the Navy in 1814. Gray and Crowninshield are also representative of presidents of "political" (Republican) banks.

It has been mentioned in another connection that only in exceptional cases can the entrepreneur, that is the actual leader of his enterprise, be found among the bank presidents of the first period. Nevertheless there were a few cases prior to about 1820 in which experts were elected to head banks and where as such they must have exerted influence on their concerns. One of these experts was Gulian Verplanck[84] (1751-1799), fourth president of the Bank of New York (1791-1799); he was a nephew of Daniel Crommelin, one of the leading Dutch bankers of the eighteenth century in whose firm (Crommelin and Son in Amsterdam) young Verplanck had received his commercial education. A relative of Verplanck was Daniel Ludlow[85] (1750-1814), for some time New York's largest merchant and importer, whose maternal grandfather, Charles Crommelin, had founded the Crommelin and Son house in Amsterdam, mentioned above. In that firm Ludlow had been educated, just as had Verplanck, and when later he was active in founding the Manhattan Company and became its first president (1799-1808) the knowledge of banking which he had acquired in his youth must have stood him in good stead. Probably more than any other bank president of his period he was the entrepreneur of the bank he headed. These men were the forerunners of the expert bank presidents of the second period.

Directors

Nothing would be gained in the understanding of American banking history if lists or biographical sketches of early bank directors were inserted at this point. Suffice it to say that probably most of the leading merchants in those decades were at one time or another members of bank boards. The director of the American city bank between 1781 and 1814 was typically a successful merchant, a leader in society and endowed with a sense of public responsibility manifested in political or charitable activities. Of course, the same characterization can be stated in the less friendly language of the radicals of the 1790's who thought of bank directors as belonging to an aristocratic group, if not clique, dominating or at least trying to dominate business, society, and politics. Instead of listing the names of bank directors, the author refers the reader to earlier paragraphs on bank presidents. Many of them were bank directors before being elected presidents and represent the contemporary type of bank director as well as of bank president.[86] It will also be remembered that Alexander Hamilton was a bank director just as was his deadly enemy, Aaron Burr, or Brockholst Livingston or Rufus King. A later crop of city banks, however, the one chartered to compete with the very first banks, possessed a different type of directorate consisting of small businessmen, such as shopkeepers and mechanics; and the composition of the boards of the early country banks included farmers as well as shopkeepers and mechanics and, in many cases also, quite a few scoundrels. Many of these men, in contrast to their colleagues in the early city banks, were adventurous borrowers and upstarts, not wealthy capitalists of social standing.

There were a few real banking leaders among the early bank directors and they alone are of interest here. Since the bank cashiers rose but slowly to importance in their enterprises, as will be described later, and since the average president did not determine the fate of the bank over which he presided, as already shown, the enterpreneur or entrepreneurs must be looked for among the bank directors. That much is certain; but only in exceptional cases does the material exist which enables the historian to decide who was the real leading personality on the board in question.

Professor Wettereau has given some thought to the question: Who were the leading men in the First Bank of the United States? He has come to the conclusion that William Bingham (previously a founder and director of the Bank of North America, whom Wettereau characterizes as "perhaps the ablest banker of the period"), Isaac Wharton, Rufus King (who had worked hard to launch the Bank of the United States), and Samuel Breck determined the policy of that bank. Since the personnel· of the board of the First Bank of the United States remained extraordinarily steady, these men (and perhaps still other directors) could grow into expert bankers.[87]

Regarding the early years of the Bank of North America, in this author's estimation William Bingham and John Nixon were the entrepreneurs who determined policy. Bingham's role is deduced from that which he played later in the First Bank of the United States, and that of Nixon from the confidence which Robert Morris reposed in him when the bank was still in its founding stage.[88] As a final example may be cited the Providence Bank; John and Moses Brown were among the first sets of directors and undoubtedly exerted

a strong influence in the administration.

However, it is not only entrepreneurs who may be looked for among the members of early bank boards. For the first period one may also expect to find creative managers there, that is, men who were able to build up the internal organization of a new type of enterprise, with practically no examples to draw on. This ability they shared with some of the early bank cashiers. In one case at least the director who became a creative manager can be identified: Edward Payne, a director on the original board of the Massachusetts Bank, was the head of a leading Boston marine insurance office which took a considerable interest in the establishment of that bank (the third in this country). He was the chairman of a committee to consider the proper methods of keeping the accounts of the new bank and assisted the accountant in opening the books set up in line with the committee's proposals. He also headed a committee which determined the original discount policy of the Massachusetts Bank and which made all arrangements preparatory to the opening of the enterprise.[89]

Cashiers

The very first bank cashier was Tench Francis (1730-1800), whom Oberholtzer has characterized as Morris's "trusted friend," and who as late as the 1790's acted as the latter's confidential purchasing agent.[90] Prior to the Revolution Tench Francis had been for many years the agent of the Penn family in connection with their proprietary interests. In 1780 he became the factor of the Pennsylvania Bank, employed to purchase materials and ship them to the army. When that purchasing agency was being liquidated and its backers founded the Bank of North America Francis was taken over as the cashier. His first job in connection with the preparation of the new enterprise was the management and supervision (under Morris's detailed instructions) of the transport from Boston to Philadelphia of the specie imported from France in 1781, which specie made possible the Bank of North America. Morris himself had selected Francis for the task for reasons which he set forth in his diary:

I thought the proposal was pleasing to him and afforded him an opportunity to show his

firm attachment to the cause of America which
some few of his actions early in the contest,
flowing from an uncommon warmth of temper, had
rendered dubious in the eyes of many people;
but for my part, I am fully convinced of his
zeal and attachment to the interest of the
United States, I employ him with pleasure, having full confidence in his fidelity, integrity,
and abilities.

After the safe arrival in Philadelphia of
the ox train which carried the specie, and
after having disposed of it, Tench Francis
started on his new job, which he retained
down to 1792. (Incidentally he rented to
the Bank the premises in which it opened
and which later it bought.) Francis was
probably a creative manager, but it is likely that he played no part in shaping the
policy of the Bank of North America.

A director of the Bank of North
America (elected as early as 1781) became
the first cashier of the Massachusetts
Bank: Samuel Osgood (1748-1813). Osgood,
however, was of too high a calibre to remain permanently a bank cashier and after
about nine months' service he resigned; he
had the stuff to made a bank director
rather than a cashier. A sketch of his
career is given here to show the type of
man to whom one of the earliest cashierships
in this country was offered. A descendant
of one of the first settlers of this
country he had studied for the ministry at
Harvard, but became instead a merchant.
Later he joined the Revolutionary army
advancing to the rank of colonel and to
assistant quartermaster. By that time he
had also gained legislative experience,
first on the local level, then as a member
of the Continental Congress (1780-1784),
and in the latter year as a member of the
Massachusetts state legislature. After his
short cashiership in the Massachusetts Bank
he became a commissioner of the United
States Treasury board (1785-1789) and the
United States' very first postmaster-general (1789-1791). In 1791 he removed to New
York where he held various public offices
and where he was connected with the Manhattan Company as a director.[91]
More of a real bank cashier was
William Seton (1746-1798), a Scotsman of
good family who, coming to this country at
an early age, had settled in New York and
married into the Carson family, a leading
commercial family of colonial New York. He
was engaged in the shipping and importing
business under the firm names of Carson

and Seton, and later Seton, Maitland and
Company. An Episcopalian and loyal to the
Crown he remained in New York during the
British occupation. Since his business
suffered because of the war, in 1777 he
accepted an appointment as assistant ware-
house keeper. In 1779 he became a notary
public and 1782 secretary to the Superintendent of Police. Nevertheless he belonged to those Loyalists whose property
escaped confiscation, and in 1783 when a
new line of French packets was established
he became its deputy agent and the supervisor of the American end of the business.
In 1784 Seton (whose brother, by the way,
was a banker in Edinburgh) was appointed
cashier of the newly-founded Bank of New
York. He seems to have been a high type
of man, enjoying the confidence of Hamilton
who, when Secretary of the Treasury, corresponded with Seton. Obviously the relation between Morris and Francis parallels
that between Hamilton and Seton. It has
been described above how Seton received his
training for the new job from Tench Francis.
He retained the position until 1794, in
which year he resigned and took a trip to
Europe. A few years later he was dead.[92]
Seton's successor was Charles
Wilkes (1764-1833), also an immigrant. Born
in London he came to this country in 1784 on
the advice of Seton who was acquainted with
the Wilkes family. Soon after Wilkes's
arrival he entered the service of the Bank
of New York and advanced so quickly in the
profession that in 1792 the cashiership of
the New York branch of the First Bank of
the United States was offered to him.
Declining that job he stayed on in the Bank
of New York and became not only its cashier,
but, in 1825, even its president. Thus he
was the first man in this country to round
out a complete career in banking.[93]
George Simpson (1759-1822) was for
many years the cashier of the First Bank of
the United States. Young Simpson, whose
father had immigrated from England in 1753,
had been appointed Assistant Commissary
General at Corryell's Ferry. Later upon
the creation of the Bank of North America he
was made an officer of that bank, a position
which he left to become an officer and a
few years later the cashier of the Bank of
the United States.[94] It is not clear what
role he played in this bank. Earlier
authors considered him the actual head of
that enterprise; while Professor Wettereau
seems to be inclined to depreciate his
standing. In fact he was an entrepreneur

by character, showing his capacity when, upon the dissolution of the First Bank of the United States, he became the cashier and, until his death, the de facto head of Stephen Girard's Banking House.

A similar career was that of Jonathan Burrall, the original and only cashier of the New York branch of the First Bank of the United States. In 1811 he became the cashier of the Bank of America which succeeded that branch much as Girard's banking house succeeded the parent bank. Burrall (1753-1834) had previously been an assistant paymaster in the Northern Army and at the close of the war he became a member of the commission to settle the accounts of the quartermaster's department. Later he was assistant postmaster general and manager of the New York State lotteries.[95] From 1815 to 1816 he was president of the Bank of America.

The first cashier of the Hartford Bank of 1792 was of lesser calibre. Earlier he had been an apothecary, a bookseller, and a dealer in public securities. Later, upon his retirement from the bank in 1799, he opened a grocery. However, Normand Knox (?-1821), his successor, lived up to the high standard of the city bank cashier of the first period. He had been a leather merchant and belonged to that group of men who were interested in underwriting marine and fire insurance before any special enterprise was organized for that purpose in Hartford. Subsequently in 1803 when the Hartford Insurance Company was originated for dealing in marine insurance, he became its secretary. At the same time he retained his job as cashier of the Hartford Bank until 1814 when he resigned to become president of the Phoenix Bank in the same city, the first competitor of the Hartford Bank.[96]

Incomplete as this material may be, it yet depicts clearly the ancestry of the American banking profession: of the eight men whose careers have been sketched above, four rose to become the heads of their respective banks thereby proving that they possessed entrepreneurial capacity. Furthermore, Tench Francis, William Seton, and George Simpson, at least, must have been creative managers, for they did a managerial job for which there were no precedents in this country. There can be little doubt on the other hand, that the early country bank cashiers represented a different type, but no reliable material in his respect has come to the attention of this author.[97] On the whole, founders and personnel of

the very first American city banks lived up to a rather high standard. This seems to have been true also for the second and third banks in each of the main trade centers and for some of the first banks in the smaller ports. With what has been characterized above as the fourth crop of banks, this situation began to change.

Among the country bankers of this latter class, there was at least one man who deserves notice, a man who ended up an impostor, to be sure, but one with a touch of business genius. This man was a Boston lawyer, Andrew Dexter, Jr., who after having read law at Lunenburg, Massachusetts, had been admitted to the bar in Suffolk County in 1802.[98] In the course of his banking activities, Dexter became the founder of the first chain of banks in America. In addition, he was apparently the first to see the possibilities of corporate business organization and to develop methods which later became notorious in the field of corporation finance. Dexter acquired a stock majority in the Berkshire Bank of Pittsfield, in the Bangor Bank of Bangor, then in Massachusetts, and in the Farmers' Exchange Bank of Glocester, Rhode Island.[99] After having done so, he took complete control of the management of the respective corporations, putting dummies on the boards of directors to whom he transferred a few shares to make them eligible. It is remarkable that at this early stage of banking he looked upon the various banks of his chain as belonging to a superior unit: they had to work hand in hand and were run for his profit, not for that of the individual units. One Dexter bank had to give its bills to and receive in exchange the bills of another Dexter bank and pay them out over the counter.[100] This chain of banks was coupled with the Boston Exchange Office (to be discussed in a later chapter). With the help of this latter office Dexter tried to control the New England currency, a goal to be achieved later by the Suffolk Bank. He made the mistake, however, of using the short-term funds of this enterprise for a long-term investment, and so was forced into committing fraud to avoid bankruptcy. In spite of his efforts he broke down financially and had to flee. His blunders and manipulations, however, had far-reaching consequences. They caused the first wave of bank failures in this country and demonstrated to its business community that banks were as liable to failure as other business enterprises.

Diagram
(Referring to page 36)

Chapter III

SECOND PERIOD

GENERAL CHARACTERISTICS

American banking in the second period (1815-1840) still consisted essentially of what it had in the first, namely, of discounting indiscriminately real and accommodation paper, of lending to the national or to state governments, of issuing notes, and of keeping deposits. Nevertheless, certain other features clearly distinguish the second period from the first.

To begin with, the decades between 1815 and 1840 saw, besides regular bank notes, a great variety of other credit instruments circulated by banks, such as post notes, notes payable at places other than the place of issue, branch drafts (of the Second Bank of the United States), certificates of deposit and, in addition to these credit instruments, scrip which was much used as a medium of exchange.[1] Such a diversity of credit instruments had not circulated before 1812, and after 1840 they were to disappear, leaving the field to the regular bank note and to the check.

While legislators and even bankers themselves during the first period hardly understood which functions were indispensable to this business, other then issuing notes, a better understanding of the essentials of banking developed in the second period. After 1820, definitions of banking formulated for practical purposes were written into bank charters, as, for instance, (in 1825) into that of the Dutchess County Bank in the state of New York. In that charter banking powers were defined as including the discounting of bills, notes, and other evidences of debt, the receiving of deposits, the buying of gold and silver (bullion and foreign coins), the buying and selling of bills of exchange, and the issuing of bills, notes, and other evidences of debt.[2]

Regardless of this progress toward a better understanding of banking, Mercantilist tradition was still very much alive in the decades under investigation: banks were widely considered to be public blessings and therefore were multiplied all over the countryside. Thus through the extension of country banking, the trend toward lower standards in banking begun with the first wave of bank charters in the middle of the 1790's was not only not arrested, but even accelerated; and in the 1820's and 1830's American banking reached its moral and managerial nadir. During the second period state banks were created not because capital was seeking investment nor because places with established commerce and manufacture needed bank accommodations, but because men without capital and credit wanted loans.[3] And since, according to Mercantilist banking theory, capital was superfluous for banking, while on the other hand banks enabled men to create credit, "to melt down property into money," the founding of banks seemed to be a legitimate means to the desired end. Thus except in a few seaboard towns and inland trade centers American banking in this period was still Mercantilist "banking on private credit," with but a thin veneer of commercial banking. This can be seen at every turn. As late as 1838, when Arkansas chartered her first banks, they were supposed to "quicken industry," to "supply capital to everybody," and to "raise the value of land" by "coining the wild lands of Arkansas into money." In the same year a senate report by Felix Grundy, a representative of the back country also, thus expounded a theory which was actually Sir James Steuart's on the role of the capital of banks: "For the security of these [notes]...the capital stock was created."[5] Such statements prove, merely by their phraseology, the true character of American country banking in the 1820's and 1830's. The coexistence of essentially Mercantilist land banks with more or less modern commercial banks was the source of specific problems during the second period, problems which were carried over into the next one.

Since to honest, traditional, and significant, although unsound banking was added dishonest and fraudulent enterprise in this field, the foremost task of progressive leaders in this second period was to make it safe beyond doubt. Attempts in this direction became the _leitmotif_ in the late 1820's and 1830's and the coexistence of recklessness and backwardness, on the one hand, and keen striving for reform by legislative action, on the other, distinguishes these decades from those preceding. Numerous recipes were recommended toward the desired end. Banks were supposed to be made safe by a limitation of the total amount of notes in relation to the banks' capitals, an old Mercantilist panacea;[6] by the prohibition of small notes,[7] a measure recommended by the classical economists; by enforcing the regular redemption of circulating notes;[8] by making banks mutually responsible; and, finally, by basing notes on first class security which was to be set aside outside of the issuing bank. It did not occur to the legislators or bankers of this period that even after all these requirements were complied with, honest banking enterprises would still be unsound unless they were liquid. This discovery was left to the following period,[9] for down to the 1830's the concept of liquidity was still enveloped in that of security.[10] Actually in the 1820's and 1830's the average American bank was nonliquid. In line with Mercantilist tradition many of them still considered specie as almost superfluous for banking; almost all of them practiced a combination of long (better: medium) and short term credit; and all of them issued notes, that is to say, short term obligations, on the basis of accommodation paper (i.e., medium term loans), as was the accepted practice. Even the Second Bank of the United States made large accommodation loans in the South and West after it had begun its expansion in 1830.

The great achievements of this period were central banking (as practiced by the Second Bank of the United States), the Suffolk Bank System, the New York Safety Fund System, and Free Banking. Each of them aimed at making American banking safer and sounder by one means or another, and each of them will be examined in detail. Of these four main achievements, the first two were the work of entrepreneurs; while the other two were due to the activities of legislators. Most of them were but short-lived. By 1840, when the period drew to its close, central banking had become the victim of politics and the Safety Fund System was crippled beyond repair. To be sure, the Suffolk Bank System flourished in 1840, but was not to survive the next period. The ideas underlying Free Banking, however, were to dominate American banking for many decades to come and those behind the Safety Fund Act also remained alive until about one hundred years after their inception, they were embodied in a national act, the Act of 1933 which created the deposit insurance system. By contrast when central banking was again fitted into American institutions after decades of bitter experience, its exponents could not revive the old tradition: it had been utterly destroyed. They were forced to erect their building with imported stone. But although three of the four main achievements of the second period were not permanent successes (whatever may have been the value of their underlying ideas) much ground was broken in the 1820's and 1830's and much seed broadcast which was destined later to bear fruit.

I

Banking Transactions

The lending operations of banks in the 1820's and 1830's to be discussed first can be classified according to the following criteria: according to borrowers; according to the character of the loans; according to the security; and according to the length of credit. According to borrowers one can distinguish between loans to merchants, to stock traders, to manufacturers (mechanics), to agriculturists, to the national and state governments, and to corporations. According to the character, there were "accommodation" and "transactions" loans,[11] the former in contrast to the latter not resulting from any particular business transactions. According to the security pledged, distinction can be made between loans on "personal security;"[12] loans on property of all kinds (including those secured by mortgage); and loans on the security of stock. Finally, according to the term of the loans, there can be found medium and long term loans (loans on renewable "accommodation paper," largely identical with loans on property); thirty to one hundred and twenty days short term loans (i.e., discounts of "real paper," identical with the above-mentioned loans on the security of trade paper); "temporary loans" for less than thirty days; demand loans (both these latter categories being in most cases loans on the pledge of stock); and overdrafts.[13]

The borderline between medium and short term credit was fluid in the years under investigation. The Second Bank of the United States, for instance, considered sixty and ninety day bills as "bills on short terms," but discounted trade paper at five, six, eight, and occasionally even nine months. Furthermore, by 1830 when the Bank had difficulties in finding employment for its funds because of the repayment of government loans, it invested in one to three year accommodation paper, payable at New Orleans and secured by mortgage.[14] To be sure, the Bank was severely criticized for such a policy as, for instance, by the New York group which was anxious to set up a national bank in New York City after the expiration of the charter of the Second Bank of the United States. Probably it was Isaac Bronson who wrote into the plan for the new bank the clauses: No note or bill to be discounted and no loan to be made for more than ninety days; every note and bill to be paid bona fide when due; renewals to be granted only when indispensable in the interest of the bank and upon depositing additional security. It seemed to the backers of the plan that the long term lending of the Second Bank of the United States had caused the unsound business conditions of the early 1830's and they intended in their lending policy to follow the examples of the Bank of England and the First Bank of the United States.[15]

Most city banks of the 1820's and 1830's, let alone the country banks, were even less conservative than the Bank of the United States and on an average, paper was discounted at longer terms than in the first period, when the early genuine mercantile banks discounted at thirty and sixty days only.[16] There were various reasons for this development. From lack of experience the earliest American banks had been overcautious. Furthermore during the second period, especially in the early 1820's and late 1830's, banks were beginning to prefer bills of exchange to local notes, partly because

they could circumvent legal interest requirements by charging exchange[17] and partly because such bills were often sounder than local notes. Those who discounted bills of exchange labored under the disadvantage of being forced to grant longer terms for such paper because of poor transportation facilities. Finally, the competition of country banks, which lived by lending on medium term, must have played its part in the trend toward lengthening the average time for loans and discounts.

Thus progress in the field of short term credit to merchants, manufacturers, and agriculturists, was not impressive in the second period. Little, if anything, was done in the 1820's and 1830's to made banking safe by restricting its activities to the discounting of short term "real," to the exclusion of accommodation, paper; i.e., only a few attempts were made to abandon the combination of medium and short term credit in the same banking enterprises, a combination by that time already traditional.

The protagonist of commercial banking pure and simple was Isaac Bronson. Bronson (1760-1838) was the son of a Connecticut farmer who was repeatedly a member of the Connecticut state legislature. Young Bronson, without having attended college, studied medicine and became a junior surgeon during the Revolutionary War. After the war, abandoning medicine, he made a voyage to India and traveled in Europe. About 1792 he was settled in Philadelphia, whence he removed to New York about two years later. There, as in Philadelphia, he engaged in private banking and in addition became a founder of the Merchants Bank of New York. After a few years he dissolved his partnership and in 1807 joined the Bridgeport Bank of Bridgeport, Connecticut, founded in 1806, of which he became the controlling stockholder and president. In this capacity he proved to be a creative entrepreneur, being one of the first, if not the very first, banker to make his notes payable at the counters of a bank in the city (in this case, New York) to which his notes tended. Be that as it may, he seems to have devised that method of remunerating the redeeming city bank which was later adopted by the Suffolk Bank. Somewhat later Bronson deposited most of his specie with his New York City correspondent and subsequently ran into serious difficulties when specie payments were stopped in 1814.[18]

Having extricated himself from these difficulties after the resumption of specie payments, Bronson made of the Bridgeport Bank an enterprise unique for the period. According to James Alexander Hamilton[19] Bronson's theory was that banks should "furnish a medium of trade and not capital;" that is to say, he thought in terms of commercial banking as then practiced in England. Consequently with but one exception discussed below he would discount only sixty day paper, and would allow no renewals. In gauging this achievement one should keep in mind, however, that for a short while immediately after the War of 1812 there was a more general tendency to build up strictly commercial banking in America. In 1816 some of the Philadelphia banks started to discriminate against accommodation paper and in 1820 the Secretary of the Treasury suggested the desirability of banks discounting trade paper only.[20] Thus the idea of strictly commercial banking was in the air for some years after 1810; but Bronson seems to have been the only banker who took it seriously and made it the basis of his business policy.

Bronson's argument for discounting short-term trade paper exclusively ran as follows: If we suppose a bank discounts notes at sixty days only and that it discounts every day one-sixtieth of the total, it becomes every day repossessed of one-sixtieth of its issues or of their value. Consequently if danger is apprehended, such danger could be easily avoided by refusing to discount for some time, a policy, which, as we would say, would make the bank more liquid each day. Although not familiar with the concept of liquidity as yet, Bronson, as one of the very first American bankers, was actually thinking in such terms.[21] Some years after Isaac Bronson's death his biographer, still writing in the spirit of the second period, well described the late banker's theory and practice as follows: The circulating notes of his bank "were issued only in exchange for business paper representing commodities in transitu... Once in sixty days the whole debt due the bank was cancelled by payment ... Its circulation vibrated largely [i.e., it was elastic]. At certain seasons when the products of the country were coming

forward to market it expanded; at others it shrunk within very narrow limits." But actually this is not the whole story, as will be shown later.

Through his success in business, his interest in sound banking, and his literary activities, Bronson gained prestige among businessmen as well as with far-sighted financiers and economists, and became influential with politicians. One of Carey's Essays on Banking was addressed a "Mr. Bronson," although one cannot be certain that Carey's addressee was Isaac Bronson. In the winter of 1828-1829 when the Safety Fund plan came up in Albany, a scheme of Bronson's was discussed as an alternative and tentatively combined with Forman's suggestions, as will be described below.[22] By that time Bronson had gained influence also on C. C. Cambreleng, the New York congressman and chairman of the Ways and Means Committee. Some years later, in 1833, his advice was sought regarding the consequences of the contemplated removal of the public deposits from the Second Bank of the United States. His answers show a broad, analytical mind and an ability to think in economic, as opposed to business, terms. His role as adviser in this connection came about because J. A. Hamilton considered him among New York's "distinguished bankers" whom he was charged to consult by McLane, then still Secretary of the Treasury.[23] Probably the fact that he took interest in the question of a national bank, (first as a friend and after the close of 1832, as a foe of the existing Bank of the United States) played its part also. In the former period even Nicholas Biddle was willing to take his advice.[24] In 1832, in which year he withdrew from the Bridgeport Bank, Bronson was on the New York committee of merchants which drafted the plan for a new national bank intended to replace the Second Bank of the United States, and apparently for some years to come he was the driving force behind this and similar schemes. The new national bank, as contemplated by the New York committee, was to be restricted to commercial loans pure and simple, and in this connection Bronson was able to expound once more his fundamental ideas on the functions of banks.[25] Later, in the 1830's Condy Raguet, who held him in high regard and had already published his paper quoted below, printed some of his letters.

In the meantime Bronson had gained an influence on the development of American banking by practicing and broadcasting a banking theory, the first public expression of which was made by MacVickar (under Bronson's influence) in the Hints on Banking, especially the idea that banks should loan their credit only and should invest their capital permanently in mortgages and stock as a security for the noteholders.[26] This was a novel idea for that time,[27] as Condy Raguet stressed, the adoption of which seemed to contradict Bronson's life-long fight for strictly commercial banking; but this idea embodied in the Free Banking Acts of the 1830's, 1840's, and 1850's was to triumph in America.[28] Bronson, as described above, regularly discounted short term business paper which would not be renewed under any circumstances; but under a resolution passed on September 28, 1821 he invested the capital of his bank in first class, well secured, medium-term loans, so that he could accommodate two classes of customers without endangering his liquidity. This type of banking gained wide importance in the next period.[29]

However, Isaac Bronson's struggle for commercial banking did not succeed at that time. When, in 1816, as alluded to above, the leading Philadelphia banks (the Bank of North America, the Farmers and Mechanics Bank, and the Bank of Pennsylvania) attempted to discriminate against accommodation loans and to eradicate what they considered a "pernicious abuse," they were violently attacked by Mathew Carey. He argued that a large portion of the community could not "possibly have access to banks in any other form."[30] When, by 1840, the second period drew to a close the situation had not changed much in comparison with its beginning and an attempt of the Connecticut banks to discount exclusively business paper and paper "subject to no renewal" was deemed "a great innovation" at that time. A contemporary British author describing American banking in 1837 thus stated the difference between banking in the two countries:

Their rule is our exception, our rule is their exception. They [the Americans] prefer accommodation paper, resting on personal security and fixed wealth, to real bills of exchange, resting on wealth in transition from merchants to manufacturers to consumers.[31]

In other words while England at that time already possessed commercial banking of the nineteenth-century type, America still adhered to an older banking philosophy because of her very different economic conditions.[32]

Industrial credit was not recognized as a specific type of credit in the second period. The small industrialists of the 1820's and 1830's, like the farmers, could borrow short and medium term funds alike from the same banks; namely, short term funds on real paper and medium term funds on accommodation paper secured by the pledge of property. However, mechanics and manufacturers were handicapped because they rarely received bills and notes from their customers and, when they did, such paper was mostly at so distant a date that it could hardly be discounted.[33] Thus, as the above quoted writer put it, "ships and steamers [were] built with the proceeds of three months accommodation paper, manufactories, mills, breweries, distilleries erected; the borrower thinking himself sure of a renewal of the bill when it falls due."[34] There was a tendency, at least at the beginning of the second period, to guarantee the so-called "productive classes" their fair share in the available bank credit. In Pennsylvania the three banks established in 1814 had to lend one-fifth of their capital to farmers, manufacturers, and mechanics in their districts (Article 9 of the charter). In banks which had the word Mechanics in the title (Mechanics Bank, Farmers and Mechanics Bank, Merchants and Mechanics Bank) the percentage of industrial loans must have been pretty high; and there is at least one example in which legislation tried to safeguard the character of a Mechanics Bank as an institution for industrial credit. The Pennsylvania Act of 1814 regulating banks ruled that no person was eligible for the position as a director in the Mechanics Bank of Philadelphia unless he was a mechanic actually engaged in his mechanical employment or occupation and had followed the same for at least one year previous to his election (Article 1).[35]

Very little is known about the credit facilities which were enjoyed by the capitalistic industrial sector of that period, especially the New England textile industry. Fundamentally they should not have had any special features; but before the turn of the period textile industrialists were acquiring control of banks.[36] There is one interesting case on record, that of the Litchfield and Torrington Manufacturing Company of Connecticut which produced woolen and cotton cloth. In 1821 it received a loan of $40,000 from the Litchfield branch of the Phoenix Bank of Hartford and had to give a mortgage on its plant as security. The loan could not be repaid and the bank had to take possession of the factory and stock and run the enterprise.[37] A few years later the Boston branch of the Second Bank of the United States lent to a manufacturing company $30,000 secured by the guarantee of the president of the "office."[38] Another credit transaction, one between the Bank of New York and the North River Steam Boat Company, a capitalistic transportation enterprise, may also be illuminating in this connection: this latter concern received credit on the pledge of its steamboats.[39]

Industrial bank credit in the 1810's, 1820's, and 1830's was, as already indicated, akin to agricultural bank credit, and this kinship stemmed from their common descent from Mercantilist "banking on private credit." To be sure, a part of the agricultural credit which was extended in the second period, like a portion of the industrial, was short term credit for the movement of crops based on sound trade paper.[40] But most of it was investment credit and with respect to this type of agricultural loans America underwent, in the decades under investigation, experiences which Great Britain had undergone in the eighteenth century. As the Secretary of the Treasury described in a report of 1820:[41] American agriculture was being developed with the help of bank credit. But in many cases improvements resulted in the ruin of the agriculturists in question. For their earnings did not increase by such improvements to such an extent as to enable them to pay the high interest and to discharge their debts. Thus when the banks were forced to call the loans in time of stress, the farmers were liable to become bankrupt.[42] The very interesting attempt made by the South in the 1830's to put agricultural credit on a sounder basis will be discussed in some detail in a later chapter. During the decades under investigation farmers and their representatives

still complained, as in the late eighteenth century, that banks had deprived them of access to loanable private funds.[43]

In all the lending operations discussed so far banks relied for their security either on the character of the discounted paper which represented actual business transactions and therefore carried two names, or on the pledge of property. However, there were in the second period still other possibilities for securing bank loans. It will be remembered that during the first period American banks adopted the practice of loaning on the basis of their own stock and that the First Bank of the United States borrowed in England, pledging United States stock as collateral. Thus it was in line with tradition when as early as 1817 the board of the Second Bank of the United States[44] resolved to loan on bank and government stock as collateral. In the years to follow such loans were to become rather common all over the country although some banks kept aloof from this practice.[45] The lending by banks on the basis of their own stock (on so-called stock notes) became notorious in the 1810's, 1820's, and 1830's.

Loans made on the pledge of stock were partly short and partly medium term loans. Those of country banks on the pledge of their own stock were of the character of accommodation loans; while loans made by large city banks on the pledge of government bonds and stocks of various enterprises (including their own) were in most cases of the nature of short term loans.[46] According to the Philadelphia practice established in 1822, loans on stock of various descriptions took two different forms. They were either bills discounted on the pledge of stock or "bills receivable" secured by stock. The latter[47] were loans as opposed to discounts and they were "temporary," that is to say, they would run for periods of less than thirty days.[48] In the case of such "temporary" loans, stock was not formally hypothecated, but only transferred into the possession of the lending bank which at the same time received a promissory note or sometimes a post dated check from the borrower.[49] In the early 1820's the Second Bank of the United States took a further step by granting, on the pledge of stock, demand loans which were treated as cash in the bookkeeping procedure. "Temporary" as well as demand loans seem to have resulted from the needs of stock trading. When in the 1820's the Philadelphia stock market decayed while that in New York grew, demand loans on the pledge of stock were no longer applied for in Philadelphia.[50]

By the end of the second period, however, they also came into existence in New York where leading bankers were undoubtedly informed about the Philadelphia procedure. In New York demand loans on stock collateral seem to have resulted alike from the necessities of stock trading and from those of the pet banks. In a later chapter the origins of the pet bank system will be sketched and it will be shown that the state banks which became public depositories in the 1830's faced a dilemma: they received public deposits to be kept on call and at the same time to be made available to the business community, At least two of them located in the city of New York, the Mechanics Bank and the Bank of the Manhattan Company, found a way out by lending such funds on demand on the basis of stock collateral. Thus here as previously in Philadelphia the old practice of loaning on stock collateral was altered with regard to the length of the loans, i.e., in one essential point, and when this new method became permanent and widespread in the 1830's, the call loan market was born.[51] It will be shown later how the practice of making demand loans on stock collateral received a new impetus in the next period from the growth of bankers' balances and the custom of paying interest on such balances.

Akin to lending on stock collateral was a type of lending by banks which occured in the second period, as it had in the first, and which looks strange to the modern observer; namely, the lending on the basis of bullion and specie. Nevertheless such loans can be easily explained: importers or other merchants, who were collecting specie for special objects for which no other medium of exchange would do and who in the meantime needed funds for other purposes, preferred not to part with their specie, the accumulation of which was difficult, but instead to borrow bank money on that basis.[52]

So far, lending to individual borrowers has been discussed. Corporations could, as a matter of fact, get short term credit on the same basis as private businessmen. But in the field of medium term credit other possibilities opened up. In the 1820's, for instance, the Morris Canal and Banking Company, a New Jersey improvement bank which became important as a banking enterprise in the 1830's, needed funds for building its canal. It issued two series of post notes of $300,000 and $500,000, respectively, which were bought by the Bank of New York. They were repaid when the issuing enterprise got an intermediate loan in Europe and was able to float its stock there.[53] A similar case of intermediate financing is recorded for the year 1837 in which the same Bank of New York took from the New York Commissioner of the Canal Fund $200,000 worth of five per cent transferable certificates of stock which were sent for sale to London. This transaction, however, touches the borderline of medium and long term (investment) credit as well as that of corporation and public credit.

In line with the tradition established during the first period, American banks in the second went on lending considerable sums at short and medium terms to the various American governments, including those of cities. Occasionally charters or other laws required banks to loan a certain percentage of their capital to the commonwealth from which they received their charter.[54] Such short and medium term lending to the federal, state, and city governments should be clearly distinguished from the investment by banks of part of their capitals in government stock and even in stock of other corporations, as that of turnpikes, canals, and even other banks. Investment of bank capital in government stock was traditional, for the early American banks, as has been described, were modeled on the Bank of England which had invested all its capital in obligations of the government; and the capitals of both the First and Second Banks of the United States were partly paid in government stock. When the second period opened, seven out of the nine Philadelphia banks, including the Banking House of Stephen Girard, had invested $3,648,689 out of a capital of $7,734,000 in government stock, treasury notes, and corporation stock. In addition they had loaned $327,221 to the city of Philadelphia and to the state of Pennsylvania on medium and short terms.[55] In the years to follow the percentage of government loans to the total tended to diminish.

While short and medium term lending to various governments went on in the established way the subscribing of government stock by banks changed its significance. This change became obvious when the Bank War broke out and certain loan transactions of the Second Bank of the United States were under fire. The Second Bank of the United States had taken from the Federal government $4,000,000 worth of five per cent stock in 1821; $5,000,000 worth of four and a half per cent in 1824; and $5,000,000 worth of four and a half per cent in 1825. When these loans were investigated by a congressional committee in 1832 a difference of opinion came into the open. There was a good deal of disagreement between conservatives and progressives as to what banks could legitmately do with government stock thus acquired.[56] Conservatives thought a bank should be entitled to buy government stock for permanent investment until it was redeemed but should not become a middleman in such stock. Progressives, on the other hand, took it for granted that a bank was entitled to sell to the public stock which it had taken over from a government, i.e., that it was legitimate business for a bank to act in the capacity of what was then called a loan contractor. During the War of 1812 merchants such as John Jacob Astor, Stephen Girard, David Parish, and Jacob Barker had acted as loan contractors, but in the decades under investigation that branch of the mercantile business was shifting into the hands of banks. There was general agreement throughout the second period that banks should not be entitled to trade in government stock in the open market. Toward the end of the second period the development took a new turn. The New York Free Banking Act made the investments of bank capital in government stock obligatory. But at the same time the views of the progressives as to proper functions of banks in connection with long term government loans became more widely accepted. Some leading commercial banks, as the Bank of the United States of Pennsylvanis, the Morris Canal and Banking Company (of New Jersey), the Phoenix Bank, and the Bank of the Manhattan Company (both of New York), developed investment banking as a line of their regular business. They bought security issues outright or on commission, sold them to the public, and in addition

serviced the loans as required.[57]

Turning now to the other side of the banks' balance sheets, the deposit business will be discussed first. As it was cultivated by the large Eastern city banks in the second period it was still essentially a business in time deposits, as it had been in the first. Mathew Carey estimated in 1816 that one half of the deposits held by the Philadelphia banks were "in sums below 2,000 dollars due to persons who are constantly receiving and paying away money and whose balances fluctuate daily from this sum to as low as 100 dollars," while the other half was "due to large capitalists in sums from 5 to 20, or 30,000 dollars."[58] Or, in modern language, he estimated that 50 per cent of the total were demand deposits and the other 50 per cent time deposits. If his estimate was correct for Philadelphia, at the opening of the second period, one can assume for the country as a whole 75 per cent time deposits and 25 per cent demand deposits. In 1820 the Secretary of the Treasury estimated the total of deposits in American banks to be $18,000,000, and in the 1830's they were stated in Congress to amount to about $50,000,000.[59] The trend during the period was toward the supplanting of time deposits by demand deposits. Created deposits, although not yet recognized as a specific type, were gaining in importance as compared to lodged deposits. Finally more and more there came into existence deposits of banks with other banks (bankers' balances, to use the modern term) in addition to the growing deposits of private capitalists. All these threads in the development will be discussed presently in more detail.

As could be expected, the Bank of the United States, the largest American bank of its time, with America's greatest contemporary business genius at its helm, contributed much to the development of the demand deposit business in this period. More than this, statements emanating from its friends show a clear understanding of this line. Horace Binney, for instance, in a speech delivered before Congress in January 1834, remarked: "We have, it may be, one hundred and forty to fifty millions of bank notes and bank deposits performing in part the same office." And later in the same speech he described how loans called in by the Bank would be paid to a certain extent by drafts on "herself" and "as her line of discounts goes down so does her line of individual deposits."[60] A mechanism such as described here presupposes of course thoroughly modern credit methods and extensive demand deposits; and in this respect the Second Bank of the United States did not stand alone. As a matter of fact it was the city banks and not the country banks which were beginning to develop the business in deposits; but they still did it reluctantly. As Biddle expressed it: if deposits come they are welcome, but they are not paid for.[61] In the crisis of 1837, at least in Boston, deposits increased. Because of general lack of confidence, businessmen who received notes of banks unknown to them were anxious to convert them into obligations of institutions with which they had regular dealings and which therefore they trusted.[62]

The use of checks, as a matter of fact, increased parallel with the growth of demand deposits; but the check was still in its infancy. Not even Biddle could then (in 1832) foresee its future. He believed that checks were not well suited to become substitutes of coin and bank notes "because they would represent only individual responsibilities, not those [of] recognized corporations established by law or of... the government."[63] Actually, however, such substitution was already being practiced, as can be seen from a description of 1831:[64] "The quantity of currency required in a business community is...diminished by the habit of substituting for gold and silver or paper money drafts or checks on bankers drawn against previous deposits. Where banking establishments exist individuals in the immediate neighbourhood are enabled to dispense with keeping on hand either specie or notes...and this circumstance explains why the institutions in the cities always surpass those of the country in the amount of their deposits while they fall far below them in circulation."[65] The words "checks on bankers drawn against previous deposits" seem to indicate that created, as opposed to lodged, deposits were not yet known to the American public in 1831; but they did exist, as already mentioned.[66] The rules and regulations of 1816 of the Second Bank of the United States, for instance, contain a section 3 stating that the value of a bill or note discounted should be passed to the credit of the applicant and might be withdrawn.[67]

Although the Second Bank of the United States was leading in the development of lodged and created demand deposits, it was not interested in the keeping of bankers' balances[68] which, as mentioned above, also gained importance in the second period. Many documents of the 1830's speak of specie funds, which were defined as deposits of country banks with city banks, serving the same purpose as specie. In the 1830's such specie funds were estimated at five million dollars.[69] This definition implies that specie funds were essentially of the same character as demand deposits and they were, of course, held in places like Boston, New York, Philadelphia, New Orleans, and so on. In Boston the Suffolk Bank system, as is generally known and as will be described in detail later, specialized in keeping "specie funds" for the banks of New England. But it had no monopoly of that business, and numerous New England banks kept funds with other Boston banks out of which their notes were paid on presentation by the Suffolk Bank. Such funds were not necessarily, and those with the Suffolk Bank never were, demand deposits liable to draft by check, i.e., they were not bankers' balances in the modern sense, although on the way to becoming such. Specie funds also came into being when banks in the country made arrangements with city banks by which their notes were made payable with their city correspondents instead of at the counters of the issuing bank. Such arrangements were not uncommon in the 1830's.[70] But again, bank deposits by other banks originating from this type of contract were not yet identical with modern demand deposits liable to draft by check. Truly modern bankers' balances, however, came into existence in the networks of correspondents which some New York banks built up in the second half of the 1820's and in the first half of the 1830's.

Correspondent relationships, as have been described, had already been created in the first period, but they did not gain real importance before the second. To be sure, the term "correspondents" was still unknown when the second period opened, and the word "connexion" was used instead;[71] but in the early 1830's variations of the word were used.[72] As an example of correspondent relationships in that decade, the network of the Mechanics Bank of New York is given in a footnote.[73] In 1833 that

CARNEGIE LIBRARY
LIVINGSTONE COLLEGE
SALISBURY, N. C. 28144

bank had fifty-four correspondents (including the branches of banks) in seventeen states; while at the same time the Union Bank of New York had sixteen correspondents in eight states, and the Bank of the Manhattan Company twenty-six correspondents in ten states (including the District of Columbia). Such correspondent relationships were often enough used for illegitimate ends, as, for instance, when banks lent specie to other banks so that they could comply with legal requirements at their opening or at times of examination. A contemporary foreign observer remarked in the 1830's: "The mutual accommodation system extends amongst banks as completely as amongst their customers."[74]

There was no city in this country in which the correspondent system was developed to such an extent as in New York and consequently no city in which deposits of banks with other banks (bankers' balances) showed an equal growth. The development[75] was due to the fact that New York was becoming the emporium of the North and New York funds commanded a premium all over the country. This meant that inland banks which kept reserves in New York not only possessed funds just as valuable as specie, but in addition could profit occasionally from selling exchange on New York. (Receiving interest on those funds hardly played a part in the second period.) Furthermore, the fact that bank notes being made payable in New York circulated at par everywhere gave an additional incentive for keeping funds in New York. Thus in the period under investigation, bankers of New York State, Ohio (1820's), Indiana and Illinois (1830's) kept part of their reserves in the form of bankers' balances in New York City. Banks in Boston and Philadelphia developed a similar business in the same decades, Philadelphia banks (especially the Girard Bank) keeping considerable funds for Southern institutions. In the 1830's bankers' balances and correspondent relations among banks had become so extensive and widespread that in New Orleans they were considered a danger to financial stability since they were supposed to put the banks of that city under the control of foreign (out-of-state) banks in case the latter suddenly withdrew their funds.[76] In 1838 the state was almost on the point of legally restricting New Orleans banks to being merely collection agents of out-of-state banks. Correspondent relationships at that time had developed to a point that caused Amos Kendall to expect that banks in the interior would become more or less offices of discount and deposit for the Eastern city banks. These banks in turn would control the specie of the country and through their credit in Europe would regulate the banking system of the country in time of stress.[77]

It was in the second period that in connection with the deposit business a development started which was later to result in one of the most serious problems of American banking: the paying of interest on deposits. Although there was one exception to the rule (The Farmers Bank of Maryland paid interest on deposits since 1804)[78] it would hardly have occurred to the average bank director in the first period to pay such interest.[79] Providing a safe place of deposit for capitalists was considered one of the main functions of banks,[80] and the question rather was whether or not banks should charge a fee for such service. This question was generally decided in the negative, but the Massachusetts Bank and perhaps some other early banks followed, at least temporarily, the example of the Bank of Amsterdam which charged a fee on deposits (payable probably at withdrawal).[81]

When the second period opened the situation had not changed. As early as 1816, however, the Philadelphia banks made a move, strange for that time, which was severely criticized by Mathew Carey.[82] They agreed among themselves to pay interest on balances due to each other, balances which had originated because notes were not redeemable in specie at that moment. This and similar agreements in other cities may well be considered as early steps toward a change in attitude and policy. Actually the paying of interest on deposits seems to have begun in the late 1810's in cases where the deposits in question were time deposits by contract and therefore amounted to loans to the banks taking them. In Massachusetts the new policy of paying interest on deposits came into being when the first savings banks were founded and deposited with banks a large percentage of the funds of the savers. Special contracts were made stipulating among other terms the interest rate, which varied between 5 and 6 per cent, and the maximum amount of such interest-bearing deposits. At least in Massachusetts some banks seem to have specialized in this sort of business, and after the use of savings by commercial banks in their regular business had proved a success, one of the Boston banks in 1825 also acquired insurance funds by paying interest. This bank concluded a contract with an insurance office by which the bank paid 4 1/2 per cent interest on funds up to $100,000 while the insurance office had to serve thirty days notice in case of withdrawal.[83] By 1825 the custom of paying interest on deposits had already become so important that a Massachusetts law of that year required separate returns for deposits bearing interest. We are less well informed about the beginnings of the new practice in New York; but it is known that witnesses queried during an investigation of 1820 were aware of it.

In 1825 a transaction took place which was later much discussed and criticized and which throws additional light on the origin of the policy under investigation. During the crisis of that year when the Second Bank of the United States was badly in need of increased metallic reserves, Nicholas Biddle succeeded in attracting specie into the coffers of the Bank. He induced a broker to deposit about $100,000 metallic money of which he was in charge, offering him interest thereon. This deposit was a genuine demand deposit. The transaction was so unique at that time that the cashier had to ask for instruction in charging the interest.[84] Biddle's act can be considered a second stage in the development. Just as in the cases described earlier, it was to the bank's interest to receive the deposit and therefore it was willing to pay for it. On the other hand and in contrast to the Massachusetts transactions where interest was paid only on time deposits, the Second Bank of the United States in this case paid interest on a demand deposit, thereby opening up a road fraught with danger. Competition, however, had played no part in its decision.

The paying of interest on demand deposits seems to have received an impetus under English influence. In the 1820's the Second Bank of the United States and other American firms received interest on their cash balances with the Barings in London[85] and other English merchant bankers

must have followed the same practice. Probably under such stimulus, by the middle of the 1820's the Second Bank of the United States was hard pressed by its large customers, e.g., Nathaniel Prime of New York, to pay interest on their deposits. Such applications, however, were turned down at the time. After 1834 the English joint stock banks paid interest on deposits, as became known in America. In so doing, however, they distinguished between "current accounts" (demand deposits) and "interest accounts" (time deposits), a distinction which unfortunately was not taken over here. The Commercial Bank of New Orleans in the early 1830's, to be sure, tried to establish a special kind of interest-bearing time deposits. "Persons depositing with the intention of receiving interest on their deposits" had to have them entered in a special pass book. They were at any time entitled to have these deposits transferred to their current accounts, but would receive interest only on amounts left for at least thirty days in the special account.[86]

The paying of interest on real demand deposits seems to have spread in connection with the growth of networks of correspondents. In New York the Bank of America was said to have paid interest on a deposit of the Planters Bank of Georgia at an early date. A Philadelphia bank paid in the early 1830's to the Union Bank of Tennessee[87] 3 per cent interest on a deposit of a million dollars on the basis of which it redeemed the notes of the latter bank, made payable at its counters. In Massachusetts the paying of interest on bankers' balances was considered legitimate even by the legislators[88] who were hostile to the trend as such, and frowned on interest payment to individuals. As early as the 1830's the development had reached the point that not only city but also country banks paid interest even on small deposits of individuals, as can be seen from the annual returns alluded to above.[89] Nevertheless when the period closed the paying of interest on deposits of individuals had not yet become the established practice in Massachusetts and most of the interest-bearing deposits belonged to the Commonwealth and savings banks. Special contracts were probably made in cases where interest was paid on deposits, and the more conservative banks, for instance the Massachusetts Bank in Boston, had not adopted a practice which they considered unsound, and which, for a few years, even became illegal, except for deposits of the Commonwealth and savings banks and for inter-bank balances.[90]

In the second period, as in the first, lodged deposits were considered as funds deposited for safe keeping and the notion that actually they were borrowed funds had hardly entered the minds of bankers. Their outlook could not but change, however, when banks began to take interest-bearing time deposits as described above. However, taking such interest-bearing time deposits was not the only method by which banks could borrow funds between 1815 and 1840. As in the first period, it was a Bank of the United States which took the lead in transactions of this type. For the purpose of acquiring metallic money to help the country resume specie payments the Second Bank of the United States effected in 1817 a joint loan from two English houses, Baring Brothers and Company and Reid, Irving and Company, for £745,000 (about $3,195,000) hypothecating United States government stock. That is to say, the transaction was essentially identical with that concluded some twenty-five years earlier by the predecessor bank except that the term of the loan was shorter (it was due January 1, 1819).[91] Again in 1818 the Bank had to borrow funds in Europe to enable the government to repay the Louisiana loan,[92] and by 1820 it owed the Barings, then its only credit connection in Europe, about $750,000. It recognized that it had reached the limit of its credit line.[93] Later under Biddle, however, the Second Bank of the United States received a much larger running credit from the Barings and so entered into an essentially modern credit relationship with a foreign bank.

The Bank of the United States was not the only American bank which borrowed abroad in those years. In the 1820's the Bank of New York borrowed from the Barings to repay a domestic loan,[94] handing over certificates of indebtedness in denominations of £50 to £4,000, which undoubtedly were sold by the Barings to English investors. In the same decade the Morris Canal and Banking Company placed a loan in Holland. In the next, after the New York

Safety Fund Banks had been authorized by law in 1836 to borrow abroad, the Bank of New York concluded a loan of £112,500 for thirteen months at 5 per cent from Morrison, Cryder and Company through the latter's New York agent, Richard Alsop. This loan, however, was, like that of the same bank, described above, of an intermediary character. The London house received 2, 3, and 4 years post notes which were sold in the London money market.[95]

Other American banks, which had no access to the European money market, borrowed at home[96] on the pledge of stock, as in the first period. In 1824 even Biddle intended to consummate such a sixty-day transaction in Boston. (Rediscounting was still very rare and "discountenanced.")[97] For small banks a more important method of borrowing throughout most of the second period was the issuing of post notes, which the Second Bank of the United States had not disdained to use in the 1810's.[98] Its charter permitted this use, restricting it only with regard to denominations and terms of such notes (nothing under a hundred dollars and with no more than sixty days to run). To give another example, in 1819 the young Suffolk Bank, upon entering the foreign exchange business, borrowed the necessary capital by issuing post notes. In fact, at one time or another between 1815 and 1830 banks in at least the following Northern states borrowed with the help of circulating post notes: Massachusetts, Rhode Island, Connecticut, New York, Indiana, and Ohio.[99] (Statistics giving the amount of such borrowings exist for Massachusetts.) This method of borrowing funds by issuing circulating post notes in small denominations was meaningful indeed. Since there was no organized money market, smaller banks had to go straight to the community at large if they needed funds. With the help of post notes they were more or less able to force it to supply their credit needs. During the depression following the crisis of 1837, that is, at the end of the period under investigation, Southern banks indulged in the same type of borrowing. Soon thereafter, however, the post note and thereby this specific method of borrowing by banks passed out of existence.

Of very different character were the large interest-bearing post notes. They were actually medium-term bonds, and with their help the leading banks of this country, such as the Bank of the United States of Pennsylvania, the Morris Canal and Banking Company, the Manhattan Company, and the Girard Bank, borrowed abroad in the late 1830's to mitigate the impact of the crisis. It is not accidental that on the whole (disregarding the South) the use of large interest-bearing post notes followed that of the small circulating type, predicating as they did the existence of and access to a well-organized money market in Europe.

It is highly probable that the development of networks of correspondents which has been described above led to new methods by which country banks borrowed funds from their city correspondents.

II

Banking Organization

At the opening of the second period the boards of directors in banks (as in other corporations) were what they had been in the first: namely, administrative bodies[100] and even as late as the 1830's a "discreet" and intelligent board of directors was considered essential for good management.[101] The charter of the Second Bank of the United States, to give an example, stated "that for the management of the affairs of the said Corporation there shall be twenty-five directors;" and it is typical of the status of directors as managers that in some banks they had to give bond before entering upon the duties of their office.[102] As can be seen from the pamphlet literature of the late 1810's and 1820's, public opinion recognized the boards as what they were intended to be. For example, when Mathew Carey, then himself a bank director, was giving advice in matters of banking, he did so by publishing a Letter to the Directors of the Banks.[103]

It had become customary during the early years of American banking for bank directors not to receive any emoluments, and clauses to that effect were inserted in numerous bank charters. Nevertheless it was expected that merchants of good standing would covet these positions, a not unreasonable expectation. Banks were considered semi-public enterprises and service as bank director was deemed a sort

of public service. In addition it was taken for granted that their interest in banks would be sufficient to make large investors enter the boards to run the enterprises to protect their own funds. However when the second period opened a different situation existed. Banks had by that time become business enterprises like others and efficient bank managers could easily be hired. In spite of this change the tradition of unpaid service was upheld and bank directors as such did not receive any remuneration.

At the opening of the second period, a new type of bank director was already in existence, besides those elected by the stockholders as their representatives. This new type consisted of men who represented the commonwealths which had invested in the banks. One who knows the ethical level of early nineteenth-century state politicians can easily envisage how the selection and election of state directors of banks took place, and such reports as have survived confirm the expectations.[104] On the other hand, the functions of the directors determined their selection by the stockholders. There was disagreement on whether or not state, or government, directors had functions different from those of the directors elected by the stockholders (Daniel Webster and Andrew Jackson representing the different points of view.)[105] The following contemporary statement gives a good picture of the functions of the latter:

> They [the directors] should have remembered that they act for others and not for themselves; and, of course, are bound by more rigid obligations than would be required in the exercise of their individual rights or in the management of their own property. They are the mere agents of the stockholders, appointed to protect all the rights, perform all the duties, and to use all just and honorable means to secure the advantage granted by the act of incorporation.[106]

This description, however, tells only half of the story and must be read along with the following suggestion of 1820 regarding the ideal bank director:[107]

> The directors...ought to be...of undoubted credit, great experience, and extensive business. Neither integrity, nor abstract

talent, nor both are enough. They ought
...to be men extensively engaged in business and well acquainted with men of business. Such men not only are better qualified to govern the affairs of the bank,
but give to it their own business, which is
valuable not merely on account of its extent
but also on account of its character, and
attract to it numerous customers like themselves; and thus secure to it in the aggregate business to a greater extent and of a
better character than men of different description can do. Not to obtain the services of such men is to fail in managing the
institution.

The ideal bank director, unfortunately, seems to have been rather rare; and,
as might be expected, those who were anxious to become bank directors were impelled
by the desire for capital,[108] or profit[109]
or prestige,[110] or all of these. Since no
emoluments were paid to them, as described above, the temptation was great,
all the more so since the "production of
convertible paper money," as Opdyke in
retrospect put it a few decades later,[111]
resulted in "demoralizing tendencies."
There were reasonable people in the second
period who would have agreed with Opdyke.
A businessman of Zanesville, Ohio, a director of the local bank, who was trying to
liquidate it in 1819, wrote to the Secretary of the Treasury: "Making a virtue of
necessity I have...lent my aid to an honest [italics in the original] closing of
the concern (which has always been respectable) so far as bankers can lay claim to
the character of honesty."[112]

While average directors of leading
Eastern city banks probably lived up to
the ethical standards of other businessmen
of their time and of their section of the
country, the morals of the average country
bank directors were notoriously low.[113]
They preempted the credit facilities of the
bank which they controlled[114] and in addition were supposed very often to have used
their position for dubious private gain.
In some banks they were said to have extracted 1, 2 to even higher percentage as
a consideration for the endorsing of bills
or notes which were refused by the banks
in question-unless endorsed by one of the
directors.[115] The foreign observer who
reported this practice doubted if American
legislatures would ever be able to control

bank directors and made them restrict
themselves to "just and honest" dealings.[116]

In this connection the following
description drafted at the end of the
second period is of unusual interest:

The directors must necessarily be placed in
the hands of a few men who have comparatively
but little interest in the bank. Most of
them are selected among men in active business, in order that they may be able to
judge of the solidity of the paper offered
for discount; and as they are not paid it is
impossible to expect that they should attend
without deriving some compensation for the
sacrifice of a portion of their precious
time. This may consist in part from the discounts they obtain for themselves which may
always be kept within reasonable bounds.
But the power and consideration attached to
the office can be obtained only by granting
favors; whilst on the contrary a refusal
renders the directors unpopular. To this
may be added a want of sufficient moral responsibility. The honorable merchant who
would feel disgraced by his own individual
failure is not affected by that of the bank
of which he may be a director.... The most
prolific source of the errors of bank directors is the natural sympathy which they feel
for men who are engaged in similar pursuits
to their own. It may upon the whole be affirmed that banks though money lenders are
in fact governed rather by the borrowers
than by the lenders.[117]

These various quotations give a good idea
not only of the prevailing practice, but
also of the motives which between 1820
and 1840 induced businessmen to become
bank directors. The most important incentive, however, is not mentioned in this
passage, but it has been alluded to before,
briefly, and will be noted more fully
later,[118] namely, the possibility of gaining control of the bank in question.

It has been described in a previous chapter how, as early as the 1790's,
it became common practice among bank
boards to appoint committees to deal with
specific administrative problems or tasks
and how toward the end of the first period
some of these committees were attaining
some sort of semi-permanent status.
Regardless of this development, however,
when the second period began such committees of the boards had not yet reached

the point where they were taking over virtually the whole administration of banks; the bank boards as such were still administrative bodies.

In the second half of the 1810's however, the first deviation from the established organizational practice took place and there started a long and slow process, first in one bank, but soon to be copied and to become general, by which the bank boards lost their administrative functions. It is not accidental that this change began in the Second Bank of the United States, for this enterprise was a national banking institution whose directors came from different parts of the country. Consequently, while boards of directors of local banks could administer their enterprises, the board of the national bank was not able to do so because of inadequate means of transportation and communication. Therefore the administrative functions of the board had to be shifted either to the officers or to local committees. The latter plan seems to have been intended by the framers of the charter who inserted the clause that seven directors could form a quorum for the transaction of business, and this was the direction in which the development actually turned first.[119]

In the 1820's the board of the Second Bank of the United States had set up the following committees: an Exchange Committee, a Standing (Monthly) Committee, Committees on the State of the Bank, on the Offices, on Elections, and a Dividend Committee. Special Committees were appointed occasionally for special purposes, for instance, when forfeited stock was to be sold or a loan in Europe negotiated. This type of organization persisted, and it was described by a Congressional Committee of 1833 as a "well established [practice] that the most important business of the bank [was] done by committees," which, incidentally, acted rather informally. "The usual practice [was] for the president to communicate any matters relating to the bank orally [to the board] and recommending the course to be pursued. This being done, some gentleman, generally a member of the exchange committee or committee on the offices move[d] that the subject be referred to a committee."[120]

The Bank of the United States was not an exception, however, and such

administrative committees of bank boards, especially exchange committees, standing committees, and committees on the state of the bank,[121] could be found in many banks during the second period. As a matter of fact, administration of banks by committees can be considered as typical of the years between 1820 and 1840 and as a second stage in the development of bank administrations[122] (the first stage being administration by full boards). Since in the 1830's certain other organizations in the economic field which started at that time copied contemporary political organization,[123] one can conclude that the expansion of "bank government" by committees was at least inspired by our political institutions.

Two of the above-mentioned committees of the Second Bank of the United States are of particular interest, namely, the standing or monthly committee and the exchange committee. The former was appointed monthly in rotation to attend daily at the bank "to afford aid and advice." That is to say, this committee symbolized the concept of the board as an administrative body, after it had become practically impossible for the board as a whole to do an administrative job. It is not surprising that this committee passed out of existence in 1828: there was no longer anyone on the board who could have given "aid and advice" to Nicholas Biddle, the president of the Bank and one of the world's leading contemporary bankers. The exchange committee, on the other hand, grew in importance, and similar committees, as already indicated, came into existence in many of the larger American banks in the 1830's. Banks which discounted mostly accommodation paper, i.e., country banks, could easily stick to the established practice, discounting once or twice a week during a meeting of the full board, and making the applicants wait until the next discount day. Such procedure was impossible, however, if a bank wanted to build up a considerable business in bills of exchange.[124] These bills were payable at places other than the seat of the discounting bank, and in figuring the price a varying rate of exchange had to be added to the legal interest. If only because of the fluctuating exchange rate, businessmen would have been unwilling to wait for days. There was, furthermore, competition among

banks for good bills of exchange, and
therefore the cumbersome traditional procedure of a full board passing leisurely
on the offerings was no longer feasible.
Thus especially during the 1830's the discounting of bills of exchange and later
notes in general tended to shift to committees meeting daily.[125]   In 1821 the
Second Bank of the United States went even
further, adopting a rule that in the absence of the Exchange Committee the president and the cashier were authorized "to
purchase exchange which may be offered for
sale if an immediate answer be desired and
report such purchase to the Exchange Committee in its next meeting."[126] With a
time lag, other banks followed suit. In
the 1830's the directors of the Second
Bank of the United States asserted that
discounting was "in truth...a power exercised very generally by the officers of
banks throughout the United States."[127]
The directors of the Massachusetts Bank,
to give an example, adopted a rule in 1831
that any two directors could discount bills
and notes, and in 1840 authorized the
president to perform this function and to
report his actions to the board.[128]

        However, in the 1830's there was
still doubt in the minds of many bankers
as to whether the discounting by committees
of the board, let alone by the officers,
was proper procedure. The by-laws of the
1830's of the Girard Bank of Philadelphia,
for instance, ruled that "no committee
shall be invested with the power of making
discounts when the appointment shall be
opposed by one fourth of the directors,"
and even the Board of the Second Bank of
the United States was reluctant to permit
its branches to proceed along the new
lines which it had adopted for itself.[129]

        In the Second Bank of the United
States the exchange committee extended its
functions far beyond the original limits,
until it finally was in charge of "all the
large monied operations of the Bank requiring confidential and prompt action."[130]
The committee, set up first as a foreign
exchange committee,[131] was in charge of the
exchange department, handling domestic and
foreign exchange, the foreign loans then
in existence, the sale of forfeited stock,
and the negotiations with the federal
government regarding the two five-million-
dollar loans of 1824 and 1825; but for a
long time it did not discount. However,

as soon as the Bank started to build up
an extensive business in domestic exchange, the functions of the exchange committee widened to include discounting
bills of exchange. Thence it proceeded to
discounting notes on the days between the
meetings of the board. The proceedings
of the exchange committee were entered in
a book and laid, but not read, before the
board. In the early 1830's the exchange
committee of the Second Bank of the United
States was in charge of all matters relating to the operations of the parent bank
and its branches in foreign and domestic
exchange and bullion, acting at the same
time as a daily committee for the purchase
of domestic exchange.[132]

        By that time the character of the
Second Bank of the United States as a
high-capitalistic, large-scale enterprise
was definitely established, and therefore,
earlier than in other American enterprises,
it became evident that its business could
not be run by committees. Thus by force
of circumstances, but accelerated through
the personal factor (the existence of a
powerful leader at the head of the Bank)
decisive organizational progress took
place. Through a small change in the
appointing procedure the exchange committee
that had acted previously as an authority
now became a screen for Biddle, the entrepreneur, who ran the Bank admirably,
albeit autocratically. This term is not
used to express a value judgment, for
Biddle became but the exponent of a secu-
lar trend. Instead of appointing the
exchange committee in rotation, the president of the Bank appointed its members
every three months at will.[133] Since he
himself was at the same time an _ex-officio_
member of the committee, he controlled the
most important part of the Bank's business.
It was nominally still entrusted to that
committee which at the end, however, would
not even make regular reports to the board.
The directors of the Bank considered,
probably rightly so, that such a set-up
was necessary for a successful administration of the Bank.[134]

        Thus in a particular case, that of
the Second Bank of the United States, a
development came to a close which had
started in the late 1810's when banks began to grow into large scale enterprises
and management by boards of directors
became unwieldy. The administration by

committees represented only a temporary solution of the problem, a solution which gave way when the development of banks and of the American national economy as a whole progressed further toward high-capitalistic forms. The necessity of keeping certain large transactions secret arose in all banks and this necessity alone worked for the change in organization.[135]

Thus the administration of banks by the president and officers came into being and the third stage of the organizational development of banks was reached. The change was comparatively easy because this organizational possibility had existed from the outset as, again, can be seen most clearly in the Second Bank of the United States. The latter's Rules and Regulations of 1816 distinguished clearly, but without using adequate terms, between the board of directors as an administrative and as a policy-making body, respectively. While the functions of the board in the former capacity were circumscribed in sections 3, 5, and 13, the "proceedings of the Board of Directors when conducting their business as a deliberative body" (policy-making body, as we would say today) were described in detail in section 28.[136] Thus the board could and actually did develop into a policy-making body. On the other hand, section 11, paragraph three of the charter became the starting point for that organizational development which deprived the committees of the board of their status as pillars of the administration. This section permitted the corporation to "make a compensation to the president for the extraordinary attendance at the bank as shall appear to them reasonable."[137] On this basis the president in time could become the well-paid chief executive officer of the Bank.

Originally, of course, the functions of the president of the Bank of the United States were traditionally those of trust and confidence. According to the Rules and Regulations of 1816, section 5, the president was to take into his custody plates, paper moulds, and bank paper; he was to superintend the printing of bills and notes ordered by the directors to be printed; and to keep a regular account of the paper in his custody and of the paper ordered to be printed. He was to sign all bills and notes and to keep the seal of the corporation. Under the same Rules and Regulations of 1816 the cashier had managerial functions: countersigning bills and notes; supervising the personnel; examining the daily settlement of the cash account; taking charge of the cash in case of deficiencies; attending the meetings of the board and keeping the records of its proceedings; consulting with the committees of the board; and reporting to the president whenever necessary.

The ascendancy of the president in the Second Bank of the United States dates from the appointment of Langdon Cheves. When Cheves was elected president he was not meant to be merely a figure-head; he was called to save the Bank from disaster and to reorganize it. But the influence of the example he set was such that it is probably permissible to go a step further and to date the trend toward a change in functions of the bank presidents in America from that day in 1819 when Cheves took over the presidency of the Second Bank of the United States.[138] It was then that there began in American banks the ascendancy of presidents who were to become administrators.

The fact that Cheves did not correspond to the type of bank president to which American business was accustomed in the period after the War of 1812 can be ascertained from a pamphlet of 1821 which has already been quoted. Discussing the set-up in the Second Bank of the United States after the appointment of Cheves the anonymous author says: "No communication was made by the directors [italics in the original] but...whatever the President was pleased to make known proceeded from himself without the authority or sanction of the board. Doubtless the stockholders expected to have been met by the directors or at least by their committee, and to have received a communication previously digested and agreed to by the board. But not being consulted by the President they with lamb-like submission took no measures for the exercise of their right or the performance of their duty. Voluminous documents were indeed presented; and the committee found the President from an early hour in the morning to a late hour in the evening always ready [italics again in the original] to make a speech against the former administration and in commendation of the present or to explain the causes of difference between himself and the cashier."[139] That is to say, Cheves, being on the job all day, administered his bank without attempts at interference on the part of the board. As can be seen from the quotation this procedure seemed strange at that time.

The author of the passage was not only critical of, but even hostile to Cheves; and he aimed at replacing him as head of the Bank. His hostility was partly due to the fact that Cheves was overstepping the traditional limits of his position. But it proves the strength of the trend toward the ascendancy of presidents in the bank administrations that his suggestions, when adopted in part, even accentuated the development which Cheves had inaugurated. The pamphleteer suggested as president "a man familiar with accounts, habitually conversant with extensive money operations, readily and accurately perceiving the effect of every financial measure; perfectly acquainted with the various interests of commerce, the course of exchange, and the complicated means of a great moneyed institution." Such a president would, according to the author, "be pleased to meet the directors as equals in deliberation and action."[140] That is to say, the author no longer thought in terms of a figure-head or of a man of public confidence as bank president, such as had been typical of the first period. He wanted an expert financier at the head of the Bank, and Cheves did not live up to this standard. But modern as was that suggestion, at that point he wanted to arrest the development. Believing in a tradition established in the First Bank of the United States and in other early American banks he wanted his expert banker at the head of the bank to be a _primus inter pares_.[141] However, when Biddle, one of the first modern bank presidents in America, who in many respects conformed to the pamphleteer's ideal, succeeded Cheves he did not become the _primus inter pares_. Due to his superior abilities, his character, and the force of circumstances, he became the entrepreneur surrounded by directors who were at the best policy makers, and he set the example after which the presidents of the big Eastern city banks were patterned after the 1840's.[142]

The rules and regulations of the Girard Bank of Philadelphia and of the Union Bank of Louisiana at New Orleans,

both of the early 1830's, show well what functions were entrusted to presidents of city banks at the end of the second period.[143] According to the rules of these banks the president still possessed all the functions which he had had in the first period, namely, keeping the seal of the corporation in his custody, taking care of bank paper, paper moulds, and plates, signing all bills and notes, and presiding over the board. But in addition he was now also to exercise supervision over all the concerns of the corporation, to superintend the official conduct and the duties of all persons employed in the bank, and to perform all such functions and duties as properly belonged to his place as president and such as were entrusted to him by the board. However, he did not yet appoint the cashier and other employees of the bank. Such appointments were still in the hands of the board, as they had been in the first period.[144] Summing up, one can say that the presidents of reputable banks in the advanced sections of the country in the 1830's were more akin to modern bank presidents than to the typical bank presidents of the first period. If not yet the chief executives of their enterprises they were at least on the way to becoming such. The Union Bank of Louisiana went so far as to designate its president the "head of the corporation,"[145] an essentially modern aspect of his position.[146]

The rise of the bank president, exemplified in Biddle's rise to power in the Second Bank of the United States, was facilitated by the custom of proxy voting by stockholders. Thereby concepts as to the proper (approximately even) distribution of power among the stockholders held in the first period and embodied in many early charters were becoming obsolete in the second period. Early bank charters often restricted[147] the number of votes which could be cast by any one stockholder, but since they did not forbid voting by proxies a concentration of power over banks in the hands of a few took place regardless of such restrictions. The use of proxies, however, opened up an even more dangerous road. Because it became customary to give proxies to the president and other directors and because the president at the same time was developing into the chief executive officer, a two-pronged move began: the bank administrations, at least nominally still represented by the board of directors, tended to become autonomous, i.e., independent of the stockholders; and in the second instance, the president became equally independent of the board as an organ of the corporation. The board was nominally elected by the stockholders, but actually by the president and his friends on the board who commanded the proxies. The development was in full swing as early as 1824, as Biddle's letters show, and in 1832, for instance, he controlled 504 votes from Massachusetts, 194 from New York, 144 from Virginia and North Carolina, and 177 from various other states. In addition he had received, jointly with other directors, proxies for some more votes, and his close second, General Cadwalader, controlled 538 votes from Massachusetts. (One T.P. Cope, another director, voted 93 shares.)[148] In other banks the development may not have gone to the same length, but it was undoubtedly under way elsewhere also.

In the preceding description of the rise of committees of the bank boards to the position of pillars of the administration and in turn of the substitution of the bank officers in this capacity, the concomitant change in the functions of the bank boards as a whole has been alluded to repeatedly. In this case, as in that of the rise of the president's office to importance, the change was facilitated because the stage had been set since the 1810's. In that decade the Rules and Regulations of the Second Bank of the United States, as already mentioned, made a distinction between two functions of the board, one of which was called the "deliberative."[149] In the 1830's a committee of directors of the same Bank mentioned "directive" and "legislative" functions of the Bank board, that is to say, in present-day language, administrative and policy-making functions. When administrative development which has thus far been described from one angle, is viewed from the other, one of the functions of bank boards (the "directive") can be seen as decaying as the other (the "legislative" or "deliberative") grew in importance. Where the latter was not the case, the bank boards by the 1830's tended to decline into powerless representatives of the stockholders. As is typical of transitional periods, there could be found in the 1830's side by side bank boards which were policy-making bodies pure and simple, such as the board of the Second Bank of the United States;[150] others, in the process of change, which were working through committees and were being guided by strong, expert presidents at the same time, as, for instance, those of the Girard Bank of Philadelphia and of the Suffolk Bank in Boston; and finally, others which still largely ran the banks.[151]

Again the development can be observed in the Second Bank of the United States as in a test tube. As explained by a friend of the administration, the board had the right to execute any business for which authorization had been given to the corporation in its charter, but the board voluntarily restricted its own performance to a certain part thereof. Otherwise, the carrying on of its extensive business would have been impossible.[152] In 1833, in fact and in the eyes of the directors of the Second Bank of the United States, the board was already a policy-making body, having become a body of that character in the Cheves era. In his period of the Bank's history the board was split into two parties, a conservative and an enterprising one. The former was led by Cheves; the latter, after a contest in November 1822, elected Biddle president of the Bank.[152a] A genuine question of policy was hereby settled, namely whether, as the conservatives wanted, the forfeited bank stock should be canceled and the Bank's capital reduced or whether, as desired by the enterprising faction, the forfeited bank stock should be sold and the Bank's liquid capital restored. The latter policy was bound to lead to credit expansion, while the conservative group preferred a rather restricted business. Another question of policy, one which came up before the board in Biddle's time, was settled by the resolution of December 2, 1823 when the board decided to go extensively into the exchange business. This decision had far-reaching economic consequences. Once more, in 1832, the board of the Second Bank of the United States acted as a policy-making body on a vital question. After the reelection of Jackson the nonresident members of the board were called to meet with the resident directors in special session. In this session the board decided that the Bank should not contract in preparation of winding up its affairs, that it should proceed with its business as usual, but that it should at the same time invest its means in such a way that it had better command over them, that is to say, in self-liquidating paper.[152b]

In the 1830's Jackson and his followers, represented in the Bank itself by the government directors appointed in 1832, still thought along traditional lines and looked at the board as a sort of collective administrator of the Bank. In the paper read to the Cabinet on September 18, 1833 Jackson complained that "the most important business, even that of granting discounts" was no longer executed by the board. To this reproach the directors of the Bank answered that the business of the board was "not exclusively nor primarily to make loans: --its business is to govern the whole Institution... The business of the Board is to prescribe how the details of the operations of the Bank are to be made."[153] The government directors objected that "the great body of the correspondence [was] never seen at the table or in the room where the board meets." "The real business is not there [by the board] transacted nor its real authority there exercised...there exists beyond its control a power that can be and is exerted promptly, secretly, and efficiently from one end of the country to the other;...the just instrumentality of the directors has been curtailed either by the mode of operations, gradually introduced, or by positive regulation, from time to time prescribed."[154] Disregarding the value judgment embodied in this statement, it is a correct description of a typical historical process by which in a specific high-capitalistic concern an adequate administration developed which fitted the needs of modern times and modern banking enterprise. At the same time the board of directors moved into a position where it could perform a useful function under the new conditions.[155]

However, the change in the _functions_ of bank boards, just described, was accompanied by still another change. The control of banks by individuals and families during the first period has been discussed in an earlier chapter. There was an increased tendency toward such control in the second period; and, as already indicated in another context, in the 1830's directors of some banks had developed from being the servants of the stockholders to

being their masters. They had obtained control of their banks by buying up shares or through the instrumentality of proxy voting or _de facto_ because of apathy on the part of the average stockholder. In 1831 Nathan Appleton referred to this matter when mentioning the "private use" of bank funds by "the principal stockholders" which "object [had] been sometimes accomplished by buying up a majority of the stock so as to control the choice of directors."[156] (As a matter of fact stockholdings in banks were at that time, as later, so widely distributed and the average stockholder took so little interest in the administration of his bank that control could be exercised on the basis of a very small percentage of the shares.)[157] A few years later, in a report to the Louisiana legislature of 1838, Edmond J. Forstall considered as one of the most serious defects in contemporary Louisiana banking: "the monopoly by eighteen to thirty firms or individuals, chiefly bank directors, of the active means of the banks,...thus identifying public and private credit with that of a few individuals and jeopardizing the interest of a whole community."[158]

The role of the cashier in banks during the first period has been discussed in detail, and in this chapter the change in his functions in the Second Bank of the United States has been mentioned. As a matter of fact, the rise of the bank presidents not only implied a decline in the importance of the board, but also in that of the cashiers.[159] While during the first period the cashier had been the only banking expert in his enterprise, he now came to share that expertness with the president, who of course remained his superior. But compensatory factors were involved in this change. In the second period the president was moving closer to the cashier since he was on the way to becoming _de facto_ an officer of the bank, thus bridging that gap between the board and the cashier that can be sensed during the first period. While the wording of the charters of the first and second periods indicate clearly that the president was meant to be a director and not an officer of his bank, by 1830 the public must have begun to take a new and more realistic view. A passage from Jackson's message of 1829 in which the Bank's "officers" were commended was understood by everybody, including Biddle himself, as a commendation of Biddle, the Bank's president, who was thus aligned with the officers.[160] As a matter of fact, by 1832 Biddle considered himself the "chief officer" of the Bank. Furthermore to the extent that the bank administrations became autonomous, as described before, and to the extent that banks became large scale and indispensable enterprises, the cashiers rose together with the presidents.[161] Finally, in contrast with the first period, the cashiers had now good chances to become bank presidents themselves, as will be described shortly. The Rules and Regulations of 1832 of the Union Bank of Louisiana thus described the functions of the cashier: he countersigns bills and notes; observes the conduct of the personnel and reports thereon to the board; he examines daily the settlement of the cash accounts and reports, if necessary; he lays before the board on discount days a statement on the accounts; he attends all the meetings of the board and keeps records of its proceedings; and finally he keeps in his custody the seal of the bank.[162]

Since the change in the position of the cashiers resulted from that of the bank presidents its beginnings can be expected to go back to the late 1810's. It is indicative of the incipient change that in 1820 the very important correspondence between the Secretary of the Treasury (Crawford) and certain banks regarding public deposits (deposits of receipts from the sale of public lands) were in some cases addressed to and answered by the cashiers, in others to or by the presidents.[163]

The change in the functions of the presidents, cashiers, and directors could not but be reflected in the personalities of those holding these positions.[164] To give a few examples: Richard Varick (1753-1831), the president of the Merchants Bank of New York, resigned in 1820. He was a typical old-style bank presidents. In the Dictionary of American Biography he is characterized as a soldier; and his career has been described in detail. It may be added that in the early 1790's he cooperated with Hamilton and that in the years to follow he played a role in the social life of his city, for instance, as the president of the New York Society of the Cincinnati. Thus in the first period he

was the right sort of man for the position of bank president. His successor, however, was Lynde Catlin (1768-1833). Catlin had been trained at Yale University to become a lawyer; had been the cashier of the Merchants Bank from 1803 to 1817; then, on solicitation of his friend John Jacob Astor, served as the cashier of the New York branch of the Second Bank of the United States from 1817 to 1820, in which latter year he succeeded Varick. That is to say, an expert banker replaced a figurehead, thereby automatically shifting the administration of the bank in question from a board of merchants, superior to a president like Varick, to the expert bank president, superior in turn to a board of merchants without special training or experience in the field of banking.[165]

A few years later the same development took place in the Bank of New York. Between 1784 and 1825 this bank had seven presidents, all of whom were elected prior to 1812 and all of whom were either men with remarkable war records or public-spirited, successful merchants with wide family connections among the New York upper classes. The last of these men, Matthew Clarkson (1758-1825), has been characterized as "living the life of a public-spirited citizen of means and leisure." During all those same years the bank had only two cashiers. When Clarkson resigned in 1825 it was his cashier, Charles Wilkes, who became his successor as president of the bank, and after the latter's death in 1832 he, in turn, was succeeded by his cashier, Cornelius Heyer.

To give a third example and at the same time one for Boston, let us cite the case of Henry B. Stone. He had been a teller in the Suffolk Bank when it opened; had then become a cashier of the Eagle Bank; and from that position he had advanced to that of president of the Suffolk Bank.[166] It was definitely against the trend when, as late as 1837, the old-fashioned Massachusetts Bank of Boston appointed as president a director, John James Dixwell, a merchant with outside business interests, who was no expert in banking and who received a salary not higher than that of his cashier.[167]

In the 1830's the stockholders, like the bank boards and bank presidents, were moving into an essentially modern position within their enterprises, a position which is so familiar today that that it does not need description. But in reliable banks in backward sections of the country there still survived the concept of the stockholder as a more or less responsible proprietor of his bank. In 1833 when applying for admission into the ranks of the pet banks, the stockholders of the Maine Bank in Portland were willing to pledge themselves individually for the performance of the government business if it were entrusted to them. And again during the crisis of 1837 the Suffolk Bank was able to extract bonds of indemnity, not only from directors, but even from prominent stockholders of certain banks in the state of Maine.[168] In the crisis of 1857 such actions would no longer have been possible.

III

Banking Philosophy

Between 1815 and 1840 America possessed what most of her citizens desired, namely what would be called today inflationary banking. It would have been impossible, or possible only to a lesser extent, if contemporary banking had been based rigidly on specie. Therefore in those decades large sections of public opinion still clung to the Mercantilist theory that specie was superfluous for banks. As late as 1833 representatives of New York business, including such an able banker as Isaac Bronson, were not ashamed to claim as an evil the fact that the whole capital of the Second Bank of the United States consisted of money, because they felt that this led the Bank to overtrading. According to these men such an evil was avoided by the Bank of England because it conducted its business without any monied capital whatsoever.[169]

The imaginary needs of business were, of course, rationalized and reflected in a specific banking philosophy which, in turn, was reflected in the actions of individual bankers and legislators. In the first period, as has been described before, the mercantile banks in the cities were expected to bank only on their capital and deposits; while the country banks, adhering to Mercantilist banking theory, issued notes in multiples of their capitals (from one and a half to three), at the same time considering capital superfluous for banking. The former theory was disappearing in the second period. At the same time the latter remained at the root of all average banking.[170] However, the theory was refined during those years and was (in line with Mac Vickar's Hints on Banking) usually expressed in the following way: Banks should not bank on their capitals, but on their credit and keep their capital intact as a security for the noteholder.[171] This theory, which will be discussed in some detail later, came to prevail in American banking with the introduction of Free Banking of the New York brand.

To put it in another way: what the third period generally recognized as an essential of banking, namely, the swapping of promises to pay between businessmen and banks,[172] had not been widely recognized as such in the second period. In the words of Clibborn: American bankers, unlike British bankers, considered "themselves lenders of paper currency and not discounters and changers of private into public debts."[173] The phrase "public debts" is rather misleading in this connection, referring as it does to banknotes; but it is meant to convey the same meaning as that embodied in Biddle's designation of notes as obligations of "recognized corporations."[174] For the generation which was in its prime in the 1830's, note issue was still the conditio sine qua non of banking. "Some persons calling themselves bankers do not issue any notes of their own.... These are not bankers at all, for they get the bills discounted by others who are bankers properly so called."[175]

Inflationary banking, as a matter of fact, had undesirable results. When the second period opened Mathew Carey gave warning that the directors of banks had a responsibility to their communities "to proceed with care and caution and to preserve a steady and systematic career." He considered it a "most serious and awful truth" that the banks had become "literally masters, in a very high degree, of the destinies of those of their debtors not in tolerably independent circumstances. They may at pleasure reduce some to bankruptcy, by abrupt requisitions for the amount of their debts; and may by undue accommodations enable others to make great fortunes out of the distresses of the public. When money is plenty banks are servants and useful servants of the community... When money is scarce they...become absolute masters of their fellow citizens."[176] But Carey's warnings were not heeded and inflationary banking took its course.

The passage just quoted shows that by 1815 the social dangers of such banking had been realized; by 1830 they were surprisingly well understood. It was recognized that banks were "manufacturing bank note capital for the use of trade" which diminished with every reaction and almost vanished with every panic. It was seen that bank notes were often "representatives of nothing but legislative power."[177]

The evils caused by inflationary banking were comprehended but not the remedy, and in this connection a typical feature of banking in the second period which did not contribute to its improvement should be discussed, viz., the wide participation of states in banking. Such participation began in the first period, as described in a previous chapter, and took two different forms: either the state in question would own a bank outright and manage it through electees of the legislature (in the language of that period it would have been a bank "entirely public, both as respects capital and direction").[178] Or the state in question would hold shares in certain banks sending a corresponding number of state directors into the boards. The state acquired such shares sometimes in lieu of a bonus, sometimes by investing available and/or expected funds in bank stock, sometimes by handing over state bonds, and sometimes by a combination of these methods. A question which should be investigated is: to what extent did state participation in banks and especially the outright ownership of banks represent a development of the eighteenth-century loan offices. This author feels that such connection may well have existed. (He has gained this impression, for instance, from the fact that in the case of the Bank of the State of Alabama the loanable funds were distributed among the counties in a way reminiscent of that used by the old loan offices.[179]) There can be no doubt that experience in one state influenced actions in another. When the governor of Alabama suggested the Bank of the State of

Alabama, he referred to the State Bank of South Carolina as his model. The philosophy back of state participation in banks underwent a change, however, when it was adopted by the western states.[179a] The intention of making the advantages of banking available to the common man and to exclude mischief wrought by untrammelled and unsupervised banking, were, in contrast to the first period, probably the most important reasons for such participation in the western states in the 1820's and 1830's.

The ownership of banks and the participation in banks by states only aggravated the evils; and other panaceas had no better effects because of lack of understanding of the essentials of sound banking. In 1816 Carey rightly complained that even after many years of experience bank directors had not grasped the principles of banking or, in his words, they had "no precise idea of the system that ought to be followed."[180] But he himself had nothing to offer except a repetition of the Mercantilist recipe that note issues should be properly related to the banks' capitals. Furthermore in recommending this policy he himself got mixed up. He recognized that the banking capital employed by an individual or a community should have a proper relation to the trade and commerce of that individual or community. From that correct presupposition, however, he jumped to the doubtful conclusion that the amount of bank credit should equally be brought into a proper relation to the volume of trade and commerce. It had not yet dawned on him that the volume of trade and commerce might have been influenced just by the volume of credit available at a previous period.[181] Such statements make it clear that the banker at the opening of the second period was still steering without compass.

Another contemporary author,[182] who wrote about twenty years after Carey, stressed the inability of the American banker to control his customers in the use which they made of the credit received. Scottish bankers, who confined their business to the discounting of trade paper, could draw valid conclusions as to the prudence or lack of wisdom with which these men ran their businesses from the conduct of their clients and from general mercantile information. American bankers,

in contrast, would not do so, dealing mostly, as they did, in accommodation paper.
These therefore lacked the beacon which
guided their Scottish colleagues.

But this same author felt that
American bankers in the second period were
not altogether without guidance. As a
matter of fact as early as 1818, President
Jones of the Second Bank of the United
States wrote to the Secretary of the
Treasury: "It is a fact corroborated by
the experience of all banks that their
operations must necessarily be regulated
by those of the banks in their immediate
vicinity otherwise those which are the
most prudent and parsimonious will become
the creditors of those who are the most
liberal or extravagant, the consequence of
which is an immediate specie responsibility."[183]   Later, in the 1820's and 1830's
many of the better-managed banks all over
the country were guided in their lending
policy by their balances with the Bank of
the United States, just as banks today
are guided by the clearing house balances.
For instance, according to a report of
the Second Bank of the United States in
1833, it had been forced to increase its loans
in the fall of 1832, because the state
banks were largely indebted to the Bank
and therefore were afraid to expand their
discount line.[184]   At that time the most
advanced bankers were learning also to use
foreign exchanges as a compass.[185]   To be
sure at that very time England was already
taking a more advanced step so that the
American bankers who at home were in the
vanguard still remained backward in comparison with the best English practice.

Unsound as banking was in the
period under investigation it served the
purpose of most of its backers outside the
commercial centers: it contributed to the
development of capital resources. Banking
as practiced in the second period amounted
to a continuous process of inflation
through which, as in every inflation, purchasing power was transferred from the
economically less active to the more active part of the population. These men,
entrepreneurs, used the borrowed funds,
i.e., the purchasing power created more or
less out of nothing, for investments, a
process which took place at the expense of
the recipients of fixed incomes and of those
who lost through bank failures and through
the decreasing value of numerous bank
issues. This sort of economic progress,
brought about by bank inflation, was, of
course, very wasteful; but it can hardly
be doubted that the American national
economy through unsound, inflationary banking was developed more quickly than would
otherwise have been the case. Contemporaries, to be sure, were unable to understand the process of capital formation
through inflation which was taking place
before their eyes;[186] but we possess from
the period next following, during which
the process continued, an exact although
cynical description of the way that capital
was created by this process of bank inflation (as then practiced under a system of
Free Banking):[187]

"A number of men get together... They
want to build a railroad; they have no money...
They employ John Thompson, to purchase state
bonds for them, and pay therefor, trusting
them for his pay till the first batch of bank
notes, founded on them, is issued. They issue their railroad bonds, hypothecate them in
Wall Street, and pay John Thompson for the
State stock. They are then ready with a
state-stock secured circulation, to commence
the road. The only trouble is to keep the
bills afloat. But this is managed very easily.
The bank need only be located where it will
not pay the brokers to run on it, either in
Rhode Island or Maine... The people take
the money as long as it goes; while the
Chicago and other bankers...are afraid to
run upon it, for fear of breaking it and
thus creating a panic."

Chapter IV

THE PROBLEM OF COUNTRY NOTES AND
THE SUFFOLK BANK SYSTEM

The first fifteen years of American banking, as has already been described, were characterized by the fact that the large Eastern seaports were each getting one "money bank." These enterprises were administered reasonably well by leading merchants of the cities in question and carried on what today would be called a commercial banking business. Although, of course, considerable business acumen was necessary for success in the new field the difficulties connected with this type of banking were not insurmountable. The situation changed, however, when in the 1790's banks multiplied and banking enterprises were founded also in country towns. As already stressed, country banks represented a veiled renascence of Mercantilist "banking on private credit" and they caused serious economic and business problems which took decades to solve satisfactorily. One of these problems, the fight between city and country banks for their share in the total circulation, its implications, together with the outstanding solutions of the various problems resulting therefrom form the subject matter of the present chapter.

Country bank notes first became a problem around 1800.[1] Since at that time farmers and country shop-keepers were generally indebted to city capitalists and merchants, the issues of country banks, dubbed "foreign money," tended to flow to such places as Philadelphia, New York or Boston.[2] Notes of country banks had to be taken by city merchants in the course of their trade and in the 1790's city banks were inclined to take them on deposit.

The Boston banks seem to have first become concerned about "foreign money" in 1796 when country money was accumulating in the city. In March of that year the Massachusetts Bank appointed a committee to confer with committees of the Union Bank and the Boston branch of the Bank of the United States on the subject of whether or not country bank notes should be taken by the Boston banks. Not much seems to have resulted from that move. Three years later, in July 1799, the board of directors of the Massachusetts Bank once more took the initiative in this matter by appointing another committee "to meet any committees which might be appointed by the other banks to confer with them" on the circulation of out-of-town bills. This committee met with the committees of the two banks above-mentioned and the delegates decided unanimously to make the following recommendations to their respective boards of directors: bills of certain enumerated country banks to be taken on special deposit and if tendered in payment of debts due the banks at 1/2 per cent discount. On the basis of these recommendations received in August 1799 the board of the Massachusetts Bank resolved as late as September 1800 to take the bills of the enumerated banks on special deposit only if turned in in amounts larger that $400 and to deduct 1/2 per cent discount if deposited in smaller amounts or if passed to the credit of the depositor "absolutely." In October 1800, that agreement was abrogated. In 1803, however, the three banks again joined hands and systematically sent back for redemption country notes which had come into their possession.[3] They met with such obstacles, however, that, changing their policy, they refused for the future to take country bank notes on deposit. For some time thereafter the vacuum was filled by money brokers, who found temporary use for country notes until the supply became so large that again nothing could be done except to present them for redemption, an exceedingly difficult operation.

This situation was especially inconvenient for the smaller merchants in Boston who lived from their trade with the country; and consequently some of these men made another attempt in 1804 to deal with country money without forcing the country banks to redeem it in specie. In that year with their backing the Boston Exchange Office was chartered.[4] The idea was to create a depository for country money since, as mentioned before, the existing Boston banks at this juncture would not touch these notes. Country money once deposited in a bank could, as the founders conceived, be used for making loans to the same businessmen who currently deposited it and who would thereby get cheaper accommodations than they could have from the established banks. These same businessmen in their capacity as stockholders finally would draw profit from these funds which could hardly be used in any other way. The flaw in this reasoning is obvious: a kind of bank money for which there is no use does not become useful by being collected and reissued. Nevertheless the Boston Exchange Office[5] came into being as a corporation entitled to set up a fund consisting of $150,000 in Massachusetts currency (i.e., notes of Massachusetts country banks) and $50,000 specie. The charter of this bank is remarkable for its mixture of preposterous and wise clauses. The Office was not allowed to issue notes of its own; it was not allowed directly or indirectly to demand specie from other banks. It was debarred from asking or receiving a premium for exchanging the bills of one bank for those of another or for specie and from purchasing notes at a discount. It was entitled, however, to receive deposits and to make discounts, paying out bills "promiscuously as they were received." The discounts of the Boston Exchange Office were limited to a "proportion not exceeding 33 1/3 per cent of the amounts of bills and specie actually deposited in the bank at the time of discount."

If we can trust the anonymous contemporary pamphleteer who dealt with this corporation,[6] the Boston banks were originally friendly to the Boston Exchange Office since, in the first instance, the city was cleared of country notes. As a matter of fact, the collection of country notes to pay up its capital resulted for a limited timé in a sort of local deflation which made room for Boston issues. However after the capital had been paid in and the new bank started discounting, the older ones felt the competition and tried

to gain power over the new enterprise. When unsuccessful they met under the leadership of the Union Bank and decided to fight the Exchange Office by collecting country notes and sending them home for redemption. Thereby they embarrassed the country banks and indirectly sapped the strength of the former.[7] Caught thus between the hostility of the Boston banks and the lack of cooperation on the part of the money brokers who felt their domain invaded, the growth of the concern was quickly checked, if ever it had been possible; and when in 1805 it failed in its attempt to get a legal monopoly for this sort of business by an amendment to its charter it was doomed. By that time the Boston Exchange Office had come into the hands of Andrew Dexter, Jr., who has been discussed above[8] and who with its help made the first, unsuccessful, attempt to control the New England currency.[9]

After these various experiments at dealing with Massachusetts country money had failed, that money necessarily depreciated; and nothing could be done by the recipients except to enforce its redemption regardless of popular feeling in this matter. Nathan Appleton (1779-1861), a pioneer of American textile industry and a merchant in Boston, who had been a factor in Dexter's downfall, now took action in this direction. In 1808 he tried to stop the nuisance of "evasion and delay" practiced by the country banks.[10]

In those days Massachusetts law regarding bank notes was not yet stringent and a bank which failed to redeem its notes had to be sued. Hence the only way to embarrass a non-specie-paying bank was to institute proceedings and multiply suits in the law courts. Nathan Appleton therefore decided to organize about a hundred of his fellow sufferers, (many of whom were probably also to sign the Circular of 1809 to be discussed shortly). Every participant in the scheme contributed $100 to a war chest, notes were acquired, and the Boston broker, William Cochran, was employed to carry out the following plan: his agents would appear with the acquired notes at the counters of the various country banks. By threatening to return each day with a new batch of notes and to start a law-suit for a new party for every case of non-compliance with their demand, they forced redemption of the notes. The plan succeeded for the time being, and some of the weaker banks were forced out of existence. Thus it came about that Nathan Appleton first began to take an interest in banking [11] on which he soon was to gain influence.

It was in all probability Nathan Appleton and his friends [12] who in 1809 again took the lead in another step in the same direction. In a circular letter to the country banks, signed by such firms as those of S[amuel] and N[athan] Appleton and Ebenezer Francis, an attempt was made to induce the country banks to provide for the redemption of their notes. In order to afford every facility and convenience to their country customers, as described in the letter, the Boston merchants had accepted notes of the various country banks. Their confidence in these banks, however, had been abused "within the last two years" since the latter had refused to pay their notes on presentation, or at least, by the use of all sorts of chicanery, had made redemption exceedingly difficult. [13] This attempt at educating the country banks was a failure.

Around 1810 country money presented a problem only for the Boston merchants, while the Boston banks kept aloof. The latter did not take country notes on deposit, thus refusing to have anything to do with them; but by such a policy they made country money a serious problem for themselves. [14] Since the notes of city banks could be easily redeemed while country notes could neither be deposited nor converted into specie without much trouble, country notes became the customary medium of circulation in Boston and the issues of Boston banks could not be kept afloat. Or, in other words, the policy of the Boston banks contributed to the extensive circulation of country notes at their very doors. Thus they were finally forced to change their stand in this matter. To put it differently: since the Boston merchants controlled the city banks they became concerned with the problem of country money not only in their capacity as merchants, but also in that of stockholders and directors of city banks.

By that time, the time of the War of 1812, the activities of the early note-brokers, mentioned above, had developed into the domestic exchange business

characteristic of America down to Civil War times. Those note-brokers built up a lucrative business by acquiring "foreign" bills, i.e., bills of country banks, at a discount and by sending them home for redemption. Furthermore some of the brokers were employed by country banks to circulate and redeem their notes in Boston. [15] So profitable became this business that after the War of 1812 the domain of the brokers was invaded for the first time by an incorporated bank, the New England Bank, [16] which had been founded in 1813 as the fifth in Boston. Founders and stockholders of that bank were well-known Boston merchants, such as the Appletons, Cabots, Goddards, Patrick T. Jackson, and Francis C. Lowell. On behalf of their stockholders and other customers, shortly after having been set up, this bank undertook the collection of country notes at cost within and outside the state. Furthermore, after 1814 it built up a regular business in buying and collecting country money and drafts. In this connection the bank wrought a change in the New England collection business by indicating its willingness to buy country notes at all times at the fixed discount of 1 per cent while the brokers bought at varying rates as cheaply as possible. When the Manufacturers and Mechanics Bank of Boston, later the Tremont Bank, temporarily followed the example of the New England Bank, competition between these two banks and the brokers reduced the discount for country money to 1/4 per cent until the two banks came to terms and 1 per cent became for some time the standard discount for country money in Boston. At the same time the New England Bank began to specialize in collecting New York notes and in transporting specie thence to Boston, thereby eliminating New York notes from the New England circulation.

The New England Bank not only stabilized the discount for country money in Boston and excluded New York notes from circulation in that section of the country, but it also attempted to regulate the New England currency. As a means toward this end the New England Bank offered to take bills of all New England banks of good standing at a graduated rate which varied with the cost of sending the notes home for redemption. Alternatively, the

country banks were offered an arrangement
by which the New England Bank would redeem
their notes in Boston and credit them with
the discount at which the notes were acquired. Many made use of this offer. [17]

At this juncture there were the
following possibilities for handling the
foreign money situation. Country money
could be taken in the cities at a discount
or at par. The former policy meant that
the public had to pay the expense of redemption including a certain profit for
the redeeming agent. Brokers or city
banks could act as such agents, profiting
from the transactions; but when the issuing bank itself provided for redemption of
its notes in the city it took the whole or,
by splitting it with an agent, a part of
the profit connected with the redemption
of its notes. In the second case, redemption at par, the cost could be borne by
the city banks if they agreed among themselves on such policy (as was apparently
done for some time in New York) or the
issuing banks could keep funds in the city
for the purpose of redemption, thus absorbing the cost, as was essential in the
Suffolk Bank system. The road which
actually was taken in the various commercial centers depended partly on the vision
and actions of the leading bankers in the
city concerned and partly on the actions
of the legislature in question.

As mentioned above, the New
England Bank did a thriving business in
New York bank notes. Therefore it must
have been well informed on the monetary
conditions in that state, and it is quite
possible that its arrangements with the
New England country banks were modelled on
those developed in New York. This city,
of course, experienced, after about 1800,
the same influx of country money, in this
case notes of banks in New York State and
Connecticut. The branch of the First Bank
of the United States sent them home for
redemption and was bitterly assailed for
this "unreasonable practice." [18] The situation is supposed to have been different
from that in Boston because country money
was at par in New York City before the
War of 1812. In those years the Bridgeport
Bank, managed by Isaac Bronson, [19] and the
Mechanics Bank of New York City made a
contract by which the former bank opened a

special deposit in the latter, the full
amount of which was to be maintained for
the duration of the contract. The Mechanics Bank in return was to redeem the bills
of the Bridgeport Bank, made payable in
New York with the former bank, whenever
presented. All the money thus advanced
by the Mechanics Bank was to be reimbursed
weekly by the Bridgeport Bank without recourse to the special deposit. There is
no doubt that Bronson intended to increase
his circulation to such an extent that the
profit thereof overcompensated him for the
loss of interest on the deposit. This was
perhaps the very first contract of the type
which the Suffolk Bank used later, and it
seems to have been copied by other New York
banks after the War of 1812. [20]

In that period the New York City
banks required the country banks to keep
funds in the city "equal to the redemption
of all their paper." That is to say,
country banks were forced to keep permanent
deposits in the city amounting in some
cases to as much as ten or twenty thousand
dollars, and at the same time to redeem
promptly every note which might be received. They had to give the city banks
the use of their permanent deposits as
compensation for backing and redeeming
their issues. This scheme worked, for the
following reason: at that time the
Connecticut banks were anxious to make
their notes payable in New York City,
hoping thereby to build up a circulation
in that place. Under the strict legislation of Connecticut they had to pay interest on notes payable, but not actually
redeemed, in that state. Such interest
charges, of course, made business unprofitable if based on circulation payable
at their own counters. In 1817, however,
after resumption, there no longer existed
this incentive to comply with the conditions of the New York City banks. At the
same time the New York country banks, except those in the "head market towns" of
Albany, Troy, and Lansingburgh, resolved
"with almost one accord to shake off the
yoke," and the system collapsed. [21] Nevertheless it is important to keep in mind
that for some time in the 1810's New York
possessed a country note redemption system
which was, except in one point, essentially
similar to that which later was to become
famous as the Suffolk Bank system.

Probably during the same years after the War of 1812 when country money was at par in New York City and at 1 per cent discount in Boston, the New York arrangement of remunerating city banks for the redemption of country notes was introduced into Boston by a Connecticut bank.[22] Connecticut notes circulated in both cities and at that period became a convenient and profitable means of remittance from Boston to New York, so that their discount in Boston dropped to 1/2 per cent. Consequently the Connecticut banks were on the point of losing their circulation in New England so that their chances for profit were decreased. One of these Connecticut banks decided to deposit $50,000 with one of the Boston banks for one year without interest while that bank (the New England Bank?) undertook to redeem its notes at a discount and to reissue them.[23]

This was the situation in 1818 when the Suffolk Bank came into existence. As early as 1819 its directors decided to enter the "foreign money business," i.e., the business in country money, thus providing competition for the New England Bank. The decision as such was no creative achievement; it was just an incident in the competitive struggle between two banks. However the success of the Suffolk Bank and its victory over the older competitor, were due to several moves. One was the decision to make the acquisition and collection of country money a cooperative venture of the Boston city banks. It is important to keep this in mind, for later when the country banks made that business a cooperative venture of their own this line of the Suffolk Bank was abandoned. The methods applied by the Suffolk Bank during the first few years of its activity in the foreign money field were not revolutionary, but became so when its leading men hit on an ingenious idea through the application of which what had originally been a collection business became a clearing of country notes. The tremendous success of the Suffolk Bank as well as its importance for the American national economy resulted from that highly creative, unheard-of achievement, and it was brought about in the simplest way. At the moment when, instead of being forced to settle in specie, the country banks

were allowed to settle by turning in those New England notes which they themselves had received in the course of their trade, the decisive step was taken. Thereby what was conceived in the interest of the city banks became palatable also to the country banks, regardless of all the grumbling; and the system that had failed in New York became a success in Boston. It is noteworthy that as early as 1832, in a letter to a recalcitrant country bank, the Suffolk Bank incorrectly claimed that the permanent deposit was a consideration for "receiving from you bills of all the other banks in the New England States in exchange for your own at par."[24] However, the final success was due also to a supplementary move which gave the Suffolk Bank power over the country banks. The Suffolk Bank, although not insisting on the payment of all country bank notes in specie, nevertheless rose to domination over those banks by becoming their creditor whenever they were unable to redeem their note obligations promptly. The Suffolk Bank would then charge 2 per cent interest per month on the overdrafts and sometimes would discount the paper of the country banks, keeping their notes as collateral. Regardless of a published interpretation to the contrary, it was as a creditor and not as a debtor of the country banks that the Suffolk Bank was able to keep the former under control. Whenever the amount of notes redeemed for any one bank exceeded the funds to its credit plus its permanent deposit, the Suffolk Bank had the right to send the excess home for redemption.

In the preceding paragraph the ideas behind the development of the Suffolk Bank have been sketched. The men who evolved these ideas, made them the basis of the policy of the Suffolk Bank, and thus laid the foundation of a system of the highest economic importance must be looked for in certain committees of the board of the Suffolk Bank. The earliest one was appointed in February 1819 and consisted of the bank's president, Ebenezer Francis,[25] Ebenezer Breed, and William Appleton. It will be remembered that the latter had cooperated with Nathan Appleton in connection with the circular letter of 1809 discussed above, as had Ebenezer Francis. Undoubtedly a line leads from that action of Nathan Appleton to the committee of 1819 of the Suffolk Bank. It was this committee which brought the Suffolk Bank into the promising field; but the policy which it recommended remained within established, although not widely-established, practice. The committee recommended that the bank enter the business in foreign money which is "now received at the New England Bank and at the same rates. That if any bank will deposit with the Suffolk Bank five thousand dollars as a permanent deposit with such further sums as shall be sufficient from time to time to redeem its bills taken by this bank, such bank shall have the privilege of receiving its own bills at the same discount at which they are purchased." Those country banks which were already correspondents of the Suffolk Bank should be allowed the same privilege without the permanent deposit of five thousand dollars if they would make all their deposits at the Suffolk Bank.[26] In accordance with these proposals a committee of the board of directors, consisting of Ebenezer Francis, Ebenezer Breed, and one John Belknap, administered the foreign money business of the Suffolk Bank in competition with the New England Bank without spectacular success. Competition between the two banks and the brokers lowered the discount on country money to such an extent that the business was hardly profitable.

In the spring of 1824 the circulation of country notes in Boston once more represented a serious problem for all of the banks of the city. They were unable to keep in circulation an amount of notes which was proportionate to their share in the banking capital of New England. The notes of the city banks were presented for redemption whenever specie was needed, while the notes of the country banks served as a medium of exchange. It will be remembered that by that time the circulation of most banks was still limited legally to a certain proportion of the banks' capitals.[27] "The maximum note issue permitted being far in excess of the aggregate amount of currency which could be kept outstanding, it was directly to the interest of each bank to secure for itself as much of the field as possible and therefore to pay out its own notes rather than the notes of its neighbours, thus making a field for its own circulation

by withdrawing from the channels of trade and presenting for redemption the notes of other banks which came into its possession." The Boston banks furthermore suffered from the fact that the city agents of the country banks made call loans (to be exact, loans "payable in three or five days after demand") in country notes at reduced rates of interest, thus depriving the Boston banks of much "valuable business."[28]

At this juncture, the decisive step was taken toward what today is called the Suffolk Bank system: in 1824 there came into being, in order to check "the enormous issues of country...paper" and to make room for their circulation, the cooperative venture of the Boston banks.[29] The decisive step must be attributed to two New England textile merchants who until then had not participated in the development. They had experienced all the disadvantages of an unregulated note issue and the difficulties associated with the disposal of country bank notes received in the regular course of their trade. They were connected with the Suffolk Bank as directors and therefore were acquainted with the note collection and domestic exchange business of that time as practiced by the Suffolk and New England Banks. These two men were William Lawrence (1783-1848) and John Amory Lowell (1798-1881). Lawrence, like Nathan Appleton, is famous as a leader in the early New England textile industry, being one of the founders of the first corporation for the manufacture of woolen goods, and his creative ability had been proved in more than one venture. Lowell was a less important man and his participation in the formation of the Suffolk Bank system is his main contribution to American economic life. Undoubtedly it was these two men who conceived the idea of concerted action on the part of the Boston banks with regard to country money. Consequently the Suffolk Bank appointed them a committee to confer with the other Boston banks concerning measures which might be accepted in common. The cooperation of other banks could be expected since they had all suffered alike from the situation.

On April 10, 1824 Lawrence and Lowell addressed a letter to each of the Boston banks drawing attention to the situation described above and inviting cooperation for the purpose of ameliorating it.

They proposed that a fund be set up to be assessed in proportion to the capitals of the participating banks and to be put at the disposal of one or several Boston banks for the purpose of acquiring "eastern" money, i.e. notes of the banks of Maine, at 1/4 per cent discount and sending it home for redemption. Profit and loss were to be proportionately distributed. Reference was made in this letter to the corresponding "experiment" of the New York banks (mentioned above) which took foreign money even at par and yet profited from the increased issues made possible by the creation of a vacuum in the circulation through the regular redemption of country money.

This proposal referred exclusively to Maine notes and envisaged cooperative action in buying them up and sending them home for redemption. (At that time Maine possessed a banking system which actually represented land banking pure and simple and which thereby was particularly bothersome to the more modern city banks of Massachusetts.) In the ensuing negotiations, the scope of the scheme was widened. Funds were assessed, collected, and deposited with the Suffolk Bank, for dealing not only in Maine notes, but in notes of all the New England banks. Furthermore, instead of buying foreign money in the open market, the agent of the Associated Banks, i.e., the Suffolk Bank, was to procure it by taking it over from the Boston banks at the best rate given by the New England or any other city bank. The Boston banks, in turn, acquired it in the course of their regular business dealings.[30]

The alliance of the Boston banks was at once correctly sensed by the New England country banks as an attempt to decrease the circulation of the latter in order to make room for the notes of the former. Therefore some of the country banks attempted a counterstroke intended to crush the alliance of the Boston banks by one composed of country banks.[30a] On January 16, 1826, stockholders of the country banks met in Boston with Henry Shaw of Lanesborough in the chair and Thomas Rotch of New Bedford acting as secretary. The meeting, which was not too well attended, appointed a committee to draft resolutions. The resolutions offered by this committee read substantially as follows: Since a number of Boston banks have formed a combination contrary to the spirit and meaning of their constitutions, injurious to town and country, only wanting in sufficient power to destroy every monied institution within its reach, the participants of the meeting pledge themselves to produce a cooperation of country banks in a system counteracting that of the Boston banks. For this purpose the participating banks are advised to withdraw their deposits from the Suffolk and allied banks, and to redeem at their own counters only. They are furthermore advised to exchange notes among themselves to lessen the accumulation of bills in Boston. Although not embodied in the resolutions, the representatives of the country bank seem to have thought also of collecting Boston notes with the view of "running" on the city banks. These resolutions were not too well received and came to naught.[31]

The letter of April 10, 1824, quoted above, was important as the first decisive step toward the building of one of the most fruitful institutions in the field of American banking down to 1840. Yet, surprisingly, a scrutiny of its contents reveals not a single new idea: A proposition was made for concerted action in buying up and sending for redemption country money which circulated in Boston, as had been tried as early as the 1790's and early 1800's and again a few years later when the Boston banks fought the Boston Exchange Office. To collect funds for this purpose was put forward as another suggestion; it may well have been contributed by Nathan Appleton since it is identical with his plan of 1808 for a "war chest."[32] (Incidentally, Nathan Appleton actually became a supporter of the Suffolk Bank system.) Finally, the proposal was influenced by what its backers knew of similar actions in New York. Creative ideas were contributed only in a later stage of the development.

The importance of the agreement concluded on the basis of that letter of April, 1824[33] lies in the following facts: first, by gaining the backing of the Boston banks for its foreign money business the Suffolk Bank rose in its competitive struggle with the New England Bank;

furthermore, the capital now set aside for that business was so large that it could not only be extended further than ever before, but could even be monopolized; finally, since the Suffolk Bank could be certain of the moral backing of the whole trading community it could make use of its power and of the possibilities resulting from the contract with the associated banks.

The methods applied by the Suffolk Bank in its now expanding collection business were at first not influenced by the arrangement. In fact they were identical with those applied before, except that notes of Maine banks were included for the first time. But in 1825 a further step was taken and with it something revolutionary came into existence in the field of American banking. In that year the Suffolk Bank established a par collection system and it was probably in this connection that the clearing idea was inserted, as already stressed. It seems from the wording of the Directors' Records (June 16, 1825) that the incentive for collecting at par did not originate in the Suffolk Bank itself, but came from one or several of the associated banks. Since the clearing idea now became the pivot on which rested much of the economic importance of the whole system it would be of the greatest value, from the point of view of this research, to know just who contributed it. However, the material which survives does not answer this question.[34]

Thus was set up the Suffolk Bank system viewed by its contemporaries as a device to enforce the redemption of country notes whereby the latter circulated at their face value all over New England. Historically speaking, an equal importance lay in the fact that the Suffolk Bank system was the first regional clearing system[35] to be successfully established; and this took place eighty years before the problem of regional and national clearing of checks was tackled in this country. Lawrence and Lowell not only made the first decisive moves, but also became the creative entrepreneurs who determined the policy of the new business through the agency of a Foreign Money Committee of the board of directors of the Suffolk Bank in which they were the dominating figures. Henry B. Stone, the president of the Suffolk Bank from 1825 through

1849, is supposed to have contributed to the success of the system as the able executor of their policy, but it is impossible to determine whether his achievements lay more on the entrepreneurial or managerial side. Under Stone's control, but on his own responsibility, worked the redemption teller, William Grubb (who died in 1862), the prototype of the creative manager. Without any example to draw on, he managed with spectacular success what was actually America's first clearing house, a managerial achievement of the first rank. In the appendix to this chapter may be found the by-laws of the foreign money department of 1856 which actually were but a "description of the present mode of conducting that department in the form of by-laws."[36]

At this point it may be interesting to look at the development from still another angle, that is, as an example of the working of capitalism in its era of greatness. The Suffolk Bank system originated from the striving for profit on the part of the Boston banks and as the result of the competitive struggle between two rival enterprises. The result, however, deeply influenced the economy of a whole region. To begin with the least important results: While in the 1810's deposits made by country banks in consideration of the redemption of their notes by city banks amounted to ten, twenty, or even fifty thousand dollars, in the 1820's competition had brought them down as low as two thousand dollars (for small banks) and this, too, for better service.[37] While in the 1800's and early 1810's the discount of country notes varied from day to day and was as high as 4 per cent, competition brought it down to as low as 1/4 per cent. When competition was excluded a standard rate of 1 per cent prevailed for some time. After that, competition was renewed through the entrance into the field of a new enterprise. Thereupon again the rate was brought down until finally, after the creation of the Suffolk Bank system, the discount on New England country money disappeared altogether and the latter circulated freely at par all over New England. In the course of that development, which was identical with mild deflation since it kept the country banks constantly under check, country money rose from being a nuisance to becoming a valuable part of the national circulation. During the more than two decades in which this economic process took place prior to the definite establishment of the Suffolk Bank system, exponents of that process thought only of profit and competition. So much is certain from the sources. By applying what to these men was sound and sane business reasoning the Suffolk Bank system was made the representative of wholesome nineteenth-century banking, with specie as its basis and redemption of all obligations in specie as its backbone. Thus they contributed to the elimination, at least in New England, of the last vestiges of Mercantilist "banking on private credit" with its different philosophy.

The purpose of this chapter is not to write a detailed history of the Suffolk Bank system.[38] Suffice it to say that because of the gigantic difficulties in building up an enterprise of that size and character, the results were at first somewhat disappointing and the organization was in danger of being discarded by about 1830.[39] Especially the expectation of the Boston banks that the device would increase their circulation did not materialize. Indeed Nathan Appleton who blamed the establishment of banks just outside the city for the failure was for some time rather pessimistic about the future. It is quite possible, of course, that the incipient check business played a part.[40] All in all, it was only after 1830 that the Suffolk Bank system was firmly established; but then so firmly that it survived even the crisis of 1837. At that moment, because of the suspension of specie payments, there was a strong temptation for the country banks to withdraw. They would have profited from extended circulation, but not a single one succumbed to the temptation, and without exception they remained members of a system which enabled them to make use of all New England money[41] received in the course of their regular business.[42]

The Suffolk Bank system, as already mentioned, had a mildly deflationary effect on the New England currency. To express it differently, the New England country banks could not issue as many notes nor make as much profit as they would otherwise have done. At that time Mercantilist land-bank tradition still

lingered, especially in Maine and Vermont.[43] That is to say, numerous country banks did not recognize that redemption of their notes in specie was a moral as well as a legal obligation, let alone a matter of course. Therefore, the Suffolk Bank system was exceedingly unpopular with many of its members. Moreover, the country banks realized that the Suffolk Bank made large profits in the redemption and clearing business, or, as they saw it, out of them. So the feeling grew among them that, if it was impossible to discard the system, then at least it should be conducted exclusively in the interest and to the profit of the country banks themselves. Thus they finally decided to set up an organization of their own on a cooperative basis, an idea fundamentally sound and progressive.[44]

James G. Carney was the leader in this movement against the Suffolk Bank, a movement in which creative ideas played an equal role with meaner emotions on the part of disgruntled and irritated members of the system. According to his own statement, since 1828 Carney had advocated the establishment of a bank in Boston to be owned by the New England country banks and managed in their interests. At that time, while cashier of the Lowell Bank, Carney's feelings and interests had been outraged when the Suffolk Bank demanded that his bank make a deposit of $5,000 on a paid-in capital of only $50,000 or face the consequences. In the next decade (in 1835), according to Lake,[45] a petition was presented to the Massachusetts legislature to establish a bank to be owned by the country banks which should perform functions similar to those of the Suffolk Bank. Whether Carney had something to do with that petition (which was tabled) is not known. Be that as it may, in the end Carney was successful in getting the indispensable backing of a Boston bank when the Suffolk Bank clashed with the young Exchange Bank (founded in 1847). Today when one reads the correspondence between the two banks one recognizes that the Suffolk Bank was right, although its letters and actions were unnecessarily dictatorial and threatening and of the sort to create enemies.[46] This alliance of country bank interests with a Boston bank led to a successful termination of plans which otherwise would probably have remained unsuccessful. Thus in 1855[47] the Bank of Mutual Redemption was chartered "to redeem our [the country banks'] currency at par in Boston," and began operations in the summer of 1858.

The Bank of Mutual Redemption was a remarkable enterprise indeed, being, as it was, America's first bankers' bank. Its stock was to be subscribed and held exclusively by New England banks which in this case were permitted to hold stock in another corporation. This permission represented one of the early steps toward the modern holding company and at the time was almost revolutionary.[48] Carney, then president of the Lowell Bank and treasurer of the Lowell Institution for Savings (which he had helped to found in 1829), became the president of the new bank. His cashier was Henry P. Shed of Roxbury, one time bank commissioner of Massachusetts; and one C. B. Bradbury, formerly clerk of the Foreign Money Department of the Suffolk Bank, became superintendent of the corresponding department of the new enterprise. Through the latter official the experience of the Suffolk Bank in the redemption and clearing business was transferred to the competing concern.[49]

The Bank of Mutual Redemption began its activities in the summer of 1858, and immediately tried to come to terms with the Suffolk Bank. Letters reprinted below[50] show clearly its intentions: Each of the banks should clear and redeem for the members of its system and should exchange with its rival such notes as were redeemable with it. The Suffolk Bank, as these letters indicate, was first willing to go along with these suggestions, but suddenly changed its mind, resolved to fight, and obviously solicited the help of other Boston banks. Thereupon it refused to accept specie for notes of country banks if tendered in Boston by the Bank of Mutual Redemption. Such notes were collected and presented at the counters of the banks in question.[51]

This was the situation when on September 29, 1858 a meeting of representatives of country banks was held in Springfield, Massachusetts, at which it became apparent that the new enterprise could already muster considerable strength among the New England country banks. In consequence of this meeting the backers of the Bank of Mutual Redemption started to withdraw their permanent deposits from the Suffolk Bank. In Boston a number of younger institutions joined in the fight which became in a way one between a younger and an older generation.[52] The Suffolk Bank continued the struggle into October, but decided to yield when it discovered that the Boston banks were not presenting a united front for its protection. The fact that the Massachusetts Bank Commissioners, fearing a derangement of New England monetary concerns, elected to take an interest in the matter may have contributed to this decision also.[53]

On October 9, 1858 the Board of Directors of the Suffolk Bank resolved (9 to 3) to send out the following letter to the New England banks:[54]

For the expenses of the foreign money system of the Suffolk Bank the Bank finds its remuneration in the use of the deposits of the various Banks in New England. As no other general mode of compensation has ever been thought of, the maintenance of the system depends upon the continuance of these deposits. To place the Banks withdrawing, on the same footing as before withdrawal is obviously inconsistent with the plan of keeping up the system by means of deposits. The Suffolk Bank system has been conducted for 30 years on the principle of sending home for payment in specie the bills which we receive of those Banks which have withdrawn their deposits. We consider this indispensable to the system, and that it would be futile to attempt to carry it on without the power of enforcing it. In continuing this redemption system, the Suffolk Bank has had for many years no motive beyond that of securing to the community a continuance of its acknowledged benefits. The labor expense and risks of the business have been equal to any remuneration received from the use of the deposits. We cannot consent any longer to have the Bank placed in the position, as is charged against us of carrying on this business merely for its profit, nor can we be expected to stand out against public opinion, prejudiced and excited, in sustaining a system however beneficial to the public, after it has become unremunerating and hazardous to the stockholders of the Bank.

The Suffolk Bank system is now conducted theoretically and practically, precisely as it has been in the past. - If public sentiment is now against it, and if it is less appreciated by the trading community and the City Banks than heretofore, the cause is not to be found in the mode of pursuing it. The time has arrived to surrender our agency in the system as heretofore conducted, our responsibility in it must now cease, because its main feature, the right to send bills home for specie cannot be given up without destroying its efficacy, - because our exercise of this right is effectually made use of by those hostile to the Suffolk Bank system to place the Bank in a false attitude! before the public, and because under existing circumstances, the Bank does not wish to stand in the way of a trial of the attempted experiment of a foreign money system to be conducted on less stringent principles.

We shall continue to receive country money from the Banks as heretofore subject to conditions that it may perhaps be found necessary hereafter to make.

A few days later the Suffolk Bank, probably as a tactical move, threatened to withdraw completely from the foreign money field, but actually it came to terms with the Bank of Mutual Redemption, both banks exchanging such foreign bills as had come into their possession.[55] However, in 1860, after losing ground constantly, the Suffolk Bank practically gave up the foreign money business. Its defeat was caused mainly by the fact that when once it had gained a monopoly it became dictatorial and highhanded. Unwilling to adapt itself to changing conditions it became unable to find its way back when the business again became competitive.

Nevertheless, the quick victory of the Bank of Mutual Redemption is somewhat of a surprise. Its president, Carney, although shrewd and aggressive, did not represent the highest type of business leadership. Fond of sharp practices,[56] he was distrusted by the other Boston bank presidents, and being an autocrat he ran into many difficulties. His bank was rent by dissensions between him and the cashier, it had to go through fights (perhaps unavoidable) with the Suffolk Bank and the clearing house, and also drew fire from the Massachusetts Bank Commissioners because of malpractices.[57] On the other hand, the bank was well secured against loss by a

clause in its charter as amended in 1859 (chapter 100, sec. 1) according to which the subscribed stock was held to be pledged against the indebtedness of the member banks. While the Suffolk Bank handled the foreign money business in a dignified, routine fashion, the Bank of Mutual Redemption pushed it with a very undignified aggressiveness.[58] In so doing it promised more than it could carry out: Banks were promised interest on their permanent deposits at rates which differed for Boston and for country banks, those of the latter being graduated according to their size. However this promise was withdrawn as of April 4th at the suggestion of Thayer by a decision of the board of directors on March 16, 1859. All permanent deposits were lower than those required by the Suffolk Bank. In lieu of permanent deposits New England banks could subscribe the corresponding amounts to the stock of the Bank of Mutual Redemption thereby sharing in the profits of its business. The Bank of Mutual Redemption quickly extended its business beyond the limit of its members and of the New England region. Following the example of the Suffolk Bank it organized a more or less independent note-clearing system for Rhode Island with the help of the Bank of North America in Providence. At the same time it made arrangements with the Albany "assorting house" and the Metropolitan Bank in New York, the redemption systems of which will be discussed shortly, and finally it indicated its willingness to take at par from any party the notes of banks which kept their accounts with it and the notes of all other New England banks at a rate of twenty cents per thousand dollars.[59] Under these circumstances its foreign money business grew rapidly. While on October 13, 1858 it held foreign money to the amount of $78,750.02 and in clearing house packages (i.e., ready to be presented at the clearing house to the Boston correspondents of the country banks in question) $81,579.03, the corresponding figures on February 23, 1859 were $1,002,076 and $170,069.34.[60] In one respect, however, the policy of the new enterprise seems to have been more cautious than that of the Suffolk Bank; while the latter bank permitted overdrafts its younger competitor required a special agreement before they were allowed.[61]

As has been stressed, the first regional redemption system was established in

New York and in all probability it served as a model for Boston. In the latter city the device was developed by combining redemption with clearing features so that the system became firmly rooted in New England. After this achievement the ideas migrated from Boston back to New York. In the meantime, however, the banks in the state of New York experimented on their own. By the middle of the 1820's the New York City banks permitted country banks to redeem their notes in New York funds instead of in specie when such notes were presented at their (the country banks') counters.[62] The country banks, of course made use of that advantageous possibility. But in consequence thereof most payments by country banks were not made out of funds actually available, but instead their notes (their promises to pay) were paid out of the credit which they had with their New York City correspondents. Thus the system collapsed quickly; and Lake[63] suggests that it was this experience of the New York banks which induced the Suffolk Bank to insist on payment in specie of the notes of the New England country banks.

In the 1830's the Albany banks exerted some pressure on the banks of the surrounding country, forcing them to redeem their notes regularly in specie or in drafts on Albany or New York which were available because of the trade in produce, e.g., flour.[64] Some of them purchased the country banknotes at a moderate discount, and sent them home by messengers

employed by them. The pressure which occurred previous to the suspension [of 1837] contributed to derange this system of redemption, and the Legislature, by an act of May, 1837, as a condition of waiving the forfeiture, provided that during the suspension each bank should receive the notes of other banks at par in payment of debts.

This produced an agreement between the [New York] city and country banks, by which the former received the country paper at par, allowing time, according to distance, for the country banks to redeem; the latter being at the expense of the messenger employed for taking it home, and the risk of transmission. This arrangement operated admirably well, and continued until the resumption of specie payments, when it became no longer the interest of the parties to continue it; the city banks

being relieved from the legal obligation to participate in the sacrifice requisite to carry it on. A voluntary arrangement was, however, substituted, by which certain of the city banks undertook to purchase the country paper at a half, and afterwards at three-quarters per cent discount, and hold it a stipulated time, at the expiration of which the banks in the country were required to redeem it in funds current in New York, and take it home at their own risk and expense.

The operation of this arrangement was very favorable; but, owing to the circumstances above alluded to, the redemptions during the last summer [1839] were unusually heavy, and, when the pressure came on in the fall, it was found that the capital required to carry it on was more than the banks engaged in the purchase could devote to that object in such a critical juncture, consistently with their paramount obligation to sustain themselves in the payment of specie. The consequence of breaking off this arrangement at such a crisis, when the capital required to effect any other was not to be had, was to sink the paper of the country banks down to an extravagant rate of discount, as well as to break off in a great measure other means of intercourse between the city and country, of great importance to men of business, such as the collection of notes payable in the country, and the remittance of drafts from the country to the city.

Consequently the country banks made an arrangement among themselves to exchange their notes at the State Bank in Albany. In this exchange other banks and individuals could participate if they contributed toward the expenses of the messengers who cashed the balances and returned the cleared notes. But this arrangement left country notes which were circulating in the City of New York still unprovided for. Since no city bank was willing to devote enough capital to setting up a duplicate of the Suffolk Bank system and thus incur the hostility inevitably resulting from such action, the New York legislature had to tackle the problem in 1840. Many suggestions were offered at that time, actually the law of April 4, 1840 relative to the redemption of bank notes required the banks of the state to redeem their notes at 1/2 per cent discount either in New York City or in Albany (or by a later amendment also in Troy). This Act had an undesirable effect. Since New York banking at that time worked under the Free Banking principle it became profitable under the law of 1840 to issue notes without running a regular banking business. These notes could be circulated by a redemption agent in one of the above-mentioned cities and the redemption discount could be split between him and the would-be bank. To prevent this type of business the redemption discount was reduced to 1/4 per cent in 1851.

The law of 1840 did not lead to satisfactory arrangements regarding country notes circulating in New York City. Finally, after various proposals had come to naught, the Metropolitan Bank of New York was chartered in 1851 for the purpose of copying the Suffolk Bank system in that city, James McCall[65] being its first president. Whether or not he was also the man who provided the basic idea is not certain, however, for the leading spirit of the bank from the outset was its cashier, John E. Williams, who as president of the Metropolitan Bank later became one of New York's leading bankers. He himself has described how the bank came into being; the business of bona fide bankers was being damaged badly through the circulation of irresponsible note issuers who profited solely from the redemption discount or from loaning batches of their notes to Wall Street brokers.[66] These bona fide bankers of course knew the Suffolk Bank. In fact, as early as the 1840's the Suffolk Bank had made arrangements with them and with other businessmen to take New England notes from them at one-tenth of one per cent discount. The new bank followed this model and so the idea back of the Suffolk Bank system came to be tried out also in New York City: by enforcing regular redemption of country notes a certain percentage of them were to be driven out of circulation. The Metropolitan Bank, so Williams claimed, was an immediate success and forced thirty to forty wildcat banks to close their doors. At the same time its actions purified the atmosphere of Wall Street and gave the legitimate city bankers a fairer share in the note circulation of the state.[68] The Metropolitan Bank acted as the redemption agent for those banks which kept deposits

there. First it claimed the whole redemption discount but later split with its country bank depositors which thus profited at the rate of one eighth of one per cent on the redemption of their notes. The latter step, sharing the profit of the redemption business with the issuing country banks, was due to the fact that, in contrast to New England practice, the note redemption and clearing in New York was neither a cooperative venture of the city banks nor did it become a monopoly. The American Exchange Bank of New York City[69] seems to have followed suit (or cooperated?); and after 1858 the Metropolitan Bank competed also with an "assorting house" which was organized in Albany under the joint management of the Merchants' Bank and the Bank of the Interior, both of that city. This latter redemption agency, which incidentally was known of in Boston,[70] redeemed the notes of New York country banks at the legal discount of one quarter of one per cent, New England notes at one eighth of one per cent, Pennsylvania and New Jersey notes at one quarter of one per cent. Country banks which kept deposits with the organization paid ten cents per one hundred dollars of redeemed notes, i.e., the legal discount was split at the ratio of three to two between issuing banks and redemption agent. Notes presented for redemption were paid in Albany, Troy or New York City on the morning following receipt.[71] How this organization came into being will be described shortly.

Both the New England and the New York enterprises of this type were de facto clearing houses, as was clearly realized by the end of the 1850's. At that time an official source explained that the actions of the Metropolitan and American Exchange Banks had established the clearing of country notes in New York City, a precedure which was highly beneficial to business. And it went on to explain that the only difference between this note clearing system and the New York check clearing house was the following: according to the custom of the latter, a debtor bank could meet its creditor and borrow the balance due; while in the country system the debtor without sufficient funds on deposit was posted and suspended simply because the parties were so isolated that they could

not avail themselves of the aggregate
credit balances.[72]

      The differences between the New
England and New York systems on the other
hand are obvious: there, exclusively an
achievement of private enterprise; here,
very much the result of legislative actions
which determined business policy. There,
a par collection system; here, a system of
collection at a discount. There, a monopolistic; here, a competitive business.
There, the issuing country banks alone
bore the burden, while the monopolistic
clearing house (the Suffolk Bank) alone
made a profit, although the cooperating
city banks enjoyed considerable indirect
advantages;[73] here, a wider public bore
the burden, while issuing banks and redemption agents made some profit. In consequence of these differences the issuing
banks in New England grumbled against
their monopolistic clearing agent, while
in New York it was the banks which had to
take country notes on deposit that felt
aggrieved. The result was similar: hardly
had the Bank of Mutual Redemption come
into existence, when the underlying idea
migrated from New England to New York.

      With reference to a circular of
the Bank of Mutual Redemption one D. H.
Rasbach of the Chittenango Bank in 1855
suggested the establishment of a similar
institution in the State of New York. It
was to be set up on a cooperative basis
like the Bank of Mutual Redemption, but
the cost of redemption was to be borne by
the members pro rata to the notes redeemed
"to their debit." This plan won the backing of numerous other country banks, which
expected that the cost of redemption would
be lowered considerably. During the ensuing discussions the original plan was
changed. A new one followed more closely
the Suffolk Bank scheme in that members
were supposed to keep deposits with the
new redemption agency and clearing house.
The amount of deposits was to be based on
the circulation of the depositing bank,
the minimum to be two thousand dollars and
the maximum two per cent of the circulation. This was a sounder policy than that
of the Suffolk Bank which rigidly based
the amount to be deposited on the capitals
of the country banks. The plan, as in all
the New York schemes, did not aim at par
collection. The agency was to receive
notes of members at one-fifth of one per

cent discount. The scheme failed because
it was not ratified by a sufficient number
of country banks.[74]

      In the fall of 1857 the plan was
taken up again, this time George W. Coyler
of Palmyra being the driving force, and
the Superintendent of the New York Banking
Department backing the proposal in his
report of December 31, 1857. That feature
of the Metropolitan Bank set-up, by which
a solvent country bank could be seriously
embarrassed or even broken for no greater
fault than a temporary lack of funds with
its New York agent, was obnoxious to the
New York official.[75] With this backing
the plan succeeded and the Albany "assorting house" described above came into being.

      By that time the matter had ac-
quired a new aspect in New York City, because the New York clearing house (established in 1856) cleared not only checks
but also notes of city banks and notes of
such country banks as had a redemption
agent in the city. This scheme worked
satisfactorily until state bank notes
passed out of existence under the tax features of the amended National Banking Act.
But the problem of foreign notes did not
disappear: since national banks could not
count the notes of other national banks as
reserves, they were interested in getting
rid of the latter as quickly as possible.
This was easy in brisk times, but in slug-
gish times the notes accumulated in the
city. At first, therefore, they were
taken care of by the clearing house; but
when the assorting proved too expensive
the Park Bank took over the job for an
annual consideration from each bank that
chose to avail itself of the service.[76]
These activities of the Park Bank continued until the redemption organization of
the United States Treasury came into being
in the 1870's and made superfluous local
and regional note redemption and clearing
arrangements for national bank notes.

      There can be no doubt that the
New England note redemption and clearing
system was superior to that of New York,
while the latter in turn was better than
that of Philadelphia. As can be inferred
from certain entries in the minutes of the
Philadelphia Board of Presidents, a considerable number of Pennsylvania country
banks redeemed their notes at par in
Philadelphia through correspondents. Occasionally the presidents resolved not to

take notes on deposit which were not re- deemed at Philadelphia. Not before 1858, however, did the Pennsylvania banks begin to cooperate in the matter of country money. On August 16, 1858 Singleton A. Mercer, president of the Farmers and Mechanics Bank of Philadelphia, then the most important bank in the city, made a proposal which was unanimously adopted, namely: "that the Farmers and Mechanics Bank will receive at par from the banks of Philadelphia the notes of all non-redeeming banks that are solvent east of the Allegheny Mountains (according to a list agreed upon from time to time between the said bank and the other banks) and cause the same to be redeemed provided that the said banks will pay to the Farmers and Mechanics Bank one quarter of one per cent upon the amount of the same and defray the losses and expenses arising therefrom and provided further that the banks hereby agree with the Farmers and Mechanics Bank that they will receive the said notes at par from the Community...."[77] This system was actually put into practice for some time as can be seen from the elaborate statistics in the minutes of the Clearing House Association. In September and November of that year, e.g., the Philadel- phia banks sent for redemption to the Farmers and Mechanics Bank $795,225 and $524,410 in country bank notes, respect- ively. In June 1859 the Farmers and Mechanics Bank proposed a further step; to extend the redemption scheme so as to in- clude also the non-redeeming banks of Pennsylvania west of the Alleghenies. Three-eighths of one per cent was proposed as the charge to the Philadelphia banks for that service. Although this offer was passed by the Associated Banks by a vote of nine to seven, it was considered as re- jected because the motion was not carried

unanimously. Since the vote indicated con- siderable dissatisfaction with the plan as it stood, in July 1859 the Farmers and Mechanics Bank dropped it altogether.[78] One can surmise that a commission of one- quarter of one per cent in addition to defraying the expenses and making good the losses of the business seemed too high to many of the Philadelphia banks.

By such action, of course, the problem of country money not redeemable in the city regained its original importance. On October 10, 1860 President Smith of the Bank of North America offered a resolution "that the notes of the banks of this Commonwealth received by the banks of this City and not redeemed here shall be re- turned for redemption in coin and that the expense shall be borne in proportion to the amount of their business with the Clearing House." This motion was discussed, amended, and tabled. In Pennsylvania as in New England and New York the matter soon lost its significance.

What distinguished the Pennsylvania system from those in the two other sections was the fact that it was not all-embracing. Some of the country banks redeemed their notes at par in Philadelphia, bearing the burden of the redemption as did the ones of New England, and only those institutions which did not do so voluntarily were to be forced by cooperative action. As in New England but unlike New York[79] the public was to benefit from the activities of the Philadelphia city banks. However, while the latter were willing to bear the ex- pense, the Boston city banks forced that burden upon the unwilling New England country banks. Finally, in contrast to both New England and New York where note redemption was combined with note clear- ing, Pennsylvania was backward, aiming at most at a redemption system.

APPENDIX I

The following bill was presented to the grand jury of Windsor County, Vermont, in 1808. The basis for the legal procedure was a demand on the Vermont State Bank to pay its notes in specie.

STATE OF VERMONT,
Windsor county, ss

At the honorable supreme court of judicature now sitting at Woodstock, for and within the county and State aforesaid, the jurors within and for the body of the county of Windsor aforesaid, in court here duly empannelled and sworn, upon their oath, present: That Jireh Durkee, late of Royalton, in the county of Windsor aforesaid, and now residing in Boston, in the Commonwealth of Massachusetts, being an evil-disposed person, and not minding to get his living by truth and honest labor, but contriving how he might injuriously obtain from the State of Vermont, and the good citizens thereof, and from the good citizens of the neighboring States, money to support his idle and profligate way of life, and diminish and destroy the resources of the State of Vermont; and rendering it difficult and impossible for the good citizens thereof to obtain money or current bank notes for the payment of their just debts, and thereby to increase the profits of his injurious speculations; heretofore, to wit, on the 27th day of April, 1808, with force and arms, at Woodstock, in the county of Windsor aforesaid, with intent to draw from the Vermont State Bank, at the office of discount and deposite thereof, at Woodstock aforesaid, the specie there deposited by the directors thereof, for the purpose of redeeming the notes by them issued, and with intent thereby to prevent the president and directors of said bank from making loans of money or bank notes to the good citizens of this State, by which a benefit would accrue to the said citizens in their commercial interests, and in the payment of their just debts, and by which an interest would accrue to this State, enriching the treasury thereof, and with intent to exchange the specie which he should so draw from said bank for bank notes at an amount below their nominal value, that he might thereby realize a filthy gain to himself, at the expense and loss of this State, and with intent to continue and repeat the draughts upon said bank for specie, and the exchange of the same specie for bank notes as aforesaid, so often as he should be able so to do, did sort, collect, and get into his possession bank notes, which had before been issued by the president and directors of said bank, payable at their said office of discount and deposite at Woodstock, to a large amount, to wit: to the amount of $9,000; and having the intent aforesaid, he, the said Durkee, did then and there present the same bank notes last aforesaid at the said office of discount and deposite where the same were made payable as aforesaid: the said president and directors have been obliged to pay, and then and there did pay, to said Durkee, in specie, as aforesaid; which doings of the said Durkee are to the great injury and oppression of the good citizens of this State, who, from time to time have been, still are, and hereafter may, be, in need of obtaining loans of money or bank notes at the bank aforesaid, to the great obstruction of benefit of the laws of this State, establishing said bank and the branches thereof, "to the great diminution of the established revenue of this State, to the evil example of all others in like cases offending, and against the peace and dignity of the State.

Reprinted from U.S. 25th Congr., 2d sess., House Executive Document 79, 110, 111. This is apparently the indictment to which Nathan Appleton refers in Examination, 4.

APPENDIX II

ORGANIZATION OF THE FOREIGN MONEY DEPARTMENT OF THE SUFFOLK BANK

The Superintendent of the Foreign Money Department shall have charge of, and account of, all business of the department.

He shall receive all Bank Bills, checks &c. delivered to this department, and account to the Cashier for the same.

He shall at the close of each days business, receive the Trunks containing Bank Notes, which may have been assorted during the day, from the several sections, with the keys thereto, and place them in the Vaults of the Bank, as also all other property belonging to the Bank in his department, and shall lock them in said Vault and deliver the keys to the Cashier. He shall in the morning of each days business receive from the Cashier, the keys of the Foreign Money Vault, and deliver therefrom, the Trunks containing the Bank Bills of the several Sections, to the same Clerk whose duty it is to assort, prove, and place the same in packages.

He shall have the general supervision of the persons employed in the Department, and he shall immediately inform the President, if any one is inattentive, or neglects the duties assigned to him or if he knows or has suspicion of a want of integrity in any one employed in his department. And if he should neglect to report the same to the President he shall be held answerable to the Bank, for any loss which it may sustain by negligence or want of integrity in such persons.

He shall have at the close of each days business all accounts of his department made up, and correctly balanced.

He shall require the persons who receive the money from the Boston Banks to carry with him a Trunk, in which he shall place the money he receives and keep it carefully locked until delivered.

1st Assistant Clerk, Foreign Money Department

It shall be his duty, under direction of the superintendent to receive and receipt for all packages of Bills, checks &c. delivered to the Department, to open them; and take therefrom, all letters addressed to the Cashier, and deliver the same to him, the Bank Bills he will divide among the several sections, to be counted and assorted.

He shall keep a record of all Bank bills delivered to the sections, or officers of the Bank.

He shall render each day, at the close of business, an account of all these Receipts and Payments to the Superintendent.

He shall have the supervision of the Foreign Money Department in the absence of the Superintendent unless otherwise ordered by the President.

He shall report immediately to the President, any neglect, or inattention to their duties, or any want of integrity, or any suspicion of it, in any person employed in the Department, and he shall be held accountable for any loss which the Bank may sustain from those causes, if he fails to give such information to the President.

2nd Assistant Clerk, F. M. Department

He shall give the Bills of this Bank in exchange for Foreign money to parties as directed by the Superintendent.

He shall at the close of each days business render an account to the Superintendent of all money received and paid by him.

He shall attend to other duties of the department assigned to him by the Superintendent.

He shall report immediately to the President any neglect, or inattention to their duties, or any want of integrity, or suspicion thereof, in any person employed in the Department, and he shall be held accountable for any loss which the Bank may sustain from these causes if he fails to give such information to the President.

Clerks of Sections, F. M. Department

It shall be the duty of the Clerk of the second Section, in the morning of each days business, to receive the Bank Bills of the different sections from the Superintendent, to assort and prove the correctness of the same, by an account made up from the return of the several Sections. To see the whole

strapped up and delivered to the Cashier or
Teller, with a list of the same.

The Clerk of each section, shall have
the general supervision of those employed in
his Section. He shall receive such packages
of Bank Bills as the distributing Clerk may
deliver to him to examine, sort, and count.

He shall immediately return to the Superintendent all packages in which he finds any
error.

He shall balance his cash, at the close
of each days business, and pack all Bills
into Trunks and lock the same. The Trunks
and keys he will then deliver to the Superintendent.

He will require of those employed in his
Section, to place their initials on the
straps of each parcel of Bills that they may
count, and cause lists of them to be made
and placed on file.

He shall keep order in his Section, and
report immediately to the President, any re-
missness, negligence, or misconduct of any
person employed therein.

APPENDIX III

The fight between the Suffolk Bank
and the Bank of Mutual Redemption was carried into the Boston Clearing House
Association and in consequence the minutes
of the Clearing House Association and of
the Clearing House Committee throw some
interesting sidelights on the matter.

Early in 1858 the Boston banks
seem to have become uneasy, and on the 9th
and 13th of February the Association and
its Committee, respectively, discussed the
methods of dealing with foreign money and
the possibilities of improving them, but
without coming to any conclusions. The
struggle began in earnest when the Bank of
Mutual Redemption asked to be admitted to the
facilities of the clearing house.[80] Since
the Clearing House Committee itself did
not dare decide that question, on July 13,
1858 it brought it before a session of the
Association. The incipient fight could
mean survival or destruction of the New
England par collection and note clearing
system, and its vital importance to the
interests of the whole Boston banking fraternity was immediately recognized. As a
matter of fact, the question agitated and
irritated the Associated Banks almost more
than the panic of the preceding year, as
can be seen from the length of the minutes
and from the heated discussions recorded
therein.

The attitude of the associated
banks was vacillating, but their sympathies
were with the Suffolk Bank system. They
felt that before any injury was inflicted
on that system the Associated Banks as
well as the community at large should be
well informed as to the malcontents and
the validity of their objections to the
system as such and to its present management. The Boston banks, as a matter of
fact, could not consider as valid any complaints on the part of country banks about
the check exerted by the Suffolk Bank on
their circulation, nor about the amount of
specie they were forced to hold. At that
time Massachusetts bank paper was circulating to the amount of 17.5 million dollars;
while the specie reserves of all Massachusetts banks amounted to 10.8 million.
Of these sums the Boston banks had 5.5
million dollars in circulation and held 9
million dollars in specie, whereas the
country banks had 12 million dollars in circulation and held 1.8 million in specie. Of
the four hundred and fifty banks in New
England at that time three-fourths were
located in Massachusetts.

Notwithstanding their sympathy with
the Suffolk Bank system the Associated Banks
were very reluctant to unleash an open war
and so they invited President Carney of the
Bank of Mutual Redemption to state his case.
He was asked what country banks were backing his enterprise and whether he intended
to compete or to come to terms with the
Suffolk Bank. These questions Carney could
not answer without jeopardizing the interests which he represented. When he refused
to answer, the Clearing House Association
was unable to take a strong stand since not
even John Amory Davis,[81] the president of
the Suffolk Bank, then a member of the

Clearing House Committee, manifested much fighting spirit. He figured the cost of the redemption business of his bank at $65,000 per annum, while the interest on all the permanent deposits was barely sufficient to cover these expenses. He maintained that the Suffolk Bank was not anxious to continue the redemption and clearing business, but on the contrary was willing to relinquish it, when the Association thought such action would be beneficial to the community. It is impossible to gauge if he was sincere or merely tactically taking the best line. To make things worse for the Suffolk Bank, the ranks of the Associated Banks were not closed. G. W. Thayer, one of the founders of the Boston Clearing House, although not an influential member of it, and Andrew T. Hall, one of its founders and leaders, backed the new enterprise among whose incorporators they had been.[87] Again, the Granite Bank, because of a misunderstanding, or so its president Alpheus Hardy claimed, had also subscribed to the Bank of Mutual Redemption. Thus after much discussion the question of admission of the Bank of Mutual Redemption to the Clearing House was referred back to the Clearing House Committee.

When the Committee again took up the matter it was joined by the leaders of the two contending groups, a fact which indicates the sense of fair dealing typical of the Boston Clearing House in those years.[83] While Thayer represented the interests of the new concern, Caleb Stetson, one of the early directors and then (1857-1868) president of the Shoe and Leather Bank, fought for those of the old. With the backing of Thomas Lamb, Stetson drew up the committee report which is still of interest as setting forth the whole problem lucidly. The drafting of this clear and well-formulated report was facilitated by a circular letter sent out in the meantime by the Bank of Mutual Redemption. The letter contained the plans and purposes of the institution.

The committee report which follows considered some of Carney's intentions "new and untried in the science of banking." (It is probable that Stetson referred to the bankers' bank feature of the scheme.)

The real questions for consideration are: Shall the banks of Boston adopt a new principle as basis for redemption or maintain the Suffolk System? Are the banks of Boston and New England ready to become partners, assume the risk, and adopt a new and untried principle, and abandon at once the Suffolk System?... Have we duly considered the consequences which may arise out of the new relation which would exist among the Associated Banks of Boston by having two banks of redemption conducting their business upon such a basis of action as they propose? Will the banks of redemption, somewhat antagonistic in the principles of action, be conducive of harmony to the New England banks generally, or will it only be the beginning of a war of extermination upon one or the other of the combattants?

Do not the Associated Banks of Boston when admitting a new member pledge it assistance and support and by such act give it a public credit?

Are the banks of New England who do not wish to try an experiment prepared to contribute to the new Bank of Mutual Redemption and to the Suffolk Bank an equal amount of money in order to induce harmony of action? Can the members of the Clearing House consistently admit a new member upon the avowed principle to compel the banks of Boston to support both institutions? Have the banks of New England only considered the importance of public confidence and harmony in the action of the banks in times of stringency and contraction of the issues....

Is not the charter of the Bank of Mutual Redemption peculiar in its character, objectionable in many of its features, being inconsistent with important provisions of the Banking Laws of Massachusetts, and therefore does not stand in the same relation to the Associated Banks of Boston and other banks incorporated in Massachusetts and other New England States?

Your Committee are of opinion that harmony of action and unity of purpose is an essential element in banking and that the commercial interests are always in jeopardy when ever a war exists upon the currency. We are of opinion that want of harmony in the action of two banks attempting to do the business of one will tend to disturb the whole business of New England.

Your Committee believes that the banks and the public have entire confidence in the general management of the Suffolk Bank as a bank for the redemption of the currency of New England.

From these considerations it is the

opinion of your Committee that unless some
mutual arrangement shall first be entered
into between the Suffolk Bank and the Bank of
Mutual Redemption upon which they will act in
harmony in their business of redemption it
will be unwise, impolitic [underlined in the
minutes] and inexpedient for the Association
of Banks in this City to admit at present such
new bank as a member of the Clearing House.

The Committee therefore suggested
that the Suffolk Bank be supported and
that the admittance of its new competitor
be postponed.

This report was adopted with eighteen yeas and four nays. Fortunately for
the historian some officer of the Clearing
House noted in pencil how the various
banks voted. The "Nays" came from the
Exchange Bank (i.e., George W. Thayer),
the Webster Bank (i.e., William Thomas),[84]
the Howard Banking Company (presided over
by Charles Ellis), and the Maverick Bank.
All of them were young enterprises, in
contrast to most of the friends of the
Suffolk Bank, and were probably interested
in the experiments of the Bank of Mutual
Redemption.

During the summer of 1858 the mat-
ter was discussed by the presidents of the
Boston banks outside of the Clearing
House.[85] A meeting took place in which a
committee was appointed consisting of
Thomas Lamb of the New England Bank,
Andrew T. Hall of the Tremont Bank, Caleb
Stetson of the Shoe and Leather Bank,
William Thomas of the Webster Bank, and
George W. Thayer of the Exchange Bank. Its
purpose was to inquire into the Suffolk
Bank System and to determine whether actions in support of that system were feasible. The first three men were friends of
the Suffolk Bank, the last two its enemies. The majority of this Committee reported to a meeting of the bank presidents
held on October 8, 1858, coming out strongly in favor of supporting the Suffolk Bank:
They doubted if the Bank of Mutual Redemption would be able to fill its place. In
the discussion of the report, however, the
other two members of the committee voiced
their dissent. Thomas felt that those
banks which wanted to withdraw from the
Suffolk Bank should be allowed to do so
without any molestation, since many bankers
had condemned the recent course of that
bank. Thayer agreed with Thomas, but

suggested the establishment of a New
England bank-note clearing house. The
meeting ended nowhere, the matter being
referred back to the committee for further
investigation into the working of the systems of both banks. Apparently this meeting influenced the Suffolk Bank, which
gave in, announcing its decision in a circular letter dated October 9.

Under these circumstances it was a
foregone conclusion that when the matter
of admission of the Bank of Mutual Redemption came up again before the Clearing
House Association on October 9 the bank
would be admitted as a member. But now
the form of admission became a subject of
etiquette. The friends of the Bank of
Mutual Redemption wanted the stigma of the
former non-admittance erased by an invitation to join the Clearing House Association
(motion by Mr. Ellis of the Howard Company),
whereas most of the banks refused to concede that much. Andrew T. Hall and Waldo
Flint, their spokesmen, defeated the motion; but the latter immediately moved that
the Bank of Mutual Redemption be admitted.
Hall and Thayer, opponent and friend of
the Bank of Mutual Redemption, respectively,
seconded the motion. Then the Bank of
Mutual Redemption was admitted by unanimous
vote and, as far as the Associated Banks were
concerned, the fight ended. Carney became
at once a very active member of the Clearing House.

Some years later, Carney became
involved in another fight with the Boston
Clearing House. Since his conduct in this
struggle was typical of the character and
methods used by the man who destroyed the
Suffolk Bank system it is here described.
After having subscribed to the loan of
7-30's (treasury notes) in 1861 the Associated Banks of Boston resolved[86] to use these
notes as the basis of clearing house loan
certificates which in turn were to be used
in the settlement of clearing house balances. Although the issue of the 7-30's
subscribed by the Associated Banks was
delayed, the Bank of Mutual Redemption in
some way had obtained possession of a certain amount of them, probably issued to
private investors. These Carney was determined to use, since his bank was then
in straightened circumstances. The controversy started when he applied for the
issue of $90,000 worth of clearing house
loan certificates against his 7-30

treasury notes. The Clearing House Committee replied that as no other bank had as yet received any treasury notes and as it was unlikely that any such notes would be received by them in the near future no date for the issue of certificates could be set.[87] A few days later Carney repeated his request and received the same reply. Hardly a week elapsed before he again demanded clearing house loan certificates against his 7-30's and this time the matter was brought before a meeting of the Clearing House Association. Thomas Lamb, as a member of the Clearing House Committee, stated the case, whereupon Carney rose and declared it mandatory for the Committee, under the vote of August 27, 1861, to issue clearing house certificates against his treasury notes. If the banks had acted in good faith he was entitled to have them. He was not altogether wrong in this argument for the New York and Philadelphia clearing houses actually issued clearing house loan certificates under the original agreement before the treasury notes were received by the banks. To checkmate Carney, John Amory Davis, president of the Suffolk Bank, moved that the aforementioned original arrangement should apply only to treasury notes received under the agreement entered into by the Associated Banks of New York, Boston, and Philadelphia; and this motion was carried. However there was no quorum at this meeting of October 23, nor was there a quorum at the next meeting on October 30.

New trouble arose on Friday, January 10, 1862, when the Bank of Mutual Redemption refused to pay its balances in specie, using demand notes in lieu thereof, although at that moment it was the established policy of the clearing house associations not to use them in the settlement of balances.[88] At a meeting of the Association on January 13 this action was declared a gross violation of the rules of the Clearing House Association and it was stated that under the constitution the case warranted suspension of the bank concerned. At this point the banks became suspicious. At a Clearing House Committee meeting of February 13 the reports of the Bank of Mutual Redemption were discussed. Lack of liquidity was obvious, although otherwise the bank was sound. At that moment the State Bank Commissioner applied to the court for an injunction to stay certain proceedings of the Bank of Mutual Redemption which he considered illegal. In March 1862 once more demand notes were tendered by Carney at the Clearing House in settlement of the balance of his bank, and once more they were refused. Thereupon on April 3 a meeting of the Associated Banks voted to expel the Bank of Mutual Redemption. It is worth noting that the Suffolk Bank was among the few who voted in favor of its former rival. One cannot fail to sense through the dry phraseology of the minutes, the strong feelings of those concerned. Consequently, on April 2, 1862 the Bank of Mutual Redemption by request withdrew from the Clearing House; only to be readmitted on January 19, 1863.[89]

Carney himself gave the following explanation of his actions in this matter:[90] as long as specie was the only legal tender, Carney conceded that the Clearing House banks were within their rights when they requested the settling of all balances in specie. However, when the United States issued legal tender notes, he felt that the situation was changed and that, being legal tender, these notes could not be refused by anyone when tendered in payment of lawful obligations. This question was of vital importance for the Bank of Mutual Redemption. It could not refuse to accept legal tender notes in its redemption and note clearing business and yet it was forced to buy specie with them at a loss, in order to settle its obligations at the Boston Clearing House. For a few days prior to demand notes becoming legal tender, the Clearing House permitted the settlement of balances with them because the Boston banks were still under the necessity of paying for their subscriptions of 7-30's, which could be done either in specie or in demand notes. During those few days, so Carney claimed, some of the Boston banks unloaded demand notes on his bank, which was a creditor bank at the Clearing House at that moment, while shortly thereafter when it was a debtor they refused to take back the same notes because the policy of the Clearing House Association in the meantime had been rescinded.

Chapter V

THE SAFETY FUND SYSTEM

While the Suffolk Bank System was built up exclusively by entrepreneurs and full-fledged central banking, to be discussed in the next chapter, was developed by one great business leader during the years in which he possessed the backing of the federal government, the other two main achievements of the second period were, as already mentioned, due to state legislators. Both of them, but especially the earlier one, the New York Safety Fund System, had an importance far beyond the immediate practical results. In passing the Safety Fund Act of 1829 or, to be exact, the Act to create a fund for the benefit of the creditors of certain monied corporations and for other purposes,[1] American legislators for the first time recognized an obligation on the part of the public authorities to protect the creditors of banks. In the last analysis this attitude and the resulting policy may have sprung from the concept of banks as chartered for the public benefit, a concept which was characteristic of the years during which most of the legislators of the 1820's had been growing up.

I

The purpose of the act, the protection of bank creditors, was to be attained in two different ways. First, it introduced the insurance principle (which implied mutual responsibility) into the field of banking; and, secondly, it established permanent bank control by special, qualified officials (bank commissioners). While the adoption of the former principle was an innovation as far as banking was concerned, the latter progress was but one more step in a development which was already more than fifty years old, as will be discussed later in more detail. From these two main features of the act were derived two different lines of the future development of American banking.

The New York Safety Fund System sprang from the brain of Joshua Forman,

whom Van Buren characterized as "a plain, but practical and farseeing man," but who, in the eyes of contemporary representatives of business, was "a certain fanciful visionary."[2] Forman (1777-1848), a native of New York State, after a college education read law and settled in Onondaga Hollow. Thence in 1819 he removed to a small clearing in the woods, the present site of Syracuse, of which he is considered the founder. Like other lawyers in similarly insignificant places, he made a living out of the confusion of land titles at that time.[3]

But Forman also took a keen interest in business and public affairs. In business he seems to have possessed a touch of creative genius. Besides building a tavern and gristmills, the usual accompaniments of young communities, he organized a company to work the gypsum deposits of that region and improved the methods of manufacturing salt. Most important, however, in this early period of Forman's life was his connection with the Erie Canal. Although not the first to conceive of a canal linking the Atlantic Ocean with the Great Lakes, he probably hit on the idea independently. He fostered, promoted, and advocated the canal in press and legislature and procured the first legislative action in connection with it.[4] In this promotion he showed himself to possess that moral courage which he would need later when suggesting his unheard-of banking scheme. Forman's connection with the Erie Canal is interesting; for this canal had first been conceived by the father of American country banking, Elkanah Watson; and in the Middle West, too, there were certain men interested in both sound banking and canals.

In order to comprehend Forman's achievement[5] and his influence on the development of American banking the background against which he acted must be understood. In 1828 the state of New York possessed forty incorporated banks. The charters of thirty-one of them would expire within the next few years. Consequently, they made a concerted effort to obtain from the legislature an unconditional renewal. They secured the election of legislators favorable to their plans and brought about an alliance with the exponents of internal improvements. However, besides the strong opposition of public opinion they faced an unfavorable legal set-up: under the New York constitution of 1821 a two-thirds majority in both houses was required for granting bank charters. Therefore their attempt failed. In this situation Forman submitted his constructive suggestions to Martin Van Buren (1787-1862), then governor of New York. It was, in turn, Van Buren's contribution to the development of American banking that he saw the merits of Forman's ideas and that after they had won the approval of his financial advisers he transmitted them to the legislature.

In this case as in many others in history, it is difficult to decide what actually prompted Van Buren's actions. In his Autobiography[6] he states that he had always been opposed to the multiplication of banks, but that he could not at that time see any possibility of arresting the trend. Therefore, so he claimed, he had shifted his attention to the problem of how to protect the helpless public against bank failures. Apprised of Van Buren's general views, Joshua Forman submitted his scheme which so impressed the governor that he presented it, together with his own views on the subject, to those whom he regarded "as the most competent and trustworthy bankers of New York and Albany."[7] After a full discussion they settled on a plan which was submitted to the legislature in the annual message of January 6, 1829.

This account, however, is contradicted in the contemporary literature by a "communication" from one who was characterized as a well informed man without official capacity and who was obviously bitterly hostile to the governor.[8] This person claimed that on presentation of Forman's plan Van Buren discovered immediately that it could become "a mighty engine of political power" through the control of the whole banking system of the state by commissioners, if these men were only "of the right political stamp." Regardless of the fact that the source is unreliable, the master politician, Van Buren (whose autobiography at every turn

shows his incapacity to think along economic lines, as well as the overgrowth of politics in his reasoning), might well have been influenced in part by the motives which his enemies imputed to him.

Van Buren's message of January 6, 1829, in which he submitted Forman's scheme, starts out by surveying New York banking.[9] The governor recognized that the state could not do without banks and also that it could not rely on the Bank of the United States alone. Consequently two courses were open. The state could recharter the old banks, if they were shown to be sound, or it could replace them by new institutions of another type. The only other type of bank in existence at that time was the state bank with branches, either financed and managed exclusively by the state or financed and managed by the state and private capitalists in cooperation. Van Buren while abhorring the existing banks was not averse to a single state bank with branches. On the other hand, he recognized that change from one banking system to another would inevitably result in loss so that it would be wiser to retain the existing chartered banks, if in connection with the renewal of their charters, measures of "safety and stability" could be imposed on them. For this purpose Forman's "sensible and apparently well considered" plan seemed to open up possibilities, and therefore the governor outlined this proposal in his message, without, however, mentioning the name of its author.

Forman's plan, as put forward by Van Buren "propose[d] to made all the banks responsible for any loss the public [might] sustain by the failure of any one or more of them...." "The idea is not entirely new to the commercial world," he went on, "although it has not heretofore been applied in this form.... It is confidently believed by competent judges that the form in which it is proposed to enforce the responsibility, being an annual and adequate appropriation of a part of their income towards a common fund, to be placed under the control of the state - the complete supervision over the institutions...in connection with the authority of the state - the consequent high character and correspondent circulation it would give to our paper... with other advantages would make" the plan acceptable to all concerned.

As already indicated, Van Buren did not suggest the scheme without being certain of the support of at least a part of the banking fraternity. Forman, who in the meantime had come to Albany upon invitation, seems to have been sent to New York City in order to sell the plan. [10] (It cannot be ascertained whether this trip took place, if it ever did, before or after the sixth of January, 1829, the date of the governor's message.) Be that as it may, in January Forman worked in Albany on the formulation of his plan and on the 24th of that month he addressed the following letter to Van Buren: [11]

I have at length succeeded in getting the exposition of my Bank project in a state that I am willing to submit it to investigation without fear of any of its principles being successfully attacked - although from having paid more attention to the matter than the manner the language may be more assailable - as a whole while it points to the public good for its object it furnishes inducements for all the parties in interest to unite in its support except perhaps those who expect to be paid for in hand....

The influence of banks upon the property and morals of a free people is only exceeded by that of the press - and their proper regulation with that view an object of primary importance in the eyes of wise and reflecting men - Even many of the bank managers have at length come to see the evils of their old system and are changing their policy and if the exposition of the causes of those evils would do no more good than by opening the eyes of those concerned and produce a better practice just good will be attained by the latter part, which I read carefully to [illegible initials, probably an Albany banker] who admitted every statement of it true but thought having things as they are he could make more money.

The "exposition" which Forman mentions in this letter was made public when on January 26, 1829 the governor followed up the pertinent part of the annual message by a special letter to the Assembly. [12] Probably such a letter was badly needed at that moment since in the meantime bank officers and stockholders, especially in New York City, had become alarmed and were organizing a strong opposition to the plan. [13] They considered, or at least pretended to consider, it as designed "to cast on solvent banks an immediate and unqualified responsibility for all those that might become insolvent." In his letter Van Buren brushed aside this argument. He gave the discussion tactically a new turn, thereby dodging the issue. It was taken for granted at that time that banks in consideration of the charters, i.e., of the privileges which they received through their charters, would pay bonuses to the commonwealths which chartered them. Therefore Van Buren claimed that the scheme proposed "to substitute for the payment of a gross sum [bonus] to the state, which has some time been exacted as a consideration for the exclusive privilege, the creation of a permanent fund, to be held as a security against all losses which our citizens may hereafter sustain through the failure of banks."

As already mentioned, this communication by Van Buren was accompanied by Forman's "exposition" [14] which gives a clear picture of his motives and ideas. In contrast to Van Buren he did not dodge, but clearly defined, the fundamental issue, describing at the same time the origin of his reasoning:

The propriety of making the banks liable for each other was suggested by the relations of the Hong Merchants in Canton, where a number of men, each acting separately, have by a grant of the Government the exclusive right of trading with foreigners, and are made liable for the debts of each in case of failure. The case of our banks is very similar; they enjoy in common the exclusive right of making a paper currency for the people of the State and by the same rule should in common be answerable for that paper. The abstractly just principle, which has stood the test of experience for seventy years, and under which the bond of a Hong merchant has acquired a credit over the whole world not exceeded by that of any other security, modified and adapted to the milder features of our republican institutions, constitute the basis of the system. [15]

So far the basic principle. The ends which Forman hoped to achieve by its application were threefold: he wanted to produce good bank management, to secure the public against loss from bank failures, and to furnish a sound and well-regulated currency. In order to reach these goals he was not afraid "to interfere with the interests and policy of the existing banks where they interfere with the public good." This advanced point of view was not in line with Forman's general economic creed emphatically stated at the end of the memorandum. However, he did not see this inconsistency while he was elaborating his specific banking theory: Paper currency is convertible into specie at all times and if well secured is as good as specie. Superabundance of such currency, however, causes rising prices and has serious consequences, (as does lack of convertibility and of security back of bank issues). Since therefore banks can deeply effect the interests of the community they ought to be considered and treated as public institutions and to be put under regulations in order to prevent their injuring the community. It was not enough that their issues were regulated by their charters, because charter clauses could easily be disregarded. Corporative property (general assets, to use a modern term) was not security enough for circulating notes, especially since banks acted independently of, and often were even hostile to, each other.

On the basis of such principles and banking theory, Forman drafted his elaborate reform program. Some points of this program are not pertinent to this chapter, since they were in line with the usual reform proposals of that time.[16] One point is of great interest, but only in another context:[17] Forman added to his basic program the suggestion that the capital of the banks be invested in government stock "or [be] put...out on bonds and mortgages." However, he himself doubted whether the suggestion, intended to "render the system perfect," could be accomplished at that time, and in all probability he was more or less forced to embody it in his memorandum. The essentials of this proposal, alien to the original scheme, were contributed by Isaac Bronson, who presented them to James Alexander Hamilton. The latter, in turn, proposed the combination of Bronson's and Forman's ideas to Van Buren as early as December 1828. Or more correctly, he recommended Bronson's plan, and suggested that one "superadd" Forman's basic idea. The opposite took place. Bronson's ideas were added in the memorandum to Forman's original plan, which actually became the pivot of the reform.[18]

Since Bronson's pet idea of restricting banks to the discounting of short term "real paper" was also included in Forman's "exposition," and also because Bronson was influential at that time, it can be assumed that he was one of Van Buren's financial advisers.[19]

Turning now to the essentials of Forman's plan, one finds them to consist of the two suggestions already mentioned.[20] A safety fund was to be raised by annual payments by each bank chartered under the proposed act according to its capital. The fund was to be applied to the payment of the debts of such participating banks as should fail, and was to be replenished when diminished by such payments. It was to accumulate until it amounted to $500,000 or $1,000,000. This proposal became the law of the land except that the upper limit of the fund was _de facto_ set at 3 per cent of the combined capitals of the banks operating under the act. The proposal referred to debts of banks in general not only to debts arising from note issues. It can be taken for granted that Forman and the legislators, who were no experts in banking although they were the ones who passed on the plan and adopted it, for practical purposes identified notes and bank debts, an identification which later proved to have been a serious error. Nevertheless they can hardly be blamed. If even Biddle could not foresee the development of the deposit and check business, such vision was not to be expected of Forman and the other men concerned here. The sponsors of the plan, on the other hand, intended to secure noteholders and depositors alike.[21] Thus from the outset the germ of decay came to be implanted in the Safety Fund System by which the otherwise well-devised institution was doomed to an early death.

Forman's second important suggestion, through which he gained considerable influence on the development of American banking, was the proposal to establish a board of bank commissioners with supervisory and reporting functions. Forman himself did not claim any originality in this idea and perhaps did not even realize the progress implied therein. The Banking Committee of the Assembly, when reporting on the scheme, was anxious to show that supervision of banks was a well-established practice. In so doing it referred to the

charters of the Bank of North America and
of the First and Second Banks of the
United States and to the banking laws of
Vermont, Rhode Island, and South Carolina.

In fact, when Forman suggested a
board of bank commissioners to examine
banks, he took but one forward step, albeit a very important one, in a development of many decades. In America charter
obligations which required banks to make
reports and to submit to examinations
resulted originally from federal or state
investment in banks. As late as 1837 two
New Orleans banks refused to permit an
examination on the ground that "as the
State held no stock in the bank and no
direct interest therein the board of
directors...would not recognize the right
of the legislature to inspect the books
of the bank,"[22] a point of view held by
Robert Morris as early as 1786.

Bank examinations were imposed on
many early American banks, however, and
the typical form of such examinations indicates their Mercantilist origin. They
grew out of the eighteenth-century suggestion that "banking on private credit"
should be open to everyone. In return for
the freedom to engage in the business of
banking (as contemplated, for instance,
in Sir James Steuarts' work), the enterprises in question should be obliged, according to this theory, to keep their
books open for inspection. "However, the
inspecting officials were not supposed to
make all-round examinations. Their
power, according to Steuart, was to be
limited, and such limitation, as proposed,
was completely in line with his basic
ideas on this type of bank and the function of capital in banking. The public
should know the amount of notes issued and
the extent and nature of security pledged,
but the examining authorities 'have no
business to examine the state of the bank
cash.' 'The bank may be without a shilling in its coffers and still its paper be
so good as if it had a million.' In this
way seems to have come into the charter of
the First Bank of the United States that
clause which permits the examination of
certain general accounts in the books of
the bank and nothing else."[23] Incidentally, the fact that this specific form of
bank examination was adopted for the first
American banks seems to this author to
be another proof of the thesis that early
American banking was influenced by Mercantilist "banking on private credit."

Wilfred Stanley Lake,[24] in his
excellent Ph.D. thesis, has shown convincingly that the first step toward modern
bank examinations was taken in the 1792
charter of the Union Bank of Boston which,
in contrast to the Mercantilist type of
bank-book examinations, permitted all
round bank examinations such as were
adopted in the following decades all over
America. However, the right to examine
banks, down to Forman's proposal of a
board of bank commissioners, rested customarily in the legislatures or, as in the
case of the Second Bank of the United
States, with the Secretary of the Treasury.
If examinations were to be conducted, a
committee was appointed by the legislature
or, as in the case of the examination of
the Second Bank of the United States of
1833, an agent was named by the Secretary.[25]
This procedure implied that although in
the first decades of the nineteenth century banks were often forced to report
regularly, they were not as yet obliged
to submit to regular examinations. Forman's
proposal and the work done by the legislative committee of the New York State
Assembly which shaped that proposal resulted in making examinations both periodical
and, at the same time, the work of expert
officials appointed for that very purpose.

The extent to which bank control
was habitually exerted when the second
period opened can be seen from the 15th
article of the 11th section of the charter
of the Second Bank of the United States.
It provided "that the officer at the head
of the Treasury Department of the United
States shall be furnished from time to
time, as often as he may require, not
exceeding once a week, with statements of
the amount of the capital stock of the
said corporation and of the debts due to
the same; of the moneys deposited therein;
of the notes in circulation and of the
specie in hand; and shall have the right
to inspect such general accounts in the
books of the bank as shall relate to the
said statement: Provided, that this shall
not be constructed to imply a right of
inspecting the account of any private
individual or individuals with the bank."[26]
If one compares section 15 of the New York
Safety Fund Act with the above clause of
the charter of the Second Bank of the

United States one recognizes forthwith the achievement:[27] "Three persons to be styled the Bank Commissioners of the State of New York shall be appointed...whose duties...it shall be, once at least in every four months, to visit every monied corporation upon which the provisions of this act shall be binding; and thoroughly to inspect the affairs of the said monied corporations; to examine all the books, papers, notes, and bonds and other evidences of debt of said corporations, to compare the funds and property of the said corporations with the statements made by them as hereinafter provided; to ascertain the quantity of specie the said corporations have on hand; and generally to make such other inquiries as may be necessary to ascertain the actual condition of said corporations and their ability to fulfill all the engagements made by them."[28] This section 15 of the act was supplemented by section 17 which gave the commissioners the power to examine, upon oath, officers, servants, and agents of the banks and any other person in relation to their affairs and condition.

Forman himself considered the establishment of a permanent board of officials who were to control banks regularly as a decisive feature of his plan. He proposed the election or appointment of such a board or the cooperation of electees and appointees on such a board to supervise the activities of banks, which he distrusted, as is shown by the following justification of his suggestion: "No mechanism can be so arranged as long to keep in order...much less a moral machinery in which human passions and frailties have so great an influence." After this statement, which would be logical for an exponent of state interference in business, one is somewhat surprised to find him recommending his plan as a whole on contrary grounds, thereby making concessions to contemporary public opinion and to the "Weltanschauung" of the business groups which he had to win over for his plan. These opposite grounds were thus stated: "This natural, safe, and easy mode of banking is founded on the immutable laws of circulation and commerce - certain in their operation as the laws of attraction and gravitation, which regulate the motion of bodies on the earth and chain it in its orbit."

Forman's plan was submitted to the Committee on the Incorporation and Alteration of the Charters of Banking and Insurance Companies of the Assembly.[29] The chairman of this committee was Alonzo C. Paige (1797-1868), a lawyer and judge in good standing who is supposed to have drafted Forman's plan into a workable bill.[30] At the same time Forman himself seems to have been in touch with the committee during the decisive weeks. The bill was characterized by a contemporary New York official concerned with banking as a compromise to obviate the necessity of enacting personal liability of bank stockholders as envisaged in the New York constitution.

When the committee submitted its bill to the plenum of the Assembly the chances of its passing were doubtful. The New York City and Albany banks were very much opposed to the scheme, an opposition which lasted for years after the act had been passed. A few years later an anonymous pamphleteer thus summed up their main objection:

The gravest objection to the system, is the creation of the Bank fund, by the half per cent annual contribution of the banks. This is represented by the "Union Committee," as being one of those defects "endangering the soundness of the currency," and also "unjust," inasmuch as it renders banks responsible for others, over which they have no control; as offering a "premium in favor of misconduct, at the expense of those which are wisely and cautiously managed;" and "more particularly unjust, in reference to the city of New York, inasmuch as the tax is laid in proportion to the capital and not to the circulation."[31]

The parliamentary situation was confused at that moment. In the preliminary conversations, the New York City and probably also the Albany banks had made the diversion of the existing half-per cent capital stock tax and the permission to charge more than 6 per cent interest for short-term loans, conditions for their taking charters under the law to be enacted.[32] However, most of the legislators were unwilling to divert the capital stock tax into the safety fund[33] and at the same time they were afraid that the imposition of an additional contribution of one-half

per cent would increase the cost of loans
for borrowers. Thus there was danger that
the bill would be killed through the concerted action of the New York City and
Albany banks.

     The bill was saved, however, by
Abijah Mann, a member of the Assembly who
detected strategical possibilities in the
proposed increase of the legal rate for
short-term loans,[34] although he himself
would have preferred the enactment of personal liability of bank stockholders, he
fell in with the plans of the friends of
the measure whose only chance lay in breaking up the alliance of the New York City
and Albany banks against the bill. (The
country banks were in favor of the bill
anyway because it promised to give their
notes a better standing.) To that end,
Mann intimated to Judge Paige that he himself would offer an amendment to the effect
that all banks in the state be permitted
to charge 7 per cent on discounts having
more than sixty-three days to run.

     The clause thus suggested already
had a history. In 1829 when the bill was
under discussion country banks in the State
of New York were permitted by their charters to charge 7 per cent, while the New
York City and Albany banks were restricted
to 6 per cent. This differentiation had
had meaning years before, but no longer
made sense. As early as 1817 the discrimination against the city banks had come
under attack, and section 2 of the Act of
April 15, 1817 to incorporate the stockholders of the Bank of Orange had provided
that all incorporated banks in the State of
New York be entitled to charge 7 per cent
on loans and discounts made for more than
sixty days, regardless of the conditions
of their charters. However this section
of the act of 1817 had been repealed by
the Restraining Act of 1818.[35] It is not
surprising, therefore, that this matter
came up again in 1829 in the preliminary
discussions with the banks and that the
amendment was passed without difficulty.
As section 33 it became a part of the act
and reads: Every monied corporation subject to this law shall be entitled to receive the legal interest [i.e., 7 per cent]
but on all notes and bills by them discounted or received in the ordinary course
of business which shall be mature in sixty-
three days from the time of such discount

the said monied corporation shall not take
or receive more, at and after the rate of
6 per cent per annum. Since according to
Chapter 43 of the session laws of 1805,
rates for short term loans were fixed at
6 per cent, Section 33 of the Safety Fund
Act was equal to an official definition of
the phrase "short term loan."

     By offering this amendment Abijah
Mann split the opposition. The Albany banks
figured that the increased interest would
overcompensate them for the half per cent
contribution to the Fund, and they abandoned
their allies. The latter, i.e., the New
York City banks, were left holding the bag.
Permission to raise the interest rate had
no practical value for them, because some
of the banks in New York City had charters
running for another fifteen years, two had
permanent charters (the Manhattan Company
and the Dry Dock Bank), and there was the
branch of the Second Bank of the United
States. These, because of charter limitations, would go on charging 6 per cent interest, forcing the rest of the New York
City banks to follow suit regardless of
the permission granted in section 33 of the
Safety Fund Act. In addition, the city
banks[36] had to hold larger specie reserves
and their note issues in comparison to
their capitals were smaller than those of
the country banks. Thus the burden and
risk involved in seeking charters under the
new act were relatively larger for the New
York City banks than for the Albany or the
country banks.[37]

II

     The first indication that the
Safety Fund idea was to migrate can be
found as early as 1830 in Massachusetts.
In February of that year the Committee on
Banks and Banking of the Massachusetts
legislature was ordered to inquire into the
expediency of establishing "a fund for the
redemption of the bills of any bank which
shall fail."[38] Such migration may have
been intended by the backers of the New
York act. At least the theory was held by
some at that time that if the Safety Fund
System was approved in one state it "would
most likely...become general." State banks,
thus organized into a mutual insurance
system, would become "a safe channel for
all government purposes" and make it easy

to dispense with the Second Bank of the United States.[39]

Nothing came of this first move in Massachusetts and the influence of the Safety Fund Act as a whole was not far-reaching. It was copied in only two states, Michigan and Vermont. The Vermont Safety Fund Act was passed in 1831.[40] It copied from the New York Safety Fund Act the two main features of that act, the fund out of which creditors of insolvent banks were to be paid and the bank commissioners with their examining functions. The differences in the essentials were only slight. In Vermont each bank chartered under the act was required to pay into the fund a sum equal to 4 1/2 per cent of its capital stock in six annual installments, that is to say, the contribution was higher than in New York; but, as in that state, the fund had to be replenished if reduced by bank failures. In regard to the bank commissioners, section 15 of the Vermont act was a verbatim repetition of the respective section in the New York act, except that Vermont established yearly examinations in place of the quarterly examinations of New York. The Vermont Safety Fund Act was confirmed in 1840 by the Act relating to banks,[41] but this act gave the directors of banks a choice between participation in the safety fund, and personal liability for the notes and deposits of their banks. This remained the legal set-up regarding Vermont's Safety Fund System until after the Civil War. Actually, by 1839 the state had ten "safety fund banks," while the largest number is supposed to have been twelve.[42]

The migration of the Safety Fund Act from New York to Vermont is explicable as a case of "contact migration," for Vermont neighbors on New York. Just as easily understood, is the migration of the act to Michigan, which was settled at that time by emigrants from the western counties of New York. These settlers were bound to be influenced by the development of institutions in their home state. Thus it is not surprising that the New York Safety Fund System was copied almost verbatim in the Michigan Act to create a fund for the benefit of the creditors of certain moneyed corporations, approved on March 28, 1836.[43] However, the Michigan Safety Fund System never gained any practical importance.[44]

From Michigan the system was on the point of migrating to the Territory of Wisconsin, originally a part of the Territory of Michigan. Therefore, again the migration of the idea is easily explained. In November and December, respectively, of 1836 two banks (the Bank of Milwaukee and the Bank of Mineral Point) were chartered in the Territory of Wisconsin. In both charters, the legislature retained the right to amend them so as to make them conform to a safety fund system, if the latter were enacted. Actually the matter came up in 1837, in which year a bill was proposed which would "create a fund for the benefit of the creditors of certain monied incorporations and for other purposes." (It will be remembered that this was the title of the New York Safety Fund Act also.) However, the bill failed to become a law because of minor disagreements between House and Council.[45]

Although the migration of the Safety Fund System as such was not impressive, the influence of its two main features was of the greatest importance. In 1833 the idea of mutual responsibility was back of the first pet-bank scheme as devised by Amos Kendall;[46] but the original plan was not put into effect. It is probable that Kendall adapted earlier and far-reaching projects which have been alluded to before.[47] That he devised his proposals inspired by the New York Safety Fund act cannot be doubted. How the concept of mutual responsibility of banks was taken up again in the second half of the nineteenth century will be described in another context.

Not much has to be said about the importance in modern times of periodic bank examinations by experts. Regular bank examinations are taken for granted today, and it has long been forgotten how they were introduced into American practice. This feature of the Safety Fund Act started independently to migrate in the 1830's, at a time when knowledge of the origin of the measure was still alive. As early as 1834 Levi Woodbury, the Secretary of the Treasury, recommended bank examinations by "committees or commissioners."[48] In 1839 George Tucker,[49] well aware of the beginnings of periodic bank "visitations," described them as copied by Maine, Connecticut,[50] Rhode Island, and Mississippi. He could have added Vermont, Michigan, and Massachusetts.[51] By and by regular bank examinations by experts became adopted all over the country and were a "must" of sound banking legislation.[52]

Chapter VI

EARLY AMERICAN CENTRAL BANKING

American banking confronts the economic historian with two major problems, if not riddles: First, how could it come about that this country which possessed extensive branch banking at an early moment and in this respect was matched only by Scotland, in modern times became the country of unit banking? Secondly, how did it happen that the United States which developed full-fledged central banking earlier than any other country in the world except Great Britain was the last to adopt it definitely in its modern form? The answer to the first question will be given in passing in its proper place; that to the second is the subject of the present chapter.

I

The Beginnings

In order to avoid confusion in studying the beginnings of American central banking one must distinguish between two phenomena: first, the rise of a controlling bank within a system of banks and, secondly, the development of those functions which today are customarily fulfilled by central banks, such as acting as the fiscal agency of the government, guarding the soundness of the currency, intervention in times of distress, and so on. This chapter is not so much interested in tracing the beginnings and early distribution among various agencies of these functions as in analyzing and describing the rise in America of a controlling bank assuming certain functions, so that in retrospect, it can be characterized as a central bank regardless of how rudimentary a central bank it may have been at times.

In so doing, the historian must keep in mind that the term "central bank" was not even known in England by the middle of the nineteenth century. Professor Hayek has recently drawn attention to the fact that the term was probably first used in Europe around 1830 by Saint Simon for the depository of all wealth in a socialist community.[1] But the expression can be found also in an American publication of David Henshaw of the same period (1831) connoting in a conditional sentence and a theoretical context the single (monopolistic) bank of a country.[2] This and similar definitions seem to have been the starting point for the modern term which is based on the connotation that one bank of issue holds a position of predominance over the other banks in the country in question so that it can exercise control over them.[3] As a matter of fact, as early as 1837 Nicholas Biddle stated in a letter that "public sentiment" recognized the necessity of "a large central controlling institution; while in England Lloyd used at that time the term "central issuer." Regardless of the fact that a precise term for the new phenomenon had not crystalized as yet, both in England and America a central bank was in the making prior to the turn of the eighteenth century.

The existence of a central bank in any country is predicated on a certain maturity of banking therein: certainly there can be no central bank in the above sense before there is a banking system. In this context it should be remembered that the Bank of England had a banking monopoly for many years in the eighteenth century. Influenced by this precedent, certain sections of American public opinion during the 1780's and 1790's also aimed at setting up a national banking monopoly or at least regional ones, as has been described previously. If this possibility had become an actuality no central bank could have developed in America as early as it did, although the monopolistic national bank or the monopolistic regional banks would by necessity have fulfilled functions which are today considered typical of central banks.

Therefore, in the opinion of this author, early central banking cannot be defined or understood merely as a bundle of functions,[4] especially since modern central bank functions all over the world developed piecemeal and were brought together slowly over a period of many decades. Early central banking can be understood only when viewed from a different angle: it presupposed, as already indicated, the existence of a banking system; that is to say, it could come into existence only at a comparatively advanced stage of banking development. Within the banking system in question the early, embryonic central bank did a banking business like the other banks and competed with them; while at the same time a distinct difference existed. This embryonic central bank was larger than average banks and towered above them, for the rudimentary central bank, like its modern counterpart, either controlled the other banks more or less or the latter were becoming dependent on it. Although as a private enterprise bound to be profitable, the early central bank was being guided by economic as well as business motives: although making profit, it did not consider its maximization as the ultimate goal as was that of the other banks of the same system.

If one simply keeps in mind the fact that the idea of a central bank presupposes the existence of a banking system, it is self-evident that the First Bank of the United States cannot have been conceived as such since it was only the fourth bank in this country. It was actually planned by Hamilton as just a "money bank" among others and a "political machine." However, when the Bank of the United States was set up in 1791 the Bank of England was already on the way toward becoming its country's central bank. As early as 1781 Lord North could describe it as from habit and usage of many years a part of the

"Constitution." By that time it had risen de facto, not by law, to be the banker to the state and to most of the departments of the government; it made the interest payments on the public debt and took care of the transfers thereof; in short, it was the fiscal agency of the British government. Thus one of the basic central banking functions had crystalized in England before the Bank of the United States was even founded. Furthermore, in Great Britain the conditio sine qua non of central banking, a banking system, had come into existence prior to that year. Between 1750 and 1765 England and Scotland experienced the first great expansion of banking activities, comparable to that which America saw later in the 1790's, so that as early as 1765 Great Britain had come to possess a banking system such as America was to have only by 1800. (That the British banks, except in Scotland, were almost exclusively private banks while the American banks around 1800 were almost exclusively chartered ones is immaterial in this connection.) At that time (1765) the Bank of England as the senior institution and their model and advisor claimed the right to exert a certain control over the chartered banks in the secondary capitals (those of Scotland and Ireland). Such control had to be conceded by the latter since the Bank of England possessed a vastly greater strength; because it had better contacts with the government; and because it was holding large metallic reserves on which the chartered banks of Scotland and Ireland relied as their last resort. The latter is true also of the English private bankers who after the 1750's and 1760's had come to provide local currencies. Finally the suspension of specie payments during the Napoleonic era contributed to strengthening the central position of the Bank of England whose notes then acquired the character of a national currency. Before the century closed, even the London bankers became dependent on the Bank of England by abandoning their own issues and by handling instead Bank of England notes, which they also used in their extensive clearings as the medium of settlements.[5]

To sum up, in the decade when the Bank of the United States was chartered as just one bank among a few others for the support of the public finances and the promotion of private enterprise, the Bank of

England, having become a rudimentary central bank, had reached the point of exercising control over other banks. It fulfilled or was soon to fulfill at least three of those functions which today are considered central bank functions: It was the fiscal agency of the government; it provided a national paper currency; and it held a considerable part of the metallic reserve of the country. To what extent these facts were known to Hamilton when he worked on his "Report on a National Bank" is difficult to decide; if they were, it would be even more difficult to gauge to what extent he understood their significance. So much is certain, that by charging the First Bank of the United States from the outset with being the fiscal agency of the Federal government and thus making the national bank "a political machine of the greatest importance to the state" he put it on a road which may have led further than he foresaw.

The speed with which the First Bank of the United States moved into a central position almost simultaneously with the emergence of an American banking system in the 1790's is truly astonishing, for the leading directors of the Bank had hardly any acquaintance at all with the business of banking prior to their election to the board. First of all, they considered the enterprise entrusted to their care as just a bank; they competed with other banks as did the Bank of England in that period, too. Repeatedly their policy was shaped with regard to the competitive struggle.[6] The board of the parent bank, for instance, was split for some time on the question of whether the legal discount of 6 per cent or a lower one of only 5 per cent should be charged in order to attract business from competing banks; and the Boston branch decided to deviate from the established policy of discounting double-name paper only and to discount single-name paper if secured by public stock since such action was deemed necessary to meet competition. On the other hand, the directors of the Bank subordinated profit to stability and public duty, thereby developing an attitude necessary in central banks, but distinct from that prevailing throughout the nineteenth century in well administered commercial banks. This attitude which did much to put the First Bank

of the United States into a central position within the American banking system was hardly considered as a great achievement by such leaders of the Bank as William Bingham, Isaac Wharton, or Samuel Breck. It has been shown in another chapter that before the first multiplication of banks took place in the 1790's banks were generally considered semi-public enterprises, and service on bank boards as some sort of public service. The directors of the First Bank of the United States may well have felt that their attitude was the proper one for all bank directors and that it should have been shared by all bank boards. But, de facto, because they adopted and upheld a standard which was being generally abandoned in those decades (if it ever was adopted) and because of their unusually wise, honest, and efficient administration, which went hand in hand with the command over a large capital, they were able to make their Bank an embryonic central bank. The stage was set: the Bank was the government's fiscal agency. (It was a depository of public funds; it assisted in the collection of the public revenue and in foreign exchange operations; transferred the funds of the government; made loans to it; and, incidentally, also helped the importers to meet their debts to the government arising from import duties.) As fiscal agent of the government the Bank possessed the closest contacts with the Secretary of the Treasury, with whom it cooperated in emergencies; and, in contrast to other banks, it functioned on the basis of a national charter, a fact which gave its currency a national character, a character emphasized by the recognition of its notes as legal tender in all payments to the government.

A feature which greatly helped the Bank in achieving its central position was its then almost unique character as a branch bank. As is generally known, the policy of establishing offices of discount and deposit was not promoted by Hamilton, but adopted at the suggestion of Oliver Wolcott (1760-1833), then an official of the Treasury. By introducing branches into American banking practice he won a lasting influence on its history. A memorandum on the expediency of what he dubbed "departments" and a plan of establishing such "departments" seem to have been submitted by him to the Secretary of the Treasury,

Alexander Hamilton, in September 1791. Both documents[7] are strictly technical and legalistic and of no particular interest from the point of view of this study. In establishing branches the Bank acted on a clause inserted in the charter, at Hamilton's suggestion, for some remote contingency. However, the Bank made use of the possibility without asking the advice of the Secretary who, obviously under the influence of his model, the Bank of England, was against the policy. As he wrote on November 25, 1791 to Seton, the cashier of the Bank of New York, "the whole affair of branches was begun, continued, and ended not only without my participation, but against my judgement...I never was consulted...the steps taken were contrary to my private opinion of the course which ought to have been pursued."[8] However, this statement seems to go too far when one remembers the memorandum and plan supposedly submitted to him by Wolcott.

An interesting question arises in this connection: What is the source of the influence which was brought to bear on this country through Wolcott. There are two possibilities: Branch banking may have been adopted under Scotch influence or under that of the English pamphlet literature[9] of the eighteenth century, which contained several suggestions to this effect. For instance, one pamphlet, entitled An Essay on Paper Circulation and a Scheme...(London, 1764) aimed at replacing the Bank of England by a Parliamentary Bank with branches. This author is inclined to consider English influence more probable than the Scotch. The monopolistic and semi-monopolistic state-owned banks, which slightly later were adopted in America and which have a fundamental similarity with the English proposals of parliamentary or "truly national" (state-owned) banks just alluded to, were typically endowed with branches. However, since the charter clause permitting the First Bank of the United States to set up branches went back to certain passages in Hamilton's "Report on a National Bank" and since Hamilton had read widely, especially in Adam Smith, and was well informed, the question must remain on open one.

The unusual combination of the qualities of the creative entrepreneur with the mental attitude of the public servant enabled the leaders on the board of directors of the First Bank of the United States to tackle problems, economic in nature, which today are under the care of central bank presidents.[10] In an age which had hardly begun to understand the question of specie reserves, the board of the Bank not only guarded its own reserves by restricting its note issues in times of stress, but, working hand in hand with the mint, even tried to protect those of the American banking system as a whole. Consequently the specie holdings of the First Bank of the United States, like those of late nineteenth-century central banks, came to reflect the economic activities of the country and especially those in foreign trade. In close cooperation with the Secretary of the Treasury who, as Mrs. Taus has shown convincingly, considered intervention in times of stringency as one of his functions,[11] the Bank tried to relieve occasional difficulties of the money market. Discount policy was not yet devised at the time under investigation, and one can only regret that the proposal to discount below the legal interest rate, alluded to before, was turned down by the board of the First Bank of the United States. Otherwise regardless of the limitations due to the existence of a legal interest rate it might have discovered before the directors of the Bank of England did that a money market can be controlled by raising and lowering the discount rate. Failing to make this discovery the directors of the Bank of the United States could exert that control only by deliberate and carefully dosed expansion and contraction of their note issues and by presenting promptly for redemption such notes of other banks as came into their possession. Controlling the money market, of course, implied gaining influence over the activities of other banks. The Bank was able to exert such influence because of its (for the time) large capital and its very cautious policy which made the other banks its debtors, as a matter of course. (When the board of the First Bank of the United States believed that the other banks had overexpanded their loans and issues, heavy specie demands were made on them.) In order to appreciate this achievement, one should keep in mind that the First Bank of

the United States was in many respects
less fitted to act as a central bank than
its successor, the Second Bank of the
United States. It had no monopoly on the
public deposits and did not receive currently from the Collectors the notes of
other banks, two facts which gave the
Second Bank of the United States much of
its power of control.

That the First Bank of the United
States was not just a bank, but that it
had put itself into the commanding position of a rudimentary central bank, was to
a large extent back of the fight against
it when its charter came up for renewal in
1810-1811. This commanding position was
one of the reasons for its downfall. That
friends and foes of the Bank were not very
articulate on this point should not mislead the historian, for the truth of that
assertion is evident if one studies contemporary documents and the pamphlet literature of those years on the renewal of
the charter of the Bank. The stockholders
of the Bank in their memorial of December
10, 1810 praying for the renewal of their
charter pointed out that it had acted as
the general guardian of commercial credit
and had taken care that an adverse balance
of trade did not result in a deficiency
of money in the state concerned. It had
protected the state banks in time of pressure and, as a matter of fact, the Philadelphia Chamber of Commerce felt that the
interest and concerns of the state banks
were so interwoven with the existence of
the national bank that the renewal of its
charter was needed.[12] (In lending banks
about one-tenth of its capital the First
Bank of the United States had started on a
road which might have led to its becoming
a real bankers' bank.) The Bank of New
York, in the same vein, in January 1811
submitted a petition[13] to Congress praying
for a renewal of the charter since the
Bank of the United States had proved its
usefulness to the state banks. Through
its branchs and "from the protection of
the government" it facilitated remittances
all over the country; it "equalize[d] the
balance of specie capital among the different cities;" finally, it could aid the
merchants better than any state bank, and
was able to assist "any state institution
which from peculiar circumstances [i.e.,
in time of stress] may require" aid. The
petition implies that the Bank of the
United States was considered by the Bank of
New York as different from other banks, as
a central bank, as we would express it
today. Years later Albert Gallatin, looking at another aspect of its activities,
correctly stated that the First Bank of the
United States if not dissolved would have
kept the state banks within proper bounds.[14]
As a matter of fact, its ability to do so,
as mentioned before, was an important
reason for its downfall. Its enemies
claimed that if the First Bank of the
United States were rechartered "all the
state banks [would] become subservient to
its views and as thoroughly subject to
its influence," and one writer doubted
"whether [in this case] any state bank
from Georgia to Maine would for beneficial
purposes exist another day." ("Beneficial"
meant, of course, for the purpose of increasing the available loanable funds.)
Another argument against the Bank was that
through its agency the government was gaining power over "the metallic medium of the
whole country." All these statements imply
an intuitive, although inarticulate, understanding of the fact that the First Bank
of the United States had risen from being
one out of many money banks to being what
is called today a central bank. The only
argument which a defender like Mathew
Carey could put up was the assertion that
the state banks in fact were not dependent
on the Bank of the United States and could
not be so because together they had more
capital. If it is taken for granted that
Carey was honest in his statement, one sees
how little even such a good economist knew
about the mechanism of monetary (central
bank) control which the board of the Bank
had put into operation.[15]

The fact that America's first central bank was destroyed by the vote cast
by Vice-President Clinton, a personal
enemy of its champion, Gallatin, provides
a striking example of the personal element
in economic development.

Intermediary Period

The First Bank of the United States had hardly been destroyed when the struggle for a new bank of similar character began. Aware of the importance of the defunct Bank, Stephen Girard seems to have hoped that his banking house, founded to take the place of the Bank of the United States, would become its full-fledged successor. In this expectation he was disappointed. He should have foreseen that a private uncharted bank under no circumstances could attain a central position within the American banking system; it is doubtful whether he really understood the true character of the First Bank of the United States. Be that as it may, shortly after Girard, cooperating with John Jacob Astor and David Parish, had turned loan contractor and subscribed much of the sixteen million dollar war loan of 1813, these men, and especially Girard as the heaviest of the three investors, were forced to become promotors of a new national bank. The loan was selling at decreasing prices and, due to the gloomy political and economic outlook, heavy loss seemed probable. Thus as early as the spring of 1814 the three associates started discussing among themselves the possibility of a national bank as the way out of both their private and the public financial troubles.

It is not the intention here to describe in detail the contribution of individuals to the creation of the Second Bank of the United States. Several recent publications[1] have shown beyond doubt that the Bank came into being through the concerted effort of a few business leaders and statesmen and only the relative importance of one of them (Stephen Girard) is a moot question. The prime movers among the former were John Jacob Astor of New York, Stephen Girard of Philadelphia, and David Parish of Hamburg, Germany, two Germans and a Frenchman. Astor and Girard are so well known to historians that they need not be characterized here. David Parish, on the other hand, was one of the most interesting personalities in both European and American business in the period between from 1800 to 1820; but his biography remains to be written.[2] (As the agent of the Barings of London and the Hopes of Amsterdam he came into this country and returned to Europe at the end of the Napoleonic era.) These three men cooperated closely in the matter of a new (second) national bank, and their interest, as already mentioned, resulted from their previous investment in the war loan of 1813. If a new national bank were chartered government stock would be needed for subscriptions, its price would rise, and the holders would not only be protected against loss but make a handsome profit. Besides these three men, Jacob Barker, the New York banker, repeatedly played the part of the catalyzer. He will be discussed in another context; suffice it here to say that in those years he was a loan contractor like the three associates abovementioned and a personal enemy of Astor. To the extent that these four men, all friends of the Madison administration, shared in the final success by organizing pro-bank sentiment in the business world and by supporting Alexander James Dallas (perhaps even as Kenneth L. Brown puts it by "engineering" his appointment as Secretary of the Treasury), America's second central bank was the result of business considerations and of the attempt of a few big businessmen to avoid loss from loans to the government.

As a matter of fact, businessmen could not have set up a new Bank of the United States. This could be done only by Congress. Consequently the creation of the new national bank was actually the achievement of statesmen. Among these, two stand out, namely Alexander James Dallas and John C. Calhoun, (the former being the star actor, the latter playing the supporting role). It was Dallas's merit "by dogged persistence and persuasive pleading," as Raymond Walters has it, to have won President Madison, a majority in

Congress, and a large portion of public opinion over to the idea.

Alexander James Dallas (1759-1817), the Philadelphia lawyer and Democratic-Republican politician, had become interested in banking problems first as Stephen Girard's legal counsel. Dallas had early advised the Philadelphia merchant in matters of admiralty law. Then he was retained to straighten out difficulties arising from Girard's banking activities, as, for instance, when in 1813 Congress imposed a stamp duty on bank notes which discriminated against private bankers,[4] or when in 1814 Pennsylvania, following the example of other states, passed a restraining act forbidding private banking. But even prior to thus gaining familiarity with banking problems Dallas had possessed good contacts with Philadelphia bankers. He had acted as unofficial go-between for his friend Gallatin and David Lenox, president of the First Bank of the United States, when in 1808 the former thought it wise for the Bank to submit an application for a new charter. Later when the eleven million dollar loan of 1812 was pending Dallas convassed his banker friends in the interest of the Treasury. Similarly when these men wanted to convey their wishes to the Secretary of the Treasury they in turn used Dallas as an intermediary. In March 1812, for instance, he transmitted a suggestion of the agents of the foreign stockholders of the defunct First Bank of the United States that its charter should be renewed for at least a few years. With all this experience Dallas was prepared to understand what was involved when it became his task to work for a new national bank.

Dallas's share in the creation of the Second Bank of the United States is clear beyond doubt. But it seems to this author that an interesting question demanding additional research still remains unanswered: the extent to which Dallas, in working for a new national bank as the Secretary of the Treasury, was in reality an exponent of business interests, the exponent of the Girard-Astor-Parish combine. There are quite a few reasons which arouse suspicions: Close cooperation between Dallas and the three associates throughout the year of 1814 is certain; Dallas took a keen interest in their bank plans. It is equally certain that he

conferred with Girard and Parish on the subject of a national bank before he drew up his own plan in October 1814 and that subsequently Girard made a few suggestions some of which were adopted by Dallas, suggestions which were in the interest of the three associates in their capacity as holders of government stock.[5] When Dallas's original plan had been presented to Congress in the fall of 1814 Parish and Astor came to Washington on Dallas's invitation to support the bill, and in December 1814 when a similar bill was pending before the Senate, Dallas wrote Girard a letter which was tantamount to suggesting a bribe to a certain senator. Finally when Congress had given the go-by to his plan and had replaced it by another, the Webster-Calhoun-Lowndes bill, Dallas successfully urged Madison to veto it for many good reasons. However, one of the reasons, and actually the first in the veto, was that the amount of government stock which could be used for subscriptions was not sufficient to raise its price in the market,[6] an argument which must have highly gratified Girard, Astor, and Parish.[7] This statement is not meant to imply that Dallas was bought, but that the erstwhile organizer of a radical party had come to identify himself thoroughly with the interests of big business. (It is noteworthy in this context that as soon as the chartering of the Second Bank of the United States was assured, Dallas resigned from his appointment.)[8]

But there is still another important reason for the suspicion that Dallas was an exponent of business interests when struggling for a new Bank of the United States. In February 1814 he refused to accept an appointment as Secretary of the Treasury because the salary was insufficient to meet his current expenses, and yet in September of the same year he was willing to take the job.[9] How was the difference between salary and current expenses going to be made good? Walters' description shows that Dallas lived just as lavishly in Washington as he had in Philadelphia; in fact, he must have lived more expensively there because he had three homes in those years, instead of the previous two, one in Philadelphia and one in the country. Where did the money for such lavish living come from? Not from his salary, nor from law practice, nor from accumulated wealth, since he had spent whatever he had earned. It is therefore suggested that Girard's account books and especially his private account books be examined regarding payments and loans to Dallas or members of the latter's family in the years 1814-1817. If Dallas can be proved to have been an exponent of business interests while working as Secretary of the Treasury for the Second Bank of the United States it would be an early and exceedingly interesting case of business influence on the national government.

But even if it could be proved that there were closer connections between the Astor-Girard-Parish combine and Dallas than is known at this moment, Dallas's personal honesty as well as his political and patriotic motives would probably remain unquestioned. He was certainly convinced that he was working for the benefit of his country, as actually he was. His was indeed a great achievement. When he submitted his original plan to Congress shortly after his arrival in Washington on October 13, 1814, he stressed his opinion that a national bank was the "only efficient remedy for the disordered condition of the circulating medium" and that after the war a national bank would serve as a safe depository for the public funds and an "auxiliary" to the public credit. It would promote the general welfare and was "necessary and proper for carrying into execution" important constitutional powers of the government. There is no indication that at that moment Dallas was thinking in terms of what one would call today a central bank. Nor did he at the moment when the matter of a national bank was taken up again, after his attempts of 1815 to induce the state banks to resume specie payments had come to naught. While the First Bank of the United States (as mentioned before) was chartered as one money bank among others, and as a "political machine," the Second Bank was intended by Dallas[10] to be an instrument for the restoration of specie payments and of the currency. It was meant to be a tool for facilitating the otherwise almost impossible resumption and the creation of a new circulating medium "coextensive with the Union" and "of equal value and use in every state."[11]

However, the bill of 1816, drawn on the basis of Dallas's suggestions to be quoted forthwith, tended in the direction of a central bank. (As a matter of fact, the resistance put up by the state banks during all the stages of the struggle indicates their intuitive understanding that a new central bank was in the making which would exert the same kind of control which the First Bank of the United States had exerted to their discomfiture.) Dallas himself was now articulate regarding the salient point. In his "Proposition relating to the national circulating medium" embodied in his annual report (the Report on the State of the Finances of December 6, 1815),[12] he suggested a national bank established on the principles of responsibility, but also of independence from the government, the former being an essential characteristic of every central bank. This national bank would issue notes of national circulation, would, in cooperation with the government, restore the metallic currency of the country, would be the depository of the government, would enhance the value of the public stocks, and, last but not least "eminent in its resources and in its example" would "conciliate, aid and lead the state banks in all that is necessary for the restoration of credit, public and private." Nothing is lacking in this program for a central bank, except the term.[13]

The annual report was followed by a letter from Dallas to Calhoun, chairman of the "Committee on that part of the President's message which relates to a national currency," written at the committee's request on December 24, 1815.[14] In this letter Dallas was as articulate in his drive for a central bank as he had been in the annual report, although some lapses show the early stage of the development toward central banking. The national bank was to act as the fiscal agency of the government (the term is not used, of course); it was to restore and maintain the national currency; and, one of the lapses, it was to accommodate "commerce, agriculture, manufactures, and the arts," i.e., to act just as a bank. In the performance of these duties the cooperation of the state banks with the "independent, though not... discordant" national bank was expected. The national bank was to compete with the state bank, again a lapse; but "competition does not imply hostility." It would be incumbent on the national bank "to conciliate the state banks, to confide to them,

liberally, a participation in the deposites
of the public revenue; to encourage them
in every reasonable effort to resume the
payment of their notes in coin." Dallas
concludes: "The national bank ought not to
be regarded simply as a commercial bank.
It will not operate upon the funds of the
stockholders alone, but much more upon the
funds of the nation. Its conduct, good or
bad, will not effect the corporate credit
and resources alone, but much more the
credit and resources of the government.
In fine, it is not an institution created
for the purposes of commerce and profit
alone, but much more for the purposes of
national policy...," a central bank, as
we would characterize it today.

Not much understanding of this aspect of the matter was manifested in the
debates on the charter of the Second Bank
of the United States.[15] But in giving the
new national bank the character of a central bank Dallas was backed by certain
sections of public opinion at least, as
can be seen from the contemporary pamphlet
literature and practical measures taken at
the time. Especially one suggestion,
which was not generally adopted, aimed in
the same direction. In order to give the
deranged bank-note currency a uniform
value and to provide an effectual check
against excessive issues for the future
Eric Bollmann wanted to make the state
banks redeem their obligations not in
specie, but in notes of the new national
bank,[16] as the English banks redeemed
their notes in notes of the Bank of England.
In 1818 the Kentucky legislature actually
made it optional for her banks to pay
their obligations in notes of the Second
Bank of the United States.[17] Although
Bollmann had not understood the central
bank character of the First Bank of the
United States, as can be seen from his
Paragraphs on Banks, and although he disliked Dallas' plan, in one respect he now
wanted to go even further than the latter.
He wanted to make the new Bank of the
United States a genuine bankers' bank.
Consequently he suggested the exclusion of
branches in order to avoid local competition. The new national bank, according to
his proposal, was to do a general discounting business only at its seat and make its
profit by discounting for banks, from its
fiscal agency for the government, and
through the interest-bearing government

bonds which were to form most of its capital. He wished the bank to exert some control over the state banks and felt that
the latter would submit to " a legitimate,
paternal, sovereign institution in order
to thrive under its wings with steadiness."
But he expected, and correctly so, strong
opposition from the state banks against a
new national bank set up under the Dallas
plan.[18]

William Jones (1760-1831), the
Philadelphia shipping merchant, formerly
Madison's Secretary of the Navy and acting
Secretary of the Treasury, for political
reasons became the first president of the
Second Bank of the United States in 1816,
although he was actually a bankrupt.[19] In
spite of this latter fact, Jones was at
that moment the logical choice for this
office. For years he had been known as
the stout friend of a national bank for
this country. As early as the spring of
1814 when Dallas wanted to advance plans
for a new Bank of the United States which
were then being promoted by his friends,
he corresponded with Jones. And when in
the fall of the same year he drafted his
own plan Jones's name was inserted as president. David Parish agreed that Jones was
the man for the job and so did Stephen
Girard.[20] This fact may well explain why
Girard, who, incidentally, was talked about
as a possible choice, finally voted for
Jones in 1816 although he was at that juncture already very suspicious of the latter's
qualifications. Dallas, on the other hand,
was much pleased by his election, having
retained his high opinion of Jones.

It is not surprising that the in-
competent William Jones was unable to grasp
fully the essential character of the tool
which Dallas had shaped. Nor was he the
man to learn from the precedent that the
First Bank of the United States had established. It is unnecessary to repeat the
story of his incompetence; but it is proof
of a strong trend that in spite of all his
bungling the Second Bank of the United
States rapidly took the character of a new
central bank even during his incumbency.
It helped the state banks to resume specie
payments, for that purpose importing specie;
and soon the state banks contracted the
habit of replenishing their specie when
needed by presenting United States Bank
notes.[21] It provided a national paper
currency; it was the fiscal agent of the

government and as such for some time selected banks as intermediary depositories
of government funds. The contemporary,
oft-quoted statement that the rigorous
policy of 1819 had saved the bank and
ruined the people is an implied recognition of the former's character as a rudimentary central bank attained under the
Jones's administration. No other bank by
a policy of contraction could have broken
the country. However, this position of
the Bank was not the result of a superior,
wise, and honest administration as had
been the corresponding one of the First
Bank of the United States. It was thrown
into the lap of William Jones, the central
bank president, _malgré lui_. It was due
to the size of the Bank; to the fact that
the frozen government deposits were transferred from the state banks to the Second
Bank of the United States; to the charter
clauses which made it the sole depository
of government funds and gave it the character of a branch bank; and to the Joint
Resolution of Congress of April 29, 1816
under which the Collectors were entitled
to accept notes of specie-paying banks for
deposit with the national bank. There was
no conscious action toward making the Bank
what we call a central bank today. Jones
did not force the state banks to settle
their note obligations regularly and the
board of the Bank refused to make it the
center of a national collection and clearing system, although that was suggested at
the time.

There is, of course, no excuse for
William Jones's shortcomings, especially
for his conniving with the stock speculators on the board.[22] But it seems to be
customary to condemn him for _mismanagement_
without a fair trial. As a matter of fact,
he could have offered extenuating circumstances. His was a task as hard as that
faced by any central banker in the nineteenth century; his situation was "extremely difficult and delicate," as Biddle
expressed it. He had to build up a bank
which was larger than any that had previously existed in this country, while at
the same time possessing different features.
On top of that he was expected to restore
a depreciated currency to its par value in
a much shorter time than that considered
necessary in England in the same period
and for the same purpose. In so doing, he
could not make use of any previous

experience. Although earlier centuries had
gone through the restoration of debased
coin currencies, there was no example as to
how to appreciate a debased bank-note currency. The contemporaneous British actions
were not of much help as a model, since
they were far from being completed and
since England was a creditor nation in
international trade,[23] while America was a
debtor. To make matters worse, the administrative confusion which had marred the war
effort from 1812 to 1815 now thwarted the
endeavors of the Bank to restore the currency to its par value.[24] Immediately after
the war there was a short-lived expansion,
followed by contraction and the concomitant
economic sufferings.[25] Therefore when the
Bank came into existence it was urged by
the government and forced by public opinion[26] to expand credit in order to alleviate the distress. Thereby the ultimate
goal, the restoration of the currency,
became more difficult to attain, for to
attain that end a steady deflationary policy
would have been the proper one. The reduction of issues "ought to have been moderate
and gradual," as Mathew Carey put it.[27]
The policy of the government to repay loans
out of its funds previously frozen with the
state banks and now taken over by the
Second Bank of the United States equally
tended to counteract the goal. It meant
that frozen purchasing power was reactivated and counteracted the deflationary
policy which was expected from the state
banks. Besides making such fundamental
errors, the Treasury was inconsiderate.
It induced the Bank to open branches where
convenient for the government, but not
justified by the needs of business; it drew
without forewarning on the Bank's branches
in any part of the country in which it had
to make payments regardless of where its
funds actually were deposited at that
moment; and it forced the Bank to take as
cash the notes of doubtful country banks.
Finally, Crawford's fight against the Bank
when it started to charge exchange on
domestic bills indicates that the Secretary
tried to force it to do what was impossible
under the given circumstances.

But even if the financial policy of
the government had been more in line with
its avowed main objective, the restoration
of a currency redeemable in specie, and
even if the Secretary of the Treasury had
been more considerate, that objective would

have been extremely hard to attain; and the struggle to that end was bound to lead to severe economic sufferings. The local currencies, the only ones then in existence, were inflated in different degrees from 7 to 25 per cent. Under these circumstances the definite return to specie payments could be achieved only after a reduction of the bank-note currency from about 110 to about 50 million dollars between 1816 and 1819,[28] a cruel deflation which no modern statesman would advocate. For many months the chief exponent of speedy resumption of specie payments, Dallas, hardly understood the implications of the policy which he pushed; and the remark of a banker after a conference with the Secretary regarding the latter's "ignorance" in matters of finance had probably more weight than his biographer assigns to it.[29] The theory of the Treasury that resumption would cure all evils was simply naive; and at least some of the banks were justified in feeling bitter when they were requested to redeem government deposits at their face value when they had been made in depreciated treasury notes or depreciated bank currency.

This was the set-up under which Jones had to work. His knowledge of banking was that of an average merchant of his time, that is to say, very limited; and since there was no continuity between the First and the Second Banks of the United States the experience gained in the former was lost for the latter. Jones is blamed especially for not having assigned a definite capital to the branches, as had been the policy of the First Bank of the United States. But regardless of the fact that his policy was erroneous there was some reasonable thinking behind it. In this respect Jones was rather ahead of his time. He looked at the Bank with its branches as a whole, as one enterprise, and not as a mere bundle of banks, as was customary locally. According to Jones the Bank was "integral in its organization and indivisible in its interest...and the apparent interest of any particular office [branch] must necessarily be subordinate to the general interest."[30] But he omitted to institute that strict control[31] which is the natural complement of his basic concept; and under the existing means of transportation and communication his reasoning was premature. He is furthermore blamed for having made the notes of the

branches redeemable not only at the place of issue, but at the parent bank and at the other branches also. In instituting this policy, however, Jones acted under the pressure of public opinion. It had been one of the points of attack on the First Bank of the United States that it paid its notes only at the place of issue,[32] and the Pennsylvania legislature had passed a law requiring its branch banks to redeem the notes of the branches at the parent offices. Thus Jones's policy, regardless of the fact that is was unsound, was not unjustifiable. In what is supposed to be his own defence[33] he claimed that that policy was considered only temporary as a simple method of transferring capital to the West in spite of its indebtedness to the East; and the free selling by the branches of drafts on each other was in fact stopped as early as August 1818. There is no excuse, however, for the discount policy of the Jones administration, i.e., the preference of stock notes to legitimate business paper. On this point alone his defence breaks down completely.[34] Jones deserves blame not so much for specific mistakes, as for his general lack of administrative ability, a lack which did not permit him to control his enterprise, especially the branches, or to check the misconduct of his collaborators. (However, in the light of what has been said in a previous chapter on the position of the bank president in the first period, one may ask: Was Jones, as president of the Bank of the United States, expected to possess administrative abilities? But in the same light he was culpable for having violated his trust as bank president.) On the other hand, when the danger became acute it was Jones who enacted the rigorous policy of contraction which was a first step to saving the Bank.[35] Jones was certainly not the man to administer a central bank, but neither was his successor Cheves.

From the outset Stephen Girard, the largest individual stockholder of the Second Bank of the United States, had opposed the Jones administration, but with the charter limitations on the voting power of large stockholders he had been unable to block it. Subsequently, in his capacity as one of the government directors, he had tried to steer the administration, but was finally forced to give up his attempts to bring it onto a sounder road.

He therefore resigned in January 1818.
However, he remained the large stockholder
which he had been before and was elected
chairman of the stockholders; in this
capacity he was soon to become instrumental in having the Jones administration replaced by that of Langdon Cheves. Girard's
aim was "a complete change of management
and system," and to reach his goal he used
indirect methods. Prevailing on important
Charleston, South Carolina, stockholders
he started the movement that led at a
meeting of local stockholders in October
1818 to the nomination of Cheves to the
presidency of the Bank and to the appointment of a committee of correspondence.
The latter was expected to consolidate
hostility against the Jones administration
in the various sections of the country and
it asked Girard for his aid in obtaining
a change. His aid was requested also when
for political reasons another movement
was set up in Boston to change the directorate of the bank. Thus Girard was
largely influential in bringing about the
change which put Cheves at the helm of the
Bank, a man for whom he had the highest
regard.[36]

It was characteristic of contemporary public opinion regarding the position of bank presidents that the politician William Jones was succeeded as president of the Second Bank of the United
States by the politician Langdon Cheves.
After having been admitted to the South
Carolina bar Langdon Cheves (1776-1857)
rose to prominence first in his state and
later in national politics until he became
the speaker of the Thirteenth Congress.
As such he cast the decisive vote which
defeated Dallas's original bank bill of
1814. This occasion probably provided
Cheves with his first contact with the
problem of a national bank. What distinguished the politician Cheves from the
politician Jones was the former's strong
personality, his administrative abilities,
and the fact that he was a good politician.
But Jones may have had a better notion of
banking: he had been a shipping merchant;
while Cheves, the uneducated son of a poor
Indian trader and storekeeper, had been a
lawyer in a society of planters. As the
contemporary sources agree, Cheves was
what is called in the vernacular a "big
talker."[37] He loved to make speeches and,
incidentally, excellent ones. The very

excellence of his speeches and especially
that of the "Exposition" of 1822 still
seems to color the judgment of historians.[38]

In that year Cheves claimed nothing
less than that within seventy days he had
restored a bankrupt enterprise not only to
health, but even to power. To be sure, the
word "bankrupt" was not used by Cheves.
He used the terms "prostrate" and "utterly
prostrate;" he claimed that the Bank was
on the point of stopping payments in the
spring of 1819; he stated that everybody
in Philadelphia expected that calamity and
asserted that he had "hourly proof of the
probability of this event." If we can
trust Jones, Cheves felt as though he had
saved the Bank from "ruin and disgrace."
However, anyone versed in business administration will agree that is impossible
to reorganize a bankrupt enterprise of the
size of the Second Bank of the United
States within a few weeks. In fact, one
must discount Cheves' statements. Nicholas
Biddle when writing a few months later to
Robert Lenox[39] of New York undoubtedly gave
a better balanced and more correct judgment
when remarking that the Second Bank of the
United States had been "crippled" and
almost destroyed by banking in the interior.
Actually the Second Bank of the United
States was not bankrupt as Cheves seems to
have thought when he took over, but only
"crippled," to use Biddle's better term,
through lack of liquidity. Its losses during the Jones era were more than 3.5
million dollars, a very heavy loss indeed,
but amounting only to about 10 per cent of
the capital of 35 million dollars. A loss
of that proportion, of course, does not
break an enterprise. Consequently Cheves
could not claim truthfully to have saved
the Bank from bankruptcy; he does deserve
credit for having nursed it back to health,
but in the opinion of this author he does
not even deserve all the credit for the
restoration of the Bank's soundness, as will
be discussed shortly. All the measures for
which Cheves claimed credit in the
"Exposition" were ones which would make an
illiquid enterprise liquid, but would not
reorganize a bankrupt one or, in other
words, make an insolvent enterprise solvent
again. Regardless of these facts Cheves'
erroneous claims were undoubtedly made in
good faith since, as will be mentioned
later, the term "liquid" as distinct from
"solvent" was not then known.[40] On the

other hand, their able presentation gave them unwarranted credit and made William Jones[41] very bitter.

How could Cheves come to the conclusion that the Second Bank of the United States was actually bankrupt when he became its president on March 6, 1819? This author suspects that he, like many of his contemporaries and especially the radical agrarians, such as John Taylor of Caroline County and later Andrew Jackson, considered a bank bankrupt if it could not redeem at once in specie all its outstanding demand obligations. Jones at least hints in this direction in his defence.[42] Furthermore Cheves seems to have considered the Bank bankrupt because he looked at the parent bank alone and not at the enterprise as a whole. It has already been mentioned in passing and here needs to be stressed that the main difference between Jones' and Cheves' outlook was that for the former the Bank of the United States plus its offices was one big enterprise, while for the latter it was a bundle of local banks. Jones in his defence[43] chided Cheves, probably with reason, for judging the Bank's status on the basis of its Philadelphia funds alone. He felt that Cheves had acted like an anatomist who tried to explain a human body by showing a single limb. Finally, Cheves claimed that the bookkeeping of the Bank was in such shape that he could not gain a clear picture. It is possible that he may not have understood double-entry bookkeeping when he entered on his job, since at that time this system was not yet common with banks.

So much about Cheves' claim that the Bank of the United States was bankrupt when he took over. As to his merits for having saved it, one must keep in mind that a policy of contraction had already been started in the summer of 1818 while Jones was still the president of the Bank upon recommendation of the committee on the state of the Bank. Slightly later on the suggestion of the same committee the board resolved to limit the payment of deposits and notes to the places of deposit and the places designated in the body of the notes, except when deposited by the government. Furthermore and still during the incumbency of Jones, the offices were restricted in drawing on the parent bank and other branches except if they had

bought bona fide bills of exchange on such places originating from real business transactions. Finally a credit had been opened in London on the basis of government stock to provide the Bank with a means of payment which was as good as specie. This credit, of course, being a medium term credit, contributed to better liquidity in the short run and gave the Bank a breathing spell. That is to say, some of the causes which had sapped the Bank's strength were in the process of being removed prior to Jones's resignation, and the administration pro tem which bridged the gap between Jones's resignation and Cheves' taking office in March 1819 had stuck to the policy of contraction.[44]

But it is possible that because of the weakness of the administration prior to Cheves' taking the reins, some of the offices may not have held strictly to the line of this policy. In any case, Cheves undoubtedly put teeth into whatever policy was determined upon. On the other hand, his claim that the Bank was worse off after contraction than it had been before is neither understandable nor is it explained to the satisfaction of this author who is inclined to discount the assertion. In some respects Cheves immediately went much further than his predecessors: as a temporary emergency measure he forbade the southern and western offices to issue any notes, and somewhat later, as a matter of permanent policy, he enjoined them from issuing notes when the domestic exchange was against the issuing office. This was in principle a sound and, for the time, a very modern policy, as will be explained later when it can be seen within a broader context.[45] (It would be most interesting to know which board member suggested it.) Furthermore he forbade all offices to draw on each other unless they had arrived previously at an understanding to that effect or unless they had transmitted in advance funds to meet such drafts. He stopped the buying and collecting of exchange on the South and West and advised the branches to collect their balances from the state banks.[46] He finally induced the Secretary of the Treasury to refrain from drawing on the Bank without advance notice and without giving time to transfer funds to the place where they were needed. It will be realized that with few exceptions (for instance, contracting a foreign loan) all of Cheves' measures were negative; he forbade, he enjoined, he stopped; but he did not build.

The historian should not rely too much on Cheves's "Exposition."[47] It is a masterpiece of oratory and an adroit "going on record" of the politician on the way out. At that moment Cheves had already announced his intention to retire, and his administration was under fire. Being marred by ugly discrepancies[48] the "Exposition" is not as trustworthy as if it were a document. At one point Cheves speaks of the "immense and rapid curtailment" ordered by his predecessor amounting to 7 million dollars for the southern and western offices, which does not keep him from claiming later that the southern and western branches when he took office had not been restrained from issuing their notes which they did most profusely. The explanation of this latter statement is hazy and unconvincing. In one context he enumerates curtailment among those measures through which his administration saved the Bank; while in another he violently disclaims all responsibility for curtailment, an exceedingly unpopular policy of which the politician wished to wash his hands. At one moment Cheves severely criticized Jones for having sacrificed productive capital by borrowing funds in London, but a little later he takes credit for having done exactly the same. ("I proudly say I suggested and advised" the foreign loan.) In fact under the given circumstances that policy of sacrificing earning assets for the sake of restoring the liquidity of the Bank was correct for both Jones and Cheves, not right for Cheves and wrong for Jones.[49]

Cheves deserved credit for two main achievements. He did a thorough house-cleaning job and he took the reins into his own hands. Through the force of circumstances and the strength of his personality, as has been described in another context,[50] he created a new type of bank president and set an example which was soon to be followed all over the country. Thus he paved the way for the business genius who was to succeed him after a few years. But Cheves himself was not a business leader. His general administrative policy was strong: the policy of contraction initiated by his predecessor with its logical consequences he saw through to the bitter end, going probably further than necessary; he paid no dividends and later kept the dividends low, regardless of all clamor, until the capital of the Bank was restored. But, in contrast, his banking policy was weak and timid. This fact, strange for such a strong personality, may have a psychological explanation. A contemporary of Cheves[51] reports that "for many years after his admission [to the bar] he was very diffident about writing anything for publication in consequence of his defective education." Just as at that time he was conscious of his lack of general education he may now have been conscious of his lack of banking knowledge. To Cheves, the Second Bank of the United States seemed just a big, actually a much too big, bank. He claimed its capital could not be employed in banking operations and therefore he wanted a reduction of it. The mere concept of this bank as a central bank, or more accurately, as a bank controlling and guiding the American banking system, was beyond his reach. This much-too-big bank had in Cheves' eyes much-too-many offices and he tried his best to get rid of some of them.[52] To be sure, he had an instinct for what is called today liquidity, although the term was not known in his time, but in his mind liquidity seems to have been identical with being able to liquidate at any moment. Cheves was haunted by the fear that the notes of the branches would be used in payments to the government and turn up at an unpropitious moment at some Eastern office not prepared to redeem them. Therefore, as mentioned above, he began by completely stopping note issues at certain offices. Instead he sent to the branches in question notes of sound banks in their neighborhood (deposited by the collectors) and advised them to reissue these notes when they made discounts. That is to say, the Bank devised for a position of command made itself a servant, the voluntary and unpaid agent for the circulation of country notes. (As a matter of fact, the circulation of notes by agents was always bitterly condemned as unsound throughout the first half of the nineteenth century.)[53] That objectionable policy was not an emergency measure passed during the critical months of 1819, but, as Biddle's letters of 1823 show, a permanent policy throughout Cheve's regime. At the same time Cheves did his best to convince the Secretary of the Treasury and Congress that the Bank should be relieved from the obligation of taking the notes of the parent bank and its branches wherever they were presented by the collectors. That the existing regulation made the circulation of the Bank co-extensive with the limits of the Union, that it made its notes a substitute for domestic exchange, and that it guaranteed their soundness making them superior to the notes of the state banks, all this did not impress Cheves. That this regulation was a blessing for the Bank, put it into the commanding position for which it was designed, and could be made a pillar of strength by a real banker, such as was Nicholas Biddle, was not recognized by the lawyer and politician at its helm.[54] Cheves suggested that the notes of the branches should be received by the collectors only where payable, but that the notes of the parent bank and the Washington office should be received everywhere and the notes of the parent bank and all branches in those states and districts which had no branches. He claimed that the regulation which was so obnoxious to him "greatly diminishe[d] the mass of sound currency in which the payments to the government [could] be made" (because under this regulation he refused to issue branch notes), "[brought] the Bank of the United States into frequent collision with the local banks...and by perpetually destroying the equilibrium of the currency produce[d] real embarrassment."[55] These moves show clearly Cheves' limitations when compared with Biddle's successful leadership under the same regulation which, fortunately for the Bank, was not rescinded. It did not occur to Cheves, as it had not occurred to Jones, but as it was beginning to dawn on Biddle (who had become a director of the Bank by that time), that there existed a simple safety valve: the regular presentation for redemption of the notes of state banks deposited by the collectors.

III

Nicholas Biddle and the Heyday of American Central Banking

When Nicholas Biddle (1786-1844), the descendant of a prominent colonial family with Quaker background, took the reins of the Second Bank of the United States in 1823, he could already look back on a distinguished career. There were not many Americans in the nineteenth century who could compare with Biddle in the brilliancy of their minds or the ability to master fields essentially widely apart.[1] The qualities of a profound student and of a great administrator are not often combined in the same person; but they were in the case of Biddle. Moreover Biddle had not only a brilliant mind, but one which matured early, a fact which explains his becoming president of the Second Bank of the United States at an early age. After a very successful college career, he studied law and in 1804 became a secretary to General John Armstrong, then the American minister in Paris. Later he joined James Monroe's staff at the London legation, whence in 1807 he returned to the United States. These years were decisive for Biddle's future. Traveling extensively in Europe, he acquired broad experience and that national outlook whibh became typical of his thoughts and actions. He made friends for life, and his connection with Monroe was later to determine his joining the board of the Bank of the United States and consequently his rise to being America's great early central banker and business leader.

How Biddle first became acquainted with banking is not known; perhaps through his father who was a director of the Bank of Pennsylvania;[2] perhaps in Paris where he took a part in the financial transactions necessitated by the Louisiana Purchase; perhaps in the course of his studies. Be that as it may, by 1810 his knowledge in this field was remarkable, as evidenced by his long speech in the Pennsylvania legislature (his maiden speech, in fact), which was the maturest expression of banking knowledge to be found in America in that period. This speech foreshadowing the future central banker was occasioned by the Holgate Resolutions, put before the Pennsylvania House of Representatives in 1810. Mr. Holgate, himself a representative, felt that it was incumbent on the state legislature to express its hostility to the rechartering of the First Bank of the United States since it involved state rights and, in his mind, would have been unconstitutional. On the other hand, Nicholas Biddle, one of the representatives of the City of Philadelphia, made himself the champion of the national bank when taking the floor. The young representative, who tackled the problem both from the legal and the economic angle, considered the state legislature entitled to express its opinion on the question then under discussion; but for him the Bank was constitutional. The power of Congress to charter a national bank was implied in its power to collect taxes: for the transfer of funds from where they were collected to where they were to be disbursed, a national paper circulation was indispensable and it could be provided only by a national bank. That power of Congress was also implied in the commerce clause of the Constitution and in the right of the general government to borrow money; "banks [were] the natural, the usual, and the best means of borrowing," and the general government could not rely on the state banks subject to the whims of state legislatures. Finally the power of Congress to charter a corporation was deduced from its power to make needful rules and regulations respecting the territories or other property belonging to the United States. Congress undoubtedly had the power to incorporate political bodies for governing the territories and Biddle could see no difference "between the right to incorporate respective public lands and the right to incorporate respective public money." For him there was no logic to the contention that Congress was undeniably entitled to establish bodies politic with the power to charter corporations while it was denied the power to charter a private corporation itself, a point stressed earlier by James Wilson in his Considerations, which Biddle may have known. He argued last but not least that a power which had been exercised for a long time without opposition, as in the case of

the Bank of the United States, could be considered as established, an argument which was soon to play a large role in the discussions on the problem of a national bank. So far Biddle, the lawyer.[3a]

Biddle, the monetary and banking theorist[4] - he had not become a practical banker as yet - was, as his speech betrays, then under the influence of Sir James Steuart, whom he quoted as "one of the most intelligent political economists;"[5] he neither mentioned Adam Smith nor indicated any familiarity with the Wealth of Nations. Although Biddle's speech was undoubtedly the maturest expression of contemporary banking thought which could be found in America on the eve of the War of 1812 no progress can be registered in comparison with Hamilton's thinking of 1790. For young Nicholas Biddle, the First Bank of the United States was just a bank and regardless of his high opinion of its directors he did not yet understand that they had made of the First Bank of the United States more than just a bank: namely, a rudimentary central bank.[6]

Biddle's discussion of the economic aspect of banking and of the Bank of the United States is not systematic, but rather rambling, since, following legal practice, he takes up one objection after the other, tearing them to pieces. First of all, banks, and the Bank of the United States among them, had been attacked as detrimental to the lower classes. Biddle claims that banks protected them, because they helped the farmer to reserve his crop for a better market and formed a defence against the usurer. For the well-to-do the Bank of the United States was especially useful. Through good faith and punctuality it had created such confidence that it had become a safe depository for the wealth of the country while at the same time it had attracted foreign funds. Those enemies of the Bank who, following Mercantilist and especially David Hume's obsolete reasoning,[7] dreaded foreign loans of every kind (as Jackson was to do twenty years later) were given a lecture on the advantages of capital import from abroad.[8] They were told that capital import made additional funds available for investment in this country. The dividends paid on these foreign funds were in fact earned by the ultimate borrowers over and above their incomes which were increased by such borrowings. Although the dividends amounted to 8 per cent, the foreign investor received a yield of only 6 per cent (our legal rate) since most of the Bank stock abroad had been sold by the government at a price of $145 for $100 face value. (The term yield was not used, of course.) Furthermore, since the heart always follows the treasure, foreign investors in American bank stock would work in our interest all the more, since in case of war their property could be confiscated in retaliation for injuries suffered by American citizens.

The young, vigorous, and adventurous American nation needed a convenient medium of exchange for its extensive and expanding foreign trade. The precious metals chosen because of their durability and portability as media of exchange all over the world were themselves articles of trade. In fact, since they were the only ones on the basis of which we could trade with certain countries, foreign commerce might at any time deprive us of our metallic means. Therefore we needed for our internal trade a medium not liable to be drained away, and bank paper furnished such a medium. It answered every purpose of domestic trade and at the same time was cheaper and more easily transmitted than metallic money. Through its adoption precious metals were released for foreign commerce, and the wealth of the country was increased by our ability to carry more money to foreign markets. What proportion of specie should be kept to answer the calls of paper was not as yet determined.

Biddle recognized that bank paper might become dangerous because "exuberant" issues might increase the price of our products, but such a tendency, as he hoped, might be counterbalanced by a low interest rate resulting from large issues [sic!]. Biddle was not afraid that our paper issues might exceed our store of metallic money - that was the purpose of paper issues - for our paper money had not exceeded our property, i.e., our landed, commercial, and manufacturing capital.[9] "Or rather, is there not in our possession solid and even convertible funds infinitely beyond the whole circulating paper?" Danger might come, however, from another direction. As

long as bank paper enjoyed the confidence of the people and foreign commerce supplied us with specie, all was well. But the delicate structure of credit had to be handled gently. Paper now occupied the place of gold and silver which was exported and could not be produced immediately. When confidence ceased (as it would in case of the dissolution of the Bank of the United States) and metal was requested in exchange for notes, banks would become embarrassed because they had tied up their funds in less convertible investments and had reserved only such metallic means as answered the ordinary demands of trade. Therefore the banks would be forced to contract. Such contraction was bound to follow anyway in the wake of the dissolution of the Bank of the United States, and dire consequences were foreseen and described by Biddle in the most realistic way.[10]

There can be no doubt that his participation in the debates of 1810 and 1811 on the fate of the First Bank of the United States represented an invaluable experience which was to influence Biddle in later years. As late as 1831 he referred to this experience and "well" recollected "the total ignorance" on the subject of banking[11] and the triumph of demogogery over reason. That this should not happen again was his goal thereafter.[12]

During the decade which lay between this speech which established his reputation and his becoming a director of the Bank, Biddle had little opportunity to develop his knowledge of banking. He practiced agriculture, served in the state senate in war time, devoted himself arduously to studies and in 1818 and 1820 ran, unsuccessfully, for Congress as the Democratic candidate of the city and county of Philadelphia. Regardless of his lack of experience in the banking field, he was offered by the stockholders a seat on the board of directors of the Second Bank of the United States, an offer which he declined; but when his old friend James Monroe nominated him as a government director in 1819 he accepted the appointment, being unwilling to shun a public duty for which the President selected him. His decision was influenced by the fact that he looked on the Bank as "of vital importance to the finances of the government and an object of great interest to the community."[13] Up to that time he had had "little concern with banks," as he expressed it, and planned to submit to the labor and hostility which the directorship entailed only "until the character of the institution was reestablished."

Once a director Biddle threw himself into the fray, and through study and the natural ability of a born financier soon became one of the most influential directors, especially since he seems to have been President Monroe's confidante on the board.[14] Biddle entered the board of the Bank at the same time that Cheves became its president. What he thought of the South Carolinian at that time is not known; by 1822 he was rather critical. He neither considered the Bank quite as prosperous as did Cheves in his "Exposition," nor did he deem the direction efficient or the officers experienced.[15] As he saw the situation there was a big task ahead for the new president.[16] Whether he worked for his own election to that position or, as expressed in a letter to Calhoun,[17] neither sought nor shunned the situation "of so much responsibility," is not certain. In fact, in the fall of 1822 when asked for his opinion regarding the qualifications of the future Bank president, he gave in answer more or less a portrait of himself: in his opinion the future president needed talent for business without necessarily being a businessman; he should enjoy the confidence of the government without being a party man, let alone an active partizan; and he should, if possible, be a Philadelphian so as to overcome the odiousness which the Bank had excited in that city and because it had to depend on the local directors rather than on those from other parts of the country.[18]

Once Biddle was nominated for president of the Second Bank of the United States he formulated his program. Recognition of the fact that the Bank, regardless of its own embarrassments, had sustained the national currency and rescued the country from the domination of irresponsible banks and their depreciated circulation implied an understanding that it had become what one would characterize today as an embryonic central bank, and praise of this development as an achievement meant a willingness on his part to assume the role of a central banker. In addition, "The time ha[d] perhaps arrived," as Biddle thought, "when it [the Bank] [might] combine its own and the country's security with a more enlarged development of its resources and a wider extension of its sphere of usefullness."[19] This was the program which the new president would actually put into effect, after he had entered upon the duties of his office in January, 1823.

Biddle, the Chief Executive

It would have been impossible to carry out such an ambitious program without building up an efficient administration.[20] In so doing Biddle relied on three pillars: confidential officers, as he styled them; directors both in the parent bank and in the offices;[21] and unofficial advisers. Confidential officers, in Biddle's terminology, were the cashiers of the parent bank and of the branches and the branch presidents. Biddle made no distinction in rank between the cashiers of the former and those of the latter. Thomas Wilson, cashier in Philadelphia when Biddle took over, was shifted to New Orleans and for the vacancy the cashier of the Boston office was at least considered.[22] Later Samuel Jaudon, cashier of the New Orleans office became cashier in Philadelphia. The cashiers of the parent bank and of the branches were appointed by the parent board, de facto by Nicholas Biddle, who in so doing followed a well-considered personnel policy.[23] As he stated it, it was the policy of the Bank "in the appointment of confidential officers [who were] to live at a distance and to execute...important trusts" to prefer men "brought up in the parent Bank under our own eyes" so that their character and conduct and their capacity to carry the policy of the Bank into effect were well known.[24] This policy implied a system of promotion from within the administration which was beautifully described by Biddle himself: "With a view to secure the best talents... and to reward the meritorious officers the rule of the Bank is that whenever any vacancy occurs it is filled by promotion... The person last introduced takes his place at the foot of the list and is gradually advanced if found deserving. The salary of the officers on their first entrance into the Bank is...$700 a year. A comparatively small compensation, but as it is known to lead to more lucrative situations it is sufficient to attract to the service of the Bank a great number of applicants of respectability. When a vacancy takes place a selection is made from these by a ballot at the Board."[25]

When a deserving man was sent to a branch as the cashier he received detailed instructions regarding his relations to both the local president and the local board. Much tact was necessary for the position, since the cashier of the branch was more than an employee of the office in question. He was the local confidential officer of the parent board and as such was entitled even to give his opinion on the election of directors and the qualifications and conduct of branch presidents.[26] Under these circumstances conflicts between presidents and cashiers could arise; but they were rare. The cashier was relied on, and held responsible, for the execution of the orders of the parent board. The degree of consideration and influence which he could have with his own board depended on his talent and personality; but whenever the orders of the parent bank were questioned by a local board, he was expected to act decisively and energetically. If, for instance, an instruction came to limit the amount of the loans of the office the cashier would have been considered derelict in his duty if he permitted a single dollar more to be loaned out, although he must not interfere with the distribution of the discounts. For the express purpose of giving the cashier a full share in the responsibility, to him and to the president of the New York office, for instance, was confided the purchase of foreign exchange and an absolute veto on the purchase of domestic bills.

A few years after Biddle had written these instructions the cashier designate of the Natchez office received the following advice:[27] Since most of the directors of the branches were appointed without being personally known to the board; since they had comparatively little interest in the Bank and were subject to periodical changes; and, finally, since in making loans they were exposed to local and personal feelings, it was the cashier who was the repository of the confidence of the Bank. He was charged with the execution of the rules and orders of the board

which kept the institution from being thrown into confusion. He was to take care that there was no deviation which could make these rules and orders ineffective. In his actions the cashier could always rely on prompt and cordial support on the part of the parent board which looked to him as the one responsible for the prevention or correction of such measures as were inconsistent with the regulations, or injurious to the interests of the Bank. He was to report to Biddle with utmost frankness and without reserve and could be sure that such frankness would be reciprocated. The parent board was anxious to protect its local officers from being exposed to local feelings and excitement, and was willing to cooperate when they reported that an office was coming under the control of an individual board member. In one case, upon the report of a cashier to that effect, an investigation of the Committee on the Offices actually took place.[28] The exalted character which was assigned to the position of cashier becomes evident time and again: for instance, from a letter of Biddle to the cashier of the Mobile office, according to which Biddle relied on the latter, as well as on the older board member, to see that a newly appointed director did not become an "injurious" one;[29] from the way in which the cashiers were kept informed (the one in New Orleans was promised that he would have the "best correspondence" in the city);[30] from the fact that in one case Biddle not only adopted the suggestion of a cashier as national policy, but also stressed that fact;[31] or, finally, from the procedure adopted in opening new branches. In some cases the preliminary investigations were conducted by cashiers of older offices, while as a rule the new one was opened by the cashier designate with or without the cooperation of one of the Philadelphia cashiers.[32]

The salaries of the cashiers were graded according to the amount of capital, business, and profit of the office in question and of the labor connected with the position. The cashiers of the parent bank and of the largest offices received $4,000 in 1824 after they, as all their colleagues, had had to take a cut when Cheves administered the Bank.[33] Biddle was anxious not to disturb the proper relationship among the compensations of the officers, but in exceptional cases he was willing to pay a special remuneration for extra services rendered by a cashier[34] and to give an "outfit" on behalf of the bank to deserving officers when sent to distant places.[35] In at least a few cases Biddle used attractive titles which gave prestige to the office-holders when he was unwilling to pay an adequate salary.[36] On the whole, however, the salaries of the cashiers were liberal, and in return the Bank required an exclusive devotion to its affairs. Cashiers were not permitted to engage in any private business, since it might affect injuriously the absolute independence of the officers, an independence which Biddle considered necessary to the fulfillment of their functions.[37] They had no access to the funds of the Bank as borrowers as, to the detriment of the enterprise, the cashiers had had in the Jones era,[38] and as they were to have again when the Bank functioned under the Pennsylvania charter. On the other hand, Biddle was thoughtful of his officers as was especially manifested when the Bank was closing its branches by 1835.[39]

The cashiers appointed under Biddle represented a high class of men,[40] a fact which testifies to Biddle's qualities as a man and his capacities as a chief executive officer. An especially good example of such appointments is that of Joseph McIlvaine, cashier of the parent bank between 1826 and 1832, whom Catterall[41] rightly characterized as an able officer, devoted to his chief, conservative, tactful, and attentive to the interests of the Bank. McIlvaine was a well-to-do man, fond of his family and his books, who found his job so "laborious" after six years of "slaving" that in 1832 he resigned. Later, in 1836, as his lobbyist in Harrisburg he was to help Biddle in getting the Pennsylvania charter.[42] Samuel Jaudon (1796-1874), McIlvaine's successor, who had risen in the Bank, probably did not rank as high as his predecessor, but was more of a bank expert and businessman. At the time of his appointment Biddle, who admired his intelligence, considered him the best man available for the job.[43] Jaudon had gained experience in the parent bank as the second assistant cashier (appointed in 1826) and subsequently (1828-1832) as the cashiers of the New Orleans office, one of the most important branches of the Bank. He, like McIlvaine, possessed Biddle's full confidence, and in a letter of introduction to McDuffie,[44] was spoken of by Biddle as his friend. In addition to the routine work of his position, Jaudon was charged with all sorts of difficult missions. In 1826, as the second assistant cashier of the parent bank, he was dispatched to Washington to have certain offenders arrested and prosecuted.[45] In 1829, while the cashier of the New Orleans office, he was ordered to Washington to see William B. Lewis, who in turn introduced him to President Jackson. Jaudon tried to convince the latter that the New Orleans board "acted only on the strictest banking principles without the least reference to party views or partialities."[46] In 1833, at a very critical period of the Bank's career, he was again sent to Washington where Biddle obviously tried to make use of his connections. He was, as Biddle expressed it, the son-in-law of the "lady" (the second wife) of Senator Hugh Lawson White.[47] Several years later, Jaudon went to London as the representative of the Bank of the United States of Pennsylvania, and his activities in the days of the Bank's agony have been described repeatedly.[48] While Biddle occupied the station of the chief executive in the Second Bank of the United States, the cashier of the parent board was the general manager who was aided by assistant cashiers as functional officers. One of them supervised the accounts between the branches and the exchange business, while a second took care of the suspended debts and the Bank's real estate.[49]

It is difficult to evaluate the importance of the position of the branch presidents in comparison with that of the cashiers, although they undoubtedly played an important part in the organizational set-up of the Bank. Nominally, branch presidents were elected by the local boards; in fact, they were appointed by Biddle. Cashiers and local confidantes, to be discussed shortly, advised Biddle with regard to persons recommendable for the positions of branch presidents. On the basis of such recommendations Biddle made suggestions to the local boards (which did the actual electing) putting at the head of the list the name of the preferred candidate.[50] He felt that the acceptability of a candidate to the parent board should be considered important by those who made the immediate elections, since the branch president was, in fact, a confidential officer of the parent board. If the election was doubtful Biddle permitted his candidate, prior to the election, to make suggestions for directors. This amounted to packing the local board with the friends of the candidate. It was very rare that such control over the local boards did not work,[51] since Biddle could exclude an undesirable man, put into the president's chair against his will, from reelection to the local board. This exclusion was possible because the presidents of the offices had to be their directors and local directors were elected annually by the directors of the parent board which, in turn, was under the control of Biddle and his close friends.

The main function of branch presidents was general supervision of the affairs of the office. They were especially relied on to select suitable local boards of directors.[52] In addition they fulfilled functions which varied with the circumstances. Consequently while Biddle's statements regarding the functions of branch presidents seem at times inconsistent, the fact is that the position was flexible. In some cases the president of a branch was expected to devote his full time to the office since the business was too large to be handled by the cashier alone, and cooperation of an active president with an efficient cashier was deemed indispensable. The situation at the Washington office (in 1824) is a case in point; and the president of the New York branch, the retired, wealthy merchant, Isaac Lawrence,[53] probably devoted most of his time to the bank's business. (Biddle's correspondence with Lawrence shows the latter as participating in the actual management of the office.) In another case, however, Biddle encouraged a branch president to have an extensive business of his own, a fact which implied that the president in question could give very limited time to the business of the branch.[54] Interesting in this context is the case of Jeremiah Mason, president of the Portsmouth office. He was a lawyer called to the position to straighten out a tangle left by his predecessor when the latter ended his career as an impostor. For some time Mason seems to have devoted

much or even most of his time to the office, receiving a fixed amount of $1200 for professional services over and above his salary. But once the affairs of the branch were in good shape again, his work load decreased and his remuneration was changed to a fee for professional services in addition to the base salary, a change which amounted to a cut in his total income from the Bank. As in the case of the cashiers, the salaries of the presidents were based on the size of the branch in question. While this author has not found any material regarding salaries of the presidents of the large offices such as New York, Boston, or Baltimore, the salaries paid in the smaller offices of the north are known. They were as follows: Burlington, Portland, and Utica, $500 per annum;[55] Hartford, Providence, and Portsmouth, $800 per annum. That is to say, to use Biddle's expression, the presidency of a branch was "considered rather an honorary than a lucrative situation."

The third pillar of Biddle's administration of the Bank was, as indicated above, a group of confidential local advisers who at times, were or were not members of the local or parent boards. Catterall[56] saw this aspect of Biddle's administration clearly and nothing is needed but to repeat his remarks: When Biddle took office Robert Lenox, a leading New York merchant and director of both the First and Second Banks of the United States, suggested that Biddle select local confidential advisers to keep him informed. The latter, adopting the suggestion, covered the whole country with a network of such advisers, men like Robert Lenox[57] himself in New York, James Lloyd and Daniel Webster in Boston, John McKim, Robert Oliver, and Roswell L. Colt in Baltimore, John Potter in Charleston, and others, serving in this capacity in other places. These men, in addition to the branch presidents, were especially relied upon when it came to the selection of directors.[58]

As previously described Biddle selected directors in the same manner as all reliable banks of the period did:[59] directors of the Bank of the United States were high ranking businessmen with wide connections who were expected to inspire confidence and to bring their own business and that of their friends to the Bank. They represented certain "interests" (a word often found in Biddle's letters), and this fact was evidenced, for instance, in the practice of electing friends or relatives of important directors to the board when the latter had to leave for a year under the principle of rotation.[60] Often directors were appointed with a view to widening the interests tied to the Bank,[61] and to having a greater variety of interests represented on the boards, so as to avoid the appearance of exclusiveness. In one case, when Biddle was swamped with complaints about an office, he decided to put friends of the complainants on the board in question to put an end to the trouble.[62]

When Biddle entered upon the duties of his office it was not easy to get suitable directors, for the Bank had become "odious" in the Jones era,[63] and good men were reluctant to become directors. But this difficulty was overcome because of Biddle's honest leadership and the strict impartiality of his selections, aimed at getting the very best men in the community.[64] Thus Biddle was soon able to select everywhere from among a number of candidates. He preferred what he called "independent,"[65] respectable businessmen who, on the whole, were reelected whenever they proved satisfactory. If unsatisfactory, on the other hand, it was easy under the rule of rotation to get rid of them without much ado. By independent businessmen Biddle meant well-to-do men who traded on their own funds, borrowed only occasionally, and were therefore not likely to abuse the Bank's means on their own behalf or that of their friends. Biddle did not expect any conflict of interest as long as the directors were really independent, and habitual borrowers were dropped.[66] "Integrity, independence, and knowledge of business" were "the first considerations," and there was only one group of businessmen excluded from the directorate, namely the competing exchange brokers, such men as Alexander Brown of Baltimore or Nathanial Prime of New York.[67] To be sure, during the Bank War other considerations entered into the selection of directors.[68]

As has been described before, nominations for directors of branch boards were made by the branch presidents, by local confidantes, and, to a smaller extent, by cashiers. Outside nominations (or, better, recommendations) were not rare. As a rule they were submitted to the officers mentioned above whose advice was relied upon when action was taken.[69] But final decision on and responsibility for nominations rested with Biddle, and occasionally he departed from local advice.[70] The nominations for the parent board were probably decided upon in a conventicle consisting of Biddle and his close friends on the board, including the cashier of the parent bank.

Politicians were excluded from the board and political considerations were only secondary in the selection of directors. In this respect Biddle's administration represented a great improvement over that of William Jones, while it is difficult to gauge the advance over that of Langdon Cheves. The selection of directors throughout the Jones era seems to have been made in the same political atmosphere in which his administration (meant to be a Republican one) had come into being. To illustrate, two items from the William Jones Papers are reprinted in Appendix III to this chapter. This atmosphere found expression also in the fact that President Monroe continuously recommended his proteges for jobs and directorships in the Bank.[71] In one case he even made himself the spokesman for local interests.

At the first election of directors in 1816 the stockholders established a precedent when they elected ten directors from each of the two parties, and from then on it became customary to divide the directorates evenly between members of the two parties.[72] That is to say, in the prevailing political atmosphere the practice of keeping an arithmetical balance between the two parties seemed the only way out. This practice Biddle threw overboard. He followed other methods of steering the Bank clear of party politics, the old practice being inacceptable to him since it was liable to force undesirable and inefficient directors on the Bank. In the Biddle era nominations were made strictly for business reasons; but when equally good candidates were available from both parties, political considerations were admitted. Although "secondary," they were "not to be overlooked." Thus, in 1824, a member of the Republican Crowninshield family was substituted for a Federalist parent-board member from Boston to "assuage" feelings which

otherwise might develop into hostility.
A few years later (in 1827) the cashier of
the New York office was asked how the New
York board members were "ranged as to their
political sentiments in regard to the government" of the state of New York; that is
to say, Biddle was alert.[73] In 1829 and
1830 after the election of Jackson and
after having, as he felt, successfully defended the Bank from being made part and
parcel of the spoils system, Biddle went
almost out of his way to have elected
directors friendly to the new administration.[74]

Prior to the Bank War it was
Biddle's practice not to make any difference between government directors and
those elected by the stockholders, as long
as they were in office.[75] Nevertheless while determining the election of the
latter, he abstained for reasons of principle from seeking influence on the appointment of the former. Consistently
with such a policy he felt no obligation
toward government directors once they were
dropped.[76] Even if they had proved useful
he would not, by suggesting their election
to the stockholders, continue government
directors who were not reappointed by the
President. But although he made no distinction between classes of directors as
long as the men were in office, he distinguished very much between director and
director. The terms "injurious director,"
"useful and influential director," "most
prudent directors," "leading directors"
with whom he had to consult can be found
in his correspondence.[77] On the whole, he
did not think very highly of the directors
most of whom gave only "occasional and
superficial attention to the concerns" of
the Bank, who had only a comparatively
small interest therein, and entered and
left the boards periodically. In one case,
the cashier of an office was advised to
keep certain information to himself and
the president of the office, an order
which is indicative of the status assigned
to the directors.[78] But others were highly esteemed because of their capacity,
character, or connections, and these became a sort of permanent directors. They
were reelected time and again, and when
they had to leave under the principle of
rotation their places were kept open, more
or less.[79]

So much for the directors as such:
as individuals they might or might not
become influential; as boards they played
no part whatsoever in the organizational
set-up of the Bank. Attendance at board
meetings, as in others in that period and
thereafter, was so poor that the boards
could not have acted as administrative
bodies. At a critical period Biddle had
to write special letters to directors urging them to attend board meetings lest the
hostile government directors get control of
the board.[80] Under these circumstances,
taking the situation realistically as it
was,[81] Biddle would not even request regular attendance at board meetings from his
candidates for directors.[82] The fact was
that under Biddle the administration of the
Bank became autonomous, that of the parent
bank by proxy voting as described in another context;[83] that of the branches through
the election of branch directors on recommendation by branch presidents and cashiers
through the parent board, the latter controlled by the chief executive. Such
autonomy of the administration did not work
to the detriment of the Bank as long as it
did business under its national charter
although later it proved disastrous.[84]

In the center of this administration
as the entrepreneur stood Nicholas Biddle,
the prototype of the modern business executive. He was forceful and strong-willed,
but at the same time urbane, even-tempered,
and considerate of the well-being and interests of his collaborators and subordinates.
Biddle considered a certain harshness of
disposition, which he undoubtedly possessed,
as indispensable for dealing with debtors
and employees.[85] Difficulties did not depress him, but instead spurred him to action.[86] He was able equally to grasp a
total situation and to master a detail, and,
being a man of both thought and action, he
was an unusual specimen of the genus
business administrator. In contrast to
Cheves, Biddle, like most men of undoubted
strength of will and character, could
afford to execute powerful leadership
gently and firmly, as he expressed it. He
would not sacrifice business principles:
rather would he let a director resign in
protest;[87] and a branch president who probably needed prodding was ordered to act
strongly without giving any indication of
weakness. On the other hand, he advised

his cashiers to act "without harshness and precipitation," "without wounding the feelings" of those with whom they had to deal, but nevertheless to look after the interests of the institution as their first duty.[88] All movements of the Bank were to be gentle, almost imperceptible, except in the results, so as to avoid all shocks and all jars.[89] After having decided on contraction in the winter of 1832 while issuing the pertinent orders to the branches, Biddle advised one of the presidents not to create unnecessary uneasiness in executing them, a policy which the parent bank was following.

In contrast to Cheves, Biddle looked at the Bank and its branches as one enterprise and, in contrast to Jones, with whom he shared the same outlook, he developed methods which combined centralized policy formation with local responsibility. According to Biddle the function of the central board was to direct the general state of the operations of the parent bank and the offices, but not to give detailed directions to the latter.[90] At the same time the "executive department" in Philadelphia was so organized that the chief executive kept himself informed on all details of the business of the branches and could establish a reasonable policy for the whole enterprise. Thus when Biddle discovered that he had not enough information on the accounts of the offices with each other, a special officer was appointed to watch these very accounts, and the central office was reorganized to cope with the situation.[91] At the end Biddle was very successful in combining command with flexibility in its execution, and his success was undoubtedly due to the fact that he understood the fundamentals of organization. Never did he issue orders over the head of the responsible subordinate: Outside nominations for directors were submitted to branch presidents and cashiers, as described above; debtors were not permitted to appeal to the parent bank, but referred back to the branch under whose management the debt had been incurred;[92] applications for loans were referred to the branch in whose district the applicant had his domicile or the security was located; when local matters were to be determined upon, as for instance the removal of the Connecticut office from Middletown to Hartford, the question was not only

investigated from all angles, but the local representatives were consulted all the way through. There is in the correspondence only a single case in which Biddle tried to force his policy on a local board; but when the latter in a very clever tactical move shifted the responsibility back to the parent board, Biddle immediately gave in.[93]

Under the then existing means of transportation and communication, Biddle had to give a good deal of latitude to the men who administered the offices. He used the word "latitude of discretion."[94] It was essential that his confidential officers understand his policy and be loyal in executing it.[95] Mutual understanding he considered more important than exact stipulations. Again and again within this framework he advised them to act as the local situation demanded[96] and was even big enough to change his plans when he recognized as valid local objections to them.[97]

As far as the organization of his enterprise was concerned, Biddle had two main functions: control and co-ordination. Control was exerted, first of all, through an extensive and elaborate system of reporting which went into such details that Biddle was able to take exception to individual accounts.[98] The letter books are in fact filled with Biddle's invitations, requests, and demands for information; and important offices, at least in critical times, reported daily.[99] One cashier, who fell short on this part of his obligations, was admonished that constant and frequent communications from all offices were essential to good administration since accurate knowledge was required as the basis of decisions.[100] Incidentally, information of a general nature was requested just as information on matters of the offices,[101] and all reports were closely watched by Biddle himself and by functional officers employed for that purpose. It goes without saying that figures so reported were evaluated by comparison.[102] A second method of control was that of inspections. These were executed by one of the cashiers of the parent bank[103] or by Biddle's second, Thomas Cadwalader,[104] or (in 1829) in a critical case, that of the Portsmouth office, by Biddle himself.[105] Prior to the trip to Portsmouth, in 1826, Biddle had conducted a personal inspection of the northern offices; but it can be taken for granted that this trip was as much an educational venture for Biddle as a means of control.[106]

In consequence of such control, depredations on the Bank were kept at a minimum. It is a high testimony to Biddle's knowledge of men and his ability to inspire loyalty that none of the confidential officers whom he appointed or whom he had elected, respectively, disappointed the confidence reposed in him. But a certain number of frauds were commited in the offices, and there was a certain amount of negligence and inefficiency. Catterall has described these cases correctly in every detail, but the description as a whole leaves an incorrect impression.[107] Probably never in his life was Catterall connected with public or business administration and so lacks an appreciation of the fact that no administration is 100 per cent efficient, that the large percentage of all dealings which run smoothly never come to the desk of the chief executive, while the small percentage of cases which give trouble fill his letter books and files (the source of research). Furthermore it should be kept in mind that Biddle's method of banking on the basis of bills of exchange against the crop in an agricultural area was so new and so revolutionary a mode of banking that mistakes and losses were unavoidable. All circumstances considered and especially the contemporaneous means of communication and transportation and the then available experience in large scale administration, Biddle's administration of the Bank was on the whole admirable. He mastered difficulties which neither Jones nor Cheves had been able to solve; forbidding the branches to function, as Cheves almost did, is no solution of an organizational problem.

Biddle's success was due partly to his methods of control and partly to those of co-ordination, which remain to be described. While control was based on a stream of information flowing from the offices to the center, a corresponding stream running in the opposite direction made for co-ordination. In one instance Biddle promised a cashier that he would have the best "correspondence" in the place.[108] Inspection trips, as a matter of fact, could be used for purposes of co-ordination as well as for those of control.

Another measure worked in the same direction: new branches, as described before, were set up mostly by a cashier of the parent bank in co-operation with the cashier designate of the office in question, who theretofore had been a clerk of the former. Such action was taken after investigations of the suggested places by some of the personnel of the parent bank or branches. In addition, co-ordination was achieved by making the non-resident (i.e., the non-Philadelphia) directors of the parent bank ipso facto directors of the branches in their respective sections and by authorizing them to speak freely to the local boards since in this way the actions and policy of the central office could be explained to the local group.[109] The same end was attained also by shifting valuable directors from the parent to the branch boards and vice versa;[110] and the occasional invitation of local officers to visit the parent bank must have had the same result.[111] In cases where methods of control and co-ordination did not work automatically or where mistakes were made, Biddle was not afraid to reprimand the men responsible for the failure, writing letters which while polite must have been very embarrassing to the recipients.[112]

An outstanding trait of his character, namely, his loyalty, contributed to Biddle's success as a chief executive. He was considerate of his collaborators and employees, as mentioned above, and he stood firmly behind them when difficulties arose.[113] When a certain cashier unjustly accused of infidelity was cleared by an investigation, not a trace of suspicion remained in Biddle's mind, and he backed him when attacked a second time.[114] With the same loyalty he stuck to the "old tried friends" of the Bank in the directorates, to use his own term: He would not permit Robert Lenox's enemies to push the latter aside although he recognized the man's shortcomings, and he refused to drop Roswell Colt of Baltimore, for fourteen or fifteen years a director in both parent and local boards, when other of his confidantes upon sending their proxies instructed him to vote for one of two other nominees.[115] Finally, Biddle was equally loyal to his predecessors, refusing to be shown in a favorable light by contrast with them. He recognized the difficulties under which they had labored and, although he did not think highly of Cheves, he invited the latter into the parent board to give him some satisfaction.[116] Cheves himself had adopted a lower method of achieving reputation; but Biddle's way undoubtedly raised the prestige of his enterprise, while Cheves had endangered it. In a lawsuit in which the counsel for a branch had placed the Bank in an attitude "disavowing the proceedings of Mr. Cheves and [Mr.] Oliver" Biddle preferred to lose the case rather than win it on that point.[117]

It is customary to denounce Nicholas Biddle as an autocrat, but this is true only if taken cum grano salis. To the contemporaries who took as the norm the administration of the First Bank of the United States or the administration of banks by committees of the board, Biddle's way of running his enterprise must in fact have appeared dictatorial. To the modern historian, however, aware of the development of business administration during the nineteenth century, Biddle's methods are seen in a different light. For the modern historian Biddle is just an early example of a typical nineteenth-century business executive managing a large-scale enterprise as the head of an autonomous administration. It would have been ridiculous for this man, one of the greatest bankers of his time, to poll the members of his board, ignorant in the particular field in comparison with himself, to find the answer to a banking problem; and Biddle did not do it. Neither did he wait for a decision of the board (which would sanction whatever he did) if quick action was needed.[118] Nor was he afraid of taking responsibilities. It is the wish of the board to turn from you personally, so Biddle wrote substantially to the president of a branch, and from the gentlemen of the office as far as possible any local feelings by assuming all the responsibility of our measures and by transferring to ourselves the odium attached to our proceedings.[119] On the other hand, although possessed of extreme self-confidence and contemptuous of public opinion as expressed in newspapers,[120] by mass meetings, and by politicians representing the wishes of constituents, as a rule Biddle did not act on important matters without seeking advice and suggestions. A large portion of the thousands of his letters

which have survived show Biddle asking a small group of trusted men for their opinions on burning questions. And he not only asked for advice, he also took it. Before deciding whether or not to apply for a new charter in 1832, his closest confidante was sent to Washington to explore the ground; and the final decision was made after much deliberation with scores of people. The renewal of the charter was, of course, a political question and Biddle's action in this case may not prove anything as to his behavior as a business executive. But in fact he acted similarly in the latter capacity, as will be described shortly.

To be sure during the Bank War another Biddle emerged, as will be described later, who does deserve to be labeled an autocrat much more than the Biddle of the 1820's. It was in this later period (beginning about 1833) that he wrote letters like the following, full of the first personal pronoun:

> For myself nothing would give me greater delight than to afford any relief to the suffering country and the moment when I think such a measure proper I will embrace it, but on my deliberate judgement the time has not yet come.[121]

Or, writing with regard to the approval by the senate of Jackson's nominations for government directors he indicated his preference to the incumbents hanging on to their jobs because new ones would have to be drilled into the same state of insignificance before they would give as little trouble.[122]

In the earlier period, however, Biddle was no dictator. Again and again he consulted local people as to the result of central office policy;[123] as to the impressions gained on a trip and the conclusions drawn therefrom;[124] and especially as to personalities. These requests for information indicate open-mindedness, especially since the cashiers were repeatedly advised to be frank in their reports and since numerous letters indicate an appreciation of a frankness which was not always pleasant. But what is really significant is the fact that Biddle consulted with his subordinates and individual board members before determining matters of policy.[125] In one case, which has already been mentioned, he was big enough to acknowledge that he had adopted the advice of a cashier

as the basis of national policy; in another he shelved a policy which met with objections; and in a third case, although
dissatisfied he gave in when he could have
overruled a local decision just by an order. As a rule he made suggestions and
avoided orders. If, in addition, one takes
all cases, like the one in which Biddle
announced a measure as having been arrived
at by Thomas Cadwalader and himself or
like another in which he delayed taking a
stand before he had consulted with the
leading directors of the Bank,[126] one certainly does not get an impression of
Biddle as a dictator or "Czar." A dictator would certainly not have accepted such
serious criticism, as that expressed in
the following letter from Thomas Cadwalader, in many respects a most important
one, without a break in the friendly relations:

                    Arch St. 14 March 1832

        You must have perceived, in our first
conversation respecting the Loans to printers, my surprize at their great amount. The
earliest intimation I had on the subject
was about a fortnight ago, from one of the
Board who said he was afraid they had been
carried too far. My memory then recurred to
all of which I had at any time heard, consisting of an accommodation to Gales and
Seaton of several years standing, which I
deemed an ordinary business transaction, one
to Duff Green, which had been granted I
think before I heard of it, and of which I
recollected nothing but the terms of a correspondence in which he had stipulated for
the entire freedom of his press upon the
Bank question - and some accommodations to
J. Harding, of which I had heard talk of a
mortgage or some similar security on his
part to the Bank. Of the amount and particulars of these loans I have no recollection.
I could not I think have been at the Board
at any time when large sums have been offered
by Harding - tho' the contrary is possible
as you are aware that I seldom attend to the
discounts, knowing little of the standing of
our dealers - supposing that the remark of
the Director, to which I have alluded, applied
to some one of these persons, I was induced
to enquire of you whether the Board had gone
farther in its Loans to Printers than might
be deemed prudent. The information which

you then gave me was of an entirely different
kind from any that I had before received: -
it related to the New York case - of which I
was, until the time utterly ignorant: - from
the memorandum made by you it appears that
those Loans were made on the 9th of Augt.
(while I was at the Sea shore) and 2d Jan.y
(the day after I was disabled by my accident).
The confidential footing on which we have
stood, and my supposed privity with all the
concerns of the Bank have placed me in a relation to the Institution different from that
of any other Director - and no censure can
fall upon any of its proceedings without affecting me in an especial degree: - even if
absent it would hardly be supposed that such
measures could take place without my knowledge subsequently at least so as to enable me
to prevent their repetition or further extension; as w.d certainly have been my strenuous
endeavour. I have, then, great reson to complain that no information has been given to
me of matters which may be unpleasant in
their consequences, to myself individually.
My dissatisfaction on this head has been increasing, from day to day. To resign would
be an extreme measure - and perhaps, at this
critical period, not a proper one towards
the stockholders, as my place cannot be supplied until the next election - on this head
however I am still somewhat unsettled. In
the meantime you will I am sure do me the
justice to acquit me of all knowledge of or
participation in the transactions to which I
have adverted - as I from the bottom of my
heart do acquit you of any wrong intention -
attributing as I do what has taken place to
the warmth of your zeal for the interests of
the Bank - to which you have been so earnestly devoting your time and talents.
        If I remain in the Baord until the end
of my term, the requisite attention shall be
paid to my duties - but, under no circumstances, will I, in the event of your occasional absence, act in any other situation
than my ordinary one at the table.
        Having thus given utterance to feelings
which I cannot disguise, - I am the more free
to assure you of my undiminished regard

        The final verdict on Biddle as
the chief executive of the Bank cannot be
reached before more extensive information
about "General" Thomas Cadwalader is available. A study of this man, for which
material is available,[128] should investigate

especially his relations with Biddle and his activities in the Second Bank of the United States. Cadwalader has been treated somewhat disparagingly, and erroneously, as the "paid lobbyist" of the Bank, whereas he was, in fact, next to Biddle (whose trusted confidante he was) the most influential member of its board. The decisive question for the evaluation of Biddle's personality is the extent to which Cadwalader kept his independence. In fact, the above letter from Cadwalader to Biddle shows him as holding his own and retaining his private opinions.

Thomas Cadwalader (1779-1841) was the scion of a socially prominent Philadelphian family which (rightly or wrongly) has been compared with the Livingstons in New York.[129] He had an honorable military record during the War of 1812, after which he held the rank of Major-General in the militia. How Cadwalader happened to become a friend of Biddle and how he came to join the Bank are still unanswered questions; although it is a fact that he was connected with the Biddle family by marriage. By the middle of the 1820's we find him rather active in the Bank both as a board member and on special missions. A letter from Biddle in 1824[130] shows that as early as that year Cadwalader possessed his full confidence and wielded considerable influence. A few years later, in 1827, we find him establishing the Nashville office[131] (a difficult task for business and political reasons) and then it was that Cadwalader became acquainted with Andrew Jackson. (As a matter of course, as soon as Jackson was elected president, Cadwalader, the social leader, offered his services.) On the same trip of 1827, Cadwalader also inspected the agency of the Bank in Cincinnati and investigated the feasibility of a branch in St. Louis.[132] In 1828, having thus become the channel of communication of the wishes of the people of Missouri, he was instrumental in the establishment of a branch in that state. By that time or shortly thereafter his status in the institution had become such that whenever Biddle was absent Cadwalader acted as president pro tem.[133] Under these circumstances, he was the logical person to be sent to Washington in December 1831 when Biddle wished to explore the ground prior to applying for a new charter. Cadwalader's reports leave no doubt about his capacities. He certainly did not disappoint Biddle who praised his "prudence" as one of the most striking qualities among his numerous "excellencies." Cadwalader had no opportunity to "lobby" for the Bank after the decision had been made to apply for a new charter.[134] In January 1832 he was laid up in Philadelphia with a collar bone and two ribs broken after an accident.[135] The extent to which Biddle relied on his advice is proved by bedside conferences which took place at that time. Biddle's letters to Cadwalader written from Washington in the spring of 1832 when he led the Bank's forces there himself show again the high opinion in which he held the "general."

Thus Cadwalader retained his influence not only in political but in matters of bank policy also. He seems to have been the one who felt strongly that the 3 per cent government bonds called up for payment in 1832 should be postponed by negotiations with the holders; and, therefore, he was sent to England. Once in London he acted like a soldier on the battle field; when difficulties arose, he took responsibilities and overstepped his instructions in order to win the day. Unfortunately his actions led to serious embarrassments for the Bank and for Biddle personally in whose interests he had tried to act.

The preceding paragraphs should have given a picture of Biddle's administrative technique. It was applied to the administration not of a bundle of local banks (Cheves' point of view), but of one branch bank, the offices of which had a good deal of independence and yet were held responsible for their dealings and forced to work for the common good. The offices were supposed to bank on the capital assigned to them; they could use their credit with other offices when the exchanges were high, but not in a way which would amount to a permanent addition to their capital (at the moment the exchanges were again favorable the accounts had to be balanced);[136] the parent bank itself was considered by Biddle as a part of the whole not as the whole itself, so that at times he stopped transactions favorable for the parent bank when they became detrimental to a branch.[137] On the other hand, when necessary he would order a branch to give up funds which were needed more urgently elsewhere; and whenever new branches came into existence a redistribution of the capital among all of them must have taken place.[138] In connection with domestic exchange transactions there must have been a continuous flow of short term funds back and forth, which welded parent bank and all the branches into a unit. The specie reserve of the Bank, which Biddle considered as an indivisible whole and which he shifted wherever the specie may have been at the moment of need, contributed to the cementing of that unit.

Biddle the Banker

So far the story has been confined to Biddle as the chief executive responsible for the organization and for the functioning of his enterprise. Just as important, if not more so, were, of course, his activities in determining the banking policy proper of his institution. In describing these, the picture of the chief executive will of necessity be rounded out.

Biddle began his career as the president of the Bank with a program of making it emphatically a commercial (a "mercantile") bank. For this purpose the available funds were to be shifted to those places where they could be given a maximum of employment in commercial banking, with country banking pursued only if it could be done with safety. (It will be described later how this policy was changed in the early 1830's.) However the Bank was not only to be just one "business bank," to use Biddle's term;[139] it was to be the leading one in the country. This goal implied that he saw the Bank as one among competitors, an outlook significant for the man who was more than a big commercial banker, actually the country's central banker.[140]

This program necessitated a policy of expansion through which Biddle developed the Bank to "power and usefulness." When Cheves resigned, the "active," or as one would say today, the liquid, capital of the Bank consisted of about eight million dollars. The rest of the total (amounting to $35,000,000) was invested in government securities, forfeited stock, and frozen debts. Consequently the funds for the

expansion of the Bank's business had to come from these three sources. First of all, forfeited bank stock was sold and, in fact, at very favorable prices. In addition, for years government stock was sold quietly, Nathaniel Prime in New York being obviously the most important sales agent.[142] By 1828 these sales were stopped or at least curtailed. On top of that, the Bank worked hard to unfreeze the frozen (or, as it was then called, suspended) debt, so that between 1823 and 1829 millions of liquid funds became available and expansion made possible.[143]

Expansion was to be practiced, as a matter of fact, both in the parent bank and in the branches, which Biddle wanted to see at the head of the business in their respective communities. The means to the end had, of course, to be adapted to the particular circumstances of the place in question. The large Eastern offices had to be freed from the encumbrance of large state-bank balances by daily exchange of notes and frequent liquidation of the balances. New York had to be relieved also of debts from the Southern offices, while the latter and those in the West had to be enjoined from issuing state-bank notes as they had previously done by order of Cheves.[144] In certain Southern and Western offices the abandonment of the reissue of state-bank notes almost meant a revolution and had to be achieved by tact and with caution,[145] after the office in question had been made strong enough to face every emergency.

The policy of expansion would have led into disaster had it not been supplemented by a wise discount policy. Thus Biddle had to determine both the character of the loans and the limit to which he wanted to carry the extension of credit. As to the latter, he was guided by what were, at the time, modern yardsticks, unknown to almost all American bankers: the movement of specie and the course of the exchanges.

The theory that note issues should be regulated by the course of the foreign exchanges had at that time a history of its own. It was first contained in Thornton's An Inquiry into the Nature and Effects of the Paper Credit of Great Britain, originally published in London in 1802. In this book Thornton explained the mechanism by which expansion and contraction of note issues by the medium of price changes acted on the exchanges. Since at the same time he denied the validity of the principle that note issues should be reduced when the gold of the Bank of England lessened and dissented from the belief that banks could issue notes without limit if they discounted business paper alone, the theory under investigation was the only one that remained.[146] A few years later David Ricardo took up Thornton's arguments in his High Price of Bullion, quoting Thornton with agreement.[147] Soon thereafter the theory was ventilated in the Bullion Report and the Select Committee on the High Price of Bullion was, in fact, emphatic on this point. It stated as its opinion that "in the present artificial condition of the circulating medium of the country it is most important to watch the foreign exchanges..." Representatives of the Bank of England were examined to see if they held the same opinion; but they did not. Nevertheless the committee pointed to examples in which the rule had been followed by the Bank of England, as Thornton had contended; it stressed that in addition to the price of bullion, the course of the exchanges was the best criterion by which inference could be drawn as to the sufficiency or excess of paper currency in circulation.[148] When the Bullion Report was taken up in the House of Commons, Thornton once more elaborated his theory.[149]

Thornton's book, mentioned above, was reprinted in Philadelphia as early as 1807 so that his ideas migrated to America very soon after their inception;[150] and the Bullion Report was eagerly read here soon after it was published.[151] In the 1820's and 1830's the Bank of England's fight for its existence was closely watched. The ensuing discussions revealed that for some time (in the 1820's) the Bank had followed the policy suggested by Thornton, Ricardo, and the Bullion Report. In this country, this policy was applied at an early moment, for it is pretty certain that Cheves' order of 1819, previously cited, forbidding the branches of the Bank from issuing notes when the exchanges were against them, was actually prompted by this philosophy.[152] On the whole, however, it took more than three decades from the year in which Thornton's book was first published for his fundamental rule to be

generally adopted in America; and Biddle probably helped to pave the way for that general adoption.[153]

Such is the history of the principle which guided Biddle in his issue policy and with respect to which he became more and more articulate as his experience and knowledge increased.[154] During the difficult year of 1825 we find him watching the movement of specie and counseling caution and prudence in view of the large and unsatisfied demand.[155] In the following year, on the other hand, he encouraged expansion because there was no foreign demand for specie.[156] In 1828, during the recession, he felt surprised and bitter that, regardless of the pressure for specie existing for several months, the New York City banks had not diminished their discount line, but had gone on lending as freely as before, thereby furnishing the means for the very demand about which they were complaining.[157] Biddle himself kept a special eye on the shipments of coin and remained "within his income."[158] (This term is very typical and was often used; it meant discounting only to the extent that other discounts fell due and were paid.) All this is to say that while Biddle was looking at the movement of specie and the foreign exchanges to guide his issue policy, the New York City banks were still far from adopting the same principle.

In a paper[159] written in 1828 Biddle explained his policy theoretically along Thornton's lines, stressing the influence of the note issues on the exchanges by way of the price mechanism. He pleaded for short-term loans of banks which would enable the latter, upon realizing coin demand from abroad, to choose the right moment, first, to cease expanding and, secondly, to begin contracting until the exchanges had taken a turn for the better. From that time on this yardstick became adopted more and more in America. For example, McDuffie, under Biddle's influence, came out with the statement that "the foreign exchange [was] an infallible barometer to indicate the soundness or unsoundness of our currency;" and James Alexander Hamilton in his memorandum of 1829 on banks and banking suggested to Van Buren that the bank commissioners to be appointed under the Safety Fund Act should watch the imports, exports, exchanges, and "the general range of the prices of commodities" and warn the banks as soon as they saw indications of an overissue of bank paper.[160]

Since even the Bank of England at that period was not consistent in the use of yardsticks for determining the total of its loans, such consistency should not be expected of Biddle; and, in fact, he is supposed to have been guided in his issue policy also by the ratio of specie in his vaults to notes in circulation. This latter policy of his will be explained, criticized, and compared with that of the contemporary Bank of England in another context.[161] It was bound to conflict at times with the policy resulting from the application of the yardstick previously described; but there is no indication that Biddle realized the difficulty. But neither did the Bank of England. Thus in the 1820's the course of the foreign exchanges and the inflow and outflow of specie determined the total of Biddle's loans, while in the 1830's the ratio of specie in his vaults to issues was professed to do so. On what he would do when the two policies conflicted Biddle was not articulate, but he seems to have inclined toward the latter one.

In the same period, the Bank's investment policy developed similarly: while it was regulated in Biddle's grand period by a set of consistent rules, in the early 1830's inconsistencies started creeping in even here. The first rule, forgotten during the expansion of the 1830's, was not to discount any accommodation paper but to restrict the Bank's dealings to business paper. Investments were to be "flexible" and "convertible" and not of permanent character.[162] In the earlier period Biddle cautioned his confidential officers regarding stock loans,[163] because they were liable to tie up the Bank's funds while business paper kept the latter "in motion." They were not excluded completely, however, and were made whenever they seemed desirable.[164] Biddle's policy regarding the length of time for which eligible paper could run has been explained in another context and needs no restatement at this point.[165] For reasons that will be explained later, bills of exchange were preferred to local paper; in fact, Biddle aimed at some sort of division of labor between local banks and branches: The former to be considered the proper agents for local loans, while the Bank was to monopolize more or less the dealings in bills of exchange both as regards discounting and collecting. What disposition the borrower made with the money lent to him did not concern the Bank, Biddle felt; but it was his policy, before determining on a loan, to make sure that the funds would not go to another bank or be used in a way detrimental to the institution or injurious to its customers.[166] He was exceedingly cautious in lending to country banks, never relying on their assets and good will, but always requiring tangible and convertible security, making loans, for instance, in the form of rediscounts.[167] In times of stringency the paper of merchants and mechanics was discounted first, that of brokers and auctioneers last.[168]

While Biddle was building up the business of the Bank in the middle of the 1820's the possibility of long and short term loans to other American countries loomed over the horizon. In 1825 the envoy from Colombia proposed to the Bank of the United States a loan of $200,000 which was to be distributed in amounts of $5 to 10,000 among the landowners of the state. Biddle, of course, refused to make such a loan since long-term loans on the security of land would not be made even to citizens of the United States, because of the extremely high expenses of such a loan, and because of the high risk; the proposal did not even offer joint liability of the landowners. (The historian immediately thinks of the joint liability established a few years later when Southern landowners borrowed with the help of their plantation banks.) At the same time, however, Biddle made a short-term loan to the Mexican government, a loan which was not without risk; Biddle was obviously anxious to initiate business relations with that state. The Mexican government had negotiated a loan with the London house of Barclay, Herring, Richardson and Company, the funds of which were not as yet available. In this situation it drew on its previous London connection, B.A. Goldsmith and Company, although the latter's Mexican agent announced in the newspapers that the drafts would not be honored. In answer the American representative of Barclay's endorsed the drafts so that they would be paid by the latter house if dishonored by the former. Although the guaranteeing house was not known in America, Biddle declared these bills with certain reserves and asked the Barings for information on which to base his final decision. The bills were actually honored by Goldsmith's who disapproved of the action of their Mexican agent.[169]

During the first decades of the nineteenth century American commercial banks, as described above, invested a considerable part of their means in securities,[170] and so did the Second Bank of the United States. Down to the 1830's it had millions of dollars tied up in "funded debt." The significance of this investment has already been mentioned and will be discussed further;[171] this significance explains Biddle's refusal at one time to sell government stock, when asked to do so, since that stock had to be reserved for the exigencies which its payment by the government or the expansion of the Bank's business might create.[172] To other securities the Bank was not entitled to subscribe; but, as he was always inclined to do, Biddle tried to cut corners here also. He advanced money to the Chesapeake and Ohio Canal Company on a note secured by its stock; he inquired if the Chesapeake and Delaware Canal Company was willing to borrow at 5 per cent on its 5 per cent Maryland stock;[173] he made arrangements with friends, for instance with Roswell L. Colt, under which they subscribed to issues of securities with the help of funds provided by the Bank on the pledge of such securities.[174] Finally, by 1830 Biddle considered using political means to get from Congress permission to subscribe to a Pennsylvania loan.[175]

Biddle's lending and investment policy will be scrutinized later on from a different angle;[176] his attitude toward deposits and checks has been touched on previously and needs no further discussion here.[177]

It was not customary in the early nineteenth century for banks to set aside reserves; but Biddle began to do this as early as 1823 for he considered them of utmost importance. He did not believe in "ostentatious" dividends, but in husbanding the resources of the Bank. Reasonable as was such a policy, courage was needed to put it into effect since a strong group of dividend-hungry stockholders did not approve. In fact, Biddle's presidency is said to have been put in jeopardy and he

was forced to go further in paying out profits than he would have liked to go.[178] Establishing reserves was of itself an achievement, but by tying together reserve and dividend policy Biddle made another acvance, unheard of before he conceived this tie. He resolved to increase the dividends, which were in fact very low when he took over, but not to advance a single step which he might be obliged to retract.[179] That is to say, he aimed at a policy of steady dividends. Consequently, through 1825 he did not pay as high a dividend as was warranted by the profits, although under pressure he raised it by 1/4 per cent to 2 3/4 per cent for six months. He increased it again to 3 per cent in July 1826 and to 3 1/2 per cent in July 1828, a rate which was held from then on. Thus Biddle accumulated a surplus for guaranteeing steady dividends, as was to become customary in twentieth century corporations. The funds set aside from profit seem to have been put originally into one over-all reserve account. However, when the latter amounted to more than $1,500,000, the account was separated and a surplus fund (a dividend reserve, as one would say today) was carried, besides a contingency reserve into which the excess over and above $1,500,000 was transferred, while further accumulation on the former account was stopped.[180] The question as to whether or not Biddle set aside hidden reserves, this author has not been able to answer.

Biddle, the Central Bank President

So far Biddle's activities have been discussed in his capacity as the chief executive of a large commercial bank. But, as a matter of fact, the Bank of the United States was more than a big commercial bank; it was this country's central bank and as such had to develop specific policies.

Biddle's movements in this connection were influenced by his intimate knowledge of the Bank of England and perhaps, to a lesser extent, by that of the Bank of France.[180] He knew, of course, what Adam Smith and Ricardo had to say on the Bank of England, and once cited the latter's posthumous Plan for the Establishment of a National Bank, of which he did not think very highly and which he considered unsuitable for America. His knowledge, however, went far beyond what could be taken from secondary sources. He studied the current parliamentary documents on the Bank of England and was so familiar with the details that he discovered a mistake in the Wealth of Nations.[182] He recommended to friends the perusal of certain of these documents and knew where they could be found by those who had no access to the originals.[183] Another friend was referred[184] to monographs on the Bank of England as, for instance, the book of McKay (which the author has been unable to identify) and the one in Abraham Rees' Cyclopaedia[185] (of which an American edition was then in the process of being printed in Philadelphia). The latter essay is particularly noteworthy because it stressed the central bank character of the Bank of England describing the English "system of banks" "with the great national bank at their head," which exercised a wholesome check on all of them. At the same time the essay quoted the review of Thornton's An Inquiry into the Nature and Effects of the Paper Currency of Great Britain, published anonymously in the first issue of the Edinburgh Review. This review of Thornton's book, written by no less a person than Francis Horner,[186] described the Bank of England as a "national establishment" guiding the commercial activities of the country "according to views of public policy."[187] Biddle not only read such material, but he learned his lesson.

Thus it is not surprising that such a thorough student as Biddle was aware of the central bank character of the enterprise whose destiny he guided. In fact he was much more conscious of being a central banker than his counterparts at the head of the Bank of England: perhaps he was the world's very first conscious central banker. More surprising is the fact that, inarticulate as they were, the stockholders sensed this. One of them bitterly complained that Biddle's object was "to keep in check the state banks and to regulate the currency of the country at their [the stockholders'] cost;"[188] that is to say, that he fulfilled central banking functions instead of maximizing the Bank's profits. In the last section of this chapter it will be shown how public opinion during the 1830's and 1840's came to understand the concept "central bank" without using the term.[189]

The character of the Bank of the United States as the country's central bank found expression in the performance of certain functions. First of all, the Bank was the fiscal agent of the government, as the First Bank of the United States had been before and as the Bank of England was at the same time. Not much need be said on this point, except that Biddle was aware of his responsibilities which he described as embracing those of the commissioners of loans, pension agents, and transfer agents.[190] In this capacity as the head of the government's fiscal agency he acted occasionally as a trustee for the government: at one time he bought secretly, by request of the Treasury and on account of the government, 3 per cent funded debt in the open market, purchases which gave advantages not otherwise to be obtained.[191] Up to the first years of Jackson's presidency Biddle considered himself an adviser of the Secretary of the Treasury in matters of finance, an attitude which culminated in his elaborate plan of 1829 for the discharge of the public debt, a plan which will be discussed in more detail in another context.[192]

None of the central banking functions performed by the Bank of the United States was more important than that of providing a sound currency. This goal had to be achieved without acquiring a note-issue monopoly such as modern central banks possess. Consequently it necessitated both a policy of keeping sound the state-bank issues and one of putting into circulation a currency of uniform value all over the nation. Charged, as the Bank was, with the "preservation" of the currency it became a "regulator" of the state-bank issues.[193] It acted as a "check" upon the state banks, to use the term applied by Lord Liverpool with regard to the Bank of England when he described its control over the country banks.[194] In other words, the relation between the Bank of the United States and the state banks was primarily "one of control and restriction," and Biddle was proud that, in spite of his occasional "recalling" the state banks to their duty of accommodating their business to their means, the relations with the solvent institutions were friendly. They realized that without such control the currency would relapse

into a confusion which ultimately would
overwhelm them.[195]

The methods applied by the Bank in
its capacity as the "regulator" of the
state-bank issues have been described by
Biddle himself, whom W. B. Lawrence quoted
as follows:[196]

> The great object is to keep the State
> banks within proper limits, to make them
> shape their business according to their means.
> For this purpose they are called upon to set-
> tle, never forced to pay specie,[197] if it can
> be avoided, but payment is taken in their bills
> of exchange or suffered to lie occasionally
> until the bank can turn around; no amount of
> debt is fixed because the principle we wish
> to establish is that every bank shall always
> be ready to provide for its notes.

Through this policy Biddle, as he expressed
it on another occasion, "melt[ed] down into
one uniform and healthy mass all the depreciated currencies with which some parts of
the country were afflicted."

However, as already indicated,
this was only one aspect of the problem of
"preserving" the currency. The other was
for the Bank itself to issue a currency of
approximately uniform value all over the
country. The difficulty lay in that the
course of trade and the indebtedness of
the younger (Western) parts of the country
to the older (Eastern) ones made all the
notes of the Bank flow automatically to
the Northeast where they were presented
for deposit or redemption regardless of
where issued. Every note of the Bank was
liable to be used as a substitute for domestic exchange. In consequence thereof
the notes of many branches had to be backed
almost exclusively by bills of exchange
drawn on those places to which the notes
tended, so that funds would await them on
their arrival. Natural as was Biddle's
extensive interest in domestic bills of
exchange, therefore, nevertheless it was
rather revolutionary. A few years earlier,
in 1818, when queried, the cashier of the
Bank of the United States knew of only one
bank besides his own which dealt in domestic exchange, namely, the Schuylkill
Bank.[198]

The fact that the Bank acted as
the fiscal agent of the government worked
in the same direction.[199] "If the Bank is
bound to transfer the whole public revenue
throughout the Union," Biddle said,[200]

and to furnish a currency payable in various
and distant places it must obviously provide
funds at these places and these can, of
course, be obtained only by purchasing bills
of exchange, payable at the points to which
the course of trade naturally directs the
notes. There these bills having reached
their maturity await the coming of that proportion of the notes which having performed
for a time the functions of a circulating
medium, are carried by the demand for duties
out of the immediate sphere of their issue.
The greater proportion of its funds, therefore, which the Bank can employ in these operations, the more readily can it sustain the
notes issued in the course of them. It is
indeed thus, and thus alone, that a circle of
sound banking operations founded on sound commercial operations contains within itself the
means of its own defence at home, and of providing for its notes which the demand for
duties may carry to a distance. These operations too are fortunately of the highest benefit to the community; they give the most direct encouragement to industry, by facilitating the purchase and interchange of all its
products, they bring the producers and consumers into more immediate contact by diminishing the obstacles which separate them, and
they specially adapt the Bank to the wants
and interests of each section of the Union,
by making it alternately a large purchaser
among the sellers of bills, and a large seller among the purchasers.

Thus Biddle's function as a central banker determined both his lending
and investment policy in his capacity as a
commercial banker and his large-scale entry
into the market in bills of exchange, then
considered the domain of brokers and private bankers. Prior to Biddle's activities
in this field the business of the Bank in
domestic exchange had been very restricted,
although Jones had entered it, probably
copying the First Bank of the United
States.[201] In comparison with his era this
line of business showed some increase in
the last years of Cheves' presidency.[202]
Whether or not the Bank should enter the
field was argued back and forth during all
those years and as early as 1819 Lowndes
was one of the main proponents of the new

policy. Later Biddle quoted him as having said, in a speech of February 18, 1819, that dealing in exchange "is the business for which the charter especially provides; it is perhaps for the country one of the most useful operations in which a national bank can be engaged."[203] Biddle himself considered the business in domestic exchange the only resource by which the Bank could sustain a circulation universally receivable without endangering its own security,[204] and he developed[205] it to the point of virtual monopoly.

However, Biddle felt that dealing in domestic exchange was not sufficient to give the country a sound currency; that extensive dealings in foreign exchange must be added thereto. It may be that his policy was the logical consequence of his conviction that issues should be made to depend on the course of the foreign exchanges and that the soundness of a currency was measured thereby.[206] Be this as it may, this step, too, was revolutionary since dealing in foreign exchanges was considered the domain of merchants and not that of chartered banks, even the Barings looking askance at these activities.[207] To be sure, as early as 1817, a committee of the Bank had contemplated entering the field because it would lead to the regular quotation of American currency in Europe, facilitate government remittances abroad, and be profitable for the Bank and enhance the value of its issues,[208] a rather superficial outlook when compared with that of Biddle to be discussed forthwith.

Biddle himself thus explained his entry into the foreign exchange market:[209]

A participation also in the foreign exchanges forms an essential part of the system, not merely as auxiliary to the transfer of funds by which the circulating medium is accompanied and protected, but as the best defence of that currency from external influences. It is the peculiarity of our monied system, that in many parts of the country the precious metals are excluded from the minor channels of circulation by a small paper currency, in consequence of which the greater portion of these metals is accumulated in masses at the points of most convenient exportation. - Now with a widely diffused metallic currency, the occasional demands for exportation are more gradually felt, the

portion exported bearing a small relation to the whole, occasions less inconvenience, and the excesses of exportation can be more readily corrected without injury. But when the great mass of the precious metals of the community lie thus accessible in the Banks of the Atlantic cities, liable to be immediately demanded on notes previously issued in the confidence of a continuance of the same state of things which caused the abundant issue of them; at the first turn in the tide of the foreign exchanges - when the supply of foreign exchange is unequal to the daily demand, the vaults of the Banks may be exhausted before any precautions can prevent it. These very precautions too, consisting as they do almost exclusively of curtailments in their loans, made suddenly - mostly without concert, and always under the influence of anxiety if not alarm, may fail with oppressive weight on the community, by the pressure on which alone can be produced the necessary re-action. This re-action moreover is necessarily slow, since our distance from Europe makes it less easy to restore the equilibrium than between adjoining countries in the same hemisphere. As this defect in our monied system, depends on the legislature, the bank has no power to remove it, and can only strive to guard against its dangers. Its tendency is to produce abrupt transitions, and violent shocks injurious to private credit, and which might prove subversive of the currency. It belongs then to the conservative power over the circulating medium which devolves on the Bank, not to be a passive observer of these movements, but to take an ample share in all that concerns the foreign exchanges. It may thus foresee, and either avert or diminish an approaching danger - it can thus break the force of a sudden shock, and supplying from its own accumulations or its own credits in Europe the more pressing demands, enable the State Institutions to provide for their own safety, and thus produce the necessary alteration in the state of the exchanges with the least possible pressure upon the Banks or the community.

At another time Biddle gave the following explanation of why the Bank had to enter the foreign exchange market: the state of the American currency depended largely on her commercial relations with Europe. In the course of the business between the two continents the balance of payments became adverse every so often, so that coin would flow out of the country. Such drain was liable to occasion abrupt dislocations in the business of the Bank which, in turn, affected the trading community. Therefore the "conservative power" of the Bank over the currency necessitated its ability to interfere on such occasions in order to break the shock of a sudden demand and to give time to the state institutions to adopt protective measures for their own security. This ability could be acquired only by large scale participation in foreign exchange operations so that in any emergency the Bank could supply the most urgent needs of commerce out of its own accumulations and credits abroad.[210] Thereby, at the same time, fluctuations of the exchange market could be prevented.[211] Two reasons stand out clearly: Biddle entered the field of foreign exchanges in order to protect the currency from foreign influence and to counteract possible disturbances of business. The former goal finds its explanation in the Bank's obligation to "preserve" the currency, the latter in the fact that Biddle took upon himself the function of keeping the country's business activities on an even keel, as will be discussed shortly in detail.

The first step into the new field was easy and must have seemed most natural. When taking it Biddle can hardly have realized that he was going to bring about a revolution. Credit transactions with large merchants, the best customers of the Bank, brought the Bank into the possession of cotton and other produce bills, drawn in the South on European houses, as Professor Hidy points out.[212] They were sent to London and their proceeds sold to importers in the form of drafts on the Barings, its London correspondents. Since this business worked well, correspondents were also appointed in Amsterdam and Paris, and the business in foreign exchange expanded.[213] Soon thereafter, however, having received an open running credit in London, Biddle gave the foreign exchange business of the bank a new turn. While the Barings, conservative as they were, expected that every draft of the Bank on its London credit would be made good almost instantly, Biddle, the "bold navigator" developed the sort of business which was to become customary among large banks all over the world in the later nineteenth century. Since the season in which the "crop" of bills of exchange,[214] as Biddle loved to express it, came into the market and the one in which the importers had to pay their bills did not coincide, Biddle drew on his credit with his European correspondents when the exchange rate was seasonally unfavorable and covered his drafts when it became favorable again. This method was considered speculative by the Barings and by American conservatives, while in fact it was based on the knowledge of a seasonal rhythm. Moreover the risk was limited by the two gold points, and Biddle was always in command of specie. At the same time he was able to exert some influence on the foreign exchanges by his issue policy. In fact, his operations were not dangerous for a powerful enterprise of the character and the capital and with the earning capacity of the Second Bank of the United States.[215] The economic implications of this policy will be discussed shortly.

To sum up, Biddle based a reliable paper currency on bills of exchange and a specie reserve which, although not sufficient for a central bank,[216] was larger than customary. This was, for America, a new method of banking, soon to be copied in various parts of the country by advanced banking leaders.

Part of this circulation consisted (after 1827) of the so-called branch drafts which seem to have been developed by Biddle under the inspiration of a suggestion made by John Forsyth in 1818.[217] These branch drafts, i.e., standardized checks of $5, $10, and later $20 drawn by the president or cashier of an office on the cashier of the parent bank payable to some officer of the branch and endorsed by the latter to bearer, have often been described. They were seriously criticized and condemned by enemies of the Bank during the time of the Bank War.[218] Many of those who attacked the credit instrument, which circulated like any bank note, did not even understand its character, as, for instance, Roger B. Taney. Its high quality was undeniable; branch drafts were considered indispensable for the operations of the Bank since the charter did not permit the signing of notes by special officers and the president was physically unable to sign a large enough number. They were beneficial to the community. Nevertheless Biddle was unwise when he introduced them.

In this case he acted as the chief executive of his enterprise rather than as the responsible central banker. In putting into circulation what were de facto checks he opened a road frought with danger. Branch drafts were copied by the Bank of Pennsylvania,[219] and slightly later circulating checks made their appearance in the state of New York.[220] (For reasons which are not clear to the author the tempting opportunity to avoid the legal restrictions of the note business by issuing standardized cashiers checks for circulation was never seized upon by any large number of state banks. It was only good fortune.) The responsible central banker should have shown more awareness of the danger which he was creating, although in turn he could have blamed Congress, and in fact did, for failing to understanding the situation and to give relief to the Bank.[221] Maybe the correct way out of the dilemma could have been found in a development of money transfers of the Dutch brand and of the business in demand deposits and in promoting and advertising the use of checks by businessmen; but, as stated previously, Biddle never recognized the great possibilities of this instrument.[222]

One important question with respect to the Bank's currency remains unanswered, but may be answerable by statistical methods:[223] Were the issues of the Second Bank of the United States prior to the Bank War elastic, in the sense that they reflected the seasonal demand for currency? Biddle himself knew the term "elastic" and used it for connoting deliberate expansion and contraction of the currency, and an astute anonymous author of 1837 emphatically claimed "elasticity" as one of the sources of power of the late Bank. The latter writer defined that term as the ability of the Bank to increase its issues from time to time: it furnished funds in the North in summer for the buying of wool, in the West in the fall for the buying of provisions, and in the South in winter for the buying of cotton. Its actions enabled the state banks in the respective sections to follow suit.[224]

It is possible that de facto elasticity of the Bank's issues did not so much find expression in seasonal expansion and contraction of the total amount of issues of the Bank which, however, is discernible in the figures, as in an automatic shifting of the notes of the Bank from section to section. Since the seasonal peaks and troughs did not coincide in the various parts of the country, elasticity may well have found expression in a rhythm of the following type: At a certain time of the year (the off-season) the notes of a particular branch accumulated in its vaults; in a succeeding period they were issued and circulated, at first in the particular section, and somewhat later were carried away by the current of trade to another section, a process identical with contraction in the former and expansion in the latter. Finally, in a last phase of the cycle, the notes were redeemed by some branch in the latter section and returned to the issuing branch in the former. Thus the cycle was completed, ready to begin all over again.

Domestic and foreign exchange transactions grew originally from the Bank's obligations as transfer agent of the government and as the responsible regulator of the country's paper currency. They soon gained importance independently therefrom. The Bank as a "national establishment," a central bank as one would say today, was expected to "equalize the domestic exchanges," a somewhat sloppy expression, the meaning of which was not without ambiguities. As a matter of fact, the Bank's business in domestic exchange pertained not only to buying (discounting) and collecting, transactions which would have been sufficient to back the Bank's issues and to provide for their uniform value; it also included the selling of domestic exchange whenever there was a legitimate demand. In consequence thereof, and in conjunction with actions previously described, the great mass of the American currency not only became more uniform than ever before and than it was to be for many years after the destruction of the Bank; it not only became more uniform than most of the contemporary European currencies which circulated over smaller areas; but the rates of domestic exchange at the same time were reduced to a negligible minimum. They were perhaps on the point of disappearing, regardless of the fact that Biddle objected to universal redeemability of branch notes as impractical.[225] In the late 1820's and early 1830's they oscillated around 1 per cent.[226] Whatever the Bank's enemies had to say on this point[227] the domestic exchanges were actually "equalized" to the full extent possible in the first half of the nineteenth century.

As Biddle "equalized" the domestic exchanges, he stabilized the foreign ones. Such stabilization resulted partly from his policy of buying foreign exchange during the season when it came into the market and selling it whenever it was needed. The Bank "as a large and constant purchaser of bills prevent[ed] fluctuations in the demand, and as seller of them, in the supply."[228] But more important was Biddle's bridging temporary disequilibria between supply of and demand for foreign exchange by short-term loan transactions of the type normally concluded by modern central banks all over the world. As Biddle himself expressed it, he prevented mischief in the foreign exchange market by the temporary use of foreign credit.[229] It is significant of the thinking of the time that a man like Condy Raguet took exception to this wise and well-executed central banking policy. He blamed Biddle for having destroyed "the most free and unrestricted competition" in the exchange market which "would be the best calculated to prevent overtrading in the banks, as well as individuals; for from such free competition the earliest indications of an excess of imports or of a depreciating currency would show themselves. That the operation of the Bank of the United States [was] to interfere with and to a certain extent to destroy this competition and consequently the check which ought to be suffered to operate monthly, weekly, and even daily with its warning" was, as Raguet pointed out, admitted by Biddle.[230] Why should the Bank be the "arbiter" of the exchange market, Raguet asked; and in the spirit of laissez-faire he felt that its power to deal in foreign exchange was injurious to the public.

As the years progressed, Biddle became a past master in the field of foreign exchanges[230a] and in a later stage of his career, as the president of the Bank of the United States of Pennsylvania, he

took a step never attempted before: he proceeded from stabilizing the foreign exchanges to controlling and manipulating the foreign exchange market. His first action in this direction was the issue in 1837 of interest-bearing post-notes of that Bank to American debtors in international trade. Thereby he created an additional international medium of exchange, acceptable because it could be sold to European investors. The issue of these bonds was bound to be reflected in the course of the foreign exchanges. But soon thereafter needing foreign exchange to pay the former Biddle went even further. Realizing that in America the foreign exchanges depended on the course of the cotton trade, he hit on the idea of controlling the latter in order to manipulate the former and in order both to revive the market of this staple commodity and to fight a prolonged and serious economic crisis.[231] Local corners of raw materials had been practiced long before Biddle's time, but it was unheard of for an enterprise to pool the export market of a staple commodity on an international scale as Biddle did in July and again in the fall of 1837. In so doing he inaugurated the type of price stabilization which since the days of the Brazilian coffee valorization before World War I has been attempted repeatedly by modern governments. The mere attempt was an amazing feat for its time, but it also succeeded. Only when attempted again in 1838 and 1839 did the transactions lead to disaster. In a period when Nathan Rothschild, queried before a Parliamentary committee in London, doubted if it were possible to "rule" for foreign exchanges of a nation for any length of time, Biddle had actually done so for many months,,by controlling the export of that commodity on which the American exchange market depended.[232]

Closely connected with its role as the regulator of the country's currency was the Bank's function as the holder of the ultimate specie and foreign exchange reserves of the national economy. Thereby a difficult task was entrusted to the Bank, entailing the control of both American and foreign (Spanish and South American) silver coins to the extent that the latter came into the United States. They were preferred in the foreign, especially the

China, trade. At the same time trans-actions in American gold coins had to take place. When during the Bank War the Bank was attacked for dealing in American coin its attackers did not understand that such dealings were the unavoidable and legiti-mate concomitant of American bi-metallism which could not work because of the over-valuation of the gold coins.[233]

Before the Bank could acquire in-fluence on the specie holdings of the national economy it had to have a firm hold on its own. For this purpose, as already indicated, the specie reserves of the Bank were considered as one indivisible fund wherever they were located. They were under Biddle's immediate control and were shifted by him from branch to branch wherever they were most needed.[234] Fur-thermore it was necessary for the Bank to attain a dominant position in the specie market. Mexican silver and Mexican coin were then imported through New Orleans as commodities at their bullion value. From the economic point of view, it was a most important function of the Bank to carry this specie, by its exchange operations, to the North, to "its appropriate markets." "This operation [was] carried out by the Bank, instead of being left to individuals, to the undoubted advantage of the commun-ity."[235] The American specie market was a seasonal one at that time and became tight every spring when the China expedi-tions were leaving the various American ports.[236] Spanish and South American coins were then in special demand and had to be husbanded. They were sold at a premium (in fact, different coins at dif-ferent premiums) and were protected against being used for inland circulation by keeping a sufficient quantity of American coin "in front." During the off season, however, they were often sent to the mint for recoinage, an operation which resulted in a small profit for the Bank.[237]

Always interested in big things, Biddle had far-reaching plans. He intend-ed to make the United States "the channel of communication" between Mexico and Europe. In fact, he aimed at wresting the silver trade of the western hemisphere from the British merchants who then con-trolled it. By 1824 an agent was sent to Mexico to enter into a combination of

exchange and bullion transactions; but the mission was not successful.[238] A few years later, for the purpose of attaining a dom-inant position in the Mexican silver trade, he proposed always to have an American man-of-war in a Mexican port ready to load specie. Furthermore he wanted the United States Navy to establish intercourse with the Pacific and to provide protection there so that he could intercept the trade in South American bullion at its source, buying it with bills on Europe. Finally he wished the mint enlarged and improved, since its inefficiency hampered the American bullion trade; for the Bank acquired bullion and foreign coin by paying the value thereof instantly, but lost the use of the money, i.e., the interest, for many months since the mint needed a good deal of time for coinage or recoinage, respectively. In-creased efficiency of the mint, as is evident, would have enabled Biddle to save interest and consequently to bid better prices for bullion or foreign coin.[239]

Although these plans did not mate-rialize Biddle was able to influence the movements of specie in this country: at one time he contracted to counteract a drain;[240] at another he lowered the exchange rate to the same end,[241] fortified by the state of his European credit. On the whole he considered the widening of the metallic basis of the country his great objective. It is in this context that one should see his often-discussed device for introducing into the East Asia trade bills on London in-stead of specie, resulting as it did in a husbanding of the country's metallic re-serves.[242] For this purpose he was also in favor of a prohibition of small notes if concerted action of the various state legislatures could be brought about.[243] As a matter of fact, the widening of the country's specie basis was urgent if only for the reason that its banking system was expanding. This expansion without the simultaneous increase of the country's specie holdings would have meant that specie was simply drawn from one vault into an-other,[244] that the reserves of the national economy became more scattered, and that the total of issues, still based on the banks' capitals not on their reserves, were less secure than before.

On the basis of a firm hold on the Bank's own treasures, with an almost controlling position in the foreign exchange market, and as a strong factor in the specie market, Biddle was able to act as the holder of the ultimate specie and exchange reserve of the country. The reserves of the state banks were so small that even a slight reduction was liable to strain them to the utmost. Any larger demand of coin for export cleaned them right out and it was therefore automatically and immediately directed against the vaults of the Bank of the United States. Often the specie situation became tight in the great Eastern seaports for no other reason than that before the sailing of the packets good bills did not present themselves in sufficient amounts.[245] As early as 1826 Biddle realized that the Bank had become "the great depository of specie," so that it was bound to be called upon as soon as demand arose;[246] and during the critical months in 1828 he expected to bear the whole burden of providing foreign bills.[247]

In addition to providing a uniform currency of national circulation, to establishing the soundness of the state bank issues, to equalizing the domestic and stabilizing the foreign exchanges, and to holding the ultimate specie and foreign exchange reserves of the national economy, Biddle considered it his duty to counteract cyclical as well as seasonal fluctuations and occasional disturbances of business. This program found expression in 1834 in a report of its Committee on the Offices, in which the Bank asserted that with the responsibility for the general condition of the currency of the country "was mingled the duty of avoiding every calamity and mitigating every shock that might, by deranging the currency, injure the community. It was for this...that at all times and under all circumstances the currency and the exchanges were objects of its constant solicitude."[248] Biddle's attitude was predicated on the following philosophy:

A mixed currency is eminently useful in prudent hands but a tremendous hazard when not controlled; and the practical wisdom in managing it lies in seizing the proper moment to expand and contract it - taking care, in working with explosive materials, whenever there is doubt to incline to the side of safety.[249]

This statement is of the highest interest, showing as it does that Biddle saw himself in the role of "managing" the currency.

Since neither discount policy, open-market policy, nor the modern policy of varying reserve ratios had yet been devised, a statement which should be taken cum grano salis, Biddle did not possess a tool to stimulate business in dull times. In such periods he could do nothing but think of the future and keep his enterprise ready to meet the problems of a new upswing. In dull times (down to 1830) it was his policy to put the funds which were no longer required in the banking business proper "in investments which though yielding small profits [were] readily convertible and from which it [the Bank] [could] immediately disengage them [the funds] at any moment when the reviving business of the community...demand[ed] the more active and useful employment;"[250] i.e., in government stock. After 1830 when the "General" government not only made no new loans, but repaid the old ones, such a policy could not be followed, and instead Biddle entered the field of accommodation loans, as will be discussed later.

More conspicuous was Biddle's intervention in time of an acute crisis on the one hand and of a boom on the other; i.e., his actions in 1825, 1828, and 1832. There is general agreement among those who have studied and described Biddle's actions before and during the crisis of 1825 that he handled the situation masterfully. He sensed the coming storm long before it broke and prepared in time for difficulties.[251] As early as April 1825 Biddle realized that the Bank of the United States was weakened through having parted with too much of its specie for the benefit of the China trade. Consequently he began to distribute the remainder so as to have it available at strategic points, and especially drew specie from Boston and New Orleans for New York.[252] At the same time he endeavored to make the Bank "strong" and "secure," impregnable, to use a modern term: he improved its liquidity by selling government stock; he strengthened the offices by sending them bills of exchange and bank notes payable at the respective places. But they were warned not to be too strict with the debtors in case the expected crisis should actually break. Some of the branches were authorized to

sell government stock if necessary, others
to sell drafts on the Barings.[253] Such
sales of foreign exchange were possible,
fortunately, for Biddle, since the crisis
came to England later than to this country.
Thus he could relieve the situation here by
drawing on London.[254]

In this stage of preparation for an
event which was then only a possibility,
Biddle was anxious not to precipitate what
he wished to escape. Therefore the state
banks were not to be pressed lest they become uneasy and diminish their discounts.
If they should they would be liable to accumulate large balances against the Bank of
the United States, which was not yet girded
for action and which had become their debt-
or through the repayment of seven millions
of government stock. Biddle especially
tried to avoid a situation where the Bank
of the United States and the state banks
from mutual dread of each other reduced
their discounts and became unable to accommodate the public. Therefore he advised
the offices to be gentle with the state
banks, but to turn the balances slowly
against them. This goal, of course, could
be achieved only by a process of contraction. Once the creditor position was attained, it could be upheld only by a very
cautious lending policy, going as far as
to decline even good business paper.[255]
Biddle was not willing to be carried away
by the current and, in the hope of doing
better or getting more business, to risk
the prosperity and safety of the institution.[256] (In fact the Bank cleared in 1825
$393,000 on a capital of $35,000,000.)[257]

When the crisis actually broke
Biddle took action in different directions.
Since New York was the center of the disturbance he rushed there "in order to
separate the danger from the alarm."[258]
He found two dangerous transactions under
way: one, a demand for specie for Canada
on the part of the British government, and
the other, a similar demand of a private
capitalist for setting up a bank in New
Orleans. The latter was induced to take
bills of exchange on New Orleans instead
of withdrawing funds from New York banks,
thus diminishing the total demand for
specie in New York. At the same time
Biddle attracted metallic money into the
parent bank by paying interest on a large
specie deposit made by the leading

Philadelphia brokerage firm, Thomas Biddle
and Company, which held certain funds in
trust for a foreign government. Payment
of interest on a deposit was a unique
transaction at that time, the significance
of which has been described in another context.[259] Once the danger of a specie drain
in New York had passed Biddle advised that
branch to expand its loans.[260] It was to
afford every proper facility to the trade
of the city without changing the creditor
status of the branch and it was to draw
specie from the state banks only if specie
demands were made on the branch itself.[261]
Thus confidence was restored and the impact
of the crisis broken. In the fall of 1826
the situation was in hand again to such a
degree that Biddle preferred paying out
specie to declining good business paper.[262]

There can be no doubt that for some
critical weeks in 1825 Biddle acted as the
lender of last resort, thereby fulfilling
a true central banking function. This fact
is of particular interest since thereby he
developed a precedent established as early
as 1817 when the Bank of the United States
had hardly come into existence. In Section
8 of the "Propositions respectfully submitted to the convention of state banks on
the part of the Bank of the United States,"
the latter offered the following price for
immediate resumption of specie payments:
in any emergency that might menace the
credit of any of the state banks it would
contribute its resources to any reasonable
extent in their support. Vera Smith has
correctly recognized that this stipulation
was a very early declaration of the lender-
of-last-resort-principle and that it thereby established a precedent.[263]

When Biddle advised the New York
office to go to the rescue of the business
community he was reluctant to make hard and
fast rules and to "direct" loans. He realized that new loans had to be decided
upon from day to day by the officers of the
branch on the basis of the state thereof.
If the situation permitted, the branch was
expected to make new loans, without, however, increasing those on personal security.
New loans were to be made on government-
stock collateral, preferably on the basis
of the "1812's."[264] Great care was to be
taken that the office did not relapse into
a debtor status and that its store of
Spanish dollars be husbanded. On the other

hand, Biddle was prepared to sell the Bank's 4 1/2 per cent government stock for cash although this willingness was not to be given public notice.[265]

This latter policy is of unusual interest since it was the opposite of the one which a modern central bank president would adopt in a crisis and depression. The latter would buy, not sell, government bonds in order to improve the reserve situation of the banking system under his care. However, in Biddle's time banks were not guided by their reserve situation, as has been described before and as should again be stressed.[265a] Although different from present-day methods under similar circumstances, Biddle's policy was reasonable and in line with the thinking of his time, especially with Sir James Steuart's philosophy. The latter had considered it one of the main advantages of government debts that they lured money out of hoards, and it was exactly this goal which Biddle tried to achieve by selling government stock against cash. As a matter of fact his action was an attack on the hoards into which funds of wealthy capitalists had fled from lack of confidence.[266] Biddle was certain that selling stock for credit would not achieve this goal since the parties who received the stock would pledge it with other banks for loans. Thereby no new funds would be made available. For the same reason he was unwilling to lend stock to banks, since he was doubtful whether such a measure would give relief.[267]

It is probable that Biddle's actions were influenced by still another contemporary line of argument. In the 1810's Mathew Carey had expressed the opinion[268] that the investment of bank funds in government stock made it impossible for the banks in question to lend a corresponding amount to businessmen. On the basis of this theory, just as on the basis of the one expounded by Sir James Steuart, it was again meaningful to sell government securities in a crisis and in the depression following thereafter in order to make additional purchasing power available to business.[269]

In 1825 Biddle had to protect the country in a crisis; in 1828 he had to check a boom and subsequently to deal with a recession which began in the spring of that year.[270] As Biddle saw the situation

during the winter months of 1828, imports from England and France had been excessive and were wont to prove disastrous since prices of American articles of export were low and the "crop of exchange" (incidentally a pet expression of Biddle's) was coming in from the South only tardily. He was surprised that regardless of these facts and regardless of continuous pressure for foreign exchange which had existed for several months, the New York and Philadelphia banks had not diminished their discounts, but had gone on lending as freely as before. Overbanking had led to overtrading, the banks themselves being responsible for the situation of which they complained.[271]

It was in February that Biddle first became alarmed by the constant demand for bills, regardless of the fact that the Bank had furnished them to an "immense" amount. Since it was the obligation of the Bank to keep the moneyed affairs of the country in sound condition and since it was especially its "business" to guard against "the train of ruinous consequences" which was bound to follow overtrading, it advised the New York office to take adequate action.[272] That is to say, the latter was to contract gradually and to distribute the restrictions in such a manner as to produce a minimum of inconvenience for the business community. The Baltimore branch was kept informed, although it was so strong that contraction in Baltimore did not seem necessary at that moment. But Biddle contemplated making use of the creditor status of the branch and of the fact that the Baltimore banks were well stocked with specie by drawing metallic money from them for the purpose of reinforcing New York.[273]

When one keeps in mind that money remained plentiful until spring, one realizes that, just as in 1825, Biddle sensed the coming difficulties at an early moment. Once again he recognized his responsibility as the country's central banker and once more he took action. It is open to question, however, whether this time he sensed the brewing trouble early enough. It is possible that he did not make the Bank strong enough in time to assist business in the recession of 1828 to the extent he had assisted it in the crisis of 1825.[274] Be that as it may, the following actions were taken: In February and March 1828 Biddle

began to place the Bank in a position of
security and strength so that it could
intervene whenever that might become
necessary to protect the community. The
precise point of intervention, however,
was, as Biddle felt, difficult to determine, and it seemed to him not feasible
to throw on the stockholders of the Bank
of the United States the burden of protecting the state banks against their own
improvidence as long as they persevered
in their easy money policy. It seemed
fairer that the Bank reserve its strength
and that it let the state banks for a
time feel the pinch for which they were
responsible through their own thoughtless-
ness. Therefore early in March the Bank
kept within its limits, discounting cautiously and, by presenting claims against
them, turning over to the state banks
every demand for specie. Thereby first
the Philadelphia and slightly later the
New York banks were made uneasy and were
induced to adopt a more prudent course.
The immediate purpose of these actions of
February and March was to reduce the rate
of exchange and put an end to the export
of specie. Biddle was willing, once this
goal was reached, to intervene for the
benefit of business in case his operations
led to great inconvenience. In March,
however, he still refused to do so. Such
intervention at the first sign of embarrassment would have been premature and
would have thwarted the ultimate goal by
enabling the state banks to pursue their
unwise course.[275] Early in April, however, Biddle saw the state banks following suit. By the end of the month he saw
their means exhausted so that it would be
easy to keep them within reasonable
limits.[276] He now counseled the New York
branch to discount on the basis of stock
collateral, good business paper, and
short term notes, the payment of which
was certain; and he was now willing to
intervene whenever the situation required
it.[277]

When Biddle undertook to check
the country's business activities the next
time, in 1832, the situation was completely different, for in the meantime he himself had led the country into an unsound
expansion. Regardless of the fact that
through the technical progress achieved
in the 1820's and especially through the

extension of steam navigation the stage
was set for a boom, Biddle shares the re-
sibility for an unfortunate development.
It was in this excessive expansion of 1830
and 1831 that Biddle, unbeknown to himself,
for the first time betrayed his trust as
the country's central banker. Nevertheless
while acting carelessly he did not act
criminally, when he made this first of the
many mistakes which were to follow. He
must especially be absolved from the blame
of having engineered this expansion for
political purposes, i.e., for making political friends through an easy money policy
and for obtaining a strategical position
in anticipation of his application for a
renewal of the charter.[278] Expansion was
not a "reckless step" as Jackson claimed;
nor was it managed with a view of making
the whole country the Bank's debtor and
thus compelling it to force the President
to choose between rechartering the Bank or
seeing the country going down in utter ruin.
Biddle did not go to the West to make a
breach in Jackson's stronghold.[279] Actually Biddle's policy was determined, on the
one hand, by the fact that the government
was paying back large amounts of public
stocks and was even beginning to discharge
the obligation with which it had paid its
shares in the Bank. (Such payments alone
were bound to lead to expansion.) On the
other hand, it was determined by the lack
of good investment opportunities typical
of those years. This dearth created difficulties for the young savings banks;[280]
it was reflected in Biddle's continuous
lookout for investment possibilities;[281]
it was to bring him into the field of investment banking after the Bank had lost
its national charter (as will be described
in a later chapter of the second volume);
and now it forced his hand to a certain
extent, for Biddle had to pay a satisfactory dividend to keep the stockholders
satisfied and could not afford to leave a
large part of the Bank's capital unemployed.
(There was something in Cheves' assertion
that the capital of the Bank was too large.)

The preceding paragraph should
have made it clear beyond doubt that the
expansion of the early 1830's originated
from economic and business and not from
political motives. Even when it was carried on into a time when Biddle applied
for a renewal of the charter of the Bank,

political motives played no part whatsoever. In fact at the very moment when the
discussions on the renewal of the charter
were in full swing the situation became
dangerous and Biddle started contracting:
in February 1832 the inland offices were
advised to settle their debts with the
parent bank and the New York office, to
discount exclusively bills of exchange on
Atlantic cities, and to stop lending on
accommodation paper.[282]

In the first half of 1830 Biddle
began his policy of expansion. In fact
ominous words can be found in the correspondence of those months. On the 23rd of
July, Biddle wrote to Albert Gallatin:
"But there has never yet been tried and
no one has scarcely yet imagined in this
country the elasticity, the expansive
power, of a well regulated bank conducted
on true business principles." He derived
that conviction from the fact that the
Bank had been able to expand its circulation from about four and a half million
dollars in 1823 to about fifteen million
in 1830 without encountering any difficulty. Somewhat later, on September 9 of
the same year, Biddle again wrote Gallatin
that the circulation of the Bank could be
increased with profit to the Bank and
safety to the community if the business of
the country demanded it, for the circulation of the Bank of the United States was
below that of the Banks of England and
France.[283] The latter issued notes redeemable in one city only so that its notes
could be brought to bear on the Bank of
France in time of panic in a more dangerous way than the circulation of the Bank
of the United States could, issued and redeemable as it was at numerous places all
over the country. This was especially
true since the American government was the
only large holder of Bank of the United
States notes and this large holder was a
partner of the Bank and interested in protecting it.

It has already been described how
Biddle was guided in his issue policy by
the course of the foreign exchanges and by
the movement of his specie holdings. Unfortunately for him, these two barometers
did not work in 1830 and 1831 because of
unusual disturbances. The European revo-
lutions of 1830,[284] as a matter of course,
resulted in the flight of capital to America,
a fact which Biddle saw, but which he did
not take into account.[285] Actually, the
statements of the Bank for the period between
January 1830 and January 1831 clearly show
the temporary inflation of the Bank's
specie holdings,[286] which was undoubtedly
the result of capital flight. It is possible, furthermore, that hazy theoretical
thinking on the consequences of increased
issues of the Bank played a trick on
Biddle. Although it conflicted with other
theories he held, he never broke through
the clouds resulting from a then widely
held heresy that overissues were impossible
as long as notes were redeemable: if issued
in excess they would return for redemption,
for the total circulation of a country was
fixed by economic laws and determined by
the volume of its transactions. Biddle
drew the conclusion that increased issues
of the Bank would result in a corresponding
decrease of state-bank issues, since the
former enjoyed a better standing.[287] He
did not see that the expansion of the central bank made general expansion possible
and that this possibility would be seized
upon quickly by the state banks. So much
can be said in Biddle's defence.

Expansion as such was probably indicated in 1830; but the extent to which
Biddle actually carried it was unjustifiable
and was severely criticized at the time.
One of the critics, who stated that the
officers of the Bank had "acted like mad-
men" and deserved "to have conservators
appointed over them" has often been
quoted.[288] And it was probably this expansion which induced Nathan Appleton to describe Biddle as a bold navigator who relied on his ability to take in the sails
in case of a squall.[289] He correctly
added: "now a regulator [i.e., a central
bank] should go for security, rather than
profit [as Biddle did in the expansion of
1830 and 1831][290] - with much ballast,
carrying light sail."

It was under these circumstances
that Biddle shifted large funds to the
West and Southwest and engaged them partly
in accommodation loans, partly in the domestic exchange business. Regarding the
former type of investment, it is not impossible that Bronson's ideas, which were
well known to Biddle, made this policy

seem undangerous. Maybe Davis Rich Dewey's comment is correct and Biddle actually tried to develop those sections of the country which provided raw materials, the export of which in turn provided the Bank with foreign exchange. But in so doing, Biddle, in a way, acted against his better insight. In 1823, he had had "more than enough" from country banking; yet now he entered this field again. To be sure, banking in the West, Southwest, and South on the basis of bills of exchange drawn against the crop was different from that banking on accommodation paper which Jones had practiced (and Biddle's accommodation loans in 1830 and 1831 were not excessive). But his own new and essentially sound mode of country banking was not conducted cautiously enough. By discounting too willingly bills of planters on factors who were apt to loan too high a percentage on the crops, these discounts were liable to degrade into accommodation loans, as in fact they did.

But such lack of caution was not the only reproach which one can justly make against Biddle. In 1828 he had correctly stressed that the explosive character of a "mixed currency," i.e., one consisting of coin and bank paper, made it obligatory in case of doubt "to incline to the side of safety."[291] This wisdom was now forgotten. One must furthermore blame Biddle for not having drawn the necessary conclusions from his own success in developing the business in demand deposits which is clearly reflected in the Bank statements.[292] It has been described in a previous chapter[293] how the movement of the Bank's deposits had come to indicate modern credit methods, i.e., the deposits of the Bank were not only mostly demand deposits but to a large extent created ones. Nevertheless Biddle looked only at the ratio of specie in his vaults to issues, a ratio which he deliberately kept at about 1 to 3.[294] He should have looked at the ratio of specie to circulation and deposits. This ratio in January 1832 was only about 19 per cent, that is to say, much too small for a central bank, the lender of last resort, and the ultimate specie reserve holder of the country. It is no excuse for a man of Biddle's caliber and for a thorough student of the Bank of England, as Biddle was, to say that he did not

understand the essential character of deposits better than most of his contemporaries. He must have realized that the Bank of England with which he vied, aimed at that time at a specie reserve of 1/3 of circulation plus deposits.[294a] It is here that Biddle's negligence lay, and his defence therefore was very lame: in Mercantilist fashion he compared his issues with his capital, and the ratio thus obtained with the corresponding ones of the Banks of England and France.[295] While there can be no valid excuse for the lightheartedness with which the expansion of 1830 and 1831 was staged, one should not overestimate its detrimental effects. The losses from banking in the West and Southwest were not exorbitant and were easily absorbed. The liquidity of the Bank could be restored, and since the state banks, of course, gladly followed suit in expanding the Bank did not lose its ability to control them.[296] Biddle's mistakes of 1830 and 1831 neither broke the Bank, nor did they deprive it of the power to fulfill central bank functions. By the fall of 1832 the situation was again in hand[297] through a policy of contraction, as described above.

The question of elasticity of the issues of the Bank, which is identical with that of counteracting seasonal fluctuations, has been dealt with previously,[298] and does not need to be taken up again. What remains is to describe Biddle's fight against such irregular disturbances of business as were caused by the repayment of government securities, a policy which was again in line with that of the contemporaneous Bank of England.[298a] The methods applied in this connection need to be seen in a broader context.

Discount policy of later nineteenth-century style, that is to say, the deliberate varying of the interest rate by the central banker for the purpose of controlling economic activities, was, of course, unknown to Biddle. In fact, he did not even see possibilities in this direction because he was accustomed to being restricted by a legal interest rate of 6 per cent. Under such restrictions checking a boom by raising the rate was impossible. It was possible on the other hand to lower the rate below 6 per cent, but this Biddle was reluctant to do. He looked at the matter not in his capacity as the central banker, but from the point of view of the chief executive of his enterprise. In 1825 he was glad that the Bank had resisted the temptation in the preceding boom time.[299] Nevertheless in 1830 he was tempted again to lower the rate when the Bank was unusually liquid and no investment opportunity was in sight. At this time he asked the cashier of the Boston office if he could increase his loans and particularly his discounts of domestic bills of exchange in case the discount rate was lowered. Frothingham was also asked for his general opinion about a measure of such a character, while Biddle himself confessed to having no definite idea on the subject as yet.[300] In fact he was loath to embark on a policy of a character which would stir up the hostility of the state banks and which would lead to a reduction of profits which could be made good only by a considerable increase in business.

In 1831, however, the business and also the profit of the Boston office had fallen off so badly that on June 7 Gardiner Greene, the president, was advised to reduce the interest rate, but with as little publicity as possible. "It is enough to say," so the advice ran, "that you have a capital which you cannot employ at 6 per cent and are therefore willing to lend it at a lower rate for some time" as a temporary and experimental operation. Back of this decision were special circumstances as well as the general increase of capital in America, but Biddle in taking action was not thinking in terms of a business principle nor did he act in order to gain influence on the country's or the section's business activities.[301]

Nevertheless Biddle did make use of a lower interest rate to preclude occasional disturbances which might easily have been caused by the repayment of government securities. Such repayments once announced forced the Bank to accumulate funds in preparation of the disbursement. Or, in other words, a certain percentage of the government deposits formerly loaned out had to be withdrawn, an action which was, of course, identical with contracting. Consequently, whenever the holders wished to anticipate the proceeds, Biddle was glad to assist them in order to avoid contraction. He went so far, in fact, as to

invite applications for loans of that character by offering therefor a lower interest rate. It goes without saying that a piecemeal anticipation of the disbursements over a longer period of time helped to smooth an otherwise dangerous transaction.[302] It is not clear when this policy was inaugurated, but the resolutions of the board of July 9 and 17, 1830 authorizing the exchange committee to lend on collateral security of approved public stock at a rate of not less than 5 per cent and 4 1/2 per cent, respectively, at least implemented it.[303]

Thus in his capacity as his country's central banker Biddle continually intervened in its business activities. Except when he expanded in 1830 and 1831 this intervention was beneficial. Later, as is generally known, in the contraction of 1834 and 1835 Biddle went on interfering, but now for selfish reasons. He tried to force Congress to compel the President to renew the charter of the Bank. It is hard to understand how the man who had felt so strongly his responsibility toward his country came to forget so completely that his power was due to his semi-official status or how he could abuse it so badly for non-official ends. The only explanation seems to be that Biddle, identifying himself with the Bank and the Bank (to a certain extent, correctly) with the commonweal,[304] believed that the end justified the means. When this period of struggling and fighting had begun Biddle's statements no longer were as sincere as they had been previously. Especially he wanted to make the country forget his ability to shape its business. In this period John Quincy Adams cited Biddle as describing

the extremely delicate position in which the institution stands toward the commercial community:.... So long as the Bank keeps within the line of safe operations upon its own funds it leaves those of commerce to regulate themselves. It neither seeks to increase nor diminish them. When, from whatever cause, there is among the merchants a tendency to overtrading it is not the province of the bank directly to interpose against it, for that would be to exercise an invidious and improper control over business with which it has but a remote concern. Its general duty is to grant facilities while it has disposable funds uninvested. The point at which it ought to stay its hands is a matter of difficulty to determine.[305]

In the same period Biddle claimed that it was "the duty of the Bank to take the state of the country as the country had chosen to make it." "If there was a demand for money and the Bank had the means of supplying it, why should it not? The object of its creation was precisely that." That is to say, he suddenly disclaimed all central banking functions, presented his institution as a big commercial bank, and claimed that it was his function to remain perfectly passive.[306] Dissimulation could hardly have gone further.

Although efficient in most respects, Biddle, of course, fell short in a few. He developed the attitude typical of the successful businessman: that the setup in which he had succeeded was well-nigh perfect[307] and did not need fundamental change. Not all of his policies were sound: his issue policy was not consistent; and his specie reserves were too small in view of the development of the Bank's deposit business and of the fact that it held the ultimate specie reserves of the country. Biddle did not foresee the future of the check; consequently when cornered by unreasonable charter conditions he created a potential danger in the branch draft.[308] Biddle did not recognize as an obligation of the Bank of the United States the building of regional clearing systems around the branches, topped by a national one headed by the parent bank: therefore in New England this central bank function came into the hands of the Suffolk Bank. Finally, he did not see that a central bank should be more or less a bankers' bank. His relations with the state banks were marked by distrust and the feeling of superiority. Biddle himself regarded them as "delicate" because of the excited feeling of the persons interested in these banks,[309] and he never overcame the idea of competing with them. He considered the bringing of the state banks into a condition of soundness without employing "any harshness or unnecessary constraint," his foremost task.[310] It is against this background that one should see Biddle's often quoted unstatesmanlike remark that it had been in the power of the Bank of the United States to break any state bank, but that he had never abused it.[311]

Biddle's policy toward the state banks was vacillating. On the one hand, it was the accepted practice of the parent bank and of the branches to back state banks which, although sound, were temporarily in distress. This policy was followed especially in 1825 when rediscounting seems to have been used to that end.[312] Furthermore there were numerous occasions in which Biddle assisted banks informally by advising the branches not to make demands on them if they were not pressed themselves.[313] Finally, at times assistance was lent in an indirect way by liberal loans to merchants (who otherwise would have demanded accommodations from local banks), by getting money out of hoards, and by temporary import of short-term capital. With such cases in mind, Biddle could point out that if there was trouble among the banks (he meant, if there was a crisis) their only security was the Bank of the United States, which held its power as a trust for the ultimate protection of the banking system whose fate was involved in the fate of the Bank.[314] But on the whole, checking the state banks came before assisting them; competition played a certain part, as mentioned previously;[315] in his dealings with country banks, Biddle was rather suspicious[316] and in those with the city banks, reluctant. (It should not be forgotten that the Bank of England also dealt with banks only indirectly.) In fact, in its early years the First Bank of the United States was nearer to becoming a bankers' bank than the Second Bank ever was during its career. Instead of leading in the building of networks of correspondents and instead of making the Bank the central reservoir of bankers' balances, Biddle let it fall far behind certain New York banks in this respect.[317] Thus he permitted the latter to build up a type of organization which allowed them collectively to fulfill central banking functions to a certain extent after the Bank of the United States had been destroyed.

There was one more serious shortcoming in Biddle's thinking. He who had become the country's central banker did not visualize his position as a quasi-officer of the government. His theory was that the influence of the government on the Bank was predicated on its stockholdings;[318] that it was a "partner" in the Bank. He considered the independence of the Bank's president from all executive influence as a vital principle.[319] One can grant Biddle this much, that the American government of the 1830's was not so constructed as to permit an American central bank to listen to its wishes as a matter of course (as the Bank of England could); but a more correct view of his status would have kept Biddle from his moral downfall during the Bank War.

The successful execution of central banking functions by the Bank of the United States was predicated on the possession by Biddle and his officers of a specific attitude and outlook, in fact the same which had distinguished the board of the First Bank of the United States and which had been exhibited by Dallas when he fought for a second national bank. These Biddle continuously practiced at the peak of his career and he abandoned them only when the heat of battle during the Bank War carried him away. Two elements are essential for the spirit in which central banking had to be conducted, then as now: a feeling of responsibility for the national economy[320] and the curb of the profit motive.

When the Bank was chartered such ideas had been expressed not only by Dallas but also by other participants in the debate, as, for instance, Representative Telford from Georgia; and Biddle had hardly become the president of the Bank before he exhibited the spirit required of the central banker. When he embarked on his original course of expansion he took pains to watch the effect of his policy on the circulation and on business in general and the impression made thereby on the mercantile community.[321] It was in this spirit of responsibility that the crisis of 1825 was handled,[322] and the policy of 1828 conceived: the monied affairs of the country were to be kept in sound condition, and the methods used to that end were not to cause unnecessary alarm.[323] In this same spirit Biddle was currently and keenly interested "in the financial concerns of the country with which the Bank [was] so much connected," as he wrote in 1825.[324] He wished the value of the services of the Bank to the community impressed on the latter, that is to say, he looked for its backing; while on the other hand he was willing to do what he considered his duty to the country even in opposition to state banks and state legislators, although in a

manner perfectly respectful and concilatory to both.[325]

Responsibility of the Bank to the country was implicitly recognized by Biddle during the Bank War at the very moment when he was repudiating it. In a report of a committee of the Bank made in that period the following telling words can be found:

On the 1st of October 1833 the violation of the charter of the Bank put an end to all that responsibility. On that day the Bank of the United States as a component part of the financial system established by Congress [i.e., as a central bank]...ceased and ...[its lending policy] became a matter for them and for them alone to decide.[326]

As to the second essential component part of the typical central banker's attitude, the curb of the profit motive, a letter of Biddle's in 1828 may be cited: the situation of the country seemed to him so critical at that time that, as he wrote, the Bank had to sacrifice some of its profit to advance the great purpose of saving the community from serious inconvenience.[327] It has been described before how some stockholders accused Biddle of not maximizing the Bank's profit and of performing central banking functions instead. In 1831 and 1832, on the other hand, striving for profit enticed Biddle away from the true obligations of his semi-public status.

Biddle's attitude and outlook can be justly appraised only if seen against the background of contemporary thinking. The phenomenon of a central bank was still so new that it could not be readily understood, and contradictory views were held on the obligations of the national bank. During the debates preceding the chartering of the Second Bank of the United States two points of view were represented: some of the proponents wanted the national bank established for national purposes and for the public benefit. For these men the employment of private interests in a national bank was only incidental and, in fact, an evil which they were willing to accept only for convenience's sake and in the interest of more efficient management. In thus compromising they intended nevertheless that the elements of public and private interests should be combined in the national bank in such a way that the

former was secured "a control of the latter." "The interest of this bank should
be made subservient to the interest of the
public;" it was not to be a "great money
machine, but an institution of a national
character."[328] This outlook survived; and
during the time of the Bank War found expression in a statement of the government
directors of the Bank appointed by Jackson:
"We have regarded that institution not as
a source of profit by individuals, but as
an organ of government established by the
nation for its own benefit."[329] In contrast, the other group among the original
exponents of a national bank considered it
primarily as a means toward furthering the
economic interests of the commercial classes, thought of by themselves as being
identical with those of the country.
Their enemies, however, imputed to them a
desire to strengthen the arm of wealth
thereby.

Once the Bank was organized the
decisive question was: how should it, the
business corporation endowed with quasi-
public functions, act in the case of a
conflict of interests. On this point
Crawford wrote in 1819: "The first duty of
the board is to its stockholders, the
second to the nation."[330] This opinion
although coming from a Secretary of the
Treasury represented, of course, a very
early stage in the development of central
banking. A later step found expression in
Ingham's words of 1829 which probably
embody also a quotation from a letter of
Crawford's: "The Board has a duty to the
nation to fulfill; whether in a conflict
between that duty and their duty to the
stockholders the one or the other ought to
yield and be secondary, although patriotism would not doubt, I submit to sounder
casuists than you or me."[331] At the height
of his career Biddle had solved the problem
de facto by recognizing responsibility
toward the national economy and by voluntarily cooperating with and servicing the
government.[332] Notwithstanding this outlook Biddle did not permit any interference by the Secretary of the Treasury in
the conduct of the institution; while
Ingham, then filling that station, considered it an obligation to suggest his official views as to its proper management.
For Biddle, the Bank belonged to the nation, and its prosperity and usefulness

would have been destroyed the moment it
lost its independence from party strife.
It was a tragic situation in which early
American central banking collapsed: it
broke down because of conflicting economic
interests and because American government
was party government. There was a national
bank, but no real nation; instead of a
nation there were interests bitterly opposed to each other, parties locked in a
deadly struggle, with local feeling and
sectional prejudice on top of all. Down
to about 1831 Biddle was many years ahead
of his time; but when he was forced to
struggle for his advanced goal by adapting
himself to the methods of his period he
not only failed, but even dropped below
its ethical level.

Biddle committed a serious mistake
when he tried to uphold the central bank
status of his enterprise, once it had lost
its national charter.[333] For that purpose
the resourceful man devised a new type of
bank organization. The branches of the old
Bank of the United States had to be sold,
of course, but in their place Biddle built
up what one would call group banking today,
besides establishing some branches in
Pennsylvania.[334] As early as the fall of
1832 Matthew St. Clair Clarke had suggested
that Biddle apply for a Pennsylvania charter and yet bank on a national scale by
making use of agencies instead of branches.
While adopting the suggestion in principle,
Biddle went further. In the spring of
1836 he managed to receive from the legislature an amendment to his Pennsylvania
charter. This amendment (An Act requiring
the Banks of this Commonwealth to make
quarterly statements to the Auditor General
and for other purposes, approved April 1,
1836) in section 2 permitted the Bank of
the United States of Pennsylvania "to purchase and hold any bank stock."[335] Consequently in September 1836, the Bank of the
United States of Pennsylvania purchased
the Merchants Bank of New Orleans which
had a capital of $1,000,000; in November
of the same year the Insurance Bank of
Columbus, Georgia was bought up. At that
time the acquisition of a bank in Alabama
was at least under contemplation. By 1838
Biddle tried to set up a Free Bank in New
York, a plan which came to naught because
of strong political opposition; but, instead, friends of the Bank established the

Bank of the United States in New York with a capital of $200,000, allegedly an independent enterprise but de facto one under the control of Chestnut Street. (M. Robinson, formerly cashier of the New York branch of the Bank and later the New York agent of the Bank of the United States of Pennsylvania, seems to have become its president.) Finally in August 1839 the charter of the Hamilton Bank of Baltimore passed into the possession of the Bank of the United States of Pennsylvania. In addition the former cashier of the Washington branch of the Bank of the United States was employed as the agent of its successor, and it is very probable that similar arrangements existed elsewhere, for instance, in Richmond, Mobile, Charleston (?), and Kentucky. These agencies seem to have circulated the notes of the Bank by buying bills of exchange. That is to say, a remarkable bank organization on a national scale was in the process of being built up again.[336]

The building of this organization as well as the policy thereof betrays Biddle's strategy: he still hoped that the national charter, and, thereby its old place in the national economy, could be restored to the Bank; and by going on fulfilling the old central banking functions as before he tried to keep the road open.[337] It was unfortunate that many members of the commercial community were so accustomed to considering Biddle as the central banker that as late as 1837 they urged him to go on as before.[338] At the same time, to follow their suggestions and intervene in the crisis of that year, appeared a personal triumph to a man as vain as Biddle. But such a policy was in fact an abuse of the prestige and credit formerly acquired and of the large capital of the Bank of the United States of Pennsylvania which had become just one of the many state banks. That futile strategy explains Biddle's actions of 1837, through which once more and for the last time he did a great service for his country: he discounted the notes of merchants in need of foreign exchange and handed them in lieu thereof interest-bearing post-notes of the Bank of the United States of Pennsylvania. These were an acceptable international medium of exchange, since they were saleable on the European exchanges. Furthermore he stabilized the rate of foreign

exchange by upholding the cotton market. His ultimate goal also explains his resistance to an early resumption of specie payments, for which it is customary to blame him. Biddle was correct in his assertion that the time for nation-wide resumption had not yet come in 1838; his opponents looked to the regional (New York) picture rather than to the national. In addition he had a correct, although only intuitive, feeling for the difficulties resulting from the downward trend of the price level, the downward swing of what we call today the Kondratieff-wave. He understood better than his opponents the dangers of deflation and the inequities resulting therefrom to the creditors.[339] But price level and exchange market were no longer Biddle's responsibilities.[340] Nor did he possess the ability to deal with such problems once his enterprise had lost its national charter, the financial power resulting from command over government funds, the backing of the government, and the confidence of wide strata of the American people. Under these circumstances his attempts to master the depression of the late 1830's were bound to fail although they prove deep economic understanding and although they were technically masterful; they only made a bad situation worse, and tainted as they were by self-interest, ultimately brought nothing but dishonor to the man who devised them.

Biddle, the Politician

As one reads Biddle's letters in the thousands of pages of his letter books, into which they were copied day by day, the Bank War approaches with the inevitability of fate in a Greek tragedy.

When Jackson's administration took office Biddle showed no apprehension, let alone hostility. There are indications that he may even have been favorably inclined to it. This is all the more possible since his close friend Cadwalader not only voted for the General, but even promoted the latter's election.[341] Partisan feeling was essentially alien to Biddle[342] and, however he may have voted in the presidential election of 1828, he was not only willing, but anxious to cooperate with the new President and his men, just as he had with the Adams administration. The Bank was willing to "give its aid cordially and sincerely to every administration," without being partisan of any.[343]

Although political considerations had never been completely excluded by the Bank, as described previously, Biddle had done his best to steer the institution clear of politics. Just as money was neither Whig nor Tory, as Biddle loved to quote from Dean Swift, the Bank was neither a Jackson man, nor an Adams man; it was just a bank which was "cautiously and fastidiously" kept from entering a field in which it had no concern.[344] In the case of the Kentucky offices, which were to a certain extent actually under political influence, Biddle did his best to give them a strict business character.[345] The officers of the Bank were advised and admonished that neutrality in political contests was their obligation.[346] If any officer had been found guilty of such an abuse of power as to make it either promote or fight the election of the humblest politician it would have been the last act of authority which he would have been permitted to exercise, as Biddle wrote.[347]

Such were Biddle's feelings and intentions when exponents of the incoming Jackson administration tried to interfere with the elections and appointments of the Bank, attempts which culminated in letters written in the summer of 1829 by Jackson's first Secretary of the Treasury, S. D. Ingham.[348] Later Biddle interpreted these efforts, probably correctly, as attempts to include the Bank in the spoils system.[349] When they took place he obviously acted[350] according to the rule principiis obsta, but he answered in a way which was not only not statesmanlike, but even unbecoming to a business executive: his answers smack of the lawyer. At the same time, emotions got the better of Biddle, who could not "notice" some passages in Ingham's letter "without violence to [his] taste and temper."[351] Jackson, on the other hand, considered the essential point of Biddle's letters to be the statement that the board did not acknowledge the slightest responsibility to the Secretary of the Treasury regarding the political opinions and conduct of the officers of the Bank and that it considered their political opinions and conduct a subject on which it never consulted and never desired to know the views of any administration.[352]

Having defended the principle of the freedom of the Bank's administration from government interference Biddle went far to bring friends of President Jackson into the directorates, as mentioned previously,[353] and he did his best not only to cooperate with, but even to strengthen the President. No document seems to show better Biddle's eagerness to cooperate with Jackson than the letter of November 16, 1829 to William B. Lewis with which he introduced his plan for the repayment of the public debt[354] in conjunction with a continuation of the charter:

There is one glory which I should rejoice to see Gen. Jackson possess - a glory in which he can have no equal and no rival. In the history of the world, no nation has ever paid off its debt - no chief Magistrate therefore has ever enjoyed the great distinction of freeing his country's industry from that burden. This Gen. Jackson can now do. He may make the 8 [th] of Jan. 1833 as illustrious as the 8th of Jan. 1815 - on the first beating off his country's enemies - on the second paying off his country's debts. What a day of Jubilee that would be for him - what a fine medal might be struck to commemorate so unexampled an event. He might be almost tempted to go over to the Branch Bank & pay off the last dollar in person. Only think of a message to Congress announcing that the whole debt of the U.S. including all that was borrowed in the revolution - and amounting to little short of two hundred millions - was finally discharged. Such a State paper would be read in every corner of the civilized world. All this can be accomplished I believe, without any difficulty. I have thought a great deal of it & see my way very clearly. It depends only on Gen. Jackson to say that it shall be.

What is a great satisfaction too, I think is, that this clearing off the debt can be accomplished, not by any straining of the resources of the country - not by any taxation, but by a measure which in itself alone is a great public benefit, I mean the simple continuance of the Bank. As the end of its charter approaches, a thousand schemes will be agitated and after keeping the country in a fever of confusion & anxiety & speculation for two or three years it will be found essential to continue the Bank in some shape - and probably none better than the present can be

devised. All these evil[s] may be avoided if
Gen. Jackson after perfectly satisfying himself on the subject would take it up in his
independent & energetic way - and carry through
the measure of paying off the whole debt during
his first term by rechartering the Bank. How
it can be done, the enclosed paper will explain - whether it shall be done must depend
on the General himself.

This letter and the plan submitted
therewith resulted in a meeting of the two
men in Washington by the end of November,
1829.[355] The sketch of this interview
which Biddle drew up has been discussed
and reprinted repeatedly.[356] It did not
take place under a lucky star, but led to
a tragic misunderstanding. Biddle was
warned of the President's hostility toward
the Bank by such men as Alexander Hamilton
and Roswell L. Colt.[357] Nevertheless he
left Jackson highly gratified, and convinced of the friendly inclination of the
President toward the Bank.[358] Jackson,
on the other hand, could not understand
how Biddle ever conceived such an idea,
inasmuch as Biddle had "acknowledged [his]
[Jackson's] frankness to him on this subject to Major Lewis and others."[359] This
complete lack of understanding, which became worse and worse, contributed to making the Bank War the bitter strife it was
to become.

Under these circumstances the unfriendly passage in Jackson's first message, that the Bank had "failed in the
great end of establishing a uniform and
sound currency" came to Biddle like a
thunder clap.[360] He was utterly surprised
by the unexpected attack and deeply hurt,
but, as was his way, he immediately girded
himself for action. In the very days following the publication of the first message of the President, the incipient
struggle already had taken on that character which was to distinguish it to the
bitter end. The characteristic features
resulted, to a large extent, from Biddle's
personality. First of all, he did not understand what was going on in the camp of
the enemy. To him the President had acted
bona fide and was just ill-informed. "I
do not feel the least anxiety about the
sortie of the President who, I am sure,
with the best intentions has erred from
want of information."[361] To him, the step

was a measure of the President "himself
exclusively," "not a measure of the cabinet
or his party," resulting from "the remains
of old notions of unconstitutionality."[362]
Although he was approximately correct, he,
a strong personality himself, failed to take
the personal factor into account. His lack
of understanding of Jackson was really astonishing, and his expectation that the
President could be induced to confess that
he had not sufficiently studied the matter
and so would leave it to Congress was
naive.[363] Biddle cannot be blamed, however, for not having realized early enough
where Van Buren stood. Who ever did?
Biddle thought that he was opposed to the
obnoxious passage;[364] in fact he liked
Van Buren, and it was not until the winter
of 1830/1831 that one finds traces in the
correspondence that he considered the New
Yorker as an enemy.[365] Thus when the
struggle was beginning Biddle did not sense
correctly what to expect from those who
were to decide the issue: while he under-
estimated his most dangerous enemies, he
overestimated the strength of his friends,
as for instance, that of Calhoun.[366]
Sanguine as he was, he not only found consolation in considering the first skirmish
a private affair of the President, but was
even satisfied with the turn things had
taken.[367]

Biddle saw two chances: either to
convince the erring President or, if this
was not possible, to have the matter decided on its own merits. Since the bank question was not a party matter, since the accusations were obviously inaccurate, and
since the President's alternative, the
"treasury bank," would be unpalatable to a
nation proud of its liberties, such an objective decision seemed possible to Biddle,
and he tried to keep the question from assuming a party character.[368] These serious
misconceptions and certain blind spots
which Biddle possessed early led to ineffective strategy and tactics, which were
never given up. The initial strategy for
the Bank to keep quiet while its friends
in Congress carried the ball was mistaken.[369]
Thereby the matter was shoved too early
onto a political track, an error which may
well have resulted from Biddle's propensities. It should be kept in mind that in
1807 he had envisaged for himself a political career,[370] that he had been a state

representative and state senator, that he
had twice run for Congress: no wonder that
he thought immediately of political possibilities for solving the conflict. But
thereby he played into the hands of his
enemies, carrying the incipient fight into
the very field where they were strongest.
At a later period of the struggle his plan
was to defend the Bank with the help of
the press. Back of that plan were his convictions that the Americans were a newspaper reading people[371] and his personal
experiences of 1810 and 1811, when he
fought for the First Bank of the United
States in the Pennsylvania legislature.[372]
As late as 1831 when the Bank War was taking shape, Biddle referred repeatedly to
that episode and to the ignorance evidenced by the men who were his colleagues
at that time. A repetition of that disaster he was going to avoid. But his strategy led, as is generally known, to the
accusation that he "corrupted" the press
and it made him, since it proved unsuccessful, vulnerable rather than strong.
In fact it was equivalent to an appeal to
the sovereign people over the heads of
their representatives,[373] an action which
explains some of the bitter feeling on the
part of the latter.[374]

Biddle's tactics were as mistaken
as his strategy. At much too early a moment did he make a display of force. "I
think it right to bring up all the strength
we can to repeal the attack," so he wrote
to John Potter as early as December 18,
1829. But thereby he did just the sort
of thing to which Jackson's warrior instinct responded. Thus while, on the one
hand, anxious not to wound the feelings of
the President,[375] on the other he invited
warlike actions.

Long before the Bank War Biddle
had recognized the possibilities of publicity. As early as 1824 in cooperation
wich such men as Mathew Carey, John Sergeant, Richard Peters, Jr. (who played a
certain part in the introduction of savings
banking into America[376]), and others he
had issued an address to wealthy citizens,
in which the latter were invited to form
a society for the promotion of internal
improvements.[377] The society was to collect and disseminate information on canals,
roads, bridges, railways, steam engines,
and other advancements which tended to
increase national wealth and individual
prosperity. It was to publish and distribute gratuitously six or eight times a
year pamphlets of thirty to forty pages
each. The advertising methods later used
by Biddle were foreshadowed in this program. Because of his familiarity with the
principles of publicity, advertising offered itself to Biddle as a means of defending the Bank when Jackson first attacked it in his annual message of 1829.

The methods and goal of Biddle's
advertising show him as the typical son of
the eighteenth century: he firmly believed
in reason as a decisive motive in human
actions. He was convinced that nine-tenths
of all errors resulted from ignorance.
Time and again he expressed the conviction
that legislatures did not err because they
had evil designs, but because they were
misinformed; and in the same vein when the
first clouds appeared over the horizon he
considered the President's actions as
caused by lack of knowledge. Thus he
planned his publicity as an "appeal to the
reason of the country from the passions of
the party leaders."[378] Trusting in the
sober sense of the people he felt assured
of success in the impending struggle if
only he were able to disseminate correct
views on the nature and operations of the
Bank and to put within the reach of each
citizen the material by which he might form
his own opinion. This he vowed would be
done;[379] and it was done, but in vain.[380]
Biddle could neither see the irrational
basis of human decisions, actions, and
dissensions; nor did he then understand
the changes which had taken place through
the enfranchisement of the broad masses.
Thus he deceived himself regarding the
effectiveness of his publicity,[381] even
after it had started. The masses could
not or would not read, or, if they did,
would not assimilate the fare which Biddle
wanted them not only to swallow, but even
to enjoy. (To be sure, by 1832 he tried
to adapt his material to the comprehension
of the prospective readers.)[382] His material was cogent for contemporary businessmen as it is for the economic historian,
but it was not translated into language
understandable by the frontiersman, the
farmer, and the mechanic. However, it was
these strata which, in the full-fledged
democracy which America was becoming, would

decide the issue once it became a political one.[383] Thus Biddle's tactics were
doomed to failure. Too late did he recognize his error, as evidenced in his speech
of 1835 before the Princeton Alumni.[384]
(This speech will be discussed later in
detail as a most important document for
showing Biddle's thinking and feeling.)
That Biddle used the most unpleasant colors
with which to depict the political change
which had caused his failure goes without
saying; the essential point is that by
that time he saw it.

Biddle can be blamed not for having made use of publicity, but for having
wasted the Bank's funds ineffectively.
As already indicated he circulated exclusively informational material, technical
in character, which the common man could
not understand; but even more foolishly
he disseminated highly efficient propaganda
emanating from his enemies, as, for instance, Jackson's veto message, because he
thought that the unreasonable arguments
used therein would of themselves make his
foes appear ridiculous.[385] Or, in other
words, he did not know what advertising
material to circulate; he did know how to
circulate it. In doing so he used most
of the methods which are applied today by
modern advertisers, direct and indirect
methods alike. He possessed lists of addresses[386] in all parts of the country to
which he mailed his material. The cashiers of the branches and confidential
agents (such as P. P. F. Degrand who understood advertising, wrote newspaper articles
on behalf of the Bank, and more or less
managed Biddle's publicity campaign in
New England)[387] received hundreds, if not
thousands, of copies of various items
which they mailed to whomever they saw fit.
Certain offices were advised to put pamphlets on outgoing steamers so that the
travelers would read them and take them
home.[388] Finally, publishers were paid
for inserting articles, congressional
speeches, state papers, and the like and
for printing and disseminating special
issues on the Bank question. When official documents or other papers were inserted in newspapers and magazines, Biddle was
anxious to have editorial comments thereon.[389] The goal was to reach almost
everybody who could read.[390]

Biddle started this publicity campaign with a clear conscience. He first[391]

disseminated the McDuffie and Smith Reports
of 1830, reports emanating from the House
of Representatives and the Senate, respectively. Since he believed that Jackson
had erred because of misinformation this
very first publicity of Biddle had no warlike intentions. He still hoped to convince the President himself. Moreover,
although there was disagreement, Congress
was just as much a part of the government
as the President: it was official material
which he circulated. On top of that he
acted in self-defence. The President had
undertaken to say about the Bank what was
wholly without foundation, Biddle wrote
on April 19, 1831 to G. A. Marshal, the
newly appointed cashier of the Natchez
office. The influence of the administration and the press subservient to it were
being employed in endeavoring to break the
Bank. In this situation the Bank could
not find safety, except in explaining its
proceedings to the people and in satisfying
the country that it had been unjustly assailed and that its operations were in fact
highly beneficial to the nation.[392] Such
explanation could be given through no other
medium than the press, the only existing
channel of communication with the people.[393]
This letter is of great importance showing
as it does the very moment when Biddle's
publicity was acquiring a changed significance. Originally applied simply for
disseminating information,[394] in the spring
of 1831 it was becoming a weapon in an incipient bitter struggle. It was then still
a weapon of defence; but as the struggle
progressed it would unavoidably become one
of tactical attack in the strategy of defence. While Biddle began with the dissemination of informational state papers, he
soon proceeded to that of private high
class papers, like those of Albert Gallatin
and William B. Lawrence, who were more or
less influenced by Biddle himself.
Controversial speeches and campaign documents were to follow. This step-by-step
change will be understood later. Biddle
had no instinct for knowing where to draw
lines; he did not see that changed situations had to be tackled with changed
methods and that what was innocuous at one
moment could become highly debatable at
another.

Biddle was one of the country's
first large-scale advertisers and as such
he necessarily gained influence on the

press: in his case a relationship which
has ever since been a major problem first
came into the open. That he went much
further than absolutely necessary through
the instrumentality of loans to publishers
and through lavish payments made him culpable. In the important letter of
Cadwalader's, reprinted above, this point
comes out clearly: Cadwalader, the insider,
was no less shocked than the enemies of
the Bank. What is really pathetic in this
connection is that Biddle became culpable
against his better instinct. Before he
was drawn into the fight for the existence
of the Bank he had refused to make loans
to a publisher for other than business
reasons in order to sustain him in business
simply because of his usefulness as an
organ of the Bank.[395] He felt that no distinction should be made between editors
friendly and hostile to the Bank and he
was afraid that the "Bank might place itself in the very unbecoming attitude of
sustaining at the seat of government a
paper opposed to the existing administration." One wonders if a few years later
Biddle really could not see the difference
between the advertising of a grocer announcing his wares[396] and the publicity
of the Bank. There was a fundamental difference, of course. His was institutional
advertising, promoting a semi-public
institution condemned by the government.
This fact should have induced Biddle not
only to avoid certain methods which he
actually used, but also to change the
source of his publicity funds when the war
had started in earnest. By not avoiding
the pitfalls he was found guilty before
the nation and the court of history. Moreover, by using ineffectual advertising he
made himself responsible to the stockholders.

Few of Biddle's moves during the
Bank War are as controversial as his application for the renewal of the charter
in 1831. It has been argued that this
move led to his defeat and that the outcome would have been different if he had
waited until after the presidential election of 1832. Although unbeknown to himself, nobody has written a stronger defence of Biddle in regard to that tactical
decision than Martin Van Buren in his
Autobiography:[397]

These intimations and declarations
[in the First and Second Annual Messages of
the President] went no further than to announce objections to the bank under its existing charter, but Mr. Biddle was too sagacious
and too well acquainted with the ways of the
world not to find in them evidence of a strong
and in all likelihood an unyielding opposition
to any national bank of the description desired by him and his associates. Having made
this discovery and being himself a man of
resolute and persistent spirit he dismissed
on the instant all hopes of assistance from
the President and looked only upon him as
upon one whose power and influence he was
destined to encounter at every step in his
efforts to obtain a new charter for the institution over which he presided.

That is to say, Van Buren conceded that the
President and the inner circle around him
were set as early as 1829 to destroy the
Bank, and were convinced that Biddle had
grasped the situation. They expected a
last ditch fight from him and consequently
looked upon every one of his actions as a
move in a deadly struggle. "From that
moment...nothing was thought of by the
management of the bank, but preparation of
the struggle."

This interpretation of Biddle's actions is totally erroneous for the years
1829 to 1831, although it shaped the thinking and reactions of his enemies. It has
been shown previously how anxious Biddle
was to cooperate with Jackson and his
friends. During those years he deceived
himself with regard to Jackson's feelings
toward the Bank, but in fact many neutral
observers were equally deceived. By 1831
he finally confessed that "on the subject
of the determination of the President towards the Bank [he] had heard so much and
such various opinions that [he] had ended
by knowing nothing."[398] In that period
Biddle was not preparing for a life and
death struggle for the very reason that he
did not expect one. His policy was conceived for the benefit of the Bank and the
capitalistic sector of the national economy whose interests he identified with the
interests of the whole, and he continuously tried to reach an agreement with
Jackson and his administration even at a
time when the Bank War had already started
in earnest. Jackson, however, imagined

sinister intentions behind every one of
Biddle's moves. The latter's bona fide
assertions, if ever made, that he believed the Bank would be rechartered could
not but arouse Jackson's suspicion, since
they seemed dishonest on the basis of his
presupposition that Biddle had understood
him. He suspected stock gambling back of
them.[399] Thus grave misunderstandings
marked the beginning of the fight.

At one time Biddle complained bitterly about what he considered Jackson's
ambiguity[400] and in at least one phase of
the struggle Jackson was actually as insincere as was Biddle in a later one.
According to the annual message of 1831
the President, without reversing himself,
left the Bank question "for the present to
the investigation of an enlightened people
and their representatives." Regardless of
the "weasel words" used in this passage
(the history of which is evident from
Biddle's memorandum of Oct. 19, 1831 and
further details of which are described in
Taney's Bank War manuscript) it was widely
understood as a retreat on the part of the
President, and was so understood by Taney
when it was first read to him. He took
the passage to mean that the President was
prepared to acquiesce with whatever decision the new Congress should make.[401]
Consequently, although unsuccessfully,
Taney opposed the insertion of this clause.
Jackson, however, did not consider it necessary at that time to say what he would
do if confronted with a bill for recharter.
It may well be that Biddle was led into
some sort of trap by this insincere passage and that it played a considerable part
in his decision to apply for the renewal
of the charter in January 1832. The passage may have been a tactical move by the
President to keep the question from being
taken up in the coming election, a move
which, however, precipitated what he intended to preclude. Be that as it may, on
Biddle's part "the determination to apply
was formed with great deliberation and
with the clearest conviction of duty."[402]

When the Bank War developed Biddle
proved to be a magnificent fighter. But,
in view of his semi-official status, one
may ask: should he have fought as valiant-
ly and bitterly as he did? However that
question may be answered, this much is
certain, that the heat of the battle carried him away and that the struggle

resulted in Biddle's severe demoralization.
Human greatness, of course, becomes evident
in adverse circumstances, and human greatness was not among the many "excellencies"
of this man's character, to employ a term
which Biddle himself would have used. One
can determine almost to the day when the
peripetia took place. It was between
December 1830 and January 1831 that Biddle
first realized Jackson's genuine hostility
and even perhaps his intention to destroy
the Bank.[403] In April 1831 he recognized
that the Bank was becoming a party
question.[404] At that time it would have
been necessary for Biddle to deliberate
with his confidential advisers and to set
the limits to which the Bank as a semi-
public institution could go in its defence
against hostile public authorities. Actually such ideas occupied Biddle at that time:
at an earlier moment he had written to
R. M. Johnson, who was to become the Vice-
President of the United States under Van
Buren:[405]

But this I do know that if he [the
President] will not do justice to the Bank we
will take the only revenge of which I hope
we are capable by doing justice to him and
his administration.

This wise program was soon to be
abandoned step by step. In a letter to
Enoch Parsons of February 28, 1831[406]
Biddle expressed regret that the President
had taken a hostile course. "We must endeavour as much as possible to counteract
its effects," he added. The weapons to
that end were "truth and reason," i.e.,
the dissemination of correct views on the
nature and operations of the Bank. Further
than this the Bank ought not to go; and
especially its officers should not be enticed into violating that perfect neutrality
which was their obligation. Advantages
derived from such efforts would be over-
balanced by the evils. "Nothing which can
be done shall drive the Bank from its perfect [sic!] neutral position," he wrote a
few days later.[407] In May he recognized
that there was a severe temptation to depart from political neutrality, but he
still resisted it.[408] This resistance,
unfortunately, was getting weaker and
weaker. A few weeks later he wrote that
although the Bank was neither for nor
against Jackson, it had to defend itself

and if in so doing the assailant, i.e., the President, suffered it was his own fault.[409] Soon thereafter he was even gratified by comments of the "Sentinel" and of the "Enquirer" on his publicity as an efficient weapon. "I have no concealment and fear on that subject for the very outcry proves the force of the blow."[410] This was a far cry from the point of departure. Now Biddle was abandoning his neutrality. "While therefore I would suppress no individual opinion and would capitulate to no vulgar prejudice I would endeavour to give no unnecessary excitement...by an ostensible and active agency in public affairs which is so liable to misconstruction."[411] Thereafter he paid only lip service to what he had originally considered his duty.[412]

The development of Biddle's publicity, as previously shown, is but an expression of this about-face which was so complete that ultimately Biddle considered it his mission to free the country from the "miserable people" who were misguiding it.[413] In other words, Biddle was clever enough to see the way, but not big enough to follow it. Pride in his work, justifiable determination to do all he could to save it, vision of the economic consequences of its destruction, on the one hand, and love of power, over-optimism, and over-confidence in his own abilities, on the other, made it psychologically impossible for him to do what he knew was right. In the last analysis he did what almost every great builder does: he identified himself with his work and his work with the interest of his country.[414]

Because he did this, he carried the fight to its extreme, and just as he did not recognize that there were limits to be observed, he did not see when it was necessary to acknowledge defeat. He came to hate and to despise his adversaries to such a degree that he could not and would not give in. He seems to have believed that the real reason for the Bank War lay in his resistance to the inclusion of the Bank into the spoils system.[415] Thus by the middle of 1832 the President and his advisers had come to be considered as "enemies," as a gang of "miserable people." The President himself against whom Biddle "defended" the Bank was in the latter's eyes that "meek and worthy man, the chief magistrate," and his entourage "mere

adventurers and gamblers," "a gang of bankrupts and gamblers," or "rotten timber." Biddle was convinced that their actions, such as engineering runs on the branches of the Bank and the removal of the deposits, were dictated by the desire to bring to a profitable conclusion bearish speculations in Bank stock.[416] (This assumption is not an impossible one with regard to men like Ellicott and Reuben M. Whitney[416a] who were then hovering about Taney and playing the roles of the villains in the drama.) Biddle believed the temper of the country to be such that any Secretary of the Treasury who would order the removal of the deposits would be impeached at the next session of Congress.

A Biddle would not give in to such a contemptible crowd, particularly since there was only one man, the President, between the Bank and success, and this one acted in opposition to the will of the country.[417] Instead of giving in he pitched power against power and in that process destroyed his better self. "Macht ist böse," to quote Friedrich Nietzsche.[418] It cannot be ascertained whether at the time of the Bank War Biddle, in the spirit of a political system of checks and balances, still believed as in 1810 that the government and the Bank mutually controlled each other. In the 1830's, McDuffie, Biddle's friend, actually did think along such lines, namely, that "upon principle... the present Bank of the United States and all future banks of a similar kind should be habitually opposed to the Executive Government. It would be an admirable balance in our system and would check the fearful tendency of Executive encroachment."[419] Such opinions would, of course, embitter Jackson, and rightly so.

When the fight began in earnest Biddle threw all the power he possessed into it, and he had ample. First of all he possessed that power which flows from unusual abilities and a superior personality.[420] Furthermore, as the president of the country's central bank he was bound, of course, to be powerful; but many other factors contributed to making him one of the most powerful Americans of his age. There was his wide range of acquaintances: Biddle knew almost everybody who counted in his time. His official position in conjunction with this wide range of friends put him into the possession of a wealth of information which in turn was used to strengthen his position. He was sitting in some sort of "whispering gallery" as he explained it, "where every calumny and every idle piece of gossip that is spoken in an undertone at any home between Portland and New Orleans is borne full and distinct upon my ear."[421] In fact, this was obviously what he wanted; for he considered it his business to know as much and to speak as little as possible about other people's affairs.[422] He must have been a reliable recipient of confidential information, otherwise it would have dried up quickly at the sources.

It has been described previously how Biddle required his cashiers to report continuously and extensively about whatever seemed to be of interest. To such reports were added newspaper clippings and copies of official documents relating to banking in the respective states.[423] Such reports were supplemented by extensive newspaper reading on Biddle's part,[424] to whom, finally, even unprinted documents circulating in Congressional committees were accessible.[425] On top of all that, regular correspondence was carried on with branch presidents and confidential advisers, and every friend of the Bank, wherever located in the country, who tendered information was thanked and encouraged to continue. Biddle was never tired of eliciting detailed information, and the recipients of his letters must have correctly gained the impression that theirs were welcome. In many cases knowledge was derived from political figures in high places. Information was often so confidential that the letters were burned after the recipient had made himself familiar with the content.[426] Biddle was anxious to make the Bank the depository of all material that could be obtained on banking operations in Europe and America[427] and he considered such information a "weapon" in the struggle for a new charter. Since, as will be described shortly, Biddle was an efficient student in every field which he tackled and especially in that of economics, whatever information he received was absorbed in scholarly fashion and thereby was given its full weight.

Such knowledge enabled Biddle to become the adviser of government officials, as mentioned before,[428] and of congressmen, who asked for his advice when legislative

actions on monetary and banking matters were pending.[429] Thereby influence accrued to Biddle automatically. His standing with these men became strong enough for him to suggest corrections in official documents, and on the eve of the Bank War he more or less coached the formulation of the congressional reports on the Bank. Such far-reaching influence was partly due to some sort of personal union between the Bank, on the one hand, and Congress and government, on the other, a tie not unnatural in the case of a semi-public central bank. Thus important congressmen and senators were bank directors,[430] and Edward Jones, at one time chief clerk of the Treasury, was a member of the board of the Washington branch. These men, always important sources of information, occasionally recommended friends for directorships. Adoption of such recommendations and other little services[431] were bound to cement good relationships with influential men and thereby to increase Biddle's own power, so that he could be of considerable service to ex-politicians. Richard Rush, Secretary of the Treasury under John Quincy Adams, was for a short while thereafter almost a protege of Biddle,[432] and in a later period Louis McLane is supposed to have owed to Biddle his presidency in the Morris Canal and Banking Company. Biddle's influence exerted in his capacity as large-scale advertiser has been discussed earlier.

Last, but not least, there was the power which flowed from Biddle's command over funds to be loaned to men of influence. McGrane has published a list[433] made up in Biddle's own hand showing the loans of the Bank to congressmen and government officers. "While you are taking care of the country...your friends must take care of you," Biddle wrote to Louis McLane,[434] when renewing a note of the latter. Among debtors of the latter category was Ashbury Dickens, for some time the chief employee of the Treasury; although, to be sure, Biddle himself had not made that loan. It came into the possession of the Bank when the latter took over some of the assets of a debtor bank. In at least one case Biddle held out a loan as an inducement to cease hostilities against the Bank.[435] With many of these men favorable debt settlements were made, as for instance with Dickens,[436] or with ex-President Monroe. The latter was so relieved by his

settlement[437] that he promised to do everything in his power to promote the interest
of the Bank "not only as a matter of justice but with a view of his own ultimate
interest." But loans and favorable settlements did not always work out this way.
Quite a few politicians borrowed from the
Bank and fought it at the same time; and
much misfortune came to the Bank through
politicians whose power secured to them
unwarranted facilities.[438]

         Most remarkable is the fact that
during the whole time when Duane was
Jackson's Secretary of the Treasury and
while the removal of the deposits hung
fire there was a line of communication between Biddle and Duane.[439] Biddle knew
in advance what stand Duane would take,
"relied" on his firmness, and went so far
as to invite him into the Bank to learn
about its history and operations if he
thought such a visit advisable. The connection was, on the whole of course, an
indirect one, but Biddle sent a publication of his directly to Duane as a courtesy.[440] After Duane had been dismissed,
Biddle obviously had his hand in the publication of the former's generally known
booklet.[441]

         When this powerful man became
deeply wounded, and with reason, by what
he could not but consider unjustifiable
attacks of the President and his friends
and by their lack of candor; when he became exasperated through the failure of
all his many attempts at compromise; and
when he saw his lifework going to pieces,[442]
he allowed himself to be dragged down
into that atmosphere of hatred and contempt of the "enemy" which has been described above. In this atmosphere the
struggle for a new charter became bitter
war where power was pitched against power;
where the end seemed to justify the means;
where Biddle became more and more stubborn[443] as it progressed; and where his
sanguine temperament, formerly a source of
strength, became one of weakness.[444] Thus
he could not and would not acknowledge defeat, and for the first time in his life
became culpable: he abused the power which
he held in trust to engineer the depression of 1833/1834 in order to force his
will on the administration and the country. By such display of power he gambled
away whatever chance was left. When this

gamble, this breach of trust, led to disaster instead of triumph, then at least for
some time Biddle seemed willing to acknowledge defeat. By the middle of 1835 he was
starting on a bona fide process of liquidation[445] and, as he expressed it himself,
was in full retreat in the face of the
enemy.[446] The basic idea behind this
liquidation was to collect the capital of
the Bank into large masses. For this purpose most of the branches were sold on long
credit to new banks, founded to take their
place; on these Biddle exerted some influence because, as a rule, they took over
the personnel of the office in question.
Since at the same time loans of the remaining branches were made preferably on stock
security the funds of the Bank quickly
came to consist of obligations of a few
banking institutions and of loans on stock
security. That is to say, at any moment
when the Bank wished to turn around again
and in one way or another apply for a new
charter, the capital would be intact and
easily accessible while the stockholders
would pocket a considerable profit through
the increase in the value of the stock.[447]
And in fact Biddle suddenly did turn, obtained a Pennsylvania charter for his enterprise, and started out on the last
stretch of his career showing himself once
more as the brilliant bank technician. In
the end it brought him nothing but disgrace.
Had Biddle been big enough to acknowledge
defeat he would have been the victor before
the court of history. But Biddle did not
recognize that he was far ahead of his
times. He had built a modern central bank
and as such his enterprise could exist
only while the government was willing to
cooperate. It was not his fault that the
existing administration refused to do so.
At this point it was his moral duty to give
up, as had the directors of the First Bank
of the United States, when after having
done a similarly splendid job they were
abandoned by Congress.

         The Bank War must have been a ter-
rific strain on Biddle[448] and the often-
quoted statement of Senator Frelinghuysen
that the latter (during the depression of
1834) was sitting in his office calm as a
summer morning was both tactless and non-
sensical. It did mischief to Biddle who
himself was inclined to be tactless.[449]
In fact, at that time he was "nearly broken

down by work," "fagged to death,"[450] and at least played with the idea of resigning.[451] During the engineered panic of 1833 and 1834 while Biddle felt certain that he had the backing of his friends[452] they first began to desert him, and such men as Ingersoll, Rush, and Sutherland turned enemies. The sudden attack of Governor Wolf of his own state, previously a supporter, came to him like a thunderclap, and initiated a mass flight of former friends. Moreover one can easily imagine what it must have meant to him when he had to barricade himself in his home during the elections of 1834, and to fill it with armed men in order to safeguard his family. By that time the situation had become such that he could not go to Washington himself without fear of serious repercussions, and although he spoke jokingly about it he obviously felt very bitter.[453] On top of all this some of his closest confidantes died, leaving gaps which could not be filled.[454] Since self-criticism was markedly absent, Biddle hardly saw to what extent his fate was of his own making. Was his sickness[455] of the winter of 1835 a flight?

After having gone through these experiences, on the 30th of September 1835, Biddle addressed both the alumni and the graduating class of his alma mater at Princeton in a speech which may be a psychological document of great interest. Perhaps he felt subconsciously that he was still standing on a pedestal, where in reality he no longer belonged. He who was always cheerful and good humored, as John Quincy Adams described him,[456] gave to this address not only a sombre, but even a morbid note, and he inserted remarks which permit a glimpse into his mind.[457] "To live without wrong and to die without fear is the great lesson of our moral nature." Did Biddle's conscience tell him that he had neglected that lesson? Speaking of the former classmates who were already lying "in lowlier beds" he was reminded of "our own absolute nothingness. They make us pause and ponder on that which in the tumult of life is too often forgotten - that which no human eye has seen, yet is worth all that human eye has ever seen - the deep, the dark, and unfathomed mystery of the human soul. They make us look inward, too, for self-examination and if that

scrutiny may suggest many things which might have been better done or more wisely left undone, we may rejoice in being spared to repair them." These words were more than rhetoric. They were a confession of the man who for selfish ends had spread disaster throughout the land and who had not even succeeded so that he could repair the damage that he had done; a confession of the man who not long before had been an example of honesty and forthrightness, who had never borrowed from the Bank, nor endorsed a note to avoid a conflict between interest and duty,[458] but whose actions were now becoming shady; a confession of the man who once had been reliable but whose statements were now becoming so insincere[459] that historians hardly know when to credit him. This interpretation of Biddle's Princeton speech finds its justification in the way in which Biddle closed it and in which he obviously found his catharsis: he incited the listeners against the hostile power to which he owed defeat and frustration, their own representative government; he misused lofty words and comparisons with classical examples (misunderstood as well) to lead up to a cry for vengeance; and he ended with vile name-calling: "These banditti will be scourged back to their caverns - the penitentiary will reclaim its fugitives in office."[460] The "aristocrat" who called the graduating class to aristocratic statesmanship and scourned the rabble had actually dropped to the very level which he despised.[461]

Whatever can be said in defence of Biddle was said a hundred years ago by MacVickar.[462] MacVickar rightly stressed the fact that the Bank became political only when attacked; that it was driven against its will into a hostile position against the administration; that it fought a "war of justifiable self-defence;" and that it was "driven mad" in the "death grapple" until it forgot its duty and, in desperation, abused its power "as a tyrant over the currency, rather than its regulator." MacVickar held the then dominant party responsible for the uncalled-for strife and for converting "a purely financial into a purely political question." "Its [the Bank's] tenacity of life was but the test of the value of its life to the country and a proof that the nation would

not willingly let it die;" its power resulted from its necessity and was an argument for its existence.[463]

Those who condemn Biddle, on the
other hand - and condemned he must be -
should nevertheless keep in mind that the
building up of pressure in order to force
a selfish policy on Congress or the administration is common practice among representatives of both capital and labor
today (A.D. 1946), and defying the President of the United States seems also to be
becoming a popular game. Even in his sins
Biddle was far ahead of his time.

The fact that Biddle, the politician, lost the Bank War should not make
one forget that he was a very efficient
one. He came near to success under the
most difficult conditions and possessed
prestige among the leading statesmen of
his time. He gave advice and they took it,
and in one case even Daniel Webster asked
Biddle what tactics he should follow.[464]
In fact, Biddle could be as shrewd, wily,
and cunning as any one of the guild, as
he evidenced, for instance, in his relations with the New York Union Committee or
in the struggles for the Pennsylvania
charter and against the Specie Circular
and the Subtreasury, in 1836 and 1838, respectively.[465]

In 1835 when Biddle was on the
point of acknowledging defeat it seemed as
if he might take once more to the plans of
his youth and, after fifteen years of successful financial leadership, round out
his career as a political leader. The
erstwhile Democrat,[466] who, of course, had
become a Whig, first turned "president-
maker," and in 1835 took an interest in
the possibility of defeating Van Buren
through General Harrison in the coming
presidential election.[467] Later he himself became an aspirant for the presidency,
and Thomas Cooper was a sort of campaign
manager for him in South Carolina.[468]
When these aspirations did not materialize,
a plan was ventilated for Biddle to become
the Secretary of the Treasury in a Whig
cabinet and in this position prepare his
ascent to the presidency in the elections
of 1844. How serious Biddle took these
schemes is difficult to decide.

Biddle's Personality and his End

In the prime of life, Biddle must
have been a fascinating man. Handsome,

clever, self-possessed, courageous, well-
educated, with the bent of a scholar,
accustomed to move in the most exclusive
social circles[469] of two continents,
Biddle was a very late example of that fine
cosmopolitan and encyclopedic civilization
of the eighteenth century, of which
Jefferson had been an earlier American representative. From the frontiersman and
from that rabble, which celebrating the
election of its hero at Jackson's first
inauguration all but wrecked the White
House, he was separated by a world. But
shadows were not lacking and as the going
became rough in a later period of Biddle's
life they became darker and darker; by
that time Thomas Wren Ward, the American
agent of the Barings, could describe Biddle
as "clever, but not sound - vain, and selfish, and avaricious of praise in an extraordinary degree, and bold and confident."[470]
At the end, the change was so complete
that the historian feels as though he were
dealing with two distinct personalities.

Biddle's Eulogium on Thomas
Jefferson not only betrays his admiration
for the country's great leader, but also an
awareness of a geistige kinship. Perhaps
Jefferson had become young Biddle's ideal.
He praised Jefferson because "all his actions were imbued by his learning, [because],
to use his own expression, 'his long life
was as much devoted to study as a faithful
transaction of the trusts committed to him
would permit' and [because] his peculiar
genius enabled him to unite the retired
love of science with the practical energy
of the world."[471] Biddle obviously felt,
and rightly so, that he possessed the same
"peculiar genius."

Biddle's activities as a business
executive, as a banker, and as his country's
central bank president, have been described;
and those as a politician at least touched
upon. But, as is generally known, Biddle
was also a writer and editor and between
1809 and 1814 he had lived as a man of
letters. The story of the Lewis and Clark
expedition (History of the Expedition of
the Captains Lewis and Clark) was Biddle's
work, and for several years he was the
editor of the Portfolio. In fact almost
every letter of his is a stylistic masterpiece, and his command of the written word
reminds one of Jefferson's. Biddle was,
furthermore, an orator of the grand eloquence of his age with its many classical

allusions.[472] Like Jefferson, Biddle had received a legal training, and he was moreover the compiler of a collection of foreign laws.[473] Again like Jefferson, he was a farmer, and even a farmer of great repute. (He was the president of the Agricultural and Horticultural Society of Pennsylvania.) He introduced pure bred Alderney cattle into the country and took an interest in the breeding of Jersey cows; making use of "forcing houses" (greenhouses) he built up a large size grapery and sold grapes in the Philadelphia market; and he finally investigated the possibility of improving the breed of American horses by crossing them with prairie horses. In 1835, when he was liquidating the Bank of the United States, his interest in this field showed a considerable increase.[474] As Jefferson took a keen interest in the broad dissemination of knowledge, so did Biddle; and as a state legislator (in 1810) he sponsored a system of public schools with very cheap, but not gratuitous, instruction.[475] Just as Jefferson had been instrumental in establishing West Point and the University of Virginia, so Biddle organized Girard College. Just as Jefferson was an amateur architect of great talent whose designs were embodied in his home in Monticello and in the buildings of the University of Virginia, so Biddle introduced into Philadelphia the early nineteenth-century so-called classical architecture, and his ideas, in turn, found expression in his country home at Andalusia, in the Bank building, and in Girard College. Just as Jefferson, all his life, but especially when he was in France, took a keen interest in whatever might be useful in developing the productive capacities of his country, so Biddle sponsored internal improvements, especially the young railroad.[476] (He claimed to have promoted the one between Philadelphia and Baltimore.)

Just as Jefferson was a scholar,[477] so was Biddle. As a matter of fact, he was the forerunner of those modern central bank presidents who at the same time have been monetary economists of repute, such as Gerard Vissering of the Nederlandsche Bank, especially. Biddle was a keen student of the economic literature of his time. That he admired Hamilton's writings and achievements all his life goes without

saying.[478] In an earlier period of his career, by 1810, he was influenced by Sir James Steuart's great work, an influence which was later, of course, superseded by that of the classical economists, Adam Smith[479] and Ricardo. But, of course, the central banker raised in Mercantilist tradition did not become a laissez-faire man, although, in line with their thinking, he believed in the harmony of the social universe.[480] But Biddle's knowledge of economic literature went much further. He was acquainted with Sir Henry Parnell's Observations on Paper Money, Banking, etc.,[481] a book which was widely read in America at that time and which, through its description of Scotch banking, influenced American public opinion. Biddle did not think highly of the book dubbing it a "party work." He quoted Thomas Tooke's Thoughts and Details of the High and Low Prices of the Last Thirty Years and Robert Mushet's A Series of Tables Exhibiting the Gain and Loss of the Fund-Holder Arising from the Fluctuations in the Value of the Currency from 1800 to 1821, all of which were published in the 1820's.[482] Such difficult books were read in the way of the scholar so that Biddle was able to cite pages, and the historian can be certain that Biddle actually read this material. Thornton and the Bullion Report were also well known to him, as can be deduced from his banking policy which has been described above. Of the important law literature of his time he knew and quoted Chitty's standard work on bills of exchange. When one keeps in mind that in addition Biddle read numerous items of the economic and political pamphlet[483] literature of the day, such as Nathan Hale's Remarks on the Bank and Currency of the New England States, Thomas Law's pamphlets,[484] William Jones' Brief Review of the Origin, Performance and Administration of the Bank of the United States,[485] and many others including Gouge's well known booklet,[486] one cannot but reach the conclusion that the amount of his reading was tremendous for a practical banker.[487] On top of all this, he watched the leading magazines of the day,[488] and, whenever special problems came up, sought information from books and articles.[489]

Such a background enabled Biddle to study and to write on particular economic problems like a trained economist. His correspondence of 1830 with Albert Gallatin on the latter's paper, "Banks and Currency," reads like one between two scholars. Moreover one finds in his letterbooks true economic treatises as, for instance, on the English crises of 1745, 1793, 1797, and 1825; on the organization and the policy of the Bank of England; on the history of English, Spanish, and American coins; on foreign exchanges and the like.[490] In the course of these studies, like many of his contemporaries and later economists, he came to bemoan the lack of statistical information.[491] Biddle understood the essentials of bi-metallism[492] (he used the words "two standards," in lieu of the modern term); he preferred mono-metallism and, for America, the silver standard. He was one of the first to recognize the phenomenon of elasticity which he defined as the power of alternate expansion and contraction of the currency to meet the state of the community.[493] He was aware of the limitations of the quantity theory of money which was then still accepted in a rather crude form: he rightly stressed the possibility that an inflationary tendency toward higher prices could be offset by an expansion or improvement of the productive forces of the country brought about by that very inflation.[494] That there were flaws in Biddle's economic reasoning has been mentioned before.[495]

It is remarkable for a keen economic thinker in the Ricardian era as was Biddle to possess historical interest as well as theoretical acumen. The mere fact that he, again like Jefferson, kept all his correspondence proves an interest in his own history and this historical sense comes out in the correspondence time and again. He sent a document back to the Treasury for correction so that it, as he put it jokingly, "may not puzzle the future historians."[496] He encouraged historical writing[497] and not only backed Matthew St. Clair Clarke when the latter in cooperation with D. A. Hall compiled his Legislative and Documentary History of the Bank of the United States, but wrote that he himself had compiled a legislative history of the Bank in the form of a manual.[498]

Whatever Biddle tackled was tackled scientifically. This is especially evident in the correspondence which he had in connection with the establishment of Girard College.[499] But even when he had

to defend his unwise step in charging damages on the "French bills" (the government bills drawn on France) protested in Paris for lack of payment, he fortified himself by studying official documents to support his claims.[500] Had Biddle become a statesman, as he might well have, he would undoubtedly have become a thinker developing Hamilton's political philosophy.[501] This statement is justified regardless of the fact that Biddle's main achievement as a Pennsylvania state senator in the 1810's had been his report on the Hartford Convention, in which he defended the Constitution as it then stood. Be this as it may, he distinctly aimed at making the Secretaries responsible to Congress, thereby following the English pattern. As a statesman he would have been a peer of the great parliamentarians of his age, of the Websters, Calhouns, and Clays; but together with them at the peak of his career he would have been on the losing side. As a statesman he would not have understood the upsurge of the masses any better than as the country's central banker.

The breadth of Biddle's interests was, as a matter of fact, reflected in the way in which he found relaxation from his arduous duties. The weekends he spent at his country seat; in one letter he spoke of the "weekly allowance of fresh air and farming."[502] When he was in the city, studying must have provided a welcome change, as did social intercourse with the leading men of his time. In both cases the borderline between duty and pleasure must have been fluid. Intellectual society was to Biddle's liking. By 1809 he was a member of Joseph Dennie's Tuesday Club[503] which embraced the contributors to the Portfolio. Later when the friends of the physician, Caspar Wistar, brought into being the so-called Wistar parties in his memory and to carry on the intellectual gatherings which had been customary at his house during his lifetime, Biddle participated.[504]

For about twenty years Biddle stood at the focal point of American civilization, and his correspondence mirrors contemporary life and history. Living in the years between the Revolutionary and the Civil Wars he appears like a connecting link between two periods. He knew President Monroe and Albert Gallatin as well as James Gordon Bennett and Thaddeus Stevens. Most of the leading Americans of his time are

represented in his correspondence as writers and recipients of letters, a few by
references only but by such references as
indicate some contact. There were repre-
sented Presidents Madison, Monroe, John
Quincy Adams, Jackson, Van Buren, Harrison,
and Tyler; the great statesmen of his time,
the Cheves, Calhouns, Clays, Websters,
McDuffies, and Livingstons, besides
Secretaries of the Treasury, Gallatin,
Crawford, Rush, Ingham, McLane, and Duane.
There were represented the host of politi-
cians, such men as Benton, Cambreleng,
Clayton, George M. Dallas, Everett,
Forsyth, Grundy, Hemphill, Ingersoll,
Silsbee, Samuel Smith, Watmough, and Hugh
Lawson White, besides the Jackson crowd.
There were, of course, contacts with the
foreign business leaders, the Barings in
London, the Hopes in Amsterdam, and the
Hottinguers in Paris, and with American
businessmen such as Nathan and William
Appleton, the Crowninshields, and Thomas
H. Perkins of New England; Astor, Lenox,
Hone, Nathaniel Prime, Thomas Wren Ward,
Isaac Bronson, and Jacob Barker of New
York; Girard of Philadelphia; the Browns
and Olivers of Baltimore; and E. J.
Forstall of New Orleans. Then came the
journalists, James Gordon Bennett, Francis
Blair, Duff Green, Joseph Gales, and
Robert Walsh; the great jurists of the
time such as Horace Binney, Rufus Choate,
Reverdy Johnson, Chancellor Kent, John
Sergeant, and Roger B. Taney; the econo-
mists, Thomas Cooper, William Beach
Lawrence, Francis Lieber, George Tucker,
and Henry Vethake. And finally there were
represented among Biddle's acquaintances
celebrities like Lafayette and Fanny Kemble
and even such a character as David Crockett.

A man like Nicholas Biddle was
bound to make many friends and many enemies at the same time. Disregarding
Jackson and his followers, who simply could
not understand a man like Biddle, there
were only very few who genuinely distrusted
him, and these few, as, for instance, the
Barings, the directors of the Bank of
England,[505] or Nathan Appleton, were
guided by instinct rather then by knowledge of Biddle's shortcomings As for the
others who disliked him, he could not help
making himself unpopular with many people.
Biddle, the elegant aristocrat with the
refined taste and the superior culture,

could not but become an object of suspicion
in the era of the rising masses, especially
since he was an adept in the field of high
finance, always understandable to a few
only. The man who considered the fear of
being unpopular the great American weakness[506] did nothing to counteract his un-
popularity. No one can practice the business of money lending, as he put it himself,
and occasionally say "No," without becoming
unpopular;[507] and it has been described
previously that Biddle's policy was to take
to himself the odium for any unpopular measures of the board, thereby protecting the
men who stood in the local firing line.

The process of electing directors
was another source of personal enemies.
Year after year some men had to be preferred to others in the elections or re-
elections or in the retention of directors,
in the process of rotation. Not every ambitious businessman who wanted to become a
director of the Bank could be taken into
its administration. Moreover, the provisions of section 11, paragraph 2, of the
charter could not but lead to disappointment and hostility on the part of disgruntled former directors. This section
prescribed that one-fourth of the directors
had to leave the [parent and branch] boards
every year and that no director could hold
his office for more than three years out of
four. When in any year the number of directors whose terms had expired constituted
one-fourth of the board in question there
were no difficulties; but when it was otherwise some directors could not be dropped
without hurting their feelings, since some
of their colleagues who had come into the
board at the same time would remain.
Biddle's correspondence is full of letters
indicating how ticklish a subject it was to
drop directors whose terms had not as yet
expired.

Biddle became the president of the
Bank after it had become widely obnoxious
through the mismanagement of Jones and the
tight-fisted policy of Cheves. Moreover
the very success of the Bank under Biddle
engendered hostility: since the state banks
were forced to keep within their means in
doing business, their profits were curtailed to the dismay of the stockholders
and their "movements restrained," i.e.,
their business reduced,[508] to the disappointment of greedy directors and needy

borrowers. At the same time the "equalization" of the domestic exchanges threw
out of business scores of brokers who formerly had waxed fat on the high rates of
domestic exchange and their fluctuation.[509]
These groups Biddle considered the most
dangerous and active opponents of his institution.

In the execution of his functions
Biddle labored continuously under difficulty: every one of his major actions influenced the national economy, and consequently every time someone was bound to be
affected detrimentally. There were, furthermore, quite a few people who, as
Biddle knew, were always inclined to find
fault with the Bank. Consequently whatever he did, some people would imagine
sinister intentions. One day when in good
humor Biddle himself charmingly expressed
his predicament. He had just established
a branch in Utica for business reasons.
"Nevertheless," so he wrote, "I presume it
will be ascribed to some great machina-
tion - some design to elevate or depress
the Masons or anti-Masons, or Mr. Clay or
Genl Jackson - or the Workers or the Agrarians
- or the Albany Regency - or the Swamp or
the Pewter mug - or the Living Skeleton
or - but this brings me to the end of my
vocabulary.... I shall rejoice...that both
the Swamp and the Living Skeleton fill up.
I have no preference between the Pewter
mug and Mr. Pitcher and for me the Regency
of Albany and of Orleans are alike extra-
neous."[510]

Biddle's activities in the Bank of
the United States of Pennsylvania have
been generally misunderstood. They will
be explained in detail in a chapter of the
second volume of this work. Suffice it
here to say that the Bank of the United
States of Pennsylvania was essentially no
longer a commercial bank. The Committee
of Investigation of 1841, sensing this
fact, expressed it by saying[511] that the
funds of the Bank were engaged in such a
way that it could no longer aid businessmen. Actually Biddle made the institution
the first modern investment bank, thereby
anticipating the Crédit Mobilier by a good
many years. But this type of enterprise
was of so distinct a character and so different from any that had existed before
that the first attempts in the direction
were bound to failure. Biddle and the
Pereires nevertheless stand side by side as
the creative entrepreneurs who brought
modern investment banking into being. A
second reason for Biddle's ultimate downfall has been described before: it was the
pooling of a raw material on an international scale and the attempt to control
the exchange market. In this respect he
attempted more than anyone could expect to
achieve in the middle nineteenth century.
Many other reasons contributed to the sad
results, as will be described forthwith.

When Biddle left the Bank in 1839
it was sick through and through, regardless
of what he may have thought of it. The
securities which it held were entered in
the balance sheet at inflated values, even
if they were not higher than the purchase
prices or the prices at which loans had
been made thereon. A semblance of soundness was upheld thereby although the Bank
was in fact loaded down with overvalued
securities and security loans which were
not convertible because of the depression.
Soon after Biddle had left, property had
to be sacrificed, in consequence of this
grave illiquidity,[512] to pay the most urgent
obligations and to uphold the credit of the
institution. Thus the typical road which
leads from illiquidity to bankruptcy was
entered. Biddle himself, the unusually
resourceful master financier, might have
been able to sustain the Bank a few more
years, or even to pull it through; his
successors could not. As Joseph Gales correctly expressed it to John Quincy Adams,
the spirit of the enterprise had gone when
Biddle resigned.[513] Thus the question
comes up: did Biddle have the moral right
to quit once he had brought the Bank into
the predicament in which it was at the time
of his resignation. As the London _Times_
correctly put it, Biddle first raised the
Bank, then deserted it and left it "to
flounder on as it could in a state of bankruptcy."[514] With his customary sanguinity
Biddle may have deceived himself with regard to that predicament, as he had done
so often during the Bank War with regard
to the true situation.

Be that as it may, there were many
more sins committed by Biddle for which
there is no possible excuse. When Biddle
used dubious methods for getting the
Pennsylvania charter he only followed what
was general practice at that time (a fact
which led to Free Banking, as will be described in the following chapter). That he

paid much too high a price for the charter
is the real sin for which he deserves
blame. The experienced business leader
should have foreseen the consequences
thereof, particularly since the Bank of
the United States of Pennsylvania was already illiquid on the very day when it
opened. This was the consequence of the particular policy of liquidating its predecessor which Biddle had followed in his capacity as the president of the latter.[515]
Once more his over-confidence and boldness
deceived him. That Biddle was really happy with this charter may be doubted. He
repeated too often how excellent it was,
at the same time conceding that "to[516]
European eyes it [would] seem a strange
composition," a composition which, however,
found its explanation in the difficulty of
making arrangements with state legislatures. Once the Bank had begun business
under its Pennsylvania charter it was its
dubious practice to issue notes with the
same name, the same engravings, and of the
same appearance as those of its predecessor.[517] But worse things followed. By
reissuing the notes of the defunct Bank of
the United States; by not keeping corporation and private business strictly
apart;[517a] by making the entries of a dangerous enterprise in the account of a firm
which had no connection therewith;[518] by
computing the profit of an uncompleted
transaction, drawing it out, and not making immediate restitution when that transaction had led to loss, by all these actions Biddle violated the mercantile code
of honor, if nothing more.

On this point no excuse or explanation will ever avail. It was a deep moral
downfall, all the deeper because Biddle,
imagining a sinister conspiracy, attacked
the directors of the Bank in public for
the ignominious bankruptcy of which he
himself was the cause.[519] At that time in
connection with the threatening repudiation of the American state debts Biddle had
already assumed the role of the "defender
of American integrity," as McGrane puts
it.[520] This role was certainly not becoming to a man whose escutcheon was no
longer without spot, and in playing it
Biddle used tactless and even outrageous
language. A few years later he devised
plans for the foreign bondholders to sue
the defaulting American states.[521] One
almost doubts if Biddle was then still in
the possession of his senses. Anyway, his

egotism, vanity, and absence of self-
criticism must have made things appear
strangely distorted to him. As late as
December 1840 the discredited man wished
to be appointed American minister to Vienna,
thus showing that he had no realization of
his own downfall.[522]

In 1844 the end came. One cannot
describe the circumstances under which
Biddle died better than by quoting substantially from Philip Hone's diary entries[523] of 1841 and his "necrology" of
1844:

> 1841. Bills of indictment have been
> found by a grand jury of Philadelphia against
> Nicholas Biddle, erstwhile president of the
> Bank of the United States, he who so lately
> was incumbered with the load of his greatness,
> ...and who is now so fallen that there are
> "none so poor to do him reverence." The
> great financier, the golden calf of Chestnut
> and Wall Streets, at whose approach the well-
> brushed hat of the cosey millionnaire, or the
> businesslike cap of the money-broker, instinc-
> tively came down from its empty eminence, and
> the pliant knee could with difficulty restrain
> its idolatrous genuflection, the "monster" of
> General Jackson's imagination, and the very
> "Old Nick" in the path of Locofoco politicians,
> - "fallen, fallen, from his high estate"...
> [Indicted for] robbery, cheating, swindling,
> and all the other crimes, true and technical,
> known to the criminal law, and described in
> its exuberant phraseology. Indicated for high
> crimes and vulgar misdemeanors by a secret
> conclave of greasy householders.

> 1844. The Great financier is no more.
> He whose appearance in Wall Street at a cer-
> tain period broke like a ray of sunshine
> through the clouds of financial difficulty;
> he whose word established and overthrew banks,
> whose fiat governed the rate of exchange and
> regulated the price of cotton, [died].

And in the very hour of his death his memory was thus persecuted by Bryant's "viru-
lent and malignant" pen:

> Died at his country seat [Nicholas
> Biddle]; he passed the last of his days in
> elegant retirement which if justice had taken
> place would have been spent in the peniten-
> tiary.

This author knows of no tragic downfall in
the field of American economic and business-
history which compares with that of Nicholas Biddle.

IV

Andrew Jackson and the Destruction of
American Central Banking

To the student of economic history who is familiar with the development of capitalism in the nineteenth century, the Bank War of the 1830's seems at the same time anachronistic and up-to-date. In order to understand it thoroughly one must overstep the boundary of economic history to study the event also from the point of view of Geistesgeschichte. Only when one looks at it as one of the various clashes between the two early American economic and ideological systems, or in other words, only as one recognizes the Bank War as an episode in the continuous fight between capitalistic and anti-capitalistic forces characteristic of American history throughout the first half of the nineteenth century can one arrive at a thorough understanding of that conflict.

The geistige world in which Biddle lived is familiar to every economic historian and if his presuppositions and ideals are accepted no flaw can be found in his reasoning. After another century of capitalistic development in America these presuppositions and ideals are taken for granted by conservatives and less doubted by the geistige descendants of Biddle's enemies than by social classes which had hardly come into existence in his day. Consequently, for the modern economist it is rather difficult to understand and appraise justly the arguments and sincerity of those who fought and destroyed the Bank and who were led to a fateful and unfortunate victory by Andrew Jackson. Their geistige Welt was still that of Jefferson and John Taylor (1753-1825) of Caroline County, the radical Virginia statesman and political writer whose ideas will be discussed in detail. Their strength lay in the fact that they used ideological weapons tempered in the forge of agrarian liberalism. Thus their ideas were rooted in a tradition which in large parts of the country still represented reality. If one does not question their agrarian and equalitarian ideals and if one concedes that the freeholders in the American backwoods could foresee a

capitalistic future no more than they could understand contemporaneous capitalism in a few seaboard towns and industrial villages unknown to them, one cannot but appreciate the force of their arguments. Just as there was no flaw in Biddle's reasoning, neither was there any in Jackson's. Because the ideals and goals of these two men and their followers were different, neither of the antagonists could make any impression on the other by logic and reason.[1]

There is agreement among historians that the Bank War not only was Jackson's work but that his own moves decided the outcome, a remarkable case of personal influence on economic development. Jackson's actions in turn resulted, of course, from an interplay between his character and the geistige world in which he lived on the one side and the external world on the other. Jackson's character, mentality, and intellectual horizon have been described repeatedly by able writers. One of them dubs the President surprisingly ill-read, naive in political matters, and as almost wholly lacking in political and social philosophy. The present author, however, feels that there is perhaps a better way to make Jackson understandable. It will be shown shortly that he was the typical representative of the radical wing of his group of coevals and as such an exponent of the philosophy of agrarian radicalism embraced by that generation. Jackson was not lacking in political and social philosophy, rather he clung too tenaciously and uncritically to the one which he had embraced as a young man and which by forty years of economic development was already outdated when he came into power. Like Jefferson, Jackson had set his face like flint against the forces of capitalism which he did not understand and which of course he could not stop. Minor factors made the situation extremely difficult. Jackson was indifferent to the influence of the so-called dignified classes because he believed in the common people as the source of political authority. This man of "iron will" and "inflexible purpose," emotionally stubborn whenever his antipathy was aroused, was at the same time overconfident in himself and in his cause.[2] Thus twenty to forty years after his ideological ancestors, Thomas Jefferson and John Taylor, had evolved radical agrarianism and secured its temporary victory, Jackson fought the last battle of a lost fight to save the old agricultural order. In the Bank War he won the last victory in a lost cause.

The origin of the philosophy of Jackson and his followers becomes evident when one studies merely the history of two of the slogans which they delighted to use.[3] In the eyes of the Jacksonians the Bank of the United States was a monster. At least since the seventeenth century this expression had been used in political discussions in England and America to attack institutions considered outrageous by their enemies. Around 1700 the American "village democrat" John Wise had given this epithet to monarchy; while vice versa for the American Tories of 1770 democracy was a "Hydra headed monster." Later the Federalist fought for a sovereign unitary state to avoid the "political monster of an imperium in imperio;" while in the opposite camp John Taylor applied the term to the First Bank of the United States as early as 1794, styling it " a monstrous contrivance."[4] Two decades later, in 1810 and 1811, the term monster was widely used in attacks on the Bank when it sought a renewal of its charter. Mathew Carey ridiculed this method, speaking of the "frightful all-devouring monster, the Bank of the United States," but the term now stuck. At the end of the same decade when the new Second Bank of the United States had made itself dangerously unpopular, Kentucky newspapers, for instance, dubbed it the "mammoth monster" (1818).[5] Here originated the predilection of Jackson and his followers for the use of the word monster with regard to the Second Bank of the United States.

The other pet slogan of the anti-Bank men was the designation of the Bank as an aristocratic institution. Statements of this kind do not sound very convincing today, but they were significant and meaningful since the term aristocracy, as used by Jackson and the Jacksonians, had a connotation different from that which the word always had in Europe and has in present day America. The specific color was given to the term in the American political debates of the 1790's which shaped Jackson's political and economic thinking. In 1794 John Taylor defined aristocracy as "names and wealth united with exclusive privileges."[6] Later he developed this idea. He recognized that power was

"attracted by wealth,"[7] and came to consider the state as controlled by a dominant economic group which was supposed to call itself aristocracy. John Locke and traditional Whig thinking are back of such statements. In America, according to Taylor, an aristocracy of credit was rising, founded on monopoly and incorporation. It would prove much more dangerous than the feudal aristocracies of Europe. The origins of that aristocracy of credit dated from Hamilton's funding system and his national bank. It lived on exploitation and through the manipulation of credit: that is to say, through the expansion and contraction of paper currency, it affected the price system and thus took a heavy toll from the national production.[8] However, this materialistic interpretation of aristocracy was not confined to its radical antagonists. On the other side of the fence John Adams, at about the same time, elaborated the term, and as it came from his study it was almost identical with what we call plutocracy today, for as an exponent of Whig tradition Adams tied social standing and political influence to property and wealth.[8a] It was this materialistic interpretation of the term aristocracy, or, in other words, the association of aristocracy with the control of economic life, which Jackson inherited and which he and his followers used in their fight.[9]

However, Jackson did more than inherit a tradition: an exponent of the radicals of his group of coevals, he tried to realize much of their ideals. His contemporaries were well aware of this fact. Van Buren, describing the uneasiness of the friends of the Bank of the United States after the elevation of Jackson to the presidency, remarked: "This presentiment had its origin in their knowledge of the school in which he had been taught the rudiments of his political education, of the earnestness with which he had in early life sustained its doctrines, and of the stability...of his character."[10] Under these circumstances it is important to study step by step the growth of this element of Jackson's geistige Welt.

In 1829, in his conversation with Biddle, the President made a statement which, although it has been quoted repeatedly, possesses more interest in this connection than has heretofore been ascribed to it. Said Jackson:

"I do not dislike your Bank any more than all banks. But ever since I read the history of the South Sea Bubble I have been afraid of banks."

This assertion contains an obvious mistake since no banks were involved in the South Sea Bubble which pivoted around government debts. As a matter of fact, Jackson confounded the South Sea Bubble with John Law's Mississippi scheme. These two speculative manias of the early eighteenth century were still generally known in American when Jackson grew up and thus they belonged to the geistige environment of his generation.[11] John Taylor, born in 1755, described them correctly in his main work in the chapter on Funding.[12] Alexander Hamilton, born in 1757, only ten years before Jackson, was not less influenced, although not so persistently, by his knowledge of the events than was the latter.[13] The fact that Jackson confounded them did not detract from the importance of that influence. For the historian the confusion is of particular interest, showing as it does the source of Jackson's knowledge. This confusion came down from William Douglass' Summary of the British Settlements published in 1749.[14] In that book Douglass, who mentioned these events repeatedly in his writings, thus described the history of the South Sea Bubble:

It came by way of France, where it was called Mississippi, with us it was called South Sea; laying aside allegory, it is the notorious instance of the bad constitution of paper effects, I mean paper common currency and transfers; and as it has some affinity with our plantations currency I hope it may be of political use with the contemporary Mississippi and French banking history annexed by way of annotations.

And in these annotations Douglass gave a history of the "Royal Bank of France which (linked with the Mississippi Bubble) projected paper currency for France [and] may be a proper warning or beacon to our American paper money colonies." These quotations, proving, as they do, Jackson's truthfulness in his statement to Biddle, show the former again as the bearer of geistige tradition.

Jackson's earliest impressions with regard to banking cannot be dated. It is easier to show when and how he came to embrace agrarian radicalism. In 1788 Jackson settled in Nashville. About twenty years old he was just at the age when men are formed for the rest of their lives by their environment and experiences. In Nashville Jackson first fell in with the middle class and tried to acquire wealth by capitalistic means. He speculated in lands, traded in horses and slaves, and opened a general store; but in the end he was unsuccessful. He lost heavily, was forced to abandon the idea of becoming a capitalist, and applied the remnants of his fortune to running his plantation. Thereby his mind became receptive to agrarian ideology which was then being worked out in Virginia, whose influence was dominant in Tennessee at that time.[15]

The Virginian radicals attacked what they called the "paper system" (in modern terms: credit economy or capitalism) and Jackson had his own experience with it during these years. In 1795 he had bought goods in Philadelphia and paid for them with the notes of a wealthy Philadelphia merchant, who in turn had bought land from him. Shortly afterwards the crisis of that year forced this merchant into bankruptcy and Jackson as the endorser of the notes had to pay them. He was able to do so only by involving his property in a complicated system of mortgages and other debts. This experience made Jackson suspicious. The fact that the failure of an Eastern merchant, who had bought from him, deprived him of 6000 acres of land and almost all of his whole fortune without any fault of his own was beyond his understanding.[16]

Another experience with Eastern capitalists came on top of the first. After Jackson had overcome, more or less, the consequences of the disaster of 1795 he returned to his earlier plan and opened another general merchandise business. Again, however, he found that his success was subject to actions by the financial powers in the eastern cities. He exchanged goods imported from Philadelphia for local products and then shipped the latter to New Orleans, selling them there for bills of exchange on banks in Philadelphia, Baltimore, and New York. In consequence thereof he was in the power of bill-brokers at both ends of the game.

As a result, Jackson distrusted the moneyed East more and more. He felt that no matter how careful, industrious, and intelligent he was and that even if every other bit of luck was in his favor, yet if the exchange should be against him, his profits would vanish. He realized that a firm could continue in business only at the will of bankers. To Jackson this control by alien bankers was bitter indeed, and so he began consistently to oppose the power exercised over the hinterland by the financiers in the East.[17]

Regardless of whether or not a less erratic man and a better manager would have succeeded in his venture, the description shows well how Jackson must have felt when he sold out his share in that enterprise. Those experiences profoundly influenced his thinking with regard to banks. What Jackson actually experienced during the 1790's and early 1800's was the working of modern credit economy, the "paper system," and for him, as for all his radical friends, banks were its principal exponents.

Thus it is not surprising to find Jackson around 1820 an avowed enemy of banking. At that time he opposed the charter of a state bank in Tennessee which was sponsored by Felix Grundy and a few years later he joined the fight against the repeal of a state law which kept the Second Bank of the United States from opening a branch in Nashville. Considering Jackson's character this attitude is the less surprising since in the meantime he personally had had an unpleasant experience with the Bank itself. In 1821 its New Orleans branch had refused to cash a draft of his on the State Department since the parent bank had forbidden the cashing of any drafts.

During the period when Jackson underwent the above-described business experiences which made him susceptible to an anti-capitalistic philosophy he had already come under such influence, namely, that of radical agrarianism. This can be clearly discerned in his actions, enunciations, and phraseology down to the time of the Bank War. Although Jackson was not conscious of how his thinking was shaped, it was in fact molded by Philip Freneau, the journalist, and by John Taylor, the statesman. Philip Freneau's influence on the minds of agrarian Americans in the 1790's has been described rightly as very strong and persistent. His biographer, Samuel E. Forman, states that Freneau's National

Gazette (published October 1791-October 1793) was circulated in every state of the Union, that in every Democratic paper of that time one will find quotations from the publication, and that most of these contained attacks on the (first) Bank of the United States. Freneau's influence was all the stronger since American public opinion was then still in its formative stage. The hatred against the Bank by wide strata of the population was thus aroused by Freneau and, according to the above-quoted author, no other influence contributed more to its downfall in 1811. Since there can be no doubt that Jackson was among those who were deeply influenced in this way, one can perhaps go a step further and claim that Forman's assertion is true even with respect to the downfall of the Second Bank.[18]

John Taylor's influence, on the other hand, came to bear on Jackson in 1795 when he came to Philadelphia as a member of the House of Representatives. He not only joined the radical wing of the Republicans but made friends with some of their outstanding men. John Taylor, whose hatred of the Bank of the United States was probably not less intense than that of Freneau, in matters of finance was the intellectual leader of that group. When Jackson came to Philadelphia John Taylor had already left Congress, but his influence persisted.

For Taylor, banking was only a fraud,[19] its profits represented a tax upon the community[20] by which labor, the creator of all wealth, was deprived of its hard-earned fruits. "Calculated" only for the admission of the rich, intended to "enrich individuals," it tended to accumulate great wealth in the hands of a few,[21] at the expense of the exploited poor. Through the Bank of the United States a group of merchants had received the exclusive right of issuing the circulating medium and they could thereby raise and diminish the prices of all commodities, and this enormous power was exercised for profit.[22] That exclusive right amounted to no less than a "monopolizing conspiracy" which was the more dangerous since land could not be increased, while paper could. Therefore landed property could not strengthen its influence, whereas property based on paper could, at the expense of all other kinds of property.[23] Foreigners, and among them Englishmen, "our late most malignant and inveterate enemy" had obtained bank stock and thus a share in the conspiracy."[24]

This economic development, according to Taylor, had serious political repercussions. "Papermen" got into Congress and the Bank governed them. Since the Bank was interested in large deposits of government money, which in turn came from taxes, legislators became interested in high taxation. Thus the Bank so undermined the morals of the legislators that freedom was destroyed. But even worse, since the Bank at any time might be controlled by a majority of foreigners, foreigners might one day guide the legislature of the United States.[25] This development had been made possible by flagrant violation of the Constitution. The Constitution did not give the right of establishing a paper currency to the Federal government, and in taking it expressly from the states the Constitution intended to secure society against the frauds and vices of paper tricks.[26]

Jefferson himself has not been cited so far, because his ideas on banks in general and on the Bank of the United States in particular were hardly known to a wider public.[27] To be sure, he later confessed to Adams that his zeal against banks was so warm at the time of the establishment of the First Bank of the United States that he was "derided a maniac by the tribe of bank mongers." He considered the Bank of the United States as being "of the most deadly hostility existing against the principles and forms of our Constitution." But later Jefferson's thoughts on this subject, practically identical with those of Freneau and Taylor, were buried in his correspondence. Thus they cannot have exerted the same influence on a young man like Jackson, as did the utterances of the other two men. With Taylor, Jefferson was convinced that at the time when Congress was still meeting in Philadelphia those members of both houses who were directors of the Bank, together with other stockholding Congressmen, exerted an improper influence on the decisions of Congress. Although Gallatin could not see any such danger, Jefferson expected obstruction in time of war by the Bank's withdrawing financial aid to government or by its dictating the terms of peace. Therefore he argued that the government should bring "this enemy to a perfect

subordination under its authorities." To this end Jefferson made some suggestions different from Taylor's. He wanted to reduce the Bank of the United States to a footing equal to that of other banks by having all share in the favors of the government, especially in the public deposits. The idea of distributing the public deposits among all banks was expressed repeatedly by Jefferson; and one of his reasons was that the state banks were owned by Americans, while a considerable portion of the stock of the Bank of the United States was owned by foreigners. Since Jackson's policy of 1833 with regard to the public deposits suggested by Taney, was along the lines of Jefferson's suggestions we should like to know whether or not Jackson or his adviser knew of them.

Such were the ideas which Jackson imbibed in the 1790's. They were expressed by members of the Democratic-Republican party repeatedly in the following two decades, especially in the years 1811, 1815, and 1816 when the bank question came up in Congress. Thus they came to dominate Jackson's mind for the rest of his life to the exclusion of all others on the subject of banking. In the 1830's they still determined him in his fight against the Second Bank of the United States whose very purpose and strategy were foreshadowed in Taylor's writings: inhibitions upon monopoly and incorporation are the remedies for an aristocracy founded on paper wealth, as the latter wrote.[28] Almost all of the ideas described above were repeated in the Bank War and embodied in the Bank Veto, which regardless of whoever actually formulated it, is representative of Jackson's intellectual world and that of his entourage.

The Bank Veto started from the conviction already to be found in Taylor's writings, but expressed often and widely held since the 1790's, that "some of the powers and privileges possessed by the existing bank are unauthorized by the Constitution;" and a later pronouncement of Jackson makes it clear that this statement represented the President's own conviction. (As late as 1837, in a letter to Senator Benton, almost quoting Taylor he wrote: "My position now is and has ever been since I have been able to form an opinion on this subject [probably during the time of his being a member of the House of Representatives] that Congress has no power to charter a bank and that the states are prohibited from issuing bills of credit or granting a charter by which such bills can be issued by any corporation or order."[29] That sentence from the Bank Veto goes on to stress that the President considered some of the powers and privileges of the Bank of the United States as dangerous to the people's liberties. This fact implies that that one sentence of the Veto contains two ideas taken from Taylor who, in his early pamphlet, deemed it superfluous to "consider how the Bank will effect liberty at its extremities" since this was too obvious for mention.[30] Taylor had considered the Bank a "monopolizing conspiracy," the Bank Veto spoke of its "monopoly" and "exclusive privileges" (which are the same since the word "monopoly" in that period meant "exclusive privileges" as opposed to "equal rights and privileges"). Such exclusive privileges, according to the Bank Veto, were granted at the expense of the public. This statement is similar to Taylor's idea of the Bank "taxing" the community.[31] The Bank Veto claimed that through a new charter a new monopoly would be bestowed on the few who had been fortunate enough to secure bank stock; ("why should not the Government sell out the whole stock and thus secure to the people the full market value of the privileges granted?"). It went on to denounce the application for rechartering the Bank by which the rich had "besought us to make them richer by Act of Congress;" and the new charter which would make "the richer more rich and the potent more powerful." All this reminds one of Taylor's idea that the Bank was calculated only for the admission of the rich.[32] However, the dependence of Jackson and his friends on Taylor becomes perfectly obvious in the paragraphs of the Veto which attack the Bank because of its dependence on foreign influence. Jackson and his friends "tremble[d] for the purity of our elections in peace and for the independence of our country in war." This is an almost parrot-like repetition of Taylor's fears[33] and the arguments to that effect presented generally in the fight against the First Bank of the United States in 1810 and 1811. This line of reasoning had already been exploded at that time by such men as Mathew Carey and Nicholas Biddle.[34]

In 1833 the latter must have felt very bitter at Jackson's repetition of what had been proved erroneous in 1811. Besides the lack of logic manifested in the passages in question, there was, in Jackson's time, only a kernel of truth in the assertions because the charter of the Second Bank of the United States carefully excluded the possibility of foreign influence on that institution (section 11, topics 3 and 16). At most such influence could have been exerted in an indirect way and only to a small degree.[35] In this respect it is difficult to judge the true significance of the Veto message. Did Jackson himself believe what he said or did he apply shrewd propaganda in flag-waving and reviving a lingering tradition which had once before proved effective?[36]

Of those objections[37] to the charter contained in the Bank Veto which are not taken from the Virginian's fight against the First Bank of the United States, one more is derived at least from the philosophy of that exponent of states' rights and local democracy: the Veto objected to the charter as submitted to the President because it would take away rights scrupulously reserved to the states. One must concede that Jackson who had lived in frontier society and under the influence of the men who were then developing the theory of local decentralized government could not but be suspicious of the Bank. For here arose an institution with centralized powers adapted to the needs of the coming capitalistic order, but contrary to the ideals and traditions of that world which had its exponent in Jackson, the typical representative of the agrarian youth whose impressionable years fell in the 1790's. As late as 1858, Governor Wise of Virginia hailed the destruction of the Bank of the United States by Jackson as "a great conquest of...an instrument of centralization."[38] What has done much harm to Jackson before the judgment of history was exactly what also destroyed Taylor's reputation as a political thinker: that is, his inability to become articulate and to express in clear and exact words and terms his fears, suspicions, and intentions.[39]

In the preceding paragraphs an attempt has been made to explain Jackson's attitude in the Bank War in the light of the theory of generations. It is questionable how much genuine economic reasoning was back of the President's actions.[40] Be that as it may, the repetition of the standardized agrarian formulas on the subject of banking, embraced by his generation, must have satisfied his conscience: once certain presuppositions were accepted the reasoning was logical and consistent indeed, as will be shown shortly. Actually banking was beyond Jackson's comprehension as it had been beyond that of Taylor;[41] and the President's dislike and hatred of the Bank were mainly emotional. Yet, how could an American agrarian of Jackson's generation be expected to stand behind the Bank of the United States when even in England at that time public opinion was still divided with respect to the Bank of England. To be sure, in England opposition did not come from agrarian circles.

Through coincidence the charters of the two central banks came up for renewal about the same time. In all probability the strong antagonism to the Bank of England which was manifested in the 1820's and 1830's was known at least to some of Jackson's advisers.[42] No less a person than David Ricardo had expressed himself as against the Bank of England, and his posthumous Plan of a National Bank of 1825 was reprinted, recommended, and commented upon by Samson Ricardo as late as 1838.[43] The Bank of England was attacked because the combined character of a bank of issue and a bank of discount and deposit was incompatible with a well-regulated paper circulation and because the interests of the Bank of England and of the public were constantly at variance. Hostility to the Bank of England was not only expressed in the British pamphlet literature of that period, but also in the hearings of 1832 before a parliamentary committee on the renewal of the bank charter.[44] At these hearings it was claimed that the Bank of England had a secret and despotic influence and control over the destinies of English commerce, that price fluctuations were due to expansions and contractions of the Bank of England, that such power was too great to be held by any one enterprise, and that the Bank of England was the cause of panics. There were complaints that the exclusive privileges of the Bank were injurious to the public interest and altogether unsound, or at least there were doubts whether or not the interest of the Bank was coincident with that of the public.[45] It was suggested that "open competition" in banking should replace its exclusive privileges. As a matter of fact, in contrast to their American counterpart the English antagonists to their central bank did not succeed; but for the understanding of the history of American banking in the 1830's it is important to keep in mind that during those years hostility to the Bank of England existed and found strong expression.[46]

The preceding quotations indicate that in some respects and even with regard to the very language the English discussions on the Bank of England were not dissimilar to the American debates on the Bank of the United States. A few additional quotations will strengthen that impression: Lord Liverpool writing to the Governor of the Bank of England on the 13th of January, 1826, stated that: "with respect to the continuation of their [the shareholders of the Bank of England] exclusive privileges in the metropolis and its neighbourhood [after 1832]...Parliament will never agree to it. Such privileges are out of fashion, and what expectation can the Bank, under the present circumstances entertain that theirs will be renewed."[47] And when in 1833 the rumor cropped out that Bank of England notes would be made a legal tender, a committee of the country bankers remonstrated thus: It would give the Bank an arbitrary power and "would expose the pursuits of agriculture, manufactures, and commerce to the control of a set of men who have no intercourse with the country, no sympathy with the people, no knowledge of their wants and circumstances - who are not identified with their prosperity," etc.[48]

Regardless of his dislike of the Bank of the United States, Jackson was at least at times inclined to recognize that the country needed an institution of that type. During the early years of his presidency he aimed at the very thing which many Englishmen of the same period were also attempting, namely, to replace the existing Bank of England, controlled by capitalists, by a similar bank under government control. In England, as mentioned before, those attempts gained momentum in the 1820's when David Ricardo wrote his Plan for a National

Bank.[49] The Currency School of monetary theorists had similar leanings and in the 1830's Torrens proposed a national bank to replace the Bank of England.[50] Thus even in England in the early 1830's it was not a foregone conclusion that the Bank of England would be allowed permanently to control the English monetary and banking system, and as late a year as 1839 was notable for a violent attack on this Bank in the House of Commons.[51]

It is in the light of such events that one should regard Jackson's repeated endeavors toward replacing the Second Bank of the United States by a similar institution but of different characteristics. These endeavors show up in his correspondence with Felix Grundy in 1829, his suggestion to create a "national bank" in the first annual message of December 1829, the assignment to James A. Hamilton of the job of devising the scheme of a non-objectionable bank to replace the existing one, his continuous thinking about a "National Bank of Deposit" in 1830, and, later in his second term, his approval in principle of a bank in the District of Columbia with branches by the consent of the states concerned.[52] If these attempts are seen in the light of contemporary English struggles, Jackson's position before the court of history becomes stronger. For the time being, however, it cannot be definitely established whether or not, and if so to what extent, Jackson was actually influenced by those contemporary English events. His policy may have been shaped exclusively by his recollections of the debates of 1811 when the renewal of the charter of the First Bank of the United States hung fire. At that time it had already been suggested that the existing Bank of the United States be replaced by a "national bank," a national bank being defined as one which "belong[s] in whole, or at least in a considerable degree, to the nation" and "whose trustees or managers or directors [are] wholly or chiefly appointed by the nation, in the same manner as it appoints other agents." Such a bank to be established in the District of Columbia with branches in the various states was then proposed in Congress and out.[53] But such plans were abandoned by Jackson as early as 1833, probably under the influence of Taney.[54]

What Jackson actually fought, as his biographer saw correctly,[55] was what is now called a central bank, owned by Eastern and foreign capitalists who would be able thereby to exert political influence. Bank stock "naturally imbibes political power," he had learned from Taylor.[56] It was especially galling to the President that the control of the Bank of the United States over the state banks was derived from its character as the depository of the public revenue. For Jackson, the Bank question was at least as much a matter of domestic as of economic policy; and nothing shows better the sincerity and seriousness of his thinking than the following passages written apparently by or under the influence of Taney and which appear in a memorandum of June 1833 to Duane and in a statement of the spring of the same year.[57]

A corporation of individuals deriving its powers from Congress, pervading every section of the Union, will in the general, by controlling the currency and leading men of the country, be more powerful than the government and may seriously thwart its views and embarrass its operations. This is one of the dangers of the present bank. But any substitute which should concentrate the same or a like power and be put entirely under the control of the general government might by the union of the political and money power give the administration of the general government more influence and the government itself more strength than is compatible with the safety of the states, the liberties of the people, and the purity of our republican institutions. Having considered the subject in all its bearings the President has come to the conclusion that all idea for any substitute for the present bank in the shape of a new institution ought to be abandoned, at least for the present.

Therefore such an institution ought not to be recommended until after a full and fair experiment to carry on the fiscal affairs without a national bank of any description.... The state institutions are therefore competent to perform all the functions which the United States bank now performs or which may be required by the government. At the same time they cannot so effectually concentrate the money power, they cannot be so easily or effectually be used for individual, political, or party purposes as a bank of the United States under any form or of any character.

Jackson's ultimate intentions with regard to banking in American are not clear. His assertion to Biddle that he did not dislike the Bank of the United States more than other banks is corroborated by later statements and was undoubtedly correct.[58] Senator Benton reported that Jackson had adopted his hard money philosophy, and so to a certain extent had Taney who at that time exerted a strong influence on the President. However, during the Bank War temporizing was unavoidable, and for tactical reasons it was necessary to have the support of at least a section of the banking fraternity and the ultimate goal, if any, had to be veiled.[59] Thus in the early 1830's Jackson became first some sort of protector of the state chartered institutions against the "monster," and later their benefactor. If one holds his statements of this period against those alluded to before, Jackson's attitude and that of his party toward the American banking system appear very inconsistent.[60] Whatever his true feelings, not only as destroyer of the Bank of the United States did Jackson gain profound influence on the development of American banking, but also through arousing public opinion against it. It will be described later how the hostility which Jackson kindled against the Bank of the United States was quickly directed against all chartered banks by a radical wing of his party. Thus, in a roundabout way through the moves of these radicals, Jackson became instrumental in bringing about Free Banking in New York.[61]

There was some element of genuine tragedy in the situation created by the Bank War. In consequence of the introduction of capitalism America had been almost split in two. Taylor had already realized this when he asserted in the 1810's that the paper system had divided the "nation into two groups, creditors and debtors" and that an "order of paper" was "created" and a "separate stock interest established by law."[62] Translated into modern language this means that the incipient capitalism had divided the nation into two parties, the beneficiaries and the victims of the new system. The fight for and against the renewal of the charter of the First Bank of the United States had been fought along the very lines of this new class alignment. Many people considered the struggle against the Bank as a "war

of the middle and poorer classes of society against the rich" and believed that in case of success the interest of the former would be promoted at the expense of the latter.[63] This tradition apparently lingered on during the next decades. Thus when Jackson honestly took the side of those who rightly or wrongly considered themselves the victims of capitalism and who had elected him President, and when he called upon them to fight the exponent of the oppressive system, he was certain to find enthusiastic response.[64] He would find this response in the emotions of the anti-capitalistic groups, and the response would be all the stronger because of the perfect consistency (although not much economic knowledge) in his arguments. It is useful in this connection to read a publication by an obscure citizen of the Mississippi Valley written a few years after the Bank War, for thereby one can understand the wide appeal of Jackson's approach not only to the uneducated backwoodsman, but also to thoughtful people in the newer sections of the country. When one reads the following deductions (disregarding any doubtful presuppositions) one recognizes Biddle's error in thinking that with his superior knowledge and insight he could enlighten the people and thus win the victory.

In the publication alluded to[65] the author thus analyzes the banking situation of the 1830's.

The business of banking was originally founded on the supposed necessity of money, as the only possible medium of effecting the exchanges of society.... It professes to supply wants supposed to be natural, but which in reality are artificial.... Experience in banking business has shown that the accommodation which by its means can be rendered to society is of a very limited extent. The extent is determined not by the real wants of a community...but by the quantity or amount of paper which the banker finds it practicable to put out and keep out consistently with his own advantage.... But it is also true that the privilege of banking, being of a kind with the power of making money, or rather of creating it, is a power that cannot be lodged in any individual or in any company without great danger.... In a new country where a great portion of its lands are unappropriated such a privilege is far more dangerous than in old ones. The

power of making money where lands are offered
for sale confers a power of purchasing and of
monopolizing them to an immense extent....

[Thus banking] is now the stepping
stone to aristocracy in these states. It has
already introduced the superfluous capital and
the overgrown influence of British aristocracy
to absorb our wealth and to expend, in foreign
lands and on foreign individuals, the profit
of the labor of the American citizen. If not
arrested in its early bud it will undermine
the free institutions of our country, prostrate its energies, and reduce the bulk of
our people to that state of degradation and
misery which prevails among the congregated
thousands of British and Irish laborers in
their native country.

The only way out was not discovered
and could not be; and in this connection
the personal element became the decisive
factor. Instead of being determined on
its own merits the matter became a foot-
ball in the struggle for power between such
men as Jackson, Van Buren, McLane, Calhoun,
and Clay. Essentially however, the Bank
War was a fight between two powerful personalities, men who were equally inclined
to be autocratic and who, as exponents of
two antagonistic views, were unable to
understand each other. Jackson, the emotional, stubborn old man, without statesmanship but with political instinct, unable to articulate his real and justified
fears, imbued with the thoughts of an older
generation, could not master the situation:
he could only destroy. A true statesman
with the same anti-capitalistic convictions, but one who understood the realities
of his time and its trend, would have preferred to check an unavoidable capitalistic development by strengthening the existing brakes instead of smashing them to
pieces and thereby letting the mechanism
run wild. Such checks would have resulted
from the policy suggested by the moderates
in the President's official family; but
their advice was in vain. The President
could not understand banking; but at the
same time his instinct told him that there
was something wrong with it. He would
even have deemed himself clever in case he
remembered Taylor's assertion that "money
...regulates itself better than it can be
regulated by the doctors, despotism, monopoly, or banking."⁶⁶ Viewed historically

Jackson's guilt lies in the fact that he
did not listen to reasonable advice.

In this fight between the two great
historical personalities, Jackson and
Biddle, the loser lost not because he backed
the worse cause nor because he was the less
capable man; it was simply that he possessed
less power. The power of the President of
the United States was greater than that of
the president of the Bank of the United
States, the former being upheld by the
broad masses. These masses, then as now,
did not understand a complicated issue but,
trusting in their champion and "hero," voted
accordingly. It would be a serious mistake,
however, if one should view the Bank War
simply as a fight for power or as a contest
between two persons. Issues were at stake
in the Bank War and the two contestants and
their backers so understood. But the battle lines were strangely drawn. Biddle
stood for the coming economic order (capitalism) which Jackson did not understand;
while Jackson (backed by certain business
groups) represented the socio-political
order of the future, which, in turn, Biddle
did not grasp. Unfortunately in fighting
at the same time for and against what the
future had in store both men also stood for
the excesses thereof: Biddle for plutocracy,
the rule of wealth, and Jackson for ochloc-
racy, mob rule.

Regardless of the fact that the
personal element was decisive for the outcome of the Bank War the downfall of the
Bank has a deep historical meaning: it was
in the 1830's that laissez-faire conquered
America and the most advanced minds of the
time inclined to the belief that free competition and immutable economic laws would
regulate the monetary concerns of the Union
much better than any national bank. It
should not be forgotten that a decade after
the Bank War the Peel Act was passed in
England. By this act the Bank of England
was to be relieved of all responsibilities
for the economy of the country; it was to
conduct its business like any other commercial bank, the British banking system as a
whole being regulated imperceptibly by the
forces of supply and demand for money and
credit. As a matter of fact, it was probably the alliance of representatives of
traditional American radicalism with those
of modern cosmopolitan laissez-faire philosophy which made the anti-bank forces irresistible.

The men who were most important in backing Jackson in his fight against the Second Bank of the United States were Amos Kendall, Francis P. Blair, and Roger B. Taney. For all three men the Bank War was principally a matter of domestic policy or rather a matter of constitutional rights and civil liberties.[67] While for Jackson, who was ten to twenty years their senior, it was a question both of domestic and of economic policy. Amos Kendall (1789-1869), like Andrew Jackson, fought the Bank under a lasting impulse born during the most impressionable years of his life. But while Andrew Jackson's youth fell into the 1790's (into the heroic age of the American party struggle, if you please) in which the basic principles of our political system were worked out, Amos Kendall was influenced for the rest of his life by the 1810's, no great decade in American history. Furthermore, whereas Jackson gained his impressions on the frontier and in Philadelphia, Amos Kendall acquired his in New Hampshire and especially in Kentucky, then no longer a frontier nor yet a mature state. Thus Jackson with all his shortcomings reflected the frontier and the great 1790's, while Amos Kendall was always a man matured in a dull period and in the narrow environment of the back country, a man whose formative experience was the War of 1812. Kendall was a representative of democracy and states rights, but the greatness and passions of the Jeffersons, Taylors, and Freneaus can no longer be discerned in his fulminating journalism. He has stated repeatedly that his antagonism to the Bank of the United States stemmed from his experience with its branches in the late 1810's in Kentucky where in his words its failure was "perhaps more signal" than anywhere else. He deemed it necessary to stress that his opposition "originated in motives higher than party spirit, self interest, and personal ambition," but qui s'excuse and he admitted that it was the Bank War which made him Postmaster-General eral.[68]

Amos Kendall has left a clear outline of his banking theory. To him (in 1819) "the very thought of these institutions [was] disgusting," while (in 1820) he understood their business as being essentially a swapping of promises to pay, those of the banks becoming currency.[69]

Experience has shown how fallacious is the idea of regulating the currency by means of a National Bank. Indeed the scheme of sustaining a paper currency of uniform value throughout a country so commercial and extensive as the United States is an absurdity. If there be a paper currency equivalent to gold and silver at the commercial centers, as in New York, it will be worth more than gold and silver at distant points as at Chicago and St. Louis. The obvious reason is that the difference of exchange between distant points and New York is always in favor of that city and bank notes equal in value there to specie can be transmitted more cheaply than gold and silver.... In an extensive community therefore a paper currency of equal value everywhere is impracticable. Most absurd is the attempt to establish such a currency in a country full of local banks whose notes, though equal to gold and silver in their own immediate neighborhood, are below the par of specie at the commercial centers and cannot be used as bills of exchange.[70]

So much for Kendall's general banking theory. The working of the Bank of the United States, which he dubbed an "infernal institution,"[71] he never understood, since he looked at it from the Kentucky angle. He seems to have thought that the branches were intended to regulate the state banks in their respective sections and was far from recognizing them as more or less the tools of the parent bank, as they actually were in the second half of the 1820's, the Bank's great period. He probably deemed himself clever and witty when he stated that the branches of the Bank of the United States in Kentucky had "no more power to control the local banks and restore a sound currency than stranded whales have to control the motions of the little fish which swim around them."[72] Kendall claimed that if in 1812 a National Bank had existed "it would have been under the control of men whose feelings and interests were averse to the war and instead of strengthening the government it might have added greatly to its embarrassments."[73] Here can be found in a popular form Jefferson's, Taylor's, and Jackson's previously described theories on the role of the Bank in wartime.

Amos Kendall made it perfectly clear that for himself the Bank question was not a matter of economic policy, but a matter of constitutional rights and civil liberties.

He looked at the destruction of the Bank as "essential to the preservation of a purely republican government."[74] Thinking along these lines as a member of Jackson's Kitchen Cabinet Amos Kendall gained a most powerful influence during the Bank War. It was he who, backing Jackson in his intention to veto the new Bank charter, drew up most of the propagandistic part of the Veto Message, analyzed above. After the charter was vetoed he went on shaping Jackson's policy with regard to the institution. Kendall and his friend Blair (to be discussed shortly) were afraid that if the Bank were left intact until the election year of 1836 it would be rechartered after all, since Jackson's tremendous popularity with the masses alone guaranteed the power to defeat it. Therefore it had to be destroyed prior to that year, and therefore in the Globe they propagandized the removal of the public deposits. After the soil was well prepared Kendall planted the seed of Jackson's letter to Duane of June 26, 1833 which represented the first actual move toward that removal. By that time the enemies of this policy tried to convince the President that the state banks would not willingly take the public deposits for fear of the Bank of the United States. But again Kendall, who as an auditor in the Department of the Treasury had the contemptible job of spying on Duane, the Secretary of that Department, pushed on. He suggested to Jackson that he (Kendall) should be sent into the field to investigate the attitude of the state banks. Following this advice Jackson ordered Duane to draw up instructions for Kendall, but Duane's draft was turned over to the latter who revised it to fit his own policy; and Jackson returned Kendall's changes to Duane as his own. Thus Kendall, self-instructed, acting against his superior's intentions went to Baltimore, Philadelphia, New York, and Boston and hired state banks to be future depositories for the public funds. That is to say, the system of pet banks was to a large extent Kendall's work.[75]

Kendall was also instrumental in bringing to Washington his bosom friend, Francis Preston Blair (1791-1876), who has been mentioned above. Belonging to the same group of coevals and having experienced the events of the 1810's in the same environment in Kentucky, the same influences had come to bear on these two men. This fact explains the similarity of their attitudes. But Blair had had practical experiences of his own with banking, having been the president of the Commonwealth Bank of Kentucky, at which time he contributed articles to Amos Kendall's Argus of Western America. When Jackson became president Blair started to attack the Bank of the United States in widely read articles charging it with intending to ruin his bank for being "Democratic." Later as the editor of the Washington Globe and as a member of the Kitchen Cabinet he backed Jackson in his anti-Bank policy and through his paper exerted a powerful influence on the public against the "monster." In cooperation with Kendall, as described above, he devised and propagated the eminently successful policy of destroying the Bank before the end of Jackson's presidency through the removal of the public deposits.

While Kendall and Blair in unofficial capacity were very much the driving forces in the Bank War, Roger B. Taney (1777-1864) as the attorney-general can be characterized as Jackson's most faithful second. This statement does not overlook the fact that Taney spurred the President repeatedly and successfully urged him to act against the Bank. Taney's age put him between Jackson and Kendall. Not as old as Jackson he was nevertheless mature enough in the 1790's to react to the political struggle of that decade as an adolescent. In an autobiographical sketch[76] he described how between 1792 and 1795, when a student at Dickinson College, he and his classmates, even when they were Federalists, reacted against the anti-republican statements of a very popular professor: his "opinions were monstrous heresies" in the eyes of the youngsters. However, more important than the party struggle of the 1790's as a source of influence was the War of 1812. Years later, Taney, the former leader of the Maryland pro-war Federalists, still bitterly assailed Federalist hostility to the war and the spirit of disunion manifested in the Hartford Convention.[77] Thus he was early attracted to Jackson in the presidential campaign of 1824 when the latter's correspondence of 1816 with Monroe was published. In one of these letters Jackson had pleaded for those

Federalists who had supported the government during the War of 1812 and had called on Monroe "to exterminate the monster called party spirit." It was under such circumstances that Taney joined the Jackson crowd.[78]

According to one of Taney's biographers the latter was called into Jackson's cabinet in 1831 as attorney-general to back the President in his policy of decentralization which the former Federalist had embraced as his own. As the scion of Southern plantation owners it was easy for Taney also to fall in with Jackson's anti-capitalistic economic policy. Thus by 1832 he had won the President's regard to such an extent that he "had become his most trusted and confidential adviser."[79]

As the only member of Jackson's cabinet Taney not only favored the veto of the Bank charter in 1832, but also urged Jackson to go ahead. He did this in the long letter of June 27, 1832 which, read today, leaves a rather painful impression, since his advice implied that Jackson should override the counsel of all his other constitutional advisers.[80] Taney was successful; and when Jackson vetoed the charter according to his advice it fell to him to draw up the legal and perhaps also to revise the political part of the Veto Message. Its gist, the very doubtful proposition that the Bank of the United States represented the instrument of a class and a section by which other classes and other sections were made to pay tribute, was, according to one of Taney's biographers, contributed by the latter[81] who, in so doing however, drew mostly on older thoughts, as described above.[82] Taney's real motive lay in the field of domestic policy. He considered it "a fixed principle of our political institutions to guard against the unnecessary accumulation of power over persons and property in any hands. And no hands are less worthy to be trusted than those of a moneyed corporation." As late as 1849, when he recorded his share in the Bank War, he made it clear that his aim was to destroy a center of irresponsible power.[83]

Taney seems to have considered himself an expert in banking. Actually, as revealed by his own record mentioned above, his insight did not go deeply,[84] although his interest in currency and

banking was of long standing.[85] During his career in the Maryland legislature he had been a member of a committee on a bank in Baltimore and had sponsored a bill to charter the Frederick County Bank as well as legislation aiming to prevent the circulation of bank notes below par and the deliberate depreciation of country notes, as supposedly practiced by Baltimore bankers and brokers. Between 1810 and 1815 he had been a director of the Frederick, Maryland, branch of a state bank; from 1818 to 1823 a director of the Frederick County Bank; and later a director and counsel of the Union Bank of Maryland in Baltimore. That is to say, Taney had gained most of his experience in banking in the legislature of an agricultural Southern state and in country banks with their lingering tradition of Mercantilist "banking on private credit" and with their atmosphere of hostility toward incipient central banking with its completely different philosophy. It is not surprising therefore that Taney, originally a friend of the national bank, became its enemy. While a member of the Maryland legislature he had voted against taxing the Baltimore branch of the Bank of the United States, but later he became alienated by the scandals caused by that branch. In his capacity as counsel in a case against the Bank and as the attorney of the Union Bank he realized the Bank's power and became definitely antagonistic to what he considered its tendency to ruthlessness. For some time (in 1831) he thought of renewing its charter only if it was forbidden to set up branches without consent of the states concerned.[86] It will be explained later under what influence he embraced the policy of destroying the Bank.

To repeat: Taney was instrumental in securing Jackson's veto of the Bank charter. He became important a second time in the development of American banking when the question of the removal of the public deposits was brought up by Blair and Kendall. At that time, like Jackson, Taney believed that the Bank was not only corrupting public opinion, but also risking bankruptcy in adventurous enterprises. So, once more, he whipped Jackson into action against the Bank.[87] In April 1833 he suggested the making of a "full and fair experiment" in order to find out whether or not the fiscal affairs of the Federal government could be conducted without the help of a national bank. At the same time he advised Jackson that the government's right to remove the public deposits still existed regardless of the report of the Committee on Ways and Means that they were safe in the custody of the Bank of the United States. The letters of April were followed up by official correspondence, and finally, on August 5, 1833, by a very important private letter. In this letter, in repetition of earlier suggestions, Taney urged Jackson to withdraw the public deposits from the Bank "provided a safe and convenient arrangement could be made with the state banks for the collection and distribution of the revenue." Playing up to Jackson and playing ball with Kendall, he admonished the President: "if your administration closes without having established and carried into operation some other plan of collection and distribution of the revenue the Bank will be too strong to be resisted by any one who may succeed you." But this danger should be prevented, for Taney was convinced "that the continued existence of that powerful and corrupting monopoly will be fatal to the liberties of the people." This letter of Taney's together with Jackson's answer are of particular interest showing as they do that Jackson and his friends used the same arguments and the same phraseology in their private letters which they used in their official pronunciamentos. That is to say, this correspondence proves at the same time their honesty and (however understandable and justifiable their political ideals) their narrowmindedness and their not too high intellectual level. Once the die was cast it fell to Taney to formulate the "Paper read to the Cabinet" of September 18, 1833 in which the President ordered the removal of the public deposits and initiated those steps through which he definitely destroyed the Bank, thereby retarding the development of efficient central banking in this country for more than seventy years. It fell to Taney as the Secretary of the Treasury, to put the President's policy into practice and to create the system of "pet banks" which resulted in so much loss to the government and contributed so much to the seriousness of the crisis of 1837.

In building up that scheme of state banks as public depositories, Taney at the same time revealed his ignorance of banking and the fact that the astute politician was anything but a statesman. He was unable to gauge in advance the low ethical standard of the men to whom he entrusted thousands of dollars of public funds. It speaks volumes that the two institutions which were most anxious to have state banks appointed public depositories, namely the Union Bank of Maryland in Baltimore and the Girard Bank in Philadelphia, within a few months of the receipt of public funds grossly abused the confidence reposed in them and used public money in private speculations. But it is noteworthy that their eagerness contributed to stiffening Taney and Kendall in their policy of destroying the Bank. These two men had no appreciation of the stand taken by Gallatin when fighting for the renewal of the First Bank of the United States. Gallatin had then recognized that state banks could afford assistance to the government in its financial operations, but added "that the general government should in respect to its own operations [not] be entirely dependent on institutions over which it has no control whatsoever." The impudence with which in 1837 after the breakdown of the pet-bank system a man like Reuben M. Whitney, one of Kendall's henchmen, denied to Congress the right of "visitation" and inquiry, is like dotting the i of Gallatin's unheeded prudence.[88]

Since Taney's honesty is beyond question he must be characterized as naive in banking matters. While he was convinced that the Bank of the United States could not provide a sound currency[89] he expected that local banks, once entrusted with public funds, could do so, because they would check each other, a fantastic idea under the circumstances. Actually after a few months many of the pet banks were on the point of refusing to take further deposits if they had also to take the responsibility for the face value of the notes deposited by the collectors. In order to have the collection of the revenue run smoothly the Treasury was forced to guarantee the notes of certain Eastern banks. Among notes thus guaranteed were those of the thoroughly unsound Union Bank of Maryland which will be discussed shortly.[90]

In a circular letter sent to the selected banks Taney admonished them to "adopt the most liberal course which circumstances will admit toward other moneyed institutions," at the same time stipulating that the government deposits could be withdrawn at any moment. The banks, of course, could do only one of two things, namely, either follow a liberal lending policy or keep the government funds available on call. Since the money market was tight they gladly took the advice to expand. They expected that the government deposits would be permanent[91] and were almost aghast when they were advised after the exhaustion of the funds in the Bank of the United States that the government would withdraw money. Taney's main objective in the winter of 1833-34 was, of course, to checkmate Biddle who at that moment was trying to force the government into submission through a policy of contraction. However, even if Biddle had not contracted loans to a larger extent than was necessary to make up for the withdrawal of the public deposits, Taney's policy would have led to contraction automatically. It is obvious that a certain amount of funds deposited in one branch bank of very large size can be the basis of a larger sum of loans than the same amount deposited in numerous weak local banks. Thus while the pet banks were spurred on to an unsound expansion, the total of their loans could under no circumstances equal the total of sound loans possible under the previous set-up.

Hard as must be the verdict on Taney's actions it must also be conceded that the original ideas with regard to a system of state banks as public depositories were not put into practice.[92] The atmosphere of contemporary banking and the legal set-up, as Taney should have known, were such that the proposals, sound as they were, were impracticable. That Taney did not see this in advance and stuck to the scheme after it had become unsound through a fundamental change, is another proof of his lack of statesmanship. Following the example of the New York Safety Fund System it was planned, probably on the basis of Kendall's suggestions, to merge the various state banks selected as public depositories into a genuine system of banks which would mutually guarantee each other.[93] However Kendall had hardly started on his journey to select state banks as public depositories when he recognized and reported that this plan was impracticable. The state banks were not willing to come into a scheme of such character, and if they had

been willing, in many cases the charters would have made it impossible.[94] Since at that time only one such mutual guaranty system existed, namely the Safety Fund System of New York, the adoption of which on a national scale had been expected by some as early as 1830, and since Van Buren had so much to do with its creation, it is certain that it served as a model. As a matter of fact, Kendall first proposed the mutual guarantee plan to Van Buren,[95] expecting him to recommend it to Jackson who finally adopted the proposal. The planned system of public depositories was to be headed by the Bank of the Metropolis at Washington; Amos Kendall was to become its president and thereby the coordinator of the public depositories. As mentioned before, the plan did not materialize, although such a closely-knit system of banks in all parts of the country, mutually responsible and strongly coordinated, could well have taken the place of the Bank of the United States, developing into a genuine central bank. But it may be doubted very much whether Kendall would have been able to take Biddle's place, even if the plan had succeeded.[95a]

During the time when Taney fought for the destruction of the Bank of the United States and was setting up state banks as public depositories, he was under the influence of a man of dubious character who thus gained a not unimportant influence on the development of American banking. During the years when Taney was the counsel of the Union Bank of Maryland, its president was Thomas Ellicott who became so close to Taney, that the latter considerd him one of his "oldest and confidential friends."[96] In his early years Ellicott (1777-1859) was an imposing personality and a shrewd and ambitious man. He had the reputation "of considerable talent and energy," as Biddle wrote. Before the latter became president of the Second Bank of the United States, Ellicott was discussed in Baltimore as possible candidate for that position. As John H. B. Latrobe, who was on the board of the Union Bank together with Ellicott and Taney, wrote in his Recollections, Ellicott originated or at least promoted the idea of state banks taking the place of the Bank of the United States as public depositories, and Swisher's research bears out the truth of Latrobe's statement. Ellicott's conception of that idea, of course, did not mean much since anyone in those years could still have remembered the period after the dissolution of the First Bank of the United States. But it seems that at a time when Jackson was still thinking of replacing the Bank of the United States by a national bank of another character, Ellicott suggested to Taney, who then thought along much the same lines as Jackson, the possibility of a different policy. In turn, Taney seems to have induced Jackson to substitute Ellicott's suggestion for his original plan. In those months of far reaching importance in the history of American banking honest Taney unwittingly became the tool of a dishonest man whose actions were influenced possibly by the fact that Biddle had been preferred to him as America's leading banker.

This much is certain: Ellicott was consulted by Taney in the spring of 1833 at which time Ellicott urged a system of state banks as public depositories and gave technical advice on how to avoid certain difficulties. When Kendall went on his previously-mentioned mission of selecting the first depositories Ellicott had already offered the services of the Union Bank of Maryland, and since those of the Girard Bank were also promised Kendall knew in advance that his mission could not be a total failure. During Kendall's visit in Baltimore Ellicott gained some influence also over this member of the Kitchen Cabinet. Then, by the middle of September, 1833, when the decisive steps were taken, Ellicott was in Washington and had an interview with Taney, who was all the while a stockholder of the Union Bank. Because of this latter fact, Taney left it to Jackson to select that bank as one of the depositories.

At that time when Ellicott's bank first received public funds he had already become involved in speculations and when he urged the matter on Taney he undoubtedly hoped to get relief from his embarrassments through receiving national deposits. As a matter of course he not only received public funds but also, like the other early depositories, contingent drafts, so-called transfer drafts, on the Bank of the United States in order to be protected against a possible run engineered by Biddle. Although not entitled to do so, Ellicott cashed these drafts, and the public funds thus withdrawn from the Bank of the United States into the custody of the Union Bank were applied to his private speculations. When the matter was on the point of becoming a scandal and of leading to an early collapse of the pet-bank scheme, Taney, who naively had fallen into the trap set for him by Ellicott, could not help bolstering up the Union Bank in order to save his face and his policy. In this connection he answered an inquiry in Congress by a false though technically correct statement. Ellicott, on the other hand, in despair and trepidation also applied to Biddle for help, pressed Taney to recharter the Bank of the United States, and was willing to state publicly that the pet-bank scheme had proved a failure.[97]

Taney's role in the history of American banking can perhaps be characterized as follows: When he became a member of Jackson's cabinet, American banking had arrived at a fork in the road. Three ways were open: to recharter the existing Bank of the United States; to charter a new national bank of similar or of different character; to set up a system of state banks as depositories for the public funds. In the first two cases, incipient central banking would perhaps have taken root in this country and become at that time, in the 1830's, part and parcel of the American institutional set-up. American banking history would in any case have been very different from what it turned out to be. It was Taney who guided the President to the road which was actually taken, but at the given moment Jackson alone was able to force the pursuance of the road suggested by Taney under the influence of Ellicott.

V

<u>The Debates of the 1830's and 1840's on the
Need of a National Bank and their
Significance</u>

It is not within the scope of this
chapter to describe the short career of the
Bank of the United States of Pennsylvania
or Van Buren's struggle for an Independent
Treasury or the fight for a new national
bank during Tyler's presidency. Nothing
new could be added to what is already known
nor could the description contribute to a
better understanding of the events. But it
was during the Bank War and during these
struggles that the real problem was clearly
brought to light, namely, whether or not
America needed a central bank. As Catterall expressed it: in the middle of the
1830's "for the first time parties clearly
divided on the issue of bank or no bank."[1]
This is the significance of the debates and
it is for this reason that they warrant further treatment.

In order to understand the significance of the public discussions of the bank
question in the 1830's and 1840's, one must
be aware of the true meaning of the terminology used therein, the understanding of
which hinges on that of the words "national
bank." The English pamphlet literature of
the eighteenth century had developed this
phrase until it came to mean a government-
owned bank to fulfill functions theretofore performed by the privately owned Bank
of England. It was in this sense that
Ricardo used the term in his posthumous
booklet. This meaning was adopted in
America temporarily only, in the years between the fight for the renewal of the
charter of the First Bank of the United
States and the first years of Jackson's
presidency.[2] In the meantime, however,
America had seen the independent evolution
of a different meaning. When Robert Morris
applied the term "national bank"[3] while he
was promoting the Bank of North America, he
meant: a bank for the struggling young nation. A decade later, however, when
Hamilton used the words again their meaning
had changed. The expression now connoted a
bank chartered by Congress, not by any one
state, to serve as the fiscal agency of
the "general govenment." This meaning
prevailed down to the 1820's. By that time
the two banks chartered by Congress in 1791
and 1816, respectively, partly because of
their character as branch banks, had been
able to perform functions not filled by
state-chartered institutions. This fact
became generally known and consequently
the term "national bank" became associated
with these specific functions which were
really central banking functions. Thus by
the 1830's the term "national bank," as
used in America, connoted exactly what is
called today a central bank, and it is in
this light that the discussions of the
1830's and 1840's on the subject should be
examined.[4] The question was not whether
or not America needed a bank chartered by
Congress, although the strict construc-
tionists were inclined to make it appear
as that, but whether or not America needed
a central bank.

The decisive point was argued, as
happens so often in public discussions, on
two different levels. The friends of a
central bank brought forward strong economic reasons which from their point of view
were irrefutable. Its foes, on the other
hand, answered along economic lines only
in exceptional cases and when they did,
they argued on the basis of the "weltanschauung" of <u>laissez-faire</u> to which they
adhered as to a religious dogma. Most of
the foes of central banking, however, completely disregarded the economic aspect of
the matter and treated the problem from the
social and political angles with arguments
which could not be answered to their satisfaction by the champions of the other
side.

Of all the items written by friends
of a national bank Mathew Carey's anonymously published pamphlet, <u>Outline of a
System of National Currency</u>, is perhaps the
most interesting. It contains a **logical**
and cogent development of the idea that
America needed a central bank and it refers repeatedly to the Bank of England,
that is to say, to that Bank which with
rapid strides was attaining uncontestable
central-bank status.[5]

A national bank was urged by its
friends in order that it might perform certain functions. Although the enumerations

to be found with the various authors differ
in details and in formulation the functions
themselves with a few exceptions can be
subsumed under the following heads: a national bank was needed as the fiscal agency of the government, as the regulator of
the currency, and as the guarantor of both
a cheap and a convenient system of the domestic exchanges and of a stable price for
the foreign ones as near as possible to
the "real par."[6] In addition, one author
saw a connection between the existence of
a national bank and a firmly established
public credit abroad;[7] others thought of
the national bank as of an ultimate holder
of the foreign exchange reserves of the
nation and as a lender of last resort in
times of crisis,[8] and some people wanted
such an institution for the purpose of
equalizing the fluctuations of business.
P. P. F. Degrand was most articulate on
this latter point:[9] a national bank was
needed to watch the course of the foreign
exchanges "so as to prepare to avert coming storms and allay a panic." "A national
bank has been found to act as the balance
wheel of the money market giving to the
local banks a public warning of coming
danger." It is noteworthy that Degrand
had been one of Biddle's close friends.
Finally, there were a few who looked at
the bank question as one partially connected with foreign policy. The interest and
dignity of the United States demanded that
the country should not be exposed beyond
necessity and the legitimate influence of
monetary and commercial operations to the
actions of foreign banking institutions,
which would be the case if the United
States had to face Britain and the Bank of
England without the agency of a national
bank of its own. Or, in other words, the
fact that other great nations possessed
such institutions forced the same policy
on this country.[10] In the words of Ogden
whose thought was along these same lines:
"To anticipate the effect of any violent
or restrictive measure which the Bank of
England might think proper to adopt and to
counteract such measures if necessary" was
the business of the American national bank.
It is evident that the ideas of all its
proponents pivoted around central banking
functions.

The friends of central banking were
divided into three main groups. One group
wanted a renewal of the charter of the Bank
of the United States and in a later stage
a restoration of the Bank of the United
States of Pennsylvania to central bank
status. A second wished a national bank
of similar character, but not the Bank of
the United States itself;[11] while the third,
in line with an English school of thought,
wanted a central bank of different character, namely, a government-owned bank, as
proposed by Ricardo. There were additional
minor points of disagreement as to the location of the central bank (Philadelphia,
New York, Washington, and, even Boston were
proposed) and as to whether or not state
permission should be requested for the
erection of branches (or of new branches).
The first group was represented by Biddle
himself, the men who during the Bank War
wrote in the interest of the institution,
such as Gallatin, William B. Lawrence,
George Tucker, Thomas Cooper, and P. P. F.
Degrand,[12] and the politicians who worked
for it, the Websters, Clays, Calhouns,
McDuffies, Samuel Smiths, and many others.
Later when during the Bank War the "other"
Biddle emerged and when the Bank of the
United States had lost its national charter,
most of these men joined the second group,
for only Biddle himself and a few diehards
continued to want the Bank of the United
States of Pennsylvania restored to central
bank status.[13]

The second group had originally
been small and had centered in New York,
which some of her citizens considered a
better seat for the national bank than
Philadelphia. Conspicuous among these was
Isaac Bronson and even he had originally
been pro-Bank of the United States. In
contrast, the petition for the charter of
a national bank of fifty million dollars
capital presented to Congress in 1832 by
David Henshaw, the Massachusetts Democratic
boss, is said to have been a political
maneuver for the purpose of splitting the
friends of central banking and of permitting Jackson to destroy the Bank to which
Henshaw was bitterly opposed.[14] The proponents of a new national bank other than
the Bank of the United States met with
favor among some friends of Jackson's, whom
Biddle characterized as wanting to sell the
national bank to the highest bidder in the
auction room;[15] an attitude which proves
that they hardly understood the character
of the Bank of the United States as a central bank with semi-public functions. The

second group, as indicated above, was to receive succour from the first[16] and, in the early 1840's embraced all those who really fought for American central banking.

The third group, finally, consisted of the proponents of what was then called a "treasury bank," i.e., a bank based on the funds of the treasury, owned and managed by the "general government." These men probably agreed with Taney that "the existence of the Bank [was] justified and depended solely upon the ground that the agency of such an institution [was] necessary to enable the government to carry on its fiscal operations."[17] Of the true character of the Bank of the United States these men had no conception. Jackson's efforts made in this direction by 1830 have been sketched and James Alexander Hamilton's draft of such an institution mentioned. By that time David Henshaw, then collector of the port of Boston, who was acquainted with Ricardo's posthumous pamphlet came out for such a bank.[18] The weaknesses of American government were too well known to permit a larger number of men to work for these plans. One can take it for granted, however, that the Independent Treasury appealed to this group, although there were among the backers of Van Buren's scheme old friends of the Bank of the United States such as Charles Jared Ingersoll.[19]

Those among the opponents of a national bank who cared to fight on economic grounds were, as mentioned above, adherents of laissez-faire and had a simple answer to the problem involved: State banks or an independent treasury, respectively, could act as the fiscal agency of the general government. On the other hand, a regulator of the currency and a guarantor of cheap domestic and stable foreign exchanges was not needed since the immutable laws of trade would perform the job infinitely better than could any national bank. Hildreth and Raguet were representative of this line of reasoning, a line which was gaining in importance in the late 1840's and 1850's when the laissez-faire doctrine became generally accepted.[20] Bancroft went so far as to deny that the Bank of the United States had ever regulated the currency and he claimed that "in the nature of things" it could not possess "any special and peculiar powers" to do so. "The National Bank has no influence at all except as a competitor." "Assuredly the Bank of the United States

cannot undertake the instruction and discipline of all the local banks in the country."[21] That is to say, unrealistically and regardless of the facts he refused to believe that there could be what is called today a central bank with its own specific functions. Oversimplified as was the outlook of these men it was modern for the time and, what is of real importance, the ideas back of the Peel Act immigrated in this connection into America.[22]

Most of the men, however, who fought first against the Bank of the United States and later against any project to set up a new national bank argued along other than economic lines. Their point of view was expressed during the Bank War by Jackson and his friends. It was represented in statements like that of Amasa Walker that the Bank was "a great central despotism dangerous to the liberties and injurious to the pecuniary interests of the people;" or of that of Bancroft in whose mind "the great objection to the continuance of the...Bank of the United States [lay] in its tendency to promote extreme inequalities in point of fortune."[23] Public opinion, to the extent that it was hostile, held the objection that a national bank by necessity would become an engine of party; that it was not safe to trust any group of men with so vast a power as was a bank of several millions; that if it came into the hands of ambitious politicians it was liable to rule the politics of the country;[24] and, finally, that unavoidably it would be managed in the interest of a few to the detriment of the many. In the midst of the excitement created by the removal of the deposits and by Biddle's contraction, A. B. Johnson, a New York country banker, blurted out: "I care not whether the Bank be constitutional or unconstitutional; a necessary fiscal agent or unnecessary;...these questions are... merged in the greater issue of whether the country shall be coerced to grant the Bank a recharter."[25] That is to say, these men removed the question of Bank or no Bank from the economic into the socio-political field.

Thus the disputants never met on common ground and the whole question of whether or not America needed central banking was not decided on its merits. It was decided at an early stage by the weight of votes of a people divided into friends and foes of capitalism, into believers in regulation of economic life, as taught by Mercantilism, and adherents of extreme _laissez-faire_, and into equalitarians and believers in social stratification. It was ultimately settled for many decades to come through political constellations and all sorts of accidental events. As a result Taney who had fought the idea that "a Bank of that description [a central bank] should be engrafted on our institutions and be considered as a settled and permanent establishment to be renewed by charter from time to time" won a victory that lasted for eighty years.[26]

Dear Sirs,

After a long struggle through years of eventful obstacles such as I believe few men under similar circumstances have so long contended with, my affairs have at length attained a crisis which admits of no other just alternative but the immediate termination of a hopeless and fruitless pursuit, and the surrender of my effects to my creditors; among whom unhappily but unavoidably are my personal friends.

A conviction of the inevitable necessity of this step impelled me at a critical moment to withdraw from the conspicuous station which I recently held, and with feelings at all times too acute for my happiness, it is for myself alone to comprehend the deep anxiety which these afflictive incidents have cost me.

I have no active funds either to meet the principal or interest of my obligations: my bank discounts and family expenses have for some time past been paid out of the proceeds of my household effects sold at Washington, the residue of which alone remains to pay several small family debts and to bear my necessary expenses for a short time until better auspices I hope may enable me to provide for the future. A retrospect of the difficulties I have encountered which are but too well known to you, will supersede the necessity of a particular detail.

On the 1st May 1808 when I arrived in the Lion [?] from Calcutta had not the political obstacles occurred which then existed, and could not have been foreseen, I should not only have paid all my debts but would have had a capital to ensure my subsequent prosperity - but my engagements at that time having absorbed all my credit I have been deprived of the power of any material effort (other than that of making the best of my then situation) during a period of nearly seven years in which commerce has been either suspended or the sport of every adverse vicicitude.

The entire proceeds of my Indigo per the Lightning to Russia, have been applied to discharge my obligations on account of that adventure and considerable sums in addition from other sources on the same account, particularly between nine and ten thousand dollars paid by Gray & Taylor on my account in part of the Respondentia Bonds, which sum I was so fortunate as to make on a purchase of teas and Russia goods jointly with them: there is still about $10,000 due on those bonds one of which has just been put in suit.

For the state of my affairs I refer to the enclosed schedule of my debts and assets, the result of which exhibits a deficiency of $29,692.

This deficiency would not appal me if the property I possess was not a dead and unproductive capital and consequently being without active funds and destitute of the means of acquiring the use of monied capital by extending my Bank accommodation (if indeed such a step would be at all justifyable, or practicable) and moreover our commercial prospects being in my view by no means flattering, I have no resource or hope but in the immediate assignment of my property for the use of my creditors and the consequent release from my debts.

I have deemed it unnecessary to swell the schedule of my effects with old and desperate claims or to enter into the history of losses which no prudence could have foreseen or prevented. I have constantly endeavoured to pursue the safest course of business and to avoid as much as possible all hazardous speculation - had I been less circumspect it is possible this explanation would have been unnecessary, but in a reverse of fortune I should have been deprived of the consolation I derive from conscious rectitude and indefatigable exertion to meet my obligations.

Your liberality and justice will see in this inevitable result its true character of adversity, and will preserve for me the esteem which you have hitherto cherished; for as no pressure of misfortune can ever divert me from the path of strict honor, I shall never cease to deserve the regard of those who candidly appreciate my motives and my actions.

With sincere regards and respect I am

Your Obd[t] Serv[t]
W. Jones
April 13th, 1815

To Messrs. Savage & Dugan[2]

Phila. 7th Nov. 1819

My dear Sir:

Yours of the 25 Ult° disappointed us much. I had hoped it would have been convenient for you to have been here at the time of the Stockholders meeting, not only in regard to the exposition then to be submitted, but that you might have mixed with the individuals and ascertained their views and opinions with more precision than they are exhibited in the report. The committee have upon the whole pursued a correct course and I see nothing exceptionable in their report unless it be the labored and inapposite compliment to the existing board and their president which was I have no doubt dragged in by the Chairman of the committee and a few other of the satellites of Mr. C[heves] in order to forestall the opinions and votes of the Stockholders at the ensuing election and to counteract the silent but menacing discontent which prevails where his conduct and measures are best known. I hope his honors may sit easy upon his brow. I have no desire to pluck a single leaf from the wreath, but I wish to give him a Direction that will substitute for his crude theories and narrow views, a practical and rational system such as will ensure to the stockholders a reasonable dividend and to the public all that they have a right to expect and no more. I understand it is not the fault of Mr. C[heves] and his friends that the report has not denounced his predecessors and exalted the fame of himself and his subservient colleagues upon the ruin of their reputation. It is said that he addressed the committee in a set speech of two hours exhibiting his individual views of the retrospective and present administration of the Bank, the former as having brought the institution to the verge of bankruptcy and the latter as saving angels who have resuscitated and placed it in safety and honor. If he had said this nothing can be more false and impudent.

The public documents exhibit the state of the Bank at large just before the election of the present Board, and the records of the Bank exhibit the efficient measures recommended by the Committee on the State of the Bank of which I was Chairman from time to time during the preceding summer which were adopted by the Board and in a train of vigorous execution before he took his seat and from which he has derived the greater part of the resources of which he boasted. He has done little more than depress the stock, oppress the community and minister to his own disgusting vanity and egotism. It is said Mr. Gales took down his speech in shorthand I should hope not for publication - nothing could be more unfair. I have the satisfaction to know that in the committee and among the stockholders generally the most respectable gentlemen when my name has been mentioned sustained it with the warmest declarations of entire confidence in my honor and integrity, and one gentlemen (Mr. Willing, my colleague) declared that he had witnessed the rectitude of my whole conduct, my zeal and devotion to the institution, and that I had been most unjustly and cruelly treated by the committee of the House of Representatives in their report. As to the malpractices and delapidations at Baltimore it is proved that they were wholly unknown to the old Board which cannot be held responsible for the usurpation of authority by its agents. It is unnecessary to say anything of the Report of the committee, as you will have seen it in print ere this reaches you. This business has detained me in the city ever since my arrival. Tomorrow Mrs. J-- and myself go to Trenton to prevail on sister Betsey to consent to the placing of my brother in a most excellent and comfortable asylum for persons deprived of their reason, established near Frankford [two words deleted] by and under the judicious direction of the Religious Society of friends. Present us affectionately to Ellen and her little darling, and to your sister Julia

Sincerely yours
W. Jones

E. W. Duval, Esq.

Phila. 29 Nov., 1816

Sir[3]

I have read with attention your letter to General Mason and have felt not less sensibly than yourself the importance of preventing the powerful influence of the Bank of the United States from falling into hostile hands, particularly in your section of the union, where that species of power is almost exclusively in the hands of our political adversaries.

If unhappily that influence should preponderate in the Direction which was chosen on the 27th instant for the Branch in your town, we acquit ourselves of all blame. We have given you a majority of republican Directors, and a republican cashier who if they are true to themselves and to the principles they profess, cannot fail to keep all right, altho' they may be associated with some of the most prominent, influential and determined, adversaries of our principles. In all the appointments we have made, the principle of a republican majority had prevailed, and this is sufficient for every legitimate purpose, unless those who have been selected as such shall prove supine or faithless. But it may be asked why did we admit some of the most obnoxious of our adversaries instead of moderate men of the same party? The answer is no less simple than conclusive: we could not help it. These men have great influence, extensive mercantile connexions, and social friendships, which excite predelictions, extremely difficult to overcome, even in the minds of those who reprehend their political conduct. How is all this, I am asked? Had you not a powerful majority in the late election for Directors of the parent Bank, 57,000 to 14,000? Yes I answer but that was not a republican majority alone; it was the result of a combination with the best of the opposite party; - with real American federalists, who love their country and as Directors will always act with us in support of its honor and credit; but when it is a question of personal choice it assumed a character of considerable delicacy and difficulty. Politically classed the Directors (by the Stockholders) stand 10 to 10 and you will of course think that the vote of the five public Directors gives to us a decided preponderance. It ought to be so! but perhaps it may be as well not to provoke the issue!!

I wish however to be distinctly understood that I would not, had I the power, give an exclusive republican Direction; it would be contrary to justice and to the principles we profess. I would give a republican majority because I believe justice and moderation are more likely to prevail under their administration than under that of their opponents of whose intolerance we have had ample proof. I have never known the republican members of our Legislatures so vigilant and so faithful to their principles as when they had a bare majority. Political comparisons are not however strictly analogous in the case of a monied institution, the administration of which is predicated upon the rates of interest; and here let me remark that the republicans of Boston have shown great supineness in respect to the Bank as the subscription book will show. Many of the most distinguished and leading republicans have not even a single share to qualify them for the Direction.

The Directors for the Branch at Boston are:

1st William Gray	Israel Thorndike
John Parker	George Blake
Nathl Silsbee	Arnold Welles
Tho. H. Perkins	Amos Binney
Tristram Bernard	Gardner Green
John C. Jones	Jesse Putnam
Barney Smith	

Cashier
Samuel Frothingham

The measures of the Direction have given universal satisfaction in this quarter; the prospects of the Bank are exceedingly auspicious, and with a just prudent and liberal course of conduct, we may perpetuate the administration of its affairs in safe and friendly hands.

With great respect

I am Sir your Obdt Servt

W. Jones

James Prince, Esq.
Boston.

Portsmouth. February, 11, 1817

The Honb. William Jones. President of the
            Bank of the U. S. Philadelphia

The time is drawing near that you
named to me when in your City that the Branch
which was intended to be established in this
place, would probably be organized - as you
gave me liberty to write you on the subject
freely. I shall make a few observations,
which you will appreciate as you think they
may deserve - That a Branch of the U.S. Bank
in this Town is considered by myself and political friends as a desirable thing as well
as necessary to counteract the overwhelming
interest of the three Federal Banks in this
place - altho' its for the interest of the
whole (politicks aside) that we be on the
most friendly terms - yet true it is the N.H.
Union Bank (the only Democratic Bank in this
place) cannot nor has not been able to keep
in circulation exceeding 25 to 30,000 D^r say
Thirty-thousand Dollars of its Bills for
years. These Federal Banks continuing has
been hostile to the N.H. U. Bk for years. As
we have not so much excitement at this time
by reason of Peace - we do not see so much
opposition. Yet we are two distinct parties
- which we have reason to regret. The establishment of the Bank, and appointment of the
first board of Directors will be to us of the
greatest importance, and of infinite consequence to the Institution as from this it
will date its character. And as you observed
to me, it would be advisable that a majority
of the Directors be Republican and at the
same time that we show a liberal disposition
towards our political opponents, by naming a
portion of that discription for Co-directors,
which to do understandingly would be absolutely necessary that such of them be pointed out
to you, so as to enable you to cause such
characters chosen as the Co Directors may conduct the business of the Institution with
pleasantness - and not be associated with
such as we know has been openly hostile to
the Administration, and to all those who have
supported it.- Of these there are among us
many influential characters of the true Boston
stamp - with such persons very few of our
friends would willingly associate - nor do we
believe you would wish to have such appointed
as Directors. These sentiments are not mine
only, but of a number of our friends in this
place.

Should W. Loyd bring forward a List
of Directors for this Town, they will probably
be of his politicks or a mixture of Democrats
who are of little weight in order to give a
show of magnaminity, but eventually to make
the institution Federal - W. Loyd lives in
Boston 60 miles hence, knows but little of
our Town, and but few of any but those of his
own politicks, and I am informed does not
visit it 3 times in 20 years, of course must
take his List from hearsay. And I will hazard
an opinion they are principally of his School.
As I have not had the pleasure of a letter
from you since I wrote you and inclosed the
powers, I can easily conceive that the Multiplicity of business: in commencing and extending the various Branches which has been put
in motion in so short a time, must have been
the cause. As I feel much interested that
the Institution succeed in this place on its
commencement I will proceed to hand you a
List of as reputable characters as any among
us - fully competent to conduct the banking
business should they be Intrusted with it.
They are all original Stockholders, altho the
names of some do not appear on the first subscription list, the most of the Repub. as
well as myself are large Bank holders in the
N.H.U. Bk and Union Insurance Co of this
place, who in the worst of times, came cheerfully forward and advanced the Government our
Cash (in War). The N.H. U. Bk. particularly
advanced One full third of our capital, and
were willing to rise and fall with the Government (no other Bk would advance Gov^t a
cent). We have risen. if there is any merit
in what we have done the List now annex'd are
the characters Republicans. As you requested
that the List handed you should be in the
order which we wished them chosen, I have so
done, and will comment on their standing and
property. In placing myself at the head of
the List, I feel a reluctance, but it is the
express desire of our friends that I have
done it, and beg you to excuse it - for my
friends sake.

Over is the List, and are decidedly
of oppinion that Nine be appointed. If so,
Six Republicans to Three Federalists.
            Lists for Directors in the Branch
Bank - Stockholders
1. George Long
2. Titus Salter Esq. $50,000 always firm sup-
   porter of the administration
3. Thomas W. Venhallow, Esq. $30,000 - do -
   Whole sale Importer Hard Ware
4. John Langdon [illegible] Esq. $50,000 -
   do - Ship Owner
5. John Pitman Esq. Lawyer of first standing
   - always Rep.
5. Wm. H. Richardson Esq. Chief Justice Supreme Court of the State - Rep.
6. Peter Pierce Esq. 50,000 - stock in funds
   various - a Rep. moderate

7. E. G. Parrot. Esq. 50,000. Merchant.
   Shipowner Rep. do.

----

1. James Rundlet, Esq. 75,000 principally
   U.S. Stock & U.S. Bk moderate Federalist
2. Sam Larkin Esq. 50,000 - Auctioneer -
   moderate Fed.
3. Jacob Cutter Esq. 50,000. Merch. has been
   a warm Fed.
4. Wm. Jones Jurd Esq. 25,000. Dry goods merchant - moderate Fed.

Also H. S. Langdon Esq. one of your Commis^{er}
(a defalcation found when he was Cash^r in N.H.
   John F. Parrott Esq. a Commi^s chosen to
   Congress
   A. W. Prescott Esq. a Commi^s very poor -
   late appointed Judge of Inferior Court
Should any Gentlemen by Name of Haven be
nominated they are all violent in their

politicks and of the Real Boston stamp. One
is President of Bk, two Directors in the 3
Federal Bks (are reputable as Merchants).
All the Sheafe's, Goddards, Ladds, Lord,
Garland, with Edw. Cutts, Esq. a Lawyer with
Wm. Hale & John McClintock are all violent
leaders of the Federal Bank. John Goddard
and J. McClintock were the year before the
War violent democrats.

Thus Sir you see I have delineated
the most prominent Characters of our Town
that are Stockholders, and as I confide this
to you as private, its my wish that this
leafe be destroyed when the Directors is
chosen, for its by these means we are to distinguish our friends from our Political enemies.

With sentiments of respect I am

Your Ob. Servt
Geo. Long.

The idea of Free Banking[1] was
neither of American vintage nor did it become a driving force in this country before
the middle of the 1830's. Its roots, however, can be traced back at least to the
eighteenth century and its history must be
kept in mind if one wishes to understand
the development which the concept underwent in America. The thought that banking
(with note issue as its characteristic
feature) might be free, that is, "entire
liberty be allowed to every one to take up
the trade of banking" had already been expressed by Sir James Steuart. But the idea
was born even before the 1760's when
Steuart published his book, for prior to
this time it had been embodied in the
Scotch banking system. Nevertheless the
concept of Free Banking, that is de facto
freedom of bank note issue, never gained
much popularity or importance in the old
world, outside of Scotland. Only after
having been transplanted to America did it
find conditions favorable for growth. In
this country the imported basic notion,
combined with other ideas of various origins and adapted to the existing external
world, came to serve as the proper solution to the difficult banking problems of
the 1830's. While that process was under
way, the sources of the basic idea were
generally unknown, as can be inferred from
a Michigan court decision which declared
in 1835 that Free Banking was unheard of.
As a matter of fact the earlier history of
the concept has remained almost forgotten
ever since, so that a modern author could
erroneously characterize Free Banking as a
truly Jacksonian idea.

What then, were the social conditions in which the concept of Free Banking
could mature in America? Free Banking was
an alluring idea to the pioneers of the
1830's who generally were debtors and who
could achieve success only with easy credit. Indebted pioneers (or pioneering

have-nots) were by necessity equalitarians.
Although politically influential, these
hard working farmers and small folk in
frontier towns were, of course, inarticulate. Their feelings and wishes had to be
formulated and expressed for them by their
representatives. These men in turn could
not but look to Europe for suitable ideas,
since intellectually at that time America
was still a European province. Thus the
desires of our pioneers had to be met with
the help of imported concepts framed into
rules of behaviour and into laws.

The popular drive toward Free
Banking crystallized but slowly and stemmed
from another movement very different in
character which has been described by Bray
Hammond. When the fate of the Second Bank
of the United States was sealed, the
founding of new banks appeared not only
desirable to debtors and have-nots, but
also safe beyond doubt to investors and
would-be capitalists. Consequently the
State of New York, then leading in many respects, was flooded with applications for
bank charters; and the incorporators could
proceed without fear of failure backed as
they were by a public eager to buy bank
stock. This state of the public mind was,
of course, sensed by the legislators, who
saw chances for filling their own pocketbooks and for promoting their political ambitions. General corruption followed in
the wake of this movement.[3] To render banking free, that is, the issue of bank notes
free, seemed to be the only way out. In
1835 a bill was introduced in the New York
Assembly which aimed at the repeal of the
so-called restraining acts passed earlier
in the nineteenth century and directed
against private, that is, unincorporated,
banking. However, this bill of 1835 was
not the first in which Free Banking was
proposed in America. A bill to that effect
had already been passed by one branch of
the New York legislature about 1810, while

the Maryland legislature in 1831 debated a
Free Banking bill entitled "An act to regulate private banking."[4] However, in spite
of these precedents, most of the New York
legislators in 1835 were still strongly in
favor of individually chartered banks.
Many of these men may have thought along
the lines of an Ohio legislator who reported in 1838 or 1839: Free Banking "is the
wildest scheme of Utopian speculation prevalent on this subject. It is founded on
the fallacious supposition that the business of banking should be conducted solely
with a view to private gain and in total
disregard of the public interests."[5] Thus
the first attempt of the 1830's at providing Free Banking in New York proved abortive. The early sponsors of that measure
needed more than inarticulate popular approval. They needed the backing of a
strongly organized political movement such
as came to be provided by the Equal Rights
Party.[6]

        This much can be said about the
early history of Free Banking in America
down to the time when the realization of
the underlying idea became a possibility.

                    II

        It has been mentioned that the
idea of Free Banking pure and simple was
expressed in economic literature at least
as early as the 1760's. A few years later
no less a person than Adam Smith, the admirer and advocate of Scotch banking, took
up the notion and elaborated it as follows:
"If banks are restrained from issuing and
circulating bank notes or notes payable to
the bearer for less than a certain sum; and
if they are subjected to the obligation of
an immediate and unconditional payment of
such bank notes, as soon as presented,
their trade may, with safety for the public
be rendered in all other respects perfectly
free." This conviction of Adam Smith probably stemmed from his experience with
Scotch banking. _Vice versa_, in the process
of interaction between ideas and the external world, once stated in Smith's influential book, the suggestion became one of
the ideological starting points of the development toward Free Banking in America.
The Bank War of the 1830's, on the other
hand, set the stage on which the idea could
be realized in this country. The fact that
Scotch banking not only had persisted up to

that moment, but that the idea of Free Banking had been transplanted also into England,
was of no small importance. The Scotch
banking system and English country bankers
and joint stock banks, permitted outside of
London under the law of 1825, could serve
as models for the American exponents of
this type of enterprise. The existence of
those models and the knowledge of their
practices inspired American economists and
statesmen[7] while they were developing their
fundamental notions. However, when they
set up a Free Banking system of their own
it proved to be very different from both
the Scotch and the English prototypes, regardless of the identity of the underlying
idea in Great Britain and America. It is
the combination of the basic with certain
accessory ideas which is specifically
American, and which was due to the particular economic and social environment of this
country.

        A discussion of the historical set-
ting may well precede the detailed description of the ideological development; and
thereby a previous thread is picked up. As
has been mentioned before, the realization
of Free Banking became possible in the wake
of the Bank War. When in the fateful decade of the 1830's President Jackson waged
war against the "monster," in the first instance (whatever his ultimate intentions
may have been)[8] he intended to kindle hostility only against the Second Bank of the
United States. However, the emotions which
he excited and the reasoning of his followers turned against all chartered banks; and
some of these men now reached the conclusion,
not fostered by the President himself, that
banking, or in other words the issue of
notes, should be open for all. In the language of the time, they felt that individuals
should be entitled "to multiply indefinitely
monied corporations." Thus the old European
idea of Free Banking suddenly became a driving force in America. It is one of the
ironies of history that the scheme, although
fitting perfectly into the intellectual and
social milieu of Jackson's disciples and
backers, was not put into practice by faithful Jackson men. Against the resistance
and votes of the Democrats Free Banking was
brought into being by the Loco-Focos, the
radical wing which had broken away from
that party and had become independent from
and even hostile to the mother organization.
The Democrats themselves were unable to

draw the consequences from their ideologies, for in the fight against the Bank of the United States Jacksonian democracy had become allied with the state chartered banks. These now clamored for protection and the Democratic party could not abandon officially its old allies. Byrdsall, the first secretary of the Loco-Focos, takes pains to make clear that bankers were the leading figures[9] in the Democratic party machine during the turbulent meeting of October 29, 1835 which gave the Equal Rights Party its nickname.

This was the setting in which Free Banking could become an actuality. Public opinion which found expression in the bitter discussions between the exponents and enemies of the proposed measure came to provide backing for the movement, the second element needed for its success. It is noteworthy that both friends and foes of the plan, Loco-Focos and Democrats, respectively, stood on the same ideological ground, the natural rights philosophy of the eighteenth century as, incidentally, was to be expected because of their common ancestry. In becoming the possession of the common man, however, the noble ideas of the Lockes, Humes, and Rousseaus had become debased and were passed about like small coin in the market.

The arguments of the Equal Rights men, the friends of Free Banking, ran about as follows: The sovereignty of the people has passed from the legislature into the hands of chartered institutions; such corporations possess monopolies which are offensive to freedom, contrary to the genius and spirit of democratic institutions, and subversive to the great and fundamental principles of equal rights and privileges asserted in the charter of our liberties. "The rightful power of all legislation is to declare and enforce only our natural rights and duties and to take none of them.... The idea is quite unfounded that on entering into society we give up any natural right." To this the conservative friends of chartered banks answered in similar language. Governor Marcy of New York (1786-1857), then still their spokesman, explained that the claim to issue paper currency stood upon a foundation quite different from property rights. The restrictions imposed by all governments on coinage had never been considered the

invasion of a property right and consequently the right to issue notes could not be considered as a common right withheld by legislatures and to be restored.[10]

In the struggle[11] of the Equal Rights men against monopolies and specifically against chartered banks, as representing banking monopolies, their ideas developed. In 1835 they resolved: "That we are opposed to all bank charters granted by individual states, because we believe them founded on and as giving an impulse to principles of speculation and gambling, at war with good morals and just and equal government, and calculated to build up and strengthen in our country the odious distribution of wealth and power against merit and equal rights."[12] And in the Declaration of Principles of 1836 one may read that the party holds: "unqualified and uncompromising hostility to bank notes and paper money as a circulating medium, because gold and silver is the only safe and constitutional currency." They therefore demanded that the state governments no longer authorize the issue of bank notes "in open violation of the constitution of the United States."

However, in 1836 the development of the party program took a turn toward Free Banking when Edward Curtis (1801-1856) was nominated candidate for Congress. Curtis, a lawyer, was later Collector of the Port of New York, and the supposed author of a series of anti-Bank essays. In a letter to be read if his name ever came up as a candidate for any office, he tried to teach the extremists a lesson in banking. "It is my opinion that the rights of the people to compete with the incorporated banks in dealing in money and credit...ought to be restored. The repeal of existing restraints in this respect is a measure which the advocates of equal rights may well insist upon.... A reformation of the banking system [that is to say: not its abolishment!] is becoming a prominent point among the lessons of the political reform of the day." It is not surprising that at first this letter produced dissatisfaction among the Equal Rights men, but after some additional correspondence the candidate was confirmed without recanting his opinions on banking. In consequence the party abstained from instructing its prospective representatives to wage war on the existing banks. They were asked only if they would advocate the exclusion of all bank notes of $10 and under that amount from circulation as currency. Thus an important step toward Free Banking was taken, and there can be no doubt that Curtis had rightly gauged public opinion. First, there was a general craving for credit and, secondly, many people did not want to destroy the banks. Besides the credit to be had, they hoped for a share in the golden harvest which they expected in the form of profit and from speculation in bank stock.

Under the pressure of the popular movement resistance now crumbled, as can be seen best in the messages of Governor William L. Marcy.[13] In his annual message of 1837 Marcy ascribed the bad times to the facts that banks possessed the exclusive privilege of furnishing the circulating medium and that "the business of loaning money [was] embarrassed by restraints imposed on other associations and on individuals." That is, of course, the cheap money argument typical of depressions. He, therefore, considered the so-called Restraining Act "so far at least as it denies to individuals and associations the right of receiving deposits and making discounts as unquestionably injurious." In this respect he suggested modifications of the law, whereas, with regard to the issue of bank notes he still wanted to sustain all prohibitions. This program was in line with the demands of the Loco-Focos, as expressed in the State Convention at Utica in September 1836,[14] and it was actually embodied in a law in 1837. However, after a short time the Governor was forced to go even further. In his annual message of 1838 he recommended reserve requirements for notes and deposits alike, an exceedingly sound and modern proposal. At the same time, since the November elections of 1837 had resulted in a landslide for the Whigs backed by the Loco-Focos, he could not but drop his resistance to a general banking law.[15] More than this, he had now to favor exactly the system which he had fought the year before. Thus he proposed to "discontinue the present mode of granting charters and to open the business of banking to a full and free competition, under such general restrictions and regulations as are necessary to insure to the public a large and sound currency."[16] This could be done either by passing a general banking law or by an entire repeal of the restraining laws

which forbade the business of banking to unauthorized individuals and associations. Allaying doubts as to the constitutional competency of the Legislature, the Governor expressed his conviction that it had the power to pass a general banking law, conferring corporate powers. But he added that according to the spirit of the constitution of the State of New York a two-thirds majority would be necessary. This message is interesting not only for what it said, but also for its terminology, which shows the influence of the Equal Rights Party. The Governor introduced the paragraph in question as follows: "Monopolies are undoubtedly incompatible with that equality of civil right which is the great object of a free Government to secure to all its citizens." He then proceeded to state that banks, although not strictly monopolies, possessed privileges withheld from individuals and associations and that they therefore shared in the odiousness with which monopolies were justly regarded.[17]

After the public has accepted Free Banking in principle, the only objection which could be raised was that such a course would impair the soundness of the circulating medium. This argument weighed heavily indeed, and not everybody was willing to brush it aside as lightheartedly as Samuel Young whose activities will be discussed shortly. The latter did not fear that Free Banking would produce redundancy of currency and that spurious bills would be forced into circulation, for, according to his optimistic views, reflecting typically eighteenth-century philosophy, "the great mass of mankind are industrious, economical, and attentive to their own interests and know how to manage their own affairs in their own way much better than legislation can guide them."[18] Most people, however, thought otherwise; and the Free Banking concept pure and simple had to be combined with another idea, in order that safety might be guaranteed to the note holder. The outcome of this process marks the change from the general-asset bank-note to the government-bond-backed bank-note, and here entered the third element of the development, the creative mind.

III

One cannot stress too strongly that the government-bond-backed bank-note was neither a high capitalistic device nor was it rooted in classical economic theory. It was a posthumous child of Mercantilism, adopted and developed by one of the great classical economists, as will presently be shown. The government-bond-backed bank-note originated when an old scheme was revamped to secure the notes of free banks.

The connection of banking with public debt, that is, public creditors obtaining the privilege of banking, is an old device which even antedated Mercantilism and which was generally known in America. This plan, as practiced for instance by the Bank of England, had come into this country when the first Bank of the United States was chartered with only one-fourth of its capital to be paid in specie, and the rest in stock of the United States. Nothing was needed now except the reshaping of the measure in such a way that an unlimited multitude of banks, instead of one privileged bank, would become tied up with public credit, this time not with a view to the public creditors, but for the benefit of the note-holders, that is, the creditors of the banks.

This reshaping was done in America by John MacVickar,[19] who at an early date elaborated the Free Banking idea while combining it in one plan with the idea of the government-bond-backed bank-note. However, one should not overestimate his achievement, since the development of the latter idea was not his work and since the same combination of ideas had also been arrived at about the same time in England.

The Free Banking idea and the idea of the government-bond-backed bank-note alike are of royal ancestry. The former, as mentioned above, was promoted by Adam Smith; the latter was enunciated by David Ricardo, who undoubtedly derived his inspirations from the note issue privilege of the Bank of England and who may have known that similar plans were "favorably entertained by Mr. Pitt who was obliged to relinquish only an account of the difficulties occasioned by the War."[20] In his Proposals for an Economical and Secure Currency, published in 1816, Ricardo wrote:[21] "What objection can there be against requiring of those who take upon themselves the office of furnishing the public with a circulating medium to deposit with government an adequate security for the due performance of their engagements.

...those whose habits and pursuits are little suited to explore the mechanism of trade are obliged to make use of money and are in no way qualified to ascertain the solidity of the different banks; accordingly we find that men living on limited incomes, women, labourers, and mechanics of all descriptions are often severe sufferers by the failures of country banks. ...Against this inconvenience the public should be protected by requiring of every country bank to deposit with government or with commissioners appointed for that purpose funded property or other government security in some proportion to the amount of their issues."[22] It is this Ricardian idea which MacVickar combined with the one promoted by Adam Smith.

MacVickar (1787-1868) came from a well-to-do New York family. His father, a ship-owning merchant and immigrant from Ireland, was one of the first in New York to engage in the China trade. A director of the Bank of New York, he was also connected with several insurance companies.[23] John, the son, studied at Columbia College in New York, became an Episcopal clergyman, and in 1817, professor of moral philosophy at his alma mater. In this capacity he became one of the early American teachers of political economy, then considered a branch of moral philosophy, as it had been in England at the time of Adam Smith. MacVickar is interesting to us as the author of an anonymous pamphlet: Hints on Banking in a Letter to a Gentleman in Albany; by a New Yorker, dated February 17, 1827, and published in New York in the same year. Written to an influential member of the New York legislature, this letter, according to a leading New York banker, actually contributed to the subsequent development.[24] It contains in fact the first proposal of that Free Banking system which was to be established a decade later.

MacVickar's plan is understandable as the outgrowth of his "Weltanschauung" and his theoretical conceptions of banking, both of which he preaches in the flowery language of his generation. "The principles of banking are much less mysterious in their nature than is generally supposed, and may be mastered by any man of common understanding. Everything depends on looking at it in its original simplicity, since the mysteries of its operations are almost entirely the fruit of legislative interference

which in Credit[25]...has obscured those natural processes which, like all the other
movements of Nature, are clear, simple,
and harmonious." "One has to look at banking as one of the natural and obvious provisions of trade; one of the simple, but
beautiful, contrivances, by which men,
united together by the bonds of mutual
confidence, economize the precious metals
and anticipate future funds by taking
promises in lieu of immediate payment.
This is the essence of the whole matter."[26]

    Such opinions on the principles of
banking are put into a larger framework.
Nature is uniform, instinct is always wise,
and self interest left free to competition
will reach the mark of public good with a
precision beyond all the wisdom of the
wisest law givers. MacVickar's "fundamental position" is that evils flow from
needless and unwise regulation. Let law
then secure the integrity of contracts
[which is imperiled by the fluctuations in
the value of money], and credit will take
care of itself; or in other words, credit,
like every other business left to itself,
will regulate itself. Legislatures are
unable to do it; they have granted to individuals and corporations monopolies and
privileges that belonged to the community,
and they should learn from experience.
The thing for them to do is to give up
credit into the hands of those whom alone
it concerns and who will certainly care
sufficiently for their interests. This
will be done anyway, if not by our own
generation then by our children, since the
prejudices against freedom are destined to
be worn away soon.[27]

    What would be the consequence of
acting in the proposed manner? Error and
fraud in banking would be limited within
the narrowest possible bounds, as soon as
credit is put under the sharp sighted control of self-interest. Credit would then
be able to obtain power only through the
voluntary confidence of society, which
would rarely be bestowed except upon integrity and wealth. Thus society would be
furnished with credit at the cheapest rate
and in precisely the quantities which it
demands.[28]

    The preceding quotations picture
clearly MacVickar's philosophy, and his
theories on banking must be viewed against
this background. He distinguished between
two forms of bank credit. Banks either

lend their own credit or they lend their
capital. In the former case the businessman is enabled to anticipate his funds by
discounting commercial paper which has originated in actual business transactions,
"by the real exchanges of society." What
takes place here is just a swapping of
credit. The bank lends the businessman the
credit of its name, as MacVickar has it.
However, when banks discount accommodation
paper for investment purposes (that is,
bills which have not originated from previous business transactions) the bank then
lends its capital to the businessman: it
"creates him funds." The former is a legitimate function of banking; the latter "is
an irregular operation, the business of the
money lender." Thus the decisive point is
reached: If the banks should be confined to
lending credit they could not go beyond the
real needs of commerce. The banks would be
safe and the currency secure. The interest
of the banker and that of the public would
be one and the same. The discounts would
rise and fall with the pulse of trade. But
when the banks are able to lend out their
capital, such harmony does not exist. They
lend their capital when they have a surplus,
not when commerce requires it. Here lay,
for MacVickar, the root of the evil, for the
banker needed capital only to support his
credit. That the exclusive use of capital
to this end would be best attained when it
was "vested" and "from under his [the banker's] control," is a strange argument from
such a stout believer in natural economics.[29]

    This flaw in MacVickar's reasoning,
however, can be explained easily as a relapse into Mercantilist thought. Sir James
Steuart in his once famous discussions of
banking had expressly maintained that the
capital of a bank served only as collateral
security for the notes issued and its purpose was to establish for the bank in question credit and confidence with the public.[30]
Thus it was Mercantilist tradition from
which MacVickar derived this suggestion,[31]
and in this connection one needs to study
another ideological line which tied in here.
This line, as far as America is concerned,
started from that feature of the Bank of
England's charter which gave its "proprietors" banking privileges in consideration of
their advancing funds toward the carrying
on of the war with France. Or, in other
words, banking privileges were given because the recipients thereof invested in

government obligations, the capital which they raised for the projected Bank of England. Such investment implied that the bank had no liquid capital for its banking business proper, but in line with the theory, then developing and just mentioned, capital was not necessary for banking. Following the policy of the Bank of England some of the early American money banks, as described previously, invested considerable parts of their capital stock in government obligations, and such and other similar investments of the capitals of banks were common by 1816. The American country banks, on the other hand, the successors of Mercantilist "banking on private credit," spread all over the country the idea that, in banking, capital was not needed at all.[33]

If capital was not necessary for banking, what was? In the eyes of many banking theorists of the eighteenth and early nineteenth centuries, it was "credit" which was essential for banking. This line of reasoning also came down from the Mercantilist era, exactly from the late seventeenth century. Clapham has made the statement[34] that the Bank of England, when founded, was considered as drawing purchasing power out of that "fund of credit" to which "almost magical qualities" were assigned by contemporaries. This tradition was developed in this country and, in the words of another modern author,[35] by 1800 people believed that there was "something called credit" "somehow and somewhere in the corporate personality of a bank" on which to issue a circulating medium. Robert Morris asserted that "paper money was the child of credit" and again that the public would deposit money in the bank to be established "availing themselves of its credit."[36] In the newspaper language of that time this fundamental idea was expressed, in one instance as follows: "Nothing is necessary to make this representative of money [bank paper] supply the place of specie, but the credit of that office or company who delivers it, which credit consists in its always being ready to turn it into specie whenever required."[37] Consequently when Rhode Island legislators in 1809 tried to remedy an unsound banking situation they did so by improving the credit basis of the banks of the state.[38]

In this setting the distinction between banking on capital and banking on credit was developed.[39] By 1829 a writer in the Free Trade Advocate[40] (probably Condy Raguet himself) distinguished between banks of discount and banks of circulation according to whether they lent their capital or their credit. But the differentiation was already contained in nuce in the Report of 1820 of the Secretary of the Treasury. If the banks followed a certain policy "and if they should retain an absolute control over one half of their capital and the whole of the credit which they employ by discounting to that amount nothing but transaction paper payable at short dates ...the remaining part of their capital might be advanced upon long credit to manufacturers and even agriculturists without the danger of being under the necessity of calling upon such debtors...if emergencies... occur." It has already been described that Isaac Bronson (however he himself may have acquired it) made this idea the cornerstone of his business policy and how he promoted it in public: banks should bank on their credit only and use their capital for safe long-term investments, thereby securing their creditors.[41]

It was from Bronson that MacVickar took the idea which did not fit at all into his own general philosophy and which he expressed as stated above. This fact is known through the fortunate discovery by Abraham H. Venit[42] of a letter written by MacVickar to Isaac Bronson. This letter shows that MacVickar was not only dependent on Bronson, but that he was conscious of that dependence. But when it came to motivating his suggestions based on Bronson's notions, MacVickar reasoned as Ricardo had done: If the evils of present banking could be confined to the commercial classes all could be left to be "regulated by the necessary laws of Credit." But bank money is not so confined: it is issued in small denominations and thereby passes into the hands of people who do not consider notes as promises to pay, but as an "equivalent for value." Thereby the notes come to be a substitute for coin and so originate new evils. Therefore and therefore alone, legislature acquires the right to interfere in order to guard the interests of the many and ignorant.[43]

Thus MacVickar arrived at his proposals, which played such an important part in the development of American banking.

Not all of the proposals are interesting, but two are essential:

1. Banking is to be a free trade, in that it may be freely entered by individuals and associations under the provisions of a general statute.

2. The amount of bank capital is to be freely fixed by such individuals or associations, but only one-tenth to be invested at the discretion of the banks, the remaining nine-tenths in government stock. From the latter the banks in question would receive interest, while the principal would remain in pledge for the redemption of their notes.[44]

While there is documentary proof for the dependence of MacVickar on Isaac Bronson,[45] his dependence on Ricardo is evidenced by the similarity of the arguments used by both men. This theory is all the more probable since MacVickar, as an economist, was thoroughly familiar with the discussions on monetary questions which were taking place in England in the 1820's and especially with the writings of the Ricardian John Ramsay McCulloch. It was McCulloch's opinion that banks should be prevented from issuing notes unless they had previously given security.[46] According to him it was not enough that all notes were made payable on demand by law. Compliance with this wise rule should be enforced by compelling bankers to give security for their issues and by prohibiting them from issuing notes before satisfying the government of their ability to honor them. Such security was to be proportioned to the issues and not to the capital. (This proposal, of course, was modern and fundamentally different from MacVickar's antiquated Mercantilist thought.) Incidentally by the same measure McCulloch wanted to force the banks to have at their disposal resources over and above the capital required for conducting their business.[47]

MacVickar's ideas were known to at least a small circle in Albany in 1827. About two years later they were more widely spread since, as already described,[48] Joshua Forman included them in his legislative proposals which in turn led to the New York Safety Fund Act of 1829. It is not certain but highly probable, that the incentive to combine in one proposal the two sets of ideas came from James Alexander

Hamilton. In a letter to Martin Van Buren, supposed to have been written in December 1828, he suggested this combination to the Governor of New York. To be sure, in this connection, Hamilton did not refer to MacVickar, but to "Bronson," i.e., Isaac Bronson, the New York banker, and as mentioned above, the original source of a good part of MacVickar's ideas. He thus described Bronson's plan:

> The capital ought, before the bank can commence its operations, to be invested in the United States or State Stocks - and these securities ought to be placed beyond the control of the bank; that they may be a fund in reserve, and never to be used or to be available for any banking operation; and the amount of the notes to be issued never to exceed the amount of this fund; and as a mean of preventing any excess let it be provided that after the bank shall have given security for its notes, they shall be countersigned and stamped by the proper officer or commissioner within whose control the stock is placed. [Ricardo's idea!] ... By this provision the capital of the bank would be secured to the public as a fund to be applied in payment of the notes in circulation, and these could not at any time exceed the amount thereof. It would also be incapable of being loaned to dealers [bank customers], and consequently not liable to be lost; but above all the bank would thus be compelled to loan its credits... [Follows the suggestion that banks loan on short term paper only.][49]

A few months later Bronson himself published his plan anonymously in the article "General Propositions..." in the Free Trade Advocate of July 11, 1829,[50] an article which at the same time contains an elaborate theoretical justification. The plan amounts to a suggestion to provide security against the failure of banks by "requiring their capital to be paid in full and to be permanently loaned in mortgage security or vested in stock, prohibiting by proper penalties the employment of any part of it in banking operations and limiting the issues...to the amount of capital."[51] It will be seen at a glance that Bronson's plan contains only one aspect of MacVickar's scheme. He is not concerned with the question of Free Banking.

Having cleared up this link between

MacVickar's (or Bronson's) and Forman's reasoning, a comparison of the latter's proposal with that of MacVickar may follow: With MacVickar the notion of a bank note backed by special security resulted from consistent reasoning based upon definite opinions on banking. In Forman's scheme, the same device stood disconnected from the main train of thought. It was added to the main ideas at the end of his memorandum "to render the system perfect," and was coupled with the suggestion to confine the banks to the discounting of short term business paper, i.e., Bronson's pet proposal. Actually, Forman did not believe in the possibility of realizing these ideas for the time being, as he himself says. He recommended the plan in the same way as MacVickar had, but although he even elaborated the arguments, in the new context their cogency was lost. Forman reasoned: banks should loan their credit and not their capital; they should be compelled to invest the latter "in safe public stocks or put it out on bonds and mortgages...and not to employ it in their ordinary business." To emphasize the difference between the two authors note should be made that while MacVickar had suggested the investment of bank capital in government stock alone, and thereby had based his proposal on precedents (Bank of England) and recent English ideas, Forman was thinking of all sorts of safe investments, including mortgages. This latter idea was traditionally American, and a step back toward Mercantilist "banking on real and personal estates" as it had been practiced by the colonial land banks.[53] This feature of Forman's "exposition" was undoubtedly due to Bronson's and/or James A. Hamilton's influence.[54] Free Banking, of course, was not mentioned by Forman for his was fundamentally a scheme not compatible with Free Banking. Thus only one of MacVickar's two basic ideas can be found in Forman's plan. This adaptation, however, was important and helped prepare the way for the later realization of MacVickar's scheme. For thus at least one aspect of it became widely known in Albany, being published in the Assembly Journal as a suggestion by Forman. It is strange irony that Forman, through his action, himself helped pave the way for a plan destined to supplant his own scheme after the lapse of a decade; although he was undoubtedly forced to take such action.

MacVickar's and Forman's proposals of 1827 and 1829, respectively, were followed in 1829 by those of Eleazar Lord who aimed in the same direction. The latter (1788-1871) had originally studied for the ministry, but had to give up that vocation because of serious eye trouble. He became a very successful businessman in New York City, where he was founder and first president of the Manhattan Fire Insurance Company and repeatedly president of the New York and Erie Railroad, which he guided during difficult years. Lord published in 1829 a pamphlet Credit, Currency and Banking in which he made suggestions very similar to those of MacVickar. However, there is a decisive difference in their arguing. Attention has already been drawn to inconsistencies in MacVickar's and Forman's reasoning. Regardless of their belief in laissez-faire, they arrived at the proposition that the freedom of the banking business should be restricted, at least as to the use of its capital. Lord, however, set the same proposal into a modern framework. Says Lord:[55] "The object of all conventional regulations of the currency should be to secure an adherence to the principles which naturally govern it." So far Lord is in agreement with MacVickar. But after this statement he goes on: "for though the operation of these principles cannot be superseded or hindered permanently, yet they may be temporarily violated and resisted." On the basis of such opinions it is consistent to force the businessman to invest his capital in a way prescribed by law. The redemption of bank notes in coin is, according to Lord, not a sufficient check; it does not make the currency definitely safe and uniform. There is too much temptation to profit from the fluctuations due to expansion and contraction. The system therefore must be changed in such a way that no banker is able to make excessive issues. As to the rest, Lord thinks along the lines of MacVickar. Excessive issues are due to the fact that banks loan their capital and credit alike. Thus Lord with consistent logic arrived, as MacVickar had inconsistently, at the conclusion that the capital of the banks should be invested in "permanent securities," whereas their credit should be "employed in the operations of discounting to an extent not exceeding the amount of capital invested."[56] Thereby the banking system would become self-regulating; all banks would secure their

notes in the same way, all bank paper
would be uniform in value, and the temptation to overissue notes would disappear.
Once the security of the notes to be issued was provided for, there could obviously be no objection to the establishment
of as many banks as individuals were willing to set up, provided they possessed the
requisite capital. Or, in other words,
there was no longer any reason to resist
Free Banking, just as there was no reason
to object to the multiplication of other
enterprise. The more, the better!

A comparison of the three proposals of MacVickar, Forman, and Lord is
interesting: MacVickar starts with the intention of making Free Banking possible,
foresees difficulties, and suggests a
scheme to overcome them so that competition may be introduced into the field of
banking. Forman does not think of Free
Banking at all and connects MacVickar's
safety valve (the government-bond-backed
bank-note) with a machine (Safety Fund
System), which already possessed a safety
valve of its own. Lord, finally, elaborates a scheme which is supposed to do
away with expansions and contractions of
bank currency; and it seems so propitious
that he finally does not see any reason
why, after its introduction, Free Banking
should not be permitted. He starts
where MacVickar ends and ends where Mac-
Vickar had taken his departure.

Did Lord know of MacVickar's ideas
and especially had he read the Hints on
Banking? It is not impossible that the
two men had social contacts. Lord was a
leading New York businessman, as was
MacVickar's father. Lord, as proved by
numerous publications, was interested in·
economic problems; MacVickar taught economics. The first edition of Lord's treatise has a chapter VIII (which was not reprinted in the second edition of 1834)
entitled: "Popular Errors respecting Currency and Banking," and pages 120-121 in
that chapter could be a criticism of
MacVickar's sanguine expectation that banking once left alone would be self-regulating. However, nothing of this can be
proved; and both these men may have started
from the same set of experiences and may
have arrived at the same conclusions independently. Born in 1787 and 1788, respectively, they belonged to the same

generation; and this alone may explain
their common ideas.[57]

IV

So much about the emergence of the
ideas essential for American Free Banking.
The legislative actions of the 1830's already mentioned should by now be understandable. It will be remembered that
Governor Marcy in his annual message of
1838 suggested the enactment of Free Banking in the State of New York; but although
the soil was well prepared the measure
would hardly have become an actuality but
for the crisis of 1837 and the collapse of
American banking which followed in its
wake. Free Banking was a piece of reform
legislation caused by a national calamity
and as such parallels the Louisiana Banking
Act of 1842.[58]

Samuel Young (1789-1850) was the
champion of the measure in the upper house
of the New York legislature. He had been
a leading Democrat in the Assembly for
many years and had taken part in the Bank
War by a series of articles in the Saratoga
Sentinel in 1831-32, written under the
pseudonym of Umbra.[59] In these articles
he attacked Albert Gallatin's just published
Considerations on the Currency and Banking
System of the United States and the
McDuffie Report. In 1835, after having
become state senator, he promoted the repeal of the restraining acts and thereby
may have attracted the attention of the
young Equal Rights Party, then still called
Anti-Monopoly Party. In 1836 the party
sent him a copy of the Declaration of
Principles and offered him the nomination
as governor of New York if he would sign
that document. In a very long and wordy
letter Young declined the honor because he
considered it wrong to provoke a split in
the party; and in addition he took issue
with the radical views on monetary questions expressed in the Principles. He
thought it impossible to exclude paper circulation altogether and instead proposed
as his program the repeal of the usury and
of the restraining acts, a proper limit of
bank issues, and the exclusion of all notes
of less than twenty dollars. He attacked
"odious and detestable monopolies," which
laid a tax on the population; but internal
improvements seemed even worse to him,

because they inflicted slavery and taxation on a future generation.[60]

In 1837 and 1838, when the question of Free Banking came up in the legislature, Young fostered in the Senate the
General Banking Law, as the pending reform
legislation was originally called.[61] He
was then the chairman of a committee, consisting of one senator from each senate
district, to report "on sundry petitions
for the passage of a law creating a general
system of banking." The two decisive reports, from which the following is quoted,
were probably his work. He saw three dangers in the existing banking system; viz,
demoralization of the public through the
process of getting charters, unmitigated
inequity in the distribution of stock, and
monopoly. Therefore he recommended the
repeal of the restraining acts, a measure
which would have led automatically to free
banking. In doing so he referred to the
Scotch banking system with which he had
already been acquainted when he wrote the
newspaper articles of 1831-32. Sir Henry
Parnell's Scotch System of Banking[62] was,
according to his own statement, his source
of knowledge. In those articles he had
praised that system because the Scotch
banks by their "active competition" had
maintained the value of their notes at par
when the Bank of England suspended. In
his report of 1837 he went into more detail.[63] In Scotland, he explained, note
issue was regulated by competition alone;
consequently, supply and demand, and the
spirit of free competition among the banks
supplied the country with a circulation
not disgraced by any failures.

The ideal Scotch set-up was then
compared with the Safety Fund System of
New York. This latter system Young criticized for its inability to free the state,
as Van Buren had put it, from the two cry-
ing sins committed by banks, namely fraud
and failures. Lack of success in this respect was supposed to be due to the fact
that under the Safety Fund System the banks
were "connected together by the bonds of
fraternal feeling, mutual sympathy, and
identity of interest.... And to the same
extent that this unity of feeling and action exists, is that free competition
neutralized which is the only safe and salutary regulator of all pecuniary dealings."[64] The interest attached to this
assertion needs no comment but the fact

should be stressed that Young shared his
Weltanschauung with Forman, the creator of
the hated Safety Fund System. Young stated,
in words almost identical with those of
Forman, what was the generally accepted
'truth' in those days: "The monetary laws,
the laws of trade, and indeed all the laws
which appertain to national, civic, and
social intercommunication among men are as
determined and fixed in their general results as the laws of light, heat, and grav-
vitation. If the various elements which
enter into problems in political economy
were fully and justly appreciated the result in all cases could be as accurately
ascertained as in mathematical sciences....
And if the legitimate principles of government and the effect of the exercise of its
powers upon the affairs of life were accurately understood by all, there would for
the same reason be no parties in politics."[65]

Young added to his report of 1837
a bill for a Free Banking act. Impressed,
as he was, with the Scotch system of joint-
stock banking his bill did not embody the
ideas of MacVickar and Lord, but went back
to the Scotch model and to the English proposals described above.[66] The underlying
idea of the Young bill was to permit banking to anyone willing to protect the creditors of his bank by pledging some property
in addition to the paid-in capital. Or in
the language of the bill:[67]

Section 1. Any person or association of persons may establish banks of discount, deposit
and circulation upon the terms and conditions
and subject to the liabilities hereinafter
prescribed.
Section 3. Three trustees shall be appointed
by the person or persons establishing such
bank, who shall not be interested therein...
to whom each person or shareholder establishing such bank shall execute a mortgage of unincumbered real estate situated in this state,
or make a conditional transfer of personal
property, which shall in the opinion of the
said trustees be of the value of at least one
and a half the amount of such shareholder's
interest in the capital stock of such bank, as
security...for the payment of all debts and
the redemption of all notes, bills and evidences of debt to be issued by such banking
association.
[Section 2 traditionally limits the circulation to one and a half times the bank's capital.]

Section 16. In case any circumstances shall
render a resort to the security held by the
trustees...necessary to insure the payment of
the debts of such association...such trustees
may make application to the court of chancery...; and the said court may thereupon
grant an order requiring the president...to
show cause why an attachment should not issue,
attaching the property of such association and
transferring the same to the trustees, with
power to collect the dues and to dispose of
the property of such association, together with
the securities previously pledged to such trustees...or of so much of the said property and
securities held as may be necessary for such
purpose;...

Commenting on this bill, Young stressed as
its main advantages the compulsory paid-
up capital, publicity of the names of the
shareholders (the respective sections are
not quoted), and their personal responsibility as established in sections 3 and
16.[68] As a matter of fact, these sections
contain some sort of compromise, for
Young's ideal was the unlimited personal
liability of the shareholders[69] as established in the Scotch joint stock banks,
whereas in this bill an additional, but
only limited, guaranty was made available
over and above the shareholder's interest
in the bank.

     Young seems to have derived his
inspiration mainly from McCulloch's article
in the Edinburgh Review mentioned above.[70]
The similarities are striking, so that one
can go as far as to say that the basic
ideas of the article were shaped into a
bill by the New York senator. The purpose
of the bill according to Young, was to correct the ruinous contractions and expansions of the circulating medium; and this
was also McCulloch's intention. Young
wanted to reach this goal by excluding
small notes from circulation and by opening banking to competition, in the "wholesome spirit" of which he and his generation
believed with religious fervor. The author
of the Review article, however, trusted
less to free competition than to the deposit of securities. By compelling bankers to increase the deposit of securities
as soon as they intended to add to their
circulation McCulloch believed that excessive issues could be stopped. This latter
idea was not embodied in the Young bill,

since, as has been mentioned, free competition was supposed to prevent overissues.
However, the main feature of section three
of the bill, the deposit of security over
and above the paid-up capital was apparently
derived from the Review article which proposed that banks which wanted to issue
small notes were "to hold a supplemental
capital as a security over and above the
capital that was required for the active
conduct of the business." This measure was
considered justifiable since "supplemental
capital would not be unproductive," but
would draw interest from the government
stock in which it was to be invested.[71]
The proposal to use real estate as security,
incorporated in the Young bill, was of
course traditionally American. However,
the bill was against the trend in too many
respects to become the basis of the Free
Banking Act of 1838.

                    V

     Legislative action which finally
resulted in the famous New York Free Banking Act of 1838 began in that year with two
bills, the one originating in the Assembly,
the other in the Senate. The Senate bill
was not only brought in by Guilian.
Verplanck (1786-1870), but was also supposed to have been his work.[72] Verplanck
was familiar with banking problems since he
had played a certain part in the Bank War.
As Democratic chairman of the Ways and Means
Committee of the House of Representatives
in Washington he had written the well known
report that, in the opinion of the House,
the government deposits were safe in the
custody of the Bank of the United States.
Thereby he had taken a stand against
President Jackson, and was forced to withdraw from the Democratic party.[73] Joining
the Whigs he ran unsuccessfully for Mayor
of New York, but in 1837-1841 was a member
of the New York Senate.

     In contrast to the Young bill
Verplanck's bill embodied the essence of
MacVickar-Lord thinking; consequently it
came much nearer to the Free Banking Act,
as finally passed, than Young's bill of the
preceding year. According to section I,
any number of persons may form a joint stock
company for the purpose of discounting notes,
receiving deposits, dealing in exchange,
making loans on real and personal securities,

issuing notes, and for some other transactions habitually performed by banks,
Such joint stock companies, by their articles of association, were entitled to
limit their liability to the joint funds
of the company, a clause which was necessitated by the fact that the common law
joint stock company is characterized by
the unlimited liability of the partners.
For constitutional reasons the bill did not
establish corporations, but joint stock
companies instead; however, in sections 19
and 20 the word corporation crept in.
Joint stock companies, as envisaged by
this bill, could issue notes of denominations higher than fifty dollars without
special limitations (section 10); but notes
of smaller denominations could be issued
only if they were secured by bonds. This
clause will be recognized as being in line
with Ricardo's original idea. However,
section 20 which established this rule was
actually dangerous and would have invited
orgies of wildcat banking. Any of the following securities could have been pledged:
public stocks of the United States, the
State of New York, or of any of the states
of the Union, or of any of the cities of
the State of New York. All these securities could be deposited at 90 per cent of
the market value of such stock in the city
of New York. Unsatisfactory as this was,
mortgages at least were not included in
the securities envisaged by Mr. Verplanck.
Sections 23 and 24 are of particular interest. The bank commissioners, who were to
hold the stock as security for the redemption of the notes to be issued, would also
have to procure such notes and the plates
from which they were to be printed, to
keep them, and to issue such bills to the
companies pledging stock under the law.
This clause deserves some comment.

MacVickar was mainly interested in
stating principles and was less concerned
about putting these principles into practice. Lord, however, thought of details;
and it occurred to him that the public
would have to be secured against fraudulent
issue of notes over and above the limitations set by law. For this purpose he
proposed that the notes be stamped by public authority and that the circulation of
unstamped notes be prohibited. This idea
had already been set forth in Ricardo's
pamphlet quoted before.[74] In the second
place, however, Lord went a step further:

It would be a great achievement, he felt,
not only to have the notes stamped by the
government, but to have them all supplied
from the same plates under public authority,
with convenient blanks left for the insertion of the names of the respective banks
and for other details. This feature, with
its advantage of making bank notes uniform,
was first embodied in the Verplanck bill.

The day after the Senate bill had
been entered, a similar bill was introduced
in the Assembly by one W. G. Patterson.
This bill was said to have been drawn by
John Canfield Spencer (1788-1855), a lawyer
and politician of many years experience in
bank matters. As a member of Congress in
1817-1819 he was on the committee which
examined the affairs of the Second Bank of
the United States and the Committee report
was his work. His interest in banking persisted, and fifteen years later, when Jackson attacked the Bank, he was among its defenders. Since the 1820's he had been constantly active in state politics. In 1827,
for instance, he was on the board appointed
to revise the statutes of the state. To
prevent abuses by moneyed corporations this
board proposed certain regulations which
were enacted into law in December of the
same year.[75]

Although the Spencer bill was, like
the Verplanck bill, based on the MacVickar-
Lord train of reasoning, there were some
important differences. Section I of the
Spencer bill established the principle that
any person or association of persons might
create banks of discount, deposit, and circulation. Here, as in the Senate bill, the
creation of corporations was carefully
avoided for constitutional reasons. However,
section 13 of the Spencer bill contained an
idea alien to the Verplanck bill: It made
shareholders or partners of banking enterprises to be created, jointly and severally
liable for the payment of all notes put
into circulation. Such unlimited liability,
to be sure, could be avoided if and when
any banking association, for the purpose of
securing the bill-holders, invested any portion of the capital (not exceeding one-half
of it) in stocks of the United States, the
State of New York, or of any other state
designated by the comptroller (Section 14).
This clause meant upholding the connection
with older Mercantilist tradition through
the link between capital and security to be
deposited for the benefit of the noteholder.

Here, as in the Verplanck bill, mortgages were not included in the eligible securities. The sound sections 23 and 24 of the Verplanck bill have very weak counterparts in the sections 9 and 15 of the Spencer bill, which provided that all notes should be countersigned by some state officials. Both bills were unsatisfactory with regard to the security to be pledged.

This latter shortcoming was clearly seen by a politician who had already been instrumental in setting up the New York Safety Fund Act, Abijah Mann, Jr. (1793-1868). In both cases he played the same part. Entering the stage at a strategic moment, he did not contribute any basic ideas; but his critical mind possessed the ability to gauge necessary tactical moves and to sense politically possible combinations. From 1828 to 1830 he was a member of the New York State Assembly; for the next two years postmaster, appointed by President Jackson; a Democratic member of Congress, 1833-1837; again in 1838 a member of the State Assembly. Here he served on two committees dealing with banking matters, having been prepared for this work by his membership in the congressional committee which examined the Bank of the United States. He tells us in his own words how he came to act in the decisive moment in 1838.[76]

Beginning with his experiences in Congress during the Bank War, he wrote: "I was appointed a member of the committee sent by the House of Representatives to examine that institution in the panic session of 1834, when the Bank, in violation of its charter, refused to submit to examination, and its directors refused to testify, through fear that they might criminate themselves.[77] In the course of performing that duty I came into much free discussion with the late Colonel Benton, and also with Mr. Biddle,[77a] who were both accomplished and intelligent on banking and finances generally. The English joint stock system, as it was called, was then recently in limited operation with individual banking, with occasional disasters. I was told that the individual banker in England, when he organized his business, always invested the largest share of his capital in the securities of the Government, reserving sufficient for his current business, as he soon learned by experience

that, with a small cash capital and his bills receivable, he could always protect himself under ordinary circumstances, and in extraordinary circumstances he could always take up money with those securities in the market at home or on the continent on terms not ruinous to himself." Mann did not understand that this policy of the English banks was possible only because the Bank of England had already become a central bank, the American counterpart of which his party was just then destroying by refusing to recharter the Second Bank of the United States.

Mann continues by describing how the Verplanck and Spencer bills were introduced in the New York legislature and then goes on: "Both were specially referred to the same committee of the whole in the Assembly, and in due course came under discussion and consideration, for about a week, with a great variety of views and opinions upon the details. I did not participate in it until the close, when I pointed out some of the defects in the practical pperation of the material provisions of both bills, until I think there were not ten men in the house who would have voted for either bill. I then stated to them, in conclusion, that if they were determined to pass a general banking law, which I did not think was necessary, I thought one could be framed which could be endured, and which would, perhaps, essentially improve and simplify the whole system, and I mentioned the principle of taking the securities by State stocks of the State of New York, into the hands of the financial officer of the State to redeem the currency, and limiting the issues of the notes to the amount of securities, so that every bank note should be simply a certificate in effect, in the hands of the holder, that he was entitled to a share in the bond equal to the amount of the note; so that a bank note, of a broken bank, should be a little better after broken than before, because it should draw interest after demand and refusal of payment. The suggestions seemed to infuse new hopes into the drooping minds of many of the Whig paper system men, who composed the whole body, except twenty-three democrats, who were of the hard money persuasion of Mr. Benton. Mr. David B. Ogden, who was a leading and able member, immediately moved to refer both bills to a select committee

of nine, to report a new bill, which was
adopted; and on that same Saturday, with
hasty zeal, the committee was appointed
and notified to appear at a meeting that
evening.... The committee, under the advice of Mr. Ogden, immediately desired me
to draw up the bill I had suggested in the
conclusion of the debate...."

"I drew the bill with your [i.e.,
Flagg's][78] valuable suggestions, except
those sections to provide for the formation of associations. It was my intention
to have placed the business of banking in
the hands of large capitalists, as in
England, or in the hands of corporations."
However, Mann was in doubt whether corporations for the purpose of banking were permissible under the New York constitution
and therefore did not provide for them in
the first draft of his bill. David B.
Ogden discovered the omission.[79] He made
it clear to Mann that he desired to have a
large bank in New York which could act as
a substitute for the defunct Bank of the
United States. It can not be ascertained
whether what later became the Bank of
Commerce was projected at that time and
whether Ogden was thinking of the project,
even though he was not among its founders.

Mann and Ogden then made a deal.
Although the former was of the opinion
that under the New York constitution banking corporations could be authorized only
by a "two-thirds vote on each singly and
separately," he was willing to drop his
scruples if Ogden would accept the 100 per
cent backing of notes by securities. The
outcome was, in the words of Millard
Fillmore, "a species of corporation" depositing securities to the full amount of
their issues.[80] The associations thus
created could contract, sue, and be sued
in the name of their president; the shares
were transferrable, and the shareholders
not individually liable for the debts of
the association.

As to the rest, Mann built his bill
with stones taken from both the Verplank
and Spencer bills. His section 1 corresponds to sections 23 and 24 of the Verplanck bill which thus came into the final
Act. Sections 2, 3, and 9 embody the
principles both of Free Banking and of bond
security to be pledged for the benefit of
the note-holder. The security was to consist "of certificates of public stock

issued by the proper authority of this
state, or either of the several states, or
by the Congress of the United States, at
the par value thereof." This last clause
was copied from the Spencer bill, but the
superfluous tying together of bank capital
and security for notes issued was dropped.
With this exclusion the Mercantilist element in the underlying set of ideas was
also abandoned, and the result resembles
Ricardo rather than MacVickar and Lord.[81]
There was certainly no telling improvement
over the two earlier bills, and Mann's
claim indicates a braggart's gross over-
estimation of his own importance.

Neither of the three bills envisaged
the use of mortgages among the securities
to be deposited. This proposal, Mercantilist in its origin[82] and in line with traditional American banking thought, was contributed by Charles Brook Hoard (1805-1886),
a young local politician and a postmaster
of Jackson's and Van Buren's appointment.
Through an amendment it came into the engrossed bill (as section 7) against Mann's
better vision. Much wiser was a second
amendment proposed by Daniel Dewey Barnard
(1797-1861). A well educated and widely
traveled lawyer, he later became American
minister to Prussia. Possibly under
European influence he suggested a 20 per
cent specie reserve against the banks'
notes, in addition to the deposited bonds.
Accordingly, section 33 of the Act prescribed a 12 1/2 per cent specie reserve
against circulation (a clause which was
dropped again in 1840).[83]

VI

Thus the New York Free Banking Act
came into being, as the result of a long
ideological development.[84] Not too successful at first, it became the object of discussion and the subject of numerous amendments. The basic ideas, however, survived
unaltered for many years to follow; viz.,
that banking should be a free trade, but
that at the same time no bank should be
allowed to supply a circulating medium
which was not secured outside of the bank
and independent of it.[85]

Free Banking once put into practice
was one of those institutions which spread
like wildfire, although with a lag of time
during which the Act was made workable by

various amendments. In New York itself no less than 134 free banks were chartered between April 1838 and the end of 1839; but most of these were unsound and went down quickly enough. It was a genuine achievement, therefore, to develop the first successful business organization on the basis of the new ideas, the Bank of Commerce, which for some time towered above all the other banks in the city of New York. This bank was created by a number of merchants, bankers, capitalists, and jurists, with Chief Justice James Kent drawing up the charter; but the leaders in this group were the partners Samuel Ward and James Gore King of the banking house of Prime, Ward and King. Ward became the first president and until he retired shaped the policy of the bank during its early years; whereas King was among the signers of the articles of association and sold a substantial portion of the original stock to the public. The bank found in George Curtis an exceedingly competent cashier and to him as the actual manager much of the success was due.[86]

In the 1840's the idea of Free Banking won minds all over the United States (although not to the exclusion of all other notions on banking). Percolating westward, particularly after a period of slow growth, it suddenly became the banking idea of the day. Free Banking represented so perfectly the underlying spirit of the period that everybody seemed to have been just waiting for the formula.

Among those who contributed to the victory of the Free Banking idea were Henry Charles Carey, who advocated the principle of free banking,[87] Condy Raguet, and Richard Hildreth. The writings of the latter two men familiarized the American leaders in this field with the new system of banking. Raguet repeatedly discussed it in his Financial Register, going so far as to declare New York Free Banking "the greatest improvement of banking which has yet been introduced in our country." In his Treatise on Currency and Banking of 1840, he reprinted the New York Free Banking Act, and devoted a whole chapter to commenting thereon. He also reproduced the Report of the Comptroller of 1840 on the "Operations under the Act to Authorize the Business of Banking" together with amendments to that act. Already in the

Treatise he expressed his expectation that the "legislatures of the different states ...may...adopt the New York system," which was identical to a suggestion that they do so.[88]

At an earlier stage, on the other hand, Hildreth had propagated the idea of free competition in banking, for in 1837 he published his History of Banks to which is added a Demonstration of the Advantages and Necessity of Free Competition in the Business of Banking.[89] Here he pleaded that "the monopoly of bank charters must be abolished altogether and not in one or two states only but in all." "Capitalists must be left as much liberty to invest their money in a bank as in a cotton mill." Hildreth expected that free competition introduced into the field of banking would result in the "Laws of Trade" controlling the currency. Thus Hildreth promoted the idea of free banking. His hazy and radical ideas could not provide the basis of an act; but once Free Banking had become a reality in New York, Hildreth logically joined its defenders. He became convinced that the principle of "requiring security from banks" (not originally embodied in his conception) was "the only legislative measure with respect to the currency which the government could reasonably and advantageously adopt."[90] Consequently in his Banks, Banking and Paper Currencies[91] of 1840 (in which his book of 1837 is substantially reprinted) he embodied in his earlier reasoning those essential features of the New York act, thus becoming one of the promoters of the New York brand of Free Banking. Like Condy Raguet, he felt impelled to reprint the whole act.[92]

Thus promoted by leading thinkers on banking and backed by public opinion, Free Banking was adopted by one state after another, by New Jersey in 1850, Ohio, Illinois, and Massachusetts in 1851, Indiana and Tennessee in 1852, Louisiana in 1853, Wisconsin in 1854, Mississippi in 1856, Michigan (for the second time) in 1857, Iowa and Minnesota in 1858, and finally by Pennsylvania and Kansas in 1861.[93] All the state laws in question were more or less copies of the New York law, except for Louisiana which engrafted certain features of the Banking Act of 1842 onto the New York ideas.[94] The fact that Free Banking in its original form was abused in many states, especially in the Middle West, does not detract from its importance nor did it destroy the persisting influence of its underlying ideas.

One interesting detail remains to be considered: viz, the fact that the Free Banking idea started to migrate from New York even before it had been put into practice in that state. Actually Michigan took over the principle as early as 1837 when the final New York act had not even been drafted. The explanation is simple. The Michigan settlers in the early 1830's came mostly from the western counties of New York and were imbued with the spirit prevailing in that state; that is, they were against monopolies, but in favor of banking, as described previously. Such notions migrated West in the minds of the pioneers of Michigan, and when a situation developed quite similar to that in the mother state, they looked for suggestions to that more developed commonwealth. Thus in 1836 the Michigan legislators copied the New York Safety Fund Act; and when the debates on Free Banking were scarcely under way in Albany, they eagerly embraced the basic ideas of the new scheme.[95] Just as had been the case in New York, so in Michigan the legislature was swamped in 1837 with applications for bank charters and could see no way out except by embodying the principle of free banking in an act.[96] At that time in New York only the Young bill was drafted, and its influence can be traced in the Michigan act. The Young bill as well as the Michigan Free Banking Act of 1837 (the first Free Banking law passed in America) established in section one the Free Banking principle. The Young bill provides in section 3 that each shareholder shall execute a mortgage on unincumbered real estate or make conditional transfer of personal property, which in the opinion of a trustee is of the value of at least one and a half of the amount of such shareholder's interest. This security is to be pledged for the payment of all debts and the redemption of notes and similar evidences of debt. Section 2 of the Michigan Act closely corresponds to the above-quoted section 3 of the Young bill, reading as follows: "The president and directors of such association shall before commencing operations furnish good and suf-

ficient securities to the auditor general, for and in behalf of the people of the state, to be held as collateral securities, when all other liabilities of such association shall fail, or prove to be insufficient for the purpose intended,...and for the redemption of all notes, which securities shall be in the full amount which such association shall at any time have in circulation or be indebted, and shall consist either of bonds or mortgages upon real estate within the state, or in bonds [that is, personal bonds] executed by resident free holders of the state, and shall forthwith lodge in the hands of the bank commissioner."

In both the New York bill and the Michigan act, just as in the older Safety Fund acts, no distinction is made between note-holders and other creditors. In all these proposals in line with Mercantilist tradition, security is supposed to consist of mortgages on real estate and personal property or personal bonds executed by the free holders, respectively. One essential difference between the New York bill and the Michigan act should be stressed; and in this respect Michigan took a forward step. Young wanted to have security given over and above the invested capital, and there was to be no connection between securities pledged and outstanding liabilities. In the Michigan act the connection between capital and security to be pledged was severed and replaced by a link between security and liabilities. Nevertheless Young's idea of a security over and above the invested capital was also incorporated in the Michigan act, in that a director was liable to the extent of his individual property and a stockholder to the amount of stock held by him. It is not surprising that this sort of land-bank-open-to-all ended in disaster, all the more so because business could be started when only 30 per cent of the capital had been paid up, whereas the Young bill required the full paying-in of capital. In addition, in Michigan real estate mortgages were taken "at true cash value" during boom times; while certain restricting clauses were circumvented, examination evaded, and the liability clauses rendered ineffective by court decisions.

It is difficult to trace with certainty the Michigan pioneers who first put the idea of Free Banking on a statute book.

In January 1837 Edwin H. Lothrop, member of the Committee on Banks and Incorporations, a leading farmer and Democrat, reported in the House of Representatives the "bill to organize and regulate banking associations." In the Senate Edward D. Ellis moved "that the Committee on Incorporations be instructed to inquire into the expediency of providing by law for a uniform and equal system for the regulation of banking associations and that they be instructed to report by bill or otherwise." A few days later a "bill to regulate banking associations" was brought in by Ellis himself, a newspaper editor, who also reported the bill. The biographies of these men mention no connection with the Michigan Free Banking Act of 1837, perhaps because the fate of this law was such that its authorship gave no reason for local or family pride. On the other hand, this silence of the biographies cannot be taken as proof either for or against the leadership of the two men in this matter.[97]

So far the westward migration of the Free Banking idea has been traced from New York to Michigan. When it came to the enactment of the idea in New York in 1838 the already existing Michigan Free Banking Act was known in New York,[98] and it is not impossible that the direct relationship between notes and securities pledged (characteristic of the New York act) was adopted, at least partly, under Michigan influence. If this was the case, then the idea originated in New York, journeyed to Michigan and then back home, improved in this one important point.

Chapter VIII

THE SOUTHERN PLANTATION BANKS

One of the subjects in the field
of banking which awaits thorough investigation is that of the Southern plantation
banks of the 1830's. These banks are of
unusual interest ideologically, but because
of the lack of adequate factual research,
the present chapter can only sketch some of
the problems involved.

The Southern plantation bank represents an attempt at modernizing Mercantilist land banking. In the colonial era the
credit needs of agriculture had been satisfied in one of three ways: by private lending on mortgage, by loan offices, and by
land banks. In the case of loan offices,
as they were established for instance by
Pennsylvania and New Jersey,[1] the colony
in question issued a certain amount of
paper money. This was allocated to the
counties according to the taxable assessment, and the alloted sums were handed to
commissioners who loaned these funds on
mortgage. The loans were to be paid back
in installments including interest (which
interest was to defray the loan office expenses of the colonial government in question) and the installments were to be lent
out again for the remainder of the period
for which the office was established.[2]
Such loan offices were still set up or at
least proposed during the first half of
the nineteenth century.[3] Land banks were
similar to loan offices except that they
were private enterprises. A number of
landowners combined, mortgaged their estates, paying interest, of course, on the
mortgages, and received bank notes. Details
as to how the loans were to be paid back
are of no importance in this context; they
have been alluded to in a previous chapter.[4]

The first suggestion aiming at
what today is called mortgage banking was
made as early as 1786 by no less a person
than Robert Morris. When the question of
loan offices came up in the Pennsylvania
legislature during the debates on the fate
of the Bank of North America and the

representatives of agriculture complained
that the bank worked exclusively in the
interest of commerce while at the same time
precluding the establishment of a loan office on which farmers could rely for their
credit needs, Morris answered: "If the
country gentlemen are willing I will freely
join in the creation of a capital in hard
cash for the establishment of a loan office.
The interests of the bank [of North America]
can never interfere with theirs."[5] That is
to say, he wanted to develop the contemporary loan office in the direction of mortgage banking, forbidding the issuance of
notes by the proposed institution. He suggested a tax in hard money on real estate
in order to establish a fund for the purpose of lending to farmers for the improvement of their lands, and he believed that a
farthing per acre would soon accumulate
into a sufficient fund. Unfortunately for
the development of American banking, the
representatives of agriculture did not see
the soundness of this suggestion because
they could not discard the idea of paper
issues as the only means of satisfying
large scale farmers' credit needs. Nor did
the merchants see the light. Sullivan
fought in vain for commercial banking pure
and simple, and preached also in vain that
banks were not meant to loan on landed security, that loans of money banks to farmers on mortgage were inadmissible.[6] His
advice was not heeded. On the contrary, by
1800 it was becoming common for charter
clauses to force banks to lend a certain
percentage of their capital or of the total
of their loans to farmers on mortgage.[7]
Thus the combination of mortgage banking
and commercial banking in the same type of
enterprise became the typical feature of
American banking, as described before.

Once this unfortunate combination
of incompatible functions was established
it was very difficult to get out of the
vicious circle. Keeping in mind this un-
happy situation the student will surely
concede that the plantation bank, regardless

of its failure as a type, was an attempt which deserves admiration. Its founders proved to possess more than usual resourcefulness and they developed new ideas, some of which were destined to become important for capitalistic development. What they actually established were land banks with a specie working capital. The recognition that one could not establish a bank by just "melting down" property and issuing notes on that basis distinguished them from the land-bank founders of the eighteenth century. This achievement becomes clearer when one remembers that even under the New York Free Banking Act of 1838 genuine land banks could be set up and, indeed, one actually was.[8] The combination of two transactions, of getting money through "melting down" property (by issuing bonds on the basis thereof) and of using this money for the purpose of banking, must be characterized as ingenious; and equally ingenious were developments in the field of security issues which resulted from the endeavors to set up this type of bank.

Disregarding minor differences and leaving the two most interesting features of the plantation bank to be discussed shortly one can characterize this type of bank as follows: Only plantation owners could become stockholders of the plantation banks. They subscribed to the capital of the bank in question by mortgaging their plantations or parts thereof. They received the corresponding amount in bank shares and this fact, i.e., that they received bank shares not bank notes, distinguished the plantation bank from the eighteenth-century land bank. The stockholders, like the members of the earlier land banks, had first claim on loans and would get such loans on the basis of their stock to an amount of 50 per cent, which was identical with lending them 50 per cent on the appraised value of the mortgaged property, an interesting development of the traditional American stock loans. The amounts borrowed had to be returned in fixed installments to meet the bonds, a rule which was perfectly in line with the traditional repayment of accommodation loans in installments; but de facto, through the tie between stock and mortgage, this rule represented a step toward self-liquidating mortgages. Profits were retained as a sinking fund to provide additional security for the payment of the bonds.

The Southern plantation bank, also called "property bank" or "mortgage bank," is a typical example of economic development through the combination of various elements all of which had existed separately before.[9] Two main ideological lines were brought together in this particular case. The participation of states in banks had been traditional in America since the 1790's, as mentioned before. Thus when the Bank of Louisiana was chartered in 1824 it was a typical American bank in that the State of Louisiana held shares in it. However, in one detail it marked progress, if you please. To understand this progress, one must remember[11] that the federal government, when investing in the First and Second Banks of the United States, gave them its bonds on which to bank like the Bank of England. In the 1820's the question whether or not banks which acquired government bonds should keep them in their portfolios became a moot one.[12] However, when Alabama and Louisiana in 1823 and 1824, respectively, obligated themselves to give their bonds to the Bank of the State of Alabama and the Bank of Louisiana, respectively, it was understood that these bonds were to be sold in order to raise a specie capital on which to bank. This stipulation seems to have been something new at that time.[13] The handing of state bonds to banks for sale to the public or the guarantee of bank bonds by the state to make them salable became one element of the Southern plantation bank. By interesting European investors in these bonds and selling thousands of them in England and Holland, the plantation banks became one of the most important agencies for capital import into the United States for about a decade.

It must be kept in mind that the Bank of Louisiana was not a plantation bank although paving the way for that new type of bank.[14] The plantation bank characteristically embraced still another element. A modern author[15] has suggested that this type of bank may have been modeled on the Prussian Landschaften, agricultural credit institutions set up first in the eighteenth century in Silesia.[16] Although it can be proved that the Landschaften were known in America[17] by that time, this author is inclined to discount this influence since the elements which make the plantation bank (except one perhaps?) can easily be explained as the development of American ideas, and since the Prussian Landschaften and the

Southern plantation banks were essentially very different enterprises. The former were mortgage institutions pure and simple; the latter were the typical hybrid American banks of that period which fulfilled two functions, in the words of Forstall, as loan offices on mortgage and otherwise and as banks of discount for the industrial and commercial interests. To be sure, the essential feature of the Landschaften, joint and individual liability of the borrowing landowners, can be found in the plantation banks. Section 4 of the charter of the Citizens Bank of New Orleans, for instance, stipulated that the "mortgages to be given by the stockholders by virtue of this act shall remain as a perpetual pledge to the holder or holders of the said bonds." It is doubtful, however, to what extent this feature was understood. The name of the first plantation bank (Consolidated Association of Planters) and the name "Union Bank," which became popular for this type of bank, indicates that the promoters knew what they were setting up. But it is doubtful whether the mass of the stockholders or many of the legislators who enacted the charters of these banks understood the implications which, in the case of the Prussian Landschaften, were generally recognized.[18] On the other hand, the complicated tying together of government bonds (or government guarantee for bank bonds), stock loans, and mortgages, characteristic of the plantation banks, as will be discribed forthwith, was strictly American and totally alien to the Landschaften with their feudal character.

The typical plantation bank was first developed in the Consolidated Association of Planters of New Orleans, chartered in 1827. The name of the man who devised the scheme and promoted it was enthusiastically pronounced by one of his collaborators, Hugues Lavergne, who in 1828 was in England in order to sell the state bonds issued to the bank. On September 6 he wrote home:

> The inhabitants of Louisiana will, without doubt, be thankful toward the man as modest as able who in the midst of all the obstacles has furnished them with the most efficient means to augment their prosperity. You have guessed, gentlemen, that I wish to speak of Mr. J. B. Moussier.[19]

Unfortunately not a single piece of information could be unearthed to throw light on Moussier's life and business activities.

Although intensive research on the plantation banks will undoubtedly reveal details now unknown, it is possible even now to sketch in broad lines how the idea of the plantation bank became an actuality. What has been described in the theoretical analysis as the second element represented the first step in the historical development. The founders of the Consolidated Association of Planters originally created mortgage bonds in order to raise a working capital for their land bank. Only when these bonds were unsalable did the directors prevail on the state government to issue state bonds in favor of the bank. While originally a straight mortgage bond was issued it was replaced in the second instance by a sort of collateral trust bond.[20] The state was secured by a pool of mortgages and thus it acted as a trustee for the bondholders who received a security over and above that which they possessed, through the state's pledging its faith for the redemption of the bonds.[21]

The first of the plantation banks, the Consolidated Association of Planters, was chartered in 1827, as mentioned before. The new type of bank was soon copied in Louisiana by two more banks, the Union Bank (chartered in 1832) and the Citizens Bank (chartered in 1833). From Louisiana the plantation bank started migrating. As early as 1833 this sort of bank was set up for the first time outside of Louisiana, namely in the Territory of Florida. The fact that the Florida enterprise of this character was called "Union Bank" indicates the line of influence. The Union Bank of Florida was the work of John G. Gamble, a native Virginian of good reputation, who was a resident of Tallahassee and who became not only one of the largest stockholders, but also the president of the bank. As such he personally took care of negotiating the bonds issued by the territory in behalf of the bank, and for this purpose Gamble traveled extensively both in America and in Europe. However, he hardly proved to be a good salesman and negotiator although, or perhaps because, he used high pressure methods. The bank came to an ignominious end, but it cannot be ascertained whether the failure was due to Gamble himself or to mismanagement during his absence in Europe. It would be worth the effort to investigate the life and the business activities of this man who was undoubtedly a business leader of his region at that time.[22] Slightly after Florida, Arkansas (1836)[23] and Mississippi (1837)[24] chartered plantation banks, the Real Estate Bank and the Union Bank, respectively, whose fates are of no interest in this context. Both cases were typical of contact migration since both Arkansas[25] and Mississippi border on Louisiana. Surprising, however, is the fact that the Territory of Wisconsin chartered a full-fledged plantation bank (the State Bank of Wisconsin). The act was not approved by Congress and was repealed.[26]

Regardless of the fact that much sound and shrewd business thinking was incorporated in the plantation bank, all banks of that type, except the Union Bank of New Orleans, met with disaster. The founders of these banks did not create modern mortgage banks because they did not break through tradition. To the contrary they remained within tradition by combining mortgage banking for the benefit of their stockholders with the usual hybrid business of lending both on trade and accommodation paper. Thus they were liable to all the losses and difficulties which the traditional American bank was bound to encounter and in addition to another specific source of danger. Plantation banks started with one hundred per cent borrowed capital. Their future depended on a very high net-profit rate which permitted them to earn the whole capital in the period during which the bonds matured, and during which the profits accumulated in a sinking fund. This point was clearly seen by the Barings in 1828 when they undertook to sell the bonds of the Consolidated Association of Planters. The representative of that bank reported home: "Messrs. Baring are of the opinion that the plan of the Consolidated Association is as new as ingenious and well conceived. They have taken pains to calculate that with a good administration the profits ought to be about equal the capital at the end of the charter."[27] These profits resulted from the difference in the interest rates between Europe and America, between two different types of loans, and between wholesale and retail borrowing. But what would happen if the administration of these banks was not good or if a crisis interfered with the anticipated net-profit rate? The result would necessarily be the failure of the bank in question. In this case the bondholders depended on the faith of the state which had guaranteed or issued the bonds with the help of which the capital of the banks had been raised. Unfortunately the states in question had undertaken obligations which they were unable to make good or, at least, to make good promptly.

Chapter IX

SAVINGS BANKS

Before leaving the second period one more of its remarkable achievements should be examined, the introduction of the savings bank into this country. As is generally known, the first institutions approximating modern savings banks were founded in Switzerland and in Germany during the eighteenth century. It was felt that the poorer classes needed secure depositories for their savings and, if worthy, a source of credit to protect them from the usurer in time of distress. In Great Britain a similar sort of institution planned to relieve the poverty of the working classes and to lighten the burden of poor relief came into being slightly later, but still before the close of the eighteenth century.[1] In contrast to the early continental ones, however, these British institutions (called Friendly Societies) were rather insurance schemes and were not meant to be sources of credit for the poor, although having in common with the former that they gladly accepted the support of well-to-do philanthropists or public agencies. In 1810, however, there was founded in Scotland by the Rev. Henry Duncan the first self-supporting modern savings bank. This final stage of the early development had been reached in the old world before savings banks were adopted in America. They were then considered here as formed for benevolent purposes, to keep the earnings of the poor and to return them plus interest when the necessities of the depositors required it.[2]

I

The beginnings of American savings banking are of particular interest from the point of view of this research, because here is one of those cases in which one can study particularly well the migration of the basic ideas behind modern institutions from the old continent to the new. In the case of the savings banks several lines of influence can be discerned. One,

to be taken up first, led from Patrick Colquhoun of London to Thomas Eddy of New York. Colquhoun (1745-1820) was a very intelligent London police magistrate.[3] After a start in business in Glasgow, where he was interested in administrative and legislative measures beneficial to the commerce and trade of that city and of the British cotton industry in general, he moved to London in 1789. Three years later he became a justice when the metropolitan police was reorganized. In this capacity he acquired a familiarity with social problems and wrote a number of books and papers on related subjects, one of which was his Treatise on Indigence of 1806.[4] In this book, which aimed at educating the poor to help themselves and started from the above-mentioned Friendly Societies (parochial societies),[5] he suggested a national deposit bank with branches for the benefit of the latter. His somewhat hazy scheme pointed toward social insurance rather than toward a modern savings bank and is distinguished from the latter also by his willingness to accept the donations of opulent philanthropists. But Colquhoun's idea that institutions of such character should be established on a national scale with governmental sanction and backing was creative since it overcame the then still prevailing local aspect of the matter.[6]

Colquhoun had been a correspondent of Thomas Eddy of New York since 1802 Eddy (1758-1827) was the son of Protestant immigrants from Ireland who had joined the Society of Friends. He grew up in a religious atmosphere and, after some abortive attempts in business elsewhere, became a succesful insurance broker in New York, making money in connection with the funding of the national debt and by insurance underwriting. Once on the road to business success Eddy turned his interest to reforms, and while his share in prison reform was his greatest single achievement, he was, in fact, connected with most of the progressive movements of his time.

Thus it is not surprising that the letters exchanged between the two men covered a wide range of subjects, such as prison reform, education of the poor, instruction of the deaf and dumb, questions of political economy, the personality of Napoleon, and so on. On April 19, 1816, in the course of this correspondence,[7] Colquhoun informed his New York friend of the establishment of savings banks in the British Isles:

> Among other philanthropic establishments which are yearly rising in the great metropolis we are now anxiously engaged in forming a Provident Institution or Saving [sic!] bank in the western district of the city upon the principle suggested and explained in my Treatise on Indigence, published in 1806 [this is a mistake], but on a far limited scale. The practical effect of these establishments was first manifested in Scotland since which they have been extended to several towns in England and are likely to become very general. Their utility scarcely requires explanation. The object is to assist the labouring poor to preserve a portion of their earnings and to give them provident habits. I send you under cover the plan of our institution which has just commenced and which has been the result of much discussion and deliberation.

There can be no doubt that this latter claim was true, for the "Provident Institution for Savings established in the Western Part of the Metropolis," the "plan" of which Eddy received, was a remarkable enterprise indeed, since among its founders and managers there were, besides Colquhoun himself, such men as Ricardo, Malthus, Torrens, Sir Thomas Baring, and Wilberforce. It is probable that the "plan" was identical or at least essentially identical with the "Regulations" reprinted by Hume,[8] and the dependence of the New York on the London institution will be discussed in all detail shortly.[9]

Colquhoun's letter of April 19, 1816 is supposed to have been the incentive which moved Eddy to action, at least so he wrote to the former on April 9, 1817. However, it has recently become known from John Pintard's correspondence that before Colquhoun's letter was even written the erection of a savings bank was under discussion in New York.[10] As early as April

3, 1816 John Pintard (to be characterized presently) wrote to his daughter that he was aiding the promotion of an association for the purpose of "inducing habits of economy by receiving the savings of labourers and domestics and putting them out on interest." Whether Eddy, whom Pintard later considered his friend, was a member of this group is not known, nor whether it was this group whose backing Eddy gained before calling a meeting of citizens for November 29, 1816.[11] Be that as it may, when the meeting took place it was known that similar attempts at setting up savings banks were under way in Boston and Philadelphia.[12]

The meeting was a full success through the efforts of John Pintard (1759-1844), just mentioned, the New York merchant and philanthropist who was also a successful promoter. In the words of Scoville,[13]

> there never lived that man in the city who could start great measures as John Pintard could do.... He could call a meeting with the pen of a poet and before the people met he would have arranged the doings for a perfect success. He knew the weak points of every man and he would gratify the vanity of men and get their money and accomplish his good purpose without any of them suspecting that they were the respectable names and moneyed tools that Mr. Pintard required.

Thus he engineered the first meeting presided over by Thomas Eddy to establish a savings bank in the city of New York. "All the men were fixed," and a resolution to establish a savings bank was quickly passed, whereupon Zachariah Lewis[14] submitted a constitution prepared by John Pintard, which will be discussed presently. The responsibility for this description must rest with Scoville, although Pintard himself wrote on December 5, 1816 that he had been "instrumental in promoting" the plan of a savings bank.[15]

The plan that was submitted and adopted was intended to enable the laboring classes to deposit their savings on interest and with the understanding that they were at liberty to withdraw the whole or part of the deposits whenever necessary. Its details are interesting for various reasons.[16] Following on the whole the plan of the London savings bank it nevertheless envisaged a typical American bank administration. A board of directors of thirty members was to be elected "for the examination of the accounts of the Bank and to adopt such measures, rules, and by-laws as they...may think necessary for the better government of the Institution." That is to say, the board was to have the character of a supervisory and policy-making body. The wording of the plan is not consistent, however: bank boards were then still generally considered administrative bodies, consequently when the plan speaks later of the "management during the recess of the board" a concession to public opinion is implied. The directors, six of whom were sufficient to form a quorum, were to elect a president and three vice-presidents, and to appoint a cashier. They were also to appoint three of their number "an attending Committee whose duty it shall be either together or singly to attend at the Bank during the time it shall be open and to have the general superintendence and management of it during the recess of the Board."[17] The attending committee was to keep minutes and to submit them to the board at the latter's monthly meeting. Thus the New York savings-bank plan of 1816 envisaged the administration of the enterprise by what was called in contemporary commercial banks which were using the same device, sitting directors or monthly committee.

Turning to the regulations of business proper one discovers that the plan of 1816, following its model, contains the pass book[18] which had to be presented in making deposits and withdrawals as is still true today. The plan, furthermore, established an interest rate (not payable on fractional parts of calendar months) of 5 per cent on all deposits from five to forty-nine dollars and of 6 per cent on all of fifty dollars and more, a rule for which there was no parallel in the model. Only whole dollars and multiples thereof were to be taken on deposit. This rule, however, again paralleled the London example and its general adoption by American savings banks gave rise in the 1850's to the "penny" or "five cents" savings banks.[19] The accounts were to be balanced and the interest entered once a year. The interest was to be derived from investment in United States or State of New York

or City of New York securities or in such other funds as the directors might see fit. Incidentally, it is noteworthy that the original plan was less dependent on the Regulations of the London institution, than was the later charter.

As already mentioned, this plan was adopted at the meeting of November 29, 1816, but the institution could not commence operations at once. The promotors realized, as Thomas Eddy wrote to Colquhoun on April 9, 1817[20] that they could not go into operation without prior incorporation. As a matter of fact, as early as December 10, 1816, the directors, elected in the November meeting, appointed a committee to seek incorporation. However, in applying to the New York legislature the committee made a tactical mistake. In choosing the term "saving bank" for the enterprise under consideration the antagonism of all those who were against "banks" was stirred up. The different and specific character of savings banks as opposed to commercial banks could not easily be understood by the average legislator of that day since no such savings bank as yet existed in America. This tactical error proved fatal. Amending the bill from "An Act to Incorporate the Saving-Bank [sic!] of the City of New York" to "An Act to Incorporate an Association by the name of the Saving Corporation of the City of New York" did not avail and the bill was lost. Among the objections raised, however, there was a very reasonable one, the claim that the cost of running the enterprise would lessen, if not defeat the purpose. It might be wiser "to allow one of the clerks [of an existing New York bank] to transact the business for a small extra allowance." In other words, it was suggested that some sort of savings department be set up in a commercial bank instead of incorporating a special savings bank.[21]

After this defeat the promoters of the New York savings bank had to change their strategy and to pursue their goal by a roundabout way. They met again in public on December 16, 1817, this time under the chairmanship of Matthew Clarkson,[22] the bank president, whose sanction of charitable and public spirited enterprises, as De Witt Clinton expressed it, was deemed essential and "a pass book to public approbation." In this meeting they took up the matter of pauperism, and resolved to constitute themselves into a Society for the Prevention of Pauperism. In so doing they again adopted British methods. In that country similar societies had served, so to speak, as midwives for savings banks, such as the Society for Bettering the Condition and Increasing the Comforts of the Poor in the Town and Neighbourhood of Liverpool which established the Liverpool Mechanics', Servants' and Labourers' Fund of 1813; or the London Society for Bettering the Condition of the Poor which brought into being the above-mentioned institution in the Metropolis and perhaps a few others; or the Edinburgh Society for the Suppression of Mendicity which fostered the Edinburgh Savings Bank.[23] In the New York meeting of 1817 which thus followed the British pattern a committee of eight was appointed to prepare a constitution and a statement on the causes of pauperism. Five of these men had previously been directors-elect of the projected savings bank of 1816. This committee included Thomas Eddy, John Griscom (to be characterized presently), Brockholst Livingston (the politician and co-founder of the Manhattan Company, then judge on the United States Supreme Court) and Zachariah Lewis. On February 6, 1818 this committee presented its report which contained a clause that the Society should work for the establishment of savings banks. Thereupon John Griscom (1774-1852), the Quaker teacher and philanthropist, moved that a savings bank be organized, repeating exactly his actions of November 1816, an indication of the same careful preparation. Subsequently, a special committee, of which John Pintard was a member, was appointed to report on the expediency of so doing.[24]

By that time the situation had become much more favorable. De Witt Clinton, one of the directors of the projected savings bank of 1816 and in fact an active one,[25] had become governor of New York in 1817. In his message of January 27, 1818, he elaborated on the evils of pauperism and, among other remedies, suggested the establishment of savings banks, a suggestion which had been well received by the legislature. (In these passages[26] he was especially concerned with lowering the tax burden resulting from poor relief.) Furthermore

savings banks had been or were then being organized also in Boston, Salem, Philadelphia, and Baltimore, respectively, so that the New York legislators could draw on experience in other American cities besides the European one. As a matter of fact, the New York Society for the Prevention of Pauperism collected information on American savings banks and spread it by publishing it under the title Documents relative to Savings Banks....[27] Finally in December 1818 the society held a meeting with members of the state legislature from the city, and John Pintard explained to them the nature of savings banks,[28] becoming so enthusiastic that he elicited smiles from the faces of those present, as he himself realized. Thus when in January 1819 a new petition for the incorporation of a savings bank, this time a petition of the Society for the Prevention of Pauperism under the signature of Matthew Clarkson, came up before the New York legislature, the latter acted quickly and the Bank for Savings came into being. Among its incorporators were William Bayard, Thomas Eddy, Brockholst Livingston, Philip Hone, Zachariah Lewis, and John Pintard.[29]

The continuity between the plan of 1816 and the corporation of 1819 is evidenced both by the personalities involved and by objective factors. William Bayard, president-elect, and Noah Brown, the steam boat builder, a vice-president-elect of 1816, are to be found in the same capacities in the charter of 1819. In addition, of the remaining twenty-eight directors of 1816,[30] fifteen became trustees under the charter of 1819.[31] The essential similarities between the plan of 1816 and the charter of 1819 will be obvious when the latter is discussed in detail later.

While Thomas Eddy, John Pintard, and their friends were busily engaged in promoting the first savings bank in New York they knew, as has been mentioned before, that similar attempts were also under way in Philadelphia and Boston. The one in the former city, to be considered next, showed a surprising similarity in all essentials to that in New York. In both cases the attempts did not grow out of the very first suggestion in this direction. As has been stressed, Pintard worked in New York for a savings bank several months before Eddy took the matter up. In

Philadelphia, on the other hand, the successful promotion of November and December 1816 had been preceded by the very interesting suggestion of setting up a "Chest of Savings" which can be characterized as a communal savings bank, very similar to the type which Germany developed in the nineteenth century. As early as October 1810 James Mease (1771-1846), the physician, scientist, and author, published in his Archives of Useful Knowledge[32] an article entitled "Bank of Industry." In this article he suggested that the Treasurer of the City of Philadelphia, acting through a clerk, should take on deposit the savings of the poor in amounts of even less than one dollar. He was to repay them on request without formality except presentation of the passbook, and all sums deposited for more than sixty days were to draw five per cent interest. The motivation of the proposal was identical with that which became common both in Britain and America in those years: the institution would be beneficial to the morals of the poor, would save the city "poor rates," and would provide an example that would soon be followed in other American cities. Mease was, according to his own acknowledgment, inspired by the example of a similar institution created by law in Paris at the beginning of the French Revolution, (the title of which he translated by "Bank of Savings")[33] and by the British "Benefit Societies" copied in Philadelphia by the "mechanics of several branches." However nothing came of this suggestion, reasonable though it was.

The man to whom Philadelphia owes its first savings bank, a mutual one as in New York, was Condy Raguet. Like Eddy, he received the incentive straight from England, but while the modern savings bank migrated to New York through the medium of an individual as source of influence, it came to Philadelphia by the impersonal medium of pamphlets. When in November 1816 Condy Raguet (1784-1842), the influence recipient, was impressed by accounts on British savings banks he was not yet the eminent editor and economist which he was to become. But he had gained experience as a merchant, had published his first treatise on monetary matters, was taking an interest in the law, and was soon (1818) to become a state senator. It was such broad experience which made him susceptible

to the influence of the British publications on savings banks when in one way or another they fell into his hands. The following were the pamphlets which Raguet received:[34] Henry Duncan's An Essay on the Nature and Advantages of Parish Banks, Second edition (Edinburgh, 1816); George Rose's Observations on Banks for Savings, probably third edition (London, 1816), and slightly later there came into his hands the Observations on the Utility and Management of Savings Banks with a View to Establishing one for the Townships of Stretford and Chorlton with Hardy, in the Parish of Manchester (Manchester, 1817). Raguet was influenced especially by the description of the Southampton Saving Fund contained in the pamphlet by Rose, its founder and president: the Philadelphia Saving Fund Society, Raguet's work, was modeled on the Southampton savings bank.

So impressed was Raguet by these pamphlets that "with the subject fresh in his mind"[35] he at once discussed the matter of establishing a similar enterprise in Philadelphia with Richard Peters. Peters (1779-1848), a lawyer, for several years United States district attorney, and later law reporter, who was already acquainted with the subject and thinking along similar lines, agreed instantly. At that early moment, if Raguet's memory is trustworthy, it was agreed to use the name "Saving Fund Society" for the institution to be proposed, that name which is so indicative of the lines of influence. Thereby Philadelphia avoided the use of the unpopular term "bank," the adoption of which contributed to delaying the similar accomplishment in New York. Once Raguet and Peters had agreed between themselves as to the desirability of creating a mutual savings bank in Philadelphia, the cooperation of other respectable and public-spirited men was secured, and although the earliest extant records disagree as to minor details it is certain that the banker Clement C. Biddle (1784-1855) and the broker Thomas Hale[36] were the next to join.

These men and their friends associated to form the Philadelphia Saving Fund Society, and on December 13, 1816 they published their Articles of Association and an Address to the Public in Freeman's Journal and Philadelphia Mercantile Advertiser. The former are almost identical with the charter of 1819 which will be discussed later in its proper place. The address, on the other hand, is interesting as an indication of how carefully the associates had studied various British plans and how aware they were of some of their essential differences. In contrast to the founders of the New York Bank for Savings they did not wait for incorporation, but went into business almost immediately, thus getting a head start over both New York and Boston.[37]

During the very days when high-minded men in both New York and Philadelphia were working on savings bank projects in their respective communities, action was also being taken in Boston. Here the move was initiated by James Savage who, as he himself acknowledged in a letter,[38] received his incentive from the plan, perhaps a broadside, of the same London savings banks which was then the model in New York also. He had seen the plan posted over a fireplace in Gardiner, Maine. Savage (1784-1873), Harvard bred, was a lawyer active in state politics and public life (connected with the Massachusetts Historical Society, overseer of his alma mater), in short, a public-spirited, far-seeing man like many of those who were responsible for the creation of the earliest savings banks in this country.[39] Savage who was not only the actual founder, but the guiding spirit of the bank for many years to come as its first "clerk" (secretary) and later, as its treasurer, chairman of its investment committee, and its president, was able to gain the backing of a very wealthy and influential clique of Boston aristocrats. It was headed by William Phillips (Jr.) (1750-1827), then lieutenant governor of the state and at the same time president of the Massachusetts Bank, "one of the most generous benefactors of his time."[40] Another member was John Phillips, his distant cousin (1770-1823), a lawyer, Massachusetts state senator for almost twenty years, president of the state senate for a decade, Boston's first mayor, influential member of the inner circles of the Federalists, president of the Manufacturers and Mechanics Bank of Boston,[41] and an active participant in all sorts of civic affairs. The Phillips cousins were joined by the latter's neighbor and close friend from the days of Andover and Harvard, Josiah Quincy (1772-1864), who was later to become Boston's second mayor and president of

Harvard. (Moreover he was a nephew of William Phillips.) With these men cooperated John Lowell (1769-1840), again an Andover and Harvard man (son of Judge John Lowell, who with the older William Phillips, the father of the lieutenant governor, had been a cofounder of the Massachusetts Bank), lawyer, pamphleteer, and man of public life.[42] And finally there should be mentioned among the rest Richard Sullivan (1779-1861), Harvard bred Federalist politician and state senator (son of James Sullivan, the Massachusetts statesman who has been described as the "richest, ablest, and most powerful" of all the Democratic Republicans).[43] Richard was the son-in-law of Thomas Russell, associate of the older William Phillips when the Massachusetts Bank was set up in 1784. Thomas Russell has been discussed in another context,[44] but it may be mentioned here that he was also the brother-in-law of Judge John Lowell (the father), who was his executor. This biographical and genealogical detail shows what a closely-knit group it was that obtained the first savings-bank charter in America and helps to explain some of the distinctive features of Massachusetts savings banking down to Civil War times: these men stood so high in the esteem of their fellow citizens and were so powerful that it seemed unnecessary and was perhaps impossible to hold them down to strict regulations, a fact which was reflected in later savings bank charters to the detriment of Massachusetts savings banking.

This group, won over in or after a meeting of November 21, 1816, with additional friends, on December 5, 1816, submitted the following petition to the Massachusetts legislature:[45]

Humbly represent the subscribers, citizens of the town of Boston, that in their opinion an Institution, by which all classes of the community may be encouraged to the practice of frugality, and especially industrious mechanics, either journeymen or masters, seamen, laborers, and men of small capital, widows, and others, may receive from their savings of wages or profits, regularly deposited and systematically invested in public stocks or otherwise, a profit proportional to the success of the institution and prosperity of the country, is highly desirable: - that similar benevolent institutions have been eminently successful in other countries, and are now contemplated in Philadelphia and New York; - that they do not expect or desire any benefit or profit to themselves, other than what is enjoyed by every individual in the community, from the success of such a design; - that they are willing to devote a part of their time, without reward, to the management of such a charity, and give the profits of the establishment in due proportion to the depositors; - that they desire not to have the authority, but only as above supposed, to receive deposits, in sums as small as one dollar, and to divide among the depositors, the profits arising from these funds, invested in the most secure stocks, or from loans; and to ensure more effectually these useful ends, they pray that they may be incorporated into a company by the name of "The Provident Institution for Savings in the Town of Boston;" with such immunities, restrictions, rights and privileges, and duties, as to your Honors may seem meet - and as in duty bound will ever pray.

[Signed.]

WILLIAM PHILLIPS,
JOHN PHILLIPS,
JOHN LOWELL,
RICHARD SULLIVAN,
JAMES SAVAGE,
Dec. 5, 1816.   JOSIAH QUINCY, and others.

Only three weeks after the decision to set up a savings bank in Boston and within two weeks of the date of the application, the Provident Institution for Savings in the Town of Boston came into legal existence. But then the trouble started.[46] While the promotors of the New York and Philadelphia savings banks had first done the thinking and then taken action, the Bostonians acted first and began thinking secondly. They had been swayed by the enthusiasm of James Savage who, according to his own confession, had read only half of the broadside of the London savings bank before deciding to promote one in Boston. His original proposals were probably immature. Consequently while the New York and Philadelphia merchants who were back of their respective and well-thought-out schemes clung to them steadily and tenaciously with considerable personal sacrifices of time and effort, the Boston backers were blowing hot, blowing cold, and almost blowing out. When at last they

started thinking they hit on a problem which had already been clearly seen in England. When the deposits in a savings bank were invested in funded securities and at the same time the depositors were free to withdraw them at any time, difficulties could easily arise. In England several solutions had been found for the problem, and in the literature which was at that very moment on Condy Raguet's desk they were described in detail.[47] The Philadelphia gentlemen, in fact, worked out a very simple method of excluding the personal liability of the managers. In Boston the matter was brought to a head in a meeting of the trustees on December 24, 1816. At that meeting some of them, for instance, John Phillips and Josiah Quincy, doubted the feasibility of opening the bank with the original by-laws (adopted on December 18) and a committee was appointed to seek a remedy. The plan reported on December 31, however, was so awkward and complicated that, fortunately for the institution, it was not adopted. It would have excluded all risk, but could not have been understood by the simple minds for whose benefit the institution had been created; it would not have inspired confidence and would probably have led to failure.

There was still another problem. The political and social leaders who were responsible for chartering the Boston Provident Institution wanted to do good. They were perfectly willing to set up their brain-child in the world, but were much too busy and engrossed in their own interests to nurse it; therefore, nurses had to be found. Savage was obviously willing to do the actual work and on December 20, 1816 he became the "clerk" of the bank.[48] But since he was a lawyer and not a businessman, and a whimsical man besides, it was obviously considered necessary to have him supervised by a "treasurer." In the above-mentioned meeting, heated discussions took place about the treasurer's position which was not to draw any emolument, and the first man chosen for the position declined.

Regardless of these difficulties the bank opened for business after an agreement was reached in February, 1817. Its character can be deduced from a broadside[49] to the public dated February 19, 1817 (the day of the opening), and the arrangement can actually be found embodied in the

by-laws as printed in 1818. In that broadside prospective investors were informed
that they would be allowed to withdraw
their deposits on four specified dates per
year on one week's notice, a timid regulation which, of course, destroyed much of
the value of the institution. (What could
a poor fellow do when he needed his few
dollars between two withdrawal dates?)
None of the other early savings banks had
contemplated any such limitations. Another
(complementary) feature of the compromise
which might be inferred did not find expression in writing. The ambitious investment plans embodied in the original by-
laws were dropped altogether. The deposits
of the customers were not invested at all,
but redeposited on interest with commercial
banks so that no difficulties from withdrawals could arise. Whether this policy
was part of the compromise, whether it was
copied from the investment policy of the
Scotch savings banks, or whether it was
due to timidity on the part of the trustees are open questions. Be that as it
may, a precedent was thus established which
was soon to determine the character of
Massachusetts savings banking for decades
to come and which was to gain great economic importance.

II

In the first section of this chapter attention has been focused on the men
who were instrumental in setting up the
first savings banks in this country. In
the following section they will be shown
again as members of social groups. The
Provident Institution for Savings in the
Town of Boston has been described previously as the work of a ruling aristocratic
group: its incorporators included, besides
the lieutenant governor and the United
States marshal, two judges, four lawyers,
three clergymen, thirty-two merchants and
tradesmen, and five mechanics.[50]   It is
not possible to make an equal breakdown of
the incorporators of the New York Bank for
Savings, but a sociological analysis of the
first board of trustees (including the
president and the three vice-presidents)
is possible. This board was made up of
fifteen merchants (including two tradesmen),
four members of the legal profession, five
craftsmen (including two shipbuilders, who
were rather industrialists), one journalist,

one physician, one gentleman of leisure
(Matthew Clarkson), and one unknown. Although this board represented the New York
upper classes it was not as aristocratic
as the clique which was behind the Boston
institution. Of these New Yorkers at least
five were connected with commercial banks
(the Bank of America, the Bank of New York,
the Mechanics Bank) thus corresponding to
the representatives of the Massachusetts
Bank and the Manufacturer's and Mechanic's
Bank who were so conspicuous among the savings bank founders in Boston. Regarding
Philadelphia, it is known only that the
founders of the Saving Fund Society were
leaders in the city's commercial, professional, and social life; while the Baltimore
Savings Bank was the work of mercantile,
religious, and educational leaders, the
latter playing little part elsewhere.[51]

Not all, not even the majority, of
those who founded the earliest savings banks
in America were philanthropists. The majority, in fact, consisted of level-headed
businessmen and men in public life who
could see advantages in helping the poor to
help themselves and in fitting them better
into a social order in the soundness of
which they, of course, believed. Thus the
burden of poor relief would be reduced.
The latter argument weighed heavily, for
instance, with De Witt Clinton, a fact
which may indicate familiarity with contemporary English thought on the subject. But
the philanthropic element, Christian in
character, was strong and even conspicuous
everywhere except in Philadelphia. It was
represented in New York by Quakers such as
Eddy and Griscom, by John Murray, Eddy's
friend, and last but not least by John
Pintard. In his case the philanthropic
background of his actions is evident from
the Bible verse which he had framed and
hung over his desk in the savings bank:
"Blessed is he that considereth the poor
and needy...."[52] In Boston the philanthropic element was represented by William
Phillips and several ministers, among whom
was William Ellery Channing (who, incidentally, was a classmate of Richard Sullivan
before mentioned). There is also a tradition in the Boston savings bank that Boston's
first catholic bishop, de Cheverus (1768-
1836), took an interest in getting the venture started. In Baltimore, finally, the
leading Episcopalian clergyman, later
Bishop Kemp (1764-1827), took an active

interest in the establishment of its first savings bank.[53]

When the founders of the earliest savings banks set out to elect the first presidents they were guided by the same principles which prompted contemporary bank boards in making their selections. They chose men who possessed the confidence of their fellow citizens and therefore seemed to be fit to execute a trust. Among men of that type bank presidents were preferred. As early as 1816 the New York founders elected William Bayard (1761-1826), the merchant prince and president of the Bank of America; and he actually became president when the Bank for Saving was finally established in 1819. In Philadelphia his remote cousin, Andrew Bayard (1761-1832),[54] president of the Commercial Bank of Pennsylvania, was the choice; while in Boston William Phillips, president of the Massachusetts Bank, accepted the appointment. There is no doubt that business considerations influenced neither the choice nor its acceptance, but the precedent thus established was soon to gain importance for business, as will be shown later.[55]

III

The pioneer savings banks of Philadelphia, Boston, and New York had hardly come into existence (they opened for business in this sequence) when they typically became in their respective sections of the country centers of influence and patterns on which other savings banks were modeled. The second crop of savings banks consisted of those in Baltimore, Salem, Hartford, Newport, Rhode Island, Providence, and Albany, which opened for business in this sequence prior to 1821. Some even overtook that of New York, but they were not achievements comparable with those in the three pioneer cities for they no longer transferred under the influence of original sources a new type of institution from the old continent to the new. Some of them, especially those of Salem and Albany, were simply copies of the ones in Boston and New York, respectively.[56]

Among this second crop of savings banks the Baltimore Savings Bank is noteworthy as the first one set up under the influence of preceding actions in this country. Two lines of influence crossed each other here. The first one emanated from Philadelphia.[57] On the same day (December 16, 1816) on which the Articles of Association of the Philadelphia Saving Fund Society were published in Philadelphia they were also printed in the American and Commercial Daily Advertiser in Baltimore. Immediately interest in the establishment of a savings bank in Baltimore was awakened, but nothing came of it. Action was taken, however, in January 1818. At a public meeting it was decided to establish a "provident bank," and a committee was appointed to draft a constitution, which was, in fact, modeled closely on the Philadelphia Articles of Association, without going so far as merely to copy them.[58] The policy of going into business without waiting for incorporation also followed that of Philadelphia. However, when it came to drawing up the charter, that of the Boston Provident Institution for Savings was consulted and exercised some influence. As a type, the short Baltimore charter leaving almost all important matters to be settled in the by-laws at the discretion of the directors is much nearer the Boston charter than it is to that of Philadelphia, and incidentally the Boston investment policy was also adopted in Baltimore for some time.[59]

Once this second crop of savings banks had come into being the development took a strange turn. While the banks in New York and Boston and those modeled on them remained sources of influence in their sections of the country, those at Philadelphia and Baltimore were not copied in their regions for decades to come, a fact for which this author finds no explanation. The pioneer savings banks as well as those of the second "generation" were bound to invite imitation by their mere existence. They "led the way and inspired confidence," as Pintard had it.[60] In addition, at least some of the promotors personally became influence-carriers, as Henry Duncan had been in Britain throughout the 1810's. This is true of Thomas Eddy who as early as January 15, 1819 recommended in a letter a "Farmers' Saving Fund."[61] It is equally true of John Pintard. In 1825 he met and corresponded with New Orleans people who intended to set up a savings bank in that city. Just as New York had onne received the plan of the London savings bank, so now (in 1827) "documents" of the New York Bank for Savings were forwarded to

Louisiana, although they probably arrived too late to be of influence. More than that, Pintard and the other trustees of the New York Bank for Savings in 1829 backed the promotion of the Seamen's Bank for Savings in the same city.[62] The idea behind this promotion was that since the New York Bank for Savings was so far from the port, one nearer the river would more easily induce the sailors to deposit a share of their earnings. Consequently the trustees of the Bank for Savings "approbated" the project in order that it could not be objected to as a rival institution. Pintard himself became a trustee of the new savings bank, while Najah Taylor, another founder and trustee of the Bank for Savings, became the first president of the new bank.[63]

IV

A comparison of the charters of the five earliest American savings banks[64] is interesting because of their similarities as well as their differences. Basically, of course, they were all very similar, but those of New York and Philadelphia represent one group and those of Boston, Salem, and Baltimore, a second.

It has been stated that the American pioneer savings banks, those in New York, Philadelphia, and Boston were modeled on English institutions, a fact which had important implications, for some essential differences in their charters can be explained as the result of their different ancestries. To be sure, none of them copied the Rules and Regulations of the very first modern British savings bank, those of Henry Duncan's Dumfries Parish Bank Friendly Society of 1810, although these were known at least in Philadelphia.[65] All three of them followed later ones which, depending on the former, nevertheless marked progress by simplifying Duncan's very complicated scheme, while on the other hand replacing a democratic by a paternalistic administration. These early British savings banks, launched between 1810 and 1816, had developed the original scheme in two different directions, which were originally represented by the (English) Provident Institution of Bath[66] and the (Scottish) Edinburgh Savings Bank. The former was the model of the Provident Institution for Savings established in the Western Part of

the Metropolis which, as described above, was back of the New York and Boston institutions. The latter, on the other hand, influenced the Southampton Saving Fund on which the Philadelphia Saving Fund Society was patterned. It was not accidental that the institution in Philadelphia was styled Philadelphia Saving (sic!) Fund Society while that in Boston was called the Provident Institution of Savings for the Town of Boston.

At that time, the 1810's, one distinguished in Britain between savings banks and provident institutions for savings, the former type belonging rather to Scotland,[67] the latter to England. This distinction, which was not a very clear-cut one, was known in America, as can be seen from an article in the (Boston) Christian Disciple, of December 1816.[68] As a matter of fact, it was impossible for it to have been clear-cut, for even the British savings banks were still in an experimental stage and were, therefore, developing and adopting features without attaining as yet, anything like standardization. On the whole one can thus characterize the two types: the Scottish savings banks put the deposits which they received out on interest with commercial banks. In England such redepositing was not feasible because of the different character and policy of her commercial banks. Consequently the deposits made with her provident institutions were funded in government securities. The latter policy was taken over in New York and Philadelphia, while the Massachusetts savings banks and, during its first years, that of Baltimore (under Massachusetts influence) adopted the same system as the Scottish savings banks, although it is not certain that this was done consciously. Other differences between the two types consisted in whether or not individual deposits were unlimited, whether the interest was to be fixed and surplus earnings to be distributed as extra dividends once in so many years or whether all earnings were to be distributed during the year in which they accrued. These various features, as will be seen, can also be found in the earliest American savings banks which, like their British models, were eclectic in drawing up their charters and by-laws.[69]

With these essentials in mind, one is able to take an interest in and to understand a comparison of the New York,

Philadelphia, Boston, Salem, and Baltimore charters.

The similarity between the New York and Philadelphia charters is striking. Both, in contrast to the others, contain details for which one would consult by-laws rather then charters.[70] Both banks were administered by boards consisting of the whole body of self-perpetuating incorporators who in New York were called "trustees," in Philadelphia "managers."[71] In New York they elected the president and three vice presidents; in Philadelphia only a president. In both charters vacancies on the board were to be filled by ballot of the remaining trustees (managers), a clause which was derived from British practice. (Incidentally the New York organization was set up more formally than that in Philadelphia.) Trustees or managers were forbidden to receive emoluments in line with stipulations in the models.

The two Massachusetts charters and the Baltimore charter which was influenced by the Boston one, as mentioned previously, differed from the New York and Philadelphia charters with regard to the administrative set-up. Both envisaged an unlimited number of "members as distinct from the administrators. Additional or new members to replace withdrawing ones were, in the case of Boston, elected by the annual meeting of the members, while in Baltimore they were elected either by the directors or by a majority of members attending any meeting. These members corresponded to the stockholders of a corporation, except that they did not have any pecuniary interest in their concern. In Boston, as set forth in the by-laws, they elected one president, twelve vice-presidents, and twenty-four "other" trustees (later twenty-five), while in Baltimore they elected, according to the charter, twenty-five directors (one of whom was to become president). These officers, if you please, or a quorum thereof, were to administer their banks as did the twenty-five Philadelphia managers or the twenty-four New York trustees (plus one president and three vice-presidents). To stress the essential difference: in New York and Philadelphia a comparatively small number of incorporators acted at the same time as administrators of their respective institutions, while in Boston and Baltimore an unlimited number of members elected the administrations.

The latter form of organization was soon to be taken over by the early savings banks in other states, as, for instance, Connecticut and Rhode Island.[72]

As to the business proper, all the early banks under investigation took on deposit only full dollars or multiples thereof, a regulation copied from the corresponding British practice; none of the five would pay interest on deposits smaller than five dollars nor for part of calendar months, clauses which again were adapted from British models.[73] However, while, according to section 2 of the New York charter, deposits had to be returned on request, the Philadelphia Saving Fund Society was bound by its charter to return them only after two weeks' notice, and no sums of less than five dollars could be taken out except to close the account (section 2, article 4). In contrast, Massachusetts and Maryland left it to the administrators of their pioneer savings banks to make the rules for withdrawals. In its original by-laws the Boston bank permitted immediate withdrawals, while the Savings Bank of Baltimore required notice. As early as 1818 the latter abandoned this requirement,[74] while Boston changed its original rule and permitted withdrawals only on specified days as described above.

It is surprising that, both in New York and Philadelphia, such an important matter as that of investments was not regulated in the bodies of the charters. Investment policy was alluded to in the preambles, a dangerous procedure since it made doubtful whether or not the passages in question were binding without any counterparts in the enacting clauses.[75] According to the preamble of the New York charter of the Bank for Savings, the Society for the Prevention of Pauperism had petitioned an incorporation "for the laudable purpose of encouraging in the community habits of industry and economy by receiving and vesting in government securities 'or stock created and issued under and by virtue of any law of the United States or of this state and no other way'" the savings of tradesmen, mechanics, etc.[76] In the body of the charter (in sections 1 and 2) the institution was forbidden to issue notes, to make discounts, or to transact any business which was that of commercial banks, other than that specified in the charter, and nobody connected with the

administration of the Bank for Savings was
entitled to borrow from it. (The charter
of the Savings Bank of Baltimore similarly
forbade in section 2 the issue of bank
notes and loans to directors.) As early
as 1820 the New York Bank for Savings,
recognizing the preamble as binding, petitioned for permission to invest also in
loans to the City of New York and in loans
on real estate. Regardless of the endorsement of Governor Clinton permission for
real estate loans was refused; but the bank
was expressly allowed to invest in government securities and to loan to the City of
New York.[77] It is possible that in its
application of 1820 the Bank for Savings
was guided by the example of the Philadelphia Saving Fund Society (although the
reason for the application was the high
price of stock);[78] the charter of the latter savings bank refers in the preamble to
the Saving Fund Society as having existed
for some time "for the sole purpose of
receiving and investing in public stock
or substantial security on real estate"
the savings of tradesmen, mechanics, etc.

In contrast to the New York and
Philadelphia charters, those of the early
Massachusetts and Maryland savings banks
embody some regulation of investment policy
in the enacting clauses, their charters
having no preambles. However, the Massachusetts clauses are the equivalent of no
regulation, for the deposits, according to
section 3 of the charter of the Provident
Institution for Savings in the Town of
Boston, were "to be used and improved to
the best advantage." Thus the promise regarding investments, made in the application for the charter,[79] was not upheld in
the charter itself. The range of investments envisaged in section 7 of the original by-laws was consequently very wide:
There were contemplated investments in
stock of the United States and of the
State of Massachusetts, stock of Boston
banks and of the national bank, and private securities; but it was expressly stated that no trustee or officer could be a
borrower. For years to come, however,
these clauses were not put into effect, as
mentioned before. The Savings Bank of
Baltimore, finally, was limited to investment in public stock and other securities,
whatever this may have meant. To sum up:
both the New York and Philadelphia charters

envisaged a reasonable limitation of investments, but by putting the clauses into the
preambles they acted unwisely, although in
the case of the New York Bank for Savings
the mistake was quickly remedied by additional legislation. In contrast, the
Massachusetts and Maryland charters "regulated" the investment policy of their
earliest savings banks, but in a wholly inadequate way.

There is one remarkable difference
between the New York and Philadelphia charters which is due to the fact that they
followed different models. In line with
the London pattern the New York Bank for
Savings was to "regulate the rate of interest to be allowed to the depositors so
that they shall receive a rateable proportion of all the profits" after deduction
of the expenses. In Philadelphia such procedure was considered unwise and a fixed
interest rate (4 8/10%) was preferred in
line with the Southampton model.[80] This
regulation necessitated an interest rate
below what was warranted by the anticipated
earnings so that a surplus had to be distributed every so often. Triennial distribution was contemplated in the Philadelphia
articles of association, but not embodied
in the charter. The Baltimore charter
under the influence of the Philadelphia
articles of association adopted this rule,
while, in contrast to Philadelphia, it did
not establish a fixed interest rate in the
charter but left that determination to the
board. As to the distribution of profits,
the wording of the two Massachusetts charters seems to align them with that of New
York, but in the original by-laws "as an
experiment" the Boston institution adopted
the Philadelphia pattern. Four per cent
interest was set for all deposits above
five dollars which were in the bank for at
least three months. However, at the end
of every five years an extra dividend was
to be distributed out of all profits which
had accrued within that period, to those
who had owned deposits for at least one
year preceding the given date. The extra
dividend was to be made pro rata to the
amount of such deposits and the length of
time during which they had remained in the
bank.[81] However these clauses were never
put into effect. They were changed before
the bank opened for business and replaced
by one which ruled that extra profits

would be paid to those who kept deposits
for full five years. This precedent was
soon widely adopted by Massachusetts savings banks and led to injustice and many
crises. The original by-laws also promised that the annual interest rate would
be raised as soon as experience permitted,
and actually from January 1820 to January
1822 regular dividends of five per cent
per year were distributed.[82]

Before leaving the discussion of
the charters, some minor points should be
mentioned. The New York and Philadelphia
institutions in contrast to those of
Massachusetts and Maryland were subject to
some sort of public control. The Philadelphia charter was unique among the early
ones in that, through the action of legislators, the maximum that could be deposited by any one person was set and the total
of deposits which the bank was entitled
to take was limited. The Provident Institution for Savings in the Town of Boston
voluntarily adopted the former type of
limitations in its by-laws.[83] They were
to be taken over soon in the State of New
York and were later widely adopted all
over America in charters and general acts,
as in English law also.

Thus from the beginning the
American savings banks, although essentially copies of the British, assumed some distinct features, in consequences whereof
the history of savings banks in the two
countries became different. While in
Britain many early savings banks were
branch banks, those in America had no
branches. Furthermore, while the British
pioneer savings banks were set up as voluntary associations, the American institutions were from the start chartered corporations. Thus while in England savings
banks could be regulated by a general law
as early as 1817, in America they were to
carry on for years under individual charters. These charters were not even standardized within the various states, so
that in Massachusetts and New York for many
decades, for instance, savings banks existing side by side had differing rights
and obligations because of the fancy of
the legislators, the pressure brought to
bear on the latter by incorporators, and
the period in which they had been chartered; for of course, the thinking about
savings banks developed over the years.

Furthermore, while in England savings banks
under the law of 1817 were restricted to
investment in government securities, in
America savings banks for years were comparatively free to choose among numerous
investment opportunities. Thus the
American savings banks, as will be described later, were, during the periods
under investigation in this chapter (second
and third), in danger of becoming mere
business enterprises trading on the savings
of the poor, an aberration from their true
purpose and from the spirit in which they
were founded.

V

The spirit[84] in which the first savings banks were brought into being persisted for a number of years. It was a blend
of paternalism and the tenets of Poor
Richard. Paternalism was evidenced, for
instance, in the preambles of the New York
and Philadelphia charters discussed previously, in the application of the Boston
promoters reprinted above, in the first
report of 1820 of the New York Bank for
Savings, and in numerous remarks of John
Pintard when writing on his activities.
It can be seen from the first circular of
1818 of the Baltimore Savings Bank in which
ministers, teachers, heads of families,
masters of vessels, master mechanics, and
the "Friend of the Widow" were invited to
take an interest in promoting and recommending the purpose of the institution.[85]
Finally it permeated the Documents relative
to Savings Banks of 1819, the earliest collection of American material on the subject, compiled for the purpose of promoting
such an institution in New York. The other
component of the spirit in which the earliest savings banks were set up and run is
just as evident: The moral influence of
savings was stressed repeatedly, as, for
instance, in the Documents relative to
Savings Banks (page 4) or in the first report of 1820 of the New York Bank for
Savings which seems to have been written
by John Pintard.[86] Quoting from Benjamin
Franklin was common: the advertising
pamphlet of 1817 of the Philadelphia Saving
Fund Society quoted Poor Richard at great
length and the first circular of the
Baltimore Savings Bank above-mentioned
cited Franklin "on the subject of saving."

Finally, the New York Bank for Savings distributed in 1826 a thousand copies of Poor Richard's Almanac.[87]

The paternalistic and philanthropic spirit in which the earliest savings banks were founded and the type of people to which they catered explain why it became a basic principle in mutual savings banks (in contrast to the much later credit unions) that the saver himself had no voice in the administration of his savings. This spirit was furthermore reflected in the attitude of the founders and trustees toward their own and other savings banks. They were imbued with the feeling of responsibility toward their depositors. This feeling found expression, for instance, in the opposition of certain Boston trustees to the opening of the Boston institution under by-laws which might result in losses; or in Pintard's letters. In one of these he commented on the timidity of his fellow trustees who "trembled" for their responsibility.[88] In regard to other savings banks, every new one was welcomed. Pintard "rejoiced" at the opening of the Greenwich Savings Bank in New York and wanted to have similar institutions brought near prospective depositors just as churches were to be brought near believers. The idea of competition between savings banks was totally alien to him. Thus the trustees of the Bank for Savings, as described before, helped in founding the Seamen's Savings Bank of New York, and Pintard considered the former the "mother bank."[89] But already in his lifetime this attitude was changing, and competition entered the field of savings banking.

The spirit described before as typical of early savings banks was reflected as a matter of fact, in their administrations also. Their objective was to afford security and interest to the savings of the lower classes, as expressed in both the New York and Philadelphia charters, while their organization was closely modeled on contemporary bank administration. The opening of the early savings banks like that of commercial banks of the same period was prepared by committees of the incorporators. In Boston, for instance, we find a committee to secure and furnish offices, another to provide books, and a third to draw up a scheme of office

regulations.[90] In New York, disregarding the committees set up in connection with the abortive plan of 1816,[91] the following committees were appointed in 1819: a committee to draft an address to the public, one to devise the mode of operations, one to provide the account books, one to draft the by-laws and to devise the seal, one to seek a suitable banking room, and one to make the final arrangements with the "City Corporation" with respect to the place of business. Later in 1819 a committee was set up to draft the first annual report, of which committee Pintard was probably the decisive member.[92] In Philadelphia, finally, there were committees "to wait upon the President and Cashier of the Bank of the United States to request their acceptance of the situation of Trustees of the Institution;" to obtain books and stationery; to draft by-laws and to prepare and publish an address to the public; and, finally, a committee on elections.[93]

Once the savings banks were opened for business they were managed in one of the two ways in which contemporary commercial banks were also managed: that is to say, either by a rather independent officer, a treasurer, who corresponded to the bank cashier, or by committees of the trustees (managers). The former type of organization was set up in Boston[94] for reasons which have been stated previously. (The rotating attending committees of the Boston Provident Institution were merely supervisory, not managing, committees; they were intended to be investment committees at the same time, but there was no real investing done in the early years of that savings bank.) The other form of organization, management by committees of trustees, envisaged already in the New York plan of 1816 described above, was adopted in New York, Philadelphia, and Baltimore. Again in line with contemporary banking practice such committees were of two different types: they were either (rotating) attending committees which did the management job or special committees. Attending committees existed in New York, Philadelphia, and Baltimore where the twenty-four trustees were divided into twelve monthly committees.[95] By attending in rotation, all the trustees would become familiar with the business problems as well as with the human angle of their institution and would be able to gather important information. In New York, these attending committees worked pretty efficiently with the assistance of a few employees. As Pintard reported, they served two people per minute in 1827 and two and a half in 1830.[96] In Philadelphia, by contrast, the attending committees soon neglected their duties, so that the business was actually managed by a secretary-treasurer, similar to the Boston set-up.[97] He received a remuneration of two hundred and fifty dollars "for his services and the use of his office."[98] After 1833 the functions formerly performed by the "committee of the month" devolved on the president who from then on received a salary, a development paralleling that in contemporaneous commercial banks.

The second type of committees were special committees which possessed either standing status or were set up for the occasion. New York had a standing funding committee, a law committee, and a (probably standing) auditing committee.[99] Philadelphia set up standing Committees of Finance and of Accounts (the former was later called the Investment Committee, but later 1825 and 1846 the whole board in weekly meetings actually determined the investments). In Boston, finally, a "board of investment," consisting of one vice-president, three trustees, the treasurer, and the secretary, was established in 1820. To give examples of non-standing special committees there may be mentioned the one of the Philadelphia Saving Fund Society to draft an act of incorporation or the one of 1825 of the Boston savings bank set up to apply to the General Court for permission to subscribe to new issues of bank stock.[100] Other such committees were appointed to revise the methods of doing business, to purchase sites, or to supervise the erection of buildings.

With the rise of savings banks from semi-charitable institutions to business enterprises the character of savings-bank administration was bound to change. Trustees and managers moved into the position of policy-making bank boards and the actual administration, as in the contemporaneous commercial banks and also in British savings banks, became the work of a salaried staff, a development which began in America as early as the 1830's.

VI

In contrast to the rapid development of the British savings banks immediately after their inception, savings banks developed but slowly in this country during the first twenty years. By 1835 deposits in all of them amounted only to about $7,000,000.[101] But progress differed among the various institutions and this difference reflected to a large extent the diverse character of leadership in the various enterprises.

No other of these institutions had a leader comparable to John Pintard who determined the fate of the New York Bank for Savings down to the 1830's. His letters give the most interesting insight into his work and the spirit in which it was carried on. In 1819 he considered himself an "oarsman" in the savings bank; in 1820 he called it his "everlasting spinning wheel;" in 1825 he was almost "prostrated" by his duties in his office and the institution; in 1830 he reported that he was "so linked" with the savings bank that his attendance was indispensable; in 1831 he was "over head and ears in savings bank duty" which increased rather than diminished; and in 1833 he spoke of the savings bank as the "child of his old age" which was so near to his heart.[102] Having headed the attending committee for the first month he attended the bank regularly and scrupulously all those years, often taking the turn of a fellow trustee who was unable to do so. Besides his activities on other committees he was the determining member of the decisive funding (investment) committee for more than a decade and wrote its reports to the board.[103] (He seems also to have drafted many of the reports of the Bank for Savings to the legislature.) Scoville did a disservice to Pintard when he claimed that the latter withdrew from the administration of the institution once it was firmly established, as was his habit. This was indeed his habit,[104] but for the savings bank he made an exception. As to the motive behind Pintard's exertions and actions which led to the building of a million-dollar enterprise (for such was the Bank for Savings even before Pintard died), he himself opened his heart when he wrote in June 1826: "If no other I shall at least leave this [the New York Bank for Savings],

I hope, a monument of my useful existence,"[105] one of the most interesting
testimonies, known to this author, as to
the real incentives of business leaders in
the era of high capitalism.

While Pintard carried the burden
in the New York Bank for Savings, Savage
was the guiding spirit in the Boston
Provident Institution. Less clear is the
matter of leadership in the Philadelphia
Saving Fund Society. It is certain that
Condy Raguet who had been on the first
"acting committee" withdrew shortly thereafter because he left the city. On the
other hand, Thomas Hale, mentioned previously as one of the founders, was for
about a decade at the helm of the Committee
of Investment, became president, and was
succeeded in this position by the first
salaried president of the institution.
These facts permit the conclusion that
Hale together with the secretary-treasurer,
George Billington, carried the load during
the first one and a half decades.

The personalities of these men and
especially Pintard's, together with their
devotion, were reflected in the rise of
their respective enterprises. Pintard and
his friends set up the Bank for Savings in
the expectation that $1000 would be depos-
ited every week, or $52,000 during the
first year. They hoped that they would
reach the million dollar mark after seven
years. In fact, instead of the hoped for
$1000, $2,807 was actually deposited on
the day of opening, the deposits amounted
to $153,000 after only six months, and the
half million mark was reached after only
eighteen months. Ten years later the bank
had two million and in another two years
two and a half million dollar deposits;[106]
twenty-five thousand accounts had been
opened in all up to 1830. Progress in
Boston and Philadelphia could not keep this
pace. In the former city the deposits
amounted after one year to about $67,600,
in itself not a bad figure, but after ten
years they were no higher than $737,000.
There was no cumulative progress from year
to year. In Philadelphia, finally, growth
under the articles of association had been
only very moderate. Not even $9,000 were
deposited during the first year and when
the funds were transferred to the corporation on March 31, 1819, i.e., after more
than two years, they amounted to but
$45,000. But from then on greater strides

were taken: as early as 1824 and 1828 the
charter limitations on the total of deposits
($300,000 and $600,000, respectively) had
to be raised to reach $1,100,000 in the
latter year, and as early as 1833 a further
rise to $1,500,000 was necessary.[107] But
then progress slackened and came to reflect
the critical conditions in the Philadelphia
of the 1840's. Not before the 1850's was
the two million dollar mark reached in the
latter city. Thus in Philadelphia, just
as earlier in New York, savings banks had
begun to become an "index of the prosperity
or distress of the working class," as
Pintard expressed it in 1832.[108]

VII

The founders and initial trustees
of the early savings banks had a number of
difficult business problems to face. The
very first was: how to earn the overhead
costs until the deposits had reached a certain point.[109] For this purpose the founders and trustees everywhere seem to have
made deposits for themselves, for their
children or grandchildren and domestics,
actions which also served to instil confidence in this unknown type of enterprise.
Such deposits were very useful at first,
but later became the source of difficulties.
In Philadelphia, as described above, the
total of deposits was limited by law and
consequently at a relatively early moment
(1823) the Saving Fund Society had to request certain depositors to withdraw their
funds. In New York similar action had to
be taken for lack of adequate investment
opportunities, although Pintard opposed the
measure. Another method for covering overhead expenses was for the founders and
trustees to contribute a fund, as was the
practice in the early British savings banks
also.[110] This was the method adopted in
Philadelphia. And finally there was the
possibility of the trustees doing even low
type clerical work gratuitously: the New
York trustees even performed the job of
porter themselves.[111]

The second problem which soon came
up was whether or not to limit the range of
depositors and, if so, by what criteria.
The savings bank was originally conceived
as a means of helping the poor, as clearly
expressed, for instance, in the preambles
of the New York Bank for Savings and the
Philadelphia Saving Fund Society. Section

I of the Boston by-laws, on the other hand, did not draw such a narrow line, but established as the object of the institution the providing of a safe and profitable mode of enabling "industrious persons of all descriptions" to invest their savings in a manner which afforded profit and security. If one wanted to follow the former line of thinking, limitation of individual deposits offered itself as a feasible method to retain the distinctive character of savings banks.[112] This problem had also to be met in Britain. In that country the various pioneer savings banks followed differing policies. The bank in Edinburgh limited individual deposits to £10; that in Bath knew no limitation whatsoever; while, finally the one in Southampton set a limit of £25, but permitted the trustees to extend the limit if they considered it desirable. Later, from 1817 on, British savings bank legislation is full of clauses limiting annual and total deposits of any one person.[113] The difference in attitude just described can be found in America too. The Philadelphia Saving Fund Society, as mentioned previously, alone of all early savings banks was bound by law to limit the deposit of any one individual to $500; but such limitation was dropped in 1824 in an amendment of the charter. In fact, it was convincingly shown at that time that any strict limitation of deposits was unsound from the social point of view. The Provident Institution for Savings in the Town of Boston, on the other hand, contemplated a limitation of individual deposits in its by-laws: when the amount of $1000 was reached the trustees had the right to request withdrawal. Finally, the trustees of the New York Bank for Savings considered $500 a reasonable limit, but regarded "more the character and circumstances of the depositor than the sum, making the most liberal construction in favor of ministers, widows, and orphans."[114] In 1831 the closing of all accounts exceeding $1000 was under consideration. In this connection a special interest policy was devised. The Bank for Savings differentiated by 1831 between large and small deposits, paying five per cent per annum on all deposits below and only four per cent on all deposits above $500.[115] By introducing this policy the bank gave a hint to large depositors that their funds were not welcomed. In addition to the limitation of

the total of any one account, the maximum that could be deposited at any one time or in any one year was subject for discussion. The same amendment to the charter of the Philadelphia Saving Fund Society that dropped the limitation for any one individual account enacted an annual limit of $200, while the Provident Institution for Savings in the Town of Boston voluntarily restricted any single deposit to $100 unless offered by seamen.

Another set of business problems for the savings banks resulted from the need for safety and liquidity. To guarantee the former, the Philadelphia Saving Fund Society as early as 1819 established a contingent fund,[116] while the New York Bank for Savings did not receive legal permission to do so before the 1830's.[117] Thereafter reserve funds became common features of New York savings banks. Massachusetts savings banks, however, were not permitted, even as late as 1860, to establish reserves. The second type of problems, on the other hand, was instinctively felt rather than clearly seen. Regardless of charter and by-law conditions, it was soon realized that to be useful savings banks had to return the deposits upon demand. Therefore limitations on withdrawals were quickly dropped, and, as a matter of fact, without any serious trouble. Savings banks developed so fast that recent, still uninvested deposits were always on hand to meet any possible demand.[118] That there was a real problem was not seen everywhere at the beginning. The original charter of the New York Bank for Savings, for instance, compelled the bank to invest all deposits, and it was doubtful whether it was permitted to use commercial banks even as temporary depositories. But it actually did so and its practice received legal sanction in the 1830's. Soon thereafter the problem was widely recognized as such and in the State of New York the requirement of an "available fund" was inserted in numerous savings bank charters. These "available funds," liquid reserves, were to be kept either as deposits with commercial banks or in the form of easily convertible loans. That New York savings banks thereby came to enter the call-loan market was an undesirable effect growing out of a reasonable regulation.

However, of all the problems with which early savings-bank trustees were faced none was as difficult as that of investments. It has been mentioned previously that two policies could be adopted. American savings banks could either redeposit their funds on interest with commercial banks or they could invest them in funded securities.[119] To the extent that they did the former they followed Scottish practice; to the extent that they did the latter they took over English savings bank policy. The Provident Institution for Savings of the Town of Boston in its early years and the Baltimore Savings Bank during its first months were representatives of the former policy, adopted for part of their funds by all Massachusetts savings banks, while the New York Bank for Savings and the Philadelphia Saving Fund Society at the beginning, exemplified the latter. This policy did not preclude, of course, the latter two institutions from using commercial banks as temporary depositories, and, in fact, the Mechanics Bank in New York and the Schuylkill, and later the Commercial Bank of Pennsylvania, served as such for the New York and Philadelphia savings banks, respectively.

The New York Saving Fund Society was distinguished by the admirable execution of its investment policy. In the very beginnings it bought securities in the open market. However, the unexpectedly quick development of the institution at an early moment, made it a power in the capital market and enabled it to bid on security issues as early as 1821. In so doing it was in a good competitive position. Its depositors were accustomed to a rate of interest below the current one and, as described before, it did not pay interest on the total of deposits, but only on deposits above five dollars which had been in the bank for a minimum time and within a certain period. Consequently the bank could afford to pay high premiums and make "bold" bids, as Pintard expressed it, in order to get a share in the then tight market of first-class securities.[120] The courageous policy of subscribing for new security issues was obviously the child of Pintard's brain and he had difficulties in getting it adopted by his fellow trustees. But finally he succeeded, and in June 1821 the Bank for Savings laid out a bid for the first time, namely for $200,000 six per

cent New York Canal Stock. The bank was not bold enough, however, and was outbid, and the securities went to an Albany bank from which the Bank for Savings attempted to buy a share. In 1826, anticipating receipts from the paying-off of a large sum of United States stock, it made an offer for a New York five per cent Canal Commissioners loan which it got at a premium of six per cent. Since this loan was subscribed in anticipation of an expected need, short term funds were borrowed from the Mechanics Bank, an example of the business-like and far-seeing way in which the concern was administered. In 1827 $100,000 six per cent Ohio Canal Stock was purchased and in 1829 $200,000 was loaned to the City of New York. When this latter loan was concluded the Bank for Savings had invested a total of about two million dollars in funded public securities. In 1830 further funds became available and we find the bank negotiating a loan of $150,000 Pennsylvania stock, a loan which was actually concluded. In the same year $66,000 New Orleans stock was purchased from an agent, but the bank had intended to buy as much as $200,000. Consequently a few months later it was again in the market taking up $100,000 six per cent Ohio stock at more than seventeen and a half per cent premium. In this case the funding committee once more anticipated a need and borrowed $50,000 from the Mechanics Bank to pay for the securities. In fact this bank loan must have been repaid very quickly, for about two months later, in January 1831, the Funding Committee successfully negotiated a purchase of $100,000 Alabama six per cent stock. Again, a year and a half later, the Bank for Savings had an uninvested balance of more than $100,000 with the Mechanics Bank. By that time, 1833, it became necessary to consummate a rather complicated transaction. $600,000 of New York Canal stock payable in 1837 and still having a nine per cent premium in the market was sold and the same amount reinvested in five per cent Pennsylvania stock redeemable in 1857. This transaction was the expression of continuous fear on the part of the trustees that not enough eligible securities would be available. The tight market in first-class securities during all these years hampered the development of savings banking, was sometimes rather embarrassing, and as far as the New York Bank for Savings was concerned was reflected in its interest policy and its attitude toward large deposits.

This situation of the capital market repeatedly forced the bank to apply to the legislature for a widening of the scope of permissible investment. The application of 1820, previously mentioned, for permission to loan on bonds and mortgages which was turned down finds its explanation in the lack of investment possibilities, and Pintard was bitter that the application was refused at that time.[121] Permission was given in 1830, however, after which time investment in bonds and mortgages became a permanent feature of New York savings banking. The scarcity of good investment opportunities, furthermore, helps one to understand why the regulations on investments embodied in New York savings bank charters became continuously broader between 1819 and 1860.

The investment policy of the Philadelphia Saving Fund Society[122] was very different from that of the New York Bank for Savings, a difference due at least partly to charter conditions. The Philadelphia savings bank was at liberty, according to section I of its charter, to choose any investment it saw fit, a latitude which that of New York did not possess. Although the articles of association had held the Philadelphia institution down to investment in public stock[123] and substantial security on real estate, and although the preamble of the charter implied at least a certain moral obligation to adhere to such limitation, its managers did not feel bound by these limitations in view of the wording of the enacting clauses. In 1817 the very first investment of the Philadelphia Saving Fund Society was one in United States stock, and soon holdings in Philadelphia city loan were added to its portfolio. Two years later the United States stock was sold in order to reinvest the proceeds in the latter type of securities. In the meantime, as early as 1818, i.e., even before the Society was incorporated, the original articles of association, permitting only investment in government securities and other substantial public stock, had been amended so as to permit real estate loans, and real estate loans were soon to play a large part in the investments of the institution. The procedure under which these loans were made was

for many years rather light-hearted. Funds were even loaned on second mortgages and to religious corporations on the security of their places of worship. Consequently real property had to be taken over in various cases and it is miraculous that no heavy losses were sustained before the latter types of investment were taken off the eligible list. By 1822 the board had authorized collateral loans which were restricted by 1825 to three-months loans on the basis of United States and City of Philadelphia stock and stock of banks in the city and county of Philadelphia. Prior to this restriction loans had been made on all sorts of collateral which today would be considered completely unfit as security for loans made from savings-bank deposits; and the lending on corporation stock, also fundamentally unsound for savings banks, was not abandoned before 1839.

The investment policy of the Baltimore Savings Bank was essentially similar to that of the Philadelphia Saving Fund Society, but the execution of the policy resulted in an investment portfolio of a different composition. As mentioned above, Baltimore started with a policy copied from its Boston model, but the redepositing of its funds with commercial banks was soon abandoned. In 1819 this type of investment, if it can be called investment at all, still amounted to 31.77 per cent of its funds, but later it became negligible and deposits with commercial banks were probably made for the same purposes as in New York and Philadelphia. However, in the early years of the Baltimore Savings Bank[124] collateral loans on the basis of bank stock were built up so that by 1827 they amounted to 83.08 per cent of all investments, while the rest was invested in United States, City of Baltimore, and bank stock. Real estate loans, on the other hand, were not made before the 1830's and did not attain an importance similar to that in Philadelphia. Collateral loans remained the backbone of the investments of the Baltimore Savings Bank down to Civil War times.

VIII

While the earliest savings banks were the work of high-minded men whose philanthropic and unimpeachable motives cannot be doubted, the same cannot be said about many of the institutions which were to follow. Savings banks quickly outgrew the comparatively narrow purpose of the founders, and business and politics entered the field. To a certain extent this development may have been the reaction to certain undesirable aspects of early savings banking. The very spirit in which it had been conceived proved not undangerous in the long run. During the period between its inception and its becoming an established fact in the economic set-up, especially after the original idealistic impulse had worn away, there originated in at least some of these institutions a spirit of "official arrogance," on the one hand, and of "timid servility" in recognition of favors bestowed, on the other.[125] Such mental attitudes did not fit into the American scene, all the less since the character of the depositors was undergoing a change. Instead of "indigent poor" whose meager savings the first institutions were meant to preserve and protect, the customers soon came more and more from the rank of industrious and thrifty workers. Consequently savings banks by and by relinquished their status of semi-charitable organizations. The road to rapid progress was opened and the total of deposits held in all American savings banks rose to about $43,000,000 in 1850 and to $150,000,000 in 1860.[126]

Business entered the field of savings banking in two different ways. In Pennsylvania and Maryland for decades to come no mutual savings banks were set up after the pioneer institutions had come into being, but business enterprises of the character of stock savings banks were founded. These cultivated interest-bearing deposits of small investors; and with capital and deposits thus obtained they carried on a more or less commercial banking business.[127] Under these circumstances James Mease repeated in a new setting his suggestion for establishing communal savings banks.[128] In New York and New England, on the other hand, mutual savings banks continued to dominate the field, but the spirit in which these newer mutual savings banks were set up and run was not comparable with the original one. In details the development was different in the various states in question and it seems useful to describe those in New York and Massachusetts.[129]

In Massachusetts, as has been mentioned before, the founders of the earliest savings banks were authorized in their charters to invest the accumulating deposits as they saw fit, but when they first redeposited them on interest with commercial banks of their choice, neither they nor the receiving banks can have realized that a new and important type of business relationship was thus initiated. Hardly a decade after these beginnings the tie between commercial and savings banking was becoming as important for Massachusetts as the combination of commercial banking and insurance had been around 1800. While the paying of interest on the deposits of savings banks was originally considered by bank boards as a more or less philanthropic act, it soon became a highly important procedure to make savings banks tenders of commercial banks and sources of capital for them. In numerous cases members of bank boards became founders and trustees of savings banks and members of their investment committees, and the office of cashier in a commercial bank and of treasurer in a savings bank was often held by the same person. The perfect freedom which the earliest Massachusetts savings banks possessed in the selection of investments taken in conjunction with the alliance between savings and commercial banking established as early as about 1820 led, after a little more than a decade, to the following distribution of investments: in 1834 the total investments of the Massachusetts savings banks amounted to about $3,400,000, out of which about $1,192,000 or 34 per cent was invested in bank stock, about $588,000 or 16 per cent in loans on bank stock, while $521,000 or 15 per cent was redeposited with commercial banks.[130] In other words, savings banks had become part and parcel of the Massachusetts banking system and powers therein, and the situation was similar, although not so pronounced, in Connecticut and Rhode Island which in establishing their savings banks had followed the Massachusetts model.[131] Savings banks in both states held investments in bank stock.

By that time (the 1830's) deposits in savings banks had become "so considerable that the Commonwealth [of Massachusetts] assumed a more immediate guardianship of them" and in the general savings bank act of 1834 prescribed definite methods of investment. The alliance between savings and commercial banking received legal sanction. (Consequently by 1860 seventy-two savings banks were located in the same rooms with commercial banks and managed by the same officers; and the Boston Provident Institution in 1856 owned fifty per cent of the capital of the Webster Bank and held a considerable interest in the Merchants.) Moreover, investments in public stocks and mortgages and collateral loans on the basis of the former were authorized. Finally, if it was not possible to invest all of their funds profitably as prescribed, savings banks were entitled to loan no more than one-fourth of their funds on personal security ("upon the credit of individual names"). It is a sad commentary on the spirit prevailing in Massachusetts savings banks in the 1840's and 1850's that these regulations, liberal as they were, were observed carefully only by a few institutions and that some, in violation of the law, ran more or less a commercial banking business. They went so far as to discount business paper and to deal in domestic exchange and to lend on business paper refused as unfit for discount by commercial banks. Some of the older savings banks which possessed charters dating back to before the passing of the general act of 1834 refused to abide by it. In line with the legal thinking of their day, but not with the spirit in which savings banking had been conceived, they insisted on the contract character of their charters. It is not surprising that under these circumstances by the middle of the century there was keen competition among Massachusetts savings banks and between her savings banks and "voluntary associations" which had sprung up in some of the manufacturing villages of the state to fulfill similar functions.

But the abuses did not end even here. It will be remembered that the first Massachusetts savings bank adopted a fixed interest rate with the proviso that profits accruing over and above that rate were to be distributed as an extra dividend every five years, a principle which was adopted generally by Massachusetts savings banks. Regular plus extra dividends soon proved so high that deposits in savings banks became an attractive investment for wealthy people. This was due to the fact that

extra dividends were paid only on those amounts which had been kept intact for the last five consecutive years prior to the date on which the extra dividend was declared and, of course, many of the savers could not comply with that condition. Wealthy people took advantage of this situation and deposited large amounts with savings banks in different names (thereby avoiding legal restrictions on individual deposits), and so pocketed the money earned with the savings of the poor who were unable to keep them intact for five years.[132]

The situation in New York differed in details but was similar in essentials. We find in the 1830's, 1840's, and 1850's the same overgrowth of business spirit in a field in which it should have been pruned, and the same competition among savings banks and between savings banks and competing outsiders, here represented by private bankers issuing interest-bearing transferable certificates of deposit. That the incorporation of new savings banks was justified only when the new one could be expected to collect savings which would not have been reached by other institutions, was completely forgotten; and the willingness of the legislature to charter new institutions, often enough for political reasons, to gratify the ambitions of individuals or their need for jobs for themselves or family members, contributed to the unsoundness of the set-up. Finally, we find in New York also too close an alliance between savings and commercial banks, although the methods of establishing that alliance were different because of the different investment policy. Investment in bank stock was an exception in New York; besides public securities, investments in bonds and mortgages, permitted at a time when good public securities were scarce, had become the backbone of New York savings-bank investments after 1831. But investment in corporate securities, as for instance in railroad stock, was permissible under some mid-century New York savings-bank charters. The improper alliance between commercial and savings banks was brought about in the following way: a sufficient number of trustees to form a quorum in a certain savings bank were at the same time directors of a commercial bank; or, trustees of a savings bank unwilling themselves to transact the business of the institution entrusted to their care, contracted with the board of a commercial bank to take over the actual administration of the savings bank, so that the latter became subordinate to the interests of the former; or, finally, trustees of certain savings banks were chiefly or wholly directors of certain commercial banks so that the savings banks in question became mere tenders of the commercial banks concerned. There were cases where this connection was unblushingly made known to the public by giving the savings bank the name of the commercial bank which controlled it.[133]

Thus within a period of barely fifty years American savings banks in the northern and middle Atlantic states experienced a development which the Eddys, Pintards, Raguets, and Savages could not have foreseen in their brightest dreams. Conceived as philanthropic institutions they had developed into enterprises of economic importance and powers in the capital and money markets. On the other hand, those men would not have been delighted by many of the features which American savings banking had acquired between 1830 and 1860, although the absence of bad failures and heavy losses would have gratified them. While the original purpose, keeping the savings of the poor, had undergone a change, the original spirit was not dead but found new expression to fit a new era. In the 1860's the savings bank was defined by one of the foremost experts in this field as "not merely a bank that pays interest on deposits, but as an institution in the hands of disinterested persons, receiving deposits for the purpose of investment in those securities which experience has demonstrated to be the most reliable and safe."[134]

INTRODUCTION

1. The words "capitalism" and "capitalistic" are used in this book in the sense of Werner Sombart's Der Moderne Kapitalismus.
2. In the same vein the author of a recent publication (using the term business leader synonymously with entrepreneur) has described him as "giving direction and unity" to the efforts of those who contribute to economic activities and as making such plans and decisions as "transform economic effort into particular goods and services." (Gordon, R. A., op. cit., 3).
3. The word "creative" is used to imply that these men are leaders on new ways, and thereby influence economic history.
4. The term "Geist" along with the term "Geistesgeschichte" will be used repeatedly in this book because there is no single English word which covers the specific phenomenon. The phenomenon has been seen and defined clearly by William James who, in "Great Men and their Environment" (op. cit., 191), distinguishes between two strata of the human mind, one which it "possesses in common with the brutes" and one which is "highest," "most characteristically human." For this higher stratum of the human mind, the possession of which distinguishes the human being from the animal, the word Geist is used in this book.
5. "Lauderdale's Oversaving Theory" in American Economic Review, XXXV (1945), 283.
6. Kessler, Harry Graf, Walther Rathenau, Sein Leben und Sein Werk (Berlin-Grunewald, 1928), 46.
7. For examples, see pp. 51, 96, and Chap. III, footnote 9.

Chapter I

FIRST PERIOD - GENERAL CHARACTERISTICS

1. Bullock, op. cit., 32. Land banks must be clearly distinguished from colonial loan offices.
2. An early quotation of this chapter can be found in the Pennsylvania debates of 1786 on the Bank of North America: "Several writers have treated on the subject of banking---one a writer of great repute, Mr. Smith, who treated on the wealth of nations" (Fitzsimmons). Carey, Debates, 106.
3. Reprinted under the title Principles of Banks. The quotation is taken from the Introduction to the edition of 1812.
3a. It is noteworthy that even Ricardo quoted Sir James Steuart: See "High Price of Bullion" in Ricardo, Works (edited by McCulloch), 274, 275, 279.
4. Essays in American Economic History (New York, 1944), 107 ff.
5. Gras, op. cit., 210
6. Thomas Willing, Letters and Papers, Introduction, 11.
7. Parts of the memorandum are reprinted by Konkle, op. cit., 96 ff.
8. P. 13 "The name of any man how great soever will not have much weight with me when I perceive that in any instance he has mistaken his subject." Professor Dorfman describing in his recent book the period following the end of the Revolutionary War remarks that all of the participants in the discussion of the great controversial economic issues seem to have known Sir James Steuart; (op. cit., I, 243, also 257).
9. Reported by W. Hamilton, printed by the Reporter, 18
10. III, 231.
11. Op. cit., 53, footnote.
12. Goddard, op. cit., 43.
13. See this author's Essays, 113 ff.
14. Steuart, Principles of Banks, 239.
15. Davis, Currency and Banking, II, 49, 50.
16. Steuart, op. cit., 188, 189.
17. Ibid., 242.
18. Ibid., 290, 186.
19. Davis, Currency and Banking, contains descriptions of earlier unsuccessful attempts to create money banks on this continent. F. C. James ("Bank of North America," 58, 59) refers to other examples. See also the same author's Money, Credit and Banking (3d. ed.), 173 ff.
20. This progress was probably due to Robert Morris's fear that it would be dangerous to base the bank on government securities because of lack of confidence. However, the passage in question in Morris's letter

to Hamilton is not clear. (Sparks, _Dip-lomatic Correspondence_, XI, 366).

21. A typical statement of young Hamilton to the effect is quoted below, see p. 29.

22. The charter of the Bank of Pennsylvania contained a preamble: Whereas the establishment of a bank "will promote the regular, permanent, and successful operation of the finances of this state and be productive of great benefit to trade and industry in general" (quoted from Biddle's speech in the _Debate in the House of Representatives of Pennsylvania...relative to the Bank of the United States_, 11). It probably follows the preamble to the charter of the First Bank of the United States: "A bank for the United States will be very conducive to the successful conducting of the national finances...and will be productive of considerable advantages to trade and industry in general." See also the preamble of the Providence Bank.

23. It is also evidenced by an institution peculiar to Rhode Island called "bank process," which was devised by the founders of the Providence Bank. When an obligation fell due to a bank and was not paid, the president or three directors after having served notice on the debtor, made an oath to that effect before the clerk of court. Thereupon the latter was required to enter judgment against the defendant and issue execution without trial. If the debtor denied the legality of the debt, however, he had all the privileges of a regular trial. (Stokes, _op. cit._, 264). A legal institution of this character is, of course, predicated on the conceptions of banks as public affairs, of punctuality as a virtue, needing special protection, and of bank directors as semi-public officials. See also, Davis, _Essays_, II, on the semi-official character of the Union Bank of Boston.

24. Lewis, _op. cit._, 61 ff.

25. Gras (_op cit._, 212 ff.) reprints the application. His comment is on pages 22 and 23.

26. Domett, _op. cit._, 33, 34. See also the applications of 1811 and 1812 for a bank in Worcester (Chase, _op. cit._, 9 ff.); the Memorial of March 1811 of the subscribers to the Bank of America (_Bank of America_, 105); the petition of 1814 for the Phoenix Bank in Hartford (Burpee, _op. cit._, 135 ff.).

27. Clarke and Hall, _op. cit._, 39, 40.

28. See below p. 91.

29. State of New York, _Messages of the Governors_, II, 700.

30. U.S. 23rd Congr., 2nd sess., _Senate Document 13_, 29, 36. In the 1830's Condy Raguet wrote: "Banks are private speculations intended for profit and they are not called upon by any consideration of public duty any more than individuals are." (_Financial Register_, II, 8.)

31. Gouge, _Journal of Banking_, 209.

32. See Dewey, _State Banking_, 33.

33. The Federal government participated in the Bank of North America, and First and Second Banks of the United States; Pennsylvania, in the Bank of Pennsylvania, in the Philadelphia Bank, and a few others; Massachusetts, in the Union and Boston Banks, etc. See also Davis, _Essays_, 107; Callender, _op. cit._, _passim_; Scroggs, _Banking Progress_, 88 ff; Holdsworth, _Empire_, I, 143.

34. Nevins, _op. cit._, 38. Soon thereafter it became the more or less general practice of the states to finance education by participation in banks or bank profits in one way or another. Muscalus has devoted a dissertation to the material (_op. cit._, _passim_, see especially the summary on pages 177 ff.), but it deals exclusively with facts and figures and does not investigate the motives and the philosophy back of this policy.

35. See p. 43. To give another example: the Philadelphia Bank applied for a charter in 1803 because banks were supposed to be "very powerful instruments of the public good" and fit objects of "legislative favor and protection." In the case of this bank the specific advantages were to be: small shares so that even less opulent citizens could become stockholders, and a particular lending policy. The bank promised to deal with a group of customers which was not "generally admitted to the benefits of banks." See _The Philadelphia National Bank_, 31. As to country banking see, for instance, the preamble to the charter of the Washington Bank, Westerly, Rhode Island (1800) in Stokes, _op. cit._, 273.

36. This idea was clearly expressed in Peletiah Webster's _Essay on Credit_ of 1786, 12, 17. When in 1792 the Hartford Bank was to be chartered it was recommended in a newspaper article because it would do away with barter, "the father of fraud and the instrument of knavery." The applicants promised that the bank would facilitate commercial operations limited by the smallness of commercial capitals, that it would bring into operation money not used in commerce

(Hamilton's idea), and that it would
"combine mercantile capital and exertion."
(Woodward, op. cit., 14 ff.)

37. U.S. 23rd Congr., 2nd sess., Senate Document 13, 42.

38. "Many of these towns whose wishes were gratified have found by dear bought experience that the expected and long-sought-for blessings [italics in original] have proved "curses in disguise" [italics in original]. Carey, Letters to the Bank Directors, Introduction, v. See also his Letters to Seybert, 53.

This outlook stems also from Mercantilist economics which embraced two schools of thought, one friendly and one hostile to banks, the latter being the geistige ancestor of the ideas to be discussed. David Hume was one of their exponents. (See "Banks and Paper Money from Essays, Moral, Political, etc., published in 1752" in McCulloch, J. R., A Select Collection of Scarce and Valuable Tracts and Other Publications on Paper Currency and Banking, (1857), 57 ff.

39. Inquiry, 356. The earliest statement to that effect is probably that of 1786 in Carey, Debates, 75.

40. Path to Riches, 52.

41. Raymond, op. cit., 408, 409.

42. Hardenbrook, op. cit., 87. See also Address to the People of Maryland, 3.

43. Op. cit., 85.

44. Davis, Essays, II, 44 ff.

45. E. S. Sparks (op. cit., 285 ff.) has collected and commented on the pertinent material. The most representative primary source is Carey, Debates, passim. See also, Governor Daniel D. Tompkins's speech of January 28, 1812, in New York, Messages of the Governors, II, 698.

46. Hammond, Bray, "Long and Short Term Credit," passim.

47. U.S. 25th Congr., 3d sess., House Executive Document 227, 535.

48. Essays in American Economic History, 116.

49. Clapham, op. cit., I, 112.

50. One only needs to cite the name of Adam Müller.

51. "That the punctuality of payments is principally due to banks is a fact generally acknowledged." (Gallatin in 1811) American State Papers, Finance, II, 481.

52. Carey, Debates, 65.

53. Hardenbrook, op. cit., 87.

54. Carey, Letters to Seybert, 54.

55. Mercantilism as a system of thought is considered by this author as the ideological expression of early capitalism; while classical theory is that of high-capitalism; these terms being used in the sense of Sombart.

56. The Bank of Vermont, for instance, was founded without any capital whatsoever.

Some of the early American banks not only had sufficient capital, but were even overcapitalized. Therefore during the first and at the beginning of the second period several cases of capital reduction, actual or planned, are noticeable. Transactions of this character took place in 1785 in the Massachusetts Bank (Gras, op. cit., 25, 52) where the capital was cut from $255,500 to $100,000. In 1813 the Bank of America reduced its capital from five to four millions, and in 1819 from four to two. (New York Laws, 1813, chapter 76; 1819, chapter 24; U.S. 23rd Congr. 1st sess., Senate Document 73, 12, 14. The reasons for the capital reduction of 1813 are discussed in Bank of America, 49 ff.) The Bridgeport Bank of Bridgeport, Connecticut, lowered its capital in 1816 from $200,000 to $100,000, i.e., by 50 per cent; and in the same year the directors of the State Bank of Boston suggested a capital reduction from 3 to 1.8 million dollars. (Gouge's Journal of Banking, 210; Stetson, op. cit., 33, 34.) Last, but not least, it should not be forgotten that as late as the 1820's a party within the board of the Second Bank of the United States (led by Langdon Cheves) desired a capital reduction in that bank.

Professor Gras, describing the earliest case of this type, has posed the question why that reduction took place in the Massachusetts Bank. Since, as shown above, such a transaction was not unique, a correct explanation would be of value. In the Massachusetts Bank and the Bank of America, as far as this author can see, actual profit or chances for profit were below the rates which investors expected from banks; in the former bank because it was too cautious in extending credit and in the latter because note issues were limited to the actually paid-in capital. Consequently in the latter case subscribers were reluctant to pay up their subscriptions. This reluctance is quite understandable when one realizes that it was generally known at that time that banks made profits over and above legal interest by lending a multiple of their capital. For some cases (perhaps including that of the Massachusetts Bank) the above quoted article in the Journal of Banking gives the clue. According to the banking theory of the time expressed in the article (by the son of the president of the bank involved) "the possession of capital was of no use for banks except to inspire confidence." "This being once fully established...[capital] was found of great inconvenience, a source of real annoyance, because its investment involved a responsibility which it was thought could be discharged with equal safety and greater advantage by the stockholders in their individual capacities... It was therefore determined to restore it to them, retaining only so much as was deemed adequate to the security of those holding the engagements of the bank." This business policy is a perfect expression of Mercantilist banking theory. In the contemporaneous case of the Boston State Bank the reduction was suggested because the bank had most of its capital invested in government loans, which could not be converted into cash, so that this portion was not available for banking purposes anyway; while, on the other hand, stockholders were anxious to have funds for investment in stock of the Second Bank of the United States. Finally the state bank-capital tax levied on that part of the capital which was not used in the business of banking was so burdensome that it contributed to the desire for reduction. (Stetson, op. cit., 33, 34.)

57. Op. cit., 31. See also Raguet, Inquiry, 8, 9 and Carey, Desultory Reflections, 9, 10. The four Philadelphia banks existing in 1811, in addition to the First Bank of the United States, had on an average $200,000 specie in their vaults. Incidentally, the Bank of England kept about forty per cent reserves in the peace years of the mid-eighteenth century. See Clapham, op. cit., I, 155.

58. Although belonging in the second period, the development of the specie reserves of the Second Bank of the United States which dropped practically to nothing in 1819, exemplifies the spirit of the first period also.

59. For the Bank of New York, see Domett, op. cit., 19 ff. and Nevins, op. cit., 15; for the Bank of North America, Lewis, op. cit., 39 ff.; for the First Bank of the United States, Holdsworth, op. cit., 27, 133 ff. and Wettereau, op. cit., passim; for the Bank of Massachusetts, Gras, op. cit., passim, esp. 222 ff., 273 ff.

60. The term "real paper" seems to have been an abbreviation for "bills or notes founded on real business transactions."

(American State Papers, Finance, III, 326.) Mathew Carey in Desultory Reflections (of 1811) defines "real notes" as bona fide notes given for value received (page 13).

61. Carey, Debates, 31. The limitation of discounts to thirty and sixty-day paper was in line with the policy of the Bank of England. See Clapham, op. cit., I, 124.

62. Gras, op. cit., 46.

63. Carey, Debates, 36.

64. As early as 1784 the directors of the Massachusetts Bank resolved that discounts when due could be charged to the account of the promisor (Gras, op. cit., 235). In 1811 the board of the same bank decided that checks on other banks would not be taken in payment of discounts payable at the bank (ibid., 402). In 1818 a committee of the New York legislature reported the following method of paying discounts when due: Applicants receive credit "on condition that they will pay their note when due in what is called current money (meaning notes of such of the banks as are current throughout the state...) which compels the borrower, during the time his note is to run, to lay by him all the current money he can collect, which of necessity he must lose the use of, and for which he is obliged to pay for the sum he may be deficient of as of the time draws near a close, a premium..." (New York Assembly Journal, 1818, 308.)

65. The first rules of the Bank of New York contained a clause that no note or bill would be discounted to pay an earlier one. See Nevins, op. cit., 15.

66. Myers, M. G. (op. cit., 47) referring to British Parliamentary Papers, 1819, III, 140, quotes the following statement: "The term accommodation paper "is, where two or more individuals agree to draw, indorse, and accept bills of exchange for each other, there being no real transaction of business between them and the whole operation being intended for the sole purpose of raising money." Such transactions were very common between European merchants throughout the eighteenth century. Today one speaks of racehorse bills.

67. A contemporary definition can be found in the Rules and Regulations of the Second Bank of the United States, sec. 4. The Secretary of the Treasury in a Report on the Bank of the United States of 1820 defined accommodation paper as "fixed or permanent loans" (page 13). The term was still so new in 1816 that Mathew Carey

explained that "the Bank of North America and the Farmers' Bank made considerable reductions on what are called accommodation notes." [Italics mine!] (essays on Banking, 39). A later source explained the term "accommodation paper" as "deriving its name from the fact that the debtors [were] to be accommodated by repeated renewals and extensions." Report of the Massachusetts Bank Commissioners for 1839, 15.

68. Reminiscences, 83.

69. Referring to accommodation paper, Mathew Carey wrote in 1811 (Desultory Reflections, 13), "Every well regulated bank considers itself as in some measure bound by almost universal practice to renew as large a part as possible, if not the whole."

70. See Rule 11 of the Rules and Regulations of the Worcester Bank of 1804: notes not to be renewed for more than four-fifths of the original sum (Chase, op. cit., 8, 9). For the Hartford Bank, see Woodward, op. cit., 88; for the Massachusetts Bank, see Gras, op. cit., 350, 351, 352, 353 (1792); for the State Bank of Illinois, see Garnett, op. cit., 11. See also footnote 82.

71. Carey, Desultory Reflections, 8.

72. Stokes, op. cit., 277.

73. Nevins, op. cit., 15; Gras, op. cit., 274.

74. Again Mathew Carey in 1815 reported extravagant accommodations to a few persons. Essays on Banking, Introduction, iv.

75. For the Massachusetts Bank in 1785, see Gras, op. cit., 273, 274; and in 1811, ibid., 401.

76. The Philadelphia Bank adopted the lending on merchandise in 1808; The Philadelphia National Bank, 51. The Bank of England hardly engaged at all in this type of business, see Clapham, op. cit., I, 113.

77. As to the Massachusetts Bank, see Gras, op. cit., 222 ff., 273 ff., "Laws" of 1784, Rules and Regulations of 1785, The Philadelphia National Bank, 28 (1803).

78. The Bank of North America in the 1780's temporarily resolved not to lend on government securities. James, "Bank of North America," 65.

79. The Bank of England had lent on its own stock by 1720, see Clapham, op. cit., I, 84.

80. To give a few examples of loans to local governments: In 1811 the Philadelphia Bank lent $100,000 to the City of Philadelphia on the pledge of taxes, the loan to be repaid in installments of $500, while the note of the city was to be renewed every sixty days. (The Philadelphia National Bank, 38). In 1811 the Massachusetts Bank made a loan to Suffolk County.

81. The Bank of North America had insisted on the repayment of government debts in 1783 (James, "Bank of North America," 65). Holdsworth, op. cit., 45 ff., 124. Wettereau, op. cit., 270, 271.

82. The directors of the Massachusetts Bank resolved in 1789 "to loan the Treasurer of this Commonwealth five thousand dollars to enable him to continue paying the civil list." Gras, op. cit., 32. As to the Bank of America see New York Laws of 1812, chapter 78.

83. James, "Bank of North America," 63; Woodward, op. cit., 15, 66. See also the quotation from the Connecticut Gazette of September 6, 1792, to be found in Duncombe, op. cit., 129.

84. Circulars of October 14 and November 20, 1789 advising the collectors to take notes of the Banks of North America, New York, and and Massachusetts. U.S. 23rd Congr., 1st sess., House Document 312, 40, 41.

85. Nevins, op. cit., 15; Catterall, op. cit., 382; Rafinesque, op. cit., 44. In 1819 the Bank of Muskingum in Zanesville, Ohio, was crippled by "over-drawing of a few individuals." American State Papers, Finance, IV, 733. The Bank of England occasionally permitted overdrafts. See Clapham, op. cit., I, 121.

86. Perhaps the earliest suggestion is to be found in Peletiah Webster's Essay on Credit (1786), 11.

87. Paragraphs on Banks, 15 ff., 32, 33.

88. Essays on Banking, 105, 162. Carey refers to an article in a New York paper suggesting the substitution of bank credit for bank notes.

89. Woodward, op. cit., 80

90. For the history of post-notes see this author's "American Bank Money in the Eighteenth and Early Nineteenth Centuries," in Southern Economic Review, X, (1944), 212 ff.

91. Gras. op. cit., 263, 264.

92. See. p. 6.

93. They are recommended by Mathew Carey in Essays on Banking, 175, 182, 184. At that time facility notes were fought in New York. In 1818 a Committee of the New York legislature reported: "...Other banks, by a different stratagem, but no less contrary to the intent and meaning of their charter, have issued a species of paper called facility notes, purporting to be payable in either money, country produce, or any thing else that has body or shape, and thereby rendering their name appropriate

only but by facilitating the ruin of those who are so unfortunate as to hold them." (New York Assembly Journal, 1818, 308.) Previous to this report, in 1816, the following "Act Concerning Banks," had been passed on November 12, 1816: "Be it enacted and declared by the people of the State of New York, represented in Senate and Assembly, That no banking company shall issue, or cause to be issued, any bills or notes, other than for the payment of money; and that the sums which may be expressed in any bills or notes, which any bank shall issue, or cause to be issued, which are according to the terms thereof receivable only in payment of debts due to the bank, shall be recoverable by the bearer of such bills or notes, in like manner as if the same contained an express promise for the payment of money." (New York Laws, 1816, chapter 14.) Facility notes are reproduced in The Philadelphia National Bank opposite pages 52 and 56. As to Connecticut, see Woodward, op. cit., 116.

94. The Philadelphia National Bank, 34.
95. Stetson, op. cit., 28.
96. See p. 49 for Philadelphia.
97. Gras, op. cit., 37, 416; The Philadelphia National Bank, 39. For the investment activities of the New London Bank, see Woolsey, op. cit., 16.
98. The Philadelphia National Bank, 192. The appendix to Mathew Carey's Desultory Reflections (p. 18), testifies to the practice at the end of the first period of setting aside reserves to meet losses from bad debts.
99. As late as 1834 the depositing of money in banks was considered by no less a person than Daniel Webster primarily a matter of safe-keeping. (U.S. 23rd Congr., 1st sess., Senate Document 72, 8.)
    It is possible that some of the founders of the Bank of North America and of the Massachusetts Bank aimed at deposit banking, Continental style; but that was not the road American banking took. See the letter of 1780 of John Nixon and George Clymer, directors of the Pennsylvania Bank, to Washington: "What we principally rested on [in the Pennsylvania Bank of 1780] was the convenience the trading people would find in lodging their money in the Bank." (Sparks, Diplomatic Correspondence II, 71,72.) In the Massachusetts Bank the intention alluded to can be seen in the charging of a fee to depositors, a practice of the Continental deposit banks. See below p. 15.

100. See Clapham, op. cit., I, 5, 20, 21.
101. See, e.g., Free Trade Advocate, II (1829), 1 ff. This article distinguishes between banks of deposit, banks of discount, and banks of circulation.
    One of the illuminating documents of the first period is a report of the Secretary of the Treasury (Albert Gallatin) to the senate regarding the application of the First Bank of the United States in 1807 for a renewal of its charter. (American State Papers, Finance, II, 351, 352, and Clarke and Hall, op. cit., 116 ff.) This report of 1809 shows how little even a man like Gallatin then knew about the principles of American banking, and it is all the more important since it is presented with the air of a schoolmaster. The secretary explained to the senators that profits of banks arose from the 6 per cent interest which they received on their loans, but that their profit amounted to more than 6 per cent on their capital, because not only did they lend their capital but also part of the deposits entrusted to them. However, this policy of the very first American banks had already been widely abandoned. Gallatin did not realize, what became common knowledge a few years later, that with a few exceptions American banks created purchasing power by lending multiples of their capitals. Confounding European certificates of deposit (and perhaps the earliest bearer notes of the Bank of England - see Clapham, op. cit., I, 21, 22) with American bank notes, he drew the conclusion, totally erroneous for America, that "bank notes and credits in the books of the bank arise...equally from deposits;" but he understood that the "aggregate of these [book] credits and of the bank notes issued constitute the circulating medium contributed by the banking operations." Gallatin believed, again with some confusion in his mind, that "experience had taught the directors what portion of the money thus deposited they may lend: or in other words [sic] how far they may with safety extend their discounts beyond the capital of the bank and what amount of specie [it] is necessary they should keep in their vaults." In a balance sheet embodied in this memorandum the secretary presents the following items: "Moneys deposited, viz, 1 credit in the bank books commonly called deposits, including the deposits both by the government and big individuals;

2. bank notes in circulation." That is to say, bank notes in circulation are presented here as deposits!

The mistake which Gallatin made in 1809 was the same one committed by James Sullivan in 1792. Both of these men failed to see the difference between Continental deposit banks and the Bank of England and both considered English and American bank notes as essentially certificates of deposit. Sullivan believed that the value of Bank of England notes depended on the certainty with which note holders could get "the real money for their paper evidential of the deposit." Consequently he wanted to limit note issues to capital and deposits and to exclude the creation of purchasing power by banks. (Path to Riches, 19-21, 34, 36, 66, 71.)

There remained a good deal of confusion in the first half of the nineteenth century regarding the differences between banks of deposit, banks of discount, and banks of circulation. It was generally understood that the Banks of Amsterdam and Hamburg were banks of deposit (or "offices of deposit and transfer." Journal of Banking, 308). It was not always understood that the taking of deposits by American banks did not make them banks of deposit by character. Even greater confusion existed regarding the differences between banks of discount and banks of circulation. This author is convinced, without at this time being able to prove his contention, that originally these terms paralleled those of "money banks" and "land banks." Only the former discounted bills and notes, while the latter issued a circulating medium on the basis of landed and other security without ever making discounts. However, this original distinction, if ever clearly made, was forgotten in America in the nineteenth century. In this country probably a bank which lent its capital and its deposits only was considered a bank of discount, while such banks as created purchasing power over and above capital and deposits were considered banks of circulation (see the above-quoted article in Free Trade Advocate and chapters IV and V in Gouge's Short History). See also Miller, op. cit., 13, on the distinction between banks of deposit, banks of discount, and banks of circulation.

102. Gras, op. cit., 37, 214.

103. There was (with perhaps one exception), no paying of interest on private deposits in the first period. In spite of the fact that it was unheard of at that time, the Bank of New York in 1792 paid 6 per cent interest on three-months deposits of the State of New York (Nevins, op. cit., 24). Even for 1810 it was a radical move when Gallatin suggested, during the discussion of the renewal of the charter of the First Bank of the United States, that it should pay interest on government deposits. For this subject see below pp. 52, 53.

104. For the First Bank of the United States see Holdsworth-Dewey, op. cit., 27; for the Hartford Bank, Woodward, op. cit., 21: "And they will receive deposits of ingots of gold, bars of silver, wrought plate or other valuable articles of small bulk and return the same on demand to the depositor." (Rules and Regulations of 1792.) For the Massachusetts bank, see Gras, op. cit., 61, 94.

In 1792 the treasurer of the state of New York deposited with the Bank of New York almost two million dollars of United States debt certificates on which the bank was to collect interest (Nevins, op. cit., 24).

Incidentally to give an example from the second period, the Union Bank of Louisiana in the 1830's took gold, silver, plate, and valuables on "special deposit" at the risk of the depositor (Rules and Regulations, Rule 38. U.S. 23rd Congr., 1st sess., House Exec. Document 73, 30). The term "special deposit" had then acquired a meaning different from the accepted meaning of the first period (see below).

105. There is one case on record in which (in 1800) the New Haven Bank returned to a customer notes of the First Bank of the United States and of New York banks which he had deposited. In 1802, however, the New York branch of that bank had become the collection agent of the New Haven Bank and notes of the above description were received on deposit. (Woolsey, op. cit., 9, 10.)

106. Directors Records, Massachusetts Bank, see Gras, op. cit., 74, 376, 378, 387, 413. From a letter by Crawford of April 23, 1817 one can draw the conclusion that, at that time at least, everything was taken on special deposit that did not circulate at par. (American State Papers, Finance, II, 307; IV, 509, 520, 524, 626. This volume is full of references to special deposits.)

107. "Voted that the cashier [of the Massa-
     chusetts Bank] be directed to receive as
     a special deposit the bank bills issued
     by the several incorporated banks of the
     New England states and that the persons
     depositing said bills be allowed to draw
     by checks for the same, - the bank re-
     taining the option to pay such checks in
     identical bills deposited or in any bills
     of the above description - the depositor
     to present a list of the bills deposit-
     ed." November 19, 1804. (Gras, op. cit.,
     387.) See, for instance, the list of
     notes held on special deposit in American
     State Papers, Finance, IV, 851, 852.

108. Gras, op. cit., 376.

109. U.S. 23rd Congr., 1st sess., Senate
     Document 13, 15. Still another alterna-
     tive was not to touch certain notes at
     all. In 1804, for instance, the cashier
     of the Bank of Philadelphia was advised
     not to take notes of banks to the south
     of Alexandria, and to the east and north
     of New York. The Philadelphia National
     Bank, 30. As to the similar policy of
     the Boston banks regarding New England
     country notes see below p. 69, and Gras,
     op. cit., 393, 394.

110. A contemporary writer reports that banks
     took notes on special deposit for safe-
     keeping (Gordon, T.F., op. cit., 71),
     which latter phrase also implies that
     they were taken as a depositum regulare.

111. American State Papers, Finance, IV, 712,
     713.

112. In 1815 the directors of the Lynn Mech-
     anics Bank resolved that the depositors
     receive "such money as they deposit or
     that which is as good, but no better."
     Burrill, op. cit., 42.

113. See the very interesting quotation from
     a contemporary almanac in Hubert, op.
     cit., 16 (original source not given).

114. Gras, op. cit., 245. This author cannot
     agree with Professor Gras's comment,
     ibid., 38.

115. See Domett, op. cit., 37, 38; Harden-
     brook, op. cit., 91; Nevins, op. cit.,
     18, 21. Nevins reproduces on a plate
     opposite p. 32, a check of 1791 reading:
     "Cashier of the Bank [the Bank of New
     York] Pay to [blank space] or Bearer
     [blank space] Paper."

116. See page 67.

117. See page 68.

118. Gras, op. cit., 413; The Philadelphia
     National Bank, 40. The Bank of England
     had taken specie on special deposit as
     early as 1696. (See Clapham, op. cit.,
     I, 37, 38.)

119. American State Papers, Finance, IV, 509.

120. As to special deposits in the crisis of
     1837 see below p. 51.

121. In using eighteenth-century sources one
     must keep in mind that the verb "deposit"
     was then equivocal. If applied in state-
     ments on banking it has one of two dif-
     ferent meanings: It either refers to
     what is expressed today by "deposit" or
     "make a deposit in a bank;" or it is
     identical with the modern term "invest"
     or "pay up," or "pay in." The meanings
     of the word "deposit" are well exempli-
     fied in the following single sentence
     taken from James Sullivan's Path to
     Riches of 1792, p. 50: "All other banks
     are confined in their credits to the
     stock actually deposited [i.e., to the
     stock actually paid in] and to the de-
     posits of private individuals," which
     phrase is self-explanatory. Again on
     p. 32, speaking on the beginnings of
     the Bank of England, Sullivan states
     that the £1,200,000 lent by its sub-
     scribers to the government "was the
     stock in real money deposited by the
     subscribers" (i.e., invested, as one
     would say today). In the following pas-
     sage from the 1792 charter of the Mass-
     achusetts Bank, the term deposit is
     again used synonymously with "pay in:"
     Directors were made liable in the case
     that notes and other debts exceeded
     "double the amount of their capital
     stock in gold and silver actually de-
     posited in the bank and held to answer
     the demand against the same."

122. The tenor of these early checks was:
     Pay to [blank space] or Bearer. See
     examples in the collections of the
     Pennsylvania Historical Society and re-
     productions in Woodward, op. cit., op-
     posite pages 49 and 57 (1793, and 1792);
     Philadelphia National Bank, opposite
     page 60. (This sample of 1814 is es-
     pecially interesting since the word
     "bearer" is scratched out and replaced
     by "order.") Domett, op. cit., oppo-
     site page. 48. Hubert, op. cit., 88.
     The reproduction of a check blank of
     the Salem Merchants Bank shows that
     checks of this tenor were used as late
     as 1830: see Dennis, op. cit., 12.
         In 1821 a Savannah lawyer gave the
     following opinion regarding a check made
     out to AB or order: "It is not a check.
     It is payable to order [italics in or-
     iginal] and checks, says Chitty [famous
     English law authority] are always pay-
     able to bearer." The draft on a bank

made out to AB or order was considered a bill of exchange by the lawyer. *American State Papers*, *Finance*, IV, 1072.

Incidentally, some of the earliest American checks were handwritten on a plain piece of paper (like the English "drawn notes" of the early eighteenth century) or in other words, without the use of printed forms. Samples are in the Historical Society of Pennsylvania. Regarding the English drawn notes, see Clapham, *op. cit.*, I, 142, 143.

123. The Bank of Columbia in Washington took notes of Maryland, Pennsylvania, and Virginia banks on deposit and issued checks on certain banks in those states. See Holdsworth, *op. cit.*, 93.

124. Gras, *op. cit.*, 43; *Philadelphia National Bank*, 37.

125. Gras, *op. cit.*, 401. Noah Webster's guess that one-fourth to one-third of all loans by the "principal" banks took the form of created deposits was certainly too high (*op.cit.*, 47).

126. Gras, *op. cit.*, 37, 39.

127. *Op. cit.*, 47. Clapham (*op. cit.*, I, 221) stresses that in the second half of the eighteenth century the use of checks was still rather exceptional even in England.

128. *American State Papers*, *Finance*, I, 223; *U.S. 23rd Congr.*, *2nd sess.*, House Executive Document 13, 2; Gras, *op. cit.*, 37, 60. Another list of depositories of Federal funds in *American State Papers*, *Finance* IV, 783.

129. Gras, *op. cit.*, 60; Nevins, *op. cit.*, 25; *Philadelphia National Bank*, 37. In 1803 the Hartford, New Haven, and Middletown Banks offered to act as depositories for the State of Connecticut and to pay 6 per cent interest on the deposits. However, the state preferred to become a stockholder in these banks. Woodward, *op. cit.*, 82.

130. Gras, *op. cit.*, 37.

131. *Op. cit.*, 344 ff.

132. *Philadelphia National Bank*, 29.

133. Hubert, *op. cit.*, 193.

134. McMaster, *op. cit.*, 240, 242; Wildes, *op. cit.*, 212.

135. Interesting in this connection is the following piece of information: In the 1800's the "principal stockholders" of the State Bank of Charleston, South Carolina, intended to establish a credit and to enter into mutual arrangements with the Manhattan Company in New York so as to give a better standing to the post notes of the two banks. The arrangement, however, did not meet with approbation of the legislature and the bank was forbidden to give credit to any bank outside the state of South Carolina (*American State Papers*, *Finance*, II, 519).

Temporarily after resumption in 1817 the Second Bank of the United States possessed a unique network of correspondents, which by its character belongs to the first, rather than to the second, period. Before the Bank had built up a system of branches it became necessary in the interest of the Treasury to employ state banks "as places of intermediate deposit" in certain parts of the country. Under an arrangement between the Secretary of the Treasury and the Second Bank of the United States the latter selected a number of state banks at suitable places as intermediate depositories and the public funds deposited in these banks were payable upon draft of the cashier of the Bank of the United States. The contracts between the Bank of the United States and the state banks gave rise to so much trouble that the former soon withdrew from its arrangement with the Treasury. (Incidentally, in a letter the Secretary of the Treasury spoke in this context of the "connexion [italics mine] between the Bank of the United States and Tennessee banks," a term which then conveyed the same meaning as the modern phrase "correspondent.") The relationship between the Bank of the United States and the selected state banks is odd from the modern point of view: the central bank kept accounts with country banks, a reversal of the usual correspondent relationship. (See *American State Papers*, *Finance*, IV, 552, 558, 582.)

136. Gras, *op. cit.*, 224.

137. Wettereau, *op. cit.*, 269, especially footnote.

138. Webster, Noah, *op. cit.*, 9.

139. Atwater, Jesse, *Considerations on the Approaching Dissolution of the United States Bank in a Series of Numbers* (New Haven, 1810), 16. A unique credit transaction of the Bank of New York in 1797 should be mentioned. In that year the bank bought from the state of New York United States stock to be paid in installments and settled at par in 1809, in which year, however, the due date of the debt was extended to 1832. Since the securities were sold by the bank the transaction amounted to a loan from the state of New York. It was paid in 1823 with funds borrowed from the Barings.

(See below p. 54; Domett, op. cit., 54;
Nevins, op. cit., 24, 38, 39.)

140. As to the First Bank of the United
States, see its charter Section 7, IX;
Holdsworth-Dewey, op. cit., 129 and 20;
as to Rhode Island, see Stokes, op. cit.,
273.

141. Woodward, op. cit., 80, 68.

142. In 1802 Noah Webster states that "in
general the notes in circulation do not
exceed the amount of the capital stock."
Op. cit., 46.

143. As to the Massachusetts Bank, see Gras,
op. cit., 369 (referring to 1797), 379
(referring to 1801). The Rules and
Regulations of 1792 of the Hartford Bank
contain the following clause: "Bills and
notes left at the office for collection
will be presented for acceptance and the
money collected or demanded without expence, except in case of protest..." It
is not quite understandable why the
service was provided free of charge.
(Woodward, op. cit., 21.)

144. See this author's "American Bank Money
...," 213.

145. See the transaction described in footnote 139 and Nevins, op. cit., 24.

146. East, op. cit., 305. Hubert (op. cit.,
37 ff.) gives illuminating biographical
sketches of early stockholders of the
Merchants Bank of New York.

147. The term "proprietors" can be found for
the subscribers of the Bank of North
America in a letter of 1781 by William
Duer to Robert Morris (East, op. cit.,
289); for the subscribers of the Massachusetts Bank, in its charter of 1784
(Gras, op. cit., 215); and for the stockholders of this bank, in the Directors'
Records of 1794 (Gras, op. cit., 336).
In 1791 the stockholders of the Providence Bank were called proprietors in
the charter (Stokes, op. cit., 264); in
1792 James Sullivan used this term for
bank stockholders continuously (Path to
Riches, 45, 47, 48, 53, 72); and in 1811
and 1814, respectively, the stockholders
of the Merchants Bank in Salem and of the
Lynn Mechanics Bank were designated as
"proprietors and associates" (Dennis,
op. cit., 15; Burrill, op. cit., 161).
Incidentally the shareholders of the Bank
of England were also called proprietors.

148. See the quotation from the Providence
Gazette of 1791 referring to the sub-
scription to the Providence Bank in
Davis, Essays, II, 62.

149. However there were differences in degree.
The list of original stockholders of the
Bank of New York (as published by East,
op. cit., 327 ff.) shows that only one
stockholder had taken twelve shares;
three had ten shares each; twelve had
six to eight shares each; seven held
five shares each; and all the rest had
less, most of them only one share. The
lists of original stockholders of the
Providence Bank of 1791 and of the
Hartford Bank of 1792 show a similar
pattern (Providence National Bank, 41
ff.; Woodward, op. cit., 170; Hartford
National Bank, 64.) In the Massachusetts
Bank in 1785, on the other hand, William
Phillips owned forty-two shares; two
insurance offices held forty each;
thirteen men held ten to twenty shares
each; and eight men, six to nine; the
rest held five and less, and again most
of them only one share (Gras, op. cit.,
538 ff.). The list of original subscribers of the New Haven Bank follows
the same pattern (Mitchell, Mary, op. cit.,
9). The original lists of stockholders
of the later banks of the first period
which had shares of small face value
look very different. See, for instance,
that of the New York Merchants Bank of
1803 (Hubert, op. cit., 202 ff.), or of
the Plymouth Bank of 1803 (Plymouth Bank
21 ff.).

150. See Holdsworth-Dewey, op. cit., 36 and
footnote 135. In 1812 the stockholders
of the State Bank of Boston appointed a
committee to negotiate with the Secretary of the Treasury regarding public
deposits; (Stetson, op. cit., 18); in
1814 the local stockholders of the Lynn
Mechanics Bank determined the site of
the bank building (Burrill, op. cit.,
16) as had done those of the Plymouth
Bank in 1802 (Plymouth Bank, 39) and of
the New Haven Bank in 1809 (Woolsey,
op. cit., 14). One is inclined to draw
the conclusion that such activities
belonged, typically, to the stockholders.
In 1816 the stockholders of the Hartford
Bank authorized the issue of facility
notes (Woodward, op. cit., 199).

151. Carey, Debates, 36.

152. See Murray, James H., A New English
Dictionary on Historical Principles.

153. Carey, Debates, 87, 33, 31. In the
debates on the charter of the First Bank
of the United States in Congress in 1791
Stone of Maryland claimed that the bill
gave a few stockholders the right to
"institute banks in particular states."
See Clarke and Hall, op. cit., 68.

154. Path to Riches, 37.

155. In 1786 the full board of the Massachusetts Bank decided on the requisition of ten cords of firewood; and a few days later on paying for them (Gras, op. cit., 291, 292).

156. Gras. op. cit., 228. The president received $200.

157. The Ordinance is reprinted by Holdsworth. Regarding the Massachusetts Bank, see Gras, op. cit., 222 ff.

158. James Wilson in the Bank of North America, Alexander Hamilton in the Bank of New York, John Lowell in the Massachusetts Bank (for the latter, see Chapter IX, page 224), and Peter Jay Munro (1767-1838) in the Merchants Bank of New York (see Hubert, op. cit., 24).

159. Nevins, op. cit., 32.

160. Regarding the committees of the Bank of England, see Clapham op. cit., I, 109; and R. D. Richards, op. cit., 266 ff.

161. Gras, op. cit., 253.

162. Gras, op. cit., 345, 346, 355; Dennis, op. cit., 25; Philadelphia National Bank, 37, 38, 41, 42, 43. Between 1792 and 1795 all preparatory steps before opening the New Haven Bank were taken by committees; Woolsey, op. cit., 7.

163. Gras, op. cit., 297. 303.

164. Ibid., 308, 320, 367, 399.

165. Philadelphia National Bank, 37; Gras, op. cit., 293, 313, 320, 338, 367, 372; Stetson, op. cit., 24, 25 (for State Bank of Boston). In the New Haven Bank on the request of the cashier a committee of audit was appointed first in 1798 and regularly thereafter; Woolsey, op. cit., 8.

166. Lewis, op. cit., 39; Gras, op. cit., 311.

167. "History of the Bank of.." in Gouge's Journal of Banking, 225.

168. Philadelphia Bank (1804), cashier: $2250; president: $2000. State Bank in Boston (1815), cashier: $2000; president: $1000. See Philadelphia National Bank, 38; Stetson, op. cit., 44. In other banks it was just the opposite. For instance, in the Merchants Bank of New York (1803) cashier: $2500; president: $3000. Finally there were banks were the presidents received nothing, e.g., the Bridgeport Bank. The latter policy was in line with Robert Morris's original ideas. In the New Haven Bank the president received the first salary in 1817 - $200 for six months (Mitchell, Mary, op. cit., 13). The president of the Mechanics and Farmers Bank of Albany had no salary, but received five per cent of the issues for his trouble in signing the notes.

169. Hubert, op. cit., 14; Woodward, op. cit., 85, 77; Burpee, op. cit., 31; "History of the Bank of --," 209, 225. As to the salary of the cashier of the New Haven Bank, see Mitchell, Mary, op. cit., 11 and Woolsey, op. cit., 13. It is characteristic of the trend that Lynde Catlin, the cashier of the Merchants Bank in New York, resigned in 1816 because the New York branch of the Second Bank of the United States offered him a salary higher than the $3500 which he was receiving at the time. (Hubert, op. cit., 86.)

170. Gras, op. cit., 315; Philadelphia National Bank, 40. As to the New Haven Bank, see Mitchell, Mary, op. cit., 11.

171. Gras, op. cit., 400 (Rules and Regulations of 1811). The Lynn Mechanics Bank is another example of the employment of a sitting director. "That each of the Board be a Director for the week in turns." (June 1, 1827.) "That each Director in his turn is appointed as a Director for a week commencing with the oldest whose duty it shall be to meet with the President...on each day of the week for which he is a director, except discount days, and they are hereby authorized to transact all such business as may come before them." (October 8, 1830.) The cooperation between sitting director and president is noteworthy. (Burrill, op. cit., 27.) The Rules and By-Laws of 1803 of the Plymouth Bank provide for a "director of the week" (Plymouth Bank, 35 ff.).

172. Gras, op. cit., 254, 402.

173. Ibid., 417.

174. Reprinted in Sparks, Diplomatic Correspondence, VII, 439 ff.

175. The plan provided under section 8: that the board of directors determine the manner of doing business and the rules and forms to be pursued." Furthermore it was to appoint the officers, to "dispose of the money and credit of the bank," and to declare dividends.

176. Ibid., 445, 446. When following the practice of the Bank of North America the Massachusetts Bank adopted the device, the term "inspector" was dropped and replaced by "sitting director." Gras (op. cit., 248, 250) has a different interpretation.

177. Clapham, op. cit., I, 109.

178. See also article I of the by-laws of the Merchants Bank of New York (Hubert, op. cit., 21, 22); Rules and By-laws of 1803 of the Plymouth Bank (Plymouth Bank, 35 ff.).

179. See below p. 38.

180. Gras, op. cit., 373, 374, 372.

181. Wettereau, op. cit., 276, 277.

182. Gras, op. cit., 253 (referring to 1784), 347 (referring to 1791), 380 (referring to 1802); Hardenbrook, op. cit., 102; Woodward, op. cit., 111. About the remuneration of bank presidents, see footnote 168.

183. In the Hartford Bank no person, copartnership, or body politic, except the State of Connecticut, could hold more than thirty shares. (Woodward, op. cit., 17.)

184. Op. cit., 18.

185. East, op. cit., 260. In the Bank of New York concentration of shareholdings took place in 1792.

186. Ibid., 300; Providence National Bank, 13 ff., 18.

187. Burpee, op. cit., 104, 113, 114.

188. Letter of Seton to Hamilton (1784), Works of Alexander Hamilton, (John C. Hamilton, ed.) I, 417, 418. The letter is also to be found in Domett, op. cit., 115.

189. The Life and Correspondence of Rufus King (New York, 1894), I, 400, 401.

190. Madison was also an opponent of the idea of a single bank for the country. See his speech of February 2, 1791. Clarke and Hall, op. cit., 40.

191. Writings (Putnam edition), VIII, 158. As early as 1791 Congressman Stone of Maryland had voiced the same fear (Clarke and Hall, op. cit., 68). The idea that the country should or could possess only one incorporated bank was long lived. As late as 1837 a pamphleteer considered it a "capital error" that every state bank charter had not been repealed after the adoption of the Constitution. (Mayo, op. cit., 25).

192. Lewis, op. cit., 52; Hamilton's letter to Seton of January 18, 1791, reprinted in Domett, op. cit., 43. See also Webster, Peletiah, Essay on Credit, 26.

193. Domett, op. cit., 40; Davis, Essays, II 54.

194. Path to Riches, 65.

195. Davis, Essays, II, 96.

196. Davis, Essays, II, 81 ff. The Bank of the United States and its branches are not counted because of its special status as the national bank.

197. Stokes, op. cit., 275, 277.

198. The question of banking monopoly in that period is treated in detail in Davis, Essays, II, 54 ff.

199. A late expression of this idea is quoted on p. 96.

200. The Providence Bank of 1791, the Union Bank of Boston of 1792, and the State Bank in Boston of 1811 each played a considerable role in this respect.

201. As to Massachusetts and New Hampshire, see Davis, Essays, II 102, 103; as to New York, Cleaveland, Introduction, xvii ff. As to Pennsylvania, Philadelphia National Bank, 55. As to Rhode Island, Stokes, op. cit., 280.

202. Gras, Business and Capitalism, 169. The reason is given by Condy Raguet. He explained that merchants could buy cheaper with cash than on credit and that country merchants therefore preferred borrowing from country banks to borrowing from city merchants whenever country banks existed in their home towns. (Circulating Medium, 49.) That is to say, the local bank lent at cheaper rates or on better terms than the city merchant, and it could do so easily since, in contrast to the merchant, it could create credit.

203. For instance, Union Bank, Boston or State Bank, Boston. (See Stetson, op. cit., 10, 455) or Farmers and Mechanics Bank, Philadelphia (Holdsworth, Empire, I, 199).

204. The Lynn Mechanics Bank, for instance, was founded in 1814 by the Lynn shoe manufacturers. They explained in their petition to the Massachusetts General Court that they sold the shoes in the middle and southern states on 3, 6, 9, and 12 months credit and that without a bank they were obliged to pay excessive brokerage in the South in order to meet punctually their payments for leather. (Burrill, op. cit., 12, 14.)

205. Bank of America, 29.

206. See, for instance, Hubert, op. cit., 60 (reprint of a Communication in the Evening Post of March 17, 1804); Dennis, op. cit., 11 (reprint of an article from the Salem Gazette of September 10, 1811).

207. Hubert, op. cit., 52 ff.

208. Letter to Gallatin of July 12, 1803, Writings (Putnam edition), VIII, 252.

209. Bank of America, 38, 39; New York State, The Messages of the Governors, II, 708 ff.

210. This telling phrase was used as late as 1834 by Silas Wright of New York. (See page 8 of his senate speech as quoted in the list of references.) In 1803 Jefferson had styled a certain bank in Providence the "Republican Bank in Providence." (Writings, Putnam edition, VIII, 252.)

211. Stetson, op. cit., 10, 11.

212. Stetson, op. cit., 1ff. The quotation is on page 19; the memorial goes on in this same vein, see pages 19, 20.

213. In Connecticut the political bank made its appearance in a different guise. By 1810 the Hartford Bank, then the only bank in that city, was considered as an exponent of the dominant (Congregational) church. When the Phoenix Bank came into existence in 1814 as the second one in Hartford it was considered and called the "Episcopal bank" and so became the symbol of the fight against the old regime. (See Burpee, op. cit., 15.) During the War of 1812 in at least some parts of the country, banks manifested their political affiliations by subscribing or not subscribing to the war loans (Stokes, op. cit., 276, 277).

The atmosphere in which the political bank was almost taken for granted is shown by the following episode: When the stockholders of the Merchants and Farmers Bank of Albany discovered in the first annual meeting in 1802 that all the directors were Republicans they insisted that at least two should be Federalists and action was taken accordingly.

214. Letters to Seybert, 45.

Chapter II

BANK FOUNDERS AND BANK PERSONNEL IN THE FIRST PERIOD

1. See Lewis, op. cit., 17 ff; Holdsworth, Financing an Empire, 44 ff; James, "Bank of North America," 59 ff.; East, op. cit., 287 ff.; Sumner, Financier, II, 21 ff.

2. The following chapter unavoidably contains a great number of names, many of which will not be so familiar to the general reader as they are to those historians versed in American eighteenth-century history, or to the author. But nothing would be gained by presenting biographical sketches of a few dozen of these men, especially since most of them are named in this particular chapter only to exemplify a social type. The author hopes that the few real leaders are clearly pointed out and explained.

3. Carey, Debates, 37; Davis, Essays, II, 35.

4. To what extent his experience with circulating notes (which his firm is supposed to have issued first in 1780) contributed to his decision of 1781 is unknown to this author.

5. Sparks, Diplomatic Correspondence, VII, 438 ff.

6. Carey, Debates, 48.

7. Sparks, Diplomatic Correspondence, VII, 438 ff.; XI, 364, 366, 374, 378. It is interesting to compare the sentence above with the following written to Morris in 1780 by Alexander Hamilton: "the only certain manner to obtain a permanent paper credit is to engage the moneyed interests immediately in it [a bank] by making them contribute the whole or part of the stock and giving them the whole or part of the profits." That is to say, the basic thinking of both men ran along the same lines and Morris may well have been influenced to a certain degree by Hamilton. But he broadened the aspect of the matter. What was for Hamilton only a means of public finance became for Morris a matter of national policy.

8. Jensen, op. cit., 367.

9. Op. cit., 288.

10. In 1813 the Mechanics and Farmers Bank of Albany adopted an oath of secrecy for its directors. See the anniversary publication of this bank (not paginated). Gallatin wrote in 1831: "The mystery with which it was formerly thought necessary to conceal the operations of those institutions [banks] has been one of the most prolific causes of erroneous opinions on that subject and of mismanagement on their part." (Considerations in Writings III., 318).

11. Sparks, Diplomatic Correspondence, VII, 444ff.; XI, 376 ff.

12. Gras, op. cit., 212.

13. Diary and Letters, I, 15.

14. Morris to Hamilton, May 26, 1781, in Sparks, Diplomatic Correspondence, XI, 365 ff.

15. See page 6.

16. See the place assigned to them in the original plan by Robert Morris (Sparks, Diplomatic Correspondence, VII, 444, 447).

17. Willing, Letters, 49 ff, 59.

18. Holdsworth-Dewey, op. cit., 26.

19. See chapter I, page 20.

20. Quoted from Dictionary of American Biography.

21. List of original subscribers in Lewis, op. cit., 133 ff.

22. Works, (Lodge, ed.), III, 73 ff, 81.

23. See page 164.

24. For the subscribed amounts the government

was to guarantee a fixed exchange rate
of 20:1 for Spanish milled dollars payable at the dissolution of the bank.

25. This basic idea of Hamilton's can be
found again in Daniel Webster's speeches.
He considered it the object of the Second
Bank of the United States "to connect the
public safety and convenience with private interests." Speech of July 7, 1832
on the Veto of the Bank Bill. (Works,
III, 424.) On the other hand, this alliance of wealth and government was bitterly assailed as early as 1810 by the
agrarian radicals, who "fear[ed] the consequences which would result from uniting
in one common bond of pecuniary interest
our national government and our monied
men." Debate in the House of Representatives of Pennsylvania...relative to the
Bank of the United States (1811), Introduction, 7.

26. Works, (Lodge, ed.), III, 101, 104, ff.

27. Works, (Lodge, ed.), III, 107. The formulation makes it probable that Hamilton
was not yet aware of Sir James Steuart's
work.

28. Reprinted in Domett's History of the Bank
of New York, ii, ff.

29. Works, (Hamilton, ed.), I, 414 ff. Regarding the beginnings of the Bank of
New York see Davis, Essays, II, 44.

30. The Bank of New York began business on
June 9, 1784, barely preceding the
Massachusetts Bank's opening on July 5 of
the same year.

31. Works, (Lodge, ed.), III, 128.

32. Heckscher, op. cit., 231.

33. Typical, for instance, is the limitation
of the totality of the debts to the capital stock (Article VI).

34. Normano, op. cit., 43, 46.

35. The meaning of this assertion can be seen
but from Fitzsimmons' lively description
of the business practices of merchants.
Carey, Debates, 101, 102.

36. Hamilton, Works (Lodge, ed.), III, 127;
Smith, Adam, (Cannan, ed.), 303, 304.

37. Hamilton, Works (Lodge, ed.), II, 165;
Smith, op. cit., 303.

38. Hamilton, Works (Lodge, ed.), III, 162,
163.

39. Most important from the point of view of
this research is chapter IV, 80 ff. of
East's Business Enterprise in the American Revolutionary Era.

40. See the list of subscribers to the Bank
of North America, Lewis, op. cit., 133 ff.

41. East, op. cit., 285. Besides Wadsworth
and Church (Carter), Robert Morris (98
shares) and William Bingham (95 shares)

must be characterized as creative capitalists. It is noteworthy that at the
same time or slightly later all these
men were also creative entrepreneurs in
the field of banking.

42. Typical of the political activities of
the earliest bank founders are those of
Elkanah Watson in connection with the
Bank of Albany; typical of those in the
second half of the period are the same
man's lobbying and bribing of legislators in order to get a charter for the
State Bank of Albany. Equally typical
of the latter part of the first period
are the activities of George Newbold,
the founder of the Bank of America.

43. Claiborne, Official Letter Book, II, 22,
23, 29-34, 41, 42, 160 ff., 181 ff.
Incidentally, a few years later, (in
1811), Claiborne was willing to charter
another bank because it promised "advantages to commerce and agriculture."
(Ibid., V, 124.)

Professor Ralph W. Hidy suggested to
this author that it may have been Edward
Livingston, who coming to New Orleans
(in 1804) provided the ferment and the
personal link between New York banking
experience and the New Orleans petition
for the incorporation of the Bank of
Louisiana. (This bank, incidentally,
lasted for only some fifteen years.) As
a matter of fact, Claiborne placed
Livingston on the committee which received subscriptions to the stock of the
bank. (See Hatcher, op. cit., 109 ff.)

44. Stokes, op. cit., 261 ff; Davis, Essays,
II, 60 ff.

45. State of New York, The Messages of the
Governors, II, 697. The speculative
element in the early New York bank promotions is stressed by Davis, Essays,
II, 90.

46. Burpee, op. cit., 135 ff.

47. Gras, op. cit., 18 ff.; East, op. cit.,
303, 304.

48. Op. cit., 21 ff.

49. Gray, op. cit., 12, 25.

50. Woodward, op. cit., 89, 90.

51. Stokes, op. cit., 274 ff.

52. Woodward, op. cit., 94; Gras. op. cit., 69.

52a. Atlantic Magazine, II (1824-1825), 174.

53. Pound, Native Stock, 197 ff., especially
page 250; Watson, Elkanah, op. cit., 332,
339, 340.

54. Pound, op. cit., 252, 254 ff. Watson
started the bank promotion like his
other projects by inserting an anonymous
"piece in the paper."

55. "The Leaders of the German Engine

Industry in the First Hundred Years,"
Journal of Economic History, IV, (1944),
121 ff.

56. Gras, op. cit., 9; *Path to Riches*,
Introd., iv.

57. Reprinted in Gras, op. cit., 209 ff.,
237.

58. For details see Gras, op. cit., 10.

59. The material on Russell is taken from
East's book. (See its index.) As to
Robert Morris's participation in the
Massachusetts Bank, see Gras, op. cit.,
539. See also Warren, John, *An Eulogy
on the Honourable Thomas Russell, Esq...
delivered May 4, 1796 before the several
societies to which he belonged* (Boston,
1796). Russell lived in Cambridge, but
was not a Cambridge merchant.

60. It may be mentioned in passing that
among the original promoters of the idea
of a bank for Maryland were some business associates of Morris. (East, op.
cit., 304.)

61. Warren's *Eulogy* (see footnote 59), 17;
Russell's position as "president of the
National Bank" is also alluded to in
Thacher, Peter, *A Sermon preached to the
Society in Brattle Street, Boston, April
17, 1796 and occasioned by the Death of
the Hon. Thomas Russell, Esq.* (Boston,
1796), 26.

62. Gras, op. cit., 237, 238, 531, 532.

63. Davis, *Essays*, II, 59, 102.

64. Lists of early banks are to be found in
Webster, Noah, op. cit., passim; Gouge,
Short History, 42 ff; *U.S. 24th Congr.,
2nd sess.*, House Executive Document 65,
210 ff.

65. It should be kept in mind that in England
this first multiplication of banks took
place between 1750 and 1765. (See Clapham, op. cit., I, 158).

66. The Bank of the Northern Liberties in
Philadelphia, founded in 1810, seems to
have been the first suburban bank in
this country. (Simon, op. cit., passim;
Holdsworth, *Empire*, I, 303 ff.)

67. George Clymer, one of the original stockholders of the Bank of North America became the president of the Philadelphia
Bank.

68. See pages 31, 33.

69. Gras, op. cit., 22.

70. Gray, op. cit., 12, 67.

71. About Varick see below page 37.

72. Hubert, op. cit., 30.

73. The Phoenix Bank depends on the Hartford
Bank; the Hartford Bank on the Bank of
New York; the Bank of New York on the
Bank of North America. (Woodward, op.
cit., 103, 104.)

74. State of New York, *Messages of the
Governors*, II, 697.

75. Gras, op. cit., 26.

76. An example of the public man elected
bank president in the second period is
General Nathaniel Terry, who in 1819
became president of the Hartford Bank.
(See *Hartford National Bank*, 24, 25).
Incidentally, he was Jeremiah Wadsworth's
son-in-law.

77. Public personalities - Federalists -
were also the two earliest presidents of
the New Haven Bank (chartered 1792,
opened for business 1795). The first
was David Austin (1732-1801). He was one
of the most prominent citizens of New
Haven and a wealthy, public-spirited man
who had no profession or business, but
dealt in real estate. He had become a
deacon of his church when still very
young, had served during the Revolution
on Committees of Inspection and Correspondence, became one of New Haven's first
aldermen, was twice a deputy to the General Assembly, a collector of customs
(1793-1801), and president of the New
Haven Bank (1795-1798). His successor,
Isaac Beers, president 1798-1812, was
also a member of a wealthy and leading
family. He had been a tavern keeper and
one of the largest early book importers
and, in the course of his lifetime, was
councilman, alderman, deputy to the General Assembly, president of the Chamber
of Commerce. (See Woolsey, op. cit., 6;
Mary Mitchell, op. cit., 26.) These men
seem to exemplify pretty well the type
of president in the earliest banks of
small trade centers.

78. *Philadelphia National Bank*, 45, 46.

79. East, op. cit., 127.

80. Regarding Clymer, see page 37.

81. Gras, op. cit., 18.

82. Hill, Hamilton Andrews, "William Phillips
and William Phillips, Father and Son,
1722-1827." (Reprinted from *New England
Historic Genealogical Register*, April
1885), 5 ff. Wisner, Benjamin B., *A
Sermon occasioned by the Death of Hon.
William Phillips* (Boston, 1827), 46.

83. When the sugar refiner Isaac Roosevelt
(1726-1794) became the third president
of the Bank of New York (1786-1791) he
was the first manufacturer to become a
bank president. However, again it is
doubtful whether he became a bank president because of his success in business or because of his public career
as a noted patriot, state senator, and
delegate to the New York State Convention
which ratified the state constitution of

1788. (Whittlesey, Charles B., The Roosevelt Genealogy, 1649-1902, [Hartford, 1902], 26-28; Nevins, op. cit., 27).

84. National Cyclopedia of American Biography, XI, 345; Daly, op. cit., 15, 16; Domett, op. cit., 58; Nevins, op. cit., 27.

85. Dictionary of American Biography and the various monographs on the Manhattan Company.

86. See also the chapters on the original directors of the New York Merchants Bank (Hubert, op. cit., 24 ff.); of the Hartford Bank (Woodward, op. cit., 31 ff); East, op. cit., 90 ff.

87. Wettereau, op. cit., 276, 277. William Bingham (1752-1804) was director from 1791 to 1801, and Rufus King from 1791 to 1793. Samuel Breck (1771-1862), a prominent Philadelphia merchant, originally from Boston, was director from 1793-1809; while Isaac Wharton served from 1797 to 1809. Biographies of the first three are to be found in the Dictionary of American Biography. For William Bingham's business activities, see also East, op. cit., 141 ff.

88. Sparks, Diplomatic Correspondence, VII, 438 ff.

89. Gras, op. cit., see under "Payne" in index and especially pages 27, 230, 241, 242.

90. For what follows, see Oberholtzer, Morris, 104 ff., 305; Appleton's Cyclopedia of American Biography; Sparks, Diplomatic Correspondence, III, 72; Lewis, op. cit., 37, 119.

91. Biographical Directory of Congress, 1774-1903. Gras, op. cit., 12.

92. Domett, op. cit., 16, 17; East, op. cit., see index; Stevens, John Austin, Jr., Colonial Records of the New York [State] Chamber of Commerce, 1768-1784 with historical and biographical sketches Part II, Colonial New York, Sketches Biographical and Historical, 1768-1784, (New York, 1867), 161-163.

93. Hardenbrook, op. cit., 95.

94. Simpson, Henry, The Lives of Eminent Philadelphians (Philadelphia, 1859), 890 ff.

95. Hardenbrook, op. cit., 141; Walters, op. cit., 15.

96. Woodward, op. cit., 76, 77, 111; Burpee, op. cit., 103, 104.

97. It can hardly be doubted that systematic local research could fill the gap and would prove to be a nice subject for a master's thesis.

98. Davis, William Thomas, History of the Bench and Bar of Suffolk County; Boutwell, op. cit., I, 15.

99. It is possible that Andrew Dexter is also identical with that Mr. Dexter who got control of the first territorial Bank in Michigan, i.e., the Bank of Detroit; he turned up there and disappeared again with a batch of notes in his pocket. (See the amusing contemporary history of that bank in Farmer, op. cit., 854 ff.) Dexter seems also to have had some connection with the Bank of Marietta, Ohio (Stokes, op. cit., 279.)

100. Dexter's methods which are both criminal and ingenious can be seen from excerpts from his correspondence with the Farmers' Exchange Bank, Glocester, Rhode Island, samples of which follow.

Andrew Dexter, jun, to John Harris and William Colwell, Esquires.
Boston, October, 8th, 1808.
"I have dispatched Mr. Edward [his clerk] to Glocester, in order to bring me such amount of bills as may now be ready, in order to send them to Berkshire by one of the directors of the Pittsfield Bank who will be ready and waiting to receive them on his return... I presume you will be able by this time to deliver him a very large amount..."

Andrew Dexter, jun. to William Colwell Esq. Boston, December 2nd, 1808.
"Besides, I wish you to employ yourself constantly in signing bills, except during the time you are naturally in the bank. I should conceive you may work in the daytime as well as night, provided you shut yourself up between the bank hours in your private chamber, letting no-one know or suspect your business. I shall send a person to you immediately to receive the other bills, in order that you may remain at the bank..."

Draft of a letter from William Colwell to Andrew Dexter jun, Glocester, December 12, 1808. (Apparently in answer to the preceding letter.)
"...The bills I shall sign as fast as I can, but I think it will be best at present to work as privately as possible, mostly in the evening. I believe I can finish fifty thousand a week..."

Andrew Dexter jun. to William Colwell. Boston, December 20, 1808.
"...I am very sorry you have signed no more bills, and beg you to sign at least twice as many more during the next week. I wish you would work day and night so as to sign if possible seventy thousand dollars a day..."

(See Report of the Committee to inquire into the...Farmers Exchange Bank in Glocester, 32, 36, 37.) A description of the affair is to be found in Stokes, op. cit., 278 ff.

Incidentally Dexter is the inventor of the oft-quoted cynical receipt: "I, Andrew Dexter, jun, do promise the President, Directors and Company of the Farmers' Exchange Bank to pay them or order — dollars in two years from the date with interest at two percent per annum; it being, however, understood that said Dexter shall not be called upon to make payment until he thinks proper, he being the principal stockholder best knowing when it will be proper to pay the same."

Chapter III

SECOND PERIOD - GENERAL CHARACTERISTICS

1. See this author's "Bank Money in the United States during the First Half of the Nineteenth Century," The Southern Economic Journal, X (1944), 212 ff. About the circulation of postdated checks in Boston, see Gras, op. cit., 91, 440. Similarly when small notes became forbidden in the State of New York small checks began circulating. Annual Report of the New York Bank Commissioners for 1836, 23. The notes of the State Bank of Illinois (of 1831) approximated state paper money redeemable by the state at a future date (Garnett, op. cit., 12).

2. Myers, Margaret, op. cit., 82. (Incidentally the last phrase is typical of the second period, referring as it does to the multiplicity of credit instruments issued by banks as mentioned above.) In 1832 MacDuffie defined a bank as "an institution established for the purpose of dealing in money." U.S. 22d Congr., 1st sess., House Report 460, 298. At the same time (1831) Nathan Appleton wrote: "The business of banking may properly be defined, the trade or traffic in money, or in securities for the payment of money, excluding all trade in merchandize other than bullion and foreign coins." (Examination, 6.)

3. Report of the Secretary of the Treasury on the Bank of the United States, 1820, 4.

4. U.S. 35th Congr., 1st sess., House Exec. Doc. 107, 216; and the interesting report of a legislative committee of 1836, reprinted in Worthen, op. cit., 41 ff.

Benjamin Franklin had considered notes secured by land as "coined land." Spahr, op. cit., 38.

5. U.S. 25th Congr., 2nd sess. Senate Doc. 179, 1.

6. See this author's Essays in American Economic History (page 121), for an understanding of this proposal.

7. See, for instance, Secretary of the Treasury's Report on the Bank of the United States of 1820, 15 (incidentally, he wanted to see banks established only in "the principal commercial cities of each state"). Gallatin, Considerations in Writings, III, 200 ff. Biddle also pleaded for a prohibition of small notes (U.S. 22nd Congr., 1st sess., House Report 460, 367) and so did Levi Woodbury (U.S. 23d Congr., 2nd sess., Senate Document 13, 35 ff.); Report of the Boston Committee (of 1834), 5. See also Miller, op. cit., 142 ff.

8. Crawford in a letter of 1819 defined "sound circulation" as "bank notes convertible into specie at the will of the holder." Biddle suggested severe punishment for non-payment of notes. Some charters, as that of the Bank of the United States, provided in this case for the payment of high interest; others for forfeiture.

9. Even advanced thinkers in the second period were so far from understanding the concept of liquidity that they could not even express the idea in a simple form. Mathew Carey, by way of quotation of what he apparently considered a good formulation, thus expressed the fact of merchants being non-liquid: Calculating on the continuance of the "usual discounts" they had formed "engagements that were far from exceeding their property, but in the present state of the pecuniary negociation exceeded their convertible effects." Essays on Banking, 80, Quotation is from Bisset's History of George III (Philadelphia, 1811), IV, 76. About twenty years later Daniel Webster made the following statement: "The true question in all our [banking] institutions was not the ultimate means of meeting all its liabilities, but the present means for present calls," i.e., not ultimate solvency, but liquidity. (Register of Debates in Congress, X, Part I, 737.) As late as 1840 the term liquidity was still uncommon. The Massachusetts Bank Commissioners wrote in their Report for 1839 the following awkward sentences in place of this simple term: "It is not enough that a bank is abundantly able to

meet all its liabilities ultimately. The funds of a bank should be in such a situation that its bills shall never be discredited even temporarily." (page 9.)

Toward the end of the period there can be found the first proposals to relate note issues to specie, but the proper relationship is still obscure. (See, for instance, George Tucker's book of 1839, op. cit., 207, 132; U.S. 23d Congr., 2nd sess., Senate Document 13, 7, 15; and the following passage from a report of the Committee of Ways and Means in 1834: "The main object of legislation should be to enlarge the basis of specie on which the paper circulation of the state banks is to depend for support." U.S. 23d Congr., 1st sess., House Document 312, 30; Report of the Boston Committee, 5, 9.)

10. See, for instance, Nathan Hale, op. cit., 39, 40. Actually to the extent that regular redemption of bank obligations was enforced in the second period banks tended to become more liquid.

11. The latter telling expression is used in the Report of the Secretary of the Treasury on the Bank of the United States (1820), 15.

12. I.e., loans without special collateral and probably mostly identical with loans on "real paper" or trade paper, as we call it (bills of exchange and promissory notes representing actual business transactions and therefore carrying two names, "double name paper" in the language of that time. For examples of the use of this term, see American State Papers, Finance, III, 261, 312, 313.

13. Overdrafts were considered an irregular sort of loan and so were loans "upon memorandum checks" whether or not these were secured by collateral. The latter were supposed to represent "accommodation of the borrower...as a matter of personal favor without receiving the sanction of an ordinary loan." Such loans were made especially to directors and officers and were becoming unpopular by 1840. (Report of the Massachusetts Bank Commissioners for 1838, 21; for 1839, 13.) Regarding overdrafts, see also American State Papers, Finance, IV, 733; and chapter III, footnote 50.

14. U.S. 22nd Congr., 1st sess., House Report 460, 525, 541, 547, 555, 562, 564.

15. Outline of a Plan of a National Bank, 13, 14.

16. Gras, op. cit., 47.

17. Trotter, op. cit., 35; Report of the Massachusetts Bank Commissioners for 1838, 11, 12.

18. Bronson, Appeal., passim. See also page 70.

19. Op. cit., 83.

20. Carey, Essays on Banking, 131. Secretary of the Treasury, Report on the Bank of the United States (1820), 15. Venit has recently published the most interesting material on Bronson, but his interpretation (op. cit., 202) seems erroneous.

21. Appeal, 6. Incidentally, Nathan Hale (op. cit., 39-40) expressed similar ideas in 1826. The following quotation is from Bronson, Henry, op. cit., 372, 373. Henry Bronson in turn depends on the article "History of the Bank of ----" (in Gouge's Journal of Banking, 209 ff., 225 ff.) which article describes the history of the Bridgeport Bank. Venit (op. cit., 201, footnote) identifies Bronson's son Arthur as the author.

22. See below, page 91.

23. Hamilton, James A., op. cit., 253 ff. An obvious reference to Bronson and his theories can be found also in the Annual Report of the New York Bank Commissioners for 1832, 5.

24. In addition to the material quoted by Venit (op. cit., 207) see Biddle's letters of January 26, 1830 to Charles A. Davis and of March 18, 1831 to M. Robinson in Biddle's Letterbooks. The copy of Biddle's letter of February 7, 1830 to Bronson, which Venit found in the Bronson Papers, is in the former's letter books, III, 171.

25. Outline of a Plan for a National Bank, 13, 14. This plan is in many other respects antiquated and clearly the work of an old man or written under the influence of one.

26. This aspect of Bronson's theory is elaborated in an article entitled "General Propositions Explanatory of the Elementary Principles of Banking" in Free Trade Advocate, II (1829), 24 ff. The paper is identified as Bronson's work by a later statement of Condy Raguet, the editor of the periodical, in his book, A Treatise on Currency and Banking, 204, footnote. The article which is of particular interest showing the roots of Bronson's thinking in Mercantilist theory, will be alluded to repeatedly. Similar ideas were current in England at that time, see Mints, op. cit., 48, footnote 27. It is unknown whether Bronson conceived his ideas independently or under such influence.

27. *Financial Register*, II, 7 ff. The biographical data on Bronson previously given are taken from an obituary published in *ibid*., 15, 16; and from Bronson, Henry, *op. cit*., 370 ff.

28. See page 193 ff.

29. See Chapter XI, second volume of this book.

30. *Essays on Banking*, 131.

31. Clibborn, *op. cit*., 29; *Connecticut Bank Commissioners*, *Annual Report*, 1841, 6, quoted by Margaret Myers (*op. cit*., 55).

32. A memorial of citizens of Albany of 1826 shows that they considered it a function of banks to provide merchants with capital. *U.S. 23d Congr*., *2d sess*. *Senate Document 17*, 251 ff. This outlook survived as late as 1857 (see Walker, Amasa, *op, cit*., 54).

33. Carey, *Essays on Banking*, 132.

34. Clibborn, *op. cit*., 26.

35. *U.S. 23rd Congr*., *1st sess*., *Senate Doc. 16*, 142 ff.

36. Stokes, *op. cit*., 308

37. Hall, *op. cit*., 247, 248.

38. Biddle to Jeremiah Mason, August 28, 1829. On April first of the same year Mason, president of the Portsmouth branch, was advised to get rid of Great Falls Manufacturing stock if it could be done gradually and imperceptibly. This letter may indicate an industrial loan on the basis of stock which was later forfeited. *Biddle Letterbooks*.

39. Domett, *op. cit*., 74. Gras (*op. cit*., 107) mentions comparatively large loans by the Massachusetts Bank to a canal corporation. The earliest large scale industrial loan on record is the loan of the 1790's of the Bank of New York to the Society for the Establishment of Useful Manufactures amounting to $45,000 and secured by government stock.

40. See the report on the portfolio of the Nashville branch of the Second Bank of the United States in *Report of the Bank of the United States to the Committee of Ways and Means* (1835), 19.

41. *Report...on the Bank of the United States*, 16. On page 15 the Secretary alluded to the kinship of industrial and agricultural credit.

42. As to the corresponding British experience, see this author's *Essays in American Economic History*, 117.

43. Raguet, *Financial Register*, II, 8.

44. See Chapter VI.

45. *U.S. 22d Congr*., *2d sess*., *House Report 121*, 66.

46. When the board of the Bank of Pennsylvania resolved to loan on stock at a cheap rate it expressly included corporation stock. (*U.S. 22nd Congr*., *1st sess*., *House Report 460*, 153). The Second Bank of the United States loaned on stock of insurance companies, banks, railroads, and canal companies (*Ibid*., 192, 193).

47. It should be mentioned that credit was also given on the strength of letters. Bankers distinguished between letters of introduction (recommendation) and letters of guarantee. If there was a misrepresentation in a letter of introduction, on the strength of which credit was given, the writer was considered "liable in law, in honor, and by the custom of merchants." Usually, but not always, the writer of a letter or recommendation or guarantee was informed about every loan made on the basis of his letter (*U.S. 22nd Congr*., *1st sess*., *House Report 460*, 558, 559). An early forerunner of these letters dating as far back as 1785 reads as follows: "This certifies that John R. Livingston Esqr. has had many Negociations with the Mass^a Bank and has in all of them conducted himself with Punctuality and Honour." (Gras, *op. cit*., 264). A certain business man in Lexington, Kentucky, was in the habit of recommending to the Lexington branch of the Second Bank of the United States those who made applications from Fleming County (about 1830). See *U.S. 22d Congr*., *2d sess*., *House Report 121*, 137.

48. *U.S. 22d Congr*., *1st sess*., *House Report 460*, 131, 136.

49. *Ibid*., 125, 128. Thomas Biddle and Company, the largest borrowers of this type, reserved the right to repay such loans at their convenience within the stipulated time. (*Ibid*., 156.)

50. *Ibid*., 129-131. Incidentally still another type of short term loans existed in the second period. During the administration of Jones, the Second Bank of the United States permitted brokers and merchants to overdraw their accounts during the day with the understanding that they would be made even again before closing hour. Cheves tried to stop this method, but when the Bank lost customers it was reintroduced. Other banks in the same period seem to have fought the custom also. The Franklin Bank of Cincinnati forbade overdrafts in its bylaws of 1833 and the Girard Bank contemplated strict measures against offenders whose names were to be reported on the next discount day. *U.S. 23rd Congr*., *1st sess*., *Senate Doc. 16*, 115 ff., 170 ff.

51. Myers, Margaret, _op. cit._, 127 ff. In Boston a rudimentary call loan market existed in the 1820's for completely different reasons; see page 72 below. It was apparently revived in the 1840's, and 1850's (Gras, _op. cit._, 124). _Report of the Massachusetts Bank Commissioners_ for 1838, 21.

52. _U.S. 22nd Congr._, _1st sess._, _House Report 460_, 133. As to lending on bullion in the first period, see Gras, _op. cit._, 50.

53. Domett, _op. cit._, 80, 86.

54. As one example out of many, see the Pennsylvania act of 1814 for regulating banks (_U.S. 23rd Congr._, _1st sess._, _Senate Doc._, _16_, 142 ff).

55. Carey, _Essays on Banking_, 69 ff. Carey was very critical of this policy.

56. _U.S. 22nd Congr._, _1st sess._, _House Report 460_, 5, 6, 298, 299, 358 ff. Dallas's plan for a national bank of 1814 provided limitations as to the alienation of public stock received by way of subscriptions (_American State Papers, Finance_, II, 867). The New York plan of 1833 for a national bank expressly made irredeemable and inalienable (except in case of need and with consent of the federal government) the stock subscribed by the federal and state governments to the projected bank. But even in case of need it was only to be hypothecated for money borrowed for one to three years. (_Outline for a Plan for a National Bank_, 7, 8.)

57. E.g., the Bank of the Manhattan Company. Myers, Margaret, _op. cit._, 23, 26.

58. _Essays on Banking_, 168.

59. _Report of the Secretary of the Treasury on the Bank of the United States_, 12; Gordon, _op. cit._, 83.

60. _Op. cit._, 4, 9. The Boston Committee of 1834 distinguished between bank notes and bank currency. See its _Report_, 5.

61. _U.S. 22nd Congr._, _1st sess._, _House Report 460_, 363.

62. Adams, Charles Francis, _Further Reflections_, 28, 29. It is characteristic of the situation that the banks did not grasp the chance to develop their deposit business. They reacted by compelling the depositors either to withdraw their deposits or to sign a pledge that they were willing to receive in payment of their deposits, notes of the same or a similar description to those which they had originally deposited.

63. _U.S. 22nd Congr._, _1st sess._, _House Report 460_, 363.

64. _Bank of the United States_ (Reprint from the _North American Review_, disseminated by the Bank of the United States), 15.

65. Incidentally this explanation holds good also for the fact that the circulation of the Second Bank of the United States was principally in the South and West. Gallatin, _Writings_, III, 453.

66. See above, page 50.

67. _An Act to Incorporate the Subscribers of the Bank of the United States._

68. Myers, Margaret, _op. cit._, 111; see also below, footnote 73.

69. Gordon, _op. cit._, 83.

70. For examples, see _U.S. 23rd Congr._, _1st sess._, _Senate Document 17_, 17. Levi Woodbury, as Secretary of the Treasury, recommended such arrangements (See _U.S. 23d Congr._, _2d sess._, _Senate Document 13_, 16). Similar arrangements were common in England where a large proportion of all country notes were payable in London (Wood, _op. cit._, 18).

71. _American State Papers, Finance_, III, 332, 333, IV, 508; _U.S. 23d Congr._, _2d sess._, _Senate Document 17_, 50.

72. "The banks with which the Manhattan Company corresponds." "We have correspondence and reciprocal accounts with..." (Union Bank, New York), 1833. (_U.S. 23rd Congr._, _1st sess._, _Senate Document 17_, 60, 74.) This author found the earliest American examples for the use of the noun "correspondent" in 1834 ("bills of exchange furnished by banks or private bankers on their correspondents in distant cities") in _U.S. 23rd Congr._, _2d sess._, _House Exec. Document 13_, 16. See also in _U.S. 23rd Congr._, _1st sess._, _Senate Document 72_, 16, Report of Daniel Webster "by a correspondent abroad." The term can be found a few years earlier in Britain in Rees's Cyclopaedia (article of 1819 on Bank of England) and in one of the "supplementary dissertations" of J. R. McCulloch to Adam Smith's _Wealth of Nations_, (Edinburgh, 1828), IV, 293.

73. "_Banks in Correspondence with the Mechanics Bank of New York_" in 1833.
New York State
   Bank of Newburgh, Bank of Troy, Bank of Utica, branch of Bank of Utica at Canandaigua, Brooklyn Bank.
Connecticut
Thames' Bank; Winahener County Bank; Tolland County Bank, Connecticut River Banking Company; Connecticut Bank, Bridgeport; Phoenix Bank, Stratford; Branch of do. at Litchfield; Middleton

Bank; Mechanics' Bank, New Haven.

Rhode Island
Merchants' Bank at Providence.

Massachusetts
New England Bank, Boston; Commonwealth's Bank, do; Merchants' Bank, New Bedford; Fall River Bank.

New Hampshire
Piscataqua Bank, Portsmouth.

New Jersey
State Bank at Newark; Mechanics' Bank, Newark; Newark Banking and Insurance Company; Commercial Bank, Perth Amboy; Orange Bank; and Bank of New Brunswick.

Pennsylvania
Farmers and Mechanics' Banks, Philadelphia; Bank of Northern Liberties, do; Southwark Bank, do; Harrisburgh Bank.

Maryland
Farmers and Merchants' Bank, Baltimore.

District of Columbia
Bank of Washington.

Virginia
Bank of Virginia, Richmond; Office of do., Petersburgh, do. do. do., Fredericksburgh; do. do. do., Norfolk; do. do. do., Lynchburg; do. do. do., Kanawha.

North Carolina
State Bank, Newbern; do. do. at Edenton; do. do. at Tarboro; Bank of Cape Fear, at Fayetteville.

South Carolina
Planters and Mechanics' Bank, Charleston; Commercial Bank, at Columbia.

Georgia
State Bank at Savannah, Branch of do. at Augusta, Augusta Insurance and Banking Company, Branch of State Bank at Macon, Mechanics' Bank at Augusta, Farmers' Bank of Chattahoochee at Columbus.

Louisiana
Louisiana State Bank, New Orleans.

Alabama
Bank of Mobile.

Ohio
Bank of Chillicothe.

Mississippi
Bank of Mississippi at Natchez. (U.S. 23rd Congr., 1st sess., Senate Document 17, 75 ff.)

The Louisville, Kentucky branch of the Second Bank of the United States reported in 1832: "The State banks with which we correspond are as follows, viz., the Commercial Bank of Cincinnati; Bank of Chillicothe, Ohio; Bank of Marietta, Ohio; Farmers and Mechanics' Bank of Steubenville; Lancaster, Ohio, Bank; Branch of Bank of Virginia, at Charleston; Northwestern Bank of Virginia, at Wheeling; Bank of Pittsburgh; Monongahela Bank, Brownsville, Pennsylvania; Evan Poultney's Bank, Baltimore; Girard's Bank, Philadelphia; Hartford Bank, Connecticut; Phenix Bank, New York. With these banks we have no other business than to collect for them; except the Northwest Bank of Virginia, at Wheeling, which acts as our agent in collecting bills payable there." (U.S. 22nd Congr., 2nd sess., House Report 121, 145.)

74. Clibborn, op. cit., 15.
75. Myers, Margaret, op. cit., 103 ff. For figures see the Annual Reports of the New York Bank Commissioners for 1834 and following years.
76. U.S. 25th Congr., 2d sess., House Exec. Document 79, 619, 656; U.S. 25th Congr., 3d sess., House Exec. Document 227, 493.
77. U.S. 23rd Congr., 1st sess., Senate Document 17, 18.
78. Myers, Margaret, op. cit., 120.
79. However, in 1809 the Secretary of the Treasury suggested that in case of renewal of the charter the First Bank of the United States should pay interest on the government deposits whenever they exceeded a certain sum. American State Papers, Finance, II, 352.
80. See, for instance, the petition of 1784 for the charter of the Massachusetts Bank, Gras, op. cit., 214.
81. The Massachusetts Bank charged 1/10 of 1 per cent between 1786 and 1790, ibid., 23, 37. Rules and Regulations of 1786, 4th section, ibid., 227. Regarding the Bank of Amsterdam see ibid., 43; also van Dillen, op. cit., 53.
82. Essays on Banking, Introduction, xix.
83. Gras, op. cit., 94, 95; Suffolk Bank, Directors' Records, December 1, 1819 and January 29, 1820. (Baker Library, Harvard University).
84. See U.S. 22nd Congr., 1st sess., House Report 460, 135.
85. Hidy, "House of Baring," 271.
86. By-laws of the Commercial Bank of New Orleans, Sec. 26. U.S. 23rd Congr., 1st sess., Senate Document 16. 235.
87. U.S. 23rd Congr., 1st sess., Senate Document 17, 17.
88. See Sec. 57, chapter 30, Revised Statutes of 1836.
89. Report of the Massachusetts Bank Commissioners for 1838, 20; for 1840, 8. The Report of the Connecticut Bank Commissioners to the General Assembly,

May Session, 1839 (House of Repr. Doc. 7) mentions (on page 10) the paying of interest on deposits by Connecticut banks. Rafinesque, on the other hand, blamed banks in general for not paying interest on deposits (1837); op. cit., 46.

When the renewal of the charter of the Second Bank of the United States hung fire its paying interest on government deposits was contemplated; see, for instance, Biddle to Horace Binney, Feb. 13, 1832 (Biddle Letter Books).

90. Report of the Massachusetts Bank Commissioners for 1850, 8. Gras, op. cit., 94, 95.

91. Hidy, "House of Baring," 270, footnote 3.

92. Report of the Bank of the United States to the Committee of Ways and Means (1833), 6, 30 ff.

93. Bank of the United States, Report of 1822, 42.

94. See Chapter I, footnote 139.

95. Domett, op. cit., 54, 74, 75.

96. In the 1830's considerable amounts of the New York Canal Fund were loaned to or deposited on interest with banks in the state. Annual Report of the New York Bank Commissioners (1832), 12; (1843), 23.

97. Ibid. (1836), 14. Rediscounting is mentioned in Biddle's letter of June 13, 1829 to A. Davis, New York (Biddle Letter Books).

98. U.S. 22nd Congr., 1st sess., House Report, 151; American State Papers, Finance, III, 367.

99. In 1837 the State Bank of Illinois was authorized to borrow $250,000 (Garnett, op. cit., 28).

100. The administrative functions of the bank boards were stressed in the bank charters adopted as the second period progressed: The charter of the Bank of America in New York (passed in 1812, that is to say, just before the first period drew to a close), enacted in section 5 "that for the well ordering, managing, and conducting of the stock, property, concerns, and affairs of the said corporation the same shall be ordered, managed, and conducted by eighteen directors." The charter of 1818 of the Bank of Burlington, Vermont stated in very similar form in section 5 "that the stock, property, and concerns of said bank shall be managed and conducted by seven directors a majority of whom shall constitute a quorum." Toward the end of the second period the charter of 1833 of the Farmers and Mechanics Bank of Hartford, Connecticut, charged the thirteen directors of the bank with the task of "well ordering the affairs of the corporation" (section 4); and in the same year that of the Franklin Bank of Cincinnati ruled in section 5 "that the real and personal estate, business, property, funds, and prudential concerns...and the administration of its [the bank's] affairs shall be under the direction, management, and control of a board of...directors" which clause was repeated literally in the charter of the Louisville Bank of Kentucky. (U.S. 23rd Congr., 1st sess., Senate Document 73, 9, 5, 3; Senate Document 17, 108, 118.)

101. Annual Report of the New York Bank Commissioners (1833), 19.

102. For example, the Bank of Burlington, Vt., Charter of 1818, sec. 21 (U.S. 23rd Congr., 1st sess., Senate Document 73, 6). See also the suggestions of Duncombe op. cit., 110, 122.

103. See also Plain Truth, 6, 11, 13: "and probably the directors are not now so proud of the measure to be desirous to blazon the circumstances." "The directors miscalculated when they pronounced that the losses were repaired." "I deny that I have arraigned the motives of the directors."

104. Scroggs, "Pioneer Banking," 413 ff. An Alabama law of 1839 provided for the compensation of the directors of the state-owned Bank of the State of Alabama to keep them from recompensing themselves to the detriment of the bank, ibid., 420. See also Garnett, op. cit., 15, 33.

105. U.S. 23rd Congr., 1st sess., Senate Document 72, 14. See also Jones, William (Friendly Monitor), op. cit., 42, 43.

106. Plain Truth, 25. See also the amusing rules and regulations of 1827 of the Lynn Mechanics Bank (Burrill, op. cit., 26).

107. American State Papers, Finance, III, 588; U.S. 23rd Congr., 2nd sess., Senate Document 17, 36. The opinion expressed in the quotation tallies with the principles applied by Biddle in the selection of directors; see letter to Robert Lenox, New York, October 27, 1823, in Letter Books. He asks for the names of men who would attract customers "without reference to their political and personal predilections." The Annual Report of the New York Bank Commissioners (1833, 19)

points to the lack of suitable directors at many places.

108. "They see that bank directors, of all others, are the most favorably situated for obtaining the use of capital; and, of course, they desire to become bank directors themselves." Amasa Walker in in his satirical "History of the Wickaboag Bank," op. cit., 53.

109. Rafinesque (op. cit., 39, 44) claims that directors borrowed at better terms and were often permitted to overdraw their accounts.

110. "One word from a director of the only bank in the place is sufficient to give a man credit or ruin his prospects." Duncombe, op. cit., 78, 79.

111. Treatise, 290, 292. It "has been found to stimulate the dishonest propensities of so many of the managers and clerks." John Pintard in a letter of July 5, 1820 mentions three cases of defalcations in New York banks since 1814 (Mechanics Bank: $120,000; Merchants Bank: $210,000; Phoenix Bank: $147,000); (op. cit., I, 302, 303.)

112. American State Papers, Finance, IV, 733.

113. The way in which they elbowed themselves into the boards has been discribed as follows: "Of course, the gentlemen who have performed all the labor of getting the stock subscribed and have taken the precaution to get 'proxies' of all the 'widows and orphans' who could not well attend in person are elected Directors 'for the ensuing year.'" Amasa Walker, op. cit., 55.

114. David Henshaw, (Banks and Banking, page 43), remarked that bank directors were compensated for managing the affairs of their institutions by the facilities which they received. As the Massachusetts Bank Commissioners put it in their Report for 1838: "whether the directors sit down to the full table themselves and bestow the crumbs only on the starving multitude" can be found through examination only. A Massachusetts act of April 25, 1838 (section 6) tried to limit loans to directors. See also Stokes, op. cit., 303, 304.

115. Such methods were probably a distortion of the then customary business of large commercial firms of guaranteeing business paper for a del credere commission of 2 1/2 per cent. U.S. 22nd Congr., 2nd sess., House Report 121, 4. Rafinesque (op. cit., 50) complained that banks were not allowed to charge a del credere commission and that they were even prevented from the establishment of companies to insure their credit

risks, as had often been proposed.

116. Clibborn, op. cit., 6, 7, 34, 35. In 1839 another contemporary observer (Joshua Forman) thus described what was common practice among this type of businessmen. Banks started by "well meaning men" were afterwards bought by knaves, who after circulating large amounts of notes withdrew what capital was left so that the public had to bear the loss. In other cases banks, whose capital was lost in wild speculations, kept up their credit by paying dividends until the insiders had sold out. Or banks, after expanding credit recklessly for profit's sake, suddenly and violently called in their loans thereby spreading disaster. (New York Assembly Journal, 1829, 174.) The earlier Reports of the Massachusetts Bank Commissioners are full of warnings that dividends could be paid legally only out of profits. A similar warning can be found in the Report of the Connecticut Bank Commissioners (1839), 5. This report contains on pages 17 ff. material regarding the behavior of bank directors. Rafinesque, (op. cit., 40) claims that bank directors were interested in directing their banks so as to be able to acquire notes at a discount and to repay large loans with depreciated paper.

117. Gallatin, Suggestions in Writings, III, 380, 381.

118. See page 62.

119. Rules and Regulations of 1816, section 13; also U.S. 23rd Congr., 1st sess., Senate Document 2, 23, 24. Non-resident directors were assembled in special meetings. The following statement by one of the directors is illuminating: "When the propriety of inviting the non-resident directors was suggested by the president, as called for by the peculiar state of the Bank, and for the purpose of recommending a course for the future operation of the bank, I remarked at that time that I could not see the utility of inviting gentlemen to direct the operations of the bank who must necessarily be comparatively ignorant of the state of the Bank and its general operations." U.S. 22nd Congr., 2nd sess., House Report 121, 62.

120. U.S. 22nd Congr., 1st sess., House Report 460, 115. See ibid., 210 ff. for the reports of the dividend committee. See also Report of the Bank of the United States to the Committee of Ways and Means, (1833), 6; U.S. 22nd Congr., 2nd sess., House Report 121, 41, 61, 68; and U.S. 23d Congr., 1st, sess., House Document 312, 26.

121. Illustrating the beginnings of such committees on the state of the bank is an entry of May 10, 1790 in the Minute Book of the Directors of the Massachusetts Bank of Boston: "The board will resolve themselves into a committee... to consider generally the state of the bank." Gras., op. cit., 330. As to this committee of the Girard Bank, see its by-laws, art. 10, (U.S. 22nd Congr., 1st sess., Senate Document 16, 172). For the working of this Committee in the Second Bank of the United States, see U.S. 22nd Congr., 1st sess., House Exec. Document 8, 26, 27.

122. See, for instance, Rules and By-laws of the Franklin Bank of Cincinnati, section 14, U.S. 23rd Congr., 1st sess., Senate Document 16, 114 ff; Rules and Regulations of the Union Bank of Louisiana, rules 17, 36, U.S. 23rd Congr., 1st sess., Senate Document 73, 27-31. The redemption and clearing business of the Suffolk Bank was administered by a foreign money committee (see below page 74). The very conservative New York Committee which was planning for a new national bank in the 1830's contemplated its administration by an Executive Committee elected yearly by the board and including the president and cashier ex officio. (Outline of a Plan for a National Bank, 10.)

123. Schlesinger, A. M., op. cit., passim; see also below page 167. The term "bank government" was used by Dallas in his bank plan of 1815. American State Papers, Finance, III, 61. In 1834 Congressman Ben Hardin stressed that the method of transacting business in Congress paralleled the method used by the Bank; op. cit., 30. See also U.S. 23rd Congr., 2d sess., Senate Document 17, 5, 6.

124. Some banks seem to have kept rather aloof from the business in bills of exchange, e.g., the Massachusetts Bank (Gras., op. cit., 125).

125. In the Suffolk Bank of Boston, for instance, as early as 1819, (Whitney, op. cit., 8); in the Massachusetts Bank in 1821, (Gras., op. cit., 432). For the Franklin Bank of Cincinnati, see U.S. 23rd Congr., 1st sess., Senate Document 16, 115; U.S. 23rd Congr., 2d sess., Senate Document 17, 52. As to Daniel Webster's opinion on the legality of bank administration by committees and the necessity of their discounting bills, see U.S. 23rd Congr., 1st sess., Senate Document 72, 13.

126. Report of a Committee of Directors, 31, 32. This policy followed precedents established as early as 1817 or 1818 when under an order of August 8, 1817 of the board of the Second Bank of the United States the president and cashier started renewing stock notes, and soon also occasionally granting new discounts. (American State Papers, Finance, III, 368.)

127. Report of a Committee of Directors, 31.

128. Gras, op. cit., 108. In 1828 the Bank of Pennsylvania was criticized by a legislative committee because of its president discounting bills and notes (Holdsworth. Empire, I, 145).

129. U.S. 23rd Congr., 1st sess., Senate Document 16, 170 ff; U.S. 23rd Congr., 1st. sess., Senate Document 2, 23, 24.

130. American State Papers, Finance, III, 332; U.S. 22nd Congr., 2nd sess., House Document 121, 51, 160 ff. Report of the Bank of the United States to the Committee of Ways and Means (1833), 6. This and the following pages give a good idea of the development of the Exchange Committee.

It is of considerable interest that the organization of the Second Bank of the United States in the 1820's paralleled that of the Bank of England in the 1780's. The Bank of England possessed in the second half of the eighteenth century a Committee in Waiting, a Treasury Committee, a House Committee, and a Committee of the Exchanges. The Treasury Committee actually controlled the business of the Bank of England just as, a few decades later, the Exchange Committee of the Second Bank of the United States controlled that of the latter bank. Public reaction to the organizational change in England had been very similar to that in the United States. One William Pickett wrote in his pamphlet, An Apology to the Public for a Continued Intrusion, etc. (1788), "by whom, when, and by what contrivance the dark and concealed system of management by a Treasury Committee without the deliberation of the Whole Court [board of directors] has been established is a consideration of the first magnitude for the Proprietors." Clapham, op. cit., I, 200.

131. Its title seems to have changed in 1823 or 1824. (U.S. 22nd Congr., 2nd sess., House Report 121, 163, 164).

132. Ibid., 23, 24; U.S. 22nd Congr., 1st sess., House Report 460, 115; U.S. 22nd Congr., 2nd sess., House Report 121, 65.

The Exchange Committee of the Franklin Bank of Cincinnati consisted of the president and two members appointed monthly in rotation. It passed on all offerings of bills of exchange daily and fixed the rates and terms of bills of exchange to be sold (U.S. 23rd Congr., 1st sess., Senate Document 16, 115).

133. In the 1830's the committees of the Second Bank of the United States were appointed by the president, except the committee on the state of the bank which was appointed by ballot (U.S. 22nd Congr., 2nd sess., House Report 121, 54, 65).

134. U.S. 23rd Congr., 1st sess., Senate Document 2, 23, 24; House Exec. Document 12, 8, 10, 16, 17. "Indeed it seems that the exchange committee themselves consider the president of the bank as concentrating in his hands the whole power," (U.S. 22nd Congr., 2nd sess., House Report 121, 28). About the procedure of the Exchange Committee and its relations to the board see ibid., 51, 55, 65, 67, 73, 74, 77.

135. U.S. 22nd Congr., 2nd sess., House Report 121, 68.

136. The Rules and Regulations of 1823 have a section 25 corresponding to the old section 23; but the juxtaposition of functions is blurred by the insertion of the words: "The discounts shall be settled and". The Rules and Regulations of the Union Bank of Louisiana (chartered in 1832) also deal (in rule 26) with the proceedings of the board as a "deliberative body." (U.S. 23rd Congr., 1st sess., Senate Document 73, 29.)

137. A similar clause is to be found in the charter of 1833, section 6 of the Hartford, Conn. Farmers and Mechanics Bank. "No director shall be entitled to any emolument...excepting the president who shall receive such compensation as the board of directors may judge reasonable for his extra services, beyond the directors." (Ibid., 36). In contrast article 11 of the charter of the Arcade Bank in Rhode Island states that the president and directors as such are not entitled to any compensation (U.S. 23rd Congr., 1st sess., Senate Document 16, 127).

138. It is significant that on March 19, 1818 William Gray, president of the Boston branch of the Bank of the United States, signed a latter to the parent bank "per order of the directors." American State Papers, Finance, III, 325.

139. Plain Truth, 38, 39.

140. Ibid., 52.

141. The idea of the president of a bank as being a primus inter pares seems to have been rather widespread. Dallas's plan of 1814 for a national bank contains the following clause: that the directors of the national bank shall appoint seven persons, one of whom to preside [italics mine], as the managers of each office of discount and deposit. American State Papers, Finance, II, 867.

142. The then old-fashioned Massachusetts Bank, by contrast, had a paid sitting director between 1836 and 1839, probably a very rare case (Gras, op. cit., 88).

143. U.S. 23rd Congr., 1st sess., Senate Document 16, 170 ff; Senate Document 73, 28.

144. Bank of Burlington, Charter of 1818, section 7: function of the board "to appoint one of their number president and also to appoint all other officers and servants necessary for the management of the concerns" of the bank (U.S. 23rd Congr., 1st sess., Senate Document 73, 3). Union Bank of Louisiana: "all officers and persons in the employ of the bank are chosen or appointed by the board of directors." (Rule 18 of the Rules and Regulations of 1832, ibid., 25 ff.) Farmers and Mechanics Bank of Hartford, Charter of 1833, section 7; a cashier and such other officers and agents as may be necessary shall be appointed and their compensations shall be regulated by the board of directors, (ibid., 36).

145. Rules and Regulations, Rule 19, ibid., 28.

146. There can be no doubt that Biddle was the chief executive officer of and entrepreneur in the Second Bank of the United States. However, the Rules and Regulations revised in 1833 during his incumbency did not bring that fact out; they were apparently designed to disguise it. The public still clung to certain conceptions of what a bank president should be. Jackson and members of his administration represented and voiced those popular opinions, although they were antiquated. It was probably wise that the administration of the Bank was not too outspoken about the far reaching organizational changes which were taking place. Thus section 16 of the Rules and Regulations of 1833 described the president's functions as keeping the seal of the corporation in his

custody, signing notes and bills, and presiding over the board. This job description, as one would call it today, makes Biddle's position look like a sinecure, especially since he did not even sign all the circulation of the Bank. (It will be remembered that after 1827 a considerable part of the circulation of the Bank consisted of branch drafts not signed by him.) On the other hand, according to the Rules and Regulations of the Bank of the United States of 1833, the cashier would seem to have risen to the position of the chief executive officer, while in fact he was only Biddle's tool. The cashier retained all the functions which he had possessed under the previous rules and in addition took over all the functions of the president as described in the rules of 1816 and not assigned to him in those of 1833. He was supposed to correspond with the foreign agents and the branches "as an organ of the committees of the board," that is to say, the fiction of the board as an administrative body was upheld. He was furthermore supposed to direct the stock, bullion, and foreign and domestic exchange operations of the Bank, which were, in fact, Biddle's domain. These Rules and Regulations of 1833 are really a remarkable piece of dissimulation.

147. Such clauses were still passed in the second period, e.g., Bank of Burlington (1818), sec. 15 (U.S. 23rd Congr., 1st sess., Senate Document 73, 41); Arcade Bank, Rhode Island (1831) (U.S. 23rd Congr., 1st sess., Senate Document 16, 127).

148. Biddle's Letterbooks; letters to Isaac Lawrence, October 3 and 25, 1823, January 4, 1824; to Prime, Ward, and Sands, November 21, 1823; to John McKim, Jr., December 17, 1823; to Enoch Parsons, January 7, 1824; to William S. Nichols, January 7, 1824. U.S. 22nd Congr., 1st sess., House Report, 460, 284, 505. The Reports of the Committee of Inquiry (page 41) give different figures. The total number of proxies was given as 4533, out of which 1436 were held by Biddle exclusively, and 1684 in conjunction with others. The New York plan of a National Bank forbade the voting by proxies. "It is believed that the rejection of proxy votes is indispensable to the election of high-minded independent men who would be able advisers of the president..." since it was repugnant to highly qualified men

to hold the place of a director at the will of an individual who controlled the votes by proxies. (Outline of a Plan of a National Bank, 9.)

149. In the early 1830's, the Rules and Regulations of the Union Bank of Louisiana spoke of "the proceedings of the board of directors when conducting their business as a deliberative body;" Rule 26. (U.S. 23rd Congr., 1st sess., Senate Document 73, 29.)

150. In this connection it is interesting to read a statement of that decade from New Orleans that banks were left for months with only three or four directors and in some cases with the president and cashier alone (U.S. 25th Congr., 3d sess., House Executive Document 227, 536).

151. The atmosphere in bank boards of the latter type is illustrated by the fact that when in 1833 the directors of the Bank of America in New York were interested in having their bank become a depository for public funds, they were willing to pledge their private fortunes for the security of such deposits (U.S. 23rd Congr., 1st sess., Senate Document 17, 85).

152. Gordon, op. cit., 126; Binney's speech, op. cit., 44, 45. Legally, the stockholders delegated their power to the board of directors which in turn delegated most of it to the president.

152a. See also Biddle to A. Dickens, Dec. 22, 1831; Biddle Letterbooks.

152b. See Biddle's letters to Perkins, Crowninshield, Rathbone, Carow, Campbell, Gilmor, McKim, and McElderry of November 9, 1832; to Rathbone of November 21 and Perkins of November 26, 1832. (Biddle Letterbooks.)

153. Report of a Committee of Directors.

154. U.S. 23rd Congr., 1st sess., House Executive Document 12, 19.

155. There was much confusion in the 1830's. The Second Bank of the United States was at that time administered by Biddle, the president. But when the Congressional Investigating Committee of 1834 came to the Bank it was received by a committee of the board of directors, "the chosen and legal agents of the Bank." Thereupon the majority of this Congressional Committee complained that the exhibition of the books and documents had not been committed to the more appropriate agents, the president and cashier, an almost amusing statement, since it came from Jackson men (U.S. 23rd Congr., 1st sess., House Report 481, 4, 5). A contemporary pamphleteer

commented that the Bank had resisted firmly "every effort of illegal search made with a view solely to criminate the directors," who, as the "responsible agents" of the Bank are "charged with a most cruel and perfidious design to bring universal distress upon the country for paltry and selfish ends." (Gordon, op. cit., 59, 60, 61.) A few years prior to the irate paper of 1833, quoted above, Jackson himself by implication had already recognized the change of functions within the Bank. In his message of 1829 he had praised the treasury for some transactions which it had consummated "aided by the judicious arrangements of the officers of the Bank of the United States." There was no mention of the directors, as the official phraseology of the time would have required.

156. Examination, 20.

157. Opdyke, Treatise, 291. As to a typical case of buying up the control of a bank in the 1830's see Correspondence relating to the Affairs of the Bank of Maryland, 2ff. especially 8, and Biddle's letter of April 14, 1832 to McDuffie on this case in which one Poultney bought up nearly all of the shares, (Biddle Letterbooks).

158. U.S. 25th Congr., 3rd sess., House Executive Document 227, 536. Sidelights on the control of Connecticut banking in the second period can be found in Hall, op. cit., 244 ff.

159. See on page 59 the quotation from the pamphlet of 1821: Cheves explains "the difference between himself and the cashier" to bewildered conservative businessmen.

160. See footnote 155 and Biddle's letters to Samuel Smith of June 14, 1832 and to Charles Jared Ingersoll of February 25, 1832 in Biddle Letterbooks. It is characteristic of the old point of view that as late as 1832 the charter of the Union Bank of Louisiana (section 13) stated that the president remains in office for the time for which the board has been elected (U.S. 23rd Congr., 1st sess., Senate Document 73, 20).

161. See the high class correspondence of the cashier of the Second Bank of the United States with those of the branches (U.S. 22nd Congr., 1st sess., House Report 460, 517 ff).

162. U.S. 23rd Congr., 1st sess., Senate Document 73, 30.

163. American State Papers, Finance III, 724 ff.

164. The change was also reflected in salaries. The cashier of the State Bank of Boston, for instance, received in 1820 a salary of $2,000. In 1829, however, the salary of the cashier of this bank was fixed at $1,400. The president of the State Bank, on the other hand, received $1,000 in 1820, $1,400 in 1825, and $2,000 in 1832. That is to say, in the year 1832 the president's salary was increased so as to equal that salary which had been typical for cashiers in city banks in 1810. See Stetson, op. cit., 44, 49, 50.

165. For data on Catlin, see Hardenbrook, op. cit., 217 ff.

166. Whitney, D. R., op. cit., 16.

167. Gras, op. cit., 128, 143.

168. U.S. 23rd Congr., 1st sess., Senate Document 17, 71; Whitney, D. R., op. cit., 29. As late as 1839 the Massachusetts Bank Commissioners contacted the principal stockholders of an unsound bank (Report for 1839, 22).

169. Outline of a Plan of a National Bank, 7, 8. In 1826 Nathan Hale attacked an article in the Rhode Island American because the author suggested that the security of banks be judged by the ratio between specie in the vaults and bills in circulation. See also Free Trade Advocate II (1829) 4. The author of this article contests the opinion that the "power of expansion in a bank" depends upon the quantity of coin in its vault.

170. Very interesting in this regard is a letter of July 9, 1819 from Crawford, in his capacity as Secretary of the Treasury, to Israel Pickens, president of the Tombigbee Bank. After having stressed the small amount of specie available and the demand for specie by importers, Crawford finds it "difficult to conceive that any bank can be managed with prudence which extends its discounts more than fifty per cent beyond its capital actually paid in." He censures the Tombigbee Bank for having extended its discounts to three hundred per cent of its capital and closes his lecture: "It would be difficult to define the extent to which it might with prudence have extended its discounts upon the public money in its possession," i.e., on its deposits. (American State Papers, Finance, III,768). Incidentally Crawford mistook the signs of the times when he claimed that banks would no longer be able to issue notes to the extent of three times their capital.

171. A foreign observer with considerable American business experience thus formulated this theory: "A banker must be a capitalist to give the public security who take his notes at par, yet...he is not a lender of capital - he borrows more capital than he lends." This latter statement refers apparently to note issues which the author considers as loans from the public (Clibborn, op. cit., 12). In 1838 the Alabama Bank Commissioners thus expressed the same theory: "The object proposed in creating bank capital is to sustain the credit of the bank paper and to enable banks to lend a larger amount of their credit. It is therefore a perversion of that purpose when they lend their capital; and every dollar of their capital loaned disables them from lending at least two of their credit." (Report of the Alabama Bank Commissioners of 1838, U.S. 25th Congr., 3rd sess., House Executive Document 227, 445 ff.)
According to Harry E. Miller (op. cit., 174) the theory was disseminated also by Lord, Gallatin, Raguet, and Gouge. Very important in this connection is Isaac Bronson's article in the Free Trade Advocate, II (1829), 24 ff; incidentally he elaborates a theory very similar to Clibborn's.

172. An early statement of this theory is to be found in Free Trade Advocate, II (1829), 2.

173. Op. cit., 24.

174. See page 51.

175. Clibborn, op. cit., 19, footnote.

176. Essays on Banking, 33, 34, 161.

177. U.S. 22nd Congr., 1st sess., House Report 460, 364, 366.

178. Governor Pickens of Alabama, quoted by Scroggs, "Pioneer Banking," 408. While the Bank of Vermont of 1806 is an early example of this type, it was represented in the second period by the Bank of the State of Alabama of 1823.

179. Ibid., 410 (apportioned according to the representation of the counties in the general assembly). Incidentally the writings of Thomas Law in the second period represent a development of the loan office idea.

179a. As to the reasons for state participation in banks in the first period see page 8.

180. Essays on Banking, 106.

181. Ibid., 49, 53.

182. Clibborn, op. cit., 25.

183. American State Papers, Finance, III, 289.

The point was also stressed by Isaac Bronson: see Hamilton, J.A., op. cit., 255.

184. Report of the Bank of the United States to the Committee of Ways and Means, 15.

185. Hamilton, J. A., op. cit., 84. Outline of a Plan of a National Bank, 15. The backers of this plan were hostile to the foreign exchange business of the Second Bank of the United States. Its regulation they felt should be left to the actual operations of trade, otherwise the course of exchange was no longer a "sure and faithful monitor" which it was expected to be. This idea may have been contributed in both cases by Isaac Bronson. See the latter's "General Propositions," 26.

186. See, for instance, Free Trade Advocate, II (1829), 6. On the other hand, Duncombe, (op. cit., 75, 76) ascribes the rapid economic growth of the United States to the use of credit.

187. The description is reprinted by James, Chicago Banks, 261. See also Hare's article in Hunt's Merchants' Magazine for 1852.

Chapter IV

THE PROBLEM OF COUNTRY NOTES AND THE SUFFOLK BANK SYSTEM

1. Appleton, Examination, 9 ff; Winthrop, op. cit., 284 ff; Mass. Publ. Doc. No. 8 (1865), 49.

2. The accumulation of country notes in the cities is described and explained by Condy Raguet in his Inquiry of 1815, pages 49 ff. As to Philadelphia, see Carey, Essays on Banking (1816), 151. Three fourths of all the remittances made to or money received in that city consisted of country bank notes "which our citizens are too often obliged to receive at par."

3. Massachusetts Bank, Directors Records, reprinted in Gras, op. cit., 368, 385 ff, 74.

4. Massachusetts Sess. Laws, 1804, ch. 40.

5. The "allegoric memoir" by Perspective, the anonymous author of which must have been close to the enterprise, is the most important source for its history. (It has been used also in Lake's unpublished Harvard Ph.D. thesis.) See especially pages 9, 10, 13.

6. See footnote 5.
7. Perspective, op. cit., 32. Lake, (op. cit., 191) mentions still another method of the Boston banks to embarrass the Exchange Office. (He refers on page 192 to the later history of the enterprise.) The Massachusetts Bank refused to receive checks on the Office in 1807 (Gras, op. cit., 68, 392).
8. See page 41.
9. Andrew Dexter, Jr.'s methods are portrayed in his correspondence with the Farmers' Exchange Bank, Glocester, Rhode Island. See Report of the Committee appointed by the General Assembly of the State of Rhode Island and Providence Plantations...to enquire into the situation of the Farmers' Exchange Bank in Glocester. (1809.) Dexter wrote to "the President and Directors of the Farmers' Bank" (op. cit., 29):

Boston, December, 1807

I take the liberty to propose to you on behalf of the Boston Exchange Office, that in case that concern who owes [sic] a majority of the stock in the office, can own one half of the stock in your bank, the office will agree to receive by loan or deposit, from 50 to 100,000 in their bills, and will pay therefore [sic] at the rate of 3% per annum, for two or more years, stipulating that the bills shall either be kept from circulation entirely, or be paid out in such manner as will be most likely to prevent their return to the Bank, and in any case any of them should remain the Office will be at the expense of returning them. This may be done by the Cashier drawing on the Office drafts, payable in specie for the amount of the bills so returned to be accompanied by bills to the same amount; for which purpose the bills may be marked so as to be identified by the Bank. The Office will also agree, in such case, to accept any other drafts of the Bank, accompanied as afore-said and to give a general and extensive circulation to all bills of the Bank as far as in their power....

[This offer was accepted.]
To the cashier, William Colwell, he wrote (op. cit., 30):

Providence, May 21st, 1808

I take the liberty to mention some ideas which myself and friends have respecting the manner of managing the concerns of the bank. The general rule should undoubtedly be to pay punctually; but in this there are important exceptions, such as when we are run upon by brokers, or any persons whatever merely for the purpose of making a profit out of the injury and loss of the Bank. These ought to be paid only by drafts on the Exchange Office at forty days sight. The Providence Banks should, in my opinion, be plagued as much as possible, by detaining them as long as it will naturally take to count out all kinds of specie change, intermixed in the most deliberate manner. The change is very important and ought to be husbanded as much as possible....

10. See in Appendix I a contemporary document showing the methods applied by country banks in 1808; also Carey, Letters to Seybert, 66 ff.
11. About a decade after these events, in 1818, Nathan Appleton fostered the foundation of a country bank, the Agricultural Bank of Pittsfield, Mass. His motives are not clear. Possibly as the leader of the early American textile industry he envisaged some such industry in Berkshire county and looked upon the founding of a bank there as a preparatory step. Maybe he wanted to get experience in country banking. Most probably, however, personal reasons were decisive, for his father-in-law, Thomas Gold (1760-1827), a lawyer in Pittsfield, became the first president of the Agricultural Bank.

Appleton's associates in this venture were John Bellows, a wealthy merchant, William Cochran, mentioned above, and his cousin, William Appleton (1786-1862), later president of the Boston branch of the Second Bank of the United States and president of the Provident Institution for Savings. These three men were also among the incorporators of the Tremont Bank of Boston in 1814, and two of them, Bellows and Cochran, participated in 1816 in founding the Provident Institution for Savings in Boston, one of the earliest American savings banks.
12. William Appleton, Cochran, and Bellows (mentioned in footnote 11) were among the signers of this circular letter. See Mass. Hist. Soc., Proceedings, XI (1869-1870), 306-308.
13. Documents elucidating the methods of country banks are reprinted by Chadbourne,

op. cit., 23, 40 ff. See also Appendix
I to this chapter.

14. Hale, op. cit., 10 ff. As to the
Massachusetts Bank see Gras, op. cit.,
393, 394, 397. At about the same time
(1808 and 1809) the New Haven Bank
resolved not to take the bills of the
banks in Bridgeport, Norwich, and New
London (Woolsey, op. cit., 10, 11).

15. Chadbourne, (op. cit., 41, 42) reprints
a contract to that effect. See also
Bangor Bank, 12, 13.

16. Second Report of the Bank Investigating
Committee of 1836, 16 ff.; History of
Suffolk County, 241 ff.; Mass. Publ.
Doc. No. 8, (1865), 51; Lake, op. cit.,
194 ff.; Felt, op. cit., 217.

17. It is difficult to put a finger on any
one man who was responsible for the
achievements of the New England Bank.
Its president from 1813-1823 was the
East India merchant, Nathaniel Goddard,
and its cashier, 1813-1824, Ebenezer
Frothingham, Jr. About Goddard, see
Forbes and Greene, op. cit., 29.
Aristocracy of Boston characterizes him
as a large shipowner in the Baltic and
freighting business, a man of great
energy and stern will.

18. Myers, Margaret, New York Money Market,
5.

19. About Bronson, see pages 45 ff.

20. Bronson, Isaac, Appeal to the Public
(1815), 18 ff.

21. Publicola, Vindication, 10, 11.

22. As mentioned above, this arrangement
meant keeping a permanent deposit in the
city banks by country banks.

23. Hale, op. cit., 18, 19.

24. Whitney, D. R., op. cit., 22.

25. He "began poor, East India merchant.
Now [1850] retired to take care of his
immense wealth." Forbes and Greene, op.
cit., 28.

26. The manuscript records of the Suffolk
Bank are now in the Baker Library of
Harvard University. See especially
Stockholders Records, 1818-1864;
Directors Records, 1818-1831, 1831-1843,
1843-1852, 1852-1859; Miscellaneous
papers, volumes (boxes) 33, 34, 35.
D. R. Whitney's book on the Suffolk
Bank is reliable and reports the most
important events without much evaluation.
In his repeatedly mentioned thesis Lake
gives a good history of the bank on the
basis of the records.

27. Report of the Indianapolis Monetary
Commission, 307, 332. See also pages
227, 228.

28. Suffolk Bank, Letter of April 10, 1824,
reprinted in Whitney, op. cit., 12.

29. Letter of October 4, 1824 (ibid., 11).
See also Spahr, op. cit., 74.

30. Incidentally the foreign money business
of the Suffolk Bank remained a cooperative venture only for a limited time.
After 1827 it was conducted on the
Suffolk Bank's exclusive responsibility.
The Boston banks from then on had, in
consideration of their deposits, if they
kept any, the right to receive from the
Suffolk Bank the par value of all New
England country notes when presented.
Some of them retained correspondent
relationships with country banks whose
foreign money and notes they transmitted
to and from the Suffolk Bank. The relation between the New England Bank of
Boston and the Lynn Mechanics Bank serves
as an example (see Burill, op. cit., 43,
44). As to the relations of the Suffolk
Bank with other Boston banks, see
Stetson, op..cit., 46-48 (State Bank
1824-1828).

30a. Hale op. cit., 23 ff.

31. Hale, Nathan, op. cit., 23-24. Lake
(op. cit., 213) quotes an article in
the Boston Daily Advertiser of May 3,
1825 reporting on this matter.

32. Nathan Appleton had been a director of
the Suffolk Bank from October 1822
through January 1823 (See Whitney, op.
cit., 69).

33. See Whitney, op. cit., 14. The Union
and Massachusetts Banks withdrew from
the arrangement as early as September
and December 1824, respectively. The
latter bank received comparatively little
foreign money in the course of its business (Gras, op. cit., 436, 117).

34. In Rhode Island the collection and clearing business was conducted differently
from what it was in the other New England
states. All but four Rhode Island banks
participated in an arrangement with the
Merchants Bank of Providence, an arrangement which was essentially identical to
that of the Suffolk Bank with New England
country banks, other than those of Rhode
Island. Rhode Island country banks kept
permanent deposits ranging from $1,000
to $3,000 with the Merchants Bank, the
total amounting to about $60,000. In
consideration of these deposits the
Merchants Bank collected without charge
items payable in New York and Boston,
while 1/8 to 1/4 per cent, 1/4 per cent,
and 1/2 per cent were charged for collections on Philadelphia, other places in

Rhode Island, and Baltimore, respectively; (the charges for collections in Massachusetts, other than in Boston, were identical with those of the Suffolk Bank). Furthermore, the Merchants Bank received at par notes of all New England banks except those which kept aloof and those which were located in the same town as the depositing bank. When the balance was against a participating bank, so that the permanent deposit was impaired, interest was charged against it. Interest accounts were closed and balances carried forward once a month.

The direct clearing system of the Merchants Bank extended to Rhode Island notes only. All other New England notes were transmitted to the Suffolk Bank which in turn transmitted all Rhode Island notes received in its clearing business to the Merchants Bank of Providence. However, while the Suffolk Bank charged the Merchants Bank interest whenever the latter was the debtor, the Merchants Bank was not entitled to the corresponding charge, when it was the creditor. (U.S. 24th Congr., 2nd sess., House Executive Document 65, 44.) The description refers to 1836.

35. The Suffolk Bank System was recognized as such as early as 1857 by Amasa Walker, op. cit., 67.

36. Records of Board of Directors, March 22, 1856.

37. The permanent deposits of the country banks with the Suffolk Bank were graded according to their capitals.

38. See Whitney, Lake, and also Stackpole, op. cit., 71 ff.; Root, New England Bank Currency, 24 ff.; Magee, op. cit., passim.

39. Defense of Country Banks, 7 ff. Appleton, Examination, 18.

40. See page 51.

41. Incidentally, Rhode Island money was cleared and redeemed by the Merchants Bank in Providence, which closely cooperated with the Suffolk Bank and exchanged with it bank money issued in the other New England states against Rhode Island bank money. (As to details see footnote 34.) The Suffolk Bank took from New York bankers and businessmen New England bills at 1/10 per cent discount (Whitney, op. cit., 38).

42. U.S. 25th Congr., 3d sess., House Executive Document 227, 110. Some of the New England states were then beginning to back up the Suffolk Bank system. The Vermont Act relating to banks of 1840 (Public Acts, chapter 1) established in section 24 a two per cent capital stock tax from which such banks were exempted which uniformly caused their bills to be redeemed at par in Boston.

43. Report of the Bank Commissioners of Maine in U.S. 25th Congr., 2d sess., House Executive Document 79, 29, 30; also History of Suffolk County, II, 343-345.

44. The idea of establishing a redemption agency the capital of which was to be drawn proportionately from the existing banks was discussed in New York as early as 1839. Annual Report of the New York Bank Commissioners for 1839, 12.

45. Op. cit., 215; the source is the Boston Daily Advertiser, March 25, 1835.

46. Correspondence between Suffolk and Exchange Banks, passim. The clash is described by Whitney, (op. cit., 46 ff.) and by Lake, (op. cit., 219 ff.). George W. Thayer was president of the Exchange Bank during the years in question. He became a director of the Bank of Mutual Redemption and was connected with the beginnings of the Boston Clearing House.

47. See Bankers Magazine, X, 57, 58.

48. Massachusetts Private and Special Statutes, 1855, chap. 450, sec. 2; 1856, chap. 126, sec. 1.

49. For what follows, see Directors Records of the Bank of Mutual Redemption, preserved in the Baker Library of Harvard University.

50.

Bank of Mutual Redemption
No. 13 Exchange Street
Boston, Massachusetts
September 2nd, 1858

To the President and Directors
of the Suffolk Bank:
Gentlemen,

I am in receipt of your Cashier's letter of 31st ult., addressed to myself and the Directors of this Bank, respecting your construction of the terms upon which the Foreign Money System is carried on by your bank, so far as the liability of Boston Banks, keeping Country Bank Accounts, is concerned.

The letter shall be laid before the Board at its meeting next Wednesday. Meanwhile, that no inconvenience may occur, to any Bank doing business with your Bank, or this, in consequence of any delay in the final settlement of the question, I am authorized to propose and do propose, that the Bank of Mutual Redemption

and the Suffolk Bank, do each become answerable to the other, until Thursday next,
and for such further time as may elapse,
after that day, previous to the written
notice of one to the other to the contrary, in the manner and to the extent
following; viz:- The Bank of Mutual Redemption to be answerable to the Suffolk
to redeem, at the Clearing Hour, each
day, all the Notes of Country Banks keeping their account with it, until previous
notice is given to the contrary, and the
Suffolk to be answerable to this Bank to
redeem, at the Clearing Hour, each day,
all the Notes of Country Banks keeping
their account with the Suffolk Bank,
until previous notice is given to the
Contrary, also. As every consideration
stated by your Cashier, as operating to
make the request a reasonable one on your
part, applies to its utmost extent to making the proposition right for us to make
to you, I hope the arrangement may be
made.

                    Respectfully Yr. M. Ob.
                    James G. Carney
                    President

                    September 8, 1858

J. Amory Davis, Esq.,
    President Suffolk Bank:
Dear Sir,
    I have received your note of 4th instant,
which, together with your Cashier's letter
of 31st ultimo, I have laid before our
Directors, who instruct me to reply, that
they do approve, confirm, and adopt the
reply to your Cashier's letter made by me
under date of 2nd instant, the receipt of
which reply you acknowledge in your note.
    I am instructed further to say, that if
there is any other understanding, provision.
or arrangement, which your Board desire to
impose upon, or make a part of, the general
settlement of the manner in which and of the
responsibilities under which, the business
between the two Banks is to be conducted,
so far as the Foreign Money System is concerned, it will be very cheerfully acceded
to by this Bank, as in the present instance,
if it, also, can be made mutually acceptable
and reciprocal; and is not likely to be
injurious or annoying to the other Banks
or to the Community; these being the only
conditions which this Bank desires to
attach to its acceptance of any proposition which may be submitted to it.

                    Respectfully Yr. M. Ob.
                    Jas. G. Carney, Prest.

(Source: Directors Record, Bank of Mutual
Redemption, September 8, 1858.)

51. See Appendix III to this chapter;
    Bankers Magazine, XIII, 348 ff.
52. See Appendix III to this chapter. The
    four Boston Banks which fought against
    the Suffolk Bank were all chartered
    between 1847 and 1854.
53. See their Report (1858), 133, 134.
54. Records of Board of Directors.
55. In this period the Massachusetts Bank
    made an arrangement with the Suffolk
    Bank under which the latter took over
    "foreign money" from the former at a
    charge of 25 cents per thousand dollars,
    (Gras, op. cit., 507).
56. See Appendix III and Shed, op. cit.,
    especially pages 7, 8, 10, 17. An
    application by Carney in his capacity
    as the secretary of the Lowell Institu-
    tion for Savings to the Massachusetts
    House of Representatives throws an
    unfavorable light on his character be-
    cause of its insincerity. See Massachu-
    setts House Document 140 (1856).
57. Shed, op. cit., passim; Reports of the
    Massachusetts Bank Commissioners for
    1855 and the pamphlet The Injunction
    which was obviously Carney's work.
    Chadbourne (pages 84 ff.) and Helderman
    (page 33) deal with the Bank of Mutual
    Redemption, and the publication of the
    Lowell Institution for Savings contains
    a few data on and a picture of Carney.
58. The directors decided on July 7, 1858 to
    make a suitable compensation to an agent
    who had solicited subscriptions.
    (Records of Board of Directors.)
59. Records of Board of Directors, October
    27, 1858 and March 16, 1859.
60. Records of Board of Directors under the
    dates mentioned.
61. Ibid., May 25, 1859.
62. This practice may have been widespread
    at that time. President Jones of the
    Second Bank of the United States in a
    letter of October 4, 1817 advised the
    Lexington branch to present the notes
    of state banks for redemption in specie
    or bills of exchange on the East or New
    Orleans (American State Papers, Finance,
    III, 321). The taking of bills of
    exchange in settlement of balances due
    from the state banks became the general
    practice of the Second Bank of the
    United States (U.S. 22nd Congr., 1st
    sess., Senate Document 50, 25).
63. Op. cit., 204. He quotes the Boston
    Daily Advertiser of August 1, 1826.

64. U.S. 26th Congr., 1st sess., House Executive Document 172, 117, quoting from the Annual Report of the New York Bank Commissioners for 1839, 6, 7, also 10. See also U.S. 22nd Congr., 1st sess., House Report 460, 357. The Annual Report of the New York Bank Commissioners for 1833 (page 12) also refers to the redemption system of the 1830's.

65. McCall was a wealthy drygoods merchant of Irish origin (Beach, op. cit., 20; Scoville, op. cit., 366). He stands first on the list of incorporators and among those who formed the first board of directors. (Art. 3, sec. 4 of the Articles of Association of 1851.)

66. See U.S. 30th Congr., 1st sess., House Executive Document 77, 222, 310. The lending of batches of notes to brokers was practiced also in Boston: see page 72. The corresponding practice of Illinois free bankers is described in Huston, op. cit., 124: most of them made no loans nor discounts; they simply secured the right to issue notes and lend them to brokers. See also James, Chicago, 232.

67. Whitney, op. cit., 38.

68. Williams, New York View, 3; Scroggs, op. cit., 57. Report of the Comptroller of the Currency, 1870, 138; Report of the Indianapolis Monetary Commission, 343. The success of the Metropolitan Bank may have been due at least in part to the above-mentioned change in the law.

69. U.S. 35th Congr., 1st sess., House Executive Document 107, 121.

70. Lake, op. cit., 235. He quotes the Boston Transcript of October 16, 1858.

71. In the 1850's the State Auditor of Indiana suggested that a bank note redemption system should be set up which followed the examples of Massachusetts or New York. U.S. 33d Congr., 2d sess., House Executive Document 82, 209.

72. U.S. 35th Congr., 1st sess., House Executive Document 107, 121.

73. In figuring these advantages the loss of interest on their deposits with the Suffolk Bank should be deducted.

74. Bankers Magazine, X, 54, 140, 244, 306, 570.

75. U.S. 35th Congr., 1st sess., House Executive Document 107, 121; Bankers Magazine, XII, 424, 631, 839, 919.

76. Cornwallis, op. cit., 49.

77. Philadelphia Clearing House Association Minutes, August 16, 1858.

78. Philadelphia Clearing House Association Minutes, June 22 and September 5, 1859.

79. In New York, as has been shown, the whole matter was handled more as a business proposition for both country and city banks, while the public paid the bill.

80. The Records of the Board of Directors of the Bank of Mutual Redemption on June 30, 1858 contain a notice to this effect.

81. John Amory Davis, president of the Suffolk Bank from 1849 to 1865, died in the latter year. The obituaries in the Boston Daily Evening Transcript of May 5 and in the Boston Post of May 6, 1865 do not contain any biographical information.

82. Thayer was a director of the Bank of Mutual Redemption and its steadfast friend, while Hall seems to have lost his interest in this enterprise. In the later 1850's he was rather among the friends of the Suffolk Bank.

83. Other examples of fair dealing are as follows: John Amory Davis, president of the Suffolk Bank, retired from the Clearing House Committee during the discussion of the subject. Thayer also asked to be excused and only when its report came before the meeting of the Association did he join the fight again. James H. Beal, president of the Granite Bank, asked to be excused, because his policy was not identical with that of his predecessor, Alpheus Hardy.

84. Thomas (1808-1872) was the president of the Webster Bank (1853-69) and the first Secretary of the Clearing House; he was scarcely heard in the discussion.

85. Bankers Magazine, XIII, 384 ff.

86. Clearing House Committee Minutes, August 26; Clearing House Association Minutes, August 27, 1861.

87. Clearing House Committee Minutes, October 8, 10, 11, 15, and 21, 1861. New York received the first notes on January 13, 1862 (Report Loan Committee, 127).

88. Mitchell, Wesley C., op. cit., 151.

89. Besides the Minutes, see the contemporary diary by an officer of the clearing house, probably Mr. Ruggles, which records interesting events.

90. Bank of Mutual Redemption, Statements and Explanations, passim.

Chapter V

THE SAFETY FUND SYSTEM

1. New York Public Laws, 52d sess. ch. 94.
2. Van Buren, Autobiography, 221, 222; Root, Erastus, op. cit., 10.
3. Leavenworth, op. cit., passim.
4. Hawley, op. cit., 251 ff.
5. Knox (op. cit., 399 ff.) gives the best description of Forman's share in the introduction of Safety Fund banking. Chaddock's monograph is uninteresting from the point of view of this research.
6. Op. cit., 221, 222.
7. It is unfortunate that Van Buren did not give the names of these men.
8. Moulton, op. cit., 67 ff. Erastus Root expressed very similar ideas, op. cit., 10.
9. State of New York, Messages, III, 239 ff.
10. Moulton, op. cit., 67 ff.
11. Library of Congress, Van Buren Papers. Forman's activities in Albany in the winter of 1828-1829 are described by Leavenworth, (op. cit., 262) and again by Dickinson, (op. cit., 406).
12. State of New York Messages, III, 259-261.
13. Nicholas Biddle was asked for his opinion at that time, but preferred to keep aloof; see his letter to Albert H. Tracy, Albany, (Feb. 3, 1830), Biddle Letterbooks. On March 3 of the same year, however, in a letter to the same gentleman he expressed criticism of the act and opposition to both the principles of mutual responsibility and the supervision by bank commissioners.
14. Reprinted in Assembly Journal, (1829), 173 ff.
15. Ibid., 179.
16. See page 44.
17. See chapter VII.
18. Hamilton, J. A., op. cit., 83, 84, 86.
19. The wording of a passage in J. A. Hamilton's letter of December 1828 indicates familiarity between Van Buren and Bronson. Hamilton refers to "a plan Bronson has submitted to me." Another passage of the same letter reads: "as Mr. Bronson expresses it." (Ibid., 83, 82.)
20. See page 88.
21. J. A. Hamilton, op. cit., 82, 84. The Vermont legislation, which copied that of New York, also proves this point: Section 39 of the Act of 1840 relating to banks (Public Acts, ch. 1), exempted such banks from payments into the Safety Fund whose directors recognized personal liability for both notes and deposits of their banks. Statements to the effect that the New York legislators intended to secure noteholders only and that a broader coverage came into the act by inadvertence can be found in the literature, but are erroneous; e.g., Miller op. cit., 151.

The error may well go back to a remark in the Annual Report of the New York Bank Commissioners for 1840, 16. The commissioners claimed that the "peculiar" feature of the act to secure all debts "does not seem until recently to have been generally understood either by the public at large or even by those engaged in the business of banking." The commissioners were uninformed on the history of the act.
22. U.S. 25th Congr., 2nd sess., House Executive Document 79, 622; Carey, Debates, 85, 118.
23. See this author's Essays in American Economic History, 123. Regarding the First Bank of the United States, see American State Papers, Finance, II, 260.
24. Op. cit., 23.
25. See U.S. 22nd Congr., 2d sess., House Executive Document 8, 1 ff.
26. Ibid., 1, 2.
27. This section, as a matter of fact, embodies the ideas of experienced legislators and probably also of financiers, in addition to those of Forman.
28. See also the contemporary description of this section of the act in Lawrence's North American Review article of 1831, reprinted under the title Bank of the United States, 35. How revolutionary this clause was in the eyes of contemporaries can be deduced from the violent attack on pages 18 ff. of the pamphlet Examination of Some Provisions.
29. N.Y. Assembly Journal (1829), 434 ff. In the Senate the bill was passed with but one amendment. Its history in that body is uninteresting. See Senate Journal, (for 1829), 330, 346, 372, 381-393.
30. Flagg, op. cit., 5, 32 ff.
31. Origin, Provisions and Effect, of the Safety Fund Law of the State of New York (Albany, 1834), 11. An attack on the act is Examination of Some Provisions of the Act to Create a Fund...(New York, 1829).
32. Moulton, op. cit., 67 ff.
33. Erastus Root claimed to have defeated

this proposal, op. cit., 12.

34. For biographical data, see page 200. Mann was a braggart, and his claims must be taken cum grano salis. They are contained in his letters to A. C. Flagg, reprinted by the latter, op. cit., 40 ff. The decisive passage has been reprinted by Knox, op. cit., 403. See also the pamphlet of 1829 (quoted in footnote 31), 16.

35. New York Session Laws, (1817), 306; (1818), 242.

36. Chaddock, op. cit., 267-269, 296-7.

37. The history of the Safety Fund System is not within the scope of this book; it is to be found in Chaddock, op. cit., passim, and in an article by Root on "New York Bank Currency," op. cit., 4 ff. It is interesting that Albert Gallatin, then himself a New York City bank president, was a leader of the City opposition against the act. He had critized it as early as 1831 in his Considerations (Writings III, 318). Later he was a backer, if not the author, of the Report of the Union Committee (1834) which primarily was a plea for the Second Bank of the United States, but which, probably for political reasons (see below footnote 47), also contained an attack on the Safety Fund System. This attack was answered in the pamphlet Origin... of the Safety Fund Law (see footnote 31). Gallatin's authorship is suggested in a review of the "Report" in the American Quarterly Review, XV (June 1834), 498 ff., last paragraph. Later in his Suggestions (Writings, III, 418, 419, 423), he took a somewhat friendlier stand; but again in 1842, he was pleased by the fact that the system had broken down; (Writings, II, 588 ff., especially 591).

The relinquishment of passive resistance by the New York City banks after 1830 against the act needs clarification. See annual message of Governor Throop of January 1830 issued after negotiations with the New York City banks and Chapter 71 of the Session laws of 1830, repealing sections 11-18, Title 2, Article 1, Chapter 18, part 1 of the Revised Statutes of 1827, which sections were objectionable to the banks.

38. The driving force seems to have been Representative Allen Tillinghast, a cotton manufacturer, born in 1768. Boston Daily Advertiser, February 24, 1830.

39. Charles August Davis to Biddle, May 21, 1830, in McGrane, Correspondence of Nicholas Biddle, 102.

40. Acts passed by the State of Vermont, 1831, chapter 20 (see especially sections 2, 4, 15, 16); also Revised Statutes of the State of Vermont, 1839 (Burlington 1840), chapter 80.

41. Vermont Public Acts, 1840, chapter 1, especially section 39; U.S. 35th Congr., 1st sess., House Executive Document 107, 31.

42. U.S. 20th Congr., 1st sess., House Executive Document 172, 37; Davis, William T., The New England States (Boston, 1897), III, 1479.

43. Acts of the Legislature of the State of Michigan, First and Extrasession of 1835 and 1836, 157 ff. Also, An Act to reorganize and regulate banking associations, ibid., 1837, No. XLVII (approved March 15, 1837).

44. The migration of the safety fund to Ohio and Iowa will be discussed in a chapter of the second volume.

45. Root, Wisconsin, 315, 325; Wight, op. cit., 147.

46. See page 176.

47. See pages 94, 95. J. A. Hamilton speaks of a "combination of banks" to replace the Second Bank of the United States, and Isaac Bronson answers him: "If anything like a safety-fund system should be attempted...." (Hamilton, J. A., op. cit., 253, 256.)

48. U.S. 23d Congr., 2nd sess., Senate Document 13, 37.

49. Theory of Money and Banks, 213.

50. See Woodward, op. cit., 140, 141.

51. In Massachusetts, regular bank investigations by a permanent board were first suggested in 1836, but it took the crisis of 1837 to make the legislators pass the Bank Commissioners Act of 1838. (Laws of the Commonwealth of Massachusetts, 1837/38, Chapter XIV. Regarding the bills of 1836, see Massachusetts Senate Documents 36 and 46 of that year.) As to Louisiana, see the various bills discussed in 1838 (U.S. 25th Congr., 3d sess., House Executive Document 227, 489 ff.) and the Act of 1842.

52. Research on a minor question, the question as to what extent the Safety Fund System was responsible for the Bank War, would be desirable. Many contemporaries considered Van Buren the Bank's worst enemy and believed that there was some such connection. For instance, in 1832, Erastus Root, in an exaggerated way, described the connection as follows:

(op cit., 6, 7, 10 ff. Erastus Root, 1773-1846, a leading New York politician was then on the point of breaking with Jackson. See also above page 89) "Gentlemen...who did not know the management and machinery which was brought to bear upon that question - who were ignorant of that stupendous power in a combination of banks connected together under the specious but delusive pretext of a safety fund, all moved by the same impulse and directed to the same object by a great central power might infer that the people of that state desired the destruction of the United States Bank. The stockholders [and] the directors of these banks, thus connected, have deep interest in its prostration. All the banks in this connection are authorized by the law creating the safety fund and, as an inducement for them to come into the scheme, to take 7 per cent on all discounts for more than sixty days." It seems that in the negotiations conducted after the act had been passed, for the purpose of inducing the New York City banks to give up their resistance Democratic politicians promised to destroy the Bank of the United States; and it was claimed that at that time (1829-1830) a "Government bank founded upon the credit of the government and its revenue was established as the orthodox creed of the party." (Moulton, op. cit., 67 ff.) In fact, once the New York branch of the Bank of the United States was out of the way, it would be easy for state legislation to permit all banks of the state, not yet entitled to charge 7 per cent on loans and discounts for more than 63 days to do so. Thereby the New York City banks which renewed their charters under the Safety Fund Act would have been compensated, because they could actually have charged that rate. This set-up made it clear that the New York Union Committee of 1834 defended the Bank of the United States by attacking the Safety Fund System. (See footnote 37.) See also Catterall, op. cit., 166, American Quarterly Review versus the State of New York, passim.

The hostility of the safety fund banks to the Bank of the United States may in part go back to events in 1829. At that time the New York City banks, unwilling to come into the new system, tried to force the hands of the state government by pretending to wind up their affairs. In this connection they contracted, and thereby inflicted hardship on the business community claiming the need of withdrawing their funds preparatory to going out of business. In this situation Biddle stepped in and advised the New York branch of the Second Bank of the United States to expand their loans both to New York merchants and reliable country banks, thereby filling the gap intentionally created by the city banks. This action contributed probably to the breakdown of their resistance. See Biddle's letters of May 28, 1829 to Robert Lenox and M. Robinson (the cashier of the New York office) in Biddle Letterbooks.

Chapter VI

EARLY AMERICAN CENTRAL BANKING

I

The Beginnings

1. Economica, May 1941, 1945.
2. Remarks upon the Bank of the United States, 38. It is noteworthy that the state-owned and state-managed bank which Georgia established at Milledgeville in 1828 was styled Central Bank (Govan, op. cit., 171, 172). In 1841, while writing on the subject of what is called today central banking, MacVickar ("National Bank," 433) used the term "central bank" in the sense of central office as opposed to branches.
3. Smith, Vera, op. cit., 3. Her statement that central banking originated in the establishment of partial or complete note issue monopolies does not hold for America. (Ibid., 147.) (It is regrettable that Chapter IV, "The Organization of Banking in America" of her interesting book is deficient. It contains awkward statements, misinterpretations, and outright mistakes, due to the fact that the range of American sources used is much too small to permit a balanced description.) The following quotation is taken from Biddle's letter to Joseph Vance, June 13, 1837 (Biddle Letterbooks). As to Loyd see Wood op. cit., 31.
4. In this context Mrs. Taus's book on the Central Banking Functions of the United States Treasury comes in for criticism when it treats the earlier period up to

1840; the chapters on the later decades are unimpeachable. At the same time the book is a good example of how economic historians can be led astray if they do not understand the age which they describe. The author deals with a very significant problem, but she uses as a tool a definition derived from familiarity with a comparatively late stage of the development. Mrs. Taus considers as central banking functions of the United States Treasury those powers and activities which influenced the reserve position of the commercial banks. This definition is very useful indeed for understanding certain activities of the Treasury in the second half of the nineteenth century, but it is meaningless if applied to an earlier period because prior to 1840 American banks were not guided in their policy by their reserve position, as has been described in a previous chapter. In order to understand both reality and historical development it would have been necessary to apply either a broader conception or two basic conceptions instead of one, each of which should have been derived from the banking practice of the decades which it was used to explain.

5. Clapham, op. cit., I, 101-103, 158, 166, 167, 170; II, 141. See also Smith, Vera, op. cit., 10 ff.
6. Wettereau, op. cit., 280.
7. Oliver Wolcott Papers, vol. 21, no. 10, in the Connecticut Historical Society. The documents were first mentioned by Professor Wettereau (op. cit., 277). He was good enough to make copies available to this author. See also Davis, Joseph S., op. cit., II, 53.
8. Works, Lodge ed., VIII, 237.
9. Clapham, op. cit., I, 104 ff.
10. The data on which the following analysis is based are taken from Wettereau, op. cit., passim, and Holdsworth-Dewey, op. cit., passim.
11. Incidentally, the English government followed a similar policy in 1793 and 1811, but abandoned it in the emergency of 1825; see Morgan, op. cit., 8. Regarding the actions of 1793 see also American Quarterly Review, VIII (1830) 459.
12. Holdsworth-Dewey, op. cit., 80, 84, 125.
13. The petition is reprinted by Hardenbrook, op. cit., 143, 144.
14. American Quarterly Review, VIII, (1830), 480, 482.

15. Carey, Letters to Seybert, 31, 33, 35, 37.

II

Intermediary Period

1. See especially Walters, Raymond, Jr., "Origins," passim and his biography of Dallas, 184 ff., 191 ff., 209 ff. Porter (Astor, II, 958-968) and Kenneth L. Brown (in "Stephen Girard, Promoter of the Second Bank of the United States") discuss Astor's and Girard's respective shares in the achievement. Walters claims that Brown has exaggerated Girard's contribution.
2. Regarding David Parish, see Ehrenberg, Richard, Das Haus Parish, 2d edition (Jena, 1925) and Walters, Philip G. and Walters, Raymond, Jr., "The American Career of David Parish" in Journal of Economic History, IV, (1944). This essay comes in for some criticism, however, because the authors, having overlooked Ehrenberg's monograph, provide incorrect information on Parish's background; furthermore his character seems to be misunderstood, and there is at least in one point a misinterpretation of his main American business activities. See also this author's "Payments between Nations in the Eighteenth and Early Nineteenth Centuries" in Quarterly Journal of Economics, L (1935-36).
3. "Origins," 130.
4. Walters, Dallas, 170, 173.
5. Brown op. cit., 129, 130.
6. Clarke and Hall, op. cit., 594.
7. Walters, op. cit., 189, ff.; Brown, op. cit., 128.
8. Walters, op. cit., 232.
9. Walters, op. cit., 182, 186.
10. American Quarterly Review, VIII (1830), 483.
11. Dallas, Annual Report of the Secretary of the Treasury, 1815, as reprinted by Clarke and Hall, op. cit., 612, 613.
12. The whole report is to be found in American State Papers, Finance, III, 19.
13. It might be mentioned that the interpretation back of this chapter is the opposite of that presented by Davis Rich Dewey, see Holdsworth-Dewey, op. cit., 148.
14. American State Papers, Finance, III, 57 ff. and Clarke and Hall, op. cit., 613 ff.
15. Clarke and Hall, op. cit., 630 ff. For

an exception see the quotation from a
speech of Representative Thomas Telfair
from Georgia; Ogden Remarks, 52.

16. Plan, 39, 40.

17. Stickles, op. cit., 56.

18. Plan, 51, 52.

19. See the important letter reprinted in
Appendix I.

20. Walters, "Origins," 119, 121, 123, 130;
Dallas, Dallas, 462, 464, 468, 471.

21. Jones [Friendly Monitor], op. cit.; 17,
25.

22. Jones's correspondence confirms his
interest in stock speculation; see his
letters to E. W. Duval of Dec. 25, 1818
and Mar. 7, 1819 (William Jones Papers).

23. Biddle stressed this point (Questions,
6).

24. U.S. 22nd Congr., 1st sess., House
Report 460, 351.

25. Carey, Essays on Banking, Introduction,
passim, and pages 21, 22.

26. Ibid., 124 ff. are illuminating if one
wants to understand the reasons for some
of Jones's unfortunate actions. (See
also Biddle, Questions, 9, 10).

27. Ibid., Introduction, v, footnote.

28. Hepburn, op. cit., (rev. ed. of 1924),
127.

29. Walters, op. cit., 214; Holdsworth-Dewey,
op. cit., 162.

30. American State Papers, Finance, III, 335,
quoted also in Holdsworth-Dewey, op.
cit., 197.

31. It is noteworthy that the then notorious
failure of the Bank of Ayr in Scotland
was also caused in part by lack of control of the branches. Kerr, op. cit.,
109.

32. Carey, Letters to Seybert, 58.

33. Jones [Friendly Monitor], op. cit., 18.

34. Ibid., 34.

35. See also the unpublished letter of Sept.
7, 1818 to McCulloch, cashier in
Baltimore; William Jones Papers,

36. Kenneth Brown, op. cit., 142, 143, 146
ff.

37. The following quotation seems to be indicative of Cheves' way of talking: "A
ship without rudder or sails or mast, on
short allowance of provisions and water,
on a stormy sea and far from the land,
will afford a figure by no means too
strong to express the hapless condition
of the Bank of the United States," when
he took over.

38. The "Exposition" was published in the
Report on the Condition of the Bank of
the United States of 1822 and reprinted
by Goddard, op. cit., 106 ff.

39. Letterbooks of Nicholas Biddle, in the
Library of Congress (hereafter referred
to as Biddle Letterbooks), February 3,
1823. Biddle, Questions, 11, 12; Jones
op. cit., 36. Bassett (op. cit., 586)
comments that, when Cheves became president, bankruptcy was imminent.

40. See Volume II, Chapter X.

41. See his letter to E. W. Duval reprinted
as Appendix II of this chapter.

42. Op. cit., 38.

43. Ibid., 37.

44. Jones's point of view is presented in
the letter reprinted in Appendix I.
The present author hopes to publish
new material on Jones's resignation in
the near future.

45. See page 124 ff.

46. "Exposition," Goddard, op. cit., 114,
115.

47. Certain passages of the "Exposition"
could have been in answer to Jones's
previously cited pamphlet. Incidentally,
Haskell's paper on Cheves is an example
of an uncritical repetition of Cheves's
claims as presented in the "Exposition."

48. Goddard, op. cit., 109 ff. The matter
of foreign loans was correctly evaluated by Lawrence, "Bank of the United
States," 549.

49. The following characterization of Cheves
written by a contemporary, if true,
would explain some features of the
"Exposition." According to this source
Cheves was "the most self-willed man....
He relied on the judgment of no one and
was influenced by no one's opinions
where they were contrary to his own.
But notwithstanding this firmness, self-
will, and self-reliance he was sensitive
as a woman to the criticism and censures
of the world. He was terribly annoyed
whilst president of the bank by the
complaints and charges made against him.
He determined to pay no dividends to
the stockholders till the finances of the
bank were in better condition. There
were hundreds dependent on their dividends for their support. The clamor
against him became furious, but he knew
the salvation of the bank depended on
the course he was pursuing...and [con-
sequently] could not be driven from
his purpose." (Actually, of course,
this was not the only question of policy
that was moot.) Perry, Benjamin F.,
"Reminiscences of Public Men, Langdon
Cheves," in XIX Century (Charleston),
I, (August 1869), 224.

50. See pages 59, 60.

51. See footnote 49; XIX Century, I, 224.

52. The only branch which Cheves actually closed (in October 1820) was the one in Cincinnati where large tracts of real estate had to be taken in payment of debts in consequence of an uncautious lending policy. Since the values increased later, however, no heavy loss was sustained in the end. The cashier of this branch was Gorham A. Worth (1783?-1856), son of a Dutchess County, New York, farmer, who later moved his family to Hudson, New York, where he taught school. Worth started his career in 1809 in the Bank of Hudson; in 1811 he was appointed cashier of the newly-founded Mechanics and Farmers Bank in Albany whence in 1817 he transferred to Cincinnati as cashier of the branch of the Second Bank of the United States. When Cheves became president of the bank Worth was fired, as he claimed, when "all the liberal and honorable part of the Board was absent." Although he seems to have been on very good terms with his (local) board Cheves charged him with "improper proceedings" in connection with the renewal of notes which Worth had given for loans of the office. In addition the renewal of bills of exchange and their transformation into accommodation paper as the general practice of the branch were under fire. It is obvious that while cashier of the branch Worth had business interests of his own, probably speculative in character. In December 1819 Worth went to Philadelphia to defend himself and in fact was reinstated. Later he became a wealthy and successful New York City banker, president of the City Bank; but the unpleasant experience of 1819 left a deep imprint on his life and when he wrote his Recollections of Cincinnati thirty years after these events the old bitterness came into the open again: "Then [after Jones] came conceit, vanity, and a withering sort of tyranny, at war with common sense, that dried up all its [the Bank's] resources leaving it like a strong man in the lap of the harlot." (page 34.)

While in Philadelphia in the winter of 1819 Worth wrote a number of letters to Thomas Sloo, Jr., a director of the branch and a prominent politician and businessman besides. These letters throw some light on Cheves even when one remembers that the dismissal was rankling in the writer. "I reached here this morning," he wrote from Philadelphia on December 18. "The vanity, and conceit, and pride and haughtiness, and pretended purity of the Great man [Cheves] are not to be imagined; no concessions, no admission of error will be made." According to Worth, Cheves practiced a "system of hyprocrisy and persecution and damnation to the Institution." On the 22d: "Cheves is at present Lord of the Ascendant...[he] is hated, as Hell ought to be, by some and worship'd, as the Devil is, by Others-!" (On his way to Philadelphia Worth had met a broker who "talked of Mr. Cheves in high terms, said he was amazing [sic!] popular.") There was apparently much worship of the "rising sun;" but for Worth, Cheves was "deal[ing] damnation round him! all the Old System is to be changed - right or wrong - and though a man of some talent, [he] is too crooked a devil and has too much malice to perceive or pursue the Interests of the Institution. If he is not overruled the Bank is dam'd." He felt that "several members of the board [like himself] looked upon the system pursued with sorrow and disgust." These racy statements may be taken for what they are worth; at least they are interesting. Of course, Worth lost his job when the Cincinnati branch was closed, went to New York in 1821, and labored for years to pay his debt to the Bank of the United States. (Cox, I. J., op. cit., 22 ff., 60 ff.) The biographical data were taken from the publisher's note in Worth's Random Recollections of Albany. Regarding the Cincinnati branch, see Catterall, op. cit., 79, 80; Biddle to Samuel Smith, Nov. 30, 1830.

In Biddle's era Worth was on good terms with the Bank. During the critical months of 1828 the New York branch offered to uphold his enterprise if he needed assistance (to Gorham A. Worth August 23, 1828). See also Biddle's letters to Worth of Jan. 29 and Febr. 28, 1834; of Jan. 19, 1836 and Jan. 21, 1838; (Biddle Letterbooks).

53. An early condemnation of the practice is to be found in Witherspoon, op. cit., (1786) 48.

54. Biddle refers to his arguments with Cheves in his letters of March 1, 1830 to John McKim and of July 29, 1830 to Albert Gallatin.

55. American State Papers, Finance, III, 589 ff., especially 592; IV, 931.

III

Nicholas Biddle and the Heyday of American Central Banking

1. It is an amazing fact that this great American has not been fully understood so far by any American historian, a fact which is due perhaps to the breadth of his activities and interests while nineteenth-century scholarship was synonymous with specialization within narrow bounds. The mere size of the article in the Dictionary of American Biography and the length of the list of references thereto as compared with others in the same handbook are most telling. An early biographical sketch can be found in Encyclopedia Americana, edited by Henry Vethake, Supplementary volume XIV (Philadelphia, 1847).

2. As to Nicholas Biddle's father, Charles Biddle, see the latter's Autobiography (Philadelphia, 1883).

3. Debate in the House of Representatives of Pennsylvania on Mr. Holgate's Resolutions, 9 ff; (Conrad, op. cit., 7, and Dorfman, op. cit., 341, 342, deal with this speech).

3a. Biddle had practiced law for some years upon his return to America in 1807.

4. Debate on Mr. Holgate's Resolutions, 28 ff.

5. Ibid., 18.

6. Ibid., 50.

7. E. A. J. Johnson, op. cit., 177, 178,

8. A similar lecture for the purpose of being used by Joshua Nichol in a conversation with Jackson is to be found in the letter of August 3, 1830 to Nichol, Nashville (Biddle Letterbooks).

9. These passages show very clearly that Biddle's thinking on monetary questions in 1810 was still essentially Mercantilist. But he was on the point of developing his ideas in the direction of the modern claim theory of money: "A farmer will sell his lands for notes, not because he can get dollars for them, but because they will enable him to buy other land or to procure merchandise." (Ibid., 49.)

10. America had had her first experience of this type when the Bank of North America contracted upon losing its Pennsylvania charter in 1785 (see Wilson, Janet, op. cit., 14).

11. To E. Parsons, Hartford, Feb. 7, 1831. From here on, the description of Biddle's activities is based largely on his letterbooks in the Library of Congress. All citations of letters refer to these letterbooks. If possible, letters which have been published by McGrane in Biddle Correspondence are cited with reference to his book.

12. To Jos. Gales, March 8, 1831, to Jas. Robertson, Apr. 8, 1831.

13. To Monroe, Jan. 31, 1819 (McGrane, 12).

14. Monroe to Biddle, Apr. 11, 1820 (McGrane, 13, 14).

15. As to his difference of opinion with Cheves, see below, pages 120, 121.

16. Draft of a letter of Oct. 29, 1822 (McGrane, 26, 27).

17. Dec. 6, 1822 (McGrane, 29).

18. Draft of Oct. 29, 1822 (McGrane, 26 ff.).

19. To Calhoun, Dec. 6, 1822 (McGrane, 29).

20. How little this administration was understood by outsiders can be seen from Henshaw, Bank of the United States, 42.

21. The branches of the Second Bank of the United States were officially designated as offices of discount and deposit. The term office is therefore used in this chapter, as it was by contemporaries, synonymously with branches.

22. According to Catterall's description (op. cit., 105), Wilson was "tactfully" shifted to New Orleans because he did not give complete satisfaction. The assertion is based on 22d Congr., 1st sess., House Report 460, 128, 129. Biddle seems to have sent Wilson to a post for which he was better qualified. See also Biddle's letters to Robert Gilmor of May 11, 1825 and January 4, 1826; to Josiah S. Johnston, Dec. 29, 1825; to Gardiner Greene, Feb. 4, 1826.

23. To the knowledge of this author there were by 1832 only a few cashiers who had come up locally; the ones of the Nashville, Lexington, and Portland offices; see Biddle's letters to John Potter, Nov. 29, 1831; to Scott Greene, Nov. 2, 1831; to Joseph Hemphill, March 27, 1830.

24. To John P. Boyd, Nov. 23, 1826 (McGrane, 40).

25. To James Crommelieu, May 7, 1827 (McGrane, 41); to W. H. Watkins, Aug. 23, 1833.

26. For the latter see the instruction of March 13, 1829 to Joseph Cowperthwait when sent to Portland for an investigation of that branch; to Samuel Jaudon, Sept, 9, 1830; to Gardiner Greene, Nov. 3, 1828; to Isaac Lawrence, Jan. 9, 1833; to Daniel Webster, Nov. 4, 1828; to M. Robinson, Nov. 28, 1828. The letter of Jan. 13, 1824 to Richard Smith, cashier in Washington, shows that a president

was selected despite the objection of the cashier. For the position of the cashier as such, see the letters to Charles S. West, cashier, New Orleans, May 17, 1823; to George Poe, cashier, Mobile, of March 17, 1830.

27. To A. Marshall, April 19, 1831.

28. To John Sommerville, cashier, Nashville, August 1, 1827.

29. To George Poe, February 16, 1831.

30. He was to be informed twice a week on the state of the foreign exchanges and the money markets in Philadelphia and New York. Duplicates of these letters would be sent to the New York cashier who was requested to add what he considered worth knowing (to Thomas Wilson, April 8, 1826).

31. To George Poe, September 22, 1832; see also to C. J. Nicholas, cashier at Richmond. Incidentally, once the cashier of an office was appointed Biddle did not interfere with its personnel policy. Only when new branches were set up and it was difficult to find competent clerks locally would the parent board send clerks and recommend them for positions; to Gardiner Greene, April 27, 1830.

32. To Isaac Carow, Apr. 12, 1831; to P. B. Porter, Sept. 24, 1819; to Nicholas Devereux, Aug. 20, 1830.

33. To Robert Gilmor, May 11, 1824; to J. Harper, May 9, 1825; to William Patterson, June 14, 1831. (The cashier of the parent bank had originally received $7,000; Samuel Jaudon received the same amount as cashier of the Bank of the United States of Pennsylvania, which may indicate that the original salary was restored before the official end of the Bank of the United States. See Bank of the United States, Report of the Committee of Investigation, 13.)

34. To Robert Gilmor, July 8, 1825.

35. To Charles J. Nicholas, Apr. 1, 1826.

36. To John McKim, March 14, 1826. The following salaries were paid in 1820 (and 1827, respectively). First tellers, $1,600 (1400); second tellers, $1,400 (1,300); loan officers, $1,200 (1,100); note clerks, $800 (750); porters, $600 (500); (to John White, July 5, 1827). In one case, that of J. Harper, cashier of the Lexington office, the original salary was restored in 1829 and the difference for the whole interim period paid. (See Biddle's letter to Henry Clay, Dec. 22, 1829.)

37. To S. Harper, cashier, Lexington, Mar. 27, 1830. Incidentally, while Biddle was anxious that a cashier should take a leave when it was needed to restore his health, regular leave was apparently not among the privileges of the cashiers. Rather complicated arrangements with the sureties of the cashiers were necessary in this case. See the letters to John White, cashier, Baltimore, June 7 and June 9, 1826.

38. See footnote 52 on Gorham A. Worth's troubles; and Bank of the United States, Report of the Committee of Investigation, 16, 17.

39. To D. Sprigg, May 13, 1835 (McGrane, 252, 253); to P. Bacot, May 13, 1835; to John Huske, Aug. 6, 1835 (McGrane, 254); to John O'Fallon, Oct. 16, 1835; to H. S. Coxe, Nov. 10, 1835; and to M. Robinson, Apr. 14, 1836.

40. Henry S. Coxe, cashier of the St. Louis office, for instance, was the son of Tench Coxe, the economist.

41. Op. cit., 105.

42. In his letter to Robert Gilmor, July 23, 1832, Biddle used the word "slave" (McGrane, 261). The note on Joseph McIlvaine in ibid., 49 is erroneous. McIlvaine was the cashier of the Bank of the United States, not assistant cashier. Furthermore he is not identical with his namesake, the recorder of the city of Philadelphia who was admitted to the bar in 1821 and died on January 16, 1838, aged thirty-eight years. (Martin, J. H., Bench and Bar of Philadelphia [Philadelphia, 1883], 290). For McIlvaine's activities in Harrisburg, see Biddle's letters to him, of Jan. 7, 10, 13, 15, 16, 17, 21, 22, 23, 30, 31, Feb. 1, 2, 4, 9, 11, Dec. 12, 15, 1836 and Mar. 7, 1837; and McGrane's description in Panic, 70 ff. As late as December 1837 McIlvaine was asked to lobby for a railroad in which Biddle was interested (Dec. 11, 1837).

43. To William B. Lewis, Oct. 10, 1829 (McGrane, 81); to Thomas H. Perkins, July 27, 1832. It seems possible that Jaudon, then cashier of the New Orleans office, was on the point of resigning from the Bank when Biddle made him its cashier. Besides Forstall he was one of the two commissioners to sell the bonds of the Union Bank of Louisiana (to Thomas W. Ward, July 30, 1832). Hidy ("Union Bank," 236) mentions Jaudon in this connection.

44. Jan. 15, 1833.

45. Instruction to Jaudon, Oct. 13, 1826.

46. To Lewis, Oct. 21, 1829; Jaudon to Biddle, Oct, 26, 1829 (McGrane, 80 ff.).
47. To J. G. Watmough, Jan. 13, 1833.
48. See, for instance, Bank of the United States, Report of the Committee of Investigation (1841), 12 ff; Jenks, op. cit., 92; Sumner, History of Banking, 276, 277, 282, 284, 304. There are a few meager notes on Jaudon in Sellers, Edwin Jaquet, An Account of the Jaudon Family (Philadelphia, 1890) and in the same author's The Jaudon Family of Pennsylvania (Philadelphia, 1924).
49. To John McKim, Mar. 14, 1826; Catterall, op. cit., 104, 105.
50. To George Hay, Jan. 30, 1824; to Daniel Webster, Aug. 10, 1828; to Francis B. Fogg, Aug. 27, 1833.
51. For instance, in Washington in 1824 where the old president was reelected against the will of Biddle (to John McKim, Feb. 18, 1824). In 1826 there were difficulties in Providence (to Seth Wheaton, Oct. 14, 1826).
52. To Richard Smith, Washington, Jan. 13, 1824; to William Wirt, Jan. 30, 1824; to James Lloyd, Oct. 4, 1824. (When a branch president like Mr. Cutts of Portsmouth disappointed the confidence reposed in him, the whole board, as a matter of fact, became suspect.)
53. Dorfman, op. cit., 721; Biddle to William Wirt, Jan. 13, 1824.
54. To Richard Anderson, July 31, 1827.
55. To Jeremiah Mason, Sept. 29, and Oct. 29, 1830; to Herman Allen, Apr. 21, 1830 and Dec. 26, 1831. A salary of $800-$1000 was contemplated for the president of the Buffalo office (to William B. Rochester, Sept. 15, 1829).
56. Op. cit., 94.
57. Incidentally in the 1830's, perhaps because of his activities as Biddle's adviser, perhaps because of peculiarities developed in his advancing age, Lenox became rather unpopular and engendered a good deal of ill will. But Biddle, admiring his outstanding qualities, stood by him as an old friend of the Bank (to Isaac Lawrence, Jan. 9, 1833).
58. To Robert Lenox and Thomas Knox, New York, Oct. 27, 1823; to James Lloyd and Daniel Sears, Boston, Oct. 29, 1823; to Henry Eckford and Thomas Knox, New York, Nov. 2, 1824, and numerous other letters.
59. See pages 55, 56.
60. To Thomas H. Perkins, Dec. 6, 1825; to Horace Binney, Jan. 31, 1832. On the other hand, Biddle avoided having father and son on a board at the same time

61. To Robert Lenox, Dec. 4, 1829, Nov. 30, 1832, and Dec. 6, 1833; to Joseph Johnson, Nov. 30, 1830; to Isaac Lawrence, Dec. 4, 1829. (In the case of Washington the directors were to be selected in such a way that the various parts of the District of Columbia would be represented; to Richard Smith, Dec. 30, 1823.)
62. To Josiah Nichol, Apr. 21, 1830.
63. To Horace Binney, Jan. 31, 1832.
64. To David Sears, Oct. 29, 1823; to Richard Smith, Dec. 30, 1823.
65. To Daniel C. Verplanck, Jan. 7, 1824.
66. To James Lloyd, Feb. 16, 1825.
67. To John McLean, Jan. 11, 1829 (McGrane, 69, 70); to Robert Lenox, Dec. 4, 1829; to George Hoffman, Nov. 24, 1830.
68. On the 20th of November 1833, Robert Lenox was asked to nominate directors who preferred the Bank and the country to that "miserable gang" in Washington.
69. See, for instance, to John Tilford, Lexington, Dec. 27, 1831; to William Patterson, Jan. 18, 1830.
70. See, for instance, to Isaac Lawrence, Nov. 28, 1828.
71. Monroe to William Jones, Apr. 29, 1816; Nov. 9, 1816; Jan. 24, 1817 (Jones Papers); to Biddle, Apr. 11, 1820 (McGrane, 13, 14). In addition to the letters reprinted in Appendix III, see also the following passage of a letter of George M. Bibb, director of the Bank of Kentucky, to William Jones, dated Dec. 21, 1816: "My apprehension of the effects of the institution as a political engine will be greatly lessened whilst you are at the head of the institution."
72. Catterall, op. cit., 22. McKim to Biddle, Jan. 8, 1820 (McGrane, 13). In a letter of Jan. 8, 1817 to William Jones, Henry Clay counseled "liberal participation of the other party" in the directorate.
73. To M. Robinson, Nov. 22, 1827; to Campbell P. White, Nov. 27, 1827; to John McLean, Apr. 10, 1829. Also Catterall, op. cit., 244 ff.
74. To Isaac Lawrence and C. P. White, Nov. 27, 1829; to George Hoffman, Nov. 22, 1829; to W. B. Lewis Feb. 24, June 11, and Oct. 31, 1830. The last letter, which is much to Biddle's credit, shows where he drew the line.
75. To Manuel Eyre, Feb. 17, 1833.
76. To Charles A. Davis, Nov. 24, 1830; to A. Dickens, Dec. 22, 1831.
77. To George Poe, Feb. 16, 1831; to

Robert Lenox, Dec. 7, 1825; to Samuel
Smith, Feb. 13, 1833; to William
Appleton, Dec. 9, 1833.

78. To William Wirt, Jan. 13, 1824 and to
M. Robinson, Feb. 11, 1825.

79. To James Lloyd, July 1, 1827; to Robert
Lenox, Nov. 28, 1828; to John Potter,
Jan. 9, 1829; to John Rathbone, Nov. 30,
1831; to Horace Binney, Jan. 31, 1832;
to Gardiner Greene, Nov. 11, 1829.

80. To John Potter, Apr. 30, and Aug. 14,
1833.

81. To Richard Smith, Dec. 31, 1823 and
Jan. 13, 1824.

82. To James Wadsworth, Aug. 10, 1829; to
B. Lewis, June 21, 1830; to John Welles,
Dec. 30, 1833; to Charles E. Dudley,
Aug. 12, 1830.

83. See page 61.

84. Bank of the United States. Report of
the Committee of Investigation, 14, 16,
17.

85. To Thomas Swann, Dec. 10, 1827. This
letter is indicative of Biddle's gentle
way of dealing with a man who had
thwarted him, although the former opponent had to take many a bitter truth.

86. See his remark after having read the
unfavorable passage in Jackson's message of 1829: better to repair it than
to regret it; (to George Hoffman, Dec.
15, 1829).

87. To John Cumming, May 5, 1829 and May 5,
1830.

88. To George Poe, Mar. 17, 1830.

89. To P. P. F. Degrand, Apr. 15, 1831.

90. To the same, June 22, 1826.

91. To Walter Bowne, Jan. 23, 1826; to John
McKim, Mar. 14, 1826 (McGrane, 39, 40).

92. To one Meredith, July 14, 1823.

93. To McDuffie, Apr. 14, 1832. This case
is quite interesting. When one Poultney
acquired control of the Bank of Maryland,
the Baltimore branch of the Second Bank
of the United States wisely refused to
take its notes any longer, although
Biddle himself did not see any reason
for such action and permitted the parent
bank to handle the notes as before.
Since he hated conflicts with state
banks he tried to induce the branch to
fall in line with his policy, but it refused and scored a victory over the
chief executive by its clever tactics.
The Bank of Maryland case was soon to
become a major scandal and the Bank of
the United States, in fact the parent
bank, sustained a heavy loss (to S. H.
Smith, Apr. 6, 1834).

94. To C. S. West, cashier of the New
Orleans office, Sept. 18, 1823.

95. To John White, cashier of the Baltimore
office, Mar. 3, 1828.

96. To M. Robinson, cashier of the New York
office, Feb. 23, 1825; to P. P. F.
Degrand, June 22, 1826; to Robert Lenox,
May 5, 1828.

97. To John White, May 1, 1826.

98. To George Poe, Mar. 17, 1830. There is
one case on record in which Biddle asked
for a list of all bills purchased and
of all domestic bills considered in
jeopardy with a detailed report on each
of them (to Joseph Johnson, Feb. 26,
1825).

99. To M. Robinson, Feb. 23, 1825.

100. To George Poe, cashier in Mobile, Oct.
10, 1827.

101. To Robert Lenox, Mar. 20, 1828; to
Walter Bowne, Mar. 25, 1828.

102. See, for instance, to George Graham,
May 31, 1823; to Isaac Lawrence, Feb. 3,
1825 and Jan. 17, 1827

103. To Enoch Parsons, July 10, 1823;
instruction to Joseph Cowperthwait,
Mar. 13, 1829. When the cashier of the
central office visited a branch its
president was invited by Biddle to discuss freely all business matters with
the former, to provide all facilities
so that he could examine the status of
the branch, and to request whatever
information he wished to acquire, since
the cashier was fully acquainted with
the opinion of the board and of Biddle
personally regarding the office (to
Enoch Parsons, July 10, 1823).

104. To Daniel Webster, Feb. 26, 1827.

105. To Jeremiah Mason, Aug. 10, 1829.

106. To John Potter, July 26, 1826.

107. Op. cit., 385 ff.

108. See page 114.

109. To Walter Bowne, Nov. 16, 1826; to
Robert Lenox, Mar. 23, 1823; to Gardiner
Greene, Jan. 6, 1830.

110. To Gardiner Greene, Nov. 11, 1829; to
Campbell P. White, Dec. 7, 1829; to
W. B. Astor, Dec. 28, 1829; to John
McKim, Jan. 1, 1834.

111. To George Newton, Nov. 29, 1826.

112. To Isaac Lawrence, Feb. 27, 1826; to
Enoch Parsons, June 17, 1826; to Campbell P. White, Nov. 2, 1826.

113. To John Huske, Apr. 17, 1828.

114. To Thomas Swann, July 2, and Aug. 26,
1825.

115. To John McKim, Jan. 1 and Jan. 8,
1834.

116. To William B. Lawrence, Mar. 24, 1821;
to John Potter, Jan. 4, 1831; to P. P. F.
Degrand, Jan. 24, 1831.

117. To John White, Jan. 11, 1830.

118. To Robert Gilmor, Jan. 4, 1826. This case shows the energy and speed with which Biddle acted. When the New Orleans cashier became suspect the matter was put before a committee of the board at 10 a.m. and at 2 p.m. an officer was on his way from Philadelphia to New Orleans to arrest the culprit.

119. To John Huske, Apr. 17, 1828.

120. To Samuel Smith, Nov. 5, 1820; to J. G. Watmough, Jan. 8, 1833; to John Sergeant, Feb. 3, 1829.

121. To S. Swartout, Jan. 2, 1834.

122. To Horace Binney, Jan. 6, 1834.

123. To John White, July 16, 1823.

124. To Robert Gilmor, Mar. 7, 1824.

125. Consultations regarding the lowering of the interest rates will be discussed later in some detail (see pages 140, 141). Other examples are to be found in the letters to C. J. Nicholas, Oct. 17, 1823; to John Huske, Nov. 28, 1827; to S. H. Smith, Aug. 9, 1833. In 1833, probably at the suggestion of the New York cashier, Biddle drafted a letter to the United States Treasurer and sent it to the cashier with the remark: "which I wish you to send with such alterations or additions as you may deem judicious." To M. Robinson, Nov. 13, 1833.

126. To Isaac Lawrence, Aug. 27, 1833; to Enoch Parsons, Sept. 6, 1833; to Samuel Smith, Feb. 13, 1833; to Horace Binney, Jan. 25, 1833; to C. J. Ingersoll, Mar. 5, 1832; to Thomas Knox, Aug. 12, 1823.

127. The author owes his knowledge of and permission to publish this important letter (preserved in the Cadwalader Papers in the Historical Society of Pennsylvania) to the courtesy of Nicholas B. Wainright.

128. The Cadwalader papers in the Historical Society of Pennsylvania are still restricted.

129. The few printed notes on Cadwalader can be found in National Cyclopedia of American Biography, XII, 269; Adams, John Q., Memoirs, see Index. Bassett. op. cit., II, 404, 590, 591, 617; Catterall, op. cit., see Index; McGrane, Biddle Correspondence, see Index (however, his biographical note, ibid., 33, footnote, is erroneous); Jordan, W., Colonial and Revolutionary Families of Pennsylvania, New Series, IV, 93, 94; Keith, Charles P., Provincial Councellors of Pennsylvania (Philadelphia, 1883), 380, 381; and an article in The North American, Sunday Edition, June 16, 1907, on "Old Philadelphia Families." The last three references were kindly given by the Historical Society of Pennsylvania.

130. To David Sears, Jan. 5, 1824 (McGrane, 33); Catterall (op. cit., 275) makes a rather naive remark regarding this important letter. He did not realize that, however charter clauses read, there will always be men who make decisions; and when a collective is charged with functions, there will, de facto, be one or two individuals who determine the will of that collective, in this case Biddle and Cadwalader.

131. To James Lloyd, Jan. 2, 1827.

132. To Daniel Webster, Feb. 26, 1827; to John Tyler, Dec. 22, 1834.

133. See, for instance, Biddle's Letterbooks, May 1832.

134. Incidentally, prior to Biddle's going himself to the capital Horace Binney acted as the representative of the Bank in Washington when the charter hung fire (to G. M. Dallas, Jan. 11, 1831).

135. To Samuel Smith, Jan. 6, 1832. See also page 122, above.

136. To John Potter, Apr. 9, 1824.

137. To Campbell P. White, Aug. 11; Thomas Knox, Aug. 12, 1823.

138. To John White, Feb. 2, 1825. In one case, when the Boston office was in difficulties, the one in New York was advised to take Boston funds from the state banks in the payment of the latter's debts so as to assist the former office which was in want of funds (to Isaac Lawrence, May 9, 1825).

139. To Richard Anderson, July 31, 1827.

140. To Robert Lenox, Feb. 3, 1823 (McGrane, 31, 32); to Campbell P. White, Feb. 3, 1823 (ibid., 30 31); to William Patterson and Robert Gilmor, Jan. 22, 1823; to John White, Feb. 19, 1823; to Samuel Lloyd, Feb. 19, 1823.

141. To Daniel Webster, Dec. 8, 1831.

142. To N. Prime, Aug. 17 and Aug. 25, 1827; Feb. 25, 1828; Feb. 6, 1829.

143. Biddle explained his policy in a letter of July 28, 1830 to Albert Gallatin.

144. To Campbell P. White, Feb. 3, 1823 (McGrane, 30, 31); to Robert Lenox, Feb. 3, 1823.

145. To Charles B. Nicholas, July 16, 1823.

146. Op. cit., (Philadelphia edition), 204 ff.

147. Works, J. R. McCulloch, ed. (New Edition, London, 1871), 276.

148. Report together with Minutes and Evidence

and the Accounts from the Select Committee on the High Price of Gold Bullion (London, 1810), 35 ff, 49, 50.

149. The author is indebted to Professor Edmund Whittaker for having put him on the track of this development.

150. An early citation of Thornton's book can be found in Thomas Law's Address (of 1825), 15.

151. An early American treatment of the Bullion Report is Eric Bollman's "Letter to Alexander Baring on the Present State of the Currency of Great Britain," in The American Review on History and Politics, II (1811). This periodical was edited by Robert Walsh who, like Bollmann, seems to have taken an Anti-Bullionist stand. Thomas Law in his Remarks of 1820, page 19, cited a publication of Walsh's entitled "Anti-Bullionist" which the present author has been unable to identify.

152. Ricardo had made clear that what was valid with regard to foreign was valid also with regard to domestic exchanges which should guide the country bankers in issuing their notes (op. cit., 283).

153. The Annual Report of the New York Bank Commissioners (dated February 1, 1834, 9 ff.) deals with the fact that the issues of the Bank of England were "professedly regulated by the state of the foreign exchanges and the price of bullion."

Incidentally, W. B. Lawrence (in his article on the Bank of the United States in the North American Review, XXXII, April 1831, 546) makes a remark which would be of great interest if it were correct. Discussing the English suspension of specie payments in the Napoleonic era he describes how the purchasing power of English bank paper fell and how this fall was reflected in the foreign exchanges. Being imperfectly understood the fall of the pound sterling in America led, Lawrence claims, to the "improvident augmentation of bank notes" in this country in 1813 and 1814. This statement would imply that American bankers by that time already looked at the exchanges in determining their issues; but probably they did not, and the passage is indicative only of the thinking of the 1830's.

154. One can appreciate the progress when one keeps in mind that by 1820 Daniel Webster considered the ability of a bank to redeem its notes in specie the criterion of whether or not its issues were

too extensive. See Law, Thomas, Remarks, 19.

155. To Isaac Lawrence, May 9, 1825.

156. To C. P. White, Nov. 2, 1826.

157. To the same, Mar. 3, 1828.

158. To Robert Lenox, Mar. 4, and to Nathaniel Prime, Mar. 5, 1828.

159. "The Currency" in the National Gazette, Apr. 10, 1828, repr. in Gilbart, History, 111 ff.

160. U.S. 22nd Congr., 1st sess., House Report 460, 310; Hamilton, J. A., op. cit., 84.

161. See page 140.

162. To Josiah S. Johnston Jan. 9, 1826.

163. To Isaac Lawrence, Oct. 13, 1823. No loans were made on stocks which were not fully paid up (to J. W. Well, Oct. 10, 1835).

164. To M. Robinson, Mar. 17, 1825; to Walter Bowne, Sept. 4, 1825. See also page 154.

165. See page 45.

166. To Gardiner Greene, Boston, Mar. 10, 1829.

167. To A. Davis, New York, June 13, 1829.

168. U.S. 22nd Congr., 1st sess., House Report 460, 129.

169. To Salazar, Jan. 27, 1825; to Rocafuerte, Nov. 6, 1824; to Baring Brothers and Company, Nov. 6, 1824; to Obregon, Feb. 1, 1825.

170. See pages 13, 49.

171. See pages 135 ff., 141, 154. As to figures, see Catterall, op. cit., 501.

172. To P. P. F. Degrand, Dec. 31, 1829.

173. To R. L. Colt, Aug. 12, 1826; to Richard Smith, Sept. 2, 1830.

174. To Samuel Jaudon, Nov. 3, 1830 and Feb. 16, 1831.

175. To George Hoffman, Dec. 15, 1829.

176. See pages 126, 129.

177. See page 51.

178. McGrane, Biddle Correspondence, 37, footnote.

179. To James Lloyd, Jan. 5 and July 5, 1824, Jan. 3 and July 5, 1825; to Robert Gilmor, Jan. 4, 1826.

180. To Samuel Smith, Jan. 27, 1830. (The letter, however, is not clear throughout.)

181. To Richard Rush, Nov. 25, 1828 (McGrane, 57); to Samuel Smith, May 2, 1828; to Horace Binney, Feb. 28, 1830.

182. To Horace Binney, Jan. 25, 1832.

183. For instance, he referred to the reprint of a document in The Museum of Foreign Literature and Science, XXI (1832), 530; to Thomas Melvill, Jan. 26, 1833.

184. To Horace Binney, Jan. 26, 1832.

185. Rees, Abraham, The Cyclopaedia; or

Universal Dictionary of Arts, Sciences, and Literature (Philadelphia, Samuel F. Bradford, Firman and Co., 1810-1842).

186. Copinger, Walther Arthur, *On the Authorship of the First Hundred Numbers of the "Edinburgh Review"* (Manchester, 1895).

187. Quoted from the English edition of Rees' *Cyclopaedia* of 1819, article "Bank of England."

188. McGrane, 51 (the letter to Biddle is dated June 17, 1828).

189. See pages 178 ff.

190. To Richard Rush, Nov. 25, 1828 (McGrane, 56 ff.); to Cadwalader Evans, Jan. 26, 1830.

191. To Horace Binney, Mar. 1, 1832.

192. See page 146.

On Nov. 20, 1823 Biddle suggested a refunding and conversion transaction to Crawford; in December of 1827 he provided foreign exchange (to Edward Jones, chief clerk of the Treasury, Dec. 17, 1824); in March of the same year he informed the Secretary of State regarding duties on cotton goods in Mexico and discrimination against American trade (to Henry Clay, Mar. 10, 1825); in 1827 again a conversion of a certain part of the funded debt was proposed (to Richard Rush, Jan. 12, 1827).

193. The term "regulator" in this context is telling. It can be found in Ricardo's *High Price of Bullion* (*Works*, ed. McCulloch, 283) applied to the Bank of England, which is called therein the "great regulator of the country paper." W. B. Lawrence, in his article on the *Bank of the United States* (op. cit., 558) pointed out that the Bank of England and the Bank of the United States were "the ultimate regulators of the currency" in their respective countries.

194. Gilbart, *History*, 64.

195. To Joseph Hemphill, Feb. 8, 1830.

196. Op. cit., 555.

197. This policy was in line with the practice of contemporary English country banks which could meet a large proportion of their obligations with London funds (Wood, op. cit., 23). There were, however, exceptions to this rule of the Bank. For many years it refused to take bills of exchange from Georgia banks, whose specie basis was so small that such a policy would have been identical with forcing the Bank of the United States to bear the burden of the import of specie into the state, which Biddle thought should be assumed by the banks. Only when the Savannah branch had become very strong did he permit it to take bills on New York and Philadelphia in the settlement of obligations of the banks. This policy provides an example of the central banker not carrying a burden which was really his (to John Cumming, Savannah, Feb. 5, 1830).

198. *American State Papers, Finance*, III, 366.

199. Gallatin explained that the obligation of the Bank to transfer government funds free of charge was equivalent to an agreement that the government could, at any time, buy from and sell to the Bank bills of exchange at par. *Works*, II, 438.

200. *Report of the Proceedings of the Triennial Meeting of the Stockholders of the Bank of the United States* (1831), 13, 14.

201. Jones to Crawford, July 20, 1817; *American State Papers, Finance*, IV, 808. See also Rules and Regulations for conducting the Exchange Business of the Bank of the United States in *U.S. 15th Congress, 2d sess, House Report 92*, 54 ff.

202. Catterall, op. cit., 140.

203. *Biddle's Letterbooks*, III, 117.

204. To Samuel Smith, Jan. 25, 1830.

205. As to figures, see Catterall, op. cit., 505.

206. *Letterbooks*, III, 157.

207. Hidy, Ralph W. "House of Baring," 272; Cole, op. cit., 394.

208. *American State Papers, Finance*, III, 333; *U.S. 15th Congress, 2d sess., House Report 92*, 57 ff.

209. *Report of the Triennial Meeting* (1831), 14, 15.

210. *U.S. 22nd Congr., 1st sess., House Report 460*, 122; see also Lawrence's comment, op. cit., 557, 559.

211. *Letterbooks*, III, 213.

212. "House of Baring," 270-272.

213. To Robert Oliver, Mar. 29 and May 5, 1826; to Robert Lenox, Sept. 6, 1827.

214. To N. Prime, Feb. 25, 1828.

215. A history of the foreign exchange business in the eighteenth and nineteenth centuries, which now is lacking, would have to show to what extent Biddle was a creative entrepreneur in this field.

216. See page 140.

217. To Edward Everett, Mar. 10, 1832. See also Catterall, op. cit., 117 ff.

218. See Catterall, op. cit., Index, under "branch drafts."

219. To Horace Binney, Jan. 24, 1832.

220. See Chapter III, footnote 1.

221. To Horace Binney, Jan. 23, 1832.
222. See page 51.
223. See the table in Catterall, op. cit., 503.
224. A New Financial Project, 19, 20.
225. To Horace Binney, Feb. 28, 1830.
226. See Catterall, op. cit., 505, and, for comparison, the rates of domestic exchange in 1842 (Hurd, op. cit., 102).
227. See footnote 37 of section IV of this chapter. Condy Raguet could not see why the price of money should be equalized; The Examiner, II (1835), 159.
228. Peabody, op. cit., 499.
229. To P. P. F. Degrand, Oct. 17, 1832.
230. Free Trade Advocate, I (1829), 339; David Henshaw (Bank of the United States, 33) took a similar stand. Incidentally in his Treatise of 1839 (120 ff.) Raguet condemned exchange dealings by banks in general.
230a. It seems that Biddle was instrumental in having exchange on New York and Philadelphia quoted in England (to John Sergeant, Apr. 6, 1838).
231. Biddle to John Quincy Adams, Financial Register, II (1838), 393. See also Trotter's comment on these transactions, op. cit.; 102, 103.
232. Report of the Secret Committee appointed to Inquire into the Expediency of Renewing the Charter of the Bank of England, Evidence, 4795; Joplin's Digest, 100, 101. Bank of the United States, Report of the Committee of Investigation, 18, 19, 61, 62.
233. To McDuffie, May 5, 1832.
234. To Gardiner Greene, Apr. 11, 1825; to John White, Apr. 14, 1825 and Apr. 27, 1826.
235. U.S. 22nd Congr., 1st sess., House Report 460, 308.
236. To John White, Apr. 27, 1826; to M. Robinson, Feb. 23, 1825.
237. To John Barney, Mar. 4, 1826; to Richard Rush, Aug. 21, 1827. The letters of Jan. 23, 1832 to George Dallas and of June 6, 1833 to Thomas Cooper are interesting because they reveal the technique of acquiring and dealing with gold bullion.
238. To Richard Rush, Aug. 21, 1827.
239. In 1837, while the president of the Bank of the United States of Pennsylvania, Biddle planned again large dealings in specie (to Joseph McIlvaine, Mar. 3, 1837).
240. To John White, Feb. 15, 1828.
241. To Isaac Lawrence, Jan. 4, 1828.
242. Report of the Triennial Meeting (1831), 15, 16.
243. To Albert Gallatin, Sept. 9, 1830.
244. To John Cumming, July 25, 1832. A party opening a new bank in Montgomery draws the necessary specie from the branches of the Bank of the United States at Savannah and Mobile.
245. To Albert Gallatin, July 29, 1830.
246. To Robert Lenox, Oct. 9, 1826.
247. To Robert Lenox, Feb. 8, 1828.
248. U.S. 22nd Congr., 2nd sess., Senate Document 17, 100.
249. "The Currency" in National Gazette, April 10, 1828; quoted also in Dialogue on a National Bank, 6. See also Biddle, Questions, second part, passim.
250. American State Papers, Finance, V, 147 (from a letter by Biddle to Crawford regarding the subscription of a Federal loan). Also see Biddle's letter to N. Silsbee, February 19, 1827.
251. On April 25, 1825 he spoke of a "squall" abroad which forced him to be very cautious (to John White, Baltimore).
252. To Gardiner Greene, April 11; to Samuel Frothingham, April 14; to M. Robinson, April 15, 1825.
253. To John White, cashier of the Baltimore office, April 15 and 19, 1825; to Gardiner Greene, president of the Boston office, April 11 and July 15, 1825.
254. In the United States the bank panic came in July, 1825, while England did not experience hers until November and December. See Thorp, Willard L., Business Annals (New York, 1926), 119, 157.
255. To Isaac Lawrence, April 22 and May 9, 1825.
256. To the same, May 12, 1825.
257. To Robert Gilmor, Jan. 4, 1826.
258. U.S. 22nd Congr., 1st sess., House Report 460, 129, 135, 484.
259. See page 52, and 53.
260. U.S. 22nd Congr., 1st sess., House Report 460, 484, 129, 135; Biddle to A. Dickens, November 30, 1818.
261. To Isaac Lawrence, February 8, 1826.
262. To Campbell P. White, November 2, 1826.
263. Smith, Vera, op. cit., 40. The "Propositions" are reprinted by Catterall, op. cit., Appendix 2; see especially, 489, 490.
264. To Robert Lenox, July 16, 1825.
265. To Isaac Lawrence, August 23, 1825.
265a. As to England, see Wood, op. cit., 35, 36.
266. On December 11, 1825 Biddle advised Robert Lenox to negotiate with "that cautious Frenchman" in order to get his specie in exchange for 4 1/2 per cent government stock to strengthen the office. If necessary a sacrifice should

be made by quoting a favorable sales
price.

267. To Robert Lenox, December 7, 1825.

268. Essays on Banking, 172, 175; Biddle to
N. Silsbee, February 19, 1827. Similar
ideas were expressed in the English
literature of the time, for instance in
Attwood, Mathias, A Letter to Lord
Archibald Hamilton, (London, 1823),
49 ff.

269. At the time under investigation the
national economy of this country was not
so unified that a crisis would break
everywhere at the same moment. Carey
envisaged in 1816 the Philadelphia banks
being helped by selling government stock
in Boston. Biddle himself, as described
above, relieved the situation by shifting some of the burden from the Northeast to New Orleans.

270. Thorp (Business Annals, 120) claims
that money remained plentiful until May.
But Biddle in his article "The Currency,"
in the National Gazette of April 10,
1828, speaks of the "present scarcity
of money."

271. To John White, March 3, 1828.

272. In 1836 Biddle considered the prevention
of a "convulsion" as in the power of the
Treasury or of a national bank, Letterbooks, (1836), 95.

273. To Robert Lenox, February 8, 1828; to
Isaac Lawrence, February 12, 1828; to
John White, February 15, 1828. See also
Biddle's article "The Currency," in the
National Gazette of April 10, 1828.
This article was answered by Condy
Raguet in the Philadelphia Gazette of
April 17, 1828, both articles being re-
printed in Free Trade Advocate, 1829.

274. It is possible that the necessity of
preparing for a repayment of government
stock on July 1 made such action impossible (to Robert Lenox, April 22, 1828).

275. To John White, March 3, 1828.

276. To Robert Lenox, April 22, 1828.

277. To John White, Baltimore, April 24, 1828.

278. Such intentions were imputed to him;
see, for instance, Taney to Jackson,
March 1833, (Jackson, Correspondence,
V, 37, 38).

279. Van Buren, op. cit., 621, 623. Taney's,
claim that during the expansion Biddle
had introduced branch drafts in the
West "a description of paper as it [the
Bank] could depreciate or raise to its
par value as best suited its own views"
was especially nonsense. Taney in his
"Report on the Removal of the Deposites"
in U.S. 23rd Congr., 1st sess., Senate
Document 2, 6.

280. See page 226. On January 3, 1831
Biddle wrote jokingly to A. Dickens,
chief clerk of the Treasury Department,
in connection with the repayment of government debts: while the President
wanted to kill the Bank, Dickens wanted
it to die from starvation.

281. To Samuel Jaudon, September 7 and Nov.
3, 1830, Febr. 16, 1831; to P. Benson,
Febr. 23, 1831. See also to A. Dickens,
September 21, 1830.

282. To Isaac Lawrence, February 4, 1832; to
Joshua S. Johnston on the same date; to
Samuel Swartout, February 2, 1832; to
Robert Lenox, February 9, 1832. This
author cannot agree with Catterall's
analysis, according to which contraction
began with the circular of October 7,
1831 (op. cit., 146 ff.). This circular did not order contraction; it advised caution and was meant to result
in a shifting of funds from the West,
Southwest, and South to New York and
Philadelphia. As Biddle's Letterbooks
show, contraction was not started before
February 1832, and the result showed up
as early as May, a quite natural time
lag, when one considers the available
means of communication.

Incidentally, this mistake in dating
the beginning of contraction resulted
in an erroneous interpretation of
Biddle's activities in the winter of
1831-1832. Believing that contraction
was ordered as early as October 1831 and
seeing the loans of the Bank increase
until May 1832 Catterall concluded that
Biddle's orders were disobeyed. The
actuality has been described above.
Furthermore Catterall came to believe
that in the spring of 1832 Biddle had
to take recourse to "frantic" efforts.
This opinion seems to have been derived
especially from assigning high importance to a letter of Biddle's of April
20, 1832 to Samuel Jaudon, cashier of
the New Orleans office (op. cit., 157).
In fact, this letter proves nothing except that Biddle's nerves were strained,
a not surprising fact since it was the
time in which the renewal of the charter
hung fire in Congress. In this letter
Biddle reprimanded Jaudon for increasing the loans of the branch in spite of
the order to contract. However, a few
days later, on April 30, 1832, Biddle
wrote an apologetic letter acknowledging one from Jaudon written before the
former letter had arrived in New Orleans
and expressing his satisfaction that
Jaudon had already fallen in line with

the policy of contraction. That there was nothing "frantic" in Biddle's actions of the period can also be seen from the fact that, although hard pressed for foreign exchange, Biddle refused to buy when he considered the offers too high. (See his letters to William G. Bucknor of September 25, 27, 29, 1832.)

283. This comparison was later offered again as justification; see, for instance, to Horace Binney, March 1, 1832.

284. Incidentally, Biddle was friendly to the régime of Louis Phillipe. (See his letter to Lafayette of October 9, 1830).

285. See his letter of October 28, 1830 to John Potter on the state of the foreign exchanges and the large funds to the credit of the Bank in Europe. On January 23, 1832 he wrote to George M. Dallas that the passengers of a single boat which had recently arrived from England were supposed to have brought $250,000 worth of gold in sovereigns. (See also the letter to M. Robinson of March 22, 1831.)

286. Catterall, op. cit., 503.

287. Biddle, Questions, 3d part, 1, 2. His thinking was in line with contemporary English thought where the problem was discussed as one of competition between the Bank of England and country bankers; see Wood, op. cit., 28, 29.

288. C. C. Cambreleng in a speech before Congress quoted these words from the letter of a dead banker friendly to the Bank, dated February 16, 1832. (See Register of Debates of Congress, X, Part II, 2380, 2381.) The statement had been ascribed to Girard, e.g., by Catterall (op. cit., 145) and lately by Wildes (op. cit., 292). The attribution is erroneous, for Girard had died in December 1831 and so could not have written a letter the following February.

289. Currency and Banking, 27; Sheppard, op. cit., 7. See also Appleton, Memoir, 287 ff. Incidentally, Appleton's critical attitude toward Biddle may well have been tainted by personal motives. In 1829 he clashed with the Boston office of the Bank and complained to Biddle who, however, upheld the branch, considering Appleton in the wrong. (See Biddle's letters to James Lloyd, March 4; to Gardiner Greene, March 10; to Nathan Appleton, August 28, 1829.)

290. Profits of the Bank were unusually high in 1831 (to Samuel Smith, June 14, 1832).

291. "The Currency."

292. Catterall, op. cit., 503.

293. See chapter III, page 51.

294. Webster, in Register of Debates of Congress, X, Part I, 737.

294a. Regarding the "Rule of 1832" see Mints, op. cit., 84.

295. To Horace Binney, March 1, 1832.

296. Catterall, op. cit., 451.

297. U.S. 22nd Congr., 2nd sess., House Report 121, 27, 140, 146. To N. Cope, October 1; to Robert Lenox, October 2, 1832.

298. See above page 132.

298a. Wood op. cit., 64.

299. To J. Harper, June 8, 1825.

300. To Samuel Frothingham, July 24, 1830 and January 5, 1831; to Samuel Smith, November 14, 1830; to W. Patterson, December 14, 1830; to Thomas H. Perkins, January 5, 1831. The Bank of England began making "special advances" at low rates in December 1833 (Wood, op. cit., 76).

301. Incidentally, Gallatin was an early friend of a variable interest rate. See his letter of August 14, 1830 to Biddle in Writings, II, 437.

302. To Francis Hopkinson, November 2, 1830; to Thomas Cadwalader June 30, 1832.

303. U.S. 22nd Congr., 1st sess., House Report 460, 123, 124, 505. Other banks seem to have followed the example of lowering the interest below the legal rate, for instance the Bank of Pennsylvania (see ibid., 153).

304. An example of this outlook can be found in the letter to William Appleton of Jan. 27, 1834   (McGrane, 219).

305. Reports of the Committee of Inquiry, 107.

306. Ibid., 118; U.S. 22nd Congr., 1st sess., House Report 460, 336, 559. See also to George McDuffie, January 9, 1833.

307. U.S. 22d. Congress, 1st sess., House Report 460, 367.

308. As to details see page 132.

309. To John Huske, Apr. 17, 1828; also to Gardiner Greene, Mar. 10, 1829; to L. M. Hinnan, Sept. 16, 1829.

310. To Joseph Hemphill, Dec. 21, 1829. Incidentally Biddle was opposed to the two fruitful principles behind the Safety Fund System, mutual insurance and bank supervision by special government officers.

311. Register of Debates of Congress, 21st Congr., 1st sess., Appendix, 103.

312. To Philip Allen, Jan. 25, 1834; to A. Davis, June 13, 1829; U.S. 29th Congr., 1st sess., House Document 226 506.

313. See above pages 135, 136.

314. To S. H. Smith, Apr. 2, 1834 (McGrane; 225).

315. See also to Thomas Knox, Aug. 12, 1823.

316. To A. Davis, June 13, 1829.

317. The Second Bank of the United States had a few correspondents as, for instance, the Consolidated Association of Planters in New Orleans and the State Bank of Mississippi (to Joseph Hemphill, Feb. 8, 1830). It was left to the board of the branch in Utica whether or not to establish correspondent relationships with state banks (to Campbell P. White, Sept. 20, 1830).

318. To John Sergeant, Dec. 15, 1827; to Edward Everett, May 12, 1827.

319. To C. J. Ingersoll, Feb. 25, 1832.

320. An unfriendly contemporary recognition of the feeling of responsibility as possessed by the Bank can be found in U.S. 23rd Congr., 1st sess., Senate Document 2, 19, where the national bank is contrasted with the state banks. It acts continuously "under the conviction of its immense power over the money concerns of the country."

321. To C. J. Nicholas, Oct. 4, 1823.

322. To Robert Lenox, Dec. 7, 1825; to Isaac Lawrence, Feb. 8, 1825.

323. To Robert Lenox, Feb. 8 and Feb. 12, 1828; to Isaac Lawrence, Feb. 12, 1828.

324. To Joseph Hemphill, Jan. 10, 1825; also to Gardiner Greene, Oct. 4, 1825.

325. To John Cumming, Jan. 12, 1825.

326. U.S. 23rd Congr., 2nd sess., Senate Document 17, 100. See also similar letters to R. H. Wilde, Feb. 24, 1834 and to Charles Hammond, Mar. 11, 1834 (McGrane, 225, 226): Since the removal of the deposits the Bank is no longer the fiscal agency of the government. Consequently the president has no right to risk private property to the public advantage. Or, as the same idea is expressed in the second letter: "The Executive, by removing the public revenues, has relieved the Bank from all responsibility for the currency and imposed upon it a necessity to look primarily to the interest of the stockholders." It is immaterial in this context whether or not these statements were sincere. The claim that a certain action had relieved the Bank of a responsibility implied a recognition that such responsibility had existed at least in the past.

327. To Enoch Parsons, Apr. 12, 1828.

328. U.S. 23rd Congr., 1st sess., Executive Document 2, 4.

329. U.S. 23rd Congr., 1st sess., House Executive Document 12, 2.

330. In this context one should note also the following passage from an unpublished letter of September 7, 1818 by William Jones, probably to the Baltimore cashier, McCulloch. Jones reported on a visit in Washington and conversations with Calhoun and Crawford: "Both approve its [the Bank's] career and both look with solicitude at the difficulties which surround it.... That this Bank should look with a steady eye to its own interest [thus in original] is what they both anxiously desire; and they have no idea that it should sacrifice any portion of them to uphold the present wretched state of things. Come what may they wish that it would keep itself above the difficulties that may for a time overwhelm other institutions." Incidentally, here one finds Cheves' policy of 1819 foreshadowed.

331. 22nd Congr., 1st sess., House Document 460, 467.

332. See the very important letter to Joseph Johnson, Sept. 27, 1830.

333. Ogden (Remarks, 25) is very strong on that point. Biddle's remarks in his "Sixth Letter to John Quincy Adams" are insincere to the extent that he denies that intention; see Financial Register, II (1838), 393.

334. To M. Allen, Nov. 17, 1837.

335. Clarke to Biddle, Oct. 30, 1832 (McGrane, 247); Pennsylvania Acts (1835-1836), No. 138, 422.

336. Bank of the United States, Report of the Committee of Investigation, 24; Financial Register, II (1838), 154 ff.; Adams, John Q., Memoirs, IX, 364. Biddle to Samuel Jaudon, May 31 and Aug. 3, 1838 (McGrane, 311, 321); to J. R. Ingersoll, Mar. 31, 1836; to J. Hunter, Apr. 25, 1836; to James Erwin, June 25, 1836; to Richard Anderson, June 29, 1836; to Samuel Patterson, Aug. 10, 1836; to George Poe, Sept. 28, 1836; to Joseph L. Robert, Jan. 3, 1837; to David Trimble, Jan. 7, 1837; to R. M. Blatchford, Jan. 9, 1837.

337. To J. Watson Webb, July 29, 1836.

338. Interesting correspondence and a contemporary article of the (London) Times are reprinted by Gilbart, op. cit., 199 ff.; Hone, Diary (entry of March 28, 1837), 248, 249.

339. "Fourth Letter from Mr. Biddle to Hon. John Quincy Adams," Financial Register, I, 342 ff.; McGrane, Panic, see Index

under "Biddle, Resumption," to John Potter, Mar. 28, 1838 and to S. Jaudon Mar. 31, 1838.

340. Occasionally Biddle recognized this fact himself (to M. Allen, July 29, 1836).

341. McGrane, Biddle Correspondence, 56 footnote; Adams, John Q., Memoirs, VIII, 355; Joseph Gales to Biddle, Nov..24, 1828; Biddle to George Hoffman, Dec. 22, 1828 (McGrane, 56, 62).

342. To Monroe, July 6, 1807 (McGrane, 3).

343. To Josiah Nichol, June 23, 1829; to A. Dickens, Sept. 16, 1829 (McGrane, 72, 76); postscript to a letter to Joseph Gales, Aug. 20, 1830.

344. To Samuel Smith, Dec. 29, 1828 (partially reprinted by McGrane, 62, 63).

345. To Edward Shippen, Feb. 12, 1829.

346. To Daniel Webster, Dec. 2, 1828; to Peter Benson, Dec. 29, 1828; to John McLean, Jan. 10, 1829; to John Harper, Jan. 9, 1829 (McGrane, 67).

347. To Henry Toland, Dec. 15, 1828; to Samuel Smith, Dec. 29, 1828 and Jan. 30, 1829.

348. U.S. 22nd Congr., 1st sess., House Report 460, 437 ff.; McLean to Biddle, Jan. 5, 1829 (McGrane, 63 ff.).

349. To John G. Watmough, May 11, 1832. In this connection see James A. Hamilton to Andrew Jackson, Dec. 9, 1833 in Jackson, Correspondence, V, 233.

350. To Samuel Smith, Dec. 29, 1828 (McGrane, 63); to John McKim, Sept. 16, 1829; to A. Dickens, Sept. 16 and 30, 1829 (McGrane, 75 ff.).

351. To A. Dickens, Oct. 19, 1829.

352. Jackson, Correspondence, IV, 84, 85.

353. To Isaac Lawrence and C. P. White, Nov. 27, 1829; to George Hoffman, Nov. 22, 1829; to W. B. Lewis, Feb. 24, May 24, June 11, Oct. 31, 1830; and other cases.

354. The plan is correctly described by Catterall, op. cit., 190, 191; Bassett, op. cit., II, 598. See also Jackson, Correspondence, IV, 90, 91.

355. On Dec. 4, 1829, Biddle wrote Robert Lenox that he had returned from Washington.

356. See, for instance, McGrane, Biddle Correspondence, 93.

357. Colt informed Biddle that Cambreleng advised selling out Bank stock since the administration was hostile (Jan. 7, 1829, McGrane, 66). Incidentally, Cambreleng had been considered for a directorship in the New York branch.

358. To Robert Lenox, Dec. 4, 1829; to Alexander Hamilton, Dec. 12, 1829; the latter to Biddle, Dec. 10, 1829 (McGrane, 88 ff.).

359. Jackson to James Alexander Hamilton, reprinted in the latter's Reminiscences, 154.

360. In a letter to Samuel Smith of Dec. 22, 1829, Biddle speaks about the need of being "cheered up a little." See also, to R. M. Johnson, Apr. 21, 1830.

361. To N. Silsbee, Dec. 17, 1829.

362. To John Potter, Dec. 14, 1829; to George Hoffman, Dec. 15, 1829.

363. To Samuel Smith, Apr. 22, 1830.

364. To Samuel Smith, Jan. 2, 1830; to Walter Bowne, May 1, 1830.

365. To M. Robinson, Dec. 20, 1830; to J. Hunter, May 4, 1831.

366. To Samuel Smith, Apr. 15, 1830.

367. To John McKim, Jan. 18, 1830 (McGrane, 96, 97).

368. To C. A. Davis, May 19, 1830; Biddle's criticism of a government bank is to be found in Letterbooks, III, 162.

369. To Samuel Smith, Dec. 22, 1829, Jan. 10 and Dec. 10, 1830; to George Graham, Dec 23, 1829.

370. To James Monroe, July 6, 1807 (McGrane, 3, 4).

371. To Thomas Cooper, Aug. 16, 1833.

372. To Joseph Gales, Mar. 2, 1831 (McGrane, 126).

373. See page 149 and footnote 380.

374. To Charles Jared Ingersoll, Feb. 12, 1831.

375. To R. M. Johnson, May 21, 1830. It was another tactical move of Biddle's to have banks memorialize Congress in order to disarm the Bank's enemies who claimed that the state banks were jealous of the latter (to Enoch Parsons, Jan. 28, 1832).

376. See page 213.

377. Address to those on whom Heaven....

378. To Nicholas Devereux, Feb. 7, 1831; to Joseph Gale, Mar. 2, 1831, (McGrane, 125).

379. To Joseph Hemphill, Mar. 12, 1830; to P. P. F. Degrand, Dec. 22, 1830; to Enoch Parsons, Feb. 28, 1831.

380. "I am preparing some machinery which will enable me to speak directly and immediately to every man in the country;" to Charles Jared Ingersoll, Feb. 12, 1831.

381. To James Robertson, Apr. 8, 1831.

382. To John O'Fallon, St. Louis, Sept. 26, 1832.

383. It will hardly be necessary to register strong disagreement with many aspects of Arthur M. Schlesinger, Jr.'s description and interpretation of the Bank War, a disagreement which will be self-evident to the readers of both books. However, in one of the impressive passages of his book Schlesinger describes how the growing importance of the common

man by 1830 was accompanied by a declining importance of Congress. The great party leader who through his eloquence and the weight of his arguments could sway his colleagues lost to the popular hero who could bid for the confidence of the masses. Biddle had no instinct for this change. He played up to and relied on the great parliamentarians who were on the point of losing their influence (op. cit., 50-52).

384. Op. cit., 13 ff.

385. Biddle shared in one correspondent's mirth over the extraordinary production which both in style and substance had scarcely a parallel; to James Dunlop, July 17, 1832.

386. Joseph Gales was asked on March 2, 1831 for a list of his subscribers (McGrane 126); a similar request was sent to John Norvall, who was asked for addresses of all reading people around Harrisburg. (This letter is not dated in the Letterbook.) See also, to J. Hunter, May 4, 1831; to E. J. Dupont, May 24, 1830.

387. Regarding Degrand, see Kirkland, Edward C., "The 'Railroad Scheme' of Massachusetts" in Journal of Economic History, V (1945), 154, and Biddle's numerous letters to him, especially those of June 14 and Dec. 22, 1830, Oct. 4, 1831, Mar. 14, 1832; also to Samuel Frothingham, May 27 and June 14, 1830.

388. To N. Benson, June 21, 1830.

389. To J. Huske, June 14, 1830; to John Norvall, June 15 and Dec. 22, 1830; to P. P. F. Degrand, Dec. 22, 1830; to John Sergeant, Feb. 7, 1831.

390. To John Norvall, no date (probably Mar. 5, 1831).

391. To James Robertson, Apr. 8, 1831; to J. G. Watmough, May 11, 1832. It is noteworthy that in 1838 Biddle declined a suggestion of Mathew Carey to appoint a publicity agent (Apr. 20).

392. For similar letters, see to William B. Lawrence, Feb. 8, 1831 (McGrane, 123); and to J. Hunter, May 4, 1831 (McGrane, 126, 127).

393. It seems rather inconsistent that the man who thought so highly of the influence of the press did not take cognizance of its attacks on the Bank or himself. But Biddle had "no taste for newspaperism" (McGrane, 132) and considered it impossible to answer every attack which appeared in the press. If once he began to refute some of them the rest, unrefuted, he felt, would be taken as conceded. On the other hand, Biddle repeatedly advised his local representatives to answer unjust charges and incorrect statements published in local papers. (To George Hoffman, Dec. 22, 1828; to G. C. Verplanck, Apr. 12, 1831; to John Tilford, and to Edward Shippen, both on June 6, 1831.)

394. To William G. Bucknor, July 13, 1832 (McGrane, 195).

395. To Daniel Webster, Oct. 2, 1828 (McGrane, 58); to John Potter, Jan. 9, 1830 (ibid., 95, 96). In the winter of 1831 a loan was made to Duff Green, editor of the Telegraph with the understanding that the borrower was "to speak his mind about the Bank just as freely as he did before" for the Bank wanted "friends from conviction" not friends "from interest" and Biddle believed in the freedom of the press; to Joseph Hemphill, Feb. 10, 1831 (ibid., 124).

396. To James Hunter, May 4, 1831; to J. G. Watmough, May 11, 1832 (McGrane, 127, 190).

397. Pages 619, 620.

398. To Leslie Combs, Mar. 23, 1831.

399. Editor's note in Van Buren's Autobiography, 647; Catterall, op. cit., 193.

Incidentally, Biddle denied having said, on coming back from the interview with the President, that the Bank would be rechartered (to John McKim, Jan. 13, 1830). But undoubtedly he wrote to Gallatin on Sept. 9 of that year that he expected the renewal of the charter without change since the President had greatly altered his opinion since the previous year.

400. To A. Dickens, Dec. 14, 1831.

401. Smith, Charles W., op. cit., 2, 3. As to Biddle's memorandum see McGrane, 129.

402. To S. D. Bloodgood, Jan. 26, 1832. As to Clay's opinion, see McGrane, 142, footnote.

403. To Samuel Smith, Dec. 10; to M. Robinson, Dec. 20; to Albert Gallatin, Dec. 28; to Jon.ª Roberts, Jan. 15, 1830 and 1831 respectively.

404. To G. C. Verplanck, Apr. 12, 1831.

405. May 21, 1830.

406. McGrane, 125.

407. To M. Robinson, Mar. 3, 1831.

408. To John Harper, May 10, 1831.

409. To Samuel Smith, June 6, 1831.

410. To Joseph Gales, June 21, 1831.

411. To William B. Rochester, Sept. 3, 1831.

412. To William G. Bucknor, July 13, 1832; to John Tilford, Sept. 26, 1832 (McGrane, 197, 198).

413. To Louis Williams, Aug. 16, 1832; to Redmond Conyngham, Sept. 24, 1832.

414. Very typical is the letter to R. M. Blatchford, Aug. 19, 1835; see also a passage in the letter to William Appleton, Jan. 27, 1834 (McGrane, 219).

415. To J. S. Barbour, Apr. 16, 1833; to J. Hunter, May 17, 1833; to Thomas Cooper, May 6, 1833 (McGrane, 209) and Aug. 16, 1833 (ibid., 215); to Daniel Webster, Apr. 6, 1835. See also in this context the speech made before the stockholders of the Bank of the United States when Biddle presented them with the Pennsylvania charter, as quoted by Conrad, op. cit., 14.

416. To Charles Jared Ingersoll, Feb. 25, 1832; to Louis Williams, Aug. 16 1832; to J. G. Watmough, Feb. 13, Feb. 24, and Dec. 23, 1833; to S. P. Carson, Feb. 28, 1833; to Joshua Nichol, Mar. 19, 1833; to J. S. Barbour, Apr. 16 and Sept. 4, 1833, July 9, 1834; to Thomas Cooper, May 6, 1833 (McGrane, 210).

416a. Besides the printed material on Whitney, see to B. Shepard, Jan. 26, 1837.

417. To William G. Bucknor, July 13, 1832 (McGrane 195, 196).

418. Biddle felt that when the Bank War began he had not permitted the Bank to be crushed by the sheer weight of power (to Thomas H. Perkins, July 27, 1832).

419. Debate in the House of Representatives of Pennsylvania on Mr. Holgate's Resolutions, 48; McDuffie's speech of December 19, 1833, quoted in Gordon, Thomas F., op. cit., 18; similarly, Hardin, op. cit., 14.

420. Daniel Webster to Thomas Cadwalader, July 5, 1832 (McGrane, 193).

421. To Thomas H. Perkins, Dec. 14, 1829.

422. To J. M. Clayton, Feb. 21, 1834.

423. To J. Hunter, June 9, 1830. On Oct. 20, 1830 Biddle asked J. Rathbone for the Reports of the New York Bank Commissioners.

424. Biddle read "habitually," for instance, the Albany Daily Advertiser (to S. Dewitt Bloodgood, Feb. 14, 1834).

425. To Richard Smith, June 22, 1838.

426. To Samuel Smith, Apr. 5, 1830; to M. Robinson, Oct. 8, 1830; and many other cases. On Nov. 3, 1830 Biddle thanked Hunter, one of the cashiers, "for the particulars of the private history of [certain] public men."

427. To Albert Gallatin, Nov. 20, 1830. The material collected for Gallatin's essay in the American Quarterly Review of 1830 was "properly arranged" and filed in the Bank when Gallatin no longer needed it.

428. See page 128.

429. To Walter Lowrie, May 13, 1824; to John Barney, Mar. 4, 1826; to Louis McLane, Mar. 6, 1826; to Samuel Smith, May 2, 1828, Feb. 27, and Mar. 4, 1829, Jan. 25, 1830; to G. McDuffie, Jan. 27, 1831.

430. For instance, Daniel Webster, N. Silsbee, Joseph Hemphill, Campbell P. White.

431. To Samuel Correy, Sept. 8, 1826; to N. Silsbee, Dec. 22, 1828; to G. McDuffie, Apr. 29, 1830; to Louis McLane, Oct. 23, 1827 and Nov. 3, 1828; to Edward Jones, Apr. 22, 1828; to S. Jaudon, June 3, 1830; to W. Tazewell, May 31, 1830.

432. To William Lehman, Mar. 5, 1829; to R. Rush, Feb. 6, 1831 (at which time Rush seems to have aspired to the position of president of the Washington branch).

433. Biddle Correspondence, 357 ff. General Harrison was also a borrower (to H. Cope, Apr. 4, 1832).

434. Mar. 4, 1828.

435. To John P. King, Oct. 4, 1832.

436. To A. Dickens, May 11, 1831..

437. To Richard Smith, Feb. 14, 1824; to Thomas Swann, May 27, 1824; to Robert Lenox, Sept. 20, 1826; to Joseph Gales, Mar. 29, 1827.

438. To John McLean, Jan. 10, 1829 (McGrane, 69).

439. To Samuel Swartout, July 30, 1833 (McGrane, 213); to Robert Lenox, July 7, 1830; to John Potter, Aug. 1, 1833; to Charles Chauncey, Aug. 2, 1833; to Thomas Cooper, Sept. 24, 1833; July 31, 1833, Aug. 16, 1833 (McGrane, 213 ff.).

440. To W. J. Duane, July 9, 1833.

441. To H. Clay, Feb. 2, 1834.

442. See the telling letter to C. J. Ingersoll, Feb. 1, 1832 (McGrane, 179).

443. To George McDuffie, Feb. 10, 1832; to J. G. Watmough, Dec. 23, 1833; to Horace Binney, Mar. 1, 1832. See also Biddle's behaviour in 1833-1834 as described in the many treatments of the Bank War. It is difficult to conceive how shortsighted Biddle became in his stubbornness: regardless of the dangerous situation, the charging of damages on the protested French bills, which played so large a part in the attacks on the Bank, was made as "not a bad addition to the income of the six months;" (to Daniel Webster, May 10, 1833). Jackson's opinion on the matter can be found in his letter to Duane, June 26, 1833 (Jackson Correspondence, V, 121).

444. To Samuel Smith, Apr. 22, 1830; to

P. P. F. Degrand, Feb. 20, 1833.

445. See, for instance, to M. Robinson, Aug. 26, 1835; to John O'Fallon, Oct. 16, 1835.

446. To R. M. Blatchford, Aug. 19, 1835.

447. To Baring Brothers and Company, Jan. 7, 1836.

448. See his "blowing up;" to William Appleton July 4, 1834 (McGrane, 240).

449. Van Buren, Autobiography, 774. Examples of Biddle's tactlessness are the victory celebration after the passage of the charter in 1832 and the statement that it had been in his power to break any state bank. See also Jackson to Taney, Aug. 11, 1833 in Tyler, Taney, 201; but the source is, of course, not reliable in this context.

450. To John Potter, Mar. 5, 1832; to J. G. Watmough, Feb. 8, 1834.

451. To J. G. Watmough, Jan. 25, 1834.

452. To John Sergeant, Feb. 12, 1834; Catterall, op. cit., 340.

453. To Daniel Webster, June 11, 1834; to J. G. Watmough, June 18, 1834.

454. To John Tyler, Nov. 27, 1834; to John McKim, Dec. 30, 1834.

455. To a committee of the Alumni Association, Princeton, Feb. 4, 1835; to Samuel Jaudon, Feb. 25, 1835; to C. A. Wickliffe, Mar. 7, 1835.

456. Memoirs, IX, 362.

457. Biddle's own comment on the speech is to be found in a letter to Edward Everett, Dec. 9, 1835. He obviously felt like apologizing for it (see to James Harper, Jan. 21, 1836).

458. To George Gibbs, Mar. 15, 1825 (McGrane, 34); to Samuel Smith, Jan. 5, 1829 (ibid., 66).

459. For examples see Ch. III footnote 146, p. 142, and the series of letters reprinted by McGrane, 228-235. See also the letter of Jan. 20, 1838; addressee omitted.

460. Address, 6, 9, 23.

461. Ibid., 14-16.

462. "National Bank," 421, 422.

463. A very similar idea can be found in the letter of Alexander Hamilton to John Woodworth, Sept. 14, 1834 (McGrane, 244).

464. To Horace Binney, Jan. 8, 1835.

465. To J. Rathbone, Feb. 14, Mar. 17, May 15, 1834; to J. G. Watmough, Mar. 25, 1834; Nathan Appleton, Memoir, 287; McGrane, Panic, 88, 231.

466. Biddle used jokingly to call himself in the 1830's "the oldest, if not the best, Democrat in Pennsylvania" (to Simon Cameron, Dec. 17, 1836).

467. To H. Cope, Aug. 11, 1835 (McGrane,

256); to Edward Everett, Nov. 12, 1835.

468. Malone, op. cit., 282 ff.; McGrane, Biddle Correspondence, 272, 278, 280, 281, 293, 296, 323, 333.

469. "His manners were kind and polished and his conversation unaffected and eloquent." Conrad, op. cit., 18.

470. Quoted by McGrane, Bondholders, 16, footnote. It is in this context that one should read a statement of the same period (in fact of 1836) which, although a joke, illuminates Ward's harsh judgment: when the negotiations for the Pennsylvania charter did not progress as Biddle desired he wrote to his representative that he was inclined to "imitate other Potentates and [to] recall our chargé." (To Joseph McIlvaine, Jan. 16, 1836.)

471. Op. cit., 6, 7.

472. Some of his speeches are cited in the list of references. On July 9, 1833 Biddle declined the invitation of the Telescopic Society to deliver the annual oration.

473. Commercial Regulations (see list of references). The compilation included treaties, laws, and regulations of the countries with which the United States had intercourse regarding imports, exports, tonnage, light-money, pilotage, port duties, bounties, drawbacks, colonial trade, navigation, national character of mariners, ships, papers, navigation.

474. Information from Nicholas B. Wainright; Hone, op. cit., II, 357 (Mar. 30, 1839); to Samuel H. Perkins, Apr. 17 and 30, 1835; instructions to his gardener, Apr. 30, 1835; to John O'Fallon, May 29, 1835.

475. Girard College Address, 9, 10; Vethake, article on "Nicholas Biddle" (see footnote 1). See also to Thomas H. Borrows, Mar. 16, 1836.

476. Address to those on whom Heaven.... To John Potter, Oct. 31, 1831 and Sept. 3, 1833; to James Neilson, Sept. 3, 1833 and many other letters. The Bank of the United States lent funds to railroads (to R. S. Colt, Apr. 14, 1831; to John White, Sept. 17, 1832; U.S. 29th Congr., 1st sess., House Document 226, 501).

477. Biddle stresses these activities in his Eulogium, 29 ff.

478. To Alexander Hamilton, son of the Secretary, Oct. 28, 1830; to G. C. Verplanck, Oct. 31, 1830.

479. On Jan. 25, 1832, Biddle speaks of Garnier's [French] translation of Adam Smith's book, "on the shelf beside me," to Horace Binney.

480. Institutions right themselves, one must patiently wait for the moment, as he wrote P. P. F. Degrand, July 24, 1833.

481. To Samuel Smith, Dec. 29, 1828.

482. U.S. 22nd Congr., 1st sess., House Report 460, 347; to Albert Gallatin, July 29, 1830. See also footnote 494.

483. A political pamphlet read by Biddle was: Proceedings, Resolutions and Addresses adopted by the State Rights Party in Charleston.

484. See list of references.

485. Biddle knew that this anonymous pamphlet was the work of his predecessor (to Albert Gallatin, Oct. 28, 1830).

486. To Thomas Cooper, Aug. 16, 1833; to J. S. Barbour, July 11 and Sept. 4, 1833.

487. Biddle was inclined to refuse reading calumnious pamphlets like those of Reuben M. Whitney (to J. G. Watmough, Jan. 8, 1833).

488. To Joseph Hemphill, Mar. 2, 1830.

489. For instance, in connection with the establishment of Girard College.

490. To Ashbury Dickens, Nov. 28, 1828; to Samuel Smith, Dec. 29, 1828; Letterbooks, III, 157 ff.

491. To A. Dickens, Nov. 18, 1831.

492. To John Barney, Mar. 4, 1826; to P. P. F. Degrand, Mar. 8, 1831.

493. "The Currency," in National Gazette, April 10, 1828; to Albert Gallatin, July 29, 1830.

494. This idea seems to indicate familiarity with Torrens' An Essay on Money and Paper Currency (London, 1812), 134 ff. U.S. 22nd Congr., 1st sess., House Report 460, 362, 363. Statements made during the Bank War often do not reflect Biddle's true opinions, see ibid., 333, 334. Referring to a statement of this character, Gouge wrote (op. cit., 217): "If a man of Mr. Biddle's great powers of mind, still thinks the embarrassments of the people are such as spring only from vibrations of trade, having their origin in natural causes, and that they are in no way increased by banking operations it must be that his situation at the head of the banking system has an influence on his judgment."

495. See page 139, 142.

496. To A. Dickens, May 11, 1831.

497. To William Carroll, June 14, 1831.

498. To M. S. Clarke, Aug. 23, 1831. Incidentally, Biddle used a historical approach in his Address of 1822 before the Philadelphia Society for Promoting Agriculture. He also took an interest in the history of his family (to M. J. Biddle, Nov. 3, 1838).

499. To James Renewick, Apr. 5 and 20, 1833.

500. To Richard Smith, June 19 and Aug. 7, 1833. For another example see Biddle's memorandum of Oct. 19, 1831 (McGrane, 131).

501. McGrane, Biddle Correspondence, 169, footnote. To S. Jaudon, May 31 and June 29, 1838.

502. To Joseph Gales, July 6, 1833.

503. McGrane, Biddle Correspondence, 170, footnote.

504. As to the Wistar parties, see Dictionary of American Biography, XX, 433. Biddle was also a member of the "Wednesday Club" which consisted of selected members of the (Philadelphia) Philosophical Society (to R. M. Blatchford, Dec. 8, 1836).

505. See the very important letter to Samuel Jaudon of Jan. 6, 1838.

506. To James Harper, Jan. 21, 1836.

507. To Josiah Nichol, Apr. 21, 1830.

508. To Joseph Hemphill, Feb. 8, 1830.

509. To Samuel Smith, Jan. 25, 1830.

510. To James G. Bennett, Sept. 15, 1830.

511. Page 14.

512. U.S. 29th Congr., 1st sess., House Document 226, 520.

513. Adams, Memoirs, X, 115 (entry dated Apr. 19, 1839). Thomas Cooper wrote to Biddle on Oct. 1, 1838: "You are the Bank" (McGrane, 333).

514. Sept. 16, 1840, quoted from McGrane, Bondholders, 44, 45.

515. To James Watson Webb, Mar. 14, 1836; to Peleg Sprague, Mar. 16, 1836; to Duff Green, Mar. 16, 1836; to John Williams, Mar. 23, 1836; to Thomas Burnside, Mar. 23, 1836.

516. For instance, to the Barings, Feb. 23, 1836; to B. M. Carter, Feb. 23; to W. Hughlett, Feb. 26, 1836.

517. To Joel B. Sutherland, Feb. 24, 1836; to Joseph Reed Ingersoll, Feb. 24, 1836.

517a. For an example see to Moses M. Rawlings, Sept. 29, 1837.

518. Bank of the United States, Report of the Committee of Investigation, 61, 62. Incidentally, Biddle treated the Bank of the United States of Pennsylvania as some sort of Biddle-Jaudon family enterprise. The Bank and its affiliates employed two Biddles and three Jaudons.

519. Letters to J. M. Clayton, originally published in pamphlet form and reprinted in U.S. 29th Congr., 1st sess., House Document 226, 475 ff. They give a completely distorted picture. (The copy of the pamphlet owned by the Library of Congress bears the following title and imprint: Reply to the Report of a

Committee of the Bank of the United
States (Paris: Printed by E. Brière, No.
55, Rue Ste.-Anne, 1841).

520. Bondholders, 42 ff.

521. Ibid., 58, 77 ff.

522. To Daniel Webster, Dec. 13, 1840
(McGrane, 338).

523. Op. cit., II, 76, 104, 206. See also
Henry Horn to Andrew Jackson, Apr. 9,
1841 in Jackson Correspondence, VI, 102.

IV

Andrew Jackson and the Destruction of American Central Banking

1. Even modern historians reflect this
situation; one should compare Catterall
(op. cit., 239) and Swisher (op. cit.,
195).

2. Parrington, op. cit., II, 145 ff;
Bassett, op. cit., I, 207; II, 451.

3. The use of the terms "monster" and
"aristocracy" as political slogans by
the Jacksonians is well characterized
in a charming parody of the Jacksonian
era by John Pendleton Kennedy, Quodlibet,
2d edition, (Philadelphia, 1860), 59,
173, 174.

4. Parrington, op. cit., I, 119, 285, 322.
Taylor, Enquiry, 17. Incidentally
Taylor used the word repeatedly, for
instance, in Government, 279, 317; and
it can even be found in a letter from
Hamilton of 1791. When a bank was
planned in this year to compete with the
Bank of New York in which Hamilton was
interested he fought it as a "newly
engendered monster." The letter is reprinted by Dommett, op. cit. 43.

5. Letters to Seybert, 35; Stickles, op.
cit., 38. The term lived on for many
years to come. It was used in 1858 by
Governor Wise of Virginia who considered
banks "money monsters" and felt that the
concentration of money power in New York
meant "danger and disaster [that do not]
differ from a national monster." U.S. 35th
Congr., 1st sess., House Executive Doc.
107, 183. In the fight of the Pennsylvania oil producers against the South
Improvement Scheme with which Rockefeller
was connected the word cropped up again
and that company was called a monster
as late as 1872 (Nevins, Rockefeller, I,
333). Finally it is almost amusing to
find the term used again in 1907 in the
struggle against the then pending
American central bank projects. The
American people were admonished not to
"yield to this alien monster." Intercollegiate Debates, 333 ff.

6. Enquiry, 30.

7. Government, 53.

8. Government, 1-74, 244-397 (especially
298 as to exploitation), 550-579. See
also Parrington, op. cit., II, 17.
Parrington comments that Taylor considered aristocracy as based on social
theft.

8a. As to John Adams's attitude toward banks
see his letter to John Taylor, Mar. 12,
1819 in Works (Boston 1856), X, 375.

9. Jackson himself developed the term
aristocracy parallel to and probably
under the influence of John Taylor.
Earlier in his life he dubbed the socially prominent families of Nashville aristocrats of Nashville, while later he
used the expressions aristocratic merchants (letter to Van Buren) and following Taylor, moneyed aristocracy. This
latter term was already common in 1810
and 1811 when the fate of the First
Bank of the United States was discussed.
Nicholas Biddle in his great speech of
1810 used it repeatedly by way of quotation. See Debates in the House of Representatives of Pennsylvania relative
the Bank of the United States, 7, 28.

10. Van Buren, op. cit., 619.

11. In addition to the quotations which follow in the text, Mathew Carey, born in
1760, mentioned the Mississippi scheme
and the South Sea Bubble in his Desultory Reflections upon the Ruinous Consequences of a Non-Renewal of the
Charter of the Bank of the United States,
2nd ed. (Philadelphia, 1810), 12; and
as late as 1841 the former scheme was
cited in connection with discussing the
question of a national bank. "At the
time of the formation of the Federal
Constitution...the recent fate of Law's
bank...induced its framers...." Reasons
for the Inexpediency of Chartering a
National Bank, 14.

12. Government, 289. Although Taylor did not
confound banking and public debt, he did
not draw clear lines between the two
economic phenomena: according to him
"all the objections against debt stocks
or paper system apply with equal...
force against banking; and the latter
subject is considered separately not as
being of a very different nature, but

for the sake of perspicuity." _Ibid._, 290-291.

13. In his first bank plan (of 1780) submitted to Robert Morris in a letter, Hamilton started from John Law and the Mississippi scheme for which he expressed some sort of admiration. _Works_ (Lodge, ed.) II, 73, 74. See above page 27.

14. The above is quoted from the second edition (London and Boston, 1755), I, 78 ff.

15. Parrington, _op. cit._, II, 4, 5.

16. John Pendleton Kennedy's parody, already mentioned, contains on page 188 a passage which looks as if it were written to lampoon Jackson's thought. Tom Crop, the Democratic constable of the Borough of Quodlibet, argues as follows: "Here was Joe Plumb, the cider-press maker, got a note from Jerry Lantern here at the crossroads, for settin' up his cider-press, and he heaved it in the bank for them to collect it - and what does the bank do, but go and purtest it! That's the way they treat a poor man like Joe Plumb, what's obliged to work for his livin': - would they 'a sarved a Big Bug so? No - don't tell me about the banks! I am sick a hearin' on 'em."

17. Campbell, _op. cit._, 27-29 (the preceding paragraphs follow closely Campbell's description); see also Bassett, _op. cit._, _passim_, Vol. I.

18. Forman, _op. cit._, 65.

19. _Public Measures_, 18. From Taylor the ideological line leads back to the fight in the Pennsylvania House of Representatives for the repeal of the charter of the Bank of North America.

20. _Ibid._, 19; _Government_, 270. The term tax is used in the sense of "burden," as was customary in the eighteenth century.

21. _Measures_, 29; _Government_, 45, 245, 272, 280.

22. _Measures_, 19, 20, 73.

23. Henry Clay voiced the same fears in a Senate speech of 1811. "Wealth is power and...its proprietor...will have a proportionate influence" regardless of whether he is a citizen or foreigner.

24. _Definition of Parties_, 9, 13.

25. _Measures_, 24; _Government_, 39, 40, 245.

26. _Measures_, 83; _Government_, 301 ff. (Jackson expressed such ideas in a memorandum of June 1833; Duane, _op. cit._, 28, 29). Taylor's ideas on banking are also treated by Mudge _op. cit._, 172 ff. and Grampp, _op. cit._, 264, 265.

27. Holdsworth, _First Bank of the United States_, has collected this material; see pages 67 ff. It is to be found in Jefferson's _Works_, IV, 439, 518, VI, 232, 305, IX, 95; Gallatin's _Writings_, I, 101, 129, 171, 184.

28. _Government_, 10.

29. Incidentally the word "order" is one of Taylor's pet words.

30. _Measures_, 84.

31. _Government_, 45, 49.

32. Denise Raymond (_op. cit._, 408, 409) expresses well what Taylor and Jackson had in mind: A man who acquired government or bank stock thereby acquired the power of compelling somebody in the world to labor for him. "The objection to these institutions, however, is not so much that they facilitate this increase of power, as that they afford this facility to the rich and not to the poor in equal proportions - that they operate as an exclusive privilege."

33. _Government_, 303. One would like to know whether Jackson was familiar with the following passage from Taylor's book: "The revival of the charter of the [first] Bank of the United States was denied upon the ground of the political power conveyed by bank stock to the subjects of England; and the highest authority declared in this denial that less than ten millions of it would vest foreigners with a pernicious portion of such power" (_ibid._, 334).

34. Carey, _Letters to Seybert_, 60; Pennsylvania House of Representatives, _Debate ...relative to the Bank of the United States_, 29, 30. Carey characterized the attacks of 1810 and 1811 as follows: the Bank is attacked as being under foreign influence and sometime styled a branch of the Bank of England. To the readers of some essays on the topic it could appear that the directors were a body of Englishmen sent over by the English government to promote the English interests and destroy those of this country.

35. But the possibility existed, as described in detail by Thomas Greaves Cary, _op. cit._, 15. See also _U.S. 22nd Congr._, _1st sess._, House Report, 460, 533.

36. According to a memorandum of Biddle's dated October 12, 1831, Jackson could not see much force in the argument that stock of the Bank was held by foreigners, as the latter confided to McLane. Biddle, _Correspondence_, 132.

37. One of the arguments used repeatedly in

the Bank War has a history of its own.
In his first message of 1829 Jackson
asserted "that...[the Bank] had failed
in the great end of establishing a
uniform and sound currency." Although
this ambiguous statement has been often
quoted, it has seldom been understood
by modern writers. First of all, it is
an almost verbatim repetition of the
assertion of Senator Smith of Maryland
made in Congress in 1810 in the fight
against the First Bank with regard to
that institution. (Holdsworth-Dewey,
op. cit., 94.) Furthermore, scrutiniz-
ing the statement one discovers that
(contrary to Biddle's and McDuffie's
understanding) it was not claimed that
the notes of the Bank and its branches
had no uniform value. What Jackson and
his followers actually claimed was that
such uniform value was not an achievement of the Bank itself, but was due to
the policy of the government, "in opposition to the policy of the Bank," as
Jackson expressed it. They stressed
that the parent bank and its branches
redeemed only those notes which had been
issued respectively by the parent bank
or by the particular branch where the
note was presented. If, in spite of
such policy, the notes of the Bank had
a uniform value all over the country,
this fact was due to their being legal
tender in all payments to the government.
Jackson and his friends knew all too
well that the Bank in 1819, during the
incumbency of Cheves, had tried to get
rid of the onerous obligation to take
all its notes and those of all its
branches at par wherever deposited by
a government collector. This scheme
failed originally because of Secretary
Crawford's resistance and later because
of that of Congress. If successful, it
would have made the issues of the Bank
and its branches local currencies.
Thus, the President and his followers
should be blamed not for an incorrect,
but for an ambiguous, statement.
(Swisher, op. cit., 169, 170; Jackson
to Duane, June 26, 1833 in Duane, op.
cit., 27-29 and Jackson, Correspondence,
V, 124; U.S. 23rd Congr., 1st sess.,
Senate Document 17, 16, 18; House Executive Document 312, 30; Henshaw, Bank of
the United States, 29; Young, Considerations on the Bank of the United States,
10, 11; Correspondence of Cheves with
Crawford in Report on the Condition of
the Second Bank of the United States,

53 ff.) Biddle, on the other hand,
claimed that since it was in the interest of the Bank to give every possible
facility to its circulation, branch
notes, though not legally receivable,
were in fact received at the parent
bank and at many, if not most, of the
branches. (U.S. 22nd Congr., 1st sess.,
Senate Document 98, 3; but see also
U.S. 23d Congr., 1st sess., Senate
Document 24, passim.)

38. U.S. 35th Congr., 1st sess., House
    Executive Document 107, 183.
39. Underlying the Bank Veto, although not
    expressed therein, there can be found
    contempt for the unproductive bankers
    and the unproductive merchants who con-
    trolled the existing and would control
    a future Bank; it came down to Jackson
    from the Physiocrats by way of Jefferson
    and Taylor who spoke of the merchants
    as "of a class unproductive," (Measures,
    78; Government, 44, 45).
40. See below page 168, 169.
41. See, for instance, Government, 296, 297,
    342 ff., 355.
42. Only a few years later, in 1837, a mem-
    ber of the American House of Representa-
    tives, referring to the English debates
    of 1832, reported that "the representa-
    tives of the great commercial and manu-
    facturing interests...protest[ed]
    against the continuance of a monopoly
    of the Bank of England to which they
    impute[d] the most sinister influence
    over their immense business" and that
    they demanded a more agreeable system
    of banking. Legaré, op. cit., 281.
43. Ricardo, Samson, A National Bank, The
    Remedy for the Evils.... (London,
    1838).
44. Report from the Committee of Secrecy on
    the Bank of England Charter (London,
    1832). [Joplin, T.], A Digest of the
    Evidence on the Bank Charter taken
    before the Committee of 1832 (London,
    1833).
45. In America this idea was expressed as
    late as 1841 in the following way: "You
    cannot divest men of their selfish pas-
    sions by making them directors of a
    national bank. The duty of such an
    institution as a regulator of the cur-
    rency would conflict with its interests
    as a bank.... It is idle to expect
    that the president and directors of a
    United States Bank would become effi-
    cient regulators of the currency at the
    expense of their own interest and that
    of the stockholders." Dialogue on the
    Subject of a National Bank, 24.

46. <u>Report</u> <u>from</u> <u>the</u> <u>Committee</u> <u>of</u> <u>Secrecy</u>,
    4206, 4293, 4442, 4450, 4501, 5782.
47. Quoted, Morgan, <u>op. cit.</u>, 89.
48. <u>Ibid.</u>, 97.
49. Passages of the <u>Plan</u> were quoted by
    Henshaw, <u>Bank</u> <u>of</u> <u>the</u> <u>United</u> <u>States</u> (of
    1831), 83 ff.
50. Morgan, <u>op. cit.</u>, 136-138.
51. <u>Ibid.</u>, 114.
52. Bassett, <u>op. cit.</u>, II, 592, 602, 603,
    631; Duane, <u>op. cit.</u>, 36; Hamilton's
    <u>Reminiscences</u>, 155 ff. The messages of
    1829, 1830, 1831 and veto message.
53. Carey, <u>Letters</u> <u>to</u> <u>Seybert</u>, 27, 29, 31.
    In 1831 Henshaw thought along the same
    lines (<u>op. cit.</u>, 45, 46). A plan con-
    ceived by John Randolph in Jefferson's
    time, which Benton sent to Jackson in
    December 1829, may have stimulated the
    latter's thinking (Jackson, <u>Correspond-</u>
    <u>ence</u>, IV, 84).
54. See Taney's paper of June 27, 1832 re-
    printed by Swisher, <u>op. cit.</u>, 193.
55. Bassett, <u>op. cit.</u>, II, 606; Swisher, 288.
    See also a passage from Taney's speech
    of August 1834 at Frederick, Maryland;
    Tyler, <u>Taney</u>, 227; and Jackson to Duane,
    June 26, 1832 (Jackson, <u>Correspondence</u>,
    V, 123).
56. <u>Government</u>, 336.
57. Duane, <u>op. cit.</u>, 16, 37.
58. Bassett, <u>op. cit.</u>, I, 430; II, 725.
    Benton, <u>op. cit.</u>, I, 158. Swisher,
    <u>op. cit.</u>, 274 ff.; Catterall, 185, foot-
    note. Henry Clay understood, or at
    least claimed to understand Jackson, as
    confining his attacks to the Bank of the
    United States "from considerations of
    policy" while he ultimately intended to
    overthrow the whole banking system.
    <u>Op. cit.</u>, <u>passim</u>, especially, 2, 4.
59. See also Seventh Annual Message.
60. The impression which the apparently in-
    consistent bank policy of Jacksonian
    Democracy made on the public is well
    described in Kennedy, <u>Quodlibet</u>, 32.
    One of the citizens of Quodlibet argues
    "that the Old Hero was an enthusiastic
    friend to State rights and especially
    to State banks, which it was the desire
    of his heart to see increased and mul-
    tiplied all over the country; that he
    was actually, as it were, making pets
    out of these banks, and was determined
    to feed them up with the public moneys
    and give them such a credit in the land
    as would forever shut out·all hope to
    friends of a National Bank to succeed
    with their purpose." Supposedly a few
    years later (pages 183, 184), "'Well,

the Globe,' replied Sam Pivot, the assessor of our county..., 'is...a little
dubious. Sometime he makes this Sub-
Treasury a smasher to all banks; and
then again he fetches it up as a sort
of staff to prop the good ones and to
knock down the cripples...and I rather
expect from what I see in the President's
message, that it isn't fairly understood
whether the Sub-Treasury is to kill or
cure the banking system.'" Supposedly
at the same time (pages 194, 195) "Mr.
Flam had received a letter from a member
of the Cabinet, apprising him that it
was deemed absolutely necessary to the
preservation of the...Democratic Party
to become extremely pointed in their
assault against the State banks, and
that the misdeeds of those institutions
should be exaggerated as much as possible, and then charged upon the Whigs."
Another description of the about-face
of the Democrats with regard to the
banking system may be found on pages 104
and 218-20. Daniel Webster spoke in
this connection of the "Janus faced"
administration. (<u>Second</u> <u>Speech</u> <u>on</u> <u>the</u>
<u>Sub-Treasury</u>, 9).
61. See page 188.
62. <u>Government</u>, 39, 51, 259, 265. Again we
    find a cartoon of this situation in
    Kennedy, <u>Quodlibet</u>, 141. "Theodore made
    a very happy hit in touching upon the
    natural hostility between the rich and
    the poor, showing with great point of
    remark, how impossible it was for these
    two classes to have any Christian feel-
    ings toward each other."
63. Carey, Mathew, <u>Letters</u> <u>to</u> <u>Seybert</u>, 54.
64. To what extent credit economy (capital-
    ism) was at stake in the fight can be
    seen by contrasting the following
    statements of Jackson and Binney, re-
    spectively. Jackson is supposed to have
    shouted to one of the many committees,
    which visited him and which pleaded for
    a renewal of the Bank in order to al-
    leviate economic distress, that he had
    always believed that those who traded
    on borrowed money would finally be the
    sufferers. Binney, on the other hand,
    in his <u>Report of 1834</u> (<u>op. cit.</u>, 16),
    asked: "What will the industrious and
    enterprising do after a scheme shall
    have succeeded which, by destroying
    paper, will infallibly destroy bank
    credit and give to the man of capital a
    monopoly of the trade and industry of
    the country?" Very similarly, Daniel
    Webster in his second speech on the

sub-treasury bill (op. cit., 9) fought the "declaration so often quoted that 'all who trade on borrowed capital ought to break.'"

65. Beck, William (pseudonym: Citizen of Ohio), Money and Banking or Their Nature and Effect Considered (Cincinnati, 1839). The quotations which are on pages v, vi, and 48 have been somewhat altered in sequence.

66. Government, 356.

67. Typical of this outlook is Van Buren's condemnation of the Bank. The economic aspect of the matter did not exist for him; for him the Bank War was exclusively a political question, (Autobiography, passim).

68. Autobiography, 201, 206, 222, 422.

69. Ibid., 224, 235.

70. Ibid., 199, 200. McDuffie expounds a similar theory but with contrary conclusions (McDuffie Report, 14).

71. Ibid., 382.

72. Ibid., 204.

73. Ibid., 199. (Exactly the same arguments are to be found in Samuel Young's Considerations, 18.)

74. Ibid., 374. Early in 1834 Kendall said to a wavering Democratic member of Congress who thought of giving in to the terrific pressure of the Bank men: "This is a struggle to maintain a government of the people against the most heartless of all aristocracies, that of money. Yield now and the Bank of the United States will henceforth be the governing power whatever may be the form of our institutions." (Ibid., 416.)

75. Ibid., 377 ff., 387.

76. Stickney, Memoir of Roger Brooke Taney, 41.

77. Ibid., 158, 159; Steiner, op. cit., 10.

78. Tyler, op. cit., 156.

79. Ibid., 175; Swisher, op. cit., 114, 201.

80. Steiner, op. cit., 107 ff; Swisher, op. cit., 189 ff.

81. Swisher, op. cit., 196.

82. See page 165.

83. Tyler, op. cit., 212; Swisher, op. cit., 115, 168, 280.

84. Swisher who on pages 167 ff. reprinted much of that manuscript of Taney's is not sufficiently at home in the field of banking to see Taney's glaringly incorrect factual statements, for instance about branch drafts or the policy of the Bank, nor does he see the fallacies in Taney's value judgments. Thus his description of Taney's share in the Bank War, although excellent in some respects, is one-sided. It is too bad that this author who gets angry with those historians who could not see the sincerity of Jackson and his friends nor their point of view, does not comprehend Biddle's aspect of the matter. See, e.g., 208.

85. Steiner, op. cit., 32; Swisher, op. cit., 83 ff.

86. Swisher, op. cit., 176.

87. Steiner, op. cit., 120 ff., 192 ff.

88. Gallatin is quoted from MacVickar, "National Bank," 414. Whitney, Protest, passim. MacVickar ("National Bank," 414) saw this point.

89. Letter to Polk, Reg. of Debates, U.S. 23rd Congr., 1st sess., Appendix, 157-161 (quoted in Swisher, op. cit., 274). Since the statement that the Bank of the United States could not establish a sound currency was made in a letter intended to influence the tactics of the Democratic party in Congress it may not represent Taney's real opinion. It is not impossible that actually he argued as follows: Since the notes of the Bank of the United States have a uniform value because of the actions of the government (see footnote 37) the same actions of the government will also make uniform the value of the notes of state banks as soon as such banks are made public depositories. Such arguing would be more logical and is actually to be found in his Report on the Removal of the Public Deposits. (U.S. 23d Congr., 1st sess., Senate Document 2, 5). But one can also read in the same report the following sentence: "The State banks can, I have no doubt, furnish a general circulating medium quite as uniform in value as that which has been afforded by the Bank of the United States - probably more so."

90. Swisher, op. cit., 267, U.S. 23d Congr., 1st sess., Senate Document 2, 33 ff.

91. Ibid., 265.

92. Swisher, op. cit., 244.

93. Jackson to Duane, June 26, 1833; Duane's instructions for Kendall; Duane, op. cit., 12, 13, 84, 85. Also U.S. 23d Congr., 1st sess., Senate Document 17, 19 and McGrane, Biddle Correspondence, 102.

94. U.S. 23d Congr., 1st sess., Senate Document 17, 10, 33, 41, 42, 48, 65.

95. Kendall to Van Buren, June 9, 1833, (Correspondence of Andrew Jackson, V, 107).

95[a]. The plan to have an association of banks act as a National Bank cropped up again in 1838; Biddle to S. Jaudon, Feb. 7, 1838 (Biddle Letterbooks).

96. Swisher, op. cit., 281. About Ellicott see Semmes, op. cit., 400; Swisher, passim, as indicated in the index of his book; Biddle to Reverdy Johnson, June 2, 1834 in Biddle Letterbooks.
97. Incidentally Ellicott was removed from the presidency of the Union Bank in 1834 and brought before the court.

V

The Debates of the 1830's and 1840's on the Need of a National Bank and their Significance

1. Op. cit., 348.
2. See page 169; and William B. Lewis to Biddle, May 15, 1830 (McGrane, 104).
3. See page 24.
4. This statement is true regardless of the fact that one finds in the contemporary literature an awkward definition like: "A National Bank, in the common acceptation of term,...is a Bank of discount and deposit chartered by the National Government with branches [italics in the original] in the several states." Hurd, op. cit., 32. Incidentally, Condy Raguet disliked the term "national bank" because it reminded him too much of the "consolidation school of politics;" he wanted it replaced by "federal bank." (The Examiner, II [1835], 141, 158, 233).
5. MacVickar's treatment of the subject is also systematic, but here as in his Hints on Banking (see chapter VII) he is inconsistent. The state banks need a "regulator," but the national bank (i.e., the regulator) is regulated by the immutable laws of trade; see especially, page 416.
6. See, for example, Raguet, Examiner, II (1835), 141; Biddle, Two Letters, 3; Gilbart, History, 38, 39; Ogden, Remarks, 51, 52; Hurd, op. cit., 32; MacVickar, "National Bank," 411, 430, 431; Henry Clay's Senate Report dated June 21, 1841 in U.S. 27th Congr., 1st sess., Senate Document 32, 5. A poorer grade of publication on the subject is Henshaw, Banks and Banking. See also Joel R. Poinsett to Biddle, May 6, 1837 (McGrane, 273, 274).
7. New York Review, VII (1840), 186.
8. Lawrence, "Bank of the United States," 558; "Public Distress," 535, 536; A New Financial Project, 20, 21. Miller, (op. cit., 165) has stressed this point.

9. Op. cit., 8. 11.
10. Clay, op. cit., 5, 6.
11. In this context see the letters of Worden Pope to Andrew Jackson, June 19 and Aug. 6, 1831 (Jackson, Correspondence, IV, 298, 299, 326, 327); Louis McLane to Jackson, May 20, 1833 (ibid., V, 78, 79).
12. Degrand wrote newspaper articles under the pseudonym of Aladdin which this author has been unable to identify.
13. In this context, see Thomas Cooper to Biddle, Oct. 1, 1838 (McGrane, 333); Biddle to Joel R. Poinsett, May 8, 1837 (ibid., 274, 275); to Robert Paterson, May 8, 1837 (ibid., 276); to John Rathbone, Apr. 14, 1837 (ibid., 282); to John Forsyth, Apr. 30, 1838 (ibid., 307, 308); to Henry Clay, May 30, 1838 (ibid., 309); to Samuel Jaudon, Aug. 3, 1838 (ibid., 320).
14. Memorial Biographies of the New England Historic Genealogical Society, I (1880), 491. Schlesinger, Age of Jackson, has a different comment (see pages 147, 148), but in fact Henshaw had just come out for a "purely government bank" as proposed by Jackson; Bank of the United States, 41, 43 ff. See also Biddle to C. J. Ingersoll and Horace Binney, Jan. 29, 1832; Biddle memorandum of Oct. 19, 1831 (McGrane, 130); to Thomas Cooper, Aug. 16, 1833 (ibid., 215).
15. To Horace Binney, Jan. 27, 1832.
16. R. Fisher to Biddle, July 7, 1834 (McGrane, 243).
17. Jackson, Correspondence, V, 35.
18. Bank of the United States, 43 ff.; Biddle to Horace Binney, Jan. 29, 1832. McLane in his letter of May 20, 1833 to Jackson discussed the possibility (Jackson, Correspondence V, 80).
19. Meigs, William M., The Life of Charles Jared Ingersoll (Philadelphia, 1897), 216, 250.
20. Hildreth, History, 137 ff; Raguet in The Examiner, II (1835), 141, 158; Miller (op. cit., 164) mentions later examples.
21. Op. cit., 43, 51 ff; Henshaw (Bank of the United States, 29, 30) takes a similar stand.
22. MacVickar, "National Bank," 424, 425, 432.
23. Both quotations were taken from Schlesinger, Age of Jackson, 174, 162. See also Alexander Hamilton to John Woodworth, Sept. 14, 1834 (McGrane, 244).
24. Henshaw, Banks and Banking, 27.
25. Quoted from Dorfman, op. cit., 608.
26. Taney to Jackson, March 1833 (Jackson, Correspondence, V, 40).

APPENDICES

1. All letters reprinted in the Appendices
   to this chapter are preserved among the
   William Jones Papers in The Historical
   Society of Pennsylvania.
2. Philadelphia merchants.
3. The first paragraph of this letter is
   omitted.

Chapter VII

FREE BANKING

1. This chapter is the revised version of
   the essay "Free Banking: The History of
   an Idea and its Exponents," first published in this author's Essays in
   American Economic History, Recently,
   Vera Smith (op. cit., passim) has treated the concept of free banking and its
   history in the various European states.
2. Inquiry into the Principles of Political
   Economy (London, 1767). Quoted from the
   reprint of Book III, published under the
   title Principles of Banks (London, 1810),
   237.
3. Proposals as to the distribution of bank
   stocks were made by the Bank Commissioners of the State of New York in a report
   of 1/27, 1837. 25th Congr., 2nd sess.,
   House Executive Document 79, 234-5.
4. Publicola, Vindication of the Currency
   of the State of New York and a Review of
   the Report...addressed to The Hon.
   Isaac Pierson (1818). Page 24 contains the following passage: To diminish
   the evils of the preseht (1810) banking
   system competition among the existing
   banks should be promoted or every citizen
   should be authorized "to bank, either
   solely or with associates, under suitable
   regulations and restrictions. The latter course is the most simple.... It
   can be done in such a manner as to render the public perfectly secure.... A
   bill to this effect was actually passed
   at the last session of the legislature
   through one branch of that body...."
   The Maryland bill is reprinted in Condy
   Raguet's Financial Register, II, 398-
   400.
5. U.S. 26th Congr., 1st sess., House Executive Document 172, 1087.
6. Hammond, Jabez D,, The History of Political Parties in the State of New York
   (Cooperstown, 1846), II, 447-8. In 1837
   the New York Bank Commissioners were
   still against Free Banking (the report
   quoted above). Albert Gallatin, in
   contrast, was a friend of free banking
   as early as 1834. Adams, Henry, The Life
   of Albert Gallatin (Philadelphia, 1880),
   651.
7. The Scotch system of banking was known
   all over America at that time. Thomas
   Hart Benton referred to it in Congress
   as early as 1831, and probably under his
   influence the matter was discussed in
   Missouri in the winter of 1834-35. It
   was a Southerner, Hugh Swinton Legaré,
   who in a speech in Congress in 1837,
   remarked: "Everybody has heard or ought
   to have heard of the Scotch system of
   banking;" Writings (Charleston, 1846),
   I, 302, 303. The system is also referred to in the Report of the New York
   Bank Commissioners of January 27, 1837,
   25th Congr., 2d sess., House Executive
   Document 79, 236, 237. Helderman,
   op. cit., 42-43, 53, 63-64 describes the
   various futile attempts to introduce
   into America during the 1830's and 1840's
   its characteristic feature, stockholder's
   liability.
       Of the publications dealing with
   Scotch banking Albert Gallatin's
   Considerations of 1831 may be mentioned.
   Its Appendix contains among "Notes and
   Statements" one on the subject extracted
   from the Report of the Select Committee
   of the House of Commons on Promissory
   Notes of Scotland and Ireland (May 26,
   1826).
8. Benton, Thomas Hart, Thirty Years' View,
   I, 158. C. J. Ingersoll to Biddle,
   Feb. 2, 1832; McGrane, Biddle Correspondence, 172.
9. George D. Strong, president of the
   Commercial Bank, and Isaac L. Varian,
   "a bank director," later state senator
   and mayor of New York. At that meeting
   the candidacy of Gideon Lee (1778-1841)
   for Congress was opposed because he was
   president of the Leather Manufacturers'
   Bank. Byrdsall, F., The History of the
   Loco-Foco or Equal Rights Party (New
   York, 1842), 21, 24, 26. See also
   Hammond, Bray, "Free Banks and Corporations: The New York Free Banking Act of
   1838," The Journal of Political Economy,
   44 (April 1936), passim.
10. Byrdsall (op. cit., 15, 27, 39, 57) re-
    prints party documents. Marcy in his
    annual message of 1837, State of New
    York, Messages from the Governors, III,
    629.
11. For the following: Hammond, Jabez, op.
    cit., II, 478 ff. and Byrdsall, op. cit.,
    27, 39, 41, 81 ff., 88.

12. This program may have been inherited from the Workingmen's Party, launched in 1828 in New York, Philadelphia and Boston. Myers, The Ending of Hereditary American Fortunes, 47.

13. New York, Messages from the Governors, III, 611 ff., 657 ff., 695 ff.

14. Byrdsall, op. cit., 73.

15. The introduction of a general banking law was facilitated by the fact that general incorporation laws had already preceded this piece of legislation, and that since the Safety Fund Act of 1828 the public no longer looked at each bank as a particular enterprise but as belonging to a class of institutions. Hammond, Bray, op. cit., 190.

16. Senate Journal, (1838), 9.

17. One should compare this phraseology with that used by Senator Young, whose role in the development will be examined shortly. Said Young in a committee report of 1837: "The monopoly characteristic of the [present banking] system, the exclusion of competition, the creation and continuance by law of a privileged order who have [sic!] the sole power of selling or lending their promises to pay in the shape of notes...are features utterly at war with equal rights and free government."

18. New York Senate, Doc. 55, 1837, 7.

19. Dorfman, Joseph and Rex Guy Tugwell, "The Reverend John MacVickar," Columbia University Quarterly, XXIII, No. 4, Dec. 1931. Seligman, Edwin R. A., "The Early Teaching of Economics in the United States," in Economic Essays, contributed in honor of John Bates Clark (New York, 1927).

20. Edinburgh Review (Feb. 1826), XLIII, 297.

21. Pages 35-6.

22. Professor Herbert Somerton Foxwell of Cambridge, England, wrote on one of Ricardo's pamphlets which is now in the Kress Collection of the Baker Library at Harvard: "The ablest of all Ricardo's writings. It is the foundation of most of the modern currency systems." Ricardo's tract is quoted by Cleaveland, op. cit., Introduction, liii. Thi proves that the essay was known in America by the middle of the nineteenth century.

23. Scoville, The Old Merchants of New York (2nd series), 281-291.

24. Williams, John Earl, "A New York View of Finance and Banking," in Old and New (November, 1873). However, Williams goes too far in his statement. Condy

25. MacVickar always writes Credit with a capital.

26. MacVickar, op. cit., 5, 6.

27. Ibid., 7, 13-14.

28. Ibid., 15.

29. Ibid., 28-31.

30. Principles of Banks, 188, 189.

31. MacVickar himself was silent in this respect, but Eleazar Lord and a New York pamphleteer knew, as the latter has it, that "this is no new expedient," for the Bank of England did not employ its capital in making discounts or in any of its ordinary business, since it was invested in government stock. Letters to the Honourable Levi Woodbury (New York, 1837), 20. (Venit, op. cit., 213, footnote, identifies Roger M. Sherman as the author of this pamphlet which was heretofore ascribed to Isaac H. Bronson.) James Alexander Hamilton (Reminiscences, 82 ff.) stressed this point. See also Gallatin, Considerations in Writings, III, 273, 319.

32. See pages 13 and 49 ff.

33. This author suspects that the idea that capital was not necessary in banking was perhaps an awkward expression of a conclusion drawn from the discovery that in payments credit could serve as money. By identifying money with capital, such a misconception could easily arise.

34. Op. cit., I, 24.

35. Stokes, op. cit., 267.

36. Carey, Debates, 37; Sparks, Diplomatic Correspondence, VII, 448. See also Sullivan, Path to Riches, 41, 51. "Paper owes its currency to the credit of the emitter." "The notes of private bankers are issued upon the credit of their reputation and private estates."

37. Providence Gazette, February 20, 1784, quoted by Stokes, op, cit., 266.

38. Stokes, op. cit., 281.

39. Banking on credit, of course, was a veiled expression of what was de facto manufacturing money or what is called today the creation of purchasing power. Opdyke in his Report on the Currency of 1858 distinguishes between a moderate and an immoderate infusion "of the fictitious or credit element" into the currency (page 14).

40. II, 1 ff.

41. As late as 1841 the New York Bank

Commissioners in their _Annual Report_ for 1840 (page 10) commented on Free Banking in terms of Bronson's philosophy.

42. _Op. cit._, 203, 204.

43. _Hints_, 38.

44. _Ibid._, 38.

45. See above, page 193.

46. As early as 1819 an American author writing under the pseudonym of Scaevola suggested that banks should give security with the courts for their notes. In case of non-payment the note holder should be entitled to sue on the bond. Amos Kendall in an article of September 1819 recommended that proposal. See William Stickney's _Autobiography of Amos Kendall_, 225. Later, substantially the same idea was expressed by Isaac Bronson in _Free Trade Advocate_, July 11, 1829. The passage is quoted by Condy Raguet in _A Treatise on Currency and Banking_, 2nd ed., 204, footnote.

    In the 1850's it was realized in Massachusetts that the New York Free Banking Act of 1838 embodied ideas of Ricardo and McCulloch (_U.S. 36th Congr., 1st sess., House Executive Document 49_, 74).

47. All these quotations from McCulloch were reproduced by an American author of the 1850's: Cleaveland, _op. cit._, Introducduction, li ff. A whole collection of similar quotations from McCulloch can also be found in Raguet, _Treatise_, 203, 204, footnote.

    It will probably be impossible to prove or disprove whether MacVickar knew the following English sources which contain ideas similar to his. One is an anonymous article in the _Edinburgh Review_ (February, 1826, Vol. 43) entitled: "Thoughts on Banking." The author (J. R. McCulloch, as a matter of fact) besides discussing the introduction of joint stock banking and the suppression of small bank notes, suggested as alternative to the latter measure "to allow private banking companies to issue notes as at present [i.e., small notes], but to oblige such as chose to avail themselves of that power to deposit securities for their payment in the hand of the government" (page 280). When he discussed his proposals in detail on pages 291-2 he made it clear that he thought primarily of security for small notes in order to protect the public. Only at the last moment he took a step further, broadening the scope of his proposal and making it apply "as well

for large as for small notes." The justification of the suggestion in the _Review_ article is permeated by a theory completely different from that of MacVickar.

Sir Henry Brook Parnell took up the ideas of the _Edinburgh Review_ article in his _Observations of Paper Money, Banking and Overtrading..._(London, 1827), a book which later influenced American thought. Ricardo's reflections quoted above, were reprinted in the _Review_ and from there were taken over by Parnell, who wanted to place English banking "under the control of continual and efficient competition." Since MacVickar's letter is dated February, 1827, he can scarcely have been influenced by Parnell, although here is the same combination of Adam Smith's and Ricardo's thoughts which we find with MacVickar.

The original ideas of both Adam Smith and Ricardo were conceived with reference to small notes. In their development, however, this connection was dropped. This was done in McCulloch's anonymous _Review_ article during the discussion; while MacVickar and Parnell no longer use that same starting point. MacVickar, following Adam Smith, wanted to forbid completely small notes below $5, but at the same time he adopted Ricardo's suggestions worked out with regard to such small notes.

Slightly later, Lord Althorp in a speech of 1833 suggested that the government should grant charters to non-issuing joint stock banks within the sixty-five miles if they deposited the paid-up capital in government securities or other equally good funds (Gilbart, _History_, 63). This English author discusses the problem of bankers depositing securities for their issues with a view to England (_ibid._, 90).

48. See page 91.

49. J.A. Hamilton, _op. cit._, 83, 84.

50. See footnote 46.

51. _Free Trade Advocate_, II, 26. One will realize the difference between the plan as presented by Hamilton and by the author himself. However, there is a discrepancy in Hamilton's letter. Actually Bronson, as described above (see page 47) invested the capital of his own bank in mortgages.

52. _New York Assembly Journal_ (1828), 182 ff.

53. MacVickar wanted to leave one-tenth of the capital to the discretion of the banks; Forman nothing.

54. Op. cit., 86.
55. All quotations are from the second edition, entitled Credit, Currency and Banking, the above is to be found on page 62.
56. Ibid., 84, 90.
57. As to the theory of generations, see the author's History of American Business Leaders, Vol. I, Ch. I.
58. Helderman, op. cit., 9.
59. Republished anonymously in 1832 as a pamphlet entitled: Considerations on the Bank of the United States, in which its repugnance to the constitution...(Albany, 1832).
60. Hammond, Jabez, op. cit., II, 447-8; Byrdsall, op. cit., 61 ff; Jenkins, John S., History of Political Parties in the State of New York (2nd ed., Auburn, 1849) gives many data on Young, easily to be found through the unusually good index.
61. For the following: State of New York, Assembly and Senate Journals, 1837 and 1838. Senate Documents 55, 1837, Report of the select committee...on sundry petitions for the passage of a law creating a general system of private banking, and Document 68, 1838, Report of the select committee on so much of the Governor's message as relates to the repeal of the restraining laws and free competition in the business of banking. Less important are Assembly Documents 303, 318, (1837).
62. He means the book quoted before in footnote 47, the exact title of which is: Observations on paper money, banking and overtrading, including those parts of evidence taken before the committee of the House of Commons which explain the Scotch System of Banking. (London, 1827). Parnell's book was widely known at that time. Thomas Hart Benton quoted him repeatedly (e.g., op. cit., 188, 202) and so did Nicholas Biddle and Samuel Young, the latter in his articles cited in footnote 59.
63. In Senate Document 55, 13, 14.
64. This argument is repeated on page 18.
65. Hon. Samuel Young, Oration delivered at the Democratic Republican Celebration of the 64th Anniversary of the Independence of the United States, July 4, 1840. (New York, 1840), 10, 11. On page 14 is an interesting elaboration of Jacksonian ideas.
66. See McCulloch, especially his anonymous Edinburgh Review article.
67. N.Y. Senate, Document 55, (1837), 21-24.
68. In his Early American Land Companies, Shaw Livermore gives the background of this proposal treating the trend toward stockholders' liability in the period 1800-1825 (261 ff.).
69. Gilbart's contemporaneous History (78, 79) contains an interesting description of the advantages of unlimited liability and especially its influence on the behavior of the shareholders.
70. See footnote 47. The article was quoted in Parnell's book.
71. Review, op. cit., 293.
72. This bill and those to be discussed presently are to be found as Nos. 65, 66, 215, and 308 in a volume without title page: Legislative Bills 1838, owned by the New York State Library, Albany, New York.
73. Daly, Charles P., Guilian C. Verplanck, His Ancestry, Life, and Character (New York, 1870). Bryant, William Cullen, A Discourse of the Life, Character, and Writings of Guilian Crommelin Verplanck (New York, 1870). Hart, C. H., A Discourse on the Life and Services of G. C. Verplanck (New York, 1870).
74. See above 191.
75. Paine, Willis S., op. cit., 25.
76. The following is taken from a letter of Mann to A. C. Flagg, reprinted in Flagg, op. cit., 40-42. Joseph Sabin in his Dictionary of Books relating to America quotes a pamphlet of Abijah Mann, Correspondence between A. Mann, Jr. and Hon. A. C. Flagg...(Brooklyn, 1868), but no copy could be located. Mann in his vanity must have told people wild stories about his share in the Free Banking Act. Bonnefoux, once a Free Banker himself, relates: "Mr. A. Mann, Jr. ...was, I believe, the gentleman who drew up the seven or eight sections which formed the groundwork of the Act to authorize the business of banking, passed April 18, 1838. The original idea, Mr. Mann told me, sprung from the example given by Mr. Stephen Girard who, when he established his bank in Philadelphia, voluntarily hypothecated his immense property for the due payment of his circulating notes." Bonnefoux, Vindication, 11.
77. A vivid description of this attempted examination is given by Benton, op. cit., 458 ff. See also U.S. 23d Congr., 1st sess., House Report 481, passim.
77a. On April 3, 1834 Biddle wrote to J. G. Watmough, "Tell me something about this Mr. Mann of New York," (Biddle Letterbooks).

78. Flagg as Comptroller of the State of New York had to carry the law into execution. His interesting report with some documents added is in U.S. 25th Congr., 3rd sess., House Executive Document 227, 201 ff.

79. David B. Ogden (1775-1849) was a famous New York lawyer and scion of a socially prominent family of ironmasters. He played no important part in public life, but in 1838 served a term in the Assembly.

80. Report of 1849, quoted from the reprint in U.S. 31st Congr., 1st sess., House Executive Document 68, 128-9. The cases arising out of the Free Banking Act are discussed by Bray Hammond, passim, and Livermore, op. cit., 287 ff. Some of these pertain to the legal character of Free Banks.

81. It was one of the doctrines of Mercantilist banking theory that capital functioned exclusively as security for the note-holder. Thence, as mentioned before, MacVickar took his suggestion that bank capital should be "vested" and "from the banker's control." Based on the same Mercantilist idea American legislatures had developed the principle of limiting the issue of notes to twice or three times the capital. MacVickar and Lord went a step further: they proposed the limitation of note issues to the amount of capital; and since both suggested at the same time its investment in securities, notes and securities were tied together indirectly. The amount of the notes was "never to exceed the amount of their pledged stock," says MacVickar (page 38), and according to Lord (page 84) the banks had to use their credit alone in discounting "to an extent not exceeding the amount of capital invested." Ricardo, who had freed himself from Mercantilist tradition, could be direct and logical from the beginning in suggesting the deposit of securities, "In some proportion to the amount of their issues." (See page 191).

82. In consequence thereof, to the extent that note issues were based on mortgages Free Banks in fact practiced Mercantilist banking on private credit. Individuals transferred mortgages to banking associations upon the condition that they received accommodation loans immediately. They melted down real property into symbolical money, as Sir James Steuart would have expressed it. (Annual Report of the New York Bank Commissioners, for 1840, 9.)

83. Laws of 1840, chapter 363, section 6. The amendments are reprinted in bill 215, 10 ff. Horace Greeley in his Recollections mentions Willis Hall as the man to whom the state is especially indebted for the Free Banking Act. (Pages 125-26.) Dixon Ryan Fox, in The Decline of Aristocracy in the Politics of New York, Studies in History, Economics, and Public Law, No. 198 (New York, 1919), 4-5, misquotes the passage. A thorough investigation by the present author as well as by the reference librarians of the New York Public and the Albany State Libraries brought nothing to light to corroborate this statement. Willis Hall (1801-1868) was a Whig politician, an Assembly man in 1838, Attorney General of the state in 1839. He wrote a few political pamphlets and after 1848 was close to the Free Soilers. A. C. Flagg (op. cit., 43) criticized his wild and vague banking theories. If there is anything at all to Greeley's statement, Hall must have played his part behind the stage and may thereby indeed have had a meritorious influence on the development. This, however, is mere guess work.

84. An Act to authorize the business of banking, passed 4/18, 1838, Laws of the State of New York, passed at the 61st session (Albany, 1838). Most important are the sections 1, 2, 3, 4, 7, and 11.

85. The history of the Act has been written by Millard Fillmore in the document quoted above and by Helderman, op. cit., 21 ff. Important are the Annual Reports of the New York Bank Commissioners, especially those of 1840 and 1841. U.S. 26th Congr., 1st sess., House Executive Document 172, 115 ff. and 2nd sess., House Executive Document 111, 122 ff. For the beginnings see also Ogden, Remarks, 28 ff.

86. Guaranty Trust Company of New York, One Hundred Years of Banking Service (privately printed, 1939), 3-10. Curtis had been cashier of the Exchange Bank in Providence, had played a part in public affairs there, and was destined to become one of the leading figures in the young New York Clearing House. The first attempt to base a Free Bank in the state of New York on exeeptionally good security was made by L. Bonnefoux, op. cit., passim.

87. Principles of Political Economy, Second Part (Philadelphia, 1838) 257 ff.

88. Financial Register, II, 10; Treatise, 201 ff, 243 ff, 308 ff, 321 ff. The

last quotation may be found on page 202.

89. See especially, pages 124 ff, 131, 132, 136.

90. Hildreth, R., _A Letter to his Excellency Marcus Morton on Banking and the Currency_ (Boston, 1840), 14.

91. See especially, pages 147 ff., 153 ff., 200 ff.

92. See also the articles on "Free Banking" in _DeBow's Review_ XII, 610 ff., XIII, (1852) 127 ff., XIV, (1853) 28 ff., 151 ff. The case for and against Free Banking is summed up in this series, the author being opposed to it.

93. Kentucky and Virginia adopted the bond-secured bank-note rather than general incorporation in 1851 and 1852, respectively, being preceded in this respect by Michigan which in 1849 incorporated this feature into bank charters. In Maryland a Free Banking bill was defeated in 1852. Helderman, _op. cit._, 149 and 97. In 1857 it was suggested by the Superintendent of the Banking Department of the State of New York to extend the principle of bond security for banknotes to the still existing Safety Fund banks. _Bankers' Magazine_, XII, 615 ff.

94. The Louisiana Free Banking Act stipulated a thirty-three and one-third per cent specie reserve against deposits and a restriction of at least two-thirds of all loans to ninety-day paper, thereby becoming the most modern banking act of that time. The progress is here due, as it is so often, to a combination of two different sets of ideas.

95. An Act to organize and regulate banking associations, No. XLVII, _Acts of the Legislature of the State of Michigan_, passed at the annual session of 1837 (Detroit, 1837), 76 ff.

96. Felch, _op. cit._, 114. The act was praised in 1837 by a contemporary author for "divesting the state of its undue control of banking." Rafinesque, _op. cit._, 37.

97. _Michigan Senate Journal_, (1837), 45, 61, 147; _Journal of the Michigan House of Representatives_, (1837), 144. Biographies of Ellis and Lothrop in _Michigan Biographies_ (Lansing, 1924), I, 272 and II, 36, respectively.

98. Hammond, Bray, _op. cit._, 196.

- - - - - - -

Chapter VIII

THE SOUTHERN PLANTATION BANKS

1. Sumner, _American Currency_, 18 ff.; Phillips, _op. cit._, 64 ff.

2. The Pennsylvania loan office of 1723 was established for sixteen years.

3. For instance in Kentucky (Parks, _op. cit._, 137), Tennessee (McGrane, _Biddle Correspondence_, 172), Missouri (Helderman, _op. cit._, 62).

4. See page 6.

5. Carey, _Debates_, 37, 38.

6. _Path to Riches_, 67, 73.

7. An early example is the charter of the Farmers and Mechanics Bank of Philadelphia. The charter (of 1793) of the Bank of Pennsylvania is of interest in this connection. The bank was required to lend the state a certain amount for the establishment of a loan office; i.e., a commercial bank was to provide funds for the establishment of mortgage banking (see Holdsworth, _Empire_, I, 134).

8. Gallatin, _Suggestions_ (_Writings_, III, 441, 442). In 1838 a land bank was set up in Selma, Alabama. Every stockholder by a deed of trust conveyed to the bank property of twice the value of the stock which he subscribed and notes were issued on this basis (Scroggs, _op. cit._, 79). Even in this case one sees a development over the original land bank.

9. At the time the plantation banks were being set up Silas M. Stilwell in his _System of Credit_ proposed a similar type of institution.

10. See pages 8, 65.

11. See page 49.

12. See page 50.

13. The problem is how this progress originated, but the author has not found the answer. The scheme was copied in Mississippi in 1830 when the Planters Bank was established. It was broached in Massachusetts in 1836 by the promotors of the Bank of Ten Millions (_Mass. Sen. Doc._ 30 [1836], 56).

14. On this bank, see Trotter, _op. cit._, 92 ff. and McGrane, _Bondholders_, 168, 169. (His comment on this bank is not correct.)

15. Sparks, E. S., _op. cit._, 6.

16. The names of these credit institutions vary, the Silesian one was called Landschaft; that in Brandenburg, Kur-und Neumärkisches Ritterschaftiches Kreditinstitut. See _Handwörterbuch der Staatswissenschaften_, 4th ed., VI, 148.

17. Pell, op. cit., 29. His information was neither correct throughout, nor did he understand the essential features of the Landschaften.

18. European investors took it for granted that such far reaching liability was established. A prospectus of 1835 announcing the sale of bonds of the Citizens Bank stressed that "the mortgaged properties afford[ed] a perpetual pledge until the true and just payment and extinction of all bonds." However, in 1843, the Louisiana state legislature passed an act which embodied a different interpretation: Whenever a stockholder of any property bank tendered any of the outstanding state bonds, he was entitled to have his property released from the mortgage given in payment of the stock of the bank and thereby serving as security for the bonds issued in favor of that bank. Such legislative action, of course, resulted in bitter reaction on the part of the bondholders. Louisiana Senate Journal, 1843-1844, Appendix, xxiii is typical of the hazy thinking on the essential question; also ibid., liii ff. and McGrane, Bondholders, 183.

19. Grenier, op. cit., 136.

20. In the words of the Louisiana Board of Currency, the mortgages were "placed in the safekeeping of the bank as a special guarantee for the reimbursement of the state bonds." Louisiana Senate Journal, 1843-1844, Appendix, xxiii.

21. The Citizens Bank also, in 1834 and 1835, tried first to sell mortgage bonds and only when they proved to be unsalable, did it sell to the investors state bonds issued under an amendment to its charter "in favor of the Citizens Bank and secured by the real estate of its shareholders."

22. Thomas, op. cit., 19, 32, 33; McGrane, Bondholders, 225 ff., 11, 12, 18; Trotter, op. cit., 344 ff.

23. John Ringold of Independence County, Arkansas, was in all probability the man who introduced the plantation bank into the young state. He seems to have come from Baltimore and was a slaveholder and one of the early merchants of Batesville. He must have possessed considerable influence for he was not only a member of the state's Constitutional Convention of 1836, but was nominated, although not elected, its president. He then became a state senator, and when the first legislature of the state assembled he moved that a joint committee of both houses be set up to introduce banking legislation. He was made chairman of that committee and his report recommended the establishment of two banks. This report determined the early policy of the state toward banking and was apparently drafted under Louisiana influence recommending, as it did, the issue of state bonds for the benefit of two banks, one of which, the Real Estate Bank of Arkansas at Little Rock, was a plantation bank. (Ringold himself became the cashier of the Batesville branch of the State Bank and participated in reckless methods.) John Wilson, president of the Constitutional Convention, speaker of the first House of Representatives, became the first president of the Real Estate Bank. (Worthen, op. cit., passim; information received from the Reference Librarian, University of Arkansas; Gough, op. cit., passim; McGrane, Bondholders, 247, ff.; U.S. 25th Congr., 2nd sess., House Executive Document 79, 684 ff.; U.S. 33rd Congr., 2nd sess., House Executive Document 82, 174 ff.

24. For Mississippi, see McGrane, Bondholders, 195 ff.

25. In Arkansas, however, the stockholders mortgaged their properties to the state, not to the bank.

26. Krueger, Wisconsin, 12. The sponsor of this bank was a son of Alexander Hamilton, William S. Hamilton.

27. Grenier, op. cit., 136.

Chapter IX

SAVINGS BANKS

1. Illuminating for the atmosphere in which the savings bank originated in Great Britain is "The Speech of J. C. Curwen, Esq. M. P. in the House of Commons on the 28th of May, 1816 on...the State of the Poor Laws," 2nd ed., London 1816, inserted as no. 14 in volume 8 of The Pamphleteer, (London, 1816).

2. Report of the Massachusetts Bank Commissioners for 1851, 17, 18.

3. See Dictionary of National Biography.

4. Copies of this book were in America at the time when the first savings banks were established here. The copy now in the Widener Library of Harvard University and used by the author was given

to that library by Dr. Waterhouse of Cambridge in 1820.

5. They collected contributions and provided relief for temporary sickness and in case of death. They were called "manages" in Scotland and were first described, but not recommended by Henry Duncan. (Duncan, op. cit., 78, 79.)

6. Colquhoun, op. cit., 110 ff. The article "On Improving the Condition of the Poor" in the (London) Quarterly Review, XII, October, 1814, 146 ff. and especially 155 ff., is representative of the same early stage in the ideological development: the problem is clearly seen, but not yet the practicable way of handling it.

7. The correspondence is reprinted by Knapp, op. cit., (London edition), 141 ff. The following quotation is to be found on page 185. There is also a short reference to savings banks in Colquhoun's letter of June 14.

8. Hume, op. cit., 7. ff.

9. Hunt, op. cit., Volume I contains a biography of Eddy, but the paragraph referring to his share in founding the first savings bank in New York (page 341) is incorrect.

10. Knapp, op. cit., 197; Pintard, op. cit., I, 7.

11. Communication in New York Post, of November 1816, reprinted in Knowles, op. cit., 16. Reports on this meeting are to be found in the New York Commercial Advertiser of December 2, 1816 and in the Evening Post of the same day. They are reprinted by Keyes, op. cit., I, 308, 309 and Hardenbrook, op. cit., 283.

12. Pintard, op. cit., I, 38, 39.

13. Scoville, op. cit., II, 237, 238; Knowles, op. cit., 53, 54.

14. Zachariah Lewis (1773-1840), Yale bred, a preacher and journalist, was editor of the New York Commercial Advertiser from 1803-1820, during which time, as later, he was interested in the distribution of religious tracts and in foreign missions. See also Knowles, op. cit., 26.

15. Pintard, op. cit., I., 38.

16. The plan is reprinted by Hardenbrook, op. cit., 283.

17. The by-laws of the London institution envisages one manager to attend to the office in rotation. Hume, op. cit., 17.

18. It is taken over from the by-laws of the London institution; see Hume, op. cit., 16.

19. In England penny savings banks started somewhat earlier (see Lewins, William, A History of Banks of Savings in Great Britain and Ireland [London, 1866] 246 ff.).

20. Knapp, op. cit., 197, 198.

21. The documents relating to the legislative history of this first attempt to get a charter are reprinted by Keyes, op. cit., I, 310 ff.; by Hardenbrook, op. cit., 284, 285; and by Knowles, op. cit., 25 ff.

22. See page 63.

23. Hume, op. cit., 3; Rose, op. cit., 3, 79; Keyes, op. cit., I, 18.

24. Pintard, op. cit., I, 153. He had joined the Society for the Prevention of Pauperism in order to promote the incorporation of a savings bank (ibid., I, 159).

25. Knowles, op. cit., 26.

26. New York, Messages from the Governors, II, 915.

27. New York, 1819.

28. Pintard, op. cit., I, 205.

29. Keyes, op. cit., I, 332 ff.; Hardenbrook, op. cit., 287 ff.

30. There is a discrepancy since two vice-presidents-elect of 1816 were not on the original board of that year. However, under the plan of 1816 they must have replaced two of the original directors prior to their election; see Knowles, op. cit., 23.

31. Hardenbrook, op. cit., 284; Knowles, op. cit., 20, 21.

32. I, 2, 125 ff.

33. Mease's knowledge of the French conditions was somewhat confused. There was created by the Convention Nationale on March 19, 1793 a Caisse nationale de prévoyance, but it did not actually come into existence. A few years later the Bank of France, however, set up under the Statuts du 28 pluviôse an VIII (February 1800) a caisse de placements et d'epargne. See Arnaud, Léopold, Manuel des Déposants aux Caisses d'Epargne (Paris, n.d.), 3, 4.

34. Raguet deposited these pamphlets with the Philadelphia Savings Fund Society in whose archives they still remain. Letter from the Society and Willcox, op. cit., 20, 21. The essay "Publications on Parish or Savings Banks" in the Edinburgh Review, No. XLIX, Vol. 25, 1815 was also known in Philadelphia at that time and is supposed to have been used as the basis of articles in Poulson's Advertiser, ibid., 75.

35. Willcox, op. cit., 18 ff.

36. As to these men, see Willcox, op. cit., 104, 106 ff. A biography of Clement C. Biddle is to be found in Henry Simpson's, The Lives of Eminent Philadelphians (Philadelphia, 1859), 83. High praise of C. C. Biddle is contained in a letter of Nicholas Biddle to John Cumming, Savannah, dated January 4, 1830 (Biddle Letterbooks).

37. Articles of Association and Address to the Public are reprinted in Willcox, op. cit., 25 ff., 205 ff. There is another interesting feature in the Articles of Association: the trustees in sections 19 and 20 were mere trustees and different from the managing trustees of the New York Bank for Savings. They were needed to protect the depositors during the period when the institution worked without a charter. Similarly, Stephen Girard, who ran an unincorporated banking business, had to appoint trustees for the deposits lodged in his bank. As soon as the Philadelphia Savings Fund Society was incorporated the trustees could be dropped and, as a matter of fact, they cannot be found in the charter.

38. Reprinted in Sherman, Franklin J., op. cit., 44.

39. His biography can be found in History of Suffolk County, I, 178; II, 401; Provident Institution for Savings in the Town of Boston, 4.

40. William Phillips' biography is easily accessible in the Dictionary of American Biography, from which the quotation is taken. See also "William Phillips and William Phillips, Father and Son, 1722-1827," reprinted from the New England Historical and Genealogical Register, April, 1885, 9 ff. and Wisner, Benjamin B., A Sermon occasioned by the Death of Hon. William Phillips (Boston 1827), 21 ff.

41. Fuess, Claude Moore, Men of Andover, Biographical Sketches (New Haven, 1928), 64 ff.

42. Greenwood, F. W. P., A Sermon on the Death of John Lowell, LL.D. delivered in King's Chapel, Boston, March 22, 1840 (Boston, 1840), 5 ff.

43. The quotation regarding James Sullivan is from Dictionary of American Biography; as to Richard Sullivan see Memorial Biographies of the New England Historic-Genealogical Society, IV, 1860-1862 (Boston, 1885), 384 ff.

44. See page 34.

45. Report of the Massachusetts Bank Commissioners (1851), 19.

46. Provident Institution for Savings in the Town of Boston, Report, Bylaws and Act of Incorporation printed for the use of the Trustees. (1817); the same, The Constitution, Plan and Bylaws of the... with Regulations of the Trustees. (Boston, December, 1818); the same, One Hundred Years of Savings Bank Service, A Brief Account of the Origin, Growth, and Present Conditions of the..., (privately printed 1916, revised and reprinted 1930). The names of the "others" in the above-quoted petition may be found on page 11 of the last item.

47. See, for instance, the constitution of the London savings bank, section 13; Willcox, op. cit., 30.

48. It would be interesting to know if he received a remuneration.

49. It is reprinted on pages 12, 13 of the anniversary publication of the Provident Institution (see footnote 46). Its description of the agreement (on page 15) does not tally with the broadside. Presumably an agreement of February 4, 1817, as described, was not put into effect.

50. Ernst, op. cit., 399.

51. Material for the analysis of the New York board of trustees has been taken from Knowles, op. cit., 49 ff., and from correspondence with Mr. Walter Hausdorfer, Librarian of the School of Business Library, Columbia University.

52. Pintard, op. cit., II, 219.

53. Among the promotors of the New York Seamen's Bank for Savings were the Bethel Union and the Society for Promoting the Gospel among Seamen in the Port of New York (see Seamen's Bank of Savings, New York, One Hundred Fifteen Years of Service, 1829-1944, [privately printed, New York, 1944], 10).

54. See his biography in Willcox, op. cit., 101.

55. Baltimore was an exception. There one Captain Daniel Howland, a former shipmaster, was selected the bank's first president. Biographical notes are not available. The Maryland Historical Society informs this author that in 1816 he was carried in the State Directories as a merchant and in 1819 as "gentleman." In 1824 he figured as president of the Phenix Fire Insurance Company of Maryland, and disappeared from the directories after 1836. He was probably a philanthropist, for in 1896 he was one of the founders of the Charitable Marine Society. (Information from the Enoch Pratt Free Library.)

56. See the Act to incorporate the Albany

Savings Bank, passed March 24, 1820,
Laws 43d sess., chap. C.

57. Thon, op. cit., 11, 12.

58. Compare the Articles of Association of
the Philadelphia Saving Fund Society
with the synopsis of those of the Savings
Bank of Baltimore in Thon, op. cit., 87,
88.

59. Baltimore Savings Bank, 9.

60. Op. cit., IV, 170.

61. Eddy's letter is reprinted in Examination into the Expediency of Establishing
a Board of Agriculture in the State of
New York, published by the New York
Correspondence Association for the Promotion of Internal Improvements.
(Brooklyn, 1819), 62 ff.

62. Seamen's Bank for Savings, New York, One
Hundred Fifteen Years of Service, 1829-
1944... (privately printed, New York,
1944).

63. Pintard, op. cit., II, 186, 352; III,
57, 58, 61; Knowles, op. cit., 82.

64. An act to incorporate an Association by
the name of a Bank for Saving (sic!) in
the city of New York; approved March 26,
1819, Laws passed in the 42d session
(1819), chap. XLII.

An act to incorporate the Philadelphia
Saving (sic!) Fund Society, approved
February 25, 1819, Laws 1819, chap LIV.

An act to incorporate the Savings
Bank of Baltimore, passed January 30,
1819; Laws 1818, chap. 93; (incidentally
the first charter to establish a "savings
bank.")

An act to incorporate the Provident
Institution for Savings in the town of
Boston, approved December 13, 1816, Laws
1816, chap. XCII.

An act to incorporate the Provident
Institution for Savings in the town of
Salem and its vicinity, approved January
29, 1818. Laws 1817, chap. LXIV.

65. Reprinted by Duncan, op. cit., 70 ff.

66. See Haygarth, John, An Explanation of
the Principles and Proceedings of the
Provident Institution at Bath for Savings
[sic!] (London, 1816).

67. However as mentioned above the Scottish
type was taken over by the Southampton
Saving Fund.

68. Reprinted in Keyes, op. cit., I, 38, 39.

69. A few other distinguishing features are
not mentioned because they were not
taken over in America and are therefore
of no particular interest from our point
of view.

70. Quite a few of the early New England
charters, especially those of Rhode

Island savings banks, following these
examples, also embodied the by-laws in
the charter. See Keyes, op. cit., II,
358.

71. Some of the contemporary British savings
banks had both trustees and managers,
e.g., London (Regulations, sec. 2) and
Southampton (Rose, op. cit., 7). The
Philadelphia original articles of association followed that example, perhaps
copying a clause in the regulations of
Duncan's Dumfries Parish Bank Friendly
Society, repr. in the latter's pamphlet
which was known to Condy Raguet (Duncan,
op. cit., 71): In Dumfries the agent of
the Bank of Scotland was ex officio
trustee and the Philadelphia articles
made the president and cashier of the
Bank of the United States trustees of
the Saving Fund Society.

72. Keyes, op. cit., I, 120, 169.

73. The New York Bank for Savings worked in
1825 under the following rules: no interest accrued until the deposit was in the
bank for at least three months and none
would be paid on deposits withdrawn between the two annual interest dates
(January 1 and July 1). Pintard, op.
cit., II, 164, 165.

74. Savings Bank of Baltimore, 15.

75. In 1818 a New York court decided: "The
preamble to an act may be used to explain an equivocal expression used in
the enacting clause, but never to control its meaning, nor supply matter not
embraced in its spirit and meaning."
Jackson ex dem Woodruff v. Gilchrist,
15 Johnson (New York) 89 (1818). As
late as 1910 it was decided: "Neither
the title of an act nor the preamble
controls the plain words thereof or
extends its purview to objects mentioned
in title or preamble, but not in the act
itself." Neumann vs. City of New York,
Vol. 137, App. Div. 55 (1910).

In Pennsylvania the following decisions were handed down: "A preamble is
no part of the law and is only to be
resorted to, where the enactment is
doubtful, to discover the intention of
the lawmakers." Erie and N.E.R. Co. v.
Casey 26, Pennsylvania 287 (1856). "The
preamble of a statute or ordinance may
be resorted to for the interpretation of
the enactment when equivocal, but as its
office is to recite the mischief to be
remedied, if it is more extensive than
the enacting part, it will not control
the effect of the legislative act."
Easton v. Easton Transit Co., 12 North
(Pennsylvania) 93 (1908).

The question actually came up in
Philadelphia in 1830, in which year such
eminent legal authorities as Sergeant
and Binney advised the Philadelphia Saving Fund Society that the limitation in
the preamble had no binding force and
that the management could make any investment it saw fit   (Wilcox, op. cit.,
161 ff.). As late as 1872 the charter
was amended, an amendment which left no
doubt that the limitations on investments contained in the preamble had no
binding force   (ibid., 164).

76. Incidentally, the preamble of the Albany
    Savings Bank of 1820 is essentially
    identical with that of the Bank for Sav-
    ings in New York. The latter's trustees
    in 1820 felt bound by the preamble; see
    the interesting discussion reprinted by
    Knowles, op. cit., 68.

77. An act concerning the Bank for Savings
    in the city of New York, approved March
    24, 1820, Laws 43d session, chap. CIX.

78. "The high price of Stocks paralyze us
    so much that we are obliged [to refuse?]
    everything like a large deposit. The
    wise-acres in our legislature refused
    our application to be permitted to loan
    on Land and Mortgage we are now liter-
    ally suffering," (Pintard, op. cit., I,
    302).

79. See page 214.

80. Section 9 of the rules of the Provident
    Institution or Saving Fund for the Town
    of Southampton (Rose, op. cit., 11).

81. See By-laws, sections 10, 12, 22.

82. Keyes, op. cit., I, 40, 41.

83. Provident Institution, 17. A limitation
    of $1000 was adopted by the Massachusetts
    Act to regulate Institutions for Savings
    of 1834, section 6. As to New York, see
    Welfling, op. cit., 13.

84. A perfect expression of this spirit can
    be found in the English pamphlet of
    William Davis, Friendly Advice to Indus-
    trious and Frugal Persons, Recommending
    Provident Institutions or Savings Banks,
    4th ed., enlarged (London, 1817). The
    author of this pamphlet was connected
    with the institution in Bath.

85. See the facsimile of the circular in
    Baltimore Savings Bank, 10.

86. The Report, an original of which is in
    the Houghton Library of Harvard Univer-
    sity, is reprinted by Keyes, op. cit.,
    I, 342 ff. As to Pintard's authorship,
    see Pintard, op. cit., II, 360.

87. Willcox, op. cit., 31, 37; Knowles,
    op. cit., 81.

88. Op. cit., II, 355.

89. Ibid., III, 100; IV, 125, 170.

90. Provident Institution for Savings in the
    Town of Boston, 15.

91. They were a committee to procure an of-
    fice, one to procure the necessary books
    and stationery, one to devise a plan for
    investing the deposits, one to give
    notice to the newspapers, and one to
    apply to the legislature for incorpora-
    tion. Knowles, op. cit., 28.

92. Ibid., 38, 39, 64.

93. Willcox, op. cit., 24, 25, 29; also 42,
    43, 45.

94. Documents relative to Savings Banks, 6.

95. In Philadelphia this committee was orig-
    inally called "acting committee" (Willcox,
    op. cit., 81). Baltimore Savings Bank,
    12.

96. Op. cit., II, 361; III, 158.

97. In contemporary British savings banks
    the actuary (secretary) became in the
    course of time the actual manager.

98. Willcox, op. cit., 50, 57, 83, 85.

99. Pintard, op. cit., III, 119, 122, 265,
    and the references to the Funding Com-
    mittee in the Index; Knowles, op. cit.,
    72; Willcox, op. cit., 81, 91, 104.

100. For other examples, see Willcox, op. cit.,
     60 ff., 87.

101. Keyes, op. cit., II, 524.

102. Pintard, op. cit., I, 235, 359; II, 170;
     III, 137, 138; IV, 125. Knowles refers
     to Pintard's activities on pages 28, 38,
     64, 72, 75, 81, 83.

103. Op. cit., III, 119.

104. Ibid., I, 197; Scoville, II, 238.

105. Pintard, op. cit., II, 278.

106. Pintard, op. cit., I, 205, 257; II, 56,
     142, 265; IV, 125.

107. Keyes, op. cit., II, 361, 362; Willcox,
     op. cit., appendices III and IV and
     table B after page 166.

108. Op. cit., IV, 73.

109. For Philadelphia see Willcox, op. cit.,
     28, 43, 45, 46; for New York, Pintard,
     op. cit., I, 203, 207, 257.

110. See, for instance, Beaumont, op. cit.,
     494; Christian, op. cit., (see footnote
     118) 2. The trustees of the newly
     founded Seamen's Bank for Savings ad-
     vanced cash for buying furniture; see
     its publication, cited in footnote 53,
     page 9.

111. Pintard, op. cit., I, 228.

112. A discussion of the problem as such is
     to be found in Keyes, Report, 116, 117.

113. Lewins, op. cit., 53, 59, 68, 124.

114. Pintard, op. cit., II, 164. Strangely
     enough in Boston one was very reluctant
     regarding deposits of ministers

(Provident Institution for Savings in the Town of Boston, Hundred Years, 17, 18). The matter of legal limitation of deposits has been mentioned previously.

115. Pintard, op. cit., III, 263; IV, 70. (The editor has overlooked a typographical error on the part of Pintard.)

116. A very early suggestion to that effect is contained in Bowles, John, Reasons for the Establishment of Provident Institutions called Savings Banks, 3d edition, (London, 1817), 18.

117. Willcox, op. cit., 158 ff.; Knowles, op. cit., 86, 92; Keyes, op. cit., I, 83.

118. An English pamphlet of 1816 (Christian, Edward, A Plan for a County Provident Bank with Observations upon Provident Institutions already established, [London, 1816], 7) recommended that a floating balance be held in the hands of the treasurer so as to enable savings banks to permit immediate withdrawals. It cannot be proved that this pamphlet was known in America, but the balances which the early savings banks outside of Massachusetts kept with commercial banks consisted not only of accumulating funds which were not yet invested, but also of liquid funds kept against possible withdrawals. (See the report of a special committee of the Philadelphia Society in Willcox, op. cit., 166.)

119. A contemporary author criticized the savings banks for investing in government securities instead of lending to needy, industrious men upon adequate securities and pledges (Rafinesque, C. S., Safe Banking including the Principles of Wealth [Philadelphia, 1837], 32, 33).

120. For the following see Pintard, op. cit., II, 51, 56, 275, 278, 358; III, 56, 138, 162, 171, 188, 209, 212; IV, 144.

121. Op. cit., I, 302; III, 119; IV, 125; Keyes, op. cit., I, 376 ff.

122. Willcox, op. cit., 152 ff., 157 ff., 173.

123. It is very interesting that in the wording of a Connecticut savings bank charter of 1821 bank stock is called "public stock" (Keyes, op. cit., I, 123).

124. Thon, op. cit., 43 ff.

125. Keyes, op. cit., II, 523.

126. Ibid., II, 528.

127. Thon, op. cit., 13 ff.; Bryan, A. C., op. cit., 110 ff.; Willcox, op. cit.,

107; Keyes, op. cit., II, 363. A contemporary condemnation of these banks by Clement C. Biddle is contained in the annual report of 1840 of the Philadelphia Saving Fund Society. See Willcox, op. cit., 109. For another condemnation, see Rafinesque, op. cit., 55, 56.

128. On the Utility of Public Loan Offices and Savings Funds established by City Authorities (1836). (This rare pamphlet is in the library of the Historical Society of Pennsylvania, and a photostat copy is in the Baker Library.) The pamphlet contains the old Continental idea that the poor should at the same time have a safe depository for their savings and a place to borrow money in time of need. Prior to Mease's suggestion of 1836 the combination of savings bank and Mont-de-Piété had been discussed in the Philadelphia Saving Fund Society as early as 1820 (Willcox, op. cit., 87). Incidentally Priscilla Wakefield's famous Tottenham scheme of 1799 had comprised a savings bank and loan fund (Lewins, op. cit., 19).

129. Reliable short sketches or New York and Massachusetts savings banking in the 1850's are to be found in Scratchley, Arthur, A Practical Treatise on Savings Banks (London, 1860), Introduction, xlvii ff. See also the slightly later pamphlets by Townsend, John Pomeroy, Savings Banks. A Paper read before the American Social Science Association at Saratoga Springs, Sept. 5, 1877 (New York, 1877) and Les Caisses d'Epargne aux Etats-Unis, Mémoire...(Paris, 1878).

130. Keyes, op. cit., I, 112. Incidentally, by 1860 only 7 per cent of their deposits could be redeposited with commercial banks by savings banks (the same author, Report, 165).

131. Ibid., 77.

132. The Reports of the Massachusetts Bank Commissioners contains reports on savings banks for every year. See especially 1838, 43; 1851, 13, 22 ff.; 1852, 29; 1853, 52 ff., 100 ff.; 1855, 90 ff.; 1856, 102 ff.; 1857, 116 ff.; 1861, 153 ff., especially 165, 166.

133. Keyes, Report, 38 ff.; 69, 78, 97 ff. (reprinted in his History, I, 363 ff.); and the latter work, I, 357 ff., 376 ff.

134. Keyes, Report, 99.

BIBLIOGRAPHY

In using the bibliography here submitted the reader should bear in mind the following facts: This bibliography neither pretends to be a complete survey of the literature on American banking history nor does it even show all that the author has read on the subject. It gives exclusively such items as have been cited or that have influenced the line of reasoning of the author even if not actually quoted. A fuller listing was deemed unnecessary because of the many good bibliographies already available to students, such as those on contemporary pamphlet literature in the books of Miller and Mints and the Bibliography of Specific Banks by John S. Muscalus (1942). Again A List of Works Relating to the First and Second Banks of the United States, published by the Library of Congress in 1908, makes it superfluous to note any but the few items most important from the point of view of the present study, or to do more than cite the pertinent public documents so that they may be identified easily. Also one might mention Ray B. Westerfield's Selected Bibliography of Money, Credit, Banking, and Business Finance (1940) for those who wish an introduction into the related literature. For the readers of this volume it is surely superfluous to insert the biographical handbooks indispensable for this type of research. One of them, the Dictionary of American Biography, cites whatever material is available on such individuals as have been treated in that book.

Manuscript sources are quoted in the footnotes alone; they do not appear in the following list. Periodical articles are inserted only if of particular interest; others appear in footnotes only.

Lastly, sources for the second volume of this work are included here together with those for the first, although a supplementary list will be added in the former at the time of its publication.

- - - - - -

Abernethy, Thomas P. "The Early Development of Commerce and Banking in Tennessee," in Mississippi Valley Hist. Rev., Vol. XIV (1927).

Acres, Wilfrid M. The Bank of England from Within, 1694-1800. London, 1931.

Adams, Charles Francis. Further Reflections upon the State of the Currency in the United States. Boston, 1837.

Adams, Herbert B. "A Sketch of Haym Salomon," in American Jewish Hist. Soc. Publ., Vol. II (1894).

Adams, John Quincy. Speech [suppressed by the previous question] on the Removal of the Public Deposites, and its Reasons. Washington, 1834.

Adams, John Quincy. Memoirs. Philadelphia, 1874-77.

Adler, Cyrus. Jacob H. Schiff. His Life and Letters. Garden City, N. Y., 1928.

Aldrich, Clara E. The History of Banking in Idaho. University of Washington, 1940.

American Academy of Political and Social Science. "Lessons of the Financial Crisis," in The Annals, Vol. XXXI (1908).

Addresses by Frank A. Vanderlip, Myron T. Herrick, William Barrett Ridgely, Charles H. Treat, George E. Roberts, George H. Earle, Jr., William A. Nash, Isaac N. Seligman, Jacob H. Schiff, Andrew J. Frame, Henry W. Gates, A. L. Mills, F. A. Cleveland, S. Wexler, Lyman J. Gage, J. M. Elliott, A. S. Frissell.

American Bankers' Association. Proceedings of the Convention...held in New York, Sept. 12th, 13th, 14th, 1877, with the Constitution and By-laws and a List of Officers. New York, 1877.

American Bankers' Association. Report of the Currency Commission of the American Bankers' Association. New York, 1906.

American Bankers' Association. Report of the Currency Commission made at a Meeting held at Chicago, Jan. 18, 1908. New York, 1908.

Andreades, Andreas M. History of the Bank of England. London, 1909.

Andrew, A. Piatt. "The Treasury and the Banks under Secretary Shaw," in Quart. Jour. Econ., Vol. XXI (1906/07).

Andrew, A. Piatt. "The Partial Responsibility of Secretaries Gage and Shaw for the Crisis of 1907" in Bankers' Magazine, Vol. LXXVI (1908).

Andrew, A. Piatt. "Substitutes for Cash in the Panic of 1907" in Quart. Jour. Econ., Vol. XXII (1907/08).

Appleton, Nathan. An Examination of the Banking System of Massachusetts.... Boston, 1831.

Appleton, Nathan. Remarks on Currency and Banking. 2nd edition, Boston, 1841.

Appleton, Nathan. Memoir of the Hon. Abbott Lawrence. Boston, 1856.

Appleton, William. Selections from the Diaries of..., 1786-1862. Boston, 1922.

Archer, Williams Segar. Speech on the Question of the Removal of the Deposites (delivered in the House of Representatives, January 29, 1834). Washington, 1834.

Armstrong, Leroy and J. O. Denny. Financial California; a Historical Review of the Beginnings and Progress of Banking in the State. San Francisco, 1916.

Armstrong, William. The Aristocracy of New York: Who they are and what they were...by an old resident. New York, 1848.

Atwater, Jesse. Considerations on the Approaching Dissolution of the United States Bank. New Haven, 1810.

Atwater, Lyman H. "Future Paper Money of this Country" in Princeton Rev. (1881?).

Backus, Charles K. The Contraction of the Currency. An Argument. Chicago, 1878.

Bailey, Dudley P. "Banking Institutions, State and National," and "Boston Clearinghouse," in Professional and Industrial History of Suffolk County, Mass. (Boston, 1894).

Baker, Henry F. Banks and Banking in the United States. 1st part, Boston, 1853. 2nd part, Cincinnati, 1854.

[Bancroft, George.] "Report of the Committee of Ways and Means to whom was referred so much of the Message of the President, as relates to the Bank of the United States," in North American Rev., Vol. XXXII (1831).

Barker, Jacob. To the Public (1819?)

Barker, Jacob. Letters, Developing the Conspiracy Formed in 1826 for his Ruin. [New York, 1827].

Barker, Jacob. The Speeches of Mr. Jacob Barker and his Counsel on the Trials for Conspiracy. New York, 1827.

Barker, Jacob, defendant. Trial of Jacob Barker, Thomas Vermilye and Matthew L. Davis. New York, 1827.

[Barker, Jacob.] Incidents in the Life of Jacob Barker of New Orleans, Louisiana with historical facts.... Washington, 1855.

Barker, Jacob. The Conspiracy Trials of 1826 and 1827. A Chapter in the Life of.... With an Introduction by R. D. Turner. Philadelphia, 1864.

Barker, Jacob. The Rebellion. Its Consequences and the Congressional Committee denominated Reconstruction Committee. New Orleans, 1866.

Barlow, Robert. A True Exposition of the Transactions which led to the Failure of the late Franklin Bank; together with a brief history of some of the detected Acts and Malpractices of its late president Samuel Leggett in relation to that institution. New York, 1831.

Barnes, James A. John G. Carlisle: Financial Statesman. New York, 1931.

Barnett, George E. State Banking in the United States since the Passage of the National Bank Act. (Johns Hopkins University Studies in Historical and Political Science, XX, Nos. 2-3) Baltimore, 1902.

Barnett, George E. State Banks and Trust Companies since the Passage of the National Bank Act. (National Monetary Commission.) 61st. Congr., 3d sess., Senate Doc. 659.

Barron, Clarence W. They Told Barron..., The Notes of the Late Clarence W. Barron. Ed. and arr. by Arthur Pound and Samuel Taylor Moore. New York, 1930.

Bassett, John Spencer. The Life of Andrew Jackson. Garden City, New York, 1911.

Bates, James L. Alfred Kelley. His Life and Work. Columbus, Ohio, 1888.

Bayley, Rafael A. The National Loans of the United States from July 4, 1776 to June 30, 1880. 2nd ed. (As prepared for the 10th Census of the United States). Washington, 1882.

Beach, George. To the Stockholders of the Phoenix Bank. Hartford, 1837.

Beach, Moses Yale. Wealth and Biography of the Wealthy Citizens of New York City.... New York, 1845.

Beard, Charles A. and Mary R. Beard. The Rise of American Civilization. New York, 1927.

Beaumont, John T. B. An Essay on Provident or Parish Banks.... London, 1816. Reprinted in Vol. VII of the Pamphleteer.

Beck, James M. Stephen Girard "Merchant and Mariner." An Oration.... Philadelphia, 1897.

Beck, William [Citizen of Ohio, pseud.]. Money and Banking or Their Nature and Effect Considered. Cincinnati, 1839.

Beckhart, Benjamin H. and James G. Smith. The New York Moneymarket (esp. Vol. II, Sources and Movements of Funds). New York, 1932.

Benton, Thomas Hart. Speech on the Resolutions offered by Mr. Clay...relative to the Removal of the Public Deposites from the Bank of the United States. (Delivered in the Senate, Jan. 2, 3, 6, 7, 1834.) Washington, 1834.

Benton, Thomas Hart. Thirty Years' View or A History of the Working of the American Government for Thirty Years, from 1820 to 1850. New York, 1854.

Benton, Thomas Hart. "On Banks and Currency" in Bankers' Magazine, Vol. XII (1857/58).

Biddle, Nicholas. Oration Delivered before the Pennsylvania State Society of Cincinnati, on the Fourth of July, MDCCCXI. Philadelphia, 1811.

Biddle, Nicholas, compiler. Commercial Regulations of the Foreign Countries with which the United States have Commercial Intercourse.... Washington, 1819.

Biddle, Nicholas. Address delivered before the Philadelphia Society for Promoting Agriculture, at its Annual Meeting of the 15th of January, 1822. Philadelphia, 1822.

Biddle, Nicholas, Mathew Carey, John Sergeant...[and others, including Richard Peters, Jr.]. Address to Those on Whom Heaven has Bestowed the Goods of Fortune and What is More Valuable, Hearts to Make Proper Use of Them for the Public Benefit. Philadelphia, 1824.

Biddle, Nicholas. Eulogium on Thomas Jefferson, delivered before the American Philosophical Society on the Eleventh Day of April, 1827. Philadelphia, 1827.

Biddle, Nicholas. Documents from..., President of the Bank of the United States to Hon. G. M. Dallas. 22d Congr., 1st sess., Senate Doc. 98 (1832).

Biddle, Nicholas. Account of the Proceedings on Laying the Corner Stone of the Girard College for Orphans, on the Fourth of July, 1833: Together with the Address, Pronounced on that Occasion at the Request of the Building Committee. And a Description of the Plan of the College, by the Architect. Philadelphia, 1833.

Biddle, Nicholas. An Address delivered before the Alumni Association.... September 30, 1835. Princeton, 1835.

Biddle, Nicholas. Two Letters Addressed to the Hon. J. Quincy Adams concerning a History of the Recharter of the Bank of the United States. London, 1837. [Four further letters to the same were published in the newspapers and are to be found in the Financial Register, Vol. I, pp. 396, 342, 400; Vol. II, p. 391.]

Biddle, Nicholas. Reply to the Report of a Committee of the Bank of the United States of Pennsylvania. Paris, 1841.

[Biddle, Nicholas.] Questions Submitted to the President of the Bank of the United States by Mr. Cambreleng with his Answers Thereto. [n.p., n.d.]

Biddle, Nicholas. The Correspondence of Nicholas Biddle dealing with National Affairs, 1807-1844, ed. by Reginald C. McGrane. Boston, 1919.

Bilbo, William N. An Address on Banks and Banking, delivered at Nashville, Tennessee, Nov. 16, 1857. Nashville, 1857.

Binney, Horace. Report of the Minority of the Committee of Ways and Means on the Removal [of the] Public Deposites. 23d Congr., 1st sess., House Rep. 313 (1834).

Binney, Horace. Speech of...on the Question of the Removal of the Deposites... January 1834. Washington, 1834.

Bishop, Joseph B. A. Barton Hepburn. His Life and Service to his Time. New York, 1923.

Blair, William Allen. Banks of Issue. Winston, N. C., 1898.

[Blodget, Samuel.] Economica; A Statistical Manual for the United States of America. Washington, 1806.

Bogart, Ernest L. "Financial History of Ohio." (University of Illinois Studies in the Social Sciences, Vol. I), Urbana-Champaign, 1912.

Bolles, Albert S. The Financial History of the United States from 1789 to 1860. New York, 1883.

Bonham, J. Ellis. Remarks of...on the Bank Question together with Governor Bigler's View on the Bank of the United States and the Debate on the Same. Harrisburg, 1852.

Bonnefoux, L. Vindication of the Free Banking System. Investigation.... New York, 1848.

Bonnefoux, L. "Consideration of the National Finances in Connection with a National Bank" in Bankers' Magazine, Vol. XVI (1861/62).

Bonnefoux, L. "Financial Policy of the Government" in Bankers' Magazine, Vol. XVI (1861/62).

Bornemann, Alfred. J. Laurence Laughlin: Chapters in the Career of an Economist. Washington, 1940.

Boucher, John N., editor. A Century and a Half of Pittsburgh and her People. New York, 1908.

Boulding, Kenneth E., "The Theory of the Firm in the Last Ten Years" in Amer. Econ. Rev. Vol. XXXII (1942).

Bourne, Edward G. "Alexander Hamilton and Adam Smith" in Quart. Journ. Econ. Vol. VIII (1893/94)

Boutwell, George S. Reminiscences of Sixty Years in Public Affairs. New York, 1902.

Breck, Samuel. Sketch of the Internal Improvements Already Made by Pennsylvania.... Philadelphia, 1818.

Breck, Samuel. Historical Sketch of Continental Paper Money. Philadelphia, 1863.

Breck, Samuel. Recollections of...with Passages from his Note-Books, ed. by H. E. Scudder. Philadelphia, 1877.

Bronson, Henry. The History of Waterbury, Connecticut. Waterbury, 1858.

[Bronson, Isaac.] An Appeal to the Public on the Conduct of the Banks in the City of New York, by a citizen. New York, 1815.

[Bronson, Isaac.] "General Propositions Explanatory of the Elementary Principles of Banking" in The Free Trade Advocate, ed. by Condy Raguet, Vol. II (1829).

Bross, William. Banking; Its History, Commercial Importance and Social and Moral Influence. A Lecture before the Mechanics' Institute of the City of Chicago,... Feb. 24, 1852. Chicago, 1852.

Brough, Charles H. "The History of Banking in Mississippi." Miss. Hist. Soc. Pub. Vol. III (1900).

Brough, Charles H. "The Industrial History of Arkansas" in Arkansas Hist. Ass. Pub. Vol. I (1906).

Brown, Ernest. New Hampshire Bank Commission (reprint from Manchester Sunday Union, Oct. 30, 1910).

Brown, John Crosby. A Hundred Years of Merchant Banking: A History of Brown Brothers and Company, Brown, Shipley & Company, and the Allied Firms...New York, 1909.

Brown Brothers and Company. Experiences of a Century, 1818-1918. 1918. Century, 1818-1918. 1918.

Brown, Kenneth L. "Stephen Girard's Bank" in The Pa. Mag. Hist. and Biog., Vol. LXVI (1942).

Brown, Kenneth L. "Stephen Girard, Promoter of the Second Bank of the United States," in Journ. Econ. Hist., Vol. II (1942).

Bryan, Alfred Cookman. History of State Banking in Maryland (Johns Hopkins Univ. Studies in Hist. and Pol. Sci. XVII). Baltimore, 1899.

Bryant, William Cullen. A Discourse on the Life, Character, and Writings of Gulian Crommelin Verplanck. New York, 1870.

[Buchanan, James, British Consul in New York.] Report and Observations on the Banks and other Incorporated Institutions in the State of New York.... New York, 1828.

Bullock, Charles J. Essays on the Monetary History of the United States. New York, 1900.

Burpee, Charles W. First Century of the Phoenix National Bank of Hartford...1814-1914. Hartford, 1914.

Burr, Anna Robeson. The Portrait of a Banker: James Stillman. New York, 1927.

Burrill, Ellen Mudge. Essex Trust Company, Lynn, Mass., 1814-1914. An Historical Sketch of the Bank for its Centennial Year. Lynn, 1914.

Burstein, Maurice J. The Ideal System of Finance. New York, 1907.

Butler, George B. The Currency Question. Some Strictures on the Pamphlet of James Gallatin. A Series of Articles Originally Published in the Evening Post and Journal of Commerce. New York, 1864.

Butler, James D. "Alexander Mitchell, the Financier." Wisconsin Hist. Coll., Vol. XI (1888).

Byars, William Vincent, editor. B. and M. Gratz: Merchants in Philadelphia, 1754-1798. Jefferson City,.1916.

Cable, John Ray. The Bank of the State of Missouri. New York, 1923.

Caldwell, James E. Recollections of a Life Time. 1923.

Caldwell, Stephen A. A Banking History of Louisiana. Baton Rouge, 1935.

Callender, Guy S. "The Early Transportation and Banking Enterprises in Relation to the Growth of Corporations" in Quart. Journ. Econ. Vol.XVII (1902/03).

Cambreleng, C. C. "Remarks on the Subject of Banking" in Debates and Proceedings of the New York State Convention for the Revision of the Constitution, 1846 (Albany [Albany Argus] 1846).

Camp, H. H. Address of...on the History of Western Banking...Annual Convention of the American Bankers' Association...1879. New York, 1879.

Campbell, Claude A. The Development of Banking in Tennessee. Nashville, 1932.

Cannon, James Graham. Clearing Houses; Their History, Methods and Administration. New York, 1900.

Cannon, James Graham. Clearing Houses. (National Monetary Commission) 61st Congr., 2d sess., Senate Doc. 491. Washington, 1910.

Cannon, James Graham. Addresses:
An Ideal Bank. 1891.
Bank Credits. 1892.
Bank Defalcations. 1894.
Profit or Loss on Bank Accounts. 1894.
Losses from Bank Debts. 1895.
Proportion of Balances to Discounts. 1895.
Uniform Statements. 1895 and 1896.
Elements of Success in Banking. 1896.
Credit, Credit-Man, Creditor. 1896.
Individual Credits. 1897.
Plan and Scope of the Union of the Credit Reform Associations of Germany. 1898.
Successful Methods in Business. 1898.
Character, the Basis of Credit. 1898.
Local Credits. 1899.
Uniform Statement Blanks and Credit Department Methods. 1899.
Bank Credits No. 2. 1905.
The Banker and the Certified Public Accountant. 1908.
Buying Commercial Paper. 1908.
Commercial Education. 1909.
The National Association of Credit Men. 1909.

Cannon, James Graham. "Clearing Houses and the Currency" in The Currency Problem and the Present Financial Situation, a series of addresses delivered at Columbia University. New York, 1908.

Cannon, James Graham. Clearing House Loan Certificates and Substitutes for Money

during the Panic of 1907. Delivered before the Finance Forum of New York City. March 30, 1910.

Capers, Henry D. The Life and Times of C. G. Memminger. Richmond, Va., 1893.

Carey, Lewis J. Franklin's Economic Views. Garden City, N. Y., 1928.

Carey, Mathew, editor. Debates and Proceedings of the General Assembly of Pennsylvania. Philadelphia, 1807.

Carey, Mathew. Desultory Reflections upon the Ruinous Consequences of a Non-renewal of the Charter of the Bank of the United States. 2d ed., Philadelphia, 1810.

Carey, Mathew. Letters to Dr. Adam Seybert...on the Subject of the Renewal of the Charter of the Bank of the United States. 2d ed., enlarged, Philadelphia, 1811.

Carey, Mathew. Essays on Banking. Philadelphia, 1816.

[Carey, Mathew.] Letter to the Directors of the Banks of the City of Philadelphia on the Curtailment of Discounts and the Effects of the Organization of the Bank of the United States. Philadelphia, 1816.

[Carey, Mathew.] Outline of a System of National Currency; and Substitute for a Bank of the United States, by Colbert [pseud.] New York, 1834.

Carlson, Avery L. A Monetary and Banking History of Texas from the Mexican Regime to the Present Day, 1821-1929. [Iowa City,(?) 1930.]

Carlson, Avery L. "Laying the Foundation of Texas Banking" in The Texas Monthly, December 1929.

Cartinhour, Gaines T. Branch, Group and Chain Banking. New York, 1931.

Cary, Thomas Greaves. Letter to a Lady in France, on the Supposed Failure of a National Bank, the Supposed Delinquency of the National Government.... Boston, 1844.

Cator, George. Trust Companies in the United States. (Johns Hopkins Univ. Studies in Hist. and Pol. Sci., XX.) Baltimore, 1902.

Catterall, Ralph C. H. The Second Bank of the United States. Chicago, 1903.

Catterall, Ralph C. H. "The Successes and Failures of the First and Second Banks of the United States," in Proc. of the Academy of Pol. Sci., Vol. I (1911).

Chadbourne, Walter W. A History of Banking in Maine, 1799-1930. (Univ. of Maine Studies. 2nd Series, No. 37.) Orono, 1936.

Chaddock, Robert E. The Safety Fund Banking System in New York, 1829-1866. 61st
Congr., 2nd sess. Senate Doc., 581.

Chapman, John M. Concentration of Banking,
the Changing Structure and Control of
Banking in the United States. New York,
1934.

Charlton, Joseph W. The History of Banking
in Illinois since 1863. Univ. of Chicago,
1939.

Chase, Charles Augustus. Worcester Bank.
Worcester National Bank, 1804-1904.
Worcester, Mass., 1904.

Christian, Edward. A Plan for a County
Provident Bank with Observations upon
Provident Institutions already Estab-
lished. London, 1816.

Cisco, John J. Letter to the Hon. E. D.
Morgan, United States Senate, on the
Finances. New York, 1868.

Claiborne, W. C. C. Official Letter Books
of W. C. C. Claiborne, 1801-1816, ed.
by Dunbar Rowland. Jackson, Miss., 1917.

Clapham, Sir John. The Bank of England.
A History. Cambridge, 1944.

Clark, Dan Elbert. Samuel Jordan Kirkwood.
Iowa City, 1917.

Clark, W. A. The History of the Banking
Institutions Organized in South Carolina
prior to 1860. Columbia, S. C., 1922.

Clarke, Matthew St. Clair, and David A.
Hall. Legislative and Documentary His-
tory of the Bank of the United States
Including the Original Bank of North
America. Washington, 1832.

Clay, Henry, Speech of Mr...of Kentucky
establishing a Deliberate Design on the
Part of the Late and Present Executive of
the United States to Break down the
Whole Banking System of the United States
...delivered in the Senate of the United
States February 19, 1838. Washington,
1838.

Clay, Sir William, Bart. M. P. Remarks on
the Expediency of Restricting the Issue
of Promissory Notes to a Single Issuing
Body. London, 1844. (Esp. ch. III: On
the recent monetary history of America.)

Cleaveland, John. The Banking System of
the State of New York, with...Adjudged
Cases; including also an account of the
New York Clearing House. New York, 1857.

Clement, John. "A Sketch of William Biddle and Thomas Biddle," in The Pa. Mag.
Hist. and Biogr., Vol. XIV (1890).

Clews, Henry. On the Necessity of an
Elastic Currency System.... Address to

the Minnesota Bankers' Assoc. at Minneapolis on June 21, 1905.

Clews, Henry. The Monetary Situation and
its Remedies. An Address to the West
Virginia Banking Assoc. June 19, 1906.

Clews, Henry. Fifty Years in Wall Street.
New York, 1908.

Clibborn, Edward. American Prosperity.
An Outline of the American Debit or Banking System.... London, 1837.

Clymer, Ernest F., editor. 1856-1917.
Some Mile-Stones in the History of the
National Park Bank of New York. [New
York, 1917.]

Clymer, Ernest F., editor. The Making of
an Institution: The National Park Bank
of New York. [New York, 1922.]

Cochran, Thomas C., and William Miller.
The Age of Enterprise. A Social History
of Industrial America. New York, 1942.

Codwin, Elliot C. Historical Sketch of
Currency and Finance. An Address before
the Citizens of Cincinnati, Ohio...1876.
Cincinnati, 1876.

Coe, George S. The Natural Road to Specie
Payments. [New York, 1868.]

Coe, George S. Addresses:
  Address to the American Bankers' Association at a Convention in Philadelphia,
  Oct. 4, 1876. New York, 1876.
  Is Resumption Complete? Address at the
  Annual Convention of the American Bankers'Association at Saratoga, August 7,
  1879. New York, 1879.
  The Silver Question. Address at the Annual Convention of the American Bankers
  Association at Saratoga Springs, August
  12th, 1880. Third ed., New York, 1880.
  The Currency of the Future. What Shall
  it be? A paper read before the American Bankers' Association at Niagara
  Falls, August 11, 1881.
  The Real Service that Banks and Bankers
  render to Society and Their Relation
  to Currency. Introductory Address to
  the Convention held in Saratoga, August
  16, 1882.
  Address of...Proceedings of the New York
  Clearing House Association. June 4,
  1884.
  The Real Service that Banks Render to
  Commerce and How They do it. Address
  at the Annual Convention of the American Bankers' Association at Boston,
  August 11, 1886.

Cole, Arthur H. "Evolution of the Foreign
Exchange Market of New York" in Jour.

Econ. and Bus. Hist., Vol. I (1928/29).

Collier, William R. An Essay on the Currency, in which is proposed the Enactment by Congress of a General Bank Law. Boston, 1834.

Colquhoun, Patrick. A Treatise on Indigence. London, 1806.

Colwell, Stephen. The Ways and Means of Payment; a Full Analysis of the Credit System. 2d ed., Philadelphia, 1860.

Conant, Charles A. "The Plans for Currency Reform" in Bankers' Magazine, LXXIII (1907).

[Congdon, James B.] A Letter to His Excellency, John Henry Clifford, on the Proposition now before the Legislature to Request the Banks of the Commonwealth to Hold on Deposit a Certain Amount of Specie, by a Practical Banker. Boston, 1853.

[Congdon, James B.] A Defence of the Currency of Massachusetts in a Letter to His Excellency Henry J. Gardner, Governor of the Commonwealth, by a Practical Banker. 2d. ed., Boston, 1856.

Conrad, Robert T. "Nicholas Biddle" in Vol. IV of The National Portrait Gallery of Distinguished Americans (James Herring, editor), Philadelphia, 1839.

Cooch, Richard L. The Record of Delaware Banks. Unpublished thesis, American Institute of Banking, 1937.

Cooke, Guy W. The First National Bank of Chicago. Chicago, 1913.

Cooke, Thornton. "The Insurance of Bank Deposits in the West" in Quart. Journ. Econ., Vol. XXIV (1909/10). (Also in Appendix B of George E. Barnett's State Banks and Trust Companies.)

Cooley, Thomas M. "Federal Taxation of State Bank Currency" in Mich. Pol. Sci. Assn. Publ., Vol. I (1893).

Cooley, Thomas M. "State Bank Issues in Michigan" in Mich. Pol. Sci. Assn. Publ., Vol. I (1893).

Cooper, Peter. The Unmeasured Importance of the Unfluctuating National Currency over which the Government has Entire Control. New York, 1875.

Cooper, Peter. Currency. Mr. Peter Cooper's Letter. Mr. Peter Cooper's Answer. Notes from S. A. Goddard. [New York] 1875.

Cooper, Peter. A Letter on the Currency. [New York], 1875.

Cooper, Thomas. A Series of Essays on the Present United States Bank. Columbia, S.C., 1833.

Coover, A. B. "Ohio Banking Institutions, 1800-1866," in Ohio Arch. and Hist. Quart., Vol. XXI (1912).

Corey, Lewis. The House of Morgan. New York, 1930.

Cornwallis, Kinahan. The Gold Room and the New York Stock Exchange and Clearing House. New York, 1879.

Coulter, E. Merton. Thomas Spalding of Sapelo. University, Louisiana, 1940.

Cowell, John W. Letter to the Right Honourable Francis Thornhill Baring on the Institution of a Safe and Profitable Currency. London, 1843.

Cox, Isaac J., editor. "Selections from the Torrence Papers" in Quart. Pub. of the Hist. and Phil. Soc. of Ohio, Vol. VI (1911).

Crockett, Walter Hill. Vermont, the Green Mountain State. New York, 1921.

Cross, Ira B. Financing an Empire: History of Banking in California. San Francisco, 1927.

Curry, J. L. M. A Brief Sketch of George Peabody and a History of the Peabody Education Fund.... Cambridge, 1898.

Curti, Merle. The Growth of American Thought. New York, 1943.

Curtiss, Frederick H. "Fifty Years of Boston Finance, 1880-1930," in Fifty Years of Boston (Boston, 1932).

Dailey, Don M. The Development of Banking in Chicago before 1890. (Abstract of a doctoral dissertation, Northwestern University, 1934.)

Dailey, Don M. "The Early Development of the Note Brokerage Business in Chicago" in Jour. Pol. Econ., Vol. XLVI (1938).

Dallas, George Mifflin. Speech of Mr. ... upon the Bill to Modify and Continue the Charter of the Bank of the United States. Senate, May 22, 1832. Washington, 1832.

Dallas, George Mifflin. Life and Writings of Alexander James Dallas. Philadelphia, 1871.

Daly, Charles P. Gulian C. Verplanck; his Ancestry, Life and Character. New York, 1870.

Davis, Andrew McFarland. Currency and Banking in the Province of the Massachusetts Bay. Vol. II. Banking. New York, 1901.

Davis, Andrew McFarland, editor. Tracts Relating to the Currency of the Massachusetts Bay, 1682-1720. Boston, 1902.

Davis, Andrew McFarland. "Boston 'Banks' 1681-1740. Those who were interested in

them" in New Eng. Hist. Gen. Reg. Vol.
LVII (1903).

Davis, Andrew McFarland, editor. "The
Prospectus of Blackwell's Bank, 1687,"
in Mass. Hist. Soc. Proc. (1904).

Davis, Andrew McFarland. The Origin of the
National Banking System. Washington,
1910.

Davis, Joseph S. Essays in the Earlier
History of American Corporations. Cambridge, 1917.

Davis, William Watson. The Civil War and
Reconstruction in Florida. (Columbia
Univ. Studies in Hist., Ec., and Publ.
Law, LIII, 1913).

Dawes, Charles G. The Present Financial
Situation. Its Causes and Lessons. An
Address, November 30, 1907.

Dawes, Charles G. Essays and Speeches.
Boston, 1915.

Dawes, Charles G. The First Year of the
Budget of the United States. New York,
1923.

Dean, Sidney. History of Banking and
Banks. Boston, 1884.

Degrand, P. P. F. Proceedings of the
Friends of a National Bank at their Public Meeting held in Boston 15th July 1841
including.... Boston, 1841.

Dehority, G. H. State Banking in Indiana.
Unpublished thesis, Indiana University,
1914.

Dennis, Albert W. The Merchants National
Bank of Salem, Massachusetts, an Historical Sketch. Salem, Mass., 1908.

Depew, Chauncey M. Speech...in the Senate
of the United States, Feb. 25, 1907 [on
the] Reform of the Currency. Washington,
1907.

De Peyster, Frederic. A Biographical Sketch
of Robert R. Livingston. New York, 1876.

Dewey, Davis R. State Banking before the
Civil War. Washington, 1910.

Dewey, Davis R. Financial History of the
United States. 7th edition, New York,
1920.

Dickinson, Ellen E. "Joshua Forman, the
Founder of Syracuse" in The Magazine of
American History, June, 1882.

Dillingham, William P. "Banking Interests
of Vermont," in The New England States
(William T. Davis, editor), Boston, 1897.

Dillon, Malcolm. The History and Development of Banking in Ireland from the Earliest Times to the Present Day. Dublin,
1889.

Domett, Henry W. A History of the Bank of
New York, 1784-1884. 3rd edition, [Cam-
bridge, 1884].

Dorfman, Joseph. The Economic Mind in
American Civilization, 1606-1865. New
York, 1946.

Dorfman, Joseph, and Rexford G. Tugwell.
"The Reverend John McVickar," in Columbia Univ. Quart., Vol. XXIII (1931).

Douglass, William. A Discourse Concerning
the Currencies of the British Plantations
in America, edited by Charles J.
Bullock, New York, 1897.

Dowrie, George W. The Development of Bank-
ing in Illinois, 1817-1863. Univ. of
Illinois Studies in the Soc. Sci., Vol.
II (1913).

Dowrie, George W. "History of the Bank of
Italy in California," in Jour. Econ, and
Bus. Hist. Vol. II (1929/30).

Dowrie, George W. American Monetary and
Banking Policies. New York, 1930.

Drew, John G. Political Economy for the
People. New York, 1874.

Duane, William J. Narrative and Correspondence concerning the Removal of the Deposites.... Philadelphia, 1838.

Duke, Basil W. History of the Bank of
Kentucky, 1792-1895. Louisville, 1895.

Dunbar, Charles F. The Theory and History
of Banking with Chapters...by Oliver M. W.
Sprague and Henry Parker Willis. 4th
edition, New York, 1922.

Duncan, Henry. An Essay on the Nature and
Advantages of Parish Banks. 2d edition,
Edinburgh, 1816.

Duncombe, Charles. Duncombe's Free Banking:
An Essay on Banking, Currency, Finance,
Exchanges, and Political Economy. Cleve-
land, 1841.

Dunn, Robert W. American Foreign Investments. New York, 1926.

Dunham, Walter L. Banking and Industry in
Michigan. Detroit, 1929.

East, Robert A. Business Enterprise in the
American Revolutionary Era. New York,
1938.

Edelman, Edward. "Thomas Hancock, Colonial
Merchant" in Jour. Econ. and Bus. Hist.,
Vol. I (1928/29).

Edmonds, Francis W. Defence of...late
Cashier of the Mechanics Bank. New York,
1855.

Edwards, George W. The Evolution of Finance
Capitalism. London, 1938.

Ehrenberg, Richard. Grosse Vermögen, ihre Entstehung und ihre Bedeutung. Jena, 1925.

Eliason, Adolph O. The Rise of Commercial Banking Institutions in the United States. Mineapolis, Minn., 1901.

Eliason, Adolph O. "The Beginning of Banking in Minnesota" in Minnesota Hist. Soc. Coll., Vol. XII (1908).

Ellicott, Thomas, Philip E. Thomas and William W. Taylor. Memorial to the Assembly of Maryland. (About 1825).

Ellicott, Thomas. Bank of Maryland. Conspiracy as Developed in the Report to the Creditors. Philadelphia, 1839.

Ensley, Enoch. Views of...on National Finances, embraced in Two Letters. Memphis, 1875.

Ernst, C. W. "Savings Banks." "Trust Companies" in Professional and Industrial History of Suffolk Co., Mass., (Boston, 1894), Vol. II.

Esarey, Logan. State Banking in Indiana, 1814-1873. Indiana Univ. Stud., No. 15 (1912).

Farmer, Silas. The History of Detroit and Michigan, or, the Metropolis Illustrated. (Especially Chapter 53, Banks and Currency.) Detroit, 1884.

Farwell, John V. "George Smith's Bank" in Jour. Pol. Econ., Vol. XIII (1905).

Federal Reserve System, Board of Governors. Banking Studies. Washington, 1941.

Felch, Alpheus. "Early Banks and Banking in Michigan," in Michigan Pioneer Coll., Vol. II (1880).

Felt, Joseph B. An Historical Account of Massachusetts Currency. Boston, 1839.

Fillmore, Millard. Extracts from the Report of Hon...Comptroller of the State of New York, 12/30, 1848. U. S. 31st Congr., 1st sess., Executive Doc. 68. (1849-50).

Fisk, Harvey E. "Fisk & Hatch, Bankers and Dealers in Government Securities, 1862-1885" in Jour. Econ. and Bus. Hist., Vol. II (1929/30).

Fite, Emerson D. Social and Industrial Conditions in the North during the Civil War. New York, 1910.

Flagg, A. C. Banks and Banking in the State of New York from the Adoption of the Constitution in 1777 to 1864. Brooklyn, 1868.

Flanagan, W. W. Security for National Bank Deposits. Submitted to the American Bankers Assn. 1885.

Flint, Charles R. Memories of an Active Life. New York, 1923.

Foot, Samuel A. An Argument in Favor of the Constitutionality of the General Banking Law of This State. Geneva, 1839.

Foote, Henry W. "In Memoriam John Amory Lowell" in The Unitarian Review.

Forbes, A. and J. W. Greene. The Rich Men of Massachusetts. Boston, 1851.

Ford, Abbie A. John Pierpont, A Biographical Sketch. Boston, 1909.

Ford, Franklin. The Country Check. It Means a Single Banking System and a Universal Check. [New York], 1899.

Ford, Henry J. The Cleveland Era.... New Haven, 1921.

Forgan, James B. Recollections of a Busy Life. New York, 1924.

"Practical Efficiency of the Present Banking Law" in North American Rev., Vol. CLXXII (1901).

Branch Banking, Address before the Bankers Club of Milwaukee, 1902.

The Currency Commission of the American Bankers Association and its Plan: A Review. Chicago, 1906.

With Joseph T. Talbert, Synopsis of a Plan for National Bank Credit Currency. 1906 (first publ. in 1903).

Currency Reform, an Address at the 185th meeting of the St. Louis Commercial Club, 1/26, 1907.

Should National Bank Deposits be Guaranteed, Address before the Annual Meeting of.... The Bankers' Association of the State of Illinois. June 11, 1908.

The Efficacy and the Limitations of Bank Supervision by Examination and the Responsible Source of Bank Management. Address, 1909.

The Mobilization and Control of the Reserves of the Country. Address before the Convention of the American Bankers' Association at New Orleans, Nov. 22, 1911.

Possibilities of Senator Aldrich's Suggestions for Legislation. Address, 1911.

Clearing House Bank Examinations. Address, 1912.

Review of the Proposed Banking and Currency Bill. 1913.

"Evolution in Banking Thought During the Past Generation" in Bulletin of the

National Association of Credit Men,
Vol. XIX (1917).

A Good Note. Address, 1920.

"Currency Expansion and Contraction" in
the Annals of the Acad. of Polit. and
Soc. Sci., Vol. XCIX (1922).

Remarks to the Old People at the Scottish Old People's Home. Chicago, 1924.

Forman, Samuel E. The Political Activities
of Philip Freneau. (Johns Hopkins Univ.
Studies in Hist. and Pol. Sci., XX),
Baltimore, 1902.

Forstall, Edmond J. Agricultural Productions of Louisiana Cotton and Sugar Interests. 1845.

Forsythe, Harold K. Growth of State and
National Banks in Indiana. Unpublished
thesis, Indiana University, 1920.

Foulds, Margaret H. "The Massachusetts
Bank, 1784-1865" in Jour. Econ. and Bus.
Hist., Vol. II (1929/30).

Fox, Dixon R. The Decline of Aristocracy
in the Politics of New York. New York,
1919.

Frame, Andrew J. Sixty Years in Banking,
1862-1922. Some Thoughts on Banking.
Waukesha, 1922.

Francis, John. Chronicles and Characters
of the Stock Exchange. Boston, 1850.

Freund, Miriam K. Jewish Merchants in
Colonial America.... New York, 1939.

Gallatin, Albert. The Writings of....;
edited by Henry Adams. Philadelphia,
1879.

[Gallatin, Albert.] "Banks and Currency"
in Amer. Quart. Rev., Vol. VIII (1830).

Gallatin, Albert. Considerations on the
Currency and Banking System of the United
States. Philadelphia, 1831.

Gallatin, Albert. Suggestions on the Banks
and Currency of the several United States
.... New York, 1841.

Gallatin, James. A Great Peace Maker: The
Diary of James Gallatin, Secretary to
Albert Gallatin, 1813-1827. New York,
1914.

Gallatin, James. "Remarks made at the meeting of Bank Officers at the American Exchange Bank, Saturday December 28, 1861"
in Bankers' Magazine, XVI (1861-62).

Gallatin, James. Leaflets:
Two letters to the Hon. S. P. Chase, Secretary of the Treasury. 1861.
Letter from...on Financial Affairs, Reprint from New York. Commercial Advertiser, Jan. 21, 1862.

Government Finances and the Currency.
Letters to Hon. David Wilmot. New York,
1862.
Letter to Hon. Samuel Hooper of Massa-
chusetts..., Reprint from the New York
Commercial Advertiser, December 20,
1862.
Letter to Hon. William P. Fessenden,
Senator of the United States. The Pro-
posed United States Banking System and
Further Issues of Legal Tender. New
York, 1863.
The New National Banking System; or,
Government Paper Money. Remarks in
Reference to the...Resolution [of the
New York Clearing House Association
held October 6th 1863...to examine into
the system of National Banking]. 1863.
The National Debt, Taxation, Currency and
Banking System of the United States....
New York, 1864.
The National Finances, Currency, Banking
being a reply to...Samuel Hooper.
New York, 1864.
Address before the Democratic Union Asso-
ciation, October 18, 1864. George B.
McClellan as a Patriot, a Warrior, and
a Statesman, Course of the Administra-
tion, State of the Finances,...1864.
The Public Debt, Banking, Currency, and
Finances of the United States. Letter
to Hon. James R. Doolittle. New York,
1866.
The Financial Economy of the United
States, with Suggestions for Restoring
Specie Payments. A letter to Andrew
Johnson.... New York, 1868.

Garris, Roy L. Principles of Money, Credit
and Banking. New York, 1934.

Gantenbein, James W. Financial Questions
in United States Foreign Policy. New
York, 1939.

Garnett, Charles H. State Banks of Issue
in Illinois. University of Illinois.
1898.

Garnett, Charles H. "Banks of Issue in
Illinois" in Sound Currency, Vol. V.
(1898).

Gibbons, James S. The Banks of New York,
Their Dealers, the Clearing House, and
the Panic of 1857. New York, 1859.

Gilbart, James W. The History of Banking
in America. London, 1837.

Gilbart, James W. The Moral and Religious
Duties of Public Companies. London,
1856.

Gilbert, James H. The Development of Banking in Oregon. Eugene, Oregon, 1911.

Gilpin, William J. and Henry E. Wallace.
Clearing House of New York City; New
York Clearing House Association, 1854-
1905. New York, 1905.

Goddard, Thomas H. A General History of
the Most Prominent Banks in Europe, particularly...the Rise and Progress of the
Bank of North America.... New York,
1831.

Gordon, Armistead C. John Tyler, Tenth
President of the United States. An Address. 1915.

Gordon, Robert A. Business Leadership in
the Large Corporation. Washington, 1945.

[Gordon, Thomas F.] The War on the Bank
of the United States. Philadelphia,
1834.

Gouge, William M. A Short History of Paper
Money and Banking in the United States
.... Philadelphia, 1833.

Gouge, William M. An Inquiry into the Expediency of Dispensing with Bank Agency
and Bank Paper in the Fiscal Concerns of
the United States. Philadelphia, 1837.

Gouge, William M. The Fiscal History of
Texas.... Philadelphia, 1852.

Govan, Thomas P. "Banking and the Credit
System in Georgia, 1810-1860." Jour. of
Southern History, Vol. IV (1938).

Grampp, William D. "John Taylor: Economist of Southern Agrarianism," in Southern Econ. Jour., Vol. XI (1945).

Gras, N. S. B. The Massachusetts First
National Bank of Boston, 1784-1934.
Cambridge, 1937.

Gras, N. S. B. Business and Capitalism.
An Introduction to Business History.
New York, 1939.

Gray, Edward. William Gray. Boston, 1914.

Grayson, Theodore J. Leaders and Periods
of American Finance. New York, 1932.

Greef, Albert O. The Commercial Paper
House in the United States. Cambridge,
1938.

Greeley, Horace. Recollections of a Busy
Life. New York, 1868.

Greene, William B. The Radical Deficiency
of the Existing Circulating Medium and
the Advantages of a Mutual Currency.
Boston, 1857.

Grenier, Emile P. The Early Financing of
the Consolidated Association of the
Planters of Louisiana. (Unpublished
thesis, Louisiana State University, 1938.)

Griffith, Elmer C. "Early Banking in
Kentucky" in Miss. Valley Hist. Assn.
Proc., Vol. II (1908/9).

Grouchy, Allan G. "A Sketch of Virginia
Banking History" in Southern Econ. Journ.,
Vol. IV (1937).

Gue, B. F. "The Public Services of Hiram
Price," in Annals of Iowa, 3rd Series,
Vol. I (1895).

Hadden, Clarence B. "History of Early
Banking in Wisconsin," in Transactions
of the Wisconsin Academy of Sciences,
Arts, and Letters, Vol. X (1894-1895).

Hale, Nathan. Remarks on the Banks and
Currency of the New England States.
Boston, 1826.

Hales, Charles A. The Baltimore Clearing
House. Baltimore, 1940.

Hall, Charles S. Benjamin Tallmadge, Revolutionary Soldier and American Businessman. New York, 1945.

Hallock, James C. Reform in Collecting
Country Items, Contemplated by the Boston
Clearing House. 1898. (Leaflet.)

Hallock, James C. "The Practicability of
a Clearing-House for Country Items," in
Bankers' Magazine, Vol. LVII (1898).

Hallock, James C. Proposed Plan for the
Clearing of Country Checks in New England,
1898. (Leaflet.)

Hallock, James C. Clearing Out-of-town
Checks. St. Louis, Mo., 1903.

Hamilton, James A. Reminiscences; or Men and
Events at Home and Abroad during Three
Quarter of a Century. New York, 1869.

Hammond, Bray. "Long and Short Term Credit
in Early American Banking," in Quart.
Jour. Econ., Vol. XLIX (1934-35).

Hammond, Bray. "Free Banks and Corporations: the New York Free Banking Act of
1838," in Jour. Pol. Econ., Vol. XLIV
(1936).

Hammond, Matthew B. "The Financial History
of Wisconsin Territory," in Proceedings
of the State Hist. Soc. of Wisconsin
(1893).

Hanaford, Phebe A. The Life of George
Peabody. Boston, 1870

Hardenbrook, William Ten Eyck. Financial
New York, A History of the Banking and
Financial Institutions of the Metropolis.
New York, 1897.

Hardin, Ben. Speech of the Hon...on the
Subject of the Removal of the Deposites,
delivered in the House of Representatives,
March 1 and 3, 1834. Washington, 1834.

Harding, William F. "The State Bank of
Indiana" in Jour. Pol. Econ., Vol. IV
(1895-1896). Reprinted also in Sound
Currency, Vol. V (1898).

Hare, Robert. Proofs that Credit as Money
...is to a Great Extent Preferable to
Coin. Abstract from a pamphlet published in 1810. Philadelphia, 1834.

Hare, Robert. An Effort to Refute the
Opinion that No Addition is Made to the
Capital of a Community by Banking.
[1834 or 1835.]

Hare, Robert. Suggestions Respecting the
Reformation of the Banking System.
Philadelphia, 1837.

Hare, Robert. A Brief Exposition of the
Injury done to the Community and Especially to the Poor by the Prohibition of
Bills under Five Dollars.... Philadelphia, 1841.

Hare, Robert. "Do Banks Increase Loanable
Capital?," in Hunt's Merchants Magazine,
Vol. XXVI (1852).

Harper, William H. and Charles H. Revell.
Fifty Years of Banking in Chicago, 1857-
1907. The Merchant's Loan and Trust
Company. Chicago, 1907.

Harris, I. G. Message of Governor...in
Reply to a Resolution of the House of
Representatives Calling for Information
Relating to the Bank of Tennessee.
Nashville, 1858.

Hart, Albert Bushnell and Edward Channing.
Documents Relative to the Bank Contro-
versy, 1816-1833. (American History
Leaflets, No. 24), New York, 1895.

Hart, Charles H. A Discourse on the Life
and Services of the Late Guilian
Crommelin Verplanck. New York, 1870.

Harter, Michael D. A Safe, Commonplace
and Efficient Remedy for Financial Ills
...A Plan to Reestablish the Rights of
the State Banks.... 1892.

Hartsough, Mildred L. The Development of
the Twin Cities (Minneapolis and St.
Paul) as a Metropolitan Market. Minneapolis, 1925.

[Harwood, James and Benjamin C. Ridgate.]
Reply to a Pamphlet Entitled a Brief Exposition of Matters Relating to the Bank
of Maryland with an Examination into
Some of the Causes of the Bankruptcy of
that Institution. Baltimore, 1834.

Haskell, Louisa P. "Langdon Cheves and
the United States Bank: A Study from
Neglected Sources," in Annual Report of
Am. Hist. Assn., 1896.

Hatcher, William B. Edward Livingston,
Jeffersonian Republican and Jacksonian
Democrat. University, La., 1940.

Hawley, Merwin S. "The Origin of the Erie
Canal," in Buffalo Hist. Soc. Publ.,
Vol. II (1880).

[Hazard, Erskine.] "Cause and Cure of
Hard Times Currency" in Hazard's United
States Commercial and Statistical Regis-
ter, Vol. I (1839/40), Philadelphia.

Hazard, Erskine. Thoughts on Currency and
Finance. Philadelphia, 1863.

Heck, Harold J. A History of Banks and
Bank Legislation in Louisiana. Unpub.
Thesis, New York University, 1939.

Heckscher, Eli F. Mercantilism. (Authorized Translation by Mendel Shapiro)
London, 1935.

Hedges, Joseph E. Commercial Banking and
the Stock Market before 1863. Baltimore,
1938.

Heinberg, John G. The Office of the Comptroller of the Currency. Its History,
Activities, and Organization. Baltimore,
1926.

Helderman, Leonard C. National and State
Banks. A Study of their Origins. Boston, 1931.

Hendrick, Burton J. The Age of Big Business. New Haven, 1921.

Henrich, F. K., O. Handlin, L. Hartz, and
M. S. Heath. "The Development of American Laissez Faire" in The Tasks of Economic History. Supplement to the Jour.
Econ. Hist., Vol. III (1943).

[Henshaw, David.] Remarks upon the Bank
of the United States, being an Examination of the Report of the Committee of
Ways and Means Made to Congress, April,
1830. By a Merchant. Boston, 1831.

Henshaw, David. Mr. Henshaw's Reply to the
Report of the Legislative Committee for
Investigating the Concerns of the Common-
wealth Bank. Boston, 1838.

[Henshaw, David.] Remarks on Banks and
Banking and the Skeleton of a Project for
a National Bank, by a Citizen of Boston.
Boston, 1840.

Hepburn, A. Barton. A History of Currency
in the United States. New York, 1915.

Herrick, Cheesman A. Stephen Girard,
Founder. Philadelphia, 1932.

Herrick, Clay. Trust Companies. Their Organization, Growth and Management. 2nd
edition, New York, 1915.

Herrick, Clay. Trust Departments in Banks
and Trust Companies. New York, 1925.

Herrick, Myron T. "The Panic of 1907 and Some of its Lessons" in Annals of the Am. Acad. of Pol. and Soc. Sci., Vol. XXXI (1908).

Herrick, Myron T., and R. Ingalls. Rural Credits, Land and Cooperative. New York, 1916.

Herzog, Peter W. The Morris Plan of Industrial Banking. New York, 1928.

Hidy, Ralph W. "The Union Bank of Louisiana Loan 1832. A Case Study in Marketing" in Jour. Pol. Econ., Vol. XLVII (1939).

Hidy, Ralph W. "A Leaf from Investment History," in Harvard Bus. Rev., Vol. XX (1941).

Hidy, Ralph W. "The Organization and Functions of Anglo-American Merchant Bankers, 1815-1860," in The Tasks of Economic History. Supplement to the Jour. Econ. Hist., Vol. I (1941).

Hidy, Ralph W. "The House of Baring and the Second Bank of the United States, 1826-1836," in Pa. Mag. Hist. and Biogr., Vol. LXVIII (1944).

Hildreth, Richard. History of Banks: to which is Added a Demonstration of the Advantages and Neccessity of Free Competition in the Business of Banking. Boston, 1837.

Hildreth, Richard. Banks, Banking, and Paper Currencies. Boston, 1840.

Hildreth, Richard. A Letter to his Excellency Marcus Morton on Banking and the Currency. Boston, 1840.

Hinchman, T. H. Banks and Banking in Michigan, with Historical Sketches.... Detroit, 1887.

Hobson, Charles K. The Export of Capital. London, 1914.

Hoggson, Noble F. Epochs in American Banking. New York, 1929.

Holdsworth, John T., and Davis R. Dewey. The First and Second Banks of the United States. Washington, 1910.

Holdsworth, John T. Financing an Empire; History of Banking in Pennsylvania. Chicago, 1928.

Homans, Isaac Smith, editor. The Banker's Common-Place Book. Boston, 1851.

Hone, Philip. The Diary of...1828-1851. New York, 1889.

Hook, Sidney. The Hero in History. A Study in Limitation and Possibility. New York, 1943.

Hooper, Samuel. "Specie Currency. The True Interests of the People." Boston, 1855. (A reprint from the Boston Transcript.)

[Hooper, Samuel.] Currency or Money; its Nature and Uses...by a merchant of Boston. Boston, 1855.

Hooper, Samuel. An Examination of the Theory and the Effect of Laws regulating the Amount of Specie in Banks. Boston, 1860.

Hopkins, Mark. A Discourse Commemorative of Amos Lawrence. Boston, 1853.

Horsefield, John K. "The Duties of a Banker. The 18th Century View," in Economica, (New Series), Vol. VIII (1941).

Hovey, Carl. The Life Story of J. Pierpont Morgan; A Biography. New York, 1912.

Hubert, Philip G., Jr. The Merchants' National Bank of the City of New York, 1803-1903. New York, 1903.

Hume, Joseph. An Account of the Provident Institution for Savings, established in the Western Part of the Metropolis. London, 1816.

Hunt, Freeman. Lives of American Merchants. New York, 1858.

Huntington, Charles C. "A History of Banking and Currency in Ohio before the Civil War," in Ohio Arch. and Hist. Quart., Vol. XXIV (1915).

Huntington, Pelatiah W. "A History of Banking in Ohio," in Ohio Arch. and Hist. Quart., Vol. XXIII (1914).

Hurd, John R. A National Bank, or No Banks; An Appeal.... New York, 1842.

Huse, Charles P. The Financial History of Boston from May 1, 1822 to January 31, 1909. Cambridge, 1916.

Huston, Francis M. Financing an Empire; History of Banking in Illinois. Chicago, 1926.

Hutcheson, Harold. Tench Coxe; a Study in American Economic Development. Baltimore, 1938.

Ingersoll, Charles J. Pennsylvania Convention, Minority Report of a Special Committee on the Subjects of the Currency and Corporations...Read May 23, 1837. Harrisbur, 1837.

Ingersoll, Joseph R. Memoir of the Late Samuel Breck. Philadelphia, 1863.

Jackson, Andrew. Messages. Boston, 1837.

Jackson, Andrew. "Letters and Papers of..." in Bulletin of the New York Public Library, Vol. IV (1900).

Jackson, Andrew. Correspondence of...,
    edited by John Spencer Bassett. Washing-
    ton, 1926.
Jackson, C. C., and A. S. Pier, "Charles
    Stebbins Fairchild" in Harvard Graduates'
    Magazine, Vol. XXXIII (1925).
James, F. Cyril. The Growth of Chicago
    Banks. New York, 1938.
James, F. Cyril. The Economics of Money,
    Credit and Banking. 3rd ed., New York,
    1940.
James, F. Cyril. "The Bank of North Ameri-
    ca and the Financial History of Phila-
    delphia" in Pa. Mag. Hist. and Biogr.,
    Vol. LXIV (1940).
James, Marquis. The Life of Andrew Jack-
    son. New York, 1938.
James, William. "Great Men and Their En-
    vironment" in Selected Papers on Philoso-
    phy. London, 1927.
Jauncy, J. J. "State Bank of Ohio" in
    Magazine of Western History, Vol. II
    (1885).
Jenks, Leland H. The Migration of British
    Capital to 1875. New York, 1927.
Jennings, Walter W. "Stephen Girard,
    Philadelphia Merchant and Banker," in
    Social Science, Vol. XVII (1942).
Jensen, Merrill. "The Idea of a National
    Government" in Pol. Sci. Quart., Vol.
    LVIII (1943).
Jewett, Isaac. Memoir of Samuel Appleton.
    Boston, 1850.
Jèze, Gaston. "Die Technik des öffentlich-
    en Kredits," in Handbuch der Finanzwis-
    senschaft, (ed. Wilhelm Gerloff and
    Franz Meisel), Vol. II, Tübingen, 1927.
Johnson, Alexander B. An Inquiry into the
    Nature of Value and Capital and into the
    Operation of Government Loans, Banking
    Institutions and Private Credit. New
    York, 1813.
Johnson, Alexander B. A Treatise on Bank-
    ing: The Duties of a Banker and his Per-
    sonal Requisites therefor. Utica, 1850.
Johnson, Edgar A. J. Predecessors of Adam
    Smith, New York, 1937.
Johnson, Reverdy. Reply to a Pamphlet en-
    titled "A Brief Exposition of Matters
    Relating to the Bank of Maryland" with
    an Examination into Some of the Causes of
    the Bankruptcy. Baltimore, 1835.
Jonas, Nathan S. Through the Years. An
    Autobiography. New York. 1940.
Jones, Breckinridge. "One Hundred Years of
    Banking in Missouri," in The Missouri
    Hist. Rev., Vol. XV (1921).

Jones, Thatcher C. Clearings and Collec-
    tions, Foreign and Domestic. New York,
    1931.
[Jones, William.] A Brief Review of the
    Origin, Progress and Administration of the
    Bank of the United States, by a Friendly
    Monitor. Philadelphia, 1819.
[Joplin, T.] A Digest of the Evidence on
    the Bank Charter Taken before the Commit-
    tee of 1832. London, 1833.

Kahn, Otto H. Reflections of a Financier.
    A Study of Economic and Other Problems.
    London, 1921.
Kahn, Otto H. Immediate Problems, an address
    delivered...December 12, 1922. Publ. by
    the Committee of American Businessmen,
    New York.
Kane, Thomas P. The Romance and Tragedy of
    Banking. 2nd ed., New York, 1923.
Kaplan, A. D. H. Henry Charles Carey. A
    Study in American Economic Thought.
    (Johns Hopkins Univ. Studies in Hist.
    and Pol. Sci., XLIX). Baltimore, 1831.
[Kellogg, Edward.] Currency: The Evil
    and the Remedy. 4th ed., improved, 1844.
Kemmerer, Edwin Walter. Seasonal Variations
    in the Relative Demands for Money and
    Capital in the United States. Washington,
    1910.
Kemmerer, Edwin Walter. "New Jersey Bank-
    ing, 1902-1927" in Journal of Industry
    and Finance (1928).
Kennedy, John P. Quodlibet containing some
    Annals thereof...2d ed., Philadelphia,
    1860.
Kent, Frank R. The Story of Alexander
    Brown & Sons. Baltimore. 1925.
Kerr, Andrew W. History of Banking in
    Scotland. London, 1902.
Keyes, Emerson W. Special Report on Savings
    Banks Made by...and Transmitted to the
    Legislature by the Superintendent [of
    Banks].... Albany, 1868.
Keyes, Emerson W. Opinion of the Attorney
    General of the United States on the Con-
    version of National Banks to State Banks
    with a Review of the Same. Albany, 1870.
Keyes, Emerson W. A History of Savings
    Banks in the United States. New York,
    1876.
King, Horatio. Turning on the Light.
    Philadelphia, 1895.
Kinley, David. The History, Organization
    and Influence of the Independent Treasury
    of the United States. Boston, 1893.
Kinley, David. The Independent Treasury

of the United States and its Relations
to the Banks of the Country. Washington,
1910.

Kinsella, Thomas. National Banks; What
shall be Substituted for Them. An
Address on Currency Reform. Brooklyn,
1882.

Knapp, Samuel L. The Life of Thomas Eddy.
London, 1836.

Knapp, Shepherd. Letter to the Stockholders of the Mechanics' Bank--in Reply to
the Defence of Francis W. Edmonds, their
Late Cashier. New York, 1855.

Kniffin, William H. Commercial Banking.
New York, 1923.

Knowles, Charles E. History of the Bank
for Savings in the City of New York,
1819-1929. New York, 1929.

Knox, John Jay. The Surplus and the Public
Debt, Address at Annual Convention of the
American Bankers' Assn. at Pittsburgh, Pa.,
October 12th, 1887. New York, 1887.

Knox, John Jay. A Permanent National Bank
Circulation. An Interview between the
Committee on Banking and Currency, House
of Representatives, and John Jay Knox on
the 16th day of January, 1890. Washington, 1890.

Knox, John Jay. A History of Banking in
the United States. New York, 1900.

Kohler, Max James. Haym Salomon, the
Patriot Broker of the Revolution, His
Real Achievements and their Exaggera-
tion. An Open Letter to Congressman
Celler. [n. p.] 1931.

Konkle, Burton A. Thomas Willing and the
First American Financial System. Philadelphia, 1937.

Krueger, Leonard B. History of Commercial
Banking in Wisconsin. (Univ. of Wis.
Studies in the Soc. Sci. and Hist., No.
18). Madison, 1933.

Kuhn, Ludwig K. Die Zeitlichkeit der
Unternehmung. Tübingen, 1938.

Lake, Wilfred S. The History of Banking
Regulation in Massachusetts, 1784-1860.
Unpub. Ph.D. thesis, Harvard Univ., 1932.

Lamont, Thomas W. Henry P. Davison. The
Record of a Useful Life. New York, 1933.

Landman, Julius. "Geschichte des Öffentlichen Kredites," in Handbuch der Finanz-
wissenschaft (ed. Wilhelm Gerloff and
Franz Meisel), Vol. II, Tübingen, 1927,

Langford, Laura C. Holloway. Famous American Fortunes and the Men who have Made
Them. New York, 1889.

Lanier, Henry Wysham. A Century of Banking
in New York, 1822-1922. New York, 1922.

Lanier, James F. D. The Financial Condition and Resources of the United States.
New York, 1865.

Lanier, James F. D. Sketch of the Life of...
(Printed for the use of his family only.)
New York, 1870.

Larson, Henrietta M. "S & M Allen--
Lottery, Exchange, and Stock Brokerage,"
in Jour. of Econ. and Bus. Hist., Vol. III
(1930/31).

Larson, Henrietta M. "E. W. Clark & Co.,
1837-1857. The Beginning of an American
Private Bank," in Jour. Econ. and Bus.
Hist., Vol. IV (1931/32).

Larson, Henrietta M. Jay Cooke, Private
Banker. Cambridge, Mass., 1936.

Laughlin, J. Laurence. "The 'Baltimore
Plan' of Bank Issues," in Jour. of Pol.
Econ., Vol. III (1894/95).

Laughlin, J. Laurence. A New Exposition of
Money, Credit and Prices. Chicago, 1931.

[Law, Thomas]. Remarks on the Report of the
Secretary of the Treasury....Wilmington,
Del., 1820.

Law, Thomas. An Address, delivered before
the Columbian Institute, Dec. 17, 1825.
Washington, 1825.

[Lawrence, William B.]. "The Bank of the
United States," in The North American
Rev., Vol. XXXII (1831).

[Lawrence, William B.]. "The Public Distress," in Amer. Quart. Rev., Vol. XV
(1834).

Leach, Josiah G. The History of the Girard
National Bank of Philadelphia, 1832-1902.
Philadelphia, 1902.

Leavenworth, Elias W. A Genealogy of the
Leavenworth Family... [containing sketch
of Joshua Forman]. Syracuse, 1873.

[Lee, Henry]. An Exposition of Facts and
Arguments in Support of a Memorial to the
Legislature of Massachusetts, by Citizens
of Boston and Vicinity in Favor of a Bank
of Ten Millions. Boston, 1836.

Legaré, Hugh S. "Spirit of the Subtreasury.
Speech....delivered in the House of Repre-
sentatives...1837," in Writings, Vol. I,
Charleston, 1846.

Lelong, A. A. Reminiscences Culled from the
Annals of the Citizens Bank of Louisiana.
New Orleans, 1911.

Lewins, William. A History of Banks for
Savings in Great Britain and Ireland.
London, 1866.

Lewis, Lawrence, Jr. A History of the

Bank of North America. Philadelphia, 1882.

Lippincott, Joanna Wharton. Biographical Memorandum Concerning Joseph Wharton, 1826-1909. Philadelphia, 1909.

Lincoln, Charles Z. The Constitutional History of New York. Vol. II. 1822-1894. Rochester, N. Y., 1906.

Livermore, Shaw. Early Land Companies, Their Influence on Corporate Development. New York, 1939.

Logan, Robert R. "Early Banking in New Mexico," in New Mexico Business Rev., Vol. IX (1940).

Lord, D., Jr. Examination of the Charges of the Board of Trade against the Phenix Bank. New York, 1838.

Lord, Eleazar. Principles of Currency and Banking. New York, 1829.

Lord, Eleazar. On Credit, Currency and Banking. [2nd edition of Principles of Currency and Banking] New York, 1834.

Lord, Eleazar. A Letter on National Currency addressed to the Secretary of the Treasury. New York, 1861.

Lord, Eleazar. Six Letters on the Necessity and Practicability of a National Currency and the Principles and Measures Essential to it. New York, 1862.

Lowell, John Amory. Review of Mr. Hooper's Pamphlet on Specie Reserves. Boston, 1860.

Loyd, Samuel Jones (Lord Overstone), Tracts and Other Publications on Metallic and Paper Currency. London, 1857.

Lutwyche, Alfred. An Enquiry into the Causes of Commercial Panics and Bad Trade. Birmingham (before 1864). [Contains the same author's A Suggestion of a Plan for Extending the Currency. Birmingham, 1857.]

Lutz, Karola. Die Geschichtliche Entwicklung der Europäischen Hochfinanz vom Mittelalter bis zum Beginnenden 19. Jahrhundert. München, 1934.

Lyford, James O. "The Savings Banks of New Hampshire," in Davis, William T., editor, The New England States, Vol. III, Boston, 1897.

McCabe, Robert L. A Central Bank of Issue for the United States. Dayton, Ohio, 1908.

McClurkin, A. J. "Summary of the Bank of North America Records," in Pa. Mag. Hist. and Biogr., Vol. LXIV (1940).

McCulloch, Albert J. "The Loan Office Experiment in Missouri, 1821-1836." (Univ. of Missouri Bulletin, XV, Social Science Series 1.). Columbia, 1914.

McCulloch, Hugh. Men and Measures of Half a Century. New York, 1900.

M'Duffie, George. Speech on the Subject of the Removal of the Deposites, Dec. 19, 1833. Washington, 1833.

M'Duffie, George. Remarks delivered in the House of Representatives on April 3 and 4, 1834 on the Resolutions taken by the Committee of Ways and Means in Relation to the Public Deposites. Washington, 1834.

McElroy, Robert. Levi Parsons Morton. Banker, Diplomat and Statesman. New York, 1930.

McFerrin, John B. Caldwell and Company. A Southern Financial Empire. Chapel Hill, 1939.

McGrane, Reginald C., editor. The Correspondence of Nicholas Biddle Dealing with National Affairs, 1807-1844. Boston, 1919.

McGrane, Reginald C. The Panic of 1837. Chicago, 1824.

McGrane, Reginald C. Foreign Bondholders and American State Debts. New York, 1935.

MacIver, R. M. "History and Social Causation," in Jour. Econ. Hist., Vol. III (1943), Supplement.

MacLeod, Henry Dunning. A History of Banking in Great Britain, (A History of Banking in all the Leading Nations, Vol. II). New York, 1876.

MacMaster, John B. "Wildcat Banking in the Teens," Atlantic Monthly, Vol. LXXII (1893).

McMaster, John B. The Life and Times of Stephen Girard, Mariner and Merchant. Philadelphia, 1918.

[McVickar, John.] Hints on Banking in a Letter to a Gentleman in Albany, by a New Yorker. New York, 1827.

[McVickar, John] "Importance of a National Bank," in The New York Rev., Vol. VIII (1841).

Madeleine, Sister M. Grace. Monetary and Banking Theories of Jacksonian Democracy. Philadelphia, 1943.

Magee, James D. "Historical Analogy to the Fight against Par Check Collection," in Jour. Pol. Econ., Vol. XXI (1923).

Malone, Dumas. The Public Life of Thomas Cooper, 1783-1839. New Haven, 1926.

Manchester, Herbert. A Century of Service. The Seaman's Bank for Savings 1829-1929. [New York], 1929.

Mann, Abijah. Correspondence between A. Mann Jr. and Hon. A. C. Flagg in Relation to the General Bank Law of New York. Brooklyn, 1868.

Marcosson, Isaac F. "The Millionaire Yield of Philadelphia," in Munsey's Magazine, Vol. XVIII (1912).

Marcosson, Isaac, F. "The Millionaire Yield of Boston," in Munsey's Magazine, Vol. XVIII (1912).

Massachusetts, Commonwealth of. Second Report of the Bank Investigating Committee...House Document No. 62 (1836).

Maynard, William H. A Speech Delivered in the Senate of New York on the 3d and 4th of February 1832 on the Resolution against Renewing the Charter of the Bank of the United States. Albany, 1832.

Mayo, Robert. A Chapter of Sketches on Finance; with an Appendix...Baltimore, 1837.

Medberry, James K. Men and Mysteries of Wall Street. Boston, 1870.

Memminger, Christopher G. Speech of...in the House of Representatives of South Carolina upon the Bill and Resolutions Relating to Bank Issues and Suspensions, December 1857. Charleston, S. C., 1858.

Merritt, Fred D. The Early History of Banking in Iowa. Iowa City, 1900.

Miller, Harry E. Banking Theories in the United States before 1860. Cambridge, 1927.

Michener, John H. The Bank of North America, Philadelphia. A National Bank Founded in 1781. The Story of its Progress through the Last Quarter of a Century, 1881-1906. New York, 1906.

Million, John W. "The Debate on the National Bank Act of 1863," in Jour. Pol Econ., Vol. II (1893/94).

Millsaps, R. W. "History of Banking in Mississippi," in Sound Currency, Vol. X (1903).

Mints, Lloyd W. A History of Banking Theory in Great Britain and the United States. Chicago, 1945.

Mitchell, Mary H. A Century and a Half of Banking in New Haven. The New Haven Bank, National Banking Association, 1792-1942. New Haven, 1942.

Mitchell, Wesley C. A History of the Greenbacks. Chicago, 1903.

Moore, Joseph, Jr. Historical Address at the Banquet...1908, to celebrate the 50th Anniversary of the First Exchange by the Clearing House Association of Philadel-phia, Philadelphia, 1908.

Morawetz, Victor. Address on the Currency Question Delivered at the Dinner of the Boston Economic Club, Dec. 19, 1907. Boston, 1907.

Morawetz, Victor. The Currency Question. 2d edition, New York, 1907.

Morawetz, Victor. Address on the Banking and Currency Problem and the Central Bank Plan, Delivered at the Finance Forum of the West Side Y.M.C.A., New York, November 24, 1909. New York, 1909.

Morgan, E. Victor. The Theory and Practice of Central Banking, 1793-1913. Cambridge, England, 1943.

Morris, Gouverneur. The Diary and Letters of..., edited by Anne Cary Morris. New York, 1888.

Morris, Henry C. The History of the First National Bank of Chicago. Chicago, 1902.

Morris, John B. Memorial to the Legislature of Maryland [regarding Bank of Maryland]. Baltimore, 1836.

Morse, John T., Jr. Memoir of Colonel Henry Lee. Boston, 1905.

Mott, T. Bentley. Myron T. Herrick. Friend of France. Garden City, New York, 1930.

Mottram, Ralph H. A History of Financial Speculation. Boston, 1929.

Moulton, R. K. Legislative and Documentary History of the Banks of the United States. New York, 1834.

Mowat, R. B. Americans in England. Boston, 1935.

Mudge, Eugene T. The Social Philosophy of John Taylor of Caroline. New York, 1939.

Murphy, Thomas F. History of the First National Bank of Scranton, Pa., 1863-1938. Scranton, Pa., 1938.

Muscalus, John A. The Use of Banking Enterprises in the Financing of Public Education, 1796-1866. (Ph.D. Thesis, University of Pennsylvania.) Philadelphia, 1945.

Mussey, Henry R., editor. "The Reform of the Currency" in Proc. of the Academy of Pol Sci., Vol. I (1911).

Myers, Gustavus. The Ending of Hereditary American Fortunes. New York, 1939.

Myers, Margaret G. The New York Money Market, Vol. I: Origins and Development. New York, 1931.

National Industrial Conference Board. The International Financial Position of the United States. New York, 1929.

Nef, John U. "What is Economic History?" in Jour. Econ. Hist., Vol. IV (1944), Supplement.

Nevins, Allan. History of the Bank of New York and Trust Company, 1784-1934. New York, 1934.

New York, State of. Messages from the Governors...edited by Charles Z. Lincoln. Vol. III (1823-1842). Albany, 1909.

New York Clearing House. Proceedings of a Meeting...Nov. 12, 1878.

New York Loan Committee. "Report...of Proceedings in Connexion [sic!] with the Government Loan of 1861," in U.S. 37th Congr., 3d sess., House Exec. Document 25.

Nicolson, Harold. Dwight Morrow. New York, 1935.

Normanno, J. F., The Spirit of American Economics. New York, 1943.

North Carolina. Report of the Joint Select Committee [of the Legislature of North Carolina, January 6, 1841] on the Suspension of Specie Payments by the Banks. Doc. No. 30.

Noyes, Alexander D. Forty Years of American Finance. New York, 1909.

Noyes, Alexander D. History of the National Bank Currency. Washington, 1910.

Noyes, Alexander D. "Methods and Leadership in Wall Street since 1893," in Jour. Econ. and Bus. Hist., Vol. IV (1931/32).

Noyes, Edward A. "The Discount Banks of Maine," and "The Savings Banks of Maine," in Davis, William T., editor, The New England States, Vol. III, Boston, 1897.

Oberholtzer, Ellis P. Robert Morris. Patriot and Financier. New York, 1903.

Oberholtzer, Ellis P. Jay Cooke, Financier of the Great War. Philadelphia, 1907.

O'Connor, Harvey. Mellon's Millions. New York, 1933.

O'Connor, Harvey. The Guggenheims. New York, 1937.

[Ogden, James De Peyster.] Remarks on the Currency of the United States and the Present State and the Future Perspective of the Community, by Publius. New York, 1840.

[Ogden, James De Peyster.] Additional Remarks on the Currency of the United States, by Publius. New York, 1841.

[Ogden, James De Peyster.] The Crisis and the Remedy, by Publius. New York. 1842.

Ohio. Auditor. Report of the Auditor of the State to the 34th General Assembly Relative to the State and Condition of Certain Banks of the State of Ohio. Columbus, Ohio, 1836.

Ohio. Report of the Joint Committee of Both Houses of the General Assembly of Ohio on the Communication of the Auditor upon the Subject of the Proceeding of the Bank of the United States against the Officers of the State in the U. S. Circuit Court. Columbus, Ohio, 1821.

O'Neall, John B. Biographical Sketches of the Bench and Bar of South Carolina. Charleston, 1859.

Opdyke, George. A Treatise on Political Economy. New York, 1851.

Opdyke, George. A Report on the Currency. New York, 1858.

Opdyke, George, and others. A Report on the Currency, May 16, 1859. New York, 1859.

Osgood, Gayton P. Speech Delivered in the House of Representatives May 5, 1834 on the Memorial of a Convention...in favor of the Restoration of the Deposites... to the Bank of the United States. Washington, 1834.

Ostrolenk, Bernhard. The Economics of Branch Banking. New York, 1930.

Pacificus, (pseud.). What will Congress Do? Philadelphia, 1837.

Paine, Thomas. Dissertations on Government, the Affairs of the Bank and Paper Money, [1786]. London, 1817.

Paine, Willis S. The Laws of the State of New York Relating to Banks, Banking... 7th Edition, New York, 1917.

Palyi, Melchior. The Chicago Credit Market Organization and Institutional Structure. Chicago, 1937.

Pargellis, Stanley. The Judgment of History on American Business. 1943.

Parks, Joseph H. Felix Grundy. Champion of Democracy. University, Louisiana, 1940.

Parnell, Henry Brooke, 1st Baron Congleton. Observations on Paper Money, Banking, and Overtrading...which explain the Scotch System of Banking. 2nd edition, London, 1829.

Parrington, Vernon L. Main Currents in American Thought. New York, 1927.

Parvin, T. S. "Thomas Hart Benton, Jr.," in Iowa Hist. Record, Vol. XVI, (1900).

Patchin, Sydney A. "The Development of Banking in Minnesota," in Minnesota History Bulletin, Vol. II (1917).

[Peabody, Oliver William Bourn.] "Bank of the United States," in The North American Rev., Vol. XXXV (1832).

Peach, W. Nelson. The Security Affiliates of National Banks. (The Johns Hopkins Univ. Studies in Hist. and Pol. Sci.,

LVIII), Baltimore, 1941.

Pearson, Henry G. Son of New England. James Jackson Storrow, 1864-1926. Boston, 1932.

Pearson, Paul M., editor. Intercollegiate Debates, Vol. I, New York, 1909.

Pease, Theodore C. The Frontier State, 1818-1848. (The Centennial History of Illinois, Vol. II), Springfield, Illinois, 1918.

Pease, Zephaniah W. The Centenary of the Merchants National Bank. New Bedford, Mass., 1925.

Pell, Ferris. Letter to Albert Gallatin, Esq. On the Doctrine of Gold and Silver, and the Evils of the Present Banking System in Effect and Tendency. New York, 1815.

Perine, Edward T. The Story of the Trust Companies. New York, 1916.

Perry, Bliss. Life and Letters of Henry Lee Higginson. Boston, 1921.

Perry, Elizabeth W. "Micajah Terrel Williams," in the 'Old North West' Genealogical Quarterly, January, 1898.

Perspective (pseud.). The Changery. An Allegoric Memoir of the Boston Exchange Office: or, the Pernicious Progress of Bank Speculation Unveiled. Boston, 1805.

Peterson, Jaffray. Sixty-five Years of Progress. A Brief History of the Continental Bank and Trust Company of New York and a Record of New York City Banks. New York, 1935.

Playfair, William. Letter to Sir W. Pulteney...on the Establishment of another Public Bank in London. London, 1797.

Plehn, Carl C. The San Francisco Clearing House Certificates of 1907-1908. Berkeley, Cal., 1909.

Phillips, Henry, Jr. Historical Sketches of the Paper Currency. Roxbury, Mass., 1865.

Pintard, John. "Letters from...to his Daughter, Eliza Noel Pintard Davidson," in New York Hist. Soc. Coll., Vol. LXX - LXXIII (1937-40).

Poage, George R. Henry Clay and the Whig Party. Chapel Hill, 1936.

Popple, Charles S. Development of Two Bank Groups in the Central Northwest. Cambridge, 1944.

Porter, Alexander. Speech in Opposition to the Motion made by Mr. Benton to Expunge from the Journal of the Senate the Resolution...disapproving of the Removal of Deposites by the President. Washington, 1836.

Porter, Henry H. H.H. Porter; A Short Autobiography. Chicago, 1915.

Porter, Kenneth W. John Jacob Astor, Business Man. Cambridge, 1931.

Potter, Orlando B. Plan for Appreciating the National Back Notes to the Values of Coin ... Also a Plan of the National Bank Currency Based upon, and Secured by the National Stocks, submitted to Secretary Chase, August 14th, 1861. New York, 1875.

Potter, Orlando B. The National Currency. Its Origin. New York, 1883.

Poultney, Evan. An Appeal to the Creditors of the Bank of Maryland and the Public generally. Baltimore, 1835.

Pound, Arthur. Native Stock. The Rise of the American Spirit Seen in Six Lives. New York, 1931.

Pound, Arthur. Murals in the State Bank of Albany ... including a Short History of the Founding of the Bank. 1943.

Prentiss, George L. "A Sketch of the Life and Public Services of Charles Butler, LL.D.," in his The Union Theological Seminary in the City of New York ... Ashbury Park, New Jersey, 1899.

Preston, Howard H. History of Banking in Iowa. Iowa City, 1922.

Preston, Howard H. "Bank of America," in Jour. of Econ. and Bus. Hist., Vol. IV (1931/32).

Price, Hiram. "The State Bank of Iowa," in Annals of Iowa, 3rd series, Vol. I (1893).

Publicola, pseud. Vindication of the Currency of the State of New York... Addressed to the Hon. Isaac Pierson. 1818.

Putnam, James William. The Illinois and Michigan Canal; A Study in Economic History. Chicago, 1918.

Quincy, Edmund. "Notice of Horace Binney," in The Report of the Council of the American Academy of Arts and Sciences, May 1876. Boston, 1876.

Rafinesque, Constantine S. Safe Banking, including the Principles of Wealth. Philadelphia, 1837.

Raguet, Condy. An Inquiry into the Causes of the Present State of the Circulatory Medium of the United States. Philadelphia, 1815.

Raguet, Condy. "Report on the Renewal of Bank Charters made to the Senate of

Pennsylvania by ... Chairman on the 15th of January 1821," in Examiner, Vol. II (1834/35).

Raguet, Condy. "Report of the Committee of the Senate of Pennsylvania, appointed to enquire into the extent and causes of the present general distress," in Financial Register, Vol. II (1838).

Raguet, Condy. A Treatise on Currency and Banking. London, 1839. 2nd edition, Philadelphia, 1840.

Randall, Emilius O. and David J. Ryan. History of Ohio; the Rise and Progress of an American State. New York, 1912.

Ravell, Charles H. Sixty Years of Banking in Michigan. Battle Creek, Mich., 1910.

Raymond, Daniel. Thoughts on Political Economy. Baltimore, 1820.

Rerick, Rowland H. Memoirs of Florida. Atlanta, Ga., 1902.

Reynolds, George M. and George E. Roberts. The Central Bank Idea. Minneapolis, 1910(?)

Ricardo, David. Proposals for an Economical and Secure Currency; with Observations ..... London, 1816.

Ricardo, David. Plan for the Establishment of a National Bank. London, 1824.

Ricardo, Samson. A National Bank. The Remedy for the Evils Attendant upon our Present System of Paper Currency. London, 1838.

Rist, Charles. History of Monetary and Credit Theory from John Law to the Present Day. New York, 1940.

Rives, William C. Speech on the Subject of the Removal of the Deposites delivered in the Senate of the United States, January 17, 1834. Washington, 1834.

Robbins, Chandler. Memoir of Hon. William Appleton. Boston, 1863.

Roberts, George E. A Central Bank of Issue. An address delivered before the Nebraska State Bankers' Assn. Omaha, Sept. 19, 1907. Chicago, 1907.

Robin, Thomas E. and William C. Smedes. An Inquiry into the Validity of the Bonds of the State of Mississippi issued in behalf of the Union Bank of Mississippi. New York, 1847.

Rochester, Anne. Rulers of America; A Study of Finance Capital. New York, 1936.

Rockwood, Charles G. One Hundred Years; a Record of the Work of the Oldest Bank in the State of New Jersey, the National Newark Banking Co. Newark, N.J., 1904.

[Ronaldson, James.] Review of the Veto, containing an Examination of the Principles of the President's Message... Philadelphia, 1832.

[Ronaldson, James.] Banks and a Paper Currency; their Effects upon Society, by a Friend of the People. Philadelphia, 1857. Originally published as Elements of a Bank Charter... Louisville, 1832.

Roosevelt, Clinton. The Mode of Protecting Domestic Industry... by Operating on the Currency. New York, 1833

Roosevelt, Clinton. The Mode of Protecting Domestic Industries... The Science of Government, founded on National Law ... Paradox of Political Economy. New York, 1889.

Root, L. Carroll. "New York Bank Currency," in Sound Currency, Vol. II (1895).

Root, L. Carroll. "States as Bankers," in Sound Currency, Vol. II (1895).

Root, L. Carroll. "New England Bank Currency," in Sound Banking, Vol. II (1895).

Root, L. Carroll. "Early Banks of Issue in Wisconsin," in Sound Currency, Vol. V (1898).

Root, Erastus. The Speeches on the Resolution of Mr. Clayton of Georgia proposing a Committee of Visitation to the Bank of the United States. Delivered March 7, 8, and 14, 1832 in the House of Representatives. 1832.

Ropes, Joseph S. "Currency, Banking and Credit," in The New Englander, Vol. XVI (1858).

Ropes, Joseph S. The Currency. Boston, 1868.

Rose, George. Observations on Banks for Savings. 3d edition, London, 1816.

Rosenberg, Hans. Die Weltwirtschaftskrisis von 1857-1859. Stuttgart, 1934.

Rowland, Dunbar. "Banking," in Vol. I of Encyclopedia of Mississippi History (Madison, Wis., 1907).

Royall, William L. A History of Virginia Banks and Banking Prior to the Civil War. New York, 1907.

Ruffin, Edmund (editor). Bank Reformer, Nos. 1-6 (Sept. 4, 1841 - Feb. 5, 1842).

Ruggles, Charles A. The Boston Clearing House Method of Handling Outside Checks and its Advantages. 3d edition, Boston, 1912.

Rutherfoord, John C. Speech ... on the Banking Policy of Virginia ... Richmond, 1856

St. Georges, A. Reflexions sur les Banques

aux Etats Unis envoyees à J.P. Poutz en Septembre 1835. Nouvelle Orléans, 1843.

Sandburg, Carl. Abraham Lincoln. New York, 1940.

Satterlee, Herbert L. J. Pierpont Morgan; An Intimate Portrait. New York, 1939.

Schlesinger, Arthur M. "Biography of a Nation of Joiners," in Amer. Hist. Rev., Vol. L (1944).

Schlesinger, Arthur M., Jr. The Age of Jackson. Boston, 1946.

Scott, James Brown. Robert Bacon, Life and Letters. Garden City, N.Y., 1923.

Scoville, Joseph A. The Old Merchants of New York City. 5 series, New York, 1863-70.

Scroggs, William O. The Financial History of Alabama, 1819-1860. Unpublished Harvard Ph.D. Thesis, 1911.

Scroggs, William O. A Century of Banking Progress. Garden City, N.Y., 1924.

Scroggs, William O. "Pioneer Banking in Alabama," in Facts and Factors in Economic History. Articles of former students of Edwin Francis Gay. Cambridge, 1932.

Seligman, Edwin R.A. "The Early Teaching of Economics in the United States," in Economic Essays, contributed in honor of John Bates Clark. New York, 1927.

Semmes, John E. John H. B. Latrobe and his Times, 1803-1891. Baltimore, 1917.

Sergeant, John. Speech ... on the Resolution Reported from the Committee of Ways and Means declaring it inexpedient to charter a National Bank. Washington, 1837.

Shepley, Ethan. Removal of the Deposites; A Speech in the U.S. Senate, Feburary 14, 1834.

Sheppard, John H. Sketch of Hon. Nathan Appleton. Boston, 1862.

Shed, Henry P. Bank of Mutual Redemption, Statement of the Cashier. Boston, 1862.

Sherman, Franklin J. Modern Story of Mutual Savings Banks. New York, 1934.

Sherman, Hoyt. "Early Banking in Iowa," in Annals of Iowa, 3d series, Vol. V (1901).

Sherman, Hoyt. "The State Bank of Iowa," in Annals of Iowa, 3rd series, Vol. V (1901).

[Sherman, Roger M.] Letters to the Honourable Levi Woodbury, Secretary of the Treasury of the United States. New York, 1837.

Simon, Lemuel C. A Century of the National Bank of the Northern Liberties of Philadelphia, Pennsylvania. Philadelphia, 1910.

Simpson, Henry. Lives of Eminent Philadelphians, now deceased. Philadelphia, 1859.

Simpson, Stephen. Biography of Stephen Girard ... Philadelphia, 1832.

Smith, Adam. An Inquiry into the Nature and Causes of the Wealth of Nations--with a Life of the Author and Introductory Discourse by J.R. McCulloch. Edinburgh, 1828.

Smith, Arthur D. Howden. Men who Run America; a Study of the Capitalistic System ... Indianapolis, 1936.

Smith, Charles W. "Roger B. Taney and Mr. Biddle's Bank," in Maryland Hist. Mag., Vol. XXXI (1936).

Smith, J. Thomas. "The National Bank of Baltimore," in Bankers' Mag., Vol. LII (1896).

Smith, Rixey and Norman Beasley. Carter Glass: A Biography. New York, 1939.

Smith, Vera C. The Rationale of Central Banking. London, 1936.

Snyder, J.F. "Forgotten Statesman of Illinois, Richard M. Young," in Illinois State Hist. Library, Publication No. 11 (Springfield, 1906).

Southworth, Shirley Donald. Branch Banking in the United States. New York, 1928.

Spahr, Walter E. The Clearing and Collection of Checks. New York, 1926.

Sparks, Earl S. History and Theory of Agricultural Credit in the United States. New York, 1932.

Sparks, Jared. The Life of Gouverneur Morris with Selections from his Correspondence ... Boston, 1832.

Sparks, Jared, Editor. The Correspondence of the American Revolution. Boston, 1853.

Spaulding, Elbridge G. A Resource of War - The Credit of the Government made immediately available. History of the Legal Tender Paper Money issued during the Great Rebellion. Buffalo, 1869.

Spaulding, Elbridge G. Address ... at the Bank Officers' and Bankers' Building, Centennial Grounds, May 30, 1876. Philadelphia, 1876.

Sprague, O.M.W. History of Crises under the National Banking System. Washington, 1910.

Stackpole, Everett Birney. "State Banking in Maine," in Sound Currency, Vol. VII (1900).

Stansfeld, Hamer. Correspondence on

Monetary Panics with Honourable Amasa Walker, late Secretary of State for Massachusetts. 1860.

Stark, W. The Ideal Foundations of Economic Thought. Three Essays on the Philosophy of Economics. London, 1943.

Starnes, George T. "Sixty Years of Branch Banking in Virginia," in Jour. Pol. Econ., Vol. XXXVI (1928).

Starnes, George T. Sixty Years of Branch Banking in Virginia. New York, 1931.

Steiner, Bernard C. Life of Reverdy Johnson. Baltimore, 1914.

Steiner, Bernard C. Life of Roger Brooke Taney, Chief Justice of the United States Supreme Court. Baltimore, 1922.

Stephens, F.F. "Banking and Finance in Missouri in the Thirties," in Mississippi Valley Hist. Assn., Proceedings, Vol. X (1920-23).

Stetson, Amos W. Eighty Years; an Historical Sketch of the State Bank, 1811-1865; the State National Bank, 1865-1891. Boston, 1893.

Steuart, Sir James. Principles of Banks and Banking of Money, as Coin and Paper.. London, 1810. (Being Book III of his Inquiry into the Principles of Political Economy, London, 1767.)

Stevens, John Austin. Albert Gallatin. Boston, 1884.

Stevens, Marshall W. History of Lee, Higginson and Company. (Unpublished thesis, Harvard Business School, 1927.)

Stickles, Arndt M. "Relief Legislation and the Origin of the Court Controversy in Kentucky," in Studies in American History presented to James Albert Woodburn. Indiana Univ. Studies, Vol. XII (1925).

Stickney, William, editor. Autobiography of Amos Kendall. Boston, 1872.

Stillman, W. Paul. The Story of a Bank and of the Community it Serves. (National State Bank of Newark, N.J., 1812-1937). Clifton, N.J., 1937.

Stilwell, Silas M. A System of Credit for a Republic, and the Plan of a Bank for the State of New York. Albany, 1838.

Stilwell, Silas M. A System of National Finance. Notes Explanatory of Mr. Chase's Plan of National Finance. Washington, 1861.

Stilwell, Silas M. National Finances; a Philosophical Examination of Credit ... New York, 1866.

Stilwell, Silas M. The National Debt-

Currency. Letters ... to the Governor of Michigan and Others. Detroit, 1868.

Stokes, Howard Kenneth. "Chartered Banking in Rhode Island, 1791-1900," in Field, Edward, editor. State of Rhode Island and Providence Plantations at the Eve of the Century. Boston, 1902.

Stone, Edwin A. A Century of Boston Banking. Boston, 1894.

Stone, Edwin A. A Second Chapter in Boston Banking... Boston, 1906.

[Sullivan, James.] The Path to Riches. An Inquiry into the Origin and Use of Money... Boston, 1792.

Sumner, William Graham. A History of the American Currency. New York, 1874.

Sumner. William Graham. The Financier and the Finances of the American Revolution. New York, 1891.

Sumner, William Graham. A History of Banking in the United States. (Vol. I of A History of Banking in All the Nations.) New York, 1896.

Swanson, William W. "The Crisis of 1860 and the First Issue of Clearing House Loan Certificates," in Jour. Pol. Econ., Vol. XVI (1908).

Swanson, William W. The Establishment of the National Banking System. Kingston, 1910.

Swisher, Carl B. Roger B. Taney. New York, 1935.

Taus, Esther R. Central Banking Functions of the United States Treasury, 1789-1941. New York, 1943.

Taylor, Amos E. "Walker's Financial Mission to London on Behalf of the North, 1863-4," in Jour. Econ. and Bus. Hist., Vol III (1930/31).

Taylor, John. A Definition of Parties; or, the Political Effects of the Paper System Considered. Philadelphia, 1794.

[Taylor, John] An Enquiry into the Principles and Tendency of Certain Public Measures. Philadelphia, 1794.

Taylor, John. An Inquiry into the Principles and Policy of the Government of the United States. Fredericksburg, 1814.

Thomas, David Y. "Banking in the Territory of Florida," in The South Atlantic Quart., Vol. IX (1910).

Thomas, David Y. A History of Banking in Florida. Ms. in Univ. of Florida.

Thompson, John. Vice-president of the Chase National Bank of New York. Comments on

Currency. _A Plan for Perfecting and Perpetuating the National Bank System._ [187-].

Thon, Robert W., Jr. _Mutual Savings Banks in Baltimore._ (Johns Hopkins Univ. Studies in Hist. and Pol. Sci., LIII) Baltimore, 1935.

Thornton, Henry. _An Inquiry into the Nature and Effects of the Paper Credit of Great Britain._ Philadelphia, 1807.

Thralls, Jerome. _The Clearing House; Facts Covering the Origin...._ New York, 1916.

Tileston, Mary W. _Thomas Tileston, 1793-1864._ 1925.

Tostlebe, Alvin S. _The Bank of North Dakota; An Experiment in Agrarian Banking._ (Columbia Univ. Studies in Hist., Econ. and Publ. Law) New York, 1924.

Trotter, Alexander. _Observations on the Financial Position and Credit of such of the States of the North American Union as have contracted Public Debts._ London, 1839.

Trufant, Samuel A. "Review of Banking in New Orleans, 1830-1840." Louisiana Historical Society _Proceedings and Reports_, Vol. X, 1917.

Trumbull, James Hammond. _The First Essays at Banking and the First Paper Money in New England._ Worcester, Mass., 1884.

[Tucker, George (?)] "Bank of the United States," _in Amer. Quart. Rev._, Vol. IX (1831).

Tucker, George. _The Theory of Money and Banks Investigated._ Boston, 1839.

Tucker, George. "Banks or No Banks," in _Hunt's Merchants' Magazine_, Vol. XXXVIII (1858).

Twitchell, Ralph E. _The Leading Facts of New Mexican History_, especially Vol. V, pp. 258-278 (Banks and Banking).

Tyler, Lyon G. _The Letters and Times of the Tylers._ Richmond, Va., 1884-96.

Tyler, Samuel. _Memoir of Roger Brooke Taney, LL.D._ .... Baltimore, 1872.

Underhill, Hershel E. _The History of Kansas Banking._ Unpublished thesis, University of Kansas. 1930.

United States. Auditor. _Report of the Committee on Failed National Banks._ U.S., 52d Congr., 2d Sess., Senate Report 1286.

Usher, Abbott P. _The Early History of Deposit Banking in Mediterranean Europe._ Cambridge, Mass., 1943.

Utley, Henry M. "The Wild Cat Banking System of Michigan," in _Mich. Pioneer Coll._, Vol. V (1884).

Van Buren, Martin. _The Autobiography of ..._ Washington, 1920.

van Dillen, J.G. _The Economic History of the Netherlands and the Bank of Amsterdam, 1609-1820._ Amsterdam, 1929.

Van Dillen, J.G., editor. _History of the Principal Public Banks...._ The Hague, 1934.

Venit, Abraham H. "Isaac Bronson: His Banking Theory and the Financial Controversies of the Jacksonian Period," in _Jour. of Econ. Hist._, Vol. V (1945).

Viner, Jacob. _Studies in the Theory of International Trade._ New York, 1937.

Waldo, Dwight B. "A Sketch of the Origin, Establishment, and Workings of the National Banking System, with Special Reference to Issues." Mich. Pol. Sci. Assn. _Publications_, Vol. I (1893).

Walker, Amasa. _The Nature and Uses of Money and Mixed Currency...._ Boston, 1857.

Walker, Joseph B. "Banking and Currency in New Hampshire," in Davis, William T., editor, _The New England States._ Boston, 1897.

Walker, Robert J. "Review of our Finances, and of the Report of Hon.S.P. Chase...," in _Continental Monthly_, Vol. III (1862).

Walker, Robert J. _American Finances and Resources._ Letters 1-5.London, 1863/64.

Walley, Samuel H. _The Financial Revulsion of 1857. An Address..._ Boston, 1858.

Walsh, John Joseph. _Early Banks in the District of Columbia, 1792-1818._ (Catholic Univ. of America, Studies in Econ., II). Washington, 1940.

Walters, Raymond, Jr. _Alexander James Dallas: Lawyer-Politician-Financier, 1759-1817._ Philadelphia, 1943.

Walters, Raymond, Jr. "The Origins of the Second Bank of the United States," in _Jour. of Pol. Econ._, Vol. LIII (1945).

Warburg, Paul M. "Defects and Needs of our Banking System," in the _New York Times_, Jan. 6, 1907.

Warburg, Paul M. _A Modified Central Bank of Issue; A Suggestion of a Bill._ New York, 1908.

Warburg, Paul M. _Essays on Banking Reform in the United States._ New York, 1914.

Warburg, Paul M. _Some Phases of Financial Reconstruction._ Address delivered at

Atlantic City, N.J., on Dec. 6, 1918.

Warburg, Paul M. Some Problems of the Investment Banker. An Address delivered before the Bond Club of New York, May 23, 1919.

Warburg, Paul M. Acceptances in our Domestic and International Commerce. Am. Acceptance Council, New York, 1919.

Warburg, Paul M. The Federal Reserve System, Its Origin and Growth. New York, 1930.

Warner, Caleb H. The National Bank of Commerce of Boston. Cambridge, 1892.

Warner, John DeWitt. "The Currency Famine of 1893," in Sound Currency, Vol. II (1895).

Warshow, Robert I. The Story of Wall Street. New York, 1929.

Warshow, Robert I. Alexander Hamilton, First American Business Man. New York, 1931.

Washburn, Charles G. The Life of John W. Weeks. Boston, 1928.

Watson, Elkanah. Men and Times of the Revolution; or, Memoirs of .... New York, 1856.

Webster, Daniel. Second Speech on the Sub-Treasury Bill, delivered March 12, 1838. Washington, 1838.

Webster, Daniel. Speech on the Currency at the Merchants' Meeting in Wall Street, New York, Sept. 28, 1840. New York, 1840.

Webster, Noah, Jr. "A Sketch of the History and Present State of Banks and Insurance Companies in the United States," in Miscellaneous Papers on Political and Commercial Subjects. New York, 1802.

Webster, Pelatiah. An Essay on Credit .... Philadelphia, 1786.

Webster, Pelatiah. Essay on Money, as a Medium of Commerce. Philadelphia, 1786.

Webster, Pelatiah. Political Essays on the Nature and Operation of Money, Public Finances and other Subjects ... Philadelphia, 1791.

Welfling, Weldon. Savings Banking in New York State... Durham, N.C., 1939.

Welton, Arthur D. "The Educational Campaign for Banking Reform," in Annals of the Amer. Acad. of Pol. and Soc. Sci., Vol. XCIX (1922).

Welton, Arthur D. The Making of a Modern Bank; An Historical Sketch of the Continental and Commercial Banks of Chicago.... Chicago, 1923.

Westerfield, Ray B. Historical Survey of Branch Banking in the United States. New York, 1939.

Wheelwright, William B. Life and Times of of Alvah Crocker. Boston, 1923.

Wettereau, James O. "New Light on the First Bank of the United States," in Pa. Mag. Hist. and Biogr., Vol. LXI (1937).

Whitney, David R. The Suffolk Bank. Cambridge, 1878.

Whitney, Reuben M. Memorial of ... to the Honorable House of Representatives ... in relation to the Charges made against him as a witness before the Committee of Investigation. Washington, 1832.

Whitney, Reuben M. Protest of ... against the Proceedings of the Select Committee of the House of Representatives, Jan. 25, 1837. Washington, 1837.

Who is Who in Finance. New York, 1911.

Who is Who in Finance, Banking and Insurance. 1920-1922.

Wickliffe, R. "Southern Bank of Kentucky," in Commonwealth Extra. Frankfort, April 30, 1839.

Wight, William W. "Early Legislation, concerning Wisconsin Banks," in State Hist. Soc. of Wis. Proc. (1896).

Wilcox, W. V. The Bankers be Damned. New York, 1940.

Wildes, Harry E. Lonely Midas. The Story of Stephen Girard. New York, 1943.

Wilkeson, Samuel. How Our National Debt may be a National Blessing. The Debt is Public Wealth ... (Issued by Jay Cooke). Philadelphia, 1865.

Willcox, James M. A History of the Philadelphia Saving Fund Society, 1816-1916. Philadelphia, 1916.

Williams, George W. History of Banking in South Carolina [and other essays]. Charleston, S.C., 1903.

Williams, John Earl. An Examination into the Prospective Effects of the National Banks upon the Public Welfare. 1863.

Williams, John Earl. Report on the National Bank Currency Act, its Defects and Effects. New York, 1863.

Williams, John Earl. "A New York View of Finance and Banking," in Old and New, Nov. 1873.

Williams, John Earl. Short Road to Specie-Currency. (Letter to Hon. John Sherman). 1874.

Williams, John Earl. The War Loans of the

Associated Banks to the Government in 1861. New York, 1876 (?).

Willing, Thomas. Letter and Papers (edited by Thomas Willing Balch). Philadelphia, 1922.

Willis, Henry Parker. The Federal Reserve System. New York, 1923.

Willis, H. Parker and Julius I. Bogen. Investment Banking. New York, 1929.

Willson, Hugh B. A Plea for Uncle Sam's Money or Greenbacks versus Bank Notes. New York, 1870.

Wilson, George. How to Abolish the National Banking System. St. Louis, 1879.

Wilson, George, compiler. Portrait Gallery of the Chamber of Commerce of the State of New York. New York, 1890.

Wilson, George Robert. Honorable George H. Proffit. His Day and Generation. [n. p., n. d.]

Wilson, James. Considerations on the Bank of North America, in The Works of the Honourable James Wilson. Philadelphia, 1804.

Wilson, Janet. "The Bank of North America and Pennsylvania Politics: 1781-1787," in Pa. Mag. of Hist. and Biog., Vol. LXVI (1942).

Winthrop, Robert C. "Memoir of Nathan Appleton," in Mass. Hist. Soc., Proc., Vol. V (1860-1862).

Wise, Henry A. Seven Decades of the Union ....A Memoir of John Tyler. Philadelphia, 1876.

Witherspoon, John. Essay on Money as a Medium of Commerce with Remarks.... Philadelphia, 1786.

Wolcott, Oliver. Remarks on the Present State of Currency, Credit, Commerce and National Industry.... New York, 1820.

Wood, Elmer. English Theories of Central Banking Control, 1819-1858. Cambridge, 1939.

Woodward, P. H. 1792-1892. One Hundred Years of the Hartford Bank.... Hartford, 1892.

Woolsey, Theodore S. The Old New Haven Bank [now] the New Haven Bank National Banking Association. New Haven, 1913.

Woolsey, Theodore S. "The Old New Haven Bank," in Papers of the New Haven Colony Hist. Soc., Vol. III (1914).

Woosley, John B. "Differential Elements in North Carolina Banking," in Southern Econ. Jour., Vol. VI (1939).

Worth, Gorham A. Random Recollections of Albany from 1800-1808. 3d edition, Albany, 1866.

Worth, Gorham A. "Recollections of Cincinnati from a Residence of Five Years, 1817-1821. Albany, 1851" in Quart. Pub. of the Hist. and Philosophical Soc. of Ohio, Vol. XI (1916).

Worthen, W. B. Early Banking in Arkansas. (Prep. at the Request of the Arkansas Bankers' Assn. for its meeting in April 1906.)

Wright, Silas. Speech on the Motion of Mr. Webster for Leave to Bring in a Bill for Prolonging the Charter of the Bank of the United States, delivered in the Senate of the United States, March 20, 1834. Washington, 1834.

Wright, Benjamin C. Banking in California. San Francisco, 1910.

Yaple, Alfred. Reminiscences of Alfred Kelley. Cincinnati, 1875.

[Young, Samuel]. Considerations on the Bank of the United States in which its Repugnance to the Constitution Albany, 1832.

Young, Samuel. Oration Delivered at the Democratic Republican Celebration of the 64th Anniversary of the Independence of the United States. July 4, 1840. New York, 1840.

Youngman, Elmer H. Credit Currency. New York, 1907.

The following anonymous books and pamphlets are arranged in two groups. The first relates to items concerning specific banking institutions and are arranged alphabetically by the name of the company. The items in the second group are arranged alphabetically by title.

Report on the Affairs of the Bangor Bank. Boston, 1822.

The Bank of America. New York, 1887.

The Bank of America. A Brief Account of an Historic Financial Institution and its Site. New York, 1918.

The Bank of America. A History of Fifty Feet in New York at Wall and William Streets, 1644-1926. [New York], 1926.

Bank of the Manhattan Company: Origin, History, Progress. [n.p., n.d.]

An Historical Sketch of the Bank of the Manhattan Company. New York, 1927.

Correspondence relating to the Affairs of
the Bank of Maryland. n.p. (ca. 1834).

Statement and Explanations of the President
and Directors of the Bank of Mutual Redemption upon the Report of the Stockholder Examining Committee, Dec. 1862.
Lowell, 1862.

Remarks on a Pamphlet entitled "Considerations on the Bank of North America."
Philadelphia, 1785.

The Bank of North America, Philadelphia.
A National Bank Founded 1781. New York,
1906.

The Charter and Renewal of the Charter of
the Bank of Orleans. New Orleans, 1823.

The Bank of Pittsburgh National Association.
The Bank Historical. Pittsburgh, 1906.

A Compilation of all the Acts, Resolutions,
Reports and other Documents in relation
to the Bank of the State of South Carolina... Columbia, 1848.

The Railroad Mania and Review of the Bank
of the State of South-Carolina. A Series
of Essays by Anti-Debt. (Publ. in the
Charleston Mercury.) Charleston, 1848.

An Exposition of Facts and Arguments in
Support of a Memorial to the Legislature
of Massachusetts, by Citizens of Boston
and Vicinity in Favor of a Bank of Ten
Millions. Boston, 1836.

Report of the Joint Select Committee Ap-
pointed to Examine and Report to the
Legislature the Question of the Bank of
Tennessee. Nashville, 1858.

Debate in the House of Representatives of
Pennsylvania on Mr. Holgate's Resolutions
relative to the Bank of the United States,
February 1811, reported by W. Hamilton.
1811.

An Act to Incorporate the Subscribers of
the Bank of the United States. Printed
by order of the Board of Directors by
William Fry, Printer. Philadelphia, 1816.

To the President and Directors of the Bank
of the United States. The Memorial of
Citizens of the Town of Lexington in the
State of Kentucky. Lexington, 1816.

Report of the Secretary of the Treasury...
[on] the Bank of the United States and its
Officers; also [on] the Different Chartered Banks.... February 24, 1820. Washington, 1820.

Report on the Condition of the Bank of the
United States by the Committee of Inspection and Investigation. Philadelphia,
1822.

Report of the Proceedings of the Triennial
Meeting of the Stockholders of the Bank
of the United States. Philadelphia,
1831.

Reports of the Committee of Inquiry appointed March 14, 1832 by the House of Representatives at Washington concerning the
Bank of the United States. (Publication
of the Second Bank of the United States.)

On Rechartering the United States Bank.
Cincinnati, 1832.

The Bank of the United States and the Veto.
(United States Telegraph Extra.) October 1, 1832.

Rules and Regulations for Conducting the
Business of the Bank of the United States.
[1833].

Report of the Bank of the United States to
the Committee of Ways and Means of the
House of Representatives. Jan. 28, 1833.

Report of a Committee of Directors of the
Bank of the United States. 1833.

Report of the Boston Committee [on the Removal of the Deposites from the Bank of
the United States]. Boston, 1834.

Report of the Select Committee relative to
the United States Bank together with the
Testimony taken in relation thereto.
Harrisburg, 1837.

Act of Incorporation of the Bank of the
United States by the State of Pennsyl-
vania. Proceedings of a Meeting of the
Stockholders. Philadelphia, 1838.

Report of the Committee of Investigation
appointed at the Meeting of the Stockholders of the Bank of the United States.
Philadelphia, 1841.

An Argument on behalf of the Defendants in
the case of Isaac Shelby, a Citizen of
Kentucky, versus...(Trustees of the Bank
of the United States). Supreme Court of
the United States, Dec., 1850. Philadelphia, 1851.

Beverly National Bank. Beverly, Mass.,
1802-1925. 1925.

Canal Bank and Trust Company, New Orleans
through Ninety-Five Years. New Orleans,
1926.

1877-1922: The Chase National Bank of the
City of New York. 1922.

History of the Chemical Bank, 1823-1913.
1913.

Report relating to the Commonwealth Bank.
[Mass.] Senate No. 35, 1838.

An Act to Incorporate the Subscribers of
the Consolidated Association of the
Planters of Louisiana. New Orleans, 1829.

Report of the Committee Appointed by the General Assembly of the State of Rhode Island and Providence Plantations...1809 to Enquire into the Situation of the Farmers' Exchange Bank in Glocester. 1809.

1784-1934. The First National Bank of Boston; A Brief History. Boston, 1934.

Banking Relations with the United States through the First National Bank of Boston. Boston, 1927.

The History of the First National Bank in the United States. A History of the First National Bank of Davenport, Iowa. Chicago, 1913.

The Girard Bank vs. George H. Boker and Charles S. Boker, Administrators of the Estate of Charles S. Boker, deceased. Argument of William L. Hine. Philadelphia, 1864.

Girard Trust Company, A Century of Financial Activity, 1836-1936. 1936.

Guaranty Trust Company of New York. One Hundred Years of Banking Service, 1839-1939. 1939.

Hartford National Bank and Trust Company. A Brief Account of Events in its History. Hartford, 1942.

Lowell Institution for Savings, At the 'Meeting of the Waters:' A Sketch of Lowell Life.... 1929.

A Century of the Institution for Savings in Newburyport and its Vicinity: 1820-1920. 1920.

Report of the Committee on the Kilby Bank. [Mass.] Senate, No. 58, 1837.

Report Relating to Kilby Bank. [Mass.] Senate, No. 34, 1838.

Report Respecting the Lafayette Bank. [Mass.] Senate, No. 51. Boston, 1838.

The Maverick National Bank Manual. Boston, 1887.

Span of a Century, 1811-1911. Mechanics and Farmers Bank. Albany, N. Y.

A Concise View of the Late Proceedings of the Leaders of the Clintonian Party in New York and at Albany for the Suppression of the Merchants Bank, by a Spectator. New York, 1804.

The Charter of the Merchants' Bank together with the Safety Fund Law and the Revised Statutes relative to Moneyed Corporations. New York, 1842.

In Commemoration of the Hundredth Anniversary of the Middletown Bank. 1901.

National Bank of Commerce in New York. An Introduction...1917.

National Bank of Commerce in New York. A Great American Bank. 1921.

June 1922. 110th Anniversary of the Founding of the National City Bank of New York. Number Eight (Monthly Magazine of the City Bank Club), Vol. XVII, No. 6, June 16, 1922.

The National Commercial Bank and Trust Company of Albany, New York. Improvements and Additions with a Brief History. Albany, N.Y., 1922.

National State Bank of Newark: One Hundred and Twenty-Five Years Ago. Newark, 1937.

Articles of Association and By-Laws of the North American Trust and Banking Company; also the General Banking Law. New York, 1838.

Report of the Committee relative to the Penobscot Bank. (Commonwealth of Massachusetts.) 1809.

Examination of the Charges of the Board of Trade against the Phenix Bank. (Prepared by the Counsel of the Bank.) New York, 1838.

The Philadelphia National Bank: A Century's Record, 1803-1903, by a stockholder. 1903.

Centennial Memorial of the Plymouth Bank and the Plymouth National Bank of Plymouth, Mass. 1803-1903. Plymouth, 1903.

The Centennial of the Providence National Bank, Providence, Rhode Island. 1891.

Second Letter to the Stockholders of the Rhode Island Central Bank. Providence, 1852.

The Savings Bank of Baltimore. One Hundred Years of Service, 1818-1918. Baltimore, 1918.

The Seamen's Bank for Savings [ch. 1829] New York, ca. 1926.

An Argument in Favor of Establishing the State Bank of Ohio; contained in a series of Five Numbers...in the Cincinnati Republican.... Cincinnati, 1833.

The Suffolk Bank and its Redemption System. Boston, 1881.

One Hundred Years of the Suffolk Savings Bank for Seamen and Others. A History.... 1933.

Reply of the Union Bank of Tennessee to a Memorial from a Portion of the Stockholders of the City of Philadelphia. 1837 (or 1838).

An Address to the People of Maryland on the Necessity of Establishing a Bank for the

Benefit of Agriculturists, by a Free-
holder. Annapolis, 1817.

The American Quarterly Review versus the
State of New York. Albany Argus Extra,
1831 or 1832.

Annalysis of Balances paid into the Boston
Clearing House from June 26 to Sept. 30
incl., 1893. [Four page folder, contains
a statistics of clearing house loan-
certificates.]

An Appeal to Banks in Particular and the
Public in General. Hartford, 1815.

The Aristocracy of Boston, who they are
and what they were..., by one who knows
them. Boston, 1898.

Bank or No Bank. Published by order of a
Committee of the Democratic Members of
Congress. [1844].

"The Banking History of New York," in
Bankers' Magazine, Vol. XVI (1861/62).

Banks and Banking, by an Old Merchant.
Newport, Oct. 27, 1857.

Banks, Banking, and Currency, by a New
York Merchant. 1856.

The Boston Clearing House Association,
1856-1936. Boston, 1936.

A Brief Notice of a Pamphlet "by a Practical Banker" on the Suppression of Small
Bills. From "The Bee." (Probably 1855.)

A Brief Review of the Recent Hearing before the Committee on Banks and Banking
upon the Petitions to Suppress Bank Bills
under Five Dollars. Boston, 1856.

Concise Observations on the Propriety of
Incorporating New Banks, submitted to the
Legislature of Pennsylvania. Philadel-
phia, 1812.

Constitution of the Boston Clearing House.
Boston, 1856.

A Correspondence between the Suffolk and
Exchange Banks, Boston on the Subject of
Redeeming the Bills of the Country Banks.
Boston, 1854.

The Crisis. Democratic Union Tract, No.
10. 1840(?) [An attack on the plan of a
(third) national bank.]

Death of Hon. Samuel Hooper. Proceedings
in the House of Representatives. 1875.

Debate on the Bill for Establishing a Bank
of the State in the Senate and House of
Commons of North Carolina in December
1829. Raleigh, 1830.

A Defence of Country Banks: Being a reply
to a pamphlet entitled an Examination of
the Banking System of Massachusetts....
Boston, 1831.

Desultory Observations on the Abuses of the
Banking System. Petersburg (Va.), 1841.

Dialogue on the Subject of a National Bank.
1841.

Discussion on the Currency Needs of Commerce between Businessmen of Wide Experience. New York Mercantile Journal,
1869. Reprinted in 1876.

Documents relative to Savings Banks, Intem-
perance and Lotteries. Publ. by the
Society for the Prevention of Pauperism
in the City of New York. New York, 1819.

Draft of a System of Banking, based on the
General Banking Bill of the State of New
York intended specially for the Use of
Three or Four Capitalists. [1846.]

An Examination of Some of the Provisions
of the Act to Create a Fund...passed
April 1829..., by a stockholder. New
York, 1829.

Federal Misrepresentations Examined, No. 1.
Democratic Union Tract, No. 12. 1840(?)

A Few Remarks addressed to Nicholas Biddle
...in answer to his Letters to the Hon.
John Quincy Adams. New York, 1836.

The Financial Revulsion and the New York
Banking System. 1857(?)

"The History of Reserve Requirements for
Banks in the United States," in Fed. Res.
Bull. Nov. 1938.

History of the New York Stock Exchange...
and the New York and London Clearing
House Systems. New York, 1887.

In Memoriam: Dr. John Andrews. Preamble
and Resolutions adopted by the Board of
Control of the State Bank of Ohio, Nov.
20, 1866. Columbus, Ohio.

The Injunction [of the Bank Commissioners
to restrain the Bank of Mutual Redemption
from borrowing specie] 1862.

"Interest on Bank Deposits. Proceedings
of the Clearing House Association, March
1858," in Bankers' Magazine, Vol. XII
(1857/58).

John Joy Edson: A Tribute.

Journal of the Bank Investigating Committee. A Select Committee of the Indiana
Senate, 1857. Indianapolis, 1857.

Loans of the United States. A series of
articles in Bankers' Magazine, Vol. LIII (1896).

Memorial of the Chamber of Commerce of the
City of New York for a National Bank.
1841.

Metallic Money, Its Value and its Functions.
Philadelphia, 1841.

Minutes of the Proceedings of the Bank
Convention held in the City of New York

on the 27th of November, 1837. New York, 1837.

The National Bank Circulation. Its Abnormal Condition and Needed Readjustment to Existing Circumstances. A Series of Editorial Articles published in the New York Daily Commercial Bulletin of Nov. 21st, 22d, 23d, 25th, and 26th, 1889.

The National Banks, Down with the Banks Forever. [n. p., n. d.]

A National Exchange, in a Series of Essays addressed to Congress on the Question of a Fiscal Agent. Philadelphia, 1842.

National Money, or a Simple System of Finance...in Three Letters. Addressed by a Citizen of Washington to the Congress of the United States. Georgetown, 1816.

A New Financial Project together with Some Remarks upon the Currency and Credit System of the United States. New York, 1837.

The New York Clearing House, Its Methods and Systems and a Description of the London Clearing House.... New York, 1888.

Origin, Provisions and Effect of the Safety Fund Law of the State of New York. Albany, 1834.

Our First Men. A Calendar of Wealth, Fashion and Gentility. Boston, 1846.

Outline of a Plan for a National Bank with incidental Remarks on the Bank of the United States. New York, 1833.

The Outline of a Plan for Regulating Domestic Exchanges, a Remedy for our Sufferings and a few Allusions to a General Banking Law. New York, 1837(?)

Plain Truth, in a Series of Numbers from the New York Daily Advertiser. New York, 1821.

A Plan for a Modified Central Bank, Nov. 12, 1907.

Proceedings of the Convention of Banks and Bankers held at Saratoga, July 20th, 21st and 22nd, 1875. New York, 1875.

Proceedings of the Friends of a National Bank at their Public Meeting, held in Boston, fifteenth July 1841. Boston, 1841.

Proceedings of the Meeting in Relation to the Establishment of a Large National Bank in this City. New York, 1863.

Proceedings of the National Bank Convention held in New York City Wednesday October 19, 1864. Syracuse, 1865.

Proceedings of the National Bank Convention held in New York City, Wednesday, June 23, 1869. Syracuse, 1869.

Professional and Industrial History of Suffolk County, Mass. Boston, 1894.

The Question of Bank Circulation as viewed by Leading New York Bankers. Reprinted from the New York Daily Commercial Bulletin. December 1883.

Reasons for the Inexpediency of Chartering a National Bank. New York, 1841.

Refutation by his Friends of the Calumnies against David Henshaw in relation to the Failure of the Commonwealth Bank.... Boston, 1844.

Remarks on Banks and Banking and the Skeleton of a Project for a National Bank, by a Citizen of Boston. Boston, 1840.

Report and Observations, on the Banks, and other Incorporated Institutions, in the State of New York. New York, 1828.

Report of the Comptroller of the Currency, 1876. [Contains a cursory history of American banking.]

Report of the Delegates of the Banks of the City of New York to the Bank Convention held at New York on the 27th of November to the 1st of December 1837. New York, 1837.

Report of the Monetary Commission of the Indianapolis Convention of the Board of Trade, Chamber of Commerce, Commercial Club and other Similar Bodies of the United States. Chicago, 1898.

Report of the "Union Committee" appointed by the Meeting of the Signers of the Memorial to Congress, held on the 11th day of February 1834 at the Merchants Exchange in the City of New York. New York, 1834.

Report on the Subject of Paying Interest on Current Deposits, presented to the Banks in New York. New York, 1858.

Report to the New York Clearing House Association of a Committee upon Reforms in the Banking Business. 1873.

The Republican Bank, being an Essay on the Present System of Banks, by a Citizen of Indiana. Madison, 1839.

"Restrictions on Banking," in The Atlantic Magazine, Vol. II (1824/25).

"Review of Edward Earle's The History of a Little Frenchman and his Bank Notes: Rags! Rags! Rags!," in Analectic Magazine, Vol. VI (1815).

"Review of the Report of the Union Committee," in Amer. Quart. Rev., Vol. XV (1834).

Six Numbers on Banking and the Shaving Operations of Directors, with General Remarks, by "Corrector," (first inserted in the Columbian Register of New Haven). New Haven, 1817.

Statue of Stephen Girard: Records of its Erection and Unveiling.... Philadelphia, 1897.

The Story of Banking in Kansas, commemorating the 50th Anniversary of the Organization of the Kansas Bankers Association, 1887-1937. 1937.

Thoughts on Banking and the Currency, by a Citizen of Western New York. Seneca Falls, 1836.

Thoughts on Banking, with References to the Trade and Currency of the United States, by a Citizen of Richmond, Va. Richmond, 1841.

What is a Monopoly, or, Some Considerations upon the Subject of Corporations and Currency, by a Citizen of New York. New York, 1835.

Written for the Governor's Reply to a Letter addressed to him by "a Practical Banker" upon the Proposed Suppression of Small Bank Notes. Boston, 1855.

HISTORY OF AMERICAN BUSINESS LEADERS

A SERIES OF STUDIES

VOLUME 2

PART II

BANKING

1840 - 1910

THE MOLDING OF AMERICAN BANKING

MEN AND IDEAS

By

FRITZ REDLICH

Part II

1840 - 1910

HAFNER PUBLISHING COMPANY, INC.

NEW YORK

1951

Copyright 1951
Fritz Redlich

PREFACE

After more than ten years of work the author is publishing the second volume of what amounts to a history of American banking, thereby completing a project which he would not have had the courage to tackle single-handed had he known in advance its magnitude and difficulties. The history of banking in any great commercial nation can be written, of course, from various angles, such as the statistical, legal, business historical, economic, and ideological angles. As far as the method goes, the presentation can be strictly positivistic or it can aim at interpretation; it can focus the attention on a process or the result thereof. These facts are stated here to make clear that the author himself is aware how much research in the field of banking history yet remains to be done and how much room is left for other publications besides his own volumes.

The author's interest lay in the process by which American banking became what it was prior to the creation of the Federal Reserve system. This process he tried to understand, and for that purpose he used traditional historical methods, supplementing them by using tools shaped in recent decades by business historians and the exponents of Geistesgeschichte. Moreover this process was to be interpreted. Naturally a guiding idea must be used if a social or historical process is to be so understood and interpreted. The guiding idea used in this research is the Schumpeterian concept of men as the carriers of economic development. Whoever rejects that concept will reject this book (and, incidentally, should not review it). Since all research in the social sciences is based on fundamental presuppositions which are mutually exclusive, justice demands that such research be judged by those who share those presuppositions, if judgment is not to be identical with outright unwarranted rejection.

As to the organization of the material presented in these volumes there was a certain difficulty. If one presents historical material strictly according to the time sequence one tears apart what belongs together and misses the sweep of development. One writes a chronicle and cannot interpret a historical process. If, on the other hand, one separates special topics, such as private banking or investment banking, one has often to go beyond the limits of the period with which one is dealing at the point at which they are presented. The dilemma is unavoidable; and so it was decided to insert a particular topic whenever the presentation had come to the period in which that topic gained special importance.

For encouragement in this research the author feels gratitude to Arthur H. Cole alone. Discouragement from other sources came at times thick and fast; but the psychological reaction to this was a source of strength, and enabled the author to carry through the self-imposed task which at times seemed to go beyond the capacity of a single, unassisted researcher, under the conditions with which he had to cope. So, many thanks to my enemies. The author would re-affirm his appreciation to Miss Ruth Crandall for her assistance in editing these two volumes. The work on the second volume was financed entirely by the author. But the Social Science Research Council contributed a considerable amount toward the cost of publication, and for this help the author wishes to express his deep appreciation.

The preface to volume I of this work expressed his indebtedness to several people who gave access to privately owned primary sources. Thereto must be added now a word of thanks to Mr. L. M. Townsend, Assistant Vice-President, who permitted the use of the records of the Bank of New York.

The author had the good fortune of meeting with an unusual degree of liberality on the part of several researchers in related fields. Dr. Muriel E. Hidy permitted him to read her manuscript on George Peabody and to use her findings to the extent that they were essential to his research. Moreover she read the pages in question. Dr. S. R. Cope permitted the use of his very valuable unprinted Ph.D. thesis on Boyd, Benfield and Company. Similarly, Dr. Irene Neu made her unprinted Ph.D. thesis on Erastus Corning available and moreover put her notes on the latter's banking activities at the author's disposal. Professors Leland H. Jenks and Thomas C. Cochran contributed some of their unprinted material. To all of them an expression of appreciation is due.

Very many local libraries were consulted and their librarians gave the most valuable information on sources and sometimes facts. Such help is acknowledged in the proper places.

The research itself has been done in Widener and Baker Libraries of Harvard University. The author is indebted to Mr. Robert H. Haynes, Assistant Librarian of the former, and to Dr. Arthur H. Cole, Librarian of the latter library, for a decade of hospitality.

An erratum should be added here. Not until a large part of the book was typed up in final form was it discovered that banknote was sometimes written as two words, sometimes as one. No special significance should be ascribed to the different spellings!

Belmont, Mass.   Fritz Redlich

Table of Contents

Chapter		Pages
X	Third Period, General Characteristics	1 - 21
XI	The Middle Western State Bank with Branches	22 - 31
XII	The Louisiana Banking Act of 1842 and Edmond John Forstall	32 - 44
XIII	The Origin of the Clearing House	45 - 59
XIV	Private Banking	60 - 84
XV	Bankers and Civil War Finance	85 - 98
XVI	National Banking (Fourth Period)	99 - 157
XVII	The Clearing House Loan Certificate.	158 - 174
XVIII	Fifth Period (1882-1910), General Characteristics . .	175 - 235
XIX	The Clearing of Out-of-Town Checks	236 - 244
XX	Cooperation among American Banks	245 - 303
XXI	Investment Banking	304 - 423
Appendix	George S. Coe, Nineteenth Century Banker and Business Leader.	424 - 447
List of References		448 - 459
Subject Index		460 - 490
Name Index.		491 - 517

THIRD PERIOD

GENERAL CHARACTERISTICS

The depression of the 1840's ushered in a new (third) period in American banking. Up to that decade, banking had been almost synonymous with issuing bank notes and the most advanced legislators and bankers had tried to make it safe beyond doubt by basing notes on first class security. After 1840, in contrast, the character of the banking business began to change, the growth of the deposit business and the struggle for liquidity becoming the keynotes of the new era.

I

The second period had hardly opened when the Second Bank of the United States practically ran out of specie; the period ended with the New York Free Banking Act of 1838 establishing a 12½ per cent specie reserve against bank notes. These two facts are indicative of the change in climate. Although the New York clause was too advanced for its time and was dropped in 1840, nevertheless specie was coming to be recognized as the indispensable basis of sound banking. Sound banking can be based on gold and silver only, as Governor Shunk of Pennsylvania put it in 1848;[1] and Governor Lowe of Iowa (on January 13, 1858) suggested a specie basis for the banking system of that youthful state. Utterances of this nature, however, did not go far enough to be really modern and may have meant nothing more than advocating banking on money as against Mercantilist "banking on real and personal estates." An action like that of Maine in 1846 requiring her banks to keep a specie reserve of 5 per cent against their notes meant little more. But even that little was progress in some parts of the country for the decades under investigation.

What counted as real progress, however, was the fight for liquidity which characterized the period. The farseeing men who struggled at that time to make banks liquid had to face an old-fashioned objection. They were told "that the solvency of a bank [did] not depend on the specie in its vault. In other words that a bank [might] be perfectly solvent with but little specie or insolvent with a large amount on hand." This contention

they could not deny; but they replied that "the real solvency of a bank [was] its immediate capacity to pay the demands upon it." That is to say, they stressed rightly, although going too far, that liquidity was the prerequisite of solvency.[2] In connection with the struggle for liquidity, banking practice and legislation progressed from establishing ratios between circulation and capital[3] (as had been common in line with Mercantilist tradition in the second period) to thinking in terms of ratios of notes to specie on hand.[4] This question will be discussed in detail shortly. To the extent that such thinking became common, a wider vista was bound to open up. More and more American bankers and legislators came to see a relation between movements of specie, and expansion and contraction of credit, while in the earlier periods this connection as a rule had been recognized only by a few, especially the most progressive exponents of "banking on mercantile credit" in the seaboard cities.[5] After the 1840's, however, that outlook typical of the later nineteenth century all over Europe became generally adopted here also. As early as 1848 Governor Shunk of Pennsylvania stated: "This increase of the precious metal [by import].... has a tendency to increase [the paper currency] by enlarging the means of the banks to extend their issues."[6]

At the same time another important change in viewpoint became possible. That bank notes represented property was an old Mercantilist idea. One of young Hamilton's bank plans[7] embodied it and, as has been described, Mercantilist land banks in general were supposed to "melt down" property. At the end of the first period Nicholas Biddle, then still under Mercantilist influence, tried to modernize this idea by claiming that bank notes represented property because they could be exchanged for property.[8] After 1840, however, when American banking came to be based more and more on specie, bank notes could be recognized as representative money in the modern sense. "This paper is but the representative of the precious metals, for it exists exclusively in promises to pay them" (1841).[9]

When the question of liquidity came up banking, as indicated, was still more or less identical with note issue, and consequently for some time the relation of specie reserves to notes became an object of discussion, legislation, and business policy. Attention seems to have been focused on the matter first in the 1830's when the fate of the Second Bank of the United States was debated.[10] In the 1840's and 1850's the interest increased; banks in the more advanced states, in line with Adam Smith's suggestion, considered 20 per cent specie reserves against their notes as very fair;[11] and the historian will recognize that that ratio would have marked progress indeed if it had been widely adopted.[12] In reality, however, such ratio existed at best only on paper[13] if deposits were disregarded, although of course they needed specie backing just as much as bank notes. Such disregard will be explained shortly. On the whole 5 to 10 per cent specie reserves against notes were customary with reliable banks outside of the Eastern trade centers.[14] In New England and the state of New York such reserves were supplemented by the funds held with the Suffolk Bank in Boston and with certain banks in New York and Albany, respectively, and elsewhere the good banks throughout the country kept "specie funds," i.e., bankers balances, in such places as New York, Philadelphia, or New Orleans, as will be discussed.[15] When, as already mentioned, Maine put her banks legally on a specie basis the state was able to enforce this clause in spite of the dire warnings of her "conservative" bankers who looked at even that little "as an onerous measure introduced by visionary theorists without any clear perception of its practical effect upon the currency."[16] Maine's success, like the drive for higher specie reserves in general, may reflect to a certain extent the increase of the precious metals following the opening of the Californian gold mines, which came at a propitious moment.

Soon after the question of higher specie reserves had started agitating public opinion a red herring was drawn across the trail in Free Banking which by that time was conquering the nation. In those states in which the government-bond-backed banknote was adopted in this connection, specie reserves against notes seemed to become less important, if not superfluous; for the idea of liquidity had not yet widely enough cut loose from that of security. Or as Helderman[17] expressed it, it was not recognized that a bond deposit was an ultimate reserve and not an immediate asset. Under these circumstances the struggle for higher specie reserves against notes was confined to such advanced states as did not take much interest in Free Banking. In Ohio the law of 1845 establishing the State Bank of Ohio required it to keep a 30 per cent specie reserve against notes, which

were also secured by a Safety Fund. Independent banks had to keep the same reserve besides backing their notes by a deposit of securities. (As to specie reserves, this law took up ideas first suggested in 1839 and 1840 by state legislative committees led by John Brough and Thomas W. Bartley, respectively.)[18] In 1848 the Connecticut Bank Commissioners suggested a 10 per cent specie reserve against circulation; and a clause to that effect was actually adopted.[19] In case of violation of the act $100 was to be paid for each week in which the provision was not complied with. At that moment, so the Bank Commissioners claimed, at least some of the banks held higher reserves accumulated in the preceding prosperous years. (When in 1852 the state passed the Act to authorize the business of banking,[20] a Free Banking measure soon to be repealed, the clause was not taken over, a fact which speaks volumes.) In 1849 a special board of bank commissioners in Massachusetts suggested that banks be required to keep in their vaults an amount of specie proportionate to their circulation; but they were afraid that it would be too difficult to formulate and enforce such a rule. So in lieu thereof they advised the legislators to pass a law requiring the banks to keep in the form of specie at all times 6 per cent of their capital and prohibiting them from making new loans and discounts if the proportion was reduced below 6 per cent.[21] Three years later, in 1852, Indiana enacted a $12\frac{1}{2}$ per cent specie reserve against notes.[22] The movement toward higher and definite specie reserves received an impetus during the crisis of 1857. In that period Governor Wise of Virginia recommended a legal specie reserve of one third against circulation and Governor Harris of Tennessee, one as high as one half.[23] In the same year Missouri by law required 33 1/3 per cent specie to be held against notes;[24] and in 1860 when Pennsylvania enacted a Free Banking measure she forced the banks to be established to keep a 20 per cent reserve against notes.

With respect to their specie reserves against notes, voluntary as the ratios were in most states, banks could establish one of two policies. Either they could "act on the principle that it [was] not necessary to keep a large amount of specie on hand, as they [were] seldom called upon for specie, and therefore regard the specie reserve.... as so much unproductive capital." Such banks kept specie only reluctantly "as though it were a drug." Or, if progressive, they could voluntarily hold a high specie reserve. Thereby they could de facto keep up a larger circulation and in addition, by creating prestige, attract deposits which, as the New York superintendent of the banking department stressed, were the main source of the banks' profits.[26] In this case their loss through the "unproductive reserves" would be overcompensated by increased profits from extended circulation and an extra deposit business. At the same time they could place themselves "on an eminence" above the contingencies arising from a so-called "tight money market on the other side" leading to extraordinary or excessive exports of specie.[27]

Regardless of some progress in the 1840's and 1850's, when the crisis broke in 1857 the proper ratio of specie reserves against bank notes was still problematic. This was particularly true since, as the crisis revealed to the public for the first time, a new line of the banking business, that in demand deposits, was forging ahead with far-reaching repercussions. In this connection the problem of liquidity acquired a new aspect, as will be shown shortly, and the development, deviating from its original course, took a turn toward legal reserve requirements for cash liabilities or deposits.

Liquidity of banks, of course, depends not only on sufficient specie reserves; it depends equally on a sound portfolio. This aspect of the matter, however, was not, and perhaps could not be, seen clearly enough, although Bronson's ideas elaborated during the second period survived and were developed by Forstall. Hooper gave their pleading a new turn: in order to make profit, banks must continuously make fresh discounts and for this reason short term paper was preferable.[28] There were a few Western banks which, following and developing Biddle's policy, lent mainly on "bills of exchange based upon produce shipped" to the market. Among these were the State Bank of Indiana, the Bank of Missouri, the State Bank of Iowa, and the banking house of George Smith and Company.[29] But, as a rule, short term and long term credit alike was extended by the American banks, or, in other words, even the best of them carried a high percentage of accommodation paper. Hedges[30] has correctly emphasized the heterogeneous character of paper in bank portfolios during the period, heterogeneous "with respect to type, purpose, and maturity date, resulting from the varied needs of the country at different times and places." Standardized commercial paper of good quality did not come into the money market in sufficient volume, so that country banks were forced to keep their secondary reserves in the form of interest-bearing bankers' balances in trade centers, while the banks in New York City resorted to call loans. During the 1850's the percentage of genuine short term business paper in bank portfolios tended further to deteriorate, because more and more banks took an interest in railroad financing which was identical with making long or at least medium term loans:

construction companies paid contractors and manufacturers with securities which were pledged with banks in order to borrow working capital, but which could be sold only slowly.[31]

In order to understand fully the struggle for liquidity in the third period, the rise of the deposit business in the advanced states such as New York or Massachusetts must be considered. A few figures may illustrate the trend. In New York State the number of depositors increased twenty times between 1849 and 1859, while circulation and deposits grew as follows.[32]

	1837 (in $1000)	1847 (in $1000)	1857 (in $1000)
circulation	$24,198	$26,237	$32,395
deposits	19,342	35,096	104,350

(figures for 1837 and 1857 each before the suspension; 1847: November 1)

That is to say, in the state of New York the ratio of circulation to deposits was 1:0.8 in 1837, 1:1.34 in 1847, and 1:3.22 in 1857. These ratios show that the deposit business in those decades expanded more than the note business; and they may even imply that the increase was at the expense of the latter.

It is not difficult to explain the trend: The mere multiplication of banks all over the country made it possible to use checks where formerly only notes or post notes would have served the purpose; and, vice versa, the increased use of checks must have led to growing demand deposits. A second factor which made for this growth was the constant and urgent demand for domestic exchange in the interior of the country. It was claimed later that in this period banks profited more from exchange than from interest.[33] To satisfy that demand in 1837 the Bank of Pennsylvania and the Girard Banks issued post notes, and Connecticut banks as late as the 1850's made accommodation loans in the West. Or they lent their notes and thus built up a circulation in that section which returned to the East whenever domestic exchange in other forms was lacking.[34] It was undoubtedly sounder policy for country banks to tie together secondary reserves and their exchange business, growing after the downfall of the Second Bank of the United States. This was done when they discovered that balances in New York and Boston, for instance, could serve equally as domestic exchange and as reserve which in normal times was just as liquid and valuable as specie in their own vaults. It goes without saying that a policy of tying together secondary reserves and domestic exchange contributed to swelling demand deposits in New York City, Boston, Philadelphia, Baltimore, and perhaps a few other commercial centers.[35]

The development of bankers' balances had been in full swing as early as the 1830's; it proceeded after a short set-back in the liquidation period following the crisis of 1837. But in contrast to the earlier decade, in the 1840's and 1850's at the expense of the previously mentioned commercial centers New York tended to concentrate most of the holdings, some of which were used to redeem the notes of country banks under note redemption contracts while the bulk was liable to draft by check.[36]

However the growth of deposits had still another (third) cause, as was clearly seen by the Massachusetts Bank Commissioners in 1859. Once demand deposits had become an established fact it became convenient for large borrowers to have their accounts credited with the proceeds of bank loans (instead of taking out bank notes), a practice existing as early as the 1830's in the Second Bank of the United States. In consequence, created deposits began to take the place of notes and large transactions tended to be settled by checks and drafts.[37] Bank notes came to serve only in retail transactions. Businessmen would no longer keep more notes than were required as till money, but would deposit the rest with their banks. The latter would present them for redemption so that the growth of the deposit business, partly caused by the creation of deposits, resulted in an increased velocity of circulation of bank notes and a decrease in the total amount which could be kept afloat. There were many bankers, of course, who did not understand what was going on. They saw their circulation falling off, became worried, and tried all means to extend it. In Boston such bankers in the morning filled their carpetbags with notes and went to State Street lending them to "sharpers and brokers."[38] The same malpractice was common also in New York and Illinois. In Connecticut, on the other hand, banks lent their notes to "parties" (banks) in the West which undertook to redeem such notes as were loaned to them and as were specially marked. If such notes were presented at the counters of the issuing bank they were returned upon the borrower for redemption. The term "protected circulation" was used for notes so loaned and early in the 1850's they amounted to about $1,500,000. The state forbade this type of business in 1854; but it seems to have been common elsewhere also, e.g., in Pennsylvania. In Massachusetts, banks rediscounted commercial paper sending their notes for circulation. (Incidentally the author is unable to date the beginnings of this type of business [lending of notes], nor is he sure to what extent banks, as opposed to brokers and the like, borrowed notes of other banks.)[39] In addition, the hypothecation of notes to secure loans from other banks was not uncommon.[40]

In the West and South the development of a modern deposit business was slow, of course; for years note issues remained far more important than deposits. This is indicated, for instance, by the balance sheet of the State Bank of Indiana, at that time one of the most progressive and best managed banks in the West. In 1847 this bank had a circulation of $3,606,452 and deposits to the amount of $555,773.42, the ratio being 1:0.15; while in the same year the ratio in Connecticut was 1:0.4 and in New York, 1:1.34. In Georgia (to give a slightly later example from the South) in the seven months from July 1854 to January 1855 the ratio was on an average 1:0.3 (6.7 million dollars circulation as against 2.03 million dollars deposits).[41] Hedges has shown that not before 1855 did the total amount of deposits exceed the total amount of circulation in the nation as a whole.[42]

Bankers, economists, and legislators, as a matter of fact, groping for an understanding[43] of the change which was under way, lit on a theoretical question: what was the character of these new-fangled demand deposits?[44] In answer the Superintendent of the New York Banking Department "unwilling to accede to the proposition that bank credits were currency" at least conceded that they performed the function of currency. The Massachusetts Bank Commissioners went further and in 1851 stated bluntly: bank currency consists of circulation and deposits.[45] They were certainly right, for simultaneously with the increase of bank deposits their very character was changing. When the first American banks came into existence in the eighteenth century it was considered one of their functions to provide safe places of deposit for funds of merchants and other capitalists, and that aspect determined the nature of most of the existing deposit business, if any, during the first two periods of American banking. As Nicholas Biddle expressed it in his great speech of 1810,[46] the American banks had become "a safe depository for the wealth of the country." By that time demand deposits were already in existence and they soon started increasing in the advanced sections of the country, as has been described.[47] Nevertheless, considering bank deposits as quasi-permanent and relying on the experience of both Mercantilist deposit banks and early American institutions, some states, even in the third period, permitted banks to issue notes on the basis of their deposits. As late as the 1850's, disregarding the change that had taken and was taking place under their very eyes, conservative bankers still looked on deposits as "quiet, stable, and reliable"; and before 1857 the idea that deposits were "dangerous" "would have stamped its promulgator a tyro in banking." Even after the panic of that year Governor Wise of

Virginia deemed it progress to allow the banks of his state "to bank upon... one half only of the deposits made in them." Or, in other words, Virginia banks in addition to the issues based on their capital were to retain the right to issue notes on the basis of their deposits, but only to the amount of 50 per cent thereof.[48] As a matter of fact a new generation of bankers and legislators in the middle of the nineteenth century had to rediscover what had been known in the eighteenth, that deposits like notes might actually be demand obligations[49] and, in the second instance, that book credits like bank notes represented to a large extent created purchasing power.[50] It took the crisis of 1857 to drive home that lesson, especially in New York. Thereafter came to an end the pyramiding of one sort of demand obligations (one sort of created purchasing power) on another, which had been possible in some states as late as the 1840's and 1850's.[51]

However, the problem had still another aspect. The rise of the deposit business was due to an increase in lodged as well as created deposits. The increase in the former, stimulated by the paying of interest thereon, resulted, according to some observers in 1857, in nothing less than a revolution in banking and business. Prior to that time laymen had thought of banks as lenders only, although in the earlier periods they had occasionally borrowed also.[52] But now suddenly the public discovered that the banks were becoming more and more borrowers as well as lenders. The borrowing of funds by banks from other banks, especially by country banks from city correspondents, partly by rediscounting, was widespread. It was equally common for out-of-town banks to sell paper in New York through brokers (who neither assumed liability nor tied up funds of their own), transactions which also amounted to the borrowing of funds by country banks.[53] The conservative Boston banker, Samuel Hurd Walley, growing alarmed, wished this practice to be forbidden altogether;[54] and for many more of his contemporaries the borrowing of banks in order to sustain a high loan (or from another angle, a transfer of lodged deposits from one bank to another or the creation by one bank of a deposit for another) was objectionable: banks should stand on their own legitimate resources. Seen in this context and in connection with the paying of interest on demand deposits, the deposit business seemed to "reverse the whole system of sound banking by making banks borrowers as well as lenders of money."[55] (Actually they paid 4 to 6 per cent on such deposits.) Capital was supposed to be diverted from its regular channels because banks borrowed "at one price to lend at a higher." Thus the whole business of the country was supposed to have been thrown into the banks. (To be sure, complaints that private

sources of credit were drying up and that businessmen were becoming wholly dependent on banks had been registered in an earlier period too, and in fact John Jacob Astor and Jacob Barker seem to have been the last large private money lenders.)[56] The change seemed so revolutionary that in New England as late as 1862 the legality of the business in demand deposits was questioned. Borrowing by banks in general and inducing the public to lend funds to banks especially, seemed to run counter to the limitation of bank capital in charters. But the Supreme Court of Massachusetts and the New York Court of Appeals[57] decided in the affirmative the question of whether or not banks were entitled to borrow money.

The discussion of the new problems did not take place on a high level; but the fact that actually a minor revolution had taken place in the field of banking could not be denied. It became perfectly obvious during the crisis of 1857. The earlier monetary panics in America had resulted from war or overspeculation leading to large imports and subsequent external drains of specie. In 1857 the country for the first time experienced a peacetime suspension of specie payments caused mainly by an internal drain. In 1857 the security of the notes of the New York Free Banks was not questioned when the money market became tighter and tighter. The crisis broke in that city when panicky depositors decided to withdraw their funds. At that moment, as it appeared to contemporaries, it became a question whether the banks or the merchants should suspend in a body. "Capital in the shape of deposits for the first time in the history of this country... sided with the businessmen against the banks."[58] Regardless of whether or not contemporary description and comment are correct they show clearly that the banking business, at least in New York and the advanced East, had undergone a radical change under the influence of the development of demand deposits.[59]

These deep reaching changes thwarted a development which was still in an incipient stage. Note issue was becoming more rationalized than ever before in America. At least New York city bankers tended to follow the policy of the Bank of England once adopted there on the advice of some of the great monetary economists of the period.[60] Biddle had taken it over in the 1820's and for Forstall it had become a "must" by 1838:[61] "Foreign Exchange...[was becoming] the barometer by which the banker sailed his barque," as the Superintendent of the New York Banking Department wrote in 1857.[62] His Massachusetts counterparts, however, noted in a critical mood in 1861 that loans and note issues were not made dependent closely enough on transactions with other countries. When the "balance of indebtedness" was against us, loans should be decreased and specie, if possible, increased. Such tendency toward more "scientific" banking, if you please, was thwarted by the rise of created deposits in addition to the lodged ones. In the late 1850's successful banking in the city of New York meant "carrying the largest debt of good paper on interest upon the smallest amount of deadweight specie and skillfully adjusting the balances daily to be struck for and against the bank in the clearing house, thus maintaining its credit and standing in that house by the balance there daily presented." Or, in other words, the banks tried to incur the greatest possible amount of debt payable on demand with a given amount of coin. These statements are of unusual interest showing as they do how slow in those decades was the change of banking policy regardless of much remarkable progress. Everywhere in the preceding two periods, and in the back country down to Civil War times, it was common usage for banks to expand credit as far as possible without regard to liquidity or other objective criteria. The preceding quotations seem to indicate that the most advanced members of the banking fraternity in the 1850's still followed that policy although in a more sophisticated way (i.e., with a view to their clearing house balances) when handling their deposit business; while at the same time they determined, or at least were admonished to determine, their note issues with reference to an objective criterion, the exchange market. Thus their misunderstanding of the basic character of deposits kept them from going far enough along the road toward sounder banking upon which they had already entered.

As indicated before, the growth of the deposit business was due in part to a practice which became rather common in the period under investigation and from which New York especially profited: namely, the keeping of their reserves with city bankers by country banks. This was no really new device. It had originated in the second period of American banking in connection with the note business. Since notes tended to flow to the centers of trade it became necessary to have them redeemed there in order to make them useful and secure at the same time. (Thus came into being the custom of making notes of banks in the interior payable at trade centers,[63] a custom which seems to have died out in the early 1840's.) For that purpose the Suffolk Bank had been created; and when the state of New York in the early 1840's enacted a law according to which its banks had to redeem their notes in New York City, Troy, or Albany, the practice conquered the most important commercial state of the nation.[64] It implied that country banks kept part of their reserves with city banks. To be

sure, public opinion at that time looked only at note redemption, and not at the concomitant keeping of reserves in places other than the domiciles of the banks concerned. The matter gained a new aspect, however, when in the third period more and more country bankers kept outside of their vaults in the form of deposits part of their reserves not only against their circulation, but also against their other current liabilities. In this connection another change came into being. Whereas in the New England and New York redemption systems, those reserves seem to have been earmarked for note redemption, and at least by the Suffolk Bank were used exclusively for that purpose, the bank reserves held in the 1840's and 1850's with city correspondents were treated by the latter as regular demand deposits. This implied that they were invested by the city banks.

Since the growth of the business in demand deposits fell in an era of fierce competition[65] it was accompanied by a fight to attract them. Therefore banks widely, and especially in New York City, adopted the policy of paying interest on deposits both of individuals and of other banks.[66] This practice, alluded to earlier, was to become one of the most serious problems in American commercial banking. Competition from private bankers and trust companies, which rather generally paid interest, played a certain part in this development, not equally serious everywhere. In Massachusetts, for instance, interest-bearing deposits represented only a fraction of all deposits; and it was not customary for the Massachusetts banks at the time to pay interest on deposits of individuals.[67]

The question whether or not interest should be paid on deposits had already arisen in the preceding period, as has been described;[68] but as must be stressed in reply to a reviewer of the first volume of this work,[69] the payment of interest on bankers' balances was not of any major importance during the 1820's and 1830's. Or to put it differently, the question of receiving interest on demand deposits played no determining role in the decision of country bankers as to whether or not they would open accounts in New York, Philadelphia, etc. In the 1830's, interest payments served to draw bankers' deposits from A to B, from the banks, still reluctant to pay interest, to competing private bankers. From the 1840's on, however, interest payments on demand deposits came to have an economic as well as a business function: they made it possible for country banks to treat balances as secondary reserves, i.e., liquid and, at the same time, productive funds. Only in the third period did interest payments determine the decision of country banks to create bankers' balances which became truly important because standardized commercial paper was still lacking. On the other hand, after the practice of paying interest on bankers' balances had spread in the 1840's and 1850's and after the experiences of the crisis of 1857, it was discovered that what was beneficial for country banks was detrimental to the banks in the centers holding their interest-bearing deposits. Moreover, the payment of interest on demand deposits was then also recognized as unsound from the economic point of view. The Connecticut Bank Commissioners suggested in 1854 that the rate should at least legally be restricted to 3 per cent; it was actually restricted to 4 per cent, but the law was repealed in 1855. On the other hand, the Associated Banks of New York, i.e., the clearing house banks, through cooperation tried to put an end to the "self-inflicted injury." The custom was considered "wrong in principle and pernicious in its consequences," tending to encroach on the necessary specie reserves and through the possibility of sudden withdrawals of the inflated deposits endangering alike the public and the banks. The phenomenon was still so young at that time that outsiders hardly knew what happened to the deposited funds on which interest was paid. In 1857 it was deemed "possible that the amount may be loaned on call in Wall Street to bull and bear the stock market."[70] The bankers, of course, knew all too well that it was just this that was being done with the interest-bearing demand deposits in order to keep them available and productive at the same time. Thus on March 16, 1858, forty-two of the New York City banks made an agreement no longer to pay interest on deposits; more seem to have joined later, but it was impossible to bring in line all of the then existing forty-six New York banks. Outside of New York there was the same trend to abandon the dangerous and unhealthy practice (for instance, in Connecticut). However, it was revived after the Civil War under the pressure of new competitors in the field of banking.

As might be expected, the rise of the deposit business not only created a whole series of new problems, as just described,[71] but at the same time also complicated some of the old ones. As has been mentioned repeatedly in passing, the use of checks expanded, and a usage spread in this connection which seems to have started in the 1830's, the certification of checks.[72] It was to become really troublesome only in the following period. During the early years of the time under investigation the certification of checks was not considered as binding upon the bank in question and it had no other function than to give clerical information. Certified checks were charged to the account of the drawer only when presented. After the establishment of the New York Clearing House in 1854 the practice was slightly changed and assumed a different character: it became customary for the paying teller on request to write his name across the face of a check (found to be good) inside a stamp bearing the date and the name of the certifying bank. If certified in this form the check was considered a legal obligation upon the bank in question which immediately charged it to the account of the drawer, although the check would be presented only on the following day through the clearing house. However, the practice was not as yet abused.[73]

Much more important for the time being was the fact that rising deposits led to a dropping ratio of specie to demand liabilities. (It is telling that in the 1850's the banks in the advanced Commonwealth of Massachusetts held in the aggregate lower specie reserves than the banks in the nation as a whole;[74] they were pitifully small.) The drop in that ratio can be clearly seen from a statistical table published in 1876 by the Secretary of the Treasury showing the principal resources and liabilities of state banks from 1834 through 1863.[75] A study of the table reveals that the ratio of specie to circulation and deposits for the banking system as a whole varied in 1835, 1845, and 1850 between about 22 and 25 per cent (in the depression year 1840 it was lower, about 18 per cent). In those same three years deposits varied between about $83,000,000 and $91,000,000 and circulation between $103,000,000 and $114,000,000. In 1853 with circulation standing at about $146,000,000 and deposits at about $145,500,000 the ratio was down to 16 per cent; and in 1855, the first year in which deposits outran circulation (about $190,000,000 as against $187,000,000) the ratio reached the low point of 14 per cent. By 1858 and 1859 it stood at about 22 per cent again. The same detrimental influence of rising deposits on the reserve ratios against demand liabilities can be seen from a sample study of twenty-six banks published by the Massachusetts Bank Commissioners.[76] Between 1850 and 1853 the consolidated statements of these twenty-six banks showed that circulation increased by 19.2 per cent, deposits by 40.7 per cent, while specie increased only by 39.9 per cent. In other words the ratio of specie to demand liabilities decreased in the period. (It is particularly interesting that the Commissioners did not even discover this fact looking, as they did, at the ratio of specie to capital.) To put it differently, under the impact of the deposit business the struggle for liquidity took on a new aspect when it had barely come into existence. At the very moment when banks first began aiming at liquidity for the sake of the note holder, another type of demand obligations became common and made two steps necessary at the same time. It was not enough now for bankers and legislators to guard the movement of specie in relation to circulation; they had to go further and look at the ratio of "immediate liabilities" ("cash liabilities") and "immediate resources" ("cash resources"). Besides struggling for a sounder bank portfolio they had to focus their attention on the ratio of specie to circulation plus deposits or, in the advanced states practicing Free banking, on the ratio of specie to deposits (at that time a new outlook in banking). This matter will be taken up in the next section of this chapter.[77]

II

There was in the period under investigation no banker equally representative of the trend toward modern banking methods and principles as Samuel Hooper. Hooper (1808-1875), born in Marblehead, was the son of a shipowning merchant and bank president of that port. After an apprenticeship in his father's enterprise he joined the Boston firm of his father-in-law, Bryant, Sturgis and Company. He left in 1843 to become a partner in the house of William Appleton and Company. This latter firm took the name of Samuel Hooper and Company in 1862. In addition, Hooper was the most influential director of the important Merchants Bank of Boston. In this capacity he accumulated valuable experience in banking which stood him in good stead when he became first a Massachusetts representative, then a state senator and finally a Congressman; for this merchant's importance for American economic development lay mainly in his influence on legislation.

At a time when most bankers were rather soft money men, Hooper took a strong stand for hard money and thereby became an early exponent of the thinking typical in banking circles in the 1880's and 1890's. A pamphlet published in 1855 gives a good idea of Hooper's starting point.[78] Disclaiming any aim at establishing novel and original doctrines, Hooper proved himself a careful student of what was then modern English banking theory, although his short-run aims were traditionally American. He advocated the principle that the power of banks to issue circulating notes should be restricted and urged that they should be required to deposit security for their issues. (Small denominations should be forbidden altogether.) That is to say, Hooper believed in the New York Free Banking principle, a fact which was soon to become important, since he was destined to play a part in the legislative struggle leading to the enactment of the National Banking system. To the extent that Hooper advocated Free Banking, however, he advocated what he considered a temporary goal. As

a country grew richer it needed a more and more substantial basis for its currency in comparison to what had been tolerable previously, until paper could be wholly withdrawn from circulation and the latter consist exclusively of metallic money. With such ideas in mind Hooper commented on the Peel Act as a temporary measure preparing the way for the abolition of paper money in England.

Hooper's ideas on the role of specie in banking were somewhat hazy when he wrote his pamphlet of 1855. He rightly saw the flaw in contemporary reasoning, that by substituting paper money for coin the national economy gained additional capital to be used for productive purposes. (He also recognized as an error the dogma that redeemable bank paper could not depreciate.)[79] He did not wish banks to lock up specie at a rate of 5 to 10 per cent of their issues. Specie should circulate so that business would be regulated by "just and correct principles," (by the "laws of trade," as one expressed it at that time), while there were no general principles and laws to control the amount of paper money in circulation. Hooper could not see how it was possible that democratic America could give private corporations the right to furnish the currency which measured all values, a despotic power used elsewhere only by autocratic governments. If the issue of notes were restricted, the profits of banks would decline; but the precious metals, providing a stable measure of value, would take the place of notes, while for certain purposes checks would serve instead.

Hooper's first great achievement, which falls into the period under investigation, was the Massachusetts Banking Act of 1858 which has been alluded to. It will be described in detail[80] how in his struggle for this act Hooper was influenced by the Louisiana banking act of 1842, the basic ideas of which through his instrumentality migrated to Massachusetts. In the latter state the question of specie reserves came to the fore by the middle of the 1850's. In 1853 the Bank Commissioners of the state reported that public attention had "of late" been drawn to this subject. Specie reserves were considered too small, but even in 1855 it was deemed impossible to fix a ratio of specie to circulation; one of specie to capital seemed attainable instead. In 1857 the commissioners gave up that antiquated point of view, but their statements conflict: one time they think of a ratio of specie to deposits and a little later they suggest legal requirements of a specie reserve related to the banks' capital or to circulation and deposits.[81] Thus the soil was prepared.

The influence of the Louisiana banking act on Hooper can be discerned as early as 1858 in a document which, as state senator he drafted in answer to a speech of Governor Nathaniel P. Banks of the Commonwealth. The latter had suggested the enactment of a law requiring a 20 per cent specie reserve against circulation and suppressing notes in denominations of $5 and below. In drafting the answer Hooper was seconded by Amasa Walker, cosigner of the paper.[82] The ideas of the two men tallied. While Hooper considered a paper currency a temporary expedient, as he now repeated, Walker in 1857 had drafted the following plan: The existing "mixed currency" of the state, i.e., the one consisting of paper and metal circulating side by side, should be gradually changed by forbidding in consecutive steps small notes, notes below $10 and notes below $25 until at last all notes were forbidden except those backed 100 per cent by metallic money.[83]

It goes without saying that Hooper and Walker in their suggestions could not go as far as they would have liked; they had the instinct to recognize what was attainable. Thus they became creative leaders. The idea that notes or deposits or that notes and deposits were to be secured by legal specie reserves was in the air.[84] In taking up the idea Hooper and Walker made themselves exponents of a trend, but they were able to put into effect in Massachusetts what for years remained but a trend elsewhere. They themselves were aware of the fact that they were blazing the trail while the public widely, but erroneously, thought that banks were required by law to keep a certain percentage of specie against their circulation.[85] Hooper's and Walker's short run aim was to increase the specie available in the Commonwealth. For this purpose they suggested, in line with ideas as old as they were incorrect, that small notes be forbidden;[86] and at the same time, under the influence of the Louisiana banking setup and in line with advanced public opinion they proposed that banks be forced to keep on reserve in specie one fifth of their circulation and deposits. A bill to this effect was presented, recommended by the Joint Committee on Banks, and became the basis of the Act to increase the amount of specie in the Commonwealth.[87]

This Massachusetts Act of 1858 (although it could be easily evaded by borrowing specie and although it had many other defects) is historically important for several reasons. First of all, it enacted a legal reserve (to be sure one of 15 per cent instead of the recommended 20 per cent). Thereby a development of several decades was brought to the point of establishing in the advanced North-East a precedent that was soon to become national practice. Although the ideological development reaches back into the eighteenth century, as will be described later,[88] it is almost certain that in America legal specie reserves were not con-

templated before the crisis of 1837 had run its course. The original New York Free Banking Act of 1838 embodied one of $12\frac{1}{2}$ per cent against bank notes, while 20 per cent had been suggested in the original amendment to the bill.[89] In the same year a committee was instructed by the Massachusetts House of Representatives to report a bill which was to include a clause requiring banks to keep a 50 per cent specie reserve against their notes. Nothing came of this Massachusetts action;[90] and the New York law was amended in 1840 so as to drop the requirement. When the New York comptroller shortly thereafter recommended 20 per cent reserves, his advice was not heeded.[91] However, in 1839 and 1840 legislative committees in Ohio recommended a 30 per cent specie reserve against notes and the suggestion was enacted in 1845.[92] Three years earlier, in 1842, Louisiana, going even further, had permanently adopted a 33 1/3 specie reserve against <u>cash liabilities</u>. At the same time a contemporary American author suggested that banks should not discount to an amount larger than three times the amount of specie in their vaults and that they should discount short term business paper only.[93]

At that point the development was reaching a fork in the road and was beginning to move on two different tracks: The first led to the enactment of legal specie reserves against notes, for instance in Ohio and Connecticut, as has been described.[94] The second, in contrast, led to legal specie reserves against cash liabilities (or against cash liabilities minus circulation, i.e., deposits). Material that is available for the 1830's and 1840's shows that people were becoming aware of this possibility, if not necessity. As early as 1834 the <u>Report of the</u> [New York] <u>Union Committee</u>, written, or at least strongly influenced by Albert Gallatin, spoke of the ratio of specie to demand liabilities.[95] In 1843 the Massachusetts Bank Commissioners reported both the ratio of specie to circulation and of specie to circulation plus deposits, proof that the problem was at least seen.[96] In 1847, the president of the Farmers and Merchants Bank of Memphis, Tennessee, suggested a 20 per cent specie reserve against bank notes and deposits. By that time it was becoming known in America that the Bank of England secured its demand obligations by a specie and bullion reserve of at least 33 1/3 per cent,[97] and soon progressive bankers and legislators "upon the highest financial authority," as Governor Harris of Tennessee put it in 1857, were aiming in the same direction.[98] (To be sure, Thomas Hart Benton complained as late as that year that the keeping on hand of an amount of hard money proportioned to the liabilities of banks seemed to be unknown "even in name.")[99] In fact, however, when Louisiana adopted a Free Banking Act in 1853,[100] it set that ratio of 33 1/3 per cent as a legal requirement. But at the same time the state veered away from the straight course which it had set itself in 1842; for the ratio of 33 1/3 per cent obtaining in the act of 1842 as reserve against cash liabilities was now required against deposits only (sec. 26). (The remaining 66 2/3 per cent were to be backed by specie funds, bills of exchange, and paper maturing within ninety days.) Notes were considered adequately secured by high class bonds. It must be stressed that this law being a concession to the popular Free Banking bias was a step backward in comparison with the act of 1842, replacing, as it did, legal reserves against cash liabilities by legal reserves against deposits. By 1858 the Louisiana set-up was becoming a model, although as will be described in another context it was hardly understood. (It was not seen that the strength of the Louisiana Act of 1842 lay in the combination of ample legal specie reserves and banking on short term self-liquidating business paper.)[101] On the whole interest concentrated on the specie reserves, and voluntary or legal ratios of from 15 to 33 1/3 per cent against cash liabilities were widely recommended, as for instance by Hooper and Amasa Walker in Massachusetts, the Philadelphia Board of Presidents,[102] Governor Harris of Tennessee, and President Buchanan.[103] But at the same time just as earlier in Louisiana the issue was becoming more and more blurred. In New York, because of the happy experience with the notes of Free Banks in the crisis of 1857, the Superintendent of the Banking Department concluded that specie reserves against government-bond-backed banknotes were superfluous, while deposits should be secured by a 20 per cent specie reserve. In the same vein Governor King of New York and Opdyke, writing for a New York businessmen's committee, recommended legal specie reserves against deposits only,[104] while a report of the New York Chamber of Commerce, very able in every other respect, did not even see that there were alternatives and consequently a problem: legal reserves against cash liabilities or legal reserves against cash liabilities minus notes.[105] To be sure, in a meeting held by the Associated Banks of New York on March 5, 1858 a committee was appointed "to consider the measure of each bank holding at all times a certain fixed percentage of coin to its liabilities," but in the end on March 16 the majority only agreed to keep no less than 20 per cent against net-deposits of every kind, including certified checks, but excluding circulating notes.[106] Thus in contrast to Louisiana and Massachusetts, progress in New York came in a diluted form and as a voluntary measure, although the

state's banking department kept urging the enactment of reserve requirements.[107] But, in fact, before the outbreak of the Civil War no New York bank kept less than 20 per cent specie against deposits, while the city banks kept almost 30 per cent. Following the New York pattern Iowa enacted in 1858 a 25 per cent reserve against deposits and left her banks to decide how much specie they considered sufficient to guarantee the redemption of their notes.[108]

The opponents of legal specie reserves (and there were many) concentrated their criticism on the point that large specie reserves would make it impossible for banks to earn fair dividends and that reserves which could not be touched in the moment of danger were useless, unless the law was to be broken as they anticipated.[109] The weakness of the latter argument will be shown shortly.

However the Massachusetts Banking Act is historically important for still a second reason. Hooper and Walker inserted a clause which guaranteed an automatic working of the legal ratio of specie to short term liabilities. In so doing they may have developed a suggestion which the Massachusetts Bank Commissioners proffered in 1850 according to which banks should be enjoined from making loans whenever their specie reserves fell below 6 per cent of their capital.[110] But it is equally possible that they copied the Louisiana law of 1853. That of 1842, Forstall's achievement, had tended in this direction although the language of that law is not too clear. Under the earlier Louisiana act banks could not lend on accommodation paper as long as their cash liabilities were not represented one third by specie and two thirds by ninety-day business paper. The Louisiana Free Banking Act of 1853 in its section 27 gave the underlying idea a classical formulation: if at any time the specie of a bank should fall below the established ratio of 33 1/3 per cent of its deposits and remain so for a period of ten days such banks were forbidden to lend or discount until the ratio was restored. Such a formulation was taken over into the Massachusetts act: if the weekly average of specie fell for two consecutive weeks below 15 percent of a bank's circulation and deposits it had to stop making new loans and discounts until the ratio was restored.[111] Thence, through Hooper, the clause was to come into the National Bank Act. It proved wholesome beyond expectation, for it resulted in higher specie reserves than legally required if a bank wished to do a continuous business. And every bank was bound to aim at that goal. This point was seen clearly and widely,[112] and much of the criticism leveled against the clause was invalid. That it worked automatically recommended it to a generation which believed so ardently in the self-regulation of economic life.[113]

In 1860 Hooper published another pamphlet on monetary and banking matters, An Examination of the Theory and the Effects of Laws Regulating the Amount of Specie in Banks. This booklet shows Hooper's thinking midway between his Massachusetts achievement, the law of 1858, and his decisive influence on national banking legislation in Civil War time, to be studied in a later chapter.[114] Hooper's ideas had developed a good deal since 1855 although he did not deviate from the course taken in the earlier publication, and they will be discussed in their proper place.[115]

III

The development of banking organization proceeded along the lines which had begun to appear in the second period. The set-up then already common in Eastern city banks[116] was adopted now in country banks also: the boards of directors ceased to be administrative bodies. Their power, especially the decision on discounts had to be and was delegated. Possible delegates were, among others, traditionally the cashiers (who in the execution of their new functions were or were not supervised by one of the directors or by the president).[117]

As an example of a cashier who thus became the general manager of his bank in the 1850's, Francis W. Edmonds may be cited. He proudly spoke of himself as the administrator to whom the success of the Mechanics Bank of New York was due. No one shared the responsibility with him, as he claimed, although he was "faithfully aided... by the subordinate officers of the bank and by [the] directors." (Italics mine). He compared his position with that of cashiers in other banks "who [had] efficient and capable presidents." (The question in this case is not to prove or disprove these statements, but to take them as an indication of administrative possibilities in the banks of the period.)[118] The public, to be sure, still thought of the cashier of a bank as a glorified bookkeeper.[119]

To the extent that cashiers did not fall heir to the administrative functions of the earlier bank boards, presidents and cashiers together might absorb them.[120] But in the Eastern city banks, as a rule, presidents now tended to rise to become administrators and general managers where that change had not taken place earlier. In some cases they had been cashiers themselves and the latter's position either lost importance[121] or it became a stepping stone for young men. The development was widely considered dangerous especially where bank officers were poorly paid. The New York Bank Commissioners, for instance, felt that the

shift of power due to the delegation of functions on the part of bank boards had contributed to the downfall of the Safety Fund System.[122]

During the period under investigation, cashiers and presidents in a number of banks were able to engraft a private business on that of the bank which they served. This development was due to the fact that charters often forbade some banks to do a business which others under more liberal charters or laws were permitted to do. In such cases cashiers and presidents acted as the agents of the bank's customers in buying and selling exchange, stocks, time bills, etc. In other cases they acted as transfer agents for corporations which held their accounts with these institutions. As a rule the customers' bank accounts were used in such operations commissions or profits on which accrued to the cashier or president, personally. Advanced opinion held that such private business of cashiers or presidents was legitimate if the boards were informed, although the public, as a rule, had no conception of when it dealt with the bank and when with its cashier or president as an individual.[123]

An early case of this type can be found in the Minutes of the Board of Directors of the Bank of New York. On June 26, 1832 the board gave permission to its cashier to accept the agency of the New Orleans Canal and Banking Company, a correspondent of the Bank of New York, for the transfer of its stock to London and to settle with the former company for such compensation as he might. In the 1850's, to give later examples, Francis W. Edmonds, the cashier of the Mechanics Bank of New York, was the transfer agent of the Canton Company. He shared voluntarily his compensation with the clerks of the bank who did the actual work. Shepherd Knapp, the president of the same bank, as he himself boasted, "bagged" $15,000 per annum through acting as the trustee to whom were made out mortgages issued as security for bonds. In such a way he acted, for instance, for the bondholders of the Parker Vein Coal Company. Another New York bank president was said to have made annually from such transactions more than from his salary. Edmonds claimed, probably truthfully, that it was usual for directors to offer such jobs to the officers of their banks as friendly acts to help them along[124]

As to individual bank directors and bank boards and as to their functions A. B. Johnson,[125] then an old gentleman and a well known New York country banker, published in Homans' The Banker's Common-Place Book (1851) an interesting article entitled "On the Duties, Omissions, and Misdoings of Bank Directors." He explained that the charters of the New York Safety Fund Banks conferred on the boards three powers, legislative (i.e., policy making), supervisory, and appointive. Under the first the boards established such offices as were necessary, regulating duties and salaries. They determined the mode of conducting business and of dealing with property, effects, and the stock of the bank. Under the appointing power they selected proper incumbents for the offices thus established, while the supervisory power found expression especially in the ability of the boards to discharge appointees at pleasure. Other contemporary sources speak of the often neglected obligation of bank directors to institute examinations[126] which, as a matter of course, belonged to their supervisory powers. Johnson stressed that the boards should legislate, appoint, and supervise, but not manage. Management should be left to the chief executive officer. A contemporary bank officer, in a booklet written for particular purposes, permits a glimpse into what was going on in boards that were not apathetic. His bank had two types of customers, mechanics and merchants. The latter required large loans in sums of ten thousands of dollars, the former small ones in amounts of a few hundred. Both groups of "dealers" were represented on the board and it was difficult at times to keep conflicts from breaking into the open.[127]

Johnson knew that cashiers had once been chief executives in banks, although as a rule, they had been excluded from the directorates.[128] Consequently, while pleading for a strong executive officer, Johnson left open whether he preferred a president or a cashier to fill that position. But executive power should be centered in one person, at all events, for divided responsibility led easily to divided vigilance. On the other hand, Johnson wished the boards to be composed of large stockholders so that the overall administration of banks would approximate that of private enterprises. If it were not possible to get efficient bank directors who would attend board meetings regularly because of their stock holdings, i.e., on the basis of their pecuniary interest in the success of banks, then compensation should be offered to them. The practice of remunerating directors by giving them a claim on bank loans seemed unsound to Johnson, especially if such loans were not properly secured. (Other contemporaries thought differently.) The indifference of certain bank boards (which met often only once a month) becomes very clear from the following sentences which were meant to convey praise rather than blame. Addressing the directors of his own bank Johnson wrote:

> Though I have been an officer of your corporation for nearly a third of a century I never saw your board but once -- the fall of 1843 -- and then I saw the same men to a

great extent who thirty years previously in the same chamber and around the same table commenced banking.[129]

It is hardly possible to show the change in the position of bank directors better than by comparing the following contemporary statements: When Thomas Willing in 1807 resigned from the First Bank of the United States whose president he had been for many years, the directors praised his "impartial conduct" observed "as well during their procedures as in coinciding with their decisions."[130] Twenty-five years later, when Charles Wilkes relinquished the presidency of the Bank of New York he wrote to his successor Cornelius Heyer: "I never can forget the uniform and unbounded confidence and support which I have uniformly received from the directors by which the path of my duty has been rendered easier while it has been cheered."[131] Again about twenty-five years later a cashier, as quoted above, could say what amounts to: La banque, c'est moi, adding that he had been "faithfully aided by the directors."[132]

It goes without saying that public opinion was slow in realizing the change. As late as the 1840's and 1850's Pennsylvania legislators, for instance, following up earlier precedents enacted the liability of bank directors in case of "fraudulent insolvency" and progressively expanded the concept.[133]

In the 1840's and 1850's, parallel with the changes in the functions of bank officers and bank boards described above, the divorce of ownership and control became a reality in an ever wider number of banks, a development which had started earlier[134] but was not easily understood even then. To the contrary, by 1850 the Massachusetts Bank Commissioners wished to establish the liability of stockholders in certain emergencies and New York introduced the double liability clause in the constitution of 1846,[135] whence it came into the National Currency Act.(The clause was implemented by chapter 226 of the New York laws of 1849.) A Wisconsin law required the guaranty of one fourth of the total outstanding currency by bondsmen[136] (presumably stockholders or stockholding directors); and as late as 1860 the Bank Commissioners of the State of Maine were pleading for the publishing of the names of the stockholders of the banks, because their reputation was supposed to be reflected in the credit standing of their banks. Actually the time of such connection had passed.[137] Bank stockholders in the 1850's would pay the installments on their subscriptions and would cash dividends but they would not even attend the annual meetings, so that often it was difficult to form a quorum.[138] The presence of numerous stockholders (other than directors) at a stockholders meeting would have been considered extraordinary, and their influence had become negligible. Only in exceptional cases did they exert some control through committees of their own choice.[139] Such indifference was partly the by-product of legislative action. The face value of shares was set extremely low in bank charters, in order to disperse the advantages that could be derived therefrom. Thereby stock went into the hands of small holders scattered all over the country, unknown to each other, and uninformed as to the conduct of the directors and officers who, according to the thought of the time, were but their agents. Moreover, the dividends to be received by many stockholders would not have been high enough to cover the cost of a trip to a stockholders meeting. Thus the same legislation which was successful in bringing about that wide distribution of bank stock which was desired, helped to destroy the power of the stockholders over the banks, except when there was a fight for control.[140] Often indifference on the part of the stockholders was reflected in the boards.

At this point earlier trains of thought must be taken up again: the boards became either apathetic[141] or, with the help of proxies self-perpetuating bodies.[142] In the former cases, the officers not only ran the banks without being controlled, but often also gained what was considered an improper influence on the election of the directors. In the latter cases the directors elected themselves, did or did not determine policies and could set the limits of their liabilities, leaving the management pure and simple to the officers. In both cases the interests of the stockholders were neglected.

IV

As always in periods of rapid change, so in the 1840's and 1850's a cross section of public opinion on banking pictures a really bewildering situation. There can be found side by side expressions of the most obsolete[143] and of the most modern ideas. It goes without saying that in the advanced states of the East, banking as such was recognized as indispensable and beyond question. As early as 1838 a Pennsylvania legislative committee stated that "no respectable portion of the community, if indeed any of our citizens, advocated" "a total overthrow" of the banking system.[144] It was not so in the South and West: Iowa agrarians, as Bray Hammond reports, were convinced that banking was a "mad, untamable beast," the "common enemy of mankind," a "withering and blighting curse," and a most successful device to swindle people.[145] The Governor of Mississippi would not go quite as far, but to him banking was still an "experiment" which, he felt, should not be repeated in his state. His colleagues

in Tennessee and Alabama, being more positive, considered the whole banking system of this country as "founded on error" or "radically wrong," respectively. The governor of the former state suggested that by-and-by his state and its neighbors should wide up all banks. Capitalists would then provide exchange for the commercial wants of the community and specie would flow in as naturally "as water finds its level." In Missouri people were convinced that the country would have been better off if banks had never been created, but that now they could no longer be dispensed with: and many in Alabama would have agreed to that statement wholeheartedly, for banking was considered a necessary evil. The chief magistrate of Kentucky in the same vein registered his opinion that the public wanted banks and preferred "bank" paper which would become inconvertible in times of crisis to no paper at all. Finally the young northwestern part of the country recognized that banks were so interwoven with business and state interest that no radical change could be made without serious detriment, as the bank comptroller of Wisconsin put it.[146]

Parallel to differences of opinion with regard to banking as such, went differences of opinion as to practical measures with regard to banking. "In the states of the Upper Mississippi Valley public policy ranged from absolute prohibition of bank credit, through state monopoly to laissez faire."[147] Moreover, when it came to making suggestions for improving the indisputable shortcomings of contemporary banking, old fashioned panaceas were recommended along with modern and sound remedies. For example, the prohibition of small notes which had been a topic of discussion in England in the 1810's and 1820's and somewhat later had come to be debated in the advanced states of America, was still being offered as a cure for the evils of the day.[148] Furthermore, the limitation of note issues relative to the bank capital, that old Mercantilist recipe, was prescribed repeatedly in this period in which banking was already essentially far advanced on the way toward modern methods.[149] Finally the question of legal interest rates was still moot. Conservatives, including such men as Samuel Hooper,[150] continued to cling to the idea that a legal interest rate was necessary and that it was illegitimate for bankers to evade it. Such evasion was practiced by forcing borrowers to make their notes payable at a place other than the domicile of the bank, so that they appeared as bills of exchange, and "exchange" could be charged over and above the legal interest rate. In figuring the rate to be charged for "exchange" considerations entered which had nothing to do with the cost of shipping specie, such as the state of the money market, the circumstances of the borrower or the length of the loan, considerations which make the spurious character of the charge evident. On the other hand, the belief in the fairness of legal interest rates was waning even in the minds of bank debtors, for whose benefit such requirements had been put on the statute books: and the infraction of the legal interest laws was general, as the Connecticut Bank Commissioners reported in 1856.[151] By that time Massachusetts country businessmen themselves often proposed making their paper payable in Boston in order to enable local banks to make what the borrowers considered a fair profit.[152] Thus by 1860 the concept of usury was ripe for discard. But only in Massachusetts was the existing usury act repealed, while in New York, beginning in 1850, it was whittled down. In the latter year a law was passed in the state prohibiting corporations from interposing the defence of usury in any action.[153]

Nevertheless the National Currency acts of 1863 and 1864 still contained clauses on legal interest rate and usury. The original act following the New York pattern set the legal rate at 7 per cent; while the version passed in the latter year[154] stipulated in section 30 that interest could be charged at the rate allowed by the state in which the National Bank was located. If the state in question had not passed any usury law the rate was limited to 7 per cent. In case of violation the interest was to be forfeited and the borrower could sue for damage to an amount of twice the interest charged. As late as 1874 this clause was reenacted,[155] and in 1875 the country's bankers, assembled at Saratoga, discussed "free trade in money," as the problem had come to be styled.[156] The regulation is still on the statute books,[157] as are usury laws in most American states where they are evaded and transgressed with no action taken by the authorities.

Many of the evils which cried for remedial action in the 1850's resulted from the adoption of the New York Free Banking system all over the country. Free Banking has been stressed as the crowning achievement of the second period of American banking: but its victory came in the third period, that is, in a time when other problems were already on the agenda in the more mature states. Consequently, the various proposals to improve on Free Banking, as advanced as they must have appeared to contemporaries, to the historian look antiquated in comparison with the struggle for liquidity, with the rise of the deposit business, with the creation of check clearings, etc. But one must keep in mind that it was the less advanced American states which were most anxious to adopt Free Banking in the 1850's. Thereby they actually made progress, but subsequently businessmen and legislators became disturbed with the working of the system. Thus in the 1850's numerous suggestions

were submitted with regard to the securities which should or should not be deposited as the basis for bank note issues. In numerous states mortgages were still among the eligible securities and to the extent that they were excluded banking gained a more modern aspect.[158] Even New York Free Banking in the late 1850's still had a truly Mercantilist feature: under the act, as it stood at that time, a land owner could mortgage his land, deposit the mortgage with the banking department, and receive bank notes in exchange.[159] That is to say, as late as 1858 he could "melt down" his property into money as Sir James Steuart had described it in the 1760's.

There was still another problem which cried for solution in connection with the introduction of Free Banking on one hand and the struggle for liquidity on the other. It was perfectly within the spirit of earlier American banking for would-be bankers under the Free Banking acts to invest all their capital in securities, or, from another point of view, in bank notes, which they then lent out in a more or less legitimate way. Such a policy was no longer in line with modern ideas of liquidity and thus there could be found in the 1850's complaints that banks were run without "working capital" (Vermont 1855; Wisconsin 1858) and suggestions that banks be restrained from investing more than 50 per cent of their capital in notes with the other 50 per cent kept in the form of specie and what we call secondary reserves today.[160]

The various proposals just described can be characterized as patchwork. They were supplemented by really modern suggestions, some of which, namely those regarding liquidity, have been discussed above in detail. Other modern propositions of the 1840's and 1850's referred, for instance, to the creation of contingency reserves, uniform dividend policy, and the prohibition of banks from owning their own stock.[161]

If one keeps in mind to what extent by 1860 leading citizens of this country disagreed with regard to the nature and need of banking and with regard to fundamental questions of banking policy, one will not be surprised to find the same disagreement on the question of what constituted legitimate and sound banking.[162] For advanced thinkers in some of the older states legitimate banking was the swapping of promises to pay between banks and businessmen. However, in those states in which Free Banking influenced the thinking, it was not easy to arrive at this point of view though it became typical later. In those states note issue on the basis of first class government paper, in combination with complete freedom of banking in every other respect, was considered the best possible if not the perfect kind of banking, and it appeared as the solution of its main problems, a solution which was supposed to correspond to the separation of the issue and banking departments of the Bank of England.[163] Once bank notes were issued exclusively on first class government securities there was for the conservative exponents of Free Banking no objection to the combination of long and short term credit in the same type of enterprise. Nor was there any objection to such combination nor to the indiscriminate issue of notes on the basis of both short and long term obligations of bank borrowers in the states which had not succumbed to the fashion of Free Banking, except in Louisiana. The essential difference between promises to pay originating from short term business transactions and from long term loans for the development of capital resources, respectively, was well understood by advanced businessmen. On the other hand, the incompatibility of these two types of transactions, if combined in one enterprise, did not become common knowledge before the decades following the Civil War.

It has been stated in detail that many conservative bankers and legislators in the advanced states, let alone those in the interior, had much difficulty in recognizing the importance of the young demand-deposit business, certain aspects of which were held to be illegitimate even as late as 1860. On the other hand, it developed rapidly and, finally, at the end of the period, was recognized as legal. There was one accessory feature of this new type of banking, however, which generally came to be considered unsound by the end of the 1850's, namely, attracting deposits by paying interest thereon.

In the Free Banking states there was agreement that the mere issue of notes without running at the same time a full-fledged banking business was illegitimate.[164] Actually, in many cases, securities were deposited and notes taken out for no other purpose than to be lent in batches to speculators. In other cases, in New York, notes were handed to brokers and money lenders and the "bank's" only profit besides the interest on the deposited securities was the one-half of one per cent redemption

discount which was split with the redemption agent. However, this sort of business was made impossible by 1850 through an amendment to the New York Free Banking Act, which reduced that discount to one-quarter of one per cent.

Another set of differences of opinion as to what constituted legitimate banking resulted from the fact that by 1860 American banking was still regional, if not local, but on the point of taking a more national aspect. Consequently there were many conservatives who still objected to banks overstepping local borders, not to mention state lines. They were justified in that up to their time inter-community and interstate banking had tended to be fraudulent banking;[165] but times were rapidly changing. In 1871 Charles Francis Adams wrote: "One fact must be accepted to begin with, the railroad has burst through the state limits... Capital does not recognize the territorial divisions of the common country...; it destroys them.[166] It is in this light that one must look at the actions and reactions of progressives and conservatives, respectively, with regard to the new type of interstate banking which developed in the 1840's and 1850's. In these decades conservatives still objected to banks being owned by "foreigners," e.g., banks in Maine owned by Chicagoans or Bostonians,[167] or even banks discounting paper abroad in order to make either large profits (Vermont) or to build up a circulation in the West (Connecticut). In the last named state it was considered at least unsound that its bankers kept reserves abroad, i.e., in Boston and New York.[168] Around 1857 the buying of commercial paper by agents in the New York market was condemned because thereby fewer funds were available to local merchants and manufacturers, and because banks were banks and not bill brokers.[169] However, a few years later, after the outbreak of the Civil War, it was conceded that such paper was uniformly and promptly met at maturity as no local discounts were. A law then required the Connecticut banks to loan an amount equal to their capital to parties in that state before they could loan funds abroad.[170]

Chapter X

THIRD PERIOD - GENERAL CHARACTERISTICS

1. For what follows in the text see <u>U.S. 30th Congr. 1st sess., House Executive Document 77</u>, 445; <u>U.S. 35th Congr. 1st sess., House Executive Document 107</u>, 322.

2. <u>U.S. 35th Congr. 1st sess., House Executive Document 107</u>, 120. State of New York, Superintendent of the Banking Department, <u>Report</u> (for 1857), 26. See also the <u>Annual Report of the Comptroller</u> of the same state, Millard Fillmore, (for 1848) <u>Assembly Document (1849)</u>, 5,55: securities deposited against notes shall be sufficient and readily convertible into cash.

3. As late as 1868 Hugh McCulloch spoke of the "necessary relation of circulation to capital."

4. It is noteworthy that as late as 1837 the manager of the London and Westminster Bank, James William Gilbart, an authority in banking, was thinking in terms of the proportion which the capital of a bank should bear to its liabilities (notes plus deposits); but the old idea was put into a modern setting: Gilbart proposed an increase of the capital in case of an unfavorable ratio (<u>History</u>, 67).

5. See, for instance, Carey, <u>Letters to Seybert</u>, 20, 21.

6. <u>U.S. 30th Congr. 1st sess., House Executive Document 77</u>, 443; or Levi Woodbury's "Report from the Secretary of the Treasury in relation to the present system of keeping and disbursing the public money," Dec. 15, 1834 in <u>U.S. 23d Congr., 2d sess., Senate Document 13</u>, 28. See also "Currency, Banking and Credit," 28.

7. See vol. I of this work, page 27.

8. Speech of 1810, <u>Debates, Pennsylvania House of Representatives relative to the Bank of the United States</u>, 49.

9. <u>Reasons for the Inexpediency of Chartering a National Bank</u>, 8. The modern point of view can be found as early as 1830 in the McDuffie Report (<u>U.S. 21st Congr. 1st sess., House Report 358</u>, dated Apr. 13, 1830). See also Massachusetts Bank Commissioners, <u>Report</u> (for 1849), 7.

10. New York Bank Commissioners, <u>Report</u> (for 1834), 12.

11. Prior to Adam Smith, Postlethwayt (<u>op. cit.</u>, 196) has recommended a ratio of 25 per cent.

12. For Georgia (1854/55) and Tennessee (Jan. 1, 1857), respectively, see <u>U.S. 33d Congr. 2d sess., House Executive Document 82</u>, 166; <u>U.S. 35th Congr. 1st sess., House Executive Document</u> 107, 239. In 1833 Duane had written to President Jackson that "on an average of all the banks... one dollar in silver cannot be paid for six dollars in circulation" (<u>op. cit.</u>, 105).

13. Massachusetts Bank Commissioners, <u>Report</u> (for 1842), 4.

14. See <u>U.S. 33d Congr. 1st sess., House Executive Document 102</u>, 89 for Connecticut; 22-48 for Massachusetts; 15, 16 for Vermont and New Hampshire.

15. See vol. I of this work, page 79 and below.

16. <u>U.S. 33d Congr. 1st sess., House Executive Document 102</u>,3.

17. <u>Op. cit.</u>, 149.

18. Helderman, <u>op. cit.</u>, 42 ff. <u>U.S. 26th Congr. 1st sess., House Executive Document 172</u>, 1083 ff, especially 1090. John Brough (1811-1854), pioneer editor and Democratic politician, Civil War governor of Ohio. See <u>Dict. of Am. Biogr.</u>, and on his activities as the chairman of the state's committee on banking and currency, <u>Ohio State Arch. and Hist. Quart.</u>, XIII (1904), 45 ff.

    T.W. Bartley (1812-1885), Ohio lawyer and judge, Democratic member of state assembly and senate, acting governor of Ohio, 1844. <u>Ibid.</u>, XXXI (1922), 213,214.

19. <u>U.S. 30th Congr. 1st sess., House Executive Document 77</u>, 194, 196; <u>Connecticut Public Acts</u> 1848, chapter XVII; Connecticut Bank Commissioners, <u>Report</u> (1854), 6.

20. <u>Public Acts</u>, 1852, chapter XXIII.

21. Massachusetts Bank Commissioners, <u>Report</u> (for 1849), 7,12; (for 1855), 76.

22. <u>Laws of Indiana</u>, 1852, chapter 10, section 33.

23. <u>U.S. 30th Congr. 1st sess., House Executive Document 77</u>,195; <u>U.S. 35d Congr. 1st sess., House Executive Document 107</u>, 182,246. <u>U.S. 37th Congr. 3d sess., House Executive Document 23</u>, 80.

    Typical of the thinking of a time of transition was the regulation in Maine which permitted banks to issue notes to the amount of 50 per cent of their capital and in addition three dollars in notes on every dollar specie in their vaults. The total issue was limited to the amount of capital plus specie on hand (<u>ibid.</u>, 6).

24. An Act to regulate banks and banking institutions... sec. 37.

25. Laws of 1860, No. 376, sec. 31. The section seems to indicate familiarity with the Massachusetts Banking Act of 1858. Amasa Walker in <u>Bankers Magazine</u> XVII (1862/63), 838 points to the trend.

26. Report (for 1856) 20. As early as 1822 (Nov. 14) a remark was entered in the <u>Minutes of the Board of Directors</u> of the Bank of New York to the effect that "deposits [were] the great source of gain to banks."

27. <u>U.S. 37th Congr. 3d sess., House Executive Document 25,28,53.</u> Massachusetts Bank Commissioners, <u>Report</u> (1856), 78.

28. See vol. I of this work, pages 45 ff; this volume, chap. XII and Hooper, <u>Examination</u>, 27.

29. Bray Hammond in <u>Jour. Econ. Hist.</u>, VIII (1948), 15.

30. Op. cit., 85.

31. Jenks, Leland H., "Railroads as an Economic Force in American Development," <u>Jour. Econ. Hist.</u>, IV (1944), 8; Hedges, <u>op. cit.</u>, 44, 85; Connecticut Bank Commissioners, <u>Report</u> (1854), 8,9; (1856), 9. <u>Bankers Magazine</u>, IX (1854/55), 81,82.

32. <u>U.S. 36th Congr. 1st sess., House Executive Document 49</u>, 105; <u>U.S. 30th Congr. 1st sess., House Executive Document 77</u>, 212; <u>U.S. 35th Congr. 1st sess., House Executive Document 107</u>, 116.

33. Statement of the Detroit banker Philo Parsons in American Bankers Association, <u>Proceedings</u> (1881), 24.

34. Bank of North America, <u>Minutes of the Board of Directors</u>, June 19, 1837; <u>U.S. 37th Cong., 3d sess., House Executive Document 102</u>, 90; "Currency, Banking and Credit," 21. Baker (<u>op. cit.</u>, 24) reports that Indiana pork dealers sustained heavy losses through the failure of two Connecticut banks, probably the Eastern and Woodbury Banks.

35. See below page 6.

36. See Vol. I of this work page 52 and Hedges, <u>op. cit.</u>, 56 ff. The Massachusetts Bank Commissioners objected to bankers' balances as disguising inter-bank lending and befogging the banks' statements.

37. Hooper, <u>Examination</u>, 36.

38. <u>U.S. 36th Congr. 1st sess., House Executive Document 49</u>, 71, 72; vol. I of this work, pages 79, 263 (footnote 66).
    In the late 1850's Jay Cooke received loans from the Bank of Harrisburg and the Bank of Chambersburg in the form of "marked notes;" see Larson, <u>Cooke</u>, 93.

39. <u>U.S. 33d Congr. 1st sess., House Executive Document 102</u>, 90; Connecticut Bank Commissioners, <u>Report</u> (1855), 5; Connecticut, <u>Public Acts</u>, 1854, chapter VIII; Massachusetts Bank Commissioners, <u>Report</u> (1854), 81.

40. See, for instance, Connecticut Bank Commissioners, <u>Report</u> (1854), 9; Massachusetts Bank Commissioners, <u>Report</u> (1859), 106; Chaddock, <u>op. cit.</u>, 357.

41. <u>U.S. 30th Congr. 1st sess., House Executive Document 77</u>, 117,118,552,553; <u>U.S. 33d Congr.</u>

2d sess., House Executive Document 82, 166.

42. Op. cit., 23.

43. See, for instance, Amasa Walker, <u>op. cit.</u>, 60 ff.

44. <u>U.S. 36th Congr. 1st sess., House Executive Document 49</u>, 105; <u>U.S. 37th Congr. 3d sess., House Executive Document 25</u>, 52. Clapham(<u>op. cit.</u>, II, 170) has shown that the directors of the Bank of England, as late as 1840, refused to consider deposits as currency.

45. Hooper in his speech of 1863 spoke of "inscribed credit in the banks which passes in all transactions among businessmen," page 3.

46. <u>Debates, Pennsylvania House of Representatives relative to the Bank of the United States</u>, 29. Similar opinions can be found still in the third period, for instance, <u>U.S. 35th Congr. 1st sess., House Executive Document 107</u>, 323 and <u>U.S. 38th Congr. 1st sess., House Executive Document 20</u>, 104.

47. See volume I of this work, page 50.

48. <u>U.S. 35th Congr. 1st sess., House Executive Document 107</u>,115,116,182. New York State, Superintendent of the Banking Department, <u>Report</u> (for 1857), 19.

49. See Viner, <u>op. cit.</u>, 243 ff. Gallatin, when Secretary of the Treasury, had still customarily linked notes with deposits (Wettereau, <u>op. cit.</u>, 268). Later his <u>Considerations</u>, Condy Raguet's writings, and Nathan Appleton's <u>Remarks</u> contributed to the rediscovery of the truth. Stephen Colwell's book reflects in its philosophy the rise of the deposit business. A very interesting contemporary item is "Organization of Debts into Currency" in <u>Bankers Magazine, XIII</u> (1858/59), 137 ff.

50. Miller, <u>op. cit.</u>, 117 ff has described in detail the discovery of this truth.

51. See the very clear statement of the Connecticut Bank Commissioners in <u>U.S. 33d Congr. 1st sess., House Executive Document 102</u>, 90,91.

52. See vol. I of this work, pages 16,17,54,55.

53. Hedges, <u>op. cit.</u>, 86.

54. Massachusetts Bank Commissioners, <u>Reports</u> (1851), 9; (1852), 7; (1854), 78, 81; (1855), 72; Walley, <u>op. cit.</u>, 27. It may be mentioned that in France in the 1820's Jacques Laffitte was attacked for the statement that banks borrowed funds from small capitalists and lent them to large enterprises: Fazy, <u>op. cit.</u>, 113.

55. <u>U.S. 33d Congr. 1st sess., House Executive Document 102</u>,90; <u>U.S. 35th Congr. 1st sess., House Executive Document 107</u>,116; <u>U.S. 37th Congr. 3d sess., House Executive Document 25</u>, 80; <u>U.S. 38th Congr. 1st sess., House Executive Document 20</u>, 43. <u>Report on the Subject of Paying Interest on Current Deposits</u> of March 4, 1858 of a Committee on "the discontinuance of the practice of allowing interest on annual deposits;" reprinted in <u>Bankers' Magazine</u>, XII (1857/58), 822 ff and in Hardenbrook, <u>op. cit.</u>, 27.

Connecticut Bank Commissioners Report (1854), 4, 5. Letters on Banks, 7, 8.

56. Porter gives in his Astor biography examples of the lending activities of this capitalist: he lent on real estate in the city and state of New York and in those sections of the country in which his American Fur Company had traded. By 1830 he lent funds to the Mohawk and Hudson Railroad in which he was interested. In 1835 he lent to the president of the Utica and Schenectady Railroad Company and other directors $100,000 on their bond and stocks as collateral security. In 1834 he made a loan of $60,000 to a textile mill for the purpose of expansion. See pages 893, 1001, 1003, 1015 and Medbery, op. cit., 293. Such activities had ceased by the 1850's. See also the interesting paper of Tooker, Elva C., "A Merchant turns to Money-Lending" in Bull. Bus. Hist. Soc., XX (1946) 71 ff. It describes the lending activities of Nathan Trotter, a Philadelphia Quaker, between 1818 and 1853 when he died. Trotter discounted business paper and made loans to the Philadelphia and Reading Railroad.

57. See Opinion of the Court of Appeals of the State of New York, Lewis Curtis, John L. Graham, Richard M. Blatchford, respondents, against David Leavitt, Receiver of the North American Trust and Banking Company... (Albany, 1857), 19 ff.

58. U.S. 35th Congr. 1st sess., House Executive Document 107, 115.

59. In the run which took place in New Orleans in October, 1857, deposits also played a decisive part. Ibid., 203.

60. Clapham, op. cit., II, 149; vol. I of this work, pages 124 ff.

61. Report of the Committee of Investigation, 4.

62. U.S. 35th Congr. 1st sess., House Executive Document 107, 107, 108, 112. U.S. 37th Congr. 3d sess., House Executive Document 25, 50; U.S. 38th Congr. 1st sess., House Executive Document 20, 40. Hooper (Examination, 17 ff) understood remarkably well the mechanism of clearing-house exchanges and its influence on the banks' lending activities. See also Bankers' Magazine, XIV (1859/60), 133. State of New York, Superintendent of the Banking Department, Report (for 1857), 7.

63. See this author's paper on "American Bank Money," Southern Economic Review, X (1944), 217 ff.

64. In Tennessee (to give an example for a Western state) the Traders Bank at Nashville was the redemption agent of the Bank of Eastern Tennessee; the Bank of Tennessee at Nashville redeemed the notes of its branches and of other banks which kept funds on deposit for that purpose.

65. Keen competition among banks is mentioned by the Massachusetts Bank Commissioners, Report (1854), 83.

66. See also Margaret Myers, op. cit., 120, 121.

67. Gras, op. cit., 115. In the early 1840's the Suffolk Bank was urged by many country banks to allow interest on the permanent deposits and its rival, the Bank of Mutual Redemption, temporarily adopted that policy in the late 1850's. Whitney, D.R., op. cit., 36. Some of the Pennsylvania banks paid interest on deposits; see Holdsworth, Empire, 207.

68. See vol. I of this work, pages 52 ff and this volume, page 5.

69. Jour. Econ. Hist., VII (1947), 214; the author abstains from dealing in detail with this unreasonable review. The Minutes of the Board of Directors of the Bank of New York contain under August 11, 1831 a correspondentship contract which shows clearly what was expected on both sides in that year. The Bank of New York expressly stipulated that no interest would be paid on the running account, but 3 per cent would be paid on any sum not exceeding $200,000 which was left for at least twelve months.

70. U.S. 35th Congr. 1st sess., House Executive Document 107, 110, 323; U.S. 36th Congr. 1st sess., House Executive Document 49, 105; U.S. 37th Congr. 3d sess., House Executive Document 25, 5, 79. Report of 1858 on the Subject of Paying Interest on Current Deposits (see footnote 55) and several meetings of the Associated Banks of New York on this subject, reprinted in Hardenbrook, op. cit., 25 ff. Connecticut Bank Commissioners, Report (1854), 5; (1856), 7; State of New York, Superintendent of the Banking Department, Report (for 1857), 11; Hedges, op. cit., 74. In New Hampshire a bill to forbid the paying of interest on deposits was defeated in 1859; see Bankers Magazine, XIV (1859/60), 74.

71. The erection of clearing houses which resulted from the rise of the deposit business will be treated in a special chapter.

72. Bank of North America, Minutes of the Board of Directors, Mar. 10 and June 25, 1840. The latter only records a resolution of the board: "marking checks good be discontinued;" postnotes were to be issued instead.

73. Report of the Comptroller of the Currency (1882), 25. For the later development of the practice, see Hepburn, History of Coinage, 329.

74. Massachusetts Bank Commissioners, Report (1860), 144; (1861), 177.

75. Annual Report on the Finances (1876), 204, 205.

76. Report (1853), 13.

77. See below pages 9, 10.

78. Currency or Money, 5, 46, 47, 48, 78, 83, 88, 107, 108, 110, 111. See also his speech of 1863, 4.

79. It goes without saying that the discussion of this problem was de facto a discussion of definitions. Those who claimed that redeemable paper money could not depreciate measured its value by specie. Those who held the opposite opinion measured its value in terms of purchasing power.

80. See this volume, page 8 ff.

81. Reports (1853), 40,41; (1855), 76,77; (1856), 78; (1857), 78,79. See also the resumé in the Report (1860), 116 ff.

82. Address of His Excellency Nathaniel P. Banks to the Two Branches of the Legislature of Massachusetts, Senate Document No. 1 (1858), 12,13. Commonwealth of Massachusetts, Joint Standing Committee on Banks and Banking, Report on so much of the address of the Governor as relates to banks and paper currency, Senate Document No. 17 (1858), 2, 20.

83. Nature and Uses, 52.

84. See above pages 9, 10.

85. Nature and Uses, 52.

86. See index under Small notes.

87. Massachusetts Acts, 1858/1859, chapter 69. Bankers' Magazine, XII (1857/58), 782 ff. Criticism of the act is to be found in Massachusetts Bank Commissioners, Report (1858), 93 ff.; (1860), 122 ff.; (1861), 148.

88. See this volume, page 37.

89. See Vol. I of this work, page 201.

90. Massachusetts House Document, No. 18 (dated February 3, 1838).

91. Dewey, State Banking, 222.

92. See this volume, page 2.

93. Duncombe, op. cit., 17.

94. See this volume, page 2.

95. Page 3.

96. Report (of Apr. 28, 1843), 20,23.

97. An anonymous pamphleteer wrote in 1841: "The just principles that are made to govern banks in other countries -- those that distinguish the Scotch and English banks from our own -- will gradually introduce themselves here. Reasons for the Inexpediency of Chartering a National Bank, 33.

The "rule of 1832" as stated by Sir Horsley Palmer was mentioned by Thomas Hart Benton in a letter to the National Intelligencer, dated Nov. 15, 1857, Bankers Magazine, XII (1857/58), 559 ff. The policy of the Bank of England was known in 1857 even in Maine, a state which was one of the least progressive with regard to banking. U.S. 35th Congr. 1st sess., House Executive Document 107, 7.

98. Ibid., 244, 246. See also Hedges, op. cit., 130 ff.

99. Bankers Magazine, XII (1857/58), 562.

100. Acts of 1853, No. 338.

101. Typical is the article "Banks of Louisiana" in Bankers Magazine, XII (1857/58), 663,664. It does not even mention the legal specie reserves. See also this volume, page 40.

102. See this volume, page 274.

103. See this volume, page 40 and U.S. Congr. 1st sess., House Executive Document 107, 246.

104. New York State, Messages of the Governors, V, 46; New York, Superintendent of the Banking Department, Annual Report (for 1837), 31; Opdyke, op. cit. (1858), 15.

105. Bankers Magazine, XII (1857/58), 886.

106. U.S. 35th Congr. 1st sess., House Executive Document 107,108,115, 123-126; U.S. 36th Congr. 1st sess., House Executive Document 49, 104. The material is reprinted by Hardenbrook, op. cit., 25, 30.

107. Bankers Magazine, XV (1860/61), 648.

108. Iowa, Laws of 1858, chapter 114, an Act authorizing General Banking in the State of Iowa, secs. 21,22.

109. See, for instance, the report of a committee of the New York Chamber of Commerce of 1858 in Bankers Magazine, XII (1857/58), 886; "Currency, Banking and Credit," 23,24; Congdon, Letter to Clifford, passim. (Congdon was cashier of the Merchants Bank, New Bedford [see Bankers Magazine, X (1855/56), 806] and his booklet is representative of the country banker's outlook). There were, of course, other minor points of criticism.

110. Report (1850), 7,12.

111. This clause can also be found in the Missouri Act to regulate banks and banking institutions of 1857, sec. 37, where it refers to reserves against notes. Louisiana influence is highly probable in this case, too.

112. Bankers Magazine, XII (1857/58), 887. See also Mints, op. cit., 148,149.

113. One should compare the clause with the corresponding one in the Connecticut Act of 1848 (see above, page 2) and the progress is evident.

114. See chapter XVI of this volume.

115. See this volume, page 104.

116. See vol. I of this work, pages 57 ff.

117. Illuminating are the articles "On the Duties and Responsibilities of a Cashier" and that of Sabine, Lorenzo, "Suggestions to Young Cashiers on the Duties of their Profession" in Bankers Magazine, X (1855/56), 161 and VII (1851/52), 504 ff; the latter is reprinted in ibid., X (1855/56), 417 ff and in Homans' Banker's Common Place Book.

118. Prof. Raymond de Roover has informed the author that he had an opportunity in the 1940's to observe several country banks in Ohio and up-state New York. In those banks the cashier was still the chief executive. The boards met frequently and approved loans proposed by the cashier.

119. Edmonds, op. cit., 11-13,18.

120. U.S. 36th Congr. 1st sess., House Executive Document 49,69; Massachusetts Bank Commissioners, Report (1843, Apr. 28), 12,14; (1851), 12; (1859), 102,103.

Interesting is the comment of the Commissioners on a case in which a cashier controlled the bank in question: he "possessed a power and influence which do not properly pertain to that office in any bank."

121. The Maine Bank Commissioners complained in 1854 that bank presidents served without compensation. What fitted into the organizational set-up of 1800 survived in backward areas as

late as the 1850's, but seemed strange then even there. See U.S. 33d Congr. 2d sess., House Executive Document 82, 9. There is a remark in the Bankers Magazine, XI (1856/57), which may be cited for whatever significance it may possess: a bank president, according to the contemporary writer, had generally little to do with the correspondence of a bank.

122. Report, 1842 (Assembly Document 29), 5,6,8.
123. Bankers Magazine, X (1855/56), 161.
124. Edmonds, op. cit., 32, 33.
125. See vol. I of this work, page 180.
126. A committee to examine the bank was, for instance, appointed by the board of the Bank of New York in the winter of 1840, Minutes, Mar. 5, 1840.
127. Edmonds, op. cit., 15.
128. But some cashiers were directors, as for instance, Francis W. Edmonds, cashier of the Mechanics Bank of New York; see ibid., 17, 30 and also Massachusetts Bank Commissioners, Report (of April 28, 1843), 12.
129. Homans, op. cit., 138 ff. The Connecticut Bank Commissioners complained in 1860 that businessmen accepted the position of bank director for the sake of honor and neglected their duties, not realizing that their position imposed a trust on them. Many bank directors, often the president included, held little stock in the bank in question; Report (1860), 9. See also Massachusetts Bank Commissioners, Report (1841), 9; (for 1850), 12; (1851, December), 8; (1852), 8; (Directors declare dividends without examination, relying on the reports of cashiers), 16; (1854), 84; (1859), 103.
130. See vol. I of this work, page 20.
131. Bank of New York, Directors Records, Nov. 8, 1832.
132. See above page 11 for the exact quotation.
133. Hartz, op. cit., 254.
134. See vol. I of this work, pages 60,61. U.S. 25th Congr. 3d sess., House Executive Document 227, 115, as to thinly attended stockholders meetings in 1838.
135. Massachusetts Bank Commissioners, Report (for 1849), 8, 13; as to New York, see Cleaveland, op. cit., 265; Constitution of 1846, Art. VIII, Sec. 7.
136. Merk, op. cit., 192. (Rev. Statutes, Chap. 71, secs. 33-37
137. U.S. 37th Congr. 3d sess., House Executive Document 25, 5; U.S. 38th Congr. 1st sess., House Executive Document 20, 5.
138. See, for instance, Gras, op. cit., 87, 89.
139. Massachusetts Bank Commissioners, Report (1859), 104; U.S. 36th Congr. 1st sess., House Executive Document 49, 69-71. The Report (for 1840), mentions on page 9 bank examinations by committees of stockholders. They were urgently supported in later reports, obviously in vain; see Report (1855), 86; (1857), 80. For Connecti-

cut (1848), see U.S. 30th Congr. 1st sess., House Executive Document 77, 123,124. For Maine (1854), see U.S. 33d Congr. 2d sess., House Executive Document 82, 9. The earliest account on thinly attended meetings of the stockholders of Banks which this author found is in a Report of the Massachusetts Bank Commissioners of December 31, 1838. See U.S. 25th Congr. 3d sess., House Executive Document 227, 115.

140. New York Bank Commissioners, Report (1842), Assembly Doc. 29, 4,5,9,11,12.
141. Gras, op. cit., 89.
142. Massachusetts Bank Commissioners, Report (1855), 72; (1859), 103; New York Bank Commissioners, Report (1842), Assembly Doc. 29, 6,7,8; (1843), Assembly Doc. 34, 12,13.
143. As late as the 1850's messengers of the Suffolk Bank trying to collect notes of the Bank of South Royalton, Vermont, were arrested and the notes attached: Whitney, Suffolk Bank, 45. See also U.S. 33d Congr. 1st sess., House Executive Document 102, 18.
144. Hartz, op. cit., 68.
145. Jour. Econ. Hist., VIII (1948), 9.
146. For the preceding, see U.S. 35th Congr. 1st sess., House Executive Document 107, 195, 214, 242,250,254,308. Conditions in Wisconsin are particularly revealing for public opinion in the Northwest: in 1846 the voters of the state rejected a proposed state constitution which forbade banking and the private issue of currency in any form. In 1848 they adopted one which left the decision on banking to a referendum. This referendum was held in 1851 and approved banking in principle whereupon a general banking act, i.e., a Free Banking system, was passed in 1852.
147. Bray Hammond in Jour. Econ. Hist. VIII (1948), 1.
148. For instance, in Arkansas or Iowa, U.S. 35th Congr. 1st sess., House Executive Document 107, 245, 322. Even Samuel Hooper considered the prohibition of small notes important; Currency or Money (1855), 108; see above page 9.
    An anonymous writer in the New Englander was one of the few contemporaries who correctly evaluated this proposal. "Currency, Banking, and Credit," 23. A New York Chamber of Commerce report of 1858 was also skeptical; see Bankers' Magazine, XII (1857/58), 888. But as late as 1880 one can find an item such as Butler, George B., The Suppression of Small Bills (Paper read before the Union League Club's Committee of Political Reform), New York, 1880.
149. For Pennsylvania in 1848, see 30th Congr. 1st sess., House Executive Document 77, 50. The Massachusetts legislature in the 1850's received petitions every year to confine the discount line of banking corporations to once or twice their capitals. This is essentially the old recipe. U.S. 36th Congr. 1st sess., House Executive

Document 49, 98. As late as 1862 the New Hampshire Bank Commissioners compared circulation with bank capital. U.S. 37th Congr. 3d sess., House Executive Document 25, 27.

150. Currency or Money, 91; speech of 1864, 12. See also "Report of the Comptroller of the Currency," November 28, 1863 in Report of the Secretary of the Treasury on the State of the Finances for the year ending June 30, 1863, 52 ff.

151. Connecticut Bank Commissioners, Report (1856), 4, 5.

152. U.S. 37th Congr. 3d sess., House Executive Document 25, 51, 82. Most interesting in this context are the Reports of the Massachusetts Bank Commissioners (1857), 84; (1858), 98; (1860), 135, 136. See also Hedges, op. cit., 85; "Currency, Banking and Credit," 32 ff; Bankers Magazine, X (1855/56), 545 ff, 753 ff; XI (1856/57), 506 ff; XII (1857/58), 202 ff; XIII (1858/59), 12 ff, 797 ff, 963 ff; Cleaveland, op. cit., see Index "Usury."

153. Ryan, op. cit., 58 ff.

154. An Act to provide a National Currency secured by a pledge of United States Bonds and to provide for the Circulation and Redemption thereof. U.S. 38th Congr. 1st sess., Chapter 106. Statutes at Large, XIII (1864-1865).

155. Act of June 22, 1874, Revised Statutes, Sec. 5197. Quoted from U.S. 53d Congr. 3d sess., Senate Report 831, 441.

156. Hooper, speech of 1864, 12; Proceedings of the Convention... Saratoga, 15, 28.

The fight for the repeal of legal interest requirements (usury laws) is reflected in the various editions of John Whipple's, Stringent Usury Laws, the Best Defence... against Hard Times. The item was published first in 1835 and frequently reprinted for about forty years thereafter with varying introductions and notes which show in an interesting way the development of the struggle. (In the end it had become a fight of farmers and laborers against business groups.) The 1855 and 1878 editions contain on pages 11-12 and 62, respectively, a survey of the then existing pertinent legislation in the various American states. While the reasoning is not of too high a character there are important ideas back of it, for instance what is called today the claim theory of money and the theorem that Georg Friedrich Knapp elaborated in his Staatliche Theorie des Geldes, namely that money is the creation of the state.

157. Section of 5197 of the Revised Statutes (12 U.S. C. [1940] 85); information received from the Comptroller of the Currency.

158. U.S. 35th Congr. 1st sess., House Executive Document 107, 310; State of New York, Annual Report of the Comptroller (for 1850), Assembly Document (1851) 9, 41, 42; Merk, op. cit., 190 ff (for Wisconsin).

159. State of New York, Annual Report of the Comptroller (for 1847), Assembly Document (1848) 4, 60, 61. U.S. 34th Congr., 1st sess., House Executive Document 102, 124, 125 (reprinting, State of New York, Superintendent of the Banking Department, Report for 1855).

160. U.S. 33d Congr., 1st sess., House Executive Document 102, 18; U.S. 35th Congr. 1st sess., House Executive Document 107, 127, 319. Merk, op. cit., 188, 189, 209.

161. U.S. 30th Congr. 1st sess., House Executive Document 77, 195, U.S. 33d Congr. 2d sess., House Executive Document 82, 9.

162. Fraudulent banking as practiced in that period and public reaction thereto are not discussed here.

163. U.S. 36th Congr. 1st sess., House Executive Document 49, 74, 97.

164. New York State, Annual Report of the Comptroller (for 1845), Assembly Document (1846) 25, 65, 66; (for 1846), Assembly Document (1847) 5, 57; (for 1849), Assembly Document (1850) 8, 61; Merk, op. cit., 188 (for Wisconsin); New York State Superintendent of the Banking Department, Annual Report, (for 1851), 43; (for 1852), 53, 54.

165. Banks in Vermont were supposed to be acquired by outside speculators and Western brokers for the purpose of stripping them of their capitals and cheating the public by worthless circulation. U.S. 35th Congr. 1st sess., House Executive Document 107, 32.

166. Quoted by Nevins, Rockefeller, I, 299.

167. U.S. 33d Congr., 2d sess., House Executive Document 82, 8; U.S. 37th Congr. 3d sess., House Executive Document 25, 81.

168. U.S. 35th Congr. 1st sess., House Executive Document 107, 31; U.S. 30th Congr. 1st sess., House Executive Document 77, 123, 124. See also the attitude of the Massachusetts Bank Commissioners in the Reports (for 1852) 9; (1853), 39 ff.

169. 35th Congr. 1st sess., House Executive Document 107, 100.

170. 37th Congr. 3d sess., House Executive Document 25, 80, 81.

Chapter XI

THE MIDDLE WESTERN STATE BANK WITH BRANCHES

The American states existing between 1840 and 1860, when they possessed any banking, made use of different systems which can be grouped under one of the following heads or seen as combinations of two or more of the types characterized by these heads. There were:

1. States which had an unlimited number of individually chartered banks:
   with or without state participation;
   with or without branches.

2. States which had an unlimited number of banks established under a general banking act (without state participation and without branches).

3. States which had a monopolistic or semi-monopolistic state bank with branches:
   exclusively state owned;
   owned by the state and private capitalists;
   owned exclusively by private capitalists (the latter an exceptional case).

The particular type of Middle Western state bank with branches, with which this chapter is concerned, falls into the third category. It represented a development of an older type of state bank with branches, but possessed specific features which distinguished it from the latter.[1]

Regardless of whether or not the American nineteenth-century founders of monopolistic state banks were aware of the ancestry of the ideas underlying their enterprises the latter actually sprang from Mercantilist banking theory. The best expression of the philosophy which was originally back of such monopolistic state banks can be found in Eric Bollmann's Outline of a Plan of the Circulating Medium of the United States of 1816.[2] According to Bollmann, who in this respect followed Sir James Steuart and other eighteenth-century thinkers, banking did not require the possession of capital: its vital principle was confidence and credit. Specie, on the other hand, was no more essential than capital and, in fact, the main advantage derived from banking consisted in obviating the necessity for specie. If there was only a single bank in existence and its notes were considered safe beyond doubt, no specie would ever be required for use within the country possessing that one bank. But when banks multiplied, their circulation became "confined," and conse-

quently the more banks came into existence the more specie was needed; or, in other words, more specie had to be kept in the vaults of the banks in order to uphold the necessary confidence. The multiplication of banks, so Bollmann thought, defeated the purpose of banks, viz., obviating the necessity for specie.[3]

While such was the original reasoning back of monopolistic banking, the actual incentive to setting up in various American states state banks with monopolies or quasi-monopolies was derived from a prevalent social philosophy. (To what extent the earliest exponents of this type of bank were also influenced by the suggestions in the English pamphlet literature of the eighteenth century for a parliamentary bank with branches can not be determined.)[4] Since banks were the source of considerable profits and since they promised many advantages to those who owned them, it seemed advisable, in the interest of the common man, to have banks run or at least controlled by the commonwealths, which were controlled, in turn, by the common man.[5] Then the profits of the banks in question would serve to lower the common man's tax burden and the advantages would be made available to him. Thus the principle of monopolistic state banks with branches was adopted in several state constitutions, as, for instance, those of Indiana (1816), Illinois (1818), and Missouri (1820); but the early representatives of this type of bank, such as the State Bank of Vermont of 1806 or the State Bank of Illinois of 1821, enjoyed neither a long life nor a successful career.[6]

Some banks of the type, however, which were established in the 1830's and 1840's[7] met with great success. Strictly speaking this younger group of monopolistic state banks with branches embraced two different kinds of banks. The first was represented by the Bank of the State of Missouri, one of the outstanding institutions of the third period.[8] It was essentially identical with the earlier banks of the type, but was launched with stricter regulations and managed with greater wisdom. More important, however, became the second very similar kind of bank, built first in Indiana on the basis of a new and distinct organizational principle. This genus, in addition to embodying that new organizational principle, also absorbed into the traditional monopolistic state bank with branches some ideas which underlay the New York Safety Fund law.[9]

The development toward the new type of bank began in a rather strange political milieu. Indiana supported Jackson faithfully, but at the same time favored a high tariff, internal improvements, and the Bank of the United States. When the fate of the national bank was settled through the presidential election of 1832, the men in the state who had upheld Clay started to agitate for a state bank with branches able to fall heir to the Bank of the United States, which would become defunct in 1836. In his message to the legislature of 1832-33 the then governor of the state, Noah Noble, who had been a private banker himself,[10] stated the case as follows:

> You are no doubt aware of the severe pecuniary embarrassments, under which, almost every class of our citizens are laboring; and of the complaints of distress heard in many parts of the state; and it is presumed you are apprised of the fact, that among the remedies spoken of, to prevent the further aggravation of the evils of a decreasing circulation, to mitigate the existing distress, the establishment of a State Bank and branches seems to be concentrating the largest share of public attention.... In other states such institutions have been successful and beneficial, but it will be your place to determine as to the practicability and policy of the measure, taking into consideration the situation and circumstances of the country, when it is matured and brought before you....[11]

The governor's proposal of a state bank with branches was embodied in two bills, similar in character, which were introduced simultaneously in 1832 in both houses of the Indiana legislature. These bills did not represent progress. Indiana had possessed a bank of the proposed type in the defunct Bank of Vincennes, chartered in 1815. When its charter was amended in 1817 it became by and large a state bank with branches, modeled on the State Bank of Kentucky. However, one new element found its way into the House bill:[12] each branch of the proposed bank was to be a separate corporation. Thus the bill suggested a group of banks rather than a bank with branches. This system of banks was to be coordinated (section 15) and to be supervised by three men "to be styled the Bank Commissioners of the State of Indiana" whose duty it was to inspect and examine the system at least twice a year (Section 63, article II). Although the bill did not become law, this clause provided the starting point for what became later the board of control of the State Bank of Indiana, to be copied by the other

banks of the same type. The influence of the New York Safety Fund Act, on the other hand, can be recognized in the section establishing bank examinations by public officials.

Typical of the social background and the thinking of the men who were connected with the beginnings of this important piece of banking legislation were those of John Ewing. Ewing (1789-1858) was born in Ireland, but had come to America at an early age, his parents settling in Baltimore. In 1813 he moved to Vincennes, Indiana, and engaged in mercantile pursuits, whence he drifted into politics. First, in 1819, he represented his county in the State House of Representatives. At that time he must have been familiar with the Bank of Vincennes since it was located in his home town. At any rate, he took an interest in the problems of banking, as can be seen from an article he wrote for a local paper.[13] Being a politician of Whig affiliations, he must have been stirred in the 1830's by Jackson's fight against the Bank of the United States. At that time he had advanced into the State Senate, where he remained for several sessions. Finally, from 1833 to 1835, as well as from 1837 to 1839, he represented his state as a Whig in Congress. Ewing, later a popular speaker in the hard cider campaign of 1840, was a lonely man, possessed of a brilliant mind, but of an "excitable disposition," which kept him from accomplishing what he might otherwise have done. Before his death he had lost his whole fortune and become an object of charity.[14] This was the man who became a leader in the early stages of the Indiana banking legislation of the 1830's.

In 1832 Ewing was made chairman of the Senate committee which was to report on the Senate bank bill paralleling the House bill, characterized above. In his report he showed himself to be well-informed but without creative imagination. He described the various possibilities for securing a sound circulating medium, one of them being granting a new charter to the Bank of the United States which he, as a Whig, favored. A national bank with national affiliations and with wider power than any state bank could possibly possess, would guarantee a uniform currency. But, in case a new charter could not be secured for the Bank of the United States, Ewing was in favor of a "public bank," in Indiana, i.e., one owned exclusively by the state, as opposed to what he called a "copartnership bank," that is to say, a bank in which both private capital and the state participated. Nevertheless in the course of the ensuing discussion he was won over to the idea of a "copartnership bank" and he himself drafted a bill for such an enterprise.

However the stepping stone for the further development, as already indicated, was the original

House bill and the clause contained therein which envisaged making the branches of the bank independent corporations. When this bill was under consideration, George H. Proffit, one of the legislators who well exemplifies the type of men responsible for the reform legislation in Indiana and later in Ohio, made a move which although unsuccessful and unimportant in itself nevertheless contributed to paving the way for the future.[15] He moved "to remodel the charter so as to make the mother bank and branches equal participators of the profits and losses of each institution, or rather that each of the branches shall be merely offices of discount and deposit." Since Proffit apparently did not object to the previously proposed legal independence of the branches, his plan pointed in the direction of control of the branches by the parent bank and of mutual liability. His motion was lost, but, since the bill as a whole failed to pass in the Senate, it made little difference.[16]

Ewing's bill did not come up for discussion in the Senate, but it was referred to a select committee. It sympathized with Proffit and in its report elaborated the idea of mutual responsibility of parent bank and branches. This plan may have presented itself as a compromise, bridging the difference of opinion between those who wished an old-type state bank with branches and those aiming at a group or chain of independent banks. The report of the select committee, dated January 29, 1833, was signed by one William Graham, a lawyer, but to what extent he was responsible therefor is not known.[17] In his report Graham proposed "that each branch should share its own dividends, reserving an ultimate liability in the bank and branches, in case of the insolvency or failure of either of them." Although mutual liability was clearly proposed in this report, the other two important features of the new type of bank (to be discussed presently) were not yet suggested.

All the bills and proposals of the session of 1832 to 1833 came to naught. In the next session (1833 to 1834), however, the matter of bank legislation was again taken up, this time with better success. Ewing, who would have been the natural leader, had faded out of the picture when he went to Washington as a member of Congress. The lawyer, George H. Dunn (1778-1854), who was the key figure in the House committee on the banking question, now became instrumental in the further development.[18] Dunn was a native of New York who had come to Indiana in 1817 and may well have acted as the "influence carrier" who contributed to making the idea of mutual liability acceptable to Indiana.[19] His "constructive mind" seems to have combined into one consistent scheme traditional ideas with new, native with imported.

Thus the State Bank of Indiana came into being by the act of January 28, 1834. It represented a new type of banking which today one would characterize as group banking rather than as branch banking. Or to use Hugh McCulloch's words, it was a bank of branches in contrast to the Bank of the United States which was a bank with branches. The achievement was due to the development of the bank commissioners (New York style) of the original House bill into an efficient board of control which itself became a body politic. Thus the loosely coordinated set of banks of the early bills became actually a group of banks, for the State Bank of Indiana consisted of a number of independent banks tied together by the parent bank (which was de facto a board of control) and by mutual liability. A formal safety fund, however, was not set up in Indiana. According to Section 26 of the act, it was the duty of the directors of the State Bank to provide for the payment of those debts of a failing branch that remained after all its own property had been applied. For this purpose they were authorized to call on the other branches for their respective shares. The new type of bank became a great success not only because of its inherent qualities but also because of the men who put it into practice and shaped its early destiny. Almost all the outstanding business leaders of early Indiana participated in the bank which became at the same time a training ground for bankers who later were to gain national importance.

The state appointed Samuel Merrill the first president of the new institution, or more correctly, the president of the Bank Board which, as described above, was actually a board of control. Merrill (1792-1855), after an education at Dartmouth College had immigrated into Indiana where he became a member of the bar and a leader in the young community. As a tax assessor he made the rounds of his county on foot, thus gaining experience and knowledge which stood him in good stead when he (also as a Whig) was elected to represent his county in various sessions of the General Assembly. Merrill was a conscientious man who took his job as president of the State Bank of Indiana seriously, exercising that control over the so-called branches which the law had contemplated. He personally examined all thirteen of them twice a year, analyzed their reports, and forced them to adopt a uniform system of bookkeeping which made such control possible. He had to resign when his party lost control of the legislature in 1843.[20]

While much of the initial success of the State Bank of Indiana was due to Merrill he found valuable cooperators. The state, according to law, appointed in addition to the president four members to the Bank Board which also included one representative of every branch. The most important among these state directors and a close second of Merrill was Calvin Fletcher, like Merrill a native of Vermont.[21] Men like Hugh McCulloch, later the first Comptroller of the Currency, organiser of the National Banking system, and Secretary of the Treasury, and J.F.D. Lanier, who gained national importance as a private banker and promoter in New York, as presidents of the Fort Wayne and Madison branches, respectively, contributed to the success of the group. Outstanding men using a well-shaped tool made the State Bank of Indiana one of the best banks of its period and a center of influence, as will be shown forthwith.[22]

The migration of the new type of bank began a few years after the establishment of the State Bank of Indiana, and Michigan was the first state to contemplate adopting it. This fact is full of meaning. Michigan neighbors Indiana so that the interest in the scheme was due to contact migration of the underlying ideas. Furthermore in the 1830's the new state was constantly on the lookout for prototypes after which to model its banking system. That Michigan also copied the New York Safety Fund Act and an early New York bill embodying the Free Banking principle has been described in earlier chapters.[23]

In Michigan the development began in 1838 when Governor Stevens T. Mason in a message of January 4 proposed a state bank, a suggestion which he followed up a year later in the message of January 7, 1839. In neither one of these message did he refer to any particular models.[24] However, when in the latter year the matter came up for consideration in the legislature, one of the representatives (one A. Allen) moved that one hundred copies each of the charters of the State Bank of Indiana and the State Bank of Tennessee be printed.[25] This move is of particular interest: when the Michigan legislators contemplated a state bank their choice lay between one of the new and one of the old type, although they themselves, of course, could not have thought in such terms. The original bill, presented by the Committee to which the pertinent part of the governor's message had been referred, shows Indiana influence; and the Act to establish the State Bank of Michigan, approved on April 2, 1839, de facto copied the State Bank of Indiana.[26] Like the latter, it had branches, and one half of the capital was contributed by the state. Just as in the State Bank of Indiana the branches of the Michigan bank were mutually liable for their debts; like the Indiana enterprise it was directed by a board, seven members of which were elected jointly by both houses of the legislature, while the remaining members were delegated by the branches (one by each branch). The Michigan copy of the Indiana

model was never put into operation, it seems that the inability to raise the necessary capital made it impossible to set up the bank.[27]

While the migration of the new type of bank into Michigan did not have any practical results the opposite was the case with Ohio. Again, as in the case of Michigan, we meet contact migration; and fortunately the process of migration can be studied here in detail. As a type, the State Bank of Ohio was identical with the State Bank of Indiana, but there were noteworthy differences. While the Indiana bank was established on the principle of mutual liability, the Ohio bank possessed a formal safety fund. While in the former bank mutual liability covered all debts, the safety fund of the latter benefited exclusively the note holders and left the other creditors unprotected. That, in contrast to Indiana, there was no state participation in the State Bank of Ohio was another important difference, which, however, is of no interest for this study.

The State Bank of Ohio was the work of Alfred Kelley (1789-1859). Kelley, an in-migrant from New York, was a broadminded, public-spirited man, possessed of a clear and orderly mind, creative both as legislator and entrepreneur; or, in the words of his biographer, he was a man who "had the originating talent which is so rare among men."[28] Kelley had experienced a successful public career in Ohio before he set out to rebuild her banking system along modern lines. He had been the driving force in building the canal linking the Ohio River with Lake Erie, and almost single-handed had kept the state from repudiating its debts in the early 1840's. However, he retired from office in March 1843 when the Board of Canal Fund Commissioners, of which he was a member at that time, was reorganized.

Kelley's withdrawal from public life did not last long, for in 1844 he was elected a State Senator, taking his seat in December of that year. The banking situation in Ohio was critical. The state still suffered from the aftermath of the panic of 1837 although specie payments had been resumed. Comparatively few banks in the Middle West were above suspicion and the rest had dubious reputations. Kelley had first gained experience in the field of banking when the Commercial Bank of Lake Erie was founded in Cleveland in 1816 and the young lawyer, incidentally the first in Cleveland, became its president.[29] Later as a man of public affairs and as a Whig he must have been stirred by the developments in banking which took place during the 1830's. It is not impossible that by this time Kelley had become acquainted with the State Bank of Indiana through personal friendship with M.T. Williams of Cincinnati, with whom he cooperated repeatedly, as, for instance, on the Canal Board. This Williams had a brother, Achilles (1795-1878), who was a state director and president of the Richmond branch of the State Bank of Indiana, and the institution may well have migrated from Indiana to Ohio through the agency of the Williams brothers.[30]

On January 7, 1845 having become the chairman of the State Senate Committee on Currency, Kelley introduced a bill "To incorporate the State Bank of Ohio and other banking companies," a bill which was his own work.[31] It aimed at "entire security to the bill-holder, reasonable security to dealers with the banks" [i.e., bank customers] and proper inducements to the investors.[32] Kelley recognized both the urgent need for sound banking legislation and the obligation of the state to provide such legislation. He felt that a legislature which gave to a company corporate powers and the right to issue notes gave it at the same time "to some extent a letter of credit" and therefore became "to some extent responsible for its correct conduct," a point of view very advanced for that time. He knew how to distinguish between the economic implications of banking and those of "other individual pursuits."

Kelley realized that two ways were open. Ohio could copy the New York Free Banking Act or it could create "a system of associated banks, each to some extent exercising a restraining power over the others... and being bound for the default of anyone so far as to prevent any loss to the bill-holder." The latter suggestion, as a matter of fact, was a modified replica of the Indiana system and the difference becomes evident from the clause: "being bound for the default of anyone so far as to prevent any loss to the bill-holder." [Italics mine]. Kelley himself did not choose between the two alternatives above mentioned, but embodied both of them in his bill. His heart, however, was with the Indiana solution of the banking problem, and the fact that her system was the work of Whigs may well have made it particularly attractive to the Ohio politicians of that creed.

One must ask why the Indiana scheme was changed upon its adoption in Ohio. The change, which clearly shows New York influence, may have resulted from the fact that both Kelley and Cowen, his collaborator in drafting the bill, were natives of that state. Through these men the safety fund feature came into the Ohio act; but it was not copied outright: while both the New York Safety Fund system and the Indiana State Bank applied the principle of mutual liability to all bank debts, the Ohio act did not. Therefore another question is posed. Why did Kelley make this change which distinguished the Ohio act from both the Indiana and New York models? In fact Kelley was in New York from the fall of 1841 to some time in February 1842, in order to raise funds, so that Ohio could

avoid defaulting on her obligations. Being a public character who was interested in questions of finance, he can be presumed to have taken notice of the blow which the Safety Fund system was experiencing that very year. It was the critical year of the system. No Safety Fund bank had failed from 1829 until 1841, when the Wayne County Bank of Palmyra broke down. On this occasion for the first time it was realized by a wider public that the law made the safety fund liable for all debts of a failing member of the system and not merely for its circulation, a broad liability which wrecked the whole system. The fact that Kelley was in New York during the critical time impels this author to believe that it is to his personal experience that the Ohio development of the Indiana scheme can be attributed.

Thus the State Bank of Ohio came into being through the law of February 24, 1845 as a system of independent private banking corporations "under the general supervision of a Board of Control, mutually liable for the redemption of the notes of a failing Branch, as security for which each Branch was required to deposit with the Central Office an amount equal to ten per centum of its circulation, which is known and designated as the Safety Fund."[34] Payments into the Safety Fund of the State Bank of Ohio had to be made either in money, or in bonds of the state, or in notes secured by real estate. When legislating regarding the payments into the safety fund Kelley improved on his model in still a second respect. While the contributions to the New York Safety Fund, and to the Safety funds of other states which took over that institution, were based on the amount of the banks' capital, in Ohio the contributions were based on the amount of circulation. Kelley was a thinker, indeed.

Kelley did not organize the state bank; this task was conferred by law upon a Board of five commissioners, the leading member of which was Judge Gustavus Swan, an old friend and associate of Kelley. The two had worked hand in hand as Canal Fund Commissioners in the critical year of 1842, and after the State Bank had been established they cooperated again on the Executive Committee of its Board of Control. Swan, who represented the Franklin Branch at Columbus, was the bank's president while Alfred Kelley was delegated to its board by the Merchants' Branch at Cleveland.[35]

The Bank of Iowa was the next of the Middle Western state banks with branches to come into existence. It did not gain any influence on the further development of American banking, but its history provides good examples both of the importance of the personal element in economic development and of the migration of ideas. The first constitution of Iowa (1846) in article IX prohibited the chartering of banks in the state. This prohibition, of course, did not result in the circulation of specie in the state as its framers had hoped, but instead in the circulation of worthless currency created in the neighboring states. To remedy this evil the new constitution of 1857 permitted the establishment of banks; and in line with the general trend Free Banks were contemplated, whose issues were to be based on government securities. However, none was set up, since other legal requirements were considered too strict by businessmen, a result which was perhaps intentional: Certain leaders in the constitutional convention came from the older Middle Western states, particularly from Ohio; it was they who favored the Indiana-Ohio solution of the banking problem, i.e., a state bank with branches, to which they were accustomed. Under their influence the creation of a state bank with branches was also made permissive under the constitution of 1857, and such a bank was actually brought into being.

Ohio influence can be traced through all the stages of the legislative development which led to the creation of the State Bank of Iowa. Discussions on a state bank may well have taken place in Iowa as early as the 1830's and 1840's when Robert Lucas (1781-1853) was (the first) territorial governor in Iowa. While governor of Ohio he had advocated a similar bank for this state.[36] Be that as it may, another governor of Iowa,[37] also hailing from Ohio and educated there (at Miami University), Robert Phillips Lowe (1805-1883), undoubtedly contributed to the introduction of the specific type of bank in Iowa. He was in office when the law creating the State Bank of Iowa was passed, and he favored it. More important for the development than Lowe, however, was another former citizen of Ohio, Samuel Jordan Kirkwood (1813-1894), who later was the war governor of Iowa. Born in Maryland he spent two decades (1835-1855) in Ohio practicing law and playing some part in her public life. He was, for instance, a member of the Ohio convention which revised the state constitution of 1802, a revision which was necessary in part because the clauses on banking had become obsolete. Thus Kirkwood came to study the problem of banking and arrived at some definite ideas on the subject. He was not opposed to banks if they were subject to strict regulation, whereby to "protect the people... from the system of bank plunder under which they have suffered so long and so grievously." After such experience in Ohio, Kirkwood came to Iowa in 1855. There he found himself face to face with similar problems when again he embarked on a public career. He became state senator and a member of the standing committee on banking just at the time when the State Bank bill

was before the legislature in 1858. To this bill Kirkwood proposed several ammendments, all of which became law when the bill was passed, so that the act embodies many of his ideas.

Thus the Act to incorporate the State Bank of Iowa was brought into existence.[38] It was a progressive law containing, for instance, the double liability of the stockholders (sec. 42) and a 25 per cent specie reserve against both notes and "current deposits" (sec. 31). This clause was undoubtedly inserted under the stimulus of the discussions resulting from the recent (1857) crisis. Disregarding minor differences the Iowa bank in its essential features was modeled on the State Bank of Ohio. Like the latter it possessed in the Board of Bank Commissioners a board of control with policy-making functions. The board could, for instance, exert an influence on the circulation and the specie holdings of the branches (secs. 2 and 3). The bank possessed a safety fund into which contributions amounting to $12\frac{1}{2}$ per cent of all circulating notes were to be paid, either in money or in securities of the United States or of the State of Iowa. Thus the branches were tied together by mutual liability, but they were mutually liable only for their note issues (secs. 7 and 12).

After having contributed to framing the law, Kirkwood participated also in organizing the bank. He became one of the founders of the Iowa City branch, was its largest stockholder, and its delegate to the board; he was elected and remained its president until 1859.[39] Many of his collaborators both on the boards of the branches and the Board of Bank Commissioners were private bankers, representative of whom was Hoyt Sherman (born in 1827), another newcomer to Iowa from Ohio and, incidentally, a brother of the Civil War general. Migrating to the former state as early as 1848 he founded one of its pioneering and later leading private banking houses, Hoyt Sherman and Company, Des Moines. Upon the establishment of the State Bank of Iowa he became the cashier of the Des Moines branch, a state director on the board of control, and its first secretary pro tem.[40]

The last state to adopt a state bank with branches of the type under discussion was Illinois. Her Act to establish a general system of banking upon a specie basis, approved as late as February 20, 1861,[41] established the Union Bank of Illinois, modeled on the State Bank of Indiana, another example of contact migration. The Union Bank possessed all the typical features of the Middle Western state bank with branches of the younger type, especially mutual liability of the branches for the debts of any failing member of the group. By not setting up a safety fund the Illinois legislature followed the Indiana example, deviating from the

Ohio-Iowa solution of the problem.[42] However the Union Bank of Illinois did not become a reality: Under section 92 of the act of 1861 it was submitted to a referendum and was voted down.[43]

Chapter XI

THE MIDDLE WESTERN STATE BANK
WITH BRANCHES

1. This author cannot agree with Bray Hammond's presentation in "Banking in the Early West" because he does not distinguish between the two types of state banks: see Jour. Econ. Hist., VIII (1948), 5 ff.
2. Passim.
3. Nothing shows better the development of thought during the period from 1815 to 1840 than a comparison of Bollmann's ideas with the following passage from Nathan Appleton's Remarks of 1841. "There is but one basis for a sound paper currency, the actual power to command coin. It is true no paper can circulate without confidence, but it is all important that this confidence should rest on a solid foundation," namely, specie; (op. cit., 8.)
4. Clapham, op. cit., I, 105 ff.
5. Trotter (op. cit., 89) explains the participation of states in banks as prompted by the desire "to afford the means of a judicious increase of the circulating medium and thereby to give impulse to agricultural labour, activity to commercial enterprise and an increased value to the lands of the state."
6. Texas planned this type of bank in 1838; see Gouge, Texas, 88, 89.
7. It may be questioned whether the younger type of Middle Western State bank with branches should be treated together with banking in the second or third period. The type of bank, of which we speak here, was undoubtedly created in the second, but since it migrated and became especially important in the third period, it is treated at this point.
8. The success of the State Bank of Missouri was largely due to its cashier, Henry Shurlds, who was one of the great bankers of his time. Shurlds (1796-1852) was born in Gloucester County, Virginia, was college bred, and had read law under William Wirt in Richmond with whom he practiced for a short period thereafter. In 1819 he went West, first to St. Louis, and about a year later to Potosi, Washington County, Missouri, then a mining center. There he practiced law, not too successfully, and upon the organization of the state government became a circuit judge. He resigned when the office of secretary of the state was tendered to him. In 1832 he became secretary to the state senate and in 1833 auditor of public accounts, thus beginning comparatively late in his life a career in the field of finance. In 1837 he was appointed cashier of the State Bank, a position which he filled with remarkable success for about fifteen years and until within a few months of his death. The personal confidence which he rightfully enjoyed seems to have contributed to the bank's remarkable career. (Bay, W.Y.M., Bench and Bar of Missouri [1878], 593 ff; Cable, op. cit., 133 ff.)
9. The background for the following can be found in the monographs of Dehority, Esarey, Forsyth, and Harding. This chapter could not have been written without the help of Miss Estella Wolf of the Indiana University Library and Mrs. Hazel W. Hopper of the Indiana State Library. They provided the author with information, excerpts, and photostats of primary and other local source material inaccessible outside of the state.
10. Esarey, op. cit., 226.
11. Indiana -- Governor -- Noble. Messages to the Legislature, 1832 -- January, 1833, 22, 23.
12. Indiana Journal, February 23, 1833, Vol. IX, no. 535.
13. Vincennes Western Sun, July 11, 1818; information given by the Indiana State Library.
14. Cauthorn, Henry S., A History of the City of Vincennes, Indiana from 1702 to 1901. (1901), 210-211.
15. Proffit (1807-1847), was born in New Orleans as the descendant of a Louisiana family. Coming to southern Indiana in 1828 he advanced during his life from bartering indigo for mink skins in his country store to the climax of his career as minister to Brazil under appointment by President Tyler. Proffit was one of the pioneer politicians and orators of Indiana. In the 1830's he represented his county for several years in the state legislature and was elected as a Whig to Congress in the 1840's after having been a prominent campaign speaker for Harrison. Proffit was interested in canals and other internal improvements, championing a railroad which, however, failed to obtain a charter. (Biographical Handbook of Congress; Wilson, Biographical Sketch on Proffit, passim.)
16. Incidentally, Proffit acted a second time on the stage of banking history, when in 1841, as one of the few stout defenders of President Tyler, he was charged with defending Tyler's veto of the National Bank bill on the floor of the House.
17. The few data on Graham which are available are contradictory. He was, apparently, of Irish descent, born 1781 or 1782, and came to this country

with his parents as a child. He grew up in Kentucky, whence he came to Vallonia, Indiana, in 1811. (Information from the Library of the University of Indiana.)

18. Dunn's activities again were typical of those of all the men who set up the new type of bank. Like them he was interested in internal improvements and, in addition, became connected with the building of the first railroad in his state. He was as instrumental in having its charter passed as in completing the actual work. After some years in the Indiana legislature he became a member of Congress and later state treasurer of Indiana. This office he held from 1841 to 1844 when the state debt agitated the public. In 1844 he became president of the Lawrenceburgh branch of the State Bank of Indiana. (Shaw, Archibald, ed., History of Dearborn County, Indiana [Bowen, 1915], 350.)

19. However, the New York Safety Fund Act had by that time already attracted wide attention. The American Quarterly Review (vol. IX of 1832), for instance, contained in the article "Report on the Currency; by a Committee of the New York Convention of the Friends of Domestic Industry, New York, 1832," (pp. 245 ff) a clear and unbiased description of the act; see especially 260 ff. Mott, Frank Luther, A History of American Magazines, 1741-1850 (New York and London, 1930), 273 evaluates the importance of the magazine.

The contemporary pamphlet Origin, Provisions and Effect of the Safety Fund Law of the State of New York (Albany, 1834), page 7, stresses that the system was generally known by 1834.

20. Merrill afterwards became president of the Madison and Indianapolis Railroad and in 1850 bought a bookstore, the ancestor of a still existing publishing house.

21. Fletcher, born in 1799, was a self-made man who had worked his way up from farmhand to lawyer and state senator. After seven years on the Bank Board he became the president of the Indianapolis branch of the State Bank of Indiana and later a successful private banker. (Knox, op. cit., 709.)

22. When the creation of a new national bank was under discussion around 1840 it was contemplated by some that the parent bank should be a sort of policy-making board of control. Jacob Barker, for instance, wrote to Henry Clay on May 13, 1841: "The mother bank should not discount; that business should be left to the branches, and for this purpose there should be a branch at the same place where the mother bank is located as well as at other places." (Incidents, 127.) It is open to question whether the Indiana example exerted any influence on such suggestions. The originators of this bank were Whigs as were the proponents of a new national bank.

23. See pages 95, 203, 204 of volume I.

24. Messages of the Governors of Michigan, (Lansing, 1925), I, 230, 231, 253.

25. House Journal (1839), 45.

26. Acts of the Legislature of the State of Michigan passed at the Annual Session of 1839 (Detroit, 1839), no. 37, 37 ff. The act is also reprinted in U.S. 26th Congr. 1st sess., House Executive Document 172, 1274 ff. See also Michigan House Documents of 1839, no. 29, 574-578; Report of the Committee on Banks... to whom was referred so much of the Governor's message as relates to the establishment of a State Bank; and Hinchman, op. cit., 45.

27. The author wishes to acknowledge the valuable assistance of the Michigan State Library in Lansing, Michigan, in getting the material for the preceding paragraphs.

28. Bates, op. cit., 201.

29. Huntington, op. cit. (1914), 134.

30. Perry, op. cit., 3; Esarey, op. cit., 256.

31. In drafting the bill Kelley cooperated with Benjamin Sprague Cowen (1792-1869), a native of New York. Cowen was originally a physician and later a lawyer and Whig politician. He was at that time the chairman of the Committee on Finance of the lower house.

32. Bates, op. cit., 132 ff. Kelley's report on the bill is to be found in Daily Ohio State Journal, VIII, January 8, 1845, p. 2.

33. It is noteworthy that Henry F. Baker of Cincinnati characterized the State Bank of Ohio as the "safety fund system of Ohio" (1854); op. cit., 12 ff.

34. This formulation is taken from the bank's pamphlet In Memoriam: Dr. John Andrews, 10.

35. It is not certain whether Kelley was also connected with the Franklin or Exchange Branch at Columbus; the list of members of the Board of Control, published in the bank's pamphlet mentioned above (pages 11-13) seems to indicate this. However, the Ohio State Archaeological and Historical Society could not find any connection, although Kelley "had no difficulties in obtaining funds from the Franklin Branch."

Incidentally Dr. John Andrews (1805-1866), in whose honor the above mentioned pamphlet was published, was also a friend of Kelley's. Originally a doctor, later a businessman, he became the principal stockholder as well as president of the Jefferson Branch of the State Bank, and was another early member of the Board of Control succeeding Swan as its president in 1855.

36. Lucas was governor of Ohio at the time of the boundary conflict with Michigan. His biography can be found in Randall and Ryan, op. cit., III, 438 ff.

37. Lowe was the first governor under the constitution of 1857.

38. Acts and Resolutions passed at the Regular Session of the Seventh General Assembly of the State of Iowa (Des Moines, 1858), chapter 87.

39. Kirkwood's successor as president of the bank was one Hiram Price, born in 1814 in Pennsylvania. He had come to Davenport, Iowa, opening a general store there. He was the typical pioneering businessman, becoming identified with the improvements of the young city, especially with an early railroad passing through that section of the state.

40. For the preceding, see the writings of D. E. Clark, Gue, Preston, Price, and Sherman.

41. Public Laws of the State of Illinois passed by the Twenty-Second Assembly (Springfield, 1861), 53 ff.

42. The decisive sections are sections 5, 9, 28, 31, 36, 51, 52. Double liability of the stock holders and the fact that the enterprise was to be strictly private without state participation may have been due to Ohio influence.

43. Huston, op. cit., I, 164.

Chapter XII

THE LOUISIANA BANKING ACT OF 1842 AND
EDMOND JOHN FORSTALL

It has been indicated that the crisis of 1837 followed by the depression of the late 1830's and early 1840's represents a turning point for American banking. The economic disaster which befell the country in those years forced legislators, bankers, and other businessmen to revise their thinking on monetary and banking matters. The outstanding results of such reconsideration were the New York Free Banking Act of 1838 and the Louisiana Banking Act of 1842. The former has been discussed in detail in an earlier chapter;[1] the latter is the subject of the present one.

Although originating at the same time and under similar circumstances the two acts differ remarkably. While the New York Free Banking Act, like the New York Safety Fund Act, was formulated outside of the banking community, the Louisiana Banking Act of 1842 was the work of a leading bank president and embodied reasoning first adopted and developed by the board of a banking enterprise. Both acts represent different stages in the development. Regardless of the fact that the New York Free Banking Act swayed state after state in the third period of American banking and was finally taken over nationally in the fourth, and regardless of the further fact that the fundamental ideas embodied in the Free Banking Act dominated American thinking down to about 1900, for the historian that act marks the end of a period. It represented the final stage in an ideological development the fundamentals of which date back to the eighteenth century. In contrast, the Louisiana Banking Act, although in some respects based on the same way of thinking, combined new elements with traditional ideas so that it became essentially modern and representative of nineteenth century thought. The Louisiana Banking Act of 1842 was the first in America which aimed not only at a specie basis, but also at liquidity and elasticity, the prerequisites of what came to be considered sound banking in modern times. Or to put it differently, the Louisiana Banking Act was the first in the United States which established by law a banking system which was liquid at all times because all cash liabilities were sustained by a fixed specie reserve in addition to short-term paper. Thus the system automatically became elastic in addition to being liquid.

I

The Louisiana Banking Act of 1842 was the work of Edmond John Forstall (1794-1873).[2] Forstall was a truly remarkable man, even if he had such undesirable traits as vanity and arrogance. A biography of this merchant, sugar planter, banker, legislator, lobbyist, and writer should, in the opinion of this author, be undertaken by an economic historian.

Forstall had an excellent background. The Forstalls were a Norman-English family which had become established in Ireland. A scion of this family entered the military service of France during the reign of Louis XIV; a son of his settled in Martinique; while a grandson, Nicholas Michel Edmond, came to Louisiana about 1750. Edmond John Forstall was the oldest son of the oldest son of this immigrant who, of noble birth himself, had become connected by marriage with the leading French families of the colony.[3] As might be expected, Edmond John enjoyed as good an education as was then obtainable in Louisiana. In 1820 he can be found as a partner of the commercial firm, Gordon and Forstall, which later became Gordon, Forstall and Company, and finally E.J. Forstall and Sons.[4] Their business soon became so extensive that in line with the mercantile practice of those years (1820's and 1830's) one of the partners, Alexander Gordon, was stationed in Liverpool. (Incidentally, he became later the managing partner of Lizardi and Company, New Orleans.) In addition to being a merchant Forstall was also a sugar planter with his plantation located in St. James Parish.[5] From figures published on Louisiana sugar production in 1844,[6] it is obvious that although not belonging to the largest sugar plantations Forstall's nevertheless was a large one. It has been impossible to ascertain whether Forstall's commercial activities preceded those as a planter or _vice versa_. Be that as it may, his interest in the state's sugar industry began while he was still young. Forstall claimed that in the early 1820's his firm imported most of the first steam engines to be installed on sugar plantations and most of the first steam-driven sugar mills; and about a decade later, in

1830, although not initiating this progress, it took part in introducing a new process, the use of the vacuum pan.[7]

Forstall's double status as planter and merchant made him eminently fit to become, in the 1830's, the president of the Citizens' Bank of New Orleans, the third plantation bank of the state, all the more since he "represent[ed] the largest interest in the institution." This statement implies that he must have mortgaged his extensive properties heavily in exchange for stock in the bank. Forstall had become interested in this new type of bank at an early stage and was one of its champions. As a matter of fact, in one way or another he was connected with all three of the Louisiana plantation banks.[8] When in 1828 a representative of the Consolidated Association of Planters, the very first of these banks, went to England to find buyers for the state bonds issued in its favor, Alexander Gordon of the Liverpool branch of Gordon, Forstall and Company put him in touch with the Barings and assisted in concluding a contract and in other transactions preparatory to the opening of the bank. A year later when that contract had led to difficulties Forstall himself was instrumental in negotiating a new agreement with Thomas Baring who was then in America; and an issue of state bonds in favor of that bank was sold by F. de Lizardi and Company of London, merchant bankers, a firm in which Forstall was interested. (It is supposed to have bought out the Liverpool branch of Gordon, Forstall and Company,[9] Alexander Gordon becoming at that time the managing partner of F. de Lizardi and Company and Forstall their New Orleans representative.) In the meantime, Forstall, while in London in 1830, and Thomas Baring had worked out the plan of a second plantation bank for Louisiana, the Union Bank. The act authorizing this bank, as well as its rules and regulations were worked out by Forstall, who in 1831 kept the Barings informed on the progress which he was making, asking also for advice regarding desirable features which would make saleable the state bonds to be issued for the benefit of the new bank. After the Union Bank had come into existence in 1832[10] Forstall became one of the two commissioners who, in that year, concluded a contract with Baring Brothers and Company and Prime, Ward, King and Company. By this contract the Union Bank sold to these firms 5,500 bonds ($5,500,000 face value) and consigned to them an additional 1,500. In that same year (1832) in connection with this business, Forestall corresponded with Thomas Wren Ward, the American agent of the Barings, regarding the credit of Louisiana.[11]

Thus it is not surprising in 1835 to find Forstall negotiating in Amsterdam with Hope and Company

regarding bonds of the Citizens' Bank. After commissioners sent out in 1834 to negotiate these bonds had been unable to conclude a sale, on September 1 of that year, Forstall arranged a conditional agreement with the Dutch banking house. Under this agreement the Hopes were willing to sell bonds for the Citizens' Bank provided that the latter could induce the state to replace the bank's bonds by state bonds, and provided further that the obligation of the bank to invest funds in the Lake Borgne Navigation Company was repealed.[12] When the State had actually issued bonds in favor of the Citizens' Bank, a contract was concluded, and the Hopes very successfully sold a part of a tranche of these bonds, the interest of which was payable at their counting house.[13]

Forstall, as mentioned above, had become by that time the president of the Citizens' Bank and controlled and administered it until 1838. In an interesting letter of September 20 of that year he described the principles which had guided him in his capacity as the bank's chief executive.[14]

> The duties devolving upon the president of a property bank carry with them a responsibility of no ordinary magnitude: the fortunes of thousands of families depend upon the good or bad management of the directory over which he presides; he is, by law, the immediate guardian of the property of the bank; he must see that the affairs of the bank are carried on according to the true intent and meaning of the act of incorporation; that expediency be not preferred to principles; that the rules laid down for the guidance of the bank be not encroached upon; that the money borrowed on the property of the stockholders be loaned out upon at least equal security; that the guaranty of one stockholder should not be lessened at the expense of another; that the guaranty of the State and bond-holders be held sacred; that the bank abstain using her deposites, unless fully prepared to meet them under all circumstances; that the other business of the bank be at all times made subservient to her functions as an issuer of currency; he must watch closely the domestic and foreign exchanges, that he may know when to expand, when to contract: in fine, his supervision and correspondence must embrace the whole sphere of action of the bank.

In the case of a businessman who was as articulate as was Forstall and a shrewd politician besides, as will be described later, it is difficult to

decide a hundred years later and without access to
the original sources whether his administration
was really as efficient as he made it appear. No
doubt it was characterized by a sense of responsibility, honesty, and foresightedness, although his
enemies on the bank board did not concede that he
possessed "any remarkably peculiar or uncommon
foresight."[15] So much is certain: contemporaries
considered him "a thorough merchant," and the
Citizens' Bank under his presidency was one of the
only two New Orleans banks which did not suspend
specie payments in 1837.[16] This success may have
been due to his "habilite tranchante" which one of
his collaborators praised,[17] who perhaps meant
Forstall's ability to think in economic as opposed
to business terms. When the actions of the Bank of
England in preparing for a coming storm became
known in New Orleans in 1836, Forstall, aware of
the importance of that city as the main American
market for the precious metals, brought about concerted action among the New Orleans banks. They
made funds available for the import of specie and
thus strengthened the position of the Louisiana
banking system. With this action Forstall became
one of the early exponents of cooperation among
American banks.

It is not known why Forstall lost his influence on
the Citizens' Bank. Political reasons, the Whig-
Democratic conflict of the decade, may have played
a certain part. There is no doubt that during the crisis
and depression of 1837/1838 actions of the hard-
pressed London house of F. de Lizardi and Company and its Paris correspondent, Lizardi Hermannos, were detrimental to his prestige. These actions included, for instance, a sale of Louisiana
bonds below the agreed-upon price, the temporary
refusal to accept drafts, and the mortgaging of certain business paper with the Bank of England. (It
will be remembered that Forstall was interested in
the London house of Lizardi's.) His obvious unwillingness to embarrass that firm by drafts which
would have been profitable to the Citizens' Bank
was liable to misconstruction: although the exchange rate on London was high and the Citizens'
Bank had funds available with Lizardi's, it did not
draw for many months during the critical period.[18]
(According to Forstall, funds were accumulated to
pay interest on the state bonds which the Citizens'
Bank was obligated to provide.)

At any rate, on August 31, 1838 Forstall decided
to place his resignation before the board of directors because the "division in the directory of the
bank" made it, as he felt, impossible for him to retain his position. Not only could he no longer rely
"upon the support of a majority" of the directors,
but he also considered them guilty of not observing
their own rules. To his decision he stuck although

a group of stockholders urgently requested him to
reconsider it.[19]

Important matters of policy were involved in
the conflict between Forstall and the majority of
the board of directors of the Citizens' Bank. First,
he wanted to eliminate all accommodation loans on
personal security while retaining such loans when
they were secured by mortgage. Thereby he wanted
to draw a clear line of distinction between trade
and accommodation paper. Secondly, he was planning to adapt the lending policy of the bank to the
specific agricultural credit needs, on the one hand,
and the bank's need for liquidity, on the other, by
making loans to agriculture in the spring and insisting on repayment after the marketing of the
harvest. (At least this seems to be the meaning of
the pertinent passage of his letter of 1839 to the
stockholders.) Thirdly, and finally, he insisted on
a certain policy regarding an issue of $3,500,000
interest-bearing postnotes, floated mostly, if not
exclusively, in Europe. Forstall insisted that these
postnotes should be bought back whenever their
market value dropped below 95 per cent so as to
uphold the credit of his institution, and for this
purpose he wished that certain funds be set aside.[20]

Forstall's resignation as indicated, was the result of a fight within the board of the Citizens' Bank,
which soon came into the open. Forstall apparently
organized a campaign to recapture control of the
bank. His enemies, on the other hand, tried to discredit the "punctiliously honorable" man[21] by instituting an examination of certain transactions of the
bank by a committee of stockholders, (mainly lawyers), appointed on October 18, 1838, and by publishing its report.[22] This report was to bring before
the public those transactions "which certain parties
believed would [reflect on] his friends," thereby
lessening Forstall himself in the estimation of his
fellow citizens. Published at a critical moment it
did much to impair the credit of the Citizens' Bank.
Moreover, malicious gossip was spread regarding
a sinister combination which Forstall was supposed to have entered into with other directors of
the bank. The fight resulted in Forstall's re-elec-
tion to the board, but without giving him control of
it, since not enough of his friends were elected at
the same time. Thus he held office only from
February to August, 1839, when he withdrew again
from the administration of the Citizens' Bank.[23]
During the few months when he was on the board in
1839 he fought for sound policy and practice, but
remained always in the minority. He objected to
putting additional credit at the disposal of the
stockholders because the bank was not liquid at that
moment; he suggested that government deposits be
set aside and kept as special deposits in liquid
form; and for reasons of principle he resisted

cotton transactions entered into for the purpose of creating funds in New York, in order to avoid the shipment of specie. (To be sure, what he suggested in place was itself a very dubious procedure, the use of kites.)[24] At that time the Citizens' Bank was already in pretty bad shape and the atmosphere on the board was determined by the open hostility between two factions.[25]

Once more Forstall became connected with the administration of the Citizens' Bank, in the fall of 1842. The State of Louisiana under the law of March 14, 1842 took possession of the assets of that bank for the purpose of liquidation and Forstall became president of the board of managers. This appointment could signify an appreciation of Forstall's activities as a banker, just as it could have been the result of political wire pulling in consequence of which a representative of the foreign creditors acquired a strategical position. However, very soon, sometime in 1843 or the early days of 1844, the presidency of that board was taken over by one Hullin,[26] and Forstall's connection with the administration of the Citizens' Bank came definitely to an end.

Forstall's business activities in the 1830's and early 1840's were supplemented by political ones. A Whig, he was in all probability a shrewd politician. In 1837 and 1838, i.e., during the session of the state's thirteenth legislature, he was in the Louisiana House of Representatives becoming a member of important committees; his share in drafting the banking reform legislation of 1842 will be discussed shortly in more detail. His intimate knowledge of the state and its economic conditions must have stood him in good stead.[27]

Forstall reached the pinnacle of his career in the middle of the 1830's. The crisis of 1837 and the depression following probably impaired his wealth;[28] the troubles of the Citizens Bank, for example, must have injured him, large stockholder that he was, at least temporarily. Even so, his business acumen, his knowledge of Louisiana, and his political affiliations made him a valuable agent for such firms as the Barings in London and the Hopes in Amsterdam who having taken a considerable interest in the flotation of American securities, for their own benefit and for that of their customers had to do their best to keep the various American states from repudiating their debts. For this purpose among others they retained Forstall, whose lobbying and propaganda activities were crowned with success at least in his home state, Louisiana.[29] Forstall seems to have been rather proud of this achievement and ascribed much of its success to the publications issued in the interest of the foreign bondholders. He was less successful in Florida where he also looked after the interests of Hope and

Company. In this case, being convinced that the Federal Government for legal reasons and in its own interest would have to assume the debt incurred by Florida while still a territory, Forstall carried the fight to Washington, but lost the battle.[30] During the time that he was struggling against Repudiation both in Louisiana and Florida, Reid, Irving and Company of London also secured Forstall's services in the interest of their clients who were holders of Mississippi bonds. Forstall made arrangements for the publication of a series of articles in a leading newspaper and its wide distribution in book form, but then discontinued his exertions. He felt that he had done all that could be done in that state;[31] but the European houses which contributed to the expenses, such as Huth and Company and the Hopes, were not satisfied. Recognizing Forstall's services in their fight against Repudiation the Barings, however, made him their agent in 1847 and in 1848 their sole agent in New Orleans, a job which he held until 1861. Nevertheless he retained his connection with Hope and Company who had appointed him their agent in 1843, succeeding one Fastenrath.[32] But an offer to represent Reid, Irving and Company of London was declined in that decade. As the agent of the London house Forstall, who developed into an expert judge of cotton, was mainly engaged in the purchase of and the advancing on cotton, paying by drafts on the Barings or a New York correspondent of theirs "as advantage dictated." He seems to have dealt for account of the Barings in other commodities and in exchange also.[33]

II

In order to understand Forstall's achievement in the field of banking it is necessary once more to sum up the ideological background of the New York Free Banking Act: The Mercantilist theory that capital was not needed for the business of banking and that it served exclusively to secure the noteholders and to establish a "credit" for the bank (on the basis of which to create purchasing power) had undergone a development in America prior to the crisis of 1837. If the above-mentioned presupposition was true, as people believed at that time, or, in other words, if the capital and the "credit" of banks served different purposes, it was possible to use the capital of banks in one way and their "credit" in another. (As will be remembered, this was the prominent and distinctive aspect of Bronson's policy which became widely known.) Thus the New York Free Banking Act provided that the capital of banks set up under the act should be invested in certain securities for the benefit of the noteholders, but it left the decision as to the banking business proper to directors and officers. For-stall, however, went a step further. He also adopt-ed the above theory, but in addition to making rules regarding the investment of the capital of banks, he devised strict regulations for the banking business proper, drawing his inspirations from the policy of the Bank of England. Forstall believed that "one of the evils of contemporary banking was the want of uniformity in the actual operations of banks so nec-essary to ensure a sound currency where there is a multiplicity of issuers of paper money."[34] This was the evil which he tried to remedy.

Forstall's influence on the development of American banking began in 1837 when he was chair-man of the Finance Committee of the Louisiana House of Representatives. It resulted originally from a report which he drafted and which in Feb-ruary, 1837, was presented to the legislature as the "Report of the Joint Committee of the Senate and House of Representatives on the banking situation of the moneyed institutions of New Orleans."[35] The report was based on the statements of all but two of the New Orleans banks, statements which were submitted upon request of the legislature. They were consolidated and Forstall analyzed them with the help of advanced concepts. As a matter of fact, just as Biddle's great speech of 1810 was in its time the maturest expression of contemporary banking thought and foreshadowed the best banking practice of the second period, so Forstall's excel-lent report of 1837 ushered in sound banking prac-tice of the third and fourth periods of American banking.

The truly modern character of Forstall's report rests in his making "cash responsibilities" the starting point for his proposals. The term, "cash responsibilities," embraced in Forstall's language both notes in circulation and deposits, and it was used interchangeably with the phrase "banking movement." The "banking movement,"[36] according to Forstall, could "only be usefully and effectually sustained by short paper payable on a fixed day and moving in a rapid circle." Long-term paper, even if perfectly secure, was of no use for banks to meet their notes and other debts payable on demand. That is to say, Forstall thought along the lines of Isaac Bronson, whose note issues, as will be re-membered, were elastic.[37] (The same was true al-so of the issues of the Second Bank of the United States to the extent that they were based on bills, especially those resulting from cotton transactions, as was clearly seen by Trotter.)[38] Forstall, by recommending the policy of banking on short-term paper, leading to elastic note issues, and on top of that by thoroughly understanding its significance and consequences, went further than the New York banker: Forstall (like Biddle) was acquainted with

and used the term elasticity.[39] Although it is open to question whether he knew about Bronson and his achievement, it is quite possible since he was wide-ly read and traveled. As a matter of fact, when Forstall in a letter of August 31, 1838 to the direc-tors of the Citizens' Bank suggested that the bank should at all times have business paper maturing within sixty days to an amount equal to circulation and deposits and that it would by such policy (in conjuncture with other measures) retain at all times the control of its operations, the passages in question sound almost like a quotation from one of Bronson's papers. (There is even a quotation mark at the decisive point.)[40] Surely Forstall was in-formed on the fact that a large proportion of the issues of the Second Bank of the United States was backed by cotton paper.

Forstall's thinking in terms of cash responsibil-ities led on the one hand to the recommendation of banking on short business paper and on the other, as will be described presently, to the suggestion of specie reserves. At the root of recommendation and suggestion was a kind of analysis which marked progress over everything that had as yet been achieved in America: In his Report of 1837 For-stall compared the cash liabilities of the New Or-leans banks with their specie and juxtaposed the ratios thus obtained with the corresponding ones for the Pennsylvania and New York banks in 1837 and with that of the Bank of England in 1836, a truly modern procedure. Equally modern was his analys-is of the portfolios of the Bank of England and of the various kinds of Louisiana banks. He found that the capital of the Bank of England was invested in government securities for the benefit of note holders and depositors, for this form of investment was the best protection against insolvency. At the same time Forstall realized that the "movement" of the Bank was sustained by bullion, by short-term business paper, and again by government securities. Starting from such an analysis of bank portfolios and from the basic ideas described above, Forstall arrived at a reform program: For the first time in American banking history a fixed ratio between cash liabilities (notes and deposits) and specie was suggested. Forstall proposed that the Louisiana banks should keep in their vaults in gold and silver at least one-third of their cash liabilities. Thus specie was to become "the regulator of banking," the "governor of a well constructed engine possess-ing within itself the power of expansion and contrac-tion."

In these suggestions the spirit of Mercantilist banking theory was definitely overcome and re-placed by the spirit of classical economics with its reliance on self-regulation of economic life.[41] For-stall recommended his suggestions, offered as the opinion of the joint committee on the banking situation, as follows: "the fixed rule which would compel the banks to use their specie on hand as the only measure of their operations would secure uniformity in our banking movement and be the best protection to currency that can be afforded." A fixed rate of specie would act as a "monitor to expand and contract." But the fixed ratio of specie to cash liabilities was not to stand alone but was to be supplemented by a sufficient amount of short-term bills to be held as a secondary reserve, to use the modern expression.[42] "A bank... should have at all times within its immediate control an amount of availables fully equal, under all circumstances, to its cash responsibilities," as Forstall expressed it in a letter of 1838.[43]

What Forstall thereby tried to introduce into American banking was the practice of the Bank of England as it had been described by Horsley Palmer and other directors of the Bank of England before the parliamentary committee of 1832: namely, that the desirable proportion against "all liabilities to pay on demand" (deposits and notes) was "about two-thirds in securities and one in bullion."[44] There can be no doubt that Forstall, the widely traveled man, possessed first-hand information and that he knew what he was proposing. It is in fact remarkable that in this case only five years elapsed before an English accomplishment was recommended in America, while in the first half of the nineteenth century, as a rule, twenty to thirty years were needed before an English or Continental achievement was sufficiently known in this country to be ready for adoption. Forstall himself, however, did not refer to the parliamentary investigation of 1832 of the Bank of England, but instead to Albert Gallatin's Considerations on the Currency and Banking System of the United States of 1831 and the practice of the Louisiana State Bank which he claimed to have operated under this principle for about eighteen years. When Forstall referred to Gallatin's Considerations, he was correct in that the idea of a certain specie reserve against circulation was contained therein. But the idea was neither worked out clearly, nor stressed, nor did it dominate Gallatin's reasoning to the exclusion of competing ideas. Actually it alternated with the traditional idea of limiting the debts of banks "to a sum bearing a certain ratio to the capital."[45] As a matter of fact, Forstall had advanced far beyond Gallatin in his knowledge of what was needed in American banking, and when one compares his plans and his final achievement with the lame clauses on specie reserves enacted by other states in the same period his greatness becomes evident.[46]

The idea that notes (or cash obligations) should be backed by a specie reserve has, as a matter of fact, a history of its own. The idea can be found in the Mercantilist banking theory of the eighteenth century, but it was then of minor importance. For Sir James Steuart the main problem was how to secure bank notes, but he realized that the founders of banks also had to provide an amount of specie sufficient to answer such notes as should return for payment.[47] While Steuart left open the question whether a fixed ratio could be established, Adam Smith tackled it, concluding that Ł 20,000 in gold and silver were a sufficient basis for Ł 100,000 circulation, i.e., he thought of a ratio of one to five.[48] In the reasoning of both these men, specie and circulation were tied together. However, when the basic idea was taken over in America this relation was blurred. This country, almost from the outset, contracted the habit of looking at the ratio of capital to note issues, thereby following the main line of Mercantilist thinking; but, what had been the side line in the eighteenth century was destined to determine sound banking policy in the nineteenth. It is meaningful indeed that when Blodget, for instance, quoted the passage just mentioned from Adam Smith's book he not only misunderstood Smith but censured him.[49]

Typical of the hazy thinking on the matter of specie reserves customary in America up to about 1830 are utterances of such men as Alexander Hamilton and Pelatiah Webster. Hamilton stated that "banks in good credit could circulate a far greater sum than the actual quantity of their capital in gold and silver" and Webster in the same vein declared that "any sum of money in the stock of the bank... is sufficient to support the credit of double or treble its amount of bank bills." It is obvious that these thinkers consciously or unconsciously blended two different lines of thought (the limitation of issues to a certain percentage of the capital in order to secure the noteholders and the keeping of a specie reserve to answer such notes as would return for redemption). Thereby the issue was befogged to the detriment of practical banking.[50]

When the New York Free Banking Act of 1838 stipulated a specie reserve, while at the same time establishing a definite security for the noteholders, the two lines of thought were separated again; but the specie reserves were dropped by an early amendment. That act, together with the writings of American thinkers like Gallatin, must have contributed to the clarification of the American mind on the problem of specie reserves. But the fact that the above described practice of the Bank of England became not only known in this country, at an early moment, but was also transplanted by Forstall, did more than anything else to bring American banking onto the road toward a fixed ratio of specie reserves to certain liabilities. In the matter of specie reserves Forstall was actually more consistent and more articulate than even the directors of the Bank of England:[51] As early as October, 1836, a suggestion was entered in the minutes of the Citizens' Bank, then controlled by Forstall, to the effect that the New Orleans institution should keep at all times one-third of their cash liabilities in specie. "A good medium would always be obtained by following the movement of the metallics."[52]

The other aspect of Forstall's thinking, mentioned earlier, which made him probably the first exponent of the "banking principle" in America, found an early expression in a letter of his to the directors of the Citizens' Bank and in a report of two of them (Hilligsberg and LeBeau). These men, being Forstall's friends and mouthpieces, recommended the adoption of a new policy by the bank, namely, banking on short-term, self-liquidating trade paper. The letter and report of 1838 belong from the point of view of this research to the most interesting documents produced by American banking in that period. The decisive passage of the former reads substantially as follows:[53]

First. Hereafter the loans of the bank shall be distributed as follows:
1. Loans on stocks, as required by the charter.
2. Loans on business paper, i.e., paper on personal security, payable in full at maturity.
3. Loans on accommodation paper, to be guaranteed by mortgage on real estate, and not to exceed two-thirds of the cash value of said estate.

Second. The bank shall hold, at all times, an amount of business paper, maturing within sixty days, equal to the amount of its deposits and circulation; every note secured by personal security shall be, de facto, considered as business paper; and every note secured by mortgage shall be considered as accommodation paper.

Third. No renewal of business paper shall take place, unless forced by extraordinary circumstances; and in all such cases, the maker or endorser of such paper shall be required to give a mortgage on real estate; and the paper thus secured, and no other, shall be considered as accommodation paper.

Fourth. The operations of the bank shall be conducted in such a manner as to discount an equal amount of accommodation paper for the country and city. Country accommodations shall be made payable from February to April, and shall be renewable, if required, on the payment of a per centum equal to the number of months for which the loan shall have been made, multiplied by five. The city accommodations shall be made payable at four

months, and renewable on the payment of twenty per cent.

Fifth. The cashier on each discount day shall lay before the board a statement showing --
1. Loans to stockholders.
2. Loans on accommodation, under the heads of 'city' and 'country,' and when due.
3. Loans on business paper, when due.
4. Cash responsibilities of the bank.

Sixth. The first rule to be applicable to all accommodation paper now held by the bank, and maturing on or after the 1st of March next.

By 1839 the various sets of ideas analyzed above had been merged by Forstall into a consistent whole,[54] and on January 23, 1839 he expounded the plan in a letter to the stockholders of the Citizens' Bank, his presentation greatly resembling the final formulation of the underlying ideas in the law of 1842. In the letter of 1839 there was put forth also, expressly and for the first time, the idea that a certain proportion of the bank's capital should be used for accommodation loans, an idea which, however, was already implied in the second and fourth suggestions of the letter of 1838. That is to say, what has been characterized above as the prominent and distinctive aspect of Bronson's policy was now also blended into Forstall's earlier train of thought.[55]

When Forstall wrote his report of 1837 (i.e., the Report of the Joint Committee of the Senate and the House of Representatives on the banking situation of the moneyed institutions of New Orleans) storm signals were raised, but the storm had not broken as yet. Several months later, however, the blow came and when the Louisiana legislature convened in December, 1837, the governor, under the impact of the crisis, requested it to devise reform legislation. For this purpose a General Bank Committee was set up of which Forstall was more than just a member: as the chairman of a subcommittee he probably did most of the work which was assigned to it. The General Bank Committee submitted a bill which both the Senate and the House amended and finally passed only to have it vetoed by the governor. Although the details of the various bills thus offered are of no interest in this context, it is noteworthy that all of them embodied a section requiring the Louisiana banks to have at least one-tenth of their capital in the form of specie by March 1, 1839; on and after March 1, 1840 they were to have at all times a specie reserve of 33 1/3 percent of their cash liabilities.[56]

The bills of 1838 represent a further step in the development which had started with Forstall's report of 1837 (the Report of the Joint Committee). As just mentioned, these bills stipulated the holdings of a certain specie reserve against cash liabilities. (Incidentally, it was not because of this clause that the final bill was vetoed.) However, the second and equally important aspect of Forstall's thinking, namely, the supplementing of specie by secondary reserves in the form of short-term paper, was not embodied in the bills. The weight of "property banks" in the Louisiana banking set-up must have made such a progressive step exceedingly difficult. The spirit dominating the legislators of 1838, who in the final (vetoed) bill attempted to force every bank to loan a certain percentage of its funds to the agrarian interest of the state, was directly opposed to this part of Forstall's thinking. However, in the report which the General Bank Committee drafted in that session and which was signed by Forstall, the latter hammered away at just this point. Analyzing the statements submitted by the various banks Forstall pointed out:

> It appears from the above data that the funds employed by our banks in loans on mortgages and long term paper amount to about $44,000,000 which may be considered as the dead weight or non availables of the banks: public credit can not be affected by it; it [the dead weight] is individual in its operation; and that the loans by discounts of mercantile paper and specie on hand amount to $15,000,000. This is the active capital or available fund retained for the purpose of sustaining the circulation; it cannot be affected without causing an immediate derangement of the whole circulating medium of the country.

Here can be found for the first time that formulation which a few years later was embodied in the act of 1842.[58] By that time Forstall saw American banks as fulfilling two different functions: as "loan offices" they lent on mortgage; as banks of discount they financed the mercantile and industrial interests, as he expressed it.[59]

The reconciliation of these functions was now becoming another one of his aims. On the basis of such ideas and as the result of such efforts there came finally into being the Louisiana Banking Act of 1842, or, to be exact, the Act to revive the charters of the several banks located in the City of New Orleans and for other purposes.[60] If and to what extent Forstall himself was instrumental in seeing the bill through the legislature seems to be unknown. Be that as it may, the act embodied his ideas as to the necessity of a fixed ratio of specie against cash liabilities and of ample secondary liquid reserves in the form of commercial paper. At the same time the act forced the New Orleans banks to adopt regarding the use of their capital and

credit a policy orginally devised by Isaac Bronson, taken over into his writings by MacVickar, later recommended by such men as Lord, Gallatin, Raguet, and Gouge,[61] and finally promoted by Forstall. Or, to put it differently, Isaac Bronson's overall policy improved by the requirement of a fixed ratio of specie reserves became Louisiana law through the instrumentality of Forstall. Thus three different lines of thought, two of which had already been combined by Bronson, were embodied in the Louisiana Banking Act of 1842.

The decisive section I of the act reads as follows:

> Each bank shall separate its loans on capital paid in from its loans on deposits; the loans on capital to be composed of accommodations on personal security or on mortgage, loans on stocks by the property banks, and of all other investments of whatever nature not realizable in ninety days.
>
> The loans on deposits and specie, representing the paper money issued by the banks shall be restricted to paper payable in full at maturity and such paper shall form a component part of the specie basis intended to meet the circulation and deposits and shall be restricted to ninety days, so as to effectually insure a rapid movement in the daily receipts.
>
> The loans and investments on the capital shall be denominated the 'dead weight'. The loans on deposits shall be denominated the 'movement of the banks'.
>
> No bank shall increase the investment in its dead weight so long as the whole of its cash liabilities is not represented in one third of the amount of such responsibilities in specie and at least two thirds in satisfactory paper payable in full at maturity and within ninety days.

These sentences are not too fortunately worded. They amounted to this: The banks had to invest their capital in medium and long-term loans just as Bronson had done. In addition, they had to invest their lodged deposits in ninety-day trade paper. Finally, whatever purchasing power they created over and above their capital and lodged deposits had to be created on the basis of such ninety-day trade paper, provided, however, that all their cash liabilities were secured at least one-third by specie and two-thirds by ninety-day trade paper. Thus the "rule of 1832" of the Bank of England was introduced into this country. At the same time loans were here for the first time legally tied to specie on hand instead of to capital (or capital plus deposits) as had been customary in America. The unfortunate wording of the law which distinguished between investment of capital and banking on deposits should not mislead the historian.

III

Louisiana banking, as organized under the law of 1842, experienced its first real test during the crisis of 1857. Since it stood that test better than the banking system of any other state it seemed destined to exert considerable influence on the future of American banking.[62] The expected development was cut short when the Civil War broke out. In the late 1850's, however, the Louisiana Banking Act of 1842 had come to be studied even in such states as New York and Massachusetts which considered themselves (and actually were) most advanced with respect to banking. That interest is all the more remarkable, because as late as 1841 Albert Gallatin had noted that the banking system of New Orleans was founded on such different principles that in other parts of the country one could not form a correct opinion of it.[63] On the other hand, when attention was first drawn thereto, the essential feature of the Louisiana Banking Act of 1842 was not understood, a proof of how advanced it was. It was not seen that its strength lay in the combination of banking on short term self-liquidating trade paper with a fixed and ample specie reserve against cash liabilities. It took almost four decades before this fact was generally recognized.[64] In the late 1850's the fixed specie reserve as such seemed to explain the success of the system.[65]

The truth of the claim that the Louisiana banking act was not understood when the attention of the country was first drawn to it in the late 1850's can be ascertained from the messages of President Buchanan on December 8, 1857 and of Governor King of New York on January 6, 1858.[66] It is equally evident from A Report on the Currency (written by George Opdyke for a committee on the currency of Weekly Meetings of Friends of a Sound Currency held in New York in the fall of 1858)[67] and from a "Report of a Committee of the [New York] Chamber of Commerce to consider changes in the Banking Laws of New York."[68] With reference to the Louisiana act these reports recommend fixed specie reserves, but there was no word on short-term trade paper supplementing the latter.

Turning from New York to Boston, one finds a similar situation. In Massachusetts it was Samuel Hooper who drew the attention of the state to the Louisiana act.[69] In contrast to Buchanan and the New Yorkers, Hooper understood that the combination of a fixed specie reserve with banking on the basis of self-liquidating short-term trade paper was the essential feature of the act. Nevertheless, he became an exponent of fixed specie reserves only. Nothing proves better the greatness of Forstall than the limitations of Hooper, who may have felt, however, that only a limited goal was attainable. In fact he wrote: "No one can doubt that the Louisiana law is safer for the banks and for the public [than the Massachusetts act of 1858]; and if experience proves that it is also more profitable to the stockholders of the banks and more beneficial to the merchants and others who are the customers of the banks it would seem to be the duty of legislators to make such the law in every state where banks exist."[70] In other words Hooper envisaged in a more remote future the adoption of the Louisiana law in its entirety; and this expectation, as mentioned above, might well have become an actuality all over the country had not the Civil War made such development impossible.

FOOTNOTES

Chapter XII

THE LOUISIANA BANKING ACT OF 1842 AND EDMOND JOHN FORSTALL

1. See vol. I of this work, page 187 ff.
2. It is Helderman's merit to have rediscovered Forstall, op. cit., 93 ff. Some information can be found in Bankers Magazine, XXXII (1877/78), 352 and in the obituary in the New Orleans Republican, Nov. 18, 1873. Ralph Hidy's opinion on Forstall (Barings, 396) is unbalanced and not in line with his own findings.
3. Arthur, Stanley C., Old Families of Louisiana (New Orleans, 1931), 112-119.
4. DeBow's Commercial Review, I, 54; Grenier, op. cit., 42, 74. As to Gordon, see Hidy, Barings, 334.
5. Forstall, Agricultural Productions, 18.
6. Reprinted in ibid., 17 ff.
7. DeBow's Commercial Review, I, 54, 55; Rightor, Henry, Standard History of New Orleans (Chicago, 1900), 668.
8. On plantation banks, see chapter VIII of vol. I of this work.
9. Grenier, op. cit., 42, 46, 55, 59, 74. About F. de Lizardi and Company, see Hidy, Barings, Index and Clapham, op. cit., II, 152, 154, 158. The firm was helped by the Bank of England during the crisis of 1837. See also Hidy, "Cushioning a Crisis...," 144 and interesting details in Report (see footnote 22), 10, 15-62.
10. Hidy, "Union Bank," 234, 236; idem, Barings, 110. Forstall saw Biddle on his way to Europe in 1832. See Biddle's letter to Thos. W. Ward of July 30, 1832, in Biddle Letterbooks.
11. McGrane, Bondholders, 71.
12. U.S. 25th Congr. 2nd sess., House Executive Document 79, 638. The negotiations are described in detail by McGrane, Bondholders, 174, 175. His source is Louisiana Senate Journal, 1843/1844, li ff.
13. Report (see footnote 22), 13, 16, 24, 35, 36.
14. U.S. 25th Congr. 3rd sess., House Executive Document 227, 564.
15. U.S. 26th Congr. 2nd sess., House Executive Document 111, 833.
16. McGrane, op. cit., p. 177.
17. U.S. 26th Congr. 2nd sess., House Executive Document 111, 833.
18. Ibid., 855 ff. Report (see footnote 22), 17, 20, 29, 33, 34.
19. U.S. 25th Congr. 3rd sess., House Executive Document 227, 564 ff; U.S. 26th Congr. 2nd sess., House Executive Document 111, 785 ff.
20. Ibid., 792 ff.
21. Hidy, Barings, 561 (footnote 7).
22. U.S. 26th Congr. 2nd sess., House Executive Document 111, 790, 793. Report of the Committee of Investigation (selected from the stockholders) Appointed by the Direction of the Citizens' Bank of Louisiana in Conformity with the Resolution of the Board of 18th. October, 1838. (Printed by E. Johns & Co. Stationers' Hall, New Orleans, 1839. 62 pages). A copy is in the Rare Book Dept., Howard-Tilton Memorial Library, Tulane University, New Orleans, Louisiana, and a microfilm in the Baker Library of Harvard University.
23. U.S. 26th Congr. 2nd sess., House Executive Document 111, 769 ff., especially 779, 785 ff.
24. Forstall suggested that the bank should draw alternately on the Paris and London agents and cover the debt to the one by the proceeds of drafts on the other (change croise, as one of his colleagues called it). This was a method widely used by merchants in the eighteenth century, but then rightly criticized as "kiting system." The cashier of the bank claimed that the European agents would under no circumstances agree to such transactions. Ibid., 823 ff., 829, 833.
25. Forstall made himself rather obnoxious by lecturing the majority of the board in elaborate papers whenever he could not win his point. This majority was later characterized by the Board of Currency as of "utter incapacity" and practicing "shameful favoritism." However, this Board seems to have been politically minded. (Louisiana State Journal, 1843/1844, Appendix, xxi.)
26. The change in the presidency was due perhaps to the fact that in 1843 a Democratic administration replaced the Whiggish one.
27. See, for instance, his anonymous article (signed "Opelousas") on "Louisiana Sugar" in DeBow's Commercial Review, I (1846), 53 ff.; and his pamphlet: Agricultural Productions of Louisiana (1845) which grew out of his answers to the questions of the Secretary of the Treasury (R.J. Walker). This pamphlet reprints Forstall's anonymous pamphlet of 1842, Louisiana and the Tarif, by a Native of Louisiana, which proves him to have been a rather ardent protectionist.
28. In his pamphlet Agricultural Productions of Louisiana he describes the critical situation of the Louisiana sugar plantations at that time (p. 7).
29. For his activities see Memorial [of February 19, 1844] of Edm. J. Forstall in behalf of Hope & Co., of Amsterdam and the holders of State Bonds issued in favor of the Citizens' Bank of Louisiana. Louisiana Senate Journal, '843-1844. Appendix, li; McGrane, Bondholders, 189, 190. McGrane

cites another (unprinted) Memorial of Forstall's of February 26, 1846. See also Hidy, Barings, 330-337, 556 (footnote 45).

30. McGrane, Bondholders, 239 ff.; U.S. 29th Congr. 2nd sess., Senate Document 163, Report of J. D. Westcott of the Committee on the Judiciary to whom was referred the memorial of Edmond J. Forstall in behalf of Hope & Company, Amsterdam and others holders (as alleged) of " $250,000 bonds of the Bank of Pensacola bearing the endorsement, to bearer, of the Territory of Florida."

31. McGrane, Bondholders, 205.

32. Louisiana Senate Journal, 1843-1844, lvi, lviii.

33. Hidy, Barings, 348, 359, 383, 400, 403, 437, 446, 561 (footnote 7). Forstall took a keen interest in Louisiana history. During a trip to Paris in 1841 he informed the then Governor of Louisiana on pertinent documents preserved there and a few publications of his were to draw the attention of a broader public to that material. See "Antiquities of Louisiana," DeBow's Commercial Review, I (1846), 238 ff. "Analytical Index of the whole of the public documents relative to Louisiana, deposited in the Archives of the Department 'De la Marine et des Colonies et [sic!] Paris'," ibid., 357 ff., 437 ff., 519 ff. Synopsis of Documents of the Department of the Marine, Paris, relating to Louisiana (1847) [I have not seen this book myself.] "An Analytical Index of the Whole of the Public Documents relative to Louisiana deposited in the Archives of the Department 'De la Marine et des Colonies' et 'Bibliothèque du Roi' at Paris," Historical Collections of Louisiana, ed. by B.F. French, Part II (Philadelphia, 1850). This publication is essentially a reprint of the articles in DeBow's Review, quoted above.

34. U.S. 25th Congr. 3rd sess., House Executive Document 227, 536.

35. U.S. 25th Congr. 2nd sess., House Executive Document 79, 609 ff.

36. The term "banking movement" was obviously derived from the French. The Bank of France then denominated its transfers of funds from one account to another as mouvements. (See Gallatin, Observations in Writings, III, 373.) When Forstall needed a handy word for notes in circulation and deposits (cash liabilities) he translated and adapted the French expression.

37. For Forstall, see U.S. 25th Congr. 2nd sess., House Executive Document 79, 619, and for Bronson, Vol. I of this work, pages 45 ff.

38. Op. cit., 34.

39. The term "elasticity" in connection with banking was hardly known in the 1810's and early 1820's. When Eric Bollmann wanted to express the idea he said: "close and reciprocal relation between trade and money [i.e., elasticity] cannot be attained with any money which trade itself does not bring into existence." (Plan of an Improved System, 12.) Bronson does not seem to have known the term although issuing an elastic currency in the 1820's. By 1830, however, it was used to characterize a sound currency expanding and contracting with the needs of trade. "All the benefits which the public derives from banks of circulation arise from their elasticity." [Italics in original] "So soon... as they exchange their promissory notes payable on demand in gold and silver not for the promissory notes of individuals payable at short periods, but for government stocks, mortgages, foreign bills of exchange intended to accumulate, and promissory notes understood... to be renewable.... they annihilate their elastic powers." Free Trade Advocate, II (1829), 6. Did Forstall know this article? (It also contains the statement that banks which loan funds on "permanent securities" act as "loan offices." This idea can be found with Forstall too.) See also chapter XIV in Gouge's Short History. Amasa Walker (op. cit. [1857], 26 ff) and others used the term in a different, derogatory sense: elastic meaning fluctuating, unstable; Miller (op. cit., 139 ff) does not keep the two meanings apart.

40. Report (quoted in footnote 22), 5.

41. Forstall's pamphlet Agricultural Productions, shows his familiarity with Adam Smith and McCulloch, whom he quotes.

42. The decisive passages were repeated in an explanation of one of the bills of 1838: see U.S. 25th Congr. 3rd sess., House Executive Document 227, 558 ff.

43. U.S. 25th Congr. 3rd sess., House Executive Document 227, 567.

44. Clapham, op cit., II, 125.

45. Gallatin, Writings, III, 253, 281, 312, 313.

46. See this volume page 9; also Dewey, State Banking, 57; Report, Indianapolis Convention, 346 ff.

47. Principles of Banks, 187.

48. Wealth of Nations, Cannon Edition, I, 276. The wording of the passage shows that Adam Smith thought along the same lines as Sir James Steuart.

49. Blodget, Economica, Statistical Manual, 162. The passage is most amusing. "We ought here to observe that Dr. Smith wrote his elaborate and highly useful work before the business of banking was well understood. It is now found that a bank to be perfectly secure ought never to loan double its capital." It is telling that the same passage from Adam Smith's chapter on money was also misunderstood by Condy Raguet who, in his Inquiry (of 1815, p. 38), claimed that Smith "supposed that in England a bank with one-fifth of its capital in specie would be able to meet all the demands." In fact Adam Smith had spoken of a ratio of specie to liabilities and Raguet so to speak transposed the passage into the American "language." As late as 1831 the passage from the

"Wealth of Nations" was quoted by Nathan Appleton; he gave it correctly, but did not mention the source (Examination, 31).

50. Webster, Pelatiah, Essay on Credit, 12. The quotation from Hamilton is from the Report on a National Bank. In the middle of the nineteenth century there was a tendency to interpret such and similar statements to the effect that the limitation of issues to twice or three times the capital actually paid-in in specie was intended to establish a fixed specie reserve against notes. Hooper (Examination, 31 ff) discusses the matter. However, this was a misinterpretation, as seen by Amasa Walker as early as 1857 (op. cit., 57, footnote). On the other hand it is undeniable that an indirect relation between specie and issues was created when issues were limited to a certain percentage of the capital and the latter was paid up in specie. But de facto, clauses of that character did not result in such a relationship since specie was either not paid in or was not held in the vaults nor were loans reduced as soon as the specie dropped below the amount of capital.

However, these clauses could have been developed into fixed specie reserve ratios as can be seen from the Missouri Act to regulate Banks and Banking Institutions and to create the office of Bank Commissioners, approved March 2, 1857 (Laws of the State of Missouri, passed by the 19th General Assembly, 1856-1857, pp. 14 ff). Article I, section 37 of the act establishes a thirty-three and one-third per cent specie reserve against notes, while at the same time limiting the issues to treble the capital (deposits are not mentioned). This blending of specie reserves with certain limitations of loans in relation to the banks' capital was rather common at that time, as may be seen in Opdyke's reform plan and even in Hooper's writings. (Opdyke, Report on the Currency, 15, 27; Hooper, Examination, 10.)

51. Clapham, op. cit., II, 181, 182, 195.
52. U.S. 25th Congr. 2nd sess., House Executive Document 79, 656, 658.
53. From a letter of Forstall's dated August 31, 1838 in U.S. 25th Congr. 2nd sess., House Executive Document 227, 564, 565. The letter is reprinted also in Report (see footnote 22), 5.
54. See the report of a committee of directors with Forstall as co-signer, U.S. 26th Congr. 2nd sess., House Executive Document 111, 798.
55. U.S. 26th Congr. 2nd sess., House Executive Document 111, 792 ff.
56. These bills, together with one submitted to the Senate by one of Forstall's former colleagues on the Joint Committee of 1837 which also embodied this idea, can be found in U.S. 25th Congr. 3rd sess., House Executive Document 227, 489 ff. For a good synopsis of the bill of the General Committee, probably drafted by Forstall

himself, see ibid., 556, 557.

57. U.S. 25th Congr. 3rd sess., House Executive Document 227, 535, 536.
58. While the term "banking movement" was translated from the French, as described above (see footnote 36), the term "dead weight" may well have been derived from the terminology of the Bank of England which used the phrase "dead weight" for an advance to the government on account of army and navy pensions. See Acres, op. cit. II, 418, and A New English Dictionary on Historical Principles III, 64. However, the term was used occasionally in the 1840's in America. The Journal of Banking (1841/42), 85 stated ironically: "Gold and silver in the vaults of a bank are dead weight to the bank." In the annual report of 1844 of the president of the Bank of Pennsylvania the following passage can be found: the bank has strengthened its position "by the sale of... unproductive real estate and stocks.... and in this way converted some of the dead weight of the Bank into active and available funds;" (Holdsworth, Empire, I, 149). The use of the term here approximates Forstall's. For a late example, see A.B.A., Proceedings (1888), 119 (mortgages were called a "dead" security).
59. U.S. 25th Congr. 3rd sess., House Executive Document 227, 535. That is to say, Forstall was aware of what Bray Hammond calls "hybridization of functions."
60. Acts passed in the Second Session of the 15th Legislature of the State of Louisiana, Number 22, approved February 5, 1842.
61. See vol. I of this work, pages 47, 193.
62. Louisiana influence on Missouri's establishing legal reserves of 33 1/3 per cent is very probable. If so, the Missouri Act of 1857 would not only be interesting as an example of the development of something new by a combination of older elements, but also as a cross of Southern and Northern influences. In requiring the banks to invest a certain percentage of their capital in state stock and by installing bank commissioners to examine the banks and to furnish them with bank notes the Act, of course, drew from the New York Free Banking Act; (Article I, section 14 and article III).
63. Suggestions, Writings, III, 407.
64. Bankers Magazine, XXXII (1877), 344 ff., especially 349, 350. Even in this article attention is not focused on the essential combination of the two features.
65. Heldermann (op. cit., 99, 141, 142) was the first to go over the material, used in the following paragraphs, but he arrived at partly different conclusions.
66. Richardson, James D., Messages and Papers of the Presidents, V, 438. State of New York, Messages from the Governors, V, 46.
67. Opdyke, op. cit., 15. Regarding the background of his thinking, see his Treatise, 286 ff.

68. Bankers Magazine, XII (1857/1858), 886-88. The same typical limitation can also be found in a speech of Thomas Hart Benton of November 15, 1857: He reports that Horsley Palmer, governor of the Bank of England, swore in 1832 before Lord Althorp's Committee: "the average proportion, as already observed, of coin and bullion which the bank deems it prudent to keep on hand is at the rate of a third of the total amount of all her liabilities, including deposits as well as issues." Ibid., 562, 563.

One cannot be surprised about these misunderstandings. The letter of December 13, 1859 of a "very intelligent gentleman in New Orleans, thoroughly versed in all matters of finance" (reprinted by Hooper, Examination, 53 ff) shows that the essential feature of the Louisiana act was not understood generally even in that state.

69. The Annual Report of the Bank Commissioners, dated September 30, 1860 (Massachusetts Public Document, No. 10) refers to both Hooper and the Louisiana banking act, the essential features of which were described (p. 127). However, the Report recommends only specie reserves and cites "economists of every stripe in England" such as McCulloch, Lord Overstone, Fullarton, Wilson, as agreeing on the necessity of large specie reserves. The Report of 1861 also referred to the Louisiana banking set-up.

70. Examination, 13.

Chapter XIII

THE ORIGIN OF THE CLEARING HOUSE

In an earlier chapter of this volume the rise of the deposit business in the 1840's and 1850's has been described.[1] As the <u>Report</u> of the Massachusetts Bank Commissioners of September 30, 1860 expressed it: "to keep a bank account was once the badge of a large mercantile business; it is now the habit of most shopkeepers, mechanics, doing a considerable business, and professional men".[2] This development was, of course, accompanied by an increased use of checks. It was not accidental therefore that the 1850's witnessed the introduction into America of the clearing house, intended to facilitate the settling of obligations arising between banks from their check business.

I

However, the clearing house was not a development <u>ab ovo</u> in this country. The organization of the first one was preceded by about fifty years of experience with, and experiments in the exchange of notes by banks and the settlement of inter-bank balances resulting from the depositing of notes by bank customers. The exchange of notes by banks and the subsequent settlement of inter-bank balances first became a problem when the early city banks were more or less <u>forced</u> to take on deposit the notes of others, especially those of second and third banks set up by 1800 in the main commercial centers. While under the then prevailing conditions notes of out-of-town banks, if taken by banks at all, had to be cashed, it was necessary to work out more convenient methods for the handling of notes of banks located in the same city.

Thus in America the development toward the establishment of clearing houses began when regular presentation for redemption of notes of out-of-town banks in the hinterland was organized in commercial centers and when in the latter a regular exchange of notes and a regular settlement of inter-bank balances, thus originating, became standardized procedures. In this process a few organizations were established which came close to the highly institutionalized clearing houses. The final step, the introduction into America of the genuine clearing house, can also be seen as terminating a development which led from the bilateral, informal exchange of notes and settlement of balances to the multilateral clearing under rigid procedure of inter-bank obligations of all sorts.[3]

The first stage in this development was preceded by the note redemption business of foreign money brokers as it was conducted in the late 1790's and 1800's.[4] When, as has been described, incorporated banks invaded this field and took notes of other banks on deposit or acquired them at a discount in order to profit from presenting them for redemption, something new was brought into existence, the importance and significance of which was not recognized immediately, namely, inter-bank obligations. Irregular presentation of inter-bank obligations for payment, taking place first, remained within the established procedure worked out by the note brokers. However, there appeared at an early moment the tendency to make a regular routine out of such presentations. The Mechanics and Farmers Bank of Albany, for instance, employed a reliable man to take the bills of "western banks," received in its regular business, once every two weeks to Buffalo where they were presented for payment. This employee occasionally cashed as much as $50,000 on one trip. In Philadelphia, in November, 1810, the then existing (very few) banks agreed to pay out their own notes only and to present those of the other city banks for redemption.[5] That is to say, prior to the War of 1812 city and country banks alike were becoming familiar with the <u>regular</u> presentation of notes for redemption by other banks.

In Boston, however, the development by that time was taking a different turn. To be sure, in December, 1792, the directors of the Massachusetts Bank had resolved to present each Saturday for redemption the notes of the branch of the Bank of the United States and of the Union Bank.[6] But prior thereto (in June, 1792) they had agreed with the directors of the branch of the Bank of the United States to deposit its notes received in the current business under the condition that such deposits be paid in silver on demand.[7] Such arrangements seem to have become common practice in Boston; otherwise the comparatively large balances which by 1810 Boston banks kept with other banks of the city would not be explicable. As a matter of fact, as late as August, 1825, the directors of the Massachusetts Bank deplored the practice of keeping balances with other banks in consequence of which "it was esteemed a most extraordinary and uncourteous proceeding to demand of any bank specie for its bills," unless after an exchange of bills the balance was ascertained. The situation was aggravating since some of the Boston banks refused to credit the account of other banks for amounts of less than $5,000. Consequently, the board of the Massachusetts Bank resolved in that year to discontinue the practice of keeping accounts with other banks and furthermore

> that the cashier be directed to assist the receiving teller in sorting and arranging the bills of the various banks which are paid in the course of the day, in order that such bills be ready to offset against demands which such banks have on the Massachusetts Bank. That if any bank refuses to receive its own bills in offset of their demands that such bank be notified that the Massachusetts Bank will refuse to receive their bills-or that specie be at once demanded, which if refused, then their bills to be refused.[8]

Disregarding the special situation in Boston, the War of 1812, or better, the suspension of specie payments caused by this war, and the establishment of the Second Bank of the United States did much to expedite the development. During suspension there was, of course, no possibility of settling inter-bank balances unless banks made specific arrangements to that effect and the only alternative to agreements of that kind was not to touch the notes of other banks. Such a radical move, however, was no longer feasible because of the relatively advanced stage which banking had reached and because of the war. Thus outside of New England, which upheld specie payments and therefore did not feel the sting of a new and urgent problem, redemption of notes for the first time became widely regulated by mutual understanding.[9]

Thus progress resulted from the disturbances created by the war; and by 1820 the city banks, or better the banks in most of the leading commercial centers, were well advanced toward regular exchange of notes and toward regular settlement of inter-bank balances. It was then claimed that in the principal cities, Baltimore, Philadelphia, and New York,[10] four-fifths of the banks representing at the same time also four-fifths of the banking capital in those cities, practiced daily exchange of notes and daily settlement of balances, a statement which may be taken for what it is worth. The banks in the smaller places and in the country were far behind the city banks, but they were being pushed forward by the Second Bank of the United

States. During the presidency of William Jones in the 1810's, to be sure, the matter was not pressed. At that time it seems to have been the policy of the branches of the Bank to present for redemption the notes of banks in their respective districts whenever a certain amount had accumulated.[11] That is to say, the presentation for redemption of notes by the Bank of the United States was still irregular in the 1810's; and Jones and the directors of the Bank were unwilling to provide clearing and collection facilities to the state banks.[12] As in every other respect Cheves when taking over in 1819 tightened up on the established procedure and tried to enforce even daily redemption in specie of notes, which was "totally without example in the intercourse of the banks" in certain parts of the country, as stressed by Savannah banks which considered that requirement a "hostile act."[13] On the other hand, by 1820 the branches of the Second Bank of the United States were not authorized to take the bills of any banks but those in their vicinity with which they had "immediate" exchanges. Under the prevailing circumstances daily settlement of inter-bank balances proved unattainable as yet. But in Biddle's era at least weekly exchange of notes was practiced and weekly settlement of balances required by the Second Bank of the United States,[14] and by the end of the 1820's through its efforts the regular exchange of notes and the regular settlement of balances had become common in large areas of the older parts of the country.[15] But even in the commercial centers note exchange and settlement of inter-bank balances were bilateral affairs; even there they did not take place often enough, and credit transactions played too large a part in the settlements. Moreover the isolated sections of the country (except in New England) were not as yet included in the mechanism of note exchanges. They hardly knew regular redemptions, and instead of settling in specie too often redeemed their notes in drafts on their city correspondents, drafts which represented credit not cash.[16] Country banks which kept bona fide redemption agents in important cities were progressive; in many cases such agents gave de facto circulation to country notes rather than being true redemption agents. In the 1830's, the dissolution of the branch system of the Second Bank of the United States resulted in a setback to the development of regular note exchanges and regular note redemptions.

However, by 1840 it was at least widely understood that American banking could be strengthened by the general introduction of regular, frequent, and "rigid" redemption of notes by isolated banks, on the one hand, and of the exchange of notes (with the subsequent settlement of balances) by neighboring banks, on the other. Nathan Appleton made a statement to this effect[17] in 1841 and believed that the stronger banks should compel the weaker ones to take appropriate action. About the same time the Louisiana legislature, as the first in this country, struggled with the task of embodying into an act requirements of this type. All the various bank bills proposed in that state in 1838 contained clauses aiming in this direction and finally the Banking Act of 1842 contained the very progressive section 12: According to this section, the New Orleans banks were prohibited from paying out the notes of other banks; they had to exchange them daily on opening their offices and had to settle the balances each Saturday in specie.[18] It is telling that this regulation referred to the New Orleans banks only. Louisiana country banks were not included in this system of daily exchanges and weekly settlements.[19]

About fifteen years prior to the Louisiana achievement, New England had already built, in the Suffolk Bank system, an institution which can be characterized as a genuine clearing house. It practiced the multilateral exchange of certain bank obligations at a fixed place, as is typical of the clearing houses. There were some features, however, which still distinguished the Suffolk Bank from the modern full-fledged clearing houses: the Suffolk Bank cleared notes alone and left checks unprovided for; it practiced country, not local clearing; it ran the clearing business for profit's sake, while modern clearing houses are cooperative, non-profit-making ventures; and finally, the procedure of the Suffolk Bank was comparatively informal, it was not yet standardized and lacked that military precision which is typical of modern clearing houses. (The clearing was, for instance, not restricted to a certain hour or certain hours per day; it filled the whole work day.) Since the Suffolk Bank system and similar organizations have been described previously in detail,[20] no further study of this subject is required at this point.

Analysis has revealed three stages of the development:
1. the irregular presentation of notes for redemption;
2. the regular presentation of notes for redemption to isolated banks or their redemption agents, respectively, or the regular exchange of notes by and the regular settlement of balances between neighboring banks;
3. the clearing house (including its predecessors, the Suffolk Bank and similar systems).

It goes without saying that these three stages of the development overlapped, or, in other words, that one and the same stage was reached at different times in different parts of the country. To take the year 1830 as an example: In that year Cincinnati merchants still had to take bank notes from their customers at par and to sell them at a discount to note brokers who presented them for redemption[21] (first stage); at the same time (1828) the Second Bank of the United States had succeeded in introducing regular settlement of balances in North Carolina[22] (second stage); but New England had at that same time already established the Suffolk Bank system, that is to say, an institution which can be characterized at least as an incipient clearing house (third stage).

II

It is in this setting[23] that one must look at the establishment in 1853 of the first full-fledged American clearing house, that of New York.[24] Prior thereto it was customary for each of the sixty New York banks to send porters every day to the various other city banks. They carried, together with a pass book, the exchanges, i.e., the notes of and drafts on other banks, received on the previous day and in the morning mail. On the credit side of the former the tellers of the debtor banks entered the items received, while on the debit side they entered the return exchanges. Since porters of several banks were apt to arrive simultaneously there was often considerable confusion and delay. The method had several disadvantages: It was both unwieldy and precluded daily settlements. Weekly settlements were attempted, but, to a large extent, they were nominal only because the weaker and reckless banks took advantage of another inherent shortcoming of the system: They borrowed informally large amounts by carrying a small debit with each of a considerable number of strong banks. They would take up sufficient funds formally on Thursday to settle their debits on Friday, the weekly settlement day, and repay the loans on Saturday by again running informally into debt as before. Thus the wealthy banks involuntarily carried their weaker competitors.

It has been stated repeatedly in the banking literature that Albert Gallatin was the first in America to suggest a clearing house for New York. His proposal to that effect, outlined in his Suggestions on the Banks and Currency of the Several United States in Reference Principally to the Suspension of Specie Payments (published in 1841),[25] reads as follows:

There is a measure which, though belonging to the administration of banks, rather than to legal enactments, is suggested on account of its great importance. Few regulations would be more useful in preventing dangerous expansions of discounts and issues on the part of the city banks, than a regular exchange of notes and checks, and an actual daily or semi-weekly payment of the balances. It must be recollected, that it is by this process alone that a Bank of the United States has ever acted or been supposed to act as a regulator of the currency. Its action would not in that respect be wanted in any city, the banks of which would, by adopting the process, regulate themselves. It is one of the principal ingredients of the system of the banks of Scotland. The bankers of London, by the daily exchange of drafts at the Clearing House, reduce the ultimate balance to a very small sum, and that balance is immediately paid in notes of the Bank of England. The want of a similar arrangement among the banks of this city, produces relaxation, favors improper expansions, and is attended with serious inconveniences. The principal difficulty in the way of an arrangement for that purpose is the want of a common medium other than specie for effecting the payment of balances. These are daily fluctuating, and a perpetual drawing and redrawing from specie from and into the banks is unpopular and inconvenient.

In order to remedy this, it has been suggested that a general cash office might be established, in which each bank would place a sum in specie, proportionate to its capital, which would be carried to its credit in the books of the office. Each bank would be daily debited or credited in those books for the balance of its account with all the other banks. Each bank might at any time draw for specie on the office for the excess of its credit beyond its quota, and each bank should be obliged to replenish its quota, whenever it was diminished one half, or in any other proportion agreed upon.

It may be that some similar arrangement might be made in every other county, or larger convenient district of the state.... the balances due by the banks in each district might be paid by drafts on New York, or any other place agreed upon.

As can be seen from this quotation Gallatin did not propose a clearing house merely as an institution for facilitating the daily exchanges of inter-bank obligations and for avoiding the "unpopular and inconvenient system" of "drawing and redrawing... specie from and into the banks." The one-time Secretary of the Treasury who had so ably handled the public finances of the young republic thought in economic rather than in business terms. This fact may have been one of the reasons why his suggestion hardly gained any influence on the

development. Another perhaps was his confounding two different problems, namely, the problem of facilitating the exchanges and that of saving specie in the settlement of balances by creating a "common medium other than specie for effecting the payment of [such] balances." Gallatin believed that the principal difficulty in the way of a clearing house was the lack of a common medium other than money. In this he was mistaken and in stressing this point he drew a red herring across the trail. A clearing house in which all balances were settled in specie was not only possible, but even feasible, and, as a matter of fact, as late as 1900, in twenty-five per cent of the American clearing houses cash was the only medium of settlements.[26] On the other hand, something like a special medium for the settlement of inter-bank balances had already been devised in Rhode Island. There, as described in a previous chapter, the Merchants Bank of Providence had established a sub-system of the Suffolk Bank system. It handled the Rhode Island note clearing business in such a way that the Suffolk Bank received from Rhode Island only the notes of New England banks outside that state, while the Merchants Bank cleared the Rhode Island notes. In order to facilitate the settlements the Merchants Bank issued most of its notes in large denominations. It was understood that if they came into the possession of any of the associated banks of Rhode Island the latter would retain these notes without presenting them for redemption. Instead they were to be used in the payment of such notes of the participating banks as were presented for redemption by the Merchants Bank.[27]

Gallatin's suggestion, as mentioned, had no immediate consequences. More than a decade later, however, the problem was tackled in earnest; and Francis William Edmonds (1806-1863) was one of the two men who deserve most of the credit for the organization of the first full-fledged American clearing house. Strangely enough, the creative entrepreneur Edmonds had become a bank executive malgré lui; he was a genre-painter whose name has a certain reputation in American painting.[28] Since he came from a large family he could not afford to pursue his main interest and so, influenced by his uncle, Gorham A. Worth, one-time cashier of the Cincinnati branch of the Second Bank of the United States and then president of the Tradesmens Bank of New York, he entered upon a banking career. After having held positions in various banks he was recommended by Shepherd Knapp, president of the Mechanics Bank of New York, for the position of cashier of that bank (1839). By that time Edmonds had acquired the reputation of being a skilled bank examiner, so that in 1840 when a committee was set up to investigate the conditions of the Manhattan

Company he was selected its secretary.[29] When Edmonds entered the Mechanics Bank it was in a pretty bad shape. Knapp's predecessor was alleged to have committed suicide and Knapp himself who had divers other interests, for example in the early trust business,[30] was unable to lift the bank from its crippled condition. Edmonds, however, quickly becoming the guiding spirit of the enterprise succeeded in developing it into one of New York's leading banking institutions. An honest man, an efficient manager with an excellent reputation and, above all, an entrepreneur with a creative touch, his career nevertheless came to an ignominious end.

Edmonds' downfall[31] throws an interesting light on the way in which reliable American banks were run in the middle of the nineteenth century: The accounting methods of the Mechanics Bank were worse than loose; they were supposed to have enabled Edmonds to circulate to his private gain notes of the bank already withdrawn and to take loans without interest. It is immaterial whether these charges were or were not substantiated; that such charges could be publicly preferred against and answered by an officer of a reputable bank is in itself an astonishing fact.[32] But there is an amusing aspect to the story: the Mechanics Bank was anxious to obtain the idle funds of the City of New York. No interest had to be paid on city deposits which, however, could be utilised in making loans to bank customers. The president, Shepherd Knapp, had managed to become the city chamberlain, while Edmonds was a member of the party in opposition. When the latter came into power and Knapp lost his job, Edmonds succeeded him as the city chamberlain and the city funds remained in the Bank. As a matter of fact, both men made contributions to their respective parties, and since such contributions were considered to be in the bank's interest, the money went from the general cash into the cashier's drawer and disappeared without being accounted for. As it happened, one day the bank hired an assistant cashier who was either unaccustomed to such loose methods or who wanted the post of cashier for himself. He brought the situation into the open and immediately Knapp took a strong stand against Edmonds which may have been motivated by jealousy.[33] Thus Edmonds had to leave the bank under suspicion of being a swindler. In reality he was merely easy-going and careless, probably identifying himself with his enterprise to such an extent that he lost sight of the fact that the bank had an individuality of its own.

This end to Edmonds' career, however, does not detract from his great merit. As mentioned above, it was he who took the initiative toward the founding of the New York Clearing House and the achievement was recognized by his being made the chairman of the first clearing house committee (a position in which he was succeeded by his collaborator, James Punnett). It is possible that Edmonds knew of Gallatin's suggestion, quoted above, since Gallatin played a conspicuous part as a bank leader in New York in the late eighteen hundred thirties, the very time when Edmonds started to rise in the banking business.

Be that as it may, there can be no doubt that Edmonds had seen a proposal published by George D. Lyman in the Journal of Commerce (1851),[34] the most important passages of which read as follows:

> Let the banks select some one bank as a medium for exchanging, to be the Exchange Bank of the city, and let an account be kept by all the city banks with this bank alone; each bank assorting and making up its exchanges as now, but all the banks sending their gross amount of exchanges to the bank so selected, at some regular hour in the morning of each day.... The entire amount of exchanges would thus be brought together and would soon be distributed with but little more labor than each bank is now subject to, made up with a slip of the Exchanging bank stating the amount of the slips of each bank, which would be footed.... They should then meet at some regular hour... at the Exchange Bank to receive from it any checks returned not good and for the correcting of any errors that may have been discovered.... Balances should be settled as now. Debtor banks should be required to pay up once a week, or every day... In this way the number of balances would be greatly reduced and specie would... stay longer in one place.

With this article Lyman, who was soon to cooperate with Edmonds, began to take an influence on the development, at the same time opening a career, although a short one, for himself. Lyman (1822-1889) was a native of Middletown, Connecticut, where he also received his banking training in the Middlesex County Bank. He went to New York in 1845 to engage in the glass business; but soon he returned to banking. In 1851 he was a clerk and bookkeeper in the Bank of North America.[35] The gist of Lyman's proposal was that the New York banks should keep accounts with one designated bank through which they all should settle their balances. As can be seen at a glance the suggestion remained within American tradition and aimed at some sort of a local Suffolk Bank system in New York. However, during the following months his ideas developed. Instead of all the New York banks keeping their accounts with and sending their exchanges to one designated bank, he came to suggest that the daily balances be settled through a special agency at a designated place. (Stuart Lyman suggests that his uncle may have been inspired by the fact that the "runners" were developing the habit of meeting at Wall Street near the corner of Nassau Street in order to effect some exchanges there.) Ultimately the latter found an opportunity to explain his suggestions to a few New York bank leaders; and during the next twelve months a number of meetings were held where the subject was thoroughly discussed amidst strong opposition. The opponents of the measure claimed that a clearing house would favor the concentration of power in the hands of its managers, who might use it for spying into the business of the participating banks or for exercising arbitrary supervision.[36] However, Thomas Tileston, president of the Phenix Bank, came to see the great possibilities in Lyman's proposal. He possessed what Lyman lacked, namely, prestige and power, and was, therefore, not only able to further, but also to accelerate, the final adoption of the plan.[37]

While Lyman's suggestions were still in the stage of discussion under the chairmanship of Tileston, a small group of bank cashiers, led by Edmonds, was taking action. Consciously or unconsciously they made an experiment along the lines which Gallatin had suggested and developed a special medium for settling inter-bank balances. They seem to have worked on the basis of a plan devised by James C. Hallock, Sr., who between the fall of 1852 and the spring of 1853 went from bank to bank selling his ideas. (Incidentally, as the result of these activities he was soon to become the first assistant manager of the New York Clearing House.)[38] In 1852, possibly under the influence of Hallock, Edmonds induced the Bank of America, the Merchants Bank, the American Exchange Bank, and the Metropolitan Bank to join with the Mechanics Bank (of which, it will be remembered, Edmonds was the leading spirit) in organizing a new system of settlements. The above-mentioned banks contributed to a $1,000,000 fund in coin which was deposited with the Mechanics Bank. This bank in turn issued certificates against the deposited coin and these coin certificates, devised by Edmonds,[39] were used by the five associated banks in the settlement of their balances. Thereby they saved themselves both the trouble of counting coin repeatedly and the risk and bother of moving it back and forth.

The men who cooperated with Edmonds in this achievement were James Punnett,[40] Augustus Ely Silliman, and John Earl Williams,[41] all of whom were soon to become leading New York bankers. The last named, cashier of the Metropolitan Bank, remained in the background, while Punnett (then cashier and later president of the Bank of America) and Silliman shared fully in the experiment. Silliman (1807-1884), then cashier and later president of the Merchants Bank, came from a prominent Rhode Island family, a fact which seems to be significant: familiarity with the note clearing business of the Merchants Bank of Providence, described above, may well have influenced his willingness to strive for a clearing house in New York.

Details are not known, but in 1853 (perhaps on April 8) the two groups joined forces. Edmonds called a meeting of bank officers for the 23d of April. It was attended by representatives of thirty-eight banks and was presided over by Thomas Tileston. Lyman thus described the atmosphere at that gathering: "Among the officers of the older banks there were several who had not met for years and quite a number of the gentlemen were wholly unacquainted. Notwithstanding this, the meeting proved remarkably harmonious. The necessity of some change in the prevailing system was fully recognized," and a committee of bank cashiers was appointed. It consisted of Edmonds (chairman), Silliman, Punnett, that is to say, the leaders of the "Edmonds" group, to whom were added Richard Berry and J. L. Everett, cashiers of the Tradesmens Bank and the Broadway Bank, respectively. They can be assumed to have been active in the "Tileston" group. The committee was "to devise and report some new method for making the exchanges and settling up the balances between the banks of this city." Lyman was not on this committee, his subordinate position as a receiving teller probably being the reason. However, the committee acted along the lines of a proposal of his which was published under his name in the Bankers' Magazine (September 1853, pages 265-67) under the title "A Plan to Simplify the Exchanges of New York City-Banks." In this article Lyman described the advantages of his plan, which was elaborated in detail so that it could be put into effect immediately. As a matter of fact, his scheme, essentially still the basis of present day clearings, was adopted at a meeting of bank officers on September 13 with but one amendment, and the first American clearing house opened in New York on October 11, 1853, Lyman becoming the first manager.

As such he proved to be highly creative, and to him belongs credit for "systematizing its [the clearing house's] details, planning its records, and bringing them to their present state of efficiency."[42] He could proudly report that in the first year of the clearing house's existence the exchanges averaged about $20,000,000 and the balances about $1,000,000 per day, while the organization was run at a cost of only $16,000 per year.[43] In spite of his contribution Lyman resigned in 1864 never again to engage in banking.[44] However, before doing so he had not only organized the New York institution but also, more or less, the Boston and Philadelphia clearing houses, as will be described later.

The New York Clearing House was at first an informal organization, directed ostensibly by the cashiers' committee of 1853 described above, but actually by its chairman, F. W. Edmonds. It had no constitution since that was considered superfluous, if not dangerous. Many of the early members, especially those who had represented the original opposition to the scheme, were reluctant to commit themselves too deeply to a new and untried venture whose consequences could not be foreseen. A constitution, it was argued, might lead to a dangerous concentration of power in the hands of those in charge of the new institution. The clearing house very soon proved its value, however, and it became obvious that formal rules were desirable to guarantee smooth sailing. Hence, in February 1854 it was suggested either that the clearing house be incorporated or at least that a set of regulations be embodied in a constitution. The task of drawing up the constitution[45] was assigned to George Curtis (1793-1856). Curtis had been the cashier of the Exchange Bank in Providence, Rhode Island, where (like Silliman) he must have acquired familiarity with the note clearing of the Merchants Bank of that city. This guess is the more probable, since Curtis had been active in city and state politics. In 1839 he had gone to New York as the cashier of the Bank of Commerce from which position he rose to the presidency of the newly-founded Continental Bank.

George Curtis, being a very intelligent man, sensed the importance of the clearing house at an early moment, although taking no part in its creation. It was at this later juncture that he assumed leadership by drawing up the constitution. Its most important feature was the organization of a formal association of the participating banks. At its annual meeting the association was to appoint a standing committee to be known as the clearing house committee to supervise the business of the organization.[46] However, Curtis did more than draft a document. He contributed to its adoption by removing objections and by inducing dissenting members to accept the necessary measure. His experience in Rhode Island politics must have made him an able leader of men for, after the adoption of his constitution, he was unanimously chosen chairman of the Committee on Suspensions. This most unpopular, unpleasant, and important position he handled so impartially that no appeals from his decisions are on record.

The contributions by members of various age groups to the foundation and initial success of the first American clearing house are significant. A teller, George W. Lyman, born in 1822 and therefore about thirty years old, conceived the plan and worked it out. Members of the preceding age group, men in their forties, provided the driving power: Edmonds born in 1806, Punnett born by 1810, Silliman born in 1807, Williams born in 1804. But even these men in the prime of their lives would not have succeeded without the backing of members of a still older generation; the cashiers in their forties would have been unable to bring doubting, recalcitrant, or uninterested members of the banking fraternity into the agreement and to enforce stringent rules on men who in line with the thinking of their time jealously guarded their independence. This could only be done by elderly gentlemen with personal and professional prestige, by the bank presidents, the men of about sixty: Tileston and Curtis, both born in 1793.

New York was followed by Boston, Philadelphia, and Baltimore which set up modern clearing houses in 1856, 1858, and 1858, respectively. In these three cases the newly-established institutions were closely modeled on the New York plan and thereby the ideas of Lyman and Curtis were being adopted in the most important commercial centers in the country. This influence exerted by Lyman and Curtis on the further development of banking, i.e., the migration of their ideas, is the most interesting fact in the next stage of the development.[47]

III

It is not possible to describe the beginnings of the Boston Clearing House as accurately as those of its New York model; (and incidentally, a good deal of interpretation would be needed to make the details of the material understandable).[48] This much is certain: Impressed by the success of the newly-founded New York Clearing House, several Boston bankers met on April 19, 1854 with the idea of establishing a similar institution in Boston. The meeting appointed a committee "to examine the practical operation of the clearing or settling house established by the banks in the City of New York." Whatever may have been the content of its report of May 1854 (which seems to be lost), it became the agency through which New York influence was carried into Boston. As a matter of fact, the committee received wholehearted cooperation from the New York Clearing House and especially from its manager whose letter, written on request of Silliman, to the cashier of one of the Boston banks has survived. In this letter Lyman explained in detail the routine and the operations of the New York Clearing House transmitting at the same time its

forms.[49] His help was highly appreciated and on
April 15, 1856 in one of the early meetings of the
Boston Clearing House Association it was resolved
to "present George D. Lyman some suitable testimonial of their appreciation of his kindness, courtesy, and aid to those with whom he has communicated in behalf of the Boston Clearing House."
This motion was presented by Andrew T. Hall,[50]
who was probably among those who had personally
experienced Lyman's courtesy.

After such preparatory steps the Boston Clearing House came into being at a meeting of bank
officers held in the Merchants Bank on September
26, 1855. That is to say, it took about one and a
half years to overcome the opposition to the "innovation upon the established order of things" considered as of "doubtful expedience." The Minute
Book of the Association reports that: "on motion
of Andrew T. Hall, Esq. [who might well have
played a part similar to that of Tileston in New
York whose contemporary of age he was], Franklin
Haven, Esq.[51] was chosen president and William
Thomas, Secretary. The president read a paper
presented by Waldo Flint, Esq. which was signed
by twenty of the Boston banks agreeing to join in
the establishment of a Clearing House." (Incidentally, it seems strange that Flint did not read it
himself.) The meeting resolved to set up a committee "to make such arrangements as they may
deem proper for carrying into effect the project."
Andrew T. Hall, Waldo Flint, and Franklin Haven
were the three leading men on the committee which
prepared a constitution (copied from that of the
New York Clearing House) and rules which were
adopted in January, 1856. The Boston Clearing
House commenced operations in March of that
year as the second in this country.

It is rather difficult to determine the share to be
attributed to each of the three leaders, two of
whom -- Hall and Flint -- became members of the
first Clearing House Committee, while the third,
Haven, was elected the first president of the Clearing House Association. Hall seems to have contributed administrative ability and personal prestige, Haven the backing of Boston's largest bank,
and Flint[52] driving power, an impression for which,
however, there is no documentary proof. Flint was,
as shown by his picture and by his conduct in the
young clearing house, a forceful, self-willed, uncompromising, and stern man,[53] apt to withdraw
his cooperation when things did not work out quite
as he wanted. Such a man, if possessed of driving
power, can easily blaze the trail, but he cannot become a leader in an organization which depends on
voluntary cooperation among equals jealous of
their independence. Thus the function of guiding
genius of the young organization did not fall to the

elderly Flint, who a few years later was no longer
able to understand his time.[54] Andrew T. Hall, his
contemporary of age, became the first chairman
of the Clearing House Committee and retained that
key position for many years.[55]

The development which led to the Philadelphia
Clearing House was different from that in both New
York and Boston, except for the influence of George
D. Lyman. While the New York Clearing House
represented in that city the first case of permanent
and institutionalized cooperation among banks
(whose administrators hardly knew each other prior
to 1854) and while the same was true of Boston, the
Philadelphia Clearing House was itself the outgrowth of previously organized cooperation among
banks. Moreover the Philadelphia Clearing House
is of interest since it provided an example of the
personal element as a retarding factor in economic
development.[56]

The parent organization, so to speak, of the
Philadelphia Clearing House was the "Board of
Presidents" which had existed since 1853. This
most interesting body (de facto, periodical meetings
of the bank presidents of the city and county of
Philadelphia established to talk over topics of common interest) will be discussed in more detail in a
later chapter. At the time when the "Board of
Presidents" was brought into being, the Philadelphia
banks were practicing informal exchanges of their
obligations in the bank room of the Philadelphia
Bank. For years, balances had been settled bi-
weekly, but tri-weekly settlements were introduced
in that very year of 1853.

The Board of Presidents had hardly come into
existence when it took up the matter of exchanges,
and on October 5 it appointed a committee to provide a suitable place to house the daily exchanges
(and incidentally to provide a home for the meetings
of the board of cashiers). From then on, the question of improving the exchanges and the settlement
of interbank balances came to occupy the interest
of the Board of Presidents almost continuously for
years. Since obviously the committee appointed in
November, 1853, did not succeed in finding a suitable
place, a year later, in November, 1854, C. S. Boker,
president of the Girard Bank, was authorized to
have a room fixed up in his bank for the accommodation of the daily exchanges. By that time, however,
the New York Clearing House was already attracting
the attention of the Philadelphia bank presidents;
and Thomas Robins,[57] president of the Philadelphia
Bank, seems to have become the prime mover in
adopting the New York device, a project which was
fought for years by an opposition led by Thomas
Allibone. Allibone, an unscrupulous businessman,
had been anxious to become the president of the
Philadelphia Bank in 1852 and when defeated by

Robins he succeeded in 1853 in getting control of the then sound Bank of Pennsylvania. He became its president and wrecked it in the next few years. Resentment towards his successful competitor for a desired appointment and the weakness of his own bank, caused by his own mismanagement, alike played their part in Allibone's attitude toward the reform movement.[58]

Robins had been on the committee of 1853 (mentioned above) together with J. B. Mitchell,[59] president of the Mechanics Bank, and John Jordan, Jr., president of the Manufacturers and Mechanics Bank, who were, respectively, president and secretary of the Board of Presidents. This composition of the committee of 1853 indicates both the importance assigned to it and to Robins personally. When the matter of adopting the New York clearing methods was taken up in earnest, Robins and Jordan were again on a three-man committee, appointed on November 1, 1855, to obtain information on the operations of the New York Clearing House and to report thereon. Two of the members of the committee, probably including Robins, went to New York and on the 15th of the same month the latter submitted a report on "a clearing house and absolute payment of balances between banks." The report indicates a clear understanding of the essentials of the New York scheme and at the same time shows Robins as possessing a touch of the politician. In fact he suggested that all the important features of the New York Clearing House be copied, namely, that daily settlements be introduced, that a manager be appointed to supervise the exchanges and to take care of the settlements, and that a depository be chosen to issue coin certificates to be used in the settlements. But at the same time he tried to make this plan palatable to the conservatives by concluding "that our present system of exchanges be continued with such modifications as will tend to the saving of time and the exact settlements between the banks daily." After extensive discussions, Articles of Association were drawn up (or better, copied from the New York Clearing House constitution) by the Robins committee. They failed to receive a two-thirds majority, however. It is noteworthy that the leading Philadelphian bankers (Mercer, Mitchell, Patterson, and Borie) voted in the affirmative.

The collapse of Allibone's bank during the crisis of 1857 almost two years after this abortive attempt cleared the road for the adoption of the New York plan by getting the main opponent out of the way. On December 14, 1857 on motion of Robins the project was revived by the Board of Presidents and Robins became a member of a five-man committee[60] appointed to prepare a plan and a set of rules to govern the clearing house to be established. The

crisis of that year and the robbery of a messenger of the Bank of the Northern Liberties had provided good object lessons for the need of cooperation. (As early as September 28, 1857 the Board of Presidents had stressed "that there should be union and concert of action by the several banking institutions of the city.") The committee mentioned above, appointed in December, went to work, and on January 25, 1858 Robins submitted on its behalf to the Board of Presidents Articles of Association which were substantially identical with those proposed by him in 1855. This time they were quickly adopted by the Board of Presidents and ratified by a sufficient majority of the banks (although two articles had to be slightly amended as early as May, 1858).

Thus the Philadelphia Clearing House came into being on February 1, 1858.[61] Mitchell and Jordan, mentioned above as president and secretary, respectively, of the Board of Presidents, became president and secretary likewise of the new organization, thus linking the two organizations. Robins' influence, however, became evident by the fact that his son-in-law, George E. Arnold, became the first clearing house manager.[62] The organizers of the institution were well aware of their dependence on the New York achievement. On May 10, 1858 it was resolved to express gratitude to Lyman, since "the system recently put into operation by the banks of Philadelphia owe[d] its origin to the genius and perseverance of George D. Lyman, Esq., of New York who established it in that city and whose influence has been exercised in its introduction in other cities." This was, undoubtedly, a high testimonial to Lyman's work and one to which the historian will subscribe.

The Baltimore Clearing House followed on the heels of that of Philadelphia[63] and since its beginnings have been described by Hales[64] it is not necessary to go into detail here. Hales' material seems to permit the conclusion that Robert Mickle, the cashier of the Union Bank of Maryland, where informal daily exchanges took place prior to the establishment of the Baltimore Clearing House, was the driving force during the decisive months. His bank, as will be mentioned shortly, took charge of the clearings, while he himself became the first manager of the Baltimore Clearing House and the chairman of the Board of Cashiers which supervised the clearing business as did the meetings of Clearing House Associations in the other cities.[65]

A comparison of the achievements in the four cities, all of which, of course, possessed informal and imperfect exchanges and settlements prior to 1853, 1854, and 1858, respectively, seems to be worthwhile. First of all, Lyman was back of the organization of the clearing houses in New York,

Boston and Philadelphia; the Baltimore Clearing House was the first to be established without his assistance. But the New York Clearing House, Lyman's work, was the model used by Baltimore as well as by Boston and Philadelphia, and Curtis's Constitution of the New York Clearing House was more or less copied in Baltimore as it was in the other cities. While the first three clearing houses of this country were conceived prior to the crisis of 1857, that of Philadelphia became an actuality only under its impact. That of Baltimore was an outgrowth of the crisis. The two earliest clearing houses were instrumental in first establishing permanent organized cooperation among banks in their respective cities; this was not true for Philadelphia and Baltimore. But while the clearing house in the former city was the work of an organization of bank presidents, that in the latter was the work of the cashiers who, when they formed the clearing house, were already cooperating, although rather informally. Only the Baltimore banks made a trial before committing themselves to the establishment of permanent clearing arrangements. Last, but not least, the first three cities organized special institutions for the clearing of inter-bank obligations and the settlement of balances. In Baltimore, however, the Union Bank of Maryland conducted the clearings and settlements for a fixed remuneration. These took place on the premises of the bank, its cashier acting <u>ex officio</u> as the clearing house manager. The same bank also became the coin depository of the clearing banks, issuing coin certificates to be used in the settlements; while in each of the other three cities the depository was separate from the clearing house proper (Bank of America in New York, Merchants Bank in Boston,[66] Farmers and Mechanics Bank in Philadelphia). The Baltimore set-up is somewhat reminiscent of that of the Suffolk Bank and of other similar organizations described in a previous chapter.[67]

IV

Lyman's own proud, almost forgotten, description of his achievement, the result of which "far exceeded the expectations of those who projected the establishment," should receive the attention which it deserves.[68] Discussing the advantages of the New York Clearing House Lyman made a distinction between those accruing to the banks and those "more general in their nature and less direct," the economic advantages as one would call them today. The former were enumerated as follows:

First: The condensation for each bank of forty-eight balances into one, and the settlement of that balance without a movement of specie.
Secondly: The avoidance of numerous accounts, entries, and postings.
Thirdly: Great saving of porters' time and risk in making exchanges and settlements from bank to bank.
Fourthly: Relief from a vast amount of labor and annoyance to which the great army of cashiers, tellers, and bookkeepers were subjected under the old system.
Fifthly: The liberation of the associated banks from all injurious dependence on each other.
Sixthly: The absolute facility, afforded by the books of the Clearing House, for knowing at all times the management and standing of every bank in the association.

As to the economic advantages, Lyman stressed the enlarged specie basis forced upon the banks through the daily settlement of the balances, and he expressed the expectation that the daily clearings would prevent violent expansions and contractions. In this respect he was mistaken, of course. The clearing house, in Lyman's words "has strengthened the entire banking system of the city...; makes the business of banking more uniform, regular and safe, while the banks themselves are really more independent. Each bank now regulates its affairs by the daily position of its balances with the Clearing House.... As the daily movements of each bank in the association can be known by inspecting the accounts of the clearing house, every bank knows how to govern its exchanges with its associates and may conduct its own business with entire independence of other banks." Lyman was even so far-sighted as to anticipate the most important change which the clearing house as an institution was to effect: becoming, as it did, the platform for permanent cooperation of banks in an era of reckless competition and rugged individualism, it served to prepare the way for a new kind of inter-bank relations.

Chapter XIII

THE ORIGIN OF THE CLEARING HOUSE

1. See this volume, pages 3 ff.
2. See page 130. The advanced American states of the East were about twenty years behind England. In the latter country as early as the 1830's even farmers had begun to keep bank accounts and to make payments by check. Clapham, op. cit., II, 149.
3. In the 1850's clearing included notes.
4. See vol. I of this work, pages 67 ff.
5. Philadelphia National Bank, 42. For other and even earlier cases, see this volume, page 246.
6. Gras, op. cit., 360.
7. Ibid., 355.
8. Ibid., 438 ff.
9. For details see this volume, page 246.
10. Boston was erroneously included in the list; American State Papers, Finance, IV, 933.
11. The Lexington branch of the Bank, for instance, on October 4, 1817 was advised to present the notes of banks in its district whenever $20,000 had accumulated.
12. Letter by Jones (June 28, 1817) to J.J. Astor, president of the New York branch, American State Papers, Finance, III, 328, 329. This letter has been correctly interpreted by Catterall, op. cit., 441.
13. American State Papers, Finance, IV, 1055, 933, 935.
14. Catterall, op. cit., 441, 444; Trotter, op. cit., 276. In 1824 the New York office practiced daily exchange of notes and weekly settlements. Biddle to Isaac Lawrence, January 6, 1824; Biddle Letter Books.
15. The fact that the Merchants Bank of Providence, which cleared Rhode Island notes under an agreement with the Suffolk Bank, did not clear notes if turned in by banks of the same place, led to the establishment of local note exchanges all over that state.
16. One of the Rhode Island banks (in 1809) redeemed its notes with post-dated checks on New York, paying interest for thirty days in advance (Stokes, op. cit., 284). An agreement of Alabama banks of 1836 with regard to their note issues can be found in U.S. 26th Congr. 2d sess., Executive Document 111, 534.
17. Remarks, 46. See also Trotter, op. cit., 108, 109.
18. An Act to revive the charters of the several banks located in the City of New Orleans. See chapter XII of this book. As to the four bills of 1838, see sections 10, 6, 8, 8, respectively, in U.S. 25th Congr. 3rd sess., House Executive Document 227, 492, 497, 513, 521. In 1859 an act approved on March 17, required the New Orleans banks to furnish every Saturday a statement regarding their balances with each of the other banks of the city.
19. To give another example illuminating the situation in the 1850's: The Bank of Tennessee, the Union Bank of Tennessee, and the Planters Bank, all of Nashville, exchanged their notes and the notes of their branches daily and settled the balances by sixty-day drafts on New York, computing interest. Thus they had ample time to obtain the aid of their branches if necessary. By the end of the 1850's this arrangement was supplemented by an agreement that no bank should ever be indebted to another participant in the arrangement for more than $100,000; the surplus was payable in gold. At about the same time Governor Johnson of Tennessee suggested a regional note clearing system. (See Report of the President and Directors of the Bank of Tennessee to the General Assembly of the State, October 3, 1859 and U.S. 35th Congr. 1st sess., House Executive Document 107, 241.
20. See vol. I of this work, pages 71 ff.
21. Clibborn, op. cit., 10.
22. Catterall, op. cit., 441.
23. For purposes of comparison, it is useful to keep in mind that in England in the late 1840's it was suggested that the joint stock banks and the Bank of England should join the bankers' clearing system. The Bank of England actually "entered the clearing" in 1864. In 1858 there was established in England the country clearing which resulted in the universal use of checks to the exclusion of notes and coin; see Clapham, op. cit., II, 215, 254.
24. Cleaveland, op. cit.; 266 ff. (This account was written by George D. Lyman, the first manager of the New York Clearing House). Cannon, op. cit. (1910), 148 ff; Gibbons, op. cit., 328 ff; Hardenbrook, op. cit., 1 ff. The primary sources as to the origin of the New York Clearing House, if they still exist, have never been used outside of the Clearing House and access has been refused to the author.
25. Writings, III, 424. However, Gallatin was not the first to draw attention to the London clearings. They were mentioned as early as 1831 in William B. Lawrence's anonymous and widely distributed article in the North American Review (The Bank of the United States. An Article re-

printed from the North American Review for April 1831 [Boston, 1831], 13.) They were mentioned again by the same author in the same magazine in 1834 (op. cit., 510). Moreover the Scotch note clearings were known in America; see Gallatin, Considerations (of 1831) in Writings, III, 350 and Journal of Banking (1841/42), 147 ff.

26. Cannon, op. cit., (1910), 46.

27. Stokes, op. cit., 285; Indianapolis Report, 833, 834. The president of the Merchants Bank was William Richmond, a director of the bank since its foundation in 1818. The surviving material, however, does not permit any conclusion as to whether or not he was responsible for this scheme. (Information from the Providence Public Library. Providence Directory of 1830.)

28. His self-portrait hangs in the New York Clearing House. It shows the typical sensitivity of an artist's face and particularly beautiful eyes.

29. U.S. 26th Congr. 2nd sess., House Executive Document 111, 108 ff.

30. Perine, op. cit., 83, 109. Beach (op. cit.) characterizes Knapp as follows: "From New England and self-made. He was formerly in the leather business with Jacob Lorillard and thus acquired his property." Later he did business under the firm Shepherd Knapp and Company, Bankers at Wall Street.

31. The following is based on the pamphlets by Edmonds and Knapp. See list of references.

32. The Massachusetts Bank Commissioners found in 1850 that in many banks of the state the cashiers were the only ones to keep records as to note issues, a practice which opened the possibility of fraudulent dealings. In other banks inadequate bookkeeping systems were used or the cashiers were negligent in having the books posted; Report for 1851, 12.

33. A picture of Knapp hangs in the New York Clearing House, since he was its president in 1860-61. It shows a hard, almost brutal, and unusually ugly man. Another picture of him is reproduced by Gilpin and Wallace.

34. The article is entitled: "Bank Exchanges," New York Journal of Commerce, Daily Edition, November 21, 1851, p. 2, column 3, signed Bank Bo Keeper [sic!].

35. See "The Clearing House of the New York Associated Banks," in Commercial and Financial Chronicle, January 11, 1896, 58, 59. The author of this unsigned article was Stuart Lyman, a nephew of George D. Lyman. By letter Stuart Lyman gave some information about his uncle. Knox (op. cit., 423) refers to Lyman; and a biographical note is to be found in Hardenbrook, op. cit., 39.

36. Cornwallis, op. cit., 45.

37. Thomas Tileston (1793-1864) had started his career as a printer and editor in Haverhill, Massachusetts. During the War of 1812 when that town became an industrial center and outlets had to be found for its products, Tileston moved to New York, like other New Englanders of that time, and started an export business. Taking produce and goods in exchange for the manufactures of Haverhill he became a shipping merchant and, after he had achieved considerable success, a prominent figure in financial New York. In 1840 he was elected president of the Phenix Bank, once a pet-bank which had run into trouble when the government deposits were withdrawn. Tileston restored the impaired capital and put the bank again on a sound basis. Thus he became an experienced banker and as such was instrumental in setting up the New York Clearing House, whose president he was for nine years. (Hunt's Merchants' Magazine, Vol. L, 93, 94; Tileston, op. cit., passim.)

38. Hallock, op. cit., Preface and p. 52.

39. Cannon, op. cit., (1910), 45.

40. James Punnett (about 1810-1870) entered the service of the Bank of North America by 1830; he became its cashier by 1846, a director in 1855, and its president in 1858. He served in that capacity until 1870. See the obituary in the New York Evening Post of May 31, 1870.

41. For biographical data, see this volume page 150.

42. Gibbons, op. cit., 328. Lyman in his account of the New York Clearing House (in Cleaveland, op. cit., 266 ff) describes in detail the working of the young institution, the account books used, etc.

43. The expenses of the Boston Clearing House were $11,000 during the first year; those of the Philadelphia Clearing House were $3,500 between March 1, 1859 and January 1, 1860, that is to say, $4,200 on a yearly basis; while the Baltimore clearing house was managed at an annual cost of $2250. (Records of the Philadelphia and Boston Clearing House Committees, July 18, 1859 and April 13, 1857, respectively; Hales, op. cit., 11.)

44. The New York Clearing House records may contain material on this resignation. Lyman removed to New Jersey and later was engaged in buying up part of the right of way for the West Shore Railroad; (Letter of Stuart Lyman).

45. The original constitution of the New York Clearing House is reprinted by Cleaveland, op. cit., 278 ff. Hardenbrook (op. cit., 5 ff) reprints numerous amendments.

46. New York Constitution, section 8; Boston Constitution section 5; Philadelphia Articles of Association, section 4.

47. It is not within the scope of this chapter to give a synopsis of the three earliest clearing house constitutions, i.e., those of New York, Boston, and Philadelphia, although it would not be without interest. The constitution of the New York Clearing House is reprinted by Cleaveland (see footnote 45); that of Boston was printed at the time of its adoption and a copy is among the papers of

the Boston Clearing House. A photostatic copy thereof was kindly presented to this author, who passed it on to the Baker Library of Harvard University. The first constitution ("Articles of Association") of the Philadelphia Clearing House is to be found on the first pages of the Minute Book of the Philadelphia Clearing House Association. The manager of the Philadelphia Clearing House had the kindness to have these pages copied for this author. These also are deposited in the Baker Library.

48. Minute Books of the Clearing House Association and the Clearing House Committee. Page 1 of the former is reproduced in the pamphlet, The Boston Clearing House Association. See also Cannon, op. cit., 240 ff; Martin, Century of Finance, pages 50 aa-51 (sic!); Bailey, passim; Gras, op. cit., see Index under Clearing House. The earliest description of the Boston Clearing House is to be found in the Annual Report of the Massachusetts Bank Commissioners (1856) which is reprinted also in U.S. 34th Congr. 3d sess., House Executive Document 87, 67.

49. This letter is reprinted by Hardenbrook, op. cit., 39, 40.

50. Andrew T. Hall (1798-1875) was originally a crockery dealer who as early as 1824 started to branch out. In that year he became one of the incorporators of the Boston and Sandwich Glass Company. Later he took an interest in an insurance company and became president of the Tremont Bank. In the same year of 1855 in which he worked toward the establishment of the Boston Clearing House he helped to incorporate the Boston and European Steamship Company and was active in soliciting subscriptions. Hall possessed a sense of team play and community of interest in an era of reckless competition. As early as 1834 when the removal of the deposits from the Second Bank of the United States led to a stringency in the Boston money market he became a member of a committee set up to protect both debtors and creditors against the evil consequences of the "unequal and oppressive" bankruptcy laws of New England. (Obituary in Boston Advertiser, November 23, 1875; Bailey, op. cit., 128 ff, 149, 150, 247, 248, 293, 395.)

51. While Hall was the contemporary of age of Tileston, Franklin Haven (1804-1893) was that of Edmonds and Silliman. Born in Cambridge, Haven started his career as a teller in the Globe Bank, and when the Merchants Bank was founded became its cashier, advancing to the presidency in 1836. Under his leadership the Merchants Bank of Boston, set up as a "pet bank," became probably the largest bank in New England. The bank was distinguished by an extensive system of correspondents, and its notes were redeemed not only in Boston, but also in New York, Philadelphia, Baltimore, and Washington. In addition to being a bank president Haven took an interest in

public life. His public activities will be discussed later in connection with his participation in early Civil War finance. Incidentally, he was one of the incorporators of the Illinois Central Railroad and from 1858 or 1859 through 1875 a director of the Eastern Railroad, being also a member of its finance committee.

In spite of having taken a considerable interest in the establishment of the Boston Clearing House of which he was an early advocate Haven did not take a leading part in its administration. He was not even regular in attending its meetings.

See Haven's obituary in the Boston Transcript Oct. 31, 1893; Bailey, op. cit., 280; Martin, Century of Finance, 51 a (sic!); Committee on Railroads... on the Eastern Railroad, Massachusetts Senate Document 169 (1876), 125, 126, 134, 136; this volume, see Index under Haven.

52. Waldo Flint (1794-1879) was a Harvard graduate who became a lawyer in Boston and later (after 1828) in Leicester, Massachusetts. He represented his town in the State Legislature in 1833 and 1834, became a bank commissioner for one year (1838), and in 1839 entered the banking business upon his appointment as cashier of the Eagle Bank of Boston, of which he became the president in 1840. (Biographical data were provided by Miss Marion G. Eaton, librarian of the Federal Reserve Bank, Boston. The Report of the Massachusetts Bank Commissioners of 1838, signed by Flint, is reprinted in U.S. 25th Congr. 3rd sess., House Executive Document 227, 129.) His contribution to the creation of the Boston Clearing House has been alluded to. He may have been on the committee of 1854; he was on that of 1855 which was appointed to take action, his name standing in the second place. Again, as mentioned above, he became a member of the first permanent clearing house committee whose sessions he attended regularly and conscientiously. On June 9, 1856 still a leader, he addressed a meeting of the Associated Banks on the proposed bylaws and moved their adoption. After one year of service, however, he refused reelection in 1857. Yet his name is to be found frequently thereafter in the minute book of the association. He repeatedly made proposals, which were adopted, but refused (for instance, on May 10, 1859) to be a member of committees formed to work them out, with but one exception: during the Civil War he was on the committee appointed to fit the legal tender notes into the Clearing House mechanism. Actions such as the following seem to have been typical of the man: On October 14, 1857 when the news of the suspension of specie payments in New York reached Boston he moved that a committee be appointed to decide on the course of action to be adopted by the associated banks of Boston. But he was neither on that committee, nor did he come to the meetings

of the banks called to deliberate on the subject, and he even stayed away when a special invitation was extended to him (Minutes of October 15 and 16, 1857). In the controversy over the admission of the Bank of Mutual Redemption to the Clearing House, he first fought a motion to invite it to become a member and then moved to have it admitted (Minutes, October 9, 1858). As to this episode, see vol I of this work, pages 84 ff.

53. The minutes of the session of November 22, 1858 are signed by Flint as secretary pro tem. The signature is indicative of his character. The letters are small and precise, the first letter of the family name does not connect with the remaining letters. The l's and t's are distinguished only by the t-stroke.

54. In 1864, for instance, he moved to reintroduce specie in the clearing house settlements.

55. The minutes show him in the chair at almost every meeting of the Clearing House Committee in the 1850's and 1860's.

56. For the following see the Minutes of the Boards of Presidents, of the Clearing House Association, and of the Clearing House Committee, preserved in the Philadelphia Clearing House. These minutes had to be used differently from those of the Boston Clearing House. In Boston all important decisions were prepared by the Clearing House Committee and presented to the meetings of the Association. Parallel reading of both sets of minutes is required in order to understand the development. In Philadelphia, the minutes of the presidents are most important, except for one year in which the Clearing House Association took the place of the Board of Presidents. Thereafter, however, the latter again became the decisive organization which determined the policy of the Clearing House in all important matters. The Minutes of the Clearing House Association deal mostly with technicalities, but contain the first constitution and its amendments (not the original bylaws). The minutes for the early years of the Clearing House Committee are almost without interest. However, when the Board of Presidents passed out of existence in the 1880's the Clearing House Committee gained the same importance as it possessed in other American cities. A good description of the beginnings of the Philadelphia Clearing House may be found in the speech of Moore, passim (see list of references); also Holdsworth, Empire, 745 ff.

57. Thomas Robins (1797-1882), the son of a Maryland plantation owner, was born on his father's plantation in Worcester County, Maryland. After having enjoyed a college education in his home state, he went in 1815 to Philadelphia where he entered a dry goods jobbing house, becoming partner after a few years. Later he established a dry goods firm of his own which did business as auctioneers or jobbers under various firm names. It had a branch in New York and for many years the agency of John Bright of Manchester, England.

Robins' banking career started in 1852 when he became the president of the Philadelphia Bank, then in straitened circumstances. However, prior to this appointment, he had already been a director of the Bank of North America and one of the assignees of the Bank of the United States of Pennsylvania. Robins became a very successful bank president and when he retired in 1879 he left the bank in prosperous condition. (Appleton's Cyclopedia; In Memoriam Thomas Robins, a pamphlet in the Historical Society of Pennsylvania; Philadelphia National Bank, 114.)

58. Allibone had been a member of Allibone and Troubat, dealers in oil and other commodities. Persuasive and hypocritical, he hoodwinked his contemporaries and colleagues on the board so that, unsuspected, he could dissipate the assets of the bank. After the failure he was indicted for criminal conspiracy to defraud the stockholders, but was acquitted in spite of incriminating disclosures. (Holdsworth, Empire, I, 153, 154; Hidy, Barings, 452.)

59. No biographical data have come to the attention of this author. Mitchell died, according to the Philadelphia Clearing House records, in 1868, after having been connected with his bank for more than fifty years. He was probably born in the 1790's and had risen as a professional banker. When the Board of Presidents was set up he became its president, probably being the senior among the Philadelphia bank presidents, although without personal prestige he would not have been so elected.

60. Other important men on this committee were C. S. Boker, president of the Girard Bank, and Singleton A. Mercer, president of the Farmers and Mechanics Bank. This latter bank was then the strongest in the city, the fiscal agent of the State of Pennsylvania and of the City of Philadelphia, and the transfer agent for several bond issues. Mercer's backing was therefore indispensable. He was originally a merchant and became the president of the Farmers and Mechanics Bank in 1837. When the Board of Presidents was brought into being he became one of its most active members. We have met him in connection with the note redemption business in Pennsylvania (see vol I of this work, page 81); we will meet him again as one of the Philadelphia delegates to the bank conference of 1861 which came to the rescue of the Federal government. He died in 1867, having resigned from the presidency the previous year. (Minutes, Board of Presidents; H.A. Boardman, Address at Obsequies of Singleton A. Mercer in Tenth Presbyterian Church, November 13, 1857; Victory Almanach for 1848 [it is doubtful whether the story contained therein refers to the bank president or a relative of his]; Holdsworth, Empire, 195 ff.)

61. On the first day $2,400,000 worth of items were cleared, the balances amounting to about $150,000.

62. He also moved to appoint the Farmers and Mechanics Bank as depository.

63. Decision to make a trial came on February 18, 1858; trials began in March, and the institution was made permanent about six weeks later.

64. Op. cit., 6-12, 45, 46, 61.

65. Robert Mickle (1798-1886) was born in Baltimore. He entered the service of the Union Bank of Maryland as a discount clerk in 1819 and was its cashier from 1830 through 1886. See his obituary in the Baltimore Sun, May 11, 1886 and Howard, George W., The Monumental City, 547, 548.

66. Daniel Denny made the arrangements with the Merchants Bank. Daniel Denny (1792-1872) was a dealer in "American goods," i.e., American manufactures, a business which came into existence in the 1820's. He was a member of Denny, Rice & Gardner and one of the founders and, from 1835 to 1872, the president of the Hamilton Bank. He was also one of the founders of the Boston Clearing House and its president from 1859 to 1870. (The Clearing House records; Aristocracy of Boston; Bailey, op. cit., passim; letter of a granddaughter of Daniel Denny, Mrs. Mary Denny Williston.)

67. See vol. I of this work, chapter IV.

68. In Cleaveland, op. cit., 266 ff, especially 269, 275-277. The earliest statistics regarding the operations of the New York Clearing House covering the period from October 10, 1853 through October 8, 1855 can be found in Bankers Magazine, XI (1856/57), 477.

Chapter XIV

PRIVATE BANKING

It is not certain when the modern term "private banking" made its appearance in America, but it probably came between 1835 and 1850. In the late eighteenth and early nineteenth centuries the expression was used to connote privately-owned as opposed to public banks and consequently included banks owned by individuals, partnerhips, and corporations. It is in this sense[1] that James Sullivan used the phrase "private banks or banks for the benefit of private companies" in his Path to Riches of 1792 and it is in the same sense that we find the term "private banks" as late as 1816 in a pamphlet entitled Curtius to the Secretary of the Treasury.[2] A federal law of 1813, to be cited shortly, equally indicates that the term "private banker" in its modern connotation was not known in that decade; and as late as the early 1830's the New York Bank Commissioners spoke of "brokers" in order to label real private bankers. The men who plied the latter's trade would call themselves "stock and exchange brokers" all through the 1830's and probably 1840's; but in the 1850's the modern term can be found in the Bankers Magazine.[3]

It is easy to trace the development of the phrase, but less easy to explain its assuming the present specific meaning. It seems to the author that in order to understand it, one must remember that in America in the eighteenth and early nineteenth centuries banking was synonymous with note issue and the latter was considered a semi-public function. Consequently when businessmen started a similar trade without issuing notes they were considered "private" bankers. Moreover since the modern term denotes banking conducted by individuals and partnerships as opposed to banking conducted by corporations, another way of thinking may have contributed to the emanation of the term's present connotation: in the early days of American independence all corporations were held to be of public character.[4]

If we turn to the beginnings and the early development of the private banking business in America, we must once more keep in mind the fact just mentioned that originally in this country "banking" was synonymous with note issue. As a historical consequence thereof we must distinguish between an older and a younger type of private banker (i.e., an individual or partnership doing a banking business without being incorporated), the former issuing notes while the latter did not. The former type was dying out fast after the War of 1812, but during that war a federal law of 1813[5] laying a tax on bank notes and discriminating against those of private banks (called "bankers" in the act) implied that there were a certain number of the latter in the business of issuing notes. Their extinction, with a few notable exceptions to be discussed forthwith, was due to the passing in most of the then economically advanced states of so-called restraining acts. These forbade note issue and sometimes even discounting and taking deposits to non-incorporated enterprises.[6] Before such legislation was passed the business of old-style private bankers and that of contemporaneous incorporated banks were hardly distinguishable: "In what do Barker's, Girard's [and other private banks] differ from the other banks, except that the latter are associations of individuals represented by directors, while the former are managers and owners?" This telling question was asked by the pamphleteer of 1816, previously mentioned.[7]

I

New York's outstanding private banker of the older type was Jacob Barker (1779-1871). Barker was a Maine-born Quaker (his family hailing from Nantucket), a Democrat by political persuasion, and at his height a "remarkably driving" and "much abused" man, as Scoville expressed it. His contemporary, John Pintard, called him uneducated but possessed of uncommon talents and unbounded enterprise. His business career started in New York even before he was of age, and by the end of the War of 1812 he was a ship-owning merchant. In 1815 this man founded the Exchange Bank in Wall Street with a capital of about $250,000, a bank which was not incorporated and of which he was the sole owner. It acquired an excellent credit rating, expanding fast and encroaching on the domain of the chartered banks. The business which it did was the typical banking business of that time and its customers were especially New York mechanics and residents of the adjacent counties, men who could not get accommodations from incorporated banks in New York City. Its notes had a wide circulation among New York craftsmen, traders, and laborers, and in addition large batches were floated in Georgia. But the latter could not be kept afloat as long as was desired, since an unfavorable exchange rate caused their quick return. Barker also issued what he called "red notes". These were notes signed by him with red ink to distinguish them from his regular issues. They were redeemable exclusively in country notes and were supposed to remain in circulation longer than notes payable in the city because the brokers would take country notes only at a 3 per cent discount, while the public accepted them at par.

It is not surprising that the chartered institutions became alarmed. They allied themselves against the intruder who was, moreover, a Democratic state senator and a founder of Tammany Hall and so the political enemy of most of their directors. Besides his resources were considered "dubious, if not fictitious." The banks started a law suit claiming that Barker violated the restraining acts; but the supreme court of the state decided that those acts referred to associations only, not to individuals. So Barker went on plying the banker's trade while his adversaries in 1818 coached a law through the legislature extending the restraining acts to individuals, forbidding the taking of deposits and the discounting of bills by all but chartered banks, but exempting Barker for a limited period of time from this regulation.

While Barker was in Albany attending the senate, news reached New York in May,1819,that his Liverpool house had failed. This caused a run on his Exchange Bank which had to reduce its circulation from $500,000 to $130,000. But Barker was able to stop the run and uphold his enterprise for one more month. He abandoned the issue of its notes and instead circulated notes of the Washington and Warren Bank of Sandy Hill, which he seems to have controlled. The latter's notes were redeemed at the Exchange Bank and agreements were made with a number of country banks to draw on Barker at ten and fifteen days sight for such notes of the Washington and Warren Bank as they might receive. Those banks, however, as Barker claims plausibly, depressed the value of the notes in order to profit from a larger discount. This further undermined the credit of the Exchange Bank, which succumbed to a second run in June,1819. Thus ended New York's only important private bank of the older type.

By 1820, under the cloak of an insurance business, Barker organized again, this time illegal, banking operations: He saw chances for profit in "guaranteeing the payment of debt for merchandise sold" (whatever this may have meant), and for that purpose established the Mercantile Insurance Company of New York. When the latter proved profitable he became interested in two other similar enterprises, the Western and the Dutchess County Insurance Companies. These companies issued their "bonds" in exchange for promissory notes and "commercial assets." The bonds were discounted at the legal rate by the recipients (borrowers) or the issuing insurance companies. Later on, so Barker claimed, after having made a success out of transactions of that character, he was copied extensively by people without capital and managerial skill so that the value of insurance company bonds decreased and he preferred to withdraw from the field.[9] Instead, he backed the Life and Fire Insurance Company. The latter had its "bonds", de facto postnotes, engraved like bank notes and, by discounting, circulated them like bank currency as late as 1825. Then this kind of illegal banking was stopped by court action in the course of what was then known as "Conspiracy Trials."

So much can be said about Barker in his capacity as a private banker. It is not possible here to follow him on his erratic career in New York and New Orleans which included several ups and downs, and a trial which was quashed. The versatile and unusually resilient man was, during his life, a ship-owning merchant, a private banker, an important Wall Street broker, a lawyer, a politician, a speculator, and a capitalist (that is to say, an investor and director in corporations, including insurance companies, banks, and manufacturing enterprises). For the economic historian, however, his main claim to importance lies in the fact that he was the first American-born loan contractor, and his activities in this field will find due attention in their place.[10] Moreover it is noteworthy that the old-style (note issuing) New York private banker of the 1810's was a new-style private banker in New Orleans forty years later.[11]

While New York has its Jacob Barker, the older type of private banker was represented in Philadelphia by Stephen Girard (1750-1831). Both these men were of humble origin; both were shipping merchants; both worked against an unfavorable legal set-up and against the hostility of chartered banks whose domain they invaded; the banking business of both was practically identical with that of those institutions. But the steady and wealthy Philadelphian succeeded, while the erratic New Yorker with slender resources had to give up. While it was common in the period for banking activities to develop out of mercantile pursuits, both Barker's and Girard's were different from those of typical merchant-bankers in that theirs were not integrated into their mercantile business. Rather the Exchange Bank and the Banking House of Stephen Girard were independent enterprises.

Stephen Girard became a private banker when trade restrictions during the Napoleonic era decreased the possibilities of employing his means in sea-borne trade, and banking promised to become a profitable investment for idle funds. By 1810 Girard had come to distrust the future of the Pound Sterling, making it seem advisable for him to withdraw some of the large funds he held with the Barings. This could best be achieved by purchasing blocks of stock of the United States and of the First Bank of the United States, transactions which represented perhaps the first American case of nationalization of foreign investments. In fact, the very block of stock of the Bank which the Barings had once purchased from the federal government was taken over and additional shares were bought in the English open market at falling prices. These purchases were originally speculative in character, for Girard expected a renewal of the charter of the national bank and, on the other hand, knew that at the worst it could be liquidated without loss. But once the former expectation did not materialize and once he had become one of the Bank's largest stockholders, in December,1811,he decided to use his strategical position to go into banking himself. Upon the dissolution of the Bank he bought the bank building and the cashier's house, hired George Simpson, its competent cashier,[12] and on May 12, 1812 started operations under the style of Stephen Girard's Banking House, aiming at a kind of succession to the Bank of the United States.

Prior to so doing Girard had an interesting correspondence[13] with the Barings who, from the merchant-banker's point of view, encouraged him to go into banking. They argued that large mercantile firms would prefer dealing with a private banker to negotiating with unwieldy boards of chartered banks. But they undoubtedly expected Girard to build up a type of business similar to that which they were conducting and did not expect that he would issue notes himself in competition with incorporated banks. They advised him to take deposits, to deal in foreign exchange, and to keep his cash with one of the great Philadelphia banks.

Stephen Girard's Banking House, which during its owner's life-time was not incorporated, started with a capital of $1,305,861, a large amount for the time; but it was not very profitable at the start. That the trustees of the First Bank of the United States during its liquidation deposited its funds with the quasi-successor, that it retained some of the customs-house business and some accounts of the Bank's customers, these were fortunate happenings probably due to the prestige of Simpson, its cashier. Moreover in connection with Girard's activities as a loan contractor[14] during the War of 1812, government business developed: deposits of funds arising from the loan transactions were made in the banking house which from 1815 on for a short while received revenue deposits also. But Girard was cautious, and in November and December 1814 and in April 1815 he refused to make advances to the federal government which was not willing to meet his conditions. Girard himself considered his enterprise a bank of discount and deposit, while in fact it was a bank of issue also, to use the contemporary term. In this respect, as in its methods, it resembled closely the average contemporary city bank, except that after some time the deposits were nominally lodged with trustees to protect the depositors in case of Girard's death, possibly also because of the existing legal restrictions on private banking. The issue of notes and postnotes was the backbone of the house's business, and as far as the keeping of reserves is concerned it was just as careless as its chartered competitors, although it is claimed that at times hardly any of Girard's ships arrived from Europe without specie for his bank.[15] It goes without saying that, just as in Barker's case, the incorporated banks of the Commonwealth did all they could to break Girard's bank. They engineered runs; but Girard was protected by government deposits in his banking house and besides received currently in the ordinary course of his unusually large mercantile transactions amounts of notes of his adversaries large enough to make him a dangerous opponent.[16] On the other hand, the Commonwealth's Restraining Acts which were directed against Girard's Banking House were largely disregarded by its owner, who ultimately succeeded in having his name deleted from the official list of unlawful banking enterprises.

An extensive investigation by a trained business historian of Stephen Girard's banking activities would be desirable. So far our knowledge is very sketchy. It is probable that in the first years after the founding of Stephen Girard's Banking House it was run by George Simpson. Girard himself seems rather to have played a role corresponding to that of a bank director: he was invariably present on the discount days, but otherwise kept no regular hours. After becoming more and more familiar with banking, he seems to have influenced the determination of policy; and in this respect there developed a difference of opinion between him and his cashier. By necessity rather than choice the house did business with smaller firms and beginners: the big merchants of Philadelphia did not bank with Girard's firm. Simpson took the stand that personal reliability and a satisfactory running account should determine the total of accommodations to the individual dealer, while Girard wished to base accommodations on the average size of deposits, a well-known method of avoiding legal interest requirements. But in addition Girard may have been guided by the contemporary point of view that merchants and other businessmen should have enough capital for their normal activities and that they should borrow only to carry peak loads, a theory which implies that in dull times they should keep idle funds on deposit.

After Simpson's death Girard not only determined the policy of his banking house, but probably took a larger share in the management himself. It will be remembered that the 1820's saw a decline in American sea-borne trade. While New England merchants turned manufacturers, Girard took an increasing interest in his bank. At that period he related his discounts to the applicant's deposits and worked preferably with auctioneers, then indispensable middlemen between importers and inland traders: he discounted real paper doubly secured by the auctioneer's signature. Strictly speaking, he did not "discount" since that was forbidden to him by the Restraining Acts. He had to make loans instead, i.e., he had to put up the full amounts loaned and to charge interest to the borrower's account. His cold, impersonal way of doing business made him much disliked among the house's dealers, a fact which contributed to the many difficulties which he already had on account of the opposition of the chartered banks and the disadvantageous legal set-up.[17]

The last of the important note-issuing private bankers was George Smith (1806-1899), the Scot who came to Chicago first in 1834. Realizing the potentialities of the place and its hinterland he returned to Scotland and raised funds wherewith to exploit those possibilities. It is highly probable that Smith sponsored the first private banking house set up in Chicago in 1837 by Strachan and Scott, for Patrick Strachan was close to George Smith for years to come. As things stood at that time a large-scale banking business could be conducted in the back country only with the help of note issues, and for that purpose George Smith, copying the Chicago Marine and Fire Insurance Company founded early in 1839 the Wisconsin Marine and Fire Insurance Company of Milwaukee with a capital of $225,000, half of which was subscribed by Smith and his Chicago associates while the rest was taken by Scottish capitalists. Its model, established in 1836, was issuing in 1837 genuine certificates of deposit to an amount of about $150,000, certificates which circulated like bank notes; and it was this latter feature which Smith was planning to adopt. The Wisconsin Marine and Fire Insurance Company's original directors, elected on June 3, 1839, were (apart from two un-

important men) George Smith, Patrick Strachan, and Alexander Mitchell who, as the company's first secretary, was ultimately to become its real head. (Mitchell [1817-1887], a farmer's son and another Scot, educated for the law, but starting out as a bank clerk, immigrated in that year, having been given his job by George Smith personally who was among his family's acquaintances.)

The purpose of the Wisconsin Marine and Fire Insurance Company as originally established was to provide a currency first for Strachan and Scott, and later, after this firm had been induced to move to New York in 1841, for George Smith's own banking house established under the name of George Smith and Company, Chicago. Since the Wisconsin Marine and Fire Insurance Company in line with its model was entitled to take deposits, its charter provided a loophole through which private banking based on note issue could be entered by the man in control. The so-called certificates of deposit issued by the company were not by character genuine documents of that description as had been those of the Chicago Marine and Fire Insurance Company. They were _de facto_ bank notes. The very first to be issued in 1839 testified that Strachan and Scott had deposited $3.00 which would be paid to their order on demand. Later the majority of the obligations were made out in even amounts to E. I. Tinkham, the cashier of George Smith and Company, and like regular bank notes they bore the imprint "will be paid on demand to bearer." Extant business papers indicate that in case of failure of this scheme George Smith had a second iron in the fire: In July, 1840, one of the shareholders of the Bank of Milwaukee, founded in 1837, but obviously bankrupt soon thereafter, assigned 749 of its shares to Alexander Mitchell, while another 1250 shares were assigned for a recognition of one dollar to two persons who might have been straw men.[18] But the need for making use of this charter never arose.

George Smith's banking business based on the currency issued by the Wisconsin Marine and Fire Insurance Company assumed what were for the time enormous proportions. It was eminently healthy, and official attacks on the latter enterprise because of the extra-legal character of its operations were defeated by Mitchell's adroit moves. Besides serving the purposes of George Smith and Company the firm became the depository of several land offices and had customers of its own, mainly land buyers who borrowed at a rate of 10-12 per cent and received their loans in the form of certificates of deposit. But the concern did not become autonomous before 1854. Prior to 1852 it was owned by George Smith and some British shareholders who by the middle of the 1840's seem to have become restive, possibly because of those difficulties. Consequently, as early as 1847, Smith had offered to relieve them of their shares; but no transaction of that character was concluded before 1852. In that year Smith became the sole owner of the Milwaukee concern,[19] which he sold out to Alexander Mitchell in 1854. By that time (in 1853) it had become a regular state bank under a newly-passed Free Banking act.

Intentionally or not, George Smith's business,[20] conducted in the framework of George Smith and Company, while the Milwaukee concern acted rather as an ancillary enterprise, resembled in some respect that which Nicholas Biddle had built up between about 1825 and 1835. It rested on the acquisition of drafts of local commission merchants for produce shipments to the East. On this basis domestic exchange could be sold on a large scale. The drafts in question were acquired with certificates of deposit of the Marine and Fire Insurance Company which, as a balance sheet of 1842 shows, was at times supported by large loans from its owner. The certificates of deposit in turn for which Smith had made himself personally liable were redeemed in Milwaukee and Chicago and by certain correspondents of George Smith and Company; for a good deal of them would flow automatically to the places on which the underlying drafts were drawn, i.e., commercial centers to which the back country was indebted for capital and for the numerous consumers' and producers' goods which it currently needed. It must be kept in mind that certificates of deposit as issued by the Wisconsin Marine and Fire Insurance Company could, of course, be created just like bank notes. Based as they were on commercial paper they represented an ideal elastic currency (amounting to about $1,500,000 in 1852), which provided large profits to the issuer and nevertheless could not easily become dangerous, unless abused. And the Scotsmen Smith and Mitchell, business leaders of first rank, would not abuse them. On the other hand, it is very doubtful whether it was sound policy to redeem these certificates of deposit at a 1 per cent discount instead of at par. (Incidentally, a limited business in foreign exchange was also conducted by George Smith, drafts and bills on England were acquired and collected, and foreign exchange sold on the basis of deposits thus brought into being in Britain.)

An Illinois law of February 10, 1853 made it a felony to issue or to receive any form of paper money except bank notes legally issued under the law of Illinois or any other American state. This law put an end to the extra-legal issues of the Wisconsin Marine and Fire Insurance Company which, as mentioned before, was sold a few months later to Alexander Mitchell after having been incorporated as a state bank. However George Smith's private bank business was geared to note issue and the creation of purchasing power to such an extent that he immediately built up a new circulation, adopting one of the worst contemporary banking practices, although in a most honest and economically beneficial spirit. He acquired the Bank of America in Washington, D.C., and under the Illinois act established in Chicago a Free Bank under the same name, the notes of both banks being almost identical in appearance. While the latter as a Free Bank could not create purchasing power in the form of notes, the former could; and so could two Georgia state banks which Smith bought also. With that group of banks the State Bank in Chicago was probably connected in some way too, since Smith held a share therein. These banks together could and did float a very large amount of notes in the Middle West. Thus George Smith who had started his business career in the late 1830's as a note-issuing private banker ended it in the late 1850's as the owner of a chain of commercial banks.[21]

II

The later type of private banker was distinguished from the earlier one by not issuing notes, that is to say, de facto by not creating purchasing power. Thus the enterprise of the new-style private banker approached what contemporaries called a bank of discount.[22] His business consisted of making loans by discounting and otherwise, in taking deposits, and in a few other transactions to be discussed shortly. A few of these men tried their hands at embryonic investment banking as will be shown in a later chapter. As long as Biddle almost monopolized the domestic and foreign exchange markets the latter provided no fields for the average private banker. Only two of them, Prime, Ward and King and Alexander Brown and Sons, did an extensive business in foreign exchange and were considered competitors by the president of the Second Bank of the United States. In anticipation of its dissolution more firms entered the field by 1835.[23]

The later type of private banker originating in the 1820's had two roots. His business stemmed either from a mercantile enterprise or from that of a money broker. It seems that this difference of origin was, in the beginning at least, reflected in the organization and policies of the enterprises concerned, so that for the 1820's and 1830's one can distinguish between merchant bankers and "genuine" private bankers, basing the distinction on the origin of the concern in question. If we possessed pertinent statistical material it would undoubtedly show that prior to 1840 most private bankers in this country rooted originally in "money shaving."[24] Students familiar with European conditions would expect to find among the latter a great number of Jewish houses. But the author has found only a few, Jacob I. Cohen, Jr., and Brothers of Baltimore, L. and S. Joseph, and Joseph D. Beers and Company of New York, and (at the end of the period) August Belmont, whose case is entirely different, however, and who had a Gentile partner almost from the start.

Material published by Walsh[25] pertaining to Romulus Riggs, the most prominent exchange dealer in the District of Columbia in the first quarter of the nineteenth century, shows clearly how banking grew from those activities. Romulus Riggs in his "exchange banking house" in Georgetown, D.C., carried on at a large scale a typical domestic exchange business, including collections. In addition he offered his services for the safe keeping of money, that is to say, he advertised for deposits and promised to pay interest at the rate of 6 per cent if left for 30 days or more. To stress the point, Romulus Riggs's business was a combination of domestic exchange operations with the taking of deposits,[26] but not simultaneously with lending activities. Future investigators may be able to show if this was a typical stage in the development from "note shaving" to private banking.

By the 1830's private bankers developed to the point that they could compete with incorporated banks in various fields, while division of labor, the possible alternative, was not being worked out as yet. First of all, private bankers, especially in New York, tried to build up networks of correspondents in competition with the former and in the course of this struggle private bankers in that state began to pay interest on demand deposits. As the following quotations show it was they, not incorporated banks, who introduced that practice. (Prime, Ward and King, then the largest private banking house in the city, was among those who adopted that policy.)[27] But incorporated banks followed suit quickly. As the New York Bank Commissioners reported in 1831,[28]

The competition for these deposits in New York between some of the banks and individual bankers, has induced offers of moderate rates of interest to the country banks for their funds while undrawn, and many of them have very considerable deposits upon those terms with individuals, [underlining mine; i.e., private bankers] whose extensive and multifarious business renders their general reputation for solvency and wealth, a very uncertain test.

Upon general principles, as interest includes a premium for the risque as well as compensation for the use of money, we should expect that those would pay the highest rate in whose hands it was least secure. And the danger to be apprehended is, that the depositors may be tempted by the rate of interest, to lose sight of that unquestionable safety which to the public is certainly more important.

A few pages later:

The object of depositing with individuals [private bankers] in preference [underlining mine] to banks, being generally for the purpose of procuring interest rather than of facilitating the ordinary operations of banking

gave, as the commissioners thought, bankers' balances with the former the character of loans. But this was an error. Two years later (in January 1833) the same Commissioners reported[29] that the practice of keeping deposits with brokers, i.e., private bankers, continued and that the funds held by the state's country banks in New York City were about equally divided between banks and private bankers. The total of New York country bank funds held by the latter amounted then to about $790,000, to which an unknown, but probably small, figure for balances of out-of-state (including Canadian)[30] banks must be added to arrive at a reasonable estimate. The numerous investments of Erastus Corning, president of the Albany City Bank, in country banks make it appear possible that men in control of banks or banking houses in financial centers made such investments for the purpose of acquiring correspondents for their banking enterprises. But so far this is only a surmise.[31]

Secondly, the holding of bankers' balances led to a collection business on the part of private bankers, and in this field they competed with incorporated banks also. Extant correspondence between the New York private banking firm, Morgan, Ketchum and Company, of which Junius Spencer Morgan was a partner, and the Whaling Bank in New London, Connecticut, permits glimpses on this line of business as conducted by private bankers.[32] (Incorporated banks would not have used different methods, of course.) In 1833 (probably in October) Morgan, Ketchum and Company made the following offer to the President and Directors of the bank.

We propose to receive the Funds of the Whaling Bank, which may consist of the bills of Banks in the City of New York, United States Bank & Branches, New England Banks generally, Banks on North River, some in New Jersey, Phila-

delphia & vicinity & Baltimore, also
Drafts or notes payable in Boston,
Providence, New Bedford, New York,
Albany, Phila. & Baltimore, giving you
credit for the Bank notes as soon as
counted & for the Drafts & notes when
paid to our credit in the respective
places named, on an interest acct. at 5
pr ct. per annum.
We further propose to take up your bills
in Boston & New York delivering the same
to you at each of said places & in acct.
as taken up at each at 1/8 pr. ct. discount.
If you prefer that the amount redeemed
in Boston should be delivered in New York
we will do so at our risk & expense, delivering them there without the 1/8 discount or will deliver them at your risk &
expense & deduct the 1/8 pr. ct.
We further propose to give you satisfactory
security for your deposits in our hands,
either in approved negociable paper or in
Bank & other Stocks that shall be acceptable
& satisfactory to you.
We further propose to allow you this
priviledge if at any time desired of over-
drawing your acct. with us to a reasonable
amount we charging you the same rate of
Interest we allow on your deposits.
If desired you may forward your Eastern
money direct from the Bank to Boston or
Providence to our Broker or Bank with
which we keep an account, we allowing you
interest on same as above. The statement
of your acct. & the acct. [illegible] to be
made up & forwarded as often as may be
desired.

In the course of negotiating this proposal one of
the directors of the Whaling Bank required the following clarification:[33]

> Will you be so good as to write a line
> by the bearer (Capt. Howard) signifying if
> the President & Directors of the Whaling
> Bank in this City are to understand that
> you will & do take the Bills of sd. Bank from
> the Suffolk Bank in Boston & deliver them
> to us in N. York at your risk, dollar for
> dollar, or if we take them of you in New
> York at par will you expect that Bank to
> risk them from Boston, by answering the
> above question you will oblige a Director.

The above negotiations resulted in a contract
which the author is inclined to consider as typical
and as a good illustration of the business dealings
of New York private bankers in 1830. It was confirmed as follows:[34]

We hand you below a memorandum of
our agreement in relation to the account
of the Whaling Bank, to commence on the
first of next January. It is understood
that the whole of your account be transferred to us in this city as soon as is consistent with other arrangements or say by
the 1st of April next.
Your remittances to us to be placed to
credit on receipt at an interest of five
per cent.
We take from you the Notes of the Banks
in New England, those of the Banks of this
City, of this State on the North River, of
Peoples Bank of Paterson, of the Banks of
Newark, of Elizabeth Town & New Brunswick, New Jersey, and of the City of Philadelphia, at at [sic!] par.
We are to transmit funds to Boston at
our risk and of [sic!] funds for the redemption of your Notes there and deliver
your Notes here at our risk and [illegible]
at par.
We make your collections without charge,
in Baltimore, Philadelphia and the principal
Towns in the Eastern States and credit the
account when paid.
N.B. In addition to the above terms we
would say that if you at any time find it
necessary to overdraw your acct with us
to a reasonable amot you are privileged to
do so with the understanding you refund the
amot as soon as practicable...

It has been stated above that the later type of
private banking developed out of mercantile enterprises and those of money brokers. To begin with
the latter, it is not easy to determine exactly at
which point a broker ceased to be a broker and began to become a private banker. For the purpose
of this study he is assumed to have crossed the
dividing line at the moment he started taking deposits and making loans by discounting paper and
otherwise. Since the new-style banker could not
issue notes, he could not create purchasing power,
for the creation of purchasing power in the form of
deposits was still far in the future. Thus he discounted and loaned on the basis of his capital and
deposits and, keeping this situation in mind, one
can easily understand why he was so anxious to
attract bankers' balances. Whether prior to 1840
he himself borrowed from incorporated banks in
order to lend at a higher rate is not known, but it
is not probable when we realize that incorporated
banks and private bankers competed with each
other. Moreover legal interest requirements and
the practice of banks to evade the latter by charging exchange make it improbable that before 1840

the private banker could become a middleman between the incorporated bank and the borrower, to any great extent if at all, as he became later in Ohio.

The earliest representative private banking firm that developed from note brokerage, or note "shaving", as it was then maliciously called, was a partnership which went under several names, the best known of which is Prime, Ward and King.[35] It was founded by Nathaniel Prime (1768-1840), a man of humble origin who is said to have started as a coachman. He set up in business in Wall street in the 1790's as a "stock and commission broker" and by taking in several partners as time went on, his firm became in turn Prime and Ward in 1808, Prime, Ward and Sands in 1816, Prime, Ward, Sands, King and Company in 1825, and Prime, Ward, King and Company in 1826. The partners were the very important Samuel Ward (1786-1839), who became the head of the firm when the founder retired in 1832 and was replaced by his son Edward; Joseph Sands, who resigned in 1826; and James Gore King (1791-1853), Rufus King's son and another important business leader.[36] These details have been presented because they are typical. The early private banking firms had usually a great number of partners, and the firm names were changed whenever there was a change in the ownership, a policy in New York, at least, demanded by the law. The business of the firm, which Scoville characterized as New York's first large genuine private banking house having no rivals at its time, was in line with what has been described as typical. But in addition, as indicated, it did a considerable business in foreign exchange, a very rare phenomenon in Biddle's days. This was possible because Prime, Ward and King were the most important financial connection of Baring Brothers and Company in the city. Both firms agreed by 1830 to open credits on each other and to share commissions. On the basis of that arrangement a joint exchange account was established and the New York house enjoyed an open revolving credit of £ 50,000 for its exchange operations; (the corresponding account of the Second Bank of the United States with the Barings amounted to £ 250,000). That is to say, Prime, Ward and King could draw up to £ 50,000 on the Barings before remitting in bills of exchange, bullion and specie, or securities to be sold by the London house. So highly valued was the connection by the Barings that the joint exchange account was reopened after the crisis of 1837. In the course of its business with Baring Brothers and Company the New York house seems to have become an acceptor of drafts, a fact which permits the conclusion that such transactions, typical of contemporary merchant bankers,

belonged to its regular lines also. Moreover as will be discussed later,[37] it was one of the first, if not the first, private bank to engage in embryonic investment banking activities.

The firm of Prime, Ward and King is best remembered by a gold transaction concluded in the spring of 1838. This transaction has often been described, and the traditional presentation is a good example of a historical myth bequeathed from one generation to another because nobody takes the trouble of checking on the story's accuracy. Here are the facts: When James Gore King was in London in the winter months of 1838, "aided and abetted" by Barings Brothers and Company, he arranged with the Bank of England on March 19 for a gold loan guaranteed by the Barings for three months. T. A. Curtis, then governor of the Bank of England, in an informal farewell letter of March 20 confirming the agreement,[38] pointed to its essential clause, namely, that the gold could be sold only for bills of exchange. At the same time he warned against undue haste, lest the price of the latter be raised. According to the traditional interpretation of the transaction[39] this gold loan enabled the American banks to resume specie payments in the summer of 1838. But claims to that effect are erroneous. Philip Hone's contemporary guarded statement[40] that it "facilitated" resumption seems to go far enough, if not already too far.

The gold loan had little if any influence on actual business conditions, but it contributed to the atmosphere of confidence which prevailed that summer. What it did was to stiffen the neck of the New York banking fraternity and make it insist on a policy of early resumption which to this author's mind proved disastrous in the long run. But insisting on such a policy and succeeding in it are two different things, and success was not due to the gold loan. For the latter to be made effective per se it would have been necessary to sell the gold on long term credit which was not done; and that resumption was actually achieved at that moment was the result of Biddle's first cotton pool and his equally well handled sale of postnotes in the London money market and perhaps also to a political payment, the settlement of the 25,000,000 francs of the French Spoliation Claims. These transactions brought about that favorable turn in the exchange rates which made resumption possible. The gold loan as such could not have had that effect, because, as must be stressed once more, the bullion and coin could under the contract be sold only for bills of exchange. Of course, whoever had the bills wherewith to buy the gold, commanded gold anyway, gold loan or not, and there were in fact in the spring of 1838 "constant petty shipments" of gold from England to the United States. To put it differently,

it was Biddle who created most of the bills of exchange for which Prime, Ward and King sold the
Bank of England's gold and with which the latter
was reimbursed.

The mere fact that the whole transaction was
concluded in less than three months should make
the historian suspicious. Moreover two contemporaries, Tooke and Biddle, whose extraordinary
knowledge of financial matters is undisputed, were
very critical of the arrangement. According to
Thomas Tooke, the agreement to ship about
£ 2,000,000 -- the actual shipment fell short of
£ 1,000,000 -- was greatly applauded on both sides
of the Atlantic; but he considered it a "quixotic
measure." The Bank of England was being enticed
into making the loan because bullion was accumulating in its coffers and it could not even lend at
4 per cent after having lowered the discount rate
from 5 per cent. Tooke warned that it was not the
business of the Bank of England to accelerate a
recovery which could be brought about permanently
only by contraction, and that this loan would enable
American businessmen to renew their reckless
course, i.e., to proceed with their malpractice of
overbanking and their (in fact, Biddle's) tampering
with the cotton market. To sum up, Tooke expected
the loan to be efficient, but he feared dire results;
and this author considers it as having had by itself
no influence on business conditions to speak of.
Only in conjunction with Biddle's transactions could
it become effective, and consequently the latter's
actions brought on those repercussions which Tooke
expected of the gold loan as such and which the
latter would have had, had it been effective by itself. That the loan was ineffective was in fact
Biddle's opinion and he knew the situation better
than anybody else, for it was of his making. He
explained in a letter of April 28, 1838 that this
specie import to be sold against bills of exchange
amounted to a mere exchange of sovereigns in New
York for sovereigns in Liverpool and therefore
could not shape the economic situation.[41] It is
telling that one-third of the gold was taken up by
Biddle himself[42] and the rest by a very few firms:
Prime, Ward and King, the Mechanics Bank of
New York ($500,000), the Merchants Bank of Bos-
ton ($97,000), the Treasurer of the United States
($1,000,000), and the Girard Bank. The sale to the
Treasurer of the United States needs some clarification. He received gold for 6 per cent treasury
notes which would appear a violation of the agreement with the Bank of England unless there was
some connection with the French indemnity payment, i.e., the payment in settlement of the French
Spoliation Claims. In fact the Bank of America, a
depository of the Treasury, paid franc bills to
Prime, Ward and King which the latter remitted to
the Barings.[43]

The author is inclined to agree with Scoville
that, prior to about 1840, no genuine private banker
could stand comparison with Prime, Ward and King,
and it seems therefore hardly worthwhile to track
down many more of them. The transactions of
Morgan, Ketchum and Company previously described have familiarized the reader with that
house. Some others he will meet later herein as
being interested in early investment banking.[44] One
of them, S. and M. Allen, is well known through
Dr. Larson's research: The founder of this firm
was Salomon Allen (about 1785-1846), the son of a
Presbyterian minister, himself a printer in Albany
who, on the side, sold lottery tickets and shortly
thereafter started "note shaving." In 1812 abandoning his printing shop he set up a Lottery and Exchange Office combining with his main line of interest a curious mixture of other dealings, including the sale of patent medicines. In 1815 he formed
a partnership with his brother Moses (1789-1877)
and opened an office in New York headed by the
latter as resident partner. Besides selling lottery
tickets it did the typical business of the money
broker, including dealings in specie. As the latter
type of business expanded, the former was abandoned.
In the 1820's some branches of the concern took
up stock brokerage, a line which was growing into
genuine investment banking, as will be discussed
in a later chapter;[45] and some attempted to enter
the foreign exchange market, with hardly any success. A deposit and discount business was never
attempted.

S. and M. Allen are interesting for various
reasons: They built up a system of branches. As
early as 1817 the original Albany office became a
branch, after Salomon himself had gone to Philadelphia in 1816 opening one there. In the late 1810's
others were established in Baltimore, Pittsburg,
Washington, Richmond, Charleston, and Fayetteville.
Not all of them were upheld; but in 1826/27 the
concern worked at New York, Philadelphia, Baltimore, Washington, Albany, Richmond, Providence,
Lynchburg, Boston, Charleston, Portland, and
Savannah. This was undoubtedly a great organizational achievement, although the Allens were hardly
unique in this respect. It is known that other lottery
ticket sellers, especially the largest one, Yates and
McIntyre, built up similar countrywide organizations. The Allen business is also noteworthy because of the logic of its growth: money brokerage
developed out of the lottery business. The ticket
seller, when he wanted to do business, had to take
whatever was offered as a medium of payment and
then had to make a business out of handling the
media which came into his hand. That is to say,
here in the banking field we meet a typical and

early example of expansion by automatic integration of divergent functions. Finally, the Allens are interesting as ancestors of important private bankers. Their real successors were E. W. Clark and Company, Philadelphia, to be discussed later; the latter in turn sired Jay Cooke and Company, and the latter's successor became Charles D. Barney and Company, Philadelphia, founded by Cooke's son-in-law and joined by his son.[46] As will be shown later, the New York branch and probably some others too were badly hit in 1834 when the concern turned to full-fledged investment banking and it never recovered from this blow. It suspended in 1837 and went into liquidation.[47]

The extraordinarily important economic role of the English merchant banker was not duplicated in this country, which is the same as saying that the Anglo-American trade was financed chiefly in England. In fact, the American merchant banker played only a minor part in the 1820's and 1830's, and this for one reason alone: he did not possess capital enough to compete with the English enterprises of the same character.[48]

Alexander Brown and Sons represent the outstanding example of the American merchant banker of the period. The firm, whose total resources by 1835 amounted to about $6,000,000, was founded in 1800 in Baltimore by Alexander Brown (1764-1834) who immigrated from Ireland where he had been active in the Belfast linen business. Establishing himself in the same line in this country he developed his concern so that ultimately it had almost a monopoly in the Irish linen trade. He became a ship owner and branched out into the cotton export business and into banking. Being thoroughly informed on the credit standing of English merchants he naturally bought drafts on them, collected these drafts, and sold exchange to smaller American importers not familiar enough with English names to run the risk of buying drafts from the exporters themselves. Moreover, profits accumulated to such an extent that it was necessary to loan funds to make use thereof. It is noteworthy that Alexander Brown never took a real interest in his banking business, which, for him, remained a side line to his merchandizing, but into which nevertheless his firm grew "rapidly" if "almost imperceptibly," as early as 1820. Although, in the fifteen years or so to follow, the exchange and credit business (including the selling of letters of credit which was commenced in 1824) became an important part of the house's business, Alexander Brown never permitted it to become the dominant end as long as he lived.[49]

There were of course during the period under investigation a few more merchant bankers, but they were of limited importance only, except in the French trade. Among them were Thomas A. Biddle and Company of Philadelphia of whom more will be said in another chapter;[50] and Jeremiah Thompson, of New York, a ship-owning cotton exporter and cloth importer. In the 1820's, besides the Browns and Prime, Ward and King, Thompson was the largest bill drawer; but he failed in 1827. In the 1830's Goodhue and Company of New York, commission merchants, were on the way toward merchant banking, but never developed a full-fledged enterprise of this kind.[51] In cooperation with the Barings and Huth and Company of London they dealt in exchange and occasionally held funds for the former house. In the same decade the Fitch and the Welles concerns dominated the French business. The former consisted of Fitch and Company, New York correspondents of Fitch Brothers and Company, Marseilles; while the Welles concern (Welles and Company) centered in Paris and was represented in this country by John and Benjamin Welles, Boston, successor in 1816 to John and Samuel Welles (founded in 1802).[52] In order to receive consignments from America these two concerns of merchant bankers and their agents financed them by large credits. Thereby they not only drew water to the mills of their mercantile business, but at the same time received a larger interest on their capital than they could have otherwise. Credit was given on the basis of bills of lading. Vice versa, when French merchants wished to trade in America the houses in France advanced on the bills of lading if the goods were shipped on consignment to the American member of the concern in question. Moreover commissions were charged on the drafts which the customers were permitted to draw and with which they paid their purveyors. Since the business of these houses was very large for the time they became wealthy until the crisis of 1837 hit them as badly as it did their London confrères. These merchant bankers, as will have been recognized, practiced the financing of international trade by applying methods still general today and known in Europe under the name of "rembours credit."[53]

III

The crisis of 1837 and its aftermath so discredited incorporated banks that the 1840's and 1850's marked the rise of private banking to real importance.[54] As a contemporary source expressed it in 1843,

Mercantile banking is concentrating in the hands of private houses of known integrity, wealth and business habits, because of the superior facility they afford over associations of irresponsible men doing business in palaces at enormous expense.

Going into detail the writer explained that besides working at lower cost, the funds of private bankers were always available to reliable borrowers, while those of incorporated banks were monopolized by the directors. Private bankers worked on a strongly competitive basis, i.e., at declining rates; their standing and means were better known to the business community than those of banks (which one may doubt); and dealing with them was more pleasant. This picture is undoubtedly overdrawn, but it contained a kernel of truth.

The historian, however, would stress other points in order to explain the rise of private banking: The dissolution of the Second Bank of the United States opened new promising fields for the activities of private bankers. The markets in domestic and foreign exchange were no longer almost monopolized by the powerful central bank. Its going out of existence created a derangement of the currency which gave the domestic exchange market an importance which it had not possessed before. Although this development was most unfortunate from the economic point of view, it resulted in large profit chances to shrewd and able private bankers. In some areas they had to contend with the competition of incorporated banks, such as the State Bank of Indiana,[55] which also entered the business in domestic exchange.

Other private bankers built a considerable business in foreign exchange, to a certain extent also in competition with commercial banks such as the Bank of Commerce of New York and New Orleans banks (the Citizens and Union Banks). First-rate British correspondents were needed for this type of business, preferably houses which stood ready to extend open credits. Leaders in this field were the Browns in Baltimore and New York who drew on Brown, Shipley and Company, their English ally, who was also strongly represented in Boston. In the latter city John E. Thayer and Brother drawing on McCalmont and Company of London were big dealers in foreign exchange; in the early 1850's they encountered the competition of Blake, Ward and Company who had Baring backing. The firm's successor Blake, Howe and Company cooperated with George Peabody and Company; while Lee, Higginson and Company, although grumbling, remained in the Baring orbit until 1857. Of New York firms, Prime, Ward and King and its successors J. G. King and Sons (still later J. G. King's Sons and Company) and Prime, Ward and Company may be mentioned. They worked with the Barings; while Duncan, Sherman and Company corresponded with George Peabody and Company. Finally in Baltimore, Oelrichs and Lurman drew on the Barings. The exchange business, as Ralph Hidy has shown, was operated under uncovered credits or on the basis of covered accounts. That is to say, in the latter case the American firm in question had to send bills on England before selling exchange in the United States. Sometimes exchange transactions were handled by issuer and drawee on joint account. Because of the fact that very few English houses participated in the business, each of which had only a limited number of American correspondents (issuers of drafts), the foreign exchange market in the United States was rather dominated by an oligopoly, although it was not manipulated.[56] In fact an oligopoly succeeded the quasi-monopoly of the Second Bank of the United States.

Last, but not least, the two decades under investigation saw the first railroad boom and the reappearance of the federal government as a borrower while several state governments had to reorganize their older debts. In other words, there came into the market a large demand for long-term capital. The commercial banks which had formerly supplied long-term-credit needs were so badly shaken by the crisis and the depression of the 1840's that for the time being they more or less withdrew from that field. This meant that the private banker had to take over, and that he could do so without serious competition on the part of incorporated institutions. Since the investment banking activities of private bankers will be treated in detail in their proper place[57] this suggestion must suffice here.

The preceding analysis, however, is not representative of the whole country; special conditions obtained in several states. In Mississippi, for example, the complete collapse of banking after 1837, in conjunction with Repudiation, left the entire field to private bankers and exchange brokers. A few full-fledged enterprises of the former description were located in Natchez, Jackson, Vicksburg, and Yazoo City; while in the rest of the state note shaving was combined with taking deposits and making discounts.[58] In Arkansas, Florida, and Texas where in 1852 "no incorporated banks [were] in regular and active operation," to use the words of the then Secretary of the Treasury, the situation was probably very similar.[59] In Ohio, on the other hand, ill-advised legislation was the basis of the rise of the private banker. In order to attract foreign capital, the state passed a law in 1850 permitting a charge of 10 per cent interest on special contracts, while the legal rate which the banks must charge was 6 per cent. Consequently, bank officers stopped making local discounts and connived with brokers and private bankers, lending at 6 per cent to the latter who in turn discounted at 10 per cent and secretly remunerated officers and directors. Furthermore private bankers could pay 6 per cent on deposits and then lend the latter at 10 per cent; that is to say, businessmen could go into a private banking business almost without capital;[60] and once in the field, they could make domestic exchange another source of profit. By the middle of the 1850's the number of Ohio private bankers was estimated by a local special examiner to be about 100. A few were rather strong, working with a capital of from $150,000 to $400,000; but some of these failed in 1854.

As in the two preceding decades, so in the 1840's and 1850's, both merchants and exchange and stock brokers became private bankers; but a distinction between merchant bankers and "genuine" private bankers which is meaningful for the 1820's and 1830's is applicable no longer to this later period. Whatever their origin, once they turned bankers their business organization and policy were essentially the same. Corcoran and Riggs in Washington and Drexel and Company in Philadelphia present good examples of banking houses whose founders were rooted in mercantile pursuits and in "money shaving", respectively, and who rose as private bankers during the period under investigation. Johns Hopkins was another merchant whose enterprise is said to have developed into a banking business, but details are not known.[61] As in the preceding period the borderline between private bankers and brokers was still fluid. In a list of 1853 the Bankers' Magazine[62] lumped together bankers, brokers, and exchange dealers, at least for New York.

Many previously important houses succumbed during the crisis of 1837 and the depression following on its heels. This was the case with the Allens and with L. and S. Joseph, whom we shall meet in one of the next chapters.[63] Others survived, among the survivors being Morris Ketchum[64] (although he was no longer a partner of Junius Spencer Morgan), the Brown concern, and Prime, Ward and King (to be dissolved soon thereafter) who came out of the ordeal unscarred and with an enhanced prestige. E. W. Clark and Company, to be discussed in detail presently, can be considered the successor of the Allens; while Drexel and Company, Philadelphia, August Belmont and Company, Winslow, Lanier and Company, Carpenter and Vermilye, all of New York, Corcoran and Riggs, Washington, and last, but not least, Lee, Higginson and Company, Boston, were examples of new private banking houses with a great future ahead of them. John Thompson and John E. Thayer and Brother were important, but during the 1840's and 1850's only.

E. W. Clark and Company of Philadelphia is presented here as a typical example of a large private banking house of the 1840's and 1850's. Although reorganized later, the life span of the original firm falls into the years between the crises of 1837 and 1857, a fact which makes it all the more representative, for this is the period with which this section deals. The founder of the firm was Enoch W. Clark (1802-1856), the son of a mill owner in Easthampton, Massachusetts. He was a relative of the Allens and learned the lottery and exchange business in their concern. His early career[65] is of no interest here. The young man was at various times an employee or partner of the Allens or independent in the same kind of business, moving from Philadelphia to Providence, thence to Boston, and back to Philadelphia. In this latter city after the failure of the Allen concern he opened an exchange and stock commission business in partnership with his brother-in-law, Edward Dodge. Very quickly the firm E. W. Clark and Company became probably the largest dealer in domestic exchange in the period. Moreover the house went heavily into investment banking, as will be described in detail in a later chapter.[66]

E. W. Clark and Company started with the small capital of $15,000 which implied that at first it could do a brokerage business only. When the available means increased, due to large profits, trading on the partners' own account could be added. Both the small capital to start with and the development of brokerage into dealing as principals seem to have been typical of this kind of enterprise. Noteworthy are the house's organizational achievements. It built up a system of branches as had the Browns and the Allens earlier. These branches were established on a principle which had been very common and used, for instance, in medieval times by the Medicis. That is to say, the original partners, those of the parent office or at least one or several of them, became partners in all the branches, whereas each branch had in addition a managing partner who participated in the profits of that branch only. In this way the Clark branches were established under different firm names in the 1840's in St. Louis, New Orleans, New York, and Burlington, Iowa (the latter branch growing out of the St. Louis office). (The branch organization of Alexander Brown and Sons, Baltimore, was older; 1810: William and James Brown and Company, later to become Brown, Shipley and Company, England; 1818: Philadelphia; 1825: New York. However at the very time when the Clarks built their far-flung organization, that of the Browns was disintegrating: the Baltimore and the English offices became independent enterprises in 1839. The degree of interdependence of the remaining Philadelphia and New York offices, to which one in Boston was added in 1844, all of which seem to have worked under the name of Brown Brothers and Company, is not known to the author.)

Such an organization implies a large number of partners, a number, as a rule, far in excess of what was common in contemporaneous industrial and mercantile partnerships. However, the large number of partners remained a typical feature of nineteenth-century private banking houses, whether they were groups of branches or not, possibly in line with European practice. But the Clark concern's organization was in still another respect typical of what was to become widespread: its partners were all members of one family. The Philadelphia parent house was owned by Enoch Clark and his brother-in-law, Edward Dodge. The former's brothers, associated in a similar, but at least originally independent enterprise in Boston, participated in the St. Louis office which one of them managed. When he went to Philadelphia, a brother-in-law of Dodge's by the name of Chase took over, and the latter's brother-in-law was put in charge of the Burlington branch. The Brown concern was a family enterprise also, and so was the house of Drexel, James G. King and Sons, and Morris Ketchum's firm before its downfall; but in these cases only fathers and sons were involved. Later it will be shown that by 1900 several of the most important private banking houses were family enterprises.

The passage which has been quoted above from the Merchants' Magazine of 1843 indicates that competition between private and incorporated banks was the keynote at that moment and so it remained throughout the 1840's and 1850's. After the crisis of 1857 when the New York Clearing House banks were on the point of abandoning the paying of interest on demand deposits, that wise move may have failed because of the competition of private bankers. The former probably lost bankers' balances to the latter; anyway, the measure had to be dropped.[67] It is certain that private bankers competed with incorporated banks as lenders in the call-loan market. In one respect they were handicapped, of course. They could not create purchasing power as the incorporated banks could (unless the latter worked under Free Banking acts). But even in this case the mere fact that incorporated banks could issue a circulating medium gave them an advantage over their competitors who could not do so. George Smith's solution of the problem has been discussed at great length. He became a note issuer by stealth; note issue was the backbone of his business. The Clarks found other solutions. First they revived Biddle's circulating branch drafts; as a matter of fact, E. W. Clark and Company, Philadelphia, drew on E. W. Clark, Brothers and Company, Burlington, and the drafts were circulated by E. W. Clark and Brothers, St. Louis. But slightly later, in 1852, after the Illinois Free Banking Act was passed in 1851, the concern founded a bank of its own in Springfield, Clark's Exchange

Bank with N. W. Ridgely, a former employee of the Second Bank of the United States as its manager. By that time several Iowa private bankers controlled commercial banks too,[68] and one wonders whether similar arrangements were made in still other states by large private banks of the period. If so, they have not come to the attention of the author.

As a lender the private banker competed not only with commercial banks, but also with the wholesaler in the North, the factor in the South, and to a certain extent with the retailer everywhere. In case of wholesalers and factors lending was incidental, of course, to the fulfillment of their main function, and since both enjoyed bank credit they acted as mere middlemen at least with respect to some of their loans, distributing bank credit converted into commodities. Retailers who gave credit on the basis of credit received from wholesalers represented a further link in that chain of middlemen which distributed bank credit in the form of commodities. But retailers assumed other banking functions, too, which made them direct competitors of private bankers rather than of incorporated banks; for they can be presumed to have done so especially in small places without banking facilities. They took deposits, albeit in small amounts, which (at least in the South) were often entered in the books as received "for safe keeping," although they were handled as straight deposits (depositum irregulare). Moreover retailers made payments for customers and even small cash advances, and in places without note shaver or bank, in their own interest they determined the value of circulating bank notes[69] by establishing the rates at which they would take them in payment.

It is possible that in the 1850's division of labor between commercial and private banks tended to grow out of what was originally competition. International merchants turning bankers were apt to be especially efficient in foreign exchange dealings, and in financing foreign trade. Branch organization, national in character and supplemented by correspondents, enabled private bankers to be more skillful in the domestic exchange business than were chartered banks, while the latter could not be circumvented when the essence of a transaction was receiving a circulating medium by way of a loan. Going into investment banking was certainly not due to competition with incorporated banks. To the contrary, it resulted rather in a division of functions, that is to say, in a lessening of competition. In the case of the Browns one can date the beginning of specialization at the middle of the 1830's when the second generation took over.[70] Unbeknown to them all those private bankers who developed the exchange business and who went into investment banking were blazing the trail which led to the emergence of the specialized private banker typical of the commercial and financial centers of this country between Civil War times and 1910.

Rising as it did in the 1840's and 1850's the total number of private banking enterprises was still small and did not compare with the total number of incorporated and Free Banks in the country. The only source which makes it possible to arrive at an estimate as to numbers is the list in the Bankers' Magazine of 1854, previously mentioned, and figures derived therefrom have been quoted repeatedly.[71] Philadelphia had by that time about 20, New York about 18 (but the number of private bankers, exchange dealers, and brokers was about 240), St. Louis about 15, and Boston about 10 private bankers. The total of private bankers outside of New York, according to the list, was 269. Only a few of them had built up branch organizations. Besides those mentioned before there were, for example, the Iowa houses Weare, Finch and Company (later Greene and Weare), Hoyt, Sherman and Company, and Cook and Sargent.

The 1840's and 1850's saw the rise of private bankers not only in the Eastern trade centers but also all over the Middle West in what were then the young states. This is indicated in the figure which has just been given and which presents a minimum, as will be explained shortly. In the last named sections of the country private banking developed originally as a side line of general stores, law offices, land agencies, and commission merchants, but it became an independent business during the decades under investigation. In those parts the private banker assumed banking functions in communities still too small to carry a chartered or Free bank. His business was conducted without much capital, a few thousand dollars being sufficient; as a matter of fact, as late as 1871 the large Chicago private banks had not more than $100,000 to $150,000 with which to work.[72] Adequate statistics cannot be made up even when we have contemporary lists of private bankers in certain communities, since they include everybody from private bankers doing a real general banking business to real estate, money and pawnbrokers; but, including such men, Chicago had in 1856 about 25 and in 1861 about 80 to 90 "private bankers."[73] In that same period Iowa trading communities had probably anywhere between one and five each.

The business of these men[74] was closely tied up with the official land business of the era. All of them made investments in land for Eastern customers and paid taxes for absentee owners. Many bought land themselves at the official price and sold it at a profit to Eastern land speculators and settlers, giving one year credit. For Iowa

their profit has been estimated at 40 per cent in addition to what they made out of trading in land warrants which they used for making payment at the land offices. Other transactions were similarly connected with the land business. The private banker bought Eastern drafts from settlers and sold them to local merchants with payments to make in the East. He collected such notes as settlers might have brought to the West, for land had to be paid for in gold exclusively. Finally the settlers made some time deposits between their arrival and the purchase of land, although the total was very small.

Considering the small means with which the western private banker worked and the general lack of capital in the young sections one can readily understand how anxious he was to attract deposits. It seems to have been usual to make out certificates of deposit payable a certain number of days after demand. It is not clear if such certificates of deposit were negotiable. They cannot have circulated freely. An advertisement of the Chicago private banker, R. K. Swift, in the fall of 1849 is most interesting. This firm offered to issue certificates of deposit[75]

payable five	days after demand at	4 per cent p.a.
ten	" " " "	5 " " " "
fifteen	" " " "	6 " " " "
twenty	" " " "	7 " " " "
twenty-five	" " " "	8 " " " "
thirty	" " " "	9 " " " "
forty	" " " "	10 " " " "

One can guess how small the average deposit was when noting that the time allowed after demand was to be settled by special contract whenever the deposit exceeded $1000.[76]

Finally the western private banker did a general collection business (of drafts and notes) which was bound to make him a dealer in domestic exchange. As a result of widespread distrust, toward the end of the period under investigation (in 1856), as the historian of Indiana banking reports, a private banking house was founded in Indianapolis with the sole purpose of presenting bills for redemption to banks in the area. (It is supposed to have driven several into bankruptcy.)[77] If that presentation is correct, more private banks of this type could have existed in the Middle West. Discounting of notes and bills was very rare in the period. But by 1860, in Chicago at least, some began dealings in securities,[78] a business which expanded when private bankers all over the West, especially as Jay Cooke's agents, became interested in the placing of war bonds.

It seems to have been typical of Middle Western business in the period that those men who had originally developed a full-fledged private banking business were anxious to incorporate their concerns. As soon as the Illinois Free Banking Act was passed in 1851 a good many of the state's private bankers, including Scammon, one of the leaders, converted their enterprises into Free Banks. Some years later Iowa private banking houses became branches of the State Bank of Iowa when the latter was brought into being, while others which were equally willing to do so were turned down. Finally, it will be described in detail that private bankers played an important role in the early years of National Banking being in many places the first prepared to join the system.[79]

In California private banking started during the period under investigation, but the beginnings were different from those in any one of the earlier American states. In California, as later in Idaho, the needs of the miners determined the start of private banking. They needed places for the safe keeping of gold dust which ultimately had to be exchanged against gold coin or drafts on Eastern banks. Just as in the Middle West, merchants turned bankers here also, but in the gold mining states they met the competition of assayers going into that business. Moreover the assumption of banking functions by express companies was characteristic of early California.[80]

IV

So little work has been done on the history of private banking that nothing but the crudest sketch can be presented for the years between 1860 and the outbreak of World War I. Two periods can be distinguished, however; one from Civil War days to about 1890, and another from 1890 to 1914. In the former period private banking not only flourished, but expanded rapidly; in the latter period it began to stagnate and even to decline. Statistical information which permits the study of this process in detail is extant.

It is known from official sources that in 1883 3,391 private bankers plied their trade in the United States and that they worked with a capital of $115,255,892. Regionally they were distributed as follows:

New England, 104   with a capital of $ 7,130,196
Middle States, 1,014   " "   "   "   62,193,765
Southern States, 293   " "   "   "   6,369,701
Western States, 1,786 " "   "   "   33,127,362
Pacific States, 194   " "   "   "   5,434,868
                                       ─────────────
                                       $ 114,255,892

The City of New York possessed 506 private bankers owning a capital of $51,758,575, followed by Boston, Philadelphia, and Baltimore with 61, 44,

and 35 private bankers, respectively (capital, $5,439,589, $2,206,728 and $1,126,738, respectively). Such cities as Louisville and Albany had 3 private bankers each with a capital of about $181,000 and $91,000,000, respectively.[81] The concentration of private banking in New York is self-evident. It was due in part to the fact that the stock exchange business resulted in the development of a special type of private banker, the Wall Street banker. He was essentially a broker financing his customers' security dealings and borrowing himself in the call-loan market. To be sure, some members of this particular guild, especially some of the early ones, like John Thompson and Henry Clews, had run a real private banking business.

The development of private banking from the 1880's on has been investigated by Barnett[82] on the basis of private sources. His figures do not tally with those of the Comptroller of the Currency, but they show the same trend. According to him there were in the United States:

in 1877   2432 private bankers
in 1888   4064   "   "
in 1899   4168   "   "
in 1909   4407   "   "

That is to say, the rate of growth between 1877 and 1888 was 67 per cent, from 1888 to 1909 9 per cent. But these figures do not present the whole story. They are in fact the result of two different trends: the decrease of the number of private bankers in the small towns was counterbalanced by an increase of what the former author calls "brokers' banks" (in New York called Wall Street bankers). In New York, Pennsylvania, and Massachusetts almost all, and in Illinois the majority, of private banks were "brokers' banks", and they were rapidly increasing from 1877 to 1909 (from 929 to 2264 in the combined four states). If the private banks of these four states are deducted from the totals given above one obtains the following, approximately correct picture for private banks in the country's rural areas:

1877   1503
1888   3050
1899   2647
1909   2143

They were losing ground continuously after the first half of the 1880's because of a growing preference of small banks for incorporation under state laws; the corporate form of organization giving greater security to depositors and an enhanced prestige to the enterprise concerned. Moreover, as a matter of course, the closing of the frontier put an end to that kind of private banking which the frontier had called into existence.

Private banking developed in post- Civil-War days in two directions: Wherever the frontier moved, private bankers appeared in communities too small as yet to provide opportunities for a state bank, let alone a National Bank. The enterprises of these men were originally very similar to those of the Middle Western private bankers of 1850 which have been described above.[83] Close contacts with the borrowers and the ability to judge men counted much in their business. Moreover, they had to be versatile, to make use of every profit chance, and if necessary to combine banking with other activities which their sophisticated colleagues in the East would have scorned. In the advanced sections of the country, on the other hand, the private banker specialized: he turned investment banker and as such we will study him in detail in one of the next chapters of this volume. Or he took a special interest in large scale mortgage banking making use of mortgage bonds, as will be described shortly;[84] or he developed ancillary enterprises, such as commercial paper houses; or he filled gaps in the existing credit structure (another subject of this chapter).

Under these circumstances the competitive situation changed. Except in the 1860's and early 1870's private bankers were not competitors of National Banks, unless the latter in a few large cities (New York, Philadelphia, Chicago) went into investment banking, and even in these cases there was cooperation rather than competition with the few National Banks active in this field. Since National Banks were then forbidden to lend on mortgage, there was rather some kind of division of labor between them and the private bankers. However, generally in the younger parts of the country and everywhere for small and medium sized mortgage loans, private bankers competed with state banks;[85] in this competitive struggle they were ultimately the losers.

Certain organizational features which had been characteristic of earlier private banking experienced a development during the period under investigation. First, large private banks tended to build branch organizations. Such branches were, as before, typically semi-independent enterprises with firm names of their own. In these branches all or some of the partners of the mother firm were part owners, and in addition, there were one or several managing partners who may or may not have had an interest in the parent organization. Jay Cooke and Company, Philadelphia, with branches in New York and Washington, provides an example for the early years of the period. However, a new trend can be observed in the 1860's and early 1870's. While earlier branch organizations of American private banking houses had been national in character, a few became international after the Civil War. The earliest case of this kind, that of the Brown concern, falls into a much earlier period: Alexander

Brown and Sons of Baltimore had an English branch of the type previously described as early as the 1810's, but for years they were merchants rather than bankers. However, in the 1860's J. and W. Seligman and Company took the lead in building an international branch organization: in 1862, i.e., the same year in which the banking house was established, it opened a branch in Frankfurt, to be followed in 1864 by one in London. The Drexels followed suit, organizing Drexel, Harjes and Company of Paris in 1867. Two years later Morton, Bliss and Company of New York set up Morton, Rose and Company of London; while Henry Clews became a partner in Clews, Habicht and Company of that same city. In 1870 Jay Cooke and Company set up Jay Cooke, McCulloch and Company of London; and when shortly thereafter the Drexels and Morgans formed their alliance which later became a complete merger, the Drexel-Morgan group had houses in London, Paris, New York, and Philadelphia. To be sure, not all private banks of first rank aimed at establishing branch organizations. Kuhn, Loeb and Company exemplify a house whose basic policy was to rely on correspondents; and Lee, Higginson and Company of Boston did not set up branches before the 1900's (1905: Chicago; 1906: New York; 1906: London to which must be added also a branch in Paris which could not be upheld).[86]

Secondly, as before, big private banking houses tended to have a large number of partners. To begin with Jay Cooke and Company again, in 1866 that concern consisted of the three houses in Philadelphia, New York, and Washington, each being a separate partnership with eight partners each. In 1871 it was reorganized as one partnership with eight partners; but its London house founded in 1870 remained a separate one with ten partners.[87] In 1912 the picture was still similar, as can be seen from the following tabulation:

J. P. Morgan and Company had   11 partners
Lee, Higginson and Company had   10   "
Kuhn, Loeb and Company had   7   "
Kidder, Peabody and Company had   5   "
  (its New York branch possibly)   7   "

Thirdly, there were still a few family firms among the large private banking houses of the period, but they became too big for that type of organization. J. and W. Seligman and Company and Kuhn, Loeb and Company conform closest to that description, although in the course of time these firms and others came to consist of a family nucleus to which were added outsiders if they had proved themselves valuable. This hold true also for the beginnings of the House of Morgan whose nucleus was by 1870 a partnership of father, son, and son-in-law.

The business of the private banker was radically changed by the establishment of the National Banking system. Previously "note shaving" had been the backbone of most of those concerns; but National Banking put a final end thereto. Many private bankers in the back country must have realized the situation at once and therefore joined the National Banking system at an early moment, as must be restated at this point.[88] Instead of "note shaving," mortgage banking now became the most important line for most of those who remained private bankers, especially for those in the back country. In the course of their mortgage business, the leading members of the guild, assuming an economic function of the highest order, imported capital from the advanced Eastern sections and even from abroad into the agricultural districts of the expanding West. A leader among these was Austin Corbin (1827-1896), one of the very first to found a National Bank. Through the agency of his firm, Macklot and Corbin in Davenport, Iowa, much Eastern capital was lent on the security of Iowa farmlands as early as the 1850's; and so important became this business that in 1865 Corbin moved to New York, establishing the house of Austin Corbin and Company, in 1874 styled Austin Corbin Banking Company. (Later in his life Corbin became to a limited extent an investment banker and a railroad reorganizer.)[89]

The kind of business which Corbin had practiced after the 1850's persisted for decades to come by moving West. The autobiography of George Draper Dayton[90] who (born in 1857) was thirty years younger than Corbin, shows how it was practiced in Minnesota in the 1880's. Dayton, a native of New York State, trained in a local lumber yard to which a private bank was attached, moved to Minnesota in 1883 in order to protect Eastern capitalists to whom one Thomas H. Parsons, owner of the unincorporated Bank of Worthington, had sold Western mortgages, bonds, and warrants. In 1884 with such backing he established the Minnesota Loan and Investment Company. It negotiated mortgages on farms in Minnesota, Iowa, North and South Dakota, selling them to Eastern clients. In some cases larger mortgages were broken up and 5 per cent mortgage bonds sold instead. The latter were issued in any amount desired, running for ten years, but repayable at the issuer's option after five years. By that time the Austin Corbin Banking Company of New York, mentioned above, was lending freely on mortgage at 12 per cent, and Corbin raised capital by reselling these mortgages all over the East and in Europe. But the low ethics of the borrowers proved a heavy blow to this kind of business and numerous farms and much farm land had to be taken over by the creditors. This was the situation when Dayton started in the business. He and his friends had faith in the future and

they bought abandoned farms and mortgages from owners in the East and in Europe, and carried them for years until new settlers were found by systematic advertising. These settlers, in turn, had to be aided for years; and when the farms or lands were finally sold to them, cash and live stock had often to be included in the sales price. In the 1890's the mortgage business of private bankers ran into another crisis and thousands of acres in South Dakota, for instance, had to be taken over. To get rid of the real estate all sorts of saleable goods had to be accepted in payment, or land in one section traded against land in another. Again it was necessary to develop farms, to build houses and barns, and then to sell to settlers on easy terms. It is clear that private bankers in their mortgage business competed with state banks and with incorporated and unincorporated mortgage-loan companies. But state banks and incorporated mortgage-loan companies could, of course, not go so far in promoting business as could private bankers.

Rural mortgages became occasionally the basis for mortgage bonds, and prior to about 1900 there were one or two houses in New York which specialized in their sale to investors. Thereafter numerous firms came to take an interest in this business which in consequence thereof experienced a new turn in the 1900's; local trust and mortgage companies creating such mortgage bonds, in order to find a market therefor, had to guarantee them. That is to say, they guaranteed certainty and promptness of payment of capital and interest, besides providing relief from the details of investment management. The services absorbed an estimated one-tenth of the income which would otherwise have been obtainable from such bonds by the investors.[91]

So much can be said about the private banker located in country districts and especially in those of the still undeveloped sections of the country. The business of the American private banker in the financial centers, on the other hand, can be reconstructed for the 1860's and 1870's from advertisements in the Commercial and Financial Chronicle. In those years, as before, New York private bankers were anxious to attract bankers' balances and they paid interest thereon. It is known, for example, that Fahnestock who then headed Jay Cooke and Company's New York branch solicited such accounts all over the East and in Canada.[92] John J. Cisco, his competitor, offered 4 per cent on daily balances to prospective depositors in 1868, subject to "check at sight." He was also prepared to issue certificates of deposit payable on demand, bearing the same rate of interest. Henry Clews promoted the same line of business. All of them competed with National Banks for bankers balances and also with respect to their collection business. Moreover the big private bankers of the 1860's and 1870's usually traded in gold,[93] at least on commission, but occasionally on their own account. Some of them bought and sold foreign exchange, as, for instance, Morton, Rose and Company who drew on their London house and collected through it. It was to participate in this profitable kind of business that Jay Cooke, who had previously made use of correspondents, established his London house. Duncan, Sherman and Company, to give a final example, advertised the issue of letters of credit for travelers in the United States and abroad and the arranging of commercial credits in Europe, east of the Cape of Good Hope, in the West Indies, and South America.

Some private bankers were active in the commercial paper market; or they acted as stock and bond brokers, private banking being often an "adjunct to the brokerage business in large cities," as Barnett expressed it; or they dealt in securities on their own account. The latter is true of James Gore King's Sons, Henry Clews and Company, and again Jay Cooke and Company who traded heavily and successfully in United States bonds.[94] Last but not least, some private bankers turned investment bankers. Of course these various activities can be found in all possible combinations and remained so during the whole period under investigation, although there was a trend for certain ones to be abandoned (the holding of banker's balances, for example), while others came into the hands of specialists, such as commercial paper houses and investment bankers.

The investment banking business as conducted in the period will be studied in detail in a later chapter.

Although closely akin to investment banking, the floating of mortgage bonds became a separate line of the banking business. A pioneer in this field was S. W. Straus and Company of Chicago. The firm was founded in 1860 as Straus Brothers and Company by Frederick W. Straus, a native of Rhenish Prussia, who in the late 1850's had started with a small merchandizing business in Indiana. This enterprise he sold out in 1869 in order to become a typical small town private banker, accepting deposits and making commercial and real estate loans. In 1882 he moved on to Chicago, launching there a small mortgage loan business, and this concern of his, which was incorporated in 1905 became the basis for the creative achievements of his son, Simon William Straus (1866-1930). The latter, prior to entering his father's business, founded and ran the Citizens Bank of Ligonier, Indiana, and after his father's death in 1898 conceived the idea of financing expensive buildings, especially skyscrapers, by splitting mortgages in-

to series of mortgage bonds and selling the latter to investors. His first issue of mortgage bonds of this type was floated in 1909 and the line became so important that the handling of ordinary mortgages could be abandoned.[95] The firm soon became the outstanding originator of real estate mortgage bonds. That creative achievement was implemented by a policy deviating from what had been traditional in the mortgage business: emphasis shifted from the safety margin (the difference between the amount of the loan and the value of property) to the latter's earning capacity. Earning capacity became the yardstick by which to measure the sum that could be safely invested. (The development of the business after World War I does not concern us here.)

The third field in which specialized private bankers continued to play a role was the commercial paper market. The modern commercial paper house is the descendant of the mid-nineteenth century bill broker, also since the 1850's called note broker. His line seems to go back to the 1830's[96] and this author thinks that the bill broker was originally, to a large extent, the product of legal interest requirements. When banks adopted the policy of going beyond the borders of their communities and especially to financial centers, discounting there promissory notes and bills of exchange in order to get around legal interest rates by charging "exchange", they were forced to use middlemen in purchasing such paper.[97] Growing from such beginnings bill brokerage reached a certain importance prior to the Civil War. In New York the business was then dominated by two firms who sold commercial paper left with them for "negotiation" on a commission basis. In Boston, which by 1850 possessed a commercial paper market ranking second only to New York, it was controlled by four houses; but more firms seem to have entered the field during the decade to follow. Gilmore, Blake and Ward and its successors were leading among the four houses; the firm did a general private banking business, including the dealing in foreign exchange and a few investment-banking operations.

After the crisis of 1857 bill brokerage was revolutionized by the newly-founded firm of Henry Clews, New York. He introduced, at least in that city, what has since become common practice, namely, the outright buying of commercial paper. Through this creative change in practice, he assumed for a short while leadership in the field in which he began to specialize.[98] (To be sure, his policy had been practiced earlier by Louisiana bill brokers.)

Up to the middle of the 1870's bill brokers had their main market in New England, the state of New York, and mid-Atlantic states, a statement which does not overlook the fact that commercial paper was occasionally sold elsewhere too, especially in

Chicago. From the middle of the 1870's on, the domain of the bill broker expanded continously until finally bill brokerage became national in scope.[99] While in the 1860's and 1870's bill brokerage was usually an appendix to a general private banking business or combined with security brokerage, the specialized commercial paper house made its appearance after 1880.[100] At that time some of the older participants in the business left for general private or investment banking.

The rise and the geographical expansion of bill brokerage in the years after 1875 are due to a large extent to the working of the National Bank Act. Both the rise of bill brokerage and the combination movement (which will be described in some detail later)[101] resulted from the clause that forbade branch banking, from the fact that the majority of National Banks were small ventures, and from their being prohibited by law to lend to any one borrower more than 10 per cent of their capital and surplus. When during the last quarter of the century, industry developed larger and larger aggregates and it became impossible for the latter to deal with one bank or even a few banks in the home town, many industrial borrowers were forced into the open market. Thus they contributed to the rise of commercial paper houses which as middlemen guaranteed the genuineness, but not the quality of their stock in trade. Many banks while customers of the commercial paper houses at the same time considered them competitors, which was not strictly correct. The fact was that the commercial paper houses stimulated competition between banks in various localities and thus brought an end to local monopolies or oligopolies. On the other hand they worked for the benefit of banks in small places which depended on one or a few local industries, sometimes seasonal in character. Such banks were enabled to spread their risk and to employ their funds the year round. (As a rule country banks are supposed to have bought commercial paper when rates were high, while city banks were in the market when rates were low, i.e., when they could not find other employment for their funds.) Once an open market of considerable size in commercial paper had developed, it began to grow aided by the efforts of commercial paper houses. Each new customer decreased his borrowings from earlier bank connections which now accumulated surplus funds. The latter, in turn, were ready to be invested in the money market and so helped the commercial paper house gain new converts for open-market borrowing.[102] By 1890, according to a contemporary source, bill brokerage had "become a distinct branch of the banking business and an important auxiliary to bankers." The commercial paper house was usually remunerated by a commission paid by the borrower, although it appeared as an outright buyer of the paper in question. This practice gave it the additional chance of profiting from a price spread. By 1910, after years of keen competition, the business was concentrating in relatively few hands, as can be concluded from the result reliably reported for about 1920.

V

So far, operations of private bankers have been discussed which were either traditional or grew logically from traditional policies. However, by 1900 some genuinely new lines were developed by private banking enterprise, established business providing patterns for such new developments.

Professor E. R. A. Seligman, for example, has pointed to the essential kinship of selling bills and notes receivable in the open market and the business of the modern finance company, also called credit company. However, the essential policy of the finance company drew its inspiration from the practice of inadequately financed enterprises which had no collateral to offer, of assigning to their banks certain accounts as the basis for loans.[103] Confidence in the debtor's unqualified reliability was needed for lending on this basis, but by 1900 it existed. By developing this basis shortly thereafter, the modern finance company came into existence. First established as a private banking enterprise, this type of business came quickly into the hand of corporations.

The creative entrepreneur who devised the new activity was one John L. Little.[104] When selling the Encyclopedia Americana on the installment plan in Chicago and experiencing a quick exhaustion of his funds, he conceived the idea of establishing a concern which would finance receivables. Encouraged by a recent Illinois Supreme Court decision on the question of wage assignments, Little, with the help of a lawyer, worked out a type of contract which provided for the collection of assigned accounts by the assignor as the agent of the assignee. It is in devising this so-called "non-notification" feature that the original creative achievement lay, later supplemented by a second, the issue of collateral trust notes against the deposit of the receivables. Prior to the elaboration of the non-notification contract, debtors had to be notified of any sale or assignment of their debts by their creditors. This, of course, precluded the development of a regular business of buying of and lending on receivables, especially in connection with installment selling, as conducted by the modern finance company. On the other hand, without the use of collateral trust notes the finance company would have been unable to raise outside funds and to develop large-scale operations.

After Little had worked out the basic idea, one Arthur R. Jones, acting as the creative capitalist, joined the creative entrepreneur. In the summer of 1904 he provided capital wherewith to start a new enterprise which bought book accounts from merchants, jobbers, and publishers. When Little and Jones were successful, they incorporated their business as the Mercantile Credit Company of Chicago. It was run as a closed corporation until 1908 when Little associated himself with one Melville Rothschild to found the National Trust and Credit Company. This concern built up a still larger credit business of the new type, while Jones went on with the original enterprise. The National Trust and Credit Company further developed the new business by financing installment payments, a change in policy which came almost imperceptibly. It was applied originally in financing the Indiana and Wisconsin canning industry.

Independently of Little's work, the finance company was brought into being also in 1908 in St. Louis by one Henry Ittleson, with businessmen from a local department store acting as the creative capitalists. Ittleson's new enterprise was styled the Commercial Credit Investment Trust. It lent on accounts receivable of jobbers and manufacturers and bought their bills, drafts, and notes receivable. By this time, the idea was taken up or conceived independently in the North East of the country by one Mr. Andersen (whose Manufacturers Commercial Company of New York, however, was not much of a success) and by A. E. Duncan who in 1910 started on a successful career in the new field, to become eventually the head of the Commercial Credit Company of Baltimore. Soon thereafter the new business spread. The underlying principle was first applied to financing real estate installments by one William E. Harmon in 1912.[105]

In addition to the finance company, the 1900's saw a new development also in the field of consumers credit. For the first time it was taken out of the hands of loan sharks to become a respectable line of business enterprise. This creative achievement was the work of a Norfolk, Virginia, lawyer, Arthur J. Morris. In his case the achievement lay in perceiving and providing for the need of small, though honest, borrowers, such as salaried men and wage earners, unable to put up tangible security, but worthy to be trusted and capable of repaying their debts in installments. Arthur J. Morris was born in Tarboro, North Carolina, in 1880, the son of a general-store owner. After having graduated from the University of Virginia he began practicing law in Norfolk and while specializing in corporation and financial law he came to grips with the problem of the credit need of small borrowers. Influenced by what he knew about European credit cooperatives which did business without requiring marketable collateral, he devised what has since become known as Morris Plan banking. This system was similar to its European models, especially the German Schultze-Delitzsch and Raiffeisen Kreditgenossenschaften and the Luzatti Banks of Italy, in that moderate sums were lent at moderate rates and on personal security. But they differed in that Morris built a business enterprise on the existing need, while the Europeans solved the problem on a cooperative basis. This implies as a further difference that under the American scheme anybody could become a borrower, while under the European plan only members of the cooperatives were benefited. However, membership in the latter is wide open. But there was also an element of Scotch banking methods embodied in the Morris Plan; namely, the requirement of two endorsers. The latter, however, under the Scotch system had greater rights than those under Morris's scheme. The two systems differ also, in that the Morris banks give no revolving credit with interest paid on the balance only, as was customary in Scotland; but interest and service fee were paid in advance and the loan was repaid in regular installments.

Morris put his plan into operation in 1907 in Norfolk, and when it proved extraordinarily successful the original venture was incorporated in 1910 as the Fidelity Savings and Trust Company of Norfolk. In 1911 for the first time another bank of the same character was opened in Atlanta, Georgia, the Atlanta Loan and Savings Company (capital $50,000); and after its success additional enterprises of that type were established: in 1912 in Baltimore, Richmond and Washington, and slightly later in Denver and New York. In this process of expansion Morris's funds gave out and he decided to create a holding company, the Fidelity Corporation of America. Finally in 1914 an elaborate organization was brought into being, capital being provided by several creative capitalists (T. Coleman Dupont, Charles H. Sabin, and John Markle).[106] It was styled the Industrial Finance Corporation. Endowed with a capital of $7,000,000 it was created to control local Morris Plan banks whose establishment on a large scale was contemplated.

As the scheme worked at that early time, borrowing and education for saving were combined: the installments of the borrower (2 per cent per week) were accumulated for the purchase of a saving or investment certificate "issued by the bank in the amount of the loan." When it was paid up, the borrower could conclude the transaction by tendering the certificate for his debt; or he could borrow thereon without endorsers and by meeting the installments of that new loan could become the owner of the certificate, i.e., a saver instead of a borrower.[107]

To sum up, while traditional commercial banking was rather sterile between 1880 and 1910, progress took place outside. It was brought about by individuals who organized small ventures in the form of partnerships to develop new lines of credit. But once success was achieved, corporations took over and further development was brought about within that organizational framework. To put it differently, progress achieved in the field of private banking did not lead to permanent growth and expansion thereof. It did not give private banking a new lease of life, but led to new lines of incorporated banking instead. By 1910, the great time of partnerships in banking was approaching its apogee.

Chapter XIV

PRIVATE BANKING

1. Pages 19, 46; page 19 must be held together with pages 23 ff.
2. Page 12.
3. IX (1854/55), 19. A writer in Hunt's Merchants' Magazine spoke in 1843 of "private houses;" see the quotation below on page 69.   Incidentally Jacob Barker called a "free bank" what we call a private bank. See Conspiracy Trials, 61, 62. In England the term "private banker" must have been much older than in America; the Barings used it in a letter of 1812; McMaster, op. cit., II, 241.
4. See the good formulation by the Handlins in "Origins of the American Business Corporation," Jour. Econ. Hist., V (1945), 22. The author cannot adopt Bray Hammond's interpretation of the term in his "Banking in the Early West," in ibid., VIII (1948), 16, footnote 47.
5. Laws of 1813, chap. 581 [LII] An Act laying duties on notes of banks, bankers, and certain companies; on notes, bonds, and obligations discounted by banks, bankers... See especially sec. 2.
6. Virginia was the first to adopt this policy; her restraining act was effective as early as Jan. 1, 1787; Griffith, op. cit., 169. In 1799 Massachusetts forbade to all but incorporated banks issuing of notes, taking deposits, and making discounts; see chapter 32, 1799 (May Session) An Act to restrain unincorporated banking associations and to prevent the issuing of small notes, approved June 22, 1799. As to the Restraining Acts in Pennsylvania, see Pennsylvania Archives, 4th series, vol. IV, (Papers of the Governors, 1785-1817) (Harrisburg, 1900), 826, 827; Journal of the 33d House of Representatives of the Commonwealth of Pennsylvania (1822/1823), 621, 622. For New York, see Cleaveland, op. cit., 234, 236, 237. Rhode Island passed a Restraining Act in 1805; Kentucky in 1812, and Ohio in 1815, see Stokes, op. cit., 280; Griffith op. cit., 178; and Huntington, Charles, op. cit., 266. Maryland had no restriction of note issue prior to 1842; Bryan, op. cit., 25. Incidentally, Upper Canada passed a Restraining Act in 1837 (Breckenridge, op. cit., 74, 75); as to the less stringent regulation of private banking in Lower Canada, see ibid., 49.
7. Curtius to the Secretary of the Treasury, 13. Incidentally, this item has been ascribed to John Taylor of Caroline County which from both content and style of the booklet seems to be entirely mistaken.
8. Barker, Letter, 6. A letter of 1811 of Fitz-Greene Halleck, the poet, then Barker's clerk, gives an idea of the latter's work habits; see Brigham, op. cit., 82.
9. Barker, Incidents, 123, 124, 130; idem, To the Public, 4-18; idem, Conspiracy Trials, 61-63; Niles Weekly Register, XLIV (1833), 353; Pintard, op. cit., I, 201; Publicola, Vindication (1818), 21, 27; Scoville, op. cit., I, 208, 214, 240; Dewey, State Banking, 144/145; Lanier, Century of Banking, 98; Paine, Laws, 23, 24. For the background, see Cleaveland, op. cit., xxxi ff; Paine, op. cit., 13-19.
10. See below, page 317.
11. Bankers Magazine, IX (1854/55), 21.
12. See vol. I of this work, pages 40, 41.
13. McMaster, op. cit., II, 241, 242; also Hidy, Barings, 50.
14. See below, page 316.
15. McMaster, op. cit., II, 344.
16. Sumner, History, 102; Brown in Jour. Econ. Hist., II (1942), 44, 45. McMaster (op. cit., II, 251 ff) reprinted the correspondence between William Jones, then acting Secretary of the Treasury, and Girard.
17. The preceding sketch is based on the books of McMaster, Herrick, Leach, Simpson (especially 114 ff, 144 ff) and the article of Brown in the Pennsylvania Magazine. (This author cannot agree with the conclusions drawn by the last-named author in the first and last paragraphs of that article. There was a close connection between Girard's loan contracting and his interest in the Second Bank of the United States, but only a loose and temporary one between those transactions and the banking house. It is entirely erroneous to mention Girard in one breath with the Rothschilds.)
18. Bank of Milwaukee, Minute Book, State Historical Society of Wisconsin; a microfilm is in the Baker Library of Harvard University.
19. Adam and Anderson, Aberdeen, to Wisconsin Marine and Fire Insurance Company, letter dated Feb. 9, 1852, preserved in the papers of the latter concern, State Historical Society of Wisconsin.
20. See Dailey, op cit., 11-14; James, Chicago Banks, I, 202 ff, 226 ff; Federal Writers Project, Alexander Mitchell, manuscript in the State Historical Society of Wisconsin; selected parts of the papers of the Wisconsin Marine and Fire Insurance Company preserved in the same institution, a microfilm being deposited in the Baker Library of Harvard University. An obituary of

Mitchell is in A.B.A., Proceedings (1887), 93 ff.

21. Another firm of old-style, note-issuing, private bankers were Jacob I. Cohen, Jr., and Brothers of Baltimore; see Baroway, op. cit., 365. Their small notes circulated even at a premium in Richmond in 1840; see Niles Register, LVIII (1840), 52.

22. See volume I, page 237.

23. Hidy, Barings, 200.

24. The contemporary term "note shaving" meant the exchange of one kind of currency for another at a discount, i.e., it connoted the business of the money broker and exchange dealer. This is evident from a letter of Lowndes to Calhoun, quoted by Starnes, op. cit. (1931), 97.

25. Op. cit., 162 ff.

26. The combination of exchange operations and the taking of "special deposits" (depositum regulare) is reported for Arkansas (after 1840); see Worthen op. cit., 114 ff.

27. Scoville, op. cit., I, 16.

28. Report dated Jan. 25, 1831 (for 1830), Assembly Document 59, 54th session, 1831, 5, 12.

29. Report dated Jan. 31, 1833 (for 1832), Assembly Document 69, 56th session, 1833, 14.

30. In the 1820's and 1830's Canadian banks used New York as a source of supply for specie and as a market for £ bills. Consequently, they held part of their reserves in the form of bankers' balances in that city; see Breckenridge, op. cit., 38, 83.

31. Neu, Irene D., Ph.D. thesis, 140, 141.

32. The following material contained in the Whaling Bank papers is published by permission of the Yale University Library, a permission which has been appreciated.

33. S. R. Smith to Morgan, Ketchum and Company, 44 Wall Street, Nov. 4, 1833. The letter is addressed to Messrs. Gersoner and Morgan, but an accompanying contemporary note says that it was directed to Morgan, Ketchum and Company.

34. Morgan Ketchum and Company to C. Billing, Esq., Pres. Whaling Bank, Dec. 18, 1833.

35. Scoville, op. cit., I, 10 ff, 243, 370.

36. The article on Samuel Ward in the Dictionary of American Biography contains the incorrect information that Samuel Ward was educated in the firm of Prime and Sands. That firm did not exist and the above presentation is the correct one. The New York Historical Society kindly made a recheck based on the New York City Directories. See also Prime, Temple, Some Account of the Family of Prime of Rowley, Mass. (privately printed, New York, 1887), 7-9; Lawrence, Ruth, ed., Colonial Families of America (New York, 1932), IX, 155-156; Hidy, Barings, 95, 109, 135, 213, 260.

37. See this volume, page 333.

38. The letter is reprinted in Hunt's biography of King in Lives, I, 199, 200. See also Clapham, op. cit., II, 164, 165.

39. For a recent example, see the article on James Gore King in Dictionary of American Biography: the gold loan "resulted" in resumption.

40. Op. cit., I, 302. It was then rumored that Prime, Ward and King had deposited American stocks to secure the loan. Diary entry dated Apr. 21, 1838. Recently Ralph Hidy has given an account of the transaction based on primary sources; see his Barings, 243 ff. This author disagrees as to his interpretation of the material which, however, is most valuable and used in the following presentation.

41. Tooke, Thomas, A History of Prices (London, 1840), III, 79-81; Biddle to P. Barett in Biddle's Letterbooks.

42. Hidy comments on that action as a defeat of Biddle wherewith this author cannot agree, except in so far as Biddle was forced against his better insight to fall in line with resumption at a much too early moment. But resumption was possible only through his brilliant, if economically unsound, financial operations, a strange and almost tragic situation. Early resumption blinded the contemporaries to the real conditions and led to a new crisis in 1839 and the long depression of the 1840's which might have been avoided by a more reasonable policy. It is difficult to understand why the Barings made the mistake of backing the policy of premature resumption. In 1837 they had estimated the American debt to foreign creditors to be £ 6,000,000, of which a certain part would never be collected, another part only over a period of several years, while $1,500,000 would be covered by the 1837 crop shipments. This left £ 3,000,000 to be provided for before cash payments could be resumed in the United States with safety. An earlier resumption would be hazardous because of foreign claims. This was exactly the stand of Biddle who had always been afraid of an immature resumption. Acting against their better judgment, the Barings helped to create a fool's paradise by contributing to confidence where continuing distrust was needed. As a letter (reprinted by Hidy on page 245) shows, all they saw was New York and not the United States as a whole. They had to foot the bill in 1839. In fact their policy in 1838 and 1839 paralleled Biddle's; they also became active in the cotton market, but unsuccessfully because of Biddle's pool; and they also indulged in facilitating an extraordinarily large import into England of American securities, which were unsound through and through.

Prime, Ward and King -- and this is the most amusing part of the story -- almost lost on the gold transaction, because they engrafted a private speculation thereon. While the gold was to be sold under the contract only against bills of exchange they took some of it and bought Ohio 6 per cents. They paid the gold nominally by bills on the Barings, de facto by a shipment of securities to be sold by the latter for covering the bills. But the price of the bonds declined before the account was closed. The only one who gained from this (in the view of this author) thoroughly "quixotic" operation was the Bank of England.

43. Hidy, Barings, 244 ff, 255, 260.

44. See this volume, page 333 ff.

45. See this volume, page 335.

46. As to the Clarks, see this volume, page 350; as to Cooke, ibid., page 355 ff; as to Barney, Larson, Cooke, 421, 422; and Holdsworth, Financing an Empire, II, 833 ff.

47. Larson, Allen, passim.

48. It is necessary at this point to clear up a mistake: Stephen Girard was not a merchant banker, as one can sometimes read. The essential feature of the latter's business was that mercantile and banking functions were fulfilled in one enterprise, the latter functions growing out of the former. This was not the case with Girard's concern. As has been shown, he built a banking business which remained a more or less independent enterprise with a firm name of its own located at a distance from the owning merchant's counting house. Many merchants were then members of boards of directors, but Girard, so to speak was the whole board himself. The fact that after Girard's death his mercantile business was liquidated, while his banking house was incorporated should prove this point, especially since no merchant banker ever issued notes as Girard did. He can be characterized as a bank-owning merchant, not as a merchant banker in the specific sense of that term.

49. Kent, op. cit., 21, 41, 44, 46, 47, 49, 108, 140.

50. See page 334.

51. Hidy, op. cit., 228, 260; Scoville, op. cit., I, 23 ff; II, 111, 112.

52. John Welles (1764-1855) was the cousin of Benjamin (1781-1860) and both were related to Samuel Welles (1778-1841) who headed the enterprise in Paris. John was a great Massachusetts politician and appears in the card index of Massachusetts legislators (State Library, Boston) as "merchant and banker." John E. Thayer is supposed to have been the firm's confidential clerk. See Shaw, Isabella Pratt, The Welles Family and Wellesley (privately printed, 1925), 23, 26 ff, 34.

53. Scoville, op. cit., I, 58 ff, 119 ff, 126; IV, 218.

54. For the following see, Hunt's Merchants' Magazine, VIII (1843), 79.

55. Lanier, Life, 17.

56. Hidy, Barings, 446 ff.

57. See this volume, chapter XXI.

58. Brough, "Banking in Mississippi," 340.

59. Jour. Econ. Hist., VIII (1948), 1.

60. Huntington, op. cit., (1915), 443.

61. Thom, op. cit., 33.

62. IX (1854/55), 23, 24.

63. See page 335.

64. In the 1850's he did business under the name of Ketchum, Rogers and Bement.

65. This has been described by Dr. Larson to whom we owe the detailed knowledge of the enterprise and whose research is the basis of the following description. Larson, Clark, passim.

66. See below, page 350.

67. Hedges, op. cit., 74, 81.

68. Preston, op. cit., 62, 63.

69. Interesting material on Southern conditions are to be found in Atherton, op. cit., 28, 54, 55, 72, 112 ff, 177.

70. Kent, op. cit., 127.

71. Larson, Cooke, 52, 53; Cochran-Miller, 76.

72. Preston, op. cit., 52; James, Chicago Banks, 201, 443.

73. Ibid., 663 ff, 667 ff; as to Cincinnati, see Bankers' Magazine, V (1850/51), 882.

74. For the following, see Preston, op. cit., 48-56 and Loehr, op. cit., passim.

75. In the State of New York the private banker issuing interest-bearing transferable certificates of deposit competed with savings banks; see vol. I of this work, page 229.

76. James, Chicago Banks, 200.
This offer should be compared with one made in 1830 by the Farmers Fire Insurance and Loan Company of New York: It offered to receive money "in trust" and issue certificates therefor. No deposit under $100 would be received and none for periods under two months. Interest at the rate of three percent would be paid on money deposited for less than four months; four per cent for money deposited for more than four months, but less than one year. For deposits to be left for more than one year the interest would be agreed upon. Money not withdrawn when due, would remain deposited for an additional period of no less than 30 days. Interest was due when the deposits were withdrawn unless this "trust" exceeded one year. See Perine, op. cit., 26, 27.

77. Esarey, op. cit., 284.

78. James, op. cit., 340.

79. James, op. cit., 216 ff and especially the list on page 220; Preston, op. cit., 134; this volume, pages 110, 111.

80. Wright, Banking in California, 15 ff; as to Idaho, see Aldrich, op. cit., 13.

81. Comptroller of the Currency, Annual Report (1893), Appendix, civ, xlv.

82. Barnett, State Banks and Trust Companies, 207 ff, Table III, following page 250; the Comptroller of the Currency stopped reporting on private banks in the middle of the 1880's.

83. See this chapter, page 73. An example showing the high opinion in which private bankers were held by Western economists is given by Dorfman, op. cit., III, 74.

84. See below, page 77.

85. Barnett, State Banks and Trust Companies, 206 ff.

86. Pearson, Storrow, 100.
87. Larson, Cooke, 184, 304, 309.
88. See this volume, pages 110 ff.
89. Dict. Am. Biogr.; First National Bank of Davenport, 90 ff.
90. Op. cit., 14 ff.
91. Chamberlain, op. cit., 106/107.
92. Larson, Cooke, 226, 306.
93. See Cisco's advertisements and Larson, Cooke, 269.
94. Ibid., 227, 230; Barnett, op. cit., 206.
95. S. W. Straus and Company, op. cit., passim; Dict. Am. Biogr.; James, Chicago Banks, 966, 1386, 1387.
96. Albert O. Greef, in the historical chapters of his book, The Commercial Paper House in the United States, has tried to prove that it roots in eighteenth and early nineteenth-century practices. His presentation is erroneous, however, because he did not understand the historical sources which he used. In the eighteenth century, as is well known, wealthy merchants everywhere sold their signature to other merchants. It was a way of profiting from one's high credit rating, although in some cases the method deteriorated to become kiting. Middlemen were not used in this connection and there was no market for such paper. Moreover Greef has misunderstood the early nineteenth-century term "note broker." Note brokerage or "note shaving" referred to dealing in bank notes and not, as Greef thinks, to dealing by discounting in promissory notes and bills of exchange (see page 16). There can be no doubt as to the real contemporary meaning of the term, of which Greef himself is aware (see page 36, footnote). When these men bought promissory notes and bills of exchange, as it happened, (I stress bought, they did not discount) they did so because such paper represented domestic, and perhaps in a few cases foreign, exchange. There was in fact a combination of bank note shaving and dealing in exchange; the businessmen concerned usually called themselves "note and exchange brokers." Greef misunderstood badly the business of the Baltimore Browns who dealt in English exchange.

There was obviously a change in the terminology in the early 1850's. It is telling that the quotation from the Wall Street Journal of 1851 which Greef reprints on page 21 describes that incipient change.

Greef's first chapter is marred throughout by his inability to distinguish in the use of his sources between note broker in the sense of bank-note shaver and note broker, as the term was used from about 1850 on. Prior to about 1840 the term meant exclusively a bank-note "broker", after that time (probably not before 1850) is meant a bank-note broker or a [promissory] note broker (more often called bill broker) or a combination of both. This criticism is not meant to detract from the value of the later chapters.
97. Foulke (op. cit., 162) in contrast to Greef has a correct historical picture of the beginnings.
98. Greef, op. cit., chapter I, especially 22, 23, 31, 32; Foulke, op. cit., 100-102.
99. Greef, op. cit., 38 ff; Kingman, H.M., "On Commercial Paper" in A.B.A. Proceedings (1887), 45 ff.
100. Greef, op. cit., 112, 113.
101. See below, pages 186-193.
102. Greef, op. cit., 44-46, 49.
103. Prendergast, op. cit., 115.
104. See Seligman, op. cit., I, 35-38; Merrick, op. cit., 8, 9.
105. Academy of Political Science, New York, Proceedings, II (1912), 94.
106. The names of some of the early directors: Herbert L. Satterlee, Willard R. Straight, Charles H. Sabin (vice-president of the Guarantee Trust Company of New York) point to Morgan influence.
107. Herzog, op. cit., 12-19, 24 ff; Cycl. of Am. Biogr., Vol. E, 160; Seligman, op. cit., 39 ff.

Chapter XV

BANKERS AND CIVIL WAR FINANCE

While for the historian it is obvious that a new period of American banking was bound to begin with the Civil War, to the contemporaries the far-reaching changes which that conflict was to effect in the financial structure of the country did not become evident until it was well under way. So it was that in the early months of the war leading bankers and government administrators alike tried to handle the new financial problems in the traditional way. The principle laid down in the Subtreasury Act of 1846 -- divorce of government and banks -- was upheld, and the Secretary of the Treasury attempted to carry on along the lines by which his predecessors had worked during the wars of their regimes. Consciously or unconsciously the Secretary as well as the leading bankers followed a theory of war finance elaborated in the first quarter of the century, efficiently formulated by Albert Gallatin, and quoted by Biddle during a Congressional investigation in the 1830's:[1]

When a war takes place, and money is wanted to prosecute it, before individual capital is disengaged from the pursuits of peace, and before the war system of taxation becomes productive, as the war itself diminishes the active demand for discounts, the bank[s] [have] disposable means with which [they] at once suppl[y] the Government. This, when the war begins. As individual capital is withdrawn from peaceful occupations, it seeks investment in the funds, and the [banks] then sell the Government loan to the citizens, thus replacing [their] active capital, and preparing for the next loan. Or, if the citizens themselves wish to take the next loan, the bank[s] may make advances to them on the several instalments of the loan, so as to enable them to take the whole loan, and thus in succession during the war, or until the taxes defray its expenses. The benefit to the Government, then, is that the bank[s] [have] an accumulated capital, which [they] place at the disposal of the Government for its immediate wants, and [are] the channel by which the loans are diffused over the country. Now, as almost all banks that ever existed have made loans to Government, the operation does not appear in it-

self a very difficult or ruinous one. The whole matter is explained by Mr. Gallatin very clearly:

'We have not adverted (says he) to the aid which may be expected from that institution [Bank of the United States] in time of war, and which should, we think, be confined to two objects.

'First. The experience of the last war has sufficiently proved, that an efficient revenue must be provided before, or immediately after that event takes place. Resort must be had, for that purpose, to a system of internal taxation, not engrafted on taxes previously existing, but which must be at once created. The utmost diligence and skill cannot render such new taxes productive before twelve or eighteen months. The estimated amount must be anticipated; and advances to that extent, including at least the estimated proceeds of one year of all the additional taxes laid during the war, may justly be expected from the Bank of the United States.

'Secondly. It will also be expected, that it will powerfully assist in raising the necessary loans, not by taking up, on its own account, any sum beyond what may be entirely convenient and consistent with the safety and primary object of the institution, but by affording facilities to the money lenders. Those who, in the first instance, subscribe to a public loan, do not intend to keep the whole, but expect to distribute it gradually with reasonable profit.'

The last two paragraphs from Gallatin's Considerations of 1831 imply that Gallatin actually envisaged banks as having three (not two) functions in war finance, as will be clear once the quotation is completed. These functions were: first, to anticipate war taxation by advances to the government; secondly, to buy government loans for investment (1812 style); and thirdly, to finance loan contractors, as the Bank of England had done as early as the eighteenth century,[3] if the distribution of the securities by the former to the ultimate investor did not proceed as fast as anticipated. This type of operation was to be repeated at each successive loan. To quote Gallatin again:

> "The greatest inducement in order to obtain loans on moderate terms consists in the probability...that the subscribers [loan contractors] will not be compelled in order to pay their instalments to sell the stock and by glutting the market to sell it at a loss; and the assistance expected from the bank[s] is to advance on a deposit of the scrip, after the first two instalments have been paid, such portions of each succeeding payment as may enable the subscribers to hold the stock a reasonable length of time."

This was the theory of war finance held in America by 1860.

I

Federal loans, as will be described in detail, were floated in the decades preceding the Civil War by inviting bids and allocating the securities to the highest bidders. In line with this tradition the first loan of the Lincoln administration (6 percent twenty-year bonds) was marketed. It was authorized on February 8, 1861 and the first tranche was offered that same month. The highest bids, i.e., those from 90.10 to 96, were accepted and the loan was placed. The largest purchasers were Ketchum, Son & Company[4] and Reed, Drexel & Company, both of New York. Another eight millions were offered for public subscription in March. This time all bids below 94 were refused and only about three millions of the bonds were sold.[5] The Bank of Commerce in New York, under its president John Austin Stevens, was the largest purchaser. As early as December, 1860, Stevens, in line with the established policy of his bank, had come to the rescue of the discredited out-going administration by taking treasury notes offered for sale. Failure to raise funds would have forced the United States Treasury to default, and so Stevens, aware of the situation, increased his original subscription of 1.5 to 4.5 million dollars. But in March, 1861, when he once more tried to help by a large bid on the $ 8,000,000 tranche of that month his efforts proved vain.[6]

Thus in the opening months of the Civil War John Austin Stevens became the natural leader in war finance. He was well prepared for this role. The son of a prosperous New York importer, Stevens (1795-1874) belonged to the group of wealthy merchants and lawyers who founded the Bank of Commerce when the Free Banking Act was passed in New York in 1838. A few months after its foundation Stevens assumed the presidency of the bank which was expected to be a powerful institution and which under his guidance actually became for a time the largest bank in the country. From the beginning the Bank of Commerce took an interest in business with state and national governments. In the late 1830's and early 1840's it subscribed to securities in amounts which were considered large in those days, whereupon it became for a short while (in 1841) the sole government depository in the City of New York. With such experience Stevens was better equipped than any other banker to play a distinguished part in the trying days of 1861.[7]

Because of the failure of the eight-million-dollar tranche of March, 1861, another loan had to be attempted in April. As a matter of fact this time treasury notes convertible into 6 per-cent bonds were offered, with the expectation that they would bring better prices than bonds. (The policy was severely criticized by James Gallatin, as will be discussed shortly, who was fearful that these short-term obligations would come due at an unpropitious moment.) The notes were offered at or above par. Serious difficulties were avoided only through the intervention of Stevens. As reported later by Samuel Hooper, who himself helped in negotiating the loan,[8] James Gallatin opposed it in a meeting of New York bank officers and insisted that Congress be called in order to raise the rate of interest set at 6 per cent. Under his influence the bankers resolved not to take the securities; but after a resolution to this effect had been passed, both Chase and Stevens addressed the meeting and the decision was reconsidered. It was instantly recognized that without Stevens's intervention the loan could not have been placed at all and his "invaluable" services were publicly recognized. His Bank of Commerce again subscribed for the largest block; and incidentally, Jay Cooke, destined to become the financial leader later in the war, then for the first time took an interest in a federal loan. In May another tranche of the loan authorized in February, namely nine million 6 per-cent twenty-year bonds were offered, but the incoming bids were so slow that failure seemed inevitable. Since this would have affected the price of the previous issues, the New York Chamber of Commerce and the banks of New York and Boston came to the rescue. Such bankers as James Gallatin, August Belmont, Moses Taylor, George S. Coe, John Q. Jones, together with some business leaders, in other fields, like A.T. Stewart and William H. Aspinwall, advertised the loan.[9] In self-interest, they felt they must support the government in its effort to sustain its credit. The chief subscribers at this time were George S. Coe of the American Exchange Bank, John Austin Stevens of the Bank of Commerce, and Ketchum, Son & Company, all of New York. Simultaneously, treasury notes were offered.[10] For these Jay Cooke and the Drexels were able to secure acceptable bids, though they failed to do so for the May bonds. The low prices for the issues of that month indicated that government credit was declining.

Salmon P. Chase (1808-1873) was then the Secretary of the Treasury, and for most of the war time he was to play opposite whoever led in the business of buying and/or selling bonds and treasury notes to ultimate investors. Lincoln had appointed Chase Secretary of the Treasury for political reasons, not because he had any particular qualifications for this office. He was to represent in the administration the conservative wing of the Republican party, i.e., the antislavery Democrats. Chase brought to his task valuable experience in public life, ability as an administrator, and untiring industry. For years he had been connected with the bar in Cincinnati; he had been a senator for one term and governor of Ohio for two. However, up to his appointment as Secretary of the Treasury, his career had not given him financial experience, while his acquaintance with unsound banking in the Middle West had taught him to distrust state-bank issues. Hence the hope of harmonious co-operation between the Secretary and the bankers appeared slight.[11]

Chase's influence was first felt in the eight-million-dollar bond issue of March 1861, the failure of which was in a way due to his policy. Chase maintained that, in order to uphold the prestige of the country, government securities must not be sold below a certain price; whereas the bankers felt that they should be sold for whatever they would bring. They thought in terms of established theory. As late as 1841 Albert Gallatin had described the selling of government bonds at the highest price they could command as the correct procedure and he had added emphatically: "It is what every government which has any regard for its credit always does."[12] On the basis of such reasoning Chase's policy was severely criticized and the fact that, nevertheless, he stuck to it, later contributed to his conflict with the conservative banking fraternity. It necessitated his alliance with Jay Cooke, the only banker who knew how to implement that policy.

In the spring of 1861, however, Jay Cooke was not yet thought of as a saviour. But financial leadership was beginning to shift, first from John Austin Stevens to two of his New York colleagues, both of whom have been mentioned, namely, James Gallatin and George S. Coe. James Gallatin (1796-1876),[13] Albert Gallatin's son, had been in Europe when young as his father's secretary. (The diary he kept at that time is of considerable interest.) Then he wished to embark on a diplomatic career, but when this ambition did not materialize, by 1830 he and his brother became brokers. Their partnership lasted until 1838, when James succeeded his father as the president of the National, later the Gallatin National Bank. For thirty years he held this position, retiring in 1868 to go to Europe where he remained for the rest of his life.

At the outbreak of the Civil War Gallatin was a faithful supporter of the administration, having taken an active part in Lincoln's election. As late as May, 1861, he expressed complete confidence in Secretary Chase as the head of the Treasury, speaking publicly in defense of the government in both commercial and banking circles. On the other hand, Gallatin had his own clearly defined ideas of the financial policy that should be pursued, ideas that he expounded in two letters to Secretary Chase. His proposal was that the government should sell bonds at the market price, i.e., at about 86 to 90 per cent of par. This, he felt, would furnish the cash necessary for those payments that could not be met by treasury notes which he suggested also. The disposition of the securities was to be bolstered with efficient advertising through post offices and newspapers, the sales point to be stressed being the absolute security of the issues. Gallatin further suggested that whereas the treasury notes should be sold directly to the public, the bonds should be taken over by the New York banks for resale at such prices as would protect the latter against loss. Gallatin tried to impress on the Secretary that bank officers as trustees of their shareholders and depositors,[14] ought not to pay more than the market price even if the public credit suffered.

The idea of placing the facilities of the New York banks at the disposal of the government was a fruitful one indeed; but, with regard to the proposed method for floating the securities, Gallatin belonged to a world fast disappearing. His idea was that the government by taking bids at a fair market price (meaning at a price favorable to the jobber) would arouse competition among capitalists "to an enormous degree." Capitalists would outbid each other; the love of gain would be excited; and the large offers thereby obtained, by demonstrating the ability of the government to get larger amounts than were actually needed, would lower the morale of the enemy. European capitalists might perhaps be tempted to participate in the bids and thereby specie would be drawn into the country. Since money here and abroad was worth more than 6 per cent and private capitalists could therefore obtain higher rates than 6 per cent on undoubted security, interest on the bonds should be around 7 per cent. With the interest established at that rate Congress should authorize the Secretary of the Treasury to set a minimum bid. An extra advantage finding expression in the minimum price set for the loans (which was to be slightly lower than its value in the market) would, by promising gain, stimulate the sale. (One can easily imagine the orgy of bearish speculation which would have resulted from such regulation.) The New York Chamber of Commerce, as Gallatin pointed out, had estimated that eight hundred thousand dollars of United States securities were in demand outside of New York and Boston, while the demand in the latter cities was only about three million. These estimates were supposed to prove to the Secretary that only by disposing of the securities at a discount (i.e., slightly below market rate) would he secure the success of the issues. These arguments illustrate the thinking prevalent among the older generation of businessmen. They failed to realize that it was futile for the government to rely on the "spirit of competition" and the "promise of gain" in the struggle to maintain the Union. In this lack of vision on the part of the bankers lay one of the roots of the ensuing conflict between the latter and Secretary Chase.

Gallatin's suggestion that the New York banks be put at the disposal of the government has been characterized as fruitful, although his idea that they should take government bonds at market price has been criticized. By that time the Boston banks as a group were coming to the rescue of their state government under a different plan: Representatives of eleven Boston banks met in April, 1861, in the clearing house and voted "to tender to the Governor of [the] Commonwealth a loan of any sums of money he might require in the present emergency...to the extent of ten pr centum on the capital of each Bank." A written offer to that effect was immediately transmitted to the governor by a committee chosen for this purpose.[15] It is probable that this action became widely known. If so, it would explain why a far-reaching proposal made soon thereafter was addressed just to the Boston business leaders, Hooper, Haven. and Gray. (The first two were connected with the Merchants Bank of Boston, which headed the offer to the Massachusetts governor; the third will be characterized shortly.) The proposal was set forth in a letter written to the three by Washington businessmen who wanted the federal loan then under advertisement to be taken by New York, Boston, and Philadelphia banks.

The Washington proposal may have had a greater significance than so far has been ascribed to it: As early as May 7, 1861 Chase had suggested in a letter to Samuel Hooper that he "thought it possible..., in view of the peculiar exigencies of the present time and of the moral effects on the South

and in Europe of a negotiation at par, [italics mine] that the great moneyed institutions of Boston, Providence, New York, and Philadelphia might think fit to unite in taking this loan." That is to say, the idea which was to become the basis of the successful loan flotations of the summer and fall of 1861 was originally Chase's; and the Washington proposal may well have been a trial balloon: the Boston addressees were businessmen with whom Chase was already cooperating as his letterbook of the period shows.[16] It goes without saying that the Washington plan was immediately opposed by those bankers whose spokesman was James Gallatin. He denounced it as being impracticable and as going too far. He maintained that banks were not reservoirs of capital, but temporary channels that must keep their funds available for the needs of commerce and trade. What Hooper, Haven, and Gray thought about the scheme at that moment is not known; they were destined to play an important role shortly thereafter.

The man who took the lead among the leaders at this juncture was George S. Coe (1817-1896). Younger than Gallatin, his philosophy differed greatly from the latter's. Whereas Gallatin thought in terms of competition, Coe stressed co-operation. As early as April 23, 1861 he had written to C. H. Rogers, chairman of the Philadelphia Clearing House Committee: "The urgency of the present occasion calls for the largest co-operation in other cities."[17] The decisive moment for Coe to assume leadership came when, after the Battle of Bull Run, Chase went to New York to meet the leading bankers and to raise money. He had come to realize, as already indicated, that only by enlisting the whole-hearted assistance of the bankers could the loans recently authorized by the law of July 17, 1861 be floated and floated quickly.[18] At the same time the bankers were prepared to take large issues of government securities, having gone through a period of liquidation after the critical fall days of 1860, and, in consequence, having ample funds at their disposal.

The source of the incentive for the meeting between the Secretary of the Treasury and the New York bankers lies in the realm of the unknown.[19] Be that as it may, on the evening of August 9, 1861 an informal meeting took place at the home of John J. Cisco,[20] Subtreasurer of the United States, who during the preceding months had worked hard to make successes of the various security flotations. Here it was suggested, as modestly expressed by Coe, that the banks be organized into some sort of union, "into an efficient and inseparable body." As such they would be able to assist the government by "advancing the capital of the country upon bonds in large amounts" and by distributing the latter to the people, while in all other respects they would remain independent. The suggestion that a federation of the banks of the leading commercial cities of the Northeast be organized to assist the government was not new, as has been mentioned. But as Chase, presumably the author of the idea, had also realized, it must come from the banks themselves to be acceptable to them.[21] Thus Coe's merit lies in having adopted the proposal, in having presented it as one emanating from a banker, and in having presented it in a workable form. This he did by underpinning it, by fitting it into a framework of thought which earlier had been at the base of his well-nigh revolutionary action of 1860, the formation of a gold pool of the New York banks, which had welded these institutions into a temporary emergency unit.[22] That which he had succeeded in doing in one city, was now to be attempted on an even larger scale.

Coe's plan met with the approval of the banks represented and with interest on the part of the Secretary; and on the next morning "we met in a bank," in fact in the American Exchange Bank which Coe headed. In this, the first of the formal daily meetings which took place from August 10 to August 16, a definite plan was elaborated. It was decided to form a "league," a "confederated bank if you please," composed of the banks of New York, Philadelphia, and Boston.[23] It was agreed that the "league" would lend to the government fifty million dollars in coin at about par; and herein lay the great achievement. It would go on lending "indefinitely" (Coe) an additional fifty million whenever necessary. It was at that meeting of August 10 that the bankers tried to impress on the Secretary that it was imperative, in order to sustain the underlying coin basis, to withdraw funds by check only as they were needed. The fact that Chase, still laboring under the impact of his hard money ideas, did not take to this proposal was another cause of the impending conflict; and later the bankers, including Coe, were sorry that they had not made its acceptance an unqualified condition.

Immediately after the meeting Coe wrote to the Associated Banks (i.e., the clearing house banks) of Philadelphia and Boston, informing them of the outcome of the parleys: "that the subject of the United States Government finances presented to us by the Secretary of the Treasury in a personal interview this morning [was] referred to a committee to consider and also to confer with committees from Boston and Philadelphia, and that they [were] requested to report to an adjourned meeting of bank officers to be held on Wednesday next." The Boston and Philadelphia banks were informed that the "Committee of Finance" set up by the New York banks consisted of Moses Taylor as the chairman,

John A. Stevens, James Punnett, Thomas Tileston, R.W. Howes, James Gallatin, J.D. Vermilye, J.M. Morrison, John Q. Jones, and George S. Coe, most of whom have been or will be considered in this volume. Whatever business genius and leadership existed in New York banking at that time was included in this committee. Its chairman, Moses Taylor (1806-1882), president of the City Bank, owed his position among other reasons to the prestige acquired during the crisis of 1857, when his policy of keeping large cash reserves had made his bank impregnable. This proof of Taylor's good judgment had made him a few months earlier, in 1860, the chairman of the Clearing House Loan Committee which, in line with Coe's suggestions, issued the very first clearing house loan certificates; it now gave weight to his support of the plan of 1861. Once more the real leader of the committee was not its chairman, but Coe, who again remained in the background and co-operated closely with both Moses Taylor and John Austin Stevens.

The Associated Banks of Philadelphia and Boston responded to the call, and both cities sent their leading men to the conference. From Philadelphia came Singleton A. Mercer representing the Farmers and Mechanics Bank, then the largest in Philadelphia, John B. Austin of the Southwark Bank, and Joseph Patterson of the Western Bank. Strangely enough, the Boston delegation was not led by a banker, but by an industrialist, William Gray,[24] one of those to whom had been addressed the Washington proposal described above. Gray's position as the leader of the Boston delegation would indicate his active interest in promoting that scheme, the essence of which, as indicated, was embodied in Coe's plan which Gray was to present to the conference. The man who gave real weight to the Boston group, however, was not its chairman, but Franklin Haven.[25] President of the Merchants Bank, the largest in New England, and one of the founders and for many years the president of the Boston Clearing House, Haven (1804-1893) was a recognized leader among Boston bankers. Like John Austin Stevens, although in a different way, he had acquired experience in government finance. For almost twenty years (1837-1854) he had been the pension agent for Massachusetts; he had been instrumental in placing a loan for the Tyler administration; he had been an Assistant Treasurer of the United States (1849-1852 or 1853); and he had acted as the chairman of the Board of Commissioners for Public Lands in his state. From the foregoing account it will be seen that the largest bank in each of the three cities was represented by its president: the Bank of Commerce of New York by John Austin Stevens, the Farmers and Mechanics Bank of Philadelphia by Singleton A. Mercer, and the Merchants Bank of Boston by

Franklin Haven.

On the 14th of August the New York Committee of Finance, previously mentioned, held a short session with the Philadelphia and Boston delegates present as guests. There it was resolved that on the following day a joint meeting be held to which proposals of the Secretary of the Treasury would be submitted. The meeting, later called "Bank Conference," opened with Moses Taylor in the chair. The atmosphere was none too favorable. Government credit had been low even before the war broke out. Now, after the battle of Bull Run, the outlook was dark and the prestige both of the administration and of the army on the wane. Confusion reigned everywhere. While several months before no one had foreseen the proportions the "Rebellion" would take, now there were many who felt that it could not be subdued. To make matters worse, the assembled bankers thought of themselves primarily as businessmen and delegates of businessmen, as trustees of the funds invested or deposited in their enterprises. It appeared to these delegates that they were being asked to "depart from their usual and legitimate business and sustain the government credit and stand and fall with it."[26]

In the midst of this distrust and reluctance Joseph Patterson of Philadelphia rose and by an eloquent appeal swayed the meeting to the support of the government. Joseph Patterson[27] (1808-1887) had been engaged in mercantile pursuits until, in 1842, he became the president of the Western Bank. Even then he continued to be a dealer in anthracite coal and the owner of large colleries in Schuylkill County. Patterson was a founder of the Philadelphia Board of Presidents, one of the earliest American organizations to aim at regular co-operation among banks. When its first chairman resigned at the outbreak of the crisis of 1857, Patterson was asked to take the chair, and in April, 1861, he became a member of the committee which issued the first clearing house loan certificates in Philadelphia. At the New York meeting of August 15, 1861, this man rose to an opportunity. Realizing that the question was not whether or not to take government obligations, but only "in what form and what character to take them," he pointed out that if the bankers refused to buy government securities the administration would be forced to set the printing presses to work. Thereafter the banks would be compelled to take government paper money. Immediately Coe endorsed Patterson wholeheartedly and the efforts of the two men won the day.[28]

The delegates decided to take $150,000,000 of 7-30 Treasury Notes in three installments, namely in August, October, and December, 1861. In the words of the resolution: "The Associated Banks of New York, Boston, and Philadelphia resolved to take jointly at par 50,000,000 dollars in notes or bonds of the United States, with the privilege of taking at par additional 50,000,000 on October 15 and December 15 unless previous to these dates there should be a negotiation in Europe or a popular subscription to the amount required."[29] Having made this decision the meeting appointed a temporary committee to arrange and perfect a plan of action under the agreement, with James Gallatin as its chairman. Although the bankers had thus resolved to advance millions from their coffers they stressed their rather depressed mood by stating that "they did so without hope or expectation of profit....and they earnestly thought to obtain from the government the assurance that they should be indemnified for loss."

The New York banks ratified the agreement immediately and those of Philadelphia followed suit the next day, August 16.[30] In Boston, however, there were difficulties. On the 17th of August representatives of the Boston banks met in the clearing house to consider whether or not to endorse the action of their committee. William Gray, who had participated in the formulation of the resolutions of the Bank Conference, reported on the proceedings of the New York meeting. He explained that it had not only agreed to a subscription of treasury notes, but also on the allocation of quotas to the three cities: namely, New York, $30,000,000; Boston, $15,000,000; and Philadelphia, $5,000,000. It was their quota of fifteen million which was opposed by the Boston banks. Leaders of the opposition were James J. Carney, president of the Bank of Mutual Redemption, and Andrew T. Hall, president of the Tremont Bank, both of whom have been referred to before. These two men suggested that $10,000,000 represented a "just proportion" for Boston. Franklin Haven, the most powerful of the Boston delegates, attempted a compromise, hoping that the banks of Providence and other New England cities would make up any possible deficiency; but ultimately a motion to take only $10,000,000 was unanimously carried.[31] Even from the dry wording of the minutes, one can sense the grave disappointment and disapproval of Gray. He promised to communicate the decision of the Associated Banks of Boston to the New York Committee, at the same time stating that here his functions ended and that he would "not probably meet the bank representatives again. But he wished to say before leaving that the situation of the country so far as the government was concerned, as deduced from reliable information, was peculiar."[32] The danger created by the resolution of the Boston banks blew over, however, for the New York banks acquiesced by taking thirty-five instead of thirty million dollars of the treasury notes. The fact that they had little business at the time and large liquid funds at their disposal certainly played a part in their willingness to meet the situation.

Chase had tried to make attractive to the public the treasury notes contracted for, by having them bear $7\frac{3}{10}$ per cent interest, i.e., two cents per day per hundred dollars. He expected that this simple computation would stimulate sales. The bankers, on the other hand, anticipated considerable difficulties in placing the loan. Therefore both the New York and Philadelphia banks entered into important agreements among themselves by forming what may be characterized as embryonic syndicates. The agreements to be described forthwith are of special interest in view of the claim that Jay Cooke introduced the syndicate into the American investment business around 1870.

The Clearing House Loan Committee which had been appointed by the Associated Banks of New York in 1860 for the purpose of issuing the first clearing house loan certificates, had been revived as the New York Loan Committee at the outbreak of war, and George D. Lyman, whose role as the founder of the New York Clearing House has been examined, was chosen as the secretary of the new committee. To him as well as to Charles P. Leverich (1808-1876), then vice-president of the Bank of New York, and one A.S. Fraser[33] must go the credit for having worked out the implementation of the government contract which implied:

> "First. To apportion the award of the government loans among the banks in proportion to their capitals.
> "Second. To apportion the several payments made on account of the loans and the proceeds of sales of securities as made by the government for account of the associates.
> "Third. To receive from the Treasury Note Committee[34] and to hold for the associates the securities as received from the government, and finally to divide them among the banks as awarded to them pro rata to their several capitals.
> "Fourth. To divide and pay over at stated periods to the banks the interest accrued on the securities sold for account of the associates."

Such provisions, of course, point in the direction of a syndicate.

Actually a syndicate had been proposed on August 15 during the conference of the banks of the three cities by Joseph M. Price (1804-1868), president of the Oriental Bank and a prominent member of the New York Clearing House. His proposal, which was laid on the table, was "that the notes thus purchased shall be held in trust by a committee appointed for that purpose for the respective associated banks in the proportion that the whole amount of notes bears to the amount of capital, and that they [the committee] be empowered to dispose of the same, in sums to suit purchasers for their par value and accrued interest to date of sale."[35] Possibly under the influence of this suggestion the Philadelphia banks formed a genuine syndicate by resolving in a meeting on August 17 of the Board of Presidents that all sales of treasury notes were to be on joint account. Here, as in New York, the details were worked out by the Loan Committee, which had been set up in April, 1861, for the purpose of issuing the (first) Philadelphia clearing house loan certificates.[36] This committee apportioned the loan among the Associated Banks according to their respective capitals:[37] the Farmers and Mechanics Bank, for instance, had to take $835,000; the Philadelphia Bank, $750,000; the Bank of North America, $420,000 while the smallest amount ($60,000) was allocated to the Tradesmen's Bank. The other quotas lay in between.[38]

The New York banks set up, apart from their loan committee, the Treasury Note Committee mentioned above, the organizational features of which cannot be ascertained in their entirety from the material available to this author. It seems to have been a New York affair, originally and primarily established to supervise the actions of the loan committee. However, it also acted from time to time as the nucleus of a General Committee, i.e., an organization of the Associated Banks of the three cities, whenever it was joined by the representatives of the Boston and Philadelphia banks.[39] The chairman of the Treasury Note Committee was John Austin Stevens, undoubtedly the best man whom the banks could have chosen for the task: the elderly and respected president of perhaps the largest bank in the United States, who after years of experience with government securities had shown his goodwill toward the existing administration in the preceding months and, at the same time, saw eye to eye with the leading representative of a younger generation, George S. Coe.[40]

The General Committee represented the allied banks of the three cities in their dealings with the Department of the Treasury and coordinated the local committees. The first meeting held in New York in September, 1861, was addressed by the Secretary of the Treasury. At this meeting the Secretary, while gaining the backing of the banks for his policy, adopted their suggestions as to the management of the subscriptions. There are also indications that at this September meeting an agreement was reached under which the banks started at once to make advances on the second installment which was not due before October. The General

Committee was convoked again for the 14th, 15th and 16th of November of the same year, simultaneously with the second meeting of the Bank Conference which had become necessary because of suggested changes in the original plan: Instead of taking the third installment of the contracted $150,000,000 in treasury notes, the banks were asked to take $50,000,000 in bonds. Acceding to this request the Bank Conference (of November, 1861) resolved: "that we take at once from the Secretary of the Treasury 7 per cent twenty-year bonds of the United States at par in equivalent 6 per cent bonds. The existing option for $50,000,000 of $7\frac{3}{10}$ per cent three-year bonds [better: treasury notes] which will expire on the 1st of December proxime being extended until the 1st of January next." This resolution was not particularly well formulated;[41] it actually stipulated that the subscription of $50,000,000 be in 6 per cent bonds on a 7 per cent basis, i.e., at 89.3. The General Committee implemented this decision by an important recommendation: the banks in all three cities were to form selling syndicates for these fifty million 6 per cent bonds; the securities were to be retained undivided by the respective local committees and sold in the common interest. Thus the Philadelphia sales organization of August, 1861, described above, was adopted in November by the allied banks as the standard organization for the three cities.[42]

This decision indicates that by November, 1861, the sale of the securities had become the crucial problem. There had been a strange element in the original arrangements between the banks and the Treasury Department: the Secretary of the Treasury, while making an outright sale of treasury notes to the allied banks, undertook at the same time to sell them to the public for the account of the banks. Besides making use of the regular treasury officials he appointed one hundred and forty-eight agents, mostly bankers, to distribute the notes throughout the North.[43] Actually this sales organization sold $31,000,000 of the first $35,000,000 allotted to New York, and doubtless a corresponding percentage of the shares of Boston and Philadelphia in the so-called first installment (i.e., the first fifty millions).[44]

This policy of Chase's cannot be attributed solely to his desire to help the banks maintain the specie basis for their liabilities, but rather to avoid competition between government and banks in the disposal of the treasury notes and to secure to the people an equal opportunity with the banks in the participation in the loan.[45] In consequence of such intentions on the part of the Secretary, the allied banks of the three cities became first a sort of underwriting syndicate. For de facto they

guaranteed that the security issues would be taken over even if not sold to the ultimate investor. What distinguished their organization from a genuine underwriting syndicate was the fact that they financed the transaction. General Committee and local committees stood for the managers in modern underwriting syndicates.

However, since the sales organization of the Secretary of the Treasury did not work too well the banks were forced into considerable sales efforts of their own, especially when government sales began to lag after the disposal of the first fifty millions. In August, 1861, at the suggestion of the New York Loan Committee it had been agreed upon that no sales would be made below par. This hampered sales for some time, but a worse handicap resulted from the considerable delay in the actual issuance of the loan certificates. The first were not issued before late in January, 1862, and the last not before early in March. By that time they were already depreciating. However, in New York and Philadephia the securities could be pledged by the banks against clearing house loan certificates even before they were issued. This policy Boston refused to follow. Ultimately, to be sure, the delay worked to the benefit of the banks, since the market improved during the early months of 1862.

II

During the first weeks after the conclusion of the contract of August, 1861, both parties were gratified. The Secretary had borrowed large funds at what he considered a cheap rate, and these funds became available immediately; the banks, on the other hand, were able to utilize their idle resources. Neither had insight enough to grasp the inherent weaknesses of the plan, depending as it did for its success upon a regular flow of the paid-out coin back to the banks. Yet scarcely a month elapsed before a potential conflict loomed on the horizon, notwithstanding the fact that both parties were aiming for the same goal, i.e., the preservation of specie payments. Although the bankers thought that Chase was going to leave on deposit with them the amounts borrowed and draw by check only when bills became due, actually he withdrew the whole amount of the loans from the banks and settled the treasury obligations with specie. For this action Chase was much blamed; but he seems to have been justified. What the bankers really wanted was that their institutions should become government depositories, but despite their opinion to the contrary the law of August, 1861, did not entitle the Secretary to make them such. The Act supplementary to an Act entitled 'An Act to authorize a National Loan and for other purposes'[46] was worded very unfortunately. It reads as follows:

that the provisions of the act entitled: An Act to provide for the better organization of the Treasury....passed August 6, 1846 be, and the same are, hereby suspended so far as to allow the Secretary of the Treasury to deposit any of the moneys, obtained on any of the loans now authorized by law, to the credit of the Treasurer of the United States in such solvent specie-paying banks as he may select; and the said moneys so deposited may be withdrawn from such deposit for the deposit with the regular authorized depositories, or for the payment of public dues, or paid in redemption of the notes, authorized to be issued under this act or the act to which this is supplementary.

One sees from the text of the act that the Secretary was entitled to leave with the banks the monies raised by loans, but he was not entitled to deposit internal or customs revenue with such banks; and only in this latter case would things have worked out as the bankers hoped. It was unreasonable to blame the Secretary for his actions, since it was Congress, not he, who was responsible for this half-hearted measure. Had the Secretary done as the banks wished, within the framework of this law, the development toward suspension would at best have been delayed only for a few months.

However, even the withdrawal of specie from the banks would not have wrought much harm during the first period of the war, had there not been two additional sources of trouble. The fact that the banks could pay for a second and a third loan, and even prepare for a fourth, each of $50,000,000, shows that the disbursed specie was actually flowing back to them. The chain was broken only because the Secretary was issuing demand notes while the loan transactions were under way. These demand notes added to the existing circulation medium and were paid into the banks in lieu of specie while the specie was hoarded for lack of confidence. These facts led to a severe shortage of coin in December, 1861, when the Trent affair brought the Union near to war with Great Britain. The alarm occasioned by this event followed on the heels of the disappointment created by the publication of the Annual Report of the Secretary of the Treasury. The lack of a definite tax policy certainly warranted criticism; but in accusing the Secretary of stupidity, James Gallatin, who in those days was gradually becoming the spokesman for the banks, showed that he did not understand the true nature of the situation. This can be seen from the fact that as early as December 9, 1861 he had advocated stopping payments on the pending loan, since Chase had broken the agreement

by proposing a tax on bank notes.[47] Actually it was impossible to finance the Civil War without creating additional purchasing power. Gallatin claimed that the Secretary did not realize that the banks could have supplied bills of exchange, certificates of deposit, drafts, and checks to any amount if the circulation proved inadequate for the increased government disbursements.[48] But Gallatin did not grasp that this, too, would have been inflation: it would have been credit instead of money inflation, created by the banks instead of by the government.

Gallatin's writings are not the only contemporary source from which to learn how the conflict between the Secretary and the banks developed, and how it was mirrored in the minds of the leaders of the banking fraternity. John Earl Williams (1804-1877),[49] president since 1857 of the then important Metropolitan Bank of New York, wrote a letter to Secretary Chase on October 4, 1861 which clearly shows how the differences of opinion turned into a conflict. Williams wrote:

> What you seem to regard as a dangerous element, the bank officers look upon as essential to their safety. What you think would guard against suspension of specie payments, they think most likely to precipitate that demoralizing calamity. What you claim for the Sub-Treasury, they ask for the banks -- the disbursement of all United States funds. While you regard the payment of public dues in bank notes, convertible at the pleasure of the holder into coin, as an evil to be avoided, they hold it as convenient and safe a mode of discharging public obligations as it is, private debts....And inasmuch as the law was made to give the banks this advantage, they feel they have a right to demand it.

It is doubtful if Williams had ever read the law. If he had done so he certainly had not understood it; otherwise, he could not have claimed that the banks had the right to disburse all government funds, for the pertinent clause of the act did not give them this right. In his anger Williams even lost the sense of proportion. After having praised Chase for his courteous and considerate treatment of the banks he turned on the Secretary, whom he, like Gallatin, considered stupid:

> Yet in truth it may be said that for a man of his [Chase's] brain power his business capacity was comparatively moderate. He undoubtedly was learned in the law, skilled in political combinations, at home in Blackstone's Commentaries and in Euclid's problems. But the mysteries of the clearing house always seemed to surpass his comprehension.[50]

The good intentions of the conservative bankers cannot be questioned, and undoubtedly they rendered a great service to their country in the summer of 1861. However, because of their conservative outlook, they were unable to understand the situation in its entirety and so were unsuited for permanent financial leadership in the national crisis. It has been shown from the letter of John Earl Williams, quoted above, how the difference of opinion was stated clearly as early as October, 1861. During the September conference of the General Committee some of the bankers requested that the second installment of $50,000,000 be lent only if the Secretary stopped issuing demand notes and started drawing checks on the banks. Their opinion did not prevail, however, because just at that moment specie had begun flowing back to the banks at a rapid rate.

Later Gallatin submitted to Chase a program whose main points were reiterated during the ensuing conflict:

1. The government should issue notes in small denominations of 5, 10, and 20 dollars, bearing interest and convertible into twenty-year bonds, such notes to be used in paying contractors and purveyors.

2. Bonds should be sold at the market price, i.e., at the best price obtainable in the market.

3. The government should draw checks on the banks for the proceeds of the loans.

4. Taxation should be increased.

When the New York bankers could not induce the Secretary to adopt this program they first turned cool and later became actually hostile. The Philadelphia banks remained more friendly. On September 23, for instance, they expressed "their judgment as opposed to a request made to the Secretary of the Treasury to suspend or discontinue the emission of treasury demand notes, believing that the judicious and restrained use of said notes will not be prejudicial, but beneficial, to the design of the Treasury and the Banks."[51]

On December 28, 1861 the New York banks decided to suspend specie payments. James Gallatin, by now definitely the leader of the disappointed New York bankers, used the opportunity to make a long and violent speech. He accused the Secretary of having refused a fair market price for funded stock, of having issued demand notes, and of not having drawn checks for the proceeds of the loans. The Secretary, so Gallatin stated, had been warned that if he continued to pursue this policy he would force the banks into suspension. As matters stood, they were now loaded down with government bonds and, with their capital thus tied up, they were unable to assist the government any further. The only question left was who was to be the first to suspend: government or banks. There was something to this point of view; but Gallatin's subsequent proposals were unrealistic and doomed to failure. He demanded not only that the government should call in and cancel the demand notes already in circulation, but also rule out any further issue of government paper money. Chase had already refused to accede to this request, since neither the banks nor anyone else could provide the coin necessary to move the increased production; and, in fact, he preferred government issues to bank money, once it was necessary to go off the metallic standard.[52]

About two weeks after suspension a commission of the Associated Banks of the three cities went to Washington. On January 11, 1862 it met informally with the Secretary of the Treasury, the Ways and Means Committee of the House, and the Finance Committee of the Senate. Chase himself fostered the meeting of the bankers with the Congressional committees, in the hope that a feasible plan would be worked out. Since co-operation had given way to dissension and since Gallatin had led the movement toward suspension, he was the natural spokesmen of the bankers at this moment, though a man of much lower caliber than either Coe or Stevens. Gallatin's suggestions contained little that was new, and, in general, followed the lines of his earlier proposals: viz., heavy taxation to insure confidence in the ability of the government to pay the interest on the loans; sale of long-term bonds at the market price, which he expected to become favorable again after the introduction of adequate taxation; cessation of the issue of demand notes; issue of one hundred million two-year treasury notes, receivable for most government dues; suspension of the Sub-Treasury Act so that banks could become government depositories; and, finally, authorization of temporary loans, secured by pledges of government stock. To Chase, of course, these proposals were inacceptable, and Hooper and Spaulding of the Ways and Means Committee of the House expressed their dissent "decidedly".[53] The final rebuff, it should be noted, was administered to the bankers by the hand of a colleague, the Buffalo banker Elbridge Gerry Spaulding, who for a brief period was becoming the financial leader of the country. He objected to any "shinning" of the government through bankers and speculators, and to the knocking down of government "stock," which would be unavoidable if it were sold without price limitation. He stressed his contention that demand notes were at least no worse than unredeemable bank paper.

Under these circumstances, James Gallatin tried to avoid an open rupture by patching up a compromise with the Secretary of the Treasury. Under an "arrangement" of January 15, 1862 the banks were to receive and pay out freely the demand notes already authorized; this they had not done in the past.[54] In return the latter were not to be made legal tender and no further issues were to be authorized. Instead, Congress was to legislate the issue of 3.65 per cent one-year treasury notes to be exchanged for demand notes and convertible into 7-30 treasury notes. At least twenty millions of the 7-30 treasury notes already issued were to be used for paying public creditors. A National Currency Act, as already drafted, was to be passed. The idea back of this compromise was that the banks would accept the existing demand notes in good grace and agree to Chase's and Spaulding's pet scheme of a national currency based on United States government stock. The government, on its part, was to relieve the Associated Banks from some of their obligations, to stop issuing additional demand notes, to drop the plan of issuing legal tender notes, and to float long-term loans at the market price instead. This last suggestion, however, was inacceptable to the Congressional Committees. Consequently the compromise fell through and it was no longer possible to avoid an open break between the banks and the government.

A short interlude followed during which leadership was surrendered to the Ways and Means Committee. The sudden and unexpected suspension of specie payments bewildered Chase, who without practical financial experience of his own and imbued with hard-money ideas was now at a complete loss. Then, as indicated above, Elbridge Gerry Spaulding assumed leadership. He was the chairman of the sub-committee of the Ways and Means Committee charged with preparing the pending loan bills. In that capacity he drafted the legal tender bill and carried it through Congress.

It is one of the ironies of history that Spaulding, a New York country banker, became the financial leader of the country because the city banks were unable to retain leadership, and the responsible Secretary of the Treasury was too inexpert to keep the reins. In this situation it was the country banker who sponsored just that measure which the city bankers had dreaded and which through months

of co-operation with the government, they had tried to avoid: viz., the use of irredeemable government paper money as the legal tender of the nation. Of course, neither the city bankers, nor Spaulding, nor the Congressmen who voted for the Legal Tender Act believed that the war could be financed by paper money alone. Further loans would have to be floated, and when this point was reached Chase took back the reins, working in close cooperation with Jay Cooke.

The conflict described in the preceding pages was due to disagreement on two problems: the type of additional purchasing power which was to be issued and the method of floating government bonds. The city bankers expected first that the war could be financed like the Mexican War which they all remembered; but it was in fact one of the early modern mass wars which, like all its successors, could be financed only by the creation of purchasing power. When this fact was sensed by the Secretary and Congressional leaders as well as by the bankers, the decisive question became who should create the additional purchasing power, government or bankers. The bankers wanted the latter, Chase and Spaulding the former. The latters' choice, which prevailed, led to irredeemable government paper money; the alternative would have led to irredeemable bank notes.

With regard to the second problem, the bankers reared and living in an era of high capitalism took it for granted that even during the war business would go on as usual and that the market should decide on the value of the securities wherewith to finance the struggle. It was their legitimate function, so they felt, to finance the government by using the market mechanism. Chase, on the other hand, did not reason along these lines, and both he and Spaulding were aware of the dangerous political consequences of permitting the functioning of a public barometer to measure the falling government credit. Since the conservative bankers were unable to propose a way acceptable both to themselves and the political leaders of the country, financial leadership shifted in the later course of the Civil War to an outsider who knew the answer.[55]

Chapter XV

BANKERS AND CIVIL WAR FINANCE

1. U.S. 22nd Congr. 1st sees., House Report 460
   360,361. Biddle refers, of course, to the Second
   Bank of the United States. However, in replacing the words "bank" or "institution" (referring
   to the Bank of the United States) by "American
   banking system", one arrives at the theory held
   in 1860.
2. Writings III, 346.
3. Clapham, op. cit., II, 148.
4. During the early war-period the firm of Ketchum,
   Son and Company experienced a rather meteoric
   rise. The banking house guided by Morris K.
   Ketchum seems to have existed since the 1830's,
   Junius Spencer Morgan having been a partner for
   a short time (Gras and Larson, op. cit., 547).
   It was one of the many banking houses which
   originated from brokerage firms and by 1845
   was styled Rogers, Ketchum and Bement. Morris
   Ketchum himself was by that time an investor in
   several railroads (the Housatonic and the Hartford and New Haven) and was closely connected
   with the New York and New Haven on whose
   board he had a seat. However, to the knowledge
   of the author not before the end of the 1850's
   did the name of Ketchum appear on the lists of
   subscribers for government security issues.
   A firm Ketchum, Howe and Company (presumably
   the same concern) successfully bid on the United
   States treasury notes of 1858; (Bankers Magazine,
   XIII [1858/59], 16). In 1861 Ketchum, Son and
   Company were heavy subscribers to the bond
   issues of February and May; and in the years to
   follow the firm was generally regarded as strong.
   In 1864, for instance, in alliance with John
   Thompson and other New York firms the
   Ketchums were bidding for the 5-20's of that
   year. The firm enjoyed prestige with the Department of the Treasury and had very good connections, J.P. Morgan being a close friend of young
   Ketchum. So late in the fall of 1864 the Secretary
   of the Treasury, Fessenden, attempted to induce
   Cooke and Ketchum to form an alliance for the
   purpose of selling 5-20's and 7-30's. The proposal came to naught, however: Ketchum is
   supposed to have depressed the market in government bonds in order to get a more favorable
   contract, while Jay Cooke tried to raise the
   prices. The latter refused to cooperate, while
   the former declined the business on the proposed
   conditions. The firm broke down in 1865 because young Edward B. Ketchum forged gold
   certificates, i.e., gold checks drawn on the Bank
   of New York, the special depository of the gold
   brokers, checks which were customarily used
   as collateral for loans. The fraudulent certificates had been hypothecated with the Importers
   and Traders National Bank. On top of that Edward
   Ketchum had stolen securities from his own firm.
   Young J.P. Morgan had certainly not displayed
   good judgment when becoming a partner of
   Edward Ketchum in at least two deals, even
   though they were concluded with profit. See
   Larson, Cooke, 100, 101, 104, 163, 164; Bankers
   Magazine, XX (1865/66), 250 ff, 742; Oberholtzer, op. cit., I, 451, 459; Kirkland, op. cit., 259.
5. At that early moment of the war bankers were
   probably held back by the belief that large government loans could not be floated in America.
   Samuel Hooper had written in 1855: "It is impossible under the present system of currency
   and banking in the United States that any large
   loans can ever be negotiated at home. The pro-
   spect, only, of a large loan would at once produce
   a panic in the money market. The banks would
   immediately stop discounting, to be prepared to
   pay back their deposits. By so doing they would
   make money so scarce and raise the rates of
   interest so high that the capitalists who own
   those deposits could do better with their money
   than to take the proposed loan.
   "The moment any accumulation of money occurs
   it is deposited in the banks and is used by them
   to increase their loans. The majority of the
   bank directors are usually active business men
   and the largest borrowers of the banks. It is for
   their interest to prevent large government loans
   being negotiated at home, as they know, in that
   case, that the banks must provide the money
   by reducing their loans..." This would result in
   so high a rate of interest that the loan could be
   obtained on better terms abroad. (Currency and
   Money, 64.)
6. Larson, Cooke, 100 ff; Mitchell, Wesley C., op.
   cit., 10 ff; Oberholtzer, op. cit., I, 126,127,133.
   Examples of bids of the Bank of Commerce and
   John A. Stevens on earlier public loans can be
   found in this volume, pages 344, 346, 349, 389.
7. Guaranty Trust Company of New York, One
   Hundred Years of Banking Service, 1839-1939,
   12, 13, 16, 17.
8. Hooper, speech of 1864, 4; the passage in question
   contains an error as to the interest rate. See
   also Mitchell, op. cit., 12 and Death of Samuel
   Hooper, 37.

9. Hunt's Merchants' Magazine, Vol. XLIV (1861), 791. American Annual Cyclopedia, 1861, 297.
10. Chase's private letterbook of this period gives a good idea of the financial situation in the spring of 1861.
11. Mitchell, Wesley C., op. cit., 3,4.
12. Suggestions in Writings, III, 414.
13. Obituaries, New York Daily Tribune, May 30, 1876, 4, col. 6; The World, May 30, 1876, 5, col. 5. Adams, Henry, The Life of Albert Gallatin, 632; Gallatin, James, Two Letters to Hon. S.P. Chase, Secretary of the Treasury (1861).
14. Exactly this phrase can be found as early as 1841 in Nathan Appleton's Remarks, 19.
15. Gras, op. cit., 510-512
16. Chase's private letterbook, National Archives.
17. As to Coe see this volume Appendix. The letter of April 23, 1861 is preserved in the Historical Society of Pennsylvania.
18. Finance Report for 1861, 8.
19. For the following see Coe's speech before the Convention of the American Bankers Association in Proceedings (1877), 24, 25 and his letter of October 8, 1875 to E.G. Spaulding in the Extra-sheets to Spaulding's History of Legal Tender Paper Money (Buffalo, 1875), 89 ff. See also "The Government Loans of August 1861" in Bankers Magazine, XVI (1861/62), 161 ff; "The Banks in 1861" in ibid., XLI (1886/87), 363 ff; A.B.A., Proceedings (1886), 111 ff ("The Banks and our War Finance"); "Report of the Loan Committee of the New York Banks" in U.S. 37th Congr. 3d sess., House Executive Document 25; Minutes, Board of Presidents, Philadelphia (Philadelphia Clearing House).
20. As to Cisco, see this volume, Index.
21. Letter to Samuel Hooper of May 7, 1861; Chase's private letterbook, National Archives.
22. See this volume, pages 160 ff.
23. The original idea of including the State Banks of Ohio and Indiana had to be discarded.
24. William Gray (1810-1892), a Harvard graduate, was a cloth manufacturer who was very active in the affairs of his city and his alma mater (Harvard University Archives).
25. Gray and Haven were accompanied by John Amory Davis, president of the Suffolk Bank, and James H. Beal, president of the Granite Bank, then a comparatively young man, but destined to become a leader in Boston finance later.
26. "Report of the New York Loan Committee," 134.
27. Obituary in A.B.A., Proceedings (1887), 98 ff; Appleton's Cyclopedia of American Biography; Minutes of the Philadelphia Board of Presidents. A speech of Patterson can be found in A.B.A., Proceedings (1877), 52 ff.
28. Coe seems to refer to this episode when stating that hesitation was removed by the question: "What if we do not unite?" Spaulding, History, Appendix, 91. See also Bankers Magazine, XLI (1886/87), 365 ff. The part Patterson played on

this occasion was not forgotten. The offices of the Comptroller of the Currency and of the Assistant Treasurer of the United States were later tendered to him, but he did not accept. He was repeatedly consulted by Chase.
29. Moses Taylor and James H. Beal of Boston advocated subscribing the whole amount of $150,000,000 at once, but were unable to persuade the others to this view.
30. A folder containing the agreement and dated August 15, 1861 signed by the directors of the Bank of North America is pasted into the minutes of the board after the entry of Aug. 22.
31. The implementation of the arrangements is reflected in the minutes of the board of directors of the Massachusetts Bank; see Gras, op. cit., 513 ff.
32. "The Boston Bankers and the Government Loan," in Bankers Magazine, XVI (1861/62), 169, 170.
33. "Report of the New York Loan Committee," 127; obituary of Leverich in New York Daily Tribune, Jan. 11, 1876. No dates on Fraser could be found.
34. See below page 91.
35. Bankers Magazine, XVI (1861/62), 163, 164. An obituary of Price is in the American Annual Encyclopedia for 1868 (New York, 1869), 585.
36. The committee included C.H. Rogers, president of the Tradesmen's Bank, E.M. Lewis, representing the Farmers and Mechanics Bank, Joseph Patterson and John B. Austin, mentioned before as delegates of the Philadelphia banks to New York, and B.B. Comegys, who later became president of the Philadelphia Bank.
37. The second $50,000,000 was not apportioned according to capital, but according to resources.
38. The minutes of the Boston Clearing House Association and Clearing House Committee are silent on these transactions. Since Boston at that time had not yet adopted the clearing house loan certificate, and consequently had no loan committee, there may have been some organizational difficulties.
39. This is deduced from the Minutes of the Philadelphia Board of Presidents, August 20, 1861. The "Report of the New York Loan Committee" (page 127) speaks of the "treasury note committee of the banks of the three cities associated." However the report of the Treasury Note Committee was signed by the New York members only. See U.S. 37th Congr. 3d sess., House Executive Document 25, 137.
40. The New York members of the Treasury Note Committee were, besides Coe and Stevens, Moses Taylor; John E. Williams (to be discussed); John Q. Jones (1803-1878), the successful president of the strong Chemical Bank; and J.D. Vermilye (1817-1892), then cashier of the Merchants' Bank. The delegates from Boston and Philadelphia were Franklin Haven and Singleton A. Mercer, respectively.
41. As to the reaction of the Boston banks see the minutes of the board of the Massachusetts Bank;

Gras, op. cit., 514 ff.

42. The name of the Boston syndicate was "Associates to the Twenty Years' Loan of November 16, 1861;" ibid., 517, 518.

43. One of these agents was Jay Cooke, whose territory covered Philadelphia and its environs, including New Jersey; (Larson, op. cit., p. 111). Incidentally in August 1861, in a letter to J.B. Mitchell, president of the Philadelphia Clearing House, John A. Stevens had asked for the names of reliable institutions in Pennsylvania and Maryland which could be entrusted with the collection of subscriptions; Philadelphia Board of Presidents, Minutes.

44. "Report of the New York Loan Committee," 138, 139.

45. Report of the Secretary of the Treasury of December 9, 1861, U.S. 37th Congr. 2d sess., Senate Document 2, 9.

46. Laws of 1861, Ch. 46, sec. 6. For the background of the conflict see also this volume, page 333.

47. Chase Diaries (Library of Congress, Ms-Division), Dec. 10, 1861.

48. Gallatin, James, Letter to Hon. Samuel Hooper of Massachusetts; reprint from the New York Commercial Advertiser of December 20, 1862, 2.

49. As to Williams, see this volume, page 150. His letter to Chase is reprinted in his pamphlet: The War Loans of the Associated Banks to the Government in 1861 (New York, 1876?), 5, 6.

50. A similar attack is to be found in Hunt's Merchants' Magazine, XLVII (1862) is an article entitled: "Federal Finances Examined:" "The new Secretary of the Treasury, Mr. Chase, was placed in power as a politician, but devoid of all those qualifications which were so indispensable to the financial head of the nation at such a momentous crisis. He was a fair lawyer, but he had never been familiar with great money transactions, the principles of financial science, or the machinery by which great operations are moved."

51. Philadelphia Board of Presidents, Minutes.

52. Gallatin, Letter to Hooper, passim. His speech of December 28, 1861 is reprinted in Bankers' Magazine, XVI(1861/62), 625 ff. Spaulding, op. cit., 19 ff.; Mitchell, op. cit., 48 ff, 68 ff; Report of the Monetary Commission of the Indianapolis Convention, 406, 407.

53. Hooper felt very bitter about James Gallatin; see his speech of 1864, 4, 5.

54. For details, see Mitchell, op. cit., 150 ff; Spaulding, op. cit., 21 ff; also Hooper, speech of 1863, 5.

55. See this volume, chapter XXI.

Chapter XVI

THE NATIONAL BANKING SYSTEM UP TO 1882
(Fourth Period of American Banking)

Pains have been taken in an earlier chapter of this work[1] to describe the development of the term "national bank" and to interpret the changing meaning thereof: originally, it connoted a bank chartered by the national government; later (by 1840) the words came to be used for what today is called a central bank; but ultimately, in the 1860's, when the National Banking system came into being the phrase reassumed its original meaning. Just as there was no continuity in the terminology so there was none in reality. There is no line whatsoever leading from the old "national banks", the First and Second Banks of the United States, to the National Banking system; nor did the discussions of the late 1830's and early 1840's on the subject of a "national bank" exert any positive influence on the men instrumental in bringing about the great achievement of the 1860's. The influence, if any, was negative in that the promoters of the National Banking system wished to avoid that type of institution which had been called a "national bank" in 1840. However the older generation living at the time of the Civil War surmised some relation or at least kinship,[2] an unjustifiable suspicion which, nevertheless, retarded the adoption of National Banking. It forced the exponents to prove at great length that the latter was not comparable with the two Banks of the United States, but on the contrary would provide a uniform currency without those features which had made the two "national banks" odious to the people.[3]

The National Currency Act, or to be correct, the Act of February 23, 1863 to provide a national currency secured by a pledge of United States bonds and to provide for the circulation and redemption thereof, can be easily understood when seen as the adoption of Free Banking on a national scale. (Such adoption may have been envisaged as early as 1839 by Condy Raguet.)[4] It is telling that when writing in the New York Times in February, 1862, Robert J. Walker, erstwhile Secretary of the Treasury and a stout defender of the scheme prior to its adoption, spoke of the pending National Currency bill as "Mr. Chase's well guarded Free Banking system;"[5] and as late as 1879 Silas M. Stilwell, who had contributed to the achievement, characterized it as the "National Free Banking La   of the United States."[6]

Consequently whatever was written in an earlier chapter[7] on the geistige genealogy of Free Banking holds true with respect to the ideological ancestry of the National Banking system. However for the latter to be sired, the fundamental ideas of New York Free Banking had to be wed with another current of thought which can be traced throughout the nineteenth century; namely, that the national government in lieu of the individual states should assume control of bank currency. This idea underlay certain passages of Madison's message of December 3, 1816,[8] Alexander Dallas's thinking ("the power of the government to supply and maintain a paper medium of uniform value will not be questioned"), and the McDuffie Report of the 1830's. In the latter decade authors became articulate on this point, as for example Roger M. Sherman in the anonymously published Letters to Levi Woodbury;[9] and one can even find such an emphatic statement as the following: "If the currency of this country is to consist of bank paper this paper should be issued under the authority of the national government and under such regulations as it may prescribe."[10] When pleading for what became the National Banking system Salmon P. Chase thus formulated the fundamental idea: there was general agreement among statesmen "that the power to regulate coin is, in substance and effect, the power to regulate currency and that the framers of the Constitution so intended."[11]

Most people who thought along these lines up to the late 1840's aimed at a "national bank," i.e., a central bank, as the instrument of the federal government for regulating bank currency. But besides this main current there was a second which avoided the central bank concept. In 1815 Dallas made an "attempt to associate [the state banks] with the view" of furnishing a uniform national currency.[12] He had to acknowledge defeat. But in the same year Judge James Workman of New Orleans presented a fruitful suggestion which pointed into the future and contained the germ of a national currency issued not by one "national bank," but by a multiplicity of banks. State chartered banks were to use United States funds "as the basis and support and limit of paper currency."[13] Workman saw clearly that his plan "would go a great way towards establishing a uniform currency."

No other trace of this line of thought was found before the 1830's. In that decade, however, one William R. Collier proposed[14] the enactment by Congress of a general banking act establishing a national system of banking instead of a national bank. Nationally chartered banks with large capital should issue general-asset bank-notes, uniform in size and appearance to distinguish them from local currencies. It was proposed that each bill contain on its face a statement regarding the national character of the issuing bank and its capital. This suggestion of a national system of banks does not seem to have made much of an impression and probably wielded no influence.[15] But a few years later (in 1841), the chemist, Robert Hare (1781-1858), interested in banking and currency reform, like Workman drafted a plan of a national currency to be issued by state-chartered banks: The "general government," through the instrumentality of a board of trustees, was to receive deposits of state stocks in an office established for that purpose. The board was to issue to the depositing banks certificates to the amount of four-fifths of the face value of such state stocks in any required denomination, but not below $5. Such certificates were to circulate and constitute a universal national currency.[16] Further details are of no interest here, except that the board of trustees was to sell the deposited stocks, under certain conditions, to pay the note holders. As will be shown shortly it was actually in the direction of this proposal that the development turned first, although Hare's booklet may have remained unknown to the protagonists of the National Banking system.

With the ideological background of National Banking clear beyond doubt all that remains for the present chapter is to describe and explain the process by which the National Banking system came into being, and its working during the first two decades of its existence.[17]

I

Both Andrew McFarland Davis[18] and Helderman[19] have shown how the idea of National Banking crystallized.[20] They have especially drawn attention to the fact[21] that as early as 1848 Millard Fillmore, then the New York State Comptroller and Vice-President-elect of the United States, worked out a plan which tended toward the adoption on a national scale of the New York Free Banking principle. His proposal attracted a good deal of public attention and led to newspaper controversies.[22] It will be remembered that in 1841 Robert Hare had suggested that state banks issue a universal national currency secured by state stocks.

Fillmore in his proposal followed the same line but gave it a slight twist. If "Congress would authorize such notes [of state banks] as were secured by stocks of the United States [underlining mine] to be received for public dues to the national treasury, this would give such notes a universal credit, coextensive with the United States, and leave nothing further desired in the shape of a national paper currency. This would avoid all objections to a national bank by obviating all necessity for one." (In appraising this plan one should recall that Fillmore had refused to join Clay's fight for a third national bank [Bank of the United States] and his proposal may well have been an ex post justification of the stand taken at a critical moment.) This idea of a national currency issued by state banks (national, because it was to be based on national stocks) was in the air by 1860. It was embodied not only in several contemporary writings to be discussed forthwith, but also in Secretary Chase's first official move toward a National Banking system.

As early as December, 1857, when dealing with the crisis of that year and suggesting remedial measures, one John Williams, then editor of the Hardwareman's Newspaper and later of the well-known trade journal, Iron Age, made in the former paper the following proposal: There should be created "a national currency or at least a circulating medium issued under such sanctions and securities as would insure the currency at par in all parts of the United States." For that purpose, and believing that the founding of another "national bank" (i.e., a central bank) was impossible, Williams counseled the "establishment of a new federal department for the control and supervision of banks throughout the United States with which all securities for the issue of bills should be lodged and from which should issue duly certified by the proper officer the entire circulation of the country." The securities to be accepted would have to be "wisely considered and accurately defined;" while the notes "thus certified" should be taken by the government in payment of duties and postage fees. They would, so Williams felt, "possess a value within a fraction of par, anywhere within the jurisdiction of the United States." Williams recognized this system as "but the extension to the whole Union of the principle on which the banks of New York and other states are now based." (Incidentally the proposal was coupled with the suggestion that small notes be forbidden and "a heavy personal responsibility on the part of the stockholders" for the liabilities of banks be established.)[23]

It is obvious that Williams's plan is very similar to that of Hare's and distinct from Fillmore's in that Williams did not tie together national currency and national stocks. The plan is in fact a step backward in comparison with Fillmore's suggestion. But Fillmore's proposal can be found again embodied in Orlando B. Potter's[24] advice to Secretary Chase, submitted in the summer of 1861: "Allow banks and bankers duly authorized in the loyal states to secure their bills by depositing with a Superintendent appointed by the government United States stocks at their par value...thus making the stocks of the United States a basis of banking on which alone a national circulation can be secured."[25] The principle underlying this suggestion of Potter's (regardless of whether or not it actually stimulated Chase) was at the root of the Secretary's official move of December, 1861. Simultaneously with the latter Millard Fillmore's own proposal was revived by Laurent Bonnefoux who claimed to have influenced, and in fact had defended, the former's plan of 1848.[26] This revival of Fillmore's plan is to be found in the Bankers' Magazine of December, 1861; and in the following month (on January 20, 1862) the editor of the National Intelligencer also reminded his readers of Fillmore's proposal.[27]

To sum up, during the winter of 1861/62 the plan of a former United States President to create a national currency by permitting (or forcing) state banks to base their issues on United States stocks and to receive notes from a United States government agency was widely discussed and recommended. It was this plan which Secretary of the Treasury Chase in his Finance Report of December, 1861, submitted to Congress. Chase, as has been described in an earlier chapter, was a believer in hard money,[28] although willing to concede that large banknotes were at least useful for the convenience of commerce. He felt a great aversion to making anything legal tender except coin. But if it was not possible for the United States to have a metallic monetary system, then whatever paper system the country possessed should be national in scope. On this basis his action of December, 1861, can be understood: He wished a law passed under which notes prepared for circulation under national direction and secured by the pledge of United States bonds would be delivered to existing solvent banks which would thereupon withdraw their circulation issued under state authority. The transition from a heterogeneous, unequal, and unsafe circulation to a uniform, equal, and safe one would thus speedily and almost imperceptibly be accomplished.[29]

There is a widely held but erroneous belief that in his Report of 1861 Chase recommended the establishment of a system of National Banks.[30] It has been pointed out and should be stressed again that he did no such thing. What he proposed in fact was the issue of a national currency by the existing state banks. If there were any doubt left the material to be presented forthwith would dot the i:

First of all, the earliest contemporary reactions to the Finance Report of 1861 do not contain any suggestion of a National Banking system, while they correctly describe Chase's proposal.[31] One author explaining in detail how it would work pointed out that state banks would come into the "new system" simply by purchasing United States bonds. He objected to the current favorite phrase that the proposed law was "tampering with the currency." According to him "Congress simply [made] a general enactment to which the banks must conform." It merely asked them to loan a given sum to the public treasury instead of to individuals, and to base their own circulation upon the strength of that loan.[32]

But there is a still other proof for the thesis here presented: Elbridge Gerry Spaulding's[33] claim that he was the first to mold Chase's suggestion of December, 1861, into a bill which could be presented to Congress is generally accepted by historians as true.[34] It is known that 200 copies of this bill were printed for the use of both the Ways and Means Committee and the Secretary of the Treasury, but no earlier author has used the Spaulding bill in the course of his research and in fact it seems to be lost in its original form. It is preserved, however, in the New York Times of January 9, 1862 and is reprinted in Appendix I to this chapter.[35]

The Spaulding bill, as might be expected, starts in fact with a clause according to which existing state banks were to issue a national currency based on national stocks. Section 5 reads as follows:

> SEC. 5. AND BE IT FURTHER ENACTED. That any chartered Bank or Banking Association, whose capital is not less than one hundred thousand dollars, organized under the laws of any State, Territory, or the District of Columbia, which may elect to avail itself of the provisions of this act, shall present to the Bank Comptroller an authorized application therefor, verified by its seal and the signatures of the President and cashier, duly acknowledged before a Judge of some Court of Record or a Notary Public and the acknowledgment thereof certified under the seal of such Court or Notary; and the said application shall state the name of said bank or banking association; the place where its office of discount and deposit is located, designating the State, and also the particular city, town, or village; the amount of the capital stock, and the number of shares into which the same shall be divided; the time when its charter will expire, and a declaration that said certificate is made to enable such bank or banking association to avail itself of the advantages of this act, and consenting to comply with

all the restrictions and requirements contained therein, and the comptroller of the currency shall record and carefully preserve the said application in his office; and thereupon such chartered bank or banking association shall be vested with all the powers and be subject to all the provisions of this act, during the period limited in its charter, as fully and effectually as associations formed under this act.

To be sure, the later sections of the bill embody different ideas such as were to be found again in the National Currency Act of 1863 which actually established a National Banking system.

Thus we arrive at a decisive question: Who contributed the idea of a system of National Banks? This much is certain: up to and including December 9, 1861, the date of the Finance Report, one of the fundamental features of the act of 1863 had not as yet been broached; namely, that the federal government should establish an independent national banking system (Collier's idea of 1834, mentioned above[36]). It is telling that that act and soon thereafter the one of 1864, which replaced it, were generally called the National Currency Act, not the National Bank Act as later generations have come to style the law, after the official change of its title in 1874.[37] It is equally telling that sec. 62 of the act of 1863 still permitted existing state banks to deposit with the Treasury United States bonds to the amount of 50 per cent of their capital receiving national circulation in return. (This clause was deleted in 1864 because of McCulloch's objections; while it was in force, he seems to have refused to comply with it,[38] a wise policy, undoubtedly, but contra legem.)

It would be of the greatest interest to know exactly how the keystone was inserted in the arch, but the author can submit only hypotheses: The fact that in 1862[39] Chase claimed to have recommended in his report of 1861 that banking associations be authorized under a general [national] act when in fact he had not, may indicate that he had meant to do so, but for tactical or other reasons had abstained. That interpretation would imply that as early as December, 1861, Chase had at least thought of a National Banking system which in fact he emphatically recommended the following year.

However, there is another possibility which the author considers more probable; namely, that the idea of a National Banking system was conceived between December 9 (the date of the Finance Report) and the December holidays when Spaulding drafted his bill. To be sure, as early as November, 1861, Eleazar Lord, who had stood by the cradle of

New York Free Banking,[40] had submitted to Chase and published a plan of a national currency which belongs to the literature already discussed. He too suggested that the Treasury Department issue bills to banks on the deposit of national stocks; and his plan is slightly distinguished from all the others of the period in that he wished to make use of existing banks and new banking associations.[41] But it is very doubtful if he wished the latter to be established under a national law. Such an idea had hardly entered his mind.[42]

In contrast, there are indications in a semi-official source (Silas M. Stilwell's System of National Finance) that the idea of a National Banking system as such was contributed in December, 1861, by the latter and the solicitor of the Treasury, Jordan, as Stilwell claimed later. (Failure to make clear what his claim actually was caused it to be discounted.) That conclusion is drawn from the wording of page 3 of Stilwell's booklet. Pages 1 and 2 give a summary of Chase's original plan as presented in the Finance Report of 1861. On page 3 Stilwell starts out: "An additional plan is now proposed by the Secretary [it is conjectured: proposed by Stilwell and adopted by the Secretary] to enable all existing banks and associations for banking purposes to become national institutions." "The Congress of the United States can pass a law which will authorize all banks and associations for banking to file their applications and articles of association in the Department of the Treasury and thus make National Institutions (Italics in original) of these that now are only organized under...state laws....These banks and others that the law may authorize to be created...will naturally become the fiscal agents of the National Treasury...and act also as the disbursing agents of the Government everywhere." This plan is in fact different from the one presented in the Finance Report of 1861 and it is from this point that National Banking took its departure.[43]

It may be useful to recapitulate and thereby to stress the history of this important detail: Chase's Finance Report of 1861 suggested the issue of a national currency by state banks. The Spaulding bill started from this proposal, but it emphasized rather the establishment of an independent system of National Banks. In the course of the legislative history of the bill the idea of state banks issuing a national currency was more and more pushed into the background, so that the act of 1863 relegated it to section 62, one of the last of the whole act which possessed 65 sections. Ultimately in the revised version of 1864 the original idea was dropped altogether. Vice versa an idea that cannot be found in the Finance Report of 1861, that of an independent system of National Banks, came to dominate

American banking.

Chase's move of December, 1861, had matured at least by November. In that month he submitted the plan of a "National Bank Department" to George S. Coe with whom he had closely cooperated during the preceding months. Coe was obviously asked to discuss the matter with his New York colleagues. This he refused to do because the suggestion would hit them like a bombshell. He even expressed himself as against the plan, thereby foreshadowing the attitude which the New York banking fraternity was to take toward the accomplished fact about a year and a half later. Although Coe objected, feeling sure that the requirements of the Treasury could be met by other means, he added suggestions of his own, namely that if the plan was to be prosecuted at all, the law at which the Secretary aimed should at least prescribe a 20 - 25 per cent coin reserve and the rule that banks should have a paid-up capital besides the amount invested in stocks.[44]

Although Coe refused to submit Chase's plan to the New York bankers, rumors leaked out that proposals for an indirect issue of government paper money were being pressed on the Secretary of the Treasury, as James Gallatin expressed it.[45] Under these proposals national securities would, in imitation of the New York Free Banking system, form the basis of such paper. When Chase came to New York to attend a meeting of the Associated Banks in which the subject of the pending loan was discussed, Gallatin read a paper warning the Secretary against such action and upon request handed him a copy of the address. To his dismay, only a few days later Chase submitted to public opinion in the Finance Report of 1861 exactly the plan which Gallatin had "exposed," as he thought. That the Secretary sent a copy of the Report to him, as well as to other important bankers (Coe, Ketchum, and Williams), may have appeared as an affront to Gallatin.[46]

These episodes show Chase as receiving expert advice before inserting the pertinent passage in his Finance Report of 1861.[47] The main features of his plan have been discussed, but others must be restated at this point: It is of interest that Chase himself stressed the connection between his proposal and New York Free Banking. The plan was no untried theory, so the Secretary pointed out; it had been tested by experience in New York and other states and had been found practicable and useful. Consequently, in line with New York legislation, Chase suggested that notes be prepared and delivered to banks and that they should be secured by the pledge of bonds. Other needful regulations should be added, such as a provision for adequate specie reserves; for "security" meant "prompt convertibility into coin." Thus Chase, a hard-money man by persuasion and possibly prodded by George S. Coe, contributed to endowing the National Banking system with potential specie reserves: although the system was put into effect at a time of suspension it looked toward resumption from the very beginning. It is not known whether or not in recommending legal specie reserves Chase had any model in mind, such as the Massachusetts Banking Act of 1858 or the Louisiana Free Banking Act of 1853 or the Ohio act of 1845 or New York Free Banking as it stood prior to the repeal of the specie reserve clause in 1840. (It is known however, that Spaulding had studied the New York act of 1838.)[48] Be that as it may, banknotes properly secured were to replace the unsound (heterogeneous, unequal, and unsafe) state-bank issues. Their advantage over the latter would lie in their bearing a common "impression," by their being authenticated by a common authority, and by their being backed by both United States stock and adequate specie reserves, as just described. Once such notes were issued the country would enjoy a uniform currency backed by uniform security and consequently safeguarded against depreciation. The holders would be protected against the deduction of discount or exchange when the notes were deposited in places other than the seat of the issuing bank or when used for remittances. On the other hand, a market would be opened for government bonds, more "money" would be available for war loans, the interest rate would decline, investors in banks would profit, and still a great money monopoly would be avoided. Last but not least, the bonds of the Union would be cemented: more people in all parts of the country would become interested in its preservation in consequence of the wide distribution of government bonds to banking associations spread all over the land.[49] The new bank money would present the best paper currency which the country had ever enjoyed: being receivable for government dues, except for customs, it would have equal value everywhere. Sound as the plan was, the Secretary neither foresaw the immediate future which brought suspension of specie payments, nor was he able to forecast the reaction of the influential bankers in the Eastern financial centers.

Helderman has posed the question whether Chase's plan of 1861 originated with or was suggested to him. He came to the conclusion that the former was possible since the State of Ohio, whose governor Chase had been only recently, had possessed Free Banking of the New York brand and legal specie reserves as they were recommended in the Finance Report of 1861.[50] Helderman has overlooked the fact that Chase himself has given the answer to his question in a letter to John Williams, mentioned above. Wrote Chase: "I never claimed any originality in respect to the National Banking Law for myself. It was discussed by many before me. Providence offered me the opportunity of securing a national currency for the whole country and I seized it. This I thought my duty and claim no merit for having proposed it."[51] (This statement, of course, does not exclude the possibility that familiarity with Ohio banking made Chase responsive to certain suggestions which were "pressed" on him, to use James Gallatin's words.) On the other hand, while disclaiming any originality Chase spoke in 1863 of the National Banking system "as a measure of his own in the success of which he felt a very deep interest,"[52] an interest which lay in the establishment of a national currency rather than in creating a market for war bonds. A.M. Davis has shown this fact beyond doubt.[53]

The first man after Chase to carry the ball was the Buffalo country banker, Elbridge Gerry Spaulding. Spaulding (1809-1897), a descendant of immigrants into the Massachusetts Bay Colony, was born in the State of New York and started his career as a lawyer in Buffalo. His first contact with banking may have come with his marriage in 1837 to the daughter of an Attica banker. In any case, shortly thereafter he brought from Batavia to Buffalo the Farmers and Mechanics Bank with which he was closely connected for the rest of his life. In the 1840's Spaulding embarked on a public career the various stages of which are of no interest here except that, having earlier been a Whig in Congress, he returned as a Republican in 1860.[54] The bill which Spaulding framed in 1861 and which has been alluded to before, was unworkable and died in the Ways and Means Committee in January, 1862. That the plan of a national currency based on national stocks was taken up again was due to Chase who remained the prime mover and provided the driving force needed for ultimate success.

The parliamentary history of the National Currency bill is well known[55] and the contributions of the leading actors other than Chase and Spaulding are well established. Thaddeus Stevens was its most powerful enemy and able to block its progress for months. After having been dropped in January the measure was taken up again in July, 1862, by Samuel Hooper [56] who in so doing gave encouragement by open support at a time when both the House and Senate financial committees were incredulous and hostile, to use Chase's words. Such support possessed great weight because of Hooper's prestige as a financial statesman, a prestige acquired through his connection with the Massachusetts Banking Act of 1858. Having previously influenced the Spaulding bill,

Hooper obtained leave to submit one of his own authorizing a National Banking system, a bill which, like the former, could not be coached through Congress. Selfish interests, of course, were to a certain extent reflected in the political opposition and personal conflicts between Chase and members of Congress also played a part.[57] But by the end of January, 1863, John Sherman was, on Chase's suggestion, approached by Jay and Henry Cooke and induced to sponsor the national currency bill and to introduce it in the Senate as his measure. As such it was passed the next month. The Cookes felt that they had contributed more than any other living men to the success, a claim difficult to gauge. Chase himself felt indebted also to Robert J. Walker (1801-1869), Secretary of the Treasury under Polk, for having given in public the sanction of his approval.[58] The previously mentioned Silas M. Stilwell, on the other hand, who assigned to himself a good deal of importance was not among those for whose aid Chase expressed gratitude. In fact one can draw the conclusion from Stillwell's own confused and incorrectly dated presentation that his cooperation with the Secretary of the Treasury was not too harmonious and that the latter merely wished to make use of his pen for popularizing the plan.[59]

Ideas of different ancestry were embodied in the National Currency Act, but the New York strain prevailed. From that state came the main features: namely, the government-bond-backed banknote, the exchange of notes against bonds at the Comptroller's office, the double liability clause (taken over from the New York State constitution of 1846, Art. VIII, sec. 7); the 7 per cent legal interest rate (in the 1864 version of the act); and even such a minor detail as avoiding the term corporations and speaking of banking "associations" instead. (This detail is understandable only when one realizes the constitutional situation in New York in 1838 and the means used to get around its limitations.)[60] Since one knows that the framers of the original bill, especially Elbridge Gerry Spaulding, relied on material requested in a hurry from New York it is clear how the above features found their way into the final act. It is equally certain that it was Samuel Hooper who inserted the reserve requirements against both notes and deposits, the clause that deposits with banks in nine other places (reserve cities) could be counted as part of the reserves,[61] and the one which made for an automatic working of the reserve requirements. The section in question of the act of 1863 (sec. 41) follows almost verbatim the Massachusetts Banking Act of 1858 which was Hooper's work. Finally we know that the absolute limitation of the total of issues typical of all the versions of the National Currency act prior to 1875, was contributed by John Sherman who, as indicated, assumed leadership in the Senate when the bill was stalled in the House.[62]

The connection between the National Banking system and New York Free Banking, and Massachusetts influence on the former are generally recognized. Less well known is the fact that through John Sherman certain ideas of Lord Overstone's, embodied in the Peel Act of 1844, were brought to bear on our basic law of 1863. The fact that the latter limited the total amount of notes that could be issued in the aggregate by all National Banks points in this direction; and, incidentally, an article in the Merchants' Magazine of 1862 (supposedly written by John Jay Knox), which may well have been the first to suggest this measure, proposed the adoption of still other features of the Peel Act (especially the issue of additional notes against gold deposits).[63] The connection was brought out clearly in the debates of 1874 when amendments to the National Currency Act were under discussion. At that time Horace Maynard,[64] pointed to the "identity of the principle in the Bank of England and our National Banking system," which seemed "obvious" to him. He considered the Comptroller of the Currency as standing at the head of our "issue department" which issued circulating notes based on public credit, while our "banking department" instead of being restricted to a single establishment was distributed among two thousand independent banks. Maynard quoted Lord Overstone's statement that the banking department of the Bank of England was "a bank in every respect identical with any other bank." He did not see the central-bank character of the Bank of England which makes his comparison limp. Nevertheless that he makes the comparison at all, is interesting and telling, and points to influence lines.[65] It is of even greater importance (because it shows the prevalence of Lord Overstone's thinking in contemporary America) that in the same year, 1874, the outstanding New York banker John Earl Williams also referred to Lord Overstone's ideas. Williams wanted to do away with National Bank notes altogether, replacing them by redeemable government paper money, the quantity of which again was to be absolutely limited. Thereby he hoped to separate strictly the issue of a circulating medium from banking proper, a separation which was, as he stressed, the principle on which the Bank of England worked.[66] To compare Maynard and Williams: the former praised the National Banking system because it was in line with the fundamental ideas of the Peel Act; the latter wanted to reorganize it in order to make it so conform.

There was one really new idea in the act as McCulloch stressed in the "Report of the Comptroller of the Currency" of 1863.[67] For the first time the principle was recognized and established that the redemption of banknotes should be guaranteed by the government authorizing their issue and thereby forcing the public to accept them as money: the notes of National Banks were in the first instance secured by national securities and in the second by general assets and double liability. But if a bank failed, its notes were immediately paid by the Treasury which canceled the underlying bonds, i.e., when at that moment their market price was depressed the faith of the nation was pledged for the redemption of the notes without loss to the holder.[68] It would be of great interest to know how this clause came into the act. It was not in Potter's plan of 1861,[69] which envisaged the sale of the deposited securities if a bank failed to redeem its notes; nor can it be found in the Finance Report of 1861 nor in the Spaulding bill of the same year. But the clause is in the Hooper bill of 1862 (sec. 25) exactly as later embodied in the act.[70]

II

The National Banking system was intended to absorb not to destroy the state banks, as McCulloch, the first Comptroller of the Currency, expressed it.[71] This goal, however, was not easily reached, because of resistance both on the part of most of the states which did not pass enabling acts facilitating conversions (as did Massachusetts, Connecticut, and Pennsylvania)[72] and on the part of state banks which did not take advantage of the possibility of founding National Banks and transferring their assets to the new enterprises. In New York the question of whether or not National Banks could be organized regardless of state sanction was even a matter of discussion.[73]

F. Cyril James[74] has summed up as follows the criticism of the law of 1863 which was partly responsible for the reluctance of the banks: First of all, the redemption provisions were considered inadequate, for National Banks had to redeem at their counters only. In this respect the law deviated from Chase's suggestions which had aimed at redemption at one or several commercial centers.[75] (The redemption problem will be discussed shortly.)[76] Furthermore distrust of Congress played a certain part. A few critics, influenced by the Banking School, were aware of the inelasticity of the system; others recognized the danger of the pyramiding of reserves with which it was burdened from the outset. Again others, realizing that the existing banks would not easily convert into

National Banks, sensed an inflationary danger; McCulloch belonged to this group. Finally, it was feared that National Banks would come into unreliable hands and deteriorate into wild-cat banks. They could in fact be established with too small a capital which did not even have to be paid up before opening for business.[77] That fear was not without foundation, although in the end it proved to be unjustified. But there is at least one case on record in which a small National Bank consisted of a desk in a broker's office. The stockholders consisted of partners in the brokerage business and members of their families. Such abuse of the banking privilege was possible because the act permitted small banks to invest all their capital in government stock. (Thereby no funds would be left for keeping adequate cash reserves and for a regular banking business unless deposits were lodged immediately, in which case, however, the depositors were not so well secured as the noteholders.)[78] There were some more minor reasons for the resentment of the bankers, such as the severe criticism to which they had been exposed when the bill was being promoted and the provision of the act which required them to assume numerical titles instead of their long-established firm names. Incidentally, it was on this point that Chase and McCulloch disagreed, the latter fighting on the side of the banks.[79]

Of course, criticism of certain aspects and details of the act, correct as it was, would not have kept bankers from making use of opportunities offered had they seen such opportunities. The real reasons for the antagonism must be sought elsewhere: The typical, or if you please, natural conservatism of businessmen played a part; moreover many were opposed to the act because they felt that war time was not suitable for monetary experiments, an attitude which was not without justification. But the most important reasons were of a character that one does not put into writing: The bankers, as Dr. Larson has it,[80] resented "any move toward the establishment of a system which might encroach on their own independent and profitable preserves;" and last but not least, to many of them, and especially the New Yorkers, it was not so certain that the Union would survive the struggle. In that case, its credit would be seriously impaired and banks tied so completely to the national credit as the National Banks were to be, might well go down with the defeat and the downfall of the credit of the Union.

Thus as early as December, 1861, and throughout 1862, state and private bankers were almost solidly aligned against this bill. As early as January 14 and 15, 1862, Chase met with representatives of the loan committees from the New York,

Boston, and Philadelphia banks and the boards of trade of the three cities. An attempt was made to iron out misunderstandings and difficulties, especially with regard to the demand notes previously floated, and to receive backing for the Secretary's bank plans. An agreement was drafted and assented to by Coe of New York and Walley of Boston which included the following clause: "It is thought desirable that Congress should adopt a general law relating to the Currency and Banking Associations, embracing the general provisions recommended by the Secretary in his report."[81] This agreement was disavowed by the banks. A conference between the Secretary of the Treasury and the leading New York bankers held later in 1862 was a complete failure;[82] and so seems to have been one which took place in Boston in 1863. In the course of the latter the Comptroller of the Currency (McCulloch) is supposed to have intimated that the instinct of self preservation should induce the presidents to wind up their banks as state institutions and to organize at once under the national act.[83]

This episode alone would show that the opposition persisted to a large extent after the measure had been passed in February, 1863, although by that time at least some of the original antagonists had changed or were changing sides. Jay Cooke among the opponents in 1861 and early in 1862, who afterwards had contributed much to the legislative success of the bill through his influence over the press and certain personalities, was now selling National Banking all over the country. McCulloch, president of the Bank of the State of Indiana, who had gone to Washington to fight the bill, was to put the system on its feet. To be sure, the farseeing and cooperative young banker, George S. Coe, who in November, 1861, had politely refused even to talk about the plan to his colleagues still remained cool. What then could one expect from the conservative crowd led by such a stubborn, overweening old man as James Gallatin.[84] He became one of the heads of the opposition which centered in the New York Clearing House.

The latter seems to have taken up the matter of National Banking because the banks had received a circular letter of the Comptroller of the Currency suggesting that they wind up as state banks and join the national system.[85] (This very important document is reprinted as Appendix 2 of this chapter.) Furthermore on everybody's desk there was another circular letter (of September 23, 1863) addressed to the officers and directors of the Clearing House banks, signed "a bank stockholder and director" (in fact Augustus Ely Silliman, president of the Merchants Bank). It recommended that the Associated Banks of New York, Boston, and Philadelphia "decline all recognition [of National

Banks] directly or indirectly in their exchanges; and let them [the Associated Banks] at once at whatever expense return the notes that they are compelled to receive to their respective points of redemption." This item, preserved in the New York Public Library and reprinted as Appendix 3 of this chapter, is of great interest because it indicates that the fight, which McCulloch had tried to avoid, began in a highly emotional atmosphere.[86]

Silliman's circular letter formed the starting point for James Gallatin when he addressed the Clearing House Association in a special meeting called for October 6, 1863. In his speech[87] which was widely disseminated, Gallatin taking up Silliman's warcry sounded the keynote for the cacophony that was to follow: National Bank notes would be "subject to the natural law of depreciation" (sic!). Consequently they could not be taken by the Clearing House banks and should be treated as "uncurrent money." Such ideas were reiterated in a publication of the New York Clearing House, which has often been cited and is in fact typical of the attitude of the New York banking fraternity and its tactics.[88] This pamphlet, embodying the report of a committee appointed by the above meeting of October 6, 1863 to report on the National Currency Act, was written by another leader of the opposition, the above mentioned John Earl Williams, president of the Metropolitan Bank of New York.[89] Besides restating most of the criticism generally leveled against the act and enumerated before, Williams, anticipating present and future disaster therefrom,[90] made the following points: banks would not be able to take National Bank notes because they did not have the legal right to pay them over the counter. (He meant they were not legal tender between individuals.) That statement was a vicious one and intended to frighten the public; it was not difficult to predict that banks could not take National Bank notes when a small minority, to which the reporter belonged, had the power arbitrarily to refuse and willfully to discredit them, as in fact it did.[91] All the recipients could do, so Williams claimed, would be to hand the National Bank notes to "uncurrent-money" brokers and to submit to a discount. (He completely overlooked the fact that the notes were legal tender in almost all payments to the government.) Under these circumstances National Currency would quickly depreciate. Williams suggested that the government issue more legal tenders, a tactical move which the banking fraternity considered to their advantage, giving them a stronger strategical position for the end of the war. (If the country stuck to legal tenders these could be made to disappear quickly after the end of the hostilities, while the National Banks would

present a powerful interest in favor of a protracted suspension of specie payments.) Finally, Williams stated that the system would collapse in the first panic: as soon as banks would begin to fail all the national notes would at once be presented in Washington for redemption, and the government would of course be unable to pay them. (The historian can question if this argument was made bona fide, because it was belied by the experience of 1857.)[92] This insincere ex parte report was, like Gallatin's speech, widely disseminated.[93]

The outcome of all these moves was that the New York Clearing House banks resolved "that all National Bank currency be treated as uncurrent money unless the bank [in question] redeem[ed] at par through a member of this Association." Even checks drawn on National Banks were refused.[94] However, it seems that the New York banks shied away from a test. Their actions were guided by the hope that the next Congress would alter the entire banking situation; otherwise they would have "to burn up or dry up."[95]

The Philadelphia banking fraternity was not so hostile by far as the New Yorkers, possibly due to the fact that Chase had such a stout friend as Joseph Patterson among the city's bankers. As early as January 19, 1863, "the bill reported in Congress for the establishment of free banking" was discussed by the Board of Presidents and referred to the loan committee; (incidentally the phraseology used provides an interesting testimony as to the contemporary outlook). A few days later (on January 31), after a discussion of the proposed "United States Banking System" the Board of Presidents on motion of Joseph Patterson appointed a sub-committee which by correspondence and personal exertion was to promote the adoption of the bill "with a view to the acceptance of its provisions and the relinquishment by the Banks of Philadelphia of their charters from the State of Pennsylvania." Good as the intentions were, for some unknown reason the Philadelphia banks turned cool once the act of 1863 was passed, possibly because of its many deficiencies, possibly influenced by the attitude of financial New York. The matter was taken up again on June 6, 1864, when a committee was appointed by the Board of Presidents to consider the act in its revised form. On September 5 this committee recommended that the presidents "take into their early and favorable consideration the conditions of the bill...and be prepared to act upon it as occasion may require." Singleton A. Mercer stated in the discussion that his board had decided to make a National Bank out of the Farmers and Mechanics Bank, then a leading one. He recommended unity of action resulting in all Philadelphia banks making the change at the same time.

President J.B. Mitchell of the Mechanics Bank, another leader, cordially united with Mercer in recommending the adoption of the resolution, but on September 19 when it came to a vote only eleven banks assented to the resolution, five voted No (the Bank of North America, the Western, Girard, Tradesmen's, and Commonwealth Banks), while three banks were absent.[96] (Actually 22 banks converted in Philadelphia in 1864.)

The reluctance of such a friendly group proves that in 1863 there was in fact much reason for criticism of the act as it stood in that year. McCulloch himself in the first Report of the Comptroller of the Currency (of 1863) made numerous suggestions as to the improvement of the law which he considered "admirable in its leading features," but not "alltogether symmetrical in its arrangements," clear, and consistent.[97] Under these circumstances it is not surprising that very few and then only small National Banks were founded in 1863 and early in 1864, a fact which worried Chase. In some cases the patriotic motive of the founders is evident and explains their establishment; (we shall meet it again when discussing the conversions of 1864). In Michigan, for instance, the first National Bank was founded in 1863 in Ann Arbor, as the First National Bank of Ann Arbor, by Alpheus Felch (1804-1896). He had been a governor of Michigan and a senator from that state and was then practicing law. The Second National Bank of Detroit was set up (in 1863 also) under the leadership of Zachariah Chandler (1813-1879) who as a senator had supported the National Currency bill and had even advocated tax measures against state banks.[98]

The number of conversions in 1863 and during the first months of 1864 was negligible. One of them was that of the Safety Fund Bank of Boston (founded in 1859) which joined the national system as the First National Bank of Boston.[99] Almost immediately thereafter the Granite Bank became the Second National Bank of that city. Another conversion planned in Boston (probably by the Merchants Bank in which Samuel Hooper was influential) seems to have been abandoned since the stockholders refused to part with their established firm name.[100] In addition there were altogether six other banks in Boston which were willing to convert. Most of them were small and presided over by unknown men, except the Washington and the New England Banks, guided by Almon D. Hodges and Thomas Lamb, respectively.[101] They discussed their problems in a meeting held on December 2, 1863, but no immediate action was taken.

These circumstances forced recognition that the law must be rewritten completely; and a new version was passed which bears the date of June 30, 1864. It seems that at this stage (i.e., in connection with the revision of the act of 1863) McCulloch consulted a bankers' committee among whose members were George S. Coe, John Earl Williams, and possibly T.W. Olcott of Albany.[102] The first was undoubtedly a good choice, but the same can hardly be said about the second, unless his appointment was a tactical move to break down his resistance.[103] In addition a deputation from New York banks including James Gallatin and George D. Lyman, manager of the Clearing House, spent an afternoon advising the Ways and Means Committee.[104] The act of 1864 increased the capital requirements for National Banks; it permitted state banks which converted to national status to retain their established firm names; and required National Banks selected as depositories of public funds to give security. Note redemption was enacted in 17 centers in addition to redemption at each bank's counters: each country bank had to select a redemption agent among the National Banks of the 17 redemption cities, each of which in turn had to have a redemption agent among those in New York City. National Banks were obligated to receive from the public the notes of all other National Banks at par (a new provision without counterpart in the act of 1863).

Even this new version of the National Currency Act did not make conversions[105] universal although the changes were in line with the wishes of the banking community. The growth of the National Banking system continued at a very slow and unsatisfactory rate (by the end of 1864 there existed only 681 National Banks with a capital of about $144,000,000; not before March 1865 was the $100,000,000 mark for note issues reached). Nevertheless National Banks were largely relied upon to sell the 10-40's bonds and the 7.3 per cent treasury notes of 1864; but they were not too successful.[106] That slow development is easily explained: National Banking did not permit the creation of loanable funds in the form of banknotes which many state banking laws did. For this and other reasons banking under the law of 1864 was not as profitable as banking under state laws.[107] The only bait, the possibility of becoming a depository of public funds, did not prove adequate because government deposits were not as advantageous as expected. A promise which seems to have been made, namely, that legal tenders would be withdrawn and canceled as fast as National Bank notes went into circulation, was not kept and probably had been discounted from the outset.[108] Consequently with profit as the flywheel of the economic system, the inherent logic of the latter forbade conversions and the establishment of National Banks in large parts of the country.

Thus it is explicable that the editor of a reputable trade paper felt the need of explaining such conversions as were taking place as being speculative schemes for the purpose of selling gold, dividing the surplus, and starting again under a new system which did not require a metallic basis.[109] Unfair as that argument was, there was in fact no incentive to convert unless there were reasons other than making money or profit chances from opportunities other than a regular banking business. When Elbridge Gerry Spaulding, for instance, brought his Farmers and Mechanics Bank of Buffalo into the fold as early as 1864, he probably meant to act patriotically. He may well have felt it was the thing to do regardless of slightly lower profit expectations.[110] In that same year Samuel Hooper appealed to the state banks to yield the control of the currency to the nation as an act of patriotism,[111] and the Merchants Bank of Boston, in which he was influential, was actually the very first to convert after the passage of the act of 1864. Patriotism seems to have played a certain role with the founders of the First National Bank of Baltimore (formally organized on December 2, 1863)[112] among whose leading backers and promoters were Johns Hopkins and Thomas Swann (c. 1806-1883). The latter, as mayor of Baltimore, had taken a decided stand against Secession when the Civil War broke out and had proved an unswerving Unionist ever after. He became the bank's first president. Johns Hopkins, on the other hand, president of the Merchants Bank and a director in a half dozen others in Baltimore, had backed the city with funds in the most trying days of the war. Patriotic motives certainly influenced Jay Cooke and the owners of Winslow, Lanier and Company whose activities as founders of National Banks will be discussed.[113] But at the same time both firms must have seen advantages in connection with their security business. Finally, for John Thompson, the founder of the First National Bank of New York, the latter provided an opportunity to stage a comeback after a bankruptcy. Where none of such motives prompted successful or powerful state bankers, they kept aloof or went on showing outright hostility.[114]

From the point of view of this research the question poses itself whether or not the setting up of the first National Banks was an entrepreneurial achievement. It must be answered in the negative. Since National Banking was based on principles generally known and widely adopted, the administration of National Banks remained within the realm of routine procedure. This author knows of only one new kind of business developed after the introduction of National Banking and even that was a very minor one: correspondent relationships were established between National Banks in Washington and in other places. The former attended to the work of examining the deposited government bonds and of redeeming, counting, and destroying worn-out and mutilated notes of the latter in recognition of a deposit of $400. (As far as the remuneration goes, the mode of the Suffolk Bank was copied, of course.) Jay Cooke's First National Bank of Washington seems to have cultivated this business in the 1860's.[115]

On the other hand, courage was needed to join the new banking system, and faith in the Union was indispensable. It must have been generally known that powerful bankers in the financial centers were opposed to the system. According to the rules of the game they would try to discredit National Bank notes and their issuers as, in fact, they did. A speaker before the 1864 Convention of National Banks stated in retrospect that until recently "to avow one's self [sic!] as friendly to a National Banking system would have been somewhat perilous."[116] John Thompson's First National Bank of New York, for instance, regardless of its alliance with the Bank of the Republic was for months virtually excluded from the clearings, could not do a regular banking business; and Thompson had willy nilly to restrict his business to dealings in war bonds.

To be sure, as already indicated, not all bankers behaved like the leaders of the New York Clearing House.[117] Businessmen played a role in devising National Banking, as has been shown above, and some bankers were conspicuous among the promoters of the measure, such as Elbridge Gerry Spaulding, Samuel Hooper, and the Cooke brothers, Jay and Henry. Others provided encouragement by correspondence as, for instance, Samuel Hurd Walley, president of the Revere Bank, who carried weight in Boston banking circles, or Morris Ketchum, the New York private banker.[118] Real enthusiasm for the new banking system, however, could be found only in some states of the West where National Banking promised an improvement over what had existed before. Statistics reflect the situation.

Disregarding Pennsylvania and New York, which by the end of 1863 had 20 and 16 National Banks, respectively, only four states had more than five National Banks each; namely, Ohio, 38; Indiana, 20; Illinois, 7; and Iowa, 6.[119] The fact that Ohio led all other states in the establishment of National Banks may have been due to Chase's personal prestige as a former governor of the state and to the fact that the National Banking act had in certain respects a marked similarity to Ohio banking legislation. On the other hand, Indiana's Free Banking system after "a disastrous failure of the law" had experienced a "quick and ruinous collapse" in 1854;[120] Illinois' Free Banking had utterly broken down by 1861;[121] and in Iowa, where the very first National Bank went into operation, no banks had been set up under an existing Free Banking measure.[122] To be sure, Ohio, Indiana, and Iowa possessed well managed state banks with branches, but good as they were, they were widely disliked as representing some sort of monopolies.

In contrast to Ohio, Indiana, Illinois, and to a less extent Iowa, National Banking had a slow start in Wisconsin and Michigan, where only 4 and 2 National Banks, respectively, were set up in 1863. In the former state the adoption of the new system by the existing banks would have meant writing off heavy losses on those state bonds which were held as the basis of circulation. Moreover, the Wisconsin Bankers' Association, after creating some esprit de corps among bank officers, had the banking situation of the state well under control. As a matter of fact, the establishment of the earliest National Banks in Wisconsin proved a rather disintegrating factor.[123] In Michigan, on the other hand, the adoption of National Banking appeared impossible because the act of 1863 permitted only 7 per cent interest (the state's legal rate) while under the state law agreements could be made between contracting parties which would allow for interest up to 10 per cent.[124] On top of that, the delivery of National Bank notes, after the deposit of bonds had been effected, was so slow that a further loss of interest resulted.[125] The differential between the interest rate allowed by the National Currency Act of 1863 and the higher local rate slowed down the development of National Banking in Iowa also.[126]

Moreover, the revision in 1864 of the original National Currency Act created an additional hurdle: the fact that the version of 1864 forbade real estate loans, permitted by the one of 1863, worked to the detriment of the West as a whole and consequently retarded the adoption of National Banking. (The clause remained unchanged until the Federal Reserve system was enacted.)[127]

Bitter as were the political and economic battles all through 1862, 1863, and 1864, the constitutionality of the National Currency act was hardly questioned and never tested. To be sure, in the fall of 1863 it was expected that the Superintendent of the Banking Department of the State of New York would make that test by commencing suit against National Banks which might attempt to issue national currency in the state. The Federal government was prepared to defend the National Banks and had already approached an eminent member of the New York bar with a view to having him act for the government in this case.[128] It did not come before the courts, however; the constitutionality of the act was obviously beyond doubt because of several earlier decisions regarding the Second Bank of the United States. Nevertheless its constitutionality was affirmed later by an obiter dictum in the case of Farmers and Mechanics Bank v. Dearing.[129] The judge pointed out that the constitutionality of the act of 1864 rested on the same principles as the act creating the Second Bank of the United States. Therefore the reasoning of Secretary Hamilton and the Supreme Court in the cases, McCulloch v. Maryland (4 Wheat. 316) and Osborne v. The Bank of the United States (9 Wheat. 708) applied. And again: "National Banks organised under the act are the instruments designed to be used to aid the government in the administration of an important branch of the public service; and Congress which is the sole judge of the necessity for their creation having brought them into existence, the States can exercise no control over them, nor in any wise affect their operation except so far as it may see proper to permit." In contrast to the National Currency Act as such, the 10 per cent tax on state bank circulation (to be discussed shortly) was challenged, but upheld in the case of Veazie Bank v. Fenno (8 Wall 533). Nevertheless as late as 1877 the opinion was voiced that the National Bank Act was unconstitutional to the extent that it made banknotes legal tender for any purpose other than for payments to the bank that had issued them.[130]

We know very little of the considerations and negotiations which preceded the forming of individual National Banks in 1863 and early in 1864. In some cases there may have been a struggle between an older and a younger generation, as the historian of the Delaware County National Bank reports for that enterprise. In this case the exponent of the older generation was sure that the National Banking system would meet disaster as had the "national banks" (the First and Second Banks of the United States) before.[131] One fact stands out clearly, namely, that private bankers played a conspicuous part among the founders of the earliest National Banks. Jay Cooke, the foremost promoter of National Banking,[132] can be found connected with three of them. Jay Cooke and Company and E.W. Clark and Company founded and controlled the First National Bank of Philadelphia. The First National Bank of Washington was established by the Cooke firms of Philadelphia and Washington and "was to all intents and purposes a part of the Jay Cooke group." Finally when New York was very slow in setting up National Banks and when a large one was needed in the city for the sake of prestige, Chase and McCulloch called on Jay Cooke who secured capital in both Philadelphia and New York and founded the Fourth

National Bank in the latter city with a capital of $5,000,000.[133] In fact, he was even willing to help found another National Bank in New York, one with the large capital of $50,000,000, if the recalcitrant city bankers were not willing to join the new system. Nothing came of this latter plan.

Cooke's role in founding the Fourth National Bank of New York, the first endowed with a large capital, can be better understood if one knows the background: an earlier attempt to that effect had broken down in November, 1863. On October 21 of that year in the Fifth Avenue Hotel in New York McCulloch met a number of capitalists invited by such men as Peter Cooper, John Jacob Astor, Jr., Freeman Clarke, Morris Ketchum, George Opdyke, Jonathan Sturges, and Elisha Riggs. Bankers were remarkable by their absence, except for John Aikman Stewart, one of the men who were developing the modern trust company, then the secretary and soon to become the president of the United States Trust Company. McCulloch addressed the assembly. He explained the need for a national currency in general and especially for a large National Bank in New York City. If such an enterprise could be founded, its existence would hasten the success of the system whose ultimate victory he believed possible without an actual clash between state and National Banks. McCulloch tried to convince the capitalists that a large National Bank in New York City was bound to become a business success, needed as it was as the correspondent of the existing hundred National Banks in the interior. Thereupon the meeting resolved to organize a $5,000,000 National Bank in the city, appointing a committee to select commissioners for receiving subscriptions at the United States Trust Company. The Commissioners (including Peter Cooper, George Opdyke, and Freeman Clarke) sent out notices on November 9 that subscription books would lie open between November 23 and December 1. The members of the committee appointed in the October meeting were probably pledged to sign a certain number of shares. Notwithstanding these efforts, the attempt ended with failure, since only $1,000,000 could be raised; and Jay Cooke who had not participated in the plan had to be asked for help.[134]

Before Cooke made his sally into New York, other private bankers had already taken an interest in establishing National Banks in the city. The First National Bank of New York (capital $300,000) was, as indicated, the work of John Thompson (1802-1891) of banknote detector fame (Bank Note and Commercial Reporter). As a matter of fact, that bank has been considered the successor of Thompson Brothers, the private banking firm of his sons, which John Thompson guided more or less. Like others among the early private bankers he had started his career as a seller of lottery tickets until in 1833 he opened a brokerage business in Wall Street, becoming a so-called Wall Street banker. Being widely known in the West because of his Bank Note Reporter, Thompson was selected as the New York agent of numerous Western banks and became the leading Eastern dealer in less known Western banknotes. Unfortunately he also engaged in dangerous railroad financeering which led to his complete financial collapse in 1857. He even lost the editorship of his Reporter, which he seems to have transferred to his sons. Regardless of his failure, during the Civil War Thompson became an unofficial adviser of Secretary Chase in matters of National Banking and was able to stage a come-back into the banking field when founding the First National Bank of New York in cooperation with his sons, one of whom (Samuel) acted as the president. To be sure, being still under the cloud of his bankruptcy, John Thompson himself was neither a stockholder, let alone a director, nor was he an officer; but, in fact, he ran the enterprise. (Incidentally, in 1867 when the National Currency Act was supposed to be revised he offered his services as a lobbyist for National Banks, and later still he founded the Chase National Bank.)[135]

Shortly after John Thompson had set up the First National Bank of New York, another firm of private bankers established the Third; namely, Winslow, Lanier and Company. Their motives in so doing have been analyzed before and more will be said about this firm in its proper place.[136] It seems probable that James Winslow (1814-1874) was the partner who led in this transaction, although personal friendship between McCulloch and Lanier may also have played a part, as Jay Cooke intimated.

Professor James has shown that in Chicago early National Banking was completely in the hands of private bankers who founded all of the National Banks of that city established between 1863 and 1865.[137] Edmund Aiken, member of the private banking house of Aiken and Norton, brought together interested merchants and capitalists while the National Currency bill was still pending. He and his friends formed the First National Bank of Chicago, which went into operation as early as 1863. (The founders took from fifty to one hundred and seventy-five shares each; Aiken became president.) The Second, Third, Fourth, and Fifth National Banks of Chicago emanated in 1864 from the banking house of E.I. Tinkham[138] and Company, while Salomon Sturges and Sons founded in the same year the Northwestern National Bank, the name of which indicates that it was brought into existence after the revision of the original National Currency Act. Another early founder of National Banks in Chicago was J. Young Scammon,[139] originally a lawyer who turned banker and for years was the main antagonist of George Smith. He controlled the Chicago Marine and Fire Insurance Company, an enterprise similar to Smith's Winconsin Marine and Fire Insurance Company without being equally successful. Subsequently Scammon converted its banking department into a Free Bank, the Marine Bank, which after great initial success was severely hit in the depression following the panic of 1857. Thereupon in 1862 Scammon became a private banker until in 1864 the versatile man switched again to founding three National Banks, the Mechanics, the Manufacturers, and the Merchants National Banks. His and Tinkham's records were matched by William F. Coolbough who was soon to become the West's representative National Banker. He was the ranking partner in the private banking house of W.F. Coolbough and Company and entered the field of National Banking by founding the Union, City, and Commercial National Banks of Chicago, the first named of which was the leading bank of the city as early as 1866.[140] In Illinois outside of Chicago the brothers Harry H. and Benjamin S. Ferris (born in 1832 and 1831, respectively) gained some importance. They had started as farmers in Princeton, Illinois, in the 1850's, and in 1862 had turned private bankers, carrying on the typical combination of banking, real estate, and insurance business. In 1865 they reorganized their enterprise as the First National Bank of Princeton. (In the 1870's Harry Ferris founded additional National Banks.)[141]

Outside of Chicago the founding of Western National Banks may not have been dominated by private bankers as completely as it was there, but private bankers played a more or less conspicuous part in this respect everywhere. The very first National Bank to open for business, the First National Bank of Davenport, was the successor of the banking house of Corbin and Dow guided by Austin Corbin. He has been discussed previously in his capacity as a private banker. Suffice it to say at this point that he was the driving force in that conversion and that he probably became the very first active National Bank president.[142] In Michigan, to give an example for that state, the First National Bank of Detroit succeeded the banking firm of Parsons and Fisher, and was founded in 1863 by Philo Parsons.[143]

If we go further west to Minnesota and focus our attention on the Twin Cities, for which material is available, we again find private bankers as the founders of the first National Banks.[144] But there is a slight difference in that the private bankers involved had turned state bankers before applying for national charters. The First National Bank of St. Paul originated in 1863 through conversion of the Bank of Minnesota which in turn was the creation (in 1862) of the banking house of Thompson Brothers. The Second National Bank of St. Paul was converted in 1864 from the People's Bank which earlier, in 1858, had become the successor of the private banking house of M. Mackabie and E.S. Edgerton. Finally, the First National Bank of Minneapolis was converted in 1865 from the Minneapolis Bank of 1864, the successor of the private banking firm of Sidle, Wolford and Company. These cases show a distinct pattern.[145]

The introduction of National Banking in the South, to the knowledge of the author, has not as yet been made the subject of research, so that details are not known. It goes without saying that the development started later than in the North, but in other respects there were similarities. Here again the abilities of the creative entrepreneur were hardly required, but a high degree of courage was necessary to brave a not too friendly public opinion. As late as 1878 Southern chambers of commerce were active in marshalling public opinion for a repeal of the prohibitive tax of 1865 in order to rebuild state banking systems all over the South.[146] Both Northerners and Southerners were responsible for establishing the first National Banks south of the Mason and Dixon line; but it is not known exactly to what extent Northerners participated, to which extent their participation involved capital transfer to an impoverished region of the country, and consequently to what extent National Banking in the early years of Reconstruction contributed to the rebuilding of the South. The discussions of the early 1870's on the maldistribution of note issues[147] seem to indicate that not much Northern capital went South to form National Banks. But some undoubtedly did. It is known, for instance, that the first permanent National Bank in Florida, the First National Bank of Jacksonville, was promoted by General T.W.C. Moore, once a member of Sheridan's staff and later National Bank examiner, and his son-in-law, Francis Elias Spinner, for years United States Treasurer.[148] As an example of a Southerner who founded one of the early National Banks in his region George W. Williams (born in 1820) may be cited. He was the son of an enterprising Georgia farmer, himself a wholesale grocer in Augusta and Charleston (connected with two of the early railroad companies) who had gained banking experience as a director of the Bank of South Carolina. He became the founder of the First National Bank of Charleston.[149] After this necessary detour, the main line of thought will again be taken up.

Regardless of all the exertions by Chase and McCulloch, regardless of the activities of private bankers and other capitalists joining the system, regardless of the endeavors of patriotic bankers, such as E.G. Spaulding, the chances for National Banking were not good as late as 1865, which was due, at least partly, to the unabated hostility of powerful bankers in the East. There was even a possibility that two banking systems would permanently contend for the field. The danger inherent in this situation was clearly recognized; under such conditions it would be impossible for the government to restrain the issue of paper money.[150] Nothing remained except to bludgeon the existing state banks into the national system. Such a policy had been contemplated earlier, when coercive tax measures were recommended repeatedly. Suggestions to this effect have an interesting history of their own. As early as 1831, Albert Gallatin suggested in his Considerations[151] that Congress might lay a duty on all banknotes so as to convert the banks into mere banks of discount and deposit and to annihilate the paper currency. At least it could thus suppress small notes below $10. In this form his plan became influential. It was taken up by Senator Rives of Virginia who suggested a stamp duty on notes; while Thomas Hart Benton seems to have been the first (in 1855) to introduce in Congress a measure of this kind. His bill aimed at levying 40, 20, and 10 cents on banknotes below five, ten, and twenty dollars, respectively.[152] In 1856 in the same vein Secretary of the Treasury Guthrie in the Finance Report of that year[153] recommended the suppression of small notes by taxation at some future time, and these ideas filtered through until they were echoed in the West by 1861.

Under these circumstances it is not surprising that tax measures against state banks were contemplated while the National Currency Act was still hanging fire. As Henry Cooke reported to his brother Jay, Chase himself was planning gradually to drive state banks out of existence by a tax of 1-2 per cent on their circulation.[154] He was backed by such an eminent man as Amasa Walker and later by Hugh McCulloch who recommended prohibitive tax measures in his second report as the Comptroller; and proposals of this character were popular in the West, especially in Chicago.[155] The powerful Eastern state bankers, however, succeeded in having dropped the (identical) tax on National and state bank circulation (envisaged in the Hooper bill) as far as the latter was concerned. Or, to put it differently, there was at first discrimination against National, not against state, banks, a discrimination which was quickly remedied in the Revenue Act of March, 1863.[156] In the end Eastern opposition did not prevail and sec. 6 of the Act of March 3, 1865 "to amend 'An Act to provide Internal Revenue...' approved June 30, 1864" sounded the death knell for state banks.[157]

There is general agreement that the ultimate success of the National Banking system (its crashing through, if you please) was to a large extent due to the remarkable organizational ability of Hugh McCulloch, one of America's great financiers, who has yet to find a biographer. Hardly any details about his share in the achievement are known. McCulloch (1808-1895), born in Maine the son of a shipbuilder and West India merchant, himself bred for the law, had migrated from Boston to Fort Wayne, Indiana, in 1833. Two years later he became the cashier and manager of the local branch of the State Bank of Indiana, in which capacity he served until the expiration of its charter in 1857, having also been on the board of directors. Thereafter he became the president of its successor, the Bank of the State of Indiana. In that capacity he went to Washington in 1862 to oppose the pending bill of the National Currency Act. However, as he himself has described, shortly thereafter he changed his stand. He was satisfied with some of the amendments embodied in the bill before it was passed, but other reasons weighed even more heavily. He became convinced that the war could not be speedily concluded, that the cost would be enormous, and that the notes of state banks, imperfectly secured as they were, could not safely be accepted in the collection of public revenue. A system of internal taxes necessitated a national circulation, as he expressed it in a speech of 1863. So he was forced to conclude that banks with a perfectly secured circulation current throughout the nation were an absolute necessity. If this conclusion was cogent he must go further and concede that in time of a national emergency the government had the right to command his services in establishing such a system as was indispensable. So he accepted Chase's offer to become the country's first Comptroller of the Currency. (To be sure, he was not the first to whom the position was tendered: it had already been turned down by several Eastern bankers, Joseph Patterson of Philadelphia among them.) McCulloch assumed his duties in 1863, and although on the point of resigning in 1864 to accept the presidency of Jay Cooke's Fourth National Bank of New York, continued in office until 1865 when he became the Secretary of the Treasury.[158]

III

After the big Eastern and especially the New York banks had joined the National Banking system in 1865, the matter of note redemption was pushed into the foreground. In that year Freeman Clarke, Comptroller of the Currency, proposed that all banks redeem their notes in the great financial centers, New York or Philadelphia,[159] a suggestion which seems to have been an adaptation of McCulloch's proposal of 1864 according to which all banks except those in Philadelphia and Boston should redeem in New York.[160] The importance of the redemption problem was generally overestimated. It was not seen or it was intentionally overlooked that in a period of suspension, notes "uniform in design and appearance," issued under a national law, secured by the same national bonds, backed by a national guarantee, limited as to the total that could be issued, and controlled by the same federal agency could not easily depreciate in relation to government paper money. Nor could notes of one such bank easily depreciate in relation to those of another. There was no comparison between such issues and those floated previously under different state laws (themselves of different character) under more or less lax supervision. The fact that originally National Bank notes were not at par in New York, as predicted, does not disprove this thesis. It was easy for men to predict depreciation if they had the power arbitrarily to adopt a business policy to that end, such policy being an expression of older ways of thinking or of outright hostility. After conversion the New York banks had, of course, to change their policy; but it is not clear what it was immediately thereafter. Although they were now required by law to take all National Bank notes at par from the public, they seem to have been very reluctant to comply with this provision of the act; and when they did, going further, they seem to have agreed among themselves to take such notes at par also from each other. However such policy was not in line with that established by the Comptroller of the Currency who aimed at a differentiation between legal tenders and National Bank notes, the former alone being lawful money into which National Bank notes should be convertible. The then Comptroller (the just mentioned Freeman Clarke)[161] wrote a rather threatening letter to George S. Coe in order to whip the New York banks into line.

Under these circumstances and with the blessings of McCulloch (then Secretary of the Treasury) by the middle of 1865 the New York, Boston, and Philadelphia banks were working on plans for an improved par-redemption system. It is supposed to have originated in discussions of the New York Society for the Advancement of Social Science which counted numerous bank directors among its members.[162] National Banks, acting as redemption agents in these cities and participating in the scheme, would take all National Bank notes at par (as required under the act of 1864), sort them, and forward them to the issuer's redemption agent, who in turn would send them to the former. The proposition was fought by the country banks because it implied that larger reserves must be kept with the redemption agents; in addition, the total of notes which could be kept afloat at any time would be decreased. It was this deflationary aspect of the scheme which, in contrast, must have appealed to the big city bankers. Because of such opposition the project had to be abandoned and it was replaced by one according to which several specialized banks of redemption were to be set up, one of these in New York. On September 26, 1865 the New York banks met to consider the matter and appointed a committee headed by James Gallatin.[163] In a meeting on October 11 the latter reported a plan modeled on older examples (Suffolk Bank, Boston; Metropolitan Bank, New York).

The plan as presented in this meeting was a voluntary one. There was no intention of coercing any bank into any particular mode of redemption other than that contemplated by law, so James Gallatin stated. He stressed that the scheme did not imply hostility to the interests of any National Bank established in good faith and he expressed full confidence in the Secretary of the Treasury and the Comptroller of the Currency as to the establishment of an adequate official policy in this matter. It is probable that the promoters believed that an amendment to the National Currency Act as proposed in the Report of the Comptroller of the Currency of 1865 would make mandatory redemption of all National Bank notes at New York, Philadelphia or Boston and that they were preparing therefor.[164] Nevertheless the historian aware of the personalities involved must become suspicious. He knows that James Gallatin[165] was at that time an old man living in the past, who had shown the most uncooperative attitude toward Chase when the latter was Secretary of the Treasury, who had opposed one of the country's greatest presidents, and who belonged to those die-hards who had fought National Banking tooth and nail. The historian must furthermore consider that the meeting which Gallatin addressed was presided over by John Quentin Jones, another New York banker whose uncooperative attitude is a matter of record.[166] By contrast, New York banking leaders in whom the government had confidence and who were known as cooperative, such as John Austin Stevens and

George S. Coe, were not on the committee. Under these circumstances the historian cannot help sensing some selfishness and undisclosed ulterior motives. On the other hand, it is likely that the men concerned actually feared that under the national law wild-cat banking would grow up, a possibility they wanted to nip in the bud.

The plan itself envisaged that all National Bank notes would be taken at par in New York, as required by law. The bank receiving such notes from the public would deposit them in an "assorting house." The latter was to be under the direction of a committee of nine, elected by the member banks, and would itself become a member of the Clearing House. Through the Clearing House all notes redeemable in New York would be presented to the issuer or redemption agent in question. Such notes as were redeemable in Boston or Philadelphia would be sent to the appropriate agents in these cities unless their banks set up similar assorting houses, in which case there would be close cooperation between such houses. The rest of the notes received in New York would be presented wherever redeemed. What the various redemption agents did with the notes once redeemed, was of no interest to the New York bankers. They seem to have felt that only if underpinned by such a redemption system would National Banking work satisfactorily; otherwise the provision in the act which required the banks to take National Bank notes at par should be dropped.[167] The cost of redemption was to be borne by the members according to the amount of notes delivered to the assorting house.

This plan went further than the law: under the latter, country National Banks redeemed in one of 17 redemption cities (including New York), while National Banks in these cities redeemed in New York. But they redeemed in New York only their own notes, not the notes of the country banks whose redemption agents they were, unless by chance the country bank's redemption agent was located in New York. Under the New York plan all notes would have been redeemed at New York just as all New England notes had once been redeemed at the Suffolk Bank.[168] The plan was sound, of course, but not as necessary as the promoters thought. It could not be put into operation. The idea of redeeming all National Bank notes in New York was thoroughly unpopular in the West which labored under the impression that it was to be made tributary to New York. The Chicago Clearing House fought the scheme violently and in 1866 organized opposition thereto all over the region.[169] It was objected that central redemption in New York was onerous and would only serve to place the money of the country at the disposal of

stock gamblers through the call-loan mechanism. Instead it was suggested that all notes of the Northwest be redeemed in Chicago where reserves could be employed in a sounder way. (Incidentally, this was an early move toward making Chicago a central reserve city.) Regardless of all the lofty phrases, the West as well as New York fought for their special and antagonistic interests.

After the failure of the scheme of 1865 the question of note redemption at a central point came up again in 1867, but now the problem was gaining a different aspect. Samuel Hooper and H.R. Hulburd, the then Comptroller, were fostering the new plan. Both of them realized, as Amasa Walker had predicted as early as 1863, that there was no immediate demand for the redemption of National Bank notes and that even those of the obscurest institution were at par without central redemption. This nevertheless they wished instituted. Samuel Hooper proffered as the reason that any temporarily passive balance of indebtedness would create a demand at the point of shipment of specie, i.e., in New York.[170] Hulburd, on the other hand, hoped that redemption at a common center would regulate the circulation so that it would rise and fall in proportion to demand. He hoped that redemption would come into existence when legal tenders appreciated so as to command a premium over banknotes. How he could have expected such a development is not understandable, unless he thought, as he probably did, that the total of legal tenders would be reduced by act of Congress. Compulsory redemption at a center would then become a preparatory step for resumption of specie payments. The interest attached to this report of Hulburd's lies in the change of viewpoint.[171]

Soon thereafter a type of central redemption agency was suggested, different from what had been proposed before. Since Western banks violently objected to a central redemption agency owned by the New York City banks, it was proposed to establish an enterprise of the same character, but owned by all the banks of the country. That is to say, the idea back of the Bank of Mutual Redemption was reshaped to fit the case: a National Bank without the privilege of issue was to be established in New York with a capital of ten or fifteen million dollars which would act as the central redemption agency and clearing house for National Bank notes. It was to be owned by the banks of the country in proportion to their surplus funds and to have two departments, one for the redemption of notes and a second to carry on a regular banking business. The latter's profit was to cover the cost of note redemption and in addition to yield a revenue on the invested capital. That bankers' bank should at the same time act as the custodian of the reserves of the National Banks and do away with the vicious custom of lending them on call, for the enterprise was to be prohibited from paying interest on bankers' balances.[172] (Incidentally, the Comptroller was afraid that without such a system New York funds would demand a premium and he was inclined to consider illegal the paying of interest on demand deposits, for banks were authorized by the National Banking Act to receive, not to hire deposits.)

Again nothing came of the plan; but soon thereafter the discussion took an almost grotesque turn. It was now generally recognized that neither business nor the public desired the redemption of National Bank notes,[173] but this situation was obviously too good to go unsuspected. A speaker addressing the 1869 convention of National Banks denied for purely theoretical reasons that National Bank notes could have a nationally uniform value.[174] So in 1873 John Jay Knox, the then Comptroller, presented the fantastic idea of forcing redemption on the country by deteriorating the monetary conditions. By replacing a system of legal par redemption with a system of redemption at a discount set by law (as the State of New York had possessed prior to the Civil War) one could make redemption a business proposition. By way of the profit motive redemption would then become a reality, Knox argued. Thereby, so he hoped, note issues would be made elastic, to the advantage of the national economy. The Comptroller realized that in consequence of such a policy the rate of domestic exchange between the various cities which was then in normal times 1/10 of one per cent would rise to about 1 per cent, a rise which might well mean the downfall of the National Banking system, as was recognized. But so infatuated was the older generation with the idea of note redemption that this possibility did not keep the Comptroller from submitting the idea to Congress and to public opinion.[175]

The redemption problem was solved ultimately in 1874, and the solution of that year stood until Federal Reserve Banking was enacted and put into effect.[176] According to the act of 1874 National Banks had to deposit 5 per cent of their circulation in lawful money with the Treasury, to be held and used for the redemption of notes. The comment of the Comptroller on section 3 of the act of 1874 is most interesting: according to his interpretation the object of the act was "the purification of the circulation rather than its redemption in the proper sense of the word."[177] He had to recognize that only under rare conditions would an individual or bank desire the redemption of National Bank notes, so that the Treasury would de facto redeem mainly worn-out and mutilated notes. By that time the Comptroller assigned but one essential function to redemption proper, namely, that it forced the banks to bank on short term trade paper and to abstain from investment in accommodation paper and in loans on doubtful stocks and bonds, a complete change from the official outlook in the years after 1865.[178] Moreover he could see a second, minor advantage in redemption, namely, that the weaker banks would be continually reminded of the fact that their notes were not money, but only promises to pay money, and that they actually had to make good their promises.[179]

The Comptroller was now very proud that the notes of National Banks were the only secured currency that was redeemed at one central point[180] besides the place of issue. The banks, however, went on grumbling because under the law of 1874 they had to bear the burden of redemption. To this charge they objected. It was generally recognized as a principle, so they correctly claimed, that holders should at their own expense present notes at the point of redemption, if such was desired. They were answered that, as things stood, filthy and mutilated notes would go on circulating if the holders had to present them at their own expense, a situation which would be detrimental to both banks and public. Moreover the banks were permitted to send notes to the Treasury unsorted, thereby saving their time and money.[181] In the course of the discussion, the spokesman of the New York banks, James Buell, president of the Importers and Traders National Bank of New York and a banking leader at the time,[182] recommended again an old plan: Since the banks had to bear the expense they should at least establish a redemption system of their own which would work faster and cheaper than the official one in Washington.[183]

The question of reserves agitated the minds of early National Bankers much less than that of redemption; and, when it did, it was not the pyramiding of reserves that worried them. Legal reserves as such were still a problem and it was questionable whether reserves should be prescribed at all, and if so whether they should be prescribed for notes and deposits or for notes or deposits only.[184] Some of the bankers had not even cut loose from the age-old idea that there was a connection and consequently a relationship to be established between capital and the amount of reserves to be kept. The opponents of legal reserve requirements pointed out that directors and managers of banks could best judge how much they could loan and how large a reserve they needed. Others took the stand that the government was under obligation to protect note holders while depositors should be allowed to protect themselves.[185] Finally, it was argued that reserve requirements cut down the amount of loanable funds available for business and that reserves to be kept "at all times," as the law required, were useless. In answer John Jay Knox,[186] Comptroller of the Currency, declared the latter assumption simply absurd; and in fact the widely-held opinion to this effect did not find justification in the wording of the law. Years later such an outstanding banker as James B. Forgan currently acted on the assumption that the law allowed him to use his reserves in time of pressure. During seasonal stringency he permitted his reserves to drop temporarily below the legal minimum, but he never had any difficulty on that account.

Bankers themselves, and especially New York bankers, seem to have desired a removal of all restrictions. As early as 1872 Henry Clews (1834-1923), then still in the early stages of an honorable business career as a Wall Street broker, suggested (in a circular letter to his business friends) that an amendment to the National Currency Act be passed which would make it possible for banks themselves to determine their reserves. It was not the government's business to protect depositors, and seasonal stringencies in the money market were traceable to the legal reserve requirements.[187] An anonymous banker followed up this pamphlet in a letter to the editor of the New York Times suggesting a quid pro quo: National Banks should surrender their currency in return for entire relief from legal reserve requirements, a suggestion which was seen from the New York point of view with a disregard for the situation in the back country.[188] Two years later James Buell made himself the spokesman of the bankers' outlook before the Committee on Banking and Currency of the House of Representatives.[189] He wanted to drop legal reserve requirements and enact in lieu thereof the requirement that the banks of the larger cities make weekly, and those in the smaller places monthly, statements for publication. The banks' customers could then decide if their depositories were safe, public opinion would be brought to bear on the banks, and self interest would cause their managers to keep ample reserves. Since the banks required their "dealers" to inform them on their financial standing, it was but a fair requirement to make them publish regular statements themselves.[190]

From the historical point of view, this fight of New York bankers was directed against Samuel Hooper's achievement of 1858 and his successful move of bringing legal reserve requirements into the National Currency Act.[191] Thus the Comptroller (John Jay Knox) had to remind the bankers that reserves were meant to protect demand liabilities, or, to put it in words which he did not use, to

guarantee the liquidity of the banking system. But the bankers had a point, and relief finally came. It did not come in the way which they desired (removal of all legal reserve requirements), but by eliminating the reserve requirements for banknotes. This step was taken in the act of June 20, 1874 "fixing the amount of United States notes...," sections 2 and 3, of which the latter section established a 5 per cent redemption fund for notes in the Treasury. This regulation was well in line with New York tradition. It followed the experience of 1857 on the basis of which reserves against notes were considered superfluous. The contemporary literature shows that this tradition had lingered on, until in 1874 it was revived.[192] At the same time other problems were discussed which the historian recognizes as younger and more important ones; and, in fact, if the proposed remedial measures had passed they would to a certain extent have done away with the pyramiding of reserves. The original House and Senate bills embodied clauses, according to which country banks were obligated to keep their entire 15 per cent legal reserves in lawful money in their own vaults; while banks in the reserve cities would still have been entitled to count bankers' balances in New York among their 25 per cent legal reserves. The former clause, however, was lost during the legislative procedure and the Comptroller interpreted as the will of Congress that the previous regulation should remain unchanged; i.e., that both country banks and banks in the reserve cities could keep part of their reserves (three-fifths and one half, respectively,) in the form of balances.[193] National Banking remained saddled with the pyramiding of reserves until the establishment of the Federal Reserve system.

It should be understood that the distinction between reserve and central reserve cities did not exist during the period under investigation (prior to 1882). This distinction was introduced only by the Act of March 3, 1887 "to amend sections 5191 and 5192 of the Revised Statutes of the United States and for other purposes;" but a trend in this direction was established as early as 1864 in section 32 of that year's version of the National Currency Act. This section made New York de facto the central reserve city of the country.[194]

IV

If the historian wishes to gain a clear picture of the problems of National Banking, its structure, and its place in the national economy about a decade after its inception, he must read the debates of 1870, 1873, 1874, and 1875 which resulted from the introduction in Congress of amendments to the

National Currency Act.[195] An anonymous author, participating in those discussions, had a remarkable understanding of the basic question underlying the debates and determining to a large extent the history and status of contemporary National Banking. Why is there such a hue and cry in one section of our country against inflation, the author of 1874 asked, while in another there seems an almost unanimous voice in favor of an expansion of the currency? There must be, he concluded, some foundation for this unnatural situation.[196] None of the contemporaries seems to have fully understood the reasons why. The practical problem so important for the National Banks of the period, whether the currency should be increased, diminished or left alone, was ultimately decided by the distribution of political power among the contestants.[197] Carl Schurz's famous statement that the back country needed capital not money, which was widely accepted as revealing the fallacy of typical back country thinking and as justifying the course which was taken, is oversimplified and should not have become the classroom slogan that it did. The problem was actually very complicated.[198]

Back of the regional conflict was the fact that the North and the East, on the one hand, and the South and the West, on the other, had advanced to different stages in capitalistic development. Consequently the former were creditor, the latter debtor sections, as has often been stressed. On top of that, banking methods, reflecting those stages of economic development, were different in the various regions, a fact which was itself of importance. As a result it was impossible to frame measures which would fit equally the different sections of the country. What the West and South needed was not just capital, as Carl Schurz put it, but banks, currency, and loanable funds.

Conditions in the South and West were then still approximating those in Europe in medieval times when the available amount of a circulating medium had determined the borderlines of economic activity. Whatever plans the farmer or petty industrialist in the American back country conceived, he needed greenbacks or National Bank notes to put them into effect. Or to state the matter differently, loanable funds reached these men in the form of currency; if they had surpluses their savings were hoarded in the form of currency. (It is not surprising therefore that they confounded the latter with liquid capital.) But unfortunately for them the total of banknotes that could be issued by 1874 was allocated to their detriment: six Eastern states had a circulation of about 110.5 million dollars, five Middle states one of about 126.1, nine Western states one of about 78.8, and fourteen South-

ern and Southwestern states one of about 36.6. Amendments to the National Currency Act passed between 1870 and 1875 tended to improve this situation, but did not alter it.[199]

James A. Garfield (probably relying on material published in the fourth "Report of the Comptroller of the Currency" of 1866)[200] outlined the historical reasons for this maldistribution. According to the original National Currency Act of 1863 (sec. 17) one half of the total circulation was to be apportioned to the states and territories according to the population, the other half according to existing banking capital, business, and resources. This clause was repealed in the revised act of June 30, 1864, but restored in the act of March 3, 1865 amending it. This latter amendment, as Garfield claimed, was lost sight of, because the existing state banks (which under sec. 44 of the act of June 30, 1864 could become National Banking associations) were to receive preferential treatment under another law of March, 1865.[201] H.R. Hulburd (then acting Comptroller of the Currency) in discussing the problem in 1866 commented that the two laws of March, 1865, conflicted with one another so that the Secretary of the Treasury had to determine the policy. He felt that it was the will of Congress to absorb the existing banks rather than to organize new ones. Consequently he so interpreted the law as to permit all conversions for which applications were turned in. Garfield, however, complained that not even after the deadline for preferential conversions (July 1, 1865) had expired was the amendment of 1865 considered as mandatory by the officers of the Treasury Department: the note issue privilege was granted to every applicant until it was too late. The reasons for the disregard of the amendment of 1865 after the expiration of the deadline may be found in the fact that by July of that year only about 131.5 million dollars of notes out of the permissible total of 300 million had been taken out.

The maldistribution of note issues which thus came into existence was doubly unjust because the back country needed more currency than the advanced regions where checks and credit instruments could be used instead.[202] In fact, circulation was allocated to the various parts of the country in reverse proportion to their needs. Because of the survival of traditional business methods in the back country this unfortunate maldistribution alone was bound to impede in the less advanced sections the establishment of banking, because banking there was still identical with note issue as it once had been throughout the land.[203] Or to put it differently, unequal distribution of currency tended to lead to an unequal distribution of banking facilities. To make things worse capitalists could not even make use of such opportunities as were legally left to them, regardless of all injustice, and the issue of notes in the South and West remained below the amounts allocated under the act of 1874. This fact astonishing in the first moment is easily explained: As the law stood at that time existing loanable funds would shrink if invested in a National Bank in the back country. The funds had to be invested in government bonds which were above par (about 112 in 1874),[204] but notes could be received only to an amount of 90 per cent of the face value. Furthermore funds had to be kept against notes, amounting to 5 per cent as a minimum. When one considers in addition the then existing Federal tax of 1 per cent on the average circulation and 1/2 per cent tax on the bank's capital,[205] a load which in some states was increased by state taxation, one can readily see that only banks able to create purchasing power by way of deposit money could profit from National Banking. This was the case only in the Northeastern and Middle states.[206] So unprofitable was the note business that many National Banks invested in bonds only the legally required minimum of one third of their capital and on top of that omitted to take out the total of notes to which they were entitled.[207] The Comptroller of the Currency computed in 1878 that National Banks could make on their circulation only 2.65 per cent more than individuals could make by a straight loan of the corresponding capital.[208]

Under these circumstances the prosperous Western farmer was forced to handle his affairs in the same way in which medieval merchants had handled theirs prior to the introduction of banks: they kept as much money as they needed to take care of their peak loads or, as a contemporary writer expressed it, so much currency as would cover the total expenses of the farm from one crop to the next.[209] The appearance of National Banks in the back country did not really make things better, but only replaced one problem by another. When the farmer acted in a businesslike manner he deposited his currency surplus in summer and winter with the local bank or directly with one in St. Louis or Chicago, receiving interest which in turn, at least in part, was earned by the bank's redepositing a large percentage of the sum in New York where it was lent on call. The transfer of such funds was accomplished with different results by mailing to New York legal tenders or National Bank notes. When legal tenders were sent to New York all was well and good for the City, for they could be used as reserves, in the settlement of clearing house balances, and in the discharge of all obligations of banks. But when National Bank notes were sent, they could not be used for any one of the above purposes, could not become the basis for the creation of loanable funds, and would not be taken by Wall Street speculators, who used deposit money, i.e., checks. Thus it happened every so often for two or three weeks that there was a redundancy of National Bank note currency in New York. New York banks would then refuse to take these notes on deposit, fearful that the depositor might demand legal tenders when making use of his funds. At such times New York banks would "force" the surplus "into the country by extraordinary means," using Chicago and Cincinnati and other places as outlets. There and in other western cities regulations were not observed as strictly as in New York and National Bank notes were used in the settlement of interbank balances. At this point, we see that currency and loanable funds were tied together in a way which would be unthinkable today, a problem which we will meet again soon.[210] In addition to this unhealthy situation of current redundancies of National Bank notes in New York, the above-mentioned businesslike actions of farmers led to further trouble when they needed their funds in spring and fall. Then there was considerable trouble in New York through their being disengaged from the stock exchange.

To sum up, loanable funds in the form of currency flowed North and East every summer and winter, and flowed West and South every spring and fall. But while a trickle flowed in the first direction, a broad stream would have been needed in the second. Unfortunately this stream could not flow because the total of currency was so limited that at the given price level there was not enough to go around at the times of maximum demand.[211] Or to put it differently, New York banks could not supply currency enough to take care of the peak loads of the back country and deposit money would not do. Farmers not prosperous enough to hold on to a large percentage of their receipts from one crop to the next could get what they needed only at exorbitant rates. Stilwell's suggestion that the legal reserve requirements be suspended between September and November of each year was not unreasonable.[212]

It goes without saying that only a few farmers had enough working capital to take care of their peak loads and seasonally to hoard currency or lend it on interest. So on top of currency the back country needed loanable funds. Such loanable funds had been created even in excess by state banks all during the first half of the nineteenth century in the form of notes. But the National Currency Act made such creation impossible because securities to be deposited in return for notes were taken only at less than their market value.

The banks in the advanced sections of the country could overcome the difficulty by replacing the creation of loanable funds in the form of notes, by the creation of loanable funds in the form of deposits, since the check had become sufficiently common. It is surprising how well the true character of deposits was understood by at least some members of Congress as early as 1870. One Representative used the term "create deposits" and another, a future U.S. president, quoted from a book of McLeod that deposits were "mere credits in the books of the bank."[213] Thus regardless of the inelasticity of note issues, an elastic element was brought into the practice of Eastern and Middle States' National Banking, i.e, into National Banking of such sections as had the advantage of the improper distribution of note issues anyway and were creditors of the rest of the country. To put it differently, the burden of the inelasticity of note issues, resulting under the given circumstances in a partial inelasticity of loanable funds, fell on those sections of the country which were not sufficiently developed to find a way out by using deposit money instead of banknotes (by creating loanable funds in the form of deposits instead of in the form of notes). They had to rely on the process of saving or on dishoarding or become tributary to those sections which could create loanable funds, provided that there was enough currency available to transfer created loanable funds to the West and South. At this point the two problems of the undeveloped regions, lack of currency and lack of loanable funds, became blurred. Maldistribution of note issues and maldistribution of the ability to create loanable funds went hand in hand aggravating the evils in some sections of the country while resulting in cumulative benefits to others. It was estimated in 1874[214] that in New York 5 per cent of all payments were effected by currency, the rest by checks. In smaller cities the proportion was 10 per cent; in still smaller places 15 to 25 per cent of all transactions were settled with currency, and in rural districts 50 per cent and more. If these estimates were correct they would also be indicative of the ability to create loanable funds in various places and sections. It is certainly not surprising that there was so much regional strife and disagreement. To the contrary the historian is surprised that, regardless of all injustice, things resolved themselves so peacefully in the end.

Among all contemporaries Henry Charles Carey and Henry Carey Baird came nearest to seeing the light. They realized that the Northern and Middle States' financiers cried for deflation, but that their business policy was inflationary. Public opinion in the Northeast, as Carey saw it, waged an incessant war upon the money of the many (the circulating note) while leaving wholly out of view the money known by the name of deposits, by means of which the few were enabled to profit at the expense of the many. Regardless of this pointed statement Carey's knowledge of what was going on was still rather hazy. Looking at deposits lodged by local depositors and passed on to St. Louis or Chicago and thence to New York, Carey found that three or even four different parties gained power over the same amount, all feeling entitled to make use thereof. This process was considered inflationary.[215]

Carey's nephew, Henry Carey Baird (1825-1912), had a clearer picture. He understood in all details the process of creating loanable funds in the form of deposits as practiced in London and in the advanced sections of his own country. Thus he arrived at the pungent statement: "The entire stock in trade of the American bullionist...is 'Inflation!' The only inflation, however, which he pretends to see himself or wishes others to see is...the circulating note....He wholly ignores inflation of bank and other credit."[216]

It can be seen from the preceding that while the country was on the road to resumption the National Banking system played a very complex role. On the one hand it retarded resumption by creating purchasing power, but at the same time it cushioned the shock. Such action was possible only in the more advanced sections of the country. On the other hand, contemporary National Banking was so constructed that it acted automatically in a deflationary way; and at this point it is necessary to repeat what has been said previously in another context: circulating notes could be received only to the amount of 90 per cent of the face value of the deposited bonds, while their market value was above par; and reserve requirements against notes and deposits further decreased the amount of active purchasing power by decreasing the total of legal tenders in circulation. (From the point of view of the banker the reserve decreased the amount of loanable funds.)[217] Of course the deflationary tendency of reserve requirements was partly offset again by the pyramiding of reserves.[218] In most parts of the country the shrinking of loanable funds if used by way of note issues was not compensated or overcompensated by the power of banks to create deposit-money, because in those sections checks were not as yet customary. Heavy taxation, unbeknown to many legislators, contributed to strengthen the deflationary character of National Banking by making it unprofitable in the undeveloped sections of the country and by inducing National Banks in others not to take out all the notes to which they were entitled. In the former sections banking facilities, which would have become potential sources of created loanable funds when the section progressed, could not be established. Carl Schurz was most emphatic in stating that New York bankers and capitalists had every facility to found banks in the West. "Why do not they do it?" he asked. The correct answer, to be sure, he did not find; he saw that they remained in New York because they could do better there, but he thought they could do better because banks went to "where there is the most business."[219] Strangely enough, if National Banks made their appearance in the back country regardless of all difficulties, this very fact had inflationary consequences. Hoarded money started "pouring" in, i.e., was deposited and loaned out again, as a clever representative from Iowa described it,[220] (or, in other words, dormant purchasing power was immediately reactivated); and for that reason National Banks were urgently desired.

V

Alonzo Barton Hepburn (1846-1922), for many years closely connected with National Banking,[221] stated correctly that for many years the system "suffered a precarious existence...with strong probability of its abandonment."[222] Matters were made particularly difficult because the National Banks themselves were no enthusiastic defenders thereof. They were far from presenting that formidable combination in its defence which its enemies pictured; and they would have acquiesced gladly with a return to state status.[223] As a matter of fact, many would have preferred an abolition of National Banking and a repeal of the tax on state banknotes. As early as 1869 there was a disposition among National Banks located in the State of New York to close and reorganize as state banks under what was considered a New York enabling act, a power which the United States Attorney General denied to them.[224] Not before 1882 (when the act of July 12 " to enable national banking associations to extend their corporative existence" was passed) was the system recognized as belonging to our permanent institutions.

Attacks came from two sides: The back country wished National Bank notes to be replaced by greenbacks (while, of course, most bankers desired exactly the opposite).[225] The former policy was suggested as early as 1867[226] and in 1876 became a plank in the platform of the newly-founded Greenback Party. Exponents of this policy[227] were on strongest grounds when they argued that the issue of National Bank notes, secured as they were by the public credit, re-

presented a waste of tax funds because government paid the banks interest on the bonds which the latter held as security against notes. It would be cheaper and equally safe to issue government paper money based directly on the strength of public credit. The validity of this argument could not be denied for the time that the country was on an irredeemable paper standard. In fact it was so strong that, as John Jay Knox commented, there was even a "legal tender faction" opposing a "National Bank faction" in the Department of the Treasury.[228] This argument could be answered, however, by pointing out that this aspect of the matter would change with resumption. Furthermore, it could be objected, as James A. Garfield did, that once National Banking was destroyed the pressure of the banking interests for the repeal of the 10 per cent tax on state-bank issues (to be discussed shortly) would become irresistible. State banks with concomitant issues of state-bank circulation would raise their ugly heads again.[229]

But the opponents of Greenbackism[230] had an even stronger argument. They pointed to the undeniable fact that the adaptation of government issues to the needs of the national economy was possible only when the government went into the banking business; or to put it in modern terms, was possible only by way of a central bank. And since they abhorred government activities in business, and especially a central bank, they became defenders of National Banking.[231] As James Buell, prominent New York bank president, put it: during the war the Treasury Department had acted as a bank of issue and deposit; but subsequently public sentiment had decided that the government should go out of the banking business altogether.[232] The exponents of this point of view followed Chase who as early as 1861 had considered the advantages of government issues (uniformity of a currency which at the same time represented a permanent loan without interest) as over-compensated by the temptation to make issues in excess of needs and by the possibility of an ultimately dishonored public credit and national bankruptcy. To be sure, there were a few conservative businessmen who were willing to leave the issue of paper money to the government. The New York bank president, John Earl Williams, stood out among them.[233] But he was not the only banker to propose such a policy, as will be shown later. Another was John Thompson, then president of the Chase National Bank, who wanted government to issue all paper currency in the form of gold and silver certificates.[234]

The second corner whence attacks were launched against the National Banking system was a rendezvous of former and would-be state bankers.

It has been made clear that National Banking in the back country was unprofitable, although there were large profit chances if only banks could be organized differently, as they once had been. James Buell, oversimplifying the problem, pointed out[235] that the state bank system had been of an "inflating nature," while the National Banking system was "contractive in its operation." Consequently the former had afforded more profit to the stockholders. Those interested in a restoration of state banking found allies among unreconstructed Southerners and by 1870 began organizing. From then on every so often they launched attacks on the 10 per cent tax on state bank circulation. Their goal was to have the tax removed altogether so that the way be opened for a return to what they must have considered the golden days of banking. As late as 1892 the Democratic platform contained a plank promising the repeal of the prohibitive tax on state bank circulation. But ultimately these interests failed just as had Greenbackism earlier.

So much can be said about attacks on National Banking as such with a view to its abolishment. On top of that (and partly as a means of furthering the objective) the undeniable defects of National Banking, as practiced in the 1860's and 1870's came under fire, ultimately with remedial results. It has been stressed before that John Sherman, obviously under the influence of the Peel Act, endowed early National Banking with a legal limitation of the total of note issues, a feature which became the target of violent criticism (de facto directed against basic ideas of the Currency School and of Lord Overstone). By the end of the 1870's it was clearly recognized in this country that nobody could determine just how much currency was needed and that actually the national economy required varying amounts of currency in various years and during the different seasons.[236] As soon as this recognition dawned on the men who held the power, these could no longer resist a widespread pressure for what was then called "free banking," a term with an entirely different meaning from its connotation of the 1830's and following decades. In the 1870's "free banking" had come to mean abandoning all legal limitation of the total of note issues.

Objections to "free banking" were raised by the American "bullionists," not because they thought in terms of Lord Overstone's, but because they were afraid that "free banking" would bring an inflationary element into National Banking. They were perfectly willing to adopt the measure if legal tenders were withdrawn or at the moment of resumption.[237] It is telling that when the date for resumption was being set "free banking" could no longer be stopped,[238] although it had been defeated only the year before. Prior to its ultimate success, "free banking" and efficient note redemption were tied together by the opponents of the measure,[239] and since it seemed impossible to provide for redemption, "free banking" was rejected. Alexander Mitchell, the Wisconsin banker and business leader, considered it almost absurd to redeem one sort of irredeemable paper money (National Bank notes) by another (Greenbacks); but even if a method of redemption could have been devised to his satisfaction he would nevertheless have rejected "free banking". He felt that the total of Greenbacks was so high that the superstructure of National Bank notes could have become too large.[240] Carl Schurz was not quite so skeptical; but considered it possible to increase the value of Greenbacks relative to National Bank notes by depriving the latter of their restricted legal-tender character. If thereafter "assorting houses" were established in every part of the country where banknotes would be redeemed in treasury notes, a check would be provided, he believed, which would make "free banking" acceptable.[241]

The back country, in contrast, desired "free banking" without any strings. "Free banking" was expected to counteract deflation. Moreover it promised that additional loanable funds would become available; (to be sure, contemporary debates show that there was no consensus of opinion whether or not the opening of National Banks in the back country would take place at the expense of private bankers and brokers or provide really new facilities).[242] If "free banking," regardless of all the difficulties previously described, should result in additional banking facilities in the undeveloped districts it could be expected also to make available hoarded currency, as has already been stated. Finally, "free banking" was desired in order to break the dependence of rural districts upon the monetary centers. National Banking, as it then stood, put the industry and the products of the West and South under the control of a combination of individuals in New York and New England, as a pamphleteer had it.[243] This dependence would have existed at all events, but the contemporary National Banking was actually so constructed as to aggravate this dependence. (It was felt, for instance, but hardly brought out clearly enough, that the reserve requirements led to a concentration of loanable funds in the money centers at the expense of those places which needed them most.) In this connection the lingering anti-monopoly tradition was revived and the language used was sometimes not different from that of John Taylor of Caroline County and Andrew Jackson.[244] One could find National Banking characterized as a "monster" and the act itself as "class legislation" leading to that centralization of power which was dangerous and distasteful to the people, but valuable to tyrants. With its help the bankers were becoming a compact, dangerous aristocracy.[245] One can even read the argument that National Banks controlled the elections and sent their stockholders to Congress, a verbatim repetition of John Taylor's age-old accusations, which really were stale by that time.[246] Incidentally, as early as 1869 the case for the repeal of the existing restrictions of note issues was presented before the National Banks themselves.[247]

It goes without saying that the men who so attacked National Banking were also sure that the banks made too great profits, which in truth was not the case. National Banking had been profitable until about 1870, prior to which date some of the banks could accumulate considerable reserves.[248] But meager years followed in which earlier reserves were often used up to pay current dividends. So unprofitable was National Banking in the second half of the 1870's that between June, 1874, and December, 1878, National Banks surrendered more than $66,000,000 of their circulation, and 144 banks representing a capital of $15,517,000 went into voluntary liquidation. Thereby they could secure to the stockholders at least the large premium on their bonds, which, as has been described before, was one of the reasons for many National Banks not being profitable enough.[249]

On the other hand, it could not be denied that National Banks drew interest twice on their capital, once on the bonds in which it was invested and the second time on the circulation received on the basis of the bonds when it was paid out for loans and discounts.[250] As early as 1865 National Banking was branded as "an odious system of plundering the people by a double interest process," as James Gallatin expressed it.[251]

In connection with the fight for "free banking" one meets statements to the effect that National Banking was not elastic. This term can be found as early as 1869 in the contemporary pamphlet literature: a school of New York financiers was characterized as desiring an "elastic currency," i.e., one the volume of which varied with the demands of trade.[252] A few years later the term was used repeatedly in the United States Senate. In 1873 Senator William A. Buckingham introduced a bill to secure an "elastic currency."[253] When John Sherman discussed this bill (Senate 1113) he preferred the word "flexibility", but he meant what the economist today calls elasticity,[254] then a new term, "a latter day phrase" as another senator expressed it.[255] To be sure, the term as used in that period did not have exactly the same connotation which it was to have a few years

later.[256] Most of the men who used it thought that inelasticity was due to the fact that both treasury notes and National Bank notes were irredeemable or that the total of both kinds of currency was limited. Some people expected that any sort of efficient note redemption, and most of them that the resumption of specie payments as such, would automatically make our currency elastic.[257] The laws of trade supplied elasticity to those countries of the world which enjoyed the currency of the world; there was disagreement only on whether or not an "artificial elasticity" could be established. It remained to be discovered that a banknote currency based on government bonds was bound to be inelastic even if such notes were redeemable in gold. Such was the ignorance as to the meaning of the term elasticity that a senator from Michigan was naive enough to propose that the Committee on Finance report a measure to give "elasticity to the circulating medium through moderate increase of currency."[258] But there were others too who badly misunderstood the term.[259]

Those men, on the other hand, who saw the problem clearly, recognized that if real elasticity of National Bank note issues was wanted, something had to be done to secure the contraction of banknote currency when it seasonally became abundant.[260] For this purpose it was suggested that the government issue bonds bearing 3.65 per cent interest which were to be interchangeable with currency; (i.e., directly with Greenbacks; and, since National Bank notes were redeemable therein, indirectly with National Bank notes). Whenever currency became seasonally abundant it would be converted into these interest-bearing bonds; whenever currency was seasonally in demand, bonds would be turned in for currency. This measure meant that the treasury, or rather the taxpayer, would bear the burden of making the currency elastic. From the modern point of view it seems a very reasonable suggestion that the people bear the burden of a sound currency the advantages of which they enjoy. However, the measure was attacked as too expensive; although its friends claimed that in the long run it would pay for itself by creating a new market for government bonds and thereby reducing the rate of interest. These people were seconded by those representatives of the back country who hoped thereby to make the latter independent of National Banks: spare funds would be invested in convertible and reconvertible bonds instead of being deposited in banks. Other friends of the measure were motivated by the idea that after such bonds were created, the paying of interest on demand deposits could be forbidden.[261] Nothing, however, came of the proposal.

The idea of an inter-convertible bond was another

one imported originally from England. When it was taken up here it was of recent origin, having been proposed by one Alfred Lutwyche of Birmingham in a pamphlet, Suggestion of a Plan for Extending the Currency (Birmingham, 1857).[262] Lutwyche proposed that the British government issue legal tender paper-money in exchange for consols if requested, and at the same time sell consols without restriction taking such paper money. In a later publication Lutwyche gave credit to William Lyon McPhin of Glasgow for having broached a similar plan in a publication of 1855, Currency Self-Regulating. The latter book in turn was said to have been preceded by a pamphlet of 1849 by the Liverpool Currency Reform Association.[263] To be sure, Erskine Hazard of Philadelphia claimed in a pamphlet, Thoughts on Currency and Finance (Philadelphia, 1863), that he had proposed a similar scheme as early as 1839. His idea was that the funded debts should and could absorb any excess of legal tenders if they were redeemable in bonds and bonds could be purchased by legal tenders. One readily sees that although very similar, the American scheme was not identical with the British for which a "powerful agitation" sprang up in England and Scotland. At least, so James Gallatin put it, and he was well informed on the origin of the scheme which he fought.[264] More impressed was John Earl Williams who, as described before, became an exponent of the inter-convertible bond plan. It is possible that the idea recommended itself because the Union's early Civil War treasury-note issues had been redeemable in bonds, as presumably had been those of the Confederacy.

VI

From the point of view of this research it is important to ask whether or not during the period under investigation executives of National Banks responded creatively to the difficulties with which they were faced.[265] This question must be answered in the negative, at least in this author's opinion. The leaders in the field of National Banking were unable to rid it of the payment of interest on de-

mand deposits although that was generally recognized as unsound; they did not abandon the practice of lending the reserves of the system on call at Wall Street, although they knew it was pernicious; they did not give the back country banking facilities for which it cried, because it seemed unprofitable to do so. Yet today it is obvious that there were so many hoards in the back country that a systematic policy of "luring" money out of such hoards, as old Sir James Steuart would have called it, would have provided all the profit chances that were needed if there had been creative vision.[266] All that these men did in the 1870's was to carry on a safe and sound banking business of exactly the type that had come into existence when the creative entrepreneurs of the 1850's established the first clearing houses. That after the panic of 1873 they nevertheless thrived was due not so much to their achievements, but to the growth of the country. They successfully overcame difficulties by political pressure exerted individually or through the newly-founded American Bankers Association[267] in which they developed methods of cooperation devised earlier. Only in handling the panics of 1873 and 1884 did these men show creative abilities and their leader in this respect was George S. Coe.

When the 1880's opened National Banking was becoming an established institution, although the legislative history of the Act of July 12, 1882 to enable national-banking associations to extend their corporate existence and for other purposes, shows that hostility and reluctance still prevailed widely.[268] But the act passed and the historian is entitled, therefore, to consider 1882 as a turning point at which another period of American banking drew to a close. While National Banking was becoming an accepted fact, it proved unable to monopolize the field. As the Comptroller of the Currency reported in 1882 there were in addition to the existing 2,269 National Banks more than a thousand state and nearly 3,400 private banks.[269] This situation is explained by the development of the check, by the fact that National Banks were not permitted to lend on real estate, while there was no specialized mortgage banking, and by the existence of minimum-capital requirements.

THE SPAULDING BILL

The New York Times

Thursday, January 9, 1862.

THE PROPOSED BANKING LAW.

THE BILL NOW BEFORE THE COMMITTEE
OF WAYS AND MEANS OF THE HOUSE OF
REPRESENTATIVES.

A NEW BUREAU IN THE TREASURY
DEPARTMENT.

HOW THE NATIONAL CURRENCY IS TO
BE REGULATED.

A Bill to provide a National currency, secured by a
pledge of United States stocks, and to provide for the
circulation and redemption thereof.

BE IT ENACTED BY THE SENATE AND HOUSE OF
REPRESENTATIVES OF THE UNITED STATES OF
AMERICA IN CONGRESS ASSEMBLED, That there shall
be established in the Treasury Department a separate
bureau, which shall be charged with the execution of
this act and all laws that may be passed by Congress
respecting the issue and regulation of a National currency secured by a pledge of United States stocks. The
chief officer of the said bureau shall be denominated the
United States Bank Comptroller. He shall be appointed
by the President, by and with the advice and consent of
the Senate, and shall hold his office for the term of five
years unless sooner removed by the President; he shall
receive an annual salary of $5,000: he shall appoint a
competent deputy, whose salary shall not exceed $2,500,
and who shall possess the power and perform the duties
attached by law to the office of Bank Comptroller during
a vacancy in such office and during his absence or inability; he shall employ, from time to time, the necessary clerks to discharge such duties as he shall assign
to them, whose salaries shall not exceed $1,000 each.
Within fifteen days from the time of notice of his appointment the Bank Comptroller shall take and subscribe the
oath of office prescribed by the Constitution and laws of
the United States; and he shall give to the United States
a bond in the penalty of $100,000, with two responsible
freeholders, as sureties, to be approved by the Secretary
of the Treasury, conditioned for the faithful discharge
of the duties of his office; and he shall not, either directly or indirectly, be interested in any bank or association
issuing National currency under the provisions of this
act. The Deputy Comptroller so appointed shall also
take the oath of office prescribed by the Constitution

and laws of the United States, and shall give a like bond
in the penalty of $50,000.

SEC. 2. AND BE IT FURTHER ENACTED. That
the said Bank Comptroller, with the approval of the
Secretary of the Treasury, shall devise a seal with
suitable inscriptions for his office, a description of
which, with a certificate of approval by the Secretary
of the Treasury, shall be filed in the office of the
Secretary of State, with an impression thereof, which
shall thereupon be and become the seal of office of the
Bank Comptroller, and the same may be renewed
whenever necessary. Every certificate, assignment
and conveyance executed by the said Bank Comptroller,
in pursuance of any authority conferred on him by law,
and sealed with his said seal of office, shall be received
in evidence in all places and Courts whatsoever; and all
copies of papers in the office of the said Bank Comptroller, certified by him and authenticated by the said
seal, shall in all cases be evidence equally and in like
manner as the original. An impression of such seal
directly on the paper shall be as valid as if made on
wax or wafer.

SEC. 3. AND BE IT FURTHER ENACTED, That there
shall be assigned to said Bank Comptroller by the
Secretary of the Treasury suitable rooms in the Treasury building for conducting the business of the Bank
Department, in which shall be safe and secure fire-
proof vaults, in which it shall be the duty of said Bank
Comptroller to deposit and safely keep all the public
stocks, books, papers, plates, and other valuable things
belonging to his department; and the said Bank Comptroller shall from time to time furnish the necessary
furniture, stationery, fuel, lights, and other proper
conveniences for the transaction of the said business,
the expense of which shall be paid out of any money in
the Treasury not otherwise appropriated.

SEC. 4. AND BE IT FURTHER ENACTED. That
the term "United States Stocks," as used in this act,
shall be construed to mean all coupon and registered
bonds now issued, or that may hereafter be issued, on
the faith of the United States by the Secretary of the
Treasury in pursuance of law.

SEC. 5. AND BE IT FURTHER ENACTED. That
any chartered Bank or Banking Association, whose
capital is not less than one hundred thousand dollars,
organized under the laws of any State, Territory, or

the District of Columbia, which may elect to avail itself of the provisions of this act, shall present to the Bank Comptroller an authorized application therefor, verified by its seal and the signatures of the President and cashier, duly acknowledged before a Judge of some Court of Record or a Notary Public, and the acknowledgment thereof certified under the seal of such Court or Notary; and the said application shall state the name of said bank or banking association; the place where its office of discount and deposit is located, designating the State, and also the particular city, town or village; the amount of the capital stock, and the number of shares into which the same shall be divided; the time when its charter will expire, and a declaration that said certificate is made to enable such bank or banking association to avail itself of the advantages of this act, and consenting to comply with all the restrictions and requirements contained therein, and the comptroller of the currency shall record and carefully preserve the said application in his office; and thereupon such chartered bank or banking association shall be vested with all the powers and be subject to all the provisions of this act, during the period limited in its charter, as fully and effectually as associations formed under this act.

SEC. 6. AND BE IT FURTHER ENACTED. That associations for carrying on the business of banking may be formed by any number of persons, not less, in any case, than five.

SEC. 7. AND BE IT FURTHER ENACTED. That persons uniting to form such an association shall, under their hands and seals, make a certificate which shall specify:

1. The name assumed by such association.

2. The place where the operations of discount and deposit of such association are to be carried on, designating the State, and also the particular city, town or village.

3. The amount of the capital stock of such association, and the number of shares into which the same shall be divided; which capital stock shall not be less than $50,000.

4. The names and places of residence of the shareholders, and the number of shares held by each of them.

5. The time when such association shall commence, and when the same shall terminate; which shall not embrace a term of existence of more than 25 years.

6. A declaration that said certificate is made to enable such persons to avail themselves of the advantages of this act.

Said certificate shall be acknowledge before a judge of some Court of Record, or a Notary Public, and the acknowledgment thereof certified under the seal of such Court or Notary, and shall be transmitted, together with a copy of the articles of association which shall have been adopted, to the Bank Comptroller, who shall record and carefully preserve the same in his office. Copies of such certificate, duly certified by the Bank Comptroller, shall be legal and sufficient evidence in all Courts and places within the United States, or the jurisdiction of the Government thereof, of the existence of such association, and of every other matter or thing which could be proved by the production of the original certificate.

SEC. 8. AND BE IT FURTHER ENACTED. That at least thirty per centum of the capital stock of such association shall be paid in at the time of the commencement of its banking business, and the remainder of the capital stock of such association shall be paid in in installments of at least ten per centum each on the whole amount to which the association shall be limited, as frequently as one installment at the end of each succeeding 90 days from the time of the commencement of its banking operations, until the whole of the capital stock shall be paid in; but when any such association shall have paid in at least sixty per centum on the amount of its capital stock, and shall deem a further extension of its capital at such times unnecessary, such association may apply to the Bank Comptroller for an extension of the time for paying the remaining installments; and if, after careful examination of the facts, said Comptroller shall be of opinion that public convenience does not require an increase of such capital stock as rapidly as required by the foregoing provisions of this section, he may authorize such extension of the time for paying in the remaining installments as shall be deemed compatible with the public interest.

SEC. 9. AND BE IT FURTHER ENACTED. That if any shareholder, or his assignee, shall fail to pay any installment on the stock when the same is required by the foregoing section to be paid, the directors of such association may sell the stock held by such delinquent shareholder, at public auction, having given three weeks' previous notice thereof in a newspaper published and of general circulation in the city where the association is located, if the same be located in a city, and if not so located, then a newspaper printed, or of general circulation, in the county where the same is located, to any person who will pay the highest price therefor, and not less than the amount then due thereon, with the expenses of advertisement and sale; and the excess, if any, shall be paid to the delinquent shareholder. If no bidder can be found who will pay for such stock the amount due thereon to the association, and the costs of advertisement and sale, the amount previously paid shall be forfeited to the association, and such stock may subsequently be sold as the directors may order.

SEC. 10. AND BE IT FURTHER ENACTED, That whenever a certificate shall have been transmitted to the Bank Comptroller, as provided in the seventh section of this act, and the association transmitting the same shall notify said comptroller that at least 30 per centum of its capital stock has been paid as aforesaid, and that such association has complied with all the provisions of this act, required to be complied with before such association shall be authorized to commence the business of banking, and that such association is desirous of commencing such business, said Comptroller shall immediately proceed, in such manner as he shall by general rules prescribe, to examine the condition of such association; to ascertain especially the amount of money paid in on account of its capital stock: the name and place of residence of each of the directors of such association, and the amount of the capital stock of which each is the bona fide owner, and generally whether such association has complied with all the requirements of this act to entitle it to engage in the business of banking; and shall cause to be made, and attested by the oaths of a majority of the directors, and by the cashier of such association, a statement of all the facts necessary to enable the Comptroller to determine whether such association is lawfully entitled to commence the business of banking under this act.

SEC. 11. AND BE IT FURTHER ENACTED, That if, upon a careful examination of the facts so reported, and of any other facts which may come to the knowledge of the said Comptroller, whether by means of a special commission appointed by him for the purpose of inquiring into the condition of such association, or otherwise, it shall appear that such association is lawfully entitled to commence the business of banking, the said Comptroller shall give to such association a certificate under his hand and official seal, showing that such association has complied with all the provisions of this act required to be complied with before being entitled to commence the business of banking under it, and that such association is authorized to commence said business accordingly; and it shall be the duty of such association to cause said certificate to be published in some daily newspaper published in the State where such association is located, for at least sixty days next after the issuing thereof.

SEC. 12. AND BE IT FURTHER ENACTED, That every association formed pursuant to he provisions of this act shall be a body corporate, and may make and use a common seal, and shall have succession by the name designated in its articles of association, and for the period limited therein; by such name may make contracts, sue and be sued, complain and defend in any court of law or equity as fully as natural persons, and may make by-laws, not inconsistent with law or the provisions of this act, for the election of directors, the management of its property, the regulation of its affairs, and for the transfer of its stock; and shall have power to carry on the business of banking by obtaining and issuing circulating notes in accordance with the provisions of this act; by discounting bills, notes, and other evidences of debt; by receiving deposits; by buying and selling gold and silver bullion, foreign coins, and bills of exchange; by loaning money on real and personal security in the manner specified in their articles of association for the purposes authorized by this act; and by exercising such incidental powers as shall be necessary to carry on such business; to choose one of their number as President of such association, and to appoint a Cashier and such other officers and agents as their business may require; and to remove such President, Cashier, officers and agents at pleasure, and appoint others in their place; and all banks and banking associations issuing banks notes to circulate as money under the provisions of this act shall be banks of discount and deposit as well as circulation, and their usual business shall be transacted in banking offices located at the places specified respectively in their charters and certificates of association, and not elsewhere.

SEC. 13. AND BE IT FURTHER ENACTED, That the shares of associations formed under this act shall be deemed personal property, and shall be transferable on the books of the association in such manner as may be prescribed in the articles of association; and every person becoming a shareholder by such transfer, shall, in proportion to his shares, succeed to all the rights and liabilities of the prior holder of such shares; and no change shall be made in the articles of association by which the rights, remedies, or security of the existing creditors of the association shall be impaired.

SEC. 14. AND BE IT FURTHER ENACTED, That it shall be lawful for any association formed under this act by its articles of association to provide for an increase of its capital from time to time, as may be deemed expedient; but no such increase shall be valid until the increased capital shall be paid in, and notice thereof shall have been transmitted to the Bank Comptroller, and his certificate obtained specifying the amount of such increase of capital stock, and that the same has been duly paid to such association.

SEC. 15. AND BE IT FURTHER ENACTED, That it shall be lawful for any such association to purchase, hold and convey real estate as follows:

FIRST--Such as shall be necessary for its immediate accommodation in the transaction of its business.

SECOND--Such as shall be mortgaged to it in good faith by way of security for loans made by such association, or for moneys due thereto.

THIRD--Such as shall be conveyed to it in satisfaction of debts previously contracted in the course of its dealings.

FOURTH--Such as it shall purchase at sales under judgments, decrees, or mortgages held by such association.

Such association shall not purchase or hold real estate in any other case or for any other purpose than as specified in this section.

SEC. 16. AND BE IT FURTHER ENACTED, That every bank and banking association, after having complied with the provisions of this act preliminary to the commencement of banking business under its provisions, may transfer and deliver to the Secretary of the Treasury any number of United States Stocks bearing an interest, which bonds shall be deposited with the Bank Comptroller, and by him safely kept in his office until the same shall be otherwise disposed of, in pursuance of the provisions of this act.

SEC. 17. AND BE IT FURTHER ENACTED, That upon the making of any such transfer and delivery, the bank or association making the same shall be entitled to receive from the Bank Comptroller circulating notes of different denominations, in blank, registered and countersigned as hereinafter provided, equal in amount to the current market value of the United States stocks so transferred and delivered, but not exceeding the par value thereof; at no time shall the total amount of such notes, issued to any such association, exceed the amount at such time actually paid in of its capital stock.

SEC. 18. AND BE IT FURTHER ENACTED, That, in order to furnish suitable notes for circulation, the Bank Comptroller is hereby authorized and required, under the direction of the Secretary of the Treasury, to cause plates to be engraved in the best manner, to guard against counterfeiting and fraudulent alterations, and to be printed therefrom and numbered in oil colors, such quantity of circulating notes in the similitude of bank notes, in blank, of the denomination of $5, $10, $20, $50, $100, $500, and $1,000, as the Bank Comptroller may deem necessary to furnish to such associations, which notes shall be countersigned and registered in proper books, in the office of the Bank Comptroller, in such manner, and by such persons, as the Bank Comptroller may prescribe and designate; and all such notes shall have engraved on their face the words, "Secured by pledge of United States Stocks."

SEC. 19. AND BE IT FURTHER ENACTED, That the plates and special dies to be procured by the Bank Comptroller, for the engraving and printing of such circulating notes, shall remain under his control and direction, and the expenses necessarily incurred by him, in executing the provisions of this act respecting the procuring of such notes, shall be audited and paid as contingent expenses of the Treasury Department; and for the purpose of reimbursing the same, and all other expenses incurred under this act, the said Comptroller is hereby authorized and required to demand and receive, upon the amount of all circulating notes delivered to such bank or association as aforesaid, one per centum, to be paid at the time of delivery thereof by the banks and associations to which they are delivered respectively.

SEC. 20. AND BE IT FURTHER ENACTED, That after any such banks or association shall have caused such notes to be filled up and signed by the President or Vice-President and Cashier thereof, in such manner as to make them obligatory promissory notes, payable on demand, at its place of business, such bank or association is hereby authorized to issue and circulate the same as money; and the same shall be received at par in all parts of the United States in payment of taxes, excises, public lands, and all other dues to the United States, and also for all salaries and other debts and demands owing by the United States to citizens, corporations, and associations within the United States: and no such bank or association shall issue post notes or any other notes for circulation as money, than such as are authorized by the foregoing provisions of this act.

SEC. 21. AND BE IT FURTHER ENACTED, That all transfers of United States stocks which shall be made by any bank or banking association as security for circulating notes under the provisions of this act shall be made to the United States Bank Comptroller, with a memorandum written or printed on such stock stating that it is held by him in trust for the bank or banking association on whose behalf such transfer is made, and

as security for the redemption and payment of the circulating notes delivered to such bank or banking association; and no transfer of any such stock by said Bank Comptroller shall be deemed valid or of binding force and effect, unless the same be countersigned by the Secretary of the Treasury, or, in his absence from his office or inability to perform the duties of his office, by the Assistant Secretary of the Treasury. It shall be the duty of the Secretary of the Treasury to keep in his office a book in which shall be entered the name of every bank or banking association, from whose account such transfer of stock is made by the Bank Comptroller, and the name of the party to whom such transfer is made, unless such transfer is made in blank, in which case the fact shall be stated in said book, and in either case the par value of the stock so transferred shall be entered therein; and it shall be the duty of the Secretary of the Treasury, immediately upon countersigning and entering the same, to advise by mail the bank or banking association, from whose account such transfer was made, the kind of stock and the amount thereof so transferred.

SEC. 22. AND BE IT FURTHER ENACTED, That it shall be the duty of the Secretary of the Treasury to countersign and enter in the book, in the manner aforesaid, every transfer or assignment of any stock held by the Bank Comptroller presented for his signature; and the Secretary of the Treasury shall have at all times during office-hours access to the books of the Bank Comptroller, for the purpose of ascertaining the correctness of the transfer or assignment presented to him to countersign; and the Bank Comptroller shall have the like access to the book above-mentioned, kept by the Secretary of the Treasury, during office-hours, to ascertain the correctness of the entries in the same.

SEC. 23. AND BE IT FURTHER ENACTED, That it shall be the duty of either the President or Cashier of every bank and banking association having stocks deposited in the office of the Bank Comptroller of the United States, once or more in each fiscal year, and at such time or times during the ordinary business hours as said officer or officers may select, to examine and compare the stocks so pledged with the books of said department, and if found correct, to execute to the Bank Comptroller a receipt, setting forth the different kinds and the amounts thereof, and that the same are in the possession and custody of the Bank Comptroller at the date of such receipt. Such examination may be made by an agent of such bank or association, duly appointed in writing for that purpose, whose receipt before mentioned shall be of like force and validity as if executed by such President or Cashier.

SEC. 24. AND BE IT FURTHER ENACTED, That every bank and banking association issuing circulating notes under the provisions of this act shall make a quarterly report to the Bank Comptroller, commencing in August next, and to be continued in November, February, May and August in each year thereafter, which report shall be verified by the President and Cashier; and all willful false swearing in respect to such report shall be perjury, and subject to the punishment prescribed by law for such offence. It shall be the duty of the Bank

Comptroller, on or before the first Tuesdays of August, November, February and May in each year, to fix upon and determine some Saturday in the quarter of the year then ended in respect to which every such incorporated bank or banking association shall make said report, and shall serve notice of such determination upon every such bank and banking association, by delivering a copy of the same to some officer or clerk thereof, at their respective places of business, or by depositing the same in the Post-office in the City of Washington, directed to each of such banks and banking associations, or some officer thereof, at their places of business respectively. The report so required shall be made by each bank and banking association, within twenty days from the day of mailing such notice, and shall be in the form prescribed by the Bank Comptroller, and shall contain a true statement of the condition of the bank or banking association making such report, before the transaction of any business on the morning of the day specified in the notice of the Bank Comptroller, next preceding the date of such report, in respect of the following items and particulars, to wit: loans and discounts, overdrafts due from banks, due from the directors of the bank, or banking association making the report, due from the directors of the bank, or banking association making the report, due from brokers, real estate, specie, cash items, stocks, and promissory notes, bills of solvent banks, bills of suspended banks, loss and expense account; capital, circulation, (distinguishing that received from the Bank Comptroller from the old outstanding bills,) profits, amount due to banks, amount due to individuals and corporations other than banks, amount due the Treasurer of the United States, amount due to depositors on demand, amount due, not included under either of the above heads. And it shall be the duty of the Bank Comptroller to publish such reports together in two newspapers to be designated by him for that purpose--one in the City of Washington and the other in the City of New-York--the publication of such report shall be accompanied with a summary of the items of capital, circulation, and deposits, specie and cash items, public securities and private securities; and the separate report of each bank and banking association shall be published in a newspaper published in the county; if a newspaper is published in the city or town in which any such bank is situated, such publication shall be had in such newspaper, at the expense of such bank or banking association making such report. In addition to the quarterly reports required by this section, every bank and banking association, located and doing business in the cities of New-York, Philadelphia and Boston, and issuing circulating notes under the provisions of this act, shall publish or cause to be published on the morning of every Tuesday, in a newspaper printed in the city in which the bank making such report is located, to be designated by the Bank Comptroller, a statement, under the oath of the President or Cashier, showing the condition of the bank or banking association making such statement, on the morning of each day of the week next preceding the date of such statement, in respect to the following items and particulars, to wit: average amount of loans and discounts, specie, deposits and circulation.

SEC. 25. AND BE IT FURTHER ENACTED, That if any such bank or association shall at any time fail to redeem, in the lawful money of the United States, any of its circulating notes, when payment thereof shall be lawfully demanded, during the usual hours of business, at the office of such bank or association, the holder may cause the same to be protested, in one package, by a Notary Public, unless the President, Cashier, or Teller of such bank or association shall offer to waive demand and notice of the protest, and shall, in pursuance of such offer, make, sign, and deliver to the party making such demand, an admission in writing stating the time of the demand, the amount demanded, and the fact of the non-payment thereof; and such Notary Public, on making such protest, or upon receiving such admission, shall forthwith forward such admission or notice of protest to the Bank Comptroller; and after such default it shall not be lawful for the bank or association suffering the same to pay out any of its notes, discount any notes or bills, or otherwise prosecute the business of banking, except to receive and safely keep money belonging to it, and to deliver special deposits: PROVIDED, HOWEVER, That if satisfactory proof be produced to such Notary Public that the payment of any such notes is restrained by order of any court of competent jurisdiction, such Notary Public shall not protest the same; and when the holder of such notes shall cause more than one note or package to be protested on the same day, he shall not receive pay for more than one protest.

SEC. 26. AND BE IT FURTHER ENACTED, That in case any such association shall fail to redeem any of its circulating notes as specified in the next preceding section, the Bank Comptroller shall, within thirty days after he shall have received notice of such failure, cause the United States stocks and securities pledged by such bank or association, or so much thereof as may be necessary to redeem the outstanding circulating notes of such association, to be sold at public auction in the City of New-York, after giving notice of such sale to such association, and also advertising the time and place of sale, with a pertinent description of the bonds to be offered for sale, in two or more newspapers published in the City of New-York, for not less than ten days next preceding the day of sale; said notes to be canceled and an equal amount of bonds.

SEC. 27. AND BE IT FURTHER ENACTED, That the Bank Comptroller may, if he shall be of opinion that the interests of the noteholders of any such association failing to redeem its circulating notes as aforesaid, will be best promoted thereby, hypothecate, or sell at private sale, any of the bonds so transferred to the Bank Comptroller by such association, to any other banking association, or to any individual, person, or firm, and receive therefor either money or the circulating notes of such failing association: PROVIDED, That no such bonds shall be sold by private sale at less than the current market value thereof at the time of sale, nor shall any such bonds be sold on credit: AND PROVIDED FURTHER, That no sale of any such bonds, either public or private, shall be complete until the bonds so sold and the transfer thereof shall have been countersigned by the Secretary of the Treasury, as provided in the twenty-first section of this act.

SEC. 28. AND BE IT FURTHER ENACTED, That on receiving notice of the failure of any such association to redeem its circulating notes as aforesaid, the Bank Comptroller shall give notice in such manner as the Secretary of the Treasury shall, by general rules or otherwise, direct, to the holders of the circulating notes of such association to present them for payment at the office of said Comptroller, who shall proceed, so soon as moneys shall have been received arising from the sale or hypothecation of the bonds of such association as aforesaid, to pay, in a ratable proportion, such circulating notes; and it shall be lawful for the Secretary of the Treasury, from time to time, to make such regulations respecting the disposition to be made of such notes after presentation thereof for payment as aforesaid, and respecting the perpetuation of the evidence of the payment thereof, as may seem to him proper; but all such notes, on being fully paid, shall be canceled; and if any of the circulating notes of such failing associations shall not be presented for payment at the office of the Bank Comptroller until after the term of two years from the date of the first publication of the notice to the holders thereof to present them for payment, said Comptroller may pay, ratably, to the holder of notes previously presented, if such notes shall not have been already paid in full, whatever of the proceeds of such sale, remaining undistributed, may be needed to fully discharge the notes so presented.

SEC. 29. AND BE IT FURTHER ENACTED, That on receiving notice that any such bank or association has failed to redeem any of its circulating notes as aforesaid, the Bank Comptroller, by and with the direction and concurrence of the Secretary of the Treasury, shall appoint a special agent, who shall immediately proceed to ascertain whether such association has refused to pay its circulating notes in the lawful money of the United States when demanded as aforesaid, and report to the Bank Comptroller the facts so ascertained, and if, from the report so made, the said Comptroller shall be satisfied that such bank or association has refused to pay its circulating notes as aforesaid, and that it has been in default for ten days, he may forthwith appoint a Receiver, and require of him such bond and security as he shall deem proper, who shall proceed, under the direction of the said Bank Comptroller, to take possession of the books, records, and assets of every description of such association, collect all debts, dues and claims belonging to such association, and upon the order of a court of record of competent jurisdiction, may sell or compound all bad or doubtful debts, and on a like order sell all the real and personal property of such association, on such terms as the court shall direct, and pay over all moneys so made the Bank Comptroller, and also make report to him of all his acts and proceedings. Such Comptroller shall cause notice to be given by advertisement in one or more newspapers in the city in which such association is located, if the same be in a city, and if not, then in one or more newspapers published in the county where the same is located, for three consecutive months, calling on all

persons who may have claims against such association to present the same, and to make legal proof thereof; and after the end of one year from the first publication of such notice, the Comptroller of the currency, after full provision shall have been first made for redeeming the circulating notes of such association, shall make a ratable dividend of the moneys so paid over to him by such Receiver, inclusive of moneys arising from sales of bonds transferred to the Bank Comptroller, as by this act provided, on all such claims as may have been so proved or adjudicated in a Court of competent jurisdiction, and from time to time, as the proceeds of the assets of such bank or association shall be paid over to him, he shall make further dividends, as aforesaid, on all claims previously proved or adjudicated; and the remainder of such proceeds, if anything, shall be paid over to the shareholders of the aforesaid association, or their legal representatives, in proportion to the stock by them respectively held: PROVIDED, HOWEVER, That if any such bank or association against which proceedings have been so instituted on account of any supposed refusal to redeem its circulating notes as aforesaid shall deny having failed to do so, such association may apply to the Circuit Court of the United States, or other Court of competent jurisdiction, to enjoin further proceedings in the premises; and such Court, after citing the Bank Comptroller to show cause why further proceedings should not be enjoined, and after the decision of the Court or finding of a jury that such company has not refused to redeem its circulating notes, when legally presented, in the lawful money of the United States, shall make an order enjoining said Bank Comptroller, and any Receiver acting under his direction, from all further proceedings on account of such supposed refusal.

SEC. 30. AND BE IT FURTHER ENACTED, That the bonds transferred to the Secretary of the Treasury, as herein before provided, by any such bank or association for the security of its circulating notes, shall be held exclusively for the purpose until such notes shall be redeemed, except as provided in this act; but the Bank Comptroller may give to any such association powers of attorney to receive and appropriate to its own use the interest on the bonds which shall have been so transferred to him by it; but such powers shall become inoperative whenever such bank or association shall fail to redeem its circulating notes as aforesaid; and said Bank Comptroller may return any of said bonds to the bank or association which transferred the same, upon the surrender to him and the cancellation of an equal amount of such circulating notes: PROVIDED, The current market value of the remaining bonds which shall have been transferred by the association offering to surrender such circulating notes shall be equal to the amount of all the circulating notes retained by such association: AND PROVIDED, FURTHER, That there shall have been no failure by such association to redeem its circulating notes, and that there shall have been no other violation by such association of any of the provisions of this act, for the security of the creditors of such bank or association; nor shall said Comptroller be required to surrender such bonds in fractional sums of less than $1,000; and, if, at any time after said bonds shall be deposited with the Bank Comptroller as aforesaid, their market or cash value shall be reduced, it shall be the duty of the Secretary of the Treasury..and he is hereby authorized to demand and receive the amount of such depreciation in other United States stocks at their cash value, or in money, from the banks receiving said bills, and to hold the same for the benefit of the bill-holders, as long as such depreciation continues.

SEC. 31. AND BE IT FURTHER ENACTED, That whenever the price of any of the bonds pledged as aforesaid for the redemption of the circulating notes of any such bank or association shall be at the Stock Exchange in the City of New-York, for four consecutive weeks, at a rate less than that at which they shall have been estimated when so pledged, and such depreciation shall not have been made good by a deposit of other stocks or money, it shall be the duty of the Bank Comptroller to notify the Treasurer of the United States of such fact, and the payment of interest upon such depreciated bonds shall be suspended, and such interest shall be retained by said Treasurer until the same, when added to the current market value of the bonds so pledged, to be ascertained as before provided, shall be equal to the amount for which such bonds were pledged: PROVIDED, That it shall be the duty of the Bank Comptroller, at the expiration of every period of three months, to cause the whole of the sums so retained, and then remaining in the treasury of the United States, to be invested in United States stocks, in the name of the Bank Comptroller, in trust for the respective associations by which the stocks on which such interest shall have accrued shall have been pledged; and whenever the price of such depreciated stocks at the Stock Exchange in New-York shall rise to the price at which they were pledged, and so remain for four consecutive weeks, such investment shall be assigned to such association, and all accruing interest on such pledged stock shall thereafter be paid to such association on demand thereof.

SEC. 32. AND BE IT FURTHER ENACTED, That whenever any such bank or association, being desirous of relinquishing its banking business, shall have paid at least 90 per centum of its circulating notes, and shall have delivered the same to the Bank Comptroller to be canceled, and shall have provided means and given security, to the satisfaction of the Bank Comptroller, for the redemption of its outstanding notes of circulation at the place where such bank or association is located, and shall have given notice thereof by advertisement for six consecutive months in two newspapers of general circulation, published, one at the Capital of the State in which such association shall be located, and one in the city, town, village or county in which the same is located, if there be one published therein, it shall be lawful for the Bank Comptroller to retransfer and deliver to such bank or association all the stocks and securities pledged by it, and thereupon all the corporate powers of such association, except such as shall be necessary to close up its affairs, shall cease.

SEC. 33. AND BE IT FURTHER ENACTED, That it shall be the duty of the Bank Comptroller to receive

worn-out or mutilated circulating notes issued by any such bank or association, and to deliver in place thereof to such bank or association other blank circulating notes to an equal amount; and such worn-out or mutilated notes, after a memorandum shall have been entered in the proper books, in accordance with such regulations as may be established by the Bank Comptroller, as well as all circulating notes which shall have been paid or surrendered to be canceled, shall be burned to ashes by said Comptroller of the currency, in the presence of the Treasurer of the United States; and in case such notes shall have been delivered to said Comptroller by an officer or agent of said bank or association, then in the presence, also of such officer or agent; and a certificate of such burning, signed by said Comptroller and Treasurer, shall be made in the books of said Comptroller, and a duplicate thereof given to such officer or agent.

SEC. 34. AND BE IT FURTHER ENACTED, That it shall be unlawful for any officer acting under the provisions of this act to countersign or deliver to any such bank or association, or to any other company or person, any circulating notes contemplated by this act, except as herein before provided, and in accordance with the true intent and meaning of this act; and any officer who shall violate the provisions of this section shall be deemed guilty of a high misdemeanor, and on conviction thereof shall be punished by fine and imprisonment, at the discretion of the court in which he shall be tried.

SEC. 35. AND BE IT FURTHER ENACTED, That all fees for protesting the notes issued by any such bank [or association] shall be paid by the person procuring the protest to be made, and such bank or association shall be liable therefore; but no part of the bonds pledged by such bank or association, as aforesaid, shall be applied to the payment of such fees; and all expenses of any preliminary or other examinations into the condition of any such bank or association shall be paid by such bank or association: and all expenses of any Receivership shall be paid out of the assets of such bank or association before distribution of the proceeds thereof; and all expenses incurred in conducting the sale of any such pledged bonds, and in advertising the same, shall be paid out of the proceeds of such sales, before the application thereof to the redemption of the circulating notes of such bank or association.

SEC. 36. AND BE IT FURTHER ENACTED, That the stockholders, collectively, of any such bank or association shall at no time be liable to such bank or association, either as principal debtors or sureties, or both, to an amount greater than three-fifths of the capital stock actually paid in and remaining undiminished by losses or otherwise; nor shall the directors be so liable, except to such amount and in such manner as shall be prescribed by the by-laws of such bank or association, adopted by its stockholders to regulate such liabilities.

SEC. 37. AND BE IT FURTHER ENACTED, That the capital stock of such association formed under this act shall be divided into shares of $100 each, and shall be assignable on the books of the association in such manner as its by-laws shall prescribe; but no shareholder in any bank or association under this act shall have the power to sell or transfer any share held in his own right so long as he shall be liable, either as principal, debtor, surety or otherwise, to the bank or association for any debt which shall have become due and remain unpaid, nor in any case shall such shareholder be entitled to receive any dividend, interest, or profit on such shares so long as such liabilities shall continue, but all such dividends, interests, and profits shall be retained by the bank or association, and applied to the discharge of such liabilities; and no stock shall be transferred without the consent of a majority of the directors while the holder thereof is indebted to the association.

SEC. 38. AND BE IT FURTHER ENACTED, That no bank or association shall take, as security for any loan or discount, a lieu upon any part of its capital stock; but the same security, both in kind and amount, shall be required of shareholders as of other persons; and no such bank or association shall be the purchaser or holder of any portion of its capital stock, or of the capital stock of any other incorporated company, unless such purchase shall be necessary to prevent loss upon a debt previously contracted in good faith, on security which, at the time, was deemed adequate to insure the payment of such debt, independent of any lien upon such stock; or in case of forfeiture of stock for the nonpayment of installments due thereon, and stock so purchased or acquired, shall in no case be held by such bank or association so purchasing for a longer period of time than six months, if the same can, within that time, be sold for what the stock cost.

SEC. 39. AND BE IT FURTHER ENACTED, That in all elections of directors, and in deciding all questions at meetings of shareholders, each shareholder shall be entitled to one vote on each share of stock held by him; shareholders may vote by proxies duly authorized in writing; but no officer, clerk, teller or bookkeeper of such bank or association shall act as proxy; and no stockholder whose liability is past due and unpaid shall be allowed to vote.

SEC. 40. AND BE IT FURTHER ENACTED, That the affairs of every such bank or association shall be managed by not less than five nor more than nine directors, one of whom shall be President of the Association. Every director shall, during his whole term of service, be a citizen of the United States and a resident of the State in which such association is located. At least three-fourths of the directors shall have resided in the State in which such association is located one year next preceding their election as directors; and each director shall own, in his own right, at least one per centum of the capital stock of such bank or association up to $200.000, and the half of one per centum of its capital over $200,000. The directors of each of such banks and associations shall, collectively, own at least one-tenth of its capital stock in their own right. Each director shall take an oath that he will, so far as the duty devolves on him, diligently and honestly administer the affairs of such bank or association, and will not knowingly violate, or willingly permit to be violated, any

of the provisions of this act, and that he is the bona fide owner, in his own right, of the shares of stock standing in his name on the books of the association, and that the same is not hypothecated, or in any way pledged, as security for any loan obtained or debt owing, which oath, subscribed by himself, and certified by the officer before whom it is taken, shall be immediately transmitted to the Bank Comptroller, and by him filed and preserved in his office.

SEC. 41. AND BE IT FURTHER ENACTED, That the directors of any such bank or association first elected shall hold their places until the first Monday in January next thereafter, and until their successors shall be elected and qualified. All subsequent elections shall be held annually on the first Monday of January, and the Directors so elected shall hold their places for one year, and until their successors are elected and qualified. But any Director removing from the State or ceasing to be the owner of the requisite amount of stock, shall thereby vacate his place. Any vacancy in the Board shall be filled by appointment by the remaining Directors. The Director so appointed shall hold his place until the next annual election, and if, from any cause an election of Directors shall not be made at the time appointed, the bank or association shall not for that cause be dissolved, but an election may be held on any subsequent day, thirty days' notice thereof having been given in a newspaper printed, or of general circulation, in the city, town, or county in which the bank or association is located.

SEC. 42. AND BE IT FURTHER ENACTED, That every such bank and association shall at all times have on hand, in lawful money of the United States, an amount equal to at least 25 per centum of the amount of its outstanding notes of circulation; and whenever the amount of its outstanding notes of circulation shall exceed the above-named proportion for the space of twelve days, or whenever such lawful money of the United States shall at any time fall below the amount 25 per centum of its circulation, such association shall not increase its liabilities by making any new loans or discounts otherwise than by discounting or purchasing bills of exchange, payable at sight, nor make any dividend of its profits, until the required proportion between its outstanding notes of circulation and lawful money of the United States shall be restored: PROVIDED, HOWEVER, That any such bank or association having money deposited to its credit in any responsible bank in the cities of New York, Boston, or Philadelphia, subject to be drawn for at sight, and which is immediately available to redeem such circulating notes, shall be deemed to be a part of the lawful money which such banks and associations are required to keep under the foregoing provisions of this section: PROVIDED, That the amount of such deposit shall not exceed three-fifths of the said amount of 25 per centum required to be kept as aforesaid. And it shall be competent for the Bank Comptroller to notify any such bank or association whose lawful money reserve shall fall below said proportion of 25 per centum to make good such reserve, and if such association shall fail for thirty days thereafter so to make good its reserve of lawful money of the United States, said Comptroller may, with the concurrence of the Secretary of the

Treasury, appoint a receiver to wind up the business of such association, as provided in the twenty-ninth section of this act.

SEC. 43. AND BE IT FURTHER ENACTED, That no such bank or association shall at any time be indebted, or in any way liable, to an amount exceeding the amount of its capital stock at such time actually paid in, and remaining undiminished by losses or otherwise, except on the following accounts, that is to say:

FIRST--On account of its notes of circulation;

SECOND--On account of moneys deposited with, or collected by, such association;

THIRD--On account of bills of exchange or drafts drawn against money actually on deposit to the credit of such association, or due thereto;

FOURTH--On account of liabilities to its stock-holders, for money paid in on capital stock, and dividends thereon.

SEC. 44. AND BE IT FURTHER ENACTED, That no such bank or association shall, either directly or in-directly, pledge, hypothecate or exchange any of its notes of circulation, for the purpose of procuring money, to be paid in on its capital stock, or to be used in its ordinary banking operations, or for the purpose of purchasing bonds of the United States, to be transferred to the Bank Comptroller; nor shall any such bank or association apply, or permit to be applied, hypothecated, or pledged, any portion of its capital stock to the pur-chase of bonds of the United States, to be transferred, as aforesaid; but such bank or association may, neverthe-less, invest from time to time the whole or any portion of its capital in such bonds.

SEC. 45. AND BE IT FURTHER ENACTED, That no such bank or association shall, during the time it shall continue its banking operations, withdraw, or permit to be withdrawn, either in form of dividends, loans to stock-holders for a longer time than six months, or in any other manner, any portion of its capital stock; and if losses shall at any time have been sustained by any such bank or association equal to or exceeding its undivided profits then on hand, no dividend shall be made; and no dividend shall ever be made by any such bank or associ-ation, while it shall continue its banking operations, to an amount greater than its net profits then on hand, deducting therefrom its losses, and bad and suspended debts; and all debts due to any such bank or association, on which interest is past due and unpaid for a period of six months, unless the same shall be well secured, and shall be in process of collection, shall be considered bad or suspended debts within the meaning of this act.

SEC. 46. AND BE IT FURTHER ENACTED, That the directors of every such bank or association shall, semi-annually, on the first Monday in May and November, declare a dividend of so much of the profits of such bank or association as they shall judge expedient; and, on each dividend day, the cashier shall make, and verify by his oath, a full, clear and accurate statement of the condition of such bank or association, as it shall be on that day, after declaring the dividend; which statement shall contain:

ONE--The amount of the capital stock actually paid in, and then remaining, as the capital stock of such bank or association.

TWO--The amount of the circulating notes of such bank or association, then in circulation, specifying the amount of each denomination.

THREE--The greatest amount in circulation at any time, since the making of the last previous statement, as shall have been exhibited by the weekly statements of the Cashier, specifying the times when the same occurred.

FOUR--The amount of balances and debts of every kind due to other banks and banking associations.

FIVE--The amount due to depositors.

SIX--The total amount of debts and liabilities of every description, and the greatest amount since the making of the last previous statement, specifying the time when the same accrued.

SEVEN--The total amount of dividends declared on the day of making the statement.

EIGHT--The amount of lawful money of the United States belonging to such bank or association, and in its possession, at the time of making the statement, de-signating the amount of each.

NINE--The amount subject to be drawn at sight, in lawful money of the United States, then remaining on deposit with solvent banks or bankers; specifying the amount so on deposit in the cities of New-York, Philadelphia, Boston and Baltimore.

TEN--The amount then on hand of bills or notes, issued by other banks and banking associations, formed and doing business under this act, and the amounts issued by other banks and banking associations.

ELEVEN--The amount of balances due from other banks and banking associations doing business under this act, and the amount due from other banks, bankers and banking associations, excluding deposits subject to be drawn at sight as aforesaid.

TWELVE--The amount on hand of bills, bonds, notes, and other evidences of debt, discounted or purchased by such bank or association, specifying particularly the amount of suspended debt, the amount considered bad, the amount considered doubtful, and the amount in suit or judgment.

THIRTEEN--The value of the real and personal pro-perty held for the convenience of such bank or associa-tion, specifying the amount of each.

FOURTEEN--The amount of real estate taken in payment of debts due to such bank or association.

FIFTEEN--The amount of the undivided profits of such bank or association.

SIXTEEN--The total amount of the liability to such bank or association by the directors thereof collectively, specifying the gross amount of such liabilities as principal debtors, and the gross amount as indorsers or sureties.

SEVENTEEN--The total amount of the liability to such bank or association by the directors thereof col-lectively, specifying the gross amount of such liabilities as principal debtors, and the gross amount as indorsers or sureties.

The statement thus made shall forthwith be transmit-ted to the Bank Comptroller.

SEC. 47. AND BE IT FURTHER ENACTED. That every such bank and association may take, reserve, receive, and charge on any loan or discount made, or upon any note, bill of exchange, or other evidence of debt, such rate of interest or discount as is for the time the established rate of interest for delay in the payment of money in the absence of contract between the parties, by the laws of the several States in which such banks and associations are respectively located, and no more: PROVIDED, HOWEVER, That interest may be reserved or taken, in advance, at the time of making the loan or discount, according to the usual rules of banking in such State or Territory; and the knowingly taking, reserving, or charging, of a rate of interest greater than that allowed by this section, shall be held and adjudged a forfeiture of the debt or demand on which the same is taken, reserved, or charged; but the purchase, discount, or sale of a bill of exchange, payable at another place than such place of purchase, discount, or sale, at the current discount or premium, shall not be considered as taking, reserving, or charging interest.

SEC. 48. AND BE IT FURTHER ENACTED, That the total liabilities of any person, or of any company or firm (including in the liabilities of a company or firm the liabilities of the several members thereof,) to any such bank or association, including liabilities as acceptor of bona fide bills of exchange, payable out of the State where such bank or association is located, shall at no time exceed one-third, exclusive of liabilities as acceptor, one-fifth, and exclusive of liabilities on such bills of exchange, one-tenth part of the amount of the capital stock of such bank or association actually paid in.

SEC. 49. AND BE IT FURTHER ENACTED, That no such bank or association shall, at any time, pay out on loans or discounts, or in purchasing drafts or bills of exchange, or in payment of depositions, nor shall it in any other mode put in circulation the notes of any bank or banking company, which notes shall not, at any such time, be receivable at par, in payment of debts by such bank or association so paying out or circulating such notes; nor shall it knowingly pay out or put in circulation any notes issued by any bank or banking association which at the time of such paying out or putting in circulation is not redeeming its circulating notes in lawful money of the United States.

SEC. 50. AND BE IT FURTHER ENACTED, That all notes, bills, and other evidences of debt, excepting bills of exchange, discounted by any such bank or association, shall be made, by the terms thereof, or by special indorsement, payable solely to such bank or association; and no such evidence of debt shall be assignable, except for collection or for the following purposes:
FIRST--To redeem the circulating notes of such bank or association.
SECOND--To pay other liabilities of such bank or association, and after such liabilities shall have been discharged.
THIRD--To divide among the shareholders on their stock.

SEC. 51. AND BE IT FURTHER ENACTED, That all transfer of the notes, bonds, bills of exchange, and other evidences of debt, owing to any such bank or association, or of deposits to its credit; all assignments of mortgages, sureties on real estate, or of judgments or decrees in its favor; all deposits of money, bullion, or other valuable thing for its use, or for the use of any of its shareholders or creditors; all payments of money to either, made after the commission of an act of insolvency, or in contemplation thereof, with a view to prevent the application of its assets in the manner prescribed by this act, or with a view to the preference of one creditor to another, except in payment of its circulating notes, shall be utterly null and void.

SEC. 52. AND BE IT FURTHER ENACTED. That if the directors of any such bank or association shall knowingly violate or knowingly permit any of the officers, agents, or servants of such bank or association to violate any of the provisions of this act, all the rights, privileges, and franchises, of such bank or association, derived from this act, shall be thereby forfeited; such violation shall, however, be determined, and adjudged by the Circuit Courts of the United States, or by other Courts of competent jurisdiction, before the corporation shall be declared dissolved; and in cases of such violation every director who participated in, or assented to the same, shall be held liable in his personal and individual capacity for all damages which the bank or association, its shareholders, or any other person shall have sustained in consequence of such violation.

SEC. 53. AND BE IT FURTHER ENACTED, That the Bank Comptroller, with the approbation of the Secretary of the Treasury, as often as shall be deemed necessary or proper, appoint a suitable person to make an examination of the affairs of every such bank or association, which person shall not be a director or other officer in any such bank or association whose affairs he shall be appointed to examine, and who shall have power to make a thorough examination into all the affairs of such bank or association, and, in doing so, to examine any of the officers and agents thereof on oath, and shall make a full and detailed report of the condition of such association to the Bank Comptroller; and such banks and associations shall not be subject to any other visitorial powers than such as are authorized by this act, except as are vested in the several courts of law and chancery; and every person appointed to make such examination shall receive for his services at the rate of $2 for each day by him employed in such examination, and $2 for every 25 miles he shall necessarily travel in the performance of his duty, which shall be paid by the bank or association by him examined.

SEC. 54. AND BE IT FURTHER ENACTED, That every president, director, cashier, teller, clerk, or agent of any such bank or association, who shall embezzle, abstract or wilfully misapply any of the moneys, funds or credits of such bank or association, or shall, without authority from the directors, issue or put in circulation any of the notes of such bank or association, or shall, without such authority, issue or put forth any certificate of deposit, draw any order or bill of exchange, make any acceptance, assign any note, bond, draft, bill of exchange, mortgage, judgment or decree, or shall make any false entry in any book, report or statement of such bank or association, with intent, in either case, to injure or defraud any other company, body politic or corporate, or any individual person, or to deceive any officer or agent appointed to examine the affairs of any such association, shall be deemed guilty of a misdemeanor, and, upon conviction thereof, shall be punished by imprisonment not less than five nor more than ten years.

SEC. 55. AND BE IT FURTHER ENACTED, That the President and Cashier of every such association shall cause to be kept, at all times, a full and correct list of the names and residences of all the shareholders in such bank or association, in the office where its business is transacted; and such list shall be subject to the inspection of all the shareholders and creditors of such bank or association during business hours of each day in which business may be legally transacted; and a copy of such list, verified by the oath of such President or Cashier, shall, at the beginning of every quarter of a year, be transmitted to the Bank Comptroller, commencing on the first day of August after the passage of this act.

SEC. 56. AND BE IT FURTHER ENACTED, That the Secretary of the Treasury is hereby authorized, whenever, in his judgment, the public interest will be promoted thereby, to employ any of such banks or associations, doing business under this act, as depositaries of the public moneys, in any place except the City of Washington.

SEC. 57. AND BE IT FURTHER ENACTED, That all suits and proceedings arising out of the provisions of this act, in which the United States, or its officers or agents, shall be parties, shall be conducted by the District-Attorneys of the several districts, under the direction and supervision of the Solicitor of the Treasury.

SEC. 58. AND BE IT FURTHER ENACTED, That every person who shall mutilate, cut, deface, disfigure, or perforate with holes, or shall unite or cement together, or do any other thing to any bank bill, draft, note, or other evidence of debt issued by any such bank or banking association, or shall cause or procure the same to be done, with intent to render such bank bill, draft, note, or other evidence of debt, unfit to be reissued by said bank or banking association, shall, upon conviction, forfeit fifty dollars to the corporation who shall be injured thereby.

SEC. 59. AND BE IT FURTHER ENACTED, That if any person shall falsely make, forge or counterfeit, or cause or procure to be made, forged or counterfeited, or willingly aid or assist in falsely making, forging or counterfeiting any note in imitation of, or purporting to be in imitation of, the circulating notes issued under the provisions of this act, or shall pass, utter, or publish, or attempt to pass, utter, or publish, any false, forged, or counterfeited note, purporting to be issued by any corporation or association doing a banking business under

the provisions of this act, knowing the same to be falsely made, forged, or counterfeited, or shall falsely alter, or cause or procure to be falsely altered, or willingly aid or assist in falsely altering any such circulating notes, issued as aforesaid, or shall pass, utter, or publish or attempt to pass, utter, or publish as true, any falsely altered or spurious circulating notes issued, or purporting to have been issued, as aforesaid, knowing the same to be falsely altered or spurious, every such person shall be deemed and adjudged guilty of felony, and being thereof convicted by due course of law, shall be sentenced to be imprisoned and kept at hard labor for a period of not less than three years nor more than ten years and to be fined in a sum not exceeding $1,000.

SEC. 60. AND BE IT FURTHER ENACTED, That if any person shall make or engrave, or cause or procure to be made or engraved, or shall have in his custody and possession any engraved plate or block after the similitude of any plate from which any circulating notes issued as aforesaid shall have been printed, with intent to use such plate or block, or cause or suffer the same to be used in forging or counterfeiting any of the notes issued as aforesaid, or shall have in his custody or possession any blank note or notes engraved and printed after the similitude of any notes issued as aforesaid, with intent to use such blanks, or cause or suffer the same to be used, in forging or counterfeiting any of the notes issued as aforesaid, or shall have in his custody or possession any paper adapted to the making of such notes, and similar to the paper upon which any such notes shall have been issued, with intent to use such paper, or cause or suffer the same to be used, in forging or counterfeiting any of the notes issued as aforesaid, every such person, being thereof convicted by due course of law, shall be sentenced to be imprisoned and kept to hard labor for a term not less than three nor more than ten years, and fined in a sum not exceeding $1,000.

SEC. 61. AND BE IT FURTHER ENACTED, That suits, actions and proceedings may be had in Courts of Record of the several States and Territories by and against corporations and associations under the provisions of this Act; and such Courts, within their respective jurisdictions, and the Judges and Justices thereof, shall have concurrent jurisdiction with the Circuit and District Courts of the United States in all such suits, actions and proceedings.

SEC. 62. AND BE IT FURTHER ENACTED, That it shall be the duty of the Bank Comptroller to report annually to Congress, at the commencement of its session:
ONE--A summary of the state and condition of every bank and banking association from whom reports have been received the preceding year, at the several dates to which such reports refer, with an abstract of the whole amount of banking capital returned by them, of the whole amount of their debts and liabilities, the amount of circulating notes outstanding, and the total amount of means and resources, specifying the amount of specie held by them at the times of their several returns, and such other information in relation to said banks and associations as in his judgment may be useful.

TWO--A statement of the banks and banking associations whose business has been closed during the year, with the amount of their circulation redeemed, and the rate PER CENTUM of such redemption and the amount outstanding.

THREE--To suggest any amendment to the laws relative to banking by which the system may be improved, and the security of the bill-holders and depositors may be increased.

FOUR--To report the names and compensation of the clerks employed by him, and the whole amount of the expenses of the banking department during the year; such report shall be made by or before the first day of December in each year, and the usual number of copies for the use of the Senate and House, and two hundred and fifty copies for the use of the Department, shall be printed by the public printer and in readiness for distribution on the first meeting of Congress.

TREASURY DEPARTMENT,
OFFICE OF CONTROLLER OF THE CURRENCY
WASHINGTON, July 14, 1863.

Most of the questions presented to the Controller, in regard to the National Currency Act, have been answered in the forms and instructions which have been sent from this office, and by letters to the interrogators. There are a few, however, that can be more conveniently and satisfactorily answered in this form than in any other.

1st Question. Is there any "reasonable doubt" of the constitutionality of this Act?

Answer. The constitutionality of the Act of Congress establishing, in time of peace, a United States Bank, with power to locate in the States Branches thereof, having been affirmatively decided by the Supreme Court of the United States, the constitutionality of the National Currency Act is not considered to be an open question.

In ordinary times the constitutionality of this Act would hardly be questioned; but in the existing emergency of the Government, engaged, as it is, in a war of gigantic proportions--with specie no longer a circulating medium--with a large internal revenue to be collected in the States and Territories, such a currency as is provided for in this Act is an absolute necessity. To deny to the Government, through such agencies as Congress might create, the power to provide a currency based upon its own resources, would be not only to deny its sovereignty, but its authority to perform properly and safely its acknowledged functions.

2d Question. What are stockholders of State Banks to gain by discontinuing their present organizations, and organizing under the national law?

Answer. The chief gain will be in a circulation of notes, which cannot long be secured through the agency of State institutions. Legal tender notes have created a taste and prepared the way for a national bank note circulation. These notes, in all sections of the country, have a better credit and are in greater demand than the notes of the strongest banks. Country bankers, notwithstanding the largeness of the issue, find it difficult to supply the call for them, and are frequently under the necessity of ordering them, at considerable expense, from commercial points, to meet the demand that will not be satisfied with anything else. The preference for these notes is not chiefly to be

attributed to the fact that they are a "legal tender," but to the fact that they are Government money, and must be good, if the Government is good. I do not say that their general credit is not, in a measure, owing to the fact that they are declared to be "lawful money," or that it was not necessary to make them so, to place them beyond the influences that might, at the time, have been combined to depreciate them; but I do say, that the people, who control the currency, as they do the legislation of the country, prefer legal tenders to bank notes, because they are Government issues, are receivable for Government dues, and must, every dollar of them be redeemed, if the Government is maintained.

The National Bank Note circulation is intended gradually to take the place of the direct issues of the Government. It is not expected that it will, at once, have the credit that has been attained by the "legal tenders," nor that the notes of the National Associations, scattered from Maine to California, will be of absolutely uniform value throughout the Union; but it is expected that these notes, sustained by the credit and secured by the resources of the nation, receivable for all public dues, except duties upon imports, and in payment of all claims against the Government, and, in case of the failure of the Banks, to be redeemed at the Treasury of the United States, will challenge, to a greater degree, the public confidence, and possess more uniformity of value than can be attained by the issues of the best managed State institutions. I will go further than this: through the instrumentality of Clearing-Houses, or Redeeming Agencies, which, in due time, may become a necessary feature of the system, the notes of the National Banks, wherever situated, will be as nearly of uniform value throughout the Union as the commercial interests of the country will require.

There will not be, in my judgment, for any considerable time, two systems of corporate banking (one State and the other National) in the United States; not that there is a necessary antagonism between the two systems, but because both will not be equally acceptable to the people and equally profitable to the banker. One or the other will fully occupy the field; and, aside from the manner in which the National system is being regarded by the people, and the rapidity with which National Associations are being formed, it requires no spirit of prophecy to predict which of the two is destined to give way. The losses which the people have sustained by bank failures; the inadequate protection which State legislation, with rare exceptions, has given to the bill-holders; the fact that the good credit of the issues of the strongest and best conducted State Banks, outside of the States or the section where they exist, is not the result of public confidence in their solvency, but of the influence of bankers and money dealers, who can as easily depress that credit as they can sustain it, and who do not unfrequently depress or sustain it, as suits their own interests or convenience alone; that all the credit that State Banks have at a distance from home is artificial and unreliable: all these things have given rise to a widespread dissatis- faction with the existing bank note circulation, and created a popular desire for a circulation, of whose solvency there can be no question, and whose credit will not be at the mercy of bank note brokers.

The Government of the United States is not to be overthrown by the attempted secession of the Southern States, and the war in which it is engaged. On the contrary, it will be vastly strengthened by the severe ordeal to which it is being subjected--strengthened by the evidence, which is every day being exhibited, of its inherent power, and the conviction that is constantly spreading and deepening in the minds of the people, that their personal destinies are identified with it-- strengthened by the very debt it is contracting, and the evidences of value that are to be based upon this debt.

Banks whose issues are secured by the Government, and which are to become the financial agents of the Government, will, in my opinion, ere long, be the only ones that will be tolerated by the people; and if the banks of the older and richer States continue, as they have done, and are now to a large extent doing, to furnish the newer and less wealthy States with a bank note circulation, they will have to do it through the agency of National Banks. In availing themselves of the National Currency Act, for loaning their capital and credit to the people of the new States, they will have the satisfaction of knowing that while adding to their own wealth, they are strengthening the Government, and creating a powerful influence against repudiation, by aiding in furnishing to the people a circulation secured by the stocks, and representing the unity of the nation.

Aside from the matter of circulation, the National Currency Act is as favorable to bankers as the banking laws of most of the States. Should it prove to be too stringent, it is safe to expect that such amendments will be made to it as will accommodate it to the rea- sonable requirements of capitalists, and the want of a great and growing nation.

Question. Will State Banks be furnished with the national circulation, according to the provisions of the 63d section of the Act?

Answer. This section is a part of the law, and must be obeyed. I have hoped, however, that very few banks would claim the advantages of it. The engrafting upon a national system of banking of a provision that, to some extent, denationalizes it, was, in my opinion, a great mistake. Nor can I understand how State Banks, without the aid of State legislation, can avail themselves of the provisions of this section without violating their

charters, or the laws under which they are incorporated. But if enabling acts, authorizing State Banks to circulate the National Currency, have been or should be passed by the Legislatures of the proper States, I should still regret being compelled to furnish this currency to in- stitutions over which the Government can exercise no supervision or control. I trust that few banks will deposit bonds and claim circulation, under the 62d section, but that the stockholders of solvent banks, who desire to connect themselves with the system, will do so, by availing themselves of the priviliges of the 61st section, or, what would be better still, by winding up their present State institutions, and organizing new associations, in- dependent of the old ones. The intention of the law was to provide a national circulation through the agency of National Banks, which should be subject to Government supervision and control. Nothing would be more sure to destroy the symmetry of the system, or be more likely to bring it into disrepute, than a distribution among the banking institutions of the States, ("good, bad and indiffer- ent,") of the national currency. I must, however, obey the law, and unless prevented from doing so, by a judicial decision or an authoritative opinion, I shall furnish circulation under the section referred to as soon as it can be provided. As notes will be first sup- plied to Associations, organized under the Act, it is not likely that State Banks can be supplied, to any consider- able extent, before the early part of the next year.

Question. Is it expected that State Banks that may become National Associations under the 61st section of the Act will give up their present corporate names?

Answer. Before I entered upon the discharge of my duties as Controller of the Currency, the Secretary of the Treasury, after much consideration, had come to the conclusion, as a National Currency was to be provided through the instrumentality of National Banking Associa- tions, that all such associations should have a common name. Persons forming associations under the act have, therefore, been advised to take the names of First, Second, Third, etc., National Banks of the places in which they are established, according to the order of organization. This rule is expected to be observed by State Banks that may be converted into National Banks, under the 61st section of the Act, as well as by original associations.

If, in their new organizations, they desire to retain, in some way, their former corporate names, it must be done in such manner as will not interfere with the symmetry of the circulation which is to be furnished to them, nor render illegal their acts as National Associa- tions. All who connect themselves with this system have a common interest in making it symmetrical and harmonious, as well as national. The retention by State Banks of their present corporate names, some of them long, and differing from others only in locality, would prevent this, and interfere with the uniformity which it is desirable to maintain in the national circulation.

I know with what tenacity and pride the managers of old and well conducted banks cling to the names which their ability and integrity have done so much to make honorable; but I would suggest to them that it will be an easy matter for them to transfer to National Institutions the credit which they and their predecessors have given to State institutions; that it is not the name of a Bank, but the character of the men who conduct its affairs, and the character of its securities, that give to it the confidence of the public.

The Merchants' Bank of Boston will not lose a particle of credit by becoming the First National Bank of Boston; on the contrary, its credit will be improved by it. Nor would the stock of the Chemical Bank of New York be a whit the less valuable, nor would its reputation be in the slightest degree lessened, by its becoming the tenth or the fiftieth National Bank of New York.

H. McCULLOCH, Controller.

Appendix III

CIRCULAR LETTER OF AUGUSTUS ELY SILLIMAN[271]

New York, Sept. 23d, 1863.

TO THE OFFICERS AND DIRECTORS OF THE BANKS OF THE NEW-YORK CLEARING HOUSE ASSOCIATION:

I trust that the common interest we all have in the subject to which I am about to call your consideration will plead my apology for any apparent freedom I may seem to take in addressing you.

One of the most important progressive features of "the New-York Clearing House Association" has been, that a unity of interests has brought the gentlemen managing the various institutions into frequent contact, and thence developed a mutual feeling of kindness, respect and confidence between them, and that the recognition of principle is so decided that the smallest institution feels that its rights will be as thoroughly recognized as those of the largest. It is, therefore, on the ground of mutual confidence that I propose to request your consideration of the few suggestions I am about to make. If, after listening to them, you shall see fit to dismiss them, well; if, on the contrary, they shall arouse and determine you to action, whatever that action may be, my object is attained. If it should awaken gentlemen from apparent apathy or discouragement, I shall have achieved my end. I, therefore, approach you in perfect simplicity, and with absence of all pretension. I shall not expect criticism on the disjointed remarks, thrown together, as not covering the subject, neither your patience, if such elaboration were necessary, nor my time would allow extended examination of a system which throws out like a vine its tendrils, grasping directly or indirectly every interest within its reach. I propose to call your attention to the new banking scheme of the Secretary of the Treasury; indeed, I should not call it new, for it has not even the merit of originality; it is but the Banking Law of the State of New-York, with other mischievous features engrafted upon it.

This scheme has begun to develop itself in various parts of the country, not without much bolstering, however, and institutions are forming, or formed, in this city, which will soon, we have reason to believe, be applying for admission into the Clearing House Association; unhappily, to some extent, they have an indirect recognition already through banks, members of that body; a recognition, to my mind, more undesirable than that of direct membership, the legal difficulties, if no other, at all times hanging over us in transactions of this character being very great. We have to meet these applications squarely, firmly and decidedly, for with their acceptance or rejection possibly rests the fate of the banks of the association; and on your action the life or death of one of the two systems may be decided.

It is as well to look back on the last two years and a half, and see under what auspices this wonder of Political Economy has been brought forth, its propriety and necessity.

We can recall, all of us, our relations with the Secretary of the Treasury since the opening of the rebellion; the desperate position of the nation at the advent of Mr. LINCOLN, stripped of army and navy by the traitors, having the previous administration in their hands, and the utter helplessness of the government credit, with its Treasury plundered, and its funds squandered by the wretches who had had its custody. We all recollect the appeal made, in vain, to the public for loans; the people stood silent and aghast, as if in a waking dream; it appeared as if the whole social fabric was sinking from under them, and that property was but a name, soon to be a fiction. The fate of the nation was hanging in the balance. The Secretary of the Treasury appealed to the banks of the three great cities, and nobly did they respond; the associated banks of the city of New-York, of course, in greater proportion than the others, as was proper. Fifty million of dollars was advanced to the government, and an army and navy arose as if by magic. The nation was saved. The financial capital of the country, aroused from its stupor by the action of the banks, soon followed in their footsteps, and the credit of the United States was restored.

But not alone fifty million, but another fifty million, and another fifty million, and still other millions were forthcoming, so that up to this time the associated banks of this city alone have advanced to the government, in the way of loans, deposits and credits, at least two hundred million of dollars; and this, not taking into consideration the proportion furnished by our sisters of Philadelphia and Boston.

This aid was advanced at fearful risk. No inducement short of the devotion of patriotism could have for one instant induced the banks to depart from their legitimate sphere to afford it. It would seem then, that these institutions were entitled to the gratitude "of him ready to perish," that the property of the widow, the orphan and the aged, thrown nobly into the vortex to aid the government, and thus risked to save it, should have been held sacred by that government. The salvation of the nation under Providence was this act of the banks. Without their generous action, the flag of a conspiracy maturing for a generation would have floated over its Capitol.

140

But what has been the response to that action? It has been this, and the finger of the historian will point to it with amazement, that while the ink was yet undried, the same pen that was drawing from us these millions, was coldly and deliberately drafting the plan for our destruction. It is hard to believe; it is hard to believe it of human nature, even of political ambition, but the fact stares us grimly and sternly in the face. The Comptroller of the Treasury, its exponent, in his recent circular triumphantly asserts it in plain Saxon, in his own language, IT REQUIRES NO SPIRIT OF PROPHECY TO SAY WHICH CLASS OF THE TWO INSTITUTIONS IS BOUND TO FALL. It is well, at any rate, that the position is defined. If carried out to the extent wished by its projector in its effect upon us, it matters but little whether this scheme is the work of the politician, or the infatuation of the theorist, the result of the conflagration destroying our property is the same.

The position being defined, let us examine into its strength and our weakness. Let us inspect closely the scaling ladders with which this new system proposes to mount and carry our works; and then decide, whether after that examination, it becomes us to fight for the interests confided sacredly to our care, or to tamely submit to power unhappily most injudiciously wielded.

The scheme of the "National Banks" proposes the following features, in which they will, so far as money making is concerned, have the advantage of the existing banks in this State, and in most if not all of the other States.

1st. They are exempt from State Taxation.

2d. Their Circulation, guaranteed by the Government, has a more extended sphere.

3d. That Circulation is made a legal tender between the Government and the people, but not as between the people.

4th. Virtually abrogating the Sub-Treasury, they are to be made the depositaries of the public funds.

5th. By adroit management, the balances standing to the credit of the country banks, of similar character, in the cities of New-York, Boston and Philadelphia, and a few other large cities, are to be recognised to the extent of their balances as the required reserve to be held by them of twenty-five per cent in legal tender, thus compelling such banks as may adopt this law, to withdraw their accounts, however unwillingly, from their present friends, and to transfer them to the new banks.

Let us suppose that the reasons are sufficient to induce us to avoid the conflict, to wind up, return our capital to our stockholders, and after liquidation renew our existence under the new system, (a plan exceedingly consoling, but which, unfortunately, the laws of the State of New-York decidedly prohibit,) what do we see?

1st. The sweeping out of existence the institutions created under the laws of one of the most powerful and loyal States in the Union, whose blood and treasure has been poured out like water in the suppression of the Rebellion--the consequent additional taxation thrown upon its citizens, and the natural indignation at a wanton exhibition of power.

But, here, let me not be misunderstood. I conceive that one of the worst features of this bill is, that it is unnecessarily throwing a firebrand into the State, raising the question of State rights. Nevertheless, I deem the sovereignty of the nation so vital, that if it were necessary to its life I would assent to the entire wiping out of State lines, if that life could be only purchased at so dear a rate.

2d. We see a circulation, paper money based upon paper; a time debt reconverted into a demand debt; a circulation resting on a conventional value, which value is subject to continued fluctuations, (as see, for instance, our New-York State stocks in 1857, sinking some forty per cent., and the banks based upon them, only prevented from failure by the combined action of the city banks,) under the endorsement of the Government, aided and nursed by its deposits, sweeping over the face of the whole continent, but only redeemable-- please mark! only redeemable, and PROTESTABLE, at the points of ISSUE, whether those points of issue be in California, Texas, Georgia or South Carolina--a circulation forced upon the people in its transactions with the Government, but with which they cannot pay their debts to each other--a gigantic "uncurrent money," an uncurrent money which, if successful, in time, is to pay us our one hundred million of seven and three-tenth notes; failing our disposition to lock up our capitals in the long loans, the alternative.

The "Banking Bill" limits this circulation to three hundred million, but the same power that forced the bill through Congress can probably cause an amendment to that law, authorizing three times that amount in addition. The whole scheme of this circulation is the throwing upon individuals the responsibility of an additional three hundred million of a QUASI legal tender, which should have been done, if done at all, fairly and openly by the Secretary of the Treasury.

The fallacy of making stock the base of circulation is fully demonstrated in England, where a very limited portion of the Government debt is recognised with gold as its basis, but there, periodically, in the contractions of the credit system, we see the "Throne" compelled to come to the rescue in legalizing that which is unable to comply with the law. Unhappily, at this moment, we have Mr. Robert J. Walker rendering this country absurd in England, in proclaiming the merits of this bill to the intensely keen political economists of that country, before whose educated reasoning the whole scheme will wither like parchment in the fire.

The Secretary of the Treasury could "not recognise two currencies." He has already furnished us with three: Demand notes; Five per cent. legal tender notes, and new "National Bank" notes--all to be admitted as money in the settlement of debts with the Government, but two alone by the people. If the theory of the Secretary of the Treasury be successful, we shall have a thousand banks spread over the whole Continent, initiated and managed, in the majority of cases, by inexperienced men, without saying any thing of unprincipled adventurers, who will flood the country with a currency essentially irredeemable, banks from whom will radiate a fearful expansion in the shape of credits issued on deposits, themselves the birth of inflation, and, Proteanlike, from which elements still further inflations will emanate, with frantic speculation and elevation of prices, until some political convulsion, or the mere hint of a return to specie payments, pricking the bubble, the "system" will collapse, spreading desolation and ruin broad-cast over the land, producing such a scene of financial calamity as shall make all our previous convulsions compare with it as a child's rattle to a whirlwind.

One of the worst features of this system is the deception of ignorant and well-meaning people, who will become depositors with these institutions, and whose property in that shape the Government will seize in its efforts to make good the deficiency in their circulation; for the Government, by the bill, is made a preferred creditor of all the assets of these institutions until the currency is redeemed. Of course, there will be exceptions, cases where experienced and careful men will invest their capital in them, but they, with all of us, will be borne away helplessly in the storm which the inevitable future will prepare for us, if Providence, in its wrath, should allow this system to have full sway.

The whole scheme is the theory of inexperienced and unpracticed men. The productive resources of this country are fully competent to carry us through this war, and to pay the debt, its cost, principal and interest, within a century; but were they doubled, they could not avert the calamity to the nation that the success of this project will carry in its train. Now, why is all this? What was, what is, the necessity, in a time of domestic convulsion, when the nation is struggling for life when the government had, and has, more than all it can do to keep itself from destruction, that we must have this bold experiment in political economy? Why chill and estrange the friends who have come so nobly to the rescue, to turn them into enemies, by the endeavor to initiate, in a time of civil war, a change in the currency of the nation, which wise men would approach with fear and trembling in a period of profound peace? The banks, with the experience of a century, were becoming more and more stable, more and more firm, more and more governed by fixed and recognised laws, more and more a single piece of machinery, through the liquidation of their debts at the Clearing-Houses, in the financial centres of the great cities, subject, of course, to the occasional vicissitudes which must occur to all that deal in credit, whether nations, corporations, or individuals; and of which this scheme will furnish a fearful example, if it is successful in obtaining an existence, such as its projector sanguinely hopes.

The Secretary of the Treasury has already flooded the country with legal tender notes to the extent of four hundred million of dollars. Three hundred million of this might have been spared, if he had taken the advice of experienced men, who urged him to obtain from Congress the passage of an act authorizing the Assistant Treasurer to draw upon the Associated Banks in the liquidation of transactions between the government and the people.

If the New-York Clearing-House Association can liquidate, in one day, ninety million of dollars of the debt of the community, with a resulting balance of only one million and a half of dollars, to be paid in notes, is it not equally true that the banks, which are the clearing houses for the liquidation of debt between individuals, can, by the transferring their balances, settle their debt connected with the government with like economy of physical means? This was urged, not only strongly on the Secretary of the Treasury, but on the committees of Congress. That of the House was so impressed with the truth of the position that they inserted a section in the loan bill, authorizing the Secretary of the Treasury to make use of the banks at his discretion. It passed the House, but was thrown out in the Senate. Is it unfair for us to surmise at whose suggestion? If the machinery furnished by the banks had been adopted, ignoring, if you please, and refusing the bank notes, the issue of legal tender notes required to pay the soldiers and various mechanics, all that would have been needed, could not, by any possibility, have extended beyond one hundred million of dollars. But now the same law that obtains, compelling four hundred million of dollars, must act in continued force; and there is nothing to prevent the requisition of one thousand million of dollars, with all its direful consequences, to the future.

But I think I hear you say, to what does all this narration and argument tend? The evil is upon us. In what is this recapitulation of the past, and prognostics as to the future, to the purpose? They should have been used to prevent the passage of the law. What is your remedy? True, they should have been; and if we had used the proper energy by remonstrance and explanation at Washington by a suitable committee, it is probable that the evil would have been averted.

But still we are not without a remedy, and that is, as yet, in our own hands. It is plain, simple and direct, and if we are true to the positions we hold, as the guardians of the property confided to our care, in many cases the ALL of women, children, the infirm, of those who look to us as their only means of support, nay, if simply influenced by the law of self-preservation, are we not bound to adopt it? As conscientious men, using the same means we would were our own property in jeopardy; as men having some previous knowledge of the tempests of the currency; as men who, with that experience, foresee the desolation and calamity that looms fearfully in the distance to the welfare of the nation; as watchmen, if you please, whose duty it is to sound the alarm ere it is too late; are we not bound to use it? It is simple this. Let the Associated Banks in the three great cities of New-York, Philadelphia and Boston, decline all recognition of these institutions, directly or indirectly, IN THEIR EXCHANGES, and let them at once, at whatever expense, return the notes that they are compelled to receive from the government to their respective points of issue for redemption. In so doing, you will keep the heart of the currency at the great city centres unscathed and whole. The power of this system for mischief will not be entirely removed; still it will be so far controlled as to prevent the ruin to ourselves and the nation, that its entire success will surely ensure.

One word more, and I will trespass no longer on your patience. The idea exists that it is simply a matter of volition as to whether we will not relinquish our present charters, and renew our institutions under this law. The banks can wind up whenever they please, but it is a very different matter when they propose to renew their corporate existence under the proposed bill, which is in direct definance of the Constitution and laws of the State of New-York.

The penalties for such banking, directly or indirectly, other than under the prescribed laws of the State, are a fine of one thousand dollars each on all parties concerned, Directors, Stockholders and Officers, AND AN ENTIRE MAKING VOID OF ALL CONTRACTS BY OR WITH THEM.--[SEE CHAPTER 20, LAWS OF 1837.]

If in what I have said I shall have been so fortunate as to command your thorough examination of the subject, whatever your decision, I shall feel well repaid. I can say for myself, that in this communication I am impelled solely by a conscientious sense of duty; but before I lay down my pen I will also say, that if the success of this scheme of banking were necessary to the suppression of the rebellion by our Army and Navy, and the restoration of the flag of the United States over every inch of its territory, that my voice should be the last heard in opposition to it, never mind how severe the sacrifice to individual interest.

A BANK STOCKHOLDER AND DIRECTOR.

Appendix IV

THE NEW NATIONAL BANKING SYSTEM; OR, GOVERNMENT PAPER MONEY[272]

At a meeting of the New York Clearing House Association, held October 6th 1863, the following resolution was adopted:

Resolved, that a committee of five Bank Officers be appointed to examine into the system of National Banking initiated by the present Secretary of the Treasury, in its prospective effects upon the currency of our nation, and the National credit; and to report what action, if any, devolves upon the Banks of this association in the premises.

REMARKS OF JAMES GALLATIN, ESQ., IN REFERENCE TO THE ABOVE RESOLUTION:

Questions of serious importance, to which your attention was solicited two years ago, have lately been brought to your notice in a circular dated 23d ult., signed "a Bank Stockholder and Director."[273] It is conceded in this circular that the "flood" of paper money issued by the Secretary of the Treasury was wholly uncalled for, and that the refusal to adopt the suggestion of Bank officers and others, as to the expedience of maintaining specie payments throughout the war, has led to the evils which were then foreshadowed, and which are now coming upon us in such frightful shapes, that even those who derided the idea of sustaining specie payments stand aghast before the creations of their own policy.--Thanks to the disasters which have overwhelmed the paper issues of the insurgent Davis in ruin, all loyal men can now see whither Mr. Chase's paper money schemes are tending. No man can now doubt the folly and the madness of these schemes, nor question the practicability of conducting any conceivable amount of financial business in this country upon a specie basis; for as we know by all past experience in the Clearing House, the quantity of real money required to be moved does not amount to a twentieth part (five cents in the dollar) of the sum of the business transacted.

The Secretary's plans are defended on the ground that they have saved to the country the interest on his issues of paper money, but the increased prices of supplies are enhancing the cost of the war, and increasing our national debt to a much greater extent than the saving of this interest; and as the proposed further issues by the new banks can only aggravate the evil, without saving to the government the interest on the proposed increase of circulation, it becomes the duty of Bankers, as well as the people to look earnestly as patriots at the consequences of the extension of this new description of paper money. Does the country need it? Will it save the Government from increased expenditure? Will it save interest to the Government? Will it bring us nearer a specie standard? All these question,

in my humble judgment, demand serious investigation. If they are to be answered in the negative, what then is the possible use of this new currency? Centralization of monetary power at Washington is one. Is that desirable? Is it judicious to place the whole volume of security for the entire paper-money of the country in the hands of ONE MAN at Washington? Images of grandeur and power may be floating in this ONE MAN'S imagination,--"Those meteor-lights, which are exhaled in the stormy atmosphere of a revolution to allure the ambitious and dazzle the weak."

This new paper money of the new banks is not a legal tender by act of Congress. Government may pay it to certain of its creditors, and it is bound to receive it in payment of all debts other than duties on imports. But the notes are redeemable only where issued, and as Government may pay at New York the issues of a bank at St. Paul, in Minnesota, it follows that the currency of the new banks located out of this city will assume the character of that description of uncurrent money heretofore, and now, bought by out city brokers at a discount. I do not understand how such issues can be taken at the Clearing House, and treated as current money in this city; and as the proposed object of creating a national currency with this money will be defeated by the inevitable depreciation of the issues in places distant from the places of redemption, no efforts of ours through the New York Clearing House would avail in counteracting the natural law of depreciation inherent in the issues thus circulating. Hence it will be impossible in my humble judgment, to receive such issues at the Clearing House, and the whole of this new Banking system, being intended to maintain a certain unity of purpose, the rejection of a part necessarily involves the rejection of the whole. No injury can be done to the Government, or the holy cause of preserving our national life, by permitting this new currency to follow the natural law of depreciation inherent in such issues, because the Government saves nothing by the issues; on the contrary, Government must lose heavily by these issues if all banks receive and pay them and thus convert them into current money to increase prices, and add immensely to the national debt, by thus increasing the cost of the war. Patriotism as well as duty therefore calls upon us to avoid the error of adding them to the volume of current money, already so largely expanded.

Before the suspension of specie payments, nearly two years ago, when the question of Mr. Chase's plans created uneasiness among us all, I then remarked in an address at one of our meetings:--"That we were all desirous of knowing his plans for the future, and particularly the measures he proposed to recommend to Congress. It is customary, in all countries, to communicate such information freely to persons making great loans, and the Finance Minister of even the most despotic governments considers himself bound to furnish it on such occasions. But Mr. Chase utterly refused to give any intimation of his plans to us. Having heard rumors from the street that plans for an indirect issue of government paper money, upon national securities, in imitation of our system in this state, were being pressed upon his notice, I prepared and read to him on that occasion an exposition of the futility of resorting to such a scheme, and explained how it would fail to yield him the supply of capital which he required. He solicited a copy of the paper, which I gave him, and in the hurry of preparing his report he no doubt overlooked it, for a few days afterward he sent in his report to Congress recommending the very scheme I had exposed. It would seem evident, therefore, that either he is not very well acquainted with the nature of financial affairs, or is controlled, no doubt by well-meaning persons, who advocate the policy of a suspension of specie payments, and a vast issue of paper money. In either case the results of his policy will be the same, and the influence upon us is no longer a matter of conjecture."[274]

We all now know what Mr. Chase's plans were, and we are also familiar, from daily observation, with the enormous fortunes that have been realized by individuals within these two years from the successful carrying out of those plans. While the poor have been made poorer, and the industrial and producing classes are loaded down by high prices incident to the inflation which "floods" of paper money create. But all remonstrance has been in vain, and now it is highly probable that the failure which bids fair to attend these new bank issues upon their emerging into circulation will lead to their being made a legal tender by Congress at the approaching session, or to some attempt of that kind; for it seems no longer doubtful that the paper-money advocates are determined to push their opportunity to the very last desperate resort, exactly in imitation of the famous bubble of the great prince of paper money, the celebrated John Law.

In view of this course of events, in January last I wrote to Senator Fessenden:

"There is a certain positive limit to our capacity for expenditure as a nation. Our savings (in the loyal states) have been shown in our last census, and although some estimate them as continuing even during the present struggle at a rate equal to that of the most prosperous year of the decade which closed with an aggregate wealth computed at twelve thousand millions, it is by these that our course in the war should be regulated as to expenditure, and whether they amount to four hundred, or seven hundred millions, it must be borne in mind that the regulating power of the currency over these savings is one of the most important elements of our economical calculations. If we continue to add to our paper measure of prices, we shall continue to lessen the power of the people to save, because we shall drive out of the country the real money UPON WHICH ALL PRICES AND VALUES DEPEND! No legislation nor device of man can prevent that. Specie is now near fifty per cent. premium; prices of every thing but government stocks are rising, and gold is flowing out of the country in a steady stream. More legal tender will increase the prices of all property and commodities, except government stocks, and render it more and more difficult to fund the national debt in long loans.

These phenomena are not new. They have always accompanied excessive issues of paper money. Fright has as much influence as the love of gain, in producing them. When there is an abundance of money, and every thing is rising, people find it more profitable to use the money to speculate with than to invest in permanent loans. Vast issues of government paper money create fears of national bankruptcy. All this fear, and alarm, and speculation may be, and no doubt is, very foolish and very unpatriotic. But we cannot change human nature. Our statesmen must deal with it as it is, if they would make it serviceable to the great and holy object of preserving our nationality and perpetuating our liberties."

And in view of the hostility evinced at Washington toward all existing Banks, I added in the same letter to Senator Fessenden:

"Since the foregoing was written, my attention has been called to the state of feeling and opinion existing at Washington upon the financial affairs of the Government. A persistent hostility seems to prevail against the banks, on the part of the very gentlemen who desire to create NEW BANKS. Now, I would ask, is this a time for such machinations? It was impossible for the Secretary of the Treasury to have gone on, in the early progress of the rebellion, had not the banks come to the aid of the Government. Indeed, many believe that the rebellion would probably, at first, have been successful, if the banks of the loyal States had not volunteered their aid, as they did, long before the Secretary was able to mature any plans for the relief of the Treasury. Although the banks supplied him with resources, he neglected the provisions of the law authorizing him to draw direct upon them, preferring to make his drafts through the sub-treasury, thus draining them of their coin, and from this cause has arisen very many of our financial troubles. It produced the suspension of specie payments, and caused the inflation of the currency, which (together with legal tender issues) have tended to reduce our material power, thus favoring the designs of the rebels."

The hostility to which I thus referred has now been openly avowed by the Comptroller of the Currency in his circular letter dated last month. He has declared his desire to have all the banks now in existence wound up and transformed into banks which shall be known by simple numerals, as "one," "two," "three," "four," &c., so that no distinctions shall remain to mark those of high credit and good standing (as the Bank of New York, Bank of Commerce and like institutions) from those which may have neither. I can find no warrant in the Act of Congress for his arbitrary attitude[?] against the old banks retaining their former names when reorganized under the new law: he says:--"Before I entered upon the discharge of my duties as Comptroller of the Currency, the Secretary of the Treasury, after much consideration, had come to the conclusion, as a National currency was to be provided through the instrumentality of National Banking Associations, that all such associations should have a common name. Persons forming associations under the Act have, therefore, been advised to take the names of First, Second, Third, &c., National Banks of the places in which they are established, according to the order of organization. This rule is expected to be observed by State Banks, that may be converted into National Banks under the sixty-first section of the Act, as well as by original associations."

It is not the Act of Congress, therefore, but a "conclusion" of the Secretary of the Treasury, which is to prohibit a bank from retaining its name, under which it may have attained a high degree of credit, as valuable to it, probably, as a large portion of its capital; and, indeed, the Secretary might with as much justice require men employed in these new banks, to be known by their numbers, instead of their names, so far as any authority that I can find in the law of Congress has conferred that power upon him.

The Comptroller of Currency says: "I know with what tenacity and pride the managers of old and well conducted banks cling to the names which their ability and integrity have done so much to make honorable; but I would suggest to them, that it will be an easy matter for them to transfer to National Institutions the credit which they and their predecessors have given to State Institutions; that it is not the name of a bank, but the character of the men who conduct its affairs, and the character of its securities, that give to it the confidence of the public. The Merchants Bank of Boston would not lose a particle of credit by becoming the First National Bank of Boston; on the contrary, its credit will be improved by it. Nor would the stock of the Chemical Bank of New York be a whit the less valuable, nor would its reputation be in the slightest degree lessened, by its becoming the tenth or the fiftieth National Bank of New York."

It is true that "a rose by any other name will smell as sweet," but I doubt very much the possibility of transferring the credit of old banks, as he proposes, to the new ones, under new names, especially as the names he proposes are not real distinctive NAMES, but simple NUMERALS! In the case of members of Congress, or the members of the Cabinet, for example, how ridiculous for the Speaker of the House, or the President to insist upon having them known by their numerals! or for the Secretary and the Comptroller to be compelled to select NUMERALS for themselves! A "centralization of power" at Washington, to enforce such a "regulation," would be no more absurd than this proposed "regulation," as part of the financial "centralization of power," to compel banks to be known by THEIR NUMERALS! Indeed, there is a serious question involved in this numbering of banks, involving the credit of the whole system. I refer to the great danger of the organization of bogus banks under the new law, as was the case under similar laws in several of the Northwestern States some years ago, and it is possible that the Secretary as well as the Comptroller may live long enough to witness the serious blows to the credit of the new banking system from abandoning distinctive names for NUMERALS.

Among all the deplorable consequences increasing the prices of commodities, by this proposed increase of paper-money through the new banks, none is so injurious to our national wealth as the transfer of our public debt into the hands of foreign capitalists at the most extraordinarily low prices. Persons not conversant with financial affairs are shamefully deceived, and misled on this question. Because the stocks of the United States are quoted at or above par, no matter what may be the price of gold and other commodities, they consider our financial policy to be founded upon the wise teachings of experience. Now, for example, let us take a case, similar to those which occur every day on the street, and in the New York Stock Board. We will suppose gold to be at fifty per cent. premium, as it has been more than once within a year, and a capitalist residing in London or Paris, wishes to buy one thousand dollars worth of our government stock-- say "five twenties." This stock is at par in our paper-money, one hundred dollars of "greenbacks" being worth one hundred dollars in "five-twenties." The capitalist has sent one thousand dollars in gold (or bills of exchange payable in gold) from London or from Paris, and this sells in New York for about fifteen hundred dollars in green-backs, there being a slight charge for expenses; so that every thousand dollars sent from other countries, when gold is about fifty premium in New York, buys about fifteen hundred dollars of our government stock, bearing six per cent interest in gold and in reality Mr. Chase gets less (in real value) than one thousand dollars for his fifteen hundred of stock, because his issues of paper money have increased the prices of every thing so much that the fifteen hundred dollars he would have received in paper, in the example just referred to, would buy far less in commodities than the thousand dollars under a specie currency. He pays interest on fifteen hundred dollars annually in gold, being ninety dollars a year, although he has received in real value only one thousand dollars. In this way every foreign capitalist when gold is at fifty premium, gets our government securities at about sixty-six cents on the dollar, so that his capital yields him more than eleven per cent. interest, while our poor people, as well as all persons having fixed incomes, are made to pay fifty per cent. more for the necessaries of life, and our own capitalists are compelled to pay fifty per cent more than foreigners for our own national securities. To impoverish a nation, and discourage the labor and savings of its people, no system is so effectual as this of paper-money; and it is this system, so ruinous to the nation and the people, which we are requested to render active and efficient by admitting its engines into the Clearing House, that they may destroy and supplant the specie paying system upon which our New York city banks are founded, and establish upon its ruins that of the notorious John Law, which has exploded in every country which has tried it, leaving a succession of awful warnings and admonitions, which are to be read in almost every chapter of the history of nations, during the last and present centuries.

Chapter XVI

THE NATIONAL BANKING SYSTEM UP TO 1882
(Fourth Period of American Banking)

1. See vol. I of this work, page 178.
2. See, for instance, Ashmead, op. cit., 73.
3. See Helderman, op, cit., 148; Scudder, op. cit., 24, 25; Potter, Plan, Appendix, iii; Finance Report (1864), 49, 51; Oberholtzer, op. cit., I, 334, 335; James, Chicago Banks, I,309; McCulloch's letter reprinted by Kane, op. cit., 24.
4. A Treatise on Currency and Banking (Philadelphia, 1839), 212. The passage is not conclusive: Raguet considers it possible that the principles of New York Free Banking might be made general. He may have thought only of adoption by the various states. See 2d ed. of 1840, 202.
5. Davis, A.M., National Banking, 64.
6. Private History, 3. See also below page 103; Gallatin, James, Letter to Fessenden, 14; U.S. 37th Congr. 3d. sess., House Executive Document 25, 93.
7. See vol. I of this work, pages 191 ff.
8. See Messages and Papers of the Presidents, ed. by James D. Richardson, I (Washington, 1896), 578, 579.
9. Pages 12 ff. Prior to that pamphlet Roger M. Sherman wrote a letter to Elisha Phelps, Controller of Public Accounts of the State of Connecticut, which was published on request of the latter. It contained the suggestion that no notes be issued by any new bank unless they were first endorsed and stamped by a public officer. That officer was not to give his sanction to any paper unless the bank had previously deposited with him stock of the United States or of any other American state bearing 6 per cent interest or mortgages on real or personal estates. One sees at first glance that all the elements of New York Banking of 1838 are contained in the proposal, except free banking as such.
10. Pitkin, op. cit., (1835), 458.
11. Finance Report (1862), 21. In fact there was no general agreement on this point. Brooks (op. cit., 55) claimed as late as 1893 that Congress was not authorized to provide a national circulation of paper money, much less to monopolize the creation of such circulation by suppressing state bank notes.
12. Clarke and Hall, op. cit., 612. Dallas seems to have suggested that the notes of certain banks which lent funds to the general government would be made receivable by the collectors. All the participating banks, wherever located, would then open accounts with each other and would take each others' notes at par from both collectors and depositors. See Bank of North America, Minutes of the Board of Directors, Apr. 12, 1815.
13. Analectic Magazine, VI (1815), 503, 517, 518.
14. Op. cit., 8, 10.
15. In the same decade Thomas Mendenhall suggested a national currency to be issued by Federal loan offices to state loan offices; the latter would lend it on the pledge of real property; op. cit., 17 ff.
16. Brief Exposition, 9 ff.
17. The following description is based to a large extent on the contemporary pamphlet literature which is so ephemeral that it is hardly worthwhile to insert the titles in the list of references. This has been done only if the items are of broader interest or the works of important authors or of bankers. The ephemeral character of this literature, however, does not detract from its value as a source in the present context.
Extensive use has been made of the Reports of the Comptroller of the Currency, in future cited R.C.C. Those between 1863 and 1871 were used as inserted in the Report of the Secretary of the Treasury on the State of the Finances for the year in question (quoted as Finance Report). For the later years the independent issues of the Comptroller's Reports were used and are so cited.
18. National Banking System, 10. In this connection Davis has mentioned the previously-quoted article in the Analectic Magazine, VI (1815), 489 ff, signed W. as the first proposal suggestive of National Banking. I have dealt with the article in another context and have identified it as written by Judge James Workman of New Orleans. See my Essays in American Economic History, 56, 104 (footnote 137). The essential point in Workman's proposal was to make the bills of the banks, which had suspended specie payments at that time, convertible into either coin or government bonds (at the option of the banks), the interest on the latter being paid in coin. The proposal is suggestive of the original legal-tender issues, convertible into 5-20's bonds whose interest was paid in gold; (pages 508, 513). It is noteworthy that in 1875 Orlando B. Potter suggested exactly the same measure that Judge Workman had proposed in 1816 and which Eric Bollmann had taken up. Potter suggested that National Banks should be forced to redeem their notes at their option, either in coin or in U.S. government bonds bearing gold interest. See his Plan, 6, 10 ff.
19. Op. cit., 134 ff. See also R.C.C. (1875) in Finance Report (1875), 191 ff.
20. Helderman (op. cit., 134) mentions in this

connection Roger M. Sherman's anonymously published Letters to Levi Woodbury. This pamphlet, which breathes Isaac Bronson's spirit and promotes his basic ideas, proposes (pp. 16 ff) a "national bank" whose issues were to be collaterally secured by government stock deposited with some outside agency. The item does not seem to belong to those which prepared the way to the National Banking System.

21. See State of New York, Annual Report of the Comptroller (for 1848), Assembly Document 5, 57; also U.S. 31st Congr. 1st sess., Executive Document 68, 131, 132.

22. Bonnefoux, "Financial Policy," 431.

23. This author has been unable to locate a copy of the December 1857 issue of the Hardwareman's Newspaper. But the passage is reprinted in Iron Age, January 1863, as the New York Public Library discovered when searching for the original source. Williams dealt with the episode in his pamphlet of 1868 (see list of references), passim.

24. Orlando Bronson Potter (1823-1894), born in Massachusetts, the son of a farmer of Colonial ancestry, was admitted to the bar in Boston in 1848. In 1853 he moved to New York and engaged in manufacture. In 1883-1885 he was a Congressman.

25. Potter, Plan, Appendix, page i ff; points 4 and 6 (paragraph 4) of the Plan show conclusively that Potter suggested the issue of a national circulation by state banks.

26. Laurent Bonnefoux belonged to those who boundlessly overestimate their own importance. He appeared in the New York City Directory of 1826 as an importer and in the late 1830's as a banker, while in 1849/50 we find him in Washington. He was, so he claimed, one of the first to defend New York Free Banking in public, publishing under the signature L.B. articles in the New York Evening Post in the fall of 1838. He was critical, however, of the admission of mortages and bonds of states other than New York as the basis of note issues and, drawing the conclusion therefrom, founded in the same year a Free Bank whose issues were based exclusively on New York State stock (New York State Stock Security Bank which existed until about 1850). In 1848 he wrote a pamphlet Vindication of the Free Banking System... which, as he claimed later, influenced Millard Fillmore's proposal, a very shadowy, at least far-fetched, claim (one should compare his Vindication, 25, with the latter's report); but as mentioned above he defended Fillmore's plan during the newspaper controversy of 1849 in "A Sound National Paper Currency" in the New York Evening Mirror, Mar. 23, 1849. (Prior thereto he had written an article "Investigation of the True Principle that Paper Money ought to be based upon", published 1847 in the New York Evening Post and reprinted in the Evening Mirror and Bankers Magazine.) Bonnefoux also published a few political items, Exposé des éventualités et des conséquences d'une guerre entre les Etats

Unis et l'Angleterre... par un Citoyen de New York (Paris, 1845); The Constitution expounded respecting its Bearing on the Subject of Slavery (New York, 1850). In the early 1860's Bonnefoux, then an ardent Republican and admirer of Lincoln, was in Paris and wrote a treatise which was published in parts as follows: two numbers in the Bankers Magazine, XVI (see list of references); four parts in the London American; the seventh and eighth parts appeared first in the New York Evening Post, then independently under the title: Extracts from a Treatise on the Constitution of the United States (New York, 1863). The ninth part, finally was published under the queer title The Constitution No. 9 (New York, 1864).

27. Cited from Helderman, op. cit., 138, footnote 2.

28. See this volume page 87 and James, Chicago Banks, I, 301.

29. Finance Report (1861), 18 ff.

30. One can read, for instance: "In his first annual report Mr. Chase would have a general law under which associations could be formed and incorporated as banks" (Cooley, "Federal Taxation," 43); other examples can be found in Brooks, op. cit., 34; Oberholtzer, op. cit., I, 328; and even James (Chicago Banks, I, 305) claims that in December, 1861, Chase "recommended the creation by the federal government of national currency associations..."). The presentation in R.C.C. (1875) in Finance Report (1875), 197 is correct, but its author did not point out that Chase in 1861 and 1862 made de facto two different proposals.
The error may go back to a confusing statement of Chase's. In his Finance Report of 1862 (page 17) he expressed his preference for a national circulation, issued by banking associations under a general act authorizing the organization of such associations as proposed in his previous report (of 1861). But such a proposal is not contained in the report of 1861. If we turn to Andrew McFarland Davis's book, The Origin of the National Banking System, we find on pages 36 and 37 a correct presentation of Chase's plan of 1861 under an erroneous headline. This headline and another passage of the same book (pages 51 and 52) show that Davis took it for granted that Chase had proposed a National Banking System as early as December, 1861. In the former passage Davis states correctly that Chase had proposed "the preparation and delivery to institutions and associations of notes prepared for circulation under national direction." But the headline reads "National Banks Suggested." This caption is not the correct one for the passage quoted which must be seen together with other statements in the Report of 1861; namely, that one of the principal features of the plan was the "circulation of notes bearing a common impression and authenticated by a common authority" (p. 19). That common authority was called National Bank Department by George S. Coe in a letter of November, 1861, to be discussed shortly. To return to

the Report of 1861, "solvent existing institutions" [underlining mine] were to "withdraw the circulation issued under State authority and substitute that provided by the authority of the Union" (pp. 19, 20). Through "voluntary action of existing [underlining mine] institutions" the transition was to be accomplished. There is no word of a National Banking system in the Report; but Coe's description of the plan as that of a National Bank Department is striking, namely a department of the Federal government to issue a national currency to "solvent existing institutions."

31. See, for instance, Bankers Magazine, XVI (1861/62), 543 (issue of January, 1862). It is remarkable that this periodical took no notice of the Spaulding bill and evidenced very little interest in the project.

32. "A National Authenticated Currency" (the title alone would prove our point) in Hunt's Merchants' Magazine, XLVI (1862), 119 ff, especially 119, 127. See also the articles "A National Currency and Banking System" in ibid., 113 ff, which is supposed to have been written by John Jay Knox (Dict. Am. Biogr.), and "A Uniform National Currency, by a Western Banker" in ibid., XLVIII (1863), 28.

33. As to E.G. Spaulding, see below page 104, and his History of Legal Tender Paper Money, 12 ff; Address, 55.

34. Davis, A.M. National Banking System, 55, 56; R.C.C. (1875) in Finance Report (1875), 197.

35. The author is indebted to the New York Public Library for the successful search for the bill. There is no copy in the Library of Congress, nor in the National Archives.

36. See above, page 100.

37. Act of June 20, 1874, sec. 1.

38. Some Strictures, 11.

39. Finance Report (1862), 17.

40. See vol. I of this work, pages 195, 196.

41. A Letter on National Currency, 6.

42. As his Six Letters show, Lord's ideas were thereafter veering away from that which became National Banking: by March 1862 he had switched to recommending the issue of legal tender treasury notes and their circulation by banks depositing national bonds into which that "national currency" was to be convertible, (op. cit., 6, 11, 12, 45).

Similar ideas can be found also in Ruggles, A.G., A National System of Finance suited to a War or Peace Establishment, Regulating Exchange and Making Specie Plenty (n.p., n.d. [1862?]). Ruggles suggested that bonds be issued to a Bureau of National Currency which would issue on that basis interest-bearing circulating treasury notes. For a similar plan see also Fraley, Frederick, Plan for the Graduate Resumption of Specie Payments and the Establishment of a System for a National Currency (n.p., n.d. [1877?]), passim.

43. It is not doubted that Stilwell worked hand in hand with the solicitor of the Treasury, Edward Jordan, whose name is given as Jordon in Stilwell's Private History. (The spelling Jordan, as used by Helderman and in the article on Stilwell in Dict. Am. Biogr., is correct as the records of the Treasury Department show [correspondence with the latter]).

44. George S. Coe to Salmon P. Chase, November 14, 1861 (Pennsylvania Historical Society).

45. The New National Banking System...(folder). reprinted as Appendix 4 of this chapter.

46. Chase Diary (Libr. of Congr., Ms. Div.), Dec. 10, 1861.

47. Pages 17 ff.

48. Spaulding, History, 12.

49. This idea played a part in Jay Cooke's advertising of war loans.

50. Op. cit., 133. Local Ohio source tend to overstress Chase's dependence on Ohio's banking set-up; see Randall and Ryan, op. cit., III, 355, IV, 501, 502.

51. The letter is reprinted in John Williams's pamphlet, op. cit., 4. In January, 1862, one Russell, for example, suggested a Board of the Exchequer which was to receive bonds and to issue a circulating medium to the amount of 80 per cent of the face value. Additional notes should be issued to any depositor of U.S. bonds to the amount of 75 per cent of their face value. See Chase, Diaries, Jan. 9, 1862 (Library of Congress).

52. McCulloch, Men and Measures, 165, 166.

53. The public usually held an erroneous belief to the contrary. See, for example, U.S. 52d Congr. 2d sess., House Committee on Banking and Currency, Hearings and Arguments on Proposed Currency Legislation, 1906/07, 21.

54. The biographical data were taken from the article in Dict. Am. Biogr. which does not refer with a single word to Spaulding's connection with the beginnings of National Banking.

55. Swanson, op. cit., 58 ff describes in detail the debate on the Sherman bill.

56. Spaulding, History, 12; Death of Hon. Samuel Hooper, 37.

57. James, Chicago Banks, I, 307.

58. For the preceding, see Davis, A.M., National Banking, 75, 78, 87, 89, 99. For an example of Walker's publicity, see his "Review of our Finances...", passim.

59. Stilwell, Private History, passim, especially 7, 9, 10; idem, A Report of Two Interviews, 12, 13.

60. See vol. I of this work, page 201.

61. A very early move in this direction is contained in a Report of the Alabama Bank Commissioners of 1838. They recommended that banks should be compelled to keep their entire capital in specie and allowed to issue notes to the amount of twice the capital, which, of course, meant a 50 per cent specie reserve. They then went on to suggest that funds held in Eastern cities on which a bank could draw at sight should be considered equal specie "to a certain percentage." U.S. 25th Congr., 3d sess., Executive Document 227, 445, 446.

The dependence of the National Currency Act on the Massachusetts Banking Act of 1858 is generally known; see Bankers Magazine, XXXII (1877/78), 351; Report of the Indianapolis Convention, 349 (the latter contains on pages 197 ff a history of the National Banking system).

62. Helderman, op. cit., 138, 139; Davis, National Banking System, 55 ff; Hooper, Banking Associations and Uniform Currency Bill, passim. The Sherman bill was reprinted in Hunt's Merchants' Magazine, XLVIII (1863), 314 ff.

63. The original limitation was $300,000,000; the law of July 12, 1870 added 54 millions; and the law of June 20, 1874 set the limit at $382,000,000. The laws are easily accessible in U.S. 53d Congr. 3d. sess., Senate Report 831, 381 ff. The limitation of the total of issues to $200,000,000 was suggested as early as January, 1862, in the article, "A National Currency and Banking System" in Hunt's Merchants' Magazine, XLVII(1862), 116, 117. The article seems to have been influential.

64. Horace Maynard (1814-1882), Congressman from Tennessee and ardent Unionist during the Civil War. He was a member of the Ways and Means Committee when the Spaulding bill hung fire; see Spaulding, History, 12.

65. Maynard, Horace, The Currency-Free Banking. Speech of ... in the House of Representatives, March 26, 1874 (Washington, 1874), 15, 16.

66. Short Road (1874), 10, 11. References to the Peel Act are very common in the contemporary pamphlet literature dealing with National Banking. An anonymous author of 1873 wrote: "The first great feature of this system is the entire separation of the department of issue from the department of discount and circulation;" (A Plan for Resuming Specie Payments without Changing the Volume of the Currency by X [New York and Chicago, 1873], 11). Praise of the Peel Act can be found in Plunkett, Thomas F., Money-Panics and Specie Payments, A Paper ... (Pittsfield, Mass., 1873), 11, 12; Bronson, Henry, The Money Problem, Inquiries concerning.... (New Haven, 1877), 15; (Bronson did not understand how the Peel Act actually worked).

67. Finance Report (1863), 57, 58. See also his remarks in Proceedings of a Meeting in relation to the Establishment of a Large National Bank, 3; (this item will be quoted later as Proceedings).

68. According to sec. 26 the holders of notes of a National Bank failing to redeem them will be directed "to present them for payment at the treasury of the United States; and the same shall be paid as presented, whereupon said comptroller may ... cancel an equal amount of bonds pledged by such association, equal at current market rates, not exceeding par, to the notes said..." In case of deficiency in the proceeds of the bonds the United States had a first lien on all assets of the association in question.

69. Plan, Appendix, ii.

70. Hooper, Banking Associations and Uniform Currency Bill, 9.

71. R.C.C. (1864) in Finance Report (1864), 50. See also Hooper, speech of 1864, p. 13. Contemporary sources are full of statements that Chase wanted to destroy the banks. This is correct only cum grano salis: He wanted to destroy them as state banks while he welcomed them with open arms into the national system. On top of that, in 1863 he pledged that the government would wage no war on the state banks. At least some of the state bankers saw the situation correctly. One of them spoke of Chase's intention to "swallow up the banks;" Oberholtzer, op. cit., I, 329. See also Gallatin, James, The New National Banking System ..., passim, and McCulloch's remarks in Proceedings, 6.

72. Knox, History, 98. As to the Massachusetts act see Bankers Magazine, XVII (1863/64), 995, 996.

73. Proceedings, 5.

74. Chicago Banks, I, 317 ff. See also McCulloch, Men and Measures, 168; Some Strictures..., passim.; Hunt's Merchants' Magazine, XLVI (1862), 125 ff; ibid., L (1864), 220, 221.

75. Finance Report (1862), 18.

76. See below pages 114-116.

77. R.C.C. (1864) in Finance Report (1864), 48. Amasa Walker ("New Currency," 834) severely criticized the fact that National Banks could be too easily established; and so did the New York Clearing House.

78. Hooper, speech of 1867, 12. James Gallatin made this latter point in 1866, Letter to Doolittle, 22.

79. The disagreement between Chase and McCulloch regarding the numerical firm names can be found expressed between the lines. McCulloch stated that before his assuming the office of Comptroller, [underlining mine] the Secretary of the Treasury had determined upon the assumption of numerals by converting state banks. Gallatin considered this policy an expression of hostility on the part of the Secretary.

80. Cooke, 137. McCulloch in Men and Measures (pages 168/69) reports what he used to answer when bankers made objections along the above lines.

81. Chase Diary, Jan. 14, 15, 20, 1861.

82. James, Chicago Banks, I, 308.

83. Some Strictures, 11.

84. Gallatin became more amenable in 1864 when he made reasonable suggestions for an improvement of the act (see his National Debt, 14 ff, 36, 42).

85. Gallatin, James, The New National Banking System.

86. The sentence is quoted in Proceedings of the National Bank Convention ... 1864, 42. As to McCulloch's attitude, see Proceedings, 6.

87. The National Banking System..., four-page folder (Appendix 4 to this chapter). The copy used by this author, now owned by the Boston Public Library, was mailed originally to a Boston State Street banker.

88. Report on the National Bank Currency Act...

89. Williams (1804-1877) was born in Newport,

Rhode Island. He entered banking as early as about 1825 when he was made cashier of the Newport Bank. Later we find him as the cashier of a bank in New Bedford and in the early 1870's for a few years in Florida as the agent of an express company (see his Letter to A.B.J., 4). In 1844 he became the cashier of the City Bank of Boston whence he transferred to the same position in the newly-founded Metropolitan Bank of New York whose president he was to be from 1857-1877. During the Civil War Williams seems to have been strongly pro-Union (see the above pamphlet). He was obviously an expert money raiser for the Unitarians as indicated by his pamphlet Money Raising. (Obituaries in New York Tribune, Sept. 21, 1877 and Unitarian Review, VIII (1877), 561-563. This information was kindly provided by the New York Public Library.)

In the early days of the war Williams believed that the real savings of the country set a limit to its war expenditures. Slightly later he belonged to those New York bankers who fought Chase as having been responsible for the suspension of specie payments in 1861. In 1862 we find him an exponent of the so-called interconvertible-bond plan declaring the "reconvertible feature" of the 5-20's his "pet scheme;" (Spaulding, History, 25, 26; Williams's statement to that effect is to be found also in Drew, op. cit., 8). After the crisis of 1873 he accused the government of having caused it by first undertaking and then failing to supply the necessary currency. In the 1870's Williams was one of the very few bankers who wished National Bank notes replaced by redeemable government paper money, which at the same time was made elastic by being tied to interconvertible low-interest-bearing bonds. (Save the Savings Banks, passim); Williams, who loved vigorous language, declared in 1876 before the A.B.A. that it was "humbug" to speak of specie payments when notes and deposits were not 100 per cent backed by specie; (ibid., 2). As to Williams's writings, see list of references, both in vol. I and II.

90. Report, 23. Williams's authorship of this item was generally known; see A Reply to the Report..., 4.

91. See below page 142.

92. However a similar argument can be found also in Hunt's Merchants' Magazine, XLVI (1862), 114, 115.

93. Williams's Report was answered in the thin and lame Reply to the Report of a Committee of the New York Clearing House.... Since we know from Oberholtzer (op. cit., I, 339, 340) how angry Jay Cooke was about that publication and that he adorned his copy with marginal notes, it seems highly probable that the Reply was disseminated, if not paid for by the latter. The fact that the Reply refers repeatedly to "Mr. Opdyke's bank," i.e., to the Fourth National Bank of New York, founded by Cooke and presided over by Opdyke, lends weight to this view.

94. Hunt's Merchants' Magazine, L (1864), 220.

95. Proceedings of the National Bank Convention... (1864), 42 ff.

96. Minutes of the Philadelphia Board of Presidents; R.C.C., (1882) 12.

97. Finance Report (1863), 49 ff. In a New York meeting in which the establishment of a large National Bank in the city was discussed on Oct. 21, 1863, McCulloch criticized the lack of nationally uniform legal interest rate, the unnecessarily strict usury clauses making discount policy on the part of the New York banks impossible, and the lack of adequate redemption procedures; see Proceedings, 5, 6.

98. Harris, Wilmer C., Public Life of Zachariah Chandler, 1851-1875 (Lansing, 1917), 70-72; A.B.A., Proceedings (1880), 29; Hinchman, op. cit., 136, 137; Grant, Claudius B., "Life and Character of Alpheus Felch" in Michigan Pioneer and Historical Collections, XXVIII (1900), 103. In Pennsylvania one of the early founders of National Banks was William Henry Rhawn (1832-1898). Starting in a country store he became a bookkeeper and in 1857 entered the employment of the Philadelphia Bank with which he remained connected for seven years. In 1863 and 1864, respectively, he organized or helped organize the Second National Bank of Frankford-Philadelphia and the Central National Bank whose cashier he became. Resigning, he became the president of the National Bank of the Republic of Philadelphia which in 1870 absorbed the National Exchange Bank. He played a certain role in the Philadelphia Clearing House and the American Bankers Association where he took an interest in the education of bank clerks. Moreover he was instrumental in organizing the Pennsylvania Bankers Association. See Cycl. Am. Biogr., XII, 532.

99. Gras, op. cit., 161.

100. Some Strictures, 7. McCulloch's circular letter of 1863 (see below, pages 137-139).

101. Hodges, op. cit., 260.

102. As to Olcott see index.

103. A.B.A., Proceedings (1876), 33. It is possible that this committee resulted from a suggestion of Jay Cooke. In January, 1864, the latter proposed to George S. Coe that government and banks should "unite their counsels." Coe, however, cold-shouldered Cooke because he, like the other bankers, felt the initiative should come from the government. He intimated that John J. Cisco, head of the New York Sub-Treasury, was the man to secure a conference with the "certainty of a hearty response." No conference was ever called, but, so the author suspects, the bankers' committee of 1864 may have had some connection with this move. See Oberholtzer, op. cit., I, 350-52 for the correspondence between Cooke and Coe.

104. Swanson, op. cit., 88.

105. As to the process of converting see, for instance, Gras, op. cit., 522-527; Burnham,

op. cit., 36, 37; Bank of North America, Minutes of the Board of Directors, Nov. 21, 23, 28, Dec. 1, 5, 1864.

106. Larson, Cooke, 161, 163.
107. A speaker at the National Bank Convention of 1864 compared the profitability of National and state banks in New York as follows: the latter could obtain notes to the amount of 100 per cent of the face value of United States 6 per cent bonds regardless of the size of their capital; the former only 90 per cent and limited to the amount of their capital. The latter were allowed 1/4 of one per cent for the redemption of their notes at distant places, the former had to redeem at par in a reserve city without compensation. The latter were not bound by any reserve requirements, the former were so bound. The same speaker explained why government deposits were not too advantageous. Proceedings of the National Bank Convention ... 1864, 16, 17.
108. James Gallatin, speech of Oct. 11, 1865 in Constitution of the National Bank Note Redemption Association, 9; the mention in Samuel Hooper's speech of 1862, 1, 2; and McCulloch's reference in his circular letter of 1863 (reprinted below as Appendix 2). See also Hepburn, History of Coinage, 321, 328.
109. James, op. cit., I, 327.
110. Incidentally an attack on Spaulding as a banker can be found in Drew, Political Economy for the People, 33.
111. Speech of April 1864, 14; R.C.C. (1882), 12. The Merchants Bank was followed by 28 others converting in the same year.
112. An Historical Sketch of the First National Bank ... 1864-1914 (Baltimore, 1914); (the author is indebted for this information to the Enoch Pratt Free Library, Baltimore). This history refers to the old First National Bank of Baltimore which was absorbed in 1915 by the Merchants-Mechanics National Bank, not to the present one which resulted from a merger of 1928; information provided by the latter to the Baker Library of Harvard University.
113. James F.D. Lanier's assistance to his home state, Indiana, in the political crisis caused by the Civil War is a matter of record.
114. Neu, (op. cit., 154) describes the reluctance of Erastus Corning, president of the Albany City Bank, and of its cashier to convert that bank.
115. Burnham, op. cit., 36, 37.
116. Proceedings of the National Bank Convention... 1864, 12.
117. See above, page 107.
118. Davis, National Banking System, 66. As to Ketchum, see chapter XV, page 98.
119. R.C.C. (1863) in Finance Report (1863), 49.
120. Esarey, Logan, A History of Indiana from its Exploration to 1850, vol. I (Indianapolis, 1915), 412, 413.
121. James, Chicago Banks, I, 284 ff.
122. Preston, op. cit., 80, 84.
123. Krueger, op. cit., 99, 102, 103; Merk, op. cit.,

213, 214.
124. Verified by correspondence with the Reference Librarian of the Michigan State Library, Lansing.
125. There seems to have been a good deal of disagreement in the Department of the Treasury as to whether or not the national currency should be printed in the Treasury from plates produced there. McCulloch decided against this proposal and made contracts with private banknote companies; see Clark, S.M., op. cit., 32, 33, 95 ff.
126. Reports of one of Jay Cooke's agents to the latter, Oberholtzer, op. cit., I, 335, 357. Sec. 46 of the act of 1863 entitles National Banks to charge an interest or discount "as is for the time the established rate of interest for delay in the payment of money, in the absence of contract between the parties, by the laws of the several states in which the associations are respectively located, and no more..."
127. Kane, op. cit., 85, 86. For a contemporary criticism of the act of 1864 see Colwell, Remarks, 16 ff.
128. McCulloch in Proceedings, 5.
129. In U.S. Reports, Supreme Court, vol. 91 (1875), 29, 33.
130. A.B.A., Proceedings (1877), 25.
131. Ashmead, op. cit., 73.
132. Larson (op. cit., 138, 139) describes his methods in promoting National Banking; also Oberholtzer, op. cit., I, 329 ff.
133. Larson, op. cit., 139-141. The first president of the Fourth National Bank was George Opdyke (1805-1880), the clothes manufacturer, retailer, and economic writer. In 1862/1863 he had been mayor of the City of New York. His methods did not suit Cooke who expressed deep dissatisfaction, but he possessed financial abilities. He became a private banker in 1869 and his firm, George Opdyke and Company, weathered the crisis of 1873.

  Opdyke was succeeded by Philo C. Calhoun (1808-1881), a native of Bridgeport, for years active in the saddlery and harness business in Charleston, in 1863 vice-president of the Fourth National Bank. Bankers' Magazine, XXXV (1880/81), 801.
134. Proceedings, passim, especially 4, 8. Jay Cooke's recollections in Oberholtzer, op. cit., I, 345.
135. Dict. of Am. Biogr.; James, Chicago Banks, I, 265, 266, 373; Paine, Baker, 55ff, 103, 104; Dillistin, Banknote Detectors, 78ff; Bankers Magazine, XLV (1890/91), 989. John Thompson was reestablished in 1869 and in 1870 became the vice-president of the First National Bank.
136. See this volume, pages 353-355. Oberholtzer, op. cit., I, 344.
137. For the following see James, Chicago Banks, 341 ff, especially 351. That book contains much material on the firms and men to be mentioned. See its Index.

138. Tinkham had once been George Smith's cashier.

139. Dailey, "Smith and Scammon," 15 ff.

140. William F. Coolbough (1821-1877), born in Pennsylvania, began his business career as a porter in a dry goods house in Philadelphia, rising to become its Western agent. In 1842 he went into business for himself in Burlington, Iowa, establishing first a mercantile house and later (in 1850) a private bank under the name Coolbough and Brooks. This house was appointed loan agent of the State of Iowa and negotiated its first loan. In 1862 Coolbough moved to Chicago and founded W.F. Coolbough and Company, Shortly after having set up his National Banks he rose to prominence. In the 1860's he became a dominating personality in the National Banking Association (see index of this volume) through his position on the executive committee and through his being the greatest banker of the Northwest. His Union National Bank towered over every other one in the region. During the panic of 1873, however, Coolbough clashed with Lyman J. Gage, then heading the First National Bank, regarding the policy to be pursued by the Chicago banks. He was for suspension; Gage, for paying the depositors in full. While Coolbough's proposal was reasonable and Gage suggested taking chances, the latter won both his point and the battle. Coolbough's abdication as Chicago's banking leader put his bank into an informal voluntary liquidation from which it never recovered. Loss of prestige, failing health, and fear of paralysis induced the great banker to end his life in 1877. See Huston, op. cit., I, 591; James, Chicago Banks, 350, 399, 506, 507.

141. Huston, op. cit., III, 340. The First National Bank of Shawneetown was organized in 1865 by Thomas S. Ridgeway (1826-1897), a local produce merchant, ibid., IV, 486.

142. History of the First National Bank of Davenport, 5, 32-35, 90 ff, 99.

143. Hinchman, op, cit., 137; a level-headed statement of Philo Parsons can be found in A.B.A., Proceedings (1881), 24.

144. Popple, op. cit., 22, 24, 28, 30.

145. Founder of the First National Bank of Toledo was Hinman Barrett Hurlbut (1819-1884), a lawyer who had switched to banking in 1850 after having gained some experience on the board of control of the State Bank of Ohio. In 1852 he opened a private bank under the firm of Hurlbut and Company, Cleveland, but soon thereafter gained control of the charter of a state bank, the Bank of Commerce, which he reorganized. In the fall of 1863 he appeared as the president of the First National Bank of Toledo and participated in the abortive attempt to establish a large National Bank in New York which was to act as the correspondent of the National Banks in the interior. (See Cycl. Am. Biogr. and Proceedings, 1, 7.) As in the Minnesota cases we find an entrepreneur engaged successively in private, state, and National banking.

146. R.C.C. (1878), xxiv.

147. See below, pages 118 ff.

148. Thomas, History of Banking in Florida, 137.

149. See his History of Banking in South Carolina, 95, 96, 102.

150. R.C.C. (1864) in Finance Report (1864), 54.

151. Page 75; see also his Writings, II, 432.

152. Opdyke, Report on the Currency, 22, 23.

153. Page 28.

154. Letter dated Nov. 26, 1862, repr. by Oberholtzer, op. cit., I, 330.

155. Ibid., 185; James, Chicago Banks, I, 312, 328, 329; Holdsworth, Empire, II, 618.

156. James, Chicago Banks, I, 312.

157. It reads: And be it further enacted that every national banking association, state bank, or state banking association shall pay a tax of 10 per centum on the amount of notes of any state bank or state banking association paid out by them after the first day of July, 1866. Chapter LXXXVIII, laws of 1865. The legislative history of the clause can be found in Knox, History, 99.

158. McCulloch, Men and Measures, 113, 130, 163 ff; Proceedings, 2, 3; Kane, op. cit., 23 ff; Oberholtzer, op. cit., I, 350 footnote. McCulloch's circular letter to the banks of December, 1863, is indicative of the spirit in which McCulloch tackled his task. It is reprinted in Men and Measures, 195 ff. See also R.C.C. (1875) in Finance Report (1875), 202.

    An interesting detail is stressed in the Proceedings of the National Bank Convention... 1869, 7. The title of the chief officer of the Bank Department was in earlier bills of the National Currency act "Bank Comptroller," This title seemed to imply that he was meant to control the banks' operations, as well as the currency. In order to avoid such misunderstanding, it was changed to Comptroller of the Currency.

159. Finance Report (1865), 64.

160. R.C.C. in Finance Report (1864), 54.

161. Incidentally Freeman Clarke (1809-1887), the second Comptroller, was, like McCulloch himself, a banker. Over the years he was connected with several country banks in the State of New York as cashier or president, respectively, and later was a director of Jay Cooke's Fourth National Bank of New York and vice-president of the Union Trust Company. Moreover he was connected with railroad companies and a politician as well. Kane, op. cit., 27.

162. Hunt's Merchants' Magazine, LIII (1865), 56. Nothing seems to be known about this Society; correspondence with the New York Historical Society.

163. For the following, see the booklet Constitution of the National Bank Note Redemption Association, passim. Incidentally the remaining members of the committee were rather unknown

men, except for Shepherd Knapp.

164. Finance Report (1865), 64.
165. See this volume, pages 86 ff.
166. See this volume, page 300. John Q. Jones (1803-1878) of Huguenot ancestry, was born in New York and started his career in a mercantile house of the city. In 1834 he entered the service of the Chemical Bank as its factory agent, but in 1839 rose to become its cashier while his cousin, Isaac Jones, presided over the bank. In 1844 he became its president, and in this capacity developed out of an unprofitable institution one of the most profitable in the city. From 1865 to 1871 Jones was the president of the Clearing House Association. History of the Chemical Bank, 87 ff.
167. Constitution, clauses 2, 5, 7, 8, and page 9.
168. E.G. Spaulding was against an assorting house as expensive and risky. He would have preferred an amendment to the act by which every bank was to have a redemption agent in New York instead of in one of the 17 redemption cities. Letter to J.U. Orvis, Sept. 30, 1865 in Spaulding's History of Legal Tender Paper Money, Appendix, 9-13.
169. James, Chicago Banks, I, 372, 374.
170. Speech of 1867, 3, 8, 11.
171. R.C.C. (1867) in Finance Report (1867), 5, 20.
172. R.C.C. (1868) in Finance Report (1868), 19; also R.C.C. (1869), ibid., (1869), 31, 32; R.C.C. (1870), ibid., (1870), 29.
173. R.C.C. (1869) in Finance Report (1869), 28.
174. Proceedings of the National Bank Convention... 1869, 24.
175. R.C.C. (1873), xvi.
176. Act of June 20, 1874. Fixing the amount of United States notes ..., sec. 3.
177. R.C.C. (1874), xii.
178. R.C.C. (1874), xiii.
179. Ibid. (1875), 220.
180. Ibid. (1878), xi.
181. Ibid. (1875), 221.
182. Buell (1820-1881), born in Glen Falls, New York, started as a clerk in a dry goods store in Troy and at 24 entered business for himself. Eight years later he accepted the position of cashier of the Central Bank of Troy whence in 1857 he transferred to the Importers and Traders Bank of New York whose president he became in 1865. He was also a director in the Fifth Avenue Bank and the United States Life Insurance Company. Welles, Albert, The History of the Buell Family (New York, 1881), 380 ff; Bankers Magazine XXXVI (1881), 912.
183. A.B.A., Proceedings (1875), 23. The bankers seem to have expected a repeal of the clauses in the law of 1874 which had established the latter (p. 26).
184. See this volume, pages 9, 10.
185. See, for instance, Edward Pierrepont, Letter of ... to Senator Sherman on the Finances (New York, 1874), 6.
186. R.C.C. (1873), xvii, xix. See also Hooper's speech of 1867, 9.

187. Our Monetary Evils. Some Suggestions for their Remedy (privately printed, New York, 1872), 7-12, 16. See also Seligman, Henry, op. cit., 21.
188. Our Currency and the Banks. Suggestions from an Experienced Banker. To the Editor of the New York Times (privately printed, 1872), passim.
189. Op. cit., 13.
190. A minor problem which irked the National Banks by 1870 was the difficulty of exchanging one type of securities against another; see Oberholtzer, op. cit., II, 137.
191. See this volume, page 104.
192. See, for instance, "The Credit System and the Currency" in Penn Monthly (December 1873), 827. The author of the article considered it absolutely necessary to keep reserves against deposits while there was "surely" no need for reserves against circulating notes which were secured by a deposit of United States bonds, by double liability, and a guarantee of the United States.
193. R.C.C. (1874), xv.
194. The underlying philosophy was clearly expressed by Samuel Hooper in Examination, 44, 45.
195. See also the paper of George Walker read before the 1878 meeting of the ABA at Saratoga, entitled, "The National Banking System of the United States as Compared with Other Banking Systems Here and Abroad," in A.B.A. Proceedings, (1878), 19-26; and Knox, History, 112 ff.
196. Our Finances. "Inflation," Expansion or Contraction, which shall it be? The East versus the West and South, by a Western Farmer (Hartford, Conn., 1874), 3, 4.
197. As an example of the discussions going on at that time see Proceedings at the Mass Meeting of Citizens in the Cooper Institute, New York... March 24, 1874 on National Finances ....(New York, 1874), passim. For the inflationist point of view see, for instance, the writings of Timothy Harrington Carter of Boston: Inflation, an Argument in its Favor (n.p.,n.d. [about 1875]); Plain Talk about Resumption (n.p.,n.d.[about 1875]); The Currency Question. A Plan of Permanent Relief (n.p. [Boston], 1875). Jay Cooke was against contraction and even an advocate of moderate expansion; see Larson, Cooke, 203, 205.
198. The statement is to be found in Carl Schurz's speech, Currency-National Banks. Speech of... of Missouri in the United States Senate. February 27, 1874 (Washington, 1874), 12.

Carl Schurz's economic knowledge was limited, although he knew Adam Smith, Ricardo, John Stuart Mill, Bonamy Price, whom he mentioned, as well as others. He had a remarkable knowledge of inflation with all its characteristic features, and the distinction between money and capital was familiar to him. On the other hand, he had a blind spot for the injustice of deflation and for all the suffering which years of deflation were bringing over the country. The distinction between debtor and creditor sections was nothing but "mischievous" to him, although it was, of course, a bitter reality. That banks could create loanable funds he could not and would not see. For him such could be created only by saving. For this shortcoming he can be blamed, for, as will be described, other members of Congress knew better. For the historian it is rather painful to see the cocksureness with which errors were propounded and the contempt with which men were treated who saw what the great senator himself could not see, regardless of how good or bad their remedies may have been. Typical are the pages of the February speech, 12-14, 22 ff, 29, 31 and the Speech of ... of Missouri in the Senate of the United States, January 14, 1874 (Washington, 1874), 19, 22 ff, 26, 28, 29.

199. The above figures were given by Maynard, op. cit., 16, the original source being probably one of the Reports of the Comptroller.

The matter was widely discussed in the contemporary literature see, for instance, Our Finances (as quoted in footnote 196), 5; Carl Schurz in his speech of Feb. 1874 (see footnote 198), speaks of the "vicious diffusion" of the currency (page 19). Dewey, Financial History, 385 ff gives the background.

200. Finance Report (1866), 72.

201. An Act to amend an Act entitled "An Act to provide Internal Revenue..." U.S. Statutes at Large, XIII (December, 1863 to December, 1865), Chap. LXXVIII, sec. 7.

202. Alexander Mitchell, the Wisconsin banker, saw these things very clearly, op. cit., 5, 6.

203. See vol. I, page 12.

204. Knox, op. cit., 116.

205. The tax on deposits can be disregarded here.

206. Buell, (op. cit., 10 ff) gives a profit computation and comments thereon; also R.C.C. (1875) in Finance Report (1875), 202 ff.

207. Dewey, Financial History, 390. (Contemporary statistics bring out that fact very clearly; see, for instance, ibid., 384).

208. Knox, John Jay, Remarks, 11 ff, especially 13.

209. Deshler, John G., A Financial System for the "Granger" with the Argument (Columbus, 1874), 16; see also Garfield, op. cit., 7.

210. See below page 120. The preceding description is based on Buell, op. cit., 4, 5, 6, 8.

211. Buck, op. cit., 6.

212. A Report of Two Interviews, 15.

213. Cox, Samuel S., Currency-Funding-Gold and Silver. Speech of ... delivered in the House of Representatives June 7, 1870 (Washington, 1870), 7; Garfield, op. cit., 5.

214. Buell, op. cit., 15.

215. Carey, Henry Charles, Currency Inflation: How it has been produced and how it may profitably be reduced. Letters to the Hon. B.H. Bristow, Secretary of the Treasury (Philadelphia, 1874), 7, 12, 13.

216. The British Credit System. Inflated Bank Credit as a Substitute for "Current Money of the Realm" (Philadelphia, 1875), 2, 6; idem, Letters on the Crisis, the Currency and the Credit System (Philadelphia, 1873), 4.

The point is also well taken by Esterly, George, A Consideration of the Currency and Finance Question (Whitewater, Wisconsin, 1874), 3, 4. He considers the "credit system" of the country "inflated" and contrasts the "contracted currency" with the "expanded credit." Even such an obscure item as Drew's Political Economy for the People (p. 35) treats deposits as created.

217. For an example, see Buell, op. cit., 10. Carl Schurz stressed the deflationary element in National Banking in his speech of February 1874 (see footnote 198), 15, 16.

218. An early attack on the pyramiding of reserves can be found in State of New York, Chamber of Commerce, Memorial to the Honorable the Senate and House of Representatives of the United States of America in Congress Assembled [submitted by A.A. Low and Sam. D. Babcock] (n.p. [New York], n.d. [1869]), 7, 8. It was suggested that a uniform rate of 25 per cent be held by all banks in legal tenders in their own vaults, probably for the deflationary effects of such measure.

219. Speech of 1874, 17.

220. Kasson, John A., Currency and Free Banking. Speech of ... of Iowa in the House of Representatives, April 9, 1874 (Washington, 1874), 3.

221. 1889-1892 as a National Bank examiner in New York City, 1892-1893 as Comptroller of the Currency, 1893-1897 as president of the Third National Bank, 1897-1899 as vice-president of the Citizens National Bank, 1899-1922 connected in various capacities with the Chase National Bank.

222. A History of Currency (New York, 1924), 313, 334. Dewey describes the fight against National Banking in his Financial History (8th ed.), 389-391, a description which does not belong to the best sections of his book. See also Knox, History, 132 ff.

223. R.C.C. (1878), xxiv; (1880), 10.

224. Keyes, Opinion, passim.

225. See, for instance, Seligman, Henry, op. cit., 21; Larson, Cooke, 203, 206; Oberholtzer, op. cit., II, 138, 139.

226. R.C.C. in Finance Report (1867), 7.

227. The following contemporary pamphlets give an idea of the arguments made in favor of replacing National Bank notes by legal tenders: Winder, W. H., The Problem of Fiscal Economy [New York, 1875], 6, 14; Taylor, James, American Currency, The Political Issue of the Day (Chicago, 1876), 8, 29; Greene, William B., Resolutions submitted to the Executive Committee of the New England Labor-Reform League and proposed for Discussion at the coming Convention of the League ... November, 14 and 15, 1875 [n.p.,n.d.] (he wanted to replace

National Bank notes by U.S. due-bills without legal tender character); Ewing, Thomas, Speech of ... delivered at Ironton, Ohio, July 24, 1875 (Columbus, 1875), passim; idem., Speech of ... delivered at Findlay, Ohio, August 14, 1875 [n.p.,n.d.], passim; Letter from a Working Man to the Treasurer of the United States (Leaflet of the National Executive Committee of the Independent Party, No. 4) [n.p.,n.d.], 6, 8; Wilson, Hugh Bowley, A Plea for Uncle Sam's Money or Greenbacks versus Bank Notes (New York, 1870), passim. Wilson, George, Jr., How to Abolish the National Banking System (St. Louis, 1879), is a shrewd piece of propaganda aiming at making proselytes for state banking among the followers of Greenbackism.

228. Quoted from Dewey, op. cit., 391.
229. Garfield, op. cit., 12; Knox, Remarks, 4; R.C.C. (1878), xii ff; (1879), 21, 22.
230. Jay Cooke was an active one, for instance; see Larson, Cooke, 203.
231. See, for instance, Bayard, Thomas F., The Currency-Specie Payments. Speech of ... of Delaware in the United States Senate, January 28, 1874 (Washington, 1874), 19, 20, 21, 22; Phelps, William W., Sound Currency. Speech of ... of New Jersey in the House of Representatives, April 1, 1874 (Washington, 1874), 14; Morrill, Justin S., Resumption of Specie Payments. Speech of ... of Vermont in the Senate of the United States January 6, 1876 (Washington, 1876), 16, 19; How to Determine the Proper Quantity of Currency? Reprint of an editorial in The Financier, New York, Mar. 7, 1874. McCulloch had thought along these lines as early as 1864; R.C.C. in Finance Report (1864), 50, 51.
232. "Remarks" in Proceedings of the Convention of Banks and Bankers held at Saratoga July 20th, 21st and 22d, 1875 (New York, 1875), 25.
233. In the anonymous pamphlet Views on Currency and Specie Payments (n.p.,n.d. [about 1874]) "a banker" (provided that the author really belonged to the guild) proposed an exclusive legal tender currency redeemable in coin; pages 3, 4.
234. Proceedings (1880), 57, 62, 63.
235. Op. cit., 16, 18, 19.
236. See, e.g., the Report of the Comptroller of the Currency (Hulburd) (1869), 38.
237. Richardson, D.M., Policy of Finance. A Plan for Returning to Specie Payments and Free Banking, February 23, 1874 (Washington, 1874), passim; [London, D.H.], The Exchequer Explained and Vindicated in a Series of Letters... (New York, 1873), 6.
238. Act of January 14, 1875 to provide for the resumption of specie payments, sec. 3.
239. In 1865 Freeman Clarke, Comptroller of the Currency, had suggested an increase of the permissible total of note issues from $300,000,000 to $400,000,000 with obligatory par redemption at New York, Boston, or Philadelphia. R.C.C. in Finance Report (1865), 67.

240. Op. cit., 12.
241. Speech of February 1874 (see footnote 198), 20, 21; "A Banker" in Views on Currency and Specie Payments (n.p.,n.d.), 7 considered redemption of one paper currency by another "preposterous;" Finance Report (1868), xxx; R.C.C. (1869) in ibid. (1869), 39; R.C.C. (1871) in ibid. (1871), 34. See also Buell, op. cit., 3, 8; Phelps, op. cit., 14, 25; Clews, op. cit., 16; Proceedings at the Mass Meeting... (see footnote 197) 3, 20; Potter, Plan, 5 ff.
    Henry Carey Baird objected to "free banking" because it permitted the creation of additional bank credit (which was the source of panics). Letters on the Crisis, the Currency and the Credit System (Philadelphia, 1873), 15.
242. Garfield, James A., Debate on the Currency Bill, Speech of ... of Ohio in the House of Representatives, June 15, 1870 (Washington, 1870), 2.
243. Governor Dix on the Currency (n.p., n.d.[about 1873]), 1.
244. See Bayard, op. cit., 20, 26; Mitchell, op. cit., 12. Carl Schurz denied that "free banking" would break the New York "monopoly," (the quotation marks being his); see his speech of February 1874, 17.
245. Drew, John G., Political Economy for the People - Our Money Muss. (sic!) A History ... with full directions to start and run National Banks ... (New York, 1874), 31; Wilson, George, Jr., How to Abolish the National Banking System (St. Louis, Mo., 1879), 13.
246. Quoted from Dewey, Financial History (8th ed.), 390.
247. Proceedings of the National Bank Convention ... 1869, 22.
248. R.C.C. (1875) in Finance Report (1875), 202 ff.
249. R.C.C. (1878), viii.
250. See, for instance, Drew, op. cit., 33, 35.
251. See his speech of October 11, 1865 in Constitution of the National Bank Note Redemption Association, 9.
252. Tatham, W.P., On the Restoration of the Standard of Value and the Proper Limit to the Use of Bank Credit as Money (Philadelphia, 1869), 15.
253. The Currency -- Specie Payments, Speech of ... of Connecticut delivered in the Senate of the United States, January 10, 1873 (Washington, 1873), 3.
254. The Currency -- Specie Payments, Speech of ... Ohio in the Senate of the United States, January 16, 1873 (n.p. [Washington], n.d., 1873), 1, 3, 8.
255. Bayard, op. cit., 22. In fact when dealing with the problem in 1869 Comptroller of the Currency Hulburd had spoken of the desirable "self-adjusting system of currency;" (Secretary of the Treasury, Report of the State of the Finances [1869], 36). A few years later a contemporary pamphlet used side by side the terms "fluid" and elastic; Governor Dix on the Currency (n.p., n.d. [about 1873]), 2 ff; and an editorial writer in the Financier, New

York, Mar. 7, 1874, using the term "elasticity" with respect to treasury notes, put it into quotation marks.

256. A thoroughly modern presentation of the problem can be found in A.B.A., Proceedings (1882), 19 ff; and later an excellent one by James B. Forgan in U. S. 52d Congr. 2d sess., House Committee on Banking and Currency, Hearings and Arguments on Proposed Currency Legislation (1906/07), 12, 13.

257. Very typical is a statement of the Wisconsin banker, Alexander Mitchell, op. cit., 15. See also Morrill, Justin S., Free Banking and Specie Payments, Speech of ... of Vermont in the Senate of the United States, December 4, 1873 (Washington, 1873), 10; Phelps, op. cit., 3; Buell, "Remarks" 24.

258. Schurz, Carl, Speech of ... of Missouri in the Senate of the United States, January 14, 1874 (Washington, 1874), 3.

259. Hawley, Joseph R., Sound Currency, Speech of ... of Connecticut in the House of Representatives, March 1, 1874(Washington, 1874), 24. As to the use of the term by Nicholas Biddle fifty years earlier, see vol. I of this work, page 139.

260. Clews, op. cit., 16.

261. See Morrill, Justin S., Resumption of Specie Payments. Speech of ... of Vermont, in the House of Representatives, January 6, 1876 (Washington, 1876), 6; Bayard, op. cit., 3; "The Credit System and the Currency" in Penn Monthly, IV (1873), 827; Baird, Letters on the Crisis..., 15; Letter from a Working Man (see footnote 227), 8; Cooper, Peter, A Letter on the Currency [New York, 1875], 5 and 16 (on the latter page Cooper quotes Baird who in turn quotes one Wallace P. Groom); Opdyke in Proceedings at the Mass Meeting, 45, and in Chamber of Commerce of the State of New York, Memorial, Minority Report of the Chamber of Commerce Committee (n.p.,n.d. [1869?]), 4; R.C.C. (1872), xx, xxi and (1873), xxxiii.

262. The item is reprinted in the same author's Enquiry, see List of references, vol. I.

263. Lutwyche, Enquiry, 37. The pamphlet of 1849 could not be identified and no copy of McPhin's book was located.

264. Letter to ... Fessenden, 20-21.

265. As to this term, see Schumpeter, Joseph G., "The Creative Response in Economic History" in Jour. Econ. Hist. VII (1947), 149 ff.

266. Sherman, John, National Finances --Specie Payments. Speech of ... of Ohio in the Senate of the United States, March 3, 1876 (Washington, 1876), 17.

267. See this volume, chapter xx.

268. R.C.C. (1881), 6 ff, (1882), 9ff; A.B.A., Proceedings (1880), 32 ff.

269. R.C.C. (1882), 18; the figure of state banks included trust companies.

270. Reprinted from Hunt's Merchants' Magazine XLIX (1863), 401 ff.

271. Original in the New York Public Library.

272. The original is in decaying condition in the Boston Public Library.

273. See Appendix 3 to this chapter.

274. These meaningless quotationmarks are in the original.

Chapter XVII

THE CLEARING HOUSE LOAN CERTIFICATE

Among the few important developments which took place in the field of American banking between the introduction of National Banking and the adoption by Congress of the Federal Reserve System, that of the clearing house loan certificate ranks probably first in importance.[1]

Clearing house loan certificates should not be confused with coin certificates, the device of F.W. Edmonds. While prior to the introduction of the Federal Reserve system coin certificates were used in normal times in the daily settlements of numerous clearing houses, clearing house loan certificates were applied during emergencies only. While the former emanated from the depositories of clearing houses and were based on coin deposits, the latter were issued by committees of clearing houses on the basis of collateral security other than coin. Clearing house loan certificates were withdrawn and replaced by coin or coin certificates as soon as the crisis had passed which had given rise to their issue. However, it is evident at a glance that clearing house loan certificates could easily be developed from coin certificates once the latter had been adopted, since the only essential difference is the character of the underlying security.

I

The first crisis to occur after the foundation of the American clearing house was the panic of 1857. Consequently in that year clearing house associations (those in New York and Boston) for the first time were confronted with the necessity of organizing concerted action among their members. Lacking such common action, every bank would have been forced to make itself impregnable by calling its loans. Contraction, in turn, would have resulted in additional failures of enterprises intrinsically sound and so would have made the crisis all the worse. Cooperation among banks, therefore, had to aim at counteracting retrenchment and this could be achieved only by making available new media of exchange to replace such as had disappeared through hoarding. Only if new media of exchange of undoubted security were created, could banks go on lending and even increasing their loans to worthy borrowers. The clearing house loan

certificate was the specifically American solution to a problem with which central banks in the other great commerical nations of the world were faced at every crisis throughout the second half of the nineteenth century.

The clearing house loan certificate was not as yet devised in 1857. In that year as an emergency measure the banks of America's leading financial centers used notes in the settlement of interbank balances; but in so doing New York conceived an intermediary instrument. In New York (as in Boston) banks were already accustomed to settling their balances in coin certificates; but when prior to the descent of the storm specie was becoming scarce the total of coin certificates had to be reduced. On the other hand when the crisis broke and suspension came, the New York country banks refused to redeem their notes in the City (at the Metropolitan Bank) as they normally did. In lieu of specie the city banks seem to have accepted from the Metropolitan Bank for country notes turned in certificates testifying to "loans" made to the country banks. The latter paid 6 per cent interest on such of their notes as they did not redeem, once the presentation was testified in the "loan" certificates of the Metropolitan Bank.

Under these circumstances the New York Clearing House Committee, headed by James Punnett, developing a precedent established during the crisis of 1837,[2] decided to permit the use of those certificates in the settlement of clearing house balances. It "issued a Circular suggesting to the Associated Banks the propriety of including [in the settlements] the certificates received for uncurrent money deposited at the Metropolitan [Bank] under the head of loans," as expressed in the Journal of Commerce of December 8, 1857.[3] In order to understand this action, one must remember that in the crisis of 1857 New York country notes were not questioned, backed as they were by first class security.[4] Consequently a majority of the Associated Banks adopted that advice: in the first instance the latter converted into certificates the notes of New York country banks which would not be redeemed. Having done so they used those certificates in the settlement of clearing house balances. As a result the City banks were enabled to apply more of their own notes for the payment of depositors and for extending credit to customers. But at the height of the crisis the Associated Banks not only used certificates based on New York country notes, but also the notes themselves bundled in sealed packages of $5000 each. Such bundles as well as certificates were tendered and accepted in the daily settlements of the New York Clearing House. As early as November, 1857, however, the Associated Banks started to return country-bank notes which had accumulated in the city. They sent them home at the rate of one-fifth of the total each month, and the certificates of the Metropolitan Bank based on those notes were retired accordingly.[5] If one keeps in mind that the notes of the New York Free Banks were de facto certificates testifying that certain securities were deposited with a state authority, the "loan certificates" of 1857 issued by the Metropolitan Bank were essentially alike to the later clearing house loan certificates. The only important difference was that the latter were based directly, and the former indirectly, on securities deposited (indirectly because the certificates of 1857 were based on banknotes which in turn were based on securities deposited).

In that decade the Massachusetts banking system was distinctly different from that of New York, a fact which was reflected in the emergency measures of 1857. The Boston[6] Clearing House Committee of that year consisted of Andrew T. Hall, chairman (who, as described before, had been a leader among the founders of the Boston Clearing House and was then its guiding genius), Almon D. Hodges, Thomas Lamb, Benjamin E. Bates (all of whom had been among its founders), and J. Amory Davis (president of the Suffolk Bank). Under the impact of suspension in New York this committee met on October 14, 1857 to discuss the emergency, and it decided to recommend to the Associated Banks the following plan "as aid for the daily settlement of balances;" "The bills of any of the Associated Banks may be received in liquidation of their daily balances instead of specie to the extent not exceeding" certain stated amounts. These amounts were related to the capitals and corresponded roughly first to five and later to ten per cent thereof, with the smaller banks favored over the larger. Special amounts were allotted to the Suffolk Bank and to the Bank of Mutual Redemption.

The plan was suggested on October 15 to a meeting of the Clearing House Association by Andrew T. Hall while Thomas Lamb[7] presented the draft of the following agreement which was adopted:

> The Associated Banks of the Clearing House severally agree each with the other, that the Bills received instead of Specie, at the Clearing House, from the Debtor Banks, and paid instead of Specie for balances to the Creditor Banks, shall be sent in with the next day's settlement at the Clearing House; that such Bills so received shall in the meantime, be and remain at the joint risk of all the Associated Banks, in proportion to the amount of their Capitals respectively.

> And it is further agreed, as above, that the Clearing House Committee may at any moment call upon any bank for satisfactory collateral security, for any balance thus paid in bills instead of Specie; and each Bank hereby agrees with the Clearing House Committee, and with all and each of the other Banks to furnish immediately such security when demanded.

Two days later, on October 17, this accord was amended: Since notes paid in the settlement of balances were put into the clearing again on the following day, the banks agreed to pay one day's interest on their daily balances to the extent to which these were paid in notes. Furthermore, as notes could be used in the settlement of balances only up to a certain amount and as it was expected that the stronger banks voluntarily (for prestige's sake?) would go on paying specie, it was resolved "that the manager of the Clearing House keep an account of the specie paid by each bank and in subsequent settlements repay to creditor banks in specie, so far as it may be paid in, the amount which each bank may have previously lost; the banks first paying specie to have the prior claim to be reimbursed from the amount received."[8]

An analysis of the Boston emergency measures of 1857 is of considerable interest. In the first instance the banks looked out for their own interest, not, as in later crises, for that of the business community at large; but the latter exerted enough pressure on the banks to gain protection, as will be described later.[9] Furthermore, there was a collectivistic element in the action of the banks because the notes received in the settlement of balances were to "remain at the joint risk of all the Associated Banks in proportion to the amount of their capitals, respectively." Finally, the Boston bankers came pretty near to the basic concept underlying the clearing house loan certificate: they agreed to give collateral security for the balances paid in notes, if demanded.

In contrast to New York and Boston, Philadelphia did not have a clearing house in 1857 when the crisis broke. But it possessed in its Board of Presidents[10] a permanent organization which could easily be made the platform for emergency cooperation like the clearing houses in the above-named two cities.[11] In fact, as early as September 25, 1857 the Board of Presidents foreseeing the imminent suspension of specie payments resolved that in this event the city banks should mutually take their notes in the settlement of inter-bank balances. A committee, including Singleton A. Mercer, president of the Farmers and Mechanics Bank, was appointed to call on the Governor and to request that he legalize the intended measure. On the next day (September 26) the board met again and Mercer submitted for its approval the blank form of a check. It was to be drawn on a depository to be appointed by the banks against securities lodged therein. These checks were to be accepted by the banks "agreeably to the terms of our said contract." As indicated by the clause to be embodied in the tenor: "good and payable agreeably to the special contract with and receivable for all debts due the banks" they were not to be paid in specie. Nevertheless they were expected to circulate and thereby to increase the existing media of payment. The plan was approved in principle.

The contract alluded to in both the proposed check and the acceptance was actually concluded on September 28, on which day the presidents resolved to sign the following document submitted by Mercer:

> The undersigned agree on the part of their respective banks that they will discontinue the payment of specie on all their liabilities and [that] they will pay out their notes of the smaller denominations for the purpose of supplying a currency and [that] they will recommend to their respective Boards of Directors that they shall increase the facilities of the cummunity by a reasonable increase of loans.

It is doubtful whether Mercer's checks were ever issued. If they had been, they would have anticipated by decades the circulating clearing house loan certificates of the early twentieth century.

Be that as it may, in addition to the attempt at creating a new medium of exchange, another problem had to be tackled. The banks which, under the agreement of September 25, had to take the notes of other Philadelphia banks must be protected against any possible loss therefrom. To that end a committee for regulating the exchanges was appointed on September 28, the day of suspension, and it found a solution for the problem involved similar to that adopted in New York and envisaged in Boston. On September 29, C.H. Rogers, president of the Tradesmens Bank and chairman of the committee, recommended

> the passage of a resolution for instructing that Committee to demand of each bank securities for amounts named, to be placed in their hands, and to demand additional

securities whenever the indebtness of any one bank exceeds the volume of its securities thus deposited. The said securities for safe keeping to be in the vaults of the Farmers and Mechanics Bank.

This suggestion was adopted by the Board of Presidents and the agreement thus reached also determined the value of the securities to be deposited by each bank. The amounts varied between $200,000 (Farmers and Mechanics and Girard Banks) and $40,000 (Consolidation Bank), the total being set at $1,450,000.[12]

A comparison of the Boston, New York, and Philadelphia emergency measures of 1857 reveals the following similarities and differences: In Boston and Philadelphia notes of city banks could be used in the settlement of balances; but, while in Boston the total for every bank was limited, in Philadelphia it was not. In Boston the banking community bore the risk, each bank sharing it according to its capital; consequently the demanding of securities was optional only, and actually none seem to have been demanded. In Philadelphia every bank had to bear its own risk and was therefore protected by deposits of securities, deposits which were graded according to the size of the banks. The New York situation was fundamentally different. New York possessed at that time government-bond-backed banknotes, while Massachusetts and Pennsylvania used general-asset notes. The New York banknotes, as has been stressed, represented certificates of deposit. Therefore no extra security was needed when the New York City banks decided to use, in the settlement of clearing house balances, temporarily irredeemable New York country notes. Such notes, in turn, were the basis of the "loan certificates" of the Metropolitan Bank, and it was from these that the full-fledged clearing house loan certificate took its start.

II

George S. Coe was the creative business leader to whom America owes the development from such beginnings of the important new credit instrument. When the crisis broke in November, 1860, Coe, backed by John Austin Stevens,[13] who presided over the decisive meeting of the New York Clearing House Association, presented what proved to be the saving idea. He suggested that a committee be appointed for the purpose of receiving in trust securities from banks needing assistance and for the further purpose of issuing certificates based thereon. At the same time he proposed "the equalization of ready money." Because of the great importance which Coe's device gained for the history of American banking the proceedings of the Association in the meeting of November 21, 1860 are here reprinted to the extent that they refer to Coe's proposals.[14] They read as follows:

In order to enable the Banks of the City of New York to expand their loans and discounts, and also for the purpose of facilitating the settlement of exchanges between the Banks, it is proposed that any Bank in the Clearing House Association may, at its option, deposit with a Committee of five persons -- to be appointed for that purpose -- an amount of its bills receivable, United States stocks, Treasury notes, or stocks of the State of New York, to be approved by said Committee, who shall be authorized to issue thereupon to said depositing Bank, certificates of deposit, bearing interest at seven per cent. per annum, in denominations of five and a thousand dollars each, as may be desired, to an amount equal to seventy-five per cent. of such deposit. These certificates may be used in settlement of balances at the Clearing House, for a period of thirty days from the date hereof, and they shall be received by creditor Banks, during that period, daily, in the same proportion as they bear to the aggregate amount of the debtor balances paid at the Clearing House. The interest which may accrue upon these certificates shall at the expiration of thirty days, be apportioned among the Banks which shall have held them during the time.

The securities deposited with said Committee as above named shall be held by them in trust as a special deposit, pledged for the redemption of the certificates issued thereupon.

The Committee shall be authorized to exchange any portion of said securities for an equal amount of others, to be approved by them, at the request of the depositing Bank, and shall have power to demand additional security, either by an exchange or an increased amount, at their discretion.

The amount of certificates which this Committee may issue as above shall not exceed $5,000,000.

This agreement shall be binding upon the Clearing House Association when assented to by three-fourths of its members.

Resolved, that in order to accomplish the purpose set forth in this agreement, the specie belonging to the associated Banks shall be considered and treated as a common fund for mutual aid and protection, and the Committee shall have power to equalize the same by assessment or otherwise.

For this purpose statements shall be made to the Committee of the condition of each Bank on the morning of every day, before commencement of business, which shall be sent with the exchanges to the Manager of the Clearing House, specifying the following items, viz:
1. Loans and discounts.
2. Deposits.
3. Loan certificates.
4. Specie.

The Chairman [John Austin Stevens] appointed the following named gentlemen as the Committee:
Moses Taylor, of the City Bank.
James Punnett, of the Bank of America.
R.W. Howes, of the Park Bank.
A.S. Fraser, of the Seventh Ward Bank.
Charles P. Leverich, of the Bank of New York.[15]

It is hardly necessary to stress the twofold aspect of Coe's plan[16]: He not only devised a new credit instrument to be used in the settlement of clearing house balances, but also supplemented its introduction. Pooling and equalizing the specie reserves of the banks were added as a means of avoiding suspension and with a view to consolidating the banks into a "body" for the time of the emergency. The suspension of specie payments which seemed impending in the fall of 1860 was thus actually avoided.[17]

The "loan committee" mentioned above, appointed to implement Coe's device by working out the necessary details, did a highly satisfactory job (holding no less than seventy-three meetings between November 20, 1860 and March 15, 1861). It was through this committee's exertions that Coe's plan became a great success at its very first application. Therefore, upon the outbreak of the Civil War, as early as April 24, 1861 the New York banks, seeing trouble ahead, prepared in a time "of ease and strength" for another issue of clearing house loan certificates, if and when needed. For this purpose the original loan committee was reappointed. And, as a matter of fact, what was the second issue of clearing house loan certificates in the city became necessary very soon. Envisaged under an agreement of August, this issue was determined upon on September 19, 1861, being considered unavoidable for the following reason: When, after an adjournment of seven weeks, the loan committee met again on the second day of that month, it found that the payment of the first installment on the $50,000,000 government loan of August, 1861, had reduced the specie reserves of some of the Associated Banks below 25 per cent. This situation appeared undesirable since (at the meeting of November, 1860, in which they adopted Coe's plan) the New York banks had also agreed on that percentage as a fixed reserve ratio. Under these circumstances the committee resolved that the specie reserves of the banks were again to be considered a pool and that every bank whose reserves fell below 25 per cent of their net liabilities (exclusive of circulation and the amounts held to the credit of the United States Treasurer) had to pay interest on the daily deficiency. The interest was to be paid to the banks holding the largest percentages of specie reserves in excess of the required 25 per cent. The "Committee continued to apportion the specie held by the associates in this manner until the 21st of September when the account was closed. Thereafter the allocation was made by requiring the banks to exchange loan certificates for specie whenever their metallic reserve dropped below 25 per cent of their "net deposits, exclusive of the amount to the credit of the government."[18] From September 21 to December 30, 1861 (on which day the New York banks suspended specie payments) specie was thus apportioned each and every day.

But there was still another problem to be solved: the issue of clearing house loan certificates of September, 1861, was based on the 7-30 Treasury Notes which the New York banks had taken as their share from the Secretary of the Treasury under the latter's contract with the Associated Banks of the three cities in August, 1861, described in chapter XV of this work. As soon as the banks had paid specie to the government on account of this loan, their reserves became depleted, as indicated above, and some of them badly needed loan certificates in order to uphold their discount line. The government, on the other hand, did not deliver any securities before January, 1862. Consequently John A. Stevens, chairman of the so-called Treasury Note Committee which supervised the Loan Committee in those months, authorized the latter to issue loan certificates without waiting for the actual delivery of the Treasury Notes.

The following complicated arrangements had to be made: The chairman of the Treasury Note Committee transferred to the chairman of the Loan Committee, Moses Taylor, the receipts given by the Assistant Treasurer of New York for the installments paid by the several banks. They had previously been endorsed to the chairman of the Treasury Note Committee and were accompanied by the original drafts of the Secre-

tary of the Treasury. After having received these documents the Loan Committee issued to the banks in question clearing house loan certificates based upon "the receipts for payments on account of government securities to be received." These loan certificates were doubly secured by "the deposit of the duplicate receipts for their [the banks'] payments on account of the loans, with the usual guarantees, and certificates of deposits, payable on presentation for an amount equal to the loan certificates issued to them," that is to say, additional security was given by the banks taking out clearing house loan certificates. Original and duplicate receipts and drafts were returned to the Assistant Treasurer after the Treasury Notes had been received in January, 1861, by the Loan Committee. The total of clearing house loan certificates authorized under the agreement of August, 1861, was originally limited to $10,000,000, but it was later increased to $20,000,000; and the latter amount was actually issued.[19]

However, even with the working out of these complicated transactions, the worries of the Loan Committee did not end. Under the agreement of August, 1861, the committee was authorized to issue clearing house loan certificates to the amount of 90 per cent of the Treasury Notes deposited. It construed this clause to mean 90 per cent of the cost price of the securities. Unfortunately, the market value of the 7-30's declined in the latter part of 1861 so that in January, 1862, the requirement was changed to 80 per cent of the face value in order to have a better margin of safety. This change, of course, involved much re-calculation, labor, and increased responsibility for the Loan Committee just as the figuring and apportioning of the interest on the certificates had been "of extreme difficulty."

III

The application of the newly-devised clearing house loan certificate remained restricted to New York during the critical months of 1860. Coe's device, and especially one of its aspects, the pooling of the specie reserves, leading to the consolidation of all banks of the City of New York into an emergency body, was too revolutionary to be adopted quickly by the very conservative banking fraternities in the other leading financial centers. The telegraph was still too young and the older generation of bankers still too unaccustomed to using it. Thus while instantaneous mutual information among the banks of various cities was already possible, parallel action could not as yet be achieved; and the banks in the other large cities of the Northern and Middle states handled their problems more or less in the traditional way.

As is generally known, the crisis of 1860 resulted from the fact that after Lincoln's election the Southern states girded for secession and their businessmen withdrew funds from the North. Baltimore was among the first to be hit because of its extensive Southern connections, and at that time it experienced its first crisis since the establishment of its Clearing House. On November 21, 1860, the very day when the clearing house loan certificate was born in New York, the Baltimore banks under the chairmanship of Johns Hopkins decided to suspend and, for dealing with the emergency, drew up a plan which was in principle identical with that used in 1837 and 1857.[20] The only difference was that the banks were debited or credited, respectively, with the balances originating because of suspension, in a book kept at the Clearing House instead of in their own books. Debtor banks paid interest on their balances; while collateral security was required only if the debit balance exceeded ten per cent of the capital of the bank concerned. This was the last application of this special Baltimore method.[21]

The Philadelphia banks, in contrast to 1857 now also organized in a clearing house, on November 22 resolved to suspend as had those of Baltimore. Like the latter they were forced to take a step which was avoided in New York through Coe's action. As in Baltimore, the Philadelphia banks in meeting this situation readopted an old measure (the above-described plan of 1857), making it a little more flexible. Instead of determining the amounts of securities to be deposited by each bank, as they had done in the former year, the banks authorized the Clearing House Committee to demand and receive collateral for the debit balances in such proportions as it considered proper;[22] and the matter was actually handled in this way.

In Boston the Clearing House Committee met two days after the date of the bank meetings in New York and Baltimore and one day later than the Philadelphia banks, i.e., on November 23. It decided to call a meeting of the Clearing House Association for the following day, November 24.[23] Here, as in Philadelphia and Baltimore, it was proposed (by Andrew T. Hall, chairman of the Clearing House Committee) to follow the tradition of 1857. This suggestion, however, met with opposition on the part of a minority which wanted to adopt the New York method. Three days had been sufficient for the migration of Coe's ideas from New York to Boston! Franklin Haven, mentioned repeatedly as one of the founders of the Boston Clearing House and president of Boston's

strongest bank, backed by Samuel Hooper,[24] its largest stockholder and director, presented a substitute for Hall's proposal. His suggestion "embod[ied] the same features with the plan adopted by the New York banks;" but what he actually wanted was the introduction into Boston of the clearing house loan certificate only. Carney, president of the Bank of Mutual Redemption,[25] in contrast, wanted to go further and to take over the New York plan it its entirety. He "proposed that the specie held by the Associated Banks be turned into a common fund and be loaned to each bank as it may be wanted under the supervision of a committee, the banks to discount to bona fide traders and not to speculators, the loans to be made for the accommodation of the greatest number." Both Haven's and Carney's motions were lost, however, when the vote was taken. The arguments brought forward against them do not sound very convincing today. Some of the bankers felt that Boston, in contrast to New York, was a debtor city and would be drained "in several directions." In answer, President Davis of the Suffolk Bank presented a telegram received from New York that Coe's scheme was working satisfactorily in that city and that the balances due New York would be allowed to remain in Boston as far as possible. In spite of this assurance, what appeared to some of the bank presidents as a new-fangled device was turned down (28 to 10) because of conservatism and lack of vision on their part; but a specific Boston shortcoming in the method of settling balances contributed to the outcome. At that time a large percentage of the Boston Clearing House balances was not settled in cash, but loaned or borrowed, respectively, by the creditor and debtor.[26] Since the introduction of the clearing house loan certificate would immediately have revealed the weakness of certain banks, the latter objected to the motions of both Haven and Carney and, allying themselves with the conservatives, defeated the suggestions.

To repeat, during the crisis of 1860 New York alone progressed along a new road; Philadelphia and Baltimore were hardly informed of the New York measures, while some of the leaders among the Boston bankers, although in vain, suggested following suit. Only a few months later, however, the advantages of Coe's scheme had become so evident that the Philadelphia Board of Presidents adopted it on April 30, 1861, thereby taking the lead over Boston. It is probable that C.H. Rogers, president of the Tradesmens Bank of Philadelphia, who had been a leader during the crisis of 1857, was the driving force. The plan as it was presented to the meeting of that Board on April 30, had been worked out in detail and embodied not only the new credit instrument, the clearing house loan certificate, but also the equalization of the specie reserves: Point 5 stipulated that "the specie belonging to the Associated Banks shall be considered and treated as a common fund for mutual aid and protection and the loan committee shall have power to equalize the same by assessment or otherwise at their discretion." After the adoption of the plan, the banks had to make daily statements showing loans and discounts, liabilities, loan certificates, and specie. As in New York, a Clearing House Loan Committee put the measure into effect.[27]

A few months later the Boston bankers also changed their minds, being forced to adopt the clearing house loan certificate at least in principle.[28] Their (incidentally, half-hearted) revision of policy resulted from their participation in the government loan transactions of 1861. The Boston bankers' conversion is easily understood when one remembers that the New York banks had made the contract with the Secretary of the Treasury dependent on the condition that "their proportion of the fifty million dollars of government securities... should be received by their loan committee at 90 per cent as a basis for the issue of loan certificates."[29] Similarly the Philadelphia banks had resolved that their loan committee should advance 90 per cent on the 7-30 Treasury Notes subscribed as their share. The era of parallel action of the banks in various cities was dawning! But, in fact, Boston did not fall in line.

On August 26, 1861, President Davis of the Suffolk Bank moved in the Clearing House Committee that a plan be presented to the Association regarding the adoption of the clearing house loan certificate. "Any bank entering into the arrangement made by the banks of New York, Philadelphia, and Boston with regard to the national loan may deposit with the Clearing House Committee Treasury Notes of the loan aforesaid and receive certificates therefore to an amount not exceeding 90 per cent of the par value of such treasury notes and scrip." This plan was adopted by the Clearing House Association the next day and the Clearing House Committee was authorized, once such certificates were taken out, to assign them to other banks in the settlement of balances, the recipients being entitled to use them again in the settlements of the following day. The banks in whose interest loan certificates were issued were to pay 6 per cent interest which was to accrue to those banks to which they were assigned. Any loss caused by an ultimate non-payment of loan certificates was to be assessed upon all Boston banks according to their capitals. So far, so good! But immediately

thereafter resistance came into play and, while clearing house loan certificates were issued (for the second time) both in New York and Philadelphia under arrangements of September 19 and November 4, 1861, respectively, none was issued in Boston in that year.[30]

Endeavors to do so in 1863 also met with failure. On November 5, of that year Samuel H. Walley,[31] president of the National Revere Bank, who had been an opponent of the proposal in 1860, moved in a meeting of the Clearing House Association that the Clearing House Committee be instructed to prepare a plan for the settlement of balances with clearing house loan certificates. Thereupon the Clearing House Committee, enlarged by four guests, met on November 9 and came to the conclusion that it could not recommend the measure because of unsurmountable difficulties. (It seems to the historian that the age of the committee members was the only unsurmountable difficulty.)[32] Andrew T. Hall, chairman of the Clearing House Committee, reported to this effect to the Association on November 14.

These Boston events are indicative of another attempt at organizing parallel action of the Associated Banks in the country's Eastern financial centers, but in the end only New York (on November 6) and Philadelphia (on December 7) went hand in hand and resolved once more to issue clearing house loan certificates.[33] Prior to the issue of 1863, however, and following on the heels of that of November, 1861, Philadelphia had already issued her third series. This was done upon the receipt of a telegram on December 30, 1861 signed by George D. Lyman, manager of the New York Clearing House, stating that the New York banks had stopped specie payments. In consequence thereof, the settlement of clearing house balances was made permissible in either clearing house loan certificates, to be issued on application, or in banknotes secured by collateral (which was in line with the emergency measure of 1860). To stress the essential point, the use of clearing house loan certificates was optional only, and in resolutions adopted by the Philadelphia Clearing House Association on March 24 and April 7, 1862, this optional aspect of the regulation was reaffirmed: balances were to be settled in specie, legal tender notes, or loan certificates; and the Clearing House manager was to distribute the daily receipts of these various media as nearly proportionately as possible. On the other hand, by spring of 1862 the earlier Philadelphia emergency medium for the settling of inter-bank balances, collaterally secured banknotes, had been dropped, as evidenced by the omission in the above list. They had been abandoned in favor of clearing house loan certificates of the New York brand.

When on December 7, 1863 the Philadelphia banks resolved once more to issue clearing house loan certificates, as mentioned above, they made a new agreement, the more important points of which may be repeated here, showing as they do the stage reached at that time in the development of the new credit instrument. Any bank at its option could deposit with a committee of five officers (the loan committee) bills receivable, as well as Pennsylvania State and Philadelphia City loan certificates. Thereupon the committee was to issue certificates of deposit (clearing house loan certificates) bearing 6 per cent interest to an amount equal to 75 per cent of the face value of such deposits. If the bank in question chose to deposit United States bonds, treasury notes, or other interest-bearing obligation of the United States it could receive certificates of deposit to an amount of 90 per cent of the face value. However, no bank could receive and have outstanding clearing house loan certificates in excess of 25 per cent of its capital. Each bank receiving clearing house loan certificates had to send each morning a statement of its condition to the manager of the Clearing House. The expenses resulting from the issue of the credit instruments were to be borne by the banks pro rata to their capitals.[34]

IV

The crisis of 1873 marked a new step in the conquest of the country by the clearing house loan certificate and at the same time the end of the first stage of its development. In that year Boston and Baltimore gave up their resistance. Baltimore now abandoned its traditional method, as Philadelphia had done in 1861, and followed the New York example, although without equalizing the specie reserves of its banks. In Boston the personal element played a decisive role in the change of policy as can be seen from the composition of the Boston Clearing House Committee of 1873 which voted to adopt the measure. James H. Beal, who seems to have been one of its most active friends in 1863 was now in the chair. Samuel H. Walley who in that year had worked for the adoption of the instrument, was still a member and so were Lamb, Hodges, Bates, all of whom had been members of the committee in 1863, and one John Cummings. A new generation was in power which did not suffer from the inhibitions of an earlier one. In addition to these two cities, Cincinnati, St. Louis, and New Orleans made use of the clearing

house loan certificate now for the first time. In New York Coe, approaching the pinnacle of his career, was most influential and under his influence his device was applied for the last time in its original form, i.e., combined with the pooling of the city's specie reserves.[35]

It was in 1873 that a second personality, Frederick D. Tappen, began to gain a decisive influence on the development of the emergency credit instrument. Tappen (1829-1902), a descendant of a Dutch colonial family, had started his career as an engineer of the Erie Railroad after having studied civil engineering. Very soon, however, he abandoned this profession and in 1850 joined the National Bank of New York (later the Gallatin Bank) as a specie clerk. When the Clearing House opened Tappen represented his bank as its "settling clerk," thus gaining an insight into the working of its mechanism. During the panic of 1857 he rose to be the cashier, and in 1868 was elected the president of the bank. Tappen was one of the most influential leaders of the Clearing House, and almost no year passed between 1872 and his death in which he did not hold some office in the organization. In 1873, 1880, 1894, 1898, and 1901 he was the chairman of the Clearing House Committee and in 1882/1883 as well as 1891/1892 he presided over the Clearing House Association. Having shown his talent for leadership in 1869 during the excitement caused by Wall Street's Black Friday, Tappen in 1873 became for the first time the chairman of a loan committee charged with the issue of clearing house loan certificates. Thereafter he was nominated to a similar position whenever during his lifetime clearing house loan certificates were issued in New York (1884, 1890, 1893). Tappen's selection by the banking community is of particular interest since in his case the actual reasons why leadership was bestowed on him are known. Tappen was courageous, fair, faithful, and a man of integrity; in other words, he possessed the necessary qualifications. He was highly praised, for instance, because, regardless of the insight which he acquired officially during those emergencies into the affairs of other banks, none ever lost an account to his institution. But other equally important motives for his selection had nothing to do with his qualifications. First of all, his personal fortune was so conservatively invested as to be beyond the reach of booms and panics. This fact gave him the equanimity necessary in times of crisis to exert leadership, when everyone else was losing his head. Furthermore Tappen was not a money-maker in the New York sense from whom one would need to keep one's affairs secret; and, last but not least, he was not at the head of one of the leading New York banking enterprises. Thus his appointment to a job which implied temporary dictatorial powers did not meet with "professional jealousies." In the end Tappen learned by experience to manipulate the clearing house loan certificate with such masterliness that it could gain the status of a standard device. Nevertheless he did not lose sight of the necessity of using the efficient credit instrument with "the greatest care and caution." His policy was based on the conviction that no solvent bank should be allowed to fail in a crisis, that at such a time the most urgent demands had to be satisfied first, and that urgency was to be measured by the willingness to pay the highest interest rates. Tappen led the New York banking fraternity not only in times of major panics, but equally during minor disturbances, such as those created by the Venezuela message of 1895, the Northern Pacific panic, and the days of uneasiness due to the death of President McKinley.[36] But his name did not become known to a wider public until he had handled the panic of 1893, that is, in fact, only after Coe's death.

After 1873 the issue of clearing house loan certificates in times of emergency became a matter of routine, (although in 1893 the application was still limited to a few large clearing houses). Therefore the history of further issues of the credit instrument is without interest from the point of view of this research, except in one respect. It will be remembered that in the crisis of 1857, Singleton A. Mercer had suggested that the Philadelphia Board of Presidents approve checks to be drawn on a depository against securities lodged therein. These checks were not to be payable in specie, but receivable for all debts due the banks; and they were expected to circulate. However, when the clearing house loan certificate was brought into existence and widely adopted, the development took a different turn. Up to the 1880's clearing house loan certificates were issued in large denominations only; they were used exclusively in the settlement of clearing house balances, and did not circulate. In 1893, however, what had originally been Mercer's idea came up again in Atlanta, Georgia, where the Clearing House issued, during the panic of that year, the first circulating clearing house loan certificates in small denominations.[37] The incentive seems to have come from the cotton merchants who needed currency to move the cotton crop, and the bankers responded to their suggestions by devising the circulating clearing house loan certificate. This author has been unable to determine if or to what extent the three men appointed as trustees for the issue of the

certificates were responsible for the innovation.[38]

In the crisis of 1907 those circulating clearing house loan certificates were either copied or devised independently in numerous other places. The San Francisco Clearing House, for example, issued them on November 1 on the basis of deposits of clearing house loan certificates of large denominations, and they circulated widely in California, Nevada, and South-East Oregon. Similar "scrip" was issued by the clearing houses in Seattle, Tacoma, and Portland with the difference that it was not even based on such deposits.[39]

V

Parallel with the introduction and extended use of the clearing house loan certificate goes an interesting development of public opinion, or more correctly, of the opinion of the business community, as to the obligations of banks in time of crisis. In 1825, 1837, and even to a large extent in 1857, bankers had considered the security of their enterprises when handling the emergency and not their responsibility toward panic stricken business. They were not yet aware of obligations to the public, obligations resulting from their key position in the economic life of the nation. Although they recognized the dependence of business on banking, it was a well established practice, in order to become impregnable, to curtail loans indiscriminately, regardless of the consequences for business at large. However, in 1857 that outlook was changing in the commercial centers of the East. Certain statements made and actions taken during the crisis of that year are indicative of a new attitude.[40] When, on October 15, 1857, Andrew T. Hall suggested cooperation among the Boston banks in dealing with the crisis, he introduced his plan "as aid for the daily settlements of the clearing house." However, on the next day leaders of the Boston business community, such men as William and Nathan Appleton, Samuel Hooper, and George B. Upton, whose interest in banking was only secondary, but who were well informed in matters of finance, met in private conference with members of the Clearing House. After this meeting they were invited to a session of the Association, where William Appleton addressed the bankers. He impressed on them the businessman's need for help, or, in other words, for additional loans. Thereupon Hall, who may have been back of the invitation, moved to double the amount of bank notes which could be tendered by each bank in the settlement of clearing house balances.[41] This action implies that the Clearing House bankers saw the connection between facilitating the settlement of clearing house balances and increasing the loans to business. The Philadelphia bankers were less articulate, but their reasoning also moved in the right direction. They gave their motive for cooperative action in the same year 1857 as follows: "Whereas it is desirable in the present condition of the circulating medium for the convenience of business that there should be union and concert of action by the several banking institutions of the city..."

Coe, when creating the clearing house loan certificate in 1860, was ahead of his time, but close enough to it to gain an influence thereon. The new instrument was suggested by him "in order to enable the banks of the City of New York to expand their loans and discounts and also for the purpose of facilitating the settlement of exchanges between the banks." A comparison with Hall's motivation of the emergency measures of the Boston banks in 1857 is illuminating; what came first in Boston in 1857, came last in New York in 1860.[42] Following the same line of thinking, the Associated Banks of New York, preparing for an anticipated emergency, on April 24, 1861 formulated the following preamble to their resolution: "Whereas the agreement between the banks entered into on the 21st of November last was productive of very beneficial results in enabling them to extend needed facilities to the community....." By this time Philadelphia was becoming almost as articulate as New York and in April,1861,adopted the clearing house loan certificate "for securing harmonious and united action in maintaining our lines of discount and facilitating the settlement of our exchanges." That is to say, as in New York the business interests were thought of first and the technical aspect of the matter (the settlement of the balances) second.[43]

To sum up, after about 1860 the associated banks in the leading financial centers, New York, Boston, and Philadelphia, had recognized their responsibilities toward the business community, at least in times of emergency. This attitude however, had not yet become the accepted one all over the country. The Chicago banks as late as 1893 were unable to agree among themselves on this point, as will be described shortly.[44] In New York, on the other hand, the new spirit became firmly entrenched in that very decade: in 1890 the Clearing House Association of New York authorized the issue of clearing house loan certificates and advised the banks of the city to consider a policy of forbearance regarding loans to parties in good standing. Thereupon Abiel Abbott Low (1811-1893), a leading New York merchant and president of the Merchants Bank,

in disregard of the established traditional policy of his bank, took out clearing house loan certificates although the bank did not actually need them. Thereby he intended to encourage weaker banks (which for prestige's sake might be afraid of so doing) to make use of the opportunity for the benefit of their customers.[45]

VI

As long as the issue of clearing house loan certificates remained restricted to a few clearing houses in the financial centers and as long as these certificates were used exclusively for settling clearing house balances they were highly beneficial although extra-legal, and did not represent any danger.[46] In 1907, however, clearing house loan certificates were issued by 51 clearing houses, and some were issued in small denominations for the purpose of serving as a circulating medium. Thereby these certificates ceased to be extra-legal and became illegal, and new dangerous problems loomed over the horizon.[47] Action had to be taken and the Aldrich-Vreeland Act of 1908 resulted. In this act an ideological development of about twenty years was brought to a conclusion and, although the law was of a temporary character only, it is of interest to the historian. On the one hand it is a composite of numerous perennial minor reform proposals of the period and on the other hand the outcome of several years of struggle to legalize the clearing house loan certificate.

In the 1890's the ideas of legalizing the clearing house loan certificates or of making clearing houses the agents in the issue of an emergency currency were in the air. Theodore Gilman, the Wall-Street broker,[48] was a leader in the former movement. Success for either one of these proposals was predicated on the incorporation of clearing houses under a federal law, a question which was much discussed up to the time of the Money Trust Investigation.[49] Under Gilman's influence several bills were presented to Congress in which he proposed that in case of an emergency banks should hand assets to their clearing houses which would issue on that basis a circulating medium to be withdrawn as soon as possible. This is the gist of the bills H.R. 3338 (54th Congr. 1st sess. [1895], sec. 9), H.R. 9279 (55th Congr. 2d sess. [Mar. 17, 1898] sec. 10) and H.R. 7950 (57th Congr. 1st sess. [1902]).[50] A very similar proposal emanated from Edward Atkinson (1827-1905), industrialist, financier, and free-lance economist;[51] and others were presented before the American Bankers Association in 1893 by

D.G. Ambler and in 1895 by William H. Rhawn.[52]

The second very similar proposal was promoted especially by Joseph H. Walker who will be characterized later in this volume.[53] It was distinguished from Gilman's in that clearing houses would not issue any emergency circulation of their own, but would on application to the Comptroller of the Currency receive government paper money and act as agents in circulating it. Walker submitted this plan in the bills H.R. 171 (53d Congr. 2d sess. [Sept. 6, 1893]) and H.R. 10289 (55th Congr. 2d sess. [May 13, 1898]).[54]

With the knowledge of the reform proposals[55] of the 1890's and 1900's in mind and against the background of the activities of Gilman, Walker, and some of their contemporaries, the historian can easily understand the place which the Aldrich-Vreeland Act holds in the history of American banking. When it passed, the exponents of an emergency currency won a temporary victory; (in 1909 the label "emergency currency" was attached to the act in a speech before the American Bankers Association).[56] At the same time by establishing currency associations the act developed the Gilman-Walker line of thought except that instead of clearing houses, special associations of banks became the bearers of the measure.[57] In fact Walker was victorious over Gilman: Clearing house loan certificates were not legalized nor issued as a circulating medium, but an emergency currency was issued by the government for circulation through National Currency Associations. On the other hand the basis of such circulation was almost the same as that which had been behind the traditional clearing house loan certificates, namely bank assets. Thus the exponents of an asset currency also got a pleasant morsel. At the same time the assets to be used as the basis of the Aldrich-Vreeland emergency currency would please all those who in the preceding two decades had fought for broadening the range of special security back of National Bank notes: Those assets were, besides commercial paper, real estate mortgages (to the delight of the last land-bank Mohicans!),[58] railroad and industrial stocks, railroad, industrial, state, city, town, and county bonds, as well as other municipals. Finally, as in many of the earlier reform bills, joint and several liability was established for the Aldrich-Vreeland currency; that is to say, basic ideas of the safety fund system, recommended by the contemporary exponents of an asset currency, were also embodied in the bill. It was really the wildest piece of legislative compromise in the field of banking of which the author is aware.

It is noteworthy that the Aldrich-Vreeland Act turned its back on the clearing house loan certificate instead of legalizing it. As has been pointed out, changes wrought in 1907 had made further applications of the traditional credit instrument appear risky. Moreover certain experiences of that year had caused a good deal of criticism which was reflected in the hearings of the Pujo Committee. In its Report[59] this sub-committee of the Committee on Banking and Currency declared the power to issue loan certificates dangerous as long as clearing house associations were not under government control: Small committees determined when the former were to be issued and to whom they were to be delivered, while those detrimentally affected had no possibility of applying for redress and of demanding revision of the decision of the clearing house loan committee concerned. As a matter of fact, in 1907 at least two cases, those of the Mechanics and Traders and the Oriental Banks, were badly bungled by the New York Clearing House.

Because of the great importance of Chicago as a money market, the introduction of the clearing house loan certificate in that city should be sketched. The Chicago Clearing House was founded in 1865 as the first in the Middle West. Leading among its founders seem to have been George Sturges, J. Young Scammon, and Lyman J. Gage. The latter, later McKinley's Secretary of the Treasury, became the first manager, but held that office only for a short time. Thereafter however, as a member of the Clearing House Committee, he exerted for many years a decisive influence on its policy.

When the question of clearing house loan certificates came up first in 1873, opinion was divided. One party was in favor of following the example of the Eastern clearing houses, while another was opposed to such policy. This latter consisted of George Sturges (1838-1890), president of the Northwestern Bank, Solomon A. Smith (1815-1879), president of the Merchants Savings, Loan and Trust Company, and Chauncey B. Blair (1810-1891), president of the Merchants National Bank,[60] all three representing strong institutions and two of them belonging to the same age group which in 1863 had defeated the clearing house loan certificate in Boston also. These men wanted to adopt a policy which had been successfully applied after the great fire, when Sturges had opposed any delay on the part of the banks in meeting their obligations. At that time his advice had been justified by the events. However, a policy which had been bold then, was "weak and timorous" now and it had disastrous consequences. The record of failures of large banks during the crisis of 1873 was far worse in Chicago than in any of the great Eastern cities. As a matter of fact, the exponents of that strategy did not understand that the situation in 1873 was very different from the set-up after the fire; the fire had been a local disaster during a national boom, while the crisis of that year was a national emergency; the fire had been a singular, while the crisis was a typical event: so different policies were required to meet exigencies different in character. Their idea was that Chicago's strong position in the country's food business would enable most of its banks to pull through without resorting to emergency measures. Regardless of whatever decision other banks might make, these powerful business leaders were determined to meet their obligations, an unwarranted prestige policy. When the vote was taken Lyman J. Gage joined the opposition and cast the decisive vote against the issue of clearing house loan certificates.[61] It is understandable that the Middle West stood for rugged individualism; nevertheless, the decision is surprising, since the first regular clearing house certificates used in Chicago in 1865 had been based on currency or government bonds.

The negative attitude toward the new credit instrument thus became a tradition which, for years to come, determined the policy of the Chicago Clearing House. In 1893, again, no clearing house loan certificates were issued and the fight which took place pro and con within its walls and which has been described by F. Cyril James,[62] is of considerable interest: In 1893 the suggestion to issue clearing house loan certificates came from leaders of the business community and was ventilated amid strong opposition in a meeting of the Clearing House Association. Under the pressure of those interests, the association was forced to adopt the clearing house loan certificate in principle, and the Clearing House Committee was authorized to issue these credit instruments. However, since three out of five members of the committee were opposed to the resolution of the Association none was actually issued although applications were submitted. Chicago's policy of 1893 was strikingly similar to that of Boston in 1861. Undoubtedly a great number of enterprises were unnecessarily sacrificed through that policy and the strong banks had to uphold weak ones by other means.

The generation which controlled the Chicago Clearing House in 1893[63] was different from that in charge in 1873, and most of the leaders were comparatively young (men in their forties and fifties), so that the traditional policy could easily have been revised as it was in Boston in 1873. Of all the leading actors of 1873 only Lyman J. Gage was on the Chicago Clearing House Committee of 1893. While he had cast the decisive vote against the clearing house loan certificate in 1873, now he was in favor of the measure fighting the very tradition which he had helped to establish. On the other hand, among the opponents was Chauncey Justus Blair, whose father had been one of the main opponents of the plan in 1873, and it is possible that sentiment determined his antagonism.

Professor James has stressed correctly that back of the debates of 1893 was the question whether or not banks were business enterprises like others which had to take care of themselves alone. The protagonists of the clearing house loan certificate felt that theirs were broader responsibilities, all the broader since Chicago was a central reserve city.

A few years later James B. Forgan, about whom more will be said later, was chosen the chairman of the Clearing House Committee and in place of Lyman J. Gage he became the acknowledged leader of the Chicago bankers. Practically every important decision emanating from the Chicago Clearing House in the first decade of the twentieth century is said to have originated with him or to have been the result of his endeavors.[64] With Forgan, a third generation of Chicago bankers came to the fore in the Clearing House, a generation which thought in broader terms than their predecessors. It was not willing to defer to the Chicago tradition regarding clearing house loan certificates; nor did Forgan wish the decision to be postponed until the outbreak of the next crisis with its inevitable atmosphere of excitement and confusion. Therefore in 1901 he suggested that the matter be taken up immediately, as was done. The Associated Banks confirmed their resolution of 1893 which authorized the issue of clearing house loan certificates and which was now ratified by the boards of directors of the various banks. Thus when the crisis broke in 1907 Chicago, falling in line with the other large clearing houses, issued certificates for the first time, but as a matter of course.

Chapter XVII

THE CLEARING HOUSE LOAN CERTIFICATE

1. This chapter deals only with certain aspects of the history of the clearing house loan certificates. As to other aspects, see the writings of Andrew, Cannon, Plehn, and Sprague, as quoted in the list of references, and the articles "Clearing House Certificates Issued during the Panic of 1907" and "Clearing House Certificates Issued during Crisis of 1914" in Commercial and Financial Chronicle of May 30, 1908 and February 13, 1915, respectively. See also Comptroller of the Currency, Reports (1891), 12 ff and (1893), 15-17.

2. As to the use of country notes in 1837, see the Annual Report of the New York Bank Commissioners (for 1837), 10, 11.

3. Page 2, col. 4.

4. See this volume page 5.

5. Myers, Margaret, op. cit., 98; "Report of the Superintendent of the Banking Department of the State of New York," in U.S. 35th Congr. 1st sess., House Executive Document 107, 117, 118.

6. The following is written on the basis of the Boston Clearing House records.

7. Thomas Lamb (1796-1887) was the son of a prominent shipping merchant, member of the firm of James and Thomas Lamb. In this firm, which was interested especially in North Western trade, the younger Thomas Lamb started his career, switching his interest to China and later to Holland and the Baltic Sea. He was instrumental in the development of Boston harbor, being for some time president of the Boston Pier and Long Wharf Corporation. Moreover, he engaged in insurance and banking, being president of the Washington Marine Insurance Company, of the New England Bank, of the Suffolk Savings Bank for Seamen, and others. Professional and Industrial History of Suffolk County; Suffolk Savings Bank; Aristocracy of Boston.

8. Association Minutes, October 17, 1857.

9. See page 166.

10. See index of this volume.

11. The following description is based on the Minutes of the Philadelphia Board of Presidents.

12. While Boston, New York, and Philadelphia applied during the crisis of 1857 essentially the same principle, Baltimore followed a precedent established twenty years before. Each bank kept a record of its balances with the other banks, and interest was paid by the debtor banks at the end of each month. Creditor banks had the right to require the settlement of balances in checks on other banks or in securities satisfactory to them. In this respect, Baltimore was also moving in the direction which was soon to be taken all over the country. See Hales, op. cit., 87, 88.

13. Stevens' backing is claimed in the publication of the Guaranty Trust Company, p. 16.

14. Report to the New York Clearing House Association of a Committee upon Reforms in the Banking Business, Presented November, 1873. (W.H. Arthur and Co., Printers and Stationers, 55 Liberty Street, New York), 56, 57, 58. See also Bankers Magazine, XV (1860/61), 500.

15. Biographical notes on Taylor and Punnett can be found in this volume on pages 89 and 56, respectively. An important man on this committee was C.P. Leverich, who became the custodian of the securities deposited. Leverich (? - 1876) was originally a merchant and had received his training in the shipping firm of Peter Remsen and Company. In 1845 in partnership with his brother he opened a business in cotton and other Southern products, an enterprise which gained wide repute in the South. In 1853 he became the vice-president of the Bank of New York bringing to it his extensive Southern business connections. In 1863 he assumed the presidency of the bank which owed its growth after the Civil War to his activities. In 1864 Leverich was the president of the New York Clearing House; (Nevins, Bank of New York, 84).

16. Sprague, History of Crises, 273.

17. The Mercantile and the Chemical Banks were not represented at the meeting mentioned above and a committee appointed to ask for their concurrence succeeded only so far as the former bank was concerned. The very strong Chemical consented to the issue of clearing house loan certificates but refused to participate in the pooling of the specie reserves, and so was excluded from the clearing house for a short period.

18. "Report Loan Committee," U.S. 37th Congr. 3d sess., House Executive Document 25, 126.

19. "Report Loan Committee," 131-133. Not quite twenty banks were borrowers in October and November, 1861; almost forty in the first quarter of 1862.

20. See footnote 12.

21. Hales, op. cit., 87 ff, 101.
22. The preceding is based on the records of the Philadelphia Clearing House. On March 18, 1861 a meeting of the Clearing House Association decided to return to the respective banks the securities deposited under the resolution of November 22, 1860.
23. The following is based on the Boston Clearing House records.
24. Incidentally, Amasa Walker's booklet The Nature and Uses of Money was dedicated to the Boston banking leaders Hooper, Hall, and Denny, among others.
25. As to Carney, see the index of this volume.
26. Cannon, op. cit (1910), 250, 251.
27. The committee consisted of Rogers, E.M. Lewis, representing the Farmers and Mechanics Bank, Joseph Patterson, president of the Western Bank, John B. Austin, president of the Southwark Bank, and B.B. Comegys, the coming man of the Philadelphia Bank.
28. When the Boston banks decided to suspend (Dec. 30, 1861), they unanimously resolved to continue using specie in the daily settlements; see Gras, op. cit., 516, 517.
29. "Report Loan Committee," 125.
30. It has been described in another context how President Carney of the Bank for Mutual Redemption applied in vain for loan certificates in October 1861; see pages 86 and 87 of vol. I of this work.
31. Walley wrote an interesting paper on the crisis of 1857.
32. The committee in that meeting consisted of Andrew T. Hall, aged 65; Thomas Lamb, 67; Almon D. Hodges, 62; John Amory Davis, ? ; Benjamin E. Bates, 55; and the following guests: Daniel Denny, then at the head of the Clearing House Association, aged 71; Waldo Flint, 69; Caleb Stetson, 60; and James H. Beal, 40. Although the minutes do not record the stand which the various men took, it is rather certain that Denny, Flint, and Stetson were leaders of the opposition while Davis and Beal fought for the measure.
33. It was New York's third and Philadelphia's fourth issue.
34. Source: Minutes of the Philadelphia Clearing House Association. Incidentally the Clearing House Loan Committee was still identical with that appointed in 1861, except that John B. Austin had been replaced by one Thomas Smith. A circular letter setting forth the conditions of the issue, dated December 7, 1863, is pasted into the Minutes of the Board of Directors of the Bank of North America.
35. Regarding Baltimore, see Hales, op. cit., 97. Philadelphia again followed the above-described rules of 1863, reformulating them; (see Minutes of the Philadelphia Clearing House Association,

September 24, and October 6, 1873); Cannon, op. cit. (1910), 83. Hepburn (op. cit., [1915] 353) describes the development of the collateral used in New York in the various issues between 1860 and 1873.
36. New York Clearing House Association, Proceedings ... in Memory ... Tappen, especially 12, 13, 15, 16, 23, 25, 35, 45, 49, 52, 53. Gilpin and Wallace, op. cit., 47; "Hundred Years," 160, 161. The article in the Dictionary of American Biography, while correct as far as the dates go, does not put Tappen into his correct historical place and overestimates his achievements.
37. Mr. W.C. Adamson, secretary of the Atlanta Clearing House, in a letter of December 21, 1940, gave the following information: (The quotation marks are Mr. Adamson's who, however, did not give his source.)

"At a called meeting of the Atlanta Clearing House Association held on August 15, 1893, the following communication from the Chamber of Commerce, dated August 14, 1893, was read:

'Capt. R. J. Lowry, President
Atlanta Clearing House Association
Atlanta, Georgia

Dear Sir:

At a very largely attended meeting held at the Chamber of Commerce today, the following resolution was adopted:

WHEREAS in view of the importance of providing ample funds for handling the cotton crop tributary to this market, and owing to the present financial conditions the money centers heretofore furnishing the required currency cannot be relied on for the usual assistance,

BE IT RESOLVED, that the associated banks of Atlanta be requested to issue Clearing House Certificates in such amounts as may be found necessary to provide ample funds for handling this business.

I am instructed to forward same to you with the request that your body take action in the premises as suggested.

Respectfully,
H.G. Saunders, Sec'y.'

"After consideration of this communication, the Atlanta Clearing House adopted a resolution providing for the issue to members of the Association, certificates in such amounts as might be necessary. In connection with this issue of certificates, Messrs. R.J. Lowry, Paul Romare, and C.A. Collier were appointed Trustees, and the provisions governing the issue of these certificates provided that certificates could be issued for 66 2/3% of the face value of the bills receivable or securities deposited by the respective banks as approved by these Trustees, and each member bank obligated itself to take out such proportion of the certificates as might be assigned to it by the Trustees and to submit to such readjustment and redistribution of such certificates so issued as the necessity of any bank or banks might in the judgment of the Trustees require from day to day, until all certificates were called and cancelled..."

38. During the crisis of 1907 the Chicago banks developed a device which was still closer to Mercer's plan of 1857 than the circulating clearing house loan certificates in small denominations. At the suggestion of Byron L. Smith (born in 1853), president of the Northern Trust Company and also president of the Chicago Clearing House Association, any bank could surrender the clearing house loan certificates issued to it, and receive in place thereof checks in denominations of 2, 5, and 10 dollars. These checks were drawn by or under the direction of the Clearing House Committee on the bank in question and were payable on application through the Clearing House. (Cannon, op. cit. [1910], 121, 122; Forgan, Recollections, 189.)

39. Plehn, op. cit., 9. 11.

40. For the following, see Boston Clearing House Records, and Minutes of the Philadelphia Board of Presidents.

41. See above page 159.

42. In that year the Boston Clearing House adopted the following preamble to its emergency measures:" ... and whereas the extension of that limit [of the use of notes in the settlement of balances] would greatly facilitate the banks in rendering assistance to the business community which is so much needed at the present time." (Minutes, Boston Clearing House Association, November 24, 1860.)

43. Report to the New York Clearing House Association (1873), 56; "Report of the New York Loan Committee," 126; Minutes, Philadelphia Board of Presidents, April 30, 1861.

44. See below page 169.

45. Guaranty Trust Company, op. cit., 23.

46. Nevertheless Leslie M. Shaw, the Secretary of the Treasury, was strongly opposed to clearing house loan certificates as early as 1905; see Hull, op. cit., 399.

47. This situation was clearly seen by the Canadian banker B.E. Walker; see Abnormal Features, 8 ff.

48. See this volume, index.

49. See the writings of Gilman, passim; Meyer, Carl, "The Legal Status of the Clearing House" in A.B.A., Proceedings (1913), 531 ff; Money Trust Investigation, 291, 540, 548, 1391, 1392, 1886, 1887. Congressman Fowler's bill H.R.

13363 (57th Congr. 1st sess.) ties in here and so does a discussion of 1907 in the American Bankers Association, Proceedings (1907), 144. As to Fowler's bill, see Horace White in ibid. (1902), 121 ff, especially 125, reprinted in Hull, op. cit., 290 ff, especially 295.

50. See Gilman, Graded System, 98 ff; idem, Federal Clearing Houses, 23 ff; U.S. House Committee on Banking and Currency, Hearings and Arguments, 1896/97, 88 ff; Hull, op. cit., 304.

51. Gilman, Graded System, 213 ff; Atkinson, Address on Finance and Banking, 10, 11. In the 1900's Andrew J. Frame was among the backers of this plan; see Hull op. cit., 336.

52. Ambler was the president of the National Bank of the State of Florida at Jacksonville. His speech was entitled "An Adaptation of the English System of the Treatment of Panics to American Needs -- or Clearing-House Loan Certificates Issued as a Circulating Medium under Governmental Control" in A.B.A., Proceedings (1893), 98 ff, especially 103, 104, reprinted in Gilman, Graded System, 217 ff. Rhawn's address under the title "The Utilization of Lawful Money Reserves through Bank Clearing Houses in relieving Monetary Stringencies and preventing Panics" appears in A.B.A., Proceedings (1895), 29 ff. Rhawn did not go as far as Gilman and Ambler. He wanted banks to be permitted to use legalized clearing house loan certificates as reserves so that money would be freed for disbursements.

  The discussion in ibid. (1907), 145 also follows the Gilman line, as does a suggestion in American Academy, Annals XXXVII (1910) 611.

53. See index and also Bankers Magazine, LII (1896), 313 ff.

54. As to the former, see Gilman, Graded System, 222 ff, especially sec. 17 of the bill and the Hearings and Arguments (1896/97) before the Committee of Banking and Currency (see footnote 50), 326, 327; as to the latter see U.S. 55th Congr. 2d sess., House Report 1575, Part 2, 241 ff. The "Curtis plan" of 1906 follows the same line; see A.B.A., Proceedings (1906), 189.

55. See this volume, pages 207 ff.

56. Proceedings (1909), 73.

57. Victor Morawetz proposed the establishment of a permanent association of banks without capital of its own, similar to the clearing house associations, which would issue to the banks asset notes backed by a high specie reserve. It was to be guided by a committee of which the Secretary of the Treasury would be an ex officio member; Banking and Currency Problem, 87 ff.

58. As late as 1873 a land bank scheme was published in Boston; see Spooner, op. cit., passim.

59. Pages 26 ff.

60. Incidentally, Chauncey B. Blair was another of those leading bankers who came originally from the State Bank of Indiana. When the latter was rechartered as the Bank of the State of Indiana he secured a controlling interest in the La Porte branch and became its president; (see Huston, op. cit., III, 18 ff).

61. Huston, op. cit., I, 229; James, Chicago Banks, 369 ff, 447 ff.

62. Ibid., 595 ff.

63. The leaders of the Clearing House Association in that period were: Orson Smith (1841-1923), Isaac G. Lombard (1835-1910), C.J. Blair (1845-1916), J.J.P. Odell (1847-1910), and last but not least, Lyman J. Gage (1836-1927).

64. James, Chicago Banks, 708.

Chapter XVIII

FIFTH PERIOD
(1882-1910)

GENERAL CHARACTERISTICS

I

The American banking business between 1882 and 1914 was determined by three basic facts. First, the country possessed (by 1905) approximately 16,000 banks, of which about 6,000 were National Banks and the rest state banks, trust companies, and private banks. What little coherence existed among these banks was brought about by clearing houses (the most powerful of which was that of New York), correspondent relationships, and, in times of stringencies, measures of the Secretary of the Treasury. (Cooperation during the crisis of 1907 due to dictatorial actions of J. P. Morgan was only an exception to the rule.) Secondly, the typical size of American banks was small, the majority working with capitals of from $25,000 to $300,000. Thirdly, many of these banks were adjuncts to industrial concerns in smaller communities and were dominated by their owners. They served special interests rather than the community at large and whatever they did was strictly local in character. Banking appeared to be "a local question."[1] By contrast the larger and best managed banks remained independent until about 1900 when some of the more important ones came under the control of investment bankers.

Conservative public opinion wished banks to be restricted to a purely commercial business facilitating the movement and exchange of commodities. It considered their function to be the lending of money and credit on the basis of their own capital and the temporarily idle funds of the community which were assembled by way of deposits in order to satisfy short term demands (1902).[2] Or to quote a successful country banker: the "business of a bank is that of promoting the interests of the community in the handling of commodities [by] extending credit and not [by] financing enterprises."[3] Frank A. Vanderlip of the National City Bank, one of New York's leading bankers, went further. He emphasized that the swapping of credits was the legitimate business of banks.[4] Their essential function was neither

the safekeeping nor the lending of money, but just the exchange of credits.[5] If one compares this outlook of a leading banker of the 1900's with earlier banking philosophy, the change experienced by American commercial banking over about 125 years becomes evident. In the process of swapping credits, so Vanderlip explained, banks created credit and the customer exchanged a deposit balance [or banknote] for evidence of his indebtedness. Thus credit and deposits were clearly seen as closely tied together, and reserves appeared as having a function not seen by American bankers in earlier periods: they served as a check on inflation. Vanderlip criticized the widely held belief that banks first took deposits and then loaned them out, and he was aware that public opinion was very slow in apprehending what appeared to him the true nature of the contemporary banking business.[6] In contrast, the historian feels as if he were transferred back into the eighteenth century in view of the stand which Charles G. Dawes was taking: according to him "the most important function which banks exercise[d] in any community [was] that of producing purchasing power."[7]

The character of banks and especially of National Banks as commercial banks was officially stressed throughout the period. As early as 1888 the then Comptroller of the Currency (Trenholm) commented that National Banks constituted "a body of bankers exclusively devoted to the collection, the safekeeping, and the employment in temporary loans of the private capital of the country."[8] Consequently the Comptroller was against any dealings in real estate securities and in general against the investments by National Banks in bonds other than those of the United States, let alone in stock. (The later conflict between some of the banks and the Comptroller's office was thus foreshadowed.)[9]

Banks which did business strictly in line with such a program took deposits and lent funds in the form of notes or by creating deposits. Note issue was continuously losing ground[10] although still remaining more important than in contemporaneous England. The deposit business, in contrast, was the backbone of banking, at least in the advanced sections of the country. It was supplemented by exchange transactions, both domestic and foreign, by the purchase and sale of bullion, by the safe-keeping of and the lending on securities, and in some cases by a few other transactions. These might or might not rise to importance in particular banks, such as the servicing of correspondents.

The unprofitability of note issues, about which more will be said later, worried National Banks in the less developed parts of the country; and there was danger that note issues might become extinct because of the steady redemption of bonds. In 1884 two bills were before Congress, one of which would have permitted the issue of notes up to the par value of the deposited bonds and up to 100 per cent of the banks' unimpaired capital. The second would have exchanged 4 per cent against 3 per cent bonds and would also have permitted note issue up to the par value thereof. The bills did not pass, and the circulation of National Bank notes decreased steadily over the next few years.[11] Under these circumstances the Comptroller recommended a repeal of the legal requirement demanding bond deposits of at least one third of the capital of National Banks or of one fourth (or at least $50,000) of National Banks with a capital of more than $150,000. The Comptroller hoped thereby to draw additional state banks into the National system and to enable men of property to establish banks of large capital.[12] Actually the year 1886 saw a minor crisis when 3 per cent bonds were called for redemption, and the National Banks had to replace them by 4 and 4-1/2 per cents. The day was saved only by the fact that the wording of the law was ambiguous and permitted delays, and by the lucky circumstance that no information leaked out which would have induced speculators to corner the banks.[13] After 1900 notes were issued on the basis of 2 per cent bonds up to their par value.

Figures given earlier indicate that by 1905 only about 6,000 out of about 16,000 American banks belonged to the national system. In many respects the business of National and state banks, including trust companies doing a banking business, was very similar, but there were some distinct differences: only National Banks issued notes; only state banks lent on real estate and mortgages. State banks were usually smaller than National Banks, a fact which had some influence on the kind of business they could undertake. It goes without saying that, while National Banks were supervised by the Comptroller of the Currency, state banks were, if at all, under state banking departments where the supervision was

less strict. Less strict supervision coming on the top of more lenient banking laws widely determined business policy and the competitive situation.

That both public and official opinion assigned the role of strictly commercial banks to the country's national institutions and that these widely adhered to that pattern is, however, much less significant for the historian than the contemporaneous trend to expand banking activities beyond the scope of commercial banking proper. This trend can be fully understood only when one knows the details of the competitive situation in which the banks operated. This was quickly changing because numerous leading bankers, especially of the then younger generations, aimed at replacing competition by what they called cooperation.

The word cooperation as used by bankers of the period connoted two different things: first, working together in the interest of the common weal or at least in the interest of the banking fraternity as a whole. Cooperation among banks in this sense will be treated in detail in a later chapter of this volume.[14] But secondly, cooperation also meant abandoning competition. A representative of cooperation in the former sense was George S. Coe; while J. P. Morgan, the private banker, stood for non-competition sans phrase as the hearings of the Pujo Committee brought out:

> Q. You are opposed to competition? Are you not?
> Morgan: No, I do not mind competition.
> Q. You would rather have combination, would you not?
> Morgan: Yes.
> Q. You are an advocate of combination and cooperation as against competition, are you not?
> Morgan: Yes, cooperation I should favor.[15]

In view of Morgan's influence over some of the most powerful commercial banks of the country, his attitude was important, of course, in the field of commercial banking. It was clearly reflected in Henry P. Davison's thinking.[16] James Stillman, the president of the National City Bank, who in the early 1900's was rather close to Morgan, thought along very much the same lines. In 1904 he gave an address of welcome to the annual meeting of the American Bankers Association, in which he stressed that the "deeper significance" of those meetings lay in the "spirit of cooperation which [was] being nurtured" at these occasions. He admonished the bankers to learn from the great progress which industry had made in "harmonizing divergent interests" and "in the greater appreciation of the rights of competitors." In the field of finance, as he pointed out, "there [was] not yet such general recognition of the value of cooperation," not sufficient understanding "for the great economic value of cooperation" through excluding that "waste which follows unintelligent competition."[17] Among the commercial bankers, the clearing house leaders were usually exponents of what was for them the most important aspect of "cooperation," namely, the setting of uniform rates for services rendered. This type of "cooperation" will be treated later in detail.[18]

To the extent that belief in "cooperation" grew, that in competition declined. As early as 1896 a statement was made before the American Bankers Association by the vice-president of the National Bank of the Republic of New York[19] (then the president of the association) that "competition in business [was] its life within well defined limits, but beyond those limits it [was] far from profitable and wise."[20] A year later James H. Eckels, then the Comptroller of the Currency and soon to become an influential Chicago banker, explained from the same platform:

> There is a point in competition between banking institutions which lies beyond the danger line and when touched invariably results in complete collapse... When [a bank] abandons, on the plea of being pressed by competitors, the gaining of the legitimate profits of banking...

it invites losses.[21]

It is certain that such views were held by many leading bankers of the period, but the majority, or at least very strong minorities, still stuck to the traditional concept of price competition as healthy or even God-ordained. Such a minority, for example, made it impossible in New York and elsewhere to do away with the paying of interest on demand deposits,[22] a practice generally considered unsound. In fact, it was this policy and that of par collections which the speakers above had in mind when complaining about the ill effects of competition. In Pittsburgh, as late as 1911, such a minority consisting of three banks, the Mellon, the Farmers Deposit National, and the Lincoln Banks, filed a bill in equity to prevent the carrying out of a resolution of the clearing house association establishing certain charges and penalties in case of violation.[23] Another similar conflict arose in Salt Lake City where in 1910 and the following years the National Copper Bank insisted on soliciting

business by underbidding the other banks.[24] This case is particularly interesting, because the latter refused to be enticed into following suit and entering into an old-fashioned price war. Instead they applied power, excluding the believer in price competition from the clearing house privileges and making life miserable and overhead high in an effort to whip him into line.

Bank customers profited from the competition among banks in various ways: without it, they would not have received interest on demand deposits, as mentioned before, and there would not have been collections at par of out-of-town items. Moreover keen competition among city banks for correspondents in smaller places permitted the latter to play off one city bank against another. "We love the country bankers," as a witty speaker expressed it before the American Bankers Association, "but they are the masters of the situation. We dance at their music and pay the piper." In fact by 1900 such accounts were "openly and ostentatiously" solicited by circulars, letters, and even traveling representatives of banks. Inducements were offered to the correspondents and other customers of competing banks to make them change their allegiance, and such aggressiveness was widely considered smart.[25] The overabundance of commercial paper and the keen competition among commercial paper houses contributed to upholding the competitive aspect of National Banking, in spite of the trend toward "cooperation" under the impact of a changing "climate of enterprise." So also did the new practice of "banking by mail" favored especially by Pittsburgh and Cleveland banks which at the same time believed in financial advertising.[26]

Unpleasant as was the competition among themselves to National Banks, much more galling was that provided by the same or a similar kind of institution, working under another and in a way more favorable legal set-up. During the years between 1882 and 1910 a keen rivalry existed between National Banks, on the one side, and state banks and trust companies, on the other; while state banks competed with savings banks and private bankers in the mortgage field. Trust Companies came to the fore as banking enterprises only after about 1890, as will later be described in more detail.[27] In that struggle with state banks and trust companies the National Banks were losing ground relatively all the time and for many years at an accelerating rate.[28] In the 1860's when note issue was still indispensable for banking they had taken over the business and by the end of that decade only about 300 state banks were left. But when shortly thereafter checks came to take the place of notes in ever widening areas new possibilities for state banks opened up. Their main chance lay for years in the clause of the National Bank Act which required a minimum capital of $50,000 ($25,000 after 1900). But new communities were often unable to carry a bank of that size and so in many cases they chose instead to establish a state bank. The inability of National Banks to extend mortgage credit and the lack of strong specialized mortgage banking added to the state banks' chances as also occasionally did lax laws and supervision.

Nevertheless state banks could not defeat the National Banking system. National Banks possessed greater prestige because of the stricter law under which they operated and because of the supervision by federal agents, and they were actually safer than state banks. This latter fact found expression in a smaller number of failures and better bankruptcy dividends. Moreover, as long as there were National Banks at all, other National Banks were needed in the reserve and central reserve cities to take care of the reserves;[29] and the right to issue notes, although not profitable, gave a slight advantage in at least some cases.

The following figures[30] give an idea of the result of the competition between National and state banks.

Year		Number	%	Capital	%
1882	National Banks	2,269	76.3	$ 483,100,000	81.0
	State Banks & Loan	704	23.7	113,361,931	19.0
	& Trust Companies				
	TOTAL	2,973	100.0	596,461,931	100.0
1892	National Banks	3,788	53.0	693,868,665	68.8
	State Banks & Loan	3,359	47.0	314,397,143	31.2
	& Trust Companies				
	TOTAL	7,147	100.0	1,008,265,808	100.0
1902	National Banks	4,535	43.8	701,465,554	60.8
	State Banks & Loan	5,814	56.2	453,056,168	39.2
	& Trust Companies				
	TOTAL	10,349	100.0	1,154,521,722	100.0

By 1900 the rising trust companies had become the National Banks' keenest competitors. In fact the latter felt they had a "trust company problem" on hand. Trust companies had been in existence ever since the 1820's, but originally they were not devised to be banking enterprises and so their early history is not within the scope of this work.[31] In the first half of the nineteenth century the trust business was usually combined with insurance underwriting, but a few banks, such as the Morris Canal and Banking Company,

were entitled by their charters to handle trusts. As a rule, legislators did not believe in this combination of functions, and with the notable exception of the Ohio Life Insurance and Trust Company which until 1857 conducted an extensive banking business, trust companies did not enter that field until late in the nineteenth century. In the 1880's, however, trust companies began to assume banking functions. In 1887 the Superintendent of the New York Banking Department reported to the legislature that trust companies, originally devised to insure property, to grant and buy annuities, to make contingent contracts, and to execute trusts, were being run in such a manner that there was practically no difference between their business and that of National and state banks. (It was at that period that they abandoned the taking of deposits on the "certificate of deposit plan" and to receive them subject to check instead.)[32] The relatively large demand for trust company charters in the state, so he explained, was due to the equivocal and unsettled terms thereof which gave trust companies not only the right to do a banking business for which they had not been set up, but even powers beyond those of regular banks.[33] The Pennsylvania Banking Department and its successor, the Commissioner of Banking, tried, although in vain, to stop the move of the trust companies toward assuming banking functions. In 1892 what was presumably the earliest attempt in the state could be nipped in the bud: the company in question agreed to desist and a court order was obtained as a warning. Nevertheless the battle was lost soon thereafter.[34]

The National Banks felt specifically aggrieved because they had to meet burdensome reserve requirements, while trust companies were not saddled with any such requirements until the 1900's,[35] and public opinion supported them in their quest for remedy. Moreover, the "trade mark" trust company attracted a considerable patronage among naive depositors, especially in New York and Philadelphia. Only in the business with correspondents and in the handling of out-of-town items were the big trust companies behind the National Banks of comparable size.[36]

The banks tried to meet that competition in various ways, New York providing the main battle ground. Through the medium of the New York Clearing House the big New York trust companies were to be forced to compete at least without unfair advantage. For that purpose the New York Clearing House Committee resolved in the early 1900's that all institutions clearing through that organization were bound after a certain date to hold the same reserves as were required from National Banks. Thereupon about 17 trust companies which were members of the New York Clearing House seem to have walked out in a body.[37] The breach was healed only after the crisis of 1907 when (in 1912[?]) they joined again after a reasonable compromise had been reached. Moreover the big bankers tried to return the blow and to invade the trust business. Henry P. Davison (1867-1922) was instrumental in devising a plan which led to the foundation of the Bankers Trust Company of New York. Davison had begun his banking career in Troy, New York, the town of his birth. He was the son of a dealer in farm implements, and the bank in which he started was owned by his mother's family. In 1888 he became a bookkeeper in a bank at Bridgeport, Connecticut, whence he transferred in 1893 to be a receiving teller of the new Astor Place Bank of New York. A year later he was taken as an assistant cashier into the Liberty National Bank founded by outstanding New York bankers such as Dumont Clarke, president of the American Exchange Bank, and on whose board were George F. Baker of the First National Bank and his close second, Harris C. Fahnestock, as well as Daniel G. Reid,[38] and Edmund Cogswell Converse. The latter, always willing to promote and push bright young men, took an interest in Davison who rose in the Liberty National Bank to the position of vice-president in 1900 and of president in 1901. In 1902 Baker brought him as a vice-president into the First National Bank. A few years later he was to become a Morgan partner. This was the man who developed the idea of fighting the trust companies by founding a strong one with a capital of $1,500,000, to which bankers all over the country could give their fiduciary business without fear that the enterprise would compete for their active accounts as the regular trust companies did. The plan aroused the greatest interest of and the

backing by outstanding bankers. In 1903 the Bankers Trust Company was brought into existence with Converse as the president and an unusually strong board of directors, among whom were Davison, Hepburn, Perkins (the Morgan partner), Robert Winsor (the head of Kidder, Peabody and Company), James G. Cannon, Albert H. Wiggin, and others.[39]

Besides state banks and trust companies, the express companies by organizing a money order business became in the 1890's and 1900's irksome competitors of both National and state banks, especially those located in the interior. Express company money orders became rather popular with the public so that they encroached on the exchange business of the banks. In this competition the express companies had advantages considered unfair by banks especially as long as the latter were hampered by a tax, levied because of the Spanish-American war. These express companies could rely on branches which were forbidden to National Banks and they possessed a mechanism which could transport money at little or no cost to themselves. When the 59th Congress put the express companies under the jurisdiction of the Interstate Commerce Commission the American Bankers Association lodged a complaint with the latter. The Association's lawyers pointed out that the express company money orders were in fact drafts or bills of exchange and that the express companies did not provide for the payment at the places on which the orders were drawn, but depended on banks to cash them. The latter in turn could not refuse to pay them lest they lose the good will of the public.[40] It will be shown below that the bankers fought back by organizing money-order and travellers-check plans of their own.[41]

It must be mentioned in passing that by 1910 the finance companies were also becoming very irksome to commercial banks. They themselves borrowed from the latter receiving cashiers' checks. These were passed on to their customers who were thereby enabled to disguise before their regular bank connection that they were selling their receivables.[42]

Generally speaking it was their limited power which kept National Banks at a disadvantage at a time "when the demands of the public for savings banks, trust companies, and other financial agencies... largely increased the field of banking operations, so that instead of being far and away the leaders in financial affairs they [were] struggling for place and [were] obliged to ally themselves with institutions of the trust company class to maintain a fair position with the leaders in the financial world." An expansion of powers on the part of the National Banks seemed to their officers to be urgent. Authorization of long term loans, especially long term loans secured by real estate, and of the acceptance and execution of trusts was wanted by National Banks so as to free them from the necessity of doing that business, if at all, through affiliates.[43]

After having studied the competitive situation of the 1890's and 1900's we shall be able to understand the trend toward expansion previously characterized from the historical point of view as one of the most important features of banking in that period. Actually throughout those decades National Banks continuously tried to expand the scope of their activities beyond traditional commercial banking. As late as 1897 Eckels, then the Comptroller, chided them for the departure from a strictly commercial business "in order to pay high interest." "Fixed loans and fixed investments [for example, were] the province of trust companies and savings institutions."[44] The banks thought otherwise. Vanderlip, for instance, felt that the enormous development of corporations warranted that departure.[45]

Thus some banks organized bond departments, for example, to handle their investments in various classes of bonds and other securities. The aggregate was considerable. Disregarding investments in U.S. bonds held as the basis for note issues, the National Banks held in 1909,

State, county, and municipal bonds	$155,811,290
Railroad bonds	342,525,242
Other public service bonds	151,999,513
All other American bonds	70,650,569
TOTAL	$720,986,614

(To this figure must be added about $20,000,000 of foreign securities and about $34,000,000 of stocks.)[46]

Bond departments, once established for the above purpose, were often developed by making them act for customers, and some of them went into full-fledged investment banking, as will be described later in detail.[47]

This brings us to the business which some banks did directly or indirectly with the stock exchange. It consisted of the following transactions: the use of stock exchange securities as collateral for discounts and personal loans; the financing of syndicates and individual syndicate participants by lending on new securities; the investment by banks in stock exchange securities; the financing of bond houses and stock brokers by loans on stock exchange collateral by other than call loans, i.e., loans for a few days under agreements to that effect; and finally the financing of stock speculation by lending on call.[48]

As is generally known, the call-loan market was the most important outlet for funds accumulating in New York, and a contemporary source estimated that by 1910 $14,000,000,000 were loaned in that market yearly. The same source estimated that one third of all loans made in New York were brokers' loans.[49] The repayment of call loans could be demanded at any time. In fact, however, according to the usage of the market, the so-called call loan was a one-day loan and if recalled before 1 o'clock the following day, was payable by 2:15 p.m. This usage should not be misunderstood, however, as implying that call loans were actually given for one day or for very few days only. If brokers' loans were well secured and the money market easy, call loans might run for weeks and even months before being called.

It has been described[50] that loans to brokers were originally made temporarily by the over-certification of checks and that such temporary loans were transformed later the same day into straight call or short term loans secured by collateral. During the period under investigation that practice had to be abandoned by National Banks because it became evident that checks could not be certified legally unless the amount in question was actually on deposit. This legal situation, however, did not obtain for trust companies and private banks which continued to follow the traditional practice of overcertification. In contrast, after the change in practice, brokers, borrowing from National Banks, received in the morning one-day unsecured loans on their personal notes and the amount in question was put to their credit. Thereupon their checks were certified and the rest of the daily routine remained unchanged: i.e., before the close of the business day the unsecured one-day loan was transformed into a collaterally secured call or short term loan.[51]

While a few call-loan transactions, especially on days which threatened to become hectic, might be concluded earlier, the "loan crowd" (on any one day 50 to 100 brokers charged with lending and borrowing, respectively) assembled traditionally by 11 o'clock at the loan desk of the New York stock exchange.[52] The large banks and banking houses which appeared as lenders each employed one broker, although in a few cases, as for instance in that of the Bankers Trust Company, several brokers were used. These were charged with placing whatever funds the principals wished to put out on call that day. Four or five brokers all told did most of the lending in the call-loan market which on busy days amounted to a total of forty or fifty million dollars. This statement implies that the same brokers represented several banks and banking houses. Only the National City Bank required the exclusive services of its broker.

Some brokers, such as Griesel and Rogers, acted for lenders as well as for borrowers; others worked for lenders only. The firm just mentioned averaged at least $10,000,000 worth of transactions a day, but its daily business reached at times the $25,000,000 mark for lenders and an additional $10,000,000 for borrowers. The lenders' brokers, as must be understood, dealt with other brokers charged with raising funds by their customers, not with the borrowers directly. Usually during the first few minutes after 11 o'clock several million dollars were lent and borrowed, respectively, whereupon very informally the average was figured and the "renewal rate" posted between 11 and 11:30. The banks and trust companies were informed immediately. Trading at the loan desk was done for several hours until about 3 o'clock in the afternoon.

When the market was normal, rates ranged between about 2 1/2 and 6 per cent, but, as is generally known, they might run much higher. But whatever they were, the National City Bank, the largest lender on call, followed the policy of not going above 6 per cent. Once the contract was concluded the borrower sent the collateral to the bank concerned where it was examined by the loan clerk and after having been approved by an officer the borrower received his money. The value of the collateral, as a rule, had to exceed the amount loaned by at least 10 points, i.e., 20 to 30 per cent; and there were a definite number of securities, namely 65 railroads and 35 industrials, which were eligible as the basis for call loans. Among them U.S. Steel common stock was preferred during the 1900's. Lenders on call were commercial banks, both New York and out-of-town institutions, and banking houses. When out-of-town banks lent they usually did so through their New York correspondents which in turn followed one of two practices. Either they announced the name of the lender, as did the Hanover and the Park Banks, the latter being the largest lender on call for out-of-town banks. Or they did not do so, as was the policy of the First National and the National City Banks. The National City Bank, the Chase National Bank, the National Bank of Commerce, and the Hanover National Bank were in this sequence the four largest lenders on call among the commercial banks. Kuhn, Loeb and Company, Goldman, Sachs and Company, and Speyer and Company took the lead in lending on call among the banking houses. Kuhn, Loeb and Company lent at times as much as any one of the above banks, namely whenever they had the temporary use of funds which were accumulating in the course of large investment banking transactions. The House of Morgan did not appear regularly as lender in the call-loan market, but helped out in time of stress.

Special attention must be drawn to the fact that it was the biggest investment bankers who as lenders dominated the call-loan market. Nothing need be said here to characterize as such the National City Bank, Kuhn, Loeb and Company, and the Speyers. But it must be remembered that the Chase National Bank was for years controlled by George F. Baker and later by the First Security Company. Moreover, the House of Morgan, Kuhn, Loeb and Company, and the security affiliate of the First National Bank, just mentioned, held interests in the National Bank of Commerce and were strongly represented on its board on which also sat the president and vice-president of the National City Bank.[53]

There were still other fields outside of commercial banking proper which National Banks wished to invade,[54] one being that of savings banking.[55] But before this latter business could be entered several vexing legal questions had to be cleared up, one of which was the question of whether National Banks could pay interest on deposits. It will be remembered that by 1860 high courts in Massachusetts and New York had held that banks were entitled to borrow money.[56] Nevertheless this right was questioned again as far as National Banks were concerned. In the 1880's several court decisions seemed to indicate that it was unlawful for National Banks to borrow money in order to lend it again and to receive deposits payable at fixed future dates with interest thereon. This interpretation of the law, if it had become the accepted one, would have implied that National Banks could take non-interest-bearing demand deposits only. Since it was common with state and private banks as well as National Banks to "purchase deposits" by paying interest, that trend of the jurisdiction threatened discrimination against National Banks;[57] but in the end it did not prevail.

It is obvious that this legal situation had a bearing on the question of whether or not National Banks could do a savings banking business; for there was no express authorization to that effect. Consequently James B. Forgan, president of the First National Bank of Chicago which under the pressure of competition was especially anxious to acquire such business, in the early 1900's founded an affiliate for that purpose among others.[58] Or to give another example, the Farmers' Deposit National Bank of Pittsburgh held 900 shares in the Farmers' Deposit Savings Bank of which further shares were held by directors under an agreement to transfer their stock to the National Bank in case of death or resignation. The directors of the latter were the directors of the savings bank.[59] By that time, however, the Comptroller of the Currency took the stand that since the right of National Banks to pay interest on deposits no longer was questioned, it was left to the boards of such banks to decide whether or not to conduct a savings or interest department.[60] But already prior to that decision some National Banks had vindicated that right for themselves and had gone ahead.[61] Immediately a new problem loomed: Should National and state banks taking savings deposits separate them from their commercial deposits or not? If the former policy was adopted it followed that assets in which savings deposits were invested must be kept separate also. Although there was some opposition, the separation of savings deposits from others and a segregation of assets was considered sound policy,[62] if commercial banks took time deposits at all.

Another new field which was invaded by banks with the help of affiliates was the trust business, although moves in that direction were restricted to the financial centers. The same holds true of attempts or at least desires of a few leading banks, especially in New York, to go into foreign banking. Such expansion of their activities would have necessitated the establishment of foreign branches and the authorization to accept or otherwise guarantee commercial paper.[63] In the less developed parts of the country National Banks would have liked to go into lending on mortgage.[64] In 1887 Trenholm, while the Comptroller of the Currency, favored an amendment to the National Bank Act establishing exceptions to the absolute prohibition of mortgage loans. In fact the introduction of mortgage bonds was changing the situation somewhat; but the law remained unchanged until the Federal Reserve System came into existence.[65]

Among the minor fields into which banks expanded or wished to expand was the lending to consumer-credit agencies. The First National Bank of Chicago under the influence of Arthur William Newton was a pioneer in this field entering it in the 1900's.[66] By that time, owing to the increased use of personal checks, banks were losing more and more of their domestic exchange business, and postal and express money orders made further inroads. Thus banks in some states (especially Missouri, Texas, and Georgia) with the help of their state bankers associations tried to organize a movement to "recapture" the money-order business. So important became the move that the American Bankers Association took hold of it. In the course of its endeavors it initiated a money-order system handled by the American Surety Company. In 1909 some 890 banks were using these money orders. In April of the same year the Association also put into effect a Travellers' Cheque plan, in the execution of which it cooperated with the Bankers Trust Company of New York. These travellers checks were sold by the banks in their own name and represented drafts drawn by the issuing bank on the Bankers Trust Company. The banks paid a charge of $10 for a thousand checks and remitted the face value whenever they actually sold them. Since banks generally agreed to cash these checks free of charge if issued in America the Bankers Trust Company waived any request for a commission. These checks were advertised widely both in the United States and in Europe.[67]

To sum up, America's banks before the end of the period were well under way toward what came to be called department-store banking in the 1920's.

The business resulting from correspondent relationships is, of course, a very old one, but it was developed during the period under investigation. Or, as F. Cyril James has it, an elaborate business was being built on the foundation of reserve holdings in larger financial centers. Banks in the latter handled the clearings and collections of their country correspondents. They sold them domestic, especially New York, and foreign exchange; they purchased bonds and commercial paper for them and performed the many functions which the parent office of a branch system was accustomed to fulfill. Last but not least the city correspondents would extend credit to the country or small-town bank in case of need, especially during seasonal stringencies, usually on the basis of a collaterally secured note. If a country bank wished to increase its note issues the city correspondent would purchase the bonds (on credit if necessary) and send them to Washington. When the notes received on that basis and transmitted to the country bank were no longer needed after the end of the season they were returned to the city correspondent. The latter placed them to the credit of the country correspondent's account thereby extinguishing the credit. In some cases loans were extended by permitting overdrafts and taking a collaterally secured certificate of deposit of the correspondent in question; or securities were bought from the correspondent with the understanding that they would be sold back to the latter if desired. This method, of course, approached rediscounting which itself took place rarely.[68] At times loans were extended to correspondents on the basis of personal notes of officers and/or directors.[69]

There were a few city banks which specialized in the business for correspondents. The Continental and Commercial National Bank of Chicago under George M. Reynolds led the parade: in 1912 it had 4,500 to 5,000 correspondents. In New York by that time the National Park Bank worked for about 4,200; while the Chase National Bank under Hepburn was developing that business so that the number of correspondents increased from 2,000 in 1899 to 3,198 in 1912. These figures reveal their full significance only when compared with the 589 correspondents of the First National Bank of New York, although the latter may have had large accounts only.[70] They should also be placed beside the 6,000 National Banks which then existed. One may ask if there was an oligopoly in that kind of business? As a matter of fact, in 1911 George M. Reynolds made the following statement: "I believe the money power now lies in the hands of a dozen men; and I plead guilty to being one, in the last analysis, of those men." In fact he reiterated this in 1911 and 1912 "fifty times." What he meant to say was: under the system of reserve holdings in the three central reserve cities which, as pointed out, was at the root of the correspondent relationships, there was "a natural concentration of... the power to issue credit against reserve, which they would carry, in the hands of a few men." This strong statement was made by Reynolds to indicate that he was aware of his responsibility.[71]

Thus the extension of credit by banks in the principal financial centers to banks in minor ones and in the country, formed the core of correspondent relationships, and inter-bank borrowing reached considerable proportions during the period under investigation. Nevertheless in the early years of the period the Comptrollers were not in favor of the borrowing by banks from other banks, and a sector of public opinion was also critical of the policy. On the other hand, the National Banks from the inception of the system took it for granted that inter-bank lending was a legitimate business; but in view of public and official opinion it was sometimes disguised, taking the form of loans to directors and officers of banks. As to the magnitude of inter-bank borrowings, it has been estimated that the average on any single day was below $9,000,000 between 1869 and 1882; that it rose to about $16,500,000 between 1883 and 1892 and to about $38,000,000 between 1893 and 1914.

So much can be said about the business which banks conducted between about 1882 and the outbreak of World War I. With regard to its profitability, one must distinguish between small banks in small places and the big ones, especially those in the central reserve cities of New York and Chicago. The chances of small banks for profit were limited, and there was a high death rate among them, as is generally known. That is to say, the death rate was high in comparison with that of banks in the advanced European countries and in Canada. Medium-sized banks, when well managed, probably made no more than what was common in business at the time.[72] In contrast the profits of some of the biggest banks were tremendous, especially of those which entered investment banking. For example, the First National Bank of New York and the National City Bank under George F. Baker and James Stillman, respectively, were huge money-making machines. The high profits which big city banks made came into the open in the 1900's when several of them founded affiliates under the so-called Chicago plan and paid up the latter's capital, amounting to several millions of dollars, by extra dividends out of accumulated surplus.[73] Such flowing over of profits was due to a policy widely adopted by successful big banks to keep their capital low, but to plough back profits, and to transform them into hidden reserves besides accumulating a considerable surplus. The First National Bank of New York, for example, carried its securities far below their real value. "We used to charge 4 per cent depreciation... and we gradually brought them down until we closed them out, and when we closed them out we carried it up to profit and loss."[74] That same bank kept its capital until 1902 at a $500,000 level while its surplus (disregarding the hidden reserves) amounted to $11,641,124 or 2,100 per cent of the capital. Then the latter was increased to $10,000,000 by a dividend of $9,500,000, i.e., a 1,950 per cent dividend, whereupon there still remained $3,415,000 in the surplus. Thereafter the dividends on the increased capital were 20 per cent each in 1902, 1903, and 1904; 21 1/4 per cent in 1905; 26 3/4 per cent in 1906; 32 per cent in 1907; 129 per cent in 1908; and finally 28 per cent in 1909 and 1910; and 38 and 33 per cent in 1911 and 1912, respectively. A really amazing record of profitability.[75] (The 100 per cent extra dividend of 1908 was made for the purpose of establishing a security affiliate, as mentioned before.) The Chase National Bank followed essentially the same policy. By 1900 its capital was $1,000,000. Shortly thereafter (in 1906) this was increased out of surplus to $5,000,000.[76] The policy of the Corn Exchange Bank, when increasing its capital in line with the necessities of the time, was a different one. By 1900 its capital was $1,000,000, dividends varying between 4 and 12 per cent, from 1890 on increasing up to 16 per cent. Moreover a surplus of about $5,600,000 was established. But this surplus was accumulated only partly from earnings, and partly from premiums received when selling new stock for the purpose of increasing the capital. In fact that part of the surplus which was the result of ploughed-back earnings amounted to about $2,400,000, while $3,220,000 had its origin in premiums.[77] Different as this policy was from that of the First and Chase National Banks it is equally indicative of the tremendous earning capacity of the big city banks of the period. Even a medium-sized bank, the Oriental Bank of New York (organized in 1853 and destroyed during the panic of 1907 through the inept and possibly selfish actions of some of the clearing house leaders) earned 25 to 30 per cent in the 1900's and paid 12 per cent dividends. Its shares sold in the market at $270 to $275.[78] From the point of view of the present research one needs to point out that highly efficient, if not creative, entrepreneurs were back of such profit records. The First National Bank was guided by George F. Baker and such assistants as Fahnestock and Garland, all of whom were among the leaders of modern American investment banking. The Chase National Bank was being developed by Hepburn; and the Corn Exchange Bank was presided over by William A. Nash, one of the pioneers of New York intra-city branch banking.

Of course the earning capacity of the leading banks was reflected in the quotations for bank stock and the following list, compiled at random, gives some idea of the situation.

to 54.75 in 1903.[80] There were a few National Banks which did not issue notes at all. Most of these non-issuing banks were in New York City, namely, the Chemical, Mechanics, and Merchants National Banks, and the National City and the National Park Banks. But in 1892 there were six more in other parts of the country.[81]

The profitability of average National Banks depended on their creating deposits or, seen from another angle, on their check business which developed rapidly. Official statistics of 1894 to which almost all the National Banks contributed showed that there were 1,929,340 depositors who commanded $1,647,017,129 deposits (the actual figures being slightly higher). State banks and trust companies had 1,436,638 depositors commanding $1,225,452,821 deposits. The two sets of figures are not strictly comparable since the latter contained a large percentage of time deposits. As to the deposits in National Banks we should like to know the percentages of lodged and created deposits. Questions to that effect were not asked and hardly could have been asked in view of what was the economic knowledge of the day. But the breakdown of the total as to the size of deposits permits certain conclusions. It is permissible to assume that most small deposits were lodged ones, while the largest category contained most of the

Quotations on Bank Stock
from
May issues of Commercial & Financial Chronicle
(Bank and Quotation Section)

	1905		1910	
	Bid	Ask	Bid	Ask
Chase National Bank, N.Y.	650		430	465
Merchants National Bank, N.Y.	175	185	175	181
Cleveland National Bank	112			105
First National Bank of Boston	262 3/8		400	
Commercial National Bank of Chicago	360	375	223	236
Girard National Bank (Philadelphia)	250	255		307 1/2[79]

As all contemporary sources indicate, note issue was not profitable because of the high price of bonds and the tax on issues. The evil was aggravated by the requirement that notes could be issued only up to 90 per cent of the face value of the bonds. When the limit was raised to 100 per cent profit chances hardly improved because issues came to be based on lower interest bonds. The unfavorable situation was reflected in the fact that the highest percentage of the permissible circulation ever issued was brought out in 1882, amounting to 81.6 per cent. The percentage dropped to 27.54 in 1892 and rose again

created deposits. There were in fact 1,724,077 depositors in National Banks whose total deposits amounting to $293,269,861 were each smaller than $1,000, and 22,738 depositors whose deposits amounting in all to $874,347,253 were each $10,000 and over.[82]

II

The great problem with which American banking was faced between 1880 and 1910 and which carried over into the post-World War I period was organizational in character. Banks had to be organized or reorganized, respectively, so as to be able to serve large-scale industry and transportation which were in the making.[83] Any one of three roads toward that goal could be taken: new large banks could be founded, existing banks could be made to grow by ploughing back profits[84] and/ or by issuing new securities, and last but not least existing banks could expand by consolidation. The last two methods could be, and actually were, combined in many cases. Hand in hand with the basic problem of growth went a second one, namely that of finding ways of organization whereby larger territories could be covered by strong, centrally located institutions. Both problems will be treated in the present and the following sub-chapters.

The need for growth was especially urgent since the National Bank Act forbade banks to lend more than one-tenth of their capital to any one borrower. Around 1900 the Comptrollers of the Currency[85] every so often recommended in their Reports an amendment to the act, permitting loans to any one borrower up to one-tenth of the resources of the lending bank. Since there was still at that time some confusion as to the character of deposits it is not quite clear what the various Comptrollers really had in mind, but ultimately the law was revised so as to limit loans to any one borrower to one-tenth of capital plus surplus. And yet the urge for larger banks continued. As late as 1912 there were only thirteen banks in the country whose capital and surplus were large enough to lend $1,000,000 or more to any one borrower and an additional forty to fifty who could so lend $500,000 and more. Of course, in the era of industrial combinations by way of trusts and holding companies, it was easy to evade such limitations by lending to several firms which were in fact part and parcel of one embracing concern.[86] To the extent that this was not done, large firms borrowed from several banks and entered the commercial paper market.

Those banks which grew and developed a large scale business had to change what had been their traditional internal organization. Two new departments were introduced: a transit department to deal with foreign checks and a credit department. The former will be discussed in detail in a later chapter.[87] The credit department, on the other hand, became necessary since as a rule borrowers were no longer intimately known to one or several of the directors. Moreover many of those borrowers were large-scale enterprises whose operations were not easily understood by outsiders. Consequently credit departments were established and the leader along the new ways was James G. Cannon[88]. Those credit departments

were to rate all applicants for loans on the basis of objective criteria. From then on large loans were given only if statements were regularly submitted; but it was discovered that not even such a policy protected the large lender. Consequently in many cases banks required that such statements as were submitted by applicants for loans must be audited by certified public accountants. Another set of problems was created by the spreading custom of buying commercial paper in the open market. Statements would be of no great help in that case as long as the total amount of paper floated by any one borrower remained unknown. As a remedy it was suggested that, like bonds, notes of open-market borrowers should be registered with a trust company and information as to the total amount outstanding be made available to banks. This movement did not succeed, however, partly because open-market borrowers often employed more than one or two brokers. Neither was a second suggestion adopted, namely, the proposal that the American Bankers Association establish a department to which all banks reported whatever paper they bought in the open market and which in turn upon request would inform potential lenders of the totals outstanding.[89]

The establishment of two new departments was, of course, not the only important change in the internal organization of banks when the growth of industrial enterprises demanded their increase in size and when a development in that direction became possible through telephones, typewriters, and stenographers. In the process of internal reorganization Charles M. McKay played a leading part. As the transit manager of the First National Bank of Chicago his achievement in developing the numerical classification of banks for clearing purposes facilitated the introduction of accounting and calculating machines and the invasion of banking by cheaper, female labor. (To be sure, as early as 1908, prior to McKay's feat, the Hibernia Bank and Trust Company of New Orleans had begun to use a numerical system for their transit letters.)[90] Such changes, however, were but late and conspicuous steps in a long process which had begun shortly after the Civil War. By that time the business of the larger banks had grown far beyond what had been known before and it became necessary to save time, labor, and expenses. This need led to a far-reaching modification of the methods by which clerical work was being done. As late as 1870 the ledger was still a record of all the details of the business, especially of the details of each account. The correspondents' remittance letters were, for example, copied into the ledger and all checks appeared to the debit, charged separately. In contrast, by 1900 the ledger in the advanced banks had become a condensed record which showed only the total of remittances from correspondents and the total of checks drawn by any one depositor. The details of each account would appear on monthly or semi-monthly statements prepared by clerks other than bookkeepers; and with the help of those statements the exchanges were proved. The monthly or semi-monthly statements were copied in letter presses, bound, and thereafter constituted the only record of the individual accounts. Parallel with this development, dealers' pass books were no longer balanced,[91] the intermediary books began to disappear, and the ledger was posted on the basis of the original papers. "Foreign," i.e., collection items, were treated correspondingly by the collection departments. Under the new system each correspondent bank and each depositor received a number which appeared in every incoming or outgoing letter, a number under which the account was known. This was the system which was further developed by McKay, as indicated above.[92]

Last but not least it should be mentioned in passing that the period under investigation experienced the first attempts at computing the exact cost of certain banking operations, such as the collection of out-of-town items,[93] or the keeping of individual accounts and the like. Again Cannon played a role in this progress.

The external growth of banks, to which we now turn, met with specific difficulties besides representing an innovation. The wording of the National Bank Act, as it was interpreted, made mergers rather cumbersome procedures. Three methods could be adopted: the absorbing bank could purchase the assets of the institution which it wished to take over, assuming at the same time its liabilities. It paid the shareholders of the latter the value of the assets minus the liabilities. Or it issued new stock to an amount equal to the stock of the bank to be liquidated. The new stock so issued was sold to the latter's stockholders whose consent had previously been obtained. A direct exchange of assets against stock, however, was not permissible: the shareholders of the absorbed banking association were paid in money, obtained by the sale of new stock of the absorbing bank to the same people who received that money. The shareholders of the liquidated bank thus came into the possession of their pro-rata share in the combination. In rare cases both banks went into liquidation and a new institution was created which acquired both businesses which were to be merged, the advantage being that the promoters of the combination were free to sell the new stock to whomever they saw fit. The Comptroller of 1902 who was in favor of consolida-

tions suggested an amendment under which National Banks would be permitted to merge in the way in which other enterprises could merge under the New York law. The latter permitted the directors of concerns to be merged, freely to negotiate and agree on the terms and conditions of the merger, after having been authorized to act by the stockholders of the respective corporations.

Bank mergers first attracted attention in the 1890's. In 1894, for example, consolidations were mentioned by the Comptroller of the Currency as having taken place in Louisville, Indianapolis, Denver, Dallas, and elsewhere. He considered them a means of restoring profitability to competing banks, but he had no premonition as to the importance and significance which the trend was to assume shortly thereafter.[94] By 1900 the consolidation movement among banks seems to have been in full swing. In 1902 alone 46 National Banks were reported as having been absorbed by other National Banks, and 11 additional ones by state banks and trust companies. Consolidations took place in that year in New York, Chicago, St. Louis (the central reserve cities), and in Albany, Boston, Baltimore, Cleveland, Detroit, Omaha, New Orleans, Newark, and Lowell.[95] The crisis of 1907 gave the movement a new impetus. Reliable statistics for the decade 1900-1909 are not available, but the total of bank mergers in that period all over the country has been estimated at 600 to 800.[96]

In order to gain an adequate picture and an understanding of the consolidations of the 1900's it seems necessary to distinguish between three kinds: one was the consolidation of small and medium-sized banks in smaller places. Such consolidations had little economic significance, except as indications of keen competition ending in cooperation and of the trend toward larger banks (some examples will be presented later). The second kind was consolidation for the purpose of acquiring branches and it can be observed especially in New York and California. Finally, the third kind consisted of consolidations of large banks in the financial centers of the country, such as New York and Chicago. While numerically by far not the largest group in the total, consolidations of that character possessed the greatest significance and marked only the beginning of the trend toward the giant bank which found its strongest expression in the 1920's.

It is this third class of consolidations with which the following paragraphs are mainly concerned. First of all, it seems to be of interest that in the 1900's the leaders in the consolidation movement of this character were investment bankers. The men who were then financing the building of trusts had as a second step to provide banks powerful enough to satisfy the current financial needs of those giants in industry and transportation which they had helped to bring into existence. On the other hand, in that process they had acquired the technical knowledge and organizational experience necessary to accomplish consolidations; and the technique which they had at the tips of their fingers could be applied to consolidating banks just as well as to consolidating steel works and railroads. Thus it is not surprising to find J.P. Morgan back of the most important segment of New York bank concentration both by mergers and interlocking directorates.

In New York, as elsewhere, the movement began by 1900. As early as 1897 the Third National Bank was absorbed by the National City Bank.[97] J. P. Morgan was at that time interested in the National Bank of Commerce,[98] the control of which he acquired in 1910. In 1900 this bank absorbed the National Union Bank and increased its capital from $5,000,000 to $10,000,000. The National Bank of Commerce thus enlarged merged in 1903 with the Western National Bank which had previously absorbed the National Bank of the United States (the former Hide and Leather National Bank). The result of these mergers was an institution with $25,000,000 capital and $10,000,000 surplus, representing no fewer than four older banks.[99] By that time (1901) Morgan's close friend George F. Baker absorbed the National Bank of the Republic into the First National Bank of New York.[100]

Another most important nucleus of mergers besides the National Bank of Commerce was the Bankers Trust Company which was also in the Morgan orbit. It will be remembered that it was founded in 1903. In 1911 and 1912, respectively, it absorbed the Mercantile and the Manhattan Trust Companies.[101] The former whose control had been acquired in 1908 by the Equitable Trust Company had been like the latter under the domination of the Equitable Life Assurance Society the controlling interest in which (i.e., 51 per cent of the stock) J. P. Morgan bought in 1909 from Thomas Fortune Ryan.[102] Under the New York legislation resulting from the Armstrong investigation, insurance companies had to divest themselves of their holdings in bank stock by 1911; but the time was later extended. Thus the absorption of the Mercantile Trust Company is easily understood and possibly in part also Morgan's acquisition of the Equitable control although that was never really explained. The two absorbed trust companies had been prosperous concerns and the rise of the Bankers Trust Company through

these mergers was simply spectacular. Within nine years the deposits increased from $5,000,000 to $168,000,000,[103] its capital from $1,000,000 to $10,000,000, its surplus from $500,000 to about $15,000,000 including undivided profits.

In the meantime the Guaranty Trust Company had also come under Morgan influence originally for the purpose of being merged into the Bankers Trust Company. When that plan was abandoned it started on a similar career of expansion by mergers. The enterprise had been founded in 1864 as the New York Guaranty and Indemnity Company (with a capital of $100,000 which was increased in 1865 to $2,000,000), and it was organized by Samuel D. Babcock (1822-1902). The latter was a native of Connecticut, trained in New York, and had worked his way up in the Peabody concern, being for some while a New York junior partner of George Peabody. In 1853 he organized in that city his own private banking firm, styled B. F. Babcock Brothers and Company with an affiliated house in Liverpool, B. F. Babcock and Company.[104] The charter of the Guaranty corporation of 1864 gave it very broad powers, and it started with lending on merchandise, stocks, and bonds and with the financing of international shipments. For reasons unknown the concern did not develop, however. Its capital was reduced, and its charter lay dormant. For fifty years Babcock was the chairman of the finance committee of the Mutual Life Insurance Company (besides being for seven years the president of the New York Chamber of Commerce and connected with numerous corporations including banks). At that time the president of the Mutual, in turn, was Richard A. McCurdy (1835-1916), a man of very dubious ethics and a typical Robber Baron who barely missed being put into jail. In 1891 McCurdy and Babcock took up the dormant charter and made a modern trust company out of the old Guaranty corporation whose name in 1896 was changed to Guaranty Trust Company. (It was one of the earliest banks to own a foreign branch.) Again, in 1910, when the insurance companies had to get rid of their investments in banks, 6,000 shares each of the Guaranty Trust Company were acquired from the Mutual and from Mrs. Harriman by two Morgan partners in association with others, and soon thereafter a process of expansion started. In 1910 the Morton Trust Company and the Fifth Avenue Trust Company were absorbed, the former itself having absorbed the State Trust Company in 1900. In 1912 the Standard Trust Company was also merged into the Guaranty Trust Company. Acting with the approval and frequently at the suggestion of J. P. Morgan, Henry P. Davison was the "engineer in chief" of those consolidations of the Bankers and Guaranty Trust Companies, the necessity for which he was one of the first to see. The result was banking units of the size needed for the times.[105]

While these consolidations were under way, one planned by George F. Baker was being abandoned.[106] The latter had acquired the control of the Chase National Bank with the idea of merging it ultimately into the First National Bank, but its business became too big and too valuable to do this and the control was sold. Albert H. Wiggin became its guiding spirit at that time.[107] But Baker seems to have merged into the First National Bank the Astor and the Sixth National Banks.[108] Of course, other mergers took place outside of the Morgan-Baker orbit too. The Atlantic Trust Company, for example, merged with the Metropolitan Trust Company, Benjamin Strong becoming the secretary of the enlarged institution. Before long, Strong became connected with the Bankers Trust Company and began to rise in the Morgan sphere of influence.[109] Moreover, the Gallatin National Bank was absorbed in 1912 by the Hanover National Bank which by interlocking directorates was tied to the National City and First National Banks. The Irving National Bank merged in 1907 with the American Exchange National Bank (which also by interlocking directorates had some contact with the ruling clique) to form the Irving National Exchange Bank which in turn in 1912 absorbed the Mercantile Bank. Finally, the People's Trust Company of Brooklyn in 1905 absorbed the Wallabout Bank and in 1910 the Home Bank, both of Brooklyn.[110]

The mergers of the Corn Exchange Bank which took place during the same decade represent the distinctly different type of consolidations aiming at the acquisition of branches mentioned above. Consequently the number of mergers was larger and the units absorbed smaller. Among the institutions absorbed were the following banks: in 1896 the Empire State Bank; in 1899 the Astor Place, the Queens County, and the Hudson River Banks; in 1900 the Home Bank; in 1902 the Eleventh Ward Bank, the Mechanics and Traders Bank of Brooklyn, and the Union Square Bank of the City of New York; in 1913 the Mount Morris Bank; and finally in 1914 the Washington Trust Company of the City of New York.[111] William A. Nash and later Walter E. Frew were the builders of the enlarged Corn Exchange Bank. Of the same character was that set of consolidations by which the Fourteenth Street Bank which had once been under Morse control absorbed the Nineteenth and Twelfth Ward Banks, changing the name to Security Bank. James G. Cannon, president of the Fourth National Bank, and his friends had their hands in these consolidations which took place by 1911. The Fourteenth Street Bank had branches as did the banks taken over, so that a relatively good-sized branch bank with $1,000,000 capital and $250,000 surplus thus came into existence.[112] To be sure, in the end this type of merger also led to large-size banking, but to units of a different character, to be discussed later.

Parallel with these New York consolidations went combination by interlocking stock ownership and interlocking directorates, as is well known and as has been described often. Very detailed material is available, and will not be presented again except in broad outlines.[113] The following few highlights may suffice: J. P. Morgan and Company had 23 directorates in 13 banks and trust companies, namely, the Astor, Bankers, Guaranty, and New York Trust Companies; the Chemical, First, and Liberty National Banks; the National City Bank and the National Bank of Commerce. In Philadelphia, the Fourth, Franklin, and Philadelphia National Banks, as well as the Girard Trust Company had Morgan directors. The Morgan-controlled Bankers Trust Company, in turn, had directorships not only in many of these banking enterprises, but also in the Illinois Trust and Savings Bank of Chicago, and the Bank of the Manhattan Company, the Chase, the Chemical, the Corn Exchange, the Fourth, the Hanover, the Liberty, the Mechanics and Metals, and the National Park Banks and in the Equitable and the United States Mortgage and Trust Companies, all of New York. Altogether the Bankers' people held 59 directorships in 19 banks and trust companies. Turning to the Guaranty Trust Company, also Morgan-controlled, we find it represented in numerous of these same banking enterprises and in addition in the United States, Union, and the Farmers Loan and Trust Companies (68 directorships in 19 banks and trust companies).

George F. Baker's First National Bank, which had gone hand in hand with the House of Morgan since the 1870's and on whose board Morgan sat, had directorships in the United States, New York, Guaranty, Bankers, Astor, and the Farmers Loan and Trust Companies as well as in the Liberty, Hanover, Chemical, Chase National Banks and the National Bank of Commerce. It had directorships in 14 banking enterprises all told, if one includes the directorships in the Illinois Trust and the First Trust and Savings Banks and the First National Bank, all of Chicago. Finally the National City Bank, which under the guidance of James Stillman was by 1910 also cooperating with Morgan, had 32 directorships in 16 banks and trust companies; namely, in New York, in the Bank of the Manhattan Company, the Hanover National Bank, and the National Bank of Commerce, and in the Central, New York, United States, and the Farmers Loan and Trust Companies; in Chicago, in the Central Trust Company, the Continental and Commercial National Bank, the Continental and Commercial Trust and Savings Bank, and the Merchants Loan and Trust Company; in Pittsburgh and Washington, in two banks each, the Mellon and the Riggs National Banks among them. One could go on analyzing the situation with respect to the National Bank of Commerce, the Hanover and Chase National Banks, and the Astor and New York Trust Companies. But that seems unnecessary and we may conclude with the following presentation: J. P. Morgan and Company, the First National Bank, the National City Bank, and the Bankers and Guaranty Trust Companies, taken together, held 118 directorships in 34 banks and trust companies with total resources of $2,679,000,000. Or to look at it from another angle, New York commercial banking was to an overwhelming extent influenced if not controlled by three men, Morgan, Baker, and Stillman, the latter two being essentially investment bankers like Morgan, and not commercial bankers pure and simple. What "control" actually meant will be discussed later in detail.[114]

At the same time, whatever control insurance companies may have exerted over banks and trust companies by 1905 was being lost to the investment bankers. This holds true of the Mercantile Trust Company which the Equitable had to abandon, of the Guaranty Trust Company which slipped from the control of the Mutual, while both insurance companies had to sell large parts of their stockholdings in the National Bank of Commerce to George F. Baker and James Stillman, respectively.[115] There were more transactions of a similar character the details of which have not come to the attention of the author for, according to the Pujo Committee Report, stock of five of the largest trust companies of the country had been held by insurance companies. Those trust companies which Morgan merged into the Bankers and Guaranty Trust Companies are supposed to have been taken over from insurance companies.

The public, of course, was horrified when sensing and later learning[116] what was going on in big city banking. The mere fact of a "Money Trust Investigation" is indicative of public opinion, which, as usual, saw ghosts as well as realized the dangerous trends. The bankers themselves were not apologetic. On the contrary, they felt that "this cooperation, this concentration in New York is not only not a peril or a menace, but it is a benefit," a protection, as Henry P. Davison expressed it.[117] A "proper, strong, scientific

banking system" would make the problem disappear anyway, so he thought. Moreover, in line with the prevailing thinking of the time the bankers had a strange concept of their role in this process of banking concentration: The latter was (as they seem to have thought or at least pretended to think) "not due to the purposes and activities of men, but primarily to the operation of our antiquated banking system [i.e., an objective factor] which automatically compels interior banks to 'concentrate' in New York hundreds of millions of reserve funds; and next to the working of the economic laws which in every country create some one city as the great financial center."[118] That is to say, in their minds, Morgan, Baker, Stillman, and all the other dii minorum gentium were just exponents of the economic law. The author is inclined to consider them entirely honest in making such statements; and when they pointed out that New York did not have as many large banks as London, Berlin, and Paris, they were right, except that they probably counted the central banks.

There are not many documents in existence which permit as deep an insight into businessmen's thinking of a period as the Letter from J. P. Morgan and Company from which the above passages have been quoted. "Just as grain and cotton and manufactures are commodities," so the Letter explained, "subject to the unchanging laws of supply and demand, so in the same way money and credit are commodities subject to the same unvarying laws, but far more intensely. It follows therefore that such 'concentration' as exists in New York (except that caused by our archaic banking system...) is due simply to the law of demand and supply." Whoever in the Morgan firm wrote that memorandum contrasted with his own belief the one which prompted the Pujo Committee, "that for their own selfish ends certain men... [had] succeeded in transcending the laws of supply and demand (which operate all over the world) and in establishing new commercial laws." "We [the House of Morgan] venture to point out that since the beginning of organized industry and commerce ... men never yet have succeeded in overriding economic law; and further that such an achievement is impossible..." This Morgan way of thinking was based on "axioms which it seem[ed] almost idle to repeat." One of them was the belief that it was the public which entrusted the bankers with business influence and powers; and another that there was some sort of divine wisdom with that public which neither would let Congress fall into the hands of "rascals" nor the financial affairs of the country into those of a "a set of clever rogues."[119]

In Boston the outstanding leader in the consolidation movement was Robert Winsor, the senior partner of Kidder, Peabody and Company whose activities in the field of investment banking will be studied in some more detail. In 1898 he organized a powerful National Shawmut Bank with a capital of $3,000,000 by merging into that enterprise (which had existed for several decades) the Columbian, National Eagle, North, Hamilton, Market, Boston, Howard, and Revere National Banks and the Bank of North America, nine banks all told. Further expansion was brought about by acquiring in 1901 the National Bank of the Commonwealth, in 1902 the Third National Bank, in 1906 the National Exchange Bank, in 1908 the Republic National Bank, and in 1912 the Eliot National Bank, all of Boston. The result was a bank of $10,000,000 capital and more than $6,000,000 surplus. In merging into the National Shawmut Bank a large percentage of Boston's banking enterprise Winsor cooperated with his Harvard classmate, William Alexander Gaston (1859-1927), lawyer and son of a Massachusetts governor, who became a director and a member of the Executive Committee of the Bank. Incidentally, in 1902 Winsor consummated another consolidation in Boston, merging the Washington National Bank into the Suffolk National Bank. The latter in 1903 was merged into the Second National Bank which may mean one of two things. Either Winsor abandoned his original plans or at that time he had his hand in the Second National Bank of Boston also.[120]

The second important set of consolidations in Boston was the work of investment bankers, too, namely of Hornblower and Weeks, founded in 1888; (Lee, Higginson and Company may well have cooperated).[121] The leading man in the firm of Hornblower and Weeks was George Wingate Weeks (1860-1927). Born on a farm in the upper Connecticut Valley, Weeks had planned for a career in the navy. When that did not materialize, he became a surveyor. Henry Hornblower, upon the death of one of his partners and the retirement of his own father, took Weeks into his Boston banking and brokerage business which the latter was soon to develop.[122] Weeks became a director in the Massachusetts National Bank in 1895 and when that institution became involved in 1898 and 1899 in the general distrust following the failure of the Globe and Broadway National Banks of Boston, Hornblower and Weeks, with other capitalists, saw the Massachusetts Bank through. In 1900 Weeks became president of the latter. By that time his firm and its friends had bought their way into this bank as well as into the First National Bank so that in June 1903 a consolidation of both could be effected: the First National Bank

acquiring the Massachusetts National Bank, the latter's leading personnel taking over the consolidated enterprise. In 1903 this combination doing business as the First National Bank of Boston absorbed the National Bank of Redemption, then the fourth largest in the city, which in 1901 had itself absorbed the Shoe and Leather National Bank. (The National Bank of Redemption was the old Bank of Mutual Redemption which was discussed in the first volume of this work.) While Weeks conceived those consolidations and made them financially possible, Daniel Gould Wing (1868-1936) was the administrator who effected them. Born in Iowa, Wing began his career in the State National Bank in Lincoln, Nebraska, became the cashier of the American Exchange National Bank of the same city, and was appointed a National Bank examiner in 1897. In 1899 he became the receiver of the two bankrupt Boston banks mentioned above (Globe and Broadway National Banks), and his ability manifested in this capacity opened the way for his further rise to leadership. He became the vice-president of the Massachusetts National Bank under Weeks whom he succeeded and the president of the enlarged First National Bank.

Later in the same period, namely, in 1912, the Merchants National Bank of Boston absorbed the State National Bank of that city;[123] and there were also some mergers into the Old Colony Trust Company (incorporated in 1890). In 1910 the latter absorbed the City Trust Company (in business since 1902) which itself had previously taken over the Mercantile Trust Company. This enterprise, in turn, had merged earlier with the Massachusetts Loan and Trust Company and with the Bunker Hill National Bank. The latter had been merged, before its absorption, with the Monument National Bank. Finally in 1914 the Bay State Trust Company was consolidated with the Old Colony which thereby became the largest institution of the kind outside of New York City.[124] (The inactive Copley Trust Company had been acquired also.)

Boston's leading investment bankers, Lee, Higginson and Company and Kidder, Peabody and Company, are supposed to have interlocked 33 of 42 banks in Boston and to have linked with them an additional 42 banks and trust companies in 35 other municipalities. The Shawmut and First National Banks and the Old Colony Trust Company were in their orbit.[125] In contrast to the New York set-up those two firms of investment bankers held only relatively small amounts of the stock in the latter three enterprises. Nevertheless they were considered the dominant or at least the most potent force therein. (Probably the remainder of the stock was widely scattered.) They also had their hands in the important Boston National Bank of Commerce.

Consolidations in Chicago have been described in detail by F. Cyril James.[126] According to the latter the pioneer in the field was the American National Bank which was brought into existence in 1898 by the amalgamation of the National Bank of America and the American Exchange National Bank. The American National Bank, in turn, was absorbed in 1900 by the Corn Exchange National Bank which that same year acquired the Northwestern National Bank and slightly later the Merchants National Bank which the First National Bank had been expected to absorb. These mergers must be assigned to Ernest Alfred Hamill (1851-1927), the son of a doctor and a native of Indiana. Turning grain broker after a training in the wholesale hardware business he associated himself as early as 1889 with the Corn Exchange National Bank whose vice-president and treasurer he became in 1896 and 1905, respectively. From then on he was the guiding spirit of the bank.[127] A second center of consolidation was the Continental National Bank[128] which between 1896 and 1900 absorbed the Haymarket Produce Bank, the Globe National Bank, and the International Bank, its capital being increased by that process to $3,000,000. During an emergency in 1904 it took over the National Bank of North America which led to a further capital increase to $4,000,000. In 1909 and 1910 a third Chicago Bank entered the road of external growth, the Commercial National Bank. For several years it had been presided over by James Herron Eckels (1858-1907), a native of Illinois, lawyer and politician, being one of the so-called gold-democrats. He was the Comptroller of the Currency from 1893-1897 and a prominent Chicago businessman thereafter.[129] His bank absorbed the Bankers National Bank and created an affiliate, the Commercial Trust and Savings Bank. At the same time the American Trust and Savings Bank took over the Mutual Bank. The two enlarged institutions, i.e., the Commercial National Bank and the American Trust and Savings Bank, were amalgamated in 1910 with the Continental National Bank to form the Continental and Commercial National Bank (capital $20,000,000) with its affiliate the Continental and Commercial Trust and Savings Bank. In 1911 the trustees for the stockholders of the Continental and Commercial National Bank, who held in trust for the latter the shares of the affiliate, also purchased the stock of the Hibernian Banking Association. The presidency of the latter was assumed by the president of the Continental and Commercial National Bank. By 1912 this closely knit group of institutions had an aggregate capital of $30,000,000 and deposit liabilities in excess of $239,000,000, that is to say, the

mergers had led to a truly modern large-scale banking enterprise.

The head of the Continental National Bank to whom we must look as responsible for this remarkable achievement in organization was George M. Reynolds. Reynolds (1865-1940) was the son of an Iowa small town banker and one of three brothers, all bankers. One stayed on in Iowa country banking. The second prior to World War I was the president of the Des Moines National Bank in Des Moines, Iowa. (In 1913 he was president of the American Bankers Association.) The third, George M., forsook the presidency of the last-named bank in 1897 for a cashiership in the Continental National Bank of Chicago of which he became a vice-president in 1902 and the president in 1906. After the merger he transferred in the same capacity into the Continental and Commercial National Bank. (He was the president of the American Bankers Association in 1908.)[130]

In the meantime the First National Bank of Chicago under James B. Forgan's able leadership had developed into another big modern bank, although it did not quite reach the size of the Continental and Commercial group. In 1900 it absorbed the Union National Bank (headed by Forgan's brother David) which had previously taken in the Hide and Leather National Bank. In that case the deposit liabilities were taken over together with an appropriate portion of the assets, while the stockholders of the Union National Bank were paid off. In 1902 the Metropolitan National Bank was absorbed by the First National Bank through an exchange of stock. By 1910 capital and surplus of the latter amounted to $20,000,000 while the deposit liabilities of the bank and of its affiliate were $150,000,000 in the aggregate. Through these consolidations Forgan made the First National Bank of Chicago one of the top ranking American banks.

If one wishes to evaluate the figures here presented by comparing them with those representative of big New York banks, one must keep in mind that the capital of the Chicago giants was to a much larger extent employed in truly commercial transactions and to a much smaller one on the stock exchange and in the financing of security flotations.

Chicago consolidations were not confined to National Banks: the American Trust and Savings Bank (capital $1,000,000) absorbed the South Park Bank and the Federal Trust and Savings Bank, increasing its capital to $3,000,000. Charles G. Dawes, founder in 1902 of the $4,000,000 Central Trust Company of Illinois, took over the Commercial Savings Bank and the private banking house of Henry Siegel and Company. Finally the Chicago

Title and Trust Company (capital $1,500,000) absorbed the Security Title and Trust Company (itself the result of a merger of 1898) and the Title Guaranty and Trust Company, increasing its capital in this process to $5,000,000.

As has been pointed out before, consolidations were not restricted to the primary financial centers. Wherever they took place they were apt to create banks large enough and therefore better fit than before to serve the credit needs of an expanding industry. To be sure, this was not always their purpose (as will be shown forthwith in a particular case). We are informed, for example, about the development in the Twin Cities.[131] The Northwestern National Bank of Minneapolis assumed in 1908 the assets and liabilities of the National Bank of Commerce, increasing its capital to $2,000,000 and adding another million to its surplus. Later that same year it acquired the Swedish American National Bank, while in 1908 the Minnesota Loan and Trust Company was taken over as an affiliate under the "Chicago Plan." Expansion was financed by a special dividend and the capital increased from $2,000,000 to $3,000,000. It is not clear who was the leading personality in these consolidations. A few years later, in 1913, the First and Second National Banks of St. Paul were merged by James Jerome Hill who acquired the latter bank and then threatened to withdraw his patronage from the former in which he had held an interest without being able to become the sole owner. The threat sufficed, however, and the stockholders of the First National sold out so that the merger could be effected. In the same year, 1913, the First National Bank of Minneapolis in a complicated transaction acquired the Minneapolis Trust Company with which it had cooperated before.

Another of the smaller financial centers which experienced a wave of consolidations in the 1900's was New Orleans. It began in 1902/03 when the recently-founded Southern Trust and Banking Company consolidated with the Union National Bank (organized 1871, reorganized 1896, with a capital of $300,000) and the Hibernia National Bank (organized in 1902) to form the Hibernia Bank and Trust Company: that is to say, in the course of this consolidation two National Banks became state banks. This consolidation was followed on March 1, 1904 by one between the Algiers Savings Bank and the Interstate Trust and Banking Company, two young institutions established in 1901 and 1902, respectively. The former sold its assets to the latter whose vice-president was Solomon Wexler. He was probably an important force in some of the New Orleans

consolidations of the 1900's, and more will be said about him later.

In 1904 the movement seems to have reached a climax: the State Banking department reported that "consolidation and expansion seem[ed] to be the favorite program in New Orleans and upon the streets of our metropolis you [could] hear of nothing but mergers and rumors of mergers." In fact the Louisiana National Bank of 1866 (capital $500,000) was consolidated with the Canal Bank and Trust Company to form the Canal Louisiana Bank and Trust Company. (Incidentally, the Canal Bank was one of the city's old banking enterprises [founded in 1831] which had been reorganized in 1895 and transformed into a trust company in 1903.) Somewhat later (May, 1904) it absorbed the Provident Bank and Trust Company, thus becoming with its increased capital of $2,500,000 one of the city's outstanding commercial banks. Moreover in June, 1904, the Central Bank and Trust Company was organized by Wexler with a capital of $1,000,000 and a paid-up surplus of $500,000. Before it opened its doors for business it was consolidated with the Germania and the Whitney National Banks to form the Whitney-Central National Bank with a capital of $2,500,000. Thereby another strong financial institution was brought into existence. (The Whitney National Bank organized in 1883 had at the time of the merger a capital of $400,000 and a $975,000 surplus.) Finally, in December, 1904, the Commercial Trust and Savings Bank of 1902 (a branch bank) consolidated with the Germania Savings Bank and Trust Company (organized 1881, capital $100,000) hard hit by a successfully withstood run which had been instigated by an unjustified malicious newspaper article. The consolidated institution took the name of Commercial-Germania Trust and Savings Bank.

In 1906 the assets and liabilities of the Security Bank and Trust Company, a small bank of 1905, was taken over by the German-American National Bank which seems to have had or established later an affiliate, the German-American Savings Bank and Trust Company. The latter two banking enterprises consolidated on December 31, 1913 with the Canal Louisiana Bank and Trust Company which then reassumed its old firm name, Canal Bank and Trust Company. The new institution had a capital of $2,000,000 and a surplus of $400,000. In the same year the Whitney Central Trust and Savings Bank, an affiliate of the Whitney Central National Bank, founded in 1908, purchased the assets and paid the liabilities of the Third District Savings Bank and Trust Company. That is to say, the Whitney Central concern and the Canal Bank and Trust Company vied with each other in the career of mergers and, incidentally, went on doing so as late as 1919.

It is evident from the material here presented that by the policy of consolidations three New Orleans banks of $2-3,000,000 were brought into existence. This was obviously the capital then needed in New Orleans for running a large-scale modern and efficient banking business.[132] (Before the era of consolidations large banks in the city had usually a capital of about $500,000.) As indicated, Solomon Wexler may have been a driving force in the expansion of the Whitney-Central National Bank and its affiliated Whitney Central Trust and Savings Bank. Born in 1867 in Natchez, Mississippi, probably as the son of immigrants, he started as a clerk in a drygoods business and later was a traveling salesman, until in 1893 he transferred to New Orleans (J. Weis and Company). By 1900 he became connected with New Orleans banking, acting after 1904 as a vice-president and in 1914-1916 as the president of the Whitney-Central concern. He played a certain role, too, in the American Bankers Association.[133]

That one or several powerful personalities were back of each and every consolidation should now have been made clear. However the personal element not only played a role in that individual business leaders became exponents of bank consolidation, but also in another way. The growth of banks made it more and more difficult to find suitable executives and it became occasionally necessary to effect a merger in order to gain the services of an outstanding banker. This is true, for example, for the merger of 1899 of the Corn Exchange Bank with the Queens County Bank of Long Island, New York, the purpose of which was to draw Walter E. Frew into the former bank. In Boston, the National Bank of Redemption permitted its absorption in 1904 by the smaller First National Bank because it could find no suitable chief executive except Daniel Gould Wing, who was unwilling to leave the latter bank. In Chicago, finally, similar reasons played a role in the absorption in 1900 of the Union National Bank by the First National Bank whereby the former's president, David R. Forgan, became the ranking vice-president in the latter bank which was presided over by his brother, James B. Forgan.[134]

III

So much may be said about the trend toward establishing larger banks by way of consolidations. But in many cases more was needed than simply growth of an existing enterprise, namely territorial expansion. It became clear by 1900 that correspondent relationships, valuable as they were, were no proper solution of the problem in question. In many cases the country correspondents de facto controlled the city bank rather than vice versa;[135] and when they did not, the relationship was not sufficiently close to permit the establishment by powerful city banks of needed overall policies. To be sure, in some cases, as in Chicago, very extensive nets of correspondents with the concomitant holding of bankers' balances kept some leading banks from aiming at a change which others desired.[136] Two solutions were possible, branch banking on the one hand and chain or group banking on the other.

In fact in the first half of the nineteenth century America had been a country of branch banks rather than of unit banks, and as such had been advanced over every other country in the world, save perhaps Scotland. It has been described[137] how the branch feature came into the charter of the First Bank of the United States, and branches were actually established by that Bank; the branch organization of its successor, the Second Bank of the United States, has been studied also.[138] After these beginnings, branch banking spread to Massachusetts (1792), Pennsylvania (1793), Virginia (1804), Maryland (1804), Vermont (1806), Kentucky (1806), Tennessee (1807), Delaware (1807), North Carolina (1810), South Carolina (1812), Georgia (1815), Indiana (1816), Illinois (1821), Alabama (1823), Louisiana (1824), Connecticut (1824), Rhode Island (1830's), Missouri (1837), and Mississippi (1838).[139] (The Middle Western state banks with branches of the younger type are not considered in the above list because, in the opinion of the author, they represent group banking, rather than branch banking.)[140]

Of course branch banking did not gain equal importance in all the states enumerated above. In the Northern and Middle Atlantic states it never obtained a real foothold. This fact has been explained by a wider distribution of capital within that region, as compared with others where it was concentrated in a few commercial centers, and by the specific form of local government.[141] These explanations do not seem too satisfactory. But the fact remains that the State Bank of Vermont broke down, a failure which put an end to branch banking in that state. In Massachusetts where the branch feature was embodied in the charter of the Union Bank of Boston it did not spread. In Connecticut and Rhode Island the early attempts of banks at setting up agencies which might have developed into branches were nipped in the bud by the bank commissioners and the legislature, respectively. In Pennsylvania the Banks of

Pennsylvania and Philadelphia, authorized to establish branches, did not make full use of their right; and the Bank of North America and the Farmers and Mechanics Bank, existing at the same time, never tried to obtain the same privilege. Finally in Maryland branch banking never developed. The real explanation for this lack of interest may be found in certain contemporary material which shows that the establishment of branches was not profitable under conditions as they then prevailed in the region from the Canadian border to the Mason and Dixon line. According to a New York bank president writing in the 1810's,

> The establishment of branches in the country by city banks is... by no means advantageous for the latter. The deposits in the branches are inconsiderable and the money [i.e., the bank notes] they loan flows into the city and compels the parent banks, in order to adjust with other city banks which have no branches, to reduce their discounts.[142]

In contrast, where there was a monopolistic or semi-monopolistic state bank with branches or numerous branch banks, as in the Middle West and South, the situation was different; and it was in these regions that branch banking flourished between about 1820 and 1860. But even in those sections of the country there were remarkable differences. Branch banking experienced its greatest success in Virginia;[144] it was widespread in Louisiana; more or less successful in the other Southern states above-mentioned; but the Union Bank of Mississippi never made use of its right to establish branches. As to the Middle West, on the other hand, disregarding the state banks with branches of the younger type, only in Missouri was branch banking a real success.

A few figures will show the picture prior to the Civil War. According to investigations of the Comptroller of the Currency, in 1848 the United States possessed 27 branch banks located in 14 states operating 143 branches; while in 1860 there were 39 branch banks in 13 states operating 222 branches (figures which include the Middle Western state banks of the younger type).[145] Of still greater value is the statistical material compiled by Chapman and Westerfield.[146] It shows that in the 1830's and 1840's the total number of branches, fluctuating between 100 and 180 amounted to anywhere between 20 and 27 per cent of all plants in operation (varying between 400 and 725). The situation changed considerably in the 1850's when Free Banking started to conquer the nation. For historical reasons Free Banking was synonymous with unit banking and so the percentage of branches to all plants dropped steadily from 20.3 per cent (139 branches out of 685 banks in operation) in 1850 to 12.2 per cent (174 branches out of 1427 banks in operation) in 1861. This drop in percentage, as can be seen at first glance, took place regardless of the increase in the absolute number of branches.

When the South lost the Civil War and the North adopted in the National Banking system the principle of Free Banking (as developed in New York and spread to numerous other states) the United States turned into a country of unit banks. Only then did unit banking become one of the characteristic features of our national economy. Whatever were the merits or demerits of this kind of banking, one must concede that it fitted well into typical American thinking in the political sphere and into the stage of economic development reached between 1860 and 1890. As a matter of course, the unit bank was then considered a local institution, i.e., one locally financed and managed, drawing funds from local depositors, and using its financial resources for the development of local enterprise. Banking was widely considered a "local question." No need for regional integration through branch banking was felt up to about 1890, and the Comptrollers of the Currency interpreted the National Bank Act as forbidding branches by implication.[147]

By 1890 the climate started to change and big banks became interested in branch banking for the first time. Besides their general desire to expand their business they wished especially to tap the outlying communities (suburbs) of the metropolitan district in the center of which they were domiciled. Moreover they hoped to exploit the hinterland not yet sufficiently developed to carry efficient banks of its own. Undoubtedly better service at lower cost could be provided by branches of strong banks located in the financial centers. Last but not least, in connection with the development of industrial consolidations new problems of finance came up which could have been solved easily through branch banks. A characteristic concomitant of consolidations in industry was that local plants of trusts did not demand as much banking service for the financing of current needs as they had when still independent enterprises. This situation forced local banks into the call loan and the commercial paper markets, thus providing additional competition in financial centers. Such competition could have been met by absorbing aggressive local banks as branches or by fighting them in their home territory through branches.

While Scotch and English experience with branch banking had been common knowledge in America for decades, Canadian, German, and to a lesser extent French success with this type of banking only now came to be known. In 1877, 1886, and 1891 prominent Canadian bankers spoke before the American Bankers Association thereon; and in the last named year a Buffalo banker urged that this example be followed. Two years later, in the 1893 convention of the Association, Horace White argued for branch banking in the United States. In the meantime, in fact as early as 1887, W. L. Trenholm, then the Comptroller, had officially taken up the question. He had wished to rescind the clause in the National Currency Act of 1864 permitting state banks to join the national system while retaining their branches, if any.[148] On the other hand he had suggested that National Banks in large cities be permitted to establish city-wide branch systems.[149] In the 1890's, interest in the matter becoming widespread, as indicated, branch banking was officially recommended on various occasions. J. H. Eckels, the Comptroller, having conducted a survey of banking all over the world in 1895, had accumulated much material on the subject. On that basis he recommended[150] for small places not exceeding 1,000 inhabitants branch banking restricted to a commercial business. President Cleveland backed this proposal in a message of 1895; and both in that year and in 1896 it was taken up also by the Secretary of the Treasury, Carlisle.[151] At that moment branch banking was officially favored because the minimum capital requirement of $50,000 excluded National Banks from working in small communities. Thus another Comptroller, Charles G. Dawes, suggested in 1898 that branches be permitted in communities of less than 2,000 inhabitants; but, on the other hand, in contrast to Trenholm, he was against intra-city branch systems. (Incidentally, he was also for foreign and colonial branches of large banks.)[152]

Those who were then in favor of unrestricted branch banking hoped that if adopted it would stabilize the discount rates which in America were wildly fluctuating, while in the leading European countries they were rather stable.[153] Among them was Professor Laughlin, the author of the Report of the Indianapolis Monetary Convention of 1897 which recommended branch banking (under rules and regulations to be prescribed by the Comptroller with approval of the Secretary of the Treasury). The abortive so-called McCleary bill, embodying the recommendations of that report, contained clauses to this effect.[154]

Such keen and widespread interest in branch banking was, of course, reflected in the American Bankers Association which thoroughly discussed the pros and cons in the course of the conventions of 1898, 1899, and 1902.[155] Strong opposition made itself felt. In 1899 a speaker "simply" wanted to say: "If any political party fathers the plan of branch banking and carries it to conclusion, with the feeling in this country against monopolies, the result will be the doom of the country banker's individualism and the downfall of the party responsible for the law." And in 1902 Charles G. Dawes expressed his opinion in equally strong language, namely, that at a time when the whole country was agitated concerning the effects of trusts, there was no chance that Congress would approve branch banking. That is to say, the then most cogent arguments against branch banking were political ones. From the economic and business points of view nothing could be said against it; but amidst such political opposition nothing could be said for it that would prevail. It was undoubtedly good tactics for the big bankers to sidetrack the issue temporarily, as they did in the Currency Commission of the American Bankers Association. The smaller bankers, especially those in the back country, on the other hand, organized for defence. It was the undoubted efficiency of branch banking which frightened them.[156]

Thus in the 1900's the climate turned unfavorable again, all the more so since business was reviving; and Congress, officials, and public opinion in most cases took a stand against branch banking. Among the factors contributing to the change was the amendment to the National Bank Act permitting National Banks to be established in small communities with a minimum capital of $25,000. This measure took care of certain complaints leveled against the existing system. Moreover it proved to have been a tactical error for the proponents of reform[157] to have tied together asset currency and branch banking, a combination which represented more than the public was able to digest.[158] The Report of 1902[159] of the Comptroller of the Currency and an opinion of the U.S. Attorney General in 1911 are indicative of the then prevailing official hostility.[160] But the issue was by no means dead. James B. Forgan, the Scotsman with Scottish training and Canadian experience, was the protagonist of branch banking in the 1900's;[161] while in 1908 Woodrow Wilson, then still the president of Princeton University, recommended it in a speech before a bankers' convention.[162]

It has been mentioned that the legal situation with regard to branch banking was not explicit. The National Bank Act was thought by implication to forbid National Banks to establish branches; and when there was silence in state laws on this point it was interpreted in many parts of the country as a prohibition.[163]

Regardless of such an unfavorable set-up on the national scene and in many of the states,[164] in at least some of them the basis was being laid for successful and comparatively extensive branch banking systems in the 1900's. These states were Michigan, New York, and California.[165] In the former two, city-wide branch systems were being developed before the period closed; in the latter, state-wide branch systems were being initiated. In Michigan[166] branches were established by a few banks as early as the 1880's and in 1909 the state's attorney general ruled that banks could set up agencies in the cities or towns in which they were located for "receiving and paying out deposits and issuing exchange." In that year most of the Detroit banks had "outlying branches" and there were also a few branches in Grand Rapids. Undoubtedly the pioneers acted under Canadian influence, a case of contact migration.

In the meantime, in 1898, New York had abandoned the absolute prohibition of branch banking which had been in effect since 1844 by permitting branches in cities with more than 1,000,000 inhabitants. The law in question was passed on the suggestion and through the efforts of Richard Aldrich McCurdy, president of the Mutual Life Insurance Company.[167] The first to see the opportunities and to make use of the act was William A. Nash, president of the Corn Exchange Bank. Nash (1840-1922) who had entered the employ of the Corn Exchange Bank in 1855 had risen to become its cashier in 1872 and its president in 1883. As early as 1899 he suggested to the board of his bank that it make use of the recent legal authorization; and after the plan had been sanctioned in February, 1899, at a stockholders' meeting, the Corn Exchange Bank was developed into a branch bank. In taking these steps, as he pointed out himself, Nash did not act under the influence of foreign examples. He had come to see the advantages of branch banking in 1893 while on the New York Clearing House Loan Committee that issued clearing house loan certificates to the members of the Association during the crisis. At that time the plight of the non-members of the Clearing House was especially difficult. They existed, so to speak, on sufferance only; unable to obtain direct help from the Clearing House they depended on such assistance as their correspondent member bank was willing to give. This, so Nash claimed, taught him a lesson and proved to him the advantages of providing banking facilities to the less active parts of the city through branches which although small would

be just as strong as the parent bank. Once the new policy was established Nash forged ahead: early in 1902 the Corn Exchange Bank owned ten branches (while five had been established by the Colonial and four by the New York Produce Banks). By the end of that year the Corn Exchange Bank had fourteen branches, seven of which had been set up by the acquisition of existing banks, while seven had been created "de novo," as it was to be called in the 1920's. In 1906 the number of state banks in New York City owning branches had increased to 23, controlling 91 branches in all. Thereafter prior to World War I the number of branches is supposed to have increased by about 10 every year.[168]

Nash's close second was Walter E. Frew. Under the former's influence he became the leading exponent of branch banking in New York City when he succeeded Nash as the president of the Corn Exchange Bank. (To be sure, earlier in his life he had been bitterly opposed thereto.) Frew (1864-1941), who had started his career in the office of the Wall-Street bankers, Shepherd Knapp and Company, whence he transferred to the Eleventh Ward Bank, rose in the Queens County Bank after 1889 until he became its president in 1895. His creative achievement in organizing one of the earliest country check clearing systems will be described later. As mentioned before, Nash drew him into the Corn Exchange Bank by acquiring the Queens County Bank. In contrast to Nash, Frew acted under European influence having studied branch banking in England, Scotland, and France.[169]

At least as important as the start of branch banking in New York was its beginning in California. California branch banking goes back to 1884, but it developed very slowly so that in 1905 there were only five branches operating in the whole state. In 1909, when a law giving statutory authority for state-wide branch banking was passed, California possessed 30 branches out of a total of 450 banks in the state system. The development remained slow for a few more years, but among the branches then existing and being established prior to World War I were the first plants of the Bank of Italy. The latter was the tool of Amadeo P. Giannini, the first American banker to build a state-wide branch banking system.

Giannini (1870-1949) was the son of poor Italian immigrants. His father operated a hotel and later an orchard in California, but was killed while Amadeo was still a child. The latter began his career in the produce business of his stepfather, once a teamster. After having made a good deal of money Giannini resigned as early as

1901 to engage in real estate speculation. By that time the legacy of his well-to-do father-in-law made him a director in a building and loan association. He withdrew from it because of differences of opinion with the other directors on matters of policy. In 1904 with a capital of $150,000 he opened in the Italian quarter of San Francisco the Italian Bank of California, soon rechristened Bank of Italy. It grew with extraordinary rapidity so that by 1912 its total assets amounted to $9,000,000. This growth is all the more impressive since in that short time it had had to weather two storms, the earthquake and the crisis of 1907. As early as the latter year, Giannini organized his first branch; three others followed in the San Francisco area between 1909 and 1912; while in 1913 he invaded Los Angeles, thereby developing his concern from a city-wide into a state-wide branch banking system. It is not quite clear how expansion was achieved in those early days; at least it is certain that Giannini at that time established the policy of buying existing banks rather than of establishing new branches. He and a clique close to him seems to have bought the stock in such banks as he wished to acquire, paying the stockholders in cash or Bank of Italy stock or both. If necessary he and his friends were financed by the Crocker National Bank on the basis of personal notes, with stock of the purchased bank pledged as collateral. The assets of the bank acquired were then sold to the Bank of Italy which absorbed its business by making it a branch.[170]

Giannini's initial rise is not sufficiently explained by merely pointing to his business acumen and to the fact that he was one of the first in California to perceive the opportunities of state-wide branch banking. (If he was really inspired by what he knew about Canadian banking, as his biographer claims, that fact remains to be documented.) Among the contributory reasons for his success may have been his ability as an extraordinarily shrewd trader who had won his spurs among the rough and ready Italian commission merchants in the San Francisco fruit and vegetable market. He certainly owed some of it to the undignified aggressiveness of the upstart who used personal solicitation of accounts and display advertising, both of which were considered unethical among the conservative bankers of the day.[171] Helpful, too, must have been his numerous contacts within the Italian colony. Last but not least it must be remembered that while those were the days of William Jennings Bryan and of a widespread distrust of bankers among the uneducated folk in the back country, here came a man who was one of them. He appealed to the national group to which he originally catered, spoke their language, and knew their ways. It is telling that prior to World War I the board of directors of the Bank of Italy consisted of Italians only, except for one lonely Irishman. In the mind of the common man of Italian extraction this bank must have appeared different from all other banks, especially as its policy was to serve the small businessman and since Giannini was an extraordinarily good showman.

Wherever branches were and remained strictly forbidden, geographical integration could be achieved by chain or group banking. These two closely related kinds of banking, if honestly conducted, typically covered wider areas within well defined regions, and to the knowledge of the author there are only a few exceptions to the rule: The most important one was James B. Forgan's establishment of two outlying banks in Chicago (the Security Bank of 1906 and the Second Security Bank of 1911). These banks must be interpreted as creative attempts at developing some sort of intra-city chain banking, corresponding to intra-city branch banking in states in which the latter was permitted. The capital of those two banks was subscribed partly locally and partly by directors and officers of the First National Bank. Its chief executive as the chairman of the boards of directors of those banks took an interest in their administration.[172] The achievement, hardly copied prior to World War I, may have been intended as a preparatory step to a city-wide branch system, if and when that were permitted in future.

For the purpose of distinguishing between the two closely related kinds of banking the author is going to follow a terminology widely adopted: He will consider as chain banking any number of banks controlled by a single man or several individuals; while the term group banking will be used whenever such control was institutionalized and exerted, for example, by a holding company.[173]

Both chain and group banking are much older in America than is usually recognized. Andrew Dexter was probably the one who built and abused the first chain of banks in the 1800's.[174] Nicholas Biddle, on the other hand, while president of the Bank of the United States of Pennsylvania in the late 1830's, organized what can be considered the first bank-group in this country. The institutions which he brought together were owned by that Bank.[175] A kind of group banking was what was practiced in the 1840's and 1850's by the Middle Western "state banks with branches" of the younger type, the organization of which has already been described in detail.[176] Finally, what were usually called "branches" of American private banks, existing between 1820 and 1910, were in fact semi-

independent enterprises with firm names of
their own, coordinated by one or several partners in both parent bank and branches. They
were managed, however, by resident partners
who usually were not interested in either the parent organization or in other branches. These
"branch" concerns of private bankers, in fact,
stand essentially between branch and chain banking. Such houses as the Browns of Baltimore,
the Allens, Clarks, and Cookes of Philadelphia,
the Drexel-Morgan concern, are prominent examples.[177] When the partners in such "branch"
systems at the same time controlled or at least
held an interest in commercial banks, as some
of them did (for example, the Clarks and the
Cookes), the chain character of the banking concern in question becomes even more evident.

In the 1850's George Smith, the private banker,
ended his career as the owner of a chain of banks,
as has been stressed;[178] and at the same time
Joel Aldrich Matteson, the businessman-politician
of Illinois, built up another chain. Matteson (1808-
1873), born in New York State as the son of a
well-to-do farmer, settled in Illinois in 1833 and
after a short career as a farmer went into business, becoming one of the contractors for the
Illinois and Michigan Canal. In the early 1840's
this very active man went into politics ultimately
to become for a few years (1852-1857) the governor of the state. He was a man of dubious ethics,
becoming notorious through his attempt at defrauding the state by stealing redeemed scrip
somehow and presenting it for redemption a
second time. Besides everything else that he did,
Matteson organized a chain of banks, at whose
center stood the State Bank of Illinois at Shawneetown and to which also belonged the Central Bank
of Joliet, the Bank of Bloomington, the Bank of
Quincy, and the Rhode Island Central Bank. The
notes of these banks were used to finance
Matteson's activities in Illinois railroading. The
chain did not survive the crisis of 1857.[179] Little
more than a decade later one Henry Greenebaum
built a chain of banks in Chicago. In the 1850's and
1860's he was the leading spirit of the private
banking house of Greenebaum Brothers, Chicago,
and in 1871 incorporated his banking enterprise
as the German National Bank of Chicago, of
which he became the president. Affiliated to
what was established as the parent organization,
Greenebaum and Company, Chicago, were also
the German Savings Bank in Chicago and Greenebaum Brothers and Company, New York. The
chain broke down in 1877 and the owner was indicted for embezzlement on several accounts.[180]

Modern chain banking, characterized by the
trend to develop into group banking, seems to have
started simultaneously in the Middle West, Northwest, and South. It has been pointed out correctly
that there is not much of a revolution (and not
much of a creative achievement) involved when a
man who owns the controlling interest in one bank
acquires also that in one or a few others located
at a small distance.[181] But when chains grew to
cover wider areas, new organizational problems
came into being; for geographical integration which
under the given circumstances could not be
achieved by branch banking was to be brought
about by building extensive chains of banks. In
this connection loose agglomerations of banks were
to be welded into embracing concerns. Thus in
the 1900's, almost imperceptibly, an innovation
was being brought into existence by creative enter-
preneurs. Shortly thereafter a further step was
being taken: while the first modern chains were
built around individuals using their own funds and
credit, later corporations were founded by the
owners or would-be owners of bank chains for
the purpose of holding the stock majority in those
banks which they controlled or wished to control.
Early holding companies in the field usually continued to capitalize on the personal prestige and
experience of an individual country banker. Then,
having easier access to the capital market, they
were able to expand further, and ultimately group
banking tended to replace chain banking after having developed out of it.

The Twin Cities are generally credited with
having become a center of chain and group banking in the 1900's. One of the early leaders in this
field was Adam Hannah, a native of Scotland who
came to this country in 1881. From 1885 on he
was engaged in the banking and farm loan business,
being the treasurer and later the president of the
Savings Bank of Minneapolis.[182] Backed by
Scottish capitalists whose funds he had previously
invested in farm loans, he organized the Adam
Hannah Company of Minneapolis and invested
some of its capital in country-bank stock.

By that time Floradora Hauser Wellcome was
entering the field. Wellcome (1858-1920) was a
native of Wisconsin and originally a practicing
physician. After having organized the Yellow
Medicine County Bank as his first banking venture,
he gradually relinquished his medical practice.
Besides holding for several years a directorship
in the National Bank of Commerce of Minneapolis,
he founded in 1903 (or 1904?) the Union Investment Company of that city which came to control
an increasing number of country banks, while at
the same time it engaged in farm loans.(Wellcome's
later activities are of no interest here.)[183] Shortly
thereafter one H. S. Helgerson organized the
Continental Securities Company in Minneapolis as

the center of a group of banks. He was a North Dakota banker who had wide backing in the state and probably over a larger region.

As a matter of fact, North Dakota seems to have played a special role as a cradle of modern chain banking. One David H. Beecher, born in 1852 in New York State as the son of a farmer, went in 1884 to Park River, North Dakota, after a start in the wholesale supply business in New York and in the wholesale and retail drug business in Minnesota. In cooperation with a partner he organized in North Dakota a small state bank which in 1885 merged into the First National Bank of Park River.[184] Other banks, such as the State Bank of Milton (established in 1889) or the Forest River State Bank of Forest River, were soon added; and in 1902, acting as their chief executive, he operated seven banks. By that time C. H. Ross of Minneapolis and Charles H. Davidson of Carrington, North Dakota, owned the majority of the stock in twelve banks and on top of that had organized the Farm Mortgage Loan and Trust Company in the last named city; in 1910 they controlled 22 banks.[185] Davidson, born in Minnesota in 1867, a man of Scotch-Irish descent, had been engaged in banking in that state earlier. By 1900 he made Carrington, North Dakota, his home, becoming one of the important figures in the state, interested in land, lumber, and elevator companies and in irrigation projects. The centers of his banking kingdom were the above-mentioned farm loan institution and the First National Bank of Carrington, whose president he was.[186]

Still further to the West, chain banking began by 1880 also, not reaching any importance, however, before the 1900's. One of the pioneers was a German immigrant, John P. Vollmer (1847-1916). Having started out in Idaho with a mercantile establishment and thereafter having gone into private banking, Vollmer founded the First National Bank in Walla Walla in 1878. In 1883 he founded a second bank, the First National Bank in Lewiston; but not until the 1900's did his chain grow, all his banks being located in Idaho.[187]

In the same decade (the 1900's) J. E. Cosgriff, president of the Continental National Bank of Salt Lake City, organized a chain of banks in Idaho, Utah, and Wyoming; and D. W. Standrod built another one centering in Idaho.[188] The latter (born in 1859 in Kentucky) came to Idaho in 1880 shortly after his graduation from a law school in the former state, and took up the practice of law in Nalad. He became the executive head of the First Savings Bank in Pocatello and with some partners was interested in eleven banks in the "inter-mountain country."[189] No biographical data are available for J. E. Cosgriff, but one wonders if there was some connection between him and Thomas Andrew Cosgriff (1854-1914) who was a bank-chain builder in Wyoming. Born in Vermont, the latter had started out in Burlington, but in 1877 migrated to Denver, Colorado, becoming a clerk in a country store. Five years later he went on to Carbon County, Wyoming, where he became an outstanding sheep raiser. He also established supply stores and banks along what was then the frontier. His first large banking venture was the First National Bank of Rawlins, purchased in 1896; in 1903 he acquired the First National Bank of Cheyenne, whose president he was until his death. In 1910 going back to Denver, Colorado, he organized there the Hamilton Bank of which he became the president. He was identified moreover with the First National Bank of Newcastle, the Rocksprings National Bank, and state banks in Saratoga, Wheville, Green River, Pine Bluff, GlenRock, and Guernsey, all in Wyoming.[190] Finally there existed in Spokane, Washington, the Union Securities Company, a holding company which by 1910 controlled about twenty-five country banks in the states of Washington and Idaho. (Chains are supposed to have been active also in Oregon.)[191]

In passing it may be mentioned that there is record of a bank group centering in Iowa. One James F. Toy of Sioux City was interested in 24 banks, of which the Farmers Loan and Trust Company of that city held the controlling interest.[192] Toy (1850-1937) was born in Wilmington, Delaware, the son of an immigrant from Northern Ireland, and a Quaker mother. He later (in 1867) moved to Iowa. There young Toy began his career in mercantile enterprises. He became identified with the banking interests of the state first by organizing the Storm Lake State Bank in 1877 in association with a firm of private bankers [?]. He became the cashier; but the following year withdrew to go into private banking. He bought an existing enterprise whose name was changed to the Banking House of James F. Toy which he was to develop. In 1881 he is supposed to have organized a bank in Alta, and later others in Sioux Rapids and Fonda thereby laying the foundation for a chain of banks soon to be reorganized as a group. In 1883 he founded the Farmers Loan and Trust Company (mentioned above) with a capital of $300,000, an enterprise which was transferred to Sioux City in 1889. Toy was an innovator. He set up a private telephone system between the early members of his chain, public telephones not existing as yet in the area. This is a noteworthy case which shows the direct connection between means of communication and business organization.

The group of banks expanded as follows (the list not being complete, however):

As the member banks' financial agent Witham received a remuneration from each, which is sup-

1887 - German Savings Bank, Remsen, Iowa.
1891 - First National Bank of Akron, Iowa (purchased).
1892 - First National Bank of Randolph, Nebraska (purchased).
1893 - First National Bank of Aurelia, Iowa (purchased).
1895 - First National Bank of Hudson, South Dakota (purchased).
1898 - First National Bank of Charter Oak, Iowa.
1901 - State Savings Bank of Hornick, Iowa (purchased).
1901 - German Savings Bank, Ricketts, Iowa (organized).
1901 - Sioux County Savings Bank, Maurice, Iowa (organized).
1902 - First National Bank of Emerson, Nebraska (purchased).
1903 - Iowa Trust and Savings Bank, Varina, Iowa (purchased).
1903 - First National Bank of Fonda, Iowa.
1905 - Citizens National Bank, Norfolk, Nebraska (purchased).
1906 - Dakota State Bank, Oldham, South Dakota (purchased).
1908 - Farmers State Bank, Osmond, Nebraska (purchased).
1909 - National Bank of Commerce, Sioux City, Iowa (purchased).[193]
1910 - Truesdale Savings Bank, Truesdale, Iowa (purchased).

It seems that the Toy National Incorporation served as the holding company of the group.

In the South, actually in Georgia, chain banking started also in the 1880's. Here the founder of the first chain of banks was William Stewart Witham (1853-1934), about whom almost nothing is known except that he was born in LaGrange, Georgia, and that he began his business career in New York in the millinery line.[194] Thence he returned to Georgia in 1886 with slender funds but with the idea of providing the state with country banking. Two years later he established his first bank in Jackson, Georgia, and meeting with immediate success acquired additional ones. Within ten years the organization had grown to about 25 banks; in 1906 it consisted of some seventy; in 1911 of about 125. By that time it was invading Florida. Witham himself was the financial agent and president of all the banks, the stockholders' meetings being so arranged that he could actually attend every one of them. Moreover he appeared in the role of the "guardian" of the banks, whatever this may have meant. By 1895 the Country Bank Security Company stood in the center of the organization; that is to say, Witham himself seeing the advantage of corporate control transformed the chain very early into a group of banks. The Country Bank Security Company was later replaced by the Bankers Financing Company which was owned and controlled by Witham. Between June 1, 1905 and May 30, 1906, for example, it handled funds totaling $6,800,000, while its capital was $650,000. It subscribed as a rule, three-fifths of the capital of each country-bank member (usually $25,000), while the remaining two-fifths was contributed locally.

posed to have amounted to $750 per annum by 1910. He appointed most of the cashiers and through them, and by way of the three-fifths interest held by the Country Bank Security Company (later the Bankers Financing Company, and still later the Bankers Trust Company) controlled them firmly. He determined their policy, issued instructions, and organized educational meetings for the cashiers who ran the units under the supervision of the local boards of directors. The latter decided on all loans save those for trifling sums. Whenever a member of the group had surplus funds it lent them on demand to the parent organization which in turn loaned them out to other members temporarily in need of capital. The parent organization's own capital served as a cushion in case of sudden withdrawals by the member-bank lender. The latter could demand the funds by letter or wire and immediately thereafter draw a check on the Bankers Financing Company. By 1905 the latter had secured the control of some small banks around New York City, usually having surplus funds available which could not be lent profitably in the New York area. These members served as lenders, i.e., as a current and secure source of capital to implement the policy just described. After 1903 there was also a Depositors Insurance Company (capital $250,000) attached to the group. Nothing is known about its work and procedures except that all members of the group insured their deposits with it. Nor is it known whether or not it gained any practical importance. But it was successfully used for advertising purposes and as an effective sales point to attract depositors. The establishment of the Depositors Insurance Company was at least a clever appraisal of the typical back-country thinking of a period in which the first attempts were made to set up deposit insurance systems in various Western and Southwestern states.[195]

Witham's close second was one W. D. Manley who succeeded the founder of the organization. Under his administration, after having expanded into several Southern States, it collapsed in 1926 having become tied up with the notorious Florida land boom.[196] But in pre-World War I days and under Witham's guidance the organization seems to have been reasonably well run, successful, and beneficial from the economic point of view.

Another Southern state which possessed a group of banks whose origin is of particular interest was Texas. When a state law of 1905 forbade branch banking, an existent branch bank was induced to convert its branches into separate banks, controlled by a trust company in Fort Worth.[197]

In the Northeastern and Middle Atlantic States, chain and group banking did not take root prior to World War I, but attempts in that direction are on record. In the 1900's New Hampshire possessed an unsuccessful chain of banks owned by one Eastman.[198] A remark of the Pennsylvania Commissioner of Banking in his Report for 1904[199] permits the conclusion that irresponsible chain banking was then being tried in this as well as in a neighboring state. It was nipped in the bud, however, as far as Pennsylvania was concerned.

The material presented at great length in the preceding paragraphs shows a distinct pattern. The very beginning of the modern chains of country banks goes back to the 1880's, but not until the 1900's did the chains experience real growth and a rise to importance. At the same time, there was a tendency to switch from chain to group banking, i.e., using corporations for holding control of the set of banks in question. As early as 1902 A. B. Hepburn pointed to holding companies and trust companies established with the avowed purpose of holding stock in different banks throughout the country.[200] The majority of the founders of modern chains and groups of country banks seem to have been born in the 1850's, a fact which should be viewed in the light of the theory of generations although that cannot be done at this point. The coincidence of birth dates is certainly not an accident. Where branch banking was prohibited, chain and group banking presented the creative solution for the urgent problem of geographical integration. This problem of geographical integration in turn resulted from technological development in the field of communication. It is telling that one of the pioneers of chain banking was one of the earliest

telephone users in his state. If this interpretation of chain and group banking is adopted, the rapid development of this type of banking is understandable. In that part of the country in which it took its firmest hold, i.e., in the Northwest, about 300 banks were included in chains and groups operated in 1916 from Minneapolis alone, while in 1920 there were in the Northwest 10 to 12 major "lines of banks" each controlling from 10 to 35 members, and 30 to 40 or more smaller ones controlling from 2 to 10.

What little information we possess seems to indicate that the policy and the organization of the early Northwestern "lines" were similar to those developed by Witham in Georgia. Part of the capital of the units was usually provided by local interests which were represented on the boards. The man in control, however, influenced the selection of the banks' employees and himself held the position of president in most, if not all, the units. The latter, while in close contact and under the supervision of the man or holding company in control, were independent of each other in the sounder "lines," whose members had either existed before and had been acquired, or were newly-founded institutions. There was obviously the trend to bind together "surplus banks" and others which were currently in need of funds.[201]

Fundamentally sound as was chain and group banking if practiced with a view to serving the back country, in financial centers these types of banking were indefensible (except when, as in Forgan's case, they were used as substitutes for intra-city branch banking). Chicago especially underwent very unpleasant experiences in this field. At almost the very moment (1887) when Witham was laying the foundation for his organization, Zimri Dwiggins[202] established the United States National Bank of Chicago. In 1891 it was reorganized as the Columbia National Bank. The next year Dwiggins acquired the control of the United States Loan and Trust Company, which was interested in the farm mortgage business. These two banks were financed by the flotation of $250,000 income bonds (out of a total of $500,000 that had been planned). Then ten small banks in Illinois and Indiana were acquired, each managed by one of the partners of Dwiggins, Starbuck and Company as its president. Moreover thirty additional banks were induced to designate the Columbia National Bank as their correspondent and reserve agent. This scheme, unsoundly financed, broke down with the collapse of the Columbia National Bank in 1893.[203]

Several years later John R. Walsh, a respected Chicago banker and politician, acquired the control of the Chicago National Bank, the Equitable Trust

Company, and the Home Savings Bank, all of Chicago. This small chain did not fail because of unsound financing, but because too much of its funds was tied up in Walsh-controlled enterprises other than banks and in loans not strictly business in character. The chain was bankrupt in 1905.[204] In 1909, however, Chicago possessed two bank chains, one consisting of two National and three state banks controlled by one William A. Tilden and another consisting of one National and three state banks controlled by one S. R. Flynn.[205]

In the same year of 1909 two politicians, by the names of Lorimer[206] and Munday, got a charter for the La Salle Street National Bank of Chicago. The former became its president, the latter vice-president. Clearing through one of the Chicago Clearing House members, it was examined by that organization and distrusted from the beginning. In 1912 it abandoned its national charter because of stricter regulations and control and assumed the status of a state bank under the title La Salle Street Trust and Savings Bank. After this reorganization it built a chain of banks in Chicago and Southern Illinois, twenty all told. Whatever capital could not be raised locally was contributed by the parent bank and withdrawn immediately after the initial examination by the state bank examiner. Disaster came in June, 1914.[207]

New York's experience with chain banking was just as unfortunate as Chicago's. Two financiers of the worst type were the first to build a chain of banks there, Charles Wyman Morse and F. Augustus Heinze. Morse (1856-1933), after success in the ice and lumber transportation business in Maine, went to Wall Street in 1897. In New York he founded the American Ice Company, a corrupt and overcapitalized promotion, and then turned to shipping. Actually he came close to monopolizing the coastwise shipping of the Atlantic Coast. Morse's partners in the banking ventures, mentioned above and carried on simultaneously with the former business, were Heinze and E. R. and O. F. Thomas, the two latter chief owners of the Mechanics and Traders and of the Consolidated Banks. Heinze (1869-1914), whose reputation was just as bad as Morse's, was a trained mining engineer who rose to fortune in Montana. In his contest with the Standard Oil group over some Amalgamated Copper mining properties he had used the most dishonorable methods and had made himself odious. The Morse-Heinze gang gained control of a number of moderate-sized National and state banks in the city. Heinze was the president of the Mercantile National Bank and Morse a director in seven banks, three of which he seems to have completely controlled. The Mercantile National Bank and the National Bank of North America were the most important ones in the chain. These banks, of course, were used to finance the schemes of the men in control, which was largely exerted on the basis of mere stockholding on margin. This is the chain whose breakdown in 1907 precipitated the panic of that year.[208]

IV

That the administrative mechanism of successful banks had to keep pace with their growth goes without saying; but, as will be shown, no perfect solution was found for the problems involved. By 1900 in the larger banks of the financial centers the presidents were modern full-fledged and highly-paid[209] chief executives; while in smaller ones in less important places they were rather general managers. But there were also banks in which the presidents were not even that. Successful small-town businessmen who had risen in trade or manufacturing and had founded banks as sources of credit for their own enterprises became the presidents thereof. In such cases that office signified mainly control, and the cashier ran the bank in question, as had been common many decades before. It is reasonable to assume that in at least some cases community leaders were elected presidents to give respectability to the bank. Such a policy would also have been in line with tradition.

The older generations of bankers active prior to 1900 usually considered the president of a bank as its general manager; and incidentally, the contemporaneous discussion as to whether banking was a profession or a trade paralleled a difference of opinion as to the true function of the president. Those who saw in the president the chief executive were prone to adopt the former point of view, those who considered him a general manager, the latter.[210] Among the bankers looking at the president as a general manager, one may cite B. B. Comegys.[211] He deemed it necessary for the president of a bank to be familiar with all its departments, their operations, and their interrelation. In the same spirit a contemporary speaker before an assembly of bankers described the duties of the man in charge of a bank as consisting in "the management of his officers and his office," "the management of his reserves," and "the management of loans and discounts." Comegys himself drew a different line: the president should leave the management of the clerks to the cashier. It was logical for Comegys to demand that the president not only be in harmony with his directors, but also to inform them on "every piece of paper discounted and every loan of money made," so that the board knew everything "that was done 'between boards'."

These statements are taken from a speech which Comegys made before the American Bankers Association, a speech which is interesting in other respects too, for one can assume that where a need is stressed there must actually be a lack. The bank president, according to Comegys, must be prepared for his job, but not necessarily through rising in a bank. Activities as a bank director or as an accountant were considered as equivalents. (The latter ties in with his concept of the president as a general manager.) He should be an educated man, able to speak and write correct English. (Such a need would certainly not have been stressed in any Western or Central European country at that time and the proposition speaks volumes.) The president was to be a "gentleman," a demand which rounds out the picture, a popular gentleman with an analytical mind, on good terms with bill brokers and private bankers, a man who would not speculate, who would not appropriate to himself commissions on transactions in which funds of his bank were involved. He was to keep in mind that banks were not just money-making machines, but had economic functions.[212] One can draw the conclusion that by 1900, at least in some cases, the president of a bank was an uneducated man, hardly able to speak correct English, on doubtful terms with his directors, hated by many people in the community, and a speculator of dubious ethics. Moreover he was all too often hard on his overworked and underpaid bank clerks some of whom were his superiors as men and professionals.[213] In many cases presidents and other bank officers had time-consuming outside interests and neglected those of the institution which was under their care. (In this context one should note the perennial problem of officers borrowing from their banks.[214]) It is, of course, impossible to estimate the percentage of all bank presidents to whom such an unfavorable picture applies; but in general the bankers were aware of the lack of respect for their trade, in contrast to the high esteem in which it was held in Europe, and of the hatred of broad strata of the population manifested beyond doubt in the McKinley campaign.[215] Since it was widely recognized "that the cashier or president [of a bank] had the fate of many of his customers wholly in his hands,"[216] the exhortation to higher ethics and better behavior was common. One speaker before the American Bankers Association warned his colleagues in the most unmistakable terms: "Let us avoid being stigmatized as a 'Society for Mutual Piracy'."[217] And another, the cashier of the North Western National Bank of Minneapolis, cried out:

> What we need in the banking business more than anything else is some... men with high ideas of honor and integrity who will give their entire attention to the business of running the bank in the interest not of themselves or a clique with whom they happen to be associated, but in the interest of the people who place their savings with them.[218]

As to the educational level of bank officers the following material is pertinent, for as late as 1895 it could be stressed that "from office boy to president probable promotions are often realized."[219] "Hundreds of bank clerks," so a report states with regard to potential recruits,[220] "are denied promotion because they write poor hands. Hundreds of clerks who write rapidly and legibly are promoted beyond [what they deserve] when measured by other standards." "If to the disgrace of poor penmanship there is added the vice of misspelled words and on top of it the crime of bad grammar, all exemplified in the letters which the bank clerk writes, how can he hope for promotion?" By 1890 some bankers were becoming aware of this most unfortunate situation, unfortunate both because of the low educational level of the personnel from which, in line with tradition, leading bankers were supposed to rise, and because of the lack of a yardstick by which to measure qualifications for advancement. Amidst considerable initial opposition the bankers themselves helped to remedy these defects by taking an interest in university schools of business administration[221] and in setting up courses for their clerks. These courses were organized through the newly-founded American Institute of Bank Clerks, which later became the American Institute of Banking.[222] It was modeled on the Institute of Bankers of England, except for its local chapters.[223]

Unsatisfactory as was the personnel situation in small and many medium-sized banks both in the top and lower echelons, at the head of the leading banks were businessmen of the highest caliber. Some had risen in banking, such as George F. Baker and his close seconds, Fahnestock and Garland, or James B. Forgan and his brother David, or James G. Cannon. It can be assumed that such men were more apt to take an interest in bank techniques than their colleagues who had entered banking originally from the outside.[224] Forgan, for example, devised in 1904 a new form of internal bank organization, assigning to individual officers the care and management of the accounts of all customers in specific lines of business.[225] He played an important part in developing bank examinations;[226] and he addressed bank clerks on what was to be considered a "good note."[227] Of course, chief executives who had not themselves risen in banks could not be expected to do this kind of thing. Such men were James Stillmann, originally a merchant; or Frank A. Vanderlip, his successor in the National City Bank, financial editor and assistant Secretary of the Treasury before becoming the bank's vice-president; or Edmund C. Converse (1849-1921) who, after a successful career in steel and as a trust builder (National Tube Company), became an important New York financier (president of the Liberty National Bank from 1903 to 1907, president of the Bankers Trust Company from 1903 to 1913, and president of the Astor Trust Company from 1907 to 1917). From the point of view of this research Converse is especially interesting, since he discovered and developed young banking talent, such men as Davison, Strong, and Prosser who became outstanding leaders in a later period beyond the scope of this volume.

It is noteworthy that the office of the Comptroller of the Currency, which was at the time a political office, was the training ground for several high-ranking bank presidents. One of these was John Jay Knox (1828-1892) who held minor positions in several banks before becoming the Comptroller in 1872 and who resigned in 1884 to take the presidency of the Bank of the Republic in New York. Another was Alonzo Barton Hepburn (1846-1922), New York legislator, Superintendent of the State Banking Department, independent operator in the real estate and lumber business, National Bank examiner in New York (1889-1892), Comptroller (1892-1893), and thereafter, president of the Third National Bank of New York (1893-1897), vice-president of the Chase National Bank (1899-1904), its president in 1904, its chairman of the board in 1911, and chairman of its advisory board in 1918. A third was Charles G. Dawes (born in 1865) who became Comptroller in 1898 and upon resigning in 1902 organized the Central Trust Company of Chicago which he guided and developed as its president. The erstwhile Comptrollers, James H. Eckels and Edward S. Lacey, also became Chicago bank presidents.[228] These details show a pattern and for that reason are presented.

Although far from being standardized, the status of the bank president was reasonably well understood and in fact easily to be understood. The opposite holds true with regard to the places which stockholders and directors filled in late nineteenth and early twentieth-century banking enterprises. The figment that the stockholder of a bank managed it through the board of directors was upheld in 1892. As late as 1905 a Supreme Court decision was handed down which accorded a bank stockholder the right to inspect the bank's books. This decision was based on the proposition that stockholders of corporations were the owners of the property whose agents the officers were, a totally unrealistic outlook for the time.[229] The judges neither understood the role of the stockholder in the modern corporation nor did they realize that contemporary banking enterprise was already much too complicated to be examined intelligently by a single stockholder, even though he was a businessman.

The examination problem was urgent throughout the period and had its bearing on the status of bank directors: Traditionally, the Comptrollers expected the directors to examine their banks and considered them derelict in their duty if they did not. In reality, however, as just explained, the directors were unable to do so, until James B. Forgan, the creative business leader with a thorough understanding of the banking business of his time, found the proper solution. About 1900 he hired for the First National Bank of Chicago an auditor who was officially the employee of the directors. From then on the books of the Bank were audited by a professional, and thereby the directors were protected.[230]

The position of the bank directors individually and collectively was really the crux of the organizational problems of the period. When it opened the then Comptroller of the Currency published a fairy tale. To be sure, he did not begin with the standard phrase, "once upon a time," nor did he tell his readers that what he considered the correct procedure had fifty years earlier been the much maligned organizational innovation of Nicholas Biddle. According to the Comptroller, National Banks usually adopted by-laws containing a clause by which an exchange committee was to be appointed by the board every six months. It had the power to discount and purchase bills and notes and to buy and sell bills of exchange; it was obligated to report at each regular meeting of the board. The latter under the by-laws also appointed every three months a committee to examine the bank, count its cash, compare assets and liabilities with the ledger entries, and to ascertain that the books were correctly kept. The purpose was to keep the directors informed on the discounts and to establish a check on cashiers, tellers, and bookkeepers. (One gets the impression that pretty dusty blank forms of these by-laws were lying in a certain drawer in the Comptroller's office and were crammed down the throat of the board of each and every new National Bank.) Pursuing his fairy tale the Comptroller described how the stockholders elected as directors [probably fair-haired] men of high character who held large amounts of stock in the bank so that they were personally interested in its prosperity and sound management. The depositors, again according to the tale, confided their funds to the bank because they believed that the directors would manage its affairs honestly and diligently and would employ honest and faithful "servants" for that purpose.[231]

A decade later the outlook in the Comptroller's office had hardly changed. The incumbent of 1891 remarked that, as a rule, banks prospered "just in proportion as their directors [were] intelligent and faithful," an absurd statement for the time, except perhaps in small places.[232] Under this concept the officers took care only of the details of the business and their selection was one of the foremost obligations of the board. That the president might control the directors did not occur to this Comptroller who drew the conclusion from Supreme Court decisions that the obligations, duties, and responsibilities of the directors were ill-defined in the law. According to him, "upon the directors... properly rest[ed] the responsibility of management" [sic!]. Any plan relieving them from their responsibility of management was "false in principle and would be found vicious in practice." The directors could not delegate their power, so the Comptroller of 1891 felt; they should not be allowed to plead ignorance when something went wrong, i.e., when losses were incurred through transactions not allowed by the National Bank Act. He felt the inattention and neglect of the directors must be overcome; they must be forced to do more than select officers and determine dividends, and they should even be punished for complete abdication of their powers. A year later it was pointed out that the directors gave direction to the business and controlled it, a seemingly reasonable statement tending to characterize the board as what we call a policy-making body. But at the same time in line with an outlived philosophy it was again claimed that the management of the banks was vested in the directors who acted through the officers, leaving only the details to the latter.[233] In this vein it went on: the Comptroller of 1896[234] stated that "directors should know whether the best bookkeeping methods were used in their banks, whether precautionary measures in the verifying of entries upon ledgers and passbooks [were] taken and whether employees from president to bookkeeper [were] engaged in speculative

enterprises and employing the bank's funds..." The Comptroller worried about the double delegation of powers, from the directors to the officers and from the officers to simple employees, which was becoming a matter of course in the large-scale banking corporation.

As late as 1905 the then Comptroller of the Currency placed the responsibility for bank management on the directors and felt that the chief executive should make to them full and complete reports, indicating all loans and important transactions. Notes and securities should be submitted for personal inspection (a simply absurd demand in view of the existence of ten or twenty-million-dollar banking enterprises). Loans to officers and directors should be scrutinized by the directors with great care. An examining committee should check the work of every clerk and officer. In line with that outlook a change in procedure was established in the Comptroller's office. The latter had formerly communicated only with bank officers. It was now to forward any letter containing severe criticism of a bank's administration to the directors requesting a formal acknowledgment.[235] As late as 1912 the Comptroller "insisted upon the boards of directors managing the National Banks,"[236] a figment without any parallel in reality as far as large-scale banking was concerned.

In view of the fact that legal concepts and what was actually possible no longer tallied, bank directors could in extreme cases, which were not too rare, become real dangers to their banks. Abusing their trusteeship for personal gain some directors recklessly speculated with other people's money and borrowed unwarranted sums upon insufficient security. The Comptroller of the Currency who pointed out these danger spots in the banking system as late as 1909, considered it one of his functions to foster a keener sense of responsibility among bank directors and to eliminate the incorrigibles from the control of banking institutions.[237]

Contemporary bankers, in contrast to the Comptrollers, held very different notions as to the function of directors. According to a description in 1899 by one of the guild, whenever a new bank was established a board of directors was selected from the different lines of trade "in order to keep track of all the paper that might be presented." A few years later, in the same vein Professor Sprague stressed as the main function of bank directors their acting as local informants. For this purpose bank boards were composed of successful men in various occupations, in the East merchants and manufacturers, in the West merchants and prosperous farmers.[238] But banks usually had difficulties in finding suitable directors, and suitable meant, according to contemporary sources, experienced businessmen with extensive businesses of their own who knew the credit rating of a great number of firms. That difficulty was due in part to the fact that large sectors of public opinion were hostile to the borrowing by directors from their own banks. The principle of selection described above worked well as long as all paper discounted or acquired was local and directors had an intimate knowledge of each party in their line. But the system had ceased to work in large banks by 1900 and so by that time the directors lost another one of their real functions.[239]

In view of such a divergence between the official attitude and the bankers' own outlook what can one expect to find in popular treatises? In a book of 1903 one can read that the "legal management of banks" was vested in "officers called directors."[240] They supervised the business and directed it. A booklet of 1907, however, while still repeating the traditional figment, at least pointed out that the delegation of power by the boards (in which the management was vested) was the real problem and that it ran the gamut between the officers being in full control of the business of banks and their having to execute routine duties only, while all important matters were discussed with the board. In the former case the boards had assumed the function of control, while abandoning that of management.[241]

In fact, in the tremendously large territory covered by the United States the various sections were in such different stages of the development by 1900 that no one picture could be drawn of bank boards which would fit equally the $25,000 state bank in some new Western state and the $20,000,000 bank in New York or Chicago. Even in banks of the same size the functions of the boards must have differed according to the stage of the development which the section had reached. There were undoubtedly some boards which actually performed the function of management and others in which the board members were informants on the credit standing of local applicants for loans. In other cases they may have had no real function whatsoever, the directors having been put into their positions by the man or men in control because they were good friends or pliant admirers. In the country as a whole there was undoubtedly less awareness of the possibility of boards acting as policy-making bodies than had been the case in the 1830's.[242]

What then were in the 1900's the functions of the boards of directors in the big city banks, especially those in New York or Chicago? To this question the author can give no precise answer. First of all, because of the process of

consolidations, the boards of some outstanding banks had up to fifty directors. (It seems to have been standard practice to retain the directors of the liquidated institution in the absorbing one. Undoubtedly good will was thus retained which might otherwise have been lost.) But of course, an assembly of fifty men can neither administer nor determine policy and in such cases executive committees on which officer-directors were strongly represented took over the affairs.[243] But even if the boards had no more than ten to fifteen members, a number considered sound at the time, their functions are not clear. That the directors were no longer informants on applicants for loans has been described earlier.[244] To repeat, few traces were found in sources of the period to indicate that there was any real understanding for the function of policy determination which is actually the appropriate one for modern boards of directors. But at least unconsciously this function must have been performed by some boards. The best contemporary statement to that effect seems the one made by the cashier of the Northwestern National Bank of Minneapolis. He stressed that the board of banks did not manage, that it "advised" and "consulted." It was the function of the officers to "carry out the policy outlined by the board of directors." If the former felt they could not, they must resign for "it is the directors to whom the depositors are looking for the safety of their funds."[245]

As in Biddle's time there certainly were important and unimportant directors. The former, who must be assumed to have been among those representing the groups in control of a bank, set the course (in some cases in an executive committee, as for example in the National Shawmut Bank of Boston). The full board merely sanctioned the course by routine action. In the era of interlocking directorates some of the directors probably had the function of looking out for peaceful solution of dangerous, potential frictions. Moreover, the boards as such were possibly platforms on which the members of certain ruling cliques met and discussed all sorts of business. The author would not be surprised if board meetings had certain social functions. What else can one expect, for example, from the boards of the Morgan-controlled Bankers and Guaranty Trust Companies, headed by a three-man voting trust each, the voting trustees being close to J. P. Morgan and appointing each and every director?[246] It is telling that Morgan himself could not or would not state what the functions of a bank director were.[247] "Call him a figure head if you like," was in the end all Morgan had to say. Probably directors in Morganized banks really had none to speak of, and existed mainly because they were required by law, gaining significance and importance only when there were struggles for or changes in control, or when executives were to be ousted or installed.

What directorships in many banks really signified was influence, although this does not necessarily imply the influence of the director himself. Even in Chicago in the 1890's a first-rate bank was in danger of losing its best customers if it was not willing to attach them to the bank by stock ownership which meant influence through directorship. This was the situation which Forgan faced as president of the First National Bank of that city and which he met by acceding to such desires.[248] As to the individual directors, there are innumerable possibilities. They might be the men in control or their true representatives or they might be mere friends and they might be relatives without any weight of their own, or outsiders grudgingly admitted in order to keep them happy and out of mischief or what seemed to be mischief from the point of view of the controlling group. For many of them directorships were highly desirable as strategical positions, for making contacts, for business advantages of all sorts, and for the prestige which went along with them.

The really important phenomenon is veiled in this confusing picture: power and functions assigned to the bank boards in the eighteenth and early nineteenth centuries had vanished in a long process. They had actually gone to the chief executives who according to legal lore were the servants of the boards. Or they had gone to controlling outsiders, such as insurance companies or investment bankers or local manufacturers who, outside of the bank concerned, determined its major policies and transmitted the decisions through their representatives on the boards or even directly to the officers. In the Morgan orbit, for example, consolidations, participation in security flotations, the investment in certain securities, the financing of syndicate securities, or the bolstering of the stock exchange through increased call loans, etc., were undoubtedly determined in the Morgan office for the National Bank of Commerce or the Bankers Trust Company and such decisions were final, a statement which does not imply that the interests of those banks were disregarded in making those decisions.

Moreover whenever the clearing houses assumed Kartell functions, as they did by setting exchange charges or determining uniform interest rates, policy determination also shifted from the individual banking enterprise and its functionaries (boards, officers) to outsiders. The members of the clearing house committee, on which the chief executive of a particular bank may or may not have had a seat, determined to a large extent the latter's price policy, and it had to abide by such decision. This aspect of clearing house activities was plainly seen by some bankers and even by outsiders.[249]

The conclusion which may be drawn from the material here presented can be formulated thus: In view of the rapid change to large-scale banking enterprise its administrative problems were satisfactorily solved only with regard to internal organization and the status of the chief executive. For the traditional top organ of the banking corporation, the board, and for its individual members no new fruitful functions had been found as yet. This lag parallels the lag in the development of business ethics remaining far behind what the tremendous responsibilities of oligopolies and giant concerns required. It was this lag which makes the era that of the Robber Barons who were represented among the bankers, albeit in their least objectionable personifications.

V

Public opinion and the bankers themselves were divided as to the merits of American banking. For some of them the National Banking system was "the best and most democratic of any age or any country."[250] But this and similar phrases were standardized to such an extent and one finds them so often that it is difficult to decide how seriously they are to be taken. Nevertheless it would be going too far to discount that outlook completely. For some of the bankers who had been extraordinarily successful under the existing conditions, the American Banking system was really well-nigh perfect as it was, as for instance, George F. Baker's opinion: "Take your national banking act. For 50 years it has been run the same and it has been run finely."[251] Or, to give another example, a businessman from Omaha, who had helped to organize one of the earliest National Banks in the West, thought that our system was "exactly adapted to American ideas and American manners and that it ha[d] accomplished for American commerce and American industry what no other system could ever have supplied for them or has ever supplied to any other country in the world."[252] In contrast, thinkers among the banking leaders and a large segment of public opinion became increasingly aware of the need for thorough-going reform.

In this struggle both the bankers and public opinion were handicapped by the tenacity with which outdated concepts survived and dominated the thinking of the time. One of them was the concentration of interest on note issues, a notion coming down from the time when banking in America had been synonymous therewith. Another was the belief that there was "a necessary and logical relation between a bank's capital and its circulation," rather than one between capital and deposits. "We have accepted without question or examination the doctrine that the note liabilities of a bank should be restricted to the amount of its paid capital or to some proportion less than its capital," so Horace White explained.[253] Again this idea was nothing less than an old superstition coming down from Mercantilist days but still finding expression in the reform bills of the 1890's and 1900's and so detracting attention from the essentials.

If one wants to bring contemporary criticism into the shortest possible formula one could say: bankers and public opinion realized that the American banking system was inelastic, a fact which found expression in seasonal stringencies and seasonal lack of currency on the one hand, and wildly fluctuating interest rates on the other. Moreover it lacked coherence. The so-called American banking system was no system at all, as one businessman expressed it.[254] Lack of elasticity and lack of coherence, so it was argued, resulted in severe recurrent panics. In comparison with the emphasis put on these two defects, the scattering and pyramiding of reserves and their concentration in New York in financially strong, but inappropriate, hands was usually neglected, although the last point was often stressed by the radicals of the day.

The discussion of the system's inelasticity, the beginnings of which have been described in an earlier chapter,[255] suffered from an over-emphasis on note issues. It was usually overlooked that it was possible by short-term loan transactions to draw gold into the country when needed and that notes were continuously losing ground to checks, that is to say, to elastic deposit money. But there remained enough reason for complaint. Inelasticity was implied in the principle of the bond-backed banknote; while elasticity of deposit currency, although mitigating the evil,[256] could not make it disappear. This was because of the undeveloped stage of large parts of the country in which only coin and currency were used. The National Bank Act, as it stood after 1882, contributed to the evil. Banks could reduce their outstanding note obligations only by paying to the Treasury in lawful money the full amount of the notes to be withdrawn. For six months thereafter they could not take out any currency at all. Under these circumstances the note supply could not expand or contract with the needs of trade. Moreover, as has been discussed, because of the high price of government bonds note-issue was not attractive from the business point of view.

While the discussion of inelasticity was marred by overemphasis of what was only one aspect of the total problem, the debate on the lack of coherence was made difficult because emotions came into play whenever that debate started. The period under investigation was still one of extreme individualism and belief in both laissez-faire and the blessings of competition, the latter supposed to be the best regulator of banking. If, however, one wanted to do away with the dangerous lack of coherence, which could not be denied, one had to give the American banking system a real master. A few men thought of developing the clearing houses so that they could assume leadership, as has been described in another context,[257] but actually the solution of the problem lay in central banking. The latter, however, was widely considered to be un-American, undemocratic, and not adapted to our republican institutions. The spectre of the Second Bank of the United States still haunted bankers and representatives of the people alike. But while it will be considered our task to present the development of the central bank idea between 1840 and about 1907, the introduction of the Federal Reserve system will not be taken up in this work. It has been described by able authors[258] and nothing new could be added here. For this reason this book leads only up to about 1910.

There were additional reasons why it was difficult to achieve reform: value judgments were involved which could not be reconciled and which divided the reformers into two camps. Conservatives considered security more important than elasticity and were unwilling to risk the former for the benefit of the latter. "We have the safest currency on earth," as a Mid-western savings-bank president proudly expressed it; or "our currency is sound beyond question and good beyond peradventure," to quote the chief executive of a National Bank.[259] That is to say, they stuck to the government-bond-backed banknote and in lieu of thorough-going reform suggested patchwork. The progressives, in contrast, wished to do away with the government-bond-backed banknote and to replace it by the asset note, also called credit currency. At this point both the main problems merged: many conservatives realized the advantages of asset notes, but only under strictly defined conditions as they prevailed elsewhere both in Europe and America, conditions which will be described shortly and which those conservatives abhorred. The progressives, on the other hand, were willing to adopt a credit currency without what the conservatives considered indispensable prerequisites for its soundness; those prerequisites being inacceptable to them also.

In a way the situation was similar to that which had prevailed between about 1820 and 1835 in that it was widely understood that our banking system was unsatisfactory. But while in the former period a great number of original and creative solutions were suggested and tried, the decades from 1882 through 1910 were remarkably sterile: old recipes were recommended over and over again and very little if anything was done, except some little patchwork. Only the end of the pre-World War I period brought a creative achievement, the introduction of the Federal Reserve System which, as already pointed out, is beyond the scope of this work.

By 1887 when bankers and other experts were asked what remedies they suggested, their proposals fell into the following categories: elimination of the note issue function of banks; additional inducements for issues by the removal of the banknote tax and by permitting issues up to the par value of the deposited bonds; provision by the United States of new low-interest-bearing bonds and the use of other securities besides United States bonds as the basis of issues; and, finally, the replacement of the government-bond-backed banknote by what was called "credit currency." The latter proposal, radical for the time, soon became the center of attention.

The discussion of reform started in earnest only after the crisis of 1893 had taught both the banks and the public a lesson. That something had to be done was clear, but what it was remained a moot question. This chapter will not survey in detail all the proposals which were broached.[260] The main ones can be classified as follows: currency reform, central banking, and deposit insurance.

For those who are familiar with typical businessmen's thinking and behavior it is not surprising that the great majority of the bankers stood aloof. If they participated at all in the debate, they usually promoted currency reform. Only very slowly did they warm up to the idea of central banking, as it was presented in the Aldrich plan; and nothing is more illuminating than the hostile attitude of the Annual Convention of 1913 of the American Bankers Association to the pending Federal Reserve Bank legislation.[261] Deposit insurance was anathema for most of them. As late as 1907 it was remarked at a meeting of the American Bankers Association that "indifference to currency reform [had been] doggedly displayed by bankers throughout the last twenty-five years" and that even in that year hardly 10

per cent had given the subject serious attention. In fact the important discussion at that meeting of the proposal of the Currency Commission of the Association seems to have been badly attended, most bankers whiling their time away on the Atlantic City board walk. On the other hand, traditionally Congress paid little attention to recommendations of the banking interests, so the bankers complained.[262] But that claim was true only if taken cum grano salis. In the 1900's such financial statesmen as Aldrich or Fowler listened, at least at times, to bankers' advice. Fowler, for example, framed the proposal of the Currency Commission of the American Bankers Association into a bill (H.R. 23017, 59th Congr. 2d sess.)[263] and the original Aldrich bill of an American central bank was the work of bankers.

Turning our attention first to currency reform we discover that its adherents were divided into two camps: those in the one wished a highly-taxed emergency currency,[264] those in the other a low-taxed credit currency.[265] But there were also schemes current which aimed at an untaxed emergency currency more or less kept in check by certain concomitant measures.[266] Leslie M. Shaw, the Secretary of the Treasury, seems to have had them in mind when speaking of an emergency currency "in the popular acceptation of the term." Consciously or not the exponents of an emergency currency seem to have looked at banknotes as different from deposits, a view which led to their objection to asset notes as inflationary.[267] Those who proposed a credit currency, in contrast, considered deposits and notes as essentially alike.[268] Moreover one suspects that the former belonged rather to an older, the latter to a younger group of coevals.

But there was a further difference in viewpoint. The adherents of a credit currency pure and simple took it for granted that it could be safely issued by any sound bank. The opponents, not denying the value of a credit currency when issued by central banks, as in England, Germany, and France, or large branch banks, as in Canada, considered it utterly dangerous if it were to be issued by about 6,000 unit banks.[269] The opponents of a credit currency usually thought in terms of early nineteenth-century experience; but it is significant that at least one of them suggested a "national reserve bank," i.e., an embryonic central bank as an alternative.[270] In consequence of that fundamental disagreement, all important reform proposals emanating from businessmen and especially bankers had to compromise and to combine credit currency and emergency currency in one and the same plan. This they did by distinguishing in various ways between a certain amount of credit notes, to be issued up to a fixed percentage of the banks' capital tax free or at least at a low tax and an additional amount of heavily-taxed credit notes to be issued up to a certain higher percentage thereof. This characteristic pertains to the three outstanding currency reform plans: the Baltimore Plan, the Plan of the Indianapolis Monetary Convention, and that of the Currency Commission of the American Bankers Association.[271] The three plans have one more feature in common: all of them recommended the establishment of a safety fund. That is to say, an old American device, which recently, in 1890, had been adopted by Canada, came to be reconsidered in this country, ultimately in vain, of course, as were all the plans with which it was coupled.[272]

The Baltimore Plan of 1893, the details of which are of no interest here, emanated from the bankers themselves. Information regarding the men who devised it will be presented shortly. In contrast, the Indianapolis Monetary Convention of 1897, although inspired by bankers, was rather a platform for business in general than one for bankers who, however, were represented. Charles C. Homer, for example, was sent by the Baltimore Board of Trade. Other bankers who can easily be identified among the delegates were R. J. Lowry of Atlanta (one-time president of the American Bankers Association), Henry Lee Higginson of Boston, John J. Mitchell of Chicago, George Foster Peabody of New York; and there were undoubtedly others. The last of the three outstanding proposals for currency reform pure and simple was, like the Baltimore Plan, the work of bankers acting in 1906 through the Currency Commission of the American Bankers Association. Being well in line with the Baltimore and Indianapolis suggestions it presented but a slight development of the ideas embodied therein. In the Currency Commission plan, for example, asset currency could be issued only by banks which had government-bond-backed banknotes outstanding, a feature which, as early as 1903, had been characterized by William B. Ridgely as most conservative and practical.[273] (Incidentally the plan was re-recommended in 1908.) In the meantime, however, the climate was changing. The disagreement between the exponents of a low-taxed credit currency and a high-taxed emergency currency lost some of its pungency. New fronts were being drawn and the contest came to rage on the question of a central bank or not. In this struggle many of the old adherents of an emergency currency joined the anti-central-bank forces developing and aiming at a program of their own giving the clearing house loan certificate legal and official status.[274]

F. Cyril James[275] severely criticized the bankers for their reform proposals of the 1890's and 1900's, and rightly so. He blamed them for overlooking the structural defects of the American banking system. He accused them of overstressing the inelasticity of note issues. Comptroller Ridgely, for example, made the statement in 1903 that in our system "all the elasticity" had to be supplied by banknotes.[276] Moreover, so James pointed out, the seasonal lack of notes in the 1900's was caused by the wild boom (inflation) of the decade which ultimately led to the panic of 1907. By being unduly impressed by the inelasticity of notes the bankers forgot entirely the urgent problem of reserves. Last but not least, Professor James showed that the theory which underlay the bankers' plans, namely, that note issues based on commercial paper could not act in an inflationary way, was obsolete, having already been revealed as fallacious.[277] That remarkable man and exponent of the bankers' plan of 1906, Forgan, became more and more doubtful the deeper he delved, and his disillusionment by 1908 explains his role in fostering the Aldrich plan but a few years later.

Prior to 1907 Alonzo Barton Hepburn stood out among the bankers fighting for currency reform. One could hardly go wrong in considering him, then the president of the Third National Bank of New York, as the man who, with Horace White and Charles Christopher Homer, did most for framing the Baltimore Plan of 1893. Hepburn was the chairman of a subcommittee of the executive council of the American Bankers Association, charged with preparing its Baltimore convention. In this capacity he suggested to the Baltimore Clearing House banks that they draft a currency reform plan. This was done by a committee of that Clearing House under the chairmanship of Homer (1847-1914). The latter, in Hepburn's opinion "one of the most competent bankers of the country," was the son of a prosperous businessman and immigrant from Germany, and after a college education had started his career in the provision business. In 1886 he became the vice-president and three years later the president of the Second National Bank of Baltimore, being also for many years the chairman of the Baltimore Clearing House Association. Once the plan was drafted by the gentlemen in Baltimore it was submitted by Homer to Hepburn, White, and others, redrafted, and in its final form presented to the 1893 Convention of the American Bankers Association by Homer, Hepburn, and a few other speakers.[278]

Hepburn retained his leadership in the bankers' movement toward reform after 1900; as late as 1906 he was made the chairman of the Currency Commission of the American Bankers Association.[279] But new men came to the fore among whom

James B. Forgan stands out. When that commission was established in 1906 Forgan had already risen so high that his appointment thereto appeared perfectly natural. He himself was reluctant to accept it. He was not satisfied with the geographical balance achieved in the membership of the commission which he had wished to make a panel of real experts. Moreover his ideas were fixed at that time and he had gone on record as to what he considered desirable, having published in 1903 a pamphlet in cooperation with the Chicago banker Joseph T. Talbert.[280] In the end, having accepted, his personality, his knowledge in the field, and his status as one of the country's biggest and greatest bankers gave him enough weight to swing the commission so that the recommendation of the Currency Commission of the American Bankers Association differed only slightly from Forgan's original plan of 1903.[281] Later, as indicated, Forgan was "one of the original advisers of Aldrich" and "exercised an important influence on shaping [the Aldrich] plan," his counsel being "continuously solicited in regard to its... modifications." Once the plan had been published it was logical for Forgan to endorse it enthusiastically and thereby contribute to its wide acceptance by the banking fraternity.[282]

While Forgan was still in the zenith of his career a group of younger bankers began to assume influence. Important among them was Frank A. Vanderlip, James Stillman's close second in the National City Bank of New York. As a former Chicago editor and Assistant Secretary of the Treasury under Lyman J. Gage he had qualified as an adviser in matters of banking reform. He acted in that capacity first as an appointee of the New York Chamber of Commerce to its committee on finance and currency of 1906, becoming also one of its two delegates to the meetings of the Currency Commission of the American Bankers Association. Then he was a member of the small group which drafted on Jekyll Island the Aldrich bill of 1910, the first bill to include the central banking feature.[283] The other members of the group were (besides A. Piatt Andrew, then Assistant Secretary of the Treasury) Paul M. Warburg, Schiff's partner in Kuhn, Loeb and Company who was soon to become instrumental in setting up the supporting National Citizens' League for the Promotion of a Sound Banking System,[284] Henry P. Davison, the Morgan partner,[285] and Benjamin Strong who rose to real importance only after the close of the period under investigation.[286]

This discussion has already brought us to the second group of main reform proposals, those

pertaining to central banking. In fact central banking had by no means been a dead issue between the 1840's and 1907 when it was again pushed into the foreground. The debate of the 1840's on the subject has been presented in this work in detail[287] and that presentation must form the point of departure for the study of the central banking idea as it developed in the following decades. The experience which the United States had gained in the field exerted both a positive and a negative influence. As to the latter, a grossly distorted concept dominated public opinion:[288] not what American central banking had been in Biddle's great years, but the picture which Jackson and his henchmen had drawn thereof, and the memory of William Jones's inefficiency and of Biddle's misdeeds at the time when a central bank was no longer in existence. Moreover the central bank concept did not fit into the intellectual climate of an era ardently believing in laissez-faire; and it must be remembered that in the 1840's its adherents in Britain had intended to destroy the Bank of England in its capacity as that country's central bank by making it just another large commercial bank. Last but not least, for many Americans central banking did not seem to harmonize with our "republican" institutions.[289] Under these circumstances the central bank idea came to react on many American businessmen, especially bankers, and politicians like a red rag on a bull, as Paul M. Warburg expressed it.[290] Such men even loved to apply the rabble-rousing terminology of Jackson's days: a speaker at the 1881 convention of the American Bankers Association, for example, posed the question whether for the third time we should "establish a monster regulator of the currency."[291] Undoubtedly there were many reasonable and moderate people who did not rely on bygone experiences or fall prey to emotional language and an appeal to misguided patriotism. But whatever they may have thought on the desirability of central banking in principle, it appeared politically unattainable or not feasible.[292]

While for the casual observer this negative line stands out, positive influence nurtured by what Americans came to learn about the working of the European central banks was continuously brought to bear on the minds of financiers, economists, and financially interested politicians. Had it not been so, the about-face of public opinion between 1907 and 1913 would not be understandable. There was actually no decade in which that positive influence did not make itself felt in a more or less subtle way: sometimes the need for the execution of certain central banking functions was pointed out; occasionally a regional central bank was recommended which fitted well into the stage of economic development which the country had reached by about 1880; and last but not least, full-fledged central banking was recommended. But this particular term cannot be expected in such recommendations. Between 1880 and 1900 the meaning of the term seems to have varied, connoting in the American language occasionally the parent office of a branch banking system.[293] The historian must be able to look through an awkward terminology to understand certain important sources.

As a matter of fact, there was never a complete break in the positive tradition of central banking. In December, 1857, for example, a governor of Kentucky stated in his message:[294] "Call it by what name you please... but let there be some fiscal agent which shall give us a national currency, [a fiscal agent] with power to regulate and restrain the local banks in their issues and avert... the ruinous vibrations and fluctuations in our trade and commerce." These words were written under the impact of the crisis of 1857. Among the reform proposals caused by this crisis there was actually one which aimed at an "enormously large bank."[295] Although no details have come to the attention of the author, it is safe to assume that, translated into modern language, it was a central bank that was desired. The same period brought forth also two essays, "The Financial Crisis" and "Currency, Banking and Credit," published anonymously in 1857 and 1858 in the New Englander. Their author felt, just as did the governor of Kentucky, that a banking system could not function without "centralization." Consequently he was for a "U.S. Treasury [Bank] or Bank of Issue" which would enjoy national confidence, determine what minimum circulation was required, and ensure universal convertibility of banknotes. But considering this goal unattainable he turned to a recommendation of what one could interpret as a regional "central bank" for New England, located in Boston (it is interesting that the modern term "central bank" was used here). That institution should sustain an agency in New York for the purpose of par redemption of New England notes in the city which was becoming the national financial center. It should be a bankers' bank controlled by the New England member banks which owned it. It should discount for their members only and act as what one would call today a lender of last resort. Deposits might be taken, however, from whomever offered them. Whether or not this bank was expected to have a note-issue monopoly is not clear;[296] but it was to issue notes backed by high specie reserves. What makes this proposal especially interesting is the idea of a regional central bank,

an idea which was to grow over the years until it found expression in the Federal Reserve System.

While the author of the article just quoted was planning a regional central bank, several of his contemporaries aimed at organizations to fulfill specific functions, now typically central banking functions. George Opdyke, for example, proposed in 1869 (?) that the National Banks of the City of New York set up a committee with power to establish a uniform discount rate, and to change it whenever in their judgment the general interests of commerce and finance demanded it. The banks, on the other hand, should be entitled to charge the set rate, a plan which implied that they should be freed from the restrictions imposed on them by the existing usury legislation.[297] In Opdyke's proposal discount policy was to emanate from a committee of New York bankers as from a central bank. Another modern central bank function was to be assumed by the Treasury, according to Opdyke's contemporary, Jay Cooke. He felt that it should "relieve the market from panic and... restore confidence and... keep things in place..."[298] He envisaged some kind of open-market policy. Finally, by 1875, the suggestion was made that the government become the ultimate holder of the country's coin reserve, again a central-bank function from the modern point of view.[299] The idea that a central reserve holder was necessary can be found repeatedly in the period: in 1880, for example, this matter was stressed in a speech before the American Bankers Association. It was suggested that there be established in New York a bureau of redemption in which each bank would keep as a reserve 15 per cent of its circulation. Any drain would act first on this central reserve and withdrawals therefrom would stand out as a danger signal to the banking system.[300]

In order to understand why from the 1850's on there was a tendency to look at central-bank functions singly rather than at the whole set performed by one institution wherever and whenever there was a central bank, one must remember what happened after the downfall of the Second Bank of the United States. The functions which this American central bank had fulfilled were either dropped or taken over by different agencies among which they were distributed more or less haphazardly as the political situation required and as businessmen saw chances for profit. The Sub-Treasury system became the country's fiscal agent. The Secretary of the Treasury, making use of the latter on the one hand,[301] and the clearing houses, on the other, came to act in emergencies but less efficiently than a central bank would have done. Finally, the New York banks were forced into the role of the country's central reserve holders. As early as

1860[302] Samuel Hooper saw this clearly when he described how the New York banks as a body held a position in relation to the commercial and financial interests of the country which resembled that of the Banks of England and of France in their respective countries. Therefore like the vaults of the latter central banks, those of the New York commercial banks should be the great depositories of specie on which rested the credit of the country. Hooper knew well, of course, that such was not the case. Later in the 1880's George S. Coe was well aware of the place which the New York banks had taken without their executives and directors being aware of the resultant responsibility. The fact that one of the central-bank functions previously performed by the Second Bank of the United States had fallen automatically into the hands of commercial banks, representing a quasi-body, is of great interest, because just that had been the goal while the Bank War was raging: some of Jackson's henchmen had proposed that state banks which would mutually guarantee each other and thereby represent a "body," to use Hooper's expression, should act as the country's fiscal agency. At the same time through private compacts with each other and the Treasury Department they would regulate the currency. But that plan did not materialize.[303]

In the 1870's there were at least two proposals in which full-fledged central banking was recommended. To be sure, when the problem was discussed terms other than "central bank" were used, such as "national clearing house that will be international in its operations,"[304] or exchequer,[305] or the like. One of the exponents of central banking in the period was Joseph C. Grubb, member of the Philadelphia Board of Trade, who for a period of years continuously harped on the subject without getting much response. He considered the First and Second Banks of the United States to be the antecedents of what was by 1870 an "overwhelming necessity." Disregarding the obsolete philosophy back of his proposal we find Grubb recommending that the Bank of England be copied in this country. As early as 1869 he submitted his suggestions to George S. Coe. The latter was reluctant to support them because, as he felt, we were "deficient in the class of men such [as] are in charge of the Bank of England," men who acted solely on sound principles without regard to "self-seeking operations." If we really had such men, so Coe thought, the politicians would keep them from assuming control of the suggested central bank, once it were established. But Coe concluded that the experience of other nations proved that a "central financial institution" was a requisite of modern civilization and

that we would have to go back to it sooner or later.[306]

By that time, one D. H. London,[307] offered a bill which also aimed at copying the Bank of England. The institution which he suggested was to be a privately-owned corporation, styled "The Governor and Managers of the Exchequer of the United States" with the chief office in New York and with numerous branches in all parts of the country. Its capital was to be paid up one-fourth in coin and three-fourths in legal tenders. The latter would be handed to the Treasury which would exchange them for bonds so that for all practical purposes the legal tenders would disappear. The "Exchequer" was to be the fiscal agent of the Federal Government with which it was to cooperate closely. It was to have a banking and an issue department in the mother bank in New York as well as in every branch. The latter departments would receive both the paid-in coin and the bonds, and would issue to the banking department banknotes at the ratio of one-fourth in coin and three-fourths in bonds for the first $200,000,000 of its notes, and at the ratio of one-half in coin and one-half in bonds for all further issues. The issue departments would be run by three commissioners appointed respectively by the President of the United States, the governor of the state in which the office was located, and the governor and managers of the latter. The banking departments, however, would be managed by electees of the shareholders. They would use the notes, received from the issue departments, in their regular banking business. The "Exchequer," according to this plan, would not have had an issue monopoly. National banks would have remained note issuers if they so desired, but in this case the total of their loans was to be limited to twice their capital. If they abandoned their issue privilege they would remain free as to the total amount they could lend. The author of the bill expected that many banks, especially those in New York, would cease to be banks of issue in order to avoid such legal limitation of their loans. Since notes were to be issued by the banking departments on the basis of short-term business paper the currency would become elastic.[308]

By far less articulate and reasonable than Grubb's and London's proposals was one discussed in the Bankers Magazine in 1875[309] according to which the National Banking system was to be more or less replaced by one gigantic "national bank" with a capital not exceeding $500,000,000 (sic!) with branches all over the country and certain exclusive privileges, note issue among them.

All the proposals so far discussed emanated from private individuals. But, interestingly enough, there is also one official plan on record which would de facto have established an embryonic central bank, although it appeared in the garb of a redemption agency. In 1868 and 1869 the Comptroller of the Currency recommended[310] that the National Banks establish a bankers' bank as their financial agency in New York. It was to act as their redemption agent and correspondent for all such business transactions as the banks would have in the country's financial center. It would automatically become a clearing house for all the banknotes of the United States and thereby keep them at par. But at the same time it was to be the central reserve holder of the banks which would thus be assured that their funds would not be used for Wall Street operations. The proposed institutions would be controlled by the member banks and managed by their electees and appointees; but this scheme did not materialize.

The author is unable to point to any important sources which would show the development of the central-bank idea between 1875 and 1895. It seems to have lain dormant. By 1895, however, interest awoke again. At that time Theodore Gilman (1841-1930), a Wall Street broker,[311] wanted to develop the clearing houses into quasi-central banks by incorporating them and putting them under federal supervision. They would be enabled thereby to give steadiness to our financial affairs, acting as balance wheels and enforcing concerted action among our banks. Such substitutes for central banks would be in harmony with our republican institutions and acceptable to those who would not stand for another commanding Bank of the United States or counterparts of the modern Banks of England or of France.[312]

Akin to Gilman's plan was one submitted by Joseph Henry Walker, Congressman from Massachusetts, and embodied in the H.R. bill 10,333 of May 13, 1898 which was developed from his earlier bill H.R. 171 of 1895. According to Walker's suggestion clearing houses were to be incorporated and entitled to create one "national clearing house" or several regional "national clearing houses." (From his wording his real intention does not become clear; see sec. 10 of the bill.) This national association or these national associations were to be entitled to buy securities from and sell them to clearing houses, and to loan and borrow. That is to say, they were obviously intended to be lenders of last resort as were central banks, besides performing their main function of being agents in the issue of an emergency currency.[313] The usury laws were not to be applicable and thus the new institution or institutions if brought into existence could have deliberately established a discount policy.

At the time when Gilman was promoting his proposal a plan was presented before the American Bankers Association to found a central bank with branches. It was to have a note-issue monopoly and to take over the gold reserves held by the federal government against the legal tenders which would be withdrawn. Its notes would be floated by rediscounting for the commercial banks of the country.[314] Transposed into modern terms, the suggested central bank was to be the ultimate reserve holder and the lender of last resort.

After 1900 there was not only an increase in the number of central-bank proposals, but the plans presented show also an increasing understanding of the problems involved. In 1901, for example, the railroad president A. B. Stickney stated bluntly that "a banking system for a great nation like the United States require[d] a central bank" with branches which would act as the financial agency of the government and as the central reserve holder of the national economy. That central bank was to be a bankers' bank.[315] Similar was a plan which Lyman J. Gage broached at that time, a "central or federated bank," a bankers' bank to replace the sub-treasury system.[316] In 1902 Joseph C. Hendrix, president of the National Bank of Commerce of New York, spoke of the lack of a "bank of ultimate reserve" (i.e., of a central bank) as a "glaring defect of our banking system."[317] Finally a few years later the scheme of a $50,000,000 bank in Wall Street was brought up. It was to serve the stock exchange and at the same time to act in many respects like the Bank of England, i.e., as a central bank, for example, by regulating the interest rate. Henry Clews fought this plan as being a revival of the Bank of the United States: that kind of institution would oppress the existing banks; and, as a matter of principle, copies of the Bank of England or of France did not belong in this country.[318] Through such preliminary debates in the late 1890's and early 1900's public opinion and bankers were being prepared for the moment when, after the crisis of 1907, central banking became the dominant issue of the day.

It is noteworthy, however, that according to several proposals cited above central banking was to be performed by a bankers' bank. This term has two different connotations: first, a bank working mainly with banks. In this sense it was stated in the first volume of this work that the First Bank of the United States was well advanced toward becoming a bankers' bank, while Nicholas Biddle did not see that the Second Bank of the United States having become a central bank should have become more or less of a bankers' bank also.[319] In the same sense big banks in the central reserve cities specializing in the business for correspondents have been called bankers' banks. But secondly, the term if used in a narrower sense connotes a bank owned exclusively by banks, such as our present Federal Reserve Banks. In this sense the bankers' bank seems to have been devised in America.

A bankers' bank in the narrower sense of the phrase was planned as early as 1815 by Maryland country banks and again in 1839 in New York when a bankers' bank was suggested for the purpose of note redemption.[320] Actually when the Bank of Mutual Redemption was incorporated in 1855 the first genuine American bankers' bank came into existence. It is not surprising therefore to find another bankers' bank proposed in the central-bank scheme of the New Englander of 1857 and 1858; while the plan of the Comptroller of the 1860's was in line with the New York plan of 1839 of a bankers' bank as a redemption agency, although there could have been hardly any line of influence leading from the older to the later scheme. Gilman's, Walker's and other plans to develop clearing houses in the direction of central banks imply the bankers' bank feature, since the clearing houses were bankers' organizations; but Stickney's and Gage's plans of the 1900's aim expressly at a bankers' bank. That is to say, this feature of our Federal Reserve System was well prepared by a long ideological development.

Currency reform and central banking having been discussed, attention can now be focused on the last of the main sets of reform proposals, deposit insurance. Suggestions along this line were first broached in the 1880's. In 1886, for example, there was a bill before Congress making the federal government the ultimate guarantor of deposits in case of final liquidation of National Banks.[321] Such and similar propositions, while emanating from the West, appealed to the East also. The original plans to that effect seem to have aimed at making hoards available for lending purposes: If banks were made safe beyond doubt, so the argument ran, hoarded money would be deposited and could then be made available as the basis for additional bank credits. Thus the chronic lack of capital would be alleviated in the West. In the East, on the other hand, where deposits were then becoming as indispensable as banknotes had been in the 1820's, bank failures and losses resulting therefrom were hitting those unable to make a reasonable selection between competing banks. Just as in the 1820's the safety fund system had been suggested to protect small folk, so in the 1890's the western idea of guaranteed bank deposits appealed to the corresponding strata in the advanced sections of the country.

The proposal appeared in two different forms: either straight state or national guarantee of deposits, as in the above-mentioned bill of 1886,[322] or safety funds. In the latter case, banks were to make regular contributions until those funds had reached a certain size and to replenish them whenever necessary. The former type of plan seems to have appeared earlier than the latter, although persisting to a certain extent into the 1900's.

In that decade the idea of guaranteeing bank deposits was in the air and William Jennings Bryan[323] especially backed it with all his prestige. Among those working out specific proposals Alexander H. Revell (born in 1858) may be mentioned. He was a prominent Chicago merchant and politician, and suggested a plan of that character to J. H. Eckels, Comptroller of the Currency during Cleveland's second presidency.[324] Another early scheme is supposed to have been elaborated by one C. W. Mosher while in jail after having ruined the Capital National Bank of Nebraska as its president. Such sets of ideas very soon reached the stage of realization. In 1893 the governor of Kansas, addressing the Kansas Bankers Association, made a remark regarding government guarantee of bank deposits, and five years later (in 1898) the state's bank commissioner recommended the enactment of a deposit guarantee law.[325]

Most bankers and especially the National Bankers were horrified[326] by such suggestions, and their emotional and vituperative language shows how uneasy they felt. Henry Clews, for example, was "strenuously opposed" to the scheme which was to him "unsound in principle," and "fraught with great danger;" attempting to put it into effect would be "one of those blunders that are worse than crimes." For Festus Wade, a reputable St. Louis banker, the plan was "the rankest kind of financial heresy and an absolute fallacy;" and even the far-seeing James B. Forgan publicly denounced the "proposal [as] abhorrent to business sense as well as justice and equity and [as] opposed to the principles and laws of political economy."[327] (In a personal interview with Theodore Roosevelt he did much to stop the movement.)[328] For all of the bankers, deposit insurance was "paternalism" and "socialism," bynames given ever since to everything that business dislikes.[329] What was really repugnant to these men was the possibility that the position in the competitive struggle of strong and well-managed banks would be undermined because their credit rating would be leveled off. They also expected (and rightly so) that wherever state banks would work under guarantee schemes National Banks would lose business to them, and they were afraid that laws to that effect would lead to overbanking and reckless banking. But only in a very few publications of such outstanding bankers or lawyers as James B. Forgan[330] and Victor Morawetz[331] can one find the really cogent argument against deposit insurance as then proposed. They pointed out that the majority of all deposits were created and represented credit; or as the men expressed it, deposits originated in the process of swapping the credit of the merchant and manufacturer for that of the bank.

Usually instead of emphasizing the valid argument, a specious one was stressed: in the spirit of caveat emptor the bankers claimed that it was up to the depositors to select strong and reliable banks as their depositories. Even disregarding at this point that the underlying philosophy was becoming untenable under the changing economic and social conditions, the attitude was unrealistic. Its exponents overlooked the extent to which the check had spread as a medium of payment and the fact that many people were forced to accept checks and consequently to keep bank accounts. Such small folk were unable to distinguish between the credit of two banks even if they had any choice. To put it differently, the bankers overlooked the fact that what we call deposit money was conquering the country. As early as 1894 the Comptroller of the Currency reported that there were many communities in which it had become customary to pay wages by checks. This held true especially for New York and Pennsylvania where about 50 per cent of the total wage payments were already made that way. The currency famine of 1893 contributed greatly to the spread of the new practice. An investigation of the former year seemed to indicate that about one half of the wage checks were being presented directly to the banks, while the other half reached them by way of retailers.[332]

In order to kill the proposals for deposit insurance Republican politicians promoted the idea of a postal savings bank to take care of small depositors.[333] The bankers, of course, were opposed to this scheme too, all the more since many National Banks were anxious at that time to enter the field of savings banking. Anti-propaganda ran along lines with which the observer of 1950 is still very familiar.

> To establish Postal Savings Banks would be contrary to the general plan of our government, wherein the originators of the Constitution sought to leave the largest measure of liberty and freedom to the people to transact their own affairs. Establishment of Postal Savings Banks would be a movement of the part of the Government to take from intelligent and progressive citizens the Savings Bank business and place its control in the hands of the [obviously the gentlemen were too kind to put down what they meant: unintelligent and backward] office holding class.[334]

For the purpose of obviating deposit insurance the banks proposed stricter supervision of banks, especially by way of clearing house examinations,[335] and cooperation in case of bank failures, as had been practiced in Chicago when the Walsh banks broke down.[336] Moreover some were willing to acquiesce if guarantee funds were put under their own administration and supervision. This attitude was logical, for at that time several insurance companies stood ready to insure deposits not exceeding a specified amount, if the risk was offered either by the bank in question or by the depositor himself. The usual rate was one-fourth of one per cent, although by 1909 there was an inclination to double it. It was suggested at that time that the companies interested in the field should combine to issue a joint policy. Moreover in Kansas, leading National Banks established the Kansas Bank Deposit and Surety Company which, however, does not seem to have gone into actual operation.[337]

This action of the Kansas National Banks leads to the question: Why did not the bankers themselves make a business out of deposit insurance? In the debates of the 1900's it was repeatedly pointed out that every risk was insurable and that the risk of loss sustained by depositors through the failure of banks could be insured on a strictly business basis. The reason that it was not done was probably twofold: there were the created deposits of extraordinary size which presented a problem of their own; and well-managed strong banks may have found occasional failures of small banks and losses sustained by depositors quite helpful to their own business. (There was, of course, another aspect to bank failures, general loss of confidence which hit the fraternity as a body.) In fact as early as 1895 one John Wheeler of Buffalo proposed to George S. Coe the establishment of deposit insurance as a business venture. The plan, which has survived in the George S. Coe papers,[338] seems interesting enough to warrant reprinting it in the appendix to this chapter. Moreover the author came across one proposal of mutual deposit insurance by banks under government control or, alternatively, of a corporation to insure bank deposits.[339]

The earliest deposit-guarantee schemes of the 1890's were devised to cope with Western conditions and when the Populist movement which had originally fostered them petered out, the pressure to enact bills of that character lessened for some time. Nevertheless, deposit-guarantee legislation became a national possibility in 1893, when Bryan introduced in Congress a bill to that effect, and again in 1908 when he was instrumental in having a deposit-guarantee plank put into the platform of the Democratic party. With the party's defeat at the polls the guarantee scheme faded out of the national picture for more than three decades.

The plan was first put into effect in certain Western states. In the 1890's bills proposing the guarantee of bank deposits were introduced year after year in Nebraska, undoubtedly under Bryan's influence.[340] But only after the panic of 1907 did the idea also sway public opinion in Arkansas, Colorado, the Dakotas, Iowa, Kansas, Louisiana, Mississippi, Missouri, Montana, New York, Oklahoma, Ohio, Texas, and Wisconsin.[341] At that juncture it was Oklahoma, not Nebraska, which took the lead and in 1908 passed the first American deposit-guarantee act.

Prior to World War I Oklahoma was followed by Kansas, Nebraska, South Dakota, and Texas. Details are of no interest here, except for underlying principles: none of the acts established a state guarantee; all of them were in fact insurance schemes similar to the New York safety fund act of 1829. Two of the acts, those of Oklahoma and Nebraska, were compulsory, while two were voluntary, Kansas and South Dakota. The Texas scheme differed from the others by giving its banks the choice between participating in a guarantee fund and furnishing a "guaranty bond" to be bought from a fidelity insurance company.[342] Whatever disaster these schemes met later, during the period under observation they led in the states concerned to a growth of state banking both as to the numbers of banks and the amount of deposits. Such rise took place at the expense of National Banks, the total number and deposits of which did not grow in the same proportion.

VI

The influence which the bankers gained on the reform movement of the 1890's and 1900's was limited because there was no measure on which they could agree among themselves. As a matter of fact, Professor Parker Willis stressed that self-interest was an obstacle to reform.[343] The conflict between the adherents of a high-taxed emergency currency and a low-taxed credit currency has been sketched, just as has that between the proponents and opponents of branch banking and central banking, respectively. In all these

cases there were bankers on both sides. These disagreements were not between the leading and the obscure bankers. The leaders fought among themselves. Opposition to the Baltimore plan, for example, came from such men as George G. Williams, president of the Chemical National Bank of New York, and John R. Walsh, president of the Chicago National Bank, whose ignominious end was still far in the future.[344] Jacob Schiff objected to both emergency and credit currencies and instead proposed that banks be entitled to encroach on their reserves in case of emergencies, paying a 6 per cent tax.[345] Charles G. Dawes, a Chicago banker in the 1900's, was against almost all proposals which were backed by the majority of his colleagues.[346]

This situation can be easily explained. When bankers discussed reform proposals they did not do so impassionately, but first of all thought of their own interests. And of course there were within the banking fraternity serious conflicts of interests: those between large and small banks; between city and country banks; between those in various regions and in developed and undeveloped sections of the country; between National Banks and state banks and trust companies; between country banks and those in reserve and central reserve cities; and even banks in the latter two may have had conflicting points of view at least at times. To make things worse, the belief in the "invisible hand" was still lingering and, if replaced at all, was replaced by the doctrine of the survival of the fittest. These tenets made irresponsible representation of interests appear justifiable. "If I were a banker and if I believed that branch banking would injure my business I should be opposed to it," as Horace White expressed it.[347] In passing it may be mentioned that disagreements can be explained in part by the rhythm of generations. The main exponents of central banking belonged obviously to a younger group of coevals than those of currency reform pure and simple. The former were Frank A. Vanderlip (born in 1864), Henry P. Davison (born in 1867), Paul M. Warburg (born in 1868), and Benjamin Strong (born in 1872); the latter were A. B. Hepburn (born in 1846), James B. Forgan (born in 1852), and Charles C. Homer (born in 1847). Last but not least, value judgments played a role when it came to the central banking discussion. It was clear that a central bank would encroach on the freedom of bankers although bringing order into our banking system which was really no system. Therefore the value scale of the individual, i.e., whether he valued order higher than freedom or vice versa, was reflected in his stand on the respective reform proposals.

In order to show how country bankers represented

their interests in the struggle for banking reform the activities of Andrew J. Frame (1844-1932) will be analyzed, all the more since they are also indicative of the intellectual level of American country bankers in the 1900's. Frame, their spokesman, can be characterized as a big frog in a small puddle, to use the vernacular. The son of a blacksmith of Scotch ancestry, Frame was born in Waukesha, which was then a pioneer village in the Territory of Wisconsin. He started his career in the Waukesha County Bank. When the latter in 1865 was converted into the Waukesha National Bank with a capital of $50,000, Frame was appointed its assistant cashier, becoming in 1866 its cashier; in 1880 he rose to the presidency and retained that position until his retirement in 1919. By 1900, when Frame, "Republican, Baptist, Mason," Elk, became some sort of public character his bank had a capital of $150,000 and $65,000 surplus.[348] He was not a great banker. Had he been, he would undoubtedly have found his way to Minneapolis or Chicago or even New York. But he made a success out of his small venture. Living all his life in a little town which he himself had seen and helped develop from pioneer conditions, he was the typical town booster and optimist. His outlook was narrow, although as a spokesman for regional and country bankers' interests he played a role in the Wisconsin and to a certain extent even in the American Bankers Association. The study of such a man's mind is important for the historian.

Frame had become interested in currency questions as early as the 1890's. He was then, like many others, an exponent of an emergency currency, submitting a specific proposal. He recognized that the lack of elasticity of the American banking system was detrimental, referring to German, English, French, and Canadian conditions in contrast. He was against an asset currency as issued in Canada although it was elastic in character. Canadian banks were large corporations, controlled by conservative financiers, while in the United States the vast number of small unit banks could not be expected to be managed with the same wise conservatism, a very reasonable outlook indeed. He conceded defects and recognized strong points elsewhere, arriving at sensible conclusions and proposals.[349] All this took place in 1897.

Shortly thereafter, however, the exponents of an asset currency committed the unpardonable sin of tying together asset currency and branch banking, and at that moment Frame's interests as a small unit banker became endangered. Then he began to fight and at first was quite frank about his motive: "For one after forty years of arduous labor in building up a bank, and as self-preservation is the first law of nature, I must respectfully decline to be accessory to my own hanging." From then on he became more and more the representative of special interests. He had one major goal, namely, to defend his vested interest in the American "splendid independent system" of banks.[350] These independent banks should be burdened as little as possible; their reserves should be small; there should be no redemption of notes at financial centers because it would be onerous. One of Frame's main objections to the Federal Reserve bill seems to have been that it required too large a part of the banks' capital to be invested in stock of the Federal Reserve Bank of the district.[351]

Frame's methods were those of the propagandist: the same speeches were offered more than once;[352] and even when the speeches were not the same the same ideas, formulations, and phrases were used over and over again.[353] Typical were "oxteams versus twentieth century progress," "great central [i.e., parent] banks with 10,000 [or 12,000] banks as tails to their big kites," or "it would take a powerful glass to spy out a gallery of bankers that would stand such ridiculous rules as those." These examples alone would indicate that Frame's language was emotional and often rabble-rousing.[354] His unselfishness and patriotism were stressed too often:[355] _qui s'excuse, s'accuse._ When a claim became entirely untenable the propagandist felt no compunction in misquoting himself and shifting his claim to safer ground: What in 1903 had been the prerequisites of elasticity became in 1907 the prerequisites for "quick redemption." He incorrectly explained that "in former addresses I have declared there are three things necessary to bring about quick redemption [Italics in the original]. I recede not one jot or one tittle from that position." In fact, he had claimed something different and had actually entirely receded from his original position.[356] This example indicates intellectual dishonesty, and dishonest Frame was, like every propagandist. In all his denunciations of an asset currency as a wild-cat currency and as I.O.U's[357] Frame never mentioned that in the pertinent plans asset currency was coupled with guarantee schemes and high reserves. The above characterization of branch banks as "big kites" was contained in an article in the Bankers Magazine of 1901. Reprints of this paper were widely circulated with a rubber stamp on the cover: "To the bankers of the United States. Branch banking means monopoly. Monopoly means revolution in banking. Are you ready to surrender?"[358]

Usually Frame's speeches follow the same pattern; the goal is predetermined; and undigested and unrelated statistical data, historical "facts," and quotations from the Bible, economic authors, and historians as well as from current newspapers and periodicals are presented to prove the point. The real problems of contemporaneous American banking he did not understand: Professor Sprague's exhortation to do away with the payment of interest on demand deposits looked good "theoretically," but he, the banker, knew better that "practically the plan [would] not work." The creation of deposits Frame never understood, and therefore statements to the effect that deposits and notes were essentially alike appeared "absurd" and ridiculous to him. The total of 14,000 millions of dollars of deposits in the United States were for Frame an evidence "that surplus capital [was] abundant."[359] Obviously Wisconsin country banks had not advanced to the point of creating deposits; and "theorists" were despised by this small-town businessman. His attitude toward the inelasticity problem is of special interest. In the 1890's Frame had recognized that American banking was inelastic. But by 1900 the concept did not fit into his propaganda line any longer: elasticity now became a "delusion and a snare," "a sweet morsel to play upon the credulity of an innocent public."[360] That the problem of inelasticity was overworked, that it had become a "hackneyed subject," as a leading Canadian banker expressed it,[361] has been pointed out earlier, but what Frame had to offer in explanation was entirely untenable. According to him "to obtain any elasticity whatsoever one of three conditions [was] necessary:" distrust of the note holder, a compulsory law to enforce the presentation of notes, and a high tax. That was Frame's opinion in 1903. Thereafter he shifted his stand again and advocated giving "as much elasticity to the circulating medium as could be safely attained."[362] To give a last example of Frame's lack of insight into contemporary banking, he had discovered "the blighting effects of [the Canadian] branch bank system."[363]

More interesting even than his shift in the matter of elasticity is Frame's complete about-face with regard to central banking. He was originally one of its exponents. As early as 1902 and 1904 he could not see any objection to a "great central bank" as the fiscal agent of the government and as a "bank of banks." He regarded the Bank of England and the Reichsbank as models. Such a bank was to issue the high-taxed emergency currency which Frame promoted. "But I suppose the banks holding government deposits would object," so he closed his recommendation of 1904.[364] Once more the start was very reasonable, and so it remained for some time. In 1907, influenced by the plan of the New York Chamber of Commerce Committee,[365] he again suggested a National Reserve Bank, similar to the Reichsbank, to issue an emergency currency whenever needed. That bank with a capital of $50,000,000 was to be superimposed on the existing banking and Sub-Treasury systems which would retain their function as holders of government deposits.[366] In 1908 Frame still stuck to the proposal when he addressed the American Academy of Political and Social Science[367] and went on doing so until about 1911. But in a paper of 1910, published in the Proceedings of the Academy of Political Science in the City of New York[368] it comes out clearly that Frame wanted to make the National Reserve Bank the "servant" of "our present splendid independent banking system," not its master. Consequently when the Federal Reserve bills came to show that a real central bank was in the making, i.e., a master of the American banking system which the latter so badly needed, and when certain sacrifices were demanded from the banks joining it, there came a complete about-face, vested interest first! Now, before it had actually been brought into existence, this exponent of central banking came to call hysterically for another Andrew Jackson to destroy the Federal Reserve system.[369] But the story does not end at this point. In the note in Who was Who (which, of course, goes back to information provided by Frame himself) it is stated that he was invited by Congressional committees as "an expert in formulating the Glass-Owen bill." It may be perfectly true that he was invited to have his say, but the implication of this sentence is that he claimed to have exerted an influence on the Federal Reserve System, a claim which borders upon the pathological.

Frame had not enjoyed a formal education and whatever knowledge he possessed was acquired in a process of self-education, a process which often has its shortcomings. "A little knowledge is a dangerous thing." In that respect Frame was typical of the nineteenth-century American businessman, the bankers included; and that the latter were aware of a deficiency, has been mentioned. Lack of a formal education replaced by self-education is a phenomenon which belongs to the American social scene of that century and is easily understood as the reverse of the supreme task with which the nation was confronted. But what makes the case of Frame painful, like that of Carnegie, is the false pretence of a learning which in fact did not exist. Frame commanded only a few picked-up, undigested, and largely misunderstood morsels of information. Learning did not mold his personality, his scattered knowledge covered cultural nakedness like a garb of rags. Nevertheless, and this is the second reason which makes his case painful, the little bit of information which he possessed, continuously repeated and twisted to suit his purpose, impressed his contemporaries who were as uneducated and uncultured as Frame himself.[370] Frame used Latin phrases, but their grammar does not bear inspection.[371] His historical concepts were of the queerest: his dictum "Britain after a campaign as long as and as bitter as ours over the Gresham Law..." is an example. It may be added that he berated the outstanding achievements in American pre-Civil-War banking, such as the Suffolk Bank system, the Louisiana Banking Act of 1842, and the State Bank of Indiana, because he did not understand them and because his adversaries praised them.[372] He revealed his utter poor taste in thanking God for the untimely death of Harriman. "Even the Lord is on our side. It is not many moons since the popular chorus was loudly singing the song that Mr. Harriman was to eat us all up. The Lord suddenly called him home." Finally, the Federal Trade Commission and Interstate Commerce Commission represented autocracy and socialism to Frame.[373]

Frame's activities have been presented and analyzed although his actual influence seems to have been nil. What makes his case interesting and worth studying is the fact that such a man could become the leader of Middle-Western country bankers. He obviously represented their interests and spoke their language, and his personality appealed to them. Regardless of his glaring deficiencies, the historian cannot withold a certain degree of understanding sympathy for this man. He was the exponent of an economic order which was disappearing and he fought a losing battle. He stood where the hand weaver had stood a hundred years earlier. Small enterprise in the field of banking which Frame defended was no longer able to compete with large-scale institutions. The uneducated, utterly narrow small-town businessman was no match (irksome as he may have been at times)[374] for the real banking leaders who became the dominant figures in Frame's lifetime. But by their very creative achievements, they were more and more undermining the traditional capitalistic order for which Frame stood and which rests on the existence of a great number of independent businessmen.

One last question remains to be studied in this chapter, the problem of influence lines which made themselves felt in the various reform proposals of the 1890's and 1900's. In the earlier periods of American banking only English and Scottish models had been observed by both American bankers and politicians; consequently only English and Scottish influence had made itself felt in American banking. This situation changed in the last quarter of the nineteenth century when the banking business as conducted in all the advanced countries came to be examined.[375] From then on to World War I, Canadian and German banking legislation and practice began to exert considerable influence while English and Scottish influence persisted.[376]

Beginning in the late 1870's, a continuously growing interest in Canadian banking can be observed in the United States, and there were three areas which represented excellent vantage grounds for observation. One was New York City whose money market was so intensely used by Canadian banks for holding reserves, lending on call, and operating in foreign exchange, that Sprague described Canadian banks as being "in a sense an outlying dependency of the New York money market."[377] The second was the Northwest which possessed close contacts with Canadian banks. Some of them had branches or agents in important American cities or made loans there without being formally represented. The Merchants Bank of Canada, for example, in the 1890's temporarily had a branch in Chicago which lent on grain in Duluth and Minneapolis, in the latter city American banks guaranteeing such loans. The Bank of Nova Scotia, to give another example, had an agent in Minneapolis in the 1880's. In fact, it was in this capacity that James B. Forgan came to the United States.[378] Finally, the third vantage point was Detroit: the fact that branch banking developed in Michigan at a relatively early moment can be considered the result of close contract with Canadian banks across the Detroit River.

But the interest in the banking structure of our North American neighbor was much more than local: as early and as often as 1877, 1881, 1886, and 1891 papers on Canadian banking were read before the American Bankers Association;[379] in 1894 and thereafter numerous witnesses before Congressional committees referred to Canadian banking and praised it;[380] and in 1895 the American Economic Association published a volume on the same subject.[381] From that time on references to Canadian banking in the literature and documents of this country were legion,[382] and even the newspapers of the period drew the attention of a wider public thereto.[383] It is significant that in the introduction of the book published by the American Economic Association, it was pointed out "that from the account of the Canadian banking system an American [would] obtain instructive contrasts."[384] As characteristic features of Canadian banking the author noted the small number of banks, their large capital, their branch organization, the competitive issue of notes, the frequent exchange of inter-bank obligations, and the payment of interest on demand deposits. The notes which the Canadian banks issued and which from 1890 on were secured by a safety fund were, as the author went on to describe, general asset (credit) notes. Their total not being rigidly limited either directly or indirectly Canadian issues were elastic and the country's interest rates did not fluctuate as violently as was common in the United States. Obviously there really was much to learn from such a set-up, and interest was focused on the issue of elastic general-asset banknotes secured by a safety fund and the branch system.

That Canadian banking thus began to exert a certain influence on the development in the United States is of particular interest, for in the 1800's Canadian banking had started under American influence.[385] The first Canadian banks were modeled on the First Bank of the United States. It was from the charter and the practice of the latter institution that Canada adopted the branch feature and the general-asset note. Moreover, not Canada, but certain American states devised and developed the safety fund. When by 1890 all these features began to attract the attention of Americans and when, in view of their satisfactory working in Canada, their adoption by the United States was recommended, a typical back-migration of ideas was under way.[386]

Several men can be traced through whose instrumentality Canadian banking exerted influence in the United States. One of them was George Hague (1825-1915). Born in England where he had his first banking experience with the Sheffield Banking Company, 1840-1851, he went to Canada in 1854. There, from 1856 through 1876 he was an accountant and later a manager of the Bank of Toronto, but in 1877 rose to become the general manager of the Merchants Bank of Canada, a position which he held until 1902.[387] As early as 1886 Hague took an interest in the work of the American Bankers Association and addressed one of its annual meetings "on the system of branch banking."[388] Other Canadians who can be proved to have had contacts with American bankers were Sir Francis Hincks (1808-1885), the financial statesman, and Sir Byron Edmund Walker (1848-1924), the leading man in the Canadian Bank of Commerce.[389]

The foremost carrier of Canadian influence, however, was the often-mentioned James B. Forgan, one of the great American bankers and business leaders of the period.[390] Forgan (1852-1924) was a Scotsman who had received his training in the Royal Bank of Scotland. After having completed his apprenticeship there he accepted a

job with the Bank of British North America, emigrated, and went to work in Montreal. After interrupting his banking career for a short while, he returned to it as a paying teller of the Bank of Nova Scotia, and soon was employed by that bank as an auditor of its branches. In that capacity he familiarized himself with conditions in Minneapolis with which city the Winnipeg branch of the Bank of Nova Scotia had close relations. Impressed therewith he recommended the setting up of an agency of his bank in Minneapolis, and when this was done he was put in charge of it. Naturally he became acquainted with Minneapolis bankers, and in 1887 was hired to be the cashier of the Northwestern National Bank which he subsequently reorganized. He revised its bookkeeping and clerical records and standardized jobs and operations so that division of labor and assignment of responsibilities to specific employees became possible. When he resigned in 1891 to become the cashier of the First National Bank of Chicago he left a reputation of being a "strict disciplinarian, a hard worker and driver, and a man of terrific tempers, although absolutely fair and always prepared to reward achievement with a free hand." It was in Minneapolis that Forgan trained two younger employees of the bank who were destined to rise in the Twin Cities' banking to the point of "affecting" its course, steeping them in Scotch-Canadian methods. They were Edward Williams Decker (born in 1887), the son of a prosperous farmer, and Clive Talbot Jaffray (born in 1865), a Canadian of Scotch origin. The former became the president of the Northwestern National Bank, while the latter rose to the top in the First National Bank of Minneapolis.

In Chicago Forgan became the president of the powerful First National Bank and rose to the very top in American banking. (Many of his activities have been presented earlier in this chapter.) His permanent position as the chairman of the Chicago Clearing House Committee was the source of extraordinary power,[391] but, of course, he would not have held that position without those qualities which made him a natural leader. In Chicago, just as before in Minneapolis, his early Canadian training and experience were continuously brought to bear on his bank and on Chicago banking, and to the extent that Forgan became a national figure the scope of that influence widened still further.

As to German banking[392] attention was first attracted to that clause in the act establishing the Reichsbank which permitted the issuance of notes over and above a fixed maximum, such notes to be heavily taxed so that they would be used in emergencies only. This seemed to many American financiers and financial statesmen a proper solution for American problems and all those who by 1900 promoted a highly-taxed emergency currency, consciously or not, acted under German influence. Later there were other features of German banking which were of wide interest such as the existence of a strong central bank issuing a highly elastic credit currency, the prevalence of a few big banks with branches, the importance of credit cooperatives, and the independence of specialized mortgage institutions. Because it indicates the strength of the German influence it must be repeated at this point that a committee of the New York Chamber of Commerce in the 1900's recommended the copying of the Reichsbank, and Senator Aldrich went so far as to state that to his mind "the system of Germany is for us the most interesting of any because the German Empire has very largely the same industrial and commercial interests that we have in the United States."[393]

After 1900 the brothers Felix and Paul M. Warburg, the German-born and German-trained members of Kuhn, Loeb and Company, were most important influence carriers. They worked for a strong American bill market with a central bank at its center which would enable American banks to keep their secondary reserves by rediscounting, instead of putting such funds into the call-loan market. They wished American banks to be authorized to accept drafts for their customers which would thus become first class short-term investments. Central bank and bill market were of course nothing specifically German, but it is certain that the Warburgs in recommending these institutions for America acted under German influence having in mind the development which the then very strong German banking system had given thereto.[394]

Moreover in the 1900's personal contacts between American and German bankers became wider. In 1907 a prominent representative of the Centralverband des deutschen Bank- und Bankier-Gewerbes, the German organization corresponding to the American Bankers Association, attended the latter's meeting,[395] and in 1910 personal statements of a leading director of the Deutsche Bank of Berlin and of the president of the Reichsbank were quoted before an American audience.[396]

The interest in and the influence of foreign banking culminated in the studies made abroad and published here by the National Monetary Commission of 1910 and it is of great interest that as early as 1911 a popular booklet was issued which explained the foreign banking systems to a broader American public.[397]

A P P E N D I X

Deposit Insurance as a Business Venture
A Plan of 1895
(George S. Coe Papers)

167 Park Street,
Buffalo, N.Y., Sept. 30th, 1895.

Mr. George S. Coe,
    Prest. American Exchange National Bank,
    New York,

Dear Sir:—

Accompanying I hand you for your consideration a quasi outline of a plan for the insurance of the accounts of depositors of National Banks, and also state banks, having in view more particularly banks west of the Missouri River, and would be pleased to have an expression of opinion from you regarding the same, and the possibility of forming a company for that purpose.

Respectfully, yours,

John Wheeler.

P R O P O S E D   P L A N
for the

Organization of an Insurance Company, with a Capitalization of $25,000,000.00, for the purpose of Insuring the Deposits of National and other Banks, at a Cost of One Per Cent, to be paid by the Bank.

The Thirty-two year's experience of our National Banks is the criterion upon which all the facts and figures hereinafter contained are based, and, in the opinion of the writer, with few exceptions, the same will apply to state banks.

Since June 20th, 1863, two hundred and sixty-seven National Banks have passed into the hands of receivers, of which twelve were restored to solvency, making the total number of failures up to December, 1894, the date of Comptroller's last report, two hundred and fifty-five, and the aggregate liabilities of these banks were $109,936,458 (p. 14, Comptroller's Report '94), with a total of cash collected of $75,044,773, and when the effects and settlements are added to this amount it gives a total of $96,916,595 (p. 14, C. R. '94) which, taken from the total of liabilities, leaves a deficiency of $13,019,763, but to which must be added the cost of collections, or expenses of the receiverships, $5,857,727 (p. 14, C. R. '94), which would give a deficency as between assets and liabilities of $18,877,490, or an actual average loss of $629,249 per annum, which, when compared with the average of deposits (estimated from best data so far obtained) $1,300,000,000, during the same period, and which includes the disasterous year of 1893,

gives us an average annual loss, from all causes, such as depression of securities, embezzlement, fraudulent banking, etc., of one-twentieth of one per cent, or within an infintesimal fraction of a per cent thereof, and this after paying for expensive receiverships and costly litigation.

With the foregoing the case, we have an unoccupied insurance field with immediate obtainable risks of several hundred million of dollars, and these risks being the choicest an insurance company could handle, as there is no question or dispute that the men who occupy the positions of officers and directors of National Banks, and most of the state banks, are possessed of the highest order of intelligence, business integrity and reliability, and whose individual fortunes are often at stake and wrapped up in the business of the institutions with which they are connected.

It is not at present moment in the imagination of the writer that any exceedingly large amount of business could be derived and obtained from the New England and Eastern states, but still, such a rate might be made for banks in the first and second divisions, and portions of the third, fourth and fifth divisions, as would make it to their interest to insure, i.e., for the purpose of obtaining and drawing the accounts of timid depositors and others onto the books of the banks that insure their customer's accounts, and upon further and more mature consideration, or after some experience, it may be found advisable to have a capital of fifty, or even one hundred million dollars, in order to handle the business of the above mentioned divisions; but in the sixth, seventh and eighth geographical divisions of National Banks, and portions of the third, fourth and fifth divisions, we have deposits in National Banks alone, susceptiable of insurance, in the neighborhood of $230,000,000 to $240,000,000, and which can be brought to insure, and at the suggested premium of 1%, and as matters now stand, it would give the company an income on simply $200,000,000 of insurance of $2,000,000 per annum, which, with the assets of the company to the extent of $22,000,000 or $23,000,000 invested in government bonds carrying 3%, and which in the event of organization it might be provided should be the only thing in which the capital of the company could be invested, in order to always have a security capable of being converted into cash at an hour's notice, would give an additional income of $690,000, or an aggregate income of $2,690,000. But, now, to make assurance doubly sure, let us double the prospective annual loss of one-twentieth of 1%, and make it one-tenth, which will give us as the company's loss on $200,000,000 of business $200,000 for the year, and allowing $150,000 for expenses of management, leaves a net balance to the

223

company of $2,340,000, or about .09 1/3 per cent profit, and if we do not double our losses, but leave them at what the statistics show them to be, one-twentieth of one- per cent, leaves the gain to the company in the neighborhood of and close onto ten per cent.

That the organization of such a company as proposed would redound to the benefit, not only of the company itself, but also its clients, there is no question. The writer interviewed a number of bankers in the northwest, and met none who did not give the plan above outlined their unqualified approval and sanction, and stated that the banks could readily afford to pay the proposed tax or premium of one per cent, for not only would it make their institutions more secure in the eyes of their customers and the public, and thereby increase their lines of deposits, by bringing to their counters money for deposit on open accounts, and for interest bearing time certificates of deposit, that is now locked up in safe deposit vaults, buried in the ground, and tied up in old stockings and hid away, but would also bring into insuring banks a large portion of the money deposited in other institutions, and would also be the means of obviating runs against a bank, and with the revival of business and improvement of the times, it would admit of a bank loaning down closer to the twenty-five per cent limit than it would otherwise be inclined to do, on account of the severe strain experienced during the late panic or unfortunate year of 1893, without having the nightmare of a long line of depositors waiting to draw their money continually before them, and again, it would be to a bank's advantage to insure, for the reason that its correspondent would the more quickly loan money on collateral when accompanied by a certificate of deposit that was insured, than on the mere collateral of hypothecated notes alone.

In a foregoing paragraph it was suggested that the banks could be brought to insure--outside of the fact that it can be seen at a glance it is to a bank's interest to insure its depositor's accounts, it can also be seen, that where one bank insures, and so advertises, its neighbor necessarily must,for in the event it did not it is reasonable to suppose that an intelligent man would naturally place his funds in the keeping of and do business with that institution where he had the greatest security and protection, and where (as the company would arrange for), if for any reason the bank closed its doors, that within twenty-four hours thereafter, when his account could be verified by wire into New York, or the head or home office of the company, instead of checking against the bank containing his account, he could check against an insurance company that would honor his checks and liquidate his balance in full, why, with such inducements held out to a man having money for deposit and need of a bank, the neighboring bank would absolutely be forced to insure or go out of business; and in the event of a one bank town where the officers refused to insure, two or three instances of inducing a competitor to enter the field that did insure, and refusing the first mentioned bank a line, or its correspondent refusing accommodations unless its certificates were insured, would speedily bring the balance, if any, of non-insuring institutions to a realization of their error in not affording their depositors every protection in their power. The company after having paid, or assumed to pay the accounts of depositors, would then become the owner and holder thereof, and stand in depositors shoes and position as far as the bank was concerned, and as before stated, having paid or assumed the accounts, it would then proceed to take charge of and wind up the affairs of the defunct institution as quickly, cheaply and economically as possible, and having men who were trained and experienced in the business, would undoubtedly save large sums which are now being and have been lost by ignorant receivers, whose interest it is to retain their positions as long as possible; or in case the company was notified or ascertained that an an insured bank was in a precarious condition, it could, if deemed advisable, have the then existing board of directors resign, and elect its own officers or agents in their stead, and continue the business of the bank.

That the men at the head of and controlling an institution such as proposed, would be possessed of and able to wield great power and influence can readily be appreciated, and it being vital to their interests to watch over and scan closely the affairs of such banks as were insured in the company, more so than it is to the officers and examiners of the government, so that the company might cancel the risk or policy of a bank it had reason to mistrust, in which event it would simply be a notice and advertisement to the world that such bank was deemed unsound, or in case the company refused to insure a bank, the same situation would exist, in either of which, a bank so blacklisted would speedily have to reinforce itself or close its doors.

The writer heretofore suggested that government bonds should be the only thing in which the capital of the company could be invested, but with any surplus the company might see fit to lay up, and which should be everything over and above 6%, such surplus could undoubtedly be invested to better advantage, and with the retention of all earnings over 6%, such a surplus would soon accumulate as to make the company one of the most powerful, if not the first financial factor in the land.

As it is apparent that unscrupulous persons organizing and conducting such a company could dispossess and deprive honorable competitors of business, and as it is also apparent that the status of such a corporation would depend largely upon the personality of the men who managed it, it should therefore be organized upon the broadest basis, and officered by the most experienced men of the banking and insurance worlds, and who possess such national reputations as George S. Coe, H. W. Cannon, George G. Williams, James G. Cannon, George N. [?] Baker, E. H. Pullen, Edward H. Simmons, J. J. P. Odell, M. M. White, John F. Whitelaw, P. W. Hayes, John Walsh, Lyman J. Gage, William C. Cornwall, J. H. Millard, William Alvord, Richard A. McCurdy, John A. McCall, Henry B. Hyde, etc.

With the organization of such an institution as suggested, loss and annoyance to depositors by failure of banks would soon become a thing of the past, the business of the country expanded to a measureable degree, and honor and credit be reflected upon the charter organizers. [Original spelling retained throughout.]

CHAPTER XVIII

FIFTH PERIOD (1882-1910)
GENERAL CHARACTERISTICS

I

1. Henry W. Yates in Hull, op cit., 277.
2. Sprague, "Branch Banking," 247; American Academy, Lessons, 135; Hull, op. cit., 23.
3. Witham Bankers Association, Proceedings (1906), 41.
4. I can distinctly remember that this was what I was taught in the early 1910's at the University of Berlin.
5. See also the attractive formulation of A. B. Stickney, president of the Chicago and Great Western Railway Company: "The merchant creates the credit--the bank fructifies it and makes it available as a medium of exchange; Hull, op. cit., 207.
6. "The Modern Bank" in Currency Problem, passim, especially 4,5,8,9. See also A.B.A., Proceedings (1901), 110,111.
7. Quoted from Cleveland, Frederick A., op. cit., 58. The original source is not given, but the quotation tallies with the spirit of Dawes's pamphlet of 1894 (op. cit., passim); perhaps it is a speech of 1903, see Dawes's Essays and Speeches, 303.
8. Comptroller, Report (1887), 8; (1888), 97.
9. See this volume page 393.
10. Boissevain, op.cit., 27.
11. Comptroller, Report (1884), xiv; (1885), xviii; (1888), 4.
12. Ibid. (1886), xviii; (1887), 5.
13. Ibid. (1887), 70, 71.
14. See this volume, chapter XX.
15. Money Trust Investigation, 1050.
16. Money Trust Investigation, 1879. As to data on Davison, see below, page 179.
17. A.B.A., Proceedings (1904), 5,6.
18. See this volume, pages 241ff.
19. E. H. Pullen, see A.B.A., Proceedings (1896), 17.
20. Money Trust Investigation, pages 537, 538 are most interesting for the complete lack of understanding of the changing climate in banking on the part of rabid believers in competition, while they also show how for certain bankers the competitor becomes a "fellow."
21. A.B.A., Proceedings (1897), 80.
22. Interest was paid on demand deposits at the rate of 2 to 4 per cent; Gras-Larson, op. cit., 516 and Kilburn in Hull, op. cit., 81. Under the sponsorship of the Superintendent of the Banking Department the Albany banks agreed not to pay interest on deposits of less than $10,000. See also Pennsylvania Commissioner of Banking, Report (1904), viii.
23. Money Trust Investigation, 542 ff. The obnoxious clause reads: "In computing interest on balances ... time deductions shall be made on such local items as are not available for the day's clearings and for all items while in transit." (A schedule of minimum deductions follows.) "Any member violating this rule, directly or indirectly, shall upon the first offense be subject to a fine not to exceed $1000... and upon further violation shall, in addition to the above fine, be subject to such penalty as the association may prescribe;" (ibid., 545, 546).
24. Ibid., 563 ff, 1215 ff.
25. E. H. Pullen, vice-president, National Bank of the Republic, New York, in A.B.A., Proceedings (1898), 91, 92. See also the address of Frederick D. Kilburn, ex-Superintendent of the New York Banking Department, in Hull, op. cit., 79; and A. J. Frame in ibid., 166.
26. Hull, op. cit., 145.
27. See below page 178.
28. In Massachusetts, National Banks competed with savings banks too. The latter lent to manufacturing corporations taking personal notes of two or three officers and/or directors as collateral security; see Atkinson, One Function, 16.
29. A. B. Hepburn made this point; see Hull, op. cit., 225.
30. The figures are derived from the Reports of the Comptroller. They show the trend reliably although they are not very satisfactory. It was currently difficult for the Comptroller to get at the figures for state banks, and those for National Banks refer only to a particular date of the year. For the former, see Report (1897), xxxiii; (1898), xlviii. William B. Ridgely, the then Comptroller, presented this kind of statistics in American Academy, Annals, XXIV (1904), 22, but his figures which include savings banks seem to be misleading.
31. See Smith, James G., op. cit., 238 ff; Perine, Story passim.
32. Certificates of deposit were payable either on short notice or at a time stated, not exceeding one year. The rate of interest varied between two and six per cent; usually it was less then four. See Hull, op cit., 466, 468.
33. State of New York, Superintendent of the Banking Department, Annual Report, (transmitted Jan. 4, 1887), 16, 17.

34. Pennsylvania Banking Department, Report (1892), 10; Commissioner of Banking, Report (1906), viii, ix; (1908), 9; (1909), 8.
35. American Academy, Lessons, 163 ff; idem, Annals, XXIV (1904), 36. Very illuminating is the debate of 1909 in the trust company section of the A.B.A. on "Limitations of the Functions of the Trust Company;" A.B.A., Proceedings (1909), Trust Company Section, 41 ff. Some of the trust company officials recognized practically no limits to their business (see, for example, page 46), while others did.
36. Money Trust Investigation, 309, 230.
37. Money Trust Investigation, 630.
38. Daniel G. Reid (1858-1925), tin-plate producer and organizer of the tin-plate industry, became an important New York financier after having sold out his concern to the United States Steel Corporation; see Cycl. Am. Biogr., XIX, 392.
39. Lamont, op. cit., 2, 15, 26, 36, 41, 47; Bankers Trust Company, op. cit., 5, 7, 32, 33.
40. A.B.A., Proceedings (1909), 19; "The Competition of the Express Companies" in Bankers Magazine, LXIII (1901), 938 ff; Swaine, op. cit., II, 86 ff.
41. See this chapter, page 182.
42. A.B.A., Proceedings (1913), 571, 572.
43. A.B.A., Proceedings (1904), 131 ff.
44. A.B.A., Proceedings (1897), 81.
45. Currency Problem, 12.
46. Comptroller, Report (1909), 9; see also (1910), 56; (1911), 59; (1912), 15, 16. The Reports of the Pennsylvania Commissioner of Banking (1909-1912, passim) give a good idea as to the securities held by Pennsylvania state banks and trust companies.
47. See this volume, chapter XXI.
48. Hollander, op. cit., 4.
49. Nourse, op. cit., 210, 216.
50. See this volume, pages 7, 10.
51. Nourse, op. cit., 215.
52. For the following see Money Trust Investigation, 743 ff, 753 ff, also 346, 347, 640, 641, 797.
53. Pujo Committee, Report, 59, 60, 68, 69, 73, 78.
54. See for example, A.B.A., Proceedings (1909), 250.
55. In the Western states the trust companies ran departments for savings and had assumed the role of savings banks in the East; see Hull, op. cit., 460.
56. See this volume, page 5.
57. Comptroller, Report (1884), lviii.
58. Recollections, 140 ff.
59. Money Trust Investigation, 1958.
60. Report (1912), 11.
61. As early as 1905, to give an example, the Northwestern National Bank in Minneapolis had opened a savings department; Popple, op. cit., 51.
62. A.B.A., Proceedings (1910), 59, 310 ff, 546, 603 ff; Pennsylvania Commissioner of Banking, Report (1906), x.

63. McRoberts, Samuel (vice-president of the National City Bank), "The Extension of American Banking in Foreign Countries" in American Academy, Banking Problems, 24 ff; also A.B.A., Proceedings (1910), 54.
64. The mortgage business as conducted in the 1880's is described in A.B.A., Proceedings (1888), 116 ff; see also ibid., (1905), 81, 82; Hull, op. cit., 404.
65. A.B.A., Proceedings (1888), 117.
66. James, Economics of Money, 346; Huston, op. cit., III, 21. Newton (born in 1868) was an Englishman who came to America in 1887 settling in Chicago. He entered the service of the First National Bank, and became its auditor in 1906 and vice-president responsible for administrative direction and executive control in 1910.
67. A.B.A., Proceedings (1903), 68, 69; (1904), 8, 112 ff, 118; (1907), 156, Appendix, 90 ff; (1909), 21, 111 ff; (1910), 206 ff; (1911), 448 ff; (1912), 175 ff.
68. Horace White in Hull, op. cit., 264.
69. James, Chicago Banks, 731; Lockhart, op. cit., passim, especially 138, 142, 143, 146, 223, 224, 239.
70. Money Trust Investigation, 305, 1641, 1966.
71. Ibid., 1657.
72. The Comptrollers of the Currency published figures regarding average earnings and average dividends of National Banks. These figures are not very illuminating since the ranges were not published simultaneously. Those to be found in the Report of 1905 (page 18) may be quoted for what they are worth: Between 1869 and 1876 the National Banks paid on the average 10 per cent dividends on their capital. The next twenty years were much less profitable, the rate being, for example, 7.5 per cent in 1892 and 6.7 per cent in 1897. Thereafter there was a new upswing and the rate was 9.9 per cent in 1904. If dividends are related to capital and surplus the rate for thirty-six years was 5.87 per cent. But the average net earnings related to capital and surplus during the same period (1869-1905) were 8.08 per cent.
73. For details and figures see this volume, page 393.
74. Money Trust Investigation, 1534. The policy of accumulating a high surplus was strongly recommended, see Kilburn in Hull, op. cit., 85, 86.
75. Money Trust Investigation, 1420-1422. The financial record of the First National Bank can be found in ibid., 1479, 1480; (it is reprinted in Gras-Larson, op. cit., 522, 523).
76. Ibid., 1429.
77. Ibid., 613,614.
78. Ibid., 236.
79. National-Bank-of-Commerce stock was quoted 205 in 1912; see Money Trust Investigation, 1326. Stillman's 47,498 shares in the National City Bank and Baker's 20,000 shares in the

First National Bank were worth $18,000,000 and $20,000,000, respectively; Brandeis, op. cit., 29. The shares of the Chemical National Bank had a book value of $2,450 and a price of more than $4,000; Kilburn in Hull, op. cit., 86.

80. Ridgely, Comptroller, in American Academy, Annals, XXIV (1904),19.

81. Comptroller, Report (1892), 51.

82. Ibid., (1894), 25.

83. This point is well taken in J. P. Morgan & Co., op. cit., 12, 13.

84. As an example of a bank which developed to importance by internal growth the Third National Bank of St. Louis may be cited. Its master mind was Charles H. Huttig (1864-1913). Born in a small Iowa town as the son of a manufacturer, he was trained in a local private bank and, after having worked in the family enterprise, in 1885 removed to St. Louis where he founded a sash and door company. In 1890 he was elected a director of the bank above-mentioned whose vice-president and president he later became. He was the president of the St. Louis Clearing House and active in the A.B.A., whose president he became in 1912. See A.B.A., Proceedings (1913), 65.

85. Report (1898), xxx ff; (1899), xix.

86. Money Trust Investigation, 1403, 1404.

87. See this volume page 236.

88. For Cannon see this volume, index, and his writings in the bibliography in volume I of this work, especially Bank Credits (1892) and the item of 1905 under the same title. The latter is reprinted in Hull, op. cit., 43 ff. The item Uniform Statement Blanks and Credit Department Methods appeared first in A.B.A., Proceedings (1899), 170 ff.

Incidentally, one of the first bankers to change the traditional method of relying on the opinion of directors and outsiders in extending credit seems to have been James H. Beal, president of the Second National Bank of Boston, who retired as early as 1888. His success seems to have been due in part to observing closely his debtors' credit on the basis of objective criteria. See Wheeler, Alexander S., The History of the Second National Bank 1860-1896, mimeographed copy, 1932.

89. A.B.A., Proceedings (1908), 195 ff; (1910), 58, 59; (1911), 526 ff, 700, 701, 703. As early as 1897 a credit bureau had been suggested to inform banks lending to other banks on the quality of paper offered for rediscount and of local collateral; see ibid. (1897), 86 ff. See also American Academy, Annals, XXXVII (1910), 610, where the author suggests the registration of commercial paper with clearing houses.

90. A.B.A., Proceedings (1909), Clearing House Section, 22.

91. The change was made in the First National Bank of Boston, for example, on June 1, 1904.

See an item in the Scrapbook regarding the consolidation of the Shoe and Leather National Bank and the National Bank of Redemption, Baker Library, Harvard University.

92. A.B.A., Proceedings (1898), 91, 92; (1913), 516. As to McKay, see James, Chicago Banks, 906, 907. A report of his on the numerical system is in A.B.A., Proceedings (1913), 191, 192, 543.

93. See this volume, page 238.

94. Report (1894), 10.

95. Ibid. (1902), 18 ff. The scrapbook regarding the consolidation of the Shoe and Leather National Bank and the National Bank of Redemption, both of Boston, is informative.

96. Chapman (op. cit., 52, 53) presents statistics of a very limited value; they cover only 27 states and the important state of New York is left out completely, although numerous mergers are on record.

97. Money Trust Investigation, 304.

98. Ibid., 1324, 1462; Pujo Committee, Report, 84, 85.

99. Guaranty Trust Company, op. cit., 27 ff.

100. Gras-Larson, op. cit., 512.

101. Money Trust Investigation, 214, 215, 602 ff.

102. Ibid., 1325; Swaine, op cit., II, 120.

103. Money Trust Investigation, 1056; Pujo Committee Report, 57 ff.

104. Cycl. Am. Biogr., XII, 289; Who was Who in America; Guaranty Trust Company, op cit., 20, 24.

105. Money Trust Investigation, 1560, 1871; Lamont, op. cit., 2, 3, 62; Guaranty Trust Company, op. cit., 30-32; Allen, Morgan, 271 ff.

106. Money Trust Investigation, 1439.

107. Albert H. Wiggin born in 1868 in Massachusetts as the son of a minister held several minor positions in Boston banking until he transferred in 1899 to New York as a vice-president of the National Park Bank. In 1904 and 1911, respectively, he became a vice-president and the president of the Chase National Bank. See Who's Who in America.

108. Money Trust Investigation, 1567; this information could not be verified in Dillistin, Banks of the State of New York, but the latter seems to have an erroneous concept regarding the last-named two banks.

109. Lamont, op. cit., 59, 60.

110. Dillistin, op. cit., 30, 37, 76; Money Trust Investigation, 126.

111. Money Trust Investigation, 576; Dillistin, op. cit., 23.

112. Money Trust Investigation, 200 ff.

113. See Money Trust Investigation, Interlocking Directorates, passim. Money Trust Investigation, 974 ff; Pujo Committee, Report, 57 ff, 89, 90; 130 (pointed summary). A. B. Hepburn thought in 1902 that interlocking ownership was the result of the prohibition of branch banking, but that was probably an error; see Hull, op.

cit., 226.

114. See this volume, page 378.
115. For the latter transactions see Money Trust Investigation, 1313 ff, 1323 ff, 1461 ff; Pujo Committee, Report, 135.
116. See, for example, de Kay, op. cit., passim; Brandeis, op. cit., passim.
117. Money Trust Investigation, 1967.
118. J. P. Morgan and Company, op. cit., 2, 3, 12 ff; (passages from this item are reprinted in Gras-Larson, op. cit., 564, 565).
119. Ibid., 4, 25 ff. See also a telling remark of Morgan in Money Trust Investigation, 1056.
120. Harvard College Class of 1880, Fiftieth Anniversary Report, 146 ff; Hodges, op. cit., 265; The Book of the Shawmut Bank (p.p., 1923), 14; Money Trust Investigation, 1997.
121. By 1912 they were allied with the First National Bank; Money Trust Investigation, 1999.
122. Washburn, op. cit., 5, 12-16; Gras, op. cit., 159 ff.
123. Money Trust Investigation, 1957, 1958, 1997, 1998.
124. Corporation records, Baker Library of Harvard University.
125. Pujo Committee, Report, 75 ff; Brandeis, op. cit., 38, 39.
126. Chicago Banks, 691 ff, 786, 787; Welton, op. cit., passim; Money Trust Investigation, 1639, 1640.
127. Who Was Who in America; Cycl. Am. Biogr., XXIV, 175.
128. James, Chicago Banks, 1212-14; Welton, op. cit., passim.
129. Huston, op. cit., IV, 156 ff.
130. Reynolds had started as a clerk in the Guthrie County National Bank where he worked from 1879-1886. From 1886-1888 he was engaged in the farm loan and real estate mortgage business in Nevada whence he returned to the former bank as cashier and manager. In 1893 he went to the Des Moines National Bank and worked there first as cashier and from 1895-1897 as president. Who was Who in America; Welton, op. cit., 17 ff; U.S. 52d Congr. 2d sess., House Committee on Banking and Currency, Hearings and Arguments on Proposed Currency Legislation, 1906/07, 132.
131. Popple, op. cit., 52 ff.
132. The author is much indebted to Miss Evangeline Thurber, Reference Librarian of the Howard-Tilton Memorial Library of Tulane University, for this material, contained in Louisiana State Banking Department, Reports (1902/03), viii; (1904), vi; (1905), vii; (1906), ix; (1912/13), 8, 9; (1918/19), xi.
133. Who was Who in America. However the note seems to be unreliable and in case of conflicting information the Reports of the Banking Department have been followed.
134. Forgan, Recollections, 130.
135. See this chapter, page 177.
136. James, Chicago Banks, 956.
137. See vol. I of this work page 98, 99.
138. Ibid., pages 113 ff.
139. Chapman, op. cit., 98; Westerfield, op. cit., 8; Southworth, op. cit., 5, 6. The final and presumably complete presentation of the material is to be found in Chapman-Westerfield, op. cit., 37 ff.
140. See chapter XI of this volume.
141. Chapman-Westerfield, op. cit., 46.
142. Carey, Letter to Seybert, 79.
143. As late as 1838 it was recommended that "independent village banks" be done away with and a monopolistic state bank with branches established in every state: Letters of Publius, 39, 51 ff. The anonymous author of this pamphlet points to a similar proposal in the Richmond Enquirer of May 16, 1837.
144. See the writings of Starnes.
145. Quoted from Chapman-Westerfield, op. cit., 3.
146. Ibid., 47, 48.
147. Southworth (op. cit., 11, 12) shows that under the act of 1863 branch banking may have been possible and that only the version of 1864 made it impossible by implication. See also Chapman-Westerfield, op. cit., 85, 86; Hull, op. cit., 277.
148. A very short list of state banks joining the national system and retaining their branches is in American Academy, Banking Problems, 30.
149. Chapman-Westerfield, op. cit., 64, 65.
150. Comptroller of the Currency, Report (1895), 25; Chapman-Westerfield, 66, 67.
151. Finance Report (1895), lxxxiii, lxxxiv; (1896), lxxix.
152. Comptroller of the Currency, Report (1898), xl, xli; and the criticism by Breckenridge in Jour. Pol. Econ.,VII (1898/99), 262 ff, reprinted also in Sound Currency, VI (1899), 55, 56.
153. Ibid., VI (1899), 1 ff, article of Breckenridge reprinted from Bankers Magazine, LXIII (1899), 38 ff.
154. Indianapolis Report, 71, 370 ff; U.S. 55th Congr. 2nd sess., House Report 1575, 30 and H.R. bill 10289, sec. 35; Chapman-Westerfield, op. cit., 67-71; Chapman, op. cit., 118 (footnote); also Hull, op. cit., 254 ff.
155. See A.B.A., Proceedings (1898), 111 ff, 125 ff; (1899), 13 (reference to an address on branch banking by a leading Canadian banker); (1899), 210; (1902), 109, 110, 119.
156. See also the illuminating paper by Eckhardt, H.M.P., "Branch Banking Among the State Banks" in American Academy, Banking Problems, 148 ff; Hull, op. cit., 271 ff.
157. The reform movement of the period is discussed below, pages 207 ff.
158. Chapman-Westerfield, op. cit., 71 ff.
159. Pages 45-47.
160. See also Representative Vreeland's attitude,

quoted in A.B.A., Proceedings (1909), Clearing House section, 12.

161. Branch Banking, passim (reprinted in Hull, op. cit., 238 ff).

162. A.B.A., Proceedings (1908), 232.

163. Comptroller, Report (1895), 40; James, Chicago Banks, 954.

164. In 1896 thirteen states forbade branches, twenty permitted them, while ten were non-committal. In 1910 the figures were 9, 12, and 27. But the 12 states permitting branches represented 25 per cent of the population of the United States. See Chapman-Westerfield, op. cit., 4, 85. A survey regarding the legal situation in the various states is in the Report of 1902 of the Comptroller, 45 ff.

165. Eckhardt (op. cit. [see footnote 156], 155) reports on the successful Tennessee Valley Bank which had 12 branches besides the parent office. It was built up by one S. S. Broadus with a capital of $200,000.

166. Southworth, op. cit., 113 ff.

167. Incidentally the law was drafted by the New York lawyer, Joseph S. Auerbach. As to McCurdy, see above, page 187.

168. For the background see Southworth, op. cit., 130 ff. The main source for the preceding paragraph is the address of Nash, Branch Banking, passim (reprinted in Hull, op. cit., 282 ff), and Ketchum, Corn Exchange Bank, 25, 26, 61, 62.

169. Obituary in New York Times, May 20, 1941, and editorial in ibid., May 21, 1941.

Shortly after the close of the period under investigation Louis G. Kaufman (1872-1941) gained importance for the development of branch banking. Kaufman was the son of a banker, and his mother was related to the Livingston family of New York. He started out in his father's bank, the Marquette County Savings Bank in Michigan, becoming cashier in 1898. Thence he transferred to the First National Bank of Marquette (1901) to become its president in 1906. By that time the young man had attracted the attention of his colleagues by his extraordinary ability and had already been the president of the Michigan Bankers Association. In 1910 he was called to New York City as the president of the Chatham National Bank which through several consolidations he built up until as the Chatham Phenix National Bank and Trust Company it became one of the largest in the nation. When in 1915 he absorbed the Century Bank (a state bank with branches) his enterprise became the first National Bank to operate intra-city branches. See his obituary in New York Times, Mar. 11, 1942, and Barron, op. cit., 30, 31.

170. Obituary of Giannini in New York Times, June 4, 1949; Dowry, "Bank of Italy," passim; Dana, Giannini, passim and especially 50, 66, 67, 71, 72,

74, 80. For the background, see Southworth, op. cit., 29 ff; Chapman, op. cit., 149 ff; Chapman-Westerfield, op. cit., 87 ff.

171. As to the advertising of contemporary banks, see Hull, op. cit., 134 ff, 141 ff, 580 ff.

172. James, Chicago Banks, 722, 723, 788, 789, 957; Forgan, Recollections, 169 ff.

173. As to the terminology, see Ostrolenk, op. cit., 53, Cartinhour, op. cit., 54, 55; Chapman, op. cit., passim. Much finer distinctions are made in A.B.A., Study of Group and Chain Banking, passim.

174. See vol. I of this work, page 41.

175. Ibid., 144, 145.

176. See this volume, chapter XI.

177. See this volume index.

178. Ibid., page 64.

179. James, Chicago Banks, 174, 224, 225, 269; and the biographies of Matteson in Dict. Am. Biogr. and Cycl. Am. Biogr., XI, 47.

180. James, Chicago Banks, see Index.

181. Palyi, op. cit., 194 ff; the passage alluded to is on page 197.

182. Book of Minnesotans, a Biographical Dictionary, ed. Albert Nelson Marquis, vol. I (Chicago, 1907); information kindly provided by the Library of the University of Minnesota.

183. Cycl. Am. Biogr., XVIII, 340, 341.

184. Compendium of History and Biography of North Dakota (1900); a copy of the note on Beecher was kindly provided by the Public Library Commission, Bismarck, North Dakota.

185. Hartsough, op. cit., 145, 146.

186. Hennessy, W. B., History of North Dakota (1910); the note was kindly provided by the Public Library Commission, Bismarck, North Dakota.

187. Aldrich, Clara, op. cit., 17.

188. Ibid., 82, 83.

189. Information kindly provided by the Idaho State Traveling Library, Boise, Idaho. The names of Drew W. Standrod's partners were J. N. Ireland, W. G. Jenkins, D. L. and L. L. Evans.

190. Cycl. Am. Biogr., XIX, 147.

191. Cartinhour, op. cit., 83.

192. A.B.A., Proceedings (1910), 473; Cycl. Am. Biogr., XXVIII, 226, 227. The following is based in part on information kindly provided by the Sioux City Public Library from the term paper of a student. The reliability cannot be vouched for. Incidentally, Horace White knew in 1902 of a chain of banks in Missouri and Kansas; Hull, op. cit., 261, 262.

193. According to another version, this bank was organized in 1912 and became the Toy National Bank in 1920.

194. Atlanta Journal, Nov. 15, 1934, page 7, col. 3; (information kindly provided by the Georgia State Library, Atlanta).

195. See this volume, pages 215 ff.

196. Witham Bankers Association, Proceedings (1906), 10, 56, 57, 127 ff. Witham himself

addressed the American Bankers Association, but his address of 1898 consisted only of commonplaces and jokes; that of 1907 of "bla, bla." See A.B.A., Proceedings (1898), 126 ff; (1907), 61 ff; also (1897), 188, 189; Cartinhour, op. cit., 84, 85; Georgia Country Bankers' Handbook, 9 ff (this rare item is in the State Library in Atlanta and a microfilm is in the Baker Library of Harvard University).

197. Cartinhour, op. cit., 90, 91.
198. See this volume, page 241.
199. Page ix.
200. Hull, op. cit., 226.
201. Hartsough, op. cit., 144 ff; Cartinhour, op. cit., 82, 83.
202. He was a partner and the guiding spirit of the private banking house of Dwiggins, Starbuck and Company, Chicago.
203. James, Chicago Banks, 583 ff.
204. Ibid., 714 ff.
205. Thomas, "Concentration," 4. Thomas also mentions a small chain consisting of two banks, and characterizes the First National Bank of Chicago plus its security affiliate, established under the so-called Chicago plan, plus one outlying bank controlled by Forgan as a chain. This seems to be erroneous. Affiliates under the Chicago plan (see this volume, index) were of a distinct character and a bank establishing such affiliates built an organization which must be distinguished from chain or group banking.
206. Lorimer, after having been one of Yerkes's henchmen, was temporarily a United States senator.
207. James, Chicago Banks, 831 ff.
208. Kane, op. cit., 271 ff, 280, 281; Sprague, "Branch Banking, " 247 ff.
209. The matter of high salaries is discussed in A.B.A., Proceedings (1898), 96.
210. As to this discussion, see, for example, A.B.A., Proceedings (1898), 13; (1900), 158.
211. Benjamin Bartis Comegys (1819-1900) born in Delaware, the son of a governor of that state, started in the dry-goods business, but early entered the service of the Philadelphia Bank in which he rose. His religious interests make his "sermon" before the bankers quite understandable; Cycl. Am. Biogr., XV, 254, 255.
212. A.B.A., Proceedings (1894), 36 ff; (1900), 162.
213. A.B.A., Proceedings (1898), 89, 90, 95, 96.
214. See, for example, Comptroller, Report (1900), xvi.
215. A.B.A., Proceedings (1897), 96. See also such contemporary items as those of Clagett, op. cit., passim or Hill, op. cit., passim; (the latter wanted to replace the existing banks by "government banks").
216. A.B.A., Proceedings (1900), 164.
217. Ibid. (1896), 18; see also (1897), 94 ff.
218. Chapman, Joseph, in Hull, op. cit., 105.

219. A.B.A., Proceedings (1895), 13.
220. Ibid. (1901), 59 ff, especially 63, 64.
221. See Clews, Henry, "Business Education and Commercial and Banking Methods" in Hull, op. cit., 3 ff; A.B.A., Proceedings, (1890), 20 ff, (1891), 19 ff, (1892), 18 ff, (1893), 16, 17. As to Coe's activities, see this volume page 434.
222. A.B.A., Proceedings (1900), 158 ff; (1901), 58 ff; (1902), 57 ff; (1903), 48 ff, 167 ff; (1904), 95 ff, 102 (an example of the very low educational level); (1905), 100 ff; (1906), 73 ff; (1907), Appendix 7 ff. By that time the annual reports of the American Institute of Banking (to be found in the Proceedings of the A.B.A.) were becoming mere routine.
223. Ibid. (1913), 194.
224. As to Cannon, see this volume, index; and, for example, his speech "Uniform Statement Blanks and Credit Department Methods" in ibid. (1899), 170 ff.
225. Recollections, 148.
226. Efficacy, passim.
227. Good Note, passim.
228. James, Chicago Banks, 647, 690, 717; see also Chapman, Joseph, in Hull, op. cit., 98.
229. Comptroller, Report (1892), 40; (1905), 55.
230. Forgan, Recollections, 149. For the background, see Walton, Seymour, "Bank Audits" in Hull, op. cit., 56 ff; (according to this man, speaking in 1905, public accountants had come into prominence "only within the last few years").
231. Comptroller, Report (1881), xxxv, xxxvi.
232. Ibid. (1891), 72, 73.
233. Ibid. (1892), 40, 41.
234. Ibid. (1896), 35.
235. Ibid. (1905), 71 ff.
236. Money Trust Investigation, 1393, 1402.
237. A.B.A., Proceedings (1909), 170, 171.
238. A.B.A., Proceedings (1899), 94; Sprague, "Branch Banking," 248, 249.
239. Comptroller, Report (1891), 73; (1892), 41; (1900), xiv, xvi. See also the discussion before the Pujo Committee in Money Trust Investigation, 2040, 2041.
240. Coffin, op. cit., 103, 104. Pages 104 ff contain an enumeration of the functions of all the bank personnel from the president downward; see also Bolles, op. cit., passim.
241. Crawford, John J., op. cit., 6, 10, 15-18.
242. See vol. I of this work according to index entries under Boards of Directors as policy-making bodies.
243. Money Trust Investigation, 1640, 1641, 1686, 1870, 1871.
244. See this chapter, page 185.
245. Chapman, Joseph, in Hull, op. cit., 104.
246. Pujo Committee, Report, 57-59; Money Trust Investigation, 596-598, 607, 1560, 1561.
247. Ibid., 1048.
248. Forgan, Recollections, 122.

249. Money Trust Investigation, 530.
250. Andrew J. Frame in A.B.A., Proceedings (1913), 95. Our banking system was "the greatest in the world;" Charles G. Dawes, Present Financial Situation, 8. The "United States has the best currency system in the world;" Leslie M. Shaw in Hull, op. cit., 396.
251. Money Trust Investigation, 1518.
252. Henry W. Yates in Hull, op. cit., 280; see also ibid., 314, 315 for Ridgely's praise of the National Banking system.
253. Hull, op. cit., 300, 301; vol. I of this work, see Index under "Issue of notes in multiples of capital." For other examples showing the survival of old ideas, see A.B.A., Proceedings (1880), 103 [a safety fund is recommended again]; (1881), 54. [Is the issue of currency an individual or a sovereign right?]
254. Stickney in Hull, op. cit., 211.
255. See this volume, page 123.
256. See Lockhart, op. cit., 138.
257. See this volume, page 167.
258. See especially the books of Willis and Warburg.
259. Hull, op. cit., 149, 302.
260. To the extent that the various Comptrollers of the Currency identified themselves with reform proposals they can be found in the Reports. Dunbar surveyed them in "National Banking System," passim, and especially in the summary on page 25. A list of minor proposals is in A.B.A., Proceedings (1910), 347. A few suggestions may be mentioned specifically: the earlier proposals to permit state banks to issue notes persisted (Hull, op. cit., 304). For some years the plan to permit state, county, municipality, and railroad bonds as the basis of note issues played a certain role; (see Harter, op. cit., passim; Hull, op. cit., 268, 305). After the crisis of 1907 it was felt that National Banks in the reserve and central reserve cities should be permitted to accept drafts; see A.B.A., Proceedings (1910), 54, 347. The branch banking controversy has been treated earlier; see above, pages 194, 195.
261. A.B.A., Proceedings (1913), 75 ff.
262. A.B.A., Proceedings (1907), 116, 144; (1910), 311.
263. See also Horace White in Hull, op. cit., 295.
264. See, for example, the paper by Pugsley, "Emergency Circulation" in A.B.A., Proceedings (1902), 134 ff, reprinted also in Hull, op. cit., 302 ff. He claimed (p. 306) Charles G. Dawes as an exponent of the measure, as he actually was, see A.B.A., Proceedings (1902), 134 ff.
265. See the papers of William B. Dean and Horace White in Hull, op. cit., 187 ff, 290 ff. What the proponents of a credit currency were desiring was brought out very well in a popular booklet by Youngman, op. cit., passim.
266. Hull, op. cit., 399, 401 ff, 420.
267. Hull, op. cit., 399, 430.

268. This came out very clearly in a discussion between the Wisconsin country banker, A. J. Frame, and Representative Fowler, in A.B.A., Proceedings (1907), 119, 131. See also Fowler's statements in Hull, op. cit., 418, 419.
269. U.S. 53d Congr. 3d sess., House Document 1508, 366; Dawes in A.B.A., Proceedings (1902), 114.
270. A.B.A., Proceedings (1907), 141.
271. The "Minutes of the Meetings of the Credit Currency Commission" in A.B.A., Proceedings (1907), Appendix, 105 ff show clearly the clash of opinion among the bankers and the way in which the compromise satisfactory to all of them was reached. Incidentally, the so-called Lovering bill (H.R. 13303) of 1901 fits into the same pattern; see U.S. 56th Congr. 2d sess., Committee on Banking and Currency, Hearings and Arguments (1901), passim.
272. These features were also embodied in 1893 in plans of the Secretary of the Treasury and the Comptroller of the Currency; see U.S. 53d Congr. 3d sess., House Report 1508, 1 ff, 57 ff; and for the latter also, Report (1894), 32 ff. For the Baltimore Plan see A.B.A., Proceedings (1894), 69 ff; U.S. 53d Congr. 3d sess., House Report 1508, passim; Chapman-Westerfield, op. cit., 65, 66. As to the Indianapolis Monetary Convention see History of the Movement for the Monetary Convention, passim; Report of the Monetary Commission of the Indianapolis Convention, especially 45 ff, 53 ff, 60 ff; Chapman-Westerfield, op. cit., 67 ff; Breckenridge, R.M., "The Report of the Monetary Commission to the Executive Committee of the Indianapolis Monetary Convention" in Journal of the Canadian Bankers' Association (1898), 291 ff; Vorhis, op. cit., 275. Finally, the most important source regarding the plan of the Currency Commission of the American Bankers Association is A.B.A., Proceedings (1907), 109 ff, Appendix, 100 ff. Charles N. Fowler's bill H.R. 23017 was accompanied by 59th Congr. 2d sess., House Report 5629 which is reprinted also in A.B.A., Proceedings (1907), 123 ff. The discussion of the bill is to be found in U.S. 59th Congr. 2d sess., Hearings and Arguments before the Committee on Banking and Currency, passim. See also Forgan, Currency Commission, passim; James, Chicago Banks, 727 ff. For a contemporary treatment of the reform movement see Cleveland, op. cit., 265 ff, 291 ff; and numerous papers in Hull, op. cit., see Table of Contents.
273. Hull, op. cit., 316.
274. See this volume, pages 167, 168.
275. Chicago Banks, 727 ff.
276. Hull, op. cit., 316.
277. The radicals of the period saw this point, see Vorhis, op. cit., 94, 366.
278. As to the Baltimore Plan, see footnote 272 and

Hales, op. cit., 104 ff. A biography of Homer is in Cycl. Am. Biogr., XVI, 299. Additional material on his activities is in Hales, op. cit., see Index; U.S. 53d Congr. 3d sess., House Report 1508, 101 ff, 112.

279. See his presentation of the plan in A.B.A., Proceedings (1907), 109 ff (also his report in ibid. [1913], 75 ff) and his introductory statements in U.S. 59th Congr. 2d sess., Hearings (see footnote 272), 1 ff.

280. Synopsis of a Plan for National Bank Credit Currency, passim. Forgan also recommended an asset currency in 1903 in a speech before the Texan Bankers Association: "The Money Supply of the United States;" it is reprinted in Hull, op. cit., 307 ff, see especially, 311. Joseph T. Talbert (1866-1920), born in Mississippi, held various banking positions in Texas until he became a National Bank Examiner in 1894. When in 1898 James H. Eckels assumed the presidency of the Commercial National Bank of Chicago he made Talbert its cashier. Until 1909 he was connected with the bank whose vice president he became. Who was Who in America; Welton, op. cit., 17.

281. James, Chicago Banks, 744.

282. A.B.A., Proceedings (1912), 62, 63; James, Chicago Banks, 799.

283. Vanderlip remained an exponent of central banking in America; see Patterson, Raymond, op. cit., 61 ff.

284. Data on Warburg can be found in this volume, see index. See also A.B.A., Proceedings (1911), 208 ff; James, Chicago Banks, 801; Warburg's writings in the bibliographies to vols. I and II of this work.

285. Davison was very active in promoting the Aldrich plan; see Lamont, op. cit., 94.

286. Strong (1872-1928) started as a clerk in a private banking house in New York, became connected with the Atlantic and Metropolitan Trust Companies, and after the latter's absorption rose in the Bankers Trust Company whose president he became. In 1914 he was appointed Governor of the Federal Reserve Bank of New York. See Dict. Am. Biogr. and Who was Who in America.

287. See vol. I of this work, 178 ff.

288. See, for example, Bankers Magazine, XXX (1875/76), 297 ff.

289. Bankers Magazine, XXX (1875/76), 298. The radicals of the 1850's expressed this idea by saying that a "national bank" was becoming only a pure despotism or a limited monarchy. The Banks of England and France, for example, were auxiliaries of despotism. See Bilbo, op. cit., 55.

This way of thinking, typical of Jackson's days, survived for decades. In the Intercollegiate Debates of 1908 on central banking and related subjects we find the following statements: a central bank of issue was contrary to the American theory of government because it centralized power and would result in a monopoly of the banking business. This would be particularly undesirable since there was so much graft and corruption in high places. A central bank might fit into imperial governments, it did not belong into a republic (page 34). See also pages 333 ff: Imperfect as our banking system might have been, it was in accord with American institutions, while central banking was "foreign to our free and independent spirit of commercial progress." It was a death blow to Americanism, it would paralyze our energy, entangle us in red tape, etc., etc.

290. A Modified Central Bank of Issue, 8.

291. Proceedings (1881), 54.

292. Charles G. Dawes in A.B.A., Proceedings (1902), 119; idem, The Present Financial Situation, 7, 8; Morawetz, Banking and Currency Problem, 52 ff. (Much material on Morawetz can be found in Swaine, op. cit., see Index.) Other men who took the same stand were Jacob Schiff (see Adler, op. cit., I, 284, 285), Secretary of the Treasury Leslie M. Shaw and Representative Fowler (Patterson, Raymond, op. cit., 39 ff, 44 ff; he also reports, pages 89 ff, on an interview with Dawes in which the latter repeated the ideas expressed in his above-quoted publication).

293. As early as 1845, the board of control of the State Bank of Ohio was called "central office;" see this volume, page 26. A.B.A., Proceedings (1886), 73, 74; Comptroller of the Currency, Report (1898), xxiii (Canada with its 38 "central banks of issue"). But the same Report (page xxii) speaks of "central governmental banks of Europe."

294. Gov. Morehead, see 35th Congr. 1st sess., House Executive Document 107, 250, 251.

295. Bankers Magazine, XII (1857/58), 888.

296. As to the former paper see New Englander, XV (1857), 712, 713 and as to the latter, the reprint pages 18, 19, 22. In this connection attention must be drawn to George Tucker's The Theory of Money and Banks of 1839, 328 ff. He recommended the establishment of two or three "national banks" with branches all over the country which would compete and mutually check each other. Of course, he did not understand that there cannot be competing central banks. Moreover one cannot trace actual influence lines emanating from this suggestion.

297. Chamber of Commerce of the State of New York, Memorial, Minority Report of the Chamber of Commerce Committee [signed George Opdyke] (n.p., n.d. [1869(?)]), 5. This plan was repeated as late as 1906 by Henry Clews in the speech "The Monetary Situation and its Remedies," see Hull, op. cit., 409. He thought of the New York Clearing House Committee or of a

298. Larson, Cooke, 220.
299. Views on Currency and Specie Payments by a Banker (n.p., n.d. [about 1875]), 2.
300. A.B.A., Proceedings (1880), 103.
301. Taus, op. cit., passim. In 1906 Jacob Schiff stressed that in America the Sub-Treasury played a role like the Bank of England; Adler, op. cit., I, 279.
302. Examination, 43, 44. See also the contemporary quotations in Miller, Harry E., op. cit., 211, 212 which show the earlier steps in that direction.
303. Gordon, Thomas F., op. cit., 91, his source (reprinted in full) being a minority report of the Ways and Means Committee.
304. Grubb, op. cit., 1.
305. London, op. cit., passim; London is mentioned by Knox, History, 115.
306. Grubb, op. cit., passim. He reprints two letters from George S. Coe (pages 6 ff). Joseph Caldwell Grubb (1818-1879), a leader in the business and social life of Pennsylvania, was widely traveled in America and Europe. He was first connected with a firm trading in firearms, later in business for himself. A director of the Bank of Pennsylvania he was considered an authority on the money market; see Jordan, Wilfred, ed., Colonial and Revolutionary Families of Pennsylvania, New Series (New York, 1939), 794.
307. Daniel H. London (1818-1875) was born in Amherst County, Virginia, and was a dry goods wholesaler in Richmond. He was an ardent supporter of Calhoun and state rights. After the Civil War he moved to New York. See his obituary in Richmond Dispatch of December 8, 1875 and Hiden, P. W., "The London Family" in William and Mary College Quarterly, Second Series, XII (1932), 265 ff. This information was kindly provided by the Virginia State Library, Richmond.
308. London, Exchequer, passim, especially 6-8, 12, 13, 31, 32, 37, 39, 40; also the address of 1874.
309. Vol. XXX (1875/76), 297 ff, 450 ff.
310. Report (1868), xxi, xxii; (1869), xii, xiii.
311. Who was Who in America.
312. Gilman, in Walker, J. H., Argument, 50, 51; U.S. House Committee on Banking and Currency, Hearings (1896/97), 60 ff, 95; Gilman, Graded Banking, 102, 103, 115, 298, 303.
313. Joseph Henry Walker (1829-1907) was a politician and a shoe and leather manufacturer. For the above, see U.S. 55th Congr. 2d sess., House Report 1575, Part 2, 241 ff, especially 246, 259.

314. A.B.A., Proceedings (1895), 66.
315. A.B.A., Proceedings (1901), 113, also reprinted in Hull, op. cit., 219. Such a keen foreign observer as Boissevain, op. cit., 30, took a similar stand.
316. Hull, op. cit., 230, 231.
317. New York Clearing House, Proceedings in Memory of Tappen, 35.
318. Monetary Situation, 7; reprinted by Hull, op. cit., 408.
319. See vol. I of this work, pages 100, 142.
320. See this volume page 115 and vol. I of this work, page 261.
321. A.B.A., Proceedings (1886), 9.
322. Another proposal of straight government guarantee is embodied in a plan of the Oklahoma Bankers Association meeting in Guthrie in the fall of 1907; see Cooke's article of 1913 in Barnett, State Banks and Trust Companies, 263.
323. See his pamphlet, passim.
324. Cycl. Am. Biogr., I, 233; see his Guaranty of Bank Deposits, passim.
325. Cooke in Barnett, op. cit., 303, 304.
326. But not all of them; see A.B.A., Proceedings (1905), 139 ff. For the attitude of the majority see ibid. (1908), 42 ff, 260, 261, 274 ff; (1909), 246 ff; Dawes in a paper of 1908 in Essays and Speeches, 95 ff.
327. Quoted from James, Chicago Banks, 774.
328. Recollections, 189 ff.
329. Clews, No Government Guaranty, 3; Wade, op. cit., 426 ff.
330. Should National Bank Deposits be Guaranteed, 4.
331. In Bank Guaranty Scheme, 8.
332. Report (1894), 17 ff, 23.
333. Bank Guaranty Scheme, 12, 13. The idea of a postal savings bank was very popular in the country; see Patterson, Raymond, op. cit., 100 ff.
334. A.B.A., Proceedings (1909), 248, 249. Incidentally this passage is a remarkable contribution to the understanding of businessmen's propaganda and the working of businessmen's minds. See also the items of Depew and Stevenson on the subject.
335. Forgan, op. cit., 5; Wade, op. cit., passim.
336. See this volume, page 285.
337. Cooke in Barnett, op. cit., 309 ff, 331.
338. Baker Library, Harvard University. It has been impossible to identify Wheeler.
339. John Schuette in Hull, op. cit., 149 ff.
340. Watson, Frank, op. cit., 3; Cooke in Barnett, op. cit., 315.
341. James, Chicago Banks, 780, 781.
342. As to details see the table prepared by Cooke and reprinted by Barnett, op. cit., facing page 264.
343. "Necessary Changes," 56.
344. U.S. 53d Congr. 3d sess., House Report 1508, 240, 241, 300 ff.
345. Adler, op. cit., I, 282.

346. See his address of 1903 in Hull, op. cit., 344 ff. In view of Dawes' great reputation one is surprised at the role which he played in the 1890's and 1900's. His outlook on banking in the 1890's was just one hundred years behind his time (see this chapter, page 175). He was against every comprehensive reform proposal of the day: against asset currency, against branch banking, against central banking (see Present Financial Situation, passim).   But he did not come out with any important proposal of his own. He was for a high-taxed emergency currency, in fact for patchwork. Dawes himself was apologetic; "I do not want to be considered an obstructionist," he said in 1903 (Essays and Speeches, 316).

347. Hull, op. cit., 255.

348. Cycl. Am. Biogr., X, 150; Frame, Sketch of his Life (in future to be cited Sketch), 7, 8; Who was Who in America.

349. Panics, passim; reprinted in Sketch, 11 ff. See also a speech of 1899 in ibid., 28.

350. Sketch, 38, 124, 168.

351. Ibid., 63, 65, 176; A.B.A., Proceedings (1913), 94.

352. Sketch, 103.

353. Ibid., 32 and 61; 36 and 120; and ibid., 40 and Bankers Magazine, LXIII (1901), 1017.

354. Sketch, 38, 63, 104, 107, 149, etc., etc.

355. A.B.A., Proceedings (1907), 142; Sketch, 52 and numerous other places.

356. Compare Sketch, 64 and 122.

357. Ibid., 77, 104, 105.

358. "Branch Banking and Asset Currency," 1017, 1023. The rubber stamp is on the reprint in the Baker Library of Harvard University.

359. Sketch, 114, 125, 149, 163, 176.

360. Ibid., 39, 145.

361. Walker, E. B., Abnormal Features, 14.

362. Sketch, 64 (speech before the Wisconsin Bankers Association, 1903); 135 (paper of 1908); and similarly 170 (paper of 1910).

363. Ibid., 123 (speech of 1907).

364. Speech of 1902 before the Michigan State Bankers Association in Sketch, 52; A.B.A., Proceedings (1904), 124, reprinted in Hull, op. cit., 171, 172.

365. See above, page 211.

366. A.B.A., Proceedings (1907), 140, 141; also Sketch, 128 ff.

367. "Diagnosis of the World's Elastic Currency Problems" in American Academy, Lessons, 77 ff (reprinted in Sketch, 134 ff, especially 156 ff) and his paper, "Advantage of a Central Bank" in Moody's Magazine of 1910, reprinted in Sketch, 159 ff.

368. Vol. I (1910/11) under the title, "How to Prevent Cash Suspension by Banks," reprinted in Sketch, 167 ff, especially 168, 180, also 185 (speech of 1912).

369. A.B.A., Proceedings (1913), 94.

370. Frame's writings and Caldwell's Recollections belong to the most important sources for the cultural level of American nineteenth-century bankers.

371. Sketch, 163.

372. Ibid., 55, 61, 62, 119, 120.

373. Ibid., 161, 216. It is indicative of the vainglorious, self-deceived, and uncultured man that these writings and speeches were reprinted and disseminated as late as 1931 instead of being permitted to sink into oblivion. In order to gain the right perspective one should view them together with the contemporaneous essays and speeches of Dawes, Forgan, and Hepburn.

374. After having made one of his typical speeches at the 1907 meeting of the A.B.A. Frame was treated unmercifully and cut a pitiful figure; Proceedings (1907), 146 ff. See also U.S. 52d Congr. 2d sess., House Committee on Banking and Currency, Hearings and Arguments (1906/07), 160.: On the question whether he had read a certain speech of Frame, the Chicago banker, Talbert answered: "No, I have not, but I know Mr. Frame," an answer which has certain implications.

375. In 1895 the Reports of the Comptroller of the Currency began systematically to contain information on foreign banking; the Report of 1894 (pages 32 ff) is full of references to English, Scottish, Canadian, and German banking.

376. It would, of course, be impossible (and entirely meaningless besides) to cite a great number of references to English and Scottish banking in the period. Official documents, scholarly publications, and popular works abound with such references. Those who wish may inspect, for example, U.S. 53d Congr. 3d sess., House Report 1508 (1894), 25, 58, 122, 144; U.S. 59th Congr. 2d sess., House Report 5629, passim; U.S. 59th Congr. 2d sess., House Committee on Banking and Currency, Hearings and Arguments on Proposed Currency Legislation 1906/1907, 2, 7, 16, 21 ff and numerous other pages; A.B.A., Proceedings (1901), 113; (1905), 118 ff; (1906), 91, 93; (1907), 132, 146; Report of the Indianapolis Monetary Convention, see Index.

377. "Branch Banking," 244.

378. Hague, op. cit., 378, 379; Forgan, Recollections, 96.

379. A.B.A., Proceedings (1877), 13 ff; (1881), 98 ff; (1886), 76 ff; (1891), 82 ff. See also B. E. Walker's papers read before American bankers by this outstanding Canadian colleague of theirs.

380. U.S. 53d Congr. 3d sess., House Document 1508, 58, 67, 101, 103, 125, 144, 175.

381. Breckenridge, op. cit., passim.

382. References to Canadian banking can be found, for example, in the following documents: U.S. 59th Congr. 2d sess., House Report 5629 (Issue and Redemption of National Bank

Guaranteed Credit Notes) or U.S. 52d Congr. 2d sess., House Committee on Banking and Currency, Hearings and Arguments on Proposed Currency Legislation 1906/07, 7, 10, 16, 21 ff, 45, and numerous other places; Senator Aldrich in U.S. 61st Congr. 2d sess., Senate Document 406, 23, 24. A.B.A., Proceedings (1906), 91, 93; (1907), 143, 146, 149, 151; (for references in the earlier Proceedings of the A.B.A., see Table of Contents and Index to the Proceedings of the A.B.A. from 1875 to 1892 inclusive compiled by William T. Brannt [New York, 1893]); Report of the Monetary Commission of the Indianapolis Monetary Convention, see Index. For references in private publications see, Cornwall, op. cit., passim; Sound Currency, VI (1899), 55. Jacob Schiff's interest in Canadian banking is mentioned by Adler, op. cit., I, 273; etc., etc.

383. Breckenridge, op. cit., 21.

384. Ibid., 6, 15, 18.

385. Shortt, op. cit., passim.

386. The migration of banking ideas between the United States and Canada is of great interest. Originally Canadian banking, as mentioned above, was created under American influence and modeled on the First Bank of the United States. By 1850 Canada adopted Free Banking, New York style, which not taking root was abandoned. By the end of the 1860's the copying of the National Banking system was widely recommended in Canada, but ultimately defeated. While in the following two decades Canadian banking in the form which it had developed out of what had been common in America by 1800 re-influenced the United States, Canada herself introduced the safety fund system which is, of course, an American device. In turn the success of this adoption re-recommended the safety fund system to the United States bankers and politicians.

387. Who is Who in Finance (1911), 1021; Hague, op. cit., 315 ff.

388. A.B.A., Proceedings (1886), 76 ff.

389. See the latter's addresses in the bibliography to this volume.

390. See his Recollections, passim, his various writings, and the numerous references to his activities in James, Chicago Banks, Index. Also Popple, op. cit., 44, 45.

391. Dawes, Essays and Speeches, 67.

392. Again it is impossible to give anything like a complete survey of the innumerable references to German banking which can be found in the period under investigation in official documents in professional publications, and in the popular literature. The following are a few examples: U.S. 53d Congr. 3d sess., House Report 1508, 24, 25, 122, 144, 242, 259; U.S. 54th Congr. 1st and 2d sess., House Committee on Banking and Currency, Hearings and Arguments, 1896-1897, 118, 158, 167; U.S. 59th Congr. 2d sess., House Committee on Banking and Currency, Hearings and Arguments on proposed Currency Legislation, 1906/07, 13, 16, 21 ff, 71, 75, 84; U.S. 59th Congr. 2d sess., House Report 5629, passim; Comptroller of the Currency, Reports (1885), xxvi; (1895), 29; (1906), 75; A.B.A., Proceedings (1902), 129; (1906), 91, 159, 162, 164; (1907), 113, 133, 141; Sound Currency, VI (1899), 55; Report of the Monetary Commission of the Indianapolis Monetary Convention, see Index; etc., etc.

393. An Address before the Economic Club of New York on the Work of the National Monetary Commission; U.S. 61st Congr. 2d sess., Senate Document 406, 8.

394. This is evident, for instance, from Warburg, Paul M., Defects and Needs, passim and idem, Discount System, 19, 28. In the address, "American and European Banking Methods and Banking Legislation" (in Currency Problem, 135), Warburg criticizes the German banks for "taking it all," i.e., for assuming too many functions. In the same series of addresses (in ibid., 17) Frank A. Vanderlip (National City Bank, New York) recommended the German central banking system combined with the Canadian system of branch banks as the proper solution for America. For German influence, see also Jacobs, L. M., in U.S. 61st Congr. 2d sess., Senate Document 569, 5.

395. A.B.A., Proceedings (1907), 57 ff.

396. American Academy, Banking Problems, 52, 87.

397. See Miles, op. cit., passim.

Chapter XIX

THE CLEARING OF OUT-OF-TOWN CHECKS

The collection of out-of-town items was a problem which baffled American bankers throughout the nineteenth century. It originated when banknotes first came to be circulated over wider areas within which they gravitated to trade centers, and when notes were issued purposely at places remote from that of their redemption. In earlier chapters of this work it has been described how the collection business was handled by the banks between about 1800 and 1860.[1] During Biddle's era difficulties in this respect were less serious than either before or after; for during his incumbency the Second Bank of the United States was de facto a central bank watching over the solvency and liquidity of the whole American banking system by enforcing frequent and regular redemption of notes. At the same time the comparatively few out-of-town checks which came into the hands of banks could be disposed of easily. They were treated as domestic exchange, and as such were taken by the Bank of the United States which possessed the mechanism to deal with them. However, when the check business expanded after 1840 the Bank no longer existed and so the redemption of out-of-town checks became a problem separate from that of the redemption of out-of-town notes. While the latter was solved after the introduction of National Banking, the cashing of out-of-town checks remained difficult for decades after the redemption of out-of-town notes as well as the clearing of local checks had become matters of routine.

By 1900 the use of checks for payments in places other than the place of issue had assumed such proportions that out-of-town checks were becoming a real puzzle for the large banks in the trade and financial centers. They had to reshape their internal organization in order to cope with the new difficulties: transit departments, so-called, were the answer. The latter grew rapidly and came to be among the largest and most important departments of city banks. But they were sore spots because of their ever increasing expense and constant demand for more help; and yet they hardly ever paid their way and were dreaded by the bank personnel because of their long hours and hard work. Thus it was in the transit departments that mechanization of banking procedures, i.e., the use of labor saving devices, was first introduced. But before such devices were adopted, other labor saving changes had been made: the name of the drawer of a check was dropped in registering it, while at the same time, the carbon copy replaced the copy book. These innovations helped, but they helped for a short time only, until a further increase in foreign items made the task of handling them as hard as it had ever been. "The remedy appeared in the form of a typewriter or billing machine with a tabular attachment. The amounts were printed in a column by means of a tabulator which spaced automatically. This marked the introduction of mechanical means for registering." The new method, while economizing time and labor, was still far from being satisfactory. But when adding attachments came into the market the problem was considered as really solved, until the introduction of numerical systems, i.e., the designation of accounts by numbers instead of names, showed that there had been room for further improvement. Numerical systems made it possible to write transit letters on specially constructed adding machines with keys for certain standard instructions.[2]

Banks could handle the collection of out-of-town checks in one of two ways: they could either try to make it a source of profit or, looking at the indirect advantages resulting from an increased check business, they could facilitate the latter by making regional par-collection arrangements, ultimately to be topped by a national par-collection system.[3] Aiming at such an all embracing system was nothing but the logical development of the basic ideas underlying the creation of the American clearing house. As early as 1857, George D. Lyman had written: "Possibly the time is not remote when a voluntary system of par exchanges and redemption of bank issues will exist among all the banks of the United States."[4]

Actually both methods (collection at a profit and the building of par-collection systems) were being tried by 1900; (and in addition in some cities such as Philadelphia, Newark, Jersey City, Albany, Troy, and Providence, banks absorbed collection charges without organizing formal collection systems). In the first case banks charged their depositors exchange for out-of-town checks; but competition tended to lower the rates until ultimately they no longer remunerated the banks for the cost of the service. It also forced them to designate numerous cities as co-called par-points, i.e., places for checks on which no collection charges were debited. The system of par-points in turn led to the queerest and most unsound routing by banks of out-of-town checks in order to save those charges. In the end keen competition for accounts, typical of the period, resulted in the general adoption of the alternative policy mentioned above. But before this was done, serious attempts were being made throughout the 1900's in numerous cities (91, in fact, in 1912) to fix collection charges at a remunerative level. The earliest plan of this type is supposed to have been put into effect in Buffalo in 1881 when the worst rate cutter, and at the same time the most efficient one, himself proposed uniform collection charges. His suggestion was gladly accepted and the scheme worked in that city for a number of years.[5]

A decade later Western clearing houses became interested in the matter of collection charges, the very first being that of St. Joseph, Missouri. When the St. Louis Clearing House followed suit, this fact attracted general attention; and when in 1899 the New York Clearing House Association took a hand in the establishment of uniform and compulsory collection charges on out-of-town checks "it created the greatest stir in the banking world."[6] It was James G. Cannon (1858-1916), then vice-president and later president of the Fourth National Bank of New York, who assumed leadership when the matter became pressing:[7] Prior to the 1890's, inland merchants had been accustomed to buy New York funds from their banks and to pay bills due in New York in checks on the city. However with the expansion of checking accounts all over the country, more and more of them found it convenient to pay their debts with personal checks which their purveyors could not refuse, and these checks, of course, were deposited with New York banks. While the latter usually required a fair remuneration for collecting the items, strong customers whose accounts were valuable could easily force their banks to desist from making such charges. Under these circumstances, rules and regulations regarding collections outside the City of New York, embodying compulsory collection charges, were adopted by the New York Clearing House on April 3, 1899.

In the years to follow attempts were made to coordinate the respective actions of the various clearing houses so as to make the move toward adequate collection charges a national one. The A.B.A. was to be the platform. A Committee on Conference of Clearing Houses of the United States was established which at its first meeting in September, 1899, in Cleveland resolved "that the practice of charging exchange for the handling of out-of-town items [was] just and proper and within the scope of legitimate banking." It therefore recommended that all the clearing house associations of the country adopt suitable by-laws or amend their constitutions. Thereby they were to assume appropriate powers to establish rules and regulations regarding collection charges, at the same time providing for their enforcement. The Committee on Conference, reorganized as a committee of the newly established Clearing House Section of the American Bankers Association, held annual meetings, but in 1906 it had to concede that progress had been slow.[8]

Shortly thereafter a new drive was organized. "Letters were written to the secretaries of the various State [Bankers] Associations and with them a form of letter [was mailed] and the request that they send this letter out to their various members asking for information as to whether they would or would not favor a plan for a uniform charge of, say one dollar per thousand on all out-of-town items, and urging the smaller banks in turn to levy this charge of one dollar upon all their customers... After analyzing carefully [the] replies it was found that it would not be practicable, for the reason that the banks in nearly all of the smaller towns absolutely declined to make any change or establish any uniform rate or to submit to a charge of one dollar per thousand to be made upon them by their correspondents. They raised the point that if they [were] obliged to charge their own customers in the small towns that there [would] be no inducement to the small customer to carry his account in the smaller towns and that he [would] carry his account in the large centers and that they [would] therefore lose the business. They furthermore claim[ed] that they [were] carrying their deposits in the large cities and receiving no compensating benefit in the way of interest. On the other hand, the banks in the large cities, who [were] compelled to bear the burden, [were] naturally all willing to enter into an arrangement to make a uniform charge of one dollar per thousand."[9] In view of this reaction nothing could be accomplished in the way of this proposal.

The New York rules and regulations of 1899, however, remained in effect unchallenged until 1912.[10] In the latter year on motion of Alonzo Barton Hepburn, then chairman of the board of the Chase National Bank, a special committee of the Clearing House was set up to make a thorough investigation "of the subject of inland exchange and collections and the methods pursued by other clearing house associations."[11]

There were two problems involved in the collection of out-of-town checks; first, the cost of collection and, secondly, the amount of time consumed in making that collection. The special committee of the New York Clearing House, abovementioned, investigated the matter on the basis of interviews with leading bank officers and of questionnaires. It found that in 1911 on a total of about $4,859,187,900 worth (or a daily average of $16,284,346) of foreign checks collected by New York banks the latter under the rules of 1899 made a small profit. Here is how the committee figured:

Collection charges in 1911		$2,139,551.00
Cost	$1,176,162.00	
Proportionate share of overhead	569,461.78	
Estimated loss of interest	296,460.00	
		2,042,083.78
		$ 97,467.22

Of course these figures represented estimates rather than exact findings and it is not surprising that the private estimates of individual bankers differed widely.

In judging the computation one must keep in mind that the New York Clearing House banks distinguished between discretionary points, 1/10 points, and 1/4 points. The first named were Boston, Providence, Albany, Troy, Jersey City, Bayonne (home office of Standard Oil!!), Hoboken, Newark, Philadelphia, and Baltimore, and also New York City and Greater New York to the extent that banks were neither members of the Clearing House nor affiliated as "non-members." Banks were free to charge or not to charge for collections on those "discretionary" places. On the two last-named points they had to charge ten and twenty-five cents per thousand, respectively. In 1911 71 per cent of all foreign checks were drawn on discretionary, and 24 per cent and 5 per cent, respectively, on 1/10 and 1/4 points.

As a result of the investigation the committee recommended that the rules and regulations of 1899 remain unchanged except in special areas. It was proposed that charges be discretionary on items on banks and trust companies in the states of Massachusetts, Rhode Island, Connecticut, New Jersey, and New York if they would engage themselves in writing to remit upon receipt of checks drawn on them in par and New York funds. What was envisaged was the making of whole sections of those states into discretionary points if all the local banks agreed to those conditions; and

perhaps as a later step the organization of a foreign check department in the New York Clearing House and so to "go down to a par basis." Incidentally, the New York policy led in the first instance to keen competition of banks located in discretionary points (especially Newark). They solicited business from New York merchants who thus saved the collection charges and nevertheless had their own checks collected at par.

As has been mentioned before, James G. Cannon was the exponent of the policy of compulsory collection charges for out-of-town checks. This attitude of his was well in line with his general interests. Cannon had turned to a thorough study of banking practices at a time when this line of business was still dominated by experience and rule-of-thumb. He was among the first to see the importance of exact accounting methods for banks and he became one of the originators of what was then called the "scientific credit movement." Its exponents, and Cannon among them, aimed at credit analysis which would aid in basing credit on objective criteria. In connection with such endeavors he established in the early 1890's the first credit department in any metropolitan bank, and his interest in clearing methods and policies, a field in which he became the outstanding expert, dated from that time. In short, he was a man who may well be characterized as the prototype of the creative manager. From his observations of cost accounting Cannon came to the conclusion that collection charges were necessary for banks, and since these charges could be upheld only in the framework of agreements among the banks concerned, he became the exponent of such agreements.[12]

Being a man of strong convictions Cannon soon became the main antagonist of those who, adopting the opposite view, tried to build up an extensive regional par-collection system for out-of-town checks. Such systems had first come into existence on a restricted scale in the last quarter of the nineteenth century. One was in effect in Pittsburgh, without formal rules or formal agreement, between 1875 and 1885. Another was established in 1896 in Sedalia, Missouri, where collections were made at par from twenty-three banks within a radius of thirty miles. Finally, by 1900 Walter E. Frew[13] (who later was to play an important role in New York banking as the president of the Corn Exchange Bank and who was at that time the president of the small Queens County Bank on Long Island, New York) was busy organizing a par-collection system for checks on banks on Long Island outside of Brooklyn. None of these systems was of great consequence. Of real importance, however, was the par-collection system which was organized in Boston in the early years of the present century.[14] It seems to this author that it is not an accident that this remarkable achievement was attained in New England with its tradition of the Suffolk Bank System. This theory is all the more probable since the plans to establish country-check clearings in Boston go as far back as 1877. At that time, of course, every New England banker was familiar with the country-note clearing system of that bank, even though that system was already defunct.

In 1877 a committee of the Boston Clearing House Association reported to that body that the collection of New England checks was effected with unnecessary labor and risk and at an expense of about $229,000 per annum. The committee expected that the inconveniences would increase with the expansion of business. Therefore it recommended the establishment of country-check clearings. The desirability of remedying the above evil was generally conceded, and there was even a majority in the Clearing House Association willing to take action. However, this majority bowed to a strong minority. The latter opposed any change because it would sever business connections long established; because the clerical force to handle the proposed country clearings would be so expensive that it would offset any possible savings; and finally, because the Clearing House Association was too loose an organization to be charged properly with so difficult a task. The minority was, rather, for setting up a new National Bank, of which the existing banks should become stockholders and which would practice country-check clearing as its special business. It was quickly recognized that under the existing laws this project was illegal, and after one of the committee members started to fight the plan root and branch it came to naught.[15]

However, the idea of clearing out-of-town checks did not lie dormant for long. As early as 1883 it was again taken up and another committee was appointed which reported that the problem had become more serious than ever. The receipt of out-of-town checks by Boston banks had doubled since 1877 and the cost of having them redeemed had increased to $400,000 per annum. The committee suggested that some sort of clearing house be established in Boston to handle the collection of out-of-town checks. This time measures were taken to put the scheme into operation; but at the last it failed again, as did a few later attempts which did not reach even that advanced state.

Success came at last, through the efforts of an outsider, one James C. Hallock, Jr., whose father had played a minor role in setting up the New York Clearing House, as has been mentioned above.[16] Hallock, thoroughly familiar with the principles of clearings, had a casual conversation in May, 1898, with a Providence, Rhode Island, banker, from which he came to the conviction that something had to be done to facilitate the collection of out-of-town checks. Upon presenting a plan, he was told, however, that Providence was not the right place for an experiment of that character; at the same time he was encouraged to try elsewhere. Thus he brought his ideas to the attention of a group of Connecticut bankers; he investigated the possibilities in New York; and finally, in June, 1898, he came to Boston where, as described above, the soil was well prepared. Submitting his suggestions to one bank after another he won the backing of leading executives and especially of Francis B. Sears who became strongly interested in solving the problem. In consequence of Hallock's endeavors the matter was taken up from where it had been left in 1883; but instead of going back to the plan of that year which only needed ratification, a majority of the banks (forty-two out of fifty) endorsed Hallock's proposals.

At this stage the Association of Boston Bank Presidents appointed a committee to look into the matter. It recommended that the Clearing House Association undertake the collection of out-of-town checks. (Whether or not it was recognized at that early moment that the recommendation implied the establishment of a regional par collection system cannot be determined.) As a result, Hallock's plan was submitted at a special meeting called for December 7, 1898, and was adopted in principle. A five-man committee was appointed for the purpose of putting it into effect; but for reasons unknown, this group did not succeed and in April, 1899, a sub-committee was charged with the task. It consisted of Francis Bacon Sears, then vice-president of the Third National Bank[17] who became an acknowledged leader in the matter of collections, and Thomas P. Beal (1849-1923), president of the Second National Bank. This sub-committee worked effectively and the clearing of out-of-town checks was established along the lines of Hallock's suggestions.[18]

Hallock and the bankers looked to the country clearings effected by the London correspondents of the English country banks as a possible model. However, they found that because of the strong opposition of some powerful Boston banks the system could not be adopted in Boston without change. Those banks fought the innovation which, they felt, threatened the stability of their correspondent relationships. In vain did Hallock point out that according to the London experience country clearings favored the concentration of accounts in a few banks rather than their dispersion in many, and that the three Boston banks then especially interested in this type of business and holding thirty-nine per cent of the accounts would be benefited by the change. (One of these three kept aloof from the country clearings for more than two years.) In view of such opposition, it was necessary to devise a method which would work regardless of whether or not a one-hundred-per-cent participation of the Boston banks could be attained. Hallock solved the problem by suggesting that the participating banks should clear according to the London system, sending clerks to the Clearing House daily to exchange the checks drawn on their respective New England correspondents. The checks thus received by each participating bank were to be settled two days later in the regular city clearings (two days being considered time enough to obtain advice of the payment of a check or the unpaid check itself as an uncollectable item). The non-cooperating minority of the Boston banks, however, would be represented in the country clearings by the Clearing House manager, and therein the Boston plan deviated from the London model. The Clearing House manager was to receive the checks drawn on correspondents of non-cooperating banks. He was to collect these items and pay them upon receipt through the regular city clearings.[19] Hallock rightly foresaw that this scheme would work in spite of the relatively large number of non-cooperating banks and the number of their correspondents. It actually worked so well that it seemed unnecessary to complicate the clearing procedure by applying two methods at the same time. Thus the London method of clearing through correspondents was dropped and what had been considered as a temporary measure only (clearing through the agency of the Clearing House manager) became the established practice and was generally known under the name of "Boston plan."

Thus the Foreign Department of the Boston Clearing House came into being, with Hallock providing the ideas and Francis B. Sears and Thomas P. Beal the driving force. Charles A. Ruggles (1849-1922), "an experienced bank clerk" and "executive officer of signal ability," was the creative manager who successfully put the scheme into effect.[20] He, for instance, developed the blank forms to be used out of those employed for city clearings. In April, 1899, the matter had matured to the point that the participating Boston banks could submit the plan to a committee of the Massachusetts country banks. Although it was expected that the country-check clearings would ultimately embrace the whole of New England it was considered wise to begin in Massachusetts alone. As the result of this meeting a conference was called of the Boston Clearing House Committee and the Massachusetts National Bank Cashiers Association, a conference which revealed a deep-reaching difference of opinion between the two groups. The country banks felt that the proposal implied the redemption in Boston of checks drawn on them, instead of at their own counters, an interference with their established methods which they resented. The Boston Clearing House Committee, on the other hand, while not wishing to dictate to the country banks how they should run their business claimed for themselves the right to manage theirs as they pleased. Aiming at the establishment of a par collection system they impressed upon the country banks that if the latter should charge exchange for their remittances to Boston, checks drawn on them would not be accepted at par in the city and would have to be collected by an express company. As a result, most opposition vanished before the meeting ended. In a second conference the country banks requested the privilege of settling in either Boston or New York funds at their discretion, a concession which was gladly made. Furthermore the Boston banks conceded that specie would be transported to Boston at their expense, if and when country banks chose to pay that way. After an agreement had thus been reached, the clearing of Massachusetts country checks started on June 8, 1899; Maine, Connecticut, and Rhode Island were included in the same year; while New Hampshire and Vermont joined in the following year. During the first years 541, 565, and 607 million dollars worth of checks, respectively, were cleared at an expense of 10, 8, and 7 cents, respectively, for a thousand dollars, at which latter level the cost remained stable. The advantage of the system for the city banks was undoubted; the country banks, however, were somewhat disappointed. They had hoped that once their checks became redeemable in Boston they would be taken at par not only there but also in New York. This expectation did not materialize.[21]

The "Boston Plan" of collecting the checks of country banks was simple. Each day the members of the Clearing House turned in such checks as they had received in the course of their business, after having endorsed them to the manager of the Clearing House. The latter had them assorted and every evening sent them to the country banks on which they were drawn. The drawees, in turn, remitted the proceeds without delay in Boston or New York funds. Finally, the Boston banks, on the morning of the second day following, charged their original receipts for country checks to the Clearing House, a system which implied that the manager of the Clearing House was himself a member of the Clearing House. New York funds received in the settlement of country checks were distributed at par among the members in proportion to the volume of their business.[22]

The Foreign Department of the Boston Clearing House did not have smooth sailing all the way,[23] but quickly ran into a storm when a number of recalcitrant small banks in New Hampshire and Vermont refused to remit at par. This storm corresponded to that which once had raged when weak banks fought against the Second Bank of the United States and the Suffolk Bank, respectively. Even the methods applied by the warring banks in 1825 and 1900 were pretty much the same.[24] The "insurgents" were banks which shunned every sort of control that would expose their weakness, which could not afford to lose even pennies, which tried to snatch advantages from their competitors by fair means or foul, or which were just shortsighted. The more selfish their purposes, the loftier were their arguments. They found their leader in one Albert H. Eastman, cashier of the Berlin National Bank in Berlin, New Hampshire, who had begun his banking career in Colebrook, New Hampshire, in 1890, had later founded a National Bank in Berlin, and by 1900 was building up a chain of banks. He founded institutions in various places in New England and gained a foothold even in Boston. Eastman was the most ardent enemy of the Foreign Department of the Boston Clearing House. In 1899 he called a meeting of the "insurgents" and suggested organized resistance.[25] All checks should be stamped "payable if desired in Boston and New York funds less exchange." At the same time, he proposed that the country banks should acquire the control of an existing National Bank in Boston or organize a new one which would not join the Clearing House but would look out for the interests of the country banks (or rather the Eastman chain?). (It would be interesting to know whether the Bank of Mutual Redemption was remembered by the participants in this meeting.) Like others of the chain builders of those years, Eastman met a bad end. Early in 1904 he was arrested for irregularities (which his friends claimed to be "purely technical offences") and died a few months later (a suicide?).

With Eastman out of the way the backbone of the resistance was broken, but the Foreign Money Department of the Boston Clearing House had had to put up a tough fight in which it was not wholly successful.[26] Lack of success was due to an error in judgment and to the fact that it was being double-crossed by some of its members. The department could have applied two efficient weapons: it could have refused to cash checks of non-par-paying banks, as had been done in London in the middle of the nineteenth century when the country clearings were established there. Or it could have charged exchange for all checks turned in by non-par-paying banks. Instead of using either of these methods, the Clearing House chose to collect the checks of such banks by express companies. In establishing this policy, however, its exponents overlooked that government would transport silver free of charge to the country banks. Consequently the latter paid the checks presented in silver which had to be transported to Boston at great expense to the associated banks. It was the "insurgents'" Boston correspondents, themselves members of the Clearing House, who put the Subtreasury to work and helped to defeat their own organization. All that remained to be done thereafter was the adoption of an exchange charge on the checks of non-par-paying banks.

More serious were difficulties which developed in the intercourse with New York, since the systems of the two cities (Boston par collections versus New York compulsory exchange charges) were incompatible. For some time attempts were made to convince New York of the advantages of a par-collection system. Hallock, having been successful in Boston and possessing the backing of the Connecticut banks, strove for that goal. His endeavors were in vain, and an awkward situation developed as far as Connecticut checks were concerned. When these were deposited in New York, exchange was deducted; then they were sent to Boston by the New York banks and collected at par. This procedure so aggravated the Connecticut banks that they almost withdrew from the Boston par-collection system, and the Boston banks began to waver. In the spring of 1899 they discussed whether or not they should abandon their system and adopt that of New York; but Thomas P. Beal, chairman of a subcommittee to report on this question and a stanch friend of the "Boston Plan," reported against any change and won the day.

New York, accustomed to leadership, would have liked to whip Boston into line. In the eyes of the New York bankers their own procedure recommended itself because it avoided coercion of country banks, resulted in concerted action among the city banks, and gave the former that profit for which they hankered.[27] Since the measure was conservative, it caused less friction than the very progressive "Boston Plan." To be sure, the New York banks had troubles of their own. Their set-up implied that they taxed the bank customers for the benefit of the country banks and, because the city newspapers were hit thereby, they opened their columns for a campaign against the system of compulsory exchange charges. Under the impact of these attacks the rates were lowered considerably.

Although this was denied at that time, James G. Cannon went to Boston and tried to induce its associated banks to change their policy. He spoke in a meeting of the Boston bank presidents nearly succeeding in his purpose; but a compromise was reached. Boston retained its par-collection system and came close to making one hundred per cent of the New England cities and towns par-collection points. For items on almost all places outside of New England, however, and for non-par-paying banks within the latter area the New York model of compulsory exchange charges was adopted.

Seen in retrospect, Boston's achievement was truly remarkable. Its exponents had the satisfaction of seeing par-collections adopted in Atlanta, Kansas City, Nashville, Oklahoma City, St. Louis, Richmond, Detroit, and finally even in New York City;[28] and Ruggles was rather active in promoting them. Boston's triumph was evident when in 1911 the president of the clearing house section of the American Bankers Association acknowledged defeat by stating that the attempts at establishing uniform collection charges had failed. Each collection center had to work out the matter to its own satisfaction. At the same time the plan for collecting New England checks then in operation in the Boston Clearing House was recommended as satisfactory.[29] Soon thereafter recognition of what had been achieved in Boston led to a movement, especially fostered by Connecticut banks, which aimed at establishing national check clearings. These activities, in turn, although unsuccessful, helped to pave the way for the nation-wide check clearing system of the Federal Reserve Banks. Their struggle and ultimate success, however, do not fall within the scope of this book.[30]

Chapter XIX

THE CLEARING OF OUT-OF-TOWN CHECKS

1. See Volume I of this work, Chapter IV, and this volume, Chapter XIII.
2. McKay, C. R., "The Numerical System in the Transit Department" in A.B.A., Proceedings (1909), Clearing House Section, 21 ff; (1910), 664, 709 ff. On the numerical system see also this volume, pages, 185, 186.
3. An early suggestion of a national par-collection system is to be found in Hildreth, History of Banks, of 1837, 138. Gallatin, on the other hand, considered this country too large for a national clearing system; (Suggestions, in Writings, III, 425). See also Collier, op. cit., 14.
4. Cleaveland, op. cit., 276.
5. Cannon, op. cit., (1910), 15. The question of uniform exchange rates was discussed in the Baltimore Clearing House as early as 1884; see Hales, op. cit., 172 ff.
6. A.B.A., Proceedings (1906), 104.
7. Cannon, the son of a small businessman, was born in New York state. He rose in the Fourth National Bank to become its vice-president in 1890 and its president in 1910. He resigned in 1914.
8. A.B.A., Proceedings (1906), 103; (1910), 651, 652.
9. Ibid., (1910), 666, 667.
10. The following is based on Money Trust Investigation, 217-220, 279, 374-378, 615-620, 627, 670, 821-823. The last-named pages contain the very important Report of the Committee on Inland Exchange to the Clearing House Committee, November 4, 1912; A.B.A., Proceedings (1906), 103-105.
11. The committee consisted of James G. Cannon, Walter E. Frew, Joseph T. Talbert, Edward Townsend, and John W. Platten. They represented the Fourth National Bank, the Corn Exchange Bank, the National City Bank, the Importers and Traders National Bank, and the United States Mortgage and Trust Company.
12. See the list of references for Cannon's writings.
13. For a description of the scheme, see A.B.A., Proceedings, (1897), 104.
14. Minutes of the Boston Clearing House Association and Clearing House Committee, Scrapbook of Charles A. Ruggles, manager of the Boston Clearing House, who was closely connected with the achievement. Hallock, op. cit., 50 ff, "Proposed Plan for the Clearing of Country Checks in New England" (four-page folder dated November 15, 1898).
15. Regardless of its failure the minority plan is interesting from the point of view of this research since it shows the longevity of ideas which have once taken root. What the minority wished to establish in 1877 was another Bank of Mutual Redemption, a cooperative venture of banks for the special purpose of collecting out-of-town checks. Moreover the plan was in line with one recommended by the Comptroller of the Currency in 1868 for the redemption of National Bank notes and may have been influenced by the latter. See Comptroller of the Currency, Report (1868), xxi, xxii; Kane, op. cit., 55, 56; and this volume page 214.
16. See page 50.
17. Sears (born in 1849) later became a vice-president of the National Shawmut Bank. In 1899 he represented the Boston banks in the "conference of clearing houses called to discuss the unsatisfactory and confused condition of collection and exchange charges (to be held during the meeting of the American Bankers Association)." Minutes of the Boston Clearing House Association, August 8, 1899.
18. That it was actually Hallock's plan which was adopted in Boston may be seen from the Minutes of the Clearing House Committee of May 1, 1899. In this meeting the Clearing House Committee resolved to table a letter from him, in which he had obviously asked for a remuneration, until the country clearing was actually in operation. Additional evidence lies in the copy of Hallock's book used by this author, which was dedicated to Mr. Ruggles, the Clearing House manager, a strong indication that Hallock's claims remained within the bounds of truth.
19. The committee report of March 29, 1899 recommending this step was signed by Sears.
20. Ruggles was active in the executive committee of the clearing house section of the American Bankers Association and the president of that section in 1910/11.
21. Minutes, Boston Clearing House Committee, May 29, 1899. The collection schedule of the Boston Clearing House Association of July, 1900, with the whole of New England as par points and in addition 1/10 and 1/4 points, is preserved in a scrapbook on the Consolidation of the Shoe and Leather National Bank and the National Bank of Redemption in the Baker

Library of Harvard University.

22.   As to the technique of foreign check collections, see, for instance, Thralls, op. cit., 125 ff.

23.   The material for the following paragraphs is taken from Mr. Ruggles' scrapbook cited before. See also Hallock, op. cit., 69, 123 ff.

24.   See, for instance, a circular "Boston Clearing House's Tyrrany exposed! The unprincipled attack on the Country Banks explained. A Vermont Banker gives thirteen reasons for not Remitting at par to the Boston Clearing House." The circular is signed by Luther B. Harris, Cashier of the Lyndenville National Bank.

25.   Letter of June 7, 1899, published in the American Banker.

26.   By that time the Kansas City Clearing House was also establishing country clearings. A collection department was opened by the Clearing House in June, 1905, and, in order to give the plan a thorough test, items on the most expensive points in the tributary territory were immediately sent by the Kansas City banks for collection. The result was so favorable that before long the area of collections was expanded, so that in June, 1909, it covered the States of Missouri, Kansas, and Oklahoma, all told about 3,000 banking institutions. Further expansion was contemplated. The Kansas City country-clearing house worked very much like the transit department of a bank, the clearing house members being the depositors. The total cost per hundred dollars dropped from 26.57 cents in July, 1905, to 12.8 cents in July, 1909. The plan was different from the Boston plan in that charges were made by the banks according to a schedule. See A.B.A., Proceedings (1909), clearing house section, 41 ff; (1912), 508 ff; (1913), 579 ff.

27.   Ford, Franklin, op. cit., passim.

28.   The New York set-up is described by Joseph Byrne, secretary of the New York Clearing House, in Bulletin of the National Association of Credit Managers, October, 1917, 986. As to Atlanta's experience, see A.B.A., Proceedings (1910), 715 ff.

29.   Ibid. (1911), 682.

30.   For the very beginnings, see Strong, op. cit., 7 ff.

Chapter XX

COOPERATION AMONG AMERICAN BANKS

I

The earliest American banks (except the Bank of North America), as was described in the first volume of this work,[1] were devised as regional monopolies. Therefore cooperation, not competition, determined the attitude of the men who ran the new enterprises. Cooperation among them was all the more natural since they had worked hand in hand during the Revolutionary War and were bound together, if not by family ties and friendship, then at least by the same political creed and identical interests within society and the body politic. Thus both the Massachusetts Bank and the Bank of New York were set up with the assistance of the Bank of North America (which, incidentally, in 1791 transmitted to the newly founded Bank of Maryland a "benign greeting," as Professor Wettereau expressed it).[2] The president of the Bank of North America sent advice to the Boston promoters of the Massachusetts Bank who appointed a director of the former bank as their first cashier. The cashier of the Bank of New York, on the other hand, received his training in the same bank during a visit to Philadelphia.[3]

Such a cooperative attitude did not change when the "national bank," the First Bank of the United States, came into being. The Massachusetts Bank and the Bank of New York acted as its agents to receive local subscriptions, and the Bank of North America welcomed it in the friendliest spirit. As a matter of fact, if Hamilton had had his way, the Bank of the United States instead of opening branches would have made already existing banks its local agents. Although this plan did not materialize, several of the latter invested in the stock of the national bank thereby creating a community of interest. Similarly, the Bank of New York reserved some of its own stock for the national bank in case the latter desired to subscribe.[4] It is not surprising, therefore, that on March 20, 1792 the board of the New York branch of the First Bank of the United States appointed a committee to confer with the directors of the Bank of New York upon the best means of promoting friendly intercourse between the two institutions, and that formal letters were exchanged promising cooperation in "any measure calculated to inspire mutual confi-

dence or public accommodation."[5] As a result, by 1792 the Bank of New York and the New York branch of the First Bank of the United States paid out indiscriminately their own notes and those of the other institution, and slightly later a regular exchange of notes, three times a week, was organized. Even the establishment of second and third local banks, regardless of initial opposition thereto, did not disturb the harmony. The Massachusetts Bank, for instance, in 1794 put its "Hall at the Service of the Proprietors of the Union Bank" and the latter reciprocated in 1809 by allowing the Massachusetts Bank to use one of its vaults. In 1811 the latter bank leased the basement of its building to the directors of the State Bank with permission to make alterations, and in the same year the Merchants Bank of Salem appointed a committee "to procure the loan of one of the vaults of the [older] Salem Bank to deposit the money of the Merchants Bank."[6] Occasionally such cooperative spirit may have been due to the fact that banks owned stock in other banks: it has been mentioned that several local banks invested in stock of the First Bank of the United States. Moreover the Bank of Maryland in 1795 owned stock in the Bank of Baltimore, and the Massachusetts Bank held shares in the Portland Bank and in the Manufacturers and Mechanics Bank of Boston.[7] That early American banks were considered, especially by their founders, as semi-public institutions contributed to the cooperative attitude.

In many cases community of interest and harmony in general facilitated the establishment of uniform policies. The sources for the 1790's and 1800's show numerous cases in which committees were appointed by bank boards in order to meet with similar committees from other banks. As a result of common deliberation, suggestions were presented to the various boards of directors and, subsequently, although not always, adopted as the policy of the individual banks. In case of the adoption of such suggestions uniform policy resulted through parallel action by different bank boards. This method was typical of the way in which cooperation by early American banks took shape. Their administrators conferred and cooperated as opportunity and necessity arose; but regular joint meetings of committes of two and later even three banks, such as took place in Philadelphia in 1792 and a few years thereafter, were probably very rare. To be specific, in that year the directors of the First Bank of the United States appointed a committee to confer with a committee of the Bank of North America once a week "for the purpose of communicating freely upon the business of both, as well as to prevent improper interference with each other as to promote the accommodation of the citizens."[8] These regular meetings were probably dropped after a few years, for in 1804 the board of the Philadelphia Bank appointed a committee "to confer occasionally [italics mine] with committees of the other banks in this city when appointed upon subjects of a common interest and for the purpose of maintaining harmonious intercourse between them."[9]

As a rule conferences of inter-bank (joint) committees were called to deal with specific subjects. Important among these was the exchange of notes and the settlement of balances, that is to say, a matter of inter-bank relations.[10] A New York arrangement to that effect has been mentioned above. In Philadelphia the Bank of North America and the First Bank of the United States agreed in 1792 to exchange notes and to settle the balances daily, and the Bank of Pennsylvania, upon establishment in 1793, was included in the arrangement. Or to give a third example, in 1810, on recommendation of a joint committee, each of the Philadelphia banks resolved to pay out its own notes only and to return the rest to the other banks for redemption.[11] However, not always were such and similar actions taken by agreement: the Massachusetts Bank, for instance, in 1793 and 1802 determined independently its policy as to the cashing of notes and checks drawn on other Boston banks.[12] (It should be kept in mind that England and Scotland developed elaborate clearing arrangements in that period.)

A second important field in which banks cooperated was the war against counterfeiting. Although documentary proof is lacking, common action in this respect may well have been established under English influence. As early as the 1790's there existed in London an informal Society of Bankers (meeting in the London Coffee House at Ludgate Hill) set up to prosecute forgers.[13] Cooperation against counterfeiting took place in Philadelphia in 1794, in Boston in 1797 and 1804, and in New Haven by 1810.[14] The Boston cooperation of 1804 took the form of an association of the banks in Essex County. The necessary funds were assessed according to an agreed-upon ratio ("one third on the corporations severally in an equal ratio and two thirds in the ratio of their

specie capital"). They were expended by a committee of seven bank directors, four of whom represented city (Boston) banks and three, country banks in the county.

An even more ambitious attempt at fighting counterfeiters by cooperation of banks of a whole region was launched in Philadelphia in September, 1813. In that month a committee was appointed[15]

by the Bank of North America - the Bank of Pennsylvania - the Philadelphia Bank, and the Farmers & Mechanics Bank to carry into operation a Plan of Union between the Banks of Virginia, Baltimore, Philadelphia, New York and other Places for the Discovery & Conviction of Persons concerned in Counterfeiting the Notes of those Banks...

Soon after the Banks of New York, Philadelphia, Baltimore and the District of Columbia had acceded to the Plan, a Select Committee in each Place, consisting of one Member from each Bank was appointed to Superintend its execution.

These sub-committees and their agents did a good job in detecting "a great number of culprits and by the seizure of a large amount of couterfeit bank notes;" and their continuous cooperation greatly facilitated the work which was to be done. A register was kept of those who were known to be notoriously employed in defrauding the public and the banks by counterfeiting notes and distributing them. On the whole the plan worked satisfactorily although there was lack of cooperation on the part of some judges. Funds seem to have been assessed and in case of need borrowed from banks in anticipation of assessment. In 1816 it was recommended that the original committee of 1813 be replaced by a new one consisting of one representative for each bank and that $500 per bank should be contributed, but the organization seems to have been discontinued.

The third field in which banks cooperated was that of public policy in its broadest sense, matters of weight and coin (including the import of change [subsidiary coin]), of stamp duties and taxes,[16] "the prevailing distress of mercantile interests" caused by yellow fever epidemics,[17] and the drawing up of memorials to legislatures as for instance in support of the First Bank of the United States.[18] In Boston, George Cabot (1752-1823), merchant, senator, and leading Federalist, seems to have been active in this type of cooperation; at least we find him repeatedly as the chairman of joint committees dealing with questions of public policy.[19]

Last but not least there was a wide field of business policy toward third parties which was discussed in common, with a view to establishing uniformity. As early as March, 1797, the then existing Philadelphia banks agreed that bills made payable at sight or on demand had to be paid the same day on which they were presented. At the same time they resolved not to discount any notes in which the words "without defalcation" or "without set-off" were omitted.[20] It has been described in another context[21] how around 1800 the Boston banks in joint committees evolved a common policy toward "foreign money" (notes of out-of-town banks). Moreover in 1801 they agreed upon the uniform treatment of firms "the owners of which were not individually known;" and in 1802 they established rules for handling "notes upon which the promissors became bankrupt." Finally, in 1813 they conferred on time limits for notes to be discounted.[22] The Baltimore banks, to give a last example, concurred in 1796 regarding the procedure to be followed in making accommodations.[23]

Uniform policies were established in the Eastern financial centers by arrangements as late as the 1810's: In 1816 the Philadelphia banks cooperated in an attempt to stop overdrafts.[24] In that year the directors of the Bank of North America, of the Farmers and Mechanics Bank, and probably also some others resolved on the basis of a recommendation of a joint committee: that if overdrafts were not made good within six days, the names of the offenders should be made available to all banks participating in the agreement. The New York banks aimed in the same direction. In June, 1817, they received from their then still existing General Committee (about which more will be said shortly)[25] the following recommendation: inasmuch as they had suffered losses from the overdrawing of accounts, it should be made a condition between the banks and their "dealers" that overdrafts were not permitted. If they happened nevertheless, banks should insist on their being paid plus interest and cost. In case overdrafts were not made good within a set number of days, the name of the offender should be circulated among the banks which would then refuse to have any further business with him. Offenders should be admitted to further dealings only by a majority vote of the banks and upon payment of the balance including cost and interest or upon satisfactory explanation.[26] (It is not certain if these rules were put into effect.) In Boston where no suspension (and consequently no break in the tradition) took place during the War of 1812, the practice of establishing uniform policies survived longest. In the latter city as late as 1816 the banks conferred "on the propriety of establishing a uniform system of receiving checks" and in 1821 on the matter of lowering the interest rate below the legal rate.

In view of the fact that the establishment of uniform policies and other kinds of cooperation came into existence as early as the 1790's, it is surprising that cooperation among banks was lacking just when it was needed most, namely, during the emergency of the 1790's: at least it is known of New York that in 1796 the Bank of New York and the New York branch of the Bank of the United States looked out each for itself.[28] Only when Hamilton pressed Wolcott, then Secretary of the Treasury, and the latter promised assistance, can there have been a change in the policy of the Bank of the United States.

In the 1800's the cooperative spirit began to break down. Various reasons contributed thereto. First of all more banks had come into being than the earlier ones considered sound. Under these circumstances genuine and wholesome cooperation degenerated into alliances for fighting the newcomers. The older banks lobbied in common, staged runs in common, and occasionally, as described above, adopted uniform policies which made life difficult for the "intruder." By 1800, for example, the Browns of Providence[29] agreed with the promoter of the Bristol Bank that the latter would join the Providence Bank and the other then existing Rhode Island institutions in fighting any attempts at setting up new banks. Similarly, in Philadelphia in 1803 the First Bank of the United States, the Bank of North America, and the Bank of Pennsylvania objected to the chartering of the Philadelphia Bank, and having been unsuccessful, they agreed not to accept its notes.[30] The same policy was established in Philadelphia again in 1812 when the Banking House of Stephen Girard came into existence. The Banks of North America and of Pennsylvania, the Philadelphia Bank, and the Farmers and Mechanics Bank appointed committees which in a joint session of June 15, 1812 resolved not to take the notes of the new concern.[31] The laws of the Commonwealth of Pennsylvania forbade private banking, and the incorporated banks, favoring this regulation, did not wish a precedent to be established.[32]

Secondly, the appearance of country banking undermined the possibility of cooperation. As has been stressed, country banks and city banks represented de facto two different types of enterprises the former being disguised land banks, the latter money banks.[33] It was perhaps unavoidable that hostilities flared up between these two incompatible kinds of enterprises[34] called by the same name, "bank."

Thirdly, but not least, the geistesgeschichtliche situation was changing and the business community began to adopt the belief that competition was a blessing, if not divinely ordained. Thus the truly cooperative spirit which had characterized the first years of American banking and that working together in the common interest which resulted therefrom were fast disappearing by the time of the War of 1812.

II

But under the impact of that war and of the monetary derangements which followed in its wake, cooperation of a different type was forced upon the banks: they learned to cooperate in order to cope with the grave emergency caused by the war. It is noteworthy that modern cooperation among banks started in just that field of emergency cooperation which the earliest bank leaders had neglected.

Banks were drawn together in the spring and summer of 1814 when panic threatened. As early as April an extraordinary drain of specie was taking place in New Orleans. Under these circumstances suspension was agreed upon in a joint meeting of the various bank boards. (This author does not know of any other case in which bank boards met jointly.) The event was commented upon at that time as the first deliberate stoppage of specie payments in this country, and the need for it was assigned in part to "the unfriendly disposition of the banks to each other."[35]

The Philadelphia and New York banks were soon to follow suit and, as in New Orleans, suspended by agreement. The Philadelphia banks arrived at this decision after joint committee meetings between the 26th and 29th of August. In New York the modus procedendi was similar: On August 20 committees of the Bank of the Manhattan Company, the Mechanics, and the City Banks invited the other banks of the city to appoint committees too. These were to meet at the Manhattan Company on August 22, in order to consider the state of the banks and of commercial credit in general and to take such measures as seemed advisable for the relief of the merchants. The committees actually met that day and held another session on August 31. In consequence of letters received from the cashiers of several Philadelphia banks (which, as indicated, had previously taken concerted action) suspension of specie payments was agreed upon for New York also.[36] The following reason was given therefor: suspension in Philadelphia would lead to an increased demand for specie in New York, partly because of "diminished" confidence, and partly because the merchants and bankers of the former city were at that moment indebted to the New York banks to a considerable amount. Further debts were accumulating.[37]

The decision of the New York banks is historically important: it represents the first case in which joint action in one city (Philadelphia) led to parallel action in another (New York). At the same time, the modus operandi is indicative of the early stage of the development: it was not the Philadelphia banks as a group which corresponded with an organization of the New York banks, but individual banks in one city communicated with individual banks in the other.

It is very probable that these cooperative actions in New Orleans, Philadelphia, and New York provided the incentive for similar proceedings in the back country, as is known, for example, for Kentucky and Ohio. In October, 1814, the directors of the Bank of Kentucky called a meeting of the banks of that state and of the principal banks of Ohio to be held at Frankfort. It was agreed by the banks' representatives to contract and to prepare for an expected emergency.[38]

Once the banks had suspended new problems arose in connection with the treatment of interbank balances which were bound to come into existence. Claims of one bank against another arising from the deposit of notes in banks other than the issuing enterprise could no longer be paid, and unless satisfactory arrangements could be made the circulation of notes would be seriously impaired, to the detriment of all concerned. Consequently, almost immediately after suspension, banks in New York as well as in Philadelphia started to cooperate on the matter of inter-bank balances, but those in the former city were quicker in arriving at satisfactory arrangements. As early as September, 1814, joint committees of the New York banks drew up a plan which was submitted to the several boards for ratification and favorable action was taken forthwith by the latter. Thereafter, the agreement was considered binding upon the institutions for three months or until 20 days' notice was given by any one bank to the contrary or until seven banks at any time resolved to dissolve the association without delay (article 8).

Under this agreement[39] the New York banks continued to take each others' notes in the payment of loans and discounts and when tendered for deposit, and exchanged them daily as before. Commencing September 1, 1814, they charged each other interest on balances at the rate of 5 per cent, and paid the accrued interest once per month. It was agreed that balances would be left intact from one morning's exchange to the next. Furthermore the banks received from the public and from each other, as theretofore, the notes of any out-of-town bank which held adequate funds for the redemption of its notes with any one bank of the city. However, remittances from country banks were to be watched by the cashiers personally (article 2). The notes of country banks were also to be exchanged daily by their correspondents; but the sums sent by one city bank to any other was not to exceed $2,000 per day. A credit in any city bank was considered as constituting an adequate redemption fund. The banks agreed in principle that balances thus originating were payable in specie or in mutually agreeable equivalent and that they were to be treated as preferred debts. Any bank was at liberty to discharge them or parts thereof in specie; while on the other hand payment could be demanded on three months' notice. (At least this seems to be the meaning of the words: inter-bank debts "shall be considered as entitled to be discharged after three months' notice in specie;" article 4.) Supplementing their policy regarding notes and balances the banks bound themselves not to increase the total of their loans without the consent of the "General Committee" (to be discussed forthwith). An exception was made for such institutions as were creditor banks and whose loans did not amount to a sum equal to 50 per cent above their capital and for banks which were required by law to lend to the state government, or in case it was considered necessary to lend for the defence of the city. Debtor banks were to reduce their loans and discounts if and when recommended by the General Committee.

This important General Committee appears in the records of the Bank of New York first as "the general meeting of committees" (Sept. 2), later as "general meeting" (Sept. 27), and finally throughout as the General Committee (abbreviated from General Committee of Banks in the City). It was to supervise the execution of the agreement and met once a week, every Wednesday; occasionally it appointed a special committee.[40] The cashiers were bound to report every Tuesday to each other the amount of specie in their vaults and the gross totals of their loans, of bills and notes discounted, and of all debts bearing interest, separating the debts due from other banks in the city. One may take it for granted that the General Committee on the day following discussed these statements. This committee in which votes were taken by banks, and in which five banks constituted a majority, represented an organizational development of the joint committees described in the previous section of this chapter.

On the whole the agreement seems to have worked fairly well. Regardless of new loans to the City of New York and to the state and national governments, it was claimed that the total of New York bank loans was approximately stable from suspension to the summer of 1815, a statement which should be taken cum grano salis.

Commercial loans are supposed to have been reduced in the same period by $3,000,000.

The Philadelphia banking community in contrast was slow in reaching a satisfactory solution of its problems, although cooperation was contemplated at the very moment of suspension. Immediately thereafter it seemed as if a semipermanent organization, a "General Committee," would develop out of the joint committees of the incorporated banks of the city assembling "to consider and report on the expediency of suspending the payment of specie and in case that measure was adopted to meet... from time to time to concert such measures as circumstances might render necessary." In fact the committees met several times and the Bank of North America through this medium tried hard to induce the banks to cooperate. Its directors considered restraint indispensable; they wished to keep the banks of the city from over-extending their issues and to force them into a gradual contraction, since otherwise bank paper was liable to depreciate and the return to specie payments to become more difficult. Moreover, correctly sensing the inter-dependence of all banks, they were afraid that without a formal agreement the less conservative institutions could frustrate the policy of the more cautious ones, which would be engulfed in any reckless expansion of the former.

Consequently as early as September 22, 1814 the Bank of North America submitted the following plan, predicated on the fact that the banks had proceeded after suspension to take each others' notes: the banks were to open interest accounts for each other as of October 1, 1814, on which interests on balances were to be credited or debited, respectively, as they accrued in the daily settlements. When a bank became indebted to another for more than a set amount, the excess was to be made good and if the debtor bank declined to do so, the creditor bank concerned was to refuse its notes. A sub-committee was to be appointed which would meet at the Bank of Pennsylvania every Monday noon for the purpose of recommending a transfer of balances, so as to equalize them as far as possible. For this purpose every member of the subcommittee would be expected to bring to each meeting an account of the balances of his bank due to and from every other one. But the consideration of this plan was postponed by the general committee; and after having been brought before the several bank boards it was rejected. The Bank of North America found only one ally, the Philadelphia Bank. The Bank of Pennsylvania through its committee declared that the object of the latter's appointment was completed so that further meetings of the general committee were unnecessary.

Thereupon the general committee was dissolved. The majority of the banks desired to pursue their own course "without concert and uncontrouled."

As expected, trouble was brewing before long and the Bank of North America once more tried to assume leadership. Once more it invited the other banks of the city to appoint committees to meet and to take the situation into consideration. When they actually met the following resolution was submitted to them for adoption: the banks were formally to resolve to take each others' notes in the discharge of debts and if tendered on deposit, provided that the depositor agreed to receive in payment of his checks or drafts at the option of the bank concerned its own notes or those of other banks of the city. An agreed-upon announcement to that effect was to be posted in each bank. The committees adjourned, consulted their respective bank boards, and in another meeting dealt the plan the fate of the earlier proposition, although the atmosphere was changing. The meeting adjourned with the understanding that in subsequent ones the debtor banks would present their own suggestions as to how to diminish their balances. Measures were in fact proposed and tried out, the debtor banks started reducing their discount lines, and their debt balances did not increase, at least for some time. On the other hand, it was impossible to arrive at a formal agreement; some banks preferred the evils of an increased circulation to the sacrifices needed if the balances were to be equalized and resumption to be prepared. Since concerted action was not possible, the second general committee was dissolved also (probably in January, 1815).[41] Until late in August of that year there seems to have been no cooperation among the Philadelphia banks; in June the Bank of North America, for instance, decided to relieve itself from all responsibility for the notes of other banks which it held after having accepted them regardless of suspension.[42]

In August, 1815, the Bank of Pennsylvania took the lead by inviting the other banks to appoint committees for the purpose of meeting and discussing a reduction of the existing inter-bank balances.[43] When the committees met jointly on August 30, 1815, the following plan was offered by the inviting bank: the banks were to be free to pay out the notes of other banks and return the remainder at stated terms. Only if the debt balance of any one bank with any other exceeded $100,000 could the creditor bank demand payment. Such payment should be made in drafts on any third bank to which the creditor bank might be indebted, in United States treasury notes and funded debt at the fair market value as of the day on which payment was demanded, or in any other

way acceptable to both parties. Instead of making an actual payment the debtor bank was to be entitled to secure that part of the balance which was called, by a deposit of United States stock or treasury notes, the interest on such securities accruing to the creditor bank until the debt balance was reduced to $100,000. This plan was to be supplemented as follows: each bank in Philadelphia should select a correspondent in New York and Baltimore with whom an agreement should be concluded mutually to take each other's notes, as had been usual prior to suspension. Balances between the banks of the three cities were to be verified on the first of each month and if more than $100,000 had accrued the excess was to be paid or at least secured immediately, as contemplated in the proposal to regulate the intercourse of the banks of the city. Thus it would be possible to take New York and Baltimore notes indiscriminately, for the respective Philadelphia correspondents of the various New York and Baltimore banks would stand ready to handle these notes.

This time it was the Bank of North America which refused cooperation, because the proposal would facilitate the issue of bank paper, whereas the Bank considered a policy of contraction and of gradual return to specie payments indispensable. Examining point after point of the proposal the Bank arrived at a scathing condemnation (which, however, was due at least in part to its previous unwillingness to buy war bonds and to take its share in financing the war just ended).[44] The Bank proposed to substitute its old plan therefor; namely, that mutually interest accounts be kept by the banks, to be settled at least in part at the first Monday of each month when the accrued interest was due also: whenever on the day of settlement the balance exceeded a certain amount the excess should be paid in specie.[45] The ball was kept rolling for some time. On September 6 and September 13 the "Committees from all the incorporated banks of the City of Philadelphia and the Northern Liberties" met by adjournment and the plan of the Bank of Pennsylvania was discussed. Several amendments were inserted but they did not change the essentials. There was neither a majority for this proposal, nor for that of the Bank of North America; and since no substitutes were offered the (third) general committee was dissolved on the last-named date.[46]

About four weeks later concerted action in New York forced Philadelphia to follow suit and a new general committee met first on October 11, as will be referred to again.[47] In the course of its deliberations it was bound to discuss not only resumption, but also the intercourse between the banks of the City of Philadelphia in general; and interest-bearing accounts so long desired by the Bank of North America were finally consented to in a meeting of this (fourth) general committee held on November 10, 1815. The agreement reads as follows[48]

Resolved. That whenever the Amount due from One Bank to another Bank in the City of Philadelphia or Northern Liberties shall exceed 25,000 Dollars, and Payment shall be demanded, the Debtor Bank shall comply with the Demand or pay Interest thereon until the Debt is reduced below $25,000 Dollars.

Resolved. That any Debtor Bank may pay its Debt or any part of it by drawing on any Bank in this City or Northern Liberties which shall have agreed to these Resolutions, or by Funded Debt of the United States at the Rate of two per Cent below its fair Market Value on the Day of Payment, and if the Parties disagree as to the fair Market Value it shall be settled by the Cashiers of two other Banks (one to be selected by each of the Parties) who may select an Umpire if necessary.

Resolved. That on the 1st Monday of every Month, each Bank shall furnish to the other respectively an exact account of the Balances due to it from all those who shall agree to these Resolutions.

Resolved. That no Bank shall pay out any Notes for Ten Dollars and upwards of the other agreeing Banks, but each Bank shall at every stated Period for exchanging Notes return to every other agreeing Bank all those Notes or Drafts for Ten Dollars and upwards which it may have on such other Bank.

Resolved. That these Resolutions shall go into operation and become binding on the 1st Monday of December next, if Six Banks shall previously agree to them and shall afterward become null and void whenever a Majority of the Parties shall so determine.

Ratifications of this agreement came in fast, the first were those of the Banks of North America and Pennsylvania, the Philadelphia and the Farmers and Mechanics Banks, and the Bank of the Northern Liberties. Consequently it was put into effect as of November 15, 1815 with the understanding that banks holding out would be entitled to become parties to the agreement prior to the first Monday in December. When we hear thereafter about a general committee it must be assumed that it consisted only of committees of the banks cooperating under the agreement of November 10, so that we deal de facto with a (fifth) general committee. On November 27 it resolved to recommend that the participating banks should not pay out the notes of the rest, but accumulate and present them for payment in notes of those cooperating;[49] and later the arrangement was tightened still further.[50] Yet two of the older banks (the Commercial and the Schuylkill) and some of the newly-founded institutions still refused to come into the agreement until a meeting of the cooperating banks on the 4th of March, 1816, decided to refuse their notes. This threat forced the dissenters to fall into line and the scheme ultimately embraced all the banks in the city and county of Philadelphia.[51]

In the meantime, by the turn of the year 1815, the Philadelphia banks had resolved also on concerted action for the purpose of reducing the amount of bills discounted in order to prepare for the resumption of specie payments. But in so doing they had failed to agree on a uniform policy for reaching that goal. Two of the banks (the Bank of North America and the Farmers Bank) made considerable reductions on accommodation paper warning their customers by circulars and announcing reductions by percentages. The other banks refused to discount new business paper or at least severely restricted such transactions.[52] In a way the Philadelphia banks were now less efficient cooperators than banks had been in the 1790's when a uniform modus operandi would have been established in such a case.

The monetary troubles of the period were of such a magnitude that they could not be solved by local cooperation only, and so for the first time it became necessary to bring together for common ends banks located in various cities and regions. Cooperation had even to be forced on some banks as time went along. The difficulty lay, as William Jones explained it,[53] in that resumption of specie payments could be achieved only "by the faithful execution of a liberal, well concerted, plan of mutual forbearance and support," while "reciprocal responsibility" was not acceptable to the banks. The spirit of competition had replaced that of cooperation to such an extent that no bank was willing to forego advantages which it possessed ! In contrast, any bank could be expected to make ruthless use thereof. Under these circumstances, at the moment of resumption those banks which were public depositories by receiving notes of other banks would automatically become the masters of the latters' fate, a situation dreaded

by the weaker banks. To make things more complicated, suspension not only had resulted in local
inter-bank balances, but had also made some
cities creditors or debtors, respectively, of
others.

In this situation, which cried for inter-bank
cooperation on a national scale, the Secretary of
the Treasury repeatedly acted as a catalyser.
This role of his seems to have started after the
flotation of the first treasury notes when he suggested that the banks receive them on deposit
when tendered and upon request exchange freely
their own against treasury notes and vice versa.
He threatened to order collectors not to accept
notes of such banks as refused to cooperate. The
Secretary was not too successful. The eight then
existing New York banks, for instance, appointed
a select committee to consider the proposal, but
refused to comply therewith. However, three of
them (those which were indebted to the others),
without the knowledge and consent of the latter,
dispatched agents to the Secretary and signed an
agreement.[54] It is evident that uniform policy of
the whole banking system in an important matter
would have been the result if the Secretary had
fully succeeded.

In 1815 the Secretary of the Treasury (Dallas)
once more fostered nation-wide bank cooperation.
On March 13, he mailed a circular letter[55] to
twenty-one banks along the Eastern seaboard from
Boston to Savannah. They were invited to form
an association and to assist the government in its
fiscal operations by paying interest on the public
debt and by negotiating federal loans when needed.
They were to open accounts with each other for
the accommodation of the Treasury and in return
would become the government's depositories.
This suggestion was bound to fail because of the
different situations of the specie-paying New
England banks and the banks in the Middle and
Southern states which were suffering in varying
degrees from overexpanded and fluctuating bank
currencies. In his report of 1815 to Congress
the Secretary acknowledged the "failure" of his
attempt to "associate" the banks with a view of
furnishing a uniform national currency. Charter
restrictions, "mutual relation and dependence
of the banks of the same state and even of the
banks of different states, and the duty which the
directors of each bank conceive they owe to their
immediate constituents upon points of security
and emolument interpose an insuperable obstacle
to any voluntary arrangement, upon national considerations alone, for the establishment of a national medium through the agency of [cooperating]
state banks." Thus Dallas wrote.[56]

Again on June 24 and October 12, 1815, Dallas

tried to needle the banks into nation-wide cooperation. On the former date he inquired by circular
letter whether they would receive, reissue, and
circulate treasury notes or else have their notes
refused by the collectors. On the latter he tried
to prod them into resumption by proposing to pe-
nalize those who refused to do so: they were to
pay 6 per cent interest on notes and deposits,
commencing on the day of refusal. These attempts
were of no avail, however. Another notification
emanated from the Secretary of the Treasury on
July 22, 1816: banks were informed that the Secretary would attempt to facilitate the collection of
revenue in lawful money and that they ought to do
their best to resume by October 1, 1816.[57] It goes
without saying that the mere mailing of identical
letters to banks all over the country was bound to
stimulate cooperation.

Cooperation so stimulated found expression,
for example, in at least two bank conventions. One
was held by Ohio banks in Chillicothe on September 6, 1816. It was agreed not to resume at that
moment, but to do so when it was ascertained that
the resumption of specie payments was general
along the Atlantic coast. A copy of that resolution
was sent to the Secretary of the Treasury "as the
answer to his circular letter of July 22, 1816."
Another similar convention of twenty-three Pen-
sylvania country banks took place on September 12
in Harrisburg, having been called by the officers
of the Harrisburg Bank. It was resolved that the
Pennsylvania country banks would resume on the
same day on which the banks of New York, Philadelphia, and Baltimore took that step. A committee
was appointed to communicate with the banks of
those cities and to effect an arrangement to that
end, while a copy of the resolution was sent to the
Secretary of the Treasury.[58]

In fact, by that time the soil for nation-wide
cooperation was being prepared. As early as July
7, 1815, a convention of committees of Connecticut
banks had met in Middletown to consider the "embarrassed state of the paper currency" and "the
expediency of taking measure to persuade or compel the New York banks to resume specie payments
at such a period as may be deemed proper." Some
of the Connecticut banks seem to have been owners
of frozen deposits with New York banks and all of
them were plagued by a stiff state law. Their
leader was probably Isaac Bronson,[59] president of
the Bridgeport Bank. The group, which the New
York General Committee styled the "convention of
sundry banks in Connecticut," formulated a proposal to that committee which was presented by
delegates on July 19.[60] The Connecticut banks
suggested that the New York banks "redeem their
loans [sic] at a rate of two per cent until specie

payments [were] resumed." The New York General Committee refused to comply with this request: the banks of the City of New York alone were competent to decide on the rate of reduction and they were not willing to make a special pledge. It is particularly interesting that in this case (probably for the first time) committees of two local bank groups communicated with each other; a second case of the same type will be presented shortly.[61]

A few months later a sub-committee of three appointed by the General Committee of the New York banks to report on a proposal of the Bank of America regarding resumption made a report the substance of which was unanimously approved by all the city banks.[62] The report of October 4, 1815 stressed correctly that resumption depended on the reduction of loans, and, in turn, the date for resumption on the extent and rapidity of such reduction. The date depended equally upon "whether the banks of Philadelphia and Baltimore [would] cooperate in measures for this purpose." It was recognized clearly that cooperation would enable the New York banks to reach the goal with a smaller total of reduction than would be necessary if they acted alone. The committee of three proposed that in preparation of resumption the aggregate debt of any New York bank to all the other banks of the city on or after January 1, 1816 should be no more than $400,000; on and after March first, no more than $250,000; on or after May first, no more than $100,000; while resumption should take place on July 1, 1816. The proposal to reduce loans was based on the above described agreement of 1814 which contemplated such reduction to be recommended by the General Committee.

Reasonable as was that plan, it did not meet with enthusiasm, but quite the opposite. As Isaac Bronson made clear in his Appeal, the crux of the matter was that many banks were loaded down with government bonds. In order to resume they had to sell, and the bonds could be sold only at a loss. But the banks concerned considering themselves as having acted patriotically when buying war bonds (incidentally, with purchasing power which they themselves created in the form of notes) were unwilling to incur such loss. They fought a rear guard action for delay.[63]

At the time when the above report was presented in New York, the Philadelphia banks were at least moving. As an all too optimistic contemporary observer incorrectly stated with reference to the above described negotiations of their (third) general committee, they had already "jointly taken resumption into consideration." Only the Baltimore banks were far behind. Thus the New York

report[64] of October 4, 1815 regarding contraction and subsequent resumption in July, 1816, was forwarded to the chairman of the General Committee of the Philadelphia banks (which, not then existing, was reestablished instantly). At the same time the latter were invited to concur "in the adoption of measures for the requisite and fair reduction of loans" and in common with the New York banks to set a definite date for resumption. The report was presented in Philadelphia on October 11 and discussed on October 20. Thereupon the banks[65] of the city, not sticking to the truth, replied that measures as suggested had been taken and were in operation; that the various banks in the City of Philadelphia had already reduced their circulation considerably; and that they would be able to resume at as early a moment as the banks in the neighboring states.[66] As to Baltimore, the New York report of October 4, 1815 was to be made available to any committee which the Baltimore banks might set up. This they did some time thereafter: early in 1817 a General Committee of Banks at Baltimore was actually in operation.[67]

In the months to follow it became evident to every single bank director and officer, as it is in retrospect to the historian, that resumption of specie payments could be achieved only by the concerted action of all the banks of the country. This condition made it necessary for banks to meet in order to come to agreements, and therefore during the years 1816 and 1817 a series of genuine bank conventions took place. The very first were probably those of 1815 and 1816, respectively, of the Connecticut and the Ohio and Pennsylvania country banks, mentioned above.[68] Another convention met in September, 1816, in Steubenville, Ohio, where representatives assembled from seventeen "western banks," that is, banks located in the western parts of Pennsylvania and Virginia and the eastern districts of Ohio. The convention appointed a committee to give notice to the banks concerned as to the proper time for resumption. (This committee seems to have met in the spring of 1817 in Steubenville, possibly under the chairmanship of one Bazaliel Wells of that city.) Moreover the convention established a uniform policy with a view to resumption, as becomes evident from the almost identical answers of the banks to the circular letter from the Secretary of the Treasury of July, 1816. On March 10, 1817, another convention was held, in Cincinnati. Here members of numerous Ohio banks, of the Kentucky banks, and of one Indiana bank discussed a date for resumption as well as their relationship to the Cincinnati branch of the Second Bank of the United States. A few days later, on March 15, a convention of banks of western

Pennsylvania and eastern Ohio demanded aid from the Bank of the United States in connection with resumption.[69]

The most important of these conventions, however, important because they brought together the banks on whose policy resumption actually depended, were held in Philadelphia. The earlier one took place on August 6, 7, and 8, 1816.[70] It was undoubtedly stimulated by the repeatedly mentioned circular letter of the Secretary of the Treasury of July 22, 1816. Representatives of the New York, Philadelphia, and Baltimore banks assembled and declared it impossible to resume before the first Monday of July, 1817, in view of the complicated financial situation, especially since the Second Bank of the United States and its branches could not be expected to be in full operation prior to that date. The banks were obviously loath to reduce loans abruptly at the "period of extreme pressure" for fear of seriously embarrassing their "dealers." Furthermore they wished to obtain a unanimous vote for resumption and to avoid a possible failure of the attempt. In their own words, they wished to gain "the requisite security against a disappointment." Selfish motives, if any, would not of course be reflected in the records. Thus the delegates disregarded the joint resolution of Congress of April 29 of that year, setting February 20, 1817 as the date of resumption. A committee consisting of one representative from each city (Messrs. Nicholson, Few, and Milnor) was appointed to wait on the Secretary of the Treasury and to inform him of the decision. The committee reported back to the convention on August 8, its report indicating the deep disappointment of the Secretary; but it did not impress the delegates enough to change their attitude. They resolved to adjourn.

When the winter approached, the banks were becoming more cooperative. At that time the Second Bank of the United States was trying to induce the Philadelphia, Baltimore, and Washington banks to participate in the acquisition of specie in Europe, the quotas of the banks of the last named two cities being $500,000 each. It is known that the Bank of Baltimore agreed to take $200,000 and that in December, 1816, several Philadelphia institutions consented to authorize John Sergeant to negotiate specie for them too on the pledge of United States stock. (Sergeant was the agent whom the Bank of the United States was sending to Europe.) Since the participating Bank of North America did not possess any, it borrowed $140,000 United States stock from the Farmers and Mechanics Bank.[71]

Shortly thereafter, with better prospects than ever before, another bank convention was called to Philadelphia by the Second Bank of the United States. It met on January 24 and 25, 1817; in addition to all the banks of New York (save the Manhattan Company of that city), Philadelphia, and Baltimore, those of Virginia (Richmond and Norfolk) were now also represented.[72] The purpose of the meeting was to set a date for a general and simultaneous resumption of specie payments. After a "threatened rupture" of the negotiations had been avoided, the delegates unanimously consented, on the basis of suggestions of the Second Bank of the United States, to resume on February 20, 1817. Thereafter the proposals of this Bank were backed by the general committees of the cities of New York, Philadelphia, and Baltimore. They recommended the adoption of those proposals to the boards of the banks which they represented and the latter ratified the agreement. That is to say, resumption of specie payments in 1817 was de facto the result of a bank convention.[73] It is noteworthy that the banks also exchanged pledges of good faith and friendly offices. It was no longer taken for granted, as it had been in the early 1790's, that they would automatically cooperate.

The chairman of the convention of the New York, Philadelphia, Baltimore, and Virginia banks was the Quaker Robert Waln (1765-1835), a leading Philadelphia merchant, engaged first in the West Indies, and later in the India and China trade. As a merchant he was second only to Stephen Girard in his city, while he outshone the latter by being also one of the early industrialists of the region. He was interested in the Phoenixville iron works, founder of the first cotton mill in Trenton and a very active director in the Bank of North America. A one-time member of the Pennsylvania legislature and of Congress and a president of the Philadelphia Chamber of Commerce, he possessed experience in public life also which, together with his high standing in the business community, made him the man for the difficult task of chairman of the convention.

Waln was also the chairman of the committee through which the convention did its actual work. His colleagues thereon were Charles Wilkes, Henry Payson, and Andrew Stevenson who represented the New York, Baltimore, and Virginia banks, respectively. Charles Wilkes of New York, then cashier but soon to become president of the Bank of New York, has been treated previously.[74] He was prepared for his work in the convention by having been the secretary of the General Committee of the New York banks. Of no less a caliber was Henry Payson (about 1761-1845). He was a native of Roxbury, Massachusetts, who in 1778 went to Baltimore where he settled as a merchant. By 1800 he was assuming a leading role, being very active in community affairs and instrumental in starting the first Unitarian Church of the city. Payson's connection with banking may have begun in 1804 when he was one of the original directors of the Bank of Maryland whose president he became by 1815. Slightly later he appeared as one of the incorporators of the Savings Bank of Baltimore.[75] The representative of the Virginia banks on the committee of the convention, Andrew Stevenson (1784-1857), was a politician rather than a banker. From 1809 to 1821 (except for the year 1817) he was a member of the Virginia House of Delegates, and later became a member of Congress and a minister to Great Britain. In 1817 he was a director of the Richmond branch of the Second Bank of the United States and he may well have been elected to that position because of his activities during the convention.

III

After resumption was achieved, cooperation among banks became exceptional. Especially rare was the establishment of uniform policies by concerted action in the years between 1817 and 1837, although a few cases from Philadelphia, New York, Boston, and New Orleans are on record.[76] Rather were these two decades characterized by a wild scramble for profit under conditions of reckless competition. In 1827 a Massachusetts legislative report spoke of the "want of harmony [that] has often appeared among the banks of this Commonwealth injurious to such institutions and of evil tendency to persons in any way connected with them."[77] However, cooperation among banks did not cease completely. In 1839 Tucker[78] pointed out that during the existence of the Second Bank of the United States banks had been accustomed to "give and expect mutual forbearance, partly because they [had been] responsible to a common head and [had been] thus led to seek a common safety in concert and unity of action; and partly because if any one [had] undertake[n] to check the operations of another it would necessarily [have led] to contention--in which case each party would have [had] its friends and supporters and as these chanced to prevail either [might have] suffer[ed] and perhaps both." In other words, banks in the 1820's and early 1830's were willing to cooperate for fear of the "national" bank and for fear of starting hostilities which would have led to alliances and possibly to ultimate defeat.

If one may draw conclusions from the almost complete absence of information on this matter, there was not much, if any cooperation in the

critical years 1819, 1825 or 1834, with a few exceptions as reported from Baltimore,[79] New York, and New Orleans. In the first named city, the banks passed a resolution on February 18, 1819 in which they pledged mutual aid. The cashiers of the state banks were authorized to ask the branch of the national bank for assistance, while the cashier of the latter could call on any bank for specie to answer demands made on the Bank of the United States. This is all that is known regarding cooperation in 1819 which seems to have been entirely lacking in 1825. In 1834, however, the New York city banks set up an emergency organization which in the records of the Bank of New York appears as the "meeting of the several banks in this city" and as the "meeting of delegates from the banks." This "meeting" of which almost nothing has come to the attention of the author made Albert Gallatin its chairman. He was at the same time also the chairman of a committee of seven appointed by the so-called Union Committee. (The latter in turn was appointed by the "meeting of the signers of the memorial to Congress held on the 11th day of February, 1834, at the Merchants' Exchange in the City of New York" for the purpose of influencing the attitude of the state legislature fighting against the Second Bank of the United States.) The above-mentioned "meeting" of banks resolved that a committee of three consisting of Albert Gallatin, Cornelius Heyer (president of the Bank of New York), and George Newbold (president of the Bank of America) be furnished by each bank with statements regarding loans and discounts, circulation, deposits, etc. These statements were to be kept secret, but consolidated for the purpose of being made known to the several bank boards. In consolidating the statements those of the New York branch of the Second Bank of the United States, of the three pet-banks, and of all the rest were to be kept separate.[80] That is to say, the banks tried to gain reliable information on the cause of their worries. The "meeting" seems to have appointed other committees also. One, for instance, communicated with the banks on March 24, 1834 and requested them to write individual letters to Congressmen (in line with suggestions of the Union Committee with which the banks seem to have cooperated). The Representatives were to be asked that Mexican and South American silver coins be made legal tender and that the mint by additional appropriations be enabled to pay coin upon delivery of silver bullion and uncurrent foreign money.[81]

It is evident from this material that the crisis of 1834 led to some loose cooperation in the City of New York. This cooperation did not serve, however, to meet the emergency by the establishment of uniform policy, but rather the banks tried to gain information and political influence. For this attempt they cannot be blamed, the crisis being political in origin.

More important, because of different character, was the cooperation in 1834 of the New Orleans banks. The latter really worked hand in hand in order to overcome their common trouble, the stringency prevailing in the money and exchange markets. For the purpose of "relieving the existing pressure in the money market," they resolved to renew the notes of trustworthy parties which would become due "with a reduction of 10 per cent every sixty days." Two committees were appointed, one to request the Second Bank of the United States to authorize its New Orleans branch to make discounts up to a certain amount, and a second to carry the above resolution into effect. This decision of the New Orleans banks was in line with previously described precedents: uniform policy was established by group action and a committee appointed to supervise its execution. The banks seem to have been satisfied with the result of this, for in 1836 they again cooperated to avert, if possible, the coming of that storm which was in the air. This time it was necessary to replenish the specie reserves of the local banking system which was continuously drained by an unfavorable rate of exchange. The banks resolved not to compete for Eastern and foreign exchange, but to pay a certain percentage above the par value; nor to pay any premium on specie, but in common to import silver from Mexico.[82]

Moreover, the New Orleans banks also made in 1836 an abortive attempt at establishing uniform policy. Recognizing the "solidarity" existing between the banks of the city, the latter agreed to submit comparable statements of their assets and cash responsibilities. On the basis of these reports it was suggested by the board of the Citizens Bank, de facto by Edmond J. Forstall,[83]

1. That the banks owing balances shall confine their discounts to the amount of their receipts.
2. That the banks to whom balances are due shall gradually increase their discounts to the amount of said balances.
3. That this agreement shall terminate on the 1st January proximo.

In order to prevent the banks out of this State from having, in future, any control over our local institutions, it is suggested that the following be the basis of any contract with them:

1. That no discount shall be allowed them, except for investment in exchange, and that to a limited amount.
2. That no cash balances shall be suffered to accumulate in their favor, over and above $5,000, without the privilege of remitting the same by checks or exchange.
3. That no notes above the denomination of $5 shall be redeemed here.

This proposal did not prevail, as can be seen from the following entry in the minutes of the Citizens Bank:

The Consolidated Association, the Improvement and Banking Company, the Louisiana State Bank, the Gas-Light and Banking Company, the Carrollton Bank, the Bank of Louisiana, and the Canal and Banking Company, have given their concurrence to the measures proposed by this bank on the 11th instant; and the City Bank having adopted the resolutions relative to the local discounts only, the cashier was instructed to communicate the fact to the above-named banks, and to state that the Union, Commercial, Mechanics and Traders', and Atchafalaya Banks, had not acknowledged the receipt of the circular.

(At that time, as later, there were always some banks who could see the advantages, if not the necessity, of cooperation. Others tended to thwart such attempts, thriving if they could by keeping aloof and enjoying the advantages without bearing the burden of the cooperation of other banks. The Massachusetts Bank in Boston and the Chemical Bank of New York were at times remarkably uncooperative, to give two examples.)[84]

These New Orleans cooperative actions of the 1830's were truly remarkable for the time. Since no comparable ones can be found in any other banking center in the decade prior to 1837 the author is inclined to assign the difference to the personal factor: no doubt E. J. Forstall played a leading part in promoting the policy of cooperation.[85]

Since banks in the 1820's and 1830's hardly cooperated even in emergencies, it is not surprising that in normal times they did so only to a very limited extent and under special circumstances. In Maryland, for instance, three banks (the Union Bank of Maryland, the Mechanics Bank, and the Commercial and Farmers Bank) united in 1825 in sending a memorial to the legislature regarding the capital tax levied on banks.[86] In both the State of

New York and the Commonwealth of Massachusetts, when whole batches of charters expired (in 1827 and by 1830, respectively), the banks concerned cooperated with regard to their renewals.[87] That is to say, at that moment a temporary community of interest came into existence in view of pending legislation. The tactics applied in New York consisted of consultations of the banks with each other through the medium of a committee, separate petitions to the legislature, and common lobbying. Because of tactical moves of the sponsors of the Safety Fund Act the united phalanx of the New York banks broke up, however, and was replaced by two separate fronts, those of the city and of the country banks of the state.[88] So the common efforts did not prevail; the banks did not receive such charters as they desired, but had to go into the newly established Safety Fund System which was soon to become a landmark in the field under investigation: The act of 1828 for the first time regulated banks as a species of enterprise and it brought into being a permanent community of interest resulting from mutual responsibility. Most of the New York banks hated this feature not less than certain Western banks had when mutual responsibility was proposed to them in 1817 when the Second Bank of the United States took over the frozen government deposits.[89] Nevertheless mutual responsibility once established could not fail to exert a deep influence on the attitude of the banks concerned. In addition sections 20 and 21 of the Safety Fund Act were bound to draw them together. They were required to elect two of the three bank commissioners. For this purpose those located in the 1st, 2d, and 3d senate districts sent one delegate each to meet at a date designated by the governor in convention in New York City, while the banks which had their seats in the remaining five districts met in Auburn. Each delegate cast one vote for every $5,000 paid-in capital.[90] In view of this situation Daniel Webster characterized the Safety Fund banks as "leagued together by legal provisions," a comment to which Senator Silas Wright objected: The banks did not represent a "league" because they had retained independent managements,[91] he thought. But Daniel Webster actually saw the salient point: a community of interest was coming into being as the by-product of legislative action; and consciousness of common interest was bound to spread with the migration of the safety fund legislation. The new spirit created by mutual dependence was bitterly denounced by those who believed in competition, if not as a law of God, then at least as a panacea.[92] In fact, however, neither the Safety Fund Act itself nor the new spirit which it engendered could sway the American banking system as a whole. That spirit remained rather the exception; and it is indicative of the one prevailing at the time that the pet banks, which as a group undoubtedly possessed strong bonds of common interest, never developed even a loose organization of their own although attempts were made in this direction. That they instantly refused mutual responsibility when it was suggested to them has been mentioned;[93] and distrust over community of interest prevailed to such an extent that they would hardly take each others' notes.

Besides community of interest created by legislative actions, there also existed in those years what might be characterized as "natural" communities of interest. These originated, for instance, in trade centers in which country notes accumulated and in which the local banks could not keep their own notes afloat. But only in Boston did such community of interest lead to successful cooperative action, as embodied in the original Suffolk Bank system.[94] Attempts of the Savannah and Augusta banks to make permanent arrangements for the settlement of inter-bank balances did not avail, because the banks in the interior would not cooperate.[95] There may be an explanation for the fact that Boston banks succeeded where those in other cities faced with identical problems failed: It has been shown before that in Boston the cooperative spirit of the first period of American banking carried over to a certain extent into the 1820's, because no suspension of specie payments interfered with traditional attitudes. As a matter of fact, when one reads about the first steps taken toward the creation of that system, as they appear in the directors' records of the Massachusetts Bank, the continuity is evident. Those steps appear to the historian as just another attempt at establishing uniform policies (in order to reduce the amount of foreign bills in circulation).[96]

To be sure, the Suffolk Bank System had still another aspect. Regardless of its eminently healthful consequences, it was originally a warlike alliance of some banks against others, all of which were engaged in the competitive struggle for their share in the circulation of notes. In its warlike character the Suffolk Bank System had its counterparts in the pre-War of 1812 period also, and as soon as it had come into existence the country banks saw it for what it really was. A convention was called for the purpose of organizing a counteralliance and numerous country banks actually met in Boston on January 16 and 18, 1826.[97] The phraseology used in this convention is indicative of the spirit of the period; and it was, in fact, a far cry from the cooperative attitude prevailing in the 1790's to the combative spirit back of these alliances and would-be counteralliances.[98] In this context may be mentioned an agreement of the Baltimore bank presidents of 1838 to recommend to their respective boards that no notes of any private banks be renewed nor accounts opened for such enterprises.[99]

Cooperation with respect to foreign notes was unsuccessfully attempted in 1836 in New Orleans also. On the 22d of October the board of the City Bank adopted resolutions, the preamble of which reads substantially as follows:

> that the circulation of the paper of the Mississippi banks is rendered more permanent than ours, because they are not redeemed in this city; whilst the notes of our banks are paid by the Mississippi banks, and immediately returned to us: hence the cause of our small circulation.

The proposal in question was not adopted. The Citizens Bank, for instance, rejected it and made the following counterproposal:

> Resolved, that the banks of this city hereby bind themselves to close the account of every bank out of this State, having agencies in our banks, that may, directly or indirectly, accumulate funds in this place for the purpose of withdrawing suddenly from them such an amount of specie as may effect the current operation of this place.
>
> Resolved that the above resolution shall be binding upon all the banks of this city, as soon as agreed to by the said banks.[100]

A "natural" community of interest also existed with regard to counterfeiters, just as it had in the preceding period. Again it was combative in character. On November 22, 1832 representatives of the Boston banks met to consider measures for securing the banks and the public alike against counterfeiters. A committee was appointed consisting of one delegate from each bank; this committee in turn appointed a subcommittee of five to "carry into effect the object of this association," namely, to prevent, detect, and punish counterfeiters. The participants had to put up $100 each and were liable to further assessment. Whether these are the very beginnings of what became later the [New England] Association of Banks for the Suppression of Counterfeiting is not clear.[101]

Thus the dominance in the 1820's and 1830's of the spirit of competition led to alliances rather than to true cooperation and, as a rule, community of interests was recognized only when these interests clashed with those of others. Regardless of this fact, however, a new type of genuine cooperation originated in the period under investigation, a type which was to become more and more important as the century progressed. Banks came to realize that they belonged to a community when even a solid one without serious fault of its own was in danger of collapsing. If, under such conditions, one bank were permitted to succumb to a run, all the others in the same locality would be endangered through the break-down of their credit. Therefore, under certain exceptional circumstances, banks were willing even to uphold a competitor. The earliest case of this type seems to have occurred in Massachusetts, where, during the War of 1812, a wavering bank was saved. A second case is reported from New York. There, about 1825, the Fulton Bank was bolstered up by others when endangered by a run.[102]

One can thus sum up the situation as it presented itself between 1817 and 1837: banks, as a rule, competed and kept aloof from each other except when there was some trouble, local or regional in character. Then under exceptional conditions they were willing to cooperate for specific ends, or to form alliances against specific evils.

IV

The suspension of specie payments in 1837, just as that in 1814, led to cooperation among banks on a scale not reached before. At the same time, new forms of organization were developed: while the suspension of 1814 marked the beginning of regional cooperation which resulted in coordination on a national scale, that of 1837 saw the emergence of the first truly national bank convention. The idea of bank conventions had not died out after the experiences of 1815, 1816, and 1817, although during the years that followed it lay dormant. At least two conventions are on record. The one of 1826 of country banks meeting in Boston in order to build up an alliance against the Suffolk Bank System has been mentioned.[103] Another one took place in Providence on August 19 of the same year; it seems to have recommended certain policies.[104] Moreover when the pet-bank system was to be set up, it was suggested that one bank each in Baltimore, Philadelphia, and Boston be appointed the government depository, while two banks were made depositories in New York; and that the government reserve the right directly to appoint one depository each in Savannah, Charleston, Norfolk, New Orleans, and Alabama. Thereafter these banks should have the right "by a convention of their presidents or otherwise" to select banks at all the other points of the country in which the public funds would be deposited.[105] Nothing came of this plan.

Group action within each city preceded the suspension of 1837: this fact is evident from the dates alone. New York suspended on May 10, Philadelphia, New Haven, Providence, and Hartford on May 11, and Boston on May 12.[106] There can be little doubt that almost everywhere the banks united in making the decision or at least in announcing it, as they did in New York, Philadelphia, Boston, and Hartford. In the last named city, for instance, on May 11 the five then existing banks agreed on sending out a circular in common. Therein they announced suspension, and committees elected by each bank from among their officers and directors, men whose names carried weight, pledged their honor that the bank in question was "safe and sound beyond contingency." The circular announced at the same time that the banks would go on taking each other's notes on deposit and in the payment of discounts.[108]

Suspension, once it had taken place, necessitated a good deal of cooperation, at least in the financial centers of the country. Under the pressure of circumstances such cooperation was uniformly patterned, as will be shown in detail in the following paragraphs: notes were taken as before, interest was paid on balances, debts owed to other banks were usually limited to certain amounts, and in some cases creditor banks received the right to demand payment or security. Emergency organizations were brought into existence in order to provide platforms for cooperation and to supervise and put into effect whatever was agreed upon. But such arrangements were local in character and, as an anonymous writer in the Financial Register stressed,[109] there was never any chance that they would cover all the banks of one state, let alone banks in different ones.

The New York banks began to meet when storm signals threatened in April, 1837, and by upholding tottering competitors tried to stave off the disaster that was in the air. In a meeting of May 4 in which thirteen banks participated it was resolved to back the Mechanics Bank. Demands on the latter were to be postponed for six months upon payment of 7 per cent interest. In order to equalize the burden resulting from this action the sum was to be apportioned among the banks at the rate of 6 per cent of each bank's capital. Soon thereafter similar action became necessary with regard to the Dry Dock Bank; this time fifteen banks participated. A committee headed by Albert Gallatin was appointed which put under the

care of the cashier of the Merchants Bank the notes of the Dry Dock company to the extent that they had been found in the possession of the officers of this bank. On the 8th of May the committee reported that in consequence of this action the total circulation of the Bank, including the amount held by the participating New York City banks, amounted to $198,705. Thereupon the cooperating banks decided, on the recommendation of the committee, to redeem the outstanding notes of the Dry Dock Bank (save those held by the participating banks) and to apportion them among the latter according to each bank's capital.[110]

In view of the world situation such local attempts at saving the day were of no avail and in the session of May 9 the New York banks resolved to suspend specie payments. On the following day, May 10, a meeting of bankers and merchants took place in the Exchange where James G. King, partner of the eminent banking house of Prime, Ward and King, proposed that bank notes should pass current as before until resumption was practicable.[111] About two weeks later the banks agreed on a series of rules and regulations which were to remain in force during the period of suspension.

These "Rules and Regulations adopted by the banks of the City of New York in reference to their business transactions with each other during the suspension of specie payments" contained the following provisions: The banks would continue to take each other's notes in payment and on deposit unless notice should be given to the contrary. Exchanges of notes would continue as usual every morning and interest at the rate of 6 per cent would be charged upon balances, such interest to commence as of May 9. No bank was allowed to hold back in the exchanges the notes of any other bank to which it was indebted. No bank was permitted to increase its loans or discounts if its aggregate indebtedness to the other banks of the city exceeded a sum equal to 10 per cent of its capital. To the contrary such banks were obligated to reduce their loans and discounts upon requisition of the "General Committee" (to be discussed forthwith). No bank was at liberty to discontinue the receipt of the notes of any other bank which was a partner to this agreement without giving three days notice to the bank whose credit was thus questioned and without at the same time sending a copy of that letter containing the reasons therefor to the "standing committee." All regulations agreed upon in the General Committee would be submitted for approval to the boards of the participating banks and would become binding by subscription after approval.

When forming their emergency association the banks set up two organs: the above-mentioned standing committee and the "general meeting of the officers of the banks of the City of New York," called the General Committee. The standing committee of three which had the power to call the General Committee (consisting of delegates from each bank) received a statement from each participating bank every Saturday. The banks had to report their loans and discounts including every item that bore interest; the balances due to and from every other bank in the city; the amount of specie on hand and the amount of current bank notes of every other bank in the city; and the amount of their own notes in circulation. In addition each bank had to report on the first business day of every month its circulation before and after the exchanges of that day had been made. These reports were open for inspection by the president and cashier of each participating bank.

The General Committee assembled frequently and was obviously the policy-making organ of the association. In the usual way it appointed committees for special purposes (for instance, a committee of correspondence and a committee on the resumption of specie payments). The assignment of the last-named committee was soon to become the main topic with which the General Committee was concerned. On August 15 and October 10, 1837, for instance, the bank officers discussed inviting delegates to a national bank convention to be called for November. On December 15 they heard the report of their own delegates to that convention. On February 28, 1838 they listened to the report of their committee on the resumption of specie payments; and the ultimate decision to resume on May 10, in spite of the opposition met in the national convention, must have been made by the same body.[112]

In Philadelphia (just as in New York) the banks associated after suspension had taken place and acted through the instrumentality of a joint or general committee. First (at the very moment of suspension) they set up a "committee of conference from the several banks of the city and county of Philadelphia" which a few days later was replaced by the more permanent general committee which appeared under various names, "Committee of Banks," "Delegates of the banks of the city and incorporated districts of the county of Philadelphia" (1837) or "Association of the delegates of the banks of the city of Philadelphia and districts" (1838).[113] It consisted of one representative from each bank, probably the president in most cases; Manuel Eyre, Biddle's confidante, was the first chairman. The purpose of the committee was to devise such measures as were deemed necessary to promote harmony of action among the various banks, and to make suggestions to regulate their intercourse.[114] After the initial excitement had quieted down, the committee met once a month.[115] Special meetings were called when subjects of importance had to be discussed immediately, as, for instance, the New York invitation to send delegates to a national convention (August 29, 1837). In the meetings of this committee, as McClurkin has phrased it, policies were established which led to closer and closer cooperation among the Philadelphia banks during the years under investigation.[116] That the committee appointed occasionally sub-committees for special purposes, goes without saying.[117]

When suspension was determined upon it was recognized that the banks of the city and county of Philadelphia must act in concert and so the following principles were laid down: the banks should receive each other's notes but pay out their own notes only, while those of other banks were to be exchanged daily; (i.e., in every day's exchange the notes received the day before would be presented). However the joint committee of the banks which was to mold these principles into rules resolved (probably on May 15) that instead of exchanging their notes daily the banks should open interest-bearing accounts for each other, accounts which were to be settled on the last day of each month. Whenever (after the exchange of notes) at the end of the month a bank was indebted to another bank for more than $30,000 the creditor bank could require payment in such a manner as was acceptable to it. Discounting or rediscounting of the debtor bank's bills receivable was contemplated as a satisfactory mode, in which case the debtor bank was to guarantee the assets which had been used to liquidate its balance.[118] These early resolutions were supplemented later in May: the general committee resolved that the banks had to report regularly by what amount the total of their loans had increased or decreased since suspension. In addition they were bound to report the aggregate balance of interest received or paid during the preceding month.[119] Such reports were actually submitted and made known to all the banks which were enabled thereby to judge the standing of each other. The next natural step was concerted contraction which was agreed upon in July, 1837.[120]

Of course when the day of resumption actually approached it was prepared for by agreement: on May 7, 1838 the general committee resolved that fractional parts of dollars were to be paid in coin; that all scrip under $1.00 issued by the city and county of Philadelphia should be redeemed by the banks pro rata to their capital and exchanged with the proper authorities. A sub-committee of seven banks was to take care of this latter transaction. The original idea that such scrip once redeemed should circulate among the banks was abandoned.[121] Slightly later a revision of the rate payable on inter-bank balances was under discussion by the general committee[122] with the aim of increasing it to 6 per cent. The moves leading to resumption will be discussed later.[123]

The Boston banks also went far in organizing cooperation for the emergency. When the news of suspension in New York reached Boston on May 11, the bank officials were hastily called to meet the same evening. They decided to suspend, as was in fact unavoidable, and to form an association which would uphold mutual confidence among the banks and sustain that of the public, prerequisites to the proper functioning of the banks. The temptation was great, so the Massachusetts Bank Commissioners[124] commented, "for the strong banks to adopt the unsocial principle that it belonged to each one to take care of itself. Such a course, to be sure, might and probably would have been suicidal in the end for the whole business community; but it is nevertheless true that many reasons might have been urged for adopting it." The Boston banks did not succumb to the temptation, but immediately laid down some principles to guide the new association. A committee thereof was to be set up to examine once a month the status of the participating banks and to report thereon, a measure which was expected to prevent over-expansion. Notes of non-participating banks (the Massachusetts Bank was to be the only one) were not to be taken on deposit by the other banks. Uniform policies were to be established regarding the payment of checks in banknotes, the opening of special specie deposits, the paying of specie to such special depositors, and the relations with the country banks.

This program was put into effect when on May 16 an organization called the "Associated Banks" was brought into existence "to prevent over-issues of bills and to provide security for balances." One of its first actions was the publication of a memorial explaining the need for suspension.[125] At the same time articles of agreement were drawn up which stipulated: that each bank would be represented by one officer; that the Associated Banks would set up a committee which would examine once a week, or oftener if needed, the circulation of each member bank and report both to the Associated Banks and the public, as in fact it did; that in case of over-issues the banks would refuse to take the notes of the offender[126] or require security for their redemption; that the committee was empowered to organize the daily settlement of inter-bank balances (an attempt made in this direction was unsuccessful); that bills of other than the Associated Banks would not be

received in Boston during the emergency, except that the relations with the New England country banks would not undergo any change (i.e., the Suffolk Bank System was upheld).

At the end of the year 1837 the governor of Massachusetts gave his opinion on the Association of the banks, formed "for the purpose of exercising a mutual control over each other and of laying before the public a weekly statement of the aggregate condition of the associated institutions. This association [so the Governor thought] has no doubt served as a salutary check on the tendency to an undue extension of bank paper and bank credit..."[127]

In fact, however, useful and indispensable as the Association and the above-described arrangements were, they did not eliminate all over-expansion nor all distrust on the part of the community which resented especially the indiscriminate re-issue of notes agreed upon by the Associated Banks. But, as indicated, the alternative, daily exchange of notes and settlement of balances, although proposed, was not put into operation. The situation was further complicated because several Boston banks failed in 1837 and 1838, and three (the Commercial, Fulton, and Hancock Banks) had to be upheld by their competitors, an action which must be stressed at this point; its significance being explained later. These events led to a supplementary agreement among the Associated Banks according to which the members had to bring their specie reserves up to 25 per cent of their issues. To sum up, the Association was undoubtedly of great value to the business community, but it was far from being perfect, a fact which is reflected in the balanced judgment of the governor of Massachusetts, already mentioned. The main deficiency of the Association lay in its inability to examine more than the circulation of its members and to gain influence over their policies and management.[128]

In New Orleans an emergency organization was built up in the years 1837 and 1838 which was hardly less elaborate than those in the northern cities. E. J. Forstall, who had been instrumental in devising what may be considered in retrospect as preparatory steps, was active therein although not always wielding the decisive influence.[129] The New Orleans set-up centered in a Board of Presidents which may have met regularly. It dealt with the emergency and, as will be described shortly, determined the date of resumption. It was probably this board which resolved that the circulation of the New Orleans banks should be related to capital and accumulated profits, and which set a ratio (ranging from 25 to 50 per cent) for each institution, undoubtedly according to whether it was a creditor or a debtor bank.[130]

Outside of the commercial centers, cooperation is known to have been attempted in Ohio. On June 5, 1837, 32 of the 33 existing chartered banks met in Columbus. They agreed not to part with their specie; to conduct their affairs with a view to early resumption; and to receive the notes of the participants to the agreement. They also resolved that each bank should pay out the notes so received in preference to its own, a measure which was expected to reduce the total circulation. Finally, each participating bank was to furnish a statement of its conditions to each of the others every sixty days.[131] If similar actions were taken by country and small-town banks in other states, they have not come to the attention of the author.

Local activities, as described, were soon topped by cooperation on a national scale. It started when, in a meeting of New York bank officers held on August 15, 1837, a committee of three was appointed to correspond with leading banks throughout the country for the purpose of "ascertaining at which time and place a convention of the principal banks should be held for the purpose of agreeing on the time when specie payments should be resumed and on the measures necessary to effect that purpose."[132] One member of this committee was George Newbold, an experienced banker; he had been the cashier (1815-32) and was at that moment the president of the Bank of America which owed its existence to his lobbying activities of 1812. The other members were Cornelius VanWyck Lawrence (1791-1861), president of the Bank of the State of New York, and Albert Gallatin, who acted as the chairman.[133] Gallatin owed this chairmanship to his personality and his prestige as a financial statesman. The other two men provided that power which flows from the command over large capital; and Newbold had cooperated with Gallatin before. Lawrence brought into the committee political influence too: he was a Tammany man and later became a chamberlain and mayor of New York.[134] On August 18 the committee sent a circular letter to "designated" banks all over the country proposing a conference and at the same time laying down in rather strong language what the committee considered their moral obligations and the rules that should guide the actions of the banks. Resumption was believed possible before the spring of 1838.

The circular letter was not too well received.[135] In the first instance it served only to crystallize opposition to the proposal and its backers, an opposition which was both economic and political in character. Enemies of Van Buren's administration adopted the strategy of tying together resumption and the chartering of a new "national" bank, a new central bank, to use the modern term. Nicholas Biddle became the natural leader of this group; and by the fall of 1837 the banks were more or less consolidating into two antagonistic camps led by Gallatin and Biddle, respectively.

It has been customary to look at their contest as one between the righteous New Yorkers and the wicked Philadelphians deceived by the selfish Biddle.[136] Such presentation is, of course, an oversimplification. The problem to be solved was, in fact, an exceedingly complicated one, as is every controversial one in economic life. Rivalry between New York and Philadelphia played a part. Philadelphia, accustomed to leadership within the nation, would not let its supremacy pass to the capital on the Hudson without a struggle. The mere fact that New York banks came out with a proposal, made that proposal unacceptable to the Philadelphians. In addition, the question of central bank or no was an important one which separated the parties. Finally, it must be understood that various interests reacted differently on suspension. Followed as it was by inflation, it stimulated exports and was therefore popular in such sections of the country as depended on the world market for their staples: while vice versa it was detrimental to the importers, the majority of whom were located in New York. Moreover the inflationary trend resulting from suspension was beneficial to the new parts of the country chronically suffering from a lack of capital. We all know today that it is possible to create real capital by a process of inflation which at the same time is so hurtful to capital owners, especially in a country with limited capital resources, since it undermines the supremacy of these owners. Under these circumstances the Philadelphia banks answered that it would be inexpedient to send delegates to a meeting, since resumption depended on the actions of Congress. They meant that it depended on the re-erection of a central bank which, like the Second Bank of the United States in 1817, would take the necessary steps to facilitate resumption (under Biddle's leadership, as many would have added as a mental reservation). The Baltimore and Boston banks joined those of Philadelphia. In Boston, to be sure, opinion was divided.[137] Some bankers were strongly for early resumption, especially Franklin Haven who later was to play an important role in the Boston Clearing House. Soon the banks of the various sections of the country were to become exponents of regional interests.

To understand the alignment fully the personal factor must be taken into consideration also. One side, as already mentioned, was led by Albert

Gallatin whose earlier achievements as Secretary of the Treasury need no comment. In 1837 he was a resident of New York and a bank president. However, he presided over a rather small bank with only $750,000 capital so that this position as such would not have entitled him to leadership. This is especially true since his connection with practical banking was of relatively recent origin. At the request of John Jacob Astor he had assumed the presidency of the National Bank, later renamed Gallatin National Bank, which under the leadership of Albert Gallatin's son, James, became important. Astor, in turn, had entered the scene when certain promoters, who had received a bank charter in 1829, approached him when unable to secure enough capital. He had furnished the needed funds on the condition that Gallatin should be made president.[138] By that time, in close cooperation with Biddle, Gallatin was writing his <u>Considerations on the Currency and Banking System of the United States</u>, one of the maturest items of the contemporary banking literature, thereby acquiring a good deal of theoretical knowledge in the field. Thus prepared, Gallatin quickly became a leader of the New York banks in the several cooperative actions previously described[139] and in matters of monetary policy: in 1837 he was their spokesman in submitting a memorial to Congress dealing with the ratio of gold and silver in the American standard coins and with problems created by the import of foreign coins; in April, 1837, he headed a committee which warned Congress against paying out the Treasury surplus to the states.[140] All his life Gallatin had been a rather dogmatic metallist and old age probably made him less flexible than he had ever been[141] while his moral fiber was strengthened. For Gallatin, banknotes were promises to pay money and suspension meant the breach of a sacred promise,[142] a breach which was bound to have dire consequences.

On the other side of the fence stood Nicholas Biddle, Gallatin's erstwhile friend and his peer. If Gallatin was dogmatic and a moralist, Biddle's attitude was tainted by self-interest and a belief in his own infallibility. What he desired was restoration to his previous status as what one would today call a central bank president; but it would be incorrect to claim, as has been done, that he was trying to uphold a tottering enterprise. The Bank of the United States[143] of Pennsylvania was at that moment solvent, although illiquid. As the country's central-bank president for over ten years Biddle had gained a clearer picture of the total situation than had the New Yorkers who looked too much at the regional aspect. In addition he was more familiar than anybody else with

the foreign exchange situation, on which in the last instance resumption depended, and with the conditions in the southern and western states which at that period provided the "crop" of exchange. At the very moment when the discussion started Biddle worked hard to restore that stability in the foreign exchange market which was the prerequisite of the New Yorkers' goal. Moreover he was already in correspondence[144] with the New Orleans banks aiming at concerted action by Philadelphia and New Orleans similar to that which his counterplayers considered necessary also. Bray Hammond, the only writer besides the author to do justice to Biddle, refers to the latter's policy as an attempt to introduce into this country a monetary system less inflexible than the one based on specie, and similar to that which the Bank of England had provided in the Napoleonic era. This aim was determined by Biddle's ultimate goal: in contrast to Gallatin who preferred security to growth, Biddle, according to Hammond, not only wished to avoid contraction, but intended to sustain a continuous expansion of the national economy. To that extent his policy was "patriotic," as even the London <u>Times</u> acknowledged. It was a difference in value judgments that resulted in the promotion of different economic and business policies by Gallatin and Biddle. As one sees it in retrospect, the question was whether a new equilibrium could be reached on the price level of 1837/1838 or whether severe contraction and a concomitant fall of prices was needed before a new equilibrium could be established on a lower level. After events have taken a certain turn it is, of course, no longer possible to ascertain what would have happened if another course had been pursued. However the author is inclined to think that whatever Biddle's contributory guilt may have been, the happenings of 1839 prove that he possessed a better insight into the national situation than did his antagonists.[145] On the other hand, price history seems to indicate that the price level of 1837 was not tenable.

Under the influence of the two personalities-- Gallatin and Biddle--the alignment which took place in the fall months of 1837 was so sharp that the delegates came to the convention more or less pledged to uphold one side or the other. In fact, the New York banks had not been discouraged by the frosty reception of their original circular letter, but after another meeting of their officers on October 10, in a second letter of October 20, 1838, invited the banks all over the country to send delegates to a convention to be held in New York on November 27. Sending out this invitation regardless of the unfavorable reaction to the original circular letter was a clever tactical move. It forced the Philadelphia and Boston banks to yield lest New York act independently, as it later actually did. A sub-committee of the joint committee of the Philadelphia banks reported against accepting the invitation, but when it came to a vote, it was accepted 14 to 1.[146]

The author has not come across much material indicating how the delegations were brought into existence,[147] but methods used in 1838 must have shaped up in the preceding fall. As in all the reform movements of the 1820's and 1830's which in their structure resembled the Federal political system,[148] there must have been a tendency to link together the banks of the various states and to have loose state organizations send delegates to the national convention. This modus procedendi was actually used in Georgia. Her banks met early in September, 1837, in Milledgeville,[149] then the state capital, and appointed to the convention three delegates whose expenses were to be paid by the "banks in Georgia in proportion to their capital paid in." They were "instructed to urge upon the convention the simultaneous resumption of specie payments by the first of June next [1838] or earlier if practicable."[150]

While Gallatin headed the New York delegation and was the moving spirit of the convention, Biddle was not even a delegate. William Meredith, president of the Schuylkill Bank of Philadelphia, led the Pennsylvania delegation in which Biddle's close friend Manuel Eyre played an important role. Acting as Biddle's lieutenant, Eyre represented that delegation on the decisive committee of the convention and drew up the minority report.

The convention of November, 1837 (it actually lasted from November 27 to December 2, 1837) was attended by 135 delegates from 18 states. When it opened, the question was not whether to resume or not; it was whether resumption should be conditional or unconditional. The task was to choose the expedient moment, that is to say, the moment at which specie payments could be resumed without the danger of a relapse. These were the decisive problems.[151] Through the mouth of the Pennsylvania delegation Biddle stressed the injury which a premature resumption would inflict, and the Boston and Baltimore banks adopted his line of reasoning. Gallatin, on the other hand, answered by pointing out the moral obligation involved and by putting his finger on the reserve situation of the banks and the favorable exchange rates. That the latter had become favorable by exchange manipulation on the part of Biddle, Gallatin did not see; neither did he realize that there was an artificial element in the picture. It is rather odd that Biddle who had worked admirably in the interest of the national

economy in those months when Gallatin had written only letters, had thereby undermined his own strategic position. The majority of the convention was decidedly against early resumption, being against contraction, its prerequisite, at a moment when the country was in the throes of a severe depression. Whatever selfishness entered into the considerations they made better sense than earlier "sound money" writers have been willing to concede. The atmosphere at the convention must at times have been very tense, and the withdrawal of the Pennsylvania, Boston, and Baltimore banks was contemplated. At that point Biddle, who was in contact with his locum tenens, Manuel Eyre, suggested that in such a case the withdrawing banks should unite in a sober, argumentative, and clear declaration of their position.[152]

The convention adjourned on December 2, without having reached a decision, to meet again on April 11, 1838. Gallatin and his colleagues on the New York delegation made a report in December, 1837.[153] They stressed the dangers and evils that prevailed and the need for cooperation on a national scale. In a later report of a committee of the New York bank officers, Gallatin declared early resumption to be possible.[154] The clue to this attitude can be found in the fact that in order to avoid political trouble the New York banks had to resume regardless of whether or not cooperation of the banks in other states was forthcoming. There is no evidence that they ever tried to take such steps in the state legislature as would have opened the road for true cooperation and compromise, and for this they are here criticized. As a matter of fact, the New York act that sanctioned suspension had set May 10, 1838 as the date for resumption in the state and so political pressure (which they did not oppose) made the banks' decision a foregone conclusion. Before the convention reassembled, as early as February 28, 1838, the New York banks announced their intention to resume on or before May 10. Thus their actions were tainted with selfishness just as much as were those of their opponents; and Biddle, who is not a reliable witness in this connection, had considered the circular letter of August, 1837, as a mere stratagem to procure the restoration of the public deposits to the New York banks. He rightly remained suspicious throughout. In fact, all the leading participants in the struggle represented special interests.

Under these circumstances the Philadelphia banks refused to send delegates to the adjourned (second) convention which met from the 11th to the 16th of April, 1838. Their decision was made in a meeting of the joint committee (the "association of the delegates of the banks of the City of Philadelphia and districts") assembled on April 4, 1838.[155] The

Pennsylvanians had a point: the adjourned convention was not recalled in a spirit of compromise in order to find, by free discussion, a solution for the problems involved. When it convened, nevertheless, the New England delegations took the lead,[156] while the New York banks were in a hopeless minority. But their delegates did not budge. All they offered in the way of compromise was resumption on July 1 instead of on May 10, the date they had resolved upon before the convention met. Disregarding the attitude of the New Yorkers, the convention agreed by majority vote to resume on the first Monday in January, 1839, (meaning the 8th of that month). This date was well selected[157] and took into consideration the rhythm of the cotton trade, which provided in that period most of the foreign exchange which became available in the United States. Biddle was angry that the convention had set any date at all. His policy had been to wait for its closing and for the adjournment of Congress, and thereafter to call a conference of the Boston, Baltimore, and Richmond banks to Philadelphia in order to determine a date for resumption.[158] His friends had apparently been unable to sell this policy to the majority of the convention. But the decision of the latter was immaterial anyway. Its resolution was framed so as to leave a loophole: it did not preclude "an earlier resumption on the part of such banks as [might] find it necessary or deem proper." Thus the New York banks could have their way without losing face. Having contracted while the Boston and Philadelphia banks had not, as a group they had become creditors and they had nothing to fear at that moment, especially since Biddle's actions had turned the tide of the foreign exchanges. So after having met locally immediately after the close of the national convention they confirmed their earlier resolution. After they had succeeded in resuming on May 10, 1838, Boston followed suit in July, 1838, and Philadelphia and the rest of the country soon thereafter.

Great interest attaches to the meetings of 1837 and 1838 as being the first national conventions (or convention, if the student prefers), even though they did not meet with success: they did not lead to concerted action on a national scale. To the contrary, when the powerful New York banks could not make their policy palatable to the rest of the country they took unilateral action against the wishes of all the other regions as expressed in the conventions. The sources indicate that there was a good deal of ill feeling toward the New Yorkers while the meetings were proceeding. In the end the latter forced their policy on the rest of the country, probably to the detri-

ment of the national economy as a whole. That unilateral action of theirs, however, was foreshadowed as early as November, 1837. The majority report of the convention drafted under New York influence recommended a date for resumption, but did not preclude earlier resumption by some banks. It even proclaimed it as the duty of each and every bank to resume as quickly as possible. The resolution of April, 1838, as has been shown, was in this respect essentially identical with the pertinent clause of the 1837 majority report. In contrast the minority report of 1837, influenced by Biddle, stressed correctly the need for simultaneous action and the dependence on the exchange situation which, in turn, was influenced by the cotton crop and foreign indebtedness.[159] The majority report and the resolution of 1838 are important illustrations of the geistesgeschichtliche situation. They indicate that the conventions were mere experiments in cooperation in an era of extreme individualism. The guiding idea was: let us cooperate, but each one must be free to do as he pleases. Thus the conventions were doomed to failure and the calling of them appears a stratagem rather than an honest attempt at free discussion and compromise.

Regardless of their failure the national conventions of 1837 and 1838 fostered new organizational developments: a whole series of regional conventions of the type held in 1815-1817 followed in their wake. Gallatin's first circular letter, that of August 18, 1837, tended to stimulate such conventions. The letter was directed only to selected banks, "designated" therein, which were invited "to collect and ascertain the opinions of the others [in the same city or state] and to communicate the general result as soon as practicable."[160] In fact, as early as August 29, the Philadelphia banks met in order to discuss the circular letter. (They came to the conclusion that a convention was superfluous, if not injurious.) Further meetings must have taken place, although details have not come to the attention of the author. The Milledgeville Convention of the Georgia banks also resulting from the circular letter has been discussed already and similar meetings were probably held elsewhere too in the late summer and fall of 1837. But local research has not been focused on these events, and large gaps in our knowledge remain to be filled.

We are better informed on a whole set of regional conventions which took place in 1838. All were held with a view of setting the exact date for resumption and many also for the purpose of establishing cooperation to that end. In the first instance they sprang from the New York convention of April, 1838, which, as will be remembered, had decided to recommend January, 1839, for resumption. What may have been the earliest of these conferences took place on May 22 and 23 in Charleston where the South Carolina and Georgia banks ratified the resolution of the New York convention.[161]

Meanwhile the picture was changing because of New York's unilateral action. Thus when the Ohio banks met at Columbus on the 6th and 7th of June, probably called in order to ratify the New York resolution as had the Georgia and South Carolina banks, they had to make independent decisions in order to cope with a new situation. According to the custom of the period of suspension,[162] the statements of the various banks were laid before the convention at its opening. A committee was appointed to consider the latest actions of Congress relating to the currency and the propriety of setting a date for resumption in Ohio. The banks were faced with a state law requiring them to resume on or before July 4, 1839 if the banks of New York, Philadelphia, and Baltimore had resumed by that time. The committee recommended that this law be obeyed, provided the two last-named cities had resumed by that time (those of New York having resumed already). Other committees were appointed to keep the banks of the state informed on actions that might be taken in those cities and to confer with the banks of Indiana, Kentucky, western Virginia, and western Pennsylvania inviting their concurrence in the matter of resumption. However, the convention was not content with preparing resumption; it took additional steps: it appointed a committee to recommend a statewide system of note exchanges and of settling balances and another to memorialize Congress and exert pressure for the repeal or revision, respectively, of certain clauses regarding public deposits.[163]

Very similar to the Columbus convention of the Ohio banks seems to have been that of the Kentucky banks which met on June 8, 1838 in the Bank of Louisville. The meeting resolved to resume on July 16, 1839 provided the banks of Philadelphia, Baltimore, Pittsburgh, Cincinnati, Indiana, and Illinois resumed on or before that date. A committee of three was appointed to negotiate with the banks of Tennessee, and of western Virginia and such other banks as they might deem proper with a view of inducing them to concur in that resolution. Furthermore it was to correspond with the banks of the cities and states on whose actions resumption in Kentucky was made to depend in order to ascertain their intentions.[164]

Of a different character and of greater importance was the Philadelphia convention of July 23, 1838, which gathered at the invitation of the joint committee of the associated banks of the city and county of Philadelphia. This invitation had been contemplated as early as March, when the Philadelphia banks declined to participate in the New York convention of April of that year.[165] So delegates of banks from Pennsylvania, Delaware, Maryland, Virginia, Kentucky, Missouri, Connecticut, Rhode Island, and Massachusetts met at the Bank of Pennsylvania in July, 1838. This meeting, as indicated, was indirectly the outgrowth of the New York convention of April; although contemplated earlier it represented in fact the answer to the New York resumption and was a belated attempt of Biddle's and the Philadelphia banks' to reassume leadership. But the initiative had slipped to New York once and for all; and in resolving to resume on August 13, 1838, the banks of the states concerned had to acknowledge New York's lead.[166] The meeting was semi-national rather than regional and in this respect was unique.

Just as the New York convention of 1838 led to a series of regional conferences (and would probably have led to even more had not unilateral New York resumption interfered), so that in Philadelphia caused another series. They were held in the South, which at that moment still depended on Philadelphia rather than on New York. Considering the key position of Louisiana within the area and in turn the key position of New Orleans within that state it is not surprising that the matter of resumption in the South was not determined by a state or regional convention, but by meetings of the New Orleans board of presidents. One of these took place on June 16, 1838. The presidents felt that in the matter of resumption they should be guided by the condition of the country in general and of the southwestern region in particular and that unnecessary embarrassment by precipitate action should be avoided. The prevailing opinion, as was expressed at that meeting, considered indispensable the cooperation of the Bank of the United States of Pennsylvania, which was still thought of as some sort of a central bank. Its agency in New Orleans should provide a generally acceptable currency until a new national bank was chartered or other remedial steps were taken by Congress to insure the country against the evils of a relapse. A committee was appointed to correspond with Biddle to that effect. If the above conditions were met the banks were willing to resume on the first Monday in January, 1839, that is to say, they ratified de facto the resolution of the New York convention of 1838. (Forstall was against the decision, but could not impose his will on the other bank presidents. He felt that New Orleans should lead in the matter of resumption, not wait for leadership. Located at the main export center for the cotton which provided most of the country's foreign exchange and at the port of entrance of Mexican bullion, to it belonged the obligation to start the ball rolling. In this his thinking approximated that of Gallatin's.)[167] As a matter of fact, the correspondence between the New Orleans committee and Biddle led to the decision of the board of presidents in a meeting of September 18 to resume in January as originally contemplated.

In the meantime, in the late summer of 1838, a conference had been held by the Alabama banks at Mount Blount Springs, but for lack of agreement another meeting had to be scheduled for October 1. By that time the Union Bank of Mississippi was sending out invitations to the banks of Tennessee, Arkansas, and Alabama to join those of Mississippi on the first Monday in December in Vicksburg in order to agree in convention on a date for resumption. At a conference of delegates of the Mississippi banks[168] taking place in Vicksburg on November 5 the above invitation was accepted. In preparation of the December meeting the banks represented at that conference were requested to submit their conditions to a committee of three. This measure was expected to "produce harmony of action" among the Mississippi banks at the regional convention, where a condensed statement was to be submitted. It was also resolved in Vicksburg to "introduce and put into circulation" "U.S. dimes and half dimes" in place of "bits and half bits."[169] In view of all those efforts and attempts at cooperation the very articulate E. J. Forstall spoke of "the solidarity [italics in original] forced upon the banks among themselves by the power given them of receiving deposits and creating currency."[170]

The material presented in the preceding paragraphs reveals a pattern: while the time of national cooperation had obviously not come as yet, that of mere local cooperation had passed. The economic life of the country had become so closely knit and the banks had become to such an extent part and parcel of banking systems that even state lines were no longer dividing. Regional cooperation in a national crisis had become indispensable. As a contemporary bank president expressed it: "those who have the management of this institution [the Bank of Tennessee] are of the opinion that the return to specie payments should be the result of united effort on the part of all the banks of this state and those south of us."[171] Therefore we find joint meetings of the banks of various states or even of various adjoining states and the tendency to establish communications with those in the surrounding ones. While in the first instance it was an emergency that brought the banks together, once they met they were inclined to take up matters of more permanent interest. Such matters were, for instance, note exchange and the settlement of balances, problems which ranked high among matters of common interest then as before, and legislative questions, today typically the subject of trade associations.

Careful study of the events between 1837 and 1841 has led the author to adopt a rather unorthodox point of view: it seems to him that the unilateral action of the New York banks in resuming in line with a New York state law against the will of all other sections of the country was most detrimental. The New Yorkers were, in his opinion, far from being the "saints" that "sound money" authors made them appear. They upset the apple cart, if one may use the expression. They unilaterally discarded a nationally adopted policy, to resume by January 1, 1839. That policy was in keeping with the rhythm of the cotton trade which provided the exchange on which resumption ultimately depended. The New York policy led instead to scattered resumptions at inconvenient dates. Instead of ratifying a reasonable agreement it forced the banks in the various regions to start fresh negotiations on matters which they thought had been settled by the work of their delegates. New York's procedure was, besides being detrimental, dictatorial rather than democratic.

As a matter of fact, after they had been resumed prematurely and piecemeal, specie payments could not be maintained except in a few regions. As early as 1839 another suspension took place in numerous sections of the country and in this connection we meet again the by-now-familiar pattern of cooperation. In Philadelphia, for instance, the banks held a special session on October 9, 1839 to consider the local money market. Suspension was suggested, but not adopted. Nevertheless a great number of banks suspended the following morning,[172] as will be discussed forthwith in detail. Baltimore followed suit; and when the intelligence reached New Orleans the Consolidated Association of Planters, the Citizens, Louisiana State, and Union Banks called a meeting of the bank presidents which decided to take the same action.[173]

The Philadelphia suspension of 1839, as indicated above, was not the result of concerted action; it deviated from the pattern established in 1814 and 1837. The minutes of the board of directors of the Bank of North America give an unusually vivid picture of how it came about: Early in October the Philadelphia Board of Trade sent an invitation to all the banks to appoint committees to meet with one of the Board to discuss the commercial situation. When the committees appeared on the 8th, as requested, they found no committee of the Board of Trade, but were left to themselves. In the ensuing meeting the Schuylkill Bank which, as contemporary sources show, was almost always overexpanded, suggested suspension, a proposal which was voted down nine to five. While the board of the Bank of North America was assembled the next day (the 9th of October) to listen to the report of its delegate (who had voted against suspension) official notice was served by the Bank of the United States of Pennsylvania that it had suspended "temporarily." A few minutes later a delegation of the Farmers and Mechanics Bank called with the information that it had followed suit. Before long the board of the Bank of North America, still in session, received the visit of a committee from the Philadelphia Bank announcing the latter's decision to stop specie payments, and soon news came that the Bank of Pennsylvania as well as the Girard, Mechanics, Western, and Moyamensing Banks had suspended also. Thereafter no choice remained. The difference between the orderly suspensions of 1814 and 1837 and the disorderly Philadelphia event of 1839 is easily explained: in 1814 and 1837 national calamities forced the banking communities to act; in 1839 (although in the last analysis caused by what the author considers the lack of a nationally-established policy) the Philadelphia suspension resulted from a local disturbance emanating from the Bank of the United States of Pennsylvania.

On the other hand, as soon as suspension had become a reality, emergency cooperation was organized again which followed the established pattern: First, there was a meeting of cashiers (probably on October 13) at which the matter of small notes was discussed; namely, whether they should be redeemed and reissued as before, or whether after redemption they were to be replaced by notes of distant banks. The latter course was decided upon.[174] Shortly thereafter the Bank of Pennsylvania invited the other banks of the city and county of Philadelphia to appoint committees to meet jointly. The first meeting of what was to become a new general committee actually took place on October 19. The chairman of the meeting stated as its object the working out of arrangements for the liquidation of balances among the banks and the discussion of their common problems. After the introductory remarks the following resolution was presented and adopted: the banks were to take each other's notes and exchange them daily; they were to keep interest-bearing accounts with each other on which 6 per cent per annum would be charged and

paid at the first of each month; balances exceeding $30,000 were to be made good; deposits were to be taken only with the understanding that specie could not be required by the depositor; a general committee consisting of one delegate from each bank was to be established to promote harmony of action among the banks and to regulate their intercourse.[175]

A general committee actually met on October 23 when most delegates reported that the proposed agreement was acceptable in principle to their banks. It was rephrased in that meeting and a subcommittee appointed to wait on those banks who had not been represented or had disagreed.[176] During the days following there were repeated meetings and negotiations in order to make the plan acceptable to all the banks. It was supplemented, for instance, by the obligation of the banks to report regularly so that their standing could be gauged, and it was resolved that there would be a stated meeting of the general committee on the first Wednesday of each month. By the beginning of November, fourteen banks had given their assent to both preamble and resolutions and more were falling in line.[177] This agreement was probably in effect until resumption in 1841.

As is generally known, specie was paid by the Philadelphia banks only during the short period from January 15 through February 5, 1841 when the downfall of the Bank of the United States of Pennsylvania led to another suspension. Again cooperation along the traditional lines became necessary. By that time there existed a loose organization of Philadelphia banks meeting as the "delegates of the several banks participating in the loan to the Bank of the United States." They met on February 5 for the purpose of devising some plan of action which would govern the future operations of the banks. It was resolved to call a convention of all the Philadelphia banks, and on February 6 a meeting was held in the Philadelphia Bank.[178]

The following resolution was presented and adopted by the convention: the Philadelphia banks were to issue postnotes in various denominations to run for twelve months. They were also to issue certificates of deposit receivable on deposit and for all dues, but not payable in specie like regular banknotes. Interest at the rate of 5 per cent was to be computed on daily inter-bank balances beginning February 9 and was to be paid once a month. Whenever a bank became indebted to any other bank for an amount of more than $20,000 the creditor bank was entitled to demand payment for the excess in bills receivable of the debtor bank guaranteed and endorsed by the latter. No money was to be accepted on deposit and no item to be taken for collection unless an agreement was made with the depositor that payment could not be demanded in specie but had to be received in notes current in Philadelphia. A general committee consisting of one representative of each bank was to be established for the purpose of promoting harmony of action and of recommending such regulations as seemed necessary; and a committee of three was to be appointed to repair to Harrisburg in order to negotiate with the legislature and administration. Banks which were unwilling to comply with the agreement which was unanimously adopted would be required to pay their balances in specie.[179]

This agreement was in effect for approximately one year and when resumption came in sight it was replaced by another adopted on February 10, 1842:[180] The banks resolved to pay out their own paper only, in denominations of $20 and upward. They agreed to exchange notes daily, every bank being under the obligation to return all the notes of all the other banks at the close of the business day. Balances were to be settled once a week or whenever required by a creditor bank. During February such balances were to be liquidated in specie or bills receivable not having more than sixty days to run; in March in specie or in bills receivable having no more than forty-five days to run, in April in specie or in bills receivable having no more than thirty days to run; and finally in May in specie or bills receivable having no more than fifteen days to run. Such bills receivable were to be approved by the creditor and guaranteed by the debtor bank. In case of default by the debtor bank punitive action was contemplated: Every bank was to place securities to the amount of $75,000 with a board of trustees consisting of one member appointed by each bank which was a party to the agreement. If a debtor bank became a defaulter with regard to the settlements agreed upon and described, the trustees were to dispose of such amount of security hypothecated by the defaulting bank, as would cover the deficiency, and to pay the amount in question to the creditor bank. Thereafter the cooperating banks would refuse the notes of the defaulter unless it immediately made good the deficiency in its securities. If they saw fit the trustees were entitled to call for additional security, to consist of specie, United States Treasury notes or other values acceptable to the trustees, who were also to be arbiters to settle and determine all matters of controversy between the banks. They were at the same time empowered to investigate the participating banks. On the other hand, any bank accused of defaulting could demand a hearing before the board of trustees. If a bank refused

compliance with any decision of the board of trustees it was no longer considered a party to the agreement and its notes would be refused by the rest. The trustees were entitled to lodge the securities in some place of safety without becoming liable therefor if in so doing they had acted in good faith. They were entitled to convert all securities deposited into specie. The cost of their trust was to be levied proportionally on the participating banks and in case of default of any of them on their respective portion of deposited securities.

Any party to the agreement was entitled to withdraw from it on July 1, 1842; but it was intended to remain in effect until August 31, 1842, unless abrogated earlier by a majority of the associated banks. It was understood that the plan was considered as a preparatory step toward general resumption of specie payments on or before August 1. The agreement was unanimously adopted and ratified by the Philadelphia banks and represented the last of the long series of cooperative actions necessitated by the crisis of 1837 and the succeeding depression.

V

It is indicative of the early stage of the development that none of the local associations and none of the regional conventions of the 1830's led to the establishment of permanent platforms for interbank cooperation. On the contrary, after all the promising attempts at organizing cooperation, the movement experienced a marked set-back. This set-back is evidenced, for instance, by certain Philadelphia events of 1842 to be described shortly. It is also manifest in the blundering way in which, in 1842 just after having resumed specie payments on May 18 and 19, the New Orleans banks through disagreement among themselves created distrust and a panic which forced most of them to stop specie payments once more. On May 31 the Citizens Bank and the Louisiana State Bank announced suspension until December 15; the Consolidated Association, the Canal, and Commercial Banks succumbed on June 1; while the City Bank gave in on June 2. A few other banks, with hardly any notes outstanding, went on paying specie, a fact which, however, had no practical consequences.[181]

Responsible for this set-back was the spirit which prevailed in the period and which found expression in such events as the following: In the fall of 1839 the Bank of the United States of Pennsylvania, (then no longer guided by Biddle) unsuccessfully tried to maneuver the New York banks into suspension; in this connection a meeting was called in the latter city on October 23, 1839, for the purpose of inciting the public to embarrass its banks through peremptory withdrawals and demands for discounts.[182] In 1841, on the other hand, the New York banks retaliated in kind. When in that year the necessity for a new suspension was discussed in the latter city its leading banks were set to avoid the calamity. So far, so good. But George Newbold, the repeatedly mentioned president of the Bank of America, went personally to Philadelphia exacting there $400,000 in coin, an action which alone enabled the New York banks to uphold specie payments.[183] That is to say, for lack of both a central bank and a truly cooperative spirit a basic question of policy, which was to determine the course of the national economy, became the subject of regional strife. Just as banks competed recklessly with each other, so cooperation of local banks deteriorated into reckless fights between banks in various localities; or, in other words, cooperation of local banks led to warlike alliances against other equally cooperating groups of banks. (We have previously met and will meet again similar alliances directed against individual banks.)

Regardless of this set-back of the movement toward organized cooperation, a set-back caused by the prevailing uncooperative spirit just described, the time was almost ripe for permanent platforms for inter-bank cooperation. As will be described shortly, the period between about 1840 and the outbreak of the Civil War saw the first organizations of that character actually come into existence. Moreover, during this period the same types of cooperation reappeared which had been common in the decades prior to the outbreak of the crisis of 1837. In New York, for example, the law of 1840 relative to the redemption of banknotes led to an alliance of the four then existing Albany banks (the State, City, Mechanics and Farmers, and Canal Banks). An arrangement was entered into under which the Albany City Bank acted as the "corresponding agent" informing each country bank "on each alternate Monday" of the amount of their notes "sealed up the Saturday previous by each of the four banks." It is possible that the sealed packages were exchanged among the four banks each of which under the law must have been the redemption agent of some of the country banks concerned. The set-up may well represent the beginning of what was known in the 1850's as the Albany assorting house, possibly its predecessor.[184]

Common actions against counterfeiters, another example, proceeded as before. These counterfeiters were a real curse and their criminal actions included the raising and altering of genuine banknotes, the issue of spurious ones, and counterfeiting proper.[185] In order to fight these outlaws there was, for instance, a [New England] Association of Banks for the Suppression of Counterfeiting, founded in 1853, which under a law of 1852 received assistance from the Commonwealth of Massachusetts and to which each bank paid an assessment of $5 for each $100,000 capital. There existed also an Eastern Banking Association for the Detection of Counterfeiting,[186] which probably covered New Jersey, Pennsylvania, and Delaware. The New York banks were not active in this field, but were admonished by the superintendent of the state's banking department to follow the example of the New England association.[187] As late as 1860, acting on that suggestion, the Albany banks by circular letter invited all banks of the State of New York to aid and cooperate in establishing The New York State Society for the Detection and Punishment of Counterfeiters and Alterers of Bank Notes. The contribution was to be $10 per annum, assessments while permissible would not exceed $5 for each $100,000 capital. (Incidentally, in 1881 the American Bankers Association assumed functions of this character. It organized a Standing Protective Committee of three in order to inform the members of the association regarding certain crimes usually committed against banks, such as forgery, burglary, and defalcation, and in order to prosecute the offenders.)[188]

The [New England] Association of Banks for the Suppression of Counterfeiting seems to have had considerable importance as a training ground in cooperation for Boston bankers. It came into existence in February, 1853, in a convention of banks at Boston, after the Massachusetts legislature had resolved to participate in the expenses of any organization set up for the purpose of protecting the community against counterfeiting. The convention adopted a formal constitution which established a board of managers and an executive committee. The association not only held meetings of members, but also arranged meetings of non-members as, for instance, in Providence in order to solicit participation there. Moreover heads of different banks working on committees toward common goals must have been drawn together. It seems meaningful that the same men who were leading in the association stood out also as leaders in the Boston Clearing House and in the first loose organization of National Banks to be studied later, such men as Andrew T. Hall, president of the board of managers of the association, Almon D. Hodges, its treasurer and later its president, George W. Thayer and Daniel Denny, presidents, and Charles B. Hall, its secretary for almost the whole time. James G. Carney, the founder of the

Bank of Mutual Redemption and destroyer of the Suffolk Bank System, was for many years the chairman of the association's executive committee whose secretary was again Charles B. Hall.

That there were warlike alliances of some banks against others has already been indicated. Some Chicago and Detroit banks, for example, joined in 1849 to break George Smith and his Wisconsin Marine and Fire Insurance Company;[190] and the Vermont banks formed a pressure group to force the Suffolk Bank to whip the South Royalton Bank into line. In this connection must be mentioned the setting up in Boston of the Bank of Mutual Redemption in the 1850's. It represented a border case, being a warlike alliance of numerous banks against the Suffolk Bank, and at the same time a truly cooperative venture just as the Suffolk Bank System had been when it started. Moreover, as has been described,[191] the movement in favor of that bank gave rise to regional bank conventions not only in New England, but also in the State of New York where certain banks aimed at a similar organization.[192] In this connection the "unity of feeling and action" of the banks of the state was successfully invoked and the result was the establishment of the Albany "assorting house."[193] (Other bank conventions of the period will be mentioned in their proper places.)

Attempts at agreeing on uniform policies were extraordinarily rare in the period under investigation, prior to and in the first years after the establishment of permanent platforms of cooperation. To be sure, in 1852 some of the New York banks drew up an agreement to abolish the practice of paying interest on deposits; it was disregarded.[194] Slightly later (1853-1855) an arrangement was in effect in that city to keep on an average 20 per cent specie reserves on "weekly balances;" it was abandoned.[195] A convention of Indiana banks on January 7, 1855, held for the purpose of "classifying" the bills of the various banks, can be viewed in the present context; little could be achieved. Notes of a few banks were declared "gild edge," while nothing was said as to the rest.[196] Finally in the early 1860's, prior to the founding of the Chicago Clearing House, the few then-existing National Banks of that city consulted repeatedly with a view of securing uniformity in policy. In 1864 all of them closed on Washington's birthday; in the same year, in order to improve the local currency, they resolved to throw out the notes of the Union Plank Road Company of Michigan. A few weeks later, under public pressure, they had to go much further: Originally, after a real battle they patched up an agreement according to

which they would bank at par on legal tenders, National Bank notes, and state bank notes, redeemed in Chicago; while others would be received and paid out at certain discounts. But when this decision did not satisfy the business community it was replaced by another under which the banks agreed to take and pay out the first-named three categories of paper only.[197]

Most important during the early years of the period was the development in America of a type of emergency cooperation the beginnings of which have been traced.[198] Banks were forced to uphold tottering competitors lest the loss of confidence on the part of the public should lead to a general disaster.[199] Cooperation of this character took place in London on a large scale during the crisis of the 1830's, and the knowledge of this fact may have stimulated similar developments in this country. In London, just as in America, such methods were not new at the time. As early as 1798 the Bank of England had lent £80,000 to the endangered firm, Boyd, Benfield and Company, sixteen persons guaranteeing £5,000 each.[200] In 1801 the Bank again made a large loan to a certain enterprise on the guarantee of thirteen other firms. But not before the crisis of the 1830's did similar actions become widespread in England. As early as December, 1836, Timothy Wiggin & Co., one of the Anglo-American merchant bankers, called for aid from its six leading competitors, and the latter gave it without appealing to the Bank of England. An agreement was signed by which each of the firms declared its willingness to accept drafts up to an amount of £30,000 each. Slightly later the banking firm of Sir James Esdaile, Esdaile, Grenfell, Thomas & Co., was supported to an honorable liquidation by the Bank of England, while other bankers put up guarantees. Again when Wildes & Co., another of the Anglo-American merchant bankers, needed help, the Barings and Overend, Gurney & Co. made a joint loan of £50,000 for one week so that its affairs could be investigated. When the investigation proved the firm's solvency, the Bank of England made a loan guaranteed by several other firms. When all attempts to help proved futile, the Bank of England ultimately agreed to give large credits to Wiggins, Wildes, and Wilson & Co. (the third of the large Anglo-American merchant bankers and equally affected by the crisis) so that all of them could liquidate quietly. These facilities again were given over the guarantee of mercantile and banking houses, especially in London and Liverpool. Finally, Morrison, Cryder & Co., F. de Lizardi & Co., and W. and J. Brown & Co., were supported by the Bank of England after having put up security and after having found solvent guarantors among mercantile and banking houses. Professor Ralph W. Hidy, to whom we owe a detailed description of these events,[201] states that "through cooperative effort three key firms were supported long enough for the impact of their failure to be lessened," while "aid given to three other merchant bankers prevented their suspension and permitted an early, orderly return to normal operations." A few years later Gilbart, the general manager of the London and Westminster Bank, a leading London banker, and an influential author on banking matters besides, wrote in an amazing little volume[202] that such actions were demanded by the teachings of the Bible.

It is against this background that one must look at the attempts of the Philadelphia and Boston banks to assist the Bank of the United States of Pennsylvania. On the other hand, to understand their actions one must keep in mind that a Pennsylvania law of 1840 had set January 15, 1841 as the date for resumption under penalty of forfeiture of the charters of non-complying banks. The Bank of the United States of Pennsylvania, as the largest bank in the state, held the key to the situation and, under these circumstances, it was quite natural that private conversations between directors of this and other banks should have taken place as early as 1839. One of them was between Richard D. Wood (1800-1869) and James Martin. The former was a Philadelphia merchant and manufacturer and for many years a director of the Philadelphia Bank. The latter was a director of the Bank of the United States of Pennsylvania. They set the ball rolling. Both men agreed that concerted action was needed and, having also agreed on a modus procedendi they brought the matter before their respective boards which appointed committees to deliberate in joint session. The latter, in turn, were informed at their meeting that the Bank of the United States of Pennsylvania could not resume on the date set by law unless its indebtedness to the other banks was permitted to remain intact. Consequently a joint committee, one of eleven city banks, was brought into existence to consider the matter and the banks thus united agreed to loan $5,000,000 to the Bank of the United States of Pennsylvania by extending its indebtedness for thirteen and a half months taking its post notes as security. The New York and New England banks were invited to lend their aid by sharing one half of the sum required, so that the action of the Philadelphia banks would not lead to local stringency and pressure on their individual debtors to repay loans. The joint Philadelphia banks appointed a committee which, under the leadership of Richard D. Wood, negotiated to that

effect in Boston and New York and the sum of $2,500,000 was actually made available. Individual banks in the North lent to individual banks in Philadelphia at 6 per cent specified amounts payable in installments nine to eighteen months from the date of the loan. Six Philadelphia banks received from 14 Boston banks $945,000; from 7 Massachusetts country banks, $130,000; from Providence banks, $338,000; from Hartford banks, $100,000; from New York banks, $800,000; and from individual capitalists in Boston, $187,000.[203] As to individual banks, it is known for instance that the Suffolk Bank lent $150,000 to "certain banks in Philadelphia... preparatory to a resumption of specie payments" on terms as proposed in a circular, to be divided as follows: Bank of Pennsylvania, $50,000; Philadelphia Bank, $30,000; Farmers and Mechanics Bank, $30,000; Mechanics Bank, $10,000; Bank of North America, $20,000; and Manufacturers and Mechanics Bank, $10,000. The State Bank of Boston, to give another example, lent $150,000 to the Farmers and Mechanics Bank of Philadelphia against its post notes secured by post notes of the Bank of the United States of Pennsylvania as collateral security. Although the latter bank had claimed that the action would enable it to resume, it unexpectedly made new demands on the various Philadelphia banks on the day preceding resumption, demands which were acceded to reluctantly. As is generally known, these attempts at saving the Bank of the United States of Pennsylvania were of no avail. A bankrupt, it suspended in February, 1841; and the other Philadelphia banks were forced to follow suit.[204]

Hardly a year later a similar action by the Philadelphia banks became necessary. At the end of January, 1842, the Bank of Pennsylvania informed the other banks of the city that it would be unable to meet the interest payment on the state debt unless it was aided. Responding to the call, a number of banks united and granted the necessary help upon satisfactory security on the condition that it was applied to that special purpose.[205]

On March 12, 1842, the solvent Philadelphia banks resumed, but soon thereafter the Girard and Pennsylvania Banks had to suspend once more. The latter applied for help, but its available securities were so poor that assistance was refused. At that moment the remaining city banks expected a run and nine of them together with the Bank of Camden (N.J.), which had a redemption agency in Philadelphia, formed a "bank league" for mutual support, each contributing $75,000 to $500,000, according to its capital, into a common fund pledged for the redemption of the notes of the participating banks. In fact, shortly thereafter a run started on the Moyamensing Bank (later called

Bank of Commerce); but the bank was upheld with the help of that fund and so stood the drain. But when the Pennsylvania legislature ordered immediate universal resumption the banks were unable to work out a common plan of action, and three of them succumbed to a run.[206]

A few years after these remarkable, although ultimately unsuccessful, attempts at cooperation, the Pennsylvania banks held a regional convention in the fall of 1845. By accepting the conditions of the so-called Relief Act of May 4, 1841, most of them had bought freedom from penalty and the forfeiture of their charters which had hung over them since their suspension in 1841. Under this act they had subscribed $7\frac{1}{2}$ per cent of their capitals to a 5 per cent state loan. They had paid with an equal amount of notes called "relief notes" which were receivable for all dues to the Commonwealth. The latter paid the banks interest at the rate of 1 per cent on their circulation of "relief notes" which were reissued by the banks and the State Treasurer whenever received. "Relief notes" had to be redeemed by the banks in the underlying loan certificates at the request of the holder, in which case the banks assumed the liability for the punctual payment of the interest on those certificates. In 1845, however, the state stopped paying the 1 per cent interest on the "relief notes." Thereupon the banks which had issued such notes appointed delegates to meet in convention. No definite course of action was established.

It was recommended that each of the banks concerned appoint one or more delegates to "attend" at Harrisburg and to urge upon the legislature the enactment of a measure absolving the banks from all liability in connection with the "relief notes."[207]

After the auspicious beginnings in the 1830's and 1840's one would have expected that cooperation and especially aid to endangered banks in time of emergency[208] would have become standard practice if for no other reason than self-protection. In fact, in 1855 Boston banks, as well as merchants, tried to rescue the tottering Grocers Bank.[209] But the historian meets with disappointment when studying the events of 1857. The geistesgeschichtliche situation, which had already found expression in the early 1840's in the set-back of cooperation previously described, made it impossible for the banks to act rationally. Agreements to expand, concluded by the New York banks in the summer of 1857, came too late and were, moreover, disregarded. No attempt was made collectively to help the Ohio Life Insurance and Trust Company;[210] and when the crisis actually broke, "instead of reciprocal aid and cooperation it became a strife who would endure most and longest," as Governor King of New York remarked in his message of January 6, 1858?[211] The events which took place in the New York Clearing House and which will be described shortly were thus correctly characterized. The New York bankers of the period were, in the words of McCulloch, "high-toned and able men," prone to view broad questions in the light of their interests and never able to reach an agreement in matters of public policy.[212] Consequently, in case of emergency everybody acted for himself without regard to the opinions and actions of others. In 1857 the banks were pulling and hauling in different directions, as Thomas Tileston told McCulloch, then still the president of the Bank of the State of Indiana; and the latter felt compelled to suggest that they had better have met and elected a king with full power to enforce unity of action. Those measures which were actually taken not only in New York, but also in Boston and Philadelphia have been described in another context.[213] (It is idle to speculate in view of the remarkable recuperative forces shown by the American economy in 1857 what course events could have taken if the banks had resorted to cooperative actions at the decisive moment instead of paving measures after the crisis had broken.)

Steps such as would have been needed in New York were actually taken in New Orleans which in 1857, upheld specie payments on notes, as is generally known. Three of the banks (the Bank of Louisiana, the Louisiana State Bank, and the Canal Bank) heeded an appeal from the Citizens Bank for assistance and an equally strong request from an agency of the state government to consider their "devoir envers la communauté," and to show their "égard pour les intérêts et l'honneur de l'Etat" as well as their "esprit éclairé." Through individual loans amounting to $400,000 they enabled the Citizens Bank to uphold the redemption of its notes,[214] while it suspended specie payments from October 15 through November 3 on deposits.

VI

Philadelphia can be proud of having set up the first permanent platform for inter-bank cooperation. The student would like to know exactly why it was Philadelphia that blazed the trail. His first reaction after having asked this question is to look for Quaker influence; for both in the English iron industry and the American spermaceti production Quakers were instrumental in getting competitors together as early as the eighteenth century. However the list of bank presidents connected with the achievement contains no typ-ical Quaker names, and Quakers are not sup-posed to have played a decisive role in Philadel-phia banking. Therefore one must rather look for a hidden line leading from the intensive emergency cooperation of the late 1830's and early 1840's to the organization under investi-gation, even though there was an interval of sev-eral years between the two. Such connection is all the more probable since Philadelphia had had a board of presidents during the emergency and since its permanent organization was also one of the bank presidents. Through the medium of these officers the personal element must have been important although one cannot put a finger on any one man as the influence carrier. Pro-ceedings of the new organization were intended to "promote stability and regularity in the business of banking." In other words, instead of joining after a collapse the gentlemen decided to practice preventive medicine.[215]

The Philadelphia Board of Presidents was or-ganized in 1853. On September 28 of that year the following agreement was drawn up: "The un-dersigned being of the opinion that periodical meetings [italics mine] of the Presidents of the several banks of the City and County of Philadel-phia for purposes of conference and interchange of views on such topics pertaining to the banking interests of this locality as will be considered proper subjects of discussion and action will pro-mote stability and regularity in the business of banking, do hereby agree to meet on Wednesday, 28th current, at the Philadelphia Bank at one o'clock and thenceforward at such time and place as may be decided on." The fact that this first meeting took place in the Philadelphia Bank and that its president, Thomas Robins, was a strong personality and later instrumental in establishing the Philadelphia Clearing House, make it per-missible to assign much of the achievement to his endeavors. To be sure, he did not become the first chairman of the new organization. That position was tendered to the senior among the Philadelphia bank presidents, J. B. Mitchell of the Mechanics Bank. The latter resigned when the crisis of 1857 broke and he would have been required to assume leadership.[216]

The very first resolution of the board indicates that it meant business: On motion of C. S. Boker,[217] president of the Girard Bank, it was resolved that the banks should turn in weekly information on their discounts and their indebtedness to New York. At the second meeting a committee was appointed to provide for a suitable place for the meetings of the Board of Cashiers and for the Exchanges. That is to say, there must have

been an organization of the cashiers as well as one of the presidents. Nothing is known, however, about that board, and it is possible that the name covered the informal organization supervising the banks' tri- and later bi-weekly meetings for set-tling interbank balances.[218] At that second meeting the presidents also discussed the figures relating to discounts and indebtedness to New York sub-mitted in compliance with the earlier resolution. A week later the question of foreign notes was on the agenda, and the scope of the weekly reports was broadened. However the reports were still unsatisfactory for the purpose or coordinating the activities of the local banking system; and be-ginning in November, 1853, the reports pertained to "immediate" means and liabilities, i.e., to current assets and liabilities, as one would say today (loans and discounts, gold and silver in the vaults, circulation and deposits, net balances due to other banks). These reports and the state of the domestic exchanges were from then on the main topics of discussion of the Board meetings: it provided indispensable information for decisions and for coordination based on the mere fact that all of the presidents possessed identical informa-tion even if they drew different conclusions there-from. In October, 1853, an arbitration committee was set up to settle such differences between the banks as might arise (motion of Singleton A. Mercer). In 1855 another committee was appointed to obtain information on the working of the New York Clearing House, and after some difficulties which have been described, the Board took action and adopted the new type of institution. It ab-sorbed the Board's functions in the period between August, 1857, and March, 1859. The Board was then revived, but from that time on its work and that of the Clearing House overlapped and it is difficult to separate the actions of the respective bodies. For this reason the cooperative achieve-ments of the Philadelphia banks in 1857 and at the beginning of the Civil War are not treated here but in other chapters.[219] Later the Philadelphia Board of Presidents began to decline; its functions were taken over by the Clearing House committee; and it was disbanded in 1882.

It goes without saying that this first attempt at permanent organization of banks could not have had a systematized program. Problems were tackled and tasks taken up as they came along. Two of these were organizational in character: the adoption of modern clearing practices and the participation, together with the New York and Boston banks, in the flotation of the early war loans of 1861, although that participation was more than an organizational achievement. In addition, the Board aimed at standardizing banking practices:

it proposed the holding of a 25 per cent specie reserve against liabilities and suggested rules for the deposit business. Finally, like a modern trade association, it discussed tax and legislative questions.

The only city which, to a certain extent, copied the Philadelphia inter-bank organization was Baltimore. It possessed a board of cashiers which developed out of irregular meetings of the latter during the emergency of 1857. Under the chairmanship if Robert Mickle, cashier of the Union Bank, it met regularly from 1858 until 1864 and occasionally thereafter. Confining its activities on the whole to the daily exchanges and the settlement of balances, it acted as the government of the Baltimore Clearing House, established in 1858. That is to say, in Baltimore this institution was left to the care of the cashiers, which may have been due to the fact that the latter had recommended its establishment in that year when suggesting the resumption of specie payments. At any rate, in contrast to New York, Boston, and Philadelphia, the banking leaders of Baltimore do not seem to have recognized at that early date the great importance of clearing houses as platforms of inter-bank cooperation. It is possible that this lack of understanding was due to the fact that the Baltimore Clearing House was not set up under the influence of George D. Lyman, as were the other three.

In addition to the then already existing board of cashiers a board of presidents came into existence in 1860 when its first action was to vote a suspension of specie payments. Not until 1864 did the Baltimore Board of Presidents begin to meet frequently, and it did not meet regularly before the early 1870's. By 1875 it had its first permanent chairman (H.A. Thompson) who in 1880 was succeeded by Enoch Pratt, president of the National Farmers and Planters Bank. The secretary of the Board was for many years W. W. Taylor, president of the National Union Bank. In 1885 the Board of Presidents adopted a new constitution which, in fact, put an end to the board of cashiers and under which it began to function as the government of the Clearing House. Prior to that time the Board of Presidents had discussed subjects of common interest (other than the exchanges and the settlement of balances), such as tax questions and matters of legislation; but as long as the board of cashiers existed there was no clear cut division of functions: in 1861 the board of cashiers resolved to suspend, while the year before, as mentioned above, this action had been taken by the presidents. In 1862 the cashiers took up questions of taxation; on the other hand in 1873 the Presidents passed on

the adoption of the clearing house loan certificate. This action of theirs is understandable because of the importance of the measure, but strictly such business should have fallen to the cashiers. One would like to know whether or not the committee which represented the Baltimore banks at the convention of the National Banks of 1869 originated in the Board of Presidents, whose secretary, W. W. Taylor, appeared among the delegates to that convention.[220]

Boards of Presidents and cashiers according to the Philadelphia-Baltimore pattern had no time to spread, for the clearing houses after their establishment in the 1850's almost immediately became media of united action among the banks, as Cannon expressed it, although they were conceived as labor saving devices only.[221] The trend in this direction was strong indeed. Banks at that time were accustomed to reduce their loans whenever the exchanges were against their city. Hooper made it clear that no special arrangements to that effect were necessary, but that united operations resulted from the same influence acting simultaneously on all the banks.[222] Under the impact of the new institution (the clearing house) such automatic concert of action tended to become conscious cooperation. To use the words of a bank officer, clearing houses came to develop "into a great conservative force mutualizing the interests of [their] members and harmoniously subordinating them to the general good."[223] In fact, however, the subordination of the individual bank to the general good was not always achieved "harmoniously." To the contrary, the importance of the clearing houses with respect to inter-bank cooperation lay in the fact that they were the earliest permanent organizations able to force banks to cooperate. The Massachusetts Bank of Boston may have been the first to undergo an experience of this character: When on October 14, 1857 the Boston banks decided to suspend specie payments, the directors of the Massachusetts Bank resolved to continue to pay specie on its bills. But it took the directors only one day to reverse their stand and to put on record the following motivation: "it was suggested as highly important that this bank should conform to the rule adopted by other banks and hold our right to claim daily settlements with the other banks at the Clearing House, which right would no doubt be denied if we did not follow the rule adopted by the other banks--in view of this fact [and some others] voted--to suspend..."[224]

It is a remarkable fact that George D. Lyman, the founder of the New York Clearing House, recognized that clearing houses would develop from labor saving devices to platforms for inter-bank cooperation, when this institution had hardly come into existence.[225] "In the bank association of the New York clearing house," so he wrote, "there is a common bond of union. All have an equal voice in its management. All share alike in its privileges and benefits. In an important sense the interest of each is thus made the interest of all. Nor is it a slight advantage that it brings together and makes acquainted the officers of the several banks and thus leads to harmony both of feeling and action. While each institution still seeks for itself the highest profit consistent with security, all are brought to feel that they have a common interest in maintaining the credit of the banking system. All must be aware that the prosperity of the city of New York is largely dependent on the credit of its banks. Through the facilities which they afford or withhold they give tone to its business which they not only represent, but to a great extent sustain and control. How important that their management should be right and safe!" So it came about that the history of inter-bank cooperation in Civil War time and thereafter are but chapters in the history of the clearing houses.[226]

It is understandable that the very first attempt of the New York banks to use the clearing house as a platform for cooperation in time of crisis was not too successful. On October 13, 1857, the day on which suspension actually took place in New York, a night meeting of the banks was called. Twenty members were unable to appear since they had closed their doors; the remaining twenty-nine had struggled through the day although some had been subjected to runs. In spite of the feeling of the majority that it was necessary to suspend, a minority of ten banks, led by James Gallatin, president of the National Bank (later the Gallatin National Bank), voted against that proposal. Shortly thereafter two of them joined the majority; but the remaining eight organized separately for mutual aid and in an endeavor to "keep faith with the public." In consequence instead of becoming a platform for cooperation, the clearing house became a battle-field in civil strife. The exchanges were immediately so deranged that the minority had to give up the battle; and general suspension had to be announced on the morning following (the 14th of October). There was some feeling at that time that suspension could have been avoided had the banks "combined" instantly.[227] But they learned their lesson, although the generation of bankers then in power was less trained to cooperate than any preceding one.[228]

VII

After the Civil War this country came to possess two platforms for inter-bank cooperation: the clearing houses gained more and more importance in this respect as they matured; and in addition organizations of trade-association character made their appearance. Since in the banking field the latter were historically the younger, there was some overlapping of functions. When trade associations of bankers came into existence, clearing house committees had in many cases already taken on jobs usually performed by trade associations, and they were loath to restrict their activities.[229]

Trade associations in the field of banking could be formed on a state, on a regional, and on a national level; and by 1860 the development turned in all three directions. On August 5, 1851, a convention of 45 Wisconsin banks took place in Milwaukee; it discussed plans for establishing a bankers' association and a central redemption system. But it needed the panic of 1857 to make the plan come to life. On September 8, 1858, another convention of 45 banks adopted the constitution of the Association of the Banks of Wisconsin; or, to use the words of a contemporary report, the banks "united in [a] system of regulating their currency." The new organization, which held special meetings on July 20 and August 11, 1859 and which for a number of years was to hold annual conventions, elected nine directors. Alexander Mitchell, the outstanding Wisconsin banker, became its president, shaping its policy to a large extent. The original intention was to force the state's wildcat banks out of existence by providing for the redemption of the members' notes in Madison or Milwaukee. The notes were to be redeemed at their face value minus the current selling price for exchange [on New York?] (to be set by the directors of the Association), so that the legitimate banks were enabled to "convert" all Wisconsin banknotes into exchange without loss. Or, to put it differently, the Wisconsin Bankers' Association established for its members a uniform policy in matters pertaining to the redemption of their notes, an attempt well in line with other contemporaneous actions,[230] but distinguished by using the form of an association. It proved impossible to establish a Mutual Redemption Bank modeled on that of Boston, as had been planned originally; but the agitation and publicity given to the matter resulted in a constructive amendment to the Wisconsin banking law of 1852.

When the political situation became critical in 1861 the Association had to go further and to protect the interests of the Wisconsin banking system endangered because its note issues were based largely on the securities of Southern states. In April of that year, the Chicago banks, realizing the difficulties which threatened, threw out the notes of 40 of the 109 Wisconsin banks. Those in Milwaukee, with the approval of the executive committee of the State Bankers' Association,[231] followed suit, but refused the notes of only 19 of the 40 institutions. The confusion which followed in the wake of these actions led to a state-wide suspension of specie payments and forced the Association to call a special convention to meet at Milwaukee on April 26. It was attended by representatives of all the banks and the private bankers of Milwaukee and by representatives of 45 country banks. The convention discredited the notes of a number of additional banks, but at the same time took positive action also: each member of the Association agreed to take at par the notes of the 70 odd banks remaining in good standing until the date of resumption of specie payments set by the legislature. In a statement issued at the same time to the people of the state the Association vouched for those 70 banks. Although the panic subsided for the moment new trouble lay ahead. With the value of Southern securities falling continuously the Comptroller issued a depreciation levy in line with the law, but 18 of the guaranteed banks refused to respond. The guarantors were thereby forced to exchange dollar for dollar U.S. lawful money for about $355,000 of discredited bills. Moreover banks in the interior of the state, becoming panicky, violated the agreement by sorting out such notes as they received, paying out the poorest and hoarding what they deemed the best. The Milwaukee banks were hard hit by such procedure: their customers now deposited mainly poor bank paper and demanded credits at par, thereby forcing the former to break their pledge in order not to succumb later: on June 22 they met and agreed to refuse the notes of another set of banks, previously guaranteed, unless they were tendered on special deposit. The announcement of this action led to a riot, but in the meantime successful negotiations had gotten under way between a committee of Milwaukee bankers and state officials. During the meetings on June 21 and 25 a suggestion of Alexander Mitchell was discussed and adopted, according to which the banks received permission to buy a pending state loan on easy terms and to deposit the bonds with the Comptroller in exchange for the depreciated Southern securities. A bankers' committee was organized to put the plan into effect. At the same time, the banks assumed the obligation jointly to maintain all then-current Wisconsin bank paper until the date of state-wide resumption. Supplementing this arrangement and aided by Milwaukee merchants, the banks collected a $100,000 fund with which they gradually redeemed the notes of the banks originally guaranteed but later dropped. These actions put Wisconsin banking on a sound basis.

When the Association held its third annual meeting on September 19, 1861, it could adopt (although in vain) a resolution recommending that the banks voluntarily resume prior to the date set by the legislature. At the same time its activities were given a new turn: it was decided to discountenance for the time being the organization of new banks, while the existing ones were to increase their circulation only by special consent of the Association's board of directors. When the date set for resumption, December 1, 1851, approached a special convention of the Association had to be called. There on November 15 a committee was appointed by the Milwaukee and about 50 country banks represented with powers to wind up any bank unable to resume. The circulation of such banks was to be paid by the committee dollar for dollar and any deficiency was to be made good out of the funds of the Association or by assessments levied on the capital of the solvent banks of the state. Notes of delinquent institutions were actually sorted out by the banks receiving them and sent to the committee of the Association at Milwaukee where they were exchanged against interest-bearing certificates of deposit; $400,000, or more than one-sixth of the Wisconsin circulation, was thus funded. In addition when resumption brought runs on some of the banks the members of the Association agreed not to demand payment from each other until the crisis subsided.

The preceding shows that up to 1861 the Wisconsin Bankers' Association in most respects remained within the best established tradition; in others it went even further: for the winding up of failing banks by an organization of the solvent ones there was no precedent. In the following year (1862) the Association worked against undue expansion; and in 1863 it passed a resolution which can be interpreted as an attempt at what one would call a Kartell today. The resolution reads as follows:[232]

> Whereas, all classes of citizens of Wisconsin, and especially its responsible bankers have suffered severely in the past from the issue of bank notes by irresponsible parties, and whereas, the suspension

of specie payments, and the stimulus given to all forms of business and trade by the immense expenditures of the national government, and the large amounts of legal tender notes it has been necessary to issue, furnish at the present time an inducement to those engaged in banking, to issue a larger circulation than their actual capital would justify, while an opportunity is also offered to parties of little or no responsibility or capital to organize banks with scarcely any other object in view than to set afloat a currency, which, however well it may keep up for a time, may, on the decline of the value of its security, or the resumption of specie payments, eventually become depreciated, thereby causing a recurrence of all those troubles and losses which the business interest of our state so recently experienced; and whereas, the present time is unusually favorable for the issue of bank notes by persons of doubtful responsibility, we believe such a currency must now be discouraged in every legitimate way, and that it behooves every responsible banker in the state to cooperate with and strengthen the wholesome restraints imposed by law to check the evil, and ward off its deplorable results; we therefore feel impelled by our duty to the business community and citizens generally, as well as our regard for the character and safety of the banking institutions of our state, to adopt the following resolutions: –

Resolved, That we, the members of the Bankers' Association of Wisconsin, will not receive the notes of any banking institution which may be hereafter established in this state unless said bank shall first have been sanctioned by a majority of the directors of the Association.

Resolved, That no banking institution now in existence in this state shall add to its circulation without having received the written consent of a majority of the directors of this Association, and in case any bank shall do without such consent, we agree not to pay its notes out, but to proceed to wind it up by protest.

Resolved, That when a majority of the directors of this Association decide to sustain the establishment of a new bank, or an increase in the circulation of an old one, they shall publish a notice to that effect over their own signatures for two weeks in

two of the daily papers of Milwaukee, and a new bank or the new circulation of an old one shall not be considered to have received the approval of a majority of the directors of the Association until such notice has been given.

Resolved, That the directors of this Association be instructed, and are hereby instructed to carefully and impartially scrutinize the character and condition of the existing banks of this state, and if any of them are found in their judgment to be in a condition so unstable and unreliable as to render their continuance incompatible with the public good, and as likely in time of financial trouble to bring loss on the community and injury to the more stable banks of the state, they shall proceed to wind up all such banks without delay, inasmuch as they can now do so without loss to the public; and their attention is more especially called to those banks which have no office, and are not engaged in the transaction of a regular local business, but are exclusively banks of circulation.

Resolved, That whenever the directors of this Association shall deem it advisable to wind up any bank, as contemplated in the foregoing resolutions, they shall notify the several banks of this Association, and upon the receipt of such notice we hereby severally agree to assent and to send to our correspondents in Milwaukee the circulation of such bank.

With this attempt at a cartellization of Wisconsin banking, the Association seems to have attained the pinnacle of its power. When in 1865 the first two Milwaukee banks secured national charters the Association seems to have broken up. Those banks determined independently their policy toward Wisconsin currency and forced the remaining banks of the city which were still working under the state law into a reorientation of theirs. The latter acting in common released several public statements; such steps were taken outside the Association which could do nothing except put blame on the national institutions.[233]

In the year following the breakdown of the Bankers' Association of Wisconsin a temporary regional bankers association was brought into being namely, the National Bankers' Association for the West. This organization developed out of a convention of National Banks of Ohio, Indiana, Michigan, Illinois, Iowa, Missouri, Kansas, Wisconsin,

Minnesota, and the Northwestern Territories. It was called by the Chicago Clearing House to meet on September 12, 1866, for the purpose of consulting on such measures "as may be deemed proper for the protection of their interests." In fact, the convention was intended to exert pressure against the enactment of central redemption for all National Bank notes in New York.[234] Edmund Aiken, president of the First National Bank of Chicago, who had attended the first convention of National Banks in 1864, is credited with having been the driving force in 1866.

It was about two years prior to the convention, just mentioned, that the movement toward trade associations in the field of banking was taken up on the national level. The incentive came from Thomas Coleman of Troy, New York, then president of its First National Bank, among whose founders he had been.[235] In September, 1864, he addressed a circular letter to numerous National Banks all over the country. In view of the concerted and persistent hostility to the National Banking system manifested in Congress during the previous session and elsewhere, he sounded out the banks as to whether or not they considered it "expedient for the friends of the system to meet by delegates at some central point." If so, they should assemble for "consultation" and for the purpose of taking such action as might be deemed advisable to maintain and perfect the National Banking law. The recipients of the circular were asked to join the writer in an invitation to such a meeting to all National Banks.[236]

The response to this letter was so favorable that on October 4 invitations were sent out asking delegates of the friends of the National Banking system to meet in New York on October 19. They were to assemble for the purpose of consulting and, if considered feasible, of taking action to maintain the system, to perfect the underlying legislation, to consider financial aid to the government, and to ensure to the country the uniform currency contemplated in the law. The convention was to be strictly a business meeting on the National Banking system and on the management of National Banks; "show or parade" and, if possible, even "all publicity" were to be avoided.[237]

When the meeting assembled, delegates from banks of 16 states were present representing $35,000,000 of banking capital. It was, in fact, a conference of little known people and only the names of Bunce of Hartford and Thompson of the First National Bank of New York[238] stand out as being widely known in the banking field. Most of the men were obscure bankers, presidents or cashiers, hailing from small places.[239] The object of the meeting was formulated in a speech of Coleman: "I was fully convinced," so he stated, "... that hostile attempts would be made at the last session of Congress by those opposed to the National Banking system to procure such changes in the law as would weaken and cripple the system, destroy its power for usefulness, efficiency, and profit, render it undesirable to organize new banks under it, and thus virtually destroy the whole system in its infancy. I thought then that there was urgent need of a co-operation of National Banks by means of a convention to protect the system and their interests from such hostile movements." (Thus Coleman let the cat out of the bag: the convention was meant to become a platform for the representation of business interests, the nucleus of a trade association, as the historian would be inclined to view it.) Coleman went on to describe the lobbying activities of the enemies of the system while no countermove had been organized by its friends. Under such pressure the original act was amended, and the speaker expected new hostile amendments to be introduced in the next session of Congress. He urged the delegates to consult together on the management of their type of enterprise and on desirable amendments to the Act. He also urged that they provide for organized opposition to further unfavorable legislation if such should be attempted.[240]

Coleman was undoubtedly one who knew the value of cooperation, "united action," "associated effort," and "associated interest," all of which words he used in the convention.[241] But he did not win an easy victory. There were actually two problems with which the delegates were faced: one was whether or not they should organize themselves into a pressure group; the other the problem of taxes and interest rates. As to taxes all of them felt that nationally chartered as they were, they should be taxed only by Congress, except for their real estate. Thereby taxes on National Banks would be uniform all over the country. The fact that Sec. 41 of the National Currency Act gave the states the power to tax National Banks was obnoxious to them: they met with hostility on the part of local assessors, with discrimination as they claimed; and they were afraid that the states by their taxing power would be able to cripple the system at will.[242] In this respect there was unanimity. But the delegates were divided as to whether or not they should fight for the establishment of a uniform interest rate. Some could not see why "money" should be worth more in one part of the country than in another; (we should not forget that these men were accustomed to legal interest rates). Others objected thereto; but some of these opponents would have been satisfied if a higher interest rate were to be established for the West than for the East.[243]

Much more difficult to solve was the organizational problem. There was one party in the convention which considered it wise to keep quiet and take no action whatever. These men wished to avoid arousing opposition and were afraid of being dragged into the political arena. The majority could not see it that way, but permitted the minority to gain a victory in that the convention desisted from formulating resolutions. On the other hand, the majority felt strongly that some sort of permanent organization was needed to look after the interests of the National Banks, a "permanent organization under the watchful eye" of a committee, a representative body to whom power of action was given in all matters pertaining to the advancement and perfection of the National Banking system, as it was expressed. Thus a General Committee of twenty-five was set up, the nucleus of which consisted of one delegate from each state represented. The committee was entitled to appoint further members. This General Committee in turn appointed an executive committee of seven. This latter committee was charged with looking after matters of banking legislation (especially as to whether or not the National Currency Act was uniform in operation in the various states) and with taking such actions as were considered expedient. It was also endowed with the right to call another convention of National Banks if it deemed proper. E. B. Judson, president of the First National Bank of Syracuse,[244] became the president and Coleman the vice-president of the General Committee, whose secretary-treasurer was J. U. Orvis, president of the Ninth National Bank of New York. Orvis, with Coleman, seems to have been one of the guiding spirits of the convention. These three men were also ex officio members of the executive committee of the organization which was known as the National Banking Association.[245]

The executive committee of the National Banking Association functioned like the organ of a trade association. In conjunction with the General Committee, which was the policy making body, it secured court decisions on doubtful provisions of the Act. It contested several clauses regarding taxation and certain claims under the U.S. revenue laws in respect to which there were differences of opinion. A large amount of information concerning banking laws and court decisions was printed and furnished to the banks, and there was extensive correspondence on questions affecting the interests of the National Banks. Between 1864 and 1869 J. U. Orvis[246] was the guiding spirit of

the General Committee. He also did the actual work of the executive committee; by steering clear of sectional influence and avoiding any "false and unwise move," he greatly benefited the members of the system. Loose as was the organization it was not only called, but thought of as an association, a word which was used repeatedly when the organization held its second meeting in 1869.[247] Its contact man in Congress seems to have been Theodore M. Pomeroy (1824-1905), representative from New York and a director of the First National Bank of Auburn.

On May 20, 1869, the executive committee held a meeting and resolved to call another convention. The number of National Banks had so increased after 1864 that the General Committee elected in that year could no longer be considered representative. Consequently the new convention, which met in New York on June 23, 1869, was meant to elect a representation which would embrace all of the then-existing National Banks. Or, as a speaker expressed it, the "association [was to be made] as comprehensive as the system itself." When the delegates assembled the situation was very different from what it had been in 1864 in that the National Banking system was no longer fighting for its existence in a hostile world; it had become a well established fact. The situation, however, was similar in other respects: Again the convention was a business meeting of men having a common interest; again it was not the cream of the profession who were present. Present were those who had been leaders in the convention of 1864 and had carried the load ever since, such men as E. B. Judson, Thomas Coleman, Charles B. Hall, cashier of the Boston National Bank, and F. W. Cronenbold, president of the First National Bank of St. Louis. Two new names stand out among the participants, those of Elbridge Gerry Spaulding, president of the Farmers and Mechanics Bank of Buffalo, and George Fisher Baker, representing the First National Bank of New York, who was to leave the convention as the secretary-treasurer of the newly appointed general committee or "the Committee of Seventy-five," as it was to be styled. The convention, like that of 1864, had to face a major problem, this time what was called "free banking"[248] in the period. As to its procedure, as in 1864, the assembly abstained from passing resolutions although several were presented. It wound up by forming a new association through electing the above-mentioned Committee of Seventy-five. The latter, in turn, appointed E. B. Judson, president, Coleman, Hall, and P. C. Calhoun (president of the Fourth National Bank of New York) vice-presidents, and an executive committee, of which

William F. Coolbaugh,[249] president of the Union National Bank of Chicago, and Henry D. Cooke, president of the First National Bank of Washington and Jay Cooke's brother, are the ones best known to the historian. Charles B. Hall seems to have done much of the actual work of the organization, the costs of which were assessed among the participating banks.[250] Its goal was to protect the common interests and to aid in perfecting the system, or, to use the phraseology of the convention, the Committee of Seventy-five was to "watch over and protect the interests of the National Banks; give timely notice of any proposed legislation adverse to their interests either by Congress or under State authority, with suggestions as to the best mode of averting such action and to secure such proper amendments to the National Currency Act as will be alike beneficial to the National Banks and to the business of the community."[251]

The organization was active as late as the spring of 1876 when it presented the need for the reduction of bank taxes to the first session of the 44th Congress and its executive committee attended a hearing of the Ways and Means Committee on this subject.[252]

After these first attempts at organizing a body able to represent the interests of the National Banks, the American Bankers Association (A.B.A.) came into existence in 1876.[253] From the historical point of view the question is important of whether or not there was any connection between the conventions of 1864 and 1869, and the executive bodies set up by these conventions, on the one hand, and the A.B.A., on the other. If such a connection should be discovered, its exact character would be of great interest. The author has been authoritatively assured that no unprinted primary material covering the founding of the Association is extant, so that the above problems cannot be solved conclusively by the use of documents. Nevertheless enough contemporary material has survived in printed form to permit at least glimpses on the subject.

This much is certain: the A.B.A. is not the successor of the conventions of National Banks in 1864 and 1869 and of their executive organization, described in the preceding paragraphs. It is equally certain that it was not the outcome of hostility to the earlier bodies. While the latter were led largely by New York country banks, the new one originated in the Mississippi Valley.[254] After preparatory steps an obviously self-appointed committee of seventeen dominated by James T. Howenstein of St. Louis held a meeting in New York at which it was decided to call a convention of bankers to meet at Saratoga. The role which George S. Coe played at this time will be discussed

in detail.[255] The promoters of the meeting considered it wise to be cautious in the beginning, so the invitation stressed the social functions of the gathering.

The convention took place on the 20th, 21st, and 22nd of July, 1875. When one studies its records it is obvious that there was a line leading from the old organization to the new one about to be founded. Of the men who had played a leading role in the old body, Charles B. Hall, Joseph U. Orvis, and George Fisher Baker attended the Saratoga convention. In fact, its permanent organization indicates that the representatives of the old and the new movement were going to cooperate: it seems like a conscious program of broadening the old body when one sees Charles B. Hall[256] become the president, James T. Howenstein,[257] the secretary, and George F. Baker, one of the vice-presidents of the convention. In addition, several references to the older organization can be found in the records of the convention. They indicate criticism, but no hostility. Hall himself referred to the "National Executive Committee which [the National Banks] now [had],"[258] and speaking on the question of a permanent bankers' association felt that more than a "convention of National Bankers" should be set up which could go with their grievances only to Congress. A broader organization was needed (a "general organization" as this speaker expressed it) which would include the banking interests all over the country.[259] That the young organization's "leading object" was to be the fight against oppressive taxation was conceded only later.[260] In 1876 when the bankers met again in Philadelphia (a meeting which is considered the first one of the American Bankers Association) they were informed of the actions of the executive committee of the earlier body[261] which was still functioning, but which seems to have gone out of existence in the fall of the year. At that time the first Executive Committee of the A.B.A. recognized the "valuable services" of the executive committee of National Banks in "promoting the banking interests of the country."[262]

Going back to the Saratoga convention, we find the continuity with the earlier ones becoming evident also from the subjects discussed: once more, as in the convention of 1869, tax questions and the problem of a uniform legal interest rate (or, vice versa, of "free trade in money," as it was styled this time) were on the agenda. To sum up, the subjects discussed, the references made, and the persons in the lead strongly indicate the continuity between the conventions of 1864 and 1869, on the one hand, and that of 1875 which paved the way for the establishment of the A.B.A., on the other. As to personalities: George F. Baker, the secretary of the old body, became the treasurer of the executive council set up by the convention of 1875 "to receive advice and suggestions of bankers who may desire to unite in a permanent Bankers' Association;"[263] and in 1876 we discover Charles B. Hall as the first president of the American Bankers Association, Thomas Coleman on its first executive committee, and George F. Baker as its first treasurer.

According to the tentative program of the Saratoga Convention a "National Bankers Convention" was to be established. It was to appoint a vice-president from each state (as the convention of 1869 had appointed National Bank officers of each state to form the "Committee of Seventy-five").[264] These vice-presidents were to promote the formation of state organizations, and the national organization would thereafter consist of delegates from the former. The state organizations would handle local grievances while general questions would be brought before the convention by their delegates. Here they would be discussed, and subsequently suggestions or complaints brought before Congress by an executive council. If this plan was to be put into operation, the "National Bankers' Convention" would be organized in Saratoga on a temporary basis only and vice-presidents would be nominated who would call state conventions. The latter, in turn, would appoint delegates to set up the permanent body, whose executive council would stand in the same relation to the banking interests as the Finance Committee of Congress stood to the members of Congress. Close cooperation between the two would naturally develop. The bankers' executive council would act as a source of information for the Finance Committee and at the same time as a channel by which an association of bankers could bring grievances before Congress, instead of individual bankers communicating with individual congressmen.[265]

This original plan was not put into effect. The Saratoga convention determined only that a permanent organization could be made conducive to the interests of the banking system. Upon adjourning, it appointed an executive committee which was charged among other things with the duty of "drafting forms for a permanent organization." This the committee did and then called the adjourned convention to meet again at Philadelphia to "complete the organization of the American Bankers Association" (which name incidentally already appeared in the minutes of the Saratoga convention). This object was achieved by adopting a constitution which established a "general" organization.

Twenty-five years later, Lyman J. Gage[266] in a reminiscent mood remarked with respect to its beginnings which he had had an opportunity to observe:

"Let me name some of [the] men [who inaugurated the Association]. . . In the front rank I would place Mr. George S. Coe of New York. . . A close second to him were such men as Mr. Hall of Boston. . . . I name a few others without regard to precedence who were wise in council and prominent in influence: Mr. Buell and Mr. Vermilye of New York; Mr. Patterson and Mr. Comegys of Philadelphia; Mr. Tyler of Boston; Mr. Simonds of South Carolina; Mr. H. H. Camp and Mr. Van Slyke of Wisconsin. . .; but my list grows, and I cannot name them all."

There was a distinct difference between the American Bankers Association and the earlier one: While the organization established by the conventions of 1864 and 1869 consisted of National Banks only, the A.B.A. was to comprise National and state banks, trust companies and savings banks, and private bankers "upon a majority vote." One clause of the constitution, which remained within the framework of those of typical trade associations, provided for one vice-president from each state. Each vice-president could become the president of a state organization simply by calling a meeting of the bankers of his state for the purpose of organizing.[267] In fact, however, it took quite a few years before State Bankers Associations were brought into existence.[268]

The American Bankers Association did not have smooth sailing all the way through. In the 1890's it was widely felt that its work could be done better by delegates of state associations and something like the original organizational plan of 1875 was broached again. Not only during the San Francisco convention of 1892 was a radical reform proposal presented, but the latter's preamble also contained stinging criticism of the manner in which the business of the Association had been handled. In the following years the membership dropped by about one fourth; but ultimately the crisis was overcome in 1895. In that year the rule was adopted that the state bankers associations send to the yearly conventions of the American Bankers Association one delegate for each fifty members. In the 1900's new trouble was brewing: the rank and file was becoming restive under what they considered an unequal representation. A spirit of resentment was abroad, as it was expressed in retrospect. Organizational changes adopted in Atlantic City in 1907 restored peace. From then on the state organizations elected representatives to the Association's organs.[269]

VIII

It has been stressed that clearing houses as well as trade associations became platforms for permanent inter-bank cooperation after the 1850's. Both types of organization provided the prerequisites for continuous working hand in hand, namely, personal acquaintance among banking leaders, the clearing houses locally, the annual meetings of state bankers associations and of the A.B.A. on a state and national basis, respectively. How successful they were in this respect can be gauged by contrast: when the crisis of 1907 necessitated the cooperation of the New York trust companies, which were then not members of the clearing house, and when their administrators were called together by J. P. Morgan, they had to be introduced to each other.[270]

Cooperation of banks in the clearing houses developed originally, in the late 1850's, 1860's, and 1870's, in two directions: they dealt on a cooperative basis both with day-to-day problems and with such as resulted from emergencies. As to their actions in emergencies, reference to chapter XVII of this volume must suffice here. Cooperation on problems coming up in normal times, in turn, covered two different fields: public policy affecting banks (a field which is today the domain of the A.B.A. and of state bankers associations) and business policy. As to the latter, there was from the outset a trend toward the establishment of uniform policies in matters affecting the stability of the individual member banks and consequently that of the group as a whole and ultimately the interest of the community at large. In the end the development tended to turn toward enforcing uniformity of operations and toward introducing supervision of the members of the group by the latter in return for the indispensable services which the organization provided for its members.

With regard to cooperation in matters of public policy, examples like the following may be cited: In 1861 in a meeting of the Boston Clearing House Association, George W. Thayer, president of the Exchange Bank, moved "that the Clearing House Committee be requested to represent the Associated Banks before the legislature in reference to the law now pending regarding the specie clause." The committee was to be guided by a resolution passed at the same meeting that "a reserve of 20 per cent on deposits and circulation is as large a sum as is thought requisite for a specie basis for the Boston banks."[271]

In 1864 a committee of the same Clearing House presented to Congress a petition relating to the then pending amendment to the National Currency Act. Turning to New York we find its Clearing House Association discussing tax matters in June 1863,[273] while in the fall of the same year it disseminated a report in order to influence public opinion against the above Act which it considered detrimental to the interests of the New York banks.[274] The Chicago Clearing House (founded in 1865) assumed similar responsibilities. As early as 1866 it organized opposition to a contemplated amendment of the National Currency Act establishing note redemption at a central point (New York) and at the same time attempted to influence remedially the state's taxation of banks.[275] The Philadelphia Clearing House Association was worrying over the same kind of problems: It brought two state-tax-law cases before the courts; and as late as 1877, after having discussed grievances regarding taxation, had the Clearing House Committee submit a report, and thereupon made efforts to influence federal legislation.[276] To the extent that national matters were involved, cooperation of banks through the medium of their clearing houses was bound to lead to cooperation among the latter, as will be discussed shortly.[277]

Of much greater and permanent importance was the trend toward the establishment of uniform policies for member banks.[278] It goes without saying that originally it was exceedingly difficult to achieve success in this area because of the prevailing philosophy of rugged individualism. It was impossible even to attempt coercion of dissenting banks, and a single member of a clearing house could block the will of the rest and make indispensable reforms impossible by way of common consent. Nevertheless the trend toward uniform policies started as early as the 1850's. As a committee of the New York Clearing House reporting[279] in 1858 phrased it, banks recognized that they were mutually dependent, that they had a common interest, and could not be isolated. Weakness of one reflected on the others.[280] It followed that they could not concede to each other perfect freedom to carry out practices that were generally acknowledged to be inherently unsound and pernicious. The body as such possessed moral and financial responsibility because of the position it occupied in the national economy.

This remarkable, new spirit, of which George S. Coe became the exponent in the 1870's and 1880's, deviated widely from that prevailing between the War of 1812 and the crisis of 1857; but it was to gain ground slowly in the decades to follow. Establishment of uniform policies was tried in matters which were most urgent. In the late 1850's the question of specie reserves was one of these and for lack of adequate legislative requirements in the State of New York a uniform policy was sought by common action of New York City banks. The above-mentioned committee of the New York Clearing House recommended that the banks "keep at all times an amount of coin equivalent to no less than 20 per cent of [their] net deposits of any kind which shall be made to include certified checks and all other liabilities, excluding circulating notes, deducting the daily exchanges sent to the Clearing House." In the same year the Philadelphia Board of Presidents debated similar ratios and the banks seem to have taken action. In New York the suggestions were ratified only by 42 out of 46 banks, nevertheless they were observed.[281]

Equally important for the New York banks was a second question, that of paying interest on demand deposits; and the committee of 1858 of the New York Clearing House recommended that this practice, generally considered "pernicious," be abandoned. In fact, again 42 out of the 46 New York City banks signed an agreement to the effect that in the future none of them would allow interest on demand deposits, provided that all banks in the association (i.e., the New York Clearing House) concurred. In a meeting of this body of March 5, 1858 a committee was appointed, consisting of James Punnett of the Bank of America, James Gallatin of the National Bank, and William F. Havemeyer of the Bank of North America, to wait on the remaining four banks and to urge them to join the rest. As the result of their endeavours three more banks consented; yet the one remaining outside frustrated the will of the group and made vital reform impossible.[282] The consequence was that the same subject had to be taken up again by the associated banks in 1873, and again without success: a tiny minority blocked the road to the establishment of sound uniform policy; and the situation was no different in the 1880's.

The following statement by an author writing in the late 1870's gives a good idea of the conditions at that time:

"The New York banks are only nominally united through the Clearing House for the purpose of making their daily exchanges and settlements and enforcing sufficient discipline in matters affecting credit and solvency to protect themselves in their dealing with each other. Apart from this, there is practically no unity among them, except on special occasions when they combine for self-protection and mutual assistance, as they did at the time of the crisis of 1873, or to expel a member of their association for cause, as in the case of the Bank of the State of New York in March 1876, or in appointing a committee to advocate or remonstrate against some particular measure pending in Congress or State legislature affecting banking interests, but the latter of course very rarely. It seems nevertheless perfectly possible for them to agree upon and observe such a unity of action as would virtually make the Clearing House a power."

This interesting statement hardly needs comment;[283] the author was aware of the influence which the clearing houses were very slowly gaining over their members and which, as he saw, could easily be used to acquire power over the money market.

From such beginnings was to develop a system through which as a matter of course the clearing houses coordinated their members and regulated the conduct of those who, directly and indirectly, enjoyed their privileges;[284] for every abuse practiced by any clearing house bank and every failure would not only endanger every other clearing house bank through the losses entailed, but would also create general distrust which might easily lead to consequences more serious than direct losses. Such a situation was bound ultimately to lead to supervision. The very beginnings of this development toward supervision can be traced as far back as the 1860's. In that decade (in 1864), for instance, the Boston Clearing House Association established a rule that National Banks joining the Clearing House must make weekly returns showing their capital and average figures for loans, specie, legal tender notes, deposits, bank balances, and circulation, figures which the state banks were obliged to furnish under a Massachusetts law.[285]

As to coordination, the Chicago Clearing House Committee under the leadership of Lyman J. Gage, then cashier of the First National Bank of Chicago, is known to have done successful work between 1887 and 1893 in prescribing standards of operation and by enforcing adherence thereto. It devised reporting forms to be used by all the member banks four times a year. These forms made for comparable and correct statements and forced better accounting methods on less advanced banks, methods which permitted the Clearing House officials to gain a true picture of the position of the member banks. Moreover, no state bank was admitted to the Chicago Clearing House which was not willing voluntarily to adopt the regulations regarding liquidity embodied in the National Bank Act.[286] Parallel with the trend toward uniform accounting methods and reporting procedures on the part of the member banks went the development of uniform charges for services rendered. The former as well as clearing non-member banks were obligated to make certain charges to their customers. Some details as to the beginnings of this policy have been given previously.[287] By 1910 it had become common for clearing houses to fix uniform rates of interest on deposits and, less often, also on loans, as well as uniform exchange and collection charges.[288] That is to say, clearing houses acted as <u>Kartells</u>, and they could do so since they could punish violators by expulsion, i.e., by the withdrawing of indispensable privileges. But there were occasionally bitter fights, for instance, in Salt Lake City and Pittsburgh.

It may well be that the development turned from attempts at establishing uniform policies by voluntary consent to enforcing unity of operations and introducing supervision of member and clearing non-member banks at the time when the clearing houses as such undertook to save endangered banks in times of emergency. Such action must at least have given momentum to the trend if it already existed. Earlier[289] it has been described how banks had become accustomed to banding together occasionally in order to stave off from an individual bank disaster which might easily engulf all. It was a relatively easy step for clearing houses to act in cases of this description once they had developed into permanent platforms of inter-bank cooperation. When using the New York Clearing House mechanism for saving the depositors of the failing Metropolitan Bank in 1884, George S. Coe initiated what was soon to become standard practice. In 1891 it was adopted in Boston when the Maverick Bank broke down in a bankruptcy which entailed considerable danger and caused much excitement because of the importance of this bank. On November 2, 1891 the Boston Associated Banks decided to relieve the depositors of the Maverick Bank by advancing funds to such depositors as would assign their claims to the Associated Banks combining for that purpose. A committee was appointed to put the agreement into effect, an agreement which led to no loss for the Boston banks.[290]

The policy which Coe had originated was developed to its final consequences in Chicago under the influence of James B. Forgan who, after 1900, played in its Clearing House a role comparable to the one played by Coe between 1870 and 1890 in that of New York. As Forgan explained in words reminding one of those of George D. Lyman (written in 1857),[291] while the clearing houses were, in the first instance, voluntary associations for the convenience of their members this fact had far reaching consequences. In the process of the daily exchanges they had to trust each other for large sums and each member therefore became interested in the integrity and solvency of all the others, for every failure reflected on all of them (a common experience, as we know).[292]

Forgan's decisive action took place in December, 1905, when three Chicago banks, all controlled by John R. Walsh, met ignominious failure. These banks were the Chicago National Bank, the Home Savings Bank, and the Equitable Trust Company. It was clear from the outset that they could not be saved and that considerable loss would have to be sustained by someone. In the nineteenth century it would have been almost a matter of course to let the depositors lose. Forgan thought otherwise. The indirect loss which would result from a breakdown of confidence in general and fall on the clearing house banks as a group would be so heavy, as he could foresee, that it would be wiser for the banks to assume the actual loss of the Walsh banks. So much confidence on the part of the business community would thereby be gained that in the long run the solvent Chicago banks would get off cheaper than by letting things run their course. He won the day against much opposition from bankers who could not see as far ahead as he did.[293]

These events of 1905, in turn, brought a local Chicago development to a conclusion, the result of which was soon to be adopted nationally as standard practice. As early as 1876 Lyman J. Gage had suggested the appointment of a regular clearing house examiner. His suggestion had been turned down at that time, but the Chicago Clearing House Committee had received the right, through a committee of its members, to examine any bank which made use of the facilities of the Clearing House. This resolution of 1876, however, remained a dead letter. In 1901 Byron L. Smith,[294] president of the Northern Trust Company, once more suggested the appointment of a clearing house examiner, but this proposal was tabled although the Clearing House Committee unanimously backed it. After the experience of December, 1905, Smith repeated his suggestion in January, 1906, this time with success.

To understand the significance of this achievement the following should be kept in mind: At that time dissatisfaction with the National Bank examiners and their methods was rather widespread.[295] They and state bank examiners could at best examine only proper accounting and compliance with the law, and examinations of that kind were not sufficient to prevent disaster. The average clearing house, in the 1890's, on the other hand, was still primarily concerned with the ascertainment and settlement of the daily balances. It could not go much further and therefore did not provide such protection to the local banking system as would have been possible if it had assumed a broader responsibility. It was still an exception for clearing houses to have clauses inserted in their constitutions like that of Boston, whose Clearing House Committee was supposed promptly to investigate infractions of the law by any member bank (section 18). But even in Boston that clause remained a dead letter as did the Chicago resolution of 1876, previously mentioned. Any attempt by the Boston Clearing House Committee to investigate a member bank would have been opposed on the ground that the investigators were competitors of the bank to be investigated. This situation was well explained by bankers to a Senate committee of 1893.[296]

How unsatisfactory the situation was had been experienced repeatedly in various cities besides Chicago and Boston: it is possible for a bank to be on the road to failure when its business policy is faulty even though its bookkeeping methods are adequate and although it complies with the law. Moreover, as a contemporary Comptroller of the Currency expressed it, "bank examinations [were then] illogical and unscientific and simply impossible under the present National Banking law." It was this gap which was filled by the action of the Chicago Clearing House when establishing the office of clearing house examiner (Bureau of Examination) working with a staff of about twelve men. Forgan and Hammill, who at that time closely cooperated,[297] were charged with selecting a man qualified for the job and in 1904 they appointed James B. McDougal (born in 1866), then a National Bank examiner whom they met accidentally in the Park Bank of New York.[298] (He was destined to play a leading part in the Federal Reserve System.) Other clearing houses followed suit;[299] New York where the former National Bank examiner Hanna and a staff of twelve men were appointed in 1911 came first and by 1913 twenty clearing houses had adopted the device. Thereby they established de facto supervision of the business policy of their members; for the clearing house examiner, in contrast to the corresponding national and state officials, would examine the result of business policy as it found expression in the documents and books of a bank.[300] In so doing and in drawing attention to shortcomings at an early moment he would protect the local system. Only when Federal Reserve Bank examinations were established did the clearing house examiner become superfluous.

Almost immediately after having become platforms for local cooperation of banks, the clearing houses started to perform the same function on an inter-local basis also. This development was early foreshadowed: just as the Bank of North America had helped to set up the Massachusetts Bank and the Bank of New York, so George D. Lyman, the founder of the New York Clearing House, helped to organize those of Boston and Philadelphia.[301] Inter-local cooperation of banks with the help of their clearing houses tended to take the form of parallel action. The latter could be brought about by joint committees which recommended policies to the clearing houses concerned.[302] This method was used, for instance, in connection with the loan transactions of 1861 when the joint committee of the New York, Boston, and Philadelphia banks was called the "General Committee." The same method was contemplated in the 1870's when the banks cooperated in an attempt to influence the mode of resumption.[303] At a later stage concerted action seems to have been in many cases the result of leadership on the part of the New York Clearing House, resembling what is generally known in economics as price leadership. The New York Clearing House disseminated information about its actions, intending to provide an incentive for similar action by other clearing houses.[304]

The subject matters for inter-local cooperation were the same as those for local cooperation, namely, public and business policies. Inter-local cooperation in the former field was the earlier kind. It began in 1857, and the first move toward using clearing houses as platforms for inter-local cooperation represented a straight development of an earlier (although unsuccessful) attempt at cooperation, that of 1837/1838. Just as in 1837 and 1838 banks had tried to resume specie payments by concerted action,[305] so in 1857 Boston intended to time its resumption to coincide with that in New York. In November, 1857, Andrew T. Hall, chairman of the Boston Clearing House Committee and a recognized leader among the Boston banks, wrote a letter to A. E. Silliman who filled the corresponding position in the New York Clearing House. Hall was then under the impression that the New York Clearing House banks would resume on January 1, 1858, and he informed Silliman that Boston was willing and able to resume on that date, provided that the banks of the various cities including New York acted in concert. Detailed information on the conditions of the Boston banks was added. The attempt is of interest, even though the plan did not work because of the resistance of some of the Boston banks.[306] In those years Hall and George S. Coe of New York were becoming exponents of inter-city cooperation of banks, through the medium of clearing houses; and they were aided in Philadelphia by Singleton A. Mercer and Joseph Patterson.

In 1861, as will be remembered, the New York, Boston, and Philadelphia banks became close allies in connection with the loan transactions of that year. They even possessed in their General Committee (consisting of committees of the three clearing houses) an emergency organization. Quite naturally the latter became a platform for inter-local cooperation when the need arose. Immediately after suspension in December, 1861, the General Committee met on January 2, 1862 and resolved that a committee be sent to Washington to impress upon Congress and the government the desirability of a certain financial policy.[307] In the years to follow cooperation of the three clearing houses on subjects of public policy became a matter of course, although their emergency organization of 1861 was dissolved. The development can be studied from the Boston Clearing House records: On May 28, 1862 a communication was received from the New York Clearing House relating to the National Currency Act. On June 6 communications from the same organization, actually emanating from George S. Coe, were discussed. Coe wished a committee of delegates of the three cities to be sent to Washington to get from the Commissioner of Internal Revenue "a beneficial construction" of the terms "circulation" and "deposits" as used in the Excise Tax Law.[308] In 1866 and 1868 similar committees negotiated in Washington regarding tax returns and a pending tax bill.[309] In 1869 cooperation took place with respect to the increase and redistribution of the National Bank circulation.[310] In the 1870's the Baltimore Clearing House was included when another common action was taken: in 1878 the four clearing houses struggled in common for influence over the way in which the resumption of specie payments was to be achieved and, although they were not successful, as a group they cooperated wholeheartedly with the Secretary of the Treasury.[311] By that time they also fought the pending Bland Silver Bill in common. But public policy was becoming a matter of the A.B.A., and the clearing houses withdrew from this field soon thereafter.

Parallel with actions of clearing houses as described above went attempts at establishing uniform policies both for various clearing houses and for their individual member banks: On March 19, 1862 John Amory Davis, president of the Suffolk Bank, suggested that the Boston Clearing House follow the example of that of New York as to the use of legal tender notes in the settlement of balances. He was instructed to work out a suitable plan. In 1864 the New York Clearing House proposed to the Boston banks the adoption of a new method of making returns. The latter took up the

suggestion and the Boston Clearing House sent out a circular letter to that effect.[312] In 1865 the Boston banks were invited to confer with a New York committee regarding the redemption of National Bank notes.[313] The preceding chapter has treated in detail the fight of clearing houses for parallel action establishing uniform policy regarding collection charges. It was a failure.

Since an entire chapter (Chapter XVII) has been devoted to describing the role which clearing houses played as platforms for emergency cooperation during the major crises, a reference thereto suffices here.

The development discussed in the preceding section was scrutinized in 1912 by the Pujo Committee in connection with the "money trust" investigation. Since the committee members were imbued with the spirit of competition and laissez-faire they were very critical of those actions which have been described here as beneficial, as indeed they were. But the Pujo Committee correctly pointed to the power exerted by the clearing houses "for good or evil" and exerted through the medium of the latter by the large banks which controlled them. It showed that in several cases this power had been abused as, for instance, in 1907 when the majority of New York banks, no longer needing clearing house loan certificates ruthlessly called those that were outstanding without due regard for weaker, though solvent, banks which were thereby broken. The Committee especially objected to Kartell-like actions of clearing houses which seemed unnecessary in view of the actually tremendous earning capacity of large banks in the period; and it objected to clearing houses acting as private clubs, without being incorporated and under public control. The Committee found it obnoxious that in New York and other places only large banks could become members of clearing houses, while perfectly solvent, but small, banks could become only "non-members." That is to say, the latter were "for an annual fee permitted to enjoy the facilities of the associations through the agency of a full member, but. . .had no part in their management." On the other hand, they were "equally with full members subject to the supervision and discipline of the association" concerned.[314]

But not only was the relationship between clearing houses and non-members banks moot, but also that between the latter and their clearing correspondents. It was not doubted that these correspondents must be secured, but their power over the non-member banks was such that it could easily be abused to the detriment of all other creditors of such banks. Under these circumstances the New York legislature passed the so-called Saxe bill which was to protect bank creditors, but which made the clearing for non-member banks a rather risky business.[315]

IX

While clearing houses and bankers associations represented the most important platforms for inter-bank cooperation they did not possess a monopoly in this respect. Banks remained free, of course, to join whenever and in whatever way they saw fit and, at least occasionally, they seem to have made use of that possibility. There existed in the 1910's, for example, an Association of Reserve City Bankers in Indiana, established in 1912. It grew out of informal dinner meetings held during the conventions of the Indiana Bankers Association, meetings in which the representatives of reserve city banks participated.[316] Another, somewhat older, loose organization was the Boston Bank Presidents Association about which very little is known. It seems to have held dinner meetings, listened to speeches, and occasionally discussed matters of policy.

Moreover there were cases in which banks cooperated without making use of any established platforms and with good reasons to do so. Trust companies, for example, were not members of the New York Clearing House in the 1900's and they had no organization of their own, save the trust company section of the American Bankers Association which does not seem to have been established before 1906. Thus during the panic of 1907 when they were endangered they had to construct an emergency framework reminiscent of that built in the 1830's. It was called the Committee of Associated Trust Company Presidents and was headed by Edward King, a leader in the field and the chief executive of the Union Trust Company. Through this temporary organization the $10,000,000 reached the trust companies which the Secretary of the Treasury made available for their assistance by depositing that amount in certain National Banks.[317] In other cases established platforms for cooperation were not used because it did not appear wise to do so. The New York banks seem to have discussed informally and agreed informally on the stand which they would take before the Pujo Committee.[318]

Most important, however was the historical accident that the most powerful financier of the late nineteenth century, J. P. Morgan, was a private banker and consequently not a member of the New York Clearing House. Consequently when Morgan took the lead in cooperative actions among American banks the latter could not be used as a platform. When in 1895, for instance, Morgan and August Belmont, Jr., the representative of the

Rothschild interests, saved the country's gold standard by a sale of gold to the Treasury and solemnly and successfully promised to protect it from withdrawals of gold (which could be done only by enlisting the cooperation of the banking community as a whole), the necessary arrangements were made wholly outside the existing bankers' organizations.[319]

Because of Morgan's decisive role in settling the crisis of 1907 the New York Clearing House (which under Coe's and Tappen's leadership had been so conspicuous in dealing with the crises of 1873, 1884, and 1893) was pushed into the background. If his biographer can be trusted,[320] Morgan, the outsider, decided in 1907 whether and when clearing house loan certificates were to be issued. As a result of such distribution of power, emergency cooperation of banks was brought about in 1907 on a loose, temporary basis: On October 22, Morgan organized a group of banks which were willing to submit statements to him. On the basis of these, the banks permitted him to allocate to each one that sum of money which he felt was appropriate to make up the total considered necessary by him to carry the weaker ones through the panic. On October 23, together with the First National Bank of New York and the National City Bank, which in fact represented groups of allied banks, Morgan decided on the help to be given to the Trust Company of America. On the same day he forced the various New York trust companies to create the emergency organization for mutual aid which has been mentioned. On October 24 he brought together a number of banks to aid the stock exchange by allocating to each one a certain amount to be lent at the loan desk; and on the day following another loan to the stock exchange was forced upon the leading New York banks. A few days later, on November 2, the New York trust companies were once more compelled to cooperate in backing the weaker ones by raising a fund of $25,000,000.[321]

X

Economic development is, of course, so complicated that every systematic presentation of change over a long period of time tends to become oversimplified. Nevertheless, the following abstract seems permissible and useful, for this chapter deals with a badly neglected area of research.[322]

During the first years of American banking a spirit of cooperation prevailed among the few existing banks until the growth of country banking acted as a blight. Before that spirit was killed, however, banks assisted each other in the solution of problems, appointed committees to meet with committees of other banks, established uniform policies, and, in common, represented their interests before legislatures. Quantitative measurements of cooperative actions as compared with competitive ones are, of course, impossible. Cooperation gradually ceased in the 1800's, but toward the end of the War of 1812, when specie payments were suspended and especially when they had to be restored again, cooperation was revived on a new level. For the first time emergency cooperation was developed which was to play an important part thereafter in all crises to come. For the purpose of dealing with the emergency caused by that war the first bankers' conventions took place in the years 1815-1817. After the return of normalcy, however, cooperation was at a low ebb: there were a few war-like alliances and some concerted action before legislatures. Important attempts at establishing uniform policies were remarkably absent except in New Orleans. The Suffolk Bank system which was originally both an alliance and a truly cooperative venture was the most important achievement in our field during the period.

The crisis of 1837 forced upon the banks of the country emergency cooperation of a magnitude unheard of prior to that time. Banks cooperated locally in temporary organizations, and inter-locally in conventions. During that crisis the first national bank convention was called, but it was unsuccessful. Moreover it was in those years and especially in the depression following the crisis that the backing by competitors of failing, although solvent, banks became rather common, after sporadic cases of that sort had occurred earlier. Thus an important forward step was taken. After the end of the emergency, cooperation again became rare; to the extent that it existed it followed the pattern of the preceding period. There were few if any attempts to develop uniform policies. Interesting events were the actions of New England and New York banks by which the redemption of country notes was organized on a cooperative basis (Bank of Mutual Redemption and Albany "assorting house"); but they had no future. It marked real progress, however, when in the 1850's the first permanent platforms for inter-bank cooperation came into existence. The very first was the Philadelphia Board of Presidents. It found one successor only, because it was soon overshadowed by the earliest clearing houses, which quickly developed into platforms for cooperation although not devised as such, and by the somewhat younger bankers associations.

From that moment on, cooperation among American banks took on a new aspect: officials came to know each other personally since they met regularly. Cooperation, not only in emergencies,

but on everyday problems, became a matter of course. Everyday problems demanded occasionally the establishment of uniform policies, occasionally representation of common interests. At the same time problems often proved of so broad a character that local cooperation alone was not sufficient for their solution. Thus as early as Civil War times the clearing houses developed from platforms for local into those for inter-local cooperation. Between the clearing houses and organizations of trade-association character (the bankers associations) a division of functions was worked out although originally there had been some overlapping: the former retained certain functions; others went to the bankers associations and were developed there.

Whether or not the meeting of bank officials in clearing houses and at conventions of bankers association produced an esprit de corps, as was hoped,[323] is not clear and, in fact, the reaction of different men must have differed. This much is certain: the majority of leading bankers woke up to an understanding of their mutual dependence, although the necessary conclusions were not always drawn from that experience. Moreover the banking fraternity moved very slowly from the concept of mutual dependence to that of mutual responsibility. However, at the beginning of the twentieth century, the latter concept had been adopted to the extent that supervision of individual banks by their organizations (clearing houses) through clearing house examiners could be established.

In the three decades beginning in 1860 there was no one to compare with George S. Coe as an exponent of interbank cooperation. As a matter of fact, he was an actor on both platforms on which such cooperation took place. His activities are described in detail in his biography appended to this volume. It portrays him as prominent among the backers of the American Bankers Association (if he was not de facto among its founders) and for years as the dominating personality in the New York Clearing House. Coe's importance lies not only in his leading the banking fraternity on the road of cooperation when it was needed, especially during emergencies, but by continuously and efficiently preaching a cooperative attitude and behavior. In so doing he was instrumental in developing the existing feeling from one of mutual interdependence toward one of mutual responsibility. It is easily recognized that the former attitude was one of enlightened self-interest from which could be derived proper behavior toward the community; while the latter starts from the relationship of the individual to the community. After Coe's death James B. Forgan of Chicago took the lead in the field under investigation.

When one considers the spirit of rugged individualism prevailing in the nineteenth century, when one remembers that competition was looked upon as some sort of divine ordination, when one keeps in mind the ethical level of many business leaders in the era of the "Robber Barons," one can see that the above record of cooperation among American bankers was an impressive achievement. To be sure, what had been done was not enough by far in view of the key position of banking within the national economy and in view of the stage which American economic development had reached by 1910. Thus it was natural for the leading bankers of the period to stress what was lacking, while the historian with the record before him can be less critical. Interesting as the following statement of 1913 is, the implied value judgment appears too harsh to the historian, and the picture itself overdrawn and too gloomy. In the latter year the Currency Commission of the A.B.A. in answer to a question formulated by a subcommittee of the Senate Banking and Currency Committee as to the essential defects of the American banking system stated:[324]

> The system lacks cohesiveness there being no provision for cooperation among the banks in it. Under ordinary conditions this is not so much felt by the banks individually, but under strained financial conditions, when each bank is thrown on its own resources and must in self protection act independently of all the rest, the lack of a system under which all could co-operate through a common policy of action becomes keenly felt and it becomes evident that what is really lacking is a system.

APPENDIX*

Evening of December 10, 1816

The following Resolutions of the President and Directors of the Bank of the United States were produced and read, viz

"At a Meeting of the President & Directors of the "Bank of the United States held on Monday the 9th "of December 1816, the following Resolutions were "adopted

"Resolved   That John Sergeant Esquire be directed to "increase the contemplated Loan to an Extent not "exceeding $1,195,000 and to ship the Proceeds there-"of to the United States in Specie according to the "Terms of his Instructions, and that He be requested "to receive from the Banks of this City and Northern "Liberties the several Sums of 6 P Cent Funded "Debt of the United States with their respective "Powers to Transfer & Pledge the same as a Securi-"ty for the Loan—it being understood that the Banks "respectively are to participate in the Loan in the "proportion of Funded Debt furnished by Each.

"Resolved   That the Specie to be imported from Eu-"rope under the Agency of the Bank shall on its ar-"rival in the United States be divided with those "Banks who have united in the Loan in the proportion "which the Public Debt furnished by each may bear to "such Importation so as to place the Bank of the "United States and the State Banks on an equality on "the whole operation.

"Resolved   That all charges arising on the negotiation "of the Loan or shipment of the Specie shall be paid "pro rata by this Bank and the Institutions who have "taken an Interest in the same.

"Resolved   That the several Banks before mentioned "be required to enter into a specific engagement "with this Bank to make good upon demand any "deficiency that may happen (if any should happen) "from the Pledge of Funded Debt furnished by them "respectively not being sufficient to pay and satisfy "their respective Proportion of the Loan to be con-"tracted and charged when the same shall become "due and payable--

"Resolved   That a Copy of the Resolution certified by "the Cashier be communicated to each of the "Banks agreeing as aforesaid prior to the Receipt "from them of the Stock to be by them respectively "furnished, for a participation by them in the "importation of Specie ordered by this Bank—and "that the said Banks be requested to signify "their assent to the said Resolutions by a vote of "their respective Boards certified under the Corpo-"rate Seal of each of the said Banks.

"Extract from the Minutes

Jon^a Smith Cash"

---

*Bank of North America, <u>Minutes of the Board of Directors</u>

The author wishes to express his appreciation to the Historical Society of Pennsylvania for permission to reprint this item.

1. See page 21. The author cannot always agree with the interpretation presented in the pertinent paper of Schwartz.
2. "Branches," 68, 69.
3. See this work, vol. I, 34 and the sources there cited.
4. Wettereau, "Branches," 74.
5. Domett, op. cit., 42. The Second Bank of the United States seems to have aimed at similar cooperation, see Gras, op. cit., 426, 427.
6. Gras, op. cit., 366, 396, 397, 406; also 414. Dennis, op. cit., 15. Incidentally, as late as the 1820's the Hartford Bank tendered the Second Bank of the United States the use of its vaults when the latter's Middletown, Connecticut, branch was transferred to Hartford (Woodward, op. cit., 129); and in 1840 the Bank of New York lent one of its vaults to the Leather Manufacturers Bank (Minutes of the Board of Directors, Mar. 3, 1840).
7. Gras, op. cit., 408, 416; Bryan, op. cit., 21.
8. Holdsworth-Dewey, op. cit., 40, 41.
9. The Philadelphia National Bank, 38, 39.
10. The term "cooperation" as used in this chapter means cooperation toward common ends and excludes business relations between banks. To be sure, the border-line was fluid, especially in the early years, and both genuine cooperation and business relations between banks resulted to a large extent in the beginning from the note business. The development of the latter kind of relationship toward correspondentships has been traced in volume I of this work, pages 16, 51, 52.

   But it may be useful at this point to add the reasons why the note business led to both the establishment of business relations and genuine cooperation: First, all banks in good standing were interested in the soundness of banknote currency which led to the common fight on counterfeiters and to arrangements regarding the exchange of notes and their presentation for redemption. Secondly, banks in the trade centers had a common interest in protecting their area of circulation against the encroachment of near-by country banks. Thirdly, all banks knew that their notes would come into the hands of other banks and could be used for staging runs unless friendly relations were established and notes exchanged regularly. Fourthly, all banks were interested in widening their circulation, which could be achieved by enforcing note redemption in trade centers. This aim led to the establishment of correspondent relationships or if the banks in question were less sound to rackets, if you please: banks agreed to float each other's notes

far away from the places of redemption.
11. Holdsworth-Dewey, op. cit., 41; Philadelphia National Bank, 43.
12. Gras, op. cit., 360, 381.
13. Journal of the House of Commons, Vol. LI (1795, 1796), 337.
14. Holdsworth-Dewey, op. cit., 52; Gras, op. cit., 73, 372, 385, 386; Woolsey, op. cit., 11, 12.
15. Bank of North America, Minutes of the Board of Directors, Mar. 21, 1816.
16. Uniform values for foreign coin were established by a joint committee of the Philadelphia banks; (Philadelphia National Bank, 40). Cooperation of the Boston banks regarding weights took place in 1794 and 1803; regarding stamp duties in 1794; regarding taxes in 1813 and 1814; and regarding import of change in 1806. In the latter case the cost was assessed in the same ratio as was the cost of detecting and punishing counterfeiters. Gras, op. cit., 73, 367, 373, 383, 386, 387, 388, 389, 411, 416.
17. Holdsworth-Dewey, op. cit., 41. The Baltimore banks in 1801 even acquired a lot and were planning to erect a building out of town to which all of them could move in case of yellow fever epidemics (Smith, J. Thomas, op. cit., 623). As late as 1822 committees of New York banks conferred on the removal to Greenwich for the duration of epidemics; see Bank of New York, Minutes of the Board of Directors, June 22, 1822.
18. Philadelphia National Bank, 52, 53; Holdsworth-Dewey, op. cit., 83.
19. Cabot had been a "trusted follower and adviser" of Hamilton and one of the early directors of both the Massachusetts Bank and the First Bank of the United States. In 1803 he became the President of the Boston branch of the latter.
20. Holdsworth-Dewey, op. cit., 41.
21. See vol. I of this work, page 67.
22. Gras, op. cit., 73, 91, 373, 380, 383, 412. In 1797 the Massachusetts Bank made its policy regarding British gold coin dependent on the policy of the two other then existing Boston banks, without common deliberations having taken place.
23. No accomodation paper to be discounted after the last day of 1796; the proceeds for discounts to be paid to the last endorser only; no checks drawn on other banks of the city to be received on deposit; the circulation of notes under five dollars to be discouraged. See, Smith, J. Thomas, op. cit., 622, 623.
24. Holdsworth, op. cit., I, 202. Bank of North America, Minutes of the Board of Directors, May 9, 1816.
25. See page 251.

26. Bank of New York, Minutes of the Board of Directors, June 5, 1817.

27. Gras, op. cit., 425, 431.

28. Holdsworth-Dewey, op. cit., 41, 42.

29. Stokes, op. cit., 276.

30. Philadelphia National Bank, 30, 33.

31. McMaster, Girard, II, 245, 246.

32. For the legal background, see this volume, page 81.

33. See vol. I of this work, page 10.

34. For an example, see a letter of Andrew Dexter to William Colwell, dated May 21, 1808. "The Providence banks should, in my opinion, be plagued as much as possible by detaining them as long as it will naturally take to count out all kinds of specie change intermixed in the most deliberate manner. . ." [i.e., in case they presented notes for redemption]. See Farmers Exchange Bank, 30; and also Baldwin, op. cit., 46: "If instead of running upon their neighbours for gold and silver for the purpose of endangering their credit with the public, in the hope of increasing a monopoly that they are not entitled to, they would mutually aid and support each other, there would be little danger of failures." (1809)

35. Niles Register, VI (1814), 226; Heck, op. cit., 57, 58.

36. Holdsworth, op. cit., I, 202; Hardenbrook, op. cit., 102; Nevins, op. cit., 41, 42. According to the Minutes of the Board of Directors of the Bank of New York (Aug. 29, 1914) the latter's president and cashier were appointed on behalf of the Bank and empowered to pledge its cooperation in such measures as might be adopted.

37. Ibid., Sept. 2, 1814.

38. Griffith, op. cit., 179.

39. Bank of New York, Minutes of the Board of Directors, Sept. 27, 1814.

40. Bronson, Appeal, 10 ff; Nevins, op. cit., 42; Hales, op. cit., 88, footnote.
    Represented on this committee were the Bank of New York, the Merchants, Mechanics, and City Banks, and the Bank of the New York Manufacturing Company. The Bank of the Manhattan Company kept aloof.

41. Bank of North America, Minutes of the Board of Directors, Mar. 9, 1815.

42. Ibid., June 19, 1815.

43. Ibid., August 24, 1815.

44. The Bank of North America tried to sell out the government stock which it held; ibid., Sept. 14 and 18, 1815.

45. For the above, see ibid., Sept. 4, 1815.

46. Ibid., Sept. 16, 1815.

47. See below, page 250.

48. Ibid., Nov. 13, 1815. This is the arrangement mentioned in Philadelphia Bank, 72, 73 and Holdsworth, Empire, I, 202; II, 446.

49. Ibid., Nov. 20, 27; Dec. 18, 1815; Mar. 4, 1816.

50. In March, 1816, the General Committee prepared a plan regarding resumption in January, 1817, which, however, was not put into effect; ibid., Mar. 18, 1816.

51. Holdsworth, op. cit., I, 202, II, 446.

52. Carey, Essays, 39.

53. Op. cit., 7, 13.

54. Bronson, Appeal to the Public, 9.

55. For the following see Walters, Dallas, 202, 205, 206, 213, 214.

56. "Report on the Finances," December 6, 1815 in Reports of the Secretary of the Treasury of the United States (Washington, 1837), II, 43.

57. The Minutes of the Board of Directors of the Bank of New York on June 29 and Aug. 15, 1816 show the reaction to the circulars of June and July, respectively.

58. Niles Weekly Register, XI (1816/17), 57.

59. See Volume I of this work, pages 45 ff.

60. Woodward, op. cit., 117.

61. See this page, below.

62. On this important committee of three were two outstanding men: One was George Newbold (1780-1858), the guiding genius of the Bank of America, who was a leader among the New York bankers as late as 1837 (see below page 255). Death notices are in the New York Evening Post of Sept. 9, 1858 and in Bankers Magazine, XIII (1858/59), 311; additional information is to be found in Lee, Francis, Genealogical and Memorial History of the State of New Jersey (New York, 1910), 1303. This information was kindly provided by the New York Public Library. The other was Lynde Catlin (1768-1833); see vol. I of this work page 63.

63. Preamble and Resolutions as adopted are in Bank of New York, Minutes of the Board of Directors, Oct. 5, 1815. They are to be found also in the Directors Records of the Bank of North America, Oct. 19, 1815.

64. Bronson, Appeal, 11 ff.

65. Bank of North America, Minutes of the Board of Directors, Oct. 19, 1815.

66. Ibid., Oct. 30, 1815.

67. American State Papers, Finance, IV, 770.

68. See above page 253.

69. American State Papers, Finance, IV, 708 ff, 788; Niles Weekly Register, XI (1816/17), 57.

70. See the "Report of the Proceedings at Phila" in Bank of New York, Minutes of the Board of Directors, August 15, 1816. New York was represented at the meeting by William Few (1748-1828), a Georgia statesman, who had removed to New York in 1799, had been a director of the Manhattan Company 1804-1814, and was at the time in question the president of the City Bank. The other New York delegates were Jonathan Burrall, president of the Bank of America, and Charles Wilkes, cashier of the Bank of New York; (about the last two men see vol. I of this work, pages 40 and 41). Philadelphia was represented by Robert Waln, about whom more will be said later (see page 254), Elihu Chauncey, and

William Milnor. Chauncey (1779-1847), a native of New Haven and graduate of Yale, was a Philadelphia lawyer and for some time connected with the United States Gazette. He became a director of the Bank of Pennsylvania and for years took an interest in the flotations of public loans. Later in his life he entered the field of railroading. Milnor (1769-1848), a Philadelphian by birth, was engaged in the iron and grocery wholesale business. He repeatedly represented Philadelphia in Congress (as for instance 1815-1817) and was Mayor of Philadelphia 1829/30. (The information on the last named two men was kindly provided by the Historical Society of Pennsylvania, from Howler, William C., Memorials of the Chaunceys [Boston 1858], 146 ff; Woodward, Evan M. and John F. Hageman, History of Burlington and Mercer Counties, N. J. [Philadelphia, 1883], 173; Biographical Directory of Congress.)

Finally, Baltimore's representatives were Joseph H. Nicholson (1770-1817) and Samuel Hollingsworth (1757-1830). The former was a leading Democratic-Republican in Jefferson's era, Congressman, judge, and first president of the Commercial and Farmers Bank of Baltimore (Dict. of Am. Biogr.). The latter, born in Cecil County, Maryland, after receiving his business education in a counting house in Philadelphia and after an honorable military career during the Revolutionary War, settled in Baltimore and became a business and social leader in that city. He was one of the founders of the Baltimore Equitable Society, the first fire insurance company of the city, and was connected with the City Bank of Baltimore whose president he became by 1819. (The information on Hollingsworth was kindly provided by the Enoch Pratt Free Library of Baltimore, from Jamar, Mary H., Hollingsworth Family and Collateral Lines. . . [Philadelphia, 1944], 39; Niles Register, XVII [1819/20], 138; XXXVIII [1830], 258; Baltimore City Directory, 1819, 1822/23.)

71. Smith, J. Thomas, "The National Bank of Baltimore" in A.B.A., Proceedings (1889), 151; Bank of North America, Minutes of the Board of Directors, Dec. 9, 1816. The agreement is reprinted in the appendix to this chapter.

72. Niles Register, X (1816), 401; Walters, Dallas, 213. The reason that the Manhattan Company was not represented is to be found in the fact that it was not represented on New York's General Committee either; see Niles Register, XI (1816/17), 57.

73. American State Papers, Finance, IV, 768 ff; Nicholas Biddle in U. S. 22d Congr. 1st sess., House Document 460, 341; Niles Register, XI (1816/1817), 57; Jones, William op. cit., 14 ff; Gallatin, Considerations, 48; Bank of New York, Minutes of the Board of Directors, Feb. 6, 1817.

74. See vol. I of this work, page 40.

75. Information kindly provided by the Maryland Department of the Enoch Pratt Free Library, Baltimore, based on the following sources: Laws of Maryland passed at the November session, 1804, chapter 48, Laws of 1818/19, chapter 93. Scharf, J. T., The Chronicle of Baltimore (Baltimore, 1874); and the same author's History of Baltimore City and County (Philadelphia, 1881), 806 [information partly incorrect]; Griffith, T. W., Annals of Baltimore (Baltimore, 1833), 228, 229, 287; Howard, George, The Monumental City (Baltimore, 1881), 549; Niles Register, Dec. 27, 1817; Baltimore American, Dec. 27, 1845.

76. See this volume, pages 247, 256.

77. "Report of the Committee to inquire whether any disadvantages have resulted from the present banking system of this Commonwealth." Massachusetts Senate Document, No. 14 (1827), 2.

78. Op. cit., 276.

79. A.B.A., Proceedings (1889), 152.

80. These consolidated statements were published in the Report of the Union Committee, 3.

81. Bank of New York, Minutes of the Board of Directors, Feb. 19 and Mar. 25, 1834.

82. Grenier, op. cit., 89, 90, 97, 98.

The cooperative actions of the New Orleans banks in 1836 are so important that the entries in the minutes of the Citizens Bank referring thereto, which are reprinted in U. S. 25th Congr. 2nd sess., Executive Document 79, 652, 653, are given here in full:

Extract from the minutes of the 26th September, 1836.

The exchange committee informed the board that, in accordance with the resolution adopted on the 19th instant, they had made the following proposals in behalf of the bank, viz:

The Citizens' Bank proposes to import from Havana and Mexico three millions of dollars of specie, or as large an amount as can there be obtained.

Said importation to be on account, and at the expense, of the banks enumerated below, pro rata their capital paid in.

For the purchase of the specie, as above, the Citizens' Bank will furnish bills on London at the rate of 9 per cent. premium; said bills to bear an interest of 6 per cent, from the day of their sale in Havana or Mexico, until reimbursed here by the contracting parties, viz: on the delivery of the specie.

Extract from the minutes of the 3d October, 1836.

The exchange committee informed the board that, in conformity with the resolution of 19th September last, they had obtained orders, based upon the terms adopted on the 26th September, from the following-named banks, viz:

From the Canal and Banking Company, for	- $200,000
Bank of Orleans -	- 100,000
Consolidated Association -	- 100,000
City Bank -	- 200,000
Mechanics and Traders' Bank -	- 150,000
Improvement and Banking Company	200,000
Gas-light and Banking Company -	- 300,000
Commercial Bank -	- 100,000
Carrollton Bank -	- 100,000
Bank of Louisiana -	- 100,000
Atchafalaya Bank -	- 100,000
	$1,650,000

And had in consequence, requested Messrs. M. De Lizardi & Co., to cause to be purchased, in Havana and Mexico, specie to the amount for which orders had been received, and to request their friends to reimburse themselves by drawing upon Messrs. F. De Lizardi & Co., London, who have been notified that, in the event of the bonds remaining unsold, remittances to cover their advances would be made from this place. The exchange committee also informed the board that, in order to facilitate the operations of the banks which have entered into the above arrangement, they had, in conjunction with the Consolidated Association, which has placed $50,000 at the disposal of this institution for that purpose, offered to loan to the following-named banks, and in the following proportion, $120,000 in specie, to be returned when the specie ordered will have been received, viz:

To the Bank of Louisiana -	-$30,000
Gas-light and Banking Company -	- 20,000
City Bank -	- 20,000
Canal and Banking Company -	- 20,000
Bank of Orleans -	- 15,000
Mechanics and Traders' Bank -	- 15,000
	$120,000

83. U. S. 25th Congr. 2d sess., Executive Document 79, 651, 653, 657, 658 (extracts from the minutes of the board of directors of the Citizens Bank of October 10 and October 17, 1836).
84. As to the Massachusetts Bank, see Gras, op. cit., 436, 438, 444, 472, 493, 500, 501 (cooperation under compulsion).
85. See this volume, chapter XII.
86. As to a similar action of the Boston banks, see Gras, op. cit., 411, 416 (1813/14).
87. Nevins, Bank of New York, 48; Burrill, op. cit., 25. For a similar case in Maryland, see Ashmead, op. cit., 32.
88. See volume I, page 94.
89. American State Papers, Finance, IV, 789.
90. New York Laws passed at the 52d session, chapter 94; Bank of New York, Minutes of the Board of Directors, Mar. 22, 1836; (the president of the bank appoints the delegate). The mode of elec-

tion was changed in 1837 (acts, chap. 74). Thereafter all commissioners were appointed by the Governor and Senate; State of New York, Assembly Doc. 5, 51.
91. Wright, speech of 1834, 8, 9.
92. See vol. I of this work, page 171.
93. See vol. I of this work, page 176.
94. Ibid., 70, 72, 73.
95. Govan, op. cit., 177, 178. The collapse of a New York scheme of a similar character has been described in vol. I, page 70 of this work.
96. Gras, op. cit., 434; also 446.
97. Nathan Hale, op. cit., 23, 24.
98. A very interesting but unsuccessful alliance was organized in Maryland in 1815. The country banks of that state felt aggrieved because the Baltimore banks would not accept their notes. Consequently they secured a charter for the Consolidated Bank of Maryland to be located just outside the city limits. It was to receive the notes of country banks, charge them to the respective banks, and "after the lapse of one month" debit interest on any remaining balance. The Consolidated Bank was to be a bankers' bank with a capital of $500,000. The capital was to be paid up with notes of Baltimore banks and to be apportioned among the Maryland country banks. The latter were to appoint the directors. The capital stock of each participating bank was to be reduced by the amount of its investment in the Consolidated Bank which was to abrogate its charter if the Baltimore banks decided to receive country notes and to reissue them. However, this scheme was never put into effect. (Hagerstown Bank, 56, 57; Maryland Laws, 1815/1816, ch. 169.)
99. Smith, J. Thomas, in A.B.A., Proceedings (1889), 153.
100. U. S. 25th Congr. 2d sess., Executive Document 79, 657, 658.
101. Gras, op. cit., 91, 92; Burrill, op. cit., 45.
102. Bancroft, op. cit., 46; Buchanan, op. cit., 19.
103. See this volume, page 257 and vol. I of this work, page 73.
104. Massachusetts Bank, Directors Records, Oct. 26, 1826; Gras, op. cit., 445. The library of Brown University, Providence kindly checked the following local papers: Manufacturers' and Farmers' Journal, Microcosm, and Rhode Island American and Gazette. They do not contain any reports on this convention.
105. Jackson to Duane, June 26, 1833, Duane, op. cit., 12.
106. There is an interesting note referring to 1839 in Niles Register (LVII, 119) which shows how banks cooperated in matters of specie payments, or to be exact, how they acted in concert. On October 11, of that year the Providence banks hesitated to pay specie waiting to hear from New York and Boston. They resumed immediately

on ascertaining that the banks in these cities continued to pay specie.

107. The Virginia banks did not cooperate when they suspended in 1837 and 1839; see Starnes, op. cit., 77, 78, 93. As to Philadelphia, see Bank of North America, Minutes of the Board of Directors, May 11 and 15, 1837. The announcement of the Hartford banks is reprinted in U. S. 25th Congr. 2d sess., House Executive Document 79, 225.

108. Woodward, op. cit., 142.

109. Volume I, 225.

110. Bank of New York, Minutes of the Board of Directors, May 9, 1837. Incidentally, Cornelius Heyer, the president of the Bank of New York and two directors, Schermerhorn and Howland, were appointed to represent this bank in any meeting of delegates.

111. The following description is based on the Minutes of the Board of Directors of the Bank of New York, May 23, 1837. See also Domett, op. cit., 86; Hardenbrook, op. cit., 107; Lanier, op. cit., 205.

112. Gallatin, Writings, III, 462, 466, 471, 478.

113. Gallatin, Writings, III, 464, 483; Financial Register, II, 78.

114. Bank of North America, Minutes of the Board of Directors, May 11 and 15, 1837, June 11, 1838.

115. Biddle to Ralph Peters, July 17, 1838; Biddle Letterbooks.

116. Op. cit., 91.

117. See, for instance, Bank of North America, Minutes of the Board of Directors, Nov. 20, 1837.

118. Ibid., May 15 and 16, 1837. Financial Register, II, 78. Incidentally, Baltimore in those days adopted very similar rules: the banks there agreed to continue taking each other's notes and to pay interest on balances monthly; while the creditor banks had the right to require the debtor banks to settle by checks on other banks or in securities acceptable to the creditor; (Hales, op. cit., 88).

119. Bank of North America, Minutes of the Board of Directors, May 29, 1837.

120. Ibid., July 20, 1837. Even today the reports mentioned above give a very clear picture of the standing and management of the various banks.

121. Ibid., May 9 and 10, 1838.

122. Ibid., May 28 and 31, 1838.

123. See below, page 266.

124. Report (for 1838), 6.

125. Stetson, op. cit., 59.

126. Gras, op. cit., 466, 467. (This entry in the directors records of the Massachusetts Bank may indicate how this clause was applied.)

127. Address of His Excellency Edward Everett to the Two Branches of the Legislature on the Organization of the Government for the Political Year commencing January 3, 1838. House Document 3 (Boston, 1838), 6.

128. The above is based on Lake's thesis, 138 ff. His sources are the issues of May 15, 17 and July 8, 1837 and January 13 and 25, 1838 of the Boston Daily Advertiser. See also Gras, op. cit., 462, 465. It is highly probable that the banks of Providence also cooperated during the emergency of 1837/1838. But the description of Stokes (op. cit., 305, 306) is not conclusive, although it indicates the existence of uniform policies during the critical months.

129. See above page 256. While emergency cooperation in Philadelphia, New York, Boston, New Orleans, and certainly also in a few other places, for which information is lacking, grew up spontaneously without being fostered by public agencies, the situation may have been different in Mississippi. In a circular letter of March 31, 1837, that is to say, at a moment when storm signals threatened, the governor of the state invited the banks to attend at the seat of government (Jackson) on the third Monday in April, the day set for the meeting of the legislature. Concerted actions of banks and legislature were intended to give relief at the dangerous moment. See Millsaps, op. cit., 26. Local research on the episode would be desirable.

130. See below page 266; and for the last statement, Dewey, State Banking, 57, 58. Dewey gives no source and hardly understood the implications of his material.

131. Huntington, op. cit., (1915), 388.

132. See also above page 260.

133. Important documents relative to the national convention of 1837 are reprinted in Gallatin's Writings, III, 462 ff.

134. Both Newbold and Lawrence are mentioned in Beach, Wealth and Biography. As to Newbold see also page 255. It is not known who originally conceived the idea of a conference on a national scale.

135. As to Philadelphia's reaction, see Gallatin, Writings, III, 464 ff; regarding Boston, Gras, op. cit., 466.

136. Historians have been too much influenced by Gallatin's ex parte description of the events in his Suggestions of 1841; see Writings, III, 398 ff.

137. Lake, thesis, 148.

138. Porter, Astor, II, 971, 985 (footnote 85).

139. See above page 262.

140. Hepburn, op. cit., 57, 132.

141. Adams, op. cit., 657 ff; Stevens, op. cit., 282 ff; Hammond, Bray, "Chestnut Street," 618.

142. Forstall thought along the same lines typical of a whole school of thought which lived on for

many decades and was represented later by the sound money writers. Forstall stated in 1838 that public and private credit were "within the keeping" of the banks. They held the morals of the people in their hands, for no acts of men would sooner demoralize a people than the degradation of its standard of value. Report of the Committee of Investigation. . ., 7.

143. See the monthly statements submitted in 1837 to the joint committee of the Philadelphia banks in Bank of North America, Minutes of the Board of Directors.

144. Financial Register, I, 236, 237.

145. Incidentally Condy Raguet took Biddle's side.

146. Bank of North America, Minutes of the Board of Directors, Nov. 20, 1837.

147. The New York delegates were appointed by the "general meeting of the officers of the banks of the City of New York;" see Gallatin, Writings, III, 471. Similarly, the Philadelphia delegates were appointed by the chairman of the joint committee on request of the latter; Bank of North America, Minutes of the Board of Directors, Nov. 20, 1837.

148. Schlesinger, op. cit., 11.

149. U. S. 25th Congr. 2d sess., Executive Document 79, 502 ff contains the minutes of the convention. See also Southern Recorder, Sept. 5, 1837.

150. The Milledgeville convention appointed two committees, one to examine the statements of the banks and to "recommend terms of intercourse among" them; the other, to consider "the subject of resuming specie payments and of discounts by the several banks of this State." The convention adopted a resolution stressing the importance of a currency convertible into specie and providing that the banks should limit their circulation to the amount of capital plus specie on hand; that during suspension they would publish monthly a consolidated report on their condition; that they would turn in statements once a month to a designated bank which would consolidate them; that they would settle their balances once a month and would pay 6 per cent interest on accounts remaining open; that the participants in the agreement would take each other's notes as long as the issuer remained in good standing. Post notes would be considered payable on demand if entering interbank settlements.

It appears that Dr. Tomlinson Fort (1787-1859), president of the Central Bank of Georgia at Milledgeville (1832-1859), was the leader of the Georgia banks. He was a renowned physician and a politician besides, representing Baldwin County in the state legislature (1818-1826) and thereafter becoming a congressman for the two years 1827-1829. He was a strong personality, a popular leader, who influenced the thinking of the masses, and an ultra-conserva-

tive. See Biographical Directory of Congress; Memoirs of Georgia (Atlanta, 1895), 207 ff; also U. S. 26th Congr. 2d sess., Executive Document 111, 234. The statement in the Biographical Directory that Fort was the president of the State Bank of Georgia is erroneous.

151. For the history of the convention see McGrane, Panic, 183 ff and Sister Madeleine, op. cit., 91 ff. (This author is in disagreement with her interpretation and her implied value judgment which are the traditional ones adopted without independent criticism.) The Minutes were printed separately and reprinted in Financial Register, I, 217 ff; II, 337 ff; and in Gallatin's Writings, III, 466 ff, 480 ff.

152. Biddle to Manuel Eyre, November 29, 1837; Biddle Letterbooks.

153. Financial Register, I, 229 ff; Gallatin's Writings, III, 471 ff.

154. Ibid., 478 ff.

155. Ibid., 483. Bank of North America, Minutes of the Board of Directors, Mar. 8, 1838.

156. Condy Raguet (Financial Register, I, 334), reports a resolution of the board of the Suffolk Bank: in the opinion of the board it was inexpedient to resume unless the banks in New York and Philadelphia did the same. The cashier was requested to inform the delegates to the convention (of April, 1838) with a copy of this resolution. According to Lake (op. cit., 150) this resolution was passed in common by a number of Boston banks.

157. However there was another school of thought which suggested resumption for a date in August or September, the dead season for the cotton trade. In that way the public would become accustomed to specie payments before the crop came into the market. From the Minutes of the Citizens Bank of New Orleans, June 27, 1838, reprinted in Financial Register, II, 154.

158. Biddle to P. Barrett and H. W. Evans, July 9, 1838; Biddle Letterbooks.

159. Financial Register, II, 219, 200; Minutes of the Proceedings of the Bank Convention. . . 1837, 11 ff.

160. The letter can be found in Gallatin, Writings, III, 462-464.

161. U. S. 25th Congr. 3d sess., Executive Document 227, 387 ff; Financial Register, I, 407.
The leading personality in this convention seems to have been Abram Blanding, a native of Massachusetts and a graduate of Brown University who in the 1790's went South on invitation of former classmates. He taught first at Columbia Male Academy, but soon quit to read law. He became connected with improvements in the state and region, including early railroading, and was a director, if not president, of the Commercial Bank of Columbia and possibly later also on the board of a Charleston bank.

He succumbed to yellow fever in 1839. See The State (Columbia, S. C., newspaper), November 24 and December 1, 1941; Blanding, Address to the Citizens of Charleston Convened in Town Meeting on the Louisville, Cincinnati, and Charleston Railroad (Columbia, S. C., 1836).

162. See, for instance, Financial Register, II, 152, 338.

163. U. S. 25th Congr. 3d sess., Executive Document 227, 622 ff.

164. U. S. 25th Congr. 3d sess., Executive Document 227, 595.

165. Bank of North America, Minutes of the Board of Directors, Mar. 8, 1838. Biddle to P. Barrett, July 9, 1838 in Biddle Letterbooks.

166. Financial Register, II, 78, 79 (the report contains discrepancies); Biddle to Joseph Ritner, July 23, 1838; Biddle Letterbooks. A note in the Columbia Centinel of July 28, 1838 refers to this conference, but is unreliable.

167. Financial Register, II, 28, 152 ff, 236 ff.

168. This meeting seems to have resulted from one of the presidents of the Natchez banks held on October 5.

169. Financial Register, II, 251, 252, 255, 317, 366.

170. U.S. 25th Congr 2d sess., Executive Document 79, 613.

171. Letter dated August 28, 1838, directed to the president of the Union Bank of Tennessee: U. S. 26th Congr. 1st sess., Executive Document 172, 705.

172. James, "Bank of North America," 80.

173. U. S. 26th Congr. 2d sess., Executive Document 111, 884.

174. Minutes, Oct. 12 and 14, 1839.

175. Ibid., Oct. 21, 1839.

176. Ibid., Oct. 24, 1839.

177. Ibid., Oct. 25, 28, 31; Nov. 2, 1839.

178. Ibid., Feb. 5 and 8, 1841.

179. Ibid., Feb. 8, 1841.

180. Ibid., Feb. 10, 1842.

181. Niles Register, LXII (1842), 256. Governor Roman of Louisiana stressed the fact that the inability of the banks of the state to harmonize their differences had led them to resume six months before the date fixed by law; McGrane, Bondholders, 180.

182. Niles Register, LX (1841), 121; Hammond, Bray, "Chestnut Street. . .," passim, especially 609, 614 ff.

183. Domett, op. cit., 88.

184. J. V. L. Pruyn to Erastus Corning July 17, 1840; from Miss Irene Neu's material, by permission. See also vol. I of this work, pages 78, 79.

185. Dillistin, op. cit., 10 ff.

186. As to these associations, see Burnham, op. cit., 29; Hodges, op. cit., 254, 255; Gras, op. cit., 484; Massachusetts Bank Commissioners, Reports (1852), 15; (1853), 64; (1855), 77. A complete set of the Reports of the [New England]

Association of Banks for the Suppression of Counterfeiting covering the years 1854-1866 is in the Baker Library of Harvard University which also has its Articles of Association and Rules of the Board of Managers (Boston, 1853). Material on the association is to be found also in the Bankers Magazine, IX (1854/55), 821; X (1855/56), 798 ff, 921 ff; XI (1856/57), 129 ff, 404, 405, 526 ff. XII (1857/58), 740 ff. XIII (1858/59), 693 ff; XIV (1859/60), 705 ff; XVII (1862/63), 843 ff.

187. Report (for 1859), 16, 17; Bankers Magazine, XIV (1859/60), 702 ff. The New England association embraced in its first year 99 out of 136 Massachusetts banks, but only 11 from other states, while in a certain later year its members amounted only to 187 out of all 507 New England banks.

188. A.B.A., Proceedings (1881), 72-75.

189. Almon D. Hodges (1801-1878), born in Massachusetts of Puritan stock, rose in the grocery business in Boston and Providence. In 1845 returning to Boston he opened a wholesale business in groceries and West India goods. While in Providence Hodges had become a director in banks, an experience which must have stood him in good stead when in 1850 he was elected president of the Washington Bank of Boston. See Hodges, op. cit., passim, expecially 91, 113, 120, 227 ff, 245 ff, 255.

190. "George Smith's Money," 117; James, Chicago Banks, I, 204, 229.

191. See vol. I of this work, page 76.

192. As to the convention of New York country banks held at Syracuse on July 9 and 10, 1855, see Bankers Magazine, X (1855/56), 54, 139 ff.

193. See vol. I of this work, page 79.

194. Hunt's Merchants' Magazine, XXXVIII (1858), 328; Dewey, State Banking, 216.

195. Ibid., 222.

196. Esarey, op. cit., 284.

197. James, Chicago Banks, I, 352, 353, 356-361.

198. See above, pages 258, 259, 261.

199. Hooper wrote in 1860 (Examination, 22): "The stronger banks are obliged, for self preservation. . ., to furnish aid to sustain the weaker banks, for they could not probably themselves withstand, and dare not risk, the effect of the shock of public confidence, that would be produced by the inopportune failure of any one bank."

200. Cope, op. cit., 315, 317 ff.

201. "Cushioning a Crisis," passim.

202. Moral and Religious Duties, 19. These teachings were reprinted in Gilbart's widely read Practical Treatise on Banking and in the Bankers Magazine, VII (1851/52) 295 ff, 360 ff.

203. Massachusetts Bank Commissioners, Report for 1840, 12. Bank of North America, Minutes of the Board of Directors, Sept. 21 and 24, Oct. 12,

19, 21, 22, Dec. 17, 1840. The banks partici-
pated as follows: Bank of Pennsylvania and
Philadelphia Bank: $1,000,000 each; Farmers
and Mechanics Bank: $750,000; Bank of North
America and Mechanics Bank: $400,000 each;
Commercial Bank: $350,000; Bank of the
Northern Liberties: $300,000; four smaller
banks: sums ranging between $200,000 and
$100,000.

204. The Philadelphia National Bank, 94 ff; Stetson,
op. cit., 62; Gras, op. cit., 472, 473.

205. Bank of North America, Minutes of the Board of
Directors, Jan. 29, 1842.

206. Holdsworth, Empire, I, 186; II, 570. The
"League" also decided to refuse country notes.
These were the results of the events alluded to
before on page 270.

207. Holdsworth, Empire, I, 68; Ashmead, op. cit.,
47, 48.

208. It is noteworthy that in both 1837 and 1857 New
York savings banks cooperated with one another.
In the former year the Greenwich and Bowery
Savings Banks applied for help to the Bank for
Savings. In the latter year the Brooklyn Sav-
ings Bank appealed successfully to the same
bank. Thereafter several others asked for
loans or purchase of their investments, but
were turned down. However, the Greenwich,
Seamen's and Bowery Savings Banks set up a
joint committee to develop concerted action.
See Knowles, op. cit., 93, 118.

209. Massachusetts Bank Commissioners, Report
(1855), 79, 80.

210. Van Vleck, op. cit., 66. A weak attempt at
assisting the failing Bank of Pennsylvania was
made that year in Philadelphia.

211. U. S. 32d Congr. 2d sess., House Executive
Document 82, 157; State of New York, Messages
of the Governors, V, 43 ff; Hedges, op. cit.,
118, 136.

212. Men and Measures, 199, 200.

213. As to the measures alluded to, see this volume,
page 158.

214. See the correspondence of George Eustice,
president of the Bureau de Circulation, with the
three banks, reprinted in Rapport du Bureau de
Circulation à la Legislature de l'Etat de la
Louisiane, Janvier, 1858. (Baton Rouge. J. M.
Taylor, Imprimeur d'Etat, 1858.) See also
Heck, op. cit., 106, 107.

215. The following paragraphs are based on the
Minutes of the Board of Presidents preserved
in the Philadelphia Clearing House. The articles
of agreement signed by the presidents are pasted
into the minute book. Moore (op. cit., passim)
has used the same source.

216. According to information from the Historical
Society of Pennsylvania no biographical data
are available. Mitchell was probably born by
1790 and he died in 1868 after having been connected with his bank for more than fifty years;
eulogy in the minutes.

217. Boker (1797-1858) was a wholesale merchant
in boots, shoes and straw hats and one of the
organizers of the Pennsylvania Steamship
Company; see Leach, op. cit., 75. After Boker's
death his successor discovered fraudulent transactions; see Girard Bank vs. Boker, passim.

218. See page 52. The Philadelphia cashiers met
as early as 1839 at least occasionally; see
Bank of North America, Minutes of the Board
of Directors, Oct. 14, 1839.

219. See chapters XV and XVII.

220. Hales, op. cit., 45 ff; Proceedings of the Convention. . . 1869, 19.
    William Wallace Taylor (1821-1898) was a
descendant of Baltimore merchants of English
and German ancestry. His paternal grandfather
traded with the West; his (German) maternal
grandfather was engaged in the import trade.
Both families were for years interested in banking, the paternal grandfather as the president
of the Commercial and Farmers Bank of Baltimore, the father as a director of the Baltimore
branch of the Second Bank of the United States
and later as one of the incorporators and directors of the Merchants Bank; while the maternal
grandfather, who before his immigration had
been employed in a Vienna banking house, was
one of the incorporators of the Union Bank of
Maryland. These data have been cited because
the author knows of no other case in that period
where a whole family was engaged in banking
to such an extent. William Wallace Taylor,
after an excellent education, entered the wholesale dry-goods business of his father, and succeeded the latter as a director of the Merchants
Bank of Baltimore (1850). Withdrawing from
this bank he later became the president of the
Union Bank of Maryland (1861) and in addition
was a director in numerous corporations. See
History of Baltimore, Maryland. . . 1729-1898
(n.p., 1898), 662-664.

221. Op. cit. (1910), 1.

222. Hooper, Examination, 23. In this context it is
noteworthy that an anonymous author writing
in the New Englander of 1858 considered it
probable that the banks in every principal commercial city would by mutual understanding
adopt weekly a minimum interest rate, if the
country did not have usury laws; "Currency,
Banking and Credit," 33.

223. J. Edward Simmons, president of the Fourth
National Bank of New York, in New York Clear-
ing House Association, Proceedings. . . in
Memory. . . Tappen, 14.

224. Gras, op. cit., 500, 501.

225. Cleaveland, op. cit., 270.

226. See this volume chapters XV and XVII.
    Where there was no clearing house in 1857,

as in Providence, steps were taken in line with tradition. In that city a meeting of Rhode Island banks took place on September 28 of that year to consider suspension. Only 21 of 33 banks sent representatives: the stronger ones, typical of the spirit of the time, kept away but were forced into suspension by the others (Stokes, op. cit., 310). Thereafter the Providence banks tried to handle the difficulties in a way which had proved successful in 1837; but the attempt broke down for lack of harmony.

227. New York Clearing House, Proceedings . . . in Memory of Tappen, 32, 33. For the background, see Van Vleck, op. cit., 71-73.

228. That the Chemical Bank of New York was the only one that did not suspend specie payments in the crisis of 1857 is widely mentioned. The author confesses that he has never been able to understand how such action in a general suspension was possible. However a resolution of the Massachusetts Bank of Boston of October 14, 1857 may give the clue. On that day the Massachusetts Bank refused to suspend because its stock of coin was three times as large as its issues "and a large number of the depositors of this Bank having agreed not to call for coin in payment of their deposits." (See Gras, op. cit., 500.) The author is convinced that the Chemical Bank took similar action, i.e., made arrangements with its depositors. If so, instead of suspending by public announcement in cooperation with the other banks, it suspended by private agreement, thereby gaining an advantage in the competitive struggle at the expense of the other banks, for such private arrangements would have been impossible if the other banks had not taken the odium. Such policy seems to be mere window dressing, but good advertising, if not an advertising stunt. The other New York banks, which excluded the Chemical Bank temporarily from the Clearing House, seem to have been rather embittered, as is understandable, if the above interpretation is correct.

229. See below page 283.

230. Bankers Magazine, XII (1858/59), 317. See for comparison vol. I of this work, Chapter IV. The following description follows closely that of Merk, op. cit., 192 ff. See also Krueger, op. cit., 71-73, 80-85, 88, 89; Hadden, op. cit., 191 ff.

231. Krueger (op. cit., 80) uses in this connection the name "Central Association of Banks of Wisconsin."

232. Wisconsin State Journal, Feb. 5, 1863, repr. in Fite, op. cit., 152 ff; Krueger, op. cit., 92; correspondence with the Reference Librarian of the University of Wisconsin Library. There is no connection between this association and the present Wisconsin Bankers' Association.

233. Merk, op. cit., 215 ff.

234. James, Chicago Banks, I, 372; Huston, op. cit., I, 551.

235. Coleman was born in 1808 in Massachusetts. His father had been engaged in the coasting trade. After a scanty education in a public school Coleman started as a clerk in a store in New Bedford. In 1827 he moved to Troy where he was engaged first in the wholesale trade of oil, paint and dyestuffs, and later in the lumber business where he acquired mercantile distinction. In 1857 he entered politics as an alderman in Troy. From 1858-1861 he represented his city in the state legislature, becoming a member, and for one year the chairman, of the committee on banks. By that time he had acquired practical knowledge of banking, being a director of the Bank of Troy from 1852-1863. This bank he left upon founding the First National Bank of Troy whose first president he became. Cyclopedia of National Biography, III, 249; Sylvester, N. B., History of Rensselaer County (New York, 1880), 280, 281.

236. "Proceedings of the Convention . . . 1864," 3.

237. Ibid., 4-6.

238. Undoubtedly Samuel Thompson, John's son.

239. Ibid., 7, 8.

240. Ibid., 13, 14.

241. Ibid., 16.

242. The power of the states to tax the National Banks must have been very irksome indeed. The assessors of the City of Boston, for instance, printed a List of Stockholders in the National Banks of Boston as of May 1, 1866 [Boston, 1866] for the use of the Assessors of the Cities and Towns of Massachusetts. The book of 524 pages contains also a list of the taxable value of the shares of every Boston National Bank which in some cases was set equal, in others below the market value. See also The State and the National Banks. The Question of Taxation, etc. Important Correspondence between Bank Officers and the Comptroller (Albany, 1864), passim.

243. Proceedings . . . 1864, 18, 32, 34, 39.

244. Edward B. Judson, born in 1813 in Coxsackie, N. Y., started his business career in a local bank and afterwards was active in the lumber business. From 1839 through 1841 he served in the New York Assembly. In 1849 he moved to Syracuse and besides being active in railroading and glass manufacture became interested in several country banks in that section. In 1863 he was called to Washington with other bankers in order to give advice regarding the perfection of the National Banking system. Immediately thereafter he founded the First National Bank of Syracuse. See Bruce, Dwight H., Onondaga's Centennial (Boston, 1896), II, 53, 54 of the Biogr. Section.

245. Proceedings . . . 1864, 19, 22-26, 34, 35, 40, 41; Bankers Magazine, XXIV (1869/1870), 854, 855.

246. Joseph Upham Orvis (1816-1883), a native of New York State, started his career in the dry-goods business at Manchester, Vermont. Thence he moved to Troy where he was engaged in the same type of enterprise. There he also became interested in banking, being active in the establishment of the Mutual Bank of Troy, becoming its vice-president and virtually its manager. He also became a vice-president of the Troy Savings Bank and one of the founders of the [later?] Troy Building and Loan Association. In 1864 he organized the Ninth National Bank of New York whose president he was from 1864 to 1867. On his retirement from this position he became the manager for New York of the National Life Insurance Company of the United States. See Orvis, Francis, The Orvis Family in America (Hackensack, 1922), 57, 58. (Information kindly provided by the Reference Librarian of the New York Public Library.)

247. Proceedings of the Convention . . . 1869, 21, 30.

248. See this volume, pages 122, 123.

249. As to Coolbaugh, see this volume, index.

250. Proceedings of the Convention . . . 1869, passim, especially 6, 19-20, 21, 25, 33, 34, 35. It is not clear how the organization was financed between 1864 and 1869. The cost of the convention of 1864 was paid by the National Banks of the City of New York; see Proceedings . . . 1864, 21.

251. Proceedings of the Convention . . . 1869, 29.

252. American Bankers Association, Proceedings (1876), 4, 71. As to its activities, see also "Argument of Hon. Chas. B. Hall of Boston before the Committee of Ways and Means, Washington, March 29th, 1870 on the portion of the Funding Bill affecting National Banks" in Bankers Magazine, XXIV (1869/1870), 854 ff.

253. A history of the A.B.A. is being prepared for the organization, but will not be available before 1951.

254. Proceedings of the Convention . . . Saratoga, 14, 15, 21. Historical notes on the A.B.A. can be found in its Proceedings (1893), 69 ff; (1895), 73 ff; (1899), 11; (1909), 7 ff; (1913), 128.

255. See this volume, page 429.

256. Charles B. Hall (1815-1883) was born in Orford, N. H., the son of a farmer. He attended public schools and an academy and taught school for some years thereafter. In 1834 he started his mercantile career as a clerk in a store in Haverhill, where a few years later (in 1838) he opened a store in West India goods on his own account. It does not seem to have flourished, for from 1841 to 1849 we find Hall as postmaster in that city. By the end of that decade he entered political life: in 1850 he served a year in the Massachusetts House of Representatives, being a member of the Demo-

cratic party; in 1851 and 1852 he was the receiver-general of the commonwealth; in 1853 a member of the state constitutional convention; and as late as 1860 presidential elector.

In the meantime he had taken an interest in banking. In 1850 he had become a director of the Merrimac Bank of Haverhill and a trustee of the Haverhill Savings Bank, i.e., combining commercial and savings banking under one administration. In 1853 he became the cashier of what was then styled the National Bank of Boston (later Boston National Bank) whose director and president he became in 1878. (New England Historical and Genealogical Register, XXXVIII (1884), 91, 92; History of the Military Company of the Massachusetts, now called the Ancient and Honorable Artillery Company of Massachusetts, 1637-1888, III (1822-1865) [Boston, 1898], 347, 348.)

257. According to information received from the St. Louis Public Library, no biographical data are known. However, the St. Louis City Directories list Howenstein (1872-1877) as "Cashier, Valley National Bank" and (1882) as National Bank examiner. Later in his life he lived in Washington; he died in 1912.

258. Proceedings of the Convention . . . Saratoga, 11, 12.

259. Ibid., 17.

260. Lyman J. Gage in A.B.A., Proceedings (1891), 72.

261. Ibid. (1876), 4.

262. Ibid., 71.

263. Proceedings of the Convention . . . Saratoga, 3.

264. Proceedings of the Convention... 1869, 26 ff.

265. Proceedings of the Convention . . . Saratoga, 17.

266. A.B.A. Proceedings (1901), 122.

267. Ibid., (1876), 3 ff, 11; Proceedings of the Convention . . . Saratoga, 27.

268. According to information kindly provided by the A.B.A. the following are the years in which the respective State Bankers Associations were founded.

1885: Texas
1886: South Dakota
1887: Iowa, Kansas, Michigan, Minnesota
1889: Florida, Mississippi, Washington
1890: Nebraska, Tennessee
1891: Arkansas, California, Illinois, Kentucky, Missouri, Ohio
1892: Alabama, Georgia, Wisconsin
1893: Virginia
1894: New York, Pennsylvania
1895: West Virginia
1896: Maryland
1897: Indiana, North Carolina, Oklahoma
1899: Connecticut
1900: Louisiana, Maine
1901: District of Columbia, South Carolina
1902: Colorado

1903: Arizona, New Jersey, North Dakota
1904: Montana
1905: Idaho, Massachusetts, New Mexico, Oregon
1908: Nevada, Wyoming
1909: Utah, Vermont
1913: Delaware, New Hampshire
1915: Rhode Island

269. A.B.A., Proceedings (1892), 54 ff; (1895), 36; (1899), 14, 16; (1907), 84, 85; (1908), 109.
    In 1895 only 1,527 members of the A.B.A. had paid their dues although in that year there were 30 state bankers associations with about 3,700 members.

270. Satterlee, J. Pierpont Morgan, 468.

271. Minutes of the Boston Clearing House Assn., Apr. 8, 1861.

272. Ibid., May 20, 1864.

273. New York Clearing House Association, Proceedings of a Meeting of the . . . held June 23d, 1863 including a Report of the Tax Committee and the Opinion of Benjamin F. Silliman on the Subject of State Taxation (privately printed, 1863).

274. Report on the National Bank Currency Act . . .

275. James, Chicago Banks, I, 372, 374.

276. ABA, Proceedings (1877), 103 ff. Stuart Patterson and William A. Porter, Opinion whether the Western National Bank of Philadelphia is subject to the Tax imposed by an Act of the Legislature of Pennsylvania approved April 30, 1864 (p.p., 1864).

277. See pages 286, 287.

278. The Chicago Clearing House in 1865 adopted a rule regarding the banking hours of its members and suspended one which did not comply with the regulation; James, Chicago Banks, I, 371.

279. Report on the Subject of Paying Interest.

280. From 1867 through 1869 the members of the Chicago Clearing House had to furnish periodical statements of financial conditions; James, Chicago Banks, I, 373.

281. Report to the New York Clearing House Association, 1873, 37 ff, 54, 55; Minutes, Philadelphia Board of Presidents, Aug. 20, 1861; Report of the Comptroller of the Currency (1873), xxiv.

282. Hardenbrook, op. cit., 25, 26.

283. Cornwallis, op. cit., 39. The author felt that by setting a minimum discount rate and adhering thereto the New York Clearing House could control the money market like the Bank of England, i.e., act as a central bank, and the author was for such policy.

284. Cannon, op. cit., (1910), 170.

285. Minutes of the Boston Clearing House Assn., Apr. 28, 1864.

286. James, Chicago Banks, II, 561; Forgan, Recollections, 284.

287. See this volume, pages 237, 238.

288. Cannon, op. cit., (1910), 13 ff; Pujo Committee Report, 28-31. By 1912 ninety-one clearing houses regulated the business in foreign checks; Money Trust Investigation, 217, 218, 374 ff, 1647.

289. See pages 271-273. In 1907 in New York alone twelve financial institutions were assisted during the crisis; Satterlee, J. Pierpont Morgan, 492.

290. Minutes, Boston Clearing House Association, Nov. 2, 1891.

291. See above page 276.

292. Recollections, 284, 285.

293. James, Chicago Banks, 714 ff.

294. Byron L. Smith (1853-1914), son of Solomon A. Smith, the influential president of the Merchants Loan and Trust Company, and himself one of Chicago's representative business leaders, rose in Chicago banking circles until in 1889 he organized the Northern Trust Company. From 1904 to 1907 he was the president of the Chicago Clearing House Association.

295. Report . . . Indianapolis Convention, 358, 359; Hull, op. cit., 97 ff, 106 ff, 119.

296. U. S. 52d Congr. 2d sess., Senate Report 1286, xxi.

297. About Hammill, see index.

298. James, Chicago Banks, 499, 720, 721; Forgan, Recollections, 186 ff, 278 ff.

299. Cannon, op. cit. (1910), 137 ff; Money Trust Investigation 167, 457 ff, 1386, 1388, 1644, 1645; A.B.A., Proceedings (1909), 31 ff.

300. Thralls, op. cit., 23 ff.

301. See this volume, pages 52 ff.

302. See this volume, chapter XV.

303. See ibid., page 287.

304. For an example, see page 287.

305. See above, pages 262 ff.

306. Minutes of the Boston Clearing House Committee, Nov. 9, 1857 through Jan. 21, 1858.

307. Minutes of the Philadelphia Board of Presidents, Dec. 21, 1861 and Jan. 24, 1862; Mitchell, Wesley C., op. cit., 48. The committee consisted of James Gallatin, George S. Coe, Vermilye, and one Martin (?) from New York; Haven, Walley, and Bates from Boston; Mercer, Patterson, and Rogers from Philadelphia. Gallatin was its spokesman.

308. Minutes of the Boston Clearing House Association, June 6 and 23, 1862.

309. Ibid., Feb. 28, 1866 and Minutes of the Philadelphia Board of Presidents, Mar. 5, 1866.

310. Minutes of the Boston Clearing House Association, Feb. and Mar., 1869.

311. See this author's paper, " 'Translating' Economic Policy into Business Policy: An Illustration from the Resumption of Specie Payments in 1879" in Bulletin of the Business Historical Society, XX (1946). Minutes, Boston Clearing House Association, Jan. 7, 1878.

312. <u>Minutes, Boston Clearing House Association,</u> Oct. 19, 1864

313. <u>Ibid.</u>, Apr. 29, 1865.

314. <u>Pujo Committee, Report</u>, 18 ff; the quotation is on page 19 ; <u>Money Trust Investigation</u>, 111ff, 136ff, 147, 148, 158ff, 178, 190, 194ff. The power of the New York Clearing House was stressed as early as 1893 by George Ward, (<u>op. cit.</u>, 64, 65); Ward was a radical.

315. Cannon, "Clearing Houses and the Currency," 104, 105. During the period under investigation the New York Clearing House was led by Cannon, Coe, Hepburn, Nash, Tappen, Jacob D. Vermilye, and George G. Williams, all of whom are known to the reader of this volume. Other clearing house leaders were Edward N. Perkins (Importers and Traders National Bank), J. Edward Simmons (Fourth National Bank), Dumont Clarke (American Exchange Bank), James T. Woodward (Hanover National Bank), and Alexander Gilbert (Market and Fulton National Bank). This list was given by William A. Nash.

316. A.B.A., <u>Proceedings</u> (1913), 567 ff.

317. Boies, <u>op. cit.</u>, 681; Lamont, <u>op. cit.</u>, 75, 76; Swaine, <u>op. cit.</u>, II, 30; <u>Money Trust Investigation</u>, 230, 444, 449.

318. <u>Ibid.</u>, 209; Swaine, <u>op. cit.</u>, II, 99 ff.

319. When once more in 1896, banks had to cooperate in assisting the Treasury by raising $25,000,000 in gold, Frederick D. Tappen is supposed to have organized a number of banks to that end. In 1899 Tappen relieved the money market by loaning money put at his disposal by a number of leading banks for that purpose. It is not certain if and to what extent Tappen used the New York Clearing House in these actions; "Hundred Years," 160, 161. About Tappen, see this volume, index.

320. Satterlee, <u>J. Pierpont Morgan</u>, 477.

321. <u>Ibid.</u>, 466, 468, 474, 479, 485.

322. How neglected it has been can be seen, for instance, from a comparison of this chapter with <u>History of the Organization . . . of the American Bankers Association</u>, 3, 4.

323. American Bankers Association, <u>Proceedings</u> (1876), 6.

324. Hepburn, <u>op. cit.</u>, 397. A contemporary wrote in the same vein substantially as follows: Each bank of ours is an independent unit. In time of stress, instead of cooperating with each other for the general good, each bank is under the necessity of looking out for itself. At the critical time, when extension of credits is the very thing needed in the interest of industry, each bank feels compelled to cut down loans and strengthen its reserves. . . . In the interest of the American people it is necessary to substitute among our banks neighborliness for isolation, cooperation for antagonism. That is to say, our series of banks should be confederated into a system of banks. McCleary, James T., <u>Banking and Currency Reform. Its Necessity, its Possibility, its Method</u>. (n.p., n.d. [1911 or 1912]),10, 11.

INVESTMENT BANKING

I

It cannot be doubted that the loan contractor ranks first among the ancestors of the modern investment banker both in Europe and America, although here he did not as yet exist during the Revolutionary War. Loans were then floated by offices managed by commissioners who were appointed by state authorities and remunerated by a commission. In fact one should not expect loan contracting in America during the 1770's and 1780's. This business was predicated on a market for securities and on the availability of surplus funds looking for permanent investment for the sake of drawing interest, neither of which prerequisites came into being here until after the war.

But the war at least prepared the way for loan contracting by giving numerous American businessmen an acquaintance with the methods of contracting.[1] As is generally known, the contract system for the furnishing of supplies to the troops was established in 1782, and thereafter contracts for supplies to the public authorities became rather common.[2] Furthermore, soon after the war there developed, with very active European participation, a highly speculative market in those public securities which had been floated during the conflict. State and Continental debt certificates were traded in order to profit from short term price fluctuations and were acquired in anticipation of assumption and funding.[3]

By the 1790's this market had become highly organized: public securities had been standardized in the process of being funded; dealings on credit had become common; quotations had begun to appear in newspapers; and security brokers and auction sales had come into existence and provided easy marketability. Nevertheless from the modern point of view this market was still primitive; true investors, especially smaller ones, i.e., people who wished to buy and hold securities for longer periods in order to draw interest regularly, had hardly entered it as yet. Funds which acumulated in that period were as a rule employed in trade or sunk in land, the traditional American form of investment; and retiring merchants had opportunities as silent partners and insurance underwriters, a new business for America which gained importance in the 1780's and 1790's.[4] Although true investors were not completely absent,[5] the market was dominated by merchants, and two reasons stand out for their entering it: big business in the eighteenth century was more speculative than it is today,[6] and large scale speculation was the one motive for the security dealings of merchants. In those years public securities accumulated temporarily in the hands of relatively few men who during the war had made fortunes ready to be invested in new types of ventures and large enough to permit their holders to wait for the appreciation of the acquired stocks. Such waiting was facilitated because these stocks constituted a satisfactory collateral for bank loans and for this reason alone their possession would have been highly desirable. But, as indicated, there was still a second motive for the early participation of merchants in the security market, namely, the possibility of acquiring an interest-bearing medium of exchange.

Securities have long lost their character as media of exchange and today it is not easy to envisage them in that role. To understand it, one must keep in mind that prior to the establishment of commercial banks and to the creation of a national debt English and American merchants had to have enough coin on hand to take care of their peak loads. Or, as an eighteenth-century author expressed it, "commercial persons" must "always have an overplus or excedent quantity [of money] ready for any commercial purpose that might offer on any sudden or unexpected occasion."[7] If they locked up this surplus in their coffers it was idle and unproductive during such time. But the creation of public stocks provided a means "for the employment and circulation of this excedent quantity of money." Thus invested it produced an interest and remained "at the same time... always forthcoming by a retransfer on the most sudden occasion." Therefore by the middle of the eighteenth century public stocks first became a medium of exchange. No less a person than David Hume put his finger on the new phenomenon:[8]

Public securities are with us becoming a kind of money and pass as readily at the current price as gold and silver... No merchant thinks it necessary to keep by him any considerable cash. Bank stock or India bonds... serve all the same purposes because he can dispose of them or pledge them to a banker in a quarter of an hour... In short our national debts furnish merchants with a species of money that is continually multiplying in their hands.

By 1780 the custom of using public stocks as money was so common in England that in a theoretical context a previously quoted writer spoke of "paper money with which public stocks may (from their easy transfer) be in some degree included;"[9] and of the "axiom 'that public stocks of transferable annuities shall produce the same effects as would be produced by an increase in the quantity of circulating money.' " That is to say, the quantity theory of money was formulated so as to include public securities. (These statements are the more interesting as the author opposed them as incorrect, considering, as he did, public securities a commodity to be bought and sold in the market.) As late as the 1820's Russian, Prussian, and French stocks, originally subscribed by English investors provided "an international currency of the first importance in financing the corn trade;" after the crisis of 1837 securities were used by American merchants for remittances to England; and as late as the 1840's bonds of certain of our Southern states issued for the benefit of plantation banks were used by English businessmen for paying cotton imports into England.[10]

It goes without saying that America adopted the new and handy business method as soon as opportunity arose. During the Revolutionary War, loan office certificates, as well as other public securities, were used for the payment of supplies, and shortly thereafter, for the payment of land grants and confiscated estates.[11] At about the same time they entered American foreign trade as a medium of payments: Nicholas Brown of Providence, for instance, sent loan-office certificates to Amsterdam to be invested in goods,[12] and before long even store keepers would take them in payment.[13] Flight from Continental currency as well as speculation played a part in the fast adoption of the new kind of money.[14] Ultimately it became so firmly entrenched in the American practice that when Texas became independent her debt certificates, which her merchants received in payment from the original holders, were used by the former as a means of paying imports of merchandise from the United States. With hardly any other acceptable medium available the early Texan population was fed and clad with their help, so that a Houston merchant could claim that no country had ever derived more advantages from its public debt than Texas.[15] In the same period American securities were used currently by American banks, bankers, and merchants for remittances to English merchant bankers.[16] In fact, "bonds supplied a major export item by which Americans were enabled in the short run to pay for the excess of imports over exports of merchandise," as Hidy expresses it.

II

In England, in contrast to America, the loan contractor was known as early as the 1780's. Both prerequisites for his existence had sufficiently developed to permit his activities: by that time England possessed a well organized market[17] of public securities and at least a limited number of genuine investors. The former fact is generally known. The latter can be proved from the contemporary literature: An author writing in 1784 explained[18] that the public stocks had furnished "the industrious individuals with an opportunity of laying out their spare monies from time to time... whereby they may receive an interest for such sums as would otherwise... lay unemployed and unproductive." To be sure, he was afraid that ownership in the stocks might lead to idleness, for "as the public stocks furnish a certain and secure income free from toil and care some may be induced to place their property in the stocks and thereby live an easy and indolent life." A few years later the same author became even more explicit, distinguishing between three classes of British holders of public securities: "The first class of public creditors, to wit, those to whom the value of the capital is of more consequence than the interest or annuity, may be considered as comprehending all those that are engaged in business as bankers, merchants, and inferior tradesmen who have alternately from time to time an occasion for their capital in their respective callings and who when they have more money on hand than they have occasion for, lay it out in the stocks in order to obtain an interest for sums that would otherwise... lay idle..." In contrast the second class of public creditors consisted of those to whom the value of capital and interest were of equal importance. They needed the capital at a distant day and in the meantime lived on the interest. The author was thinking of people not in business themselves but having children to be provided for in the future. The third class, finally, consisted of those to whom the capital was of less "consequence" then the interest. If this classification is transposed into modern terms one recognizes that "public creditors" consisted of businessmen owning securities for business purposes, temporary investors, and permanent ones.[19] A publication written in 1795, although published later, makes the case watertight: its author speaks of "little annuitants who live entirely upon the interest of their capital which is sunk in the funds."[20]

The English investors' "class" in the 1780's was still in a rather embryonic stage[21] and therefore the market in securities did not cater primarily to genuine investors. Lack of maturity of this market found expression in its highly speculative character. New loans, the terms of which were "generally of a complicated nature," had to appeal rather to the speculative instinct of large subscribers and of middlemen. "A minister in 1781... observ[ed that] the then loan was indiscriminately taken and any interest to be procured by such a loan was a poor compensation for the fatigue and anxiety of the burthen and that no business could be more disagreeable than setting the terms."[22] Only through making use of the gambling instinct of the public and through the promise of high profits could English public securities be floated at that period:[23] There were "premiums," "bonuses," and "discounts." A premium was the difference between the price at which the subscriber bought and the price at which he could sell, due to the difference between the yield and the going rate of interest. Bonuses were the extras which the subscribers received in form of lottery tickets, annuities limited to a few years, and the like (the interest was usually payable from a date prior to the due date of the last installments); and discounts could be deducted if payments on the subscribed amounts were made before the agreed upon date.[24]

As early as about 1780 the loan contractor (i.e., a middleman subscribing for the purpose of resale) seems to have played a part in providing the market with new issues, a fact which can be deduced from contemporary publications. One finds, for instance, in that decade the distinction between the wholesale and the retail price of securities[25] and the remark that the "chief of the money supplied by the sundry bankers was generally the property of other people."[26] (A few years later, but only in the 1790's, an explicit statement was made to the effect that "the original subscribers to a loan parcel[ed] it out to many others.")[27] To be sure, the term loan contractor was still unknown.

For the 1780's a contemporary "expert" distinguished two (three) types of subscriptions to public loans: (1) They were either "private," "that is to say a certain number of persons of fortune... agreed to be answerable for the whole sum to be subscribed and... made the required

deposit." Or (2) they were (a) "open to the public" in which case every person known to be financially responsible was at liberty to apply as a contributor, naming in his letter the sum he desired to subscribe. Finally (b) in exceptional cases subscription books lay open to the general public at the Bank of England or the Exchequer and any person was allowed to subscribe what he thought proper.[28] When contemporary authors[29] spoke of "public" loans, they probably meant this last mentioned type of subscriptions, open to all (2,b). Loan contracting had to tie into this framework.

Although documentary proof seems to be lacking, one is able to depict with a high degree of probability the emergence of this type of business.[30] As the contemporary literature describes, participants in "private" subscriptions were assumed to subscribe not only such sums as they personally wished to keep permanently, but to include therein those of their friends and acquaintances. The latter as a rule received their shares "without any premium or for only [a] small one." In 1785 outsiders were advised to apply to participants in private subscriptions for such sums as they wanted. To the extent that such advice was followed by people having no connection with the subscribers, and to the extent that the latter saw in that practice the possibility of gain and made use of it, loan contracting must have developed out of what at an earlier time had been acts of courtesy.[31] In fact it was London bankers who first saw the chances; and in 1783 when £7,700,000 out of a £12,000,000 loan were allotted to them they began to develop and at the same time to dominate embryonic loan contracting.

And embryonic it still was in the 1780's: "When a war requires such fleets and armies as cannot be supported by the ordinary revenue," wrote Lord Effingham in 1782,[32] "it has been usual for a minister to confer in private with a few monied men as to the terms of a Loan [italics in original], that is a sum of money to be advanced to the public [authorities] in consideration of a certain interest to be paid and which is to be secured by a mortgage of certain taxes to be for that purpose imposed on the public." Another (anonymous) writer of the period[33] complained that the loan of 1781 was not "more open," that it was restricted and "distributed amongst a set of chosen subscribers." Finally, Dr. Richard Price claimed in 1783 that the government was in the hands of "rapacious money-jobbers;" (he also indicated that there were complaints about partiality in the distribution of new loans and about their being made an instrument of corruption).[34] A few moneyed men "monopolized" them and indigent ones solicited shares "with a view of traffic and gain."[35] In at least some of the "few monied men" with whom ministers conferred "in private," in the "set of chosen subscribers," in the "rapacious money-jobbers" who solicited shares "with a view of traffic and gain" the historian will recognize businessmen who soon were to be come generally known as loan contractors. The rest of the subscribers still represented older types of English public creditors: corporations, rich noblemen, wealthy merchants, and politicians, many of whom did not look at their subscriptions as investments, but rather as remuneration for services rendered or as leading to advantages other then drawing interest. They considered "their portion of a subscription as a douceur or a reward."[36]

Not before 1796 did the author find in the contemporary literature examined by him the terms "contracting a loan" and "contractor for a loan."[37] But in that year the latter phrase was used in an official document[38] almost throughout in a technical sense, a fact which by itself would be indicative of a comparatively advanced stage of the development. Moreover certain discussions which took place in the mid-1790's make it clear beyond doubt that loan contracting was then becoming an independent and established type of business enterprise: A question of principle came up in connection with the British loan for 1796; namely, whether or not a loan contractor could make an agreement with the government which gave certain advantages to him as distinct from the subscribers to whom he sold the scrip. This question involved the broader one as to whether or not the loan contractor was an independent link in a chain or a mere representative of subscribers; or, in other words, whether loan contracting was a business enterprise. Conservatives denied it, thinking of the situation described above as characteristic of the early 1780's. Walter Boyd, on the other hand, the loan contractor to be studied shortly and then under fire, broached what was supposed to be a novel doctrine, a doctrine which was well in line with the most recent development: he distinguished clearly between "subscribers" and "contractors." The latter had specific responsibilities of their own. In order to succeed they must have an "exclusive lease of the money market till the last payment [was] made on the loan for which they [had] contracted and this right [was] reserved to them even after they had parted with their script."[39] To this theory the conservatives answered that "these contractors... [were] not to be considered as more than a deputation from the great body of subscribers, entrusted for the convenience of business with the arrangement of the loans on their behalf. ...Extraordinary risk as contractors they have none; or if they have, it is their own fault inasmuch as they may require the same security from their fellow subscribers which government requires from themselves." The new type of business was thus completely misunderstood.

No less a person then William Pitt[40] had a strong influence on the form in which full-fledged loan contracting emerged. Throughout the eighteenth century it had been customary for the Chancellor of the Exchequer, guided by the market price for older issues, to fix the price, the rate of interest, and the conditions of a new loan[41] in such a way that the "omnium"[42] would be quoted above par at the stock exchange; otherwise he would have been unable to float the issue. Successive Chancellors of the Exchequer considered it wise to let subscribers to new loans make even handsome profits. (As late as 1803 when the contractors to the loan for that year were losing money, Addington, then Chancellor of the Exchequer, expressed the expectation that ultimately the loan would "turn out advantageous to [them] because the House must be sorry when honourable and public-spirited men who [came] forward to assist the nation [suffered] loss for their zeal to promote the service."[43] Thus the customary method did not work to the detriment of the subscribers to a loan, although their influence on the terms of new issues was very limited.

This practice was changed for the first time in 1784. When Pitt funded the floating debt in that year, "he took the then novel step of offering the loan for public tender and accepting the most advantageous terms."[44] When thus appealing directly to a wider public Pitt may have acted under the influence of Richard Price who was in favor of "public" loans;[45] and the fact that he asked for tenders can be explained as follows: Prior to 1784 saving of interest was considered most important by the Exchequer[46] and to achieve this end, loans were endowed with advantages appealing to speculators. Among others they were floated far below par; but successive English governments were then not much concerned about repaying the loans and they therefore were not worried by their promises to pay a larger sum than they had received. Pitt, in contrast, introduced new aims and consequently originated a new policy, which, however, he could not uphold all the way through, as will be shown forthwith. He desired an ultimate debt reduction and therefore a favorable issue price. On the other hand, he was perfectly willing to pay a higher rate of interest since at that moment the current revenue seemed to outrun the current needs. The method of asking for public tenders may have been chosen because it permitted him to feel out the market regarding the lowest possible rate of interest; it was certainly introduced to make public loans competitive ventures. A letter from Walter Boyd to Pitt speaks of the latter's "predilection in favor of public competition."[47] Such competition[48] (expected to work to the benefit of the Exchequer) was not meant to be one among loan contractors alone, but between "monied men" in general, i.e., both large investors and loan contractors. Or as Pitt expressed it in 1794, when he actually succeeded in "exciting"[49] it, he was encouraging an open and public competition among all persons who were desirous of entering into an agreement;[50] (while the preceding loan of 1793 had to be concluded with "the only set of men who had waited upon him to negotiate the loan"). In those years methods were flexible and had to be so. In December, 1794, Pitt was forced to make a contract for the following year with Boyd, Benfield and Company, since an Austrian loan then pending in London was not to be disturbed, a statement which will be understood shortly. When another loan became necessary for the year 1796, before the one for 1795 was fully paid up, competition was fostered again; but Boyd, the contractor for the latter, convinced Pitt that he should have the option on the new loan at 1/2 per cent above the highest offer in fairness, if not as a right. Thereupon the other interests withdrew.[51] Beginning with the "Loyalty Loan" of December, 1796, however, all of Pitt's remaining loans seem to have been intended to be competitive; but in reality the strongest contractors cooperated instead of competing with each other.

There may have been good reason why the business of floating public loans did not become as competitive as Pitt had meant to make it.[52] Simultaneously with the emergence of the full-fledged loan contractor the next step of the development (progress from loan contracting to genuine investment banking) peered over the horizon: individual ultimate investors were dropping out from among the original "contributors" to a loan[53] leaving the field to the middlemen. What Pitt had in mind became an actuality only in the very successful so-called "Loyalty Loan" for 1797,(mentioned above).[54] Here met, probably for the first time, traditional public loan subscribers with loan contractors in open competition: The East India Company took two million pounds; the Bank of England one; "most other public companies in smaller proportion;" while the rest went to individual investors and loan contractors.[55] But at this very moment new forces were coming into play. In his masterful contemporary treatment of the subject of public credit Nebenius showed clearly that once competition was established participation in new flotations

could come only by large concerns which not only had considerable capital themselves, but at the same time wide connections and credit and thereby access to additional funds.[56] Thus the by-product of Pitt's policy of establishing competition in the field was the undesired exclusion of the ultimate investor as a subscriber. This led in the long run almost immediately after it had come into existence to a lessening of that competition which he desired; for those powerful loan-contracting middlemen who came to dominate the field preferred cooperation to competition. By 1795 it seems to have become rather common for them to act as "joint contractors,"[57] a device in which can be seen the very beginning of what later became investment bankers' syndicates. In so doing the loan contractors developed an older practice: While the participants in earlier eighteenth-century private subscriptions and the embryonic loan contractors of the 1780's had "formed lists" of ultimate investors to back up their offers, the formers' successors of the 1790's formed lists of loan contractors, subcontractors, and ultimate investors.

The "forming" of lists which were presented with the offer or bid[58] probably served several purposes. It enabled the contractor, who was responsible to the government for the fulfilment of the contract, to shift some of his risk to wealthy and reliable people who participated in the advantages accruing to him as an original contributor.[59] The sources are not explicit as to whether or not capitalists admitted to the rank of original contributors paid the contractor a commission; but it seems possible. The government, on the other hand, through the medium of the Bank of England which examined the lists submitted by the would-be contractor, seems to have gained thereby an assurance that the party in question was reliable and strong enough to be trusted. Consequently, when alliances of contractors were as strong as those formed in 1794 and 1795 by Walter Boyd, the lists became secondary as far as the government was concerned; and the contractors themselves looked at the device from a different angle: admission to the list was, in their eyes, equal to the bestowing of a favor. And it probably was. It is known, for instance, that Abraham Newland, for many years (1778-1807) principal cashier of the Bank of England, became wealthy by purchasing shares in the various flotations of public loans directly from the government as an original contributor. His investments of that sort were characterized by his biographer as "speculations large in the sum, tolerably secure in the result."[60] Under these circumstances it was considered fair that capitalists should be on one list only. James Morgan, a loan contractor of the early 1790's, for instance, made his subscribers sign an affidavit that they were on no other list, unless they were directors of the Bank of England or known to him because of their high ethics. It is possible that he thereby also intended to weaken his competitors. Walter Boyd did not go so far: if he suspected that applicants for his list also were on another, as some undoubtedly were, he treated them less liberally.[61]

Subscribers to a list, as a rule, were not solicited: they applied to the would-be contractor by letter or "verbally."[62] Boyd, at times, seems to have been swamped by applications and to have allotted shares pro rata. James Morgan, on the other hand, venturing for the first time into the new field in February, 1794, came pretty near to soliciting subscriptions. He had blanks printed which he deposited "at the bar at Garraway's."[63] These blanks read as follows:[64]

> Sir,
> I desire to subscribe in the list you are forming for the intended loan Thousand Pounds Omnium;[65] and I promise and engage to make the deposit and not to have any concern or interest directly or indirectly in any other list; and that no person shall have any part or interest in my subscription, but on the same conditions to be declared and observed.

It was the policy of the contractors to keep their lists secret as far as the public, government, or parliament were concerned. One of the subcontractors in 1796 referred to a "general rule time immemorial not to divulge the situation of the accounts in their books without being forced so to do."[66] The reasons can only be inferred from casual statements: some of the bankers did not wish their names revealed because they were afraid that some of their customers would blame them for not having assigned a share in the new loan to them or for not having assigned a sufficiently large one. Religious objections were referred to: the author suspects that Quakers subscribed to the war loans and quite naturally wished that their names be kept secret. Finally, political reasons are mentioned: it is possible that enemies of the government in power did not wish to appear to back its success by contributing to a loan floated for purposes to which their own party was opposed. For "the difficulties which every minister met in every new loan were more in proportion to the power of the opposition than to the fairness or need of the demand. In unpopular wars these difficulties were doubly increased."[67] Some of the speculators or investors for which English subscribers acted were

foreigners, which may have been another reason for keeping the lists secret. But in 1796 the House of Commons suspected corruption on the part of the group in power and set out to discover it.[68] Fearful of such attempts some of the contractors and other subscribers played safe and, in order to keep strictly behind the scenes, contracted under the name of dummies as the Goldsmids[69] occasionally did. It also happened that clerks or relatives of contractors or subcontractors appeared on lists in order to shift the burden of endorsing the receipts from the head or heads of large firms to employees or less busy people.[70] (One is reminded of Biddle's trouble in signing notes of the Second Bank of the United States!)

There are reprinted in the Appendix to this chapter three contemporary documents, the loan contract of February, 1794, the loan contract for the year 1795, and the preliminary offer of a loan contractor (James Morgan) of November, 1795.[71] They give a very clear idea of the way flotations of loans were handled in England in the 1790's. Moreover the parliamentary report of 1796, from which the documents were taken and which represents the most important extant source in the field, contains further information which permits the historian to reconstruct with a high degree of probability the business of loan contracting: It was the first job of a would-be loan contractor, while a new loan was pending, to provide for such amounts as he needed to pay for the first installment. Since public securities were his stock in trade he must be presumed to have held at all times certain amounts which he then was anxious to sell. In fact, as soon as a new loan was announced the market of public securities tended to decline. To this decline contributed the demand by would-be contractors that subscribers to their lists, to the extent that their solvency and reliability was not beyond doubt, deposit at least five per cent of their subscriptions. Those of whom no security was demanded were advised to be prepared for the first installment. In addition the would-be contractors appealed to friends and occasionally borrowed what the former could conveniently spare.[72]

Parallel with the financial preparations for the offer went the forming of a list, as had been described before. If the list in question represented in fact an alliance of loan contractors one or a few of them acted for the group.[73] Thus was developed the older practice under which the contractor was but the agent of the subscribers. Those representatives of the "party" in question settled the terms of the loan and bound everyone on the list: once thereon, the subscriber had no influence whatsoever.[74] The contractor, or in the case of an alliance the leading contractor or

contractors, did not necessarily wait for an invitation from the Chancellor of the Exchequer, but
might go after the business. Boyd, for instance,
offered Pitt a contract for the loan for 1796, and
so did Morgan whose second offer for that loan is
to be found in the Appendix.[75] In bidding or in
negotiating with the Chancellor of the Exchequer
the contractors were influenced by the prices for
old securities, by the optimistic or pessimistic
outlook of the public on national affairs, and by
the technical market situation: if the bears had
dominated the market lately it was expected to recover. Sometimes special messengers arrived
from the city bringing the most recent quotations
to the negotiators.[76] As soon as the deal was concluded the loan came to be traded in the market
for delivery, although the law did not recognize
such transactions; for legally a loan was considered as having taken place only after Parliament had voted it.[77]

The business of loan contracting was predicated
on the difference between the price of the omnium
and its market value, a difference which was traditionally considerable. Consequently contributors
admitted to the original lists tried to get as large
a share as possible, especially since they knew
that eager speculators, too insignificant to appear
on the lists, stood ready to purchase the stock at
a favorable price. The latter in turn did not
really mean to invest their own funds, but to gain
from price rises.[78] But the transactions by no
means lacked danger; the exact opposite was true.
Silberling has described the business as it was
conducted in the Napoleonic era.[79] According to
him, the loan contractors used the stock exchange
for selling the new securities and, for obvious
reasons, represented the bulls in the market.
Their antagonists (the bears) were the stockjobbers; Mark Sprott, one of them, contributed to
Walter Boyd's downfall. Later David Ricardo
came to play a more and more important role
among them. Under the existing loose stock exchange regulations the stockjobbers were often
able through manipulations to depress the prices
of new stock so that they could buy it in at "their
own low price," "at a fair jobbing price," as they
expressed it themselves. Then they sold the
stock on time charging a high rate of interest on
their advances and maintaining a depressed market as long as possible in order to discourage the
conclusion of the holdings on margin and to benefit from high interest charges for continuations.
To be sure, by the turn of the century, the stock
exchange itself intended to turn into an alliance of
loan contractors and it formed lists for all the
loans for the years 1798 through 1802. But the
business of the jobbers was of such a character

that they could not bid high enough and therefore
did not receive the contracts, except for a share in
the £20,000,000 loan for 1800. It seems that
Mark Sprott, the stockjobber who died in 1808, was
the leader in these attempts.

But there was still another element of risk involved: the contractor was, or the allied contractors jointly and severally were, liable "for the performance of the engagements entered into and before even the first payment was made upon the
loan." So, at least, was the situation with regard
to the loan for 1795. It is not known when such
liability was first established, but one may take it
for granted that once adopted it became common
for all later loans. This measure seems to have
been one of those essential for the emergence of
the contractor as an independent link in the chain.
When making the above quoted statement Boyd went
on: The loan contractors for 1795 "remained in
that state of responsibility during a period of very
great alarm, when Holland was overrun by the
French, in so much that the omnium fell down to
par and even to a quarter per cent discount." In
such a situation there was danger that subscribers
fearing further declines would abandon their deposits and even later installments rather than fulfill their obligations. They would thus limit their
present loss and shift any possible further one on
to the contractors who were bound to pay up the
whole amount contracted for.[80]

If one takes the loans for the service of government for the years 1795 and 1796 as examples one
finds a surprisingly wide range of participants. In
the former case, £1,500,000 out of £18,000,000
were set aside for institutional investors such as
the Bank of England, the East India Company, the
London Assurance Company, the South Sea Company, etc., which in the past had provided the bulk
of funds for British loans. Competition between
contractors and public companies was thereby
avoided. The balance of the loan was taken by an
alliance of eight contractors aided by numerous
subcontractors. The latter appeared on the lists
of the contractors but made up smaller lists of
their own. While the line between contractors and
subcontractors can be drawn clearly,[81] that between subcontractors and subscribers pure and
simple is blurred. Numerous subscribers, others
than avowed subcontractors, testified before the
Parliamentary Committee of 1796 that they had
subscribed for others as well as for themselves.
If the men in question were bankers subscribing
for customers and correspondents, as they testified, they may still be considered subcontractors.
But those who subscribed for themselves and
other members of their firm only, or men like one
Jaspar Atkinson, or the Governor of the Bank of

England who subscribed for themselves and friends did so as a matter of courtesy, as had been customary in earlier decades.[82]

After having discussed the emergence of loan contracting as a type of business enterprise in the 1780's and 1790's let us focus our attention on the men who brought it into being and on their firms. In the 1780's, as previously mentioned, London bankers dominated loan contracting, then still in an embryonic stage. Outstanding among them were Sir William Curtis, Andreas Grote, and the houses of Boldero and Dorrien. Curtis (1752-1829), a supporter of Pitt and a much ridiculed person, was the son and grandson of owners of a sea biscuit business. Later in his life he became a Lord Mayor of London and a member of Parliament. He developed the inherited enterprise branching out into Greenland fisheries and banking; and the banking house which he founded (under the name of Robarts, Curtis, Were and Company and which later became Robarts, Curtis, Robarts and Curtis, and finally Robarts, Curtis and Company) took a strong interest in loan contracting and remained in the field for a long time. We will meet the firm as late as the 1790's and 1800's in connection with British loans; in the former decade it contracted also for a £300,000 loan to the Irish government. Abraham Robarts then headed the firm which in 1794 became one of the strongest allies of Boyd, Benfield and Company, to be discussed shortly. Robarts was in fact Boyd's most active ally. Sharing in Boyd's temporary monopoly Robarts, Curtis and Company had their hands in all the loans for the years 1795 through 1799, having also bid unsuccessfully and independently on that for 1794. When Boyd, Benfield and Company was becoming insolvent the firm of Robarts, Curtis and Company remaining an ally of its former associates bid unsuccessfully on the loan for 1799; successfully on a later loan for the service of the same year, successfully for that of 1801, and unsuccessfully again for that of 1802.[83]

Prior to the 1790's a keen competitor of the Robarts-Curtis firm was Andreas Grote (1710-1788), a native of Bremen. He was a general merchant who established a banking business in 1766 in Threadneedle Street under the style of Grote, Prescott and Company. The remaining two houses appeared in the 1800's as Boldero, Lushington, Boldero and Lushington, 30 Cornhill, and Dorrien, Magens, Dorrien and Mello, 22 Finch Lane, respectively.[84] The names Grote, Boldero, and Dorrien or one or the other of them can still be found in connection with the loans for 1795, 1799, 1800, and 1802; and one or several of these firms were probably also among the "bankers" bidding for the loans for 1798 and 1801.

In the 1790's when the full-fledged loan contractor emerged simultaneously with the opening of the Napoleonic era, new firms tried their hands at the game. There was a strong Jewish element among the loan contractors of the period, although not to the same extent as among the jobbers at the stock exchange. (Cobbett, who hated these men, almost identified contractors and stock dealers with Jews.)[85] The loan floated in 1793 was contracted by Thellusson Brothers and Company, while that of February, 1794, was taken by a group consisting of James Morgan (who was considered respectable in point of solidity and character,[86] and also formed lists unsuccessfully for the loans of 1795 and 1796), John Julius Angerstein, to be discussed shortly, and Godschall Johnson, probably a German Jew. The loan for the service of the year 1795 was contracted by Walter Boyd and a "party" in which Abraham Robarts of the firm Robarts, Curtis and Company stood out (as just mentioned, it had been leading among the loan contractors of the 1780's). Boyd's other allies[87] were Benjamin and Abraham Goldsmid, Thellusson Brothers and Company[88] (a Huguenot firm), and four firms of jobbers: John and George Ward, Rawson Aislabie, E. P. Salomons, and Solomon Salomons.

It is not within the province of this chapter to review the British loan contracts of the 1790's and 1800's or to present a complete list of the contractors and unsuccessful bidders.[89] But attention must be focused on the alliance under the leadership of Boyd just mentioned which came to dominate British loan contracting for most of the 1790's. In that decade Walter Boyd was actually the most important of the fraternity and perhaps, too, the creative entrepreneur who saw all the opportunities and, specializing in this type of transactions, brought the business to its full development. Boyd (about 1756-1837), a plunger, politically an ardent supporter of Pitt, was originally a Paris banker, working under the firm name of Boyd, Ker & Co.[90] During the Revolution he had to flee for his life, went to London, and in 1793 established the house of Boyd, Benfield and Company. (His partner, Paul Benfield, a very rich man, had become notorious because of some transactions concluded while he was a civil servant of the East India Company.) In December, 1794, Boyd entered the field of loan contracting; and for a few years thereafter his firm did a tremendous business contracting in cooperation with other firms for the English £18,000,000 loan for 1795, the £18,000,000 loan for 1796, the £7,500,000 of April, 1796, the £14,500,000 for 1797, the £17,000,000 for 1798, and an Irish loan. All told he probably contracted for about £20,000,000 on account of his concern. In addition, in 1795 and 1797 Boyd, Benfield and Company as the "agents" of the Emperor took two Imperial loans[91] floated in London.

S. R. Cope has written the history of Boyd, Benfield and Company in an excellent Ph.D. thesis.[92] In it he has shown in detail and explained convincingly how it was possible for a newcomer to London to acquire within a few months a quasi-monopoly in contracting for tens of millions of pounds in British loans which lasted for a lustrum. Boyd while still in Paris working under the firm name of Boyd, Ker and Company had a partner Walckiers who was close to a great mercantile house in Brussels, bankers to the Emperor. Through this contact Boyd, Benfield and Company became agents of the Emperor in London when the Austrian government was attempting to borrow English capital in 1794. While this loan was pending it became obvious to Boyd that British guarantee was necessary for the success of the flotation and that the King's government would not take such action unless it was certain that its own needs would be met. Thus Boyd allied himself with the extraordinarily strong group of businessmen and capitalists previously mentioned and managed to receive his first contract for £18,000,000 for the service of the year 1795 even without competition. The logic of the development is obvious: Boyd started with the Austrian loan and was drawn into the first British contract to make the former succeed; vice versa the first British contract was awarded to him since the Austrian loan, politically important for the British government, must not be disturbed.

The next step in the firm's expansion was equally logical: while the allied contractors waited for the ultimate consummation of the Austrian loan and grew tired of keeping idle funds, that were ready for paying the first installment, an Irish loan was advertised. In order to keep his allies together Boyd immediately went after the English part of the issue and in March, 1795, successfully bid for the group on £1,100,000 and the 40,000 tickets of the Irish lottery.[93]

Once Boyd had attained a firm foothold in the field, through shrewd strategy and unusually strong contacts and alliances he fortified his position and developed it into a near-monopoly. For this purpose he added to the original group of his allies when bidding on the loan for 1796. Daniel Giles, for many years a director and then the governor of the Bank of England, was accommodated on his list, and potential competitors, such as the most influential J. J. Angerstein (mentioned before and to be discussed shortly) and Godschall Johnson, were successfully invited to join. In astute negotiations in which he was seconded by

Abraham Robarts he succeeded in being awarded a second British contract, that of £18,000,000 for 1796, again without competition. There was something to a contemporary attack on Boyd which pointed out that he had got the loan for 1796 because he had that for 1795, and that for 1795 because he had that for the Emperor, and that this chain was liable to grow. In fact because he had the contract for 1796 Boyd received also without competition the supplementary £7,500,000 contract of April of that year, and he was also able without competition to obtain the contract for the loan of £14,500,000 for 1797. This preferential treatment was due in part to the extraordinary, valuable, and discreet services which Boyd, a past master in exchange operations, provided to the Treasury when transferring funds to the Continent.

At this point sailing became less smooth. The later £18,000,000 for the service of the year 1797 were raised by a public subscription, and there was competition for the loan for 1798. By that time Boyd's firm was already tottering. Regardless of his great gifts Boyd was always in danger, gambler that he was. He lacked sound judgment; his firm was continuously overexpanded; he always played for high stakes without hedging; and because of such methods he was unable to make friends among the leading London merchants. These pivoted around the Bank of England whose measures Boyd counteracted repeatedly. His bull operations in the funds to support the market led to heavy losses and were responsible more than any other single factor for his failure. But political and economic events over which he had no control contributed to his difficulties and ultimate downfall, the responsibility for which he himself attributed to the Bank of England. In 1798, however, backed by his old allies, Boyd was still able to secure the £17,000,000 loan for that year; but feeling insecure he cut the offer unnecessarily fine so that there was little profit in the contract. And when that for the service of 1799 was announced in December, 1798, Boyd's former allies forced him not only to give up the leadership of the group, but even to withdraw therefrom, although they were willing to give him a participation of £500,000. Nevertheless he bid once more, this time in alliance with J. J. Angerstein and the banker Devaynes,[94] but he could not secure the contract; and when he tried his luck again in June, 1799, bidding in alliance with rather unknown houses he had fallen so low that Pitt requested the representative of the group to withdraw voluntarily. Thus ended Boyd's remarkable hegemony in the field of loan contracting. His house was put in liquidation in 1799 and in 1800 declared bankrupt.

It is of particular interest to find among Boyd's

allies John Julius Angerstein (1735-1823), the "celebrated banker," to use Nolte's expression,[95] for he was one of the English business leaders of the period. Born in St. Petersburg, the scion of a respectable Hanoverian merchants' family, a branch of which had settled in Russia and traded mainly with England, he went to London as a boy and was educated in the counting house of Andrew Thompson, an eminent Russia-merchant, one of the underwriters frequenting Lloyd's coffee house. A young man of unusual brilliance Angerstein started as a broker and independent underwriter at the age of but twenty-one, procuring the capital needed in his business prior to the acquisition of a fortune of his own by forming several partnerships in which he was the undoubted head. Angerstein rose to prominence in the 1770's when the underwriters, brokers, and merchants assembling at Lloyd's were first organized into a "system of membership." To be sure, he did not initiate the organization but he did succeed where others had failed before. After another few years of experience, especially in the 1790's, Angerstein developed new methods and policies in the field of marine-insurance underwriting which were almost blindly followed by other underwriters who trusted his sagacity and integrity. In that period he was for years the chairman and leader of the "gentlemen who compose[d] the committee for conducting the affairs of the society."

That this man entered the field of loan contracting is not surprising, for he belonged to Pitt's confidential advisers and is supposed to have suggested to him in the 1780's the use of lotteries as a regular means for raising revenue.[96] Angerstein went even further: he and his "party" contracted for one half of the tickets of the first lottery launched under the new scheme which he had helped to devise. Thereafter he came to take a keen interest in the contracting of public loans, and his "lists" were supposed to have "ranked among the first" backed as he was by the most respectable merchants. Moreover he not only contracted for loans, but also invested considerable amounts therein so that ultimately there were "very few public funds in which his name [did] not stand annexed to considerable sums." Angerstein can be found[97] as a bidder in 1793, and as a stand annexed in 1794 when he cooperated with James Morgan and Godschall Johnson. During the years when Boyd dominated the field Angerstein seems to have kept aloof; but in 1798 he again appeared on the scene although as an unsuccessful bidder and an ally of Boyd who was then looking for new friends. A few months later, however, in cooperation with the Barings, Godschall Johnson, and the bankers Devaynes and Company he secured a share in the £15,000,000 contract. In 1801 he was again among the successful bidders who included the Barings, Thellussons, Goldsmids, and Robarts, Curtis and Company; while in 1802 being once more a member of this group he lost out to a competing one.

By 1800 the Barings, then styled Francis Baring and Company (but usually called Sir Francis Baring and Company), began to become important among the London loan contractors. Francis Baring had taken an interest in security dealings as early as the 1780's when he traded in certificates of indebtedness of the United Kingdom; in the 1790's he sold in England on account of the American Treasury 6 per cent United States bonds. Moreover Francis Baring was a holder of East India and Bank of England stock, through such holdings and transactions being well prepared to take a hand also in security flotations. He seems to have entered loan contracting in connection with the Loyalty Loan for 1797. A few years later his firm was forging ahead in the new field: in 1799, as mentioned above, Francis Baring and Company allied with strong houses took a share of the loan of that year; and in 1801 cooperating with J. J. Angerstein among others the firm was again successful in securing a slice of a £28,000,000 loan. It was unsuccessful, however, in 1802 when it was once more backed by Angerstein. So much can be said about the firm's early interest in loan contracting.

In the year 1802, the Barings acquired from the American government the latter's stock in the First Bank of the United States. Shortly thereafter when the Louisiana deal between the United States and France had hardly been completed, they took over, together with Hope and Company of Amsterdam, the $12,500,000 Louisiana bonds which neither French bankers, nor the Bank of France wished to handle. As a matter of fact, Alexander Baring, Sir Francis's son soon become the guiding spirit of the firm, and Pièrre César Labouchère, the head of Hope and Company, were in Paris during the summer of 1803; and, possibly on the basis of a preliminary promise to the United States government, an agreement was concluded between the French government and the two houses. They took the securities at 78½ and Alexander Baring, to accelerate the execution of the contract, embarked for the United States. There, after the ratification of the treaty, he obtained in January, 1804, one third of the bonds as security for an advance to the French treasury. They were made out in the Register's Office "unto Francis Baring and Company of London, Merchants, or their assigns." (Under the law of November 10, 1803, the bonds were to be delivered to the French government or to such persons as might be authorized to receive them.) The remainder of the bonds taken to Europe by a messenger were handed to the Hopes of Amsterdam, a firm which will be studied shortly. Out of the total, 6 1/2 million dollars were placed in London and 5 million in Holland.[98]

Not before 1810 did the Barings become leaders in the field of loan contracting. In that year they contracted in alliance with Abraham Goldsmid a £14,000,000 loan, a dangerous transaction which proved the latter's undoing. Only from then on did the house begin to dominate the business. In 1813 the Barings and their allies were allocated a £28,000,000 loan and in 1815 they carried away the £30,000,000 loan of that year in cooperation with Smith, Payne and Smiths. As in earlier cases blocks of this loan were sold through correspondents on the Continent.

Between Boyd's downfall in 1799 and 1810 not the Barings but Goldsmid and Company were in the vanguard of the British loan contractors, being the first members of the stock exchange who turned to that business. Goldsmid and Company consisted of the brothers Benjamin (about 1753-1808) and Abraham Goldsmid (about 1756-1810).[99] Their father, a Dutch Jew, had come to England by 1750, and by 1776 the two sons started as bill brokers, being, as Benjamin's biographer claims, the first in London. "Middlemen between the Merchant and the Monied Interest" were "wholly unknown on the Royal Exchange till that time." If this statement is true and they actually transferred this sort of business from Holland to England they must have been creative entrepreneurs while still in their twenties.[100] Before this time, of course, buyers and sellers of bills had been brought together by brokers, too; but prior to the Goldsmids, so it is claimed, no broker had ever specialized in the field. From bill brokerage the road was soon to lead to dealing in bills and, in fact, what later became the business of Richardson, Overend and Company was anticipated by the brothers Goldsmid by twenty years: Banks which had surplus balances bought bills from the Goldsmids; those which needed cash sold them some of the bills which had previously been discounted. The Goldsmids' business was supplemented by dealings in foreign drafts and remittances. It was hit by the outbreak of the war in the 1790's and the brothers were then forced to go into another field in which they were destined to become outstanding. In 1793 they first shifted their interest to short term government securities, such as Exchequer, navy, transport, and victualling bills. But they not only dealt in those securities; they also became government brokers and as such successfully executed extensive and difficult transactions in navy bills between 1800 and 1802.

A few years after the Goldsmids had first taken an interest in short term government securities, they also entered the field of loan contracting. Their first transaction of this character was the participation in the contract for 1795, Boyd, Benfield and Company being the leaders of the alliance. In the following years they were steady allies of that house until its decline began. In 1799 they severed this connection and bid successfully in alliance with Robarts, Curtis and Company and E. P. Salomons, receiving a share in the loan of that year; in 1800 they joined Sir Francis Baring and Company and Daniel Giles and bid unsuccessfully on a £20,000,000 loan. In 1801 Goldsmid and Company, the Barings, and Robarts, Curtis and Company succeeded in carrying away a £2,000,000 contract. A year later the Goldsmids and their allies were outbid by Smith, Payne and Smiths and in 1803 by Sir James Esdaile and Company. The latter, however, ran into difficulties and the Goldsmids took the loan off their hands. The loans of 1804 and 1805 they contracted without competition, but in 1806 for the first time they met (successfully) that of David Ricardo, soon to become their bitter rival. In 1808 Benjamin Goldsmid committed suicide and the firm was reorganized, the stock operations being taken over by the newly-founded firm of A. Goldsmid and Company. This firm in alliance with Sir Francis Baring and Company contracted for the £14,000,000 loan of May, 1810. The loan was disappointing; and while the amount retained by Abraham Goldsmid's firm was no more than £800,000, he increased his own holdings in the attempt to bolster the market. Losses adding to his depression over his brother's death and the effects of an accident, impelled him to shoot himself in despair in September of that year.[101]

When the loan contracting business of the Goldsmids became as extensive as it did, they devised methods which, new for the time, were to be further developed later. In their own interest they had to sustain the market and did so by standing ever ready to lend on consols at 5 per cent. Thus they invaded the business of the stock brokers and made bitter enemies. The funds needed for such transactions they raised themselves by borrowing from bankers on call, using government securities as collateral. It is not certain whether they introduced call loans in the London money market; if not, they certainly popularized them. There was no firm in the Napoleonic era which contributed more to the success of war finance than the Goldsmids. Moreover they seem to have done a considerable business in selling British loans outside of Britain, fostering capital flight from the

Continent. By their buying and lending policies they upheld the value of British stocks at home and abroad and gave them "circulation," a contemporary expression which probably meant that the Goldsmids contributed to the stocks being used as media of exchange in foreign countries and international trade.

Smith, Payne and Smiths, the last of the large loan contractors of the period, became important in the field by 1800 although they seem to have subscribed to earlier loans beginning with those of the 1770's. In the 1790's they were the bankers of Boyd, Benfield and Company financing to a certain extent the latter's contracts but withdrawing their support when they became suspicious of the firm's solvency. It may be assumed that this connection gave them an insight into the business of loan contracting. They appeared, for example, as subcontractors of Boyd, Benfield and Company to the £18,000,000 loan for the year of 1795. In December, 1798, they themselves bid for the first time, though unsuccessfully, on the £3,000,000 loan for 1799, one of their allies being Daniel Giles, previously mentioned. But six months later they scored their first success while bidding in alliance with Giles and Newnham, Everett and Company on a £15,500,000 loan, sharing it with two other groups of contractors. In 1801 unaided by allies they formed a list of their own and competed with Robarts and Company, the Barings, and Goldsmids who had formed an alliance; the Committee of Bankers, Newnham, Everett and Company and their friends; and the stock exchange; but they were outbid by the first-named group. A year later they were again successful and in alliance with James Morgan subscribed for the whole of the £25,000,000 loan for 1802, being victorious over the Committee of Bankers, the stock exchange, Newnham, Everett and Company, an alliance of the Barings with John Julius Angerstein, Robarts and Company, and Esdaile and Company. It was rumored at that time that Smith, Payne and Smiths had made the lowest bid because, having speculated, they had to contract for consols in order not to be at the mercy of the stock exchange. While in 1801 and 1802 Smith, Payne and Smiths appeared as competitors of the Barings, in 1804 they joined forces with them contracting for a £15,000,000 loan of that year; and in 1815 the two firms again cooperated in taking a £30,000,000 loan. As to the loans of the intervening years nothing has come to the attention of the author, but one can be certain that Smith, Payne and Smiths had their hands in some of these flotations also.[102]

Toward the end of the Napoleonic era, as indicated in passing, the business of loan contracting tended to concentrate in a few hands. The reasons were various: The business was risky, as can be seen from the failure of the two firms which were at one time or another leaders in the field, the Boyds and the Goldsmids. In fact success depended on the course of the political events, on borrowing facilities, especially the policy of the Bank of England,[103] and the ability to counteract the manipulations of hostile stockjobbers.[104] Or, in other words, success depended to a large extent on factors over which the loan contractor had no control; and it is therefore not surprising that after the failure of some, others were frightened away. On the other hand, as time went on the capital required in the business became larger and larger. Consequently by 1815 besides Smith, Payne and Smiths the Barings almost alone had survived as active participants in the field in Britain. When in 1817 Prussia thought of floating a loan in London an official representative reported home that there were only three firms able to transact this business.[105] (Undoubtedly he referred to the Barings and the Rothschilds just entering the field, while the third firm cannot be identified with certainty; he may have meant Smith, Payne and Smiths.) By that time in connection with European and American reconstruction the business was taking an international turn, as will be described later, and became so big that only the very strongest houses could participate. At least this was the case in the European game which was assuming the character of truly modern investment banking.[106]

III

An early, perhaps the very earliest, American attempt to adopt the business of loan contracting can be traced to the 1780's. It is significant that this attempt was made by some of the biggest American security speculators of the period, who acted in cooperation with European bankers. Of the Americans concerned one was Andrew Craigie (1743-1819), apothecary general of the Revolutionary Army, wholesale apothecary, financier, and speculator of Boston and New York. Another was William Duer (1747-1799), one of the leading businessmen, promotors, and speculators of the time, who after having been the secretary to the Board of Treasury in 1786, became in 1789 Assistant Secretary of the Treasury. In October, 1788, these two men concluded a contract with the French banker Etienne Clavière[107] and with Jean Pierre Brissot de Warville (1754-1793), French writer then traveling in America and soon to become a leader of the Girondists. The purpose of the contract was to obtain from the Court of France a transfer of the debt due to that crown from the United States. However these men were not the only Americans who were after the business. In December, 1788, after having reached an agreement with the Duer interests, Robert Morris sent his confidant, Gouverneur Morris, to Europe to work for such a transfer too;[108] and finally there was still another American interested in a scheme of that character, namely Daniel Parker[109] who was backed by the French banker Le Coulteux de Cantaleu.[110] Parker may even have been the first to conceive the project and he may have originally cooperated with the Duer group. In the context of the present chapter the projected transaction is of the highest interest: had it succeeded, which it did not, the successful group or groups would have originated securities for the market as modern investment bankers do; and like contemporaneous loan contractors they would have sold in small lots those securities acquired at wholesale. The contract alluded to between Duer and Craigie, on the one hand, and the two Frenchmen, on the other, went even further: it contained a clause contemplating that the allies would "negotiate all loans which by the United States in Congress may be entrusted to their negotiation." This clause indicates that with regard to additional business in American securities the group did not think of loan contracting, but of "negotiations" Continental style, to be described shortly.[111] The attempt here sketched represents one of those cases in which economic development took place imperceptibly and unbeknown to the participants. Parker, Duer, Craigie, and Morris certainly aimed at nothing they considered spectacular and undoubtedly were unaware that they were endeavoring to do something extraordinary for America. In their minds they just concocted a "speculation."

Very little, if any, progress toward loan contracting was made in the years following assumption and funding. When capital was needed by the general government in 1796, subscription books were opened; but only $80,000 was subscribed of an authorized $5,000,000 loan. More successful was the same method in 1798 when more than $6,000,000 could be so raised. In 1798 and 1799 the builders of ships for the Navy were paid with a 6 per cent stock, payable at pleasure, and with the selling of the securities left to them. About a decade later, in 1807, deferred 6 per cent and 3 per cent stock was converted into new 6 per cent securities (redeemable at the pleasure of the government) by opening subscription books at the Treasury and several loan offices. Banks did not as yet play any role in these transactions.[112] However when the loan of 1798 was approved by Congress a feature was adopted which was soon to become typical of early nineteenth-century American loan flotations and which at the same time was to influence the methods of American loan contractors: Pitt's policy described above of asking for public tenders was embodied in the loan act. The reason therefor was that it appeared impossible to obtain money if the rate of return was fixed and if the moneyed interests were not consulted at least to a certain extent.[113] There was opposition in Congress to the new device, and objections were voiced again when a similar clause was inserted in the act authorizing the loan of 1800. A decade later such opposition prevailed, and the loans of 1810 and 1812 were advertised with fixed terms. The latter loan was a failure, however, and in the $16,000,000 loan of 1813 Congress was forced again to take recourse to Pitt's policy which became standard practice thereafter.

The first full-fledged loan contractors emerged in America in the spring of 1813 when Girard, Astor, and Parish took over what had remained unsold of that $16,000,000 loan authorized by Act of Congress of February 8, 1813.[114] It seems highly significant that all three men were foreign born and that David Parish, the leader in the transaction in question, belonged to the European "haute finance" of the day, being a son of the great Hamburg banker, John Parish. (He had come to America as the representative of Baring Brothers and Company of London and Hope and Company of Amsterdam.) The new role of loan contractors was embraced very reluctantly by these men. Prior to advertising the loan of 1813 Gallatin, the Secretary of the Treasury, had suggested a "private subscription," as one would have called it in London, by which Parish, Astor, Girard, and Herman LeRoy of New York would have taken over $10,000,000 of the issue. This plan did not materialize. Only after the failure of the subsequent "public" subscription was a commission offered, such as was common on the Continent, although unknown in London. When this commission of 1/4 per cent was proposed and it was obvious to them that subscribers could be reached through business channels, Girard, Astor, and Parish saw chances for profit. Taking the remainder of the loan at a rate of 88 for ultimate resale they turned loan contractors.[115] Parish and Girard jointly subscribed $7,055,800 (of which they were able to unload $2,950,000 immediately)[116] and Astor took $2,056,000. Loan contracting was thus established in America. Slightly later the terms of the $25,000,000 loan of 1814 specified, in line with English tradition, that all subscribers, large and small alike, must meet the same conditions. Thereby would-be loan contractors who could now be expected as bidders were put on the same level as ultimate investors.

The first native American to see the profit chance and to become a loan contractor was Jacob Barker.[117] He soon provided keen competition to the Parish-Girard-Astor combine. The latter, upon the approval by Congress of the $25,000,000 loan of 1814, was once more planning to contract either for the whole loan or for parts thereof. The securities, so required, were to be sold in Amsterdam and in England (sic!). Astor submitted two alternative suggestions to the Secretary of the Treasury.[118] The one was to "negotiate" the securities for the government on a commission basis; the other was to contract them, credit to be given by the government for the time during which the securities would be sold for the account of the combine. The sale was to be effected by Parish who was to go to Europe for that purpose. This scheme was further detailed when the government seemed inclined to favor the latter method: Parish personally proposed in Washington to contract immediately $4,000,000 or $5,000,000 of the securities at 88, the proceeds to be deposited in Stephen Girard's Banking House and to be drawn upon as the government required funds. The rest was to be payable after four months, while the interest on the bonds would begin to accrue immediately. The commission was to be 1/4 of one per cent. However, if Parish were to go to Europe as he was planning, the contract was to be for $10,000,000 at 1½ per cent commission. No deal was ever concluded. As a condition of the contract, the combine required permission to ship European goods to this country both on its own account and on that of the government, the latter at 2½ per cent commission. That is to say, the plan implied the import of capital in the form of commodities, thus financing a part of the cost of the War.

That condition may have been the reason for the failure. It is possible, however, that Barker's competition played at least a contributory role. This aggressive businessman had tried to enter the new field in the wake of the combine. Hardly had the $16,000,000 loan of 1813 been completed when he started to collect subscriptions in anticipation of future needs of the Treasury. He "formed a list" like contemporaneous English loan contractors and was actually able to get commitments for an amount of $2,400,000. Thereupon he repaired to Washington and tendered a loan of $5,000,000 as "an agent... deputed by a large number of merchants." The terms of the loan were to be the same as those previously allowed to the combine. Although Barker in an old fashioned way spoke of himself as an "agent," he actually aimed at loan contracting, as can be seen

from his offer of a larger amount than the total of the commitments by which he was backed. It can also be seen from his statement that the "compensation [of 1/4 of one per cent was] dearly earned by the responsibility that would attach on the agent." All that materialized was an allotment of $1,723,000 since the $7,500,000 loan authorized on August 2, 1813 was oversubscribed.[119]

Barker again aimed at loan contracting when the $25,000,000 loan mentioned above was authorized on March 24, 1814. As in his goal, so in his methods he now copied traditional English practice. First, he felt that the loan should attract speculators: "it is the universal custom when governments contract to do it at a rate several per cent below the retail market price" for old issues, as he expressed it. Secondly, as prospects he meant to gain institutional investors, to use a modern term. These were to be banks which would become public creditors for the sake of advantages other than mere drawing interest, as had been common in Britain during the eighteenth century. "And that such incorporated banks as may assist me in carrying this contract into effect shall have the business of government at the places of their establishment," so he wrote to the Secretary of the Treasury on April 28, 1814. To the extent that banks in New York, Boston, Philadelphia, and Baltimore subscribed, their notes should be virtually the only ones to be taken by collectors and land officers "the same as specie." When this proposal was turned down as going too far, Barker demanded "that such incorporated banks established at Salem, Boston, New York, Philadelphia, Baltimore, and Charleston as should assist [him] in carrying the contract into effect [should] have one half the business of the government, especially the collection of bonds given for duties and other customhouse deposits."[120] Their notes were to be taken on deposit by all other banks with which the government did business. This offer was accepted with some modifications and as a contractor Barker provided $5,000,000 payable in installments, receiving therefor a commission of 1/4 per cent. The contract as it was actually concluded is interesting from still another angle. It contained a clause which in line with eighteenth-century practice was bound to lead to speculative maneuvres, in this case to bearish moves intended to depress the price of the stock below its real value. (Once again, as in the 1780's when security speculations were first adopted in America, "Change Alley" was to be copied on this side of the Atlantic.[121]) That clause provided that if terms more favorable to the lenders were allowed for any part of the $25,000,000, the same terms were to be extended to the holders of the $10,000,000 stock then to be sold as the first slice of the authorized total of $25,000,000. Barker had fought for this potential rebate to be allowed to the contractor, not to the holders; but he had to acquiesce.[122] The contract had hardly been concluded when Barker applied to a bank for credit on the basis of the funded stock which he had subscribed, and he received it to a limited extent. But he met with another difficulty which resulted from the just mentioned status of the early loan contractor as one subscriber among others: unless there was brisk demand for the securities the loan contractor could not sell because his prospects could buy directly from the government.

In addition to all the other difficulties which Barker faced in his short career as a loan contractor, he also met competition. As a matter of fact, competition was provided by Dennis A. Smith who can be considered this country's second native loan contractor. He had been a cashier of the Mechanics Bank of Baltimore and later became a wealthy and enterprising merchant in that city and a director of the Second Bank of the United States. In this latter capacity he was a member of that gang of gamblers who tried to run the Bank to suit their stock speculations and who almost wrecked it. In 1814 he may have led banks in Baltimore and in the District of Columbia into taking a share in the second tranche of the $25,000,000 authorized in March, 1814, the so-called $6,000,000 loan of 1814.[123] Moreover, backed by John Jacob Astor, he contracted certain amounts for himself. Astor took $200,000 of the bonds so contracted from Dennis Smith, paying with a four-months bill to be renewed for another four months. But he refused to take the contract off Smith's hands when the latter offered it for a consideration of $20,000.[124]

IV

When the eighteenth century closed, two methods for floating public loans were being used on the European continent. One of them was traditional and went back to medieval times: capitalists and businessmen (merchants, bankers) loaned their own funds to governments (courts, princes, estates [Landstände] of smaller principalities, and to cities). During the Seven Years' War, for instance, the Berlin merchants' guild financed more or less voluntarily the needs of the city and of King Frederic II of Prussia. (No securities were issued in this case.)[125] Slightly later, in 1784, the Danish court borrowed large sums from the Landgraf von Hessen, one of the richest capitalists of his time; and in 1810, to give a late ex-ample, John Parish, member of the Hamburg banking house of Parish & Co., lent a part of his own fortune to the Austrian government, seriously embarrassed after the Battle of Wagram.[126]

Besides this traditional method, private bankers especially in Amsterdam, Frankfurt and, to a lesser extent, Hamburg had come to act as middlemen; but these middlemen did not take shares in a subscription outright as did the English loan contractors. They "negotiated" whole issues on a commission basis. At an earlier period, as a reliable Dutch source of the early 1780's describes (see Appendix 2 to this chapter), there was a second middleman or group of middlemen between the loan "negotiating" firm and the ultimate investor. This second layer of middlemen, called "undertakers" in a contemporary source, is supposed to have taken whole or large parts of issues outright like the English loan contractors; but in contrast to the latter from an originating [the "negotiating"] house and not from the borrower. The "undertakers" parceled the securities out to capitalists, receiving a commission of 1 to 2 per cent. As an example the American Holland loan of 1787 may be cited: In a letter of May 18 of that year the American financial agents in Amsterdam, W. and J. Willink and N. and J. van Staphorst, indicated their willingness to "negotiate" a loan of fl. 1,000,000 after having made a preliminary arrangement with a group of "undertakers" willing to subscribe to a part of the loan (fl. 240,000) and to take further amounts if saleable within eighteen months.[127] The author has been unable to determine exactly in which period that practice prevailed and when it disappeared. Later the "negotiating" houses themselves disposed of the securities, with the sale of which they were charged, as fast as possible directly to capitalists, soliciting by letters, circulars, and advertisements. Their endeavors led either to failure or to a "completion" of the loan (in some cases only after several years). It was by "negotiating" that the loans of the Continental Congress were floated in Holland in the 1780's.[128] The then famous Frankfurt merchant bankers, Gebrüder Bethmann, a firm (founded in 1748)[129] which by the end of the eighteenth century was guided by Simon Moritz von Bethmann (1768-1826), applied the same method. Through its flotations of public loans, especially for Austria and Denmark, it won a world reputation.[130]

The Dutch or German houses operating on this basis received from the borrowing government (court or prince) what was called in German a General-Obligation (also Hauptobligation),[131] i.e., a bond testifying to the total amount borrowed. The American loan contract of 1782 deviated slightly from this practice in that five formal contracts for 1,000,000 guilders each were made up to cover the total of 5,000,000.[132] On the basis of such bond or bonds the banker issued his own obligations, so-called Partial-Obligationen (French: obligations partielles), bonds for relatively large amounts divisible by 100. The original contract for the American loan of 1784, closed in Holland, speaks of the latter securities as "bonds of participation" (to be "signed by Messrs. Wilhelm and Jan Willink, Nicholas and Jacob van Staphorst, and De la Lande & Fynje or the successors of the said gentlemen" who "negotiated" the loan);[133] while that of the Danish loan of 1821 calls them "special bonds." To give an example, in 1804 Hope and Company sold their share in the Louisiana bonds ($5,000,000 securities bearing 6 per cent interest) in the form of $5\frac{1}{2}$ per cent "aandeelen". One half of one per cent interest was kept back in order to purchase such stock as might come into the market, a very early case of market manipulation, and in order to pay a bonus after the underlying bonds had been retired by the United States.[134] However beginning by the end of the eighteenth century there was a tendency to drop the General-Obligation and have the borrower himself make out bonds in saleable amounts (as in the case of the American Holland loans of 1787 and 1790).[135] This was soon done even when the lender was a single capitalist, because the loans thereby became marketable.[136]

As early as 1780 loan "negotiations" were very common in Amsterdam and represented an important business in that city. A well informed contemporary Dutch author spoke of a mania ("manie des emprunts") which had seized the sovereigns of small states, cities and municipalities, and big joint stock companies with the result that so many securities of such different types were in the market that it was difficult if not impossible to enumerate them. He went on to describe the methods used in the business and his description seems interesting enough to warrant translating and reprinting in Appendix 2 to this chapter.[137]

Numerous firms participated in the game, but in the 1780's one of them rose to prominence, the previously mentioned house of Hope and Company. It had been founded in the seventeenth century by the Scottish merchant, Henry Hope, himself a merchant's son, and was run as a family enterprise for more than a hundred years. In 1788, when the firm broke through the monopoly which a competitor (R. S. Th. de Smeth) had held in the Russian loan business, it emerged as the strongest house in the field. Under the guidance of Pierre César Labouchère who was to assume leadership in the firm slightly thereafter it became one of the biggest concerns of merchant bankers in the

world and, as will be shown shortly, one of the houses which brought modern investment banking into being.[138]

The public credit of France was so undeveloped during the eighteenth and the first decade of the nineteenth century that one cannot expect to find in that country many moves toward investment banking before the end of the Napoleonic era. Necker's famous book does not contain anything that would be of interest in our context.[139] Such lagging behind England, Holland, and Western Germany was due to the French form of government and to heavy losses sustained repeatedly by French public creditors.[140] However, the country experimented during the eighteenth century with all sorts of public loans. First, it issued life annuities (rentes viagères) and perpetual annuities (rentes) to individuals, and the latter also to "sociétés de capitalistes." Like the British incorporations of public creditors, these "sociétés de capitalistes" tried to obtain trade advantages by their subscriptions. Secondly, "on créa sous le nom de charges et d'offices des places que l'on accorda à ceux qui, pour les acquérir, donnaient une somme déterminée qui fut nommée finance, et l'on attribua à ces offices des gages ou salaires proportionnés a l'importance... Sous un nom déguisé ces créations de charges sont des véritables emprunts; la finance est le capital et les gages sont les intérêts." Thirdly, there were in addition, at one time or another, loans in anticipation of taxes, a "caisse des emprunts" where people could make interest-bearing temporary advances, forced loans, and to a very limited extent loans payable in installments.[141] One sees at a glance that such lack of standardization precluded a regular and large market of public loans, let alone the fact that numerous other public and semi-public agencies tried to borrow funds also. To be sure, during the reign of Louis XVI loans took a few forms only, namely, those of perpetual and life annuities and of lotteries. But the public debt was not systematically reorganized and modernized. Moreover as late as that period we meet a loan of truly medieval character: Necker, the capitalist, then minister of finance, lent 2,400,000 livres to the Trésor Royal.[142]

But even in France the foundation for the business of loan contracting was being laid prior to the Revolution of 1789. By that time it was common practice for the buyer of a rente to have it divided into "actions" (shares). These he could sell after endorsement in blank, in which case they circulated like bearer documents. Paris bankers, Boyd, Ker and Company among them, entered into contracts for blocks of perpetual annuities which they sold to merchants and investors in France, England, Austria, and the Netherlands. In addition they bought such rentes for customers on a commission basis. To give an idea of the magnitude of the transactions involved it may be mentioned that in the months April through July, 1792, they contracted and placed six blocks of rentes with a capital value of 2,800,000 livres (£112,000) with twenty capitalists, mostly in London.[143] In fact, Walter Boyd thus gained his first experience in the field in which he was to become a master.

V

It seems to the author that the modern European investment banker emerged during the negotiations of the public loans floated on the Continent after the Vienna Congress. These loans were taken by merchant bankers and their allies, some of whom were English and others Continental. This fact seems to be significant, for the transactions in question represented a mixture of business methods practiced by English loan contractors and by Dutch or Frankfurt loan "negotiators." Consequently a combination of elements, developed during the eighteenth century on both sides of the Channel, was to become typical of modern investment banking. Like the English loan contractors the early investment bankers took new security issues outright and not on a commission basis, as had done the Continental bankers. But, on the other hand, they dealt with complete issues, as had been customary on the Continent, and unlike earlier eighteenth-century loan contractors they did not compete with institutional or other ultimate investors for mere parts thereof. (To be sure, the English development was already turning in this direction after 1800.) Furthermore, although acquiring the issues outright in English fashion, the early investment bankers received a commission following Continental practice.[144] Or to look at the matter from a different angle, the transactions corresponded to what would have been called "private subscriptions" in eighteenth-century England. But they differed from the latter in that only middlemen participated, i.e., bankers who meant to sell to speculators and ultimate investors[145] and who received a commission.

The statement made earlier that in the 1790's English loan contracting started to develop toward investment banking (when ultimate investors withdrew as original contributors to new loans)[146] should not be considered as conflicting with the suggestion just presented that full-fledged investment banking as a European institution emerged in the 1810's. The incipient change which was taking shape in England was hardly recognized as being of any importance, let alone having any influence on the Continental development. Business had gone on there along traditional lines. As late as 1816, for example, when Prussia, in need of funds, approached Salomon Rothschild (known in Berlin through the transmittal of the English subsidies) the latter tried to handle the proposed loan in typically Continental eighteenth-century fashion. He intended to act as a loan "negotiator," that is to say, to float the loan in Amsterdam without taking any responsibility. When this plan proved abortive he made available to the Prussian government money belonging to the Kurfürst von Hessen, i.e., funds of a single capitalist.[147] On the other hand, Prussia was still so old-fashioned that she objected to the sale of her obligations at the exchanges, to advertisement in public papers, and even to regular price quotations. As late as 1818 when Berlin bankers competed for a 20,000,000 thaler loan (which the Rothschilds ultimately consummated) they intended to take only a part thereof outright and to sell the rest on a commission basis.[148] But in the meantime, in 1817 and 1818, the Barings, the English firm more conversant with loan contracting than any other, and the Hopes, the leading Amsterdam loan "negotiators," seconded by David Parish, as allies had wrought the decisive change characterized above.

Nebenius has described in detail the methods of the investment bankers of the post-Napoleonic era: Before taking a loan they made tentative contracts with smaller houses which planned to act as middlemen too[149] (and, incidentally, these smaller houses made corresponding tentative contracts with capitalists). When the Barings and Hopes contracted for the French loans of 1817 and that of 1818, which was later canceled, they admitted French houses as subcontractors;[150] the Rothschilds were drawn by David Parish into the former loans as well as into an Austrian loan of 1818, and John Parish invited Gebrüder Bethmann to participate in several Austrian loans.[151] While competition was very limited on the top level, keen competition for a share in new issues of securities by a second layer of middlemen and by capitalists enabled one concern or an alliance of several originating houses, to use a modern term, to conclude very large deals in competition or potential competition with a few others.[152] To be sure, since the 1790's exclusion of competition had been aimed at by powerful English loan contractors also. In the 1790's as has been described,[153] Walter Boyd, trying to exclude competition as long as an earlier loan of his was not fully paid up, had offered to take a new loan at 1/2 per cent above the highest bid of any competitor. Such methods were now copied on the Continent: In 1821 when the Rothschilds negotiated the first Neapolitan loan they requested that no other loan be floated during the period of paying up the amount in question, a reasonable demand. But when the loan was actually concluded a clause was inserted that the house should have priority in case of any new loan. The following year when an Austrian loan was pending, the Rothschilds offered to contract at 1/2 per cent above the highest bid tendered.[154] But regardless of the strength of the leading houses such manipulations did not always avail and competition persisted to a certain extent. The above-mentioned Neapolitan loan of 1821 was contested by a Milan banker, Barbaia, who cooperated with French houses; in 1822 the Rothschilds had to compete for the then-contemplated Austrian loan with a group of French bankers led by Laffitte and the Vienna house of Geymüller; and the French rentes of 1823 were contracted by the Rothschilds, as the highest bidders of four groups interested in the business.[155] To sum up, there were only a very few houses strong enough to take large loans payable in a few installments and to assume the risk involved; but there were many speculators and ultimate investors as well as smaller banks all over the countries anxious to participate in flotations. As a result, there was some kind of oligopoly at the apex of the pyramid, at least in the business with the Great Powers, the originating firms being supported by chains of middlemen. In consequence, investment banking was highly profitable, especially since agreements were occasionally made not to sell new securities below a set price.[156] How profitable it was is evident from the fabulous wealth which the Rothschilds amassed and from the fact that Pierre César Labouchère, the head of Hope and Company, doubled his fortune through his participation in the French loans of 1817.[157]

It was characteristic of the flotations of the time, in contrast to those of the eighteenth century, that only a few securities came directly into the hands of ultimate investors. Most went through those of one or several middlemen into the posession of speculators who sold out only slowly to ultimate investors.[158] The strength of the trend can be gauged from the fate of the issue of 1818 of 14,600,000 francs rentes.[159] It was offered originally both to foreigners and Frenchmen; but under the pressure of public opinion only subscriptions of the latter were accepted. The loan was intended to be a popular one, the minimum subscriptions being 2,500 francs, the maximum, 150,000. By accepting the guarantee of banks for the proper fulfillment of the obligations the circle of subscribers was to be broadened. Nevertheless since the price of the loan was set below that quoted in the market for older flotations and since the yield was better

than that for English consols the only result was that French bankers acted as middlemen for the same Dutch and English houses and speculators who at that period acquired the bulk of all the new securities.[160]

Those great houses in spite of their strength neither possessed the funds to pay for the tremendously large flotations, nor did they cover themselves completely before contracting therefor. Their tactics consisted in selling continuously enough securities so that with the money received for the scrip they could always pay the installment which was coming due. They and their subcontractors also expected to be able to borrow on the basis of the scrip. The Bank of France, for instance, made available in 1818 30,000,000 francs to be lent to the subscribers of the pending loan.[161] Regardless of such assistance which could be anticipated, the originating houses and their allies had to set aside at the time of negotiation funds large enough to pay at least the first installment. Consequently the mere announcement of a new loan was prone to have repercussions in the capital and money markets. On the other hand, once it was concluded the unsuccessful competing group or groups had liquid funds on hand which were bound to be used for speculating in the new securities[162] and indirectly contributed to the success of the fortunate competitor.

Three men can be considered as the creators of modern investment banking in the field of public credit: Their leader was Alexander Baring; he was seconded by his brother-in-law Pierre César Labouchère (born in The Hague in 1772)[163] who as the ranking partner of Hope and Company had gained considerable experience in Continental loan "negotiations."[164] In 1814 Alexander Baring had acquired an interest in the Amsterdam house which thus became the closest ally of Baring Brothers and Company. David Parish was the third of the group. He has been discussed previously, especially because of the role which he played in bringing full-fledged loan contracting to these shores.[165] By 1815 he had returned to Europe and when the decisive transactions were in the making, he seems (except in the Austrian loan of 1818 which he concluded for Baring Brothers and Company) to have represented Parish & Co., Hamburg, then owned and administered by his brothers.[166] Later he became a partner in the Vienna banking house of Graf Moritz Fries & Co., one of the four Vienna "Hofbankiers." This firm had been a leading one in the time of Maria Theresa but had fallen behind, and Parish probably meant to make it an enterprise comparable with the Barings, Hopes, and the Hamburg Parishes. In this attempt he failed. These three were the men who made a success out of the tremendously large loan transactions of the 1810's by which the European states regained their financial stability. In so doing they became at the same time the creative entrepreneurs who developed a new type of business enterprise, modern investment banking.

The transactions which gave rise to the emergence of the modern investment banker started with the French loans concluded with the Barings and Hopes in 1817. The French financier Gabriel Julien Ouvrard (1770-1846), who clearly saw the possibilities for large flotations of public loans before anybody else realized them, seems to have acted as a sort of midwife in this connection.[167] The French loans[168] were followed by an Austrian loan of 1818 contracted by the Parishes, Barings, Hopes, Bethmanns, and Geymüllers. A Russian loan of 1818 was taken over by the Hopes who had controlled the Russian business since the eighteenth century, as has been indicated. Finally in the same year an abortive French loan was concluded with the Barings and Hopes. One sees at first glance the dominant position enjoyed by the two last-named firms. How dominant it was is shown by the following fact: when the French government in 1815 tried to make an arrangement with French houses, the latter themselves referred them to the Barings; and when the Frenchmen in 1818 (at the time of the Aachen Congress) actually, but unsuccessfully, competed with the latter and their allies, they did not really mean to take the then-pending French loan, but rather to form a bottleneck and squeeze themselves in as middlemen between the French government and the foreign houses.[169]

Genuine competition in the young field of international investment banking started only when the Rothschilds entered it. The earlier history of this house does not need to be described here.[170] During the wars they had amassed a fortune as exchange brokers and as such had been of the greatest value to the English Treasury. Through the transmittal of British subsidies to the Continent they had become widely known in government circles. In addition, as agents of the Kurfürst von Hessen they had gained some experience in the handling of public loans; they had acted, for instance, as middlemen between the elector, on the one hand, and the Danish Court and the Prussian government, on the other.[171] Wealth, acquaintances, and experience alike were now put to good account.

The Rothschilds began their career as international investment bankers with the Prussian loan of 1818. The following year (1819) Nathan Rothschild took a £12,000,000 English loan which gave him prestige, but hardly any profit. Because of the crisis which broke in the fall of 1818 the price of these securities dropped; it remained depressed for a long while and never rose much above that at which they had been contracted. The fact that as early as 1819 Nathan Rothschild could get hold of this issue and defeat the Barings in their domain was due to the latter's being embarrassed by the crisis which caught them with older securities still on hand. But in fact the crisis of 1818 had done even more serious harm to the London house and its Dutch ally. During the Congress of Aachen a contract[172] (previously alluded to) had been made between the French government and the Barings and Hopes according to which the two houses and their friends took French rentes representing a capital value of 165,000,000 francs. At the same time additional rentes representing a capital of 100,000,000 francs had been taken from the allies who in turn had received them from the French government in lieu of cash. When the crisis broke Alexander Baring succeeded in having these contracts canceled. This cancellation may have saved the house of Baring, but at the same time deprived it of the confidence of and the prestige with the great European powers. Thus slightly later the Barings had to yield supremacy in the field of investment banking to the Rothschilds.

This statement is not meant to imply that they lost out completely and instantly. In 1820 the Barings and Hopes contracted a 40,000,000 ruble Russian loan in which the Bethmanns of Frankfurt participated; and in 1824 they took a share in the gigantic, although finally abortive, conversion of French rentes. But in the meantime the Rothschilds had forged ahead, for some years in cooperation with David Parish, the Barings' old representative and ally. In 1820 David Parish and Salomon Rothschild contracted an Austrian lottery loan of 58,300,000 florins, the former acting for Parish and Company of Hamburg; (John Parish, then already Freiherr von Senftenberg, drew the Bethmanns into the business).[173] In 1821 the Rothschilds secured two Neapolitan loans, quickly followed by others, and in the following year a second Prussian and a Russian loan. With the latter they defeated the Hopes in their field, as previously in 1819 they had invaded the domain of the Barings. In 1823 the Rothschilds contracted for 23,000,000 francs rentes, representing a capital value of 400,000,000 francs and they led in the flotation of two issues of Austrian so-called Metalliques, i.e., securities payable in paper money with the interest to be paid in metal (the type of securities which the United States was to float during the Civil War).[174] In connection with this loan Salomon Rothschild clashed with David Parish who was now driven from the field of international investment banking, i.e., excluded from a share of further flotations.[175] (The crisis of 1825 ruined him and in 1826 he died a suicide.) On the other hand, the proud Barings did not now disdain to become the allies of the upstarts[176] who in the French and Austrian loans of 1817 and 1818, respectively, had been mere subcontractors:[177] In the year 1823 the Rothschilds invited the Barings to participate in a Spanish loan which, however, did not materialize; and in 1824, as already mentioned, the London house took a share in the abortive French conversion, conceived by Nathan Rothschild. Nothing shows better the shift of power in the young field than these facts. Incidentally, in connection with the French conversion, the brothers hedged to the detriment of their allies so that further cooperation with the Barings became impossible.[178]

The reasons for the rise of the House of Rothschild to the position of Europe's foremost investment bankers have often been described: Besides the personal factor, Nathan Rothschild's business genius, decisive elements were the close cooperation of the five brothers, working at five financial centers, London, Paris, Vienna, Frankfurt, and Naples; the secrecy with which they conducted their business dealings which often enough had important political implications;[179] and the recognition of the value of stock exchanges as tools for the floating of securities. The London and Amsterdam exchanges had been used for that purpose prior to the time of the Rothschilds, but the latter gave the business a new turn, introducing securities simultaneously at several exchanges; and Nathan was also the first to introduce foreign securities at the London Exchange.[180] The new policy of using several exchanges at the same time they devised at the very moment when they entered the field of investment banking: The Prussian loan of 1818, the first which they contracted, was introduced at the exchanges of London, Berlin, Frankfurt, Hamburg, and Amsterdam; the Neapolitan loans of 1821, 1822, and 1823 in London and Paris;[181] while the Austrian lottery loans of 1820 and 1821 were traded in Frankfurt, Augsburg, and Vienna.

A further important reason for the Rothschilds' supremacy may have been overlooked so far: If one can trust the contemporary pamphlet of Lancaster, as the author is inclined to do, the London stock exchange during the Napoleonic era had become indispensable for the flotation of new securities, for "recirculating [a] loan," as that author expressed it. (This situation may well have been an undesired by-product of the development which made the subscribing to new issues the domain of middlemen.) But thereby jobbers and brokers had come to wield extraordinary power which, as a rule, was used against the loan contractors, as has been explained before. The "stock exchange had got the minister and the country in their clutch," to use Lancaster's words. The loan contractors were rather helpless since they did not themselves trade at the stock exchange, except "by proxy," i.e., through brokers who were men of dubious ethics. The Goldsmids, who as former members of the stock exchange knew the tricks of the trade and who were permanently represented on the stock exchange by a confidential agent,[182] could to a certain extent defeat its machinations; but at the end even they succumbed to the combination of stock-exchange bears. To the present author it seems very probable that the rise of the Rothschilds is in part due to the fact that here active members of several exchanges, one of them, Nathan Rothschild, rather a past master, turned the tables on their former colleagues. When the Rothschilds became investment bankers they were able to contract loans and at the same time to put the exchanges at their service; while in the past the contractors had unavoidably had to contend with a hostile crowd at the market place.[183] As a result the Rothschilds were able not only to float loans in unheard-of amounts, but also to keep their prices high, a fact which reflected favorably on the credit of the issuing state. Thus the powers actually vied for their favors.[184]

VI

It has been shown in the preceding section of this chapter how modern investment banking originated in the field of public credit through a cross fertilization of English loan contracting and Continental loan "negotiating" and how it became firmly established in Western and Central Europe. Both English loan contractors and Continental loan "negotiators" had been merchants and private bankers who in taking over these functions became the ancestors of modern European investment bankers. In America the development took a turn toward investment banking when chartered banks entered loan contracting which, as has been shown, existed here at the time of the War of 1812. In fact it was chartered banks which did an embryonic investment banking business throughout the third and fourth decades of the nineteenth century. The difference between Europe and America may find its explanation in the fact that during the decisive years American merchants were not as wealthy as their English and Dutch counterparts[185] while, on the other hand, the institutional setup was advanced on this side of the Atlantic in comparison with what it had been on the other at the corresponding juncture. When in America security flotations first became necessary the country had a whole system of banking corporations which the European countries did not possess at the earlier moment which marked the beginning of that need in Europe.

Loan contracting of American incorporated banks developed slowly out of their investment activities. If those of the Bank of North America during the Revolutionary War are disregarded, the first step in the indicated direction was taken in 1789 when the United States borrowed from that bank and from the Bank of New York.[186] (These "public" loans, except for the lending agency, corresponded essentially to such loans as European capitalists had made to princes, republics, and cities ever since medieval times.) Soon thereafter several of the American states began to borrow from banks established within their boundaries.[187] Typically, negotiable securities were not issued. As late as 1815 the Bank of North America requested the Governor of Pennsylvania to execute and deliver to the bank proper evidences of the sums lent although the laws had not expressly prescribed their issue.[188] When the First Bank of the United States was founded and government stock could be subscribed in lieu of specie, the development was taking a new turn and was catching up with that in England in that a chartered bank (copied from the Bank of England) became the main creditor of the "general government" by holding a large portion of the securities floated by the latter. In the following decades, as described in another context and as will be discussed forthwith again,[189] it became common practice for other American banks also to hold large funds invested in public securities and in those of corporations. It must be emphasized that securities were originally acquired by banks for the sake of permanent investment. Public opinion considered such use of bank funds legitimate, provided that the banks in question did not trade in securities and used them only in case of need, especially to buy specie.[190]

A reviewer of the first volume of this work, a statistician, who seems to consider herself an expert in banking history, has taken issue with the author for having overestimated the importance of the investment of early American banks in government and corporation stocks. In contrast to the author, she considers the investment of Philadelphia banks in United States stock in 1816 (given as an example) as "atypical" reflecting "patriotic" subscriptions during the War of 1812.[191] The reviewer is ignorant of the facts, although the figures of 1816 show indeed that this type of investment was temporarily inflated. The fact remains

and must be stressed that the investment of banks in stock was very common prior to 1837, although not equally common everywhere. There were various reasons for this policy: first, a historical one. The earliest American banks were modeled on the Bank of England whose whole capital was invested in government stock; and following this example banks were often chartered here under the condition that, if required, they would be lenders of funds to their commonwealths. Secondly, when American states floated loans they not only wished them to succeed, but also desired them to be taken over by those banks in which the state in question held an equity (and there were many). In this case, at least some of the interest would come back to the state in the form of profit on its bank shares. In Pennsylvania, for instance, there was some agitation in 1829 when neither the Bank of Pennsylvania, nor the Philadelphia Bank would bid on a state loan offered for subscription.[192] Thirdly, states were, as a rule, interested in improvements, and banks were chartered and their charters renewed if they would invest in the stock of enterprises considered necessary and yet too big to be tackled by individuals. Fourthly, occasionally still other motives prevailed, such as prompted the Connecticut legislators, for instance, to pass a law in 1816 permitting the state's banks to invest in stock of the Second Bank of the United States,[193] a law which, incidentally, followed that of Massachusetts of March 9, 1792 authorizing the Massachusetts Bank to buy and sell the shares of any American bank.[194] Finally, as was discussed in the first volume of this work, a theory was elaborated in America between about 1825 and 1845 according to which banks should bank on their credit only and invest their capital in government and corporation stock (bonds, mortgages, and other long term loans also being considered permissible). This theory found acceptance with influential bankers and in some cases became the basis of legislation. Wherever adopted, it was reflected in the comparatively large security portfolios of the exponents of this policy.[195]

Maryland was foremost among those American states which not only permitted, but forced security investments on her banks (although not under the influence of the theory just mentioned). She adopted the policy of renewing bank charters on condition that the banks in question made funds available for turnpikes. In some cases the required amounts were invested in turnpike stock; in others, presidents and directors of the banks concerned were incorporated, for instance, as President, Managers and Company of the Cumberland Turnpike Road or as the Boonsborough Turnpike Company. Such transactions, as a matter of course, were reflected in security holdings which were blown up still further through war bonds subscribed between 1813 and 1815. In consequence, in 1830 eight Maryland banks held 7.5 to 26.5 per cent of their capital in the form of stock.[196] In Pennsylvania the practice of requiring by charter that banks assist transportation enterprises by stock subscriptions (besides by making loans and grants) ran wild in the charter of 1836 of the Bank of the United States of Pennsylvania, according to which it had to subscribe $675,000 to ten railroad, navigation, and turnpike companies.[197] In New York, chartered banks were also familiar with security holdings: as early as 1797 the Bank of New York, for instance, purchased about $1,366,150 of national securities from the State of New York.[198] In the New England states the policy of investing in securities seems to have been less developed than in the Middle States; but it was by no means absent. The investment of the Massachusetts Bank in stock of the Second Bank of the United States has been mentioned. Moreover Newburyport banks invested in shares of the Eastern Stage Coach Company, a New Hampshire corporation.[199] As to Connecticut, her banks were authorized to invest in stock of the Second Bank of the United States. Furthermore the Mechanics and City Banks of New Haven were chartered upon the condition that they subscribe $200,000 and $100,000, respectively, to the Farmington Canal.[200] By 1846 her banks held 1.9 per cent of their assets in the form of securities,[201] in order to make use of surplus funds. The fact that New England was opposed to the War of 1812 and its banks abstained from subscribing to war loans may have contributed to the difference in the investment policy of banks in the Northern and Middle States.[202]

It goes without saying that the policy of investing in federal and state bonds as well as in corporation stock did not lead straight to investment banking, even if the securities were acquired directly from the issuers. Its importance lay rather in making it easy for commercial banks to assume new functions and to be drawn into an embryonic investment banking business when the opportunity arose. In order to become a first step in a new direction, the purpose of the acquisition of securities had to be changed, as indeed it was in the 1820's. Such change had to be sanctioned by public opinion. As has been described in the first volume of this work,[203] prior to that decade there was general agreement that banks were entitled to subscribe to public stock for the purpose of investment, but that it was not legitimate for them to assume the role of loan contractors. Conservatives stuck to this attitude until deep in the 1830's and considered it illegitimate for banks to sub-

scribe to new security issues for the purpose of sale at a profit. The Second Bank of the United States in its charter was expressly permitted to sell government securities obtained in lieu of cash from subscribers to its stock. Similarly when the above-cited Connecticut Act of 1816 allowed the banks of that state to subscribe to stock of the Second Bank of the United States, it authorized them also to "alien" it.[204] The fact that such permission was expressly given in two acts of the same year shows beyond doubt that "alienation" was not automatically implied in the permission to receive securities in lieu of cash or to subscribe thereto.

By that time American economic life had matured so as to necessitate the development of at least embryonic investment banking. Capital was accumulating and looking for investment, while many of the states were beginning to provide a concentrated demand therefor. By 1830 the total of state debts amounted to about $27,000,000. States felt obligated to undertake tasks which individual businessmen were unable to tackle, or to finance banks which would assist private enterprise. The challenge met with response on the part of creative business leaders who went into and built up the new line of business. The magnitude of the job with which they were faced becomes evident from the following contemporary table of state loans outstanding in 1838.

STATEMENT

of bonds issued by the several States

STATES	TOTAL
Maine	$ 554,976.44
Massachusetts	4,290,000.00
New York	10,456,152.84
Pennsylvania	24,140,003.32
Maryland	8,511,980.73
Virginia	4,129,700.00
South Carolina	5,753,770.12
Ohio	6,101,000.00
Kentucky	3,185,000.00
Tennessee	789,166.66
Louisiana	19,735,000.00
Alabama	10,800,000.00
Mississippi	7,000,000.00
Indiana	5,438,000.00
Illinois	5,479,000.00
Missouri	2,500,000.00
Arkansas	3,000,000.00
Michigan	1,840,000.00
	$123,703,750.11

The whole amount of bonds issued and authorized

to be issued by eighteen States, amounted to $ 141,269,002. Of this amount, the proportion was

for internal improvements	$ 84,856,243
for banking	51,315,000
miscellaneous	5,097,759
	$141,269,002

The States of New Hampshire, Vermont, Rhode Island, Connecticut, New Jersey, and Delaware had not issued stock of any kind, and North Carolina owed no debt;[205] [but Georgia, which is not included in the above list, had issued under an act of 1837, 206 bonds for $ 500 each and under an act of 1838, 618 bonds of the same face value].

Much progress was made in the field prior to the middle of the 1830's as will be described in detail; nevertheless American investment banking remained until that time in a rather immature stage which corresponded to that of the English loan contractor of the early Napoleonic era.

In order to establish a dividing line between precursory and incipient investment banking we have previously distinguished between loan contracting and investment banking proper. The latter has been considered to have crossed the threshold whenever there was no longer competition for new securities between direct investors and individual speculators, on the one hand, and loan contractors, on the other, the latter being defined as enterprisers who currently subscribe to new security issues in order to profit from resale. But there is, as a matter of fact, another criterion showing the point prior to which the business had not reached maturity: It is clear that it is the specific function of investment banking to make long term funds available to public authorities, public utilities, and industry. However in America during the early decades of the nineteenth century several agencies in competition with loan contractors provided such long term capital, a fact, which by itself must be considered as indicative of an immature state of that type of enterprise.

First there were individual capitalists who dabbled in new securities, such as Vincent Nolte who, aided by the Barings, in 1822 lent $300,000 to New Orleans; or the men who in 1835 and 1836 negotiated loans with the young Republic of Texas (Brookfield, Triplet, Erwin, and their friends).[206] Foremost among such capitalists was John Jacob Astor. In 1822 and 1826, respectively, he contracted for a $250,000 six per cent New York canal loan and a six per cent Ohio canal loan; while in 1830 he bid on the so-called Chemung Canal loan. Like the English participants in eighteenth-century private subscriptions, besides his own funds he invested the money of his friends and even funds of business concerns as a matter of courtesy.[207]

Secondly, more important were commercial banks as providers of long term capital. Some of those that did not turn loan contractors lent, by way of book credits, medium and long term funds to states and improvement corporations (often forced to do so in consequence of charter conditions). Moreover as a rule, commercial banks made accommodation loans payable in installments to manufacturers and farmers, thereby financing the long term needs of agriculture and capitalistic industry, as was stressed in the first volume of this work.[208] Even early railroads were financed by accommodation loans of banks, as for instance the Old Colony of Massachusetts which as late as 1850 had raised 25 per cent of its costs by short term loans, i.e., accommodation loans to be transformed into securities at the earliest possible moment. Sometimes outstanding railroad leaders raised bank funds on their own notes, pledging unsaleable stocks and bonds.[209]

Thirdly, there were the so-called improvement banks: banks which were tied to canal, railroad, gas-light, industrial, and other enterprises.[210] (Unfortunately, this very interesting field has been totally neglected by research.) Objects too big to be financed by individuals were to be financed by such improvement banks which created capital for the desired enterprise by the issue of purchasing power in the form of bank notes. To give examples: New York had her Dry Dock and Chemical Banks; New Jersey, her Morris Canal and Banking Company; Connecticut, her Connecticut River Banking Company; Rhode Island, her Blackstone Canal Bank; Maryland, her Susquehanna Bank and Bridge Company; Kentucky, among others, her Sanders Manufacturing Company of 1818; Louisiana, her Canal and Banking Company, her Gas Light and Banking Company, and her Achtafalaya Railroad and Banking Company; Georgia, her Central Railroad Bank, her Monroe Railroad and Banking Company, and her Georgia Railroad and Banking Company; Mississippi, her Commercial and Railroad Bank of Vicksburg, her Grand Gulf, her West Feliciana, her Mississippi and Alabama, and her Tombigby Railroad and Banking Companies; and Texas possessed the Texas Railroad, Navigation and Banking Company while other improvement banks planned in the young republic in 1837 did not come into existence.[211]

Fourthly, during the 1820's and 1830's there existed in New York a unique organization competing with other providers of long term capital, which has been described in detail in another context.[211a] The New York Bank for Savings, guided by John Pintard, for many years bought securities directly from the issuers, especially states and communities. What distinguished this very successful experiment from modern investment banking was the sequence of transactions. While modern investment bankers through their sales efforts gather accumulated savings, Pintard used previously accumulated savings concentrated in his institution to make flotations possible. (Of course in this case there is no clear line of demarcation between what one would call institutional investing today and rudimentary investment banking.) It is not accidental that this experiment was made by John Pintard, and the personal factor probably explains why it was not copied. There were probably not many people at that time who knew as much about security dealings as did Pintard, and those who did were far from taking an active interest in savings banking. Pintard had been in the security business at the very time when an organized security market first developed; in the early 1790's he was among the leading New York security brokers. He belonged to the friends of William Duer as whose agent he acted and we find his name among the subscribers of a "manufacturing scheme," the Connecticut Manufacturing Society planned as a joint stock company in the fall of 1791, and also among the promotors of the "Million Bank" of New York. Through Pintard a line of influence leads from Duer's first attempt at loan contracting previously described to the very successful quasi-investment banking practiced by the New York Bank for Savings between about 1820 and 1835.[212]

Fifthly, the gathering for permanent investment of funds accumulating in small amounts in the hands of the little fellow was accomplished during the period under investigation by lotteries. Public and semi-public enterprises which, according to the thinking of the time, included turnpike, canal, and bridge corporations were endowed with the right to raise capital by lotteries. The tickets were, as a rule, sold by enterprises which combined this business with what was then called "note shaving" (i.e., the dealing in "uncurrent" notes), the trading in domestic exchange, collections and perhaps even other odd lines. These enterprises, as was customary also in England,[213] often "contracted" for whole issues of lottery tickets or parts thereof, occasionally in combination with other ticket sellers. In other cases they sold lottery tickets on commission, a type of transaction which corresponded to contemporary security "negotiations." Several of these enterprises, for example those of Yates and McIntyre[214] and S. and M. Allen, reached what was for the time a considerable size.

The lottery-ticket business, which had an important economic function and in a way stood for modern investment banking, was predicated on the existence of a broad market for tickets. Such a man as John Stevens, steamboat inventor and engineer, for instance, indulged "extensively in the common practice of buying lottery tickets, something he regarded as entirely distinct from betting," as his biographer puts it.[215] Just as contemporary merchants when acquiring government stock thought less of investment than of speculation, so the little man when buying lottery tickets did not think of the use to which his money was going to be put, but only of gambling.[216] However this was the way in which in the era of early American capitalism small funds could be gathered and made available for conversion into real capital.

VII

The Second Bank of the United States began to assume leadership in the new field when the Acts of 1820 and 1821 authorizing the flotations by the federal government of a three and a five million dollar loan, respectively, permitted that Bank to subscribe the whole or a part thereof. In fact Cheves, then at the helm of the Bank, obtained two and four million, respectively. As to the loan of 1820, it is not clear whether Cheves did not plan to subscribe more or whether he was outbid; but his cautiousness points to the former. With regard to the loan of 1821, however, the evidence is plain. This loan was authorized by an Act of Congress of March 3, 1821 which permitted the flotation of $5,000,000 stock bearing 5 per cent interest.[217] Consequently on March 14, the Secretary of the Treasury (Crawford) asked for public tenders for a first tranche of $4,000,000. The lowest proposal to be received was set at $10,000; payments had to be made in one sum (i.e., not in installments, as was customary); and the bids had to be submitted on or before April 4. The Secretary was later criticized because the time allowed was too short and the requirement of payments in one sum too rigid to permit a wide participation of bidders. The implication was that he meant to be partial to the Bank of the United States since the government owed it about $3,700,000, that is to say, $1,000,000 over and above the amount lent by the Bank for the payment of the Louisiana bonds. Moreover the government had invested so heavily in the Bank, whose funds were at that moment only partly productive, that it was good business for the Treasury to play into the hands of the bank, thereby increasing its own income from the shares in the Bank. This point was made by the Secretary himself and it is possible that in fact he leaned in this direction. It actually seems that originally the Bank alone was informed on the official policy established in 1820 regarding the allocation of stock to bidders.

Loan flotations were still so uncommon that neither the procedures of the Treasury nor the bid forms were standardized, a situation which was bound to lead to a conflict before long. For example, the bids were not opened at a specified day and hour, but as they arrived. Two kinds of bids could be expected, "specific" and "conditional" or "contingent" bids. The former would come from investors and small contractors, the latter from large ones. The former were bids for specific amounts at specific rates, while the latter would be bids for the whole loan or large parts thereof at rates contingent on the offers of smaller bidders. As a matter of fact, two large bidders came into the market, the Second Bank of the United States and an alliance of would-be contractors who had "formed a list" of several subcontractors whose names have not come to the attention of the author. The alliance consisted of Prime, Ward and Sands of New York, Thomas and John G. Biddle of Philadelphia, and Charles King of New York.[218] Elihu Chauncey was undoubtedly among the subcontractors on the list.

Representatives of the alliance, certainly Charles King and Elihu Chauncey and probably Nathaniel Prime, repaired to Washington and had a conference with the Secretary of the Treasury on April 3, the day before the last on which bids would be received. The following questions were put to the Secretary: Would he issue stock to the face value of $4,000,000 or as much as would bring $4,000,000? The answer was the latter. Would he receive a contingent bid? Yes, if a maximum was set, above which the offer would not rise. An offer combining specific and conditional features would also be acceptable. Representatives of the alliance were welcome to attend the opening of their tender. The latter pointed out that the method chosen was unfavorable both for the United States and the bidders, but Crawford retorted that it had worked so far (i.e., in 1820), that it had been approved by the President and some of the "heads of the departments," and that it could not be changed then.

The following is the list of the specific bids received:

Joseph Marx, Richmond	50,000 at	105
William Cochran, Boston	165,000	105
" " "	10,000	104.50
Bank of the Manhattan Co.	1,000,000	104.125
Lewis D. Carpentier, Philadelphia	20,000	104
Herman Hendricks, New York	10,000	104.45
" " " "	10,000	104.25
" " " "	10,000	104.10
" " " "	10,000	104.00
Herman Hendricks, New York	20,000	103.75
" " " "	20,000	103.50
" " " "	20,000	103.25
Israel Thorndike, Boston	100,000	104
Henry Rice	500,000	103
or	250,000	103.50
or	150,000	104
Thomas M. Willing, Philadelphia	310,000	103.50
R. L. Colt, Baltimore	300,000	105
Jno Sharp, Jun. & Company, Philadelphia	20,000	103.50
J. Sharp, Jun., Philadelphia	10,000	102.50
A. L. Gomez, New York	20,000	103
Enoch Parsons and Elijah Hubbard, Connecticut	15,000	100
Beers and Bunnel, New York	40,000	102.50
Ben. Huntington, New York	325,000	103.50

A study of this list reveals that investors and small middlemen were competing with large contractors whose conditional bids have not been yet described. Certainly Herman Hendricks of New York was a small middleman. His presumed method of taking bids from interested parties on a commission basis and submitting them, later became common practice.[219] Henry Rice's bid was conditional to a certain extent. One wonders how he expected it to work out in practice.

Even more ambiguous, however, were the tenders of the two large contractors. The alliance bid 1/100 of 1 per cent above any other offer or average of all offers (sic!) provided that it did not bring the bid above 105.26 for $100 face value. Payments were to be made of $2,000,000 in Philadelphia, $1,300,000 in New York, and $700,000 in Boston. The bid was for all or none. The Bank of the United States, on the other hand, bid 1 per cent over the average of specific offers provided that it did not bring its bid above 107.50. At least, this is probably what the directors of the Bank meant, although they did not say so. They offered in fact "to pay one per cent over the average of premiums of the highest bids at specific rates provided it does not bring the premium over 7 1/2 per cent." That is to say, this tender was just as ambiguous as that of the alliance. But the Secretary of the Treasury understood it to mean that if the loan was oversubscribed the bid was contingent on the highest offers to the extent that they fell within the $4,000,000 limit.

On April 4 the bid of the alliance was opened, their representatives being present. The latter calculated the average of all bids to be 103.786, and that so reckoned they were outbid by the Bank of the United States. The Secretary, however, figured the average as 104.147 by throwing out, for reasons unknown, the offer of Ben Huntington and the alternative offers of Henry Rice; but it is not clear if the representatives of the alliance were told that the Bank would be allocated the loan at 105.147. In the meeting Chauncey made the point that the alliance's contingent bid amounted to 105.01; but the other gentlemen present rejected this contention and Chauncey did not press the point. Laboring under a misunderstanding representatives of the alliance were convinced that the Bank had received the loan at 104.786 and they protested to Crawford and the President. What the wording of their bid "above any other offer or average of all offers" really meant was not clear then nor is it today because the clauses are mutually exclusive. The representatives of the alliance actually claimed in one breath, assuming the former, that the loan should have been theirs at 105.01 (i.e., 0.01 per cent above the highest bid) or, assuming the latter, that they were entitled to it at 104.80 (i.e., 0.01 per cent above the price at which they figured the loan would go to the Bank). The men asserted that they had meant by "above any other bid," above any other contingent bid. This contention, as Crawford felt, was not made bona fide, but if it had been accepted, as it was not, it would have entitled the alliance to the loan only at 105.157. In view of this discussion the question must be asked whether these men were naive or sharp. How could they expect that allocations were possible at all when any one bidder made his offer contingent on the contingent bids of all other conditional bidders? Since the Barings complained in their correspondence about Prime, Ward and King's "selfishness," their predecessors' behavior in this case smacks somewhat of sharp practice, especially since one of their letters to Crawford even contained veiled threats. The latter was not to be frightened, however, and the Bank's bid was accepted.

After the Bank of the United States had received $4,000,000 worth of the stock, a second tranche was floated and sold in Philadelphia, New York, Boston, and Washington; but details are not known to the author. All told $5,000,000 were received in cash and stock issued to an amount of $4,735,269.30. As to the first tranche, it is uncertain whether Cheves considered the Bank of the United States to be a loan contractor or if he meant to invest the funds of the institution permanently in the stock. The latter is quite possible. However, a few years later when Biddle took over the stock so acquired he sold piecemeal when he saw fit (for instance, during the crisis of 1825). Thereby whatever Cheves' intention may have been, Biddle made those transactions ex post loan contracting: de facto the Bank had acted as a loan contractor subscribing to issues of securities in competition with private investors and other loan contractors.[220]

When a few years later in connection with new loans Congress once more authorized the Second Bank of the United States to subscribe to the whole or a part thereof, Biddle was already the president of the Bank. In both 1824 and 1825 it actually took the complete issues of $5,000,000 $4\frac{1}{2}$ per cent stock each, and the securities were sold in the course of time. The bitter criticism of that policy has been described in another context.[221]

Although the Second Bank of the United States was blazing the trail it was not the only incorporated bank in the 1820's which by subscribing to new issues of securities for the purpose of resale became more or less consciously a loan contractor. The loan contracting activities of incorporated banks (other then the Bank of the United States) became possible when one state after another turned to the flotation of securities. New York led the way and the beginnings can be traced: As early as 1816 while the Erie Canal project was still under discussion, it was recommended that the needed money be raised by establishing a "fund," i.e., an income to be appropriated and pledged for the payment of interests and principal of such loans as it might be convenient to make. In this connection DeWitt Clinton wrote to William Bayard (1761-1828), whose firm LeRoy, Bayard and McEvers possessed a commanding position in the country's international trade after the War of 1812 and who enjoyed the confidence of Dutch capitalists, asking if money could be obtained on the credit of the state and if so, on what terms. Responding to the call the New York merchant tried to interest his Dutch friends;[222] with what success the author is unable to report, but probably none. Nevertheless it was logical for DeWitt Clinton to think of Dutch financiers as prospective lenders on canal securities, for the eighteenth-century alliance of Amsterdam bankers interested in American loans, the so-called Club of Six, had actually invested in the earliest American canals.

It would be desirable to have a detailed account of the flotations of the first New York Canal loans, especially that of $200,000 of 1817. As to the latter it is only known that there was but one offer at 2 per cent below par, tendered by an "individual" in New York; and that ultimately the loan was taken by an Albany bank. In 1818 a $1,000,000 6 per cent loan was taken by the Bank of the Manhattan Company; and few years later one of the Albany banks subscribed to the 6 per cent Canal stock of 1821, being willing to negotiate regarding the resale of a part thereof.[223] That is to say, as early as 1821 a chartered bank was, if not an actual, then at least a potential loan contractor; and it was not the only one, as will be shown later. (Incidentally, the stage of taking securities from the issuers with no definitive purpose, but with the possibility of resale [that is, loan contracting] in mind, was reached in the West in the 1830's. In that decade Illinois, for instance, issued bonds to raise funds for the Michigan and Illinois Canal, which could not be floated in the East. Thereupon the Shawneetown Bank took $900,000 of these bonds which it sold [loan contracting]; while the State Bank of Illinois subscribed $1,765,000 as a capital investment.)[224]

The question is posed whether or not American banks in assuming the function of loan contractors were influenced by British examples. This is highly probable although there is no documentary proof. It seems to the author that certain missions to Europe which put the representatives of American chartered banks in contact with the young guild of European investment bankers must have played a role in this connection. The earliest of these missions was that of 1816 when John Sergeant was charged with raising a loan for the Second Bank of the United States on the security of 6 per cent government stock. He negotiated successfully with Alexander Baring and Thomas Reid of Reid, Irving and Company and, in addition, unsuccessfully with some Continental firms unknown to this author. From Sergeant, the Philadelphia lawyer and director of the Second Bank of the United States, the line clearly leads to Nicholas Biddle.[225] Equally important probably was the successful trip in 1823 of Charles Wilkes (then the cashier, soon to become the president of the Bank of New York) who placed in England a £200,000 loan for this bank. He negotiated in London with Alexander Baring, Mr. Shaw of Thomas Wilson and Company, and Mr. Reid of Reid, Irving and Company. Conversations with Nathan Rothschild were contemplated.[226] During these trips a prominent Philadelphia lawyer and bank director and a successful New York bank official acquired first hand knowledge of the methods of leading English investment bankers. To look at it from a different angle, borrowing in England by American incorporated banks taught the directors or officers how to handle securities, for they themselves had to provide or even to originate securities as the basis of their loans. The latter was the case, for instance, in the last mentioned transaction of 1823; and as late as 1836 the Bank of New York raised funds in London from Morrison, Cryder and Company, merchant bankers, on the basis of its own four-year post notes (bonds) to be floated in the London money market.[227]

What influence experience so gained played in the City of New York remains an open question.

But it is certain that in the first half of the 1830's some of the New York incorporated banks practiced loan contracting as a part of their regular business. The Report of the Union Committee of 1834 pointed out that large amounts of stock, principally from the South-West, had been purchased in New York with a view to their sale in the English market, but that the sale had not answered the expectations of the contractors. They had been enabled, however, to borrow abroad considerable sums on the credit of such stock.[228]

To be sure, the authors of the Report did not explicitly state that incorporated banks were among those interested in the new line of banking. Rather they probably were thinking of the activities of brokers which will be described later in detail. But that chartered banks were then very active participants in the game is evident from other sources, and on the whole in America incorporated banks preceded brokers as embryonic investment bankers. Albany banks did a loan contracting business throughout the 1820's and 1830's. Two of their earliest, if not their earliest, contracts have been mentioned previously. Moreover in 1823 the Mechanics and Farmers Bank of that city took a $300,000 5 per cent canal loan; in 1830 the State Bank of Albany bid successfully for the Chemung Canal loan;[229] and in 1834 the Merchants and Mechanics Bank of Troy as well as the State and the Mechanics and Farmers Banks, both of Albany, (the latter two jointly and successfully) bid on the Chenango Canal loan of that year,[230] all loans of State of New York floated for the benefit of those canals. Entering this field in 1835 the Albany City Bank, under Erastus Corning as the president and Watts Sherman as cashier, seems to have made its first bid for the Chenango Canal loan of that year (possibly backed by John Delafield of the Phoenix Bank who had close business relations with Corning). In 1836 it bid again, this time successfully; Corning's offers on $100,000 at 101.40 and $100,000 at 101.55 were accepted, his only competitor on this issue of Chenango Canal bonds being Thomas W. Olcott who bid par for the allied State and Mechanics and Farmers Banks.[231]

In New York City, the Bank of the Manhattan Company, acting temporarily as some sort of fiscal agent of the Ohio Canal Commissioners, the Phoenix Bank (to be discussed forthwith), and the Morris Canal and Banking Company, which will be studied later, at an early moment became interested in loan contracting[232] and remained so for some time. Moreover the fact that by 1835 the Bank of America drew on the House of Baring against consignments of various securities permits the conclusion that it too participated in the game.[233] Research in the papers of the Manhattan Company would appear promising, but permission to use them was refused. All we know is that this bank contracted for a $1,000,000 New York loan of 1818 and bid unsuccessfully for $1,000,000 on the federal loan of 1821. Its close connection with the Ohio Canal Commissioners makes it highly probable that it took an interest in Ohio loans also.

In the case of the Phoenix Bank, one is able to point out the entrepreneur who brought it into the new field. The bank was originally chartered in 1812 as the New York Manufacturing Company and reorganized in 1817 when it assumed its new name. John Delafield (1786-1853) led it at the decisive moment. Son of the outstanding New York merchant of the same name, he became cashier of the bank upon his return from England where he had carried on a private banking business. Although he was considered by some of his associates an ambitious schemer he was permitted to rise to the presidency of the bank which he left in 1838 to head the New York Banking Company which broke down soon thereafter. (During his short connection with the latter enterprise Delafield contracted for $300,000 Illinois bonds.) The Phoenix Bank sold, for instance, a $100,000 Michigan loan in the 1830's and was approached by that state again in 1837 after the legislature had approved the flotation of a $5,000,000 loan. The bank was unable to handle this issue, although Delafield tried to cooperate with Prime, Ward and King.[234]

In the late 1830's almost all of the New York City banks were ready to turn loan contractors. Things began to move in this direction in 1834. In that year Governor Marcy recommended the issue of state stock to the banks in order to counteract Biddle and to alleviate the depression, whereupon "An Act authorizing a loan for the benefit of the people of this State" was passed (Laws 1834, chapter 130). Under this act several million dollar state stocks were to be lent to the banks of the City of New York, after having been issued by the Commissioners of the Canal Fund and a bank commissioner.[235] Nothing came of this plan. However in April, 1837, a number of New York City banks, authorized to do so by chapter 360 of the laws of that year, agreed to offer proposals for taking at par the whole of several loans of the State of New York offered by public notice of April 24:[236] namely, $2,000,000 canal stock, reimbursable in 1860; $800,000 canal stock, reimbursable in 1850; and $595,000 canal stock, reimbursable in 1845. Each species was to be distributed among the banks according to their capital, except in case the ratios were changed by common consent. (Together the allied banks represented a capital of $14,000,000.) Each bank was to be individually liable for its slice; payments were to be made in installments from 1837 through 1841. The Canal Commissioners were to give 90 days notice in advance, as to the sum required, whereupon each bank would pay its rateable share. No contract was concluded, however, because suspension interferred at an unpropitious moment.

Other similar negotiations were to follow. In September, 1837, the Comptroller of the State proposed selling the banks $2,700,000 state stock of which the Bank of New York, for instance, was willing to take $250,000. In October, following up that suggestion, the Canal Fund Commissioners indicated their willingness to "loan" stock to the banks. It was to be done on the condition that the latter pledged themselves to use it exclusively for obtaining specie (that is, through sale in the European capital markets). The banks were to pay the securities in specie or specie funds on certain dates or on 60 days notice, respectively, during the years 1838 through 1841. That is to say, the banks would de facto buy the stock, and the proceeds would remain on deposit with them until needed. A contract was concluded on this basis; but the circle of contractors was smaller than that of the would-be contractors or bidders of April, 1837. Eight institutions took stock as follows:

Bank of New York	$ 209,000
Merchants Bank	310,000
Manhattan Company	426,526.55
Union Bank	209,000
National Bank	160,000
Bank of the State of New York	
	416,000
	$1,730,526.55[237]

Before this transaction was concluded the Bank of America had taken $500,000 worth of securities under the same conditions paying $73,000 in specie as an advance. Otherwise the state would have defaulted on its interest payments.

A proposition very similar to that of the Comptroller of 1837 was brought before the legislature in 1838. When the New York City banks were preparing for resumption in that year, Governor Marcy in a special message of April 12, 1838 "regarding the resumption of specie payments" suggested that the credit of the state be made available to the banks. These he wanted to strengthen, so that they would be able to withstand attacks of non-specie paying banks (especially the Bank of the United States of Pennsylvania) without contracting cruelly and to the detriment of business. However no extra-state stock was to be created for that purpose. The Commissioners of the Canal Fund were to be authorized to issue in advance stock needed in the near future for certain indispensable work and to lend it to the banks on ample security for both interest payments and principal. The latter were to pay the stock in installments. A bill embodying the proposal was lost in the House.[238]

In 1839, however, the State of New York urgently needed funds in order to avoid postponing its public works and defaulting on its interest payments. All attempts at floating a sufficient amount of securities had come to naught. The New York banks on the other hand were faced with the problem of how to uphold specie payments in view of Philadelphia suspension. Their only chance was using saleable securities for remittances to London. Under these circumstances $1,500,000 worth of state bonds were sold to New York commercial banks, with the understanding that the proceeds would be deposited with the lenders and drawn out only according to the anticipated demand. Details regarding this loan and its distribution among the various banks have not come to the attention of the author,[239] except that the Bank of Commerce and the Bank of America received a credit from the Barings on the basis of these bonds (which the latter were entitled to sell), while the Bank of New York sent its share or parts thereof to Huth and Company issuing drafts against its consignment. Prior to the conclusion of the $1,500,000 contract, the Bank of the Manhattan Company had taken $500,000 state bonds by special arrangement regarding the deposit of canal funds, and slightly thereafter the Bank of America took an issue of $208,533.90[240]

The participation of incorporated banks in loan flotations was not confined to the State of New York. From testimony by Thomas Biddle before a Congressional Committee we know that in contracting for Pennsylvania loans he cooperated with some of the Philadelphia banks. One of them was undoubtedly the Bank of Pennsylvania which by 1830 began to consign Pennsylvania bonds to the Barings.[241] By 1839 the situation was approaching that in contemporaneous New York, Thomas Dunlap, Biddle's successor as the President of the Bank of the United States of Pennsylvania, assuming leadership. In a letter of April 18 of that year he invited the Philadelphia banks to unite with his bank in taking a $1,200,000 Pennsylvania state loan, thus moving in the direction toward what would be called a syndicate today. He was successful, and as the head of that alliance placed the loan. The share of the Bank of North America was $25,000 and it was sold by the latter bank forthwith so that we have here a clear case of loan contracting by an incorporated bank.[242] In 1840 when there was danger that the Commonwealth would be unable to meet the interest payments on its loans,

the Bank of North America, once more invited by Thomas Dunlap, decided to subscribe $25,000 to an $870,000 loan of that year.[243] A few months later the Secretary of the Commonwealth required the same bank to subscribe its share of $20,000 to a $3,000,000 loan authorized to cover interest payments and repair and completion of internal improvements.[244]

These facts show how near the incorporated banks of the commercial capitals of the country came to getting a foothold in the field of investment banking. It can be assumed that they lost it only because of the severe depression of the 1840's.

To what extent Western and Southern commercial banks entered the embryonic investment banking business is difficult to decide from the very scanty material available. But it seems significant that the Republic of Texas appealed to Southern commercial banks as investors in her securities or as loan contractors, by expressing her willingness to take bank notes in payment for her stock and furthermore by offering that the notes of any bank subscribing more than $100,000 would be taken in payment of public dues. (It will be remembered that during the War of 1812 Jacob Barker had tried to sell United States bonds to commercial banks on this basis. Moreover the Morris Canal and Banking Company had tried to tie together a deal in Michigan securities and the expansion of its circulation.) In fact the president of the Commercial and Railroad Bank of Vicksburg concluded a tentative contract with the Republic of Texas which, however, was disavowed by the bank. By that time the Union Bank of Louisiana and the Commercial Bank, both of New Orleans, took small interests in bonds of the State of Alabama, but it is not known if they acted as institutional investors or loan contractors. As to Western banks, The Ohio Life Insurance and Trust Company may have taken an interest in investment banking. It seems to have contracted for Ohio bonds and at a slightly later period to have had its hands in railroad finance.[245]

From the foregoing it can be seen that there were various reasons which brought commercial banks into embryonic investment banking, first among them being, of course, the striving for profit from loan contracting. This field must have appeared promising, for it was young and no specialization was necessary for success therein. However additional advantages might be derived by commercial banks from such activities. One was the previously mentioned chance of expanding their circulation in connection with floating securities. Another possibility of gain was recognized at a very early moment in New York. When this state, as mentioned earlier, tried to sell an issue of canal bonds in 1817, only one bid was tendered and this bid was below par. Then it was discovered that commercial banks were willing to acquire securities if they received the debt certificates immediately but had to pay only slowly. Or, as the first transaction of this kind was made to appear, the commercial bank in question contracted for the securities and paid therefor, while the proceeds were deposited with it and drawn out only as they were needed for the purpose for which the funds were raised. If the commercial bank was able to sell the contracted bonds faster than the proceeds were needed, it had the use of large funds for months without paying interest thereon. After its experience with the loan of 1817 the State of New York established that policy for all its loans floated between 1817 and 1826. The policy was sanctioned by implication in the Act to improve the funds and to provide for the redemption of the funded debt of this state (passed April 21, 1818). Sec. XVI of this Act permitted state funds to be deposited in whatever bank in New York City might loan to the state $1,000,000.[246] The policy was abandoned, however, in the later 1820's when canal bonds were taken eagerly; it had to be reintroduced in 1838 and 1839 when the depression made new issues otherwise unsaleable.[247] As the documents show, the Canal Fund Commissioners were very unhappy about this return to a discarded policy.[248]

VIII

The way for private bankers to enter the investment banking business was opened in the 1820's and early 1830's when their forerunners, New York and Philadelphia brokers, invaded the field.[249] The passage in the Report of the Union Committee previously-cited undoubtedly referred to these firms which to a large extent used the contracted securities for remittances to London.

Most important among the private bankers venturing into investment banking prior to the 1840's was Prime, Ward and King of New York whose history has been given in an earlier chapter.[250] Nathaniel Prime himself, the founder of the firm, seems to have made it a pioneer in the field. In 1821, as mentioned before, it bid with others against the Second Bank of the United States on the $5,000,000 federal loan of that year. In 1824 Prime himself was instrumental in inducing Thomas Wilson and Company of London to buy Louisiana bonds floated in favor of the State Bank of Louisiana. In the same decade the firm seems to have been connected with Ohio and New York issues, and in 1828 in cooperation with John Jacob

Astor it bid on New York City stock. Nathaniel Prime resigned from his firm as early as 1832 and its real heads thereafter were, first, Samuel Ward (1786-1839) and after his death James Gore King (1791-1853). To these we must look as responsible for the firm's further achievements in investment banking.[251] In July, 1833, it was among the buyers of $2,000,000 Mississippi state bonds sold in favor of the Planters Bank, its allies being S. and M. Allen, J. D. Beers and Company, John Gossler for Thomas Wilson and Company of London, Thomas Biddle and Company, James Schott (1783-1870), Philadelphia merchant and president of the Girard Bank.[252] In 1834 in cooperation with Elisha Tibbits it bid unsuccessfully on $900,000 New York state bonds issued in favor of the Chenango Canal; while in 1837 it succeeded in alliance with Thomas W. Olcott (Mechanics and Farmers Bank of Albany) in securing $525,000 worth of such bonds issued to finance the Chemung Canal. In 1838 it was connected with the sale of Indiana bonds issued in favor of the Wabash and Erie Canal and took two issues of $500,000 each of New York canal bonds. Finally in 1839 it acquired first $310,000 and later that year $1,500,000 New York Canal bonds. It is not certain, however, if Prime, Ward and King's interest in the New York Life Insurance and Trust Company was prompted by its investment banking activities or if it had other reasons. Shares of that company were bought, partly on joint account with the Barings, in 1832 and 1833 and sold in London through the latter.

By that time Prime, Ward and King's strength had come to lie in their acting as allies, subcontractors or at least correspondents of the Barings who valued them as reliable tenders, well-informed correspondents, and strong potential participants in risk-taking. The Barings currently sold securities for Prime, Ward and King on commission or on joint account. In 1831, for example, the Barings seem to have shared with the New York house in a purchase of Mississippi bonds. In 1832 Prime, Ward and King as allies of the London merchant bankers participated in a deal concerning the $5,500,000 Louisiana state bonds issued in favor of the Union Bank of Louisiana. They contracted for $1,800,000 thereof in cooperation with the three New York firms, Beers, Joseph, and John Ward. In 1833 Thomas Wren Ward, representing the House of Baring, agreed verbally with Prime, Ward and King and a few other firms interested in loan contracting to cooperate in bidding on first class loans; but bids actually submitted for a $2,500,000 Pennsylvania loan of March and for a $200,000 Virginia loan of June were not high enough. In 1835, however, Prime, Ward and King, T. W. Ward, and William Appleton were joined by the Barings in acquiring $600,000 of a $3,000,000 Maryland loan. Moreover in December, 1835, the New York firm had large quantities of the following securities for sale with Baring Brothers and Company: first, on their own account, New Orleans 6 per cent and Florida 6 per cent; secondly, on joint account, shares of the Bank of Louisiana, of the Louisiana State Bank, the (New Orleans) Canal and Banking Company, the Bank of the United States, Ohio 6 per cent and Maryland bonds; thirdly on "various accounts" Kentucky 5 per cent bonds. (Of course, not all of those securities were contracted, some were acquired second or even third hand.) Finally, in 1837, during a trip to London James Gore King attempted to sell $300,000 Michigan securities to the Barings, an attempt which came to naught because the state had, in the meantime, disposed of the bonds to the New York broker Edward R. Biddle.[253]

The alliance of Prime, Ward and King and the Barings persisted after the crisis of 1837. The former firm on joint account or consignment sent to London, New York state and city bonds, and bonds of Alabama, Ohio, Michigan, and of the New York Merchants' Exchange. In 1838 Ohio, Indiana, New York, and Alabama bonds followed. In the same year the Barings expected Prime, Ward and King to participate in security transactions for which the house had allied itself with Hope and Company of Amsterdam. Again it is not possible to determine to what extent the securities before mentioned had been acquired by contracting and to what extent they had been purchased in the market. However, it becomes clear beyond doubt that during the 1830's rudimentary investment banking and large scale trading in securities went hand in hand. Even the Barings were as much loan contractors and "negotiators" as they were security dealers. They bought securities directly from the long term borrower as well as second hand, and they sold on a commission basis for the former just as well as for the latter. The same was undoubtedly true both of the American private bankers competing with Prime, Ward and King and the London houses competing with the Barings.

Regardless of such close connection between Prime, Ward and King and the Barings the New York house occasionally had other allies. It joined certain English houses in bidding (unsuccessfully) on a Maryland loan, and in alliance with N. M. Rothschild and Sons it contracted for a Missouri issue.

Thomas Biddle and Company of Philadelphia was another early leader in the field. It is hard to say whether in the 1820's and 1830's this was a firm of brokers or private bankers. Be that as it may, it had developed out of a commercial enter-

prise, founded in 1764 by John Biddle, a shipping merchant trading with Europe and the West Indies. Through his son Clement, who seems to have taken an interest in security dealings, the firm came down to the latter's son Thomas (1776-1857) who joined his father as early as 1791. He developed the enterprise until in the 1830's the members of Thomas Biddle and Company were considered "the most accomplished brokers" in Philadelphia and as "more prompt and skilfull" than their competitors. Thomas Biddle had first become acquainted with loan contracting as a subcontractor of David Parish when the latter acquired a considerable slice of the $16,000,000 federal loan of 1814, his (Biddle's) share amounting to $2,000,000 (?). Shortly thereafter he was connected with "Dallas's loan" of 1815, but only as an agent of European capitalists and of Richard Bache. From that time on Thomas Biddle and Company remained in the field. In 1821, as has been described in detail, they "formed a list" with Prime, Ward and King and Charles King of New York for the purpose of bidding against the Second Bank of the United States on the $5,000,000 federal loan of that year; and soon thereafter they began contracting for state loans also. They took, for instance, an Ohio loan, probably in competition with the Bank of the Manhattan Company. Cooperating again with Prime, Ward and King they shared in a contract for the previously mentioned issue of Mississippi state bonds (authorized for the benefit of the Planters Bank); and in 1835, together with Samuel Jaudon and Elihu Chauncey, Thomas Biddle purchased $500,000 worth of bonds of the Bank of Pensacola, guaranteed by the Territory of Florida. As was natural for a firm of this type, located in Philadelphia, Thomas Biddle and Company, in conjunction with other houses, including commercial banks, took shares in almost all the contemporaneous Pennsylvania loans, several million dollars worth of stock of the state, all told. This enumeration hardly covers all their transactions in the investment banking field.[254]

Those private firms which, besides Prime, Ward and King and Thomas Biddle and Company, took an interest in security flotations prior to 1840 had certainly not overstepped the borderline between brokerage and private banking proper. J. D. Beers and Company stands out among them. In 1831 the firm seems to have taken a slice of $500,000 Mississippi state bonds issued in favor of the Planters Bank. In 1832 it handled a $100,000 issue of Indiana state bonds floated for the benefit of the Wabash and Erie Canal; it was accused of sharp practices in this connection. In the same year we find it along with others as an ally of Prime, Ward and King in the purchase of Louisiana bonds authorized in favor of the Union Bank of Louisiana. Slightly later (in 1833) in the same capacity it became connected with another tranche of Mississippi bonds issued in the interest of the Planters Bank. In the same year in cooperation with Thomas Wren Ward, acting for the Barings, and others it bid unsuccessfully on Pennsylvania and Virginia bonds. Finally in the late 1830's the Beers firm seems to have subscribed $1,000,000 worth of Arkansas bonds, later taken over by the North American Trust and Banking Company.

Another firm trying its hands in the new game was S. and M. Allen whose career has been sketched in an earlier chapter.[255] The Allens had previously contracted for lottery tickets and after the 1820's some branches of the house ran a stock brokerage business. By 1833 they were ready to become full fledged loan contractors: they not only participated in the purchase of the Planters Bank bonds of that year just mentioned, but also contracted for a complete issue of Pennsylvania state bonds amounting to $3,500,000. This transaction proved their undoing during the engineered depression of 1834, although they could have had the backing of the Rothschilds the year preceding and were closely connected with Wilson and Company, the London merchant bankers. Incidentally, the Baltimore private bankers, Jacob I. Cohen, Jr., and Brothers, who like the Allens had started as tellers of lottery tickets and note shavers tried to enter the promising field too.[256]

In the flotation of Union Bank bonds alluded to there participated also John Ward and Company (about whom more will be said) and J. and L. Joseph, both of New York. The latter firm represented the Rothschilds who may have taken an interest in the Louisiana bonds through their agents. Previously, in 1831, the Josephs had taken besides, or perhaps in alliance with Joseph D. Beers, a share in the issue of $500,000 Mississippi state bonds;[257] and in 1836 they subscribed to an abortive Texas loan offered in New York. They were large land speculators besides, interested in a Staten Island real estate development and, like J. D. Beers and Company, were associates in the American Land Company (established by New York and Boston capitalists to purchase cotton lands in the Southwest). Moreover they took a hand in the Texas land gamble, especially financing Texas scrip. They broke down in 1837; and Scoville remarked in retrospect that while they had the qualities to succeed as merchants, private banking was beyond their capacity.[258]

American merchant bankers we have not met so far among those interested in investment banking prior to 1840, a situation which stands in noteworthy contrast to the English. There merchant bankers were leading in the field. To be sure, in the 1830's Alexander Brown and Sons of Baltimore, administered by George Brown (1787-1859), the son of the founder, took a flyer into the field. In cooperation with Jacob I. Cohen, Jr., and Brothers of that city and others he contracted for a $2,000,000 issue of Maryland bonds which were sold abroad.[259] There was logic to that attempt at investment banking. The Brown concern had previously always held "a good lot" of securities, because it enabled them to manage their exchange operations to greater advantage and prevented the occasional accumulation of idle funds.

Besides the Browns, established merchant bankers, one local merchant tried his hand in the new game, namely, Oliver Newberry (1789-1861). Of Puritan New England stock he was the son of an up-state New York farmer and started his career as a store owner in Buffalo and later in Detroit where by 1822 he had founded a forwarding and commission business. After these humble beginnings he became a wealthy merchant and owner of Lake ships. A branch which he established in Chicago went into the packing business and took first place among the grain carriers on the Upper Lakes. In 1837 Newberry bought $100,000 worth of Chicago bonds which he sold in New York; but when he tried to "negotiate" $500,000 worth of Michigan bonds in the winter of 1837/1838 this slice proved too big: he sold only $200,000 and had to return the rest. The attempt of this local merchant to go into the investment banking business, even though unsuccessful, is truly remarkable.[260]

Thus, besides the Bank of the United States of Pennsylvania to be studied shortly and the incorporated banks previously discussed, it was a motley crowd of unspecialized firms, among whom highly speculative New York brokers and bankers held first place, which represented in the 1820's and especially the 1830's what later became the specialized investment banking business.

In order to understand the competitive situation which obtained in our field in the 1830's, it is necessary to anticipate what will be said in the next section of this chapter on the Bank of the United States of Pennsylvania and its head, Nicholas Biddle. This Bank, regardless of its strength and regardless of its specializing in investment banking activities, was far from dominating the field. The mere amount of securities coming into the market would have made any attempt at cornering it abortive. In fact, the Bank competed on two levels: first, with New York commercial banks and private bankers in securing bonds and selling them to American investors and speculative dealers; and secondly, with the London bankers, such as the Barings, Rothschilds, Palmer, MacKillop,

Dent and Company, Magniac, Smith and Company, Huth and Company, and others in the sale to European ultimate investors and dealers. The Bank encountered the Barings and Rothschilds or their correspondents and agents, respectively, on both levels. Biddle's main entrepreneurial achievement in this field lay in making the Bank grow beyond the status of a national enterprise and of a mere American tender of the London investment bankers. He made it their peer and competitor when with the help of his London agency he began to deal directly with European capitalists, the ultimate investors. (That he did not make friends among those London houses whose field he invaded goes without saying.)

But the business was competitive in still another respect. Particular borrowers were not tied to particular investment bankers as was to become customary later: Illinois, for instance, did business with the Phoenix Bank of New York, the Bank of the United States of Pennsylvania, and directly with Magniac, Smith and Company of London; Indiana dealt within one decade with J. D. Beers and Company of New York, the Morris Canal and Banking Company, and Prime, Ward and King. Michigan worked with the Phoenix Bank and Oliver Newberry, the above mentioned local capitalist who was unable to do the job he had promised; she also negotiated through Prime, Ward and King with the Barings; and finally concluded a contract with the Morris Canal and Banking Company.[261] Florida bonds, finally, were sold or offered in New York, London (Samuel Jaudon, Palmer, MacKillop, Dent and Company), Amsterdam (Hope and Company), and the German Hanseatic cities. In consequence, as Ralph Hidy points out, portions of the same loan were often held by different parties in London which depressed the market for such securities.

The specific form which competition took was determined by the prevailing practice of the borrowing states. Only in exceptional cases did a state advertise for sealed bids, as New York and Ohio did,[262] thereby aiming at a public subscription, to use the English eighteenth-century term. As a rule the states first authorized loans and then started negotiating with a limited number of firms interested in the investment banking field. That is to say, they followed the example of English eighteenth-century private subscriptions with one difference: in England the negotiation preceded the loan act; in America the sequence was the opposite.

It goes without saying that at least a limited percentage of all American bond issues of the period was sold in the United States. As a matter of fact, by 1840 not only were there individuals in the market, but also institutional investors, savings banks and insurance and trust companies. In 1833 the New York Life Insurance and Trust Company, for example, had funds invested in banks, insurance companies, railroads, utilities, and in state stock of Ohio and Alabama.[263] In fact the domestic market must have been comparatively strong. When securities became unsaleable in London in the early 1840's large amounts were returned to the United States and were ultimately absorbed so that they did not become worthless. The Barings, for instance, sold in Charleston, S.C., South Carolina bonds undigestable in London.[264]

However with regard to the lion's share of all bond issues the American participants in the business, with the sole exception of the Bank of the United States of Pennsylvania, were national middlemen playing into the hands of a second layer of English middlemen, among whom the Barings were the leaders. Beginning in 1833 N. M. Rothschild and Sons became interested in American securities also and they were estimated to have held about $5,000,000 worth in 1835.[265] These English middlemen as wholesalers or commission merchants in securities served the British, Dutch and, to a less extent, French, Swiss, and Danish capital markets. For example, the North American Trust and Banking Company of New York, to be studied later, took bonds of the State of Arkansas issued in favor of the Real Estate Bank and the State Bank of Arkansas and sold slices to Frederick Huth and Company and to Palmer, MacKillop, Dent and Company, both of London; while the remainder was to be "negotiated" by the former firm. The Barings "negotiated" Ohio bonds for the Ohio Life Insurance and Trust Company; Ohio and Alabama bonds for Prime, Ward and King, and so on. The chains were often rather long: Michigan bonds bought from the state by Oliver Newberry found their way into the portfolio of New York banks which certainly meant to unload them on English middlemen.[266] Moreover, Hidy reports that several smaller American firms interested in security dealings, such as Coster and Carpenter, Dorr and Tappan, Shipman and Corning, and Macalester and York, continuously sent securities to the Barings for sale, sometimes in connection with exchange dealings. When this house in 1833 became reluctant to proceed with the sale of American securities, blocks were sent to the London merchant bankers Wiggin and Company and Wilson and Company.[267] To the extent that the houses above mentioned and other smaller houses, consigning securities to London, were not contractors themselves, but mere dealers buying from contractors, which appears possible, and in some cases even probable, the chains were lengthened too. As a matter of fact, the role which American commercial banks and private bankers played in the field between about 1820 and 1860 was very similar to that of the French private bankers between 1817 and 1821 in their relation to the Barings and Hopes; and it is telling for the strength of the contemporaneous American national economy that a stage which lasted about four years in France lasted about forty in the United States.

American middlemen were not even able to form a really efficient bottleneck. Many securities reached the European capital markets directly, as for instance certain quantities of Louisiana and Maryland bonds which were contracted by the Barings, or a portion of the Boston loan of 1834, taken jointly by the Barings and Hope and Company. The last named two firms in 1838 purchased $1,000,000 5 per cent bonds of South Carolina; Illinois bonds were offered directly to Frederic Huth and Company of London; and N. M. Rothschild and Sons contracted for a slice of a Missouri issue in 1838. Other issues were "negotiated" for the issuers or the first hand[268] without having been touched by American middlemen, as for example Louisiana, Maryland, and Massachusetts loans by the Barings for the Union Bank of Louisiana, the Baltimore and Ohio Railroad, the Chesapeake and Ohio Canal Company, and the Western Railroad, respectively. Such issues as were traded in the European markets without having been handled by American middlemen or without having been "negotiated" in Europe for the issuers or the first hand were either acquired with the help of the American correspondents or agents of European investment bankers or from American salesmen traveling abroad in behalf of American issuers. Washington, Georgetown, and Alexandria, authorized by law to raise funds for subscriptions to the Chesapeake and Ohio Canal, sold their bonds to Dutch houses through the intervention of the latters' New York representatives; Louisiana banks, benefited by state bonds, approached the Barings and Hopes either through the latters' American representatives or in Europe through duly authorized commissioners. Illinois, Texas, and Florida bonds were sold in Europe by traveling salesmen, if you please. Such men were, for instance, W. F. Thornton, president of the Illinois Board of Canal Commissioners who while in Europe in 1840 sold bonds of that state to Magniac, Smith and Company; or James Hamilton who tried to sell Texas bonds in England and France; or John Gamble who hawked Florida bonds all over Europe; or the notorious Samuel Swartout who negotiated abroad a loan for the Cumberland Coal Company.[269] This method of floating new securities by charging an agent with their sale does not seem to have died out in the 1840's and 1850's when American investment banking became somewhat stronger. Dr. Larson

reports a case of the 1850's. In that decade an agent was appointed to sell Philadelphia bonds issued in favor of the Sunbury and Erie Railroad. He was to receive $1\frac{1}{2}$ per cent commission and a traveling allowance, and was not to sell the bonds below certain prices which differed for the United States and Europe.[270]

As to the methods used by America's early investment bankers, it must be pointed out that in this country loan contracting[271] preceded the "negotiating" of securities. No case of the latter type of transaction concluded by any native American firm (commercial or private bank) prior to 1836 has come to the attention of the author. However American securities were very often "negotiated," when handled by Dutch or English firms, as, for instance, in 1834 the bonds of the Citizens Bank of Louisiana through W. Willinck of Amsterdam, an abortive "negotiation," to be sure. In the same year $1,500,000 worth of Louisiana state bonds assigned to the Union Bank were consigned to the Barings to be "negotiated;" and in 1839 Frederick Huth and Company of London undertook to handle Arkansas bonds that way for the account of the contractor, the North American Trust and Banking Company.[272] Such transactions, of course, familiarized American firms with the method of "negotiations." It was introduced into the practice of American firms by Nicholas Biddle when he brought the Bank of the United States of Pennsylvania into the field of investment banking.[273]

IX

Nicholas Biddle, after having been this country's first central banker and after having met defeat in this capacity, became its first full-fledged, almost specialized, investment banker by developing the Bank of the United States of Pennsylvania into a new type of enterprise. Most scholars today dealing with that concern (like the Bank's contemporaries) have completely misunderstood its character and have measured it according to commercial banking standards. But passing judgment on that basis is both erroneous and unjust. To be sure, the Bank of the United States of Pennsylvania failed, but it failed at least in part because it was too far ahead of its time, combining commercial and investment banking, but pushing the latter activities. The first great business leader to make the corresponding attempt in Europe, Jacques Laffitte, died (fortunately for him) before his enterprise collapsed. He could not have saved it. His Caisse Laffitte was, like Biddle's Bank of the United States of Pennsylvania, a combination of commercial and investment banking with the emphasis on the latter.[274] But the time had not yet arrived for such a combination of functions which at that early moment was not a conscious integration, but was due to the growth of a new function in old-line enterprises. Only after Biddle's and Laffitte's failures and after additional experiences had been gained in the equally unsuccessful Crédit Mobilier were the German Grossbanken able to make a great success out of the type of enterprise which Biddle had been the first to envisage.

As happens so often in social history, in this case also, the new came into existence merely by a small change in emphasis. Throughout the 1820's, 1830's, and early 1840's, as described above, commercial banks, especially in New York, Albany, and Philadelphia, had conducted embryonic investment banking as a side line of their regular commercial banking business. By shifting the emphasis of the concern's activities to investment banking while commercial banking functions were permitted to decline, a new type of enterprise came into being in the Bank of the United States of Pennsylvania.

It is of great interest to watch step by step how Biddle was drawn into the field of investment banking. As has been mentioned before, it began when he contracted for the federal loans of 1824 and 1825. In these transactions he was more than the traditional loan contractor, for he no longer competed with investors. The Second Bank of the United States like a modern investment banking firm took for resale whole issues of new securities from the government in need of long term funds. There is no doubt that from the outset Biddle had resale of the securities in his mind. As early as 1827 he mentioned with some pride to Richard Rush, then Secretary of the Treasury, that of $28,000,000 funded debt originally in the possession of the Bank only $17,000,000 remained at that moment.[275] A few weeks later he wrote to a United States Senator and director of the Bank that he would sell out his government stock as soon as business revived and that he would invest in discounts the funds thus made liquid, a type of investment which was more profitable for the Bank.[276] In the summer of the same year Biddle actually embarked on such a policy using Nathaniel Prime of New York as his sales agent. The minimum sales price was set by Biddle himself and the agent was bound not to divulge the information that the Bank was selling its government stock.[277]

A second type of transaction which brought Biddle into the field of investment banking was that of security loans. In 1828, for instance, the Bank made loans on Chesapeake and Ohio Canal stock. As a holder of Washington real estate acquired in the settlement of bad debts it was in-

terested in the canal's success. Moreover Biddle was convinced that Rush, then embarking for Europe, would succeed in negotiating bonds of the City of Washington which was authorized by an act to subscribe $1,000,000 canal stock with funds raised by such an issue. So Biddle lent funds on a note of the City of Washington secured by certificates of canal stock.[278] Similarly in 1830 Biddle was willing to lend the Chesapeake and Delaware Canal Company at the rate of 5 per cent on its 5 per cent Maryland stock unless the company meant to sell the latter.[279] Such transactions, on the one hand, and Biddle's continuous striving for being well informed, on the other, made him thoroughly familiar with the limited number of security issues then coming into the market. His correspondence shows that he tried to keep abreast of the development. In 1830 he requested information on a pending Mississippi loan[280] and gave advice as to federal, Ohio, and Pennsylvania bonds.[281]

By that time Biddle was contemplating a further step: the intention of the Secretary of the Treasury to pay off two million dollars of the last seven million of federal bonds which the Bank possessed forced him to look around for new possibilities. Interested as he was in the Southwest he scouted that territory for suitable investments. He thought of Louisiana state stock (if it could be had in large quantities), of the bonds of a new plantation bank planned in Louisiana (the Union Bank), and of a loan to the State of Mississippi.[282] However in entering this type of business Biddle ran against charter limitations. The Bank was not permitted to lend to states or to purchase public debts, i.e., debts of any state of the Union. But typically Biddle found a way of cutting corners. His close friends, such as Thomas Biddle or Roswell L. Colt, of Baltimore, would buy the securities in which Biddle wished to invest the funds of the Bank and borrow the purchase price from it, pledging the acquired securities. In November, 1830, for instance, Biddle offered to fund a debt of the State of Louisiana. The latter was to draw on Colt, while the debt certificates were to be sent directly to the Bank. Colt would then obtain a loan on his own responsibility, collaterally secured by the stock. Conditions of concluding the deal were a rate of interest of no less than 6 per cent, an issue-course of no more than par, and a duration of the loan of several years.[283] What Biddle meant to do with the state stock thus purchased through a dummy is not clear. He probably wished to sell the securities in Colt's name or through Colt so that the proceeds covered the "loan" to the latter. One wonders who would have received the profits from an appreciation of the securities, who would have borne losses from depreciation, and how Colt was to be renumerated for lending his name. In 1832 Biddle loaned Thomas Biddle and Company funds wherewith to contract for Pennsylvania bonds, and it is probable that he had a similar transaction in his mind when in the same year he wrote to several men in Tuscaloosa. They were informed that Biddle was willing to help them dispose of $300,000 newly created stock of the State of Alabama by submitting their proposals to capitalists who could be expected to be interested in the loan. The correspondents were advised to make the interest payable in Philadelphia or New York and to determine in advance whether the loan was to be paid back in installments or in one sum at a specified date.[284] In July of the same year we find Biddle keenly interested in the Louisiana bonds assigned to the Union Bank of that state and speaking of a party which had submitted a proposal for the whole issue. This "party" may well have had the Bank's backing, to put it mildly, and the purchase in 1835 of bonds of the Bank of Pensacola by Thomas Biddle, Samuel Jaudon (the Bank's cashier), and Elihu Chauncey was in all probability a transaction of the same type.[285] Finally, Biddle's own heavy investments in such securities as Delaware and Raritan Canal, Camden and Amboy, and Baltimore and Ohio Railroad stocks may have represented disguised activities of the Bank which lent Biddle the purchase price.[286] But it is equally possible that in the 1830's Biddle was America's earliest great railroad financier at a time when this line was not as yet institutionalized. Certain research indicating that Philadelphia was this country's first center of railroad finance points in this direction, but the hypothesis needs verification.

The charter limitations just described did not extend to loans to cities, however, so that the latter were the wedge through which the Bank of the United States could enter forbidden hunting grounds. In 1830 Biddle was interested in loans to the cities of Mobile and New Orleans.[287] In 1831 through the cashier of the Bank's branch at Cincinnati he advised the latter city regarding a loan and offered to take it if his conditions were met and the better ones which the city wished could not be obtained elsewhere.[288] It is noteworthy that in contrast to Biddle's eagerness the Barings were very selective when considering American municipal issues.

There can be no doubt that when working for the Pennsylvania charter of the Bank of the United States Biddle aimed at a release from such limitations in order to do a full-fledged investment banking business. The legislators themselves with whom his men dealt at Harrisburg unwittingly paved the way. In line with tradition, as has been described, they forced the Bank to invest considerable amounts of its capital in stock of various improvement companies. Such was the magnitude of these investments that they alone were bound to determine the future policy of the enterprise thus burdened. On top of that, Article IV of the Act to repeal the state tax on real and personal property and to continue and extend the improvements of the state railroads and canals and to charter a state bank to be called the United States Bank reads: The said corporation shall not be at liberty to purchase any stock whatever, except their own stock, treasury notes or public stocks, created by the government of the United States, or of this state, or stock of, or loans to any of the incorporated companies of this state, for the construction and improvement of roads, bridges, canals or inland navigation, or other stocks which may be bona fide pledged as security for debts to the Bank, and not duly redeemed. Thus the stage was set, regardless of the queer negative form in which the authorization of investment banking was couched.[289]

The original charter of the Bank of the United States of Pennsylvania, however, was still not what Biddle wanted, and it had hardly been accepted when we find him working on an amendment. This amendment was to remove all impediments to the Bank's doing a full-fledged investment banking business in every possible field. In March, 1836, an amendment to the Bank's charter was before the legislature authorizing it to buy bank stock. Biddle suggested that it read "bank and other stock," explaining slyly that other companies such as insurance companies were doing a banking business also and that it might be useful to employ and possess such enterprises. He obviously veiled his ulterior motives.[290] To be sure, Biddle was not successful: sec. 2 of An Act requiring the Banks of this Commonwealth to make quarterly statements to the auditor-general and for other purposes reads: "for the more convenient management of the affairs of the Bank of the United States the said corporation is hereby authorized... to purchase any bank stock."[291]

Nevertheless the authorization was broad enough to permit Biddle to develop an investment banking business; (and incidentally the fact that from 1837 on the Rothschilds and their agent August Belmont, appear as correspondents in Biddle's letterbooks is indicative of the development).[292] In building up his new business Biddle used the traditional methods of "contracting" and "negotiating" securities. As examples of the first mentioned type of transaction one may cite the subscription of the Bank of the United States of Pennsylvania of $250,000 stock of the Little Schuylkill and Susquehanna Railroad. In fact it subscribed to "loans and stocks" of nineteen improvement corporations "including those embraced in the charter." To the extent that it "subscribed" to such loans (bonds), it actually contracted for them. But with regard to state issues charter limitations, described above, forbade contracting. When nevertheless the Bank contracted de facto, as in the case of the $5,000,000 Mississippi state bonds floated for the benefit of the Planters Bank, it had to do so by stealth. (In this case Biddle himself appeared as the contractor while the Bank guaranteed the payment. Later the securities were taken over by the Bank in settlement of the debt incurred by Biddle when paying the installments.) As a rule, however, in order not to violate the spirit of the law Biddle introduced into the American practice loan "negotiating" of the Dutch type which, as mentioned above, does not seem to have been used earlier in this country.[293]

The Bank's remuneration for the "negotiation" of securities was in general $1\frac{1}{2}$ per cent commission, which included "the expenses of brokerage and any incidental disbursements." In addition, for paying dividends on the "negotiated" securities 1 per cent was billed. The $1\frac{1}{2}$ per cent commission was in excess of what competing commercial banks would charge for the "negotiation" of securities, but the rate seems to have remained below that of the Barings who demanded 2 per cent if drafts were made in advance of sales.[294] Biddle felt that he was entitled to charge more than his American competitors, because the Bank had in Samuel Jaudon its own representative in the London capital market and so could give services over and above what was customary. Moreover the Bank was desirous "to connect itself with such operations," or, to put it in modern terms, the Bank was to specialize in security flotations which would so increase its efficiency that an extra charge was justified. Payment was made to the borrowers or their accounts were credited against earlier advances as soon as the securities entrusted for "negotiation" were sold. Payment was based on the rate of exchange of 60-day bills on London as of the day on which the notice of the deposit of the value in London was received by the Bank.[295]

If Biddle had conducted loan "negotiations" in the way which was common in Amsterdam in the eighteenth century he would hardly have run much risk. However he established the dangerous policy of lending on the securities which he was going to sell on commission, although not in all cases. In several instances he strictly refused applications to that effect;[296] but on the whole he would rather loan than refuse to loan.

For Biddle this policy was the logical development of the "lending on stock securities" which he had practiced while he was still the president of the "national bank." He continued and preferred it to every other type of loan during the period after his defeat by President Jackson when he was preparing for liquidation.[297] By giving it a slight turn, that old policy of his was revamped: the Bank of the United States of Pennsylvania tied together the "negotiation" of securities and the lending thereon before they were sold. To be sure, Biddle did not devise this policy; it was also practiced in England by the leaders in the field of investment banking such as Baring Brothers and Company.[298] But, as usual, Biddle went to extremes. Thereby the combination of loan "negotiating" and advances on securities by which nineteenth-century "negotiating" was distinguished from eighteenth-century transactions of the same type became an exceedingly dangerous procedure. This was particularly so, since the Bank, possibly under Biddle, certainly under Dunlap, compensated too often for a lack of loanable funds by itself borrowing, profiting from the difference between interest rates in England and America and those for borrowers with first and second class credit ratings. The very bonds on which the Bank lent were often hypothecated in England. If ever the bottom should drop out of the security market, as in fact it did, and securities on which advances had been made became unsaleable, the issuer would, of course, be unable to repay what he had received. What was planned to be loan "negotiating" would then ex post become loan contracting, for nothing would remain except to take over the securities in the hope that they would later appreciate. In consequence the enterprise concerned would first become illiquid and thereafter proceed on the usual road from illiquidity to insolvency. This was the one which America's first real investment bank was actually going to travel; and it was Biddle's policy of tying together lending with security "negotiations" which in addition to other mistakes broke the Bank of the United States of Pennsylvania.[299]

Until fate caught up with the Bank there was no type of American securities in the floation of which it was not willing to lend a helping hand. (To be sure, Biddle declined to have anything to do with the flotation of loans for Spain, as was suggested to him.)[300] The "detailed statement" as of December 21, 1840 prepared by a committee of stockholders and the accompanying "detailed account of stock" show the breadth of the Bank's activities in the security field.[301] At that time the Bank held state loans amounting to about $15,000,000 (Illinois, Indiana, Maryland, Michigan, Mississippi, Pennsylvania, and even Texas bonds and treasury notes from which Biddle originally had shied away).[302] It owned city bonds (Harrisburg, Lancaster, Mobile, Pittsburgh).[303] It had invested in shares of more than 20 banks (especially in Louisiana and Mississippi), the largest single investment of this type being in the Morris Canal and Banking Company. To be sure, most of these holdings in bank stock had no connection with investment banking activities proper, except for the controlling share in the last-named New Jersey improvement bank. (The origin and the significance of shares held in such enterprises as the Farmers Loan and Trust Company, the American Life Insurance and Trust Company, and the Ohio Life Insurance and Trust Company are not certain, but it is possible that control of security buyers was intended.)[304] Last but not least the Bank held shares in forty to fifty railroad, canal, bridge, turnpike, navigation, land, coal, salt, iron, copper, and manufacturing corporations and through some of these holdings had a strong foothold in Pennsylvania coal mining.

It must be distinctly understood that not all of these security holdings resulted from investment banking proper and that many were involuntary. There were two ways in which securities came into the possession of the Bank: by investment banking activities (contracting as well as "negotiating" with the concomitant lending on the securities to be floated, as described above) and by straight lending on securities. A clear dividing line cannot be drawn; however, one may take it for granted that small holdings in securities indicate as the basis of acquisition straight loans that had remained unpaid. But even straight loans may have been disguised investment banking activities, so that the figures given below for securities subscribed and received in the settlement of debts are not illuminating in this respect. So much is certain from a balance sheet made out as of March 1, 1841, that of more than 91.5 million dollar assets of the bankrupt Bank of the United States of Pennsylvania almost 31.2 resulted from the Bank's activities in the field of securities; while only a little more than 20 million dollar assets were those typical of commercial banks.[305] Besides those accounts whose origin in security transactions is beyond doubt there were others which cannot be clearly recognized as being of such origin, but which in all probability, at least in part, stemmed therefrom. Biddle tried to have the Bank become the fiscal agent of corporations or the depository of states whose long term capital needs it satisfied,[306] all of which must have resulted in deposit accounts of the type which was common in late nineteenth-century investment banks, such as the House of Morgan.

As to details, the committee of investigation appointed by the stockholders after the collapse of the Bank of the United States of Pennsylvania found[307] among its assets $5,154,027.12 worth of both corporation shares and state and corporation bonds received from individuals in the discharge of debts; plus an additional $1,459,003.58 worth of securities so received from corporations (including 3,891 corporation shares). The Bank held securities previously subscribed amounting to $1,391,455, and previously purchased in the market amounting to $1,911,269.29. It held [Pennsylvania?] state loans representing $380,988.12 and its own stock amounting to $2,471,400. All told when suspending it possessed $11,038,700.11 worth of securities. To make these figures representative there must be added an estimated $12-15,000,000 of securities which the Bank lost in London by not redeeming debts for which such securities were pledged. Actually in 1839 Jaudon's loans in London had tied up Pennsylvania, Mississippi, Michigan, Indiana, Maryland, and Illinois bonds amounting to $12,200,900. The Bank's total investment-banking business from 1836 through 1841 can be estimated to have amounted to $40-50,000,000.

Besides the Bank of the United States of Pennsylvania there were two other banks which for some years (between about 1837 and 1840) approached the status of genuine investment banks. These were the Morris Canal and Banking Company, a typical New Jersey improvement bank (which conducted its banking business in an office in New York City), and the North American Trust and Banking Company. The former's charter of 1824 permitted it to buy stocks and thereby predestined it for that role. Unfortunately, very little is known about the banking business of the concern, which was carried on with a capital of $900,000 (out of the total paid-up capital of $4,000,000). In one way or another at an early moment Biddle had gained a good deal of influence over it; at least he was able to make his friend, Louis McLane, the president of the enterprise when the latter left the cabinet in 1834. By 1837 in connection with a reorganization of the Morris Canal and Banking Company, when additional stock was floated at fifty cents on the dollar face value, the Bank of the United States of Pennsylvania seems to have acquired the controlling interest. Thomas Cadwalader, Biddle's confidante, and Edward R. Biddle were elected directors and represented the controlling bloc of stock amounting to almost $1,000,000. Consequently Biddle came to back the Morris Canal and Banking Company to the hilt, and his relative, Edward R. Biddle, a New York stock broker, rose from a director, first to vice-president and later, in January, 1839, to president. There were continuous security transactions between the two investment banks, the smaller of which acted as a sort of tender of its big brother.

Best known of those dealings is the one in Michigan stock which led to disaster for the holders; but the Morris Canal and Banking Company was also active in the flotation of Indiana bonds, and toward the end of its banking career it took an interest in $5,000,000 Texas bonds. It was all but bankrupt in 1840.[308]

The North American Trust and Banking Company of New York, on the other hand, belonged to the early American trust companies and is supposed to have been established in 1838 under the New York Free Banking Act, one Strong being the "strong man" therein. Its capital of $2,000,000 was large for the time. When going into investment banking it adopted the policy of contracting; it does not seem to have "negotiated" securities. Once they were purchased they were consigned to correspondents in London who "negotiated" them for the New York firm. Only small amounts could have been sold in the United States. The aggregate of state stocks acquired prior to its breakdown in September, 1841, amounted to $5,915,000 face value, of which Palmer, McKillop, Dent and Company of London "negotiated" prior to April 1, 1840 about $1,200,000. Moreover between May, 1839, and January, 1840, Roskell and Company, Jas. B. Murray, and Huth and Company, all of London, "negotiated" for account of the New York firm sundry state securities, the proceeds of which amounted to $908,777.77. The following table compiled from the accounts and preserved in court records is of unusual interest because of the many details contained therein. It speaks for itself:

Sales of State Stocks by Palmers & Co., prior to 1st April, 1840 compiled from their accounts C, Nos. 1, 2, and 3, London Commission

Date of sale.	State Stocks.	Par value.	Price sold at.		Proceeds, less brokerage.
1838	C, No. 1, London Commission				
Oct. 26	New York Stocks,.............	£ 7,425 at	93 per cent		£ 6,886 03 3
1839					
Feb. 26	Alabama, (dollar)............	1,125	82	"	919 13 9
28	....	1,125	83	"	930 18 9
Mar. 4	Indiana, (sterling)............	4,500	95	"	4,263 15 0
4	(dollar).............	1,125	83	"	930 18 6
6	Alabama, ...	2,250	82	"	1,839 07 6
May 14	Indiana, ...	1,125	81 3-4	"	916 07 6
16	(sterling)...........	11,250	92 1-2	"	10,378 02 6
1839	C, No. 2, London Commission				
July 2	Indiana Stock, (sterling)........	1,125	90	"	1,009 13 9
15	Ohio,.....................	11,250	92	"	10,321 17 6
15	Indiana, (sterling)............	2,700	90	"	2,395 16 0
Aug. 5	Arkansas, ...	1,125	95	"	1,075 08 0
10	....	3,375	95	"	3,228 08 9
Sept. 10	Ohio, ...	2,250	90	"	5,019 07 6
23	Indiana, (sterling)............	9,450	80	"	7,536 07 6
24	Ohio, ...	2,250	88	"	1,974 07 6
30	Indiana, (sterling)............	80,100	75	"	60,075 00 0
Oct. 1	Ohio, ...	1,125	87	"	975 18 9
3	....	2,250	87	"	1,951 17 5
4	....	6,750	86	"	5,788 02 6
12	....	10,125	86	"	8,682 03 9
15	....	4,500	86	"	3,858 15 0
17	....	3,375	86	"	2,894 01 3
17	....	1,125	85 1-2	"	959 01 3
17	....	1,125	86	"	964 13 9
21	Indiana, (sterling)............	12,150	75	"	9,082 02 6
24	Ohio, ...	2,250	85	"	1,906 17 6
29	....	2,250	85 1-2	"	1,918 02 6
31	....	1,350	85	"	1,144 02 6

Oct. 31	Indiana, (sterling).............	900	80 per cent	717 15 0
Nov. 1	Ohio,.....................	1,125	85 1-2 "	959 01 3
2		2,250	85 1-2 "	1,918 02 6
Dec. 7	New York, $2,000,............	450	82 "	360 00 0
8	Ohio,.....................	450	85 1-2 "	385 17 7
14	....	2,250	89 "	1,996 17 6
	....	1,125	89 "	998 08 9
17	....	9,000	89 "	7,987 10 0
20	....	1,575	90 "	1,413 11 3
26	....	1,125	90 "	1,089 13 9
31	....	2,250	86 "	1,929 07 6
1840	C, No. 3, London Commission			
Jan. 6	Arkansas, (sterling).........	1,124	91 1-2 "	1,021 00 0
Feb. 18	Indiana, ...	6,075	82 "	4,966 06 3
28	....	3,375	82 "	2,759 01 3
Mar. 9	....	45,000	80 "	36,000 00 0
		£270,000 eq'l to $1,200,000		£221,259 04 9

Less Palmers' commission on par value, 1 per cent
on $270,000 ....   2,700 00 0

Proceeds, cash, in London 218,559 04 9

Add 1½ per cent for 90 days interest, for the time it would take a
bill of exchange, drawn in New York in 1840, at 60 days sight, to
mature in London....................................   3,268 07 9

Net proceeds in London, for which the Company could draw at
10 per cent exchange, would realize in New York: £221,837 12 6

$1,084,539 50

Being a loss of about 9½ per cent on the par value of the state
stocks, sold by Palmers.

It goes without saying that the concern borrowed heavily to carry its purchases. The most important of its sources of credit were the Palmers in London who, as was customary, permitted the firm to draw against the securities transmitted for "negotiation." Other sources of credit were Thomas Wilson and Company from which $300,000 were borrowed and Holford and Company of London who lent $300,000 on $500,000 Arkansas bonds. Finally the Bank of the United States of Pennsylvania and the Girard Bank were heavy lenders. Of course when American states began to default on their interest payments in 1841 and the Bank of the United States of Pennsylvania met its Waterloo, the North American Trust and Banking Company became hopelessly bankrupt; but it had hardly ever made money. On $3,100,000 worth of state securities, sold in Europe prior to April 1, 1840, it claims to have lost 18 per cent on an average, the total loss then amounting to $870,000. On October 1, 1840 it had on hand unsold state securities having a face value of $1,954,040. During its career it had handled Ohio, Indiana, Maryland, South Carolina, Florida, Alabama, and Arkansas bonds; of the latter $1,000,000 were taken over from J. D. Beers and Company.

X

A new beginning had to be made after the depression of the early 1840's, during which collapsed not only the Bank of the United States of Pennsylvania, the Morris Canal and Banking Company, and the North American Trust and Banking Company, i.e., the quasi-specialized investment banking houses, but also several of the non-specialized private bankers interested in the field. At the same time commercial banks were generally withdrawing therefrom. But this new beginning was delayed. The flotation of large issues of American securities was impossible at that time without the cooperation of European capital because of the then still small rate of accumulation in this country. However European capital was temporarily frightened away in the wake of Repudiation. Under these circumstances Free Banking came as a godsend, creating as it did a market for federal and state securities. Thereby, however, it was bound to retard the emergence of specialized investment banking. In fact, Free Banks can be found between 1840 and 1860 on numerous, if not all lists of subscribers to new state and federal issues.[310] As such they had appeared first in March, 1839, when the New York Canal Fund Commissioners floated a $1,000,000 loan. Besides a private banker currently interested in the field and an Albany chartered bank, we find as successful bidders on this issue the Bank of Commerce of New York ($500,000) and two other (obscure) Free Banks taking $50,000 and $40,000, respectively.[311]

To the extent that investment banking existed in this country between about 1840 and 1860 it was the domain of private bankers who sold the contracted securities to both American speculators and investors and European middlemen. They fulfilled an important economic function, assuming a considerable risk, as had the English contractors and subcontractors of the Napoleonic, and the Continental ones of the post-Napoleonic era. Identical functions made for similarity of many of their transactions. On both continents and in both the corresponding periods subcontractors were admitted by contractors to shares in contracts at the original price and conditions. When, as in the case of the so-called Union Bank bonds (bonds of the State of Louisiana issued in the latter's favor) the subcontractors left the sale of their slices to the contractors, the function of risk-assuming becomes evident at first glance.[312]

While the previously mentioned pioneers disappeared almost completely during the depression following the crisis of 1837, a good many new private bankers entered investment banking in the 1840's and 1850's. To be sure, Prime, Ward and King survived the crisis and flourished until the concern was dissolved in the late 1840's. Neither did Thomas Biddle and Company succumb, but no trace of the latter's activities in the field of investment banking during those decades has been found, except ten bids for $10,000 each on the Mexican War loan of 1848 and a paltry $1,000 subscription to the Pennsylvania loan of 1861. Moreover, the tradition of some of the old firms survived for years to come in younger ones, as for instance, that of the Allens in E. W. Clark & Company of Philadelphia and that of Prime, Ward and King in both James Gore King and Sons and in August Belmont's firm, as will be shown later. Enterprises active in the field in the period 1840-1860 dealt in federal, state, county, and municipal securities, on the one hand, and in railroad bonds on the other; but they do not seem to have touched the first securities of manufacturing enterprises and coal companies which were then making their appearance in the national market.[313] Corporation stock was still floated almost exclusively in the traditional way by opening subscription books to[314] local investors.

Anyone wishing to get an idea of the magnitude of the job of the investment banker in the field of state securities should look at the tabulation of the indebtedness of the American states in 1846 or 1847 in the Bankers Magazine,[315] a tabulation which should be compared with that for 1838, reprinted above.[316] The total debt of American states at the later date amounted to about $224,000,000, but single flotations of more than $1,000,000 were still exceptional.

The business in federal and most state securities was conducted in the following manner: the amount of the loan and the interest rate were set, and bids were invited for a particular date. Those who offered the highest price or (in the case of the federal government which in this period did not float its loans below par) those who offered the highest premiums were successful. The flotations of 1843, 1847, and 1848 are examples of federal loans issued as described.[317] But the method could not be upheld all the way through. When a reissue of treasury notes, authorized by law, became necessary in May, 1858, John J. Cisco, the United States Sub-Treasurer in New York, "contracted" treasury notes at $4\frac{1}{2}$ per cent with various banks and savings banks of the city without the formality of an advertisement or invitation for bids. (The Bankers Magazine[318] praised the negotiation since the securities were thus taken "by first hands instead of being hawked about the streets by brokers and speculators.") A few years later, on December 17, 1860, Congress authorized an issue of $10,000,000 treasury notes which were to be awarded to those who bid the lowest interest rates, provided that the bids were not so low as to be unacceptable.[319] On top of this deviation from the standard practice, the first bond issues of the year 1861 were floated below par.

The State of New York had adopted the method of floating its securities by competitive bidding as early as 1818, when sec. 2 of the Act to improve the funds and to provide for the redemption of the funded debt of the state, passed on April 21, 1818, made it optional for the state authorities to float a $1,000,000 6 per cent loan either in the traditional way by opening subscription books or by advertising for bids in public newspapers.[320] Just as in the case of the federal government the state could not uphold this method in time of depression. In 1837 and 1839, for example, loans were floated by direct negotiations with commercial banks, as described above; later, securities were exchanged for temporary loans previously made by such banks, and some others were probably floated by being used as a medium of payment to contractors.[321] Other states followed the examples of the federal government and the State of New York as, for instance, Wisconsin in 1853 when it invited bids on a $50,000 loan and received offers of $220,000;[322] or Ohio (where, however, the method had been used earlier) in 1850[323] and 1856; or Missouri and Pennsylvania in 1853 when $200,000 and $1,000,000, respectively, were involved;[324] or North Carolina in 1854 when one tranche of $500,000 was subscribed by a firm of New York bankers, while a later one of $260,000, for which no bids were received from New York, went to local parties.[325] City bonds were floated at least in some cases by competitive bidding, as, for instance, the Detroit bonds of 1855.[326] But the method of bidding was different, being identical with that used for most railroad bonds, which will be described later. Usually city bonds, like those of counties (e.g., Ohio county bonds) were contracted or "negotiated," as seem to have been some state issues.

Subscriptions to federal and state bonds (to the extent that the latter were sold publicly) were still essentially identical with the English public subscriptions of the Napoleonic era. Loan contractors, speculators, and individual and institutional investors competed on the same level; and consequently bids ranged between a few hundred or a few thousand dollars and several millions.[327] In the case of state loans, the ranges tended to be smaller; to give examples, the bids on the New York State loan of 1853 ranged between $10,000 and $175,000 and on that of 1855 between $3,000 and $1,500,000.[328] Returning to the comparison between English subscriptions of 1800 and American ones of 1850, we find the place of the Bank of England, the East India Company and other corporations taken in this country by chartered and Free banks, savings banks, and insurance companies. The names of Jacob Little or Jay Gould (bidding, for instance, on the Mexican War loan of 1848 and the Ohio State loan of 1850 or the New York State loan of 1853, respectively)[329] represented the speculative element; while the various private bankers, who will be discussed shortly in more detail, stand for the loan contractors. However, a trend toward truly modern investment banking can be discerned: in some cases bids were tendered with the clause "all or none," as for instance, in the case of the Ohio loan of 1855 ($2,400,000) or the Pennsylvania loan of 1852 when C. H. Fisher bid the whole $3,000,000 for the Barings and their friends.[330] The latter case is most interesting. Although other bids were higher, the loan was awarded to Fisher since otherwise the total would have been sold less favorably. That is to say, this type of clause tended to eliminate both speculators and investors (individual and institutional alike), and to pave the way for the modern investment banker.[331]

A study of the distribution of the federal loan of 1843 is illuminating in this context since this distribution is typical of the federal and of many of the state loans of the period:[332]

UNITED STATES LOAN OF 1843.

Statement of Persons to whom was awarded the Stock of the Loan for seven millions of dollars, at five per cent interest, payable in ten years from July 1, 1843, with the terms

OFFERS ACCEPTED.				
Names of Subscribers	Amount	Rate of premium	Rate of interest	Amount of premium
John Ward & Co.	6,498,000	101.01	5 per cent	$65,629.80
Secretary of War, in trust for Indian tribes	50,000	101.01	"	505.00
Southwark Bank	200,000	101.01	"	2,020.00
Bank of Potomac	40,000	101.01	"	404.00
Piscataqua Bank	30,000	101.01	"	303.00
Charles Davies, Treasurer Military Academy, West Point	16,000	101.01	"	161.60
Daniel Parker	10,000	101.01	"	101.00
Philadelphia Savings Fund Society	100,000	102.37½	"	2,375.00
Pennsylvania Company for Insurance on Lives and Granting Annuities	56,000	101.55	"	868.00
	7,000,000			$72,367.40

OFFERS NOT ACCEPTED.

Patapsco Bank	20,000	101.00	5 per cent
George Curtis	50,000	101.00	"
John A. Stevens	50,000	101.00	"
J. G. Fendi	30,000	101.00	"
Bank of Baltimore	100,000	100.75	"
Horace Binney	16,000	100.75	"
J. E. Thayer & Brother	30,000	100.75	"
Corcoran & Riggs	100,000	100.75	"
Franklin Haven	2,000,000	100.90	"
Corcoran & Riggs	350,000	100.25	"
Corcoran & Riggs	1,000,000	100.00	"
Bernard W. Campbell	10,000	100.00	"
Massachusetts Fire and Marine Insurance Company	60,000	100.00	"
Josiah Bradlee & Co.	68,000	100.00	"
William Pratt	100,000	100.00	"
Phineas Upham	25,000	100.00	"
Middletown Bank	30,000	100.00	"
Bank of Charleston, S. C.	100,000	100.00	"
James Camak	30,000	100.00	"
Bowery Savings Bank	125,000	100.00	"
Timothy C. Leeds	10,000	100.00	"
Provident Institution for Savings, Boston	123,000	100.00	"
John W. Tredwell	20,000	100.00	"
Thomas P. Hoopes	10,000	100.00	"
John J. Swift	10,000	100.00	"
Bank of the Metropolis	500,000	"Most favorable terms."	
Henry Toland	1,000,000	103.10	5 per cent

The two last bids were not received until after the time for making offers had expired, and the arrangement had been closed with those whose offers were accepted.

Among the nine successful bidders on this loan of 1843 we find one outstanding loan contractor, John Ward and Company of New York, a large brokerage house. As will be remembered, it was active in investment banking as early as the 1830's, but seems to have lost its importance before 1850. (The firm, characterized by John Thompson as one of the "most solid houses" of the period, seems to have been among the forerunners of modern commercial paper houses.)[333] Moreover, there were two government agencies, three commercial banks which can be assumed to have subscribed in order to use the securities as the basis of note issues, two institutional investors (one savings bank and one insurance company) and (probably) one individual investor. The twenty-five unsuccessful bidders included five commercial banks. (One of them, the Bank of the Metropolis of Washington, may have aimed at loan contracting.) Then there were three institutional investors, at least seven (but probably more) individual investors

and at least two would-be loan contractors. These were Corcoran and Riggs, about whom much will be said later, and Henry Toland, bidding for $1,450,000 and $1,000,000 respectively. (Originally Henry Toland [1791-1865] had been a prominent Philadelphia merchant engaged in the China trade; in 1843 he was conducting a stock brokerage business in New York in partnership with his son.)[334] As to the rest, their intentions cannot be discerned: Franklin Haven, for instance, president of the (Boston) Merchants Bank, who submitted a bid for $1,000,000, may have acted in trust for Boston capitalists or for his bank; and John Austin Stevens, when bidding for $50,000, may have done so for himself or again for his bank, the Bank of Commerce of New York over which he presided. The rest may have been investors, agents of investors, dummies of loan contractors, or loan contractors themselves.

When one examines the lists of bidders on the various federal and state loans of the period one will almost always find a few firms bidding for various amounts at various rates.[335] There are two possible explanations of this practice: either they were bidding as agents for different parties or their bids represented some sort of demand schedule: they were willing to take additional securities if they could be had at lower prices. A casual contemporary remark that bidders to the United States loan of 1858 (in which case the practice described is particularly evident) desired the securities "for home account," makes the former interpretation the more probable one.[336] It would imply that the investment bankers of the period circularized their prospects prior to new flotations and collected their orders, receiving a commission in case of success. That method, if actually applied, would have approximated the one which was common in England in the 1790's, except that the American participant in subscriptions determined the price, while his English counterpart left the determination to the contractor.[337]

The most important transactions in the field of government flotations during the period under investigation resulted from the Mexican War. The issues of war bonds in 1847 and 1848 far exceeded in size all earlier flotations and they were the first which the country experienced in an era of an undoubted gold standard and with no "national bank" in existence. Thus they posed new problems, and new firms rose in the field whose owners were creative and courageous enough to find proper solutions for those problems and to stake capital and reputation on the execution. The Washington private bankers, Corcoran and Riggs, and to a less extent E. W. Clark and Company of Philadelphia contributed to and consequently profited most from Mexican War finance.

Mexican War finance provides a rather bewildering picture. Suffice it to say, that both treasury notes and bonds were issued and that the former could be exchanged into the latter and reissued when once redeemed. Large amounts of securities were exchanged rather informally at par for specie and drafts on New Orleans and paid to creditors of the government. The earliest flotations were authorized under an act of July 22, 1846 under which both $5,000,000 bonds and $3,000,000 treasury notes were advertised for bids. As to the latter it is noteworthy that bids as low as $1,000 were declared eligible, although earlier no bids below $25,000 are supposed to have been acceptable. The change meant a step toward those popular loans which were in the offing. Among the bidders, both investors and contractors, we find Corcoran and Riggs offering cautiously on treasury notes sums of not exceeding $20,000 at a time and taking in addition $350,000

worth of bonds mostly at par for investment. N. M. Rothschild and Sons went heavily into the Treasury notes and, out of the total of $4,000,000 subscribed, converted $500,000 into 6 per cent stock. The Rothschilds must have worked through dummies: the name of Belmont their agent, cannot be found on the lists of subcribers. The Barings did not risk more than $100,000 on these treasury notes which they, too, converted into bonds later.

On February 9, 1847 $18,000,000 worth of 6 per cent stock authorized under the law of January 28 of that year was advertised. This loan was meant to be, but did not become, a popular loan: bids as low as $50 were acceptable. (In fact the lowest amounts tendered were $400 and $500, but the prices proposed were not high enough and the offers were rejected.) The bidders were expected to offer at least par and it was left to them to decide on a premium. An aggregate of more than 57.5 million dollars were brought forward, of which more than 54.8 millions were above par. Bids with premiums ranging from 1/8 to 2 per cent were accepted; and Corcoran and Riggs who tendered a bid for the whole $18,000,000 received the lion's share. Still as in the eighteenth-century English public subscriptions, investors (individual and institutional) and loan contractors competed. Among the latter (besides Corcoran and Riggs) John Ward[339] and M. Morgan, and Winslow and Perkins stand out, the former two bidding for $12,000,000, the latter two for $11,333,333 ("two thirds of loan not absolutely subscribed for"). They had another bid in for $1,000,000. It is not certain whether "John Ward & M. Morgan" were a firm or an alliance in which John Ward partook. As to Winslow and Perkins, the first named partner was the broker Richard H. Winslow who later became Lanier's associate in the once famous partnership which will be studied in detail.[340] Other conspicuous subscribers were savings banks, insurance companies, and commercial (including Free) banks; and among the latter we find the Bank of North America (New York), the Bank of the Northern Liberties (Philadelphia), the Bank of the Metropolis (Washington), and Bonnefoux's New York State Stock Security Bank. Some of the commercial banks may have aimed at loan contracting.[341]

Prior to proceeding with the description of Mexican War finance the main actors in the field deserve study, the firm of Corcoran and Riggs. By that time (early in 1847) it began to attract attention. The concern was headed by William Wilson Corcoran. Corcoran (1798-1888), the son of an Irish immigrant, was born in Georgetown, D. C., where he started his business career in the drygoods store of this brothers. In 1817 he established himself in this line under the firm name

W. W. Corcoran and Company, which in 1819 branched out into the commission and auctioneering business. Young Corcoran was unsuccessful, however, and had to suspend in 1823. Between 1828 and 1836 we find him in charge of the real estate of the Bank of Columbia at Washington which brought him into contact with the Washington branch of the Second Bank of the United States; the latter being a heavy creditor of the former had taken over many of its assets. In 1837 Corcoran set up a stock brokerage business in Washington and in 1840 formed a partnership with George Washington Riggs (1813-1881). The latter, a son of Elisha Riggs (once a partner of George Peabody) had received his training in his father's mercantile business in Baltimore and with Peabody in London.

The partnership of Corcoran and Riggs went into investment banking soon after it had come into existence. We have found it among the subscribers to the federal loan of 1843; and its activities in the early months of the Mexican War have been touched upon. It is at this point that the discussion of Mexican War finance must be taken up again: The above mentioned subscription of Corcoran and Riggs to the $18,000,000 loan of 1847 was both audacious and successful; moreover their operations of 1848 became a landmark from the historical point of view. In bidding for the loan of the latter year Corcoran and Riggs appeared as the allies of the Barings and as the American members of an embryonic international syndicate. A bid for the whole loan of $16,000,000 was placed by this group and $14,065,550 was allocated to it.[342] Of this amount $1,250,000 were for account of Baring Brothers and Company, $250,000 for James Gore King and Sons, and $1,400,000 for foreign account other than the Barings. Of the last named sum $750,000 was taken by George Peabody on joint account for himself, Elisha Riggs, and W. W. Corcoran. (Later another $3,000,000 of Corcoran and Riggs's share went to a group of London merchant bankers led by the Barings, who supported the American house still further in the months to follow.) The syndicate, if you please, enjoyed the tacit cooperation of the Rothschilds, although the latter had refused to join. They advised their American agents not to buy federal securities at that moment, in order not to disturb the bid by causing a rise in the market.

After this success in 1847 and 1848 it was only natural that Corcoran and Riggs should expand their interest in the field of investment banking, especially since they had won such valuable connections. As early as 1849 they entered railroad finance, bidding on an issue of Chattanooga and Nashville Railroad bonds. In 1851 and 1852 we

again find them active in government finance. As allies of the Barings they acquired shares in a $600,000 federal loan in favor of Texas and in Massachusetts issues. Independently, at that time they took Tennessee securities which the Barings sold for them on commission.[343]

If we turn from the flotation of federal and state securities to that of railroad bonds, and focus our attention on the way in which they were floated, we find a much broader range of policies applied in connection with the issue of American railroad securities. The common methods of marketing the latter were contracting and "negotiating". But in addition some new issues were auctioned off, a very unsatisfactory procedure which aroused the ire of Henry Varnum Poor. Nevertheless there were several New York firms which specialized in this business, and auctions of new railroad securities took place regularly. In addition good railroad bonds were often floated on the basis of bids. But such bidding was different from that on federal and on state bonds. In the latter cases sealed bids had to be submitted on a particular date, when they were opened and the issues distributed among the highest bidders. In contrast, the wording of announcements[344] of the flotation of railroad bonds, namely, that bids had to be offered <u>until</u> a certain date indicates where the essential difference lay. As in the case of security auctions, the method opened the door for dubious reporting, leaving the public in the dark, or (worse) deceiving it, as to the true value of the issues concerned; and again Henry Varnum Poor fought the custom and promoted the adoption of that mode of bidding which was common for federal and state stock. According to Alfred Chandler, Winslow, Lanier and Company, who closely cooperated with Poor, were the first to follow the latter's advice for some of the railroad issues which they floated for the borrowers. That is to say, they required sealed bids to be opened at a specific date, reporting the result of the allocation as was common for government securities (see the announcement above on page 345).[345] As examples of railroad bonds floated by inviting bids the following may be cited: Michigan and Southern Railroad bonds of 1850; $1,200,000 Baltimore and Ohio Railroad bonds of 1853 ($4,000,000 were offered by subscribers and would-be subscribers); and Chicago, Burlington and Quincy Railroad bonds of 1857.[346] It is suspected that the bids on most railroad bonds were below par.

But even with this enumeration of the customary methods of floating railroad securities the list is not exhausted: Once in a while railroads sent agents to Europe to sell their bonds, as had been common for state bonds in the 1830's. The Mobile and Ohio and the Sunbury and Erie Railroads may be cited as examples.[347] Often railroad securities were pledged with commercial banks for loans and it was left to the latter to transform them into money, i.e., to act as quasi-investment bankers. (Some commercial banks seem to have subscribed even to railroad stock, as did the Phoenix Bank of Hartford which for a short time owned shares in the Hartford and New Haven and in some western railroads.)[348] Finally, at least one case is known in which Massachusetts banks agreed to finance the subscribers to a railroad (the Old Colony), a situation which implies that commercial banks enabled a railroad to eliminate the investment banker.[349] (Railroad stock, in contrast to bonds, does not seem to have been handled by the investment bankers of the period.)

After the collapse of the first three quasi-specialized investment banking firms in the early 1840's, advance toward specialization was slow in our field. To be sure, Drexel and Company, Philadelphia, founded in 1838 as an uncurrent money brokerage house by the former Austrian portrait painter, Francis Martin Drexel (1792-1863), was on the way toward that goal. Francis' son Anthony J. (1826-1893) was coming to the fore in the firm when the period under investigation drew to its close.[350] Since specialization was not needed a few commercial banks could remain in the field choosing to do so when the majority of those formerly interested therein withdrew. Whenever we find the name of Thomas W. Olcott in subscription lists we are entitled to suspect as the real principal in the transaction the Mechanics and Farmers Bank of Albany, whose president Olcott[351] was from 1836 through 1880. Rufus Howard King may have acted similarly for the State Bank of Albany, as will be discussed later. The Bank of Commerce of New York City which is supposed to have specialized in government finance from its start subscribed in 1858 for $1,500,000 worth of 4½ per cent treasury notes and $1,500,000 worth of federal bonds.[352] Finally, the Bank of the Metropolis of Washington, to give a last example, appears so often as a bidder on securities that we must assume it to have acted as a loan contractor or at least on a commission basis.[353]

Since there was no specialization even on investment banking as such, one cannot expect interested firms to have specialized on federal and state securities, on the one hand, or railroad bonds, on the other. But just as we found in the case of the Drexels a trend in the former direction, so we can discern a trend in the latter also, exemplified by Corcoran and Riggs and by Winslow, Lanier and Company, a firm which will be discussed later. While the former emphasized the one line, the latter stressed the other.

Whoever went into investment banking in either field in America between 1840 and 1860 had to reckon with European capital and its representatives as allies, potential customers or competitors. Except for lack of information we would be able to arrange the participants in the game according to their dependence on European houses. They ran the whole gamut from local bankers who took an occasional interest in securities of their states or nearby municipalities and railroads and small New York brokers putting in bids once in a while on limited shares in larger flotations (both classes having no European connections), through large genuine American houses with less or more backing from across the Atlantic, to mere agents of European houses which, finally, appeared themselves in rare cases, i.e., under their own names, in the American capital market.

Among stronger American houses which started originally without European backing were such firms as the Clarks and, possibly, the Drexels and that of Thompson, the "Bank Note Detector." Material on both E. W. Clark and Company and John Thompson can be found in earlier chapters. Thompson appeared in the investment banking field as early as 1847 when he was keenly interested in the federal treasury notes issued in pursuance of the Act of July 12, 1846. Shortly thereafter he bid successfully on $500,000 of the War loan of 1847. In 1849 he bid $50,000 on a New York state loan and five years later (1854) on $235,000 worth of North Carolina securities, competing with Carpenter, Vermilye and Company about whom more will be written. In 1855 he carried away $1,050,000 of a New York Canal loan of $1,500,000, and the whole $1,250,000 of a second canal loan of that same year. When his bankruptcy disqualified him from doing business on his own account he established as brokers his two sons, Samuel C. and Frederick. Steered by their father they did business as Thompson Brothers and we find them, for instance, as bidders on $1,000,000 of the 3¾ per cent treasury notes of 1858, receiving $125,000.[354] In 1860 they bid $625,000 on the federal loan of that year.

Another name found repeatedly during this period in the list of subscribers is Rufus Howard King of Albany; but it is doubtful what role he played. King (1794-1867) was a Connecticut lad who started in Albany as a dry-goods merchant in partnership with his brother-in-law. Early in his life he was elected a director of the State Bank of Albany whose president he became in 1860. An able financier he was also active (ultimately as the president) both in the Albany Savings Bank and the Albany Insurance Company. All three institutions succeeded remarkably well under his guidance, a fact which testifies to his executive ability.[355] Because of these different affiliations of his we are unable to judge if his subscriptions represented disguised investment banking activities of the State Bank of Albany (in which case he would have played a role similar to that of T. W. Olcott) or if he acted for institutional investors (savings bank and insurance company). He bid, for instance,[356] on a New York Canal loan of 1849; he took $30,000 City of Buffalo bonds in 1852 and a share in the New York state loans of 1853 and 1854; he subscribed $200,000 worth of the $1,500,000 New York Canal loan of 1855 while bidding unsuccessfully for another $800,000 of the same issue and on $750,000 of the $1,250,000 Canal loan of that year. As late as 1860 he bid $100,000 on a federal loan.

E. W. Clark and Company of Philadelphia, which has been alluded to above, first embarked on investment banking activities[357] in 1847, when they became subcontractors of Corcoran and Riggs, participating in the latter's bid on the whole issue of $18,000,000 federal bonds of that year. In 1848 they were again on the Corcoran and Riggs list, but also bid independently on a share in the $16,000,000 loan, receiving on their own offer close to $1,000,000. Having once obtained a foothold in the investment banking business they expanded their interest therein, and throughout the 1850's prior to the crisis of that decade they "negotiated" and contracted state, municipal, and railroad securities, such as bonds of the City of St. Louis (their "first striking effort of this kind"), of Quincy (Illinois), Keokuk and Burlington (Iowa), and of the states of Illinois and Missouri. Moreover, they sold Allegheny County bonds (floated to aid in the building of a bridge for the Pittsburgh and Connelsville Railroad) and a good many railroad securities: for the Pennsylvania Railroad, the Pittsburgh, Fort Wayne and Chicago; the Philadelphia and Reading; the Chartiers Valley; the Northern Central (Baltimore-Harrisburg); the Sunbury and Erie; the Vermont Central; and the Atlantic and Pacific Railroad in Missouri. While these railroad bonds were "negotiated," the Clarks contracted for the Philadelphia City bonds issued in favor of the Sunbury and Erie and for some Atlantic and Pacific bonds. A contract for State of Missouri bonds by the Boston house (J. W. Clark and Company) of the group proved the concern's undoing. The Boston Clarks had borrowed on these bonds. When, during the panic of 1857, the loans were called they had to suspend, and the whole set of Clark banks had to follow suit.[358] The New York and Philadelphia houses became inde-

pendent enterprises during the reorganization after the suspension of the group in 1857; and as early as 1858 both E. W. Clark and Company of Philadelphia and the new firm Clark, Dodge and Company of New York were active in the field again. The former bid on $200,000 federal treasury notes and were awarded $25,000; the latter bid successfully on $300,000 federal bonds.[359]

Among the houses with old and strong European connections on which attention will now be focussed, James Gore King and Sons stands out. Its head, once the leading spirit of Prime, Ward and King, had inherited the Baring backing from that firm after its dissolution in 1847. Ralph Hidy has shown that King had a good deal to do with the Barings' decision to reenter the American capital market which they had neglected after the disappointment over Repudiation. He advised the London merchant bankers to go into the treasury notes of 1847 and induced them to sell other federal securities on joint account. In 1848 the Kings shared in the successful bids of "Corcoran and Riggs for selves, Baring Brothers and others" on the Mexican War bonds of 1848, as must be restated at this point. In 1850 James Gore King and Sons, again in cooperation with the Barings, took a share in an Ohio loan which was sold on joint account. In 1852 they shared equally with the Barings in a $2,000,000 New Orleans issue and later in the year, in alliance with the Barings, Rothschilds, and the American C. H. Fisher, they took a $3,000,000 Pennsylvania loan subscribed under Fisher's name. Moreover the Kings secured New York City and Jersey City bonds which the Barings sold on commission. Not content with flotations of federal, state, and city loans the Kings branched out into railroad securities and, again as an ally of the Barings and Charles H. Fisher (who placed the bid), took a share in Pennsylvania Railroad bonds.[360]

Outside of New York and Philadelphia the firms Oelrichs and Lurman in Baltimore and Gilmore, Blake and Ward (or, respectively, its successor Blake, Ward and Company) had Baring backing. These firms were admitted as allies in connection with the purchase of Maryland bonds from the Baltimore and Ohio Railroad; and in 1850 and 1851 they cooperated with regard to Massachusetts bonds and issues of the City of Boston in which George Peabody and the Hopes also participated.[361]

George Peabody in competition with the Rothschilds had dominated the trading in American securities between 1842 and 1848 and had remained strongly interested therein when the Barings reentered the American field. He became the backer and ally of an American firm, Duncan, Sherman and Company. Moreover even while residing in London, Peabody remained an American and toward the end of his life gained influence on this country's investment banking both through his own activities and through the selection of his successor.

To be sure, Peabody's activities as a loan contractor were small in comparison with his other interests on the wider stage of merchant banking. He was no innovator in our field and did not enter it prior to the Mexican War, that is to say, late in his life, and even then only reluctantly and first as a subcontractor and on joint account. Rather was Peabody a shrewd investor and an extraordinarily able security dealer. As such he was important from the economic point of view in that he facilitated the flow of European capital to America. His main contribution to American investment banking lay in his building an enterprise which was so structured and so well known that it could easily become, under proper guidance, a leading investment banking house. Moreover, as already indicated, Peabody discovered the man (Junius Spencer Morgan) who was to use the instrument which he had forged. Peabody's life work is of a particular interest in our context, however, because it shows how investment banking could grow logically, although slowly, from other activities. As in the case of the Barings and the early American commercial banks pioneering in the field, Peabody's investment banking business developed at least in part from private investments. Certainly the gestation period, if you please, was long in this case.[362]

George Peabody (1795-1869) came from a poor family of Puritan stock. As a mere youngster he began to work in a grocery store in a small Massachusetts town (now Peabody). He rose rapidly and by 1814 was the manager and soon thereafter the partner of Elisha Riggs, running the latter's dry goods house in Georgetown, D. C. In 1815 Riggs and Peabody moved to Baltimore; in 1829 the latter became the head of the firm from which he withdrew in 1837 when he settled in London.

Prior thereto Peabody had had his first experience with the flotation of securities; he was one of the three Maryland commissioners appointed to sell in England bonds issued by the state to assist internal improvements. Shortly after having transferred his headquarters to London he undertook the agency of the Chesapeake and Ohio Canal Company to dispose of Maryland state bonds assigned to that corporation. The sales transaction became rather complicated because of credit given on the basis of the securities and because of threatened underselling. (Maryland bonds having been assigned to various firms were offered in the London market by several houses.) Ultimately Peabody unloaded on the Barings those

securities for which he was responsible. It was baptism by fire, if you please; and soon Peabody was to become an outstanding expert in the field of American securities and of security dealings. His knowledge was acquired by investments of his own funds, for Peabody, like other businessmen in this country, believed in the intrinsic value of many American securities which in the early 1840's were utterly depressed in the English market. Under these circumstances some of them became an advantageous medium of payment for imports from America. Peabody used them himself for that purpose and acquired them on commission for others. When his experience and reputation as a security trader grew, securities were consigned to him for sale on commission or on joint account. Trading in securities on his own or on joint account was also undertaken.

By that time the son of Peabody's old partner, George Washington Riggs, trained in Peabody's counting house in London, had become Corcoran's partner in the firm of Corcoran and Riggs, previously described. This fact led to close cooperation between the two firms and to Peabody's being drawn into the investment banking field. Jointly with Corcoran and Riggs and Elisha Riggs, he became a subcontractor of the Washington firm and the Barings to the tune of $750,000 when these firms acquired the lion's share of the Mexican War loan of 1848 (although as late as 1847 Peabody had believed that no large amounts of federal bonds could be sold in Britain). Moreover he personally assisted Corcoran in his sales efforts in England, accompanying him on his travels, and he took up war bonds over and above the amount for which he had made himself responsible in the subcontract just mentioned: he acquired another $770,000 jointly with Corcoran and Riggs.[363] It is noteworthy that Peabody and the Barings marketed their shares (to the extent that they were taken to England) "in perfect union". They even took a block of the 1847 bonds from the Rothschilds when the latter started underselling them. Many of the securities were marketed through agents on the Continent, selling especially to small investors in Germany.

In the years 1849 through 1851 Peabody increased and diversified his security holdings and in this connection participated in the flotation of new securities, such as Illinois Improvement and Wabash and Erie Canal bonds and Bay State Mills stock; but he acted as an investor, not with resale in his mind. Nevertheless thereby he came nearer to the status of an investment banker, especially since in those years he also became a joint contractor for a few state issues and those of first-class cities, such as Boston. (He participated in an unsuccessful bid for the New York City bonds of 1849.) It is telling that when Peabody concluded a partnership agreement in this period, the articles of association, contemplating "operations" in "American and other stocks," did not distinguish between dealing in securities and contracting. Those articles of association are interesting for still another reason: Peabody reserved the right to operate in securities on his own account, aside from the firm. This fact may throw light on the unsolved question of how the important contemporaneous banking firm of John E. Thayer and Brother was organized, for it seems that the influence of Nathaniel Thayer (1808-1883) on early American railroads and his activities in railroad finance were rather private activities, and not those of the head of a banking house.

By 1850 interest in America was generally shifting from state to railroad securities, and again Peabody entered the new field only slowly. He did a considerable business in railroad iron, but throughout the 1840's refused to take railroad bonds in payment therefor, as was customary. By 1850, however, he had changed his policy and, since his business in railroad iron and the acceptance of railroad bonds were bound to make him familar with both the roads and their securities, it was natural that he should become a full-fledged investment banker in this very field. With his last and decisive achievement Peabody followed on the heels of the Barings and Rothschilds who, as mentioned above, had contracted for Pennsylvania Railroad bonds in 1852. That fact is indicative. Never in his life was Peabody an innovator, but he grasped possibilities as soon as a creative entrepreneur had revealed them.

In the last period of his life and in his capacity as a full-fledged investment banker Peabody closely cooperated with the New York firm of Duncan, Sherman and Company, his correspondents. The house of Duncan, Sherman and Company was founded in 1851[364] by Alexander Duncan who as a poor lad had come to America from Scotland and had fallen heir to the business and fortune of an outstanding Providence merchant. His partner, Watts Sherman,was considered by contemporary businessmen a "small town merchant", not a designation of high regard. Duncan soon withdrew to enjoy the rest of his life in Scotland and was succeeded by his son, W. Butler Duncan, Sherman being the actual head of the firm. The latter (1809-1865) was born in Utica. He received his training in the Ontario County Bank and became by 1830 the cashier of the Herkimer County Bank at Little Falls, N.Y. When in that capacity he visited Albany in 1833 to open an account with the State Bank of that city he attracted the attention of Erastus Corning, hardware dealer and iron manufacturer, who at that time was an influential director of that bank. A year later when Corning founded the Albany City Bank Watts Sherman became its cashier. As a matter of fact, he was very anxious to land the job as can be seen from a letter in which he promised that in this case he would bring to the new institution at least two country banks as correspondents. Sherman remained as cashier of that bank under the rather autocratic Corning as president until he became a partner in Duncan, Sherman and Company.[365]

The function of the latter firm as the ally of Peabody and Company in the investment banking field was the bidding and contracting for American issues under their name, but on joint account. Since Watts Sherman had received much of his advanced training in one of those Albany banks which (under the leadership of Thomas W. Olcott, Rufus H. King, and Erastus Corning, respectively) had been very active in New York state securities, he was undoubtedly well prepared to handle such assignments. Part of the securities so acquired were sold in the United States and the rest sent to the London house. The latter had by that time built up an efficient sales organization for securities, selling both in England and on the Continent. In Switzerland and Germany, especially, railroad securities had a market, provided the roads were constructed in areas with German settlements.

One of Peabody's first joint transactions with Duncan, Sherman and Company was one in Virginia bonds. It was followed by one in Pennsylvania securities: the allies took in 1852 a complete issue of $850,000 bonds of that state. In the fall of that year, lacking encouragement from its London ally, Duncan, Sherman and Company still shied away from railroad flotations. However when Peabody changed his policy the field was quickly invaded. Peabody himself bought $100,000 Illinois Central bonds from the agent of the company in England; and both firms jointly acquired slices of issues of the Ohio and Pennsylvania, the North Western Virginia, and the Belvedere Railroads. Finally in 1853 the London banker took the last step on his long and slow road toward full-fledged investment banking: he contracted in his own name for a total of 1,844 7 per cent convertible first mortgage bonds of the Eastern Division (Cincinnati-St. Louis) of the Ohio and Mississippi Railroad of which Duncan, Sherman and Company were the bankers. These securities he brought out in the London market under his own name and sole responsibility. The bonds sold so satisfactorily that Peabody took up an option for another block of 600 bonds; and on joint account with Page and Bacon of St. Louis, contractors of the road, he also handled bonds of the Western Division.

The Rothschilds worked in this country not through native American houses, but through a foreign born agent, August Belmont. Belmont (1816-1890), of German-Jewish descent, came to this country after having received his business training in the Frankfurt and Naples branches of A. M. Rothschild und Söhne. In 1837 he was sent to New York after the previous representatives of the concern, J. and L. Joseph, had failed during the crisis.[366] Belmont was clever enough to look for a first class American partner whom he found in the person of Charles Christmas, considered by contemporaries as one of the best brokers and bankers of the City of New York. For years Christmas had been the chief clerk of Prime, Ward and King; and upon leaving the latter concern in the 1830's he had done business on his own account first as Christmas and Livingston and later as Christmas, Livingston, Prime and Coster. The firm's name alone would indicate its social background; as a matter of fact, one of the partners was Rufus Prime, Nathaniel Prime's son.[367] Thus one may see some of the tradition of Prime, Ward and King, pioneers in American investment banking, as surviving in the house of Belmont.

August Belmont does not appear as a subscriber to security flotations as often as might be expected from his and his principals' importance. One can surmise that in many more cases dummies did his bidding to veil his operations. His name can be found, however, as a bidder on the New York stock of 1849 and the Ohio stock of 1850.[368] Later in that decade he appeared with a bid of $1,000,000 on the list of subscribers to the treasury notes of 1858.

Before closing this section of the chapter (treating the decades between 1840 and 1860) attention must be devoted to a New York house which has been mentioned in passing and which was the most creative one among the investment bankers of the period dealing in railroad securities: Winslow, Lanier and Company. The firm was originally composed of James F. D. Lanier (1800-1881) and Richard M. Winslow (ca. 1806-1861) who were joined later by the latter's brother James, whose role in early National Banking has been mentioned. Lanier, who was of Huguenot ancestry and had been a lawyer by profession practicing in Madison, Indiana, laid the basis for his rise in business as the clerk of the state's House of Representatives. Retiring from this appointment he became connected with the State Bank of Indiana as a large stockholder, president of its Madison branch, and later as a member of the parent board. By 1838 he was influential enough to appear as one of the Indiana delegates to the New York bank convention

of that year. There he cooperated with Albert Gallatin whom he rightly considered the moving spirit of that convention.

In order to understand the achievements of Winslow, Lanier and Company the early history of railroad finance must be kept in mind. Although it is not possible to date exactly the entry of investment bankers into the field of railroad securities, once more we meet Nicholas Biddle as a leader who blazed the trail. When the Bank of the United States of Pennsylvania closed its doors in 1841 it had in its portfolio "loans" to seven roads ranging between $17,000 and $501,592.76. (These loans will be commented upon later.) It held bonds of five roads and stock in eighteen. All told it had made investment credit available to twenty-two roads.[369] That is to say, by 1840 the investment banker had already made his entry into the railroad field, even though Biddle was certainly several years ahead of his time.

In fact large scale investment banking activities in the field were predicated on the development of the bond as a regular means of financing railroads. Originally, the latter, like other corporations, were financed by locally offered and subscribed stock; although, to be sure, such stock was spread some times among investors in a larger number of communities along the future line of the road. Like subscribers to government loans, subscribers to railroad stock were expected to pay their subscriptions in installments and in many cases only when such installments were called, or to put it differently, when assessments were levied. Often installments were paid by stock notes, as was customary in contemporaneous banking also. The financing of railroads by stock subscriptions was considered conservative as late as 1850; but stock exchanges were then also used for selling railroad shares which did not find subscribers in the traditional way.

In the meantime difficulties had arisen whenever construction costs outran the original estimates or subscribers were unwilling or unable to fulfill their obligations toward the corporation in question; (forfeited stock was sold at auction). First, it seems that bank loans were resorted to, loans of the kind that can be found in the balance sheet of the Bank of the United States of Pennsylvania; and later, by the middle of the 1830's, there were developed two new types of securities, the preferred stock and the railroad bond. As to the former we are well informed through the research of Professor George Heberton Evans.[370] He has shown that, following English precedents, preferred stocks were created in 1836 by Maryland improvement companies to facilitate state subscriptions and that by the early 1840's securities of that type were first issued directly to individuals. It seems safe to say that the preferred railroad stock was originally a means of raising funds within the country when otherwise it was impossible. In contrast, the railroad bond was probably created in order to appeal to the English capital market. Professor Leland H. Jenks (who has kindly shown his material on early railroad bonds to the author) knows of three issues of the 1830's: Camden and Amboy £/$ bonds of 1834 floated through the Barings; about $400,000 worth of Philadelphia and Reading 5 per cent £ bonds of 1836 brought out by McCalmont, Bros. and Company of London, relatives and correspondents of a New York house which promoted the road; and Louisville, Cincinnati and Charleston Railroad[371] bonds of 1837 guaranteed by the State of South Carolina, floated through Palmer, Dent and Company. (By that time the Rothschilds were taking an interest in Erie Railroad bonds.) Moreover in 1838 the American Life Insurance and Trust Company of New York contemplated taking $150,000 worth of Hartford and New Haven Railroad bonds, raising the necessary funds by floating its own securities in London. Nothing came of this scheme, to be sure, but in 1841 the Bank of the United States of Pennsylvania (which did all its financing with a view to the London capital market) had no less than five different issues of railroad bonds in its portfolio.[372] At first a "revolutionary means of railroad finance" (Kirkland), in the 1850's, if not earlier, bonds became an element in the original financial plan instead of being used in emergencies only. The first ones are supposed to have been medium term securities running for about five years, but they were soon standardized as ten to twenty years first mortgage bonds. By 1850 bonds had become so common with railroads that legislatures were called to regulate their issues.

Prior to the regular use of standardized railroad bonds, investment bankers could not take more than an occasional interest in the field, but details about their entering it are unknown. Still other questions remain unanswered at this time, for example, how the railroads disposed of the city and county bonds which they received in aid? Were investment bankers employed in distributing these securities and also in distributing railroad securities used for payments to contractors, land sellers, and purveyors? If so, to what extent were they used? There is at least one case on record in which two New York brothers, George L. and Robert Schuyler, were railroad contractors and promoters as well as brokers and private bankers,[373] and there is hardly any doubt that their banking enterprise fulfilled quasi-investment banker's functions for the brothers in their capacity as railroad promoters. We should also like to know how well and to what extent the exchanges served as outlets for those who as contractors, etc., came into the possession of railroad securities; or, to put it differently, if the exchanges enabled those concerned to avoid the investment banker and so retarded the development of a specialized business of that character in railroad securities.

It is against this background that one must look at the achievements of Winslow, Lanier and Company who, as indicated, were probably the first to come near to specializing as investment bankers in the railroad field. Their light will shine even brighter if their activities are compared with those of another contemporary leader in railroad finance, John Murray Forbes. Forbes, the great Boston merchant, was born in 1813 and consequently younger than either Winslow or Lanier; nevertheless he represented an earlier stage in the development. He financed the building of railroads such as the Michigan Central in the 1840's and a few others (the Chicago, Burlington and Quincy or the Hannibal and St. Joseph); but in contrast to the professional investment banker he did not appeal to the market. He knew that because of the decline of the China trade capital lay idle in Boston, and that because of falling profits in whaling New Bedford Quakers were ready to embark on new ventures. Through personal and family connections, individuals were approached and the railroads thus financed.[374] To be sure, Forbes succeeded where others failed, but his were personal triumphs, not creative achievements in finance that opened new roads. Therefore the railroad financier Forbes bears no comparison with Winslow and Lanier.

Lanier first took an interest in railroads during the 1840's, "resuscitating," as he expressed it, the Madison and Indianapolis road. According to the findings of Alfred Chandler, the bonds of this road were sold in New York through the brokers, Winslow and Perkins. Thereby a personal contact was established from which grew Lanier's later business affiliation. Moreover while gaining familiarity with railroading and railroad finance Lanier became convinced that capital could be safely invested in the securities of Western roads. By that time, in fact in 1847, Lanier made a successful trip to Europe for the purpose of refunding the debt of the State of Indiana. There he met Horsley Palmer, Nathan and James Rothschild, Labouchère of Hope and Company, making contacts which may well have given him that insight into investment banking methods which he came to need soon thereafter. Thus prepared, late in 1848 he went to New York for the purpose of embarking in railroad promotion or construction in the West. On January 1, 1849 he formed his partnership with Winslow whose earlier activities have been touched upon. The partnership was intended to carry on a private banking business besides its main objective of negotiating Western railroad securities.

When the firm started out on this venture, Western railroad bonds were unknown in the New York capital market and the firm at first had pretty rough going. It had to take on its own account a large share of the issues which it tried to "negotiate" and to guarantee those securities which it actually sold first to a very limited circle of investors. The earliest bonds brought out by Winslow, Lanier and Company were those of the Madison and Indianapolis Railroad. These were followed by bonds of the Little Miami, the Columbus and Xenia, the Cleveland, Columbus and Cincinnati, the Cleveland, Painesville and Ashtabula, the Ohio and Pennsylvania, the Michigan Southern, the Lake Shore, and other railroads. According to Alfred Chandler's findings large parts of the various issues were sold to New York jobbers. Some of them were houses of foreign origin, such as von Hoffmann and Company, Meyer and Stucken (both German), Camman and Whitehouse (English)[375] De Lannay, Iselin and Clark, and De Coppet and Company (Swiss) which sold the securities in Europe where investors frightened by the revolutionary movements of those years provided a ready market. Unfortunately material is lacking with which to reconstruct the entire chain of distribution. On top of their business in railroad securities, Winslow, Lanier and Company introduced into the capital market Ohio county bonds which for years became the favorite investments of cautious capitalists. After the initial distrust had been overcome by extensive advertising in the form of newspaper articles and pamphlets written by Lanier, the investment business of the firm grew by leaps and bounds until it became "enormous," as Lanier tells us in his autobiography; i.e., the firm sold at times a total of $1,000,000 worth of bonds per day. For years it was without a competitor in the field which it had opened, and the profit was accordingly large. The commission for the "negotiation" of railroad bonds was 5 per cent, a figure which should be compared with the $1\frac{1}{2}$ per cent which Biddle had charged for his "negotiations" of state bonds. But in many cases the firm "contracted" for whole issues and in these cases must have pocketed even larger profits. "Negotiations" and "contracts" were often coupled with arrangements to act as the roads' purchasing agent for rails, besides becoming their transfer and fiscal agents. This latter function

implied the paying out of interest on the securities floated. Thus an extensive general banking business developed out of the investment banking activities of the firm; and the uncanny intuition of the owners can be seen from their gradual withdrawal from the latter after 1854. When the crisis broke in 1857 they were safe, for by that time they had switched to conservative private banking, especially serving those enterprises which they had helped to bring into existence. Lanier often participated in reorganizations when necessary, one of the first being that of the Pittsburgh, Fort Wayne and Chicago Railroad (1859).[376]

XI

A new turn was given to American investment banking during the Civil War through the brilliant activities of Jay Cooke. Jay Cooke (1821-1905), the son of a frontier lawyer and politician at Sandusky, Ohio, had become acquainted with investment banking methods while he was connected with E. W. Clark and Company, first as a clerk and later as a partner. The business of this firm in the decade from 1847 through 1857 has been sketched above. Cooke left the Clark concern when it suspended during the crisis of 1857 and in the years to follow became some sort of free-lance, small scale investment banker. Without having a firm of his own he "negotiated" new security issues for several railroads in whose reorganization he took a hand. He sold, for instance, bonds of the Sunbury and Erie, the Franklin and the Ironton Railroads, being remunerated therefor by stock. Occasionally he cooperated with the reorganized house of E. W. Clark and Company. In addition to such activities he bought and sold in the market a variety of transportation stocks and bonds.[377] The relative youth of American investment is evident, regardless of the greater maturity it had reached between 1840 and the crisis of 1857. Here was a man in his thirties, sitting at a desk lent by the Clarks who themselves had just gone through a reorganization, who was bond salesman, security speculator, and a little bit of an investment banker, "negotiating" new issues of securities, not with wealthy European capitalists (in the style of the 1820's and 1830's), but with small local banks and local capitalists. Thus he started out on the road which was bound to lead him to become the champion of popular loans.

In order to understand his great achievement in Civil War times the history of "popular" loans in Europe must be sketched. In an earlier part of this chapter it has been described how the idea of popular loans originated in England as early as the last quarter of the eighteenth century. But at that time the term connoted only a public subscription in the course of which tenders would be taken from anybody. As things stood, the range of contributors would be widened thereby so as to include smaller capitalists; broad strata of the population were not yet sufficiently advanced on the road of saving to take any interest in what was then called a "public subscription." The Loyalty Loan came nearest to what could then be expected of a popular loan. Not much progress was made in the Napoleonic era, but immediately thereafter France assumed leadership in the indicated direction and it is meaningful that the St. Simonists became exponents of the idea of popular loans: Henri Rodrigues suggested one of 120,000,000 francs in 1831. But the attempt proved unsuccessful, and a bankers' alliance had to rescue the issue. The Emprunt National ordered on March 9, 1848 met with no better success.[378] In the same period, as will be remembered, the Mexican War loans of this country also aimed at a broadening of the range of participants. The goal was not reached here either, although the American tradition of floating federal loans by public subscriptions instead of by dealing with middlemen, lent itself to a development toward popular loans. But in Europe by 1850 the time was becoming ripe for the latter to succeed. Only a few years after the failure of 1848, the French Crimean War loans (rentes) of 250,000,000 and 500,000,000 francs, respectively, were floated as popular loans in March and December, 1854. These and another similar issue of 750,000,000 francs of 1855 were highly successful. So also was that of 500,000,000 francs of rentes of 1859 raised to finance the Italian War. The Pereires and their friend Napoleon III were exponents of the policy of "democratizing the rente" or of "souscriptions nationales," as popular loans were called in France.[379]

There can be no doubt that Cooke acted under the inspiration of such developments. In order to succeed, however, the exponent of popular loans in this country had not only to work for a change of the regulations traditionally underlying subscriptions, introducing a general sales agency, but he had also to revamp the methods of distribution and to devise a new appeal to such prospects as he intended to reach. It became necessary to build up a new type of organization, namely, a network of agents all over the country, controlled and coordinated from a center; and the whole apparatus of modern advertising had to be put at the disposal of that sales organization. That Jay Cooke was able to envisage what was needed and, in addition, to put it into effect showed his creative ability. There was no American parallel on which he could rely; and while he was familiar with the French model[380] he redevised it in a creative spirit. Thus Cooke was able to sell hundreds of millions of bonds, a feat which nobody had achieved in this country before, or had even dreamed of doing.

It has been indicated above how Jay Cooke's activities after 1857 were educating him for his role as a creative entrepreneur and, in fact, we can observe step by step how he assumed it. Cooke established his own house, Jay Cooke and Company, in Philadelphia on January 1, 1861. No definite capital was assigned thereto, but the two partners (Cooke and his brother-in-law) were worth together about $650,000. That a partnership with so small a capital could go into investment banking on so large a scale is another indication of the still undeveloped state of this type of enterprise. The first Civil War loans, being floated in the traditional way by competitive bidding, left little room for the young concern. But its way was being prepared through close contracts with both Salmon P. Chase, Secretary of the Treasury, and John Sherman, the influential financial statesman in Congress; and the first opportunity opened up in connection with the flotation of treasury notes in April, 1861. Cooke seized it, and became one of the few large subscribers whose bids were high enough to be accepted. His share was $200,000, a respectable amount. His firm also participated in a small way in the later federal loans of that year.[381]

Cooke took the next step on the road toward his achievement when in the same year, 1861, he convinced the treasurer of the Commonwealth of Pennsylvania to sell at par, on an appeal to patriotism, a $3,000,000 state loan. This implied an attempt at a popular loan, for such an appeal would sway the rank and file rather than hard-headed businessmen and financiers. Jay Cooke and Company and Drexel and Company were made general agents for selling the loan. They succeeded in disposing of it to large and small banks, railroad and insurance companies, and to individuals in amounts as low as $50 regardless of the fact that most bankers thought that the loan was not worth par.[382] Under these circumstances the success was a personal triumph for Jay Cooke, proving as it did that the aggressive sales method which he proposed was efficient and feasible. The state treasurer reported and recommended it to the Secretary of the Treasury.

Cooke's great hour came when Chase ran into trouble with the conservative banking fraternities of New York, Boston, and Philadelphia which had financed the needs of government all through the second half of 1861.[383] But only a man like

Jay Cooke would have grasped the chance. He was a man of an extreme self-confidence (which reminds the historian of Nicholas Biddle). On the other hand, he was a newcomer in the field of investment banking so that he would not lose prestige through failure; and he had not as yet accumulated large wealth which would be endangered by errors of judgment. The case shows well why so often young firms are the cells from which springs economic development.

It must be repeated that the original Civil War loans were floated in the traditional way by advertising for bids. Prospects were bankers and capitalists who were interested in buying at prices which promised profit through an appreciation of the securities. Therefore bankers strongly opposed the flotation of federal securities at par. Nevertheless, when in the summer of 1861 they were inveigled into taking at par $150,000,000 worth of securities without competitive bidding the Secretary (thereby deviating from all established practice) had to help them sell the bonds for which they had made themselves responsible. A system of 148 agents all over the loyal North was organized for that purpose. Jay Cooke was one of these agents, his area being Philadelphia and environs, including New Jersey. He was highly successful, advertising on his own account much more than contemplated by the Treasury.[384] In the meantime there came the conflict between the Secretary and the banks of the three cities. Since Chase insisted on selling bonds only at par, since he refused offering them at the market price (as potential loan contractors demanded), and since there was no machinery to provide for price control of newly floated securities, nothing was left but a popular loan, or, from a different point of view, collecting funds by selling at high pressure to smaller investors. This was the policy which Jay Cooke had recommended since early in 1861. He was to put his suggestions into practice in March, 1862, when he was appointed special agent for selling the 5-20's. Since the retail distribution of securities was undeveloped prior to that time, both the basic task and the creative achievement (including the sale of "baby bonds" by traveling salesmen) lay in that field. Supplemented by suitable advertising Cooke's sales methods worked.

It is not necessary here to present in detail the organization and the advertising used in the successful sales campaign for the 5-20's.[385] The ideas underlying the campaign have been described by Dr. Larson as follows: Cooke recognized that small investors would become buyers if an appeal was made to their patriotism. He saw that they would hold the bonds once acquired so that previous sales would not interfere with further issues. Finally he guessed correctly that because his was a new method of distribution (reaching new strata of potential investors) his campaign would not disrupt the established financial mechanism of the country. Cooke's thinking proved valid, but his success on this basis needs additional explanation: it has been ascribed by Cooke's biographer "first and foremost" to his buoyant, enthusiastic, and optimistic personality. It was undoubtedly equally due to his ability as an organizer and to his instinct for advertising. Cooke knew the value of an emotional appeal. His only predecessor in the field of publicity, Nicholas Biddle had never understood it, imbued as he was with the rationality of the eighteenth century.

When, after having been dropped by the Treasury in 1864 for political reasons, Jay Cooke was charged again in 1865 with selling the so-called 7-30's Treasury notes (three-year notes bearing 7.3 per cent interest) he used methods and organization tested in the 5-20's campaign. Improved as they were, they were used with excellent results.[386] But there were occasional difficulties and Cooke repeatedly had to support the price of the 7-30's in the New York market, a method which he had sparingly used already in the 5-20's campaign. An old European method was thus first introduced into America.[367] "With these loans," as Dr. Larson puts it, "security distribution in America entered its modern phase. The old system of selling ⌊limited⌋ issues through bankers who ⌊contacted⌋ only a relatively small number of ⌊larger⌋ investors had proved inadequate. In its place came large-scale, high pressure selling through an aggressive sales force which reached into the savings of ⌊the little fellow⌋ and which was supported by ⌊measures of price control in⌋ the New York market. The era of the baby bond, the door-to-door salesman, and the 'pegging' of the market was in its beginning."[388]

XII

The years that followed the close of the Civil War experienced a number of deep reaching changes in the field of American investment banking. The technique of flotations was revolutionized; but one has to keep in mind that such revolution was foreshadowed by European developments and by Cooke's activities during the war. The loan contractor of old,[389] bidding against investors and speculators, the type which had come down from late eighteenth-century English practice and had been characteristic of America before Jay Cooke brought the popular loan onto the American scene, was disappearing. He was being replaced by the modern investment banker, taking whole issues of securities from the borrower, alone or in cooperation with other houses. While this method might appear like a return to that of earlier English eighteenth-century private subscriptions, the modern American investment bankers, as they emerged in the 1870's, were of course entirely different from the kind of men who were their remote ancestors and even their fathers. And so was the environment in which they worked. The firms engaged in the line once more changed almost completely. As a matter of fact, when one compares the names of those active in any earlier decade with those in the field between 1840 and 1860, 1860 and 1880, and thereafter, respectively, one gains the impression that about every fifteen to twenty years investment banking was rejuvenated with only a few survivors remaining in business. Only after the final victory of big enterprise was achieved after 1880 did the composition of investment banking become relatively stable.

Dr. Larson has drawn attention to the fact that the revolution in investment banking was in part due to the unwillingness of the London capital market to handle the war bonds of the Union. This refusal weakened Anglo-American financial relations at a time when the death of Joshua Bates, the New England born and bred senior partner of the Barings, and the retirement of George Peabody had severed important personal ties. Consequently lessening dependence on London and the emergence of specialized investment banking firms with a technique of their own characterize the new period.

Of all the new techniques adopted during and after the Civil War the syndicate stands out as especially important.[390] The syndicate has been defined by Dr. Larson as a "device whereby strong banks jointly undertake to distribute a loan, maintaining a price by rigging the market." The "syndicate," as defined, did not exist in America prior to the Civil War. But its beginnings, in Europe at least, can be traced back into the eighteenth century, and American business had been moving in this direction since the early nineteenth. The modern syndicate developed in a long process out of the "lists" of would-be subscribers to English public loans. We have examined before how during the Napoleonic era these lists, which originally included both contractors and ultimate investors, came to exclude the latter. By the end of the era they were lists of loan contractors and represented alliances of leading firms. These alliances of English contractors in the late Napoleonic era, those of the Barings, Hopes, and French bankers in 1817 and 1818[391] or those of the French bankers of the 1820's and many others can be considered

as the roots from which stemmed the first embryonic syndicates. As such can be seen joint account transactions and arrangements of leading investment bankers, such as the Barings and George Peabody or the Barings and the Rothschilds in 1848 and 1853, respectively, not to sell certain securities below certain prices,[392] for the essential characteristic of the modern syndicate is cooperation in the selling as opposed to cooperation in the buying, only, of securities as in the old-time alliances. On the other hand, "rigging of the market" started in the 1790's. It was in 1794 that Walter Boyd, then the Emperor's financial agent in London, suggested to Pitt rigging the market for the first tranche of the first Imperial loan of ₤3,000,000; but the plan was not executed.[393] However on his own he supported the market for the British loans which he contracted with disastrous results for his firm, in fact. At that time the Goldsmids began to interfere in the market successfully and on a large scale to protect their interests as loan contractors, as has been described. On the Continent Hope and Company of Amsterdam carried on the same kind of business. When in 1804 they floated their share of the Louisiana bonds they did not sell the American securities, but in line with contemporary Dutch practice issued their own certificates of participation, keeping the original debt certificates in their vaults. The certificates of participation, however, bore one half of one per cent less interest than the underlying American securities and the difference was to be used for buying up such certificates as might come into the market.[394] Slightly later, i.e., between 1820 and 1860, the Rothschilds continuously rigged the market for the securities which they floated.

In America the foundation for the syndicate was laid at the time when American investment banking came into existence. As early as 1813 Stephen Girard and David Parish sold on joint account more than $2,000,000 of the government stock which they had acquired. In 1814 the cashier of the Farmers and Mechanics Bank of Philadelphia invited the other banks of the city to appoint committees for the purpose of conferring on the application of the Secretary of the Treasury for a loan. A few months later the Pennsylvania governor's request for a loan led to a meeting of the Philadelphia banks which discussed what share each bank should take.[395] These earliest steps in the direction of what later became the syndicate remained without lasting influence. However the alliances of investment bankers of the 1830's for the purpose of handling particular flotations represented a second step in the American development. Such alliances among incorporated banks and private bankers in their capacity as loan contractors have been described and two of them are of the greatest interest. One is a verbal agreement between Thomas Wren Ward, representing the Barings, and Elihu Chauncey, Thomas Biddle and Company, J. D. Beers and Company, and Prime, Ward and King. It was concluded in the winter of 1833 and stipulated that with regard to certain carefully selected public loans there "should be a concert of action to prevent competition and secure a better profit on smaller interests by division." However the arrangement failed to function.[396] The second agreement was that of the New York banks negotiating with the Canal Fund Commissioners in April, 1837. The banks were not only willing to take about $4,000,000 securities of the state, sharing in proportion to their capital, but they also made arrangements with respect to the distribution of those securities. The parties pledged themselves to dispose of the bonds only through remittances to Europe, not to part with them below par, and to act in concert in all matters of disposition. If at the end of an agreed upon period, securities remained unsold, the banks were bound to dispose of them under whatever arrangements would then be made.[397] This business, to be sure, came to naught. Agreements of the Philadelphia banks on loans to their Commonwealth and to the Bank of the United States of Pennsylvania represent the corresponding stage for that city. In the latter case the banks received post notes of the Bank, i.e., medium term securities which they sold individually if they did not wish to keep them as investments.

In the 1840's alliances of investment bankers became more numerous. We have mentioned that of Corcoran and Riggs and the Clarks with regard to the War loan of 1847 and of the former firm with the Barings and their friends in connection with that for 1848. In the latter we may find the first example of a real international alliance, in which American firms were participants. (In earlier similar cases they had acted only as subcontractors of foreign houses.) It must be kept in mind, however, that in almost all the American alliances of the period and those to follow during the Civil War (with a few exceptions) there was no joint sale. Once the purchase was concluded each firm took its share and disposed of it independently. One of the exceptions is a contract on joint account of Vermont Central bonds concluded in 1860 by Jay Cooke and Anthony J. Drexel.[398]

The $150,000,000 loan transactions of 1861, which have been described in chapter XV, mark the last step in the American development prior to the emergence of the full-fledged modern syndicate. In fact the arrangements of the New York, Philadelphia, and Boston banks with the Secretary of the Treasury closely approached it in character. The banks made themselves responsible for the total of $150,000,000 worth of securities. But the Secretary set up a sales organization and appealed through it to a broader market than the quasi- underwriting banks could reach themselves. He disposed of as much as he could of the contracted bonds all over the country (the banks themselves also selling independently). Thereby the strain on the money markets of the three cities was relieved.[399] The Secretary of the Treasury, as must be stressed, sold for the joint account of the "underwriting" banks; responsibility and distribution were thus to a certain extent separated as in the modern genuine underwriting syndicate. Moreover the Philadelphia banks independently pushed the development toward the syndicate. On August 17, 1861 they resolved that all sales of the securities subscribed as the share of the city would be on joint account, and this plan was adopted in November, 1861, by the General Committee of the banks of the three cities with regard to the last tranche of $50,000,000 of the $150,000,000 total. These arrangements, except for rigging the market, bore almost all the characteristics of a real syndicate.[400]

Shortly thereafter rigging the market was introduced into American practice when, first in connection with the sale of the 5-20's and much more so in connection with that of the 7-30's in 1862 and 1865, respectively, Jay Cooke repeatedly entered the New York capital market in order to sustain the price of the securities. He himself spoke of "managing the market."[401]

After the War closed, the trend toward the modern syndicate persisted. Security issues were becoming so large that many could be handled only by alliances of investment bankers. On the other hand, because of the sums involved, ultimate investors could now easily be squeezed out. The borrowers had to rely on the bankers in command of large funds who were able therefore to set the conditions. Thus the loan contractor once and for all gave way to the modern investment banker. The development of alliances took place both in the field of government and railroad securities. In 1867, for instance, Jay Cooke and Company, the Clarks, and the Drexels cooperated in selling a $23,000,000 Pennsylvania state loan;[402] and in the same year the same group distributed loans for the Lehigh Coal and Navigation Company and the North Missouri Railroad. By that time the Cookes and the Clarks also made a joint account venture in Lake Superior & Mississippi Railroad stock and in stock of a subsidiary land company. This particular transaction is of interest as showing a development in the methods used by cooperating investment bankers. The agreement regarding the

sale of Lake Superior & Mississippi Railroad stock reminds one of an area pool, one firm reserving New York, the other Boston, while in the Philadelphia area there was to be cooperation. Sales price and commission to agents were agreed upon. (Incidentally, Budge, Schiff and Company, about whom more will be said were among these agents.)[403]
Thus by 1870 this country was further advanced toward what was later called a selling syndicate, rather than toward the underwriting syndicate in the strict sense of the term, the latter being characterized by the separation of underwriting from purchase and sale. Or, as Dr. Larson defines the underwriting syndicate, "for a group to guarantee the sale of a specified amount of an issue... with the understanding that if the bonds were not sold [by whatever organization was charged with the task] the syndicate members would be responsible to the extent of their underwriting."[404]

The various elements which characterize the modern syndicate were probably first in the 1860's combined in Europe; and through the agency of Jay Cooke the new device was brought to these shores. He first employed it in connection with the $2,000,000 bond issue of 1870 of the Pennsylvania Railroad Company. Eight concerns underwrote the issue. Besides the leader, Jay Cooke and Company, there were the Fidelity Trust Company, S & W. Welsh, Stuart & Brothers, E. W. Clark & Company, Drexel & Company, C. & H. Borie, and W. H. Newbold Son and Aertsen. The selling job was to be done by five of the eight houses under the management of Jay Cooke and Company. The sales were for "general account" (joint account), the profit being distributed proportionally to the amounts for which the several parties were responsible. The cost of advertising the bonds was to be charged in the same proportion. The firms chosen to sell the bonds were the Cookes, the Drexels, the Clarks, and, in addition, the Borie and Newbold firms.[405]

The next and even more important syndicate organized by Jay Cooke was established in connection with the refunding of the Civil War loans. It will be discussed in its proper place.[406]

The second great change which American investment bankers brought about between 1865 and 1880 has been characterized by N.S.B. Gras as the shift from the passive to the active phase of investment banking.[407] In the former era the investment banker provided capital using such care as could be expected of a money lender; but once he had done so, he became passive in his relations both to the investing capitalists and to the administration of the capital-using concern in question. Such was the status of all the investment bankers providing capital for the young railroads prior to

about 1860, as exemplified by Winslow, Lanier and Company when they were in the railroad field. The new phase, in contrast, was characterized by the investment banker's taking an active interest in the affairs of the corporation whose securities he had floated. His interest was manifested not only by his becoming a director, but even by being an influential member of the boards. He thus shared the responsibility for the use to which were put those funds which through his activities had been made available by capitalists and smaller savers. It was in all probability Jacques Laffitte who first developed the new type of investment banker as early as the late 1830's and early 1840's while he was at the head of the Caisse Laffitte.[408]

The change from the passive to the active type of investment banker may well have been prepared by the practice of some railroads to form permanent affiliations with certain investment bankers: for example, the Drexels became in that period the bankers of the Pennsylvania Railroad; the newly-founded firm of John J. Cisco & Son, headed by the former United States Sub-Treasurer in New York, became allied with the Union Pacific and the Chesapeake and Ohio; Fisk & Hatch with the Central Pacific; and Henry Clews with the Rock Island.[409] Jay Cooke and Company followed in 1869 by becoming the banker and fiscal agent of the Northern Pacific. To the extent that investment bankers, thus allied with railroads, were paid for their services with stock in addition to whatever cash remuneration they received, the change in status was facilitated. When Jay Cooke and Company, for instance, concluded their contract with the Northern Pacific in 1870 to sell the road's $100,000,000 bonds, they received a potential claim to three-fifths of the stock.[410] (For each $1,000 bond sold, Jay Cooke and Company was to receive $200 in stock.) After this contract had been executed, difficulties arose because of lack of cooperation on the part of the railroad's executives who made commitments without due regard to the financial necessities of its bankers. Protests were unavailing. Such lack of consideration on the railroad's part for the standing and obligations of the financial agent led to the latter's downfall.[411]

Jay Cooke's experience with the Northern Pacific could hardly have been unique, and similar ones must have forced investment bankers into assuming an active role. But even when the relationship between the administration of the industrial or transportation enterprise and its banker was satisfactory, the latter, by selling securities, assumed certain responsibilities toward the investors who bought on the strength of his prestige and recommendations. In an era of low business ethics, this situation provided another incentive to share in the administration or at least policy determination of the client. Thus control of enterprises by investment bankers, which at a later stage was to become dangerous and an expression of financial power, originally was rather an act of self-defence on the part of the bankers. To be sure, sometimes it was the outcome of a personal union of investment banker and promoter; Jay Cooke, for instance, being one of the promoters of the Northern Pacific.

Of all the investment bankers leading in post-Civil War days only the Clarks, Drexels, and Vermilyes were older firms; and of these the Clarks had undergone a reorganization and the Vermilyes were hardly important when the era began. Jay Cooke and Company, founded in 1861, who had carried the load of war finance and had remained in the vanguard for several years thereafter, struggled hard to survive, but succumbed to the panic of 1873. Besides Jay Cooke and Company other new firms were coming to the fore in the 1860's among which several groups can be distinguished. One of them consisted of Jay Cooke's leading New York agents for the sale of the 5-20's who had received their education in the field of investment banking in that connection, namely, Vermilye and Company, Henry Clews and Company, and Fisk and Hatch.

Very little is known about Vermilye and Company, except that the firm was founded in New York as a typical brokerage and private banking house in 1830 by Washington Romeyn Vermilye (1810-1876), a man of Huguenot descent, and one George Carpenter. The original style of Carpenter and Vermilye was changed to Vermilye and Company in 1844; but not before the Civil War did the house rise to importance, accumulating capital which amounted to about $1,000,000 at the end of the war. Vermilye, whom Jay Cooke one time intended to make the president of his Fourth National Bank, enjoyed a great reputation as did his partner, Wood. (The firm existed under the name assumed in the 1840's until 1904 when it became Mackay and Company.)[412]

Henry Clews and Company, the second firm of the group, was founded by Henry Clews (1834-1923), an Englishman who came to this country at an early age and had received his business training in New York in a firm of woolen importers. He became independent in Wall Street as a broker and private banker, working with various partners under the consecutive firm names of Stout, Clews and Mason, Livermore, Clews and Company, and Henry Clews and Company (assumed by 1870). Clews's activities in the investment banking field were not of long duration; for most of his life he was a stock trader and broker and a typical Wall Street banker, financing his clients' trading on margin.

Henry Clews entered investment banking by 1860. In that year he bid $119,000 on the federal bonds of October and shortly thereafter he took an interest in some of the early Civil War flotations, an interest which developed into his becoming one of Cooke's New York agents. Following the trend in the post-War era he became connected with a railroad (the Rock Island), a partner in a London house (Clews, Habicht and Company), and a member in Cooke's refunding syndicate of 1871. His interest in the field was bound to lead to a large security portfolio and he had to suspend in 1873.[413]

The same fate befell Fisk and Hatch. This firm was founded in 1862 by Harvey Fisk and Alfrederick Smith Hatch, both Vermont boys (born in 1829 and 1831, respectively). They had gained experience in banking before, the latter in Connecticut and New Jersey where he had been the cashier of the Bank of Jersey City, the former in New York City. (Fisk had worked first in the Mechanics Bank and later in the Bank of the Commonwealth.) Their initial success is interesting: it shows once more that one could go into investment banking at that time with very little capital. When establishing their business the young men raised $15,000 from relatives and friends and themselves invested hardly more than about $25,000, as can be concluded from their property during a reorganization of their firm three years later. On the other hand, the profit rate was tremendous: the original partnership of 1862 made $408,000 in the three years in which it existed. The firm became illiquid through uncautious railroad financing, remained sick after the troubles of 1873, and suspended again in 1884. It was liquidated in 1885.[414]

In the course of the few years following the Civil War during which Fisk and Hatch flourished, the firm was a member of Cooke's refunding syndicate of 1871. In addition, it was very active in railroad securities, selling government bonds issued in favor of the Union and Central Pacific Railroads to the amount of $27,855,000 and also $53,000,000 Central Pacific Railroad bonds. From these activities grew a connection with the Chesapeake and Ohio Railroad in which Huntington and his associates were interested too. Fisk and Hatch made temporary advances to the road and sold its first mortgage bonds. Just as Jay Cooke and Company broke down because of their alliance with the Northern Pacific, so Fisk and Hatch suspended because of frozen assets resulting from their loans to the Chesapeake and Ohio, loans secured by unsaleable stocks and bonds. After its reorganization the firm marketed government bonds issued in the process of refunding the Civil War 5-20's.[415]

After the liquidation of Fisk and Hatch was completed Harvey Fisk (who died in 1890) established in association with his sons the firm of Harvey Fisk and Sons. Pliny Fisk (born in 1860) became its leading spirit. Prior to World War I the house was important among the small investment bankers. Being on very good term with J. P. Morgan and Company, Harvey Fisk and Sons were repeatedly participants in the formers' flotations, and appear in a few cases also as allies of Kuhn, Loeb and Company. More often they bought for distribution securities from both houses, especially the Morgans. We are not informed about such business as they did independently although the American Locomotive Company and the Hudson Company are mentioned as having been dominated by Pliny Fisk.[416]

John J. Cisco and Son, may be considered as belonging to the same group of investment bankers regardless of their slightly different origin. John J. Cisco (1806-1884), the descendant of a Spanish family and originally a cloth dealer, was ambitious politically. Appointed Assistant Secretary of the Treasury by President Buchanan, during the latter's administration he was the United States Sub-Treasurer in New York and in that capacity gained the confidence, if not admiration, of the New York banking fraternity. His masterpiece seems to have been the reissue in 1858 of $3,000,000 of treasury notes which he negotiated with New York commercial banks and savings banks. The incoming Lincoln administration recognized his worth, and Secretary Chase retained him in office. Chase usually dealt through Cisco with the New York banks. When, for instance, in March, 1862, $3,000,000 were needed to move the Army of the Potomac, Cisco raised the amount by quietly selling 7-30 treasury notes to New York banks, instead of throwing them into the open market. After having contributed much to whatever success the early war flotations had and to that of the later ones also (in spite of being no friend of Jay Cooke), Cisco resigned as of the end of the fiscal year of 1864. He was prevailed upon to remain a few more months and then went into business for himself under the name of John J. Cisco and Son, private bankers. His firm was soon taking an interest in investment banking. As special agents of the Union Pacific (a position which Jay Cooke and Company had turned down in 1867) the firm successfully sold $100,000,000 Union Pacific bonds.[417]

Secondly, the Civil War marked the rise of the German Jewish investment bankers in America.[418] Outstanding among them was the firm of J & W. Seligman & Company, New York, which grew from several mercantile concerns owned by the various Seligman brothers and scattered all over the country. In 1857 they united their capital to form a New York house which was to import clothing and in the early 1860's was still doing business in this line with the army. In 1862, however, the Seligmans turned bankers, in the course of time opening branches in Frankfurt, London, Paris, San Francisco, and New Orleans with the various brothers as resident managers. Almost immediately upon its change in character the firm attained considerable importance buying up quietly and busily, and selling through its Frankfurt branch, especially in Germany, about $200,000,000 worth of war bonds, few of which were then saleable in England and France. (The Rothschilds are supposed to have done a similar business.) Joseph Seligman (1819-1880) was the undoubted head of the firm in that early period. Born and educated in Bavaria, he had come to this country in 1837 and has been for some time the secretary of Asa Packer, the financier. He was succeeded by his brother Jesse.[419]

A second firm similar to the Seligmans which started in the period under investigation was Kuhn, Loeb and Company of New York. It was founded in 1867 by Abraham Kuhn and Solomon Loeb who had been partners first in Lafayette, Indiana, and later in Cincinnati in a general merchandise business, a business which traditionally included the extension of merchandise credits. Retiring from that enterprise in 1865 they moved to New York where, after some months of leisure, they established a private banking firm which was soon to enter the investment banking field. Kuhn, Loeb and Company in the 1870's dealt in government and railroad securities, but their spectacular rise falls into the two last decades of the nineteenth century and was the work of Jacob Schiff. This will be discussed at its proper place.[420]

In contrast to the two preceding firms the Speyers (L. Speyer-Ellisen of Frankfurt) remained more of a European concern which, however, was strongly represented in the United States by Philip Speyer and Company (called after 1878, Speyer and Company), New York. The founder, Philip Speyer, came to this country in 1837 and was first a dealer in foreign exchange and an importer of European merchandise. When in 1845 his brother Gustavus immigrated, the partnership of Philip Speyer and Company was formed. It is claimed that this firm was the first to open the German market for American Civil War bonds. Be that as it may, it was certainly very active in the sale of those securities in Germany.[421] Although not among the leading American houses the Speyers were important investment bankers prior to World War I, cooperating regularly with Kuhn, Loeb and Company and with the First National Bank of New York.

Moreover they were large lenders on call at the stock exchange and had their hands in several financial and other corporations, especially trust companies.

The Seligmans, Speyers, and Kuhn, Loeb and Company in their beginnings depended on Frankfurt connections, that city being at the time the chief capital market in Western Germany. From the economic point of view, their function was capital import. In their activities they remained closer to American financial tradition than did Jay Cooke who had shown outright hostility to the idea of floating war loans abroad,[422] and who was the first investment banker in this country to rely for large flotations on American strength rather than on European correspondents.

Last, but not least, there was in the period under investigation a third group of investment bankers, Yankee firms working out of New York. In fact the future belonged to them and by 1870 they were laying the foundation for their successful careers. The economic historian is reminded of a remark of Scoville's that New England Yankees coming to New York as youngsters did so much better than New York lads.

Let us begin the survey of this group with the one least important as a businessman, Levi P. Morton. Morton (1824-1920), a Vermont boy, started his business career in country stores. The failure of one of them, a branch of which he was running very efficiently in Hanover, New Hampshire, resulted in his acquaintance with James M. Beebe of Boston, an outstanding dry goods merchant of the period. The latter, a creditor of the bankrupt firm, took over and permitted the branch to proceed as an independent enterprise under Morton's management. Shortly thereafter the latter was able to buy out Beebe. So impressed was Beebe by this incident that in 1849 (by which time Morton had made $12,000 to $13,000 in his little store) he invited the young man to join James M. Beebe and Company as a junior partner. In the same year (1849) Junius Spencer Morgan also became a Beebe partner. Thus Morton became acquainted with the later Peabody partner, an acquaintance which was soon more or less to determine Morton's becoming a banker; but for another few years he remained in the dry goods business in Boston and New York. Becoming a victim of the Civil War he had to suspend in 1861 and to compromise with his creditors.[423]

In 1863 Morton started a private banking business in Wall Street, L. P. Morton and Company, and among his partners was Walter H. Burns, Junius Spencer Morgan's son-in-law. By the late 1860's Burns became the resident partner of a London branch (L. P. Morton, Burns and Company)

while the New York house was reorganized as Morton, Bliss and Company, George Bliss bringing $2,500,000 into the firm. Morton was now able to attempt big business.

In contrast to his competitors Morton was a politician rather than a businessman. Brebner characterizes him as the "suavely aggressive banker-politician from Vermont." Because of this combination of interests he was soon to drop out from the race of the great investment bankers. But in the 1870's as a close ally of J. P. Morgan, he was in the front rank. Much of his initial success against Jay Cooke was due to that combination and to his close contacts with President Grant, among whose substantial backers he was. As early as 1869 after the dissolution of L. P. Morton, Burns and Company he allied himself in London with a Canadian politician, John Rose, forming the firm of Morton, Rose and Company. His partner had earlier in his life made a fortune in business and law in Montreal, a fortune which he invested in the London partnership. Rose had his hands in such enterprises as the Grand Trunk Railroad, the Hudson's Bay Company, and in some of the transcontinental railroads in the United States. His career in politics was equally successful although the able, discreet, but somewhat acquisitive man was not overpopular with leading Canadian politicians. While Rose was a representative his name became connected with the abolition of the usury laws in Lower Canada. As a commissioner he negotiated with the United States the settlement of the Oregon claims. As an exponent of Protestant interests he participated in the London conference of 1867 which settled the details of the Canadian Federation and he became the Dominion's first minister of finance. As such he went to England in 1868 to float a loan for the completion of the inter-colonial railway. This must have been Rose's first experience with investment bankers. In 1869 he went as a special commissioner to Washington in order to negotiate on the questions of fisheries, trade arrangements, and the Alabama claims; and he contributed much to the conclusion of the Washington Treaty of 1870. By that time he was already Morton's partner, and in 1871 and 1872 these two men were most active in working for peace on the basis of a reasonable American attitude with regard to the "indirect claims" arising from the Alabama issue.[424] His and Morton's political success made the allied New York and London firms, Morton, Bliss and Company amd Morton, Rose and Company, extraordinarily strong competitors for the then pending funding transactions; and the two firms contributed much to Jay Cooke's downfall.

To be sure, ruining another man's business and

succeeding in one's own enterprises are two different things; and while Morton and his ally, J. P. Morgan, were able to deprive Jay Cooke of the control of government flotations, neither in 1870 nor in 1873 were they able to make their own operations succeed. In the former year Cooke had to take over; in the latter the attempted flotation became a dismal failure. Nevertheless because of his political affiliations Morton became a fiscal agent of the government in London and one of the bankers charged with the transfer from London to America of the $15,500,000 awarded to the United States by the Court of Arbitration on her Alabama claims.[425] Later in the 1870's the Morton firms together with the Morgan concern became the mainstay of refunding; but details on the business of the Morton firms thereafter seem to be unknown. They were not among those who blazed the trail after 1880. The senior partner, as a politician, certainly brought business to his enterprise, which was run by his partner George Bliss (1816-1896). The latter, like Morton, had grown up in the dry goods business and had with uncanny intuition speculated in that field on a price rise during, and a price fall immediately after, the War. Creative ability he probably lacked, but he took advantage of America's rise in the late nineteenth century "in... regular banking transactions." Bliss seems to present a good example of success in business without the exertion of leadership.[426]

The second New England Yankee who began to rise in New York investment banking during the period under investigation was George Fisher Baker. His activities exemplify the combination of commercial and investment banking typical of Germany and possible under American law, although only rarely realized. Baker's career will be described in detail when the role of commercial banks in late nineteenth-century investment banking is discussed.

Thus we can turn to the third and most important of the New England Yankee investment bankers of New York, J. P. Morgan, Levi P. Morton's ally of the 1870's. He also will be studied in more detail later. At this point, however, it is necessary to explain his rise in the 1870's. To do this, attention must be directed to the Drexels of Philadelphia.

In fact, a permanent alliance in 1871 of the Morgan and Drexel firms contributed much to the rise of J. P. Morgan, then a member of Dabney, Morgan and Company of New York. That alliance can easily be explained and actually has been explained[427] by the different areas in which lay the strength of the two firms. J. S. Morgan and Company, London, the successors of Peabody and Company and the English correspondents of the Drexels after the 1860's, were very active in Europe, while the Drexels were powerful in America. Consequently the merger of the New York members of the two groups of banking houses, and additional arrangements which are unknown, must have appeared feasible to both. At that time the Drexels had a house in New York, Reed, Drexel and Company, headed by Mr. Reed, an accomplished banker and special friend of John J. Cisco. (That house in turn seems to have developed out of the firm J. T. Van Vleck and Reed, later styled Van Vleck, Reed and Drexel, active in the 1850's.)[428] Reed, Drexel and Company, like Dabney, Morgan and Company, disappeared when Drexel, Morgan and Company, New York, came into existence in 1871. The latter's senior partner was first Joseph William Drexel (1833-1888), the third son of the founder of the house of Drexel and Company, Philadelphia. Having been in business in Chicago independently for some while, he returned to Drexel and Company in 1861 and six years later was sent to Paris to guide the concern's European member, Drexel, Harjes and Company. Joseph William Drexel retired from Drexel, Morgan and Company as early as 1876 when J. P. Morgan became its head. Junius Spencer Morgan was at least the nominal head of the Morgan-Drexel alliance of banks until he died in 1890 and he was succeeded as such by Anthony J. Drexel until the latter's death in 1893. At that time J. P. Morgan, the senior partner in the New York firm, became the ranking partner of Drexel and Company in Philadelphia, until finally in 1895 what had by that time become J. P. Morgan and Company, New York, and Drexel and Company, Philadelphia, merged without abandoning the established firm names. To what extent the actual command of the Drexel-Morgan group of banking houses had shifted to J. P. Morgan prior to 1893 cannot be gauged by an outsider. Probably it had shifted to a considerable degree.[429]

In the early 1860's the Drexels had worked hand in glove with the Cookes, who even borrowed from the former, pledging securities for their loans. In 1861, for example, both firms were agents for the sale of a $3,000,000 Pennsylvania state loan; and they were contemplating opening in common a private banking house in Washington. But when Jay Cooke started his spectacular rise the very conservative Drexels became suspicious or jealous or both, and somewhat antagonistic. Nevertheless Anthony J. Drexel cooperated with the Cookes and Clarks in establishing the First National Bank of Philadelphia in 1863. There was by no means a break as yet. In 1867 we find the Drexels, Clarks, and Cookes as allies in selling a $23,000,000 Pennsylvania loan and security issues for the

Lehigh Coal and Navigation Company and the North Missouri Railroad. As late as 1870 the Drexels participated in Jay Cooke's syndicate for the sale of $2,000,000 Pennsylvania Railroad bonds.

At this juncture the Drexels, rising steadily, began to turn their backs on the less conservative Jay Cooke who recognized the hostility of his former allies and friends. When the funding operations started in earnest in 1870 the two houses were in different camps. The Drexels now went so far as to refuse cooperation in Cooke's syndicate of 1871 and became bitter critics of the latter's Northern Pacific venture.[430]

By the time the Drexels consummated their permanent alliance with the Morgans they already possessed a valuable investment banking business, exporting some securities to Germany. When they first entered the field is not certain, but it can hardly have been much before 1850. By the middle of that decade, however, they were very active in the railroad field. They were connected, for instance, with the Sunbury and Erie and the Vermont Central; and in the second half of the 1860's they became bankers for the Pennsylvania Railroad. By the end of the 1850's they were taking an interest in government finance also. In 1858 we find the previously mentioned firm of Van Vleck, Reed[431] and Drexel taking $400,000 worth of $4\frac{1}{2}$ per cent treasury notes and bidding on another $1,000,000 worth of $4\frac{3}{4}$ per cent treasury notes of which they were allotted $137,000. The same year Drexel and Company of Philadelphia took $500,000 United States bonds.[432] When the Civil War broke out the Drexels, by then commanding a capital of about $2,000,000, went heavily into federal securities. Reed, Drexel and Company were among the few large subscribers to the federal bonds floated in February, 1861, and slightly later the Philadelphia Drexels took a keen interest in the treasury notes of May. As a matter of fact, they backed Jay Cooke (who went after bids) and placed $141,000 with banks and one individual. They were unable to get satisfactory bids on the May bonds, however. To what extent they participated in the later Civil War flotations is not known.

XII

The outstanding set of transactions during the 1870's was the refunding of the Civil War loans, which was planned as early as the 1860's and, quite naturally, promoted by Jay Cooke. But a bill which he backed and which would have resulted in an attempt to float a loan in Europe was lost. Had the bill succeeded Cooke would have had allies in young J. P. Morgan, then representing J. S. Morgan

and Company, and in certain New York brokers who had the backing of German-Jewish houses, such as Bischoffsheim and Goldschmidt. However, instead of launching an ambitious refunding program, McCulloch, Secretary of the Treasury, to whom Congress had left the decision, preferred to live from hand to mouth, selling new securities cautiously when old ones fell due and could not be redeemed from current surplus. Cooke assisted the treasury in transactions of this type.[433]

In 1870, however, the job was tackled in earnest. American investment banking was by that time slowly becoming an oligopoly, at least with regard to large operations; and its methods were in a state of rapid transition. All the leading firms of the period, discussed in the preceding section of this chapter, were in one way or another interested in the business. It began in July, 1870, when Congress passed a law[434] authorizing the sale of $1,500,000,000 worth of securities of different types bearing 4 to 5 per cent interest. They were to be exchanged for 5-20's or sold, the proceeds being used to buy up a corresponding amount of the latter. This act was amended in January, 1871, so as to permit an issue of $500,000,000 (instead of $200,000,000) worth of 5 per cent bonds. The operation was delayed because of the outbreak of the Franco-Prussian War, but Jay Cooke worked on the Secretary of the Treasury trying to get hold of the business. His main opponent at that moment was the house of Morton, Bliss and Company, an opposition which made Jay Cooke angry, since he considered the firm as a brokerage house "just fledgling into bankers and selling government loans." But August Belmont (with Rothschild backing, of course), the Drexels, and the Seligmans were also competing. Jay Cooke's firm planned an aggressive, strongly centralized sales organization which would permit liberal remuneration to the loan agents as an inducement to devote all their efforts to the job.

That competition and political pressure forced Boutwell, the Secretary of the Treasury, when offering the first tranche of $200,000,000 in March, 1871, to establish a loosely structured organization. (Earlier, in 1863, Fessenden had unsuccessfully tried the same method when he was the Secretary of the Treasury.) Under the original plan of 1871 National Banks and a great number of private bankers were to sell the loan. The latter included Jay Cooke and Company, Fisk and Hatch, Vermilye and Company, the Clarks of New York and Philadelphia, Winslow, Lanier and Company, and Kidder, Peabody and Company of Boston. In London the sale of the securities was entrusted to Jay Cooke, McCulloch and Company, Morton, Rose and Company, Seligman Brothers, and J. S. Morgan

and Company. The Barings and Rothschilds kept
aloof. An unusual method was going to be tried
here a second time, regardless of the earlier failure, a method which was different alike from
everything that was traditional and everything that
had promise. Its adoption was, in fact, not the
outcome of business considerations, but the result of oligopolistic competition typically taking
the form of political pressure and wire pulling. It
was meant to be a compromise and was bound to
fail. Securities amounting to about $130,000,000
remained unsold.

Under these circumstances Jay Cooke took preparatory steps for the organization of a syndicate
and approached the Secretary with definite proposals.[435] At first they were turned down, since
Cooke requested that the proceeds of the flotation
be deposited with National Banks for a certain
period of time to which Boutwell would not agree.
But ultimately the latter was forced to turn to the
Cookes, and they organized two syndicates for taking the loan, one in New York and one in London.
Each was to be responsible for selling a certain
amount of securities, $10,000,000 and $15,000,000,
respectively; and both of them together would receive an option on what remained of the tranche of
$200,000,000. A clause in the agreement that the
proceeds of the loan would remain on deposit for
a period of 90 days with the banks concerned without drawing interest increased de facto the compensation set by law. When Cooke went to work to
organize the syndicates, he ran into difficulties,
a hostile alignment of his competitors taking place.
The strongest houses stood aside; the Barings and
Rothschilds refused cooperation and so did the
Morgans. Morton, Rose and Company followed
suit for fear of the Barings, and the Drexels declined an invitation to join. As a matter of fact,
Jay Cooke was never recognized by the titans in
finance; whatever prestige he possessed was with
smaller financiers. Under these circumstances
he was forced to rely on his old allies and friends
from Civil War times, such firms as Fisk and
Hatch, Vermilye and Company, Clews, Livermore
and Company, and Clark, Dodge and Company.
Moreover he found support among the National
Banks, the Firsts of Washington and Philadelphia
and the Fourth of New York (all founded by Cooke)
and John Thompson's First National Bank of New
York then already strongly influenced by its
cashier, George F. Baker. The cooperating European syndicate was led by Jay Cooke, McCulloch
and Company and consisted mainly of German-
Jewish bankers in London, Frankfurt, Hamburg,
Berlin, and Brussels. After the two syndicates had
contracted for the $25,000,000 of the loan, sub-
scription books were opened and within an extra-

ordinarily short time all that remained of the
tranche had been taken. The success was due in
part to pegging the market of the securities.

It is not surprising that after this success Jay
Cooke tried to induce the Secretary of the Treasury
to announce the issue of a second tranche in 1872.
He thought in terms of a flotation of $600,000,000
of securities of $4\frac{1}{2}$ and 5 per cent types through
Jay Cooke and Company, Jay Cooke, McCulloch
and Company, and the Rothschilds. The plan was
blocked by Cooke's enemies. The Mortons, Morgans, and Drexels wished to have a hand in the
business, and the National Banks wanted to sell a
share in the loan on commission. Again the Fes-
senden-Boutwell plan of 1863/1871 was to be tried
which incidentally, was promoted before the youthful American Bankers Association. Joseph Patterson, whose role in connection with the $150,000,000
loan of 1861 will be remembered, made himself
the spokesman of the plan and is suspected of having acted in behalf of the Drexels.[436]

In consequence, a broad alliance of bankers was
brought into existence which was to negotiate the
sale of $300,000,000 worth of United States securi-
ties. It subscribed outright for $10,000,000 with
an option on the remainder. The members of the
syndicate were to receive for the "negotiation"
one per cent commission and they were accorded
the right to hold the proceeds of their sales for
three months, which was equal to another one and
one half per cent. Jay Cooke and Company, representing Jay Cooke, McCulloch and Company and
N. M. Rothschild and Sons, subscribed for one
half of the $10,000,000, while L. P. Morton and
J. P. Morgan, representing the Barings, J. S. Morgan and Company, Morton, Rose and Company,
Morton, Bliss and Company, and Drexel, Morgan
and Company, subscribed for the other half. Subscription books were opened in February, 1873,
both in New York and London. Jay Cooke and
Company took most of the share offered in New
York; response in Europe, however, was very slow.
In order to create a demand for the securities, Jay
Cooke without consulting his allies advised the
Secretary of the Treasury to call $100,000,000 of
old securities; but he was disavowed by the other
members of the alliance who possibly sensed his
intention of getting control of the operation. Under
these circumstances the original call was rescinded
and replaced by one for only $50,000,000; and in
the end sales remained far below the $300,000,000
goal. There were several reasons for the failure.
The fact that the syndicate had an option on the
whole loan and contracting for the securities at a
later moment promised better profit than "negotiating" them at an earlier date may have been one of
the reasons. Another possibly was the antagonism

of the former members of the successful syndicate of 1871 who this time were shoved aside. They are supposed to have formed what at the Paris Bourse would have been called a contremine, selling United States securities for the purpose of breaking the market and discouraging potential buyers of new securities. Finally, lack of centralized control of the operation, as Jay Cooke felt, contributed to the dismal failure. At its root was the fact that firms were coupled together whose character and policies were mutually exclusive and could not be reconciled: the loud-mouthed, aggressive, typically American upstart, Jay Cooke, and the conservative, somewhat aristocratic, cautious, slow-moving Europeans who having nothing to gain from speed, but much to lose from possible mistakes, could not pull together at one rope.[437] Jay Cooke failed soon thereafter.

When Secretary Bristow took over the Treasury in June, 1874, $178,548,300 of the $500,000,000 5 per cent ten year bonds authorized in 1870 were not floated as yet. Preliminary negotiations with bankers regarding this block led nowhere, although there were originally three syndicates competing for the business, each of which was willing to take "firm," i.e., to contract for a large amount of bonds. But their offers were so pressing and the money market so bright that the Secretary of the Treasury decided to invite tenders in order to avoid favoritism and secure the advantages of competitive bidding. Thus in July a public subscription of the traditional character was announced. Once more there was competition between investors and loan contractors, large and small. But the strongest members of the original and competing syndicates now united and formed an alliance which was superior "in promise and influence" to all previous syndicates. This alliance of investment bankers, led by N. M. Rothschild and Sons, London and J. and W. Seligman and Company, New York, bid for $55,000,000 under the condition that no other bids were accepted and asked for a twelve months option on the remainder. However, the government had received smaller bids amounting to more than $20,000,000 of which $10,113,550 were above par and which it therefore wished to accept. (The rest seems to have represented bids of American would-be loan contractors requesting a 1/4 per cent commission on their bids at par.) Consequently the $55,000,000 bid lapsed. Shortly thereafter, however, private negotiations were opened between Bristow on the one side and August Belmont and Company acting for the Rothschilds and J. and W. Seligman and Company on the other. It was agreed that their syndicate would contract for $45,000,000 of which $15,000,000 was to be paid on or before August 1,

1874, the rest at their pleasure before January 31, 1875. Moreover the contracting firms received an option on the rest of the tranche, amounting to $122,680,550 to be made use of prior to the last named date. They were to receive a commission of one fourth of one per cent on the total amount subscribed.[438] One half of the contracted-for $45,000,000 was taken by the various houses of the Rothschild concern and August Belmont and Company, New York. Of the remainder one moiety was subscribed by the Seligmans acting for the Crédit Foncier of Paris and about ten to fifteen other continental houses, while the other moiety went to the First National Bank of New York acting in cooperation with McCulloch and Company (successor to Jay Cooke, McCulloch and Company). This information permits a conclusion as to the original three competing syndicates above-mentioned.

The contract of July 28, 1874 was "renewed" on January 29, 1875, August Belmont and Company acting for N. M. Rothschild and Sons; Drexel, Morgan and Company for J. S. Morgan and Company;[439] and J. and W. Seligman for Seligman Brothers of London. That is to say, these firms, their London allies, and their associates on both sides of the Atlantic took up the option, receiving 1/2 per cent commission. The result of this transaction was that all the remaining 6 per cent bonds were refunded into 5 per cent securities.[440]

The next refunding transaction took place in 1876. On August 24 of that year the Secretary of the Treasury entered into a contract with August Belmont and Company on behalf of the Rothschilds and their associates, J. and W. Seligman and Company for themselves and their allies, and Drexel, Morgan and Company on behalf of J. S. Morgan and Company and Morton, Bliss and Company and allies for $40,000,000 worth of $4\frac{1}{2}$ per cent bonds. The contractors received an option for the remaining $260,000,000 worth of $4\frac{1}{2}$ per cent bonds authorized by the acts of July 14, 1870 and January 20, 1871. However the Secretary had the right to cancel the contract at any time after March 4, 1877, giving 10 days notice. The contractors received a commission of 1/2 per cent. Payments were to be made at par plus accrued interest in gold coin, U.S. gold certificates, or 6 per cent bonds (5-20's).[441]

Under this contract $90,000,000 worth of $4\frac{1}{2}$ per cent bonds had been sold by March 1, 1877. At that time a favorable turn in the money market induced the Secretary to work for a termination of the contract expecting that he could sell 4 per cent instead of $4\frac{1}{2}$ per cent bonds at par. However when the contract was actually terminated an additional total of $100,000,000 $4\frac{1}{2}$ per cent was left to the syndicate, and a new contract was promised to its members who in return abandoned their option for the remaining $100,000,000 4½ per cents. Subsequently, on May 11, it was decided to sell an amount of $200,000,000 bonds at 4 per cent, authorized under the Resumption Act and to apply $185,000,000 thereof for redemption purposes. On June 9, 1877 a contract was concluded with some of the members of the old syndicate; namely, August Belmont and Company (acting for the Rothschilds, of course), Drexel, Morgan and Company (for themselves and J. S. Morgan and Company), J. and W. Seligman (for themselves and Seligman Brothers), Morton, Bliss and Company (for themselves and Morton, Rose and Company), Drexel and Company (Philadelphia), and the First National Bank of New York. The contract was to terminate on June 30, 1878 while it could be canceled by the Secretary of the Treasury after December 31, 1877. In fact the syndicate took $25,000,000 worth of 4½ per cent and $25,000,000 worth of 4 per cent bonds receiving 1/2 per cent commission on its sales. The public criticized the syndicate for lack of faith and the Secretary for not insisting on its taking a larger risk by buying a greater amount of 4 per cent bonds. It had an option, however, for further sums. Under the contract the syndicate had to open a public subscription at par in the United States. Such a subscription was actually open between June 14 and July 16, 1877. The public was entitled to subscribe coupon bonds in denominations of $50 and $100 and registered stock in denominations of $50, $100, $500, $1000, $5000 and $10,000. Payment had to be made within a period of three months. Objections were raised because coupon bonds could be subscribed only in unusually small denominations. That is to say, there was a complaint that the interests of larger American capitalists had not been protected by the Secretary of the Treasury. Nevertheless $75,496,550 worth of 4 per cent bonds were taken. The success of the public subscription was such that another one was being planned, but the idea was later abandoned.[442]

The reason for abandoning a second public subscription may have been that the syndicate was entitled to raise the price of the bonds above par both in America and Europe after the subscription books were closed. Under these circumstances its members were anxious to avoid another par-subscription after the "reasonable period" stipulated in the contract had elapsed. Some of the success of the public subscription may be ascribed to the fact that the National Banks were interested therein. Since the bonds were payable in gold and very little of the metal was in the hands of the public, the banks had to be used for buying gold or remitting currency to the associates in New York.

It seems also that the National Banks' interest was protected to the extent that they wished to subscribe themselves.

But the transaction did not have smooth sailing all the way through. It will be remembered that this contract for 4 per cent bonds grew originally from a cancellation of an earlier one for 4½ per cent bonds; and that the new syndicate was composed of the investment banks which had handled the business before. Nevertheless the syndicates were not identical. In the earlier one Morton, Bliss and Company represented, besides themselves, the interests of the United States Trust Company, the Merchants, American Exchange, and Third National Banks, and of Kuhn, Loeb and Company and Winslow, Lanier and Company, an example of how broad was the range of allies (subcontractors) of the individual houses which participated in the various refunding syndicates. The above-named old subcontractors of Morton, Bliss and Company were not represented in the new syndicate, however, and demanded proper participation. The quarrel which arose because Morton, Bliss and Company gave no notice to its old subcontractors when going into the new syndicate seems to have been settled by arbitration. The syndicate of 1877 is supposed to have sold a total of $235,000,000 worth of 4 and 4½ per cent bonds, of which $40,000,000 were used for securing gold.[443]

In April, 1878, Secretary Sherman concluded[444] another contract for the sale of $50,000,000 worth of 4 per cent bonds at 101½. The same syndicate agreed to take "firm" $10,000,000 with an option on the rest; but it was required to subscribe not less than an average of $5,000,000 per month. Again the syndicate received 1/2 per cent commission. The Secretary was bound not to sell any other bonds except a few specified ones, during the life of the contract.[445]

According to the Finance Report of 1879[446] a new public subscription was opened on January 1, 1879 for 4 per cent bonds. The sales proceeded rapidly in this country, but it was necessary to take care of the European bondholders who either had to or wished to convert. Therefore on January 21, 1879 a contract was concluded with a syndicate consisting of the London houses N. M. Rothschild and Sons, J. S. Morgan and Company, Morton, Rose and Company, and Seligman Brothers (who seem to have acted through J. and W. Seligman, New York). The syndicate had the exclusive right to sell United States 4 per cents in Europe; and it was understood that it would not interfere with the popular sales in America, at least not prior to July 1, 1879.[447]

With the intention of promoting the pending sale of the 4 per cents the Secretary of the Treasury

issued a circular letter on March 4, 1879 announcing that as soon as the 6 per cents of 1867 and
1868 were refunded, he would offer less favorable
terms for the refunding of the 10-40's. Stimulated
by this announcement, a syndicate represented by
the Bank of Commerce on April 4 took up all that
remained of the 5-20's by concluding a contract
for $40,000,000 worth of 4 per cent bonds.[448]

A few days later the Secretary of the Treasury
actually made a new and less favorable offer. He
required of applicants for a new issue a premium
of 1/2 per cent and fixed the commission uniformly
at 1/8 per cent for all subscriptions exceeding
$1000, although heretofore it had been graded.
Under these conditions he offered another issue of
$150,000,000 4 per cents and was successful, an
American syndicate accepting his offer as early
as April 18. If the Commercial and Financial
Chronicle is correct this syndicate originated with
Fisk and Hatch but it was represented by the First
National Bank of New York. It not only bid on the
offered $150,000,000 but also on $44,556,300 refunding certificates of $10 denominations. The
latter offer was declined, since it seemed to be
the will of Congress that the $10 certificates were
reserved for small investors who actually received an opportunity to buy them from the post-
masters, from designated National Banks, and
directly from the United States Treasurer and
the Assistant Treasurers. Of the $150,000,000,
the syndicate received $121,000,000, the remain-
der having been taken up by earlier bids, some of
which had been tendered by members of the syndicate individually. The First National Bank and
Fisk and Hatch each took $25,000,000 worth of the
securities. These transactions concluded the refunding of the 10-40's.[449]

The preceding description shows the importance
of European investment bankers in the refunding
process which between the collapse of Jay Cooke
and May, 1877, was pretty much controlled by a
small clique of London houses with strong representation in this country. By that time, however,
the situation became more favorable from the
American point of view. The Secretary of the
Treasury in the spring of 1877 was strong enough
to force the foreign investment bankers to offer
a part of their bargain at favorable prices to the
American public prior to going before the international capital market. Moreover the last flotations, to the extent that they were not offered in
public subscriptions, were taken by American
syndicates instead of being gobbled up by those
houses which between 1874 and 1877 had possessed
a sort of monopoly.[450]

XIII

With the end of the refunding operations[451]
American investment banking entered a new era.
For about the first fifteen years railroad securities
dominated the market, but in the second half of
the 1890's industrials began to come to the fore.
Federal flotations were important only during a
few years in the 1890's; but they will be discussed
first. A continuous outflow of gold then made it
imperative to replenish the Treasury's holdings if
the gold standard was to be preserved; while a few
years later the Spanish-American War necessitated
the raising of extra funds. Both of these ends
could be accomplished only by the issue of securities.

In the 1890's the federal government floated its
securities by competitive bidding again, or at
least it tried to do so. On January 17, 1894
$50,000,000 worth of 5 per cent bonds were publicly
advertised, the lowest price being set at 117.223
which meant a 3 per cent yield on the bonds. Of
the bids received $9,295,300 were above the limit;
$52,292,150 bids received at 117.223 were scaled
down by 5.331 per cent so as to complete the authorized issue, while further bids for $55,705,100
were rejected for various reasons. So, at least,
was the transaction described officially. But this
presentation was entirely misleading. Only through
personal negotiations between the Secretary of the
Treasury, Carlisle, and representatives of the
New York bankers (as in 1860-61) forty-eight hours
before the subscription books were closed was the
transaction saved from becoming an utter failure.
Responsible for the ultimate success was John A.
Stewart (1822-1926), one of the creators of the
modern trust company business, and then president
of the United States Trust Company. He was aided
by James Stillman, James Thomas Woodward
(1837-1910), the very successful president of the
Hanover National Bank, and Edward King of the
Union Trust Company. Stewart alone subscribed
for $30,000,000 of the issue.[452]

As early as November of the same year another
issue of $50,000,000 became necessary and again
a public subscription was attempted. This time
Carlisle took no chances, but negotiated early with
the New York bankers, although it was generally
held that the public subscription, advertised on
November 14, would be a success. The legality of
this issue was not in doubt as had been that of the
earlier one. Public opinion was being built up to
consider it unpatriotic to withdraw from the
Treasury the gold needed for paying the subscriptions. Consequently 486 bids totaling $178,836,050

were received. Among these was one by a New York syndicate for the whole amount at 117.077. This bid turned out to be more favorable than the aggregate of all the others which would have had to be accepted in case of its refusal, and so the syndicate was awarded the whole issue of $ 50,000,000.[453] It sold only slowly, however. When in February, 1895, the contract was concluded with the Morgan-Belmont syndicate (which will be discussed forthwith), the syndicate of November, 1894, still held large amounts of undigested securities selling three points below the purchase price.[454]

These two flotations of 1894 were followed by the well known "private contract" (as J. P. Morgan significantly called it himself) between the Treasury and the latter's American and European syndicates, known as the Morgan-Belmont syndicates, for the delivery of 3,500,000 ounces of gold to be paid by $62,315,400 worth of 4 per cent 30 years coin bonds yielding $3\frac{3}{4}$ per cent. August Belmont, Jr. (1853-1924) who in 1890 had taken over his father's firm (representing as before the House of Rothschild) played the leading role aside from Morgan in the transaction. It was concluded on the basis of the Revised Statutes, Sec. 3700.[455] Well known and often described the transaction needs mention only,[456] except that it seems worthwhile to restate the main participants in the American syndicate which took $31,157,000 worth of the total issue. These were:

August Belmont and Company taking	$2,753,875
J. P. Morgan and Company	$2,678,825
First National Bank of New York	$2,600,000
Harvey Fisk and Sons	$2,600,000
United States Trust Company	$1,800,000
National City Bank	$1,500,000
Fourth National Bank	$1,000,000
Chase National Bank	$1,000,000
Hanover National Bank	$1,000,000

and smaller firms taking the rest.[457]

From the point of view of this research it is important to keep in mind that the incentive for the transaction came from N. M. Rothschild and Sons in London by way of J. S. Morgan and Company to the New York house of the Morgan concern. But J. P. Morgan himself bore the brunt of the negotiations (regardless of whether he or Carlisle hit on the saving idea of making use of sec. 3700, still a moot question); and he was responsible for the successful execution of the contract. He took a tremendous risk; his interest and that of the national economy were identical, as the historian can see, and his action was highly beneficial. On the other hand, he, a private banker, was de facto for a time not only the master of the exchange market, but also of the gold in the Treasury, and to a certain extent supervised the national finances in a way which was rather irksome to those who were officially responsible therefor.[458]

Regardless of the success of the private contract of February, 1895,[459] the gold reserves of the Treasury needed replenishing again by the end of the year when (on December 23) J. P. Morgan discussed the situation with the President. He offered a new contract for $200,000,000 worth of gold, an amount which was estimated by the government to be sufficient until Congress met in 1897. Although no commitments were made on the part of the government, Morgan immediately organized a syndicate for bidding not less than $100,000,000 and not more than $200,000,000 privately or in public subscription, with the understanding that no participant would withdraw gold from the Treasury. The London market being closed at the time to American borrowers because of the tight political situation (Jameson Raid and Venezuela), Morgan made the necessary arrangements in Germany and France and also solicited participation in the smaller Western continental states (Holland, Belgium, Switzerland). The Rothschilds, on the other hand, refused cooperation.

In organizing the syndicate Morgan cooperated closely with John A. Stewart, Pliny Fisk of Harvey Fisk and Sons, and Edward D. Adams, the New York representative of the Deutsche Bank, Berlin. Participation was very widely distributed, and the syndicate was composed of European banks and private bankers, ready to ship gold for their shares; of American banks, savings banks, private bankers, and individuals owning gold and willing to exchange it for bonds; of New York, Chicago, Boston, and Philadelphia banks possessing gold and willing to put it at the disposal of the government, although intending to replenish their coffers later by selling the bonds so acquired; and finally of institutions and individuals not owning gold, but expecting to be able to get hold of it without drawing on the Treasury. When the syndicate organization was completed, Morgan wrote on January 4, 1896 to the president offering a contract for 11,500,000 ounces of gold equal to approximately $200,000,000 on the terms of the contract of February 8, 1895. If, however, under the pressure of Congress (so Morgan hinted) the government should decide on a public subscription, Morgan would do his best to assist the administration and to make such a subscription a success.

While financial New York expected another private subscription the government decided on a public subscription of only $100,000,000 worth of 4 per cent bonds. If the syndicate were to become active under these circumstances it would have been bound by its own internal arrangements to bid for "all or none." Such action, however, was not considered wise and on January 14, 1896 Morgan dissolved the syndicate. Its standing ready may have contributed to the success of the public subscription which was advertised on January 6. Morgan, after having abandoned his original syndicate, formed a second one to participate in the bids and actually submitted a bid for the whole issue. His partners in the new syndicate were the National City Bank, Harvey Fisk and Sons, and the Deutsche Bank; and the price offered was 110.6877. Another syndicate participating unsuccessfully in the bidding was led by John A. Stewart who, representing 180 bidders, offered 110.075 for $76,000,000 worth of bonds. Incidentally, in the end, Morgan gave Stewart's United States Trust Company a participation of $1,800,000 in his syndicate. As a result of those moves more than $66,000,000 were allotted to individuals, while the Morgan syndicate received an allocation of $33,179,250, later raised to $37,915,850. The total of eligible bids amounted to about $527,000,000.[460]

The $200,000,000 war loan of 1898 is of no interest in our context since the investment banker had no share therein. It was a popular loan sold at par with statutory preference for the small bidder. The loan was highly successful, because it was sold below its market value, and it was estimated that the government had sacrificed no less than $4,000,000 and possibly more by not having asked for bids but selling the loans at a fixed price. Nevertheless the method selected for political reasons was justified "on high grounds of public policy." $100,000,000 was supposed to have been tendered in offers amounting to $500 each, another $100,000,000 in offers of such a magnitude that all bids exceeding $5000 could be excluded from allocations. In fact, however, the loan was so favorable that wealthy people undoubtedly got their shares by bidding through dummies. Regardless of the fact that an overwhelming success was taken for granted two syndicates stood ready: one headed by Morgan bid on the whole loan, while a second (the participants of which are unknown to the author) offered $100,000,000 at 1 per cent premium.[461]

XIV

Between 1880 and 1910 the business of floating securities was done in one of three ways:[462] there was either contracting or "negotiating" or underwriting or there was a combination of these various types of transactions. For example J. P. Mor-

gan and Company "negotiated" an issue of Louisville and Nashville bonds for the issuing railroad with a syndicate consisting of Lee, Higginson and Company, Kissell, Kinnicut and Company, and Moffet and White who bought these bonds on joint account (combination of "negotiating" and contracting). Or to give another example, in March, 1912, an issue of $25,000,000 Virginia Railway first-mortgage bonds was sold by the National City Bank (which must have contracted them first) to Lee, Higginson and Company and Kissell, Kinnicut and Company who took them on joint account; but the National City Bank acted as an underwriter (combination of contracting on two levels with underwriting).[463]

As to underwriting, to be taken up first, there was some confusion. The reason therefor was lack of distinction between two different phenomena: the bankers spoke of underwriting only[464] when an individual house or a syndicate as such guaranteed the success of an issue to the borrower without selling it, which is, of course, entirely different from that sort of "underwriting" which was the function of participants in a syndicate, especially one based on previous contracting. In the latter case the specific relationship is one between syndicate manager and participants. To put it differently, the public loosely called "underwriting" what was de facto syndicating of an issue, i.e., handling securities by a syndicate, as will be described shortly. The bankers, however, used the term underwriting in a specific sense as did, for instance, George F. Baker. Before the Pujo Committee, he described this business method correctly, and interestingly enough did not understand what the counsel of the committee was talking about when the latter used the term underwriting in the broader, popular sense. Here is Baker's definition:[465]

"... if a company was going to sell a million of bonds, or to offer them to their stockholders, as often has been done, they would go to a banking house and say, 'We are going to offer these securities, and we want to sell them and to be sure that they are sold, will you underwrite them?' or, in other words, take all that the stockholders do not take for, say, 1 per cent commission [on the whole issue], or whatever they agree on. That is the substance of it,"

except that the underwriters usually received those securities which they had to take over at a more favorable rate than the public. To stress the point once more, it is essential of underwriting proper that the borrower himself sells the securities, but in case of failure is covered by the underwriting house or syndicate. Selling and risk bearing are in the first instance entirely separated. (Rarely, as in the above cited case, a contractor could become an underwriter when selling to retailers.)

Secondly, there was "negotiating," i.e., selling of securities by the investment banker on a commission basis with the concomitant lending on the securities to be sold. On the 16th of December, 1908, for example, several railroads, the New York Central, the Michigan Central, the Lake Shore, the Michigan Southern, and the Cleveland, Cincinnati, Chicago and St. Louis Railroads wrote identical letters to J. P. Morgan and Company, appointing the House of Morgan their fiscal agent. They proposed that the latter should act whenever the railroad in question wished to dispose of new securities. The sales price and the commission were to be agreed upon between the fiscal agent and the finance committee of the road and the former was to advance 75 per cent of the agreed upon sales price on the securities, to be held as collateral. The roads received a short letter of acceptance which was revised in 1911. In that year a commission of $1\frac{1}{2}$ per cent of the face value of the securities to be negotiated was established by the House of Morgan as the remuneration for its efforts, except in the case of securities which ran for less than six years. In the latter case, the commission was to be 1 per cent for each year of the life of the security. At the same time the House of Morgan offered to advance 90 instead of 75 per cent of the agreed upon sales price. It must be stressed that the above roads wrote the identical letters on the same date and received identical answers which in 1911 were revised again by identical letters. These facts indicate that the action emanated from the Morgans who (whatever the degree) possessed control over the roads.[466] It must be emphasized that we meet here modernized, eighteenth-century loan "negotiations" with the concomitant lending on the securities to be "negotiated," a combination which Biddle had once promoted in America to his own undoing. It is probable that the "negotiating" house usually guaranteed the success of the flotation, i.e., underwrote the issue.

Thirdly, there was contracting, and this business in turn appeared in various forms: Either an individual firm contracted, as had been done throughout the nineteenth century;[467] or several investment bankers contracted on joint account, as the Morgans, the First National Bank, and the National City Bank did very often;[468] or the contracting was done by a syndicate, the issue was syndicated. It has been described before how the

syndicate was introduced into the American practice, and details as to the working of syndicates by 1900 will be presented shortly.[469]

The question poses itself: in which cases were securities underwritten (in the strict sense of that term), sold on commission, or contracted. A detailed study would be required to find the answer, and it is very doubtful whether it could be made anywhere except in the archives of the leading investment bankers of the 1900's, which are not open to research. A second pertinent question is: when was it customary to work through a syndicate? The latter could be engrafted on all three kinds of operations. If a syndicate contracted, it did not underwrite, of course, in the strict sense of the term, for risk taking was implied in the outright purchase of the securities in question and the distribution of the risk assumed among the participants was an internal affair of the syndicate. Only from the point of view of the syndicate manager, as opposed to that of the borrower, did the participants underwrite. In line with an author writing[470] in the 1920's one can distinguish between selling syndicates and underwriting syndicates proper according to which group was the seller of the securities in the first instance. If the syndicate's manager sold on the latter's account or on commission we deal with a selling syndicate; if the issuer sold, with an underwriting syndicate proper. Taking up again the question posed above, one would think at first glance that the reason for organizing a syndicate would be the intention to find participants in risk taking or the high costs of flotations, costs which could be recovered only slowly, as the securities moved into the hands of ultimate buyers. Consequently one would expect syndicating for risky and especially for large flotations (the United States Steel syndicate, for example, was a $200,000,000 syndicate) and syndicates as tools of smaller firms. As a matter of fact, one of the partners of Lee, Higginson and Company explained[471] that syndicating was used by his firm for dividing the risk and for gaining assistance in the distribution of securities which was "another form of insurance." In reality, however, the situation was much more complicated. It seems certain that issues were syndicated even when the risk involved was very small and the syndicate managers would have been strong enough to handle the issues themselves. In such cases syndicating did not mean much more than having favored people participate in certain and large profit. Vanderlip, James Stillman's successor as the president of the National City Bank, remarks in his autobiography[472] that participations especially when the "participants" were connected both with the floating enterprise and its investment banker were "the means of some of the worst abuses that occurred in Wall Street." There is, for instance, a case on record in which the syndicate managers had sold all the securities before the invited participants to the syndicate in question had even time to answer, and all the latter did was to cash checks for their profits four weeks after the due date of those answers.[473] The element of power in business can be sensed in such cases, and it becomes evident when William Rockefeller, for instance "declared himself in," as Vanderlip expresses it,[474] on 25 per cent of the profits from a New York Central Railroad flotation handled by the National City Bank. It is this power element which seems to explain much of the raison d'être of many contemporary syndicates.

While in numerous cases very large profits were made by participants in syndicates the business did not lack danger, not even for firms as strong as the Morgans. A case in point is the unsuccessful International Mercantile Marine flotation. By 1903 when the market was glutted with undigested securities the danger to the investment bankers became obvious, and in 1907 the so-called Morse banks broke down, in part because they were overloaded with syndicate participations.[475] In that same year, Kuhn, Loeb and Company underwrote $75,000,000 Union Pacific bonds, but only $2,000,000 worth could be sold; the rest had to be taken over by the underwriters.[476] In other cases the risk lay in an unexpectedly slow sale of securities, as for example when the Great Northern and the Northern Pacific Railroads floated bonds for financing the acquisition of the Chicago, Burlington and Quincy Railroad. These bonds could not be disposed of for more than a year.

Participation in syndicates were open or silent.[477] In some cases, participants enjoyed the same terms as the originating houses; in others, less favorable ones. It depended on the terms of the agreement, but the latter practice seems to have prevailed. At any rate the house or the houses managing the syndicate received a commission.[478] Participants were banks, bankers, and trust companies, (prior to 1906) insurance companies, and in addition "prominent and influential" individuals. It often happened that besides a bank and trust company there were some of its officers and directors individually on a syndicate. (In a particular case of a $5,000,000 syndicate, twenty-four officers of banks were individually underwriters.)[479] This practice was severely criticized during the hearings of the Pujo Committee; Jacob Schiff disapproved it; and a few years later (in 1919) Frank O. Wetmore, since 1916 president of the First National Bank of Chicago, became so disgusted with it that he

founded a special affiliate, the First National Investment Company, later renamed First Chicago Corporation, to take up the offers for participations received by the officers of the First National and the First Trust and Savings Banks. Through this affiliate the profits of such participations became profits of the banks while the officers were enjoined from personally gaining improperly.[480]

The making up of a syndicate in New York in 1900 must have been very similar to the making up of a "list" in London in 1800. When an issue was going to be popular, Morgan made allotments to his friends and regular allies without any previous application, and Schiff seems to have followed a similar policy. On the other hand when it was difficult to form a syndicate applications were invited,[481] and those houses and men who had been benefited before were expected to take a share.[482] Some investment bankers, including Schiff and especially the smaller ones, had lists called "underwriting lists," containing the names of banks, corporations, and wealthy capitalists interested in certain types of securities. It was considered an "enviable privilege" to be on such lists from which the investment bankers selected their allies.[483] They varied according to the character and size of the flotations and their number was occasionally rather large, more than 100. This was probably not the case in regular Morgan syndicates. Neither that house nor the First National Bank made use of lists in selecting syndicate participants, probably because the number of those who were eligible was so small that it could be kept in mind. Moreover the records of earlier transactions showed the participants. When new business with the same company came along these men or firms were invited again if there had been no trouble.[484] Regular participants in Morgan's flotations after about 1900 were the First National and the National City Banks of New York; their agreement to that effect will be quoted.[485] Others were Lee, Higginson and Company and Kidder, Peabody and Company of Boston and, in the flotation of certain securities, the First National Bank and the Illinois Trust and Savings Bank, both of Chicago (headed by James B. Forgan and John Mitchell, respectively).[486] Usually for large and important issues, participations were allotted also to English, French, and German banks and bankers. It is evident that widening the market as well as distribution of risk was the function of the syndicate in such cases. After their spectacular fight against the allied Hill-Morgan interests for the Northern Pacific control, Kuhn, Loeb and Company won recognition, so that from then on they also participated in numerous Morgan flotations and vice versa invited the Morgans into theirs. Besides such regular allies there seem to have been some participants who appeared only occasionally as subscribers to issues of a particular kind floated by the big houses.

In numerous cases when European cooperation was desired there were set up two syndicates working hand in hand, an American and a European one. Such organizational set-up may have been devised first by Jay Cooke; at least it appeared in connection with his refunding operation of 1871. Thereafter we find the same method applied repeatedly by the big houses which undertook the later refunding operations in the 1870's; and it played a part again in 1895 when under Morgan's leadership an American and a European syndicate floated bonds with the proceeds of which they replenished this country's dwindling gold reserves. As late as about 1910 we find two syndicates cooperating in floating industrial securities. It seems however that on the whole in a later stage of the development single syndicates with European members were preferred, at least by the leading houses.

A certain agreement of 1912 which has been published[488] gives a good idea of the way in which new securities to be contracted were syndicated, i.e., handled by selling syndicates. To be sure, the agreement is not one among the leading firms, but between smaller Wall Street bankers (William Salomon and Company[489] and Hallgarten and Company, syndicate managers) and it does not necessarily follow that the big firms used identical methods. But in essentials there cannot have been much difference, and the agreement was selected at random by the Pujo Committee referring as it did to what was then the last security introduced at the New York stock exchange. The following are the most important provisions: The parties to the syndicate bought preferred and common stock of the California Petroleum Corporation at certain prices, each subscriber indicating the amount in cash for which, together with accrued dividend, he wished to be responsible. The subscription implied that the subscriber was liable to make pro rata payments to the syndicate managers for specified purposes. The managers of the syndicate were to have "the sole direction and management and the entire conduct of the transactions and business of the syndicate." The subscribers especially authorized the managers to buy and sell the securities concerned and to manipulate the market at the expense of the syndicate, which implied the repurchase, if necessary, of securities once sold. The managers were bound, however, not to sell below a certain price. They were authorized by the contract to borrow funds by pledging the securities to be sold or themselves to lend thereon (charging interest to the syndicate) and to

fix the compensation for brokers, counsels, etc. Moreover the subscribers irrevocably granted the discretionary right to the managers "to consent to any modifications of and to settle the form and terms of the certificate of incorporation of the corporation and the certificates of said stocks [preferred and common]..., the voting trust agreement, the name of the corporation and the state of incorporation..." (One wonders if the large investment bankers in their syndicate agreements went as far as that.) The syndicate managers were actually entitled to do each and every thing without being held responsible at all except for want of good faith and wilful negligence. Subscribers were not entitled to receive any securities or the proceeds therefor prior to the termination of the syndicate. If, on the other hand, the managers chose to hand them securities in compensation for payments required, such securities were to be held by the subscribers subject to the control of the managers, to be returned on request for sale on account of the syndicate. Such was obviously a widely adopted practice,[490] regardless of occasional exceptions to the rule. Morgan, for instance, stated before the Pujo Committee that participants in his syndicates did not receive securities. These were marketed by the House of Morgan in their capacity as the syndicate managers. After the termination the subscribers to Morgan syndicates received their share in the profits or had to take their pro rata share in the unsold securities (as, for example, in the case of the International Mercantile Marine flotation). Morgan made it very explicit that the sale of securities by different parties was to be excluded because "then the market is apt to be bad."[491] The syndicate agreement under investigation contained a clause to the effect that "upon the complete performance of all his undertakings and the termination of the syndicate each subscriber shall be entitled to receive his ratable portion of the syndicate stocks or the proceeds of so much thereof as may have been sold by the managers, less his pro rata share of the syndicate expenses. The net profits shall be divided among the subscribers in proportion to their respective subscriptions" and losses, accordingly. (No contemporary syndicate agreement regarding underwriting proper has come to the attention of the author.)

While Morgan never permitted participants in his syndicates to sell independently parts of the flotations in question this was sometimes allowed or even requested by other investment bankers organizing syndicates. Kuhn, Loeb and Company and Lee, Higginson and Company seem to have been exponents of the latter policy. This practice implied that the sellers received brokerage over and above the syndicate commission. But, whatever they sold, they were not released from their obligation to take, if necessary, a pro rata share in the securities remaining unsold. Contracts to the contrary were introduced only after World War I.[492]

In many agreements covering selling syndicates, i.e., syndicates whose managers undertook the original selling of the securities to the public, it was stipulated that payments were to be made to the issuing corporation on specified dates or when needed, regardless of the amount of securities sold at that moment. In such cases syndicate members had to make advance payments on call; but if such obligation was assumed the commission for the "negotiation" was higher than when this was not the case.

Market manipulation was considered essential for the successful flotation of new securities. Just as, in the eighteenth century, public stocks could not be floated in England unless the gambling instinct was called into play, so in the 1900's it was impossible in America to float corporation securities without so doing. Consequently, syndicate managers and investment bankers acting for themselves or on joint account charged a leading stock exchange firm with such manipulation of the market as seemed necessary, or did the job themselves. The manipulator, in turn, employed brokers who bought and sold the new security according to plan, their orders usually being matched. Buying orders by outsiders coming into the market were executed, of course, from the pool of securities to be floated; but if the market became weak, outside sales orders would be automatically absorbed by the investment banker's brokers. Market manipulation had several purposes: first of all, the market was to appear active because speculators would go only into an active market. Secondly, the market was to be so handled that securities could be sold at what was considered an adequate price by the investment bankers concerned. Thirdly, bona fide buyers and speculators were to be protected while the flotation was in full swing. The Pujo Committee was much concerned about the question of whether market manipulation for the purpose of floating new securities was legitimate, and it was inclined to answer the question in the negative. Market manipulation means, seen from one possible angle, misleading the public as to the market price, no longer freely established by supply and demand; and this was the aspect of the matter which was stressed. However one can look at it from a different point of view: security flotations were indispensable as a means of building up the gigantic productive apparatus with which our national economy is working today; and it might appear that speculation when called into play performed the economic

function of making possible such large security flotations as were needed. If one argues along these lines methods appealing to speculators appear sensible if applied with responsibility. In fact, however market manipulation went very far, and had to do so because watered securities had to be floated. The original United States Steel flotation is an example: the market was manipulated to an extent that prices of United States Steel securities collapsed almost immediately when the purpose of the manipulation was achieved and the latter ceased. In the case of the California Petroleum Corporation above-mentioned whose capital consisted of 121,000 shares of which 105,729 were listed, 362,270 shares were traded within the first month; i.e., the stock was sold three and a half times within one month[493] due to manipulation contemplated in the syndicate agreement. It was, in fact, a highly successful flotation.

Past master in the field of market manipulation was James Robert Keene (1838-1913), an Englishman who had come to America as an adolescent and had started humbly in California. From 1876 on he worked in Wall Street making and losing fortunes. It was he who handled, for instance, the United States Steel flotation and that of Amalgamated Copper.[494]

Besides the above type of market manipulation practiced by the investment banker there was a second which was called "steadying the market." It was applied not only while new securities were being floated, but also for a long time thereafter. The purpose of this type of manipulation was to forestall violent price fluctuations and to make the securities in question move with the market. For this purpose the investment banker or the managers of a syndicate that had floated those securities gave daily to brokers what were called "selling orders on a scale up and buying orders on a scale down." That is to say, the orders were not matched. To the contrary, in a steady market at what was considered the desirable price they would not be executed at all, for the buying orders were at prices below those which prevailed in the market and the selling orders above. Only when the market price deviated from the one considered desirable, was the scale so set as to influence it moderately. At all events when, for some reason, it came to move in the "wrong" direction, the orders went into play immediately since the scale was established with great deliberation. Moreover if a bona fide outside order should come into the market the brokers working for the investment banker were ready to take it up. Therefore small orders to buy or sell could not create excitement in the market for the simple reason that there was not available at that moment the corresponding order to sell or buy, respectively. It must be stressed, that contemporary investment bankers themselves did not call such operations manipulations. They seem to have been very common and were organized and carried out regardless of whether they brought profit or loss.[495]

The retail distribution of securities was rather undeveloped prior to World War I. In a great many cases the syndicate heads or the individual investment bankers who undertook the flotation opened subscription books as had been traditional throughout the nineteenth century. An advertisement ("offer for public subscriptions") of the National City Bank for 750,000 shares of the Amalgamated Copper Company of New Jersey, dated April 28, 1899, which may be used as an example, stated: "Subscriptions [at the rate of $100 per share] must be addressed to the City Bank of New York and accompanied by a certified check to its order for 5 per cent of the amount of such subscription, the balance to be payable 10 days after notice of allotment."[496] How much of the publicly offered securities was actually allocated to the public is a different question as is how much was taken up by insiders for sale at a profit. In the case of the Amalgamated Copper flotation only 20 per cent of the securities are said to have gone to investors directly.[497] If they did not open subscriptions investment bankers fed the new securities slowly into a carefully manipulated market. Sometimes they used both methods, besides selling some of the securities to large institutional investors and to "bond houses" about which more will be said shortly. Occasionally a subsyndicate was organized for the purpose of retail distribution[498] in which bond houses took large shares. However only after World War I did it become common practice for securities to be contracted by a syndicate of investment bankers which sold them immediately at a slightly higher price to a syndicate of dealers.[499] At all events, as indicated before, speculation was used to a considerable extent as an intermediate link in the distribution of securities.

But there were a few firms which specialized in the selling end of the business. For example, White, Weld and Company and Kissel, Kinnicut and Company are supposed to have marketed limited quantities of securities, mainly those floated by the House of Morgan,[500] acting as some kind of jobbers. At the same time they floated issues of small corporations themselves, taking risks cautiously by contracting piecemeal for one part of an issue after an earlier one was sold. By 1900 N. W. Harris and N. W. Halsey developed new methods of security retailing using bond salesmen, while Lee, Higginson and Company of Boston

seem to have been the first of the big investment bankers to build, as early as the 1900's, an efficient retail sales organization of their own.[501] The consequence was that besides handling their own flotations they had to buy, to satisfy their regular customers, popular securities, in the flotation of which they had no share, as for example from J. P. Morgan and Company securities of a subsidiary of the United States Steel Corporation.[502] Not quite as advanced but yet elaborate for the time was the sales organization of the First National Bank of Chicago which not only sold the securities in whose origination it participated to banks in the Western states, but also tried directly to reach individual investors by circularizing prospects among its customers and others whose names were selected from taxpayers lists.[503] Whenever bond salesmen were used the latter regularly visited banks, savings banks, trust companies, insurance companies, colleges and universities, trustees of estates, and even individual investors.[504]

It was to the smaller firms above-mentioned that the word "bond house" was originally applied, although after World War I the terms "investment house" and "bond house" seem to have been used synonymously.[505] But the terminology was not clear cut. One contemporary author stated that the term applied to houses "which endeavor[ed] to sell bonds strictly on the investment value by advertisement, circular letters and personal solicitation, as distinguished from banking houses which accept deposits and deal in other securities as well as bonds."[506] But actually bond houses often had small banking departments. Another author stressed that the sales function was cultivated by the bond house which dealt directly with investors through personal solicitation. In dealing with their purveyors, so he reports, they devised a specific practice, buying on "underwriters option," that is to say, retaining the right to return to the former that part of the issue which they could not sell.[507] The same author contrasted bond house and international investment banker; but again there was no clear line of demarcation. At least several hundred of those "merchants of securities" existed by 1910, competing keenly with each other and at the same time facing competition from the bond departments of commercial banks then coming into vogue. Nevertheless consolidations were not taking place in the line as yet. Some of the bond houses, as has been mentioned before, had small banking departments which kept customers' deposits subject to draft by check (a few houses even paying interest thereon); some acted as fiscal agents for corporations and municipalities. They were especially active in the field of municipals and quasi-municipals (county and tax-district bonds) working at a gross profit margin of 3/4 to 1 per cent. Under their influence the business in municipal bonds was standardized on a higher level than had been common prior to 1875, the securities being subjected to the stricter requirements of bond attorneys. Most bonds of smaller communities were contracted on the spot, the houses having professional "buyers on the road;" but some of the larger communities proposed bids. In these cases the bond house competed with institutional investors and individual capitalists, as the loan contractor had once competed with such bidders in the Napoleonic days in London and in the 1850's in this country. Circumstances being equal, methods were often used by bond houses similar to those which had been applied by loan contractors when bidding for state issues in the middle of the nineteenth century: bids were tendered for "all or none."

Some of the bond houses also took an interest in railroad mortgage bonds; but they could handle only those of small lines, since the large ones were in the orbit of the leading investment bankers.[508] However, they could compete successfully for equipment bonds for which there was no interest on the part of the big houses. If bond houses wanted to deal in railroad bonds of the large lines they had to ally themselves with the investment bankers and act as participants in flotations, i.e., as subcontractors and "sub-underwriters" ("secondary underwriters"). But they were then at the mercy of their big brothers who used (or abused) them, forcing them to take over, at a small concession of about $1\frac{1}{2}$ points, securities which remained in the hands of syndicates after the public subscription had come to an end ($1\frac{1}{2}$ points concession meaning $1\frac{1}{2}$ points below the price at which the securities had been offered to the public).[509]

Industrial and public utility securities provided for the bond house a wider field than railroad bonds. By 1910 competition for public utility bonds was already keen although these securities were still new on the market, but that for industrial bonds was slight. Buyers' resistance to both types was giving way, but not fast enough to impair chances for large profit. The gross profit rate for both types of securities was 5 to 15 per cent, very often with a stock bonus on top of that; but the high cost of distribution must be kept in mind.[510] Shortly before the outbreak of World War I some houses began distributing collateral trust bonds, secured by issues of companies acting in special fields, known as collateral trust water bonds, collateral trust lighting bonds, collateral trust real estate bonds, and the like.

The leading investment bankers of the period were of the active type, to use Professor Gras's expression. The type, as will be remembered, had come into existence in an earlier period and its spread became now almost unavoidable.

A banking house that has organized a great industrial or railway [corporation] or that has offered its securities to the public is represented on the board of directors and acts as its fiscal agent; [it] thereby assumes a certain guardianship over that corporation. In the ratio in which that corporation succeeds or fails, the prestige of the banking house and its capacity for absorbing and distributing future issues of securities is affected. If competition is threatened it is manifestly the duty of the bankers, from their point of view of the protection of the stockholders, as distinguished from the standpoint of the public, to prevent it if possible.[511]

It has been described previously that originally becoming "active" was a matter of self-defence for the investment banker, and so it remained to a certain extent during the period under investigation. Whatever one may think of the business ethics of the investment bankers of 1900, they were as a rule higher than those of many other big businessmen who had hardly outgrown the era of buccaneering. Investment bankers when planning and acting did not think of the public, of course, but at least a minimum of consideration for the investor was safe and sound policy, if they wished a permanent business; and this they certainly did. Thus after 1880 the scope of the investment banker's participation in corporation boards broadened; the defence element remained important, but what was aimed at was now indirect rather than direct self-defence: the investment banker had to defend the goose which laid the golden eggs.

The "active" status of the investment banker (reached by the 1870's) became the starting point after 1880 for still further developments of the greatest significance. The activities of the investment bankers of that time made possible truly modern large scale enterprises. Fixed capital began to gain a greater importance relative to circulating capital than ever before. Atomistic "beneficial" competition approached its apogee. If gigantic enterprises with fixed capital prevailing competed in the traditional way, such competition was bound to lead to disaster. So it was again in the first instance in self-defence that the leading investment bankers of the period tried to stop competition, that is to say, actually to stop the attendant dangers thereof. Atomistic "perfect" competition was replaced under their influence in large scale enterprises by imperfect competition, co-operation, and interlocking interest.

The tremendous power which accrued after 1880 to J. P. Morgan and to the other great investment bankers was accumulated in two steps: first by the logical development of their earlier acquired status of "active" investment bankers, and second-ly by their achievement in making themselves the key figures in the national economy. The result of this process is usually called investment bankers' control, a correct, but badly misunderstood term. To be sure, a contemporary statement that in-vestment bankers as fiscal agents of corporations "being responsible for [their] welfare and fi-nances" "controlled" and "directed" those finances, is a good description of the situation.[512] In every other respect control by the investment banker was negative rather than positive. In other words, voting trusts[513] and directorates in corporations were to keep out undesirable people, whatever this may have meant, and to preclude detrimental policies. The only positive aspect of control was very often the selection of the chief executive and perhaps of other leading officers, as comes out in a letter of Schiff's written in 1912. With respect to some railroad he wrote to a European ally: "but the recent management has evidently been a very poor one and must be thoroughly changed."[514] Morgan, for instance, made Elbert H. Gary the head of the United States Steel Corporation and sustained him in a fight with Charles Michael Schwab, very much to the detriment of the enter-prise concerned. He made the very unfortunate selection of such a nonentity as Charles S. Mellen to head the New York, New Haven and Hartford Railroad. George F. Baker, on the other hand, selected Theodore Newton Vail as the head of the American Telephone and Telegraph Company when by a pool he developed a concern of national im-portance out of the previously Boston-controlled corporation. But once the "right" men were in and as long as they ran the enterprise in question in line with an understood over-all policy and with profit, the investment banker in control in effect did absolutely nothing. Industrially, to use Veblen's term, what appeared as investment banker's con-trol meant de facto autonomous administrations.[515] But they were autonomous only in return for suc-cess and good behavior, and the continuously re-current need for additional funds in an expanding national economy made the captains of industry vassals of the investment bankers. These things are too well known to need further detailed atten-tion.

Investment bankers' activities led, as indicated, to diminishing competition in the fields which they controlled. Consequently those contemporaries whose gospel was the Wealth of Nations and who believed with their long deceased master in the magic power of competition as the regulator of economic life and vehicle of progress were horri-fied. Untermyer, the New York lawyer and counsel of the Pujo Committee, was among these, and his questioning of such investment bankers as Morgan or Baker took all too often a turn toward the pa-thetic. He acted on the basis of a semi-religious creed, on the basis of certain value judgments, as the modern social scientist would express it; con-sequently he could not understand the fact state-ments, the basic thinking, and the value judgments of those whom he questioned. His remarkable factual knowledge, on the other hand, made him in many respects their superior. There was, of course, much dissimulation and lack of cooperation on the part of the bankers, but not always when the counsel suspected it. He and the members of the Pujo Committee, spellbound by their belief in competition, saw the powerful investment bankers as "striking at the very vitals of [even] potential competition." By throttling this institution under which the country had grown and prospered the bankers had violated the spirit of our legal system. The Pujo Committee thought there was still time to smash by legislative action the obstructions to competition which the investment bankers had erected; and that when the "arteries of credit" were no longer "clogged," large enterprises would be-gin to compete again. Much understanding for facts and trends the legislators did not possess, but they sensed rather correctly that the "money power" (i.e., the control of economic life by the investment banker or "financial capitalism") might fall by its own weight.

The second step, in the accumulation of this control of economic life by the investment banker, alluded to previously, remains to be discussed. Domination of railroads, industrial corporations and, to a less extent in that period, of public serv-ice corporations would not have been possible if the investment banker had not been ready at all times to finance their legitimate needs. For this purpose some of the investment bankers, espe-cially the House of Morgan, assumed the functions of fiscal agents of the corporations whose securi-ties they floated. This implied that they became their depositories and, in fact, extraordinarily large deposits were involved. One of the Morgan partners conceded before the Pujo Committee that a part of these deposits was invested in securities[516] that is to say it was used in the course of the in-vestment banker's business. The situation was blurred, of course, when investment banking ac-tivities were performed by commercial banks, such as the First National and the National City

Banks of New York; but essentially it was the same. (Here and in many other respects one sees clearly how serious problems were arising by 1910, problems which had to be solved in the 1930's.) Moreover for the purpose above-mentioned of being always ready to serve the capital needs of the largest corporations the investment banker had to acquire control of the main customers for securities and of sources of credit for himself. As to the former, we find the leading investment bankers attempting to gain influence over the large insurance companies.[517] A detailed investigation of this relationship does not fall within the scope of this research. But it may be mentioned that by 1913 J. P. Morgan held a majority in the Equitable Life Assurance Society and that his partner George W. Perkins (1862-1920) was between 1901 and 1905 simultaneously a vice-president of the New York Life. George F. Baker, on the other hand, was a trustee and member of the Finance Committee of the Mutual Life Insurance Company. Finally, prior to 1905 Schiff was a director in the Equitable, and at that time the Speyers seem to have had their hands in the Mutual Life Insurance Company.[518] More interesting from the point of view of this research is the control of commercial banks by investment bankers. It implied access to short term funds in the form of lodged deposits,[519] especially bankers' balances, and in the form of created deposits. Such funds could be used for two purposes: first as call money, that is to say, as a prop for speculation in securities. (It will be remembered how important was the role of speculation in the flotation of the gigantic security issues of the 1900's.) It is not accidental that those commercial banks which were interested in investment banking themselves were among the largest lenders on call.[520] Secondly, the banks so controlled were made to develop a business in what was called "syndicate securities," that is to say, lending on securities not yet listed on the stock exchange, but still held by syndicates.[521] Since National Banks were by law hampered in entering the business in securities, the investment bankers took an additional interest in building up large trust companies which, working under state laws, were free to act in that field as their masters saw fit. It is not necessary here to enumerate all the banks and trust companies in which the Morgans, Bakers, Stillmans, Schiffs, etc., were interested. Morgan is said to have had "a powerful voice" in banks and trust companies whose resources amounted to $723,000,000. Among them were such banks as the National Bank of Commerce, the Chemical National Bank, and the Bankers and the Guaranty Trust Companies. George F. Baker, on the other hand, held at one

time, in the interest of the First National Bank of New York, the majority of the stock of the Chase National Bank which was later transferred to the former's security affiliate, although the motive of acquiring this control was not in the field of security dealings. Finally Lee, Higginson and Company and Kidder, Peabody and Company together were the most potent forces in the three leading Boston banks which held more than one half of the city's banking resources, the First National Bank, the National Shawmut Bank, and the Old Colony Trust Company.[522]

The important question remains, to what extent was there concerted exertion of control on the part of the leading investment bankers, or to what extent did they compete among themselves, regardless of their policy of abandoning the competitive struggle in the sectors which they came to dominate. The situation was obviously different in several decades of the Morgan period. In the beginning (the 1870's) there was keen competition between Jay Cooke, the German-Jewish bankers, and perhaps the Rothschilds, on one side, and the Morgans-Drexels-Mortons-Barings, on the other. In the railroad field, the Morgans and Belmonts seem to have gone their own way in the 1880's and also in the 1890's, as did Stillman and Schiff, while Baker was always Morgan's "unswerving" ally.[523] There is documentary proof that Morgan's endeavors in January, 1895, to provide gold for the Treasury by a private bond issue were prompted to a certain extent by fear that the business might otherwise go to "Speyer and Company and similar [i.e., the German-Jewish] houses."[524] In the end, the terrific clash during the Harriman-Hill war of 1901 between two rivaling houses of investment bankers, the Morgans and Kuhn, Loeb and Company, showed that competition of investment bankers did not work any better than that between railroads. Thus thereafter the big houses appeared definitely arm-in-arm and hand-in-glove; but if one reads between the lines (for instance, in Vanderlip's recollections[525]), Schiff was hardly ever considered by Morgan an ally without reservation in contrast to Stillman who after 1907 was so accepted. Schiff cooperated with the latter rather than with Morgan and Baker.

When investment bankers abandoned competition they did so by "recognizing" each others' clients. It was not considered "good form," as Schiff expressed it, "to create unreasonable interference or competition... After the negotiation has once begun [a banking house] should not endeavour to get it away from somebody else."[526] As a matter of fact, however, the established investment bankers went further. They recognized certain corporations as belonging to the domain of certain houses and so would not compete for their business. But, if we can believe Schiff whose upright behavior before the Pujo Committee makes an excellent impression on the historian, there was interference and attempted interference in what were probably borderline cases.

According to Professor Cochran's material the beginnings of the tying of certain corporations to certain investment bankers can be dated back to the 1880's. In that decade, strong roads whose securities were popular and in demand could still float them by asking for bids, without taking punishment later. This was the case, for instance, with the Chicago, Burlington and Quincy Railroad. Weaker roads, in contrast, had to abandon the method even against their will. The Northern Pacific is a case in point. In 1880 a syndicate, with the Morgans and Winslow, Lanier and Company as the leading members, took up the financing of the road at the point at which Jay Cooke had left it when he failed. A few years later, when a new flotation became necessary, the members of the earlier syndicate considered it their right to have the new securities; but the company asked publicly for bids. It received only one which was tendered by August Belmont and Company. Thereupon J. P. Morgan lodged a strong protest with its president. He denounced asking for bids as a breach of faith with the syndicate.[527]

The investment bankers of 1900 do not seem to have relied on the loyalty of their colleagues and potential competitors, but to have aimed at regular tying contracts, as can be guessed from the following extract from a meeting of the reorganization committee of the Northern Pacific Railroad held on March 14, 1896:

> The chairman stated that "it had been considered desirable that the bankers who had charge of the reorganization should, if possible, continue their friendly relations with the reorganized company for further ten years upon terms and conditions set forth in an agreement" which was ratified by the committee and declared binding upon the railroad.

In this agreement dated March 16, 1896, the banks in question (J. P. Morgan and Company and Deutsche Bank, Berlin) agreed for ten years to market the road's securities, if it desired, upon such terms and for such compensation as might be agreed upon, without being bound to do so. The company during that period was under the obligation of informing the bankers regarding "accounts, operations and conditions of the company and its property."[528]

In consequence of such policies and tactics, the great investment bankers, Morgan, Baker, Stillman, Kuhn, Loeb and Company, Lee Higginson and Company, and Kidder, Peabody and Company, controlled large transactions almost to the complete exclusion of outsiders, i.e., minor houses which they did not approve. Between about 1900 and 1910 there was only one issue exceeding $10,000,000 that was floated without their participation, and even that (an issue of $13,500,000) had the Morgan blessing. But dominance did not mean monopoly. There were other investment bankers[529] besides those belonging to the inner ring, such as the Speyers, Seligmans, Fisks, Blairs, Hallgartens, Salomons, and others, at least two commercial banks in Chicago, and several trust companies in New York which were interested in the field and will be discussed later. Dominance, however, meant that no important business in the area could be done without participation by the leading houses.

And still not all avenues were closed to newcomers, and not all doors to competition were slammed. This becomes evident from the remarkable rise of new investment banking firms after World War I. To a certain extent, the mere extension of capital needs would have made it impossible to uphold a tight control permanently. In fact, local investment houses made their appearance in the 1900's and so testified to the growing capital accumulation in secondary banking centers. But the true reason for the rise of new firms, which started on their careers between 1900 and 1910 when the power of the allied investment banking leaders was without match, lay in the latter's shortsightedness, the nemesis of their creativity, to use Toynbee's term. Small issues of industrials they could leave to outsiders without fear of punishment. For example, Harvey Fisk and Sons, which was on good terms with the House of Morgan, financed Bethlehem Steel.[530] But what the great men of the period, with perhaps one exception, did not see was that two main gaps were left wide open through which, somewhat later, new blood and vigorous competition could make their entrance again. These gaps were in the fields of public utilities and of retail distribution of securities. As to the former, utility bonds were then not in favor with the public and the big houses were rather reluctant to establish connections in this field. Stillman of the City Bank and Storrow of Lee, Higginson and Company seem to have been the only ones who came near to gaining a foothold therein.[531] On the beginnings of efficient retail distribution of securities a few words have already been said.

Thus, prior to World War I, the foundation was laid for the rise of the firms Harris, Forbes and Company and Halsey, Stuart and Company. The former was founded by Norman Wait Harris (1846-

1916) who had started as a soliciting agent for a life insurance company in Cincinnati, in which he rose and which he developed. In 1881 he founded the banking house of N. W. Harris and Company in Chicago[532] which specialized in state, county, city, and public utility bonds. He was the first to emphasize the need for and to build an efficient sales organization for securities. Noah W. Halsey (1856-1911), on the other hand, started his firm, N. W. Halsey and Company, in New York in 1901 after having been employed in Harris's organization as the New York branch manager. In 1903 he opened a Chicago office with H. L. Stuart in charge. Like Harris he took an interest in municipal bonds and entered the public utility field at a very early moment: In 1907 H. L. Stuart made the firm's first contact with Samuel Insull; and Halsey brought together in the 1900's the early constituents of the Pacific Gas and Electric Company and took a share in the founding of the Tri-City Railway and Light Company. Moreover he was one of the innovators in security retailing. Jay Cooke's security selling from house to house had been long forgotten, when Halsey, following on the heels of Harris, again adopted this method. In 1904 he also started national advertising of securities, advertising of the so-called "educational" type, and three years later, in cooperation with other bond houses, called a conference to discuss the possibilities of creating a broader market for securities.[533] (N. W. Halsey and Company ran into difficulties in 1916. The New York house was absorbed by the National City Company while the Midwestern offices became Halsey, Stuart and Company.) One readily sees that a younger generation of creative business leaders was here, between about 1900 and 1907, turning in new directions of which the accomplished leaders of the period hardly thought. But spectacular success was to be theirs only in a period beyond the scope of this book.[534]

When the Money Trust Investigation took place in 1913 financial capitalism was at the acme of its career, indeed, but the seed of decay was implanted and would soon sprout. The work of the Morgans, Bakers, Stillmans, and Schiffs was necessitated by the growth of enterprises in the fields of transportation and industry and, vice versa, it made their further growth possible. Thus their activities were meaningful and highly beneficial in the first instance. But, of course, the development had the undesirable aspect of power concentration for which a remedy was in the making at the expense of the investment banker as an institution. The growth of industry, assisted by the investment banker, was soon to reach a point at which big enterprises could to a certain extent dispense with the former's activities. Moreover,

after the collapse of high pressure selling of securities in the 1920's the range of potential customers narrowed down. Thus the investment banker was caught between two millstones, self-financing by industry out of oliogopoly profits and elimination of the middlemen by the largest institutional security buyers who acquired securities directly from the issuing borrower. Financial capitalism did not fail, but, to that extent and to the extent that government entered the scene as a financing agency in the 1930's, it fell from its dizzy height and lost that control over the national economy which its great nineteenth-century representatives had built.[535]

XV

In America financial capitalism, the organization of the large-scale sector of the national economy under the guidance and to the advantage of the investment banker, was the work of no more than half-a-dozen firms and hardly twice as many men. Outstanding among the former were: J. P. Morgan and Company, the First National and the National City Banks of New York, Kuhn, Loeb and Company, and to a smaller extent the two Boston houses, Lee, Higginson and Company and Kidder, Peabody and Company. The leaders of these firms, with the single exception of the German Jew, Jacob Schiff, were the descendants of New England Puritans, although some of them had not themselves grown up as Puritans. These men were first of all: J. P. Morgan, descendant of Connecticut pioneers, although himself educated in England and Germany; James Stillman, Texas-born Yankee; and George F. Baker who grew up on a Massachusetts farm in a strictly Puritan atmosphere. (The Yankee, Levi P. Morton, was in the beginning very close to this set of men, but fell behind because of his political ambitions.) Morgan and Baker, born in 1837 and 1840, respectively, belong to the generation of the Robber Barons,[536] while Schiff and Stillman, born in 1847 and 1850, respectively, were ten years their juniors. The Bostonians, Robert Winsor, Gardiner M. Lane, and James J. Storrow, who were about twenty years younger than Morgan and Baker, no longer belonged to the pioneers of financial capitalism, and yet came early enough to play a part in its creation through their Boston firms above-mentioned.[537]

This list of leading firms and men should be a warning for the scholar not to adopt the widely-held but erroneous belief, that in America in the nineteenth and early twentieth centuries, investment banking was the exclusive domain of private bankers. As to sheer numbers private bankers undoubtedly exceeded commercial bankers in the field. But when one looks at the small number of men who by 1910 were at the apex of the pyramid, Morgan, Baker, Stillman, and Schiff, one finds two commercial bankers among the four top men. The activities of commercial banks in our field during the period under investigation will be discussed later in more detail.

The creative achievements of the men who brought financial capitalism into being were rooted in their organizational ability as well as in their capacity to think in magnitudes which would have made dizzy their lesser contemporaries. But organizational ability and vision alone would not have led to such staggering results as they actually achieved, had these bankers not been ruthless, brutal, and domineering. Theirs was the era of criminal buccaneering by businessmen. Without those qualities they would not have succeeded in bringing order into the chaos caused by reckless competition of large-scale enterprises. They were intellectually and morally superior to those with whom they dealt and whom often enough they fought a outrance; they were no buccaneers, but from our point of view their standard of ethics remained low because of their failure to recognize national or social responsibility. Theirs was the era of laissez-faire which, once embraced as a matter of creed, foredoomed any feeling for responsibility. If, as these men believed, the natural law ruling social life demanded the fight for the survival of the fittest, there was no room for what today would be called high business ethics. Thus these men were both magnificent builders and ruthless destroyers and their creative concentration on the organizational and financial side of transportation and industry, while overlooking the human and strictly industrial aspects, gives their destructiveness "daimonic" character.

It goes without saying that Morgan was the real leader among the leaders. John Pierpont Morgan (1837-1913) was the son of Junius Spencer Morgan (1813-1890), Peabody's partner and creative successor. He grew up in Hartford, London, and Vevey (Switzerland) and as a teen-ager spent some time in the Azores, experiences which were bound to give him an international outlook with a European tint. The American West was unknown to him until after the Civil War. The environment in which young Morgan's personality was shaped was typically bourgeois and, in line with American tradition, church-influenced. As a matter of play, the boy formed a partnership with a cousin keeping books as to income and expenditure. For his own use and for his own satisfaction, beginning as a child and for many years as an adult, he accounted strictly for his own expenditures.

Rechenhaftigkeit, as Sombart calls the trait of the bourgeois, the enjoyment of accounting and of translating everything into figures, was typical of this man.

After having finished his general education by studying a few semesters at the University of Göttingen, young Morgan spent a short while in his father's counting-house and in 1857 was sent for additional training to Duncan, Sherman and Company in New York. There he was just an apprentice, notwithstanding much that has been written to the contrary. Needless to say, everything was done to facilitate the broadest possible business education of the youngster, who in 1859 went to New Orleans and Cuba. Returning, he opened an office of his own, and in 1860 with a relative he founded the firm of J. P. Morgan and Company, New York, which took over the agency of the London Peabody firm. (This, incidentally, implied a change in the policy of the latter house which previously, and in contrast to the Barings and Rothschilds, had worked through American correspondents.) The beginnings of J.P. Morgan and Company which fell into the opening years of the Civil War were not satisfactory all the way through. To be sure, by that time the young man was showing traits of independence, decisiveness, and willingness to tackle what for him were still big affairs. But when thrown into the maelstorm of Civil War business he became associated with "dirty deals" (the Hall carbine affair and certain gold dealings) and with doubtful personalities, such as Edward Ketchum, associations which show lack of caution, injudiciousness, and poor judgment of character. Indeed, Morgan never became a good judge of men, as he himself knew. As his latest biographer[538] hints, the fact that J. P. Morgan and Company became Dabney, Morgan and Company in 1864 might indicate that Junius Spencer Morgan preferred to have a reliable older supervisor for his son. When the Civil War ended Dabney, Morgan and Company flourished so that J. P. earned more than $50,000 a year and thus, as has been described, could come to play the orthodox role of an active young businessman, citizen, and church member.

In 1871, that is to say, at the time when Junius Spencer Morgan put his London house in the front rank of European investment bankers through the successful termination of the very risky French loan flotation, Drexel, Morgan and Company was formed by the merging of Reed, Drexel, and Company and Dabney, Morgan, and Company. This merger, which has been mentioned before, seems to have been conceived by Anthony J. Drexel and was highly beneficial for both concerns.

Prior to the merger J. P. Morgan's business had consisted of buying and selling bills of exchange and securities (the latter mainly on a commission basis) and of dealing in foreign exchange and gold. As a matter of course he served as a source of information for his father. Investment banking seems to have been entered cautiously.[539] By that time J. P. Morgan was having an experience which, being extraordinary but nevertheless characteristic of the period, was of the type to form a young man's attitude for the rest of his life. It was one of those experiences which, being general, form whole groups of coevals. J. P. Morgan had an orderly mind and was by upbringing a gentleman with a standard high for that time of lowest American business ethics. By 1870 he clashed with the Erie ring when backing the administration of the Albany and Susquehanna Railroad. In this connection he saw reckless competition and political corruption at their worst, and he met the situation ruthlessly and successfully. But he must have been shocked, a shock which may have contributed, on the one hand, to the choice of a creative life work of bringing order into the railroad field deranged by unbridled competition. On the other hand, it contributed to his developing that negative attitude toward government which became unrealistic and untenable during the later years of his life and a source of bitter personal disappointment toward its end.

In the 1870's, however, Morgan's main efforts were not spent in railroad financing. In that decade he became connected with the Refunding transactions, gigantic for the time. From Morgan's point of view these activities must have appeared in the beginning as a hard struggle against Jay Cooke's dominance over government finance, a struggle in which Morgan himself was not even the leader. At the start Levi P. Morton, his ally, better qualified for the job by his political affiliations, assumed leadership. It is significant that as late as 1877 a Refunding syndicate went under Belmont's name rather than Morgan's.

Having successfully made his entrance into large-scale investment banking in the field of government loans, Morgan was bound to be drawn into railroad finance after the conclusion of the Refunding transactions. Experience, connections, character, and wealth were making Morgan a leader, once he had reached the prime of his life, and railroads provided then the most attractive prospects for the coming financier. His first big transaction in the railroad field was the sale of a large part of William Vanderbilt's holdings in the New York Central Railroad. For this purpose Morgan organized a syndicate consisting of Drexel, Morgan and Company, August Belmont and Company, Morton, Bliss and Company, and Jay Gould. The operation was so successfully conducted that it

brought him reputation and a firm foothold in this line of business. In going on the board of the New York Central Morgan, following advanced business experience of his time, became an "active" investment banker. Thereby he started out on a road which led ultimately to the creation of financial capitalism in America, as has been indicated above. The New York Central transaction was important for Morgan for still other reasons. It was rounded out by an alliance of the New York Central with the Morgan-dominated Wabash, St. Louis and Pacific Railroad. Experience gained in establishing this alliance tended to assist him further in developing his activities in the direction toward what is called financial capitalism today.

In order to understand Morgan's role in railroad finance in the 1880's and 1890's one must remember that his extraordinarily strong personality made him the dominant figure among business leaders even of the highest order. He was awe-inspiring to his close cooperators, and terrifying to many with whom he came into occasional contact. In contrast to most contemporary businessmen he had a goal which went far beyond mere money-making, a goal which was highly beneficial to the national economy. He meant to put an end to buccaneering, the robbing of enterprises by the entrepreneur, and to unbridled, cutthroat competition; he intended to replace these defects of contemporary business by orderly and responsible administration in a cooperative system of interlocking interests. To be sure, what Morgan called responsibility was not what one is accustomed to call social and national responsibility today. Morgan was utterly devoid of understanding such terms.[540] Responsibility for him was financial responsibility and fair dealing with business associates and large investors who bought securities on the strength of Morgan's prestige as an investment banker. But even in this respect he was not wholly consistent: he thought of the large and foreign investor rather than of the small American fellow who was making his appearance as a security buyer toward the end of Morgan's life, to a large extent on the strength of the latter's actions and those of the other leading investment bankers of the time. Farseeing as Morgan was as a banker, his social vision was narrow, that of an aristocrat and gentleman of the Victorian era; and while his ethical standard was above that of his group of coevals it was below that of younger men coming to the fore by 1900. Morgan's success, at least in the 1880's and 1890's, was largely due to his ability to be à un corsair corsair et demi and when his interests were really endangered, as in the case of Harriman's Northern Pacific onslaught in 1901, he fought without any regard to the economic consequences of his actions.

This powerful personality, able to speak authoritatively to railroad presidents and financiers who in line with the standard of their time were rugged individualists of doubtful ethics, was backed by the command over millions of dollars, the most valuable European contacts, and a remarkably strong organization. Until 1890 Junius Spencer Morgan was still at the helm of the London house, then leading among the European investment bankers. In his own organization (Drexel, Morgan and Company until 1894) J. P. could rely on a first class team. Foremost among his collaborators was Charles Coster whom Morgan himself admired for his complete mastery of detail, combined with an immediate and comprehensive grasp of problems, and for his astonishing ability for sustained work. It was he who managed the exacting details of the railroad reorganizations of the 1890's. Coster was seconded by Samuel Spencer (a former railroad president who, however, did not become a Morgan partner) and by another partner, Francis Lynde Stetson, an outstanding legal expert.

The methods used by Morgan in his railroad reorganizations and, mutatis mutandis, in his other flotations, have been correctly described a follows:[541] The minimum earning capacity of the road in question was determined, and fixed debts were so scaled down that even under the worst circumstances interest on bonds could be paid. The stockholders of the road to be reorganized were assessed to provide the reorganized enterprise with enough working capital. New stock was issued lavishly to keep everybody happy or, to put it differently, stock was recklessly watered, a policy which was bound to create difficulties at a later moment. When, for instance, more real capital was needed by a "Morganized" enterprise such capital could often be raised only by new bond issues which might throw the original well-balanced fixed-debt structure out of gear. Furthermore, the House of Morgan charged very heavily for its services: it received cash, a sales commission when securities were "negotiated," and stock. Morgan took care that for a reasonable period of time reorganized enterprises could not come under reckless or hostile control, and for this purpose he devised the voting trust.[542] It was a creative achievement for the time, although Schiff did not like it, being the result of bitter experience in connection with some of Morgan's earlier reorganizations, namely, those of the Baltimore and Ohio and the Reading Railroads. These policies came under fire in the later years of Morgan's life.

It goes without saying that attacks on Morgan because of high profits were absurd. Profit was then, even more than today, the flywheel of the economic system; and in the institutional set-up in which he worked, his was the correct behavior pattern. Moreover Morgan provided services which only very few men and concerns were able to provide, and those services were highly beneficial in the first instance both from the economic and the business points of view. But in due time Morgan came to pay for his achievements. He, too, experienced the "nemesis of creativity." By 1900 when he had reached the age of sixty he was losing the understanding for, and his grip on, the changing world in which he had to work. From the creator he descended to the status of technician. By 1900 when the sexagenarian entered industrial finance he thought he knew all the answers, to use the vernacular. Or, to put it differently, he applied the methods which had proved their worth in an earlier period and in a different field to a new stage of the development and in an area which would have required adaptation of policies and procedures by creative achievements. Thus in the last decade of his life Morgan erred repeatedly. His policy of stock watering was permissible, if at all, alone on the basis of that boundless optimism which was typical of the time of his youth and justified by the continuous expansion of the national economy, but only as long as, and in such regions where, it lasted. However after an extended period of expansion such as America had experienced after Civil War times, the percentage rate of further growth was bound to decline, and what had been without danger earlier became dangerous then. When Morgan started on his career, chaos in railroading was such that no price was too high to bring in order. But success once attained could easily make the same price for further similar achievements too high when seen from the economic point of view.

Cooperation and combination were proving profitable and economically satisfactory when Morgan entered the railroad field by 1880. But this was so only under the special circumstances that then prevailed. The aging man, however, mistook combination and interlocking interests as panaceas and did not see any limitation to those organizational patterns. By 1910 they had to a large extent became profitable rather than economically desirable; and capitalistic rhythm, not tempered by economic considerations, made Morgan proceed full speed on a road long after it was time to slow down. All of Morgan's major mistakes came after he had passed sixty. United States Steel was recklessly watered and its securities floated with such a degree of stock market manipulation that its common stock, once market support was withdrawn, fell from about 58 to about 8. Although United States Steel recovered and, in the long run, proved sound after all, International Mercantile Marine Company of 1902 was an outright failure. The Hill-Harriman fight could have been avoided if Morgan had preferred a competent partner to one who was an athlete and an Adonis (as was Robert Bacon). Put to the acid test the latter was not up to his assignment, because he could not read the signs. But he mistook them because Morgan himself hardly recognized that by 1900 he no longer possessed that undisputed position which he had held in 1895. He did not gauge correctly and in time the competitive position which Schiff had won when he acquired backing by Rockefeller money and began working hand-in-glove with the business genius Harriman, Morgan's inveterate adversary.

If Morgan had retired at the age of sixty he would stand out as a shining example of creativity, responsibility in business, and uprightness in an era of reckless buccaneering. To be sure, we would have missed the magnificent picture of Morgan handling the crisis of 1907. But we would have been also saved from seeing an old Morgan going from mistake to mistake. From those mentioned above the road led to the New York, New Haven and Hartford hodge-podge which, after Morgan's death, brought into court its directors, including Morgan's friend Baker.[543] Moreover, in the same period the House of Morgan refused to reorganize General Motors and permitted an independent flotation of $13,500,000 securities of Studebaker in order to recover a loan to that firm. That is to say, neither Morgan nor his partners sensed the future of the automobile industry, just as they had neglected public utilities.

On the whole Morgan's actions led to an unwise accumulation of power and one bound to call up antagonism, investigation, and interference. One may ask the question as to what extent the errors in judgment which the elderly Morgan committed and which were permitted to become the basis of gigantic transactions were due to the fact that the original partners, who as a team guided by Morgan had made his house the first of its kind in America, were worn out by 1900 and were succeeded by a second set which regardless of its worth was not comparable to the Costers, Fabbris, and Wrights. If this question were answerable in the positive it would follow that there was more teamwork in the House of Morgan prior to about 1900 than the few publications on Morgan and his firm show. Moreover, knowing that Morgan was not a good judge of men and suspecting that his

later partners were not as well qualified as the earlier ones, one may be inclined to see Junius Spencer Morgan's influence in the selection of those masterful partners which his son, John Pierpont, had in the first twenty-five years of his career. To be sure, coming into the firm at a time when J. P. had already acquired tremendous prestige and had become also an old gentleman, the new partners were probably unable to be as independent and to speak up as freely as had the men who had grown up with him. Thomas Lamont, a Morgan partner himself, states that some of the latter's associates "stood in such awe of him that they were sometimes hardly at their best with him."[544] But the thesis remains to be proved. If it were found to be correct it would enable the historian better to attribute to the various Morgan partners the share in and the glory for the House's great achievements of the 1880's and 1890's.[545]

There was no banker and especially no private banker who could bear comparison with J. P. Morgan during the years in which the latter flourished. But Jacob Schiff (1847-1920), the German Jew, stood probably second in importance among the private bankers active in the investment banking field, although he did not rank as high as Baker and Stillman, the commercial bankers, who will be discussed later. The beginnings of his firm, Kuhn, Loeb and Company, have been touched upon. Schiff entered it in 1875 when he came to America for a second time and for good, marrying shortly thereafter the daughter of Salomon Loeb. (He had been in New York before from 1865 to 1872, working first as a clerk in a brokerage house and from 1867 on as a partner in Budge, Schiff and Company.) One Abraham Wolff joined Kuhn, Loeb and Company in the same year of 1875 and was Schiff's close cooperator after Loeb's retirement. In the 1890's the firm attracted a set of younger partners who were extraordinarily able men; namely, in 1896 Felix M. Warburg (born in 1871) who had received his business education in his father's banking house, M. M. Warburg and Company, Hamburg, and had thereafter done business in Frankfurt; Otto H. Kahn (born in 1867) who had been educated in his father's private banking business in Mainz, had had broad business experience in England, and had been connected with Speyer and Company when he came to New York first in 1893; and finally Paul M. Warburg (born in 1868), Felix's brother who joined Kuhn, Loeb and Company in 1902 and is widely known because of his connection with the establishment of the Federal Reserve system.[546] Although younger members of the founders' families were admitted as partners also, the firm had a distinctly German-Jewish character prior to World War I.

Much of Schiff's success was due to this friendship with Ernest Cassel which started in 1879 when the two men became acquainted through a common friend.[547] Both were contemporaries (born in 1847 and 1852, respectively); both were of humble German-Jewish origin, the places of their birth being Frankfurt and Cologne, respectively. Both left Germany at an early age to live in the Anglo-Saxon world. Both their beginnings in business were rather obscure. Schiff's first independent enterprise in America, as mentioned before, was as a partner of Henry Budge under the name of Budge, Schiff and Company. (The firm was discontinued in 1872 at which time Schiff returned to Germany.) Henry Budge[548] was a Frankfurt Jew also, and his family's firm in that city did not have a good reputation. In the early 1870's it was considered "very fifth rate" by the directors of the rising Darmstädter Bank, while Vienna bankers felt it was "just honest enough to keep out of the hands of the police."[549] As a matter of fact, Jay Cooke's association with the Frankfurt Budges was one of the reasons of his downfall, for no decent firm in Europe would touch a security which had been handled by that firm. Cassel, on the other hand, had been the chief clerk of the London investment bankers, Bischoffsheim and Goldschmidt, which by 1875 went out of business in the midst of scandal. A Commons Committee then recommended that "a remedy [for their undoings] ought to be found in the tribunals of the country."[550] To be sure, these beginnings do not reflect on the men personally. Schiff had other very close European connections besides Cassel, namely Edouard Noetzlin, honorary president of the Banque de Paris et Pays Bas, and Robert Fleming who first founded in Dundee the American-Scottish Investment Company and later, working in London, made a business out of securing English funds for investment in America.

In essentials Schiff's business must have been very similar to Morgan's. Like Morgan he took an interest in railroad finance at an early moment (i.e., in the 1870's). Like Morgan he came to control a number of roads[551] which implied participation in railroad reorganizations. But Schiff attained prominence later than his great rival. Only with the reorganization of the Union Pacific Railroad, which Morgan had declined and in connection with which Harriman rose to prominence, did Schiff become an investment banker of first rank; and that reorganization took place as late as the 1890's. Like Morgan, too, Schiff took a hand in the export of American capital. In 1899 Morgan converted the Mexican debt and in 1900 and 1901 he floated English loans. Schiff, on the other hand, besides taking an interest in Mexico and Central

American finance floated German and Austrian treasury bills and financed the Japanese government during the Russo-Japanese War.[552] Again like Morgan, Schiff took an interest in industrial flotations, as for instance in those of the American Beet Sugar Company, of Armour, and of Westinghouse.[553] But in many respects there seem to have been important differences in policies. Schiff disapproved of the voting trust and was not as anxious as Morgan, Baker, and Stillman to sit or to have his partners sit on the boards of enterprises which he financed. He considered it possible to protect himself without being so represented. Schiff did not become the depository of the corporations whose securities he floated. His average deposits during five years did not amount to much more than $17,000,000 as against the $162,491,819 deposits which Morgan held on November 1, 1912 of which almost $82,000,000 were deposited by 78 interstate corporations. (On the directorates of 32 of these Morgan was represented.)[554] Unlike Morgan, Schiff did not control a group of banks, but relied on correspondents. The most important ones have been mentioned, but he had many more as, for example, the Warburgs of Hamburg, although he avoided "standing alliances," as he expressed it.[555] He regularly cooperated with the Speyers who on the other hand were his rivals; and there were also a good many joint transactions with the National City Bank.[556] Schiff's syndicate policy also had distinct features. Only in exceptional cases did he give participations to individuals; every participant in his syndicates was expected to help place the securities which he underwrote. Instead of forming syndicates for the purpose of contracting, Kuhn, Loeb and Company often contracted first and afterwards formed a syndicate, composed of banking houses, financial corporations, and their foreign correspondents.[557] Schiff's business seems to have had an even more international character than Morgan's. In many cases he formed foreign syndicates only, i.e., syndicates without American participants. This implied that the issues in question were sold exclusively abroad, and when Schiff formed American syndicates his foreign correspondents usually participated with a large percentage, about one third. Finally, Schiff seems to have taken a larger interest in industrial processes than Morgan, Baker, and Stillman. His son as a youth received a thorough training in railroad enterprises, a type of education which neither Morgan nor Stillman considered necessary for their sons. (However, Schiff's biography, written by an admiring author without an understanding of business history, may be misleading.) Although Schiff's business was not as large as Morgan's (who between 1902 and 1912 floated $1,950,000,000 worth of securities of interstate corporations and, in addition, unknown millions of government bonds, both American and foreign), it was extraordinarily large: between 1907 and 1912 Kuhn, Loeb and Company floated, alone, corporation securities amounting to $530,862,000 and, in conjunction with other investment bankers, an additional $704,777,708; while in the period 1897-1906 the firm had purchased in conjunction with other bankers securities to the amount of $821,289,000.[558]

The two Boston houses of Lee, Higginson and Company and Kidder, Peabody and Company also belonged "to the principal banking agencies through which the greater corporate enterprises of the United States obtain[ed] capital for their operations," to use the word of the Pujo Committee's Report.[559] They were, as the Report goes on to describe, not so closely allied with Morgan, Baker, and Stillman as the latter were among themselves. However they acted "rather in unison and cooperation" with those men. In no way was there competition and antagonism as there had been at least at times between the House of Morgan and Kuhn, Loeb and Company.[560]

Lee, Higginson and Company was originally one of the typical private banking houses which grew from a brokerage firm, theirs being established in 1848 by John Clarke Lee and George Higginson (1804-1877 and 1804-1889, respectively). By the time of the Civil War it was still in the brokerage business, but had already gone into private banking and especially had entered the investment banking field. Quite naturally it first took an interest in local issues, such as those of the Vermont Central and the Connecticut Railroads, the Merrimac Manufacturing Company, and the Massachusetts Cotton Mills. After the war the field broadened, Calumet and Hecla Copper Mining Company, the Atcheson, Topeka and Santa Fe and the St. Louis and San Francisco Railroads, the American Bell Telephone, and the American Writing Paper companies belonging to those financed by the Boston house. Who was really responsible for the start and the early development of this branch of their business is not clear to the outsider. In the last two decades of the century the senior members were George Cabot Lee, a partner since 1853 and the son of one of the founders, and Henry Lee Higginson, the son of the other, a partner since 1868. The former was according to the description of one of the younger members of the house, "of the old Salem and old Boston counting house type," that is to say, he kept his own books and wrote his letters himself; but he represented a very valuable brake on his adventurous partner, Henry Lee Higginson. Higginson (1837-1920), who had entered business only with great reluctance

after having attempted to follow the calling of an artist and after a very honorable military career during the Civil War, was one of those businessmen whose success it is difficult to explain. He was neither a born business leader nor even a good judge of men. Many of his colleagues on State Street did not consider him to have any special talent for finance. On top of that he was obviously a high strung man who during the daily routine of his office "endured much anxiety and almost agony," and in the course of his life went through long series of personal disappointments and frustrations. But he was venturesome, and, since ultimately he succeeded so well, he must have been able to see chances and to initiate and follow through large transactions. Moreover he was often lucky, as in his connection with the Calumet and Hecla mines, the control of which was originally secured by his brothers-in-law, and he was fortunate in his partners. As a personality and a man of culture he stood far above the business leaders and wealthy barbarians of his group of coevals, the Robber Barons.

By 1900 the investment banking business of the House of Lee, Higginson and Company which was suffering from lack of team work among its partners was a little old-fashioned. The firms which it financed were usually intimately known because their officers or directors were friends or relatives; and whatever securities were taken over for sale were distributed among rich capitalists in comparatively large blocks. John Murray Forbes's methods come to mind, and one can look at the firm of Lee, Higginson and Company as it presented itself by 1895 as a stage or a link in the development between the business as conducted by Forbes and Nathaniel Thayer and full-fledged investment banking as handled by the House of Morgan. Yet times were changing, the number of actual and potential investors was increasing, and each of the former would now take on an average a smaller total of securities, aiming also at a fair distribution in the portfolio.

The real upswing of the firm's investment banking business began by 1900 and was probably due to two outstanding business leaders, Gardiner Martin Lane and James Jackson Storrow. The former (1859-1914), the son of a Harvard professor, started his business career with the firm, went (invited by Charles Francis Adams) into the Union Pacific Railroad where he became a vice-president and whence he returned to Lee, Higginson and Company as a partner in 1891. Storrow (1864-1926), on the other hand, the son of a lawyer, bred for the law at Harvard, and a practicing lawyer himself, became a partner in 1900. These men knew what the times demanded and under their influence Lee,

Higginson and Company expanded its investment banking activities which were now conducted on a national scale. Between 1907 and 1912 this business of theirs reached a total of over one hundred issues for corporations at an aggregate value of upward of $1,000,000,000. The firm thereby joined the ranks of the leading investment banking houses of the country.

For those who know the period it goes without saying that originally railroad securities stood first among those floated by the House. In fact by 1900 95 per cent of its investment banking business was in railroad bonds. (Besides it had its hands in the Calumet and Hecla mines, in the American Telephone and Telegraph Company, and in General Electric.) But the profit on railroad issues was decreasing; and so when assuming leadership Storrow went after industrial securities, as did his competitors also. Among others, the United States Smelting, Refining and Mining Company, the United Fruit Company, the United Shoe Machinery Corporation, and last but not least General Motors were brought at least temporarily into the orbit of Lee, Higginson and Company. Storrow seems to have possessed more understanding of industrial processes than most other contemporary investment bankers, as shown by his activities as the chairman of the voting trustees and reorganizer of the last-mentioned firm.[561] Sales resistance to the not-yet-standardized industrial bonds was considerable, but it was still stronger against bonds of public service corporations, and to have gone into this latter field, as Storrow did, was a creative achievement. He realized that if this sales resistance could be overcome that field would become a source of large profits, as it actually did. By 1913, as a result of his policy, 75 per cent of the House's business was in industrial and public service bonds.

Storrow is credited with two organizational feats both of which were rooted in his aims and in his understanding of the needs of his time. If his house was to do a national business, the traditional method of collecting information would be insufficient. As a remedy an efficient statistical department was built up. Secondly, Storrow organized the retail distribution of securities following closely on the heels of N. W. Harris. This latter step appears to have developed logically from the attempt at introducing into the market new types of securities. After what has been said on this subject before it will be easily recognized that that these were great achievements indeed. Storrow anticipated what became the general trend in the 1920's.[562]

Lee, Higginson and Company's rival, though at times its ally, was Kidder, Peabody and Company. That firm was really the successor of John E. Thayer and Brother, the once important Boston firm which has been mentioned before. In 1865 it was reorganized by one of its partners and some of its clerks, H. P. Kidder and Francis H. and Oliver W. Peabody. We know very little about the beginnings of the new firm except that its senior partner, Henry Purkitt Kidder (1823-1886), began his career in a dry goods auction house and was thereafter connected with the Boston and Worcester Railroad, until he entered as a clerk the service of John E. Thayer and Brother. In recognition of his work during the panic of 1857 he was made a partner in 1858. In 1866 the young firm, Kidder, Peabody and Company, became an agency of the Barings; thereafter it rose quickly to become one of New England's foremost private banking houses, doing a considerable business in foreign exchange. When and how it first took an interest in investment banking is not known.

The head of Kidder, Peabody and Company during the decades under investigation was Robert Winsor. Winsor (1858-1930), born in Salem, was the son of a doctor, who saw service during the Civil War, and thereafter settled in Winchester. Young Robert was prepared at Phillips Exeter Academy and graduated from Harvard. In 1880 he entered the employ of Kidder, Peabody and Company as a clerk and rose to be invited to join as a partner in 1894. Becoming the representative of the Morgan interests in New England he was bound to be drawn more and more into investment banking. Since Winsor thoroughly disliked personal publicity we know extraordinarily little about his activities which must essentially have corresponded to those of the other great investment bankers of the period. He was connected with the financing of numerous railroads and other enterprises, including the United States Steel Corporation and the American Telephone and Telegraph Company and also with combining existing enterprises into what became the Boston Elevated Railway and the Boston Consolidated Gas Companies.[563] Between 1908 and 1912 Kidder, Peabody and Company took an interest in the contracting or underwriting and marketing of more than 100 issues of corporations aggregating in excess of $1,100,000,000.[564]

XVI

Commercial banks had never withdrawn completely from the field of investment banking. The New York Bank of Commerce, for instance, is said to have done a restricted business in securities throughout the 1840's and 1850's and it can actually be found as a bidder for $1,500,000 of the 4½ per cent treasury notes of 1858.[565] When the Civil War approached, this bank and others in commercial centers were extensively drawn into the handling of government securities. The Merchants Bank of Boston, for example, and the Merchants and Traders Bank of New York each appeared with three bids totaling $138,000 and $50,000, respectively, on the list of subscribers to the first tranche of $10,000,000 of the loan authorized by Congress on June 22, 1860.[566] Early in 1861 we find, along with John Austin Stevens (Bank of Commerce), George S. Coe (American Exchange Bank) as a large bidder on the federal loans offered, as were also such bank presidents as James Gallatin (National Bank), Moses Taylor (City Bank), and John Q. Jones (Chemical Bank). In the summer of 1861, as has been described in another context, all of the commercial banks of New York, Boston, and Philadelphia were over head and ears in investment banking in connection with the $150,000,000 government loan transaction. Moreover almost everywhere banks had to aid the governments of their states. Many Pennsylvania banks, for example, subscribed to the $3,000,000 state loan of 1861; the large Philadelphia banks taking amounts ranging from $100,000 to $300,000; the smaller ones, sums from $20,000 to $50,000; and country banks correspondingly less. There is no doubt that the loans of other Northern states were equally subscribed in part by local banks; but it is impossible, of course, to decide what percentages were taken as the basis of note issues, for investment, and for resale, respectively. It seems certain, however, that at least some of the securities were acquired with resale in mind. After the National Banking system had come into being in 1863, banks working under national charters were, as a matter of course, expected to sell war bonds, and they did so on commission to a limited extent. Only in exceptional cases may they have done a relatively considerable business therein, as is known of John Thompson's First National Bank of New York.[567]

The interest of National Banks in the flotation of government securities by no means ended with the Civil War. As will be remembered, some took a share in the Refunding transactions of the 1870's and appeared as participants in various syndicates from that of 1871 on. There even seems to have been a feeling among them that they had been squeezed out a bit. Again we found National Banks taking a hand in the federal flotations of the 1890's. It will suffice here to refer to material already presented.[568]

The legal basis for investment banking activities of National Banks can be found in a clause of the National Currency Act of 1864, section 8, according to which those banks were authorized to discount and negotiate "evidences of debt" in general. Court decisions elaborating on that clause made it clear that National Banks had the undoubted power to invest their funds in, to distribute, and to deal in U.S. government obligations. Moreover it was decided that they had the implied power to invest their funds in obligations of municipalities and business corporations, but not in stock of the latter. (However there are cases on record where banks acted ultra vires.) For many years the Comptroller of the Currency, going still further, allowed National Banks to participate in the distribution of new securities and generally to deal in securities to the extent that the banks were entitled to use them as an investment.[569] Since National Banks almost without exception bought bonds of all types as secondary reserves occasionally, if not regularly, it was a natural step for the larger ones to participate in syndicates which enabled them to acquire at a favorable rate what they would have acquired anyway. Bond departments, originally established for investing funds of the bank in question, began to act for customers and especially correspondents and finally wound up in investment banking activities. It is probable that more National Banks took syndicate participations than the few which had a special interest in investment banking and which will be discussed shortly. This seems to be indicated by the fact that the holding of securities by National Banks increased continuously over the years from 0.59 per cent of their total resources in 1863 to 9.45 per cent in 1912.[570]

Among those commercial banks which carried on the American tradition and acted as investment bankers as well as doing a regular commercial banking business, the First National Bank of New York stands out preeminently. This was not accidental. In an earlier chapter of this volume it has been described how the First National Bank of New York was founded by John Thompson who, prior to his failure in 1857, had conducted sizeable investment banking activities. Moreover after that bank had been established it met with such hostility on the part of powerful New York state banks that commercial banking was impossible for many months, and it had to concentrate its interest on the sale of war bonds. So advantageous was this business that in 1864 the First National Bank made a profit of $267,000, i.e., more than 50 per cent on its capital ($500,000). From then on, the bank remained in the security field. Originally it lent only on government securities as collateral.

Later it contracted for a complete $4,000,000 issue of District of Columbia bonds which it sold at 2½ per cent profit to the Seligmans who in turn sold the securities in Germany. In 1871 participating in Cooke's Refunding Syndicate it was underwriting $1,000,000 worth of the 5 per cent funding loan, a figure which was matched by only one other commercial bank, the Fourth National of New York. There was a good deal of contact between Jay Cooke and Company and the First National Bank of New York, which at the time of Cooke's downfall carried Northern Pacific securities for the former. The bank was also a heavy creditor of Fisk and Hatch.[571]

By that time George F. Baker (1840-1931), the powerful business leader with the Midas-touch, had begun to rise in the First National Bank. Baker had grown up in a strictly Puritan environment on a farm in Massachusetts. His father, a New York politician, brought the sixteen-year-old youngster into the New York Banking Department at Albany where he worked as a clerk for a number of years. There he gained some experience with such securities as the New York Free Banks deposited for their note issues. On his trips to the Banking Department John Thompson met the young man and when he founded the First National Bank of New York he invited young Baker to join as a stockholder and paying teller. Baker invested his $3,000 savings in First National Bank stock and took the job, quickly rising to become in 1865 an assistant cashier and later cashier. In 1873 when Jay Cooke and Company failed and the First National Bank survived the earthquake, Baker was already influential enough to bring three former Cooke partners into the First National Bank: Harris C. Fahnestock, the head of Cooke's New York branch; James A. Garland, an experienced security trader; and Francis O. French, who was to build a foreign exchange department for the bank. These men raised funds from their relatives and friends and cooperated with Baker in acquiring a block of stock from president Samuel Thompson, whose successor Baker became in 1877.[572]

By 1873 Baker must have been thoroughly convinced of the value of investment banking, otherwise he would hardly have brought Fahnestock and Garland into the Bank, men whose strength lay in their experience with securities. The rise of the First National Bank to one of the country's leading investment banks was, from then on, Baker's and Fahnestock's work, the latter guiding the bank's bond department. Fahnestock (born in 1840) had first been discovered by Jay Cooke while he was a teller in the Bank of Harrisburg (the fiscal agent of the Franklin Railroad in which Cooke was

interested). The bank was an active seller of the Pennsylvania $3,000,000 loan of 1861 for which Cooke was one of the sales agents. Recognizing the young teller's ability Cooke offered him a partnership, and Fahnestock soon became the most important of Cooke's partners, ranking second only to Jay Cooke himself. At the head of the New York office he became an experienced security trader and shared his firm's tremendous, although not always fortunate, experience in the investment banking field. In cooperation with Levi P. Morton and J. P. Morgan he handled the American end of the abortive flotation of federal bonds of February, 1873.[573]

Only with access to the archives of the First National Bank would it be possible to describe its rise in the investment banking field. For lack of such access most of what is known was established by the Pujo Committee in 1912 and in addition we can catch from other sources a few glimpses on the development. To what extent the bank's success in the field was due to the friendship between Baker and Morgan dating back to 1873 cannot be gauged. However, it seems that the First National Bank was less of an originator of issues than a most powerful ally.[574] As early as the 1880's while Morgan had already embarked on his spectacular activities in the railroad field, Baker, certainly seconded by Fahnestock, became a railroad financier and reorganizer also. He started with the Richmond and Danville Railroad, and thereafter was active in the reorganization of the New Jersey Central. By 1910 in cooperation with Morgan the First National Bank had become a factor in the anthracite coal industry through its affiliation with the Delaware, Lackawanna and Western, the Lehigh Valley, the Central of New Jersey, the Reading, and a few smaller roads which together controlled 88 per cent of Pennsylvania's anthracite deposits. Baker and Morgan were associated also on several other railroads, such as the Southern (where they represented together the majority of the voting trustees), the New York Central, and the New York, New Haven and Hartford.

Important reasons for the rise of the First National Bank were its strength in the field of government flotations and Baker's policy of acquiring bank stock in the interest and with the funds, but not always in the name, of the Bank. While seemingly identical with that of the Morgans and Schiffs that policy in Baker's case was essentially a different one; for bank stock was here acquired by the head of a commercial bank, not by a private banker. Most important among such holdings was the block of more than 50 per cent of the stock of the Chase National Bank and smaller equities in the National Bank of Commerce, the

Bankers Trust Company, the Guaranty Trust Company, the Liberty National Bank, the Astor Trust Company, the New York Trust Company, the Brooklyn Trust Company, and two banks in Minneapolis.[575] Last, but not least, Baker played a certain role in the early attempts at consolidating the country's steel industry, backing as he did, William C. Moore in his abortive negotiations with Andrew Carnegie. That he cooperated with Morgan in the organization of the United States Steel Corporation goes almost without saying. The bank was among the underwriters of the original stock and bond issues and among Morgan's allies in subsequent flotations.

The second commercial bank which assumed leadership in the investment banking field was the National City Bank of New York which after 1900 was the largest in the country, having resources amounting to $275,000,000. It was dominated by James Stillman who owned almost one fifth of its capital, while J. P. Morgan and Company, William and John D. Rockefeller, Kidder, Peabody and Company, Jacob H. Schiff, and Robert Bacon, the former Morgan partner, were other important stockholders. James Stillman owed his presidency to the Rockefellers and was generally considered the representative of their banking interests. James Stillman (1850-1918) was the son of a pioneer Texas merchant of Puritan stock. He started his business career in the enterprise of his father who toward the end of his life was a cotton and hide merchant in New York City. After his father's death the son became a partner in the firm (Woodward and Stillman) which banked with the National City Bank. The latter was the bank of New York's raw material interests; it financed cotton and Cuban sugar, metal and leather dealers, anthracite and gas producers, and a few railroads.

The young merchant's rise in business was acknowledged by his becoming a director of the National City Bank and of the Chicago, Milwaukee and St. Paul Railroad, on whose board he met William Rockefeller. All his life Stillman was a strange personality, shy, stiff, taciturn, and formal; and when he attained power the small, elegant, hawk-like man whose "shyness and myopia increased his inborn reticence to an almost morbid degree" made a crude and terrifying impression on many people. As death approached, however, he became almost human. Stillman's rise to power is the work of the Standard Oil crowd. William Rockefeller recognized the unusual financial acumen of the then still unknown merchant, and it was probably due to the former's influence that in 1891 Stillman became the president of the National City Bank. With its raw material affiliations it was the logical bank connection for

Standard Oil which, however, would transfer its account only if a persona grata, if not its representative, became the bank's chief executive. Thus was Stillman put into power; and he made good.

How the National City Bank entered investment banking is hardly known. Certainly Stillman took a keen interest in the Spanish-American War loan. In that connection he met Frank A. Vanderlip (1864-1937), a Chicago journalist and financial editor for whom Lyman J. Gage, the newly appointed Secretary of the Treasury, had such regard that he brought him to Washington in 1897 and made him Assistant Secretary of the Treasury. In 1901 Vanderlip joined the National City Bank as Stillman's protege and vice-president. Vanderlip, who succeeded Stillman in 1909, when the latter assumed the position of chairman of the board, claims for himself the merit of having made an investment bank out of the National City Bank. But some of his statements in this connection are so palpably incorrect that one becomes suspicious. No doubt he played a role in that respect, although the Bank was well along the road before he entered it. During the middle of the 1890's Stillman cooperated in the Union Pacific reorganization made possible by Standard Oil funds. In 1899 the Amalgamated Copper Company was launched under National City Bank auspices when the Standard Oil crowd wished to take an interest in Anaconda copper. In the same year Stillman played a part in the merger of the Consolidated Gas Company of New York and the Edison Illuminating Company which put New York's gas and light business under Rockefeller-Stillman control. Somewhat later the National City Bank floated a $30,000,000 bond issue for Armour and Company, and built a railroad in Bolivia cooperating with Speyer and Company. The importance which the Bank attained in the investment banking field is[576] evident from the fact that for some years there was an agreement between the Morgans, the First National, and the National City banks that of any issue originating with any of the three enterprises the originating house was to have 50 per cent and its two allies 25 per cent each.[577] The participants to this arrangement called it the pool.

There seems to have been only one city besides New York in[578] which commercial banks undertook large scale investment banking operations during the period under investigation, namely Chicago.[579] During the Civil War, war bonds were sold in Chicago by several firms, among which Preston, Willard and Kean was outstanding. In the early 1880's its successor, Preston, Kean and Company reorganized as S. A. Kean and Company, entered investment banking; but it broke down in the 1890's, probably for lack of capital. At about the time when S. A. Kean and Company tried their hands in the new game (actually in 1882), N. W. Harris and Company did the same with better success, remaining in the field permanently. Out of N. W. Harris and Company there developed Halsey, Stuart and Company when N. W. Halsey of the New York office of that firm and Harold L. Stuart from its Chicago office founded Halsey and Company, to become Halsey, Stuart and Company after the former's death. These firms have been mentioned before.[580] The business of these first Chicago investment bankers was originally small and rather primitive. They purchased municipal bonds all over the West and South, and sold them in small amounts to banks, insurance companies, and estates in Chicago. The bonds were acquired personally on the spot by the same men who did the selling to their restricted clientele. This must be kept in mind if one would understand the entry of the Chicago commercial banks into the field.

In the late 1880's the First National Bank of Chicago, blazing the trail, but followed by a few other commercial banks, went first into the bond business. This bond business was handled by its foreign exchange department which became a foreign exchange and bond department. By 1891 the bank was sufficiently familiar with the new line to take over and distribute a complete issue of $1,276,000 Chicago 4 per cent bonds. Its total investment banking business amounted in that year to $7,000,000, the profit on which was about $80,000; while in 1892 turnover and profit had risen to $11,000,000 and $160,000, respectively. Yet by 1900 Chicago's investment banking was still local in character. Not before 1892 was the first issue floated, the interest on which was payable in Chicago instead of New York, as had been usual before, Blair and Company of New York being the buyers of these bonds of the Sanitary District of Chicago. In the 1890's the field of interest broadened: in 1900 Chicago banks and bankers had gone beyond municipal and state bonds, floating in that year eleven other issues (out of which ten were for local utilities). The great industrial mergers of the period in the Middle Western industrial areas, however, were still financed in New York, but Chicago banks began to participate in New York syndicates. The First National Bank of Chicago still led, originating and distributing local bonds and taking blocks of Eastern securities for sale among its customers. The Union Trust Company and the Metropolitan National Bank were also in the field which in 1899 was invaded by the first powerful competitor of the First National Bank, the Merchants Loan and Trust Company. In 1904 at least five and probably more commercial banks and trust companies of the city were in the

bond business; by 1910 some of them were active in stocks also.[581]

Between 1900 and 1910 two Chicago commercial banks gained a certain importance in investment banking: the First National Bank of Chicago (or its security affiliate, respectively) and the Illinois Trust and Savings Bank.[582] The first was headed by James B. Forgan, who has been studied; the second by John Mitchell (1853-1927), another of Chicago's outstanding bank presidents. Both banks were among those which the House of Morgan would offer participations, although its business with Western banks was limited. (Less clear is the role which the Continental and Commercial National Bank or its affiliated trust company, respectively, played in our field.)[583] Between 1907 and 1912 the Illinois Trust and Savings Bank took participations amounting to $53,000,000, more than one half of which were for securities of railroads and public utilities. But it also financed the Jones and Laughlin Steel Corp. The participations of the First National Bank or its security affiliate, on the other hand, amounted to $76,618,000 between 1907 and 1914; the total amount of the flotations in which the bank participated was $1,316,114,000. In addition it sold municipal bonds as follows:

1907	$ 3,200,576
1908	5,894,534
1909	6,826,375
1910	3,787,900
1911	4,906,646
1912	4,812,883
1913	5,981,240
Total	$35,410,154[584]

As to its participations, it took an interest in the financing of utilities, railroads, and industrial enterprises. Among the latter were Morris and Company, Swift and Company, the International Harvester Company, and the Jones and Laughlin and the Inland Steel companies. However only one issue was handled independently in this period, an issue of $2,150,000 worth of securities of the American Refrigerator Transit Company. This fact alone, together with a comparison of the magnitudes of the Chicago participations with those cited before for the investment banking business of the leading New York firms, shows the relative position of the Chicago leaders in the field.

Nevertheless an important organizational problem which came up after 1900 was solved right in Chicago. Prior to the early 1900's the holding of stock by and the broadest investment banking activities of commercial banks working under national charters were considered legal; and as mentioned before, National Banks which were engaged on this kind of business entrusted it to so-called bond departments, a term which may go back to Civil War days. However by 1902, stirred by some court decisions, the Comptroller of the Currency adopted a different attitude toward such broad activities and ruled that they were not authorized by the National Bank Act, although the right of National Banks to hold bonds (except mortgage bonds) and to participate in bond flotations was not contested. Consequently the banks in question had to take action, and a way out of the difficulty was developed in the First National Bank of Chicago (guided, as will be remembered, by James B. Forgan).[585] In 1903 he organized the first security affiliate of any National Bank, the First Trust and Savings Bank in Chicago, under a plan which was soon to become widely adopted and known as "Chicago Plan." The security affiliate of the First National Bank of Chicago was established as a state bank with a capital of $1,000,000 and was to be permanently owned by the stockholders of the former. The president, vice-president, and cashier of the First National Bank as trustees were to hold the stock of the affiliate, the First Trust and Savings Bank, and the latter's profit was to go to the stockholders of the First National Bank pro rata of their equity therein. No stockholder in the affiliate could transfer his shares without at the same time transferring those in the First National Bank, that is to say, ownership in the First National Bank and the First Trust and Savings Bank could not be separated. The original capital of the affiliate was supplied by a special 12½ per cent dividend of the parent bank.[586]

This scheme started to migrate soon after its inception, for the problem was the same whereever National Banks did an investment banking business. Thus in 1908 and 1911 the First National and the National City Banks of New York established security affiliates, the First Security and the National City Companies, respectively, and so did the Continental and Commercial National Bank in Chicago,[587] whose affiliate was the Continental and Commercial Trust and Savings Bank, founded in 1910. These security affiliates were "officered and directed" by the men who were the officers and directors of the parent National Bank.

Regarding the establishment of the security affiliate of the First National Bank of New York, the First Security Company, we know a few details: When it seemed possible to George F. Baker that the First National Bank of New York might be forced to give up its investment banking business as previously conducted, he could choose between two alternatives. Either he could organize an independent enterprise owned by the small coterie which controlled that bank and sell to the new firm, on the stock exchange or by auction, the securities no longer permissible as an investment of the old concern. Or he could follow the Chicago plan, an action which would benefit the minority stockholders of the First National Bank. He chose the latter mode, and like the First National Bank of Chicago paid up the capital of the affiliate by a special 100 per cent dividend which gave the First Security Company a capital of $10,000,000. The trustees holding the stock of the affiliate were bound to elect the same board as headed the parent bank.[588] Shortly thereafter in the establishment of the security affiliate of the National City Bank the identical policy was followed; its capital of $10,000,000 was provided by a special dividend of 40 per cent. It seems highly probable that these two security affiliates had as their main function the task of holding stock and especially bank stock in the interest of the parent banks concerned, a practice which involved the National City Bank in a controversy with the Comptroller.

To sum up, security affiliates as they came into existence in the 1900's were state-chartered institutions owned pro rata by the stockholders of National Banks. They had powers to do a financial business not permitted to the parent bank. Original security affiliates were so organized that their stock was held in trust by officers of the bank in question. These would manage the affiliate and elect the same board of directors that was at the head of the parent bank. No shares of stock came into the hand of the public and no share of the affiliate could be sold except with the share of the parent National Bank. During the period under investigation security affiliates were usually organized under state banking laws, but before its close the first seems to have been established under a general business corporation act as later became common. The name of the security affiliate typically resembled that of the parent bank with which it usually shared the same building.[589] To what extent the early security affiliates of the 1900's were actually in the investment banking business and to what extent they were mere holding companies, this author has been unable to determine. The emphasis undoubtedly shifted later in the former direction. It is very possible that only in the second instance did what were conceived as holding companies became investment banking enterprises, a development which falls into the post-World-War I period.

The problem now was whether the Comptroller would consider as an evasion of his rulings this solution which enabled the banks concerned to do a "business which was not specially authorized by the banking act." But he did not. He took the stand that the security affiliates were "organized in accordance with a statute of [a] state. [Officers were] elected by the stockholders of those concerns. They [were] entirely distinct, absolutely, from the National Bank[s]. The National Bank[s], as such, as... corporations [were] not interested... in them at all. The line of cleavage [was] clear and distinct." It is well known that in the 1930's the thought on the problem had changed.[590]

Private bankers and commercial banks engaged in investment banking had to meet new rivals when trust companies entered that field in the 1890's. That entry was quite natural: the corporate trust business provided some of them with an intimate knowledge of corporation affairs and with valuable contacts. Moreover in some cases it may have been just a matter of course to help finance such corporations as were serviced by the particular trust company in other respects anyway. Nevertheless, it was a moot question even among trust company officers whether or not investment banking was a suitable field for this type of enterprise; and the New York Superintendent of Banks was much opposed to such activities as late as 1904. The funds which trust companies could use for that purpose were their capital, trust deposits and general deposits, lodged and created alike; the danger lay in the possibility of an improper use of trust funds, i.e., at least in their being tied up in undigested or undigestible securities. Some of the trust companies of the 1900's became very largely engaged in investment banking activities, while others abstained therefrom "absolutely."[591]

Almost no details of the beginnings of those activities are known, but the author suspects that they started with participation in federal and state, perhaps also municipal, flotations. We have met the United States Trust Company of New York as a subcontractor of Morton, Bliss and Company, taking a share in the Refunding transactions of the 1870's; and if we had complete lists of participants in those transactions we might find a few more. In the early 1890's the same United States Trust Company, led by John A. Stewart, and the Union Trust Company under Edward King[592] played a rather prominent part in aiding federal flotations. Moreover among the subscribers to the first federal loan of 1894 were the Manhattan Trust Company ($250,000), the Astor Trust Company ($250,000), the United States Trust Company ($2,500,000), the State Street Trust Company ($250,000), the Farmers Loan and Trust Company ($2,000,000), and the Knickerbocker Trust Company ($500,000).[593] In November of that year the Knickerbocker and the Brooklyn Trust Companies, as well as the United States and the Union Trust Companies, were participants in the successful

syndicate taking a $50,000,000 federal loan. Again a few months later, as mentioned before, J. P. Morgan gave the United States Trust Company a participation in his syndicate of February, 1895.

A genuine research problem remains to be done, namely, to clear up how some of the trust companies were drawn into a general investment banking business and which companies blazed the trail. The development must have started after about 1895, and a theory explaining their entry into the broad field will be presented shortly. Whether the Morgan-dominated trust companies played a leading role in this respect is unknown to the author. It is certain that they were active as originating houses or at least participants in flotations. These statements pertain to the Guaranty, Bankers, and Astor Trust Companies of which the first named had a very active bond department.[594] It is an open question to what extent the United States, the New York, and the Farmers Loan and Trust Companies, which were in the orbit of the National City Bank,[595] assisted Stillman in his investment banking activities or were drawn by him into the field. It would certainly have been a most natural procedure for the United States Trust Company, which actually can be found[596] as an ally of the National City Bank and Kuhn, Loeb and Company in a $35,000,000 flotation of the Chicago, Milwaukee and St. Paul Railroad. Moreover the Trust Company of the Republic,[597] the Central Trust Company,[598] and the United States Mortgage and Trust Company, all of New York can be found in the field. The last named had affiliations with Kuhn, Loeb and Company. It can be taken for granted that the Morton Trust Company was active therein too, for it was the successor to Morton, Bliss and Company, and Thomas Fortune Ryan who dominated it personally appeared as a syndicate manager in the period.[599] The Knickerbocker Trust Company headed and controlled by Charles T. Barney, originally a real estate operator, even concentrated its efforts on syndicate participations. In 1907 it had most of its deposits thus tied up. Its failure, as is generally known, precipitated the crisis of that year, and Barney ended as a suicide in November.[600]

Outside of New York there were at least two trust companies in Chicago (beside the security affiliates of Chicago National Banks) which were extensively in the investment banking field,[601] and in Boston the Old Colony Trust Company[602] participated in flotations of Kidder, Peabody and Company and Lee, Higginson and Company in whose orbit it moved. The participation of trust companies in flotations outside the financial centers was probably rare, but the Worcester Trust Company and the Union Trust Company of Springfield took small participations in flotations of Kidder,

Peabody and Company which were represented in their directorates.[603]

If it is true, as it probably is, that trust companies began with participation in government and municipal bonds, and only in a later stage proceeded to go after railroad and other securities, they would have moved from undoubtedly legitimate to doubtful transactions. Nothing can be sounder than the investment of trust funds in the former securities. But in many cases trust companies may have been enticed by syndicate managers to leave the path of safety by taking an interest in the latter; for their participation in flotations was considered by the public a recommendation of the securities in question and almost a guarantee of their soundness.

XVII

By way of conclusion, the growth of the investment banking business will be described quantitatively. By 1820 the earliest New York Canal loans amounted to several hundred thousand dollars each, and this was the usual magnitude prior to 1840. The federal flotations of the 1820's ranged between three and five million dollars and were large for the time, but the Bank of the United States would have been or was, respectively, strong enough to contract therefor. Toward the end of the period some of the state flotations reached and overstepped the $1,000,000 mark, as for instance those of New York; but in most cases American banks and bankers, if they handled such issues at all, handled them in cooperation with others. Only a very few American houses were strong enough to deal with an issue exceeding $1,000,000. Most interesting as to the magnitudes involved is the list of issues handled by the North American Trust and Banking Company, reprinted on page 342 of this chapter. The latter firm, one of the largest in the field, did an investment banking business of about $6,000,000 during its existence (probably five to ten years). The Bank of the United States of Pennsylvania, as mentioned previously, in the fall of 1840 held state bonds alone to the amount of about $15,000,000, many of which were pledged for loans, of course. Since the trouble of the bank resulted in part from its inability to sell the securities taken over, these bonds may have represented a comparatively large percentage of the total dealt with during its existence of almost five years. Thus it seems conservative to estimate its investment banking business during that period at about $40,000,000 or $50,000,000. It was probably larger.

Between 1840 and Civil War times state flotations usually, although not always, exceeded $1,000,000 and railroad bond flotations amounted to several hundred thousand dollars each. The $16,000,000 and $18,000,000 Mexican War loans were extraordinarily large for the time but, as has been described, there were several bidders for the whole loans or the largest parts thereof. Winslow, Lanier and Company, the main distributors of Western railroad bonds in the 1850's, handled up to $1,000,000 securities per day, a business considered enormous.

Disregarding the Civil War flotations, in the period immediately following we find flotations of several million dollars common, while flotations of between $10,000,000 and $20,000,000 did not surprise the guild. But when Jay Cooke planned to float $100,000,000 worth of Northern Pacific bonds the figure was so high that it caused suspicion, and Jay Cooke broke down in the course of his endeavors. The conversion syndicates of the period were able to handle securities to the amount of more than $100,000,000, but they made themselves responsible only for sums of $10,000,000 to $25,000,000 and took up options in case the business developed favorably.

Two decades later these magnitudes in turn were shrinking to insignificance. By 1900 the House of Morgan handled several hundred million dollars worth of securities per year, although Morgan himself considered the $200,000,000 United States Steel flotation an exceptionally large one. The total of syndicated issues of the dominant group of investment bankers (excluding issues made singly or on joint accounts) amounted to more than $3,000,000,000 in six years of the first decade of the twentieth century.[604]

In order to get the right perspective for the figures last given one must look beyond the period under investigation. Between 1927 and 1931 there were 37 American houses each of which during those five years handled $100,000,000 or more of new issues. Leading among these houses was the National City Company, the security affiliate of the National City Bank, which as syndicate head and participant floated $5,807,078,020 worth of securities. Harris, Forbes and Company in the same capacity floated $5,521,432,600 in four and one-half years (before its consolidation with the Chase Securities Corporation); the Guaranty Company followed with $4,874,420,270, and Halsey, Stuart and Company with $4,115,542,300 floated in a period of five years. J. P. Morgan and Company stood in the fourth place as a syndicate head (with $1,631,052,000 worth of securities), but since the firm followed the policy of not appearing as a mere participant in flotations, it was no longer among the leading houses with respect to the total of flotations handled during the period of 1927 through 1931. To put the whole matter differently, while the flotation of several hundred million dollars worth of securities was considered colossal prior to World War I the leading firms at the end of the 1920's floated about one billion worth of securities per year.[605]

February 3d 1794.

We hereby engage on our own Parts, and on the Behalf of the Gentlemen authorizing us to sign for them, to subscribe Eleven Millions in Money for the Loan of the present Year on the following Terms; viz'. for every £. 100 subscribed to receive

£. 100 of £. 3 per Cents. to be consolidated with
  the present £. 3 per Cent. Consol.
£. 25 of £. 4 per Cents.
A Long Annuity of 11s. 5 d. to determine with the
  present Long Annuities.

A Discount to be allowed of £. 3 per Cent. on the whole Money advanced beyond the Instalments up to the latest Period of them: - the Dates of Payments to be as follow:

1794 - February	11th	- a Deposit of	- £.	10 per Cent.
April	15	- a Payment of	-	10
June	6	- D°	-	10
July	18	- --	-	10
August	29	- --	-	15
October	17	- --	-	15
November	28	- --	-	15
1795 - January	13	- --	-	15
			£.	100

The Interest on the 3 per Cent. Consols. to commence from 5th January. - On the 4 per Cents. from 10th October 1793, and the First Half Yearly Payment on the Long Annuity to be made on 5th April 1794.

(Signed)

John Julius Angerstein,
James Morgan,
Godschall Johnson,
Nesbitt and Stewarts.

We the undersigned undertake and agree, that we will make good the Payments on a Loan of £. 18,000,000 for the Service of Government for the Year 1795, in case the same shall receive the Sanction of Parliament, and likewise on a Loan of £. 6,000,000 for the Service of the Emperor, in case Parliament shall think proper to make Provision, that if the Whole, or any Part of the Dividends, payable on the said Loan in May and November respectively in each Year, shall not be punctually paid on the Part of the Emperor, the Sums so due shall be payable on the 5th Day of July and the 5th Day of January respectively following, out of the Consolidated Fund, or out of the Supplies of the Year: The said Loan (if both of them take place) to be on the Conditions following; viz'. That for every £. 100 of Money advanced on the Loan of £. 18,000,000, the Subscribers shall be entitled to:

£. 100 - - 3 per Cent. Con. Ann[s].
  33 6 8 4 per Cent. Ann[s].
  -- 8 6 Long Ann[s].

That the Interest on the 3 per Cent. Annuities shall commence from the 5th Day of January 1795, and the Interest on the 4 per Cents. and the Long Annuities on the 10th Day of October 1794.

That £. 10 per Cent. shall be paid on or before the 6th Day after the Terms of the Loan shall have been approved by a Resolution of the House of Commons; that the next Three Payments shall be of Ten per Cent. each; and the Four following Payments shall be of Fifteen per Cent. each; the last to take place on the Friday succeeding the 10th Day of January 1796.

And that every Person, making any Payment in Advance for compleating his Contribution, shall be entitled to an Allowance at the Rate of £. 3 per Centum on such Sum so advanced, from the Day of compleating the Contribution to the Friday succeeding the said 10th Day of January 1796.

And that for the Austrian Loan, such Conditions shall be stipulated on the Part of the Emperor as were stipulated for the Loan of £. 3,000,000, which are to make Part of the £. 6,000,000 above-mentioned.

We further undertake and agree, that if the Loan of £. 18,000,000 should receive the Sanction of Parliament, and Provision should not be made for guaranteeing the Austrian Loan, as aforesaid, we will make good the Payments on such Loan of £. 18,000,000 on the Terms above-mentioned, with the Addition of 4 s. per Ann. to the Long Annuity, making such Annuity in the Whole 12 s. 6 d. per Annum.

It is understood that an Option will be given to the several Public Companies hereinafter mentioned, to subscribe for the Sums set against their Names respectively; and that the Dividends upon the Austrian Loan shall be made payable at the Bank of England.

The Governor and Deputy Governor of the Bank.	100,000
The Bank.	400,000
The East India Company.	300,000
The London Assurance Company	200,000
The South Sea Company	200,000
The Royal Exchange Assurance Company	200,000
Corporation of the Trinity House	100,000
	£. 1,500,000

And we further agree to execute any Instrument that may be thought necessary for binding us, jointly and severally, to the due Performance of this Agreement.

London, 12th December 1794.

(Signed)

Boyd, Benfield, and Co.
Abraham Robarts,
Peter Thellusson,
Thellusson, Brothers, and Co.
B. and A. Goldsmid,
John and George Ward,
Rawson Aislabie,
E. B. [sic!] Salomons.

Witness:
Godfrey Thornton, Governor
of the Bank.
Daniel Giles, Deputy Governor
of the Bank.

Kensington Gore, Nov. 16, 1795.

Sir,

I have the Honor to acquaint you, that, considering it to be your fixed Principle in all possible Cases to dispose of Loans by Competition; I have formed a List to enable me to offer for the ensuing Loan, to the Amount of 15 Millions, and to be extended if necessary - The Subscribers are about 400 real Stockholders, and monied Men, and are prepared to make the Payment. I have at my Banker's upwards of £. 300,000, and can have £. 200,000 more at a Moment's Notice, to deposit as a Security. - It has been my Aim to have no Subscribers for large Sums, but to diffuse the Subscription; and I can with Confidence assure you, Sir, that the List is compleat and proper for the Purpose, and will tend to advance the Price of the Contract. - And considering, that in conducting so important a Concern, it is proper for me to be prepared to meet all possible Events; and reflecting, that Circumstances may make it necessary, and Parliament may agree to guarantee a further Loan to be raised in England for his Majesty the Emperor; in that case, I am ready, on Behalf of my List of Subscribers, to conform to your own Conditions, by a positive or eventual Agreement; having entire Confidence that you always act with the best Intentions, and conformable to Justice. - I have the Honour to be,

SIR,
Your most

[signed: James Morgan]

The R^t Honble Wm Pitt.

Appendix II

Translation of page 210 of Samuel Ricard's Traité Général du Commerce contenant... (Amsterdam, 1781) describing loan negotiations in contemporary Amsterdam.

The mercantile house charged with such a negotiation [of securities] first deposits in the hands of a notary the power of attorney furnished by the state for the account of which it is supposed to raise the loan, say 4,000,000 florins. Immediately thereafter it publishes a prospectus setting forth the plan according to which the operation is to be conducted. In order to facilitate it, 4,000 bonds are issued with a face value of 1,000 florins each payable to bearer: in these bonds the borrowing state affirms the terms on which it will repay the capital, for example, 5, 10, 15, 20 years or more or less. Furthermore, it states the interest rate of 4 per cent (or more or less) per annum which it will pay punctually every six months at the office of the house charged with the negotiation until the entire capital is repaid.   Consequently the necessary number of coupons are attached to every bond: [in our example] each amounting to 20 florins for every date on which this sum must be paid by the house charged with the negotiation, as the interest accruing on each bond of 1,000 florins every six months. In case the interest is made payable only once per year the coupons would be made out for 40 florins if the interest is 4 per cent.[607]

The transaction opens when the operating house has the 4,000 bonds negotiated through its broker. The latter finds sur le champs[608] entrepreneurs who advance the 4,000,000 for a commission of one to two per cent or more or less. These entrepreneurs in turn place these 4,000 bonds for their own account with capitalists who want nothing but to invest their money in such securities since they have confidence in the operation.

The costs of such an operation to the state which floats the loan are not considerable in view of the nature of the negotiation; for if the loan is to run twenty years they do not amount to more than one-fourth or at most one-third of one per cent. As a rule the costs consist of two to two and a half per cent commission for the house responsible for the operation, one to two per cent for the entrepreneurs who take over the issue in order to place it with capitalists on their own account, and one per cent for the remaining costs including brokerage fees. In addition, the house charged with the negotiation[609] requires a commission of one to two per cent on the total amount of interest paid out at every term, the rate varying with the trouble that has to be taken in making the payment.

To be sure, these costs are subject to modifications according to the difficulty and complication of the operation; and the endeavors necessary to make it a success serve as a yardstick for the profit of those engaged in the flotation[610] and other agents.

Chapter XXI

INVESTMENT BANKING

1. The English Dictionary on Historical Principles (James A. H. Murray, editor, Oxford, 1908) describes a "contract [as] a business agreement for the supply of certain articles or the performance of specified work at a certain price, rate or commission." The earliest example of the use of the word in this sense dates from 1602, which fact implies that the type of business was known in England at that time. Since public loans were paid in installments over a period of time a genuine "contract" was involved. See, for example, the wording of David Parish's letter to A. J. Dallas of March 16, 1813 (Letterbooks IV, New York Hist. Soc.) in which he indicates his willingness under certain conditions to enter into an arrangement with the Secretary of the Treasury to furnish at stated periods the whole amount wanted that year.

   Before a subscription was fully paid up it was called scrip, which is but an abbreviation of subscription; see Hales, Charles, op. cit., 35.

2. Davis, Essays, I, 127, 128.

3. The development of this market is described in ibid., 185 ff, especially 193; see also East, op. cit., 270 ff.

4. East (op. cit., 20, 22, 218) describes the investment opportunities in the late colonial era of "men of fortune who live[d] upon their income" and of others unable or unwilling to employ their funds in trade, to have consisted of land, personal notes, bonds, and mortgages. Some merchants invested in British public stocks, "funds" of the Bank of England, and securities of American municipalities. He states that moneyed men, because of their experience in the era of inflation caused by the war, had lost faith in personal loans and by the 1780's were looking for other investment opportunities.

5. See East, op. cit., 278, footnote, 279.

6. Nolte, born before the eighteenth century closed, wrote in his recollections (op. cit., 312): "It is the speculative spirit alone which marks the real merchant." See also Handlin, op. cit., 61.

7. Gale, An Essay, 91.

8. "Essay of Public Credit," in Essays and Treatises on Several Subjects, (new edition, London, 1760), 138, 139.

9. Gale, op. cit., 3, 7, 8; see also Carey, George G., op. cit., 3. The following statement can be found in a Dutch publication of 1781: "les effets peuvent circuler et circulent en effet aussi facilement que des lettres de change ou des billets payables au porteur;" Ricard, op. cit., 208.

10. Jenks, op. cit., 62, 107. As late as the 1850's the following definition can be found: "Cash, in commerce, means the ready money, bills, drafts, bonds and all immediately negotiable paper in an individual's possession." McCulloch, John R., A Dictionary Practical, Theoretical, and Historical of Commerce and Commercial Navigation. New edition. (London, 1856), 268.

11. East, op. cit., 39, 155, 281, 43, 225, 317; Davis, Essays, I, 139, 199, 142. Davis (ibid., 141) describes how even the shares of the Scioto Land Company "afforded the insiders a currency which could be and was traded off for all sorts of assets and advantages."

12. East, op. cit., 39. Samuel Blodget wrote in his Economica of 1806 (page 158): "We all know that the stock thus created [i.e., for internal improvements] would in lieu of specie serve for remittances to Europe."

13. East, op. cit., 269.

14. In 1798 the United States' first men-of-war were paid for with 6 per cent stocks (see Bayley, op. cit., 43). As to the use of United States bonds in international trade in the 1790's, see Huth, op. cit., 10, 11, 127.

15. Gouge, Texas, 155.

16. Hidy, Barings, 109, 110, 135, 167, 168, 182.

17. As to the securities traded in this market, see, for instance, Fairman, op. cit., passim, especially the introductory pages 1-3.

18. Gale, An Essay, 9, 32. The author of this item, Samuel Gale, was a native of Hampshire in England who came to this continent in 1770, served as the assistant paymaster of the British forces in North America, and later went to Canada where he died in 1826. Some of his writing, here quoted, was done while he was stationed in St. Augustine, Florida. See Wallace, W. Stewart, Dictionary of Canadian Biography (Toronto, 1926).

19. Gale, Essay III, 32, 37, 38, 43. Sinclair (op. cit., 32) stated at that time that "those who [bought] into the public stocks in order to make family settlements or to provide for remote futurity... [were] the principal buyers and holders of stock."

20. Tooke, John Horne, op. cit., 39. Considerable progress toward genuine investment must have been made between about 1750 and 1780. In the former year Andrew Hooke in An Essay on the National Debt and National Capital... (London, 1750) proposed to change the debt into Tontine

annuities. He expected full success from such a measure because it would appeal to "striking and interesting motives" of "adventurers" as manifested in the popular passion for lotteries. The use of the term "adventurers" in this context is telling, of course. In fact the genuine investor was disregarded, although the author realized that his scheme competed with the purchasing of land in fee. On the other hand, he was thinking of people subscribing 250 pounds sterling which indicates the existence of at least a potential demand for genuine investment by 1750.

21. See also the following quotation regarding the emergence of an investor "class": "When those who had acquired a competency wished to disengage themselves from the fatigues of business they realized their property by laying it out in the purchase of land or by lending it to the country on the faith of government. This circumstance gave rise not only to an additional number of Land Owners but likewise to a description of people whose claims to the national property are equally well founded; I mean the Public Creditors." (Peel, National Debt, 14.) A decade later one could read: "The regular payment of the interest on the government-funds and the number of persons in this country preferring the interest they afford to the hazardous profits of trade occasion continual purchasers" for public loans. (Fairman, op. cit., 2.)

22. On the Debt of the Nation, 112; see also Mortimer, op. cit., passim.

23. Sinclair, op. cit., 27.

24. Effingham, op. cit., 17 ff; Hartley, op. cit., 3; Price, op. cit., 24; Gale, op. cit., 106, 151 ff, 193 ff; Mortimer, op. cit., 33; Sinclair, op. cit., 83; Carey, George G., op. cit., 9. When America entered the European capital market it had of course to adapt itself thereto and to rely heavily on bonus and "gratifications;" (see the contract of 1784 in Bayley, op. cit., 18, 19).

25. Gale, An Essay, 191.

26. Guardian of Public Credit containing a Variety of Important Observations... (London, 1788), 25.

27. Tatham, op. cit., 47. See also an interesting comment of 1797: "The government subscriber contracts only for an annuity in lieu of his principal and seeks the reinstatement of the capital by selling the annuity he stands entitled to under the denomination of stock;" Observations on the National Debt and An Enquiry into its Real Connection with the General Prosperity (Norwich, 1797), 8. And ibid., 9: "The original contractors, depending upon the advantage of their bargain, in general subscribe for much larger sums than they can provide, in the expectation that they can sell their scrip immediately or between the different installments with a premium."

28. Mortimer, op. cit., 169 ff; also Hales, Charles, op. cit., 34. As to the corresponding distinction for modern times, see the article "Loans, Public" in Palgrave's Dictionary of Political Economy, ed. by Henry Higgs (London, 1926), Vol. II, 621.

29. On the Debt of the Nation, 112; Price, op. cit., 24.

30. According to Francis, op. cit., 120, the number of applicants for the loans floated during the American war increased as follows: 1778--240, 1779--600, 1780--1,100, 1781--1,600. Applicants were bankers, merchants, and members of the stock exchange.

31. Mortimer, op. cit., 170; Francis, op. cit., 152.

32. Op. cit., 3.

33. On the Debt of the Nation... (1781), 112.

34. For examples, see Francis, op. cit., 118, 119, 150 ff.

35. Price, op. cit., 23.

36. On the Debt of the Nation, 112; Mortimer, op. cit., 168. One meets the oldest type of public creditor in the pamphlet literature of the 1720's: "and the greatest part of the proprietors of the public debts have been at different times incorporated for the purpose of carrying on certain trades;" (Gould, Nathaniel, An Essay on the Public Debts of this Kingdom wherein..., 2d ed. [London 1726], 61, 62). See also Pulteney, William, Earl of Bath, A State of the National Debt... (London, 1727), 59, 60. One is reminded immediately of the Bank of England and the South Sea Company, but one should also keep in mind that the charter of the former was continued under Queen Anne and George II in consideration of additional loans and so was that of the East India Company. Consequently by 1785 a large proportion of the British public debt was held by corporations.

37. Morgan, William, (Additional Facts Addressed to the Serious Attention of the People of Great Britain respecting the Expences of the War and the State of the National Debt [London, 1796], 29) speaks of "contractors for the loan" in a technical sense.

38. "Report of the Select Committee appointed to enquire into the Circumstances of the late Loan," Journal of the House of Commons, LI (1795/1796), 309 ff; in future cited as "Report." But even this report once uses the words "contractors or subscribers," i.e., both terms synonymously (310), while the most important witness stressed the distinction: "the right of the contractors (not of the subscribers);" (325). After 1800 the term loan contractor was generally accepted as a technical term; see, for instance, Alexander, op. cit., 106; Cobbett, Paper against Gold, 111, 122, 123; Lancaster, op. cit., 3, 13, 14, 20, and numerous other passages. In a later stage of the development the term "contractor" came to mean what one calls

investment banker today. In this sense the term can be found as late as 1866; see Bourne, op. cit., II, 258, 259.

39. A Letter to the Right Honourable William Pitt, 22 ff. It is very interesting that at the root of the debate of 1796 was the same problem which in America as late as 1814 led to a controversy between Jacob Barker in his capacity as loan contractor and the Secretary of the Treasury. The United States in 1814 was at the point at which England had been in 1796; Barker, Incidents, 52.

40. Newmarch, William, On the Loans Raised by Mr. Pitt... (London, 1855), passim.

41. "It is the immediate province of the Chancellor of the Exchequer to treat with individuals or the public for such sums as the different services require and to procure them on the best terms." Observations on the National Debt, 9. After having made a preliminary agreement with men willing to advance money on such terms, the Chancellor proposed them to Parliament; see Carey, George G., op. cit., 9.

42. As to this term, see footnote 65.

43. Cobbett, Preliminary Part, 10.

44. Dict. of Nat. Biogr. For a contemporary comparison of both methods, see Nebenius, op. cit. (2d ed.), 397.

45. Price, op. cit., 24 and Morgan, William, Review, passim.

46. Ibid., 16, 17. This was especially the policy of Lord North; see Morgan, William, Facts Addressed to the Serious Attention of the People of Great Britain respecting the Expence of the War and the State of the National Debt, 4th ed. (London, 1796), 13, 16.

47. "Report," 353, 354; reprinted in A Letter to the Right Honourable William Pitt, 18.

48. The way that competition worked out may be seen from the example of the Irish loan of 1795. Every subscriber of £100 was to receive £100 in 5 per cent stock and an annuity for fifteen years. Those who would offer to take the smallest amount of annuity would get the loan; ibid., 12, footnote. See also Newmarch, op. cit., 72, 74.

49. Newmarch, op. cit., 10, 11.

50. A witness before a Parliamentary Committee of 1796 stated that a private loan "was expected to be a great Bonus and on that account I considered competition to have been first established;" "Report," 322.

51. "Report," 323; A Letter to the Right Honourable William Pitt, 3, 14 ff; Newmarch, op. cit., 13, 14.

The following was the crux of the matter. Before 1794 no payment on a new loan had ever begun to be made prior to some months subsequent to the last payment on the preceding loan. The contractors of 1794 were afraid of some change in that practice, for they made it a condition of the loan that there should be no other borrowing or money-raising by public authorities that same year. (They actually intended to prevent a loan to the Kingdom of Sardinia.) When in spite of this agreement the Imperial "private" loan was brought forward that year, the contractors gave public notice of their arrangement with the Chancellor of the Exchequer, at the same time competing for the loan. Thus these contractors (Morgan, Angerstein, Johnson) seem to have established a precedent, although in December, 1794 (i.e., prior to the last installment of the loan that was due in January, 1795) they did not object to the negotiation of a new loan for 1795 since they considered their loan practically completed. Following up that precedent of 1794, when competing for the loan for 1796, Morgan intended to induce Pitt to state that the contractors and original contributors to this new loan would be entitled to the contract for the then-pending second loan to the Emperor if guaranteed by Parliament. Under these circumstances, while the loan for 1795 and the first Imperial loan, both of which Boyd had contracted, were not as yet completed, he undoubtedly had a point in opposing competition for the loan for 1796; ("Report," 312, 318, 319, 320, 321, 332, 335, 337, 342, 353, 354).

52. One of Pitt's enemies accused him of "praising so much and practicing so little" the "principle of negotiating a loan by open competition;" Maitland, James, the 8th Earl of Lauderdale, Thoughts on Finance Suggested by the Measures of the Present Session, 3d ed., (London, 1797), 23. See also Grellier, op. cit., 381, 387, 388, 416.

53. This term is to be found in the Letter to the Right Honourable William Pitt, 21.

54. Newmarch, op. cit., 16 ff. See also Morgan, William, A Comparative View of the Public Finances from the Beginning to the Close of the Administration (London, 1801), 35 ff.

55. Grellier, op. cit., 401.

56. Op. cit., 2d ed., 397.

57. Letter to the Right Honourable William Pitt, 22; Newmarch, op. cit., 72 ff.

58. Nebenius, op. cit. (1st ed.), Appendix, 37.

59. A source of the 1810's speaks of "contractors and those on the original list;" The Art of Stock-Jobbing, 26.

60. [Collier, John Dye], The Life of Abraham Newland, Esq., late Principal Cashier of the Bank of England (London, 1808), 99.

61. The material embodied in the preceding paragraph is to be found in "Report," 315, 329, 332, 337, 340, 342.

62. Ibid., 333.

63. Garraway's, located in Exchange Alley, was one of the greatest and earliest of the London coffee houses, founded in the seventeenth century and clustering around the Royal Exchange. The leading London merchants were accustomed to gather

in these places for business and social purposes. In the eighteenth century Garraway's
became one of the chief resorts of the stock
brokers. See Wright, Charles and C. Ernest
Fayle, A History of Lloyd's (London, 1928), 10,
15, 59, footnote.

64. "Report," 315.
65. "Omnium" is a technical term widely used in
the period under investigation. English eighteenth-century loans consisted as a rule in the
combined sale of various securities. Consequently "omnium," as a contemporary writer
put it, meant "the articles which form a loan
in the aggregate." "If the omnium is brought
to market it is disposed of separately;" Hales,
Charles, op. cit., 35; Art of Stockjobbing, 136.
That is to say, a contractor and the original
subscribers may have received for £100 a
certain amount of 3 per cent consols and an
annuity for, say, sixteen years. Consols and
annuity represented the omnium, but by 1800
they were sold separately at the exchange.
Later the custom seems to have changed and
the contractor sold prior to the last installment either the omnium or the various articles
(Carey, George G., op. cit., 46). Incidentally,
what was actually traded prior to that date
were the receipts for the earlier installments.
66. "Report," 337. But at least some lists have
survived; ibid., 350 ff.
67. Francis, op. cit., 149.
68. "Reports," 335-349.
69. Alexander, op. cit., 106.
70. "Report," 336,337.
71. Ibid., 358, 359, 350.
72. Ibid., 315, 317.
73. Ibid., 354. Boyd and Robarts, for instance,
represented the contractors for the loan for
1795.
74. Ibid., 322, 329.
75. Ibid., 323, 350, and this volume, page 397.
76. "Report," 317, 319. A perfect description of
the way in which a loan contractor negotiated
with the Chancellor of the Exchequer in a
"private negotiation" is to be found ibid., 323;
while the way in which a bidding started out
can be seen ibid., 310, 311.
77. Ibid., 328.
78. Art of Stock Jobbing, 70; see also the slightly
earlier contemporary statement quoted in
footnote 27.
79. Op. cit., 427 ff; Art of Stock Jobbing, 20;
Newmarch, op. cit., 72-74; Cope, op. cit.,
437-442. A contemporary description of the
business of loan contracting can be found in
Cobbett, Paper against Gold, 19, 20, 111. See
also Brickwood, John, Iun., A Plan for Reducing the Capital and the Annual Charge of the
National Debt.., 2d ed., (London, 1820), 34:
"And it should be recollected also that from
the capital so employed in the trade of public

securities [at the stock exchange]... our national necessities have always been readily supplied in the first instance." As to Mark Sprott
see Cope, op. cit., 319, 376, 440, 444; and
Francis, op. cit., 200, 201. In 1799 he had participated in a contract for the lottery of that
year.
80. "Report," 327,332.
81. To be sure, the Goldsmids appeared both as
contractors and subcontractors for the loan for
1796.
82. See above, page 306.
83. Cope, op. cit., 431, 432, 433, 434, 435, 438,
439, 441, 442.
84. Dict. of Nat. Biogr.; Bailey's list; Francis,
op. cit., 161; Cope, op. cit., 432 ff; Grellier,
op. cit., 404. Some details on the history of
the Boldero firm can be found in Price, Handbook, 15, 16.
85. Preliminary Part, 14, 46, 70.
86. "Report," 372, 321; Cope, op. cit., 431.
87. Cope, op. cit., 77, 78.
88. In the eighteenth century two brothers Jacques
and Peter de Thélusson established houses in
Paris and London. Peter(1737-1797), who went
to London in 1762, was naturalized under the
name of Thellusson. Starting as the agent of
large Continental houses he soon began trading
on his own account and from such beginnings
became a typical merchant banker. In his lifetime he was rather considered a merchant. He
acquired such fame that as late as 1880 he was
styled in a speech before the American Bankers
Association: "the great English private banker;"
Proceedings (1880), 39. Capefigue, op. cit.,
I, 242; III, 76, 77; Cope, (op. cit., 430, 431, 432,
433, 439, 441) shows the Thellusson firm as
participating in the loans for 1793, 1794, 1795,
1796, 1799, 1801; Dict. Nat. Biogr.
89. The most reliable and complete material regarding those flotations can be found in Cope's
thesis, 430 ff. See also Grellier, J. J., The
Terms of All the Loans... (London, 1799), 42;
Newmarch, op. cit., 72 ff (not correct throughout). A list of the loan contractors of the
period is in Escott, T.H.S., The Story of British Diplomacy, Its Makers and Movements
(Philadelphia, 1908), 183.
90. Bouchary, op. cit., II contains a chapter on
this firm.
91. Clapham in "Loans and Subsidies," 496, 497,
498 gives information on the fate of the Imperial
loans.
92. The author is indebted to Dr. Cope for having
made this unpublished thesis available to him
and for permitting him to quote therefrom.
The following paragraphs are based on Cope's
work. Printed material on the firm can be
found in Dict. Nat. Biogr.; Silberling, op. cit.,
404 ff; Grellier, op. cit., 383; Lancaster, op.
cit., 25 ff; Ehrenberg, op. cit., II, 38 ff, 65,
75 ff; "Report," 327, 333.

93. As to this Irish loan, see also Letter to Pitt, 12, footnote; "Report," 333, 334.

94. As to Devaynes and Company, see Price, Handbook, 48/49.

95. Op. cit., 252. Regarding Angerstein see Public Characters, 1803-1804 (London, 1804), 385 ff, especially 390, 391, 397, 398, 399; Dict. of Nat. Biogr; Martin, Frederic, The History of Lloyd's and of Marine Insurance in Great Britain (London, 1876), see Index and especially 145, 146, 178, 227, 241, 336; Wright and Fayle, op. cit. (see footnote 63), Index and especially 114, 115, 201, 274.

96. Prior to the 1780's lotteries in England were spasmodic and held in connection with the flotation of public loans. In that decade, according to John Ashton (op. cit., 89 ff), they first became a regular institution, dissociated from loans, a sort of voluntary taxation appealing to the taste for gambling. The methods used in floating a lottery were essentially identical with those used in floating public loans: The Chancellor of the Exchequer invited a few leading stock brokers to a conference in which he proposed a lottery, naming an amount the total of which was to be distributed in prizes and asking those present, which price they would tender for the concession. In the ensuing negotiation a price would be agreed upon which gave the government a clear profit without any risk whatsoever. Those who received the concession, as a matter of course, set the price for the tickets high enough so as to be repaid for the concession plus a handsome profit. The method clearly resembles a so-called "private" subscription for a loan. In fact, lottery contracting may have branched out from loan contracting.

By 1800 when private subscriptions had been more or less replaced by bids, this method was adopted also for contracting public lotteries: Sealed bids were turned in; at the opening date the bidders assembled; the Chancellor of the Exchequer would state the lowest price at which the government was willing to dispose of the lottery; whereupon the bids were opened; (contemporary description of the lottery of 1807; ibid., 147, 148). The most successful lottery contractor of the period was one T. Bish who was prominent in every lottery from 1799 to 1826, originally as a partner of the stock broker and lottery-office keeper, John Branscomb (ibid., 127). One gains the impression that nobody was strong enough to get all the tickets of any one lottery, but that several "parties" took shares.

97. From Cope's material.

98. Hidy, Barings, 18, 19, 21, 26, 31-34, 52, 53; Francis, op. cit., 203 ff; Bourne, op. cit., II, 235, 239 ff; Escott, op. cit., 86 ff; Capefigue, II, 271, 273, 335, 336, 340; III, 29. As to the Louisiana-bond transaction, see Labouchère, op. cit., 441 ff; Bosch, op. cit., 35 ff; Cobbett, William, Political Register, IV (1803), 954, 883, 884; V (1804), 404 ff. The last passage cited is reprinted in his Preliminary Part, 47 ff. It is interesting that Cobbett tried to make his readers understand the functions of the Barings in the Louisiana-bond transaction. According to him, they were "mere dealers," "wholesale dealers," "merely the speculators" who would sell the stock "just as loan mongers sell slices of the omnium." See also Lyon, E. Wilson, Louisiana in French Diplomacy, 1759-1904, (Norman, 1934), 248 and Bayley, op. cit., 45. According to information received by the author, there is no material regarding this transaction in the National Archives.

99. These data were taken from Dict. Nat. Biogr.

100. Alexander, op. cit., 16.

101. Cope, "Goldsmids," passim; Alexander, op. cit., passim, especially, 106 ff; Lancaster, op. cit., 40; Silberling, op. cit., 428; Francis, op. cit., 160 ff; Bourne, op. cit., II, 235 ff. An attack on the Goldsmids is contained in Cobbett, Paper against Gold, 99 ff. It is based on "Report from the Select Committee on the Manner of Funding Exchequer Bills... 14th May, 1810" in Hansard's Parliamentary Debates, XVII, May 18-June 21, 1810, Appendix, cxciv.

102. Easton, op. cit., 91 ff; Hidy, Barings, 28, 53; Cope, op. cit., 314, 432, 438, 439, 441, 442; Price, Handbook, 123. The firm was established by Abel Smith, Jr. (1711-1788), (the grandson of a Nottingham banker) who moved to London in the 1760's and founded the banking house, Smith and Payne. His son Robert (1752-1838), the first Lord Carrington (1796), Boyd's banker, retired from business upon receiving the peerage, being succeeded by his brother Samuel (1754-1834). As to Payne, see Easton, op. cit., 65, 66.

103. Boyd, Benfield and Company received a blow from which they never fully recovered when in 1796 the Bank of England suddenly curtailed lending. (The notice of December 31, 1795 is reprinted in Gilbart, History and Principles, 37.) Slightly later, the suspension of specie payments had considerable influence on loan contracting. "It now remains no longer," wrote a contemporary author, "a matter of concern or anxiety with the Loan-monger that he is unable to fulfil his engagements. If he can pay two or three installments of his subscription, the Bank, on the credit of these, advances the greater part of the remainder; and thus by preventing the necessity of an immediate sale of the whole keeps up the price of the new stock and invariably assures a profit to the original subscriber. This reliance on the support of bank paper encourages every moneyless adventurer and of course increases

the number of competitors for a share in the public spoils." (The last words say enough about the outlook of the pamphleteer!) Morgan, William, A Comparative View of the Public Finances from the Beginning to the Close of the Late Administration (London, 1801), 39, 40.

104. The Art of Stock-Jobbing, 19, describes how the loan contractors "in their turns" were ruined by the stockjobbers.

105. Ehrenberg, op. cit., I, 83.

106. A parallel process can be observed in Vienna. While during the Napoleonic Wars local bankers such as Arnstein & Eskeles, J. H. Geymüller & Co., Graf Moritz Fries & Co., and Melchior Steiner & Co. had financed the needs of the Austrian government, the first big Austrian loan floated thereafter came into the hands of Parish and Company, Hamburg; Hope and Company, Amsterdam; Baring Brothers and Company, London; and Gebrüder Bethmann, Frankfurt; while only one firm in Austria, the Geymüllers of Vienna, participated. That is to say, the strongest international houses took the business away from local financiers of limited strength.

The development in Frankfurt seems to have been similar: by 1790 besides Gebrüder Bethmann there were other bankers, such as the Gontards, Rüppell & Harnier, Metzler, and Willemer interested in loan "negotiating." After 1815 the Bethmanns alone were left in the field and even they were able to play only a very minor role; (Ehrenberg, op. cit., I, 76, 136).

107. Clavière (1735-1793), one of the foremost stock gamblers of his time, Necker's antagonist by 1790, and minister of finance in 1793, was one of the Genevese, i.e., Swiss Protestant, bankers who dominated this business in Paris in the late eighteenth century. Before emigrating to Paris he had been a merchant in Geneva which he left after the so-called aristocratic revolution of 1782. See Bouchary, op. cit., I, 11 ff; Capefigue, op. cit., I, 242, 282. The various French encyclopedias contain articles on Clavière.

108. Davis, Essays, I, 152 ff, especially 159, 166, 170.

109. The many notes on Parker to be found in East (op. cit., see Index) and in Davis (Essays, I, 140, 141, 148, 149, 152, 153, 157, 161, 164 ff) permit one to piece together a pretty good picture of the man and his business activities. A merchant from Watertown, Mass., during the war he was a contractor in partnership with Duer and fled from his creditors by going to Europe in 1784. In Europe he worked to interest European capital in speculations in American land and securities. His connection with Le Coulteux dated from 1783. He does not seem to have been too scrupulous.

110. Le Coulteux is characterized by Capefigue (op. cit., II, 244) as "financier remarquable, associé à une maison de banque très active." He was one of the early French potential loan contractors (see this volume, page 319). He became a senator under the consulate.

111. See this volume, pages 318, 319.

112. Pitkin, A Statistical View (1817), 326, 332, 334; Myers, Margaret, op. cit., 13 (her source could not be identified).

It is possible that agents were used in collecting subscriptions, for Jacob Barker, who did this in 1813, spoke (Incidents, 40, 75) of "the commission of the quarter of one per cent on the... sum furnished which government was in the habit of allowing to the agent by whom subscriptions were obtained." This statement is not too trustworthy, however. According to Walters and Walters (op, cit., 160, 161) a commission of ¼ per cent was first offered on March 18, 1813 because of the failure of the sixteen million dollar loan. In fact, if a commission was customary why did Barker in 1812 "prevail on many of [his] friends to furnish [Mr. Gallatin] considerable sums" instead of making a business out of collecting subscriptions as he did later (Incidents, 39)?

113. Bayley, op. cit., 43 ff.

114. See also Vol. I of this work, pages 102, 103.

115. Walters and Walters, op. cit., 160 ff; Walters, Dallas, 178 ff.

116. Vol. IV of David Parish's Letterbooks (in the New York Historical Society) gives a good idea of how Girard and Parish handled this business. Out of the seven millions they kept on joint account two and a half millions and in so doing acted like wealthy English people throughout the eighteenth century who loaned their funds to the government. They speculated on a price rise and probably successfully. For the remaining four and a half millions they acted as loan contractors, although in fact David Parish himself subscribed in the name of Oliver Wolcott for one and a half million of the latter sum, i.e., to that extent he speculated for himself as distinct from his joint adventure with Girard. The installments for this private purchase of Parish's were financed by the Bank of America of New York which discounted Parish's notes, endorsed by Minturn and Champlin, and held the certificates as an additional security. Only the remaining about three millions were unloaded at once. "We will take care to deliver before the 15th day of this month... the names of the persons embraced by our proposal together with the sums respectively payable by each," so Girard and Parish wrote to Gallatin on April 8, 1813; (Letterbooks, IV, 259, 260). At the same time they requested that the cashiers of certain designated banks be advised

to take subscriptions from any persons authorized by Girard and Parish or either of them. Finally Gallatin was to send blank certificates for subscriptions to the cashier of Stephen Girard's Banking House where they were obviously made out to the subscribers.

See especially the letters to A. J. Dallas, Mar. 16, 1813; to Albert Gallatin, Apr. 8, 1813; to Dennis A. Smith, Apr. 12, 1813; to Oliver Wolcott, Apr. 14, 21, 24, 1813; to Vincent Nolte, Apr. 15, 1813; to Jon^a Burrall and H. Kuhl (cashiers of the Bank of America, New York, and the Farmers and Mechanics Bank, Philadelphia, respectively) of Apr. 13, 1813; to Richard Parish, May 8, 1813.

117. For details of Barker's life, see pages 60, 61 of this volume. David Parish uses in his letter of May 7, 1814 to Prime and Ward the very term, stating that for an amount of about four millions a "contract" had been made with Barker and Company; (Letterbooks, V, 236). Barker himself would have preferred to conduct his loan contracting more or less in the name of Oliver Wolcott and was disappointed when the latter declined. He did not know that Wolcott was supporting David Parish; see footnote 116.

118. Walters and Walters, op. cit., 162, 163; Porter, Astor I, 333 ff.

119. Barker, Incidents, 40-44. If one examines the the list of subscriptions which Barker collected (ibid., 40, 41; also Scoville, op. cit., I, 331 ff) one sees that the amounts ran from $1,200 to $50,000. Only Isaac Clason, Theodore Fowler, Henry A. & John G. Coster, and one bank subscribed larger amounts. Thus the question comes up whether these men too aimed at loan contracting. A remark of Scoville's regarding Clason (op. cit., II, 365) would testify against this interpretation.

120. Barker, Incidents, 47 ff.

121. As to bullish and bearish moves with respect to public loans at the London Stock Exchange in the Napoleonic era, see Silberling, op. cit., 427.

122. Barker, Incidents, 52; for the following see ibid., 58, 68.

123. Barker, Incidents, 80; Bayley, op. cit., 90, 91. As to Dennis A. Smith see the following references kindly provided by the Enoch Pratt Free Library at Baltimore: Neal, John, Wandering Recollections of a Somewhat Busy Life (Boston, 1869), 157; Griffith, Thomas W., Annals of Baltimore (Baltimore, 1824), 214; Niles Register, XIII (1817/18), 377 and XV (1818/19), 59; Caterall, op. cit., 40, 43, 45-50.

124. Porter, Astor, I, 335 ff.

125. See this author's "Payments between Nations..." in Quart. Journ. Econ., L (1935/36), 695, 696, and the sources cited therein.

126. See Ehrenberg, op. cit., I, 46, 47, 50 ff., 77.

The situation was the same in contemporary Prussia; consequently the sources, such as Eichborn, op. cit. (see Index under Anleihen) and Lenz-Unholtz, op. cit., 40, 41, 70, 71, 231, 236, 238, 262, 263, are full of examples of this type of public borrowing which was the only one open to that state until the end of the Napoleonic era. The bankers Eichborn & Co. in Breslau, for instance, made loans to the Silesian cities of Breslau, Neustadt, Landeshut, and Waldenburg. They also lent to the cities of Greiffenberg, Friedland, Gottesberg, and Schweidnitz, being secured by the Solidarhaft (joint and several liability) of the merchants' guilds of these cities. On the other hand, the financial needs of the Prussian government after the defeat of Jena were taken care of by the merchants' guilds of her leading commercial cities, Berlin, Breslau, Königsberg, Stettin, and Elbing. To the extent that coin was not available the merchants lent their credit in the form of drafts on one another, in fact in the form of kites. In these and similar emergencies, loans to cities and governments alike easily took the form of forced loans. Besides the cases cited by Eichborn, Pallmann (op. cit., 156) reports one for Frankfurt, the "Patriotische Anlehen" of 1796; and Cohen (op. cit., 139) mentions forced loans raised by the French in occupied Hanover in 1807.

Genuine investors were not expected to contribute to Prussian loans prior to that of 1815 which in this respect marked a departure and real progress from older principles (Eichborn, op. cit., 255). As late as 1807 in connection with a loan which the city of Breslau floated in the form of 5 per cent Obligationen it was expressly stated that the merchants had to bear the burden "da auf die reichen Particuliers doch nicht zu zählen sei;" Eichborn, op. cit., 122, 123. The Prussian attempt of 1809 to issue an "Anleihe auf Prämien," i.e., to raise funds by a loan combined with a lottery was a complete failure, although the merchants acting as agents tried to sell the tickets.

Much detailed material on Prussian loans in the first three decades of the nineteenth century can be found in Rachel, Hugo and Paul Wallich, Berliner Grosskaufleute und Kapitalisten, vol. III (Übergangszeit zum Hochkapitalismus 1806-1856) (p.p., Berlin, 1939), 1 ff, 294-296.

127. The letter is reprinted by Bayley, op. cit., 20.

128. Edler, op. cit., 78, 82, 83, 211, 212, 214, 215. Bayley (op. cit., 17) shows that the three Dutch firms which floated the American loan of 1782 received $4\frac{1}{2}$ per cent commission plus 1 per cent for paying the annual interest. The commission was reduced to 4 per cent when the

loan of 1790 was floated; this rate was low for the time and equal to that which Austria paid for her loans (ibid., 23).

129. Helbing, op. cit., 8, 31 ff, 41, 44, 45.

130. A list of its flotations between 1754 and 1826 can be found in Pallmann, op. cit., 567 ff. For the following, see Landmann, op. cit., 510, 511; Ehrenberg, op. cit., I, 49, 50; von Gönner, op. cit., 51, 52.

131. Cohen (op. cit., 145 ff) reprints that for the Danish loan of 1821. In this document the term "general bond" is used.

132. Bayley, op. cit., 17. For a late example of this mode in the early nineteenth century, see Cohen, op. cit., 149.

Recently one of the three copies of a General-Obligation has come with the Wallich collection into the Kress Room of the Baker Library of Harvard University. It refers to a 200,000 Thaler loan of the Elector of Saxony (Friedrich August, Herzog zu Sachsen, Jülich, Cleve, Berg, Engern und Westphalen, etc, etc). It was negotiated in 1778 by the Frankfurt bankers, Gebrüder Bethmann and Jacob Friedrich Gontard und Söhne, and repayable in four installments on May 1, November 1, 1785, May 1 and November 1, 1786.

Incidentally, Cope found the term "octroi" used for what was undoubtedly the General-Obligation of the Imperial Loan of 1794 floated in London; thesis, 56.

133. Bayley, op. cit., 18; Cohen, op. cit., 145. On pages 24 and 25 of Bayley's book one finds reprinted the contract for the American loan of 1791 concluded in Antwerp. This "contract" is identical with the General-Obligation. It contains the following clause: The American chargé d'affaires "consents that... three thousand copies of this contract shall be printed each of which containing at foot a receipt of one thousand florins, Brabant exchange money, with a name or in blank, at the option of the money lenders, signed by the [chargé d'affaires], numbered from one to three thousand, and countersigned by C.J.M. De Wolf [banker and negotiator of the loan] for the sake of certifying that the number of partial contracts [Partial-Obligationen] issued by virtue of this consent does not exceed that of three thousand." See also the facsimile of a prospectus of the Spanish loan of 1807 negotiated by Hope and Company, Amsterdam, in Wolff, op. cit., after page 124.

The Austrian lottery loans of 1820 and 1821 were handled similarly. A General-Obligation was made out to the Rothschilds who at the same time received for sale Partial-Obligationen au porteur; see von Gönner, op. cit., 183. The same form was used once more in connection with an 1826 loan of the Duchy of Parma taken over by the Rothschilds; see Corti, Aufstieg, 380.

134. Bosch, op. cit., 36.

135. Bayley, op. cit., 20, 23. Thousand or three thousand bonds, respectively, of 1000 fl each were handed to the "negotiators." As late as 1818 Nathan Rothschild at least countersigned every Prussian Partial-Obligation; see Ehrenberg, op. cit. I, 95. The latter method was also used in connection with the Danish loan of 1821; see Cohen, op. cit., 145.

136. Ehrenberg, op. cit., I, 53. According to Lotz (op. cit., 414, footnote) a "General Bond" was used as late as 1890 in connection with loans of certain undeveloped non-European countries.

137. Ricard, op. cit., 204, 210. The author is indebted to Professor Herbert Heaton for having drawn his attention to the important source.

138. See Baasch, Ernst, Holländische Wirtschaftsgeschichte (Jena, 1927), 192 ff; the Dictionary of National Biography contains material on several members of the Hope family who were active in the firm. Clapham("Loans and Subsidies," 498) provides information on the fate of the Russian loans negotiated by the Hopes in the 1780's. See also Nolte, op. cit., 156.

139. A Treatise on the Administration of the Finances of France, translated by Thomas Mortimer (London, 1784), Vol. II, ch. XI. Necker himself arranged for several public loans while he served as a minister; Hennet, op. cit., 266 ff, esp. 284.

140. Such losses resulted, for instance, from John Law's transactions and later in the course of the Revolution; see Nebenius, op. cit., (1st ed.) 19, 30; von Gönner, op. cit., 109. For a concrete example of such losses, see Lenz-Unholtz, op. cit., 190, 191. Sir James Steuart laid much stress on the different development of public credit in England and France.

141. The preceding is based on Hennet, op. cit., 24 ff, the quotation being on page 27.

142. Ibid., 283-287, 296, 300. Vührer (op. cit., I, 356) writes: "Rien de plus bizarre, de plus disparate et de plus incohérent que le régime sous lequel se trouvait placée, avant la Révolution, la Dette constituée."

143. Cope, op. cit., 8,9; cited by permission.

144. The contract for the French loan of 1817 granted $2\frac{1}{2}$ per cent commission, that for the Austrian loan of 1818 4 per cent (Nebenius, op. cit., [1st ed.], 27, 59, 60). The Rothschilds received 4 per cent commission on the Prussian loan of 1818 (Ehrenberg, op. cit., I, 90), etc.

145. Nebenius calls these firms "Wechselhäuser" (see op. cit., [1st ed.], 27, 73, 75, 76, 77 ["Wechsler"]; [2d ed.], 509). As late as 1835, the Rothschilds themselves used this term for characterizing their enterprise; Corti, Blüte, 105. Less often the term "Bankier" or "Bankierhäuser" is used synonymously (see [1st ed.], 76, 77; [2d ed.], 402). It is telling that in the years after the Napoleonic wars the term loan contracting came into the German language

replacing the eighteenth-century term "eine Anleihe negociren;" (Nebenius [2d ed.], 406; von Gönner, op. cit., 10, 63, footnote). Nebenius speaks of "Contrakte" and "contrahieren" (e.g., [1st ed.], 9, 87; [2d ed.], 401, 402, 406); and so did the Rothschilds in their business correspondence: "zu kontrahierende Anleihe" (Meyer Amschel Rothschild & Söhne to Pillersdorf, Apr. 12, 1822, Salomon Rothschild to Metternich, Oct. 22, 1822; see Corti, Aufstieg, 294, 299).

146. See page 308.

147. Ehrenberg, op. cit., I, 80, 81.

148. Ibid., 89.

149. Nebenius speaks of "Uebernehmer und deren Untertheilhaber," op. cit.,(1st ed.), 8; (2d ed.), 509, 510; Lancaster calls them loan-contractors and sub-contractors (op. cit., 23). Von Gönner speaks of the former as "Unternehmer," op. cit., 71, 79.

150. For details see this author's "Jacques Laffitte and the Beginnings of Investment Bankers in France" in Bull. Bus. Hist. Soc. XXII (1948), 143 ff.

151. Nebenius, op. cit., (1st ed.), 107, footnote; David Parish to Salomon Rothschild, repr. in Ehrenberg, op. cit. I, 117; Laffitte, Mémoires, 115. The Gontards of Frankfurt are mentioned as early allies of the Rothschilds (Corti, Aufstieg, 315).

152. Nebenius, op. cit. (1st ed.), 257, 261, 262; (2d ed.), 397. For a very typical example, see the letter of Meyer Amschel Rothschild & Söhne to Pillersdorf, Apr. 12, 1822 in Corti, Aufstieg, 294.

153. See page 312.

154. Corti, Aufstieg, 266, 268, 294, 318.

155. Ibid., 265, 311, 318.

156. Von Gönner, op. cit., 79.

157. Thorold, op. cit., 13.

158. Nebenius, op. cit., (1st ed.), 8, 9; (2d. ed.), 81, 82, 509, 510; The Art of Stock Jobbing (1816), 18, 66. Cobbett (Preliminary Part, 130, 131) states that the loan contractor sold "out in little parcels to subaltern speculators who would have made the loan themselves if they could." The investors of the post-Napoleonic era are well characterized by Nebenius, op. cit., (2nd ed.), 521 ff.

159. The French system was different from those of the other European countries in that the public creditor bought a "rente perpetuelle." The capital value thereof was determined by the market and quoted for rentes of 5 francs; Nebenius (2nd ed.), 23, 24; Hennet, op. cit., 24 ff.

160. Nigohosian, op. cit., 142, 144, 145; Nebenius, op. cit.,(1st ed.), 63 ff, 67, 68.

161. Ibid., 71, 72; also 255.

162. For a typical case see ibid., 65.

163. Labouchère, of Huguenot ancestry, had been apprenticed to his uncle, a French cloth merchant by 1785. In 1790 he entered the House of Hope as a "French clerk" and soon became a partner and its head. Described as shrewd and of quick perception, a perfectionist in many respects, and possessing the manners of a gentleman, nevertheless he lacked a "refined education" and the power of wit. Thorold, op. cit., 1 ff; Nolte, op. cit., especially 50 ff. Labouchère's likeness is to be found in Wolff, op. cit., after page 154. Regarding the firm of Hope, see Bourne, op. cit., II, 243, footnote; Hidy, thesis, 8; Escott, op. cit., 97; Nolte, op. cit., 50, 262; Baasch, op. cit., 207.

164. Wolff, op. cit., after page 124, reproduces the facsimile of a prospectus of 1807 of Hope and Company advertising a Spanish loan. See Baasch, op. cit., 197, 198, 205, 206.

165. Vol. I, pages 101 ff, vol. II, page 316.

166. Fisher (op. cit., 303, 307), is misinformed on the part which the various personalities played in connection with this loan.

167. Wolff, op. cit., 182 ff; Lévy, op. cit., 214 ff; Marion, op. cit., IV, 412; Nigohosian, op. cit., 23 ff, 48 ff. See (op. cit., 148) discounts Ouvrard's contribution.

168. See the documents reprinted by Nigohosian, op. cit., 193 ff and his description, ibid., 64 ff.

169. Nolte, op. cit., 264; Nigohosian, op. cit., 45, 46; Nebenius, op. cit., (1st ed.), 24, 73, 75; Marion, op. cit., IV, 413, 414; Nervo, op. cit., 242 ff, 303 ff. Disregarding the loans to be discussed later, mention should be made of a few more in those years especially a Dutch, a Swedish, and a Danish loan. The latter amounting to Mark Banko 6,000,000 was floated by Hamburg houses (Nebenius, op. cit.,[1st ed.], 124).

170. See Corti, Aufstieg, passim; Ehrenberg, op. cit., I, 41 ff; Berghoeffer, Christian Wilhelm, Meyer Amschel Rothschild, der Gründer des Rothschildischen Bankhauses (Frankfurt, 1922).

171. For the early relations between Prussia and the Rothschilds, see also Nigohosian, op. cit., 70.

172. For details, see ibid., 166 ff, 205 ff.

173. The unsavory story of this loan, floated in two issues in 1820 and 1821, respectively, is to be found in von Gönner, op. cit., 61 ff.

At that time the stock exchange practices as originally developed in Amsterdam and London were adopted in Germany also. Interesting in this connection is Der Kluge Kapitalist (Wien, 1824). (A micro-film of this item, which is in the Library of the University of Heidelberg, is in the Baker Library of Harvard University.) The booklet is especially valuable for its explanation of the technical language then used, the language of the five brothers Rothschild.

174. This type of securities had been created in 1815

when Fl. 50,000,000 were floated, the interest of which (2½ per cent) was payable in "Conventionsmünze." See Nebenius, op. cit., (1st ed.), 42; and for further details see Fischer, op. cit., 278.

175. Four or three allied houses, respectively, took the Austrian issues of 1823: the Rothschilds, Barings, and Reid, Irving and Company of London took both of them; while David Parish was probably in on the first; (Corti, Aufstieg, 320 ff).

176. Incidentally P.C. Labouchère so disliked the Rothschilds that the Hopes would not have any dealings with them.

177. However as early as 1815 and 1816 the Rothschilds had at least negotiated with the French government; see Nigohosian, op. cit., 29, 30.

178. Ehrenberg, op. cit., I, 108, 111, 112; Nolte, op. cit., 303 ff; Corti, Aufstieg, 314, 315, 339. The Barings and Rothschilds also cooperated in 1824 in the foundation of the Alliance, British and Foreign Fire and Life Assurance Company, which was conceived by Nathan Rothschild. Reid, Irving and Company of London participated. Not before 1847 did the Barings and Rothschilds cooperate again. In that year they floated a £8,000,000 British loan; see Corti, Blüte, 270.

Very little has come to the attention of the author regarding Reid, Irving and Company and its head, John Irving, who became the first president of the Alliance and died in 1845. The participation of the firm in the Austrian loans of 1823 has been mentioned in a footnote. Nolte had a very low opinion of both the firm and its head: He remarked that the former "although very undeservedly, as the sequel has shown, stood in great repute," while the latter "had one of the most narrow business minds I have ever known." (Maybe Nolte was disappointed by the way the firm handled and disentangled his bankrupt affairs in the early 1840's.) John Irving as well as his partner Sir John Rae Reid, bart. were members of Parliament. See Nolte, op. cit., 284, 432; Dod's Parliamentary Companion, 1839, 1840, 1841; Martin, op. cit., 292, 293; Schooling, Sir William, Alliance, Assurance, 1824-1924 (London, 1924), 2 ff, 12 (Irving's picture is to be found opposite page 25); Hidy, Barings, see Index.

179. Corti, Aufstieg, 373.

180. Prior to his time two Imperial (Austrian) loans had been floated in London in 1795 and 1797, respectively, and a Portuguese loan had followed in 1809. But political moves were back of these flotations; see Nebenius, op. cit., (1st ed.), Appendix, 55; Hennet, op. cit., 426.

181. Corti, Aufstieg, 291.

182. Their representative was one Nathan Solomons; see Cobbett, Paper against Gold, 122. As "Nathan" he is often mentioned by Lancaster, op. cit., passim.

183. Lancaster, op. cit., passim and especially 12, 24, 43.

184. While in the post-Napoleonic era the floating of loans for the Great Powers was more or less monopolized, a large number of firms, most of them domiciled in London, entered this field to the extent that it was neglected by the Barings and Hopes as well as by the Rothschilds. There were some areas from which these firms shyed away, namely, South America, the European North, and the Pyrenean and Balkan Peninsulas.

As to South America, as early as 1825 the Rothschilds took an interest in Brazil which was unable to meet its obligations toward another London house, and in 1829 in cooperation with T. Wilson and Company they loaned this state £800,000. The Barings, on the other hand, floated a loan for Buenos Ayres in 1824. This was, however, all the business which the Barings and Rothschilds did in South America prior to 1830; the rest was left to smaller houses. In 1822 a loan was floated for Colombia by Herring, Graham and Company, although in 1821 the Barings had negotiated with Bolivar through their agent, Eric Bollmann; (see this author's Essays in American Economic History, 65). In the former year Chile received a loan through Hullett Brothers and Company, and Peru one through Frys and Chapman who took further loans of this state in 1824 and 1825. In 1824 B.A. Goldschmidt and Company provided Colombia and Mexico with funds, while T. Wilson and Company dealt with Brazil. The following year Mexico switched to Barclay, Herring and Company, while Guatemala and Guadaljava were financed by I. and A. Powles and W. Ellward, Junr, respectively.

Turning to the states in Northern Europe we find A. F. Haldimand and Sons launching in London the Danish loan of 1821. (The very interesting General-Obligation, here called "general bond," is reprinted by Cohen, op. cit., 145 ff.) In the 1810's this state had floated a loan with Hamburg houses. The loan of 1821 is of particular interest since two-thirds of the total of £3,000,000 were issued in Pounds Sterling, the rest in Mark Banko to facilitate the sale on the Continent. The interest on the £ tranche was payable by B. A. Goldschmidt and Company. In 1825 Denmark switched to T. Wilson and Company. In the same year Norway contracted a loan of 1,500,000 Mark Banko with Hambro and Sons, then still a Danish firm; although an earlier loan of that country, that of 1818, had been placed through Gebrüder Benecke in Berlin and Averdieck & Co., Hamburg.

The Spanish loans of the 1820's have been studied in Bull. Bus. Hist. Soc., XXII (1948), 155. In 1823 we find J. Campbell and Company as financiers of Spanish needs, while Portugal in the same year had dealings with B. A. Goldschmidt and Company.

Greek loans were floated in 1824 and 1825 by Loughman and Company and the Ricardos, respectively.

See Gilbart, James William, History and Principles of Banking (London, 1834), 59 (the material is [unreliably] reprinted in Bourne, op. cit., II, 259); Cohen, op. cit., 145 ff, 149, 192; Corti, Aufstieg, 329. The South American transactions are touched upon in volume I of this work, page 126.

185. Talleyrand stressed the fact that American merchants were commonly borrowers; op. cit., 28.

186. For details see Bayley, op. cit., 29. Of the same character were the temporary loans of 1791 from the Bank of North America, of 1792 and following years from the Bank of the United States, and of 1794 and 1796 from the Bank of New York; see ibid., 36 ff.

187. During the War of 1812 the Governor of Pennsylvania borrowed repeatedly from the Bank of North America for the use of the Commonwealth and even of the Federal government. See Bank of North America, Minutes of the Board of Directors, Oct. 10 ($25,000), Dec. 5, 1814 ($100,000), May 15, 1815 ($50,000 to be put to the credit of the United States).

188. Bank of North America, Minutes of the Board of Directors, Apr. 12, 1815. Temporary loans of banks to state governments which did not involve the issue of securities persisted for decades to come. In Virginia, for example, the banks advanced to the state $200,000 in 1840 and increased this amount to $350,000 by 1843; (Starnes, op. cit. [1931], 101). In that period New York banks made a loan of the same type to their government; see New York Canal Fund Commissioners, Report (dated Jan. 17, 1842) Assembly Doc. 18 (64th session), 24.

189. See vol. I of this work, page 13.

190. This early stage of the development was reflected as late as 1843 in the opinion expressed by the attorney of the Bank of New York that it was entitled to subscribe to Canal Loans for the purpose of investment; Minutes of the Board of Directors, May 2, 1843.

191. Jour. Econ. Hist., VII (1949), 213; this work, I, 49.

192. Hartz, op. cit., 98.

193. Public Statute Laws of the State of Connecticut, Book II, (May Session, 1816), Chap. V.

194. Gras, op. cit., 219, 344, 345.

195. See vol. I of this work, pages 47, 91.

196. Bryan, op. cit., 45-47, 76; Hagerstown Bank, 46, 49, 50.

197. Hartz, op. cit., 46. In 1814 the Delaware County Bank at Chester, Pa., decided to invest part of its capital in bank stock, and selected shares of the Commercial and Schuylkill Banks and of the Bank of the Northern Liberties as desirable. Actually Schuylkill Bank stock was bought. In 1815 a committee of the same bank was authorized by the directors to buy United States 6 per-cent bonds. In the 1840's it owned stock in the Girard Bank and of the State of Pennsylvania (which latter it was anxious to sell); at that time it acquired shares in the Chesapeake and Delaware Canal Company and United States 5 per-cent bonds; (Ashmead, op. cit., 15, 16, 25, 45, 46). The Bank of Chester County, to cite another Pennsylvania bank, prior to 1837 depended for its prosperity more or less on an investment in Schuylkill Navigation stock and its appreciation. In 1843 it owned Union Canal, Chesapeake and Delaware Canal, and Susquehanna and Tidewater Canal bonds; (Burnham, op. cit., 24).

198. We learn from a contemporary pamphlet that in the late 1820's a bill was before the state legislature according to which all banks chartered in New York thereafter were to be compelled to loan three-fourths of their capital to manufacturing enterprises. This bill might have resulted in large security holdings of banks if it had been passed. See Examination of some Provisions, 9, 10.

199. Kirkland, op. cit., 52.

200. Ibid., 78.

201. U.S. 30th Congr. 1st sess., House Executive Document 7, 7, 118. In 1839 the Connecticut Bank Commissioners reported various banks as holding Farmington Canal and Northampton Company stock, Connecticut River Company stock, and Norwich and Worcester Railroad stock, respectively. Report to the Assembly, May session, 1839, House of Representatives, Document 7, 7. As late as 1860 Connecticut banks had invested in government, state, and other stock; Connecticut Bank Commissioners, Report (1860), 12.

202. Regarding the contemporaneous investment policy of Southern banks, nothing has come to the attention of the author.

203. See pages 50 and 250 (footnote 56).

204. As late as 1818, the New York Act to improve the funds and to provide for the redemption of the funded debt of this state (passed Apr. 21, 1818) authorizing the banks to subscribe to a Canal loan, also authorized them from time to time to sell and dispose of any stock (sec V). State of New York, Laws in relation to the Erie... Canals, I, 389 ff.

205. The table is adapted from one in the Annual Report of the Comptroller of the State of New York to the Legislature, Jan 3, 1838 (Albany, 1839), 89. As to Georgia see Report of the Commissioners appointed by Authority of the

Legislature on the subject of the State Finances (Milledgeville, 1839), appended documents, 54.

206. Gouge, Texas, 42, 50, 273; Hidy, Barings, 70.

207. Porter, Astor, 996, 997, 1014; Niles Register, XXIII (1822/23), 96.

208. Page 47.

209. Kirkland, op. cit., I, 177, 252, 328.

210. A pamphlet of 1832 by Richard Ronaldson (op. cit., 8) shows that public opinion saw some connection between banks and internal improvements.

211. As to Maryland, see Bryan, op. cit., 47; as to Connecticut and Rhode Island, see Kirkland, op. cit., 74, 82; as to Kentucky, see Griffith, op. cit., 180; for Georgia, see State of Georgia, Report of the Commissioners appointed by the Authority of the Legislature on the Subject of the State Finances (Milledgeville, 1839), appended documents, 59; for Mississippi, see Brough, "Banking in Mississippi," 325, 326; for Texas, see Gouge, Texas, 66. See also the remarks of Bray Hammond, "Long and Short Term Credit," 86.

211a. See Vol. I, pages 226, 227.

212. Davis, Essays, I, 274, 283, 284, 287.

213. See this chapter, footnote 96.

214. Research on Yates and McIntyre is being conducted in the Research Center in Entrepreneurial History by Hugh Aitken and Irene Neu.

215. Turnbull, Archibald D., John Stevens: An American Record (New York, 1928), 112.

216. Martin, op. cit., passim; Larson, "S. and M. Allen," passim; State of New York, Laws in relation to the Erie and Champlain Canals, I, 328, 329.

217. Bayley, op. cit., 62, 63; Finance Report of 1821 in Reports of the Secretary of the Treasury, II (1815-1828), 214. The following is based on Correspondence and Documents, passim.

218. Charles King (1789-1867), the second son of Rufus King, educated in the counting house of Hope and Company, Amsterdam, was at that time the partner of Archibald Gracie, New York.

219. See this volume, pp 347, 365 and footnote 112 of this chapter.

220. Bayley, op. cit., 62; Holdsworth-Dewey, op. cit., 211; Cheves' own comments on these transactions in the "Exposition" of 1822 (see Goddard, op. cit., 126) are hazy, perhaps intentionally misleading.

221. See vol. I of this work, page 50.

222. Public Documents relating to the New York Canals which are to connect the Western and Northern Lakes with the Atlantic Ocean with an Introduction (New York, 1821), 240, 242 ff; Bosch, op. cit., 30.

223. See vol. I of this work, page 226; Domett, op. cit., 73, 74; New York Canal Fund Commissioners, Report, dated Jan. 17, 1842, Assembly Doc. 18 (64th session), page 21.

224. Garnett, op. cit., 30.

225. Boyd, op. cit., passim; Hidy, Barings, 71.

226. Mayer and East, op. cit., passim.

227. Bank of New York, Minutes of the Board of Directors, Mar. 18, 1836.

228. Page 8.

229. Niles Register, XXIII (1822/23), 290; Porter, Astor, 996.

230. New York Canal Fund Commissioners, Report dated January 7, 1835, Assembly Doc. 4 (58th sess.), 24.

231. Watts Sherman to Erastus Corning July 29 and Aug. 11, 1835; G. Hawley to the same, July 9, 1836; Erastus Corning Papers, from Miss Neu's material, by permission.

232. Myers, Margaret, op. cit., 24, 26; Domett, op. cit., 73, 74.

233. Hidy, Barings, 198.

234. Jenks, William, op. cit., 578; McGrane, Bondholders, 107, 144; Scoville, op. cit., I, 389; Dict. of Am. Biogr.

235. New York Assembly Doc. 15, 64th session (1842), 25, 26.

236. Bank of New York, Minutes of the Board of Directors, Apr. 27, 1837; New York Canal Fund Commissioners, Report, dated Jan. 4, 1858, Assembly Doc. 5 (61st session), 16, 17.

237. Ibid., 18; Bank of New York, Minutes of the Board of Directors, Sept. 14 and Oct. 31, 1837.
    Incidentally, the Bank of New York consigned this stock and some acquired in 1839 to Morrison, Cryder and Company and Frederic Huth and Company of London; see ibid., Jan 22, 1839 and Feb. 2, 1840. The block of $160,000 worth of bonds contracted by the National Bank were consigned to the Barings, as Hidy has shown; Barings, 161.

238. New York, Senate Journal (1838), 416 ff, especially 421; New York, Assembly Doc. 15, 64th session (1842), 27, 28.

239. New York Canal Fund Commissioners, Report, dated Feb. 3, 1840, Assembly Doc. 74 (63d sess.), 36, 37, 38; Hidy, Barings, 282; Hunt, op. cit., I, 201 mentions the flotations.
    The $1,000,000 Massachusetts state securities ("scrip") floated in 1837 for the benefit of the Western Railroad as well as the $2,100,000 state bonds of 1838 and the $1,200,000 of 1839 transferred to the same road served the identical function of defending the specie of the Massachusetts banking system, although not intentionally. See Western Railroad, Proceedings (Nov. 23, 1837), 8ff; (Jan. 27, 1841), 9, 10; Kirkland, op. cit., I, 130 ff.

240. From the material surviving in the Erastus Corning papers, as gleaned by Miss Neu, it appears highly probable that the Albany banks too, by way of private negotiation, took on joint account New York state stock in 1839 or 1840. Erastus Corning, then president of the Albany City Bank, in November, 1840, embarked for Europe in order to sell $150,000 worth of

securities out of the bank's share of $250,000 in what had been subscribed by the presumably allied Albany banks. The correspondence between Watts Sherman, the cashier of the bank, and its president shows how stock was taken to Europe: "The proper way to prepare such of the stock as you take out," so the cashier writes to the embarking president, "is to place it in my name as cashier of the Albany City Bank or individually, in certificates of $5000... & give power of Atty with cash certificate in blank, you taking the certificates & sending the power of atty by another packet to your address." When Corning left, Palmer, McKillop, Dent and Company were already selling for account of the allied banks $250,000 worth of the securities and had disposed of $20,000 or $25,000 at 92 although the limit, at least originally, had been 93.

When Corning arrived in England he left on commission $35,000 of the stock with the Barings who authorized the Albany City Bank to draw at the rate of 80 per cent of the face value and in addition he succeeded in disposing of $65,000 worth of bonds. Nothing is known as to the rest, but it is certain that the transaction was in the end unprofitable.

In order to make good this loss, one of the directors of the bank in 1842 suggested to the president that the bank take some of the then pending issue of New York State stock, which he expected to rise, especially with the view that some of it could become the basis of circulation. (Incidentally, the Albany City Bank also tried to sell some New York State stock through the Merchants Bank of New York. Possibly it was a subcontractor of the Merchants Bank in connection with an earlier issue.)

Watts Sherman to Erastus Corning, Nov. 12, 1840 and Feb. 26, 1841; J.V.L. Pruyn to Corning, May 7, 1842; (from Miss Neu's material, by permission).

241. U.S. 22d Congr. 1st sess., House Report 460, 136; Hidy, Barings, 96. The participation of the president of the Girard Bank in a contract for the Mississippi bonds of 1833 might indicate interest by that bank in loan contracting.

242. Bank of North America, Minutes of the Board of Directors, Apr. 18, 22; May 6, 13, 16, 1838.

243. Ibid., Feb. 4 and 6, 1840.

244. Ibid., Jan. 18, 1840.

245. Gouge, Texas, 81, 95; Jenks, William, op. cit., 583; Hidy, Barings, 274; U.S. 26th Congr. 2d sess., Executive Document 111, 535.

246. State of New York, Laws... in relation to the Erie... Canals, I, 389 ff.

247. New York Canal Fund Commissioners, Report dated Jan. 18, 1842, Assembly Doc. 18, (65th sess.), 21; dated Feb. 3, 1840, ibid. 74, (63d sess.), 38, 39.

248. Incidentally, it is against this background that one must look at the clash between the Associated Banks of New York, Boston, and Philadelphia and the Secretary of the Treasury in 1861, which has been described in chapter XV of this volume. The banks then tried to make the Secretary adopt the above policy developed in New York and traditional there, although it was not in line with federal procedure and was sanctioned on this level only by a recent law. That is to say, the old New York policy established in 1817 was to be adopted in 1861 nationally so as to determine the privileges of commercial banks acting as investment bankers under agreements of that year. The unwillingness of the Secretary to go beyond established national tradition, led to the clash.

The question of whether or not the investment banker should be allowed to profit from the deposit of the proceeds of loans which he floated troubled statesmen and bankers again in 1872. Boutwell, then Secretary of the Treasury, had permitted Jay Cooke and Company, leaders of the syndicate of 1871, to keep the proceeds of its bond sales for three months without interest. Consequently, he was accused of having allowed a compensation exceeding the maximum set by the refunding act; but the Ways and Means Committee and the House of Representatives upheld him. (See Larson, Cooke, 360.)

249. McGrane, Bondholders, 194, 228; Hidy, Barings, 134, 135.

250. See this volume, pages 67 ff.

251. Bankers Magazine, XVIII (1863/64), 91; New York Canal Fund Commissioners, Report, dated Jan. 7, 1835, Assembly Doc. 4 (58th sess.), 24; ibid., dated Jan. 4, 1838, Assembly Doc. 4 (61st sess.), 15; ibid., dated Jan. 3, 1839, Assembly Doc. 26 (62d sess.), 5, and dated Feb. 3, 1840, Assembly Doc. 74 (63d sess.), 36.

252. Leach, Girard National Bank, see index and especially p. 75.

253. Hidy, "Union Bank," 234 ff; Scoville, op. cit., I, 131, 391, 392; Porter, Astor, 1014; McGrane, Bondholders, 132, 144 ff. Hidy, Barings, 70, 110, 111, 149, 151, 168, 199, 260 ff.

254. U.S. 22d Congr. 1st sess., House Report 460, 136, 154, 156; Holdsworth, Empire, II, 811, 812; McGrane, Bondholders, 131; Hidy, Barings, 116, 168.

255. See this volume, pages 70, 71.

256. The Diary of Philip Hone, 1821-1857, Allan Nevins ed., I, 114; Larson, "Allen," 431 ff; Hidy, Barings, 521, footnote 12; Baroway, op. cit., 364; this chapter, footnote 259.

257. Brough, "Banking in Mississippi," 322. The firm is called in this source J. L. and S. Joseph and Company. Its ally is named Joseph D. Burs and Company. This author is sure that Brough refers actually to the Beers'.

258. Bankers Magazine, XVII (1863/1864), 90, 91;
      Hidy, "Union Bank," 238; Scoville, op. cit., I,
      16; Sakolski, op. cit., 223, 224, 243, 252;
      Larson, "Allen," 431, 432.

259. Kent, op. cit., 133, 122 (Letter of Alexander
      Brown, dated June 25, 1833). The Cohens were
      undoubtedly the same firm which in 1835 bid
      on the $500,000 Chenango Canal loan of the
      State of New York. See New York Canal Fund
      Commissioners, Report, dated Jan. 6, 1836,
      Assembly Doc. 4, (59th sess.), 21, 22. Maybe
      the Browns were back of this bid on Chenango
      Canal stock also.

          This transaction is rather interesting show-
      ing, as it does, the informal way in which the
      business was handled. The Cohens were allo-
      cated $400,000 worth of the securities while
      $100,000 were to go to one Herman Hendricks
      in New York. However, the Cohens refused
      to accept the allocation claiming their bid was
      "for all or none," as the standardized formula
      was later. Thereupon Hendricks was pre-
      vailed upon to withdraw and the whole amount
      was allocated to the Cohens. In the meantime
      the latter had discovered that their bid of 112
      had been unreasonably high and they declined.
      A letter of Watts Sherman to Erastus Corning
      of August 11, 1835 refers to the transaction.

260. Catlin, George B., "Oliver Newberry" in Mich.
      Hist. Mag. XVIII (1934), 5 ff; Jenks, William,
      op. cit., 519; McGrane, Bondholders, 146.

261. McGrane, Bondholders, 107, 113, 131, 132,
      144 ff, 198, 228, 233; Hidy, Barings, 263.

262. Margaret Myers, op. cit., 26; as to New York,
      see below, page 344.

263. Smith, James G., Trust Companies, 257.

264. Hidy, Barings, 290, 291.

265. As to the sale of American securities in the
      United States, see ibid., 197, 199, 265, 283; as
      to the Rothschilds, ibid., 195, 197.

266. McGrane, Bondholders, 294, 251, 252; Jenks,
      William, op. cit., 574, 607.

267. Hidy, Barings, 167, 168, 170, 172, 528 (foot-
      note 39), 200, 283, 289, 290.

268. "First hand" is intended to connote such enter-
      prises as received state bonds in aid; as to
      such transactions, Hidy, Barings, 261, 281.

269. McGrane, Bondholders, 89, 106, 107, 113, 171;
      Hidy, "Union Bank," passim; Gouge, Texas,
      107; Myers, Margaret, op. cit., 25; Scoville,
      op. cit., III, 258.

270. Larson, Cooke, 89; for other late cases see
      below, page 349 and Oberholtzer, op. cit., II,
      104.

271. It is telling that Philip Hone used the term
      "contractor" for what we would call investment
      banker; see his Diary, Allen Nevins ed., I, 114.

272. Hidy, "Union Bank," 236; McGrane, Bond-
      holders, 174, 252.

273. A hybrid between contracting and "negotiating"
      of securities was the contract of 1838 between
      Michigan and the Morris Canal and Banking
      Company. The latter sold Michigan bonds as
      the state's agent for 2½ per cent commission,
      but at the same time guaranteed the sale at
      par and payment according to a certain schedule;
      ibid., 146, 147.

274. See the author's "Jacques Laffitte and the Be-
      ginnings of Investment Banking in France" in
      Bulletin of the Business Historical Society,
      XXII (1948), 153 ff.

275. Biddle Letterbooks, Jan. 12, 1827.

276. Ibid., Feb. 19, 1827 to Hon. N. Silsbee.

277. Ibid., Aug. 17 and 25, 1827, Feb. 6, 1829, to
      Nathaniel Prime; also Dec. 31, 1829 to P. P. F.
      Degrand.

278. Ibid., Aug. 12, 1828 to R. L. Colt.

279. Ibid., Sept. 2, 1830 to Richard Smith.

280. Ibid., May 25, 1830 to Stephen Duncan, Natchez.

281. Ibid., May 13, 1830 to L. W. Tazewell.

282. Ibid., Sept. 7, 1830 to Samuel Jaudon.

283. Ibid., Nov. 3, 1830 and Feb. 16, 1831 to Samuel
      Jaudon, then cashier of the New Orleans office
      of the Bank.

284. Ibid., Feb. 29, 1832; Hidy, Barings, 116.

285. McGrane, Bondholders, 224, 225.

286. Biddle Letterbooks, July 30, 1832 to Thomas
      Wren Ward; Nov. 9, 1833 to James Neilson;
      July 20, 1834 to P. E. Thomas.

287. Ibid., June 24, 1830 to George Poe; Sept. 7,
      1830 to Samuel Jaudon.

288. Ibid., Feb. 23, 1831 to P. Bensen, Cincinnati;
      Hidy, Barings, 151, 152.

289. Pennsylvania Laws, 1835/36, No. 22, approved
      Feb. 18, 1836.

290. Biddle Letterbooks., Mar. 26 to Thaddeus
      Stevens; Mar. 29, 1836 to C. B. Penrose.

291. Pennsylvania Laws, 1835-1836, No. 138, ap-
      proved Apr. 1, 1836.

292. Nov. 15, 1837 to R. Niles, Vienna (Jaudon's
      mission to London was not meant to interfere
      with the business of the Rothschilds); Jan. 29,
      1838 to John Sergeant (Bank of the United
      States was disposed to encourage the friendly
      disposition of the Rothschilds); Mar. 16, 1838
      to J. Hamilton (the Rothschilds are recom-
      mended as possible sellers of Texas bonds);
      Aug. 27, 1838 to August Belmont; Sept. 22,
      1838 to Joseph Cowperswait (the letter indi-
      cates close cooperation with August Belmont).

293. Ibid., Aug. 15, 1836 to Joseph Paxton; Aug.
      31, 1838 to S. Jaudon; Sept. 29, 1838 to C. A.
      Davis; McGrane, Bondholders, 197; Report of
      the Committee of Investigation, 55; Bankers
      Magazine, I (1846/1847), 338.

294. Hidy, "Union Bank," 236; idem, Barings, 153.
      In general the commission for "negotiations"
      seems to have varied with the urgency of the
      borrower's need and the difficulties involved.
      The commission required by the Morris Canal
      and Banking Company in 1838 for selling Mich-
      igan bonds was 2½ per cent (Jenks, William,
      op. cit. 582).

295. **Biddle Letterbooks**, Oct. 5, 1837 to Lewis Rogers; Dec. 5, 1837 to P. P. F. Degrand; May 7, 1838 to Richard Anderson; June 5, 1838 to James M. Porter.

296. _Ibid._, Mar. 8, 1838 to George Poe; May 7, 1838 to Richard Anderson; June 6, 1838 to Jacob Barker.

297. Report of the Committee of Investigation, 11, 14.

298. Hidy, "Union Bank," 236. It is noteworthy that in Scotland a special kind of bank was developed by that time to lend on securities, the so-called Exchange Banks or Exchange Companies. American bankers were informed about this type of enterprise in the Bankers Magazine, VI (1851/52), 207 ff.

299. A case illustrating the essential point is the Michigan loan transaction, although originally it did not concern the Bank of the United States of Pennsylvania itself but its "tender," the Morris Canal and Banking Company. In January, 1838, the Governor of Michigan entrusted the Phoenix Bank of New York with the "negotiation" of $1,000,000 of her bonds and slightly later was authorized by it to draw an amount up to several hundred thousand dollars. But the bonds proved unsaleable and were returned from Europe. Unable to refund the advances the state was forced to make the ill-fated contract with the Morris Canal and Banking Company which was later transferred in part to the Bank of the United States of Pennsylvania. See Jenks, William, op. cit., 579-581.

300. **Biddle Letterbooks,** June 15, 1838 to Don A. Calderon.

301. Report of the Committee of Investigation, 26 ff, 54 ff.

302. **Biddle Letterbooks**, Oct. 3, 1838 to F. W. Gilmer; Jan. 23 and Mar. 16, 1838 to James Hamilton; Sept. 6, 1838 to Daniel Webster. Arkansas and Alabama loans were offered to Biddle also, see Oct. 3, 1837 to S. B. Carson; Aug. 24, 1838 to Commissioners of the State of Arkansas; June 7, and June 9, 1838 to William R. King and F. L. Lyon; Oct. 9, 1838 to J. J. Palmer.

303. Biddle was also interested in bonds of Cairo and Savannah; see _ibid._, Oct. 16, 1838 to C. W. Anderson; Jan. 3, 1839 to E. R. Biddle.

304. _Ibid._, W. H. Seward to Nicholas Biddle, Jan. 17, 1838.

305. Report of the Committee of Investigation, 40.

306. **Biddle Letterbooks**, Mar. 26, 1836 to T. G. McCulloch; Aug. 31, 1838 to Samuel Jaudon.

307. Report of the Committee of Investigation, 54 ff; Hidy, Barings, 545, footnote 11.

308. Jones, Chester L., op. cit., 111 ff; Jenks, William, op. cit., 581 ff; Myers, Margaret, op. cit., 26-28; McGrane, Bondholders, 131, 146 ff; Report of the Committee of Investigation, 28; Biddle Letterbooks, Nov. 6, 1838, Jan 16, and

18, 1839, Feb. 24, and Mar. 9, 1840 to E. R. Biddle; May 2, 1839 to Roswell L. Colt. The correspondence between the two Biddles in 1838 and 1839 is full of proposals regarding the exchange of securities. They seem to have been significant, for Hidy has found that the Barings also practiced such transactions to keep their portfolio moving; "Union Bank," 249, Barings, 169, 528 (footnote 39).

309. The information is derived from various court documents to be found in the Baker Library of Harvard University under K.D.X., L. 439; the item is mentioned in Larson, Guide as no. 675. See especially, the first document of the collection, 11, 23, 26, 37-39, 41, 42, 61. The table is on pages 38,39. Some data on the enterprise can be found in Perine, op. cit., 69, 74, 76-78 and in Smith, James G., op. cit., 275.

310. To give examples, in 1850 Ohio banks took a considerable slice of a loan of that state and in 1852 a whole Virginia loan was bought "for the use of one of the Chicago banks;" Bankers Magazine, V (1850/51), 83; VII (1852/53), 83.

311. New York Canal Fund Commissioners, Report dated Feb. 3, 1840, Assembly Doc. 74, (63d sess.), 36.

312. Hidy, "Union Bank," 238, 239; idem, "Leaf from Investment History," 68.

313. Bankers Magazine (VII [1852/53], 752) reports the introduction at the New York stock exchange of coal company stock; _ibid._, 83 mentions flotations of manufacturing corporations.

314. _Ibid._, VIII (1853/54), 91.

315. Volume I (1846/47), 659.

316. See page 325 of this volume.

317. Reports of the Secretary of the Treasury, IV (1837-1844), 629; VI (1846-1849), 162 ff, 215 ff, 325 ff.

318. XIII (1858/59), 15.

319. Oberholtzer, op. cit., I, 127, 128.

320. Laws of the State of New York in relation to the Erie and Champlain Canals..., I, 389 ff.

321. New York Canal Fund Commissioners, Reports (1835), 24; (1836), 21, 22; (1837), 19; (1838), 16, 17; (1840), 36 ff; (1843), 12. Bankers Magazine, IV (1849/50), 82; VII (1852/53), 752, 926; IX (1854/55), 319; X (1855/56), 64 ff; XIII (1858/59), 10.

The Massachusetts act of 1837 (chapter 172) contemplated in sec. 2 the sale of $1,000,000 state securities by public auction or otherwise. How the issue was actually sold is unknown to the author. But in December, 1842, the Western Railroad sold £100,000 state bonds authorized in its favor and transferred to it, "called" $480,000, at auction at an average rate of 84¾; see Martin, Century of Finance, 177.

322. Bankers Magazine, VII (1852/53), 927.

323. _Ibid._, V (1850/51), 83; XI (1856/57), 416.

324. _Ibid._, VIII (1853/54), 90, 91.

325. _Ibid._, VIII (1853/54), 843; IX (1854/55), 406.

326. *Ibid.*, IX (1854/55), 919.
327. See, for instance, the list of subscribers to the Mexican War loans of 1847 and 1848, Reports of the Secretary of the Treasury, VI (1846-1849), 215 ff, 325 ff.
328. Bankers Magazine, VII (1852/53), 927; X (1855/56), 64 ff.
329. *Ibid.*, V (1850/51), 83; VII (1852/53), 927.
330. *Ibid.*, XI (1856/57), 416; VII (1852/53), 335.
331. For an early case of this type in which the borrower tried to straighten out the situation by negotiations and in which the loan miscarried in consequence, see New York Canal Fund Commissioners, Report (1836), 59th sess., Assembly Doc. 4, 21, 22.
332. Finance Report, 1843 in Reports of the Secretary of the Treasury, IV (1837-1844), 629. The distribution of the Pennsylvania loan of 1861 still followed the same, by that time traditional, pattern; see Larson, Cooke, 107.
333. Scoville, op. cit., II, 167; Bankers Magazine XLV (1890/91), 990.
334. Scoville, op. cit., II, 296; III, 322.
335. See, for instance, Finance Reports, 1843, 1847, 1848; Bankers Magazine, X (1855/56), 64 ff; XIII (1858/59), 15, 16, 224.
336. *Ibid.*, XIII (1858/59), 223, 224. But in the case of the Bowery Savings Bank's several bids on the federal loan of 1860 totaling $600,000, the latter is probable, each bid for $100,000 being exactly 0.25 or 0.1 per cent higher than the next lower one; Finance Report (1860), 483.
337. See this chapter, page 309.

Occasionally state and federal agencies interfered with investment banking activities. In New York, for instance, in the 1830's the Canal Fund Commissioners currently accumulated large funds, but were unable to buy up canal stock because of its unreasonably high price and because the owners would not part with it before the due date. The canal commissioners therefore lent the accumulating funds to banks on interest or invested them in other New York state stock which was thereby kept out of the hands of investment bankers and the public, or lent them to the State Treasury on application of the Comptroller. This policy was contemplated as early as 1825; (8th Report of the Canal Fund Commissioners, State of New York, Laws... relating to the Erie and Champlain Canals, II, 294). Moreover in 1838 the Canal Fund Commissioners lent about $1,600,000 to the state treasury, and for many years they held City of Albany bonds. The Reports of the Canal Fund Commissioners from 1831 on are full of information on this matter. See, for instance, Report dated Jan. 2, 1833, Assembly Doc. 4, (56th sess.), 1, 2, 14, 19 ff; Report dated Jan. 3, 1839, Assembly Doc. 26, (62d sess.), 5; dated Feb. 3, 1840, Assembly Doc. 74, (63d sess.), 20, 21; dated Jan. 6, 1841,

Assembly Doc. 5, (64th sess.), 10; also dated Feb. 2, 1831, Assembly Doc. 102, (54th sess.), 1.

In 1839 the Commissioners of the New York School Fund took $20,000 Chemung Canal bonds and the Bank Fund, $25,000; New York Canal Fund Commissioners, Report, dated Feb. 3, 1840, Assembly Doc. 74, (63d sess.), 41.

In 1853 an issue of $500,000 6 per cent North Carolina bonds was taken by Alabama Commissioners as an investment for the funds of the defunct State Bank held in trust as a sinking fund for the debts of the state; Bankers Magazine, VIII (1853/54), 443.

Federal agencies appeared as bidders on the federal loan of 1843; see the list of subscribers to this loan, above page 345.

338. From Muriel Hidy's material, by permission.
339. It is not clear who this John Ward was; possibly the New York broker above mentioned, but Muriel Hidy suspects that he was the brother of Samuel Ward, the deceased partner of Prime, Ward and King.
340. In 1848 Winslow and Perkins bid successfully for $50,000 and unsuccessfully for $1,600,000 of the war bonds of that year. The name of M. Morgan can be found as that of a large buyer of treasury notes in 1847.
341. Reports of the Secretary of the Treasury of the United States, VI (1846-1849), 134, 162 ff, 215 ff, 224. See also Bayley, op. cit., 70 ff.
342. The loan was payable in five installments. No bid was accepted unless one per cent of the offered amount was deposited in advance. The lowest bid to be accepted was $50. See Reports of the Secretary of the Treasury, VI (1846-1848), 336, 337.
343. Hidy, "Investment History," 68-71; Bankers Magazine, IV (1849/50), 251.
344. See, for instance, Bankers Magazine, IX (1855/56), 920; Pearson, op. cit., 62-64.
345. The preceding is to a certain extent based on information received from Alfred Chandler whose research can be expected to throw much new light on early railroad finance. Examples of auctions of new issues are in the American Railroad Journal, XXV (1852), 269, 798. In ibid., XXIII (1850), 695 an advertisement of Winslow, Lanier and Company can be found which shows the introduction by this firm into the railroad practice of the way of bidding usual for government securities.
346. Bankers Magazine, VII (1852/53), 752; V (1850/51), 515, 516; XII (1857/58), 592.
347. Bankers Magazine XI (1856/57), 78; VII (1852/53), 1019. The agent was R. Hallett, formerly president of the Bank of Mobile.
348. Burpee, op. cit., 55, 60.
349. Pease, Merchants National Bank, 32.
350. Dict. Am. Biogr.; Larson, Cooke, 42, 99.

351. Thomas W. Olcott (1796-1880) rose in the Mechanics and Farmers Bank of Albany whose cashier he was in the 1820's. This bank was considered by contemporaries as identified more or less with Van Buren's interests. The then Governor regarded Olcott highly and the latter is supposed to have approved the Safety Fund idea at an early moment and to have co-operated on the draft of the bill.

Olcott can be found as an ally of Prime, Ward and King in acquiring about $525,000 worth of the Chemung Canal bonds of 1837. Later he was a bidder on a New York loan of 1854, on the New York and Harlem Railroad bonds of the same year, and on a New York canal loan of 1855. In the last mentioned case he was unsuccessful with two bids for $410,000 and $1,000,000 worth of the securities; (in addition the name of J. J. Olcott can be found as that of a bidder on another canal loan of the same year). See Bankers Magazine XXXIV (1879/80), 820 containing a death notice and ibid., IX (1854/55), 319; X (1855/56), 65, 66; New York Canal Fund Commissioners, Report dated Jan. 4, 1838 Assembly Doc. 5 (61st sess.), 15; Starr, op. cit., 7.

352. Bankers Magazine, XIII (1858/59), 15, 224. As to an early transaction of the Bank of Commerce, see this volume, page 344.

353. The bank appeared as a bidder on the federal loan of 1843 with $500,000; in 1847 it bid $100,000 on the Mexican War loan of that year. As late as 1858 we find it as a bidder on $200,000 United States treasury notes of which $112,500 were awarded to it; while in the fall of that year it was awarded $59,000 United States bonds on two bids. See Bankers Magazine, XIII (1858/59), 15, 16, 224.

The Bank of the Metropolis was at that time neither fish nor fowl. Its charter not having been renewed in 1844 at its expiration, the bank was run by a board of trustees, headed by John P. Van Ness. It was reorganized as a National Bank in 1865. See Washington, Past and Present, John Claggett Proctor, ed. (New York, 1930), I, 297.

354. Reports of the Secretary of the Treasury, VI (1846-1849), 162 ff, 216. Bankers Magazine, IV (1849/50), 332; VIII (1853/54), 843; X (1855/56), 64; XIII (1858/59), 16; Finance Report (1860), 481; Paine, Baker, 55.

355. Reynolds, Cuyler, Genealogical and Family History of Southern New York and the Hudson River Valley (New York, 1914), III, 1017 ff. (The author is indebted to the New York State Library for this reference.)

356. Bankers Magazine, IV (1849/50), 332; VI (1851/52), 1018; VII (1852/53), 927; IX (1854/55), 319; X (1855/56), 64, 65, 66; Finance Report (1860), 481.

357. Larson, "E. W. Clark & Co." passim, and her Cooke, 26 ff, 69; Holdsworth, Empire, II, 624.

358. Larson, Cooke, 73-74, 81. In view of the previously mentioned activities as land speculators of several of the embryonic investment bankers of the 1830's, it is noteworthy that the Clarks engaged in land speculation also; ibid., 75.

359. Bankers Magazine, XIII (1858/59), 16, 225.

By the end of the 1850's the then famous firm of Howland and Aspinwall, at that time a brokerage and banking house rather than a trading concern, dabbled in investment banking. They appeared as bidders on the federal bonds of 1858, tendering five different bids totaling $450,000; ibid., 224.

360. Hidy, "Investment History," 68, 71, 73; Bankers Magazine, V (1850/51), 83; VII (1852/53), 167; Hunt, op. cit., I, 201.

361. Hidy, "Investment History," 69.

362. The following is based on Muriel Hidy's material, by permission.

363. It was well within tradition that an original loan contractor should spread his risk by making subcontracts with alliances of firms, himself becoming one of the allies.

364. Bankers Magazine, VI (1851/52), 423. The following circular letter of May 13, 1851 of the newly founded firm of Duncan, Sherman and Company has survived in the Erastus Corning papers. It is reprinted in full, because it gives a good idea of the business of contemporary New York private bankers of the type that was active in investment banking: "The undersigned have the honor to inform you that they have entered into Association as private bankers in the City of New York under the name and style of Duncan, Sherman & Co., and will open an office of discount, deposit, and general Banking business, on the first day of October next. They will act as Agents for country and distant Banks and for individuals. Also for States, Cities, Railroad and other companies, in paying interest or dividends, registry of transfers, etc. Will deal in Foreign and Domestic Exchange and be prepared to arrange credits and furnish circular notes and letters for travellers, available in the principal cities of Europe, the United States, and Canada. They will also effect purchases and sales in all Government and other stocks and securities of the United States." (Signed Alexander Duncan, Watts Sherman, William Butler Duncan.) From Miss Neu's material, by permission.

365. From Miss Neu's material, culled from the Corning papers, by permission; see her thesis, pages 126 ff. Information kindly provided by the New York State Library, based on Weeks, L. H., Prominent Families of New York (1898), 506; see also Hall, Henry, America's Successful Men of Affairs (New York, 1895), I, 594.

366. Belmont's original name seems to be unknown. The author suspects it was Schoenberg, a German-Jewish name whose correct translation would be Belmont.

367. Scoville, op. cit., II, 196.

368. Bankers Magazine, IV (1849/50), 82; V (1850/51), 83; XIII (1858/59), 15.

369. Bank of the United States of Pennsylvania, Report of the Committee of Investigation, 29 ff.

370. Op. cit., passim. As Professor Evans told the author recently, there may have been a few earlier issues of preferred stocks than those mentioned in his paper.

371. The road was later renamed South Carolina Railroad.

372. The issuers were the Little Schuylkill Navigation, Railroad and Coal Company, the Raleigh and Gaston, the New Orleans and Nashville, the Lexington and Ohio, and the Philadelphia, Wilmington and Baltimore Railroads. The Hartford and New Haven was at one time planning to contact Biddle regarding the sale of its bonds.

373. Kirkland, op. cit., I, 326 ff; for specific cases, see ibid., 112, 126, 127, 175, 202; Martin, Century of Finance, 163.

374. Pearson, op. cit., 28, 29, 75, 76, 87.

375. To a certain extent these firms themselves tendered bids on securities too. This is especially true of Camman and Whitehouse who appeared as bidders on the Mexican War loans of 1847 and 1848, on a $50,000 New York Canal loan of 1849 and an Ohio state loan of 1850. In 1849 they also bid for Chattanooga and Nashville Railroad bonds. In the 1850's we meet a firm, Camman and Company, presumably successors of the above firm. It secured the North Carolina bonds of 1853 and bid on the New York Canal loan of 1855, acquiring $50,000 worth of the securities. A second bid of $600,000 and one on $200,000 of another tranche were lost. In 1858 the firm offered $750,000 on the $20,000,000 federal loan. A firm E. Whitehouse, Son and Morrison, which we meet in the same period may have descended from Camman and Whitehouse also. It bid $100,000 on a New York state loan of 1858; in the same year it went heavily into the $20,000,000 federal bonds of which it secured $450,000 and in 1860 it bid $100,000 on the $10,000,000 of October. See Bankers Magazine, IV (1849/50), 251, 332; V (1850/51), 83; VII (1852/53), 927; X (1855/56), 64-66; XIII (1858/59), 10, 224; Reports of the Secretary of the Treasury, VI (1846-1849), 216, 326; Finance Report (1860), 482.

376. Lanier, Sketch (1871 edition), passim, especially 10-12, 15, 17ff, 24 ff, 56, 38, 39.

377. Larson, Cooke, 89, 91, 92.

378. Vührer, op. cit., II, 173, 244, 245, 282, 284, 285, 289, 293. (The figures for the flotations of the 1850's given below refer to capital values.)

379. Corti, Blüte, 309.

380. Larson, Cooke, 121.

381. Ibid., 96, 101, 103, 104.

382. Ibid., 106, 107.

383. See this volume, chapter XV.

384. Oberholtzer, op. cit., I, 150; Larson, Cooke, 111, 114, 117 ff.

385. Ibid., 120-132; Oberholtzer, op. cit., I, 234 ff. Intensive research on Confederate war finance would be desirable, our knowledge being very limited. As to the flotation of war loans, there were distinct differences: while in the North all Civil War loans were domestic loans and it was left to private enterprise to export the securities, thereby importing capital for the prosecution of the war, the Confederacy went directly to the European capital markets. There was floated in 1863 at 90 per cent of par the 7 per cent £ 3,000,000 cotton loan. The securities were convertible into cotton, the French tranche, for example, at the rate of 54 centimes per (English) lb. while the price for cotton was at that moment 2.20 francs. Under these circumstances subscribing to the loan amounted to a term speculation in cotton. The Cotton Loan was floated by J. Henry Schroeder and Company of London and Emile Erlanger and Company of Paris. It was five times oversubscribed. In the same year there was issued in Europe an 8 per cent loan authorized by the Act of February 2,1863. See Bosch, op. cit. 132 ff.

386. Oberholtzer, op. cit., I, 478 ff.

387. Ibid., I, 195, 196, 459, 505.

388. Larson, Cooke, 174, 175.

389. Cooke himself used the term; see Oberholtzer, op. cit., I, 161.

390. Larson, Cooke, 105, 216-218, 223, 245, 247, 314, 315, 325.

391. See my article "Jacques Laffitte," 143-145.

392. Hidy, "Investment History," 72, 73.

393. Cope, thesis, 66, 67, 173, 376.

394. Bosch, op. cit., 36.

395. Bank of North America, Minutes of the Board of Directors, Dec. 5, 1814, Apr. 12, 1815; for the last mentioned transaction see this chapter, footnote 187.

396. Hidy, Barings, 168.

397. Bank of New York, Minutes of the Board of Directors, Apr. 27, 1837.

398. Larson, Cooke, 95.

399. Larson, Cooke, 111.

400. Finance Report (1861), 8.

401. Larson, Cooke, 173.

402. Ibid., 223, 245, 247, 250, 251.

403. Ibid., 252.

404. Ibid., 315.

405. Ibid., 315-317.

406. See below, page 366.

407. Larson, Cooke, Introd., xiii.

408. See the author's essay on "Jacques Laffitte," 154.

409. Larson, Cooke, 245, 248, 257, 260, 276; Fisk, op. cit., 712, 713.

410. Larson, Cooke, 277.

411. Ibid., 349, 373, 374.

412. In order to avoid misunderstandings, it is pointed out that there were three brothers Vermilye, sons of the printer, William W., active in New York banking during the nineteenth century. See Riker, James, Harlem (City of New York): Its Origin and Early Annals... (New York, 1881), 550.

The oldest of them appears as the secretary of the temporary Association of the New York banks of 1837; see Gallatin's Writings, III, 471, 480. The name is given there as W. H., but the author thinks this is an error and that it was actually William Montgomery Vermilye (1801-1878). He is also mentioned in Oberholtzer, op. cit., I, 298.

The next was Washington Romeyn Vermilye, the private banker. About him, see Larson, Cooke, Index; Oberholtzer, op. cit., Index, especially I, 347, II, 11, 19; Cycl. Am. Biogr., XIV, 455.

Younger still was Jacob D. Vermilye (1817-1892). He rose in New York commercial banking and was connected with various banks until in 1858 he became the cashier and in 1868 the president of the Merchants Bank of New York. He was for several years chairman of the Executive Committee of the New York Clearing House Association and in 1872 and 1873 its president. As a director he was connected with some twenty banks and insurance companies; see Hubert, op. cit., 154, 155, 167.

413. See article, "Clews" in Dict. Am. Biogr.; Larson, Cooke, 124, 257, 309, 323, 409; Oberholtzer, op. cit., see Index; Finance Report (1860), 482, 483. Numerous advertisements of Henry Clews can be found in the Commercial and Financial Chronicle, for example in vol. X (1870). The statement in the Dict. Am. Biogr. that the firm name was changed in 1877 is erroneous.

414. Cyclop. Am. Biogr., XI, 261; XIV, 525; Fisk, op. cit., passim.

415. Ibid., 712 ff; Larson, Cooke, 248; 257, 322, 409. The Commercial and Financial Chronicle (XIII [1870], 237) contains in the text a disguised advertisement of the firm for Chesapeake and Ohio bonds. It belongs to the genus which the French called at that time "réclames," an unsound and misleading advertising method.

416. Money Trust Investigation, 2124, 2125.

417. Obituary in New York Daily Tribune, Mar. 24, 1884; Larson, Cooke, 247, 248; Oberholtzer, op. cit., I, 134, 261, 417, 418, 426, 432; II, 102; Bankers Magazine, XIII (1858/59), 15; Ketchum, op. cit., 15. Numerous letters from Chase to Cisco can be found in Chase's private letter-books. Cisco and Cooke disliked each other thoroughly: the former would not recognize Cooke as a "financier," but praised him as a "good advertiser for patent medicines;" Cooke in turn castigated Cisco's political ambitions and his overestimating his own importance. The Commercial and Financial Chronicle contains numerous advertisements of the Ciscos for Union Pacific bonds.

418. About this group, see Jenks, British Capital, 267 ff.

419. About the Seligmans, see the biographies of Joseph, Jesse, and Isaac Newton Seligman in Dict. Am. Biogr.; Larson, Cooke, 208, 217, 218.

420. Adler, Schiff, I, 11, 12.

421. Obituary of James Speyer in New York Times, Nov. 1, 1941; Money Trust Investigation 745, 1541, 1765, 2205, "Interlocking Directorates," Exhibit 134A; Who is Who in Finance (1911); Fisk (op. cit., 707) mentions cooperation of Fisk and Hatch with the Speyers. The Speyers can be found as bidders on a federal loan as early as 1860; see Finance Report (1860), 481.

422. Oberholtzer, op. cit., I, 285.

423. McElroy, op. cit., 31, 33, 36, 39, 42.

424. Brebner, John Bartlett, North Atlantic Triangle. The Interplay of Canada, the United States and Great Britain (New Haven, 1945), 188, 189. Articles in Dictionary of National Biography and Dictionary of Canadian Biography (Toronto, 1945). Breckenridge (op. cit., 229, 239 ff) described the role which John Rose played in the Canadian banking-reform movement of the late 1860's.

425. McElroy, op. cit., 55, 67.

426. Dict. of Am. Biogr.

427. Gras-Larson, op. cit., 551.

428. Bankers Magazine, IX (1854/55), 24; XIII (1858/59), 16.

429. Drexel and Company, op. cit., 39 ff; Gras-Larson, op. cit., 555.

430. Larson, Cooke, 89, 93, 95, 104, 106-109, 131, 222, 223, 245, 247, 257, 315, 319, 321; Oberholtzer, op. cit., I, 546; II, 134.

431. The spelling Reed is the correct one.

432. Bankers Magazine, XIII (1858/59), 15, 224.

433. Larson, Cooke, 178, 208 ff, 214, 218, 219. A detailed description of the flotation of Southern state bonds during the Reconstruction era would be interesting.

434. As to the basic legislation, see Dewey, Financial History (8th ed.), 352 ff, 429; also Bayley, op. cit., 93 ff. A short review of the transactions can be found in A.B.A., Proceedings (1879), 105 ff.

435. Finance Report (1871), xvii, xviii.

436. The preceding and some of the following is based on the masterful description of the transactions in Larson, Cooke, 317-27, 360, 393-96.

437. See the thin remarks in Finance Report (1873) ix, x.
438. Finance Report (1874) ix, x; Bankers Magazine, XXIX (1874/75), 180 ff.
439. Not quite clear is the role of the Morgans in the original $45,000,000 syndicate.
440. Finance Report (1875), xi, xii.
441. Ibid. (1876) xi; Bankers Magazine, XXXI (1876/77), 497, 498.
442. Finance Report (1877) viii, xi; (1878) xvii-xix; Bankers Magazine, XXXII (1877/78), 1 ff, 72, 73, 239, 841.
443. Corey, op. cit., 124.
444. Comm. and Fin. Chronicle XXVI (1878), 351, 405.
445. Bankers Magazine, XXXII (1877/78), 841; A.B.A, Proceedings (1887), 21.
446. Pages xv-xx.
447. Bankers Magazine, XXXIII (1878/79), 652.
448. Ibid., 841 ff.
449. Finance Report (1879) xv-xx; Bankers Magazine, XXXIII (1878/79), 841 ff; XXXIV (1879/80), 316.
450. Finance Report, (1879, xviii, xix) shows the result of the refunding transactions. See also, ibid., (1881) 462; (1882) viii ff.
451. The refunding transactions in the years following 1879 are of no interest in our context, see Finance Report (1880) xii; (1882), x; Refunding of National Debt. Statements before the Committee on Finance, U.S. Senate, with regard to the bill (H.R. 4592) to facilitate the refunding of the national debt [Washington, 1881]; John Jay Knox in A.B.A. Proceedings (1887), 21, 22. A refunding act was not signed by the President and without special legislation $563,000,000 in 6 and 5 per cent bonds were continued with the consent of the holders at 3½ per cent payable at the option of the government. The exchange of bonds seems to have been almost exclusively a concern of the National Banks. See Bankers Magazine, XXXVII (1882/83), 308.
452. Barnes, Carlisle, 315 ff; Finance Report (1894), xxxiv; U.S. 54th Congr. 2d sess., Senate Document 187, 5, 6, 32 ff. A list of subscribing banks culled from this source is to be found in footnote 453. These were probably also the subscribers marshalled by Stewart.
453. Finance Report (1895), xxvii; Barnes, Carlisle, 357 ff. The syndicate consisted of the United States Trust Company (John A. Stewart); Drexel, Morgan and Company; the First National Bank of New York; the Union Trust Company (Edward King); and Harvey Fisk and Sons, all of whom signed the bid; and in addition of the following: Drexel and Company, Philadelphia; J. S. Morgan and Company, London; the National Bank of Commerce; the Chase National Bank; the National City Bank; the Hanover National Bank, all of New York; the First National Bank of Chicago; the Mutual Life Insurance Company; the Gallatin National Bank; the Merchants National Bank, both of New York; the Bank of the Manhattan Company; Morton, Bliss and Company; Heidelbach, Ickelheimer and Company; I. and S. Wormser; J. and W. Seligman, and Company; Blair and Company; Vermilye and Company; F. G. Smithers and Company; Edward Sweet and Company; Kountze Brothers; Laidlaw and Company; the Bowery Savings Bank; the Knickerbocker Trust Company; the Greenwich Savings Bank; Cooper, Hewitt and Company; A. R. Eno; A. E. Orr for a Brooklyn Savings Bank; Brewster, Cobb and Estabrook, Boston; Winslow, Lanier and Company; Brooklyn Trust Company; E. Rollins, Morse and Bro., Boston; Blake Bros. and Company, Boston; Fourth National Bank, New York. See U.S. 54th Congr. 2d sess., Senate Document 187, 40, 44. A short description of the transaction is in ibid., 6, 7.
454. Commercial and Financial Chronicle, LX (1895), 325.
455. Act of March 17, 1862 (An Act to authorize the purchase of coin and for other purposes), c. 45 sec. 1, 12 Stat. 370, 31 U.S. Code Ann. sec. 734 (Money and Finance).
456. Barnes, op. cit., 371 ff; Satterlee, op. cit., 280. Allen, Morgan, 106 ff, the latest description, adds details previously unknown. But his statement regarding Morgan's profit from the transaction is unsatisfactory, since that of his London house in the European syndicate is omitted. Incidentally, this is a good example of correct, but incomplete, information which is misleading and therefore worse than no information at all. The contract can be found in Commercial and Financial Chronicle, LX (1895), 282/283. See also ibid., 205, 206, 236, 274, 322, 324, 325, 331, 332, 409 ff, 1033; Finance Report (1895), xxvii; U.S. 54th Congr. 2d sess., Senate Document 187, 7 ff, 222 ff; Morgan's own story on pages 292 ff.
457. Allen, Morgan, 124.
458. Barnes, op. cit., 392.
459. The syndicate opened subscription books in the United States on February 20, 1895. Payments were to be made in cash or certified checks to J. P. Morgan and Company. It was announced simultaneously that at least one half of the issue would be allotted to London and sold there by N. M. Rothschild and Sons and J. S. Morgan and Company. See Commercial and Financial Chronicle, LX (1895), 332.
460. U.S. 54th Congr. 1st sess., Senate Document 221, passim (this report is referred to in the Finance Report (1896), xxix); Commercial and Financial Chronicle, LXII (1896), 3, 54, 56, 68, 108, 110, 111, 117, 252, 295, 296, 303, 340, 846; Finance Report (1896), xxix; Barnes, op. cit., 410 ff.

The Bankers Magazine contains very little information on the loan transactions of 1894, 1895, and 1896; see XLVIII (1893/94), 569; L

461. (1894/95), 12 ff; LI (1895), 272 ff; LII (1896), 10, 11.

461. Commercial and Financial Chronicle LXVII (1898), 47, 92, 147; Bankers Magazine, LVII (1898), 17 ff.

462. For comparison with European business methods, see Lotz, op. cit., passim.

463. Money Trust Investigation, 2006, 2013.

464. But, of course, there is also genuine underwriting of the same character when a house or syndicate "negotiates" securities, at the same time guaranteeing the success of the flotation.

465. Money Trust Investigation. 1546.

466. Ibid. 1013, 1014. J. P. Morgan himself was a member of the finance committee of the New York Central, the organ through which in case of new security flotations that road was to negotiate with J. P. Morgan and Company.

467. As to the contracts of Kuhn, Loeb and Company "made in the first instance without any associates," see ibid., 1758, 1759. Or, to give another example, Lee, Higginson and Company contracted alone for a $8,750,000 issue of the Western Electric Company (January, 1910); ibid., 2012.

468. Money Trust Investigation, 1033, 1548, 1550, 1557, 1830. As to the joint contracts of Kuhn, Loeb and Company, see ibid., 1761-1765; but it is possible that the word "jointly" was used here in a broader sense and does not mean; "on the joint account."

469. For examples see ibid., 1717, 1737.

470. Gerstenberg, op. cit., 328; Raymond, op. cit., issue of May 31, page 20. According to the former author (op. cit., 332) underwriting commissions ranged between $2\frac{1}{2}$ and 10 per cent.

471. Money Trust Investigation, 2013, 2014.

472. Op. cit., 273.

473. Money Trust Investigation, 1277 ff.

474. Op. cit., 273. William Rockefeller was connected with the railroad and the bank.

475. Money Trust Investigation, 1411.

476. Adler, Schiff, I, 113; Nourse, op. cit., 103. To give another example, the Chicago Street Railway Syndicate of 1905 was a signal failure; see Comptroller of the Currency, Annual Report (1915), I, 35 ff.

477. Money Trust Investigation, 1269.

478. Ibid., 2018.

479. Ibid., 1982.

480. Ibid., 1871; James, Chicago Banks, II, 961.

481. Money Trust Investigation, 1031 ff, 1273, 1276, 1547, 1662, 1663. An example of an invitation to join a syndicate ("we have reserved for you a participation... of $230,000") can be found in ibid., 969.

482. Allen, Lords, 80.

483. Gerstenberg, op. cit., 329. Schiff's list comprised 85 to 125 names.

484. Money Trust Investigation, 1848, 1849.

485. Money Trust Investigation, 1545, 1548, 1552, 1553, 1849, 1854.

486. For examples see ibid., 1541, 1545, 1549, 1553.

487. There is a tremendous amount of information regarding individual flotations in the volumes covering the Money Trust Investigation, but unfortunately it is not balanced. For instance, while Lee, Higginson and Company and Kidder, Peabody and Company reported the names of the participants in their flotations, Morgan, Kuhn, Loeb and Company, the First National, and the National City Banks did not. In other respects also the reports of the various banks and banking houses lack uniformity. The greatest deficiency lies in the fact that in most cases only joint issues are reported, not transactions in which the firm in question had no allies. Consequently, whatever material is presented here regarding issues is given by way of example. Completeness is impossible on the basis of the sources used, but could probably be achieved by painstaking research which would go far beyond the scope of a chapter in a history of American banking. See Money Trust Investigation, 2208, and the lists prepared by the leading investment bankers to be cited in their proper places.

488. Money Trust Investigation, 965 ff.

489. William Salomon had been a partner of the Speyers and went into investment banking independently in 1901; see Swaine, op. cit., I, 707.

490. See Money Trust Investigation, 877.

491. Ibid., 1033.

492. Gerstenberg, op. cit., 330.

493. Money Trust Investigation, 940; as to the manipulation of the Amalgamated Copper issue of 1899, see ibid., 1592, 1593.

494. Allen (Lords 33, 71) gives a good description of Keene's methods; see also 355-356. The Money Trust Investigation (pages 708 ff) throws a very unfavorable light on this man.

495. Money Trust Investigation, 1282, 1283, 1286.

496. Ibid., 1590; for another example see Sammis, op. cit., 250.

497. Money Trust Investigation, 1592. For details on the Amalgamated Copper flotation, see Lawson, op. cit., 342 ff.

498. Money Trust Investigation, 1673.

499. Ashmead, Graham, op. cit., 232.

500. Money Trust Investigation, 1540, 1667, 1668. In 1912 J. P. Morgan and Company purchased $5,500,000 debentures of the Illinois Steel Company and immediately resold them to Kissel-Kinnicut and Lee, Higginson and Company; (ibid., 1846, 1847).

501. But only the 1920's saw the building of large scale retail distribution organizations of investment banks. The leader in that period was Charles Edwin Mitchell, president of the National City Bank; see Allen, Lords, 304 ff, especially 312.

502. Money Trust Investigation, 1842, 1843, 1846, 1847; Pujo Committee, Report, 134.
503. James, Chicago Banks, 697.
504. The Pennsylvania Commissioners of Banking reported in the early 1900's that "quite recently the State [had] been invaded by the representatives of so-called bond houses and kindred corporations;" Report (for 1902), ix.
505. Willis and Bogen, op. cit., 8.
506. Nourse, op. cit., 100.
507. Ibid., 107.
508. For an example, see Chamberlain, op. cit., 62.
509. The preceding description is based on ibid., 18, 20, 21, 23, 24, 47-50, 57-61, 67, 113, 119, 125, 127.
510. Ibid., 83, 86, 129.
511. Pujo Committee, Report, 159, 160.
512. Money Trust Investigation, 313, 316.
513. Ibid., 1816, 1824. Much material on voting trusts can be found in that publication with the help of the index, pages 2196, 2197. For voting trust agreements, see 1092, 1093, 656 ff.
514. Adler, Schiffs, I, 140.
515. Money Trust Investigation, 1019, 1020, 1453-1455, 1561. The discussion before the Pujo Committee and in public is marred by lack of distinction between management and policy determination; see ibid., 1963, 1964.
516. Money Trust Investigation, 1984, 1985.
517. Of $1,360,000,000 worth of securities floated between about 1900 and 1905, Schiff sold about $100,000,000 to the Equitable, the New York Life, and the Mutual Life; Adler, Schiff, I, 192. As to those affiliations, see Money Trust Investigation, 984, 988; Pujo Committee, Report, 60, 69, 78, 135; Brandeis, op. cit., 15, 16.
518. Adler, Schiff, I, 185 ff.
519. By 1870 Jay Cooke used deposits lodged in his banking house for advances to the Northern Pacific Railroad; Larson, Cooke, 432.
520. For details see this volume, page 181.
521. Money Trust Investigation, 347.
522. For details, see Pujo Committee, Report, 57, 106.
523. For example, see Money Trust Investigation, 1525, 1686; Allen, Lords, 79.
524. Allen, Morgan, 107.
525. Op. cit., 195.
526. Money Trust Investigation, 1665, 1666, 1668, 1669, 2045.
527. With Professor Cochran's permission.
528. Money Trust Investigation, 1341, 1342.
529. The names of other smaller houses can be found in ibid., 1698. The above mentioned Blair and Company financed, for example, the Republic Iron and Steel Company.
530. Money Trust Investigation, 1554, 1563, 1564, 1669.
531. Stillman (National City Bank) financed Consolidated Gas; ibid., 1673.
532. His son Albert Wadsworth Harris (born in 1867) entered his father's firm in 1888 and became managing partner in 1907. By the time he entered N. W. Harris and Company (actually in 1891), Allen Boyd Forbes (1866-1923) joined it also. Forbes was a lawyer and had started in the legal department of Swift and Company of Chicago. He became a partner of the Harris firm in 1901, but only in 1909 was the firm rechristened Harris, Forbes and Company. See Huston, op. cit., III, 34 ff.
533. Bryson, op. cit., 6, 7; Commercial and Financial Chronicle, CIII (1916), 708, 709.
534. In contrast, the strength of Dillon, Read and Company did not root in preliminary achievements in pre-World War I days. It was due to the activities of Clarence Dillon which fall entirely into the post-War period. Dillon (born in 1882) was the son of a clothing merchant and small banker in San Antonio whose original name was Samuel Lapowski. Young Dillon went to Harvard, graduating in 1905, and after having had a few minor jobs went to Europe where he is supposed to have studied fine arts. This at least was gossiped in his firm. After his return he became the president of a machine tool factory in the Middle West and in 1916 joined the New York banking firm of William A. Read and Company whose founder, William A. Read, born in 1858, died that same year. (Read had come up in the banking house of Vermilye and Company. Being an able bond man he had cooperated occasionally with Stillman and Schiff and after falling out with the former had been financed by the Hanover National Bank, dying a wealthy man.) Dillon became senior partner of his house in 1920 and changed the firm's name to Dillon, Read and Company in 1921. See Barron, op. cit., 29; Allen, Lords, 370; Who is Who in Finance, Banking and Insurance, 1933-35 (Philadelphia, 1935).
535. Pujo Committee, Report, 159 ff; Sweezy, op. cit., passim.
536. See this author's forthcoming paper "The Business Leader as a 'Daimonic' Figure."
537. Since the Cravath law firm in New York acted for Kuhn, Loeb and Company, Speyer and Company, Hallgarten and Company, J. and W. Seligman and Company, Harvey Fisk and Sons, and William Salomon and Company, much information on the legal aspect of the investment bankers' business can be found in Swaine's book on that firm.
538. Allen, op. cit., 237, 27, 29.
539. Corey, op. cit., 88.
540. Allen, Lords, 94.
541. Allen, Morgan, 85 ff. As to Morgan's railroad reorganizations, see Campbell, op. cit., 145 ff.
542. The voting trust agreement of the stockholders of the Bankers Trust Company can be found in Money Trust Investigation, 656 ff.

543. Paine, _Baker_, 269.
544. _Op. cit._, 142.
545. The sources for Morgan's activities are extraordinarily unsatisfactory. Corey's book is totally unreliable; Satterlee's is irksome because of its lack of criticism. Allen's book, better balanced than any of its predecessors, adds very little to what was known before. Good is the article on Morgan in Gras-Larson, _Case Book_ although it lacks critical appraisal. Important, of course, is the _Money Trust Investigation_, 1003 ff, 1808 ff, 1959 ff, 2126 ff.
546. The dates are from _Who's Who in Finance_; Adler, _Schiff Life and Letters_, I, 15 ff.
547. _Ibid._, II, 329.
548. He is supposed to have become later a partner of Hallgarten and Company, New York.
549. Oberholtzer, _op. cit._, II, 214, 215; Larson, _Cooke_, 295 ff.
550. Jenks, _op. cit._, 292.
551. See Pujo Committee, _Report_, 78-80.
552. Adler, _op. cit._, I, 197 ff.
553. As an ally of Lee, Higginson and Company and the Seligmans, Kuhn, Loeb and Company took an interest in the issues of General Motors; _Money Trust Investigation_, 1689.
554. Pujo Committee, _Report_, 57.
555. _Money Trust Investigation_, 1663.
556. _Ibid._, 1698, 1760 ff.
557. For a list of securities purchased without associates in the first instance, see _ibid._, 1758, 1759.
558. Pujo Committee, _Report_, 78; _Money Trust Investigation_, 1660 ff, especially 1661, 1662, 1663, 1668, 1671, 1677, 1684, 1695-1698, 1757 ff; Adler, _op. cit._, I, _passim_, especially 27, 28, 91 ff, 151.
559. Page 90.
560. Incidentally, Brown Brothers and Company whom we have met before as merchant bankers took an interest in investment banking, beginning about 1880 when Eugene Delano took charge of the Philadelphia office. But they did not belong to the leading houses in the field. We find them as allies of the Morgan group of banks when in 1887, for instance, they cooperated with Drexel, Morgan and Company in the flotation of securities of the Philadelphia and Reading Railroad. In the 1900's they appear repeatedly as allies of Kuhn, Loeb and Company, Kidder, Peabody and Company, and Lee, Higginson and Company. See Brown Brothers and Company, _Experiences_, 53, 54; _Money Trust Investigation_, 1698, 1760, 1926-1929, 1932, 2073, 2074, 2078, 2083. Incidentally the Baltimore house, Alexander Brown and Sons, also appears as a participant in a flotation; see _ibid._, 1698.
561. The Central Trust Company, J. and W. Seligman and Company, and Kuhn, Loeb and Company cooperated in the reorganization of General Motors; Pearson, _op. cit._, 124.
562. The preceding is based on Stevens's manuscript, _op. cit._, _passim_, especially 1-7, 22, 28, 32; Pearson, _op. cit._, _passim_, especially 97 ff; Perry, Bliss, _op. cit._, 239, 268 ff; Pujo Committee, _Report_, 75, 76; _Money Trust Investigation_, 1898 ff, 2003 ff.
563. Harvard College Class of 1880, _Fiftieth Anniversary Report_ (Report X-1930), privately printed, 1930, 146 ff.
564. Pujo Committee, _Report_, 76, 77; _Money Trust Investigation_, 1995 ff, 2051 ff.
565. _Bankers Magazine_. XIII (1858/59), 15.
566. Secretary of the Treasury, _Report on the Finances_ (1860), 481.
567. Oberholtzer, _op. cit._, I, 112 ff.
568. Among the subscribers of the first federal loan of 1894 were the following: American Exchange National Bank: $2,500,000; Chase National Bank: $500,000; Gallatin National Bank: $400,000; National Park Bank: $1,000,000; Seaboard National Bank: $200,000; Hanover National Bank: $1,500,000; Bank of the Manhattan Company: $500,000; Importers and Traders National Bank: $1,000,000; Merchants National Bank; $500,000; Bank of America: $500,000; Mechanics National Bank: $500,000; Chemical National Bank: $1,000,000; Central National Bank: $1,250,000; National Bank of Commerce: $1,000,000; Fifth Avenue Bank: $500,000; Fourth National Bank: $1,000,000. It is, of course, impossible to decide what proportion of these subscriptions were, respectively, for investment and for resale (investment banking). The list of subscribers can be found in _U.S. 54th Congr. 2d sess., Senate Document 187_, 34, 35. Again one can find numerous banks as subscribers to the loan of 1896; see the list of subscribers in _U.S. 54th Congr. 1st sess., Senate Document 221, passim_.
569. Peach, _op. cit._, 38 ff, especially 50; Comptroller of the Currency, _Annual Report_ (1915), I, 35 ff.
570. Hollander, _op. cit._, 796, 813, 814; Peach, _op. cit._, 75, 76.
571. Paine, _Baker_, 69, 70, 84, 90, 91, 94, 95. A scholarly biography of Baker would be highly desirable.
572. The date is not certain. In some sources 1874 is given as the year in which Baker became president.
573. As to Fahnestock, see Larson, _Cooke_, 92, 107, 113, 114, 227, 256, 307, 308, 313, 421.
574. _Money Trust Investigation_, 2031, 2032.
575. Pujo Committee, _Report_, 66 ff, 80 ff; Paine, _Baker_, 125, 129; _Money Trust Investigation_, 1019, 1419 ff, 1895 ff; pages 2205 ff contain a list of joint, syndicate, and pool transactions of the First National Bank over a period of ten years.
576. As to the joint account and syndicate transactions of the National City Bank, see _ibid._, 2111 ff.

577. Burr's Stillman biography is so naive that it is most telling. See passim and especially 44,82; Vanderlip, op. cit., passim, especially 156 ff, 190; Pujo Committee, Report, 71 ff; as to Vanderlip, see also Who was Who in America I (1897-1942). With regard to the term "pool" see Money Trust Investigation, 2205, 2206.

578. Except that the National Shawmut Bank of Boston participated in Kidder, Peabody's flotations (ibid., 2074, 2076, 2079, 2083); and the First National Bank of that city in Lee, Higginson's (ibid., 1938).

579. For the following, see Huston, op. cit., I, 536 ff; James Chicago Banks, 340, 494, 516, 563, 564, 695, 697, 699, 785, 789, 790, 791, 1115 ff; Money Trust Investigation, 1032, 1848; Pujo Committee, Report, 91 ff.

580. See this chapter, page 381. Incidentally from S. A. Kean and Company stemmed two more firms in the investment banking field, Farson, Leach and Company, dissolved in 1906 when A. B. Leach and Company and John Farson and Son came into being.

581. Lee, Higginson and Company seem to have cooperated closely with Chicago institutions, including trust companies, which appear as participants in numerous of their flotations, especially of Western corporations; see Money Trust Investigation, 1926, 1929, 1930, 1933, 1935.

582. See ibid., 1848, 1854, 1927, 1930, 1933, 1934, 1935.

583. We find it, for example, as an ally of Lee, Higginson and Company; Money Trust Investigation, 1926, 1930, 1933.

584. James, Chicago Banks, II, 791.

585. See his Recollections, 140 ff. However, one gains the impression that the affiliate originally aimed at a business in savings deposits rather than at investment banking activities. It seems that the bank's keen competition with John J. Mitchell's Illinois Trust and Savings Bank played a role in making the decision.

586. James, Chicago Banks, II, 693, 694, 787, 1109 ff; Peach, op. cit., 54.

587. Money Trust Investigation, 1406. There were in 1913 eight other banks with one to three million dollars capital who had also established affiliates the stock of which was saleable or purchaseable only together with the shares of the parent bank, but in those cases the state bank affiliates may not have been in the investment banking business at all. See also Peach, op. cit., 61 ff.

588. Money Trust Investigation, 1423, 1430-1434.

589. Peach, op. cit., 52, 53, 66.

590. Money Trust Investigation, 1406-1408, 1411-1413.

591. Herrick, op. cit., (first ed. of 1909), 43, 44; Kirkbridge, op. cit., (first ed. of 1905), 6, 94, 95; Smith, James G., op. cit., 150-152. State of New York, Superintendent of Banks, Annual Report for the Year 1903 (Albany, 1904): the "right [of trust companies] to engage in underwriting schemes [should be] unqualifiedly denied."

592. Edward King (1833-1908) was the son of a private banker and Rufus King's grandson. He was a Harvard graduate and joined his father's banking business which he ran until 1861. He then became a member of the New York stock exchange and was its president 1872/73. In the latter year he became the president of the Union Trust Company, a position which he held until his death. Cyclopedia of American Biography, XV, 282; see also Who's Who, 1903 edition.

593. U.S. 54th Congr. 1st sess., Senate Document 221, passim.

594. Money Trust Investigation, 1698, 1762, 1849, 1853, 1856.

595. Pujo Committee, Report, 72, 73.

596. Money Trust Investigation, 1698, 1761, 2078.

597. Sammis, op. cit., passim. The Trust Company of the Republic, founded in 1902, went into investment banking immediately and tried to float the securities of the ill-fated United States Shipbuilding Company. But the underwriting contract ran to the Mercantile Trust Company. See also Pujo Committee, Report, 78.

598. The Central Trust Company can be found as an ally of Kuhn, Loeb and Company and Lee, Higginson and Company; Money Trust Investigation, 1698, 1761, 1932. As to an unsuccessful transaction of the Central Trust Company, see Banking Law Journal, XVIII (1901), 91 ff.

599. Money Trust Investigation, 2077.

600. Boies, op. cit., passim.

601. Money Trust Investigation, 1646, 1647.

602. Ibid., 1859, 1933, 1998, 2073, 2074, 2076, 2079, 2084; Pujo Committee, Report, 75, 76.

603. Ibid., 77, Money Trust Investigation, 2078, 2082.

604. Ibid., 1020, 2209; Pujo Committee, Report, 160.

605. Bryson, op. cit., 24, 25.

The preceding chapter represents the only existing attempt at writing a history of investment banking for any one country. Plenge's ambitious project came to naught years ago and the two chapters on the Crédit Mobilier alone were published. Sketches on the subject exist such as the entirely unsatisfactory chapter VII in Willis's and Bogen's textbook on investment banking or Muriel Hidy's chapter XIV in the Growth of the American Economy, ed. Harold F. Williamson (New York, 1946). These circumstances should be kept in mind when judging this performance. Starting therefrom the next student certainly should be able to do a better job.

606. For an explanation of this appendix and its source, see page 318 of this chapter.

607. This, for us, unnecessarily elaborate description shows how new the business must have been; otherwise it would not have been necessary to explain it in such a cumbersome way to the merchants expected to read the book.

608. Literally "in the field;" on the exchange?

609. The terms operation and negotiation seem to be used synonymously in the source.

610. The source uses the word Commissionaires; it probably means those engaged in the negotiation and the entrepreneurs.

Appendix

GEORGE S. COE

NINETEENTH CENTURY BANKER AND BUSINESS LEADER

To the economic historian who has taken a fancy to studying the role which entrepreneurs have played in economic development it is surprising that in America some of the most creative business leaders have been neglected by students and forgotten by the public. Interest has centered on spectacular businessmen, even if they were scoundrels rather than true leaders. Among the forgotten men who deserve the careful attention of economists and historians is the New York banker, George S. Coe.

I

George Simmons Coe[1] was a descendant of one Matthew Coe who had come to this country by 1645, probably from Suffolk, England. The immigrant settled first in Portsmouth, N.H., and later led a roving life which took him to various places in Massachusetts, including what today is Maine, until he died in Falmouth, Mass.[2] George S. Coe himself was born in 1817 in Newport, R.I. His father was a cabinet maker who could afford for his son nothing more than a scanty education in a public school. Thus Coe was destined to become one of those self-made men who dominated American business during the nineteenth century. At fourteen years of age he started his career in a country store of his native town; but only four years later in 1835, at the age of about eighteen, he transferred as a "general clerk" into a country bank, the Rhode Island Union Bank of Newport.[3]

Coe had hardly come of age when Newport seemed too small for his ambitions; and New York with its immense possibilities lured him away. He obviously had several irons in the fire. William Vernon, a son of the great colonial merchant and a leading citizen of Newport, took an interest in the young man and (on August 22, 1838) wrote the following letter of introduction to James Boorman, head of the important New York mercantile house of Boorman and Johnston:[4]

It may be that in your extensive operations you require the services of a young gentleman qualified in all respects for a business man. As such, I have great pleasure in recommending Mr. George Coe of this town to your patronage. You may place implicit confidence in his integrity & if received into your service; or that of any of your friends, he will not need my recommendation; his ability and industry will recommend your favor.

It is probable that Coe did not make use of this letter for otherwise it hardly would have survived among his own papers. Be that as it may, in the same year in which it was written, Coe landed a job with Prime, Ward and King, the leading New York firm of private bankers, which in that very year was playing a part in what they thought was liquidating the crisis of 1837. It may well be that such business experience as well as the observation of inter-bank cooperation established for the emergency exerted a deep influence on the young man and many years later determined those of his actions with which he was to make history.

In 1844 (?) Prime, Ward and King sent Coe to Cincinnati to take care of their banking and commission business in this western trade center. (As a matter of fact, Coe appears in the Cincinnati directory of 1846 as "com. mer.," commission merchant.)[5] However he did not stay there long. He obviously made business or personal contacts with the leading men of the then flourishing Ohio Life Insurance and Trust Company which did an extensive banking business, and which before the end of the decade made Coe the cashier of its New York branch.[6] Once more Coe remained in the service of the firm only a few years; and in this case it would be interesting to know in detail what reasons induced him to leave. Be that as it may, about 1852 Coe joined as a partner an existing banking house which thereupon assumed the firm name of Gilbert, Coe and Johnson. It failed shortly thereafter.[7]

II

The years up to Coe's failure in the middle of the 1850's can be considered as the apprenticeship of the coming business leader. Regardless of that failure which cannot have reflected on his character and abilities, late in 1854 or early in 1855 the young banker was appointed cashier of the American Exchange Bank. At the same time he was a trustee of the Ohio Life Insurance and Trust Company and as such early in the summer of 1857 examined its New York branch without discovering that the balance sheet was forged. The American Exchange Bank seems to have had close business relations with that branch and when the latter's ignominious end approached Coe was called on August 21, 1857. He helped it along for a few more days but was unable to stave off disaster.[8]

In 1860 Coe became the president of the American Exchange Bank and remained in that position until his resignation in 1894. When he entered it New York commercial banking was just making a tremendous step forward by organizing the first clearing house of the country (thus creating the platform for some of Coe's future activities and achievements); and George D. Lyman, its first manager, was already recognizing that it would become an instrument for permanent cooperation among banks as indeed Coe was to make it.

It goes without saying that Coe could not have become a leader among the New York bankers had he not been an eminently successful banker himself. And actually he was one, although the honor of being the most successful one, at least in the judgment of his contemporaries, he had to leave to president George J. Williams of the Chemical Bank.[9] Unfortunately, as is the case so often, there seems to be no material extant on the basis of which one could study Coe's entrepreneurship within the American Exchange Bank, which, incidentally, upon receiving a national charter was styled American Exchange National Bank; (it was later absorbed by the Irving Trust Company). The secret of Coe's success is not known unless it be that he was a master in dealing with men[10] and an able administrator who inspired and held the confidence of the business world. He was not matched by many "in the rapid and correct dispatch of business," as expressed in a private letter to Coe.[11]

Coe died in 1896. During the last years of his life he was "shut out by impaired mental and physical health from contact with his fellows and business affairs." Consequently his activities "had in a large measure passed out of the mind"[12] of the younger generation of bankers which was then taking over.

III

The speed with which by 1860 the newcomer assumed leadership among the members of the New York banking fraternity is truly astonishing and proof not only of his unusual abilities, but equally of his tact. In fact it is characteristic of the man that in the early 1860's he tried to keep behind the scenes and to leave honor and the appearance of leadership to what were then the "grand old men" of the profession, especially to Moses Taylor, president of the City Bank, and John Austin Stevens, president of the Bank of Commerce, with whom he cooperated closely. Although not among the founders of the New York Clearing House, his understanding of the essentials and possibilities of the new type of institution must have been unusual for the times, and as early as 1861 his name appears (for the first time) on a committee appointed by the organization.

Prior to this appointment to his first official station in the Clearing House, Coe, using it as a platform, had already made history by devising the clearing house loan certificate, as has been described before.[13] That he did not become a member of the committee that he had suggested and that put his proposal into practice is indicative of Coe's character as well as of his standing at that moment.

In this case the scholar is in the unusually fortunate position of knowing how the business leader who devised a successful business tool of the greatest economic importance looked on it after the lapse of many years. In 1884 Coe described clearing house loan certificates as equivalent to supplemental currency, issued for local use by clearing house associations. He considered them at the same time as representing a mechanism by which bills receivable, as well as negotiable securities, could be conveniently transferred from one bank to another in exchange for money or as a ready substitute therefor. Coe recognized that his device at its inception stood "outside of law" or, in other words, that it was a device conceived and brought into being by businessmen and neither anticipated nor regulated by law.[14] By creating this credit instrument, later generally used as a means of handling panics, Coe became de facto a leader of the American banking community in every crisis prior to the establishment of the Federal Reserve System. But by institutionalizing his leadership at the very moment when it began, Coe paved the way for the forgetfulness of posterity. He disappeared behind his work so that to the superficial observer the course typical of American crises of the late nineteenth and early twentieth centuries seems to have been determined by objective factors alone. However, in fact, Coe's achievement shaped the modus operandi of the solvent banks and to a certain extent made out of crises as typical sociological and economic phenomena the particular historical events (e.g., the American crisis of 1884). That Coe could be thus forgotten is the more surprising since his contemporaries were well aware of his leadership;[15] but a contributory factor must be found in the supplementary role which Frederick D. Tappen played in the crises of the late nineteenth century and which has been described in an earlier chapter.[16]

A few months had hardly passed after the creation of the clearing house loan certificate when for a second time Coe exerted influence on the country's financial history. By that time he was taking an interest in the flotation of government bonds.[17] These were then sold to the highest bidder at market prices, a procedure which in the first half of the year 1861 Coe considered the correct one. But when this method (for good reasons) became inacceptable to "leading members of Congress"[18] Coe, as has been described in an earlier chapter of this volume, played a decisive role in organizing the banks of New York, Philadelphia, and Boston into a "league" which lent the government at par $150,000,000 all told. But this bankers' syndicate (as one might call it) did not, as Coe expected, become the sole source of intermediary funds and consequently the almost monopolistic sales agent, besides the Treasury, for government loans. The device worked very successfully for several months, but then broke down for reasons which lie beyond the scope of this present investigation.[19]

There was a straight line leading from Coe's first to his second great achievement. The fundamental idea was in both cases the same: cooperation of competitors for important ends. Just as in 1860 for the period of the financial emergency he had united the commercial banks of New York, so now he merged the commercial banks of the three Eastern trade centers "into an efficient and inseparable body, for the purpose of advancing the capital of the country upon government bonds in large amounts, and through their clearing house facilities and other well known expedients to distribute them in smaller amounts among the people in a manner that would secure active cooperation among the members in this special work, while in all other respects each bank could pursue its independent business."[20] Approximately forty years earlier on the old continent the Rothschilds had discovered how stock exchanges could be used to float government securities in amounts unheard of before; now an American banker had enough vision to see how clearing houses could be used for the same purpose, again an insight which had been beyond the comprehension of every other contemporary. "To insure full co-operation and success," Coe went on to

explain, "the expedient of issuing clearing-house certificates and of appropriating and averaging all the coin in the various banks as a common fund which had been invented but the year before was applied to that special object with good effect."[21] That is to say, Coe himself saw and stressed the connection between his first and his second achievements.

However there was still another important idea back of his action of 1861. It is generally known that after the destruction of the Second Bank of the United States, which was de facto a central bank, the New York City banks as a whole assumed certain central banking functions, and Coe as early as 1861 may have had an intuitive understanding of that fact. In England and France, as he knew, the capitals of the Banks of England and France, respectively, "had been found sufficient for the gigantic struggles of those great nations." He figured that because the capitals of the commercial banks of New York, Philadelphia, and Boston, combined, were larger than those of the Banks of England and France their emergency organization in the American political crisis of 1861 should be able to achieve financially what the two European central banks had accomplished in the past.

Regardless of Coe's eminently successful leadership in the summer of 1861 he lost his influence before the winter began. When the loan transaction of the year resulted in a conflict between the New York bankers and the Secretary of the Treasury, Coe withdrew into the background, and James Gallatin, a man of very different caliber and of an older generation, became their spokesman. But Coe's inability to retain leadership had a deeper significance. He represented too conservative an outlook for the terrific contest which the Civil War was to become. He was convinced and remained convinced throughout his life that the conflict could have been financed essentially in the same way as had been the Mexican War and the minor European wars of the middle of the nineteenth century. He thought, too, that the American people would have been willing to submit to that rigid taxation which "sound" finance would have entailed. The historian who knows the actual behavior of many businessmen and of large strata of the population, easily sees the flaw in Coe's reasoning. In fact, the Civil War, like the many major ones to follow, could not be financed by an increased velocity of circulation (as Coe's idea was, expressed in modern terms) plus taxation, but only by taxation plus the creation of additional purchasing power. Coe, as just indicated, did not realize this fact; but as if he had understood the situation he himself pleaded for the creation of about $200,000,000 of irredeemable bank paper as backing for which the existing coin reserve of the banks (about $40,000,000) and government bonds were to be set aside. (It will be shown later that for reasons of principle Coe detested any government currency. The idea of a coin reserve, even if held only in the background, was attractive to him since he felt that banks needed constantly to look out for the future redemption of their issues and thus would be surer guardians of irredeemable paper money than would the government.) The above proposal was not his originally, but he promoted it and was disappointed when Chase discarded the plan in favor of a system of National Banks. Never in his life, although himself having given advice (probably in 1864 rather than 1863)[22] and although working under a national charter, did Coe become reconciled to the system. He never abandoned that antagonism which was typical of the New York bank leaders of the 1860's. In this respect he exhibited a blind spot, for regardless of its early shortcomings the creation of the National Banking system as such was a great achievement which would have been missed had the above-sketched plan been adopted and state banks permitted to provide for the unavoidable inflation.[23] Coe also criticized the policy under which the conversion privilege of the early legal tender issues was not bestowed on the later ones, so that the indirect connection with gold (by way of the interest payment on the bonds into which legal tenders first could be converted) was broken. Otherwise, he claimed, the notes could have been absorbed automatically.

Although Coe increased his prestige during the decade that followed his great achievements of 1860 and 1861, he had no other opportunity to exert widely visible leadership prior to the outbreak of the crisis of 1873. In that year the mere fact that clearing house loan certificates had again to be resorted to caused him to be the outstanding figure among the New York bankers. His prominent influence is evident at first glance, for simultaneously with the flotation of the certificates in 1873 that measure was again adopted by the New York banks which Coe considered their indispensable supplement, namely, the pooling of the gold reserves.

Coe's leadership in the emergency of 1873 is also attested by his becoming the chairman of a committee of nine to consider reforms of the practical operations of banks with each other and the public.[24] As a matter of fact, the report of this committee of November 11, 1873, which Professor Sprague[25] characterized as "the ablest document which has ever appeared in the course of our banking history," was Coe's work. As far as the historian can see, in this report Coe began preaching that lesson which he was to preach for the rest of his life: Experience had taught him that the associated banks were mutually dependent in time of peril and in the trust which the daily dealings in the clearing house imposed. (One cannot sufficiently stress the point that, in 1873, this outstanding banker considered business a trust !) Consequently every member was bound to suffer from the errors and indiscretions of every other member. From that fact Coe deduced that no clearing-house bank had the moral right to conduct its affairs in defiance of the convictions of its associates or to deal with its customers in terms which were in conflict with the common interests. Bank officers had no right to be sharp competitors and to consider themselves only laborers for dividends for their constituents. They were trustees of the whole community and public administrators, holding positions within the national economy which forbade departure from sound principles.

On the basis of such presuppositions Coe arrived at certain recommendations which remained near to his heart all his life and which were repeated by him time and again: the payment of interest on demand deposits was to be strictly prohibited (thereby the lending of such deposits to Wall Street which Coe considered unsound would be stopped); only member banks should enjoy the advantages of the Clearing House (the suggestion was here couched in the words that "only checks drawn upon the Associated Banks should be received on deposit"); banks which did not strictly observe the rules adopted by the Association should be expelled from the Clearing House. (Making the Clearing House a strong and tight organization was one of Coe's permanent aims.) The second of these three points needs further comment: Coe was much too good a businessman not to find it galling that non-members through the assistance of members enjoyed privileges for which they did not pay, thereby gaining unearned competitive advantages. But even more important for Coe was the fact that non-members were then not subject to that control which made the clearing-house banks relatively secure. Through their relative instability, as Coe realized, non-members endangered the strength of those members through which they worked with the Clearing House, and thereby unavoidably that of the Associated Banks as a body.[26]

The next crisis through which the country passed was the so-called Metropolitan Bank crisis of 1884 which, as Coe himself described,[27] developed after the failure of the Marine and the difficulties of the Second National Banks of New York. To avoid serious trouble the issue of clearing house loan certificates was once more decided upon almost as a matter of course, one may assume. Soon thereafter, however, a run on the Metropolitan Bank began and the clearing house committee was called together. Upon examination it found that this bank had eight to nine million dollars deposits, most of which represented the reserves of interior banks so that the latter were in danger of having to stop payments because of temporary illiquidity and in anticipation of the loss of a large percentage of their reserves. Such suspension of numerous country banks was bound to lead to failures of businessmen everywhere and, on the other hand, to heavy drafts on the New York City banks which singly were bound to succumb. Ruin would thus spread throughout the land. At that moment of danger for the national economy Coe suggested successfully that the Associated Banks take possession of the Metropolitan Bank, pay the depositors, and share in the possible loss of one or two million dollars rather than permit the conflagration to run through the country.[28] It was not the very first time that solvent banks backed an insolvent rival to avoid a major disaster; but here for the first time a clearing house association as such took action in a form which soon was to become standard in cases of such character.

On the basis of this experience Coe's ideas developed far beyond the immediate emergency and the prevalent thinking of the day. For him there could be no return to the methods of keen rivalry once the crisis had blown over. First of all, it had taught him "the power and importance of this voluntary association," i.e., the clearing house association, and he came to understand its place within the national economy. Coe now recognized that the New York Clearing House was not simply a place of meeting for bank officers without responsibility, utterly independent of each other, and indifferent to their brethren's welfare and business habits. It was especially galling to him that twice, in 1857 and 1873, the opposition of two or three members had defeated the wishes of the overwhelming majority of the Clearing House Association so that the abolition of interest payment on deposits could not be made a binding obligation of all members thereof. But Coe's vision went still further. It has been mentioned previously that his action of 1861 may have implied that he already saw the combined New York banks as standing in America where the Banks of England and France stood in their respective countries. In 1884 he saw clearly in this respect. The New York banks, he said in his address, are the holders of the ultimate reserves of the country; and then he adds a somewhat awkward phrase which may have meant what today is called the lenders of last resort. Later in his speech he characterized

them as "refuges in commercial commotion!" That is to say, he recognized the New York banks as a cohesive system of the character of a central bank, believing that this system was better suited to our constitution than was a central bank, an argument which was soon to play some part in the fight against the legislation which led to the enactment of the Federal Reserve system. Consequently he felt that the New York banks should become a homogeneous body and that the burden and responsibility of the great trust of being a quasi-central bank should be shared by the adoption of uniform conditions with special regard to the public welfare.

From the fact that in a grave emergency no New York bank singly could ride out the gale and that combined they took the place of a central bank he once more drew the conclusion that no one of them could claim the right to pursue its own business selfishly, disregarding the delicate situation in which the Association found itself. He saw the New York banks

> so inextricably bound together by the daily transfer of portions of the nation's deposits from one bank to another, by the difficulty of recovering checks upon defaulting members..., by the univers[al] distrust which one failing member cast upon its associates, and by the urgent demand made upon the stronger in time of troubles to combine their resources for the protection of the weaker to avert general disaster that an identity of interest [was] created by the very existence and necessity of the Association.

Coe recognized the New York banks as a "federated community" whose members were mutually responsible for each other so that it was not only the privilege, but even the duty of each bank to conduct its business with a view to the stability of the Association and the welfare of the nation and to scrutinize the conduct of the other members in this respect. None of the banks could be insensible to the ignorance, selfishness, and unethical conduct of any other. Coe could see no sense in an attitude which made the banks responsible partners in time of stress and eager competitors and antagonists in days of prosperity.

Therefore he introduced the following resolution: Since the experience of the Associated Banks in the recent panic had again shown that in times of financial disturbance every member of the Association was compelled to make common cause with every other member in the risk of giving relief, it was proper and necessary to inquire whether the business methods of the various members were uniform and correct, and equitable to all the banks bound together in the Clearing House. In order to gauge the meaning of this resolution one must remember the general business situation of the period (1884). It was a time of reckless competition, the time of the "Robber Barons," the time in which Spencer's philosophy was appealing to American businessmen. And there stood a financial leader of first rank who, being convinced that the New York banks were "custodians of a public trust," preached cooperation, responsibility; nay more than that: interference with other people's business, i.e., interference with the freedom of enterprise in order to win greater ends. For him the necessity of performing an economic function came first, before business and before absolute freedom; and so he stood for what is today called "control" of business. (To be sure, Coe strove for self-control: the mere thought of government-control would have horrified him.) With this approach to the banking problems of his day Coe seems to have been a child of the twentieth century rather than of the nineteenth.

What Coe proposed at that moment were the following measures. First, he called for the abandonment of the paying of interest on demand deposits. This was, as already indicated, an old demand of Coe's and of other far-seeing New York bankers. Secondly, he asked that checks drawn on banks out of the city should not be credited as ready cash to the banks' customers. At that time there were at any one moment items to an amount of ten millions in the process of collection. (The question of out-of-town checks was bound to become a more troublesome one somewhat later.) Thirdly, he wished the settling of all stock-exchange transactions by check to be replaced by clearing arrangements since the former method was putting an unnecessary burden on the Associated Banks. In this very sound proposal spoke the champion of the clearing house as an institution.

Coe's proposals were referred first to a committee of five, the majority of whom, under his chairmanship, reported favorably; then to a committee of eight, seven of whom concurred in a report dated July 29, 1884. This report again was Coe's work. But his endeavors were in vain; he was blocked by a minority headed by Octavius D. Baldwin, president of the Fourth National Bank and a member of the latter committee.[29]

It seems to the author that one of the high points in Coe's lifelong struggle for cooperation among the banks of the country was his participation in 1875 and 1876 in the foundation of the

American Bankers Association (A.B.A.). To be sure, since no primary material relating to the pre- and early history of the association is supposed to be in existence there is no documentary proof for the importance and exact character of his contribution. So much is certain: the obituary in the 1896 Proceedings of the A.B.A. characterized Coe as "one of the organizers of this body;" and the author is convinced that the tradition which assigns the achievement to country bankers was planted. It seems impossible that the A.B.A. could have come into existence without active cooperation of the New York City banks; while on the other hand it might well have been impossible to achieve the goal if they had been in the foreground. It should be kept in mind that the decision to organize the movement was made by a group of bankers meeting in New York City; that the convention which resolved to establish the association was held not far from New York in Saratoga; and that the second convention of the A.B.A. took place in New York City. Coe himself came to the fore as soon as the association was in the throes of being established. He was not present at the 1875 meeting of bankers which resolved to form a permanent organization. But it has been shown previously that Coe knew how to stay in the background when that was necessary.[30] On the other hand, when the first convention of the A.B.A. was called his participation was widely advertised[31] and at that very meeting he assumed a leading role. He made one of the key speeches[32] (and, incidentally, from then on he addressed every convention up to that of 1886). Furthermore, he became the first chairman of the executive council of the youthful organization, a position which he held for many years. As early as the 1880's a journalist stated that in this capacity he was "really the controlling spirit" thereof.[33] Moreover, from 1881-1883 Coe was the (third) president of the A.B.A., declining reelection in the latter year.[34]

Contemporary newspapers claimed[35] that the association developed quickly into a pressure group. In fact, the bankers assembled in Saratoga in 1875 had aimed at a permanent bankers' organization believing that grievances such as the taxation of banking capital and deposits, usury laws, and others under which the banking interests suffered could be removed by securing the proper legislation. In 1879, the secretary of the association gave "an encouraging account of the influence exerted by the organization [on] shaping legislation."[36] Such development would not have been against Coe's intentions. To the contrary, he was the chairman of the A.B.A's first executive council which organizing the banks and bankers all over the country and advising them to use pressure group tactics brought the new body on to that road.[37] Thereafter, in his fight for sound money Coe repeatedly used such tactics. It will be shown later that, as early as 1877, he organized the clearing houses in the Eastern trade centers for the purpose of memorializing Congress and warning it against radical silver legislation. Later in his life, in 1886, together with Cornelius N. Bliss[38] and one Charles S. Smith,[39] he became one of the treasurers of the so-called Fairchild Fund, raised by H. J. Fairchild, member of H. B. Claflin and Company (New York, Manchester, Paris) "for the promulgation of facts indicating the danger of the continued coinage of the 412½ grain dollar." The three treasurers were to disburse the collected money at their discretion for the above purpose.[40] Finally in 1893 Coe proposed the establishment of a National Monetary Committee of members of the American Bankers Association. This body was to become one representative of the industrial, commercial, and financial interests of the country for the purpose of formulating and reporting for adoption by Congress and state legislatures a sound American currency and banking system.[41]

Remarks made by Coe[42] in public permit the conclusion that he originally considered as the purpose of the A.B.A. the freeing of the banks from the "special taxes" imposed during the Civil War.[43] He felt that the Association had rendered "most important" service to that end by diffusing information and by the personal influence of its members. From that point on he wished the A.B.A. to become an educational venture, by serving as a platform for the exchange of views between bankers, facilitated by personal contact and social intercourse. Being conscious of his own lack of formal education, he was aware of a need for "higher education" of the profession, much more in this country than in Europe. (Coe's remarks also show that the A.B.A. was first considered as a temporary organization, or at least presented as such, possibly in order to overcome the active resistance of the many rugged individualists in the trade.) Those statements of Coe's may be taken for what they are worth, because in cases like the one under investigation, frankness may easily defeat the purpose, and Coe was a sort of diplomat. He genuinely felt that through the instrumentality of the A.B.A. the bankers should voluntarily organize themselves "into a more compact system for the greater security and facility of trade" and that they would thereby "elevate the tone, dignity, and usefullness" of their profession.

IV

So far Coe's leadership of the banking community in matters of business has been studied, although with the description of his role in 1861 this line has been overstepped. In the following paragraphs his influence on the country's monetary policy will be reviewed.

The two great problems which arose in this field after the conclusion of the Civil War were the resumption of specie payments and the silver question; and Coe took a keen and active interest in both. As early as 1868 he came out with his first publication, The Natural Road to Specie Payments, a Letter to Representative John V. L. Pruyn.[44] In this paper Coe objected to the policy of returning to specie payments by a gradual withdrawal of the legal tenders. He objected because the withdrawal of a part of this "unsound" currency would not change the character of the rest. He believed that resumption and maintenance of specie payments would thus be delayed until enough coin was available to redeem all notes in specie, i.e., all that had not been absorbed in the meantime by bond issues. Instead he proposed that the legal tender act be amended so as to legalize gold contracts, or, in other words, so as to permit the payment of coin or its equivalent for new contracts expressly made payable in coin. He expected that that measure would lure coin out of hoards, that it would stop the export and even cause the import of specie, and that it would restore the broken link between national and international money. He was not afraid that this measure would lead to two different currencies existing side by side since the banks would immediately adapt themselves to the new condition. But he wished the measure supplemented by a policy of absorbing legal tenders by bond issues.

After the publication of his first pamphlet Coe continued his interest in the problem of resumption, and, once the date was set, threw himself into the fray in order to make it a complete success. During the summer of 1877 he offered a plan of his own, by which he intended to duplicate his achievement of 1861, namely, organizing the banks of the Atlantic trade centers into a sort of syndicate, this time for the purpose of achieving resumption. Baltimore was now to be included in the group; in 1861 the cooperation of its banking community had been impossible owing to the prevailing sentiment of its citizens.[45] This plan was presented by Coe to the convention of the A.B.A. held at New York in September, 1877.[46] According to this suggestion the National Banks should combine "in ratio of capital in the purchase" of 50 to 100 million dollar bonds to be sold by the banks or the Treasury to the public. The banks would credit the Treasurer immediately for the whole amount "as gold deposit," subject to his orders, while in the meantime they would count the gold as part of their reserves and in case of need could draw thereon, depositing bonds, coin, or legal tenders as security for the government. The banks would gather gold into their coffers by the sale of the bonds and, simultaneously, surrender legal tender notes previously held. (It has been indicated and will be shown later in detail that Coe considered permanent resumption impossible without the complete withdrawal of the greenbacks.) The banks should be permitted, on the other hand, to exchange one type of security for another so that they could reissue legal tender notes to counteract any too rapid contraction. Thereby the return to specie payments would be achieved through the "ordinary financial agencies" and by conservative methods. Or, in other words, Coe wished that banks and business, not the government, as contemplated by law, would be instrumental in achieving resumption; for the latter mode might lead to a dangerous locking up of large amounts of specie in anticipation of the first of January, 1879.

Coe's plan of 1877 was not adopted. Nevertheless he led the banking fraternity in the fall of 1878 when the New York Clearing House Association, making itself the mouthpiece of the banks of the country, sent a delegation to Washington to offer their cooperation to the Secretary of the Treasury.[47] This mission has been described by the author elsewhere in some detail.[48] Suffice it to say here that as its outcome the New York Clearing House banks passed resolutions which were adopted by all members and which "obliterated" all differentiation between gold and paper currency and, at the same time, relegated silver to the place of subsidiary coins, as will be described later.

Once resumption was achieved Coe fostered the official policy of the Republican Party whose program was to go further than the administration was planning, not only by redeeming the circulating treasury notes in gold but by withdrawing them completely.[49] If and to what extent Coe had influenced the adoption of this party policy is unknown to the author. Undoubtedly it was in line with his thoughts of 1868, and the possibility of his influence should not be discounted. Public opinion considered him at least a "representative Republican"[50] and a private letter from Francis Elias Spinner to Coe seems to indicate that at one time the latter was even considered for the

position of Secretary of the Treasury.[51] In the 1870's, in line with his pamphlet of 1868, Coe suggested that the legal tenders be made convertible into bonds as they had been at the beginning of the war, and he expected that thus they would be absorbed gradually, or in other words that they would thus be funded automatically.[52]

At the very moment when resumption of specie payments was in the process of being achieved a new monetary problem was born in America, the silver question. Coe caught a glimpse of the problem during those months when he led the National Banks in the implementation of the official monetary policy of the nation; a few years later he saw it clearly. He recognized that the Bland-Allison Act of 1878 which required the Treasury to buy at least two million dollars worth of silver every month and to coin it into silver dollars was a radical error. But he conceded that when this law was enacted simultaneously with the return to specie payments it was regarded "indifferently" because it appeared in association with that happy event.[53] This concession of Coe's makes it the more remarkable that in 1878 and 1879 he acted as if he then had a clear picture of the situation, namely, that a policy regarding silver was being forced upon the government which was liable to endanger the maintenance of specie payments, once resumption was achieved.

Coe's actions to meet the danger took two different directions: First, he organized the banking fraternities of the leading Eastern commercial centers into a body, applying the tactics which he had so successfully used in 1861 and which he had planned to use again to achieve the resumption of specie payments. In a meeting of the New York Clearing House Association of January 9, 1878, a committee was appointed consisting of five bank officers from New York, three from each of the cities of Boston, Philadelphia, and Baltimore, and three merchants and representatives of trust and insurance companies. The committee was to memorialize Congress against the passage of the contemplated silver legislation and to petition for authorizing the coinage of silver, except as subsidiary money, only if the value of silver coin was regulated by its bullion content. The committee was also to communicate with the several banks and other institutions represented and, through the clearing house associations all over the country, with other financial institutions, inviting and requesting them to join in such a memorial and petition, and through them to urge merchants, traders, and manufacturers to place their affairs on a gold basis. It was contemplated that, in case the committee wished to submit proposals to the constituent bodies, simultaneous meetings would be called in the four participating cities. (Parallel action of clearing house associations was a new device at that time which Coe had helped to develop.)[54]

Coe's second activity was of a very different character: He was instrumental in inducing the New York Clearing House Association (through clause 5 of its Resolutions of November 12, 1878) to prohibit the use of silver coins and silver certificates in settling balances, except as subsidiary currency in amounts of less than ten dollars. Contemporary public opinion recognized that Coe was responsible for this clause. The Daily Graphic, a popular paper championing silver, made Coe a target of its dissatisfaction with that measure. On December 5 of that year its first page showed Coe with other bankers lying dead under the wreckage of the National Banking system destroyed by the Bland bill which provided for free and unlimited coinage of silver and the ultimate adoption of which the cartoonist anticipated. A few days later, on December 9, in a cartoon again covering the whole first page Coe was shown as a vendor of balloons trying to save his merchandise, the National Banking system, in a gale created by the passage of the bill; and the caption read "A breath has made them and a breath may destroy them." In both cartoons a reference in the picture to the obnoxious resolution 5 of the Clearing House Association made clear to the reader who and what were under fire.

The majority of Congress could not but consider this resolution 5 of the New York Clearing House Association as an unwarrantable interference with the economic policy of the land. Therefore by a law of August 12, 1882, it denied the extension of their charters to all National Banks that continued membership in a clearing house which refused silver in the settlement of balances.[55] Thereupon the New York Clearing House took evasive action, and, because Coe explained and defended its policy in an anonymous pamphlet one can hardly go wrong in assigning to him the responsibility for devising it or at least putting it into effect.[56] In his defense Coe started characteristically from the idea that a responsibility rested on the Clearing House, namely, that of determining "whether or not the unit of value [should] be retained at par with other civilized nations." If the doors of the institution were opened to silver the aggregate reserves of the banks would begin to deteriorate and there was no point at which this deterioration could be arrested. Gold would quickly be expelled. Therefore the banks had no desire to be released from their voluntary obligation of 1878 to settle balances in gold and treasury notes only. Since none of them offered silver certificates, none could

be refused, and so the act of 1882 was not violated. There was no legal requirement, however, which demanded that silver certificates actually tendered in the settlement of balances by the Treasury as a member of the Clearing House be merged with the funds which passed between the banks. Those silver certificates were treated as a special fund payable to such banks as had tendered drafts on the Treasury for clearing. Thus the clearing house settlements were preserved "unadulterated," the bank reserves maintained intact, and the strongest assurance of security was given to depositors. Every reason for withdrawing deposits and for hoarding gold coin was thereby removed. (Incidentally, it is interesting to observe how here the need of self-preservation obviously forced the banks by a contradictory business policy to counteract the economic policy established by Congress.)

It was probably through his interest in the resumption of specie payments that Coe was impelled to join the forces battling against silver. His first moves in this direction of 1877 and 1878 must be seen as attempts to protect that achievement against the anticipated dangers arising from faulty silver legislation. The pamphlet of 1885, just discussed, and the policy described therein were defensive measures too. From that point, however, Coe progressed; he developed a monetary program and even took offensive action to rescue the endangered gold standard when it became necessary.

Coe's monetary program was formulated in 1880. In a speech of that year he suggested that the coinage of silver dollars of 412½ grains be stopped and "that the Treasury receive and pay out silver bullion as nearly as possible at its market value in gold, and issue certificates of deposit in denominations for circulation." Such silver certificates should be redeemable in gold or the equivalent amount of silver at the pleasure of the government.[57] This proposal of Coe's had various purposes: it was to arrest a danger and provide the country with the badly needed paper currency "of absolute and unquestionable value" destined to replace the obnoxious legal tenders and indirectly to create a new market for silver.

The hour for Coe's offensive action, on the other hand, came in 1885. Without access to the minutes of the New York Clearing House it is not possible to evaluate the extent to which Coe was instrumental in devising certain transactions which took place in that year. But the resolutions adopted by that body on July 13, the subsequent measures, and a circular letter sent out on July 20 to banks all over the country, all bear so much the stamp of Coe's personality and of his very phraseology that the historian is inclined to assign him a large share therein. It was in July that the New York banks were first told that the gold reserves of the Treasury were running low and were in danger of being exhausted, in which case the government would be forced to make its payments in silver. Consequently, at any moment the country might slide into a silver standard. The banks were asked what actions they were willing to take to avoid such a calamity. They resolved to come to the rescue. The circular, mentioned above, bearing among others Coe's signature, went out to inform the country's banks about the agreement of their New York colleagues with the Treasury. Under this agreement the New York banks were handing to the Treasury $10,000,000 in gold in exchange for fractional silver coin and currency, which was to be apportioned among these banks in the ratio of their gold reserves. If this sum should prove insufficient a further sum had been promised, not to exceed another $10,000,000; and in this case the banks in Philadelphia, Boston, Chicago, and other cities were to be invited to share the burden. Immediately one sees Coe's fundamental ideas translated once more into policy: First the New York banks acted as a body and apportioned among themselves the burden and risk connected with the rescue of the gold standard. In the second instance (just as in 1861) the banks of the other leading commercial centers would be invited to participate if the New York banks alone could not achieve the goal.[58]

In the years 1877, 1878, and 1879 when Coe was working to crystallize opposition against the danger threatened by the silver policy being promoted by certain groups, the spokesmen of the latter knew that Coe was himself interested in silver mining. In its issue of November 25, 1878 the Daily Graphic pictured Coe holding in his hand Resolution 5 of the Clearing House Association and at the same time picking the pocket of another Coe perusing the balance sheet of the Silver Islet Mining Company, in which he was in fact interested.[59] The caption reads: Picking his own pocket. But Coe's thinking on monetary matters may actually have been influenced by his business interests; for later in his life he became a bimetallist and as such by 1890 saw eye to eye with President Harrison's Secretaries of the Treasury, Windom[60] and Foster. To be sure, Coe's earliest publication on the silver question in 1880[61] does not contain anything which would indicate that at that time he was a bimetallist, nor does his Introductory Address of 1883. A passage in the former speech even seems to repudiate bimetallism.[62] When he actually adopted the creed is not known to the author, but it was probably between 1883 and 1885, for in the latter year he presented to the

Chicago Convention of the A.B.A. a paper of S. Dana Horton on "The Internationality of the Silver Question" which promoted international bimetallism.[63] Coe was clever enough to see that no nation by itself could establish and uphold a workable brand of bimetallism; but he felt that the remonetization of silver and a fixed ratio of the values of the two precious metals could be achieved internationally.[64] Under these circumstances Coe became one of the backers of the attempts to organize international bimetallism and took a keen interest in S. Dana Horton's mission to Europe in 1891, a mission which aimed in this direction.[65]

The fact that Coe was actually a bimetallist distinguished him from many American businessmen, economists, and politicians who fought for "sound currency" in the 1880's and early 1890's and whom Coe joined. But, whatever his ultimate intentions were, he realized that America alone could not stem the tide against silver and that therefore it was necessary in the first instance to uphold the gold standard which was the monetary standard of the leading commercial nations of the world. As he expressed it in a letter of December 12, 1890[66] to Secretary Windom, since there existed a "unity of financial interest" among the leading nations of the world, uniform and internationally interchangeable money was indispensable and America must hold "fast to the recognized... money medium until by international agreement the two precious metals [could be] restored to their ancient parity and universal use." Free coinage of silver autonomously established by America would in his eyes be a case of "national conflict with higher commercial law." Thus while cooperating with the gold men his convictions induced Coe to retain a certain independence. For example, he did not sign the 1891 anti-silver declarations of the New York Chamber of Commerce,[67] although he was on the committee which was to urge on Congress the necessity of repealing the silver law.[68] On the other hand, in his public declarations of the last decade of his life he was careful not to stab in the back the men who fought for the gold standard pure and simple, although he did not disguise his bimetallistic point of view. Very typical in this respect are the statements in his Chicago speech of 1885 which may be quoted here:[69]

> It remains to be seen whether European nations will find it necessary to review the question in their own interest which from our point of view seems clearly to point to a substantial restoration of the former conditions of the two metals. It was with them that the disturbance began and it is there that the experience

should be fully tried and the final
conclusion reached... Is it not reasonable to believe that the two precious
metals which mankind in all ages of
the world have used together as money
must both continue to be, as they have
ever been, the indispensable servants
of social life? They are found together
in the mines and to dispense with one
will necessarily increase the cost of
the other... Ages of common use have
given them both the stamp of Divine
ordination. 'What God has joined together let no man put asunder.'..."

It was Coe's opinion that this country had an immense interest at stake, but that it could afford
to wait for the progress of the European investigation of and experience in the matter.

V

Coe was a rare specimen of the genus business leader in that he loved to study and to reflect on his business and his other pursuits. As
a contemporary columnist expressed it, Coe was
a man of "student-like appearance and of con-
templative nature,... one of the rare bankers who
find a great enjoyment in the speculative study
of financial subjects as [they] find in practical
banking itself... The study of finance as a science
is to him a greater pleasure than the practical
application of the science in the banking house."
According to this writer the New York bankers
considered him "the ablest theoretical banker in
the city."[70] Another journalist wrote a little later
that Coe was "a student of the vast interests with
which banking... is concerned," "a thinker of rare
penetration and power of careful and accurate
generalization. Probably there is no one in his
calling who has a clearer and more comprehensive and more practical knowledge of the principles of his business."[71]

Under these circumstances it is not surprising
that Coe was among the leaders of the movement
which aimed at the establishment of what became
academic schools of business administration.
He was on a committee appointed by the American
Bankers Association in 1890 to look into the matter of "schools of finance and economy."[72]

It will be shown that the above statements
describing Coe as a thinker need to be taken cum
grano salis; but no doubt Coe was a "thinker" and
an articulate one, and thus from his enunciations
the scholar is able to study in detail the intellectual world of a nineteenth-century American

business leader, albeit an atypical one for his
time. Coe possessed a consistent weltanschauung
which can be characterized as laissez-faire on a
Puritan background, with "Providence" taking a
considerable interest in business. On the whole it
was the same weltanschauung to which conservative businessmen try to cling even today, except
that it has grown somewhat stale since Coe's
time.[73]

For Coe, social reality was regulated by the
same laws which ruled the cosmos. "Is there [not]
a higher law prevading business affairs as truly
as there is one regulating the stars?" Coe asked;
and in another speech he proclaimed:

"There are ultimate truths and laws in
economic science as sacred and as obligatory as are those of the decalogue,
with which they are inseparably allied
in all the business of every-day life,
and while we may except to either of
these laws in practice, we cannot modify
their beneficent conditions nor abate
their universal claim upon men. It is
the highest function and duty of government to guard the people from the inevitable consequences of the infraction
of both these moral and material obligations."[74]

Coe's belief in natural laws as ruling society had
religious roots. He was an elder of the Presbyterian Church and an exponent of protestant ethics,
and therefore a believer in work as such having
a moral value. "Work is the condition of all
progress, the promoter of all virtues, the bond
and regulator of all social life."[75] For Coe "all
men [were] under a vital obligation to their
Creator, the world, and themselves diligently to
labor in some useful way... and to interchange
with others the fruit of their labor for mutual
benefit. Thus only can they fulfill the law of their
own nature and promote the general good." (There
is, of course, a good deal of Adam Smith in this
statement: Smith's idea of the human propensity
to truck and barter has, in Coe's language, become a divine obligation and Smith's idea of society
as being coordinated by the market is equally embodied.) Civil progress and "the largest development of humanity" were for Coe the result of
division of labor.

Besides being convinced of the existence of
immutable economic laws, Coe believed in "natural
rights which belonged to men," among which was
the "pursuit of happiness which means... property."
(This phrase is telling for those who know how
Jefferson once coined the trinity: life, liberty,

and pursuit of happiness, to replace the proposed phrase life, liberty, and property; and John Locke and English Whigs become evident as Coe's geistige ancestors.) Our privilege as citizens he believed to consist in that we could go everywhere and anywhere with our property unabated by government interference. To abate it would be infringement of natural rights. Thus in Coe's eyes the question of a government-issued currency could become "a moral as well as a financial question."

It goes without saying that in this world of Coe's the state (government) played a minor role compared with the "immutable" economic laws and natural rights, as is already indicated in statements previously quoted.

> The truth cannot be too often reiterated that all material values are governed by influences far beyond the reach of human vision and legislation, and every clumsy intervention of Government in a subject of such world-wide relations simply illustrates the impotence and the limitations of human law.[76]

Government stood for Coe "in the same financial relation to society as others, simply [as] exchangers of its service"[77] for the production of the country. He looked at government, as is still customary among businessmen, as some sort of enterprise to be judged with business yardsticks. By issuing legal tender notes the Treasury had become for Coe a kind of bank, and a bankrupt one since it held only about 40 per cent of its issues as a metallic reserve. The place which Coe assigned to government becomes evident in his statement that government could draw from the producers by taxation "such portion of the fruits of their labor as can be spared [underlining mine!] for the national administration and protection." National administration and protection were a sort of luxury, when compared with the needs of business, a point of view which shows how wide were the Atlantic and Pacific oceans in Coe's time and how far in the future was the atomic bomb. But in contrast to many of his contemporaries Coe was not hostile to the government nor did he show that contempt which one finds all too often in contemporary sources. He took for granted that the government should strictly abstain from any interference with business and he went very far in this respect, as will be shown shortly when Coe's monetary views are discussed. But in line with his general outlook he worked continuously for cooperation between banking and government in matters of monetary policy, provided, of course, he considered such policy sound. (For the historian it is obvious that here the borderline between unselfish service and the prosecution of selfish interests becomes shadowy.) For Coe the obligation to act unselfishly went far, at least at times. He considered it "a duty which everyone owe[d] to this country to hold himself in readiness... to be sacrificed on the altar of patriotism." (Old Judge Mellon in Pittsburgh and many others of Coe's generation would have disagreed wholeheartedly.) Coe's patriotism was distinctly national in character. He was imbued with "the idea of nationality," "this National [sic!] sentiment, now so potent and all prevailing" which, as he saw it, was strengthened by the history of the last few years and the expansion of modern transportation and communication.[78]

It can readily be seen that most of the elements which determined the thinking of this nineteenth-century business leader were essentially of eighteenth-century origin. Coe was immune to a typically nineteenth-century idea which proved most alluring to American businessmen: he had no use for Herbert Spencer's absorption of Darwinism into the field of sociology. For him business did not become a fight for the survival of the fittest as it did for many of his contemporary colleagues.[79] On the contrary, Coe's importance in American economic history lies in the fact that he was far ahead of his time as the exponent of voluntary cooperation between businessmen for business as well as economic ends. Coe believed in "social progress,"[80] but he did not state explicitly whether he considered cooperation as replacing competition in the course of that social progress. Be that as it may, in his attitude toward competition his ideas had veered away from those commonly held at his time. In a report of 1873 he condemned "sharp and degrading competition;" while in an address of 1884 he demanded that competition should be one of superior character, fidelity, and intelligent management. Banks, especially, as he expressed it in 1883, could not permit any member of the fraternity "to compete for business by introducing unsound and vicious practices which if adopted by all would impair the entire system and endanger the community."[81] There is to be found in Coe's writings hardly any trace of a belief that prosecution of his interest by everyone would result in social harmony, that typical eighteenth-century thought.[82] In contrast he even stood for group interference with the business of individuals for the common good.

Coe's important actions pertinent in this context have been described, and at this point the question arises: what theoretical and philosophical concepts prompted those actions. The answer seems to be that Coe acted intuitively and that later in his life he was guided by experience. Whenever he acted in the spirit of cooperation he did what seemed to him at that moment the thing to do and, like a true man of action, did not reflect. With his scanty education Coe was not an original and independent thinker, and therefore he was not articulate as to such moves as were for the moment almost revolutionary. But in advance of his time he possessed a clear insight into human interdependence. For him the "whole world [was] practically merged into one community as well of material as of moral interest;" and there was for him mutual dependence both of men and nations. Economics confirmed Christian teaching, and commerce and inventions contributed to making the world one "compact and vital organism."[83]

The conclusion to be drawn is this: Coe's weltanschauung served for preparing speeches; his actions which made history and the behavior which he practiced and preached to the business community were both based on inclinations, intuition, and experience; and he never realized the contradiction between his weltanschauung and his actions. It especially never occurred to him that his belief in immutable economic laws and his striving for cooperation, responsibility, and self-control of business did not quite jibe.

Turning from Coe's weltanschauung to his monetary theories one meets with a disappointment: some of the latter smack of contemporary undergraduate economics; platitudes were presented with too much emphasis and in language too flowery;[84] and the banker was not even up-to-date. The quantity theory of money, for example, was considered by Coe as a "mathematical truth" and was restated in its crudest, even then long-antiquated, form.

Coe distinguished between money and currency. Money, an "unvarying object,"[85] was what had an intrinsic value, and the adoption of the precious metals as such was due to "human instinct and necessity tantamount to Divine ordination." "Money cannot be made from paper. Any human attempt to create it is only a weak and ineffectual encroachment upon the Divine prerogative."[86] "Money is a mineral substance." It was its function to serve as an ultimate arbiter of commercial values and as a means for settling balances. Money being "itself the product of industry and the expressed value measured by the hours or days expended in its production" had an "inherent right to be what it is, the criterion of labor bestowed by men upon all other forms of labor."[87] "Convertibility into coined money [was] the ultimate claim for justice... on the trial of all commercial obligations."

Paper instruments which served as media of exchange were not money, but currency; and currency included notes, checks, bills of exchange, and deposits. That deposits were essentially different from notes was a long accepted belief, but one which Coe fought, and rightly so. Transactions not settled in money but in currency were barter, according to Coe.[88] Currency was "the declaration and testimony of labor existing elsewhere;"[89] "its total vitality resulted from the labor which preceded it." Currency derived its "power and significance from the property it conveyed." It was the "shadow of money" and supposed to be "true," that is to say, to be based on bills of exchange and notes representing goods moving from the producer to the consumer.[90] Notes and bills issued on credit alone were "empty vehicles, commercial kites, representatives without constituents." Currency was brought and was to be brought into existence in the wake of business transactions by commerce itself and by commerce alone.[91] That, if thus brought into being, there could never be too much currency in circulation, was a belief widely held by leading economists and representatives of commercial banking pure and simple. How much currency was needed in a national economy depended on "industrial work done;" thinking in terms of per capita ratios seemed absurd to Coe.

The creation of currency on any other basis than that described above was bound to lead, so Coe thought, to an unwarranted increase of purchasing power and, in the second instance, to an abandonment of specie payments. To use modern terms, Coe clearly understood the confiscatory character of any creation of additional purchasing power;[92] while, vice versa, he was blind to the economic dangers and injustices of deflation,[93] a typical business attitude of his time.

Coe took for granted that currency was backed by an adequate reserve,[94] but he objected to the rigid reserve requirements contained in the National Bank Act. It seemed "absurd" to him that the law compelled the banks to keep a definite ratio of money to liabilities. It was the function of reserves to be used in an emergency and consequently for him there was no sense in requiring that they be kept intact permanently. That would be the same as requiring a general to keep his reserves untouched in a battle.[95] But, like most of his contemporaries, he really misinterpreted the wording of the act.

On the basis of his presuppositions it is not surprising that Coe completely failed to understand the essentials of a government-issued currency. He could not and would not see how greenbacks could ever exist along with other "sound" currency; and the weaker his arguments the more emphatic became his denunciation of the treasury notes.[96]

He denied that the government could ever have any other function in the monetary field than stamping pieces of gold and silver. It had no legitimate right to issue currency (legal tenders, for instance). In so doing, it "impaired the Divine order of things" and "trespassed" on the private rights of the citizens.[97] It was admonished to withdraw the legal tenders completely, thereby leaving the monetary field to commerce, where it belonged. That Coe was against the National Banking system, as it stood, followed from the above theoretical presuppositions, for National Banks issued notes based on government debts. In the 1880's he considered American banking "by no means well established," but on the contrary, as being in a "chaotic condition." Obviously by 1890 he was pleased by the expectation of the approaching disintegration of the National Banking system because of the rapid reduction of the public debt. America had "yet to meet the currency question in all its phases," as he thought. As a matter of fact, he did not suggest a return to state banking; but felt that our currency should "go on bear[ing] the impress of nationality." What he proposed was the issue of general-asset banknotes by banks that were limited in their issues to a certain percentage of their capitals ($\frac{1}{2}$-$\frac{1}{4}$). Such notes should be preferred debts in case of bankruptcy and draw interest if not promptly redeemed.[98] (Coe was not aware that with these suggestions he was decades behind his time.) Such notes would be elastic, in contrast to National Bank notes which were not; and in this respect Coe was undoubtedly correct. Erroneously, however, he claimed that debt certificates had never served and never could serve as media of exchange in international trade. He did not know that in the late eighteenth and early nineteenth centuries, debt certificates had so served, as has been described in an earlier chapter,[99] and that they were not, as Coe would have expected, "instinctively repelled by merchants."

The preceding paragraphs show that aside from his vision regarding the need of cooperation and his insight into practical problems Coe on the whole had absorbed the basic economic thinking of his time uncritically and not without misunderstandings, due probably to his lack of formal education. There was one question, and in fact a very important one, which occupied his mind and on which he tried to think independently: What was the economic function of the commercial banker? The answer given in textbooks did not satisfy him, but in attempting to fill the gap Coe, as could be expected, fell into confusion. In a committee report of 1873[100] he had traditionally stressed the thought that banks were the "natural depositories for the current capital of the nation;" that their functions were to preserve the funds entrusted to their care, to "prevent them from falling into inactivity." In 1875 he had repeated the eighteenth-century theory that it was the function of banks to economize the use of money.[101] Thereafter cutting loose from the textbooks he conceived of banks and bankers as the "world's accountants."[102] He defined a bank as a depository of the money's worth of a variety of articles which its dealers produced and exchanged through the bank. Deposits in turn were the money's worth of existing commodities continually changing and moving about in kaleidoscopic variety from one form, from one person, and from one bank to another. Bankers bills receivable were chattel mortgages upon goods held in custody for the banks by their customers.[103]

It is evident that Coe cannot be compared with those men who were both successful bankers and influential banking theorists, such as Isaac Bronson in America, James W. Gilbart in England, and E. Albert Hahn in Germany. Coe's power of economic analysis was in fact very limited; he was an amateur in this field, but an amateur to whom the American banking community would listen year after year. What has been said previously about the relationship of Coe's weltanschauung to his most important actions finds a parallel in that between his monetary theories and the fiscal stratagems which he occasionally proposed. An analysis of his address of 1877 yields interesting results in this connection.[104] For approximately an hour Coe must have presented a naive monetary theory, and thereafter he proposed a financial plan, the underlying ideas of which, however, were not derived from the theoretical presuppositions, but from naive interpretation of his experience and from his interest as a businessman. The line of reasoning was as follows: The issue of legal tender notes antedated suspension; consequently they were the cause of suspension; consequently, if permanent resumption was desired, the original cause, the legal tenders, must be removed. Furthermore, banks are the legitimate issuers of currency, they have a vested right in so doing; and the government which interfered with that right should beware. Coe's theories unfortunately did not prove his recommendation and realizing this, perhaps subconsciously, he became emotional every time that he touched upon the sore spot.

Coe, the thinker, was at his best in his reports to the New York Clearing House Association, that is to say, when his thinking was directed toward business problems and business policy. In these reports it was guided by the feeling of responsibility and really was of "rare penetration." He was at his worst, in contrast, in his thinking on economic policy. Unbeknown to himself his personal business interests tainted it; and while he considered it to be based on "scientific" presuppositions the latter too often contained hidden value judgments and begged the question.

VI

In 1878 a columnist presented Coe in an editorial as the president of a large banking institution, chairman of the Executive Committee of the American Bankers Association, author of valuable speeches and essays on financial matters, and one of the men who endeavored, though in vain, to keep Secretary Chase from committing the blunders made by him in the years 1861-1863.[105] While the historian would not agree to the last

passage, he in turn would characterize Coe as the man who devised the Clearing House Loan Certificate, as the man who was foremost among those determining the country's financial policy during the first year of the Civil War; as a leader of the American banking community in the 1860's, 1870's, and 1880's (his platforms being the New York Clearing House and the American Bankers Association); and as the man who in an era of reckless competition and rugged individualism stood for responsible business administration, cooperation, and the self-policing of business.

When Coe died in 1896 there was nobody in New York on whom his mantle fell. The ideals for which he had striven, however, were by no means dead, and the torch with Coe had carried was taken over by James B. Forgan, the president of the First National Bank of Chicago, to whose activities so much space has been devoted in this volume.

Appendix

Letter of S. Dana Horton to George S. Coe
(from the George S. Coe Papers)

Vevey. 27. May/91

Dear Mr. Coe

I have just got your letter and am very grateful to you for it--

It is rather lonely business trying to steer so big a ship as a syndicate of nations, and your letter relieves that feeling wonderfully.

I am glad to know all is well with you, and greatly cheered about things generally by this friendly "hail"--

I have just telegraphed my good and true friend in Washington who is my intermediary there with [Senator Nelson W.] Aldrich and [Senator William B.] Allison -- Frank W. Hackett,[106] 486 Louisiana Av. -- as follows "Coe wrote Foster, Aldrich might see Coe."

April 5th I got a telegram from [James G.] Blaine [Secretary of State] at Rome saying the President [Harrison] had fixed April 15 as the termination of my official duties and saying I might send my report from Paris May 15.

That blunder is not yet rectified. The idea of taking away the official character from a man who is on the point of winning a battle!

That single blunder may defeat us for the year. (Excuse pencil) I telegraphed Hackett, and Aldrich and Allison saw [Secretary of the Treasury] Foster but it was the President's doing and he was away and Foster knew little or nothing of the matter. I should have written Foster but technically I have no business to write to anyone but Blaine.

You see?

Now it was supposed when Foster came in[107] that Aldrich and Allison would make it all right for me with Foster. Apparently there was something omitted! Now they want me to come home and educate the President I suppose. I am to tell him that he is a barbarian ignoramus? The resources of civilization are at a pretty low ebb -- when that is necessary!

I enclose some copies of letters[108] on the mere subject of my leaving Europe to visit America -- not on the subject of my giving up the mission. I am keeping that idea in the background. They could not conceive of America letting me give it up!

I am with my family for a few days after seven weeks absence plus the influenza but I have all the wires in my hand, and shall be back in the fight when my bodily presence in London is important.

Suppose Goschen, [Chancellor of the Exchequer] in answer to a question in the House of Commons, should reply "yes" to the idea of changing the Bank Act so as to take Silver Bullion equally with gold bullion as deposit provided other nations gave Free Coinage to Silver.

That would put England on the inclined plane would it not? It would start the movement on the Continent.

Now I have been striving for that ever since I got on this side in September. It can be done -- before August. England can be committed to joint action before the Farmers' Alliance Congress gets into the subject of Silver and upsets everything. But it is only on my lines that it can be done. I have worked, but only at half speed since April 5th -- Mr. [President] Harrison's order has cut down my 'horse-power' to that extent.

I sent my "report"[109] May 15th showing why extension is necessary. Foster ought to telegraph my 'extension' and tell me "to do the best I can." My position is not that of a diplomat under orders, not [that] of a subordinate official. It is that of proficient counsel in the midst of litigation. But then the President did not "see it" in March and April and who is to make him see it now?

Your letter is a reinforcement of most salutary purport. And as I said before I am very grateful for it--

Just to show you what I am doing I will ask you to read a note of some little things done lately. I went to Holland from London with Lord Reay[110] whom I have long endeavored to induce to take hold of the cause diplomatically from England as I do for the U.S. He is the one Member (of the House of Lords) who knows the ropes of European capitals and his character position and all are a mighty reinforcement. Arriving at 12 I dined with the Gov. of the Bank of Holland and Van der Berg ex Gov. of the Bank of Java, and [Gideon Maria] Boissevain, a strong man in Holland.[111] I wanted them to understand that it would not do for them to throw cold water on the idea that other nations would be content to give Free Coinage if England offered to take bullion. They must "lay low" and encourage Goschen in any start he can be got to make. Otherwise a cry from Holland might scare him off altogether.

Next day I went to Paris not stopping in Belgium because the men I wanted to see were away. There I dined among others with the French Minister of Commerce and showed him how things were and fixed him up with the idea I came with, viz., that "City opinion" in Paris discreetly used could work up "City opinion" in London, that if Goschen knows that "City opinion" in London would stand his coming out for something to encourage other nations in restoring silver he would be clay in the hands of the potters, to include [Sir William Harry] Houldsworth and [Henry] Gibbs [Baron Aldenham].[112] The Ministers at once proposed to send a Commissioner -- this is confidential under seven time locks -- to work the thing up. Now if I could Keep at them in Paris I could get that Commissioner started and be a "Dutch uncle" to him in London! Next day I went at the Gov. of the Bank of France on the same line to use his influence with Baron Rothschild. I enclose you a letter to and from Lord R. in London. I _sent_ a copy of the first with the pamphlet to Baron R. (Paris) saying if he wanted to talk of the matter I would be at the Continental Hotel in Paris on certain days. I heard nothing nor did I much expect he would say anything. But that can be put through too -- with perseverance and tact. You see I know him, I took his measure and he is the ablest of all the Rothschilds.

I wrote Gibbs that the same tactics ought to be used with Bleichröder[113] in Berlin, and he thinks my suggestion "very valuable" and will do what he can. But he _cannot do much._ I could do it if I could go to Berlin. But as matters stand I cannot do that. So it goes.

In short I have done service of which this is a little specimen since April 5 (as well as before) but my combinations are foiled by the act of the Government. The full concentration I had planned is defeated. The whole _point_ lies in taking the "7" [?] fullest advantage of the squeeze that is "on" in Europe.

Will it last?

Who can be sure? My idea is to strike while the iron is hot and there is no one on this side who can swing my hammer.

The bad harvest here plus the good harvest in America will help to maintain the pressure here -- if all turns out as it promises now.

But! How about paying for wheat with American securities? How about 20 millions of Silver that "in the normal course of business" we used to export. That stays at home now. Gold must go in its place and _stay._ You see?

The return flow of gold to America _may_ not take place!

And so the European scare may be calmed till Free Coinage agitation in Congress turns all Europe into spectators, waiting till America sets its gold free.

But! The way the Government have botched this whole business by preventing me from doing what I had set out to do! 5 months in Washington in 1889. 8 months in Washington in 1890. And now recall -- when if I had been allowed to work, as any common sense business man would be only to glad to let me I could have had the whole thing started by this time--
You understand that the good things you [illegible] say of me have their complete justification if only in this, that I am the _only man_ in the field of influence _from nation to nation all around the circle._ And when I think of all I have accomplished in England I wonder the Silver leaders are not more restive at my influence.

I say this because I want to add how harmful it would be for me to show any vainglory on that subject.

By the way I got them to concentrate their fire on [William] Lidderdale,[113] [governor of the Bank of England] and the lecturing I have done about their tactics in approaching Gladstone -- Whew!

I won't go on!
This is too much already -- but you are very good!

You know I would have appealed long ago to you and James (a Fairchild) if I had not felt that I had no business to weary you with well-doing -- _your_ well-doing, not mine!

If men like you were not so scarce! The fact is this -- if Windom's plan of letting me do my best with a _free mind_, with money enough to feel I could be justified in giving my prime of life, and labor without stint, to my work and yet be laying up something for the future -- if this be carried out Silver can be remonetized in Europe. And the money is appropriated $20000 last June and the same amount again in February, and I have received only part of the first 20000.

But if you ask _what will happen without me,_ I tell you I don't know. I know the men in each country and I know there is not a man who will not do his work better if I am there to stimulate him. There is no way of duplicating me. I am one of the founders [of the Bimetallic League], as [Enrico] Cernuschi is and [Emile, Baron de] Laveleye, [the Italian and Belgian economist, respectively] and I am the only man of them all who has tried cases, and fought his way to verdict and judgment and I speak their languages.

So I am a link in the chain. The chain does not hold if there is a link gone.

There is an illusion universal in America, and very natural, that is against me. Even Wm B. Dana has it. It is that there is such a 'person' as England, or France, etc. that _does_ this or that. There is no such person.

There are some Englishmen and Frenchmen and I alone know them all. They have their good points and their weak points. Add my _vis viva_ to them and they produce certain results.

I am not the road, nor the waggon, nor the horses nor the driver, but I am the right hand that grasps the whip and uses it.

Being that and knowing as I do the importance of my cause as an element of good government in my country I am not unconscious of the _barbarian_ quality of the way I have been treated. The mental qualities and character that my mission asks for are without precedent in our foreign relations, and if a parallel were sought at all one would have to go to Benjamin Franklin to get into the neighborhood of it.

Of course I do not mean to represent myself in magnificent proportions, but I do mean to say that half my strength in this matter is that I need no introduction to cabinet circles in any country in Europe because my name is known already as one of the masters in my specialty, and as an international, not a local, publicist, and as a man who can be trusted.

I ask myself how can we expect next winter to overcome the wild men in Washington when there is not virtue enough in the country to enable me to finish the good work now begun.

Your letter to Foster was to me pathetic as a cry for civilization from out of the depths of New York the pattern and foremost example of what American institutions have produced.

The bitterness is here --
I do not believe there is a power in Europe where a man like me could be located as I have been.

Mark, the whole thing is so _asinine._
If they wanted to haggle on the money let them do it -- let them say they are not disposed to give me the money that has appropriated for me -- etc. But that is not all that they do. They withdraw my official character, abruptly -- an act which is as if one should pull the tree up by the roots to see if it was growing.

And that is our Statesmanship as to Silver after the

struggle of 1889-1890-1891 with the storm cloud of the Farmer's Alliance on the horizon ! and when, meanwhile, Europe is still waiting to see the United States turn into a Silver country and leave its gold for Europe -- to bolster up the reputations of the gold men who have ruled so far!

The future of sound finance at stake, and Mr. Harrison is allowed to break down as far as he can the man who is in position to do what I can do --

Selah!

Remember me to Mrs. Coe and to your daughter-in-law and son. My wife is better this year than last and my boy is a comfort to his parents and looks like my father.

Yours faithfully

S. Dana Horton

FOOTNOTES

Appendix

GEORGE S. COE

NINETEENTH CENTURY BANKER
AND BUSINESS LEADER

1. This biographical sketch is based to a large extent on what remains of the papers of George S. Coe. Miss Mary P. McLean, Librarian of the American Bankers Association, was very helpful in tracking the papers down; and the owners, Coe's granddaughters, Miss Alice Stanley Coe of Englewood, N.J., and Mrs. Clinton H. Blake of Great Barrington, Mass., volunteered to deposit the material in the Baker Library of Harvard University. The material given by Miss Coe is cited as Coe Papers (C.P.); the gift of Mrs. Blake as Coe Scrap Books (C.S.B.).

2. Coe, Henry F., Descendants of Matthew Coe (Boston, 1894), 5, 40.

3. More or less reliable biographical sketches on Coe can be found in Dict. of Am. Biogr.; Cyclopedia of Am. Biogr., II (1892), 553; Hall, Henry, America's Successful Men of Affairs, I (New York, 1895), 145; Bayles, Richard Mather, History of Newport County, R.I. (New York, 1888), 585 ff; and in [Boston] Herald, Supplement, July 26, 1886. Obituaries were published in New York Times and Evening Post of May 4, 1896; in Bankers Magazine, LII (1896), 579 (this item is remarkably thin for a man like Coe); and in the Proceedings of the American Bankers Association (1896), 137a.
   Coe lived in Englewood, N.J., and Adeline W. Sterling's The Book of Englewood (Englewood, N.J., 1922) contains a few notes which permit glimpses into Coe's activities for the community in which he lived (see index). Pictures of Coe were published in the books by Bayles, Sterling (109), and in Hardenbrook, op. cit., 20.

4. A biography of Boorman can be found in the Dict. of Am. Biogr. The letter, which was obviously prized highly by Coe himself, is preserved in C.S.B.

5. Letter from the Ohio Philosophical and Historical Society.

6. Coe first appears in the New York City directory in 1849/1850 as "cashier of life ins. and trust co. 45 Wall," and is listed in this capacity through 1852/53. In 1853/54 and 1854/55

he appears as "banker;" 1855/1856 as "cashier," then as "vicepresident." His home was in Brooklyn.

7. This firm appeared in the New York City directories from 1847/48 through 1850/51 as Gilbert, Cobb and Johnson, brokers, 52 Wall. Then it became Gilbert and Johnson, brokers, 52 Wall (and later 41 William). In 1853/54 it is listed as Gilbert, Coe and Johnson, bankers, William c. Exchange Place. The firm was still listed in 1855/56. It can be found also in the list of New York bankers, brokers, and exchange dealers in Bankers Magazine, IX (1854/55), 23. (The data contained in this and the preceding footnote were kindly provided by Mr. Paul North Rice, chief, Reference Department, New York Public Library and by Mr. Edward H. Fenner, Reference Librarian, Business Library, Columbia University.) The following dates are usually given in the biographical notes on Coe: Gilbert, Coe and Johnson failed in 1854; Coe joined the American Exchange Bank the same year; and became its vice-president as early as 1855.

8. Bankers Magazine, L (1894/95), 3 ff. The assertion of the obituary that Coe played a leading part in 1858 in the attempt at abandoning the paying of interest on demand deposits is very doubtful.

9. "Bankers in Hot Debate" in Philadelphia Press, June 21, 1890, clipping in C.S.B. As to Williams, see Cycl. of Am. Biogr., I, 261, and History of the Chemical Bank (New York, 1913), 65 ff.

10. An example of the enthusiastic response of his collaborators is a letter of James M. Morrison to Coe, dated Sept. 23, 1879 (C.S.B.).

11. Elias Francis Spinner to Coe, April 2, 1875, C.S.B. The Coe papers indicate that he took a keen interest in Western and Canadian mining enterprises and he is known to have been a director in numerous corporations, most important among which were the Mutual Life Insurance Company of New York and the Postal Telegraph and Cable Company. This fact may indicate that Coe was a leader in financing corporations, but it may testify only to his possessing the confidence of the community and therefore to his being a desired director of reputable corporations. (Coe's trusteeship from 1856-1896 in the Mutual Life Insurance Company, an office which brought its holders a "considerable amount of prestige," is mentioned by Clough,

Shepard B., A Century of American Life Insurance: A History of the Mutual Life Insurance Company of New York [New York, 1946], 111, 349.)

12. Commercial and Financial Chronicle, LXII (1896), 848.

13. Coe's obituary in the American Bankers Association Proceedings (1895) states that he was "influential in securing the issue of clearing house loan certificates in times of panic." For details, see chapter XVII of this volume.

14. Address of 1884 before the New York Clearing House Association.

15. "... And his council and expedients have been so frequently followed by the associated banks during the special crises through which the country has passed..." "Commerce, the Maker of its own Currency" in The Chronicle, November 14, 1891.

16. See this volume, pages 165, 166.

17. See King, op. cit., 186.

18. So much can be deduced from a letter dated May 22, 1861 from Salmon P. Chase to James Gallatin and George S. Coe, who represented a committee of the New York Chamber of Commerce; Chase's private letterbook, Treasury Department Arch. in National Archives, Washington.

19. For a detailed description of the achievement and its collapse, see this volume, pages 88 ff.
    Coe's own version of the story is contained in a letter to Elbridge Gerry Spaulding, dated October 8, 1875, and contained in the latter's History of the Legal Tender Paper Money (Buffalo, 1869), Appendix, 89 ff. This letter is reprinted by Hardenbrook, op. cit., 11 ff. Coe referred to the transactions also in speeches before the American Bankers Association; see Proceedings (1876), 45; (1877), 34.

20. Letter to Spaulding, in Spaulding, op. cit., 89.

21. Ibid., 90.

22. A.B.A., Proceedings (1876), 33.

23. Letter to Spaulding, in Spaulding, op. cit., 93-95.

24. The report is reprinted by Sprague, Crises, 91 ff and by Hardenbrook, op. cit., 16 ff.

25. Op. Cit., 90.

26. One more suggestion of Coe's may be mentioned at least in a footnote since it gained importance later, that of charging exchange on out-of-town checks when deposited by customers.

27. Proceedings of the New York Clearing House Association, June 4th, 1884. Address of George S. Coe, President of the American Exchange Bank (printed by the New York Clearing House), reprinted in Bankers Magazine, XXXIX (1884), 43 ff, and by Sprague, op. cit., 371 ff, Report of a Special Committee appointed by the New York Clearing House Association to Recommend Reforms in the Practical Business of Banks (printed by the New York Clearing House). This report, which can be found reprinted in Bankers Magazine, XXXIX (1884), 129 ff, in Sprague, op. cit., 381 ff and in Hardenbrook, op. cit., 36, 37, was undoubtedly Coe's work.

28. That Coe devised and executed the policy of mobilizing the Clearing House Association for the purpose of making available immediately the securities of the Metropolitan Bank, and thereby averted disaster, is stressed in the previously cited article in the Boston Herald (see footnote 3). An enthusiastic private letter by Spinner to Coe, dated June 22, 1884 (preserved in C.S.B.) praises Coe for "resuscitating the Metropolitan Bank" and thereby saving the Jacksonville Bank and its depositors.

29. Coe preserved among his papers a printed sheet signed by Baldwin addressed to E.H. Perkins, Jr., Chairman of the Clearing House Association, in which Baldwin fought the plans for forbidding the receiving of checks and drafts on other cities as cash and the paying of interest on deposits. The main function of banks, he claimed, was the gathering together of idle funds so as to make them useful to the community and the above methods served that purpose. This way of arguing is typical of certain widely used tactics: Baldwin means business and talks economics. This document is reprinted by Sprague (Crises, 385, 386).

30. It is characteristic that in 1861 the important letters regarding the pending loan transaction were addressed by Chase to John Austin Stevens, those on details to Coe; Chase's private letter books, National Archives.

31. Proceedings (1876), 3.

32. Ibid. 34 ff.

33. Boston Herald, July 26, 1886. Coe was the chairman of the executive council from 1876 to 1881 when he became the president of the association. Upon refusing reelection in 1883 he again became the chairman of the executive council and remained so until 1886. From 1886 to 1889 and 1890 to 1893 he was a member of the council.

34. Proceedings (1883), 71, 72, 74.

35. See for instance Cincinnati Enquirer, October 8, 1879 (clipping in C.S.B.).

36. History of the Organization and Annual Conventions of the American Bankers Association (n.p., 1888), 4, 7; also in Proceedings (1888), 25, 26, 28.

37. A.B.A., Proceedings (1876), 70.

38. Cornelius Bliss (1833-1911), merchant, manufacturer, was in 1892 and following years treasurer of the Republican National Committee, and in 1896-98 Secretary of the Interior.

39. Charles Stewart Smith (1832-1909) was a New York drygoods merchant who retired from business in 1886 to devote his time to municipal

improvements and political reforms. He was a founder of the Fifth Avenue Bank and a director in several banks, savings banks, trust companies, and insurance companies. See Cycl. of American Biogr., XXIV, 252.

40. The fund (meant to reach at least $15,000, if possible $25,000) was originally organized by a number of enterprises, mostly private banks in New York, Boston refusing to cooperate. Besides H.B. Claflin and Company, drygoods merchants, these were Drexel, Morgan and Company; Morton, Bliss and Company; Brown Bros. and Company; Winslow, Lanier and Company; Blake Bros. and Company; Bliss, Fabyan and Company (of which Cornelius Bliss was a member); Smith, Hogg and Gardiner; Edward S. Jaffray and Company; and Phelps, Dodge and Company. Their contributions ranged from $250 to $500. They were joined by commercial banks and a few large companies. The banks were the First, Third, and Fourth National Banks, the National Bank of Commerce, the Merchants National Bank, the Bank of America, the National Bank of New York, the Republic National Bank, and the Importers and Traders National Bank. Arnold Constable and Company, Tiffany and Company, the United States Trust Company, and Lewis Brothers and Company were the other members of the group. They worked in Washington mainly through Representative Darwin R. James (1834-1908), a New York importer and Congressman (1883-1887); and the fund paid the campaign against another Bland bill for the free coinage of silver. The group had a special disbursing agent. Material on the Fairchild Fund is in C.P. Especially interesting is a letter from James to Coe dated April 5, 1886.

Incidentally, H. J. (probably Horace Jones) Fairchild, although belonging to the same family, was no close relative of Charles Stebbins Fairchild, in 1886 Assistant Secretary of the Treasury. See Fairchild, Timothy March, The Name and Family of Fairchild, (Iowa City, 1940).

41. See Proceedings (1893), 36, 37.
42. Introductory Address of..., President of the American Bankers Association to the Convention held in Louisville, Ky., October 10, 1883, 1-3. Also in Proceedings, (1883), 5 ff. The Proceedings of the early conventions of the A.B.A. are bound together in two volumes where they are easily accessible. Reports of the Proceedings at Conventions of the American Bankers Association from its Organization in 1875 to 1889, Vol. I, contains Conventions of 1875-1882, Vol. II, those of 1883-1889. The volumes are not currently paginated, but the page numbers run within the Proceedings of each convention. These volumes will be cited in future as Proceedings.

43. The taxes imposed in 1862 were those on bank capital, bank deposits, and checks. They were repealed by the Act of March 3, 1883; see Dewey, Financial History, 301, 419-420.
44. New York, 1868. The letter was first published in the Journal of Commerce and widely commented upon in the press (see collection of clippings in C.P.). Coe preserved among his papers numerous letters which he received approving his proposal, including those from James M. Morrison, president of the Bank of the Manhattan Company, Francis Elias Spinner, Samuel H. Walley, Elbridge Gerry Spaulding, J. Winslow, member of Winslow, Lanier and Company, and last, but not least, one from Pruyn himself.
45. An anonymous four-page folder dated June, 1877, and entitled "Resumption of Specie Payments," preserved in C.S.B. The essential section of the proposal is reprinted in the author's essay " 'Translating' Economic Policy into Business Policy" in Bulletin of the Business Historical Society, XX (1946), 190 ff.
46. Proceedings (1877), 40. On August 24, 1877, Coe asked President Hayes for an interview, presumably to discuss this plan. The letter is preserved in the Hayes Memorial, Fremont, Ohio.
47. The prevailing sentiment among the bankers was in fact for cooperation between banking community and government; see Proceedings (1877), 42 ff; (1878), 48.
48. Bulletin of the Business Historical Society, XX (1946), 193, 194.
49. Proceedings (1876), 48, (1877), 35. Coe seems to have recommended this policy also in an address delivered before the Merchants Club of Boston on December 7, 1878. He pointed out that the resumption of 1878 was not identical with that contemplated in 1866 and 1869 when complete withdrawal of the greenbacks was planned. Reports on this speech are to be found in The World of December 10 and in the New York Herald of December 8, 1878. (The latter report is entitled "Resumption. Mr. George S. Coe's Address on the Return of Specie Payments.")
50. New York Evening Post, November 12; Independent, November 14, 1891. (Clippings are in C.S.B.)

Coe was, of course, no narrow-minded partisan. On November 9, 1885 he wrote to William Lee Trenholm, the newly appointed (Democratic) Civil Service Commissioner: "Strange as it may seem for a Republican I find my highest enthusiasm kindled by the great measures of the present [Democratic] government..." A few months later he congratulated Trenholm upon his being appointed Comptroller of the Currency (March 20, 1886). The letters are in the Library of Congress.

51. Spinner (1802-1890) was U.S. Treasurer during Lincoln's presidency and many years thereafter (1861-1875). The letter in question is dated April 2, 1875, and the passage reads: "I have a thousand times thought what a pity it was that your services could not be secured as the Secretary of the Treasury." (C.S.B.)

52. Proceedings (1876), 49; (1877), 37. The above was also the salient point in the Saratoga speech of 1879 (see footnote 73). An encouraging letter from one Trowbridge dated October 7, 1879 is in C.S.B.

53. Remarks... upon the Silver Question (1885); also in Proceedings (1885), 33 ff.

54. This memorial to Congress signed by all members of the Committee, and by Coe in the first place, was published under the title The Silver Question, Memorial to Congress, January, 1878 (New York, 1878). It was obviously the work of Henry Varnum Poor, the railroad journalist and economist, who at that time wrote on monetary questions and whose assistance is acknowledged in the pamphlet. There was a good deal of cooperation between Poor and Coe: "at the instance" of the latter Poor was "called upon by the chair" during the 1877 convention of the A.B.A. and addressed the gathering [Proceedings (1877), 67]; and in the same year Poor dedicated his book, Money and its Law embracing a History of Monetary Theories and a History of the Currency of the United States (New York, 1877) to "George S. Coe, President of the American Exchange Bank and Chairman of the New York Clearing House Association, in token of esteem for his character and in acknowledgement of his earnest and intelligent labors for the reformation of our currency." Incidentally, there is in C.P. a letter from Poor to Coe dated November 25, 1891 dealing with monetary matters in which Coe is addressed as "My dear Friend," in which reference was made to an "old friendship," and in which the writer signed as Coe's "very warm, sincere friend."

On January 31, 1878 Coe sent a copy of the draft of that memorial to President Hayes. The accompanying letter is in the Hayes Memorial, Fremont, Ohio.

55. Dewey, Financial History, 408.

56. New York Clearing House Association. Its Relation to Gold and Silver Currency, 1878 and 1885 (privately printed). Coe's authorship is proved by his correspondence in C.P. Among the letters which Coe received upon the publication was one from August Belmont.

57. The Silver Question, 14, 15, 6.

58. The circular is reprinted by Hardenbrook, op. cit., 34. Coe himself proudly reported on this transaction to the American Bankers Association in a speech: Remarks of Geo S. Coe upon the Silver-Question, before the American Bankers Association at a Meeting in Chicago, Sept. 23d, 1885 (printed for private distribution). The speech is to be found also in Proceedings (1885), 33 ff. The passage reads as follows: "The temporary danger which existed until income... overtook expense was satisfactorily arranged by concert with the Clearing House Committee in New York whose earnest efforts at that critical moment preserved the gold standard and were enlisted in behalf of the commercial community which is their privilege to specially represent." The theory that the transaction was to a large degree Coe's work gains strength from the following fact: The Committee on Coinage, Weights and Measures which was then dominated by silver men instructed their chairman, Representative Bland, to submit a report to the House in which implicitly Coe was strictured for the actions of which he was so proud, but which looked so differently from the point of view of the exponents of silver. "Whereas at the Convention of the American Bankers Association held at Chicago, Ill., in the month of September 1885 Mr. George S. Coe, a member of the executive council of said association and the president of the American Exchange National Bank of New York City, made in an address delivered before the said convention the following statement..." the Secretary of the Treasury was asked whether or not any such agreement as referred to by Coe was made and carried out and by what authority of law. See Congressional Record, House, 49th Congress, 1st session (Feb. 3, 1886), XVII (1886), 1100. There is a lengthy report on this matter in an article "The Silver Question," dispatch to the Journal of Commerce, Feb. 2, 1886, in an unidentified issue of the latter; (clipping is in C.S.B.).

59. Material on this enterprise is in C.P.

60. Windom's Annual Report of the Secretary of the Treasury of 1889 (pp. lxvii, lxviii) expresses bimetallic ideas which are very similar to those held by Coe. As a matter of fact, there is a letter of Windom's in C.P. in which the Secretary thanked Coe for commending his plan for the solution of the silver question (Windom to Coe, December 6, 1889).

Incidentally the New York Historical Society possesses three letters of Coe's to Charles S. Fairchild, President Cleveland's Secretary of the Treasury, dated April 2, 1887, November 27, and December 8, 1888. In the first letter Coe expressed the gratification of the City at Fairchild's appointment and praised the latter's "commercial views and instincts." In that of November 27, 1888 Coe expressed the "cordial thanks of the New York Clearing House Association" for the authority given to the Treasury Department to issue certificates of deposit for gold endorsed "payable only to any Bank member of the Clearing House Association." Thereby a safe medium for the payment of clearing house balances both among the banks and between the banks and the treasury department was created, and the risk of transporting gold "through the crowded streets of New York" avoided. The third letter is uninteresting, a mere matter of courtesy.

61. The Silver Question. Address...at the Annual Convention of the American Bankers Association at Saratoga Springs, August 12th, 1880. This speech was widely circulated: the author has come across three editions. The speech is also to be found in Proceedings (1880).

62. Silver Question (p. 9) refers to European economists of widely recognized ability and experience regarding bimetallism "as entirely impracticable if not utterly inconsistent with natural law."

63. Proceedings (1885), 37 ff.

64. Coe expressed bimetallic views in public in his address of 1891: An Inside View of the Financial Situation, An address delivered at the Bankers' Convention in New Orleans, November 12th, 1891 (n.p., n.d.) and also contained in the Proceedings (1891), 43 ff. Coe's bimetallistic position is stressed by the reporters on the address in the Journal of Commerce of November 13, the Chronicle of November 14, and the Springfield Republican of November 19, 1891. (Clippings are in C.S.B.) A paper of this period can be found in Forum, XII (1891/92), 611 ff under the title "Why the Silver Law should be Repealed."

65. There is in the C.P. a letter of Horton's, the renowned American economist, which is so interesting both by describing Horton's activities and by reflecting on Coe's personality and interests that it is reprinted in the Appendix to this chapter.
Coe knew that funds for this mission were appropriated to the State Department. But, as Horton wrote to Coe on June 6, 1891, Blaine, the Secretary of State, turned over Horton and his mission to the Secretary of the Treasury, Mr. Windom. "Mr. Blaine ha[s] recognized by act, speech, and writing that the silver question and my [Horton's] work belonged to the Treasury and that the money appropriated for this purpose to the State Department was therefore indirectly held at the disposal of [the Secretary of the Treasury]."
The mission was so secret that Horton was instructed to write from time to time only confidential personal letters to Secretary Windom.
It was terminated by telegram as of April 15, 1891 since Foster, succeeding Windom upon the latter's sudden death, was not informed on the matter. So, at least, it appeared to Horton. In fact, the termination may well have been due to

a fundamental change in policy on the part of President Harrison. (This possibility may be deduced from a letter of Horton's to Coe of June 4, 1891.) For further details see Appendix and a pamphlet of S. Dana Horton without title page Report on the Remonetization of Silver in Europe, dated May 15, 1891, printed by the Imprimerie de la Société Anonyme de publications périodiques, Paris. Circular letter of June 10, 1891 from Horton to Senator Aldrich (copy in C.P.).

66. Copy is in C.P.

67. Incidentally Coe joined the New York State Chamber of Commerce in 1859; he became a member of its Committee on Finance in 1880 and the chairman in 1884. Annual Report of the Corporation of the Chamber of Commerce of the State of New York, 1896-97, 19.

68. Evening Post, November 12, 1891, clipping in C.S.B.

69. Remarks of Geo S. Coe upon the Silver Question before the American Bankers Association at a Meeting in Chicago, Sept. 23, 1885 (printed for private distribution); also in Proceedings (1885) 33 ff.

70. Philadelphia Press, June 21, 1890 (clipping in C.S.B.). The Independent in 1879 characterized Coe as "not only a practical banker, but also a scientific economist" (which, of course, he was not).

71. New York Times, December 23, 1891 [?], (clipping in C.S.B.).

72. A.B.A., Proceedings (1893), 77; idem, Education of Business Men (New York, 1892), 8.

73. Especially interesting are the Saratoga speech of 1878, the Boston speech of 1886, and the New Orleans speech of 1891. The following analysis is based on these sources if others are not cited in footnotes. The Saratoga speech was printed repeatedly: Is Resumption Complete? Address at the Annual Convention of the American Bankers' Association at Saratoga, August 7, 1879 (New York, 1879); Resumption, The Currency and the Banks, Address... (New York, 1879); it is printed also in Proceedings (1879), 38 ff. The address was widely commented upon in the press, e.g., The World, August 22, 1879; Cincinnati Enquirer, October 8, 1879; and others (clippings are in C.S.B.). The Boston speech, "Address on the Real Service that Banks Render to Commerce and How they do it," is to be found in Proceedings, (1886), 27 ff. The New Orleans speech finally was printed separately under the title, An Inside View of the Financial Situation, an Address delivered at the Bankers' Convention in New Orleans, November 12, 1891 (n.p., n.d.). (This edition was obviously for private distribution.) It is to be found also in Proceedings (1891), 43 ff.

74. Introductory Address of 1883, 11. In the same address Coe speaks of the "general perfection

of natural law" (p. 13), of "natural law of higher and universal power" (p. 18), "the greater law of supply and demand" (p. 20), and the "law of labor" (p. 22); but as to the latter he was hazy and did not explain what he meant. See also Proceedings (1877), 33. In 1879 Coe stated his conviction that immutable economic laws demanded the resumption of specie payments: It was the order of Providence against which we may not rebel that commerce should resume its normal conditions. (It would be totally erroneous to consider this statement hypocritical.)

75. "Address" of 1876, Proceedings (1876), 34.
76. The Silver Question, 8, 9.
77. Proceedings (1876), 51.
78. Introductory Address of 1883, 12. Very characteristic of Coe's national feeling is a speech on October 20, 1885, the manuscript of which is in C.P.
79. See Cochran and Miller, op. cit., 124 ff.
80. Introductory Address, 22; Silver Question, 4.
81. Introductory Address, 2.
82. The nearest statement is to be found in the Address of 1876 [Proceedings (1876), 34], that on the whole human society proceeded "regularly and harmoniously."
83. "Address on the Real Service that Banks Render to Commerce, and How They Do It," Proceedings (1886), 28.
84. See, for instance, his presentation of the labor theory of value in Proceedings (1875), 35, 36.
85. Proceedings (1877), 32. A short reference to Coe's opinions on monetary matters is in U.S. 53d Congr. 3d session, House Report 1508, 364.
86. The Real Service that Banks and Bankers Render to Society and their Relation to Currency. Introductory Address to the Convention of the American Bankers Association at Saratoga, August 16th, 1882 (New York, 1882). It may be found also in Proceedings (1882), 5 ff. For similar statements see ibid. (1875), 36.
87. Introductory Address of 1883, 9; also Proceedings (1883), 8.
88. See, for instance, Proceedings (1876), 37.
89. Ibid., 43, 44.
90. Proceedings (1877), 32.
91. See the tirade in Proceedings (1876), 40, 41.
92. His description of the economic consequences of a run-away inflation in Proceedings (1877), 36 is masterful and could be used today as classroom reading.
93. Proceedings (1877), 38.
94. See, for instance, Proceedings (1875), 43.
95. Report of the New York Clearing House Committee, November 11, 1873 (Sprague, op. cit., 95).
96. See Proceedings (1877), 35, 37; (1878), 49, 50; (1879), 41 ff.
97. Such ideas are to be found in the letter to Spaulding (Spaulding, op. cit., Appendix, 95, 96),

and are implied in the "wild" economic analysis of the legal tender issues in Proceedings (1876), 46, 47.
98. The Currency of the Future. What Shall it Be? Paper read before the American Bankers Association at Niagara Falls on August 11, 1881; also to be found in Proceedings (1881), 29 ff. Similar ideas were expressed in his "Remarks" made to the convention of the A.B.A. in Saratoga Springs in 1884, see Proceedings (1884) 94; The Question of Bank Circulation as viewed by Leading New York Bankers (re printed from the New York Daily Commercial Bulletin, December, 1883), 1, 2.
99. See this volume, p. 304.
100. See page 427. Similar ideas are to be found in the Introductory Address of 1883, 6. As to Coe's naive conceptions of the history of banking see Proceedings (1876), 37, 38, 40, 41. (The country store has all the essential elements of a bank!)
101. Ibid., 39.
102. The Real Service that Banks and Bankers Render to Society and their Relation to the Currency. Introductory Address to the Convention of the American Bankers Association in Saratoga, August 16, 1882. For the confusion in Coe's mind see also his "Address" of 1877 (Proceedings [1877], 32) and Introductory Address of 1883, 7 ff.
103. One must concede that Coe thought along the lines of Arthur Dahlburg; (see monograph 54, T.N.E.C., 54-58, 72, 73).
104. Proceedings (1877), 30 ff.
105. The World, New York, Dec. 10, 1878.
106. Then a lawyer, later Assistant Secretary of the Navy.
107. I.e., became Secretary of the Treasury upon Windom's sudden death in 1891.
108. They are in the Coe Papers.
109. "Remonetization of Silver in Europe," May 15, 1891. (Imprimerie de la Société Anonyme de publications périodiques.) The copy in the Widener Library of Harvard University (Econ 4470.55) is catalogued as Horton, Samuel Dana, Confidential Notes on Silver Diplomacy, A Letter.
110. Donald James Mackay, eleventh Baron Reay, Dutch diplomat, later naturalized English citizen, Governor of Bombay.
111. Boissevain, scion of a patrician family, (1837-1925), was a banker, economic writer, and bimetallist.
112. Houldsworth, a "landed proprietor" and M.P. took a keen interest in monetary matters. He was a member of the gold and silver commission, and a delegate to the Monetary Conference at Brussels, 1890. Gibbs was a merchant, scholar, M.P., president of the Bimetallic League.
113. Influential private banker.

LIST OF REFERENCES

Volume II

To be used in addition to the bibliography in Volume I. Each author's writings are arranged chronologically.

A.B.A. See American Bankers Association

Academy of Political Science in the City of New York. "The Reform of the Currency" in Proceedings, I (1910/11), No. 2.

Adams, Henry. The Life of Albert Gallatin. Philadelphia, 1880.

Adams, L. R., compiler. The Georgia Country Bankers Handbook. The Official Textbook of the Witham Banks. p.p., about 1920.

Adler, Cyrus. Jacob Henry Schiff. A Biographical Sketch. New York, 1921.

Alexander, Levy. Memoirs of the Life and Commercial Connections Public and Private of the Late Benj. Goldsmid, Esq. of Rochampton, Containing... London, 1808.

Allen, Frederick Lewis. The Great Pierpont Morgan. New York, 1949.

-----. The Lords of Creation. New York, 1935.

American Academy of Political and Social Science. "The Government Regulation of Banks and Trust Companies," in The Annals, XXIV (1904).

-----. "Banking Problems," in The Annals, XXXVI (1910).

-----. "The Need for Currency Reform," Supplement to The Annals, XXXVII (1911).

American Bankers Association. First Report of the Executive Council of the... for the year 1877, including the Addresses and Proceedings before the Committee of Ways and Means. 2nd ed. New York, 1877.

-----. History of the Organization and Annual Conventions... (Report of the Secretary... at the Convention held at Cincinnati, Ohio, October 3d and 4th, 1888). n.p., 1888.

-----. A Study of Group and Chain Banking: a Survey... New York, 1929.

-----. Economic Policy Commission. The Guaranty of Bank Deposits. A Historical Account... New York, 1933.

Ames, Gaston W. Gaston Griffin. A Country Banker. Port Jervis, New York, 1900.

Ames, Gaston W. Gaston Griffin. A Country Banker concluded. New York, 1901.

Ashmead, Graham. "Syndicate by Arrangement and Operation. The Machinery for Distribution and Marketing of Industrial Securities," in Trust Companies, XXXIII (1921).

Ashmead, Henry G. History of the Delaware County National Bank. Chester, Pa., 1914.

Ashton, John. A History of English Lotteries. London, 1893.

Ashton, T. S. "The Bill of Exchange and Private Banks in Lancashire 1790-1830," in Ec. Hist. Rev., XV (1945).

-----. "The Relation of Economy History to Economic Theory" in Economica, New Series, XIII (1946).

Atherton, Lewis E. The Southern Country Store 1800-1860. Baton Rouge, 1949.

Atkinson, Edward. What is a Bank? What Service Does a Bank Perform? A Lecture given before the Finance Club of Harvard University, March, 1880. Also... Boston, 1880; another edition, New York, 1881.

-----. "Address on Finance and Banking" at the Dinner of the Boston Boot and Shoe Club, December 17, 1890, in The Shoe and Leather Reporter of December 25, 1890.

-----. "The Banking Principle; or, Banking in its Relations to Currency," in New York Journal of Commerce and Commercial Bulletin, April 1, 1895.

-----. One Function of the Savings Bank; its Importance as a Lender or Distributor of Capital. Address... before the Savings Bank Association of the State of New York, May 20, 1897. n.p., 1897.

Austin, Edna Page. A Gallant Gentleman. The Life of Chellis A. Austin. New York, 1932.

Baasch, Ernst. Holländische Wirtschaftsgeschichte. Jena, 1927.

Bailey, T. A Correct Alphabetical List containing all the Country Bankers residing in England, Scotland and Wales with the Names of the Bankers in London upon which they draw... 6th ed., London, 1806; 9th ed., London, 1811.

Baird, Henry Carey. American and English Banking Contrasted. An Issue for Mr. Carnegie... Philadelphia, 1908.

Bank of Lexington. Charter and By-Laws. Philadelphia, 1838.

Bankers' Trust Company [New York]. Twenty-
five Years... 1903-1928. p.p., 1928.

Barker, Jacob. Letter from... to his Friend at
Bristol, Pennsylvania, in relation to the late
Conspiracy to Destroy the Exchange Bank.
New York, 1819.

Baroway, Aaron. "The Cohens of Maryland," in
Maryland Historical Magazine, XVIII (1923) and
XIX (1924).

[Bayne, S. G.] The Bankers Hall of Fame. [A Collection of Cartoons]. p.p. [New York], 1905.

Bentham, Jeremy. Defence of Usury shewing the
Impolicy of the Present Legal Restraints on the
Terms of Pecuniary Bargains. Philadelphia,
1796.

Blocker, John G. The Guaranty of State Bank De-
posits. [University of Kansas] Bureau of
Business Research, Kansas Studies in Business,
No. 11. Lawrence, Kansas, 1929.

Boies, William J. "Trust Companies and the
Panic" in American Review of Reviews, XXXVI
(1907).

Boissevain, Gideon Maria. Money and Banking in
the United States. Translated from the Dutch.
Amsterdam, 1909.

Bolles, Albert S. Bank Officers: Their Authority,
Duty and Liability. New York, 1890.

Bosch, Kornelis Douwe. De Nederlandse Beleg-
gingen in de Verenigte Staten. Amsterdam-
Brussel, 1948.

Bourne, H. R. Fox. English Merchants: Memoirs
in Illustration of the Progress of British Commerce. London, 1866.

Bouchary, Jean. Les Manieurs d'Argent à Paris
à la fin du XVIIIe siècle. 3 vols. Paris, 1939-
1943.

Boyd, Julian P. "John Sergeant's Mission to England for the Second Bank of the United States,"
in Pa. Mag. Hist. and Biog., LVIII (1934).

Brandeis, Louis D. Other People's Money and
How the Bankers Use It. New York, 1914.

Breckenridge, Roeliff Morton. "The Canadian
Banking System," in American Economic Asso-
ciation, Publications, Vol. X, Nos. 1-3. New
York, 1895.

-----. "The History of Banking in Canada." National Monetary Commission. U.S. 61st Congr.,
2d sess., Senate Document 332. Washington,
1910.

Brigham, Johnson. The Banker in Literature.
New York, 1910.

Brinkmann, Carl, ed. Zur Wirtschaftsgeschichte
der deutschen Unternehmung. Schriften der
Akademie für Deutsches Recht, Gruppe Wirt-
schaftswissenschaft, No. 5. Berlin, 1942.

Brooks, Francis A. Objections Legal and Practical to our National Currency System. n.p.,
n.d. [1893].

Bryan, William Jennings. Guaranteed Banks.
Topeka, Kansas, August 27, 1908, Chicago, 1908.

Bryson, A. E. Halsey, Stuart and Co., Inc. 1901-
1937. A History of the House with Observations
on the Bond Market and its Economic Background since the turn of the Century. (Typewritten copy in Baker Library of Harvard University.)

Buell, James. Statement of... [before] Committee
on Banking and Currency, February 9th, 1874.
p.p., 1874.

Burnham, Smith. First Hundred Years of the National Bank of Chester County 1814-1914. p.p.,
1914.

Campbell, E. G. The Reorganization of the American Railroad System, 1893-1900. New York,
1938.

Capefigue, Jean. Histoire des Grandes Opérations
Financières. 4 vols. Paris, 1855.

Carey, George G. Every Man his own Stock-Broker;
or a Complete Guide to the Public Funds. 2d
ed., London, 1821.

Carey, Henry Charles. Currency-Inflation. How
it has been produced and how it may be profitably
reduced. Letter to the Hon. B. H. Bristow.
Philadelphia, 1874.

Chamberlain, Lawrence. The Work of the Bond
House. New York, 1912.

Chapman, John M., Ray B. Westerfield, [and
others]. Branch Banking. Its Historical and
Theoretical Position in America and Abroad.
New York, 1942.

Chazotte, Peter Stephen. A New System of Banking Developed and Exemplified in a New Scheme
to Establish a Merchants Bank of General Deposits and also in a Scheme to Establish a Grand
National Bank. Philadelphia, 1815.

Cisco, John J. A Letter to the Secretary of the
Treasury from the Assistant Treasurer of the
United States at New York... New York, 1862.

Citizens Bank of Louisiana. Report of the Committee of Investigation... Appointed by the Direction of the Citizens Bank of Louisiana in
Uniformity with the Resolution of the Board of
18th October, 1838. New Orleans, 1839.

Clagett, W. H. Money, Banks, Panic and Prosperity.
No. 25. Farmers' Reading Circle Library.
Chicago, 1898.

Clapham, John H. "Loans and Subsidies in Time
of War," in Economic Journal, XXVII (1917).

Clark, S. M. Report to the Secretary of the
Treasury from the First Division National
Currency Bureau showing its Origin, Growth
and Present Condition. n.p., November, 1864.

Cleveland, Frederick A. The Banks and the Treasury. New York, 1905.

Clews, Henry. Our Monetary Evils. Some Suggestions for their Remedy. New York, 1872.

-----. No Government Guaranty of Bank Deposits and No Ownership of Railroads by the Government. An Address... p.p., 1908.

Cobbett, William. Paper Against Gold. [London, 1817.]

-----. Preliminary Part of Paper against Gold. London, 1821.

Coe, George S. Introductory Address of... President of the American Bankers' Association to the Convention held in Louisville, Ky., October 10, 1883. [n.p., 1883.]

[Coe, George S.] New York Clearing House Association. Its Relation to Gold and Silver Currency 1878 and 1885. [p.p., 1885.]

Coffin, George M. The A.B.C. of Banks and Banking. New York, 1903.

Coffinière, Antoine Siméon Gabriel. Stockbörse und der Handel in Staatspapieren... Aus dem Französischen... herausgegeben mit einem Nachtrage vom Geheimen Rath Schmalz zu Berlin. Berlin, 1824.

Cohen, Bernhard. Compendium of Finance, containing... London, 1822.

Colwell, Stephen. Remarks and Suggestions upon the State and National System of Banks, upon the Expansion of Currency, and Advance of Gold and the Defects of the Internal Revenue Bill of June, 1864. Philadelphia, 1864.

Commercial and Rail Road Bank of Vicksburg. Charter and By-Laws. Philadelphia, 1838.

Conant, Charles A. "The Growth of Trust Companies," in Review of Reviews, November, 1912.

Cooke, Jay and Co., Bankers. How to Organize a National Bank under Secretary Chase's Bill. Philadelphia, 1863.

Cooke, Jay. How our National Debt can be paid. The Wealth, Resources and Power of the People of the United States. Philadelphia, 1865.

Cooke, Thornton. "The Insurance of Bank Deposits in the West," in Quart. Jour. Econ., XXIV (1909/10).

-----. "Four Years more of Deposit Guaranty," in Quart. Jour. Econ., XXVIII (1913/14).

-----. "The Collapse of Bank-Deposit Guaranty in Oklahoma and its Position in other States," in Quart. Jour. Econ., XXXVIII (1923/24).

Cope, S. R. "The Goldsmids and the Development of the London Money Market during the Napoleonic War," in Economica, New Series, IX (1942).

-----. The History of Boyd, Benfield and Co. A Study in Merchant Banking in the last Decade of the Eighteenth Century. Typewritten Thesis, University of London, 1947.

Cornwall, William C. The Currency and the Banking Law of the Dominion of Canada Considered with reference to Currency Reform in the United States. New York, 1895.

Corti, Conte Egon Cesar. Der Aufstieg des Hauses Rothschild, 1770-1830. Leipzig, 1927.

-----. Das Haus Rothschild in der Zeit seiner Blüte, 1830-1871. Leipzig, 1928.

Crawford, John J. Bank Directors; their Powers, Duties and Liabilities. New York, 1907.

Dailey, Don M. "Smith and Scammon. Early Chicago Bankers," in Bull. Bus. Hist. Soc., XI (1937).

Dana, Julian. A. P. Giannini. Giant in the West. A Biography. New York, 1947.

Dana, Richard H., Jr. Usury Laws. Speech of... in the House of Representatives of Massachusetts, February 14, 1867 on the Repeal of the Usury Laws. New York, 1872.

Davis, Robert M. Public and Private Credit and Banking and their Abuses. New Orleans, 1869.

Dawes, Charles G. The Banking System of the United States and its relation to the Money and Business of the Country. Chicago, 1894.

De Kay, John W. The People's Money. A Brief Analysis of the Present Position in America. London, 1913.

Depew, Chauncey M. Postal Savings Banks. Speech of... in the United States Senate, December 15, 1908. Washington, 1909.

Dew, Thomas R. Essay on the Interest of Money and the Policy of Laws Against Usury. Shellbanks, Va., 1834.

Dietzel, Carl. Das System der Staatsanleihen im Zusammenhang der Volkswirthschaft betrachtet. Heidelberg, 1855.

Dillistin, William H. Bank Note Reporters and Counterfeit Detectors, 1826-1866 (Numismatic Notes and Monographs No. 114). New York, 1949.

-----. Directory of New Jersey Banks, 1804-1942. New Jersey Bankers Association, 1942.

-----. Historical Directory of the Banks of the State of New York. New York, 1946.

Drexel and Co. A New Home for an Old House. p.p. Philadelphia, 1927.

Dorfman, Joseph. The Economic Mind in American Civilization. Vol. III, 1865-1918. New York, 1949.

Dunbar, Charles F. "The National Banking System," in Quart. Jour. Econ., XII (1897/98).

Easterbrook, W. T. "The Climate of Enterprise," in Am. Ec. Rev., XXXIX (1949).

Easton, Harry Tucker. The History of a Banking House (Smith, Payne and Smiths). London, 1903.

Eckels, James H. [and others]. The Baltimore Plan for the Creation of a Safe and Elastic Currency. Addresses of... delivered at the Convention of the American Bankers Association at Baltimore, Oct. 11, 1894. Baltimore, 1894.

Edler, Friedrich. The Dutch Republic and the American Revolution. Johns Hopkins University Studies in Historical and Political Science Series XXIX, No. 2. Baltimore, 1911.

Effingham, Thomas Howard, 3d Earl of. An Essay on the Nature of a Loan, being an Introduction to the Knowledge of the Public Accounts. York, 1782.

Eichborn, Kurt von. Das Soll und Haben von Eichborn und Co. in 200 Jahren. 2d ed. München und Leipzig, 1928.

Escott, T. H. S. City Characters under Several Reigns. London, 1922.

Emerson, Thomas. [Letters]. [Windsor, Vermont, 1839?]

Evans, George Heberton, Jr. "The Early History of the Preferred Stock in the United States," in Am. Ec. Rev., XIX (1929).

-----. "The Entrepreneur and Economic Theory: A Historical and Analytical Approach," in Am. Ec. Rev., XXXIX (1949).

Fairman, William. The Stocks Examined and Compared: or a Guide to Purchasers in the Public Funds, containing... London, 1796.

Fazy, J. J., Opuscules financiers sur l'effet de privilèges, des emprunts publics et des conversions sur le crédit de l'industrie en France. Paris, 1826.

Fischer, Erich. "Der Staatsbankerott von 1816 und die Sanierung der österreichischen Finanzen nach den Napoleonischen Kriegen," in Zeitschrift für Volkswirtschaft und Sozialpolitik, Neue Folge, IV, (1924/25).

Fisk, Theophilus. An Oration on Banking, Education, etc. delivered at the Queen Street Theatre in the City of Charleston, S.C., July 4th, 1837. Charleston, 1837.

[Flint, Waldo]. Some Strictures on an Act to Provide a National Currency... Boston, 1863.

Foote, Allen Ripley. A Sound Currency and Banking System. How it may be Secured. New York, 1845.

[Fortune, E. F. Thomas.] Fortune's Epitome of Stocks and Public Funds; containing... 10th ed., London, 1820.

Foulke, Roy A. The Commercial Paper Market. New York, 1931.

Fowler, William W. Ten Years in Wall Street or Revelations of Inside Life and Experience on 'Change. Chicago, 1870.

Frame, Andrew J. Can the Severity of Panics be Ameliorated. Address... delivered at Waukesha, Wis., Friday, July 9, 1897. p.p.

-----. "Branch Banking and Asset Currency," in Bankers Magazine, Vol. LXIII (1901).

-----. "Shall we have a National Reserve Bank... A Monograph." Reprint from the American Bankers Convention Edition of The Wall Street Summary, Sept. 14, 1909.

-----. Conservatism our Watchword. This Criticism... p.p. Waukesha, Wis., 1911.

-----. Diagnosis of the National Monetary Commission Bill. Address... p.p., 1912.

Francis, John. Chronicles and Characters of the Stock Exchange. London, 1849.

Freeman, Pliny, and Hugh McCulloch. The National Standard Rate of Interest as a Regulator. Correspondence between... New York, 1872.

Gale, Samuel. An Essay on the Nature and Principles of Public Credit. London, 1784.

-----. Essay II on the Nature and Principles of Public Credit. London, 1784.

-----. Essay III on the Nature and Principles of Public Credit. London, 1786.

Gallatin, James. The Proposed United States Banking System and Further Issues of Legal Tenders. p.p., 1863.

Galston, Arthur. Security Syndicate Operations. Organization, Management and Accounting. New York, 1925.

Garraty, John Arthur. Silas Wright. New York, 1949.

Gerstenberg, Charles W. "The Underwriting of Securities by Syndicates," in Trust Companies, X (1910).

Gilbart, James William. History and Principles of Banking. The Laws of the Currency, etc. London, 1866.

Gilman, Theodore. Graded Banking System Formed by the Incorporation of Clearing Houses under a Federal Law with Power to Issue a Clearing House Currency by Pledge of Bank Assets... Boston and New York, 1898.

-----. Federal Clearing Houses. Boston and New York, 1899.

Gönner, Nicolaus T. von. Von Staatsschulden, deren Tilgungs-Anstalten und vom Handel mit Staatspapieren. München, 1826.

Gras, N. S. B. and Henrietta M. Larson. Casebook in American Business History. New York, 1939.

Greene, William B. Equality. West Brookfield, Mass., 1849.

-----. Mutual Banking. West Brookfield, Mass., 1850.

Greene, William B. Mutual Banking, showing the Radical Deficiency of the Present Circulating Medium... The Anti-interest League, [1896].

Grellier, J. J. The History of the National Debt from the Revolution in 1688 to the Beginning of the Year 1800... London, 1810.

Grimes, William H. The Story of Commercial Credit Company, 1912-1945. p.p., 1946.

Groom, Wallace P. Currency Needs or Commerce. National Paper Money, interchangeable with Government Bonds, advocated. New York, 1873.

[Grubb, Joseph C.]. A Plea for a Regulator of Finance by a Philadelphia Delegate to the National Board of Trade at its Meeting held in Baltimore, January 14, 1874 to which is added... p.p., [1874].

[Hagerstown Bank, Hagerstown, Md.] Hagerstown Bank at Hagerstown, Maryland, Annals of One Hundred Years, 1807-1907. n.p., 1910.

Hague, George. Banking and Commerce. A Practical Treatise... New York, 1908.

Hales, Charles. The Bank Mirror or a Guide to the Funds in which is given... London, 1796.

Hall, F. G. History of the Bank of Ireland. Dublin, 1949.

Halm, George N. Monetary Theory. A Modern Treatment of the Essentials of Money and Banking. Philadelphia, 1942.

Hamilton, Earl J. "Origin and Growth of the National Debt in Western Europe," in Am. Ec. Rev., XXXVII (1947).

Hammond, Bray. "Banking in the Early West: Monopoly, Prohibition, and Laissez Faire," in Jour. Econ. Hist., VIII (1948).

-----. "The Chestnut Street Raid on Wall Street, 1839," in Quart. Jour. Econ., LXI (1946-47).

-----. "Jackson, Biddle, and the Bank of the United States," in Jour. Econ. Hist., VII (1947).

Handlin, Oscar, and Mary Flug Handlin. Commonwealth. A Study of the Role of Government in the American Economy: Massachusetts, 1774-1861. New York, 1947.

Handy, William Matthews. Bank-systems of the World... also Postal Savings Banks... Chicago, 1897.

Harter, Michael D. American Banking and the Money Supply of the Future. Publications of the American Academy of Political and Social Science. No. 81. Philadelphia, 1893.

Hartley, Winchcombe Henry. An Address to the Public on the Subject of the late Loan. London, 1781.

Hartz, Louis. Economic Policy and Democratic Thought: Pennsylvania, 1776-1860. Cambridge, 1948.

Heaton, Ernest. The Trust Company Idea and its Development. Buffalo, 1904.

Helbing, Claus. Die Bethmanns. Aus der Geschichte eines alten Handelshauses zu Frankfurt am Main. Wiesbaden, 1948.

Helm, Florence. Banking Developments in Missouri, 1920-1936. Sedalia, Mo., 1939.

Hennet, Albin Joseph Ulgrien. Theorie du Crédit Public. Paris, 1816.

Hepburn, Alonzo Barton. History of Coinage and Currency in the United States and the Perennial Contest for Sound Money. New York, 1903.

Hibbert-Ware, Samuel. Remarks on the Facility of Obtaining Commercial Credit... Manchester, 1806.

Hidy, Muriel E. "The George Peabody Papers," in Bull. Bus. Hist. Soc., XIII (1938).

Hidy, Ralph W. The House of Baring and the American Trade 1830-1842. Unpubl. Ph.D. Thesis, Harvard, 1935.

-----. "Cushioning a Crisis in the London Money Market," in Bull. Bus. Hist. Soc., XX (1946).

-----. The House of Baring in American Trade and Finance. English Merchant Bankers at Work, 1763-1861. Cambridge, 1949.

Hill, Thomas E. Money Found: Recovered from its Hiding Places and Put into Circulation through Confidence in Government Banks. Chicago, 1894.

Hirst, Francis W. "The Credit of Nations" in U.S., 61st Congr. 2d sess., Senate Document 579. Washington, 1910.

Hodges, Almon D., Jr., ed. Almon Danforth Hodges and his Neighbors. An Autobiographical Sketch of a Typical Old New Englander. p.p. Boston, 1909.

Hollander, Jacob H. "Bank Loans and Stock Exchange Speculation," in U.S. 61st Congr. 2d sess., Senate Document 589. Washington, 1911.

-----. "The Security Holdings of National Banks," in Am. Econ. Rev., III (1913).

Homans, Isaac S., ed. The Banker's Almanac for 1851. Philadelphia, 1851. (Appeared from 1852 on as The Merchant's and Banker's Almanac.)

Hooper, Samuel. Banking Associations and Uniform Currency Bill with Extracts from the Reports of the Secretary of the Treasury submitted to Congress December 1861 and December 1862. n.p., n.d. [1863].

Hooper, Samuel.
Speeches delivered in the House of Representatives:
    On the Treasury Note Bill, Feb. 3, 1862. (Also circulated in a German translation.)
    On the Finances, Jan. 19, 1863.
    On the Necessity of Regulating the Currency of the Country, Apr. 6, 1864. Washington, 1864.

On the Loan Bill, Feb. 1, 1866. Washington, 1866.

On the Bill to Amend the National Banking Law, Feb. 5, 1867. Washington, 1867.

On the Necessity of Regulating the Currency of the Country, Feb. 5, 1867. Washington, 1867.

On the Necessity of Resuming Specie Payments, Feb. 5, 1869. Washington, 1869.

Hope, John. Letters on Credit. 2d ed., London, 1784.

Howe, M. A. De Wolfe. "A Great Private Citizen. Henry Lee Higginson," in The Atlantic Monthly, March, 1920.

Hull, Walter H., ed. Practical Problems in Banking and Currency being a Number of Selective Addresses delivered in Recent Years by Prominent Bankers, Financiers and Economists... New York, 1907.

Huth, Hans, ed. Talleyrand in America as a Financial Promoter, 1794-1796... Washington, 1942.

Indianapolis Monetary Convention. See Report of the Monetary Commission of the... [list of references, Vol. I of this work].

Jenks, William L. "Michigan's Five Million Dollar Loan" in Mich. Hist. Mag., XV (1931).

Jones, Chester Lloyd. The Economic History of the Anthracite Tidewater Canals. Publications of the University of Pennsylvania, Series in Economy and Public Law No. 22. Philadelphia, 1908.

Kapp, K. William. "Teaching of Economics: A New Approach," in Southern Economic Journal, XII (1945/46).

Kerr, Winfield S. John Sherman. His Life and Public Services. Boston, 1908.

Ketchum, William H. History of the Corn Exchange Bank, New York City, from the Time of its Organization in 1852 to March 1923. p.p., 1923.

Kirkbridge, Franklin B., and J. E. Sterrett. The Modern Trust Company: its Functions and its Organization. 1st ed. (New York, 1905), 4th ed. (New York, 1913).

Kirkland, Edward C. Men, Cities and Transportation. A Study in New England History, 1820-1900. Cambridge, 1948.

Kretschmer, Ernst. Geniale Menschen. Berlin, 1929.

Knox, John Jay. Remarks of... Comptroller of the Currency before the Committee on Banking and Currency, House of Representatives on the Substitute for a Bill to Retire the Circulating-

Notes of the National Banks, and for other Purposes... February 19, 1878. Washington, 1878.

Labouchère, G. "L'Annexion de la Louisiane aux Etats-Unis et les Maisons Hope et Baring," in Revue d'Histoire Diplomatique, XXX (1916).

Laffitte, Jacques. Mémoires. ed. by Paul Duchon. Paris, 1934.

Lake, Wilfred S. "The End of the Suffolk System," in Jour. Econ. Hist., VII (1947).

[Lancaster, J.] The Bank--The Stock Exchange--The Bankers--The Bankers' Clearing House--The Minister, and the Public. An Expose... London, 1821.

[Larson, Henrietta M.] "The Brighton Market Bank," in Bull. Bus. Hist. Soc., XII (1938).

Larson, Henrietta M. Guide to Business History. Cambridge, Mass., 1948.

Lawson, William John. History of Banking with a Comprehensive Account of the Origin, Rise, and Progress of the Banks in England, Ireland, and Scotland. London, 1850.

Lawson, Thomas W. Frenzied Finance. New York, 1905.

Lenz, Friedrich and Otto Unholtz. Die Geschichte des Bankhauses Gebrüder Schickler. Berlin, 1912.

Lockhart, Oliver C. "The Development of Interbank Borrowing in the National System, 1869-1914," in Jour. Pol. Econ., XXIX (1921).

Loehr, Rodney C. "Jason C. Eaton, Territorial Banker," in Minnesota History (Publ. Minn. Hist. Soc.), XXIX (1948).

[London, Daniel H.] The Exchequer explained and vindicated in a Series of Letters by the author of the Bill. New York, 1873.

London, Daniel H. [The Currency, Address of...] to the Members of the General Assembly of Virginia and the Friends of a Stable Currency... [New York, 1874.]

Löwitt, Karl. "The Theological Background of the Philosophy of History," in Social Research, XIII (1946/47).

Lotz, Walther. "Die Technik des deutschen Emissionsgeschäftes," in Schmoller's Jahrbuch, N.F. XIV (1890).

[Lowndes, pseud.] Plan of a Currency Agent to Obviate the Honest Objections of all Parties and to Meet the Views of Moderate Men. [n.p., 1843.]

Luxon, Norval Neil. Niles' Weekly Register. New Magazine of the Nineteenth Century. Baton Rouge, 1947.

Lyman, Rollo L., ed. Government Insurance of Bank Deposits. Reprint of Portions of Articles of... Material Collected by the Extension Division of the University of Wisconsin, F. A. Hutchins, Secretary, Department of Debating. [Madison, Wis.], 1908.

[Mackworth, Sir Humphrey.] Proposal for Paying Off the Public Debts by the Appropriated Funds... London, 1720.

McCleary, James T. Banking and Currency Reform. Its Necessity, its Possibility, its Method. An Address. n.p., n.d. [1911 or 1912].

McCulloch, Hugh. Our National and Financial Future. Address of... at Fort Wayne, Indiana, October 11, 1865. Fort Wayne, 1865.

McPherson, Logan G. The Monetary and Banking Problem. New York, 1896.

Marion, Marcel. Histoire financière de la France depuis 1715. Paris, 1914-1931.

Marshall, Alfred. "The Social Possibilities of Economic Chivalry," in Economic Journal, XVII (1907).

Martin, Asa Earl. "Lotteries in Pennsylvania prior to 1833," in Pa. Mag. Hist. and Biog., XLVIII (1924).

Martin, Joseph G. A Century of Finance. Martin's History of the Boston Stock and Money Markets, One Hundred Years from January 1798 to January 1898. Boston, 1898.

Mayer, Josephine and Robert A. East. "An Early Anglo-American Financial Transaction," in Bull. Bus. Hist. Soc., XI (1937).

Mendenhall, Thomas. A New Plan for a National Currency. Philadelphia, 1834.

Merk, Frederick. Economic History of Wisconsin during the Civil War Decade. Publications of the State Historical Society of Wisconsin, Studies, Vol. I. Madison, 1916.

Merriam, Clinton L. Banking and Currency. Speech of... of New York in the House of Representatives, March 27, 1874. Washington, 1874.

Merrick, Robert G. The Modern Credit Company. Its Place in Business Financing. Baltimore, 1922.

Miles, Herbert D. The Science of Currency and Centralized Banking... Chicago, 1911.

Miller, Alphonse B. Thaddeus Stevens. New York and London, 1939.

Miller, Addison C. "Historical Sketch of the Savings Bank of Utica, New York," A.B.A., Proceedings of the Convention... held at Kansas City, Mo.,... 1889. New York, 1889.

Mitchell, Alexander. Currency and Free Banking. Speech of... of Wisconsin in the House of Representatives, March 27, 1874. Washington, 1874.

-----. Papiergeld und Freibankwesen. Rede des Herrn... aus Wisconsin gehalten im Repräsentantenhause am 27. März 1874. Milwaukee, 1874. (A German translation of the preceeding item.)
for biography, see United States Works Progress Administration.

Money Trust Investigation. See U.S. Congress, House. Committee on Banking and Currency.

Moran, Charles. A Reply to "Mutual Banking." New York, 1871.

Morawetz, Victor. The Banking and Currency Problem in the United States. New York, 1909.

Morgan, J. P. and Co. Letter from Messrs... in Response to the Invitation of the Sub-Committee ... of the Committee on Banking and Currency in the House of Representatives. p.p. [New York], 1913.

Morgan, William. A Review of Dr. Price's Writings on the Finances of Great Britain... 2d ed., London, 1795.

Mortimer, Thomas. Every Man his Own Broker or A Guide to Exchange Alley. 10th ed., London, 1785.

Muhleman, Maurice L. Monetary and Banking Systems. A Comprehensive Account... with Complete Statistical Information... New York, 1908.

Myrick, Herbert. Co-operative Finance. An American Method for the American People... New York, 1912.

Nash, Bradley D. Investment Banking in England. Chicago, 1924.

Nash, William A. Branch Banking. An Address to Convention of New York State Bankers Association held at New York Clearing House, October 9th and 10th, 1902. p.p. 1902.

National Bank Note Redemption Association. Constitution adopted October 11, 1865. New York, 1865.

National Bank of America, Salina, Kansas. Letters from National Banks in Oklahoma upon the "Guaranty Law." p.p., 1909.

Nebenius, Friedrich. Der öffentliche Credit dargestellt in der Geschichte und in den Folgen der Finanzoperationen... Carlsruhe und Baden, 1820.

-----. Der öffentliche Credit. 2d ed. 1st part. Über die Natur und Ursachen des öffentlichen Credits, Staatsanlehen... Karlsruhe u. Baden, 1829.

Neu, Irene D. A Business Biography of Erastus Corning. Unpubl. Ph.D. Thesis, Cornell, 1950.

Newmarch, William. On the Loans Raised by Mr. Pitt during the First French War, 1793-1801 with... London, 1855.

New York Clearing House. Report on the National Bank Currency Act, its Defects and Effects. New York, 1863.

New York Clearing House Association. Proceedings of a Meeting of... held in Memory of Frederick D. Tappen..., March 10, 1902. [n.p., n.d.]

New York State Chamber of Commerce. Currency Legislation Pending in Congress. Report on the Subject by the Committee on Finance and Currency of the... New York, 1908.

New York, State. Laws of the... in relation to the Erie and Champlain Canals together with... Documents requisite for a Complete Official History of those Works. Albany, 1825.

[New York State, Legislature, Assembly] Report of the Committee appointed to inquire into the official conduct of the Hon. William W. Van Ness made in Assembly, April 5, 1820. Albany, 1820.

Niebyl, Karl H. Studies in the Classical Theories of Money. New York, 1946.

Nigohosian, V.A. La Libération du Territoire Français après Waterloo, 1815-1818. Thesis, Paris, 1929.

Nolte, Vincent. Fifty Years in Both Hemispheres or Reminiscences of the Life of a Former Merchant. Translated from the German. New York, 1854.

Nourse, Edwin G. Brokerage. New York, 1910.

Noyes, Alexander D. "The Trust Companies: Is There Danger in the System?" in Political Science Quarterly, XVI, (1901).

Paine, Albert Bigelow. George Fisher Baker. A Biography. p.p., 1920.

Paine, Thomas. The Decline and Fall of the English System of Finance. Philadelphia, 1796.

[Pallmann, Heinrich]. Simon Moritz von Bethmann und seine Vorfahren. p.p., Frankfurt a/Main, 1898.

Patterson, J.W. Observations on the Report of the Committee of the Senate of the United States respecting the Credit Mobilier of America. Washington, 1873.

Patterson, Raymond. The Central Bank Controversy [Letters republished from the Chicago Tribune, October, 1909] n.p., 1910.

Pearson, Henry Greenleaf. An American Railroad Builder, John Murray Forbes. Boston, 1911.

Pebrer, Pablo. Taxation, Revenue, Expenditure, Power, Statistics and Debt of the Whole British Empire. London, 1833.

[Peel, Sir Robert, 2d bart.] The National Debt Productive of National Prosperity. Warrington, 1787.

Penrose, Boies. "The Early Life of F. M. Drexel, 1792-1837. The Peregrinations of a Philadelphia Painter-Banker," in Pa. Mag. Hist. and Biog., LX (1936).

Percy, H.C. Our Cashier's Scrap-Book, being Bank Notes New and Old for General Circulation. A Portfolio of Bank Anecdotes... New York, 1879.

Pitkin, Timothy. A Statistical View of the Commerce of the United States... New York, 1817.

-----. A Statistical View of the Commerce of the United States of America including also an Account of Banks... New Haven, 1835.

Plenge, Johann. Gründung und Geschichte des Crédit Mobilier. Tübingen, 1903.

Poindexter, J. Carl. "Some Misconceptions of Banking and Interest Theory," in Southern Economic Journal, XII (1946/47).

Poor, Henry Varnum. Money and its Laws embracing a History of Monetary Theories and a History of the Currencies of the United States. New York, 1877.

-----. The Money Question. A Handbook for the Times. New York, 1898.

-----. Resumption and the Silver Question. New York, 1878.

Postlethwayt, Malachy. "Remarks on Banks and Banking," in The Universal Dictionary of Trade and Commerce. London, 1751.

Price, F. G. Hilton. A Handbook of London Bankers. [London, 1876].

Price, Richard. The State of the Public Debts and Finances... with a Plan of raising Money by Public Loans and for redeeming the Public Debt. London, 1783.

Prüfer, Walter. Methodologie zur Erforschung des Unternehmertums. Thesis, University of Leipzig, 1934.

[Pujo Committee] Report of [subcommittee of] Committee [on Banking and Currency] appointed pursuant to House Resolutions 429 and 504 to Investigate the Concentration of Control of Money and Credit. February 28, 1913. U.S. 62d Congr. 3d sess., House Report 1593.

Putney, Albert H. Currency, Banking and Exchange. Chicago, 1909.

Ramon, Gabriel. Histoire de la Banque de France d'après les sources originales. Paris, 1929.

Raymond, William L. "Investment Banking in the United States. Its Historical Background and Development," in Barron's The National Financial Weekly, VI (1926).

Revell, Alexander H. Guaranty of Bank Deposits. Chicago, 1908.

Reynolds, Arthur. Some Aids to the Solution of the Financial Problem. Address delivered before the Kansas Bankers Association, Wichita. n.p., 1909.

Reynolds, George M., and George E. Roberts. The Central Bank Idea. Minneapolis, n.d.

Reynolds, George M. Safeguards against Recurring Panics. Address before the... Texas Bankers Association... n.p., n.d. [1911].

Ricard, Samuel. Traité Général du Commerce contenant... Amsterdam, 1781. (edition by Thomas Antoine de Marion.)

Robb, Thomas Bruce. The Guaranty of Bank Deposits. Boston and New York, 1921.

[Ronaldson, Richard]. Banks and a Paper Currency: Their Effects on Society, by a Friend of the People. Philadelphia, 1832.

Ryan, Franklin W. Usury and Usury Laws. Boston, 1924.

Sakolski, Aaron M. The Great American Land Bubble. New York and London, 1932.

Salz, Arthur. "Vermögen und Vermögensbildung in der vorkapitalistischen und in der modernen kapitalistischen Wirtschaft," in Grundriss der Sozialökonomik, Sec. IV, Part I. Tübingen, 1925.

Sammis, L. Walter. "The Relation of Trust Companies to Industrial Combinations, as illustrated by the United States Shipbuilding Company," in Annals of the American Academy of Political and Social Science, XXIV (1904).

Satterlee, Herbert L. The Life of J. Pierpont Morgan. p.p., New York, 1937.

Schumpeter, Joseph A. "The Creative Response in Economic History," in Jour. Econ. Hist., VII (1947).

Schwartz, Anna Jacobson. "The Beginning of Competitive Banking in Philadelphia, 1782-1809." Jour. Pol. Econ., LV (1947).

Scudder, M.L., Jr. National Banking. A Discussion of the Merits of the Present System. Economic Monographs, No. XII, Honest Money League of the Northwest. New York, 1879.

Seay, George J. On the Fowler and Aldrich Bills. Address before the Convention of the Virginia Bankers Association at Lynchburg, Va., June 19, 1903. n.p., n.d. [1903].

Seligman, Edwin R.A. The Economics of Installment Selling. New York, 1927.

Seligman, Henry. The Financial Question. p.p., New York [1874].

Sherman, Roger M. [Letter to] Hon. Elisha Phelps, Controller of Public Accounts, Hartford, Conn. dated March 22. 1832 [broadside] "published at the request of the Controller." (The item is in the Baker Library of Harvard University.)

Shortt, Adam. "The Early History of Canadian Banking. Origin of the Canadian Banking System," in Journal of the Canadian Bankers' Association, IV (1896/97).

Silberling, Norman J. "Financial and Monetary Policy of Great Britain during the Napoleonic Wars," in Quart. Jour. Econ., XXXVIII (1923/24).

Sinclair, Sir John. The History of the Public Revenue of the British Empire. 2d ed., London, 1790.

Smith, Howard R. "The Role of Science in the Formulation of Economic Policy," in Southern Economic Journal, XII (1945/46).

Smith, James E. The Development of Trust Companies in the United States. New York, 1928.

Spooner, Lysander. A New Banking System. Boston, 1873.

Sprague, O.M.W. "Branch Banking in the United States," in Quart. Jour. Econ., XVII (1902/3).

-----. Banking Reform in the United States. Cambridge, 1913.

Starr, Chandler. An Address delivered at the Whig Convention held at Utica the 10th of September, 1834. New York, 1834.

Stevenson, Charles W. Postal Savings Banks. Address delivered before... the Missouri Bankers Association, October 20, 1909. p.p., [Warrensburg], 1909.

Stillwell, Silas M. A Report of Two Interviews with Hon... A Philosophical Explanation of the Laws that Control Free Banking, Exchange and Currency... Chicago, 1874.

-----. Private History of the Origin and Purpose of the National Banking Law and System of Organized Credits for the United States with Comments by the Author. New York, 1879.

Straus, S.W. and Co. Forty Years without Loss to Any Investor. p.p., 1922.

Strong, Benjamin, Jr. Seven Months of the New Banking System. Address before the New York State Bankers Association Convention... 1915. p.p., [1915].

Stubbe, Adolf. Organisation und Arbeitsteilung des Amerikanischen Bankwesens. Ph.D. Thesis, University of Berlin, 1906.

Swaine, Robert T. The Cravath Firm and its Predecessors. p.p., [New York], 1946.

Swanson, William Walker. The Establishment of the National Banking System. Ph.D. Thesis, University of Chicago, 1910.

Sweezy, Paul M. "The Decline of the Investment Banker," in Antioch Review, I (1947).

Tatham, Edward. A Letter to the Right Honourable William Pitt, Chancellor of the Exchequer, on the National Debt. n.p., 1795.

Tead, Edward L. An Address on Banking and Money. 1880.

Thom, Helen Hopkins. Johns Hopkins. A Silhouette. Baltimore, 1929.

Thomas, R.G. "Concentration of Banking Control through Interlocking Directorates as Typified by Chicago Banks" in The Journal of Business of the University of Chicago, VI (1933).

Thorold, Algar L. The Life of Henri Labouchere.
New York and London, 1913.

Tilton, Cecil G. William Chapman Ralston. Courageous Builder. Boston, 1935.

Tooke, John Horne. The Causes and Effects of
the National Debt and Paper Money... to which
is added an Appendix containing a Just and Impartial Review of the Funds of England... by the
late Dr. Price. London, 1818.

Turin, Guido. Der Begriff des Unternehmers.
Mitteilungen aus dem handelswissenschaftlichen
Seminar der Universität Zürich. Neue Folge.
Heft. 84. Zürich, 1947.

[United States Congress.] Memorial Addresses
on the Life and Character of Samuel Hooper
(a Representative from Massachusetts) delivered in Senate and House of Representatives,
February 20, 1875. U.S. 43d Congr. 2d sess.,
1875.

U.S. Congress. Sale of Bonds. Testimony Taken
by Committee on Finance. Investigation of the
Sale of Bonds during the years 1894, 1895, and
1896. U.S. 54th Congr. 2d sess., Senate Doc.
187. Washington, 1896.

U.S. Congress. House. Committee on Banking
and Currency. Hearings and Arguments before
the... 54th Congr. 1st and 2d sess., 1896-97.
Washington, 1897.

-----. Hearings and Arguments before the...
U.S. 56th Congr. 2d sess. Washington, 1901.

-----. Hearings and Arguments before... on Proposed Currency Legislation. U.S. 59th Congr.
2d sess., Dec. 11-15, 1906. Washington, 1907.

-----. Money Trust Investigation. Investigation
of Financial and Monetary Conditions in the
United States... Washington, 1913.

-----. Report of the... together with Hearings
thereof on Bill H.R. 8149. 53d Congr. 3d sess.,
1894. Washington, 1894.

-----. Report of the Special Subcommittee consisting of Hon. James T. McCleary, Hon. George
W. Prince, and Hon. John Murray Mitchell of
the... on the Bill... entitled a bill to provide...
for the amendment of the laws relating to National Banking Associations. March 23, 1898.
U.S. Congr. 2d sess., 1898.

United States. Laws. Laws... relating to Loans,
Paper Money, Banking, and Coinage 1790-1895.
U.S. 53d Congr. 3d sess. Senate Report 831.
Washington, 1896.

United States National Monetary Commission.
Vol. XX. Miscellaneous Articles. Washington,
1911.

United States Works Progress Administration.
[Biographical Sketch of Alexander Mitchell]
Typewritten manuscript, prepared by the Fed-
eral Writers' Project, in the State Historical
Society, Madison, Wis.

University of Illinois. Bureau of Business Research, Bulletin No. 39. Investment Banking in
Chicago. Urbana, 1931.

Vanderlip, Frank A. and Boyden Sparkes. From
Farm Boy to Financier. New York, 1935.

Van Vleck, George W. The Panic of 1857. An
Analytical Study. New York, 1943.

Van Vorhis, Flavius J. The Currency Trust Conspiracy. Indianapolis, Ind., 1910.

Vreeland, Edward B. Banking and Currency Reform. Address to the Pennsylvania Bankers'
Association at Bedford Springs, Pa., September,
1908. n.p., n.d.

Vührer, A. Histoire de la Dette Publique en France.
Paris, 1886.

Wade, Festus J. "How to Nullify the Bank Deposit
Guaranty Fallacy," in Trust Companies, IX
(1909).

Walker, Amasa. "The New Currency of the United
States," in Bankers Magazine, XII (1862/63).

Walker, Sir Edmund [Byron E.] Address at Meeting of New York State Bankers Association,
Saratoga, 10th July 1895. Toronto, 1895.

-----. Banking in Canada. Paper read before
the Congress of Bankers and Financiers,
Chicago, 23rd June, 1893. Toronto, 1896.

-----.The Relation of Banking to Business Enterprise. Address delivered at the Meeting of the
Louisiana Bankers Association... 1904 and before the Bankers Club of Detroit... 1904. n.p.,
n.d., (1904).

-----.Abnormal Features of American Banking.
Address... given at the Meeting of the American
Bankers Association, Denver, Colorado, 30th
Sept. 1908. n.p., n.d. [1908]

-----.Banking as a Public Service. Address before
the New York State Bankers Association. p.p.,
1912.

Walker, Joseph H. Argument of... in Exposition of
the Financial and Banking Situation of the Country
and in Explanation and Advocacy of his Bill.
(H.R. 171)... Washington, 1896.

-----. [Speeches and Addresses of] 1898-99.

Warburg, Paul M. A Central Bank System and the
United States. Address before the American
Bankers Association 1908.

-----. The Discount System in Europe. U.S. 61st
Congr. 2d sess., Senate Doc. 402 (1910).

Warburg, Paul M. A Plan for a Modified Central Bank. p.p., 1907.

Ward, George G. A Better Financial System or Government Banks. Boston, 1894.

Wasson, R. Gordon. The Hall Carbine Affair. A Study in Contemporary Folklore. New York, 1948.

Watt, Donald B. Investment Banking as a Career (American Council on Education, Vocational Monograph Series, No. 3), New Haven, 1929. (Chap. III, Outline of a History of Investment Banking).

Watson, Frank. A History of the Nebraska Bank Guaranty Law. Written and Submitted to the Federal Reserve Board, March 21, 1933. p.p., 1937.

Wettereau, James O. "The Branches of the First Bank of the United States," in The Tasks of Economic History, in Jour. Econ. Hist., II (1942).

[Whipple, John.] Jeremy Bentham and the Usury Laws, by a Rhode Islander. New York (?), 1836.

------. Stringent Usury Laws the best Defence against "Hard Times." n.p., n.d.

Whipple, John. Free Trade in Money or Noteshaving, the Great Cause of Fraud, Poverty and Ruin... An Answer to Jeremy Bentham. Boston, 1855.

------. Free Trade in Money, the Great and Principal Cause of Fraud, Poverty and Ruin... An Answer to Jeremy Bentham... with an Introduction by Nahum Capen. New York, 1878.

Wilder, S.V.S. Records from the Life of... New York, 1865.

Williams, John Earl. Letter to A.B.J., author of the Pamphlet Entitled "The Union as it was and the Constitution as it is." New York, 1863.

------. Letter to Hon. Robert C. Schenck, M.C.... on the Origin, Object, and Effect of the National Banking System of the United States with some Suggestions for its Improvement. New York, 1868.

------. Raising Money: A Paper by... of New York. Read at a National Conference of Unitarian and other Christian Churches. Boston, 1872.

------. Short Road to Specie Currency. Letter to Hon. Sir Francis Hincks. p.p., 1875.

------. Short Road to Specie Currency. Letter to the Hon. John Sherman and Hon. Sir Francis Hincks. p.p., 1875.

------. Save the Savings Banks. Remarks of... on Savings Banks, National Banks and National Currency at the American Bankers Association in Philadelphia, Oct. 4, 1876. New York, 1876.

Williamson, Harold F. The Growth of the American Economy. New York, 1944.

Winter, P.J. Het Aandeel van den Amsterdamschen Handel aan den Opbouw van het Amerikaansche Gemeenebest. The Hague, 1927.

Willis, Henry Parker. "Necessary Changes in the National Bank Act," in the George Washington University Bulletin, IV, 4 (1905).

Witham Bankers' Association. Proceedings of the Annual Convention... at Warm Springs, Ga... 1906. Successful Ways, Methods and Plans for Conducting a Country Bank. Atlanta, Ga. [1906].

Worley, Ted R., "The Control of the Real Estate Bank of the State of Arkansas 1836-1855," in Miss. Vall. Hist. Rev. XXXVII (1950/51).

Youngman, Elmer H. Credit Currency. New York, 1907.

Yuille, George Allen. The Confession of a Trust Magnate. Chicago, 1911.

ANONYMOUS

The Art of Stock-Jobbing Explained, exposing... 4th ed., London, 1816. 7th ed., London, 1819.

Bank Guarantee Scheme. Democratic Plan Condemned as Taxing the Honest and Prudent in favor of the Dishonest and Imprudent and Threatening the Basis of Business. p.p., 1908.

The Character of the National Government of the So-Called Free America of 1890. Boston, 1890.

"The Commercial Paper Business," in Federal Reserve Bulletin, VII (1921).

The Correspondence and Documents relating to the Proposals for Five Millions of Five per Cent Stock of the United States Created under the Act of Congress of the 3d of March, 1821. Philadelphia, 1822.

"Currency, Banking and Credit," in The New Englander, May, 1858.

The Currency Problem and the Present Financial Situation. A Series of Addresses delivered at Columbia University, 1907-1908. New York, 1908.

Curtius to the Secretary of the Treasury of the United States on the Subject of National Currency. New York, 1816.

A Familiar View of the Operation and Tendency of Usury Laws... being a Reply in Part to the Essay of a "Rhode Islander." New York, 1837.

"The Great Bond Conspiracy," from the New York World. [New York, 1904 (?)].

The History of the Movement for the Monetary Convention at Indianapolis, January 12th and 13th, 1897, and the Report of its Proceedings. n.p. [Indianapolis], n.d. [1897].

Henry Purkitt Kidder, Born Jan. 18, 1823 Died Jan. 28, 1886. p.p., Boston, n.d. [1886].

The Impolicy of Returning Bankers to Parliament in the Ensuing General Election... by a Friend of the Poor. London, 1802.

Intercollegiate Debates. See Pearson, Paul M. ed. in Bibliography to Vol. I of this work.

Investment Banking in Chicago. University of Illinois. Bureau of Business Research, Bulletin 39. Urbana, Ill., 1931.

Der Kluge Kapitalist oder Praktische Darstellung der verschiedenen Arten Geschäfte und Spekulazionen in Staatspapieren mit Vortheil zu machen. Ein nützliches Taschenbuch für Kapitalisten, Käufer und Verkäufer von Staatspapieren und für alle Personen welche in Geschäften mit öffentlichen Fonds zu thun haben. Wien, 1824, im Schrämblischen Bücherverlage.

A Letter to the Right Honourable William Pitt, Chancellor of the Exchequer, on his Conduct with respect to the Loan concluded on the twenty-fifth of November last... London, 1796.

The Letters of Publius on the Subject of Reforming the Banking System and Currency of the United States and of Providing a Substitute for a National Bank and a Sub-Treasury System. Washington, 1838.

Letters on Banks and Banking Containing an Account of the Operations of the Special Banking System of New England by Silex. Boston, 1853.

Observations on the National Debt and An Enquiry into its Real Connection with the General Prosperity. Norwich, 1797.

On the Debt of the Nation compared with its Revenue and the Impossibility of carrying on the War without Public Economy. London, 1781.

"100 Years of Banking in New York," in Banking Law Journal, XVII (1900).

Remarks on the Projected Abolition of the Usury Laws... Edinburgh, 1818.

The Remedy in a National Bank of the People versus a Treasury Bank and a National Bank of a Party: An Appeal to the People of the United States with a Plan, by an American Citizen. New York, 1838.

A Reply to the Report of a Committee of the New York Clearing House Association on the National Bank Currency Act. n.p., 1864.

"Report of the Select Committee appointed to enquire into the Circumstances of the late Loan," in Journal of the House of Commons, LI (1795/96).

Thoughts on Banking and the Currency; by a Citizen of Western New York. Seneca Falls, 1836.

A Treatise on the Currency and the Exchanges, proposing a Remedy... by the Establishment of a General Exchange Office which shall also be the Fiscal Agent of Government. New York, 1841.

World's Congress of Bankers and Financiers, comprising Addresses upon Selected Financial Subjects and also a Series of Papers on Banking... Chicago, 1893.

A Peep into the Banks and a Glance at the Consequences of Creating Monied Institutions; by an Observer. New York, 1828.

Principles of Safe Banking Applied to Trust Companies. n.p., n.d.

SUBJECT INDEX

FOR VOLUMES I AND II

Absorption of banks by others, see Mergers.

Acceptances, see Drafts, accepting of...

Accomodation paper, accomodation loans 10-12, 43-48, 57, 66, 126, 135, 139, 140, 142, 192, 206, 208, 224, 235, 269, 296; II, 3, 34, 38, 39, 116, 251, 292, 326

Accomodations, see Bank loans

Accounting, accounts 16, 30, 39, 53, 59, 60, 63, 77, 83, 92, 103, 115, 119, 123, 127, 161, 211, 219, 224; II, 4, 7, 11, 24, 45, 46, 48-50, 54, 56, 62, 63, 66, 67, 70, 78-80, 177, 179, 182, 183, 185, 186, 197, 204, 216, 223, 224, 236-240, 247, 249-252, 258, 260, 268, 284, 285, 297, 309, 341, 380, 382

Accountants, see Employees

"Active Capital," productive capital 29, 109, 124; II, 39, 437

Administration of banks

administrative staff 18-20, 36-41, 55-65, 85, 90, 105-109, 113-119, 123, 146, 150, 159, 169, 183, 184, 202, 255; II, 11-13, 202-207, 213, 214, 257, 415

autonomy of 61, 63, 118, 121; II, 12, 378

by committees, see Committees

in the sense of bank management 9, 17-20, 29, 34, 39, 41, 55-67, 74, 79, 83-85, 89, 90, 93, 98, 105-107, 113, 114, 116, 117, 119-121, 123, 143, 144, 180, 208, 211, 222; II, 12, 13, 33-35, 47, 54, 63, 109, 117, 138, 194, 197, 201-207, 218, 261, 267, 276, 279, 339, 393, 438

Administration of savings banks 210, 211, 212, 215, 216, 218, 219, 220, 222, 223, 229, 230, 302

Administrative control, 106, 116, 118-120, 134, 271, 273

Advantages of banks, disadvantages 7, 8, 9, 28, 29, 31, 43, 65, 111, 232

Advertising (publicity), propaganda 9, 132, 141, 148-153, 167, 221, 222, 244; II, 35, 65, 73, 76, 87, 88, 177, 182, 197, 200, 216, 218, 219, 224, 279, 300, 316, 318, 320, 336, 344, 347, 355-357, 360, 369, 371, 376, 381, 398, 417

Affiliates II, 180, 181, 182, 183, 191, 192, 193, 230, 373, 379, 392-395, 422

Agents, agencies

of banks 21, 70, 72, 73, 93, 109, 124, 145, 149, 156; II, 193, 212, 214, 220, 221, 245, 254, 258, 266, 270, 336, 348

of English merchant bankers and of investment bankers 54, 101, 126, 127; II, 33, 35, 333, 335-337, 349, 353, 370, 388

Agrarian radicalism (liberalism) 108, 162, 164, 165, 167, 168, 171, 244; II, 13

Agreements among banks, see Cooperation

Agriculture, agricultural, see also Credit, agricultural, 9, 25, 48, 103, 112, 129, 168, 174, 205; II, 34, 326

Aldrich Plan II, 209-211

Aldrich-Vreeland Act II, 167, 168

Alliances of banks, bankers, see also Investment bankers, alliances of... 68, 70, 73, 75, 76; II, 96, 109, 247, 255, 257, 258, 270, 271, 289, 295

American Bankers Association II, 124, 151, 167, 168, 176, 177, 179, 182, 185, 191, 193, 195, 203, 209-212, 214, 218, 220-222, 227, 237, 242, 270, 281-283, 287-289, 302, 366, 429, 430, 433, 434, 438, 443, 445

American banking likened to Bank of England II, 15, 105

American Institute of Bank Clerks, American Institute of Banking II, 203

Annuities II, 306, 397, 400-402

Antagonism to banks, attacks on banks 8, 9, 18, 65, 106, 111, 118, 165-172, 188, 211, 287; II, 13, 27, 145, 197, 279, 280

Anti-Capitalistic, see Capitalism

Anti-Monopoly Party,... tradition 196; II, 122

Aristocracy, aristocratic 22, 38, 155, 159, 163, 166, 171, 214, 216, 286, 290; II, 123, 367, 383

Armstrong investigation II, 187

Articles of association 35, 36, 199, 202, 213, 217, 224, 227, 300; II, 102, 352

Arts, artisan, see Crafts, craftsman

Assayers turning bankers II, 74

Asset currency, see Security behind bank notes, general assets

Assets

current II, 2, 274

earning, see Active capital

frozen 105, 115, 124; II, 257, 361

immediate, see current

in general 13, 126, 153; II, 182, 186, 191, 192, 197, 204, 223, 256, 260, 325, 341, 348

Assignment of property 182; II, 58

Associated banks, see also Clearing house member banks, Bankers' associations, in emergencies, 73, 74, 84-86; II, 7, 10, 48, 50, 54, 57, 89-91, 106, 107, 140, 158, 159, 162-164, 167, 170, 242, 283-285, 411, 427-429

...of New York, Boston and Philadelphia (1861) 87; II, 87-95, 103, 140, 142, 162, 286, 287, 426

"Assorting house" 77, 79, 80; II, 115, 122, 154, 270, 271, 289

Attorney General 173, 174, 296; II, 195, 196

Auctioneers 126, 186; II, 58, 63, 348

Auditing, see Accounting

Austrian loans, see Imperial loans

Automatism, see Self-regulation

Automobile industry II, 395

"Baby bonds" II, 357

Balance of trade, balance of payments, balance of indebtedness 100, 130; II, 6, 115, 265

Balance sheets of banks 13, 15, 160; II, 4, 341, 425

Balances, see Bankers' balances, Inter-bank obligations

"Baltimore Plan" II, 210, 217

Bank

administration, see Administration of banks

boards, see Boards of directors

charter, national 45, 98, 102, 104, 111, 118, 121, 123, 130, 131, 138, 143-146, 150, 159, 167, 168, 173, 174, 179, 181, 200; II, 23, 193, 221, 325

charters, see also Charter 7, 8, 12, 13, 20-22, 25, 28, 31-34, 36, 43, 47, 49, 54, 55, 57, 60-62, 68, 77, 78, 85-95, 115, 144, 145, 189, 190, 197, 202, 203, 207, 208, 211, 232, 252, 294, 297, 298; II, 5, 11, 12, 22-25, 33, 38, 63, 101, 103, 107, 112, 113, 138, 142, 178, 187, 202, 257, 263, 272, 273, 295, 325, 339-341; renewal of ... 89, 100, 102, 111, 121, 138, 139, 141, 146, 147, 150, 151, 153, 154, 163, 167-170, 173-175, 177-181, 200, 282, 287, 289; II, 23, 39, 62, 257, 324, 415, 432

commissioners and similar public officers (comptroller, superintendent of banking department, etc.); see also Comptroller of the Currency 76, 77, 80, 87-89, 91-94, 125, 144, 191, 194, 197, 199, 200, 203, 297; II, 2, 4, 5, 7-14, 23, 24, 26, 27, 43, 57, 60, 65, 100, 101, 110, 147, 178, 192, 193, 204, 215, 257, 261, 270, 277, 331, 339, 390, 394, 414

conventions, conferences, meetings 73, 76, 136; II, 89-92, 106, 108, 114, 116, 195, 209-211, 222, 240, 241, 248, 252-255, 257, 258, 260, 262-271, 273, 275-283, 288, 289, 297, 301, 353, 381, 429, 430, 433, 445

credit, see Bank loans, Book credits

currency, see Bank notes, Circulation, Currency

customers, "dealers" 11, 22, 47, 52, 53, 56, 65, 69, 122, 126, 131, 194; II, 12, 13; 40, 45, 49, 60, 62, 63, 73, 78, 117, 158, 167, 175, 179, 180, 186, 192, 207, 222-224, 237, 241, 247, 251, 254, 277, 285, 309, 310, 376, 389, 392, 427, 429, 437

debtors, see Borrowing from banks, Debtors

directors 11, 13, 15, 16, 18-20, 22, 25, 26, 28, 30-32, 34-40, 52, 55-65, 69, 71, 72, 82, 85, 98, 99, 107, 110-114, 116-118, 120-123, 153, 154, 159, 161, 166, 169, 174, 184, 186, 191, 200, 207, 211, 229, 230, 232, 253, 256, 257, 261, 262, 266, 269, 287, 288; II, 8, 11, 12, 20, 34, 36-38, 45, 46, 56, 58, 60-66, 96, 106, 109, 111, 112, 114, 116, 132, 133, 140, 143, 144, 153, 154, 163, 181-183, 185, 188-190, 197, 198, 202-207, 213, 222, 223, 225, 227, 233, 245, 246, 248, 249, 252-255, 259, 272, 275, 280, 292, 293, 295-301, 309, 312, 318, 324, 328, 330, 338, 341, 349, 352, 373, 391, 411, 417; abuse of their position 11, 22, 56, 117, 253; II, 13, 70, 205, 318; functions of... 55, 56, 58-60, 63, 64, 82, 85, 95, 98, 116, 117, 120-123, 203, 232, 243, 253; II, 11, 12, 24, 204-207; incompetence, negligence of... 65, 118; II, 12, 20; reasons for becoming, for being made 37, 47, 55, 56, 98, 116, 117, 253; II, 20, 207; records 15, 59, 63, 74; II, 257, 267; remuneration of... 18, 25, 55, 56, 252, 255; II, 12; representing "interests" 116, 117; II, 207; rotation in office 117, 118, 159; selection of ..., election of ...55, 62, 114, 116-120, 159, 169, 184, 185, 252; II, 13, 25-27, 205, 206

examinations, ...examiners: (in general) 52, 92, 95, 203; II, 48, 204, 224, 261, 286, 425; by clearing houses, see Clearing house examinations; by directors or their committees or employees or by stockholders 18; II, 12, 20, 24, 204, 205; by legislative committees or public officers 92, 93, 95, 200, 203, 265; II, 23, 202

failures 41, 56, 66, 68, 69, 80, 89-91, 94, 95, 107, 108, 161, 174, 191, 194, 197, 200, 202, 207, 208, 215, 230; II, 24, 58, 107, 111, 129, 130, 137, 141, 178, 183, 190, 193, 201, 202, 215-217, 223, 261, 268, 272, 285-287, 289, 293, 337, 338, 341, 342, 353, 363, 380; 390, 391, 395, 424, 425, 427, 428, 437; actions taken by solvent banks in case of... (see also Clearing houses, emergency actions) II, 277, 428; threaten the banking community II, 258, 284, 285, 298, 428

founders, incorporators 6, 8, 20, 24-37, 39, 45, 69, 76, 85, 136, 187, 201, 206, 208, 212, 214, 232, 242, 244, 259, 263; II, 27, 37, 108-112, 151, 153, 198-202, 299-301

in the sense of fund 15, 24

loans, lending activities of banks, see also Call loans, Demand loans, Policy of banks, lending, 6, 7, 11-13, 27, 32, 33, 35, 43-50, 62, 65, 66, 68, 74, 82, 94, 99, 100, 103, 114, 119, 122, 124-127, 130, 131, 136, 137, 141, 142, 150, 153, 154, 159, 176, 182, 187, 194, 195, 198, 205, 206, 208, 215, 220, 227, 228, 239, 248, 249, 253, 266, 269, 282, 297; II, 2, 4, 5, 12, 13, 38, 39, 43, 47, 49, 63-66, 69, 70, 72, 75-78, 96, 116, 121, 123, 132, 158, 160, 161, 163, 164, 166, 167, 175, 180-183, 200, 202, 203, 205, 206, 213, 215, 220, 224, 227, 245-249, 252-255, 259-261, 271, 274, 284, 285, 295, 299, 303, 304, 325, 338-340, 349, 353; calling of ... 48, 50, 64, 193; II, 158, 166, 180,

calling of ... (cont'd.) 249-251, 259, 260; cost
of ... 94, 126; distribution of ... 47, 49, 114;
II, 39; limitation of total 68, 195, 257, 296;
II, 2, 3, 20, 39, 42, 78, 133, 213, 249; limitation
of to any one or certain borrowers II, 131, 185;
payment, settlement of ..., see Debts, payment
of ...; security behind ..., see Security behind
bank loans

management, see Administration of banks in the
sense of bank management

money, see Bank notes

note companies II, 152

note detectors II, 111, 349

note issue the characteristic feature of banking,
... synonymous with banking, notes identified
with bank debts 12, 13, 43, 64, 91, 187; II, 1,
60, 118, 208

notes, bank money, bank paper, see also National
Bank notes, Small notes, 6-9, 11-18, 21, 24, 27,
28, 33, 41, 43, 44, 46, 49, 50-52, 59, 60, 63-70,
72-75, 77, 78, 80-83, 91-95, 97-100, 102, 104-
106, 108-110, 112, 124, 125, 128-130, 132, 135,
139, 140, 145, 161, 165, 167, 168, 172, 174, 175,
187-191, 193-197, 199, 205, 206, 219, 220, 234,
236, 237, 238, 246, 250, 253, 258, 259, 264, 273,
275, 288, 293, 295, 296; II, 1, 3-6, 8-10, 13-15,
22, 36, 37, 42, 45-49, 56, 60, 61, 63-66, 72, 73,
84, 87, 93-95, 99-103, 105, 108, 110, 111, 113,
120-123, 128, 137, 138, 142, 147-149, 152, 158-
160, 164, 166, 175-178, 194, 198, 208-210, 213-
215, 219, 221, 245-252, 257-263, 268-271, 273,
275-278, 284, 292, 295-297, 309, 317, 332, 346,
389, 390, 427, 436; acceptable by collectors,
see Collectors of Internal Revenue; assorting
of ... 80, 83, 84; II, 46, 114, 116, 277; buying
of ... 16, 69, 72, 73, 78; character of ... 193;
II, 1, 116; issued by private bankers II, 60, 61,
63-66; issued without a regular banking business 79, 263; II, 15, 278; exchange of ... 71, 73,
76-78, 124; II, 45-48, 55, 245, 246, 248, 249,
251, 259-261, 266-270, 274, 292; interest bearing ... 27; "marked" 259; II, 4; packages of ...
83, 84; II, 129, 159, 270; payment of ..., redemption of .. see Redemption; worn-out and mutilated
18; II, 109, 116, 131; see also Circulating of
notes, Circulation, Clearing, Country notes, Currency, Hypothecation of notes, Lending of notes,
National Bank notes, Redemption of notes, Small
notes

officers, see also Cashiers, Presidents 19, 34
40, 57-59, 61-63, 83, 90, 93, 113-120, 126, 131,
139, 143, 146, 255, 257; II, 11-13, 36, 49, 50,
52, 70, 86, 89, 93, 106, 110, 111, 132, 140, 143,
144, 181-183, 185, 190, 197, 198, 202-205, 207,
223-225, 238, 253, 259-264, 275, 282, 330, 373,
394, 427, 428; functions, obligations of ... 58,

83, 84, 114, 115, 117, 119, 136, 151, 154, 274; II, 202,
206; salaries, compensation of ... 113-115; II, 11

organization 17-20, 25, 34, 36, 55-64, 106, 115,
118, 119, 120, 144, 145, 255; II, 11-13, 22, 23, 71,
72, 74, 75, 184-202; internal, see also Foreign
money department, 39; II, 185, 186, 203, 204, 207,
221, 236, 388, 392

paper, see Bank notes

personnel, see Bank officers, Cashiers, Employees, Presidents of banks

process 232

statements 92, 93, 139, 140, 144; II, 7, 36, 39,
117, 133, 161, 164, 165, 186, 249, 255, 256,
260-262, 266-268, 284, 288, 297, 339, 340

stock, shares 8, 9, 12, 13, 16-18, 21, 26-28, 30,
32, 33, 36, 41, 48, 57, 62, 65, 76, 77, 152, 154,
167, 169, 183, 184, 187, 201-203, 206, 220, 223,
227-229, 234, 287, 298, 303; II, 12, 33, 62-64,
66, 111, 132, 139, 181, 183, 184, 186, 187, 190,
191, 197, 198, 201, 205, 207, 218, 305, 313, 324,
327, 334, 336, 339, 341, 390, 393, 399; forfeited
57, 58, 61, 124; held abroad 112, 166, 169, 287;
II, 62, 63, 313; held by states, by federal government, see State and federal participation in
banks; its distribution 17, 26, 197, 232, 240,
242; II, 12, 13; of other banks held by banks 13,
18, 49, 76, 144, 259; II, 181, 245, 295, 324, 325,
339, 341, 393, 409; prohibition of banks from
owning their own stock II, 14; quotations II, 184,
226, 227

veto 166, 167, 173, 174, 288

war 50, 117, 118, 121, 131, 132, 134, 143-145,
147-156, 160, 162, 163, 165-167, 170-174, 178-
180, 188, 196, 198, 200, 265, 266, 281, 288, 290;
II, 23, 213

Banker (term) 17, 64

Bankers'
associations, see also American Bankers Association II, 110, 182, 215, 218, 229, 237, 246,
252, 258, 270, 271, 276, 280, 281, 283, 288, 289,
301, 302; in emergencies, see also Joint committees II, 259, 260, 261, 264, 266, 269, 272,
278, 417; internal organization of ... II, 270, 280,
282, 283; officers of ..., organization of ... II,
276-278, 280-282, 429; policy of ... II, 276, 280

balances, for short term ..., see Inter-bank obligations 16, 22, 49-54, 70, 71, 73-79, 142, 262;
II, 2-4, 6, 7, 45, 65, 66, 72, 76, 77, 117, 132,
133, 141, 193, 239, 240, 248, 250-252, 256, 259-
261, 268, 269, 284, 295-297, 379, 428

banks 75-77, 85, 100, 104, 142, 261; II, 115, 212
214, 215, 219, 239, 241, 295

Banking
and monetary theory, ... philosophy 5, 7, 8, 11,
26-29, 43, 46, 47, 64-66, 75, 91, 92, 111, 112,

124, 125, 129, 137, 139, 143, 158, 169-172, 174,
191-196, 198, 201, 202, 233, 234, 270, 275, 279,
294, 296, 297; II, 4, 8, 14, 22, 29, 32, 35-37,
105, 175, 208, 210, 216, 263, 305, 324, 436, 437;
Isaac Bronson's 46, 47, 91, 139, 193-195; II, 3,
36, 38, 39

business 10-17, 44-54, 69, 72, 98, 109, 170, 172,
193, 200; II, 5, 36, 54, 61, 121, 124, 127, 175,
176, 180-183, 213, 220, 274, 339; of private
bankers II, 61, 63-66, 73, 75, 76

by mail II, 177

capital of a city or region 65, 72; II, 46

legislation, see also National Bank Act, Safety
Fund Act, 8, 13, 21, 44, 47, 53, 54, 68, 70, 78,
79, 82, 85, 89, 91-95, 104, 106, 144, 153, 165,
174, 188, 190, 193, 194, 196, 197, 199, 201-204,
208, 220, 221, 224, 225, 227-229, 236, 248, 261,
264, 266, 297, 298; II, 1, 2, 6-15, 23-28, 32, 35,
37-40, 43, 47, 60, 61, 64, 70, 74, 78, 92, 93,
100-103, 108-110, 113, 114, 116, 121, 137, 138,
141-143, 145, 146, 167, 176, 178, 195, 196, 212,
215, 217-220, 229, 247, 252, 257, 266, 270, 273,
276, 278, 280-285, 287, 324, 325, 327, 331, 332,
339, 364, 379, 394, 429, 432; determines business policy 79, 80; II, 15, 67, 78, 110, 187, 201,
207, 239, 249, 264, 267, 270, 272, 324

movement II, 36, 37, 39

on bills of exchange 120, 129, 131, 140; II, 3

on capital, see also Capital, banks lend their...
64, 193

on credit, see Credit of banks, to be lent

on land and merchandise, see Land banks

on mercantile credit, see Money banks

on "private credit," see Land banks

on real and personal estates, see Land banks

policy, see Policy, public toward banks

principle, school II, 38, 105

profession, ... expertness 19, 41, 62, 63; II, 430

profession or trade? II, 202

statistics II, 74, 109, 175, 178, 183-186, 194, 196,
223, 224

system 20-23, 52, 89, 96, 98, 99, 101, 109, 128,
134, 137, 142, 170, 171, 176, 189, 197, 228, 289;
II, 13, 32, 54, 117, 256, 267, 274, 276, 277, 282,
286, 290, 303, 410, 428

Bankruptcy, failures, involvency, bankrupt, insolvent, see also Bank failures, 33, 41, 48, 56,
64, 90, 104, 107, 108, 160, 164, 182, 183; II, 12,
26, 36, 57, 61, 63, 69, 71, 73, 96, 109, 121, 145,
158, 247, 311, 312, 315, 335, 340, 342, 348-350,
353, 361, 363, 367, 386, 389, 435

Banks

of circulation, of issue 13, 96, 168, 193, 197, 199,
237; II, 62, 121, 213, 278

of deposit 13, 27, 168, 169, 197, 199, 209, 237,
291; II, 4, 62, 113, 121

of discount 9, 13, 168, 193, 197, 199, 207, 237,
291; II, 39, 62, 64, 113

of redemption 72-87; II, 114

viewed as public or semipublic institutions, see
Public and semipublic character of banks

Bar, see Jurists

Bears II, 310, 317, 323

Bids, bidding on securities, see Loan contractors,
Investment bankers, business methods, Subscriptions, "public"

Bill brokers II, 15, 77, 78, 84, 203, 314

Bill drawers II, 67, 69, 70

Bills

legal term 93-95, 102, 107, 151, 174, 187, 188,
197-201, 203, 204, 211, 290; II, 9, 23-27, 29,
38, 39, 47, 95, 99, 101, 102, 104-108, 111, 113,
117, 123, 141-143, 167, 168, 176, 195, 208, 209,
211, 213-216, 287, 365, 409, 415

of exchange, see also Banking on..., Domestic,
Foreign exchange 10, 11, 18, 27, 29, 43, 45, 47,
51, 56-58, 94, 108, 114, 126, 129, 131, 133-137,
139, 141, 145, 157, 164, 172, 234, 237, 239, 254,
262, 269, 276; II, 10, 11, 13, 36, 64, 67, 68, 70,
73, 77-79, 82-84, 93, 140, 161, 165, 168, 179,
204, 222, 247, 249, 251, 294, 314, 340, 343, 436

of lading II, 69

Bi-metallism 134, 158; II, 433, 439-441, 445, 446

Bland-Allison Act, Bland bill II, 431, 432, 444

Boards

of cashiers (Philadelphia, Baltimore) II, 52, 53,
274, 275, 299

of control of state banks with branches II, 23-27,
30

of directors 17-19, 30, 32, 34, 38, 39, 41, 55,
57-61, 63, 67, 92, 98-100, 105, 107, 110, 112,
113, 115, 117-123, 143, 144, 146, 153, 159, 176,
183-185, 211, 217, 228, 230, 254, 256, 257, 262,
263, 269, 273; II, 11-13, 32-35, 38, 46, 62, 83,
107, 160, 170, 179, 182, 196, 197, 200, 201, 203,
204, 206, 207, 224, 245, 246, 248-250, 254-256,
258, 259, 268, 272, 294, 295, 297, 393, 395;
appointing power 18-20, 56, 57, 60, 67, 113, 114,
123, 211, 241, 255; II, 12, 204, 205; as administrative bodies 11, 18, 20, 55, 57-59, 61, 62, 118,
121, 211, 241, 252, 255, 256; II, 12, 132, 200,
204-206; as policy making bodies 18-20, 59, 61,
62, 105, 108, 141, 211, 223, 241, 256; II, 11-13,
205-207; chairman of ..., see Chairman; con-
troling, examining, supervisory power 18, 19,
117, 118; II, 12, 204-206; functions in general
18, 61, 62, 65, 67, 76, 211, 241, 255; II, 11, 12,
205-207; meetings 11, 18, 19, 57-59, 61-63, 118,
122, 211, 261; II, 12, 203, 204, 291; meetings
jointly with those of other banks II, 248; of
branches 114-117, 119, 120, 153, 159; II, 27

of presidents and their committees 80; II, 52, 53,

of presidents and their committees (cont'd.) 58, 90, 91, 107, 159, 160, 163, 166, 261, 266, 267, 274, 275, 284, 289

of trade, see Chamber of Commerce

Bond

departments of banks II, 180, 376, 389, 390, 392, 394

holders (in general) 207, 208, 298; II, 11, 33, 317, 318, 342; American 141; II, 305; foreign 161; II, 35, 342, 368

houses II, 180, 376, 377, 381, 420

salesmen II, 355, 357, 376

Bonds of corporations

(in general) 54, 133, 203, 206-208, 271; II, 11, 61, 175, 180, 182, 185, 187, 305, 339, 341, 359, 360, 371, 376, 389, 392, 393

specified: Bank..., see also Post notes, 49, 54, 93, 133, 203, 206, 207, 271; II, 33, 201, 330, 334, 337, 338; Government..., see Public stock; Industrial..., see Industrial securities; Municipal ..., see Municipal securities; Personal..., 11, 90, 91, 93, 182, 195, 203, 227, 229; II, 76, 317, 399; Railroad..., see Railroad securities; State..., see Public stock

Bonus 65, 90; II, 306, 319, 376, 400, 401

Book

credits 12, 13, 235, 236; II, 4, 5, 120, 140, 326

transfers 132, 164

Bookkeeping, see also Accounting 15, 18, 39, 48, 53, 108; II, 24, 185, 186, 205, 221, 286

Boom 137-141, 203

Borrowing

from banks, borrowers, bank debtors 6, 9, 31, 32, 35, 39, 44, 47-49, 56, 64, 94, 111, 112, 117-119, 126, 135, 153, 155, 160, 193, 220, 226, 232, 242; II, 4, 13-15, 49, 61, 63, 67, 70, 75, 78, 79, 96, 131, 133, 158, 179, 180, 181, 185, 203, 205, 206, 246, 272

of banks 16, 17, 52, 54, 55, 70, 79, 200, 208, 239, 252, 258; II, 5, 46, 47, 64-66, 181-183, 200, 224, 268, 272, 273, 291, 343, 414; abroad 16, 27, 48, 49, 54, 55, 57, 58, 108, 109, 111, 133, 200; II, 330, 332, 340, 341, 343; from a central bank 100, 129; of specie, see Lending of specie

"Boston Plan" of collecting country checks II, 240, 241

Branch

banking, branches, see also State banks, 14-17, 21, 31, 34-36, 41, 48, 52, 58, 63, 67, 82, 94, 96, 98-100, 104-106, 108-110, 113-121, 123-126, 129, 131, 132, 134-137, 139, 141, 142, 144-146, 149, 152-154, 160, 165, 169, 172, 174, 176, 178, 179, 184, 185, 209, 221, 239, 255, 266, 269, 273, 274, 276, 280, 288, 291, 298; II, 18, 22-27, 30, 45, 46, 48, 55, 74, 78, 137, 186, 192-198, 201, 213, 214, 217-222, 227, 229, 232, 235, 245, 247,

253-256, 292, 299, 339, 348, 353, 424, 425; foreign II, 182, 187, 195; intra-city II, 184, 188, 195-197, 201, 229

drafts 43, 131, 132, 142, 256, 278, 290; II, 72

notes 106, 108-110, 129, 132, 288; II, 65; redemption of ... 106, 109, 132, 288; II, 26, 55

Branches

coordination of ..., control of 119, 120, 271; II, 23, 24

of enterprises other than banks II, 32, 33, 68, 179, 335, 363

of private bankers II, 33, 71-73, 75, 197, 198, 350, 362, 363, 381, 390, 392, 421

British consols, loans, securities II, 124, 305-315, 321, 322, 324, 356, 358, 375, 397-404

Brokers, incl. stock brokers, see also Money brokers, Bill brokers 53, 55, 124, 126, 136, 213, 249, 263; II, 4, 5, 15, 60, 61, 66-68, 71, 73, 74, 77, 78, 87, 96, 106, 111, 122, 180, 181, 185, 190, 191, 214, 304, 314, 323, 326, 330, 333-335, 341, 344, 346, 348, 349, 353, 361, 365, 374, 375, 385, 387, 398, 402, 403

banks, see Wall Street bankers

loans II, 180

Building and Loan Associations II, 197

Bullion, precious metals 14, 43, 49, 58, 112, 125, 130, 134, 189, 192, 275; II, 8, 36, 37, 67, 68, 74, 146, 176, 208, 255, 267, 287, 288, 370, 379, 382, 383, 431-434, 436, 439, 440

trade, ... market, specie market, see also Specie movements, 112, 134, 135; II, 34, 77, 432, 440

report 5, 125, 157

Bulls II, 310, 312

Business

cycle 130, 131, 135

interests 9, 22, 28, 60, 85, 102, 103, 116, 117, 143, 144, 169, 170, 171, 192; II, 167, 169, 201, 217-220, 245, 258, 264, 273, 275, 277-284, 289, 430, 433, 435, 437, 438

leader, business leadership (entrepreneur, entrepreneurship) 1, 2, 20, 26, 33, 38-41, 44, 58, 60, 66, 74, 77, 79, 88, 101, 109, 110, 118, 159, 161, 208, 223, 224, 231; II, 24, 25, 64, 67, 76, 86, 88, 109, 169, 188, 190, 191, 193, 198, 203, 204, 220, 313, 331, 336, 352, 364, 383, 387, 424, 425, 434

man 15, 26, 29-32, 39, 46, 49, 51, 56, 57, 64, 68, 78, 79, 101, 113, 115-117, 132, 137, 142, 148, 159, 160, 192, 195, 196, 215, 216, 269; II, 14, 15, 27, 30, 32, 33, 88, 90, 96, 106, 109, 163, 202-204, 206, 208-211, 219, 220, 304-307, 312, 315, 317, 318, 325, 351, 352, 356, 363, 377, 382, 383, 387, 424-429, 433-435, 440

men's thinking 88, 142; II, 63, 87, 88, 159, 166, 167, 189, 209, 215, 217, 218-220, 272, 283, 428, 429, 434-438

By-laws
  of banks 18, 34, 58, 74; II, 204
  of savings banks 210, 211, 215-222, 225
Call loans, call loan market 49, 72, 225, 250;
    II, 3, 7, 72, 74, 115, 116, 119, 124, 180, 181,
    194, 207, 220, 222, 288, 314, 363, 379, 427
Canals, Canal Commissioners, canal funds, canal
    stock 49, 88, 127, 148, 226, 249, 252; II, 25, 26,
    29, 33, 198, 326, 327, 329-333, 337-339, 341,
    344, 349-351, 359, 395, 409, 414-416
Capital
  (in general) 7, 8, 11, 31, 32, 43, 46, 54, 56, 65,
    66, 74, 78, 109, 112, 141, 182, 228, 290, 293;
    II, 2, 3, 5, 8, 15, 61, 63, 64, 69, 70, 73, 76, 79,
    85, 88, 110, 118, 119, 140, 142, 146, 154, 175,
    193, 202, 215, 219, 223, 262, 278, 305, 306, 308,
    313, 315, 316, 319, 322, 325-327, 329, 331, 341,
    343, 347, 349, 354, 360-362, 375, 376, 380, 384,
    387, 398, 402, 426, 437
  export 126; II, 386
  flight 139; II, 314
  import 111, 142, 171, 206; II, 76, 198, 317, 351,
    363, 416
  increases II, 183, 378, 379
  market, market for securities 226, 227, 230;
    II, 198, 304-306, 310, 312, 316, 319, 321, 327,
    331, 334-338, 340, 341, 344, 348-351, 354, 355,
    357-359, 362, 363, 369, 370, 373, 375, 377, 381,
    399, 416
  of banks 6, 7, 10, 13, 15, 27, 28, 30, 61, 64, 65,
    68, 75, 78, 91, 92, 94, 98-100, 106, 107, 109,
    114, 123, 124, 131, 136, 138, 141, 144, 145,
    154, 179, 192-198, 200, 201, 203, 205-208, 228,
    233, 234; II, 5, 14, 25, 26, 39, 42, 48, 62, 69,
    71, 73, 74, 79, 100, 101, 106, 108, 111, 115, 123,
    132, 133, 138, 141, 146, 175, 176, 178, 179, 183,
    185, 187, 188, 190-193, 195, 197, 199, 200, 208,
    213, 218-220, 226, 249, 263, 279, 284, 295, 331,
    341, 342, 356, 365, 389, 391, 393, 394, 426, 429;
    as the basis of taxation and contributions of all
    kind 73, 80, 91, 93, 95, 194, 234, 261; II, 88,
    91, 119, 159, 160, 164, 165, 176, 185, 210, 246,
    257, 259, 260, 264, 270, 272, 273, 277, 294, 331,
    359, 431; investment of ... (see also Policy, in-
    vestment ...): in business paper 62; in govern-
    ment securities, loans to a government 10, 13,
    16, 47, 49, 50, 91, 104, 124, 137, 185, 193-195,
    198-200, 234, 293, 294, 296; II, 14, 35, 36, 39,
    43, 94, 102, 103, 106, 119, 123, 152, 324, 330,
    409; in mortgages and personal bonds 47, 91,
    194, 195, 205, 324; otherwise or not specified
    13, 22, 47, 49, 124, 192-195; II, 2, 14, 33, 35,
    38, 149, 218, 325, 339, 409; to be paid up, how
    to be paid up (see also Public Stock used for
    subscriptions to banks) 27, 49, 68, 191, 194,
    198, 203; II , 43, 106, 213; reductions 20, 61,

    109, 233, 234; II, 187
  role of banks in the formation of ... 7, 8, 11, 29,
    31, 66
  role of ... in banking 7, 28, 43, 64, 92, 98, 106,
    123, 192, 193, 200, 234, 258, 296; II, 35, 66, 71;
    basis of credit 7, 192, 234, 258; II,35; sets
    limits to the amount of loans, see Bank loans,
    limitation; security for note issues, see Secur-
    ity behind bank notes, Capital lent (... and de-
    posits lent) 64, 100, 192, 194, 195, 236, 258;
    minimum required II, 124, 195; not needed
    (superfluous) 7, 12, 43, 64, 193, 293; II, 22, 35;
    resources over and above ... considered neces-
    sary 194, 198, 203; II, 103; sets limits to total
    amount of loans, see Bank loans,
    limitation
  transfer, 106; II, 112
Capitalism, capitalistic, precapitalistic, high-
    capitalistic, anti-capitalistic 1, 9, 10, 29, 47,
    58, 59, 62, 74, 150, 162, 164, 165, 167, 170, 171,
    174, 180, 191, 206, 224, 231, 233, 289; II, 95,
    118, 220, 326, 327, 378, 384
Capitalists, moneyed men 9, 13, 15, 25, 27, 30, 39,
    50, 52, 67, 89, 111, 136, 137, 164, 168, 169, 187,
    201, 202, 214, 289; II, 4, 13, 22, 61, 63, 76, 87,
    96, 111, 113, 118, 121, 138, 146, 190, 198, 262,
    272, 306, 308, 312, 316, 318-320, 324, 326, 329,
    334-336, 339, 346, 355-357, 360, 368, 373, 377,
    387, 398, 404
Cash Liabilities, see Demand obligations
  resources, see Resources
Cashiers 14, 18, 19, 20, 21, 34, 35, 36, 39-41, 53,
    58, 60, 62, 63, 75, 76, 77, 79, 99, 113-121, 129,
    141, 145, 149, 184, 186, 202, 211, 222, 228, 269,
    271, 274, 296, 298; II, 11, 12, 20, 27, 29, 46,
    48-51, 53, 54, 56, 57, 59, 62, 63, 113, 151, 153,
    154, 165, 179, 190, 196, 199, 200, 204, 206, 218,
    221, 228, 229, 232, 245, 248, 254-256, 260, 262,
    268, 275, 279, 284, 291, 297, 301, 308, 318, 330,
    331, 339, 353, 358, 366, 390, 393, 404, 411, 415,
    417, 424, 425
  as borrowers 115, 269; II, 203, 205
  become presidents 19, 20, 36, 40, 41, 63, 79,
    269; II, 151
  functions of 19, 34, 59, 62, 63, 83, 84, 113-115,
    117, 119, 131, 153, 256, 259, 273; II, 11, 38, 56,
    101, 202, 249, 251, 259
  salaries of ... (remunerations of ...) 19, 63, 114,
    115, 241, 257, 271
Cashiers' checks 15, 132; II, 179
Central bank
  (in general) 96-100, 101, 103-106, 109, 111, 113,
    127, 128-131-133, 139, 140, 143, 152-154, 168,
    169, 176, 178-180, 200, 280, 286; II, 70, 99, 100,
    105, 121, 158, 189, 208-215, 262, 266, 270, 426,
    428

Central bank (cont'd.)
  Aid to other banks, cooperation with... 100, 103, 104, 142, 239
  checks the other banks 100, 126, 128, 138, 140, 142, 159; II, 212
  competes with other banks 97, 98, 103, 124, 139, 142, 180
  control, mutual by .. and government 152, 166
  control of banks 96-99, 103, 104, 109, 110, 128, 140, 169, 172, 180, 291; II, 212, 255
  control of the national economy 140, 141, 168
  controlled itself 142, 166-168, 169, 172, 180, 288; II, 213
  cooperates with the government, tries to... 98-100, 103, 105, 108, 128, 144-146, 150, 154
  functions 96-100, 104, 105, 128, 136, 140, 142, 143, 145, 160, 171, 178-180, 267, 276, 280; II, 211, 212; collectively performed by a system of commercial banks 142, 176, 290; II, 212, 213, 302, 426, 428; equalizes, the domestic exchanges 132, 133, 135, 160, 179, 180; fights seasonal and irregular disturbances of business 98, 99, 132, 135, 140, 141; fiscal agency of the government, see this entry; in case of war 166, 167, 172; influences cyclical movements of business activities 96, 130, 131, 135-138, 141-143, 168, 179; II, 212, 214, 428; issues a national currency 97, 98, 103, 104, 110, 111, 113, 128-131, 135, 139, 147, 175, 288, 290; II, 212; lender of last resort 97, 136, 140, 179; II, 212, 214, 428; regulates the currency 96, 128-133, 135, 139, 155, 169, 172, 179, 180, 280, 288; II, 48, 211-213; stabilizes the foreign exchanges 133, 135, 179, 180; ultimate reserve holder 97, 98, 133, 135, 140, 142, 179; II, 212-214, 428
  idea 97, 102; II, 208, 211, 214
  policy 98, 99, 104, 105, 127-129, 133, 135-143, 150, 158, 288; II, 247, 315
  president, central banker 99, 104, 105, 110, 113, 124, 127-145 (Biddle, the Central Bank President) 152, 157, 158, 168, 171, 176, 269, 276, 288; II, 213, 263, 337, 340
  regional II, 211, 212
  term 96, 266; II, 212, 213
Central banker, see Central-bank president
Central Banking 44, 88, 96-186; II, 208, 209, 211-215, 217, 219, 235
Central redemption, central redemption agency, see also Redemption Fund, II, 115, 116, 212, 214
Central Reserve Cities II, 115, 117, 169, 178, 183, 186, 214, 217
Certificates
  of deposit 43, 229, 236, 237; II, 63, 64, 73, 76, 83, 93, 160-162, 165, 178, 182, 224, 225, 268, 277, 432
  of indebtedness 54; II, 437
  of saving or investment II, 79, 80
Certified public accountants II, 185
Chain banking, see Group banking
Chairman of the Board of Directors II, 197, 204, 241, 391
Chamber of Commerce, Board of Trade 100; II, 10, 86, 88, 106, 112, 172, 187, 210, 211, 213, 219, 222, 254, 267, 268, 433
Chancellors of the Exchequer II, 307, 310, 401, 403, 439
Charter clauses, ... conditions 22, 28, 43, 49, 54, 55, 60, 68, 77, 91, 92, 94, 95, 99, 105, 106, 130, 142, 159, 167, 192, 205, 207, 224, 252, 255, 297, 298; II, 252, 324-326, 338, 340
Chartered banks
  as opposed to Free Banks 97, 130, 170, 188, 189; II, 100, 102, 344, 345
  as opposed to private banks, see Incorporated banks
Chartering, establishing, incorporating of banks 7, 22, 31, 33, 35, 36, 39, 43, 79, 91, 95, 97, 102, 103, 111, 143, 167, 191, 206-208, 215, 221, 244, 291; II, 26, 27, 64, 99, 198, 215, 247, 262, 266, 324, 325, 331
Charters, see Bank charters
Cheap currency, cheap money 112, 190
Checks, see also Circulating of... 15, 43, 51, 74, 75, 80, 83, 91, 127, 131, 132, 142, 234, 238, 239, 247, 248; II, 3, 4, 7, 8, 45, 47-49, 76, 89, 92-94, 107, 118-120, 124, 171, 177, 178, 182, 184-186, 208, 216, 224, 236-238, 240, 241, 246, 247, 250, 256, 261, 292, 296, 373, 376, 427-429, 436
  certification of... II, 7, 10, 180, 284, 376
  out-of-town..., foreign II, 177, 179, 185, 186, 236-244, 429, 443
"Chicago Plan" see Affiliates
Chief executives, executives, general managers, managers of banks, administrators , see also Administration of banks (in the sense of administration staff) 19, 33, 35, 59, 60, 63, 74, 90, 113-127, 132, 141, 146, 169, 255, 256, 273; II, 11, 12, 33, 48-50, 60, 61, 72, 124, 138-141, 146, 193, 197, 199, 202, 204, 205, 207, 208, 213, 221, 239, 272, 283, 301, 350, 391, 425
Circular letters 68, 69, 80, 85, 86, 175; II, 106, 107, 117, 137-145, 158, 251-254, 256, 259, 262-265, 270, 272, 279, 287, 296, 318, 369, 376, 432, 433
Circulating
  medium, see Currency
  of checks 132; II, 160, 166, 173
  of notes 16, 17, 28, 41, 69, 71-74, 78-80, 84, 91, 92, 109, 124, 128, 132, 145, 161, 174, 188-190, 194, 199, 205, 206, 253; II, 4, 26, 46, 49, 61, 62, 66, 99, 101, 138, 236, 261, 262, 268, 273, 292

Circulation
  check on..., limitation of... 84, 194-196, 198-200, 233, 240, 257; II, 8, 37, 43, 99, 104, 105, 113, 115, 122, 123, 150, 156, 221, 261
  in multiples or percentages of capital or capital plus deposits 16, 17, 28, 44, 64, 65, 72, 134, 140, 194, 197, 233, 257, 296; II, 1, 4, 5, 13, 16, 37, 43, 297, 437
  in the sense of circulating medium, see Currency
  ratios issue to capital 94, 140, 194, 233, 296; II, 37, 43, 149, 208, 278
  total of notes issued by all banks or any individual bank or a number of banks 10, 29, 46, 51, 67-73, 75, 79, 80, 85, 89, 93, 94, 99, 110, 112, 126, 131, 134, 139, 140, 143, 170, 185, 198, 199, 201, 203; II, 2-4, 6-8, 12, 15, 22, 26, 27, 36, 38, 39, 48, 61, 93, 113, 114, 118, 119, 123, 141, 142, 144, 162, 212, 248, 250, 253, 255, 257-262, 274, 277, 278, 284, 287, 292, 300, 332
Cities, borrowing of..., see Municipal loans
City banks 10, 19, 21, 22, 35, 38, 39, 45, 48, 50, 51, 53, 55, 56, 60, 69-74, 77-81, 93, 94, 142, 266; II, 5-7, 11, 45-50, 62, 78, 95, 141, 146, 158-160, 177, 182-184, 189, 193, 194, 217, 236, 240, 241, 246, 247, 249, 255, 257, 428
Civil War, Civil War time 11-13, 95, 158, 214; II, 6, 7, 11, 14, 15, 27, 40, 57, 73-75, 77, 85-87, 90, 96, 99, 106, 109, 111, 116, 137, 138, 140, 142-146, 151, 161, 185, 194, 220, 270, 274, 276, 289, 355-359, 361-366, 382, 384, 387-389, 391, 392, 395, 426, 430
Civil War Finance II, 57, 85-98, 107, 113, 124, 144-146, 322, 355-362, 365, 395, 416, 438
Clearing ("exchanges")
  in England 97; II, 48, 55, 239, 241, 246
  of out-of-town checks 74; II, 196, 236-244
  outside of established clearing houses 71, 73-81, 84-87, 105, 142, 260-262; II, 46-48, 50-53, 55, 221, 429
  within clearing houses II, 14, 45, 48, 50, 53, 54, 107, 109, 142, 159-161, 166, 179, 182, 185, 186, 202, 236, 239, 240, 274-276, 284, 285, 288
Clearing house
  associations 81, 84-87; II, 51-53, 107, 140, 142, 144, 158-164, 167-169, 172-174, 177, 196, 237, 239, 283, 284, 287, 302, 417, 425, 427, 428, 431-433, 437; constitution and rules (by-laws) 87; II, 51-54, 57, 58, 237, 286, 427, 428, 432, 433; policy of..., 87; II, 58, 92, 164-167, 169, 237, 238, 241, 242, 285-287, 432
  balances 66, 79, 80, 86, 87; II, 6, 50, 119, 158-161, 163, 164, 166, 167, 432
  coin certificates II, 50, 53, 54, 158, 169
  committee 84-87; II, 49-52, 57, 88, 158, 159, 163-165, 169, 173, 179, 207, 221, 240, 274, 276, 283, 285, 286, 427, 428, 445

depositories II, 53, 54, 158, 160, 166
examiners, examinations II, 202, 216, 285, 286, 289;
leaders (managers, officers, presidents, secretaries) 86; II, 50-54, 57, 89, 108, 154, 159, 161, 164, 165, 169, 172, 173, 177, 184, 210, 221, 227, 240, 284, 303, 425
loan certificates 86, 87; II, 89-92, 158-174, 196, 275, 287, 288, 425-427, 438; circulating II, 160, 166, 167, 172, 173; legalization of... II, 167, 168, 173, 210
loan committee II, 89-92, 106, 107, 158, 160-165, 168, 196
member banks, members, see also Associated banks 85; II, 72, 106, 107, 115, 140, 179, 196, 202, 210, 238, 240, 241, 244, 276, 283-287, 427, 428, 431, 432; non-members II, 196, 238, 285, 287, 288, 427
minutes (records) 4, 81, 84; 87; II, 50, 52, 57, 287, 432
national II, 214
rules and regulations, see Clearing house associations, constitution and rules
Clearing houses 74, 77, 79-81, 84-87, 97, 261, 296; II, 7, 45-59, 88-91, 93, 106-109, 115, 124, 137, 140, 142, 144, 146, 151, 158, 159, 163-170, 172, 173, 175, 179, 208, 210, 212-215, 227, 233, 236-242, 262, 270, 271, 273-276, 279, 283-289, 299, 300, 303, 425-430, 432, 438
clear notes besides checks 77, 80; II, 115
cooperation of... 286
emergency actions, other than issue of clearing house loan certificates, II, 285, 287, 428
establish uniform service charges II, 207, 237, 238, 241, 242, 244, 285, 287, 302
foreign check department II, 238, 240-242, 244
incorporation of... II, 51, 167, 214, 287
special committees, joint committees II, 284-287, 425, 429, 431
Clerical work 83, 84; II, 185, 186, 239
Clerks, see Employees
Coal, see Mining
Coffee houses II, 309, 313, 401, 402
Coin, see Specie
  subsidiary II, 246, 267, 292, 431-433
Coinage, recoinage 134, 189; II, 255, 430-433, 437, 439, 440, 444
Coins, foreign 133, 134, 136, 158; II, 255, 263, 292
Collateral, see Security behind bank loans
  trust bonds 207; II, 377
  trust notes II, 78
Collection
  agents 52, 237, 251
  charges, see also Exchange, charging of... II, 236-238, 241, 244, 287
  systems (national, regional) 105; II, 236, 238-242

Collections, collecting 17, 69, 71, 72, 74, 78, 105, 108, 126, 165, 240, 251, 260, 261; II, 20, 45, 46, 64-66, 69, 73, 76, 78, 182, 186, 223, 236-239, 269, 285, 317, 327, 429
  Par ... 74, 80, 84; II, 177, 236, 238-242
Collectors of Internal Revenue, of Ports 100, 105, 109, 110, 175, 180, 189, 288; II, 113, 147, 252, 317, 332
Colleges, college education, universities 37, 40, 45, 63, 88, 110, 155, 158, 173, 191, 214; II, 24, 27, 57, 58, 79, 195, 203, 210, 294, 297, 376, 382, 387, 388, 420, 422, 434
Colonies, colonial 12, 17, 24, 25, 29, 40, 110, 164, 195, 205; II, 165, 399, 424
Combination
  movement in banking, see Control of banks by investment bankers, Concentration of money power, Interlocking directorates, Mergers
  of heterogeneous functions by banks, of long and short term credit by banks 9, 11-13, 27, 44, 45, 205, 207, 208; II, 3, 15
Combinations in industry and transportation II, 185-187, 194, 195, 383, 384, 391, 392
Commerce, commercial, mercantile, see also trade, 7-9, 25-27, 30, 31, 33, 38, 60, 65, 82, 93, 100, 103, 104, 111, 112, 128-131, 141, 143-145, 168, 172, 179, 182, 192, 193, 205, 207, 209; II, 13, 32, 39, 45, 71, 88, 90, 101, 189, 207, 212, 213, 222, 246, 304, 399, 430, 433, 436, 437
Commercial
  banking, banks 7, 8, 10-12, 21, 22, 24, 28, 30, 32, 36, 43, 45-47, 50, 53, 64, 67, 98, 104, 124, 127, 142, 160, 171, 205, 211, 216, 218, 219, 222, 223, 225, 226, 228-230, 267, 297; II, 6, 45, 64, 69, 70, 72, 80, 175-177, 179-181, 189, 195, 198, 211, 213, 214, 248, 304, 325, 326, 332, 337, 341, 344, 345, 349, 425, 426, 436, 437, 444
  banking combined with: insurance 32, 33, 35; II, 187, 189; investment banking II, 328-338, 340, 344, 346, 347, 349-351, 358, 359, 362, 364, 370, 376, 378-380, 382, 385, 388-394, 411; private banking II, 72; savings banking, see Savings banking, combined ...
  center, see   Trade Centers
  paper, ... houses, ... market, see also Bills of exchange, II, 3-5, 14, 15, 39, 64, 66, 75, 77, 78, 177, 182, 185, 194, 210, 227, 346
Commission 50, 81; II, 11, 67, 69, 77, 78, 203
  merchants, see Merchants
Commissions paid in connection with the flotation of loans, see Securities, commission paid ...
Committees
  occasional II, 50, 52, 53, 57, 88-91, 107, 108, 111, 114, 115, 142, 144, 160
  of bank boards, see also Exchange committees 18-20, 39, 56-59, 61, 71, 72, 74, 108, 114, 121,
  130, 135, 143, 183, 211, 241, 254-256, 274; II, 20, 26, 190, 204-206, 245, 259, 268, 409
  of bank conventions, of cooperating banks II, 252-255, 266, 267, 297; confer with such committees of other banks, see also Joint Committees, 18, 20, 67, 72; II, 245-248, 250, 252, 253, 358
  of clearing houses, see Clearing house ...
  of savings-bank boards 214, 215, 222, 223, 224, 226, 228, 302
Communication, means of 57, 106, 119, 120; II, 162, 199, 200, 201, 435
Community of interest among banks 197; II, 57, 140, 245, 246, 257, 258, 276, 283, 285, 289, 427, 428
Competition 28, 29, 171, 192; II, 57, 87, 88, 92, 177, 273, 350, 377-379, 382, 383, 429, 435, 438
  belief in ... 197, 198; II, 87, 88, 208, 247, 257, 258, 287, 290, 378
  in banking 16, 21, 23, 31, 41, 45, 53, 57, 58, 68, 69, 71-80, 84, 86, 94, 97, 98, 103, 104, 124, 133, 168, 180, 190, 196-198, 202, [222, 229 (among savings banks)], 292-294; II, 6, 7, 47, 54, 64, 69, 70, 72, 74-76, 78, 112, 176, 177, 179-181, 186, 194, 215, 220, 221, 224, 225, 237, 238, 241, 245, 251, 255, 256, 257, 270, 286, 289, 300, 334, 422, 426-428, 435; between incorporated and private banks 117; II, 6, 62, 65, 66, 70, 72, 75, 76, 258; between National Banks and state banks II, 176-178; between National Banks and trust companies II, 177-179
  in the flotation of securities 226; II, 308-312, 314, 315, 318-322, 326, 328, 330, 334-336, 338, 340, 344, 347, 349, 351, 355, 359, 363, 365-367, 376, 377, 379, 380, 385, 387, 388, 398, 401
Competitors upheld II, 258, 259, 261, 271-273, 285, 289, 298, 299, 428
Comptroller of the Currency II, 25, 74, 102, 104-106, 113-119, 124-135, 137-139, 141, 145, 146, 153, 155, 156, 168, 175-177, 180, 182, 185, 186, 191, 194, 195, 204, 205, 210, 214-216, 223, 286, 389, 393
Concentration
  in banking, see Interlocking directorates, Mergers
  of bankers balances, reserves II, 4, 183, 189, 208, 239, 240
  of certain transactions II, 78
  of "money power" 169; II, 50, 123, 144, 146, 183, 189, 381
Confederacy II, 124, 416
Confidential advisers to bank executives 113-116, 151, 153
Conflicts of interest among banks, see Inter-bank fights
Congress, Congressional (House of Representatives, Senate) 25, 29, 31, 40, 50, 57, 100-103, 105, 107,

Congress, Congressional (cont'd.)
110-112, 121, 127, 132, 141, 143, 146-149, 151,
152, 154, 156, 158, 165-167, 169, 175, 177-179,
186, 189, 201, 208, 282, 288, 290, 292; II, 23,
29, 85-87, 93, 95, 100-102, 104-107, 110, 113,
115-118, 123, 137, 141, 142, 144-147, 158, 167,
176, 179, 189, 195, 209, 215, 217, 246, 252, 255,
262, 263, 265, 266, 279, 281-284, 287, 294, 316-
318, 329, 344, 365, 369, 370, 389, 430, 432, 433,
440
Congressional Committees 46, 50, 57, 103, 153,
175, 183, 198-200, 256; II, 94, 95, 101, 104, 108,
117, 123, 142, 150, 168, 219, 220, 281, 286, 290,
332, 411, 445
Congressmen (Representatives and Senators) 46,
102, 107, 115, 121, 151, 153, 154, 165, 166, 170,
198-200, 282, 290; II, 8, 23, 24, 30, 87, 95, 108,
120, 123, 148, 150, 155, 214, 254, 255, 280, 282,
297, 338, 426, 439, 444
"Connection" (old fashioned term for correspond-
ent) 51, 239
Conservative, Conservatism II, 2, 106
Consolidations, see Mergers
Consols, see British loans
Constitution, constitutional, unconstitutional
English 97
Federal 38, 111, 147, 158, 166, 172, 174, 180,
189, 286; II, 99, 110, 137, 216, 428
State 38, 89, 93, 190, 199, 201, 298; II, 12, 22,
26, 27, 104, 143
Consumers credit II, 74, 182
Continental
Congress, see Congress
currency 24, 26, 27; II, 305
debt certificates II, 304
Contingency reserves, see Reserves, contingency
Contraction, see Expansion and Contraction,
Policy of banks, issue
Contractors, contracting, see also Loan contractors, Securities, contracting of ..., 29, 34; II, 3,
198, 304, 345, 352, 354, 399, 404
Control
of banks: by a central bank, see Central Bank,
control; by business enterprises, corporations
48; II, 79, 187, 189; by individuals 17, 20, 22,
32, 35, 41, 45, 48, 52, 56, 58, 60-62, 69, 114,
116, 166, 247, 257, 273; II, 13, 33, 34, 38, 61,
65, 72, 110, 112, 137, 192, 198, 199, 201, 202,
206, 207, 285, 390, 391, 393
of business II, 429, 438; by investment bankers
II, 175, 181, 187-190, 206, 207, 341, 379, 386,
390; by other banks, see also Bankers' banks,
52, 68, 71, 145, 146, 255, 256, 261; by public
authorities, see Supervision
of enterprises (other than banks) by investment
bankers II, 361, 362, 372, 378, 381, 384, 386,
387, 391
of the currency, monetary control 8, 41, 52, 68,
69, 100, 104, 128, 135, 202; II, 99, 109, 114
Conversion of state banks into National Banks
II, 105, 107-109, 112, 118, 138, 145, 152, 425
Convertibility of
bank notes and government paper money into coin,
see Redemption
government paper money into bonds, see Government paper money, Interconvertible bond plan
Cooperation
of banks 21, 67, 69-73, 75, 78-81, 85, 89, 94, 197,
260; II, 7, 34, 45-47, 51-55, 75, 88-90, 107, 124,
158, 170, 176, 177, 186, 189, 214, 216, 238, 245-
303, 426, 429, 430, 435-438; in emergencies
II, 247, 248-256, 259-269, 271-274, 276, 277,
283, 287-289, 296, 303, 424, 426, 430, 433
of investment bankers, see Investment bankers,
alliances
Coordination of banks II, 274, 275, 278, 283-285
"Copartnership bank" see State and federal participation in banks
Corners, cornering 133; II, 335
Corporation securities, not specified (for specified
securities, see Securities) II, 313, 324, 333, 339,
341, 344, 353, 354, 360, 365, 375, 376, 387, 388
Corporations (private), corporate 7, 12, 41, 44, 49,
51, 55, 60, 64, 68, 72, 76, 88, 91, 93-95, 111,
127, 144, 161, 163, 166, 167, 169, 174, 188, 190,
192, 199, 201, 219, 221; II, 11, 14, 23, 24, 26,
57, 60, 74, 78-80, 104, 142, 143, 180, 186, 187,
204, 216, 246, 299, 307, 308, 310, 324-327, 339,
341, 345, 353, 360, 363, 371, 373-379, 386, 387,
393, 394, 400, 442
Correspondents 16, 46, 51-55, 70, 72, 76-78, 80,
131, 142, 239, 250, 251, 260-262, 280; II, 5, 6,
11, 34, 35, 46, 57, 64-66, 69, 70, 72, 75, 77,
109, 111, 141, 153, 175-177, 179, 181-183, 185,
186, 193, 196, 201, 214, 215, 224, 237, 239-241,
249, 250, 278, 287, 292, 310, 314, 333, 336, 337,
342, 352, 354, 363, 364, 382, 386, 389
Cost computation in banking II, 186, 238
Cotton industry, market, trade 131, 133, 145, 161,
202, 209; II, 35, 36, 67-69, 82, 166, 171, 172,
254, 265, 267, 297, 305, 391, 416
Counterfeiting II, 155, 246, 258, 270, 292
Country
banks, bankers, banking 9-12, 16, 19, 21-23, 33,
35, 39, 41, 43, 45, 48, 51-53, 55-57, 64, 67-74,
76-78, 81, 84, 88, 94, 124, 126, 128, 140, 142,
172, 174, 180, 193, 239, 242, 259, 260, 262, 266,
275; II, 3-7, 11, 45-47, 61, 65, 78, 95, 104, 108,
114, 117, 137, 141, 151, 175, 177, 182, 183, 191,
193, 195, 198-201, 215, 217-220, 240, 241, 246-
249, 252, 257, 258, 261, 262, 270, 272, 281, 288,
292, 295, 300, 352, 355, 389, 424, 429

Country banks (cont'd.)
  in England 168, 188, 191, 276; II, 239
  checks, see Checks, out-of-town
  clearings, see Clearing of out-of-town checks
  indebted to the city 67, 71; II, 38
  money, notes 15, 67-87, 105, 109, 174, 258, 260,
    261; II, 61, 115, 158-160, 249, 257, 289, 295;
    buying of ..., see Bank notes, buying of ...
  stores, see Stores
County bonds II, 180, 345, 350, 354, 355, 376, 381
Courts 37, 68, 82, 87, 198, 212, 232, 294; II, 61,
  110, 178, 283
  decisions 187, 203; II, 5, 61, 78, 110, 137, 181,
    204, 205, 280, 389, 392
Craftsmen, see Mechanics
Created deposits, see Deposits, created
Creation of purchasing power II, 93, 95, 119, 121,
  155, 175, 183, 426, 436
  in the form of deposits, see Deposits, created
  in the form of notes 7, 8, 10, 28, 29, 30, 43, 65,
    66, 100, 170, 171, 193, 236, 237, 242; II, 35,
    39, 64, 66, 72, 108, 119, 120, 253, 267, 326
Creative
  achievements, ideas, innovations 7, 33, 47, 71,
    73, 75, 88, 190, 209; II, 9, 77-79, 124, 166, 186,
    196-198, 201, 204, 209, 220, 236, 239, 323, 354,
    356, 357, 378, 382-385, 388
  capitalist 1, 30, 34, 244; II, 79
  entrepreneur 1, 26, 30, 38, 45, 72, 74, 88, 99,
    160, 231, 244; II, 48, 49, 77-79, 112, 124, 160,
    184, 198, 199, 204, 311, 313, 314, 321, 322,
    325, 347, 351, 353, 356, 381, 382, 424
  manager 39-41, 74; II, 50, 238, 240
Credit 6, 7, 9, 16, 24, 25, 27, 32, 43, 44, 62, 67,
  71, 90, 100, 103, 108, 110, 112, 130, 131, 137,
  163, 171, 190, 192, 193, 248; II, 46, 100, 141,
  142, 175, 189, 198, 213, 216, 238, 297, 304,
  308, 317, 330, 343, 362, 378, 379, 436
  agricultural, see also Land banks, Plantation
    banks 9, 22, 48, 126; II, 34, 73, 76, 198, 199,
    201, 228
  companies, see Finance companies
  cooperatives, credit unions 222; II, 79, 222
  currency, see Security behind bank notes, gen-
    eral assets
  department of banks II, 185, 227, 238
  facilities, see Credit need
  instruments 32, 43, 131; II, 73, 118, 160, 161,
    163, 165-169, 319, 425
  movement, scientific II, 238
  need and facilities 31, 32, 47, 54, 56, 192, 205,
    209; II, 192, 201, 341
  of banks 7, 28, 52, 54, 78, 104, 123, 130, 131,
    134, 136, 145, 160, 192, 193, 293; II, 6, 22, 34,
    35, 39, 61, 138, 139, 146, 249, 258, 259, 276,
    284, 292; to be lent 47, 64, 192-195, 258, 296;

    II, 138, 175, 324, 405
  policy, see Policy of banks, lending
  rating, ... standing 55; II, 12, 54, 60, 69, 84, 146,
    206, 215, 216, 227, 340
  revolving, running 51, 131; II, 67, 70, 79
  structure, system 112, 164, 165
Creditor
  banks 66, 71, 79, 136, 137, 261; II, 171, 249, 250,
    256, 259, 260, 262, 268, 269, 296 ; at the clear-
    ing house 79, 87; II, 159, 161, 163
  nations 105
  sections of a country 106; II, 118, 120, 155, 252,
    265
Creditors 9, 18, 145, 170, 191; II, 76, 78, 363, 390,
  404
  foreign 35; II, 82
  of banks, see also note holders 88, 95, 193, 197
    203; II, 25, 142, 287, 348
Crises, in general, see panics
Crisis
  of 1825 53, 135-137, 142, 143; II, 166, 323, 329
  of 1834 154, 155, 200; II, 255, 256, 335
  of 1837 51, 54, 55, 64, 75, 145, 175, 196; II, 9,
    25, 32, 34, 35, 38, 67, 69-71, 158, 166, 259-265,
    269, 270, 289, 299, 300, 305, 334, 335, 344, 353,
    424
  of 1857 64, 84; II, 2-5, 7, 10, 27, 40, 53, 54, 71,
    72, 77, 89, 90, 100, 107, 112, 141, 158, 160, 163,
    165-167, 198, 212, 273-276, 283, 286, 299, 300,
    350, 355, 388
  of 1860 II, 160, 161, 163, 167, 275
  of 1873 II, 124, 151, 153, 165, 169, 284, 288, 361,
    427
  of 1884 II, 124, 288, 426-428
  of 1893 II, 166, 169, 209, 216, 224, 288
  of 1907 II, 166, 167, 169, 172, 175, 179, 184, 186,
    197, 202, 210, 214, 217, 283, 288, 385, 394
Currency, circulating medium, in contrast to
  specie 24, 25, 41, 51, 56, 64, 68, 72, 75, 76, 85,
    90, 91, 93, 100, 103-106, 110, 113, 125, 128-
    132, 135, 158, 163-166, 168, 170, 172, 174, 175,
    189-193, 196-198, 201, 202, 236, 237; II, 1, 2,
    4, 8, 9, 27, 33, 36, 37, 39, 63, 64, 70, 72, 82,
    93, 99-103, 105, 113, 118-120, 122-124, 137,
    138, 141, 142, 144-146, 160, 166-169, 172, 208,
    213, 216, 218, 219, 252, 267, 276, 278, 305, 368,
    399, 430-433, 436, 437
  Commission of the American Bankers Associa-
    tion (1906) II, 195, 209-211, 290
  control of ..., see Control of the ...
  deficiency of ... 30, 118-120; II, 208, 210
  depreciation of ..., restoration of a depreciated
    27, 66, 68, 103, 105, 106, 113, 129, 133, 174;
    II, 8, 18, 103, 107, 114, 144, 249, 252, 278
  elasticity of ..., see Elasticity
  emergency, see Emergency currency

local 97, 106, 288; II, 100, 271, 425
management of ... 135
mixed 135, 140; II, 9
national, see National currency, Central bank
　issues a ...
redundancy, superabundance 91, 190; II, 119,
　123
reform, see Reform
regulated by the central bank, see Central bank,
　functions, regulates the currency
regulation, see Regulation of the currency
restoration of a depreciated ..., see Currency,
　depreciation of ...
School 169; II, 122
seasonal demand for ... 132; II, 119, 122, 123
security behind ..., see Security behind bank notes
sound, see Sound Currency
uniform, uniform value of...104, 128, 129, 132,
　135, 147, 172, 195, 196, 199, 288, 290; II, 23,
　99, 100, 101, 103, 114, 116, 121, 137, 252, 279
Darwinism II, 435
Dead weight, dead stock 29; II, 6, 39, 43
Dealers, see Bank customers
Debtor
　banks 66, 79, 99, 136, 153, 261; II, 47, 171, 249-
　　252, 256, 259, 260, 262, 268, 269, 296; at the
　　clearing house 79, 87; II, 159, 163
　nation 105
　sections of the country 7, 67, 106, 129; II, 118,
　　155, 163, 252, 262, 274
Debtors (for bank debtors, see Borrowing from
　banks) 9, 71, 99, 133, 170, 187; II, 78
Debts, see also Bank loans, 9, 28, 90, 92, 98, 115,
　119, 124, 164, 198, 201, 232; II, 249, 384
　of banks (liabilities, obligations), see also Bor-
　　rowing of banks, 6, 91, 93, 104, 197, 198, 201,
　　203; II, 24-26, 92, 160, 186, 192, 204, 223, 248,
　　251, 253, 259, 284, 437; limited to the amount
　　of capital 244; II, 16, 37
　payment, settlement 6, 11-13, 45-48, 78, 82, 87,
　　91, 98, 153, 154, 205, 206, 234, 253, 269, 274;
　　II, 34, 38, 79, 142, 144, 160, 166, 182, 247-250,
　　256, 257, 272, 326, 338, 340, 341
Defalcations, see Frauds
Definitions of banking 43, 247, 267; II, 14
Deflation, deflationary 68, 74, 75, 105, 106, 145;
　II, 114, 120, 122, 154, 155, 436
Defraudations, see Frauds
Del-credere commission 253
Delegates, delegations to bankers' associations,
　conventions, meetings II, 264, 265, 267, 268,
　273, 275, 279, 280, 282, 297, 431
Demand
　deposits 15, 50, 51, 53, 132, 140; II, 3-6, 15, 116,
　　123, 124, 181
　loans 45, 48, 49, 72

notes, see Bank notes, Treasury notes
　obligations 50, 66, 108; II, 1, 3, 5, 32, 36-40, 117,
　　141, 256, 274, 297
Democratic Republicans, Democrats, Democracy
　22, 23, 33, 37, 38, 102, 112, 117, 156, 165, 166,
　172, 173, 179, 184-186, 188, 189, 196, 198, 200,
　204, 214, 266, 289, 290; II, 34, 60, 61, 87, 122,
　191, 217, 294, 301
Department-store banking II, 182
Dependence of banks
　on a central bank 97, 100, 142
　on each other 23, 66; II, 249, 252, 257, 283, 289,
　　427, 428
Department of the Treasury, see Treasury
Deposit
　business 13, 15, 50-54, 91, 142, 250; II, 1, 3, 4-7,
　　14, 15, 60-62, 68, 70, 175, 275
　eighteenth century term 238
　insurance 44; II, 200, 201, 209, 215-217, 223, 224
　money II, 119, 120, 208, 216
Deposits
　created 15, 50, 51, 140, 239; II, 4-6, 66, 119, 120,
　　142, 184, 216, 219, 379, 394
　demand, see Demand deposits
　in savings banks, see Savings banks, deposits
　interest bearing 49, 51-54, 77, 136, 228, 237,
　　239, 251, 252; II, 3, 5-7, 15, 18, 65, 66, 70, 72,
　　76, 116, 119, 123, 124, 177, 181, 182, 219, 221,
　　249-252, 259, 260, 268, 271, 284, 285, 376, 427-
　　429, 443
　lodged 15, 50, 51, 54; II, 2, 5, 6, 39, 106, 120,
　　184, 379, 394
　of banks in other banks, see Bankers balances
　of country money in city banks 67-69, 238, 239
　of federal, state and city governments, see
　　Public deposits
　of savings banks in commercial banks 216, 218,
　　225-228, 303
　permanent, see also Time deposits, 70-77, 80, 85,
　　176, 260, 261; II, 4
　special 14, 15, 67, 70, 237, 238; II, 34, 82, 161,
　　261, 277
　time, see Time deposits
　withdrawal of ... 52, 53, 76; II, 270
Deposits, depositors 7, 10, 13-17, 24, 35, 43, 50-
　54, 64, 67, 68, 79-81, 91, 92, 95, 105, 108, 127,
　129, 140, 176, 177, 190, 193, 198, 211, 213, 226, 236,
　237, 250, 259, 260, 264, 300; II, 3-7, 33, 36, 38,
　39, 45, 62-66, 72-74, 76, 77, 83, 87, 90, 93, 96,
　104-106, 109, 116, 117, 119-121, 123, 140, 142,
　158, 161, 162, 175, 178-180, 182, 184-187, 191,
　194, 196, 200, 205, 206, 208, 209, 212, 215-217,
　219, 223, 224, 237, 241, 248, 250, 252, 255, 259,
　261, 267-269, 273, 274, 277, 284, 285, 287, 292,
　300, 317, 340, 341, 376, 378, 386, 394, 427-429,
　432, 436, 437

Depositors, see Deposits

Depositories 68, 96, 111, 135, 209; II, 96, 216,
    269, 378, 386
    of public funds 16, 22, 49, 98, 103-105, 169, 173,
    175-177, 239, 256, 290; II, 63, 68, 86, 92-94,
    108, 135, 141, 251, 252, 258, 259, 341, 437

Depositum regulare,... irregulare 14, 237, 238;
    II, 72

Depreciation
    charged on securities II, 183
    of notes (currency), see Currency, depreciation
    of ...

Depression, see Stringencies
    following the crisis of 1837 54, 145, 160; II, 1, 4,
    7, 32, 70, 71, 82, 269, 289, 344

Directors, see Bank directors

Disadvantages of banks, see Antagonism to banks,
    Advantages of banks

Discount
    days 11, 57, 63, 241, 249; II, 38, 62
    on banknotes 14, 67-74, 77-80, 82, 253, 261;
    II, 45, 47, 61, 64, 66, 103, 107, 144, 271
    policy 39, 99, 135, 140; II, 151, 212, 214, 299,
    302
    rate, see Interest rate

Discounting, discounts 10, 11, 15, 18, 19, 22-24,
    45-48, 51, 56-58, 62, 64-66, 71, 91, 94, 98, 99,
    104, 109, 114, 122, 125, 126, 132, 136-141, 145,
    182, 190, 192, 193, 195, 198, 219, 229, 234, 237,
    254, 266, 293; II, 11, 15, 18, 30, 39, 48, 60, 61,
    63, 64, 66, 68, 70, 73, 84, 85, 96, 123, 134, 161-
    164, 167, 180, 194, 202-204, 206, 212, 247-251,
    255, 256, 259, 260, 270, 274, 292, 297, 314, 338,
    389

Discretionary points II, 238

"Discounts" (specific English term of the eight-
    eenth century) II, 306

Dishoarding 137; II, 120

Dividends, see also Policy, dividend 18, 111, 112,
    127, 138, 183, 253, 268; II, 10, 12, 13, 24, 123,
    133, 183, 184, 205, 226, 340, 427
    special, extra II, 183, 192, 393

Division of labor in banking 21, 22, 33, 126; II, 65,
    72, 75

Divorce of ownership and control 62; II, 12

Domestic exchange 52, 58, 69, 72, 78, 105, 108,
    114, 123-125, 129, 130, 132-134, 139, 141, 165,
    198, 229, 274-276; II, 3, 13, 64, 65, 70-73, 84,
    176, 182, 236, 256, 274-276, 285, 327
    notes of certain banks serve as substitutes for
    ... 110, 129; II, 3

Double liability, see Liability of stockholders,
    limited

Double-name paper 10, 48, 98, 248; II, 63

Drafts 78, 131, 136, 165; II, 34, 35, 41, 64, 66, 69,
    73, 74, 79, 93, 179, 428, 432

accepting of ... II, 34, 67, 182, 222, 271
    drawn by branches on each other or parent
    office 106, 108
    drawn by a government 17, 105, 108, 126, 158,
    177; II, 317, 347
    drawn on banks, bankers, see also checks, 14, 51,
    69, 108, 239, 259; II, 4, 46-48, 61, 67, 182, 250,
    251, 295, 330, 332, 338, 340, 343, 405

"Drawn Notes" 239

Dry goods houses II, 153, 154, 193, 230, 233, 301,
    347, 349, 351, 363, 364, 388, 443, 444

Economic
    development, progress 2, 3, 66, 162, 166, 206;
    II, 194, 316, 357, 424
    law, see Natural law in banking

Economists, economics, political economy 6, 9,
    44, 46, 100, 111, 153, 157-159, 162, 188, 191,
    194, 196, 197, 209, 213; II, 4, 5, 36, 123, 140-
    142, 152, 167, 211, 219, 433, 434, 436, 440, 446

Editors, see Journalists

Education of bank employees, see Employees,
    education of ...

Educational institutions benefited by banks 8

Elasticity, inelasticity 7, 46, 132, 139, 140, 158,
    192; II, 32, 36, 42, 64, 105, 115, 116, 120, 123,
    151, 208, 210, 213, 218, 219, 221, 222, 437

Emergency currency II, 167, 168, 209, 210, 214,
    217-219, 222

Employees of banks (accountants, clerks, tellers,
    etc) 19, 34, 36-41, 59, 60, 63, 74, 76, 83, 84,
    93, 113, 118, 120, 154, 211, 213, 253, 271; II, 7,
    11, 45-47, 49, 50, 54, 57, 59, 63, 71, 72, 132,
    151, 165, 177, 179, 181, 185 (female) 186, 201-
    205, 221, 232, 236, 240, 309, 353, 355, 381, 385,
    386, 388, 390
    education of ... 34, 38, 40; II, 151, 200, 203, 245,
    430, 434

Endorsements, endorser 56, 126, 131, 155, 164;
    II, 38, 79, 268, 292, 309, 319

Entrepreneur, entrepreneurial, see Business
    leader

Enterprises, types of ... 18, 26, 33, 37, 41, 48, 55,
    58, 60, 62, 63, 69, 74-77, 80, 86, 97, 98, 106-
    108, 119, 121, 124, 131-133, 141, 145, 160, 165,
    168, 196, 205, 207; II, 169, 175, 185, 187, 194,
    202, 245, 247, 257, 263, 271, 279, 307, 311, 322,
    324-327, 338, 339, 344, 350, 351, 355, 356, 358,
    360, 361, 363, 364, 377, 378, 381-384, 386, 388,
    391, 393, 394, 429

Equal Rights Party (Loco-Focos) 161, 188-190,
    196, 293

Equalization of specie resources, see Specie pool

Equipment bonds II, 377

Ethics, ethical 55, 56, 175; II, 76, 165, 167, 169,
    187, 197, 198, 202, 203, 207, 290, 297, 309, 323,
    360, 377, 382-385, 427, 428, 434

Examinations, see Bank examinations

Exchange, see Domestic exchange, Foreign exchange

banks, companies (Scotland) II, 413

brokers, see Money brokers

business, dealers 17, 54, 60, 61, 115, 130, 131, 198; II, 3, 11, 65, 71, 176, 179, 196, 415

charging of ... 45, 52, 105; II, 3, 13, 66, 77, 103, 207, 236, 237, 240-242, 443

committees of bank boards 57, 58, 141; II, 204, 294, 295

dealers, see Exchange business, Money brokers

domestic, see Domestic exchange

foreign, see Foreign exchange

market 131, 133, 137, 145, 160; II, 6, 64, 70, 256, 263, 370

of inter-bank obligations, see Bank notes, exchange of ..., clearing

rate (both domestic and foreign) 57, 123, 131-134, 138, 145, 160, 161, 165, 172, 244; II, 34, 61, 67, 116, 256, 264, 340, 343

Exchanges

(french: bourses), see Stock exchanges, Wall Street

in the sense of clearings, see Clearing

items to be exchanged with other banks II, 47, 49, 50, 284

"Exchequer" II, 213

Exchequer (British) II, 306-308, 314

Expansion

and contraction, see also Policy of banks, issue, Overexpansion, 61, 65, 66, 85, 99, 105, 108, 109, 112, 119, 124-127, 130, 132, 134-141, 143, 158, 163, 168, 176, 180, 195, 196, 198, 257, 266, 275, 278; II, 1, 33, 37, 54, 68, 123, 141, 142, 158, 248-254, 256, 259, 260, 263-265, 273, 277, 303, 331, 431

of an enterprise, see Growth

of the scope of banking activities II, 179-182

territorial II, 193-202

Exports, exporters 133, 137, 140; II, 69, 262, 267, 305, 416

Express companies II, 74, 151, 179, 182, 240, 241

Facility notes 13, 235, 236, 240

Factors 32, 39, 140; II, 72

Families in banking 17, 20, 26, 37, 38, 62, 63; II, 72, 75, 111, 179, 191, 229, 245, 299, 319, 363, 385

Farm loan business, see Credit, agricultural

Farmers, farms 9, 32, 39, 44, 45, 47, 48, 67, 111, 148, 157, 158, 187, 193, 204, 205, 269; II, 14, 63, 71, 112, 118, 119, 190, 198, 199, 205, 301, 326

Farmers' Alliance II, 439, 441

Federal

government, see Government

Reserve System II, 110, 116, 117, 158, 182, 208, 209, 212, 215, 218, 219, 232, 242, 286, 385, 425, 428

Trade Commission II, 220

Federalists 21-23, 25, 33, 117, 173, 174, 184-186, 214; II, 246

Fee charged to depositors 13-15, 52, 236

Finance companies II, 78, 79, 179

Financial

capitalism II, 381-383

centers II, 65, 73, 76, 77, 103, 109, 114, 122, 142, 158, 167, 172, 182, 183, 186, 189, 192, 194, 201, 202, 212, 214, 218, 236, 247, 256, 259, 323, 332, 380, 394

officers of states, included with Bank commissioners

Financiers 46, 60, 113, 160, 161, 165; II, 113, 120, 123, 167, 202, 211, 218, 221, 226, 288, 315, 322, 354, 356, 362, 366, 383, 384, 429

Fines II, 2, 143, 225

Firm names II, 67, 71, 75, 83, 106, 108, 138, 139, 146, 198

numerical ... of National Banks II, 106, 138, 139, 145, 146

Fiscal agencies

of corporations 33; II, 340, 341, 355, 360, 365, 372, 376-378, 390

of the federal and state governments 96-98, 103, 104, 108, 128, 129, 132, 169, 174, 175, 178-180, 280; II, 58, 102, 138, 153, 212-214, 219, 252, 364

Forced loans II, 319, 405

Foreign

banking 179; II, 182

coins, see Coins, foreign

exchange, ... operations, ... dealers 17, 28, 29, 54, 58, 66, 98, 114, 125, 130-137, 140, 145, 158, 179, 258, 275, 277, 279; II, 35, 62, 64, 67-70, 72, 77, 84, 176, 182, 220, 256, 263, 265, 267, 294, 312, 314, 335, 336, 362, 382, 383, 388, 390; market 130, 133, 135, 145, 160; II, 64, 68, 70, 264; quotations 130, 277; policy of banks guided by the course of ... 124-126, 130, 135, 139, 140, 258, 275; II, 5

loans (American lending abroad), see also Borrowing of banks, abroad, 126; II, 386

money (notes of out-of-town banks) 16, 67, 69-74, 76, 77, 80, 260-262; II, 45, 107, 141, 144, 158, 236, 247, 248, 257, 258, 274, 327; department 74, 76, 83, 84

Frauds, fraudulent banking, defraudations, defalcations 19, 41, 43, 44, 116, 120, 186, 190, 192, 197, 199, 253; II, 15, 58, 96, 198, 223, 241, 270, 299, 425

Free banking 44, 47, 64, 66, 79, 144, 160, 187-204, 296; II, 2, 5, 8, 10, 14, 15, 20, 22, 27, 64, 73,

Free banking (cont'd.)
74, 99, 100, 102, 103, 105, 107, 109, 110, 112,
145, 147, 148, 159, 194, 235, 343-345, 347, 390
acts 50, 79, 170, 187, 188, 190, 194, 197, 198,
200-204, 206, 293-297; II, 1, 2, 9, 10, 15, 25,
26, 32, 35, 37, 43, 64, 72, 74, 86, 103, 140, 342
(as used in the 1870's) II, 122, 123, 280
"Free trade in money" II, 14
Freedom of banking, freedom of note issue, freedom of the banking business 92, 187, 188, 190,
192, 194-197, 201-203, 292; II, 14, 429
French
loans II, 305, 320-322, 356, 382
spoliation claims II, 67
"Friendly Societies" 209
Frontier 172, 187; II, 74, 355
Frozen assets, see Assets, frozen
Functions of banks 7, 8, 9, 11, 13, 43, 46, 52, 56,
65, 66, 111, 205, 206; II, 4, 22, 33, 39, 95, 175,
176, 325, 437
Funding of the public debt, "Funding System,"
Refunding 27, 163, 164, 209; II, 145, 304, 307,
316, 338, 354, 360, 361, 363-369, 374, 383-390,
394, 411, 418, 431
"Funds," see Public stock
Geist, geistig, Geistesgeschichte 2, 10, 162, 163,
164, 231; II, 99, 247, 265, 273
Genealogy of enterprises II, 67, 69-71, 112, 353
General
asset bank notes, ... currency, see Security behind
bank notes, general assets
banking laws, see Free Banking Acts
committees, see Joint committees
managers of banks, see Chief executives
obligation II, 318, 319, 406
stores, see Stores
Generations 2, 3, 31, 36, 64, 76, 162-164, 167,
171-173, 191, 192, 196-198, 217; II, 51, 58, 88,
91, 99, 110, 116, 165, 169, 176, 201, 202, 209,
217, 276, 381, 383, 386, 387, 425, 435, 436
Gold, see Bullion, Specie
certificates, gold checks II, 96, 121, 367, 444
contracts II, 430, 431
mining, mines, see Mining
standard, see Metallic standard
Government
federal, "general," national 8, 12, 22, 24, 25,
27, 50, 51, 54, 58, 88, 94, 98, 100, 103, 105,
109, 111-113, 118, 128, 132, 135, 138, 139, 142-
146, 149, 150, 152-155, 166-169, 172-176, 178,
180, 185, 206, 244, 255, 288, 290, 291; II, 35,
62, 70, 85-95, 99, 100-102, 105, 107, 110, 113,
114, 117, 121, 123, 137, 138, 140-142, 144-146,
162, 168, 212, 214-216, 224, 241, 252, 258, 287,
313, 316-318, 324, 327, 339, 346, 367, 370, 371,
381, 383, 427, 431, 432, 434, 435, 437, 440

aid given to ... by banks, see Government loans
banks, public banks (state owned and managed)
21, 65, 89, 99, 147, 168, 169, 178-180, 266, 291;
II, 22, 23, 60
bond-backed bank notes 66, 190, 191, 196, 199, 201,
297; II, 2, 10, 14, 15, 95, 99, 100, 101, 103, 104,
110, 114, 116, 119-123, 127, 128, 138, 141, 145,
160, 176, 208, 209, 210, 277, 437
bonds, see Government-bond-backed bank notes,
Public stock, Security behind bank notes, special
business influence on ... 103, 169
credit, see Public credit
debts, see Government loans
deposits, see Public deposits
directors, state directors 55, 62, 65, 106, 112,
118, 121, 144, 184, 252; II, 24-27
disbursements, expenditures 105, 110, 111, 130,
141; II, 93, 278
drafts, see Drafts, drawn by a government
funds 25, 98, 105, 111, 145, 175, 177, 239, 257,
276, 289; II, 93, 140
interference with business 91, 93, 99, 146, 191,
193, 202; II, 175, 212, 288, 414, 435, 437
investments in banks, see State and federal participation in banks
loans to ..., see also public stock, 7, 8, 12, 13, 16,
24, 27, 43-45, 49, 50, 58, 98, 101, 102, 105, 111,
126, 137, 164, 185, 220, 235; II, 62, 85, 88, 93,
94, 101, 138, 140, 141, 144, 147, 153, 162, 164,
249, 279, 286, 287, 303, 324, 327, 338, 344, 345,
358
obligations, their role in banking, see also Public
stock, used for subscriptions 10, 13, 49, 54;
II, 14, 15, 92
paper money, see also Legal tender notes and
Redemption 15, 24, 27, 167, 189, 205; II, 90, 94,
95, 103, 105, 114, 121-124, 137, 144, 145, 151,
168, 322, 427, 435, 436
participation in banks, see State and federal
participation
Governments
foreign 29, 30, 96, 97, 126, 133, 136, 189, 209;
II, 8, 124, 144, 306-310, 312-314, 318-320, 322,
324, 397, 403-405
state ..., see States
Governors 8, 22, 30, 31, 33, 36-38, 89, 90, 155,
189, 190, 194, 196, 212, 214, 220; II, 23, 25,
27, 38, 87, 88, 103, 108, 109, 160, 190, 198, 212,
213, 215, 230, 257, 261, 273, 296, 324, 331, 358,
409, 413, 415
of the Bank of England and other central banks
II, 310, 312, 397, 398, 439, 440
Grants II, 325
Greenback Party, "Greenbackism" II, 121, 122
Greenbacks, see Legal tender notes
Group banking, chain banking 41, 144, 145, 259;

II, 23-25, 64, 72, 110, 193, 197-202, 230, 241
Groups of coevals, see Generations
Growth, expansion of an enterprise II, 69, 185-
     194, 197-202, 217, 227, 312, 334, 336, 338, 381
Guarantee 48, 126, 175, 206-208, 249, 253; II, 12,
     33, 67, 76, 77, 105, 141, 182, 215-218, 220, 260,
     268, 269, 271, 277, 312, 321, 334, 340, 354, 355,
     360, 371, 372, 395, 397, 398, 401, 412
Guidance of banks in establishing policy, see also
     Foreign exchange, policy..., Policy of banks,
     issue, lending, 66, 108, 124-126, 130, 131, 135,
     137, 275; II, 33, 36, 37, 54
"Hard Money" philosophy 170, 200; II, 89, 101, 103
Haupt-Obligation, see General Obligation
High capitalism, high capitalistic, see Capitalism
Hoarding, hoards, see also Dishoarding, 24, 137,
     142; II, 93, 118, 119, 121, 122, 124, 215, 224,
     277, 430, 432
Holding company 76; II, 79, 185, 197-201, 393
Hong Merchants 90
Hypothecation of notes 71; II, 4, 133
  of securities, business paper 16, 48, 54, 66;
     II, 34, 96, 132, 340
Ideas
  in banking 6, 21, 25, 27, 33, 44, 46, 68, 71-74,
     79, 95, 154, 188, 189, 193, 198, 202, 203, 206,
     207, 218; II, 24, 32, 37, 50, 99, 100, 102, 104,
     105, 107, 114, 115, 124, 160, 167, 179, 243, 260,
     265, 357, 426-428, 433
  on banking 7, 8, 28, 29, 36, 46, 47, 89, 90, 91, 92,
     143, 165, 166, 167, 169, 174-176, 178, 179, 181,
     187-207, 209; II, 13, 22, 27, 32, 38, 39, 105, 113,
     116, 123, 183, 203, 205, 215, 218, 432, 437
  their role in history 1, 2, 162, 189
Ideas, institutions
  migration of... 36, 42, 78-80, 94, 95, 125, 180,
     187, 188, 191, 193, 194, 197-199, 201-204, 207-
     215, 217-220, 294; II, 8, 25-27, 32, 37, 39, 40,
     51, 79, 103, 104, 115, 124, 163, 196, 213, 221,
     232, 235, 257, 314, 355, 356, 360, 393
Illegitimate, illegal, unsound, wild cat banking
     12, 41, 44, 52, 54, 66, 79, 109, 193, 199, 202;
     II, 15, 61, 62, 87, 106, 115, 116, 167, 177, 218,
     276, 283
Illiquidity, illiquid, see Liquidity
Immigrants 40, 101, 191, 209; II, 23, 29, 63, 69,
     77, 104, 193, 196, 198, 199, 210, 221, 226, 316,
     347, 349, 353, 361, 362, 424
Imperial loans II, 308, 312, 358, 397, 398, 401
Importers 22, 38, 49, 98, 131, 185; II, 63, 69, 86,
     262, 299, 361, 444
Imports 133, 137; II, 5, 82, 305, 317, 351, 362
  ...duties 98, II, 144
Impostors, see Frauds
Improvement banks 49; II, 326, 341
Improvements, see Internal improvements

Incorporated banks (as opposed to private banks)
     13, 21, 88, 89, 94, 97; II, 60-63, 65-67, 69, 70,
     72-74, 80, 83, 249, 250, 262, 317, 323, 324, 325,
     329, 330, 332, 335, 344, 358
"Incorporation" (for incorporating, see Chartering)
     163, 166, 211, 212, 214, 215, 217, 219, 229, 297;
     II, 319
Incorporators of banks, see Bank founders
Independent Treasury, see Treasury
Indianapolis Monetary Convention II, 195, 210
Industrial credit 22, 47, 48, 249
Industrial securities, "industrials," not specified
     II, 168, 181, 344, 369, 374, 377, 380, 384, 386,
     388, 392, 413
Industrial securities, specified
  bonds II, 337, 388, 391, 419
  stock II, 181, 341, 374, 375, 385, 391
Industry, industrial, manufactures, see also Com-
     binations, industrial, 7, 9, 30, 31, 88, 103, 112,
     129, 168, 207; II, 39, 61, 79, 175, 176, 185, 187,
     189, 192, 202, 207, 222, 254, 273, 300, 326, 377,
     378, 381, 382, 392, 409, 420, 430
Inelasticity, see Elasticity
Inflation, inflated 26, 106, 158, 160; II, 93, 106,
     118, 142, 145, 146, 154, 175, 210, 262, 427
Inflationary banking 64-66; II, 120-122, 142, 209
Influence lines, see also Ideas, migration of...,
     5, 6, 13, 26, 28, 29, 33-36, 42, 47, 53, 59, 60,
     65, 70, 71, 73, 76, 78, 79, 91, 95, 98, 99, 109,
     112, 127, 137, 157, 164-167, 169, 170, 173, 174,
     176, 177, 180, 187, 190, 191, 193-199, 201, 203,
     204, 206, 208, 209, 213, 217, 218, 220, 222, 226-
     228, 244, 245, 254, 264, 298; II, 23-27, 40, 43,
     51-54, 105, 113, 117, 195, 196, 211, 213, 215,
     219-222, 233, 245, 274, 275, 320, 324, 327, 330,
     351, 353-355, 435
  Canadian II, 195-197, 218-221, 235
  German II, 195, 218-222, 235
  Scottisch, see Scotch banking
Innovation, see Creative achievement
Insolvency, see Bankruptcy
"Inspectors" 19, 241
Installment selling II, 78, 79
Installments
  debts paid in..., see Debts, payment of...
  on stock subscriptions, see Subscriptions, pay-
     ment of...
Institute of Bankers of England II, 203
Insurance
  business, ... companies, see also Marine insur-
     ance, 32, 33, 35, 41, 53, 185, 191, 195, 228, 253,
     (of credit risk), 300; II, 61, 63, 112, 171, 178,
     187, 189, 207, 216, 217, 223, 224, 294, 301, 333,
     336, 339, 341, 345-347, 350, 354, 356, 376, 378,
     381, 392, 431
  principle in banking, see Deposit insurance,

Insurance (cont'd.)
    Safety Fund, characteristics of ...
    underwriters, ...brokers 32, 35, 37, 41, 209;
    II, 304, 313,
Integration, regional, geographical 21; II, 194-201
Interbank
    borrowing, see Borrowing of banks
    fights, ... hostility 68, 70, 73, 76, 77, 84-87, 91,
        259; II, 109, 114, 115, 217, 247, 248, 255, 257,
        270, 293, 303, 331, 389; ... between state banks
        and the national bank 100, 103, 110, 266; II, 46
    obligations, see also Bankers balances, Deposits,
        permanent, 16, 78, 79, 80, 105, 108, 124, 129,
        136, 139, 154; II, 45, 46, 48, 49, 52, 54, 119,
        142, 147, 158, 171, 221, 248, 249, 253, 256, 257,
        261, 268, 272, 274,
Interconvertible bond plan II, 123, 124, 151
Interest 7, 48, 70, 71, 85, 134, 194, 198, 205, 209-
    211, 213, 218, 222, 261; II, 3, 6, 14, 15, 49, 63,
    65, 66, 69, 76, 79, 91, 110, 121, 122, 146, 159,
    161-163, 171, 180, 237, 238, 247-250, 260, 277,
    285, 295-297, 304-307, 317, 319, 322, 324, 331-
    333, 339, 343, 366, 374, 384, 414, 427
    accounts, see Time deposits
    bearing: ... bank note, see Bank notes, interest
        bearing; ... government paper money, see
        Government paper money; ... post notes, see
        Post notes, interest bearing
    on securities 97; II, 33, 34, 94, 144, 146, 147,
        250, 252, 272, 273, 305-307, 317, 319, 329, 355,
        397, 398, 400
    paid on deposits, balances, see Deposits, interest
        bearing
    paid on notes while not redeemed 70, 200, 247;
        II, 252, 437
    rate, discount rate, see also Legal interest, 10,
        11, 52-54, 71, 72, 77, 98, 99, 112, 140, 141,
        184, 208, 211, 220, 221, 226, 259, 266; II, 7, 63,
        65, 66, 68, 70, 73, 76, 83, 87, 96, 110, 119, 158,
        161, 164-166, 181, 195, 207, 208, 212, 221, 225,
        233, 247, 248, 259, 261, 268, 272, 273, 279, 280,
        294, 297, 299, 306, 310, 314, 338, 340, 343, 397
    rate on securities II, 86, 87, 91, 103, 123, 146, 307,
        308, 316, 319, 327, 329, 334, 338, 344-347, 349,
        352, 357, 358, 365, 367-370, 389, 390, 392, 398
Interests, see Business interests
Interlocking directorates, ... interests, ... stock
    ownership 21; II, 187-190, 206, 227, 378, 383,
    384, 386
Intermediate financing 49, 54; II, 426
Internal improvements, ... companies 6-8, 48, 89,.
    148, 157, 196; II, 23, 29, 30, 297, 324-326, 332,
    339, 340, 351, 353, 399
    ... securities, see Canals, Turnpikes, Public
    utilities
International trade, see Trade, foreign

Inter-state bank relations,
    beginnings of ... 16
Interstate Commerce Commission II, 179, 220
Intervention in times of distress,
    by a central bank, see Central bank influences
        cyclical movements, fights seasonal and irreg-
        ular disturbances; by government, see Govern-
        ment interference
Investment
    bankers, ... banking 50, 138, 160; II, 64, 67-69,
        71, 72, 75-78, 91, 175, 180-184, 186-190, 206,
        207, 304-423; alliances of II, 308, 320-323, 330,
        333, 334, 337, 348-352, 355, 358, 359, 361, 363-
        368, 370, 371, 373, 374, 377-380, 386-388, 390,
        391, 394, 395, 411, 415, 421; "active and pas-
        sive" status II, 360, 361, 364, 377, 378, 383;
        business methods II, 308-310, 314, 316, 317,
        320, 321, 323, 328-330, 337, 344, 345, 347, 348,
        351, 354-360, 365, 371-380, 384, 387, 398;
        control, see Control of enterprises; German-
        Jewish II, 362, 365, 366, 379, 381, 385, 386;
        permanently allied with certain corporations
        II, 336, 360, 378-380
    credit 9, 48, 49, 192
    in banks 9, 17, 25-27, 31, 32, 43, 65, 202; II, 62,
        65, 90, 142, 336, 390; ... by state and federal
        governments, see State and federal participa-
        tion in banks
Investments
    in general, investment opportunities 9, 41, 66,
        101, 111, 138, 192, 211, 229; II, 62, 73, 76, 85,
        123, 145, 222-224, 304-308, 310, 313, 325-327,
        329, 335, 336, 339, 351, 355, 363, 378, 386, 395,
        398-400, 414
    of banks, see also Capital of banks, investment,
        Policy of banks, investment, 11-13, 21, 27, 45,
        49, 50, 112, 127, 137, 139, 141; II, 3, 6, 8, 36,
        39, 78, 85, 175, 180, 182, 207, 256, 295, 324,
        325, 329, 332, 338, 340, 341, 359, 389, 393, 409,
        421
    of savings banks 211, 214-216, 219, 221-229, 299
Investors 54, 55, 86, 101, 133, 187, 216, 228, 298;
    II, 26, 61, 76, 77, 85, 87, 92, 96, 103, 304-306,
    308, 317, 318, 320, 321, 326, 328, 329, 335, 336,
    338, 344-347, 351, 353, 355, 357-360, 367, 369,
    376, 377, 383, 387, 400, 405
    ... foreign 112, 206, 298; II, 76, 309, 383
    institutional II, 317, 320, 327, 332, 336, 341, 345-
    347, 350, 376, 377, 381
Irish Loans II, 311, 312, 401
Irredeemable, see Redemption
Issue
    of notes, see Circulating of notes
    of notes related to specie on hand, see Reserve
        ratios, specie to issues
Issuers of notes II, 33, 64, 72, 83, 110, 114

multiplicity of ... II, 36, 105
Issues, see Bank notes, Circulation, Currency
Jews, Jewish, see also, Investment bankers,
    German Jewish, II, 65, 311, 314, 353, 386
Joint
    accounts II, 67, 70, 91, 333, 334, 348, 350-352,
        358-360, 371, 372, 375, 386, 395, 404, 410
    committees of bank boards, "general commit-
        tees," secret committees, and their sub-
        committees II, 91, 92, 94, 245-264, 266-269,
        272, 277, 292, 297, 299, 359
    contractors II, 308, 351
    liability of borrowers, contractors 126, 207;
        II, 310, 398, 405
    loans II, 271
    stock banks, joint stock companies 53, 188, 197-
        200, 294; II, 55, 319, 327
Journalists, publishers, editors, printers 122, 149,
    150, 159, 165, 172, 173, 204, 213, 216, 299, 391,
    429, 434
Jurists (Judges, Lawyers) 6, 18, 26, 28, 33, 37,
    41, 63, 88, 93, 102, 107, 109-111, 116, 121,
    146, 157, 159, 174, 176, 185, 186, 189, 199, 201,
    202, 212-216, 241, 259, 296; II, 24-27, 29, 30,
    34, 57, 61, 78, 79, 86, 87, 99, 101, 104, 108, 110,
    112, 113, 153, 179, 190, 191, 199, 204, 216, 229,
    246, 294, 297, 330, 353, 355, 378, 387, 420
Kartell II, 207, 285, 287
Laborers, wage earners 209, 210, 212, 214
Laissez-faire 133, 157, 171, 178, 180, 181, 195;
    II, 13, 208, 211, 287, 382, 434
Land, landed property, see Real estate
Land
    agencies, land business II, 63, 73, 76
    banks (banking on real and personal estates,
        banking on private credit) 5-7, 9-12, 22, 24, 27,
        28, 43, 48, 67, 73, 75, 92, 174, 193, 195, 203,
        205-207, 231, 237, 296, 297; II, 1, 14, 168, 247
    offices II, 63, 73, 317
    owners, absentee, for others, see farmers,
        planters, II, 73
Landschaften 206, 207, 297
Lawyers, see Jurists
Ledger II, 185, 186, 204, 205
Legal
    interest, legal interest rate 10, 11, 45, 57, 93,
        94, 98, 99, 112, 140, 233, 266; II, 13, 14, 61, 66,
        70, 77, 110, 119, 134, 151, 247, 279, 281; eva-
        sion of ... II, 13, 14, 63, 66
    reserves (fixed reserves) II, 9, 10, 37, 40, 103,
        104, 116, 117, 122, 141, 436; automatism of
        legal reserve requirements II, 10, 132
    reserves: against demand liabilities II, 9, 10,
        38, 39, 116, 120; against deposits II, 9, 10, 116;
        against notes II, 9, 43, 116, 117, 132
    tender, lawful money 87; II, 95, 101, 117, 124,
        137, 141, 144, 145, 208, 252, 255, 277; ... char-
        acter of bank notes 98, 168, 288; II, 107, 110, 114,
        122, 128, 137, 141, 145
    tender notes (greenbacks) II, 57, 95, 107, 108,
        114, 115, 118-124, 137, 141, 142, 145-149, 164,
        213, 214, 271, 278, 284, 287, 427, 430-432, 435-
        437
Legislation, see Banking legislation
Legislators, see also Congressmen, 8, 33, 35, 40,
    43, 44, 53, 64, 88, 89, 91, 93, 94, 111, 143, 148,
    157, 158, 166, 174, 187, 188, 193, 196-198, 200,
    203, 207, 211-214, 221, 244, 298; II, 1, 2, 4, 5,
    8, 9, 12, 14, 15, 23-25, 27, 29, 30, 32, 39, 40,
    57, 61, 120, 178, 254, 255, 300, 324, 339, 378
Legislatures, see Congress, State legislatures
Legitimate banking, see Sound banking
Lending of banks
    (in general), see Bank loans, Policy of banks,
        lending
    of notes 79, 263; II, 3, 4
    of specie 52; II, 9, 67, 68, 295
    of stock 137; II, 331, 332
Letters
    as the basis of credit 249
    of credit II, 69, 77, 415
Liabilities of banks
    in general, see Debts of banks
    ... cash, current, demand, "immediate," see
        Demand obligations, Demand deposits
Liability
    in general 199, 201, 203, 249, 261, 298; II, 24, 26,
        307, 308, 310, 320, 331, 338, 351, 352, 357, 359,
        360, 366, 374, 395
    joint, see Joint liability
    personal
    ... of directors, managers 95, 203, 215, 256, 264;
        II, 12; ... of stockholders, limited (double liability
        clause) 198, 199, 203; II, 12, 27, 100, 104, 105,
        154; ... of stockholders, unlimited 93, 94, 198,
        199, 292; II, 12, 64
Limitation
    of lending, see Bank loans, limitation of
        total of ...
    of note issues, see Circulation, limitation of ...,
        Circulation in multiples of capital
    of stockholdings 20
Liquidation of banks 56, 61, 109, 154, 157, 161;
    II, 35, 62, 69, 123, 141, 153, 186, 206, 215, 271,
    312, 340, 361, 362
Liquidity, liquid, illiquid 10, 44, 46, 47, 87, 107-
    109, 124, 135, 140, 141, 160, 161, 247, 248;
    II, 1-3, 6, 7, 14, 32, 34, 117, 236, 263, 284, 338,
    340, 361, 428
"Lists" of loan contractors II, 308-310, 312, 313,
    317, 328, 334, 350, 358, 373, 398
Liverpool Currency Reform Association II, 124

Loan
  contractors, loan contracting 50, 101; II, 61, 82,
    85-87, 304-318, 320, 321, 323-332, 335, 336,
    338, 344-347, 349, 351, 357, 358, 367, 377, 397,
    398, 400-405; alliances of ... II, 308-316, 320,
    328, 329, 331-333, 347, 358; business methods,
    see Investment bankers, business methods
  offices 9, 12, 65, 205, 207, 231, 297; II, 39, 42,
    147, 304, 305, 316
  sharks II, 79
Loanable funds ("money") 9, 62, 65, 100, 142;
    II, 118-122, 279, 308, 326, 327, 329, 340, 359,
    379, 386, 414
  concentration of ... II, 122, 378
Loans from banks, see Bank loans; to banks, see
    Borrowing of banks
Lobby, Lobbying, Lobbyist 115, 123; II, 32, 35,
    111, 247, 257, 262, 279
Local character of banks II, 15, 175, 194, 259
Loco-Focos, see Equal Rights Party
Long term credit, long term loans, long term
    paper 9, 12, 33, 41, 44, 45, 49, 126, 154, 193,
    242; II, 3, 15, 36, 39, 67, 70, 141, 180, 324, 326,
    353
Losses 81, 83, 89, 90, 101, 107, 120, 140, 164,
    208, 222, 269, 273; II, 3, 90, 105, 110, 133, 177,
    215, 216, 223, 224, 247, 253, 276, 278, 284, 285,
    307, 310, 312, 314, 319, 338, 343, 374, 411, 428
Lotteries, lottery tickets 41; II, 68, 71, 111, 306,
    312, 313, 319, 322, 326, 335, 400, 403, 405
Louisiana Banking Act of 1842 196; II, 8, 9, 10,
    32-44, 47, 220
"Loyalty loan" of 1796 II, 308, 312, 313, 356
Machines in banking II, 185, 236
"Makers" of paper 10; II, 38
Malpractices, see Administration of banks, mis-
    management
Management, managerial, managers in general
    55, 74, 84, 115, 165, 202; II, 113, 116, 224,
    351, 360, 363, 374, 378, 381, 435
  ... of banks, see Administration of banks, Chief
    executives
Managing partners, see Partners
Manipulation of securities or exchange markets
    II, 70, 264, 312, 314, 315, 319, 357-359, 366,
    374-376, 385
Manufactures, see Industry
Manufacturers, industrialists 22, 32, 44, 45, 47,
    193, 216, 242, 245; II, 3, 15, 63, 71, 79, 89,
    118, 167, 205, 207, 216, 227, 254, 272, 326,
    352, 431, 443
Marine insurance 32, 39, 41; II, 313
Massachusetts
  Banking Act of 1858 4; II, 8-11, 40, 103, 104
  National Bank Cashiers Association II, 240
Mechanics 31, 32, 39, 44, 47, 126, 148, 191, 213,

    214, 216, 219-221; II, 12, 45, 60, 61, 142, 218,
    424
Media of Exchange, ... of payments 7, 8, 13, 29,
    43, 46, 49, 69, 72, 97, 112, 133, 170; II, 158, 160,
    216, 236, 237, 252, 304, 305, 436
  international ... 133, 145; II, 305, 315, 332, 351,
    437, 440
Medium term loans, ... credit 11, 12, 44-50, 108;
    II, 3, 39, 326, 354, 359
Memorandum checks 248
Memorials, petitions 100; II, 246, 255-257, 261,
    263, 266, 283, 430, 431
Mercantile banking, see Commercial banking
Mercantilism, Mercantilist 5-7, 9-13, 24, 26-29,
    43, 44, 48, 64, 65, 67, 75, 92, 111, 140, 157, 174,
    181, 191-195, 199, 201, 203, 205, 233, 234, 296;
    II, 1, 4, 13, 14, 22, 35-37, 208
Merchandise, lending on 11, II, 187
Merchant bankers 22, 53, 54; II, 33, 61, 62, 64, 67,
    69, 71, 83, 271, 272, 305, 313, 318-320, 330,
    335, 336, 348, 350, 351, 398, 402, 421
Merchants, mercantile enterprises 9, 17, 18, 21,
    22, 25, 28-35, 37, 38, 40, 41, 44, 45, 47, 49, 50,
    55, 56, 63, 67-69, 72, 100, 102, 104, 106, 107,
    116, 126, 130, 131, 141, 142, 145, 164, 165, 184-
    186, 191, 202, 205, 210, 213, 215-217, 234, 242,
    249, 259, 266, 288, 298, 300; II, 4, 5, 8, 12, 15,
    23, 32-34, 40, 47, 56-64, 66, 69, 71-75, 77, 79,
    83, 84, 86, 90, 111, 112, 113, 119, 152, 153, 166,
    167, 171, 179, 191, 197, 199, 204, 205, 210, 215,
    216, 233, 237, 238, 246, 248, 254, 259, 271-273,
    277, 294, 298-300, 304, 305, 307, 311-314, 317-
    319, 323, 327, 329, 331, 333-335, 346, 348, 352,
    354, 362, 363, 391, 399, 400, 404, 405, 420, 424,
    431, 437, 443
  Exchange, New York II, 255, 259
Mergers (combinations) in banking 21; II, 75, 78,
    176, 185-194, 197, 206, 207, 229, 364, 376, 382,
    391, 395
Messages, presidential and gubernational 62, 89,
    90, 103, 146-151, 166, 167, 169, 174, 190, 196,
    212, 288; II, 23, 25, 40, 99, 195, 273, 331
Metallic Money, see Specie
Metallic standard
  (in general) 103; II, 94, 101, 144
  bimetallic, see Bimetallism
  gold ... 123; II, 288, 347, 369, 432, 433, 445
  silver ... 158; II, 433
Metropolitan districts II, 194
Mexican War, ... loans II, 95, 344, 345, 347-351,
    356, 359, 395, 415, 416, 426
Middlemen
  in credit II, 67, 70, 72, 77, 78, 84
  in stock, see Loan contractor, Securities, middle-
    men
Migration of ideas, see Ideas, migration of ...

Migrations, internal (including those of individuals) 95; II, 23-27, 29-31, 113, 199

Mining, mines II, 2, 74, 337, 341, 344, 359, 390, 413, 433, 434, 442

Ministers, clergymen 29, 37, 40, 191, 195, 209, 216; II, 68, 227

Mint 99, 134; II, 255

Mismanagement of banks 25, 77, 105, 106, 159, 183, 192, 207, 243, 246, 247, 253, 298; II, 4, 53, 318

Mississippi scheme 27, 164, 286, 287

"Mixed Currency," see Currency, mixed

Mixed enterprise in banking (banks owned and managed by states and private capitalists in cooperation) 27, 89, II, 22

Modeling one bank on another 7, 10, 21, 26, 28, 31, 33-35, 49, 65, 79, 97, 99, 188, 206, 207, 211, 217, 218, 220, 221; II, 23, 24, 26, 27, 63, 221, 324

Monetary
  control, see Control of the Currency
  policy, see Policy, public
  theory, see Banking and Monetary theory

Money
  banks, banking on mercantile credit, banking on a specie basis 6, 7, 9-11, 13, 22, 24, 26-29, 67, 97, 100, 103, 193, 205, 237; II, 1, 2, 247
  brokers, note brokers, exchange brokers 16, 66-70, 72, 117, 129, 160, 161, 164, 174, 259; II, 45-47, 61, 64-68, 70-73, 76, 82, 84, 107, 138, 144, 322, 327, 335, 349
  international II, 430, 433
  market 54, 55, 99, 176, 179, 200, 230; II, 3, 5, 13, 78, 96, 117, 169, 180, 220, 256, 267, 284, 302, 303, 307, 314, 321, 359, 367
  orders II, 179, 182
  shaving, "money shavers," see Money brokers
  Trust Investigation II, 167, 189, 287, 381

Moneyed men, see Capitalists

Monopoly, monopolizing 11, 27, 31, 62, 74, 163, 165-167, 171, 189, 190, 196, 203, 289; II, 78, 103, 195, 306, 311, 312, 319, 369, 380, 408, 426

Monopoly of banking 21, 23, 31, 68, 96, 97, 99, 189, 190, 192, 197, 202, 242, 288, 293; II, 13, 22, 23, 110, 124, 194, 218, 228, 245, 293
  ... of particular lines of banking 51, 68, 74, 77, 79, 80, 100, 126, 128, 130, 175, 266, 293; II, 70, 212, 213, 214

"Monster" 161, 163, 173, 174, 188, 286; II, 122, 211

Morris plan banking II, 79

Mortgage
  banking 205-208, 297; II, 75-77, 178, 222
  banks (as used in the 1830's), see Plantation banks
  bonds 207, 298; II, 75-77, 182, 354, 393

loan companies II, 76

Mortgages, mortgaging, real estate loans 7, 9, 11, 27, 28, 44, 45, 47, 48, 91, 122, 164, 194, 195, 197, 199, 200-203, 205-207, 227, 229, 296, 298, 302; II, 11, 14, 33, 34, 38, 39, 75-77, 110, 124, 168, 175-178, 182, 201, 399, 437

Motives
  of bank founders 24, 25, 28-32, 43, 97, 103, 244, 259; II, 108, 109, 111
  of founders of savings bank 210, 224, 227
  of others 37, 56, 89, 90, 97, 103, 174; II, 109, 167, 254, 275, 304, 324, 379

Multiplication of banks 8, 21, 22, 35, 43, 67, 89, 98, 188, 196, 245, 289; II, 3, 22, 245, 247

Municipal Loans, ... securities 12, 49, 199, 211, 220, 226, 227, 235; II, 165, 168, 180, 249, 318, 319, 324, 326, 333-335, 337-340, 344, 345, 349-352, 354, 376, 377, 381, 389, 392, 394, 395, 399, 405, 414

Mutual
  acquaintance of bank officers II, 50, 52, 276, 283, 289
  information II, 246, 247, 262, 270, 274
  responsibility, ... liability of banks 44, 88-90, 93-95, 176; II, 24-27, 168, 213, 251, 257, 289, 428

National Bank
  (in the sense of central bank) 8, 19, 24-26, 28, 29, 31, 34, 35, 45, 46, 57, 97, 98, 100-105, 107, 111, 128, 130, 143, 144, 150, 163, 169, 171, 172, 174, 177-181, 220, 250, 286, 288, 290, 291; II, 23, 29, 30, 62, 99, 100, 137, 148, 151, 213, 232, 245, 255, 262, 266, 340, 347
  (synonymous with government bank) 168, 169, 178
  Act, National Currency Act, amendments and supplementary acts 80; II, 10, 12, 14, 78, 95, 99, 102, 104-119, 121, 124, 137, 138, 145, 146, 176, 178, 182, 184-186, 194, 195, 205, 207, 208, 279-281, 283, 284, 286, 287, 379, 389, 393, 436; ... opposition to, criticism of II, 106, 107, 113, 114, 124, 137, 140-146, 151, 283, 427, 436
  examiners II, 112, 155, 190, 204, 232, 285, 286, 301
  notes 80; II, 105, 107-109, 114, 115, 118, 119, 121-123, 137, 141, 142, 144, 145, 151, 168, 176, 180, 182, 184, 271, 437; maldistribution of ... 112, 118-120, 287; redemption, clearing of ... 80; II, 107, 108, 114-117, 151, 152, 156, 214, 279, 283, 287

National Banks, National Banking System 80; II, 8, 11, 14, 25, 74-78, 99, 157, 175-184, 186-192, 194, 195, 199, 202, 205, 207, 208, 212-217, 219, 223, 225, 229, 235, 236, 241, 270, 271, 275, 278-282, 284, 288, 300, 301, 353, 366, 379, 389, 392-394, 427, 431, 432, 437
  as sellers of and traders in government securities II, 108, 109, 365, 366, 368, 370, 389, 431

National Citizens' League for the Promotion of a
    Sound Banking System II, 211
National Currency
  Act, see National Bank Act
  Associations II, 168
  as used in the 1860's and later II, 95, 99-102,
    104, 107, 110, 111, 113, 117, 138, 144, 145, 147-149
  as used in the 1830's, see Central bank, issues
    a national currency
National economy 59, 66, 71, 133-135, 143-145,
    150, 160; II, 8, 116, 117, 121, 122, 194, 214,
    263, 264, 265, 270, 283, 290, 337, 370, 375, 378,
    381, 383, 384, 427, 428, 436
National Monetary Commission II, 222
Nationally chartered banks (prior to 1863), see
    National Bank (in the sense of Central bank)
"Natural law, " "economic law" in banking 93, 139,
    171, 180, 189, 192, 193, 195, 197, 202, 291;
    II, 8, 107, 123, 142, 144, 189, 215, 218, 382,
    433-436, 447
Navigation II, 325, 339, 341, 359, 373, 409
"Negotiating" of securities, see Securities,
    "negotiating" of ...
New York funds 52, 78; II, 116, 237, 238, 240, 241
Newspaper articles, Newspapers, see Press
Note
  brokers, see Bill brokers, Money brokers
  clearing, see Clearing
  holders 6, 28, 64, 91, 139, 203, 294; II, 7, 25,
    35, 36, 116, 219, 273; protection of ... 88, 91,
    190, 191, 199, 200, 201, 264, 296; II, 26, 37,
    100, 103, 105, 106, 116, 137
  issue the essential feature of American banking,
    banking synonymous with note issue, see Bank
    note issue
  shaving, see Money brokers
Notes, see Bank notes, Promissory notes
Numerical classification of banks and accounts
    II, 185, 186, 236
Offices of discount and deposit, see Branch bank-
    ing
Oligopoly II , 70, 78, 183, 207, 208, 222, 321, 365,
    366, 381
"Omnium" II, 307, 309, 310, 402
Open market operations, ... policy 128, 135;
    II, 185, 212
Optional clauses on bank notes 13
Organization, see Bank organization
Outlying communities, suburbs, banking in ... 245;
    II, 194, 196, 197
Out-of-town banks
  checks on ..., see Checks, out-of-town
  notes of ..., see Foreign money
Overbanking, overtrading, overissues (excessive
    issues), overexpansion 64, 91, 99, 104, 112,
    126, 133, 137-139, 141, 195, 196, 198; II, 5, 48,

68, 145, 216, 249, 252, 261, 268
Overdrafts 12, 45, 71, 77, 235, 248, 249; II, 66,
    182, 247
Pamphlet literature 5-7, 16, 35, 47, 55, 59, 60, 68,
    73, 99, 100, 104, 148, 149, 154, 157, 167, 168,
    178, 180, 191, 195, 196, 199, 213, 214, 221;
    II, 8, 11, 22, 60, 99, 107, 117, 123, 124, 211, 323,
    355, 430-432
Panics (crises) 65, 66, 136, 137, 139, 142, 155,
    158, 164, 168, 179, 200, 208, 278; II, 5, 13, 82,
    96, 107, 142, 158, 159, 163, 165, 166, 170, 208,
    212, 248, 256, 269, 271, 277, 287, 288, 322, 425,
    426
Paper money, see Currency, Government paper
    money
"Paper system" 164, 165, 166, 170, 200, 286, 289
Par
  collections, see Collections
  points II, 237
  redemption, see Redemption
Parallel actions
  ... of banks in various cities II, 162, 164, 248
  ... of clearing houses II, 286, 287, 431, 432
Parent office, ... board of branch banks, parent
    bank 35, 41, 58, 98, 106, 108, 110, 113-124,
    131, 136, 139, 142, 165, 172, 273, 288; II, 24,
    30, 71, 72, 75, 182, 194, 196, 198, 200, 202, 212,
    218, 353
Parliament, parliamentary, House of Commons
    99, 128, 133, 168, 169; II, 22, 37, 309-311, 386,
    397, 398, 401, 439
Partial-Obligation II, 319, 358, 406
"Participation" in security flotations, participants
    II, 312, 362, 368, 370-375, 380, 386, 389, 392,
    394-396, 422
Partnerships, partners 25, 29, 30-33, 142, 199,
    II, 60, 61, 67, 68, 71, 72, 75, 80, 87, 106, 112,
    179, 187, 190, 198, 199, 201, 202, 304, 310, 312,
    313, 321, 346, 348, 349, 351-353, 355, 356, 358,
    360-364, 372, 378, 379, 382, 384-388, 390, 391,
    420, 424
  Partners, managing in branch systems II, 32, 33,
    71, 75, 198, 362, 363, 385
Pass book 53, 211, 213; II, 47, 186, 205
Pauperism 209, 211-213, 216, 219
Peel Act 171, 180; II, 8, 105, 122, 150, 213
"Pegging", see Manipulation
Periodicals, articles in ... 6, 128, 156-158, 193,
    194, 198, 202, 213, 218, 294; II, 50, 60, 71, 73,
    76, 100, 101, 105, 109, 212, 213, 215, 218, 219,
    259
Permanent platforms for interbank cooperation
    II, 269, 270, 271, 273-276, 280, 283-289, 425
Personal contacts, their role in the development
    of banking 33, 34, 35, 36, 42[chart]; II, 25, 26,
    430

element (factor) in economic development 1, 2, 3, 58, 100, 162, 171, 212; II, 26, 52, 165, 193, 256, 262, 274, 327

security, see Security, personal

"Pet banks" 49, 64, 95, 173, 175, 176, 177, 289; II, 56, 57, 255, 257, 258

Physicians 45, 213, 216; II, 198, 297, 388

Physiocrats 288

Plantation banks 126, 205-208, 297, 298; II, 33, 39, 305, 338

Planters, plantations 107, 126, 140, 164, 174, 206, 207; II, 32, 33, 39, 58

Policy of banks, see also Central bank policy,13, 17-20, 36, 39, 40, 46, 47, 54, 61, 65, 77, 90, 91, 98, 99, 105, 106, 109, 110, 113, 114, 118-124, 126, 127, 129-131, 136-138, 140-142, 145, 150, 157-159, 161, 193, 200, 202, 218, 234, 273; II, 2, 3, 6, 34-39, 62-64, 70, 71, 75, 77-79, 82, 86, 89, 92, 114, 120, 124, 153, 176, 177, 182-184, 193, 196, 197, 200, 201, 207, 237, 246, 249, 250, 254, 256, 258, 260, 261 263, 265, 267, 268, 270, 278, 286, 288, 329, 339, 432, 433,437

dividend... 109, 127, 268; II, 14, 183

investment... 10, 13, 49, 50, 62, 126, 127, 129, 135, 139, 193, 200; II, 14, 324, 325, 338

issue ... 8, 17, 28, 44, 64-66, 99, 105, 106, 108, 109, 119, 124, 125, 128, 131, 140, 142, 143, 279; II, 15; ... how to be guided, how guided 108, 125, 126, 130, 139, 140, 196, 240, 248, 275; II, 5, 33, 43

lending... (... regarding discounts) 10-12, 22, 27, 39, 45-49, 64, 66, 98, 106, 122, 124-127, 129, 136, 138-141, 143, 176, 187, 193, 229, 232-236, 266, 269; II, 6, 9, 15, 33, 34, 38, 62, 63, 124, 176, 181, 183, 185, 187, 340; ... how to be guided, how guided 66, 124, 126, 137, 195, 236, 237, 257, 267; II, 1, 6, 9, 10, 39, 42, 275

personnel... 19, 83, 84, 113-115, 118, 120, 121, 154, 159, 271

regarding country notes 67-81, 109, 238, 239, 276; II, 46, 247, 257

regarding interest payment on deposits 52, 53; II, 65, 271

regarding reserves 127; II, 2, 183, 271, 284

uniformity of... (see also Uniform charges) II, 245-247, 251-253, 255, 256, 261, 271, 275-277, 283-285, 287, 289, 290, 292

Policy of investment bankers, loan contractors II, 309, 315, 323, 348, 352, 357, 367, 373, 374, 377-380, 382, 384, 386, 388, 390, 393, 395

Policy, public 8, 24, 29, 31, 105, 106, 128, 156, 169, 172, 174, 179, 232; II, 86, 87, 91-94, 145, 146, 246, 263, 273, 286, 287, 307, 308, 316, 327, 344, 356, 357, 371, 414, 427, 430-433, 435, 438, ... toward banks 29, 88, 166, 169-179, 188, 288, 289, 298; II, 13, 23, 102, 113, 114, 116, 118,

121, 144, 283, 333, 411

Political
background of ..., influence on bank organization and measures 57, 89, 166-177, 188-190; II, 23, 104, 118, 193, 208, 211, 214, 232, 264, 282

banks 22, 23, 33, 38, 117, 173, 185, 186, 242, 243

Political
economy, see Economists

ends to be achieved by founding banks 23, 24, 25, 30, 31, 97, 98, 103, 104, 243

influence exerted by banks, see Power of banks
thought 158, 162, 163, 167, 169, 171, 172, 180, 187, 189, 190, 192, 197; II, 194

Politics, political in general 22, 28, 31, 32, 38, 39, 44, 89, 107, 115, 117, 118, 121, 123, 127, 138, 139, 144, 146, 147, 148, 149, 151, 152, 155, 157, 163, 164, 166, 171-175, 178-181, 184, 185, 187-189, 197, 199, 200, 214, 215, 228; II, 23, 61, 141, 142, 195, 211, 212, 245, 256, 262, 264, 277, 280, 309, 312, 315, 323, 357, 362, 364-366, 370, 371, 381, 383

Politicians, statesmen 32, 35, 37, 38, 46, 55, 89, 101, 102, 106, 107, 109, 110, 117, 121, 145-156 (Biddle, the politician), 158, 159, 161, 162, 165, 171, 172, 175, 179, 180, 188, 199, 200, 201, 212, 214, 266, 296, 298; II, 23, 26, 29, 33, 35, 61, 83, 104, 141, 145, 153, 191, 198, 201, 202, 211, 213, 215, 216, 220, 221, 255, 262, 297, 300, 301, 307, 355, 356, 363, 364, 390, 411, 433

"Popular loans" II, 90, 321, 347, 355-357, 368, 371

Portfolio, see Investments in general, Investments of banks

Postal Savings Bank II, 216

Post-dated checks 48; II, 55

Post notes 13, 16, 17, 43, 49, 54, 55, 133, 145, 239; II, 3, 61, 62, 67, 128, 268, 272, 297
... interest bearing 24, 54, 55, 145; II, 34, 330, 359

Power of banks and bankers, influence of ... 8, 64, 65, 71, 73, 74, 90, 141, 142, 165, 166, 168-170, 174, 175, 180, 184; II, 124, 224, 255, 256, 276, 287, 288, 361, 373, 378, 380, 385

Preambles
... of charters 7, 8, 219, 220, 221, 224, 227, 232, 302
... of acts 301, 302

Pre-capitalistic, pre-capitalism, see Capitalism

Precious Metals, see Bullion, Specie

Preferred stock II, 353, 354, 374

Premium 68, 134, 226; II, 116, 145, 146, 183, 184, 256, 294, 306, 328, 344-347, 369, 371

Presentation for payment of notes, see Redemption of notes

Presidents (vice presidents) of banks, see also Board of Presidents,14, 15, 18, 20, 25, 26, 30,

Presidents...Board of Presidents (cont'd.)
32, 34-41, 45, 48, 57-63, 66, 74, 76, 77, 79-87,
102, 106-110, 113, 119, 123, 124, 127, 129, 131,
133, 143, 145, 153, 159, 161, 173, 176, 183, 186,
198, 201, 202, 207, 211, 214, 217, 222, 245, 255,
257, 259, 261, 280, 291, 292, 298; II, 8, 11, 12,
24-27, 30-35, 48-54, 56-59, 64-66, 86, 87, 89-
91, 93, 106-109, 111-113, 121, 132, 151-154,
160, 163-165, 167, 169, 171, 179, 181, 190-194,
196-205, 210, 215, 217, 218, 221, 222, 226-229,
232, 237, 239, 242, 243, 254, 255, 258-260,
262-264, 266, 267, 273-276, 279, 280, 285, 287,
293, 294, 296-299, 301, 302, 324, 329-333, 341,
346, 349, 352, 369, 373, 389-393, 410, 411, 417,
425, 429, 438
    functions, duties of...20, 36, 58-60, 63, 83, 84,
155, 198, 201, 203, 232, 241, 254-256; II, 11,
33, 101, 153, 202
    salaries, remuneration of... 19, 25, 59, 63, 116,
241, 255, 257; II, 11, 19, 202, 203
Presidents of branches 48, 113-119, 121, 131, 141,
153, 273; II, 25, 26, 30
Presidents of savings banks 212-214, 217-219,
223, 224; II, 208, 349
Presidents of the United States 22, 61, 62, 101,
102, 104, 112, 113, 115, 117, 118, 121, 123,
138, 141, 144-156, 158, 159, 161-180, 188, 198-
201, 282, 288, 289; II, 23, 29, 86, 89, 100, 101,
114, 120, 195, 213, 215, 328, 329, 340, 362,
363, 370, 433, 439, 446
Presidents of trust companies II, 111, 153, 173,
204, 369, 422
Press (newspapers) 88, 89, 121, 122, 126, 148-150,
152, 153, 160, 163, 165, 173, 196, 204, 213, 217,
282; II, 87, 99-101, 106, 117, 129, 204, 219, 220,
241, 263, 278, 294, 304, 320, 344, 429, 432,
    ... articles 35, 149, 153, 173, 193, 196, 197, 232,
244; II, 23, 35, 49, 148, 192; 355, 438
Pressure groups, activities of... 12, 156; II, 35,
124, 271, 279, 429-431, 444
Price control of securities, see Manipulation
Prices, price level, price flunctuations 8, 91, 112,
125, 133, 145, 158, 163, 165, 168, 192, 195;
II, 142, 144-146, 263, 304, 364
Printers, see Journalists
Printing of notes 59; II, 152
Private bankers, private banking 13, 35, 41, 45,
49, 53, 101, 102, 187, 188, 202, 229, 293; II, 6,
23, 25, 27, 30, 60-84, 96, 106, 109, 111, 112,
122, 124, 152, 153, 175, 176, 180, 181, 187,
190, 191, 198, 199, 203, 227, 232, 258, 277,
282, 288, 305, 343-392, 394, 415, 420, 422,
424, 444
    abroad 29, 30, 38, 40, 97, 294; II, 271, 295, 299,
305, 306, 309-316, 318, 320-323, 329, 331, 335,
336, 358, 370, 373, 385, 386, 398, 400, 402-406

older type II, 60-64, 82
younger type 64; II, 60, 61, 69-74, 82
specialized II, 73-75, 77, 344, 349, 354, 358
    their activities in investment banking II, 333-337,
343-392, 394, 395
    their role in the establishment of the National
Banking System II, 74, 76, 110-113
Private banking - term II, 60
"Private credit" (contemporary expression for
mortgage credit) 9
Privilege
    (in general) 7, 12, 163, 167, 189, 215, 427, 435
    banking or certain lines of banking considered
a ... (an exclusive right) 31, 90, 165-168, 170,
190-192, 293; II, 115, 118, 138
Private lending, private lenders 48, 103, 192, 205;
II, 15, 18, 69, 399
    ... ceases because of the activities of banks 9,
48; II, 5
Profit (in general) 31-33, 56, 68, 70, 82, 101, 144,
154, 161, 165, 171, 188, 214, 215, 225, 259;
II, 11, 49, 69, 84, 87, 88, 103, 116, 120, 145,
224, 304, 306, 307, 316, 317, 321, 322, 326, 338,
347, 354, 355, 357, 359-361, 363, 366, 372-374
376-378, 381, 382, 384, 388, 398, 400, 403
Profit of banks, profitability 6, 8, 9, 15, 30, 31,
33, 41, 52, 68, 70-80, 90, 97, 104, 114, 127, 130,
134-136, 139, 141, 143, 159, 165, 190, 195, 206,
208, 215, 232, 233, 236, 253; II, 3, 8, 14, 15, 22,
34, 40, 45, 47, 61, 62, 64, 70, 71, 73, 75, 77, 78,
106, 108, 109, 115, 119, 120, 122-124, 133, 137,
152, 154, 176-178, 183, 184, 186, 187, 194, 200,
226, 236, 238, 241, 252, 255, 261, 276, 279, 306,
307, 324, 325, 332, 338, 340, 373, 389, 390, 392,
393
    ploughed back II, 183-185
    subordinated to other objectives 8, 97, 98, 104,
128, 139, 143, 144, 215; II, 90
Prohibition of banking II, 13, 20, 26, 27
Promissory notes, single name paper 10, 11, 18,
24, 32, 45, 47, 48, 51, 58, 94, 98, 127, 138, 145,
153, 155, 164, 198, 237; II, 26, 38, 61, 66, 73,
77-79, 84, 180, 182, 185, 197, 204, 205, 224, 225,
247, 249, 256, 258, 318, 326, 399, 404
Promoters, promotion 6, 8, 25, 26, 30, 33, 34, 88,
101, 104, 178, 207, 210-212, 215, 218, 221;
II, 25, 99, 109, 112, 186, 202, 245, 283, 315, 327,
354, 355, 361, 365, 372
Propaganda, see Advertising
Property 6, 7, 43-45, 47, 48, 55, 90, 91, 93, 111,
112, 163, 165, 189, 197, 198, 203, 206; II, 1, 14,
33, 305, 306, 339, 361, 380, 434-436
"Property banks," see Plantation banks
"Proprietors" of banks 17, 18, 29, 64, 192, 240,
254; II, 245
"Protected circulation," see Bank notes, "marked"

Protection of
  creditors, see Creditors of banks, how to be
    secured;
  noteholders, see Noteholders
Proxy voting, proxies 25, 60, 61, 118, 120, 253,
  256; II, 13, 132
Public
  and semipublic character of banks 7, 8, 22, 31,
    33, 37, 43, 55, 88, 91, 98, 144, 150, 151, 153,
    179, 188, 232, [denial]; II, 60, 245
  banks, see Government banks
  credit, ... creditors 24, 27, 49, 103, 104, 179
    191, 266; II, 86, 87, 90, 95, 105, 106, 121, 140,
    144, 305-308, 317, 319, 321, 323, 324, 329, 331,
    347, 398-400
  credit (specific term by 1840), see also Govern-
    ment credit, 62, 85; II, 39, 297
  debt 97, 209; II, 25, 30, 144-146, 304, 305, 316,
    319, 344, 354; ... connection with banking (see
    also government-bond-backed bank notes 191,
    286; ... contemporary expression for bank notes
    64; discharge, redemption, reduction of ... 128,
    138, 146, 147; II, 176, 307, 319, 327, 329, 338,
    339, 344, 347, 365, 406, 414, 437
  deposits, see also Removal of the ... 15, 16, 22,
    49, 53, 54, 63, 100, 104-106, 108, 109, 141, 145,
    152, 154, 166, 173, 175-177, 198, 236, 237, 239,
    288; II, 34, 49, 55, 62, 92, 108, 141, 219, 252,
    257, 264, 266, 288, 317, 331-333, 431
  funds, see Depositories of ..., Government funds
  lands 63, 111
  loans, see Government loans, Public stock,
    States, lending to
    (eighteenth century term) II, 306, 307
  officers supervising banking, see Bank commis-
    sioners, Comptroller of the Currency
  opinion, 93, 101, 105, 121, 165, 174; II, 103, 116, 321,
    369, 432; on banking 7, 8-10, 16, 23, 28, 31,
    55, 62, 64, 65, 68, 70, 74, 76, 77, 89, 96, 101,
    102, 104, 106, 107, 111, 112, 128, 157, 163, 165,
    167, 168, 170, 171, 174, 180, 187-190, 196, 202,
    203, 205, 211, 233, 255, 287; II, 2, 6, 9, 11-15,
    20, 26, 112, 113, 117, 120, 166, 167, 175, 176,
    178, 183, 189, 195, 201, 202, 206-208, 211, 214,
    283, 324, 325, 395
  policy, see Policy, public
  revenue 98, 104, 129, 169, 175; II, 113, 252, 307,
    313, 327, 365
  stock, foreign issues, see also British loans,
    French loans, Imperial loans, Irish loans,
    II, 305, 309, 318-323, 386, 387, 398, 406, 408,
    409; issued by the federal and state govern-
    ments 12, 18, 41, 47, 50, 54, 58, 65, 66, 98, 101-
    104, 108, 123, 127, 128, 136-138, 140, 141, 170,
    185, 186, 194, 195, 198-201, 206-208, 211, 214,
    218-220, 226, 227, 229, 234, 237, 239, 277, 278,
287, 296, 298; II, 26, 27, 33-35, 62, 77, 82, 85-
    96, 99-105, 108, 109, 120, 123, 124, 141, 145,
    146, 161, 164, 165, 168, 169, 176, 184, 208, 209,
    213, 223, 224, 250-254, 273, 277, 291, 294, 295,
    304, 313, 316-319, 322-371, 374, 376, 381, 383,
    387, 389-392, 394, 395, 399, 404-406, 410, 412-
    416, 418, 426, 427, 430, 432; held or to be held
    by banks, see also Capital of banks, invest-
    ment in government securities 10, 18, 47, 50,
    90, 104, 124, 127, 135, 137, 194, 200, 206, 250,
    293, 294; II, 36, 94, 103, 110, 119, 121, 122,
    133, 175, 180, 277, 293, 317, 318, 324, 325, 327,
    329, 330, 338, 340, 341, 346, 389, 393; held or
    to be held by savings banks 211, 218, 220, 221,
    226, 227, 229, 303; lending on ..., see stock
    loans; proceeds left on deposit with the con-
    tracting banks II, 92, 331-333, 366, 411; special
    issues: Holland loan of 1787 II, 318; Louisiana
    bonds II, 313, 314, 319, 327, 358, 403; Mexican
    war loans, see Mexican War; 5-20's II, 146, 147,
    357, 359-361, 365, 367; used for subscriptions
    to banks 13, 49, 65, 101, 102, 138, 191, 206;
    II, 324, 325
  utilities, see also Canals, Turnpikes; enterprises
    II, 326, 327, 378, 385; securities 13; II, 180,
    336, 339-341, 377, 380, 381, 388, 392
Publicity, see Advertising
Publishers, see Journalists
Pujo Committee II, 168, 176, 189, 287, 371, 373-
  375, 378, 380, 387, 390
Punctuality in business 7, 9, 111; II, 233
Quakers (Society of Friends) 110, 209, 212, 216;
  II, 60, 199, 254, 273, 274, 309, 354
Railroad
  financing II, 3, 18, 111, 198, 294, 326, 332, 337,
    339, 348, 349, 352-354, 361, 365, 372, 373, 376,
    379, 380, 383, 384, 386-388, 390, 391
  reorganizations II, 355, 380, 384, 386, 390, 391
  securities (in general) II, 181, 326, 336, 349,
    352-355, 359, 361, 362, 369, 380, 388, 390, 392,
    395; ... bonds 66; II, 168, 180, 326, 344, 345,
    348-350, 352-355, 359, 360, 361, 365, 371, 373,
    376, 384, 388, 395, 415, 416; ... stock 229;
    II, 168, 325, 326, 339, 341, 349, 353-355, 359,
    360, 384, 409
Railroads 66, 148, 157, 195; II, 15, 29, 30, 31, 57,
  70, 76, 96, 112, 153, 165, 187, 214, 297, 300,
  326, 339, 349, 352, 353, 355, 356, 360, 363, 372,
  377-380, 383, 386, 391, 410
Real estate, real property 28, 43, 112, 115, 164,
  165, 170, 171, 197, 198, 203, 205, 220, 227, 269,
  298, 302; II, 26, 33, 76, 77, 79, 112, 124, 133,
  176, 180, 197, 199, 201, 204, 279, 304, 305, 335,
  338, 339, 341, 348, 359, 377, 394, 399, 400, 404,
Real estate securities, see Mortgages, Mortgage
  bonds

"Real paper," business paper, trade paper, "transaction paper" 10-12, 43-47, 65, 91, 106, 125, 126, 136, 138, 192, 193, 195, 208, 229, 234 (term), 248, 253, 297; II, 34, 36, 38-40, 63, 116, 251

Receivables 200; II, 78, 79, 179, 260, 268, 269, 425, 437

Recession, see Stringencies

Rechartering, see Bank charters, renewal of ...

Recruiting of bank officers, see also Cashiers become presidents, II, 203, 204

Redemption

  agents 16, 45, 51, 53, 69-72, 79-81, 261; II, 15, 18, 46, 47, 66, 108, 109, 114, 115, 137, 154, 214, 215, 248, 270, 272

  cities II, 108, 115, 154

  (convertibility) of government paper money in (into) specie or bonds, see also Interconvertible bond plan, II, 94, 95, 105, 124, 137, 149, 198, 368, 427, 430-432

  discount 78, 79; II, 15, 116, 152

  Fund, Washington II, 117

  of notes, see also Branch notes, redemption of ... National Bank notes, redemption 6, 16, 44, 45, 52, 63, 67-78, 81, 82, 85-87, 91, 94, 99, 105, 106, 108, 112, 129, 132, 139, 188, 193-195, 197, 199, 200, 203, 247, 248, 262, 275, 276, 288; II, 4, 6, 10, 13, 37, 45, 46, 48, 55, 57, 61, 64, 66, 73, 93, 99, 103-105, 107-109, 116, 122, 123, 129, 130, 137, 141, 142, 144, 147, 152, 158, 160, 212, 218, 236, 240, 246, 248, 251, 258, 259, 268, 270, 271, 272, 273, 276, 277, 289, 292, 293, 297, 427, 437

  of notes: at par 70, 74, 76, 80, 81, 261; II, 105, 107, 114-116, 212, 236; at places other than the place of issue 43, 45, 51-53, 69, 70, 76; II, 6, 13, 114-116, 132, 218, 249, 256; cost of ... 70, 76, 78, 80, 85; II, 115, 116; regular ... 78, 79, 110; II, 45-47; remuneration for ... 45, 70, 71, 72, 74, 76, 77, 81

  systems 70-81, 263; II, 114, 115, 116, 276

Rediscounting 54, 104, 126, 142; II, 4, 5, 182, 214, 222, 227, 260

Reform 44, 91, 196, 197; II, 9, 13, 35, 36, 38, 100, 167, 168, 173, 195, 207-218, 220, 234, 283, 427; "currency reform" II, 209-211, 215

Refunding, see Funding

Regulation

  (in general) 181, 192

  ... of banking, see also Self-regulation, 52, 90, 91, 204; II, 27, 36

  ... of banking by competition 175, 197; II, 208

  ... of the currency, see also Central bank, regulates, 8, 69, 90, 91, 171, 195; II, 48, 99

Reissue of notes, see Circulating of notes

"Relief notes" II, 273

Rembours credit II, 69, 77

Remittances, transfer of funds 15, 17, 71, 78, 100, 108, 111, 112, 129, 130; II, 66-68, 100, 103, 185, 186, 240, 241, 248, 256, 295, 305, 312, 314, 322, 332, 333, 359, 364, 368, 399

Removal of the public deposits from the Second Bank of the United States 46, 152, 154, 173-176, 180, 280; II, 57

Renewal of bank charters, see Bank charters, renewal of ...

Renewing of paper 11, 45-47, 153, 235, 269; II, 38, 256, 258, 318

"Rentes" II, 319-322

"Report on a National Bank" (Hamilton's) 28, 98, 99

"Report on Public Credit" (Hamilton's) 29

Reports, reporting

  of banks or their organizations 53, 66, 87, 92, 143; II, 24, 107, 128, 129, 144-146, 274, 284, 287, 297, 427, 429, 437

  of legislative committees on banking matters 43, 149, 153, 175, 196-199, 293, 298; II, 23, 24, 36, 38, 39, 99, 255

  of public agencies, officers on banking matters 48, 90, 91, 103, 193, 202, 236; II, 45, 93, 101-103, 105, 106, 108, 113, 118, 135, 136, 145, 178, 185, 192, 195, 201, 223, 252

Republicans II, 87, 104, 216, 431, 443

"Repudiation" 161; II, 25, 35, 70, 138, 343, 350

Reserve

  cities, see also Central reserve cities, II, 104, 117, 132, 152, 178, 217, 288

  ratios

    specie to capital II, 8, 10, 37, 116; specie to deposits 297; II, 8, 10, 162, 284; specie to issues 126, 140, 201; II, 1-3, 8, 9, 37, 43, 132, 149, 201, 212, 261; specie to issues plus deposits (demand liabilities) 10, 140, 267; II, 7-10, 27, 36-39, 44, 103, 275, 283, 436

  situation as guide to policy, see Policy of banks, issue..., how to be guided; lending ..., how to be guided

Reserves (specie reserves in general), see also Legal reserves, 52, 53, 80, 84, 92, 94, 99, 112, 124, 134, 135, 137, 142; II, 3, 6-8, 10, 15, 27, 36-38, 62, 89, 103, 106, 115-117, 119, 124, 154, 161, 162, 173, 175, 178, 179, 182, 183, 208, 210, 212, 214, 217, 218, 220, 264, 271, 283, 284, 303, 427, 428, 431, 436

  against deposits 297; II, 2, 3, 9

  against notes 6, 112, 131, 201, 234, 236, 248, 257; II, 1-3, 9, 37, 114, 117, 119, 212, 261

  against notes and deposits (cash liabilities) 10, 52, 80, 84, 94, 97, 99, 124, 134, 135, 137, 142, 190; II, 9, 32, 37-40, 42, 104, 283, 433

  contingency... 13, 32, 127, 225, 236; II, 14, 123

dividend 127
hidden 127; II, 183
metallic ... of the country, see also Central Bank functions, ultimate reserve holder, 10, 98, 99, 133, 134, 135, 137, 142; II, 7, 256, 370, 374, 410, 432, 433, 435
pyramiding of ... II, 115-117, 120, 208
secondary II, 3, 6, 14, 37, 39, 222, 389
Resources
(in general) 103, 104, 113, 127, 136; II, 69, 185, 189, 194, 202, 391
cash ... II, 37, 62
Responsibility, see also Liability, Mutual responsibility 15, 38, 64, 103, 135, 141, 143-146, 175, 222; II, 183, 207, 213, 217, 250, 255, 273, 278, 283, 286, 360, 375, 382, 383, 385, 428, 429, 432, 437, 438
"Restraining acts" 21, 94, 102, 187, 189, 190, 196, 197; II, 60-63, 81, 247
Resumption of specie payments 15, 46, 54, 70, 78, 103-106, 136, 145; II, 25, 67, 82, 103, 115, 120-123, 142, 249-255, 260-269, 272, 273, 275-278, 286-288, 295, 297, 331, 368, 430, 431, 437
Retailer, see Shop keeper
Returns, see Reports of banks
Risk 15, 76, 78, 85, 94, 126, 131, 136, 215; II, 50, 54, 65, 66, 69, 78, 140, 159, 160, 215, 216, 223, 239, 288, 307, 308, 310, 315, 321, 333, 340, 344, 347, 368, 370, 372, 373, 376, 428, 433
Robber Barons II, 187, 207, 290, 381, 429
"Rule of 1832" II, 39
Rules and regulations of banks 10, 11, 15, 18-20, 31, 34, 51, 58-60, 62, 63, 83, 84, 114, 240, 255; II, 33, 247, 259, 260
Runs (running) on banks 66, 73, 152, 177, 259; II, 61, 62, 192, 224, 247, 258, 272, 273, 276, 277, 292, 293, 428
Safe banking, making banks safe, see also Sound banking, 44, 45, 192, 195, 203; II, 178, 215, 224
Safety Fund 88-95, 194; II, 24-27, 210, 215, 216, 221
Safety Fund Act, ... banks, ... system, in and out-side of New York 44, 46, 54, 88-95, 125, 176, 194-197, 200, 203, 265, 266, 279, 293, 297; II, 2, 11, 23, 25, 26, 30, 32, 168, 215, 217, 235, 257, 415
Savers 52; II, 80, 360
Savings 53, 209, 210, 213, 214, 219-222, 225, 229, 303; II, 79, 118, 120, 145, 146, 151, 155, 203, 305, 327, 356, 357, 390
Savings banking combined with or conducted by commercial banks and trust companies 211, 228-230; II, 181, 182, 216, 226, 301, 327, 422
Savings banks (in general) II, 177, 179, 180, 181, 282, 336, 344-347, 349, 350, 362, 370, 376
communal ... 213, 228

five cents ..., penny 211, 299
mutual ... 52-54, 76, 138, 148, 209-230; II, 225, 226, 255, 299, 326, 327, 345, 346
stock... 228; II, 181
administration of ..., see Administration, Committees
business problems 224-227, 303
charters, constitution, plan, see also Preambles, 210-214, 217-222, 225, 227-229, 300, 302, 303
founders of ... 76, 210, 212-219, 221, 222, 224, 228, 259; II, 255
officers, see also Trustees, 76, 214, 215, 219, 220, 222-224, 227-229, 299
deposits, depositors 209, 210, 213-216, 218-225, 227-230, 300-302
earnings and their applications (dividends, extra-dividends, surplus) 215, 218, 220, 229
policy in general 217-221, 225, 302, 303; interest ... 225-227, 229, 301; investment ... 52-54, 215-230, 302, 303; II, 225, 345
purpose of ... 210, 212, 214, 215, 219, 224, 228, 230
spirit 221, 222, 228, 229, 230
Scotch Banking 5, 65, 66, 96, 99, 157, 187, 188, 197, 198, 292; II, 79, 195, 196, 220, 221
Scrip
(in the sense of illegal paper money) 43, 198; II, 260, 261
(in the sense of not fully paid securities) II, 86, 164, 207, 321, 335, 400
Seasons, seasonal 131-135, 140; II, 117, 122, 182, 208, 210
Secrecy 25, 59, 62, 243; II, 309, 323
Secretaries of the Treasury 8, 12, 14, 15, 17, 22, 25, 37, 40, 46, 48, 50, 56, 63, 66, 92, 95, 98, 99, 101, 102-106, 108, 110, 128, 144, 146, 152-154, 156, 159, 173, 175, 193, 288; II, 7, 25, 48, 70, 85, 87-96, 99,. 101-104, 106-108, 113, 114, 118, 138, 140-142, 144-146, 162, 164, 169, 175, 195, 204, 209, 211, 212, 247, 252-254, 263, 287, 288, 315-317, 327, 328, 338, 356, 357, 359, 362, 365-369, 391, 399, 401, 411, 426, 431, 433, 438, 439, 444, 446
Secretaries to bank boards 19, 34; II, 27, 63
Securities, see also bank stock, bonds, county bonds, corporation securities, not specified, industrials, municipal securities, public stock, public utilities, railroad securities, stocks, war bonds
(in general) 17, 19, 27, 127, 160, 206, 215, 226, 302; II, 11, 66, 67, 73, 82, 83, 109, 162, 166, 171, 172, 180, 182, 183, 205, 214, 223, 272, 296, 304-306, 318, 319, 321-325, 329, 330, 335, 336, 338, 340, 341, 343, 351, 371, 373-377, 379, 383, 386, 387, 390, 394, 395, 425
auction sales of II, 304, 348, 353, 393, 413

Securities (cont'd.)

bidding on ... by loan contractors, see Loan contractors;

bidding on ... by the public, see Subscriptions, public

commission paid or demanded for flotations II, 308, 316-318, 320, 340-343, 347, 349, 366-369, 372, 374, 375, 384, 389, 398, 405, 412

competitive bidding on ..., see Subscriptions, public

consignment of ... II, 33, 295, 330, 332, 334, 336, 337, 342, 351, 411

contracting of ..., contracts regarding ..., II, 33, 90, 92, 96, 320-323, 326, 327, 331, 333-342, 344, 345, 347, 348, 350, 352, 355, 358, 359, 366-372, 374-377, 386, 388, 390, 395, 412

dealers in ..., dealings in ..., ... traders (see also brokers) 41, 44, 49; II, 74, 304, 310, 311, 313-315, 323, 326, 327, 334-336, 350-352, 355, 361, 374-376, 379, 383, 389, 390, 392, 415

... dealings by commercial banks 17, 50; II, 73, 74, 324, 341, 389, 402

distribution-organization II, 92, 306, 318, 321, 336, 337, 342, 351, 352, 356-359, 361, 365, 372, 376, 377, 381, 386, 389, 392, 419, 426, 431

exchange of ... II, 413

flotation of ... (method not specified) 49, 202; II, 35, 86-88, 91, 94-96, 185, 207, 294, 304, 306-310, 312, 313, 315, 316, 318, 320-324, 326-329, 331, 332, 334, 337, 340-345, 347, 349-354, 357, 358, 361, 363-369, 371-380, 382, 384-386, 389-396, 398, 403, 405, 408, 411, 416, 421, 422, 426

flotations, magnitude of ... II, 344, 355, 356, 359, 386-388, 392, 395, 396

issuers of ... (borrowers) II, 325, 326, 330, 334, 337, 340, 348, 358, 359, 371, 372, 375, 376, 381

lending of ... 137; II, 254

lending on ..., see Stock loans

market in ..., see Capital market, Stock exchanges

market price of ..., see price of ...

middlemen: not specified II, 306, 318, 320-323, 328, 336, 337, 342, 344, 347, 355, 356, 371, 376; ... financing of II, 315, 318, 321, 340, 341, 343, 364, 374, 379, 390, 404

"negotiating" of ... 50, 54, 126, 207; II, 3, 34, 67, 252, 316-321, 323, 327, 334-337, 339-342, 345, 348-350, 355, 366, 371, 372, 384, 398, 404, 406, 412

"negotiating" of ... combined with advances II, 340, 341, 343, 372, 375, 411, 413

new issues in general, see ... flotations

new issues, contributors to ... II, 306, 308-310, 320, 356, 364, 401

options on II, 366-368, 395

originating of ... II, 316, 318, 320, 321, 330, 373, 376, 390-392, 394

price agreements for the sale of ... II, 321, 351, 358, 359, 374

prices of ..., price determination II, 250, 251, 306, 307, 310, 313, 315-317, 321-323, 336, 338, 341, 342, 344, 347, 357-360, 368-372, 374-377, 385, 389, 398, 403, 411, 426

quotation of ... II, 304, 307, 310, 320

retailing of ..., retailers, sale to the public II, 87, 351, 356, 357, 372, 376, 377, 380, 381, 388

sale of ... (in general) 49; II, 91, 92, 186, 306, 314, 316-318, 320, 321, 325-327, 329, 330, 332, 333, 338, 344, 354, 355, 357-360, 365-368, 370-376, 380, 381, 388-390, 392

sale of ... abroad 207; II, 33, 330, 331, 333-335, 337, 344, 348, 350, 352, 365, 366, 390, 408, 410

sale of ... directly to the public, see Securities, retailers of ...

sale on commission for the second hand II, 333, 334, 336, 337, 348, 350, 351, 398

sales agents and representatives II, 92, 337, 338, 348, 351, 352, 356, 357, 360, 361, 364, 365, 390, 426

sales methods, see Investment bankers, business methods

servicing of ... 50; II, 340, 355, 398, 415

subscriptions to ..., subscribers to ..., see Subscriptions

trading, see dealers in, ... dealings

trading for delivery II, 310

underwriting of ... II, 92, 359, 360, 371-374, 377, 386, 388, 390, 391

"underwriting lists" II, 373

... used as media of payments II, 304, 305, 315, 332, 351, 352, 399, 440

... used for payments to contractors II, 316, 345, 347, 354, 399

Security affiliates, see Affiliates

"Security" as used in the early nineteenth century 44, 113, 130, 138, 139; II, 103, 252, 276

Security

behind bank loans, see also Stock loans 6, 7, 11, 16, 27, 44, 45, 47-49, 54, 71, 77, 90, 92, 98, 108, 119, 122, 126, 127, 136-138, 141, 154, 160, 198, 207, 227, 229, 235, 248, 249, 298 ; II, 3, 4, 12, 34, 36, 38, 39, 76, 78, 79, 87, 96, 132, 158-164, 167, 181, 182, 187, 197, 205, 224, 225, 227, 250, 259, 261, 269, 271, 272, 304, 305, 313, 332; capital as ... 6, 7, 28, 43, 47, 64, 192, 194, 199, 201, 234, 258, 296; II, 35, 37; general assets, commercial assets 6, 91, 190; II, 100, 105, 160, 168, 195, 208, 209, 210, 217, 218, 221, 222, 437; government guarantee II, 105, 114, 154; special: coin, specie 6, 201; II, 427; merchandise II, 44,

187, 220; land, mortgages 6, 7, 47, 197-199, 200, 201, 203, 247, 296; II, 14, 147; not specified (incl. personal property) 6, 7, 28, 44, 91, 92, 191, 194-198, 201-204, 294; II, 1, 2, 8, 14, 168, 261, 278; public stock, see also Government-bond-backed-bank notes 47, 66, 191, 194, 199-201, 296; II, 2, 10, 27, 103, 105, 114, 147, 148, 154, 158, 159, 427
  given for deposits II, 66, 108, 431
  personal 11, 44, 47, 136, 198; II, 34, 39
Self-financing of industry II, 381
Self-liquidating paper, see also Real paper, 32, 46, 47, 62; II, 10, 38-40
Self-regulation, especially of the banking system 171, 192, 195, 196; II, 11, 13, 36, 104, 117, 124
Senate, see Congress
Senators, see Congressmen
Settlement of interbank..., clearing-house... balances 105, 129; II, 45-50, 52-55, 158-161, 163, 164, 166, 167, 171, 246, 259-261, 266, 267, 268, 269, 274, 275, 277, 284, 286, 296, 297, 432, 436
  medium used in the..., see also Clearing house coin certificates, Clearing house loans certificates 97; II, 48, 50, 158-160, 164, 169, 240, 241, 269, 287, 432, 446
Shop keepers, store keepers, retailers, tradesmen 22, 23, 37, 38, 41, 67, 107, 216, 219, 220; II, 45, 61, 63, 72, 79, 305, 335, 431
Short term credit, ... funds, ... loans, ... paper 5, 9-12, 32, 33, 41, 44-50, 91, 93, 94, 124-126 133, 138, 142, 193-195, 226, 249; II, 3, 9, 10, 14, 15, 32, 36-40, 116, 175, 180, 208, 213, 326
Signing of notes 59, 60, 63, 131
Silver, see Bullion
  certificates II, 121, 432
  coins, see Specie
  question II, 430-433, 439-441, 444, 446
  standard, see Metallic standard
  trade, ... imports, see Bullion, ... trade
Single name paper, see Promissory notes
Sinking fund 206, 208; II, 414
"Sitting director" 19, 20, 25, 211, 241
Small notes
  (in general) 130, 193, 198; II, 160, 268
  prohibition of..., 44, 134, 188, 190, 196, 198, 294; II, 8, 9, 13, 100, 113, 292
  special security for... 199, 294
Social implications of banking (social background) 17, 18, 25, 28, 37, 38, 63-65, 90, 91, 144, 170, 180, 181, 184, 187, 188, 216; II, 22, 23
Socialism (socialistic) 96; II, 215, 220
Solidarity of banks II, 267, 271
Solvency 90, 107, 128, 247; II, 1, 138, 166, 236, 263, 271, 277, 284, 285, 287, 289, 309, 315, 425, 428
Sound banking, legitimate banking 22, 46, 54, 65,

109, 129, 140, 142; II, 1, 6, 14, 15, 26, 32, 36, 37, 209, 237, 430
Sound Currency 7, 24, 90, 93, 96, 110, 125, 128, 130, 135, 147, 172, 175, 189, 190, 192, 195, 247, 289, 290; II, 23, 29, 36, 40, 42, 123, 208, 209, 292, 297, 430, 433, 436
South Sea Bubble, Bubble Act 5, 164, 286
Spanish-American War II, 179, 369, 391
Spaulding Bill II, 101, 102, 104, 105, 125-136, 149, 150
Specialization in banking, see Division of labor, Private bankers, specialized
Specie, gold coin, silver coin, metallic money 8, 10, 11, 13, 15, 16, 23-25, 27-29, 32, 40, 43-45, 49, 51-54, 64, 68, 69, 71, 72, 75-78, 81, 82, 84, 87, 91-93, 100, 104, 105, 108, 112, 124-126, 129-131, 133-137, 140, 158, 172, 191, 193, 205, 206, 257, 259, 276, 279; II, 1-3, 6-9, 13, 14, 22, 26, 27, 29, 32, 36-39, 42, 43, 45-50, 54, 62, 67, 68, 73, 74, 82, 87, 89, 92-94, 99, 101, 105, 109, 115, 137, 141, 144-147, 158-166, 208, 213, 240, 241, 246, 249, 250, 252, 254-256, 260-263, 267-270, 273-275, 284, 291, 292, 295, 297, 300, 304, 317, 324, 331, 332, 347, 367-369, 410, 427, 430-433, 436
  demand, drain 99, 125, 130, 131, 134-136, 257; II, 5, 248, 255, 256, 258
  funds 51, 52; II, 2, 10, 35, 149, 331
  holdings of a central bank 99, 124, 133, 134, 139
  holdings of a country or region 99, 100, 130, 134
  market, see Bullion, trade
  movement of ... guidance for banks 124-126, 130, 131, 139, 140; II, 1, 38
  movements: external (exports, imports, shipments) 30, 39, 104, 112, 124-126, 130, 131, 134, 135, 138; II, 1, 3, 33-35, 67, 68, 256, 263, 291, 292, 294, 430; internal 39, 134, 137
  pool II, 89, 160-165, 426, 427
  reserves, see Reserves
Speculation, speculators, speculative
  (in general) 26, 82, 131, 164, 175, 177, 182, 188, 189, 269; II, 5, 15, 61, 82, 94, 96, 109, 119, 142, 145, 163, 197, 203, 205, 304-307, 309, 312, 315, 335, 364, 399, 403, 404, 415, 416
  in bank stock 31, 105, 151, 152, 190, 244; II, 82, 318
  in securities in general 151; II, 115, 176, 180, 305, 306, 310, 315, 317, 320, 321, 326, 327, 335, 344, 345, 355, 357, 361, 367, 375, 376, 379, 400, 404
State
  and federal participation (investment) in banks 8, 13, 25, 55, 65, 92, 167, 206, 232, 239, 242, 250; II, 22, 23, 25, 29, 324, 326, 327
  bank examiners II, 202, 285, 286
  bankers associations, see Bankers associations

State (cont'd.), banks: as opposed to "national bank" 12, 43, 49, 66, 94, 100, 103-105, 108, 110, 111, 124, 128-132, 135-145, 159, 165, 166, 169, 170, 172-180, 189, 239, 251, 262, 273, 274, 289-291; II, 7, 22, 46, 87, 99-101, 148, 213, 252, 255, 291; as opposed to those in the National Banking system II, 75, 76, 101, 102, 105, 106, 108-113, 119, 121, 122, 124, 137, 138, 141, 145, 149, 175-179, 181, 184, 186, 192, 199, 202, 206, 215, 217, 223, 229, 271, 282, 284, 389, 393, 427, 437; with branches 89, 99; II, 22-31, 74, 110, 113, 193, 194, 197, 228

bonds, see Public stock

debts, see Public stock, Repudiation, States, lending to...

directors of banks, see Government directors

legislative committees 25, 91, 93, 94, 174, 197, 200, 201, 204, 298; II, 2, 9, 13, 23-27, 35-39, 300

legislatures 6, 22-26, 29, 33, 37, 40, 45, 56, 62, 65, 70, 75, 78, 88-90, 92, 94, 95, 104, 106, 110-112, 130, 134, 144, 148, 161, 174, 184, 187-193, 196-200, 202-205, 211, 212, 214, 223, 229, 239, 296, 298, 302; II, 9, 23, 24, 26, 27, 29, 30, 35, 36, 38, 39, 47, 57, 61, 138, 178, 193, 246, 254-257, 264, 269, 270, 273, 277, 283, 284, 287, 288, 296, 297, 300, 301, 331, 339, 353, 354, 430

ownership of banks, see Government banks

representatives and state senators, see Legislators

rights 111, 167, 172, 289; II, 141

States (commonwealths), state governments 7, 8, 13, 16, 22, 23, 25, 27-29, 31, 32, 35, 37, 41, 42, 52, 54, 55, 65, 69, 70, 78, 79, 81, 82, 89, 90, 94, 95, 100, 102, 107, 110, 132, 153, 161, 163, 165-167, 169, 172, 174, 179, 187, 189, 195, 196, 197, 199, 201-203, 206-208, 266, 298; II, 23, 24, 35, 86, 88, 99, 101, 103, 105, 109, 110, 112, 137, 138, 141, 144, 145, 178, 194, 197-199, 216, 217, 229, 247, 248, 252, 253, 255, 256, 258, 259, 262-267, 272, 273-283, 297, 301, 304, 324-326, 329, 331, 332, 339, 341, 343, 344, 354, 389, 435

lending to..., state debts 7, 12, 16, 43, 44, 49, 50, 53-55, 82, 118, 123, 297; II, 26, 33, 35, 70, 88, 249, 257, 272, 273, 277, 305, 324-326, 333, 341, 344, 345, 358, 389, 409

methods of borrowing II, 336, 344, 345

Statesmen, see Politicians

Stock of not specified corporations 48, 49, 227, 229, 249; II, 175, 187, 324, 325, 341, 344, 389, 392, 393

of the federal and state governments, see Public stock

brokers, see Brokers

exchanges 49, 145, 161; II, 7, 74, 119, 180, 207, 214, 288, 307, 310, 314, 315, 320, 323, 353, 354,

363, 365, 374, 375, 379, 393, 400, 402, 422, 426, 429

holders, (stock holdings) 12, 16-18, 20, 24, 25, 28, 30, 31, 35, 37, 45, 55, 59-64, 68, 69, 73, 76, 90, 94, 100, 102, 104, 106, 107, 112, 118, 122, 127, 128, 138, 142-144, 150, 154, 159, 166, 168, 177, 183-186, 198, 199, 201, 206-208, 219, 232, 234, 240, 266, 280, 288, 297, 298; II, 12, 13, 27, 30, 33-35, 38, 40, 62, 63, 87, 106, 108, 111, 122, 123, 132, 137, 138, 141, 143, 144, 163, 186, 189, 191, 192, 197, 199, 202, 204, 205, 239, 252, 353, 377, 379, 384, 390-394, 427; functions of... 17, 59, 64, 73, 112, 197, 203, 256, 257; names of... to be published 198; II, 12; personal liability, see liability, personal; power of..., voting power 20, 60, 62, 106, 117; II, 13, 204, 213

holders': committees 107, 240, 241; II, 13, 34, 340, 341; meetings 17, 18, 83, 107, 243; II, 12, 13, 196, 200

jobbers, see Securities, dealers in...

loans, stock notes, security loans, lending on securities 11, 12, 32, 44, 45, 48, 49, 54, 98, 106, 126, 127, 136-138, 141, 154, 160, 206, 207, 227, 229, 249, 254; II, 38, 39, 116, 132, 176, 254, 291, 313, 314, 318, 326, 330, 332, 338-341, 350, 351, 353, 361, 364, 372, 374, 379, 389, 395, 403, 404

market, see Capital market, Stock exchanges, Wall Street

notes, see Stock loans

traders, stock trading, see Securities, dealers in...

watering II, 384

Store keepers, see Shop keepers

Stores 164; II, 29, 31, 73, 79, 151, 154, 199, 216, 301, 347, 351, 363, 424

Stringencies, depression, emergencies, recession, times of pressure 16, 52, 78, 85, 99, 100, 125, 126, 131, 133, 137, 138, 154, 160, 190; II, 117, 175, 181, 182, 208, 212, 221, 254, 256, 264, 272, 303, 331-333, 344, 428

Subcontractors of loan contractors and investment bankers II, 308-310, 320, 321, 323, 328, 333, 334, 344, 350, 351, 359, 368, 377, 394, 411

Subscription books II, 306, 316, 344, 366, 368, 369, 376, 418

Subscriptions

collected by middlemen and submitted on a commission basis II, 317, 328, 347, 365, 404

paying of... 12; II, 86, 306, 308-310, 317, 321, 327, 328, 331-333, 340, 353, 367, 368, 376, 397-404, 414

"private" II, 306, 308, 312, 316, 320, 326, 336, 344, 358, 367, 370, 379, 401, 403, 410

"public" 226; II, 86-88, 96, 306-308, 312, 316, 327-331, 333, 334, 336, 344-348, 350, 352, 353,

356, 357, 365, 367-371, 376, 377, 380, 389, 395, 398, 403, 412, 414, 415, 426

security given for ... II, 306, 307, 309, 310, 398, 414

Subscriptions, subscribers to banks 13, 22, 25, 26, 28, 30, 34, 35, 50, 76, 77, 85, 101, 102, 184, 185, 206, 233, 240, 243, 244, 250, 297; II, 12, 111, 197, 245

to public loans 50, 86, 87, 101, 127, 226; II, 85-87, 91, 92, 95, 164, 273, 306-311, 315-319, 321, 323-325, 327, 329-333, 335, 344-350, 353, 356, 358, 359, 365-369, 377, 389, 394, 397, 398, 400, 402-404, 411, 421

to securities others than the above and not specified 127; II, 325-327, 337, 338-341, 348-350, 352, 353, 374

Subtreasury, Subtreasurer 156, 289; II, 85, 88, 93, 94, 141, 145, 151, 212, 214, 219, 241, 344, 360, 362

Sugar plantations, sugar industry II, 32, 33, 391

Supervision of banks, lack of ... 25, 65, 88-93, 175, 192; II, 22, 26, 100, 138, 168, 176, 178, 202, 216

... by clearing houses II, 283-287, 289

Surplus 127; II, 183-185, 187, 188, 190-192, 218, 224, 226

"Suspended debt" see Assets, frozen

Suspension of specie payments 10, 14, 15, 46, 52, 75, 78, 97, 197, 275; II, 3, 5, 34, 46, 57, 93-95, 103, 114, 144, 145, 147, 151, 158-164, 247-250, 252, 257-264, 266-270, 272, 273, 275-277, 287, 289, 297, 300, 331, 332, 403, 436, 437

Swapping of promises to pay between businessmen and banks 64, 172, 192; II, 14, 175, 216, 225

Syndicate securities II, 180, 207, 379

Syndicates II, 91, 92, 180, 308, 332, 348, 358-361, 365-377, 379, 380, 383, 386, 389, 390, 392, 394, 395, 411, 418, 426

managers of ... and their predecessors II, 92, 309, 371-376, 394, 395

Tax (in the sense of burden) 165, 167, 196; II, 224, 241

Taxes, taxation, tax payer 24, 80, 93, 102, 111, 146, 166, 174, 197, 205, 212, 213, 234, 261; II, 22, 24, 60, 73, 85, 93, 94, 108, 110, 112, 113, 119-123, 128, 141, 179, 184, 209, 210, 217, 219, 221, 222, 246, 256, 275, 279-281, 283, 287, 292, 300, 306, 319, 339, 376, 403, 426, 429, 430, 435, 444

Tellers, see Employees

"Temporary loans" 45, 48; II, 180

Textile industry 47, 48, 68, 72, 259

"Theorists" 111; II, 2, 141, 142

Tying contracts, see Investment bankers, permanently allied with certain corporations

Time deposits 15, 50, 52-54; II, 73, 181, 182, 184

Trade, see also Commerce, 7, 65, 67, 71, 72, 112, 129, 131, 136, 164, 191, 192; II, 202, 205, 208, 212, 278, 304, 319, 399, 400

associations II, 267, 275, 276, 279, 280, 282, 283, 289

centers 10, 15, 33, 35, 41, 43, 66, 67, 70, 172; II, 2-4, 6, 7, 45, 46, 51, 64, 73, 105, 137, 166, 193, 236, 257, 262, 267, 292, 299, 389, 424, 426, 430, 431, 433

domestic 112, 164

foreign (international) 9, 31, 34, 38, 69, 99, 105, 112, 133-135, 191; II, 62, 63, 69, 72, 187, 254, 305, 313, 315, 329, 346, 354

in produce, staple commodities 78, 133; II, 64, 196, 305, 335, 391

paper, see Real paper

Trader, Indian ...(for other traders, see Shop keepers) 33, 107

Trading company 27, 28

"Transaction loans" see Real paper

Transfer

of money, of funds, see Remittances

of securities 97

agents 128, 132; II, 11, 58

Transit department of banks II, 185, 236, 244

Transportation, transportation enterprises 45, 48, 57, 106, 119, 120, 138; II, 185, 187, 325, 381, 382, 435

Travellers checks II, 179, 182

Treasury, Treasurer, Department of the Treasury of the United States 14, 40, 80, 98, 102, 105, 106, 128, 153, 158, 173, 175, 178, 180, 239, 240, 267; II, 68, 87, 89, 91-94, 96, 100-103, 105, 112, 116-118, 121, 123, 137, 141, 142, 145, 152, 162, 208, 212, 213, 252, 263, 288, 303, 313, 316, 317, 327, 328, 357, 365, 367, 369, 370, 379, 426, 431-433, 435, 444

bank, see government bank

Note Committee (1861) II, 91, 162

notes 49, 106; II, 68, 86, 87, 93-96, 124, 161, 165, 250, 252, 269, 344, 347, 349, 350, 353, 356, 357, 362, 365, 389, 415; special issues:demand notes (Civil War) 87; II, 93-95, 106, 141; 7-30's; 86, 87; II, 90-92, 95, 96, 108, 141, 162, 164, 357, 359

Trust

business of banks II, 178-180, 182

companies II, 6, 49, 76, 111, 175-181, 184, 186-192, 201, 217, 226, 282, 283, 288, 336, 341, 342, 354, 359, 363, 369, 376, 379, 391, 394, 395, 431; active as investment bankers II, 368-371, 373, 380, 392, 394, 395, 422

Trustees, trusts, trusteeship 7, 106, 113, 128, 136, 142, 154, 169, 197, 198, 203, 207, 300; II, 11, 62, 87, 90, 100, 160, 161, 166, 172, 173, 178, 180, 191, 205, 269, 376, 379, 393, 415, 425, 427-429

Trustees of savings banks 212, 215, 216, 218-220, 222-226, 228-230, 300, 302

Turnpikes, turnpike stock II, 324, 325, 327, 341

Unconstitutional, see Constitution

"Uncurrent money" (notes of out-of-town banks) see "Foreign Money"

"Underwriter's option" II, 376

Underwriting, underwriters, see Securities, underwriting of ...

Uniform charges for services rendered by banks, see also Clearing houses establish uniform charges, II, 177, 207

"Union Committee" (New York, 1830's) 93, 156; II, 255, 330, 333

Unit banking 95; II, 193, 194, 209, 218, 219

Universities, see Colleges

Unsound banking, see Illegitimate banking

Usurer, usury, usury acts 7, 111, 196, 209; II, 14, 212, 214, 299, 363, 429

Vaults 83; II, 224, 245, 292

Velocity of circulation 29; II, 4, 61, 426

Voting trusts II, 206, 374, 378, 384, 386, 388, 390

Voyages 11, 45

"Wall Street" 66, 79, 161; II, 7, 60, 61, 66, 119, 124, 165, 202, 214, 363, 373-375, 427

bankers, brokers, 79; II, 74, 77, 111, 117, 167, 196, 361, 374

War bonds, war debt, war loans, see also Mexican War, 101; II, 73, 103, 104, 109, 142, 250, 253, 274, 325, 347, 356, 358, 360-363, 389, 391, 416

War finance, see also Civil War finance 24, 25, 29, 166, 172, 185; II, 85-98, 250, 314, 317, 426

War of 1812 5, 15, 16, 46, 59, 69-71, 105, 111, 123, 172-174, 186, 243; II, 45, 46, 60, 62, 247, 248, 257, 258, 283, 289, 317, 323-325, 329, 332, 409

Warrants II, 76

"Washington proposal" II, 88, 89

Ways and Means Committee, see Congressional Committees

Weltauschauung 93, 191, 197; II, 434, 436, 437

Wealth 17, 25, 26, 31, 37, 39, 47, 95, 102, 111, 112, 144, 148, 163-166, 171, 189, 192, 287; II, 4, 145, 146, 304, 321-323, 356, 363, 383, 387

"Wealth of Nations" 29, 111, 128; II, 37, 378

Whigs 156, 163, 190, 198, 200, 289, 296; II, 23-26, 29, 30, 34, 35, 104

English II, 435

Wholesalers, see Merchants

Wild-cat banking, see Illegitimate banking

World War I 133; II, 74, 362, 375-377, 380, 385, 393, 396

Yield 112; II, 306, 321, 369, 370

NAME INDEX

Volumes I and II

Aachen II, 322

Adams, Charles Francis II, 15, 387

Adams, Edward D. II, 370

Adams, John 163, 166

Adams, John Quincy 141, 145, 146, 153, 155, 159, 160

Addington, Henry II, 307

Agricultural and Horticultural Society of Pennsylvania 157

Agricultural Bank (Pittsfield) 259

Aiken, Edmund II, 111, 279

Aiken and Norton, Chicago II, 111

Aislabie, Rawson II, 311, 398

Alabama 65, 144, 206, 226, 252; II, 13, 55, 193, 258, 267, 301, 325, 332, 334, 339, 342, 343, 414

Alabama claims II, 363, 364

Albany, N. Y. 16, 23, 31, 33, 35, 46, 70, 77-80, 89, 90, 93, 94, 194, 195, 217, 226; II, 2, 6, 45, 61, 66, 68, 74, 108, 186, 236, 238, 270, 271, 289, 329, 330, 338, 344, 349, 352, 390, 410, 414

Albany and Susquehanna Railroad II, 383

Albany City Bank II, 65, 152, 270, 330, 352, 410, 411

Albany Insurance Company II, 350

Albany Savings Bank II, 349

Aldrich, Nelson W. II, 209, 211, 222, 439

Alexandria, Va. 35; II, 337

Algiers Savings Bank (New Orleans) II, 192

Allegheny County, Pa. II, 350

Allen (S. and M.), Moses Allen, Salomon Allen II, 68, 69, 71, 198, 327, 333, 335, 344

Allibone, Thomas II, 52, 53

Allison, William B. II, 439

Alsop, Richard 54

Alta, Ia. II, 199

Amalgamated Copper Company II, 202, 375, 376, 391

Ambler, D. G. II, 168

American and Commercial Daily Advertiser (Baltimore) 217

American Economic Association II, 220

American Bankers Association, see Subject Index

American Beet Sugar Company II, 386

American Bell Telephone Company II, 387

American Exchange National Bank (Chicago) II, 191

American Exchange National Bank (Lincoln, Neb.) II, 190

American Exchange Bank, American Exchange National Bank (New York) 79; II, 50, 87, 89, 179, 188, 223, 303, 368, 389, 421, 425

American Fur Company II, 18

American Ice Company (New York) II, 202

American Land Company II, 335

American Life Insurance and Trust Company II, 341, 354

American Locomotive Company II, 362

American National Bank (Chicago) II, 191

American Refrigerator Transit Company II, 392

American Scottish Investment Company II, 386

American Surety Company II, 182

American Telephone and Telegraph Company II, 378, 388

American Trust and Savings Bank (Chicago) II, 191

American Writing Paper Company II, 387

Amsterdam (Holland) 13, 16, 17, 38, 101, 131, 159; II, 33, 35, 305, 313, 314, 316-321, 323, 329, 334, 336, 337, 340, 358, 398

Andalusia, Pa. 157

Anderson, Mr. II, 79

Andover, Mass. 37, 214

Andrew, A. Piatt II, 211

Andrews, John II, 30

Angerstein, John Julius II, 311, 312, 315, 397, 401

Ann Arbor, Mich. II, 108

Appleton, Nathan 62, 68, 69, 71-73, 75, 82, 139, 159, 259, 279; II, 47, 166

Appleton, Samuel 69

Appleton, William 71, 159, 259; II, 166, 333

Appleton (William) and Co. II, 8

Argus of Western America 173

Arizona II, 302

Arkansas 43, 208, 298; II, 20, 70, 217, 267, 301

Armour and Company II, 386, 391

Armstrong, John 110

Arnold, George E. II, 53

Arnstein & Eskeles II, 404

Aspinwall, William H. II, 86

Association of Banks for the Suppression of Counterfeiting II, 258, 270, 271, 298

Association of Boston Bank Presidents II, 239

Association of Reserve City Bankers in Indiana II, 288

Association of the Banks of Wisconsin II, 276-278

Astor, John Jacob 50, 63, 101-103, 159; II, 5, 263, 316-318, 326, 333

Astor, John Jacob, Jr. II, 111

Astor National Bank (New York) II, 188

Astor Place Bank (New York) II, 179, 188

Astor Trust Company (New York) II, 188, 189, 204, 391, 394

Atchafalaya Railroad and Banking Company II, 256, 295, 326

Atcheson, Topeka and Santa Fe Railroad II, 387

Atkinson, Edward II, 167

Atkinson, Jasper II, 310

Atlanta, Georgia II, 79, 166, 172, 210, 242

Atlanta Loan and Savings Company II, 79

Atlantic and Pacific Railroad II, 350

Atlantic City II, 209, 283

Atlantic Trust Company (New York) II, 188, 232

Attica, New York II, 104

Auburn, New York II, 257

Auerbach, Joseph S. II, 229

Augsburg II, 323

Augusta, Georgia II, 112, 257

Austin, David 245

Austin, John B. II, 89, 97, 172

Austria II, 312, 318-323, 349, 386, 404, 406

Averdieck und Company II, 408

Azores II, 382

Babcock, Samuel D., B. F. Babcock Brothers and Company, B. F. Babcock and Company II, 187

Bache, Richard II, 334

Bacon, Robert II, 385, 391

Baird, Henry Carey II, 120

Baker, George F. II, 179, 181, 183, 184, 187-189, 203, 207, 226, 280-282, 364, 366, 371, 378-382, 385-387, 390, 391, 393

Baker, Henry F. II, 30

Baldwin County, Georgia II, 297

Baldwin, Octavius D. II, 429, 443

Baltimore, Maryland 16, 34, 116, 117, 120, 137, 145, 157, 159, 164, 173-175, 183, 212, 216-220, 222, 261, 298; II, 3, 23, 46, 51, 53, 54, 65, 66, 68-71, 74, 75, 79, 109, 133, 152, 163, 165, 171, 186, 198, 210, 238, 246, 247, 250, 252-255, 258, 262, 264-267, 275, 287, 292, 294, 295, 297, 299, 317, 318, 328, 335, 338, 348, 350, 430, 431

Baltimore and Ohio Railroad II, 337, 339, 348, 350, 384

Baltimore Savings Bank 216, 217, 219-221, 226, 227

Bancroft, George 180

Bangor Bank 41

Bank of Albany 23, 33, 244

Bank of Alexandria (Virginia) 32

Bank of America (Chicago) II, 64

Bank of America (New York) 16, 22, 35-37, 41, 42, 53, 216, 217, 232, 244, 256; II 50, 54, 68, 161, 171, 253, 255, 262, 270, 284, 293, 330-332, 347, 404, 421

Bank of America (Washington) II, 64

Bank of Amsterdam 13, 27, 52, 237

Bank of Baltimore 35; II, 245, 254, 346

Bank of Bloomington (Bloomington, Ill.) II, 198

Bank of British North America II, 221

Bank of Burlington (Vermont) 252, 255

Bank of Camden (Camden, New Jersey) II, 272

Bank of Chambersburg (Pennsylvania) II, 17

Bank of Charleston (South Carolina) II, 346

Bank of Chester County (Pennsylvania) II, 409

Bank of Columbia (Washington) II, 348

Bank of Commerce (Cleveland) II, 153

Bank of Commerce, National Bank of Commerce (New York) 202; II, 51, 70, 86, 87, 89, 145, 181, 187-189, 207, 214, 226, 332, 344, 346, 349, 350, 369, 388, 389, 418, 421, 425, 444

Bank of Commerce (Philadelphia), see Moyamensing Bank

Bank of Detroit 246

Bank of Eastern Tennessee II, 18

Bank of England 6, 7, 9-11, 13, 18, 19, 21, 26-29, 31, 33, 45, 49, 64, 96-99, 125-128, 139, 140, 142, 143, 158, 159, 168, 169, 171, 178, 179, 191-193, 195, 197, 200, 206, 234, 238, 254, 288, 293; II, 5, 9, 15, 19, 34, 36-39, 48, 55, 67, 68, 85, 105, 211, 213, 214, 219, 232, 233, 263, 271, 302, 306, 308-313, 315, 324, 345, 397, 399, 400, 403, 426, 428, 440

Bank of France 127, 139, 140; II, 213, 214, 232, 313, 321, 426, 428, 439

Bank of Hamburg 13, 27, 237

Bank of Harrisburg (Pennsylvania) II, 17, 390

Bank of Holland [sic! in a quotation] ,see Nederlandsche Bank

Bank of Hudson (New York) 269

Bank of Italy (Cal.) II, 197

Bank of Java II, 439

Bank of Iowa II, 26

Bank of Kentucky II, 248

Bank of Louisiana (New Orleans) 31, 206; II, 256, 273, 295, 334

Bank of Louisville (Kentucky) II, 266

Bank of Marietta (Ohio) 246

Bank of Maryland (Baltimore) 15, 16, 32, 34, 273; II, 245, 255

Bank of Milwaukee 95; II, 63

Bank of Mineral Point (Wisconsin) 95

Bank of Minnesota (St. Paul) II, 112

Bank of Mutual Redemption (Boston) 76, 77, 80, 84-87, 261, 262; II, 18, 58, 90, 115, 159, 163, 215, 241, 243, 271, 276, 289

Bank of New York 7, 9, 11, 12, 15-18, 20, 21, 23, 28, 30, 34-38, 40, 42, 48, 49, 54, 63, 99, 100, 191, 216, 234, 237, 239, 240, 245, 249, 252; II, 91, 96, 145, 161, 245, 247, 249, 254, 255, 286, 292, 293, 296, 324, 325, 330-332

Bank of North America (Boston) II, 190

Bank of North America (New York) II, 49, 284, 347

Bank of North America (Philadelphia) 5-7, 11, 12, 15-17, 19-21, 23-26, 30, 33-37, 39, 40, 42, 47, 81, 92, 178, 205, 231, 232, 235, 236; II, 56, 58, 91, 108, 194, 245-247, 249-251, 254, 267, 268, 272, 286, 293, 299, 324, 332, 409

Bank of North America (Providence) 77

Bank of Nova Scotia II, 220, 221

Bank of Orange 94

Bank of Orleans (New Orleans) II, 295

Bank of Pennsylvania (Philadelphia) 14, 21, 35, 47, 110, 132, 232, 297; II, 3, 53, 194, 233, 246, 247, 249-251, 266, 268, 272, 294, 299, 324, 332

Bank of Pensacola II, 334, 339

Bank of Potomac II, 345

Bank of Providence 15

Bank of Quincy (Quincy, Illinois) II, 198

Bank of St. George, Genoa 27

Bank of South Carolina 16

Bank of South Royalton (Vermont) II, 20

Bank of Stephen Girard, see Girard (Stephen's) Banking House

Bank of Tennessee (Nashville, Tennessee) II, 18, 55, 267

Bank of the Interior (Albany) 79

Bank of the Manhattan Company (New York) 16, 21, 22, 31, 35, 36, 38, 40, 42, 49, 50, 52, 55, 94, 212, 239; II, 48, 188, 248, 254, 293, 296, 328-332, 334, 418, 421

Bank of the Metropolis (Washington) 176; II, 346, 347, 349, 415

Bank of the New York Manufacturing Company (New York) II, 293

Bank of the Northern Liberties (Philadelphia) 245; II, 53, 251, 299, 347, 409

Bank of the State of Alabama 65, 206, 252

Bank of the Republic, National Bank of the Republic (New York) II, 109, 177, 187, 204, 444

Bank of the State of Indiana, successor to State Bank of Indiana, see State Bank of Indiana

Bank of the State of Missouri II, 3, 22

Bank of the State of New York (New York) II, 262, 284, 331

Bank of the State of Tennessee 14

Bank of the United States (New York) 145

Bank of the United States of Pennsylvania 50, 55, 115, 133, 144, 145, 160, 161, 178, 179, 285; II, 58, 197, 263, 266, 268, 269, 272, 325, 331, 332, 335-341, 343, 353, 354, 359, 395, 413

Bank of Toronto II, 221

Bank of Troy II, 300

Bank of Vincennes (Indiana) II, 23

Bank of Worthington II, 76

Bankers Financing Company (Atlanta) II, 200

Bankers Magazine II, 101, 344

Bankers National Bank (Chicago) II, 191

Bankers Trust Company (Atlanta) II, 200

Bankers Trust Company (New York) II, 179, 180, 182, 187-189, 204, 206, 207, 232, 379, 391, 394

Banks, Nathaniel P. II, 9

Banque de Paris et Pays Bas II, 386

Barbaia, Banker II, 321

Barclay, Herring, Richardson and Company,

Barclay, Herring and Company 126; II, 408

Baring, Alexander II, 313, 321, 322, 330

Baring Brothers and Company, London 16, 53, 54, 101, 127, 130, 131, 156, 159, 208, 239; II, 33, 35, 62, 67-70, 82, 271, 314-316, 320-323, 326, 329, 330, 332-337, 339, 340, 347, 348, 350-352, 354, 358, 359, 366, 379, 382, 388, 403, 404, 408, 411, 413

Baring, Francis II, 313

Baring (Francis) and Company II, 313-315

Baring, Thomas 210; II, 33

Barker, Jacob 50, 101, 159; II, 5, 30, 60, 61, 317, 318, 332, 401, 404, 405

Barnard, Daniel Dewey 201

Barnett, George E. II, 74

Barney (Charles D.) and Company II, 69

Barney, Charles T. II, 394

Bartley, Thomas W. II, 2, 16

Batavia, New York II, 104

Bates, Benjamin E. II, 159, 165, 172, 302

Bates, Joshua II, 358

Bath (England) 225

Bavaria II, 362

Bay State Trust Company (Boston) II, 190

Bayard, Andrew 217

Bayard, William 36, 42, 212, 217; II, 329

Bayonne, New Jersey II, 238

Beal, James H. 263; II, 97, 165, 172, 227

Beal, Thomas P. II, 239, 241

Beebe, James M., James M. Beebe and Company II, 363

Beecher, David H. II, 199

Beers, Isaac 245

Beers (Joseph D.) and Company II, 65, 333-336, 343, 359

Beers and Bunnel II, 328

Belfast II, 69

Belgium II, 370, 439, 440

Belknap, John 72

Bellows, John 259

Belmont, August II, 65, 86, 339, 344, 347, 353, 365, 379, 383

Belmont, August, Jr. II, 288, 370

Belmont (August) and Company II, 71, 367, 368, 370, 380, 383

Belvedere Railroad II, 352

Benecke, Gebrüder II, 408

Benfield, Paul II, 311

Bennett, James Gordon 158, 159

Benton, Thomas H. 159, 170, 200, 292; II, 9, 19, 113

Berkshire Bank (Pittsfield) 41

Berlin, Germany II, 189, 222, 318, 320, 323, 366, 370, 408, 440

Berlin, New Hampshire II, 241

Berlin National Bank (Berlin, New Hampshire) II, 241

Bernard, Tristram 184

Berry, Richard II, 50
Bethlehem Steel Company II, 380
Bethmann, Simon Moritz von II, 318
Bethmann, Gebrüder II, 318, 320, 322, 404, 406
Biddle, Clement II, 334
Biddle, Clement C. 213
Biddle, Edward R. II, 334, 341
Biddle, John II, 334
Biddle, John G. II, 328
Biddle, Nicholas 6, 46, 51, 53, 54, 57, 58, 60, 61,
    63, 64, 96, 105, 107, 109-164, 167, 170, 171,
    176, 177, 179, 180, 200, 247, 255, 256, 266, 270,
    271, 273, 276, 278, 283-285; II, 1, 3, 4, 5, 36,
    46, 64, 67, 68, 72, 82, 85, 197, 204, 206, 211,
    214, 236, 260, 262-267, 269, 297, 309, 329-332,
    335-341, 353, 355-357, 372
Biddle, Thomas, Thomas Biddle and Company 136;
    II, 69, 328, 332-334, 338, 339, 344, 359
Billington, George 224
Bingham, William 16, 34, 39, 42, 98, 244, 246
Binney, Amos 184
Binney, Horace 50, 159, 302; II, 346
Birmingham, England II, 124
Bischoffsheim and Goldschmidt II, 365, 386
Bish, T. II, 403
Blackstone Canal Bank II, 326
Blaine, James G. II, 439, 446
Blair, Chauncey B. II, 169, 174
Blair, Chauncey Justus II, 169
Blair, Francis P. 159, 172-174
Blair and Company II, 380, 392, 418, 420
Blake, George 184
Blake Brothers and Company II, 418
Blake, Ward and Company II, 70, 350
Blanding, Abram II, 297
Bleichröder, Gerson II, 440
Bliss, Cornelius N., Bliss, Fabyan and Company
    II, 430, 443, 444
Bliss, George II, 363, 364
Blodget, Samuel II, 37
Boissevain, Gideon Maria II, 439
Boker, C. S. II, 52, 58, 274, 299
Boldero, Lushington, Boldero and Lushington II, 311
Bolivia II, 391
Bollmann, Eric 6, 12, 104; II, 22, 42, 147, 408
Bonnefoux, Laurent II, 101, 148, 347
Boonsborough Turnpike Company II, 324
Boorman, James, Boorman and Johnston II, 424
Borie, A. E. II, 53
Borie (C. and H.) II, 360
Boston, Massachusetts 7, 12-14, 16, 19, 21, 22,
    31, 32, 34, 35, 38, 39, 41, 48, 51-54, 61, 63,
    67-73, 76-79, 81, 85-87, 92, 98, 113, 116, 117,
    135, 141, 173, 179, 180, 185, 210, 212, 214-219,
    222-227, 250, 260, 261; II, 2, 3, 4, 5, 8, 14, 15,
    40, 45, 46, 51, 52, 54, 55, 66, 68-75, 77, 86,
    88-92, 97, 106, 108, 109, 113-115, 129, 132,

133, 139-142, 146, 156, 158-160, 163-167, 169,
    172, 173, 184, 186, 190, 193, 210, 212, 227, 238-
    242, 246, 247, 255, 257, 258, 261-265, 270-276,
    282-288, 292, 295, 298, 302, 315, 317, 328, 329,
    335, 337, 346, 350, 351, 354, 356, 359, 360, 363,
    365, 370, 373, 376, 378, 379, 381, 387-389, 394,
    411, 426, 431, 433, 444
Boston and Sandwich Glass Company II, 57
Boston and Worcester Railroad II, 388
Boston Bank Presidents Association II, 288
Boston Consolidated Gas Company II, 388
Boston Elevated Railway Company II, 388
Boston Exchange Office 15, 41, 68, 73
Boston National Bank 332; II, 280, 301
Boutwell, George S. II, 365, 366, 411
Bowdoin, James 37
Bowery Savings Bank (New York) II, 299, 346, 414,
    418
Boyd, Walter II, 307, 308-314, 320, 358, 401
Boyd, Benfield and Company II, 271, 308, 311, 312,
    314, 315, 398, 403
Boyd, Ker and Company II, 311, 312, 319
Bradbury, C. B. 76
Bradlee (Josiah) and Company II, 346
Branscomb, John II, 403
Brazil 133; II, 408
Brebner, John B. II, 363
Breck, Samuel 39, 98, 246
Breed, Ebenezer 71, 72
Bremen II, 311
Brewster, Cobb and Eastabrook II, 418
Bridgeport, Connecticut II, 179
Bridgeport Bank 19, 35, 42, 45, 46, 70, 232, 241;
    II, 252, 253
Brissot de Warville, Jean Pierre II, 315
Bristol, Rhode Island 35
Bristol Bank (Rhode Island) II, 247
Bristow, Benjamin H. II, 367
Broadway Bank (New York) II, 50
Broadway National Bank (Boston) II, 190
Bronson, Isaac 35, 42, 45-47, 64, 70, 91, 139, 159,
    179, 193-195; II, 3, 35, 36, 38, 39, 42, 148, 252,
    437
Brookfield II, 326
Brooklyn, New York II, 238
Brooklyn Savings Bank II, 299, 418
Brooklyn Trust Company II, 351, 394, 418
Brough, John II, 2, 16
Brown, Alexander, Alexander Brown and Sons,
    Baltimore 117; II, 64, 69-72, 75, 198, 335, 421
Brown Brothers and Company II, 71, 421, 444
Brown, George II, 335
Brown, John 20, 31, 33, 35, 38, 39
Brown, Kenneth L. 101
Brown, Moses 31, 39
Brown, Nicholas II, 305
Brown, Noah 212

Brown, Shipley and Company II, 70, 71
Brown (William and James) and Company, Liverpool II, 71, 271
Brown family (Baltimore) 159
Brown family (Providence) 20, 21, 31, 32; II, 247
Brussels II, 312, 366
Bryan William Jennings II, 197, 215, 217
Bryant, William Cullen 161
Bryant, Sturgis and Company II, 8
Buchanan, James II, 10, 40, 362
Buckingham, William A. II, 123
Budge, Henry II, 386
Budge, Schiff and Company II, 360, 385, 386
Buell, James II, 116, 117, 121, 122, 154, 282
Buenos Ayres II, 408
Buffalo, New York II, 104, 109, 195, 216, 223, 237, 335, 350
Bunce, Russell 20
Bunce family II, 279
Bunker Hill National Bank (Boston) II, 190
Burlington, Iowa II, 71, 72, 350
Burlington, Vermont 116; II, 199
Burns, Walter H. II, 363
Burr, Aaron 22, 31, 35, 38, 42
Burrall, Jonathan 36, 41, 42
Byrdsall, F. 189
Cabot, George II, 246, 292
Cabot family 69
Cadwalader, Thomas 61, 119, 122, 123, 145, 150; II, 341
Calcutta 182
Caldwell, John 32, 38
Calhoun, John C. 101-103, 113, 147, 158, 159, 171, 179
Calhoun, Philo C. II, 152, 280
California II, 74, 137, 141, 166, 186, 196, 197, 301, 375
California Petroleum Corporation II, 374, 375
Calumet and Hecla Copper Mining Company II, 387, 388
Camak, James II, 346
Cambreleng, C. C. 46, 159
Camden and Amboy Railroad II, 339, 354
Camman and Whitehouse II, 355, 416
Camp, H. H. II, 282
Campbell, Bernard W. II, 346
Campbell (J) and Company II, 409
Canada, II, 67, 76, 183, 195, 196, 208, 210, 218-221, 235, 363, 399, 442
Canadian Bank of Commerce II, 221
Canal and Banking Company, New Orleans, see Canal Bank (New Orleans)
Canal Bank (Albany) II, 270
Canal Bank (New Orleans) II, 11, 192, 256, 269, 273, 295, 326, 334
Canal Bank and Trust Company, Canal Louisiana Bank and Trust Company (New Orleans) II, 192

Cannon, James G. II, 179, 185, 186, 188, 203, 224, 237, 238, 242, 243, 275, 303
Canton (China) 90
Canton Company II, 11
Cape of Good Hope II, 77
Capital National Bank of Nebraska II, 215
Carbon County, Wyoming II, 199
Carey, Henry Charles 202; II, 120
Carey, Mathew 11, 13, 23, 46, 47, 50, 52, 55, 64, 65, 100, 105, 137, 148, 163, 167, 178, 247
Carlisle, John G. II, 195, 369, 370
Carnegie, Andrew II, 219, 391
Carney, James G. 75-77, 84-87, 262; II, 90, 163, 270
Carpenter, George II, 361
Carpenter, Vermilye and Company, Carpenter and Vermilye II, 71, 349, 361
Carpentier, Lewis D. II, 328
Carrington, North Dakota II, 199
Carrollton Bank (New Orleans) II, 256, 295
Carson and Seton 40
Carter, John, see Church, John Barker
Cassel, Ernest II, 386
Catlin, Lynde 36, 63, 241; II, 293
Catterall, Ralph C. H. 115, 116, 120
Central America II, 386
Central Bank and Trust Company (New Orleans) II, 192
Central Bank of Georgia 266; II, 297
Central Bank of Joliet (Illinois) II, 198
Central Bank of Troy II, 154
Central National Bank (New York) II, 421
Central National Bank (Philadelphia) II, 151
Central Pacific Railroad II, 360, 361
Central Railroad Bank II, 326
Central Railroad of New Jersey II, 390
Central Trust Company (New York) II, 189, 394
Central Trust Company of Illinois (Chicago) II, 189, 191, 204
Centralverband des deutschen Bank- und Bankier-Gewerbes II, 222
Century Bank (New York) II, 229
Cernuschi, Enrico II, 440
Chandler, Alfred II, 348, 354, 355
Chandler, Zachariah II, 108
Channing, William Ellery 216
Charleston, South Carolina 16, 35, 107, 116, 145; II, 68, 112, 152, 258, 266, 297, 317, 336
Charlestown, Massachusetts 34
Chartiers Valley Railroad II, 350
Chase, Salmon P. II, 87, 88, 89, 91, 92, 93, 94, 95, 98, 99, 100, 101, 102, 103, 104, 105, 106, 107, 108, 109, 110, 111, 113, 121, 144-146, 148, 151, 356, 357, 362, 427, 438
Chase National Bank (New York) II, 121, 155, 181, 183, 184, 188, 189, 204, 227, 237, 370, 379, 390, 418, 421

Chatham National Bank, Chatham Phenix-National Bank and Trust Company (New York) II, 229

Chattanooga and Nashville Railroad II, 348, 416

Chauncey, Elihu II, 293, 294, 328, 329, 334, 339, 359

Chemical Bank, Chemical National Bank (New York) II, 97, 139, 146, 154, 171, 184, 188, 217, 227, 256, 300, 326, 379, 389, 421, 425

Chemung Canal II, 326, 330, 333, 414, 415

Chenango Canal II, 330, 333, 412

Chesapeake and Delaware Canal Company 127; II, 338

Chesapeake and Ohio Canal 127; II, 337, 338, 351

Chesapeake and Ohio Railroad II, 360, 361

de Cheverus, Bishop 216

Cheves, Langdon 59-61, 106-110, 113, 114, 117-121, 123-125, 129, 138, 159, 183, 249, 268, 269, 288; II, 46, 327, 329

Chicago, (Illinois) 172; II, 63, 64, 73, 75, 77-79, 111-113, 115, 119, 120, 153, 167, 169, 170, 172, 174, 177, 182-186, 188, 189, 191, 193, 197, 198, 201, 202, 204, 206, 207, 210, 211, 215, 217, 218, 220, 226, 271, 277, 278, 283-286, 289, 302, 335, 364, 370, 380, 381, 391, 392, 394, 422, 433, 438

Chicago, Burlington and Quincy Railroad II, 348, 354, 373, 380

Chicago Marine and Fire Insurance Company II, 63, 112

Chicago, Milwaukee and St. Paul Railroad II, 391, 394

Chicago National Bank (Chicago) II, 201, 217, 285

Chicago Title and Trust Company (Chicago) II, 192

Chile II, 408

Chillicothe, Ohio II, 252

China 31, 134; II, 254, 346, 354

Chittenango Bank 80

Chitty, Joseph 157

Choate, Rufus 159

Christian Disciple (Boston) 218

Christmas, Charles, Christmas and Livingston, Christmas, Livingston, Prime and Coster II, 353

Church, John Barker 28, 29, 30, 34, 42

Cincinnati, Ohio 123, 269; II 25, 30, 47, 48, 119, 165, 253, 266, 339, 352, 362, 381, 424

Cisco, John J. II, 76, 88, 344, 362, 364, 417

Cisco (John J.) and Son II, 360, 362

Citizens Bank (Ligonier) II, 77

Citizens Bank (New Orleans) 207; II 33-36, 38, 70, 256, 258, 267, 269, 273, 294, 295, 337

Citizens National Bank (New York) II, 155

Citizens National Bank (Norfolk, Nebraska) II, 200

City Bank (Boston) II, 151

City Bank (New Haven) II, 325

City Bank (New Orleans) II, 258, 269, 295

City Bank (New York), see National City Bank

City National Bank (Chicago) II, 112

City Trust Company (Boston) II, 190

Claflin (H. B.) and Company II, 430, 444

Claiborne, William C. C. 30, 244

Clapham, Sir John 193

Clark, E. W., E. W. Clark and Company, E. W. Clark, Brothers and Company, E. W. Clark and Brothers II, 69, 71, 72, 110, 198, 344, 347, 349, 350, 355, 359-361, 364, 365, 415

Clark (J. W.) and Company (Boston) II, 350

Clark, Dodge and Company II, 350, 365, 366

Clarke, Dumont II, 179, 303

Clarke, Freeman II, 111, 114, 153, 156

Clarke, Matthew St. Clair 144, 158

Clark's Exchange Bank II, 72

Clarkson, Matthew 63, 211, 212, 216

Clavière, Etienne II, 315, 404

Clay, Henry 158-160, 171, 179; II, 23, 30, 100

Clayton, Augustin S. 159

Cleveland, Grover II, 195, 215

Cleveland, Ohio II, 25, 26, 163, 177, 184, 186, 237

Cleveland, Cincinnati, Chicago and St. Louis Railroad II, 372

Cleveland, Columbus and Cincinnati Railroad II, 355

Cleveland National Bank II, 184

Cleveland, Painesville and Ashtabula Railroad II, 355

Clews, Henry, Henry Clews and Company II, 74-77, 117, 215, 232, 360, 361, 366

Clews, Habicht and Company II, 75, 361

Clibborn, Edward 64

Clinton, De Witt 211, 212, 216, 220; II 329

Clinton, George 100

Club of Six, Amsterdam II, 329

Clymer, George 26, 37, 245

Cobbett, William II, 311

Cochran, Thomas C. II, 380

Cochran, William 68, 259; II, 328

Coe, George S. II, 86, 87, 88, 89, 90, 91, 94, 97, 103, 106, 108, 114, 115, 124, 148, 151, 160-163, 165, 167, 176, 213, 216, 223, 281-283, 285-289, 302, 303, 389, 424-446

Coe, Matthew II, 424

Cohen (Jacob I. Jr.) and Brothers II, 65, 82, 335, 412

Colebrook, N. H. II, 245

Coleman, Thomas II, 279, 280, 282, 300

Collier, C. A. II, 172

Collier, William R. II, 100, 102

Cologne II, 386

Colombia (South America) 126; II, 408

Colonial Bank (New York) II, 196

Colorado II, 217, 301

Colquhoun, Patrick 209-211

Colt, Roswell L. 116, 120, 127, 147; II, 328, 338

Columbia College 191

Columbia National Bank (Chicago) II, 201

Columbian National Bank (Boston) II, 190

Columbus (Ohio) II 26, 262, 266

Columbus and Xenia Railroad II, 355

Comegys, Benjamin B. II, 97, 172, 202, 203, 230, 282

Commercial and Farmers Bank(Baltimore) II, 256, 294, 299

Commercial and Financial Chronicle II, 369

Commercial and Railroad Bank (Vicksburg) II, 326, 332

Commercial Bank (Boston) II, 261

Commercial Bank (New Orleans) 53; II, 256, 269, 295, 332

Commercial Bank (New York) 292

Commercial Bank (Philadelphia) 217, 226; II, 251, 299, 409

Commercial Bank of Columbia, S.C.

Commercial Bank of Lake Erie II, 25

Commercial Credit Company (Baltimore) II, 79

Commercial Credit Investment Trust (St. Louis) II, 79

Commercial-Germania Trust and Savings Bank (New Orleans) II, 192

Commercial National Bank (Chicago) II, 112, 184, 191, 232

Commercial Trust and Savings Bank (Chicago) II, 191

Commercial Trust and Savings Bank (New Orleans) II, 192

Committee of Associated Trust Company Presidents II, 288

Commonwealth Bank (Philadelphia) II, 108

Congdon, James B. II, 19

Connecticut 16, 25, 29, 30, 32, 37, 45, 48, 54, 70, 71, 95, 119, 219, 228, 239, 241-243; II, 2, 3, 4, 7, 9, 14, 15, 16, 17, 20, 49, 65, 105, 147, 179, 187, 190, 193, 238-242, 252, 253, 266, 292, 301, 324-326, 349, 361, 381, 409

Connecticut Manufacturing Society II, 327

Connecticut Railroad II, 387

Connecticut River Banking Company II, 326

Consolidated Association of Planters 207, 208; II, 33, 256, 267, 269, 295

Consolidated Bank (New York) II, 202

Consolidated Bank of Maryland II, 295

Consolidated Gas Company of New York II, 391

Consolidation Bank (Philadelphia) II, 160

Continental and Commercial National Bank (Chicago) II, 182, 189, 191, 392, 393

Continental and Commercial Trust and Savings Bank (Chicago) II, 189, 191, 393

Continental Bank (New York) II, 51

Continental National Bank (Chicago) II, 191

Continental National Bank of Salt Lake City II, 199

Continental Securities Company (Minneapolis) II, 198

Converse, Edmund Cogswell II, 179, 204

Cook and Sargent II, 73

Cooke, Henry II, 104, 109, 113, 281

Cooke, Jay, Jay Cooke and Company II, 17, 69, 73, 75-77, 86, 87, 91, 95, 96, 98, 104, 106, 109-111, 113, 151-153, 198, 212, 281, 355-357, 359-369, 374, 379-381, 383, 386, 390, 395, 411, 417

Cooke (Jay), Mc Culloch and Company II, 75, 365-67

Coolbough, William F., Coolbough and Brooks, W. F. Coolbough and Company II, 112, 153, 281

Cooper, Peter II, 111

Cooper, Thomas 156, 159, 179

Cooper, Hewitt and Company II, 418

Cope, S. R. II, 312

Cope, T. P. 61

Copley Trust Company (Boston) II, 190

Corbin, Austin, Austin Corbin and Company, Austin Corbin Banking Company, Corbin and Dow II, 76, 112

Corcoran, William Wilson, W. W. Corcoran and Company II, 347, 348, 351

Corcoran and Riggs II, 71, 346, 347, 349-351, 359

Corn Exchange Bank (New York) II, 183, 184, 188, 193, 196, 243

Corning, Erastus II, 65, 152, 330, 352, 410, 411

Corporation of the Trinity House, London II, 397

Cosgriff, J. E. II, 199

Cosgriff, Thomas Andrew II, 199

Coster, Charles II, 384

Coster and Carpenter II, 336

Country Bank Security Company (Atlanta) II, 200

Cowen, Benjamin Sprague II, 26, 30

Coyler, George W. 80

Craigie, Andrew II, 315,316

Crawford, W. H. 14, 15, 63, 105, 144, 159, 257, 288; II, 327-329

Crédit Foncier (Paris) II, 367

Crédit Mobilier (Paris) II, 338

Crocker National Bank (San Francisco) II, 197

Crockett, David 159

Crommelin, Charles, Crommelin, Daniel, Crommelin and Son 38

Cronenbold, F. W. II, 280

Crowninshield, Benjamin William 38

Crowninshield family 117, 159

Cuba II, 382, 391

Cumberland Coal Company II, 337

Cumberland Turnpike Road II, 324

Cummings, John II, 165

Curtis, Edward 189, 190, 296

Curtis, George II, 51, 346

Curtis, T. A., II, 67

Curtis, Sir William II, 311

Cutter, Jacob 186

Cutts, Edward 186

Dabney, Morgan and Company II, 364, 382

Daily Graphic II, 432, 433

Dakota State Bank (Oldham, S. Dakota) II, 200

Dallas, Alexander J. 8, 101-104, 106, 107, 143; II, 99, 147, 252, 334
Dallas, George M. 159
Dallas, Texas II, 182
Dalton, Peter Roe 34
Dana, William B. II, 440
Darmstädter Bank II, 386
Dartmouth College II, 24
Davenport, Iowa II, 31, 76
Davidson, Charles H. II, 199
Davis, Andrew Mac Farland 5, 24; II, 100, 104
Davis, Jefferson II, 144
Davis, John Amory 84, 87, 262, 263; II, 97, 159, 163, 164, 172, 287
Davison, Henry P. II, 176, 179, 187, 189, 204, 211, 217
Dawes, Charles G. II, 175, 191, 195, 204, 217, 234
Dayton, George Draper II, 76
De Coppet and Company II, 355
Decker, Edward Williams II, 221
Degrand, P. P. F. 149, 179
Delafield, John II, 330, 331
De la Lande and Fynje II, 319
Delano, Eugene II, 421
De Lannay, Iselin and Clark II, 355
Delaware II, 193, 199, 230, 266, 270, 302, 326
Delaware and Raritan Canal II, 339
Delaware County Bank, Delaware County National Bank (Chester, Pennsylvania) II, 110, 409
Delaware, Lackawanna and Western Railroad II, 390
Denmark II, 318, 319, 322, 336, 408
Dennie, Joseph 158
Denny, Daniel II, 59, 172, 270
Denver, Colorado II, 79, 186, 199
Depositors Insurance Company (Atlanta) II, 200
Derby family 38
Des Moines, Iowa II, 27, 191
Des Moines National Bank (Des Moines, Iowa) II, 191, 228
Detroit, Mich. II, 17, 108, 186, 196, 220, 242, 271, 335, 345
Deutsche Bank (Berlin) II, 222, 370, 371, 380
Devaynes and Company II, 312, 313
Dewey, Davis R. 140
Dexter, Andrew Jr. 41, 68, 246, 247, 259; II, 197, 293
Dickens, Ashbury 153
Dickinson College 173
Dillon, Clarence II, 420
Dillon, Read and Company II, 420
District of Columbia 52, 169; II, 65, 101, 246, 301 318, 390
Dixwell, John James 63
Dodge, Edward, II, 71, 72
Dorr and Tappan II, 336
Dorrien , Maggins, Dorrien and Mello II, 311

Douglass, William 164
Drexel, Anthony J. II, 349, 359, 364, 382
Drexel, Francis Martin II, 349
Drexel, Joseph William II, 364
Drexel and Company II, 71, 72, 75, 87, 349, 356, 359- 361, 364-366, 368, 379, 418
Drexel, Harjes and Company II, 75, 364
Drexel, Morgan and Company II, 75, 198, 364, 366, 368, 382-384, 418, 421, 444
Dry Dock Bank (New York) 94; II, 259, 326
Duane, William J. 154, 159, 169, 173, II, 16
Duer, William 25; II, 315, 316, 326, 404
Duluth II, 220
Dumfries Parish Bank Friendly Society (Scotland) 219
Duncan, A. E. II, 79
Duncan, Alexander II, 352
Duncan, Rev. Henry 209, 213, 217, 218
Duncan, W. Butler II, 352
Duncan, Sherman and Company II, 70, 77, 350, 352, 382, 415
Dundee (Scotland) II, 386
Dunlap, Thomas II, 332, 340
Dunn, George H. II, 24, 30
Dupont, T. Coleman II, 79
Durkee, Jireh 82
Dutchess County Bank (New York State) 43
Dutchess County Insurance Company II, 61
Dwiggins, Zimri, Dwiggins, Starbuck and Company II, 201
Eagle Bank (Boston) 63; II, 57
Eastern Bank (Connecticut) II, 16
East India Company II, 308, 310, 311, 313, 345, 397, 400
Eastern Banking Association for the Detection of Counterfeiting II, 270
Eastern Stage Coach Company II, 325
Easthampton, Massachusetts II, 71
Eastman, Albert H. II, 201, 241
Eckels, James H. II, 177, 180, 191, 195, 204, 215, 232
Eddy, Thomas 209-213, 216, 217, 230
Edinburgh (Scotland) 33, 40, 225
Edinburgh Review 128, 198
Edinburgh Savings Bank 212, 218
Edinburgh Society for the Suppression of Mendicity 212
Edison Illuminating Company II, 391
Edmonds, Francis W. II, 11, 20, 48-51, 158
Effingham, Lord II, 306
Eichborn und Company II, 405
Eleventh Ward Bank (New York) II, 188, 196
Eliot National Bank (Boston) II, 190
Elizabethtown, New Jersey II, 66
Ellicott, Thomas 152, 176, 177
Ellis, Charles 86
Ellis, Edward D. 204

Empire State Bank (New York) II, 188

England 13, 30, 46, 47, 66, 97, 105, 136, 137, 163, 168, 169, 218; II, 13, 33, 64, 69, 70, 71, 124, 141, 195, 196, 209, 211, 218, 221, 246, 273, 304, 305, 309, 313-315, 317, 319, 320, 326, 327, 330, 331, 335, 336, 340, 345, 347, 351, 355, 373, 375, 381, 385, 386, 398, 399, 403, 411, 426, 437, 440

Eno, A. R. II, 418

Ellward, W. Jr., II, 408

Equitable Life Assurance Society II, 187, 189, 379

Equitable Trust Company (Chicago) II, 201, 202, 285

Equitable Trust Company (New York) II, 187, 188

Erie Canal 88; II, 329

Erie Railroad (Erie ring) 195; II, 165, 354, 383

Erlanger (Emile) et Cie., Paris II, 416

Erwin II, 326

Esdaile (Sir James), Esdaile and Company, Sir James Esdaile, Esdaile, Grenfell, Thomas and Company II, 271, 314, 315

Essex County, Massachusetts II, 246

Essex Bank (Salem, Massachusetts) 32, 35, 42

Essex Fire and Marine Insurance Company 32

Evans, George Heberton II, 253

Everett, J. L. II, 50

Everett, William 159

Erving, John II, 23, 24

Exchange Bank (Boston) 75, 86, 296; II, 283

Exchange Bank (New York) II, 60, 61

Exchange Bank (Providence) 32; II, 51

Eyre, Manuel II, 260, 264

Fabbri, Egisto II, 385

Fahnestock, Harris C. II, 76, 179, 184, 203, 390

Fairchild, H. J. II, 430, 444

Fairchild, James II, 440

Falmouth, Massachusetts II, 424

Farm Mortgage Loan and Trust Company, Carrington, North Dakota II, 199

Farmers and Mechanics Bank (Buffalo) II, 104, 109, 280

Farmers and Mechanics Bank (Hartford) 252, 255

Farmers and Mechanics Bank (Philadelphia) 16, 47, 81, 297; II, 54, 58, 59, 89, 91, 97, 107, 160, 172, 194, 246, 247, 251, 254, 268, 272, 299, 358

Farmers and Merchants Bank (Memphis, Tennessee) II, 9

Farmers Bank of Maryland 52

Farmers Bank (Philadelphia) 255; II, 251

Farmers Deposit National Bank (Pittsburgh) II, 177, 181

Farmers Deposit Savings Bank (Pittsburgh) II, 181

Farmers' Exchange Bank (Glocester, Rhode Island) 41, 246, 247, 259

Farmers Loan and Trust Company (New York) II, 188, 189, 341, 394

Farmers Loan and Trust Company (Sioux City) II, 199

Farmers State Bank (Osmond, Nebraska) II, 200

Farmington Canal II, 325

Farson, Leach and Company, John Farson and Son II, 422

Fastenrath II, 35

Fayetteville, North Carolina II, 68

Federal Trust and Savings Bank (Chicago) II, 191

Federalist 163

Felch, Alpheus II, 108

Fendi, J. G. II, 346

Ferris, Benjamin S. II, 112

Ferris, Harry H. II, 112

Fessenden, William P. II, 96, 145, 365, 366

Few, William II, 254, 293

Fidelity Corporation of America II, 79

Fidelity Saving and Trust Company (Norfolk, Va.) II, 79

Fidelity Trust Company (Philadelphia) II, 360

Fifth Avenue Bank (New York) II, 154, 421

Fifth Avenue Trust Company (New York) II, 187

Fifth National Bank of Chicago II, 111

Fillmore, Millard 201; II, 16, 100, 101, 148

Financial Register 202; II, 259

First Bank of the United States 6, 9, 11-21, 25, 26, 28, 30, 31, 34-37, 39-42, 45, 48, 49, 60, 67, 70, 92, 97-106, 111, 112, 116, 128, 129, 142, 143, 148, 157, 163, 165-170 175, 177, 178, 191, 206, 232, 234, 237; II, 12, 62, 99, 110, 193, 213, 214, 221, 235, 245-247, 292, 313, 324

First Chicago Corporation II, 373

First National Bank of Akron, Iowa II, 200

First National Bank of Ann Arbor II, 108

First National Bank of Auburn, New York II, 280

First National Bank of Aurelia, Iowa II, 200

First National Bank of Baltimore II, 109, 152

First National Bank of Boston II, 108, 184, 190, 193, 379, 422

First National Bank of Carrington II, 199

First National Bank of Charleston II, 112

First National of Charter Oak, Iowa II, 200

First National Bank of Cheyenne II, 199

First National Bank of Chicago II, 111, 153, 181, 182, 185, 188, 191, 193, 197, 204, 207, 221, 226, 279, 284, 362, 366-370, 372, 373, 378, 379, 381, 388-391, 393, 418, 438

First National Bank of Davenport II, 112

First National Bank of Detroit II, 112

First National Bank of Emerson, Nebraska II, 200

First National Bank of Fonda, Iowa II, 200

First National Bank of Hudson, South Dakota II, 200

First National Bank of Jacksonville, Florida II, 112

First National Bank of Lewistown, Idaho II, 199

First National Bank of Marquette II, 229

First National Bank of Minneapolis II, 112, 221

First National Bank of New Castle, Wyoming II, 199

First National Bank of New York II, 109, 111, 179, 181, 183, 187-189, 227, 279, 280, 288, 362, 366-370, 372, 373, 378, 379, 381, 388-391, 393, 418, 444

First National Bank of Park River, North Dakota II, 199

First National Bank of Philadelphia II, 110, 364, 366

First National Bank of Princeton, Illinois II, 112

First National Bank of Randolph, Nebraska II, 200

First National Bank of Rawlins, Wyoming II, 199

First National Bank of St. Louis II, 280

First National Bank of St. Paul II, 112, 192

First National Bank of Shawneetown, Illinois II, 153

First National Bank of Syracuse II, 280, 300

First National Bank of Toledo II, 153

First National Bank of Troy II, 279, 300

First National Bank of Walla Walla II, 199

First National Bank of Washington II, 109, 110, 281, 366

First National Investment Company (Chicago) II, 373

First Savings Bank (Pocatello) II, 199

First Security Company (New York) II, 181, 393

First Trust and Savings Bank (Chicago) II, 188, 373, 393

Fisher, Charles H. II, 345, 350

Fisk, Harvey II, 361, 362

Fisk (Harvey) and Sons II, 362, 370, 371, 380, 418

Fisk, Pliny II, 362, 370

Fisk and Hatch II, 360-362, 365, 366, 369, 390

Fitch and Company, Fitch Brothers and Company II, 69

Fitzsimmons, Thomas 34

Flagg, A. C. 201

Fleming, Robert II, 386

Fletcher, Calvin II, 25, 30

Flint, Waldo 86; II, 52, 57, 172

Florida, 207, 208; II, 35, 70, 112, 151, 200, 201, 301, 334, 336, 337, 343, 399

Flynn, S. R. II, 202

Fonda, Iowa II, 199

Forbes, Allen Boyd II, 420

Forbes, John Murray II, 354, 387

Forest River State Bank (Forest River, N. Dakota) II, 199

Forgan, David R. II, 191, 193, 203

Forgan, James B. II, 117, 169, 170, 181, 191, 193, 195, 197, 203, 207, 210, 211, 215-217, 220, 221, 285, 286, 289, 373, 392, 393, 438

Forman, Joshua 8, 88-93, 194-197

Forman, Samuel E. 165

Forstall, Edmond J. 9, 62, 159; II, 3, 5, 10, 32-40, 256, 261, 266, 267, 296, 297

Forstall, Nicholas Michel Edmond II, 32

Forsyth, John 131, 159

Fort, Tomlinson II, 297

Fort Wayne, Indiana II, 25, 113

Fort Worth, Texas II, 201

Foster, Charles II, 433, 439, 440, 446

Fourteenth Street Bank (New York) II, 188

Fourth National Bank of Chicago II, 111

Fourth National Bank of New York II, 110, 111, 113, 151, 152, 153, 188, 237, 243, 280, 303, 361, 370, 390, 418, 421, 429, 444

Fourth National Bank of Philadelphia II, 188

Fowler, Charles N. II, 209

Frame, Andrew J. II, 218-220, 234

France, 30, 39, 137, 158; II, 69, 195, 196, 209, 218, 305, 313, 315, 319, 336, 337, 353, 362, 370, 373, 426, 440

Francis, Ebenezer 69, 71, 72

Francis, Tench 19, 34, 39-41

Franco-Prussian War II, 365

Frankfort, Kentucky II, 248

Frankfurt, Germany II, 75, 318, 320, 323, 353, 362, 363, 366, 385, 386

Franklin, Benjamin 221, 222; II, 440

Franklin Bank (Cincinnati) 249, 255

Franklin National Bank (Philadelphia) II, 188

Franklin, Ohio II, 26, 30

Franklin Railroad II, 355, 390

Fraser, A. S. II, 91, 161

French, Francis O. II, 390

Frederick II, King of Prussia II, 318

Frederick County Bank (Maryland) 174

Free Trade Advocate 193, 194

Frelinghuysen, Frederick T. 154

Freeman's Journal and Philadelphia Mercantile Advertiser 213

Freneau, Philip 165, 166, 172

Frew, Walter E. II, 188, 193, 196, 238, 243

Fries (Graf Moritz) und Company II, 321, 404

Frothingham, Ebenezer 259

Frothingham, Samuel 141, 184

Frys and Chapman II, 408

Fulton Bank (Boston) II, 261

Fulton Bank (New York) II, 258

Gage, Lyman J. II, 153, 169, 174, 211, 214, 215, 224, 282, 284, 285, 391

Gale, Samuel II, 399

Gales, Joseph 159, 160

Gallatin, Albert 6, 21, 100, 102, 139, 149, 158, 159, 166, 175, 179, 196, 236, 237; II, 9, 17, 37, 39, 40, 47-49, 55, 85-87, 113, 255, 259, 262-265, 267, 316, 353

Gallatin, James II, 86-90, 93, 94, 103, 104, 106-108, 114, 123, 124, 144, 263, 276, 284, 302, 389, 426

Gallatin National Bank, New York II, 87, 165, 188, 263, 276, 284

Gamble, John G. 207; II, 337

Gardiner, Maine 215

Garfield, James A. II, 118, 121
Garland, James A. II, 184, 203, 390
Gary, Elbert H. II, 378
Gas-Light and Banking Company (New Orleans) II, 256, 295, 326
Gaston, William Alexander II, 190
General Electric Company II, 388
General Motors Corporation II, 385, 388
Geneva 27; II, 404
Georgetown, D. C. II, 65, 337, 347, 351
Georgia 53, 100, 143, 144, 276; II, 4, 16, 61, 64, 79, 112, 141, 166, 182, 193, 200, 201, 264-266, 293 297, 301, 326
Georgia Railroad and Banking Company II, 326
German American National Bank (New Orleans) II, 192
German American Savings Bank and Trust Company (New Orleans) II, 192
German National Bank (Chicago) II, 198
German Savings Bank (Chicago) II, 198
German Savings Bank (Remsen, Iowa) II, 200
German Savings Bank (Ricketts, Iowa) II, 200
Germania National Bank (New Orleans) II, 192
Germania Savings Bank and Trust Company (New Orleans) II, 192
Germany 209; II, 195, 209, 210, 218, 221, 222, 235, 319, 338, 351, 352, 362-365, 370, 373, 381, 386, 390, 437
Geymüller (J. H.) und Company II, 321, 322, 404
Giannini, Amadeo P. II, 196, 197
Gibbs, Henry, Baron Aldenham II, 439, 440, 447
Gilbart, James William II, 16, 272, 437
Gilbert, Alexander II, 303
Gilbert, Coe and Johnson II, 424, 442
Giles, Daniel II, 312, 314, 315, 398
Gilman, Theodore II, 167, 168, 214, 215
Gilmore, Blake and Ward II, 77, 350
Girard, Stephen 16, 50, 100, 102-104, 106, 107, 159, 300; II, 60-63, 83, 254, 316, 317, 358, 404 405
Girard Bank, Girard National Bank (Philadelphia) 249; II, 3, 52, 58, 68, 108, 160, 268, 272, 274, 333, 343, 409
Girard College 157, 158
Girard Trust Company (Philadelphia) II, 188
Girard's (Stephen) Banking House 35, 41, 42, 49, 52, 55, 58, 60, 61, 175, 177; II, 247, 317, 405
Gladstone, William Ewart II, 440
Glasgow (Scotland) 209; II, 124
Glen Rock, Wyoming II, 199
Globe Bank, Globe National Bank (Boston) II, 57, 190
Globe National Bank (Chicago) II, 191
Glocester, Rhode Island 41
Goddard family 69, 186, 260
Göttingen II, 382
Gold, Thomas 259

Goldman, Sachs and Company II, 181
Goldsmid and Company, A. Goldsmid and Company, Abraham Goldsmid, Benjamin Goldsmid II, 309, 313-315, 323, 358, 398
Goldschmidt (B. A.) and Company 126, 127; II, 408, 409
Gomez, A. L. II, 328
Gontard (Jacob Friedrich) und Söhne II, 404, 406
Goodhue and Company II, 69
Gordon, Alexander II, 32, 33
Gordon, Forstall and Company II, 32, 33
Goschen, George Joachim II, 439
Gossler, John II, 333
Gouge, William M. 157; II, 39
Gould, Jay II, 345, 383
Gracie, Archibald 36, 42; II, 410
Graham, William II, 24
Grand Gulf Railroad and Banking Company II, 326
Grand Rapids, Michigan II, 196
Grand Trunk Railroad II, 363
Granite Bank (Boston) 85, 263; II, 97, 108
Grant, Ulysses S. II, 363
Gras, N. S. B. 10, 16, 20, 32, 33; II, 360, 377
Gray, William 22, 31, 32, 35, 36, 38, 42, 184; II, 88, 89, 90, 97
Great Britain 48, 97, 209, 225; II, 93, 255
Great Northern RailwayCompany II, 373
Greece II, 409
Green, Duff 159
Green River, Wyoming II, 199
Greene, Gardiner 141, 184
Greene and Weare II, 73
Greenebaum, Henry, Greenebaum Brothers, Chicago, Greenebaum and Company, Chicago, Greenebaum Brothers and Company, New York II, 198
Greenland II, 311
Greenwich Savings Bank (New York) 222; II 299, 418
Griesel and Rogers H, 181
Griscom, John 212, 216
Grocers Banks (Boston) II, 273
Grote, Andreas, Grote, Prescott and Company II, 311
Grubb, Joseph C. II, 213, 233
Grubb, William 74
Grundy, Felix 43, 159, 165, 169
Guadaljava II, 408
Guaranty Trust Company (New York) II, 187, 188, 189, 206, 379, 391, 394, 395
Guatemala II, 408
Guernsey, Wyoming II, 199
Guthrie, James II, 113
Guthrie County National Bank II, 228
Hackett, Frank W. II, 439
Hague, George II, 221
Hague, The II, 321
Hahn, E. Albert II, 437
Haldimand (A. F.) and Sons II, 408

Hale, Nathan 157
Hale, Thomas 213, 224
Hale, William 186
Hall, Andrew T. 84, 86, 263; II, 52, 57, 90, 159, 163, 164, 166, 167, 172, 270, 286
Hall, Charles B. II, 270, 271, 280, 281, 282, 301
Hall, D. A. 158
Hall, Willis 296
Hallgarten and Company II, 374, 380
Hallock, James C., II, 239
Hallock, James C., Jr. II, 50, 239-241
Halsey, Noah W. II, 376, 381, 392
Halsey (N. W.) and Company II, 381, 392
Halsey, Stuart and Company II, 380, 392, 395
Hambro and Sons II, 408
Hamburg (Germany) 13, 28, 101; II, 316, 318, 321, 323, 366, 385, 408
Hamill, Earnest A. II, 191, 296
Hamilton, Alexander 8, 12, 21, 26-30, 34-36, 38, 40, 42, 63, 97-99, 111, 147, 157, 163, 164, 178, 243; II, 1, 37, 110, 245, 247, 292
Hamilton, James II, 337
Hamilton, James Alexander 11, 46, 91, 125, 169, 180, 194, 195, 294
Hamilton Bank (Baltimore) 145
Hamilton Bank (Boston) II, 59, 190
Hamilton Bank (Denver) II, 199
Hammond, Bray 11, 187; II, 13, 263
Hancock Bank (Boston) II, 261
Hanna, National Bank examiner II, 286
Hannah, Adam, Adam Hannah Company, Minneapolis II, 198
Hannibal and St. Joseph Railroad II, 354
Hanover, New Hampshire II, 363
Hanover National Bank (New York) II, 181, 188, 189, 303, 313, 369, 370, 418, 420, 421
Hardwareman's Newspaper II, 100
Hardy, Alpheus 85
Hare, Robert II, 100
Harmon, William E., II, 79
Harriman, E. H. II, 187, 220, 379, 383, 385, 386
Harris, Albert W. II, 420
Harris, Isham J. II, 3, 9, 10
Harris, Norman Wait II, 376, 380, 381, 388
Harris (N. W.) and Company II, 381, 392, 420
Harris, Forbes and Company II, 395, 380, 420
Harrisburg, Pennsylvania 115; II, 252, 269, 273, 339, 340, 350
Harrisburg Bank (Harrisburg, Pennsylvania) II, 252
Harrison, Benjamin II, 433, 439, 441, 446
Harrison, Richard 35, 42
Harrison, William H. 156, 159; II, 29
Hartford, Connecticut 19, 20, 29, 31, 32, 35, 36, 48, 116, 119, 217, 259, 272, 279, 292, 349, 382
Hartford and New Haven Railroad II, 349, 354, 416
Hartford Bank 12, 17, 19-21, 30-32, 36, 38, 41, 42,

232, 237, 239, 240, 242-244; II, 292
Hartford Convention 158, 173
Hartford Fire Insurance Company 32, 41
Hatch, Alfrederick S. II, 361
Havemeyer, William F. II, 284
Harvard University 37, 40, 214; II, 190, 387, 388, 420, 422
Havana II, 294, 295
Haven, Franklin II, 52, 57, 88-90, 97, 163, 262, 302, 346
Haverhill, Massachusetts II, 56, 301
Haverhill Savings Bank II, 301
Hayek, F. A. 96
Haymarket Produce Bank (Chicago) II, 191
Hazard, Erskine II, 124
Hedges, Joseph E. II, 3, 4
Heidelbach, Ickelheimer and Company II, 418
Heinze, F. Augustus II, 202
Helderman, Leonard C. II, 2, 100, 103
Helgerson, H. S. II, 198
Hemphill, Joseph 159
Hendricks, Herman II, 328, 412
Hendrix, Joseph C. II, 214
Henshaw, David 96, 179, 180
Hepburn, Alonzo Barton II, 121, 155, 179, 183, 184, 201, 204, 210, 217, 227, 237, 303
Herkimer County Bank (Little Falls, New York) II, 352
Herring, Graham and Company II, 408
Hessen II, 318, 320, 322
Heyer, Cornelius 63; II, 12, 255, 296
Hibernia Bank and Trust Company (New Orleans) II, 185, 192
Hibernia National Bank (New Orleans) II, 192
Hibernian Banking Association (Chicago) II, 191
Hide and Leather National Bank (Chicago) II, 191
Hide and Leather National Bank (New York) II, 187
Hidy, Ralph W. 131; II, 70, 272, 305, 336, 350
Higginson, George II, 387
Higginson, Henry Lee II, 210, 387
Hildreth, Richard 180, 202
Hill, James J. II, 192, 373, 379, 385
Hilligsberg II, 38
Hincks, Sir Francis II, 221
Hoard, Charles Brook 201
Hoboken, New Jersey II, 238
Hodges, Almon D. II, 108, 159, 165, 172, 270, 298
Holford and Company II, 343
Holgate, Jacob 6, 111
Holland, 54; II, 310, 314, 318-323, 329, 336, 337, 340, 370, 439
Hollingsworth, Samuel II, 294
Homans, Isaac S. II, 11
Home Bank (New York) II, 188
Home Bank of Brooklyn II, 188
Home Savings Bank (Chicago) II, 202, 285
Homer, Charles C. II, 210, 217

Hone, Philip 159, 161, 212; II, 67
Hooper, Samuel, Samuel Hooper and Company
   II, 3, 8, 9, 10, 11, 13, 18, 20, 40, 104, 105, 108,
   109, 113, 115, 117, 163, 166, 213, 275
Hoopes, Thomas P. II, 346
Hope, Henry II, 319
Hope and Company, Amsterdam 101, 159; II, 33,
   35, 313, 314, 316, 319-322, 334, 336, 337, 350,
   354, 358, 404, 408, 410
Hopkins, Johns II, 109, 163
Hornblower, Henry, Hornblower and Weeks II, 190
Horton, S. Dana II, 433, 439-441, 446
Hottinguer et Cie, Paris 159
Houldsworth, Sir William Henry II, 439, 447
Houston, Texas II, 305
Howard Banking Company, Howard National Bank
   (Boston) 86; II 190
Howenstein, James T. II, 281, 301
Howes, R. W. II, 89, 161
Howland, Daniel 300
Howland and Aspinwall II, 415
Hoyt, Sherman and Company II, 73
Hubbard, Elijah II, 328
Hudson, New York 35
Hudson Company II, 362
Hudson River Bank (New York) II, 185
Hudson's Bay Company II, 363
Hulburd, H. R. II, 115, 118
Hullett Brothers and Company II, 408
Hullin II, 35
Hume, David 111, 189, 210; II, 304
Huntington, Ben. II, 328
Huntington, Collis P. II, 361
Hunt's Merchants' Magazine II, 105
Hurd, John 35
Hurlbut, Hinman B., Hurlbut and Company
   II, 153
Huth (Frederick) and Company II, 3, 5, 69, 332,
   336, 337, 342
Huttig, Charles H. II, 227
Idaho II, 74, 199, 302
Illinois 52, 202; II, 4, 22, 27, 64, 72, 74, 78, 109,
   110, 112, 191, 193, 198, 201, 202, 266, 278,
   301, 325, 330, 331, 336, 337, 340, 341, 350, 351
Illinois and Michigan Canal II, 198
Illinois Central Railroad II, 352
Illinois Trust and Savings Bank (Chicago) II, 188,
   373, 392, 422
Importers and Traders National Bank (New York)
   II, 96, 116, 154, 243, 421, 444
Improvement and Banking Company (New Orleans)
   II, 256, 295
India II, 254, 305
Indiana 52, 54, 202; II, 17, 22-30, 73, 77, 79, 109,
   110, 113, 152, 191, 193, 201, 253, 266, 271, 278,
   288, 301, 325, 333, 334, 336, 340-343, 353, 354

Indiana Bankers Association II, 288
Inland Steel Company II, 392
Indianapolis II, 30, 73, 186, 195, 210
Industrial Finance Corporation II, 79
Ingersoll, Charles J. 155, 159, 180
Ingham, S. D. 144, 146, 159
Insull, Samuel II, 381
Insurance Bank (Columbus, Georgia) 144
International Bank (Chicago) II, 191
International Harvester Company II, 392
International Mercantile Marine Company II, 373,
   374, 385
Interstate Trust and Banking Company (New Orleans)
   II, 192
Iowa 202; II, 1, 13, 20, 26, 27, 31, 71-74, 76, 109,
   110, 153, 190, 191, 199, 200, 217, 227, 278, 301
Iowa City II, 27
Iowa Trust and Savings Bank (Varina, Iowa) II, 200
Ireland II, 23, 32, 69, 199, 311, 312, 347
Iron Age II, 100
Ironton Railroad II, 355
Irving National Bank (New York) II, 188
Irving National Exchange Bank of New York II, 188
Irving Trust Company (New York) II, 425
Isle de France 34
Italian Bank of California II, 197
Italy II, 179, 196, 97, 440
Ittleson, Henry II, 79
Jackson, Andrew 55, 61, 62, 108, 111, 115, 121,
   123, 128, 138, 144-46, 148, 149, 151, 152, 154,
   159, 160, 162-80, 188, 198-201, 255, 257, 266,
   288, 289; II, 16, 23, 122, 211, 213, 219, 232, 340
Jackson, Patrick T. 69
Jackson, Georgia II, 200
Jackson, Mississippi II, 70
Jaffrey, Clive Talbot II, 221
James, Darwin R., II, 444
James, F. Cyril 33; II, 105, 111, 169, 182, 191, 210
Jameson Raid II, 370
Japan II, 386
Jaudon, Samuel 113, 115, 271, 278, 285; II, 334,
   336, 339-41
Jay, John 24
Jefferson, Thomas 21, 22, 156-158, 162, 166, 172;
   II, 294, 434
Jefferson, Ohio II, 30
Jekyll Island II, 211
Jenks, Leland H. II, 354
Jersey City II, 236, 238, 350
Johnson, A. B. 180; II, 11, 12
Johnson, Godschall II, 311-313, 397, 401
Johnson, Reverdy M., 151, 159
Jones, Arthur R., II, 79
Jones, Edward 153
Jones, Isaac II, 154
Jones, John C. 184

Jones, John Q., II, 86, 89, 97, 389
Jones, William 15, 66, 104-10, 115, 117, 119, 120, 129, 140, 157, 159, 182-85, 249; II, 46, 114, 154, 211, 251
Jones and Laughlin Steel Corporation II, 392
Jordan, John, Jr., II, 53
Joseph, L. and S., II, 65, 71, 333, 335, 353
Journal of Commerce II, 158
Judson, E. B., II, 280, 300
Jurd, Wm. Jones 186
Kahn, Otto H. II, 385
Kansas 202; II, 215-217, 244, 278, 301
Kansas Bank Deposit and Surety Company II, 216
Kansas City II, 242, 244
Kaufman, Louis G. II, 229
Kean (S. A.) and Company II, 391, 392, 422
Keene, James Robert II, 375
Kelley, Alfred II, 25, 26, 30
Kemble, Fanny 159
Kemp, Bishop 216
Kendall, Amos 52, 95, 172-77
Kent, Chancellor James 159, 202
Kentucky 104, 145, 146, 163, 172, 297; II, 13, 30, 193, 199, 212, 248, 253, 266, 301, 325, 326, 334
Keokuk, Iowa II, 350
Ketchum, Edward B. II, 96, 382
Ketchum, Morris II, 71, 72, 103, 109, 111
Ketchum, Son and Company, Ketchum, Howe and Company II, 86, 87, 96
Kidder, H. P. II, 388
Kidder, Peabody and Company II, 179, 190, 365, 373, 379-381, 387, 388, 394, 395, 421, 422
King, Charles II, 328, 334, 410
King, Edward II, 288, 369, 394, 418, 422
King, James Gore 202; II, 67, 259, 333, 334, 350
King (J. G.) and Sons, J. G. King's Sons and Company II, 70, 72, 77, 344, 348, 350
King, John Alsop II, 10, 40, 273
King, Rufus 39; II, 67, 410, 422
King, Rufus Howard II, 349, 352
Kirkland, Edward C. II, 354
Kirkwood, Samuel Jordan II, 27, 31
Kissell, Kinnicut and Company II, 371, 376, 419
Knapp, Shepherd, Shepherd Knapp and Company II, 11, 48, 49, 196
Knickerbocker Trust Company (New York) II, 394, 418
Knox, John Jay II, 105, 116, 117, 121, 204
Knox, Normand 32, 36, 41, 42
Kountze Brothers II, 418
Kuhn, Abraham II, 362
Kuhn, Loeb and Company II, 75, 181, 211, 222, 362, 363, 368, 373, 377, 379-81, 385-87, 391, 394, 421
Labouchère, Pierre César II, 313, 319, 321
Lacey, Edward S. II, 204
Lafayette, Indiana II, 362

Laffitte, Jacques, Caisse Laffitte II, 17, 321, 337, 338, 360
La Grange, Georgia II, 201
Laidlaw and Company II, 418
Lake, W. S., 75, 78, 92
Lake Borgne Navigation Company II, 33
Lake Erie II, 25
Lake Shore Railroad II, 355, 372
Lake Superior and Mississippi Railroad II, 359, 360
Lamb, Thomas 85-87; II, 108, 159, 165, 171, 172
Lamont, Thomas II, 385
Lancaster, J. II, 323
Lancaster, Pennsylvania 16; II, 340
Lane, Gardiner M., II, 381, 387
Lanesborough, Massachusetts 73
Langdon, H. S. 186
Langdon, John 25, 185
Lanier, James F. D. II, 25, 111, 152, 347, 353-55
Lansingburgh, New York 70
Larkin, Sam 186
Larson, Henrietta II, 68, 106, 337, 357, 358, 360
La Salle Street National Bank, La Salle Street Trust and Savings Bank (Chicago) II, 202
Latrobe, John H. B. 176
Laughlin, J. Laurence II, 195
de Laveleye, Emile Baron II, 440
Lavergne, Hugues 207
Law, John 27, 164; II, 145, 146
Law, Thomas 157
Lawrence, Cornelius Van Wyck II, 262
Lawrence, Isaac 116
Lawrence, William 72, 74
Lawrence, William B. 129, 149, 159, 179; II, 55
Lawrenceburg, Indiana II, 30
Leach (A. B.) and Company II, 422
Leather Manufacturers Bank (New York) 292; II, 292
Le Beau II, 38
Le Couteulx de Cantaleu II, 316, 404
Lee, George Cabot II, 387
Lee, Gideon 292
Lee, John Clarke II, 387
Lee, Higginson and Company II, 70, 71, 75, 190, 371-374, 376, 379-81, 387, 388, 394, 419, 421, 422
Leeds, Timothy C. II, 346
Lehigh Coal and Navigation Company II, 359, 365
Lehigh Valley Railroad II, 390
Lenox, David 102, 159
Lenox, Robert 107, 116, 120
Le Roy, Herman II, 316, 329
Le Roy, Bayard and McEvers II, 316, 329
Leverich, Charles P. II, 91, 161, 171
Lewis, E. M. II, 97, 172
Lewis, William B. 115, 146, 147
Lewis, Zachariah 210, 212, 299

Lexington, Kentucky 249
Liberty National Bank (New York) II, 179, 188, 204, 391
Lidderdale, William II, 440
Lieber, Francis 159
Life and Fire Insurance Company II, 61
Ligonier, Indiana II, 77
Lincoln, Abraham II, 86, 87, 140, 144, 163, 362
Lincoln Bank (Pittsburgh) II, 177
Litchfield, Connecticut 48
Litchfield and Torrington Manufacturing Company, Connecticut 48
Little, Jacob II, 345
Little, John L. II, 78, 79
Little Miami Railroad II, 355
Little Rock, Arkansas 298
Little Schuylkill and Susquehanna Railroad II, 339
Livermore, Clews and Company, see Clews, Henry
Liverpool (England) II, 32, 33, 61, 68, 124, 187, 271
Liverpool Currency Reform Association II, 124
Liverpool Mechanics', Servants' and Laborers' Fund 212
Liverpool, Lord 128, 168
Livingston, Brockholst 22, 31, 39, 212
Livingston, Edward 244
Livingston, Robert R. (Chancellor) 28, 32
Livingston family 123, 159
de Lizardi (F.) and Company, London, de Lizardi (M.) and Company, New Orleans II, 32-34, 271, 295
Lizardi, Hermannos II, 34
Lloyd, James 116
Lloyd's II, 313
Locke, John 163, 189; II, 435
Loeb, Solomon II, 362, 385
Lombard, Isaac G. II, 174
London, D. H. II, 213, 233
London, (England) 16, 40, 49, 53, 54, 97, 101, 108, 115, 123, 126, 131, 136, 159, 209, 217, 220; II, 11, 33-35, 48, 67, 69, 70, 75, 77, 189, 239, 240, 241, 246, 271, 294, 306, 308, 311-16, 320, 322, 325, 330, 332-37, 340-43, 348, 350-52, 354, 358, 361-70, 373, 376, 382, 384, 386, 402, 408, 418, 439, 440
London and Westminister Bank II, 16, 272
London Assurance Company II, 310, 397
London Society for Bettering the Condition of the Poor 212
London Times, see Times, London
Long, George 185, 186
Long Island, New York II, 238
Lord, Eleazar 195-99, 201, 293, 296; II, 39, 102
Lorillard, Jacob II, 56
Lorimer, William II, 202
Los Angeles, California II, 197
Lothrop, Edwin H. 204

Loughman and Company II, 409
Louis XVI, King of France II, 319
Louisiana 30, 54, 62, 202, 206, 208, 218, 298; II, 8, 9, 10, 15, 19, 29, 32, 33, 34, 35, 36, 38, 39, 40, 47, 77, 103, 192-94, 217, 220, 266, 301, 313, 325, 326, 333-35, 337-39, 341,344
Louisiana National Bank (New Orleans) II, 192
Louisiana Purchase 110; II, 313
Louisiana State Bank (New Orleans) II, 37, 256, 257, 269, 273
Louisville, Kentucky 251; II, 74, 186
Louisville and Nashville Railroad II, 371
Louisville, Cincinnati and Charleston Railroad II, 354
Low, Abiel Abbott II, 167
Lowe, Robert Phillips II, 1, 27, 30
Lowell, Francis C. 69
Lowell, John (Judge) 214
Lowell, John (1769-1840) 214, 215
Lowell, John Amory 72, 74
Lowell, Massachusetts II, 186
Lowell Bank 75, 76
Lowell Institution for Savings 76
Lowndes, William 102, 129
Lowry, R. J. II, 172, 210
Loyd, W. 185
Lucas, Robert II, 27, 30
Ludlow, Daniel 38
Lunenburg, Massachusetts 41
Lutwyche, Alfred II, 124
Luzatti Banks II, 79
Lyman, George D. II, 49-56, 91, 108, 164, 236, 275, 285, 286, 425
Lyman, Stuart II, 50, 56
Lynchburg, Virginia II, 68
McCall, James 79, 263
McCalmont and Company, McCalmont Bros. and Company II, 70, 354
McCleary, James T. II, 195
McClintock, John 186
McClurkin, A. J. II, 260
McCulloch, Hugh II, 16, 24, 25, 102, 105-108, 110, 111, 113, 114, 139, 151-53, 273, 365
McCulloch and Company II, 367
McCulloch, John Ramsay 194, 198, 294
McCurdy, Richard A. II, 187, 196, 224
McDougal, James B. II, 286
McDougall, Alexander 37
McDuffie, George 115, 125, 149, 152, 159, 179, 196; II, 16
McGrane, R. C. 153, 161
McIlvaine, Joseph 115
McKay, Charles M. II, 128, 185, 186
Mackay and Company II, 361
McKim, John 116
McKinley, William II, 166, 169, 203
McLane, Louis 46, 153, 159, 171; II, 341

Mc Leod, Henry D. II, 120
Mc Phin, William Lyon II, 124
Mac Vickar, John 47, 64, 155, 191-99, 201, 293, 294, 296; II, 39
Macalester and York II, 336
Mackabie (M) and E. S. Edgerton II, 112
Macklot and Corbin II, 76
Madison, James 8, 30, 101, 102, 159; II, 99
Madison, Indiana II, 25, 353
Madison and Indianapolis Railroad II, 30, 354, 355
Madison, Wisconsin II, 276
Magniac, Smith and Company II, 336, 337
Maine 73-75, 95; II, 1, 2, 12, 15, 16, 19, 60, 202, 240, 301, 325, 424
Maine Bank (Portland) 64
Mainz II, 385
Malthus, Thomas R. 210
Manchester (England) 213; II, 430
Manchester, Vermont II, 301
Manhattan Company, see Bank of the Manhattan Company
Manhattan Fire Insurance Company 195
Manhattan Trust Company (New York) II, 187, 392
Manley, W. D. II, 201
Mann, Abijah 94, 200, 201, 295
Manufacturers and Mechanics Bank (Boston), see Tremont Bank
Manufacturers and Mechanics Bank (Philadelphia) II, 53, 272
Manufacturers Commercial Company of New York II, 79
Manufacturers National Bank (Chicago) II, 112
Marblehead, Massachusetts II, 8
Marcy, William L. 189, 190, 196, II, 331
Maria Theresa, Empress II, 321
Marine Bank (Chicago) II, 112
Marine National Bank (New York) II, 427
Market National Bank, Market and Fulton National Bank (New York) II, 190, 303
Markle, John II, 79
Marquette County Savings Bank II, 229
Marseilles II, 69
Marshal, G. A. 149
Martin, James II, 272
Martinique II, 32
Marx, Joseph II, 328
Maryland 15, 52, 127, 173-77, 188, 219-21, 228; II, 27, 53, 54, 193, 194, 215, 256, 266, 294, 295, 301, 324-26, 334, 335-38, 340, 341, 343, 350, 351, 353
Mason, Jeremiah 116
Mason, Stevens T. II, 25
Massachusetts 13, 16, 21, 22, 32, 35, 37, 38, 40, 52-54, 61, 68, 75, 76, 84, 94, 95, 202, 218-221, 225, 226, 228, 229, 232; II, 2-12, 14, 16, 20, 71, 74, 89, 104, 105, 159, 160, 181, 193, 214, 225, 238, 255, 257, 258, 261, 266, 270, 272, 284,
297, 302, 324, 325, 337, 348-51, 381, 390, 410, 413, 424
Massachusetts Bank (Boston) 6-8, 10, 11, 13-21, 23, 25, 32, 34-40, 42, 52, 54, 58, 63, 67, 214, 216, 217, 232-236, 238, 240, 249, 260, 262; II, 45, 46, 245, 246, 256, 257, 261, 275, 286, 292, 300, 324, 325
Massachusetts Cotton Mills II, 387
Massachusetts Fire and Marine Insurance Company II, 346
Massachusetts Loan and Trust Company (Boston) II, 190
Matteson, Joel Aldrich II, 198
Maverick Bank (Boston) 86; II, 285
Maynard, Horace II, 105, 150
Mease, James 213, 228
Mechanics and Farmers Bank (Albany) 241, 243, 269; II, 45, 270, 330, 333, 349, 415
Mechanics and Farmers Bank (New Orleans) II, 295
Mechanics and Metals National Bank (New York) (resulted from a merger of the Mechanics National Bank) II, 188
Mechanics and Traders Bank (Brooklyn) II, 188
Mechanics and Traders Bank (New Orleans) II, 256
Mechanics and Traders Bank (New York) II, 168, 202
Mechanics Bank (Baltimore) II, 256, 318
Mechanics Bank (New Haven) II, 325
Mechanics Bank (New York), Mechanics National Bank 16, 49, 51, 216, 226, 250, 251; II, 11, 20, 48-50, 68, 184, 248, 259, 293, 361, 421
Mechanics Bank (Philadelphia) 47; II, 53, 108, 268, 272, 274, 299
Mechanics National Bank (Chicago) II, 112
Mechanics National Bank (New York), see Mechanics Bank (New York)
Mellon, Charles S. II, 378
Mellon, Thomas II, 435
Mellon National Bank (Pittsburgh) II, 177, 189
Memphis, Tennessee II, 9
Mendenhall, Thomas II, 147
Mercantile Bank, Mercantile National Bank (New York) II, 171, 188, 202
Mercantile Credit Company (Chicago) II, 79
Mercantile Insurance Company II, 61
Mercantile Trust Company (Boston) II, 190
Mercantile Trust Company (New York) II, 187, 189, 422
Mercer, Singleton A. 81; II, 53, 89, 97, 107, 108, 160, 166, 173, 274, 287, 302
Merchants and Farmers Bank (Albany) 243
Merchants and Mechanics Bank (Troy) II, 330
Merchants and Traders Bank (New York) II, 389
Merchants Bank (Albany) 79
Merchants Bank (Baltimore) II, 109, 299
Merchants Bank (Boston) 229; II, 8, 52, 54, 57, 59,

68, 88, 89, 108, 109, 139, 146, 190, 341, 389
Merchants Bank (Chicago) II, 191
Merchants Bank (New Bedford) II, 19
Merchants Bank (New Orleans) 144
Merchants Bank, Merchants National Bank (New York) 16, 22, 35-37, 42, 45, 63, 70, 241; II, 50, 97, 106, 107, 184, 259, 293, 331, 368, 411, 417, 418, 421, 444
Merchants Bank (Providence) 260, 261; II, 48, 50, 51, 55, 56
Merchants Bank (Salem) 37, 38; II, 245
Merchants Bank of Canada II, 220, 221
Merchants Loan and Trust Company (Chicago) II, 189, 302, 392
Merchants-Mechanics National Bank (Baltimore) II, 152
Merchants National Bank (Chicago) II, 112, 169
Merchants National Bank (New York), see Merchants Bank
Merchants Savings, Loan and Trust Company (Chicago) II, 169
Meredith, William II, 264
Merrill, Samuel II, 24, 25, 30
Merrimac Bank (Haverhill) II, 301
Merrimac Manufacturing Company II, 387
Metropolitan Bank, Metropolitan National Bank (New York) 77, 79, 80; II, 50, 93, 107, 114, 151, 158-60, 285, 427, 428, 443
Metropolitan National Bank (Chicago) II, 191, 392
Metropolitan National Bank (New York), see Metropolitan Bank
Metropolitan Trust Company (New York) II, 188, 232
Mexico 126, 134; II, 255, 256, 267, 294, 295, 386, 408
Meyer and Stucken II, 355
Miami University (Ohio) II, 27
Michigan 95, 187, 202-204, 246, 297; II, 25, 108, 110, 112, 123, 196, 220, 229, 278, 301, 325, 331, 332, 334-336, 340-342, 412, 413
Michigan and Illinois Canal II, 330
Michigan and Southern Railroad II, 348
Michigan Central Railroad II, 354, 372
Michigan Southern Railroad II, 355, 372
Mickle, Robert II, 53, 59, 275
Middlesex County Bank (Connecticut) II, 49
Middletown, Connecticut 35, 119; II, 49, 252, 292
Middletown Bank 239; II, 346
Milan II, 321
Mill, James Stuart II, 154
Milledgeville, Georgia II, 264, 265, 297
Milnor, William II, 254, 294
Milwaukee II, 63, 64, 276-278
Minneapolis, Minnesota II, 192, 199, 201, 220, 221
Minneapolis Bank II, 112
Minneapolis Trust Company II, 192
Minnesota 202; II, 76, 112, 144, 192, 193, 199, 279,

301
Minnesota Loan and Investment Company II, 76
Minnesota Loan and Trust Company (Minneapolis) II, 192
Minturn and Champlin II, 404
Mississippi 45, 202, 208; II, 13, 35, 70, 193, 217, 232, 258, 267, 296, 300, 301, 325, 326, 333-35, 338, 340, 341
Mississippi and Alabama Railroad and Banking Company II, 326
Mississippi Valley II, 281
Missouri 123; II, 2, 13, 22, 29, 182, 193, 194, 217, 237, 238, 244, 266, 278, 301, 325, 334, 337, 345, 350
Missouri River II, 223
Mitchell, Alexander II, 63, 64, 122, 211, 274, 299
Mitchell, Charles Edwin II, 419
Mitchell, J. B. II, 53, 58, 108, 373, 392, 422
Mobile, Alabama 114, 145; II, 339, 340
Mobile and Ohio Railroad II, 348, 349
Moffet and White II, 371
Mohawk and Hudson Railroad II, 18
Monroe, James 110, 112, 113, 117, 153, 158, 159, 173, 174
Monroe Railroad and Banking Company II, 326
Montana II, 202, 302
Monticello 157
Montreal II, 221, 363
Monument National Bank (Boston) II, 190
Moore, T. W. C. II, 112
Moore, William C. II, 391
Morawetz, Victor II, 173, 216
Morgan, James II, 308, 311, 313, 315, 397, 398, 401
Morgan, John Pierpont II, 96, 175, 176, 179, 187-89, 206, 207, 211, 283, 288, 363-366, 370, 371, 373, 374, 378-87, 390, 391, 394, 395, 419
Morgan (J. P.) and Company (of the 1860's) II, 382
Morgan (J. P.) and Company II, 75, 181, 188, 189, 198, 341, 362, 364, 366, 370-374, 376, 378-381, 384-388, 391, 392, 395, 419
Morgan, Junius Spencer II, 65, 71, 96, 351, 363, 364, 382, 384, 385
Morgan (J. S.) and Company II, 364-368, 370, 418
Morgan, M. II, 347, 414
Morgan, Ketchum and Company II, 65, 68
Morris, Arthur J. II, 79
Morris, Gouverneur 21, 25, 26; II, 316
Morris, Robert 17, 19, 20, 24-27, 29, 30, 34, 39, 40, 42, 92, 178, 193, 205, 231, 241, 243, 244; II, 316
Morris and Company II, 392
Morris Canal and Banking Company 49, 50, 54, 55, 153; II, 178, 326, 330, 332, 336, 341, 343, 412, 413
Morrison, J. M. II, 89
Morrison, Cryder and Company 54; II, 271, 330
Morse, Charles W. II, 188, 202, 373

Morton, L. P. II, 363, 364, 366, 381, 383, 390

Morton (L. P.) and Company II, 363

Morton (L. P.), Burns and Company II, 363

Morton, Bliss and Company II, 75, 363, 365-68, 379, 383, 394, 418, 444

Morton, Rose and Company II, 75, 77, 363, 365, 366, 386

Morton Trust Company (New York) II, 187, 394

Mosher, C. W. II, 215

Mount Blount Springs II, 267

Mount Morris Bank (New York) II, 188

Moussier, J. B. 207

Moyamensing Bank (Philadelphia) II, 268, 272, 273

Munday, C. B. II, 202

Murray, James B. II, 342

Murray, John 216

Mushet, Robert 157

National Bank (Chicago) II, 191

Mutual Bank of Troy II, 301

Mutual Life Insurance Company (New York) II, 187, 189, 196, 379, 418, 442

Nalad, Idaho II, 199

Nantes, France, 33

Nantucket II, 60

Naples II, 320, 322, 323, 353

Napoleon, Napoleonic II, 310, 311, 314, 315, 319, 320, 323, 326, 344, 345, 355, 358, 377, 404, 405, 408

Nash, William A. II, 184, 188, 196, 303

Nashville, Tennessee 123, 164, 165; II, 18, 55, 242

Natchez, Mississippi 114, 149; II, 70, 193

"National Bank Department" (original term for what became the office of the Comptroller of the Currency) II, 148, 149

National Bank in the City of New York, see Gallatin National Bank

National Bank of America (Chicago) II, 191

National Bank of Boston, see Boston National Bank

National Bank of Commerce (Minneapolis) II, 192, 198

National Bank of Commerce (New York), see Bank of Commerce

National Bank of Commerce (Sioux City) II, 200

National Bank of North America (Chicago) II, 191

National Bank of North America (New York) II, 202

National Bank of the Commonwealth (Boston) II, 190

National Bank of the Republic of New York, see Bank of the Republic (New York)

National Bank of the Republic (Philadelphia) II, 151

National Bank of the State of Florida (Jacksonville) II, 173

National Bank of the United States (New York) II, 187

National Banker's Association for the West II, 278, 279

National Banking Association II, 153, 280, 281

National City Bank, City Bank (New York) 16, 269; II, 89, 161, 175, 176, 180, 181, 183, 184, 187-89, 204, 211, 226, 243, 248, 288, 293, 370-73, 376, 378, 380, 381, 386, 389, 391, 393-95, 418, 419, 425

National City Company (New York) II, 381, 393, 395

National Copper Bank (Salt Lake City) II, 177

National Eagle Bank (Boston) II, 190

National Exchange Bank (Boston) II, 190

National Exchange Bank (Philadelphia) II, 151

National Farmers and Planters Bank (Baltimore) II, 275

National Gazette (Freneau's) 165

National Intelligencer II, 101

National Park Bank (New York), see Park Bank

National Revere Bank (Boston) II, 164

National Shawmut Bank (Boston) II, 190, 206, 243, 379, 422

National Trust and Credit Company (Chicago) II, 79

National Tube Company II, 204

National Union Bank, see Union Bank (Baltimore)

National Union Bank (New York) II, 187

Nebenius, Karl Friedrich II, 308, 320

Nebraska II, 200, 215, 217, 301

Necker, Jacques II, 319, 404

Nederlandsche Bank (The Netherlands Banks) 157; II, 439

Nesbitt and Stewarts II, 397

Nevada II, 166, 228, 302

New Bedford, Massachusetts 73; II, 19, 66, 151, 300, 354

New Brunswick, New Jersey II, 66

New England 47, 51, 71, 75-81, 85, 86, 142, 149, 228, 238, 260, 261; II, 2, 5, 6, 46-48, 63, 66, 77, 90, 115, 122, 212, 223, 239, 240, 242, 252, 258, 261, 263, 270-72, 289, 325, 335, 358, 363, 364, 381, 388

New England Bank (Boston) 69-73, 86, 260; II, 108, 171

New Hampshire 25, 172; II, 16, 18, 201, 240, 241, 302, 325, 326

New Haven, Connecticut 35; II, 246, 259, 294, 325

New Jersey 49, 50, 79, 202, 205; II, 66, 98, 238, 270, 302, 326, 341, 357, 361, 376

New London, Connecticut 35; II, 65

New Mexico II, 302

New Orleans 30, 31, 45, 51-53, 60, 92, 113-115, 135, 136, 144, 153, 159, 164, 165, 207, 208, 217, 226, 244; II, 2, 18, 29, 32-34, 36, 38-40, 47, 55, 61, 70, 71, 99, 147, 165, 185, 186, 192, 193, 248, 255, 256, 258, 261, 263, 266, 267, 269, 273, 289, 294, 326, 332, 334, 335, 339, 347, 350, 362, 382

New York (City) 16, 17, 21, 22, 28, 30, 31, 35-37, 40, 41, 45, 46, 49-53, 63, 64, 67, 69-71, 73, 77-80, 87, 89, 90, 93, 94, 101, 114, 116-18, 124, 125, 135-39, 142, 144, 145, 159, 164, 172, 173,

179, 189, 195, 198, 209, 210, 213-24, 226, 227,
  237, 239-41, 245, 260; II, 2-7, 10, 11, 15, 20,
  25, 40, 46-54, 60, 61, 65-77, 79, 86-97, 106-111,
  114-117, 119-123, 129, 132, 133, 139, 140-142,
  144, 146, 152-154, 156, 158, 160-168, 175, 177,
  179-84, 186-89, 191, 193, 194, 196, 198, 200,
  202, 204, 206, 208, 210-14, 217-20, 223, 224,
  227, 232, 233, 237-42, 245-50, 252-55, 257-67,
  269-76, 279-88, 292, 293, 295, 297, 299, 301,
  302, 315-17, 326, 327-39, 341-47, 349, 350,
  352-57, 359-71, 373, 376, 378-82, 385, 388, 389,
  391-94, 411, 417, 420, 422, 424-33, 437, 438,
  440, 444, 445
New York (State) 8, 16, 22, 25, 31, 36, 37, 41, 43,
  52-54, 61, 70, 80, 81, 88, 89, 92, 93, 95, 132,
  170, 187-190, 196, 199, 201-204, 212, 221, 225,
  227-29, 235, 237, 239, 244, 301; II, 2-6, 10, 12,
  14, 15, 19, 24-26, 30, 36, 40, 65, 74, 76, 77, 99,
  100, 103-105, 109, 110, 116, 121, 141, 143, 148,
  153, 154, 158-60, 178, 179, 181, 186, 194, 196,
  198, 199, 204, 215-17, 235, 238, 243, 257, 264,
  270, 271, 273, 279-81, 284, 287, 289, 300, 301,
  325, 326, 329, 330-36, 342-45, 349, 350, 352,
  353, 390, 394, 395, 409, 410, 414, 416
New York, see also Bank of New York
New York and Erie Railroad, see Erie Railroad
New York Bank for Savings 214, 216, 217, 218,
  220-227; II, 299, 326, 327
New York Banking Company II, 331
New York Central Railroad II, 372, 373, 383, 390,
  419
New York Guaranty and Indemnity Company
  (New York) II, 187
New York Life Insurance and Trust Company
  II, 333, 336
New York Life Insurance Company II, 379
New York Manufacturing Company II, 331
New York Merchants Exchange II, 334
New York, New Haven and Hartford Railroad
  II, 378, 385, 390
New York Produce Bank (New York) II, 196
New York Saving Fund Society 226
New York Society for the Prevention of Pauperism
  212
New York Society of the Cincinnati 63
New York State Society for the Detection and Pun-
  ishment of Counterfeiters and Alterers of Bank
  Notes II, 270
New York State Stock Security Bank II, 148, 347
New York Stock Board II, 146
New York Times II, 101, 117, 125
New York Trust Company (New York) II, 188, 189,
  391, 394
New York Union Committee, see Subject Index,
  Union Committee
Newark, New Jersey II, 66, 186, 236, 238
Newberry, Oliver II, 335, 336

Newbold, George 244; II, 255, 262, 270, 293
Newbold (W. H.), Son and Aertsen II, 360
Newburyport, Massachusetts 35; II, 325
Newland, Abraham II, 308
Newnham, Everett and Company II, 315
Newport, Rhode Island 35, 217; II, 150, 424
Newport Bank (Newport, Rhode Island) II, 32, 151
Newton, Arthur William II, 182, 226
Nicholson, Joseph H. II, 254, 294
Nietzsche, Friedrich 152
Nineteenth Street Bank (New York) II, 188
Ninth National Bank of New York II, 280, 301
Nixon, Henry 20, 26, 37, 38
Nixon, John 20
Noble, Noah II, 23
Noetzlin, Edouard II, 386
Nolte, Vincent II, 313, 326
Norfolk, Virginia II, 79, 254, 258
North, Lord 97
North American Trust and Banking Company
  (New York) II, 335-37, 341-43, 395
North Carolina 61; II, 47, 79, 301, 326, 345, 349
  414, 416
North Dakota II, 76, 199, 217, 302
North Missouri Railroad II, 359, 364
North National Bank (Boston) II, 190
North River II, 65
North River Steam Boat Company 48
Northern Central Railroad II, 350
Northern Liberties (Philadelphia) II, 250, 251, 291
Northern Pacific Railroad II, 166, 360, 361, 365,
  373, 380, 383, 390, 395
Northern Trust Company (Chicago) II, 173, 285,
  302
Northwestern National Bank (Chicago) II, 111, 169,
  191
Northwestern National Bank (Minneapolis) II, 192,
  203, 206, 221
Northwestern Virginia Railroad II, 352
Northwestern Territories II, 279
Norway II, 408
Oberholtzer, Ellis P. 39
Odell, J. J. P. II, 174, 224
Ogden, David B. 200, 201
Oelrichs and Lurman II, 70, 350
Ohio 52, 54, 188, 202; II, 2, 9, 16, 19, 24-27, 31,
  70, 71, 87, 103, 104, 109, 110, 217, 248, 252-54,
  262, 266, 278, 301, 325, 326, 330-34, 336, 338,
  342, 343, 345, 350, 353, 355, 416
Ohio and Mississippi Railroad II, 352
Ohio and Pennsylvania Railroad II, 352, 355
Ohio Life Insurance and Trust Company II, 178,
  273, 332, 336, 341, 424, 425
Ohio River II, 25
Oklahoma II, 217, 244, 301
Oklahoma City II, 242
Olcott, Thomas W. II, 108, 330, 333, 349, 350, 352, 415

Old Colony Railroad II, 326, 349
Old Colony Trust Company (Boston) II, 190, 379, 394
Oliver, Robert 116, 121
Olivers of Baltimore 159
Omaha II, 186, 207
Ontario County Bank, New York II, 352
Opdyke, George (George Opdyke and Company) 56; II, 10, 40, 111, 151, 152, 212
Oregon II, 166, 199, 302, 363
Oriental Bank (New York) II, 91, 168, 184
Orvis, J. U. II, 280, 281, 301
Osgood, Samuel 22, 31, 34, 36, 40, 42
Ouvrard, Gabriel Julien II, 322
Overend, Gurney and Company II, 271
Overstone, Lord II, 105, 122
Pacific Gas and Electric Company II, 381
Packer, Asa II, 362
Page and Bacon, II, 352
Paige, Alonzo C. 93, 94
Palmer, Sir Horsley II, 19, 37, 354
Palmer, McKillop, Dent and Company II, 335, 336, 342, 343, 354, 411
Palmyra, New York 80; II, 26
Paris, France 110, 131, 158, 159; II, 34, 69, 75, 146, 189, 312, 313, 319, 322, 323, 362, 364, 366, 367, 402, 404, 430, 439, 440
Parish, David 50, 101-104; II, 316, 317, 320, 323, 334, 358, 404, 405
Parish, John, II, 316
Parish, John, Jr. II, 318, 320, 322
Parish and Company II, 318, 321, 322, 404
Park Bank, National Park Bank (New York) 80; II, 161, 181, 183, 184, 188, 227, 286, 331, 389, 418, 421
Park River, North Dakota II, 199
Parker, Daniel, merchant from Watertown II, 316
Parker, Daniel II, 345
Parker, John 184
Parker Vein Coal Company II, 11
Parnell, Sir Henry 157, 197, 294
Parrot, E. G. 186
Parrott, John F. 186
Parsons, Enoch 151; II, 328
Parsons, Philo II, 17, 112
Parsons, Thomas H. II, 76
Parsons and Fisher II, 112
Patapsco Bank II, 346
Paterson, New Jersey II, 65
Patterson, Joseph II, 53, 89, 90, 97, 107, 113, 172, 282, 287, 302, 366
Patterson, W. G. 199
Payne, Edward 39
Payson, Henry II, 254, 255
Peabody, Francis H. II, 388
Peabody, George II, 187, 348, 350-52, 358, 382

Peabody and Company II, 70, 352, 364, 382
Peabody, George Foster II, 210
Peabody, Oliver W. II, 388
Peabody, Massachusetts II, 351
Pell, Ferris 6
Penn family 39
Pennsylvania 6, 7, 13, 16, 17, 24, 47, 49, 50, 55, 79, 81, 102, 106, 110, 111, 115, 127, 133, 144, 148, 154, 156-58, 160, 161, 178, 179, 202, 205, 226, 228, 232, 301; II, 1, 2, 4, 12, 13, 18, 20, 31, 36, 62, 74, 105, 109, 151, 153, 165, 178, 193, 201, 216, 233, 247, 252-54, 264, 266, 270, 272, 301, 324, 325, 332-35, 339-41, 344, 345, 350, 352, 356, 358, 364, 389, 390
Pennsylvania Bank (Philadelphia) 5, 24-26, 37, 39
Pennsylvania Company for Insurance on Lives and Granting Annuities II, 345
Pennsylvania Railroad II, 350, 352, 360, 364
Penobscot Bank 35
People's Bank (Paterson, New Jersey) II, 65
Peoples Bank (St. Paul) II, 112
People's Trust Company (Brooklyn) II, 186
Pereire Brothers 160; II, 356
Perkins, Edward N. II, 303
Perkins, George W. II, 179, 379
Perkins, Thomas H. 159, 184
Peru II, 408
Peters, Richard, Jr. 148, 213
Phelps, Dodge and Company II, 444
Phenix Bank (New York), see Phoenix Bank
Philadelphia 5, 6, 16, 20-22, 24-26, 30, 31, 33-35, 39, 40, 45-52, 58, 60, 61, 67, 80, 81, 87, 100-102, 104, 107, 108, 111-14, 119, 120, 123, 125, 128, 136-38, 157, 159, 164, 166, 172, 173, 175, 179, 185, 210, 212-24, 226, 227, 235, 260; II, 2, 3, 6, 10, 18, 45, 46, 51-54, 61, 62, 66, 68, 69, 71-75, 88-92, 94, 97, 98, 106, 107, 110, 113-15, 124, 129, 132, 133, 140-142, 153, 156, 159, 160, 163-67, 172, 179, 184, 188, 198, 213, 236, 238, 245-55, 258-60, 262, 263, 265-70, 272-75, 281-84, 286, 287, 291, 292, 294, 297, 299, 302, 317, 324, 328-30, 332-34, 337-39, 346, 347, 349, 350, 356, 357, 359, 360, 364, 365, 368, 370, 389, 411, 421, 426, 431, 433
Philadelphia and Reading Railroad II, 18, 350, 354, 421
Philadelphia Bank, Philadelphia National Bank 12, 13, 16, 19, 22, 32, 37, 232, 235, 238, 241; II, 52, 58, 91, 97, 134, 151, 172, 188, 230, 246, 247, 249, 251, 268, 272, 274, 299, 324
Philadelphia Saving Fund Society 213, 217-21, 223-27; II, 345
Phillips, John 214, 215
Phillips, William 6, 20, 32, 34, 37, 38, 214, 240
Phillips, William, Jr. 214-17
Phillips Academy 37

Phoenix Bank (Hartford) 19, 20, 31, 32, 36, 41, 42, 48, 243; II, 349

Phoenix Bank (New York) 50; II, 50, 56, 330, 331, 336, 413

Phoenixville Iron Works II, 254

Pickering, Timothy 38

Pierce, Peter 185

Pine Bluff, Wyoming II, 199

Pintard, John 210, 212, 216-18, 221-24, 226, 230; II, 60, 326, 327

Piscataqua Bank II, 345

Pitman, John 185

Pitt, William II, 307, 308, 310-13, 316, 358, 398, 401

Pittsburgh 14; II, 68, 177, 181, 188, 238.266, 285, 340, 435

Pittsburgh and Connelsville Railroad II, 350

Pittsburgh, Fort Wayne and Chicago Railroad II, 350, 355

Pittsfield, Massachusetts 41, 259

Planters Bank (Nashville) II, 55

Planters Bank of Georgia 53

Planters Bank of Mississippi II, 333-35, 340

Platten, John W. II, 243

Plymouth, Massachusetts 33

Pocatello, Idaho II, 199

Polk, James K. II, 104

Pomeroy, Theodore M. II, 280

Poor, Henry Varnum II, 348, 445

Poor Richard, see Franklin, Benjamin

Populist movement II, 216

Portfolio 156, 158

Portland, Maine 64, 116, 153; II, 68

Portland, Oregon II, 166

Portland Bank (Portland, Maine) II, 245

Portsmouth, New Hampshire 35, 116, 119, 185; II, 424

Portugal II, 409

Postlethwayt, Malachy II, 16

Potosi, Missouri II, 29

Potter, John 116, 148

Potter, Orlando B. II, 101, 105, 147, 148

Powles, I. and A. II, 408

Pratt, Enoch II, 275

Pratt, William II, 346

Prescott, A. W. 186

Preston, Willard and Kean, Preston, Kean and Company II, 391

Price, Bonamy II, 154

Price, Hiram II, 31

Price, Joseph M. II, 91

Price, Richard II, 306, 307

Prime, Edward II, 67

Prime, Nathaniel 53, 117, 124, 159; II, 67, 328, 333, 338, 353

Prime, Rufus II, 353

Prime, Ward and Company II, 70, 424

Prime, Ward and King (Prime and Ward, Prime, Ward and Sands, Prime, Ward, Sands, King and Company) 202; II, 33, 64, 65, 67, 68-70

82, 259, 328, 329, 331, 333, 334, 336, 344, 350, 353, 359, 415

Prince, James 184

Princeton, Illinois II, 112

Princeton University 155; II, 195

Proffit, George H. II, 24, 29

Prosser, Seward II, 204

Providence (Rhode Island) 15, 21, 31, 33, 35, 39, 77, 116, 217; II, 48, 50, 51, 55, 66, 68, 71, 88, 90, 236, 238, 239, 247, 270, 272, 296, 298, 300, 305, 352

Providence Bank 8, 20, 21, 31, 32, 38, 39, 42, 232, 240, 247, 258, 259, 293, 295

Providence Insurance Company 32

Provident Bank and Trust Company (New Orleans) II, 192

Provident Institution for Savings (Boston) 215-18, 220-22, 224-26, 229, 259; II, 346

Provident Institution of Bath (England) 218

Prussia II, 305, 315, 320, 322, 323, 405

Publicola 6

Punnett, James II, 49, 50, 51, 56, 89, 158, 161, 284

Putman, Jesse 184

Queens County Bank of Long Island, New York II, 188, 193, 196, 238

Quincy, Illinois II, 350

Quincy, Josiah 214, 215

Raguet, Condy 46, 47, 133, 180, 193, 202, 213, 215, 224, 230, 232, 242; II, 39, 99, 147, 297

Raiffeisen Kreditgenossenschaften II, 79

Rasbach, D. H. 80

Read, William A., William A. Read and Company II, 420

Reading Railroad II, 384, 390

Real Estate Bank of Arkansas 208, 298; II, 336

Reay, Lord (Donald James Mackay) II, 439, 447

Reed, partner in Reed, Drexel and Company II, 364

Reed, Drexel and Company II, 86, 364, 365, 382

Rees, Abraham 128

Reichsbank II, 219, 221, 222

Reid, Daniel G. II, 179, 226

Reid, Thomas II, 330

Reid, Irving and Company 54; II, 35, 330, 408

Remsen (Peter) and Company II, 171

Rensselaer family 33

Republic National Bank (Boston) II, 190

Revell, Alexander H. II, 215

Revere Bank, Revere National Bank (Boston) II, 109, 190

Reynolds, George M. II, 182, 183, 191, 228

Rhawn, William Henry II, 151, 168

Rhenish Prussia II, 77

Rhode Island 11, 17, 32, 33, 35, 54, 77, 92, 95, 193, 219, 228, 232, 246, 250, 261; II, 48, 50, 51, 55, 193, 238, 240, 247, 266, 300, 302, 326

Rhode Island Central Bank II, 198

Rhode Island Insurance Company 32

Rhode Island Union Bank (Newport) II, 424

Ricardo, David 5, 125, 127, 157, 158, 168, 178-80,

191, 193, 194, 199, 201, 210, 293, 294; II, 154, 310, 314, 409
Ricardo, Samson 168
Rice, Henry II, 328, 329
Richardson, William H. 185
Richardson, Overend and Company II, 314
Richmond, William II, 56
Richmond, Indiana II, 26
Richmond, Virginia 145; II, 29, 68, 79, 233, 242, 254, 265, 328
Richmond and Danville Railroad II, 390
Ridgely, N. W. II, 72
Ridgely, William B. II, 210
Ridgeway, Thomas S. II, 153
Riggs, Elisha II, 111, 348, 351
Riggs, George Washington II, 348, 351
Riggs, Romulus II, 65
Riggs and Peabody II, 351
Riggs National Bank (Washington) II, 189
Ringold, John 298
Rives, William C. II, 113
Roberts, Abraham II, 311, 312, 398
Roberts, Curtis, Ware and Company, Roberts, Curtis, Roberts and Curtis, Roberts, Curtis and Company II, 311, 313-15
Robins, Thomas II, 52, 53, 58, 274
Robinson, M. 145
Rochambeau 29
Rock Island Railroad II, 360, 361
Rockefeller, John D. II, 391
Rockefeller, William II, 373, 385, 391
Rocksprings National Bank (Rocksprings, Wyoming) II, 199
Rodrigues, Henry II, 356
Rogers, C. H. II, 88, 97, 160, 163, 172, 302
Rogers, Ketchum and Bement II, 96
Rollins (E.), Morse and Brother II, 418
Romare, Paul II, 172
Rome, Italy II, 439
Roosevelt, Isaac 35, 245
Roosevelt, James 35, 42
Roosevelt, Theodore II, 215
Root, Erastus 265, 266
Rose, George 213
Rose, John II, 363
Roskell and Company II, 342
Ross, C. H. II, 199
Rotch, Thomas 73
Rothschild, Alphonse Baron de II, 440
Rothschild, James II, 354
Rothschild, Melville II, 79
Rothschild (M. A.) und Söhne II, 320-23, 353, 426
Rothschild, Nathan 133; II, 322, 323, 330, 354
Rothschild (N. M.) and Sons II, 288, 315, 334-37, 339, 347, 348, 350-54, 358, 362, 365-68, 370, 379, 382, 408, 418
Rothschild, Nathaniel Meyer Baron de II, 440

Rothschild, Salomon II, 320, 322
Rousseau 189
Roxbury, Massachusetts 76; II, 254
Royal Bank of Scotland II, 221
Royal Exchange Assurance Company II, 397
Rüppell und Harnier II, 404
Ruggles, Charles A. II, 240, 242
Rundlet, James 186
Rush, Richard 153, 155, 159; II, 338
Russell, Thomas 34, 35, 42, 214
Russia 182; II, 305, 313, 319, 322
Russo-Japanese War II, 386
Ryan, Thomas Fortune II, 187, 394
Sabin, Charles H. II, 79
Safety Fund Bank (Boston) II, 108
St. Joseph, Missouri II, 237
St. Louis, Missouri 123, 172; II, 29, 71-73, 79, 119, 120, 165, 186, 215, 227, 237, 242, 281, 350, 352
St. Louis and San Francisco Railroad II, 387
St. Paul, Minnesota II, 112, 144, 192
St. Petersburg II, 313
Saint Simon, Saint Simonists 96; II, 356
Salem, Massachusetts 32, 35, 37, 38, 212, 217-19; II, 317, 387, 388
Salem Bank II, 245
Salomon (William) and Company II, 374, 380
Salomons, E. P. II, 311, 314, 398
Salomons, Solomon II, 311
Salt Lake City II, 177, 285
Salter, Titus 185
San Francisco II, 166, 197, 282, 362
Sanders Manufacturing Company II, 326
Sands, Joseph II, 67
Sandusky, Ohio II, 355
Sanford, Peleg 32
Saratoga, New York II, 14, 281, 282, 429
Saratoga, Wyoming II, 199
Saratoga Sentinel 196
Savage, James 214, 215, 224, 230
Savannah, Georgia II, 46, 68, 257, 258
Savings Bank of Minneapolis II, 198
Scammon, J. Young II, 74, 112, 169
Schiff, Jacob II, 211, 217, 362, 373, 378-382, 384-386, 390, 391, 420
Schott, James II, 333
Schroeder (J. Henry) and Company, London II, 416
Schultze-Delitzsch Kreditgenossenschaften II, 79
Schurz, Carl II, 118, 121, 122, 154, 155
Schuyler, George L. and Robert II, 354
Schuyler, Philip 25, 29, 33, 37
Schuyler family 33
Schuylkill Bank (Philadelphia) 226; II, 251, 264, 268, 409
Schuylkill County II, 90
Schwab, Charles Michael II, 378
Scioto Land Company II, 399
Scotland 97, 197, 209, 218, 299; II, 48, 63, 79, 124,

195, 196, 198, 218, 221, 246, 352, 413

Scoville, Joseph A. 210, 223; II, 60, 67, 68, 335, 363

Seaboard National Bank (New York) II, 421

Seamen's Bank for Savings (New York) 218, 222; II, 299

Sears, Francis B. II, 239, 243

Second Bank of the United States 13, 15, 23, 25, 35, 36, 43-46, 48-51, 53-55, 57-64, 66, 92, 94, 95, 100-159, 161-163, 165-180, 184, 185, 188, 189, 198, 199, 200, 206, 222, 232-234, 239, 241, 244, 249, 251, 254-257, 259, 266, 269, 273, 276, 288; II, 1-4, 23, 24, 36, 45-48, 57, 64, 67, 70, 72, 85, 99, 100, 193, 208, 212, 213, 214, 236, 241, 253-257, 262, 291, 292, 299, 309, 318, 324, 325, 327-330, 333, 334, 338, 348, 395, 426

Seattle II, 166

Second National Bank of Baltimore II, 210

Second National Bank of Boston II, 108, 190, 227, 239

Second National Bank of Chicago II, 111

Second National Bank of Detroit II, 108

Second National Bank of Frankfort-Philadelphia II, 151

Second National Bank of New York II, 427

Second National Bank of St. Paul II, 112, 192

Second Security Bank (Chicago) II, 197

Security Bank (Chicago) II, 197

Security Bank (New York) II, 188

Security Bank and Trust Company (New Orleans) II, 192

Security Title and Trust Company (Chicago) II, 192

Sedalia, Missouri II, 238

Seligman, E. R. A. II, 78

Seligman, Jesse II, 362

Seligman, Joseph II, 362

Seligman (J. and W.) and Company II, 75, 362, 363, 365, 367, 368, 380, 390, 418

Seligman Brothers, London II, 365, 367, 368

Selma, Alabama 297

Sergeant, John 148, 159, 302; II, 254, 291, 330

Seton, William 34, 40-42, 99

Seton, Maitland and Company 40

Seven Years' War II, 318

Seventh Ward Bank II, 161

Sharp, John Jr. II, 328

Shaw, Henry 73

Shaw, Leslie M. II, 209

Shaw of Reid, Irving and Company II, 330

Shawneetown Bank II, 330

Shed, Henry P. 76

Sheffield Banking Company II, 221

Sheridan, Philip II, 112

Sherman, Hoyt II, 27

Sherman, John II, 104, 105, 122, 123, 356, 368

Sherman, Roger M. 293; II, 99, 147, 148

Sherman, Watts II, 330, 352, 411

Shipman and Corning II, 336

Shoe and Leather Bank (Boston) 85, 86

Shunk, Francis R. II, 1

Shurlds, Henry II, 29

Sidle, Wolford and Company II, 112

Siegel (Henry) and Company II, 191

Silberling, Norman II, 310

Silliman, Augustus Ely II, 50, 51, 106, 107, 140, 286

Silsbee, Nathaniel 159, 184

Silver Islet Mining Company II, 433

Simmons, J. Edward II, 303

Simonds, Andrew II, 282

Simpson, George 34, 35, 40-42; II, 62, 63

Sioux City, Iowa II, 199, 200

Sioux County Savings Bank (Mauria, Iowa) II, 200

Sioux Rapids, Iowa II, 199

Sixth National Bank (New York) II, 188

Smeth, R. S. Th. de II, 319

Smith, Abel Jr. II, 403

Smith, Adam 5, 6, 13, 29, 99, 111, 127, 157, 188, 191, 231, 294; II, 2, 16, 37, 154, 434

Smith, Barney 184

Smith, Byron L. II, 173, 285, 302

Smith, Charles S. II, 430, 443

Smith, Dennis A. II, 318

Smith, George; George Smith and Company II, 3, 62-64, 112, 198, 271

Smith, Jonathan II, 291

Smith, Orson II, 174

Smith, Robert, the first Lord Carrington II, 403

Smith, Samuel 149, 159, 179; II, 403

Smith, Samuel F. 37

Smith, Solomon A. II, 169, 302

Smith, Thomas 81

Smith, Vera 136

Smith and Payne, Smith, Payne and Smiths II, 314, 315, 403

Smithers (F. G.) and Company II, 418

Society for Bettering the Condition and Increasing the Comforts for the Poor in...Liverpool 212

Society for the Advancement of Social Science, New York II, 114

Society for the Prevention of Pauperism 212, 219

Sombart, Werner 29; II, 382

South Carolina 65, 92, 107, 156; II, 112, 141, 266, 301, 325, 336, 337, 343, 354

South Dakota II, 76, 200, 217, 301

South Park Bank (Chicago) II, 191

South Royalton Bank II, 271

South Sea Company II, 310, 397, 400

Southampton (England) 225

Southampton Saving Fund 218, 220

Southern Railway Company II, 390

Southern Trust and Banking Company (New Orleans) II, 192

Southwark Bank (Philadelphia) II, 89, 172, 345

Spain II, 323, 340, 408, 409

Spaulding, Elbridge Gerry II, 94, 95, 101-105, 109, 113, 125, 154, 280

Spencer, Herbert II, 429, 435

Spencer, John Canfield 199, 201

Spencer, Samuel II, 384

Speyer, Gustavus II, 362

Speyer, Philip II, 362

Speyer (Philip) and Company, Speyer and Company II, 181, 362, 363, 379, 380, 385, 386, 391

Speyer-Ellissen, L. II, 362

Spinner, Francis Elias II, 112, 431, 445

Spokane II, 199

Sprague, O. M. W. II, 205, 219, 220, 427

Springfield, Iowa II, 72

Springfield, Massachusetts 76

Sprott, Mark II, 310

Standard Oil Company II, 202, 238, 391

Standard Trust Company (New York) II, 187

Standrod, D. W. II, 199

Staphurst, Nicholas and Jacob van II, 318, 319

State Bank (Albany, New York) 16, 23, 31, 33, 78, 244; II, 270, 330, 349, 350, 352

State Bank (Boston) 12, 13, 19, 22, 31, 35, 42, 233, 234, 241, 257

State Bank (Charleston) 239

State Bank (Chicago) II, 64

State Bank of Arkansas 298; II, 336

State Bank of Georgia II, 297

State Bank of Illinois (Shawneetown) II, 22, 198, 330

State Bank of Indiana II, 3, 4, 24, 25, 26, 27, 30, 70, 97, 106, 113, 174, 220, 273, 353

State Bank of Iowa II, 3, 27, 74

State Bank of Kentucky II, 23

State Bank of Louisiana II, 333, 334

State Bank of Michigan II, 25

State Bank of Milton, North Dakota II, 199

State Bank of Missouri II, 29

State Bank of North Carolina II, 414

State Bank of Ohio II, 2, 25-27, 30, 97, 153

State Bank of South Carolina 65

State Bank of Tennessee II, 25

State Bank of Vermont 82, 233; II, 22, 193

State Bank of Wisconsin 208

State National Bank (Lincoln, Nebraska) II, 190

State Savings Bank (Hornick, Iowa) II, 200

State Street Trust Company (New York) II, 187, 394

Steiner (Melchior) und Company II, 404

Stetson, Caleb 85, 86; II, 172

Stetson, Francis Lynde II, 384

Steuart, Sir James 5-7, 13, 26, 43, 92, 111, 137, 157, 187, 192, 231; II, 14, 22, 37, 124

Steubenville, Ohio II, 253

Stevens, John II, 327

Stevens, John Austin II, 86, 87, 89, 91, 94, 97, 114, 160, 162, 346, 389, 425

Stevens, Thaddeus 158; II, 104

Stevenson, Andrew II, 254, 255

Stewart, A. T. II, 86

Stewart, John Aikman II, 111, 369-371, 394, 418

Stickney, A. B. II, 214, 215, 225

Stillman, James II, 176, 183, 188, 189, 204, 211, 226, 369, 372, 379-382, 385-387, 391, 420

Stilwell, Silas M. II, 99, 102, 104, 119

Stone, Henry B. 63, 74

Storm Lake State Bank, Iowa II, 199

Storrow, James J. II, 380, 381, 387, 388

Story, Joseph 37

Stout, Clews and Mason, see Clews (Henry) and Company

Strachan, Patrick, Strachan and Scott II, 63

Straus, Frederick W., Straus, Simon William, Straus Brothers and Company, Straus (S. W.) and Company II, 77

Strong, Benjamin II, 188, 204, 211, 217, 232

Strong, George D. 292

Strong (North American Trust and Banking Company) II, 342

Stuart, H. L. II, 381, 392

Stuart and Brothers II, 360

Studebaker Corporation II, 385

Sturges, George II, 169

Sturges, Jonathan II, 111

Sturges (Salomon) and Sons II, 111

Suffolk Bank, Suffolk National Bank (Boston) 41, 44, 45, 51, 54, 61, 63, 64, 67, 70-80, 83, 84, 85, 86, 87, 88, 142, 260-262; II, 2, 6, 18, 20, 47-49, 54, 55, 66, 97, 109, 114, 115, 159, 163, 190, 220, 239, 241, 257, 258, 261, 271, 272, 287, 289, 297

Suffolk County 41

Suffolk, England II, 424

Sullivan, James 8, 18, 21, 33, 205, 214, 237, 238; II, 60

Sullivan, Richard 214-16

Sunbury and Erie Railroad II, 337, 349, 350, 355, 365

Susquehanna Bank and Bridge Company II, 326

Sutherland, Joel B. 155

Swan, Gustavus II, 26, 30

Swann, Thomas II, 109

Swartout, John 35, 42

Swartout, Samuel II, 337

Swedish American National Bank (Minneapolis) II, 192

Sweat (Edward) and Company II, 418

Swift, John J. II, 346

Swift, Jonathan 146

Swift, R. K. II, 73

Swift and Company II, 392, 420

Swisher, Carl B. 176

Switzerland, Swiss 209; II, 336, 352, 355, 370, 382

Syracuse, New York 88; II, 300

Tacoma II, 166

Talbert, Joseph T. II, 211, 232, 234, 243

Tallahassee 207

Talleyrand 9

Taney, Roger B. 131, 151, 152, 159, 169, 172-177, 180, 181

Tappen, Frederick C. II, 165, 166, 288, 303, 426

Tarboro, N. C. II, 79

Taus, Esther 99

Taylor, John (of Caroline County) 8, 33, 108, 162-172; II, 122, 123

Taylor, Moses II, 86, 89, 90, 97, 161, 162, 389, 425

Taylor, Najah 218

Taylor, W. W. II, 275, 299

Telfair, Thomas 143

Tennessee 14, 53, 164, 202; II, 2, 9, 13, 16, 18, 55, 193, 201, 266, 267, 301, 325, 348

Texas II, 70, 141, 182, 217, 232, 301, 305, 326, 332, 335, 337, 340, 342, 348, 381, 391

Texas Railroad, Navigation and Banking Company II, 326

Thayer, George W. 77, 85, 263; II, 270, 283

Thayer (John E.) and Brother II, 70, 71, 346, 352

Thayer, Nathaniel II, 352, 387

Thelluson, Peter II, 402

Thellusson Brothers and Company II, 311, 313, 398

Third District Savings Bank and Trust Company (New Orleans) II, 192

Third National Bank of Boston II, 190, 239

Third National Bank of Chicago II, 111

Third National Bank of New York II, 111, 155, 187, 204, 210, 368, 444

Third National Bank of St. Louis II, 227

Thomas, E. R. II, 202

Thomas, O. F. II, 202

Thomas, Wm. 86, 263; II, 52

Thompson, Andrew II, 313

Thompson, Frederick II, 349

Thompson, H. A. II, 275

Thompson, Jeremiah II, 69

Thompson, John II, 71, 74, 96, 109, 111, 121, 279, 346, 349, 366, 389, 390

Thompson, Samuel II, 111, 349, 390

Thompson Brothers, New York II, 111, 349

Thompson Brothers, St. Paul II, 112

Thorn, W. F. II, 337

Thorndike, Israel 184; II, 328

Thornton, Godfrey II, 398

Thornton, Henry 124, 125, 128, 157

Tibbets, Elisha II, 333

Tilden, William A. II, 202

Tileston, Thomas II, 50-52, 56, 89, 273

Times, London 160; II, 263

Tinkham, E. I., E. I. Tinkham and Company (Chicago) II, 63, 111, 112

Title Guaranty and Trust Company (Chicago) II, 192

Toland, Henry II, 346

Tombigby Railroad and Banking Company II, 326

Tompkins, Daniel D. 8, 22, 31, 36

Tooke, Thomas 157; II, 68

Torrens, Robert 169, 210

Townsend, Edward II, 243

Toy, James F., Banking House of James F. Toy II, 190, 200

Toy National Incorporation II, 200

Toynbee, Arnold II, 380

Traders Bank (Nashville) II, 18

Tradesmen's Bank (New York) II, 48, 50

Tradesmen's Bank (Philadelphia) II, 91, 97, 108, 160, 163

Tredwell, John W. II, 346

Tremont Bank (Manufacturers and Mechanics Bank), Boston 13, 69, 86, 214, 216, 259; II, 57, 90, 245

Trenholm, William L. II, 175, 182, 195

Tri-City Railway and Light Company II, 381

Triplet II, 326

Trotter, Nathan II, 18, 36

Troy, New York 70, 79; II, 6, 154, 179, 236, 238, 279, 300, 301

Troy Building and Loan Association II, 301

Troy Savings Bank II, 301

Truesdale Savings Bank, (Truesdale, Iowa) II, 200

Trust Company of America (New York) II, 288

Trust Company of the Republic (New York) II, 394, 422

Tucker, George 95, 159, 179; II, 255

Tuscaloosa II, 339

Twelfth Ward Bank (New York) II, 188

Twin Cities II, 192, 198, 221

Tyler, Edward II, 282

Tyler, John 159, 178; II, 29, 89

Umbra (pseud. for Samuel Young) 196

Union Bank (Boston) 16, 21, 35, 42, 67, 68, 92, 232, 260; II, 45, 59, 193, 245

Union Bank (Florida) 207

Union Bank (Illinois) II, 27, 28

Union Bank of Louisiana (New Orleans) 60, 63, 207, 208, 237, 255, 257; II, 33, 70, 256, 267, 332, 333, 335, 337-339, 344

Union Bank of Maryland (Baltimore) 174-177; II, 53, 54, 256, 275, 299

Union Bank of Mississippi 208; II, 194, 267

Union Bank (New Hampshire) 185

Union Bank (New York) 52; II, 331

Union Bank (Tennessee) 53; II, 55

Union Insurance Company (Portsmouth) 185

Union Investment Company (Minneapolis) II, 198

Union National Bank (Chicago) II, 112, 153, 191, 193, 281

Union National Bank (New Orleans) II, 192

Union Pacific Railroad II, 360-362, 373, 386, 387, 391

Union Plank Road Company of Michigan II, 271

Union Securities Company (Spokane) II, 199

Union Square Bank of the City of New York II, 188

Union Trust Company (Chicago) II, 392
Union Trust Company (New York) II, 153, 188, 288, 369, 394, 418
Union Trust Company (Springfield, Massachusetts) II, 394
United Fruit Company II, 388
United Shoe Machinery Corporation II, 388
United States Loan and Trust Company (Chicago) II, 201
United States Mortgage and Trust Company (New York) II, 188, 243, 394
United States National Bank (Chicago) II, 201
United States Smelting, Refining and Mining Company II, 388
United States Steel Corporation II, 181, 226, 372, 375, 376, 378, 384, 385, 388, 391, 395
United States Trust Company (New York) II, 111, 188, 189, 368, 371, 394, 418, 422, 444
University of Virginia 157
Untermyer, Samuel II, 378
Upham, Phineas II, 346
Upton, George B. II, 166
Utah, II, 199, 302
Utica, New York 116, 160; II, 352
Utica and Schenectady Railroad Company II, 18
Vail, Theodore Newton II, 378
Valley National Bank (St.Louis) II, 301
Van Buren, Martin 88-91, 125, 147, 150, 156, 159, 163, 171, 176, 178, 180, 194, 197, 201, 265; II, 262, 415
Vanderbilt, William II, 383
Vanderlip, Frank A. II, 175, 180, 204, 211, 217, 235, 372, 373, 379, 391
Van Ness, John P. II, 415
Van Slyke, N. B. II, 282
Van Vleck (J. T.) and Reed, Van Vleck, Reed and Drexel II, 364, 365
Varian, Isaac L. 292
Varick, Richard 35, 37, 42, 63
Veblen, Thorstein II, 378
Venezuela II, 166, 370
Venhallow, Thomas W. 185
Venice 27
Venit, Abraham H. 193, 293
Vera Cruz 30
Vermilye, Jacob D. II, 89, 97, 282, 302, 303, 417
Vermilye, Washington R. II, 361
Vermilye, William M. II, 417
Vermilye, and Company II, 360, 365, 366, 418, 420
Vermont 75, 82, 92, 95; II, 14-16, 20, 21, 25, 193, 199, 240, 241, 271, 302, 326, 361, 363
Vermont Central Railroad II, 350, 359, 365, 387
Vermont State Bank, see State Bank of Vermont
Vernon, William II, 424
Verplanck, Guilian 38, 198, 199, 200, 201
Vethake, Henry 159
Vevey, Switzerland II, 382

Vicksburg, Mississippi II, 70, 267
Vienna, Austria II, 320, 321, 323, 386, 404
Vincennes, Indiana II, 23
Virginia 60, 162, 164, 167, 297; II, 2, 5, 29, 79, 113, 193, 194, 233, 246, 253, 254, 266, 296, 301, 325, 333, 335, 352, 409
Virginia Railway II, 371
Vissering, Gerard 157
Vollmar, John P. II, 199
Von Hoffmann and Company II, 355
Wabash and Erie Canal II, 333, 334, 351
Wabash, St.Louis and Pacific Railroad II, 383
Wade, Festus II, 215
Wadsworth, Jeremiah 25, 29-32, 34, 36, 42
Walckiers, Baron de II, 312
Walker, Amasa 180; II, 9, 10, 16, 113, 115
Walker, Sir Byron Edmund (Edmund Walker) II, 221
Walker, Joseph Henry II, 168, 214, 215
Walker, Robert T. II, 99, 104, 141
Wallabout Bank (Brooklyn) II, 188
Walley, Samuel Hurd II, 5, 100, 109, 164, 165, 302
Waln, Robert II, 254
Walsh, John Joseph II, 65
Walsh, John R. II, 201, 202, 216, 224, 285
Walsh, Robert 159
Walters, Raymond 101, 102
Warburg, Felix M. II, 222, 385
Warburg (M. M.) and Company II, 385, 386
Warburg, Paul M. II, 211, 217, 222, 235, 385
Ward, John, John Ward and Company II, 333, 335, 345-47
Ward, John and George II, 311, 398
Ward, Samuel 202; II, 67, 333
Ward, Thomas Wren 156, 159; II, 33, 333, 334, 359
Washington, George 37
Washington, D. C. 110, 115, 116, 121, 123, 145, 153, 155, 173, 176, 179; II, 68, 71, 75, 79, 88, 89, 106, 109, 110, 113, 129, 135, 142, 144-146, 182, 254, 287, 300, 301, 317, 328, 329, 337, 338, 347-349, 351, 363, 364, 391, 439, 440, 444
Washington and Warren Bank II, 61
Washington Bank, Washington National Bank (Boston) II, 108, 190, 298
Washington Globe 173
Washington Insurance Company (Providence) 32
Washington, State of... II, 199, 301
Washington Trust Company (New York) II, 188
Watmough, John G. 159
Waukesha, Wisconsin II, 218
Waukesha County Bank, Waukesha National Bank II, 218
Wayne County Bank (Palmyra, New York) II, 26
Weare, Finch and Company II, 73
Webster, Daniel 55, 102, 116, 156, 158, 159, 179, 244, 247
Webster, Peletiah II, 37
Webster Bank (Boston) 86, 229, 263

Weeks, George Wingate II, 190
Weis (J.) and Company (New Orleans) II, 192
Wellcome, Floradora Hauser II, 198
Welles, Arnold 184
Welles and Company, John and Benjamin Welles, John and Samuel Welles II, 69, 83
Wells, Bazaliel II, 253
Welsh, S. and W. II, 360
West Feliciana Railroad and Banking Company II, 326
West Indies II, 77, 254, 334
West Point 157
West Virginia II, 301
Westerly, Rhode Island 35
Western Bank (Philadelphia) II, 89, 90, 108, 172, 268
Western Insurance Company II, 61
Western National Bank (New York) II, 187
Western Railroad II, 337, 410, 413
Westinghouse Electric and Manufacturing Company II, 386
Wetmore, Frank O. II, 373
Wettereau, James O. 18, 30, 39, 40; II, 245
Wexler, Solomon II, 192, 193
Whaling Bank (New London) II, 65, 66
Wharton, Isaac 39, 98, 246
Wheeler, John II, 216, 223
Wheville, Wyoming II, 199
White, Horace II, 195, 208, 210, 217
White, Hugh L. 14, 115, 159
White, Weld and Company II, 376
Whitney, Reuben M. 152, 175
Whitney National Bank, Whitney Central National Bank, Whitney Central Trust and Savings Bank (New Orleans) II, 192, 193
Wiggin, Albert H. II, 179, 188, 227
Wiggin (Timothy) and Company II, 271, 336
Wilberforce, William 210
Wildes and Company II, 271
Wilkes, Charles 40, 63; II, 12, 254, 293, 330
Williams, Achilles II, 26
Williams, George G. II, 217, 224, 303, 425
Williams, George W. II, 112
Williams, John II, 100, 103
Williams, John Earl 79; II, 50, 51, 93, 94, 97, 103, 105, 107, 108, 121, 124, 150, 151
Williams, M. T. II, 25
Willing, Thomas 5, 12, 20, 25, 26, 30, 34, 37, 38, 42, 183; II, 12
Willing, Thomas M. II, 328
Willinck, W. II, 337
Willink, Wilhelm and Jan II, 318, 319
Willis, Parker II, 217
Wilmington, Delaware 16; II, 199
Wilson, James 6, 26, 33, 111
Wilson, John 298
Wilson, Thomas 113

Wilson, Woodrow II, 195
Wilson (Thomas) and Company, London II, 271, 330, 333, 335, 336, 343, 408
Winchester, Massachusetts II, 388
Windom, William II, 433, 440, 445, 446
Windsor County, Vermont 82
Wing, David Gould II, 190, 193
Winnipeg II, 221
Winslow, James II, 111
Winslow, Richard H. II, 347, 353-55
Winslow and Perkins II, 347, 354, 414
Winslow, Lanier and Company II, 71, 109, 111, 347-49, 353-55, 360, 365, 368, 380, 395, 418, 444
Winsor, Robert II, 381, 388
Wirt, William II, 29
Wisconsin 95, 202, 208; II, 13, 14, 20, 79, 110, 122, 198, 217-219, 276-278, 282, 301, 345
Wisconsin Bankers Association II, 110
Wisconsin Marine and Fire Insurance Company II, 63, 64, 112, 271
Wise, Henry A. 167; II, 2, 4
Wise, John 163
Wistar, Caspar 158
Witham, William Stewart II, 200, 201
Witherspoon, John 6
Wolcott, Oliver 36, 37, 42, 98, 99; II, 247, 404, 405
Wolf, C. J. M. de, Antwerp II, 406
Wolf, George 155
Wolff, Abraham II, 385
Wood, Richard D. II, 272
Wood, partner in Vermilye and Company II, 361
Woodbury Bank (Connecticut) II, 16
Woodbury, Levi 8, 95; II, 99
Woodward, James Thomas II, 303, 369
Woodward and Stillman II, 391
Worcester Trust Company (Worcester) II, 394
Workman, James II, 99, 147
Wormser, I. and S. II, 418
Worth, Gorham A. II, 48, 269
Wright, J. Hood II, 385
Wright, Silas II, 257
Wyoming II, 199, 302
Yale University 63, 299
Yates and McIntyre II, 68, 327
Yazoo City, Mississippi II, 70
Yellow Medicine County Bank II, 198
Young, Samuel 196-98, 203, 293
Zanesville, Ohio 56

Ref.
332.1
R317

105719

For Reference

Not to be taken from this room

$42.00